THE MOTION PICTURE GUIDE

THIS VOLUME IS DEDICATED TO
THE MEMORY OF
DAVID WARK GRIFFITH

THE MOTION PICTURE GUIDE

Silent Film

1910-1936

Robert Connelly

CINEBOOKS, INC.
Chicago, 1986
Publishers of THE COMPLETE FILM RESOURCE CENTER

Publishers: Jay Robert Nash, Stanley Ralph Ross; **Editor-in-Chief:** Jay Robert Nash; **Executive Editor:** Stanley Ralph Ross; **Associate Publisher and Director of Development:** Kenneth H. Petchenik; **Senior Editor-in-Charge:** Jim McCormick; **Senior Editors:** David Tardy, Robert B. Connelly; **Production Editor:** William Leahy; **Associate Editors:** Oksana Lydia Creighton, Jeffrey H. Wallenfeldt, Edie McCormick, Michaela Tuohy, Jeannette Hori, Tom Legge; **Contributing Editors:** James J. Mulay (Chief Contributing Editor), Daniel Curran, Michael Theobald, Arnie Bernstein, Phil Pantone, Brian Brock; **Assistant Editors:** Debra Schwieder, Susan Fisher, Donna Roth, Marla Kruglik, Kristina Marcy, Sarah von Fremd, Wendy Anderson; **Art Production and Book Design:** Cathy Anetsberger; **Research Staff:** Shelby Payne (Associate Editor and Chief Researcher), William C. Clogston, Tobi Elliott, Carol Pappas, Rosalyn Mathis, Millicent Mathis, Andrea Nash; **Business/Legal:** Judy Anetsberger.

Associate Publishers: Howard Grafman, Lynn Christian, James and Monica Vrettos, Antoinette Mailliard, Brent H. Nettle, Michael Callie, Constance Shea, Barbara Browne Cramer.

Editorial and Sales Offices: CINEBOOKS, 6135 N. Sheridan Road, Chicago, Illinois 60660.

Library of Congress Catalog Card Number: 85-071145
ISBN: 0-933997-00-0 THE MOTION PICTURE GUIDE (10 Vols.)
0-933997-10-8 THE MOTION PICTURE GUIDE, Vol X
(A-Z, Silent Film)

Printed in the United States
First Edition
This volume contains 13,500 entries.

1 2 3 4 5 6 7 8 9 10

FOREWORD

This volume of The Motion Picture Guide is a celebration of the silent feature film, an art form that, when at its best, has been likened most closely to music with its rhythms, its contrapuntal cutaways, its crescendos. It marks that perhaps too-brief period of time when, in capable hands, "the film came nearer to being an art form, in its own right, than it has ever been since," according to historian Ernest Lindgren.

The era of the silent feature film spanned less than three decades, and many major works of art—shot on perishable nitrate film stock, and stored under less-than-archival conditions—have disappeared. Still others have been reconstructed through the painstaking work of restorers, piecing them together from multiple sources, notably partial release prints found in divergent areas of the world. Indeed, the dogged pursuits of these dedicated collector-restorers have resulted in something of a renaissance at the time of this writing: great silent movies such as Abel Gance's NAPOLEON have attained new audiences of enthusiasts who had not been born at the time of initial release. Our fervent hope is that the search-and-restoration work will continue so that these remarkable films will reach ever wider audiences.

The silent feature motion picture, so quick to depart after Al Jolson's benchmark mouthings in THE JAZZ SINGER in 1927, was a long time in coming, particularly in the U.S. Although the first nickelodeon accepted its first proffered coin in 1905, the monopoly broadly known as The Trust—which licensed the storefront theaters and policed its licensees in the name of patent protection—was highly resistant to the changeover from one- and two-reelers to features of four or more reels. Not until distributing entrepreneur George Kleine—paradoxically, one of the early members of The Trust—broke the rules of the game and *violated* The Trust by importing the Italian epic QUO VADIS? in 1913 were the floodgates opened. D.W. Griffith, acting against the explicit instructions of his employer, Biograph, quickly furthered the subversion of the once all-powerful monopoly by making the first American feature-length film, JUDITH OF BETHULIA, in the same year. Others quickly rose to the challenge, creating a body of work which, at its finest, can stand with the best of today's cinema.

For those who are unacquainted with this unique and short-lived art form, we suggest a trial without preconceptions. The silent feature film, for all its similarities to synchronized-sound cinema, is a *different* experience. Less realistic, it is no less involving. Indeed, silent cinema calls for more mental agility, more imagination. We hope that this volume may assist such viewers in selecting those silent features which are—and such judgments are highly individualistic—most worthy of viewing.

Readers will find here every U.S. and British silent feature film ever made, as well as many important ones from other lands. Roughly 3,500 such films have been profiled and more than 10,000 are listed with credits, making this volume an invaluable tool for interested laypersons and scholars alike. Many of these films no longer exist; we have had to consult numerous historical sources in order to glean plot synopses and anecdotes about such films, rather than relying on the far more pleasant experience of viewing them. In this way—less than wholly satisfying though it may be—we have in some measure prolonged the life of these works. Our hope is that readers will find many hours of pleasure herein.

As the chief author of this volume—a privilege as well as a labor, the culmination of a lifelong interest in silent pictures—it has been my pleasure to organize, compile, and pen many of these entries. This would not have been possible without the help of a number of associates. I wish especially to thank hardworking Associate Editor Oksana Lydia Creighton; my publisher and friend Jay Robert Nash; Senior Editor James McCormick and Senior Editor/Senior Writer David Tardy (who both wrote many of these entries); my friend and advisor Kathleen Crowley; and most especially my wife Linda, without whose help and support this project would have entailed far more agony than ecstasy.

Robert Connelly

HOW TO USE INFORMATION IN THIS GUIDE

ALPHABETICAL ORDER

All entries have been arranged alphabetically throughout this and all subsequent volumes. In establishing alphabetical order, all articles (A, An, The) appear after the main title (AFFAIR TO REMEMBER, AN). In the case of foreign films the article precedes the main title (LES MISERABLES appears in the letter L) which makes, we feel, for easier access and uniformity. Contractions are grouped together and these will be followed by non-apostrophized words of the same letters. B.F.'s DAUGHTER is at the beginning of the letter B, not under BF.

TITLES

It is important to know what title you are seeking; use the *complete* title of the film. The film ADVENTURES OF ROBIN HOOD, THE, cannot be found under merely ROBIN HOOD. Many films are known under different titles and we have taken great pains to cross-reference these titles. (AKA, also known as) as well as alternate titles used in Great Britain (GB). In addition to the cross-reference title only entries, AKAs and alternate titles in Great Britain can be found in the title line for each entry. An alphabetically arranged comprehensive list of title changes appears in the Index volume (Vol. X).

RATINGS

We have rated each and every film at critical levels that include acting, directing, script, and technical achievement (or the sad lack of it). We have a *five-star* rating, unlike all other rating systems, to signify a film superbly made on every level, in short, a masterpiece. At the lowest end of the scale is *zero* and we mean it. The ratings are as follows: *zero* (not worth a glance), *(poor), **(fair), ***(good), ****(excellent), *****(masterpiece, and these are few and far between). Half-marks mean almost there but not quite.

YEAR OF RELEASE

We have used in all applicable instances the year of United States release. This sometimes means that a film released abroad may have a different date elsewhere than in these volumes but this is generally the date released in foreign countries, not in the U.S.

FOREIGN COUNTRY PRODUCTION

When possible, we have listed abbreviated names of the foreign countries originating the production of a film. This information will be found within the parenthesis containing the year of release. If no country is listed in this space, it is a U.S. production.

RUNNING TIME

A hotly debated category, we have opted to list the running time a film ran at the time of its initial U.S. release but we will usually mention in the text if the film was drastically cut and give the reasons why. We have attempted to be as accurate as possible by consulting the most reliable sources.

PRODUCING AND DISTRIBUTING COMPANIES

The producing and/or distributing company of every film is listed in abbreviated entries next to the running time in the title line (see abbreviations; for all those firms not abbreviated, the entire firm's name will be present).

COLOR OR BLACK-AND-WHITE

The use of color or black-and-white availability appears as c or bw following the producing/releasing company entry.

CASTS

Whenever possible, we give *the complete cast and the roles played* for each film and this is the case in 95% of all entries, the only encyclopedia to ever offer such comprehensive information in covering the entire field. The names of actors and actresses are in Roman lettering, the names of the roles each played in Italic inside parentheses.

SYNOPSIS

The in-depth synopsis for each entry (when such applies) offers the plot of each film, critical evaluation, anecdotal information on the production and its personnel, awards won when applicable and additional information dealing with the production's impact upon the public, its success or failure at the box office, its social significance, if any. Acting methods, technical innovations, script originality are detailed. We also cite other productions involving an entry's personnel for critical comparisons and to establish the style or genre of expertise of directors, writers, actors and technical people.

REMAKES AND SEQUELS

Information regarding films that have sequels, sequels themselves or direct remakes of films can be found at the very end of each synopsis.

DUBBING AND SUBTITLES

We will generally point out in the synopsis when a foreign film is dubbed in English, mostly when the dubbing is poor. When voices are dubbed, particularly when singers render vocals on songs mimed by stars, we generally point out these facts either in the cast/role listing or inside the synopsis. If a film is in a foreign language and subtitled, we signify the fact in a parenthetical statement at the end of each entry (In Italian, English subtitles).

CREDITS

The credits for the creative and technical personnel of a film are extensive and they include; p (producer, often executive producer); d (director); sup (supervisor); w (screenwriter, followed by adaptation, if any, and creator of original story, if any, and other sources such as authors for plays, articles, short stories, novels and non-fiction books); t (titler); ph (cinematographer, followed by camera system and color process when applicable, i.e., Panavision, Technicolor); m (composer of musical score); ed (film editor); md (music director); art d (art director); set d (set decoration); cos (costumes); spec eff (special effects); ch (choreography); m/l (music and lyrics); stunts, makeup, syn sc (synchronized score); s eff (sound effects); and other credits when merited. When someone receives two or more credits in a single film the credits may be combined (p&d, John Ford) or the last name repeated in subsequent credits shared with another (d, John Ford; w, Ford, Dudley Nichols).

GENRES/SUBJECT

Each film is categorized for easy identification as to genre and/or subject and themes at the left-hand bottom of each entry. (Western, Prison Drama, Spy Drama, Romance, Musical, Comedy, War, Horror, Science-Fiction, Adventure, Biography, Historical Drama, Children's Film, Animated Feature, etc.) More specific subject and theme breakdowns will be found in the Index (Vol. X).

PR AND MPAA RATINGS

The Parental Recommendation provides parents having no knowledge of the style and content of each film with a guide; if a film has excessive violence, sex, strong language, it is so indicated. Otherwise, films specifically designed for young children are also indicated. The Parental Recommendation (**PR**) is to be found at the right-hand bottom of each entry, followed, when applicable, by the **MPAA** rating. The PR ratings are as follows: **AAA** (must for children); **AA** (good for children); **A** (acceptable for children); **C** (cautionary, some objectionable scenes); **O** (completely objectionable for children).

KEY TO ABBREVIATIONS

Foreign Countries:

Arg.	Argentina
Aus.	Australia
Aust.	Austria
Bel.	Belgium
Braz.	Brazil
Brit.	Great Britain (GB when used for alternate title)
Can.	Canada
Chi.	China
Czech.	Czechoslovakia
Den.	Denmark
E. Ger.	East Germany
Fin.	Finland
Fr.	France
Ger.	Germany (includes W. Germany)
Gr.	Greece
Hung.	Hungary
Ital.	Italy
Jap.	Japan
Mex.	Mexico
Neth.	Netherlands
Phil.	Philippines
Pol.	Poland
Rum.	Rumania
S.K.	South Korea
Span.	Spain
Swed.	Sweden

Key to Abbreviations (continued)

Switz. Switzerland
Thai. Thailand
USSR Union of Soviet Socialist Republics
Yugo. Yugoslavia

Production Companies, Studios and Distributors (U.S. and British)

AA ALLIED ARTISTS
ABF Associated British Films
AE Avco Embassy
AEX Associated Exhibitors
AFN Associated First National Pictures
AH Anglo-Hollandia
AIP American International Pictures
AM American
ANCH Anchor Film Distributors
ANE American National Enterprises
AP Associated Producers
AP&D Associated Producers & Distributors
ARC Associated Releasing Corp.
Argosy Argosy Productions
Arrow Arrow Films
ART Artcraft
Astra Astra Films
AY Aywon

BA British Actors
B&C British and Colonial Kinematograph Co.
BAN Banner Films
BI British Instructional
BIFD B.I.F.D. Films
BIP British International Pictures
BJP Buck Jones Productions
BL British Lion
Blackpool Blackpool Productions
BLUE Bluebird
BN British National
BNF British and Foreign Film
Boulting Boulting Brothers (Brit.)
BP British Photoplay Production
BPP B.P. Productions
BRIT Britannia Films
BRO Broadwest
Bryanston Bryantston Films (Brit.)
BS Blue Streak
BUS Bushey (Brit.)
BUT Butchers Film Service
BV Buena Vista (Walt Disney)

CAP Capital Films
CC Christie Comedy
CD Continental Distributing
CHAD Chadwick Pictures Corporation
CHES Chesterfield
Cineguild Cineguild
CL Clarendon
CLIN Clinton
COL COLUMBIA
Colony Colony Pictures
COM Commonwealth
COMM Commodore Pictures
COS Cosmopolitan (Hearst)

DE Dependable Exchange
DGP Dorothy Gish Productions
Disney Walt Disney Productions
DIST Distinctive
DM DeMille Productions
DOUB Doubleday

EAL Ealing Studios (Brit.)
ECF East Coast Films
ECL Eclectic
ED Eldorado
EF Eagle Films
EFF & EFF E.F.F. & E.F.F. Comedy
EFI English Films Inc.
EIFC Export and Import Film Corp.
EL Eagle-Lion
EM Embassy Pictures Corp.
EMI EMI Productions
EP Enterprise Pictures
EPC Equity Pictures Corp.
EQ Equitable
EXCEL Excellent

FA Fine Arts
FBO Film Booking Office of America
FC Film Classics
FD First Division
FN First National
FOX 20TH CENTURY FOX (and Fox Productions)
FP Famous Players (and Famous Players Lasky)
FRP Frontroom Productions

Gainsborough Gainsborough Productions
GAU Gaumont (Brit.)
GEN General
GFD General Films Distributors
Goldwyn Samuel Goldwyn Productions
GN Grand National
GOTH Gotham
Grafton Grafton Films (Brit.)

H Harma
HAE Harma Associated Distributors
Hammer Hammer Films (Brit.)
HD Hagen and Double
HM Hi Mark
HR Hal Roach

IA International Artists
ID Ideal
IF Independent Film Distributors (Brit.)
Imperator Imperator Films (Brit.)
IP Independent Pictures Corp.
IN Invincible Films
INSP Inspirational Pictures (Richard Barthelmess)
IV Ivan Film

Javelin Javelin Film Productions (Brit.)
JUR Jury

KC Kinema Club
KCB Kay C. Booking
Knightsbridge Knightsbridge Productions (Brit.)
Korda Alexander Korda Productions (Brit.)

Ladd Ladd Company Productions
LAS Lasky Productions (Jesse L. Lasky)
LFP London Films
LIP London Independent Producers
Lorimar Lorimar Productions
LUM Lumis

Majestic Majestic Films
Mascot Mascot Films
Mayflowers Mayflowers Productions (Brit.)
Metro Metro
MFC Mission Film Corporation
MG Metro-Goldwyn
MGM METRO-GOLDWYN-MAYER
MON Monogram
MOR Morante
MS Mack Sennett
MUT Mutual

N National
NG National General
NGP National General Pictures (Alexander Korda, Brit.)
NW New World

Orion Orion Productions
Ortus Ortus Productions (Brit.)

PAR PARAMOUNT
Pascal Gabriel Pascal Productions (Brit.)
PDC Producers Distributors Corp.

Key to Abbreviations (continued)

PEER	Peerless
PWN	Peninsula Studios
PFC	Pacific Film Company
PG	Playgoers
PI	Pacific International
PIO	Pioneer Film Corp.
PM	Pall Mall
PP	Pro Patria
PRC	Producers Releasing Corporation
PRE	Preferred
QDC	Quality Distributing Corp.
RAY	Rayart
RAD	Radio Pictures
RANK	J. Arthur Rank (Brit.)
RBP	Rex Beach Pictures
R-C	Robertson-Cole
REA	Real Art
REG	Regional Films
REN	Renown
REP	Republic
RF	Regal Films
RFD	R.F.D. Productions (Brit.)
RKO	RKO RADIO PICTURES
Rogell	Rogell
Romulus	Romulus Films (Brit.)
Royal	Royal
SB	Samuel Bronston
SCHUL	B.P. Schulberg Productions
SEL	Select
SELZ	Selznick International (David O. Selznick)
SF	Selznick Films
SL	Sol Lesser
SONO	Sonofilms
SP	Seven Pines Productions (Brit.)
SRP	St. Regis Pictures
STER	Sterling
STOLL	Stoll
SUN	Sunset
SYN	Syndicate Releasing Co.
SZ	Sam Zimbalist
TC	Two Cities (Brit.)
T/C	Trem-Carr
THI	Thomas H. Ince
TIF	Tiffany
TRA	Transatlantic Pictures
TRI	Triangle
TRU	Truart
TS	Tiffany/Stahl
UA	UNITED ARTISTS
UNIV	UNIVERSAL (AND UNIVERSAL INTERNATIONAL)
Venture	Venture Distributors
VIT	Vitagraph
WAL	Waldorf
WB	WARNER BROTHERS (AND WARNER BROTHERS-SEVEN ARTS)
WEST	Westminster
WF	Woodfall Productions (Brit.)
WI	Wisteria
WORLD	World
WSHP	William S. Hart Productions
ZUKOR	Adolph Zukor Productions

Foreign

ABSF	AB Svensk Film Industries (Swed.)
Action	Action Films (Fr.)
ADP	Agnes Delahaie Productions (Fr.)
Agata	Agata Films (Span.)
Alter	Alter Films (Fr.)
Arch	Archway Film Distributors
Argos	Argos Films (Fr.)
Argui	Argui Films (Fr.)
Ariane	Les Films Ariane (Fr.)
Athos	Athos Films (Fr.)
Belga	Belga Films (Bel.)
Beta	Beta Films (Ger.)
CA	Cine-Alliance (Fr.)
Caddy	Caddy Films (Fr.)
CCFC	Compagnie Commerciale Francais Einematographique (Fr.)
CDD	Cino Del Duca (Ital.)
CEN	Les Films de Centaur (Fr.)
CFD	Czecheslovak Film Productions
CHAM	Champion (Ital.)
Cinegay	Cinegay Films (Ital.)
Cines	Cines Films (Ital.)
Cineriz	Cinerez Films (Ital.)
Citel	Citel Films (Switz.)
Como	Como Films (Fr.)
CON	Concordia (Fr.)
Corona	Corona Films (Fr.)
D	Documento Films (Ital.)
DD	Dino De Laurentiis (Ital.)
Dear	Dear Films (Ital.)
DIF	Discina International Films (Fr.)
DPR	Films du Palais-Royal (Fr.)
EX	Excelsa Films (Ital.)
FDP	Films du Pantheon (Fr.)
Fono	Fono Roma (Ital.)
FS	Filmsonor Productions (Fr.)
Gala	Fala Films (Ital.)
Galatea	Galatea Productions (Ital.)
Gamma	Gamma Films (Fr.)
Gemma	Gemma Cinematografica (Ital.)
GFD	General Film Distributors, Ltd. (Can.)
GP	General Productions (Fr.)
Gray	(Gray Films (Fr.)
IFD	Intercontinental Film Distributors
Janus	Janus Films (Ger.)
JMR	Macques Mage Releasing (Fr.)
LF	Les Louvre Films (Fr.)
LFM	Les Films Moliere (Fr.)
Lux	Lux Productions (Ital.)
Melville	Melville Productions (Fr.)
Midega	Midega Films (Span.)
NEF	N.E.F. La Nouvelle Edition Francaise (Fr.)
NFD	N.F.D. Productions (Ger.)
ONCIC	Office National pour le Commerce et L'Industrie Cinematographique (Fr.)
Ortus	Ortus Films (Can.)
PAC	Production Artistique Cinematographique (Fr.)
Pagnol	Marcel Pagnol Productions (Fr.)
Parc	Parc Films (Fr.)
Paris	Paris Films (Fr.)
Pathe	Pathe Films (Fr.)
PECF	Productions et Editions Cinematographique Francais (Fr.)
PF	Parafrench Releasing Co. (Fr.)
PIC	Produzione International Cinematografica (Ital.)
Ponti	Carlo Ponti Productions (Ital.)
RAC	Realisation d'Art Cinematographique (Fr.)
Regina	Regina Films (Fr.)
Renn	Renn Productions (Fr.)
SDFS	Societe des Films Sonores Tobis (Fr.)
SEDIF	Societe d'Exploitation ed de Distribution de Films (Fr.)
SFP	Societe Francais de Production (Fr.)
Sigma	Sigma Productions (Fr.)
SNE	Societe Nouvelle des Establishments (Fr.)
Titanus	Titanus Productions (Ital.)
TRC	Transcontinental Films (Fr.)
UDIF	U.D.I.F. Productions (Fr.)
UFA	Deutsche Universum-Film AG (Ger.)
UGC	Union Generale Cinematographique (Fr.)
Union	Union Films (Ger.)
Vera	Vera Productions (Fr.)

ABIE'S IMPORTED BRIDE**
(1925) 7 reels Temple Theatre Amusement/Trio bw

Philadelphia-produced film has young Abie Lavinsky, the son of a prosperous woolen mill owner, becoming involved with the plight of starving Russian Jews and setting out to raise money on their behalf. He promotes a huge ball, featuring a jazz band, which attracts the younger crowd and brings in $100,000. Before leaving for Europe to deliver the money, his father's friend, Max, arranges a marriage between a young peasant and the elder Lavinsky. Abie, who is opposed to this, finds himself in a real pickle when he meets the girl and they fall in love. Returning to the U.S., the young man is convinced his father will disinherit him, but is delighted instead to discover that the arrangement was only a scheme to put an end to his bachelorhood.

d&w, Roy Calnek.

Comedy/Drama **(PR:A MPAA:NR)**

ABLEMINDED LADY, THE*** (1922) 5 reels PFC bw

Henry B. Walthall *(Breezy Bright)*, Elinor Fair *(Daphne Meadows)*, Helen Raymond *(Widow McGee)*.

Confirmed bachelor Henry B. Walthall (who never gave a bad performance) works as a ranch hand for a thrice-married widow, McGee. The lady has her sights set on him and finally does get him to the altar, but only after he brings a young couple together, and a bandit to justice.

d&ph, Ollie Sellers or Don Gamble; w, (based on the story "The Able-Minded Lady" by William R. Leighton).

Comedy/Drama/Western **(PR:A MPAA:NR)**

ABRAHAM LINCOLN**
(1924) 12 reels Rockett-Lincoln/AFN bw (AKA: THE DRAMATIC LIFE OF ABRAHAM LINCOLN)

Kentucky and Indiana Period: Fay McKenzie *(Sarah Lincoln)*, Westcott B. Clarke *Thomas Lincoln)*, Irene Hunt *(Nancy Hanks Lincoln)*, Charles French *(Isom Enlow)*, Calvert Carter *(Mr. Gollaher)*, Madge Hunt *(Mrs. Gollaher)*, Raymond Lee *(Austin Gollaher)*, Ida McKenzie *(Sarah Lincoln, 10-Years-of-Age)*, Danny Hoy *(Abraham Lincoln, 7-Years-of-Age)*; The New Salem Period: George A. Billings *(Abe Lincoln, as a Young Man)*, Ruth Clifford *(Anne Rutledge)*, Eddie Burns *(John McNeil)*, Pat Hartigan *(Jack Armstrong)*, Otis Harlan *(Denton Offut)*, Jules Hanft *(Mr. James Rutledge)*, Julia Hesse *(Mrs. James Rutledge)*, Louise Fazenda *(Sally, a Country Girl)*, Robert Bolder *(A Country Politician)*, William Humphrey *(Stephen A. Douglas)*, William McIlwain *(Dr. Allen)*, Fred Kohler *(Slave Auctioneer)*, Bob Milasch, George Reehm *(Southern Planters)*; Springfield and Washington Period: George A. Billings *(Abraham Lincoln)*, Nell Craig *(Mrs. Abraham Lincoln)*, Homer Willits *(John Hay)*, Jim Blackwell *(Tom)*, Eddie Sutherland *(William Scott)*, Frances Raymond *(Scott's Mother)*, Jack Rollings *(Union Sentry)*, William McCormick *(Corporal of the Guard)*, Frank Newburg *(Bixby, Union Soldier)*, William Moran *(John Wilkes Booth)*, John Steppling *(Chairman of Delegation)*, Wanda Crazer *(A Dancer)*, Walter Rogers *(Gen. U. S. Grant)*, Alfred Allen *(Gen. George Meade)*, James Welch *(Gen. Robert E. Lee)*, Miles McCarthy *(Gen. Anderson)*, Earl Schenck *(Col. Rathbone)*, Dolly McLean *(Miss Harris)*, Genevieve Blinn *(Mary Todd's Sister)*, Mickey Moore *(Willie Lincoln)*, Newton Hall *(Tad Lincoln)*, Francis Powers *(Richard J. Oglesby)*, Cordelia Callahan *(Mrs. Surratt)*, Dallas Hope *(Stable Boy)*, Dick Johnson *(Bartender)*, Jack Winn *(Ned Spangler)*, Lawrence Grant *(Actor at Ford's Theater)*, Kathleen Chambers *(Ivy Livingston, Actress)*, Harry Rattenbury *(Stage Hand)*, W. L. McPheeters *(Allan Pinkerton)*; President Lincoln's Cabinet: Willis Marks *(William H. Seward)*, Nick Cogley *(Simon Cameron)*, Charles Smiley *(Salmon P. Chase/Hugh McCulloch)*, R. G. Dixon *(Gideon Welles)*, Harry Kelsey *(Caleb B. Smith)*, Joseph Mills *(Montgomery Blair)*, Fred Manly *(Edward Bates)*, William von Hardenburg *(James Speed)*, R. J. Dustin *(William Dennison)*.

An epic biography detailing the life and the legends of the nation's 16th president from his boyhood years in the midwest through his presidency, the Civil War years, and his assassination. The picture helped to spark a revival of interest in its subject; Carl Sandburg was just beginning the first volume of his monumental six-book portrait of Lincoln. This well-meaning biographical blockbuster lacked the cinematic genius of its inspiration, THE BIRTH OF A NATION. The film did have its moments, though, especially in the battle scenes and the depiction of Lincoln's early years in Kentucky, Indiana, and Illinois. The romance with Anne Rutledge (Clifford) was particularly well done, but for the most part, the picture was rather like an unending tableau.

p, Al and Ray Rockett; d, Phil Rosen; w, Frances Marion; ph, Robert Kurrle, Lyman Broening.

Biography **(PR:A MPAA:NR)**

ABSENT*** (1928) 5 reels Rosebud Film bw

Clarence Brooks, George Reed, Virgil Owens, Rosa Lee Lincoln, Floyd Schackleford, Clarence Williams.

Historically interesting film about a shell-shocked black veteran who wanders into a mining town, is taken care of by an old man and his daughter, regains his memory after a fist fight, and is given a new start in life by the American Legion.

d&ph, Harry A. Gant.

Drama **(PR:A MPAA:NR)**

ABSENTEE-NRA, THE*** (1915) 5 reels Mutual Master/Majestic

Robert Edeson, Olga Grey.

Allegorical story of ambition, pleasure, power, extravagance, and justice set against the contemporary world of labor strife. Good action scenes between militia and workers made this an above average effort for its time.

d, Frank E. Woods, Christy Cabanne.

Drama **(PR:A MPAA:NR)**

ABYSMAL BRUTE, THE*** (1923) 8 reels UNIV bw

Reginald Denny *(Pat Glendon, Jr.)*, Mabel Julienne Scott *(Maude Sangster)*, Hayden Stevenson *(Sam Stubener)*, Charles French *(Pat Glendon, Sr.)*, David Torrence *(Mortimer Sangster)*, George Stewart *(Wilfred Sangster)*, Buddy Messinger *(Buddy Sangster)*, Crauford Kent *(Deane Warner)*, Dorothea Wolbert *(Mrs. MacTavish)*, Julia Brown *(Violet MacTavish)*, Harry Mann *(Abe Levinsky)*, Kid Wagner *(Battling Levinsky)*, Jack Herrick *(Rough House Ratigan)*, Irene Haisman *(Gwendolyn)*, Nell Craig *(Daisy Emerson)*, Will R. Walling *(Farrell)*.

Denny is convincing as the shy young man from the mountains (the son of a former prizefighter) who comes to San Francisco and becomes successful in the fight game using the monicker "The Abysmal Brute." When Denny saves a man's life, he meets socialite Scott and falls like a ton of bricks. They begin to see each other, and Denny keeps his profession a secret until he wins her love as well.

d, Hobart Henley; w, A. P. Younger (based on the novel by Jack London); ph, Charles Stumar.

Drama **(PR:A MPAA:NR)**

ACCORDING TO HOYLE***
(1922) 5 reels David Butler/Western Pictures Exploitation bw

David Butler *("Box Car" Simmons)*, Helen Ferguson *(Doris Mead)*, Phil Ford *(Jim Mead)*, Fred J. Butler *(Dude Miller)*, Harry Todd *(Jim Riggs)*, Buddy Ross *(Silent Johnson)*, Hal Wilson *(Bellboy)*.

Nice little comedy about a tramp, played by Butler, who finds a correspondence school course on how to become successful. There are three rules: "don't be a piker, put up a bluff, and think success and you will be one." Shortly thereafter, he sees the girl who inspires him to put the advice to work. While getting a shave, he kids the barber into thinking he's a wealthy western miner. Then when he leaves a big tip using up his last penny, word gets all over town that he's the real McCoy. The rest of the story deals with Butler outconning the con men (by salting some worthless land the girl had been cheated out of), making a killing, and settling down to a life which would have made Dale Carnegie proud. Interesting collaboration between Butler, who would become one of Hollywood's most prolific directors *(SUNNY SIDE UP, THE LITTLE COLONEL, ROAD TO MORROCCO, SAN ANTONIO)*, and Van Dyke (THE THIN MAN).

d, W. S. Van Dyke; w, John B. Clymer (based on a story by Clyde C. Westover, Lottie Horner); ph, Arthur Todd.

Comedy **(PR:A MPAA:NR)**

ACCORDING TO LAW** (1916) 5 reels GAU bw

Mildred Gregory, Howard Hall, E. K. James, Madison Weeks, Alan Robinson, Albert Macklin, John Reinhardt, Charles W. Travis, Helen Marten, Mathilde Baring.

Fairly played melodrama explores such issues as marriage without children, maternal death at birth, divorce, and illegitimacy. Sad themes but universal problems.

d, Richard Garrick; w, Paul M. Bryan, Joseph H. Trant.

Drama **(PR:C MPAA:NR)**

ACCORDING TO THE CODE* (1916) 5 reels Essanay bw

Lewis S. Stone, Marguerite Clayton, E. H. Calvert, Sidney Ainsworth, Florence Oberle.

This film had much going for it—good acting, impressive Civil War battle scenes, handsome costumes and sets, as well as a powerful courtroom climax inspired by MADAME X. Unfortunately, the direction was so mechanically botched that audiences of that day found it virtually impossible to follow.

d, E. H. Calvert; w, Charles Michelson.

Drama **(PR:A MPAA:NR)**

ACE OF ACTION** (1926) 5 reels Action Pictures/AEX bw

Wally Wales [Hal Taliaferro] *(Wally Rand)*, Alma Rayford *(June Darcy)*, Charles Colby *(Farber)*, Hank Bell, Charles Whitaker, Fanny Midgley, William Hayes, Frank Ellis.

Predictable B western has Wales settling a feud between rival families over a water hole, bringing the bad hombre to justice and winning the girl to boot.

d, William Bertram; w, Betty Burbridge; ph, Ray Ries.

Western **(PR:A MPAA:NR)**

ACE OF CADS, THE*** (1926) 8 reels FP/PAR bw

Adolphe Menjou *(Chappel Maturin)*, Alice Joyce *(Eleanour)*, Norman Trevor *(Sir Guy de Gramercy)*, Phillip Strange *(Basil de Gramercy)*, Suzanne Fleming *(Joan)*.

The role of an officer driven from his regiment and framed to look guilty of infidelity in the eyes of his fiancee was made to order for the suavely cool Menjou. After traveling the world for years in disgrace, he returns home to find justice, revenge, and the love of the woman who misjudged him.

p, William Le Baron; d, Luther Reed; w, Forrest Halsey (based on a story by Michael Arlen); ph, J. Roy Hunt.

Drama **(PR:A MPAA:NR)**

ACE OF HEARTS, THE (1916, Brit.) 4 reels Clarendon bw

James Willard *(James Fairburn)*, Dolly Bishop *(Lola Vane)*, Frank Sargent *(Dick Rayston)*.

British domestic drama in which an editor sets the stakes at life when he gambles on the draw of cards with his wife's paramour.

d, Charles Calvert; w, James Willard.

Drama **(PR:C MPAA:NR)**

ACE OF HEARTS, THE**** (1921) 6 reels Goldwyn bw

Lon Chaney *(Farralone)*, Leatrice Joy *(Lilith)*, John Bowers *(Forrest)*, Hardee Kirkland *(Morgridge)*, Raymond Hatton *(The Menace)*, Roy Laidlaw *(Doorkeeper)*, Edwin Wallock *(Chemist)*.

An anarchist band, advocating the murder of wealthy capitalists, selects its assassin by dealing cards. The one who gets the ace of hearts must do the deed. In this case, a bomb is to be placed under a restaurant table where the intended victim dines regularly. But the would-be killer, knowing that a pair of lovers nearby will also be killed, refuses to go through with it. For this he is sentenced to death and the cards are dealt again. This time it falls upon Chaney to execute his only rival for the woman he loves. Instead of carrying out the sentence, he performs a completely selfless act by blowing up the leaders of the society.

d, Wallace Worsley; w, Ruth Wightman (based on the novel *The Purple Mask* by Gouverneur Morris); ph, Don Short.

Drama **(PR:A MPAA:NR)**

ACE OF THE LAW* (1924) 5 reels ANCH bw

Bill Patton *(Bill Kennedy)*, Peggy O'Day *(Mildred Mitchell)*, Lew Meehan *("Black" Muller)*.

When O'Day is abducted by Meehan, Patton swings into action and saves her, as well as her herd of cattle.

Western **(PR:A MPAA:NR)**

ACQUITTAL, THE** (1923) 7 reels UNIV bw

Claire Windsor *(Madeline Ames)*, Norman Kerry *(Robert Armstrong)*, Richard Travers *(Kenneth Winthrop)*, Barbara Bedford *(Edith Craig)*, Charles Weilesley *(Andrew Prentice)*, Frederick Vroom *(Carter Ames)*, Ben Deeley *(The Butler)*, Harry Mestagyer *(The District Attorney)*, Emmett King *(The Minister)*, Dot Farley *(The Maid)*, Hayden Stevenson *(The Taxi Driver)*.

Fair mystery about the murder of a stepfather and the rivalry his two sons share for the same girl. Universal borrowed an all-Metro company to produce this marginal effort and gave full credit for such in the opening credits.

d, Clarence Brown; w, Jules Furthman, Raymond L. Schrock, Dale Van Every, John Huston, Tom Reed, Tom Kilpatrick, Anthony Veiller (based on the play by Rita Weiman); ph, Silvano Balboni.

Mystery **(PR:A MPAA:NR)**

ACQUITTED*** (1916) 5 reels FA/TRI bw

Wilfred Lucas *(John Carter)*, Mary Alden *(Mrs. Carter)*, Bessie Love *(Helen Carter)*, Carmen De Rue *(Nellie Carter)*, Sam De Grasse *(Ned Fowler)*, Elmer Clifton *(Ira Wolcott)*, W.J. Freemont *(Night Watchman)*, Spotiswoode Aitken *(Charles Ryder)*, James O'Shea *(Police Chief)*, F. A. Turner *(Police Captain)*.

Solid early film about a banker, wrongly accused of murder, who is dismissed from his job because of the notoriety he receives. When his family reaches the point of near-starvation, he decides to commit suicide so that they might survive on his insurance. At the last minute he is saved by his youngest daughter and his employer, who restores his position.

d, Paul Powell; w, Roy Somerville (based on a short story by Mary Roberts Rinehart); ph, John W. Leezer.

Drama **(PR:A MPAA:NR)**

ACROSS THE CONTINENT**** (1922) 6 reels Lasky-PAR bw

Wallace Reid *(Jimmy Dent)*, Mary MacLaren *(Louise Fowler)*, *Theodore Roberts (John Dent)*, Betty Francisco *(Lorraine Tyler)*, Walter Long *(Dutton Tyler)*, Lucien Littlefield *(Scott Tyler)*, Jack Herbert *(Art Roget)*, Guy Oliver *(Irishman)*, Sidney D'Albrook *(Tom Brice)*.

Reid, the son of automobile magnate Roberts, drives a sporty car manufactured by his father's business rival, Long. When Reid learns that Long plans to sabotage his father's entry in a transcontinental race, he demonstrates his familial loyalty by driving the car himself. An excellent action film, highlighted by a spectacular cross-country auto race. There is plenty of suspense due to a fine script, snappy titles, and superb acting and direction in this Reid winner.

d, Phillip E. Rosen; w, Byron Morgan; ph, Charles Schoenbaum.

Adventure **(PR:A MPAA:NR)**

ACROSS THE DEAD-LINE** (1922) 5 reels UNIV bw

Frank Mayo *(John Kidder)*, Russell Simpson *(Enoch Kidder)*, Wilfred Lucas *(Aaron Kidder)*, Lydia Knott *(Charity Kidder)*, Molly Malone *(Ruth)*, Frank Thornwald *(Lucas Courtney)*, Josef Swickard *(Old Abel)*, William Marion *(Gillis)*.

A family feud erupts between two brothers in a northwestern logging community. Simpson's son Mayo has divided loyalties. Torn between the pleasures of the hedonistic life style practiced by his uncle, Lucas, and his father's puritanism, he is finally straightened out through his love for a tormented amnesiac girl. Laughable melodrama with a few good fights and an exciting storm sequence. Director Conway kept things moving nicely, considering the material he had to work with.

d, Jack Conway; w, George C. Hull (based on a story by Clarence Budington Kelland); ph, Leland Lancaster.

Adventure **(PR:A MPAA:NR)**

ACROSS THE DEADLINE** (1925) 5 reels William Steiner bw

Thomas Lingham *(Martin Revelle)*, Florence Lee *(Mrs. Revelle)*, Rulon Slaughter *(Rance Revelle)*, Josephine Hill *(Shirley Revelle)*, Bud Osborne *(Ben Larrago)*, Pat Rooney *(Shifty Sands)*, Leo Maloney *(Clem Wainwright)*.

Romeo and Juliet transposed to the American West. Maloney falls hard for Hill despite a feud between their two families. When Hill's brother Slaughter is the victim of a frame-up following a stagecoach robbery, Maloney saves him from a lynch mob, ending the feud. Maloney, one of the silent screen's most popular cowboys, was never given the chance to make his mark in talkies due to his untimely death in 1929. This film about feuding clans, brought to their senses through the love of a boy and girl, was not bad, but certainly not one of his best.

d, Leo Maloney; w, Ford I. Beebe; ph, Ben Bail, Jacob A. Badaracco.

Western **(PR:AA MPAA:NR)**

ACROSS THE PACIFIC*** (1926) 7 reels WB bw

Monte Blue *(Monte)*, Jane Winton *(Claire Marsh)*, Myrna Loy *(Roma)*, Charles Stevens *(Aguinaldo)*, Tom Wilson *(Tom)*, Walter McGrail *(Capt. Grover)*, Herbert Pryor *(Col. Marsh)*, Edgar Kennedy *(Cpl. Ryan)*, Sojin, Theodore Lorch *(Aguinaldo's Agents)*.

Tormented by the revelation of his recently deceased father's dishonorable conduct, Blue enlists in the army and ventures out to fight Aguinaldo's (Stevens') guerrillas, to the dismay of his sweetheart, Winton. Wooing beautiful half-caste Loy in order to gain information about the enemy, Blue is discomfited when Winton appears on the scene, having accompanied her father, Pryor, to the same outpost. Blue gets the information and the guerrillas are routed; the lovers are reconciled at the end. Basically a western set during the unfortunate occupation of the Philippine Islands by the U.S., shortly after the Spanish-American War. Of particular interest are the performances of Loy, in an early Oriental role, and Kennedy, who was given a rare opportunity in a dramatically effective death scene.

d, Roy Del Ruth; w, Darryl Francis Zanuck (based on the play by Charles E. Blaney); ph, Byron Haskins.

Adventure **(PR:A MPAA:NR)**

ACROSS THE SINGAPORE**** (1928) 7 reels MGM bw

Ramon Novarro *(Joel Shore)*, Joan Crawford *(Priscilla Crowninshield)*, Ernest Torrence *(Capt. Mark Shore)*, Frank Currier *(Jeremiah Shore)*, Dan Wolheim *(Noah Shore)*, Edward Connelly *(Joshua Crowninshield)*, James Mason *(Finch)*, Duke Martin *(Matthew Shore)*.

Against her will, Crawford's hand is pledged to sea captain Torrence, who sets sail for Singapore with his brothers. The bibulous Torrence is left ashore in the orient by his mutinous crew led by Mason, who has Torrence's youngest brother Novarro clapped in the brig. Returning to home port, Novarro immediately sets out with Crawford to locate his lost brother. When found, Torrence senses the love that Novarro and Crawford feel for each other, so he does the decent thing. This saga of love and hate, set against life on the sea, exemplified the artistic standards which elevated MGM to the top. Sets, costumes, cast, direction, and especially the special effects made this a Hollywood studio production of the first order.

d, William Nigh; w, Richard Schayer, Ted Shane (based on Ben Ames Williams' novel, *All the Brothers Were Valiant)*; t, Joe Farnham, ph, John Seitz; ed, Ben Lewis; set d, Cedric Gibbons.

Drama **(PR:A MPAA:NR)**

ACTION GALORE** (1925) 5 reels Action Pictures/Artclass bw

Buddy Roosevelt *(Bud Laurie)*, Toy Gallagher *(Betty McLean)*, Charles Williams*(Luke McLean)*, Joe Rickson *(Gil Kruger)*, Jack O'Brien *(Strike Carney)*, Raye Hamilton *(Ma Kruger)*, Ruth Royce *(Kate Kruger)*.

A ranger, Roosevelt, is shot by Gallagher when she mistakes him for a claim jumper. Later, they are left to die in a burning cabin by the villain, but Roosevelt gets them out and captures the bad man after a good fight sequence in a deserted mine shaft.

d, Robert Eddy.

Western **(PR:A MPAA:NR)**

ACTION CRAVER, THE** (1927) 5 reels Ben Wilson/RAY bw

Dick Hatton.

Returned doughboy lands a job on a ranch and is smitten by the owner's niece. The jealous foreman accuses the newcomer of shooting a calf and deserting his European wife, but his intentions are exposed, and he is driven from the spread.

d, Victor Potel; ph, Eddie Linden.

Western **(PR:A MPAA:NR)**

ACTRESS, THE***   (1928) 7 reels MGM bw

Norma Shearer *(Rose Trelawney)*, Ralph Forbes *(Arthur Gower)*, Owen Moore*(Tom Wrench)*, O. P. Heggie *(Sir William Gower)*, Gwen Lee *(Avonia)*, Lee Moran *(Colpoys)*, Roy D'Arcy *(Gadd)*, Virginia Pearson *(Mrs. Telfer)*, William Humphrey *(Mr. Telfer)*, Effie Ellsler *(Mrs. Mossop)*, Andree Tourneur *(Clara Defoenix)*, Cyril Chadwick *(Capt. Defoenix)*, Margaret Seddon *(Trafalgar Gower)*.

Shearer is an actress in love with a man whose family refuses to accept her because of prejudice towards theater folk. After being driven from the home of his grandfather, Shearer is reduced to a state of near-starvation, but is saved in the end when the old man changes his mind and backs a play in which she is to star.

d, Sydney Franklin; w, Albert Lewis, Richard Schayer (based on the play "Trelawney of the Wells" by Arthur Wing Pinero); t, Joe Farnham; ph, William Daniels; ed, Conrad A. Nervig; set d, Cedric Gibbons.

Drama (PR:A MPAA:NR)

ADAM AND EVA****   (1923) 8 reels COS/PAR bw

Marion Davies *(Eva King)*, T. Roy Barnes *(Adam Smith)*, Tom Lewis *(Mr. King)*, Willliam Norris *(Uncle Horace)*, Percy Ames *(Lord Andy)*, Leon Gordon *(Clinton DeWitt)*, Luella Gear *(Julie DeWitt)*, William Davidson *(Dr. Delamater)*, Edward Douglas *(Lord Andy's Secretary)*, Bradley Barker, John Powers *(Eva's Admirers)*, Horace James *(Gardener)*.

Despondent about his spoiled daughter Davies' devilish ways, wealthy Lewis turns the reins of his business over to his young employee, Barnes, and disappears for a time. Despairing of his ability to handle young hellion Davies, Barnes hits on the plan of telling her that her family is financially ruined. The once-extravagant Davies straightens out, working for the support of the family. Upon Lewis' return from his unannounced self-exile, he is initially annoyed by Barnes' plan. Viewing daughter Davies' redemption convinces her father that Barnes is the man for her. Excellent comedy, with lavish sets and costumes, parallels Biblical history in that the principals descend from riches to ruin and back again. Davies (one of the screen's premier comediennes) was described by *Variety* as the "blonde beauty with the knack of carrying off breezy comedy parts with a certain jaunty chic." As with all of the films that William Randolph Hearst financed for his mistress through Cosmopolitan Pictures— the company he established for the sole purpose of showcasing Davies' talents—this picture lost money.

d, Robert G. Vignola; w, Luther Reed (based on the stage play by Guy Bolton, George Middleton); ph, Harold Wenstrom, Tony Gaudio; set d, Joseph Urban.

Comedy (PR:A MPAA:NR)

ADAM AND EVIL****   (1927) 7 reels MGM bw

Lew Cody *(Adam Trevelyan/Allan Trevelyan)*, Aileen Pringle *(Evelyn Trevelyan)*, Gwen Lee *(Gwen De Vere)*, Gertrude Short *(Dora Dell)*, Hedda Hopper *(Eleanor Leighton)*, Roy D'Arcy *(Mortimer Jenkins)*.

Excellent marital farce, in the Lubitsch tradition, with Cody providing the laughs by playing identical twin brothers in a hotel setting. Wonderful, suggestively innocent, humor is on the numbers due to fine script, titles, direction, and acting by all.

d, Robert Z. Leonard; w, F. Hugh Herbert, Florence Ryerson; t, Ralph Spence; ph, Andre Barlatier; ed, Leslie F. Wilder; art d, Cedric Gibbons, Richard Day.

Comedy (PR:A MPAA:NR)

ADAM BEDE**   (1918, Brit.) 6 reels International Exclusives bw

Bransby Williams *(Adam Bede)*, Ivy Close *(Hetty Sorrel)*, Malvina Longfellow *(Dinah Morris)*, Gerald Ames *(Arthur Donnithorne)*, Claire Pauncefort *(Aunt Lydia)*, Inez Bensusan *(Sarah Thorne)*, Will Corrie *(Farmer Poyser)*, Charles Stanley *(Seth Bede)*, Ralph Forster *(Squire)*.

In this 19th Century drama set in England, the grandson of a squire saves the niece of a poor farmer from the accusation of having murdered her illegitimate child.

d, Maurice Elvey; w, Kenelm Foss (based on the novel by George Eliot).

Drama (PR:C MPAA:NR)

ADAM'S RIB**   (1923) 8 reels FP/PAR bw

Milton Sills *(Michael Ramsay)*, Elliott Dexter *(Prof. Nathan Reade)*, Theodore Kosloff *(Monsieur Jaromir, King of Moravia)*, Anna Q. Nilsson *(Mrs. Michael Ramsay)*, Pauline Garon *(Mathilda Ramsay)*, Julia Fay *("The Mischievous One")*, Clarence Geldert *(James Kilkenna)*, George Field *(Minister to Moravia)*, Robert Brower *(Hugo Kermaier)*, Forrest Robinson *(Kramer)*, Gino Corrado *(Lt. Braschek)*, Wedgewood Nowell *(Secretary to Minister)*, Clarence Burton *(Cave Man)*.

By offering herself in her mother's stead, Garon attempts to prevent her mother Nilsson from committing adultery with deposed monarch Kosloff. When Garon's true love Dexter discovers her in compromising conditions with Kosloff, her own happiness is threatened. Grain broker Sills, Nilsson's neglectful husband, rids himself of rival Kosloff by restoring the king to his throne upon the promise of a large grain purchase from Kosloff's country. The principal players are happily reunited, and Sills' strategy proves financially fortuitous as well. Implausible, loosely constructed society drama dealing with marital infidelity. This was another of DeMille's cleverly named "modern relationship" films which, in spite of its numerous weaknesses, managed to pack them in.

p&d, Cecil B. DeMille; w, Jeanie Macpherson; ph, Alvin Wyckoff, Guy Wilky, Anne Bauchens.

Drama (PR:A MPAA:NR)

ADELE***   (1919) 6 reels United Picture Theaters of America bw

Kitty Gordon, Mahlon Hamilton, Wedgewood Nowell, Joseph Dowling.

Gordon is most convincing as a Red Cross nurse, captured by the Germans and forced to become a spy in order to save her lover. Well directed by Worsley, who is best remembered for his work with Lon Chaney in THE PENALTY, HUNCHBACK OF NOTRE DAME, etc.

d, Wallace Worsley; w, Jack Cunningham (based on the novel *The Nurse's Story* by Adele Bleneau); ph, Clyde De Vinna.

War (PR:A MPAA:NR)

ADMIRABLE CRICHTON, THE***   (1918, Brit.) 8 reels G. B. Samuelson/JUR bw

Basil Gill *(Crichton)*, Mary Dibley *(Lady Mary)*, James Lindsay *(Woolley)*, Lennox Pawle *(Lord Loam)*, Lilian Hall Davis *(Agatha)*.

This British version of the classic Barrie play about a noble family being shipwrecked and becoming completely dependent upon their butler, was later remade on a grand scale as MALE AND FEMALE by Cecil B. DeMille.

d, G. B. Samuelson; w, Kenelm Foss (based on the play by James M. Barrie).

Drama (PR:A MPAA:NR)

ADOPTED SON, THE**   (1917) 6 reels Metro bw

Francis X. Bushman *("Two-Gun" Carter)*, Beverly Bayne *(Marian Conover)*, Leslie Stowe *(Tom McLane)*, J. W. Johnston *(Henry McLane)*, John Smiley *(Luke Conover)*, Gertrude Norman *(Mrs. Conover)*, Pat O'Malley *(George Conover)*.

Fair film about feuding mountain folk who manage to work it all out through marriage. A typical outing for the popular Bushman, whom Metro made rush from set to set, playing dashing romantic roles, until his star dimmed considerably when it became known that he was secretly married to his perennial costar, Bayne.

d, Charles Brabin; w, Albert Shelby Le Vin (based on a story by Max Brand).

Drama (PR:A MPAA:NR)

ADORABLE CHEAT, THE***   (1928) 6 reels CHES bw

Lila Lee *(Marian Dorsey)*, Cornelius Keefe *(George Mason)*, Burr McIntosh *(Cyrus Dorsey)*, Reginald Sheffield *(Will Dorsey)*, Gladden James *(Howard Carver)*, Harry Allen *("Dad" Mason)*, Alice Knowland *(Mrs. Mason)*, Virginia Lee *(Roberta Arnold)*, Rolfe Sedan *(Card-Playing Guest)*.

Loving Keefe, rich girl Lee assumes another name and takes a menial job in her father's factory, one that will bring her into his proximity. When love blossoms, she reveals her true identity and invites Keefe to a party at her father's mansion. Lee's weak-willed brother steals money from her father's safe to cover gambling losses, and suspicion falls on the lowly Keefe. He clears his name, wins the lovely Lee, and assumes the command of her father's business empire. This neat little programmer about a shipping clerk who falls in love with the boss' daughter without knowing it was shot in 10 days for $10,000.

d, Burton King; w, Arthur Hoerl; t, DeLeon Anthony; ph, M. A. Anderson; ed, Anthony.

Drama (PR:A MPAA:NR)

ADORABLE DECEIVER, THE**   (1926) 5 reels R-C/FBO bw

Alberta Vaughan *(Princess Sylvia)*, Cora Williams *(Mrs. Pettibone)*, Harlan Tucker *(Tom Pettibone)*, Daniel Makarenko *(King Nicholas)*, Jane Thomas *(Flo Doyle)*, Frank Leigh *(Jim Doyle)*, Rosa Gore *(Mrs. Schrapp)*, Sheila Hayward *(Bellona)*.

Story about a princess and her ruling father who flee a European revolution and come to America. After selling the last of their jewels, the impoverished girl takes a job *impersonating* a princess. A young man hires her to play the role, as a gag, before his social-climbing mother. While doing so, she exposes a couple of jewel thieves posing as royalty and, of course, ends up with the wealthy young man. Financier Joseph P. Kennedy, father of a president and of two senators, had just purchased the Film Booking Offices of America; this picture was one of the first to be released by the company under Kennedy's imprimatur.

d, Philip Rosen; w, Doris Anderson (based on the story "Triple Trouble" by Harry O. Hoyt); ph, Roy Klaffki.

Comedy/Drama (PR:A MPAA:NR)

ADORATION**   (1928) 7 reels FN-WB bw

Billie Dove *(Elena, Princess Orloff)*, Antonio Moreno *(Serge, Prince Orloff)*, Lucy Dorraine *(Ninette)*, Nicholas Soussanin *(Count Vladimir Zubov)*, Nicholas Bela *(Ivan)*, Winifred Bryson *(Baroness Razumov)*, Lucien Prival *(Baron Razumov)*, Emil Chautard *(Gen. Count Alexis Murajev)*.

Lovely Dove and her husband Moreno are aristocrats who, separately, flee from the turmoil of revolutionary Russia. Convinced that Dove had been cheating on him with Soussanin prior to their departure, Moreno goes on a bender. Dove peddles her jewelry for sustenance and then, her money gone, takes a job as a model. Seeking her errant husband, Dove finds him working as a waiter between drinking sessions. Moreno refuses to rejoin his apparently faithless wife, but follows her when she departs. He hears Dove beg Soussanin to tell her husband the truth. The rascal refuses to do so, but the eavesdropping Moreno is convinced of his wife's innocence. This standard, but handsomely produced, Dove film afforded her the opportunity to look beautiful through countless changes of clothing.

d, Frank Lloyd; w, Winifred Dunn (based on a story by Lajos Biro); t, Garrett Graham; ph, John Seitz; ed, John Rawlins, Frank Stone; syn sc.

Drama (PR:A MPAA:NR)

ADVENTURE* (1925) 7 reels, FP/PAR bw**

Tom Moore *(David Sheldon)*, Pauline Starke *(Joan Lackland)*, Wallace Beery *(Morgan)*, Raymond Hatton *(Raff)*, Walter McGrail *(Tudor)*, Duke Kahanamoku *(Noah Noa)*, Noble Johnson *(Googomy)*, James Spencer *(Adam)*.

Good directorial work by Fleming (who went on to direct GONE WITH THE WIND and THE WIZARD OF OZ) kept this one whipping right along. The story is about an early-day, liberated woman who sails to an island inhabited by a single white man. She nurses him through a tropical fever, keeps him from being bilked by a couple of nasty traders, saves his plantation from native attack, and then cleverly marries him after he rescues her.

d, Victor Fleming; w, A. P. Younger, L. G. Rigby (based on the novel by Jack London); ph, C. Edgar Schoenbaum.

Adventure (PR:A MPAA:NR)

ADVENTURE IN HEARTS, AN* (1919) 5 reels PAR bw (AKA: CAPTAIN DIEPPE)

Robert Warwick, Helene Chadwick, Juan de la Cruz, Winnifred Greenwood, Walter Long, Howard Gaye.

Feeble fare about an American's unpleasant encounters with the officials of a small European kingdom. An Army captain in WW I, this was one of the first appearances of matinee idol Warwick after his separation from the service.

d, James Cruze; w, Elmer Harris (based on the story "Captain Dieppe" by Anthony Hope and the play by Harrison Rhodes); ph, Frank Urson.

Adventure (PR:A MPAA:NR)

ADVENTURE SHOP, THE* (1918) 5 reels VIT bw

Corinne Griffith *(Phyllis Blake)*, Walter McGrail *(Josephus Potts, Jr.)*, Warren Chandler *(Josephus Potts, Sr.)*, Priestley Morrison *(John Montgomery)*, Robert Gaillard *(Franklin Herbert)*, Freeman Wood, Victor Stewart.

Poor Vitagraph offering—in spite of the presence of beautiful Griffith—about a society youth playing "underworld" and, of course, getting involved for real. Staging was all done at Vitagraph's studio in Brooklyn's Flatbush section.

d, Kenneth Webb; w, George H. Plympton (based on the story "The Green Gullabaloo" by Bud Fisher); ph, Tom Malloy.

Crime (PR:A MPAA:NR)

ADVENTURER, THE*** (1928) 5 reels MGM bw

Tim McCoy *(Jim McClellan)*, Charles Delaney *(Barney O'Malley)*, George Cowl *(Esteban de Silva)*, Dorothy Sebastian *(Dolores de Silva)*, Michael Visaroff *(Samaroff)*, Gayne Whitman *(The Tornado)*, Alex Melesh *(John Milton Gibbs)*, Katherine Block *(Duenna)*.

This unusual McCoy film, set in South America, gave the great cowboy star the chance to show off some flashy outfits while playing an American mining engineer who falls in love with Sebastian, the daughter of a deposed Latin president. In an attempt to help her father regain his position, McCoy becomes involved in a revolution and after a number of adventures, in which he narrowly escapes with his life, the hero manages to restore the rightful ruler to his office and win the heart of the girl who captured his fancy.

d, Viachetslav Tourjansky; w, Jack Cunningham (based on a story by Leon Abrams); t, Ruth Cummings; ph, Clyde De Vinna; ed, Sam S. Zimbalist; set d, Alexander Toluboff.

Adventure (PR:A MPAA:NR)

ADVENTURES OF CAPTAIN KETTLE, THE** (1922, Brit.) 5 reels Captain Kettle Films bw

Charles Kettle *(Capt. Charles Kettle)*, Nina Grudgeon *(Pacquita)*, Austin Leigh *(Gen. Salveston)*, E. L. Frewen *(Martin Cranforth)*.

English adventure about a soldier of fortune who is crowned king of a South American plantation, and in the end saved from an armed uprising by a beautiful native girl.

p, Austin Leigh; d, Meyrick Milton, w, C. J. Cutcliffe-Hyne.

Adventure (PR:A MPAA:NR)

ADVENTURES OF CAROL, THE*** (1917) 5 reels WORLD bw

Madge Evans *(Carol Montgomery)*, George MacQuarrie *(Comdr. Montgomery)*, Rosina Henley *(Mrs. Montgomery)*, Carl Axzell *(James)*, Nicholas Long *(Beppo)*, Kate Lester *(Mme. Fairfax)*, Jack Drumier *(Marse Fairfax)*, Frances Miller *(Mammy Lou)*.

A wonderful and skillfully sentimental performance by Evans (who retired from the screen after marrying playwright Sidney Kingsley) as a lost child who, through her goodness, brings happiness to a family of stubborn adults.

d, Harley Knoles; w, (based on a story by Julia Burnham); ph, Rene Guissart.

Drama (PR:AA MPAA:NR)

ADVENTURES OF KITTY COBB, THE* (1914) 4 reels Waner bw

Marian Swayne *(Kitty Cobb)*, Jack Hopkins *(The Inventor)*, Howard Missimer *(The Spy)*.

Swayne, a simple girl from the wilds of Long Island, is so enamored by the stories inventor Hopkins tells her about Manhattan, that she journeys there in search of fame and fortune. Broke and unable to find work, she is about to be evicted from the theatrical boarding house where she has been living when a fellow lodger comes to her rescue by getting her a job as theater usher. Shortly thereafter Hopkins, whom Swayne has always secretly loved, attends a show with his mother, recognizes his old friend, and persuades her to take a job as their family secretary. Hopkins has developed a secret weapon for the U.S. government which foreign spies attempt to steal. Swayne foils the plot and is captured by enemy agents. The film ends with Hopkins saving his government, capturing the spies and getting the girl. Although inspired by Flagg's newspaper drawings, the story had little to do with the character he created.

w, (based on James Montgomery Flagg's nationally syndicated newspaper drawings from the *New York Sunday World*.)

Spy Drama (PR:A MPAA:NR)

ADVENTURES OF MR. PICKWICK, THE*** (1921, Brit.) 6 reels ID bw

Fred Volpe *(Samuel Pickwick)*, Mary Brough *(Mrs. Bardell)*, Bransby Williams *(Sgt. Buzfuz)*, Ernest Thesiger *(Mr. Jingle)*, Kathleen Vaughn *(Arabella Allen)*, Joyce Dearsley *(Isabella Wardle)*, Arthur Cleave *(Mr. Winkle)*, Athene Seyler *(Rachel Wardle)*, John Kelt *(Mr. Snodgrass)*, Hubert Woodward *(Sam Weller)*, Norman Page *(Justice Stoneleigh)*, Thomas Weguelin *(Mr. Wardle)*, Townsend Whitley *(Dodson)*, Harry Gilbey *(Fogg)*, John E. Zecchini *(Fat Boy)*.

English comedy based on the Dickens character in which a country outing with friends and club members ends up in a breach-of-promise suit by a man-starved landlady.

d, Thomas Bentley; w, Eliot Stannard, E. A. Baughan (based on *The Pickwick Papers* by Charles Dickens).

Comedy (PR:A MPAA:NR)

ADVENTUROUS SEX, THE** (1925) 6 reels AEX/Pathe bw

Clara Bow *(The Girl)*, Herbert Rawlinson *(Her Sweetheart)*, Earl Williams *(The Adventurer)*, Harry T. Morey *(Her Father)*, Mabel Beck *(Her Mother)*, Flora Finch *(The Grandmother)*, Joseph Burke.

Bow gives Rawlinson the bum's rush when he ignores her charms, concentrating instead on his airplane. Footloose, the flapper then goes on a spree of drinking and dancing, meeting adventurer Williams. When the bounder compromises and humiliates her, Bow leaps into the waters of the Niagara. As she is about to be swept over the falls, Rawlinson arrives and rushes to her rescue. With the aid of an airplane, ironically, he saves the feckless heroine. This run-of-the-mill programmer is of interest only because it features Bow before she became one of the movies' biggest stars.

p, Howard Estabrook; d, Charles Giblyn; w, Carl Stearns Clancy (based on a story by Hamilton Mannin); ph, George Peters.

Drama (PR:A MPAA:NR)

ADVENTUROUS SOUL, THE* (1927) 6 reels HM bw

Mildred Harris *(Miriam Martin)*, Jimmy Fulton *(Dick Barlow)*, Tom Santschi *(Capt. Svenson)*, Arthur Rankin *(Glenn Martin)*, Charles K. French *(John Martin)*.

In his role as a shipping magnate, French conspires to have his ne'er-do-well son Rankin shanghaied aboard one of his vessels, where the hapless lad will be subject to the stern discipline of a cruel master, Santschi. Eavesdropping, Rankin overhears the plan and flees. The press gang snatches Fulton in Rankin's stead, to the dismay of the latter's sister, Harris, who loves the abducted lad. Once at sea, shipping clerk Fulton gives a good account of himself, gaining the respect of the captain and his roughneck crew under the assumed name of his sweetheart's sibling. Ashore once more, he rejoins Harris, who makes certain that all concerned know of Fulton's valor. Inept effort on every level, which one might suspect was produced solely to exploit the marriage of Harris to Charles Chaplin.

d, Gene Carroll; sup, Harriet Virginia; w, (based on a story by John J. Moreno); ph, Jerry Fairbanks.

Adventure (PR:A MPAA:NR)

ADVENTUROUS YOUTH** (1928, Brit.) 5 reels PM/WB bw

Derrick de Marney *(The Englishman)*, Renee Clama *(Mary Fergusson)*, Dino Galvani *(Don Estaban)*, Sybil Wise *(The Vamp)*, Loftus Tottenham *(Mr. Fergusson)*, Julius Kantorez *(Father O'Flannigan)*, Harry Bagge, Harry Peterson, Lionel d'Aragon.

This English adventure was set during the Mexican Revolution and deals with a heroic British miner who surrenders in order to save the village church from being destroyed.

p&d, Edward Godal.

Adventure (PR:A MPAA:NR)

AFFAIR OF THE FOLLIES, AN*** (1927) 7 reels A1 Rockett/FN-WB bw

Lewis Stone *(Hammersley)*, Billie Dove *(Tamara)*, Lloyd Hughes *(Jerry)*, Arthur Stone *(Sam the Waiter)*, Arthur Hoyt *(The Inventor)*, Bertram Marburgh *(Lew Kline)*.

Former Follies girl Dove, forced by circumstances to go back to the stage when her husband Hughes loses his job, meets millionaire L. Stone, who falls hard for her. L. Stone, Hughes, and inventor Hoyt—who has been unsuccessfully trying to reach L. Stone to get financial aid for his latest project—have never met, although the three have lunch every day at the same restaurant. Finally introduced to one another by their waiter, A. Stone, the three converse. L. Stone recounts his joy over having the unnamed Dove accept his invitation to dinner that evening; Hughes tells the others of his having broken up with his wife; Hoyt discloses his failure to meet his potential backer. The philanthropic L. Stone advises Hughes to return to his wife and arranges a meeting with Hoyt, and all ends well. An entertaining small-world story, spiced with coincidence, having to do with differing perspectives converging.

d, Millard Webb; w, June Mathis (based on the story "Here Y' Are, Brother" by Dixie Wilson); ph, Tony Gaudio; ed, Hugh Bennett.

Drama **(PR:A MPAA:NR)**

AFFAIRS OF ANATOL, THE*** (1921) 9 reels FP/PAR bw

Wallace Reid *(Anatol De Witt Spencer)*, Gloria Swanson *(Vivian, His Wife)*, Elliott Dexter *(Max Runyon)*, Bebe Daniels *(Satan Synne)*, Monte Blue *(Amber Elliot)*, Wanda Hawley *(Emilie Dixon)*, Theodore Roberts *(Gordon Bronson)*, Agnes Ayres *(Annie Elliott)*, Theodore Kosloff *(Nazzer Singh)*, Polly Moran *(Orchestra Leader)*, Raymond Hatton *(Hoffmeier)*, Julia Faye *(Tibra)*, Charles Ogle *(Dr. Bowles)*, Winter Hall *(Dr. Johnson)*, Guy Oliver *(The Spencer Butler)*, Ruth Miller *(The Spencer Maid)*, Lucien Littlefield *(The Spencer Valet)*, Zelma Maja *(Nurse)*, Shannon Day, Alma Bennett *(Chorus Girls)*, Elinor Glyn, Lady Parker *(Bridge Players)*, William Boyd, Maud Wayne *(Guests)*, Fred Huntley *(Stage Manager)*.

An adaptation of one of playwright Schnitzler's episodic, amoral Viennese dramas about the sexual adventures of the Casanova-like Anatol (Reid), who lightheartedly deceives his wife (Swanson) with dozens of delightful ladies, including Daniels (aptly named Satan Synne), purportedly the world's wickedest woman. Daniels, he discovers to his disgust, is the pure and loving wife of a disabled WW I veteran. Trend-setting, star-studded production in which DeMille, correctly sensing the change in America's moral attitude, gives his audience a healthy dose of glamor, sex, and implied naughtiness.

p&d, Cecil B. DeMille; w, Jeanie Macpherson, Beulah Marie Dix, Lorna Moon, Elmer Harris (based on the play "Anatole" by Arthur Schnitzler; paraphrased by Granville Barker); ph, Alvin Wyckoff, Karl Struss; ed, Anne Bauchens.

Drama **(PR:C MPAA:NR)**

AFLAME IN THE SKY*** (1927) 6 reels R-C/FBO bw

Sharon Lynn *(Inez Carillo)*, Jack Luden *(Terry Owen)*, William Humphreys *(Maj. Savage)*, Robert McKim *(Joseph Murdoch)*, William Scott *(Saunders)*, Charles A. Stevenson *(Grandfather Carillo)*, Bill Franey *(Cookie)*, Mark Hamilton *(Slim)*, Walter Ackerman *(Desert Rat)*, Jane Keckley *(Cordelia Murdoch)*, Ranger, the Dog.

This very good contemporary western mixed airplanes and horses. The outstanding scene in the picture showed the hero signaling for help by skywriting. This was McKim's (HELL'S HINGES, THE MARK OF ZORRO) last film before his death.

d, J. P. McGowan; w, Ewart Adamson (based on a story by Mary Roberts Rinehart); ph, Joe Walker.

Western **(PR:A MPAA:NR)**

AFRAID OF LOVE* (1925, Brit.) 7 reels BRIT/United Kingdom Photoplays bw

Honorable Mrs. John Russell *(Rosamund Bond)*, Leslie Faber *(Anthony Bond)*, Juliette Compton *(Ruth)*, Jameson Thomas *(Philip Bryce)*, Mickey Brantford *(Tony Bond)*, Moore Marriot *(Father)*, Adeline Hayden Coffin *(Mother)*.

Poorly done British film about a woman who leaves her cheating husband to work at her former lover's dress shop. This whole mess was really nothing more than an advertisement for Russell's real-life London dressmaking establishment.

p, F. J. Nettlefold; d, Reginald West; w, Honorable Mrs. John Russell.

Drama **(PR:C MPAA:NR)**

AFRAID TO FIGHT*** (1922) 5 reels UNIV bw

Frank Mayo *(Tom Harper)*, Lillian Rich *(Harriet Monroe)*, Peggy Cartwright *(Sally Harper)*, Lydia Knott *(Mrs. Harper)*, W. S. McDunnough *(Dr. Butler)*, *Tom McGuire ("Big Jim" Brandon)*, Harry Mann *(Leonard)*, Wade Boteler *(Phillip Brand)*, Al Kaufman *("Slick" Morrisey)*, Roscoe Karns *(Bertie)*, Guy Tiney *(Fat Boy)*, Charles Haefeli *(Johnny Regan)*, Tom Kennedy *(Battling Grogan)*, James Quinn *(Slim Dawson)*.

Above average (at that time) Universal programmer about an Army vet who returns home and takes up professional boxing in order to pay his sister's medical bills. Well-staged fight scenes and an impressive performance by Mayo, who made a most believable practitioner of the "sweet science."

d, William Worthington; w, Charles Sarver (based on a story by Leete Renick Brown); ph, Arthur Reeves.

Adventure **(PR:A MPAA:NR)**

AFRAID TO LOVE** (1927) 7 reels FP/LAS bw

Florence Vidor *(Katherine Silverton)*, Clive Brook *(Sir Reginald Belsize)*, Norman Trevor *(John Travers)*, Jocelyn Lee *(Helen De Seminiano)*, Arthur Lubin *(Rafael)*.

Shallow society comedy sees the routine plot centered around a will-reading. In this case, Brook is instructed not to marry Lee under penalty of losing his late uncle's millions. He marries nice girl Vidor to get around this, but ends up falling in love with her.

p, B. P. Schulberg; d, Edward H. Griffith; w, Doris Anderson, Joseph Jackson (based on the play "The Marriage of Kitty," adapted by C. Gordon Lennox from a play by Mme. Fred de Gresac, F. DeCroisset); t, Alfred Hustwick; ph, J. O. Taylor.

Comedy **(PR:A MPAA:NR)**

AFTER A MILLION* (1924) 5 reels SUN bw

Kenneth MacDonald *(Gregory Maxim)*, Ruth Dwyer *(Countess Olga)*, Alphonse Martell *(Ivan Senine)*, Joe Girard, Hal Craig, Jay Hunt, Stanley Bingham, Ada Bell.

Tired script about the adventures of MacDonald fulfilling the stipulations of a will drawn up by an exiled Russian nobleman. Most of the movie deals with a gang of Bolsheviks attempting to stop him and, of course, failing.

d, Jack Nelson.

Adventure **(PR:A MPAA:NR)**

AFTER BUSINESS HOURS** (1925) 6 reels COL bw

Elaine Hammerstein *(June King)*, Lou Tellegen *(John King)*, Phylis Haver *(Sylvia Vane)*, John Patrick *(Richard Downing)*, Lillian Langdon *(Mrs. Wentworth)*, William Scott *(James Hendricks)*, Lee Moran *(Jerry Stanton)*.

Outside of being the first Columbia release to play a first run at a Times Square theater, there is nothing about this society drama that deserves remembering. The story concerns a tightwad husband who does not believe women should be trusted with money and forbids his wife to buy most things. This of course (as often happened in pictures of this era) drives her to shoplifting, and almost into the arms of another man. The movie ends with the husband realizing his mistake after giving the other fellow a good thrashing.

d, Mal St. Clair; w, Douglas Doty (based on the story "Everything Money Can Buy" by Ethel Watts Mumford); t, Walter Anthony; ph, Dewey Wrigley; ed, Errol Taggart.

Drama **(PR:A MPAA:NR)**

AFTER DARK** (1924) 5 reels William Steiner/Hurricane bw

Charles Hutchinson *(Billy Fisk)*, Mary Beth Milford *(The Girl)*.

As an early serial star, Hutchinson gained enough popularity to star in his own series of action-plus programmers. They were extremely low-budgeted affairs that never attempted to deliver anything beyond thrills. This one, about a woman thief and stolen bonds, lived up to its potential.

d, James Chapin; w, J. F. Natteford.

Adventure **(PR:AA MPAA:NR)**

AFTER FIVE*** (1915) 4 reels LAS bw

Edward Abeles *(Ted Ewing)*, Sessue Hayakawa *(Oki, His Valet)*, Betty Shade *(Nora Hildreth)*, Jane Darwell *(Mrs. Russell)*, Theodore Roberts *(Bruno Schwartz)*, Monroe Salisbury, James Neill, Ernest Joy, Jode Mullally, Ernest Garcia.

When a young man thinks he has lost everything on the stock market, he takes out a life insurance policy to benefit his girl and hires gangsters to do him in. When he finds out the stock has actually doubled, he spends the remainder of the film dodging the killers. Of course, all ends well.

d, Oscar Apfel; w, William C. DeMille (based on a play by William and Cecil B. DeMille).

Drama **(PR:A MPAA:NR)**

AFTER MANY DAYS** (1919, Brit.) 6 reels Progress/BUT bw

Bruce Gordon *(Paul Irving)*, Alice Russon *(Marion Bramleyn)*, Irene Brown *(Connie)*, Adeline Hayden Coffin *(Mrs. Irving)*.

This British drama is about a burglar who causes a model's pregnancy, but leads a girl to think his artist brother was responsible.

p, Frank E. Spring; d, Sidney Morgan; w, Morgan.

Drama **(PR:C MPAA:NR)**

AFTER MANY YEARS*** (1930, Brit.) 6 reels Savana/Jury-MG bw

Henry Thompson, Nancy Kenyon, Savoy Havana Band.

The son of a murdered policeman journeys to Peru where he captures the drug smugglers who killed his father.

p, Alvin Saxon; d&w, Lawrence Huntington.

Crime **(PR:A MPAA:NR)**

AFTER MARRIAGE* (1925) 5 reels SUN/Madoc bw

Margaret Livingston *(Alma Lathrop)*, George Fisher *(David Morgan)*, Helen Lynch *(Lucille Spencer)* Herschel Mayall *(James Morgan)*, Annette Perry *(Mrs. George Spencer)*, Mary Young *(Mrs. James Morgan)*, Arthur Jasmine *(Bob Munro)*.

Fisher is disinherited by his father, Mayall, when he marries a working-class girl, Lynch. In the meantime, the father is carrying on an affair with an actress, Livingston, who seduces the unknowing son. Later, Mayall is murdered and Fisher is suspected, but Livingston turns out to be the killer. The end sees Fisher return to his forgiving wife.

d&w, Norman Dawn.

Drama **(PR:A MPAA:NR)**

AFTER MIDNIGHT*** (1921) 5 reels SELZ/SEL bw

Conway Tearle *(The Stranger/Gordon Phillips)*, Zena Keefe *(Mrs. Phillips)*, Macy Harlam *(Warren Black)*, Charlie Fag *(Mock Sing)*, Woo Lang *(Toy Sing)*, Harry Allen *(Harris)*.

Well directed programmer about a look-alike lost brother taking over for his dying, derelict sibling, then saving the family fortune (which was stolen from him anyway) and falling in love with the widow.

d, Ralph Ince; w, Edward J. Montagne (based on a story by John Lynch); ph, Jacob A. Badaracco.

Drama **(PR:A MPAA:NR)**

AFTER MIDNIGHT*** (1927) 7 reels MGM bw

Norma Shearer *(Mary)*, Lawrence Gray *(Joe Miller)*, Gwen Lee *(Maizie)*, Eddie Sturgis *(Red Smith)*, Phillip Sleeman *(Gus Van Gundy)*.

As the wife of MGM production head Irving Thalberg, actress Shearer was always assigned the best directors, cinematographers, writers, art directors, etc. Her films were given top priority, and they showed it. In this case Bell, a star director at Metro, provided the script as well, and it was tailor-made for Shearer and her vast audience. The story sees her as a plain but sincere girl who toils selling cigarettes, while her roommate sister dances in a nightclub chorus line and lives to party. After much sacrifice Shearer is finally in the position to buy a $1,000 bond which she intends to give her ex-convict boy friend to start a taxicab company. Unfortunately, the lovers have a spat and when the sister returns that night with a $1,000 tip which was given her by a rich admirer, it occurs to Shearer that frugality is the diet of chumps. This provides the star with an opportunity to do the very thing her audience loved most, metamorphosize from Plain Jane to ravishing beauty, as she enters into the exciting world of jazz bands and expensive champagne. The end sees her sister die in a drunken driving accident, leaving Shearer and her repentant gentleman friend alone to contemplate the true meaning of existence.

d&w, Monta Bell; t, Joe Farnham; ph, Percy Hilburn; ed, Blanche Sewell; set d, Cedric Gibbons, Richard Day.

Drama **(PR:A MPAA:NR)**

AFTER THE BALL* (1924) 7 reels Renco/FBO bw

Gaston Glass *(Arthur Trevelyan)*, Miriam Cooper *(Lorraine Trevelyan, His Sister)*, Thomas Guise *(Mark Trevelyan, His Father)*, Robert Frazer *(District Attorney)*, Edna Murphy *(Arthur's Wife)*, Eddie Gribbon *(A Crook)*.

Wrongly convicted and imprisoned, Glass permits his family to believe he has died. After many years, he escapes from prison. The real criminal confesses his guilt and Glass is reunited with his family. Inept and boring film written by the composer of the musical standard. Even the presence of Miriam Cooper, who did some wonderful things for D. W. Griffith, could not aid this hopelessly directed, scripted, and edited mess.

d, Dallas M. Fitzgerald; w, James Colwell (based on the song and story by Charles K. Harris); ph, Ross Fisher.

Drama **(PR:A MPAA:NR)**

AFTER THE SHOW* (1921) 6 reels FP/PAR bw

Jack Holt *(Larry Taylor)*, Lila Lee *(Eileen)*, Charles Ogle *(Pop O'Malley)*, Eve Southern *(Naomi Stokes)*, Shannon Day *(Lucy)*, Stella Seager *(Vera)*, Ethel Wales *(Landlady)*, Carlton King *(Mr. McGuire)*.

This inferior backstage retread of chorus girls and seduction impressed the critics only by Paramount's nerve in releasing it as a first-run feature.

d, William C. DeMille; w, Hazel Christie McDonald, Vianna Knowlton (based on the story "The Stage Door" by Rita Weiman); ph, Guy Wilky.

Drama **(PR:A MPAA:NR)**

AFTER THE STORM** (1928) 6 reels COL bw

Hobart Bosworth *(Martin Dane)*, Eugenia Gilbert *(Joan Wells/Mary Brian)*, Charles Delaney *(Joe Dane)*, Maude George *(Molly O'Doon)*, George Kuwa *(A. Hop)*, Linda Loredo *(Malay Dancer)*.

Good action sequences in this melodrama about a ship's captain (Bosworth) who takes his young son and deserts his wife, whom he believes has been unfaithful. Twenty years pass, and it is discovered that George, the woman Bosworth has taught his son Delaney to hate, has stowed away on board ship to be near her boy. A second young woman, Gilbert, is also a stowaway and, as it turns out, she just happens to be the daughter of another lady who also betrayed Bosworth. In the end the captain forgives his former wife, gives his blessings to Gilbert and his son, and then heroically gives up his life during a storm to save the young couple.

p, Harry Cohn; d, George B. Seitz; w, Will M. Ritchey (based on a story by Harold Shumate); ph, Joe Walker; ed, Arthur Roberts; art d, Robert E. Lee.

Drama **(PR:A MPAA:NR)**

AFTER THE VERDICT** (1929, Brit.) 10 reels Tschechowa/BIFD bw

Olga Tschechowa *(Vivian Denys)*, Warwick Ward *(Oliver Baratrie)*, Malcolm Tod *(Jim Gordon)*, Henry Victor *(Mr. Sabine)*, Betty Carter *(Mrs. Sabine)*, Daisy Campbell, Winter Hall, Andy Esmond, A. B. Inlson, Ivo Dawson.

British suspense yarn about the lady friend of a tennis star who is framed for the murder of a woman who had attempted to seduce him.

p, I. W. Schlesinger; d, Henrik Galeen; w, Alma Reville (based on a novel by Robert Hichens).

Drama **(PR:A MPAA:NR)**

AFTERWARDS** (1928, Brit.) 7 reels BUS/AP&D bw

Marjorie Hume *(Mrs. Carstairs)*, Julie Suedo *(Tocati)*, J. R. Tozer *(Dr. Anstice)*, Cecil Barry *(Bruce Cheniston)*, Dorinea Shirley *(Iris Wayne)*, Jean Jay *(Hilda Ryder)*, Pat Courtney *(Cherry)*, Fewlass Llewellyn *(Sir Richard Wayne)*, Frank Perfitt *(Maj. Carstairs)*.

In this English drama, a doctor discovers that his rival for the hand of the woman he loves is actually the former fiance of a girl the doctor had killed earlier, while attempting to save her from attacking Indians.

d, W. Lawson Butt; w, R. Byron Webber (based on the novel by Kathlyn Rhodes).

Drama **(PR:A MPAA:NR)**

AGAINST ALL ODDS*** (1924) 5 reels FOX bw

Charles "Buck" Jones *(Chick Newton)*, Dolores Rousse *(Judy Malone)*, Ben Hendricks, Jr. *(Jim Sawyer)*, William Scott *(Bill Warner)*, Thais Valdemar *(Olivetta)*, Bernard Siegel *(Lewis)*, William N. Bailey *(Tom Curtis)*, Jack McDonald *(Warner's Uncle)*.

Buck Jones returned to westerns (after starring in various non-cowboy films in which his name was changed to Charles) in this story which involved saving the life of a pal who was framed for murder. This was not his best, but Jones was always good.

d, Edmund Mortimer; w, Frederic Chapin (based on the story "Cuttle's Hired Man" by Max Brand); ph, Joseph Brotherton.

Western **(PR:A MPAA:NR)**

AHEAD OF THE LAW* (1926) 5 reels B. A. Goodman/A. G. Steen bw

Bruce Gordon, Doris Prince.

Nothing out of the ordinary in this little western about a Texas Ranger who cleans up the town and wins the love of the prettiest girl in the territory.

d, Forrest Sheldon.

Western **(PR:A MPAA:NR)**

AIN'T LOVE FUNNY?* (1927) 5 reels R-C/FBO bw

Alberta Vaughn *(Helena Brice)*, Thomas Wells *(Bob Kenwood)*, Syd Crossley *(Spike Murphy)*, Babe London *(Daisy Dooley)*, Johnny Gough *(Saunders)*, Charles Hill Mailes *(John Brice)*.

Weak comedy about a girl who, during the war, pledges her heart to every soldier she meets. Vaughn's performance is the only bright spot.

d, Del Andrews; w, Doris Anderson (based on a story by Lela Gidley, Kay Clement); t, Neal O'Hara, Jack Collins; ph, Allen Siegler.

Comedy **(PR:A MPAA:NR)**

AIR HAWK, THE** (1924) 5 reels Van Pelt-Wilson/FBO bw

Al Wilson *(Al Parker/The Air Hawk)*, Webster Cullinson *(Maj. Thomas)*, Frank Tomick *(Maj. Falles)*, Emmett King *(John Ames)*, Virginia Brown Faire *(Edith)*, Lee Shumway *(Robert McLeod)*, Frank Rice *(Hank)*, Leonard Clapham *(Kellar)*.

Wilson, an ace stunt pilot, plays a Secret Service agent who breaks up a gang of crooks trying to steal Faire's platinum mine after murdering her father. There is a great stunt in which Wilson leaps from his plane onto the wing of the escaping villain's plane and whips him in a mid-air fight.

d, Bruce Mitchell; w, George W. Pyper; ph, Bert Longenecker; ed, Della M. King.

Adventure **(PR:A MPAA:NR)**

AIR LEGION, THE** (1929) 7 reels FBO/RKO bw

Martha Sleeper *(Sally)*, Ben Lyon *(Dave)*, Antonio Moreno *(Steve)*, John Gough *(McGonigle)*, Colin Chase *(Field Manager)*.

Former war ace Moreno assumes responsibility for young Lyon, son of his late commander, training him to fly the mail route. Lyon loses his courage during a rough flight, and later deliberately wounds himself to avoid having to make a mercy flight during a tornado. Lyon finally proves his real mettle by saving Moreno's life, and further demonstrates his manhood by stealing his mentor's girl friend, Sleeper. This attempt on the part of FBO to cash in on the popularity of flying movies is pretty much a small-budget affair. All of the cliches are there but Lyon and Moreno are an interesting pairing.

d, Bert Glennon; w, Fred Myton (based on a story by James Ashmore Creelman); t, Randolph Bartlett; ph, Paul Perry; ed, Archie Marshek.

Drama **(PR:A MPAA:NR)**

AIR MAIL, THE**** (1925) 8 reels FP/PAR bw

Warner Baxter *(Russ Kane)*, Billie Dove *(Alice Rendon)*, Mary Brian (Minnie Wade), Douglas Fairbanks, Jr. *(Sandy)*, George Irving *(Peter Rendon)*, Richard Tucker *(Jim Cronin)*, Guy Oliver *(Bill Wade)*, Lee Shumway *(Scotty)*, Jack Byron *(Rene Lenoir)*, John Webb Dillon *(Donald McKee)*, Lloyd Whitlock *(Speck)*.

America's fascination with aviation, and especially flying the mail, made this film a winner. Baxter plays the regenerated "I don't give a damn, just give me my joystick" ex-Army pilot, who not only learns to love the service, but flies through storms, delivers medicine, and battles sky pirates. He also makes a man out of Fairbanks, Jr. (who gives a good performance), marries Dove, and carries with a sense of sincere authority the motto of the air mail carrier, "Nor rain, nor snow, nor wind, nor night, can stop the pilot in his flight!"

d, Irvin Willat; w, James Shelley Hamilton (based on a story by Byron Morgan); ph, Alfred Gilks.

Adventure **(PR:A MPAA:NR)**

AIR MAIL PILOT, THE** (1928) 6 reels Superlative/HM bw

James F. Fulton *(Jimmie Dean)*, Earl Metcalfe *(Tom Miller)*, Blanche Mehaffey *(Ruth Ross)*, DeWitt Jennings *(Robert Ross)*, Max Hawley *(Hap Lester)*, Carl Stockdale *(Addison Simms)*.

A young air mail pilot prevents the successful robbery of the mail (by his rival for the love of Mehaffey) by jumping from his airplane onto the wing of the crook's plane, giving him a pasting before bringing the craft down.

d, Gene Carroll; w, Harriet Virginia; ph, Lew Lang.

Adventure **(PR:A MPAA:NR)**

AIR PATROL, THE* (1928) 5 reels UNIV bw

Al Wilson *(Al Langdon)*, Elsa Benham *(Mary Lacy)*, Taylor Duncan *(Capt. Carter)*, Jack Mower *(Michael Revere)*, Monte Montague *(Sid Swivel)*, Art Goebel, Frank Clark *(Aviators)*, Frank Tomick *(Kelly)*.

Seeking a mysterious gem smuggler, Wilson of the Air Patrol goes undercover to join the gang of the man he suspects, Mower. Captured by the criminals along with the beautiful Benham he breaks his bonds and pursues the escaping Mower in his plane to rescue the abducted lady and bring the gang to justice. Wilson was a good stunt pilot who wrote and starred in a series of "thrill" pictures geared to the Saturday matinee audience by Universal. This movie does not pretend to be much, and it succeeds.

d, Bruce Mitchell; w, William Lester (based on a story by Al Wilson); t, Gardner Bradford; ph, William S. Adams; ed, De Leon Anthony.

Adventure **(PR:A MPAA:NR)**

ALADDIN FROM BROADWAY*** (1917) 5 reels VIT bw

Edith Storey *(Faimeh)*, Antonio Moreno *(Jack Stanton)*, William Duncan *(William Fitzgerald)*, Otto Lederer, Laura Winston, George Holt.

Good program feature about a young American who poses as an Arab to enter the sacred city of Mecca on a bet. While there he rescues the daughter of an Englishman who had been abducted in the Damascus uprising some 18 years earlier.

d, William Wolbert; w, Helmer Walton Bergman (based on the novel by Frederick Stewart Isham).

Adventure **(PR:A MPAA:NR)**

ALADDIN'S OTHER LAMP** (1917) 5 reels Rolfe/Metro bw

Viola Dana *(Patsy)*, Robert Walker, Augustus Phillips, Henry Hallman, Ricca Allen, Edward Elkas, Nellie Grant, Louis B. Foley, Elsie McLeod.

This variation of the Arabian Nights theme has a young slave reunited with her mother after an effectively filmed dream sequence dealing with a magical lamp. A children's film with good special effects.

d, John H. Collins; w, June Mathis (based on the play "The Dream Girl" by Willard Mack); ph, John Arnold.

Comedy/Fantasy **(PR:AA MPAA:NR)**

ALARM CLOCK ANDY*** (1920) 5 reels PAR bw

Charles Ray *(Andrew Gray)*, George Webb *(William Blinker)*, Millicent Fisher *(Dorothy Wells)*, Tom Guise *(Mr. Wells)*, Andrew Robson *(Mr. Dodge)*.

Ray, one of the most popular stars of the early days, plays a bashful, stuttering clerk who loves the boss' daughter. Before the movie is over, Ray, of course, overcomes his shyness, lands a huge order, and marries the girl.

d, Jerome Storm; sup, Thomas H. Ince; w, (based on a story by Agnes Christine Johnston); ph, Chester Lyons

Drama **(PR:A MPAA:NR)**

ALASKAN, THE**** (1924) 7 reels FP/PAR bw

Thomas Meighan *(Alan Holt)*, Estelle Taylor *(Mary Standish)*, John Sainpolis *(Rossland)*, Frank Campeau *(Stampede Smith)*, Anna May Wong *(Keok)*, Alphonz Ethier *(John Graham)*, Maurice Cannon *(Tautuk)*, Charles Ogle *(The Lawyer)*.

A perfect part for Meighan, who plays an Alaskan determined to stop big business interests from taking over the land and enterprises of the long-time settlers. Meighan wins out in the end, of course, but only after taking the robber barons before a Senate Investigating Committee and holding them off in one of the most exciting fist fights ever filmed.

d, Herbert Brenon; w, Willis Goldbeck (based on a novel by James Oliver Curwood); t, H. H. Caldwell; ph, James [Wong] Howe.

Adventure **(PR:A MPAA:NR)**

ALBANY NIGHT BOAT, THE** (1928) 6 reels TS bw

Olive Borden *(Georgie)*, Ralph Emerson *(Ken)*, Duke Martin *(Steve)*, Nellie Bryden *(Mother Crary)*, Helen Marlow *(The Blonde)*.

Ferryboat crewman Emerson rescues Borden when she leaps overboard from the deck of a pleasure boat to escape the clutches of a lecherous yachtsman. He and Borden marry and share a riverfront house with Martin, a fellow crewman, who harasses the beauteous Borden with his amorous advances. Returning from a river crossing, Emerson shines his searchlight on his own home and witnesses an attempt at rape by Martin. Swimming to the riverbank, Emerson scales the palisades and saves his bride.

d, Alfred Raboch; w, Wellyn Totman; t, Al Martin, Frederick Hatton, Fanny Hatton; ph, Ernest Miller; ed, Byron Robinson.

Drama **(PR:A MPAA:NR)**

ALEX THE GREAT* (1928) 7 reels FBO bw

Richard "Skeets" Gallagher *(Alex)*, Albert Conti *(Ed)*, Patricia Avery *(Muriel)*, Ruth Dwyer *(Alice)*, Charles Byer *(Brown)*, J. Barney Sherry *(Smith)*.

Poorly done film about a Vermont simpleton, who wins both a good job and an heiress when he travels to the big city, is of interest only because it features Gallagher (who starred in D. W. Griffith's last film THE STRUGGLE) and is directed by Murphy, who was responsible for Bessie Smith's only movie ST. LOUIS BLUES.

d, Dudley Murphy; w, Murphy (based on the novel by H. C. Witwer); t, Randolph Bartlett; ph, Virgil Miller; ed, Ann McKnight.

Comedy **(PR:A MPAA:NR)**

ALF'S BUTTON*** (1920, Brit.) 7 reels Hepworth bw

Leslie Hensen *(Alf Higgins)*, Alma Taylor *(Liz)*, Gerald Ames *(Lt. Denis Allen)*, James Carew *(Eustace the Genie)*, Eileen Dennes *(Lady Isobel Fitzpeter)*, John McAndrews *(Bill Grant)*, Jean Cadell *(Vicar's Wife)*, Gwynne Herbert *(Lady Fitzpeter)*.

English comedy in which a WW I soldier discovers that a button on his field jacket is made from Aladdin's magical lamp. Of course his three wishes provide the laughs.

d, Cecil M. Hepworth; w, Blanche McIntosh (based on a play by W. A. Darlington).

Comedy **(PR:A MPAA:NR)**

ALI BABA AND THE FORTY THIEVES* (1918) 5 reels FOX bw

George Stone, Gertrude Messinger, Lewis Sargent, Buddy Messinger, G. Raymond Nye, Raymond Lee, Charles Hincus, Marie Messinger, Jack Hull.

A Fox "Kiddie Picture," in which children made up the cast and the sets were built to scale. These films were aimed at the moppet market, but never quite made it. As the title indicates, this one is about the poor woodcutter who becomes rich by overhearing the magic words "Open Sesame."

d, C. M. and S. A. Franklin; w, Bernard McConville (based on the story in the ancient tales *The Arabian Nights Entertainment)*; ph, Frank Good, Harry Gerstad.

Fantasy **(PR:A MPAA:NR)**

ALIAS JIMMY VALENTINE*** (1920) 6 reels Metro bw

Bert Lytell *(Lee Randall, Alias Jimmy Valentine)*, Vola Vale *(Rose Lane)*, Eugene Pallette *("Red" Jocelyn)*, Wilton Taylor *(Detective Doyle)*, Marc Robbins *(Bill Avery)*, Robert Dunbar *(Lt. Gov. Fay)*, Winter Hall *(William Lane)*, James Farley *(Cotton)*.

An American classic about a reformed safecracker, Lytell, who assumes a second identity and lands the position of assistant cashier at the First National Bank. There is one detective who suspects the truth and hounds him until the time Lytell must make a decision to save a child who is locked in a vault.

d, Edmund Mortimer; sup, Maxwell Karger; w, Finis Fox (based on the play by Paul Armstrong from the short story "A Retrieved Reformation" by O. Henry); ph, Sol Polito.

Crime **(PR:A MPAA:NR)**

ALIAS JULIUS CAESAR**** (1922) 5 reels Charles Ray/FN bw

Charles Ray *(Billy Barnes), Barbara Bedford (Helen)*, William Scott *(Harry)*, Robert Fernandez *(Tom)*, Fred Miller *(Dick)*, Eddie Gibbon *("Nervy"Norton)*, Tom Wilson *(Mose)*, Harvey Clark *(Monsieur Dumas)*, Gus Thomas *(Harrington Whitney)*, Milton Ross *(Police Sergeant)*, S. J. Bingham *(Detective)*, Phillip Dunham *(Billy's Valet)*, Bert Offord *(Janitor)*.

After having his clothes stolen while showering, Ray attempts to make his way home draped in a shower curtain. He is arrested for "impersonating Julius Caesar" and thrown into a jail cell with Gribbon, a society thief. After release, he attends a party where Gribbon is at work. The crook, delighted to see his former prison mate, enlists his help by slipping him the jewels as he works the room. Eventually the cops arrive, arrest the bad guy, and everyone, especially Ray's romantic interest, Bedford, hails Ray a hero. A very funny movie and one of Ray's best.

d, Charles Ray; w, Richard Andres; t, Edward Withers; ph, George Rizard; ed, Harry Decker; art d, Howard Berbeck.

Comedy **(PR:A MPAA:NR)**

ALIAS MARY BROWN*** (1918) 5 reels TRI bw

Pauline Starke *(Betty)*, Casson Ferguson *(Dick Browning)*, A. N. Millett *(Hewlett)*, Eugene Burr *(Watson)*, Sidney De Gray *(Carnac)*, Walter Belasco *(Uncle Ike)*, E. Thompson *(Gunter)*, Dick Rosson *(Weasel)*, Alberta Lee *(Mrs. Browning)*.

Nifty thriller reverses the burglar role by having the culprit assume the disguise of a *woman*. Actually, the fellow's deceased parents were impoverished and driven to the grave by the people he robs, which certainly entitles him to pull his exciting capers and live happily ever after.

d, Henri D'Elba, William Dowlan; w, E. Magnus Ingleton (based on her own story); ph, Elgin Leslie.

Crime **(PR:A MPAA:NR)**

ALIAS MIKE MORAN*** (1919) 5 reels PAR bw

Wallace Reid *(Larry Young)*, Ann Little *(Elaine Debaux)*, Emory Johnson *(Mike Moran)*, Charles Ogle *(Peter Young)*, Edythe Chapman *(Ma Young)*, William Elmer, Winter Hall, Jean Calhoun, Guy Oliver.

This film about a fortune-hunting coward, Reid, who shirks his duty to country by paying an ex-convict to take his place in the draft, was well done on all counts. After the imposter dies heroically, the shirker reforms, joins the Canadian Army, and loses a hand while fighting gallantly. Reid handles what was, for most of the picture, a very unsympathetic role with great skill.

d, James Cruze; w, Will M. Ritchey (based on the story "Open Sesame" by Frederick Orin Bartlett); ph, Frank Urson.

Drama **(PR:A MPAA:NR)**

ALIAS MRS. JESSOP** (1917) 5 reels Metro bw

Emily Stevens, Howard Hall, Donald Hall, William H. Tooker, Sue Balfour, Lillian Page, Eldean Steuart.

Another variation of the good-bad sister yarn, only this time with cousins. Nice double exposure work, and a fine performance by Stevens in a dual role, make it work well on the programmer level.

d, William S. Davis; sup, Maxwell Karger; w, Albert Shelby Le Vino (based on a story by Blair Hall).

Drama **(PR:A MPAA:NR)**

ALIAS THE DEACON** (1928) 7 reels UNIV bw

Jean Hersholt *(The Deacon)*, June Marlow *(Nancy)*, Ralph Graves *(John Adams)*, Myrtle Stedman *(Mrs. Clark)*, Lincoln Plummer *(Cunningham)*, Ned Sparks *("Slim" Sullivan)*, Tom Kennedy *("Bull" Moran)*, Maurice Murphy *(Willie Clark)*, George West *(George)*.

Hersholt, playing a professional gambler known as "The Deacon," meets two young hobos, Marlow and Graves, on a train. When other hobos discover that Marlow is a girl in boy's clothing, she is menaced, and Hersholt helps save her. In the next town, Graves is severely beaten in a prizefight in the hope of making enough money to set up housekeeping with Marlow. Cheated of his prize money by crooked promoter Plummer, Graves is arrested on a spurious count. Hersholt sets things right by besting Plummer in a card game and forcing him to confess his role in the frame-up. Dated even in its time, with action sequences added only for a bit of excitement, this film falls short of the mark despite a good performance by Hersholt.

d, Edward Sloman; w, Charles Kenyon (based on a play by John B. Hymer, Leroy Clement); t, Walter Anthony; ph, Gilbert Warrenton, Jackson Rose; ed, Byron Robinson.

Drama **(PR:A MPAA:NR)**

ALIAS THE LONE WOLF* (1927) 7 reels COL bw

Bert Lytell *(Michael Lanyard)*, Lois Wilson *(Eve de Montalais)*, Paulette Duvall *(Liane DeLorme)*, William V. Mong *(Whitaker Monk)*, Ned Sparks *(Phinuit)*, Ann Brody *(Fifi)*, Alphonz Ethier *(Inspector Crane)*, James Mason *(Popinot)*.

The third picture in the successful series (which carried on well into the sound-film years) dealing with the derring-do of reformed high-society jewel thief Michael Lanyard, alias "The Lone Wolf." Lytell plays Lanyard, who meets the glamorous Wilson aboard a luxury liner. Wilson plans to smuggle her valuable gems through customs upon the ship's arrival in New York in order to get enough money to assist her errant brother. Jewel thieves Sparks and Duvall are also aboard the vessel; plotting to purloin the gems, they inform Wilson of Lytell's criminal background. Mong poses as a customs agent in order to get the jewelry, but Lytell—actually a Secret Service agent—foils the thieves' plot. As with others in the LONE WOLF series (see Index), implausible events are somewhat redeemed by action, romance, humor, and likable characters.

p, Harry Cohn; d, Edward H. Griffith; w, Griffith, Dorothy Howell (based on the novel by Louis Joseph Vance); ph, J. O. Taylor; art d, Robert E. Lee.

Crime **(PR:A MPAA:NR)**

ALIAS THE NIGHT WIND*** (1923) 5 reels FOX bw

William Russell *(Bing Howard)*, Maude Wayne *(Katherine Maxwell)*, Charles K. French *(Amos Chester)*, Wade Boteler *(Thomas Clancy)*, Donald MacDonald *(Clifford Rushton)*, H. Milton Ross *(R. J. Brown)*, Charles Wellesley *(Police Commissioner)*, Mark Fenton *(The Nurse)*, Otto Matieson, Bob Klein, Bert Lindley *(Detectives)*.

Russell, the athletic, daredevil star of serial fame (THE DIAMOND FROM THE SKY), appeared in a number of child-oriented, action-packed progammers. In this one, he clears himself of stealing bonds.

d, Joseph Franz; w, Robert N. Lee (based on the novel by Varick Vanardy); ph, Ernest Miller.

Adventure **(PR:A MPAA:NR)**

ALICE ADAMS*** (1923) 6 reels Encore/AEX bw

Florence Vidor *(Alice Adams)*, Claude Gillingwater *(Virgil Adams)*, Vernon Steele *(Arthur Russell)*, Harold Goodwin *(Walter Adams)*, Margaret McWade *(Mrs. Adams)*, Thomas Ricketts *(J. A. Lamb)*, Margaret Landis *(Henrietta Lamb)*, Gertrude Astor *(Mildred Palmer)*.

Dissatisfied with her lower-middle-class existence, the pretentious Vidor lives in fantasy, attempting to impress her acquaintances with her posture of substantial wealth. Finally, during a dinner with Steele, she is embarrassed into a realization of her actual circumstances. She decides to get a job to help her failing father. Good re-creation of Tarkington's small-town America. Director Lee has a nice feeling for the subject matter and Vidor essays her part with humor, tempered by the right amount of pathos. One of the many films Vidor made under the aegis of her then-husband, King Vidor (they were divorced a year after this picture's release) before he attained true fame with MGM.

d&w, Rowland V. Lee; w, Lee (based on a story by Booth Tarkington); ph, George Barnes.

Comedy **(PR:A MPAA:NR)**

ALIEN, THE*** (1915) 8 reels SEL bw

George Beban, Edward Gillespie, Hayward Ginn, Andrea Lynne, Thelma Salter, Jack Davidson.

Interesting and artistically successful blending of film and live theater. Beban, a distinguished actor and playwright, used THE ALIEN, directed skillfully by Ince, as an elaborate prolog to his live performance in the play "The Sign of the Rose." Beban, the film, and his play were a great success at the Astor Theatre in New York and in subsequent showings.

d, Thomas H. Ince; w, (based on "The Sign of the Rose" by C. T. Dazey, George Beban).

Drama **(PR:A MPAA:NR)**

ALIEN ENEMY, AN*** (1918) 5 reels Paralta bw

Louise Glaum *(Neysa von Igel/Frau Meyer)*, Mary Jane Irving *(Fraulein Bertha Meyer)*, Thurston Hall *(David J. Hale)*, Albert Allardt *(Emil Koenig)*, Charles C. Hammond *(Adolph Schmidt)*, Jay Morley *(Maj. Samuel J. Putnam)*, Roy Laidlaw *(Louis Meyer)*, Joseph J. Dowling *(Baron von Mecklin)*, Clifford Alexander *(Wireless Operator)*.

Predictable wartime propaganda, with a good performance by the always excellent Glaum, the stage and screen actress who appeared in many Mack Sennett comedies.

d, Wallace Worsley, w, Monte M. Katterjohn; ph, L. Guy Wilkey.

War **(PR:C MPAA:NR)**

ALIEN SOULS** (1916) 5 reels LAS bw

Sessue Hayakawa *(Sakata)*, Tsuru Aoki *(Yuri Chan)*, Earle Foxe *(Aleck Lindsay)*, Grace Benham *(Mrs. Conway)*, J. Parks Jones *(Jack Holloway)*, *Violet Malone (Gertrude Van Ness)*, Dorothy Abril *(Geraldine Smythe)*.

Hayakawa, a rich Japanese importer, raises his best friend's daughter to believe she is a wealthy heiress. At college, she falls for a fortune-hunting American who persuades her to elope. Hayakawa learns of this, intercedes, and reveals the truth. The despondent girl's attempted suicide fails and her benefactor proposes marriage in spite of her shame. Well-acted film which could have been done more effectively in one reel.

p, Jesse Lasky; d, Frank Reicher; w, Margaret Turnbull (based on a story by Hector Turnbull).

Drama **(PR:A MPAA:NR)**

ALIMONY** (1924) 7 reels R-C/FBO bw

Grace Darmond *(Marion Mason)*, Warner Baxter *(Jimmy Mason)*, Ruby Miller *(Gloria Du Bois)*, William A. Carroll *(Philip Coburn)*, Jackie Saunders *(Betty Coburn)*, Clyde Fillmore *(Granville)*, Herschel Mayall *(Blake)*, Alton Brown *(Grey)*.

Darmond guides her husband from poverty to wealth, but when he starts playing around, she divorces him and is awarded a huge alimony settlement. Later, when his paramours leave him bankrupt, Darmond takes him back and makes a success of him again.

d, James W. Horne; w, Wyndham Gittens, E. Mangus Ingleton (based on a story by Ashley T. Locke); ph, Joseph Dubray, Pierre Collings.

Drama **(PR:A MPAA:NR)**

ALL ABOARD** (1927) 7 reels B&H/FN bw

Johnny Hines, *(Johnny)*, Edna Murphy *(May Brooks)*, Henry Barrows *(Thomas Brooks)*, Babe London *(Princess)*, Sojin *(Prince)*, Frank Hagney *(Ali Ben Ome)*, Dot Farley *(Aunt Patsy)*, James Leonard *(El Humid)*.

Fired from his job as a shoe salesman, Hines is hired as a guide for a group of tourists headed for the Middle East. He falls hard for Murphy, daughter of the group's leader. Once in Egypt, Hines is duped by Sojin into getting married to obese London, a native princess. Discovering that Murphy has been abducted by desert bandits, Hines abandons his portly bride and goes to Murphy's rescue. London's marriage to the infidel proves to be invalid, so Hines is free to marry his true love, Murphy. This Hines comedy (partially set in Egypt to provide desert thrills) doesn't quite come off. Hines was always good for a laugh, but this was not up to his standard.

d, Charles Hines; w, (based on a story by Matt Taylor); ph, George Peters.

Comedy **(PR:A MPAA:NR)**

ALL AMERICAN, THE (SEE: OLYMPIC HERO, THE, 1928)

ALL DOLLED UP*** (1921) 5 reels UNIV bw

Gladys Walton *(Maggie Quick)*, Edward Hearn *(James Montgomery Johnson)*, Richard Norton *(Percy Prack)*, Florence Turner *(Eva Bundy)*, Helen Bruneau *(The Widow)*, Fred Malatesta *(Amilo Rodolpho)*, Ruth Royce *(Mademoiselle Scarpa)*, John Goff *(Eddie Bowman)*, Frank Norcross *(Mr. Shankley)*, Muriel Godfrey Turner *(Madame De Jercasse)*, Lydia Yeamans Titus *(Landlady)*.

Good actioner about a department store salesgirl who saves a wealthy spinster from a pickpocket and later prevents her from being blackmailed. There are several exciting fights handled beautifully by the athletic Walton, who is awarded a million dollars for her efforts.

d, Rollin Sturgeon; w, A. P. Younger (based on a story by John Colton); ph, Alfred Gosden.

Adventure **(PR:A MPAA:NR)**

ALL FOR A GIRL*** (1915) 5 reels Mirograph bw

Renee Kelley, Roy Applegate, Frank De Vernon, Sue Balfour, E. T. Roseman, Robert Lawrence, Georgia Harvey, Sidney D'Albrook, Jerold Hevener, E. G. Longman, Margaret Willard, Al Brady, Bert Tuey.

Beautifully photographed, written, and acted rural drama about love, adversity, and triumph. Particularly good is the now all-but-forgotten British stage, screen, and vaudeville veteran Kelly.

d, Roy Applegate; w, (based on a play by Rupert Hughes); ph, George Condert.

Drama **(PR:A MPAA:NR)**

ALL MAN* (1916) 5 reels PEER/WORLD bw

Robert Warwick *(Jim Blake)*, Louis Crisel *(Sandy Bluebottle)*, Charles Duncan *(John Sherman Blake)*, Alec B. Francis *(John Maynard)*, Gerda Holmes *(Ethel Maynard)*, Mollie King *(Alice Maynard)*, George McQuarrie *(Gillette Barker)*, Johnny Hines *(Snap Higgins)*, Henry West *(McKin)*.

Perfectly awful western which was shot in New Jersey and looked it. In one scene, supposed to take place on a Montana ranch, a stretch of Macadam boulevard is clearly visible in the background. Marion, who wrote the script, was destined to go on to better things.

d, Emile Chautard; w, Frances Marion (based on a story by Willard Mack); ph, Lucien Tainguy.

Western **(PR:A MPAA:NR)**

ALL MAN* (1918) 5 reels VIT bw

Harry Morey *(John Olsen)*, Betty Blythe *(Belle Follot)*, Bob Gaillard *(Lt. Reilly)*, George Majeroni *(Marco Paroni)*, Carleton King *(Morris Sachs)*, Bernard Siegel *(Ryan)*.

Crime story that starts off well enough but falls apart by the end. Decent performances, though, by Morey and Blythe, considering what they had to work with. Future "Queen of Sheba" Blythe, a former stage actress in Europe and on Broadway, was making her film debut in this Brooklyn Vitagraph studio production.

d, Paul Scardon; w, Garfield Thompson (based on the story "Fiddler's Green" by Donn Byrne).

Crime **(PR:A MPAA:NR)**

ALL MEN ARE LIARS** (1919, Brit.) 5 reels Progress/BUT bw

Alice Russon *(Hope)*, Bruce Gordon *(Stephen)*, Jessie Earle *(Isobel)*, George Harrington *(Luke)*.

In this British drama, the son of a London missionary is forced to marry a woman whose only thought is of herself.

p, Frank E. Spring; d&w, Sydney Morgan (based on the novel by Joseph Hocking).

Drama **(PR:A MPAA:NR)**

ALL NIGHT**** (1918) 5 reels BLUE bw

Carmel Myers, Rudolph Valentino, Charles Dorian, Mary Warren, William Dyer, Wadsworth Harris, Jack Hull, Lydia Yeamans Titus.

Hilarious farce, often imitated over the years, has Valentino as a bright young entrepreneur—down on his luck, but with the promise of a $1 million investment from a western copper magnate—throwing a dinner party for a couple his wife has just introduced. The fun begins when the investor sends a wire saying that he is in town and on his way over to see how well his would-be associate manages his home. Lots of role switching here, as the guests pose as hosts and the hosts take on the role of servants. This was the kind of fare ideally suited for the talkies, but nonetheless worked beautifully in the silent medium. And, it must be said, in this early role Valentino proved once again he really could act.

d, Paul Powell; w, Fred Myton (based on the short story "One Bright Idea" by Edgar Franklin).

Comedy **(PR:A MPAA:NR)**

ALL OF A SUDDEN NORMA*
(1919) 5 reels B.B. Features for Exhibitors Mutual bw

Bessie Barriscale *(Norma Brisbane)*, Joseph Dowling *(Hamilton Brisbane)*, Albert Colby *(Cuthbert Van Zelt)*, R. Henry Grey *(Oliver Garrett)*, Frank Leigh *(Duke of Duffield)*, Melbourne MacDowell *(Emerson Trent)*.

This lavishly produced, capably acted nonsense is boring and completely improbable. Of interest only due to Barriscale's stature in the history of film as veteran performer and finally the head of her own production company.

d, Howard Hickman; w, Jack Cunningham (based on a story by Thomas Edgelow); ph, L. Guy Wilkey.

Drama **(PR:A MPAA:NR)**

ALL ROADS LEAD TO CALVARY** (1921, Brit.) 5 reels Astra bw

Manna Grey *(Nan Phillips)*, Bertram Burleigh *(Bob Phillips)*, Mary Ordette *(Joan Allway)*, Roy Travers *(Preacher)*, Julie Kean *(Hilda Phillips)*, J. Nelson Ramsay *(Mr. Allway), David Hallett (Arthur Allway)*, George Travers *(Editor)*, Lorna Rathbone *(Editor's Wife)*, Kate Gurney *(Landlady)*.

English drama about a member of Parliament who leaves his mistress and gives up his career when his common-born wife tries to poison herself.

p, H. W. Thompson; d&w, Kenelm Foss (based on the novel by Jerome K. Jerome).

Drama **(PR:C MPAA:NR)**

ALL SORTS AND CONDITIONS OF MEN** (1921, Brit.) 5 reels ID bw

Renee Kelly *(Angela Messenger)*, Rex Davis *(Harry le Briton)*, James Lindsay *(Lord Jocelyn)*, Mary Brough *(Landlady)*.

In this English drama, a recreational facility is built for the poor by a lord's nephew and the heiress of a brewery.

d, Georges Treville; w, Colden Lore (based on the novel by Sir Walter Besant).

Drama **(PR:A MPAA:NR)**

ALL SOULS EVE** (1921) 6 reels Realart bw

Mary Miles Minter *(Alice Heath/Nora O'Hallahan)*, Jack Holt *(Roger Heath)*, Carmen Phillips *(Olivia Larkin)*, Clarence Geldert *(Dr. Sandy McAllister)*, Mickey Moore *(Peter Heath)*, Fanny Midgley *(Mrs. O'Hallahan)*, Lottie Williams *(Belle Emerson)*.

This fair programmer was one of many films, at the time, dealing with the concept that the dead can return to visit those who believe. Very nice performance by Minter in the dual role of Irish maid and sculptor's wife.

d, Chester Franklin; w, Elmer Harris (based on the play by Anne Crawford Flexner); ph, Faxon Dean.

Drama **(PR:A MPAA:NR)**

ALL THE BROTHERS WERE VALIANT** (1923) 7 reels Metro bw

Malcolm McGregor *(Joel Shore)*, Billie Dove *(Priscilla Holt)*, Lon Chaney *(Mark Shore)*, William H. Orlamond *(Aaron Burnham)*, Robert McKim *(Finch)*, Robert Kortman *(Varde)*, Otto Brower *(Morrell)*, Curt Rehfeld *(Hooper)*, William V. Mong *(Cook)*, Leo Willis *(Tom)*, Shannon Day *(The Brown Girl)*.

Against tradition, beautiful Dove joins her husband McGregor— whom she suspects of cowardice—aboard the whaling vessel he commands. They find McGregor's lost brother, Chaney, who had been much admired by all. Chaney incites the crew to mutiny when his younger brother refuses to alter the ship's course to recover a purported hidden treasure. Blood proves thicker than the surrounding ocean as the brothers ultimately come to one another's assistance, with Chaney losing his life in the process. Dove acknowledges her husband's courage. Interesting for a view of Chaney with an ordinary face and no hump on his back. Remade— though much altered—in 1928 as ACROSS TO SINGAPORE.

d, Irvin V. Willat; w, Julien Josephson (based on the novel by Ben Ames Williams); ph, Robert Kurrle.

Drama **(PR:A MPAA:NR)**

ALL THE SAD WORLD NEEDS* (1918, Brit.) 5 reels BA/STOLL bw

Lauri de Freece *(Peep O'Day)*, Joan Legge *(Rhoda Grover)*, Lennox Pawle *(George Grover)*, Adelaide Grace *(Miss Flint)*, Cyprian Hyde *(Ernest Hanbury)*.

An impoverished violinist's music is plagiarized by a concertina player who uses it to gain fortune and fame.

d, Hubert Herrick; w, Kenelm Foss.

Drama **(PR:A MPAA:NR)**

ALL THE WINNERS** (1920, Brit.) 6 reels G. B. Samuelson/GEN bw

Owen Nares *(Tim Hawker)*, Maudie Dunham *(Dora Dalton)*, Sam Livesey *(Pedro Darondarez)*, Maidie Hope *(Picco)*, Ena Beaumont *(Daphne Dression)*.

English mystery about a prosperous sportsman who is almost forced by blackmail into making his daughter marry a criminal.

d, Geoffrey H. Malins; w, (based on the novel *Wicked* by Arthur Applin).

Crime **(PR:A MPAA:NR)**

ALL THE WORLD TO NOTHING*** (1919) 6 reels Pathe bw

William Russell, Winifred Westover, J. Morris Foster, Hayward Mack.

Exciting rags-to-riches story dealing with stock market manipulation is an impressive early directorial effort by the great King. King demanded, and received, depth of character from his players and honest detail in his sets and locations. Here, part of the excitement of the film is an account of 1919 financial skullduggery on the big market in the East. A bit of history for market players today.

d, Henry King; w, Stephen Fox (based on the novel by Wyndham Martyn).

Drama **(PR:A MPAA:NR)**

ALL THE WORLD'S A STAGE*** (1917, Brit.) 5 reels HD bw

Eve Balfour *(Lavender Lawn)*, Esme Beringer *(Delia Rackham)*, James Lindsay *(Geoffrey Daunton)*, Leslie Howard Gordon *(David Hart)*, Judd Green *(Capt. Offley)*.

Complicated English mystery about the protege of a successful London producer who marries the son of a wealthy land owner— though she thought he was only a fisherman—after having been framed for the murder of her mentor by a jealous actress.

p, Julius Hagen, Harold Double; d, Harold Weston; w, Leslie Howard Gordon (based on the novel by Herbert Everett).

Mystery **(PR:C MPAA:NR)**

ALL WOMAN*** (1918) 6 reels Goldwyn bw

Mae Marsh *(Susan Sweeney)*, Jere Austin *(Strong)*, Arthur Housman *(Dick)*, John Sainpolis *(Tupper)*, Warner Baxter, Jack Dillon, Joe Henaway, Hazel Alden, Madelyn Klare, Elsie Sothern, Lois Alexander, George White.

The wonderful but often difficult to direct Marsh is a city girl who inherits a country hotel, cleans up a depraved saloon, brings a thief to justice, helps a young couple get together, and ends up marrying the country attorney, who rightfully thinks of her as being "all woman." Another of the inferior films Marsh made under her Goldwyn contract, one which eventually drove her to a brief retirement from the screen.

d, Hobart Henley; w, (based on a story by E. Lloyd Sheldon); ph, Oliver T. Marsh.

Drama **(PR:A MPAA:NR)**

ALL WRONG*** (1919) 5 reels Pathe bw

Bryant Washburn *(Warren Kent)*, Mildred Davis *(Betty Thompson)*, Charles Bennett *(Donald Thompson)*, Helen Dumbar *(Mrs. Donald Thompson)*, Fred Montague *(Randolph Graham)*, Margaret Livingston.

The engaging Washburn portrays a young salesman so enamored by courtship that, after marrying, he elects to live alone and continue to date his bride. After a number of very funny situations in which he bounces from one jam to another, he finally comes to the conclusion that he has been "all wrong."

d, William Worthington, Raymond B. West; w, Jack Cunningham (based on a story by Mildred Considine); ph, Clyde De Vinna, Clyde Cook.

Comedy **(PR:A MPAA:NR)**

ALLEY CAT, THE** (1929, Brit.) 7 reels British and Foreign bw

Mabel Poulton *(Polly)*, Jack Trevor *(Jimmy Rice)*, Clifford McLaglen *(Simon Beck)*,

Shayle Gardner *(Inspector Fordham)*, Margit Manstead *(Melona Miller)*, Marie Ault *(Ma)*.

A man who wrongly believes he has killed a socially prominent person is taken in by a cockney girl and develops into a successful composer.

d, Hans Steinoff; w, Iris North (based on the novel by Anthony Carlyle).

Drama **(PR:A MPAA:NR)**

ALLEY OF GOLDEN HEARTS, THE* (1924, Brit.) 6 reels BPP/Motion Picture Sales bw

Queenie Thomas *(Charity)*, John Stuart *(Jack)*, Cecil Morton York *(Sir James/Paul Manners)*, Frank Stanmore *(Grocer)*, Mary Brough, Bernard Vaughn, Adeline Hayden Coffin, Judd Green, Pollie Emery.

Another English film dealing with class distinction. In this case the villagers are invited by a lonely squire to a New Year's party where they are told that he is the uncle of a peasant girl.

p&d, Bertram Phillips; w, Frank Miller (based on a story by E. P. Kinsella).

Drama **(PR:A MPAA:NR)**

ALLIES (SEE: LOVE IN A HURRY, 1919)

ALL'S FAIR IN LOVE** (1921) 5 reels Goldwyn bw

May Collins *(Natalie Marshall)*, Richard Dix *(Bobby Cameron)*, Marcia Manon *(Vera)*, Raymond Hatton *(Craigh Randolph)*, Stuart Holmes *(Rogers)*, Andrew Robson *(Marshall)*.

After believing a series of lies a vampire told her about her husband and then separating from him, Collins decides to win Dix back by doing a little vamping on her own. Dix allows May to do her act and then lets her know, in no uncertain terms, that it's a wife and not a playmate he wants. One of Dix's very early films during this, his first year in pictures following a brief Broadway career. Samuel Goldwyn left the failing production company the following year. Mergers followed, resulting in the formation of MGM.

d, E. Mason Hopper; w, Arthur F. Statter (based on the play "The Bridal Path" by Thompson Buchanan); ph, John J. Mescall.

Drama **(PR:A MPAA:NR)**

ALMOST A HUSBAND**** (1919) 5 reels Goldwyn bw

Will Rogers *(Sam Lyman)*, Peggy Wood *(Eva McElwyn)*, Herbert Standing *(Banker McElwyn)*, Cullen Landis *(Jerry Wilson)*, Clara Horton *(Jane Sheldon)*, Ed J. Brady *(Zeb Sawyer)*, Sidney De Gray *(John Caruthers)*, Gus Saville *(Jasper Stagg)*, Guinn Williams.

Rogers made a successful transition from stage to screen in this rural comedy about a country teacher who moves to a small town and, at a party, entertains the crowd by taking part in a "let's pretend" wedding with the local beauty. As it turns out, the minister is for real and a license is not necessary in that state. When the town bad guy trys to move in on her, the girl asks Rogers not to release her from the marriage. This inspires the rejected suitor to cause a run on her father's bank. Fortunately, Rogers has just sold a novel and uses his advance money to save the day. The girl, whom he of course marries, is played by Wood, a distinguished actress who earned television immortality some 30 years later for her portrayal of the kindly Norwegian matriarch in the live TV series "I Remember Mama."

d, Clarence Badger; w, (based on the story "Old Ebenezer" by Opie Read); ph, Norbert Brodine, Marcel Le Picard.

Comedy **(PR:A MPAA:NR)**

ALMOST A LADY*** (1926) 6 reels Metropolitan/PDC bw

Marie Prevost *(Marcia Blake)*, Harrison Ford *(William Duke)*, George K. Arthur *(Bob Blake)*, Trixie Friganza *(Mrs. Timothy Reilly)*, John Miljan *(Henri)*, Barney Gimore *(Mr. Reilly)*.

Any comedy with Prevost and Friganza (both veterans of the Mack Sennett laugh factory) could hardly miss, and this one about a clothes model trying to break into society was no exception.

d, E. Mason Hopper; w, F. McGrew Willis, Anthony Coldeway (based on the story "Skin Deep" by Frank R. Adams); ph, Hal Rosson.

Comedy **(PR:A MPAA:NR)**

ALMOST MARRIED** (1919) 5 reels Metro bw

May Allison, Walter E. Percival, Frank Currier, Harry Rattenbury, Wharton James, Hugh Fay.

Fair little comedy about a yodeling Swiss waitress who falls for an American tourist. She follows him to the States where she becomes a vaudeville star, and ultimately marries the young man.

d, Charles Swickard; w, June Mathis, Luther A. Reed (based on the story "His Father's Wife" by E. V. Durling); ph, William E. Fildew.

Comedy **(PR:A MPAA:NR)**

ALOMA OF THE SOUTH SEAS*** (1926) 9 reels FP/PAR bw

Gilda Gray *(Aloma)*, Percy Marmont *(Bob Holden)*, Warner Baxter *(Nuitane)*, William Powell *(Van Templeton)*, Harry Morey *(Red Malloy)*, Julanne Johnston *(Sylvia)*, Joseph Smiley *(Andrew Taylor)*, Frank Montgomery *(Hongi)*, Madame Burani *(Hina)*, Ernestine Gaines *(Taula)*, Aurelio Coccia (Sailor).

Dashing young Marmont, come to the tropics to forget his true love Johnstone, defends native girl Gray from the unwanted advances of ruffian Morey. Her native lover, Baxter, is unhappy about Gray's apparent gratitude to Marmont. The latter's lost love arrives on the island paradise with her new husband, Powell, a bibulous cad. Smitten with Gray, the lecherous Powell attempts to trick the simple girl into his bed. Powell dies during a storm, Johnstone and Marmont realize they love each other, and Gray is reunited with Baxter. Gray, who became world famous for the introduction of "the shimmie" and later became a "Follies" star performing Hawaiian and South Seas dances, made her film debut here. Her beauty and grace were magnificently captured by Tourneur, a director of genius who could make studio sets resemble oil paintings. Powell usually played villains during this period of his career; his suave, urbane style—like Baxter's—only blossomed with sound.

d, Maurice Tourneur; w, James A. Creelman (based on the play by John B. Hymer, Leroy Clemens); ph, Harry Fishbeck; art d, Charles M. Kirk.

Adventure **(PR:A MPAA:NR)**

ALONE IN LONDON* (1915, Brit.) 4 reels Turner Films/ID

Florence Turner *(Nan Meadows)*, Henry Edwards *(John Biddlecombe)*, Edward Lingard *(Redcliffe)*, James Lindsay *(Chick)*, Amy Lorraine *(Mrs. Burnaby)*.

Dated (even for its time) British crime story redeemable only by the performance of American star Turner in her first character role.

d, Larry Trimble; w, (based on a play by Harriet Jay, Robert Buchanan).

Crime/Drama **(PR:A MPAA:NR)**

ALONG CAME RUTH** (1924) 5 reels MG bw

Viola Dana *(Ruth Ambrose)*, Walter Hiers *(Plinty Bangs)*, Tully Marshall *(Israel Hubbard)*, Raymond McKee *(Allan Hubbard)*, DeWitt Jennings *(Capt. Miles Standish)*, Adele Farrington *(Widow Burnham)*, Brenda Lane *(Annabelle Burnham)*, Victor Potel *(Oscar Sims)*, Gale Henry *(Min, the Hired Girl)*.

Dana plays a city girl who moves to the country because she can't find clients for her interior decorating business. There she not only finds a general store to "enhance," but a good looking rustic lad to marry.

d, Edward Cline; w, Winifred Dunn (based on the play by Holman Francis Day); ph, John Arnold.

Comedy **(PR:A MPAA:NR)**

ALSTER CASE, THE* (1915) 5 reels Essanay bw

Bryant Washburn *(George Swan)*, John H. Cossar *(Detective Trask)*, Ruth Stonehouse *(Beatrice)*, Anne Lee *(May Walsh)*, Louise Crolius *(Miss Cornelia Alster)*, Betty Scott *(Linda)*, Arthur W. Bates *(Keith)*, Roderick LaRoque *(Allen Longstreet)*, Beatrice Styler.

Inexpensively produced effort by Essanay to enter the serious film market was too short on production values and big name players to really make the grade. Heretofore the Chicago-based company had specialized in westerns and comedies.

d, J. Charles Haydon; w, (based on a novel by Rufus Gillmore).

Drama **(PR:A MPAA:NR)**

ALTAR CHAINS*** (1916, Brit.) 5 reels LON/JUR bw

Dawson Milward *(Capt. Kerr)*, Heather Thatcher *(Alice Vaughan)*, Philip Hewland *(Harry Avery)*, Edward O'Neill *(Philip Anson)*, Minna Grey *(Mrs. Anson)*, Fred Volpe *(Harky)*, Hubert Willis *(Charles Vaughan)*, Donald Calthrop.

Bizarre early British feature in which a captain with less than a month to live forces a moneylender, to whom he is indebted, to join him in the drinking of poison.

d&w, Bannister Merwin.

Crime **(PR:C MPAA:NR)**

ALTAR STAIRS, THE** (1922) 5 reels UNIV bw

Frank Mayo *(Rod McLean)*, Dagmar Godowsky *(Parete)*, Louise Lorraine *(Joie Malet)*, Harry De Vere *(Blundell)*, Hugh Thompson *(John Strickland)*, Boris Karloff *(Hugo)*, Nick De Ruiz *(Tulli)*, Lawrence Hughes *(Tony Heritage)*, J. J. Lanoe *(Capt. Jean Malet)*.

South Seas adventure featuring Mayo as a ship's captain who saves the natives' new-found Christian faith from the opportunist who seeks to exploit them.

d, Lambert Hillyer; w, George Hively, Doris Schroeder (based on the novel by G. B. Lancaster); ph, Dwight Warren.

Adventure **(PR:A MPAA:NR)**

ALTARS OF DESIRE* (1927) 6 reels MGM bw

Mae Murray *(Claire Sutherland)*, Conway Tearle *(David Elrod)*, Robert Edeson *(John Sutherland)*, Maude George *(Kitty Prior)*, Andre Beranger *(Count Andre D'Orville)*.

Skillful direction by Cabanne, and Murray looking gorgeous in soft focus, are about the only good things that can be said about this story of a girl who goes to Paris (to acquire polish), returns a snob, and straightens out in the end.

d, Christy Cabanne; w, Alice D. G. Miller, Agnes Christine Johnson (based on the story by Martha Thompson Davies); t, Ruth Cummings; ph, William Daniels; ed, George Hively; set d, Cedric Gibbons, Arnold Gillespie.

Drama **(PR:A MPAA:NR)**

ALWAYS AUDACIOUS** (1920) 6 reels PAR bw

Wallace Reid *(Perry Danton/Slim Attucks)*, Margaret Loomis *(Camilia Hoyt)*, Clarence Geldart *(Theron Ammidown)*, J. Monte Dumont *(Jerry the Gent)*, Rhea Haines *(Denver Kate)*, Carmen Phillips *(Molly the Eel)*, Guy Oliver *(Martin Green the Reporter)*, Fannie Midgely *(Mrs. Rumson)*, Charles Bennett.

Two men look enough alike to be twins, but they are not related. One of them is honest, the other a crook. Pretty familiar stuff here, and Reid's handling of the two characters is less than impressive.

d, James Cruze; w, Tom Geraghty (based on the story "Toujours de l'Audace" by Ben Ames Williams); ph, C. Edgar Schoenbaum.

Crime **(PR:A MPAA:NR)**

ALWAYS THE WOMAN** (1922) 6 reels Betty Compson/Goldwyn bw

Betty Compson *(Celia Thaxter)*, Emory Johnson *(Herbert Boone)*, Doris Pawn *(Mrs. Adele Boone)*, Gerald Pring *(Reginald Stanhope)*, Richard Rosson *(Mahmud)*, Arthur Delmore *(Gregory Gallup, Manager)*, Macey Harlam *(Kelim Pasha)*.

Another reincarnation story, taking place this time almost entirely on shipboard. Effective ancient Egyptian flashbacks gave the lovely Compson ample opportunity to look exotic.

d, Arthur Rosson; w, Rosson (based on a story by Perley Poore Sheehan); ph, Ernest G. Palmer.

Drama **(PR:A MPAA:NR)**

AMARILLY OF CLOTHESLINE ALLEY**** (1918) 5 reels ART/PAR bw

Mary Pickford *(Amarilly Jenkins)*, William Scott *(Terry McGowan)*, Norman Kerry *(Gordon Phillips)*, Ida Waterman *(Mrs. Stuyvesant Phillips)*, Kate Price *(Mrs. Jenkins)*, Margaret Landis *(Colette King)*, Thomas H. Wilson *(Bosco McCarty)*, Fred Goodwins *(Johnny Walker)*, Wesley Barry, Herbert Standing, Frank Butterworth, Antrim Short, George Hackathorne, Gertrude Short.

Pickford, the eldest daughter of widow Price, is the darling of an East Side New York neighborhood known as "Clothesline Alley." Her boy friend, Scott, waiter at the dance hall, gets her a job selling cigarettes, and she meets Kerry, a wealthy young man on a tear with a crowd of chums. After a fight breaks out and Kerry is forcibly ejected, Pickford takes him home for repairs. This kindness is rewarded when Price is hired to do the young man's laundry. As time passes, Kerry becomes convinced that he is in love with the little East Side girl, but the young man's aunt (to bring him to his senses) invites Pickford's entire clan to attend a social gathering with her "high-bred" friends. This wonderful scene ends with Pickford leading the family back to "Clothesline Alley," where she returns to the waiting arms of Scott, who has just landed a swell job with the city.

d, Marshall Neilan; w, Frances Marion (based on a novel by Belle K. Maniates); ph, Walter Stradling.

Comedy/Drama **(PR:A MPAA:NR)**

AMATEUR ADVENTURESS, THE**** (1919) 5 reels Metro bw

Emmy Whelen *(Norma Wood)*, Allen Sears *(Oliver Morley)*, Gene Pallette *(George Goodie)*, William V. Mong *(William Claxtonbury)*, Marion Skinner *(Mrs. Claxtonbury)*, Lucille Ward *(Mrs. Sentel)*, Victor Potel *(Gregory C. Sentel)*, Rosemary Theby.

All but forgotten now, Whelen was a comedic actress of true greatness, as this delightful film illustrates. THE AMATEUR ADVENTURESS provided her with a role in which she could play it straight with dramatic power, dress and look as beautiful as any of the glamor queens, and parody the movie vamps of that day with a devastation the equal of Mabel Normand.

d, Henry Otto; w, June Mathis, Luther A. Reed (based on the story by Thomas Edgelow); ph, Arthur Martinelli.

Comedy **(PR:A MPAA:NR)**

AMATEUR DEVIL, AN*** (1921) 5 reels FP/PAR bw

Bryant Washburn *(Carver Endicott)*, Charles Wingate *(His Father)*, Ann May *(His Sweetheart)*, Sydney Bracey *(His Valet)*, Graham Pettie *(Farmer Brown)*, Anna Hernandez *(Mrs. Brown)*, Christine Mayo *(A Musical Comedy Star)*, Norris Johnson *(Her Daughter)*.

In this film Washburn (a clever light comedian in his own right) is told by his girl friend, who finds him a rich bore, to go out into the world and become a regular fellow or forget about her. This leads him into a number of comic situations which provide the audience with laughs, while teaching Washburn the ways of the real world and transforming him into the very man his sweetheart wants to marry. Probably inspired by Douglas Fairbanks' HIS PICTURE IN THE PAPERS (1916).

d, Maurice Campbell; w, Douglas Bronston (based on the story "Wanted a Blemish" by Jessie E. Henderson, Henry J. Buxton); ph, H. Kinley Martin.

Comedy **(PR:A MPAA:NR)**

AMATEUR GENTLEMAN, THE*** (1920, Brit.) 7 reels STOLL bw

Alfred Paumier *(Prince Regent)*, Gerald McCarthy *(Viscount Horatio Debenham)*, Geoffrey Wilmer *(Capt. Slingsby)*, Sydney Seaward *(Sir Mortimer Carnaby)*, Vivian Reynolds *(Jasper Gaunt)*, Dalton Somers *(Natty Bell)*, Teddy Arundell *(Digby Smivvle)*, Will Cori *(Capt. Chumley)*, Judd Green *(Jerry the Bosun)*, A. C. Fotheringham-Lysons *(Peterby)*, Sinclair Hill *(Jerningham)*, Langhorne Burton *(Barnabas Barty)*, Madge Stuart *(Lady Cleone Meredith)*, Cecil Humphreys *(Wilfred Chichester)*, Herbert Synott *(John Barty)*, Pardoe Woodman *(Ronald Barrymaine)*.

Paumier portrays a commoner who tries to pass himself off as English nobility after his uncle leaves him a hefty inheritance.

d, Maurice Elvey; w, (based on the novel by Jeffrey Farnol).

Drama **(PR:A MPAA:NR)**

AMATEUR GENTLEMAN, THE*** (1926) 8 reels INSP/FN bw

Richard Barthelmess *(Barnabas Barty)*, Dorothy Dunbar *(Lady Cleone Meredith)*, Gardner James *(Ronald Barrymaine)*, Nigel Barrie *(Sir Mortimer Carnaby)*, Brandon Hurst *(Peterby)*, John Miljan *(Viscount Devenham)*, Edwards Davis *(John Barty)*, Billie Bennett *(Duchess of Camberhurst)*, Herbert Grimwood *(Jasper Gaunt)*, Gino Corrado *(Prince Regent)*, Sidney de Gray *(Capt. Chumley)*, John Peters *(Capt. Slingsby)*.

Barthelmess is the son of an early 19th-Century prizefighter who inherits a fortune from his uncle and goes to London where, with the help of a servant, he passes himself off as a gentleman. Good performances all around, plus an exciting steeplechase finale.

d, Sidney Olcott; w, Lillie Hayward (based on a novel by Jeffrey Farnol); t, Tom Miranda; ph, David W. Gobbett; ed, Miranda.

Drama **(PR:A MPAA:NR)**

AMATEUR WIDOW, AN* (1919) 5 reels WORLD bw

Zena Keefe *(Rhoda Canby)*, Hugh Dillman *(Irving Mason)*, Jack Drumier *(James Potter)*, William Black *(Stanley Potter)*, Pauline Dempsey *(Aunt Chloe)*, Mary B. Davis *(Aunt Elizabeth)*, Eugenie Woodward *(Cousin Hepzibah)*, Florence Ashbrooke *(Mrs. Green)*, Charles Ascot.

Pedestrian programmer about an heiress who runs away from her money-grabbing relatives with the help of her black mammy. Happily, she meets and falls in love with the good-looking fellow who marries her for herself alone.

d, Oscar Apfel; w, Joseph Franklin Poland; ph, Max Schneider.

Drama **(PR:A MPAA:NR)**

AMATEUR WIFE, THE** (1920) 5 reels PAR bw

Irene Castle *(Justine Spencer)*, W. T. Carleton *(Cosmo Spottiswood)*, Arthur Rankin *(Billy Ferris)*, S. J. Warrington *(Randolph Ferguson)*, A. Saskin *(Oliver Ferris)*, Augusta Anderson *(Dodo Spencer)*, Mrs. Charles Dewey *(Loti the Maid)*, Ellen Olson *(Sara)*.

The great dancer Castle was the whole show in this less-than-original potboiler about a neglected wife who makes the transition from old-fashioned girl to high-stepping flapper and then, in turn, neglects her husband. The ending, in which she decides to stay by his side forever after he loses his fortune, is, at best, contrived.

d, Edward Dillon; w, Jane Murfin (based on a story by Nalbro Bartley); ph, Hal Young.

Drama **(PR:A MPAA:NR)**

AMAZING IMPOSTER, THE* (1919) 5 reels AM bw

Mary Miles Minter *(Joan Hope)*, Plunkett Edward Johnson *(Plinius Plumm)*, Margaret Shelby *(Countess of Crex)*, Alan Forrest *(Kent Standish)*, Henry Barrows *(Herbert Thornton)*, Carl Stockdale, George Periolat, Edward Jobson.

This showcase for childlike romantic lead Minter (Mary Pickford's only serious rival) deals with intrigue, love, and Bolshevism. The picture is nice to look at but drags and lacks purpose.

d, Lloyd Ingraham; w, Frank Howard Clark (based on a story by Joseph Franklin Poland).

Crime **(PR:A MPAA:NR)**

AMAZING LOVERS** (1921) 6 reels A. H. Fischer/Jans bw

Diana Allen, Marc McDermott, Grace Darling, Ramsaye Wallace, Sally Crute, Gustav von Seyffertitz, Robert Paton Gibbs, John Goldsworthy, John L. Shine, E. J. Ratcliffe.

Allen was a Ziegfeld beauty who never graduated to picture stardom, although she made a number of programmers like this one about a female secret agent who poses as an underworld type and breaks up a counterfeit ring.

d, B. A. Rolfe; w, Charles A. Logue (based on the novel *The Shining Band* by Robert W. Chambers).

Crime **(PR:A MPAA:NR)**

AMAZING PARTNERSHIP, THE** (1921, Brit.) 5 reels STOLL bw

Milton Rosmer *(Pryde)*, Gladys Mason *(Grace Burton)*, Arthur Walcott *(Julius Hatten)*, Temple Bell *(Stella)*, Teddy Arundell *(Baron Feldemay)*, Robert Vallis *(His Confederate)*, Harry J. Worth *(Jean Marchand)*, Charles Barnett *(M. Dupay)*.

British thriller about a girl detective who solves a crime by deducing that the stolen jewels are actually hidden in an oriental idol.

d, George Ridgwell; w, Charles Barnett (based on the novel by E. Phillips Oppenheim).

Crime **(PR:A MPAA:NR)**

AMAZING VAGABOND*** (1929) 5 reels FBO/RKO bw

Bob Steele *(Jimmy Hobbs)*, Tom Lingham *(George Hobbs)*, Lafe McKee *(Phil Dunning)*, Perry Murdock *("Haywire")*, Jay Morley *(Bill Wharton)*, Emily Gerdes *(Myrtle)*, Thelma Daniels *(Alice Dunning)*.

Western lumber camp movie, with nonstop action. Steele is a rich man's son being sent west where he becomes a man, defeats the crooks, and wins the girl.

d, Wallace W. Fox; w, Frank Howard Clark; t, Helen Gregg; ph, Virgil Miller; ed, Della M. King.

Adventure **(PR:A MPAA:NR)**

AMAZING WIFE, THE** (1919) 6 reels UNIV bw

Mary MacLaren *(Cicely Osborne)*, Frank Mayo *(Lt. John Ashton)*, Ethel Lynne *(Claire Winston)*, Stanhope Wheatcroft *(Phillip Ashton)*, Seymour Zeliff *(John Ashton)*.

Unpleasant little film about an impoverished girl (MacLaren) who passes herself off to the parents of a war hero as his widow. She is warmly welcomed into the family—until he returns.

d&w, Ida May Clark (based on the story "Whose Widow" by Elinor Chipp); ph, King Gray.

Drama (PR:A MPAA:NR)

AMAZONS, THE** (1917) 5 reels PAR bw

Marguerite Clark *(Tommy)*, Elsie Lawson *(Willie)*, Helen Greene *(Noel)*, William Hinckley *(Lord Litterly)*, Helen Robinson *(The Marchioness)*, Edgar Norton *(Lord Tweenways)*, Andre Bellon *(De Grival)*.

This rather thin updating of a Pinero play has only Clark's usual charming performance to recommend it. A story perfectly fitting Clark's innocent-maiden manner so beloved by audiences of the 1910s.

d, Joseph Kaufman; w, Frances Marion (based on a play by Sir Arthur Wing Pinero); ph, William C. Marshal.

Drama (PR:A MPAA:NR)

AMBITION*** (1916) 5 reels FOX bw

Bertha Kalich *(Marian Powers)*, Kenneth Hunter *(Robert Powers)*, William H. Tooker *(John Moore)*, W. W. Black *(James Grant)*, Kittens Reichert *(Betty Powers)*, Daniel Crimmins.

An ambitious young district attorney attempts to further his career by placing his attractive wife in the seductive company of a corrupt and powerful political boss. The scheme backfires, however, when, instead of his appointment being granted, the two fall madly in love. Morality standards in 1916 would not permit the couple either consummation or happiness so, at the last moment, the wife's daughter intervenes and the marriage is preserved. The film was well produced, written, and acted, with above-average direction.

d, James Vincent; w, Mary Murillo.

Drama (PR:A MPAA:NR)

AMERICA****

(1924) 11 reels D. W. Griffith/UA bw (GB: LOVE AND SACRIFICE)

Neil Hamilton *(Nathan Holden)*, Erville Alderson *(Justice Montague)*, Carol Dempster *(Miss Nancy Montague)*, Charles Emmett Mack *(Charles Philip Edward Montague)*, Lee Beggs *(Samuel Adams)*, John Dunton *(John Hancock)*, Arthur Donaldson *(King George III)*, Charles Bennett *(William Pitt)*, Frank McGlynn, Jr. *(Patrick Henry)*, Frank Walsh *(Thomas Jefferson)*, Lionel Barrymore *(Capt. Walter Butler)*, Arthur Dewey *(George Washington)*, Sydney Deane *(Sir Ashley Montague)*, W. W. Jones *(Gen. Gage)*, Harry O'Neill *(Paul Revere)*, Henry Van Bousen *(John Parker, Captain of the Minutemen)*, Hugh Baird *(Maj. Pitcairn)*, James Milady *(Jonas Parker)*, Louis Wolheim *(Capt. Hare)*, Riley Hatch *(Chief of Mohawks/Joseph Brant)*, Emil Hoch *(Lord North)*, Lucile La Verne *(Refugee Mother)*, Downing Clark *(Lord Chamberlain)*, P. R. Scammon *(Richard Henry Lee)*, Ed Roseman *(Capt. Montoue)*, Harry Semels *(Hickatoo, Chief of Senecas)*, H. Koser *(Col. Prescott)*, Michael Donovan *(Maj. Gen Warren)*, Paul Doucet *(Marquis de Lafayette)*, W. Rising *(Edmund Burke)*, Daniel Carney *(Personal Servant of Miss Montague)*, E. Scanlon *(Household Servant at Ashley Court)*, Edwin Holland *(Maj. Strong)*, Milton Noble *(An Old Patriot)*.

The last of D. W. Griffith's great silent epics traces the course of the American Revolution from its beginnings through the surrender of the British at Yorktown. Seen from the perspectives of young lovers Hamilton and Dempster, the latter the daughter of a family divided in the conflict (a favorite theme of the great director), the major characters are framed by characterizations of the heroic figures of the era. Griffith pulls out all the stops, using his favorite techniques—montage, vignettes, et al—to depict the stirring warning ride of Paul Revere (O'Neill) in a virtual steeplechase race through town and countryside, besting his pursuers in a ride more furious than those of many a western picture. (According to one historian, actor O'Neill got the role of Paul Revere because he was the only applicant who could ride the Irish horse Griffith had purchased at great cost; horse threw rider during the filming after all, and Griffith wisely left the fall in the picture. O'Neill remounted, so the rebels were warned that "The British are coming" after all.) The Battle of Bunker Hill (actually, Breed's Hill) is here reconstructed on a scale perhaps surpassing the original. Griffith makes strong symbols of the colors of the parties in the conflict, with the Union Jack serving as shroud for the fallen Mack, downed in the service of the patriots (a fact concealed from his royalist father by Dempster, his sister). Barrymore is the arch-villain royalist who hectors the young lovers mercilessly. Initially running 16 reels, the picture was screened with a very necessary intermission. Reportedly costing nearly $1 million, Griffith apparently intended this to be the first of a continuing series of historical documents; publicity for the film referred to it as "Series One." The sequelae never followed; Griffith got into serious financial trouble as a result of this picture and had to turn to other things. The theme of AMERICA had been suggested to the director by Will H. Hays, head of the all-powerful censorship board known as the "Hays Office," at the behest of the Daughters of the American Revolution, who wanted their organization's point of view espoused by the powerful medium of movies (their approach was successful; for years, virtually every school-age child in the cities of the U.S. was exposed to cuts from the film in a classroom setting). As was the case with many of the director's other lengthy epics, he had apprenticed on briefer works during his years at Biograph, most notably with his one-reeler, 1776, OR THE HESSIAN RENEGADES in 1909. The finished picture bore a striking resemblance to Griffith's 1907 play, "A Fool and a Girl," at least in its romantic plot line. It actually had very little to do with author-titlist Chambers' original story; indeed, Chambers—who liked Griffith, and was extremely helpful on the set—wrote another novel based on the film's plot, so different from his own original.

p&d, D. W. Griffith; w, John L. E. Pell (based on a novel by Robert W. Chambers); t, Chambers; ph, G. W. Bitzer, Marcel Le Picard, Hendrik Sartov, Hal Sintzenich; m, Joseph Carl Breil; ed, Rose Smith, James Smith; art d, Charles M. Kirk.

Historical Drama Cas. (PR:A MPAA:NR)

AMERICAN ARISTOCRACY*** (1916) 5 reels FA/TRI bw

Douglas Fairbanks *(Cassius Lee)*, Charles de Lima *(Leander Hick)*, Jewel Carmen *(Miss Hick)*, Albert Parker *(Percy Horton)*, Arthur Ortego *(Delgado)*.

America's aristocracy, according to screenwriter Loos, consisted of millionaires who manufactured everything from hatpins to malted milk. It was money that counted here, not lineage, and in this delicious satire Fairbanks plays a Virginian from a very "old" family. He manages to turn a resort infested by these *nouveau riche* upside-down, foils a plot to smuggle arms to Mexico, and wins the girl who, in the end, is almost a Democrat at heart.

d, Lloyd Ingraham; w, Anita Loos (based on a story by Loos); ph, Victor Fleming.

Comedy/Adventure Cas. (PR:A MPAA:NR)

AMERICAN BEAUTY* (1927) 7 reels FN bw

Billie Dove *(Millicent Howard)*, Lloyd Hughes *(Jerry Booth)*, Walter McGrail *(Claverhouse)*, Margaret Livingston *(Mrs. Gillespie)*, Lucien Prival *(Gillespie)*, Al St. John *(Waiter)*, Edythe Chapman *(Mme. O'Riley)*, Alice White *(Claire O'Riley)*, Yola D'Avril *(Telephone Girl)*.

Just another of those cliched yarns where a poor girl wants the best that money can buy but spurns a millionaire to accept the love of the "right man." Highlight of this programmer is a brief shot of Dove in her undies.

p, Carey Wilson; d, Richard Wallace; w, Wilson (based on a story by Wallace Irwin); t, Robert Hopkins; ph, George Folsey.

Drama (PR:A MPAA:NR)

AMERICAN BUDS*** (1918) 6 reels FOX bw

Jane Lee *(Jane)*, Katherine Lee *(Katherine)*, Albert Gran (Col. Harding), Regina Quinn *(Cecile)*, Lucille Satterthwaite *(Ethel)*, Nora Cecil *(Emily)*, Leslie Austin *(Bob Dutton)*, H. D. Southard *(Robert Duncan)*, William Hayes, Maggie Weston.

Moviegoers knew Jane and Katherine Lee as the "Baby Grands" and the "Two Little Imps," talented sisters who made a series of popular features for Fox. AMERICAN BUDS is typical in that the titles are as funny as the situations, and the appeal as strong for adults as for children.

d, Kenean Buel; w, Buel (based on a story by M. Strauss).

Comedy (PR:AA MPAA:NR)

AMERICAN CONSUL, THE* (1917) 5 reels LAS/PAR bw

Theodore Roberts *(Abel Manning)*, Maude Fealy *(Joan Manning)*, Tom Forman *(Geoffrey Daniels)*, Raymond Hatton *(President Cavillo)*, Charles West *(Pedro Gonzales)*, Ernest Joy *(Sen. James Kitwell)*.

Slow-moving, padded film about political corruption, a Central American revolution, and ultimate Yankee fair play. A veritable pre-play of the headlines in the 1980s.

d, Rolin S. Sturgeon; w, Harvey Thew, Thomas Geraghty (based on a story by Paul West).

Adventure (PR:A MPAA:NR)

AMERICAN LIVE WIRE, AN** (1918) 5 reels VIT bw

Earle Williams, Grace Darmond, Hale Clements, Claire Toner, Orral Humphrey, Margaret Bennett, Malcolm Blevins.

Good performance by Williams (a major star who died in 1927 at age 46) despite a disjointed script about a young fellow who loses his girl, takes a post in South America, and marries her in the end.

d, Thomas R. Mills; w, William Addison Lathrop (based on the story "The Lotus and the Bottle" by O. Henry).

Drama (PR:A MPAA:NR)

AMERICAN MAID* (1917) 5 reels Goodrich/MUT bw

Edna Goodrich, George Henery, William B. Davidson, John Hopkins.

This early film effort by Broadway star Goodrich was terrible on all counts. The producers (one of whom was the star) got the affair underway by showcasing the actress in beautiful attire, then apparently gave up and turned the second half of the picture into the kind of western which was popular in the nickelodeon days.

d, Albert Capellani; w, Hamilton Smith (based on a story by Julius Rothchild).

Western (PR:A MPAA:NR)

AMERICAN MANNERS*** (1924) 6 reels Richard Talmadge/FBO bw

Richard Talmadge *(Roy Thomas)*, Marc Fenton *(Dan Thomas)*, Lee Shumway *(Clyde Harvey)*, Helen Lynch *(Gloria Winthrope)*, Arthur Millett *(Conway)*, William Turner *(Jonas Winthrope)*, Pat Harmon *(Mike Barclay)*, George Warde *(Bud, the Waif)*.

Kids—and those adults who'd admit to it—did not attend Talmadge movies for edification. Talmadge was the stunt man's stunt man, and his pictures consisted of nonstop action from beginning to end. Here Talmadge returns to the U.S., after being educated in Europe, to clear his father of a smuggling charge. This movie had more than its share of incredible acrobatics by the man who, on occasion, even doubled for Douglas Fairbanks.

d, James W. Horne; w, Frank Howard Clark; t, Joseph W. Farnham; ph, William Marshall, Jack Stevens.

Adventure (PR:A MPAA:NR)

AMERICAN METHODS*** (1917) 6 reels FOX bw

William Farnum *(William Armstrong)*, Willard Louis *(M. Moulinet)*, Lillian West

(Marie Moulinet), Genevieve Blinn *(Marquise de Beaulieu)*, Allan Forrest *(Octave de Beaulieu)*, Jewel Carmen *(Claire de Beaulieu)*, Florence Vidor *(Betty Armstrong)*, Mortimer Jaffe *(Jimmy)*, Bertram Grassby, Marc Robbins, Joseph Swickard.

Nice vehicle for Farnum as an American of French descent who inherits an iron mine in the old country, beats some nasty aristocrats, and saves the situation with real American pluck. Farnum was at the peak of his career—one of the highest paid actors in Hollywood—when he made this film. Unfortunately, his great success would come to an end in 1925 when, during the filming of A MAN WHO FIGHTS ALONE, he received a serious injury which limited him to minor parts for the rest of the silent era.

d, Frank Lloyd; w, F. McGrew Willis, Lloyd (based on the novel *The Ironmaster* by Georges Ohnet); ph, Billy Foster.

Adventure **(PR:A MPAA:NR)**

AMERICAN VENUS, THE*** (1926) 8 reels FP/PAR bw/c

Esther Ralston *(Mary Gray)*, Lawrence Gray *(Chip Armstrong)*, Ford Sterling *(Hugo Niles)*, Fay Lanphier *(Miss America)*, Louise Brooks *(Miss Bayport)*, Edna May Oliver *(Mrs. Hugo Niles)*, Kenneth MacKenna *(Horace Niles)*, William B. Mack *(John Gray)*, George De Carlton *(Sam Lorber)*, W. T. Benda *(The Artist)*, Ernest Torrence *(King Neptune)*, Douglas Fairbanks, Jr. *(Neptune's Son, Triton)*.

Rival cosmetic companies vie for the valued endorsement of the "American Venus" beauty contest's winner. This exploitation film was made to cash in on the New York Graphic's sensational charge that the Miss America contest of the preceding year had been fixed. The winner in question (Lanphier) actually appears in this film and several scenes of the pageant were shot in color.

d, Frank Tuttle; w, Frederick Stowers (based on a story by Townsend Martin); ph, J. Roy Hunt; art d, Frederick A. Foord.

Drama **(PR:A MPAA:NR)**

AMERICAN WAY, THE* (1919) 5 reels WORLD bw

Arthur Ashley *(Richard Farrington)*, Dorothy Green *(Betty Winthrop)*, Franklin Hanna *(Stuyvesant Van Allen)*, Leslie Leigh *(Mrs. Van Allen)*, Carl Sauerman *(Henry Steinmetz)*, Robert Fisher *(Jerome Schwartz)*, Harry Semels *(Half Breed)*, Charles Wellsley *(Lord Farrington)*, Ed Roseman, John Ardizoni, Hazel Sexton, Stewart Fisher, Barbara Butler.

Unimaginative society drama about an American (hence the title) courting and winning an English girl. A poorly done film expressing a time when the U.S. was flaunting a newly won strength and importance in the eyes of the world.

d, Frank Reicher; w, Wallace C. Clifton (based on a story by Florence C. Boles).

Drama **(PR:A MPAA:NR)**

AMERICAN WIDOW, AN*** (1917) 5 reels Metro bw

Ethel Barrymore, Irving Cummings, Dudley Hawley, Ernest Stallard, Charles Dickson, Alfred Kappler, Arthur Lewis, Pearl Browne, George A. Wright, Hugh Wynne.

Above average programmer about a young widow (Barrymore), who marries a rather average fellow in order to earn her inheritance and the opportunity to wed a European nobleman. After the titled fellow marries an actress, however, she realizes the folly of class worship and the value of American decency, which of course is embodied in the lad she married in the first place. Much better than it sounds principally because it boasted the presence of "the first lady of the American theater," baseball lover and book collector Barrymore.

d, Frank Reicher; sup, Maxwell Karger; w, Albert S. Le Vine (based on the play by Kellett Chambers); ph, George Webber.

Drama **(PR:A MPAA:NR)**

AMERICANO, THE*** (1917) 5 reels FA/TRI bw

Douglas Fairbanks *(The Americano)*, Alma Rubens *(The Girl)*, Spottiswoode Aitken, Lillian Langdon, Carl Stockdale, Tom Wilson, Tote Du Crow, Charles Stevens, Mildred Harris.

Story of a mining engineer who falls in love with the daughter of a deposed South American president, rescues him from a dungeon and places him back in office, then marries the girl and assumes the post of commander of the armed forces. All of this was, of course, accomplished with Fairbanks' usual enthusiastic exuberance.

d, John Emerson; w, Anita Loos, Emerson (based on the novel *Blaze Derringer* by Eugene P. Lyle, Jr.); ph, Victor Fleming.

Adventure/Comedy **Cas.** **(PR:A MPAA:NR)**

ANCIENT HIGHWAY, THE** (1925) 7 reels FP/PAR bw

Jack Holt *(Cliff Brant)*, Billie Dove *(Antoinette St. Ives)*, Montagu Love *(Ivan Hurd)*, Stanley Taylor *(Gaspard St. Ives)*, Lloyd Whitlock *(John Denis)*, William A. Carroll *(Ambrose)*, Marjorie Bonner *(Angel Fanchon)*, Christian J. Frank *(George Bolden)*.

Above-average lumber camp movie with the customary log jam and dynamiting scenes. Also, a dandy fight between hero Holt and all-time great villain Love, plus the beautiful Dove.

d, Irvin Willat; w, James Shelley Hamilton, Eve Unsell (based on a novel by James Oliver Curwood); ph, Alfred Gilks.

Adventure **(PR:A MPAA:NR)**

ANCIENT MARINER, THE** (1925) 6 reels FOX bw

Clara Bow *(Doris)*, Earle Williams *(Victor Brant)*, Leslie Fenton *(Joel Barlowe)*, Nigel de Brulier *(The Skipper)*, Paul Panzer *(The Mariner)*, Gladys Brockwell *(Life in Death)*, Robert Klein *(Death)*.

Counterpoising a modern-day love story on Coleridge's poem "The Rime of the Ancient Mariner," Bow's infatuation with rich rakehell Williams is thwarted when skipper de Brulier drugs the cad, inducing a dream about an albatross. Awakening, de Brulier gives up the girl in favor of true love Fenton. Attempt to use the Coleridge poem to make a contemporary morality statement is, for the most part, a failure.

d, Henry Otto, Chester Bennett; w, Eve Unsell (based on the poem by Samuel Taylor Coleridge); t, Tom Miranda; ph, Joseph August.

Fantasy **(PR:A MPAA:NR)**

AND A STILL, SMALL VOICE*** (1918) 6 reels National Film for Exhibitors Mutual bw

Henry B. Walthall *(Clay Randolph)*, Joseph Dowling *(Col. Robert Singleton)*, Fritzi Brunette *(Mary Singleton)*, George Fisher *(Richard Dunlap)*, Charles Arling.

Another absorbing performance by Walthall as an honest bank cashier driven to a life of crime, who reforms and marries the girl he loves. Too bad the story did not allow him to show his full potential as an actor, a fate he was consigned to since leaving D. W. Griffith after his sensitive performance in THE BIRTH OF A NATION in 1915.

d&w, Bertram Bracken (based on a story by Dennison Clift).

Crime/Drama **(PR:A MPAA:NR)**

ANGEL CHILD* (1918) 5 reels Plaza bw

Kathleen Clifford *(Glory Moore)*, Leslie T. Peacocke *(Her Father)*, Rita Harlan *(Her Mother)*, Fred Church *(Richard Grant)*.

This film about the antics of a super tough and mischievous woman misfires at every level. It did, however, allow Clifford to show off some of her old vaudeville capers, though the antics are hardly moving fare for the silver screen.

d, Henry Otto; w, Harl McInroy; ph, Joseph Brotherton.

Comedy **(PR:A MPAA:NR)**

ANGEL ESQUIRE*** (1919, Brit.) 7 reels GAU bw

Aurele Sydney *(Jimmy)*, Gertrude McCoy *(Kathleen Kent)* Dick Webb *(Angel)*, W. T. Ellwanger *(Spedding)*, George Traill *(Connor)*, Cecil del Gue *(Reale)*, Florence Nelson *(Mrs. Reale)*.

This British thriller has various characters trying to figure out the combination to a safe left by a millionaire gambler as his last joke on society.

d, W. P. Kellino; w, George Pearson (based on a novel by Edgar Wallace).

Mystery **(PR:A MPAA:NR)**

ANGEL OF BROADWAY, THE**** (1927) 7 reels DM/Pathe bw

Leatrice Joy *(Babe)*, Victor Varconi *(Jerry Wilson)*, May Robson *(Big Bertha)*, Alice Lake *(Goldie)*, Elise Bartlett *(Gertie)*, Ivan Lebedeff *(Lonnie)*, Jane Keckley *(Captain Mary)*, Clarence Burton *(Herman)*.

Joy, an entertainer in a night spot, haunts a Salvation Army mission to pick up material for her show. She performs in the uniform of a lassie, complete with tambourine, to the dismay of Varconi. Ultimately, Joy is redeemed and she unites with Varconi. The films of Weber, one of America's greatest female directors, were highly personal statements dealing with such controversial subjects as divorce, race relations, and abortion. Her compassionate, almost fundamental, moral sense was, however, so much in tune with the America of the teens that the profits she brought Universal earned her the right to demand a studio of her own. But, when the 1920s roared in, and America's moral fabric began to change, Weber, a woman who refused to compromise her ideals, quickly tumbled from that lofty pinnacle. She lost the autonomy her personal studio provided, and once again found herself working for moguls who did not share her values, nor for that matter really give a care. She did, however, direct a few more films, such as this one, before disappearing completely from the scene. THE ANGEL OF BROADWAY was a tale of two cities, contrasting the world of cafe society with a lower east side Salvation Army mission. It dealt with blasphemy, redemption, and the intrinsic goodness of mankind, and it did so with such consummate skill that audiences never for a moment felt they were being preached to. Such was the neglected genius of Weber.

p, William Sistrom; d, Lois Weber; w. Leonore J. Coffee; t, John Kraft; ph, Arthur Miller; ed, Harold McLernon; art d, Mitchell Leisen.

Drama **(PR:A MPAA:NR)**

ANGEL OF CROOKED STREET, THE* (1922) 5 reels VIT bw

Alice Calhoun *(Jennie Marsh)*, Ralph McCullough *(Schuyler Sanford)*, Scott McKee *("Silent" McKay)*, Rex Hammel *("Kid Glove" Thurston)*, *William McCall ("Cap" Berry)*, Nellie Anderson *("Mother" De Vere)*, Mary H. Young *(Mother Marsh)*, George Stanley *(Stoneham)*, Walter Cooper *(Dan Bolten)*, Martha Mattox *(Mrs. Phineas Sanford)*.

Typically poor Vitagraph feature about a girl forced to work as a domestic due to her family's financial reverses. After a theft, the widow for whom she works wrongly accuses her and she is sent to reform school. When the girl gets out, she seeks revenge, joins a gang of crooks but, ultimately, falls in love with her accuser's son.

d, David Smith; w, C. Graham Baker (based on a story by Harry Dittmar); ph, Stephen Smith, Jr.

Drama **(PR:A MPAA:NR)**

ANKLES PREFERRED*** (1927) 6 reels FOX bw

Madge Bellamy *(Norah)*, Lawrence Gray *(Barney)*, Barry Norton *(Ted)*, Allan Forrest *(Hornsbee)*, Marjorie Beebe *(Flo)*, Joyce Compton *(Virginia)*, Arthur Houseman *(Jim)*, J. Farrell MacDonald *(McGuire)*, William Strauss *(Goldberg)*, Lillian Elliott *(Mrs. Goldberg)*, Mary Foy *(Mrs. McGuire)*.

Advertising man Gray gets the beautiful Bellamy a job modeling clothes at the shop owned by MacDonald and Strauss. Determined to succeed on the basis of her intellect rather than her shape, Bellamy finds herself pressed into service by the shopkeepers to garner more capital from their backer, Forrest. A glass of wine gets the silly sweetheart tipsy and she gives the plan away. When Forrest gets amorous in an auto, a chase ensues which ends in a battle between Gray and Forrest. The lissome lass decides that a well-turned ankle beats a well-rounded mind any time where men are concerned. Bellamy enjoyed great success with a series of "working girl makes good" pictures during the 1920s. In this one, she looks great, acts well, and even manages to bring happiness to two roommates.

d, J. G. Blystone; w, James Hamilton (based on a story by Kenneth Hawks, Blystone, Philip Klein; ph, Glen MacWilliams.

Comedy **(PR:A MPAA:NR)**

ANNA ASCENDS*** (1922) 6 reels FP/PAR bw

Alice Brady *(Anna Ayyob)*, Robert Ellis *(Howard Fisk)*, David Powell *(The Baron)*, Nita Naldi *(Countess Rostoff)*, Charles Gerrard *(Count Rostoff)*, Edward Durrand *(Siad Coury)*, Florence Dixon *(Bessie Fisk)*, Grace Griswold *(Miss Fisk)*, Frederick Burton *(Mr. Fisk)*.

Working in a New York City coffeehouse, upwardy mobile immigrant Brady discovers her boss Powell is the head of a gem-smuggling ring. When she confronts the villain, the resulting altercation causes her to believe she has killed him. She assumes another identity and becomes a success. Years later, to keep her sweetheart Ellis' sister from marrying Gerrard, a member of the smuggling mob, Brady confesses her complicity in the "death" of Powell. The latter proves to be alive after all. Wonderful location shots of lower Manhattan are a definite plus in this screen adaption of Brady's hit Broadway play about a little Syrian immigrant who becomes a best-selling author.

d, Victor Fleming; w, Margaret Turnbull (based on the play by Harry Chapman Ford); ph, Gilbert Warrenton.

Drama **(PR:A MPAA:NR)**

ANNA CHRISTIE**** (1923) 8 reels THI/AFN bw

Blanche Sweet *(Anna Christie)*, George F. Marion *(Chris Christopherson)*, William Russell *(Matt Burke)*, Eugenie Besserer *(Marthy)*, Ralph Yearsley *(The Brutal Cousin)*, Chester Conklin *(Tommy)*, George Siegmann *(Anna's Uncle)*, Victor Potel, Fred Kohler.

Determined that his daughter shall not fall victim to the lure of his own cruel master, the sea, Marion sends Sweet to the Minnesota farm of cousins. Mistreated there, young Sweet runs off to Chicago, where she becomes a streetwalker. Seeking redemption, she visits Marion in New York and sets up housekeeping on the coal barge he commands. There she falls in love with sailor Russell, a fate her father feared. In the ensuing argument, she confesses her clouded past, risking the loss of both her father and her lover. A reconciliation is effected at the end. It has been said that the only filmed adaptation author O'Neill liked of one of his plays was the silent version of ANNA CHRISTIE. To be sure, this was an artistically well produced-and-acted production, which producer Ince claimed he made not for the money, but rather to show the critics he could deliver art, as well as entertainment. Sweet has, in retrospect, been a bit critical of the film and her performance, but the reviewers at the time thought her superb, and perhaps she has been unreasonably harsh on herself.

p, Thomas H. Ince; d, John Griffith Wray; w, Bradley King (based on the play by Eugene O'Neill); ph, Henry Sharp.

Drama **(PR:C MPAA:NR)**

ANNA THE ADVENTURESS** (1920, Brit.) 6 reels Hepworth/N bw

Alma Taylor *(Anna/Annabel Pelissier)*, James Carew *(Montague Hill)*, Gerald Ames *(Nigel Ennison)*, Gwynne Herbert *(Aunt)*, Christine Rayner *(Mrs. Ellicote)*, Ronald Colman *(Brendan)*, James Annand *(Sir John Ferringhall)*, Jean Cadell *(Mrs. White)*.

English mystery in which a Parisian dancer assumes the identity of a twin in order to kill a crooked husband.

d, Cecil M. Hepworth; w, Blanche McIntosh (based on a novel by E. Phillips Oppenheim).

Crime **(PR:A MPAA:NR)**

ANNABEL LEE*

(1921) 5 reels Joe Mitchell Chopple "Heart Throb Feature"/Joan Film Sales bw

Jack O'Brien *(David Martin)*, Lorraine Harding *(Annabel Lee)*, Florida Kingsley *(Mother Martin)*, Louis Stearns *(Col. Lee)*, Ben Grauer *(David Martin as a Child)*, Arline Blackburn *(Annabel Lee as a Child)*, Ernest Hilliard *(David Grainger)*.

Young fisherman O'Brien agrees to absent himself from his true love Harding for a year at the request of her father Stearns. After many adventures, including mutiny and abandonment on an island, O'Brien returns and claims the waiting maiden as his bride. Independent feature film based on the poem by Poe is horrible in every way.

d, William J. Scully; w, Arthur Brilliant (based on the poem by Edgar Allan Poe).

Mystery **(PR:A MPAA:NR)**

ANNAPOLIS* (1928) 6 reels Pathe bw

Johnny Mack Brown *(Bill)*, Hugh Allan *(Herbert)*, Hobart Bosworth *(Father)*, William Bakewell *(Skippy)*, Charlotte Walker *(Aunt)*, Maurice Ryan *(Fat)*, Jeanette Loff *(Betty)*, Byron Munson *(First Classman)*, Fred Appleby.

Initially competitive, plebes Brown and Allan become friends at the U.S. Naval Academy until Brown spots Loff, Allan's girl friend. Allan goes off the base to confront Loff about her flirtatiousness despite being confined to quarters. When he gets in trouble, Brown covers up for him. When Brown is court-martialed, Allan confesses his guilt. A complete stereotype military-academy film. The subject was dear to the heart of director Cabanne, himself a graduate of the Naval Academy.

p, F. McGrew Willis; d, Christy Cabanne; w, Willis (based on a story by Royal S. Pease); t, John Krafft; ph, Arthur Miller; ed, Claude Berkeley; art d, Edward Jewell; m/l, "My Annapolis and You," Charles Weinberg, Irving Bibo; syn sc; s eff.

Drama **(PR:A MPAA:NR)**

ANNE AGAINST THE WORLD* (1929) 6 reels T/C/RAY bw

Shirley Mason *(Anne)*, Jack Mower *(John Forbes)*, James Bradbury, Jr. *(Eddie)*, Billy Franey, Isabelle Keith *(Teddy)*, Belle Stoddard, Tom Curran *(Emmett)*, Henry Roquemore *(Folmer)*, Boris Karloff.

This poorly done backstage hokum offers absolutely no surprises. It's all about a comedy-music star, Mason, who falls for and marries the dashing and wealthy Mower. A producer relentlessly pursues her, however, and her husband decides to test her fidelity by pretending he is penniless. Mason decides to leave him and return to her old life, but their love for one another overcomes all, and the two are reunited.

d, Duke Worne; w, Arthur Hoerl (based on a novel by Victor Thorne); ph, Hap Depew; ed, J.S. Harrington.

Drama **(PR:A MPAA:NR)**

ANNE OF GREEN GABLES** (1919) 7 reels REA bw

Mary Miles Minter *(Anne Shirley)*, George Stewart *(Gilbert Blythe)*, Marcia Harris *(Marilla Cuthbert)*, Frederick Burton *(Matthew Cuthbert)*, F.T. Chaillee *(Abdenego Pie)*, Leila Romer *(Mrs. Pie)*, Lincoln Stedman *(Jumbo Pie)*, Hazel Sexton *(Josie Pie)*, Master Russel Hewitt *(Anthony Pie)*, Albert Hackett *(Robert)*, Maurice Lovelle *(Diana Barry)*, Mrs. Caroline Lee *(Mrs. Barry)*, Jack B. Hollis *(Rev. Figtree)*, Mary Hall, Beatrice Allen, Harry Bartlett.

This is an average picture about the trials of an orphan girl reared by New England relatives in stark, unsmiling, never-show-affection manner. But the real historical interest here is in the pairing of the two principals in what was to become, three years later, Hollywood's most sensational scandal—the still unsolved murder of 35-year-old director Taylor and the subsequent banishment from stardom of Minter, his reputed 22-year-old paramour.

d, William Desmond Taylor; w, Frances Marion (based on the four "Anne" novels by L.M. Montgomery); ph, Hal Young.

Drama **(PR:A MPAA:NR)**

ANNE OF LITTLE SMOKY* (1921) 5 reels WI/PG bw

Winifred Westover *(Anne)*, Dolores Cassinelli *(Gita)*, Joe King *(Bob Hayne)*, Frank Hagney *(Ed Brockton)*, Ralph Faulkner *(Tom Brockton)*, Harold Callahan *(Buddy)*, Alice Chapin *(Mrs. Brockton)*, Frank Sheridan *("The" Brockton)*, Edward Roseman *(Sam Ward)*.

Forest ranger King is at odds with the Brockton clan after the government dispossesses them of the mountain area they claim as their own. Westover falls in love with her clan's nemesis but becomes jealous when King saves gypsy girl Cassinelli from a lecherous lout. The duty-ridden King arrests his girl friend's father for poaching on government property, but the charge is dropped when Westover steals the evidence. Later, the clan believe that King has killed one of their number, Hagney, and go after him with bloodhounds. Westover diverts the hounds from their intended prey by donning King's clothing and laying a false scent. Hagney proves to be alive and all turns out well. This inferior independent production, dealing with love and duty, is set in the mountains. Original release print listed neither director nor writer.

d, Edward Connor; w, Frank Beresford (based on a story by Connor); ph, John S. Stumar.

Drama **(PR:A MPAA:NR)**

ANNEXING BILL*** (1918) 5 reels Astra bw

Gladys Hulette *(Enid Barwell)*, Creighton Hale *(Billy)*, Mark Smith *(George Frayne)*, Margaret Greene *(Mrs. Frayne)*.

Fine little comedy featuring two of the silent cinema's most underrated players, Hulette (TOL'ABLE DAVID) and Hale (WAY DOWN EAST, CAT AND THE CANARY). In this story, an inherited windfall disrupts romance, but all ends well when the money is ultimately lost in the stock market.

d, Albert Parker; w, Tom Cushing (based on a story by Edgar Franklin).

Comedy **(PR:A MPAA:NR)**

ANNIE LAURIE*** (1927) 9 reels MGM bw

Lillian Gish *(Annie Laurie)*, Norman Kerry *(Ian MacDonald)*, Creighton Hale *(Donald)*, Joseph Striker *(Alastair)*, Hobart Bosworth *(The MacDonald Chieftain)*, Patricia Avery *(Enid)*, Russell Simpson *(Sandy)*, Brandon Hurst *(The Campbell Chieftan)*, David Torrence *(Sir Robert Laurie)*, Frank Currier *(Cameron of Lochiel)*.

The body of a kinsman is dumped at the doorstep of Bosworth, head of the warring MacDonald clan. The vengeance-seeking MacDonalds raid the lair of their enemies, the Campbells, capturing Avery, who proceeds to capture the heart of her captor, Striker. Kerry falls in love with Gish, daughter of the peace-seeking governor, Torrence, who persuades the MacDonalds to house some Campbell troops on their land. The treacherous Campbells attempt to sabotage the defenses of the MacDonalds, but Gish helps her man to overcome them. Clan warfare in Scotland is the subject of this big MGM production. Gish, in her autobiography *The Movies, Mr. Griffith, and Me*, recalled fans writing to ask why she didn't smile more in her films. "I did in ANNIE LAURIE," she said, "but I can't recall that it helped much"....Some of us recall otherwise.

d, John S. Robertson; w, Josephine Lovett; t, Marian Ainslee, Ruth Cummings; ph, Oliver Marsh; ed, William Hamilton; art d, Cedric Gibbons, Merrill Pye.

Drama **(PR:A MPAA:NR)**

ANN'S FINISH* (1918) 5 reels AM bw

Margarita Fischer, Jack Mower, Adelaide Elliot, David Howard, John Gough, Robert Klein, Perry Banks.

Dreadful film with a plot so confused that at one point the whole movie stops and a title card asks the audience to guess what Ann will do next. Some reviews of the day felt this was the picture's highlight.

d, Lloyd Ingrahm.

Drama **(PR:A MPAA:NR)**

ANOTHER MAN'S BOOTS*** (1922) 5 reels Ivor McFadden/ANCH bw

Francis Ford *(The Stranger)*, Harry Smith *(Ned Hadley)*, Elvira Weil *(Nell Hadley)*, Frank Lanning *(Injun Jim)*, Robert Kortman *("Sly" Stevens)*.

Ford assumes the identity of his wounded friend Smith at the latter's own request, deceiving both Smith's blind father and his lovely sister, Weil. Kortman, who wants their ranch, sees through the imposture and accuses Ford of the murder of Smith. In the nick of time, the real Smith shows up. This comeback picture for Ford—one-time serial star (and brother of director John)—worked very well for the small, action-oriented theaters. There were no director or writer credits on the original release prints.

d, William J. Craft; w, Daniel F. Whitcomb; ph, Edward Estabrook.

Western **(PR:A MPAA:NR)**

ANOTHER MAN'S WIFE** (1924) 5 reels RF/PDC bw

James Kirkwood *(John Brand)*, Lila Lee *(Helen Brand)*, Wallace Beery *(Capt. Wolf)*, Matt Moore *(Phillip Cochran)*, Zena Keefe *(Dancer)*, Chester Conklin *(Rumrunner)*.

Standard domestic-society folks yarn about a neglected wife who fakes desertion in order to re-activate her husband's libido. The ploy works, but only after the couple become involved with rumrunners, a shipwreck, and a rescue by a U.S. Navy submarine. Box office attendance at the time was given a boost by the real-life, newlywed status of stars Kirkwood and Lee.

d, Bruce Mitchell; w, Elliott Clauson, Mitchell; ph, Steve Norton.

Drama **(PR:A MPAA:NR)**

ANOTHER SCANDAL*** (1924) 8 reels Tilford/W.W. Hodkinson bw

Lois Wilson *(Beatrice Vanderdyke)*, Holmes Herbert *(Pelham Franklin)*, Flora Le Breton *(Mrs. May Beamish)*, Hedda Hopper *(Cousin Elizabeth MacKenzie)*, Ralph Bunker *(Mally)*, Zeffie Tilbury *(Brownie)*, Ralph W. Chambers *(Valentine Beamish)*, Bigelow Cooper *(Mitchell Burrows)*, Allan Simpson *(Alec Greenwood)*, Harry Grippe *('Arry 'Arris)*.

An almost naughty programmer, shot in Florida, about flirtations and male-female dominance in marriage. Everyone concerned accomplished a great deal working on a shoestring.

d, Edward H. Griffith; w, G. Marion Burton (based on the play by Cosmo Hamilton); ph, Dal Clawson.

Drama **(PR:A MPAA:NR)**

ANSWER, THE*** (1916, Brit.) 5 reels BRO/Browne bw

Muriel Martin-Harvey *(The Lonely Woman)*, George Foley *(Justin Siddeley)*, Dora Barton *(The Lost Magdalene)*, George Bellamy *(The Clerk)*, T.R. Tozer, Gregory Scott, Arthur M. Cullin.

In this British drama, a desperate man who has lost everything is brought to his senses when a spirit shows him three examples of faith overcoming despair.

d, Walter West; w, Dane Stanton (based on the novel *Is God Dead?* by Newman Flower).

Drama **(PR:A MPAA:NR)**

ANSWER, THE*** (1918) 7 reels TRI bw

Joe King *(John Warfield)*, Charles Dorian *(Robert Warfield)*, Francis McDonald *(Guidi Garcia)*, Jean Hersholt *(Shepard)*, Claire Anderson *(Goldie Shepard)*, Alma Rubens *(Lorraine Van Allen)*, Wilbur Higby, Betty Pearce.

This unusual seven-reel Triangle special did not use the customary big-name cast but had an interesting plot which favored socialism. King, the son of a political activist, runs a refuge for working stiffs in San Francisco and loves the daughter of laboring parents. He discovers his aristocratic lineage when his English grandfather dies leaving him a fortune, which he elects to share with the masses. There is a nice double plot twist in which his working-class girl friend embraces the world of wealth, while a society girl who does volunteer work at the center falls in love with him and his cause.

d, E. Mason Hopper; w, E. Mason Ingleton; ph, A. Nagy.

Drama **(PR:A MPAA:NR)**

ANTON THE TERRIBLE*** (1916) 5 reels LAS/PAR bw

Theodore Roberts *(Anton Kazoff)*, Anita King *(Vera Stanovitch)*, Horace B. Carpenter *(Gen. Stanovitch, Her Father)*, Harrison Ford *(David Burkin)*, Hugh B. Koch *(Grand Duke Ivanovitch)*, Edythe Chapman *(Babushka, Anton's Mother)*, Elia Trombly *(Olga, Anton's Sister)*.

The highly underrated elder brother of Cecil B. DeMille directed this beautifully acted and photographed story of a Cossack who revenges his sister's rape and saves his mother's life by heroically committing suicide.

p, Jesse Lasky; d, William C. DeMille; w, Marion Fairfax, Charles Sarver, Jules Eckert Goodman (based on a story by Thomas H. Uzzell); ph, Charles Rosher.

Drama **(PR:A MPAA:NR)**

ANTICS OF ANN, THE*** (1917) 5 reels PAR bw

Ann Pennington *(Ann Wharton)*, Harry Ham *(Tom Randall)*, Ormi Hawley *(Olive Wharton)*, Crauford Kent *(Gordon Trent)*, W.T. Carleton *(Mr. Wharton)*, Charlotte Granville *(Mrs. Bredwell)*.

Good showcase for Pennington, a popular Ziegfeld dancer who is credited with popularizing the dance craze "The Black Bottom." Here her elfish charm is shown to great advantage while performing a host of tomboy stunts and dance gyrations. The plot to this film really didn't matter. Audiences wanted to see this great entertainer, and Paramount gave them that chance.

d, Edward Dillon; w, Coolidge W. Streeler (based on a story by Frederick Chapin); art d, Richard Murphy.

Comedy **(PR:A MPAA:NR)**

ANY WIFE* (1922) 5 reels FOX bw

Pearl White *(Myrtle [Mrs. John] Hill)*, Holmes Herbert *(Philip Gray)*, Gilbert Emery *(Mr. John Hill)*, Lawrence Johnson *(Cyril Hill)*, Augustus Balfour *(Dr. Gaynor)*, Eulalie Jensen *(Louise Farrata)*.

White, past her prime, plays a suburban wife who runs off with her husband's employee, sinks to the gutter, and finally commits suicide by jumping from a bridge. At this point, White awakens from a dream, causing the audience to realize the unsatisfactory titillation they were receiving was even less so.

d, Herbert Brenon; w, Julia Tolsva; ph, Tom Malloy.

Drama **(PR:C MPAA:NR)**

ANY WOMAN* (1925) 6 reels FP/PAR bw

Alice Terry *(Ellen Linden)*, Ernest Gillen *(Tom Galloway)*, Margarita Fischer *(Mrs. Rand)*, Lawsun Butt *(James Rand)*, Aggie Herring *(Mrs. Galloway)*, James Neill *(William Linden)*, De Sacia Mooers *(Mrs. Phillips)*, Henry Kolker *(Egbert Phillips)*, George Periolat *(Robert Cartwright)*, Lucille Hutton *(Agnes Young)*, Arthur Hoyt *(Jones)*, Malcolm Denny *(Lord Brackenridge)*, Thelma Morgan *(Alice Cartwright)*.

Spoiled young woman returns from Europe to find her father broke and in poor health. She takes a job, avoids the advances of several mashers, and finally marries a nice young man who has started a soft drink company. Only some clever title cards keep this film from being a failure on all levels.

d, Henry King; w, Jules Furthman, Beatrice Van (based on a story by Arthur Somers Roche); t, Randolph Bartlet; ph, Ernest Hallor, William Schurr.

Drama **(PR:A MPAA:NR)**

ANTHING ONCE*** (1917) 5 reels BLUE bw

Franklyn Farnum *(Theodore Crosby)*, Claire Du Brey *(Senorita Dolores)*, Marjory Lawrence *(Dorothy Stuart)*, Mary St. John *(Mrs. Stuart)*, Sam De Grasse *(Sir Mortimer Beggs)*, Lon Chaney *(Waughnt Moore)*, H.M. Thurston *(Getting Mohr)*, Raymond Wells *("Horned Toad" Smith)*, William Dyer *(Jethro Quall)*, Frank Tokunaga *(Algernon)*.

This blatant Fairbanks imitation has a New York playboy inheriting a western ranch on the condition that he live there for 6 months. There are, of course, a villain and a pretty girl, both of whom he manages to handle breezily. Good fun, but definitely not comparable to a Fairbanks offering.

d, Joseph DeGrasse; w, William Parker (based on a story by Isola Forrester, Mann Page).

Drama **(PR:A MPAA:NR)**

ANYTHING ONCE*** (1925) 5 reels Classplay/AY bw

Gladys Walton, Harold Austin, Tully Marshal, Mathilde Brundage, Francis McDonald, Arko the Dog.

A sailor who has spent his last cent on an English-cut suit and a turn-down hat, in the manner of the Prince of Wales, is invited to the home of a man whose daughter is infatuated with a phony duke. The sailor exposes the crook and wins the girl. This was a very well done budget production.

p, Jack Weinberg; d, Justin H. McCloskey; w, Harry Chandlee (based on a story by Nate H. Edwards); ph, Charles Murphy.

Comedy/Drama **(PR:A MPAA:NR)**

APACHE, THE** (1925, Brit.) 8 reels Millar-Thompson/Napoleon bw

Adelqui Millar *(The Panther)*, Mona Maris *(Lisette Blanchard)*, Jameson Thomas *(Gaston d'Harcourt)*, Jerrold Robertshaw *(Albert d'Harcourt)*, Doris Mansell *(Armande)*, San Juana *(Mario)*, James Carrasco *(Gaspard)*.

British love story about an Apache dancer who marries the sister of his former fiancee in an act of revenge but ultimately falls in love with her.

p, Adelqui Millar, Herbert Thompson; d, Millar; w, Michael Allard.

Drama **(PR:A MPAA:NR)**

APACHE, THE*** (1928) 6 reels COL bw

Margaret Livingston *(Sonya)*, Warner Richmond *(Gaston Laroux)*, Don Alvarado *(Pierre Dumont)*, Philo McCullough *(Mons. Chautard)*.

Good little mystery, set in the Apache dens of Marseilles and Paris. Livingston, a theatrical knife-thrower, obtains a confession from her partner by threatening him with death during a performance and thus saving the man she loves from wrongly being sent to Devil's Island for a crime the partner committed.

p, Jack Cohn; d, Phil Rosen; w, Harriet Hinsdale (based on a story by Ramon Romero); ph, Ted Tetzlaff; art d, Harrison Wiley.

Mystery (PR:A MPAA:NR)

APACHE RAIDER, THE*** (1928) 6 reels Pathe bw

Leo Maloney *(Apache Bob)*, Eugenia Gilbert *(Dixie Stillwell)*, Don Coleman *(Dal Cartwright)*, Tom London *(Griffin Dawson)*, Walter Shumway *("Fang" Jaccard)*, Fred Dana *("Bit" Ward)*, Jack Ganzhorn *("Breed" Artwell)*, William Merrill McCormick *(Ray Wharton)*, Robert C. Smith *("Beaze" La Mare)*, Murdock MacQuarrie *(Don Felix Beinal)*, Whitehorse *(Ed Stillwell)*, Robin Williamson, Dick La Reno, Robert Burns, Allen Watt.

Maloney discovers that London is a thief who is stealing cattle with the help of a gang of hired thugs and rotten politicians, and he begins stealing London's cattle himself. Soon he is regarded as a bandit and London succeeds in arousing the townspeople against him. At his lynching party, with London guffawing from the sidelines, the crowd suddenly turns against the cutthroat, and he and Maloney shoot it out, with Maloney finally becoming the town's big hero. Nice paced western.

d, Leo D. Maloney; w, Ford J. Beebe; ph, Edward A. Kull.

Western (PR:A MPAA:NR)

APARTMENT 29** (1917) 5 reels VIT bw

Earle Williams, Ethel Gray Terry, Denton Vane, L. Johnston, Billie Billings, V. Stuart, Bernard Siegel, Frank Mason, Tommy Brett.

Rather interesting programmer about a theatrical producer who uses actors to stage the events of his play in order to persuade a newspaper critic to print a good review. This above-average (for Vitagraph) production owed much to George M. Cohan's "Seven Keys to Baldpate," from the Earl Derr Biggers novel, where a writer lives his novel just as he is writing it.

d, Paul Scardon; w, Edward J. Montagne (based on his own story).

Mystery (PR:A MPAA:NR)

APE, THE* (1928) 5 reels Milt Collins/Collwyn bw

Ruth Stonehouse, Gladys Walton, Basil Wilson, Bradley Barker.

Brainless little independent mystery that the producers claim is based on real police records. Shadows weave in and out, figures dance on window sills, and fights in the dark enliven but do not illuminate what is going on in the director's head in this jumbled mess, where a fleeting shot of the Hudson River is about the only recognizable feature of the picture.

d, B.C. Rule; w, (based on police records).

Mystery (PR:A MPAA:NR)

APOSTLE OF VENGEANCE, THE**** (1916) 5 reels Kay-Bee/TRI bw

William S. Hart *(David Hudson)*, Nona Thomas *(Mary McCoy)*, Joseph J. Dowling *(Tom McCoy)*, Fanny Midgley *("Marm" Hudson)*, Jack Gilbert *(Willie Hudson)*, Marvel Stafford *(Elsie Hudson)*, Jean Hersholt.

Another top effort by actor-director Hart. In this one he plays a preacher who seeks revenge without the use of a gun. A truly marvelous blend of action, romance, and sentimentality, with Dane Hersholt playing an extra in his second year in films.

d, William S. Hart, Clifford Smith; w, Monte M. Katterjohn; ph, Joseph August.

Western (PR:A MPAA:NR)

APPEARANCE OF EVIL*** (1918) 5 reels WORLD bw

June Elvidge *(Maida Brown)*, Frank Mayo *(Louis Letchworth)*, Douglas Redmond, Jr. *(Gordon Brown)*, George MacQuarrie *(Harold Brown)*, Nora Cecil *(Miss Spurgeon)*, Inez Marcel *(Elsie Quimby)*, Clay Clement, Jr., Louis Grizel, Jack Drumier.

Far-fetched but good programmer about a woman accused by small-town residents of having an affair with a man whom she cannot prove (because of lost records) is her husband. Some tense moments when they try to take her child away, and a surprise ending, helped make this one work.

d, Lawrence C. Windom; w, Clara S. Berranger (based on a story by Horace Hazeltine [Charles Stokes Wayne]); ph, Max Schneider.

Drama (PR:A MPAA:NR)

APPEARANCES** (1921) 5 reels FP/PAR bw

David Powell *(Herbert Seaton)*, Mary Glynne *(Kitty Mitchell)*, Langhorne Burton *(Lord Rutherford)*, Marjorie Hume *(Agnes, Kitty's Sister)*, Percy Standing *(Percy Dawkins)*, Mary Dibly *(Lady Rutherford)*.

This rather boring English film is about an architect and his wife who try to live in the manner of their socially "superior" associates. After her husband plays the market and loses, the wife takes a job with a lord who secretly loves her. Suspecting an affair between the two, the husband steals her $25 paycheck and alters it to read $2,500. The check is cashed by a promoter the architect owes money to, and the lord, on receiving it back from the bank, because of his affection for the wife, destroys it. The architect finally confesses, and he and his wife decide to begin a new life together in Canada. This was one of the rare English films to play American houses at the time, but scenic shots alone were not enough to put it over.

d, Donald Crisp; w, Edward Knoblock; w, Margaret Turnbull (based on a story by Edward Knoblock); ph, Hal Young.

Drama (PR:A MPAA:NR)

APRIL FOOL*** (1926) 7 reels CHAD bw

Alexander Carr *(Jacob Goodman)*, Duane Thompson *(Irma Goodman)*, Mary Alden *(Amelia Rosen)*, Raymond Keane *(Leon Steinfield)*, Edward Phillips *(Joseph Applebaum)*, Snitz Edwards *(Mr. Applebaum)*, Nat Carr *(Moisha Ginsburg)*, Baby Peggy, Pat Moore, Leon Holmes *(The Kids)*.

This story about a former pants-presser who gives up his fortune so that his daughter may find happiness with the young man she loves is rather like the Cohens without the Kellys and Abie before he met his Irish Rose. After making a fortune in the umbrella business, the former pants presser finds his daughter has fallen in love with the son of a newly rich neighbor. However, the son is accused by his uncle of stealing a large sum of money which was actually stolen by the uncle's own son. The former pants presser steps in and, by giving up his fortune, succeeds in assuring his daughter's happiness. Nutty early story of New York's *nouveaux riche* in the Roaring Twenties.

d, Nat Ross; w, Zion Myer (based on the play "An April Shower" by Edgar Allan Woolf, Alexander Carr); t, James Madison; ph, L. William O'Connell.

Comedy (PR:A MPAA:NR)

APRIL SHOWERS**** (1923) 6 reels PRE bw

Kenneth Harlan *(Danny O'Rourke)*, Colleen Moore *(Maggie Muldoon)*, Ruth Clifford *(Miriam Welton)*, Priscilla Bonner *(Shannon O'Rourke)*, Myrtle Vane *(Mother O'Rourke)*, James Corrigan *(Matt Gallagher)*, Jack Byron *(Flash Irwin)*, Ralph Faulkner *(Champ Sullivan)*, Tom McGuire *(Lt. Muldoon)*, Kid McCoy, Danny Goodman *(The Ring Managers)*.

Warm, funny, not too sentimental story of young Irish love on New York's lower East Side. Director Forman guided this film beautifully, creating a host of touching scenes, such as the one where Harlan cannot bring himself to tell his girl, Moore, he flunked the police academy exam (his father having been an officer killed on duty), and laughs it off. He goes to his mother who, in a beautifully understated moment, lets him know she understands. Harlan turns to boxing to support the family and help his kid sister out of a jam and ultimately lands a championship bout. However, on learning the fight has been fixed by gamblers to favor him, he tells the crowd. The officials elect to let the match go on anyway, and the incensed champ tears into Harlan with a vengeance and, after a great struggle, knocks him cold. The young man is forced to hang up his gloves, but the story ends happily with an appointment to the police force being granted. Moore is superb as Maggie. At the end of the film she visits Harlan in the hospital, carrying a portrait she painted after taking mail-order art lessons. An effective bit of business throughout the picture shows the sweethearts engaging in a series of playful little arguments, and upon receiving the picture, he gazes up at her and asks who it is. Expressing the perfect amount of anger Moore says "Why, don't ya recognize your own 'bog trottin' mug?" This was the kind of honestly touching film that made the audiences of that day feel truly good about each other.

p, B.P. Schulberg; d, Tom Forman; w, Hope Loring, Duryea Lighton; ph, Harry Perry.

Comedy/Drama (PR:A MPAA:NR)

ARAB, THE*** (1915) 5 reels LAS/PAR bw

Edgar Selwyn *(Jamil, the Son)*, Horace B. Carpenter *(The Sheik, His Father)*, Milton Brown *(Abdullah)*, Billy Elmer *(Meshur)*, Sydney Deane *(Dr. Hilbert)*, Gertrude Robinson *(Mary)*, J. Parke Jones *(Ibrahim)*, Theodore Roberts *(Turkish Governor)*, Raymond Hatton *(Mysterious Messenger)*, Irvin S. Cobb *(American Tourist)*.

Nicely filmed story of an Arab who converts to Christianity and saves a group of Christians from an attempted Turkish massacre. Of particular interest is a cameo role by the celebrated author, Cobb, at the beginning of the first reel.

p&d, Cecil B. DeMille; w, Edgar Selwyn, DeMille (based on the play by Selwyn); ph, Alvin Wycoff; ed, DeMille.

Drama (PR:A MPAA:NR)

ARAB, THE**** (1924) 7 reels Metro/Goldwyn bw

Ramon Novarro *(Jamil Abdullah Azam)*, Alice Terry *(Mary Hilbert)*, Gerald Robertshaw *(Dr. Hilbert)*, Maxudian *(Governor)*, Count Jean de Limur *(Hossein, His Aide)*, Adelqui Millar *(Abdulla)*, Paul Vermoyal *(Iphraim)*, Alexandresco *(Oulad Nile)*, Justa Uribe *(Myrza)*, Gerald Robertshaw *(Dr. Hilbert)*, Paul Francesci *(Marmount)*, Giuseppe De Compo *(Selim)*.

By shooting some of his scenes in Algiers and using native extras, Ingram (one of the great directors) brought a powerful sense of realism to the popular Arabian genre. Novarro is the son of a Bedouin tribe leader who is disowned by his father for raiding a desert oasis during the holy time of a feast. He becomes a guide in a Turkish city where he meets and falls in love with Terry, daughter of a Christian missionary. Jamil foils an attempt by the governor to massacre the Christians and for his skillful use of Bedouin tribesmen in the affair, his dying father appoints him leader of his tribe. Whereupon Novarro extracts a promise from Terry to return to him as she leaves for the U.S. This is a visually stunning motion picture, and the end, which leaves audiences guessing as to whether Christian and Moslem can really get together, is most effective.

d&w, Rex Ingram (based on a play by Edgar Selwyn); ph, John F. Seitz.

Adventure (PR:A MPAA:NR)

ABABIAN KNIGHT, AN*** (1920) 4 reels Haworth/R-C bw

Sessue Hayakawa *(Ahmed)*, Lillian Hall *(Elinor Wayne)*, Jean Acker *(Zorah)*, Marie Pavis *(Cordelia Darwin)*, Harvey Clark *(George Darwin)*, Fred Jones *(Aboul Pasha)*, Tom D. Bates, Roy Coulson, Fred Jones, Elaine Innescourt.

Cashing in on the interest of that day, reincarnation, the producers of this film have a modern girl imagine she loves Hayakawa, a donkey boy in ancient Egypt. The picture flashes back to that time, and some first-rate action footage unfolds as Hayakawa rescues the girl from the clutches of a lecherous Jones.

d, Charles Swickard; w, E. Richard Schayer (based on a story by Gene Wright); ph, Frank Williams.

Adventure **(PR:A MPAA:NR)**

ARABIAN LOVE****** (1922) 5 reels FOX bw

John Gilbert *(Norman Stone)*, Barbara Bedford *(Nadine Fortier)*, Adolphe Menjou *(Capt. Fortine)*, Herschel Mayall *(The Sheik)*, Robert Kortman *(Ahmed Bey)*, William H. Orlamond *(Dr. Lagorio)*, Barbara LaMarr.

This successful attempt to cash in on the "sheik" craze was, in fact, a better picture than the original. Plot has young American Gilbert joining an Arab band after killing a French officer who wronged his sister. Later, the band attacks a caravan and Gilbert rescues the widow of the man he killed. Not knowing this, the two fall in love, but upon learning the truth, the widow sets a trap for her lover. Before he is captured, however, she discovers the circumstances of her husband's crime and gives the American her heart. Of this breakthrough film for dashing Gilbert, Variety wrote, "...introducing a star in the person of John Gilbert who stands out as a comer."

d, Jerome Storm; w, Jules Furthman; ph, Joe August.

Adventure/Romance **(PR:A MPAA:NR)**

ARCADIANS, THE* (1927, Brit.) 7 reels GAU bw

Ben Blue *(Simplicitas Smith)*, Jeanne de Casalis *(Mrs. Smith)*, Vesta Sylva *(Eileen Cavanaugh)*, John Longden *(Jack Meadows)*, Gibb McLaughlin *(Peter Doody)*, Humberston Wright *(Sir George Paddock)*, Cyril McLaglen *(The Crook)*, Doris Bransgrove *(Sombra)*, Nancy Rigg *(Chrysea)*, Teddy Brown, Ivor Vintor, Lola and Luis, Tracey and Haye, Balliol and Merton, Donovan Sisters, Tiller Girls, 12 Arcadian Nymphs.

Saville, a popular English director (with a love for camera movement), failed completely with this British adaptation of a once-popular stage musical. A nightclub owner escapes to Arcadia after wrongly thinking the police are after him for his after-hours operations. When he returns to England, he gives his club an Arcadian atmosphere, rides to victory in the derby, and wins back his wife from the crooked jockey he took the place of. If this sounds confusing, bad, or both, bear in mind that there were seven vaudeville acts whose routines could not be heard in this silent picture and titles as bad as the following describing a horse race: "Gluepot will stick; Cabbage is a bit green, but may get ahead; Watertrap is sure to run; Oscar has been scratched, which made Oscar wild."

p, Maurice Elvey, Victor Saville, Gareth Gundrey; d, Saville; w, (based on the play by Mark Ambient, Alex Thompson).

Comedy **(PR:A MPAA:NR)**

ARE ALL MEN ALIKE?* (1920) 6 reels Metro bw

May Allison *("Teddy")*, Wallace MacDonald *(Gerry Rhinelander West)*, John Elliot *(Uncle Chandler)*, Winnifred Greenwood *(Mrs. Hayden)*, Emanuel A. Turner *("Gunboat" Dorgan)*, Ruth Stonehouse *(Ruby Joyce)*, Lester Cuneo *(Raoul Uhlan)*, Wilson Hummell, Harry Lamont, Bowd "Smoke" Turner, Peggy Blackwood.

An unbalanced, disjointed, unfunny attempt to produce a comedy dealing with a woman's role in a man's world. Another silent that could have been made straight from the headlines of the 1970s and 1980s.

d, Philip E. Rosen; w, A.P. Younger (based on the novel *The Waffle Iron* by Arthur Stringer); ph, Ben Bail.

Comedy **(PR:A MPAA:NR)**

ARE CHILDREN TO BLAME?*
(1922) 5 reels Chopin/Certified bw (AKA: ARE THE CHILDREN TO BLAME?)

Em Gorman *(Little Rosalind)*, Joseph Marquis *(Robert Brown)*, Alex K. Shannon *(David Granger)*, George Henry *(Judge Brown)*, Gordon Standing *(Caleb Hands)*, Tatjena Rirah *(Becky Small)*, Francis Eldridge *(Alice Hawthorne)*, Emma Tausey *(Mrs. Winslow)*, Robert Tausey *(Albert Winslow)*.

This mishmash, based loosely on George Eliot's novel *Silas Marner*, failed on every count. It's all about a little girl whose mother dies and she is left in the care of her aunt. The child, Gorman, has never met her father, Marquis, though he sends money to help provide for her care. When he is pressured by the aunt to send more money, Gorman robs the miserly village blacksmith. The child's aunt, who turns out to be a phony, then dies, and the girl somehow makes her way to the home of the blacksmith who takes her in. When authorities later try to remove Gorman from him, it is discovered that she is really not Marquis' daughter, and the orphan is left in the care of the delighted blacksmith.

d&w, Paul Price.

Drama **(PR:A MPAA:NR)**

ARE PARENTS PEOPLE?**** (1925) 7 reels FP/PAR bw

Betty Bronson *(Lita Hazlitt)*, Florence Vidor *(Mrs. Hazlitt)*, Adolphe Menjou *(Mr. Hazlitt)*, Andre Beranger *(Maurice Mansfield)*, Lawrence Gray *(Dr. Dacer)*, Mary Beth Milford *(Aurella Wilton)*, Emily Fitzroy *(Margaret)*, William Courtwright *(Freebody)*.

The marvelous acting by Bronson, and the slick direction by St. Clair, make this comedy about a young girl's successful attempt to reunite her divorce-bound parents a delight. It all comes about when Bronson, after some hectic misadventures, runs away from home and spends the night sleeping in the office of a doctor she has grown to like. Her parents, of course, are frantic. They go through countless recriminations and finally when Bronson returns home find themselves reunited through their love for her.

d, Malcolm St. Clair; w, Frances Agnew (based on a story by Alice Duer Miller); ph, Bert Glennon.

Comedy **(PR:A MPAA:NR)**

ARE THE CHILDREN TO BLAME?
(SEE: ARE CHILDREN TO BLAME? 1922)

ARE YOU A FAILURE?**** (1923) 6 reels Preferred Pictures bw

Madge Bellamy *(Phyllis Thorp)*, Lloyd Hughes *(Oliver Wendell Blaine)*, Tom Santschi *(Killdevil Brennon)*, Hardee Kirkland *(Gregory Thorp)*, Jane Keckley *(Aunt Emily)*, Myrtle Vane *(Aunt Charlotte)*, Hallam Cooley *(Emmet Graves)*, Samuel Allen *(Thaddeus Crane)*, Sport the Dog.

Satisfying outdoor yarn about the last member of a lumbering family who is raised by aunts and turned into a shop clerk pantywaist. He is the town sissy in the eyes of everyone but the lumber boss' daughter, who has just returned from finishing school. She promises her love if he can "prove" himself, which he does by taking on the town bully. A terrific logjam scene is the highlight of this one.

d, Tom Forman; w, Eve Unsell (based on a story by Larry Evans); ph, Harry Perry.

Adventure **(PR:A MPAA:NR)**

ARE YOU A MASON?* (1915) 5 reels FP bw

John Barrymore, Alfred Hickman, Charles Dixon, Charles Butler, Ida Waterman, Dodson Mitchell, Helen Freeman, Jean Acker, Lorraine Huling, Harold Lockwood, Kitty Baldwin, W. Dickinson.

Feeble comedic effort has Barrymore experiencing a series of difficulties while attempting to pass himself off as a Mason. The film was a failure on all levels.

d, Thomas N. Heffron; w, (based on the play by Leo Dietrichstein and on a German play by Lauf and Kraatz).

Comedy **(PR:A MPAA:NR)**

ARE YOU LEGALLY MARRIED?**** (1919) 5 reels Elk Photoplays bw

Lew Cody, *(John Stark)*, Rosemary Theby *(June Redding)*, Henry Woodward *(Wayne Hearne)*, Nanon Welsh *(Sue Redding)*, H.J. Barrows *(J.J. Redding)*, Roy Laidlaw *(Henry Martin)*.

This film about a woman who is divorced in one state and married again in another (which did not recognize the validity of the former decree, making her guilty of bigamy) caused a political sensation at the time. In fact, a print of this picture was shown in Congress, which inspired two measures being introduced to nationalize divorce laws, both of them losing, of course.

d, Robert T. Thornby; w, Henry Christeen Warnack (based on a story by Miles Dobson); ph, Sol Polito.

Drama **(PR:A MPAA:NR)**

ARGENTINE LOVE*** (1924) 6 reels FP/PAR bw

Bebe Daniels *(Consuelo Garcia)*, Ricardo Cortez *(Juan Martin)*, James Rennie *(Phillip Sears)*, Mario Majeroni *(Sen. Cornejo)*, Russ Whital *(Emanuel Garcia)*, Alice Chapin *(Mme. Garcia)*, Julia Hurley *(La Mosca)*, Mark Gonzales *(Rafael Cornejo)*, Aurelio Coccia *(Pedro)*.

This film, made during the height of the Valentino craze, is mainly of interest because almost everyone in the picture wearing pants (with the exception of Rennie, who plays an American engineer) is a Valentino look-alike. Daniels does well playing against this army of FOUR HORSEMEN OF THE APOCALYPSE clones, but the movie does not fare as well.

d, Allan Dwan; w, John Russell, Gerald Duffy (based on the story by Vincent Ibanez); ph, Roy Hunt.

Drama **(PR:A MPAA:NR)**

ARGUMENT, THE (SEE: EVIDENCE, 1918)

ARGYLE CASE, THE**** (1917) 7 reels Robert Warwick/SF bw

Robert Warwick *(Asche Kayton)*, Charles Hines *(Joe Manning)*, Frank McGlynn *(John Argyle)*, Arthur Albertson *(Bruce Argyle)*, Gazelle Marche *(Nan Thornton)*, Elaine Hammerstein *(Mary Mazuret)*, Frank Evans *(Mr. Hurley)*, John B. Fleming *(Inspector Doherty)*, H. Cooper Cliffe *(Frederick Kreisler)*, Mary Alden *(Nellie Marsh)*, Robert Vivian *(Finley)*, Joe Quinn.

This nifty action film, in the Sherlock Holmes tradition, was the first offering of favorite actor Warwick's production company. Film advisor William J. Burns founded the famous private detective agency.

d, Ralph Ince; w, Frederick Chapin, Ince (based on the play by Harvey J. O'Higgins, Harriet Ford, in collaboration with Detective William J. Burns); ph, Andre Barlatier.

Crime/Action **(PR:A MPAA:NR)**

ARIZONA**** (1918) 5 reels Douglas Fairbanks/ART bw

Douglas Fairbanks *(Lt. Denton)*, Theodore Roberts *(Canby)*, Kate Price *(Mrs. Canby)*, Frederick Burton *(Col. Benham)*, Harry Northrup *(Capt. Hodgeman)*, Frank Campeau *(Kellar)*, Kathleen Kirkham *(Estrella)*, Marjorie Daw *(Bonita)*, Marguerite de la Motte *(Lena)*, Raymond Hatton *(Tony)*, Robert Boulder *(Doctor)*, Albert McQuarrie *(Lt. Hatton)*, Ernest Butterworth, Tully Marshall.

Cleverly written comedy set in the Old West gives Fairbanks more than enough opportunity to stunt and charm his way to eventual triumph.

d, Douglas Fairbanks, Albert Parker; w, Fairbanks (based on the play by Augustus Thomas); ph, Hugh Carlyle, Hugh C. McClung, Glen MacWilliams.

Comedy/Western **(PR:A MPAA:NR)**

ARIZONA BOUND* (1927) 5 reels FP/PAR bw**

Gary Cooper *(Dave Saulter)*, Betty Jewel *(Ann Winslow)*, Jack Daugherty *(Buck Hanna)*, El Brendel *(Oley "Smoke" Oleson)*, Charles Crockett *(John Winslow)*, Christian Frank *(Texas Frank)*, Joe Butterworth *(Tommy Winslow)*, Guy Oliver *(Sheriff)*, Guinn "Big Boy" Williams, Flash the Horse.

In this one, Cooper, a ne'er-do-well, loves only his horse, Flash, and beautiful Jewel, who wishes he would settle down and marry and take care of her. A gold shipment robbery brings him out of his lazy ways, when Jewel is kidnaped by the robbers and Cooper saves her, the gold, and their romance. Quick moving western of primary interest because of Famous Players' decision to select a young Gary Cooper after his successful second lead part in THE WINNING OF BARBARA WORTH to compete with Metro Goldwyn's saddle star Col. Tim McCoy.

d, John Waters; w, Marion Jackson, John Stone, Paul Gangelin (based on a story by Richard Allen Gates); t, Alfred Hustwick; ph, Edgar Schoenbaum.

Western (PR:A MPAA:NR)

ARIZONA CATCLAW, THE* (1919) 5 reels WORLD bw

Edythe Sterling *(Blossom Ruggles)*, William Quinn *(Frank Stimpson)*, Gordon Sackville *(Hank Ruggles)*, Leo Maloney *(Asa Harris)*, Steve Clementi *(Zapatti)*, Pauline Becker, Leo Maloney.

Less than adequate western about the struggle between a Mexican bandit and a female rancher. Intended strictly for kids on the lower half of a double bill.

d, William Bertram; w, Charles Motimer Peck.

Western (PR:A MPAA:NR)

ARIZONA CYCLONE* (1928) 5 reels UNIV bw

Fred Humes *(Larry Day/Tom Day)*, George K. French *(John Cosgrave)*, Margaret Gray *(Kathleen Cosgrave)*, Cuyler Supplee *(Mel Craven)*, Pee Wee Holmes *(Pee Wee)*, Benny Corbett *(Benny)*, Dick L'Estrange *(Lazy Lester)*, Scotty Mattraw *(Scotty)*.

Low-grade western in which look-alike cousins (the bad one is known as the "Night Hawk") become involved in a robbery. In the end, the good one, whose identity the "Night Hawk" had assumed, saves the day.

d, Edgar Lewis; w, William Lester; t, Gardner Bradford; ph, Eddie Linden, Bill Cline; ed, Jack Jackson; art d, David S. Garber.

Western (PR:A MPAA:NR)

ARIZONA DAYS* (1928) 5 reels ED/SYN bw**

Bob Custer *(Chuck Drexel)*, Peggy Montgomery *(Dolly Martin)*, John Lowell Russell *(Dolly's Father)*, J. P. McGowan, Mack V. Wright *(Villains)*, Jack Ponder *(Detective)*.

The action moves right along in this western about a ranchers' protective association detective (Custer) who is sent to wipe out a gang of rustlers. He infiltrates the gang, finds Montgomery's father, Russell, has joined the gang unwillingly but for the protection of his herd, and after Montgomery lets it be known that she believes he is a member of the gang he turns the tables on everybody. He rescues Montgomery's father and arrests the gang leader, and Montgomery and her dad go back to the range without any more fears.

d, J. P. McGowan; w, Mack V. Wright (based on a story by Brysis Coleman); ph, Paul Allan.

Western (PR:A MPAA:NR)

ARIZONA EXPRESS, THE* (1924) 7 reels FOX bw**

Pauline Starke *(Katherine Keith)*, Evelyn Brent *(Lola Nichols)*, Anne Cornwall *(Florence Brown)*, Harold Goodwin *(David Keith)*, David Butler *(Steve Butler)*, Francis McDonald *(Victor Johnson)*, Frank Beal *(Judge Ashton)*, William Humphrey *(Henry MacFarlane)*.

More a prison picture than a western, the nonstop action must be credited to director Buckingham. Goodwin is sentenced to death for a crime he did not commit. His sister, Starke, proves that he is innocent, and reaches the governor in time to save her brother's life. Even the ending, which exploits the last-minute stay of an electrocution (a ploy beaten to death ever since director D. W. Griffith dazzled the world with its prototype in the modern episode of INTOLERANCE), was handled with suspenseful skill.

d, Thomas Buckingham; w, Fred Jackson, Robert N. Lee (based on a story by Lincoln J. Carter); ph, Starke Wagner.

Crime (PR:A MPAA:NR)

ARIZONA KID, THE** (1929) 5 reels Charles Davis bw

Art Acord *(Bill Strong, the Arizona Kid)*, Cliff Lyons *(Ned Hank)*, Bill Conant *(Sheriff Morton)*, Carol Lane *(Mary Grant)*, George Hollister *(Mandel Labor)*, Lynn Sanderson *(Bud Jenkins)*, James Tromp *(Postman Stebbins)*, Horace B. Carpenter *(Jake Grant, Mary's Father)*, Star the Horse, Rex the Dog.

The Arizona Kid (Acord), a U.S. marshall posing as a dude, infiltrates a gang who are holding a stagecoach guard and his daughter hostage, then frees them and arrests the outlaws. Star, Acord's horse, and the dog Rex add their lovable antics to a well-told and-acted story.

d&w, Horace B. Carpenter.

Western (PR:A MPAA:NR)

ARIZONA ROMEO, THE* (1925) 5 reels FOX bw**

Buck Jones *(Tom Long)*, Thomas R. Mills *(Sam Barr)*, Lucy Fox *(Sylvia Wayne)*, Lydia Yeamans *(Martha)*, Maine Geary *(Richard Barr)*, Hardee Kirkland *(John Wayne)*, Marcella Daly *(Mary)*, Harvey Clark *(The Sheriff)*, Hank Mann *(Deputy)*, Silver the Horse.

Offbeat Jones feature that goes for laughs and a tender love story, rather than shoot-em-up action. There are, however, a couple of fights and a great riding scene as Buck, wooing a woman who is running away with a man just to spite her father, gives chase after the eloping couple and from his galloping horse jumps aboard a speeding train. Once on board, he declares his love for the woman and she realizes that he is her true one after all.

d, Edmund Mortimer; w, Charles Kenyon, Mortimer.

Western (PR:AA MPAA:NR)

ARIZONA SWEEPSTAKES* (1926) 6 reels UNIV bw**

Hoot Gibson *(Coot Cadigan)*, Helen Lynch *(Nell Savery)*, George Ovey *(Stuffy McGee)*, Kate Price *(Mrs. McGuire)*, Emmett King *(Col. Tom Savery)*, Philo McCullough *(Jonathan Carey)*, Tod Brown *(Detective)*, Jackie Morgan, Billy Kent Schaeffer, Turner Savage *(McGee Kids)*.

In this one, Gibson (Universal's No. 1 cowboy star) mixes it up with rival gangs in San Francisco's Chinatown and is wrongly charged with murder. Fleeing home to Arizona with the three children of a pal back in San Francisco, he is just in time to enter the Arizona Sweepstakes, on which the fate of McCullough's ranch depends. Gibson wins the race, saves the ranch, and wins McCullough's winsome daughter. For the finale, a telegram arrives absolving him of all connections with the San Francisco murder. An affable, good humored, one-time rodeo champion, Gibson probably never gave a bad performance, and this is no exception.

d, Clifford S. Smith; w, Isadore Bernstein (based on a story by Charles Logue); ph, Harry Newmann.

Western (PR:A MPAA:NR)

ARIZONA WILDCAT* (1927) 5 reels FOX bw**

Tom Mix *(Tom Phelan)*, Dorothy Sebastian *(Regina Schyler)*, Ben Bard *(Wallace Van Acker)*, Cissy Fitzgerald *(Mother Schyler)*, Gordon Elliott *(Roy Schyler)*, Monte Collins, Jr. *(Low Jack Wilkins)*, Doris Dawson *(Marie)*, Marcella Daly *(Hellen Van Acker)*, Tony the Horse.

Highly entertaining Mix movie with a difference. In this one, the great cowboy star plays a horse breeder who sells polo ponies to the California society crowd his childhood sweetheart belongs to. When one of her brother's teammates is injured, Mix takes his place and performs some really great stunt riding. The picture's climax provides another offbeat angle with Mix chasing the villain (who has abducted the girl) on horseback through the great rooms, halls, and staircase of a sprawling California mission, a trick galloping feat that Mix's second horse, Tony, as smart as any cowboy horse in the annals of film, accomplished splendidly. This is another example of Mix's discoveries in his constant search for new settings and daredevil things to do to sharpen audience interest, not only in the genre, but in Americana itself.

d, R. William Neill; w, John Stone (based on a story by Adele Rogers St. John); ph, Dan Clark.

Adventure (PR:A MPAA:NR)

ARMAGEDDON* (1923, Brit.) 6 reels BI/New Era bw**

Interesting re-creation of the military campaign Lord Allenby waged in Palestine.

p&d, H. Bruce Woolfe.

War (PR:A MPAA:NR)

ARMS AND THE GIRL** (1917) 5 reels PAR bw

Billie Burke *(Ruth Sherwood)*, Thomas Meighan *(Wilfred Ferrers)*, Louise Bates *(Olga Karnovitch)*, J. Malcom Dunn *(Eugene)*, A. Bower *(The General)*, William David *(Martin)*, George S. Trimble, Harry Lee, May De Lacy.

The incomparable Burke's second feature for Paramount is little more than a routine affair. It tells of an American girl touring Europe who finds out her fiance has been cheating on her. She then becomes separated from her parents in Belgium when the war breaks out. It all ends well when Burke meets a handsome American engineer, whom she ultimately marries.

d, Joseph Kaufman; w, Charles E. Whittaker (based on a story by Grant Stewart, Robert Baker); ph, William C. Marshall.

Drama (PR:A MPAA:NR)

ARMS AND THE WOMAN** (1916) 5 reels Astra/Gold Rooster bw**

Mary Nash, Lumsden Hare, H. Cooper Cliffe, Robert Broderick, Rosalind Ivan, Suzanne Willa, Edward G. Robinson.

Fascinating film about a Hungarian peasant (Nash) who immigrates to America and lands a job singing in a New York dive. She is discovered by a wealthy steel manufacturer who marries her and makes her an opera star. When the war breaks out in Europe, she tries to stop her husband from selling munitions to the Allies and even becomes involved with German agents to accomplish this. The film ends on the kind of happy note which would soon be impossible since the U.S. shortly thereafter abandoned its position of neutrality. A wonderful performance by Nash, who enjoyed a distinguished career well into the talkies, playing opposite Shirley Temple in HEIDI (as Fraulein Rottermeier), Bob Hope in MONSIEUR BEAUCAIRE, and as Katharine Hepburn's mother in THE PHILADELPHIA STORY. The film is also noteworthy for Miller's breathtaking, documentary-like scenes of 1916 New York and its various ethnic faces, including a very young Edward G. Robinson.

d, George Fitzmaurice; w, Ouida Bergere; ph, Arthur Miller.

Drama (PR:A MPAA:NR)

ARMSTRONG'S WIFE** (1915) 5 reels LAS bw

Edna Goodrich *(May Fielding)*, Thomas Meighan *(David Armstrong)*, James Cruze

(Harvey Arnold), Hal Clements *(Jack Estabrook)*, Ernest Joy, Raymond Hatton, Horace B. Carpenter, Mrs. Lewis McCord.

Well-produced and acted "women's picture" set in the Canadian woods is meant to showcase distinguished Broadway actress Goodrich who, unfortunately, did not photograph well and never really made the transition to "movie star." Film also offered a rare glimpse of future director Cruze as an actor, the man who was to go on to join the movement of directors who preferred to make their films out of real incidents and with real material, called the "open-air" school, culminating in the supreme achievement of the school, Cruze's THE COVERED WAGON of 1923.

p, Jesse Lasky; d, George Melford; w, Margaret Turnbull.

Drama (PR:A MPAA:NR)

ARRIVAL OF PERPETUA, THE** (1915) 5 reels Schubert/WORLD bw

Vivian Martin *(Pet)*, Milton Sills *(Guardian)*, Nora Cecil *(Aunt)*, John Hines *(Valet)*, Alec B. Francis, Fred Truesdale, Julia Stuart.

Lightweight vehicle has a boarding school student inheriting $1 million provided she lives with one of two designated guardians. She leaves school, but finds the company of her old-maid aunt intolerable. She then moves in with the other choice—a crusty, outdoors-oriented "professional bachelor" whom she wins over and presumably marries in the end. Martin (whose career was much too short) performs with great charm, as opposed to the stage-oriented rendering of Sills, in his first screen role. Hines, who plays the part of the valet, would go on to stardom as a comedian in the 1920s.

d, Emile Chautard; w, Frances G. Corcoran (based on a play by R.H. Cochran).

Comedy (PR:A MPAA:NR)

ARSENAL**** (1929, USSR) 6 reels Vufku-Kino bw

Seymon Svashenko *(Tymish)*, Amvroziy Buchma *(German Soldier)*, Mykola Nademsky *(Official)*, M. Kuchynsky *(Petlyura)*, D. Erdman *(German Officer)*, O. Merlatti *(Sadovsky)*, A. Yevdakov *(Nicholas II)*, S. Petrov *(German Soldier)*, Mykhaylovsky *(Ukranian Nationalist)*, H. Kharkov *(Red Army Soldier)*, Pyotr Masokha.

Rarely in all of cinema has the depiction of historical events been presented with images that equal those of director Dovzhenko in this extraordinary film. By following the experiences of a lonely soldier (beautifully played by Svashenko) we are allowed to eavesdrop on those tumultuous and terrifying events which engulfed the Russian people when a world war turned into a revolution. The symbolism is profound, the images dazzling, the titles riveting—and at the film's conclusion, when Dovzhenko's Everyman is mowed down by the guns of the White soldiers, the audience is left emotionally drained and intellectually stimulated in a way which only the cinema of silence can accomplish.

d&w, Dovzhenko; ph, Danylo Demutsky; m, Ihor Belza; ed, Dovzhenko; art d, Isaac Shpinel, Vladimir Muller.

Historical Drama Cas. (PR:A MPAA:NR)

ARSENE LUPIN** (1916, Brit.) 7 reels Lon/JUR bw

Gerald Ames *(Arsene Lupin)*, Manora Thew *(Savia)*, Kenelm Foss *(Inspector Guerchard)*, Douglas Munro *(Gournay-Martin)*, Marga la Rubia, Philip Hewland.

This British thriller set in Paris deals with the escapades of a gentleman thief and the inspector who is determined to catch him.

d, George L. Tucker; w, Kenelm Foss (based on the play by Maurice LeBlanc, Francois de Crosset).

Crime (PR:A MPAA:NR)

ARSENE LUPIN* (1917) 6 reels VIT bw

Earle Williams, Ethel Grey Terry, Brinsley Shaw, Mr. Leone, Bernard Siegel, Gordon Gray, Logan Paul, Hugh Wynn, Billie Billings, Julia Swayne Gordon.

This totally inept Vitagraph feature is based on the popular play by Leblanc. This one details more adventures of the wily crook Lupin and the detective who catches him and then lets him slip away.

d, Paul Scardon; w, Garfield Thompson, Paul Potter (based on the play by Maurice Leblanc).

Crime (PR:A MPAA:NR)

ARTIE, THE MILLIONAIRE KID* (1916) 5 reels VIT bw

Ernest Truex *(Artie)*, Dorothy Kelly *(Annabelle)*, John T. Kelly *(Artie's Dad)*, Albert Roccardi *(Uriah Updike)*, William Dunn *(The Detective)*, Etienne Girardot *(The Widow)*.

This poorly made filmization of a story by American humorist and playwright George Ade deals with a college student evicted from his father's house for bad grades. The youth learns about railroad property his father must have, buys it on the sly, and holds the old man up for $1 million. The only bright spot in this retrogressive film was the performance of John T. Kelly.

d, Harry Handworth; w, William B. Courtney (based on a story by George Ade).

Comedy (PR:A MPAA:NR)

ARTISTIC TEMPERAMENT, THE** (1919, Brit.) 5 reels BL bw

Lewis Willoughby *(John Trevor)*, Margot Kelly *(Helen Faversham)*, Frank Adair *(Edward Faversham)*, Daisy Burrell, Patrick Turnbull.

English love story about a girl who, after the death of her sister, rejects the advances of a wealthy nobleman and finds happiness through her violin and marriage to a struggling artist.

p, David Falcke; d, Fred Goodwins; w, Eliot Stannard.

Drama (PR:A MPAA:NR)

ARYAN, THE**** (1916) 5 reels Kay-Bee/TRI bw

William S. Hart *(Steve Denton)*, Bessie Love *(Mary Jane)*, Louise Glaum *(Trixie)*, Charles K. French *("Ivory" Wells)*, Swallow *(Mexican Pete)*, Gertrude Claire *(Steve's Mother)*, Herschel Mayall *(Trixie's Lover)*.

One of Hart's best films, THE ARYAN tells of a man betrayed by a woman. He vows revenge and does so by murder and plunder, until he confronts a truly virtuous girl (beautifully portrayed by Love) who restores his Aryan faith in the goodness of womankind. For this picture, Hart shot 15,485 feet of negative which he edited to less than 5,000 feet. The production cost was under $14,000.

d, William S. Hart, Clifford Smith; w, C. Gardner Sullivan; ph, Joseph August.

Western (PR:A MPAA:NR)

AS A MAN LIVES*** (1923) 6 reels Achievement Films/American Releasing bw

Robert Frazer *(Sherry Mason)*, Gladys Hulette *(Nadia Meredith)*, Frank Losee *(Dr. Ralph Neyas)*, J. Thornton Baston *(La Chante)*, Alfred E. Wright *(Henri Camion)*, Kate Blancke *(Mrs. John Mason)*, Tiny Belmont *(Babette)*, Charles Sutton *(Atwill Meredith)*.

Much ado in this nicely paced film about eyes being the "windows of the soul." The eyes of the characters here revealed who was good or evil and in the end those eyes did not lie. It all begins when Hulette senses evil in the face of Frazer as he proposes to her, and she turns him down. Frazer goes to Paris where he gets involved in a fight with an apache, Baston, who kills his girl friend. Both men seek the help of a plastic surgeon, Baston for his face (to protect him from the police), and Frazer to help change his character. Abruptly, the story switches to the American West, where Hulette has been hurled into a mine shaft. Baston saves her but dies in the attempt, and Frazer finally wins Hulette. Director Dawley's interesting use of faces and atmospheric sets raised this movie to a level above melodrama.

p, Gilbert E. Gable; d, J. Searle Dawley; w, William Dudley Pelley (based on a story by Bob Dexter); ph, Bert Dawley.

Drama (PR:A MPAA:NR)

AS A WOMAN SOWS** (1916) 5 reels GAU bw

Alexander Gaden *(Loren Hayward)*, Gertrude Robinson *(Milly Hayward)*, Covington Barrett *(Boddie Hayward)*, John Rheinard *(Robert Chapman)*, Charles W. Travis *(Joseph Willoughby)*, Mathilde Baring *(Aunt Abbie)*, Yvonne Chappelle *(Georgia, Her Niece)*.

This average domestic drama has the husband wrongly suspecting his wife of cheating. Ultimately he realizes his terrible mistake when she gallantly nurses him and their child back to health after a near fatal bout with scarlet fever.

d, William F. Haddock; w, O.A. Nelson.

Drama (PR:A MPAA:NR)

AS GOD MADE HER*** (1920, Brit.) 5 reels AH/N bw

Mary Odette *(Rachel Higgins)*, Henry Victor *(Seward Pendyne)*, Adelqui Migliar *(Sir Richard Pendyne)*, Lola Cornero *(Lady Muriel Pendyne)*.

This English romance, filmed in Holland, dealt with the attempt of a noblewoman to persuade her son's common-born wife to leave him. One of many British films dealing with class distinction.

p, Maurits Binger; d&w, B.E. Doxat-Pratt (based on the novel by Helen Prothero Lewis).

Drama (PR:A MPAA:NR)

AS HE WAS BORN** (1919, Brit.) 5 reels But bw

Stanley Logan *(Felix Delaney)*, Odette Goimbault *(Ninette Monday)*, Mary Dibley *(Evelyn Garland)*, Will Corrie *(Soper)*, Athol Ford *(Dr. Twentyman)*, Stanley Turnbull *(The Mayor)*, Jeff Barlow *(The Solicitor)*.

British comedy about the trials of a not too dependable young man who is instructed, by the provision of a will, to live an entire month on his own.

d&w, Wilfred Noy (based on a play by Tom Gallon, Leon M. Lion).

Comedy (PR:A MPAA:NR)

AS IN A LOOKING GLASS*** (1916) 5 reels WORLD bw

Kitty Gordon *(Mrs. Lila Despard)*, F. Lumsden Hare *(Andrew Livingston)*, Frank Goldsmith *(Jack Firthenbras)*, Gladden James *(Lord Udolpho)*, Teddy Sampson *(Felice)*, Charles Eldridge *(Sen. Gales)*, Mrs. Woodward *(Mrs. Gales)*, Lillian Cook *(Miss Vyse)*, George Majorim *(Dromiroff)*, P. Massi *(Rowell)*.

In her first U.S. film, English beauty Gordon is triumphantly vampish as a foreign agent who turns the tables on her co-conspirators after realizing she really *loves* the American governmental official from whom she obtained valuable naval secrets.

p, Shubert; d, Frank H. Crane; w, E. Phillips; ph, Edward Horn.

Spy Drama (PR:A MPAA:NR)

AS MAN DESIRES*** (1925) 8 reels FN bw

Milton Sills *(Maj. John Craig)*, Viola Dana *(Pandora La Croix)*, Ruth Clifford *(Gloria Gordon)*, Rosemary Theby *(Evelyn Beaudine)*, Irving Cummings *(Maj. Singh)*, Paul Nicholson *(Col. Carringford)*, Tom Kennedy *(Gorilla Bagsley)*, Hector Sarno *(Toni)*, Lou Payne *(Maj. Gridley)*, Anna May Walthall *(The Duchess)*, Edneh Altemus *(Camille)*, Frank Leigh *(Watkins)*.

Sills plays an English major stationed in India who is wrongly accused of killing his superior officer after discovering the blighter had designs on his fiancee. He flees to the South Seas where he becomes rich by gathering pearls and appoints himself lord. While there, he becomes involved with a beautiful native girl, as well as some villainous types who are determined to steal his fortune. Eventually the native girl is killed, the villains are defeated, he is pardoned, and all ends splendidly, with Sills and his original love, Clifford, spending the rest of their lives back home on that smashing little island where the sun was not allowed, until recently, to ever set. Well done film, in spite of its "white man's burden" attitude.

d, Irving Cummings; sup, Earl Hudson; w, Marion Orth, Hudson (based on the novel *Pandora La Croix* by Gene Wright); ph, Roy Carpenter; ed, Marion Fairfax, Charles Hunt; art d, Milton Menasco.

Drama **(PR:A MPAA:NR)**

AS MEN LOVE** (1917) 5 reels Pallas/PAR bw

House Peters *(Paul Russell)*, Myrtle Stedman *(Diana Gordon)*, J.W. Johnston *(Keith Gordon)*, Helen Jerome Eddy *(Marjorie Gordon)*.

The message here is that friendship between men can be stronger than the love of husband and wife. Oddly, this movie was produced with the women's market in mind.

d, E. Mason Hopper; w, Adele Harris (based on a story by Lois Zellner).

Drama **(PR:A MPAA:NR)**

AS THE SUN WENT DOWN** (1919) 5 reels Metro bw

Edith Storey *("Col." Billy)*, Lewis J. Cody *(Faro Bill)*, Harry S. Northrup *(Arbuthnot)*, William Brunton *(Albert Atherton)*, E.A. Turner *(Gerald Morton)*, Frances Burnham *(Mabel Morton)*, ZaSu Pitts *(Sal Sue)*, F.E. Spooner *(Gin Mill Jack)*, Alfred Hollingsworth Pizon *(Ike)*, Vera Lewis *(Ike's Wife)*, George W. Berrell *(Piety Pete)*.

This authentic recreation of the Old West is nice but on the long side. It deals with a simple blackmail plot and misunderstood romantic intentions.

d, E. Mason Hopper; w, George D. Baker; ph, William Thompson.

Western **(PR:A MPAA:NR)**

AS YE SOW* (1914) 5 reels Brady/WORLD bw

Alice Brady, Douglas MacLean, Walter Fischer, Beverly West, John Hines, Edmund Mortimer, George Moss, Charles Dungan, Lydia Knott.

A young New Englander comes to New York where he secures employment as a chauffeur. Before long, he elopes with his employer's only child, causing the old man to suffer a fatal heart attack. It is not until their child is born that the bride discovers her husband is a hopeless, staggering alcoholic. When his treatment of her becomes deplorable, she is moved to retaliate by cutting off his cocktail funds. This angers him enough to clean out the safe and grab the child whom he deposits on his mother's doorstep back on old Cape Cod. As fate would have it; the girl visits this very same village and takes a room in the very same house where she falls in love with his brother, a minister of the cloth, when she is convinced her husband is dead. She decides to marry the minister and, as their wedding vows are being read, a ship hits the rocks and the entire town rushes to the rescue. A nifty little twist of the plot reveals the survivor to be the bride's globe-trotting husband. The rescue party carries him to his mother's cottage where he informs the astonished throng of his relationship to the bride and her child. This inspires the bride to pack up her wedding gown and return to the full-time duties of wife and mother. It is not long, however, before the one-time chauffeur returns to his carousing ways and encounters a former drinking companion. When he chooses to ignore his old acquaintance, the two men fight on a rocky ocean cliff and both fall to their deaths. The picture ends with the minister and the widow overlooking the corpse. It was not a great film.

d, Frank Hall Crane; w, Rev. John M. Snyder.

Drama **(PR:A MPAA:NR)**

ASHAMED OF PARENTS* (1921) 5 reels WB bw

Charles Eldridge *(Silas Wadsworth)*, Jack Lionel Bohn *(Arthur Wadsworth)*, Edith Stockton *(Marion Hancock)*, Walter McEvan *(Albert Grimes)*, W.J. Gross *(Peter Trotwood)*.

Message picture (from the studio which suggested years later to use Western Union when sending one) about a shoemaker, Eldridge, who sacrifices everything in life to send his son, Bohn, to college. The young man becomes a football star and is soon engaged to a beautiful socialite. Ashamed of his background, he notifies his parents of his forthcoming wedding but asks his father not to attend. When the old man lies dying of a broken heart, his future daughter-in-law secretly visits him and is truly impressed by his goodness. Through her intervention, Bohn goes to his father and there is a happy ending for all concerned.

d, Horace G. Plympton; w, (based on the story "What Children Will Do" by Charles K. Harris); ph, Jack Brown.

Drama **(PR:A MPAA:NR)**

ASHES OF EMBERS*** (1916) 5 reels FP/PAR bw

Pauline Frederick *(Agnes Ward/Laura Ward)*, Earl Foxe *(Richard Leigh)*, Frank Losee *(William Benedict)*, Maggie Halloway Fisher *(Mrs. Ward)*, Herbert J. Frank *(Daniel Marvin)*, Jay Wilson *(Detective)*.

This film with a standard plot in which a bad twin exploits a good twin until the very end when justice triumphs, is made more than worthwhile by Frederick's superb playing of the sisters.

d, Joseph Kaufman; w, Forrest Halsey (based on his play); ph, Ned Van Buren.

Drama **(PR:A MPAA:NR)**

ASHES OF HOPE** (1917) 5 reels TRI bw

Belle Bennett *(Gonda)*, Jack Livingston *(Jim Gordon)*, Jack Richardson *("Ace High" Lawton)*, Percy Challenger *("Flat Foot")*, Josie Sedgwick *(Belle)*.

This film is almost plagiaristic in its likeness to the earlier Ince-Triangle triumph THE FLAME OF THE YUKON. It suffers by comparison but is still above average, especially in direction and photography.

d, Walter Edwards; w, Thomas Ince; ph, Gus Peterson.

Drama **(PR:A MPAA:NR)**

ASHES OF VENGEANCE**** (1923) 10 reels FN bw

Norma Talmadge *(Yoeland de Breux)*, Conway Tearle *(Rupert de Vrieac)*, Wallace Beery *(Duc de Tours)*, Josephine Crowell *(Catherine de Medici)*, Betty Francisco *(Margot de Vaincorie)*, Claire McDowell *(Margot's Aunt)*, Courtenay Foote *(Comte de la Roche)*, Forrest Robinson *(Father Paul)*, James Cooley *(Paul)*, Andre de Beranger *(Charles IX)*, Boyd Irwin *(Duc de Guise)*, Howard Truesdell *(Vicomte de Briege)*, Jeanne Carpenter *(Yolande's Invalid Sister Anne)*, Winter Hall *(The Bishop)*, William Clifford *(Andre)*, Murdock MacQuarrie *(Carlotte)*, Hector V. Sarno *(Gallon)*, Earl Schenck *(Blais)*, Lucy Beaumont *(Charlotte)*, Mary McAllister *(Denise)*, Kenneth Gibson *(Phillipe)*, Carmen Phillips *(Marie)*, Rush Hughes *(Soldier Boy)*, Frank Leigh *(Lupi)*.

A lavish costume drama with outstanding performances by Talmadge and Tearle. The story is set in France during the Huguenot massacre (see INTOLERANCE) and ends after many spectacular action scenes with the love between hero and heroine overcoming generations of family hatred.

p, Joseph M. Schenck; d, Frank Lloyd; w, H.B. Somerville, Lloyd (based on the book *Ashes of Vengeance*, a Romance of Old France by H.B. Somerville); ph, Tony Gaudio.

Drama **(PR:A MPAA:NR)**

ASTHORE** (1917, Brit.) 5 reels CL/ID bw

Hayford Hobbs *(Lord Frederick Armitage)*, Violet Marriot *(Elsa)*.

English thriller set in Ireland tells of a woman who convinces the man who loves her to scar the face of her former fiance. In order to win her he obeys, but assaults her stepfather by mistake.

d, Wilfred Noy; w, Kenelm Foss.

Crime **(PR:C MPAA:NR)**

AT DEVIL'S GORGE** (1923) 5 reels Arrow bw

Edmund Cobb *(Paul Clayton)*, Helene Rosson *(Mildred Morgan)*, Wilbur McGaugh *(Clayton's Partner Dav)*, William White *(Pop Morgan)*, Max Ascher *(Tobias Blake)*, Ashton Dearholt *(Stranger in Town)*.

Cobb is held captive by his goldmining partner after beating him in a winner-take-all card game. Cobb escapes, however, brings the heavy to justice, wins the girl, and lives happily ever after as the sole owner of the mine.

d, Ashton Dearholt; w, Daniel F. Whitcomb.

Western/Drama **(PR:A MPAA:NR)**

AT THE MERCY OF TIBERIUS

(SEE: PRICE OF SILENCE, THE, 1920, Brit.)

AT THE STAGE DOOR** (1921) 6 reels R-C bw

Billie Dove *(Mary Mathews)*, Frances Hess *(Helen Mathews as a Girl)*, Miriam Battista *(Mary Mathews as a Girl)*, Margaret Foster *(Mrs. Mathews)*, Elizabeth North *(Helen Mathews)*, William Collier, Jr. *(Arthur Bates)*, C. Elliott Griffin *(George Andrews)*, Myrtle Maughan *(Grace Mortimer)*, Charles Craig *(John Brooks)*, Viva Ogden *(Mrs. Reade)*, Billy Quirk *(Harold Reade)*, Huntly Gordon *(Philip Pierce)*, Katherine Spencer *(Alice Vincent)*, Doris Eaton *(Betty)*.

Typical backstage hokum about a poor but virtuous chorus girl who finally lands a rich but decent society guy she loves. Nice performance by Billy Dove, "The American Beauty" of the silent era, who was 21 years old at the time this film was made.

d&w, Christy Cabanne.

Drama **(PR:A MPAA:NR)**

AT THE VILLA ROSE** (1920, Brit.) 7 reels STOLL bw

Manora Thew *(Celia Harland)*, Langehorne Burton *(Harry Weathermill)*, Teddy Arundell *(Inspector Hanaud)*, Norman Page *(Julius Ricardo)*, Joan Beverley *(Adele Rossignol)*, Eva Westlake *(Mme. Dauvray)*, Kate Gurney *(Helene)*, J.L. Boston *(Besnard)*, Armand Lenders *(Perichet)*.

Tepid British mystery about a gang of international jewel thieves who abduct a phony medium in Monaco and pin the blame on her for the murder of a strangled widow.

d, Maurice Elvey; w, Sinclair Hill (based on a novel by A.E.W. Mason).

Crime **(PR:A MPAA:NR)**

AT YALE (SEE: HOLD 'EM YALE!, 1928)

ATOM, THE*** (1918) 5 reels TRI bw

Pauline Starke, Harry Mestayer, Belle Bennett, Ruth Hanforth, Walter Perkins, Lincoln Stedman, Gene Burr, Tom Buckingham, Charles Force.

A well done movie with what was then referred to as "human interest value." It tells of a maid (Starke), employed in a theatrical boarding house, who secretly loves astruggling actor with an ambition to play Shakespeare. A fire at the theater puts an end to his career and he is deserted by everyone but the servant girl whom he hardly noticed before. After a time, she gets him a job with a traveling medicine show and joins him on the road.

d, William Dowlan; w, Catherine Carr; ph, Elgin Lessley.

Drama **(PR:A MPAA:NR)**

ATTA BOY!*** (1926) 6 reels Monty Banks/Pathe bw

Monty Banks *(Monty Milde)*, Mary Carr *(Grandmother)*, Virginia Bradford *(The Girl)*, Virginia Pearson *(Mme. Carlton)*, Ernie Wood *(Craven, Ace Reporter)*, Fred Kelsey *(Detective)*, Henry A. Barrows *(Mr. Harrie)*, Earl Metcalf *(His Brother)*, Jimmie Phillips *(Millionaire Kid)*, Alfred Fisher, George Periolat, America Chedister, William Courtwright, Lincoln Plummer, Kewpie Morgan.

Banks made a series of "thrill" comedies before moving to England where he became a successful director and married Gracie Fields. A small man who literally took his life in his hands performing daredevil stunts, here he ends up clinging to the top of a ladder which is planted on the back seat of a driverless car speeding through mountain roads one would be afraid to walk through. A very funny movie by a highly underrated artist.

d, Edward H. Griffith; w, Charles Horan, Alf Goulding; t, Harold Christy; ph, William Reese, Ted Tetzlaff, Blake Wagner.

Comedy **(PR:A MPAA:NR)**

ATTA BOY'S LAST RACE*

(1916) 5 reels FA/TRI bw (AKA: THE BEST BET)

Dorothy Gish, Keith Armour, Carl Stockdale, Adele Clifton, Loyola O'Connor, Fred A. Turner, Tom Wilson, Joe Neary.

This hackneyed plot about a horse race and a girl's mortgage could barely have sustained a two-reel short, much less a five-reel feature. Gish, however, is charming as she acts her way beyond the padding in the story.

d, George Siegmann; w, Tod Browning.

Drama **(PR:A MPAA:NR)**

AUCTION BLOCK, THE*** (1917) 7 reels Goldwyn bw

Ruby De Remer, Alec B. Francis, Florence Deshon, Florence Johns, Dorothy Wheeler, Walter Hitchcock, Ned Burton, Charles Graham, George Cooper, Francis Joyner, Bernard Randall, Peter Lang, Tom Powers, Joe Phillips.

Fascinating look at Manhattan's theatrical, gangster, and tenderloin life. This story by prolific adventure writer Beach was gripping, even shocking, in spite of less-than-great acting, direction, and photography.

d, Lawrence Trimble; w, Adrian Gil-Spear (based on the novel by Rex Beach); ph, David Calcagni.

Drama **(PR:C MPAA:NR)**

AUCTION BLOCK, THE*** (1926) 7 reels MGM bw

Charles Ray *(Bob Wharton)*, Eleanor Boardman *(Lorelei Knight)*, Sally O'Neil *(Bernice Lane)*, Ernest Gillen *(Carter Lane)*, David Torrence *(Robert Wharton, Sr.)*, James Corrigan *(Mr. Knight)*, Forrest Seabury *(Edward Blake)*, Ned Sparks *(Nat Slauson)*, Charles Clary *(Homer Lane)*.

Ray, the son of a millionaire, makes good on his own by opening a shoe store in the home town of his estranged wife, a North Carolina beauty contest winner who had left him after his father told her Ray was without character. Soon all the girls in town are after him, and one, O'Neil, compromises him. As she had hoped, her father tries to make Ray marry her. When the father finds out that Ray is already married, he goes gunning for the shoe store owner, who is saved when his wife forces the vamp to confess the frame-up, and the two then are reconciled.

d, Hobart Henley; w, Frederic and Fanny Hatton (based on the novel by Rex Beach); ph, John Arnold.

Comedy **(PR:A MPAA:NR)**

AUCTION MART, THE** (1920, Brit.) 6 reels BA/Phillips bw

Gertrude McCoy *(Jacqueline)*, Charles Quartermaine *(Her Father)*, Gerald Moore *(Basil Stair)*, Basil Foster *(Carver)*, Sir Simeon Stuart *(Peer)*, Moya Nugent, Henry Doughty, Minnie Rayner.

English film set in Paris about a twisted man who forces his daughter into a life of crime. In the end she finds the man who reforms her through love.

d, Duncan Macrae; w, Adrian Brunel (based on a novel by Sydney Tremaine).

Drama **(PR:A MPAA:NR)**

AUCTIONEER, THE*** (1927) 6 reels FOX bw

George Sidney *(Simon Levi)*, Doris Lloyd *(Esther Levi)*, Sammy Cohen *(Moe)*, Marion Nixon *(Ruth Levi)*, Gareth Hughes *(Dick Eagan)*, Ward Crane *(Paul Groode)*, Claire McDowell *(Mrs. Tim Eagan)*.

This story of a little Jewish auctioneer who takes over a millionaire's mansion is a clever comedy, done in good taste. It features Sidney, who lent his considerable talent to many such parts. (See THE COHENS AND THE KELLYS.)

d, Alfred E. Green; w, L.G. Rigby, John Stone (based on the play by Charles Klein, Lee Arthur); ph, George Schneiderman.

Comedy **(PR:A MPAA:NR)**

AUDACIOUS MR. SQUIRE, THE*** (1923, Brit.) 5 reels B&C bw

Jack Buchanan *(Tom Squire)*, Valia *(Constance)*, Russell Thorndike *(Henry Smallwood)*, Malcolm Tod *(Edgar)*, Sydney Paxton *(John Howard)*, Dorinea Shirley *(Bessie)*, Forbes Dawson *(Pitt)*, Fred Raines *(Jupp)*.

Good little English comedy featuring Buchanan (the musical star who was sensational in the Fred Astaire classic THE BANDWAGON) in a story about mistaken identities.

p, Edward Godal; d, Edwin Greenwood; w, Eliot Stannard (based on the play "Squire the Audacious" by Sydney Bowkett).

Comedy **(PR:A MPAA:NR)**

AUDREY* (1916) 5 reels FP bw

Pauline Frederick *(Audrey)*, Charles Waldron *(Lord Hayward)*, Margarete Christians *(Evelyn Byrd)*, E. Fernandex *(Jean Hugon)*, Helen Lindroth *(Mrs. Darden)*, Henry Hallam *(Mr. Darden)*, Jack Clark *(John Byrd)*, Rita Connolly.

Disastrous attempt by Famous Players to turn Frederick (a major star in her own right) into Mary Pickford's clone after they suspected America's sweetheart was thinking of changing studios. Pickford did change studios in this same year, accepting an astonishing $10,000 weekly and a $300,000 bonus from Adolph Zukor, while Frederick went on to portray character roles.

d, Robert Vignola; w, Harriet Ford, E.F. Boddington (based on the novel by Mary Johnston).

Drama **(PR:A MPAA:NR)**

AULD LANG SYNE** (1917, Brit.) 5 reels B&C bw

Violet Graham *(Beatrice Potter)*, Henry Baynton *(Wilton Daneford)*, Sydney Fairbrother *(Mrs. Potter)*, George Bellamy *(Luke Potter)*, Roy Travers *(Ned Potter)*, Jack Buchanan *(Vane)*.

This British drama about class distinction deals with a commoner who marries a lord and then assumes the guilt for her brother when he is caught stealing precious jewels.

d&w, Sidney Morgan.

Drama **(PR:A MPAA:NR)**

AULD ROBIN GRAY** (1917, Brit.) 5 reels ID bw

R.A. Roberts *(Robin Gray)*, Langhorne Burton *(Jamie)*, Miss June *(Jenny)*.

British film about a Scottish sailor who overcomes a number of obstacles and makes it home in time to save his fiancee from marrying a farmer.

d, Meyrick Milton; w, Kenelm Foss.

Drama **(PR:A MPAA:NR)**

AUNT RACHEL** (1920, Brit.) 6 reels G.B. Samuelson/Granger bw

Isobel Elsom *(Ruth)*, Haidee Wright *(Aunt Rachel)*, James Lindsay *(Ferdinand de Blacquaire)*, Lionelle Howard *(Reuben)*, Tom Reynolds *(Eld)*, Dalton Somers *(Fuller)*, Leonard Pagden *(Ezra Gold)*, Hubert Willis *(Earl)*, Dan Godfrey *(Isiah)*.

This English love story, set in 1850, tells of an aunt disappointed in love, who stands in the way of her niece marrying the man she loves.

d, Albert Ward; w, Roland Pertwee, Hugh Conway (based on a novel by Conway).

Drama **(PR:A MPAA:NR)**

AUTOCRAT, THE** (1919, Brit.) 6 reels RF bw

Ethel Douglas Ross *(Elsie)*, Reginald Fox *(Jack Blake)*, Ralph Foster *(Adm. Blake)*, William Brandon *(Phillip)*, Eileen Moore, Myra Aberg, Tom Coventry.

English drama about the black sheep son in a military family who, after being disowned by his father, an admiral, returns home to save his sister from abduction by the real family cad, his cousin.

d&w, Tom Watts.

Drama **(PR:A MPAA:NR)**

AUTUMN OF PRIDE, THE*½ (1921, Brit.) 6 reels GAU/WEST bw

Nora Swinburne *(Peggy Naylor)*, David Hawthorne *(John Lytton)*, Mary Dibley *(Helen Stone)*, Cecil Morton York *(Abel Lytton)*, Cecil du Gue *(Mr. Naylor)*, Clifford Heatherley *(George Pentecost)*, Donald Castle *(Willoughby)*, Hargrave Mansell *(Handley)*.

This British love story is about a young man who buys a farm for the girl who has lived on it to prevent his rich father from evicting her.

d, W.P. Kellino; w, Paul Rooff (based on a novel by E. Newton Bungey).

Drama **(PR:A MPAA:NR)**

AVALANCHE, THE*** (1919) 5 reels ART/PAR bw

Elsie Ferguson *(Chichita/Mme. Delano)*, Lumsden Hare *(Price Ruyler)*, Zeffie Tilbury *(Mrs. Ruyler)*, Fred Esmelton *(John Harvey)*, William Roselle *(Ferdie Derenforth)*, Grace Field *(Sybil Price)*, Warner Oland *(Nick Delano)*, George Dupre, Harry Wise, George Fitzmaurice, W.T. Carleton.

A first class performance is given here by the beautiful Ferguson in a dual role as mother and daughter. The story has the girl running away from a South American convent to marry a novelist. She eventually arrives at a gambling club run by a man who is married to her mother. After a while, the woman begins to suspect the relationship, and when her daughter is forced to kill the gambler, she assumes the guilt.

d, George Fitzmaurice; w, Ouida Bergere (based on the novel by Gertrude Atherton); ph, Arthur Miller.

Drama **(PR:C MPAA:NR)**

AVALANCHE*** (1928) 5 reels PAR bw

Jack Holt *(Jack Dunton)*, Richard Winslow *(Jack at 12)*, Barclanova *(Grace)*, Doris Hill *(Kitty Mains)*, John Darrow *(Verde)*, Guy Oliver *(Mr. Mains)*, Dick Winslow *(Jack Dunton at Age 12)*.

This superior western about a gambler who raises a boy as his own son was a perfect role for Holt. An honest gambler, Holt learns that his ward, Darrow, would like to study mine engineering at school. To pay for his education, Holt begins to cheat at cards but all appears to have been for naught as Darrow, after three years in school, returns to the mining town and immediately loses himself in riotous living. Intent on saving the boy, Holt determines to leave the town and his mistress, Barclanova. She attempts to thwart this by vamping the boy, and the two elope. Holt goes after them, ultimately to save their lives in an avalanche. All works out in the end as Holt and Barclanova are reunited. The avalanche at the end of the picture is beautifully staged in this satisfying film.

d, Otto Brower; w, Sam Mintz, Herman Mankiewicz, J. Walter Ruben (based on a story by Zane Grey); t, Mankiewicz; ph, Roy Clark; ed, Jane Loring.

Western **(PR:A MPAA:NR)**

AVE MARIA** (1918, Brit.) 5 reels CL/H bw

Concordia Merrill *(Margaret)*, Rita Johnson *(Helen Grey)*, Roy Travers *(Jim Masters)*, H. Manning Haynes *(Jack Haviland)*, A.B. Imeson *(Guy Fernandez)*, Sydney L. Ransome *(Providence)*, William Lugg *(Sir John Haviland)*.

An English love story about amnesia among the nobility and the tragic complications it leads to.

d, Wilfred Noy; w, Reuben Gilmer.

Drama **(PR:A MPAA:NR)**

AVENGER, THE* (1924) 5 reels AY bw

Guinn "Big Boy" Williams.

Williams thwarts the attempt of a sneaky real estate operator to railroad the brother of the girl he is lusting after, in this rather slow-moving western. Typical of the many minor westerns former football player Williams starred in before he drifted over to character parts.

d, Charles R. Seeling.

Western **(PR:A MPAA:NR)**

AVENGING CONSCIENCE, THE***
(1914) 6 reels Reliance-Majestic/MUT bw (AKA: THOU SHALT NOT KILL)

Henry B. Walthall *(The Nephew)*, Blanche Sweet *(His Sweetheart)*, Spottiswoode Aitken *(The Uncle)*, Josephine Crowell *(Her Mother)*, George Siegmann *(The Italian)*, Ralph Lewis *(The Detective)*, Mae Marsh *(Maid at the Garden Party)*, Robert Harron *(The Grocer's Boy)*.

After being prevented by the uncle who raised him from marrying the girl he loves, a young man's depression drives him to the brink of insanity. Griffith illustrated this with a closeup showing a spider spinning its web and cruelly snaring an unsuspecting fly. (This remarkable and revolutionary scene was shot by a very young Brown after several days of patient innovation.) Driven to despair, the young man strangles his uncle and bricks in the body behind a fireplace wall. Before long, however, his guilty conscience manifests itself in images of his uncle's ghost, as well as visions of heaven and hell. When a detective arrives to question him, the nephew (in a beautifully directed scene which anticipated Eisenstein's use of montage by more than a decade) begins to confuse the tapping of the policeman's foot and the thumping of the clock's pendulum with the beat of his victim's heart. Terrified, he escapes to his cabin hideaway where he attempts to hang himself. The law, however, gets to him in time and cuts him down before strangulation. Meanwhile, the girl, equally possessed by guilt, throws herself over a cliff. It is at this point that the young man awakens from his nightmare. The film ends,with newlyweds and uncle basking in a fairyland setting surrounded by cherubic children, playful animals, and the mythological god, Pan, frolicking about. Griffith's last film before his masterpiece THE BIRTH OF A NATION was more than the "filler" some critics have accused it of being. It was, to be sure, uneven in places, but its somber, brooding, psychological mood did much to influence the art of Lang, Murnau, Pabst, and for that matter, the entire German cinema of the 1920s. Marsh, here playing a lowly maid, went on to her great role as "the little sister" in THE BIRTH OF A NATION, a role for which she will always be remembered.

d&w, D.W. Griffith (based on Edgar Allan Poe's "The Telltale Heart," "Annabel Lee," and "The Pit and the Pendulum"); ph, Billy Bitzer, Karl Brown; ed, James Smith, Rose Richtell.

Drama **Cas.** **(PR:C MPAA:NR)**

AVENGING FANGS* (1927) 5 reels CHES/Pathe bw

Sandow *(The Dog)*, Kenneth McDonald *(Dick Mansfield)*, Helen Lynch *(Mary Kirkham)*, Jack Richardson *(Trigger Kincaid)*, Max Asher *(Sheriff)*.

Sandow, one of Rin-Tin-Tin's lesser rivals, leads the brother of his murdered master out West to avenge the killing by a gang of house invaders. The brother, McDonald, soon traces the gang's leaders and after some harrowing adventures helps capture the thugs and finds a bride in Lynch.

d, Ernest Van Pelt; w, George Pyper; ph, Jimmy Brown.

Western **(PR:A MPAA:NR)**

AVENGING RIDER, THE* (1928) 6 reels FBO bw

Tom Tyler *(Tom Larkin)*, Florence Allen *(Sally Sheridan)*, Frankie Darro *(Frankie Sheridan)*, Al Ferguson *(Bob Gordon)*, Bob Fleming *(Sheriff)*, Arthur Thalasso *(Dance Professor)*.

Tyler and a bevy of female extras, who must have been under contract to someone, plod through this unusual western ranch mystery plot, assisted by Darro. A mysteriously murdered ranchman leaves his estate to Tyler and Allen, and she comes West with all of her classmates to take an instant dislike to Tyler and all his western ways. However, by the time he solves the murder they have formed a mutual attachment and things are looking up for them both. Nice story but quite poorly played.

d, Wallace Fox; w, Frank Howard Clark (based on a story by Adele Buffington); t, Randolph Bartlett; ph, Nick Musuraca; ed, Della M. King.

Western **(PR:A MPAA:NR)**

AVENGING SHADOW, THE** (1928) 5 reels McConnell/Pathe bw

Ray Hallor *(James Hamilton, Young Bank Clerk)*, Wilbur Mack *(Worthington, His Assistant Cashier)*, Clark Comstock *(Sheriff Apling)*, Howard Davies *(The Warden)*, Margaret Morris *(Marie, His Daughter)*, LeRoy Mason *(George Brooks, Deputy Warden)*, Grey Boy *(Klondike the Dog)*.

Bank clerk Hallor is railroaded and sent to prison, but Grey Boy, his wonder dog, sniffs the bad guys out, and he and his master chase them down and bring them to justice. Grey Boy steals most of the scenes he is in, and those are a great many, capped by a great chase scene involving the dog and Hallor.

d, Ray Taylor; w, Bennett Cohen; t, Ray Doyle; ph, Harry Cooper, David Smith; ed, Thomas Malloy.

Drama **(PR:A MPAA:NR)**

AVENGING TRAIL, THE* (1918) 5 reels Yorke/Metro bw

Harold Lockwood *(Gaston Olaf)*, Sally Crute *(Rose Havens)*, Joseph Dailey *(Tom Pine)*, Walter P. Lewis *(Dave Taggart)*, Louis R. Wolheim *(Lefty Red)*, William Clifford *(Hale)*, Warren Cook *(Dr. Saunders)*, Art Ortega, Tom Blake, Robert Chandler.

A typical lumberjack quickie, with trees falling, men fighting and loving, and rousing comedy, shot almost entirely outdoors. Even the cliches are substandard in this one.

d, Francis Ford; w, Fred J. Balshofer, Mary Murillo (based on the novel *Gaston Olaf* by Henry Oyen); ph, Antonio Gaudio.

Adventure **(PR:A MPAA:NR)**

AVERAGE WOMAN, THE* (1924) 6 reels C.C. Burr bw

Pauline Garon *(Sally Whipple)*, David Powell *(Rudolph Van Alten)*, Burr McIntosh *(Judge Whipple)*, Harrison Ford *(Jimmy Munroe)*, De Sacia Mooers *(Mrs. La Rose)*, William Tooker *(Col. Crosby)*, Russell Griffin *("Tike" La Rose)*, Coit Albertson *(Bill Brennon)*.

A nonsensical waste of time which sets out to explain why modern (1924) girls are as good as or better than their predecessors. A newspaper reporter finds his "average woman" is the daughter of a judge, who "sentences" him to visit her once a week for following her in trying to get his story. When a blackmail attempt against her father fizzles, the average woman turns out to be some prize dame who chooses, after all, to marry the lowly reporter. Harebrained excuse for a story.

d, William Cabanne; w, Raymond S. Harris (based on a story by Dorothy De Jagers); ph, Jack Brown, Neil Sullivan.

Drama **(PR:A MPAA:NR)**

AWAKENING, THE*** (1917) 5 reels WORLD bw

Montagu Love *(Jacques Revilly)*, Dorothy Kelly *(Marguerite)*, John Davidson *(Horace Chapron)*, Frank Beamish *(Varny)*, Joseph Granby *(Prosper Chavassier)*, Josephine Earle *(Celestine)*.

Love, a French peasant with a gift for drawing, goes to Paris where he lives a life of dissipation, painting only to support his taste for wine. One night he finds a young woman who has collapsed in the snow from hunger. He takes her home, falls in love, and becomes an inspired artist. On a wager, the art colony's resident cad lures her to his garret, drugs her, and robs her of her virginity. Hearing of this and thinking the worst, Love challenges the rotter to a duel where he is shot in the arm. The film ends with him marrying the girl and experiencing more than enough inspiration to make them both wealthy for life. Love was splendid in a mature, well-conceived motion picture.

d, George Archainbaud; w, E.J. De Varnie.

Drama **(PR:C MPAA:NR)**

AWAKENING, THE*** (1928) 9 reels Goldwyn/UA bw

Vilma Banky *(Marie Ducrot)*, Walter Byron (Count Karl von Hagen), Louis Wolheim *(Le Bete)*, George Davis *(The Orderly)*, William A. Orlamond *(Grandfather Ducrot)*, Carl von Hartmann *(Sub-Lt. Franz Gerver)*, Yola D'Avril *(Cabaret Girl)*, General Wietsheslav Savitsky *(Top Sergeant)*, Ferdinand Schuman-Heink *(Officer Of Uhlans)*, Owen Corin, Paul Vasel *(Soldiers)*.

This technically superb Goldwyn production rehashed all of the WW I movie situations, with generous portions of THE WHITE SISTER and THE SCARLET LETTER thrown in for good measure. Of particular interest is the sympathetic portrayal of German soldiers a year before ALL QUIET ON THE WESTERN FRONT was released.

p, Samuel Goldwyn; d, Victor Fleming; w, Carey Wilson (based on a story by Frances Marion); t, Katherine Hilliker, H.H. Caldwell; ph, George Barnes; m, Hugo

Riesenfeld; ed, Viola Lawrence, Hilliker, Caldwell; art d, William Cameron Menzies; m/l, "Marie," Irving Berlin; syn sc; s eff.

War **(PR:A MPAA:NR)**

AWAY GOES PRUDENCE*** (1920) 6 reels PAR bw

Billie Burke *(Prudence Thorne)*, Percy Marmont *(Hewlitt Harland)*, Maude Turner Gordon *(Aunt Prudence Thorne)*, Charles Lane *(Mr. Thorne)*, Dorothy Walters *(Mrs. Ryan)*, Bradley Barker *(Michael Ryan)*, M.W. Rale [Rayle] *(Chinaman)*, Albert Hackett *(Jimmie Ryan)*.

Pleasing society comedy in which Burke is ordered by her fiance to decide between her love of piloting airplanes or him. Out of spite, she chooses the former. All ends well with a double kidnap plot and some nifty flying thrown in for good measure.

d, John S. Robertson; w, Kathryne Stuart (based on a story by Josephine Lovett); ph, Roy Overbaugh.

Comedy **(PR:A MPAA:NR)**

AWFUL TRUTH, THE** (1925) 6 reels PWN/PDC bw

Agnes Ayres *(Lucy Slatterley)*, Warner Baxter *(Norman Slatterley)*, Phillips Smalley *(Kempster)*, Raymond Lowney *(Danny Leeson)*, Winifred Bryson *(Josephine)*, Carrie Clarke Ward *(Mrs. Leeson)*.

This fair matrimonial comedy, set in a Canadian honeymoon lodge, is hampered by Ayres' inability to play comedy. She is a flirt and her jealous husband, Baxter, takes offense particularly with her vamping Smalley, a mine owner. Although innocent of any liaisons, Ayres and Smalley are caught in a compromising situation by Baxter who thereupon obtains a divorce. A year later they become friends again, but Baxter still believes she was unfaithful to him. Ayres arranges a phony tryst with Smalley and, as she hoped, Baxter comes along to save her. She then explains that there can be no love without trust, and the two are reunited.

d, Paul Powell; w, Elmer Harris (based on the play by Arthur Richman); ph, Joseph A. Dubray.

Comedy **(PR:A MPAA:NR)**

AYLWIN** (1920, Brit.) 6 reels Hepworth bw

Henry Edwards *(Hal Aylwin)*, Chrissie White *(Winifred Wynne)*, Gerald Ames *(Wildespin)*, Mary Dibley *(Sinfi Lovell)*, Henry Vibart *(Philip Aylwin)*, Gwynne Herbert *(Mrs. Aylwin)*, Valentine Grace *(Tom Wynne)*, E.C. Matthews *(Shales)*, Amy Lorraine *(Meg Gudgeon)*.

This British film, set in Wales, tells of a girl who becomes insane when her alcoholic father is killed in a landslide.

d, Henry Edwards; w, (based on the novel by Theodore Watts-Dunton).

Drama **(PR:A MPAA:NR)**

B

BABBITT*** (1924) 8 reels WB bw

Willard Louis *(George F. Babbitt)*, Mary Alden *(Mrs. Myra Babbitt)*, Carmel Myers *(Tanis Judique)*, Raymond McKee *(Theodore Roosevelt Babbitt)*, Maxine Elliot Hicks *(Verona Babbitt)*, Virginia Loomis *(Tina Babbitt)*, Robert Randell *(Paul Reisling)*, Sissy Fitzgerald *(Mrs. Zilla Reisling)*, Gertrude Olmstead *(Eunice Littelfield)*, Lucien Littlefield *(Edward Littelfield)*, Dale Fuller *(Tillie the Maid)*, Kathleen Myers *(Miss McGown)*, Frona Hale *(Mrs. Littelfield)*.

Good screen adaptation of the Sinclair Lewis novel about a middle-aged business man who has a brief fling with a beautiful young golddigger before being brought to his senses by his son. A theme so familiar in the intervening years, in American, French, British, German, and Scandinavian films, that one must begin to believe that finding a young lady to "fling" with is a universal longing of middle-aged men.

d, Harry Beaumont; w, Dorothy Farnum (based on the novel by Sinclair Lewis); ph, David Abel.

Drama **(PR:A MPAA:NR)**

BABBLING TONGUES*** (1917) 6 reels IV bw

Grace Valentine, James Morrison, Arthur Donaldson, Paul Campellani, Louise Beaudet, Gladden James, Carolyn Birch, Richard Tucker, Robert E. Hill.

A young woman married to a middle-aged man becomes the victim of malicious gossip when a dashing poet is befriended by her husband. After fighting a duel with one of her accusers, the husband, who believes the gossip, now lies near death. At this point, his poet-friend tells the dying man that the lies he thinks are true have driven his wife into his arms, and the movie fades out. But, there is a surprise ending. The picture fades up again, revealing the poet sitting at his desk. He is writing a novel, and all of the preceding action was a part of it.

d, William Humphrey; w, Humphrey, George Edwardes Hall.

Drama **(PR:A MPAA:NR)**

BABE COMES HOME*** (1927) 4 reels FN bw

George Herman Ruth *(Babe Dugan)*, Anna Q. Nilsson *(Vernie)*, Louise Fazenda *(Laundry Girl)*, Ethel Shannon *(Georgia)*, Arthur Stone *(Laundry Driver)*, Lou Archer *(Peewee, 3rd Baseman)*, Tom McGuire *(Angel Team Manger)*, Mickey Bennett *(Mascot)*, James Bradbury, Guinn "Big Boy" Williams, James Gordon *(Baseball Players)*.

Babe Ruth (in a solid performance) plays a baseball star whose weakness for chewing tobacco sparks a separation from his lady love (Nilsson) on the day before their wedding. This causes a batting slump which ends on the day of the pennant, when his girl forces her way through the crowd to present him with a major league-sized plug.

p, Wid Gunning; d, Ted Wilde; w, Louis Stevens (based on a story by Gerald Beaumont); ph, Karl Struss.

Drama **(PR:A MPAA:NR)**

BAB'S BURGLAR*** (1917) 5 reels PAR bw

Marguerite Clark *(Bab Archibald)*, Leone Morgan *(Jane Raleigh)*, Richard Barthelmess *(Tommy Gray)*, Frank Losee *(Mr. Archibald)*, Isabel O'Madigan *(Mrs. Archibald)*, Helen Greene *(Lelia Archibald)*, William Hinckley *(Carter Brooks)*, Guy Coombs *(Harry, Lelia's Fiance)*.

In this second of the "Bab" series, the boarding school darling is given a checkbook by her indulgent father. This is used to great comic advantage, as is the scene towards the end where the girl confuses her sister's boy friend (who had come to elope) with a burglar. A well-done early non-slapstick comedy feature.

d, J. Searle Dawley; w, (based on a story by Mary Roberts Rinehart).

Comedy **(PR:A MPAA:NR)**

BAB'S CANDIDATE* (1920) 5 reels VIT bw

Corinne Griffith, George Fawcett, Webster Campbell, Charles Abbe, William [Stage] Holden, Roy Applegate, Walter Horton, Wes Jenkins, Harry A. Fisher, Blanche Davenport, Frances Meller Grant.

This was not an episode of the popular Mary Roberts Rinehart "Bab" series but, rather, an uneven little drama with a political setting which is little more than a showcase of Corinne Griffith's considerable beauty.

d, Edward H. Griffith; w, Lucien Hubbard (based on the story "Gumshoes 4-B" by Forrest Crissey); ph, William McCoy.

Drama **(PR:A MPAA:NR)**

BAB'S DIARY*** (1917) 5 reels PAR bw

Marguerite Clark *(Bab Archibald)*, Nigel Barrie *(Carter Brooks)*, Leonora Morgan *(Jane Gray)*, Frank Losee *(Mr. Archibald)*, Isabel O'Madigan *(Mrs. Archibald)*, Richard Barthelmess *(Tommy Gray)*, Helen Greene *(Lelia Archibald)*, Guy Coombes *(Harry)*, Jack O'Brien *(Harold Valentine)*, George Odell *(The Butler)*.

Another story of sub-deb Bab (Clark) is a delightful romp through youthful ways. Clark comes home from boarding school for Christmas vacation and tells her parents that she is engaged to be married to a "Harold Valentine." Of course a real Harry Valentine appears and the adventure swings along from there to a touching ending, with Clark safely back at school after the foolish adventure.

d, J. Searle Dawley; w, (based on a story by Mary Roberts Rinehart); ph, Lewis Physioc.

Drama **(PR:A MPAA:NR)**

BABY MINE*** (1917) 6 reels Goldwyn bw

Madge Kennedy, Frank Morgan, Kathryn Adams, John Cumberland, Sonia Marcelle, Virginia Madigan, Nellie Fillmore, Jack Ridgway.

Clever screen adaptation of a successful Broadway comedy about a young woman whose husband leaves her after a quarrel, and all attempts to induce him to come back fail. Finally she resolves on a ruse—she tells him he is the father of a beautifully bouncing baby. The fun comes in trying to find a baby to use to put over the ploy.

d, John S. Robertson, Hugo Ballin; w, Doty Hobart (based on the play by Margaret Mayo); ph, Arthur Edeson.

Comedy **(PR:A MPAA:NR)**

BABY MINE*** (1928) 6 reels MGM bw

Karl Dane *(Oswald Hardy)*, George K. Arthur *(Jimmy Hemmingway)*, Charlotte Greenwood *(Emma)*, Louise Loraine *(Helen)*.

Good Dane comedy has the big fellow tricked into marrying a very tall and not particularly attractive Greenwood. Dane takes off the next morning, but returns a year later when told that he has a son. The movie ends with a very funny sequence in which three babies, and a cigar-smoking midget dressed in diapers, chase each other all over the place. It's so much fun that Dane overlooks the second deception and decides to stay.

d, Robert Z. Leonard; w, F. Hugh Herbert, Lew Lipton, Sylvia Thalberg (based on the play by Margaret Mayo); t, Ralph Spence; ph, Faxon Dean; ed, Sam S. Zimbalist; set d, Cedric Gibbons, Frederic Hope.

Comedy **(PR:A MPAA:NR)**

BABY MOTHER, THE (SEE: NO BABIES WANTED, 1928)

BACHELOR'S BABY, THE*** (1927) 6 reels COL bw

Helene Chadwick *(Eleanor Carter)*, Harry Myers *(Bill Taylor)*, Midget Gustav *(Mr. Boppo)*, Edith Yorke *(Mrs. Carter)*, Blanche Payson *(Mrs. Boppo)*, Pat Harmon *("Hardboiled" Hogan)*, James Marcus *(Col. Carter)*.

Before screwball comedies came into vogue, Columbia produced this little gem, which has the underrated Myers chasing all over the place looking for a baby to substantiate the lie Chadwick told a traffic cop: that she and her husband (actually, Myers was a complete stranger following her to win a date) are speeding to reach their gravely ill child. Myers finally shows up with Gustav, a midget he hires to impersonate the kid, at the same time that Chadwick's parents and the little fellow's very jealous wife all arrive on the scene. The harried couple barely manage to escape the ensuing madness in an airplane and, after a series of additional complications, discover their mutual love and are married.

d, Frank R. Strayer; sup, Harry Cohn; w, Julien Sands (based on a story by Garrett Elsden Fort); ph, J.O. Taylor.

Comedy **(PR:A MPAA:NR)**

BACHELORS' CLUB, THE*** (1921, Brit.) 6 reels ID bw

Ben Field *(Peter Parker)*, Ernest Thesiger *(Israfel Mondego)*, Mary Brough *(Mrs. Parker)*, Sydney Fairbrother *(Tabitha)*, Arthur Pusey *(Paul Dickray)*, Margot Drake *(Jenny Halby)*, James Lindsay *(Elliot Dickray)*, Sydney Paxton *(Caleb Twinkletop)*, A.G. Poulton *(Edward Halby)*, Arthur Cleave *(Warlock Combs)*, Dora Lennox *(Israfel's Sweetheart)*, Jack Denton *(Mandeville Brown)*, Alice de Winton *(Dowager)*.

Superior English comedy about a henpecked man who inherits a fortune and establishes a club for women-hating, intrinsically chauvinistic men.

d, A.V. Bramble; w, Eliot Stannard (based on the novel by Israel Zangwill).

Comedy **(PR:A MPAA:NR)**

BACHELOR'S PARADISE** (1928) 7 reels TS bw

Sally O'Neill *(Sally O'Day)*, Ralph Graves *(Joe Wallace)*, Eddie Gribbon *(Terry Malone)*, Jimmy Finlayson *(Pat Malone)*, Sylvia Ashton *(Mrs. Malone)*, Jean Laverty *(Gladys O'Toole)*.

Prizefighter Graves is nursed back to health by O'Neill after suffering an accident. Assuming he loves her, O'Neill makes plans for their wedding, but Graves gets cold feet and leaves her standing at the altar. Later, during a big fight, Graves is knocked down and O'Neill comes to him in the form of a vision. This gives him the inspiration to get up and win the bout and exchange vows with the girl he loves.

d, George Archainbaud; w, Frances Guihan, Vera Clark (based on a story by Curtis Benton); t, Harry Braxton; ph, Chester A. Lyons; ed, Robert J. Kern; art d, Hervey Libbert.

Drama **(PR:A MPAA:NR)**

BACK FIRE** (1922) 5 reels SUN/AY bw

Jack Hoxie *("Lightning" Carson)*.

"Lightning" Carson (Hoxie) drifts into town with his pal and the friend suggests that they hold up the Wells-Fargo office. The chance remark is overheard and it also so happens that the office is indeed robbed the next day. Hoxie's pal is thrown into jail and Hoxie flees. When he is finally found it is revealed that he is a Texas Ranger.

He joins forces with the sheriff and they tackle the outlaws. Pretty sticky going for the popular Hoxie.

d&w, Alvin J. Nietz.

Western **(PR:A MPAA:NR)**

BACK HOME AND BROKE*** (1922) 8 reels FP/PAR bw

Thomas Meighan *(Tom Redding)*, Lila Lee *(Mary Thorne)*, Frederick Burton *(Otis Grimley)*, Cyril Ring *(Eustace Grimley)*, Charles Abbe *(H.H. Hornby)*, Florence Dixon *(Olivia Hornby)*, Gertrude Quinlan *(Aggie Twaddle)*, Richard Carlyle *(John Thorne)*, Maude Turner Gordon *(Mrs. Redding)*, Laurence Wheat *(Billy Andrews)*, Ned Burton *(Horace Beemer)*, James Marlowe *(Policeman)*, Eddie Borden *(Collector)*.

When Meighan's father dies and leaves him swamped with debts, everyone but Lee deserts him. The plucky young man heads West, becomes an oil millionaire, and returns home in the guise of a mendicant. Under an assumed name, he buys up most of the town's property and in the end throws a lavish banquet, in which he announces his engagement to Lee and informs the turncoats they need fear nothing from him nor from the power of his money.

d, Alfred E. Green; w, J. Clarkson Miller, George Ade; ph, Henry Cronjager.

Drama/Comedy **(PR:A MPAA:NR)**

BACK TRAIL, THE** (1924) 4 reels UNIV bw

Jack Hoxie *(Jeff Prouty)*, Alton Stone *(A Tramp)*, Eugenia Gilbert *(Ardis Andrews)*, Claude Payton *(Harry King)*, Billy Lester *(Jim Lawton)*, William McCall *(Judge Talent)*, Buck Connors *(Shorty)*, Pat Harmon *(Curry)*.

Hoxie, one of the silent screen's most popular cowboy stars, could ride and fight with the best of them, as he does in this western about a man with amnesia who clears himself after being framed. A war veteran, Hoxie in his illness is induced to believe he is a criminal and he breaks his father's will in order to take over his sister's estate. Finally, his memory returned, he foils the crooks.

d, Clifford Smith; w, Isadore Bernstein (based on a story by Walter J. Coburn); ph, Harry Neuman.

Western **(PR:A MPAA:NR)**

BACKSTAGE** (1927) 6 reels TIF bw

William Collier, Jr. *(Owen Mackay)*, Barbara Bedford *(Julia Joyce)*, Alberta Vaugh *(Myrtle McGinnis)*, Eileen Percy *(Fanny)*, Shirley O'Hara *(Jane)*, Gayne Whitman *(Frank Carroll)*, Jocelyn Lee *(Flo)*, Guinn Williams *(Mike Donovan)*, Jimmy Harrison *(Charlie)*, Brooks Benedict *(Harry)*, Lincoln Plummer *(Mr. Durkin)*, Marcia Harris *(Landlady)*, Louise Carver *(Referee)*, John Batten *(Eddie)*.

Collier misinterprets the situation when his chorus girl sweetheart stays at her stage manager's apartment after her show is stranded and cast members are hungry. After a lot of situations designed to amuse, the truth of the matter surfaces, but unfortunately the intended laughs don't.

d, Phil Stone; w, John F. Natteford, Sarah Y. Mason; ph, Joseph A. Dubray, Earl Walker; ed, Leroy O. Ladwig; art d, George E. Sawley.

Comedy/Drama **(PR:A MPAA:NR)**

BAFFLED*½ (1924) 6 reels IP bw

Franklyn Farnum, Alyce Mills, Harold Austin, Andrew Waldron.

Farnum (no relation to Dustin or William) is the star of this routine western about a prominent cattleman who secretly leads an outlaw gang in an attempt to control all of the land in the territory. During the course of the film, Farnum is falsely accused by the villain of committing a crime, but he manages to clear his name and save his sweetheart's spread before nailing the crook and his henchmen.

d, J.P. McGowan; w, James Ormont; ph, Walter Griffin.

Western **(PR:A MPAA:NR)**

BAIT, THE*** (1921) 5 reels Hope Hampton/PAR bw

Hope Hampton *(Joan Grainger)*, Harry Woodward *(John Warren the Fish)*, Jack McDonald *(Bennett Barton the Fisherman)*, James Gordon *(John Garson the Game Warden)*, Rae Ebberly *(Dolly the Hooked)*, Joe Singleton *(Simpson the Bait Catcher)*, Poupee Androit *(Madeline the Minnow)*, Dan Crimmons *(Jimmy the Bullfish)*.

Gilbert's script and Tourneur's direction keep this an absorbing underworld story. A jewelry store salesgirl, Hampton, is framed for a robbery by another employee, Singleton, and another salesgirl, Ebberly. McDonald snatches her out of prison and takes her to Paris, for nefarious reasons of his own. However, a wealthy man, Woodward, whom Hampton was to set up for a blackmail scheme, turns the tables on McDonald and he and Hampton set sail for New York, falling in love on the way. Home again, Woodward manages to obtain a confession from Ebberly. He clears Hampton's name of the jewelry store robbery and wins her hand.

d, Maurice Tourneur; w, John Gilbert (based on the play "The Tiger Lady" by Sidney Toler); ph, Alfred Ortlieb.

Mystery **(PR:A MPAA:NR)**

BALLET GIRL, THE*** (1916) 5 reels Brady/WORLD bw

Alice Brady *(La Syrena/Jennie Raeburn)*, Holbrook Blinn *(Zachary Trewehella)*, Robert Frazer *(Fred Pearl)*, Julia Stuart *(Mrs. Raeburn)*, Harry Danes *(Charles Raeburn)*, Laura McClure *(Mae Raeburn)*, Jessie Lewis *(Irene Dale)*, Alec B. Francis *(Jerry Vergoe)*, George Ralph *(Maurice Avery)*, S. Wheatcroft *(Fuzz Castleton)*, Fred Radcliffe *(Joe Cunningham)*, Robert Kegerreis *(Jack Danby)*.

An excellent early Alice Brady feature, which calls for her to emote from a range of youthful vigor and joy to hopelessness and despair. Behind-the-scenes carnival life is seen in the raw as Brady struggles with both ambition and love, and the outcome of her tribulations is withheld until the very end of the picture.

p, William Brady; d, George Irving; w, (based on the novel *Carnival* by Compton Mackenzie).

Drama **(PR:A MPAA:NR)**

BANDIT'S SON, THE** (1927) 5 reels FBO bw

Bob Steele *(Bob McCall)*, Tom Lingham *(Dan McCall)*, Hal Davis *(Matt Bolton)*, Stanley Taylor *(Rufe Bolton)*, Anne Sheridan *(Helen Todd)*, Bobby Mack *(Jake Kirby)*, Barney Gilmore *(Amos Jordan)*, Finch Smiles *(Rev. Todd)*.

Steele earns the right to marry the parson's daughter after clearing his name, saving his one-time gunfighter father from the rope, and bringing the real crook to justice. This was the year dynamic little Steele, then 21 years of age, began his long career as a film cowboy. The "Ann Sheridan" in the cast is not the "oomph girl" of the 1930s and 1940s, who in 1927 was only 12 years old and who did not hit Hollywood until 1933.

d, Wallace W. Fox; w, Frank Howard Clark; ph, Nick Musuraca.

Western **(PR:A MPAA:NR)**

BANTAM COWBOY, THE** (1928) 5 reels FBO bw

Buzz Barton *(David "Red" Hepner)*, Frank Rice *(Sidewinder Steve)*, Tom Lingham *(John Briggs)*, Dorothy Kitchen *(Nan Briggs)*, Bob Fleming *(Jason Todd)*, Bill Patton *(Chuck Rogers)*, Sam Nelson *(Jim Thornton)*.

Another in the series of Barton's "Red" Hepner westerns. This time the kid cowboy saves a girl and her father from a crooked half-brother, who sets out to kill them when he learns the railroad is planning to build a spur through their property.

d, Louis King; sup, Robert N. Bradbury; w, Frank Howard Clark (based on a story by Bradbury); t, Frank T. Daugherty; ph, Roy Eslick; ed, Della M. King.

Western **(PR:A MPAA:NR)**

BAR NOTHIN'*** (1921) 5 reels FOX bw

Buck Jones *(Duke Travis)*, Ruth Renick *(Bess Lynne)*, William Buckley *(Harold Lynne)*, Arthur Carew *(Stinson)*, James Farley *(Bill Harliss)*.

Jones, at his best, saves a ranch of honest folks from cattle people who covet the valuable land. Plenty of riding, fighting, and the kind of stunt work that put the popular cowboy hero in a class by himself, as he protects Renick and her invalid brother from greedy cattle buyers who are trying to force the pair out of their ranch. An exciting finish has Jones lying in the desert after being robbed by one of the crooked cattlemen, grabbing a stray horse and hard-riding it back to the ranch to nip the badmen's plot in the bud.

d, Edward Sedgwick; w, Jack Strumwasser (based on a story by Strumwasser, Clyde C. Westover); ph, Frank B. Good.

Western **(PR:A MPAA:NR)**

BAR SINISTER, THE*** (1917) 9 reels Abrams & Werner bw

Mitchell Lewis, Hedda Nova, Victor Sutherland, Jules Cowels, William A. Williams, W.J. Gross, Florence St. Leonard, Mary Doyle, William Anderson, Frank Reilly, George Dangerfield, James Turbin, J.R. Chamberlain, Mack Wright.

This fascinating film set in the Old South deals with honor and racial purity. Here the heroine becomes acceptable only after she proves she was abducted as a child and is actually "all white." The production values were quite high for an independent and it is interesting in that respect to compare this picture with THE BIRTH OF A NATION, released just two years earlier.

d, Edgar Lewis; w, (based on the poem by Anthony Kelly); ph, Edward C. Earle.

Drama **(PR:A MPAA:NR)**

BARBED WIRE**** (1927) 7 reels PAR bw

Pola Negri *(Mona)*, Clive Brook *(Oskar)*, Einar Hanson *(The Brother)*, Claude Gillingwater *(The Father)*, Charles Lane *(The Commandant)*, Gustav von Seyffertitz *(The Neighbor)*, Clyde Cook *(Hans)*, Ben Hendricks, Jr. *(The Sergeant)*.

This film about a French girl's love for a prisoner of war is one of those rare pictures in which almost everything seems right. The faces of the extras, the sets (especially the prison camp), the photography, the acting (except for Negri, who was somewhat out of character), and the direction all excel. At the time of its making, this film was highly controversial because it was regarded by many as pro-German. Perhaps, with its strongly eloquent appeal for pacifism, it seems all the more wonderful because it was produced some three years before ALL QUIET ON THE WESTERN FRONT. Producer Pommer was offered the book the film was made from by director Lee. It was about an English girl who falls in love with a German prisoner-of-war, but Pommer wanted Negri to play the part of the girl so the locale was changed to France. It was the great German producer-director's second film after his arrival in Hollywood. For Negri, the film was a godsend, as she was in deep mourning over the recent death of Rudolph Valentino, with whom she had had a lasting romance, and the picture promised to take her mind off the tragedy.

p, Erich Pommer; d, Rowland V. Lee; w, Jules Furthman, Lee (based on a novel *The Woman of Knockaloe, a Parable* by Hall Caine); ph, Bert Glennon.

Drama **(PR:A MPAA:NR)**

BARNES MURDER CASE, THE**
(1930, Brit.) 5 reels STOLL bw (GB: THE CONSPIRATORS)

Betty Faire *(Louise Fitzmaurice)*, David Hawthorne *(Herbert Wrayson)*, Moore Marriott *(Morris/Sidney Barnes)*, Edward O'Neill *(Col. Fitzmaurice)*, Margaret Hope *(Mrs. Barnes)*, Winifred Izard *(Queen of Rexonia)*, Fred Rains *(Benham)*.

In this English thriller, a father kills a blackmailer in order to save his son, but an innocent girl is wrongly accused.

d&w, Sinclair Hill (based on the novel by E. Phillips Oppenheim).

Crime **(PR:A MPAA:NR)**

BARRIER, THE* ** (1926) 7 reels MGM bw

Norman Kerry *(Meade Burrell)*, Henry B. Walthall *(Gale Gaylord)*, Lionel Barrymore *(Stark Bennett)*, Marceline Day *(Necia)*, George Cooper *(Sgt. Murphy)*, Bert Woodruff *(No Creek Lee)*, Princess Neola *(Alluna)*, Mario Carillo *(Poleon)*, Pat Harmon *(Ist Mate)*, Shannon Day *(Necia's Indian Mother)*.

A terrific sea storm sequence, in which the ruthless Barrymore allows his halfbreed wife to die, and an ice floe sequence worthy of WAY DOWN EAST, open and close this highly polished MGM winner. In between, there's a love story involving a Virginia aristocrat, assigned to the North Woods, and Barrymore's daughter, who has been raised by Walthall as his own. The conflict arises when the brute shows up at the post and delights in telling his daughter the truth. This was the second and best filming of the popular Beach novel, and this one, like the first, has a happy ending.

d, George Hill; w, Harvey Gates (based on the novel by Rex Beach); ph, Max Fabian, Ira H. Morgan.

Drama **(PR:A MPAA:NR)**

BARRIERS OF THE LAW* ** (1925) 4 reels Independent Pictures bw

J.P. McGowan *(Steve Redding)*, Helen Holmes *(Rita Wingate)*, William Desmond *(Rex Brandon)*, Albert J. Smith *(Redding's Cohort)*, Norma Wills *(Annie)*, Marguerite Clayton *(Leila Larkin)*.

Interesting casting by a small-time production company of two former stars (Desmond and Holmes) to make the kind of movie they were famous for. Holmes is a bootlegger's daughter who destroys her father's boat before it is raided by revenue officers. Her dad is jailed, but she escapes, then quits her bootleg gang when its leader refuses to help her father. The gang leader drives her into a whorehouse, from which she escapes, into the arms of a revenue agent, Desmond. After some tribulations, she infiltrates the gang to obtain evidence against them, and winds up getting locked in a flaming boxcar. A wild chase by the revenue man ensues, and she is saved, and Desmond and Holmes prove they still have the touch.

d, J.P. McGowan; w, William Lester (based on a story by Travers Vale); ph, Walter Griffin.

Action **(PR:A MPAA:NR)**

BASHFUL BUCCANEER½** (1925) 5 reels Harry J. Brown/RAY bw

Reed Howes *(Jerry Logan)*, Dorothy Dwan *(Nancy Lee)*, Sheldon Lewis *(1st Mate)*, Bull Montana *(2nd Mate)*, Jimmy Aubrey *(Cook)*, Sam Allen *(Captain)*, George French *(Clipper Jones)*, Sailor Sharkey, "Gunboat" Smith.

Howes (who handsomely modeled for Arrow collars) is really good as Jerry Logan, a writer of sea adventures who has never set foot on a boat. He decides to remedy this by chartering a ship owned by Dwan and setting out in search of buried treasure. His crew is made up of thugs, and when they mutiny, Howes brings them under control through his impressive athletic prowess. A movie company, which just happens to be nearby, spots it all and hires him to write adventure scripts. He also wins the love of Dwan and a taste for the sea.

d, Harry J. Brown; w, King Johnson, Burke Jenkins.

Adventure **(PR:A MPAA:NR)**

BAT, THE* ** (1926) 9 reels UA bw

Andre de Beranger *(Gideon Bell)*, Charles Herzinger *(Courtleigh Fleming)*, Emily Fitzroy *(Mrs. Cornelia Van Gorder)*, Louise Fazenda *(Lizzie Allen, the Maid)*, Arthur Houseman *(Richard Fleming)*, Robert McKim *(Dr. Wells)*, Jack Pickford *(Brooks Bailey)*, Jewel Carmen *(Miss Dale Ogden)*, Sojin Kamiyama *(Billy, the Japanese Butler)*, Tullio Carminati *(Moletti)*, Eddie Gribbon *(Detective Anderson)*, Lee Shumway *(The Unknown)*.

This was the first of three filmed versions of the popular stage whodunit about a mysterious stranger who dresses as a bat, flashes a rodent shadow through the use of a special flashlight (long before Bruce Wayne got on the beam) and challenges the audience to figure out which of the many on-screen characters is really the killer.

p, d&w, Roland West (based on the play by Mary Roberts Rinehart); t, George Marion, Jr.; ph, Arthur Edeson; art d, William Cameron Menzies.

Mystery **(PR:A MPAA:NR)**

BATTLE CRY OF PEACE, THE*** ** (1915) 9 reels VIT bw

Charles Richman, L. Rogers Lytton, Charles Kent, James Morrison, Julia Swayne Gordon, Mary Maurice, Evart Overton, Louise Beaudet, Belle Bruce, Harold Hubert, Norma Talmadge, Jack Crawford, Lucille Hammil, Thais Lanton, Lionel Brehan, Joseph Kilgour, Paul Scardon, William Fergerson, Harry S. Northrup, James Lackaye.

In 1915, while war raged in Europe, film producer Blackton received permission from author Maxim (whose brother invented the machine gun) to film a book Maxim had written which passionately advocated military preparedness. The book described the invasion of New York by an army of looting, raping, and civilian-murdering monsters. Although the nationality of the invaders was never mentioned, the design of their helmets, combined with the Kaiser Bill mustaches they sported, left little doubt as to which side of the European conflict they represented. In fact, Blackton admitted that his purpose was to encourage America's entrance into the war, and that he really didn't care "which one of the Allies wins." Teddy Roosevelt thought it a "bully" picture and beat his drum on its behalf. His support encouraged his close friend, Gen. Leonard Wood, to place 2,500 marines at Blackton's disposal (they made ideal extras), and helped induce the preparedness-prone public to fill the nation's theaters. At the same time, Henry Ford, who was campaigning for peace, took out full page ads denouncing the movie and the book as propaganda for the weapons industry. One cannot overestimate the advantageous effect this all had at the box office, while on the West Coast, Thomas Ince, the consummate showman, elected to exploit the situation by producing his own epic, CIVILIZATION, which took the pacifist point of view. THE BATTLE CRY OF PEACE, along with THE BIRTH OF A NATION, ranks as one of the silent cinema's most controversial films. Unfortunately, only a few out-takes have survived, as has the rumor that an extra who worked in the mob scenes, a man named Lember Bronstein, of the Bronx, was in reality Russian revolutionist Leon Trotsky. It is impossible to actually document this, but somehow, with Teddy, Maxim, and Henry Ford all involved, it sure does *feel* right.

p, J. Stuart Blackton; d, Wilfred North; w, Blackton (based on the book *Defenseless America* by Hudson Maxim); ph, Leonard Smith.

Drama **(PR:A MPAA:NR)**

BATTLE OF GETTYSBURG* ** (1914) 5 reels KB/MUT bw

Willard Mack, Charles French, Enid Bennett, Herschal Mayall, Walter Edwards, Frank Borzage, J. Barney Sherry, Anna Little, George Fisher, Frank Burke, Enid Markey.

Ince provides a love story to add depth to this historical film, but it is all but forgotten once the fighting starts. For more than an hour on the screen the battle wages back and forth in a horrifying glimpse of man-to-man warfare, with the audience as confused as the participants as to which side in the mighty conflict gained or lost what. In the end the awesome toll of the three-day battle is tellingly glimpsed in a moonlit shot of a ravine filled with dead men and horses. Director Ince's first feature film, the BATTLE OF GETTYSBURG was directed from a scenario so highly detailed that there were even directions for the facial expressions of the actors. All the battle scenes were broken down with detailed instructions to the cameramen (eight of them) for the angles to be covered. Mack Sennett, a good friend of Ince's, used some of the props and mobs of extras in the Santa Ynez canyon where the battle scenes were shot, for a picture he was making at the time, COHEN SAVES THE FLAG.

d, Thomas H. Ince, Charles Giblyn; w, C. Gardner Sullivan.

Historical **(PR:A MPAA:NR)**

BATTLE OF LIFE, THE½** (1916) 5 reels FOX bw

Gladys Coburn *(Mary Boland)*, Art Acord *(Dave Karns)*, William Sheer *(Jack Ellis)*, Frank Evans *(Tom Boland)*, Richard Neill *(O'Leary)*, Alex Shannon *(Wentworth)*, Violet de Biccari *(Mary, Age 12)*.

Director Vincent paints a convincing picture of New York's underworld in this motion picture which has Coburn managing to grow up following the straight path—in spite of a hard-drinking gangster father and the tremendous pressures of her environment.

d, James Vincent; w, Adrian Johnson (based on a story by James R. Garey).

Crime **(PR:A MPAA:NR)**

BATTLE OF THE SEXES, THE** (1914) 5 reels MUT bw

Lillian Gish *(Jane Andrews)*, Owen Moore *(Frank Andrews)*, Mary Alden *(Mrs. Frank Andrews)*, Fay Tincher *(Cleo)*, Robert Harron *(The Son)*, Donald Crisp, W.E. Lawrence.

This was Griffith's first independent picture after leaving Biograph and cost less than $5,000 to produce. It's star, Gish, remembers it being shot in five grueling days and nights. Nevertheless it was greeted enthusiastically by critics and public alike. It tells of a wealthy middle-aged man taken in by a fortune-hunting woman and her cunningly suave paramour. When his daughter learns of the indiscretion, she goes to the woman's apartment with the intention of shooting her but, instead, is captivated by the confidence man. The father, on discovering his daughter in a position not unlike his own, realizes his error and delivers her back into the fold of his proper Victorian family. Griffith admitted from the start that this was to be a potboiler. Since it was imperative that his new company begin with a financial winner, he may have compromised a bit or cut a few corners here or there. Perhaps he had his eye on a future project—something to do with the Civil War.

d, D.W. Griffith; w, (based on "The Single Standard" by Daniel Carson Goodman); ph, G.W. Bitzer; ed, James Smith, Rose Richtel.

Drama **(PR:A MPAA:NR)**

BATTLE OF THE SEXES, THE** (1928) 10 reels UA bw

Jean Hersholt *(Judson)*, Phyllis Haver *(Marie Skinner)*, Belle Bennett *(Mrs. Judson)*, Don Alvarado *("Babe" Winsor)*, Sally O'Neil *(Ruth Judson)*, William Blakewell *(Billy Judson)*, John Batten *(A Friend)*.

Griffith, whose personal and professional life was at a low ebb, desperately needed a commercial success when he decided to remake this film which he considered a potboiler in 1914. Comedy (particularly of the sex-farce, flapper variety) was not his strong suit, and that is evident here. Sadly, the director was no longer in control. He was now expected to answer to production head Joseph M. Schenck, a man who added a musical and sound effects track without even consulting Griffith. The master did not approve of the "enhancement," the finished film, or, for that matter, what was becoming of his life.

d, D.W. Griffith; w, Gerrit Lloyd (based on "The Single Standard" by Daniel Carson Goodman); t, Lloyd; ph, Karl Struss, G.W. Bitzer; m, R. Schildkret, Hugo Riesenfeld; ed, James Smith, syn sc; s eff.

Drama **(PR:A MPAA:NR)**

BATTLES OF THE CORONEL AND FALKLAND ISLANDS, THE***
(1928, Brit.) 8 reels BI bw (AKA: THE DEEDS MEN DO)

Craighall Sherry *(Adm. Sturdee)*.

English production re-creating the naval pursuit and sinking of the ship Von Spee. In 1932, a sound track was added for a re-release booking under the title THE DEEDS MEN DO.

p, A.E. Bundy, H. Bruce Woolfe; d, Walter Summers; w, Harry Engholm, Frank Bowen, Merritt Crawford.

War (PR:A MPAA:NR)

BATTLESHIP POTEMKIN, THE*****
(1925, USSR) 5 reels Goskino bw (BRONENOSETS POTEMKIN; AKA: POTEMKIN)

Alexander Antonov *(Vakulinchuk)*, Vladimir Barsky *(Comdr. Golikov)*, Grigory Alexandrov *(Senior Officer Gilyarovsky)*, Mikhail Gomorov *(Sailor Matyushenko)*, Levchenko *(Boatswain)*, Repnikova *(Woman on the Steps)*, Marusov *(Officer)*, I. Bobrov, A. Fait *(Recruits)*, Sergei Eisenstein *(Priest)*, Alexander Lyovshin *(Petty Officer)*, Beatrice Vitoldi *(Mother With Baby Carriage)*, Konstantin Feldman *(Student Fel'dman)*, Protopopov *(Old Man)*, Korobei *(Legless Veteran)*, Yulia Eisenstein *(Lady Bringing Food to Mutineers)*, Prokopenko *(Mother of Wounded Aba)*, A. Glauberman *(Aba)*, N. Poltautseva *(School Teacher)*, Brodsky *(Intellectual)*, Zerenin *(Student)*, Sailors of the Red Navy, Citizens of Odessa, Members of the Proletcult Theatre.

Without a doubt one of the most important films in the development of the cinema, Sergei Eisenstein's POTEMKIN has been subjected to an intense amount of scrutiny and debate unprecedented in film history. Set in Russia during the failed revolution of 1905, POTEMKIN begins on board the Czarist battleship with the sailors whispering rumors of a revolutionary uprising. The cramped, inhuman conditions the sailors are forced to suffer begin to take their toll and tempers flare. When the ship's doctor claims that the maggot-infested meat the men are being served is perfectly edible, they have had enough. When a small group of sailors refuses to eat the rancid meat, the ship's officers order the guards to throw a tarpaulin over the men and execute them. The tension builds as the officer barks the sequence of orders to the firing squad. Just before the triggers are pulled a sailor, Antonov, emerges from the crowd, and urges the guards to think about whose side they're on—the officers or the sailors. The guards hesitate, then lower their weapons. The sadistic officer goes mad with rage and tries to grab one of their rifles. Suddenly all the sailors revolt and take over the ship, but Antonov is killed during the struggle. The *Potemkin* then steams to the town of Odessa. On the beach, the sailors erect a tent shrine to their fallen comrade Antonov where his body lies in state for all the citizens to see. The workers of Odessa file past the dead hero's body and his brave deeds spark a revolutionary fervor in the hearts of all who pass. The citizens of Odessa unite with the men of the *Potemkin* and all vow to rise against the Czar. One bright day when most of the people of Odessa are on the shore waving and cheering the men on the *Potemkin*, Czarist troops arrive to quell the revolutionary movement. Chaos erupts as rows and rows of soldiers advance down the stone steps that lead to the beach, firing at everything that moves. A young mother is shot and her baby carriage tumbles down the steps. An old woman tries to save the child, but is killed by a Cossack. The outraged sailors of the *Potemkin* turn their ship's huge guns on Odessa's military headquarters and destroy it. When the smoke clears the slaughter has ended, but corpses lie strewn on the Odessa steps. Back on the *Potemkin*, the sailors surmise that the rest of the Czar's fleet will be coming to quell this uprising. The men decide to leave Odessa and meet the flotilla head on. The *Potemkin* prepares for battle as she steams out to meet her destiny. Tension builds as the *Potemkin* approaches the fleet. All sailors are at their battle stations. The guns of the fleet turn toward the *Potemkin*. Suddenly, instead of violence, the *Potemkin* is met with smiles from the men of the other battleships. The fleet has decided to join the revolution against the Czar and fight alongside the men of the *Potemkin*. In March of 1925, a 27-year-old filmmaker named Sergei Eisenstein, who had recently made the film STRIKE, was commisioned to produce a film celebrating the 20th anniversary of the 1905 Revolution. Along with political activist Agadzhanova-Shutko, he drafted a script hundreds of pages in length, which attempted to cover all the important events that transpired in that historic year. They began filming in Leningrad, but ran into bad weather. Then, after shooting a few scenes in Baku, Eisenstein moved on to Odessa, where the decision was made to devote the entire film to the events which occurred in that region during the time of the *Potemkin* mutiny and use them as a microcosm of the whole revolution. Eisenstein's efforts resulted in one of the most important films ever made. Not because of its Marxist message, but because of the way in which the story was told. The Russian director had taken the basics of composition and editing and transformed them into something incredible. Eisenstein built his film almost musically by using different shots (long shots, medium shots, closeups) and cutting them in such a way as to heighten the moments and build emotions by bombarding the viewer with a whole series of conflicting images that would convey mood and feeling. By experimenting with the rhythm and tempo of his editing, known as *montage*, Eisenstein was able to affect audiences with a purely filmic style which could not be duplicated in any other medium. Though Eisenstein had always cited American director D.W. Griffith as a major inspiration, the Russian's films were of a very different nature. While both directors are known for spectacles of epic grandeur, Griffith's films were structured along traditional dramatic rules by following a main character or characters throughout the drama. Eisenstein, however, following his Marxist beliefs, concentrated on the masses—not individual characters. What is amazing about Eisenstein's films is that he is still able to convey human feeling and drama within his wider format by briefly allowing the audience to see the individuals who make up the whole. The moments he concentrates on are heightened and moving because we see only important moments in the lives of these people (Antonov deciding to fight the officers, the old woman trying to save the baby). Eisenstein's *montage* style of filmmaking has influenced countless filmmakers from Russia to Hollywood. While many directors employ his methods in brief sequences to heighten the effect (most memorably in the films of Hitchcock and Peckinpah), few use *montage* as extensively and skillfully as Eisenstein had. Though it at first seems incongruous to mention them in the same breath as Eisenstein, low-budget, independent filmmakers like Russ Meyer (VIXEN, FASTER PUSSY CAT, KILL, KILL) and George Romero (NIGHT OF THE LIVING DEAD, etc.) have employed the Russian director's visual style and made it their own. Because low-budget filmmakers haven't the time or money to spend on complex moving camera shots, they have been forced to affect audiences through skillful use of detailed composition and editing. POTEMKIN has become such an institution to filmmakers, especially the Odessa Steps sequence, that it even has been affectionately parodied in such films as Woody Allen's BANANAS and LOVE AND DEATH, and Terry Gilliam's BRAZIL. Eisenstein would forge ahead and make other remarkable films (ALEXANDER NEVSKY, IVAN THE TERRIBLE I and II), but it is POTEMKIN that he will always be remembered for.

p, Jacob Bliokh; d, Sergei Eisenstein; w, Eisenstein, Nina Agadzhanova-Shutko; t, Nikolai Aseyev; ph, Edward Tisse, V. Popov; m, Edmund Meisel; ed, Eisenstein; art d, Vasili Rakhals.

Historical Drama Cas. (PR:C MPAA:NR)

BATTLING BUTLER*** (1926) 7 reels MGM bw

Buster Keaton *(Alfred Butler)*, Sally O'Neil *(The Girl)*, Snitz Edwards *(His Valet)*, Francis McDonald *(Alfred "Battling Butler")*, Mary O'Brien *(His Wife)*, Tom Wilson *(The Trainer)*, Eddie Borden *(His Manager)*, Walter James *(The Girl's Father)*, Buddy Fine *(The Girl's Brother)*.

Keaton is sensational as the wealthy fop who passes himself off as a boxer in order to impress a girl. At the end of the film, when he fights the real "Battling Butler," the action (which is played completely straight) is almost unbearable to watch. Such is the beating the little man endures before pulling himself up from the floor and triumphing over the bully. This is perhaps the most unusual film Keaton made while a major star and, in a melancholy sense, perhaps the most autobiographical.

d, Buster Keaton; w, Albert Boasberg, Paul Gerard Smith, Lex Neal, Charles Smith (based on the musical "Battling Butler," by Stanley Brightman, Austin Melford, music, Philip Brabham, words, Douglas Furber); ph, Bert Haines, Dev Jennings.

Comedy Cas. (PR:A MPAA:NR)

BEATING THE GAME*** (1921) 6 reels Goldwyn bw

Tom Moore *("Fancy Charlie")*, Hazel Daly *(Nellie Brown)*, DeWitt C. Jennings *(G. B. Lawson)*, Dick Rosson *(Ben Franchette)*, Nick Cogley *("Slipper Jones")*, Tom Ricketts *(Jules Franchette)*, Lydia Knott *(Mme. Franchette)*, William Orlamond *(Bank President)*, Lydia Yeamans Titus *(Angelica, His Wife)*.

Good comedy drama about a safecracker who is hired to set up the "big job" by living a completely straight life for six months in the small town where the heist will be made. He pulls this off so well that they are about to elect him mayor. He also manages to fall in love with the local lovely. When the man who set it all up arrives and is told by the cracksman that he can't go through with the scheme, there is a nifty twist ending. It turns out that the boss is really a crime buff (as well as a state senator) who at last has found an honest man he can back for public office.

d, Victor Schertzinger; w, Charles Kenyon; ph, Ernest Miller; art d, Cedric Gibbons.

Comedy/Drama (PR:A MPAA:NR)

BEAU BRUMMEL**** (1924) 10 reels WB bw

John Barrymore *(George Bryan Brummel)*, Mary Astor *(Lady Margery Avanley)*, Willard Louis *(Prince of Wales)*, Irene Rich *(Duchess of York)*, Alec B. Francis *(Mortimer)*, Carmel Myers *(Lady Hester Stanhope)*, William Humphreys *(Lord Avanley)*, Richard Tucker *(Lord Stanhope)*, Andre Beranger *(Lord Byron)*, Claire de Lorez *(Lady Manly)*, Michael Dark *(Lord Manly)*, Templar Saxe *(Desmond Wertham)*, Clarissa Selwynne *(Mrs. Wertham)*, James A. Marcus *(English Inn Keeper)*, Betty Brice *(Mrs. Snodgrass)*, Roland Rushton *(Mr. Abrahms)*, John J. Richardson *("Poodle" Byng)*.

A splendid production and one of Barrymore's best silent performances. He is an English dandy whose wit and elegance win him the favors of the mighty, but whose arrogance costs him his friends, leaving him to die penniless in a French insane asylum. It was an assignment perfectly suited to the great man's flair, and he showed it at once on the set when, on meeting his leading lady, Astor, he whispered in her ear, "You are so beautiful." Astor, then 17 (Barrymore was 41), confessed later in her autobiography that they fell in love "and I am sure that he was more startled than I." She went on, "In the filming of the many romantic, delicate love scenes...we could stand there, quietly loving the closeness." Barrymore was on a first name basis with almost everybody on the set and often spoke with them about technical details. Yet he maintained a dignity that was touching, and impressive.

d, Harry Beaumont; w, Dorothy Farnum (based on the play by Clyde Fitch); ph, David Abel.

Drama Cas. (PR:A MPAA:NR)

BEAU GESTE**** (1926) 11 reels FP/PAR bw-c

Ronald Colman (Michael "Beau" Geste), Neil Hamilton *(Digby Geste)*, Ralph Forbes *(John Geste)*, Alice Joyce *(Lady Brandon)*, Mary Brian *(Isobel)*, Noah Beery *(Sgt. Lejaune)*, Norman Trevor *(Maj. de Beaujolais)*, William Powell *(Boldini)*, Victor McLaglen *(Hank)*, Donald Stuart *(Buddy)*.

Wren's epic story of honor, sacrifice, courage, and love between brothers was filmed three times but never as well as the first. Everything about this production, from the direction to the titles, is outstanding. But in the final analysis, it is Beery's portrayal of the sadistic Sgt. Lejaune that remains completely unforgettable. Contributing another term to an English language already loaded with chivalric terms, BEAU GESTE is a marvelous paean to honor among men in the face of adversity. Opening on the scene of a desert fort where only dead Foreign Legionnaires can be seen, the story flashes back 20 years to the boyhood of the Geste brothers, three sons of an honorable mother, vowing to protect her always. Then the brothers are fighting together in the Legion, not only Arabs but a commanding officer, Beery, who gives one of the finest performances of his life. Director Brenon won raves for his work in turning out a movie spectacle with large-scale Arab attacks on the desert near Yuma, Arizona, in his return to big-scale pictures after a series of whimsies. Colman considered his role as one of the brothers his greatest personal achievement in films, and he was ideally suited to give the fine and beautiful gestures the words *beau geste* today describe. Hamilton and Forbes are excellent as the other two brothers, and Brian is her lovely self in one of the feminine roles, with the mother admirably portrayed by Joyce. It is true that lip-reading, which gave birth to a new sport in the 1920s called "cuss-word puzzle," would have helped in witnessing BEAU GESTE, especially when Beery was performing, who would say things during filming that were "hot" even on the set.

d, Herbert Brenon; w, Paul Schofield, John Russell (based on the novel by P. C. Wren); ph, J. Roy Hunt; m, Hugo Riesenfeld; art d, Julian Boone Fleming.

Adventure **(PR:A MPAA:NR)**

BEAU REVEL**** (1921) 6 reels PAR bw

Florence Vidor *(Nellie Steel)*, Lewis S. Stone *(Lawrence "Beau" Revel)*, Lloyd Hughes *(Dick Revel)*, Kathleen Kirkham *(Alice Lathon)*, Richard Ryan *(Rossiter Wade)*, Harlan Tucker *(Will Phyfe)*, William Conklin *(Fred Lathon)*, Lydia Titus *(Ma Steel)*, William Musgrave *(Bert Steel)*, Joe Campbell *(Butler)*, Lydia Yeamans.

Interesting love triangle in which a father (Stone) and his son (Hughes) vie for the love of a beautiful dancer played by Vidor. Wray's direction is excellent and the closing scene where Stone commits suicide by leaping from a window to his death is a shocker.

d, John Griffith Wray; sup, Thomas H. Ince; w, Luther Reed (based on a story by Louis Joseph Vance); ph, Henry Sharp.

Drama **Cas.** **(PR:C MPAA:NR)**

BEAU SABREUR*** (1928) 67m PAR bw

Gary Cooper *(Maj. Henri de Beaujolais)*, Evelyn Brent *(May Vanbrugh)*, Noah Beery *(Sheikh El Hamel)*, William Powell *(Becque)*, Mitchell Lewis *(Suleiman the Strong)*, Frank Reicher *(Gen. de Beaujolais)*, Oscar Smith *(Djikki)*.

When three French Legionnaires overstay their leave they are thrown into jail, where one of the three, Cooper, wins the title "Beau Sabreur" when he conquers a traitor in a duel. His uncle, a general, sends Cooper into the desert to learn the customs of the people and eventually he meets American journalist Brent. Meanwhile, the traitor who had dueled Cooper tries to thwart "Beau Sabreur's" efforts at a treaty with a sheik, but Cooper escapes a trap with Brent and goes through with his assignment. The sheik he is dealing with joins Cooper in repelling an attack by the traitor, whom Cooper kills, and, after serving France, Cooper confesses his love for Brent. Good action picture which was billed as the sequel to BEAU GESTE but resembled it only in that it had a desert setting and some members of the same cast, as well as a story by Wren.

d, John Waters; w, Tom J. Geraghty (based on P. C. Wren's story); t, Julian Johnson; ph, C. E. Schoenbaum; ed, Rose Lowenger.

Adventure **(PR:A MPAA:NR)**

BEAUTIFUL AND DAMNED, THE** (1922) 7 reels WB bw

Marie Prevost *(Gloria)*, Kenneth Harlan *(Anthony)*, Harry Myers *(Dick)*, Tully Marshall *(Adam Patch)*, Louise Fazenda *(Muriel)*, Cleo Ridgeley *(Dot)*, Emmett King *(Mr. Gilbert)*, Walter Long *(Hull)*, Clarence Burton *(Bloeckman)*, Parker McConnell *(Maury)*, Charles McHugh *(Shuttlesworth)*, Kathleen Key *(Rachel)*, George Kuwa *(Tanner)*.

This liberal translation of Fitzgerald's novel is pretty much a bore. Of interest mainly because of the author, there is still a good performance by the always dependable Marshall as the grandfather of pleasure-seeking Harlan, whose wife, Prevost, has spent all of her father's money. When Marshall dies, leaving the two nothing, they try unsuccessfully to go to work, but soon return to their frantic pursuit of pleasure. A near fatal accident brings them slowly round to their senses, and they sail off together to Europe, resolving to live more circumspectly and ultimately to make good.

d, William A. Seiter; w, Olga Printzlau (based on the novel by F. Scott Fitzgerald).

Drama **(PR:A MPAA:NR)**

BEAUTIFUL BUT DUMB** (1928) 7 reels TS bw

Patsy Ruth Miller *(Janet Brady)*, Charles Byer *(James Conroy)*, George E. Stone *(Tad)*, Shirley Palmer *(Beth)*, Greta Yoltz *(Mae)*, William Irving *(Ward)*, Harvey Clark *(Broadwell)*.

The old story about the homely office stenographer who takes off her glasses, fixes up her hair, becomes a flapper, and wins the love of her amazed employer. Miller and director Clifton did the best they could with what they had to work with.

d, Elmer Clifton; w, J. F. Natteford; t, Frederick Hatton, Fanny Hatton; ph, Guy Wilky; ed, Desmond O'Brien.

Comedy **(PR:A MPAA:NR)**

BEAUTIFUL CHEAT, THE (1926) 7 reels UNIV bw

Laura La Plante *(Mary Callahan/Maritza Chernovska)*, Harry Myers *(Jimmy Austin)*, Bertram Grassby *(Marquis de la Pontenac)*, Alexander Carr *(Al Goldringer)*, Youcca Troubetzkoy *(Herbert Dangerfield)*, Helen Carr *(Lady Violet Armington)*, Robert Anderson *(Dan Brodie)*.

Fun movie has a small time motion picture company hiring press agent Myers to take La Plante, a New York shop girl, to Europe to build her up as a great Russian actress—who just happens to own the crown jewels—and bring her back a superstar. When they return home, the company throws a lavish party at a Long Island estate they know is vacant for the season, to introduce her to America. The rightful owners return, however, and are furious until they discover that their daughter is one of the bit players. So the party is not only allowed to continue, but the wealthy couple put up the money to back the production, and Myers proposes to La Plante.

d, Edward Sloman; w, A. P. Younger, Olga Printzlau (based on the story "Doubling for Cupid" by Nina Wilcox Putnam); ph, Jackson J. Rose.

Comedy **(PR:A MPAA:NR)**

BEAUTIFUL GAMBLER, THE* (1921) 5 reels UNIV bw

Grace Darmond *(Molly Hanlon)*, Jack Mower *(Miles Rand)*, Harry Van Meter *(Lee Kirk)*, Charles Brinley *(Jim Devlin)*, Herschel Mayall *(Judge Rand)*, Willis Marks *(Mark Hanlon)*.

Darmond marries Van Meter, the owner of a gambling emporium, after her father loses everything betting. Then she meets Mower, who in protecting her from Van Meter, apparently kills him. The two take off for New York, but two years later Van Meter shows up again and this time, while struggling with Mower, is shot to death. Mower is arrested and prepares to go to the chair, when a former employee of the gambler confesses to the murder. Confusion was this film's only attribute.

d, William Worthington; w, Hope Loring (based on a story by Peter B. Kyne); ph, George Barnes.

Western/Drama **(PR:A MPAA:NR)**

BEAUTIFUL KITTY*** (1923, Brit.) 5 reels Walter West/BUT bw

Violet Hopson *(Kitty)*, James Knight *(Jim Bennett)*, Robert Vallis *(Alf Brigs)*, Arthur Walcott, Follie Emery, Fred Percy.

English story about a not-too-bright working stiff who loses his winnings when he buys a broken-down racehorse.

d, Walter West; w, J. Bertram Brown.

Drama **(PR:A MPAA:NR)**

BEAUTIFUL LIAR, THE** (1921) 5 reels PRE/FN bw

Katherine MacDonald *(Helen Haynes/Elsie Parmelee)*, Charles Meredith *(Bobby Bates)*, Joseph J. Dowling *(MacGregor)*, Kate Lester *(Mrs. Van Courtlandt-Van Allstyn)*, Wilfred Lucas *(Gaston Allegretti)*.

Run-of-the-mill programmer about an office girl who is a double for a star who refuses to play a benefit. She steps in (with some coaching), passes for the actress, and finds her costar is a rich customer of her firm whom she has always cherished. She is hailed as a great comedienne for her performance, and the customer falls in love with her in spite of her duplicity.

d, Wallace Worsley; w, Ruth Wightman (based on the story "Peachie" by George Marion, Jr.); ph, Joseph Brotherton.

Drama **(PR:A MPAA:NR)**

BEAUTY AND BULLETS** (1928) 5 reels UNIV bw

Ted Wells *(Bill Allen)*, Duane Thompson *(Mary Crawford)*, Jack Kenney *(Joe Kemp)*, Wilbur Mack *(Frank Crawford)*.

When Wells breaks up a stage robbery, he recognizes one of the bandits to be the brother of the girl he loves. Wells takes the money home, but the gang sneaks up on him and steals the loot back. It doesn't take more than a couple of reels, however, before our hero tracks them down and arranges to have the misguided brother released into his custody.

d, Ray Taylor; w, George Plympton (based on a story by Carl Krusada, Vin Moore); t, Val Cleveland; ph, Joseph Brotherton; ed, Gene Havlick.

Western **(PR:A MPAA:NR)**

BEDROOM WINDOW, THE*** (1924) 7 reels FP/PAR bw

May McAvoy *(Ruth Martin)*, Malcolm McGregor *(Frank Armstrong)*, Ricardo Cortez *(Robert Delano)*, Robert Edeson *(Frederick Hall)*, George Fawcett *(Silas Tucker)*, Ethel Wales *(Matilda Jones)*, Charles Ogle *(Butler)*, Medea Radzina *(Sonya Malisoff)*, Guy Oliver *(Detective)*, Lillian Leighton *(Mammy)*.

Fortunately for Cortez, his fiancee's aunt is a mystery writer. So when the Latin from Manhattan is falsely accused of murdering his sweetheart's father, the lady steps in, puts her talent to use, and nails the family lawyer.

d, William De Mille; w, Clara Beranger; ph, Guy Wilky.

Mystery **(PR:A MPAA:NR)**

BEGGAR ON HORSEBACK**** (1925) 7 reels FP bw

Edward Everett Horton *(Neil McRae)*, Esther Ralston *(Cynthia Mason)*, Erwin Connelly *(Frederick Cady)*, Gertrude Short *(Gladys Cady)*, James Mason *(Homer Cady)*, Theodore Kosloff *(The Prince)*, Betty Compson *(The Princess)*, Frederick Sullivan *(Dr. Rice)*.

This remarkable satire pulled no punches in its observation of money-obsessed, anti-aesthetic, big-business types. A poor composer of serious music is forced to work with jazz in order to make a living. To get out of his bind, he proposes to a rich girl in spite of being in love with an equally poor painter. When she accepts, he goes into psychological collapse and then has a nightmare about money. When he awakens he returns to the painter. Owing much to the German cinema, the dream sequence showing the capitalist talking into a gigantic telephone, his women dressed in dollar sign garments, and a courtroom where almost every prop was surrealistically depicted, gave U.S. audiences a dazzling artistic, if not commercial, success.

d, James Cruze; w, Walter Woods, Anthony Coldeway (based on the play by George S. Kaufman, Marc Connelly); ph, Karl Brown.

Comedy/Drama **(PR:A MPAA:NR)**

BEHIND THE FRONT*** (1926) 6 reels FP bw

Wallace Beery *(Riff Swanson)*, Raymond Hatton *(Shorty McGee)*, Mary Brian *(Betty Bartlett-Cooper)*, Richard Arlen *(Percy Brown)*, Hayden Stevenson *(Capt. Bartlett-Cooper)*, Chester Conklin *(Scottie)*, Tom Kennedy *(Sergeant)*, Frances Raymond *(Mrs. Bartlett-Cooper)*, Melbourne MacDowell *(Mr. Bartlett-Cooper)*, Jerry Mandy *(Limburger Soldier)*, Charles Sullivan *(Soldier)*, Gertrude Astor *(French Barmaid)*.

Beery, using his wife Gloria's last name as a gag, plays a big "Swede" detective, and Hatton the pickpocket who lifts his watch, in this comedy which sees them tricked by a pretty girl into enlisting to fight the Kaiser in order to fill the ranks of her brother's volunteer company. Plenty of laughs are delivered by ace comedy director Sutherland, as the boys lampoon every aspect of doughboy life.

d, Edward Sutherland; w, Monte Brice, Ethel Doherty (based on *The Spoils of War* by Hugh Wiley); ph, Charles Boyle.

Comedy **(PR:A MPAA:NR)**

BELOVED ROGUE, THE*** (1927) 10 reels UA bw

John Barrymore *(Francois Villon)*, Conrad Veidt *(Louis XI)*, Marceline Day *(Charlotte de Vauxcelles)*, Lawson Butt *(Duke of Burgundy)*, Henry Victor *(Thibault d' Aussigny)*, Slim Summerville *(Jehan)*, Mack Swain *(Nicholas)*, Angelo Rossitto *(Beppo)*, Nigel de Brulier *(Astrologer)*, Lucy Beaumont *(Villon's Mother)*, Otto Matiesen *(Olivier)*, Jane Winton *(The Abbess)*, Rose Dione *(Margot)*, Bertram Grassby *(Duke of Orleans)*, Dick Sutherland *(Tristan l'Hermite)*.

This enormous production provided Barrymore with the opportunity to portray another of his macabre characters, poet-patriot Francois Villon, who does battle with the evil Burgundians in the service of his country and king. This was Veidt's first U.S. film and director Crosland's most ambitious. Most critics of the day disliked the film as being far too extravagant in settings and acting, and Barrymore himself practically disowned it, in spite of having the services of Veidt, who, it is said, knelt and kissed Barrymore's hand when they first met. In *The Life of John Barrymore* by John Kobler, Kobler says that Barrymore stole into the theater during one of the early showings of THE BELOVED ROGUE, and sat in silence in a rear balcony seat. At one point, no longer able to control himself, he shouted into the audience, "Call yourself an actor? My God, what a ham!" Again, most critics agreed with him.

d, Allan Crosland; w, Paul Bern; t, Walter Anthony; ph, Joe August; art d, William Cameron Menzies.

Drama/Adventure **Cas.** **(PR:A MPAA:NR)**

BELOW THE LINE*** (1925) 7 reels WB bw

Rin-Tin-Tin *(Himself)*, John Harron *(Donald Case)*, June Marlowe *(Mary Barton)*, Pat Hartigan *(Jamber Niles)*, Victor Potel *("Cuckoo" Niles)*, Charles [Heinie] Conklin *(Deputy Sheriff)*, Gilbert Clayton *(Rev. Barton)*, Edith Yorke *(Mrs. Cass)*, Taylor Duncan *(The Sheriff)*.

Rin-Tin-Tin, the most popular of all silent screen animals, is at his best as he battles alligators, villainous dogs, and a crook so low he attempts to steal the church funds, in this action-packed programmer. At the opening, Rin-Tin-Tin falls off a train and is found and cared for by a village youth, to whom the dog becomes intensely devoted. A murderer sics a pack of bloodhounds after the youth when the youth thwarts the theft of church funds, and Rin-Tin-Tin fights them off; when the thief and killer attacks the youth, the dog is there once again, fangs bared, but underneath it all the dog a whole generation loved for its sweet disposition.

d, Herman Raymaker; w, Charles A. Logue; ph, John Mescall, Bert Shipman.

Adventure **(PR:A MPAA:NR)**

BEN-HUR**** (1925) 12 reels MGM bw/c

Ramon Novarro *(Ben-Hur)*, Francis X. Bushman *(Messala)*, May McAvoy *(Esther)*, Betty Bronson *(Mary)*, Claire McDowell *(Princess of Hur)*, Kathleen Key *(Tirzah)*, Carmel Myers *(Iras)*, Nigel De Brulier *(Simonides)*, Mitchell Lewis *(Sheik Ilderman)*, Leo White *(Sanballat)*, Frank Currier *(Arrius)*, Charles Belcher *(Balthasar)*, Dale Fuller *(Amrah)*, Winter Hall *(Joseph)*.

During the reign of Imperial Rome, a young Jewish man, Novarro, develops a close friendship with a Roman centurion, Bushman. Their friendship is shattered when Bushman learns that Novarro is Jewish. The ambitious centurion pleases the governor by turning Novarro and his family over to the authorities after a loose tile falling from their house causes the death of a general. Novarro is made a galley slave and during a painful trek through the desert he meets Christ. The messiah gives the parched Novarro a sip of water, a drink which gives the enslaved Jew the will to fight against his oppressors. When the ship that Novarro is assigned to is attacked and begins to sink, he manages to save the life of its commander, Currier, and the grateful Roman adopts the slave. Suddenly possessed with wealth and status, Novarro makes a good reputation as a master charioteer. Soon he is challenged by his old nemesis, Bushman, to a race. During the intense spectacle witnessed by thousands Bushman is trampled to death and Novarro goes on to victory. Soon after, Novarro learns that Christ is to be crucified in Jerusalem. Novarro goes to witness the horrible deed, and there he is reunited with his mother, McDowell, and his sister, both of whom have leprosy. Through faith in Christ, they are both cured and Novarro and his family return to their palace. Since the publication of Gen. Lew Wallace's incredibly popular novel in 1880, *Ben-Hur* has been dramatized in the most spectacular manner possible for several generations. In 1899 the first of several stage-play versions of the material was produced. These incredible productions featured extravagant sets, huge crowd scenes, and even a chariot race on stage with real horses. The first film version of BEN-HUR was released in 1907 by the Kalem film company which had learned that a chariot race was going to be staged outdoors as an extra added attraction to a fireworks display. Director Sidney Olcott took the opportunity to set up a few cameras and film the race. Later he added some interior scenes to pad out the action and the film was released to rave reviews and large crowds. The Kalem company was sued by Gen. Wallace's estate for breach of copyright, the first such case in motion picture history. Kalem lost and the suit was settled for $25,000. Still a hot property, the rights to *Ben-Hur* were dickered over by every major studio in Hollywood. Finally, in 1922, Goldwyn studios secured the rights to film *Ben-Hur*. After a chaotic and incredibly costly beginning, which saw the entire company travel to Italy to shoot the film on location, the home office became slowly aware that they had a disaster on their hands. Director Charles Brabin, star George Walsh (who had yet to appear before the cameras), and writer-supervisor June Mathis were all unceremoniously fired, and in their places came director Niblo, actor Novarro, and writers Meredyth and Wilson. But, alas, MGM's troubles were far from over. Louis B. Mayer arrived to check on things and was somewhat relieved to find the industrious Niblo about to shoot the all-important sea battle. Just before the shoot, Niblo noticed that the Italian assistant director had divided the local extras representing the opposing forces into groups of Fascists and anti-Fascists (Mussolini had recently taken control of the country). He then discovered that the hundreds of swords and spears to be used in the scene had been sharpened to a fine point. Luckily the situation was rearranged at the last minute to avoid political bloodshed while the cameras were rolling. Deadly problems continued to plague the production. On the day of the sea battle, it was discovered to everyone's horror that when the armada of ships caught fire and began to sink most of the armor-plated Italian extras had lied about knowing how to swim. It was feared that several of the extras had sunk to the bottom of the Mediterranean before the rescue ships could get to them. To this day accounts conflict regarding the loss of lives. The company doggedly pushed on, hurdling obstacles again and again, but eventually production head Irving Thalberg demanded that they return to the U.S. (he had been against the Italian expedition from the start). It was with a sense of relief that most of the film folk returned to Culver City. There, the exciting chariot race was filmed (once again after a series of disasters and setbacks) using a combination of newly built sets and matted models. After the cameras had stopped rolling and the smoke cleared, BEN-HUR had cost just under $4 million. The finished product, with the truly spectacular chariot race as its highlight, received a great deal of popular and critical acclaim. BEN-HUR grossed $9 million on its initial release. Quite an accomplishment, but after paying the distributors and giving 50 percent of the receipts to Gen. Wallace's estate, MGM was left with only $3 million, $1 million less than the film cost, but the prestige MGM garnered was worth the price. BEN-HUR was rereleased in 1931, shortened and with music, but the public was no longer interested. In 1959 MGM remade the film starring Charlton Heston and directed by William Wyler, who, ironically, had worked as an assistant director during the chariot scene of the 1925 silent version.

d, Fred Niblo, Ferdinand P. Earle; 2nd unit d, Reaves Eason; w, Bess Meredyth, Carey Wilson, June Mathis (based on the novel by Lewis Wallace); t, Katherine Hilliker, H. H. Caldwell; ph, Rene Guissart, Percy Hilburn, Karl Struss, Clyde De Vinna, E. Burton Steene, George Meehan, Paul Eagler; m, William Axt, David Mendoza; ed, Lloyd Nosler; set d, Cedric Gibbons.

Historical Drama **Cas.** **(PR:A MPAA:NR)**

BERTHA, THE SEWING MACHINE GIRL*** (1927) 6 reels FOX bw

Madge Bellamy *(Bertha Sloan)*, Allan Simpson *(Roy Davis)*, Sally Phipps *(Jessie)*, Paul Nicholson *(Jules Morton)*, Anita Garvin *(Flo Mason)*, J. Farrell MacDonald *(Sloan)*, Ethel Wales *(Mrs. Sloan)*, Arthur Housman *(Salesman)*, Harry Bailey *(Sam Ginsberg)*.

Another undistinguished starring role for Bellamy, the sweetly innocent daughter of the dean of literature at the University of Texas, in a Hollywood career that collapsed in the mid-1930s, after only 15 years in the movies. Here she plays a girl who loses her job as a sewing-machine worker and then gets a job with a lingerie firm as a telephone girl. She falls in love with a shipping room clerk, Simpson, and is soon promoted to chief model for the firm, thanks to the company's manager, Nicholson, who hankers after her. Bertha is commissioned to go to Paris as a designer, but she is fast-talked into visiting Nicholson's home, from which he abducts her onto his yacht. After a thrilling motorboat chase by Simpson, she is rescued and it turns out that Simpson is the real owner of the lingerie company and truly desires her for herself alone.

d, Irving Cummings; w, Gertrude Orr (based on a play by Theodore Kremer); ph, Abe Fried.

Drama **(PR:A MPAA:NR)**

BETTER 'OLE, THE*** (1926) 9 reels WB bw

Syd Chaplin *(Old Bill)*, Doris Hill *(Joan)*, Harold Goodwin *(Bert)*, Theodore Lorch *(Gaspard)*, Ed Kennedy *(Cpl. Quint)*, Charles Gerrard *(The Major)*, Tom McGuire *(English General)*, Jack Ackroyd *(Alf)*, Tom Kennedy *(The Blacksmith)*, K. Morgan *(Gen. von Hinden)*, Arthur Clayton *(The Colonel)*.

History has tended to neglect Charles Chaplin's half brother Syd, who had a successful comedy career of his own. This WW I farce was one of his most popular. In it he portrays a carefree British Army sergeant who tries to prove that major Gerrard of his regiment is a German spy. To get across his message he is forced to play a German soldier, attack his own men, and nearly get shot as a spy himself. A trick ending has the firing squad shooting blanks, giving time for contrary evidence to arrive, after which Chaplin is freed.

d, Charles "Chuck" Reisner; w, Darryl F. Zanuck, Reisner (based on the play by Bruce Bairnsfather, Arthur Eliot); t, Robert Hopkins; ph, Ed Du Par, Walter Robinson.

Comedy **(PR:A MPAA:NR)**

BEVERLY OF GRAUSTARK*** (1926) 70m COS/MGM bw-c

Marion Davies *(Beverly Calhoun)*, Antonio Moreno *(Dantan)*, Creighton Hale *(Prince Oscar)*, Roy D'Arcy *(Gen. Marlanax)*, Albert Gran *(Duke Travina)*, Paulette Duval *(Carlotta)*, Max Barwyn *(Saranoff)*, Charles Clary *(Mr. Calhoun)*.

It is said that "The Chief" (W.R. Hearst) delighted in seeing his lovely protege, Marion Davies, dressed in men's clothes, and this movie gave him an eyeful. She plays an American girl who assumes the identity of her injured cousin—heir to the throne of Graustark—who must be in attendance to prevent his kingdom from being taken over by a villainous general. This film, though not her best, was still good entertainment, and the ending scene, shot in color, showed her off to marvelous advantage.

d, Sidney Franklin; w, Agnes Christine Johnston (based on the novel by George Barr McCutcheon); t, Joe Farnham; ph, Percy Hilburn; ed, Frank Hull; art d, Cedric Gibbons, Richard Day.

Drama **(PR:A MPAA:NR)**

BEYOND** (1921) 5 reels PAR bw

Ethel Clayton *(Avis Langley)*, Charles Meredith *(Geoffrey Southerne)*, Earl Schenk *(Alec Langley)*, Fontaine LaRue *(Mrs. Langley)*, Winifred Kingston *(Viva Newmarch)*, Lillian Rich *(Bessie Ackroyd)*, Charles French *(Samuel Ackroyd)*, Spottiswoode Aitken *(Wilfred Southerne)*, Herbert Fortier *(Dr. Newmarch)*.

The old story about a woman shipwrecked on an island for a year, who returns home to find her fiance married to another lady. The only thing different about this version of an old story was the use of after-life spirits to motivate the characters, as the mother of Clayton urges her to watch over her no-good twin son, Schenck, after her death. When she does die, the brother disappears, and the mother appears as a spirit to remind Clayton of her vow. A long search ensues, during which Clayton is forced to leave the man she loves. A report comes that Clayton has died in a shipwreck, and her fiance then marries another woman. Clayton finally reappears, however, without Schenck, and the lucky death of her fiance's new wife frees him for a reunion with Clayton.

d, William Desmond Taylor; w, Julia Crawford Ivers (based on the play "The Lifted Veil" by Henry Arthur Jones).

Drama **(PR:A MPAA:NR)**

BEYOND PRICE** (1921) 6 reels FOX bw

Pearl White *(Mrs. Philip Smith)*, Vernon Steel *(Philip)*, Nora Reed *(Vivaria)*, Louis Haines *(Weathersby)*, Maude Turner Gordon *(Mrs. Florence Weathersby)*, Byron Douglas *(Norbert Temple)*, Ottola Nesmith *(Mrs. Temple)*, Dorothy Walters *(Mrs. Dusenberry)*, Dorothy Allen *(Lizzie)*, J. Thornton Baston *(Mrs. Temple's Friend)*, Charles Sutton *(Cobbler)*.

White, past her prime as the queen of the serials, made a number of inferior program features for Fox—this being one of them. Within four years she would retire from the screen and move to France where she starred in vaudeville. At the time of making this film, her salary was around $100,000 a year; in France, she appeared in a revue for $3,000 a week. BEYOND PRICE was Fox's attempt to give White "real parts" in real pictures, as opposed to serials, and was one of 10 routine feature films Fox gave her to do, most of them made at the new Fox studio at 10th Avenue and 55th Street in New York City. Interestingly, White anticipated by more than 60 years a belly streamlining technique which came into wide use among the joggers in the 1980s, the wearing of a slimming belt around the waist while running. Due to an unfortunate tendency to gain poundage, White often wore rubber bloomers.

d, J. Searle Dawley; w, Paul H. Sloane; ph, Joseph Ruttenberg.

Drama **(PR:A MPAA:NR)**

BEYOND THE ROCKS*** (1922) 7 reels PAR bw

Gloria Swanson *(Theodora Fitzgerald)*, Rudolph Valentino *(Lord Bracondale)*, Edythe Chapman *(Lady Bracondale)*, Alec B. Francis *(Capt. Fitzgerald)*, Robert Bolder *(Josiah Brown)*, Gertrude Astor *(Morella Winmarleigh)*, Mable Van Buren *(Mrs. McBride)*, Helen Dunbar *(Lady Ada Fitzgerald)*, Raymond Blathwayt *(Sir Patrick Fitzgerald)*, F. R. Butler *(Lady Wensleydon)*, June Elvidge *(Lady Anningford)*.

The eternal triangle with a twist: Swanson, who married an older man for money, falls in love with a dashing young lord, played by Valentino. But when the relationship gets out of hand, she decides to break it off before her husband gets hurt. She writes letters to both her husband and lover, but they are intercepted by a woman jealous of the nobleman, who switches them. When the husband receives his, he immediately leaves on an African expedition. Swanson, full of remorse, follows him, accompanied by her mother and an equally penitent Valentino. When the husband's party is attacked by bandits, he is fatally wounded. The second party arrives just in time to receive his forgiveness and understanding, which is registered cinematically by the dying man placing her hand in the hand of the man she truly loves.

d, Sam Wood; w, Jack Cunningham (based on a novel by Elinor Glyn); ph, Alfred Gilks.

Drama **(PR:A MPAA:NR)**

BID FOR FORTUNE, A** (1917, Brit.) 4 reels Unity-Super bw

A. Harding Steerman *(Dr. Nikola)*, Violet Graham *(Phyllis Wetherall)*, Sydney Vautier *(Dick Hattaras)*.

This British mystery deals with the occult and a scientist bent on acquiring a valuable Chinese staff.

d&w, Sidney Morgan (based on the novel by Guy Boothby).

Crime **(PR:A MPAA:NR)**

BIG CITY, THE*** (1928) 7 reels MGM bw

Lon Chaney *(Chuck Collins)*, Marceline Day *(Sunshine)*, James Murray *(Curly)*, Betty Compson *(Helen)*, Mathew Betz *(Red)*, John George *(The Arab)*, Virginia Pearson *(Tennessee)*, Walter Percival *(Grogan)*, Lew Short *(O'Hara)*, Eddie Sturgis *(Blinkie)*.

Crooked cabaret owner Chaney plays it straight (that is, without grotesque makeup) in this film about gang warfare, where a rival gang is fleecing his customers of their jewels. Chaney tricks them into handing the gems over to his own gang. A naive ingenue, Day, manages to persuade Chaney and his gang members to go straight, while the rival gangsters are sentenced to jail. Good performances by Murray, leader of the rival gang, and Compson, Chaney's girl friend, who was on hand when the "Man of a Thousand Faces" first made it big in THE MIRACLE MAN.

d, Tod Browning; w, Waldemar Young (based on a story by Browning); t, Joe Farnham; ph, Henry Sharp; ed, Harry Reynolds; set d, Cedric Gibbons.

Crime **(PR:A MPAA:NR)**

BIG GAME* (1921) 6 reels Metro bw

Mary Miles Minter *(Judith Baldwin)*, Monte Blue *(Tod Musgrove)*, Willard Lewis *(Sen. Baldwin)*, Grace Goodall *(Hallie Baldwin)*, Guy Oliver *(Congressman Hamill)*, William Boyd *(Robert W. Courtney)*, Mabel Van Buren *(Mrs. Langley)*.

Predictable and poorly executed story about a married woman who pretends to make love to a man in order to bring out "the man" in her husband. It all happens in a cabin in the Canadian North Woods, where the husband socks a Canuck guide who thinks he is just irresistible to the ladies, bringing everybody to their feet in applause.

d, Dallas Fitzgerald; w, Edward T. Lowe, Jr. (based on a play by Willard Robertson, Kilbourne Gordon); ph, Jackson Rose; art d, Sidney Ullman.

Drama **(PR:C MPAA:NR)**

BIG PAL½** (1925) 5 reels William Russell/Henry Ginsberg bw

William Russell *(Dan Williams)*, Julanne Johnston *(Helen Truscott)*, Mary Carr *(Mary Williams)*, Mickey Bennett *(Johnny Williams)*, Hayden Stevenson *(Tim Williams)*, William Bailey.

Entertaining film for kids is all but stolen by little freckle-faced Bennett, as the nephew of heavyweight contender Russell. On the night before the championship fight, gamblers kidnap Bennett in an attempt to force Russell to take a dive in the fifth round. Bennett escapes during the fight, however, and rushes to ringside just in time to watch his uncle score a knockout. The new champ also scores a victory with the pretty little social volunteer who had become pals to both.

d, John G. Adolfi; w, Jules Furthman.

Adventure **(PR:A MPAA:NR)**

BIG PARADE, THE***** (1925) 13 reels MGM bw/c

John Gilbert *(James Apperson)*, Renee Adoree *(Melisande)*, Hobart Bosworth *(Mr. Apperson)*, Claire McDowell *(Mrs. Apperson)*, Claire Adams *(Justyn Reed)*, Robert Ober *(Harry)*, Tom O'Brien *(Bull)*, Karl Dane *(Slim)*, Rosita Marstini *(French Mother)*.

Vidor's famous war film began as a little six reeler and grew into an epoch masterpiece which included some Technicolor sequences. Gilbert, as the wealthy small town boy coaxed by his father and girlfriend into "joining up," gave the performance of his life. Scenes such as the one where he teaches the smitten Adoree to chew gum, and the terribly moving moment which has him giving a cigarette to the dying teenaged German soldier, as well as the picture's finale where he returns to France hobbling on a wooden leg (emulating author Stallings, who lost a limb during the conflict) and seeks out the girl he left behind, can grip audiences as much now as they did in 1925. Then there's the spectacle of 200 trucks and an army of troops (shot in San Antonio with the government's complete cooperation) pushing off to the front followed by the title "It had begun—the BIG PARADE." And the incredible march into the devastating face of enemy machine gun fire in the Belleau Wood, which Vidor choreographed with eerie slowness, using a metronome and a battalion of extras, most of whom had seen service in France. THE BIG PARADE was a success on all levels, including the financial, costing $382,000 to produce with an initial profit return of $3,485,000. For Gilbert, THE BIG PARADE was a personal achievement, beginning with the mustache (his stock in trade) which he shaved off for the film. That, together with being togged in drab khaki throughout instead of smartly tailored clothing, proved to him and to his bosses at MGM that he was a fine actor and not just a handsome suit to hang on the wall and be stared at. The picture almost became a routine programmer, and would have had it not been for Irving Thalberg, one of MGM's big shots. After seeing a preview, he was so excited by it that he convinced director Vidor that it could be made into an historic war film, and together they reshot the picture from beginning to end with a new slant. The result has been called the best picture of men at war, next to ALL QUIET ON THE WESTERN FRONT, Hollywood has ever made, in spite of its obvious anti-war propaganda and its treacle love story. Also to be said for it, like THE BIRTH OF A NATION, BEN-HUR, and INTOLERANCE, to name a few, THE BIG PARADE did a great deal in converting the American public to the ranks of film-going at a time when pictures were still almost all new.

d, King Vidor; w, Harry Behn (based on a story by Lawrence Stallings); t, Joseph W. Farnham; ph, John Arnold; m, William Axt, David Mendoza; ed, Hugh Wynn; art d, Cedric Gibbons, James Basevi.

War **(PR:A MPAA:NR)**

BIG PUNCH, THE*** (1921) 5 reels FOX bw

Buck Jones *(Buck)*, Barbara Bedford *(Hope Standish)*, George Siegman *(Flash McGraw)*, Jack Curtis *(Jed, Buck's Brother)*, Jack McDonald, Al Fremont *(Jed's Friends)*, Jennie Lee *(Buck's Mother)*, Edgar Jones *(The Sheriff)*, Irene Hunt *(Dance Hall Girl)*, Eleanore Gilmore *(Salvation Army Girl)*.

Jack Ford (brother of Francis Ford) directed this well-crafted Jones western drama in which a young man about to enter a seminary is implicated in a crime while trying to help his brother, and is sent to prison. After being released, he gives his word to carry on the work of a dying district-circuit-rider, converts his outlaw brother, and marries a Salvation Army girl.

d, Jack Ford; w, Jules G. Furthman; ph, Frank B. Good.

Western/Drama **(PR:A MPAA:NR)**

BIG TOWN IDEAS*** (1921) 5 reels FOX bw

Eileen Percy *(Fan Tilden)*, Kenneth Gibson *(Alan Dix)*, Jimmie Parrott *(Spick Sprague)*, Ion Poff *(Deputy)*, Laura La Plante *(Molly Dorn)*, Leo Sulky *(George Small)*, Harry De Roy *(Bald-Headed Man)*, Lefty James *(Warden)*, Larry Bowes *(Governor)*, Paul Kamp *(Grocer's Boy)*, Paul Cazeneuve *(Show Manager)*, Wilson Hummell *(Chef)*, Jess Aldridge *(Bodyguard to the Governor)*.

Nice combination of comedy and melodrama has small town hash slinger Percy breaking a young fellow out of prison, tracking down the real crooks, and clearing his name. Film's highlights are Percy's intelligent performance and some very funny titles, especially in the chorus of the prison show which the waitress joins in order to help the young man escape.

d, Carl Harbaugh; w, John Montague; ph, Otto Brautigan.

Comedy/Mystery **(PR:A MPAA:NR)**

BIG TREMAINE*** (1916) 5 reels Yorke/Metro bw

Harold Lockwood *(John Tremaine, Sr.)*, May Allison *(Isobel Malvern)*, Lester Cuneo *(Redmond Malvern)*, Albert Ellis *(Judge Tremaine)*, Lillian Hayward *(Mrs. Tremaine)*, William Ehfe *(David Tremaine)*, Andrew Arbuckle *(Samuel Leavitt)*, Josephine Rice *(Mammy)*, Virginia Southern *(Julia Cameron)*, William De Vaull *(John Nolan)*.

Director-screenwriter Otto did very well with this little programmer about a young man who is wrongly sent to prison for seven years because of a crime his brother committed. He returns home a social outcast, but on his brother's death a confession surfaces and his good name is restored.

d&w, Henry Otto (based on the novel *David Tremaine* by Marie Van Vorst); ph, Tony Gaudio.

Drama **(PR:A MPAA:NR)**

BIGAMIST, THE* (1921, Brit.) 10 reels George Clark/STOLL bw

Guy Newall *(George Dane)*, Ivy Duke *(Pamela Arnott)*, Julian Royce *(Herbert Arnott)*, A. Bromley Davenport *(Richard Carruthers)*, Barbara Everest *(Blanche Maitland)*, Dorothy Scott *(Mrs. Carruthers)*, Douglas Munro *(Proprietor)*.

The Stoll motion picture company of Britain released a film 10,000 feet in length to tell the story of a wife who discovers that her husband is a bigamist, but stays with him for the sake of the kids.

d&w, Guy Newall (based on the novel by F. E. Mills Young).

Drama **(PR:A MPAA:NR)**

BILLY JIM* (1922) 5 reels Fred Stone/R-C bw

Fred Stone *(Billy Jim)*, Millicent Fisher *(Marsha Dunforth)*, George Hernandez *(Dudley Dunforth)*, William Bletcher *(Jimmy)*, Marian Skinner *(Mrs. Dunforth)*, Frank Thorne *(Roy Forsythe)*.

Stage star Stone—the Scarecrow in the original Broadway presentation of "The Wizard of Oz"—was less than impressive in his movie debut, playing a cowboy on a toot, who is actually a wealthy young man who saves a beautiful girl and then her father's mining camp from claim jumpers. At the time of this film's release, Variety observed that the musical comedy star was probably only suited for character roles and he did, in fact, go on to become the ideal father type in such pictures as Katherine Hepburn's ALICE ADAMS.

p, Andrew J. Callahan; d, Frank Borzage; w, Frank Howard Clark (based on a story by Jackson Gregory).

Comedy/Western **(PR:A MPAA:PR)**

BIRTH OF A NATION, THE***** (1915) 12 reels Epoch bw

Lillian Gish *(Elsie Stoneman)*, Mae Marsh *(Flora Cameron, the Little Sister)*, Henry B. Walthall *(Ben Cameron, the Little Colonel)*, Miriam Cooper *(Margaret Cameron)*, Mary Alden *(Lydia Brown, Stoneman's Mulatto Housekeeper)*, Ralph Lewis *(The Honorable Austin Stoneman, Leader of the House)*, George Siegmann *(Silas Lynch)*, Walter Long *(Gus, a Renegade Negro)*, Robert Harron *(Ted Stoneman)*, Wallace Reid *(Jeff, the Blacksmith)*, Joseph Henabery *(Abraham Lincoln)*, Elmer Clifton *(Phil Stoneman)*, Josephine Crowell *(Mrs. Cameron)*, Spottiswoode Aitken *(Dr. Cameron)*, George Andre Beranger *(Wade Cameron)*, Maxfield Stanley *(Duke Cameron)*, Jennie Lee *(Cindy, The Faithful Mammy)*, Donald Crisp *(Gen. Ulysses S. Grant)*, Howard Gaye *(Gen. Robert E. Lee)*, Sam De Grasse *(Sen. Charles Sumner)*, Raoul Walsh *(John Wilkes Booth)*, Eugene Pallette *(Wounded Enemy to Whom Ben Gives Succor)*, Elmo Lincoln *(White Arm Joe)*, Olga Grey *(Laura Keene)*, William De Vaull *(Jake)*, Tom Wilson *(Stoneman's Negro Servant)*, Erich von Stroheim *(Man Who Falls Off Roof)*, Bessie Love *(Piedmont Girl)*, Violet Wilkey *(Flora as a Child)*, Alberta Lee *(Mrs. Lincoln)*, William Freeman *(Sentry)*, Charles Stevens *(Volunteer)*, Monte Blue, Sul Te Wan.

It has been said that President Woodrow Wilson, on viewing THE BIRTH OF A NATION at a White House screening exclaimed, "It's like writing history with lightning." Actually, it is more than that. Originally released as THE CLANSMAN (the title was changed several months later), THE BIRTH OF A NATION is, in fact, the most important motion picture ever made! With this single work of art, D. W. Griffith gave the cinema credibility, and for the first time the arcade novelty was accorded the same respect as opera, ballet, and theater. It was a motion picture which, because of its creator's historical perspective of "The Klan," sparked riots in the streets and litigation in the courts. But, above all, it was an almost flawless work of art, one in which *every* cinematic convention was put to such skillful use that millions of people were moved and manipulated as they had never been before. By tracing the fortunes of two families (one Northern and one Southern) who knew each other before the hostilities, Griffith brings to life the saga of America's most tragic period. Almost every important historical event (from the early battles to the emergence of the "Invisible Empire") is recreated with such realism that one is given the impression Matthew Brady's photographs have come to life. But the *story* also stirs the blood and touches the heart, and scenes, such as the Little Colonel's return to his beloved Piedmont, the moonstruck Yankee sentry's adoring glance at Lillian Gish when she visits the military hospital, the suicide leap of Marsh to avoid being raped by Long, the black renegade, the body-strewn battle field followed by the title, "War's Peace," and, of course, the justly celebrated ride of the Klan, which brings this mighty motion picture to a thundering conclusion, are as impressive now as they were in 1915. Griffith was quite familiar with Negrophobe preacher Dixon's play, "The Clansman," which formed the basis for the picture; the director's own wife, Linda Arvidson Griffith, had starred in a cinema adaptation made by the Kinemacolor Company in 1909 (the underexposed footage didn't print properly, so the picture was shelved). Griffith's cowriter Woods had written the earlier screen adaptation, and he was the one who suggested the project to Griffith. Brought in on a budget of about $100,000, this remarkable picture set a box-office record unsurpassed for silent films. By 1931, it had returned more than $18 million for Epoch, a company created especially for the production by Griffith and Harry E. Aitken, whose Triangle Film Corporation had recently lured the director away from American Biograph. Whole books have been devoted to THE BIRTH OF A NATION, and many more will surely follow. And that's as it should be, because in a very real sense, this is the picture which started it all.

p&d, D. W. Griffith; w, Griffith, Frank E. Woods (based on the novel and play *The Clansman* and the novel *The Leopard's Spots* by Thomas Dixon, Jr.); ph, G. W. Bitzer; m, Joseph Carl Breil, Griffith; ed, James Smith; cos, Robert Goldstein.

Historical/Drama **Cas.** **(PR:C MPAA:NR)**

BLACK BEAUTY*** (1921) 7 reels VIT bw

Jean Paige *(Jessie Gordon)*, James Morrison *(Harry Blomefield)*, George Webb *(Jack Beckett)*, Bobby Mack *(Derby Ghost)*, John Steppling *(Squire Gordon)*, Adele Farrington *(Lady Wynwaring)*, Charles Morrison *(John Manly)*, Mollie McConnell *(Mrs. Gordon)*, Capt. Leslie T. Peacock *(Lord Wynwaring)*, Colin Kenny *(George Gordon)*, Georgia French *(Flora Gordon)*, Robert Bolder *(Vicar Blomefield)*, Margaret Mann *(Mrs. Blomefield)*, George Pierce *(Farmer Grey)*, James Donnelly *(Fat Bailiff)*, Robert Milasch *(Lean Bailiff)*, Black Beauty the Horse.

This better than average Vitagraph feature combines a love story with the traditional narrative of the beautiful horse which was traded around until it won the big race. The clever convention of raising and lowering a curtain to separate the two is highly effective as are the action scenes showing the horse being raised from colt to thoroughbred and the race itself. This was the last appearance of the veteran actress McConnell.

d, David Smith; w, William B. Courtney, Lillian Chester (based on the novel by Anna Sewell); ph, Reginald Lyons.

Drama **(PR:AAA MPAA:NR)**

BLACK BIRD, THE**** (1926) 7 reels MGM bw

Lon Chaney *(The Blackbird/The Bishop of Limehouse)*, Renee Adoree *(Fifi)*, Owen Moore *(West End Bertie)*, Doris Lloyd *(Limehouse Polly)*, Andy MacLennan *(The Shadow)*, William Weston *(Red)*, Eric Mayne *(A Sightseer)*, Sidney Bracy *(Bertie's No. 1 Man)*, Ernie S. Adams *(Bertrie's No. 2 Man)*, Lionel Belmore, Billy Mack, Peggy Best.

Chaney portrays a London criminal who hides behind the disguise of a cripple, greatly respected and loved in Limehouse. This was one of Chaney's most popular performances and, perhaps, Moore's best. Another success also for director Browning, who was at the helm of many of Chaney's best films in the 1920s.

d, Tod Browning; w, Waldemar Young (based on "The Mockingbird" by Tod Browning); ph, Percy Hilburn; ed, Errol Taggart; set d, Cedric Gibbons, Arnold Gillespie.

Crime **(PR:A MPAA:NR)**

BLACK CYCLONE*** (1925) 5 reels HR/Pathe bw

Rex *(King of the Wild Horses)*, Lady *(Horse)*, The Killer *(Horse)*, Guinn Williams *(Jim Lawson)*, Kathleen Collins *(Jane Logan)*, Christian Frank *(Joe Pangle)*.

Innovative Hal Roach feature, full of suspense, action, laughs, pathos, in which horses play the major parts, supported by humans. Rex is fascinating as the wild stallion who falls in love with Lady, and they both go through myriad exciting adventures before becoming tamed and devoted to cowboy Williams and his girl, Collins. The two humans and the two horses are all rubbing noses in the end.

d, Fred Jackman; w, Hal Roach; t, H. M. Walker; ph, Floyd Jackman, George Stevens.

Western **(PR:AAA MPAA:NR)**

BLACK PIRATE, THE**** (1926) 9 reels Elton/UA c

Douglas Fairbanks *(The Black Pirate)*, Billie Dove *(The Princess)*, Anders Randolf *(Pirate Leader)*, Donald Crisp *(McTavish)*, Tempe Pigott *(Duenna)*, Sam De Grasse *(Pirate)*, Charles Stevens *(Powder Man)*, Charles Belcher *(Chief Passenger)*, Fred Becker, John Wallace, E. J. Ratcliffe.

This definitive pirate movie has Fairbanks at his best—sword fighting, walking the plank, capturing a ship single-handedly, avenging the murder of his father, rescuing the maiden from a fate worse than death, and fulfilling the calling of his noble birth. Outstanding bit of action in the film is a unique filmic event—the dueling scene with pirate Randolf—quite possibly the best swordplay ever captured on the screen, with Fairbanks at the top of his agile and graceful form. Charles Stevens, a grandson of the Indian warrior Geronimo and a friend of Fairbanks, had the distinction of being resurrected several times after he had been killed in the picture, each time bouncing up to assume the identity of another extra, yet he was credited with only one role, that of "Powder Man." THE BLACK PIRATE also is noted for using the Technicolor process, which had been marketed for the first time in 1917. Still in its infancy as a process, it gave THE BLACK PIRATE a sickly quality of pinks and oranges to human flesh, but a sort of glaring grandeur to the costumes and sets. As in all Fairbanks' films, the pirate world of the film was thoroughly researched and wonderfully mounted, and is a great exhibition of the star's boundless enthusiasm, energy, and his prodigious fascination with the role he portrayed.

d, Albert Parker; w, Lotta Woods, Jack Cunningham (based on a story by Elton Thomas, Fairbanks); ph, Henry Sharp; m, Mortimer Wilson; ed, William Nolan; art d, Carl Oscar Borg.

Costume/Adventure **Cas.** **(PR:A MPAA:NR)**

BLAZING BARRIERS (SEE: JACQUELINE, OR BLAZING BARRIERS, 1923)

BLAZING DAYS* (1927) 5 reels BS bw

Fred Humes *(Smilin' Sam Perry)*, Ena Gregory *(Milly Morgan)*, Churchill Ross *(Jim Morgan)*, Bruce Gordon *("Dude" Dutton)*, Eva Thatcher *(Ma Bascomb)*, Bernard Siegel *(Ezra Skinner)*, Dick L'Estrange *("Turtle-Neck" Pete)*.

Wyler, who would go on to direct such classics as DEAD END, JEZEBEL, and THE BEST YEARS OF OUR LIVES, got his start and learned his craft directing super low-budget cowboy programmers like this one. It is a routine story about a cowboy (Humes) who tracks down the villain about to do dirt to Humes' girl friend, Gregory. In the end, Humes captures the villain as he is escaping with the loot, and his girl friend accepts his proposal of marriage.

d, William Wyler; w, George H. Plympton, Robert F. Hill (based on a story by Florence Ryerson); ph, Al Jones; art d, David S. Garber.

Western **(PR:A MPAA:NR)**

BLAZING TRAIL, THE* (1921) 5 reels UNIV bw

Frank Mayo *(Bradley Yates/Pickins)*, Frank Holland *(Dr. Pickney Forbes)*, Verne Winter *("Chipmunk" Grannis)*, Bert Sprotte *(Hank Millicuddy)*, Madge Hunt *(Ma Millicuddy)*, Mary Philbin *(Talithy Millicuddy)*, Lillian Rich *(Carroll Brown)*, Ray Ripley *(Lewis Van Dusen)*, Joy Winthrop *(Hulda Mews)*, Helen Gilmore *(The Village Talking Machine)*.

Second rate programmer has Mayo as a young doctor suffering from a blood condition which is poisoning him. He goes to the Blue Ridge Mountains to relax, takes a job as lumberjack, and falls in love with a beautiful teacher who was sent by the state to enforce minimum educational standards. Mayo is accused of seducing the local tart, but his medical partner arrives with a corrective serum and everything is straightened out in the end.

d, Robert Thornby; w, Lucien Hubbard (based on a story by Mann Page, Izola Forrester); ph, William Fildew.

Drama **(PR:A MPAA:NR)**

BLIND ALLEYS** (1927) 6 reels FP/LAS bw

Thomas Meighan *(Capt. Dan Kirby)*, Evelyn Brent *(Sally Ray)*, Gretta Nissen *(Maria D'Alvarez Kirby)*, Hugh Miller *(Julio Lachados)*, Tom Chalmers *(Dr. Webster)*, Tammany Young *(Gang Leader)*.

Unintentionally funny story about a sea captain who, because of an auto accident, is separated from his South American bride on their first night in New York. Most of the film deals with his looking for, and just missing, her, with the inevitable happy ending.

d, Frank Tuttle; w, Emmet Crozier (based on a story by Owen Davis); ph, Alvin Wyckoff.

Drama **(PR:A MPAA:NR)**

BLIND BARGAIN, A*** (1922) 5 reels Goldwyn bw-c

Lon Chaney *(Dr. Arthur Lamb/The Ape Man)*, Jacqueline Logan *(Angela Marshall)*, Raymond McKee *(Robert Sandell)*, Virginia True Boardman *(Mrs. Sandell)*, Fontaine La Rue *(Mrs. Lamb)*, Aggie Herring *(Bessie)*, Virginia Madison *(Angela's Mother)*.

Contrary to popular opinion, Chaney made few *true* horror films, and this was one. In A BLIND BARGAIN, he plays two roles; a demented doctor and the "Ape Man," who was the result of an earlier experiment. It is always fascinating to study this great actor's art, and in this film one can unmistakably recognize the army of monsters who would stomp across the screens of movie theaters in the 1930s and 1940s.

d, Wallace Worsley; w, J. G. Hawks (based on "The Octave of Claudius" by Barry Pain); ph, Norbert Brodin.

Horror **(PR:C MPAA:NR)**

BLIND BOY, THE** (1917, Brit.) 4 reels BP/Ruffells bw

G. H. Chirgwin *(Hubert)*, Ivy Montford *(Inez)*, Evelyn Sydney *(Mary)*, Frank Dane *(Claude)*, Jack Clare *(Harry)*.

This British drama, about a violinist who adopts a blind youth, takes on a sinister note when he begins to dream that his cousin intends to murder him for his inheritance.

p, Edward Godal; d, Edwin J. Collins, Jack Clare; w, (based on a play by George H. Chirgwin).

Drama **(PR:A MPAA:NR)**

BLIND GODDESS, THE*** (1926) 8 reels FP/PAR bw

Jack Holt *(Hugh Dillon)*, Ernest Torrence *(Big Bill Devens)*, Esther Ralston *(Moira Devens)*, Louise Dresser *(Her Mother)*, Ward Crane *(Tracy Redmond)*, Richard Tucker *(Henry Kelling)*, Louis Payne *(Taylor)*, Charles Clary *(District Attorney)*, Erwin Connelly *(Chief of Detectives)*, Charles Lane *(Judge)*.

Fleming skillfully directs a fine cast in this gripping melodrama, which sees Dresser walking out on her struggling politician husband and daughter, only to return some 20 years later (when he's a powerful leader of the party) to beg forgiveness. He refuses and is subsequently killed by his partner, who had attempted to involve him in a dishonest deal and feared exposure. Dresser is accused of the murder, and when her daughter's fiance, the district attorney, learns that she's his sweetheart's mother, he resigns his office and successfully defends her in court. A dictaphone recording left by the victim points the finger of guilt to the correct party, and the mother and daughter are tearfully reunited.

d, Victor Fleming; w, Gertrude Orr, Hope Loring, Louis Duryea Lighton (based on the novel by Arthur Chesney Train); ph, Alfred Gilks.

Drama **(PR:A MPAA:NR)**

BLIND HEARTS**** (1921) 6 reels AP bw

Hobart Bosworth *(Lars Larson)*, Wade Boteler *(John Thomas)*, Irene Blackwell *(Mrs. Thomas)*, Collette Forbes *(Hilda Larson)*, Madge Bellamy *(Julia Larson)*, Raymond McKee *(Paul Thomas)*, William Conklin *(James Curdy)*, Lule Warrenton *(Rita)*, Henry Hebert *(James Bradley)*.

Absorbing film about mistaken identity which causes two business partners and friends to feud for 20 years. Their son and daughter (who were deliberately switched by a nurse as infants to satisfy the desire each set of parents had for a boy and girl) fall in love but are not allowed to see each other until a tragedy at the end of the film brings the men to their senses and permits them to honor an oath they made two decades earlier to dance at their children's weddings.

p, Hobart Bosworth; d, Rowland V. Lee; w, Joseph Franklin Poland (based on a story "Blind Hearts" by Emille Johnson); ph, J. O. Taylor.

Drama **(PR:A MPAA:NR)**

BLIND HUSBANDS**** (1919) 8 reels Jewel/UNIV bw

Erich von Stroheim, Gibson Gowland, Sam De Grasse, Francelia Billington, Faye Holderness, Jack Perrin, Grace McClean, Valery Germonprez, Ruby Kendrick, Richard Cummings, Louis Fitzroy, William De Vaull, Percy Challenger, Jack Mathis.

Von Stroheim's Teutonic bearing no doubt had much to do with convincing Carl Laemmle, head of Universal Studios, to allow him to direct his first feature film. The Austrian had learned well as an assistant to D. W. Griffith, but what he brought to the screen was the antithesis of his teacher's art. For the first time, sophisticated and cynical sex became a part of the U.S. cinema. BLIND HUSBANDS (a picture he also wrote and acted in) dealt with husbandly neglect, wifely frustration, and blatantly opportunistic seduction during a mountain climbing excursion. The film not only marked the beginning of a brilliant and controversial directorial career, but also the birth of "The Man You Love to Hate."

d, Erich von Stroheim; w, von Stroheim (based on his story "The Pinnacle"); ph, Ben F. Reynolds; art d, von Stroheim.

Drama **Cas.** **(PR:A MPAA:NR)**

BLOOD AND SAND*** (1922) 8 reels FP/PAR bw

Rudolph Valentino *(Juan Gallardo)*, Lila Lee *(Carmen)*, Nita Naldi *(Dona Sol)*, George Field *(El Nacional)*, Walter Long *(Plumitas)*, Rosa Rosanova *(Senora Augustias)*, Leo White *(Antonio)*, Charles Belcher *(Don Joselito)*, Jack Winn *(Potaje)*, Marie Marstini *(El Carnacione)*, Gilbert Clayton *(Garabato)*, Harry La Mont *(El Pontelliro)*, George Periolat *(Marquise de Guevera)*, Sidney De Grey *(Dr. Ruiz)*, Fred Becker *(Don Jose)*, Dorcas Matthews *(Senora Nacional)*, William Lawrence *(Fuentes)*.

Youthful matador Valentino becomes an idol of bull-ring *aficionados* with his skill and valor. As his career courses upward, he weds lovely Lee, who has long adored him. Flushed with victory after a bloody bullfight, he meets the passionate Naldi and is taken with her charms. Ever faithful, wife Lee handles the affair with forbearance. One afternoon, Valentino's concentration is broken by the sight of Naldi in the company of another man, and he is badly gored. As a new young hero accepts the plaudits of the bull-ring crowd, he dies in his faithful wife's arms. Valentino was celebrating his victory in a court battle involving his ex-wife, actress Jean Acker (although the marriage was apparently unconsummated, their separation was hotly contested) with a champagne party for a few friends when he got the news from Jesse Lasky that he had been chosen to play the role of Juan Gallardo, a part he had wanted very much. He steeped himself in the lore of the bull ring and did his best to catch the spirit of the role, succeeding quite well. Unfortunately, the studio seemed uncooperative. Valentino had assumed that location shooting would be done in Spain, where he thought he could readily learn all the tricks of the trade. Paramount's executives decided otherwise; the picture was shot in the studio. Originally, a costly matte process was to have been used to artifically transport the actor into the Madrid arena, but editor Arzner's experimental intercutting of stock shots was so effective that the studio chiefs decided to save money and use it (Arzner was to become the best-known woman director of all time). Angered by what he considered to be shabby treatment by the studio—especially following the enormous success of his previous picture, THE SHEIK (1921)—Valentino refused to attend the premiere. BLOOD AND SAND was well received by critics and public alike. The film made Lee a star, and gave a great boost to the career of screen vamp Naldi in a role that had originally been assigned to Bebe Daniels.

d, Fred Niblo; w, June Matthis (based on the novel *Sangre y Arena* by Vicente Blasco-Ibanez and the play by Tom Cushing); ph, Alvin Wyckoff; ed, Dorothy Arzner.

Drama **Cas.** **(PR:C MPAA:NR)**

BLOT, THE**** (1921) 7 reels Lois Weber bw

Philip Hubbard *(Prof. Griggs)*, Margaret McWade *(His Wife)*, Claire Windsor *(His Daughter)*, Louis Calhern *(His Pupil)*, Marie Walcamp *(The Other Girl)*.

Lovely Weber film that contrasts the economic conditions between the families of a poor university professor and a wealthy shoe manufacturer. Like most of the highest salaried women director's work, her message is conveyed without preaching, and the movie is filled with numerous beautiful and touching visual moments.

d&w, Lois Weber, Phillips Smalley; ph, Philip Du Bois, Gordon Jennings.

Drama **(PR:A MPAA:NR)**

BLUE BLOOD* 1/2 (1925) 6 reels CHAD bw

George Walsh *(Robert Chester, a Young Scientist)*, Cecille Evans *(Geraldine Hicks, Daughter of the Chewing Gum King)*, Philo McCullough *(Percy Horton, a Social Parasite)*, Joan Meredith *(Delight Burns, Society Debutante)*, Robert Bolder *(Leander Hicks, a Chewing Gum King)*, Harvey Clark *(Tom Riley, Hotel Detective)*, C. Howe Black *(Amos Jenkins, Scientist's Colored Servant)*, Eugene Borden *(Charlie Stevens, Horton's Chauffeur)*.

Action star Walsh plays a scientist who uses his talent with his fists to prevent Evans (better known as "the girl with the $100,000 legs"), the daughter of the chewing gum king, from marrying a rum runner, who has passed himself off as the malted milk king. Walsh, a likable performer, just can't overcome the terrible direction, script, and production values provided in this one.

d, Scott Dunlap; w, Frank Clark.

Adventure/Crime **(PR:A MPAA:NR)**

BLUE STREAK, THE*** (1926) 5 reels Richard Talmadge/FBO bw

Richard Talmadge *(Richard Manley)*, Louise Lorraine *(Inez Del Rio)*, Charles Clary *(John Manley)*, Henry Herbert *(Jack Slade)*, Charles Hill Mailes *(Don Carlos)*, Victor Dillingham *(Slade's Assistant)*, Tote Du Crow *(Pedro)*.

Action abounds in this Talmadge production, which has the great stunt star traveling to Mexico to check on his father's business interests. There, he falls in love with a local beauty and captures the crooks who have been stealing ore. Turns out the biggest crook is Herbert, the superintendent of the mine.

d, Noel Mason; w, James Bell Smith; ph, Jack Stevens, Frank Evans; ed, Doane Harrison.

Adventure **(PR:A MPAA:NR)**

BLUEBEARD'S SEVEN WIVES**** (1926) 8 reels FN bw

Ben Lyon *(John Hart/Don Juan Hartez)*, Lois Wilson *(Mary Kelly)*, Blanche Sweet *(Juliet)*, Dorothy Sebastian *(Gilda LaBray)*, Diana Kane *(Kathra Grannie)*, Sam Hardy *(Gindelheim)*, Dick Bernard *(Lem Lee)*, Andrew Mack *(P. Owers)*, Wilfred Lytell *(Paris)*, B. C. Duval *(Dan Pennell)*, Katherine Ray, Ruby Blaine, Lucy Fox, Muriel Spring, Kathleen Martyn, Diana Kane *(Bluebeard's Wives)*.

Hysterical satire about the movie business has a bank teller (Lyon) so much in love with a pancake cook that he loses count of his money and his job. In desperation, he finds work as a movie extra and, when the star is injured, the similarly statured Lyon is put in the lead to conclude the remaining shots. At this point he is discovered, and the studio machinery goes to work. First, his name is changed, then the publicity department decides he needs to be glamorized so they plant him on an incoming ship from Spain and arrange to have the press greet "the silver screen's newest lover." Afterwards, they arrange for seven marriages and divorces to transpire to create an exotic air. All of this, of course, does little to enhance him in the eyes of his little cook but, in the end, he carries her away to the country where they live happily forever after. During the course of this very funny film, everything from Latin lovers, Nita Naldi-like vamps, and studio yes men are deliciously lampooned.

d, Alfred A. Santell; w, Blanche Merrill, Paul Scofield; ph, Robert Haller; art d, Robert M. Hass.

Comedy **(PR:A MPAA:NR)**

BLUFF** (1924) 6 reels FP/PAR bw

Agnes Ayres *(Betty Hallowell)*, Antonio Moreno *(Robert Fitzmaurice)*, Fred Butler *("Boss" Mitchel)*, Clarence Burton *(Waldo Blakely)*, Pauline Paquette *(Fifine)*, Jack Gardner *(Dr. Steve Curtiss)*, Arthur Hoyt *(Algy Henderson)*, E. H. Calvert *(Norton Conroy)*, Roscoe Karns *(Jack Hallowell)*.

When her brother needs medical attention, Ayres passes herself off as the famous fashion designer, Nina Loring. Her creations cause a sensation but she is arrested, in the guise of Loring, for embezzlement. Crack lawyer Moreno gets her off, however, and then asks her to become his partner in life.

d, Sam Wood; w, Willis Goldbeck (based on a story by Rita Weiman, Josephine Quirk); ph, Alfred Gilks.

Drama **(PR:A MPAA:NR)**

BLUSHING BRIDE, THE*** (1921) 5 reels FOX bw

Eileen Percy *(Beth Rupert)*, Herbert Heyes *(Kingdom Ames)*, Philo McCullough *(Dick Irving)*, Jack La Reno *(K. Ames)*, Rose Dione *(Mrs. K. Ames)*, Harry Dunkinson *(Butler)*, Bertram Johns *(Duke of Downcastle)*, Herschel Mayall *(Lord Landsmere)*, Sylvia Ashton *(Mrs. James Horton-Kemp)*, Earl Crain *(Mr. Scanlon)*, Madge Orlamond *(Mrs. Scanlon)*, Robert Klein *(Footman)*.

Snappy little comedy has showgirl Percy marrying a millionaire who believes her to be the niece of duke Johns. The laughs come fast when she moves into her husband's house and discovers her long lost uncle is employed there as a butler. In the end, as it always happened in those frothy entertainments, everything works out.

d&w, Jules G. Furthman; ph, Otto Brautigan.

Comedy **(PR:A MPAA:NR)**

BOB HAMPTON OF PLACER** (1921) 8 reels Marshall Neilan/AFN bw

James Kirkwood *(Bob Hampton)*, Wesley Barry *(Dick)*, Marjorie Daw *(The Kid)*, Pat O'Malley *(Lt. Brant)*, Noah Beery *(Red Slavin)*, Frank Leigh *(Silent Murphy)*, Dwight Crittenden *(Gen. Custer)*, Tom Gallery *(Rev. Wyncoop)*, Priscilla Bonner *(Schoolteacher)*, Charles West *(Maj. Brant)*, Bert Sprotte *(Sheriff)*, Carrie Clark Ward *(Housekeeper)*, Vic Potel *(Willie McNeil)*, Buddy Post *(Jack Moffet)*.

This lavishly filmed, though lesser Neilan effort, has Kirkwood, an officer wrongly accused of murder, becoming a notorious gambler and gunfighter when he gets out of prison. Kirkwood joins a wagon train and saves from Indians a girl whom he later discovers is his daughter. The film ends with his name being cleared after he and his young pal Barry die in the company of Custer (Crittenden), at the Little Big Horn.

p&d, Marshall Neilan; w, Marion Fairfax (based on the novel by Randall Parrish); ph, Jacques Bizeul, David Kesson; art d, Ben Carré.

Drama/Western **(PR:A MPAA:NR)**

BOLIBAR*** (1928, Brit.) 7 reels BI/PP bw

Elissa Landi *(Francoise-Marie/La Monita)*, Michael Hogan *(Lt. Donop)*, Hubert Carter *(Col. Bellay)*, Carl Harbord *(Lt. Gunther)*, Jerrold Robertshaw *(The Marquis)*, Cecil Barry *(Capt. Egolstein)*, Evelyn Roberts *(Capt. Brockendorf)*, Gerald Pring *(Capt. O'Callaghan)*, Charles Emerald *(Colonel)*, Hector Abbas *(Artist)*.

British-produced war picture set in Spain of 1808. In this story, the attacking British forces emerge triumphant after the daughter of an artist accidentally provides them with the signal they need.

p, H. Bruce Woolfe; d&w, Walter Summers (based on the novel *The Marquise of Bolibar* by Leo Perutz).

War **(PR:A MPAA:NR)**

BORDER WOMEN** (1924) 4 reels Phil Goldstone bw

William Fairbanks *(Big Boy Merritt)*, Dorothy Reviere *(May Prentiss)*, Jack Richardson *(Gentleman Jack)*, Chet Ryan *(Cocas Kid)*, William Franey *(McGilligan)*.

In this action-packed programmer, Fairbanks (a favorite of the kids and no relation to Douglas) plays a Texas Ranger who, at the request of a dying outlaw, not only saves his sister, but marries her as well.

d, Alvin G. Nietz; w, Keene Thompson.

Western **(PR:A MPAA:NR)**

BORROWED FINERY*** (1925) 7 reels TIF bw

Louise Lorraine *(Sheila Conroy)*, Ward Crane *(Channing Maynard)*, Lou Tellegen *(Harlan)*, Taylor Holmes *(Billy)*, Hedda Hopper *(Mrs. Borden)*, Gertrude Astor *(Maisie)*, Trixie Friganza *(Mrs. Brown)*, Barbara Tennant *(Lilly)*, Otto Lederer.

Good little mystery has clothes model Lorraine taking a job with a society crook (posing as a government agent), who is after a priceless gem belonging to a woman Lorraine knows. There are a number of complications, as well as some good laughs before Crane, a real undercover cop, exposes the crook and confesses his love for Lorraine.

d, Oscar Apfel; w, George Bronson Howard.

Crime **(PR:A MPAA:NR)**

BOWERY CINDERELLA* (1927) 7 reels EXCEL/COM

Pat O'Malley *(Larry Dugan)*, Gladys Hulette *(Nora Denahy)*, Kate Bruce *(Bridget Denahy)*, Ernest Hilliard *(Ned Chandler)*, Rosemary Theby *(Mrs. Chandler)*, Pat Hartigan *(Pat Denahy)*, Pauline Carr *(Maisie Brent)*, Howard Mitchell, Leo White, John Webb Dillon, Music Box Revue Chorus.

If there was ever an example of an actress *not* getting the breaks, then the dubious honor must go to Hulette. She went from playing opposite Richard Barthelmess in TOL'ABLE DAVID (where she gave a wonderful performance) down to playing the second lead in this Poverty Row bomb, in which she is a Bowery girl who turns down riches for her real beau, a playwright, whose next work is a howling success.

d, Burton King; w, Adrian Johnson, Melvin Houston; t, Harry Chandlee; ph, Art Reeves.

Drama **(PR:A MPAA:NR)**

BOY OF MINE*** (1923) 5 reels AFN bw

Ben Alexander *(Bill Latimer)*, Rockliffe Fellows *(Dr. Robert Mason)*, Henry B. Walthall *(William Latimer)*, Irene Rich *(Ruth Laurence)*, Dot Farley *(Mrs. Pettis)*, Lawrence Licaizi *(Junior Pettis)*.

All around solid production, with just the right amount of pathos, features child actor Alexander, who would go on to play Jack Webb's partner on the "Dragnet" television series decades later. Here, he leads the way in turning his rich and uncompromisingly strict banker father into a kind and loving man after Alexander and his mother temporarily leave home.

d, William Beaudine; w, Hope Loring, Louis D. Lighton, Lex Neal (based on a story by Booth Tarkington); t, Lighton; ph, Ray June, George Richter, Richard Fryer; ed, Robert De Lacy.

Drama (PR:A MPAA:NR)

BOY RIDER, THE*** (1927) 5 reels FBO bw

Buzz Barton *(David Hepner)*, Lorraine Eason *(Sally Parker)*, Sam Nelson *(Terry McNeil)*, David Dunbar *(Bill Hargus)*, Frank Rice *(Hank Robbins)*, William Ryno *(Jim Parker)*.

Barton is a homeless kid who wanders through the West. He gets mixed up with cattle rustlers, teams up with an old-timer, and saves a girl, only to wander off in the end to his next adventure.

d, Louis King; w, Frank Howard Clark; ph, E. T. McManigal.

Western (PR:A MPAA:NR)

BRAND OF COWARDICE, THE** (1916) 5 reels ROL/Metro bw

Lionel Barrymore *(Cyril Mamilton)*, Grace Valentine *(Marcia West)*, Robert Cummings *(Col. Gordon West)*, Kate Blancke *(Mrs. West)*, John Davidson *(Navarette, a Mexican Bandit)*, Frank Montgomery *(A Mexican Indian)*, Louis Wolheim *(Cpl. Mallin)*, Tula Belle *(Rana, Idqui's Daughter)*, Marcia West.

Pedestrian programmer about a pantywaist who becomes a man and wins the girl he loves—the daughter of a U.S. colonel—by rescuing her from the clutches of Mexican bandits. Stage veteran Cummings is not to be confused with film star "Robert" Cummings of a much later date.

d, John W. Noble; w, Charles Maigne.

Adventure (PR:A MPAA:NR)

BRANDED A BANDIT** (1924) 5 reels Arrow bw

Yakima Canutt *(Jess Dean)*, Judge Hamilton *(Grandaddy Jim)*, Wilbur McGaugh *("Horse" Williamson)*, Alys Murrell *(Jeanne)*.

In reviewing this film *Variety* wrote, "Despite the first name, Yakima Canutt isn't a Jap star. He's the world's champ cowboy for achievements as a stunt man and for developing devices to protect stunt men everywhere." He was also perhaps the greatest action director in the history of the movies, as well as the recipient of a special Oscar in 1966 acknowledging his achievements as a stunt man, and made a number of routine program westerns of which this was one.

p, Ben Wilson; d, Paul Hurst.

Western (PR:A MPAA:NR)

BRANDED WOMAN, THE*** (1920) 5 reels FN bw

Norma Talmadge *(Ruth Sawyer)*, Percy Marmont *(Douglas Courtenay)*, Vincent Serrano *("Velvet" Craft)*, George Fawcett *(Judge Whitlock)*, Grace Studdiford *(Dot Belmar)*, Gaston Glass *(William Bolton)*, Jean Armour *(Mrs. Bolton)*, Edna Murphy *(Vivian Bolton)*, H. J. Carvill *(Henry Bolton)*, Charles Lane *(Herbert Averill)*, Sidney Herbert *(Detective)*, Edouard Durand *(Jeweler)*, Henrietta Floyd *(Miss Weir)*.

Society drama about a girl born to a wealthy father and a chorus girl, who is raised by her grandfather after the mother proves to be unfit. When the child grows up and marries well, she decides not to tell her husband about her background and becomes the blackmail victim of her mother's evil paramour. This first run feature was a fine vehicle for its very popular star, Talmadge, who was married at the time to producer Schenck.

p, Joseph M. Schenck; d, Albert Parker, w, Anita Loos, Albert Parker (based on the play "Branded" by Oliver D. Bailey); ph, J. Roy Hunt.

Drama (PR:A MPAA:NR)

BRANDING BROADWAY**** (1918) 5 reels PAR-ART bw

William S. Hart *(Robert Sands)*, Seena Owen *(Mary Lee)*, Arthur Shirley *(Larry Harrington)*, Lewis W. Short *(Dick Horn)*, Andrew Robson *(Harrington, Sr.)*.

In this Hart "Eastern," the great cowboy star is sent to New York (via baggage car) by the authorities of an Arizona town he tore apart after returning from the range and discovering the place had gone dry. A marvelous mixture of comedy and thrills. BRANDING BROADWAY credits carry the name of Thomas H. Ince as supervisor, but director Hillyer and star Hart both claimed that he had nothing to do with the production. In fact, Hart and Ince, once firm friends, no longer were on speaking terms, a split that began over money and ended with them enemies after a quarrel over Hart's horse, Fritz, which Ince violently disliked.

d, Lambert Hillyer; sup, Thomas H. Ince; w, C. Gardner Sullivan; ph, Joe August.

Adventure (PR:A MPAA:NR)

BRANDING IRON, THE* (1920) 6 reels Goldwyn bw

Barbara Castleton *(Joan Carver)*, James Kirkwood *(Pierre Landis)*, Russell Simpson *(John Carver)*, Richard Tucker *(Prosper Gael)*, Sidney Ainsworth *(Jasper Morena)*, Gertrude Astor *(Betty Morena)*, Albert Roscoe *(Rev. Frank Holliwell)*, Marion Colvin *(Mrs. Upper)*, Joan Standing *(Maude Upper)*, Louie Cheung *(Wen Ho)*.

A terrible film, interesting only because, in an era when the flapper was replacing traditional values, THE BRANDING IRON celebrated the belief that there were some women in the world who could not live without being totally dominated by a man. The story takes place in the Old West, and alternate spring and winter segments play as much of a role as the stars, "mood enhancers," as it were, meant to show the feelings of the woman "branded" by a man's personality (spring), and when she is not under his brand (winter).

d, Reginald Barker; w, J. G. Hawks (based on a story by Katherine Newlin Burt); ph, Percy Hilburn.

Western (PR:A MPAA:NR)

BRAT, THE* (1919) 6 reels Metro bw

Alla Nazimova *(The Brat)*, Charles Bryant *(MacMillan Forrester)*, Amy Veness *(Mrs. Forrester)*, Frank Currier *(The Bishop)*, Darrell Foss *(Stephen Forrester)*, Bonnie Hill *(Angela)*, Milla Davenport *(The Brat's Aunt)*, Henry Kolker *(A Man About Town)*, Ethelbert Knott *(Butler)*.

Less-than-adequate melodrama about an orphaned child who becomes a chorus girl, is then discovered by an author who sees in her life the makings of a great novel, and—after many complications—becomes his wife.

d, Herbert Blache; w, June Mathis, Alla Nazomova, Charles Bryant (based on the play by Maude Fulton); ph, Eugene Gaudio.

Drama (PR:A MPAA:NR)

BRAVE AND BOLD*** (1918) 5 reels FOX bw

George Walsh, Regina Quinn, Francis X. Conlan, Dan Mason, Mabel Bunyea, Mike Donlin.

Fast-paced programmer in which Walsh (a principal actor in Griffith's *Intolerance* and brother of director Raoul Walsh) performs a myriad of thrilling stunts, including the scaling of Pittsburgh's Fort Pitt Hotel. His athletics all are geared to speed along a weak plot about munitions contracts, with the result that this one is a bomb.

d&w, Carl Harbaugh (based on the story "Four-Forty at Fort Penn" by Perley Poore Sheehan); ph, Ben Struckman.

Adventure (PR:A MPAA:NR)

BRAVEST WAY, THE** (1918) 5 reels FOX bw

Sessue Hayakawa, Florence Vidor, Tsuru Aoki, Yukio Aoyama, Jane Wolff, Tom Kurihara, Winter Hall, Josephine Crowell, Goro Kino, Clarence Geldert, Guy Oliver.

Another Hayakawa saga of self-sacrifice. In this one, the distinguished Japanese actor plays a man who brings the widow and children of his best friend to America to care for them, and loses the love of his misunderstanding, half-American fiancee. All ends well with the widow conveniently passing on, and the girl, who has since become an opera singer, realizing his true worth.

d, George Melford; w, (based on a story by Edith Kennedy).

Drama (PR:A MPAA:NR)

BRAZEN BEAUTY*** (1918) 5 reels UNIV bw

Priscilla Dean *(Jacala Averill)*, Thurston Hall, Katherine Griffith, Gertrude Astor, Alice Wilson, Leo White, Thornton Church.

Good comedy about a feisty Montana heiress who comes to New York, invades a social circle (on her own terms), and finds the one fellow from that crowd worthy of her. An outstanding performance by Dean, who plays the untamed beauty with zest and displays a good right hook on a numbskull suitor who obviously is only after her money.

d, Tod Browning; w, William E. Wing (based on a story by Louise Winter); ph, Alfred Gosden.

Comedy (PR:A MPAA:NR)

BREAD*** (1918) 6 reels UNIV bw

Mary MacLaren *(Candace Newby)*, Gladys Fox *(Estelle Payne)*, Edward Cecil *(Arnold Train)*, Kenneth Harlan *(Dick Frothingham)*, Louis Morrison *(Emil Krause)*.

Highly unusual film in which a loaf of bread is used as an allegorical reflection on human values and morality, though whether it makes its point clearly or not is anybody's guess. A farm girl, MacLaren, goes to the city to become an actress and is shortly a pawn in lecherous hands. She runs away, rents a room, and is finally reduced to three pennies. Hungry, she goes out into a driving rainstorm to spend the three cents on a loaf of bread. There follow interminable, ludicrous, and absurd perils as she loses the bread in the rain and ultimately finds it—in the window of a cafe patronized by her former evil friends. The story then leaps through time to show MacLaren after her triumph on the stage, when the man of her dreams takes her in his arms.

d&w, Ida May Park (based on a story by Evelyn Campbell).

Drama (PR:A MPAA:NR)

BREAKER, THE* (1916) 5 reels Essanay bw

Bryant Washburn *(John Widder)*, Nell Craig *(Alice Treadwell)*, Ernest Maupain *(Piazzi)*.

There is a lot of padding in this drama which has Washburn as a door-to-door salesman being duped by an Italian counterfeiter into carrying home a suitcase full of "funny" money. A girl detective, who is working on the case, prevents his arrest, and together they round up the crooks.

d&w, Fred E. Wright (based on the story by Arthur Stringer).

Crime (PR:A MPAA:NR)

BREAKING POINT, THE*** (1921) 6 reels J. L. Frothingham/Hodkinson bw

Bessie Barriscale *(Ruth Marshall)*, Walter McGrail *(Richard Janeway)*, Ethel Grey Terry *(Lucia Deeping)*, Eugenie Besserer *(Mrs. Janeway)*, Pat O'Malley *(Phillip Bradley)*, Winter Hall *(Dr. Hillyer)*, Wilfred Lucas *(Mortimer Davidson)*, Joseph J. Dowling *(Mrs. Marshall)*, Lydia Knott *(Mrs. Marshall)*, Irene Yeager *(Camilla)*.

Well done and daring for its time is this story about a girl who, out of necessity, marries a hard-drinking womanizer. After five years she reaches the breaking point when her husband throws her out and threatens to give their child to his mistress, and kills him. Later, after confessing to her mother-in-law, the understanding and sympathetic soul arranges for the family doctor to make the death look accidental.

d, Paul Scardon; w, H. H. Van Loan (based on the story "The Living Dead" by Mary Lerner); ph, Rene Guissart.

Drama **(PR:C MPAA:NR)**

BREAKING POINT, THE*** (1924) 7 reels FP/PAR bw

Nita Naldi *(Beverly Carlysle)*, Patsy Ruth Miller *(Elizabeth Wheeler)*, George Fawcett *(Dr. David Livingston)*, Matt Moore *(Judson Clark)*, John Merkyl *(William Lucas)*, Theodore von Eltz *(Fred Gregory)*, Edythe Chapman *(Lucy Livingstone)*, Cyril Ring *(Louis Bassett)*, W. B. Clarke *(Sheriff Wilkins)*, Edward Kipling *(Joe)*, Milt Brown *(Donaldson)*, Charles A. Stevenson *(Harrison Wheeler)*, Naida Faro *(Minnie)*.

When a young doctor believes he has killed the husband of the woman he has forbidden himself to love, he flees to the north woods and nearly dies in a storm. Sometime later, after losing his memory, he is recognized by an actress, and the real murderer is soon exposed. The doctor then regains his sense of the past and marries the woman he had denied himself. Fine direction and a top-notch cast make this a much better picture than it sounds.

d, Herbert Brenon; w, Edfrid Bingham, Julie Herne (based on the novel by Mary Roberts Rinehart); ph, James Howe.

Drama **(PR:A MPAA:NR)**

BREED OF MEN*** (1919) 5 reels WSHP/ART bw

William S. Hart *("Careless" Carmody)*, Seena Owen *(Ruth Fellows)*, Bert Sprotte *(Wesley Prentice)*, Buster Irving *(Bobby Fellows)*.

Another fine Hart feature, this time about a Chicago land swindler who sells a huge parcel of acreage in Arizona. Hart, a bad man-turned-good whom the crook had connived into becoming his sheriff, follows him to the Windy City and brings him to justice. There were some interesting Chicago location shots in this Ince production.

d, William S. Hart, Lambert Hillyer; sup, Thomas H. Ince; w, J. G. Hawks; ph, Joseph August.

Western **(PR:A MPAA:NR)**

BREED OF THE SUNSETS** (1928) 5 reels FBO bw

Bob Steele *(Jim Collins)*, Nancy Drexel *(The Spanish Girl)*, George Bunny *(Don Alvaro)*, Dorothy Kitchen *(Marie Alvaro)*, Leo White *(Senor Diego Valdez)*, Larry Fisher *(Hank Scully)*.

Steele is in love with a Mexican girl, so on the day she is to marry a man against her will, he disguises himself as a native, abducts the girl, and wins the permission of her sympathetic and admiring father.

d, Wallace W. Fox; w, Oliver Drake (based on a story by S. E. V. Taylor); t, Randolph Bartlett; ph, Robert De Grasse; ed, Della M. King.

Western **(PR:A MPAA:NR)**

BRENDA OF THE BARGE** (1920, Brit.) 5 reels HAE/Walturdaw bw

Marjorie Villis *(Brenda)*, James Knight *(Jim Walden)*, Bernard Dudley *(Harry)*, Blanche Stanley *(Mary Brown)*, Tom Coventry *(Judd Brown)*, Rose Sharp *(Mrs. Walden)*.

Convoluted British drama about the son of a farmer who does not realize the girl he loves is, in reality, his stepsister who had been kidnaped as a child.

d&w, Arthur Rooke.

Drama **(PR:A MPAA:NR)**

BREWSTER'S MILLIONS*** (1914) 5 reels LAS bw

Edward Abeles, Joseph Singleton, Sydney Deane, Miss Bartholomew, Mabel Van Buren, James MacGregor, Dick La Reno, Baby La Reno, Baby De Rue, Winifred Kingston, Bernadine Zuber, Monroe Salisbury, Maurine Rasmussen.

This first screen version of the popular play about the man who must spend $1 million quickly if he hopes to collect a big inheritance features Abeles, who had starred in the Broadway production. Although well acted and directed, it does not have the same comedic punch Roscoe Arbuckle brought to the part some seven years later.

p, Jesse L. Lasky; d, Cecil B. DeMille, Oscar Apfel; w, Melville Stone, Winchell Smith (based on the novel by George Barr McCutcheon and the play by Smith and Byron Ongley); ph, Alvin Wyckoff.

Comedy **(PR:A MPAA:NR)**

BREWSTER'S MILLIONS**** (1921) 5 reels FP/PAR bw

Roscoe Arbuckle *(Monte Brewster)*, Betty Ross Clark *(Peggy)*, Fred Huntley *(Mr. Brewster)*, Marion Skinner *(Mrs. Brewster)*, James Corrigan *(Mr. Ingraham)*, Jean Acker *(Barbara Drew)*, Charles Ogle *(Col. Drew)*, Neely Edwards *(MacLeod)*, William Boyd *(Harrison)*, L. J. McCarthy *(Ellis)*, Parker McConnell *(Pettingill)*, John McFarlane *(Blake)*.

The second filming of the successful theatrical comedy about a man who is eligible to inherit a fortune, providing he can spend a million dollars—conditionally—within a year. This was inspired property for "Fatty" Arbuckle, who played the part beautifully without his customary baggy pants and butcher boy derby. BREWSTER'S MILLIONS was remade three more times as talkies.

p, Jesse L. Lasky; d, Joseph Henabery; w, Walter Woods (based on the book by George Barr McCutcheon and the play by Winchell Smith and Byron Ongley); ph, Karl Brown.

Comedy **(PR:A MPAA:NR)**

BRIDAL CHAIR, THE** (1919, Brit.) 6 reels G. B. Samuelson/FBO bw

Miriam J. Sabbage *(Sylvane Sheridan)*, C. M. Hallard *(Lord Louis Lewis)*, Daisy Burrell *(Jill Hargreaves)*, Mary Rorke *(Mrs. Sheridan)*, John Kelt *(Butler)*.

British love story about a man of noble birth who vows he will never allow himself to marry as long as his crippled fiancee is still alive.

d, G. B. Samuelson; w, Samuelson, Roland Pertwee.

Drama **(PR:A MPAA:NR)**

BRIDE FOR A NIGHT, A* (1923) 5 reels Syracuse Motion Picture/REN bw

Henry Hull *(Jimmy Poe)*, Mary Thurman *(Jean Hawthorne)*, William H. Tooker *(Jean's Uncle)*, Nellie Parker Spaulding, Alyce Mills, Charles Craig, Tammany Young, Billy Quirk, Marcia Harris.

The laughs are pretty thin in this comedy about a young man who inhales too much gas while at the dentist. He begins to think of himself as a real detective and actually breaks up the robbery of his sweetheart's uncle's bank.

Comedy **(PR:A MPAA:NR)**

BRIDE OF FEAR, THE* (1918) 5 reels FOX bw

Jewel Carmen, Charles Gorman, Charles Bennett, Leonard C. Shumway.

Terrible hokum about a girl who marries a crook who once saved her life. When her husband is sent to prison, she meets and falls in love with a wealthy young man who was formerly an alcoholic. After her husband's release, she assumes the guilt when the man she loves kills her spouse, who attempted to rob him.

d&w, S. A. Franklin (based on a story by Bennett Cohen).

Drama **(PR:A MPAA:NR)**

BRIDE OF HATE, THE*

(1917) 5 reels Kay-Bee/TRI bw (AKA: WANTED FOR MURDER, OR BRIDE OF HATE)

Frank Keenan *(Dr. Dudley Duprez)*, Margery Wilson *(Mercedes Mendoza)*, Jerome Storm *(Paul Crenshaw)*, David M. Hartford *(Judge Shone)*, Elvira Well *(Rose Duprez)*, Mrs. J. Hunt *(Mammy Lou)*.

Set before the Civil War, a Southern doctor seeks revenge on the man who seduced his grand-niece by introducing him to a beautiful female slave he won on a wager. The seducer falls madly in love, marries the girl, and is told by the delighted doctor that "You have married a nigger!" Well, the rotter immediately becomes a dipsomaniac, hits the skids, and ends up wandering through a section of town which has been quarantined against yellow fever. When he realizes his situation and attempts to escape the area, a soldier standing guard shoots him down. As the cad lies dying, the doctor reluctantly informs him that his bride is, in fact, actually half Spanish. This is, to be sure, *not* the film one would select to show at the annual convention of the Urban League.

d, Walter Edwards; w, (based on a story by John Lynch).

Drama **(PR:A MPAA:NR)**

BRIDE OF THE STORM½** (1926) 7 reels VIT/WB bw

Dolores Costello *(Faith Fitzhugh)*, John Harron *(Dick Wayne)*, Otto Matiesen *(Hans Kroon)*, Sheldon Lewis *(Piet Kroon)*, Tyrone Power *(Jacob Kroon)*, Julia Swayne Gordon *(Faith's Mother)*, Evon Pelletier *(Faith, Age 8)*, Ira McFadden *(Heine Krutz)*, Tutor Owen *(Funeral Harry)*, Fred Scott *(Spike Mulligan)*, Donald Stuart *(Angus McLain)*, Walter Tennyson *(Ensign Clinton)*, Larry Steers *(Commander of the USS Baltimore)*.

When their ship is wrecked in the Dutch East Indies, Gordon and her little daughter make it to a small rocky island which contains a lighthouse run by a Dutch family. The mother lives long enough only to inform them that her daughter is an heiress, and the child grows up in their care to evolve into an incredibly beautiful woman (Costello). When she becomes of age, the family plot to marry her off to their half-wit relative and snare her fortune. But, fortunately, an American ship stops nearby for repairs, and Harron, in a very nicely staged fight scene, rescues the girl and returns her safely to the land of the free.

d, J. Stuart Blackton; w, Marian Constance (based on the story "Maryland My Maryland" by James Francis Dwyer); ph, Nick Musuraca, William Adams.

Drama **(PR:A MPAA:NR)**

BRIDE'S AWAKENING, THE* (1918) 6 reels UNIV bw

Mae Murray *(Elaine Bronson)*, Lewis J. Cody *(Richard Earle)*, Clarissa Selwynne, Harry Carter, Joe Girard, Ashton Dearholt.

Leonard, Murray, and Cody may have tried hard, but were unable to do much of anything with this absurd social melodrama about a young heiress who lives with her guardian and is engaged to a bounder of a fellow who wants nothing more than to spend her money. The rude awakening saves the heiress plenty of grief.

d, Robert Z. Leonard; w, F. McGrew Willis.

Drama **(PR:A MPAA:NR)**

BRIDE'S SILENCE, THE** (1917) 5 reels AM bw

Gail Kane, Lewis J. Cody, Henry A. Barrows, James Farley, Robert Klein, Ashton Dearholt.

Early evidence of director King's greatness could be found in this trite, heavily padded story about a prosecuter's wife, which the director somehow made bearable. One of King's impossible-to-find medium-length features, but already showing the sympathy and delicacy he would pour into his silent masterpiece, TOL'ABLE DAVID (1921).

d, Henry King; w, (based on a story by Daniel Frederick Whitcomb); ph, John F. Seitz.

Drama **(PR:A MPAA:NR)**

BRIGHT LIGHTS*** (1925) 7 reels MGM bw

Charles Ray *(Tom Corbin)*, Pauline Starke *(Patsy Delaney)*, LilyanTashman *(Gwen Gould)*, Lawford Davidson *(Marty Loftus)*, Ned Sparks *(Barney Gallagher)*, Eugenie Besserer *(Patsy's mom)*.

Broadway entertainer Starke grows tired of life on the Great White Way and returns to the tranquility of her small town home. Before long she falls in love with Ray, a regular fella, but he feels inadequate around her sophisticated friends and begins to behave like a slicker. This turnabout almost destroys their romance, but a pal sets Ray straight and he wins Starke back by just being himself.

d, Robert Z. Leonard; w, Jessie Burns, Lew Lipton (based on the story "A Little Bit of Broadway" by Richard Connell); t, Joseph W. Farnham, William Conselman; ph, John Arnold; ed, William Le Vanway; set d, Cedric Gibbons, Richard Day.

Comedy **(PR:A MPAA:NR)**

BRING HIM IN* 1/2** (1921) 5 reels VIT bw

Earle Williams *(The Fugitive)*, Bruce Gordon *(The Mountie)*, Fritzi Ridgeway *(The Girl)*, Elmer Dewey *(Baptiste)*, Ernest Van Pelt *(Canby)*, Paul Weigel *(Braganza)*.

This frozen-tundra story of duty and gratitude deals with the decision a Mountie, Gordon, must make after his life has been saved by the innocent fugitive he is trailing, Williams. He decides to give him an hour's head start, but when he does catch up, deliberately fires his pistol in the air. The fugitive, however, fires straight away, hitting the officer in the chest. A title card then reads, "I shot in the air, old Pal," and the other replies, "I wish to God I had." After a gripping and well-directed series of scenes where the fugitive drags the policeman through the snow and back to a post, the Mountie, who does manage to survive, tells the settlers, "I shot myself." A very good programmer.

d, Earle Williams, Robert Ensminger; w, Thomas Dixon, Jr. (based on a story by H. H. Van Loan); ph, Jack MacKenzie.

Drama **(PR:A MPAA:NR)**

BROADWAY AFTER DARK*** (1924) 7 reels HR/WB bw

Adolphe Menjou *(Ralph Norton)*, Norma Shearer *(Rose Dulane)*, Anna Q. Nilsson *(Helen Tremaine)*, Edward Burns *(Jack Devlin)*, Carmel Myers *(Lenore Vance)*, Vera Lewis *(Mrs. Smith/Landlady)*, Willard Louis *("Slim" Scott)*, Mervyn Le Roy *(Carl Fisher)*, Jimmy Quinn *(Ed Fisher)*, Edgar Norton *(An Old Actor)*, Gladys Tennyson *(Vera)*, Ethel Miller *(The Chorus Girl)*, Otto Hoffman *(Norton's Valet)*, Lew Harvey *(Ton Devery)*, Michael Dark *(George Vance)*, Fred Stone, Dorothy Stone, Mary Eaton, Raymond Hitchcock, Elsie Ferguson, Florence Moore, James J. Corbett, John Steel, Frank Tinney, Paul Whiteman, Irene Castle, Buster West.

Another smooth man-about-town outing for Menjou, but this time as the lead and this time not the lecherous roue. He is a wealthy playboy darling of New York society circles who is attracted to Nilsson, playgirl counterpart to himself. However, he surprisingly soon tires of Nilsson's frivolity and especially her inveterate flirting with other members of their set, and through this new view of her he in turn grows tired of the superficiality of his life. Seeking seclusion, he takes a room in a boarding house filled with theatrical people and meets Shearer, a poor working girl. Shearer soon is fired from her job because it is discovered that she had previously served time in jail. Menjou immediately takes over as her guardian and attempts to pass her off as his ward in theatrical circles, but Shearer is in for another disillusionment when a detective tries to frame her. Seeing that the whole panoply of the city is working against the good life, Menjou decides to take Shearer away and begin a new life somewhere else.

d, Monta Bell; w, Douglas Doty (based on a play by Owen Davis); ph, Charles Van Enger.

Drama **(PR:A MPAA:NR)**

BROADWAY BILLY* 1/2 (1926) 5 reels Harry J. Brown/RAY bw

Billy Sullivan *(Billy Brookes)*, Virginia Brown Faire *(Phyliss Brookes)*, Jack Herrick *(Ace O'Brien)*, Hazel Howell.

Brown could really grind out the movie sausages, including this one about a boxer who continues to fight in order to support his wife's expensive tastes. But when she's seriously hurt in an automobile accident, he takes on the champion of the world and wins.

d, Harry J. Brown; w, Henry R. Simon.

Drama **(PR:A MPAA:NR)**

BROADWAY ROSE** (1922) 6 reels TIF/Metro bw

Mae Murray *(Rosalie Lawrence)*, Monte Blue *(Tom Darcy)*, Ray Bloomer *(Hugh Thompson)*, Ward Crane *(Reggie Whitley)*, Alma Tell *(Barbara Royce)*, Charles Lane *(Peter Thompson)*, Mary Turner Gordon *(Mrs. Peter Thompson)*, Mrs. Jennings *(Mrs. Lawrence)*, Pauline Dempsey *(Colored Maid)*.

This rather typical backstage drama has little to recommend it aside from some elaborate sets and Murray's costumes. And well she might have worn them, for in the story she is a dancing star who falls in love with rich Bloomer. Over his parents' opposition, the pair elope. But then, alas, Bloomer tells her that she is not worth the loss of his father's millions, and she returnes to her childhood sweetheart, Blue.

d, Robert Z. Leonard; w, Edmund Goulding (based on the popular song of the same title); ph, Oliver T. Marsh, set d, Tilford Cinema Studios.

Drama **(PR:A MPAA:NR)**

BROADWAY SCANDAL** (1918) 5 reels BLUE bw

Carmel Myers *(Nenette Bisson)*, W. H. Bainbridge *(Dr. Kendall)*, Edwin August *(David Kendall)*, Lon Chaney *("Kink" Colby)*, Andrew Robson *(Armande Bisson)*, S. K. Shilling *(Paul De Caval)*, Frederick Gamble *(Falkner)*.

This highly insulting film took the position that all French girls were *not* tramps. At least, that's what the hero of this movie learns while serving in "The Great War," where he meets a few besides the leading lady—a waitress in her father's French restaurant in New York—who becomes wrongly implicated in a crime. This one is of interest mainly because of Chaney's gangster portrayal.

d, Joseph De Grasse; w, Harvey Gates.

Drama **(PR:A MPAA:NR)**

BROKEN BLOSSOMS***** (1919) 6 reels Griffith/UA bw

Lillian Gish *(Lucy Burrows)*, Richard Barthelmess *(Cheng Haun, the Yellow Man)*, Donald Crisp *(Battling Burrows)*, Arthur Howard *(His Manager)*, Edward Peil *(Evil Eye)*, George Beranger *(The Spying One)*, Norman "Kid McCoy" Selby *(A Prizefighter)*, Wilbur Higby, Karla Schramm, Ernest Butterworth, Fred Hamer, George Nicholls *(London Policeman)*, Moon Kwan *(Buddhist Monk)*.

When a Chinese aristocrat (Barthelmess) encounters a group of skylarking Caucasian sailors and is knocked to the ground while trying to break up a fight, he decides to journey to England and deliver the peaceful message of his faith. Instead, the noble "yellow man" is reduced to smoking opium and running a curio shop in the Limehouse section of London. Lucy, the illegitimate daughter of prizefighter Crisp, is the constant victim of the boxer's abuse and, after a particularly severe beating, staggers out of his house and collapses in front of Barthelmess' store. It is a fateful incident, for he has long loved Lucy from a distance, and now takes the girl in and showers her with the only kindness she has ever known. Crisp returns from a championship fight to discover that his daughter is with a "Chink." He flies into a rage, breaks down the door of the closet where Gish (in one of the greatest performances of all cinema) is hiding with an axe, then drags her home and beats her to death. Barthelmess returns home to find the girl he loves missing and his apartment in shambles. He races to her rescue and, on encountering the terrible reality, empties his revolver into the menacing body of Crisp. The gentle Chinaman then takes Lucy to his flat, lays her body out in a silken gown, and commits suicide. Griffith shot this truly remarkable film in only 18 days and, through his intimate sense of visual poetry, lighting, and mood, may have influenced the art of motion picture making as much as he did with his grandest of spectacles, INTOLERANCE. The film opened in New York City at increased prices, and made man-about-town Barthelmess an overnight cinema sensation. Barthelmess became such a favorite of Griffith's that he could call the great director "Governor," while everybody else called him "Mr. Griffith." Technically, the picture is interesting in its simulation of London fog and the resulting soft, muted tones. The first of Griffith's features to be shot entirely on stages (the other had all used outdoor locations extensively), it was also the first in which Griffith had the film stock dyed in various sections in soft pastel colors. This was the result of a fortuitous accident involving Carol Dempster, the young dancer who did live terpsichorean prologs before the screening of many of Griffith's pictures. (At this time, Dempster was replacing star Gish in the director's personal life; according to some reports, Griffith enjoyed fomenting rivalry between his two female admirers.) During a preview performance of BROKEN BLOSSOMS, the colored stage lights used in Dempster's live performance were inadvertently left on when the picture was screened. Quick to adapt to accidents, the innovative director recognized the potential of the soft tints and incorporated them in his film. Strange to say, BROKEN BLOSSOMS—essentially a simple picture, shot on stages—cost more to produce than Griffith's complicated THE BIRTH OF A NATION. Compelled to seek additional funds from Adolph Zukor, Griffith was stunned by the tycoon's response: "You bring me a picture like this and want money for it? You may as well put your hand in my pocket and steal it. Everybody in it dies. It isn't commercial." Griffith borrowed money and bought the film back from Zukor's Artcraft for $250,000. It proved to be the only of his pictures to return a profit between THE BIRTH OF A NATION (1915) and WAY DOWN EAST (1920). Griffith was beset with casting problems prior to the start of production. Gish rebelled at her role, pointing out that she was a big girl now and ill-suited for the part. When Griffith finally cajoled her into accepting the role, she came down with influenza (a dangerous epidemic was sweeping the country at the time). Crisp was, literally, moonlighting; he was directing a film himself for Famous Players-Lasky during the day, and Griffith had to shoot all his scenes at night. Shot in only 18 days, the picture was rehearsed for an exceptionally long six-week period. At the outset of rehearsals, Griffith still had not settled on an actor for the part of The Yellow Man. Character actor George Fawcett, who was 60 years old and obviously unsuited for the part, played the part during rehearsals. When Barthelmess arrived on the set, he enjoyed the advantage of watching the talented Fawcett handle the role, later confessing that he copied that fine actor's mannerisms. In the end, everything worked. At the picture's premiere, the producers were surprised to hear no applause at the conclusion. The audience members were emotionally stunned, too touched to clap their hands. In a strange epilog to the production, in 1935 Griffith receivedan offer from England to remake the picture, with Emlyn Williams and Dolly Haas in the starring roles. Griffith traveled to London filled with anticipation, but a dispute over the casting of Haas scuttled the project.

d&w, D. W. Griffith (based on the story "The Chink and the Child" by Thomas Burke); ph, Billy Bitzer, Hendrik Sartov, Karl Brown; m, Louis F. Gottschalk, Griffith; ed, James Smith.

Drama **Cas.** **(PR:A MPAA:NR)**

BROKEN CHAINS** (1916) 5 reels PEER/WORLD bw

Carlyle Blackwell *(Harry Ford)*, John Tansey *(Harry as a Boy)*, Ethel Clayton *(Georgia Gwynne)*, Madge Evans *(Georgia as a Girl)*, Herbert Barrington *(Gen. Gwynne)*, Stanhope Wheatcroft *(Paul Fitzhugh)*, Herbert Delmore *(Dr. Tom Lincoln)*, Henry West *(Sampson)*, Louis Grisel *(Moses)*, William Sherwood *(Jefferson)*, Jessie Lewis *(Bessie Fitzhugh)*, John Tansey.

There is more than a little racism in this picture about a Northern army officer who is sent south to hunt moonshiners and is wrongly convicted of a murder actually performed by a "bad nigger." The young man is given life and sentenced to the chain gang. He escapes, however, and is harbored by a Southern girl who believes him innocent. Of course he vindicates himself and marries the girl, but not before the black villain is graphically depicted "getting his."

d, Robert Thornby; w, Mrs. E. M. Ingleton (based on a story by Clay M. Greene, Joseph R. Grismer).

Drama **(PR:C MPAA:NR)**

BROKEN DOLL, A* (1921) 5 reels AP bw

Monte Blue *(Tommy Dawes)*, Mary Thurman *(Harriet Bundy)*, Mary Jane Irving *(Rosemary)*, Les Bates *(Bill Nyall)*, Lizette Thorne *(Mrs. Nyall)*, Arthur Millett *(Sheriff Hugh Bundy)*, Jack Riley *(Knapp Wyant)*.

Heavily padded, overly sentimental tale of a man who loves all things, especially the crippled daughter of the rancher for whom he works. When the little one breaks her doll, Blue, in order to get the money to replace it, captures an outlaw to earn the reward, then marries the sheriff's daughter. A property not worthy of the talents of Dwan and Blue.

d, Allan Dwan; w, Dwan, Lillian Ducey (based on a story by Mary Jane Irving); ph, Lyman Boening, W. L. O'Connell.

Drama **(PR:A MPAA:NR)**

BROKEN HEARTS* (1926) 8 reels Jaffe Art Films bw

Maurice Schwartz *(Benjamin Rezanov)*, Lila Lee *(Ruth Esterin)*, Wolf Goldfaden *(Cantor Esterin)*, Bina Abramowitz *(Mama Esterin)*, Isidor Cashier *(Victor Kaplan)*, Anna Appel *(Shprintze)*, Charles Nathanson *(Mr. Kruger)*, Liza Silbert *(Mrs. Kruger)*, Theodore Silbert *(Milton Kruger)*, Morris Strasberg *(Marriage Broker)*, Henrietta Schnitzer *(Esther)*, Betty Ferkauf *(Benjamin's Mother)*, Louis Hyman *(Mishka)*, Leonid Snergoff *(Captain of the Cossacks)*, Julius Adler *(David Adler)*.

This story of a Jewish writer who flees Russian persecution and overcomes numerous obstacles before finally marrying the daughter of a wealthy merchant was pretty amateurish stuff. Of interest mainly because, with the exception of Lee, the entire production consisted of members of the then-flourishing Yiddish theater.

d, Maurice Schwartz; w, Frances Taylor Patterson (based on the play by Z. Libin); ph, Frank Zucker.

Drama **(PR:A MPAA:NR)**

BROKEN HEARTS OF HOLLYWOOD*** (1926) 8 reels WB bw

Patsy Ruth Miller *(Betty Ann Bilton)*, Louise Dresser *(Virginia Perry)*, Douglas Fairbanks, Jr. *(Hal Terwilliger)*, Jerry Miley *("Hop" Marshall)*, Stuart Holmes *(McLain)*, Barbara Worth *(Molly)*, Dick Sutherland *(Sheriff)*, Emile Chautard *(Director)*, Anders Randolph *(District Attorney)*, George Nichols *(Chief of Detectives)*, Sam de Grasse *(Defense Attorney)*.

Another version of the "Madame X" story, this time set in Hollywood. Dresser is wonderful as the mother who deserts her daughter for stardom, only to save her from the gallows by assuming guilt for a killing in the end. Fine performances all around and an interesting look at the motion picture industry of that time.

d, Lloyd Bacon; w, Graham Baker (based on the story by Raymond L. Schrock, Edward Clark); ph, Virgil Miller; ed, Clarence Kolster.

Drama **(PR:A MPAA:NR)**

BROKEN MELODY, THE**

(1929, Brit.) 7 reels Welsh-Pearson-Elder/PAR bw

Georges Galli *(Prince Paul)*, Andree Sayre *(Bianca)*, Enid Stamp-Taylor *(Gloria)*, Cecil Humphreys *(Gen. Delange)*, Mary Brough *(Marthe)*, Albert Brouett *(Jacques)*.

Set in Paris, this British romance has to do with an exiled prince who writes an opera for a singer with whom he is having a fling, but comes to his senses in time to return to his shopgirl wife before the marriage is destroyed.

p, George Pearson; d, Fred Paul; w, Thomas Coutts Elder, Paul (based on the play by Herbert Keith, James Leader).

Drama **(PR:A MPAA:NR)**

BROKEN ROMANCE, A** (1929, Brit.) 7 reels Parkinson/FOX bw

William Freshman *(Jack Worth)*, Blanche Adele *(Mary Davies)*, Paul Neville *(John Shund)*, Laura Smithson *(Lalla Watkins)*, Colin Crop *(Joe Davies)*.

A beautiful Welsh crippled girl allows herself to be talked into playing the lead in a movie about her life and then, to her great delight, is given the opportunity to meet the writer she is in love with at one of the screenings.

d&w, J. Steven Edwards.

Drama **(PR:A MPAA:NR)**

BRONCHO TWISTER*** (1927) 5 reels FOX bw

Tom Mix *(Tom Mason)*, Helen Costello *(Paulita Brady)*, George Irving *(Ned Mason)*, Dorothy Kitchen *(Daisy Mason)*, Paul Nicholson *(Black Jack Brady)*, Doris Lloyd *(Teresa Brady)*, Malcolm Waite *(Dan Bell)*, Jack Pennick *(Jinx Johnson)*, Otto Fries *(Sheriff)*, Tony the Wonder Horse.

Good western set in contemporary Arizona has Mix and a Marine buddy saving Costello from a forced marriage, and holding off an army of heavies from inside a Spanish mission where dynamite has been stored. Exciting action footage as Mix and his pal hurl stick after stick of the explosives at the villains like war-time hand grenades.

d, Orville Dull; w, John Stone (based on a story by Adela Rogers St. John); ph, Dan Clark.

Western **(PR:A MPAA:NR)**

BRONENOSETS POTEMKIN

(SEE: BATTLESHIP POTEMKIN, THE, 1925, USSR)

BRONZE BELL, THE** (1921) 6 reels Ince/PAR bw

Courtney Foote *(Har Dyal Rutton/David Amber)*, Doris May *(Sophia Farrell)*, John Davidson *(Salig Singh)*, Claire Du Brey *(Nairaini)*, Noble Johnson *(Chatterji)*, Otto Hoffman *(La Bertouche)*, Gerald Pring *(Capt. Darrington)*, C. Norman Hammond *(Col. Farrell)*, Howard Crampton *(Dogget)*, Fred Huntley *(Maharajah)*.

A big, expensive, and well-produced film which failed because of weaknesses in the script. The setting is revolution-torn India, as well as Long Island, and the excellent action scenes were directed by Horne, the man who would skipper some of Laurel and Hardy's best pictures. Scarcely a notable production by the once great producer Ince.

d, James W. Horne; sup, Thomas H. Ince; w, Del Andrews, Louis Stevens (based on the novel *The Bronze Bell* by Louis Joseph Vance); ph, George Barnes.

Drama **(PR:A MPAA:NR)**

BROWN OF HARVARD**** (1926) 8 reels MGM bw

Jack Pickford *(Jim Doolittle)*, Mary Brian *(Mary Abbott)*, Francis X. Bushman, Jr. *(Bob McAndrews)*, Mary Alden *(Mrs. Brown)*, David Torrence *(Mr. Brown)*, Edward Connelly *(Prof. Abbott)*, Guinn Williams *(Hal Walters)*, Ernest Gillen *(Reggie Smythe)*, William Haines *(Tom Brown)*.

Perhaps the best college picture of the Roaring Twenties, and more genuine in atmosphere than almost any college picture that preceded or has followed it. BROWN OF HARVARD smacks of authenticity all around, and is a whale of a good story, as Haines, in the title role, arrives at school as a "fresh" freshman, an average student, but a whiz with the girls. A washout in a climactic crew race, for which his classmates ridicule him, he harbors thoughts of quitting school but is talked out of it by his father, who tells him to fight it out. Returning in the fall, Haines attempts to make the football team, but can manage only to get on the second string. In the Yale game, he is sent in during the first half, but before much has happened he gets a bump on the leg and must leave the field, to the cries of "quitter" from his classmates. Finally, in the last quarter, he goes back on the field with the score 3 to 0 for Yale, and in a sensational run carries the ball the length of the field in a series of bone-smashing rushes, and then Bushman goes over for the victory. Brian, the target of much of Haines' attentions at Harvard, is simply smashing as the object of his affections, and Alden and Torrence's performances as Haines' mother and father are admirably played. The college is "location" Harvard, as is the stadium where the game is played (an actual contest, in fact, was filmed to add to the realism—it was the previous year's game between Harvard and Yale, when Yale was favored but was held to a 0 to 0 tie. Thus the celebration on the field after the game in the film actually was the real thing). Added to all this was Haines himself, a collegiate looking actor if there ever was one. A valuable film contribution from the 1920s, and worth looking at today.

d, Jack Conway; w, A. P. Younger, Donald Ogden Stewart (based on the play by Rida Johnson Young); t, Joe Farnham; ph, Ira H. Morgan; ed, Frank Davis; art d, Cedric Gibbons, Arnold Gillespie.

Drama **(PR:A MPAA:NR)**

BRUTE, THE*** (1927) 7 reels WB bw

Monte Blue *("Easy Going" Sondes)*, *Lelia Hyams (Jennifer Duan)*, Clyde Cook *(Oklahoma Red)*, Carroll Nye *(The El)*, Paul Nicholson *(Square Deal Felton)*.

Off-beat contemporary western comedy about an oil boom was novel in its depiction of *noveau riche* Indians. However, what was considered good for a laugh then, now borders on the offensive.

d, Irving Cummings; w, Harvey Gates (based on a novel by Douglas Newton); ph, Abe Fried.

Western/Comedy **(PR:A MPAA:NR)**

BUCKING THE TRUTH* (1926) 5 reels BS/UNIV bw

Pete Morrison *(Slim Duane)*, Brinsley Shaw *("Coarse Gold" Charlie)*, Bruce Gordon *(Matt Holden)*, William La Roche *(Eben Purkiss)*, Charles Whittaker *(Red Sang)*, Ione Reed *(Anne)*, O. Robertson *(Tom Bailey)*, Vester Pegg *(Sheriff Findlay)*.

Morrison was one of Universal's second string cowboys and, although he had been before the cameras since 1912, he really never advanced beyond the minor league offerings BUCKING THE TRUTH was typical of. Here he is a cowboy mistaken for a crook, who finds a smuggler's hideout where a sheriff is being held captive. He successfully frees the sheriff, gets back in town to save the real crook from a lynch mob, and wins the hand of Reed in the process.

d, Milburne Morante; w, J. I. Kane; ph, Richard Fryer.

Western **(PR:A MPAA:NR)**

BUECHSE DER PANDORA (SEE: PANDORA'S BOX, 1929, Ger.)

BULLDOG COURAGE* (1922) 5 reels CLIN/Russell bw

Bessie Love *(Gloria Philips)*, George Larkin *(Jimmy Brent)*, Albert MacQuarrie *(John Morton)*, Karl Silvera *(Snakey Evans)*, Frank Whitman *(Big Bob Phillips)*, Bill Patton *(Sheriff Weber)*, Barbara Tennant *(Mary Allen)*.

Feeble programmer about a college man, Larkin, who goes West at his uncle's request (not to mention a $50,000 reward) to lick a bully, Whitman, who gave him a beating some years before. The young man not only evens the score but captures a band of rustlers and wins Love, who didn't deserve to be in this loser.

d, Edward Kull; w, Jeanne Poe; ph, Harry Neuman; ed, Fred Allen; art d, Louis E. Myers.

Western **(PR:A MPAA:NR)**

BULLDOG DRUMMOND*** (1923, Brit.) 6 reels ASTRA-N bw

Carlyle Blackwell *(Capt. Hugh Drummond)*, Evelyn Greeley *(Phyllis Benton)*, Dorothy Fane *(Irma Peterson)*, Warwick Ward *(Dr. Lakington)*, Horace de Vere *(Carl Peterson)*, Gerald Dean *(Algy Longworth)*, Harry Bogarth *(Sparring Partner)*, William Browning *(James Handley)*.

This British mystery, based on the popular Bulldog Drummond character, was shot in Holland. This time, the dashing Drummond (Blackwell) saves a captured industrialist from foreign agents who have been holding him hostage in a nursing home.

p, Maurits Binger; d, Oscar Apfel; w, C. B. Doxat-Pratt (based on the play by "Sapper" [H. C. McNeile]).

Crime **(PR:A MPAA:NR)**

BULLDOG PLUCK** (1927) 5 reels Bob Custer/FBO bw

Bob Custer *(Bob Hardwick)*, Viora Daniels *(Jess Haviland)*, Bobby Nelson *(Danny Haviland)*, Richard R. Neill *(Destin)*, Walter Maly *(Gillen)*, Victor Metzetti *(Curley Le Baste)*, Hugh Saxon *("Pa" Haviland)*.

Custer, popular cowboy star of the silents and early talkies, has an unusual role in this one playing the town's saloon-owner who brings a stranger to justice and weds the daughter of a hard-luck family he has befriended.

d, Jack Nelson; w, Evanne Blasdale, Madeline Matzen (based on the story "Hardwick of Hambone" by W. Bert Foster); ph, Ernest Miller.

Western **(PR:A MPAA:NR)**

BULLET MARK, THE* (1928) 5 reels Fred J. McConnell/Pathe bw

Joseph W. Girard, Albert J. Smith, Lincoln Plumer, Margaret Gray, Gladys McConnell, Jack Donovan.

A wild horse trainer is framed for a bank robbery by an angry ranch foreman, whose job he has taken over. The trainer escapes and, with the help of a pretty young lady, clears himself. DUEL IN THE SUN it's not.

d, Stuart Patton; w, Joseph Anthony Roach (based on a story by Harry Wood); t, Jack Kelly; ph, Allan Davey; ed, Jack Donovan.

Western **(PR:A MPAA:NR)**

BULLIN' THE BULLSHEVIKI** (1919) 4 reels EFF & EFF bw

Marguerite Clayton, George Ross, Olive Burke, Louise Fazenda.

Rather feeble attempt at satirizing Russian communism really misses the boat by not taking advantage of Fazenda's considerable talents. Even a screen full of young ladies cavorting around in what then were called bathing suits fails to generate any excitement in this brainless tirade against the then new Soviet state.

d&w, Frank P. Donovan.

Comedy **(PR:A MPAA:NR)**

BUNTY PULLS THE STRINGS*** (1921) 7 reels Goldwyn bw

Leatrice Joy *(Bunty)*, Russell Simpson *(Tammas Biggar)*, Raymond Hatton *(Weelum)*, Cullen Landis *(Rab)*, Casson Ferguson *(Jeemy)*, Josephine Crowell *(Susie Simpson)*, Edythe Chapman *(Ellen Dunlap)*, Roland Ruston *(Minister)*, Georgia Woodthorpe *(Mrs. Drummon)*, Sadie Gordon *(Maggie)*, Otto Hoffman *(Beadle)*.

Well-acted and directed comedy about life in a small Scotch town. There are lots of laughs and suspense, as Joy (at her most charming) manages to keep her brother out of jail and get herself and her father married in a double wedding.

d, Reginald Barker; w, J. G. Hawks, Charles Kenyon (based on the play by Graham Moffat); ph, Percy Hilburn.

Comedy **(PR:A MPAA:NR)**

BURIED TREASURE*** (1921) 7 reels COS/PAR bw

Marion Davies *(Pauline Vandermuellen)*, Norman Kerry *(Dr. John Grant)*, Anders Randolph *(William Vandermuellen)*, Edith Shayne *(Mrs. Vandermuellen)*, Earl Schenck *(Joeffrey Vandermuellen)*, John Charles *(Duc de Chavannes)*, Thomas Findlay *(The Captain)*.

Handsomely produced Davies film which catered to contemporary interest in reincarnation. The film also gave the star the opportunity to play a modern-day heiress and a Spanish maiden during the days of pirates and galleons as she leads her father on a wild goose chase for treasure. Instead, she takes her lover to the treasure revealed to her in a dream, and eventually wins her father's permission for their marriage.

d&w, George D. Baker; ph, Hal Rosson; set d, Joseph Urban.

Romance **(PR:A MPAA:NR)**

BURN 'EM UP BARNES**** (1921) 6 reels Mastodon/Affiliated bw

Johnny Hines *("Burn 'Em Up" Barnes)*, Edmund Breeze *("King" Cole)*, *Betty Carpenter (Madge Thompson)*, George Fawcett *(An Eccentric Tramp)*, J. Barney Sherry *(Whitney Barnes)*, Matthew Betts *(Ed Scott)*, Julia Swayne Gordon *(Mrs. Whitney Barnes)*, Richard Thorpe *(Stephen Thompson)*, Dorothy Leeds *(Betty Scott)*, Harry Fraser *(Francies Jones)*, "Billy Boy" Swinton *(The Baby)*.

In his first feature length comedy, Hines plays the speed crazy son of a rich automaker who, after an argument about fines, decides to go out into the world on his own. Before long, he is robbed by crooks, thrown unconscious into a railroad freight car, and wakes up in a small town where he is taken in by a couple of tramps and falls in love with the daughter of the bank president. After a number of wonderful sight gags, and some intelligently constructed exposition, the movie climaxes with Hines chasing bank robbers in a car he had entered in the big race. Needless to say he catches them, gets the girl, and wins the race. A first-rate performance from one of the sadly neglected comic stars of the silent era.

d, Johnny Hines, George A. Beranger; w, Raymond L. Schrock; ph, Ted Beasley, Hal Young, Ned Van Buren.

Comedy **(PR:A MPAA:NR)**

BURNING SANDS*** (1922) 6 reels FP/PAR bw

Wanda Hawley *(Muriel Blair, an English Girl)*, Milton Sills *(Daniel Lane, a Philosopher)*, Louise Dresser *(Kate Bindane)*, Jacqueline Logan *(Lizette)*, Robert Cain *(Robert Barthampton)*, Fenwich Oliver *(Mr. Bindane)*, Winter Hall *(Governor)*, Harris Gordon *(Secretary)*, Albert Roscoe *(Ibrihim)*, Cecil Holland *(Old Sheik)*, Joe Ray *(Hussein)*.

This film was billed as the answer to THE SHEIK. It was, in fact, a good movie with plenty of gunplay and romance, as a desert man wins the heart of a colonial governor's daughter. A fine production by the man who directed the legendary Rudolph Valentino feature.

d, George Melford; w, Olga Printzlau (based on the novel by Aurthur Weigall); ph, Bert Glennon.

Adventure **(PR:A MPAA:NR)**

BY PROXY*** (1918) 5 reels TRI bw

Roy Stewart *("Red" Saunders)*, Maude Wayne *(Lindy)*, Walter Perry *(Aleck)*, Wilbur Higbee *(Cattle Buyer)*, Harry Yamamoto *(Ah Sing)*, John Lince.

The third in the "Red Saunders" series is a situation, rather than action western, with the hero (as the title would indicate) standing in for a fellow cowboy to plead marriage. He kidnaps the wrong girl to bring to his pal, and discovers his mistake only to fall in love with the victim himself.

d, Cliff Smith; w, (based on a story by Henry Wallace Phillips); ph, Steve Rounds.

Western **(PR:A: MPAA:NR)**

BY RIGHT OF POSSESSION*** (1917) 5 reels VIT bw

Mary Anderson *(Kate Saxon)*, Antonio Moreno *(Tom Baxter)*, Otto Lederer *("Bells")*, Leon D. Kent *(Trimble)*.

This is a double feature in one. The first half of the film has the principals involved in a mining story, while the second part (featuring the same romantic leads) becomes a western. Both sequences are action-packed. and both are well produced.

d, William Wolbert, w, Garfield Thompson (based on a story by Alvah Milton Kerr).

Adventure/Western **(PR:A MPAA:NR)**

BY THE WORLD FORGOT*** (1918) 5 reels VIT bw

Hedda Nova *(Truda)*, J. Frank Glendon *(Derrick Van Beekman)*, Patricia Palmer *(Stephanie Maynard)*, R. S. Bradbury *(John Maynard)*, George Kunkel *(William Woywood)*, Otto Lederer *(Hano)*, Ed Alexander, Jake Abraham.

A wealthy young man, shanghaied from his bachelor party, escapes with the help of friendly seamen, discovers an island populated by the Caucasian descendants of a long-ago shipwreck, and falls in love with a girl from that group. He is rescued finally by the very men who arranged for his kidnaping, but he chooses to stay with his new love on the island.

d, David Smith; w, Frederic R. Buckley (based on a story by Cyrus Townsend Brady).

Adventure **(PR:A MPAA:NR)**

BY WHOSE HAND?*** (1916) 5 reels EQ/WORLD bw

Edna Wallace Hopper *(Edith Maitland)*, Charles J. Ross *(John Maitland)*, Muriel Ostriche *(Helen Maitland)*, Nicholas Danaev *(Kimba)*, John Dillon *(Simon Baird)*, James Ryley *(David Sterling)*.

Unusual murder mystery, highlighted by a trial in which the witnesses, through the use of double exposures, relate the facts. At the film's conclusion, the judge turns tothe audience and (through a title) says, "All the information is in, you deliver the verdict."

d, James Durkin; w, Channing Pollock, Rennold Wolf.

Mystery **(PR:A MPAA:NR)**

BY WHOSE HAND? (1927) 6 reels COL bw

Ricardo Cortez *(Van Suydam Smith)*, Eugenia Gilbert *(Peg Hewlett)*, J. Thornton Baston *(Sidney)*, Tom Dugan *(Rollins)*, Edgar Washington Blue *(Eli)*, Lillian Leighton *(Silly McShane)*, William Scott *(Mortimer)*, John Steppling *(Claridge)*, De Sacia Moores *(Tex)*.

Not-too-exciting society thriller has Agent X-9 (Cortez) finally, with the help of insurance agent Baston, exposing notorious jewel thief Scott after briefly suspecting the girl he loves, Gilbert, of being the crook. Smart set drama presumably takes place on a Long Island estate and in a jazz age night club.

d, Walter Lanh; w, Marion Orth; ph, J. O. Taylor; art d, Robert E. Lee.

Crime **(PR:A MPAA:NR)**

CABARET, THE* (1918) 5 reels World/bw

June Elvidge, Carlyle Blackwell, Montagu Love, John Bowers, George MacQuarrie, Captain Charles, Minta Durfee.

Four struggling Greenwich Village artists and a beautiful model share their poverty and their dreams. When one of the painters becomes insanely possessive of her, the model decides to pursue a career on the stage and is an immediate success. Before long, three of the painters are told they are going to have their work exhibited, and they decide to throw a celebration party. When the actress attends and finds the fourth young man missing, she rushes to his studio, offers him hope, and poses for him once again. Needless to say, the collaboration becomes the talk of New York, and the picture ends as it began, with the five of them together again—sharing their failures and their triumphs.

d, Harley Knoles; w, Virginia Tyler Hudson (based on a story by J. U. Guisey).

Drama **(PR:A MPAA:NR)**

CABARET GIRL, THE* (1919) 5 reels BLUE/UNIV bw

Ruth Clifford *(Ann Reid)*, Carmen Phillips *(Dolly)*, Ashton Dearholt *(Ted Vane)*, Harry V. Meter *(Balvini)*.

A girl with opera-singing ambitions comes to the big city and ends up performing in a cabaret. Before long, she meets a wealthy young man and they become engaged. The fellow's mother steps in to prevent him from marrying below his class, and breaks up the relationship. In the end, however, the couple are reunited when the fellow prevents the cabaret's sleazy owner from forcing himself upon the singer.

d, Douglas Gerrard; w, Rex Taylor or Fred Myton (based on a story by Hope Loring); ph, Victor Milner.

Drama **(PR:A MPAA:NR)**

CABINET OF DR. CALIGARI, THE***

(1921, Ger.) 5 reels Decla-Bioscop/Goldwyn bw (DAS CABINETT DES DR. CALIGARI)

Werner Krauss *(Dr. Caligari)*, Conrad Veidt *(Cesare)*, Friedrich Feher *(Francis)*, Lil Dagover *(Jane)*, Hans Heinz von Twardowski *(Alan)*, Rudolf Lettinger *(Dr. Olson)*, Rudolph Klein-Rogge *(A Criminal)*.

One of the landmark films in the history of the cinema, THE CABINET OF DR. CALIGARI was one of the first self-conscious works of film as "art" and had a profound and lasting impact on the world's creative community. The film opens as two pale-faced men dressed in black, one young, the other older, sit on a park bench exchanging stories. The younger man, Feher, begins to tell a fantastic tale of horror. We are then transported to the town of Holstenwall, a bizzare-looking community filled with jagged roads and buildings with pointed rooftops that look as if they are about to engulf their residents. Into the community walks Krauss, a sinister-looking man dressed in a black cloak and top hat. He ventures to the city hall where he seeks to buy a permit for his carnival exhibit. When asked what he exhibits, Krauss replies that he is the caretaker of a somnambulist. Despite the barely restrained laughter of the city bureaucrats, the permit is granted. That night the town clerk of Holstenwall is stabbed to death in his bed by person or persons unknown. Meanwhile, Feher describes how he and his best friend, Twardowski, were in competition over the romantic affections of Dagover. Looking to have some fun, the young men visit the mysterious carnival and the recently added attraction catches their attention. Krauss ushers the crowd inside his tent to show them Cesare the somnambulist (Veidt), a man whose eternal sleep can only be interrupted by his caretaker's command. He steps over to a coffin-like box and opens it. Inside is Veidt, an extremely pale man dressed in a black leotard who seems to be asleep. Upon Krauss' command, Veidt's dark eyes blink open and he steps out of his "coffin." The crowd is taken aback by Veidt's forebidding appearance and they regard him cautiously. Krauss claims that Veidt is capable of predicting the future and asks for a volunteer to ask the sleeper a question. Twardowski immediately asks Veidt, "How long have I to live?" Without hesitation Veidt replies, "Until dawn." Shaken, Twardowski and Feher leave the carnival and meet Dagover to walk her home. Later that night as Twardowski lies asleep, the shadow of a man with a long knife rises on the wall next to his bed. Twardowski awakes and makes a futile effort to defend himself before being murdered. The next morning a shocked and angry Feher vows to investigate the murder and suspects Krauss and his somnambulist are the culprits. Though the police are a bit dubious of Feher's accusations, they agree to look into the matter. That night another murder occurs, but before the killer can escape into the night, he is caught by the police. The next morning the newspapers claim the serial killings have been solved, but upon interrogation the murderer, Klein-Rogge, only admits to the killing of the previous night, claiming he thought the mysterious killer would be blamed. On her way to meet her father and Feher at the police station, Dagover stumbles across the tent of Krauss. Seeing the girl outside his door, Krauss brings her inside and slowly wins her confidence. He then leads her to Veidt's coffin and opens it. Scared, but fascinated, Dagover moves in to get a closer look at the sleeper when he suddenly snaps open his eyes and glares at her. Pure terror sweeps over the girl as she screams and runs. from the tent. After Twardowski's funeral Feher wanders over to Krauss' tent and peeks inside. There he sees Krauss asleep in a chair with Veidt laid out in his coffin nearby. Wanting to make sure that both will sleep through the night, Feher keeps watch. Later that evening we see Dagover asleep in her bed. Outside Veidt is walking stiffly down the crooked paths that lead to the house. His gaunt figure rises at her window and he climbs inside her room. The somnambulist approaches the bed and produces a long knife. As he is about to stab her, Veidt hesitates and stares at the girl's beautiful face. Overcome with emotion, the sleeper abandons his murderous mission. Suddenly, Dagover awakens and, on seeing Veidt towering over her, screams. The somnambulist grabs the terrified girl, who faints, and carries her off over the jagged rooftops and twisted roads. Back at the tent, however, Feher reconfirms that both Krauss and Veidt are still asleep and decides to go home. Meanwhile, some of the villagers have given chase to Veidt who has been making slow progress carrying Dagover. With the villagers gaining on him, Veidt drops the girl and stumbles off. Wandering away, the exhausted somnambulist finally collapses in a ditch and dies. The villagers take the hysterical Dagover home where she claims it was Veidt who kidnaped her. Feher states that this is impossible, but upon investigation it is learned that Krauss had placed a life-sized dummy of Veidt in the coffin. Krauss escapes the police and Feher chases him to an insane asylum where he loses the trail. Feher asks the attendants if a patient named Caligari is being held there, but he is referred to the head of the asylum. Feher enters the man's office and is horrified to find that the man in charge of the insane asylum is none other than Krauss. Feher leaves the office and eventually manages to convince some of the other doctors that his tale is true. That night, while Krauss sleeps, the men search his office for clues and discover a journal in which Krauss details his evil plan. Having become obsessed with the work of a mystic named Caligari, Krauss became determined to prove that a somnambulist's mind could be controlled by others. When a somnambulistic patient is brought into the asylum, Krauss decides to fulfill his destiny and become Caligari. Feher and the doctor's reading is interrupted by a villager who announces that they've found Veidt's body in a ditch. Feher and the doctors go to the site and the next morning they confront Krauss with the corpse. Upon seeing Veidt, Krauss' veneer crumbles and he sobs with grief over the body. Suddenly Krauss' sadness turns to insane rage and he attacks the group. Three men force Krauss into a straightjacket and cart him off to a cell. We are then taken back to the opening shot of the film as Feher finishes telling his story to the old man. We then see that the bench they are sitting on is located in the courtyard of the insane asylum. Dagover sits staring into space and Veidt can be seen walking amongst the other insane, gently stroking the petals of a flower he holds in his hand. From under the arches steps Krauss, the director of the asylum. When Feher spots the man he becomes violent and tries to lunge at him screaming, "He is Caligari!" The attendants surround Feher and he is soon straightjacketed and placed in a cell. Krauss follows them and upon examining Feher declares, "At last I understand the nature of his madness. He thinks I am that mystic Caligari. Now I see how he can be brought back to sanity again." And with that chilling, somewhat ambiguous, coda, the film ends. In an age where most films were based on existing novels or legends, THE CABINET OF DR. CALIGARI was written specifically for the screen by Hans Janowitz and Carl Mayer. Janowitz was inspired by the real-life unsolved murder of a girl during a carnival and brought the story to his friend Mayer's attention. Mayer, who had had some deeply disturbing experiences with psychologists while a soldier during WW I, integrated this aspect of his life into the story and together the men wrote a bleak, pessimistic view of post-war German society which was extremely distrustful of authority. The men then approached producer Erich Pommer with their idea and suggested that settings for the film be bizarre painted canvases. Intrigued by the idea and happy to save money by painting the film's sets and shadows, Pommer bought the script and assigned it to director Fritz Lang. Lang, however, was too busy to take on the project, so it was transferred to Robert Wiene. Wiene liked the idea and hired Expressionistic designers Hermann Warm, Walter Rohrig, and Walter Reimann, all affiliated with the magazine *Sturm*, to design the sets. Distorted perspectives, twisted shapes, sharp angles, and a conscious avoidance of verticals and horizontals make up the look of both the exterior and interior sets. Not only were the settings of the film painted in the angular and bizarre style of Expressionism, but the costumes, furniture, and even the performances of the actors where integrated into the whole. Krauss and Veidt each move as if they belong in this strange world. Veidt moves slowly, almost gliding along the walls, while Krauss is hunched over and moves in sharp steps accentuated by the use of a cane. While writers Mayer and Janowitz were quite pleased with the look of the film, some reports state that they were extremely unhappy when their script was tampered with. According to some sources, their draft of the film is portrayed as reality, not the ramblings of an insane mind. Only after the film had gone into production was the framing story added to make it appear that the whole film was the product of a sick mind, much to the dismay of its authors. This move made their film "safe" by taking the edge off the material. The audience is allowed to escape this insane world because in the end it turns out to be the harmless vision of a madman, not a nightmarish reality. Despite the misgivings of Mayer and Janowitz, the film does end on a disturbing note. The final shot of Krauss' face is very ambiguous and is open to interpretation. Perhaps Ferher was right after all, and Krauss is Caligari. THE CABINET OF DR. CALIGARI exploded onto the art world with shocking impact. The film was the first motion picture that tried to expand the cinema beyond its obsession with the re-creation of reality that had dominated the movies since its invention. Whereas most films tried desperately to look realistic, THE CABINET OF DR. CALIGARI went boldly ahead and purposely tried to look as alien and unreal as possible. The film's unique vision provided the spark needed to expand the Expressionist movement in Germany and the new art school spread into every medium. German music, theater, painting, posters, literature, architecture all were inspired by CALIGARI. The film also propelled the German cinema to world prominence. Ignored by most of Europe since the war, German films had trouble being distributed outside that country's borders. When CALIGARI was released, French film enthusiasts acquired prints of the film and held secret screenings. Eventually the demand for the film was such thatthe French government finally lifted its ban on German films and CALIGARI was the first to be shown. As it had in Germany, the film greatly influenced the French artistic community and provided direct inspiration for the avant-garde film movement. In addition to providing artistic inspiration throughout the world, CALIGARI was also one of the very first horror films and set some plot conventions that would be used and reused for decades. The evil doctor who commits murder through a "monster" whose will he controls, the mysterious carnival that invades a town to cause terror, the ultimately sympathetic monster who falls in love with a beautiful girl, and of course, angry villagers giving chase to the monster, were all used regularly in every horror film since, especially the FRANKENSTEIN series. Though its influence was felt throughout the world, THE CABINET OF DR. CALIGARI had no successful imitators (director Wiene tried to repeat his success but failed miserably) and it remains a unique phenomenon in the history of motion pictures.

p, Erich Pommer; d, Robert Wiene; w, Carl Mayer, Hans Janowitz; ph, Willy Hameister; art d, Hermann Warm, Walter Reimann, Walter Rohrig; cos, Reimann.

Horror **Cas.** **(PR:A MPAA:NR)**

CABIRIA*1/2** (1914, Ital.) 12 reels Itala Film bw

Lidia Quaranta *(Cabiria)*, Umberto Mozzato *(Fulvio Axilla)*, Bartolomeo Pagano *(Maciste)*, Enrico Gemelli *(Archimedes)*, Luigi Chellini *(Scipio Africanus Major)*, Italia Almirante Manzini *(Sophonisba)*, Alex Bernard, Vitale De Stefano *(Massinissa)*, Antonio Branioni *(Bodasforet)*.

Fosco, using the pseudonym Giovanni Pastrone, began this massive 12-reel motion picture, about the war between Carthage and Rome, in 1912, and a young girl of wealthy parents who is kidnaped by pirates during the hostilities and is saved by a slave friend. It was the first film to cost more than $1 million, and its sequences—which included the Battle of Syracuse, the sacrifice of the children to Baal, the burning of the Roman Fleet (through the use of mirrors) by Archimedes, and Hannibal's crossing the Alps with his army of elephants—were impressive in scale and execution. But it was the director's brilliant use of elaborate tracking and dolly shots—a revolutionary concept at the time—and his very often powerful closeups, such as the outstretched hand of a priest during a sacrifice, which really fascinates today. CABIRIA was re-released with a sound track in 1932. Fosco, although not advancing the telling of a story via a treatment on the screen, nevertheless, did so many pioneer achievements with his directing and camera and settings that D.W. Griffith found it a major source of inspiration during his filming of INTOLERANCE. The film's grand manner is even carried over to the subtitles, which are highly poeticized to harmonize with the powerful images the screen is showing. A rich filmic experience throughout, even today.

d, Giovanni Pastrone [Piero Fosco]; w, Pastrone, Gabriele D'Annunzio (based in part on the book by Titus Livus); ph, Segundo de Chomon, Giovanni Tomatis, Augusto Battagliotti, Natale Chiusano; m, Ildebrando Pizzeti.

Historical **Cas.** **(PR:G MPAA:NR)**

CALIFORNIA*** (1927) 5 reels MGM bw

Tim McCoy *(Capt. Archibald Gillespie)*, Dorothy Sebastian *(Carlotta del Rey)*, Fred Warren *(Kit Carson)*, Lillian Leighton *(Duenna)*, Edwin Terry *(Brig. Gen. Stephen W. Kearny)*, Frank Currier *(Don Carlos del Rey)*.

McCoy was hired by MGM to fill a void in their western department and made a series of good action pictures. In this one, he plays an American Army officer who battles the Mexican (not identified as such in the titles) bad men, and wins the heart of their most beautiful senorita, in the days before California was yet a state.

d, W.S. Van Dyke; w, Frank Davis (based on a story by Peter B. Kyne); t, Marian Ainslee, Ruth Cummings; ph, Clyde De Vinna; ed, Basil Wrangell; set d, Eddie Imazu.

Western **(PR:A MPAA:NR)**

CALIFORNIA OR BUST*** (1927) 5 reels FBO bw

George O'Hara *(Jeff Daggett)*, Helen Foster *(Nadine Holtwood)*, John Steppling *(President Holtwood)*, Johnny Fox *(Mechanic)*, Irving Bacon *(Wade Rexton)*.

Tinkerer O'Hara lets his small-town garage go to the dogs as he works to perfect his invention, a new type of automobile engine. When motoring magnate Steppling passes through town with his lovely daughter Foster, his car breaks down near the garage. This gives O'Hara a chance to explain the advantages of his new design. Steppling sends for his chief engineer Bacon who, upon arriving, senses a rival in O'Hara for the affections of Foster. Bacon disparages O'Hara's design and challenges him to a race. As preparations start, a thief steals Bacon's motorcar. The others set out in pursuit—using O'Hara's marvelous motor—and catch the rascal after an exciting chase. The inventor gets a job and the girl as a result of his successful speeding. Anomalously pedestrian for an auto-chase picture.

d, Phil Rosen; w, Byron Morgan; t, Al Boasberg; ph, H. Lyman Broening.

Comedy **(PR:A MPAA:NR)**

CALIFORNIA ROMANCE, A*** (1922) 4 reels FOX bw

John Gilbert *(Don Patricio Fernando)*, Estelle Taylor *(Dolores)*, George Siegmann *(Don Juan Diego)*, Jack McDonald *(Don Manuel Casca)*, Charles Anderson *(Steve)*.

Funny romantic adventure film, in which Gilbert, with the help of the U.S. Cavalry, saves a California town from a band of desperadoes, in the days before statehood. Gilbert is all for federation—both with the U.S. and with fiery beauty Taylor—but the latter is a separatist on both counts, making for some entertaining moments.

d, Jerome Storm; w, Charles E. Banks (based on a story by Jules G. Furthman); ph, Joseph August.

Satire **(PR:A MPAA:NR)**

CALL FROM THE WILD, THE (1921) 5 Reels PFC bw

Wharton James *(The Man)*, Frankie James *(The Boy)*, Highland Laddie *(The Dog)*.

A man about to pull up stakes and move from his wilderness home plans to shoot his dog. James the younger rescues the mutt from its fate; the collie then joins aband of wolves and roves the wilderness with them. Local residents come to believe the beast to be the notorious "killer wolf" and try to hunt it down. Pressed into service as a hunter, the boy—now a man—finds the dog he had befriended caught in a trap. He frees his canine friend and the two renew their acquaintance. Later, the pooch returns the favor, seeking help when its human friend is hurt. The independent producer wisely chose to title the picture in such a way that it was bound to be confused with Jack London's famous novel *The Call of the Wild*.

p,d&w, Wharton James; ph, Floyd Jackman.

Adventure **(PR:A MPAA:NR)**

CALL OF THE EAST, THE** (1922, Brit.) 5 reels IA/Curry bw

Doris Eaton *(Mrs. Burleigh)*, Warwick Ward *(Arthur Burleigh)*, Walter Tennyson *(Jack Verity)*.

In this British drama, Tennyson runs into his old friend Ward in Egypt and discovers that Ward suffered a hunting accident which renders him temporarily insane on occasion. Tennyson, in return, confesses that some time back he had a love affair with a married woman. Of course, it turns out that she is the wife of his friend and that the passion is still there. When Ward becomes wise to the situation, he attempts to kill her but, on failing, wanders off into the desert where he conveniently dies in a sandstorm, leaving the lovers to themselves.

p,d&w, Bert Wynne (based on the novel by Esther Whitehouse).

Drama **(PR:C MPAA:NR)**

CALL OF THE NORTH, THE*** (1914) 5 reels LAS bw

Robert Edeson *(Graehme [in Prologue]/Ned Stewart, the Son)*, Theodore Roberts *(Galen Albert, the Factor)*, Winifred Kingston *(Virginia, Factor's Daughter)*, Horace B. Carpenter *(Rand)*, Florence Dagmar *(Elodie)*, Vera McGarry *(Julie)*, Milton Brown *(Me-en-gan)*, Jode Mullaly *(Picard)*, Sidney Deane *(MacTavish)*, Fred Montague *(Jock Wilson)*.

In a dual role, Edeson plays both father and son in the northern wilderness. Edeson the younger, a trader unconnected with the all-powerful Hudson Bay Company, seeks the persons responsible for killing his father after unjustly accusing him of seducing trading-post owner Roberts' wife. Caught by company minions, Edeson is sent on "La Longue Traverse," a solo journey through the wilderness without food or weapons. After many trials and tribulations, he is saved with the help of Kingston, daughter of the very man who wronged his father. On his deathbed, Roberts—seeking absolution—confesses his crimes, ending the younger Edeson's grim search. This is the great director DeMille's second directorial effort (his first was THE SQUAW MAN in the same year), and the first in which he receives solo directorial credit. His partner, Samuel Goldfish (later Goldwyn), was overjoyed with the picture's New York reception, and cabled star Edeson: "PICTURE IS GREATEST EVER." Edeson, who had starred in the stage play, had been eagerly sought for the film role. His contract with the studio was remarkable; it gave the actor control over such things as locations and minor-role casting. Edeson had specified that real Canadian locations and real Canadian Indians be used. In fact, the realities of time and budget prevailed; the picture was made in the high country near Big Bear Lake in California during the summer. Temperatures soared over the 100-degree mark and the actors worked standing in salt, a standard substitute for snow at the time. In their arctic clothing, the cast suffered terribly. This is DeMille's first collaboration with talented cinematographer Wyckoff, with whom he was to make many of his most celebrated films.

d&w, Cecil B. DeMille (based on the novel *Conjuror's House* by Stewart Edward White and the play by George Broadhurst); ph, Alvin Wyckoff; ed, Mamie Wagner.

Adventure **(PR:A MPAA:NR)**

CALL OF THE WILD, THE* (1923) 7 reels HR/Pathe bw

Jack Mulhall *(John Thornton)*, Walter Long *(Hagin)*, Sidney D'Albrook *(Charles)*, Laura Roessing *(Mercedes, Charles' Wife)*, Frank Butler *(Hal)*, Buck The Dog.

Stolen from its English home, a young Saint Bernard dog is taken to Canada to serve as a sled dog. The cruelly mistreated mutt meets Mulhall, who rescues the canine from its venomous master. The dog repays the favor when Mulhall gets into trouble. Cinematographer Jackman, noted for his work with animals, had shot the similarly titled THE CALL FROM THE WILD two years earlier. This pale film version of London's novel of the North was noteworthy only for the tricks performed by Buck the Saint Bernard.

d&w, Fred Jackman; (based on the novel by Jack London); ph, Floyd Jackman.

Adventure **(PR:A MPAA:NR)**

CALL OF YOUTH, THE*

(1920, Brit.) 4 reels FP-LAS-British Producers/PAR bw

Mary Glynne *(Betty Overton)*, Ben Webster *(Mark Lawton)*, Jack Hobbs *(Hubert Richmond)*, Marjorie Hume *(Joan Lawton)*, Malcolm Cherry *(James Agar)*, Gertrude Sterroll *(Mrs. Lawton)*, Victor Humphrey *(Peter Hoskins)*, John Peachey *(Dr. Michaelson)*, Ralph Foster *(Minister)*.

Slow-moving British film about a family in financial trouble who are assisted by a millionaire attracted to their daughter. She, of course, loves another and when the benefactor becomes aware of this, he arranges to have the young man sent off to the darkest region of Africa. The film concludes with the millionaire going to retrieve his rival, once he realizes that he has no chance of winning the girl.

d, Hugh Ford; w, Eve Unsell (based on the play "James, the Fogy" by Henry Arthur Jones).

Drama **(PR:A MPAA:NR)**

CALLAHANS AND THE MURPHYS, THE***　(1927) 7 reels MGM bw

Marie Dressler *(Mrs. Callahan)*, Polly Moran *(Mrs. Murphy)*, Sally O'Neil *(Eileen Callahan)*, Lawrence Gray *(Dan Murphy)*, Frank Currier *(Grandpa Callahan)*, Gertrude Olmsted *(Monica Murphy)*, Eddie Gribbon *(Jim Callahan)*, Turner Savage *(Timmy Callahan)*, Jackie Coombs *(Terrence Callahan)*, Dawn O'Day *(Mary Callahan)*, Monty O'Grady *(Michael Callahan)*, Tom Lewis *(Mr. Murphy)*.

Tenement dwellers Dressler and Murphy argue across the alley separating their buildings, while two of the multitudinous brood of children, O'Neil and Gray, quietly fall in love. Gray gets involved with gangsters and disappears, leaving O'Neil pregnant. Dressler, already blessed with sufficient fecundity, offers to save the situation by adopting her daughter's child. Gray returns, and he and O'Neil announce that they were married on the sly. The couple's two gregarious mothers return to their friendly fighting, this time over the new arrival. An ethnic comedy that works, due to an understated script, good direction, and the inspired casting of Dressler and Moran. The ladies are perfection as the battling Irish matrons and, although stereotypical situations abound they never offend.

d, George Hill; w, Frances Marion (based on the novel *The Callahans and the Murphys* by Kathleen Norris); t, Ralph Spence; ph, Ira Morgan; ed, Hugh Wynn; set d, Cedric Gibbons, David Townsend.

Comedy　(PR:A MPAA:NR)

CAMERAMAN, THE****　(1928) 8 reels MGM bw

Buster Keaton *(Luke Shannon)*, Marceline Day *(Sally)*, Harold Goodwin *(Stagg)*, Harry Gribbon *(Cop)*, Sidney Bracy *(Editor)*, Edward Brophy *(Man in Dressing Room)*, Vernon Dent *(Man in Bathing Suit)*, William Irving *(Photographer)*.

Keaton, a tintype portraitist, is much taken by the delightful Day, a secretary for a newsreel company. Trading in his tintype camera for a movie camera, he sets out to prove to her company that he can be a valuable asset to them. His misguided cinematic efforts result in marvelously silly shots, the screened results showing double-exposed battleships gliding majestically up the Great White Way, among other things. A date with Day at a swimming pool is a confused disaster, ending with the damsel departing with Keaton's rival, ace newsreel cameraman Goodwin. Undaunted, the tenacious tyro tries again to prove his worth in his rival's game. Tipped off to a tong war by Day, he enhances the activities of the orientals by tossing bomb-simulating light bulbs while he furiously cranks the camera; when two opposing Chinese grapple, he places a knife in the hand of one for a close-up. Next, filming a regatta—attended also by rival Goodwin, accompanied by Day—he leaves his camera unattended on the shore to rescue his love when she falls into the water. Departing to fetch medical assistance, Keaton returns to find the lady recovering in the arms of Goodwin, who claims credit for her salvation. Defeated at last (in a truly touching scene, Keaton sinks to his knees, alone on the beach), the failed photographer turns back to his tintyping. However, two reels of his film have mysteriously turned up at the newsreel company (we discover in flashback that an organ grinder's mischievous monkey had substituted one reel for another at the site of the tong war, and had—habituated to cranking the handle of his master's street organ—operated the movie camera when Keaton effected the rescue). The resulting footage is wonderful, proving Keaton's bravery, and Keaton wins the girl—and a job—after all. The picture concludes with Keaton and Day walking down a boulevard, she assuring him that people truly think well of him. Suddenly, windows on both sides open; confetti and ticker tape shower down upon the surprised couple. Convinced at last of the adulation of his adoring public, Keaton strides happily along the avenue, unaware that Charles Lindbergh—just returned from his famous flight—is in an open touring car behind him. MGM moguls thrust this story on Keaton, after rejecting several of his own proposals, because they wanted to please William Randolph Hearst (whose Hearst International Newsreel organization was the pivot around which the picture swirled), hoping for a good press in the Hearst newspapers (the newspaper tycoon was also an MGM stockholder). The picture did very well at the box office, outgrossing even Keaton's best United Artists releases. This was Buster Keaton's first film after his brother-in-law, Joseph Schenck, talked him out of independent production and into becoming an MGM star. Charles Chaplin was right when he urged the comedian not to surrender his autonomy because ultimately art *would* be sacrificed for commerce. But that sad event remained several movies away, because here, Buster had a talented and sympathetic director in Edward Sedgwick (a fellow child vaudevillian) who wisely allowed the great "Stone Face" to create much of the film's comedic business. Consequently, this story about a tintype photographer who becomes a newsreel man for the sake of a girl provided one of the world's greatest funny men with one last chance to really shine. It would take a couple of years before the calculating moguls in Culver City would set out—quite deliberately, and all too cruelly—to snuff out his unique and glorious light, but they did—making the world a darker place ever since.

d, Edward Sedgwick; w, Richard Schayer (based on a story by Clyde Bruckman, Lew Lipton); t, Joseph Farnham; ph, Elgin Lessley, Reggie Lanning; ed, Hugh Wynn or Basil Wrangell.

Comedy　(PR:A MPAA:NR)

CAMILLE***　(1927) 9 reels Norma Talmadge Productions/FN-WB bw

Norma Talmadge *(Camille [Marguerite Gautier])*, Gilbert Roland *(Armand)*, Lilyan Tashman *(Olympe)*, Maurice Costello *(Monsieur Duval)*, Harvey Clark *(The Baron)*, Alec B. Francis *(The Duke)*, Rose Dione *(Prudence)*, Oscar Beregi *(Count de Varville)*, Helen Jerome Eddy *(Camille's Maid)*, Albert Conti *(Henri)*, Michael Visaroff *(Camille's Father)*, Evelyn Selbie *(Camille's Mother)*, Etta Lee *(Mataloti)*.

The sorrowful Roland attends an auction, purchasing a portrait of a beautiful woman and her diary, as well. The shade of the subject of the portrait comes to his side, opens the diary, and commands him to read. The rest of Dumas' famous tragedy is told in flashback, recounting the rise of humble shopgirl Talmadge to the rank of the most sought-after courtesan of all Paris. Meeting young student Roland, the now-consumptive Talmadge falls in love with him but rejects him for his own good at the urging of his father, Costello. Talmadge had just separated from her husband, influential Hollywood mogul Joseph Schenck (who was responsible for establishing her independent production company), but their professional association continued. This role was actor Roland's big break, the film that firmly established him as a star. This was the sixth filming of the Dumas tragedy about the 19th-Century fallen woman dying of tuberculosis. It had been made in 1912 with Sarah Bernhardt, 1915 with Clara Kimball Young, 1917 with Theda Bara, 1920 with Nazimova, 1920 with Pola Negri, and it would be filmed again with Greta Garbo in 1936.

d, Fred Niblo; w, Olga Printzlau, Chandler Sprague, Fred De Gresac (based on the novel *La Dame aux Camelias* by Alexandre Dumas the younger); t, George Marion, Jr.; ph, Oliver T. Marsh.

Drama　(PR:A MPAA:NR)

CAMPBELLS ARE COMING, THE***　(1915) 4 reels UNIV bw

Francis Ford, Grace Cunard, Mr. Denecke, Lew Short, Harry Schumm, Duke Worne, Eddie Polo, Mark Fenton, Jack Holt.

Exciting action feature about the Sepoy uprising of 1857, in which a Scottish regiment saved an English garrison. The marvelously realistic battle scenes were directed by Ford, some two years before his younger brother, John, shot his first foot of film.

d, Francis Ford; w, Grace Cunard (based on a story by Emerson Hough).

Historical　(PR:A MPAA:NR)

CAMPUS FLIRT, THE***　(1926) 7 reels FP-LAS/PAR bw

Bebe Daniels *(Patricia Mansfield)*, James Hall *(Denis Adams)*, El Brendel *(Knute Knudson)*, Charlie Paddock *(Himself)*, Joan Standing *(Harriet Porter)*, Gilbert Roland *(Graham Stearns)*, Irma Kornelia *(Mae)*, Jocelyn Lee *(Gwen)*.

Another college film, but with girls this time. Daniels is outstanding as the spoiled, European-educated daughter of a social climbing mother who is finally sent to an American college by her level-headed father. At first her snobbish ways are met with hostility by her classmates, but when she joins the track team and excels, all of that changes. Paddock, one of the greatest runners of his day, played the part of the team's coach. Location shots were filmed at the University of Southern California. This was character actor Brendel's first feature film; strangely, he played the part of a Swede even in silents, where his famed expression "Yumpin' Yiminy" went unheard.

d, Clarence Badger; w, Louise Long, Lloyd Corrigan; t, Ralph Spence, Rube Goldberg; ph, H. Kinley Martin.

Comedy　(PR:A MPAA:NR)

CAMPUS KNIGHTS*　(1929) 6 reels CHES bw

Raymond McKee *(Prof. Ezra Hastings/Earl Hastings)*, Shirley Palmer *(Audrey Scott)*, Marie Quillen *(Edna)*, Jean Laverty *(Pearl)*, J. C. Fowler *(Dean Whitlock)*, Sybil Grove *(The Matron)*, P. J. Danby *(The Janitor)*, Leo White *(Pearl's Lawyer)*, Lewis Sargent *(The Sport)*.

McKee plays a double role in this dated (even for the time) college comedy about a sappy professor and his girl-chasing twin brother.

d, Albert Kelly; sup, Lon Young; w, Arthur Hoerl, Kelly; t, Lee Authmar, Hoey Lawlor, Young; ph, M. A. Anderson; ed, Earl Turner, James Sweeney.

Comedy　(PR:A MPAA:NR)

CAP'N ABE'S NIECE　(SEE: CAPTAIN'S CAPTAIN, THE, 1919)

CAPPY RICKS*　(1921) 6 reels FP/PAR bw

Thomas Meighan *(Matt Peasley)*, Charles Abbe *(Cappy Ricks)*, Agnes Ayres *(Florrie Ricks)*, Hugh Cameron *(Murphy)*, John Sainpolis *(Skinner)*, Paul Everton *(Capt. Kendall)*, Eugenia Woodward *(Mrs. Peasley)*, Tom O'Malley *(Capt. Jones)*, Ivan Linow *(Ole Peterson)*, William Wally *(Swenson)*, Jack Dillon *(Larsen)*, Gladys Granger *(Doris)*.

When the ship's captain dies, first mate Meighan takes over. After the boat docks, its owner, Abbe, puts another in charge and there is a fight between the newcomer and Meighan, who elects to deliver the ship to San Francisco himself. This so infuriates Abbe, who is also angered because his daughter is in love with the disobedient sailor, that he drags her along on a long ocean voyage. Then, as fate would have it, their ship crashes on the rocks with the hero arriving in time to save the day.

d, Tom Forman; w, Albert Shelby Le Vino, Waldemar Young (based on the novel by Peter B. Kyne and the play by Edward E. Rose); ph, Harry Perry.

Drama　(PR:A MPAA:NR)

CAPRICE OF THE MOUNTAINS**　(1916) 5 reels FOX bw

June Caprice *(Caprice Talbert)*, Harry S. Hilliard *(Jack Edmunds)*, Joel Day *(Dave Talbert)*, Lisle Leigh *(Maria Baker)*, Richard Hale *(Tim Baker)*, Albert Gran *(James Edmunds)*, Tom Burrough *(Tom Edmunds)*, Robert D. Walker *(Dick Deane)*, Sara Alexander *(Caprice's Aunt)*, Harriet Thompson *(Fairy Queen)*, Sidney Bracy, Robert Vivian, Zena Keefe, Lucia Moore, Genevieve Reynolds, Grace Beaumont, Leo Kennedy.

In an attempt to develop a Mary Pickford of his own, William Fox searched through his roster of female players and selected a 17-year-old girl. He named her June Caprice and featured her in a series of films blatantly imitating "America's Sweetheart." The experiment did not work, which is evident by the fact that Caprice is not exactly a household word—although this film about a love-smitten mountain girl wasn't bad.

d, John G. Adolfi; w, Clarence J. Harris.

Drama **(PR:A MPAA:NR)**

CAPRICES OF KITTY, THE*** (1915) 5 reels Bosworth bw

Elsie Janis *(Kitty Bradley)*, Courtenay Foote *(Gerald Cameron)*, Herbert Standing *(The Guardian)*, Vera Lewis *(Miss Smythe)*, Martha Mattox *(Miss Rawlins)*, Myrtle Stedman *(Elaine Vernon)*.

In this film, Janis (one of America's best-loved stage performers, and a tireless entertainer of the troops during WW I) plays a boarding school student who sneaks out to take a spin in her new auto. When it breaks down, a young man driving by stops to assist her, and there is an immediate attraction between the two. They arrange to meet the next day, are discovered, and subsequently are ordered to report to her guardian. When the young man is recognized as being a famous painter, it is explained that there exists a provision of her inheritance that says she may not see her fiance (they told the old boy they were engaged in order to make things look better) for six months prior to her wedding, unless she is willing to surrender the inheritance. This provided Janis with the opportunity to put into play her theatrical specialty—assuming a number of different roles through the use of various costumes.

d, William Desmond Taylor; w, Elsie Janis.

Comedy/Drama **(PR:A MPAA:NR)**

CAPTAIN CARELESS** (1928) 5 reels FBO bw

Bob Steele *(Bob Gordon)*, Mary Mabery *(Ruth)*, Jack Donovan *(Ralph)*, Barney Furey *(Medicine Man)*, Perry Murdock *(Perry)*, Wilfred North *(John Forsythe)*.

A girl (Mabery) is shipwrecked but makes it to an island infested by cannibals. The young man who loves her (Steele), upon hearing the news, flies to her aid and after a series of adventures, makes the rescue.

d, Jerome Storm; w, Perry Murdock. Frank Howard Clark (based on a story by Bob Steele); t, Randolph Bartlett; ph, Virgil Miller; ed, Jack Kitchen.

Adventure **(PR:A MPAA:NR)**

CAPTAIN COURTESY*** (1915) 5 reels Bosworth bw

Dustin Farnum *(Capt. Courtesy)*, Herbert Standing *(Father Reinaldo)*, Winifred Kingston *(Eleanor)*, Courtenay Foote *(Granville)*, Carl von Schiller *(Jocoso)*, Winona Brown *(Indian Girl)*.

The story takes place during the days when California was under Mexican rule. Farnum's parents (who were among the first American settlers) are murdered by wealthy Mexican landowners. He vows revenge, and gets it in the disguise of "Captain Courtesy." In the end, he not only sets everything right, but wins the most beautiful girl in the province as well.

d, Hobart Bosworth; w, Edward Childs Carpenter.

Western **(PR:A MPAA:NR)**

CAPTAIN DIEPPE (SEE: ADVENTURE IN HEARTS, AN, 1919)

CAPTAIN JANUARY*** (1924) 6 reels SL/Principal bw

Baby Peggy *(Captain January)*, Hobart Bosworth *(Jeremiah Judkins)*, Irene Rich *(Isabelle Morton)*, Harry T. Morey *(George Maxwell)*, Lincoln Stedman *(Bob Pete)*, John Merkyl *(Herbert Morton)*, Emmett King *(John Elliot)*, Barbara Tennant *(Lucy Tripp)*.

Sentimental heart tugger (later remade with Shirley Temple) about an old lighthouse keeper who finds a lost child (popular Baby Peggy) and raises her as his own. After five years, a nautical accident brings the child's uncle and aunt into the picture, and when the aunt recognizes the girl as being the daughter of her dead sister, she separates the two. Of course they are later reunited, providing an appropriately happy ending.

d, Edward F. Cline; w, Eve Unsell, John Grey (based on the novel by Laura Elizabeth Richards); t, William J. Sackheim; ph, Glen MacWilliams.

Drama **(PR:A MPAA:NR)**

CAPTAIN LASH*** (1929) 6 reels FOX bw

Victor McLaglen *(Captain Lash)*, Claire Windsor *(Cora Nevins)*, Arthur Stone *(Gentleman Eddie)*, Albert Conti *(Alex Condax)*, Clyde Cook *(Cocky)*, Jean Laverty *(Queenie)*, Frank Hagney *(Bull Hawks)*, Boris Charsky *(Condax's Servant)*, Jane Winton *(Babe)*.

McLaglen saves svelte society type Windsor from a scalding in the stokehole of a ship, and she rewards him by having him smuggle some stolen gems ashore. His pal Cook substitutes coal for the stones, getting McLaglen in serious trouble with Windsor's confederates. It's nothing the big bruiser can't handle, though, as he singlehandedly mauls the entire mob. The crooks are apprehended and the gems are returned to their rightful owner. McLaglen is the king of the ocean-sailing stokers—a giant of a man who loves 'em and leaves 'em, in this film loaded with action and oriental atmosphere. Cook is a comic stand-out as the captain's little concertina-playing pal.

d, John Blystone; w, John Stone, Daniel G. Tomlinson (based on a story by Laura Hasse, Tomlinson); t, Malcolm Stuart Boylan; ph, Conrad Wells; ed, James K. McGuinness; syn sc, s eff.

Drama **(PR:A MPAA:NR)**

CAPTAIN OF THE GRAY HORSE TROOP, THE*** (1917) 5 reels VIT bw

Antonio Moreno *(Capt. George Curtis)*, Mrs. Bradbury *(Jennie)*, Otto Lederer *(Crawling Elk)*, Al Jennings *(Cut Finger)*, Robert Burns *(Cal Streeter)*, Edith Storey *(Elsie)*, H. A. Barrows, Edward Cecil, Neola May.

A western with a conscience, which portrayed Indians as the victims of greedy white ranchers out to use Washington "red tape" to steal their land. Plenty of action in this horse opera which came closer to the truth than most.

d, William Wolbert; w, A. Van Buren (based on a novel by Hamlin Garland).

Western **(PR:A MPAA:NR)**

CAPTAIN SALVATION**** (1927) 8 reels COS/MGM bw

Lars Hanson *(Anson Campbell)*, Marceline Day *(Mary Phillips)*, Pauline Starke *(Bess Morgan)*, Ernest Torrence *(The Captain)*, George Fawcett *(Zeke Crosby)*, Sam De Grasse *(Peter Campbell)*, Jay Hunt *(Nathan Phillips)*, Eugenie Besserer *(Mrs. Buxom)*, Eugenie Forde *(Mrs. Bellows)*, Flora Finch *(Mrs. Snifty)*, James Marcus *(Old Salt)*.

Hanson, one of the screen's finest actors, was superb as the seminary graduate who returns to his 1840 New England fishing town, torn between pursuing a life at sea and a religious vocation. Once home, he befriends a fallen woman and incurs the wrath of the narrow-minded villagers. Disgusted by their intolerance, he ships out on what turns out to be a convict ship, as does the girl who has been cast out of the community. At sea, the captain (Torrence) tries to rape the girl, and Hanson comes to her defense. In the struggle she kills her attacker but soon dies herself. Her passing takes place in the hold of the ship, surrounded by the dregs of society. This experience so moves the young man that he decides to dedicate himself to his faith—sailing the seas as an evangelist.

d, John S. Robertson; w, Jack Cunningham (based on the novel by Frederick William Wallace); t, John Colton; ph, William Daniels; ed, William Hamilton; art d, Cedric Gibbons, Leo E. Kuter.

Drama **(PR:A MPAA:NR)**

CAPTAIN SWIFT* (1914) 5 reels Life Photofilm bw

David Wall *(Capt. Swift)*, George De Carlton *(George Gardner)*, William H. Tooker *(Butler)*, Frank B. Andrews *(James Seabrook)*, Harry Spingler *(Harry Seabrook)*, Thomas O'Keefe *(Detective)*, Iva Shepard *(Mrs. Seabrook)*, Maxine Brown *(Mabel, Her Daughter)*, Ethel Wayne *(Lady Stanton, Her Sister)*, Phillip Robson *(Sir James Stanton)*, Emily Loraine *(Mrs. Marshall)*.

Less-than-effective film about a bastard son who runs away to Australia, suffers great adversity, returns home to find his mother, and is shot by a group of men who do not realize his true identity.

d, Edgar Lewis; w, (based on a play by Haddon Chambers).

Drama **(PR:A MPAA:NR)**

CAPTAIN'S CAPTAIN, THE***
(1919) 5 reels VIT bw (AKA: CAP'N ABE'S NIECE)

Alice Joyce *(Louise Grevling)*, Arthur Donaldson *(Cap'n Abe)*, Percy Standing *(Cap'n Joab)*, Julia Swayne Gordon *(Aunt Euphemia)*, Eulalie Jensen *(Betty Gallup)*, Maurice Costello *(Lawford Tapp)*.

Donaldson is a storekeeper in a fishing town who bores everyone with his lies about his brother, who he claims is the world's greatest pirate. When his niece (who ran away from a very strict aunt) arrives, she decides that Donaldson needs a little excitement in his life and persuades him to impersonate his pirate kin. This he does and pulls off the stunt so well that a group of East Indians are convinced he is the buccaneer who, at one time, desecrated their temple. This leads to some real adventure, and Donaldson, with some help from his niece and her new-found beau, comes out on top.

d, Tom Terriss; w, Terris, A. Van Buren Powell (based on the novel *Cap'n Abe—Storekeeper* by James A. Cooper); ph, Joe Shelderfer.

Adventure **(PR:A MPAA:NR)**

CAPTAIN'S COURAGE, A* (1926) 6 reels Ben Wilson/RAY bw

Dorothy Dwan, Eddie Earl, Jack Henderson, Richard Holt, Lafe McKee, Al Ferguson.

A Ben Wilson cheapie which tells of the struggle between rival factions to possess an island in Lake Michigan. This film presented its audience with bad sets, bad costumes, bad direction, bad titles, bad acting, and Dorothy Dwan.

d, Louis Chaudet; w, George Pyper (based on a story by James Oliver Curwood).

Adventure **(PR:A MPAA:NR)**

CAPTIVE, THE*** (1915) 5 reels LAS/PAR bw

Blanche Sweet *(Sonya)*, House Peters *(Mahmud)*, Gerald Ward *(Milos)*, Page Peters *(Marko)*, Theodore Roberts *(Turkish Officer)*, Jeanie MacPherson, Billy Elmer, Marjorie Daw, Tex Driscoll.

During the Balkan War, a Turkish soldier (House Peters) is captured by Montenegrins and made the prisoner of Sweet to work in the fields left untended since her brother was killed in battle. After some time, her younger brother becomes fond of the captive, as does she. When the Turks retake the area, Peters saves Sweet from being raped by his fellow countrymen but is later stripped of his title and lands for doing so. The film ends with the two of them meeting again by accident—mutual victims, who now have only each other. This lovely little romance, with its exotic setting, was marred by a terrible tragedy. During a battle scene, soldiers were to fire their rifles into a door and then smash it open with their rifle butts. During the first take, one of the extra players—Bob Fleming, who ordinarily appeared in westerns—fell to the ground dead, a bullet in his brain. One of the rifles had a live round, although the players and property people claimed they had all been checked out and that all contained only blank cartridges. Responsibility for the "accident" was never assigned and the studio hushed up the incident as much as possible, keeping the dead player's widow on the payroll for a long time. THE CAPTIVE was the first film in which DeMille gave his stenographer Macpherson a co-writing credit. Macpherson was to become one of the great man's most important collaborators as well as the great love of his life.

d, Cecil B. DeMille; w, DeMille, Jeanie Macpherson; ph, Alvin Wyckoff; ed, DeMille.

Drama **(PR:A MPAA:NR)**

CAPTIVE GOD, THE**** (1916) 5 reels KB/TRI bw

William S. Hart *(Chiapa)*, Enid Markey *(Lolomi)*, P. D. Tabler *(Mexitili)*, Dorothy Dalton *(Tecolote)*, Robert McKim *(Montezuma)*, Dorcas Mathews *(Maya)*, Herbert Farjean *(Cacama)*, Robert Kortman *(Tuyos)*.

Set in Mexico during the 16th Century, this rather unusual William S. Hart opus tells the tale of a Spanish child who is washed up on the East coast of Mexico and raised by a tribe of peaceful cliff-dwelling Aztec Indians. After growing to manhood and becoming the leader of the tribe who took him in, Hart is captured by a warring tribe of Aztecs. During his captivity, McKim's daughter, Markey, falls in love with Hart. As he is of European descent, the Aztecs decide to sacrifice Hart to the gods, but Markey manages to alert the cliff-dwellers to his predicament and they rescue him after a ferocious battle. Hart's usual obsession with historical accuracy held true for this nonwestern film as well. Producer Thomas H. Ince allowed plenty of time and money to be spent on researching the life of the Aztecs, which resulted in the sculpture and set departments building an entire Aztec city based on actual carvings from the period. The epic quality of the film was evident on screen and the $50,000 production cost (more than twice what was spent on most Hart films) was justified by rave reviews and decent returns at the box office.

p, Thomas H. Ince; d, Charles Swickard; w, Monte J. Katterjohn; ph, Clyde De Vinna; art d, M. Doner.

Adventure **(PR:A MPAA:NR)**

CARDIGAN** (1922) 7 reels Messmore Kendall/ American Releasing bw

William Collier, Jr. *(Michael Cardigan)*, Betty Carpenter *(Silver Heels)*, Thomas Cummings *(Sir William Johnson)*, William Pike *(Capt. Butler)*, Charles E. Graham *(Lord Dunmore)*, Madeline Lubetty *(Marie Hamilton)*, Hatty Delaro *(Lady Shelton)*, Louis Dean *(Sir John Johnston)*, Colin Campbell *(The Weazel)*, Jere Austin *(Jack Mount)*, Frank R. Montgomery *(Chief Logan)*, Eleanor Griffith *(Dulcina)*, Dick Lee *(Quider)*, Jack Johnston *(Col. Cresap)*, Florence Short *(Molly Brandt)*, George Loeffler *(Patrick Henry)*, William Willis *(John Hancock)*, Austin Hume *(Paul Revere)*.

A love story involving rebels and royalists at the outset of the American Revolution, with young rebel colonist Collier, Jr. falling in love with Carpenter, daughter of the tory governor. Historical figures are woven into this drama, which includes the exciting warning ride of Paul Revere (Hume) and the battles of Lexington and Concord. Collier saves his sweetheart from the infamous Pike and the British are routed. Interesting mainly for the purpose of comparison with D. W. Griffith's AMERICA, released two years later, which treated the same material in far finer fashion.

d, John W. Noble; w, Robert W. Chambers (based on his novel); ph, John S. Stumar, Ned Van Buren, Max Schneider.

Historical/Drama **(PR:A MPAA:NR)**

CARMEN*** (1915) 5 reels LAS/FP bw

Geraldine Farrar *(Carmen)*, Wallace Reid *(Don Jose)*, Horace B. Carpenter *(Pastia, a Tavern-Keeper and Smuggler)*, Pedro De Cordoba *(Escamillo, the Toreador)*, Billy Elmer *(Morales, an Officer)*, Jeanie Macpherson, Anita King *(Gypsy Girls)*, Tex Driscoll, Milton A. Brown.

Carmen (Farrar), a worker in a cigarette factory, fights with jealous gypsy Macpherson and is remanded to the custody of handsome soldier Reid. Vamping Reid, she uses her feminine wiles to induce him to let her escape. Disgraced, Reid follows her to the gypsy smugglers' camp where she has found refuge. Farrar taunts Reid and leaves him for De Cordoba, a famous bullfighter. In a jealous rage, Reid stabs Farrar to death. This version of Merimee's famed novel—on which Georges Bizet's opera is based—began a long association between director DeMille and his star, Farrar, who tied with Gloria Swanson for the honor of starring in the greatest number of DeMille's films (six apiece). Studio chief Jesse L. Lasky scored a tremendous public relations coup in signing Farrar, the best-known American opera singer of her time, to play the leading part; her phonograph recording of Bizet's opera had sold a million copies. When Lasky informed the director of his plans, DeMille reportedly said: "Carmen? Without using her glorious voice?" The same sentiments were echoed by the press: "The Mona Lisa without her smile; a Stradivarius without its strings. . . ." Fortunately, the fair Farrar defied operatic convention; her beautiful face and tightly muscled, small body lent themselves perfectly to the part. In addition, she was a Hollywood *type*: flirtatious, adventurous, hedonistic, and fey, a jazz-loving, high-living natural. Lasky had offered her unheard-of terms: a royalty, a share of the profits, and two dollars for every minute she spent in Hollywood, whether on the set or not. Lasky had high hopes for the financial and artistic success of CARMEN and he quickly acceded to director DeMille's idea of a warmup project for her. DeMille reasoned that Farrar's stage mannerisms would probably have to be unlearned, necessitating many retakes. They decided to film MARIA ROSA first, using the same leading players, Farrar and Reid, but to release it after CARMEN. Farrar, nervous about the new medium, agreed to the plan. The studio accorded the diva every perquisite possible, including a two-story mansion replete with servitors, a chauffeured Hispano-Suiza limousine, a private railroad car, a pianist on the set, a bungalow with a grand piano at the studio, and a supply of handsome men. Farrar's costar, Reid, got his first leading role with her. A little-known stage actor, Reid was to star in seven DeMille films before his tragic drug-related death at the age of 30. DeMille cast his protege Macpherson—his mistress and, later, his chief screenwriter—as Farrar's gypsy rival knowing that Macpherson despised the star. The fight between the two women—the first such distaff battle in feature-film history—was considerably enhanced by this inspired casting. The wiry Macpherson went at it with a vengeance, but she emerged bruised and battered, no match for the well-muscled Farrar. The project had been threatened financially by representatives of composer Bizet, who had demanded that a huge royalty be paid for the right to screen his opera. DeMille and his writer brother, William, decided to fight if necessary, averring that they had as great a right to Merimee's novel as the operatic composer. Fearful of a lawsuit, DeMille abandoned his plan to have a pianist play selections from Bizet's opera during filming; Farrar had to content herself with other selections (she favored jazz). Rival producer William Fox had gotten wind of the production and, realizing that the warmup film would slow things down for DeMille, quickly launched his own production of the story. Released simultaneously, Fox's film—starring Theda Bara in the title role—was quickly withdrawn, no match for DeMille's detailed work. CARMEN was a cinematic benchmark of the silent screen; DeMille and cinematographer Wyckoff here established a visual style that the two were to use so effectively in many later pictures, that of extreme contrast, the commingling of highlights and deep shade. The effect may have been partly due to the director's special problems with illuminating star Farrar, whose gray eyes completely failed to register on the orthochromatic emulsions of the time under flat lighting. The star was reported to have shrieked and clawed at the screen when she saw herself pupil-less, like Little Orphan Annie during rushes. Of such strange things are cinematic styles developed.

p&d, Cecil B. DeMille; w, William C. DeMille (based on the novel by Prosper Mérimée); ph, Alvin Wyckoff; ed, C. B. DeMille.

Drama **(PR:A MPAA:NR)**

CARMEN OF THE KLONDIKE*** (1918) 7 reels Selexart bw

Clara Williams *(Dorothy Harlan)*, Herschell Mayall *("Silk" McDonald)*, Edward Coxen *(Cameron Stewart)*, Joseph J. Dowling, Jack Waltemeyer.

Intelligently filmed "great white North" movie about claim-jumping, leading logically to a sensational fight scene which left audiences limp. Photography of then "virgin" Alaska makes this one well worth viewing.

d, Reginald Barker; w, Monte M. Katterjohn.

Action **(PR:A MPAA:NR)**

CARNIVAL GIRL, THE** (1926) 5 reels AEX bw

Marion Mack *(Nanette)*, Gladys Brockwell *(Her Mother)*, Frankie Darro *(Her Brother)*, George Siegmann *(Sigmund)*, Allan Forrest *(Lt. Allan Dale)*, Jack Cooper *(Gunner Sgt. Riley)*, Victor Potel *("Slim")*, Max Asher *(The Barker)*.

Modest little film about carnival-wire walker Mack who is loved by a naval officer. The highlights of the picture were a burning ship sequence, as well as fine performances by Darro, as the kid, and Siegmann, as the heavy.

d, Cullen Tate; w, Raymond Cannon; t, Cannon, Robert Hopkins; ph, Lee Garmes; ed, Donn Hayes.

Drama **(PR:A MPAA:NR)**

CAROLYN OF THE CORNERS* (1919) 5 reels Pathe bw

Bessie Love *(Carolyn)*, Charles Elder *(Joseph Stagg)*, Charlotte Mineau *(Amanda Parlow)*, Eunice Moore *(Aunt Rose)*, Margaret Cullington, Pauline Pulliam, Prince the Dog.

Love's portrayal of a child is truly remarkable in this otherwise hokey picture about a girl believed to be an orphan, who brings a pair of estranged lovers together before being reunited with her parents who were believed drowned.

d, Robert Thornby; w, Frank S. Beresford (based on a novel by Ruth Belmore Endicott); ph, Frank B. Good.

Drama **(PR:A MPAA:NR)**

CARPET FROM BAGDAD, THE*** (1915) 5 reels Selig bw

Kathlyn Williams, Charles Clary, Wheeler Oakman, Guy Oliver, Eugenie Besserer, Frank Clark, Harry Lonsdale, Fred Huntley.

Col. William Selig's first feature film, set in Egypt, Bagdad, and New York, provides plenty of thrills as it tells of a sacred carpet's theft and the subsequent robbery of a Gotham bank vault. There was a nicely staged sandstorm, and Selig found in this film the perfect story in which to use his exotic animals. He was an enterprising fellow who not only maintained studios in Chicago and California, but owned a personal zoo as well.

d, Colin Campbell; w, (based on a novel by Harold McGrath).

Adventure/Crime **(PR:A MPAA:NR)**

CASE OF JONATHAN DREW, THE (SEE: LODGER, THE, 1926, Brit.)

CASEY AT THE BAT** (1927) 6 reels FP/PAR bw

Wallace Beery *(Casey)*, Ford Sterling *(O'Dowd)*, ZaSu Pitts *(Camille)*, Sterling Holloway *(Putnam)*, Spec O'Donnell *(Spec)*, Iris Stuart *(Trixie)*, Sydney Jarvis *(McGraw)*, Lotus Thompson, Rosalind Byrne, Anne Sheridan, Doris Hill, Sally Blane *(Other Florodora Girls)*.

Beery, the town junk man and star of the local baseball team, is spotted by a big league scout who brings him to New York to play for the Giants. When the team makes it to the World Series, a fix is instigated, with Beery being convinced he is too sick to play. The kid mascot, however, exposes the plot and Beery gets to the park just in time to face the opposing pitcher, with two outs and his team behind.

Following the spirit of the poem, "the mighty Casey" strikes out, but a title is inserted saying that a trick ball had been used and the game will be played again.

p, Hector Turnbull; d, Monte Brice; w, Jules Furthman, Reginald Morris, Brice, Turnbull (based on the poem by Ernest Thayer); t, Sam Hellman, Grant Clarke; ph, Barney McGill.

Comedy/Drama **(PR:A MPAA:NR)**

CASSIDY*** (1917) 5 reels TRI bw

Dick Rosson *(Cassidy)*, Pauline Curley *(Grant's Daughter)*, Frank Currier *(District Attorney Grant)*, Mac Alexander *(Garvice)*, Eddie Sturgis *(The Bull)*, John O'Connor *(The Bartender)*.

Grim story about Rosson, a small-time crook out West, who wants desperately to return home to New York before dying of tuberculosis. In order to finance the trip, he unknowingly burglarizes the house of the town's district attorney, who gets the drop on him. The D.A proves to be a compassionate man, however, and after hearing the story, gives the poor devil some money and sends him on his way. But Rosson is able to repay the kindness by saving a girl (who turns out to be his benefactor's daughter) from white slavers, and is mortally wounded in the struggle. The picture ends with Rosson staggering through the rain, trying to make it to the train which will take him East, but running out of time.

d, Arthur Rosson; sup, Allan Dwan; w, (based on a story by Larry Evans).

Drama **(PR:A MPAA:NR)**

CAT AND THE CANARY, THE*** (1927) 8 reels UNIV bw

Laura La Plante *(Annabelle West)*, Creighton Hale *(Paul Jones)*, Forrest Stanley *(Charles Wilder)*, Tully Marshall *(Roger Crosby)*, Gertrude Astor *(Cecily Young)*, Arthur Edmund Carewe *(Harry Blythe)*, Flora Finch *(Susan Sillsby)*, Martha Mattox *("Mammy" Pleasant)*, Lucien Littlefield *(Dr. Patterson)*, George Siegmann *(Hendricks)*, Joe Murphy *(Milkman)*, Billy Engle *(Taxi Driver)*.

Framed by the Gothic-arched back of a chair, we see the legatees presumptive of an eccentric millionaire—dead these 20 years—awaiting the stroke of midnight, the time that the deceased has decreed that his will be read. The closest relatives of the late recluse, atwitter with anticipation, are appalled to learn that they have been left nothing; the entire estate is to go to distant relative La Plante, the only one of the clan who didn't consider the old man's mind to be twisted. One stipulation: La Plante herself must be demonstrably in her right mind; otherwise, a second document will be opened naming another heir. Mysterious occurrences abound in the old mansion—the attorney disappears, secret panels open and close, a sinister hand with Fu Manchu fingernails menaces the assemblage—all serving to put La Plante's sanity in jeopardy. In a second sinister disappearance, Hale is trapped within the walls of the ancient structure. Horror is larded liberally with humor in this benchmark feature which established a genre, the haunted-mansion picture. Far more cinematic than theatrical, Willard's play (which opened on stage in the same year the film was made) works beautifully on the screen. Director Leni pulls out all the stops with vignettes, odd camera angles, and long tracking shots in this, his first U.S. helming. A long-time art director in his native Germany, Leni had directed the expressionistic masterpiece WAXWORKS in 1924, serving also as art director. In THE CAT AND THE CANARY, Leni had the advantage of another talented artist, set designer Hall, who had worked on THE PHANTOM OF THE OPERA (1925) and who was to go on to further Gothic fame with DRACULA (1931) and FRANKENSTEIN (1932). Co-scripter Hill was a talented director in his own right. A visual delight, alternating thrills with giggles, well paced and with fine characterizations all around. Remade with sound in 1931 as THE CAT CREEPS and remade again (with Bob Hope in his first big starring role) in 1939.

d, Paul Leni; w, Robert F. Hill, Alfred A. Cohn (based on the play by John Willard); t, Walter Anthony; ph, Gilbert Warrenton; set d, Charles D. Hall.

Mystery **Cas.** **(PR:A MPAA:NR)**

CATCH AS CATCH CAN* (1927) 5 reels GOTH/LUM bw

William Fairbanks *(Reed Powers)*, Jack Blossom *(George Bascom)*, Rose Blossom *(Lucille Bascom)*, Larry Shannon *(Phil Bascom)*, Walter Shumway *(Ward Hastings)*, George Kotsonaros *("Butch")*, George Chapman *(Slippery Schnitzel)*.

Low-budget programmer about the manager of a baseball team who takes the blame for throwing the game in order to protect the brother of the girl he loves. It all works out in the final inning.

d, Charles Hutchison; sup, Sam Bischoff; w, L. V. Jefferson; ph, James Brown.

Drama **(PR:A MPAA:NR)**

CAT'S PAJAMAS, THE** (1926) 6 reels FP/PAR bw

Betty Bronson *(Sally Winton)*, Ricardo Cortez *(Don Cesare Gracco)*, Arlette Marchal *(Riza Dorina)*, Theodore Roberts *(Sally's Father)*, Gordon Griffith *(Jack)*, Tom Ricketts *(Mr. Briggs)*.

Variation on the Cinderella theme which again features Bronson. In this one she plays a seamstress whom Cortez, a temperamental opera star, marries in order to discourage his army of adoring female fans. The remainder of the picture deals with Bronson winning him over and becoming the pampered bride of her shopgirl dreams.

d, William A. Wellman; w, Hope Loring, Louis D. Lighton (based on a story by Ernest Vadja); ph, Victor Milner.

Drama **(PR:A MPAA:NR)**

CAVEMAN, THE*** (1926) 7 reels WB bw

Matt Moore *(Mike Smagg)*, Marie Prevost *(Myra Gaylord)*, John Patrick *(Brewster Bradford)*, Myrna Loy *(The Maid)*, Phyllis Haver *(Dolly Van Dream)*, Hedda Hopper *(Mrs. Van Dream)*.

Good cast in a nifty comedy about a bored society girl who releases half of a $50 bill with instructions that the other half be claimed at her apartment. Moore, who plays a coal delivery man, finds it and on a whim, the girl passes him off to her society friends as an eccentric professor. Before long she falls in love, and when he informs the crowd of his true identity, they eject him from their august company. At this point, the girl is perfectly happy to ride off into the sunset in his coal wagon. Look for the part of the maid, played by Loy, who makes her film debut here.

d, Lewis Milestone; w, Darryl F. Zanuck (based on the original story by Gelette Burgess); ph, David Abel, Frank Kesson.

Comedy **(PR:A MPAA:NR)**

CELEBRATED CASE, A*** (1914) 4 reels Kalem bw

Alice Joyce, Guy Coombs, Alice Hollister, Marguerite Courtot, James B. Ross, Harry Millarde.

Story of a French soldier who is imprisoned for the murder of his wife because of the mistaken testimony of his little girl. Effective scenes of the convict's galley and battle re-creations were the highlights of this Kalem feature.

d, George Melford; w, Gene Gaunthier (based on a play by Adolphe D'Ennery, Eugene Cormon).

Drama **(PR:A MPAA:NR)**

CHAIN LIGHTNING** (1922) 5 reels Ben Wilson/Arrow bw

Ann Little *(Peggy Pomeroy)*, Norval MacGregor *(Maj. Lee Pomeroy)*, William Carroll *(Red Rollins)*, Joseph Girard *(Col. George Bradley)*, Jack Daugherty *(Bob Bradley)*.

Budget-minded programmer about a girl who is able to attend finishing school because her father takes a second mortgage on his property. Then, when he becomes ill—as well as destitute— she returns home, rides in the big race, and saves the day.

p&d, Ben Wilson; w, J. Grubb Alexander, Agnes Parsons; ph, Harry Gersted.

Drama **(PR:A MPAA:NR)**

CHALLENGE ACCEPTED, THE*** (1918) 5 reels Hodkinson/Pathe bw

Zena Keefe *(Sally Haston)*, Charles Eldridge *(John Haston)*, Russell Simpson *(Uncle Zeke Sawyer)*, Joel Day *(Steve Carey)*, Sidney D'Albrook *(Billy Murphy)*, John Hopkins *(James Grogan)*, Warren Cook *(Capt. Roderick Brooke)*, Chester Barnett.

There is an authentic feel to this film about a mountain boy who is drafted into the Army, only to desert when he becomes the victim of the camp bully. After returning home, his patriotic girl friend, Keefe, demands that he do his duty and delivers him back to the base where he is let off with a reprimand. Some time later, while on leave, the boy captures a band of draft-dodging mountain men, making a most favorable impression on both Keefe and Uncle Sam.

d, Edwin L. Hollywood; w, Donald Gordon Reid; ph, Charles Hoffman.

Drama **(PR:A MPAA:NR)**

CHALLENGE OF CHANCE, THE*** (1919) 6 reels Continental bw

Jess Willard *(Joe Bates)*, Arline Pretty *(Fay Calvert)*, Harry Van Meter *(El Capitan)*, Albert Hart *(Burr)*, Lee Hill *(Bob Edwards)*.

Heavyweight boxing champion Jess Willard gave a surprisingly good performance in his debut on the screen. It is a neat little western in which he saves a girl and her stable of race horses from a lecherous "gringo" and a small army of Mexican insurgents.

d, Harry Revier; w, Roy Somerville (based on a story by William H. Hamby); ph, Leo Rossi, Arthur Todd, Eddie James.

Western **(PR:A MPAA:NR)**

CHAMPAGNE** (1928, Brit.) 8 reels British International/W&F bw

Betty Balfour *(Betty)*, Jean Bradin *(Jean)*, Theo Von Alten *(The Baron)*, Gordon Harker *(The Father)*, Clifford Heatherly *(The Manager)*, Jack Trevor *(The Officer)*, Sunday Wilshin *(A Girl)*, Claude Hulbert *(A Guest)*, Balliol and Merton *(Dancers)*, Marcel Vibert.

Balfour plays an irresponsible daughter whose rich father, known as the "Champagne King," insists that she break off with the young man she wants to marry. She travels to Paris where she has wild parties and an affair with a middle-aged man who shows a nasty streak. When she discovers that her father has gone broke, Balfour takes a job in a cabaret to support him. Things grow unbearable and she returns to the brute she'd been seeing and asks him to take her back to the U.S. At the last minute she is rescued by her former boy friend from the lecher, who, it turns out, had been hired by the girl's father to teach her a lesson. Hitchcock considered CHAMPAGNE one of his worst films due mainly to a banal script which, according to an interviewer, he took home each night and placed between the pages of *Whittaker's Almanac* "to see if it would have absorbed something interesting by morning." The film did have its good moments, however, including a comic touch where a drunk is swerving from side to side on a docked ship until the ship begins to roll and he is suddenly walking straight while everyone else on board staggers.

p, John Maxwell; d, Alfred Hitchcock; w, Eliot Stannard, Hitchcock (based on an original story by Walter C. Mycroft); ph, John J. Cox; art d, C. W. Arnold; set d, Elstree.

Drama **Cas.** **(PR:A MPAA:NR)**

CHAMPION OF LOST CAUSES*** (1925) 5 reels FOX bw

Edmund Lowe *(Loring)*, Barbara Bedford *(Beatrice Charles)*, Walter McGrail *(Zanten/Dick Sterling)*, Jack McDonald *(Joseph Wilbur)*, Alec Francis *(Peter Charles)*.

A good action-mystery movie about a writer who becomes involved in a murder while searching out story material. There are plenty of thrills along the way as he clears the father of the girl he has fallen in love with and, in the end, brings the real killer to justice.

d, Chester Bennett; w, Thomas Dixon, Jr. (based on a story by Max Brand); ph, Ernest Palmer.

Mystery **(PR:A MPAA:NR)**

CHANG**** (1927) 8 reels PAR/FP bw

Kru *(The Pioneer)*, Chantui *(His Wife)*, Nah *(Their Little Boy)*, Ladah *(Their Little Girl)*, Bimbo *(The Monkey)*.

Following the success of GRASS, A NATION'S BATTLE FOR LIFE, and with the backing of Jesse Lasky, filmmakers Schoedsack and Cooper journeyed to Siam where they created a masterpiece. Never before had audiences seen the terror and the beauty of jungle life presented with such realism. This was, however, no mere newsreel account, but rather a carefully choreographed motion picture— made with no shooting script—which told of a family's struggle to survive in a land of man-eating tigers, deadly leopards, and stampeding elephants. CHANG was, indeed, a theatrical experience as gripping and suspense-filled as anything ever constructed within the controlled environment of a back lot. And, towards the end when the wild elephant herd began its charge, the picture blew up through a process called Magnascope to an enormous size, which left audiences breathless.

p,d&w, Merian C. Cooper, Ernest B. Schoedsack; t, Achmed Abdulla; ph, Schoedsack.

Adventure **(PR:C MPAA:NR)**

CHARGE IT** (1921) 7 reels EPC/Jans bw

Clara Kimball Young *(Julia Lawrence)*, Herbert Rawlinson *(Phillip Lawrence)*, Edward M. Kimball *(Tom Gareth)*, Betty Blythe *(Millie Gareth)*, Nigel Barrie *(Dana Herrick)*, Hal Wilson *(Robert McGregor)*, Dulcie Cooper *(Rose McGregor)*.

In this one, Young (who was a bit too old for the part) plays a young wife determined to live within her husband's income. Then, when he begins to succeed, she goes on a spending binge, charging everything. This leads to the marriage breaking up, and the entrance of a smooth-talking, fast-dancing "other man." In the end, however, the wife comes to her senses, regains her instinct for thrift, and the marriage is saved.

d, Harry Garson; w, Sada Cowan; ph, Jacques Bizeul.

Drama **(PR:A MPAA:NR)**

CHARITY?* (1916) 7 reels MUT bw

Linda A. Griffith [Linda Arvidson], Creighton Hale, Sheldon Lewis, Marie Bruce, Veta Searl, Morgan Jones, Henry Hallman, Elizabeth Burbridge, Sam J. Ryan, John Dunn.

Arvidson, who acted in and wrote the story for this picture, was obviously influenced by her husband D. W. Griffith's disdain for hypocrisy (this was the year of the director's masterpiece, INTOLERANCE), and in this film exposes the professional charity industry.

d&w, Frank Powell (based on a story by Linda A. Griffith).

Drama **(PR:A MPAA:NR)**

CHARM SCHOOL, THE*** (1921) 5 reels FP/PAR bw

Wallace Reid *(Austin Bevans)*, Lila Lee *(Elsie)*, Adele Farrington *(Mrs. Rolles)*, Beulah Bains *(Susie Rolles)*, Edwin Stevens *(Homer Johns)*, Grace Morse *(Miss Hayes)*, Patricia Magee *(Sally Boyd)*, Lincoln Stedman *(George Boyd)*, Kate Toncray *(Miss Curtis)*, Minna Redman *(Miss Tevis)*, Snitz Edwards *(Mr. Boyd)*, Helen Pillsbury *(Mrs. Boyd)*, Tina Marshall *(Europia)*.

Reid is given a tried-and-true formula for this picture. In vaudeville and burlesque, the routine was known as "seminary stuff," whereby a couple of fellows accidentally stumble into a girls' school and dress like women to remain among the lovelies. In this case, Reid is an auto salesman who becomes heir to the Bevans School for Young Women. Once settled in, he turns the institution into a charm school, replacing the standard courses with swimming, fencing, and dancing, providing the audience with plenty of cheesecake and a goodly number of laughs.

d, James Cruze; w, (based on the novel by Alice Duer Miller); ph, C. Edgar Schoenbaum.

Comedy **(PR:A MPAA:NR)**

CHARMER, THE*** (1925) 6 reels FP/PAR bw

Pola Negri *(Mariposa)*, Wallace MacDonald *(Ralph Bayne)*, Robert Frazer *(Dan Murray)*, Trixie Friganza *(Mama)*, Cesare Gravina *(Senor Allessandro Spotti)*, Gertrude Astor *(Bertha Sedgwick)*, Edward Davis *(Mr. Sedgwick)*, Mathilde Brundage *(Mrs. Bayne)*.

Negri is very good in this change-of-pace film in which she plays a Spanish dancer who becomes famous in America and is loved by two men. One is a millionaire, the other his chauffeur. In the end, she chooses the latter.

d, Sidney Olcott; w, Sada Cowan (based on the novel *Mariposa* by Henry Baerlein); ph, James [Wong] Howe; ed, Patricia Rooney.

Drama/Comedy **(PR:A MPAA:NR)**

CHASER, THE** (1928) 6 reels Harry Langdon/FN-WB bw

Harry Langdon *(Husband)*, Gladys McConnell *(Wife)*, Henry Hayward *(Her Mother)*, William Jaimison *(His Pal)*, Charles Thurston *(The Judge)*.

By the time Langdon—that wonderful comedian with the strange man-child persona—made this feature, he was already past his popular and artistic peak. No doubt it's true that this talented little man needed a Frank Capra (who directed his greatest works, TRAMP TRAMP TRAMP and THE STRONG MAN) to orchestrate the natural sense of melody which was his art, but unfortunately he became arrogant when critics and intellectuals began comparing him to Chaplin—and decided that he too could do it all. After signing a million-dollar contract with First National, he directed himself in THREE'S A CROWD, a film topheavy with pathos and "meaning." It failed, and in an attempt to retrench, he reverted to the formula which had worked so well during his days with Sennett. In fact, THE CHASER was in a sense a remake of SATURDAY AFTERNOON, his most popular comedy short of that period. But again, the laughs just weren't there. The baby in the grownup body had sadly lost his appeal. It was just too late.

d, Harry Langdon; w, Clarence Hennecke, Robert Eddy, Harry McCoy (based on a story by Arthur Ripley); t, E. H. Giebler; ph, Elgin Lessley, Frank Evans; ed, Alfred De Gaetano.

Comedy **(PR:A MPAA:NR)**

CHASING THE MOON*** (1922) 5 reels FOX bw

Tom Mix *(Dwight Locke)*, Eva Novak *(Jane Norworth)*, William Buckley *(Milton Norworth)*, Sid Jordan *(Velvet Joe)*, Elsie Danbric *(Princess Sonia)*, Wynn Mace *(Prince Albert)*.

Non-stop action as Mix, believing he has taken a poison which will kill him at the end of 30 days, races from America to Russia and through Spain in search of a professor who has the only known antidote. Completely believable and thoroughly enjoyable.

d, Edward Sedgwick; w, Sedgwick, Tom Mix; t, Ralph Spence; ph, Ben Kline; ed, Spence.

Action Comedy **(PR:A MPAA:NR)**

CHEATED HEARTS*** (1921) 5 reels UNIV bw

Herbert Rawlinson *(Barry Gordon)*, Warner Baxter *(Tom Gordon)*, Marjorie Daw *(Muriel Beekman)*, Doris Pawn *(Kitty Van Ness)*, Winter Hall *(Nathaniel Beekman)*, Josef Swickard *(Col. Fairfax Gordon)*, Murdock MacQuarrie *(Ibraham)*, Anna Lehr *(Naomi)*, Boris Karloff *(Nil Hamed)*, Al MacQuarrie *(Hassam)*, Hector Sarno *(Achmet)*.

The scene is set in northern Africa and tells of two brothers—the sons of an alcoholic father—who are in love with the same girl. She loves one of the boys but fears he may have inherited the tendency toward drink. They argue and, out of spite, she accepts a proposal of marriage from the other. Some time later, her fiance is held for ransom, and the brother, with the help of Bedouin bandits, rides to the rescue, convincing the girl that he was the right man for her all along.

d, Hobart Henley; w, Wallace Clifton (based on the novel *Barry Gordon* by William Farquhar Payson); ph, Virgil Miller.

Drama **(PR:A MPAA:NR)**

CHEATER REFORMED, THE* (1921) 5 reels FOX bw

William Russell *(Jordan McCall/Dr. Luther McCall)*, Seena Owen *(Carol McCall)*, John Brammall *("Buster" Dorsey)*, Sam De Grasse *(Thomas Edinburgh)*, Ruth King *(Mrs. Edinburgh)*.

Far-fetched, but harmless melodrama in which Russell (in a double role) plays the crusading rector of a corrupt town who is murdered in order that his twin brother, a crook, can assume his identity. In the end, the brother is regenerated, exposes the criminals, is forgiven by the townfolk, and ends up with his late brother's widow who, incredibly, never suspected the masquerade.

d, Scott Dunlap; w, Jules G. Furthman, Dunlap (based on a story by Furthman); ph, Clyde De Vinna.

Drama **(PR:A MPAA:NR)**

CHEATERS** (1927) 6 reels TIF bw

Pat O'Malley *(Allen Harvey)*, Helen Ferguson *(Mary Condon)*, George Hackathorne *(Paul Potter)*, Lawford Davidson *(Jim Kingston)*, Claire McDowell *(Mrs. Robin Carter)*, Helen Lynch *(Marion Carter)*, Heinie Conklin *(Mose Johnston)*, Alphonz Ethier *(McCann)*, Max Davidson *(Michael Cohen)*, Edward Cecil *(Detective)*, William O'Brien *(Butler)*.

Ferguson and Hackathorne are reformed crooks now working as clerk and cashier at a fancy hotel. They are approached by their former boss (whom they are trying to avoid) and ordered to assist in stealing the jewels owned by a wealthy guest. In the end, the criminal is killed, and the couple are let go by a kindly detective who understands.

d, Oscar Apfel; w, W. C. Clifford (based on a story by Harry D. Kerr); ph, Joseph A. Dubray, Allen Davey; ed, James C. McKay; art d, Edwin B. Willis.

Crime **(PR:A MPAA:NR)**

CHEATING CHEATERS*** (1927) 6 reels UNIV bw

Betty Compson *(Nan Carey)*, Kenneth Harlan *(Tom Palmer)*, Lucien Littlefield *(Lazare)*, Eddie Gribbon *(Steve Wilson)*, Cesare Gravina *(Tony Verdi)*, Sylvia Ashton *(Mrs. Brockton)*, Erwin Connelly *(Mr. Brockton)*, Maude Turner Gordon *(Mrs. Palmer)*, E. J. Ratcliffe *(Mr. Palmer)*.

Compson is a female detective who passes herself off as an ex-convict in order to infiltrate a gang of crooks who pass themselves off as high society. Actually there are two gangs, and the difficulties they share "fitting in" are played for plenty of laughs. Compson, of course, rounds them all up in the end, including the handsome fellow who was made part of the mob against his will.

d, Edward Laemmle; w, James T. O'Donohue, Charles A. Logue (based on the play by Max Marcin); t, Walter Anthony; ph, Jackson Rose.

Crime/Comedy **(PR:A MPAA:NR)**

CHECKERS** (1913) 5 reels All Star Feature bw

Thomas W. Ross.

Well known stage and screen actor Ross changed virtually nothing when he adapted his production of this popular play to the screen. The result: another static screen presentation.

p&d, Thomas W. Ross; w, (based on the play by Henry M. Blosson, Jr.).

Romance (PR:A MPAA:NR)

CHICAGO*** (1928) 9 reels DM/Pathe bw

Phyllis Haver *(Roxie Hart)*, Victor Varconi *(Amos Hart)*, Eugene Pallette *(Casley)*, Virginia Bradford *(Katie)*, T. Roy Barnes *(Reporter)*, Warner Richmond *(District Attorney)*, Robert Edeson *(Flynn)*, Clarence Burton *(Police Sergeant)*, Sidney D'Albrook *(Photographer)*, Otto Lederer *(Amos' Partner)*, May Robson *(Matron)*, Julia Faye *(Velma)*.

Set in Chicago during the Roaring Twenties, this is the story of a husband who sticks loyally by his wife, in spite of the fact that she murdered her lover. However, when the notoriety she receives through her trial (beautifully filmed) turns her into a publicity-seeking egomaniac, he tosses her out. This well produced, often gripping melodrama was remade in 1942 as ROXIE HART by William Wellman, who turns it into a very funny comedy.

d, Frank Urson; w, Lenore J. Coffee (based on the novel *Chicago* by Maurine Watkins); t, John Krafft; ph, Peverell Marley; ed, Anne Bauchens; art d, Mitchell Leisen; cos, Adrian.

Drama (PR:A MPAA:NR)

CHICAGO AFTER MIDNIGHT** (1928) 7 reels FBO bw

Ralph Ince *(Jim Boyd)*, Jola Mendez *(Betty Boyd/Mona Gale)*, Lorraine Rivero *(Betty Boyd, as a Baby)*, James Mason *(Hardy)*, Carl Axzelle *(Ike, the Rat)*, Helen Jerome Eddy *(Mrs. Boyd)*, Ole M. Ness *(Tanner)*, Robert Seiter *(Jack Waring)*, Frank Mills *(Frank)*, Christian J. Frank *(Casey)*.

Released from prison after 15 years, Ince goes after Mason, the rival gang leader who set him up for his sentence. In Mason's cabaret, Ince meets Mendez, a dancer. Ince kills Mason and implicates Mendez' sweetheart, Seiter. In order to clear the latter of a murder charge, Mendez joins Ince's mob. When gang members find out about her quest, they make things hot for her. Ince learns at the last minute that Mendez is his own daughter. He rescues her at the cost of his own life, clearing Seiter with his dying confession. Although this movie had more than its share of crooked cops, brassy chorus girls, fast cars, rattling machine guns, bootleggers, and sleazy stool pigeons, it fell far short of equalling UNDERWORLD, the film that was its inspiration.

d, Ralph Ince; w, Charles K. Harris, Enid Hibbard; t, George M. Arthur; ph, J. O. Taylor; ed, Arthur.

Crime (PR:A MPAA:NR)

CHICKEN CASEY*** (1917) 5 reels TRI bw

Dorothy Dalton *(Chicken Casey/Marvis Marberry)*, Charles Gunn *(Everett Hale)*, Howard Hickman *("Dickey" Cochran)*, Thomas Guise *(Israel Harris)*.

Chicken Casey is the name Broadway star Marvis Marberry (Dorothy Dalton) assumes when she impersonates a "cafe girl" in order to prove to a best-selling author that she is indeed the right person to play the leading character from his novel when it is made into a play.

d, Raymond B. West; w, J. G. Hawks (based on the play "Doorsteps" by Christine Silver).

Drama (PR:A MPAA:NR)

CHICKENS** (1921) 5 reels Ince/PAR bw

Douglas MacLean *(Deems Stanwood)*, Gladys George *(Julia Stoneman)*, Clair McDowell *(Aunt Rebecca)*, Charles Mailes *(Dan Bellows)*, Edith Yorke *(His Wife)*, Raymond Cannon *(Willie Figg)*, Willis Marks *(Philip Thawson)*, Al Filson *(Decker)*.

Modestly produced little comedy-drama about a wealthy playboy (MacLean) who smashes his high-powered car into a beautiful young girl's chicken farm. He immediately falls in love and purchases the adjoining farm in order to woo her but, when his guardian loses his fortune, he finds himself in the chicken-raising business for real. There is a rival who holds the deed to his farm, causing some trouble along the way but, in the end, everything ends up fine.

d, Jack Nelson; sup, Thomas H. Ince; w, Agnes Christine Johnston (based on the story "Yancona Yillies" by Herschel Hall); ph, Bert Cann.

Comedy/Drama (PR:A MPAA:NR)

CHILD FOR SALE, A* (1920) 6 reels Graphic bw

Gladys Leslie, Creighton Hale, Anna Lehr, Julia Swayne Gordon, William Tooker, Bobby Connelly, Ruth Sullivan, William Davidson, Marie Schaffer.

Heavy-handed propaganda about an artist who is driven to sell his daughter to a wealthy family but relents at the last minute because his son wants his sister back. Later, he becomes involved with another rich family and discovers that the woman of the house is actually his mother from a former marriage.

d&w, Ivan Abramson; ph, Louis Dunmyre.

Drama (PR:A MPAA:NR)

CHILD OF M'SIEU*** (1919) 5 reels TRI bw

Baby Marie Osborne *(Marie, Child of M'sieu)*, Philo McCullough *(Phillip)*, Harrish Ingraham *(Absinthe)*, Claire Alexander *(Claire)*, Katherine McLaren *(The Lace Lady)*.

This most satisfying screen translation of the Browning poem, "Pippa Passes," gave talented Osborne the chance to do some dramatic, as well as comedic, acting.

d, Harrish Ingraham; w, (based on the poem "Pippa Passes" by Robert Browning); ph, William Nobles.

Drama (PR:A MPAA:NR)

CHILDREN OF DIVORCE*** (1927) 7 reels FP/PAR bw

Clara Bow *(Kitty Flanders)*, Esther Ralston *(Jean Waddington)*, Gary Cooper *(Ted Larrabee)*, Einar Hanson *(Prince Ludovico de Sfax)*, Norman Trevor *(Duke de Gondreville)*, Hedda Hopper *(Katherine Flanders)*, Edward Martindel *(Tom Larrabee)*, Julia Swayne Gordon *(Princess de Sfax)*, Tom Ricketts *(The Secretary)*, Albert Gran *(Mr. Seymour)*, Iris Stuart *(Mousie)*, Margaret Campbell *(Mother Superior)*, Percy Williams *(Manning)*, Joyce Coad *(Little Kitty)*, Yvonne Pelletier *(Little Jean)*, Don Marion *(Little Ted)*.

Bow's follow-up to IT is just another society problem drama, full of cocktail parties and unhappy marriages. In this one, which was handsomely mounted, the effort was made to depict the plight of children who suffer parental indifference and neglect. Some sources state that Josef von Sternberg directed some of the scenes.

d, Frank Lloyd; w, Hope Loring, Louis D. Lighton (based on the novel by Owen Johnson); ph, Victor Milner.

CHILDREN OF THE NIGHT*** (1921) 5 reels FOX bw

William Russell *(Jerrold Jarvis Jones)*, Ruth Renick *(Sylvia Ensor)*, Lefty Flynn *(Alexic Trouvaine)*, Ed Burns *(Barry Dunbar)*, Arthur Thalasso *(Vance)*, Wilson Hummell *(Tankerton)*, Helen McGinnis *(Anne Mannister)*, Edwin Booth Tilton *(Mannister, Her Father)*, Frederick Kirby *(Carver)*, Herbert Fortier *(Zenia)*.

Fun movie about a bored brokerage clerk who daydreams adventures which involve the office stenographer whom he loves. His dreams are full of action and Dillon directs them with skill.

d, Jack Dillon; w, John Montague (based on a story by Max Brand); ph, George Schneiderman.

Adventure/Fantasy (PR:A MPAA:NR)

CHIMMIE FADDEN*** (1915) 4 reels LAS/PAR bw

Victor Moore *(Chimmie Fadden)*, Raymond Hatton *(Larry, His Brother)*, Mrs. Lewis McCord *(Mrs. Fadden, Their Mother)*, Ernest Joy *(Van Courtlandt, a Millionaire)*, Anita King (Fanny, His Daughter), Camille Astor *(Hortense, the French Maid)*, Tom Forman *(Antoine, the Butler-Thief)*, Harry DeRoy *(Perkins, the Butler)*, Tex Driscoll.

Moore had no trouble making the adjustment from Broadway stage to movie set. He was, in fact, marvelous as Chimmie Fadden, the Bowery roughneck who lands a job as footman to a wealthy family and is forced to serve dinner (hilariously) when the butler fails to show up. There is a robbery, and Chimmie is at first a suspect but, in the end, he clears the matter up, wins the friendship of the family and the love of their French maid.

d, Cecil B. DeMille; w, DeMille (based on the book and play by E. W. Townsend); ph, Alvin Wyckoff; ed, DeMille.

Comedy (PR:A MPAA:NR)

CHIMMIE FADDEN OUT WEST*** (1915) 5 reels LAS/PAR bw

Victor Moore *(Chimmie Fadden)*, Camille Astor *(The Duchess)*, Raymond Hatton *(Larry)*, Mrs. Lewis McCord *(Mother Fadden)*, Ernest Joy *(Mr. Van Courtlandt)*, Tom Forman *(Antoine)*, Florence Dagmar *(Betty Van Courtlandt)*, Harry Hadfield *(Preston)*.

This sequel to De Mille's CHIMMIE FADDEN, released earlier the same year (and featuring much the same cast), has Moore again recreating his stage role as the breezy Bowery tough boy who, with his family, has had the good fortune to fall in with rich folks. Moore is pressed into service by railroad tycoon Joy to carry off a publicity scheme. The city boy goes westward bearing bags of gold, intending to announce a fabulous mining strike, then is to return to the East on a train that will proceed to set a transcontinental speed record. The twain meet with mighty amusing results. Moore's restrained performance is a delight and the western scenery is wonderfully filmed.

p&d, Cecil B. DeMille; w, DeMille, Jeanie Macpherson (based on stories by E. W. Townsend); ph, Alvin Wyckoff; ed, DeMille.

Comedy (PR:A MPAA:NR)

CHINESE BUNGALOW, THE*** (1926, Brit.) 7 reels STOLL bw

Matheson Lang *(Yaun Sing)*, Genevieve Townsend *(Charlotte)*, Juliette Compton *(Sadie)*, Shayle Gardner *(Richard Marquess)*, George Thirlwell *(Harold Marquess)*, Malcolm Tod *(Vivian Dale)*, Clifford McLaglen *(Abdul)*.

This was one of the few British features from the 1920s which could compete on *any* level with the films of Germany and the U.S.. It tells of a British actress who, after being abducted by the servants of Lang, a Mandarin of great wealth, decides to marry him. After the ceremony, they send for her sister Townsend who joins them in his lavish Chinese "bungalow." When Thirlwell, an Englishman working on a nearby rubber plantation, meets the bride, there is an immediate attraction and, in spite of the sister's objections, they have an affair. Lang discovers this, vents his anger, and shortly thereafter the young man dies of a mysterious fever. When his brother arrives to investigate, he falls in love with Townsend, who has also inspired the interest of Lang and presented her with a simple choice—marriage to him or death to her sister. Gardner intervenes and is placated by the Mandarin who serves wine explaining that one of the glasses contains poison. When there is no effect, the Englishman assumes that Lang was bluffing and leaves—taking the women with him. The film ends with a very effective fadeout of the Chinaman writhing in agonyfrom the poison *he* has ingested.

d, Sinclair Hill; w, (based on the play by Marian Osmond, James Corbett).

Mystery/Drama (PR:A MPAA:NR)

CHORUS GIRL'S ROMANCE, A** (1920) 5 reels Metro bw

Viola Dana, Gareth Hughes, Phil Ainsworth, William Quinn, Jere Sundin, Sidney De Grey, Lawrence Grant, Tom Gallery, Edward Jobson, Martin Best, Anne Schaefer, Dorothy Gordon, William V. Mong.

Hollywood generally did not fare well with films based on American author F. Scott Fitzgerald's stories, and this one was no exception. Adapted from one of his short stories, it's about a college student and chorus girl who marry, only to face the hardship of poverty.

d, William C. Dowlan; w, Percy Heath (based on the story "Head and Shoulders" by F. Scott Fitzgerald); ph, John Arnold.

Drama (PR:A MPAA:NR)

CHRIS AND THE WONDERFUL LAMP*** (1917) 4 reels Edison bw

Thomas Carnahan, Joseph Burke, Peggy Adams.

The Edison Company was able to string together footage dealing with nature subjects, as well as a couple of dramatic and comedy shorts, by using the story of a boy who discovers a magic lamp. The gimmick worked, and a pretty good feature was the result.

d, Alan Crosland; w, Summer Williams.

Adventure (PR:A MPAA:NR)

CHRISTIAN, THE** (1914) 8 reels LIEBER/VIT bw

Edith Storey *(Gloria Quayle)*, Earle Williams *(John Storm)*, Harry Northrup *(Lord Robert Ure)*, James Morrison *(Paul)*, Jane Fearnley *(Vera)*, Donald Hall *(Horatio Drake)*, Edward Kimball, Charles Kent, J.J. Sandbrook, Carlotta De Felice, Alberta Gallatin, James Lackaye, Rose Tapley, Alice Joyce.

This Caine novel of life in London depicts the triumph of Christian decency and had much to do toward making the movies respectable when it opened at New York's prestigious Harris Theatre in 1914. Storey, noted for her athletic prowess, had plenty of chance to show off her form in this acclaimed picture.

d, Frederick Thompson; sup, J. Stuart Blackton; w, Eugene Mullin (based on the novel by Hall Caine).

Drama (PR:A MPAA:NR)

CINDERELLA** (1915) 5 reels FP bw

Mary Pickford, Owen Moore, Hayward Mack.

It would seem that Famous Players rushed this one in order to cash in on the Pickford name and the fairytale theme during the Christmas holidays. The film was, in almost every way, below the standards of both studio and star. Pickford plays the hard-working little cinder girl whose more fortunate sisters are off to the Prince's Ball. Just when it looks as if the put-upon Pickford is going to miss out on the fun yet again, her fairy godmother appears and works the magic necessary for this diamond-in-the-rough to attend the posh doings. At the ball, the prince himself comes under Pickford's spell, but when she disappears before the tolling of midnight turns her fine clothes back to rags, he's left with nothing to remember her by but a glass slipper. Then ensues the famous hunt to find the foot that fits the slipper, and, of course, the trail leads to Pickford and the "happily ever after" ending.

d, James Kirkwood; w, (based on the childrens fable.)

Fantasy (PR:A MPAA:NR)

CIRCUS, THE**** (1928) 7 reels Charles Chaplin/UA bw

Charles Chaplin *(The Tramp)*, Merna Kennedy *(The Girl)*, Harry Crocker *(Rex, the Tightrope Walker)*, Allan Garcia *(Circus Owner)*, Stanley J. Sanford *(Head Property Man)*, John Rand *(Assistant Property Man)*, George Davis *(Magician)*, Henry Bergman *(The Old Clown)*, Steve Murphy *(The Pickpocket)*, Betty Morrissey *(The Vanishing Lady)*, Doc Stone *(The Prizefighter)*.

In 1928, Chaplin was given an Academy Award "for his versatility and genius in writing, acting, directing, and producing THE CIRCUS." This film—about a tramp who unknowingly becomes the star clown of a small time circus, falls in love with the owner's bareback-riding daughter and, in the end, selflessly arranges for her to marry the dashing tightrope walker whom she loves—contains some of Chaplin's most hilarious and touching moments. Unfortunately, there has been a tendency on the part of some (perhaps because it was produced between his two masterpieces, THE GOLD RUSH and CITY LIGHTS) to underrate this exceptional motion picture. But make no mistake, this is great cinema, and in the 1970 revival for which Chaplin composed the score, there is a beautiful ballad, "Swing Little Girl", which the artist sings himself.

p,d&w, Charles Chaplin; ph, Roland H. Totheroh; m&ed, Chaplin; art d, Charles D. Hall.

Comedy Cas. (PR:A MPAA:NR)

CIRCUS ACE, THE*** (1927) 5 reels FOX bw

Tom Mix *(Tom Terry)*, Natalie Joyce *(Millie Jane Raleigh)*, Jack Baston *(Kirk Mallory)*, Duke Lee *(Job Jasper)*, James Bradbury *(Gus Peabody)*, Stanley Blystone *(Boss Canvass Man)*, Dudley Smith *(Durgan the Miller)*, Buster Gardner *(The Sheriff)*, Clarence *(A Kangaroo)*, Tony the Wonder Horse.

Mix had a circus to use as the backdrop for his riding, stunting, and shooting in this entertaining feature. After falling for a pretty circus performer, he joins the company and foils a plot on the part of a small-town Arizona mayor to take control of the girl and her show.

d, Ben Stoloff; w, Jack Jungmeyer (based on a story by Harold Shumate); ph, Dan Clark.

Western (PR:A MPAA:NR)

CIRCUS DAYS*** (1923) 6 reels Sol Lesser/FN-WB bw

Jackie Coogan *(Toby Tyler)*, Barbara Tennant *(Ann Tyler)*, Russell Simpson *(Eben Holt)*, Claire McDowell *(Martha, His Wife)*, Cesare Gravina *(Luigi, the Clown)*, Peaches Jackson *(Jeannette)*, Sam De Grasse *(Lord)*, De Witt Jennings *(Daly)*, Nellie Lane *(Fat Woman)*, William Barlow *(Human Skeleton)*.

Toby Tyler was the perfect role for young Coogan to play. This is the story of the boy who runs away to join the circus after his uncle abuses him. He graduates from lemonade salesman to star of the show, performing a trick riding act and, in the end, returns to escort his mother from the home of her completely rotten brother-in-law.

d, Edward F. Cline; sup, Jack Coogan, Sr.; w, Harry Weil, Cline (based on the novel *Toby Tyler; or, Ten Weeks With a Circus* by James Otis); t, Eve Unsell; ph, Frank Good, Robert Martin; ed, Irene Morra.

Comedy/Drama (PR:A MPAA:NR)

CIRCUS MAN, THE*** (1914) 5 reels LAS bw

Theodore Roberts *(Thomas Braddock)*, Mabel Van Buren *(Mary Braddock)*, Florence Dagmar *(Christine Braddock)*, Hubert Whitehead *(Frank Jenison)*, Jode Mullally *(David Jenison)*, Raymond Hatton *(Ernie Cronk)*, Frank Hickman *(Dick Cronk)*, Fred Montague *(Col. Grand)*.

Well acted, directed, written, and photographed story about a stern circus owner who overcomes a series of setbacks to finally find happiness at the end of the last reel.

d, Oscar Apfel; w, Cecil B. DeMille (based on George Barr McCutcheon's novel *The Rose in the Ring*).

Drama (PR:A MPAA:NR)

CITY GONE WILD, THE*** (1927) 6 reels PAR bw

Thomas Meighan *(John Phelan)*, Marietta Millner *(Nada Winthrop)*, Louise Brooks *(Snuggles Joy)*, Fred Kohler *(Gunner Gallagher)*, Duke Martin *(Lefty Schroeder)*, Nancy Phillips *(Lefty's Girl)*, Wyndham Standing *(Franklin Ames)*, Charles Hill Mailes *(Luther Winthrop)*, King Zany *(Bondsman)*, "Gunboat" Smith *(Policeman)*.

Veteran director Cruze must have been somewhat influenced by UNDERWORLD when he made this gangster movie about a mob mouthpiece and a prosecuting attorney who love the same girl. Plenty of fast cars, machine guns, "Chicago pineapples," *plus* Louise Brooks, in this one.

d, James Cruze; w, Jules Furthman (based on a story by Jules and Charles Furthman); t, Herman Mankiewicz; ph, Bert Glennon.

Crime (PR:A MPAA:NR)

CITY LIGHTS***** (1931) 6 reels Charles Chaplin/UA bw

Charles Chaplin *(The Tramp)*, Virginia Cherrill *(The Blind Girl)*, Harry Myers *(The Millionaire)*, Hank Mann *(The Boxer)*, Allan Garcia *(The Butler)*, Florence Lee *(Grandmother)*, Henry Bergman *(Mayor/Janitor)*, Albert Austin *(Sweeper/Crook)*, John Rand *(Tramp)*, James Donnelly *(Foreman)*, Robert Parish *(Newsboy)*, Stanhope Wheatcroft *(Man in Cafe)*, Jean Harlow *(Guest)*.

By 1931, the talking picture was a reality, and Chaplin anguished over what to do with CITY LIGHTS. Should he add dialog sequences? Should the Little Fellow speak—and if so, how should he sound? The decision was made to buck the trend, as well as the commercial odds, and release the picture as a silent. The world should be grateful for this, because it resulted in what is generally considered Chaplin's greatest work. The story tells of a tramp who falls in love with a blind flower girl and goes to prison after convincing her that he is a handsome millionaire and providing her with the funds for a sight-restoring operation. There is plenty of great comedy along the way, but it is the film's ending which stands alone in the annals of the cinema. The Little Fellow returns after his incarceration to find the woman of his dreams, radiantly beautiful, operating a thriving florist shop. A couple of boys begin to torment the odd-looking tramp, and the girl watches the scene, amused by the expression of adoration on his face as he stares at her through the shop window. "I've made a conquest," she says to her grandmother. Then, taking pity on him, she steps outside and hands him a flower and a coin . . . "You?" her title card reads. The vagabond forces a smile and shakes his head. "You can see now?" he asks. "Yes I can see now." The poignancy of this most beautiful of scenes is beautifully described by John McCabe in his biography *Charlie Chaplin*: "She does not know what to say; he does not know what to say. She is stunned, happy, unbelieving, disappointed to the heart, moved to the heart. He looks at her timidly, smiling in tender pain. He is hopeful, yet he dare not hope, yet he dare not fail to hope. As he watches her eyes, the camera moves in to him for that rarity in Chaplin films, a close-up. The scene fades."

p,d&w, Charles Chaplin; ph, Roland Totheroh; m, Chaplin; art d, Charles D. Hall; syn sc; s eff.

Comedy/Drama Cas. (PR:A MPAA:NR)

CITY OF PURPLE DREAMS, THE*** (1918) 7 reels Selig bw

Thomas Santschi *(The Derelict)*, Bessie Eyton *(The Girl)*, Fritzi Brunette *(The Anarchist)*, Frank Clark, A. D. Sears, Eugenie Besserer, Cecil Holland, Harry Lonsdale.

When a derelict is bumped into by a wealthy girl in her automobile, class tension erupts. She throws some money at him to buy soap and shouts—"Get clean, and stay clean!" This angers and regenerates the down-and-outer, who not only pulls himself up from the gutter, but gets the girl as well—much to the chagrin of a female Bolshevik, who liked him the way he was.

d, Colin Campbell; w, Gilson Willets (based on the novel by Edwin Baird).

Drama **(PR:A MPAA:NR)**

CITY OF SILENT MEN*** (1921) 6 reels FP/PAR bw

Thomas Meighan *(Jim Montgomery)*, Lois Wilson *(Molly Bryant)*, Kate Bruce *(Mrs. Montgomery)*, Paul Everton *(Old Bill)*, George MacQuarrie *(Mike Kearney)*, *Guy Oliver (Mr. Bryant)*.

Interesting if rambling story of a country mechanic who comes to the city in search of work but is framed for murder and sent to Sing Sing. He escapes to California where, under an assumed identity, he prospers. On his wedding day, however, a New York detective obsessed with tracking him down (a la Jimmie Valentine) arrives on the scene and, to prevent fingerprint detection, the desperate young man thrusts his hands into a whirling machine. The policeman is so impressed by the courage of this deed that he allows his prey to go undetected.

d, Tom Forman; w, Frank Condon (based on the novel *The Quarry* by John A. Moroso); ph, Harry Perry.

Drama **(PR:A MPAA:NR)**

CITY OF THE DEAD (SEE: FORBIDDEN ADVENTURE, THE, 1915)

CIVILIZATION** (1916) 7 reels Ince bw

J. Barney Sherry, Enid Markey, Howard Hickman, George Fisher, Herschal Mayall, Lillian Reade, Fanny Midgley, Lola May, Charles K. French, J. Frank Burke, Jerome Storm, Ethel Ullman.

As a means of cashing in on J. Stuart Blackton's BATTLE CRY OF PEACE, Thomas H. Ince produced this film which took the pacifist side during a time when Americans looked on in disbelief as the European powers cut themselves to ribbons. It told of a submarine captain whose body is taken over by Christ in order to preach against war. A pretentiously symbolic film, CIVILIZATION was much talked about in its day and actually made money for its producer, Thomas H. Ince, while D. W. Griffiths' much greater, denser, deeper, and more magnificent INTOLERANCE, also a pacifist film and released six months earlier, lost money. Part of the reason for its success was Ince's self-aggrandizing nature. Using Woodrow Wilson's re-election campaign slogan, "He kept us out of war," Ince gave the idea for CIVILIZATION to screenwriter C. Gardner Sullivan with the idea of telling about the devastating war between two mythical countries, and how both were destroyed, while the Christ figure preaches pacifism. Always self-promoting, Ince personally showed the picture to Wilson, who, Ince followers allege, praised it highly, and Ince had his photo taken with the president. Afterwards, a prominent Democrat claimed the picture helped Wilson in his election victory over Charles Evans Hughes. When it opened in New York City, actress Billy Burke "fainted" in the audience for publicity purposes. In any event, as far as Ince was concerned, his great pictures were behind him by now and this was just a part of the closing chapter on a once great career.

p, Thomas H. Ince; d, Ince, Raymond West, Reginald Barker, Jay Hunt, Walter Edwards, J. Parker Read, David Hartford; w, C. Gardner Sullivan; ph, Irvin Willat, Joseph August, Dal Clawson, O. M. Grove, Clyde De Vinna, J. D. Jennings, Charles Kaufman.

War/Drama **Cas.** **(PR:A MPAA:NR)**

CLANCY'S KOSHER WEDDING* . (1927) 6 reels R-C/FBO bw

George Sidney *(Hyman Cohen)*, Will Armstrong *(Timothy Clancy)*, Ann Brody *(Mamma Cohen)*, Mary Gordon *(Molly Clancy)*, Sharon Lynn *(Leah Cohen)*, Rex Lease *(Tom Clancy)*, Ed Brady *(Izzy Murphy)*.

The Jewish and Irish owners of adjacent clothing stores are constantly at one another's throats. Their progeny, Lynn and Lease, naturally fall in love. Lynn's father Sidney tries to force his choice—Brady, a Jewish prizefighter—on her. At an outing, the two suitors fight for Lynn's hand. The fathers place a side bet, each wagering the family business. Lease gets Lynn, and the fathers decide to join their businesses so they can keep on arguing. One of many films to take advantage of the Jewish-Irish illicit romance theme popularized by the long-running hit play "Abie's Irish Rose" written by Anne Nichols in 1922.

d, Arvid E. Gillstrom; w, J. G. Hawks, Curtis Benton, Gilbert Pratt (based on a story by Al Boasberg); ph, Charles Boyle.

Comedy **(PR:A MPAA:NR)**

CLARION, THE** (1916) 5 reels EQ/WORLD bw

Carlyle Blackwell *(Harrington Surtaine)*, Howard Hall *(Dr. Surtaine)*, Marion Dentler *(Esme Elliot)*, Charles Mason *(Dr. Mark Elliot)*, George Soule Spencer *(Norman Hale)*, Rosemary Dean *(Milly Beal)*, Phillip Hahn *(Max Veltman)*.

Pretty good programmer about an idealistic youth who purchases a small town paper and continues to expose corruption, in spite of the fact that his father is involved in an investigation and his sweetheart owns property in a slum which he has set out to clean up.

d, James Durkin; w, (based on the novel by Samuel Hopkins Adams).

Drama **(PR:A MPAA:NR)**

CLASSMATES*** (1914) 4 reels American Biograph-Klaw & Erlanger bw

Blanche Sweet, Henry B. Walthall, Lionel Barrymore, Marshall Neilan, Gertrude Robinson, Thomas Jefferson, Dorothy Bernard.

Interesting early feature about four West Point cadets, rivalry for a pretty girl, bravery, and suspense, set in the jungles of South America. Though credited with the picture's supervision, D. W. Griffith had already departed from Biograph, the company his weekly one-reelers had supported for so many years. His credit probably resulted more from his fame in the public's perception than from any work he did on the picture. His bosses at Biograph, Jermiah J. Kennedy and H. N. Marvin, had—ironically—battled with Griffith over whether his first feature-length film, JUDITH OF BETHULIA, should be made. By the time the offended Griffith departed from the studio, the moguls were already committed to features such as this one, having made a deal with theatrical producers Klaw & Erlanger to film their successful plays. (Interestingly, Griffith later was to disavow similar credits for supervising some of the productions of Harry E. Aitken's Triangle Film Corporation, his next employer.) Many of Griffith's stock-company players are featured in CLASSMATES and the successful play on which it is based was co-authored by Cecil B. DeMille's playwright brother, William.

d, James Kirkwood; sup, D. W. Griffith; w, Frank E. Woods (based on a play by William C. DeMille, Margaret Turnbull).

Drama **(PR:A MPAA:NR)**

CLASSMATES*** (1924) 7 reels INSP/FN bw

Claude Brooke *(Duncan Irving, Sr.)*, Richard Barthelmess *(Duncan Irving, Jr.)*, Reginald Sheffield *(Bert Stafford)*, Charlotte Walker *(Mrs. Stafford, His Mother)*, Madge Evans *(Sylvia Randolph, Her Niece)*, Beach Cooke *(Bubby Dumble)*, James Bradbury, Jr. *("Silent" Clay)*, Antrim Short *(James, a West Pointer)*, Maj. Henry B. Lewis *(Major Lane, Officer in Charge)*, Richard Harlan *(A Halfbreed)*, Tony Tommy *(An Indian Guide)*, Herbert Corthell *(Drummer)*.

Location shooting at West Point and a sensitive performance by Barthelmess as a cadet expelled in his third year after being goaded into punching an underclassman who wishes to secure his own release, made this picture a winner. Barthelmess pursues the young opportunist to South America, clears his name, and is married, with all the trimmings, at the military academy.

d, John S. Robertson; w, Josephine Lovett (based on the play by Margaret Turnbull, William C. DeMille); ph, Roy Overbaugh, John F. Seitz; ed, William Hamilton.

Drama **(PR:A MPAA:NR)**

CLAY DOLLARS** (1921) 5 reels SELZ/SEL bw

Eugene O'Brien *(Bruce Edwards)*, Ruth Dwyer *(June Gordon)*, Frank Currier *(Sam Willetts)*, Arthur Houseman *(Ben Willetts)*, Jim Tenbrooke *(Lafe Gordon)*, Florida Kingsley *(Mrs. Gordon)*, Tom Burke *(Buck Jones)*, Jerry Devine, *(Peter)*, Bruce Reynolds *(Village Cut-up)*.

O'Brien returns home to discover that the land his uncle willed him has been traded—through death-bed conniving—for valueless farm property by a crooked neighbor whose son covets the girl O'Brien loves. As the film moves along, he shrewdly convinces the villain that the farm is actually worth a fortune because expensive bricks can be made from the soil. This leads to the ultimate exchange of property and a happy ending. The film is not exactly action-packed.

d, George Archainbaud; w, Lewis Allen Browne; ph, Jules Cronjager.

Drama **(PR:A MPAA:NR)**

CLEAN UP, THE** (1923) 5 reels UNIV bw

Herbert Rawlinson *(Montgomery Bixby)*, Claire Adams *(Phyllis Andrews)*, Claire Anderson *(Mary Reynolds)*, Herbert Fortier *(Robert Reynolds)*, Margaret Campbell *(Mrs. Reynolds)*, Frank Farrington *(Amos Finderson)*.

A tycoon dies, leaving $50,000 to everyone who was born, bred, and still living in his town. To his nephew, he bequeaths one dollar and requests that he remain on for 30 days. The money goes to everyone's heads and the town goes to hell. But the nephew, at the suggestion of a pretty girl, takes control of the situation and saves the community. Then, to top things off, the uncle's attorney presents him with a check for $2 million which was granted on the condition that the lad would learn from the earlier object lesson. Where else could it happen but in America?

d, William Parke; w, Raymond L. Shrock, Eugene Lewis, Harvey Gates (based on a story by H. H. Van Loan); ph, Richard Fryer.

Comedy/Drama **(PR:A MPAA:NR)**

CLEARING THE TRAIL** (1928) 6 reels UNIV bw

Hoot Gibson *(Pete Watson)*, Dorothy Gulliver *(Ellen)*, Fred Gilman *(Steve Watson)*, Cap Anderson *(Dan Talbot)*, Philo McCullough *(Silk Cardross)*, Andy Waldron *(Judge Price)*, Duke Lee *(Cook)*, Monte Montague *(Tramp)*, Universal Ranch Riders *(Cowboys)*.

After learning that his father has been murdered and the ranch taken over by a couple of bad men, Gibson returns home, takes a job as cook, and finally leads his friends in a gun battle against the outlaws that sets everything straight.

d, B. Reeves Eason; w, John F. Natteford (based on a story by Charles Maigne); t, Harold Tarshis; ph, Harry Neumann; ed, Gilmore Walker; art d, David S. Garber.

Western **(PR:A MPAA:NR)**

CLEMENCEAU CASE, THE*** (1915) 6 reels FOX bw

Theda Bara, William E. Shay, Stuart Holmes, Jane Lee, Mrs. Cecil Raleigh.

Brenon's direction was fine (especially in his effective use of closeups) and Bara was quite good as the wife-vampire in this exciting screen adaptation of a lesser known work by Dumas the younger. The third picture for the legendary screen vamp Bara.

d&w, Herbert Brenon (based on a play by Martha Woodrow from a novel by Alexandre Dumas *fils*).

Drama **(PR:A MPAA:NR)**

CLEVER MRS. CARFAX, THE*** (1917) 5 reels LAS/PAR bw

Julian Eltinge *(Temple Trask)*, Fred Church *(Billy Wise)*, Daisy Robinson *(Helen Scott)*, Jennie Lee *(Mrs. Mary Keyes)*, Noah Beery *(Adrian Graw)*, Rosita Marstini *(Rena Varsey)*.

Eltinge, the foremost female impersonator of his day, plays a newspaper lonely hearts columnist who makes a bet that he can attend a luncheon dressed in female garb without being detected. At the restaurant he becomes attracted to a young woman who is in the company of a man he recognizes as being a crook. In order to protect her, he accompanies the couple (dressed in drag) on an ocean voyage where, in the end, he saves the day and wins the girl. Eltinge's ability to laugh at himself made this film a total delight.

d, Donald Crisp; w, Gardner Hunting (based on a story by Hunting, Hector Turnbull).

Comedy **(PR:A MPAA:NR)**

CLIMBERS, THE* (1915) 5 reels Lubin bw

Gladys Hanson, George Soule Spencer, Jack Standing, Charles Brandt, Ruth Brynan, Rosetta Brice, Peter Lang, Ferdinand Tidmarsh, Walter Hitchcock, Clarence Elmer, Frankie Mann, Eleanor Barry, Bernard Siegel, Walter Law, Edith Ritchie, Walter Clarke, Mildred Gregory, Florence Hackett.

Less-than-impressive drama in which a social-climbing husband ruins and causes the death of his heiress wife's father and, in the end, pays the price through personal disgrace. This film, although poorly done, was based on a popular play which was shot again in 1919 featuring Corinne Griffith.

d, Barry O'Neill; w, Clay M. Greene (based on a play by Clyde Fitch).

Drama **(PR:A MPAA:NR)**

CLIMBERS, THE* (1919) 5 reels VIT bw

Corinne Griffith *(Blanche Sterling)*, Hugh Huntley *(Richard Sterling)*, Percy Marmont *(Ned Warden)*, Henry Hallam *(George Hunter)*, Emily Fitzroy *(Mrs. Hunter)*, Josephine Whittell *(Clara Hunter)*, Jane Jennings *(Aunt Ruth Hunter)*, James Spottswood *(James Garfield Trotter)*, Corinne Barker *(Julia Godesby)*, Charles Halton *(Jordan)*.

Second filming of Fitch's popular society drama about a man obsessed with climbing to the top. His wife is content with happiness and there is another man who has been willing to stand in the shadows because of his love for her. However, after the husband kills himself by taking poison, the other man steps forward and the two begin their climb to the *true* pinnacle of success.

d, Tom Terriss; w, (based on the play by Clyde Fitch); ph, Thomas Malloy.

Drama **(PR:A MPAA:NR)**

CLOTHES MAKE THE PIRATE*** (1925) 9 reels Sam E. Rork/FN bw

Leon Errol *(Trem Tidd)*, Dorothy Gish *(Betsy Tidd)*, Nita Naldi *(Mme. De La Tour)*, Tully Marshall *(Scute, the Baker)*, James Rennie *(Lt. Cavendish)*, Edna Murphy *(Nancy Downs)*, George F. Marion *(Jennison)*, Walter Law *(Dixie Bull, the Pirate)*, Frank Lalor *(Crabb, the Innkeeper)*, Reginald Barlow *(Capt. Montague)*.

Errol, a tailor in 18th-Century Boston, is badly henpecked by his wife, Gish, and dreams of living the life of a pirate. One night, while wearing his pretend pirate outfit, real buccaneers mistake him for their captain and haul him back to their ship. Lots of laughs as the little comic blunders his way through one high-seas adventure after another, including the capture of his wife, who fails to recognize him because he has shaved his whiskers. This gives him the opportunity to get even for all of the years she dumped on him. When the picture ends, the couple are back in Boston, with the little tailor very much in command and the wife loving it.

d, Maurice Tourneur; sup&w, Marion Fairfax (based on a novel by Holman Francis Day); ph, Henry Cronjager, Louis Dunmyre; ed, Patricia Rooney; art d, Charles O. Seessel.

Comedy/Adventure **(PR:A MPAA:NR)**

CLOWN, THE*** (1927) 6 reels COL bw

Johnny Walker *(Bob Stone)*, Dorothy Revier *(Fanchon)*, William V. Mong *(Albert Wells)*, John Miljan *(Bert Colton)*, Barbara Tennant *(Corinne)*, Charlotte Walker.

Fine little programmer about a clown and part circus owner who discovers his wife making love to his partner. He intends to kill the man, but before he can a storm dislodges a beam, crushing his wife. The paramour accuses the clown of murdering her, and he is sent to prison. Years later, the circus plays the penitentiary, and the former clown sees his child as an adult for the first time. Overcome by emotion, he escapes and the film ends a la *HE WHO GETS SLAPPED*, with the old clown feeding his enemy to an unfriendly lion.

p, Harry Cohn; d, W. James Craft; w, Dorothy Howell, Harry O. Hoyt; ph, Norbert Brodin.

Drama **(PR:C MPAA:NR)**

COBRA* (1925) 7 reels Ritz-Carlton/PAR bw

Rudolph Valentino *(Count Rodrigo Torriani)*, Nita Naldi *(Elise Van Zile)*, Casson Ferguson *(Jack Dorning)*, Gertrude Olmstead *(Mary Drake)*, Hector V. Sarno *(Victor Minardi)*, Claire De Lorez *(Rosa Minardi)*, Eileen Percy *(Sophie Binner)*, Lillian Langdon *(Mrs. Porter Palmer)*, Henry Barrows *(Store Manager)*, Rosa Rosanova *(Marie)*, Natacha Rambova.

Valentino's first independent production after a long absence from the screen included a dance act which he performed with his wife, Rambova. The resulting film is pretty much a mess. It tells the story of an impoverished Italian nobleman (Valentino) who collects women as a hobby. Forced to take a job to pay off his debt-ridden palace, Valentino accepts a position from Ferguson, an antique dealer, at whose shop he meets and genuinely falls in love with Olmstead, the secretary. At the same time he is pursued by Naldi, who believes him wealthy. When she discovers that Valentino is broke, she sets her sights on Ferguson and ends up marrying him. She again tries to have an affair with Valentino, who ignores her at first but finally agrees to meet her in a hotel. At the last minute, Valentino feels a sense of guilt and leaves the hotel, which later burns down, killing Naldi. Ferguson is grief-stricken by the news, while Valentino leaves town. When he returns a year later he finds that Ferguson has regained his peace in the care of Olmstead, and despite his love for her, the Italian leaves the couple to find happiness together. According to actress Colleen Moore, who was working next to the Valentino set at the time, the area was completely closed off by curtains, so she and actor Mervyn LeRoy cut a hole in the fabric and charged the girls in the studio a nickel a peek.

d, Joseph Henabery; w, Anthony Coldeway; ph, J. D. Jennings, Harry Fischbeck; set d, William Cameron Menzies.

Drama **Cas.** **(PR:A MPAA:NR)**

CODE OF MARCIA GRAY*** (1916) 5 reels Morosco/PAR bw

Constance Collier *(Marcia Gray)*, Henry DeVere *(Harry Gray)*, Forrest Stanley *(Orlando Castle)*, Herbert Standing *(Banker Agnew)*, Howard Davies *(Crane)*, Helen Jerome Eddy *(Crane's Daughter)*, Frank Boon *(James Romaine)*.

Lloyd skillfully directed this film (based on a true situation which destroyed the Knickerbocker Bank in New York City and caused the panic of 1907) about a banker who is arrested for manipulating funds and causing the collapse of his own institution. When his faithful wife seeks bail money, she discovers that none of her socially prominent friends will get involved. She therefore pawns her jewels and, in desperation, turns to an attorney who secretly loves her. He not only comes up with the bond, but also spends the last of his funds to redeem her gems. When the husband returns home with two tickets to South America, he finds the lawyer there, flies into a rage, and demands that she make a choice between them. The wife does so by tearing up one of the tickets, and the banker storms out. The lawyer further proves his love by refusing to turn the man in (even though his skipping bail will cause near-bankruptcy) saying that he would rather start again from scratch than do anything to embarrass the only woman he ever loved. Meanwhile, the escaping fugitive is met and murdered by a depositor who was ruined because of his chicanery. This leaves the widow and her devoted attorney free to find happiness together.

d, Frank Lloyd; w, Lloyd, Elliot J. Clawson.

Drama **(PR:A MPAA:NR)**

CODE OF THE RANGE** (1927) 5 reels RAY bw

Jack Perrin, Rex the Dog, Starlight the Horse, Pauline Curley, Nelson McDowell, Lew Meehan, Chic Olsen.

Perrin is a righteous cowboy bent on revenge for the murder of his schoolteacher sister, who was seduced into becoming a dance hall girl after answering an advertisement for a teaching position. Perrin's horse and dog were used to particularly good advantage in this edition of his popular series.

d, Morris R. Schlank, Ben Cohn; w, Cleve Meyer; ph, William Hyer.

Western **(PR:A MPAA:NR)**

CODE OF THE SEA*** (1924) 6 reels FP/PAR bw

Rod La Rocque *(Bruce McDow)*, Jacqueline Logan *(Jenny Hayden)*, George Fawcett *(Capt. Hayden)*, Maurice B. Flynn *(Ewart Radcliff)*, Luke Cosgrave *(Capt. Jonas)*, Lillian Leighton *(Mrs. McDow)*, Sam Appell *(John Swayne)*.

Exciting programmer about a son (La Rocque) who overcomes the stigma of having a father who violated "the code of the sea" when he lifted anchor and escaped during a storm. The film climaxes with a terrific storm sequence in which the son not only fails to panic, but also acts heroically.

d, Victor Fleming; w, Bertram Millhauser (based on a story by Byron Morgan); ph, Charles Edgar Schoenbaum.

Drama **(PR:A MPAA:NR)**

COHENS AND KELLYS, THE*** (1926) 8 reels UNIV bw

Charlie Murray *(Patrick Kelly)*, George Sidney *(Jacob Cohen)*, Vera Gordon *(Mrs. Cohen)*, Kate Price *(Mrs. Kelly)*, Olive Hasbrouck *(Nannie Cohen)*, Nat Carr *(Milton Katz)*, Mickey Bennett *(Milton J. Katz)*.

Murray is an Irish cop who constantly bickers with Sidney, who owns a drygoods emporium. Their progeny, of course, fall in love and secretly marry. Pregnant, the Cohen girl (Hasbrouck) is cloistered from the Kelly clan. When Sidney visits an unexpected act of honesty upon his policeman adversary, the two families are united and join in a business enterprise. First in a series of popular comedies about the problems created when an Irish boy falls in love with a Jewish girl. Actually, "Uncle" Carl Laemmle, the crafty head of Universal Studios, used the play "Two Blocks Away" (from which his picture was adapted) as an excuse to blatantly plagiarize the phenomenal success of the play "Abie's Irish Rose".

p, E. M. Asher; d, Harry Pollard; w, Alfred A. Cohn, Pollard (based on the play "Two Blocks Away" by Aaron Hoffman); ph, Charles Stumar; art d, Charles D. Hall.

Comedy **(PR:A MPAA:NR)**

COHENS AND THE KELLYS IN PARIS, THE*** (1928) 8 reels UNIV bw

George Sidney *(Nathan Cohen)*, J. Farrell MacDonald *(Mr. Kelly)*, Vera Gordon *(Mrs. Cohen)*, Kate Price *(Mrs. Kelly)*, Charles Delaney *(Patrick Kelly)*, Sue Carol *(Sadye Cohen)*, Gertrude Astor *(Paulette)*, Gino Corrado *(Pierre, Paulette's Husband)*, Charlie Murray.

Hoping to prevent two of their offspring from marrying during a study tour of Paris, business partners Sidney and MacDonald travel to the City of Light to find they are too late. Instead, they find themselves helping to resolve the newlyweds' marital discord, which resulted from husband Delaney's attention to model Astor, whom he is painting. A battle with Astor's spouse Corrado nearly wrecks a bistro. The errant partners and their progeny are rescued by the parents' wives, who scoop them up in an airplane. The second of the COHENS AND THE KELLYS series (which carried on into talkies) is better than you might think.

d, William Beaudine; sup, Joseph Poland; w, Alfred A. Cohn; t, Albert De Mond; ph, Charles Stumar; ed, Frank Atkinson, Robert Carlisle.

Comedy **(PR:A MPAA:NR)**

COLLEGE*** (1927) 6 reels Joseph M. Schenck/UA

Buster Keaton *(Ronald)*, Ann Cornwall *(Mary Haines, the Girl)*, Flora Bramley *(Her Friend)*, Harold Goodwin *(Jeff Brown, a Rival)*, Grant Withers, Buddy Mason *(His Friends)*, Snitz Edwards *(The Dean)*, Carl Harbaugh *(Crew Coach)*, Sam Crawford *(Baseball Coach)*, Florence Turner *(Ronald's Mother)*, Lee Barnes *(Keaton's Double for Pole Vault)*, Paul Goldsmith, Morton Kaer, Bud Houser, Kenneth Grumbles, Charles Borah, Leighton Dye, "Shorty" Worden, Robert Boling, Erick Mack *(Themselves)*, University of Southern California Baseball Team.

Keaton—as an undergraduate studious bookworm—loses his love Cornwall to athlete Goodwin. Determined to win her back, he enrolls at the college they both attend—working as a soda jerk to pay his tuition—armed with self-help books on sports. In academe, he tries out for virtually every athletic event, to no avail: the broad jump leaves him with his head stuck in the sand, his kicking feet in evidence; during a dash, two juveniles overtake him; he knocks over every hurdle but the last, then prissily pushes that one over for the sake of neatness. His efforts at the soda fountain are equally inept. Counseled by a friendly dean, Edwards, Keaton gets the post of coxswain for the varsity crew. Despite the crew's efforts to dislodge him from the rudder, he persists and the crew wins a big race. When his true love is threatened by the lustful Goodwin, the tenacious Keaton responds to her telephoned plea for help with a characteristic burst of athletic prowess, racing to her assistance over hedges, overtaking speeding motorcars, leaping vast chasms, and, finally, pole vaulting into her dormitory window. Keaton's previous picture, THE GENERAL, had lost money, and it was to be the last of his independent productions to bear his name alone as director. Money man Aubrey Schenck had decided to pay closer attention to the finances, and installed Horne as director on this one. The prosaic story line contained some rare moments of classic Keaton visual comedy, but COLLEGE is generally regarded as his weakest feature film. It barely cleared expenses at the box office. The film marked the only time that Keaton ever used a stunt double; Olympic pole vaulter Barnes handled that one athletic activity for him.

d, James W. Horne; sup, Harry Brand; w, Carl Harbaugh, Bryan Foy; ph, J. Devereux Jennings, Bert Haines; ed, J. S. Kell.

Comedy **Cas.** **(PR:A MPAA:NR)**

COLLEGE DAYS*** (1926) 8 reels TIF bw

Marceline Day *(Mary Ward)*, Charles Delaney *(Jim Gordon)*, James Harrison *(Larry Powell)*, Duane Thompson *(Phyllis)*, Brooks Benedict *(Kenneth Slade)*, Kathleen Key *(Louise)*, Edna Murphy *(Bessie)*, Robert Homans *(Mr. Gordon)*, Crauford Kent *(Kent)*, Charles Wellesley *(Bryson)*, Gibson Gowland *(Carter)*, Lawford Davidson *(Prof. Maynard)*, Pat Harmon *(The Coach)*, William A. Carroll *(Dean)*.

Realistic look at college life in the 1920s, complete with roadhouse parties, flappers, the Charleston, and jazz. The big football game finale is sensational, perhaps because of the presence of Younger (who adapted *Brown of Harvard* to the screen) as supervisor.

d, Richard Thorpe; sup&w, A. P. Younger; ph, Milton Moore, Mack Stengler; ed, James C. McKay; art d, Edwin B. Willis.

Drama **(PR:A MPAA:NR)**

COME ON OVER**** (1922) 6 reels Goldwyn bw

Colleen Moore *(Moyna Killiea)*, Ralph Graves *(Shane O'Mealia)*, J. Farrell MacDonald *(Michael Morahan)*, James Marcus *(Carmody)*, Kate Price *(Delia Morahan)*, Kathleen O'Connor *(Judy Dugan)*, Florence Drew *(Bridget Morahan)*, Harold Holland *(Myle Morahan)*, Mary Warren *(Kate Morahan)*, Elinor Hancock *(Mrs. Van Dusen)*, Monte Collins *(Dugan)*, C. E. Mason *(Barney)*, C. B. Leasure *(Priest)*.

This heartwarming, sentimental, Celtic ballad of a movie tells the story of three generations of Irish and Irish Americans. Produced, as it was, during a time when audiences regarded kindness, loyalty, and love as virtues, this wonderful film—with its equal portions of laughter and tears—was as capable of touching the heart as the poetry of the Emerald Isle itself.

d, Alfred E. Green; w, Rupert Hughes; ph, L. William O'Connell; art d, Cedric Gibbons.

Drama/Comedy, **(PR:AA MPAA:NR)**

COMING AN' GOING** (1926) 5 reels Action/Artclass bw

Buffalo Bill, Jr. *(Bill Martin)*, Belva McKay *(Rose Brown)*, Harry Todd *(Andy Simms)*, Hal Thompson *(James Brice Brown)*, Mathilde Brundage *(Mrs. Brown)*.

When a cowboy wakes up in a girl's hotel room, her banker father forces him to marry her, even though she regards him with disdain. Later, the young man saves her mother's life in a fire and is accepted by the family.

d, Richard Thorpe; w, Frank L. Inghram.

Western Drama **(PR:A MPAA:NR)**

COMING OF AMOS, THE**** (1925) 6 reels Cinema/PDC bw

Rod La Rocque *(Amos Burden)*, Jetta Goudal *(Princess Nadia Ramiroff)*, Noah Beery *(Ramon Garcia)*, Richard Carle *(David Fontenay)*, Arthur Hoyt *(Bendyke Hamilton)*, Trixie Friganza *(Duchess of Perth)*, Clarence Burton *(Pedro Valdez)*, Ruby Lafayette *(The Nurse)*.

This send-off of melodramas is great fun from beginning to end. La Rocque plays an Australian who visits the French Riviera and falls in love with a Russian princess, beautifully played by Goudal. Beery (in a classic performance) lusts for, and is rejected by, the Princess, which leads him to kidnap and imprison her in the torture chamber of his castle fortress. When she refuses to yield to his libidinous demands, he pulls the lever which opens the floodgates. It looks like a watery end for poor Goudal, but La Rocque, in the best Douglas Fairbanks tradition, fights his way to the rescue and sees to it that Beery perishes by his own hideous device.

p, Cecil B. DeMille; d, Paul Sloane; w, James Ashmore Creelman, Garrett Fort (based on a story by William John Locke); ph, Arthur Miller; ed, Elmer Harris; art d, Chester Gore.

Satire/Adventure **Cas.** **(PR:A MPAA:NR)**

COMMANDING OFFICER, THE** (1915) 4 reels FP bw

Alice Dovey *(Floyd Bingham)*, Donald Crisp *(Col. Archer)*, Marshall Neilan *(Capt. Waring)*, Douglas Gerrard *(Brent Lindsay)*, Ethel Phillips *("The Queen")*, Russell Bassett *(Col. Bingham, Retired)*, Bob Emmons *(The Sheriff)*, Jack Pickford *(The Commandant's Orderly)*, Francis Carpenter *(The Boy)*, Olive Johnson *(The Girl)*.

Story of a young woman (Dovey) who marries an army officer (Crisp) because he is left two small children after the death of his sister, and because her father, a fellow officer, wanted her to. When Crisp becomes abusive, she turns to a former gentleman friend, and at this time evidence appears indicating that Crisp may have murdered still another of his wife's former suitors. He stands trial for the crime but is found innocent.

d, Allan Dwan; w, Theodore Burt Sayre.

Drama **(PR:A MPAA:NR)**

COMMON LAW, THE*** (1916) 7 reels SF bw

Clara Kimball Young *(Valerie West)*, Conway Tearle *(Neville)*, Paul Capellani *(Querida)*, Edna Hunter *(Rita)*, Lillian Cook *(Stephanie)*, Julia Stuart *(Mrs. Neville)*, Edward M. Kimball *(Mr. Neville)*, Lydia Knott *(Mrs. West)*, D. J. Flanagan *(Ogilvy)*, Edna Hunter, Edmund Mortimer, Barry Whitcomb, Charles Craig, Julia Stuart.

This was Young's first film for Lewis J. Selznick, the immigrant father of David O. Selznick, and it made her a super star. She plays a young woman from a prominent background who becomes destitute upon the death of her mother and is forced to model in order to survive. Young's personal beauty and bearing did much to make this character totally believable. Audiences the world over cheered for her as she sacrificed her personal happiness for the young artist she loved, defended her honor by killing a lust-filled Spanish painter and, in the end, was rewarded by marrying her sweetheart after all.

d, Albert Capellani; w, (based on the novel by Robert W. Chambers); ph, Hal Young.

Drama **(PR:A MPAA:NR)**

COMMON LAW, THE*** (1923) 8 reels SF bw

Corinne Griffith *(Valerie West)*, Conway Tearle *(Louis Neville)*, Lillian Lawrence *(Martha Neville)*, Elliott Dexter *(Jose Querida)*, Hobart Bosworth *(Henry Neville)*, Bryant Washburn *(John Burleson)*, Doris May *(Stephanie)*, Harry Myers *(Cardemon)*, Miss Du Pont *(Lily Neville)*, Phyllis Haver *(Rita Tevis)*, Wally Van *(Samuel Ogilvy)*, Dagmar Godowsky *(Mazie)*.

Handsomely produced remake of the 1916 Selznick production, updated and altered to some extent, but with Tearle reviving his role of Louis Neville.

d, George Archainbaud; sup, Myron Selznick; w, Edward J. Montagne (based on the story by Robert Chambers).

Drama **(PR:A MPAA:NR)**

COMPROMISE*** (1925) 7 reels WB bw

Irene Rich *(Joan Trevore)*, Clive Brook *(Alan Thayer)*, Louise Fazenda *(Hilda)*, Pauline Garon *(Nathalie)*, Raymond McKee *(Cholly)*, Helen Dunbar *(Aunt Catherine)*, Winter Hall *(Joan's Father)*, Lynn Cowan *(James)*, Edward Martindale *(Commodore Smithson)*, Frank Butler *(Ole)*, Muriel Frances Dana *(Nathalie as a Child)*.

Story of a neglected older sister (Rich) who marries the town hunk while her pampered younger sister is in Europe getting a divorce. When the girl returns, she sets out to steal away her brother-in-law but loses out in the end. There is a whale of a tornado scene towards the end of this movie.

d, Alan Crosland; w, Edward T. Lowe, Jr. (based on a novel by Jay Gelzer); ph, David Abel.

Drama **(PR:A MPAA:NR)**

CONFLICT, THE** (1921) 7 reels UNIV bw

Priscilla Dean *(Dorcas Remalie)*, Ed Connelly *(John Remalie)*, Martha Mattox *(Miss Labo)*, Hector Sarno *(Buck Fallon)*, Olah Norman *(Letty Piggott)*, Herbert Rawlinson *(Jevons)*, L. C. Shumway *(Mark Sloane)*, Sam Allen *(Orrin Lakin)*, C. E. Anderson *(Ovid Jenks)*, Knute Erickson *(Hannibal Ginger)*, Bill Gillis *(Hasdrubel Ginger)*.

To accommodate her late father's deathbed wish, socialite Dean goes to the timber country to live with her uncle, Connelly, a cruel and autocratic lumber lord. His jealous housekeeper, the sinister Mattox, attempts to poison Dean, who runs to Rawlinson—her uncle's adversary in a land-grabbing deal—for respite. When Rawlinson is captured by her uncle's minions, she assumes his place among the loggers and goes to his rescue. Connelly sees the errors of his ways after the two young people are nearly swept over a waterfall and all ends well. Except for the beautiful Dean, there is nothing above average in this outdoor northwoods adventure. Even the obligatory log jam sequence does not stand out.

d, Stuart Paton; w, George C. Hull (based on the novel *Conflict* by Clarence Budington Kelland); ph, Harold Janes.

Northwoods Adventure **(PR:A MPAA:NR)**

CONNECTICUT YANKEE AT KING ARTHUR'S COURT, A*** (1921) 8 reels Mark Twain-FOX bw

Harry C. Myers *(The Yankee/Martin Cavendish)*, Pauline Starke *(Sandy)*, Rosemary Theby *(Queen Morgan le Fay)*, Charles Clary *(King Arthur)*, William V. Mong *(Merlin, the Magician)*, George Siegmann *(Sir Sagramore)*, Charles Gordon *(The Page)*, Carl Formes *(Mark Twain)*, Herbert Fortier *(Mr. Cavendish)*, Adele Farrington *(Mrs. Cavendish)*, Wilfred MacDonald *(Sir Lancelot)*.

Douglas Fairbanks was offered the lead in this movie adaption of Mark Twain's wonderful satire about a modern American who is transported back to the days of King Arthur's England. He turned it down and the part went to Myers, who is best remembered as Chaplin's drunken sometimes friend and benefactor in CITY LIGHTS. Myers is fine in the role, which would subsequently be played by Will Rogers and Bing Crosby.

d, Emmett J. Flynn; w, Bernard McConville (based on the novel by Mark Twain); ph, Lucien Andriot; ed, C. R. Wallace; art d, Ralph De Lacy.

Satire **(PR:A MPAA:NR)**

CONQUERED HEARTS* (1918) 7 reels IV/Rialto bw

Marguerite Marsh, Corinne Uzzell, Emma Lowry, Eileen Walker, Richard Turner, Harry Myers, R. Paton Gibbs, Dean Raymond, Barney Gilmore, Frank Evans, Sheridan Tansey, Al Franklin Thomas.

Nothing out of the ordinary in this story of a salesgirl who makes it to the top by becoming a movie star. In the end, she turns down an Englishman of noble blood to marry her former prizefighter sweetheart. Marguerite Marsh (Mae's older sister) was quite good in this one, considering what she had to work with.

d, Francis J. Grandon; w, (based on a story by Emma Bell Clifton); ph, Marcel Le Picard.

Drama **(PR:A MPAA:NR)**

CONQUERING POWER, THE**** (1921) 7 reels Metro bw

Alice Terry *(Eugenie Grandet)*, Rudolph Valentino *(Charles Grandet)*, Eric Mayne *(Victor Grandet)*, Ralph Lewis *(Père Grandet)*, Edna Demaurey *(His Wife)*, Edward Connelly *(Notary Cruchot)*, George Atkinson *(His Son)*, Willard Lee Hall *(The Abbé)*, Mark Fenton *(Mons. des Grassins)*, Bridgetta Clark *(His Wife)*, Ward Wing *(Adolph)*, Mary Hearn *(Nanon)*, Eugène Pouyet *(Cornoiller)*, Andreé Tourneur *(Annette)*.

Ingram's follow-up to THE FOUR HORSEMEN OF THE APOCALYPSE is a beautiful and skillfully directed film and the first to present Valentino as a full-fledged star. The story told of an aristocratic Frenchman (Valentino) who is sent to live with his estranged uncle in Noyant after the family fortune is lost. The old sibling hatred between the brothers is passed on to the nephew, who has fallen in love with the cruel and miserly old man's step-daughter. In order to separate the youthful couple, Valentino is shipped off to Martinique, and all of their letters are intercepted. Eventually, the uncle (in a cinematic tour de force) experiences a horrible and solitary death in his strongroom, surrounded by his hoarded gold. Valentino, who has made good on his own, returns to be united with the woman he loves.

p&d, Rex Ingram; s, June Mathis (based on Honore de Balzac's novel *Eugenie Grandet*); ph, John F. Seitz; tech d, Ralph Barton, Amos Myers.

Drama **PR:A MPAA:NR)**

CONSPIRACY, THE*** (1914) 4 reels FP bw

John Emerson, Lois Meredith, Francis Byrne, Harold Lockwood, Dobson Mitchell, Iva Shepard, Hal Clarendon, Edward Durand.

Nifty, well-paced little mystery, which involves a writer of crime thrillers, a girl detective, a dope fiend, and just the right amount of humor to set the whole thing off. Emerson would, of course, go on to create movie magic directing Douglas Fairbanks' breezy series of action-comedies.

d, Allan Dwan; w, (based on a play by Robert Baker, John Emerson).

Crime/Comedy **(PR:A MPAA:NR)**

CONSPIRATORS, THE (SEE: BARNES MURDER CASE, THE, 1930, Brit.)

CONVOY** (1927) 8 reels Robert Kane/FN bw

Lowell Sherman *(Ernest Drake)*, Dorothy Mackaill *(Sylvia Dodge)*, William Collier, Jr. *(John Dodge)*, Lawrence Gray *(Eugene Wyeth)*, Ian Keith *(Smith)*, Gail Kane *(Mrs. Wyeth)*, Vincent Serrano *(Mr. Dodge)*, Donald Reed *(Smith's Assistant)*, Eddie Gribbon *(Eddie)*, Jack Ackroyd *(Jack)*, Ione Holmes *(Ione)*.

Heavy use of newsreel, and perhaps official government footage of battle scenes, could not elevate this picture above the programmer level. Advertised as "The Big Parade of the Navy," it tells the story of a spy (Sherman) and an American agent (Mackaill) and their romantic involvement during WW I.

p, Victor Hugo Halperin, Edward R. Halperin; d, Joseph C. Boyle; w, Willis Goldbeck (based on the novel *The Song of the Dragon* by John Taintor Foote); ph, Ernest Haller.

Spy **(PR:A MPAA:NR)**

CORNER IN COLLEENS, A*** (1916) 5 reels TRI bw

Charles Ray *(Richard Taylor)*, Bessie Barriscale *(Shamrock)*, Margery Wilson *(Rose)*, Roy Neill *(Dan Allen)*, Aggie Herring *(Annie Fahy)*, Walter Perry *(Manus McCoy)*, Alice Taaffe [Terry] *(Daisy)*, Alice Lawrence *(Hyacinth)*, Charles French *(English Commander)*, George Fisher, Jerome Storm.

Ray is an American who travels to Ireland (shortly after the Easter Uprising) to look over the estate he has just inherited. Once there, he discovers an old nurse is living on his property with four orphaned girls. At first there is hostility towards the "furriner" on the part of the prettiest of these, but after Ray takes on a squadron of British troops (who are searching for the colleen following a rebel meeting) the girl realizes that the Yankee is indeed the boy for her.

d, Charles Miller; w, C. Gardner Sullivan; ph, Clyde De Vinna.

Comedy/Drama **(PR:A MPAA:NR)**

CORPORAL KATE* (1926) 8 reels De Mille/PDC bw

Vera Reynolds *(Kate)*, Julia Faye *(Becky)*, Majel Coleman *(Evelyn)*, Kenneth Thompson *(Jackson)*, Fred Allen *(Williams)*.

Low-budget WW I picture about two female entertainers (one Jewish and one Irish) who fall in love with the same soldier in France. The doughboy, however, goes to Reynolds when Faye is killed in action.

d, Paul Sloane; sup, C. Gardner Sullivan; w, Albert Shelby Le Vino (based on a story by Zelda Sears, Marion Orth); t, John Krafft; ph, Henry Cronjager.

Comedy **(PR:A MPAA:NR)**

COST, THE** (1920) 5 reels PAR bw

Violet Heming *(Pauline Gardner)*, Edwin Mordant *(Col. Gardner)*, Jane Jennings *(Mrs. Gardner)*, Ralph Kellard *(John Dumont)*, Edward Arnold *(Hampden Scarborough)*, Clifford Grey *(William Fanshaw, Jr.)*, Carlotta Monterey *(Leonora Fanshaw)*, Aileen Savage [Pringle] *(Olivia)*, Walburton Gamble *(Mowbray Langdon)*, Florence McGuire *(Suzanne)*, Julia Hurley *(Grandma)*, Arnold Lucy, Marjorie Manning.

Curious programmer about a boarding school girl who marries unhappily and then meets the fellow she loves. Her husband, who becomes head of the woolen trust, has an affair with an associate's wife and when his wife finds out she leaves him. Shortly thereafter, the man is nearly ruined in a financial crash, and his wife rejoins him to assist in the rebuilding. He is successful, but at the height of this triumph, drops dead— freeing her to marry the man she really loves.

d, Harley Knoles; w, Clara S. Beranger (based on the novel by David Graham Phillips); ph, Philip Hatkin.

Drama **(PR:A MPAA:NR)**

COTTON KING, THE** (1915) 5 reels Brady/WORLD bw

George Nash, Julia Hay, Eric Mayne, Fred Truesdell, Julia Stuart, Lillian Cook.

An honest businessman, who saves America from a band of crooked speculators who attempt to corner the cotton market, becomes known as the "Cotton King." He moves south, purchases a mill, becomes engaged to the daughter of one of the former partners, and incurs the hatred of another partner's son who lusts for the girl. After a number of attempts to get even, the vindictive young man is finally brought to justice. The film's highlight is a scene in which the girl is bound, gagged, and deposited at the bottom of an elevator shaft, where she is left to contemplate a most unpleasant death before the hero's last-minute rescue.

d&w, Oscar Eagle; (based on a play by Sutton Vane).

Drama **(PR:A MPAA:NR)**

COUNTERFEIT*** (1919) 5 reels PAR bw

Elsie Ferguson *(Virginia Griswald)*, David Powell *(Stuart Kent)*, Helene Montrose *(Mrs. Palmer)*, Charles Kent *(Col. Harrington)*, Charles Gerard *(Vincent Cortez)*, Ida Waterman *(Mrs. Griswald)*, Robert Lee Keeling *(Mr. Palmer)*, Fred Jenkins *(Uncle Ben)*, Mrs. Robertson *(Aunt Jemima)*, Elizabeth Breen *(Marinette, the Maid)*, Robert Vivian.

Ferguson arrives at the society resort of Newport about the time that considerable sums of counterfeit money are flooding the area. She is suspected by everyone except the young man who has fallen in love with her, but in the end she turns out to be a government agent and, of course, she breaks up the ring.

d, George Fitzmaurice; w, Ouida Bergere (based on a story by Robert Baker); ph, Arthur Miller.

Crime **(PR:A MPAA:NR)**

COUNTRY KID, THE*** (1923) 6 reels WB bw

Wesley Barry *(Ben Applegate)*, "Spec" O'Donnell *(Joe Applegate)*, Bruce Guerin *(Andy Applegate)*, Kate Toncray *(Mrs. Grimes)*, Helen Jerome Eddy *(Hazel Warren)*, George Nichols *(Mr. Grimes)*, Edward Burns *(Arthur Grant)*, George C. Pearce *(The Judge)*.

Pleasant comedy melodrama about the adventures of three orphans and a wicked uncle who is out to steal their inheritance. This is one of the best-remembered of Barry, the freckle-faced teenager's, films.

d, William Beaudine; w, Julien Josephson; ph, E. B. Du Par; ed, Clarence Kolster.

Comedy/Drama **(PR:AA MPAA:NR)**

COUNTRY MOUSE, THE** (1914) 4 reels Bosworth bw

Hobart Bosworth *(Bill Balderson)*, Adele Farrington *(Addie Balderson)*, Marshall Stedman *(George Marshall)*, Myrtle Stedman *(Myrtle Marshall)*, Rhea Haines *(Mme. Pauline)*.

Bosworth and his wife, Farrington, go to Washington after he is elected to Congress, aiming to stop the railroad from plowing up his neighbor's land. Bosworth is targeted by a looker who is in the employ of the transportation lobby, but Farrington spruces herself up, becomes a knockout, and earns her husband's real passion.

d, Phillips Smalley; w, Hobart Bosworth.

Drama **(PR:A MPAA:NR)**

COUNTY CHAIRMAN, THE*** (1914) 5 reels FP bw

Macklyn Arbuckle *(The Honorable Jim Hackler)*, Willis P. Sweatnam *(Sassafras Livingston)*, Harold Lockwood *(Tillford Wheeler)*, Daisy Robinson *(Lucy Rigby)*, Mabel Wilbur *(Lorena Watkins)*, Amy Simmons *(Chick)*, Wellington A. Playter *(Joseph Whittaker)*, William Lloyd *(Elias Rigby)*, Helen Aubrey *(Mrs. Rigby)*.

Combination of love and politics set against a rural backdrop, with just enough comedy to keep the film moving nicely. This was a fine slice of Americana which improved on the original play.

d&w, Allan Dwan (based on the play by George Ade).

Comedy/Drama **(PR:A MPAA:NR)**

COURAGE*** (1921) 6 reels Sidney A. Franklin/FN bw

Naomi Childers *(Jean Blackmoore)*, Sam De Grasse *(Stephan Blackmoore)*, Lionel Belmore *(Angus Ferguson)*, Adolphe Menjou *(Bruce Ferguson)*, Lloyd Whitlock *("Speedy" Chester)*, Alec B. Francis *(McIntyre)*, Ray Howard *(Stephan Blackmoore, Jr.)*, Gloria Hope *(Eve Hamish)*, Charles Hill Mailes *(Oliver Hamish)*.

Set in Scotland, this drama of a man who serves 18 years for a murder he did not commit, and whose wife loyally stands by him the entire time, was beautifully directed and produced. It was a programmer which rose well above the limitations of its budget.

p, Albert A. Kaufman; d, Sidney A. Franklin; w, Sada Cowan (based on a story by Andrew Soutar); ph, David Abel; ed, William Shea.

Drama **(PR:A MPAA:NR)**

COURTSHIP OF MILES STANDISH, THE*** (1923) 9 reels Charles Ray/AEX bw

Charles Ray *(John Alden)*, Enid Bennett *(Priscilla Mullens)*, E. Alyn Warren *(Miles Standish)*, Joseph Dowling *(Elder Brewster)*, Sam De Grasse *(John Carver)*, Norval MacGregor *(William Bradford)*, Thomas Holding *(Edward Winslow)*, Frank Farrington *(Isaac Allerton)*, William Sullivan *(John Howland)*, Marian Nixon.

Ray grew tired of playing the country boy roles which earned him fame and fortune, left Thomas Ince, and produced this historical extravaganza about the Pilgrim settlers and the love of John Alden (Ray) for Priscilla Mullens (Bennett). Ray invested his personal fortune in this undertaking, and although the film received some very favorable reviews, audiences really wanted to see Douglas Fairbanks in costume and not their lovable hayseed. The picture was a box-office disaster and the star never regained his once-loyal following. Ray was later forced to accept supporting roles, and finally extra bits before his untimely death in 1943 at the age of 52.

d, Frederick Sullivan; w, Al Ray (based on the poem by Henry Wadsworth Longfellow); ph, George Rizard.

Costume Drama **(PR:A MPAA:NR)**

COVERED TRAIL, THE* (1924) 5 reels SUN bw

J. B. Warner *(Bill Keats)*, Robert McKenzie *(Sheriff)*, Ruth Dwyer.

Cowboy Warner tries to divert his weak-willed brother from his thieving ways and is himself mistaken for a desperado. Saved from a lynch mob by the sheriff, McKenzie, Warner prevents a robbery of the local stagecoach line and, with McKenzie, captures the men responsible. He is then cleared of complicity by the confession of his dying brother. This was the last film made by second-string cowboy actor Warner, who died in 1924 at the young age of 29. Sadly, his last picture was as ordinary as his first.

d, Jack Nelson.

Western **(PR:A MPAA)**

COVERED WAGON, THE**** (1923) 10 reels FP/PAR bw

Lois Wilson *(Molly Wingate)*, J. Warren Kerrigan *(Will Banion)*, Ernest Torrence *(Jackson)*, Charles Ogle *(Mr. Wingate)*, Ethel Wales *(Mrs. Wingate)*, Alan Hale *(Sam Woodhull)*, Tully Marshall *(Bridger)*, Guy Oliver *(Kit Carson)*, John Fox *(Jed Wingate)*.

THE COVERED WAGON was not only the first epic western, it was also so well directed, photographed, and edited, that it gave the feeling of actually being a documentary—in spite of a somewhat banal plot and obligatory love story. Originally intended to be no more than a Mary Miles Minter programmer directed by George Melford, it came to the attention of Jesse Lasky, whose grandfather had entertained the producer, as a boy, with endless stories of his adventures crossing the continent in a prairie schooner. Lasky later became caught up in Emerson Hough's book while making the long parallel trip by train to the coast, and decided that this mighty chapter in the American saga deserved much more. Lasky replaced Melford with Cruze, the Utah-raised director who knew life in the real West firsthand. The choice was perfect and the resulting film—shot almost entirely on location with a cast of 3,000, under the toughest of conditions—is fraught with images that remain in the mind as sweeping scenes of endless wagons slowly on the move, silhouetted against the horizon, struggle to cross the Platte River. Fighting off Indian attacks (Col. McCoy had 1,000 native Americans from reservations across the country under his direction here), escaping cattle stampedes, and surviving by means of a bloody (though needlessly sadistic) buffalo hunt, were just some of the challenges realistically portrayed by Cruze. The story itself is pretty much a straight western melodrama, brightened up a bit by the inclusion of real-life characters. Torrence delivers a terrific performance, and the rest of the cast—with the exception of Kerrigan who is wrong for his part and was selected out of loyalty and friendship by Cruze—is fine. When all was said and done the story mattered not as it was really just the excuse Lasky and Cruze needed to re-create an important phase of America's history which they loved and understood and believed necessary to record on film. THE COVERED WAGON was enough of a hit in its own time to inspire a clever Will Rogers parody, released the same year: TWO WAGONS—BOTH COVERED which has the settlers arriving in California to be greeted by real estate developers.

p&d, James Cruze; w, Jack Cunningham (based on the novel by Emerson Hough); ph, Karl Brown; ed, Dorothy Arzner; adv, Col. T. J. McCoy.

Western **(PR:A MPAA:NR)**

COWARD, THE** (1927) 6 reels R-C/FBO bw

Warner Baxter *(Clinton Philbrook)*, Sharon Lynn *(Alicia Van Orden)*, Freeman Wood *(Leigh Morlock)*, Raoul Paoli *(Pierre Bechard)*, Byron Douglas *(Darius Philbrook)*, Charlotte Stevens *(Marie)*, Hugh Thomas *(Maitland)*.

Playboy Baxter falls in love with socialite Lynn, who scorns him for the idler he is. Insulted by his rival Wood, Baxter challenges Wood to fight, and is soundly trounced. Ashamed, Baxter becomes a remittance man, going to the North Woods, where he apprentices himself under the tutelage of trapper Paoli. Toughening up, Baxter manages to save Wood—who has had an accident while on a hunting trip—and carry him to civilization. Later challenged by Wood, Baxter knocks the bully senseless and wins the hand of Lynn. Better-than-average filming of that tired old story about the cowardly youth who goes to the North Woods and fights his way to manhood.

d, Alfred Raboch; w, Edfrid Bingham, Enid Hibbard, J. G. Hawks (based on the story by Arthur Stringer); ph, Jules Cronjager.

Adventure **(PR:A MPAA:NR)**

CRAB, THE** (1917) 5 reels TRI bw

Thelma Salter, Frank Keenan, Ernest Butterworth, Gertrude Claire, J.P. Lockney, Thomas J. Guise.

Salter, a minor child star of the 1910s and 1920s, is quite good as the orphaned child who brings happiness into the life of a lonely, miserly man.

d, Walter Edwards; w, C. Gardner Sullivan.

Drama **(PR:A MPAA:NR)**

CRADLE, THE** (1922) 5 reels LAS/PAR bw

Ethel Clayton *(Margaret Harvey)*, Charles Meredith *(Dr. Robert Harvey)*, Mary Jane Irving *(Doris Harvey)*, Anna Lehr *(Lola Forbes)*, Walter McGrail *(Courtney Webster)*, Adele Farrington *(Mrs. Mason)*.

This is a society drama with a message. It tells of a young couple who divorce and marry others, but after their child becomes ill due to mistreatment by both step-parents, they realize their mistake and return to each other.

d, Paul Powell; w, Olga Printzlau (based on the play "Le Berceau" by Eugene Brieux); ph, Hal Rosson.

Drama **(PR:A MPAA:NR)**

CRADLE BUSTER, THE*** (1922) 5 reels Patuwa/ARC bw

Glenn Hunter *(Benjamin Franklin Reed)*, Marguerite Courtot *(Gay Dixon)*, William H. Tooker *("Blarney" Dixon)*, Mary Foy *(Melia Prout)*, Lois Blaine *(Sally Ann Parsons)*, Osgood Perkins *("Cracked" Spoony)*, Townsend Martin *(Holcombe Derry)*, Beatrice Morgan *(Mrs. Reed)*.

Hunter, who excelled at playing country bumpkins (see MERTON OF THE MOVIES) is fine as the pampered mama's boy who overcomes the constant and cruel ridicule of his fellow youths to become a man and win the heart of the town beauty.

p, Frank Tuttle, Fred Waller, Jr.; d&w, Tuttle; ph, Waller; ed, Cecil R. Snape.

Comedy/Drama **(PR:A MPAA:NR)**

CRAIG'S WIFE*** (1928) 7 reels Pathe bw

Irene Rich *(Mrs. Craig)*, Warner Baxter *(Mr. Craig)*, Virginia Bradford *(Ethel)*, Carroll Nye *(John Fredericks)*, Lilyan Tashman *(Mrs. Passmore)*, George Irving *(Mr. Passmore)*, Jane Keckley *(Miss Austen)*, Mabel Van Buren *(Mrs. Frazer)*, Ethel Wales *(Eliza)*, Rada Rae *(Mary)*.

Fascinating story of a woman who dominates and humiliates her husband because of an obsession for material possessions—especially their house—which she governs tyrannically. When her husband is suspected of a double murder, this fastidious tyrant, to whom her home is everything, tries to thwart the police investigation so as not to disturb her household. The husband, Baxter, finally is exonerated but at last, realizing the intolerableness of living with his wife, he leaves her, taking his daughter with him. Remade in 1936 with Rosalind Russell, and again in 1950 with the title changed to HARRIET CRAIG, featuring Joan Crawford.

d, William C. De Mille; w, Clara Beranger (based on a novel by George Edward Kelly); ph, David Abel; ed, Anne Bauchens; art d, Edward Jewell.

Drama **(PR:A MPAA:NR)**

CRASHIN' THRU** (1923) 6 reels R-C/FBO bw

Harry Carey *(Blake)*, Charles LeMoyne *(Allison)*, Vesta Pegg *(Saunders)*, Cullen Landis *(Kid Allison)*, Joseph Harris *(Morelos)*, Neil Craig *(Garcia)*, Myrtle Steadman *(Celia Warren)*, Vola Vale *(Diane Warren)*, Charles Hill Mailes *(Uncle Benedict)*.

Carey plays a rancher whose life is saved by his partner who is crippled in the incident. The partner's son becomes involved with rustlers, and Carey, who has been performing the house chores, arranges for a "lonely hearts" wedding to give him the freedom to protect the livestock. When the woman arrives, she brings an unmentioned daughter, which negates the deal. In the end, Carey falls in love with the daughter, the partner with the mother, and the son is killed in a roundup of the outlaws.

d, Val Paul; w, Beatrice Van (based on the story "If a Woman Will" by Elizabeth Dejeans); ph, William Thornley, Robert De Grasse.

Western **(PR:A MPAA:NR)**

CRAVING, THE*** (1918) 5 reels BLUE bw (AKA: DELIRIUM)

Francis Ford *(Carroll Wales)*, May Gaston *(Beulah Grey)*, Peter Gerald *(Alla Kasarib)*, Duke Worne, Jean Hathaway.

Ford is a recovered alcoholic who discovers a new formula for a high explosive. Gerald realizes its value and sends his ward Gaston (whom he controls through hypnosis) to steal the secret by inducing the scientist to begin drinking again. She succeeds, and Ford sinks quickly to his former level. At this point, there is a beautifully filmed nightmare sequence in which the inventor tours the battlefields of Europe and is shown the effect his formula will have on the fate of the world. He awakens a reformed man, and later in a terrific struggle, kills Gerald, which frees Gaston from his spell.

d&w, Francis Ford, Jack Ford; ph, Edward Gheller.

Drama **(PR:A MPAA:NR)**

CRAZY TO MARRY*** (1921) 5 reels FP/PAR bw

Roscoe "Fatty" Arbuckle *(Dr. Hobart Hupp)*, Lila Lee *(Annabelle Landis)*, Laura Anson *(Estrella De Morgan)*, Edwin Stevens *(Henry De Morgan)*, Lillian Leighton *(Sarah De Morgan)*, Bull Montana *(Dago Red, a Crook)*, Allen Durnell *(Arthur Simmons)*, Sidney Bracey *(Col. Landis)*, Genevieve Blinn *(Mrs. Landis)*, Clarence Burton *(Gregory Slade)*, Henry Johnson *(Norman Gregory)*, Charles Ogle *(Cement Man)*, Jackie Young *(Cupid)*, Lucien Littlefield *(Minister)*.

Top-flight comedy in which Arbuckle plays an absent-minded doctor who believes he can cure criminal instincts through head surgery. A movie full of cleverly executed sight gags by perhaps the world's most neglected and misunderstood funny man. This was Arbuckle's last film as an actor (he went on to direct a few pictures using the *nom de cinema* of William B. Goodrich). The actor's career had been ruined by the rape case in which starlet Virginia Rappe died after allegedly having been sexually assaulted while in a drunken stupor by the overweight actor. Although Arbuckle was acquitted in court, the public furor over the case resulted in the establishment of the notorious, censorious Hays Office. This was one of three Arbuckle comedies directed by Cruze (in a planned fourth, Will Rogers was hastily substituted for Arbuckle, now a pariah) just a year before the famed director made his classic THE COVERED WAGON.

d, James Cruze; w, Walter Woods (based on a scenario by Frank Condon); ph, Karl Brown.

Comedy **(PR:A MPAA:NR)**

CREAM OF THE EARTH (SEE: RED LIPS, 1928)

CREATION** (1922, Brit.) 5 reels Raleigh King bw

Dorothy Fane *(Zena Hammond)*, Frank Dane *(Faux Evermore)*, Sir Simeon Stuart *(Dr. Ganally)*, Thelma Murray, William Freshman, Kate Gurney, Raleigh King, Beryl Norton.

Better-than-average British drama about a woman with spiritualistic instincts, who is tricked into believing another man possesses the reincarnated soul of her recently drowned husband. The fortune hunter marries her, is regenerated, and dedicates his life to working with the poor. He also learns that her first husband was a rotter and a bigamist, and the film ends happily with the two of them expecting a child.

d, Humberston Wright; w, (based on the novel *The Man Who Dared* by May Edington).

Drama **(PR:A MPAA:NR)**

CRIME AND PUNISHMENT* (1917) 5 reels Arrow/Gold Rooster bw

Derwent Hall Caine *(Rodion Raskolnikoff)*, Cherrie Coleman *(Dounia, His Sister)*, Lydia Knott *(His Mother)*, Carl Gerard *(Razoumikhin Perkovitch)*, Sidney Bracy *(Andreas Valeskoff)*, Marguerite Courtot *(Sonia Marmeladov)*, Robert Cummings *(Porfiry the Magistrate)*.

This was an altogether unsuccessful attempt to bring the famous Dostoyevsky novel to the screen. The somber, psychoanalytical theme proved to be too introverted for director McGill and actor Caine to put across, as it was to be in 1935 with Peter Lorre as the intellectual killer of the pawnbroker, and Josef Von Sternberg directing.

d, Lawrence McGill; w, (based on the novel by Fyodor Dostoyevsky).

Drama **(PR:A MPAA:NR)**

CRIMSON CHALLENGE, THE**** (1922) 5 reels FP/PAR bw

Dorothy Dalton *(Tharon Last)*, Jack Mower *(Billy)*, Frank Campeau *(Buck Courtney)*, Irene Hunt *(Ellen Courtney)*, Will R. Walling *(Jim Last)*, Howard Ralston *(Clive)*, Clarence Burton *(Black Bart)*, George Field *(Wylackie)*, Mrs. Dark Cloud *(Anita)*, Fred Huntley *(Confora)*.

Dalton may well have introduced the gun-slinging woman (who would be played to perfection in the talkies) in this picture about good versus evil on the cattlelands. When her father is murdered, Dalton swears revenge and sets out to become an expert at the fast draw. Once she has mastered this, she rides into town, holds up a saloon full of outlaws, and challenges their boss to a showdown. The movie has a terrific ending with Dalton and the villain engaged in a pistol duel on horseback in which she shoots the gun out of his hand, but is then unable to kill an unarmed man. The outlaw, however, reaches for a concealed weapon and is shot to death by the girl, who breaks down and falls into the arms of her lover.

d, Paul Powell; w, Beulah Marie Dix (based on the novel *Tharon of Lost Valley* by Vingie E. Roe); ph, Harry Perry.

Western **(PR:A MPAA:NR)**

CRIMSON CIRCLE, THE*** (1922, Brit.) 6 reels KC/Granger bw

Madge Stuart *(Thalia Drummond)*, Rex Davis *(Jack Beardmore)*, Fred Groves *(Inspector Parr)*, Clifton Boyne *(Derrick Yale)*, Eva Moore *(Aunt Prudence)*, Robert English *(Felix Marl)*, Lawford Davidson *(Raphael Willings)*, Sydney Paxton *(Harvey Froyant)*, Norma Walley *(Kitty Froyant)*, Harry J. Worth, Bertram Burleigh, Mary Ordette, Joan Morgan, Henry Victor, Olaf Hytten, Victor McLaglen, George Dewhurst, Jack Hobbs, Henry Vibart, Kathleen Vaughan, Flora le Breton, Eille Norwood, Malcolm Tod, Sir Simeon Stuart.

When this film was released, it boasted having the largest number of British actors ever to appear in a British motion picture, many of them performing in cameo roles. It was actually a pretty good mystery which dealt with a gang of blackmailers, known as the Crimson Circle, who threatened a number of prominent people with murder. After producing a series of clues and presenting a number of seemingly guilty characters, the leader of the gang is revealed to be a private detective.

d, George Ridgwell; w, Patrick L. Mannock (based on the novel by Edgar Wallace).

Mystery **(PR:A MPAA:NR)**

CRIMSON CITY, THE** (1928) 6 reels WB bw

Myrna Loy *(Onoto)*, John Miljan *(Gregory Kent)*, Leila Hyams *(Nadine Howells)*, Matthew Betz *("Dagger" Foo)*, Anders Randolf *(Maj. Howells)*, Sojin *(Sing Yoy)*, Anna May Wong *(Su)*, Richard Tucker *(Richard Brand)*.

Loy, who could play exotic orientals so well, was right at home here with Wong who, for some reason, could do likewise. The story tells of a girl about to be sold into slavery to a cruel but wealthy Mandarin, who falls in love with the white fugitive who saves her. Miscegenation being a no-no at the time, Loy gives Miljan up to his occidental first love, Hyams.

d, Archie Mayo; w, Anthony Coldeway; t, James A. Starr; ph, Barney McGill.

Drama **(PR:A MPAA:NR)**

CRIMSON DOVE, THE*** (1917) 5 reels WORLD bw

Carlyle Blackwell *(Brand Cameron)*, June Elvidge *(Adrienne Durant)*, Marie La Varre *(Faro Kate)*, Henry West *(Jim Carewe)*, Edward N. Hoyt *(Jonathan Gregg)*, Louis R. Grisel *(Joseph Burbank)*, Dion Titheradge *(Philip Burbank)*, Maxine Elliott Hicks, Julia Stuart, Blanche Davenport, Mildred Beckwith, Norman Hackett.

This human drama, set in the Old West, did not unduly idealize its characters, as it told of a woman with a past who wins the heart of a minister and their struggle to find happiness.

d, Romaine Fielding; w, Frances Marion; ph, William Cooper.

Drama/Western **(PR:A MPAA:NR)**

CRIMSON RUNNER, THE*** (1925) 6 reels Hunt Stromberg/PDC bw

Priscilla Dean *(Bianca Schreber)*, Bernard Siegel *(Alfred Schreber)*, Alan Hale *(Gregory Von Krutz)*, Ward Crane *(Count Meinhard von Bauer)*, James Neill *(Baron Rudolph)*, Charles Hill Mailes *(Baron Semlin)*, Mitchell Lewis *(Conrad, the Black)*, Taylor Holmes *(Bobo, the Valet)*, Ilsa De Lindt *(Princess Cecile)*, Arthur Millett *(Captain of Police)*.

In this one, Dean, a fascinating actress to watch, plays the leader of a Viennese band of daredevil thieves, who steal from the wealthy in order that the poor might eat. She falls in love with an aristocrat, avenges the death of her father, and ends up married and honest.

d, Tom Forman; sup, Hunt Stromberg; w, Harvey Gates; ph, Sol Polito; ed, William Decker; art d, W. L. Heywood.

Crime **(PR:A MPAA:NR)**

CRINOLINE AND ROMANCE*** (1923) 6 reels Metro bw

Viola Dana *(Emmy Lou Wimbleton)*, Claude Gillingwater *(Col. Charles E. Cavanaugh)*, Lillian Lawrence *(Mrs. Kate Wimbleton)*, Betty Francisco *(Betty Biddle)*, John Bowers *(David Gordon)*, Allan Forrest *(Augustus Biddle)*, Mildred June *(Birdie Bevans)*, Gertrude Short *(Sibil Vane)*, Lillian Leighton *(Abigail)*, Nick Cogley *(Uncle Mose)*.

Dana is the granddaughter of a plantation owner who shuts her away from the world so she won't repeat the mistake her mother made by eloping. She runs away to the city where jazz, flappers, and the Charleston are in abundance. There she meets two men who fall in love with her and, when she returns to the plantation, they follow to ask her hand. When the grandfather suggests a duel, she selects the one she really loves. Dana, who approached this part with tongue-in-cheek, gave a most charming performance.

d, Harry Beaumont; w, Bernard McConville; ph, John Arnold.

Comedy/Drama **(PR:A MPAA:NR)**

CRITICAL AGE, THE*** (1923) 4 reels Hodkinson bw

Harlan Knight *(Peter Gorach)*, James Harrison *(Tom Finley)*, Alice May *(Mrs. Finley)*, Pauline Garon *(Margaret Baird)*, Wallace Ray *(Bob Kerr)*, Raymond Peck *(Sen. Morgan Kerr)*, William Colbin *(Sen. Baird)*, Marion Colbin *(Mrs. Colbin)*.

Nice little rural melodrama in which Harrison, a diamond-in-the-rough, wins the girl away from the son of a senator after an exciting, well-directed canoe rescue.

d, Harry McRae; w, (based on the novel *Glengarry School Days* by Ralph Connor).

Drama **(PR:A MPAA:NR)**

CROOKED ALLEY*** (1923) 5 reels UNIV bw

Thomas Carrigan *(Boston Blackie)*, Laura La Plante *(Norine Tyrell/Olive Sloan)*, Tom S. Guise *(Judge Milnar)*, Owen Gorine *(Rudy Milnar)*, Albert Hart *(Kaintuck)*.

Fascinating plot motivation in this adaptation of a "Boston Blackie" story. Carrigan attempts to avenge an old convict whom a mean-spirited judge would not allow to die on the outside, by steering the judge's only son towards a life of crime. The daughter of the late convict (whom Blackie is sweet on), however, falls in love with the young man and prevents his fall. Boyle's 1910 stories spawned a substantial "Boston Blackie" industry. The first of the silents was BOSTON BLACKIE'S LITTLE PAL (1918), starring Bert Lytell. The character spun into sound pictures in Columbia's 13-feature starring Chester Morris, and successful radio and television series followed.

d, Robert F. Hill; w, Hill, Adrian Johnson (based on the story "The Daughter of Crooked Alley" by Jack Boyle); ph, Harry Fowler.

Crime **(PR:A MPAA:NR)**

CROOKED STREETS*** (1920) 5 reels PAR bw

Ethel Clayton *(Gail Ellis)*, Jack Holt *(Rupert O'Dare)*, Clyde Fillmore *(Lawrence Griswold)*, Clarence H. Geldart *(Silas Griswold)*, Josephine Crowell *(Mrs. Griswold)*, Frederick Starr *(Sailor Hugh)*.

A young American woman who has traveled to China with an antique dealer is attacked by a gang of white slavers shortly before it is time to return to the States. A group of French sailors intervenes, but one of them, who is a drunk, mistakes her for a prostitute and decides to claim her for his own. This time she is saved by a handsome Englishman who challenges the sailor to a boxing match. There is an exciting fight, which the Englishman wins, and at the end we discover that the woman is really an American agent who came to the Orient to capture an opium smuggler who, as it turns out, is the antique dealer.

d, Paul Powell; w, Edith Kennedy (based on the story "Dinner at Eight" by Samuel Merwin); ph, William Marshall.

Crime **(PR:A MPAA:NR)**

CROSS BREED*** (1927) 6 reels Bischoff bw

Johnnie Walker *(Andy Corwin)*, Gloria Heller *(Marie Dumont)*, Charles K. French *(John Corwin)*, Frank Glendon *(Jacques Bereau)*, Henry Herbert *(Sam Cranister)*, Joseph Mack *(George Dumont)*, Olin Francis *(Poleon)*, Silverstreak *(Comanche, the Dog)*.

Good second feature (geared to the children's market) featuring still another Rin-Tin-Tin pretender. There was a slight twist here, however, in that both man *and* dog play cowards who prove themselves in the end. It all has to do with a lumber camp that the hero owns and the bad guys try to steal (but fail).

d, Noel Mason Smith; w, Bennett Cohen (based on a story by Wells Ritchie); ph, Ray June.

Adventure **(PR:A MPAA:NR)**

CROSSING TRAILS** (1921) 5 reels Cliff Smith/AP bw

Pete Morrison *(Jim Warren)*, Esther Ralston *(Helen Stratton)*, John Hatton *(Buster Stratton)*, Lew Meehan *("Red" Murphy)*, Floyd Taliaferro *(Peter Marcus)*, J. B. Warner *("Bull" Devine)*, Billie Bennett *(Mrs. Warren)*.

A girl, wrongly accused of murder, escapes and takes a job at Morrison's ranch. When the villain arrives and tries to kidnap her, Morrison not only saves her from a fate worse than death, but also proves her innocence.

d, Cliff Smith; w, Alvin J. Neitz, L. V. Jefferson; ph, John Thompson.

Western **(PR:A MPAA:NR)**

CROWD, THE***** (1928) 9 reels MGM bw

Eleanor Boardman *(Mary)*, James Murray *(John Sims)*, Bert Roach *(Bert)*, Estelle Clark *(Jane)*, Daniel G. Tomlinson *(Jim)*, Dell Henderson *(Dick)*, Lucy Beaumont *(Mother)*, Freddie Burke Frederick *(Junior)*, Alice Mildred Puter *(Daughter)*.

As the silent film days drew to a close, director King Vidor created this genuine American masterpiece, a brutally realistic, deeply moving look into the life of a common American man. The film opens with the birth of the main character on July 4, 1900, the infant's proud father declaring his son will grow up to be a man the world will hear from. Fueled by his father's dreams for the future, the baby grows to adolescence (now played by Murray) an idealistic, ambitious young man who has the energy and talent to take the world by storm. Then suddenly, his father dies. Feeling abandoned and alone with his source of inspiration gone, Murray is forced to make it on his own in New York City. Murray is awed by the sight of the Manhattan skyline as the ferry takes him into the city, but he is given an ominous warning by a fellow passenger, "You've got to be good in that town if you want to beat the crowd." The sobering truth of this remark is soon felt by Murray as he becomes one in the number of faceless employees engulfed by the huge office buildings which spot the city like massive beehives. Though starting at the bottom rung, Murray still retains his enthusiasm and is confident that he'll work his way to the top. The older employees have heard it all before, however, and they, too, serve as ominous signposts on the road ahead. One day Murray and a friend from work arrange a blind date at Coney Island. There he meets Boardman and soon they are married. They move into their dream house and produce two children. Unfortunately, Murray has great difficulty separating himself from the crowd of average workers in his company and the years of unfulfilled ambitions begin to take their toll. Soon the dream house is seen as nothing more than a claustrophobic tenement, the family as an unwanted hindrance. Murray's hopes get a boost, however, when he wins $500 in a slogan-writing contest, but his happiness is dashed when his youngest child is killed in an auto accident. Things go from bad to worse for Murray. His sudden lack of ambition costs him his job and he is forced to sell vacuum cleaners door-to-door. He even fails at this and is soon reduced to having to work as a sandwich board ad man walking up and down the streets of Manhattan. Pressured by her brothers, Boardman leaves Murray. Feeling like a total failure, Murray decides to commit suicide by leaping off a bridge. Before he can take the fatal plunge, his young son wanders onto the scene and the sight of his little boy gives Murray the fortitude to carry on with his life. The married couple reunite, though their sky-high ambitions are sobered by some bitter lessons and harsh realities. Seeking an evening's entertainment, the family visits a vaudeville theater where they sit laughing at the clowns, indistinguishable from the hundreds of others in the audience. THE CROWD is a realistic, bittersweet film that presents an unidealized view of the common man. Murray's character starts out full of energy and hope, but life deals him its inevitable series of blows and setbacks. He survives his fate, but at the cost of his hopes and dreams which he has been forced to abandon in order to go on living with himself. THE CROWD illustrates the day-to-day compromises average people must make if they are to survive. Vidor neither celebrates nor condemns this harsh reality, he just presents it as it is. The film is truly timeless, its message as relevant today as in 1928. Vidor's harsh, un-Hollywood view of reality so shook Irving Thalberg and MGM that the studio let it sit on the shelf unreleased for a year. Thalberg's commercial instincts were correct, for while the film was praised critically, average Americans had no interest in seeing their lives played out before them. Ironically, actor James Murray, who was a minor talent until his magnificent performance in THE CROWD, was never offered as good a role again and became a hopeless alcoholic. Refusing to take what he considered charity from Vidor when he was casting OUR DAILY BREAD in 1934, Murray disappeared. In 1936 Murray's dead body was pulled from the Hudson River, an apparent suicide.

p&d, King Vidor; w, Vidor, John V. A. Weaver, Harry Behn (based on a story by Vidor); t, Joe Farnham; ph, Henry Sharp; ed, Hugh Wynn; set d, Cedric Gibbons, Arnold Gillespie.

Drama **(PR:A MPAA:NR)**

CRYSTAL CUP, THE*** (1927) 7 reels Henry Hobart/FN bw

Dorothy Mackaill *(Gita Carteret)*, Jack Mulhall *(Geoffrey Pleyden)*, Rockliffe Fellows *(Eustace Bylant)*, Jane Winton *(Polly Pleyden)*, Edythe Chapman *(Mrs. Carteret)* *Clarissa Selwynne (Mrs. Pleyden)*.

An interesting film from the days before women's lib and gay rights. The heroine learns as a child to hate men but, when she grows up to be a ravishing beauty, she attracts a great deal of their attention. Annoyed by this, she begins to dress like, and adopt, masculine attitudes—including the ability to light a match with her thumbnail in the manner of William S. Hart. When the gossip about her demeanor becomes unbearable, she marries a young writer who agrees to live with her platonically. Before long, however, he breaks the pact and makes a pass, which she easily thwarts. The picture ends with her finding Mr. Right and returning to her natural state—being feminine.

p, Henry Hobart; d, John Francis Dillon; w, Gerald C. Duffy (based on the novel by Gertrude Franklin Atherton); t, Mort Blumenstock; ph, James Van Trees.

Drama **(PR:A MPAA:NR)**

CUB, THE*** (1915) 5 reels Brady/WORLD bw

Martha Hedman *(Alice Renlow)*, Johnny Hines *(Steve Oldham)*, Robert Cummings *("Cap" White)*, Jessie Lewis *(Becky King)*, Bert Starkey *(Stark White)*, Dorothy Farnum *(Peggy White)*.

Funny comedy in which cub reporter Hines is sent to cover the story of feuding hillbilly families, after the star reporter is taken ill. Approaching the situation like a war correspondent, he becomes involved with both factions and delivers solid laughter all the way.

d&w, Maurice Tourneur; w, (based on a play by Thomas Buchanan).

Comedy **(PR:A MPAA:NR)**

CUB REPORTER, THE** (1922) 5 reels Phil Goldstone, bw

Richard Talmadge *(Dick Harvey)*, Jean Calhoun *(Miriam Rhodes)*, Edwin Booth Tilton *(Harrison Rhodes)*, Wilson Hummel *(Mandarin)*, Lewis Mason, Ethel Hallor *(Crooks)*.

Talmadge leaped and bounded his way through this action programmer about a cub reporter who rescues the daughter of a jewel collector from Chinese Tong members who held her in exchange for a precious stone stolen from an oriental idol.

p, Phil Godstone; d, Jack Dillon; w, George Elwood Jenks; ph, Harry Fowler.

Adventure **(PR:A MPAA:NR)**

CUMBERLAND ROMANCE, A*** (1920) 5 reels REA/PAR bw

Mary Miles Minter *(Easter Hicks)*, Monte Blue *("Sherd" Raines)*, John Bowers *(Clayton)*, Guy Oliver *("Pap" Hicks)*, Martha Mattox *("Ma" Hicks)*, Robert Brower *(The Mountain Bishop)*.

Bowers, a young engineer working in the mountains, has a romance with Minter and feels obligated to marry her. Blue, who is studying for the ministry, challenges him to reveal his intentions and, on hearing them, becomes the city fellow's ally. There is a well-executed fight between Bowers and Oliver (Minter's hostile father) which Blue courageously breaks up. The wedding is set and the groom's wealthy parents arrive from the East. But before the service is finished, Oliver, who has gotten himself liquored up, starts firing into the party, and Minter throws herself in front of the bullet meant for Blue. It is then that she becomes aware of her true feelings, and the film ends on a happy note.

d&w, Charles Maigne (based on the novel *A Mountain Europa* by John Fox, Jr.); ph, Faxon M. Dean.

Drama **(PR:A MPAA:NR)**

CUPID BY PROXY***　　(1918) 5 reels Pathe bw

Baby Marie Osborne *(Marie Stewart)*, Minnie Danvers *(Mrs. Brown)*, Mary Talbot *(Mrs. Stewart)*, J. N. McDowell *(Mr. Brown)*, John Steppling *(Mr. Stewart)*, Mildred Harris *(Jane Stewart)*, Antrim Short *(Ralph Brown)*, Kenneth Nordyke *(Tommy Brown)*.

This highly entertaining picture featured a host of kids, including Harris, the future Mrs. Charles Chaplin, and the adorable Osborne. It tells the story of young sweethearts who live next door to each other, but whose romance is endangered by the girl's socially ambitious mother. Osborne, however, toddles her way to the rescue, and in the end, brings the couple together again.

d, William Bertram; w, Isabel M. Johnston.

Comedy　　**(PR:A MPAA:NR)**

CURSE OF DRINK, THE***　　(1922) 6 reels Weber & North bw

Harry T. Morey *(Bill Sanford)*, Edmund Breese *(John Rand)*, Marguerite Clayton *(Ruth Sanford)*, George Fawcett *(Ben Farley)*, Miriam Battista *(Baby Betty)*, Alice May *(Mother Sanford)*, Brinsley Shaw *(Sam Handy)*, Albert L. Barrett *(Harry Rand)*, June Fuller *(Margaret Sanford)*.

Updated version of the popular stage melodrama about an alcoholic railroad engineer who is demoted to piloting a switch engine. When he drunkenly seeks revenge by commandeering the train the railroad's president is on, his daughter and the president's son give chase in another locomotive. The girl jumps aboard the train, races atop the coaches, and stops the engine just before it crashes. For this, the son is granted permission to marry the spunky little heroine, and the old man volunteers to take the pledge.

p, Joseph M. Shear; d&w, Harry O. Hoyt (based on the play by Charles E. Blaney); ph, Harry Fishbeck.

Drama　　**(PR:A MPAA:NR)**

CYCLONE, THE***　　(1920) 5 reels FOX bw

Tom Mix, Colleen Moore, Henry Herbert, William Ellingford, Tony the Horse.

Mix plays a Canadian Mountie in this exciting movie, who battles smugglers and saves his girl from their dirty clutches. The film's highlight is the climax when Mix puts gunny sacks on his horse's hooves and rides him up the stairs in order to peek through the transom and locate the villains, a thrill a minute for Mix's tens of thousands of young hero worshippers. Another one of Mix's consistent screen roles, that of the ordinary honest cowpoke who owns, in his words, "my own horse, saddle, and bridle." That horse, in CYCLONE, was Tony the Wonder Horse, an animal faster than Mix's previous Old Blue, and smart in learning tricks, as in riding up the stairs in CYCLONE. Other tricks Tony learned were pounding down the locked door of a cabin where Mix was held prisoner, and untying the rope binding Mix's wrists when he was in a jam.

d, Cliff Smith; w, J. Anthony Roach (based on a story by Tod Hunter Marigold); ph, Frank B. Good.

Adventure　　**(PR:A MPAA:NR)**

CYCLONE OF THE RANGE**　　(1927) 5 reels FBO bw

Tom Tyler *(Tom Mackay)*, Elsie Tarron *(Mollie Butler)*, Harry O'Connor *(Seth Butler)*, Dick Howard *(Jake Darkin)*, Frankie Darro *(Frankie Butler)*, Harry Woods *(The Black Rider/Don Alvaro)*, Beans *(A Dog)*.

Tyler, who is perhaps best remembered as "Captain Marvel" in the 1940 Republic serial, enjoyed a successful career as a cowboy star in silents and talkies. In this picture, he plays a wandering cowpoke who avenges the murder of his older brother by the Black Rider.

d, Bob De Lacy; w, Arthur Statter, F. A. E. Pine (based on a story by Oliver Drake); ph, Nick Musuraca.

Western　　**(PR:A MPAA:NR)**

CYTHEREA***　　(1924) 6 reels Madison/FN bw-c

Lewis Stone *(Lee Randon)*, Alma Rubens *(Savina Grove)*, Norman Kerry *(Peyton Morris)*, Irene Rich *(Fannie Randon)*, Constance Bennett *(Annette Sherwin)*, Charles Wellesley *(William Grove)*, Betty Bouton *(Claire Morris)*, Mickey Moore *(Gregory Randon)*, Peaches Jackson *(Helen Randon)*, Brandon Hurst *(Daniel Randon)*, Hugh Saxon *(Randons' Butler)*, Lee Hill *(Groves' Butler)*, Lydia Yeamans Titus *(Laundress)*.

This rather ordinary society drama is about a man who becomes bored with his wife and two children and runs off to Cuba with another woman. After awhile he realizes the error of his ways and returns to the fold. This film was highlighted by a couple of skillfully directed dream sequences, beautifully photographed on location in Cuba in color. Producer Goldwyn's most lavish independent production to date, CYTHEREA was based on a book that few people thought capable of being brought to the screen, given the point of view of the Hays Office at the time. Writer Marion resolved the problem by forcing the story into a conventional Hollywood mold, having Rubens die of a strange tropical disease and the repentant Stone return to the bosom of his family a chastened man. The formula was sufficiently successful that writer Marion and director Fitzmaurice worked in collaboration on four other Goldwyn pictures. This was the beautiful Bennett's first Hollywood-made picture in the role of a youthful vamp, purportedly patterned after Lillian Gish.

p, Samuel Goldwyn; d, George Fitzmaurice; w, Frances Marion (based on the novel *Cytherea, Goddess of Love* by Joseph Hergesheimer; ph, Arthur Miller (Technicolor sequences); ed, Stuart Heisler.

Drama　　**(PR:A MPAA:NR)**

D

D.W. GRIFFITH'S "THAT ROYLE GIRL"

(SEE: "THAT ROYLE GIRL", 1925)

DADDY*** (1923) 6 reels FN bw

Jackie Coogan *(Jackie Savelli/Jackie Holden)*, Arthur Carewe *(Paul Savelli)*, Josie Sedgwick *(Helene Savelli)*, Cesare Gravina *(Cesare Gallo)*, Bert Woodruff *(Eben Holden)*, Anna Townsend *(Mrs. Holden)*, Willard Louis *(Impresario)*, George Kuwa *(Valet)*, Mildred *(Herself)*.

In this heart-warming story, Coogan is the son of a poor violin teacher. His parents separate and the boy is taken by his mother to live with old friends. After she dies, the boy runs away to the city where he is befriended by an old street musician. It turns out that the old man was the instructor of Coogan's father—now a world famous artist—and the two are reunited.

p, Sol Lesser; d, E. Mason Hopper; w, Mr. and Mrs. Jack Cooper; ph, Frank B. Good, Robert Martin; ed, Irene Morra.

Comedy/Drama **(PR:A MPAA:NR)**

DADDY LONG LEGS**** (1919) 7 reels FN bw

Mary Pickford *("Judy" Abbott)*, Milla Davenport *(Mrs. Lippert)*, Wesley Barry *(Her Pal)*, Miss Percy Aswell *(Miss Pritchard)*, Fay Lemport *(Angelina Wycoff)*, Mahlon Hamilton *(Jarvis Pendleton)*, Lillian Langdon *(Mrs. Pendleton)*, Betty Bouton *(Julia Pendleton)*, Audry Chapman *(Sally McBride)*, Carrie Clarke Warde *(Mrs. Semple)*, *Marshall Neilan, Fred Huntley, Estelle Evans, Dorothy Rosher.*

In this near-masterpiece, Pickford goes from playing a 12-year-old inmate of a heartless orphanage (where, as in SPARROWS, she protects her fellow charges at every turn) to a lovely young woman who falls in love with and marries her distinguished guardian. In between all of this, she and director "Mickey" Neilan created moments of comedy and pathos which will live as long as there are motion picture projectors to share them.

d, Marshall Neilan; w, Agnes Christine Johnston (based on the story and play by Jean Webster); ph, Charles Rosher, Henry Cronjager.

Comedy/Drama **(PR:A MPAA:NR)**

DAMAGED GOODS*** (1915) 7 reels AM bw

Richard Bennett, Adrienne Morrison, Maud Milton, Olive Templeton, Josephine Ditt, Jacqueline Moore, Florence Short, Lewis Bennison, John Steppling, William Bertram, George Ferguson.

The opening title of this film with a message reads: "Twenty percent of the population of this country is infected by this dread disease." Then it tells the story of a young man, Bennett, who gets drunk at his bachelor party and becomes infected with syphilis after sleeping with a prostitute. He seeks the help of a quack who claims to provide a cure, but instead Bennett passes it on to his bride and later his child. The film ends with the man who ruined three lives contemplating suicide.

d, Thomas Ricketts; w, Harry Pollard (based on the play "Les Avaries" by Eugene Brieux).

Drama **(PR:A MPAA:NR)**

DAME CHANCE* (1926) 7 reels David Hartford/American Cinema bw

Julanne Johnston *(Gail Vernon)*, Gertrude Astor *(Nina Carrington)*, Robert Frazer *(Lloyd Mason)*, David Hartford *(Craig Stafford)*, Lincoln Stedman *(Bunny Dean)*, Mary Carr *(Mrs. Vernon)*, John T. Prince *(Sims)*.

Improbable story about a wealthy man who "sponsors" a down-and-out actress to test womankind after his wife deserts him. The two fall in love and marry after she proves her fidelity to him, he his decency to her by not taking advantage, and his wife her consideration for both by conveniently departing this earth. This film's only bright spot was the presence of Johnston, Douglas Fairbanks' beautiful princess in THE THIEF OF BAGDAD.

d, Bertram Bracken; w, Frances Nordstrom; ph, Walter Griffin.

Drama **(PR:A MPAA:NR)**

DAMSEL IN DISTRESS, A*** (1919) 5 reels Pathe bw

June Caprice, Creighton Hale, W. H. Thompson, Mark Smith, Charlotte Granville, Arthur Albro, George Trimble, Katherine Johnston.

Some wonderful shots of New York complement this entertaining Caprice feature about a girl who is ordered to stay at home because she is smitten by her vacation guide. She escapes to join him, but instead bumps into a musical comedy writer who, after a number of funny situations, really wins her love.

d, George Archainbaud; sup, Albert Capellaini; w, (based on a story by P. G. Wodehouse); ph, Lucien Tainguy.

Comedy **(PR:A MPAA:NR)**

DAMON AND PYTHIAS*** (1914) 6 reels UNIV bw

Cleo Madison *(Hermion)*, Anna Little, William Worthington, Herbert Rawlinson, Frank Lloyd.

Superior early feature re-created ancient Greece skillfully. The producers claimed a cast of 3,000, and the production—with its battle scenes and chariot race—looked it. Madison, as Hermion, is particularly effective in this story about two inseparable friends, Madison and Worthington, who are condemned to death by Dionysius the tyrant. When Pythias wins leave to go home to straighten his affairs, Damon offers his life as hostage if Pythias does not return. The tyrant, seeing the depth of their friendship, pardons them both.

d, Otis Turner; w, Allan Dwan (based on the novel by Edward Bulwer-Lytton).

Spectacle **(PR:A MPAA:NR)**

DAN*** (1914) 5 reels All Star Feature bw

Lew Dockstader *(Dan)*, Lois Meredith, Gail Kane, Beatrice Clevener, George Cowl, W. D. Fisher, Hal Reid, John H. Pratt, William Conklin.

Dockstader—the foremost minstrel entertainer of his day—plays a faithful "colored" servant who saves his master's son (a Confederate officer) from the firing squad by securing entrance to his prison tent and blackening his face with charcoal. The son escapes, but Dockstader is executed in his place. The film ends on a highly sentimental note, with the elderly servant's burial in the family cemetery—right alongside his master who had been killed in a Yankee raid.

w, Hal Reid.

War **(PR:A MPAA:NR)**

DANCER'S PERIL, THE*** (1917) 5 reels WORLD bw

Alice Brady *(Vasto/Lola)*, Philip Hunt *(Grand Duke Alexis)*, Montagu Love *(Michael Pavloff)*, Alexis Kosloff *(Nicholas)*, Harry Benham, Jack Drumier, Augusta Burmeister, Cecil Fletcher, Louis Grisel, Johnny Hines, Sidney D'Albrook.

The Grand Duke of Russia falls in love with and marries the premier dancer of the Imperial Ballet. The government does not approve and the girl is sent to France, leaving behind a daughter who is raised by the mistress of the academy. The child grows up to become one of the world's foremost dancers and, as such, tours Paris. While there, the impresario abducts her and forces himself on her. The girl's mother, however, learns of this and shoots him before he can rape her. The Grand Duke, who has also learned of this, arrives on the scene just in time to take blame for the action of his wife. The picture ends with the family reunited. Brady gives an excellent performance as both mother and daughter.

d, Travers Vale; w, (based on the story "The Snowbird" by Harriet Morris).

Drama **(PR:A MPAA:NR)**

DANCING MOTHERS*** (1926) 8 reels FP-LAS/PAR bw

Alice Joyce *(Ethel Westcourt)*, Conway Tearle *(Jerry Naughton)*, Clara Bow *(Kittens Westcourt)*, Donald Keith *(Kenneth Cobb)*, Dorothy Cumming *(Mrs. Massarene)*, Elsie Lawson *(Irma)*, Norman Trevor *(Hugh Westcourt)*.

When Famous Players first released this film they provided audiences with coupons asking their opinion of its rather controversial ending. This was a jazz-age picture, which told of a neglected wife (Joyce) who sits home alone while her husband cheats and her daughter (Bow) flirts. But when she learns that her "little girl" has become involved with a notorious playboy, her maternal instincts compel her to take action. She puts on her makeup, selects her best gown, and sets out to vamp the fellow herself. Of course she completely wins him over and, after realizing that her daughter and husband are concerned only with themselves, sails for Europe with *her* new found paramour.

d, Herbert Brenon; w, Forrest Halsey (based on a story by Edgar Selwyn, Edmund Goulding); ph, J. Roy Hunt; art d, Julian Boone Fleming.

Drama **Cas.** **(PR:A MPAA:NR)**

DANGER MARK, THE*** (1918) 5 reels PAR bw

Elsie Ferguson *(Geraldine Seagrave)*, Mahlon Hamilton *(Duane Mallett)*, Gertrude McCoy *(Sylvia Mallett)*, Crauford Kent *(Jack Dysart)*, Maude Turner Gordon *(Kathleen Severn)*, Edward Burns *(Scott Seagrave)*, W. T. Carlston *(Col. Mallett)*.

Ferguson gives a splendidly understated performance as an alcoholic society girl who courageously battles her disease and refuses to marry her sweetheart until it is licked. This film, which could have been little more than anti-liquor propaganda, was elevated to a higher artistic plane because of the intelligent rendering of her part.

d, Hugh Ford; w, Robert Maigne (based on a story by Robert W. Chambers).

Drama **(PR:A MPAA:NR)**

DANGER POINT, THE*** (1922) 6 reels Halperin/ARC bw

Carmel Myers *(Alice Torrance)*, William P. Carleton *(James Benton)*, Vernon Steel *(Duncan Phelps)*, Joseph J. Dowling *(Benjamin)*, Harry Todd *(Sam Biggs)*, Margaret Joslin *(Elvira Hubbard)*.

A woman fearing that her husband no longer loves her becomes convinced of this when she phones him and is told he cannot speak to her. She is not, however, told that one of his oil tanks has just exploded, so she assumes the worst. She packs her bags and, as she leaves her house for the railroad station, runs into a former suitor who still lusts for her. He drives her to the depot, puts her on a train, and then jumps on the next car as it is pulling out. In a nice bit of cross-cutting, the husband is shown fighting his fire, while the wife fights off the former suitor who is attempting to rape her. There is a train wreck, which occurs just as the husband reads his wife's farewell note. When the victims are brought back to town, the woman is unhurt, but her husband suspects his wife has been unfaithful. The dying former suitor, however, confesses the truth, and the marriage is saved. Nice special effects in this satisfying programmer.

d, Lloyd Ingraham; w, Victor Hugo Halperin; t, Adelaide Heilbron; ph, Ross Fisher.

Drama **(PR:A MPAA:NR)**

DANGER SIGNAL, THE** (1915) 5 reels Kleine bw

Arthur Hoops *(Danny/Denis Canavan)*, Ruby Hoffman *(Beatrice Newnes)*, John Davidson *(Rodman Cadbury)*, Frank Belcher *("Boss" Havens)*, Tom Walsh *(Roscoe Newnes)*, Billy Sherwood *(Henry Cadbury)*, Della Connor *(Amy Carroll)*, Miss Coventry *(Mrs. Canavan)*.

Improbable story about a lazy young man who is instilled with ambition when he is given a red warning flag to handle on a construction site. He then—rather incredibly—climbs from precinct worker to political boss of the city, and marries a prominent society widow along the way. The film was highlighted by some effective double-exposure photography, which enabled Hoops to play both father and son.

d, George Kleine; w, (based on the short story "Canavan, the Man Who Had His Way" by Rupert Hughes).

Drama **(PR:A MPAA:NR)**

DANGER VALLEY* (1921) 5 reels Pinnacle /Independent Film Assn. bw

Neal Hart *(Doug McBride)*.

In this average Hart horse opera, the cowboy star plays an engineer who heads west to locate a missing mine and save its owner's daughter from the clutches of a villain who also is searching for the mine.

Western **(PR:A MPAA:NR)**

DANGEROUS AGE, THE*** (1922) 7 reels AFN bw

Lewis Stone *(John Emerson)*, Cleo Madison *(Mary Emerson)*, Edith Roberts *(Ruth Emerson)*, Ruth Clifford *(Gloria Sanderson)*, Myrtle Stedman *(Mrs. Sanderson)*, James Morrison *(Bob)*, Helen Lynch *(Bebe Nash)*, Lincoln Stedman *(Ted)*, Edward Burns *(Tom)*, Richard Tucker *(Robert Chanslor)*.

Stone has been dominated by his wife for 22 years, so when youthful Clifford throws herself at him while he is on a business trip, he becomes infatuated. Stone writes a letter to his wife terminating their marriage and then finds Clifford in the arms of another. Stone rushes home to intercept the dispatch but arrives too late. His wife, on reading the letter, realizes the error of her ways and, without letting on to her husband, completely changes her attitude towards him.

d, John M. Stahl; w, J. G. Hawks, Bess Meredyth (based on a story by Frances Irene Reels); ph, Jackson J. Rose, Al Siegler.

Drama **(PR:A MPAA:NR)**

DANGEROUS HOUR*** (1923) 5 reels Cliff Reid bw

Eddie Polo *(Eddie Polo, Daredevil Screen Star)*, Jack Carlisle *(Jim Crawley)*, George A. Williams *("Dad" Carson)*, Catherine Bennett *(Anita Carson)*.

The popular serial star Eddie Polo plays himself in this behind-the-scenes actioner. On location in Arizona where he is shooting a picture, Polo becomes friendly with a pretty young woman and her father. He is also made aware of mine owner Carlisle's indifference towards safe working conditions. Then, after returning to Hollywood, Polo hears about a cave-in and flies back to Arizona where he rescues a group of trapped miners, humiliates Carlisle in a fist fight, and wins the heart of the girl.

d, William Hughes Curran; w, Rena Parker.

Adventure **(PR:A MPAA:NR)**

DANGEROUS TO MEN** (1920) 6 reels Metro bw

Viola Dana *(Eliza)*, Milton Sills *(Sandy Varrell)*, Edward Connelly, Josephine Crowell, Marian Skinner, John P. Morse, James Barrows, Mollie McConnell, Helen Raymond, Doris Baker.

When her father dies, Dana, who attends a boarding school, is told she must now live with her guardian, played by handsome Sills. She imagines him to be a boring old fogy, so she decides to dress like a tomboy and annoy him into sending her back to school. When they meet, she is amazed to find he is a handsome bachelor, and falls immediately in love. Sills, of course, treats her like a child—up until the film's end when Dana saves him from a fortune-hunting actress, and her guardian sees for the first time that his charge is, in actuality, a beautiful young woman.

d, William C. Dowlan; w, A. P. Younger (based on the play "Eliza Come To Stay" by H. V. Esmond); ph, John Arnold.

Drama **(PR:A MPAA:NR)**

DANTE'S INFERNO*** (1924) 6 reels FOX bw

Lawson Butt *(Dante)*, Howard Gaye *(Virgil)*, Ralph Lewis *(Mortimer Judd)*, Pauline Starke *(Marjorie Vernon)*, Josef Swickard *(Eugene Craig)*, Gloria Grey *(Mildred Craig)*, William Scott *(Ernest Judd)*, Robert Klein *(A Fiend)*, Winifred Landis *(Mrs. Judd)*, Lorimer Johnston *(The Doctor)*, Lon Poff *(Secretary)*, Bud Jamison *(The Butler)*.

Having been ruined by his one-time friend, ruthless capitalist Lewis, Swickard sends the man a copy of the book "Dante's Inferno." Then, as the industrial king begins to read, the picture fades to a strikingly directed depiction of hell, which closely emulated the famed illustrations of Gustave Dore. At the time, these scenes—which seemed to show hundreds of naked sufferers—caused quite a sensation. Actually, the actors (except for one establishing shot of a semi-nude Starke) wore body stockings. The effect was really quite erotic, and more than made up for a banal ending in which the rotter awakens from his dream a reformed man, anxious to change his evil ways.

d, Henry Otto; w, Edmund Goulding (based on a story by Cyrus Wood); ph, Joseph August.

Drama **(PR:A MPAA:NR)**

DAPHNE AND THE PIRATE*** (1916) 5 reels FA/TRI bw

Lillian Gish *(Daphne La Tour)*, Elliot Dexter *(Phillip De Mornay)*, Walter Long *(Jamie d'Arcy)*, Howard Gaye *(Prince Henry)*, Lucile Young *(Franchette)*, Richard Cummings *(Francois La Tour)*, Jack Cosgrove *(Duc de Mornay)*.

This exciting motion picture, written by D. W. Griffith, sees Gish as a French woman transported against her will to the colony of Louisiana, where females are in short supply. When the ship full of women is attacked by pirates, Gish takes command of an unmanned cannon and mows the buccaneers down, thus saving the vessel of her homeland. There is a fascinating scene in which the ladies are being selected to make the voyage and Gish contorts her face into ugly expressions to avoid selection. This is remarkably like the slave-market sequence from INTOLERANCE, made the same year. Gish and Griffith protege Cabanne developed an excellent working relationship in their collaborations. In *The Movies, Mr. Griffith and Me*, she emphasized the director's receptiveness to her suggestions and wrote; "He had confidence in me, which gave me confidence in myself."

d, Christy Cabanne; w, Granville Warwick (D. W. Griffith).

Adventure **(PR:A MPAA:NR**

DAREDEVIL'S REWARD***

(1928) 5 reels FOX bw (AKA: $5,000 REWARD)

Tom Mix *(Tom Hardy)*, Tony *(The Wonder Horse)*, Natalie Joyce *(Ena Powell)*, Lawford Davidson *(Foster)*, Billy Bletcher *(Slim)*, Harry Cording *(An Outlaw)*, William Welch *(James Powell)*.

Another thrill-a-minute Mix western in which the hero, playing a Texas Ranger, captures a band of outlaws and wins the niece of the gang's leader after he is killed. There is a great finale in which Mix rescues Joyce from an out-of-control car which plunges down a treacherously endless mountainside. Mix also uses a number of disguises in this one, which gave him the chance to play for laughs.

d, Eugene Forde; w, John Stone; ph, Dan Clark.

Western **(PR:A MPAA:NR)**

DARING CHANCES*** (1924) 5 reels UNIV bw

Jack Hoxie *(Jack Armstrong)*, Alta Allen *(Agnes Rushton)*, Claude Payton *(Sampson Burke)*, Jack Prat *(Joe Slavin)*, Catherine Wallace *(Ethel Slavin)*, Doreen Turner *(Bebe Slavin)*, Genevieve Danninger *(Roberta Simpson)*, Newton Campbell *(Bill)*, William McCall *(Sheriff)*, Scout the Horse.

Popular cowboy star Hoxie was given plenty of opportunity to ride, shoot, and fight in this entertaining oater. It all has to do with his desire to win the big rodeo steeplechase, in spite of the ruthless efforts of the bad hombres to prevent him from doing so.

d, Clifford S. Smith; w, Isadore Bernstein; ph, Harry Neumann.

Western **(PR:A MPAA:NR)**

DARING YOUTH*** (1924) 6 reels Principal Pictures bw

Bebe Daniels *(Anita Allen)*, Norman Kerry *(John J. Campbell)*, Lee Moran *(Arthur James)*, Arthur Hoyt *(Winston Howell)*, Lillian Langdon *(Mrs. Allen)*, George Pearce *(Mr. Allen)*.

Inspired by novelist Fannie Hurst's then famous attitude about marriage ("Have breakfast together twice a week and complete freedom the rest") this was a good vehicle for talented Daniels. Daniels marries Kerry with the understanding that she must be allowed complete independence. He wisely realizes that she will "wisely come to her senses" if he just makes a point of ignoring her silliness. He does, and she does—and the picture ends with Daniels happily acting out her role as the perfect little housewife.

d, William Beaudine; w, Alexander Neal (based on a story by Dorothy Farnum); ph, Charles J. Van Enger; ed, Edward McDermott; art d, Joseph Wright.

Comedy **(PR:A MPAA:NR)**

DARK ANGEL, THE**** (1925) 8 reels Goldwyn/FN bw

Ronald Colman *(Alan Trent)*, Vilma Banky *(Kitty Vane)*, Wyndham Standing *(Capt. Gerald Shannon)*, Frank Elliot *(Lord Beaumont)*, Charles Lane *(Sir Hubert Vane)*, Helen Jerome Eddy *(Miss Bottles)*, Florence Turner *(Roma)*.

Wonderful love story about Colman and Banky, a young British couple who are unable to marry before he is sent to the front during WWI. Colman is blinded and captured by the Germans but Banky believes he is killed in action. After the war, Standing, his best friend (who has always admired Banky from a distance), asks for her hand and she accepts. But then he discovers that Colman is actually living in the North of England writing children's stories under a pen name because he refuses to be a burden on the woman he loves. Standing informs her of this, but before she can reach him her father goes to Colman, and together they work out a plan to deceive her. When she arrives, Colman has memorized the placement of furniture and is informed of what she will be wearing and its colors. In this way he courageously convinces her that he is not handicapped and no longer loves her. Brokenhearted, she leaves and he makes his way to the closet where he removes a bust of her face. Fortunately, she is still outside the door when, after caressing her likeness, he begins to weep. She hears this, realizes the sacrifice he has made on her behalf, and the two are reunited in the end. This was a beautifully directed, written, and acted work, and a triumph for Banky in her first U.S. film.

d, George Fitzmaurice; w, Frances Marion (based on a play by H. B. Trevelyan); ph, George Barnes.

Drama **(PR:A MPAA:NR)**

DARK MIRROR, THE*** (1920) 5 reels PAR bw

Dorothy Dalton *(Pricilla Maine/Nora O'Moore)*, Huntley Gordon *(Dr. Phillip

Fosdick), Walter Neeland *(Red Carnahan)*, Jessie Arnold *(Inez)*, Lucile Carney *(Addy)*, Petro de Cardoba *(Mario)*, Donald MacPherson *(The Nut)*, Bert Starkey *(Charlie the Coke)*.

This crime-society thriller was a good vehicle for Dalton, who plays twin sisters—one raised by a "leading family" and the other in the slums. Their identities and fate become interchanged, and the fast-paced action kept audiences on the edge of their seats until the last reel.

d, Charles Giblyn; sup, Thomas H. Ince; w, E. Magnus Ingleton (based on the novel by Louis Joseph Vance); ph, John Stumar.

Crime **(PR:A MPAA:NR**

DARK ROAD, THE*** (1917) 5 reels TRI bw

Dorothy Dalton *(Cleo Murison)*, Robert McKim *(Carlos Costa)*, Jack Livingston *(Capt. James Murison)*, Jack Gilbert *(Cedric Constable)*, Walt Whitman *(Sir John Constable)*, Lydia Knott *(Lady Mary Constable)*.

In this intriguing story, Dalton plays a British woman named Cleo, who is reincarnated from the Egyptian empress of the same name. She is married to Livingston, an army officer who does not know she is using her great beauty and animal attraction to get from other men the luxuries he cannot afford to provide her. When war is declared, he arranges for her to stay with relatives and then embarks for France. As soon as he is gone, his wife seduces Gilbert, the young man of the house, who falls madly in love with her as a result. The call of the flag, however, is strong and soon he too leaves for the front, taking with him a passionate love letter and the talisman Dalton's husband had given her. A short time later, McKim, an art dealer (and German agent) visits their estate to appraise some paintings and Dalton attempts to cast her spell on him. Instead, it is he who takes command, and she quite willingly moves into a London apartment he establishes. A letter her husband sends her, containing military information, is intercepted by McKim and relayed to Berlin by wireless. In Europe, meanwhile, the war bogs down and Gilbert is killed in the trenches. On going through his effects, Livingston finds his wife's letter, which is a duplicate of one she gave him. Then, when the Germans attack and are beaten back, a copy of the dispatch which McKim sent and which implicated Cleo is found on an enemy colonel. Livingston is summoned to headquarters to explain this and is given permission to return to London. Working with Scotland Yard, he locates McKim's flat and, when they crash in, he finds his wife in the arms of the spy—who is led away to face the worst. Now, alone with his wife, he hands her a dagger and orders her to save them further disgrace. She refuses and attempts to weaken his resolve through her sexual charms, but he becomes infuriated and hurls the knife at a portrait of Cleopatra—piercing its breast. His wife gasps in pain, clutching her own chest, and then falls across the divan—dead.

d, Charles Miller; w, J. G. Hawks (based on a story by John Lynch).

War **(PR:A MPAA:NR)**

DARK STAIRWAYS*** (1924) 5 reels UNIV bw

Herbert Rawlinson *(Sheldon Polk)*, Ruth Dwyer *(Sunny Day)*, Hayden Stevenson *(Frank Farnsworth)*, Robert E. Homans *("Dippy" Blake)*, Walter Perry *(Chris Martin)*, Bonnie Hill *(Rita Minar)*, Kathleen O'Connor *(Geraldine Lewis)*, Dolores Rousse *(Madge Armstrong)*, Emmett King *(Henry Polk)*, Lola Todd *(Stenographer)*, Tom McGuire *(Police Chief)*.

Falsely convicted of stealing a valuable necklace, a bank cashier allows his fellow convicts to think him guilty in order to be included in their escape. Once out, he nails the real crook and clears his name. There is one striking and highly effective scene in which a dirigible hovers over the prison to pick up the fleeing cons.

d, Robert F. Hill; w, L. G. Rigby (based on a story by Marion Orth); ph, William Thornley.

Crime **(PR:A MPAA:NR)**

DARKEST LONDON** (1915, Brit.) 4 reels Barker bw

Ivy Close *(Mabel Carstairs)*.

In this British thriller, an heiress who had been kidnaped runs away from her crooked husband to become a successful dancer. In this capacity she meets and falls in love with a nobleman who is being blackmailed.

d, Bert Haldane.

Crime **(PR:A MPAA:NR)**

DARLING MINE* (1920) 5 reels SF bw

Olive Thomas, Walt Whitman, J. Barney Sherry, Margaret McWade, Betty Schade, Walter McGrail, Richard Tucker, Anna Dodge.

Tepid, poorly organized movie about an Irish girl who is discovered by a famous playwright and is loved by his nephew. At one point in the story, she visits the house of a well-known playboy in an attempt to reconcile him with his fiancee. The nephew misunderstands her motive and flies into a mighty rage—but by the time this film mercifully comes to an end, the lassie reassures him of her virtue and, once again, completely captivates his heart.

d, Lawrence Trimble; w, John Lynch, Trimble.

Drama **(PR:A MPAA:NR)**

DARLING OF PARIS, THE** (1917) 6 reels FOX bw

Theda Bara *(Esmaralda)*, Glen White *(Quasimodo)*, Walter Law *(Claude Frallo)*, Herbert Heyes *(Capt. Phoebus)*, Miss Carey Lee *(Paquette)*, Alice Gale *(Gypsy Queen)*, John Webb Dillon *(Clopin)*, Louis Dean *(Gringouier)*.

This adaptation of Victor Hugo's *The Hunchback of Notre Dame* was made six years before the definitive Lon Chaney version. There were some great crowd scenes, but the production suffered at the time of its release because of the difficulty audiences had in accepting sex queen Bara as the innocent Esmeralda.

d, J. Gordon Edwards; w, Adrian Jackson (based on the novel *The Hunchback of Notre Dame* by Victor Hugo); ph, Phil Rosen.

Drama **PR:A MPAA:NR)**

DARLING OF THE RICH, THE* (1923) 6 reels B.B. Productions bw

Betty Blythe *(Chamrio Winship)*, Gladys Leslie *(Lizzie Callahan)*, Jane Jennings *(Jane Winship)*, Montagu Love *(Peyton Martin)*, Charles Gerard *(Torrence Welch)*, Leslie Austin *(Mason Lawrence)*, Julia Swayne Gordon *(Dippy Helen)*, Albert Hackett *(Fred Winship)*, Walter Walker *(Mike Callahan)*, A. Gorwin *(Detective)*, Rita Maurice *(The Baby)*.

A real curiosity in that a great deal of money was spent on the production values for a script so bad it's entertaining. The story is of a pure and beautiful girl who becomes involved with Wall Street tycoons, dresses in an outrageous Cleopatra costume, and auctions herself off to the highest bidder to finance her brother's operation. Incredibly, one old boy offers $1 million, while another pledges half of everything he has. In the end, however, she marries the young financier she really loves, thus ringing down the curtain on a tale which truly could only have happened in America.

d, John G. Adolfi; w, Dorothy Farnum (based on the play "The Imposter" by Leonard Merrick, Michael Morton); ph, Edward Paul.

Drama **(PR:A MPAA:NR)**

DAS CABINETT DES CALIGARI

(SEE: CABINET OF DR. CALIGARI, THE, 1919, Ger.)

DAUGHTER IN REVOLT, A** (1927, Brit.) 8 reels AA bw

Mabel Poulton *(Aimee Scroope)*, Edward O'Neill *(Lord Scroope)*, Patrick Susands *(Billy Spencer)*, Lilian Oldland *(Georgina Berners)*, Pat Aherne *(Jackie the Climber)*, Hermione Baddeley *(Calamity Kate)*, Marie Ault *(Mrs. Dale)*, Daisy Campbell *(Lady Scroope)*, Neil Curtis *(Alexander Lambe)*, Gertrude Sterroll *(Lady Erythea Lambe)*.

British comedy about a nobleman's daughter who gets into one jam after another until she is finally arrested for burglary after trading places with a chum.

p, Archibald Nettlefold; d&w, Harry Hughes (based on the novel by Sidney Gowing).

Comedy **(PR:A MPAA:NR)**

DAUGHTER OF LOVE, A** (1925, Brit.) 5 reels STOLL bw

Violet Hopson *(Mary Tannerhill)*, John Stuart *(Dudley Bellairs)*, Jameson Thomas *(Dr. Eden Brent)*, Fred Raynham *(Lord St. Erth)*, Arthur Walcott *(Mr. Tannerhill)*, Ena Evans *(Lillian)*, Gladys Mason *(Lady St. Erth)*, Madge Tree *(Mrs. Tobin)*, Minna Grey *(Mrs. Diamond)*, Mrs. Charles Beattie *(Mme. Korsikov)*.

Average British class-drama about a lord's objection to his son's love affair with a girl who was born out of wedlock, until it is discovered she is actually the daughter of a prominent society physician.

d, Walter West; w, Lucita Squires (based on the novel by Mrs. E. J. Key).

Drama **(PR:A MPAA:NR)**

DAUGHTER OF MINE*** (1919) 5 reels Goldwyn bw

Madge Kennedy *(Rosie)*, John Bowers *(Charles Howard)*, Tully Marshall *(Papa Mendelsohn)*, Arthur Carew *(Joseph Rayberg)*, Abraham Schwartz *(Rabinovitch)*.

Kennedy's orthodox Jewish father breaks up her relationship with a struggling Christian writer, and the dejected young man disappears. Shortly thereafter, she lands a job with a publishing house and convinces its owner, Carew (who is sweet on her) to allow her to read one of her boy friend's manuscripts to him, the idea being that advertising for a lost author would make a great publicity stunt. She is invited to her boss' apartment and begins to read the story, which is set in medieval times. At this point, the picture fades out and the young man's tale is told on the screen. The movie ends with Carew placing the ad and the lovers being reunited.

d, Clarence G. Badger; w, (based on a story by Hugo Ballin); ph, Marcel Le Picard.

Drama **(PR:A MPAA:NR)**

DAUGHTER OF THE SEA, A** (1915) 5 reels WORLD bw

Muriel Ostriche *(The Girl)*, W. H. Tooker *(Her Father)*, Catherine Calhoun *(Mrs. Rutland)*, Clara Whipple *(Her Daughter)*, Clifford Grey *(Jack, Her Son)*, Roy Applegate *(Alexander Gibson)*.

Poor girl from a fishing village saves a wealthy woman from drowning and, as a reward, is brought to her estate to be educated. The girl falls in love with the woman's son, but class distinction prevents their marrying until she further proves herself by taking the blame for a killing the daughter of the house committed. In the end, of course, it all works out.

d, Charles W. Seay; w, Russell E. Smith (based on the story "The Fisher-Girl" by Frances Marion).

Drama **(PR:A MPAA:NR)**

DAUGHTER PAYS, THE*** (1920) 5 reels SF bw

Elaine Hammerstein *(Virginia Mynors)*, Norman Trevor *(Osbert Gault)*, Robert Ellis *(Gerald Roseborough)*, Theresa Maxwell Conover *(Mrs. Mynors)*, Evelyn Times *(Pansy Mynors)*, Bryson Russell *(Percy Ferris)*.

Set in England, this is the story of a widowed mother of two girls (one a cripple) who lives in poverty. The eldest daughter is awarded a scholarship in London, and the mother consents to let her go—hoping that she will return with a wealthy young husband. Instead, she encounters the man her mother jilted years before, and who is determined to have her in order to reap revenge. Before long, however, the older fellow falls in love with the pretty daughter, and she with him.

d, Robert Ellis; w, Edward J. Montagne (based on a story by Mrs. Bailey Reynolds); ph, John W. Brown.

Drama **(PR:A MPAA:NR)**

DAUGHTERS OF MEN* (1914) 5 reels Lubin bw

George Soule Spencer, Ethel Clayton.

Pop Lubin, Philadelphia's pioneer film producer, advertised this early feature as being his masterpiece. It was, in fact, a boring account of the struggle between labor and management and misfired on every level.

d, George Terwilliger; w, Lawrence S. McCloskey (based on a story by Charles Klein).

Drama **(PR:A MPAA:NR)**

DAUGHTERS OF TODAY**
(1924) 7 reels Sturgeon-Hubbard/SF bw (AKA: WHAT'S YOUR DAUGHTER DOING?)

Patsy Ruth Miller *(Lois Whittall)*, Ralph Graves *(Ralph Adams)*, Edna Murphy *(Mabel Vandegrift)*, George Nichols *(Dirk Vandegrift)*, Edward Hearn *(Peter Farnham)*, Gertrude Claire *(Ma Vandegrift)*, Philo McCullough *(Reggie Adams)*, Phillips Smalley *(Leigh Whittall)*, ZaSu Pitts *(Lorena)*, H. J. Herbert *(Calnan)*, Fontaine La Rue *(Mrs. Mantell)*, Truman Van Dyke *(Dick)*, Dorothy Wood *(Flo)*, Marjorie Bonner *(Maisie)*.

Country girl Murphy becomes part of a fun-loving set after she enrolls in a swanky city college. At a party she rejects the advances of obnoxious McCullough and is accused of his murder when he is later found dead. Her country boy friend Hearn comes to town, however, and solves the case.

d, Rollin Sturgeon; w, Lucien Hubbard; ph, Milton Moore.

Drama **(PR:A MPAA:NR)**

DAUGHTERS WHO PAY** (1925) 6 reels BAN bw

Marguerite De La Motte *(Mary Smith/Sonia)*, John Bowers *(Dick Foster)*, Barney Sherry *(His Father)*.

This programmer was designed with something for everyone. De La Motte is a suburban girl who works as a dancer named Sonia in a Russian night club. A wealthy young weakling, her brother's employer, is crazy about her, but her brother has just stolen $10,000 from the company. To get him off the hook, De La Motte goes to the weakling's father to plead the case and is refused. She then returns dressed as Sonia and promises to dump the son if he agrees to drop the charges. Everything turns out fine in the end when Sonia exposes a group of Reds—using the club for cover—and reveals her true identity to the old man.

d, George Terwilliger; w, William B. Laub; ph, Edward Paul, Charles Davis, Murphy Darling.

Drama **(PR:A MPAA:NR)**

DAVID AND JONATHAN** (1920, Brit.) 6 reels G.B. Samuelson/GEN bw

Madge Titheradge *(Joan Meredith)*, Geoffrey Webb *(David Mortlake)*, Richard Ryan *(Jonathan Hawksley)*, Sidney Wood *(David as a Child)*, Jack Perks *(Jonathan as a Child)*.

This British film about a couple of friends who love the same girl they are shipwrecked with was made on the stage of a Hollywood studio.

d, Alexander Butler; w, (based on the novel by E. Temple Thurston).

Adventure **(PR:A MPAA:NR)**

DAVID HARUM*** (1915) 5 reels FP bw

William H. Crane *(David Harum)*, Kate Meeks *(Aunt Polly)*, May Allison *(Mary Blake)*, Harold Lockwood *(John Lenox)*, Hal Clarendon *(Chet Timson)*, Guy Nichols *(Deacon Perkins)*, Russell Bassett.

Broadway star Crane, under the skilled direction of Dwan, brought Westcott's beloved small town philosopher to life in the first motion picture production of DAVID HARUM. In 1934 Will Rogers remade the film, adding his own special touch.

d&w, Allan Dwan (based on the novel by Edward Noyes Westcott); ph, Hal Rosson.

Comedy/Drama **(PR:A MPAA:NR)**

DAWN*** (1917, Brit.) 6 reels Lucoque bw

Karina *(Mildred Carr)*, Hubert Carter *(Devil Caresfoot)*, Madeleine Seymour *(Mildred Caresfoot)*, Edward Combermere *(George Caresfoot)*, R. Heaton Grey *(Philip Caresfoot)*, Annie Esmond *(Mrs. Bellamy)*, Frank Harris *(Mr. Bellamy)*, George Snazelle *(Arthur Heigham)*.

Well-done British thriller about a woman who murders her paramour—after arranging his marriage to a wealthy heiress—and then discovers he has no intention of sharing the fortune.

d, H. Lisle Lucoque; w, Pauline Lewis (based on the novel by H. Rider Haggard).

Drama **(PR:A MPAA:NR)**

DAWN*** (1928, Brit.) British and Dominions/Woolf and Freedman bw

Sybil Thorndike *(Edith Cavell)*, Marie Ault *(Mme. Rappard)*, Mary Brough *(Mme. Pitou)*, Ada Bodart *(Herself)*, Dacia Deane *(Mme. Deveaux)*, Haddon Mason *(APM)*, Mickey Brantford *(Jacques Rappard)*, Cecil Barry *(Col. Schultz)*, Frank Perfitt *(Gen. von Zauberzweig)*, Edward O'Neill *(A Priest)*, Maurice Braddell *(A Flier)*, Griffith Humphreys *(The President)*.

Controversial and suppressed British film about Edith Cavell (Thorndike), a nurse who was executed by the Germans during WWI for helping British military prisoners escape.

p&d, Herbert Wilcox; w, Wilcox, Robert J. Cullen (based on the play by Reginald Berkeley).

War **(PR:C MPAA:NR)**

DAWN OF A TOMORROW, THE*** (1915) 5 reels FP bw

Mary Pickford *(Glad)*, David Powell *(Dandy)*, Forrest Robinson *(Sir Oliver Holt)*, Robert Cain *(His Nephew)*, Margaret Seddon, Blanche Craig, John Findlay.

Pickford gave her usual fine performance as a British slum waif who rescues her sweetheart from a life of crime and saves a millionaire from committing suicide. "America's Sweetheart" had signed on with Famous Players in 1912 at a salary of $500 per week. By the time THE DAWN OF A TOMORROW was completed, Pickford was such a hot item that within a year studio head Adolph Zukor raised her to an incredible $10,000 per week with a $300,000 bonus and her own studio, The Mary Pickford Company, which would be used exclusively for making her films.

d, James Kirkwood; w, Frances Marion (based on a play by Frances Hodgson Burnett).

Drama **(PR:A MPAA:NR)**

DAWN OF THE EAST** (1921) 5 reels Realart/PAR bw

Alice Brady *(Countess Natalya)*, Kenneth Harlan *(Roger Strong)*, Michio Itow *(Sotan)*, America Chedister *(Mariya)*, Betty Carpenter *(Sonya)*, Harriet Ross *(Mrs. Strong)*, Sam Kim *(Wu Ting)*, Frank Honda *(Liang)*, H. Takima *(Kwan)*, Patricio Reyes *(Chang)*.

Countess Brady, an aristocratic refugee from the Russian revolution, lands a job dancing in a Shanghai cabaret in order to support her sickly sister. She becomes involved with Itow, a royalist who opposes the new republic. He tells her he will get the money for her to escape to America if she marries a certain Chinese millionaire. Believing the ceremony will not be binding, she does so, splits the money with Itow, and escapes to America. After arriving in the U.S., she marries an American diplomat who is interested in the Chinese republic but, before long, Sotan shows up and threatens to tell her husband of the former marriage unless she obtains certain information about China for him. She refuses and the millionaire is brought over to heighten his threat. At a meeting between Brady, Itow, and the millionaire, the countess explains that the marriage was planned by Itow in order to swindle money, and the millionaire, who is actually a pretty decent sort, kills his unscrupulous countryman and returns to the Orient, leaving her in peace.

d, E. H. Griffith; w, E. Lloyd Sheldon; ph, Gilbert Warrenton.

Drama **(PR:A MPAA:NR)**

DAY OF DAYS, THE*** (1914) 4 reels FP bw

Cyril Scott, Dave Wall, Hal Clarendon.

Based on a popular Vance story, this fast-paced action film has a young tannery clerk outwit a band of crooks, an army of cops, his ruthless boss, and marry an heiress as well.

d, Daniel Frohman; w, (based on a story by Louis Joseph Vance).

Crime **(PR:A MPAA:NR)**

DEAD CERTAINTY, A* (1920, Brit.) 5 reels BRO bw

Gregory Scott *(Arthur Dunbar)*, Poppy Wyndham *(Pat Stone)*, Cameron Carr *(Henry Stone)*, Harry Royston *(Martin Mills)*, Mary Masters *(Mrs. Woodruff)*, Wallace Bosco.

This was just another of those below average British films about the sport of kings. In this one, a rotter tries to force a girl's gentleman friend to throw a race. Of course the young fellow wins, after all, and the scoundrel gets what's coming to him.

p, Walter West; d, George Dewhurst; w, P. L. Mannock (based on the novel by Nat Gould).

Crime **(PR:A MPAA:NR)**

DEAD MAN'S CURVE** (1928) 6 reels FBO bw

Douglas Fairbanks, Jr. *(Vernon Keith)*, Sally Blaine *(Ethel Hume)*, Charles Byer *(George Marshall)*, Arthur Metcalf *(Fergus Hume)*, Kit Guard *(Goof Goober)*, Byron Douglas *(Benton)*, James Mason *(Derne)*.

Fairbanks, who works for Aladdin Motors, comes in third in an auto race and discovers there is a problem with the engine. His boss blames the poor showing on cowardice, so Fairbanks quits to improve the motor on his own. He corrects the problem and unknowingly uses his former employer's daughter's money to enter the big race. He takes first place, in an excitingly photographed contest, and wins the girl as well.

d, Richard Rosson; w, Ewart Adamson; t, Randolph Bartlett; ph, Phillip Tannura; ed, Adamson.

Adventure **(PR:A MPAA:NR)**

DEBT OF HONOR* (1922, Brit.) 5 reels STOLL bw

Isobel Elsom *(Hope Carteret)*, Clive Brook *(Walter Hyde)*, Sydney Seaward *(Maj. Baring)*, Lionelle Howard *(Ronald Carteret)*, Lewis Gilbert *(Proprietor)*, Frank Goldsmith *(Col. Latimer)*, Frances Peyton *(Mrs. Latimer)*, Hilda Sims *(Ayah)*.

Just another British Empire saga, set in India, about a rotter who is blackmailing a woman due to her brother's gambling debts. In the end a python kills the scoundrel, and the woman is left in peace.

d, Maurice Elvey; w, (based on the novel by Ethel M. Dell).

Drama **(PR:A MPAA:NR)**

DECAMERON NIGHTS*** (1924, Brit.) 10 reels Graham-Wilcox-Decla bw

Lionel Barrymore *(Saladin)*, Ivy Duke *(Perdita)*, Werner Krauss *(Soldan)*, Bernhard Goetzke *(Torello)*, Randle Aryton *(Ricciardo)*, Xenia Desni *(Lady Teodora)*, Jameson Thomas *(Imliff)*, Hannah Ralph *(Lady Violante)*, Albert Steinruck *(King Algarve)*.

Wilcox, an Irish-born director who became one of England's top cinema figures, took his company to Germany, where he combined the considerable talents of Barrymore and Krauss to tell the story of a sultan's son and his love for a Moslem princess.

p, Herbert Wilcox, Erich Pommer; d, Wilcox; w, Wilcox, Noel Rhys (based on the play by R. McLoughlin, B. Lawrence and the book *The Decameron* by Giovanni Boccaccio).

Drama **(PR:A MPAA:NR)**

DEEDS MEN DO, THE
(SEE: BATTLES OF THE CORONEL AND FALKLAND ISLANDS, THE, 1928, Brit.)

DELIRIUM (SEE: CRAVING, THE, 1918)

DEMOCRACY*** (1918, Brit.) 6 reels Progress/BUT bw

Bruce Gordon *(George Greig)*, Alice O'Brien *(Diana Tudworth)*, Frank Dane *(Gerald Tudworth)*, Alice Russon *(Rose Greig)*, Alice de Winton *(Lady Tudworth)*, Wyndham Guise *(Sutton Tudworth)*, Jack Andrews *(Daniel Greig)*, Mrs. Hubert Willis *(Mary Greig)*.

This highly interesting British film, set during WWI, had a lot to say about the English class system. The story tells of a working man's son who saves the life of a young aristocrat, despite the fact that his sister was earlier seduced by him.

p, Frank E. Spring; d&w, Sidney Morgan.

War **(PR:A MPAA:NR)**

DER GOLEM
(SEE: GOLEM: HOW HE CAME INTO THE WORLD, THE, 1920, Ger.)

DER LETZTE MANN (SEE: LAST LAUGH, THE, 1924, Ger.)

DESERT BLOSSOMS** (1921) 5 reels FOX bw

William Russell *(Stephen Brent)*, Helen Ferguson *(Mary Ralston)*, Wilbur Higby *(James Thornton)*, Dulcie Cooper *(Lucy Thornton)*, Charles Spere *(Bert Thornton)*, Margaret Mann *(Mrs. Thornton)*, Gerald Pring *(Mr. Joyce)*, Willis Robards *(Henry Ralston)*.

Fair melodrama about a construction engineer accused of using inferior materials and causing a bridge to collapse. His employer's son is actually the guilty party but, out of loyalty, the engineer assumes the guilt, heads West, changes his identity, and falls in love with a girl who recognizes him but keeps his secret. In the end he is exonerated and marries the girl.

d, Arthur Rosson; w, Arthur J. Zellner (based on a story by Kate Corbaley); ph, Ross Fisher.

Melodrama **(PR:A MPAA:NR)**

DESERT FLOWER, THE*** (1925) 7 reels FN bw

Coleen Moore *(Maggie Fortune)*, Lloyd Hughes *(Rance Conway)*, Kate Price *(Mrs. McQuade)*, Geno Corrado *(Jose Lee)*, Fred Warren *(Dizzy)*, Frank Brownlee *(Mike Dyer)*, Isabelle Keith *(Inga Hulverson)*, Anna May Walthall *(Flozella)*, William Norton Bailey *(Jack Royal)*, Monte Collins *(Mr. McQuade)*, Ena Gregory *(Fay Knight)*.

Talented Moore soared high above the material she was given here. She plays a young orphan who raises a baby sister, reforms the young drunk whom she loves, and protects her personal honor from the lecherous advances of a degenerate step-father.

d, Irving Cummings; w, June Mathis (based on the play by Don Mullally); ph, T. D. McCord; ed, George McGuire; art d, Edward Shulter.

Western/Drama **(PR:A MPAA:NR)**

DESERT PIRATE, THE*** (1928) 5 reels FBO bw

Tom Tyler *(Tom Corrigan)*, Frankie Darro *(Jimmy Rand)*, Duane Thompson *(Ann Farnham)*, Edward Hearne *(Norton)*, Tom Lingham *(Shorty Gibbs)*.

Good Tyler western about a sheriff who adopts a kid (the underrated Darro), clears the father of the girl he loves, and takes on a saloon full of crooks with his bare hands.

d, James Dugan; w, Oliver Drake (based on a story by Frank Howard Clark).

Western **(PR:A MPAA:NR)**

DESERT RIDER, THE** (1929) 5 reels MGM bw

Tim McCoy *(Jed Tyler)*, Raquel Torres *(Dolores)*, Bert Roach *(Friar Bernardo)*, Edward Connelly *(Padre Quintada)*, Harry Woods *(Williams)*, Jess Cavin *(Black Bailey)*.

McCoy is a pony express rider who is robbed by a band of outlaws who are after a land grant owned by beautiful Mexican Torres. McCoy tracks down the varmints and gets back the stolen grant, thus saving her land for Torres.

d, Nick Grinde; w, Oliver Drake (based on a story by Ted Shane, Milton Bren); t, Harry Sinclair Drago; ed, William Le Vanway; cos, Lucia Coulter.

Western **(PR:A MPAA:NR)**

DESERTED AT THE ALTAR** (1922) 7 reels Goldwyn bw

Bessie Love *(Anna Moore)*, William Scott *(Bob Crandall)*, Tully Marshall *(Squire Simpson)*, Barbara Tennant *(Nell Reed)*, Eulalie Jensen *(The Teacher)*, Fred Kelsey *(The Other Man)*, Frankie Lee *(Tommy Moore)*, Wade Boteler *(John Simpson)*, Les Bates *(The Mob Leader)*, Edward McQuade *(The Sheriff)*, Helen Howard *(The Gossip)*, Queenie the Dog.

Orphan girl Love and her brother Lee are in the custody of a dishonest guardian who schemes to have his son marry her for a secret inheritance. Scott, a city fellow, arrives, becomes romantically involved with Love, and they plan to marry. At the wedding, however, a woman holding a baby steps forward and accuses Scott of being the baby's father. Later, after a well-filmed mob scene in which the townsfolk attempt to lynch the urbanite, it is disclosed that the guardian was behind it all.

d, William K. Howard, Al Kelley; w, Grace Miller White (based on the play by Pierce Kingsley); ph, Glen MacWilliams, John Meigle.

Drama **(PR:A MPAA:NR)**

DESERT'S PRICE, THE*** (1926) 6 reels FOX bw

Buck Jones *(Wils McCann)*, Florence Gilbert *(Julia)*, Edna Marion *(Nora)*, Ernest Butterworth *(Phil)*, Arthur Houseman *(Tom Martin)*, Montague Love *(Jim Martin)*, Carl Stockdale *(Gitner)*, Harry Dunkinson *(Sheriff)*, Henry Armetta *(Shepherd)*.

Jones plays a college man who comes home to his ranch to discover that the feud which exists between his family and that of a girl he is attracted to is really the fault of an outlaw band. He, of course, sets the record straight and wins the girl as well.

d, W. S. Van Dyke; w, Charles Darnton (based on a story by William MacLeod Raine); ph, Reginald Lyons.

Western **(PR:A MPAA:NR)**

DESERT'S TOLL, THE***
(1926) 6 reels MGM bw (AKA: THE DEVIL'S TOLL)

Francis McDonald *(Frank Darwin)*, Kathleen Key *(Muriel Cooper)*, Chief Big Tree *(Red Eagle)*, Anna May Wong *(Oneta)*, Tom Santschi *(Jasper)*, Lew Meehan, Guinn Williams.

Santschi is at his villainous best as an outlaw who murders an old miner for his claim but is thwarted by a young man who ultimately brings him to justice. The hero of this well-produced little western was handsome McDonald, who would go on to become one of the screen's top heavies.

d, Clifford Smith; t, Gardner Bradford; ph, George Stevens, Jack Roach; ed, Richard Currier.

Western **(PR:A MPAA:NR)**

DESIRED WOMAN, THE** (1918) 5 reels VIT bw

Harry Morey *(Richard Mostyn)*, Florence Deshon *(Irene Mitchell)*, Jean Paige *(Dolly Drake)*, Charles Hutchinson *(Jarvis Saunders)*, William Cameron *(Jeff Henderson)*, Eulalie Jensen *(Marie Winship)*, Harold Foshay *(Andy Buckton)*, Aida Horton *(Little Dick Mostyn)*, Julia Swayne Gordon *(Mrs. Moore)*, Herbert Potter *(Delbridge)*.

This episodic film suffers from the lack of a central theme in its attempt to relate the story of a man who lives and loves fully before finding security through religion.

d, Paul Scardom; w, (based on a story by Will N. Harben).

Drama **(PR:A MPAA:NR)**

DESPOILER, THE**** (1915) 5 reels TRI bw

Charles K. French *(Col. Damien)*, Enid Markey *(Sylvia Damien)*, Frank Keenan *(Emir)*, Roy Laidlaw *(The Mayor)*, Fanny Midgley *(The Abbess)*, J. Frank Burke *(Field Marshal)*.

This interesting film about the horrors of war is careful not to take sides. It tells the story of a colonel, attached to a group of irregulars, who captures a town in order to plunder money its citizens raised for the enemy. The colonel places his leader, Keenan (a man who secretly lusts for his daughter) in charge of this operation, and when all else fails, the people are told the army will be turned loose on the abbey where the women have taken refuge. Meanwhile, the colonel's daughter can't get through the military lines and goes to the abbey. When Keenan arrives with his drunken men, the daughter—confident he will protect them—lets him in. Keenan pretends not to recognize her and makes a proposal: if she will give herself to him, then he will spare the others from his lusting horde. She courageously consents, and the brute has his way with her. When the act is done, the victim distracts her abuser and kills him with his own service revolver. Meanwhile, the colonel's conscience is awakened, and he rides to the abbey to stop the atrocity. But when he arrives and finds his first in command dead, he orders the troops to be set loose and the killer be brought to him so that he might personally deal out the punishment. Within minutes his daughter, her face covered by a veil, is delivered and the officer empties his pistol into her heroic little body. It is then that he lifts the veil and discovers the terrible truth. It is also then that he is awakened from a dream by Keenan, who tells him the mayor of the town has made his decision regarding the money. "It is not necessary," the colonel declares, and then he orders his men to mount. After all, there is a *war* to fight.

d, Thomas H. Ince; w, J. G. Hawks, Ince.

War **(PR:A MPAA:NR)**

DESTINY'S ISLE* (1922) 6 reels ARC bw

Virginia Lee *(Lola Whitaker)*, Ward Crane *(Tom Proctor)*, Florence Billings *(Florence Martin)*, Arthur Housman *(Arthur Randall)*, George Fawcet *(Judge Richard Proctor)*, William B. Davidson *(Lazus)*, Mario Marjeroni *(Dr. Whitaker)*, Ida Darling *(Mrs. Pierpont)*, Albert Roccardi *(Mrs. Ripp)*, Pauline Dempsey *(Mammy)*.

This programmer (shot almost entirely in Miami) provided some spectacular scenic backgrounds in telling its story of island romance. This, combined with some better-than-average fights, and nifty motorboat and airplane stunts, made it a crowd pleaser.

d, William P. S. Earle; w, Margery Land May; ph, William S. Adams.

Drama **(PR:A MPAA:NR)**

DESTRUCTION* (1915) 5 reels FOX bw

Theda Bara *(Fernade)*, J. Herbert Frank *(Dave Walker)*, James Furey *(John Froment)*, Gaston Bell *(John Froment, III)*, Warner Oland *(Mr. Deleveau)*, Esther H. Oier *(Josine Walker)*, Master Tansey *(Josine's Brother)*, Arthur Morrison *(Lang)*, Frank Evans *(Mill Foreman)*, Carleton Macey.

Less than satisfactory Bara effort about a woman who schemes to get her new husband's wealth upon his imminent death. Fate doesn't take kindly to her plan, however, as the man dies before he can change his will in her favor, and his son outwits her next devilish plan, to kill him. One of nine pictures Bara made the year she broke into the movies and gained instant fame.

d&w, Will S. Davis (based on the novel *Labor* by Emil Zola).

Drama **(PR:A MPAA:NR)**

DEVIL DODGER, THE* (1917) 5 reels TRI bw

Jack Gilbert *(Roger Ingraham)*, Carolyn Wagner *(Fluffy)*, Roy Stewart *(Silent Scott)*, John Lince *(Ricketts)*, Anna Dodge *(Mrs. Ricketts)*, George Willis *(Bowie)*, Belle Bennett.

In this early film, Gilbert plays a sickly preacher who heads West for his health and becomes the sky pilot of a town run by gambler Stewart. After an altercation with Stewart, the preacher is nursed back to health by Wagner, a dance hall girl—and Stewart's woman. The picture ends with the preacher saving Stewart's life in a gun battle and, in his last act as a reverend, marrying the two. The bad man, of course, is regenerated, and religion is encouraged to flourish in the town he no longer chooses to rule.

d, Cliff Smith; w, J. G. Hawks.

Western **(PR:A MPAA:NR)**

DEVIL DOGS* (1928) 6 reels Morris R. Schlank/ANCH bw

Alexander Alt *(Archie Van Stratten)*, Pauline Curley *(Joyce Moore)*, Stuart Holmes *(Sgt. Gordon White)*, Ernest Hilliard *(Lt. Holmes)*, J. P. McGowan *(Capt. Standing)*.

A clone of the popular Wallace Beery-Raymond Hatton series, but without the talent or the laughs. In this one, the boys (Alt and Holmes) chase after the same girl and join the army.

d, Fred Windermere; w, Maxine Alton, Adele Buffington; t, Al Martin; ph, Robert E. Cline; ed, I. Rosen.

Comedy **(PR:A MPAA:NR)**

DEVIL TO PAY, THE* (1920) 6 reels Pathe bw

Roy Stewart *(District Attorney)*, Robert McKim *(The Banker)*, Fritzi Brunette, George Fisher, Evelyn Selbie, Joseph J. Dowling, Richard Lapan, Mark Fenton, William Marion.

Nice courtroom programmer about a district attorney and a bank president in love with the same girl. The banker is in the witness box, and the D.A. brings on a surprise witness whose identity is concealed until the end. It turns out that he is the very same man supposedly executed earlier for the murder the banker committed. This testimony and the sight of the man drive the real killer to suicide and the girl into the arms of the district attorney.

d, Ernest C. Warde; w, Jack Cunningham (based on a novel by Frances Nimmo Greene); ph, Arthur Todd.

Crime **(PR:A MPAA:NR)**

DEVIL'S APPLE TREE** (1929) 7 reels TIF/Stahl bw

Dorothy Sebastian *(Dorothy Ryan)*, Larry Kent *(John Rice)*, Edward Martindel *(Col. Rice)*, Ruth Clifford *(Jane Norris)*, George Cooper *(Cooper)*, Cosmo Kyrle Bellew *(The Roue)*.

Sebastian arrives on a tropical island where she is to marry a man she became engaged to through a matrimonial agency. Being desperate and poor, she has taken the identity of a wealthy female passenger whom she believed was dying of smallpox. Thanks to her new social standing, Sebastian is invited into the home of a prominent family and falls in love with the handsome son, Kent. Then the rich woman—who made a sudden recovery—shows up and exposes Sebastian as a fraud. Grief-stricken and humiliated, she wanders into the jungle where natives capture her and prepare to burn her alive. Fortunately, Sebastian is saved in the nick of time by Kent, who realizes he loves her for what she is.

d, Elmer Clifton; w, Lillian Ducey; t, Frederick Hatton; ph, Ernest Miller; ed, Frank Sullivan.

Drama **(PR:A MPAA:NR)**

DEVIL'S CARGO, THE* (1925) 8 reels FP/LAS bw

Wallace Beery *(Ben)*, Pauline Starke *(Faro Sampson)*, Claire Adams *(Martha Joyce)*, William Collier, Jr. *(John Joyce)*, Raymond Hatton *(Mate)*, George Cooper *(Jerry Dugan)*, Dale Fuller *(Millie)*, "Spec" O'Donnell *(Jimmy)*, Emmett C. King *(Square Deal Sampson)*, John Webb Dillon *(Farwell)*, Louis King *(Briggs)*.

Easterner Collier comes to Sacramento after the 1849 California Gold Rush, takes over the newspaper, and crusades against corruption in the town. This encourages the "decent" folks to rise up and drive the "sinners" out. In the meantime, Collier falls for Starke, not realizing that she is a cabaret entertainer. Branded a hypocrite when found in her company, Collier is imprisoned with the other "sinners" on a cargo ship and deported to sea. After a boiler explosion a group of ruffians, led by bully Beery, take over. Collier defeats the big fellow in a nicely staged fight, assumes control, realizes Starke's real worth, and marries her after they are rescued by another ship.

d, Victor Fleming; w, A. P. Younger (based on a story by Charles E. Whittaker); ph, C. Edgar Schoenbaum.

Drama **(PR:A MPAA:NR)**

DEVIL'S CHAPLAIN* (1929) 6 reels T/C/RAY bw

Cornelius Keefe *(Yorke Norray)*, Virginia Brown Faire *(Princess Therese)*, Josef Swickard *(The King)*, Boris Karloff *(Boris)*, Wheeler Oakman *(Nicholay)*, Leland Carr *(Ivan)*, George McIntosh *(The Prince)*.

A good cast helped this modest actioner about an heir to a Balkan throne who escapes to America after his country is overthrown. In the States he is befriended by a Secret Service agent who helps restore him to his throne, while at the same time winning the heart of the king's lady friend who had been posing as a revolutionist to protect her monarch.

d, Duke Worne; w, Arthur Hoerl; ph, Hap Depew; ed, J. S. Harrington.

Drama **(PR:A MPAA:NR)**

DEVIL'S MASTERPIECE, THE** (1927) 6 reels Sanford F. Arnold bw

Viginia Brown Faire, Gordon Brinkley, Fred Kohler *(Reckless Jim Reagan)*.

Fair programmer set in the North Woods about a Mountie in disguise who is out to nail a gang of dope dealers. It is not until the movie's end that he captures the bad men and convinces the girl he loves that he is not one of them.

d, John P. McCarthy; w, Mason Harbringer; ph, Lyman Broening.

Crime/Adventure **(PR:A MPAA:NR)**

DEVIL'S PARTNER, THE** (1923) 5 reels Iroquois/IP bw

Norma Shearer *(Jeanne)*, Charles Delaney *(Pierre/Sgt. Drummond)*, Henry Sedley *(Henri, Jeanne's Father)*, Edward Roseman *(Jules Payette)*, Stanley Walpole.

Shearer (whom husband Irving Thalberg would make into one of MGM's leading stars) plays the object of a ruthless smuggler's lust in this Northwest woods programmer. At the film's conclusion, she is free to marry the young man she really loves when the villain perishes in flames.

d, Caryl S. Fleming.

Drama **(PR:A MPAA:NR)**

DEVIL'S PASSKEY, THE* (1920) 7 reels UNIV bw

Sam DeGrasse *(Warren Goodwright)*, Una Trevelyan *(Grace, His Wife)*, Clyde Fillmore *(Capt. Rex Strong)*, Maude George *(Renee Malot)*, Leo White *(Amadeus, Her Husband)*, Mae Busch *(La Belle Odera)*, Jack Mathis *(Count de Trouvere)*, Ruth King *(Yvonne, His Wife)*, Ed Reinarch *(Director of Theatre Francais)*, Al Edmondson *(Alphone Marier, the Reporter)*, Evelyn Gosnell.

On the strength of his success with BLIND HUSBANDS, von Stroheim was given the green light to make his next film, THE DEVIL'S PASSKEY. No prints of this film appear to exist, but the picture does not seem to be a particular favorite of his as he rarely referred to it in later years (perhaps due to the story not being an original). Also, von Stroheim spent a mere seven months creating the picture, so one might assume the director's mind was really on his next project, the masterpiece FOOLISH WIVES. The main character of this film (Trevelyan), like his heroine in BLIND HUSBANDS, is a dissatisfied American wife living in Europe. And, like her earlier counterpart, she, too, is swept off her feet by the attentions of an army officer (at one point, von Stroheim was going to write in a part for himself but decided against it). Trevelyan's husband (DeGrasse) is a wealthy playwright who continues to have his work rejected because his plots lack punch. When his wife's indiscretion makes a gossip column (the names of the principals are of course withheld) DeGrasse finds his inspiration, and puts the story into dramatic form. The show opens, and because the in crowd realizes that he has unwittingly written a play about his own situation, the production is a tremendous success. At a party following the opening, the humiliated Trevelyan claims to have a headache, and the playwright sends her home with Fillmore, the man with whom her name has been linked. Then a drunken guest spills the beans, and, after punching him out, DeGrasse returns home fully expecting to find his wife in the arms of her paramour and intent on seeking revenge. DeGrasse does find them together, but Fillmore wrestles his gun from him and pleads innocence. DeGrasse agrees to forgive them, but they demand that he believe their story. When he claims that he can't, the couple leave him alone. DeGrasse at this point contemplates the incredible irony of his situation and places the pistol to his temple. But before he can squeeze the trigger, his wife rushes back to him and the picture ends on a happy note. Universal spent a great deal promoting the opening of this picture, and in so doing made a star of von Stroheim, in the manner of Griffith and DeMille. Curiously, one of the advertising blurbs, which appeared in "Moving Picture Weekly" made a point of cashing in on the bathtub sequence vogue, which the latter had made his own. The piece reads, "The bathroom scene of the picture features an expensive and carefully tiled reconstruction copied from the photograph of the 'natatorium' of a Parisian stage favorite before the war." There was no doubt in anyone's mind that the article was referring to La Belle Ptero, a Spanish gypsy, who was the most famous courtesan of her time.

d&w, Erich von Stroheim (based on the story "Clothes and Treachery" by Baroness De Meyer, von Stroheim); ph, Ben Reynolds; ed, Grant Whytock, von Stroheim; art d, von Stroheim.

Drama **(PR:A MPAA:NR)**

DEVIL'S PLAYGROUND, THE*** (1918) 7 reels Fraternity/Atlantic bw

Vera Michelena, Harry Spingler, Lillian Cook, Robert Cummings, W. H. Tooker, George S. Trimble, Dallas Tyler, Robert Fisher, Mrs. Adams.

Better-than-average independent film which examines the jazz dance craze which was sweeping the nation at that time. By contrasting the relationships between an innocent girl pursued by a wealthy masher, and a young society man ensnared by a woman of the world, the producer presented a lurid and commercial look at jazz, sex, and booze.

d, Harry McRae Webster; w, (based on a story by Dallas Tyler).

Drama **(PR:A MPAA:NR)**

DEVIL'S TOLL, THE (SEE: DESERT'S TOLL, THE, 1926)

DEVIL'S TOWER* (1929) 5 reels T/C/RAY bw

Buddy Roosevelt *(James Murdock)*, Frank Earle *(Tom Murdock)*, J. P. McGowan *(George Stilwell)*, Thelma Parr *(Doris Stilwell)*, Art Rowlands *(Phillip Wayne)*, Tommy Bay *(Dutch Haynes)*.

This terrible western, in which Roosevelt saves a dam from destruction, received much greater distribution than it deserved due to a shortage of silent product for the program houses during the early days of sound transition.

d, J. P. McGowan; w, Victor Rosseau, McGowan; ph, Ernest Depew; ed, Erma Horsley.

Western **(PR:A MPAA:NR)**

DEVIL'S TRAIL, THE* (1919) 5 reels WORLD bw

Betty Compson *(Julie Delisle)*, George Larkin *(Sgt. MacNair)*, William Quinn *("Dutch" Vogel)*, Fred M. Malatesta *(Dubec)*, Claire DuBrey *(Dubec's Wife)*.

Below-par Northwest Mounted Police programmer about an officer who is sent to the post at Chino Landing to track down the outlaws who captured the two daughters of that station's company commander. Compson and Larkin were all this one had going for it.

d, Stuart Paton; w, (based on a story by Frank Beresford); ph, William Thornley.

Adventure **(PR:A MPAA:NR)**

DIAMOND NECKLACE, THE*** (1921, Brit.) 6 reels ID bw

Milton Rosmer *(Charles Furness)*, Jessie Winter *(Lily Farady)*, Sara Sample *(Margaret Bayliss)*, Warwick Ward *(Ford)*, Mary Brough *(Mrs. Tudsberry)*, Johnny Butt *(Maurice Pollard)*, F. E. Montague-Thacker *(Basil Mortimer)*, John Peachey *(Mr. Bainbridge)*, Miss Fordyce *(Mrs. Farady)*.

This above-average British feature was based on the Guy de Maupassant story about a couple who live 10 years of terrible poverty and hardship to replace a lost necklace, only to discover in the end that it was a fake.

d&w, Denison Clift (based on the Guy de Maupassant story "La Parure").

Drama **(PR:A MPAA:NR)**

DIAMONDS ADRIFT*** (1921) 5 reels VIT bw

Earl Williams *(Bob Bellamy)*, Beatrice Burnham *(Consuela Velasco)*, Otis Harlan *("Brick" McCann)*, George Field *(Don Manuel Morales)*, Jack Carlisle *("Home Brew")*, Hector Sarno *(Senor Rafael Velasco)*, Melbourne MacDowell *(James Bellamy)*, Omar *(Himself)*.

In this change-of-pace movie, popular dramatic actor Williams plays an irresponsible young fellow whose millionaire father (in an attempt to make something of him) puts him to work for $50 a month on a cargo ship. The deal is that if Williams can pay back a $5,000 overdraft, a partnership in the family company will be his. Williams sets sail and takes the first step towards manhood by knocking out the ship's bully. Next, he wins a fine Persian cat in a card game which he presents to a beautiful senorita shortly after docking in Mexico. There is an immediate attraction between the two, but Williams is told that the young lady has been promised by her father to a shady character (Field). Williams and his mates kidnap the girl, subdue the bad hombre, and return to the U.S. where they learn there is a $5,000 reward for the would-be groom, a fugitive. And, as luck would have it, there is also a $5,000 reward for the return of the cat which, it turns out, has been wearing a priceless diamond necklace. The movie ends with Williams settling down with a bride and a new career.

d, Chester Bennett; w, Frederick J. Jackson; ph, Jack MacKenzie.

Comedy/Drama **(PR:A MPAA:NR)**

DIANE OF STAR HOLLOW***
(1921) 6 reels C. R. Macauley Photo Plays/Producers Security bw

Bernard Durning *(Sgt. Pat Scott)*, Evelyn Greeley *(Diane Orsini)*, George Majeroni *(Alessandro Orsini)*, Fuller Mellish *(Father Lorenzo)*, George E. Romain *(D. Crispi)*, Freeman Wood *(Dick Harrison)*, Al Hart *(Hanscom)*, Louis J. O'Connor *(Sheriff)*, Joseph Gramby *(Pietro)*, Sonia Marcelle *(Carlotta Orsini)*, Charles Mackay *(Dr. Ogden)*, May Hopkins *(Jessie)*, Julia Neville *(Jessie's Mother)*.

Lots of action in this interesting film (made before the names Mafia and Cosa Nostra were household words) about a constabulary chief who breaks up a gang of Black Handers run by the father of the girl he loves.

d, Oliver L. Sellers; w, Joseph Farnham (based on the story by David Potter); ph, Lucien Tainguy.

Crime **(PR:A MPAA:NR)**

DICK TURPIN**** (1925) 7 reels FOX bw

Tom Mix *(Dick Turpin)*, Kathleen Myers *(Alic Brookfield)*, Philo McCullough *(Lord Churlton)*, James Marcus *(Squire Crabstone)*, Lucille Hutton *(The Maid)*, Alan Hale *(Tom King)*, Bull Montana *(Bully Boy)*, Fay Holderness *(Barmaid)*, Jack Herrick *(Bristol Bully)*, Fred Kohler *(Taylor)*.

Mix abandons his western garb to play the legendary English highwayman who robbed the rich to feed the poor in this grand action movie. He also saves an aristocratic woman from a forced marriage before hanging up his pistols, mask, and sword. Mix was at his best in this handsomely mounted Fox feature.

d, John G. Blystone; w, Charles Kenyon, Charles Darnton (based on the novel *Rookwood* by W. Harrison Ainsworth); ph, Dan Clark.

Adventure **(PR:A MPAA:NR)**

DICTATOR, THE**** (1922) 6 reels FP/PAR bw

Wallace Reid *(Brook Travers)*, Theodore Kosloff *(Carlos Rivas)*, Lila Lee *(Juanita)*, Kalla Pasha *(Gen. Campos)*, Sidney Bracey *(Henry Bolton)*, Fred Butler *(Sam Travers)*, Walter Long *("Biff" Dooley)*, Alan Hale *(Sabos)*.

Great satirical comedy in which Reid stumbles into a South American revolution, followed by Long, a cab driver who wants the tab Reid ran up in the States while visiting stage doors, paid. There is plenty of action, but it's all played for laughs as the young American wins the war for the rebels and the girl he loves—despite the fact that his father's company formerly owned the country.

d, James Cruze; w, Walter Woods (based on the play by Richard Harding Davis); ph, Karl Brown.

Comedy **(PR:A MPAA:NR)**

DIE NIBELUNGEN (SEE: SIEGFRIED, 1924, Ger.)

DIE NIBELUNGEN (SEE: KRIEMHILD'S REVENGE, 1924, Ger.)

DIMPLES*** (1916) 5 reels Metro bw

Mary Miles Minter *(Dimples)*, William Cowper *(Her Father)*, John J. Donough *(His Friend Horton)*, Thomas J. Carrigan *(Robert Stanley)*, Schuyler Ladd *(Joseph Langdon)*, Fred Tidmarsh *(Welbourne Howard)*, Peggy Hopkins *(Eugenia Abbott)*, Charlotte Shelby *(Mrs. Riley)*, Harry Ford *(Tom Craig)*, William Rausher *(Minister)*, Mae De Mets *(His Wife)*.

Minter, the daughter of a miser, has a doll in which a substantial amount of money has been socked. One summer, a young man vacations nearby and is quite taken by the charming young girl, known as Dimples. Later, when he finds himself squeezed for margins on the stock market, Dimples finds the cash and cycles to town where she covers the situation with the young man's broker, and all ends well.

d, Edgar Jones; w, Harry O. Hoyt (based on a story by Mary Louise Dowling).

Drama **(PR:A MPAA:NR)**

DINTY**** (1920) 6 reels FN bw

Wesley Barry, Colleen Moore, Tom Gallery, J. Barney Sherry, Marjorie Daw, Pat O'Malley, Noah Beery, Walter Chung, Kate Price, Tom Wilson, Aaron Mitchell, Newton Hall, Young Hipp, Hal Wilson, Anna May Wong.

Neilan, one of the greatest directors in motion picture history, put together this mixture of sentiment and melodrama with an obvious sense of love. It is the story of a young Irish-born lad who is orphaned in San Francisco, becomes a successful newsboy, and ultimately, because of his knowledge of the streets, rescues the daughter of a prominent judge from the members of a Chinatown Tong. The boy's reward is adoption into this loving family and the reward of the audience is 90 minutes or so of laughter, thrills, and tears.

d, Marshall Neilan, John MacDermott; w, Marion Fairfax (based on a story by Neilan); ph, David Kesson.

Drama **(PR:A MPAA:NR)**

DISHONORED MEDAL, THE*** (1914) 4 reels Reliance-Majestic/MUT bw

George Gebhart, Miriam Cooper, Raoul Walsh, Frank Bennett, Mabel Van Buren, Dark Cloud.

In Algeria a French officer deserts a beautiful native girl (to whom he gave his Legion of Honor medal) when he discovers she is pregnant by him. The girl dies and her baby son is raised as an Algerian by a kindly old man who has another son. When the boys grow up, they fall in love with the same girl—as does the French officer who has returned to govern the province. The officer orders the girl to be brought to him, and the boys spearhead a revolution which results in heavy casualties. During the fighting the father is wounded by his son, recognizes the medal he is wearing, and informs the boy of his parentage. Crushed, the young man arranges for the girl and his friend to escape and remains behind to be with his dying father—to face certain execution.

d&w, Christy Cabanne; sup, D. W. Griffith.

Drama **(PR:A MPAA:NR)**

DIVIDEND, THE*** (1916) 5 reels TRI bw

William H. Thompson *(John Steele)*, Charles Ray *(Frank Steele)*, Ethel Ullman *(Betty Price)*, Margaret Thompson *(Maisie)*.

Thompson is one of those capitalists who takes delight in evicting tenants, chuckles at industrial accidents, and enjoys cutting his workers' wages on Christmas Eve. He is so obsessed with making money that he even misses his son's graduation from college. When the young man (Ray) comes home and asks for a job, the father hands him a broom and offers him $3 a week to sweep out the office. Somewhat disillusioned, the boy goes out and becomes an opium fiend. After the passage of some time, the father realizes the selfishness of his ways and when his son— broken and battered—is brought to him after being in a street fight, the old man breaks down and begs for forgiveness.

d, Walter Edwards; w, C. Gardner Sullivan.

Drama **(PR:A MPAA:NR)**

DIVINE WOMAN, THE*** (1928) 8 reels MGM bw

Greta Garbo *(Marianne)*, Lars Hanson *(Lucien)*, Lowell Sherman *(Legrande)*, Polly Moran *(Mme. Pigonier)*, Dorothy Cumming *(Mme. Zizi Rouck)*, John Mack Brown *(Jean Lery)*, Cesare Gravina *(Gigi)*, Paulette Duval *(Paulette)*, Jean De Briac *(Stage Director)*.

Garbo was radiant as a parentally neglected girl from Brittany who moves to Paris and becomes a famous actress with the help of a theatrical producer (beautifully played by Sherman), her mother's former paramour. She becomes involved with Hanson, an army deserter, who is jailed after stealing a dress for her. Garbo swears to wait for him but, instead, yields to the attraction of Sherman's wealth. The picture ends on a happy, if unsatisfying note, with Garbo retiring from the stage to marry Hanson after his release. Some details and surroundings in the life of the immortal Sarah Bernhardt were used in the film, most prominently Garbo's hair, done in a style Bernhardt had made famous.

d, Victor Seastrom; w, Dorothy Farnum (based on the play "Starlight" by Gladys Unger); t, John Colton; ph, Oliver Marsh; ed, Conrad A. Nervig; set d, Cedric Gibbons, Arnold Gillespie.

Drama **(PR:A MPAA:NR)**

DIVORCE** (1923) 6 reels FBO bw

Jane Novak *(Jane Parker)*, John Bowers *(Jim Parker)*, James Corrigan *(George Reed)*, Edythe Chapman *(Mrs. George Reed)*, Margaret Livingston *(Gloria Gayne)*, Freeman Wood *(Townsend Perry)*, George McGuire *(Tom Tucker)*, George Fisher *(Winthrop Avery)*, Phillip De Lacy *("Dicky" Parker)*.

When Novak's parents divorce, she and her husband, Bowers, vow that their marriage will always endure. Bowers (who works for Jane's father), however, falls into a fast crowd and becomes the plaything of beautiful vamp Livingston. Novak begs her father to fire Bowers, and when he does the back-slapping pals and Livingston all desert him. Bowers, now aware of the fool he was, returns to the arms of his understanding and forgiving wife.

d, Chester Bennett; w, Andrew Bennison; ph, Jack MacKenzie.

Drama **(PR:A MPAA:NR)**

DIVORCE GAME, THE*** (1917) 5 reels WORLD bw

Alice Brady *(Florence)*, John Bowers *(Paul)*, Arthur Ashley *(Jean le Beau)*, Kate Lester *(Mrs. Safford)*, Joseph Herbert *(Duke de Sallure)*, John Drumier *(Mendoza)*, Marie LaFavre *(Fifi Dupet)*.

Bowers (who committed suicide 19 years after this film was made and was the real-life inspiration for the film A STAR IS BORN) costars with Brady in this comedy about a titled Frenchman and his extravagant American wife who live by their wits and beyond their means.

d, Travers Vale; w, Francis Marion (based on the play "Mlle. Fifi" by Leo Dietrichstein).

Comedy **(PR:A MPAA:NR)**

DIVORCE TRAP, THE*** (1919) 5 reels FOX bw

Gladys Brockwell *(Eleanor Burton)*, Francis MacDonald *(Jim Drake)*,William Sheer *(Eddie Callahan)*, John Steppling *(Jacob Harmon)*, Betty Shade *(Marie Worden)*.

In this melodrama a telephone operator marries a millionaire's son, causing his disinheritance. She returns to her job while the young man finds another woman with whom he secretly hires a shyster lawyer and plots to terminate the union by dirtying the loyal bride's reputation. Fortunately, an honest attorney intervenes, saves the girl's honor, and wins her hand. This was the kind of material that small town audiences loved and, as such, this film worked very well indeed.

d, Frank Beal; w, Denison Clift (based on a story by Jasper Ewing Brady); ph, Fred Leroy Granville.

Drama **(PR:A MPAA:NR)**

DIXIE FLYER, THE* (1926) 6 reels T/C/RAY bw

Eva Novak, Cullen Landis, Pat Harmon.

Except for some good stunt work by Novak (in the Pearl White tradition), this programmer about a nasty railroad vice-president's attempt to steal the business from the good owner (Novak's father) has little to offer.

d, Charles J. Hunt; w, H. H. Van Loan; ph, William Tuers, Joseph Walker.

Action **(PR:A MPAA:NR)**

DO AND DARE*** (1922) 5 reels FOX bw

Tom Mix *(Kit Carson Boone/Henry Boone)*, Dulcie Cooper *(Mary Lee)*, Claire Adams *(Juanita Sanchez)*, Claude Peyton *(Cordoba)*, Jack Rollins *(Jose Sanchez)*, Hector Sarno *(Gen. Sanchez)*, Wilbur Higby *(Col. "Handy" Lee)*, Bob Klein *(Yellow Crow)*, Gretchen Hartman *(Zita)*.

This unusual and highly entertaining Mix film was a melange of comedy, adventure, and satire. As he listens to a story about the exploits of his grandfather, Kit Carson Boone, young Mix (the town boob) closes his eyes and imagines the scene. A flashback is then introduced in which Mix (who plays both parts) romps through a series of adventures where he lampoons himself in a most devastating manner. When the picture fades back to the present, the youthful clod becomes involved with a mysterious senorita and somehow finds himself in the middle of a full-blown South American revolution. Here director-writer Sedgwick turns young Mix into a hero who single-handedly saves the republic and its president, and wins his daughter, the mysterious Spanish maiden.

d&w, Edward Sedgwick (based on a story by Marion Brooks); t, Ralph Spence; ph, Dan Clark; ed, Spence.

Adventure **(PR:A MPAA:NR)**

DO YOUR DUTY*** (1928) 7 reels FN bw

Charlie Murray *(Tim Maloney)*, Lucien Littlefield *(Andy McIntosh)*, Charles Delaney *(Danny Sheehan, Jr.)*, Edward Brady *(Ritzy Dalton)*, Blue Washington *(Dade Jackson)*, Doris Dawson *(Mary Ellen Maloney)*, Aggie Herring *(Mrs. Maloney)*, George Pierce *(Capt. Dan Sheehan)*.

Inspired casting placed comedian Murray in the role of a New York cop who is wrongly convicted of drinking on duty. After being demoted from sergeant to patrolman, he is too ashamed to attend his daughter's wedding to a police officer, which is to be held at the station. However, he arrests the crooks who framed him and sets the record straight in time to give his daughter away and receive a promotion to lieutenant.

d, William Beaudine; w, Vernon Smith (based on a story by Julian Josephson); t, Gene Towne, Casey Robinson; ph, Michael Joyce; ed, Stuart Heisler.

Comedy/Crime **(PR:A MPAA:NR)**

DOCTOR JACK*** (1922) 5 reels Hal Roach/AEX bw

Harold Lloyd *(Dr. Jack)*, Mildred Davis *(The Sick-Little-Well-Girl)*, John T. Prince *(Her Father)*, Eric Mayne *(Dr. Ludwig von Saulsbourg)*, C. Norman Hammond *(The Lawyer)*, Anna Townsend *(His Mother)*, Mickey Daniels, Jackie Condon, Charles Stevenson, Richard Daniels, William Gillespie.

One of Lloyd's lesser, but still hilarious, silent features about a small town doctor who treats his patients with common sense and good cheer. When he is brought in to consult with Mayne in the case of "The Sick-Little-Well-Girl," Lloyd determines that a little excitement is all she really needs and proceeds to deliver just that. His impression of an escaped lunatic is a tour de force and, needless to say, produces a cure.

p, Hal Roach; d, Fred Newmeyer; w, Thomas J. Griser (based on a story by Sam Taylor, Jean Havez, Roach); ph, Walter Lundin.

Comedy **(PR:A MPAA:NR)**

DR. JEKYLL AND MR. HYDE**** (1920) 7 reels PAR bw

John Barrymore *(Dr. Jekyll/Mr. Hyde)*, Martha Mansfield *(Millicent Carew)*, Brandon Hurst *(Sir George Carew)*, Charles Lane *(Dr. Richard Lanyon)*, J. Malcolm Dunn *(John Utterson)*, Cecil Clovelly *(Edward Enfield)*, Nita Naldi *(Therese)*, George Stevens *(Poole)*, Louis Wolheim.

Author Stevenson's famed novel—which draws much from William Blake's Doctrine of Contraries—has Barrymore with a drug-induced dual personality, one upright, honest, and philanthropic, the other the embodiment of evil. As the good doctor, Barrymore is concerned with his experiments, which may lead to expunging evil from human nature by isolating the bestial tendencies of humankind. He develops a concoction that concentrates all of the latent evil in him, turning him into the malevolent Hyde, who lopes through the low sections of London satisfying his lusts and indulging his cruel caprices. An antidote restores him to his good persona. Gradually, the effect of the antidote lessens as the evil in him burgeons beyond his control, to the point where the virtuous part of him sees no solution other than suicide. Stevenson's cerebral story takes on lycanthropic overtones in the highly visual medium of the silent screen; Barrymore's stunning metamorphoses—accomplished largely through sheer acting technique, since makeup and time-lapse effects were minimal—seem more suitable for Lawrence Talbot/THE WOLF MAN (1941) than for this fable dealing with the extremes of human nature. His Jekyll is nattily attired, smooth, handsome, erect of posture, cool and thoughtful of mien; his evil, personified in visual terms, is crouched, with bulging eyes and hand-wringing gestures (and, unfortunately, with a formula-induced change into unkempt clothing). Barrymore's virtuosity carries the film, which is workmanlike—generally acknowledged to be director Robertson's best of his many pictures—and restrained, with fine sets and camerawork. Barrymore was no stranger to film at the time; he had starred in a number of light romantic comedies for Adolph Zukor's Famous Players between 1914 and 1919, only one of which—THE INCORRIGIBLE DUKANE—appears to have survived the years. He proved incorrigible himself in these pictures, frequently disappearing from the studio for days, to be hunted down and discovered sleeping off a drinking bout in a sleazy Bowery saloon. To Zukor's relief, after one such drinking session, Barrymore announced his intention of giving up pictures forever. When Barrymore finally became a serious dramatic star on Broadway in "Peter Ibbetson" a friend persuaded him to try the picture business again, suggesting that the now-famous actor contact Zukor again. "He'd throw me out of the place," responded Barrymore. "I was a bad boy then...." Zukor did not throw him out; the result was this, Barrymore's first serious dramatic film role. The work took a toll on the busy Barrymore, whose schedule reflected the dual role he played. By day, he worked at the studio on West Fifty-Sixth Street in New York; by night, he rehearsed William Shakespeare's "Richard III" on Broadway. He played both parts intensely physically; with a heavy copper suit of armor, Barrymore's Richard suffered contusions every evening as he fell straight backward in battle. Bathed in sweat, almost steamed by exertion and hot stage lights, he had to be hosed down with cold water before his dresser could remove the mailed suit. Between his two personae of film and stage, Barrymore would race to Atlantic City to meet his love, the poet and playwright "Michael Strange" (Blanche Oelrichs) who, when her divorce went through, became his second wife. Not surprisingly, Barrymore suffered a breakdown shortly after the film's completion, and retired to a rest home for two months. But his Jekyll-Hyde portrayal became the benchmark; the role had been essayed in pictures by six other actors to that time (indeed, Louis B. Mayer's production for Pioneer was released in the same year) and was to be remade in sound versions by such great actors as Fredric March and Spencer Tracy, yet Barrymore's performance is still remembered as a definitive visual portrayal.

d, John S. Robertson; w, Clara S. Beranger (based on the novel *The Strange Case of Dr. Jekyll and Mr. Hyde* by Robert Lewis Stevenson); ph, Roy Overbaugh.

Horror **Cas.** **(PR:A MPAA:NR)**

DR. JIM*** (1921) 5 reels UNIV bw

Frank Mayo *(Dr. Jim Keene)*, Claire Windsor *(Helen Keene)*, Oliver Cross *(Kenneth Cord)*, Stanhope Wheatcroft *(Bobby Thorne)*, Robert Anderson *(Tom Anderson)*, Herbert Heyes *(Capt. Blake)*, Gordon Sackville *(Assistant Doctor)*.

A young doctor's dedication to his child patients is resented by his socially oriented wife. After she suffers a nervous breakdown, the couple set sail on a merchant ship and the wife is attracted to the masculine demeanor of the surly captain. After a well-photographed storm scene, Dr. Jim (Mayo) and the captain engage in a terrific fight which the doctor ultimately wins. This proves to his wife the love she once doubted, and they return home to the practice she now understands.

d, William Worthington; w, Eugene B. Lewis (based on a story by Stuart Paton); ph, Leland Lancaster.

Drama **(PR:A MPAA:NR)**

DOG LAW** (1928) 5 reels FBO bw

Ranger the Dog, Robert Sweeney *(Jim)*, Jules Cowles *(Hawkins)*, Walter Maly *(McAllister)*, Mary Mabery *(Jean Larsen)*.

After Sweeney is wiped out in a crooked card game by Maly, the gambler is murdered and our hero accused. Sweeney does manage to clear himself with the help of his fiancee, Mabery, while Ranger, his faithful dog, forces the real killer, Cowles, to jump to his death from a cliff.

d, Jerome Storm; w, Frank Howard Clark (based on a story by S .E. V. Taylor); t, Helen Gregg; ph, Sam DeGrasse; ed, Della M. King.

Adventure **(PR:A MPAA:NR)**

DOG OF THE REGIMENT*** (1927) 5 reels WB bw

Rin-Tin-Tin *(Rinty)*, Dorothy Gulliver *(Marie Von Walrorf)*, Tom Gallery *(Richard Harrison)*, John Peters *(Eric von Hager)*.

This film, which is said to have been based on Rin-Tin-Tin's life, tells of an American attorney who journeys to Europe to settle a client's estate. He accuses Peters, a German lawyer, of trying to cheat his client, an heiress, and, in so doing, wins the gratitude of the girl and her dog. When the war breaks out, he returns to the continent as a flier and is shot down by the Germans. Rin-Tin-Tin, who is with his mistress (now a Red Cross volunteer), rescues him from the wreckage and they later escape the firing squad set up by Peters. The picture ends with the dog barking his approval as his mistress and his friend embrace.

d, Ross Lederman; w, Charles R. Condon; ph, Ed Du Par; ed, Charles Kolster.

War/Animal **(PR:A MPAA:NR)**

DOING THEIR BIT*** (1918) 5 reels FOX bw

Jane Lee, Katherine Lee, Franklyn Hanna, Gertrude Le Brandt, Beth Ivins, Alex Hall, Kate Lester, William Pollard, Aimee Abbott, Jay Strong, R.R. Neil, Edwin Sturgis.

Jane and Katherine Lee (popular sisters known as "The Two Little Imps") are orphaned Irish children who come to America and immediately inspire patriotism, army enlistments—and guilt on the part of the sniveling slackers they encounter. In their spare time, they round up a gang of German spies and saboteurs, intent on blowing up their uncle's munitions factory.

d&w, Kenean Buel; ph, Joseph Ruttenberg.

Spy **(PR:A MPAA:NR)**

DOLL'S HOUSE, A**** (1918) 5 reels PAR bw

Elsie Ferguson *(Nora)*, H. E. Herbert *(Helmar)*, Ethel Grey Terry *(Mrs. Linden)*, Warren Cook *(Dr. Rank)*, Zelda Crosby *(Ellen, the Maid)*, Mrs. R. S. Anderson *(Anna, the Nurse)*, Douglas Redmond *(A Child of Krogstadt)*, Charles Crompton *(A Child of Frogstadt)*.

Broadway star Ferguson and master director Tourneur produced in this fine film a rich cinematic experience which remained at all times true to the sprit of its inspirer, Ibsen.

d, Maurice Tourneur; w, Charles Maigne (based on the play by Henrik Ibsen).

Drama **(PR:A MPAA:NR)**

DOLLAR DEVILS** (1923) 6 reels Schertzinger/Hodkinson bw

Joseph Dowling *(Zannon Carthy)*, Miles McCarthy *(Hal Andrews)*, May Wallace *(Mrs. Andrews)*, Eva Novak *(Amy)*, Hallam Cooley *(Bruce Merlin)*, Cullen Landis *(Jim Biggers)*, Lydia Knott *(Mrs. Biggers)*, Neyneen Farrell *(Helen Andrews)*.

City slicker Cooley comes to a small New England town to pull off an oil discovery scam. Everyone in the community falls for the hustle except elderly Dowling and engineering student Landis, who ultimately exposes the con. In the meantime, Landis' sweetheart leaves him for Cooley, but it all turns out for the best, as her sister Novak is really the perfect girl for him.

d, Victor Schertzinger; w, Louis Stevens; ph, John Stumar.

Drama **(PR:A MPAA:NR)**

DOLLAR MARK, THE** (1914) 5 reels WORLD bw

Robert Warwick, Barbara Tennant.

This film, which featured a spectacular dam-bursting scene, a miners' strike, a run on a bank, and the presence of Broadway star Warwick, should have had a lot going for it. Unfortunately, poor direction and the use of titles to tell the story dragged down the production.

d, O. A. C. Lund; w, George Broadhurst (based on a story by Lund).

Drama **(PR:A MPAA:NR)**

DOLLARS AND SENSE* (1920) 5 reels Goldwyn bw

Madge Kennedy, Kenneth Harlan, Willard Louis, Florence Deshon, Richard Tucker.

Contrived nonsense about a moral chorus girl who is fired from her show for turning down the attentions of a banker. With only two cents to her name, she goes to a bakery to buy bread and meets its young owner, who has allowed his shop to go to pot because he spends more time pursuing culture than crescent rolls. She suggests that he allow her to straighten out the business, which she *almost* does before they run a little short of money. She then approaches the banker for a loan, explaining that she loves "the lug with the loafs" enough to do anything for him. The banker agrees to provide the cash on the condition that she pack her bags and move into his bachelor digs. She agrees and, on arriving, is pleasantly surprised to find her sweetheart—and a minister also—on hand, providing a happy but completely ludicrous ending.

d, Harry Beaumont; w, Gerald C. Duffy (based on the story "Two Cents Worth of Humaneness" by Octavus Roy Cohen); ph, Norbert Brodine.

Drama **(PR:A MPAA:NR)**

DOLLY'S VACATION*** (1918) 5 reels Pathe bw

Baby Marie Osborne *(Dolly McKenzie)*, Jack Connolly *(Joan McKenzie)*, Bob Gray *(Harry Maynes)*, Little Sambo *(Ebenezer Eczema Abraham White)*, Howard McKenzie, Bert Wilson.

Good family entertainment was provided by this engaging film in which Osborne and her little friends turn "Peaceful Acres" (her uncle's farm) into a madhouse—with the help of some cleverly trained animals. There was an obligatory romantic subplot which, fortunately, did not get in the way of the laughs.

d, William Bertram; w, Mrs. George Griffin Lee; ph, William Thornley.

Comedy **(PR:A MPAA:NR)**

DON JUAN*** ½** (1926) 10 reels WB bw

John Barrymore *(Don Juan)*, Mary Astor *(Adriana Della Varnese)*, Willard Louis *(Perdillo)*, Estelle Taylor *(Lucretia Borgia)*, Helene Costello *(Rena, Adriana's Maid)*, Myrna Loy *(Maria, Lucretia's Maid)*, Jane Winton *(Beatrice)*, John Roche *(Leandro)*, June Marlowe *(Trusia)*, Yvonne Day *(Don Juan, at Age 5)*, Philippe De Lacey *(Don Juan, at Age 10)*, John George *(Hunchback)*, Helena D'Algy *(Murderess of Jose)*, Warner Oland *(Caesar Borgia)*, Montagu Love *(Donati)*, Josef Swickard *(Duke Della Varnese)*, Lionel Braham *(Duke Margoni)*, Phyllis Haver *(Imperia)*, Nigel De Brulier *(Marquis Rinaldo)*, Hedda Hopper *(Marquise Rinaldo)*, Helen Lee Worthing *(Eleanora)*, Emily Fitzroy *(The Dowager)*, Gustav von Seyffertitz *(Alchemist)*, Sheldon Lewis, Gibson Gowland, Dick Sutherland *(Gentlemen of Rome)*.

Barrymore performed his own stunts (and there is a sensational dueling scene) in this expensive and highly entertaining film about the great lover who takes on and outwits his powerful parents, the Borgias in order live a life of true meaning with the woman he loves. This was the first Vitaphone feature film, and although it used only music and sound effects, the experiment proved so successful that the brothers Warner were encouraged to produce THE JAZZ SINGER the following year. That fact, the music and sound effects feature, has tended to overshadow the essential greatness of DON JUAN, a lively, wonderfully staged and directed early super film directed by Alan Crosland, who, after achieving spectacular fame with this picture, went on to do THE JAZZ SINGER. Filled with fun, DON JUAN is a wonderful romp through the court intrigues of the frightful Borgias, the Italian family of Spanish origin that influenced the papacy in Italy in the 15th and 16th Centuries. One of four children of Pope Alexander before he was elected Holy Father, and a Roman woman, Vannozza Cattanei, Don Juan (Barrymore), the Duke of Gandia, steals the screen from the opening reel, as orgy scenes, torture chambers, prison escapes, and romantic scenes with Astor (his offscreen romance during the filming of BEAU BRUMMEL three years before), done as only the sensitive lover and romantic Barrymore could do them. Oland and Taylor as the Borgias are excellent in support, as is Loy, playing one of her typical oriental roles, as a vampish spy. There was no doubling in Barrymore's dueling scenes, including the show-stopper battle with Love in the ornate great hall of the castle, one of the best duels the movies have ever seen, watched over from the stairs by Oland, Taylor, and Loy. In this scene, a great act of courage was performed by the star when he dove from the top of the stairs onto Love's back, with both of them sliding the rest of the way down. It was not the only act for which Barrymore would win applause from the cast: during a love scene with Astor, he entered the room through a tall window and the glass shattered into hundreds of pieces. Barrymore went right on with the scene and luckily came through it without injury. Another time, during a re-enactment of the flooding of the Tiber River, Barrymore stayed under water for 48 seconds so that a closeup could be made. When he emerged, fellow workers on the set applauded him as one. The laboriousness of the research and making of the sets defies description. In costuming and architectural design, the fidelity to the times was as true as a huge research staff could make it. The building of the Spanish-Moorish castle hall where the great duel takes place was a study in aerial beauty, and absolutely true to the architecture of the castles of the time. For the torture chamber scenes, an exact replica of the dungeons of the St. Angelo castle was fully recreated, and to capture the flooding of the Tiber, Crosland and his photographer, Byron Haskins, were caged in a watertight box made of inch-thick glass.

d, Alan Crosland; w, Bess Meredyth (based on the poem *Don Juan* by George Gordon [Lord] Byron); t, Walther Anthony, Maude Fulton; ph, Byron Haskins; m, William Axt; ed, Harold McCord; art d, Ben Carre; syn sc; s eff.

Costume/Drama (PR:A MPAA:NR)

DON MIKE*** (1927) 6 reels FBO bw

Fred Thompson *(Don Miguel Arguella)*, Ruth Cliffoer *(Mary Kelsey)*, Noah Young *(Rueben Pettingill)*, Albert Prisco *(Don Louis Ybara)*, William Courtright *(Gomez)*, Tom Bates *(James Kelsey)*, Norma Marie *(Dolores)*, Carmen Le Roux *(Carmen)*, Silver King the Horse.

Popular cowboy star Thompson was quite good as the California aristocrat who fights for his land and wins the beautiful girl. The Douglas Fairbanks tradition was well served in this nice little action film.

d, Lloyd Ingraham; w, Frank M. Clifton; ph, Ross Fisher.

Adventure (PR:A MPAA:NR)

DON Q, SON OF ZORRO**** (1925) 11 reels Elton/UA bw

Douglas Fairbanks *(Don Cesar de Vega/Zorro)*, Mary Astor *(Dolores de Muro)*, Donald Crisp *(Don Sebastian)*, Stella de Lanti *(The Queen)*, Warner Oland *(Archduke Paul of Austria)*, Jean Hersholt *(Don Fabrique)*, Albert MacQuarrie *(Col. Matsado)*, Lottie Pickford Forrest *(Lola)*, Charles Stevens *(Robledo)*, Tote du Crow *(Bernardo)*, Martha Franklin *(The Duenna)*, Juliette Berlanger *(A Dancer)*, Roy Coulson *(An Admirer)*, Enrique Acosta *(Ramon)*.

In this sequel to THE MARK OF ZORRO, Fairbanks was at his athletic and comedic best. He played Don Cesar de Vega, son of the legendary Zorro (and master of the bull whip), whom his father sends from California to Spain to be educated in the traditions of the Old World. After winning the favor of the court, due to his charming and dashing American ways, he is accused of committing murder and performs a fake suicide in order to seek out the real culprit. There is plenty of action and twice the thrills when Zorro himself (played by Fairbanks in a double role) arrives at the end to help win justice for his son and peace for the land of his birth.

d, Donald Crisp; w, Jack Cunningham (based on "Don Q's Love Story" by Hesketh Prichard, Kate Prichard); ph, Henry Sharp, E. J. Vallejo; m, Mortimer Wilson; ed, William Nolan; art d, Edward M. Langley; spec eff, Ned Mann.

Adventure Cas. (PR:A MPAA:NR)

DON QUIXOTE*** (1923, Brit.) 5 reels STOLL bw

Jerrold Robertshaw *(Don Quixote)*, George Robey *(Sancho Panza)*, Bertram Burleigh *(Carrasco)*, Sydney Fairbrother *(Terezo)*, Minna Leslie *(Dulcinea)*, Edward O'Neill *(The Duke)*, Marie Blanche *(The Duchess)*, Frank Arlton *(Father Perez)*, Adeline Hayden Coffin *(The Housekeeper)*.

This enjoyable British interpretation of Miguel de Cervantes' masterpiece was played mostly for laughs.

d, Maurice Elvey; w, Sinclair Hill (based on the novel by Miguel de Cervantes).

Comedy (PR:A MPAA:NR)

DON X** (1925) 5 reels A. G. Steen/B. A. Goodman bw

Bruce Gordon *(Frank Blair/Don X)*, Josephine Hill *(Gladys Paget)*, Boris Bullock *(Perez Blake)*, Victor Allen *(Pecos Pete)*, Milburn Morante *(Frank Paget)*, Robert Williamson *(Red)*.

Gordon plays the head of the Cattlemen's Protective Association who takes on the guise of Don X, a wealthy Mexican beef buyer, in order to bring Bullock, one of the neighboring ranchers who has been rustling, to justice.

d&w, Forrest Sheldon.

Western (PR:A MPAA:NR)

DON'T CALL ME LITTLE GIRL*** (1921) Realart bw

Mary Miles Minter *(Jerry)*, Winifred Greenwood *(Harriet Doubleday)*, Ruth Stonehouse *(Joan Doubleday)*, Jerome Patrick *(Monty Wade)*, Edward Flanagan *(Peter Flagg)*, Fannie Midgley *(Mrs. Doubleday)*.

Modestly produced but well done comedy in which a young girl (Minter) comes to town and orchestrates a series of situations in which her spinsterish cousin manages to snare the man she has always loved.

d, Joseph Henabery; w, Edith Kennedy (based on the play "Jerry" by Catherine Chisholm Cushing); ph, Faxon M. Dean.

Comedy (PR:A MPAA:NR)

DON'T GET PERSONAL*** (1922) 5 reels UNIV bw

Marie Prevost *(Patricia Parker)*, George Nichols *(Silas Wainwright)*, Daisy Robinson *(Emily Wainwright)*, Roy Atwell *(Horace Kane)*, T. Roy Barnes *(John Wainwright)*, G. Del Lorice *(Maisie Morrison)*, Sadie Gordon *(Arabella New)*, Alida B. Jones *(Jane New)*, Ralph McCullough *(Jimmie Barton)*.

Snappy comedy has chorus girl Prevost being sent by her father to visit his wealthy friend's country estate to get her away from Broadway's temptations. Once there she straightens out the romantic problems of her host's daughter and wins the heart of his misogynist son Barnes.

d, Clarence G. Badger; w, Doris Schroeder (based on a story by I. R. Ving); ph, Milton Moore.

Comedy (PR:A MPAA:NR)

DON'T MARRY** (1928) 6 reels FOX bw

Lois Moran *(Priscilla Bowen/Betty Bowen)*, Neil Hamilton *(Henry Willoughby)*, Henry Kolker *(Gen. Willoughby)*, Claire McDowell *(Aunt Abigail Bowen)*, Lydia Dickson *(Hortense)*.

To teach her strait-laced boy friend Hamilton a lesson, flapper Moran dresses up like her 19th-Century cousin and makes him look the fool at a party. After that experience, Hamilton is more than willing to do the Charleston with his little sweetie.

d, James Tinling; w, Randall H. Fay (based on a story by Philip Klein, Sidney Lanfield); t, William Kernell; ph, Joseph August.

Comedy (PR:A MPAA:NR)

DON'T MARRY FOR MONEY*** (1923) 6 reels Weber & North bw

House Peters *(Peter Smith)*, Rubye De Remer *(Marion Whitney)*, Aileen Pringle *(Edith Martin)*, Cyril Chadwick *(Crane Martin)*, Christine Mayo *(Rose Graham)*, Wedgewood Nowell *(The Inspector)*, George Nichols *(Amos Webb)*, Hank Mann *(An Explorer)*, Charles Wellesley *(Alec Connor)*.

When life with millionaire husband Peters becomes somewhat of a bore, De Remer has a flirtation with rotter Chadwick, who makes a career out of these affairs by blackmailing the wives. Peters, who has more on the ball than she thinks, subtly lets De Remer know about Chadwick and she drops him like a hot burrito.

d, Clarence L. Brown; w, Hope Loring, Louis D. Lighton.

Drama (PR:A MPAA:NR)

DON'T TELL EVERYTHING*** (1921) 5 reels FP-LAS/PAR bw

Wallace Reid *(Cullen Dale)*, Gloria Swanson *(Marion Westover)*, Elliot Dexter *(Harvey Gilroy)*, Dorothy Cumming *(Jessica Ramsey)*, Genevieve Blinn *(Mrs. Morgan)*, Baby Gloria Wood *(Cullen's Niece)*, De Briac Twins *(The Morgan Twins)*.

Routine but entertaining society comedy about a young couple, Swanson and Reid, whose secret marriage is threatened by the wife's jealousy of former girl friends, and the husband's vulnerability to the advances of a vamp. All ends well in a hunting lodge where Swanson is given graphic proof of her husband's fidelity.

d, Sam Wood; sup, Thompson Buchanan; w, Albert Shelby Le Vino (based on a story by Lorna Moon); ph, A. R. Hamm.

Comedy (PR:A MPAA:NR)

DOORSTEPS** (1916, Brit.) 5 reels Turner/Hepworth bw

Florence Turner *(Doorsteps)*, Henry Edwards *(George Newlands)*, Campbell Gullan *(Tozer)*, Amy Loraine *(Mrs. Skipps)*, Fred Rains *(Stage Manager)*.

Popular American actress Turner was brought to England to play the lead in this film about a boarding house worker who befriends a young playwright. After some time she becomes a successful actress, saves him from a killer, and marries the lucky chap.

d, Henry Edwards; w, Larry Trimble (based on a play by Edwards).

Drama (PR:A MPAA:NR)

DOUBLE LIFE OF MR. ALFRED BURTON, THE*** (1919, Brit.) 5 reels Lucky Cat/ID bw

Kenelm Foss *(Alfred Burton)*, Ivy Duke *(Edith Cowper)*, Elaine Madison *(Mrs. Burton)*, Joe Peterman *(Mr. Waddington)*, Phillip Hewland *(Lord Idlemay)*, Ronald Power *(Cowper)*, James Lindsay *(Mr. Bromford)*, M. Humbertson Wright *(Kamar Shri)*, Gordon Craig *(Alfie Burton)*.

This is a good little English comedy about a tree of knowledge and an ineffectual Cockney clerk who eats one of its magic beans and is transformed into a poet.

p, George Clark; d, Arthur Rooke; w, Kenelm Foss (based on the novel by E. Phillips Oppenheim).

Comedy (PR:A MPAA:NR)

DOUBLING FOR ROMEO**** (1921) 6 reels Goldwyn bw

Will Rogers *(Sam/Romeo)*, Sylvia Breamer *(Lulu/Juliet)*, Raymond Hatton *(Steve Woods/Paris)*, Sydney Ainsworth *(Pendleton/Mercutio)*, Al Hart *(Big Alec/Tybalt)*, John Cossar *(Foster/Capulet)*, C. E. Thurston *(Duffy Saunders/Benvolio)*, Cordelia Callahan *(Maggie/Maid)*, Roland Rushton *(Minister/Friar)*, Jimmy Rogers *(Jimmie Jones)*, William Orlamond *(Movie Director)*.

In this hilarious satire, Rogers plays an Arizona cowboy sweet on a girl who believes the only real lovers are those in the movies. After she shows him a picture of Douglas Fairbanks, he sets off for Hollywood to learn the tricks and is hired to double for the heavy in a serial. There are a number of very clever bits lampooning the picture business and a teriffic dream sequence (after the discouraged cowboy returns home), in which his friends and the girl he loves become characters in the Romeo and Juliet story with Rogers outswashbuckling Fairbanks at his best. He awakens with a renewed sense of confidence and drags the unresisting girl to the altar.

d, Clarence Badger; w, Bernard McConville (based on a story by Elmer Rice); t, Will Rogers; ph, Marcel Le Picard.

Comedy (PR:A MPAA:NR)

DOUBLING WITH DANGER*** (1926) 5 reels Richard Talmadge/FBO bw

Richard Talmadge *(Dick Forsythe)*, Ena Gregory *(Madeline Haver)*, Joseph Girard *(Elwood Haver)*, Fred Kelsey *(Avery McCade)*, Harry Dunkinson *(Detective McCade)*, Douglas Gerrard *(Malcolm Davis)*, Paul Dennis *(Arthur Channing)*, Herbert Prior *(Manning Davis)*, Joseph Harrington *(Morton Stephens)*.

Talmadge provides nonstop thrills as he tumbles, fights, and outwits a gang of crooks bent on stealing the plans for a silent airplane designed for the U.S. government. This was another fun film from the "Prince of Pep."

d, Scott R. Dunlap; w, Grover Jones; d, Doane Harrison.

Adventure **(PR:A MPAA:NR)**

DOUGLAS FAIRBANKS IN ROBIN HOOD (SEE: ROBIN HOOD, 1922)

DOWN BY THE RIO GRANDE* (1924) 5 reels Phil Goldstone bw

William Fairbanks, Dorothy Revier, Andrew Waldron, Olive Trevor, Jack Richardson, Milton Ross.

This Fairbanks contemporary western about a young man's struggle to win the ranch which is rightfully his was pretty much a tedious and actionless bore.

d, Alvin J. Neitz; w, Donald Fitch (based on a story by Julio Sabello); ph, Roland Price.

Western **(PR:A MPAA:NR)**

DOWN GRADE, THE** (1927) 5 reels GOTH/LUM bw

William Fairbanks *(Ted Lanning)*, Alice Calhoun *(Molly Crane)*, Charles K. French *(Mr. Lanning)*, Big Boy Williams *(Ed Holden)*, Jimmy Aubrey *(The Runt)*.

Action-filled programmer in which Fairbanks used motorcycles, fast cars, and an airplane to defeat a gang of crooks out to destroy his father's railroad.

p, Sam Sax; d, Charles Hutchison; w, Welles W. Ritchie; ph, James Brown.

Adventure **(PR:A MPAA:NR)**

DOWN THE STRETCH* (1927) 7 reels UNIV bw

Robert Agnew *(Marty Kruger)*, Marion Nixon *(Katie Kelly)*, Virginia True Boardman *(Mrs. Kruger)*, Lincoln Plummer *(Devlin)*, Jack Daugherty *(Tupper)*, Ward Crane *(Conlon)*, Ben Hall *(Pee Wee)*, Otis Harlan *(Babe Dilley)*, Ena Gregory *(Marion Hoyt)*.

Feeble little racetrack drama about a jockey who is forced by his sadistic trainer to nearly starve himself to death in order to make the weight for the big race. He wins and promptly passes out in the arms of the girl he loves.

d, King Baggot; w, Curtis Benton (based on the story "The Money Rider" by Gerald Beaumont); ph, John Stumar.

Drama **(PR:A MPAA:NR)**

DOWN TO EARTH*** (1917) 5 reels ART bw

Douglas Fairbanks *(Billy Gayner)*, Eileen Percy *(Ethel)*, Gustave von Seyffertitz *(Dr. Jollyem)*, Charles P. McHugh *(Dr. Samm)*, Charles Gerrard *(Charles Riddles)*, William H. Keith *(Mr. Carter)*, Ruth Allen *(Mrs. Fuller Germes)*, Fred Goodwine *(Jordan Jinny)*, Florence Mayon *(Mrs. Phattison Qiles)*, Herbert Standing *(Mr. A. D. Dyspeptic)*, David Porter *(Mr. Coffin)*, Bull Montana *(Wild Man)*.

Very funny Fairbanks movie has "Mr. Action" taking over an asylum after he learns his ex-girl friend, who suffered a nervous breakdown, is registered there. Fairbanks discovers that the various maladies the patients suffer are all imagined, and it is great fun watching him cure the hospital population and win back his girl to boot.

d, John Emerson; w, Anita Loos (based on a story by Douglas Fairbanks); ph, Victor Fleming.

Comedy/Adventure **(PR:A MPAA:NR)**

DOWN TO THE SEA IN SHIPS*** (1923) 9 reels Whaling/Hodkinson bw

William Walcott *(Charles W. Morgan)*, William Cavanaugh *(Henry Morgan)*, Leigh R. Smith *("Scuff" Smith)*, Elizabeth Foley *(Baby Patience Morgan)*, Thomas White *(Baby Tommy Dexter)*, Juliette Courtot *("Judy" Peggs)*, Clarice Vance *(Nahoma)*, Curtis Pierce *(Town Crier)*, Ada Laycock *("Henny" Clark)*, Marguerite Courtot *(Patience Morgan)*, Clara Bow *("Dot" Morgan)*, James Turfler *("Jimmy")*, Pat Hartigan *(Jake Finner)*, Capt. James A. Tilton *(Captain of the Morgan)*, J. Thornton Baston *(Samuel Siggs)*, Raymond McKee *(Thomas Allan Dexter)*.

This well-directed and quite elaborate epic of whaling life, shot in New England, has an authentic feel. Indeed the scenes of slaughter were all too real—but the "thrill" it once provided for audiences has hopefully diminished in these more enlightened times. The one thing this picture really had in its favor was the debut of Clara Bow.

d, Elmer Clifton; w, John L. E. Pell; ph, Alexander G. Penrod, Paul Allen, Albert Doubrava, Maurice E. Kains; m, Henry F. Gilbert.

Drama **Cas.** **(PR:A MPAA:NR)**

DOWN UPON THE SUWANNEE RIVER*
(1925) 6 reels Royal Palm/Lee-Bradford bw

Charles Emmett Mack *(Bill Ruble)*, Mary Thurman *(Mary Norwood)*, Arthur Donaldson *(Dais Norwood)*, Wally Merrill *(Herbert Norwood)*, Walter Lewis *(Rev. John Banner)*, Blanche Davenport *(Old Mag)*, Charles Shannon *(Hoss-Fly Henson)*.

Atheist Mack elopes with Thurman and, because of the hatred of his neighbors, signs on to work a ship which is sailing around the world. In his absence, Thurman discovers she is going to have his child and tries to kill herself. She is saved by an elderly black man and, when she returns home, finds Mack, who has discovered Christ at sea and has joined the church.

d, Lem F. Kennedy; w, Hapsburg Liebe.

Drama **(PR:A MPAA:NR)**

DOWNHILL (SEE: WHEN BOYS LEAVE HOME, 1927, Brit.)

DRAGNET, THE**** (1928) 8 reels PAR/FP bw

George Bancroft *(Two-Gun Nolan)*, Evelyn Brent *(The Magpie)*, William Powell *(Dapper Frank Trent)*, Fred Kohler *("Gabby" Steve)*, Francis McDonald *(Sniper Dawson)*, Leslie Fenton *(Shakespeare)*.

Tough von Sternberg gangster film about a dedicated cop who goes on a binge after being led to believe he accidentally killed his partner in a shoot-out with Powell's gang. The frame-up, however, is revealed to him by Powell's moll—a girl to whom he is attracted. This sobers him enough to clean up the gang and marry the girl who is wounded in the battle.

d, Joseph von Sternberg; w, Jules Furthman, Charles Furthman (based on a story by Oliver H. O. Garrett); t, Herman J. Mankiewicz; ph, Harold Rosson; ed, Helen Lewis; set d, Hans Dreier.

Crime **(PR:A MPAA:NR)**

DRAMATIC LIFE OF ABRAHAM LINCOLN, THE
(SEE: ABRAHAM LINCOLN, 1924)

DREAM MELODY, THE* (1929) 6 reels Excellent Pictures bw

John Roche *(Richard Gordon)*, Mabel Julienne Scott *(Mary Talbot)*, Rosemary Theby *(Alicia Harrison)*, Robert Walker *(George Monroe)*, Adabelle Driver *(Nora Flanigan)*, Adolph Faylor *(Signor Malesco)*, Elinor Leslie *(Mrs. Chance)*.

Dreary programmer about a starving composer who is finally granted the recognition he deserves when a famous impresario listens to his haunting composition. The nightclub songstress who made it all possible is also rewarded by receiving his proposal of marriage.

d, Burton King; w, Isadore Bernstein, Carmelita Sweeney, Hazel Jamieson (based on a story by Lenore Gray); t, Bernstein, Sweeney; ph, William J. Miller, Walter Hass; ed, Betty Davis; spec eff, Robert Stevens.

Drama **(PR:A MPAA:NR)**

DREAM STREET** (1921) 9 reels D.W. Griffith/UA bw

Carol Dempster *(Gypsy Fair)*, Ralph Graves *(James "Spike" McFadden)*, Charles Emmett Mack *(Billy McFadden)*, Edward Peil *(Swan Way)*, W.J. Ferguson *(Gypsy's Father)*, Porter Strong *(Samuel Jones)*, George Neville *(Tom Chudder)*, Charles Slattery *(Police Inspector)*, Tyrone Power *(Street Preacher)*, Morgan Wallace *(Masked Violinist)*.

This allegorical drama, based on a couple of short stories by Burke (BROKEN BLOSSOMS, 1919), was also set in the Limehouse section of London and told of a music hall dancer, Dempster, who finally finds happiness and theatrical success married to a street tough with a wonderful singing voice. Outside of the impressive sets, photography, and lighting, DREAM STREET is one of Griffith's weakest features. Portions of this film were later screened using an early synchronized sound process.

d, D. W. Griffith; w, Roy Sinclair (based on "Gina of Chinatown" and "The Sign of the Lamp" by Thomas Burke); ph, Hendrik Sartov; ed, James and Rose Smith; art d, C. Blythe Sherwood; set d, Charles M. Kirk.

Drama **Cas.** **(PR:A MPAA:NR)**

DRESS PARADE*** (1927) 7 reels DM/Pathe bw

William Boyd *(Vic Donovan)*, Bessie Love *(Janet Cleghorne)*, Hugh Allan *(Stuart Haldane)*, Walter Tennyson *(Dusty Dawson)*, Maurice Ryan *(Mealy Snodgrass)*, Louis Natheaux *(Patsy Dugan)*, Clarence Geldert *(Commandant)*.

This well-directed and -produced film, shot at West Point, suffered from too many titles. The story, however, about a young, wise-guy prizefighter who falls for a commandant's daughter, uses political pull to become a cadet, and is turned into a man by the academy, had its moments.

d, Donald Crisp; w, Douglas Z. Dotty (based on the story "Raw Material" by Maj. Alexander Chilton, Maj. Robert Glassburn, Herbert David Walter); t, John Kraft; ph, Peverell Marley; ed, Barbara Hunter; art d, Emile De Ruelle.

Drama **(PR:A MPAA:NR)**

DRIFTER, THE** (1916) 5 reels GAU bw

Alexander Gaden, Lucille Taft, Albert Macklin, Iva Shepard, Stockton Quincy.

This movie, about spiritual regeneration, told of a divinity student with a weakness for gambling who goes on a betting binge until the faith of his sweetheart inspires him to return to his studies. He does and eventually becomes a spellbinding preacher.

d, Richard Garrick; w, John B. Clymer.

Drama **(PR:A MPAA:NR)**

DRIFTIN' SANDS** (1928) 5 reels FBO bw

Bob Steele *(Driftin' Sands)*, Gladys Quartaro *(Nita Aliso)*, William H. Turner *(Don Roberto Aliso)*, Gladden James *(Benton)*, Jay Morley, Carl Axzelle.

Steele plays a good pistol-handler who is hired by Turner to protect his daughter Quartaro. But when the young couple fall in love, Steele is banished from the ranch. Later, when he saves Quartaro from the bandits, Steele is welcomed into the family.

d, Wallace W. Fox; w, Oliver Drake (based on the story "Fate of the World" by W. C. Tuttle); t, Frank T. Daugherty; ph, Allan Siegler; ed, Drake.

Western **(PR:A MPAA:NR)**

DRIVEN FROM HOME*** (1927) 7 reels CHAD bw

Ray Hallor, Virginia Lee Corbin, Pauline Garon, Sojin, Anna May Wong, Melbourne MacDowell, Margaret Seddon, Sheldon Lewis, Virginia Pearson, Eric Mayne, Alfred Fisher.

This old-time melodrama about a father who turns his daughter away because she elopes with his handsome secretary, rather than the nobleman he selected, has its hair-raising moments. There is also a Chinese dope-den proprietor who is after her, but in the end the father sees the error of his ways and embraces the young couple.

d, James Young; w, Enid Hibbard, Ethel Hill; ph, Ernest Miller.

Drama **(PR:A MPAA:NR)**

DROPKICK, THE*** (1927) 7 reels FN bw

Richard Barthelmess *(Jock Hamill)*, Barbara Kent *(Cecily Graves)*, Dorothy Revier *(Eunice Hathaway)*, Eugene Strong *(Brad Hathaway)*, Alberta Vaughn *(Molly)*, James Bradbury, Jr. *(Bones)*, Brooks Benedict *(Ed Pemberton)*, Hedda Hopper *(Mrs. Hamill)*, Mayme Kelso *(Mrs. Graves)*, George Pearce *(The Dean)*.

Entertaining-but-lesser Barthelmess effort about a college football star who comes back to win the big game after being suspected of murdering the coach. The cast also included 10 college football stars of the day from various universities.

d, Millard Webb; w, Winifred Dunn (based on the story "Glitter" by Katherine Brush); ph, Arthur Edeson, Alvin Knechtel.

Drama **(PR:A MPAA:NR)**

DRUG TRAFFIC, THE*** (1923) 5 reels Irving Cummings bw

Barbara Tennant *(Mary Larkin)*, Gladys Brockwell *(Edna Moore)*, Bob Walker *(Willie Shade)*.

There was a rash of exploitation films at this time dealing with the danger of drug addiction. In this story a doctor begins to take a fix now and then to keep up his demanding schedule. Eventually he is hooked, sinks to the gutter, and goes to prison. He escapes and burglarizes his own hospital to secure the needed dope. Finally, however, he faces the truth and spends a night in agony attempting to kick the habit. Unfortunately, he finds his only escape is in death.

p, Sol Lesser; d, Irving Cummings; w, Harvey Gates.

Drama **(PR:A MPAA:NR)**

DUCKS AND DRAKES** (1921) 5 reels Realart bw

Bebe Daniels *(Teddy Simpson)*, Jack Holt *(Rob Winslow)*, Mayme Kelso *(Aunty Weeks)*, Edward Martindel *(Dick Chiltern)*, William E. Lawrence *(Tom Hazzard)*, Wade Boteler *(Col. Tweed)*, Maurie Newell *(Cissy)*, Elsie Andrean *(Nina)*.

Fair comedy has flirtatious Daniels being taught a lesson by her fiance and a couple of chums. One of the boys lures her to a hunting camp where another cohort, posing as an escaped convict, pretends to almost steal her virtue. After her escape, she is more than willing to live a quiet, devoted life with the one fellow she really loves.

d, Maurice Campbell; sup&w, Elmer Harris; ph, H. Kinley Martin; art d, Una Hopkins.

Comedy **(PR:A MPAA:NR)**

DUDE COWBOY, THE** (1926) IP/FBO bw

Bob Custer *(Bob Ralston)*, Flora Bramley *(Doris Wrigmint)*, Billy Bletcher *(Shorty O'Day)*, Howard Truesdell *(Amos Wrigmint)*, Bruce Gordon *(Carl Croth)*, Amber Norman *(Mabel La Rue)*, Sabel Johnson *(Aver)*, Edward Gordon *(Count Duse)*.

Custer and his sidekick O'Day are on their way to take over the dude ranch he owns when they save Truesdell and his daughter from bandits. Custer takes a job as chauffeur to be near the girl (Bramley) when he learns that they are headed for the resort as well. At the film's end, Custer rescues Bramley from his crooked foreman and discloses his real identity.

p, Jesse J. Goldberg; d, Jack Nelson; w, Paul M. Bryan (based on a story by James Ormont); ph, Ernest Miller.

Western Drama **(PR:A MPAA:NR)**

DUKE STEPS OUT, THE*** (1929) 8 reels MGM bw

William Haines *(Duke)*, Joan Crawford *(Susie)*, Karl Dane *(Barney)*, Tenen Holtz *(Jake)*, Edward Nugent *(Tommy Wells)*, Jack Roper *(Poison Kerrigan)*, Delmar Davies *(Bossy Edwards)*, Luke Cosgrove *(Prof. Widdicomb)*, Herbert Prior *(Mr. Corbin)*.

Haines gave his usual competent performance as a wealthy young man who becomes a prize fighter to show his father he can make it on his own. On a train, he falls for Crawford (not used to best advantage in this film) and returns to college to pursue her. At first she is not impressed, but in the end he not only wins her heart—but the championship as well. Although a silent picture, at one point a voice is heard over a radio, and a popular song is introduced to enhance the mood.

d, James Cruze; w, Raymond Schrock, Dale Van Every (based on a story by Lucian Carey); t, Joe Farnham; ph, Ira Morgan; ed, George Hively; art d, Cedric Gibbons; m/l, "Just You," William Axt, David Mendoza; syn sc; s eff.

Comedy/Drama **(PR:A MPAA:NR)**

DULCY*** (1923) 7 reels Constance Talmadge/AFN bw

Constance Talmadge *(Dulcy)*, Claude Gillingwater *(Mr. Forbes)*, Jack Mulhall *(Gordon Smith)*, May Wilson *(Mrs. Forbes)*, Johnny Harron *(Billy Parker)*, Anne Cornwall *(Angela Forbes)*, Andre Beranger *(Vincent Leach)*, Gilbert Douglas *(Schuyler Van Dyke)*, Frederick Esmelton *(Blair Patterson)*, Milla Davenport *(Matty, Dulcy's Companion)*.

A clever comedy about a girl who invites a couple of business prospects to a disastrous dinner party in order to further her husband's career. Marion Davies made a talking version of this film in 1930 called NOT SO DUMB.

d, Sidney A. Franklin; w, Anita Loos, John Emerson, C. Gardner Sullivan (based on the play by George S. Kaufman, Marc Connelly); ph, Norbert Brodin.

Comedy **(PR:A MPAA:NR)**

DUMB GIRL OF PORTICI** (1916) 8 reels UNIV bw

Anna Pavlova *(Fenella)*, Rupert Julian *(Masaniello)*, Wendworth Harris *(Duke d' Arcos)*, Douglas Gerrard *(Alphonso)*, John Holt *(Conde)*, Miss Betty Schade *(Isabella)*, Miss Edna Maison *(Elvira)*, Hart Hoxie *(Perrone)*, Miss Laura Oakley *(Rilla)*, N. De Brouillet *(Father Francisco)*, Boris Karloff *(Extra)*.

When Universal Pictures hired Pavlova—the foremost ballerina of all time—to star in the screen adaptation of the opera "Masaniello," they did the world a great service. The contribution would have been more profound, however, if they had allowed her to dance. Unfortunately, she was permitted only a few steps, and motion picture *acting* was not her strong suit. Boris Karloff made his screen debut as an extra in this film.

d, Lois Weber, Phillips Smalley; w, Weber (based on the opera "Masaniello" by Daniel Francois Espirit); ph, Dal Clawson.

Drama **(PR:A MPAA:NR)**

DUPE, THE* (1916) 5 reels LAS bw

Blanche Sweet *(Ethel Hale)*, Ernest Joy *(Mr. Strong)*, Verda McEvers *(Mrs. Strong)*, Thomas Meighan *(Jimmy Regan)*.

A young social secretary (Sweet) is hired by McEvers, a society woman who has grown tired of her husband and interested in playboy Meighan. He, however, finds *Sweet* attractive, and the secretary steals $150 from her employer to buy a dress to impress Meighan at a reception. Her conscience aroused, she confesses the crime to McEvers who orders her to dine alone with her husband and thus provide evidence for a divorce. During their dinner, Sweet admits being part of a scheme, and the two rush back to her employer's mansion only to find it crowded with people. It is then that the playboy announces he intends to change his ways and asks the pretty little secretary to be his wife. Sweet, one of D. W. Griffith's finest actresses at Biograph, must have known she was no longer working for the master when she made this one.

d, Frank Reicher; w, Margaret Turnbull (based on a story by Hector Turnbull).

Drama **(PR:A MPAA:NR)**

DUST FLOWER, THE* (1922) 6 reels Goldwyn bw

Helene Chadwick *(Letty Gravely)*, James Rennie *(Rashleigh Allerton)*, Claude Gillingwater *(Steptoe)*, Mona Kingsley *(Barbara Wallbrook)*, Edward Peil *(Judson Flack)*, George Periolat *(Ott)*.

Lee was not at his best when he directed this dribble about Chadwick, a slum girl who attempts to commit suicide after being forced to work as a cigarette girl by her swinish stepfather. A young millionaire (Rennie), who has just been rejected by his fiancee, intervenes, however, and marries her out of spite. Some time later, the fiancee has second thoughts and breaks the couple up. But the husband, realizing he truly loves Chadwick, takes her back and gives the stepfather a good licking as well.

d, Rowland V. Lee; w, Basil King; ph, Max Fabian.

Drama **(PR:A MPAA:NR)**

DUST OF DESIRE** (1919) 5 reels WORLD bw

Rubye de Remer *(Beth Vinton)*, Thomas J. Carrigan *(Dick Thornton)*, Marion Barney *(Mrs. Jack Stevens)*, Stuart Holmes, Betty Blythe, Betty Hutchinson.

When de Remer marries, she confesses to her husband that she once had a lover but includes a little lie, saying that he is dead. The couple are happily living in South America when her former paramour shows up and threatens to make things sticky. To preserve her union, de Remer arranges for the intruder to experience an accident and for her husband to save his life. The plan works to perfection, and the grateful survivor leaves them in peace.

d, Perry Vekroff; w, Clara Beranger, Forrest Halsey; ph, Edward Horn.

Drama **(PR:A MPAA:NR)**

DYNAMITE DAN* (1924) 5 reels SUN/AY bw

Kenneth McDonald *(Dan)*, Frank Rice *(Boss)*, Boris Karloff *(Tony)*, Eddie Harris *(Sherlock Jones)*, Diana Alden *(Helen)*, Harry Woods *(Brute Lacy)*, Jack Richardson *(Fight Manager)*, Emily Gerdes, Jack Waltemeyer, Max Ascher, Frank Rice.

Another of those so-bad-it's-good movies, about a day laborer who knocks out theheavyweight champion of the world when he finds him flirting with his girl friend, a pretty finishing school student. On the strength of this achievement, the young fellow turns pro and quickly scales the pugilistic heights. The movie ends with a badly choreographed battle in which he defeats the champion for a second time—taking the crown.

d&w, Bruce Mitchell; ph, Bert Longenecker.

Drama **(PR:A MPAA:NR)**

EACH PEARL A TEAR*** (1916) 5 reels LAS bw

Fannie Ward *(Diane Winton)*, Charles Clary *(Lorillard)*, Jack Dean *(John Clarke)*, Paul Weigel *(Roger Winston)*, Jane Wolff *(Mrs. Van Sant)*, Ben Alexander.

Ward is the daughter of a confidential clerk in the employ of Clary, a ruthless stockbroker. She returns home from boarding school to take care of her ailing father, and the broker is immediately attracted to her. When the old fellow dies, Clary makes her his ward, but his intention is seduction. She, however, has fallen for his secretary (Dean) and when the broker discovers this, he fires the young man. The film ends with Dean making a killing in the market—with Ward's help—and ruining the man who gave them so much trouble.

d, George Melford; w, Beatrice C. DeMille, Leighton Osmun (based on the play by E. Lloyd Sheldon).

Drama **(PR:A MPAA:NR)**

EACH TO HIS KIND***

(1917) 5 reels LAS/PAR bw (AKA: THE RAJAH'S AMULET)

Sessue Hayakawa *(Rhandah)*, Tsuru Aoki *(Princess Nada)*, Viola Vale *(Amy Dawe)*, Ernest Joy *(Col. Marcey)*, Eugene Pallette *(Dick Larimer)*, Guy Oliver *(Col. Dawe)*.

Hayakawa plays a British-educated Hindu whose sincere affection for an insensitive white girl ends in ridicule. This drives him to hate the entire Caucasian race, and he instigates a bloody revolution in his homeland, which culminates in the capture of the offending girl. He is just about to kill her when a Hindu girl, whom he now realizes he *truly* loves, intervenes on her behalf.

d, Edward J. LeSaint; w, George Du Bois Proctor (based on a story by Paul West).

Drama **(PR:A MPAA:NR)**

EAGER LIPS** (1927) 7 reels CHAD/FD bw

Pauline Garon *(Mary Lee)*, Betty Blythe *(Paula)*, Gardner James *(Bill Armstrong)*, Jack Richardson *(Tony Tyler)*, Evelyn Selbie *(Miss Lee)*, Fred Warren *(Clancy)*, Erin La Bissoniere *(Charmonta)*.

When her mother dies, Garon is taken in by Blythe, the owner of a Coney Island attraction. Richardson, who has the show next door, offers Garon marriage and a job dancing. She innocently accepts, but Blythe, who knows a rat when she sees one, vamps Richardson and exposes him for what he is. The movie ends with Garon learning her lesson and returning to James, the boy who really loves her.

d, Wilfred Noy; w, Adele Buffington; ph, Ted Tetzlaff, Ernest Miller.

Drama **(PR:A MPAA:NR)**

EAGLE, THE 1/2** (1918) 5 reels BLUE bw

Monroe Salisbury *(John Gregory)*, Edna Earle *(Lucy)*, Ward Wing *(Bob)*.

Nonstop action in this western about a road agent who robs the rich to support the poor. This one had an exciting twist ending with Earle performing a breathtaking bareback ride to save the hero.

d, Elmer Clifton; w, Ethel Hill.

Western **(PR:A MPAA:NR)**

EAGLE, THE*** (1925) 7 reels UA bw

Rudolph Valentino *(Vladimir Dubrovsky)*, Vilma Banky *(Mascha Troekouroff)*, Louise Dresser *(The Czarina)*, Albert Conti *(Kuschka)*, James Marcus *(Kyrilla Troekouroff)*, George Nichols *(Judge)*, Carrie Clark Ward *(Aunt Aurelia)*, Michael Pleschkoff *(Capt. Kuschka of the Cossack Guard)*, Spottiswoode Aitken *(Dubrovsky's Father)*, Gustav von Seyffertitz, Mario Carillo, Otto Hoffman, Eric Mayne, Jean De Briac.

Entertaining Valentino adventure about a Cossack who spurns the advances of Katherine the Great (Dresser) and becomes a masked defender of the poor after his father's lands are stolen. His lust for revenge ends, however, when he falls in love with Banky, the daughter of the man responsible for his father's death. Made vulnerable by his love, the Czarina's troops capture him, and Banky marries him in prison on the eve of his execution. At the last minute, Dresser takes pity upon the lovers, and they are allowed to leave Russia safely.

d, Clarence Brown; w, Hans Kraly (based on the story "Dubrovsky" by Aleksandr Sergeyevich Pushkin); t, George Marion, Jr.; ph, George Barnes, Dev Jennings; art d, William Cameron Menzies; ed, Hal C. Kern, cos, Adrian.

Adventure **Cas.** **(PR:A MPAA:NR)**

EAGLE'S CLAW, THE* (1924) 5 reels Charles R. Seeling/AY bw

Guinn "Big Boy" Williams.

Williams, who became a popular character actor in the talkies, made a number of Poverty Row westerns like this one, about a young fellow who inherits a mine and then has to fight to keep it.

d, Charles R. Seeling.

Western **(PR:A MPAA:NR)**

EAGLE'S FEATHER, THE*** (1923) 7 reels Metro bw

Mary Alden *(Delia Jamieson)*, James Kirkwood *(John Trent)*, Lester Cuneo *(Jeff Carey)*, Elinor Fair *(Martha)*, George Siegmann *(Van Brewen)*, Crauford Kent *(Count De Longe)*, John Elliot *(Parson Winger)*, Charles McHugh *(The Irishman)*, William Orlamond *(The Swede)*, Jim Wang *(Wing Ling)*.

In this unusual western, Kirkwood returns home from the war, is unable to find work, and hops a westbound freight. He is thrown off the train and subsequently hired by an amazon-like rancher (Alden). Before long, she falls for him and even dreams about his asking for her hand in marriage. Therefore, when he comes to request permission to wed her niece, Alden becomes infuriated and orders them both from her property. Later she repents, searches for them in an exciting and beautifully photographed blizzard scene, and brings them home.

d, Edward Sloman; w, Winifred Dunn (based on a story by Katharine Newlin Burt).

Western **(PR:A MPAA:NR)**

EAGLE'S MATE, THE*** (1914) 5 reels FP bw

Mary Pickford *(Anemone Breckenridge)*, James Kirkwood *(Lancer Morne)*, Ida Waterman *(Sally Breckenridge)*, Robert Broderick *(Abner Morne)*, Harry C. Browne *(Fisher Morne)*, Helen Gillmore *(Hagar Morne)*, Estelle Kibby *(Myra Morne)*, R. J. Henry *(Luke Ellsworth)*, Russell Bassett *(Rev. Hotchkiss)*, Jack Pickford.

Kirkwood did well by his mentor, D. W. Griffith, in the direction of this mountain film about feuding families and the relationship between a girl from one side, and a boy from the other. Pickford, the girl in question, is kidnaped by the rival clan and, to keep her kinfolk from having to pay a hefty ransom, agrees to a wedding. The film's picturesque landscapes appear to have been shot in the West Virginia mountains where the novel that inspired the picture was set. This was one of several films that Kirkwood helmed for Pickford in 1914; he also played opposite her in three of these pictures.

d, James Kirkwood; w, Marion Michelson (based on a novel by Anna Alice Chapin).

Drama **(PR:A MPAA:NR)**

EARL OF PAWTUCKET, THE** (1915) 5 reels UNIV bw

Lawrence D'Orsay *(Lord Cardington, Earle of Pawtucket)*, Rosemary Theby *(Henriett)*, Harry Myers *(Arthur)*, Emile Hoch *(Silas Hooper)*, Helen Gilmore *(Aunt Jane)*, Flora Mason *(Ella)*, Thomas Curran.

A great deal was lost in the transition from stage to silent screen of D'Orsay's popular characterization, as the laughs were primarily in his exaggerated English vocal inflections.

d&w, Harry Meyers (based on a play by Augustus Thomas).

Comedy **(PR:A MPAA:NR)**

EARLY BIRD, THE*** (1925) 7 reels ECF bw

Johnny Hines *(Jimmy Burke)*, Sigrid Holmquist *(Jean Blair)*, Wyndham Standing *(George Fairchild)*, Edmund Breese *(The Great La Tour)*, Maude Turner Gordon *(Jean's Aunt)*, Bradley Barker *(Fairchild's Accomplice)*, Flora Finch *(Mrs. Quincy)*, Jack De Lacy *("Flyn")*.

The underrated Hines plays an independent milkman who has organized his fellows to fight the dairy trust. One morning he gives a ride to Holmquist, a pretty girl who has just left a costume party dressed as a domestic. The two fall in love and Holmquist, afraid that she might discourage him, hides the fact that she is actually the president of the trust. Some time later, the guild's manager, Standing, attempts to fix the price. Hines rushes to his office building and discovers, to his horror, that Holmquist is the president. He now believes that she had been using him and breaks off the romance. Later, when Holmquist finds out that Standing has poisoned the independent milk supply, she warns Hines, who manages to destroy it in time. There is nonstop action from this point on with Holmquist being abducted by the bad guys and Hines taking them all on in a beautifully directed fight scene. It ends with the hero—in the best Pearl White tradition—rescuing Holmquist from an ice-cutting machine.

d, Charles Hines; w, Victor Grandin, Argyll Cambell (based on a story by Richard M. Friel); t, Ralph Spence; ph, Charles E. Gilson, Neil Sullivan, John Geisel; set d, Tec-Art Studios.

Comedy **(PR:A MPAA:NR)**

EARLY TO WED*** (1926) 6 reels FOX bw

Matt Moore *(Tommy Carter)*, Kathryn Perry *(Daphne Carter)*, Albert Gran *(Cassius Hayden)*, Julia Swayne Gordon *(Mrs. Hayden)*, Arthur Housman *(Art Nevers)*, Rodney Hilderbrand *(Mike Dugan)*, ZaSu Pitts *(Mrs. Dugan)*, Belva McKay *(Mrs. Nevers)*, Ross McCutcheon *(Bill Dugan)*, Harry Bailey *(Pelton Jones)*.

Entertaining little comedy about a young married couple who live beyond their means and lose everything when they can't make the payments on their debts. However, when things look darkest, they take in a millionaire, feed him with a borrowed meal, provide him with a makeshift bed, and are rewarded with a well-paying position in his firm.

d, Frank Borzage; w, Kenneth B. Clarke (based on the story "Splurge" by Evelyn Campbell); ph, Ernest G. Palmer.

Comedy **(PR:A MPAA:NR)**

EARTH*****

(1930, USSR) 8 reels Vufku-Kino-Ukrain/Amkino bw (ZEMLYA; AKA: SOIL)

Stepan Shkurat, Semyon Savshenko, Pyotr Masokha, Mikola Nademski, V. Mikhailov, E. Maximova, Yulia Solntseva.

In 1926, Alexander Dovzhenko, a Ukranian peasant, abandoned his life as a painter and cartoonist and began directing films. After achieving much acclaim for his revolutionary epoch, ARSENAL—a film which firmly placed him in a league with

Sergei Eisenstein and Vsevolod Pudovkin—he set about making the masterpiece, EARTH. Dovshenko's native Ukraine was where Russia's collective farm program had its first test and the director wanted to pay tribute to that movement. He was also inspired by a newspaper story which told of the murder by the "kulaks" (the old guard reactionary land owners) of a young Communist, who brought the first tractor into the province. So the director wrote a somewhat sketchy plot which used this event merely as a means of producing a study of the land, the people, and the flow of nature—which was so much a part of his beloved homeland. There are countless moments of great beauty in this remarkable film, such as the wheat fields blowing in the wind and the closeups of nature's abundance being gathered at harvest time (never have such simple objects been treated with such esthetic endearment). And then those faces—rough, weather-beaten, yet indomitable. The faces of the Ukraine in Dovzhenko's tapestry cast an impression that Hollywood with all of its makeup artists could never come close to duplicating. As in the real life occurrence, the director's hero also drives his tractor onto the land possessed by the enemies of the people and he is also killed. There follows a powerful funeral sequence, where the hero's father stoically refuses a Christian service and conducts his own in the peasant tradition. To the old man (and Dovzhenko as well) this is merely part of nature's plan. Like the seasons and the crops, all things pass and return—in the Ukraine. And the only hope the people of that land can cling to, is that perhaps in time things may get better. In 1958, at the Brussels World Fair, 117 film historians voted EARTH one of the 10 best motion pictures of all time.

d&w, Alexander Dovshenko; ph, Daniel Demutski; m, L. Revutsky; ed, Dovshenko; art d, Vasili Krichevsky.

Drama **Cas.** **(PR:A MPAA:NR)**

EAST IS EAST*** (1916, Brit.) 5 reels Turner/BUT bw

Florence Turner *(Victoria Vickers)*, Henry Edwards *(Bert Grummett)*, Ruth Mackay *(Mrs. Carrington)*, W. G. Saunders *(Dawson)*, Edith Evans *(Aunt)*.

This little English romantic drama—about a cockney who loses his sense of priority after inheriting 250,000 pounds, deserts his fishmonger sweetheart but returns to her in the end—featured U.S. actress Turner.

d&w, Henry Edwards (based on the play by Philip Hubbard, Gwendolen Logan).

Drama **(PR:A MPAA:NR)**

EAST IS WEST*** (1922) 8 reels Constance Talmadge/FN bw

Constance Talmadge *(Ming Toy)*, Edward Burns *(Billy Benson)*, E. A. Warren *(Lo Sang Kee)*, Warner Oland *(Charley Yong)*, Frank Lanning *(Hop Toy)*, Nick De Ruiz *(Chang Lee)*, Nigel Barrie *(Jimmy Potter)*, Lillian Lawrence *(Mrs. Benson)*, Winter Hall *(Mr. Benson)*, Jim Wang *(Boat Owner)*.

Burns saves beauteous Talmadge from a life of slavery and sends her back to America in the custody of Warren. Before long, she adapts to the ways of the West but is coveted by powerful Chinatown figure, Oland, who attempts to kidnap her. Once again she is rescued by Burns, who takes her home and proposes marriage. Oland, who isn't really a bad fellow, agrees to this arrangement once it is disclosed that as a baby Talmadge was stolen from American parents.

p, Joseph M. Schenck; d, Sidney Franklin; w, Frances Marion (based on the play "East Is West: a Comedy in Three Acts and a Prologue" by Samuel Shipman, John B. Hymer); ph, Antonio Gaudio; art d, Stephen Goosson.

Drama **(PR:A MPAA:NR)**

EAST LYNNE*** (1913, Brit.) 6 reels Baker/Walturdaw bw

Blanche Forsythe *(Lady Isobel)*, Fred Paul *(Archibald Carlyle)*, Fred Morgan *(Capt. Levison)*, Rachel de Solla *(Cornelia Carlyle)*, May Morton *(Joyce)*, Pippin *(Little Willie)*, Doreen O'Connor *(Alfy Hallijohn)*, Roy Travers, Rolf Leslie.

This British picture, set in the 19th Century, is about a titled woman who runs off with a murderer and ultimately poses as a nurse to be with her dying child. Based on the novel of the same name and the long-running stage melodrama, this was the first six reel feature made in England.

d, Bert Haldane; w, Harry Engholm (based on the novel by Mrs. Henry Wood).

Drama **(PR:A MPAA:NR)**

EAST LYNNE** (1916) 5 reels FOX bw

Theda Bara *(Lady Isabel)*, Stuart Holmes, William H. Tooker, Claire Whitney, Stanhope Wheatcroft, Eugenie Woodward, Ben Deely, H. F. Hoffman, James O'Connor, Emily Fitzroy, Eldean Steuart.

This William Fox version of the old war-horse of a melodrama had several things going against it. One, audiences had trouble identifying movie vamp Bara with the long-suffering Lady Isabel and, two, by placing the action in a modern setting, the villainy seemed almost tame by contemporary standards.

d, Bertram Bracken; w, Mary Murillo (based on the play by Mary Elizabeth Braddon from the novel by Mrs. Henry Wood).

Drama **(PR:A MPAA:NR)**

EAST OF BROADWAY** (1924) 6 reels Encore Pictures/AEX bw

Owen Moore *(Peter Mullaney)*, Marguerite De La Motte *(Judy McNulty)*, Mary Carr *(Mrs. Morrisey)*, Eddie Gribbon *(Danny McCabe)*, Francis McDonald *(Prof. Mario)*, Betty Francisco *(Diana Morgan)*, George Nichols *(Officer Gaffney)*, Ralph Lewis *(The Commissioner)*.

An Irish-American kid (Moore) has one ambition in life: to be a New York cop. He attends the academy and is about to be disqualified for being too short when he engages in a fight which impresses the commissioner. On the strength of this, he is allowed to take the written exam, which he flunks after placing the Tropic of Capricorn in the Bronx. The commissioner does allow him to wear his uniform for one night to avoid disappointing his girl and, as he is walking with officer Nichols, they observe a robbery. The men spring into action, Nichols is shot, and Moore is wounded. In the hospital, the young Irishman is appointed to the force, and plans are made for a wedding in uniform.

d, William K. Howard; w, Paul Schofield; ph, Lucien Andriot.

Comedy Drama **(PR:A MPAA:NR)**

EAST OF SUEZ*** (1925) 7 reels FP-LAS/PAR bw

Pola Negri *(Daisy Forbes)*, Edmund Lowe *(George Tevis)*, Rockliffe Fellowes *(Harry Anderson)*, Noah Beery *(British Consul)*, Kamiyama Sojin *(Lee Tai)*, Mrs. Wong Wing *(Amah)*, Florence Regnart *(Sylvia Knox)*, Charles Requa *(Harold Knox)*, E. H. Calvert *(Sidney Forbes)*, Jesse Fuller.

Negri returns to China, after being educated in England, to discover her father dead and the Oriental maid who raised her was actually her mother. At the same time, Lowe, with whom she is in love, breaks off their relationship to pursue a diplomatic career. Shortly thereafter, Sojin, a monstrous mandarin, kidnaps her. She is rescued by Fellowes, who is really a rat. Negri marries him out of gratitude, but when he discovers that his wife is a half-breed outcast, he makes her life miserable. Meanwhile, Lowe returns and is forbidden by Fellowes to see Negri. He chooses to ignore this, and they meet at her house, where Fellowes is waiting to execute his husbandly prerogative. There is a suspenseful scene where Fellowes is about to squeeze the trigger when he suddenly falls over dead, a victim of wine his mandarin enemy had poisoned. The picture, which was nicely directed by Walsh, ends with the lovers returning to England and Sojin being punished in the Oriental manner.

d, Raoul Walsh; w, Sada Cowan (based on the play by William Somerset Maugham); ph, Victor Milner.

Drama **(PR:C MPAA:NR)**

EAST SIDE—WEST SIDE** (1923) 6 reels Principal Pictures bw

Kenneth Harlan *(Duncan Van Norman)*, Eileen Percy *(Lory James)*, Maxine Elliot Hicks *(Kit Lamson)*, Lucille Hutton *(Eunice Potter)*, Lucille Ward *(Mrs. Cornelia Von Norman)*, John Prince *(Paget)*, Betty May *(Amy Van Norman)*, Charles Hill Mailes *(Dr. Ernest Shepley)*, Wally Van *(Skiddy Stillman)*.

Wealthy Ward fires her author son's secretary (Percy) when she senses their relationship is not strictly business. But when she realizes the depth of their feelings and the sweetness of the girl, despite her lowly upbringing, she goes to Percy and asks her to return.

p&d, Irving Cummings; w, Hope Loring, Louis B. Lighton (based on the play by Leighton Osmun, Henry Hull); ph, Arthur Martinelli.

Drama **(PR:C MPAA:NR)**

EASY COME, EASY GO*** (1928) 6 reels PAR bw

Richard Dix *(Robert Parker)*, Nancy Carroll *(Babs Quayle)*, Charles Sellon *(Jim Bailey)*, Frank Currier *(Mr. Quayle)*, Arnold Kent *(Winthrop)*, Christian J. Frank, Joseph J. Franz *(Detectives)*, Guy Oliver *(Conductor)*.

Fair Dix program comedy about a radio anouncer who is fired by his father for profanity and becomes involved with an elderly bank robber. The laughs are provided by Dix's attempts to give the money back.

d, Frank Tuttle; w, Florence Ryerson (based on the play by Owen Davis); t, George Marion, Jr.; ed, Otto Lovering.

Comedy **(PR:A MPAA:NR)**

EASY GOING GORDON** (1925) 5 reels Paul Gerson Pictures bw

Richard Holt *(Gordon Palmer)*, Kathryn McGuire *(Aileen Merton)*, Gordon Russell *(Slung Williams)*, Fernando Galvez *(Beef O'Connell)*, Roy Cushing *(Judson)*, Harris Gordon *(George Elvin)*.

Holt, a millionaire's son, is completely devoid of gumption until a couple of crooks steal his fiancee's engagement ring. He becomes a changed man as he tracks them down and gets the ring back. Later, when the family business is in danger, Gordon—with the help of the crooks—steals his partner's proxies and saves the day.

d, Duke Worne; w, Grover Jones.

Drama **(PR:A MPAA:NR)**

EASY MONEY** (1925) 6 reels Harry J. Brown/RAY bw

Cullen Landis *(Bud Parsons)*, Mildred Harris *(Blanche Amory)*, Mary Carr *(Mrs. Hale)*, Crauford Kent *(Lewis)*, Gertrude Astor, Gladys Walton, Rex Lease, David Kirby, Joseph Swickard, Wilfred Lucas.

Landis, a decent young man, is arrested after committing a crime to please a nightclub dancer. He is approached by a shyster lawyer who persuades him to impersonate a lost heir. After pulling this off, he falls in love with the daughter of the family. Then the real son arrives and is accused of burglary, but Landis steps forward, sets the matter straight, and wins the girl.

d, Albert Rogell; w, Marion Jackson (based on a story by Sam Mintz); ph, Ross Fisher.

Crime **(PR:A MPAA:NR)**

EASY PICKINGS** (1927) 6 reels FN bw

Anna Q. Nilsson *(Mary Ryan)*, Kenneth Harlan *(Peter Van Horne)*, Philo McCullough *(Stewart)*, Billy Bevan *(The Detective)*, Jerry Miley *(Tony)*, Charles Sellon *(Dr. Naylor)*, Zack Williams *(Remus)*, Gertrude Howard *(Mandy)*.

Just another spooky house, hooded stranger, phony heir, crooked lawyer, secret passage, "feets git movin'" black servant movie, highlighted only by the presence of comedian Bevan.

p, Frank Griffin; d, George Archainbaud; w, Louis Stevens, William A. Burton (based on the play "Easy Pickings, a Mystery-Comedy in Three Acts" by Paul A. Cruger); ph, Charles Van Enger.

Mystery **(PR:A MPAA:NR)**

EASY ROAD, THE** (1921) 5 reels FP/PAR bw

Thomas Meighan *(Leonard Fayne)*, Gladys George *(Isabel Grace)*, Grace Goodall *(Katherine Dare)*, Lila Lee *(Ella Klotz)*, Arthur Carew *(Hemingway)*, Laura Anson *(Minnie Baldwin)*, Viora Daniels *(Laura)*.

Novelist Meighan marries society woman George and the good life makes him lazy. He begins to drink too much and is unable to write. When George sails for Europe (leaving word that he should use her bank account freely) Meighan becomes despondent and decides to kill himself. At the water's edge he finds a little waif also bent on suicide because she is slowly going blind. Meighan intervenes, gives her the will to live, and is inspired to write again. Meanwhile, George—who has rejected the advances of Carew, a former flame—returns to Meighan, who has proven at last that he is his own man.

d, Tom Forman; w, Beulah Marie Dix (based on the story "Easy Street" by Blair Hall); ph, Harry Perry.

Drama **(PR:A MPAA:NR)**

EASY TO GET*** (1920) 5 reels PAR bw

Marguerite Clark *(Milly Morehouse)*, Harrison Ford *(Bob Morehouse)*, Rodney LaRocque *(Dick Elliot)*, Helen Greene *(Pauline Reid)*, Herbert Barrington *(Talbot Chase)*, Kid Broad *(Thaddeus Burr)*, H. Van Busen *(Jim Tucker)*, Julia Hurley *(Marm Tucker)*.

Clark and her husband, Ford, are on their honeymoon train trip. He goes to the smoking compartment and after 10 minutes, missing him desperately, she follows. Outside the door, Clark overhears Ford telling another fellow that all girls are easy, including his own wife. Infuriated and hurt, Clark leaves the train and becomes involved in a series of adventures which end with her pretending to be kidnaped. It turns out the abduction is real, and this inspires Ford to appreciate his bride's true worth.

d, Walter Edwards; w, Julia Crawford Ivers (based on a story by Izola Forrester, Mann Page); ph, Hal Young.

Drama **(PR:A MPAA:NR)**

EASY TO MAKE MONEY*** (1919) 5 reels Metro bw

Bert Lytell *(James Frederick Slocum, Jr.)*, Gertrude Selby *(Ethel Wheeler)*, Frank Currier *(James Frederick Slocum, Sr.)*, Stanton Heck *(Henry Fowler)*, Ethel Shannon *(Katherine Fowler)*, Edward Connelly *(Jasper Kennedy)*, Bull Montana *(Charles "Kid" Miller)*.

Lytell accepts a bet from his millionaire father that he cannot keep from being arrested for speeding. To win the $25,000, he has himself jailed by starting a fight. After his release, his car breaks down in a small town, and Lytell becomes attracted to the pretty girl who owns an unprofitable hotel. The young man takes control of the situation, business booms, and before long he practically owns the whole town. When the father is invited to attend the wedding, he is so pleased with the situation that he gives the couple a check for half a million dollars. "Gee," Lytell says, "it's easy to make money."

d, Edwin Carewe; w, Finis Fox (based on a story by John H. Blackwood); ph, Robert B. Kurris.

Comedy/Drama **(PR:A MPAA:NR)**

EASY VIRTUE*** (1927, Brit.) 8 reels Gainsborough/World Wide bw

Isabel Jean *(Larita Filton)*, Robin Irvine *(John Whittaker)*, Franklin Dyall *(Mr. Filton)*, Enid Stamp-Taylor, *(Sarah)*, Violet Farebrother *(Mrs. Whittaker)*, Frank Elliot *(Col. Whittaker)*, Darcia Deane *(Marion Whittaker)*, Dorothy Boyd *(Hilda Whittaker)*, Ian Hunter *(Counsel)*, Eric Bransby Williams *(Correspondent)*, Benita Hume *(Telephonist)*.

Hitchcock directed this drama, inspired by the Coward play, about a divorced woman who marries a younger man. He adores her, and she propels his parents into a state of shock before deserting him.

p, Michael Balcon; d, Alfred Hitchcock; w, Eliot Stannard (based on a play by Noel Coward); ph, Claude McDonnell; ed, Ivor Montagu; set d, Islington.

Drama **Cas.** **(PR:A MPAA:NR)**

EBB TIDE*** (1922) 8 reels FP/PAR bw

Noah Beery *(Richard Attwater)*, Lila Lee *(Ruth Attwater)*, James Kirkwood *(Robert Herrick)*, Raymond Hatton *(J. L. Huish)*, George Fawcett *(Capt. Davis)*, Jacqueline Logan *(Tehura)*.

Solid cast and some fine underwater photography elevate this programmer above the average. Beery makes himself king of an uncharted island after killing his wife and best friend, who he suspects are having an affiar. He ruthlessly governs the pearl-diving natives and his daughter, until a derelict ship with a motley crew of three are deposited there by a storm. Two of the strangers attempt to steal Berry's fortune, but one of them, who has been regenerated through his love for the daughter, stands in their way. In the end, mutual greed leads to the death of everyone but the lovers, who are happy to share paradise with its liberated natives.

d, George Melford; w, Waldemar Young (based on the writings of Robert Louis Stevenson, Lloyd Osbourne); ph, Bert Glennon.

Adventure **(PR:A MPAA:NR)**

EDGE O'BEYOND** (1919, Brit.) 6 reels G.B. Samuelson/GEN bw

Ruby Miller *(Dinah Webberley)*, Owen Nares *(Dr. Cecil Lawson)*, Isobel Elsom *(Joyce Grey)*, C. M. Hallard *(Capt. Burnett)*, Minna Grey *(Dulcie Maitland)*, Fred Raynham *(Oswald Grant)*, James Lindsay *(Maj. Egerton)*.

Harsh drama set in colonial Africa about a woman who escapes her sadistic husband only after the death of her baby.

d, Fred W. Durrant; w, Irene Miller (based on the novel by Gertrude Page).

Drama **(PR:A MPAA:NR)**

EDGE OF THE ABYSS, THE*** (1915) 5 reels Kay-Bee/TRI bw

Mary Boland *(Alma Clayton)*, Robert McKim *(Neil Webster)*, Frank Mills *(Wayne Burroughs)*, Willard Mack *(Jim Sims)*.

Boland rejects her boy friend, who is a failure at business, and marries a famous criminal lawyer. However, because of his work load, she soon feels neglected and gets in touch with her former gentleman caller, who comes to her home and pleads with her to run away with him. Also in the house is a burglar, whom the husband once saved from the electric chair. The robber sees the attorney's picture on the bureau, realizes the situation, and sees his chance to repay the man. He orders the woman to tie her former beau up and takes her into another room where he gives her a good lecture. The young man escapes and calls the police, but not before the wife is made to realize her husband's decency. When the cops arrive, she hides the thief and sees to it that he escapes. Then she contacts her husband and asks him to rush to her bed.

d, Raymond B. West; sup, Thomas H. Ince; w, C. Gardner Sullivan.

Drama/Crime **(PR:A MPAA:NR)**

EDUCATION OF ELIZABETH, THE*** (1921) 5 reels FP bw

Billie Burke *(Elizabeth Banks)*, Lumsden Hare *(Thomas)*, Edith Sharpe *(Lucy Fairfax)*, Donald Cameron *(Harry)*, Frederick Burton *(Middleton)*.

The young Burke was ideally suited to play a follies girl whose wealthy boy friend brings her home to meet his horrified parents. After some time, and many comic complications, her suitor leaves on business and Burke—to almost everyone's delight—transforms his bookworm brother into the ideal mate.

d, Edward Dillon; w, Elmer Harris (based on a play by Roy Horniman); ph, George Folsey.

Comedy **(PR:A MPAA:NR)**

EDUCATION OF NICKY, THE** (1921, Brit.) 5 reels HAE/Walturdaw bw

James Knight *(Nicky Malvesty)*, Marjorie Villis *(Trixie Happinleigh)*, Constance Worth *(Chloe)*, Mary Rorke *(Lady Aberleigh)*, Keith Weatherley *(Col. Trouville)*, Dolores Courtenay *(Virginia)*, George Williams *(Mr. Malvesty)*, Winifred Sadler *(Mrs. Malvesty)*.

In this little British romance, a couple of wealthy cousins can pursue their love affair only after they both become bankrupted.

d&w, Arthur Rooke (based on the novel by May Wynn).

Drama **(PR:A MPAA:NR)**

EFFICIENCY EDGAR'S COURTSHIP*** (1917) 5 reels Essanay bw

Taylor Holmes *(Edgar Bumpus)*, Virginia Valli *(Mary Pierce)*, Rodney La Rock *(Mr. Wimple)*, Ernest Maupain *(Mr. Pierce)*.

In one of Essany's better features, director Windom worked comedic wonders with a tiny cast and a thin story line. It all had to do with an efficiency expert, Holmes, demonstrating his various innovations to his sweetheart's father to win his favor—while La Rock, his rival, does everything possible to sabotage the effort.

d, L. C. Windom; w, Charles J. McGuirk (based on a story by Clarence Buddington Kelland).

Comedy **(PR:A MPAA:NR)**

ELEVENTH COMMANDMENT, THE** (1924, Brit.) 8 reels GAU bw

Fay Compton *(Ruth Barchester)*, Stewart Rome *(John Lynton)*, Lilian Hall Davis *(Marian Barchester)*, Charles Quartermaine *(James Mountford)*, Jack Hobbs *(Robert Ransome)*, Dawson Millward *(Sir Noel Barchester)*, Louise Hampton *(Lady Barchester)*, Brian Aherne *(Norman Barchester)*.

Interesting British crime drama in which an actress saves her sister from a blackmailer by assuming the guilt for an indiscretion.

d, George A. Cooper; w, (based on the play by Brandon Fleming).

Crime **(PR:A MPAA:NR)**

ELEVENTH HOUR, THE*** (1922, Brit.) 6 reels STOLL bw

Madge White *(Doris Elliot)*, Dennis Wyndham *(Jeff Ironside)*, Philip Simmons *(Hugh Chesyl)*, M. Gray Murray *(Col. Elliott)*, Beatrice Chester *(Mrs. Elliot)*.

In this English love story, the daughter of a career officer marries a farmer in name only. After leaving him, she sees the light and returns to his home following his near suicide.

d, George Ridgwell; w, Leslie Howard Gordon (based on the novel by Ethel M. Dell).

Drama **(PR:A MPAA:NR)**

ELEVENTH HOUR, THE*** (1923) 7 reels FOX bw

Shirley Mason *(Barbara Hackett)*, Charles Jones *(Brick McDonald)*, Richard Tucker *(Herbert Glenville)*, Alan Hale *(Prince Stefan de Bernie)*, Walter McGrail *(Dick Manley)*, June Elvidge *(Estelle Hackett)*, Fred Kelsey *(Commander of the Submarine)*, Nigel De Brulier *(Mordecai Newman)*, Fred Kohler *(Barbara's Uncle)*.

There are plenty of thrills—in the serial tradition—as a U.S. Secret Service chief (Jones) uses speedboats, airplanes, and a submarine to stop the evil—and quite mad—Prince Stefan from taking over the world.

d, Bernard J. Durning; w, Louis Sherwin (based on a play by Lincoln J. Carter); ph, Don Short.

Adventure **(PR:A MPAA:NR)**

ELISABETH REIGNE D'ANGLETERRE

(SEE: QUEEN ELIZABETH, 1912, Fr.)

ELLA CINDERS*** (1926) 7 reels FN bw

Colleen Moore *(Ella Cinders)*, Lloyd Hughes *(Waite Lifter)*, Vera Lewis *("Ma" Cinders)*, Doria Baker *(Lotta Pill)*, Emily Gerdes *(Prissy Pill)*, Mike Donlin *(Studio Gateman)*, Jed Prouty *(The Mayor)*, Jack Duffy *(The Fire Chief)*, Harry Allen *(The Photographer)*, D'Arcy Corrigan *(The Editor)*, Alfred E. Green *(The Director)*, Harry Langdon, E. H. Calvert, Chief Yowlache, Russell Hopton.

Moore was ideally suited to play the comic strip slavey who enters a contest against the wishes of her stepsisters and wins a trip to Hollywood. Once there, she becomes involved in an hilarious series of comic stiutations (one of which features Langdon in a cameo role) as she tries to break into the movies. Then, believing a staged fire to be real, her panic-stricken reaction causes the studio brass to award her a contract. Now, not only is she on her way, but the hometown iceman and football star, whom she loves, shows up, turns out to be a millionaire's son, and asks her to marry him.

p, John McCormick; d, Alfred E. Green; w, Frank Griffin, Mervin LeRoy (based on the comic strip "Cinderella in the Movies" by William Conselman, Charles Plumb); t, George Marion, Jr.; ph, Arthur Martinelli; ed, Robert J. Kern; art d, E. J. Shulter.

Comedy **(PR:A MPAA:NR)**

ELOPE IF YOU MUST** (1922) 5 reels FOX bw

Eileen Percy *(Nancy Moore)*, Edward Sutherland *(Jazz Hennessy)*, Joseph Bennett *(Willie Weems)*, Mildred Davenport *(Elizabeth Magruder)*, Mary Huntress *(Mrs. Magruder)*, Harvey Clarke *(Mr. Magruder)*, Larry Steers *(Warren Holt)*.

A couple of stranded actors meet a millionaire on the train back to the city and accept his offer of $10,000 to pose as servants and prevent his daughter from marrying the wrong man.

d, C. R . Wallace; w, Joseph Franklin Poland; ph, Otto Brautigan.

Drama/Comedy **(PR:A MPAA:NR)**

ELUSIVE ISABEL** (1916) 6 reels BLUE bw

Florence Lawrence *(Isabel Throne)*, Sydney Bracey *(Luigi)*, Harry Millarde *(Hamilton Grimm)*, Wallace Clarke *(Prince D'Abruzzi)*, William Welsh *(Chief Campbell)*, Paul Panzer *(Count Rosini)*, Jack Newton *(Senor Rodriguez)*, Sonia Marcel *(Senorita Rodriguez)*.

The Latin nations of the world are plotting to take over the U.S.. They meet in Washington to sign their compact, but Secret Service agent Millarde foils their plot and captures the heart of one of the female conspirators.

d, Stuart Patom; w, Raymond L. Schrock (based on a novel by Jacques Futrelle).

Spy Drama **(PR:A MPAA:NR)**

ELUSIVE PIMPERNEL, THE*** (1919, Brit.) 6 reels STOLL bw

Cecil Humphreys *(Sir Percy Blakeney)*, Marie Blanche *(Lady Marguerite)*, Norman Page *(Chauvelin)*, Fotheringham Lysons *(Robespierre)*, Teddy Arundell *(Colet d' Herbois)*, Madge Stuart *(Juliette Marny)*, A. Harding Steerman *(Abbe Jouquet)*, Dorothy Hanson *(Mlle. Cardeille)*.

Costume adventure about an English nobleman who, disguised as The Scarlet Pimpernel, rescues French aristocrats from the reign of terror following the revolution.

d, Maurice Elvey; w, Frederick Blatchford (based on the novel by Baroness Orczy.)

Adventure **(PR:A MPAA:NR)**

EMBARRASSMENT OF RICHES, THE**

(1918) 5 reels Walker/Hodkinson bw

Lillian Walker *(Elizabeth Holt)*, Carl Brickert *(John Russell, Philanthropist)*, John Costello *(William Gildersleeve, Banker)*, Edward Keenan *(Bobby Gildersleeve, His Son)*, Henry Sedley *(Count Orloff)*, Edward Roseman *(Leighton Craig)*, Harriet Ross *(Mrs. Goodwin)*, Reeva Greenwood *(Alma)*, Peggy Lundeen *(Miss Partridge)*, Howard Truesdale *(Ted Phelan)*, John Dillon *(Jim Connors)*, Leonie Flugrath, Mrs. William Bechtel, Yale Boss, Edna Hammel, Edward Donnelly.

Walker toils in a sweatshop until her wildest dream comes true and she inherits a fortune. Unfortunately, the man she loves, a settlement worker, is an idealist and Walker is forced to pose as her own secretary to win his heart.

d, Edward Dillon; w, Roy Somerville (based on the play by Louis K. Anspacher); ph, Al Ligouri.

Drama **(PR:A MPAA:NR)**

EMERALD OF THE EAST**

(1928, Brit.) 6 reels British Pacific-BIP/Wardour bw

Joshua Kean *(Lt. Desmond Armstrong)*, Mary Odette *(Nellum)*, Jean de Kuharski *(Maharajah)*, Lya Delvelez *(Maharanee)*, Gillian Dean *(Evelyn)*, Maria Forescu *(Chieftainess)*, Kenneth Rive *(Maharaj Kumar)*, Promotha Bose *(Vaghi)*.

In this saga of the British Empire, a brave lieutenant risks his life to save that of a maharajah's son from a band of renegade killers.

d&w, Jean de Kuharski; w, (based on the novel by Jerbanu Kothawala).

Adventure **(PR:A MPAA:NR)**

EMPTY HANDS*** (1924) 7 reels FP/PAR bw

Jack Holt *(Grimshaw)*, Norma Shearer *(Claire Endicott)*, Charles Clary *(Robert Endicott)*, Hazel Keener *(Mrs. Endicott)*, Gertrude Olmstead *(Gypsy)*, Ramsey Wallace *(Montie)*, Ward Crane *(Milt Bisnet)*, Charles Stevens *(The Indian Guide)*, Hank Mann *(Spring Water Man)*, Charles Green *(Butler)*.

Shearer, a liberated flapper, is a tremendous disappointment to her wealthy father. He takes her with him on a business trip to examine some holdings in Canada, and when she is introduced to his chief engineer, Holt, there is immediate animosity. Later, as her canoe is swept down the rapids, Holt goes after her and the two become isolated in the woods. (Here, we see an update of the movie MALE AND FEMALE, where the resourceful woodman is taking care of the completely helpless jazz baby.) They gradually fall in love and later, after Shearer proves her grit by breaking off their relationship to protect his career, Holt demands that she marry him.

d, Victor Fleming; w, Carey Wilson; ph, Charles Edgar Schoenbaum.

Drama **(PR:A MPAA:NR)**

ENCHANTED COTTAGE, THE***** (1924) 7 reels INSP/FN bw

Richard Barthelmess *(Oliver Bashforth)*, May McAvoy *(Laura Pennington)*, Ida Waterman *(Mrs. Smallwood)*, Alfred Hickman *(Rupert Smallwood)*, Florence Short *(Ethel Bashforth)*, Marion Coakley *(Beatrice Vaughn)*, Holmes E. Herbert *(Maj. Hillgrove)*, Ethel Wright *(Mrs. Minnett)*, Harry Allen.

Supremely beautiful film on every level, about a crippled English war veteran, who, unwilling to face the world because of war injuries to his face, isolates himself in a remote cottage. In time he encounters an extremely homely girl, who understands his reluctance to be seen by others. They enter into a marriage of convenience but, before long, the inner beauty each possesses begins to surface, and from that point on they emerge beautiful and whole in each other's eyes. Barthelmess was wonderful and MacAvoy delivered one of the greatest performances in motion picture history.

d, John S. Robertson; w, Josephine Lovett (based on the play by Arthur Wing Pinero); t, Gertrude Chase; ph, George Folsey; ed, William Hamilton.

Drama **(PR:A MPAA:NR)**

ENCHANTED HILL, THE*** (1926) 7 reels FP/PAR bw

Jack Holt *(Lee Purdy)*, Florence Vidor *(Gail Ormsby)*, Noah Beery *(Jake Dort)*, Mary Brian *(Hallie Purdy)*, Richard Arlen *(Link Halliwell)*, George Bancroft *(Ira Todd)*, Ray Thompson *(Tommy Scaife)*, Brandon Hurst *(Jasper Doak)*, Henry Herbert *(Bud Shannon)*, George Kuwa *(Chan)*, Mathilde Comont *(Conchita)*, Willard Cooley *(Curley MacMahon)*, George Magrill *(Ist Killer)*.

Modern western in which Holt and his men use machine guns and an airplane to fight the bad fellows who are out to steal his ore-rich land. In the end, Holt wins the whole shootin' match, but villain Beery walks away with the picture.

d, Irvin Willat; w, James Shelley Hamilton (based on a novel by Peter Bernard Kyne); ph, Al Gilks.

Western **(PR:A MPAA:NR)**

ENCHANTED ISLAND, THE** (1927) 6 reels TIF bw

Henry B. Walthall *(Tim Sanborn)*, Charlotte Stevens *(Alice Sanborn)*, Pierre Gendron *(Bob Hamilton)*, Pat Hartigan *("Red" Blake)*, Floyd Shakleford *(Ulysses Abraham Washington)*.

Stranded on a tropical island for 15 years, Walthall and his daughter live an enchanted life until a shipwreck delivers three strangers. Walthall passes his daughter off as a boy and when the truth is revealed, two of the men fight over her. Fortunately, the decent one wins, and her virtue is spared. Then, when a volcano erupts, everyone is killed but the young couple who have fallen in love, and they are rescued at sea.

d, William G. Crosby; w, Kay Sherwood (based on a story by John Thomas Neville); ph, Joseph A. Dubray, Stephen Norton; art d, George E. Sawley.

Drama **(PR:A MPAA:NR)**

ENCHANTMENT* (1920, Brit.) 6 reels LFP/JUR bw

Henry Krauss *(John Desmond)*, Mary Odette *(Pat Desmond)*, Eric Barclay *(Charles Stuart)*, Edward O'Neill *(Sandy Stuart)*, Henry Vibart *(Father Casey)*, Mary Brough *(Mrs. Slattery)*, George Bellamy *(Tim Cassidy)*, Joyce Barbour *(Sophie Desmond)*, Hargreave Mansell *(Dr. O'Connor)*, Caleb Porter *(Sailor)*.

Ireland was fighting desperately for its independence from British tyranny when this film was produced in England about the son of an Irish smuggler who saves the daughter of a drunkard from entering a convent.

d, Einar J. Bruun; w, Frank Fowell (based on the novel by E. Temple Thurston).

Drama **(PR:A MPAA:NR)**

ENCHANTMENT*½** (1921) 7 reels COS/PAR bw

Marion Davies *(Ethel Hoyt)*, Forrest Stanley *(Ernest Eddison)*, Edith Shayne *(Mrs. Hoyt)*, Tom Lewis *(Mr. Hoyt)*, Arthur Rankin *(Tommy Corbin)*, Corinne Barker *(Nalia)*, Maude Turner Gordon *(Mrs. Leigh)*, Edith Lyle *(The Fairy Tale Queen)*, Huntley Gordon *(The Fairy Tale King)*.

Davies is a spoiled flapper who wraps her parents and her six boy friends from Harvard around her little finger. To celebrate his birthday, her beleaguered father attends a performance of "The Taming of the Shrew" and comes to the conclusion that his daughter needs a Petruchio of her own. He hires the actor who performed the role and arranges for him to appear with his daughter in an amateur production. After tempestuous rehearsals, in which Davies' fury goes unchecked, the play gets underway. The conclusion of act three calls for Davies (who has been asleep for a hundred years) to be kissed by Prince Charming; but this time the actor, who has fallen in love with her, gives her a smacker worthy of Rudolph Valentino. Bells ring and thunder roars as Davies, like Katherine—sees the light.

d, Robert G. Vignola; w, Luther Reed (based on the story "Manhandling Ethel" by Frank Ramsay Adams); ph, Ira H. Morgan.

Comedy **(PR:A MPAA:NR**

END OF THE GAME, THE** (1919) 5 reels Hodkinson/Pathe bw

J. Warren Kerrigan *(Burke Allister)*, Lois Wilson *(Mary Miller)*, Alfred Whitman *(Frank Miller)*, Jack Richardson *(Dan Middleton)*, George Field *(Four-Ace Baker)*, Walter Perry *(Wild Bill)*, Bert Appling *(Sheriff)*, *J. J. Franz (Hotel Clerk)*, Eleanor Fair *(Mona)*.

No surprises in this one about a young man and his sister who travel by wagon train from New England to California in search of gold. After arriving, the saloon keeper, who lusts for the girl, kills the brother. But a handsome Virginian intervenes and avenges the murder.

d, Jesse D. Hampton; w, F. McGrew Willis (based on a story by George Elwood Jenks); ph, Charles Stumar.

Western **(PR:A MPAA:NR)**

END OF THE TRAIL, THE*** (1916) 5 reels FOX bw

William Farnum *(Jules Le Clerq)*, Gladys Brockwell *(Adrienne Cabot)*, Willard Louis *(Devil Cabot)*, Eleanor Crowe *(La Petite Adrienne)*, H. A. Barrows *(Harvey Gordon)*, William Burress *(Father Le Jeune)*, Harry De Vere *(John Robinson)*, Hermina Louis *(Mrs. Robinson)*, H. J. Hebert *(Wapau)*, Ogden Crane *(Jacques Favre)*, Charles Whittaker *(Trading-Post Inspector)*.

Brockwell (who played Janet Gaynor's sadistic sister in SEVENTH HEAVEN) all but stole the show in this story of a rugged trapper's undying love for a woman, set against the hardship and danger of the frozen North.

d&w, Oscar Apfel (based on the story "Hope Rides with Me" by Maibelle Herkes Justice).

Drama/Adventure **(PR:A MPAA:NR)**

ENEMIES OF CHILDREN* (1923) 6 reels Fisher/Mammoth bw

Anna Q. Nilsson, Claire McDowell, Lucy Beaumont, George Siegmann, Joseph Dowling, Raymond Hatton, Ward Crane, Charles Wellesley, Virginia Lee Corbin, Kate Price, Boyd Irwin, Eugenie Besserer, William Boyd, Mary Anderson.

A superior cast was wasted in this melodrama about an urchin adopted by a wealthy family. By the end of this potboiler, the mystery of her parentage is solved.

d&w, Lillian Ducey, John M. Voshell (based on the novel *Youth Triumphant* by George Gibbs).

Drama **(PR:A MPAA:NR)**

ENEMIES OF WOMEN, THE**** (1923) 11 reels COS/Goldwyn bw

Lionel Barrymore *(Prince Lubimoff)*, Alma Rubens *(Alicia)*, Pedro De Cordoba *(Atilio Castro)*, Gareth Hughes *(Spadoni)*, Gladys Hulette *(Vittoria)*, William Thompson *(Col. Marcos)*, William Collier, Jr. *(Gaston)*, Mario Majeroni *(Duke de Delille)*, Betty Bouton *(Alicia's Maid)*, Jean Brindeau *(Mme. Spadoni)*, Ivan Linow *(Terrorist)*, Paul Panzer *(The Cossack)*.

Marvelous images, magnificent sets, and excellent acting, more than compensated for a contrived ending in this otherwise fascinating script. Barrymore is superb as Prince Lubimoff, an aristocratic Russian libertine who flees his country, along with lady friend Alicia (Rubens), after killing a Cossack in a duel. In Paris he finds Rubens with her son (Collier)—whose existence she has kept a secret—and, thinking he is her young lover, deserts her. They meet again in Monte Carlo where the embittered prince, having lost most of his fortune, has formed a club for misogynists called the "Enemies of Women" (a plot development which provided director Crosland with the opportunity to stage an orgy worthy of Eric von Stroheim at his decadent best). Rubens is there desperately trying to win money at the gambling tables for her son, who has been captured in the war. Finally Collier is released and he and Barrymore participate in a duel during which the young man dies of a heart attack. The prince then learns the truth and, guilt-ridden, he goes off to the war and fights heroically. At the front he meets Rubens, who is serving as a nurse, and the two somehow manage to overcome the tragedy of the past and find happiness in each other's arms.

d, Alan Crosland; w, John Lynch (based on the novel *Los Enemigos de la Mujer* by Vicente Blasco-Ibáñez); ph, Ira Morgan; set d, Joseph Urban.

Drama **(PR:A MPAA:NR)**

ENEMIES OF YOUTH** (1925) 6 reels Atlas Educational/Moeller bw

Mahlon Hamilton, Gladys Leslie, J. Barney Sherry, Jack Drumier, Jane Jennings, Burr McIntosh, Charles Delaney, Gladys Walton.

Curious little jazz-age programmer about a town so conservative—due to the older citizens who control it—that the young people are forced to go elsewhere for their entertainment, causing their involvement in drinking, and worse. Realizing how desperate the situation is, the district attorney runs for mayor as an independent, is backed by the governor, wins the race, and even influences a big company to locate a factory there.

d, Arthur Berthelet; w, Stacey A. Van Petten.

Drama **(PR:A MPAA:NR)**

ENEMY, THE**** (1927) 9 reels MGM bw

Lillian Gish *(Pauli Arndt)*, Ralph Forbes *(Carl Behrend)*, Ralph Emerson *(Bruce Gordon)*, Frank Currier *(Prof. Arndt)*, George Fawcet *(August Behrend)*, Fritzi Ridgeway *(Mitzi Winkelmann)*, John S. Peters *(Fritz Winkelmann)*, Karl Dane *(Jan)*, Polly Moran *(Baruska)*, Billy Kent Schaefer *(Kurt)*.

Gish and Forbes are a newly married Austrian couple. When the war breaks out, Forbes is drafted, leaving Gish and her baby near starvation after her professor father is fired for teaching pacifism. Forbes is reported killed and Gish turns to prostitution to feed her family. There is, however, a happy ending with Forbes, who is alive after all, returning home.

d, Fred Niblo; w, Willis Goldbeck, Agnes Christine Johnston (based on the play "The Enemy; a Play in Four Acts" by Channing Pollock); t, John Colton; ph, Oliver Marsh; ed, Margaret Booth; set d, Cedric Gibbons, Richard Day; cos, Gilbert Clark.

Drama **(PR:C MPAA:NR)**

ENEMY OF MEN, AN** (1925) 6 reels COL bw

Cullen Landis, Dorothy Revier, Charles Clary.

When her sister dies giving birth to the child of a political boss who deserted her while she was pregnant, a young woman sets out to punish all men. She becomes a popular figure at New York nightclubs, where she makes suckers of the playboy population. Later she sets up a home for girls and falls for a young doctor. She refuses to marry him until she hears the news that her late sister's husband has been murdered by one of the girls he ruined.

d, Frank R. Strayer; w, Douglas Bronston; ph, Frank B. Good.

Drama **(PR:A MPAA:NR)**

ENEMY SEX, THE** (1924) 8 reels FP/PAR bw

Betty Compson *("Dodo" Baxter)*, Percy Marmont *(Garry Lundaberry)*, Sheldon Lewis *(Albert Edward Sassoon)*, Huntley Gordon *(Judge Massingale)*, De Witt Jennings *(Harrigan Blood)*, William H. Turner *(Blainey)*, Dot Farley *(Ida Summers)*, Ed Faust *(Comte de Joncy)*, Pauline Bush *(Miss Snyder)*, Kathlyn Williams *(Mrs. Massingale)*.

Not too many laughs in this comedy-drama about a chorus girl (Compson) who rejects the favors of five millionaires (for a little "consideration"on her part) in order to nurse alcoholic Marmont back to health.

d, James Cruze; w, Walter Woods, Harvey Thew (based on the novel by Owen Johnson); ph, Karl Brown.

Comedy/Drama **(PR:A MPAA:NR)**

ENTER MADAME*** (1922) 7 reels Samuel Zierler Photoplay/Metro bw

Clara Kimball Young *(Prima Donna Lisa Della Robia/Mrs. Gerald Fitzgerald)*, Elliot Dexter *(Gerald Fitzgerald)*, Louise Dresser *(Mrs. Flora Preston)*, Lionel Belmore *(Archimede)*, Wedgewood Nowell *(The Doctor)*, Rosita Marstini *(Bice)*, Ora Devereaux *(Miss Smith)*, Arthur Rankin *(John Fitzgerald)*, Mary Jane Sanderson *(Aline Chalmers)*, George Kuwa *(Tomamoto)*.

Young is an opera star who creates a sensation when she returns to New York in the middle of her European tour, because her husband has filed for divorce. Before long, Young completely out-charms her rival and wins her spouse back.

p, Harry Garson; d, Wallace Worsley; w, Frank Bresford (based on a story by Gilda Varesi, Dolly Byrne); ph, William O'Connell.

Comedy/Drama **(PR:A MPAA:NR)**

ENVIRONMENT* (1922) 6 reels Irving Cummings/Principal bw

Milton Sills *(Steve McLaren)*, Alice Lake *(Sally Dolan/Chicago Sal)*, Ben Hewlett *("Willie Boy" Toval)*, Gertrude Claire *(Grandma McLaren)*, Richard Headrick *(Jimmie, Steve's Adopted Son)*, Ralph Lewis *("Diamond Jim" Favre)*.

Absurd premise sees Lake as a gun moll, being sent to work for Sills to pay off the money her partners stole from him. She falls in love with the big lug, but leaves anyway with a couple of crooks who come to visit her. Sills follows her, extricates her from the scene of a crime in which she was involved, and is arrested himself. Lake dries her tears, returns to Sills' country home, and promises to wait for him until he gets out of jail.

d, Irving Cummings; w, Harvey Gates.

Crime **(PR:A MPAA:NR)**

ENVY** (1917) 5 reels McClure/TRI bw

Ann Murdock *(Betty Howard)*, Shirley Mason *(Eve Leslie)*, George Le Guere *(Adam Moore)*, Lumsden Hare *(Stanton Skinner)*, Jessie Stevens *(Eve's Foster Mother)*, William Wadsworth *(Eve's Foster Father)*, Robert Cain *(Rocco Irwin)*.

This first film in a proposed series covering the seven deadly sins, tells of millionaire Le Guere, who falls for and marries rural girl Mason. Later, he becomes infatuated with stage star Murdock, who has been told she may only have two years to live. Mason is envious of the actress but, being a decent sort, welcomes her to convalesce at her country estate. Along with Murdock comes rotter Hare, who after a time repays the hospitality of his hostess by trying to rape her. Le Guere rushes to his wife's rescue and there is a whale of a fight, but for some reason the film endsthere—leaving the audience completely baffled as to what became of the characters.

d, Richard Ridgely; w, Florence Morse Kingsley; ph, George Lane.

Drama **(PR:A MPAA:NR)**

ERNEST MALTRAVERS*** (1920, Brit.) 5 reels ID bw

Cowley Wright *(Ernest Maltravers)*, Lilian Hall Davis *(Alice Darvil)*, Hubert Gordon Hopkirk *(George Legard)*, Norman Partridge *(Luke Darvil)*, George Bellamy *(Mr. Merton)*, Florence Nelson *(Mrs. Merton)*, Ernest A. Douglas *(Lord Vargrave)*, Stella Wood-Sims *(Evelyn)*, N. Watts-Phillips *(Waters)*.

In this contemporary British drama a young woman saves the life of a wealthy man from her murderous father. Later, after having a child and escaping from a cruel marriage which has been forced upon her, she meets the man again.

d, Jack Denton; w, Eliot Stannard (based on the novel by Lord Lytton).

Drama **(PR:A MPAA:NR)**

ERSTWHILE SUSAN** (1919) 6 reels REA bw

Constance Binney, Jere Austin, Alfred Hickman, Mary Alden, Anders Randolf, George Renavent, Leslie Hunt, Bradley Barker, Clara Verdera.

This curious little film, which portrayed the Pennsylvania Dutch as cruel exploiters of their women folk, depicts the daughter of one such family being liberated from this fate by a stepmother (with money in her own name) who sends the girl off to school.

d, John S. Robertson; w, Kathryn Stuart (based on the novel *Barnabetta* by Helen R. Martin and the play by Marian De Forest); ph, Roy Overbaugh.

Drama **(PR:A MPAA:NR)**

ESCAPE, THE* (1914) 7 reels Reliance-Majestic/MUT bw

Blanche Sweet *(Mae Joyce)*, Mae Marsh *(Jennie Joyce)*, Robert Harron *(Larry Joyce)*, Donald Crisp *("Bull" McGee)*, Owen Moore *(Dr. von Eiden)*, Fred A. Turner *(Jim Joyce)*, Ralph Lewis *(The Senator)*, "Tammany" Young *(McGee's Henchman)*, Lillian Gish.

Griffith's unpleasant examination of eugenics, as reflected by a family of the slums, has one character selling his wife into a life of prostitution and drunkenly crushing his baby to death. We also witness the strangling of a kitten for the fun of it, plus death by consumption and common-law promiscuity. Yet, somehow the master (in what was obviously *not* his greatest effort) managed to come up with a happy ending.

d, D.W. Griffith; w, (based on a play by Paul Armstrong); ph, G. W. Bitzer; ed, James Smith, Rose Ritchel.

Drama **(PR:C MPAA:NR)**

ESCAPE, THE** (1928) 6 reels FOX bw

William Russell *(Jerry Magee)*, Virginia Valli *(May Joyce)*, Nancy Drexel *(Jennie Joyce)*, George Meeker *(Dr. Don Elliott)*, William Demarest *(Trigger Caswell)*, James Gordon *(Jim Joyce)*.

Russell is a medical intern who loves Valli, the daughter of a bootlegger. When her father is killed, Valli goes to work at a nighclub. Russell is later fired, begins to drink to excess, and becomes a bootlegger himself. One night he delivers a shipment to the club, where he sees Valli. The two escape together, just before the place is raided.

d, Richard Rosson; w, Paul Schofield (based on a play by Paul Armstrong); t, Garrett Graham; ed, J. Logan Pearson, Edwin Robbins.

Crime **(PR:A MPAA:NR)**

ESMERALDA** (1915) 4 reels FP bw

Mary Pickford *(Esmeralda)*, Ida Waterman *(Her Mother)*, Fuller Mellish *(Her Father)*, Arthur Hoops *(Count de Montessin)*, William Buckley *(William Estabrook)*, Charles Waldron *(David Hardy)*.

This short feature—about a poor country girl who moves away from her farm and the boy she loves when precious ore is discovered on her parents' land—was not one of Pickford's better films. It had an incomplete, rushed look about it which, quite likely, was the case as Paramount wanted its top star to open the season. One of the last scenes, however, where she spots her sweetheart in the crowd as she prepares to enter into an arranged marriage, contains plenty of the Pickford magic.

d, James Kirkwood; w, Frances Marion (based on the novel by Frances Hodgson Burnett).

Drama **(PR:A MPAA:NR)**

ETERNAL CITY, THE*** (1915) 8 reels FP bw

Pauline Frederick, Thomas Holding, Kittens Reickert, Frank Losee, Arthur Oppenheim, Fuller Mellish, Jiquel Lanoe, George Majeroni, John Culow, J. Albert Hall, Macey Harlan.

Shot in Italy, this film dealing with political unrest was greatly enhanced by its locations. There was also a fine performance by Broadway star Frederick and some impressively staged mob scenes.

d&w, Edwin S. Porter, Hugh Ford (based on the novel by Hall Caine); ph, Porter.

Drama **(PR:A MPAA:NR)**

ETERNAL GRIND, THE* (1916) reels undetermined FP bw

Mary Pickford *(Mary)*, Lorette Blake *(Amy)*, Dorothy West *(Jane)*, John Bokers *(Owen)*, Robert Cain *(Ernest)*, J. A. Hall *(James Wharton)*.

At this time in her career, Pickford—the world's leading motion picture star—was publicly expressing dissatisfaction with the scripts Famous Players was providing her. This dreadful potboiler, about a girl who challenges the conditions of her sweatshop, marries the boss' son, saves her two sisters (one a prostitute, the other consumptive), and transforms the old capitalist shopowner into a thoughful human being, was certainly one of those.

d, John B. O'Brien; w, William H. Clifford.

Drama **(PR:A MPAA:NR)**

ETERNAL LOVE* (1917) 5 reels Butterfly/UNIV bw

Douglas Gerrard *(Paul Dechellette)*, George Gebhart *(Cou-Cou)*, Edward Clark *(Francois Gautier)*, Dan Duffy *(M. Blanc)*, Ruth Clifford *(Mignon)*, Miss Marvin *(Mme. Blanc)*, Myrtle Reeves *(Mimi)*.

In this first Butterfly production for Universal, an artist in Britanny paints a pretty local girl and they fall in love. He departs for Paris, vows to return for her, but becomes involved in the fast life and breaks his word. The girl goes to Paris, finds him dying, and nurses him back to health, thus providing a happy ending for an otherwise very sad motion picture.

d, Douglas Gerrard; w, E. M. Ingleton (based on her own story); ph, Jack Mackenzie.

Drama **(PR:A MPAA:NR)**

ETERNAL LOVE*** (1929) 9 reels Feature/UA bw

John Barrymore *(Marcus Paltram)*, Camilla Horn *(Ciglia)*, Victor Varconi *(Lorenz Gruber)*, Hobart Bosworth *(Rev. Tass)*, Bodil Rosing *(Housekeeper)*, Mona Rico *(Pia)*, Evelyn Selbie *(Pia's Mother)*.

Lubitsch's last silent film is a soggy one set against the Swiss Alps and tells of two lovers who, after enduring many trials, find happiness by committing mutual suicide. In spite of the presence of Barrymore, Horn, and director Lubitsch, this film was somewhat a disappointment. It lost money at the box office for producer Joseph Schenck and part of the reason was the cost of Barrymore's presence—he agreed to make the film for $150,000 and a bonus on profits.

p, Joseph Schenck; d, Ernst Lubitsch; w, Hans Kraly (based on the novel *Der Konig der Bernina* by Jakob Christoph Beer); t, Katherine Hilliker, H. H. Caldwell; ph, Oliver Marsh; m, Hugo Riesenfeld; ed, Andrew Marton; set d&cos, Walter Reimann; syn sc; s eff.

Drama **(PR:A MPAA:NR)**

ETERNAL MAGDALENE, THE** (1919) 5 reels Goldwyn bw

Charles Dalton *(Elijah Bradshaw)*, Margaret Marsh *(Elizabeth)*, Charles Trowbridge *(Paul)*, Donald Gallaher *(Macy)*, Maude Cooling *(Mrs. Bradshaw)*, Vernon Steele *(The Preacher)*, Maxine Elliot *(The Eternal Magdalene)*.

Dalton, a rural banker with an obsession for reform, brings a famous evangelist to town and begins his crusade. After becoming suspicious that his daughter is seeing one of his clerks, he drives her out of his house. Then he has a dream in which he sees his daughter giving birth out of wedlock, becoming a woman of the night, and his son being arrested for the murder of her seducer. He awakens eager to forgive and is delighted to discover that his daughter and the clerk were secretly married.

d, Arthur Hopkins; w, (based on the play by Robert H. McLaughlin); ph, Phil Rosen.

Drama **(PR:A MPAA:NR)**

ETERNAL SAPHO, THE** (1916) 5 reels FOX bw

Theda Bara *(Laura Grubbins)*, James Cooley *(Billy Malvin)*, Walter Lewis *(Mr. Marvin, Sr.)*, Harriet Delaro *(Mrs. Marvin, Sr.)*, Einar Linden *(John Drummond)*, Mary Martin *(Mrs. Drummond)*, Kittens Reichert *(Their Child)*, George Macquarrie *(Jack McCullough)*, Warner Oland *(H. Coudal)*, Frank Norcross *(Grubbins)*, Caroline Harris *(Mother Grubbins)*.

Produced at the height of Bara's popularity, Fox could not fail commercially by pairing her (the world's foremost vamp) with Sappho, one of the world's greatest lyric poets, who was the leader of a group of Greek girls who loved music and poetry and probably Aphrodite, the Greek goddess of erotic love. However, the only thing this version had in common with Daudet's then-popular book, was the stair-climbing scene.

d, Bertram Bracken; w, Mary Murillo (based on the novel *Sapho* by Alphonse Daudet).

Drama **(PR:A MPAA:NR)**

ETERNAL SIN, THE* 1/2** (1917) 7 reels Brenon/SELZ bw

Florence Reed *(Lucretia Borgia)*, William E. Shay *(The Duke of Ferrara, Her Husband)*, Stephen Grattan *(Her Brother)*, Richard Barthelmess *(Gennaro, a Young Officer)*, Alexander Shannon *(Rustighello, the Duke's Guard)*, A. G. Parker *(Maffio)*, M. J. Briggs *(Astopio)*, Edward Thorne *(Jeppo)*, Elmer Patterson *(Liveretto)*, Anthony Merlo *(Petrucci)*, William Welsh *(Gubetta, the Duchess' Confidant)*, Henry Armetta *(The Jester)*, Juliet Brenon *(Bianca, a Maid of Honor)*, Jane Fearnley *(Pricess Negroni)*, Henrietta Gilbert *(Flametta, Fisher Maid)*.

Selznick spared no expense and Brenon (one of Griffith's true rivals) directed a remarkable film dealing with the life and death of mass murderer Lucretia Borgia. With its spectacularly beautiful costumes and sets, this picture delighted and shocked its audiences.

d, Herbert Brenon; w, George Edwardes-Hall, Brenon (based on the play "Lucretia Borgia" by Victor Hugo); ph, J. Roy Hunt.

Crime Drama **(PR:C MPAA:NR)**

ETERNAL STRUGGLE, THE*** (1923) 8 reels Metro bw

Renee Adoree *(Andree Gränge)*, Earle Williams *(Sgt. Neil Tempest)*, Barbara La Marr *(Camille Lenoir)*, Pat O'Malley *(Bucky O'Hara)*, Wallace Beery *(Barode Dukane)*, Josef Swickard *(Pierre Grange)*, Pat Harmon *(Oily Kirby)*, Anders Randolf *(Capt. Jack Scott)*, Edward J. Brady *(Jean Cardeau)*, Robert Anderson *(Olaf Olafson)*, George Kuwa *(Wo Long)*.

A couple of Mounties are in love with the cafe owner's daughter. Believing she killed the man who tried to rape her, the girl flees to northern Canada. The officers follow; one to help her escape, the other to bring her in. She is captured, exonerated, and the movie ends with a twist. It turns out that the man she marries is actually the one with the sense of duty.

p, Louis B. Mayer; d, Reginald Barker; w, Monte M. Katterjohn, J. G. Hawks (based on "The Law-Bringers" by G. B. Lancaster); ph, Percy Hilburn; ed, Robert J. Kern.

Adventure **(PR:A MPAA:NR)**

ETERNAL TEMPTRESS, THE*** (1917) 5 reels PAR bw

Lina Cavalieri *(Princess Cordelia Sanzio)*, Mildred Counselman *(Angela)*, Elliot Dexter *(Harry Althrop)*, Allen Hale *(Count Rudolph Frizi)*, Edward Fielding *(Prince Estezary)*, Hallen Mostyn *(Col. Althrop)*, James Laffey *(Ambassador Lawton)*, Pierre De Matteis, Peter Barbier.

Italian opera star Cavalieri made her motion picture debut in this handsomely mounted Paramount production about a temptress who uses her power over a U.S. diplomat stationed in Italy to deliver secret information to Austrian agents. He is saved from ruin, however, when she realizes she actually loves him and stops the transaction.

d, Emile Chautard; w, Eve Unsell (based on a story by Mme. Fred de Gressac).

Spy Drama **(PR:A MPAA:NR)**

ETERNAL THREE, THE** (1923) 7 reels Goldwyn bw

Hobart Bosworth *(Dr. Frank R. Walters)*, Claire Windsor *(Mrs. Walters)*, Raymond Griffith *(Leonard Foster)*, Bessie Love *(Hilda Gray)*, George Cooper *(Bob Gray)*, Tom Gallery *(Tommy Tucker)*, Helen Lynch *(Miriam Barnes)*, Alec Francis *(Dr. Steven Browning)*, William Orlamond *(Hacienda Owner)*, Charles West *(The Butler)*, Maryon Aye *(Maid)*, William Norris *(Old Roue)*, James F. Fulton *(The Governor)*, Irene Hunt *(The Governor's Wife)*, Peaches Jackson *(The Governor's Child)*, Victory Bateman *(Mrs. Tucker)*, Billie Bennett *(Mrs. Bateman's Friend)*, Lillian Leighton *(Housekeeper)*.

Only Neilan's directorial genius could have made something of this tired story about a neglected doctor's wife who is tempted to have an affair with her husband's adopted son. The boy, however, has an accident (after seducing his foster father's secretary) and the doctor saves his life. Once recovered, the young man is punished by being sent to Europe, and the husband begs his wife to forgive his former indifference.

d, Marshall Neilan, Frank Urson; w, Carey Wilson (based on a story by Neilan); ph, David Kesson.

Drama **(PR:A MPAA:NR)**

ETERNAL WOMAN, THE** (1929) 6 reels COL bw

Olive Borden *(Anita)*, Ralph Graves *(Hartley Forbes)*, Ruth Clifford *(Doris Forbes)*, John Miljan *(Gil Martin)*, Nina Quartaro *(Consuelo)*, Josef Swickard *(Ovaldo)*, Julia Swayne Gordon *(Mrs. Forbes)*.

After saving a young American in a shipwreck, Borden, an Argentine stowaway, falls in love with him. Sometime later, she is mistakenly led to believe that he is the man who murdered her father. She sets out to kill him but discovers the truth in time, and the real killer is brought to justice.

p, Harry Cohn; d, John P. McCarthy; w, Wellyn Totman; ph, Joseph Walker; ed, Ben Pivar; art d, Harrison Wiley.

Drama **(PR:A MPAA:NR)**

EUGENE ARAM*** (1914, Brit.) 5 reels Cricks bw

Jack Leigh *(Eugene Aram)*, Mary Manners *(Madeleine Lester)*, John Sargent *(Richard Houseman)*, Stewart Patterson *(Walter Lester)*, Wingold Lawrence *(Geoffrey Lester)*, Antonia Reith *(Elinor Lester)*, Frank Melrose *(Rowland Lester)*, Lionel d'Aragon *(The Judge)*, Henry Foster *(Cpl. Bunting)*, Harold Snell *(Mr. Courtland)*, Fred Southern *(Peter Dealtry)*.

This early English feature, set in the 18th Century, tells of a scholar who was executed for a crime he did not commit.

d&w, Edwin J. Collins (based on the novel by Edward Bulwer Lytton).

Crime **(PR:A MPAA:NR)**

EUGENE ARAM* 1/2** (1915) 4 reels Edison bw

Marc MacDermott *(Eugene Aram)*, Mabel Trunnelle, Edward Earle, Bigelow Cooper, Gladys Hulette, Herbert Prior, George Wright.

Desperately poor MacDermott conspires to murder a wealthy man. However, when he arrives on the scene, the deed has already been done. MacDermott later inherits some money and is about to be married when the son of the victim appears and accuses him—on the strength of information given him by the real killer. MacDermott is tried and convicted, and after his fiancee dies (due to the shocking turn of events) he gladly goes to the gallows.

d&w, Richard Ridgeley (based on the novel by Edward Bulwer Lytton).

Drama **(PR:A MPAA:NR)**

EVANGELINE*** (1929) 9 reels Edwin Carewe/UA bw

Dolores Del Rio *(Evangeline)*, Roland Drew *(Gabriel)*, Alec B. Francis *(Father Felician)*, Donald Reed *(Baptiste)*, Paul McAllister *(Benedict Bellefontaine)*, James Marcus *(Basil)*, George Marion, Sr. *(Rene La Blanc)*, Bobby Mack *(Michael)*, Lou Payne *(Governor-General)*, Lee Shumway *(Col. Winslow)*.

Lovely filmed version of the Longfellow poem about an Acadian woman's struggle in the New World, her search for her lost love, and her sad fulfillment as a Sister of Mercy when she finds him dying in an epidemic in Philadelphia, after which, she, too, dies, and they are buried together.

d, Edwin Carewe; w&t, Finis Fox (based on the poem by Henry Wadsworth Longfellow); ph, Robert B. Kurrle, Al M. Green; m, Hugo Riesenfeld; ed, Jeanne Spencer; syn sc; s eff.

Drama **(PR:A MPAA:NR)**

EVEN AS YOU AND I (1917) 7 reels UNIV bw

Ben Wilson *(Carrillo)*, Mignon Anderson *(Selma)*, Bertram Grassby *(An Artist)*, Priscilla Dean *(His Wife)*, Harry Carter *(Saturniska)*, Maud George *(Cleo, a Harpy)*.

In this interesting Lois Weber morality film, the Devil fails to snare Wilson and Anderson through poverty, lust, and suspicion, because they are protected by honor, love, and youth. Finally, drink becomes his successful tool, and they are nearly ruined. But loyalty saves them in the end, and they begin life anew with less honor, youth and love—but more wisdom and experience.

d, Lois Weber; w, Maude Grange (based on a story by Willis Woods).

Drama **(PR:A MPAA:NR)**

EVENING CLOTHES*** (1927) 7 reels FP/PAR bw

Adolphe Menjou *(Lucien D'Artois)*, Virginia Valli *(Germaine)*, Noah Beery *(Lazarre)*, Louise Brooks *(Fox Trot)*, Lido Manetti *(Henri)*, Andre Cheron *(Germaine's Father)*.

When his wife leaves him because she is bored with country life, a wealthy French farmer moves to the city, studies the social graces, and tries to win her back. Finally, after bankrupting himself by living the high life and finding himself with only a set of evening clothes to his name, he returns to his apartment where his wife is waiting for him.

d, Luther Reed; w, John McDermott (based on a play by Andre Picard, Yves Mirande); t, George Marion, Jr.; ph; Hal Rosson; ed, Eda Warren.

Drama **(PR:A MPAA:NR)**

EVERY MAN'S WIFE* (1925) 5 reels FOX bw

Elaine Hammerstein *(Mrs. Randolph)*, Herbert Rawlinson *(Mr. Randolph)*, Robert Cain *(Mr. Bradin)*, Diana Miller *(Emily)*, Dorothy Phillips *(Mrs. Bradin)*.

Weak programmer about a jealous woman whose obsessive behavior drives her husband from her home. In the end, however, she realizes the foolishness of her ways and is reunited with him.

d, Maurice Elvey; w, Lillie Hayward (based on a story by Ethel Hill, Enid Hibbard).

Drama **(PR:A MPAA:NR)**

EVERY MOTHER'S SON** (1926, Brit.) 8 reels BRIT bw

Rex Davis *(David Brent)*, Frederick Cooper *(Tony Browning)*, Jean Jay *(Janet Shaw)*, Moore Marriott *(Nobby)*, Alf Goodard *(Bully)*, Haddon Mason *(Jonathan Brent)*, Gladys Mamer *(Minnie)*, Johnny Butt *(Tricky)*, Hubert Harben *(Sir Alfred Browning)*, Leal Douglas *(Lady Browning)*.

This English film, set against the background of WW I, tells of an Army veteran who becomes a tramp and marries his former love, in spite of the fact that she had a baby by the dead son of a squire.

p, F. J. Nettlefold; d, Robert J. Cullen; w, Lydia Hayward (based on a story by G. B. Samuelson, Harry Engholm).

War **(PR:C MPAA:NR)**

EVERY WOMAN'S PROBLEM** (1921) 5 reels Plymouth Pictures bw

Dorothy Davenport *(Clara Madison)*, Willis Robards *(Grant Williams)*, Maclyn King *("Big Bill" Deavitt)*, Wilson Du Bois *(Dan Channing)*.

After Davenport is elected to a judgeship on the feminist ticket, a sensationalist newspaper smears her to such an extent that her husband threatens the life of its editor. A gang of bootleggers, who are also targets of the paper's wrath, retaliate by bombing the paper and killing the editor. The husband is convicted of the crime on circumstantial evidence, and after Davenport is elected governor she must decide whether to grant him a pardon or allow the wheels of justice to run their course. She decides in favor of the wheels, but fortunately one of the bootleggers confesses the truth.

d, Willis Robards; w, J. F. Natteford (based on a story by Hal Reid); ed, Martin G. Cohn.

Drama **(PR:A MPAA:NR)**

EVERYBODY'S GIRL*** (1918) 5 reels VIT bw

Alice Joyce *(Florence)*, May Hopkins *(Ella)*, Walter McGrail *(Blinker)*, Percy Standing *(Bill)*, William Carleton *(Oldport)*, Victor Stewart *(Blinker's Servant)*, Bernard Siegel *(Shopkeeper)*.

Joyce and Hopkins are working girls who share an apartment on "Brick Dust Row," a tenement area. Being attractive, they meet any number of men and allow themselves to do so because they can always spot the "fresh" ones. While on their way to Coney Island one day, they meet McGrail, a millionaire who falls for Joyce.

Being a decent girl, she is put off by his money, but after he becomes a hero in a boat accident, she decides to accept his proposal of marriage.

d, Tom Terriss; w, A. Van Buren Powell (based on the story "Brick Dust Row" by O. Henry); ph, Robert Stuart.

Comedy/Drama (PR:A MPAA:NR)

EVERYBODY'S SWEETHEART ** (1920) 5 reels SEL/SF bw

Olive Thomas *(Mary)*, William Collier, Jr. *(John)*, Joseph Dowling *(The General)*, Aileen Manning *(Mrs. Willing)*, Martha Mattox *(Miss Blodgett)*, Hal Wilson *(The Corporal)*, Bob Hick *(Mr. Willing)*.

A boy and girl survive a train wreck and are sent to the poorhouse where they are treated badly. They escape and make their way to the home of a wealthy old man, who takes them in and treats them like his own children. As fate would have it, the boy turns out to be his long lost grandson. This was Thomas' last film before her tragic suicide in Paris, and the title, which bore no relation to the story line, was no doubt added to commercialize on that happening.

d, Alan Crossland; w, (based on a story by John Lynch); ph, Robert Newhard.

Drama (PR:A MPAA:NR)

EVERYMAN'S PRICE* (1921) 5 reels J. W. Film bw

Grace Darling *(Ethel Armstrong)*, E. J. Radcliffe *(Henry Armstrong)*, Charles Waldron *(Bruce Steele)*, Bud Geary *(Jim Steele)*.

Very boring business about a district attorney, Waldron, who sets out to prosecute food profiteers. His investigators determine that Waldron's future father-in-law is involved, which causes his fiancee to break their engagement. By the film's end, Waldron clears the old boy for lack of evidence, and the wedding goes on as scheduled.

d, Burton King; w, F. McGrew Willis; ph, L. D. Littlefield.

Drama (PR:A MPAA:NR)

EVE'S DAUGHTER, 1916, Brit. (SEE: LOVE, 1916, Brit.)

EVE'S DAUGHTER* (1918) 5 reels PAR bw

Billie Burke *(Irene Simpson-Bates)*, Thomas Meighan *(John Norton)*, Lionel Atwill *(Courtenay Urquhart)*, William Riley Hatch *(Marinn Simpson-Bates)*, Rose Tapley, Eulalie Jensen, Rex Hitchcock.

When an attractive young girl is left only $15,000 by her millionaire father, she goes to New York where she shortly meets two men who claim to love her. The one she selects takes her to Boston, but before long she discovers that he has no intention of marrying her. At this point, she leaves him flat and accepts the proposal of the other fellow, a decent sort.

d, James Kirkwood; w, Margaret Turnbull (based on a play by Alicia Ramsey); ph, L. E. Williams.

Drama (PR:A MPAA:NR)

EVE'S LOVER** (1925) 7 reels WB bw

Irene Rich *(Eve Burnside)*, Bert Lytell *(Count Leon Molnar)*, Clara Bow *(Rena D'Arcy)*, Willard Louis *(Austin Starfield)*, John Steppling *(Burton Gregg)*, Arthur Hoyt *(Amos Potts)*, Lew Harvey *(Agitator)*.

Rich is a career woman who owns a steel mill. Louis, her crooked competitor, arranges for an impoverished count to marry her so that he can gain control through a merger. The count, however, falls in love with Rich after he marries her and backs out of the deal. To get even, Louis brings in a flapper (Bow) who informs Rich of her husband's plot. Rich severs her relationship with the count, but welcomes him back with open arms after he steps in and thwarts a strike which was fomented by Louis.

d, Roy Del Ruth; w, Darryl Francis Zanuck (based on a story by W. K. Clifford); ph, George Winkler.

Drama (PR:A MPAA:NR)

EVE'S SECRET** (1925) 6 reels FP/PAR bw

Betty Compson *(Eve)*, Jack Holt *(The Duke of Poltava)*, William Collier, Jr. *(Pierre)*, Vera Lewis *(Duchess)*, Lionel Belmore *(Baron)*, Mario Carillo *(Prince Boris)*.

The Duke of Poltava (Holt) sends a peasant girl (Compson) to Paris where she is groomed to be his duchess. On her return, they go to the Riviera where Compson's beauty and charm attract men, which makes the Duke insanely jealous. A peasant boy from her province arrives to gamble his small inheritance and, after an innocent tryst, Holt challenges him to a duel. The nobleman is slightly wounded on the field of honor, and it is then that Compson realizes she truly loves him.

d, Clarence Badger; w, Adelaide Heilbron (based on *The Moon-Flower* by Zoe Atkins, Lajos Biro); ph, H. Kinley Martin.

Comedy/Drama (PR:A MPAA:NR)

EVIDENCE*** (1915) 5 reels Shubert/WORLD bw

Edwin August *(Lord Winborne)*, Lillian Tucker *(Lady Winborne)*, Haidee Wright, Florence Hackett, Richard Temple, Lionel Pape, Richard Buhler, Morris Walcot Stewart, Jr.

Lord and Lady Winborne (August and Tucker) are a happily married British couple who have a son. Then one night at a party, a drunken captain makes a pass at Tucker on the veranda. Her husband spots this from a distance, but after rushing to her assistance is told by the captain that she encouraged the encounter. The next day, the sober and repentant officer calls to apologize, but August, who believes the accusation, refuses to talk to him. Some time later, a mutual friend arranges a meeting, but August rejects a reconciliation and insults the captain. The angry captain writes a note to Tucker, saying that her husband has been injured and that she should go to the Red Lion Inn at once. This she does, but her husband also reads part of the message and rushes to the inn himself. As he attempts to break down the door, the captain burns the letter, leaving no evidence which Tucker can use to explain her presence in the captain's room. Her husband divorces her and their child is placed in his custody, and the mother is ordered never to see her boy again. Five years later, a family friend who learns the captain is dying in India, goes there and obtains a deathbed confession. Meanwhile, Tucker sees her boy riding in the park, can no longer stand the separation, and kidnaps him. The picture ends with the couple patching up their differences and somehow regaining the contentment they once enjoyed in the days when the double standard was never, ever challenged.

d&w, Edwin August (based on a play by J. L. DuRocher Macphearson).

Drama (PR:A MPAA:NR)

EVIDENCE* (1918) 5 reels TRI bw (AKA: THE ARGUMENT)

Audelle Higgins *(Mrs. John Corbin)*, J. Barney Sherry *(John Corbin)*, Howard Davis *(Dr. Richard Hyde)*, Pauline Starke *(Wyliss Hyde)*, Eugene Corey *(John Corbin, Jr.)*, Edwin Jobson *(Chief Fenton)*, George Chase.

A prominent lawyer formulates a theory that a man can murder his wife and convince any jury in the world that he is innocent by means of insanity. He shares the idea with a prominent doctor-friend who, on arriving home, is shocked to see a man climb out of his wife's bedroom window. The doctor, believing her unfaithful, stabs her to death and puts his formula to work. At this point, what could have become an interesting film fizzles out, with the attorney getting off, his son by a former marriage telling his fiancee (the doctor's daughter) he thinks their wedding should be postponed, and the doctor insisting that the ceremony take place on schedule.

d, Walter Edwards; w, Jack Cunningham; ph, C. G. Peterson.

Crime (PR:A MPAA:NR)

EVIL THAT MEN DO, THE
(SEE: LITTLE DOOR INTO THE WORLD, THE, 1923, Brit.)

EXALTED FLAPPER, THE*** (1929) 6 reels FOX bw

Sue Carol *(Princess Izola)*, Barry Norton *(Prince Boris of Dacia)*, Irene Rich *(Queen Charlotte of Capra)*, Albert Conti *(King Alexander of Capra)*, Sylvia Field *(Marjorie)*, Stuart Erwin *(Bimbo Mehaffey)*, Lawrence Grant *(Premier Vadisco of Dacia)*, Charles Clary *(Dr. Nicholas)*, Michael Visaroff *(Old Fritz)*.

Carol is charming as the flapper princess who refuses to marry Norton, a prince she has never seen. They meet later, while he is traveling incognito, and fall in love. Her mother the queen, not knowing who he is, has Norton abducted, but the princess rescues him. Of course the lovers and their kingdoms live happily ever after.

d, James Tinling; sup, Kenneth Hawks; w, Matt Taylor (based on a story by Will Irwin); t, H. H. Caldwell; ph, Charles Clarke; m, Arthur Kay; ed, Caldwell; syn sc.

Comedy/Romance (PR:A MPAA:NR)

EXCESS BAGGAGE*** (1928) 8 reels MGM bw

William Haines *(Eddie Kane)*, Josephine Dunn *(Elsa McCoy)*, Neely Edwards *(Jimmy Dunn)*, Kathleen Clifford *(Mabel Ford)*, Greta Granstedt *(Betty Ford)*, Ricardo Cortez *(Val D'Errico)*, Cyril Chadwick *(Crammon)*.

Haines, a vaudeville acrobat, falls in love with and marries dancer Dunn. She then enters the movies and becomes a success, while her husband continues to play the small time. After a while, he begins to suspect Dunn of having an affair with movie star Cortez. They separate, and shortly thereafter Haines falls from the high wire and loses his nerve. The picture ends with him on stage in a comeback, unable to perform until he sees Dunn, who has returned to cheer him on and prove her love.

d, James Cruze; w, Frances Marion, Ralph Spence (based on the play by John Wesley McGowan); t, Spence; ph, Ira Morgan; ed, George Hively; set d, Cedric Gibbons.

Drama (PR:A MPAA:NR)

EXCITEMENT*** (1924) 5 reels UNIV bw

Laura La Plante *(Nila Lyons)*, Edward Hearne *(Arthur Drew)*, William Welsh *(Hiram Lyons)*, Frances Raymond *(Mrs. Lyons)*, Fred De Silva *(Eric Orton)*, Margaret Cullington *(Violet Smith)*, Albert Hart *(Abner Smith)*, Rolfe Sedan *(Willie Winkle)*, Bert Roach *(Toby)*, Stanley Blystone *(Freddie)*, Lon Poff *(Roger Cove)*, George Fisher *(Chester Robbins)*, Fay Tincher *("Mammy")*.

After being abducted, stuffed into a mummy container, and delivered to a maniacal Egyptian who intends to return her to her tomb, La Plant's husband (Hearne) arrives in the nick of time. It is then that he tells her it was all a gag to get her over her craving for excitement.

d, Robert F. Hill; w, Hugh Hoffman; w, Crosby George; ph, Jack Rose.

Comedy (PR:A MPAA:NR)

EXCITERS, THE*** (1923) 6 reels FP bw

Bebe Daniels *(Ronnie Rand)*, Antonio Moreno *(Pierre Martel)*, Burr McIntosh *(Rackham, the Lawyer)*, Diana Allen *(Ermintrude)*, Cyril Ring *(Roger Patton)*, Bigelow Cooper *(Hilary Rand)*, Ida Darling *(Mrs. Rand)*, Jane Thomas *(Della Vaughn)*, Allan Simpson *(The Mechanician)*, George Backus *(The Minister)*, Henry Sedley *("Gentleman Eddie")*, Erville Alderson *("Chloroform Charlie")*, Tom Blake *("Flash")*.

Daniels gave her usual appealing performance in her portrayal of a thrill-seeking socialite flapper who is compelled to marry before turning 21 in order to earn her inheritance. She is impressed by Moreno, a gangster, falls in love, and they marry.

In the end it turns out that her husband is really an undercover agent, but Daniels accepts him anyway.

d, Maurice Campbell; w, John Colton, Sonya Levien (based on the novel by Martin Brown); ph, George Webber.

Comedy/Crime **(PR:A MPAA:NR)**

EXCUSE MY DUST*** (1920) 5 reels PAR bw

Wallace Reid *("Toodles" Walden)*, Tully Marshall *(President Muchier)*, Theodore Roberts *(J. D. Ward)*, Ann Little *(Dorothy Walden)*, Guy Oliver *(Darby)*, Otto Brower *(Henderson)*, Walter Long *(Ritz)*, Jack Herbert *(Oldham)*, Fred Huntley *(Magistrate)*.

Reid, the head of an auto company's West Coast office and a crackerjack racing driver, is married and has a little boy. His wife and her father (the president of the company) want him to quit racing, so they arrange with a judge to have his license suspended until after the big competition is over. On a bet, however, Reid takes one of his cars out, which causes his wife to leave him. The film's exciting climax comes when Reid and his father-in-law take the place of their two drivers (who have met with foul play at the hands of their competitors) and win the race. The little woman, of course, is at the finish line when their cars rush across, and all is forgiven.

d, Sam Wood; w, Will M. Ritchey (based on the story "The Bear Trap" by Byron Morgan); ph, Alfred Gilks.

Adventure **(PR:A MPAA:NR)**

EXILES, THE*** (1923) 5 reels FOX bw

John Gilbert *(Henry Halcombe)*, Betty Bouton *(Alice Carroll)*, John Webb Dillon *(Wilheim von Linke)*, Margaret Fielding *(Rose Ainsmith)*, Fred Warren *(Dr. Randolph)*.

Gilbert was on the way to superstardom as he played a district attorney who convicts an innocent girl of murder. She escapes to Tangiers and is abducted by the owner of a gambling den. After Gilbert discovers her innocence, he goes after her, executes a successful rescue, and brings her home to be his wife.

d, Edmund Mortimer; w, Fred Jackson, John Russell (based on a story by Richard Harding Davis).

Adventure **(PR:A MPAA:NR)**

EXIT SMILING*** 1/2** (1926) 7 reels MGM bw

Beatrice Lillie *(Violet)*, Jack Pickford *(Jimmy Marsh)*, Doris Lloyd *(Olga)*, De Witt Jennings *(Orlando Wainwright)*, Harry Myers *(Jesse Watson)*, Tenen Holtz *(Tod Powell)*, Louise Lorraine *(Phyllis Tichnor)*, Franklin Pangborn *(Cecil Lovelace)*, D'Arcy Corrigan *(Macomber)*, William Gillespie *(Jack Hastings)*, Carl Richards *(Dave)*.

British comedy star Lillie, in her U.S. screen debut, provides a wonderful blend of comedy and pathos as she portrays the wardrobe lady and utility person for a traveling theatrical company. She arranges for young Pickford, who has been wrongly accused of a crime, to join the troupe as stage manager and sees him through his crisis. In the end, although she loves him deeply, Lillie clears his name and delivers him to the arms of the girl he loves.

d, Sam Taylor; w, Taylor, Tim Whelan (based on an original story by Marc Connelly); t, Joe Farnham; ph, Andre Barlatier; ed, Daniel J. Gray; set d, Cedric Gibbons, Frederic Hope.

Comedy/Drama **(PR:A MPAA:NR)**

EXIT THE VAMP*** (1921) 5 reels FP bw

Ethel Clayton *(Mrs. Marion Shipley)*, T. Roy Barnes *(John Shipley)*, Fontaine La Rue *(Mrs. Willy Strong)*, Theodore Roberts *(Old Man Shipley)*, William Boyd *(Robert Pitts)*, Mickey Moore *(Junior Shipley)*, Mattie Peters *(Colored Mammy)*.

Barnes, a happily married man, becomes interested in La Rue, the notorious vamp. When he vouches for a jewelry purchase she has made, the salesman alerts his wife, Clayton, who follows them and watches as La Rue slips Barnes her apartment key. Clayton rushes over, gains entrance, and dresses in her rival's clothes. When her husband arrives, the room is dark and they embrace. It is then that Barnes comes to his senses and realizes the depth of his love—much to the chagrin of La Rue, who gets there just a little late.

d, Frank Urson; w, Clara Beranger; ph, Charles Edgar Schoenbaum.

Comedy/Drama **(PR:A MPAA:NR)**

EXPERIMENT, THE*** (1922, Brit.) 5 reels STOLL bw

Evelyn Brent *(Doris Fielding)*, Clive Brook *(Vivian Caryll)*, Templar Powell *(Maj. Maurice Brandon)*, Norma Whalley *(Mrs. Lockyard)*, C. H. Croker-King *(Philip Abingdon)*, Cecil Kerr *(Fricker)*, Laura Walker *(The Nurse)*, Hilda Sims *(Vera Abingdon)*.

U.S. film star Brent (who later enhanced the work of Joseph von Sternberg) and distinguished British actor Brook (who did the same) were fine together in this love story about a wealthy fellow who poses as his fiancee's chauffeur to prevent her from mistakenly running off with an army officer.

d, Sinclair Hill; w, William J. Elliot (based on the novel by Ethel M. Dell).

Drama **(PR:A MPAA:NR)**

EXQUISITE SINNER, THE*** (1926) 6 reels MGM bw

Conrad Nagel *(Dominique Prad)*, Renee Adoree *(The Gypsy Maid)*, Paulette Duval *(Yvonne)*, Frank Currier *(The Colonel)*, George K. Arthur *(His Orderly)*, Matther Betz *(The Gypsy Chief)*, Helena D'Algy, Claire Du Brey *(Dominique's Sisters)*, Myrna Loy *(The Living Statue)*.

Even though he was replaced as director during the shooting, Von Sternberg's first film for MGM, after the stir caused by his SALVATION HUNTERS, remains a visual poem. The story concerns an artistic boy who renounces the practical world of business in favor of a carefree vagabond life. Adoree, as the gypsy maid, was at her most charming.

d, Joseph von Sternberg, Phil Rosen; w, Von Sternberg, Alice D. G. Miller (based on the book *Escape* by Alden Brooks); t, Joe Farnham; ph, Maximilian Fabian; ed, John W. English; art d, Cedric Gibbons, Joseph Wright.

Drama **(PR:A MPAA:NR)**

EXTRA GIRL, THE*** (1923) 7 reels Mack Sennett/AEX bw

Mabel Normand *(Sue Graham)*, Ralph Graves *(Dave Giddings)*, George Nichols *(Pa Graham)*, Anna Hernandez *(Ma Graham)*, Vernon Dent *(Aaron Applejohn)*, Ramsey Wallace *(Phillip Hackett)*, Charlotte Mineau *(Belle Brown)*, Mary Mason, Max Davidson, Louise Carver, William Desmond, Carl Stockdale, Harry Gribbon, Billy Bevan, Andre Beranger.

Normand's career was shattered because of her connection with the sensational William Desmond Taylor case. She had been with the director the day of his murder and, for a time, was even a suspect. It was an era when the mere suggestion of impropriety was cause enough for the "uplifters" (as D. W. Griffith referred to such self-appointed champions of American morality in his earlier masterpiece, INTOLERANCE) to go for the jugular. Mary Miles Minter's career was also destroyed by the incident, but author Sennett happily offered a helping hand to his former sweetheart Normand, and this comic melodrama about a girl's attempt to break into the movies was made. The film is full of thrills and laughs, and the scene where Normand unknowingly leads a lion through the movie lot on a leash is classic. Unfortunately, the cinema's foremost female clown did not enjoy in real life the happy ending her last important picture provided. She died in 1930, at the age of 35, of tuberculosis and drug-related complications.

d, F. Richard Jones; w, Bernard McConville (based on a story by Mack Sennett); ph, Homer Scott, Eric Crockett.

Comedy **Cas.** **(PR:A MPAA:NR)**

EXTRAVAGANCE** (1919) 5 reels PAR bw

Dorothy Dalton *(Helen Douglas)*, Charles Clary *(Alan Douglas)*, J. Barney Sherry *(Hartley Crane)*, Philo MacDonald *(Billy Braden)*, Donald MacDonald *(William Windom)*.

This film explored the theory—which enjoyed popular vogue at the time—that dreams may have a greater effect on one's moral develpment than real experiences. In this picture, Dalton plays a woman of great extravagance who reforms after she dreams that her husband has paid for her self-indulgence with his life.

d, Victor L. Schertzinger; sup, Thomas H. Ince; w, R. Cecil Smith (based on a story by John Lynch); ph, John S. Stumar.

Drama **(PR:A MPAA:NR)**

EYE FOR EYE*** (1918) 7 reels Nazimova/Metro bw

Alla Nazimova *(Hassouna)*, Charles Bryant, Donald Gallagher, Sally Crute, E. L. Fernandez, John Reinhardt, Louis Stern, Charles Eldridge, Hardee Kirkland, Miriam Batista, William T. Carleton, William Cohill, Barry Whitcomb, Anita Brown.

Nazimova was perfectly cast as a Bedouin girl who escapes from the desert, where she was condemned to death for helping a French officer get away. Her rescuers, however, sell her into slavery, and she becomes a dancer in a traveling circus. Eventually she is seen by the officer, and he takes her home to live with himself and his wife. Quite by accident, she discovers his wife making love to another man and angrily throws a knife at them. Her Bedouin code prevents her from revealing the reason for her action and she is sent to a convent to live. After some time, an Arab who covets her informs Nazimova that her entire family has been killed by the officer she has now grown to love. As a means of revenge, she sets out to seduce his young nephew but cannot go through with it. In the end she marries the man she still loves, after his wife is killed in an automobile accident.

d, Albert Capellani; w, June Mathis, Capellani (based on the play "L'Occident" by Henry Kistemaeckers); ph, Eugene Gaudio.

Drama **(PR:A MPAA:NR)**

EYE OF THE NIGHT, THE*** (1916) 5 reels Kay-Bee/TRI bw

William H. Thompson *(David Holden)*, Marjory Wilson *(Jane)*, Thornton Edwards *(Robert Benson)*, J. P. Lockney *(Denby)*, Agnes Herring *(Mrs. Denby)*, Jack [John] Gilbert.

This sentimental tear-jerker, about a kindly old lighthouse keeper's conflict with the narrow-minded residents of an English fishing village, featured a splendid performance by the now all-but-forgotten Thompson. This marked the end of Gilbert's first year in the moving picture business.

d, Walter Edwards; w, C. Gardner Sullivan.

Drama **(PR:A MPAA:NR)**

EYES OF JULIA DEEP, THE** (1918) 5 reels AM bw

Mary Miles Minter *(Julia Deep)*, Alan Forrest *(Terry Hartridge)*, Alice Wilson *(Lottie Driscoll)*, George Periolat *(Timothy Black)*, Ida Easthope *(Mrs. Turner)*, Carl Stockdale *(Simon Plummet)*, Eugenie Besserer *(Mrs. Lowe)*.

Minter, a working girl who has risen to head the exchange desk at a department store, lives in the same boarding house as Forrest, an heir who is squandering the last of his family's fortune. The young man is on the verge of suicide when Minter enters his life and saves him from the deed, winning his love in the process.

d, Lloyd Ingraham; w, Elizabeth Mahoney (based on a story by Kate L. McLaurin).

Drama **(PR:A MPAA:NR)**

EYES OF THE HEART* 1/2** (1920) 5 reels REA bw

Mary Miles Minter *(Laura)*, Edward Burns *(Mike)*, Lucien Littlefield *(Whitey)*, Florence Midgely *(Sal)*, Burton Law *(Simon)*, John Cook *(John Dunn, the Landlord)*, Fred Turner *(Dr. Dewey)*, William E. Parsons *(Dennis Sullivan)*, Loyola O'Connor *(Mrs. Sullivan)*.

Minter delivered a fine performance in this change-of-pace role about a blind girl who regains her sight and discovers the true world is not the utopian paradise she had been led to believe. In fact, she has been protected from reality by three good-hearted crooks determined to spare her from the sordid existence they share. Disillusioned by all of this, she falls under the spell of a big-time gangster who plans to use her fine sense of touch to crack safes. Fortunately, her friends manage to save her in time, and the picture ends on a happy note, with the group living on a ranch out West.

d, Paul Powell; w, Clara Genevieve Kennedy (based on the story "Blindness" by Dana Burnet); ph, William Marshall.

Crime **(PR:A MPAA:NR)**

EYES OF THE UNDERWORLD** (1929) 5 reels UNIV bw

Bill Cody *(Pat Doran)*, Sally Blane *(Florence Hueston)*, Arthur Lubin *(GangLeader)*, Harry Tenbrook *(Gimpy Johnson)*, Charles Clary *(John Hueston)*, Monty Montague *(Gardener)*.

When a newspaper publisher is murdered by gangsters, Cody goes to his house to comfort his grieving daughter Blane. The crooks break in to find incriminating evidence, and Cody traces them to their hideout. He is captured, but manages to escape and quickly brings the killers to justice.

d, Leigh Jason, Ray Taylor; w, Jason, Carl Krusada; t, Val Cleveland; ph, Al Jones, Frank Redman.

Crime **(PR:A MPAA:NR)**

EYES RIGHT** (1926) 5 reels Otto K. Schreier/Goodwill Pictures bw

Francis X. Bushman, Jr. *(Ted Winters)*, Flobelle Fairbanks *(Betty Phillips)*, Dora Dean *(Alice Murdock)*, Larry Kent *(Maj. Snodgrass)*, Frederick Vroom *(Col. Thomas A. Davis)*, Robert Hale *(Lt. Smith)*.

Bushman works in the San Diego Military Academy kitchen because he cannot afford the tuition. One day the commandant sees him playing football and arranges for him to become a cadet. Bushman and Fairbanks, the commandant's niece, fall in love and this angers Kent, a cadet, who then frames Bushman on a drinking charge. The young man is dismissed from the academy, but Fairbanks argues his case so well that he is reinstated just in time to win the big game.

d, Louis Chaudet; w, Leslie Curtis (based on a story by Ernest Grayman); ph, Allen Davey.

Drama **Cas.** **(PR:A MPAA:NR)**

F

FACE AT THE WINDOW, THE** ½ (1920, Brit.) 6 reels BA/Phillips bw

C. Aubrey Smith *(Bentick)*, Gladys Jennings *(Marie de Brisson)*, Jack Hobbs *(Lucien Cartwright)*, Charles Quartermaine *(Lucien Degradoff)*, Ben Field *(Peter Pottlebury)*, Sir Simeon Stuart *(Henri de Brisson)*, Kathleen Vaughn *(Babette)*, Kinsey Peile *(Dr. Le Blanc)*.

Great British character actor Smith gave his usual fine performance in this unusual mystery about a dead detective who is brought back to life with electricity to reveal the identity of a crook.

p, Gerald Malvern; d, Wilfred Noy; w, Adrian Brunel (based on the play by F. Brooke Warren).

Crime **(PR:A MPAA:NR)**

FACTORY MAGDALEN, A* (1914) Sawyer 5 reels bw

Edyth Totten, Rex the Dog.

Jumpy, disconnected, and uninspired melodrama in which only Rex gave a satisfactory performance. It was renaissance woman (stage actress, author, screen writer, and stage producer) Totten's only appearance as an actress in motion pictures.

d, Elwood Bostwick; w, Edyth Totten.

Drama **(PR:A MPAA:NR)**

FAIR CO-ED, THE*** (1927) 7 reels MGM bw

Marian Davies *(Marian)*, Johnny Mack Brown *(Bob Dixon)*, Jane Winton *(Betty)*, Thelma Hill *(Rose)*, Lillian Leighton *(Housekeeper)*, Gene Stone *(Herbert)*.

Davies goes to college in order to play on the basketball team coached by Brown, a man to whom she is attracted. After an argument with him, she fails to show up at one of the big games and her team loses. Sensitive to the scorn her fellow players feel towards her and ashamed of her poor sportsmanship, she not only competes in the next game, but scores the winning goal and captures Brown's heart.

d, Sam Wood; w, Byron Morgan (based on a play by George Ade); t, Joe Farnham; ph, John Seitz; ed, Conrad A. Nervig; art d, Cedric Gibbons, Arnold Gillespie; cos, Gilbert Clark.

Comedy **(PR:A MPAA:NR)**

FAIR ENOUGH*** (1918) 5 reels AM/Pathe bw

Margarita Fisher *(Ann Dickson)*, Eugenie Forde *(Mrs. Ellen Dickson)*, Alfred Hollingsworth *(James Dickson, Esq.)*, Alice Knowland *(Mme. Ohnet)*, Harry McCoy *(Frederick Pierson)*, Jack Mower *(Carey Phelan)*, Bull Montana *("Happy" Flanigan)*.

Entertaining comedy about a newly rich family that manages to buy its way into society. The daughter (who deals exclusively in $100,000 contributions) is the target of a sissyish, fortune-hunting man-about-town, and Montana, a golden-hearted cop has placed the entire department at her disposal. In the end, and after many very funny complications, she marries one of the officers who, to her parents' relief, just happens to be a closet millionaire.

d, Edward Sloman; w, Elizabeth Mahoney (based on a story by J. Anthony Roach).

Comedy **(PR:A MPAA:NR)**

FAIR PLAY** (1925) 5 reels William Steiner bw

Edith Thornton *(Norma Keith)*, Lou Tellegen *(Bruce Elliot)*, Gaston Glass *(Dickie Thane)*, Betty Francisco *(Rita Thane)*, David Dunbar *(Bull Mong)*, Simon Greer *(Charlie Morse)*.

When criminal attorney Tellegen is wrongly convicted of murdering his fortune-hunting wife, Thornton, his devoted secretary (who loves him secretly) infiltrates the underworld and finds the evidence which clears his name.

d, Frank Crane; sup, Charles Hutchinson; w, John Francis Natteford; ph, Ernest Miller.

Crime **(PR:A MPAA:NR)**

FAIR PRETENDER, THE*** (1918) 6 reels Goldwyn bw

Madge Kennedy *(Sylvia Maynard)*, Tom Moore *(Don Meredith)*, Robert Walker *(Harcourt)*, Paul Doucet *(Ramon Gonzales)*, Wilmer Walter *(Capt. Milton Brown)*, Emmett King *(Townsend)*, John Terry *(Freddie)*, Charles Slattery *(Barnum)*, Florence Billings *(Marjorie Townsend)*, Grace Stevens *(Mrs. Townsend)*.

Amusing blend of comedy, romance, and melodrama, as a young man and woman, both posing as millionaires, meet at a big society party. Also on hand is a German spy intent on stealing some secret plans. He is ultimately captured, and the couple fall in love for all of the right reasons.

d, Charles Miller; w, (based on a story by Florence C. Bolles).

Comedy/Spy **(PR:A MPAA:NR)**

FAITH** (1920) 5 reels FOX bw

Peggy Hyland, J. Parks Jones, Edward Hearn, Winter Hall, Edwin B. Tilton, Milla Davenport, Frederick Herzog.

Very likely inspired by the success of THE MIRACLE MAN, this film told of a greatly loved teacher in a Scottish town with the power to cure and keep people well. His son, and the daughter of the community's wealthiest man, are in love, but her father has arranged for her to marry a nobleman. After the girl becomes gravely ill and the old teacher saves her life, however, the father sees the light and allows the young lovers to wed.

d, Howard Mitchell; w, J. Anthony Roach.

Drama **(PR:A MPAA:NR)**

FAITH HEALER, THE* (1921) 7 reels FP/PAR bw

Milton Sills *(Michaelis)*, Ann Forrest *(Rhoda Williams)*, Fontaine La Rue *(Mary Beeler)*, Frederick Vroom *(Matther Beeler)*, Loyola O'Connor *(Martha Beeler)*, Mary Giraci *(Little Annie)*, John Curry *(A Negro, Uncle Abe)*, Adolphe Menjou *(Dr. Littlefield)*, Edward Vroom *(Dr. Sanchez)*, Robert Brower *(Dr. Martin)*, Winifred Greenwood *(A Mother)*.

This blatant ripoff of THE MIRACLE MAN is even more deplorable because of its sanctimonious inclination to preach. The film's single innovation was making a young man the faith healer, and the reason for this was undoubtedly to permit a love interest.

d, George Melford; w, Mrs. William Vaughn Moody, Z. Wall Covington (based on the play by Moody); ph, Harry Perry.

Drama **(PR:A MPAA:NR)**

FAKE, THE*** (1927, Brit.) 9 reels Neo-ART/Williams and Pritchard bw

Henry Edwards *(Geoffrey Sands)*, Elga Brink *(Mavis Stanton)*, Juliette Compton *(Mrs. Hesketh Pointer)*, Norman McKinnel *(Ernest Stanton)*, Miles Mander *(Honorable Gerald Pillick)*, J. Fisher White *(Sir Thomas Moorgate)*, A. Bromley Davenport *(Hesketh Pointer)*, Julie Suedo *(Dancer)*, Ivan Sampson *(Clifford Howe)*, Ursula Jeans *(Maid)*.

In this British drama a member of the Parliament forces his daughter to marry a drug-addicted nobleman, who later dies when the girl's lover attempts to cure him.

p, Julius Hagen; d, George Jacoby; w, George A. Cooper (based on the play by Frederick Lonsdale).

Drama **(PR:C MPAA:NR)**

FALSE BRANDS** (1922) 5 reels WORLD/PFC bw

Joe Moore *(Joe Sullivan)*, Eileen Sedgwick *(Eileen Morgan)*, C. W. Williams *(Sam Morgan)*, Robert Kentman *(Max Schultz)*.

Moore and his college sweetheart, Sedgwick, are separated when she returns home to nurse her ailing father. Later, Moore is dismissed for some pranks and is sent by his father to a ranch as discipline. It turns out that this is the very spread which Sedgwick's father supervised and which all of a sudden is plagued by rustlers. Kentman, the foreman, convinces the neighbors that Moore is the culprit, but in the end the young man destroys the gang and exposes Kentman to be their ringleader.

d, William J. Craft; w, Harry Chandlee, William B. Laub (based on a story by Craft); ph, Joseph Mayer.

Western **(PR:A MPAA:NR)**

FALSE COLORS*** (1914) 5 reels Bosworth bw

Lois Weber, Phillips Smalley, Dixie Carr, Charles Marriott, Courteney Foote.

Good Weber film about a popular actor who quits the stage and moves to an island after his wife dies in childbirth. The infant, a girl, is neglected by the couple who are put in charge of raising her. Some 18 years later, the father returns to beg his daughter's forgiveness, but is rejected. The film does, however, end on a happy note, with the two reunited and the daughter embarking on a successful acting career.

d, Lois Weber; w, Weber, Phillips Smalley.

Drama **(PR:A MPAA:NR)**

FALSE EVIDENCE*** (1919) 5 reels Metro bw

Viola Dana *(Madelon MacTavish)*, Wheeler Oakman *(Burr Gordon)*, Joe King *(Lot Gordon)*, Edward J. Connelly *(Sandy MacTavish)*, Patrick O'Malley *(Richard MacTavish)*, Peggy Pearce *(Dorothy Fair)*, Virginia Ross *(Samanthy Brown)*.

An old Scotsman promises his little girl (Dana) marriage to a wealthy man (King). When the girl grows up, however, she prefers his impoverished cousin Oakman. One night after a dance, King attacks Dana and is stabbed and nearly killed by her. Oakman takes the blame for this and is almost lynched before Dana arrives to save him. She also promises to marry King when he recovers but, fortunately for almost everyone involved, before the ceremony can take place a tree falls on the wealthy cousin, crushing him to death.

d, Edwin Carewe; w, Finis Fox (based on the novel *Madelon* by Mary E. Wilkins); ph, John Arnold.

Drama **(PR:A MPAA:NR)**

FALSE EVIDENCE** (1922, Brit.) 6 reels STOLL bw

Edna Flugrath *(Maud Deveraux)*, Cecil Humphreys *(Rupert Deveraux)*, E. Holman Clark *(Sir Francis Arbuthnot)*, Frank Petley *(Herbert Arbuthnot)*, Eric Lugg *(Hugh Arbuthnot)*, Constance Rayner *(Marian Arbuthnot)*, Teddy Arundell *(Hilton)*, Miss Costello.

In this British drama a man struggles to prove that his father took the blame for his cousin's cowardly behavior during an encounter in a Zulu war.

d, Harold Shaw; w, Frank Miller (based on the novel by E. Phillips Oppenheim).

Drama **(PR:A MPAA:NR)**

FALSE FACES*** (1919) 6 reels ART/PAR bw

Henry B. Walthall *(The Lone Wolf)*, Mary Anderson *(Cecelia Brooks)*, Lon Chaney *(Eckstrom)*, Milton Ross *(Ralph Crane)*, Thornton Edwards *(Lt. Thackery)*, William Bowman, Garry McGarry, Ernest Pasque, William Bainbridge.

Walthall gives his usual fine performance portraying a reformed crook now working as a secret agent for the Allies. While fighting in France, he learns that the Germans are about to step up their U.S. operations, so he sets sail for the States. In New York, his cunning is pitted against that of a master German spy, played menacingly by Chaney. There are plenty of thrills in this wartime picture, which concludes with a tremendous fight between Walthall and Chaney and the destruction of the Kaiser's espionage network.

d, Irvin Willat; sup, Thomas H. Ince; w, Willat (based on a story by Louis Joseph Vance); ph, Edward Willat.

Spy (PR:A MPAA:NR)

FALSE FATHERS* (1929) 5 reels ED/Charles Davis bw

Noah Beery *(Parson)*, Horace B. Carpenter, Francis Pomerantz, E. A. Martin.

Two prospectors care for a baby who has survived an Indian attack. One of them also saves the life of a detective who has been pursuing him for a murder charge from which he is later cleared. In the end, it turns out that the baby really belongs to one of the prospectors, and a parson intervenes to prevent the authorities from taking it away.

d, Horace B. Carpenter; ph, Harry Neumann.

Western (PR:A MPAA:NR)

FALSE FRIEND, THE* (1917) 5 reels PEER/WORLD bw

Robert Warwick *(Bill Ramsdell)*, Gail Kane *(Virginia Farrell)*, Jack Drumier *(Robert Harrell)*, Earl Schenck *(De Witt Clinton)*, E. J. Rollow *(J. Carleton Clinton)*, Louis Edgard *(Byron)*, Pinna Nesbit *(Marietta)*.

Warwick, who is working his way through college, and his wealthy friend both love the same girl. The rich fellow orders his valet to drug Warwick to make him look ridiculous in front of her parents. She marries the wealthy lad, and Warwick heads West where he becomes the manager of a lumber camp. One summer, when the married couple are vacationing nearby, the valet confesses what he did to Warwick and there ensues a fight whereby Warwick knocks the stuffing out of his rival. The valet then murders his employer and commits suicide, thus opening the door for Warwick to marry the widow of his dreams.

d, Harry Davenport; w, (based on a story by Florence C. Bolles).

Drama (PR:A MPAA:NR)

FAME AND FORTUNE*** (1918) 5 reels FOX bw

Tom Mix *(Clay Burgess)*, Kathleen O'Connor *(Della Bowen)*, George Nicholls, Charles McHugh, Jack Dill, Annette DeFoe, Val Paul, E. N. Wallack, Clarence Burton.

Mix returns home after years of wandering to discover his father dead and his property in the hands of a villain who controls half the town. A provision in the will makes it necessary for Mix to prove his identity in order to have any claim on the estate. Those townspeople who do remember him are terrified to speak up, but Mix, in his inimitable, athletic manner, delivers justice—and wins the girl along the way.

d, Lynn Reynolds; w, Bennett Ray Cohen (based on the story "Slow Burgess" by Charles Alden Seltzer); ph, J.D. Jennings.

Western (PR:A MPAA:NR)

FAMILY CUPBOARD, THE** (1915) 5 reels Brady/WORLD bw

Holbrook Blinn, Frances Nelson, John Hines, Grace Henderson, Jessie Lewis, Clinton Preston, Stanhope Wheatcroft, Estelle Mardo.

A good family man falls prey to the charms of a ruthless chorus girl and his marriage is destroyed. Later, despondent and ridden with guilt, he discovers that his son has also become the victim of this treacherous vampire. The father intervenes and the family is reunited.

d&w, Frank H. Crane (based on the play by Owen Davis).

Drama (PR:A MPAA:NR)

FAMILY SECRET, THE*** (1924) 6 reels UNIV bw

Baby Peggy Montgomery *(Baby Peggy Holmes)*, Gladys Hulette *(Margaret Selfridge)*, Edward Earle *(Garry Holmes)*, Frank Currier *(Slim Selfridge)*, Cesare Gravina *(Fruit Vendor)*, Martha Mattox *(Nurse)*, Lucy Beaumont *(Miss Abigail)*, Martin Turner *(Uncle Rose)*, Elizabeth Mackey *(Aunt Mandy)*.

Earle is secretly married to Hulette because her millionaire father resents him. When the young man sneaks into his father-in-law's house to see his baby, he is arrested and sent to prison. Later, after a number of complications, he is accepted and the family enjoys real happiness.

d, William Seiter; w, Lois Zellner (based on "Editha's Burglar, a Story for Children" by Frances Hodgson Burnett and "Editha's Burglar, a Dramatic Sketch in One Act" by Burnett); ph, John Stumar.

Drama (PR:A MPAA:NR)

FAMILY SKELETON, THE** (1918) 5 reels PAR bw

Charles Ray *(Billy Bates)*, Sylvia Bremer *(Poppy Drayton)*, Andrew Arbuckle *(Dr. Griggs)*, Billy Elmer *("Spider" Doyle)*, Otto Hoffman *(Billy's Valet)*, Jack Dyer *(Wheeler)*.

When Ray reaches the age of 21 and inherits several million dollars, his six guardians lecture him on the curse of drink and inform him that his father died of alcoholism. Then, when the young man throws a party to celebrate his majority, he takes a drink of liquor and promptly becomes a dipsomaniac. His life is almost ruined by the time his girl gets the bright idea of faking a kidnaping. In rescuing her, he forgets the family curse and the two go on to lead a healthy and happy existence.

d, Victor L. Schertzinger; sup, Thomas H. Ince; w, (based on a story by Bert Lennon); ph, Chester Lyons.

Drama (PR:A MPAA:NR)

FANCHON THE CRICKET** (1915) 5 reels FP bw

Mary Pickford, Adele Astaire, Fred Astaire, Gertrude Norman, Jack Pickford, Lottie Pickford.

A witch's granddaughter is persecuted by the other children but ultimately wins the affection of the boy she loves after rescuing him from drowning, saving the life of his dimwitted brother, and nursing him through a contagious fever. By far not one of Pickford's best. The cast is historic; in addition to the Pickfords, it was Fred and Adele Astaire's debut in film as a dancing act (Fred Astaire was 16 years old at the time). Two years later they would make their bow on Broadway.

d, James Kirkwood; w, Frances Marion (based on a novel by George Sand).

Fantasy (PR:A MPAA:NR)

FANCY DRESS** (1919, Brit.) 5 reels Lucky Cat/ID bw

Godfrey Tearle *(Tony Broke)*, Ivy Duke *(Hebe)*, Guy Newall *(Earl of Richborne)*, Will Corrie *(The Guv)*, Frank Miller *(Dick Scribe)*, Elaine Madison *(8th Wonder)*, George Tawde *(Mike)*, Kitty Barlow *(Ma)*, Patricia Stannard *(Mrs. Van Graft)*, Bryan Powley *(Mr. Rong)*, James English *(Mr. Wright)*.

In this little English comedy, a touring actor is hired by an attorney to assume the identity of an aristocratic heir.

p, George Clark, Guy Newall; d&w, Kenelm Foss.

Comedy (PR:A MPAA:NR)

FANGS OF JUSTICE 1/2** (1926) 6 reels Sam Bischoff bw

Silverstreak the Dog, Johnny Walker *(Terry Randall)*, Wheeler Oakman *(Paul Orr)*, June Marlowe *(Janet Morgan)*, Frank Hagney *(Walter Page)*, Freddie Frederick *(Sonny the Boy)*, Cecile Cameron *(Trixie)*, George Irving.

Silverstreak, one of the better Rin-Tin-Tin imitators, is involved in three bite-to-the-death battles, climbs a ladder to rescue a child, and saves his master's inheritance, in this fast-paced action programmer.

d, Noel Mason Smith; w, Adele De Vore; ph, James Brown or James B. King.

Adventure (PR:A MPAA:NR)

FANGS OF THE WILD** (1928) 5 reels FBO bw

Ranger the Dog, Dorothy Kitchen *(Blossom Williams)*, Sam Nelson *(Larry Holbrook)*, Tom Lingham *(Pop Williams)*, Syd Crossley *(Rufe Anderson)*.

Kitchen's alcoholic father has promised her to Crossley, a superstitious and nasty mountain man. Crossley hates Kitchen's dog, Ranger, and attempts to kill it a number of times, but Ranger always manages to survive and comes back to protect his mistress from Crossley's unwanted advances. Nelson arrives to buy land for the railroad from Kitchen's father but Crossley steals the money and tries to murder Nelson. Fortunately, Ranger gets there in the nick of time, saves the day, and delivers the handsome stranger to his interested mistress.

d, Jerome Storm; w, Ethel Hill, Dwight Cummins (based on a story by Dorothy Yost, Cummins); t, Randolph Bartlett; ph, Robert De Grasse; ed, Pandro S. Berman.

Adventure (PR:A MPAA:NR)

FAR CALL, THE** (1929) 6 reels FOX bw

Charles Norton *(Pal Loring)*, Leila Hyams *(Hilda Larsen)*, Arthur Stone *(Schmidt)*, Warren Hymer *(Soup Brophy)*, Dan Wolheim *(Black O'Neil)*, Stanley J. Sanford *(Capt. Storkerson)*, Ulrich Haupt *(London Nick)*, Charles Middleton *(Kris Larsen)*, Pat Hartigan *(Lars Johannson)*, Charles Gorman *(Haycok)*, Ivan Linow *(Red Dunkirk)*, Harry Gripp *(Pete)*, Sam Baker *(Tubal)*, Bernard Siegel *(Aleut Chief)*, Willie Fung *(Wing)*, Frank Chew *(Ling Fu)*, Randolph Scott *(Helms)*.

After going to St. Paul Island in the Bering Sea to rob the seal hatchery, Norton falls in love with the governor's daughter Hyams. She discovers that Norton is really the long lost son of a greatly respected citizen who is now deceased. When she tells him so, Norton decides to call the job off. However, Haupt, one of Norton's henchmen, goes through with the plan. Norton stops him, and becomes a welcome member of the community. Scott's first film experience, a job he won after meeting Howard Hughes on a golf course.

d, Allan Dwan; w, Seton I. Miller, Walter Woods (based on a story by Edison Marshall); t, H. H. Caldwell; ph, Hal Rosson; ed, Caldwell; syn sc; s eff.

Drama (PR:A MPAA:NR)

FAR CRY, THE** (1926) 8 reels FN bw-c

Blanche Sweet *(Claire Marsh)*, Jack Mulhall *(Dick Clayton)*, Myrtle Stedman *(Louise Marsh)*, Hobart Bosworth *(Julian Marsh)*, Leo White *(Max Fraisier)*, Julia Swayne Gordon *(Helen Clayton)*, William Austin *(Eric Lancefield)*, John Sainpolis *(Count Filippo Sturani)*, Dorothy Revier *(Yvonne Beaudet)*, Mathilde Comont *(The Maid)*.

Sweet is quite beautiful in this expensively mounted, but rather ordinary film about a wealthy American heiress who travels to Europe where she marries and divorces a fortune-hunting swine. She is then enthusiastically courted by an oily count, as well as her former American boy friend, whom she ultimately chooses. There is approximately 15 minutes of color photography which is used to good advantage in this picture.

d, Silvano Balboni; w, June Mathis, Katharine Kavanaugh (based on the play by Arthur Richman); ph, John Boyle; ed, Al Hall; art d, E. J. Shulter.

Drama **(PR:A MPAA:NR)**

FAR FROM THE MADDING CROWD** (1915, Brit.) 5 reels Turner/ID bw

Florence Turner *(Bathsheba Everdene)*, Henry Edwards *(Gabriel Oak)*, Malcolm Cherry *(Farmer Boldwood)*, Campbell Gullan *(Sgt. Troy)*, Marion Grey *(Fanny Robin)*, Dorothy Rowan *(Lyddie)*, John MacAndrews, Johnny Butt *(Farmhands)*.

American film star Turner was featured in this British romance about a farming girl who falls in love with a bailiff after a suitor kills the cheating sergeant she mistakenly married.

d&w, Larry Trimble (based on the novel by Thomas Hardy).

Drama **(PR:A MPAA:NR)**

FARMER'S WIFE, THE*** (1928, Brit.) 9 reels BIP/W&F bw

James Thomas *(Samuel Sweetland)*, Lillian Hall-Davies *(Araminta Dench)*, Gordon Harker *(Chierdles Ash)*, Gibb McLaughlin *(Dunnybrigg)*, Maud Gill *(Thirza Tapper)*, Louise Pounds *(Widow Windeatt)*, Olga Slade *(Mary Hearn)*, Antonia Brough *(Mary Bassett)*.

Hitchcock directed this charming British comedy about a widowed farmer who searches high and low for a new mate until he comes to the realization that he loves his housekeeper.

p, John Maxwell; d, Alfred Hitchcock; w, Hitchcock, Eliot Stannard (based on a play by Eden Philpotts); ph, Jack Cox; ed, Alfred Booth; set d, Elstree.

Comedy **(PR:A MPAA:NR)**

FATAL FINGERS** (1916. Brit.) 7 reels B&C/Davison Film Sales bw

George Bellamy *(Earl of Ellersdale)*, Mary Merrall *(Irene Lambton)*, A. V. Bramble *(Member of Parliament Rollo Lambton)*, Harry Latimer *(Don Mario)*, Farmer Skein *(Home Secretary)*, Icilma Rae *(Irene, the Child)*.

In this British mystery, a nobleman pretends to commit suicide to prove that a member of Parliament was poisoned by an Italian don to stop him from presenting a bill which would exclude aliens.

d, A. V. Bramble, Eliot Stannard; w, Stannard.

Crime **(PR:A MPAA:NR)**

FATE'S PLAYTHING** (1920, Brit.) 6 reels AH/But bw

Constance Worth *(Dolores Blackett)*, Bruce Gordon *(Dr. Lucas Murray)*, Adelqui Migliar *(Hugo Amadis)*, Frank Dane *(Charles Blackett)*, Hector Abbas *(Sylvester)*, Henry Scofield *(Blackett)*.

The Butchers film company of the United Kingdom journeyed to Holland to produce this love story about a woman who is abandoned by her husband when their child becomes critically ill, and then finds salvation and true love in the arms of her former fiance.

p, Maurits Binger; d, B. E. Doxat-Pratt; w, Reginald Lawson (based on the novel *Oranges and Lemons* by C. F. Harding).

Romance **(PR:A MPAA:NR)**

FATHER O'FLYNN** (1919, Brit.) 6 reels RF bw

Ethel Douglas *(Molly O'Brien)*, Reginald Fox *(Terence O'Connor)*, Ralph Foster *(Father O'Flynn)*, Eileen Bellamy *(Eileen O'Brien)*, Little Rex *(Jim)*, Tom Coventry *(John O'Sullivan)*.

This English mystery uses the Irish setting of Killarney to tell its story of a tenant who kills the landlord who seduced his daughter and then shifts the blame to a poor peasant.

d&w, Tom Watts.

Crime **(PR:A MPAA:NR)**

FAUST*** 1/2** (1926, Ger.) 8 reels UFA bw

Emil Jannings *(The Devil)*, Gosta Ekman *(Faust)*, Camilla Horn *(Marguerite)*, Yvette Guilbert, Wilhelm Dieterle.

Murnau's last German film before coming to the U.S. is a stylized, impressively cinematic telling of the story about the old man who sells his soul for youth. Wonderful performances, sets and bizarre camera angles give one the impression of paintings by Hieronymus Bosch or Pieter Breughel come to life.

d, F. W. Murnau; w, Hans Kyser (based on German folklore and the writings of Christopher Marlowe and Johann Wolfgang von Goethe); ph, Carl Hoffman; art d, Robert Herlth, Walter Rohrig.

Fantasy **Cas.** **(PR:C MPAA:NR)**

FEAR O' GOD**

(1926, Brit./Ger.) 8 reels Gainsborough-Emelka/Artree (GB: THE MOUNTAIN EAGLE)

Bernard Goetzke *(Pettigrew)*, Nita Naldi *(Beatrice, the Governess)*, Malcolm Keen *(Fear o' God)*, John Hamilton *(Edward Pettigrew)*.

FEAR O' GOD was Alfred Hitchcock's second full directorial assignment. The film's only remains are six photographs. The story told of a store manager who yearns for a young schoolteacher. She escapes to the mountains, however, and marries the recluse who rescues her. While returning from the Tyrol region of the Alps, where the film was shot, Hitchcock suffered a severe bout of nausea. The director, who had a terror of vomiting since childhood, felt the attack was the result of a type of social claustrophobia brought on by being in an area where no English was spoken, leaving him feeling strange and displaced.

p, Michael Balcon; d, Alfred Hitchcock; w, Eliot Stannard; ph, Baron [Giovanni] Ventimiglia.

Drama **(PR:A MPAA:NR)**

FEARLESS LOVER, THE** (1925) 5 reels Perfection bw

William Fairbanks *(Patrick Michael Casey)*, Eva Novak *(Enid Sexton)*, Tom Kennedy *(Tom Dugan)*, Lydia Knott *(Mrs. James Sexton)*, Arthur Rankin *(Ted Sexton)*, Frankie Darrow *(Frankie)*.

Fairbanks plays a second generation cop who arrests his sweetheart's brother. He later learns that the lad was forced into a life of crime quite against his will by Kennedy, a notorious gangster. Inspired by love and duty, the young officer goes after the crook and secures the release of his future brother-in-law.

d, Henry MacRae; w, Scott Dunlap; ph, Allen Thompson.

Drama **(PR:A MPAA:NR)**

FEMALE OF THE SPECIES*** (1917) 5 reels Kay-Bee/TRI bw

Dorothy Dalton *(Gloria Marley)*, Enid Markey *(Marcia Dorn)*, Howard Hickman *(Carleton Condon)*, Gertrude Claire *(Mrs. Dorn)*, Roy Laidlaw *(Jim Alderdice)*, Aggie Herring *(Mrs. Alderdice)*.

Dalton is Hickman's paramour until he meets, falls in love with, and marries Markey. Sometime later Dalton and Hickman meet by coincidence on a train. There is an accident, Hickman loses his memory, and Dalton throws his coat over the body of a dead man. She then leads Hickman to believe that they are married and the two head West. Shortly after they are settled, an old friend spots them and notifies Markey, who thought her husband dead. She leaves for the West at once and wins Hickman back.

d, Raymond B. West; w, Monte M. Katterjohn (based on a story by Russell E. Smith).

Drama **(PR:A MPAA:NR)**

FICKLE WOMAN (SEE: FICKLE WOMEN, 1920)

FICKLE WOMEN*** (1920) 5 reels Schwab bw (AKA: FICKLE WOMAN)

David Butler, Eugenie Besserer, Harry Todd, Lillian Hall, Julanne Johnston, Helen Gilmore, William Sharpe, Fred Bond.

Satisfying Butler drama, about the prejudice and jealousy a small town centers on a returning soldier who is rumored to have become a gambler and drinking man. Butler overcomes all of this and takes on his two main detractors in a sensational fight scene, shot in the midst of a colorful town carnival.

d, Fred J. Butler; w, (based on the story "Sitting on the World" by Sophie Kerr); ph, Hugh McClung.

Drama **(PR:A MPAA:NR)**

FIELD OF HONOR, THE** (1922, Brit.) 5 reels British Producers bw

Felix Joubert *(Jacques de Labain)*, Percy Moran *(Thomas Que)*.

British film, set in 1445, recreates a historic duel between an English knight and a Burgundian.

p, John Bowman; d, Percy Moran; w, Felix Joubert.

Drama **(PR:A MPAA:NR)**

FIFTY CANDLES** (1921) 5 reels Willat/Hodkinson bw

Marjorie Daw *(Marywill Tellfair)*, Bertram Grassby *(Hung Chin Chung)*, Ruth King *(Carlotta Drew)*, Wade Boteler *(Mark Drew)*, William Carroll *(Henry Drew)*, George Webb *(Dr. Parker)*, Dorothy Sibley *(Mah Li)*, Edward Burns *(Ralph Coolidge)*.

Good acting, lighting, and set designs made up for negligent direction in this atmospheric mystery about a well-born Chinaman who suffers through 20 years of indentured servitude, and then murders his former master once he is free.

d, Irvin V. Willat; w, (based on a story by Earl Derr Biggers).

Mystery **(PR:A MPAA:NR)**

FIFTY-FIFTY GIRL, THE*** (1928) 7 reels PAR bw

Bebe Daniels *(Kathleen O'Hara)*, James Hall *(Jim Donahue)*, William Austin *(Engineer)*, George Kotsonaros *(Buck the Gorilla Man)*, Johnnie Morris *(Oscar the Thug)*, Alfred Allen *(Kathleen's Uncle)*, John O'Hara.

Interesting pre-womens liberation piece about a young couple (Daniels and Hall) who make a deal when they become joint owners of a gold mine. She will do the digging, he will do the cleaning and cooking, and the first one to cry uncle will lose their share. There is a nasty neighbor who tries to take over, and when his henchmen attack Daniels, she screams for help and Hall provides it.

d, Clarence Badger; w, Ethel Doherty, Lloyd Corrigan (based on a story by John McDermott); ph, J. Roy Hunt.

Comedy/Adventure **(PR:A MPAA:NR)**

FIGHTER, THE*** (1921) 5 reels SF bw

Conway Tearle *(Caleb Conover)*, Winifred Westover *(Dey Shevlin)*, Arthur Housman *(Blacardo)*, Ernest Lawford *(Caine)*, George Stewart *(Jack Standish)*, Warren Cook *(Sen. Burke)*, Helen Lindroth *(Mrs. Hawarden)*.

Tearle has risen through the ranks to become president of a railroad. Westover becomes his ward after her father dies and Tearle, through political pull (he controls the legislature), sees to it that she is accepted by society. Housman, his sworn enemy, leaks a story to the press that his ward's father was crooked. To protect the girl, Tearle takes the blame. Westover then turns against her guardian and accuses him of hiding behind her father's reputation. In the end she learns not only the truth but that she loves Tearle, who defeats his political enemies and marries Westover.

d, Henry Kolker; w, R. Cecil Smith (based on a novel by Albert Payson Terhune).
Drama **(PR:A MPAA:NR)**

FIGHTER'S PARADISE** (1924) 5 reels Phil Goldstone bw

Rex "Snowy" Baker, Andrew Waldron, Dick Sutherland, Jack Curtis, Harry Burns, Kenneth Benedict, Margaret Landis.

Because a cowardly, small town soda jerk resembles the famous boxer, Cyclone Carter, he is forced into a fight. A blow on the head turns him into a fighting machine, and he becomes the local hero and the darling of the girl he has always loved.

d, Alvin J. Neitz; w, J. F. Natteford.
Drama **(PR:A MPAA:NR)**

FIGHTING AMERICAN, THE** (1924) 6 reels UNIV bw

Pat O'Malley *(Bill Pendleton)*, Mary Astor *(Mary O'Mallory)*, Raymond Hatton *(Danny Daynes)*, Warner Oland *(Fu Shing)*, Edwin J. Brady *(Quig Morley)*, Taylor Carroll *(W. F. Pendleton)*, Clarence Geldert *(William A. Pendleton)*, Alfred Fisher *(Mr. O'Mallory)*, Jack Byron *(Alfred Rutland)*, James Wang *(Lee Yong)*, Emmett King *(College Professor)*, Jane Starr *(Lizzie)*, Frank Kingsley *(Harry March)*.

On a fraternity bet, O'Malley proposes to Astor, a girl who secretly loves him. When she discovers his motive, she joins her father at his mission in China. Later, O'Malley sails to the Orient, saves Astor from bandits, and asks her to be his wife for real.

d, Tom Forman; w, Harvey Gates, Raymond L. Schrock (based on a story by William Elwell Oliver); ph, Harry Perry.
Comedy/Adventure **(PR:A MPAA:NR)**

FIGHTING BOB*** (1915) 5 reels Rolfe/Metro bw

Orrin Johnson, Olive Wyndham.

Interesting, action-packed adventure, set in Central America, which advocated U.S. intervention to establish democracy there. The beautifully filmed battle scenes did much to offset the blatant jingoism the picture presented.

d, John W. Noble; w, Edward Rose.
Adventure **(PR:A MPAA:NR)**

FIGHTING BOOB, THE*** (1926) 5 reels R-C/FBO bw

Bob Custer *(El Tigre)*, Frank Whitson *(Clayton)*, Sherry Tansey *(Timothy Raymond)*, Hugh Saxon *(Jasper Steele)*, Violet Palmer *(Helen Hawksby)*, Andrew Arbuckle *(Old Man Hawksby)*, Sam Lufkin *(Jeff Randall)*, Tom Bay *(Bowers)*, Joan Meredith *(Dolores)*, Bobby Nelson *(Bobby)*, Artie Ortega *(Ortega)*.

Fast-paced western in which Custer takes the place of an army buddy who was gassed during the war. He arrives on the scene to help his uncle fight the gang which is trying to steal his spread. Custer not only saves the ranch, but wins the pretty granddaughter as well.

d, Jack Nelson; w, Nelson, James Ormont (based on a story by William Lester); ph, Arthur Reeves.
Western **(PR:A MPAA:NR)**

FIGHTING BREED, THE*** (1921) 5 reels Selig-Rork/AY bw

Rex "Snowy" Baker *(Brian O'Farrell)*, Wilfred Lucas *(John MacDonald)*, Ethel Payton *(Enid MacDonald)*.

Filmed on location in Australia, wealthy Baker returns to the family ranch pretending to be a tenderfoot. After a number of exciting adventures, he wins the respect of his employees and the love of a female neighbor.

d, Wilfred Lucas; w, Lucas, Bess Meredyth.
Adventure **(PR:A MPAA:NR)**

FIGHTING CHEAT, THE** (1926) 5 reels Action/Weiss Brothers Artclass bw

Wally Wales *(Wally Kenyon)*, Jean Arthur *(Ruth Wells)*, Ted Rackerby *(Lafe Wells)*, Fanny Midgley *(Mrs. Wells)*, Charles Whitaker *(Jud Nolan)*, V.L. Barnes *(Doctor)*, Al Taylor *(Cook)*.

Wales happens upon outlaw Rackerby who has been left for dead by his gang. Wales agrees to take a packet of money to the desperado's mother and falls in love with the outlaw's sister, Arthur. Later, Rackerby recovers and summons the sheriff and his men to ride to Wales' and Arthur's assistance when they are under attack by the gang.

d, Richard Thorpe; w, Betty Burbridge.
Western **(PR:A MPAA:NR)**

FIGHTING COWARD, THE*** (1924) 7 reels FP/PAR bw

Ernest Torrence *(Gen. Orlando Jackson)*, Mary Astor *(Lucy)*, Noah Beery *(Capt. Blackie)*, Cullen Landis *(Tom Rumford)*, Phyllis Haver *(Elvira)*, G. Raymond Nye *(Maj. Patterson)*, Richard R. Neill *(Joe Patterson)*, Carmen Phillips *(Mexico, an Octoroon)*, Bruce Covington *(Gen. Rumford)*, Helen Dumbar *(Mrs. Rumford)*, Frank Jonasson *(Rumbo)*.

Cruze took an ordinary play and turned it into an outstanding satire on the "Old South." Landis, who has been raised in the north by Quakers, returns home but will have nothing to do with grits, juleps, or duels. His horror-stricken family, who hold "honah" above all else, disowns him, but eventually he wins their favor by mastering the use of a pistol and sword and proving himself to be the best man on any plantation. In this wonderful spoof, Cruze orchestrates the laughs perfectly, and at no time does he overplay his hand.

d, James Cruze; w, Walter Woods (based on the play "The Magnolia" by Booth Tarkington); ph, Karl Brown.
Comedy **(PR:A MPAA:NR)**

FIGHTING CUB, THE*** (1925) 6 reels Crown/TRU bw

Wesley Barry *(Thomas Patrick O'Toole)*, Mildred Harris, Pat O'Malley, Mary Carr, George Fawcett, Stuart Holmes.

Ambitious copy boy Barry dreams only of becoming a cub reporter. Finally, his editor tells him that the job is his if he can get an interview with a famous philanthropist. The philanthropist's daughter arranges the meeting, and Barry takes a shine to the older man at once. Later, the boy stumbles on the hideout of a notorious gang called the Owls. This is the yarn of a lifetime, but to Barry's horror it turns out that the leader of the gang is none other than the philanthropist himself. He is planning on quitting the rackets and devoting the rest of his life to charitable works and had called one last meeting when the cops (on a tip from a disloyal gang member) come crashing in. Barry pleads for the older man, gets him off the hook, and kills the story which would have made him famous.

d, Paul Hurst; w, Adele Buffington; ph, Frank Cotner, Lee Humiston.
Crime/Adventure **(PR:A MPAA:NR)**

FIGHTING EDGE** (1926) 7 reels WB be

Kenneth Harlan *(Juan de Dios O'Rourke)*, Patsy Ruth Miller *(Phoebe Joyce)*, David Kirby *(Gilette)*, Charles Conklin *(Chuck)*, Pat Hartigan *(Taggert)*, Lew Harvey *(Bailey)*, Eugene Pallette *(Simpson)*, Pat Harmon *(Hadley)*, W.A. Carroll *(Joyce)*.

When a government agent is captured by smugglers, Harlan is assigned to the case. He crosses the Mexican border disguised as a halfbreed and meets the imprisoned man's daughter. They manage to free the agent but are trapped in a deserted house by the desperados. It almost looks like they are done for when the U.S. army arrives on the scene to save the day.

d, Henry Lehrman; w, Edward T. Lowe, Jr., Jack Wagner (based on a novel by William MacLeod Raine); ph, Allan Thompson, Robert Laprell; ed, Clarence Kolster.
Crime **(PR:A MPAA:NR)**

FIGHTING FOR LOVE*** (1917) 5 reels Red Feather bw

Ruth Stonehouse *(Sylvia)*, Jack Mulhall *(Jim)*, Jean Hersholt *(Ferdinand)*, Noble Johnson *(Johnny Little Bear)*, J. F. Briscoe *(Billy Guard)*, Ruby Marshall *(King's Favorite)*.

After striking gold, cowboy Mulhall and his college-educated Indian friend tour Europe and end up in one of those tiny, comic opera countries. Wishing to catch a glimpse of a queen, Mulhall scales the palace wall and meets a beautiful monarch whom he believes to be a servant. She tells him that unless her queen marries a neighboring king, her country will be destroyed by war. Mulhall quickly sizes up the situation, sends for his rough rider friends who fought in the Spanish American War, defeats the enemy army, and weds the lovely young queen—who gladly abdicates.

d, Raymond Wells; w, Fred Myton (based on a story by Wells).
Comedy/Adventure **(PR:A MPAA:NR)**

FIGHTING ODDS*** (1917) 6 reels Goldwyn bw

Maxine Elliott *(Mrs. Copley)*, Henry Clive *(Mr. Copley)*, Charles Dalton *(John W. Blake)*, George Odell *(Egan)*, Regan Hughston *(Jewett)*, William T. Carleton *(Detective Butler)*.

In her screen debut, Broadway star Elliott plays the wife of an honest auto manufacturer who is hoodwinked by a Wall Street financier, bankrupted, and sent to jail. Posing as an English woman of position, Elliott seduces the truth from the real crook and her husband is vindicated.

d, Allan Dwan; w, Roi Cooper Megrue, Irvin S. Cobb; ph, Rene Guissart.
Drama **(PR:A MPAA:NR)**

FIGHTING SMILE, THE** (1925) 5 reels IP bw

Bill Cody *(Bud Brant)*, Jean Arthur *(Rose Craddock)*, Charles Brinley, George Magrill, Billie Bennett.

Arthur, who would become one of the world's best-loved stars, got her start in modest westerns such as this one about Cody, a cowboy who returns home to find that his father's cattle are being stolen with the help of his boyhood pal. His friend is killed after experiencing a regeneration and providing Cody with the tip he needs to wipe out the rustlers.

p, Jesse J. Goldburg; d, Jay Marchant; w, William A. Burton, Harry J. Brown; ph, Brown.
Western **(PR:A MPAA:NR)**

FIGHTING TERROR, THE** (1929) 5 r eels J. P. McGowan/SYN bw

Bob Custer, Bud Osborne, Hank Bell, J.P. McGowan, Adabelle Driver, Hazel Mills, Cliff Lyons, Tom Bay.

Custer is out to get the hombres who killed his brother, but runs into a snag because the crooked sheriff of a town on the Nevada-California border keeps letting the villains cross. By the end of the fifth reel, however, Custer gets his revenge.

d, J. P. McGowan; w, Sally Winters; ph, Hap Depew.
Western **(PR:A MPAA:NR)**

FINAL CURTAIN, THE** (1916) 5 reels Kleine bw

Alma Hanlon *(Ruth Darrell)*, Arthur Hoops *(John Lord)*, Florence Coventry *(Jane Lord)*, Herbert Hayes *(Herbert Lyle)*, Frank Belcher *(John Banks)*, Beryl Mercer

(Mary), W. C. Carlston *(Henry Cole)*, Frank Norcross *(George Robbins)*, The Marvelous Sylvesters, Crimmins and Gore.

A smalltime repertory actress is discovered and makes it big on Broadway. She meets Hoops, a wealthy woolen manufacturer who recognizes her as being the young actress he once admired when her family's show played his small town years before. They marry and she retires from the stage. Before long, however, his neglect of her in favor of running his business causes a separation and she returns to her career. Hoops, convinced that his wife is having an affair with her leading man, completely severs the relationship. Later, when he realizes his error and seeks a reconciliation, he discovers that she has quit the business and disappeared. At the same time, a trust is plotting to take over his operation. His wife, who is now working as a telephone operator, overhears the scheme and wires a warning to Hoops, which reaches him in time. When the grateful woolen magnate seeks out the girl to thank and reward her, he finds the woman he has always loved and the two are reunited.

w, Channing Pollock.

Drama **(PR:A MPAA:NR)**

FINE FEATHERS* (1915) 5 reels Cosmos/WORLD bw

Janet Beecher, David Powell, Lester Chambers, Henry Gisell.

The Walter play from which this curiosity was filmed tells of a young chemist whose success provides his giddy wife with the money to buy expensive hats. The picture also strongly suggests that good wives spend money on household supplies—never on frivolous articles of clothing.

w, (based on the play by Eugene Walter).

Drama **(PR:A MPAA:NR)**

FINE FEATHERS** (1921) 6 reels Metro bw

Eugene Pallette *(Bob Reynolds)*, Claire Whitney *(Jane Reynolds)*, Thomas W. Ross *(Dick Meade)*, Warburton Gamble *(John Brand)*, June Elvidge *(Mrs. Brand)*.

A government inspector accepts a bribe from a crooked contractor to allow inferior material to be used in building a dam. Later, after going broke and facing a prison sentence for his crime, the inspector kills the man who bribed him and then commits suicide.

d, Fred Sittenham; sup, Maxwell Karger; w, Lois Zellner, Eugene Walter (based on the play by Walter); ph, Arthur A. Cadwell; art d, Lester J. Vermilyea.

Drama **(PR:A MPAA:NR)**

FINE MANNERS*** (1926) 7 reels FP/PAR bw

Gloria Swanson *(Orchid Murphy)*, Eugene O'Brien *(Brian Alden)*, Helen Dunbar *(Aunt Agatha)*, Walter Goss *(Buddy Murphy)*, John Miltern *(Courtney Adams)*.

Entertaining Swanson feature about a millionaire smitten by a chorus girl who mistakes him for being a waiter. To make her acceptable to his crowd, he arranges for Swanson to be taught "poise" by his aunt while he goes out of town on business. She proves to be such a good student that, when he returns, he finds the woman no longer to his liking. The millionaire then asks that she be herself again—and his bride. FINE MANNERS was Swanson's last film for Paramount. The star would soon begin producing her own films at her recently acquired studio, thanks to the backing of Joseph P. Kennedy.

d, Richard Rosson; w, James Ashmore Creelman; ph, George Webber.

Comedy/Drama **(PR:A MPAA:NR)**

FINGER PRINTS* (1923) 5 reels Hyperion bw

Violet Palmer.

Decidedly inferior film about a man who is murdered for a string of pearls he was going to present as a homecoming gift to his motherless daughter. Her fiance sets out to solve the case, and although the killer appears to be the butler, it turns out to be an old friend of the father.

d, Joseph Levering; w, Alton Floyd.

Mystery **(PR:A MPAA:NR)**

FINNEGAN'S BALL** (1927) 7 reels Graf Brothers/FD bw

Blanche Mehaffey *(Molly Finnegan)*, Mack Swain *(Patrick Flannigan)*, Cullen Landis *(Young Flannigan)*, Aggie Herring *(Maggie Finnegan)*, Charles McHugh *(Danny Finnegan, Sr.)*, Westcott B. Clarke *(Lawyer O'Connell)*, Kewpie Morgan *(Judge Morgan)*, Mimi Finnegan *(Danny Finnegan, Jr.)*.

The Flannigans leave the old sod for America, followed by their friends the Finnegans. Mr. Finnegan (McHugh) gets a job working for Mr. Flannigan (Swain) and their son and daughter become engaged to marry. McHugh inherits a fortune and snubs his old friend and boss, which makes it difficult for the young sweethearts. The windfall, however, proves to be bogus, and the families get together again in time for the wedding party.

d, James P. Hogan; sup&w, Max Graf (based on a play by George H. Emerick); ph, Blake Wagner.

Comedy **(PR:A MPAA:NR)**

FIRE AND SWORD*** (1914) 6 reels Kismet Feature Film bw

Isabel Rea *(The Girl)*, Tom McEvoy *(The Newsman)*.

In this interesting film, director Hunter used the beach at Coney Island, plus the people who worked the amusement park's concessions, and even the horses and camels from one of the entertainment center's shows, to tell the story of a wealthy girl's abduction by an Arab chief and her subsequent rescue by a U.S. newspaper reporter.

d, T. Hayes Hunter.

Adventure **(PR:A MPAA:NR)**

FIREMAN, SAVE MY CHILD*** (1927) 6 reels FP/PAR bw

Wallace Beery *(Elmer)*, Raymond Hatton *(Sam)*, Josephine Dunn *(Dora Drumston)*, Tom Kennedy *(Capt. Kennedy)*, Walter Goss *(Walter)*, Joseph Girard *(Chief Dumston)*.

Another good Beery and Hatton comedy. This time the boys are firemen who find themselves and their hook-and-ladder on call every time the chief's daughter needs her car towed, her laundry picked up, etc. Plenty of slapstick laughs highlight this audience pleaser, intended strictly to entertain.

d, Edward Sutherland: w, Monte Brice, Tom Geraghty; ph, H. Kinley Martin.

Comedy **(PR:A MPAA:NR)**

FIRES OF CONSCIENCE* (1916) 5 reels FOX bw

William Farnum *(George Baxter)*, Gladys Brockwell *(Margery Burke)*, Nell Shipman *(Nell Blythe)*, H. A. Barrows *(Robert Baxter)*, H. J. Herbert *(Paul Sneed)*, William Burress *(Randolf Sneed)*, Eleanor Crowe *(Mabel Jones)*, Willard Louis *(Doc Taylor)*, Brooklyn Keller *(Felix Lunk)*, Fred Huntley *(Pete Rogers)*.

Farnum heads west after killing the man who was having an affair with his wife. There he meets and falls in love with a woman who persuades him to return home and face the music. In a completely implausible turn of events, the presiding judge at his trial turns out to be the father of the slain man, who just happened to see the killing. Citing the unwritten law, His Honor dismisses the case before the jury can say Clarence Darrow, and George returns to his new love.

d, Oscar Apfel; w, Henry Christeen Warnack.

Drama **(PR:A MPAA:NR)**

FIRES OF FATE** (1923, Brit.) 8 reels GAU/WEST bw

Wanda Hawley *(Dorinne Adams)*, Nigel Barrie *(Col. Egerton)*, Pedro de Corboda *(Prince Ibrahim)*, Stewart Rome *(Rev. Samuel Royden)*, Edith Craig *(Miss Adams)*, Percy Standing *(Stephen Belmont)*, Arthur Cullin *(Sir Charles Royden)*, Douglas Munro *(Mansoor)*, Cyril Smith *(Lord Howard Cecil)*.

This English film, set in Egypt, tells the story of a British officer (Barrie) with only a year to live, who rescues a pretty young girl from a fate worse than death at the hands of an Arab prince.

d, Tom Terriss; w, Alicia Ramsey (based on the novel *Tragedy of the Korosko* by Arthur Conan Doyle and a play by Lewis Waller).

Adventure **(PR:A MPAA:NR)**

FIRES OF INNOCENCE** (1922, Brit.) 7 reels Progress/But bw

Joan Morgan *(Helen Dalmaine)*, Bobbie Andrews *(Arthur Dalmaine)*, Arthur Lennard *(Rev. Dalmaine)*, Marie Illington *(Lady Crane)*, Madge Tree *(Bella Blackburn)*, Nell Emerald *(Lydia Blackburn)*.

English village life is explored by contrasting a vicar and his family with that of the local aristocrat. At first, the clergyman's daughter is looked down upon by the locals because of her manner of dress; then the vicar himself comes under attack after quite innocently visiting a woman new to the community. But it all works out—in that British sort of way—when the daughter falls in love with the aristocrat's son.

p, Frank E. Spring; d&w, Sidney Morgan (based on the novel *A Little World Apart* by George Stevenson).

Drama **(PR:A MPAA:NR**

FIRM OF GIRDLESTONE, THE*** (1915, Brit.) LFP/JUR bw

Edna Flugrath *(Kate Horston)*, Fred Groves *(Ezra Girdlestone)*, Charles Rock *(John Girdlestone)*, Windham Guise *(Maj. Clutterbuck)*, Hayford Hobbs *(Tom Dimsdale)*, Gwynne Herbert *(Mrs. Scully)*, Molly Terraine *(Rebecca)*.

This interesting early British mystery feature was based on a Doyle novel about an elderly merchant who attempts to murder his ward in order to save his failing business.

d, Harold Shaw; w, Bannister Merwin (based on the novel by Arthur Conan Doyle).

Mystery **(PR:A MPAA:NR)**

FIRST YEAR, THE*½** (1926) 6 reels FOX bw

Matt Moore *(Tom Tucker)*, Kathryn Perry *(Grace Livingston)*, John Patrick *(Dick Loring)*, Frank Currier *(Dr. Livingston)*, Frank Cooley *(Mr. Livingston)*, Virginia Madison *(Mrs. Livingston)*, Carolynne Snowden *(Hattie)*, J. Farrell MacDonald *(Mr. Barstow)*.

Borzage directed and Marion wrote the screenplay for this fine comedy about the trials and tribulations of a young couple's first year of marriage. The film's highlight is a dinner party set up to help the husband land a big business deal in which everything imaginable goes wrong. The newlyweds have plenty of troubles and laughs throughout this beautifully acted picture, but they finish their difficult first year with hubby making good and a baby on the way.

d, Frank Borzage; w, Frances Marion (based on the play by Frank Craven); ph, Chester Lyons.

Comedy **(PR:A MPAA:NR)**

$5,000,000 COUNTERFEITING PLOT, THE** (1914) 6 reels Dramascope bw

William G. Burns, Glenn White, Joseph Sullivan, Clifford P. Saum, Hector Dion, Jack Sharkey, William Cavanaugh, Charles E. Graham, Harry Lillford, James

Ayling, John Ransom, Arthur Morrison, Frank Carrington, Harry Driscoll, Jack Drumier, Howard Missimer, Edward Walton, Ezra Walck, Georgia O'Ramie, Jean Acker, Eileen Hume.

A group of Philadelphia counterfeiters are printing hundred dollar bills. When one of the gang gives a note to his daughter, who buys a dress with it, the bill reaches the Treasury Department in Washington, where the chief of the Secret Service registers a stern expression and declares, "This looks like a job for William G. Burns." At that point, the famous private detective (playing himself) enters the picture and in, a most uncinematic manner, solves the case.

d, Bertram Harrison; w, George G. Nathan.

Crime **(PR:A MPAA:NR)**

$5,000 REWARD (SEE: DAREDEVIL'S REWARD, 1928)

FLAG LIEUTENANT, THE*** (1919, Brit.) 6 reels Barker/JUR bw

Ivy Close *(Lady Hermione Wynne)*, George Wynn *(Lt. Dicky Lascelles)*, Dorothy Fane *(Mrs. Cameron)*, Ernest Wallace *(Maj. Thesiger)*, Frank Adair *(Adm. Wynne)*, Wallace Bosco *(Villain)*.

A brave lieutenant is branded a coward by his peers who think he abandoned his post during an enemy attack by the Bashi Bazouks. The only witness to the truth is his major, who was wounded and suffers from amnesia as a result.

p, Jack W. Smith; d, Percy Nash; w, (based on the play by W. P. Drury, Leo Tover).

FLAG LIEUTENANT, THE** (1926, Brit.) 9 reels Astra-N bw

Henry Edwards *(Lt. Dicky Lascelles)*, Lillian Oldland *(Sybil Wynne)*, Dorothy Seacombe *(Mrs. Cameron)*, Fred Raynham *(Maj. Thesiger)*, Fewlass Lewellyn *(Adm. Wynne)*, Hayford Hobbs *(Honorable D'Arcy Penrose)*, Forrester Harvey *(Dusty Miller)*, Humberston Wright *(Stiffy Steele)*.

When his major becomes wounded, lieutenant Edwards gets through and brings the help which saves the fort. Unfortunately, the major loses his memory and cannot stand up for Edwards who is branded a coward for not being at his post when the Union Jack was in danger. In the end, the admiral's daughter brings out the truth and the young man is not court-martialed. It looks as if the entire British Navy was put at the disposal of the producers of this film, but that could not offset the poor direction and barely adequate acting.

d, Maurice Elvey; w, Patrick L. Mannock (based on the play by W. P. Drury, Leo Tover).

FLAMES*** (1917, Brit.) 6 reels But bw

Margaret Bannerman *(Cuckoo)*, Owen Nares *(Valentine Cresswell)*, Edward O'Neill *(Richard Marr)*, Douglas Munro *(Dr. Levetier)*, Clifford Cobbe *(Julian Addison)*.

An old practitioner of the occult trades souls with a young man, but his friends come to his rescue and force the mystic to exchange them back.

p, F. W. Baker; d, Maurice Elvey; w, Eliot Stannard (based on the novel by Robert Hichens).

Fantasy **(PR:A MPAA:NR)**

FLAMES OF CHANCE, THE** (1918) 5 reels Kay-Bee/TRI bw

Margery Wilson *(Jeanette Contreau)*, Jack Mulhall *(Harry Ledyard)*, Anna Dodge *(Mrs. Tibbets)*, Wilbur Higbee *(Frederick Armstrong)*, Percy Challenger *(Character Man)*, Ben Lewis *(John Finch)*, Eugene Corey *(Anatole)*, Lee Phelps *(Paul)*.

Wilson, a New York stenographer, volunteers to write to three prisoners of war who are being held by the Germans. Her letters give the impression that she is an elderly lady, and one night, quite by accident, Mulhall, one of the prisoners, holds one of her pages near the fire, causing secret writing to appear. When he is sent home because of a wound, Mulhall informs the Secret Service of the unusual letter and then goes to visit Wilson. It turns out that her boss is actually the spy, and Mulhall and his correspondent falls in love.

d, Raymond Wells; w, Harvey Gates, Elizabeth Haas (based on the story "Three Godsons of Jeanette Contreau" by Francis W. Sullivan); ph, Pliny Horne.

Spy **(PR:A MPAA:NR)**

FLAMES OF FEAR** (1930, Brit.) 6 reels Argyle Art/Equity British bw

John Argyle *(Bob)*, Nancy Stratford *(Mary)*, Ernest Bakewell *(Bert)*, Bessie Richards *(Mother)*.

In this British drama set in Tamworth, a once-cowardly mine-worker saves the brother of his fiancee from a disaster and earns the respect of his fellows.

p, John F. Argyle; d, Charles Barnett; w, Argyle.

Drama **(PR:A MPAA:NR)**

FLAMES OF PASSION*** (1922, Brit.) 9 reelsGraham-Wilcox/Astra bw

Mae Marsh *(Dorothy Hawke)*, C. Aubrey Smith *(King's Counsel Richard Hawke)*, Hilda Bayley *(Kate Watson)*, Herbert Langley *(Arthur Watson)*, Allan Aynesworth *(Mr. Forbes)*, Eva Moore *(Aunt)*, George K. Arthur *(Friend)*, Henry Vibart *(Lord Chief Justice)*, A. G. Poulton *(Counsel)*, Alban Atwood *(Mayor)*, Harry J. Worth *(Sheriff)*, Tony Fraser *(Agitator)*.

The great U.S. film star, Marsh, made a series of films in Britain, including this one about a married woman who is forced to admit in court that it was really her child who was killed by her drunken ex-chauffeur.

d, Herbert Wilcox; d, Graham Cutts; w, M. V. Wilcox, Herbert Wilcox.

Drama **(PR:A MPAA:NR)**

FLAMES OF THE FLESH* (1920) 6 reels FOX bw

Gladys Brockwell, William Scott, Harry Spingler, Ben Deely, Charles K. French, Louis Fitzroy, Rosita Marstini, Josephine Crowell, Nigel de Brulier.

Terrible melodrama about a girl turned bad who, in order to deliver revenge on an old man, seduces and sexually enslaves his youngest son. When the older brother arrives to rescue the lad, he and the vamp fall in love. The girl, however, realizing that she is unworthy of him, commits suicide.

d, Edward J. LeSaint; w, Dorothy Yost (based on a story by Forrest Halsey, Clara S. Beranger).

Drama **(PR:A MPAA:NR)**

FLAMING BARRIERS*** (1924) 6 reels FP bw

Jacqueline Logan *(Jerry Malone)*, Antonio Moreno *(Sam Barton)*, Walter Hires *(Henry Van Sickle)*, Charles Ogle *(Patrick Malone)*, Robert McKim *(Joseph Pickens)*, Luke Cosgrave *(Bill O'Halloran)*, Warren Rogers *(Mayor Steers)*, Claribel Campbell.

Moreno is hired to steal the patent for a fire-fighting machine Ogle invented. Instead, he falls for Ogle's daughter, and they put the machine to good use by extinguishing a burning bridge and saving hundreds of lives. This deed sells plenty of machines and earns Moreno the heart of young Logan.

d, George Melford; w, Harvey Thew (based on a story by Byron Morgan); ph, Charles G. Clarke.

Drama **(PR:A MPAA:NR)**

FLAMING WATERS*** (1925) 7 reels Associated Arts/FBO bw

Malcolm McGregor *(Dan O'Neil)*, Pauline Garon *(Doris Laidlaw)*, Mary Carr *(Mrs. O'Neil)*, John Miljan *(Jasper Thorne)*, Johnny Gough *(Midge)*, Mayme Kelso *(Mrs. Rutherford)*.

Good old-fashioned melodrama about a young man who returns home from the sea to find his mother dispossessed of her home (after buying phony oil stock) and working as a washerwoman. He goes to the oil fields to find the swindler and after a number of action-packed scenes, including a thrilling escape through the "flaming waters," he brings the villain to justice and wins the love of a millionaire's daughter.

d, F. Harmon Weight; w, E. Lloyd Sheldon; ph, William Marshall.

Drama **(PR:A MPAA:NR)**

FLAPPER, THE*** (1920) 5 reels SF bw

Olive Thomas *(Ginger King)*, Warren Cook *(Sen. King)*, Louise Lindroth *(Elmina Buttons)*, Theodore Westman, Jr. *(Bill E. Forbes)*, W. T. Carleton *(Richard Channing)*, Katherine Johnston *(Hortense)*, Arthur Housman *(Tom Morgan)*, Charles Craig, Maury Steuart, Raymond Hewitt, Barbara Butler, Norma Shearer.

Nicely acted and directed by Thomas and Crosland, this story about a schoolgirl who is raised so strictly that she can't resist getting into all sorts of innocent trouble, was the kind of fluff that 1920 Hollywood was pleasantly made of.

d, Alan Crosland; w, Frances Marion; ph, John W. Brown.

Comedy **(PR:A MPAA:NR)**

FLASHLIGHT, THE* (1917) 5 reels BLUE bw

Dorothy Phillips, William Stowell, Lon Chaney, Alfred Allen, George Berrell, Evelyn Selbie, Mark Fenton, Charles C. Jackson, Clyde Benson.

The photography was about the only worthwhile thing in this programmer, which told of mountain sweethearts wrongly accused of murder. At the trial, the young man is let off (due to evidence provided by a flashlight picture) and the girl is convicted. It, of course, all works out in the end, with the lovers returning to their home in the mountains where their hearts were free to once again "beat as one."

d&w, Ida May Park (based on a story by Albert M. Treynor); ph, King D. Gray.

Drama **(PR:A MPAA:NR)**

FLATTERY** (1925) 6 reels MFC/CHAD bw

John Bowers *(Reginald Mallory)*, Marguerite de la Motte *(Betty Biddle)*, Alan Hale *(Arthur Barrington)*, Grace Darmond *(Allene King)*, Edwards Davis *(John Biddle)*, Louis Morrison *(Mayor)*, Larry Steers *(District Attorney)*.

Civil engineer Bowers, because he has been pampered all his life, is obnoxiously conceited. Knowing his weakness for hearing nice things about himself, some crooked politicians sweet-talk him into building the new city hall with shoddy materials. Eventually he realizes the error of his ways, however, and destroys the half-completed building, manages to have the cartel arrested, and marries the boss' daughter.

d, Tom Forman; sup, Norman Walker; w, H. H. Van Loan; ph, King Gray, Harry Perry.

Drama **(PR:A MPAA:NR)**

FLESH AND THE DEVIL**** (1926) 9 reels MGM bw

John Gilbert *(Leo von Harden)*, Greta Garbo *(Felicitas von Eltz)*, Lars Hanson *(Ulrich von Kletzingk)*, Barbara Kent *(Hertha Prochvitz)*, William Orlamond *(Uncle Kutowski)*, George Fawcett *(Pastor Voss)*, Eugenie Besserer *(Leo's Mother)*, Marc MacDermott *(Count von Rhaden)*, Marcelle Corday *(Minna)*, Rolfe Sedan.

Director Brown set out to make a film in the German style and succeeded marvelously with FLESH AND THE DEVIL. It was his first picture for MGM, and it brought together the most exciting romantic team the screen had ever known—Gilbert and Garbo. The story told of Gilbert and Hanson, lifelong friends, who return home to Austria from their military academy on holiday. At the station Gilbert meets Garbo when she drops her bouquet. The handsome officer picks it up for her, but keeps one flower for himself. Later, at the grand ball, they meet again and in the darkened garden he lights her cigarette. She inhales sensually and blows the fire out. "You know," his title card reads, "when you blow out the match, it's an invitation to kiss you." This begins a torrid affair which leads to their discovery by her husband, and Gilbert (in a scene beautifully shot in silhouette) is forced to kill him on the field of honor. As punishment, the young officer is banished to the African Corps, but before leaving he asks his dear friend Hanson to fulfill his gentlemanly obligation by looking after the widow Garbo, who might now be impoverished. Three long years pass before Gilbert is finally pardoned by the emperor, and when he returns home Hanson is at the station to meet him—accompanied by his wife, Garbo. Gilbert becomes completely reclusive to avoid the temptation the presence of the woman he loves would present, but Garbo (who is becoming more satanic with every reel) ultimately seduces him and convinces Gilbert to run away with her. On the night they are due to leave, Hanson discovers them together and then another duel is arranged on their boyhood turf. Gilbert refuses to raise the pistol, desiring to be punished, but before the fatal shot is fired, Garbo, who is somewhat ambiguous in her actions at this point, rushes to the scene of the encounter, crashes through the ice, and drowns. Thus the spell is broken—the devil has departed—and the men are freed to renew their deep friendship. Not a great film, certainly, but just as certainly one to be remembered. There are shimmering photographic effects, for example, that would be hard to match today, and the sets are big, in the dramatic sense of the word, with staggering visual effects, a glamorous production in the days when Hollywood meant glamor. Gilbert and Garbo (it was the first of a series the two made as a romantic pair) added spice to their steamy love scenes by the fact that they were carrying on romantically off the screen at the time.

d, Clarence Brown; w, Benjamin F. Glazer (based on the novel *Es War; Roman in Zwei Banden* by Herman Sudermann); t, Marian Ainslee; ph, William Daniels; ed, Lloyd Nosler; set d, Cedric Gibbons, Frederick Hope.

Drama **(PR:A MPAA:NR)**

FLIRT, THE*** (1922) 8 reels UNIV bw

Eileen Percy *(Cora Madison)*, George Nichols *(Papa Madison)*, Lydia Knott *(Mama Madison)*, Helen Jerome Eddy *(Laura Madison)*, Buddy Messenger *(Hederick Madison)*, Harold Goodwin *(Jimmy Madison)*, Nell Craig *(Della Fenton)*, Tom Kennedy *(Sam Fenton)*, Lloyd Whitlock *(Valentine Corlis)*, Edward Hearn *(Richard Lindley)*, Bert Roach *(Wade Trumble)*, William Welsh *(George Carroll)*, Dorothea Wolbert *(The Cook)*.

Director Henley does a fine job in capturing the look and feel of small-town America in this motion picture adaption of a Booth Tarkington story. Nichols is doing well in the real estate business, but the size of his family makes him financially cautious. His daughter Percy is a natural flirt, and although engaged to Hearn, she is attracted to confidence man Whitlock the moment he lands in town. Nichols refuses to become involved in Whitlock's oil deal, so Percy forges her father's name to some papers, allowing the con to make a bundle and take off with the loot. When the scandal hits, Nichols takes the blame to spare his daughter and her sister marries Hearn. Finally, ashamed of her actions, the young girl confesses all, Whitlock is arrested, and a new fellow arrives who, of course, falls head over heels for the formerly flirtatious beauty.

d, Hobart Henley; w, A. P. Younger (based on a story by Booth Tarkington); ph, Charles Kaufman.

Drama/Comedy **(PR:A MPAA:NR)**

FLIRTING WITH FATE*** (1916) 5 reels FA/TRI bw

Douglas Fairbanks *("Augy" Ainsworth)*, Jewel Carmen *(Gladys Kingsley)*, Howard Gaye *(Roland Babney)*, William E. Lawrence *(Augy's Friend)*, George Beranger *(Automatic Joe)*, Dorothy Hadel *(Phyllis)*, Lillian Langdon *(Mrs. Kingsley)*, Wilbur Higby *(Landlord)*, J. P. McCarthy *(Detective)*.

A struggling young artist, Fairbanks, meets Carmen, a society girl, and falls hard. He manages, through a wealthy friend, to meet the girl, but her aunt has already arranged for her to marry a man of means. Despondent, Fairbanks hires a professional killer to end his misery. But then he receives a note from the girl of his dreams, informing him that it is he she loves, and to really make his day a distant stepmother keels over and leaves him several million dollars. It is here that the fun really begins as the athletic Fairbanks puts all of his skills to use in escaping the assassin—and, of course, claiming the girl.

d&w, Christy Cabanne (based on a story by Robert M. Baker); ph, William Fildew.

Comedy/Adventure **Cas.** **(PR:A MPAA:NR)**

FLOATING COLLEGE, THE*** (1928) 6 reels TS bw

Sally O'Neil *(Pat Bixby)*, William Collier, Jr. *(George Dewey)*, Georgia Hale *(Frances Bixby)*, Harvey Clark *(The Dean)*, Georgie Harris *(Snug)*. E.J. Ratcliffe *(Nathan Bixby)*, Virginia Sale *(Miss Cobbs)*.

O'Neil and Hale are wealthy sisters who fall for swimming instructor Collier. To get the edge, Hale arranges to have O'Neil enrolled in a floating college, but it turns out that Collier has been hired to teach on the cruise. Hale hops on board, and when they get to China she locks her sister in a hotel closet, then makes her play for Collier. At that time, a revolution breaks out, but the athletic swimming instructor saves the endangered sister, and they are married at sea.

d, George J. Crone; w, Stuart Anthony; t, Paul Perez; ph, Harry Jackson; ed, Desmond O'Brien.

Comedy/Adventure **(PR:A MPAA:NR)**

FLOOR ABOVE, THE* (1914) 4 reels Reliance/MUT bw

Dorothy Gish, Henry B. Walthall, Earle Foxe, Ralph Lewis, Estelle Coffin.

Gish did as well as she could with this flimsy little melodrama about a flirtatious married chorus girl who realizes how much she loves her husband, after nearly being accused of murder.

d, James Kirkwood; w, (based on the novel *The Tragedy of Charlecot Mansions* by E. Phillips Oppenheim).

Drama **(PR:A MPAA:NR)**

FLORIDA ENCHANTMENT, A* (1914) 5 reels Broadway Star/VIT bw

Sidney Drew *(Dr. Fred Cassadene)*, Edith Storey *(Miss Lillian Travers)*, Charles Kent *(Maj. Horton)*, Jane Morrow *(Bessie Norton)*, Ada Fifford *(Mrs. Stella Lovejoy)*, Ethel Lloyd *(Jane)*, Lillian Burns *(Malvina)*, Grace Stevens *(Miss Constancia Oglethorpe)*, Allan Campbell *(Mr. Stockton Remington)*, Cortland Van Dousen *(Charley Wilkes)*, Frank O'Neil *(Gustavus Duncan)*.

Strange little comedy about a girl who swallows a pill and turns into a man, then gives her black maid one and watches her change also.

d, Sidney Drew; w, Marguerite Bertsch (based on a story by Archibald Clavering Gunter).

Comedy **(PR:A MPAA:NR)**

FLOWING GOLD*** (1924) 8 reels Richard Walton Tully/AFN bw

Anna Q. Nilsson *(Allegheny Briskow)*, Milton Sills *(Calvin Gray)*, Alice Calhoun *(Barbara Parker)*, Crauford Kent *(Henry Nelson)*, John Roche *(Buddy Briskow)*, Cissy Fitzgerald *(The Suicide Blonde)*, Josephine Crowell *(Ma Briskow)*, Bert Woodruff *(Pa Briskow)*,Charles Sellon *(Tom Parker)*.

Fast-moving direction makes this otherwise hokey melodrama a fun action programmer to watch. Sills, a soldier of fortune, is hired by a family to work the oil field which is making them rich. Kent, the Army officer who once persecuted Sills, is out to steal their land, but Sills thwarts this scheme and also saves the rich family's son (Roche) from the clutches of ruthless vamp Fitzgerald. Toward the end of the movie, Roche's sister rescues Sills from a fire and the two marry.

d, Joseph De Grasse; w, Richard Walton Tully; ph, Gilbert Warrenton, Roy Carpenter; ed, Ed LeRoy Stone; art d, William S. Hinshelwood.

Drama **(PR:A MPAA:NR)**

FLY GOD, THE* (1918) 5 reels TRI bw

Roy Stewart, Claire Anderson, Edward Piel, Aaron Edwards, Percy Challenger, Walter Perry.

An invalid is traveling through Arizona with his wife when he is robbed of everything by a road agent. They become friendly with a man, who gets the stranger a job in a saloon. One day the robber enters, spots the invalid, and fires a shot at him. The invalid throws a hammer and kills the outlaw. It turns out that the sheriff is the brother of the man who got him a job and he arrests the invalid for murder. At the trial, all but one juror (a friend of the sheriff's brother) find the invalid guilty. The juror catches a fly and says to the others, "If this critter lands on a window pane, then he goes free." Of course it does, and the invalid is released to spend the rest of his days with his wife and their newborn baby.

d, Cliff Smith.

Western **(PR:A MPAA:NR)**

FLYING FIFTY-FIVE, THE** (1924, Brit.) 5 reels STOLL/Equity British bw

Lionelle Howard *(Reggie Cambray)*, Stephanie Stephens *(Stella Barrington)*, Brian B. Lemon *(Lord Fountwell)*, Lionel d'Aragon *(Sir Jacques Gregory)*, Frank Perfitt *(Josiah Urquhart)*, Bert Darley *(Honorable Claud Barrington)*, Adeline Hayden Coffin *(Aunt)*.

In this British adventure-romance, a nobleman disguises himself as a stableboy and rides his sweetheart's horse in the big race after her jockey is beaten up by crooks.

d&w, A. E. Coleby (based on the novel by Edgar Wallace).

Romance/Adventure **(PR:A MPAA:NR)**

FLYING FEET, THE*** (1929) 11 reels MGM bw

Ramon Novarro *(Tommy)*, Ralph Graves *(Steve)*, Anita Page *(Anita)*, Edward Nugent *(Dizzy)*, Carrol Nye *(Tex)*, Sumner Gretchell *(Kewpie)*, Gardner James *(Specs)*, Alfred Allen *(Admiral)*, The Three Sea Hawks.

Saga of six U.S. Naval Academy graduates who attend flying school, and the heartbreak and triumps they share while trying to earn their wings. Lt. Comdr. Wead, who wrote the story for this picture, was later immortalized in John Ford's biographical film WINGS OF EAGLES.

d, George Hill; w, Richard Schayer (based on a story by Lt. Comdr. Frank Wead, USN); t, Joe Farnham; ph, Ira Morgan; air ph, Charles A. Marshall; ed, Blanche Swell; art d, Cedric Gibbons; m/l, "You're the Only One for Me," William Axt, David Mendoza; syn sc.

Drama **(PR:A MPAA:NR)**

FLYING FROM JUSTICE** (1915, Brit.) 4 reels Neptune bw

Gregory Scott *(Charles Baring)*, Joan Ritz *(Winnie)*, Douglas Payne *(John Gully)*, Alice Moseley *(Mildred Parkes)*, Fred Morgan *(James Woodruffe)*, Cecil Morton York *(Rev. Lacarsey)*, Frank Tennant *(John Lacarsey)*, Jack Denton *(Pearly Tanner)*, Maud Williams *(Mrs. Baring)*, Brian Daly *(Maj. Parkes)*.

English thriller about a divinity student who becomes involved with a gang of counterfeiters.

d, Percy Nash; w, (based on the play by Mark Melford).

Crime **(PR:A MPAA:NR)**

FLYING PAT*** (1920) 5 reels New Art/PAR bw

Dorothy Gish, James Rennie, Morgan Wallace, Harold Vizard, William Black, Porter Strong, Tom Blake, Kate Bruce, Mrs. Waters, Dorothy Walters.

Funny movie featuring Gish—one of the screen's best comediennes—about a young married couple who return from France and move into a mansion she just inherited. They are a "modern" couple, and the husband decides that she should take up a career rather than live the traditional domestic existence. Gish elects to become an aviator, and when her hubby becomes insanely jealous of her dashing instructor, the laughs begin to fly.

d, F. Richard Jones; w, Henry Carr, Jones (based on a story by Virginia Philley Withey); ph, Fred Chaston.

Comedy **(PR:A MPAA:NR)**

FLYING ROMEOS*** (1928) 7 reels FN bw

Charlie Murray *(Cohan)*, George Sidney *(Cohen)*, Fritzi Ridgeway *(Minnie)*, Lester Bernard *(Goldberg)*, Duke Martin *(The Aviator)*, James Bradbury, Jr. *(The Nut)*, Belle Mitchell *(Mrs. Goldberg)*.

Murray and Sidney are a pair of barbers in love with Ridgeway the manicurist. Because she is goofy about flyers, the boys sign up for lessons. Then when their plane goes out of control and does some hair-raising stunts, the plane's owner figures them to be hot-shot pilots and induces them to fly to Europe. The duo take him up on this, which provides additional hysterics, but on their return they discover, to their disgust, that Ridgeway has married an aviator.

p, E. M. Asher; d, Mervyn LeRoy; w, John McDermott; t, Sidney Lazarus, Gene Towne, Jack Conway; ph, Dev Jennings; ed, Paul Weatherwax.

Comedy **(PR:A MPAA:NR)**

FLYING TORPEDO, THE*** (1916) 5 reels FA/TRI bw

John Emerson *(Winthrop Clavering)*, Spottiswoode Aitken *(Bartholomew Thompson)*, William E. Lawrence *(William Haverman)*, Fred J. Butler *(Chief of International Crooks)*, Raymond Wells *(His Accomplice)*, Viola Barry *(Adelaide E. Thompson)*, Bessie Love *(Hulda)*, Lucille Younge *(An Outlaw Woman)*, Ralph Lewis *(Head of the Board)*.

Fascinating film—similar to THE BATTLE CRY OF PEACE but without the sermon—about a flying torpedo which is stolen by foreign agents. The U.S. is in danger until Emerson cleverly gets hold of a model, and the government manufactures a number of them. When California is invaded and the enemy is pushing eastward, the torpedos are put into action and the war is won.

d, Jack O'Brien, W. Christy Cabanne; w, Robert M. Baker, John Emerson; ph, George Hill.

War/Science Fiction **(PR:A MPAA:NR)**

FOG, THE** (1923) 7 reels Max Graf bw

Mildred Harris *(Madelaine Theddon)*, Louise Fazenda *(Millie Richards)*, Louise Dresser *(Mrs. Theddon)*, Marjorie Prevost *(Edith Forge)*, Ann May *(Carol Gardner)*, Ethel Wales *(Mrs. Forge)*, Cullen Landis *(Nathan Forge)*, Ralph Lewis *(Jonathan Forge)*, David Butler *(Si Plumb)*, Frank Currier *(Caleb Gridley)*, Edward Phillips *(Gordon Ruggles)*, Charles Anderson.

Landis publishes a romantic poem about his ideal girl in a local newspaper. The poem's subject, who is a student, reads the verse and is deeply touched. Years later, after he has been unhappily married and victimized by the war, they meet in Siberia (where he is working for the Red Cross) and fall in love.

p, Max Graf; d, Paul Powell; w, Winifred Dunn, H. H. Van Loan (based on a novel by William Dudley Pelley); ph, John Arnold.

Drama **(PR:A MPAA:NR)**

FOLLIES GIRL, THE*** (1919) 5 reels S.A. Lynch/TRI bw

Olive Thomas, Wallace MacDonald, William V. Mong, Claire McDowell, Lee Phelps, Ray Griffith, J.P. Wild, Lillian Langdon.

A dying old millionaire is surrounded by his relatives and realizes that they are only interested in his money. He sends for the niece he has never seen (by a late daughter from whom he had been estranged), and one of the blood-sucking relations hires a chorus girl to impersonate her. But the dancer turns out to be a square-shooter, who nurses the old boy back to good health.

d, Jack Dillon; w, (based on a story by W. Carey Wonderly); ph, Steve Norton.

Drama **(PRA:A MPAA:NR)**

FOOD FOR SCANDAL** (1920) 5 reels REA bw

Wanda Hawley, Harrison Ford, Ethel Grey Terry, Lester Cuneo, Margaret McWade, Minnie Prevost, Juan de la Cruz, Sidney Bracey.

The impoverished daughter of a once wealthy family follows her sweetheart, a struggling lawyer, to San Francisco and becomes a chorus girl. They run into a rich college friend of his, who is looking for a clever attorney and a corespondent to expedite a sticky divorce case. The two are, of course, hired, but before the picture ends, the chorus girl brings the couple back together, and the lawyer is made chief counselor for his friend's firm.

d, James Cruze; w, Edith Kennedy (based on the play "Beverly's Balance" by Paul Kester); ph, H. Kinley Martin.

Drama **(PR:A MPAA:NR)**

FOOL THERE WAS, A*** (1915) 6 reels Box Office Attractions/FOX bw

Theda Bara, Edward Jose, Runa Hodges, Clifford Bruce, Victor Benoit, May Allison, Mabel Fremier.

This famous Bara movie popularized the word vamp almost overnight and was single-handedly responsible for building the Hollywood empire of William Fox. It was Bara's first movie and she played the role of a sexual vampire with such telling force that the English language gained a new word, the cinematic firmament a new star, and the directorial rolls a budding new prospect in director Frank Powell, who is credited with discovering Bara.

d, Frank Powell; w, Roy L. McCardell, Powell (based on the play by Porter Emerson Browne and the poem "The Vampire" by Rudyard Kipling); ph, Lucien Andriot.

Drama **Cas.** **(PR:A-C MPAA:NR)**

FOOLISH WIVES**** (1920) 10 reels UNIV-Super Jewel bw

Rudolph Christians *(Andrew J. Hughes)*, Miss Du Pont *(Helen, his Wife)*, Maude George *(Princess Olga Petschnikoff)*, Mae Busch *(Princess Vera Petschnikoff)*, Erich von Stroheim *(Count Sergius Karamzin, Captain of 3rd Hussars, Imperial Russian Army)*, Dale Fuller *(Maruschka, a Maid)*, Al Edmundsen *(Pavel Pavlich, a Butler)*, Cesare Gravina *(Caesare Ventucci, a Counterfeiter)*, Malvine Polo *(Marietta, His Daughter)*, Louis K. Webb *(Dr. Judd)*, Mrs Kent *(His Wife)*, C. J. Allen *(Albert I, Prince of Monaco)*, Edward Reinach *(Secretary of State of Monaco)*.

After Irving Thalberg, production head at Universal, took the authority to edit his film away from von Stroheim and turned it over to Ripley, this magnificant production was cut from 33 reels to 10. The Austrian had constructed enormous sets and hired an army of extras to serve as a backdrop for his story about a phony count who, along with his two mistresses, lives a life of total debauchery in postwar Monte Carlo. A brutal film, it is filled with glimpses of the squalor that mixes with the splendors in 1920s international society.

d&w, Erich von Stroheim; t, Marian Ainslee, Von Stroheim; ph, Ben Reynolds, William Daniels; m, Sigmund Romberg; ed, Arthur Ripley; art d, E. E. Sheeley.

Drama **Cas.** **(PR:C MPAA:NR)**

FOOLS OF FORTUNE* (1922) 6 reels Golden State/AM

Frank Dill *(Chuck Warner)*, Russell Simpson *(Magpie Simpkins)*, Tully Marshall *(Scenery Simms)*, Frank Brownlee *(Ike Harper)*, Thomas Ricketts *(Milton DePuyster)*, Lillian Langdon *(Mrs. DePuyster)*, Marguerite De La Motte *(Marion De Puyster)*.

Dreadful comedy in which Dill and a group of his cowboy friends head East to pass him off as a millionaire's son. This picture is so padded that no less than 10 titles are exchanged between the westerners and the conductor as they are boarding his train. Then, when the wealthy man in question declares he has no son, the cowboys whoop it up enough to bring in the cops. None of this is faintly amusing. But the ending, in which it is revealed that Dill is really the old boy's son by a previous marriage, is so outrageous that it almost makes the rest worthwhile.

d, A. Byron Davis; d, Louis Chaudet; w, Wilbur C. Tuttle (based on his story "Assisting Ananias"); ph, King Gray.

Comedy/Western **(PR:A MPAA:NR)**

FOR HEAVEN'S SAKE* 1/2** (1926) 6 reels Harold Lloyd/PAR bw

Harold Lloyd *(J. Harold Manners, the Uptown Boy)*, Jobyna Ralston *(Hope, the Downtown Girl)*, Noah Young *(Bull Brindle, the Roughneck)*, James Mason *(The Gangster)*, Paul Weigel *(Brother Paul, the Optimist)*.

Lloyd's first film for Paramount release doesn't have the pathos and careful plot construction of its predecessor, THE FRESHMAN, but the gags are nonstop and hilarious! It all has to do with a millionaire (Lloyd) inadvertently contributing to a skid row mission (which is named in his honor), falling in love with the preacher's daughter, and eventually making parishioners out of every tough guy in the neighborhood.

d, Sam Taylor; w, John Grey, Ted Wilde, Clyde Bruckman; t, Ralph Spence; ph, Henry N. Kohler; ed, Allen McNeil; art d, Liell K. Vedder.

Comedy **(PR:A MPAA:NR)**

FORBIDDEN ADVENTURE, THE***
(1915) 5 reels MUT bw (AKA: CITY OF THE DEAD)

Charles Ray, Louise Glaum, Herschal Mayall.

While travelling in India, a man catches a glimpse of a beautiful girl who lives in the forbidden city. He enters, finds the young lady, and they are banished to the land of the dead. This is an enormous desert area, from which they manage to escape. Once home, she immediately agrees to become his wife.

d, Charles Swickard; w, J. G. Hawks.

Adventure/Romance **(PR:A MPAA:NR)**

FORBIDDEN CARGOES***(1925, Brit.) 7 reels Granville/Western Import bw

Peggy Hyland *(Violet)*, Clifford McLaglen *(John Tredennis)*, James Lindsay *(Sir Charles)*, Guy Tilden Wright *(Philip Sutton)*, Bob Vallis *(Black Mike)*, Daisy Campbell *(Lady Tredennis)*, James Edwards Barber *(William Trefusis)*.

This British costume picture is set in 18th-Century Cornwall and tells of a smuggler who saves the life of a murdered squire's son because he is in love with the lad's stepsister.

p&d, Fred Leroy Granville; w, Mary Murillo (based on a story by Douglas Stuart).

Adventure **(PR:A MPAA:NR)**

FORBIDDEN PARADISE**** (1924) 8 reels FP/PAR bw

Pola Negri *(Catherine, the Czarina)*, Rod La Rocque *(Capt. Alexis Czerny)*, Adolphe Menjou *(Chancellor)*, Pauline Starke *(Anna)*, Fred Malatesta *(French Ambassador)*, Nick De Ruiz *(The Rebellious General)*, Madame Daumery *(Lady-In-Waiting)*, Clark Gable, Carrie D'Aumery.

The Czarina (Negri) of a mythical European kingdom is saved from revolutionaries by La Rocque, a dashing young officer. She rewards him with her sexual favors, and he falls madly in love with her. After breaking up with Starke, his former sweetheart and a lady in waiting, La Rocque learns that he is merely one of many soldiers to whom this award has been bestowed. Furious, he joins the rebels, but swears that no harm shall come to his monarch. One of the most famous examples of the Lubitsch touch occurs at this point, when the uprising is shown to be thwarted in three quick shots. First, the general's hand moves to his sword, then the chamberlain's hand presents a checkbook, and the general's hand releases its grip. For his treachery La Rocque is condemned to death, but the Czarina cannot bring herself to execute this punishment and La Rocque and Starke are allowed to pursue their happiness, while the head of state finds solace in the arms of the French ambassador. Gable's bit part, his first, was awarded to him soon after he and his dramatic coach, Josephine Dillon, whom he had recently married, settled in Hollywood.

d, Ernst Lubitsch; w, Agnes Christine Johnston, Hans Kraly (based on the play "The Czarina" by Lajos Biro, Melchoir Lengyel); ph, Charles Van Enger; set d, Hans Dreier.

Comedy/Drama **(PR:C PAA:NR)**

FORBIDDEN WOMAN, THE*** (1920) 6 reels EPC bw

Clara Kimball Young *(Diane Sorel)*, Conway Tearle *(Malcolm Kent)*, Jiquel Fanol *(Andrew De Clermont)*, Kathryn Adams *(Mme. De Clermont)*, Winter Hall *(Edward Harding)*, Milla Davenport *(Luisa)*, Stanton Williams *(Jimmy)*, John MacKinnon *(The Butler)*.

Young plays a famous French actress and star of the Paris production of "The Forbidden Woman." When she rejects an admirer because he is married, it drives the man to suicide. Young sails for America and rents a house to get over her depression before opening on Broadway. She and a novelist neighbor fall in love, but when Young learns that his sister was the wife of the Parisian who killed himself, she tells him about the tragedy. The writer is outraged and spurns Young, but when his sister returns home and tells him the truth about the situation, he realizes that he acted badly, and the two are united in the end.

d, Harry Garson; w, H. Tipton Steck (based on the novel by Lenore J. Coffee); ph, Arthur Edeson.

Drama **(PR:A MPAA:NR)**

FOREIGN DEVILS*** (1927) 5 reels MGM bw

Tim McCoy *(Capt. Robert Kelly)*, Claire Windsor *(Lady Patricia Rutledge)*, Cyril Chadwick *(Lt. Lord Vivien Cholmondeley)*, Frank Currier *(U.S. Minister Conger)*, Emily Fitzroy *(Mrs. Conger)*, Lawson Butt *(Sir Claude)*, Sojin *(Lama Priest)*, Frank Chew *(Prince Taun)*.

McCoy, assigned to the U.S. Embassy in Peking at the outbreak of the Boxer Rebellion, rescues an English lady from a band of Chinese priests and sees to it that she makes it to the barricade. McCoy holds the attacking Chinese off single-handedly but gets through to the barricade himself to inform the people there that the Allies are on the way. His reward for all of these heroics, of course, is the lady's love.

d, W. S. Van Dyke; w, Marian Ainslee (based on a story by Peter Bernard Kyne); t, Ainslee, Ruth Cummings; ph, Clyde De Vinna; ed, Sam S. Zimbalist; art d, Cedric Gibbons, David Townsend; cos, Rene Hubert.

Adventure **(PR:A MPAA:NR)**

FOREVER AFTER*** (1926) 7 reels FN bw

Lloyd Hughes *(Ted Wayne)*, Mary Astor *(Jennie Clayton)*, Hallam Cooley *(Jack Randall)*, David Torrence *(Mr. Clayton)*, Eulalie Jensen *(Mrs. Clayton)*, Alec Francis *(Mr. Wayne)*, Lila Leslie *(Mrs. Wayne)*.

Hughes, a young man of limited means, loves Astor, a millionaire's daughter. At her suggestion, Hughes goes to college and becomes a football hero. Astor's mother does not approve of Hughes' humble roots and persuades him to break up with her daughter by telling the girl that he does not care for her. The young man does this and goes off to fight in WW I, where he is wounded. Astor, in the meantime, jilts the wealthy fellow her mother selected for her, joins the Red Cross, and is reunited with Hughes in France.

d, F. Harmon Weight; w, Paul Gangelin (based on the play by Owen Davis); ph, Karl Struss.

Drama **(PR:A MPAA:NR)**

FORGIVEN, OR THE JACK O'DIAMONDS* (1914) 6 reels Stellar bw

Edwin Forsberg, Caroline French, Hector Dion, Daniel Bertona, Luke J. Loring, Ricca Allen, Fritzie Brunette, Lois Alexander, Frederick Burton.

This motion picture translation of the theatrical melodrama about a reformed gambler who finally wins the girl was about two reels too long. Filmed in Florida, it does, however, give contemporary audiences a fair look at that fabulous state before the land rush.

d, William Robert Daly; w, Bennett Musson (based on the play by Clay M. Greene).

Drama **(PR:A MPAA:NR)**

FORTUNE HUNTER, THE** (1914) 6 reels Lubin bw

William Elliot, Ethel Clayton, Rosetta Brice, Charles Brandt, George Soule Spencer, Florence Williams, James Daly, Ruth Bryan, Bernard Siegel, Gaston Bell, Ferdinand Tidmarsh.

Less-than-successful motion picture version of the popular John Barrymore play about an impoverished young spendthrift's effect on a rural American town.

d, Barry O'Neil; w, Clay M. Greene (based on a play by Winchell Smith).

Drama **(PR:A MPAA:NR)**

FORTUNE HUNTER, THE** (1927) 7 reels WB bw

Sydney Chaplin *(Nat Duncan)*, Helene Costello *(Josie Lockwood)*, Clara Horton *(Betty Graham)*, Duke Martin *(Handsome Harry West)*, Thomas Jefferson *(Sam Graham)*, Erville Alderson *(Blinky Lockwood)*, Paul Kruger *(Roland)*, Nora Cecil *(Betty Carpenter)*, Louise Carver *(Drygoods Store Owner)*, Bob Perry *(Sheriff)*, Babe London *(Waitress)*.

In this ordinary comedy, Chaplin is persuaded by a friend who married money to move to a small town where he can do the same. His benefactor, of course, plans to share in the spoils. Before long, the richest woman in town is in hot pursuit, but Chaplin has fallen for the girl who owns a failing soda fountain, which the comedian, after a number of tired gags, turns into a great success.

d, Charles F. Reisner; w, Bryan Foy, Robert Dillon (based on a play by Winchell Smith); ph, Ed Du Par; syn sc.

Comedy **(PR:A MPAA:NR)**

FORTUNE'S CHILD*** (1919) 5 reels VIT bw

Gladys Leslie, Kempton Greene, Stanley Walpole, Frances Mann, Fred Smith, Jessie Stevens, Denton Vane, Frank Norcross, Miriam Miles.

Wholesome little film about an orphan's love for a crooked prizefighter which brings about his complete regeneration. The picture's modest production values did not hurt, and may have indeed enhanced, the sweet sentiment projected by all.

d, Joseph Gleason; w, (based on the story "Beth" by Lawrence McCloskey); ph, Jules Cronjager.

Drama **(PR:A MPAA:NR)**

FORTY WINKS**** (1925) 7 reels FP-LAS/PAR bw

Raymond Griffith *(Lord Chumley)*, Viola Dana *(Eleanor Butterworth)*, Theodore Roberts *(Adam Butterworth)*, Cyril Chadwick *(Gaspar Le Sage)*, Anna May Wong *(Annabelle Wu)*, William Boyd *(Lt. Gerald Hugh Butterworth)*.

Griffith is a British secret service agent accused of stealing valuable military plans which were in the possession of his fiancee's brother, Boyd. They were actually taken by Eurasian operative Wong under orders from sinister Chadwick. Thus the stage is set for master comedian Griffith to do battle for order and justice, as only he can, in a rip-roaring, action-packed, uproariously funny action comedy.

d, Frank Urson, Paul Iribe; w, Bertram Milhauser (based on the play "Lord Chumley" by Cecil B. DeMille, David Belasco); ph, Peverell Marley.

Comedy **(PR:A MPAA:NR)**

FOUNDATIONS OF FREEDOM, THE** (1918, Brit.) 6 reels Birmingham bw

Maud Yates *(Jane Butler)*, Cecil Morton York *(Col. Washington Butler)*.

This British historical romance dealt with the love between American and English families during the time of Ben Franklin and George Washington.

d&w, Arthur Branscombe.

Drama **(PR:A MPAA:NR)**

FOUR FEATHERS** (1915) 5 reels Dyreda/Metro bw

Howard Estabrook, Irene Warfield, Arthur Ewers, Hayward Mack.

First filming of Mason's novel about an English officer who performs heroic deeds, after being branded a coward, on behalf of the British Empire. Unfortunately, the picture suffered from bad direction, casting, and production values.

d&w, J. Searle Dawley (based on the novel by A. E. W. Mason).

Adventure **(PR:A MPAA:NR)**

FOUR FEATHERS* 1/2** (1929) 8 reels PAR/FP bw

Richard Arlen *(Harry Faversham)*, Fay Wray *(Ethne Eustace)*, Clive Brook *(Lt. Durrance)*, William Powell *(Capt. Trench)*, Theodore von Eltz *(Lt. Castleton)*, Noah Beery *(Slave Trader)*, Zack Williams *(Idris)*, Noble Johnson *(Ahmed)*, Harold Hightower *(Ali)*, Philippe De Lacy *(Harry, as a Boy of 10)*, E. J. Radcliffe *(Col. Eustace)*, George Fawcett *(Col. Faversham)*, Augustin Symonds *(Col. Sutch)*.

The third filming of A. E. W. Mason's novel of cowardice overcome, during the British occupation of the Sudan, was far superior to the earlier American and English versions. Directors Cooper and Schoedsack, the daredevil helmsmen of CHANG, GRASS, and KING KONG, created some sensational battle scenes, as well as some truly magnificent location footage.

p, David Selznick; d, Merian C. Cooper, Ernest B. Schoedsack, Lothar Mendes; w, Howard Eastbrook, Hope Loring (based on the novel by A. E. W. Mason); t, Julian Johnson, John Farrow; ph, Robert Kurrle, Cooper, Schoedsack; m, William Frederick Peters; ed, Schoedsack; syn sc; s eff.

Adventure **(PR:A MPAA:NR)**

FOUR HORSEMEN OF THE APOCALYPSE, THE**** (1921) 11 reels Metro bw

Rudolph Valentino *(Julio Desnoyers)*, Alice Terry *(Marguerite Laurier)*, Pomeroy Cannon *(Madariaga, the Centaur)*, Josef Swickard *(Marcelo Desnoyers)*, Brinsley Shaw *(Celendonio)*, Alan Hale *(Karl von Hartrott)*, Bridgetta Clark *(Dona Luisa)*, Mabel Van Buren *(Elena)*, Nigel De Brulier *(Tchernoff)*, Bowditch Turner

(Argensola), John Sainpolis *(Laurier)*, Mark Fenton *(Sen. Lacour)*, Virginia Warwick *(Chichi)*, Derek Ghent *(Rene Lacour)*, Stuart Holmes *(Capt. von Hartrott)*, Jean Hersholt *(Prof. von Hartrott)*, Henry Klaus *(Heinrich von Hartrott)*, Edward Connelly *(Lodgekeeper)*, Georgia Woodthorpe *(Lodgekeeper's Wife)*, Kathleen Key *(Georgette)*, Wallace Beery *(Lt.-Col. von Richtoffen)*, Jacques D'Auray *(Capt. d'Aubrey)*, Curt Rehfeld *(Maj. Blumhardt)*, Harry Northrup *(The Count)*, Claire De Lorez *(Mlle. Lucette, the Model)*, Bull Montana *(The French Butler)*, Isabelle Keith *(The German Woman)*, Jacques Lanoe *(Her Husband)*, Noble Johnson *(Conquest)*, Minnehaha *(The Old Nurse)*, Arthur Hoyt *(Lt. Schnitz)*, Beatrice Dominguez *(A Dancer)*.

Many of the scenes in Ingram's motion picture version of the Blasco-Ibanez anti-war novel about an Argentinian family which fights on separate sides during WW I, have the look of oil paintings come to life. It was a very costly film to produce (but earned over $3 million) and, besides antagonizing the French, English, and Germans, who felt they were represented unfairly, a new star was born the moment Valentino began his electrifying tango. The story tells about the aftermath of the death of Argentine patriarch Cannon, who hated his German son-in-law and loved Julio (Valentino). When he dies the family disperses to Germany and France, with Valentino landing in France where he opens a studio. Here he paints, entertains his friends, and falls in love with Terry, the young wife of a jurist. War strikes Europe, and Terry's husband enlists, while she joins the Red Cross. As a nurse, she finds her husband has been blinded in the fighting, and she vows to resist the attentions of Valentino. On Valentino, meanwhile, descends a stranger who, invoking the symbols of the Four Horsemen of the Apocalypse—war, conquest, famine, and death—gets him to enlist. Trading his palette for a rifle, however, leads him to his doom, for, after distinguishing himself in battle he is killed in an exchange of gunfire with his cousin who went to Germany, and now has become an officer.

d, Rex Ingram; w, June Mathis (based on the novel by Vicente Blasco-Ibanez); ph, John F. Seitz; m, Louis F. Gottschalk; ed, Grant Whytock; art d, Joseph Calder, Amos Myers; makeup, Jean Hersholt.

Drama/War **(PR:A MPAA:NR)**

FOUR MEN IN A VAN*** (1921, Brit.) 7 reels Direct Film Traders/Titan bw

Manning Haynes *(Wilkes)*, Donald Searle *(Buggins)*, Johnny Butt *(Troddles)*, Gordon Hopkirk *(Murray)*, Moore Marriott *(Mudley)*.

This bright little British comedy, about the misadventures of a group of chums who spend their vacation traveling by caravan, is entertaining and amusing.

d&w, Hugh Croise (based on the novel *We Three and Troddles* by R. Andom).

Comedy **(PR:A MPAA:NR)**

FOUR SONS**** (1928) 10 reels FOX bw

James Hall *(Joseph Bernle)*, Margaret Mann *(Grandma Bernle)*, Earle Foxe *(Von Stomm)*, Charles Morton *(Johann Bernle)*, Francis X. Bushman, Jr. *(Franz Bernle)*, George Meeker *(Andres Bernle)*, Albert Gran *(Letter Carrier)*, Frank Reicher *(Schoolmaster)*, Hughie Mack *(Innkeeper)*, Michael Mark *(Von Stomm's Orderly)*, August Tollaire *(Burgomaster)*, June Collyer *(Ann, the American Girl)*, Wendell Phillips Franklin *(James Henry)*, Ruth Mix *(Johann's Girl)*, Jack Pennick *(Joseph's American Friend)*, Leopold Archduke of Austria *(German Captain)*, Robert Parrish *(Child)*, L. J. O'Connor *(Aubergiste)*, Capt. John Porters, Ferdinand Schumann-Heink, Carl Boheme, Constant Franke, Hans Furberg, Tibor von Janny, Stanley Blystone, Lt. George Blagoi *(Officers)*.

Ford traveled to Germany to shoot background footage for this picture and met the great Teutonic director F.W. Murnau, who had just signed a contract with Fox. The German was pleased to show Ford the techniques his UFA studio used, as well as a number of German cinematic classics. Fascinated by all of this, the American returned to Hollywood and made this antiwar film about a Bavarian mother who loses three sons to combat and finally settles in the U.S. with the fourth. Ford's use of the moving camera and Germanic atmosphere was masterful, and he would call upon these methods again with his 1935 masterpiece THE INFORMER.

d, John Ford; w, Philip Klein (based on the story "Grandmother Bernle Learns Her Letters" by Ida Alexa Ross Wylie); t, Katherine Hilliker, H. H. Caldwell; ph, George Schneiderman, Charles G. Clarke; ed, Margaret V. Clancy; m/l, "Little Mother," Erno Rapee, Lew Pollack; syn sc; s eff.

Drama **(PR:A MPAA:NR)**

FOUR WALLS* 1/2** (1928) 8 reels MGM bw

John Gilbert *(Benny)*, Joan Crawford *(Frieda)*, Vera Gordon *(Mrs. Horowitz)*, Carmel Myers *(Bertha)*, Robert E. O'Connor *(Sullivan)*, Louis Natheaux *(Monk)*, Jack Byron *(Duke Roma)*.

Fine performances by Gilbert, Crawford, and O'Connor, as well as good direction, make this underworld picture a cut above the rest. Gilbert plays a gangster who fights to go straight after serving a term for manslaughter. Crawford, as the East Side girl who sticks by him through it all, was well on her way to stardom when this film was made. O'Connor, as the hard-boiled detective with the heart of gold, is the quintessential New York cop.

d, William Nigh; w, Alice D. G. Miller (based on the play by George Abbott, Dana Burnet); t, Joe Farnham; ph, James Howe; ed, Harry Reynolds; set d, Cedric Gibbons.

Crime **(PR:A MPAA:NR)**

FOX FARM** (1922, Brit.) 6 reels George Clark/STOLL bw

Guy Newall *(James Falconer)*, Ivy Duke *(Ann Wetherall)*, A. Bromley Davenport *(Sam Wetherall)*, Barbara Everest *(Kate Falconer)*, Cameron Carr *(Jack Rickaby)*, Charles Evemy *(Slim Wetherall)*, John Alexander *(Jacob Boase)*.

Newall, a wealthy farmer, is scorned by his wife and adored by Duke, daughter of the local scoundrel. When Newall is blinded in an accident, Duke comes to work for and be near him. Meanwhile, Newall's wife becomes involved with Carr, giving Duke the right at last to declare her love for Newall. The film ends with the two stumbling off to find happiness on their own.

d&w, Guy Newall (based on the novel by Warwick Deeping).

Drama **(PR:A MPAA:NR)**

FRAILTY* (1921, Brit.) 6 reels STOLL bw

Madge Stuart *(Diana)*, Rowland Myles *(Charles Ley)*, Sydney Lewis Ransome *(Beverley Dacre)*, Paulette del Baye *(Felice Ley)*, H. Agar Lyons *(Harman)*, J. Edward Barber *(The Partner)*, Mrs. Gerald *(Marie Ley)*.

This cheerful little English film tells of an orphaned bastard who marries a recovered alcoholic and is seduced into becoming a drug addict by his mother's paramour.

d, F. Martin Thornton; w, Leslie Howard Gordon (based on the novel by Olive Wadsley).

Drama **(PR:C MPAA:NR)**

FRAME UP, THE*** (1917) 5 reels AM bw

William Russell *(Jeffrey Claiborne)*, Harvey Clark *(Avery Claiborne)*, Lucille Ward *(Mother Moir)*, Francella Billington *(Jane Anne)*, Alfred Ferguson *(Bud Yeager)*, Charles Newton *(Jim Vance)*, Clarence Burton *(Michael Broderick)*.

Good action comedy, in the Douglas Fairbanks tradition, in which wealthy young Russell takes a job with a cab company to be near the owner's daughter. Before the picture's end, he battles an army of crooks who are trying to take over and wins the girl.

d, Edward Sloman; w, Jules Furthman.

Comedy/Adventure **(PR:A MPAA:NR)**

FRAU IM MOND (SEE: WOMAN ON THE MOON, THE, 1929, Ger.)

FRECKLED RASCAL, THE** (1929) 6 reels FBO/RKO bw

Buzz Barton *(Red Hepner)*, Milburn Morante *(Hank Robbins)*, Tom Lingham *(Follansbee)*, Lotus Thompson *(Sally)*, Pat O'Brien *(Jim Kane)*, Bill Patton *(Bill Latham)*.

Lingham cuts off a town's water supply in a scheme to drive up its price. When Barton and a friend bring in a 20-horse waterwagon, Lingham attacks them. The boys drive him off and later Barton discovers him dying of thirst in the desert. Barton offers him a drink in return for the villain's signature on a contract agreeing to charge a fair price for water.

d, Louis King; w, Frank Howard Clark; ph, Nick Musuraca; ed, George Marsh.

Western **(PR:A MPAA:NR)**

FREE LIPS** (1928) 6 reels James Ormont/FD bw

June Marlow *(Ann Baldridge)*, Frank Hagney *(Bill Dugan)*, Jane Novak *(Flossie Moore)*, Ernie Shields *(The Fox)*, Olin Francis *(Detective Kelly)*, Edna Hearn *(Mazie)*.

Hagney, the owner of a nightclub called Free Lips, falls for Marlow, a decent girl who works as his hostess. When she is accused of murdering one of her customers, Hagney takes the blame. In the end, the real killer is found, Hagney goes straight, and he marries the small town hostess who reminds him of his Indiana-born mother.

d, Wallace MacDonald; w, Jack Kelly (based on a story by Raymond Wells); ph, Jack Fuqua, Cliff Thomas; ed, Gene Milford.

Crime **(PR:A MPAA:NR)**

FREEDOM OF THE PRESS** (1928) 7 reels UNIV-Jewel bw

Lewis Stone *(Daniel Steele)*, Marceline Day *(June Westcott)*, Malcolm McGregor *(Bill Ballard)*, Henry B. Walthall *(John Ballard)*, Robert E. O'Connor *(Boss Maloney)*, Thomas Ricketts *(Wicks)*, Hayden Stevenson *(Callahan)*, Robert Ellis *(Cyrus Hazlett)*, Boris Baronoff *(A Crook)*, Morgan Thorpe *(Organist)*, Evelyn Selbie *(Italian Mother)*, Bernard Seigel *(Italian Father)*, Wilson Benge *(Butler)*.

When his newspaper publisher father is murdered, McGregor takes over and spearheads a campaign which prevents Stone, a corrupt politician, from becoming mayor.

d, George Melford; sup, Arthur E. Shadur; w, J. Grubb Alexander (uncredited) Curtis Benton, J. G. Hawks (based on a story by Peter B. Kyne); t, Walter Anthony; ph, Ben Reynolds; ed, George McGuire.

Drama **(PR:A MPAA:NR)**

FRENCH DOLL, THE** (1923) 7 reels TIF/Metro bw

Mae Murray *(Georgine Mazulier)*, Orville Caldwell *(Wellington Wick)*, Rod La Rocque *(Pedro Carrova)*, Rose Dione *(Mme. Mazulier)*, Paul Cazeneuve *(Mons. Mazulier)*, Williard Louis *(Joseph Dumas)*, Bernard Randall *(Snyder)*, Lucien Littlefield *(Dobbs, the Butler)*.

Murray, a pretty French girl, is forced by her parents to sell fake antiques. She is brought to America where they attempt to marry her off to wealthy Caldwell. Toward the end of the picture, there is an incident at a Palm Beach party in which Murray is wounded by a gunshot. This makes Caldwell realize the depth of the love he feels for her, regardless of her past, and the two marry.

p&d, Robert Z. Leonard; w, Frances Marion (based on a play by Paul Armont, Marcel Gerbidou); t, Alfred A. Cohn; ph, Oliver T. Marsh.

Drama **(PR:A MPAA:NR)**

FRENCH DRESSING*** (1927) 7 reels FN bw

H. B. Warner *(Phillip Grey)*, Clive Brook *(Henri de Briac)*, Lois Wilson *(Cynthia Grey)*, Lilyan Tashman *(Peggy Nash)*.

Dwan directed his actors with great skill in this society comedy about a frigid wife who flees to Paris after misinterpreting her husband's innocent flirtation with a visiting friend. The "City of Light" completely transforms her, however, and after a little fling of her own, she returns to her husband's arms—a wiser *and* warmer wife.

p&d, Allan Dwan; w, J. L. Campbell (based on a story by Adelaide Heilbron); ph, Ernest Haller; ed, Terrell Morse.

Comedy/Drama **(PR:C MPAA:NR)**

FRESHIE, THE** (1922) 5 reels Frederick Herbst/Di Lorenzo bw

Guinn "Big Boy" Williams *(Charles Taylor)*, Molly Malone *(Violet Blakely)*, Lincoln Stedman *("Tubby" Tarpley)*, James McElhern *(Prof. Noyes)*, Edward Burns *(Ranch Foreman)*, Lee Phelps *(Tom)*, Sam Armstrong *(Jack)*, J. Buckley Russell *("Society Sam")*, Jules Hauft *(Mr. Blakely)*.

A ranch hand sacrifices everything to get an education. When he first arrives on campus he is the butt of merciless hazing, but after capturing a burglar, he wins the respect of his fellow students and the heart of the campus queen.

d&w, W. Hughes Curran; ph, Charles J. Stumar.

Comedy/Drama **(PR:A MPAA:NR)**

FRESHMAN, THE**** (1925) 7 reels Harold Lloyd/Pathe Exchange bw

Harold Lloyd *(Harold "Speedy" Lamb)*, Jobyna Ralston *(Peggy)*, Brooks Benedict *(College Cad)*, James Anderson *(Chester A. "Chet" Trask)*, Hazel Keener *(College Belle)*, Joseph Harrington *(College Tailor)*, Pat Harmon *(The Coach)*, Charles Stevenson *(Assistant Coach)*, Oscar Smith *(The Dean's Chauffeur)*, Grady Sutton, Gus Leonard, Charles Farrell, Mike *(Mascot Dog)*.

Full of gentle pathos and timeless gags, this wonderful film about a boy who goes to college and, after being the butt of the student body's practical jokes, wins the big game and the girl of his dreams, is one of the finest satirical comedies ever made. It earned more than any other Lloyd picture, grossing $2,651,000 on a production cost of $301,681, although, ironically, a great deal of this was lost in a lawsuit that consumed more than seven years, with a former writer friend of Lloyd's, H. C. Witwer, who claimed Lloyd and his people stole a story of his. At the end of the battle, the Harold Lloyd Corporation, after first losing the suit, finally won it on appeal, but it was an expensive ordeal. So Lloyd was thereafter always extremely careful when dealing with writers.

d, Sam Taylor, Fred Newmeyer; w, John Grey, Ted Wilde, Tim Wheelan, Taylor, Clyde Bruckman, Lex Neal, Jean Havez, Brooks B. Harding; t, Thomas J. Grey; ph, Walter Lundin, Henry Kohler; ed, Allen McNeil; art d, Liell K. Vedder.

Comedy **(PR:A MPAA:NR)**

FRIDAY THE 13TH* (1916) 5 reels PEER/WORLD bw

Robert Warwick *(Robert Brownley)*, Clarence Harvey *(Peter Brownley)*, Charles Brandt *(Judge Lee Sands)*, Gerda Holmes *(Beulah Sands)*, Montagu Love *(Count Varneloff)*, Lenore Harris *(Simone)*.

After a Southern judge is ruined by a New York stock operator, his daughter secures a job (under an assumed name) in the broker's office. She falls in love with the son of her employer, but still feeds her father the inside information which can destroy his enemy. Eventually, she confesses her actions to the young man, but he forgives her and they are married.

d, Emile Chautard; w, Frances Marion (based on the novel by Thomas W. Lawson).

Drama **(PR:A MPAA:NR)**

FRIENDLY HUSBAND, A*** (1923) 5 reels FOX bw

Lupino Lane *(Friend Husband)*, Alberta Vaughn *(Tootsie, Friend, Wife)*, Eva Thatcher *(The Mother-In-Law)*.

Few comedians could do as much with their bodies as British music hall star Lane. Unfortunately, he was unable to register more than two facial expressions, which prevented him from attaining real stardom in feature films. His pictures—such as this one about the misadventures of a family vacationing by trailer—were loaded with sight gags and breathtaking stunts, but the funny little man was obviously better suited for the variety stage, to which he would soon return.

d, John Blystone; w, Hampton Del Ruth (based on a story by Blystone); t, Ralph Spence; ph, Jay Turner; ed, Spence.

Comedy **(PR:A MPAA:NR)**

FROM RAGS TO RICHES (SEE: RAGS TO RICHES, 1922)

FROM THE GROUND UP*** (1921) 5 reels Goldwyn bw

Tom Moore *(Terence Giluley)*, Helene Chadwick *(Philena Mortimer)*, De Witt Jennings *(Mr. Mortimer)*, Grace Pike *(Mrs. Mortimer)*, Hardee Kirkland *(Carswell, Sr.)*, Darrel Foss *(Carswell, Jr.)*.

Pleasant little romantic comedy in which Moore plays a laborer who scales the ladder of success and ends up not only owning the skyscraper he once dug the foundation for, but marrying the daughter of his former employer as well. The building used for this film was the Loew's State, which was then under construction in Los Angeles.

d, E. Mason Hopper; w, Rupert Hughes; ph, John J. Mescall.

Romance/Comedy **(PR:A MPAA:NR)**

FROM THE MANGER TO THE CROSS**** (1913) 6 reels Kalem bw

Gene Gaunthier, Jack Clark, R. Henderson-Bland, Robert Vignola, Alice Hollister, Sidney Olcott, J. P. McGowan, Helen Lindroth, Percy Dyer, Sidney Baber.

Kalem specialized in shooting their pictures at actual locations (Ireland, in particular, where they made so many that at one time their productions were kiddingly referred to as O'Kalem's), and this version of the Passion Play was filmed in Palestine. The film was an enormous artistic and commercial success and was still being shown in 1938, when it was reissued with sound.

d, Sidney Olcott; w, Olcott, Gene Gaunthier (based on the New Testament); ph, George K. Hollister.

Biblical **(PR:A MPAA:NR)**

FRONT PAGE STORY, A** (1922) 6 reels VIT bw

Edward [Everett] Horton *(Rodney Marvin)*, Lloyd Ingraham *(Mayor Gorham)*, James Corrigan *(Matt Hayward)*, Edith Roberts *(Virginia Hayward)*, William E. Lawrence *(Don Coates)*, Buddy Messenger *(Tommy)*, Mathilde Brundage *(Mrs. Gorham)*, Lila Leslie *(Suzanne Gorham)*, Tom McGuire *(Jack Peeler)*.

Comfortable little comedy in which a cub reporter (well played by Horton) delivers the big story, becomes half owner of his paper, and marries the publisher's daughter.

d, Jesse Robbins; w, F. W. Beebee (based on a story by Arthur Frederick Goodrich); ph, Vernon Walker.

Comedy **(PR:A MPAA:NR)**

FRUITS OF DESIRE, THE*** (1916) 5 reels WORLD bw

Robert Warrick, Alec B. Francis, Robert Cummings, Ralph Delmore, D. J. Flannigan, James Mack, James Ewens, Adolphe Lestina, Philip Basi, George Moss, Harry C. Weir, Ezra Walck, Adolph Parina, Madaline Traverse, Harry DeVere, Dorothy Fairchild, Julia Stuart, Phyllis Hazeltine, Mildred Havens.

Story of a driven rural boy, who rises from day laborer to owner of the steel mill while stepping on everyone (including the working girl who loves him) as he claws his way to the top.

d, Oscar Eagle; w, (based on the novel *The Ambition of Mark Truitt* by Henry Russell Miller).

Drama **(PR:A MPAA:NR)**

FUGITIVES** (1929) 6 reels FOX bw

Madge Bellamy *(Alice Carroll)*, Don Terry *(Dick Starr)*, Arthur Stone *(Jimmy)*, Earle Foxe *(Al Barrow)*, Matthew Betz *(Earl Rand)*, Lumsden Hare *(Uncle Ned)*, Edith Yorke *(Mrs. Carroll)*, Jean Laverty *(Mame)*, Hap Ward *(Scal, the Rat)*.

Bellamy, a nightclub singer, is wrongly accused of murdering her boss and sent to Sing Sing by young district attorney Terry. After he helps her escape, Bellamy's innocence is determined, and she saves Terry from a gang of crooks.

d, William Beaudine; sup, Kenneth Hawks; w, John Stone (based on a story by Richard Harding Davis); t, Malcolm Stuart Boylan; ph, Chester Lyons; syn sc.

Crime **(PR:A MPAA:NR)**

FURTHER ADVENTURES OF THE FLAG LIEUTENANT**
(1927, Brit.) 9 reels Neo-Art/Williams and Pritchard bw

Henry Edwards *(Lt. Dicky Lascelles)*, Isabel Jeans *(Pauline)*, Lilian Oldland *(Sybil Wynne)*, Lyn Harding *(The Sinister Influence)*, Fewlass Llewellyn *(Adm. Wynne)*, Fred Raynham *(Col. William Thesiger)*, Albert Egbert *(Bill)*, Seth Egbert *(Walter)*, Vivian Baron *(Ah Loom)*.

For an English film of its time, the action was better staged than usual, due probably to the efforts of German director Hagen. The last time around, Edwards prevented a fort from being overrun by ungrateful colonials. This time he saves some plans, which are important to the preservation of the Empire, from falling into the clutches of a gang of spies.

p, Julius Hagen; d, W. P. Kellino; w, George A. Cooper (based on a story by W.P. Drury).

Adventure **(PR:A MPAA:NR)**

G

GALLANT FOOL, THE* (1926) 5 reels Duke Worne/RAY bw

Billy Sullivan *(Billy Banner)*, Hazel Deane *(Princess Iris)*, Ruth Boyd *(Cynthia)*, Frank Baker *(Count Danvo)*, Jimmy Aubrey *(Beaney Mulligan)*, Ferdinand Schumann-Heink *(Crown Prince Boris)*, Robert Walker *(Capt. Turgemore)*.

Sullivan, an appealing, athletic actor who deserves to be better remembered, plays the son of an American millionaire, off to Valdonia to collect a debt owed his father. He impersonates a prince, takes on the evil Schumann-Heink and his 24-man army, and ends up marrying the queen, who has also been victimized in this laughingly inept, super low-budgeted, kid-oriented programmer.

d, Duke Worne; w, George W. Pyper.

Adventure **(PR:A MPAA:NR)**

GALLOPIN' THROUGH (SEE: GALLOPING THRU, 1923)

GALLOPING ACE, THE** (1924) 5 reels UNIV bw

Jack Hoxie *(Jim Jordon)*, Margaret Morris *(Anne Morse)*, Robert McKim *(David Kincaid)*, Frank Rice *(Knack Williams)*, Julia Brown *(Louise Williams)*, Dorothea Wolbert *(Susie Williams)*, Fred Humes *(Fred)*.

Hoxie returns home from the war a hero but finds his job gone. He is given employment on a ranch owned by Morris, discovers that McKim (the owner of a nearby quarry) is about to steal her land, foils the plot, and wins the love of the girl.

d, Robert North Bradbury; w, Isadore Bernstein (based on a story by Jacques Jaccard); ph, Merritt Gerstad.

Western **(PR:A MPAA:NR)**

GALLOPING GALLAGHER*** (1924) 5 reels MON/FBO bw

Fred Thompson *(Bill Gallagher)*, Hazel Keener *(Evelyn Churchill)*, Frank Hagney *(Joseph Burke)*, Nelson McDowell *(Leon I. Berry)*, Shorty Hendrix *(Tub)*, Andy Morris *(Slim)*, Silver King the Horse.

Thompson's horse Silver King was becoming a serious rival to Tony (Tom Mix's steed) by the time this western was made, and as such was given a prominent role. The story is about a wanderer who comes to town in time to foil a robbery, is elected sheriff, and saves the girl (a female minister) from the clutches of the gang on bringing them to justice. Good, clean entertainment from Thompson, who was a Presbyterian minister in real life.

d, Albert Rogell; w, Marion Jackson; ph, Ross Fisher.

Western **(PR:A MPAA:NR)**

GALLOPING GOBS, THE** (1927) 5 reels Action Pictures/Pathe bw

Buffalo Bill, Jr. *(Bill Corbitt)*, Morgan Brown *(Chub Barnes)*, Betty Baker *(Mary Whipple)*, Raye Hampton *(Fanny)*, Walter Maly *(Outlaw Leader)*, Robert Homans *(The Banker)*, Jack Barnell *(The Ensign)*, Fred Burns *(Sheriff)*.

Fair action programmer has a couple of sailors winning a western ranch in a poker game, foiling a stage holdup, rescuing a pretty girl, and settling down where the deer and the antelope play.

d, Richard Thorpe; w, Frank L. Inghram (based on a story by Lew Collins, Sergey Sergeyeff); ph, Ray Reis.

Western **(PR:A MPAA:NR)**

GALLOPING KID, THE*** (1922) 5 reels UNIV bw

Ed [Hoot] Gibson *("Simplex" Cox)*, Edna Murphy *(Helen Arnett)*, Lionel Belmore *("Five-Notch" Arnett)*, Leon Bary *(Fred Bolston)*, Jack Walters *(Steve Larabee)*, Percy Challenger *(Zek Hawkins)*.

Gibson gives his usual winning performance as "Simplex" Cox, an easy-going cowboy hired by Belmore, the fastest gun in the territory, to keep his daughter Murphy from seeing bad guy Bary. At first, the girl's resentment leads to many humorous situations, but when Gibson proves her boy friend to be a crook out to steal her father's platinum mine, she shows her appreciation by falling in love with her chaperone.

d, Nat Ross; w, A. P. Younger, Arthur Statter (based on a story by William Henry Hamby); ph, Arthur Reeves.

Western/Comedy **(PR:A MPAA:NR)**

GALLOPING THRU**
(1923) 5 reels Sunset bw (AKA: GALLOPIN' THROUGH)

Jack Hoxie, Priscilla Brown.

Popular cowboy star Hoxie comes to the aid of some homesteaders, clears the head of the family of a crime he did not commit, brings the real crook to justice, and wins the settler's sister.

d, Robert North Bradbury.

Western **(PR:A MPAA:NR)**

GAMBLE WITH HEARTS, A**
(1923, Brit.) 5 reels Master/Woolf and Freedman bw

Milton Rosmer *(Dallas Chalfont)*, Madge Stuart *(Morag Lannon)*, Valia *(Rosaleen Erle)*, Olaf Hytten *(Dallas, Jr.)*, Margaret Hope *(Fanette Fraser)*, Cecil Morton York *(Vickers)*, George Bishop *(Inspector Duer)*, Mickey Brantford, Hargreave Mansell, Pat Fitzgerald.

In this English thriller, a man on the run is finally proven innocent of stabbing an actress by his fiancee, who had become the victim of amnesia. She also points the finger of guilt to the detective who framed him.

p, H. B. Parkinson; d, Edwin J. Collins; w, Lucita Squier (based on the novel by Anthony Carlyle).

Crime **(PR:A MPAA:NR)**

GAMBLING IN SOULS*** (1919) 6 reels FOX bw

Madlaine Traverse *(Marcia Dunning/Mme. Rouge)*, Herbert Heyes *(Duke Charters)*, Murdock MacQuarrie *(Thomas Philborn)*, Lew Zehring *(Dick Philborn)*, Mary McIvor *(Edith Dunning)*, Henry Barrows *(Latimer)*, Marion Skinner *(Mrs. Caldwell)*, William Clifford *(Robert Dunning)*.

Predictable but well-handled melodrama about a woman who avenges the death of her husband (who committed suicide after being ruined by a crooked broker) by bankrupting the man who did it at the gaming tables.

d, Harry Millarde; w, Dennison Clift (based on a story by Serge J. Warshawsky); ph, Harry Gersted.

Drama **(PR:A MPAA:NR)**

GAMBLING WIVES** (1924) 7 reels Ben Wilson/Arrow bw

Marjorie Daw *(Ann Forrest)*, Edward Earle *(Vincent Forrest)*, Baby Dorothy Brock *(Baby June)*, Lee Moran *(A Friend)*, Betty Francisco *(Sylvia Baldwin)*, Joe Girard *(Duke Baldwin)*, Florence Lawrence *(Polly Barker)*, Ward Crane *(Van Merton)*, Hedda Hopper *(Mme. Zoe)*, Buddy the Dog.

Bored with married life, Earle turns to gambling and becomes infatuated with a casino owner (played by Hopper, before becoming a super gossip columnist), who leads him on to make her partner and paramour Crane jealous. When Daw learns of husband Earle's romantic and financial indiscretions, she retaliates by throwing herself at Crane. The marriage seems all but doomed until Hopper, jealous in her own right, stabs her lover, causing the young couple to come to their senses.

d, Dell Henderson; sup, Ben Wilson; w, Leota Morgan (based on a story by Ashley T. Locke).

Drama **(PR:A MPAA:NR)**

GAME OF LIFE, THE** (1922, Brit.) 10 reels G. B. Samuelson bw

Isobel Elsom *(Alice Fletcher)*, Lilian Hall Davis *(Rose Wallingford)*, Dorothy Minto *(Betsy Rudd)*, Campbell Gullan *(Edwin Travers)*, Tom Reynolds *(Jim Cobbles)*, James Lindsay *(Reggie Walker)*, Allan Aynesworth *(John)*, Hubert Carter *(Marcus Benjamin)*, Windham Guise *(Abel Fletcher)*, Fred Lewis *(Richard Wallingford)*, C. Tilson-Chowne *(Richard Travers)*, Mickey Brantford *(Nipper)*, Mrs. Henry Lytton *(Queen of Hearts)*.

England's first 10-reel feature was this epic historical re-creation of the great events during the reign of Queen Victoria, as seen through the eyes of three girls. In spite of its size and production expenditures, the film looked like an amateur show compared to the ones produced in Germany, France, and the U.S., at that time.

d, G. B. Samuelson; w, Lauri Wylie, Samuelson.

Historical/Drama **(PR:A MPAA:NR)**

GANGSTERS OF NEW YORK, THE*** (1914) 4 reels Reliance bw

Henry B. Walthall *(Porkey Dugan)*, Consuelo Bailey *(Cora Drew)*, Jack Dillon *(Biff)*, Ralph Lewis *(Spike Golden)*, C. Lambert, O. Child, Miss A. Horine, F. Herzog, P. Riley, Miss B. Craig.

This film about underworld characters and decent folk was very much in the Griffith tradition. It was well directed by Cabanne and featured a gripping death house scene, not unlike the master's "last mile" sequence in INTOLERANCE, which would electrify the screen a year later.

d, W. Christy Cabanne; sup. D. W. Griffith; w, Anita Loos.

Crime **(PR:O MPAA:NR)**

GARDEN OF KNOWLEDGE, THE (1917) 5 reels Dal Clawson bw

Little is known about this picture, which took the position that the eugenic theory applies to the mental as well as physical, and that mental discordancy will inevitably lead to depression and doom. There was a story line about the love of a young man for a girl, his promise to remain pure, and the temptations presented by various women. There was more than a little nudity featured, which might also account for its obscurity.

Drama **(PR:O MPAA:NR)**

GARDEN OF RESURRECTION, THE**
(1919, Brit.) 7 reels George Clark/STOLL bw

Guy Newall *(Bellairs)*, Ivy Duke *(Clarissa)*, Franklin Dyall *(Cruickshank)*, Mary Dibley *(Belwottle)*, Douglas Munro *(Moxon)*, Lawford Davidson *(Fennell)*, Hugh C. Puckler *(Dr. Perowne)*, Humberston Wright *(Gen. French)*, Madge Tree *(The Aunt)*.

Depressing British drama about a wealthy, racially mixed woman who is abandoned after giving birth to a stillborn child by the man who tricked her into a mock marriage. The film does, however, have a happy ending, with the woman wedding the fellow who helped her through the ordeal.

d, Arthur Rooke; Guy Newall (based on the novel by E. Temple Thurston).

Drama **(PR:A MPAA:NR)**

GARRISON'S FINISH***
(1923) 8 reels Jack Pickford/Allied Producers and Distributors bw

Jack Pickford *(Billy Garrison)*, Madge Bellamy *(Sue Desha)*, Charles A. Stevenson *(Col. Desha)*, Tom Guise *(Maj. Desha)*, Frank Elliot *(Mr. Waterbury)*, Clarence Burton *(Crimmins)*, Audrey Chapman, Dorothy Manners *(Sue's Friends)*, Ethel Grey Terry *(Lilly Allen)*, Herbert Prior *(Race Course Judge)*, Charles Ogle *(Col. Desha's Trainer)*, Lydia Knott *(Billy's Mother)*.

After jockey Pickford is doped by a crooked trainer and loses the Melville Handicap at Belmont Park, he is suspended and later becomes involved in a barroom brawl and suffers amnesia. A couple of tramps deliver him to the horse farm of Bellamy's father, whose address they find on his person. The girl recognizes Pickford, nurses him back to health, and he repays her kindness by winning the Kentucky Derby for her family colors. The crooked trainer is then found guilty of the Belmont affair, and the exonerated jockey asks for and wins the hand of the girl he has come to love. Includes actual on-location shots of the Kentucky Derby and from the Metropolitan Handicap at Belmont Park, N.Y. "America's Sweetheart" Mary Pickford is credited with writing the titles for her brother's picture.

d, Arthur Rosson; sup&w, Elmer Harris (based on the story by William Blair Morton Ferguson); t, Mary Pickford; ph, Harold Rosson.

Sports **(PR:A MPAA:NR)**

GASOLINE GUS*** (1921) 5 reels FP/PAR bw

Roscoe Arbuckle *(Gasoline Gus)*, Lila Lee *(Sal Jo Banty)*, Charles Ogle *(Nate Newberry)*, Theodore Lorch *("Dry Check" Charlie)*, Wilton Taylor *(Judge Shortridge)*, Knute Erickson *("Scrap Iron" Swenson)*, Fred Huntley.

In the wake of the sensational Roscoe "Fatty" Arbuckle scandal (the comedian was determined innocent by the jury which heard his case in the Virginia Rappe incident) Sid Grauman withdrew this comedy, about a character who makes a fortune with a fake oil well, from his Chinese Theatre and the movie was never shown in the U.S.

d, James Cruze; w, Walter Woods (based on the story "Dry Check Charlie" by George Patullo).

Comedy **(PR:A MPAA:NR)**

GATE CRASHER, THE 1/2** (1928) 6 reels UNIV-Jewel bw

Glenn Tryon *(Dick Henshaw)*, Patsy Ruth Miller *(Mara Di Leon)*, T. Roy Barnes *(Hal Reade)*, Beth Laemmle *(The Maid)*, Fred Malatesta *(Julio)*, Claude Payton *(Zanfield, the Stage Manager)*, Russell Powell *(Caesar, the Actor)*, Tiny Sanford *(Stage Doorman)*, Al Smith *(Pedro, the Waiter)*, Monte Montague *(A Crook)*.

Tryon's good performance puts this modest comedy over. It's about a posterhanger who, after having an automobile accident involving a Broadway actress, falls in love with her. Then, when he reads that her jewels have been stolen, he goes to New York to retrieve them for her, puts the finger on her crooked press agent, and wins her love in return. There is one scene where Tryon—who began his career in Hal Roach comedies—really shines: he's trying to escape from the press agent's henchmen, and the theater curtain goes up with him on stage. Without so much as missing a beat, the terrified small town boy goes into a perfectly hilarious burlesque routine.

d, William James Craft; sup, Harry L. Decker; w, Carl Krusada, Vin Moore, Craft (based on a story by Jack Foley, Craft); t, Albert De Mond; ph, Al Jones; ed, Charles Craft.

Comedy **(PR:A MPAA:NR)**

GATEWAY OF THE MOON, THE* (1928) 6 reels FOX bw

Dolores Del Rio *(Toni)*, Walter Pidgeon *(Arthur Wyatt)*, Anders Randolf *(George Gillespie)*, Ted McNamara *(Henry Hooker)*, Adolph Millar *(Rudolf Gottman)*, Leslie Fenton *(Jim Mortlake)*, Noble Johnson *(Soriano)*, Virginia La Fonde *(Indian Child)*.

Jungle nonsense in which English railroad inspector Pidgeon, who has come to Bolivia, is saved from being murdered by the half-caste niece (Del Rio) of the crooked foreman (Randolf) who is trying to take over the road.

d, John Griffith Wray; w, Bradley King (based on the novel *Upstream* by Clifford Bax); t, Katherine Hilliker, H. H. Caldwell; ph, Chester Lyons.

Drama **(PR:A MPAA:NR)**

GAUCHO, THE* 1/2** (1928) 10 reels Elton/UA bw-c

Douglas Fairbanks *(The Gaucho)*, Lupe Velez *(The Mountain Girl)*, Geraine Greear *(The Girl of the Shrine)*, Eve Southern *(Girl of the Shrine, as a Child)*, Gustav von Seyffertitz *(Ruiz, the Usurper)*, Michael Vavitch *(Ruiz's 1st Lieutenant)*, Charles Stevens *(The Gaucho's lst Lieutenant)*, Nigel De Brulier *(The Padre)*, Albert MacQuarrie *(Victim of the Black Doom)*, Mary Pickford *(Our Lady of the Shrine)*.

This most unusual of all Fairbanks films had the great swashbuckler playing a man on the shady side of the law, a real outlaw, who shocked audiences of that day by mocking God and lusting after The Girl of the Shrine (Greear). He even tries to seduce this radiant creature, but can't go through with it because of her virginal innocence. Robert Fairbanks, the star's beloved brother, had recently died and the actor-writer (and former altar boy) was obsessed at the time by the mysteries of religion. He even had leprosy and attempted-suicide brought into the plot before the Gaucho is converted and saves Greear and a kindly priest from execution by putting his extraordinary athletic abilities to use.

p, Douglas Fairbanks; d, F. Richard Jones; w, Lotta Woods (based on a story by Elton Thomas, Fairbanks); t, Joseph B. Harris; ph, Antonio Gaudio; ed, William Nolan; art d, Carl Oscar Borg; syn sc; s eff.

Costume/Drama **(PR:A MPAA:NR)**

GAY AND DEVILISH*** (1922) 5 reels R-C bw

Doris May *(Fanchon Browne)*, Cullen Landis *(Peter Armitage)*, Otis Harlan *(Peter Armitage, the Uncle)*, Jacqueline Logan *(Lilah Deane)*, Bull Montana *(Tony)*, Lila Leslie *(Aunt Bessie)*, Ashley Cooper *(The Butler)*, Arthur Millett *(lst Detective)*, *Kingsley Benedict (2nd Detective)*, Milton Ross *(3rd Detective)*, George Periolat *(Nethercote)*.

Funny comedy has May agreeing to marry elderly but wealthy Landis in order to save her guardian from bankruptcy. Before meeting him, however, she falls for a handsome young fellow who just happens to be the old boy's nephew. Then, as a means of getting off the hook, May persuades her best friend Logan to vamp Landis, but she mistakenly picks the wrong person and does her act for the nephew. To further complicate matters, Montana, the prizefighter, goes off his beam for Logan, while May's aunt sets her sights on Landis' uncle. There is, of course, complete bedlam before the picture concludes with everyone marrying the person of their choice.

d, William A. Seiter; w, Garrett Elsden (based on a story by Charles A. Logue); ph, Pliny Goodfriend.

Comedy **(PR:A MPAA:NR)**

GAY CORINTHIAN, THE*** (1924), Brit.) 6 reels I.B. Davidson/BUT bw

Victor McLaglen *(Squire Hardcastle)*, Betty Faire *(Lady Carrie Fanshawe)*, Cameron Carr *(Lord Barrymore)*, Humberston Wright *(Sir Thomas Apreece)*, Donald McCardle *(Harry Fanshawe)*, George Turner *(Jeremy)*, Jack Denton *(Dr. Lee)*, Guardsmen Penwill *(Flaming Tinman)*, Noel Arnott *(Gentleman Jeffries)*.

In this English adventure film, McLaglen, the only man to ever win the Academy Award (THE INFORMER, 1935) and fight for the heavyweight championship of the world (against Jack Johnson, 1909), plays a man who is good with his fists and saves a lady from a band of gypsies. A radically edited and shortened version of this was reissued in 1926 with the title THE THREE WAGERS.

d, Arthur Rooke; w, Eliot Stannard (based on the novel by Ben Bolt).

Adventure **(PR:A MPAA:NR)**

GAY LORD QUEX, THE** (1917, Brit.) 6 reels ID bw

Ben Webster *(Lord Quex)*, Irene Vanbrugh *(Sophie Fullgarney)*, Lilian Braithwaite *(Duchess of Strood)*, Hayford Hobbs *(Capt. Bartling)*, Margaret Bannerman *(Muriel Eden)*, Donald Calthrop *(Valma)*, Claire Pauncefort *(Lady Owbridge)*, Lyston Lyle.

In this British domestic drama, a lord who is engaged to marry attempts to compromise a woman who discovers his romantic interlude with a duchess.

d, Maurice Elvey; w, Eliot Stannard (based on the play by Arthur Wing Pinero).

Drama **(PR:A-C MPAA:NR)**

GAY OLD BIRD, THE** (1927) 7 reels WB bw

John T. Murray *(Mr. Cluney)*, Louise Fazenda *(Sisseretta Simpkins)*, Jane Winton *(Mrs. Cluney)*, William Demarest *(Mr. Fixit)*, John Stepping *(Uncle)*, Frances Raymond *(Aunt)*, Ed Kennedy *(Chauffeur)*.

Stepping has promised his nephew a fortune on the condition that he is happily married. His nephew's wife, whom he has never met, has an argument with her husband and leaves home just before Stepping makes his first visit. A substitute wife is needed in a hurry, and it is provided by the neighbor's maid, played by two-reel comedy star Fazenda. The funny business that follows is as obvious as the film's happy ending.

d, Herman C. Raymaker; w, C. Graham Baker, Edward Clark (based on a story by Virginia Dale); ph, Virgil Miller.

Comedy **(PR:A MPAA:NR)**

GAY RETREAT, THE*** (1927) 6 reels FOX bw

Ted McNamara *(Ted McHiggins)*, Sammy Cohen *(Sam Nosenbloom)*, Gene Cameron *(Dick Wright)*, Betty Francisco *(Betty Burnett)*, Judy King *(Joan Moret)*, Jerry the Giant *(Jerry)*, Holmes Herbert *(Charles Wright)*, Charles Gorman *(Edward Fulton)*, Pal the Dog.

On the strength of the impression they made in the box office smash WHAT PRICE GLORY, McNamara and Cohen were given their own series of comedies. In this, their first, the boys play the chauffeur and valet to Cameron, a wealthy young man who has been rejected by all of the services because of his sleepwalking. Cameron joins the ambulance corps and his servant friends accompany him to France. There are, of course, the usual slapstick complications, which end with the trio capturing a contingent of Germans and returning home as heroes. Better-than-average comedy of this sort.

d, Ben Stoloff; sup, George E. Marshall; w, J. Walter Ruben, Murray Roth, Edward Moran (based on a story by William Conselman, Edward Marshall); t, Malcolm Stuart Boylan; ph, Sidney Wagner.

Comedy/War **(PR:A MPAA:NR)**

GEARED TO GO** (1924) 5 reels Harry J. Brown/RAY bw

Reed Howes, Carmelita Geraghty, George Nichols, Winifred Landis, Joe Butterworth, Cuyler Supplee, Melbourne MacDowell, George Williams.

The son of a taxicab company owner takes a job driving for an independent firm when he hears that the little guys are being crushed. Later, he and his sweetheart, who has inherited part of the company, bring peace to the warring factions.

d, Albert Rogell; w, Henry Roberts Symonds, John Wesley Grey; ph, Ross Fisher.

Drama **(PR:A MPAA:NR)**

GENERAL, THE***** (1927) 8 reels Buster Keaton/UA bw

Buster Keaton *(Johnnie Gray)*, Glen Cavender *(Capt. Anderson)*, Jim Farley *(Gen. Thatcher)*, Frederick Vroom *(Southern General)*, Marion Mack *(Annabelle Lee)*, Charles Smith *(Her Father)*, Frank Barnes *(Her Brother)*, Joe Keaton, Mike Donlin, Tom Nawn *(Union Generals)*.

Keaton's masterpiece is a wonderful combination of elements—part war, part adventure, part romance, and *all* comedy—enhanced by the most meticulous and lavish re-creations of a historic incident the cinema had ever known. A railroad engineer (Keaton) tries to enlist in the Confederate Army at the outbreak of the Civil War but is rejected because his civilian occupation is considered more important to the cause. His sweetheart, Mack, chooses to regard him as a shirker and breaks off their engagement. Later, while she is en route to visit her father and Union soldiers commandeer her train (the locomotive is Keaton's beloved "General"), it is Keaton who gives chase in another engine. From this point on, the picture becomes a comedic tour de force, as the greatest nonstop gaggle of sight gags ever assembled are unraveled one after another, perfectly timed and executed. It is also pure cinema, because when Keaton isn't moving, then the trains, props, and troops are. Keaton manages to rescue the girl deep in Yankee territory, re-commandeers the "General," and the chase begins all over again in reverse. With two Northern armies right behind him, ready to launch a big offensive, Keaton daringly pulls the "General" to a stop and sets fire to the railroad bridge he just crossed. The Union general studies the situation, weighs his position, and decides to cross it anyway. Then, in a fittingly climactic conclusion to all that has occurred, the Union supply train slowly inches its way across the flaming wooden construction, begins to tremble, sways desperately, and then crashes to the water below. The Confederate armies have been given the precious time needed to drive back the Federals, and Keaton is a hero to Mack and the South. *Sight and Sound* magazine conducted a poll in 1972, which concluded that THE GENERAL is the eighth greatest motion picture ever made. They may have been a bit conservative.

p, Joseph M. Schenck; d, Buster Keaton; w, Al Boasberg, Charles Smith (based on a story by Keaton, Clyde Bruckman, from *The Great Locomotive Chase* by William Pittinger); ph, J. Devereaux Jennings, Bert Haines; ed, Sherman Kell, Harry Barnes; prod d, Fred Gabourie; makeup, Fred C. Ryle.

Comedy **Cas.** **(PR:A MPAA:NR)**

GENERAL JOHN REGAN*** (1921, Brit.) 7 reels STOLL bw

Milton Rosmer *(Dr. O'Grady)*, Madge Stuart *(Mary Ellen Doyle)*, Edward O'Neill *(Tim Doyle)*, Ward McAllister *(Horace P. Billings)*, Bertie Wright *(Thady Gallagher)*, Teddy Arundell *(Police Constable Moriarty)*, Robert Vallis *(Sgt. Colgan)*, Judd Green *(Kerrigan)*, Gordon Parker *(Maj. Kent)*, Windham Guise *(Father McCormack)*.

Ireland is the setting for this little comedy about a rich American visitor and the local doctor who, as a gag, make the point that the nation of Bolivia was actually liberated by a man from the village.

d, Harold Shaw; w, William J. Elliott (based on the play by George A. Birmingham).

Comedy **(PR:A MPAA:NR)**

GENERAL POST** (1920, Brit.) 5 reels ID bw

Lilian Braithwaite *(Lady Broughton)*, Henderson Bland *(Edward Smith)*, Joyce Dearsley *(Betty Broughton)*, Dawson Milward *(Sir Denys Broughton)*, Douglas Munro *(Albert Smith)*, Colstan Mansell *(Alec Broughton)*, Teddy Arundell *(Jobson)*, Sara de Groot *(Miss Prendergast)*, Adelaide Grace *(Lady Wareing)*, Thomas Canning *(Lord Wareing)*, Irene Drew *(Mary Wareing)*.

In this British film about class distinction, an aristocrat finally permits his daughter to marry the man she loves—a working stiff—after the lad wins the Victoria Cross on the 1914 battlefield.

d, Thomas Bentley; w, Eliot Stannard (based on the play by J. E. Howard Terry).

Romance/War **(PR:A MPAA:NR)**

GENTLE JULIA*** (1923) 6 reels FOX bw

Bessie Love *(Julia)*, Harold Goodwin *(Noble Dill)*, Frank Elliott *(Randolph Crum)*, Charles K. French *(John Atwater)*, Clyde Benson *(George Atwater)*, Harry Dunkinson *(Uncle Joe Atwater)*, Jack Rollins *(Newland Sanders)*, Frances Grant *(Mrs. Joe Atwater)*, William Irving *(George Plum)*, Agnes Aker *(Mrs. George Atwater)*, William Lester *(Herbert Atwater)*, Gypsy Norman *(Mrs. Herbert Atwater)*, Mary Arthur *(Florence Atwater), Richard Billings (Herbert Atwater, Jr.)*.

Engaging performance by Love as a pretty girl from a small town who becomes infatuated with an older man and follows him to Chicago. When she discovers he has a wife, Love returns home to marry the boy who has always loved her.

d, Rowland V. Lee; w, Donald W. Lee (based on the novel by Booth Tarkington); ph, G. O. Post.

Drama **(PR:A MPAA:NR)**

GENTLEMAN FROM MISSISSIPPI, THE**
(1914) 5 reels Brady/WORLD bw

Thomas Wise.

Wise, who created this role in the theater, was perfect as the Southern senator, although the picture was less so. The story has to do with the senator's children, new to Washington, being taken in by a corrupt politician until their daddy saves the day by exposing the plot on the congressional floor. Good location shots and Wise's performance were the highlights of this property, better suited for the speaking stage.

d, George L. Sargent; w, (based on the play by Harrison Rhodes, Thomas Wise).

Drama **(PR:A MPAA:NR)**

GENTLEMAN OF LEISURE, A*** (1923) 6 reels FP/PAR bw

Jack Holt *(Robert Pitt)*, Casson Ferguson *(Sir Spencer Deever)*, Sigrid Holmquist *(Molly Creedon)*, Alec Francis *(Sir John Blount)*, Adele Farrington *(Lady Blount)*, Frank Nelson *(Spike Mullen)*, Alfred Allen *(Big Phil Creedon)*, Nadeen Paul *(The Maid)*, Alice Queensberry *(Chorus Girl)*.

This property was originally purchased for Wallace Reid. However, after his tragic death it was turned over to Holt, who had recently exhibited his skill at handling light comedy. It's about a brash young American millionaire who returns from England and meets a few chums at a New York cafe. He is in the process of complaining that he has not seen an attractive girl since arriving, when he spots Holmquist across the room. Failing to get her attention, he wagers his friends that within 24 hours he will have her photograph, personally autographed to him. The completion of this mission provides plenty of laughs and more than a few thrills, as Holt foils a robbery along the way.

d, Joseph Henabery; w, Anthony Coldeway, Jack Cunningham (based on the play by John Stapleton, Pelham Grenville); ph, Faxon M. Dean.

Comedy **(PR:A MPAA:NR)**

GENTLEMEN PREFER BLONDES*** (1928) 7 reels PAR/FP bw

Ruth Taylor *(Lorelei Lee)*, Alice White *(Dorothy Shaw)*, Ford Sterling *(Gus Eisman)*, Holmes Herbert *(Henry Spoffard)*, Mack Swain *(Francis Beekman)*, Emily Fitzroy *(Lady Beekman)*, Trixie Friganza *(Mrs. Spoffard)*, Blanche Frederici *(Miss Chapman)*, Ed Faust *(Robert)*, Eugene Borden *(Louis)*, Margaret Seddon *(Lorelei's Mother)*, Luke Cosgrave *(Lorelei's Grandfather)*, Chester Conklin *(The Judge)*, Yorke Sherwood *(Mr. Jennings)*, Mildred Boy *(Lulu)*.

Loos' saucy adventures of gold digger Taylor lost some of its sparkle in this 1928 screen version, in spite of a valiant effort on the part of director St. Clair. It was, however, a tremendous break for the unknown actress to be given the coveted leading role in this greatly publicized motion picture, and major stardom would have, no doubt, been hers if she had not elected to marry a successful New York stockbroker, retire from the screen the following year, and give birth to future writer-actor Buck Henry.

d, Malcolm St. Clair; w, Anita Loos, John Emerson (based on the story and play by Loos); t, Herman Mankiewicz, Loos; ph, Hal Rosson; ed, William Shea.

Comedy **(PR:A MPAA:NR)**

GET YOUR MAN*** (1921) 5 reels FOX bw

Buck Jones *(Jock MacTier)*, William Lawrence *(Arthur Whitman)*, Beatrice Burnham *(Leonore De Marney)*, Helen Rosson *(Margaret MacPherson)*, Paul Kamp *(Joe)*.

Jones rides north-of-the-border in this entertaining story about a Mountie who loves the daughter of a smuggler. Her father is murdered by Jones' old adversary, and after a long chase through a snowstorm and an exciting fight, Jones not only gets his man but the girl as well.

d, George W. Hill, William K. Howard; w, John Montague (based on a story by Alan Sullivan); ph, Frank B. Good.

Adventure **(PR:A MPAA:NR)**

GETTING MARY MARRIED*** (1919) 5 reels Marion Davies/SEL bw

Marion Davies *(Mary)*, Norman Kerry *(James Winthrop, Jr.)*, Matt Moore *(Ted Barnacle)*, Frederick Burton *(Amos Bussard)*, Amelia Summerville *(Mrs. Bussard)*, Constance Beaumar *(Matilda Bussard)*, Elmer Grandin *(John Bussard)*.

Nice performance by Davies as the stepchild of a millionaire, who is directed by a provision in his will to live with his brother's family after his death. The will also states that in the event Davies should marry, the fortune will go to his blood relative. Naturally, life is made unbearable for the girl, and she responds by marrying an enormously wealthy young man. The brother then inherits the fortune which, after the many debts are paid, consists of less than $2. Fine direction by Dwan and a nifty script by Emerson and Loos made this the best Davies picture to date.

d, Allan Dwan; w, John Emerson, Anita Loos; ph, Lyman Broening.

Drama **(PR:A MPAA:NR)**

GHOST TRAIN, THE**
(1927, Brit.) 7 reels Gainsborough/Woolf and Freedman bw

Guy Newall *(Teddy Deakin)*, Lise Bois *(Miss Bourne)*, Louis Ralph *(Saul Hodgkin)*, Anna Jennings *(Peggy Murdock)*, John Manners *(Charles Murdock)*, Agnes Korolenko *(Elsie Winthrop)*, Ernest Verebes *(Richard Winthrop)*, Rosa Walter *(Julia Price)*.

Location shooting in Germany added some interest to this British thriller about a detective who takes the part of a simpleton in order to break up a gang of gun runnners who have been using an abandoned railroad line.

p, Michael Balcon, Herman Fellner; d, Geza M. Bolvary; w, (based on the play by Arnold Ridley).

Crime **(PR:A MPAA:NR)**

GILDED BUTTERFLY, THE** (1926) 6 reels FOX bw

Alma Rubens *(Linda Haverhill)*, Bert Lytell *(Brian Anestry)*, Huntley Gordon *(John Converse)*, Frank Keenan *(Jim Haverhill)*, Herbert Rawlinson *(Courtney Roth)*, Vera Lewis *(Mrs. Ralson)*, Arthur Hoyt *(Mr. Ralston)*, Carolynne Snowden *(Black Maid)*.

Entertaining, if improbable, society drama about a girl who has been raised to seek out the finer things in life borrowing money from a friend of her late father to finance her fortune-hunting venture. She goes to Monte Carlo, falls in love with a handsome young American, and returns home broke. To avoid repaying her debt with sexual favors, she burns her wardrobe for the insurance money and is caught. On the way to the police station, however, the patrol wagon is involved in an automobile accident and a woman is killed. This gives the kind-hearted policeman the chance to switch identities, and the girl is released to join her young man.

d, John Griffith Wray; w, Bradley King (based on a story by Evelyn Campbell); ph, Frank Good.

Drama **(PR:A MPAA:NR)**

GILDED CAGE, THE*** (1916) 5 reels PEER/WORLD bw

Alice Brady *(Princess Honore)*, Alec B. Francis *(King Comus)*, Gerda Holmes *(Queen Vesta)*, Montagu Love *(Baron Stefano)*, Arthur Ashley *(Capt. Kassari)*, Sidney D'Albrook *(Nickolai)*, Clara Whipple *(Lesbia the Goose Girl)*, Irving Cummings *(Prince Boris)*, May De Lacy.

This swashbuckling romance about a beautiful young queen and a dashing prince, who love one another without realizing their true identities, was done in the PRISONER OF ZENDA tradition.

d, Harley Knoles; w, Francis Marion (based on the story "Her Majesty" by J. I. C. Clarke); ph, Arthur Edeson.

Romance **(PR:A MPAA:NR)**

GILDED DREAM, THE*** (1920) 5 reels UNIV bw

Carmel Myers *(Leona)*, Thomas Chatterton *(Jasper)*, Elsa Lorimer *(Geraldine)*, Boyd Irwin *(Frazer Boynton)*, Zola Claire, May McCulley, Eddie Dennis, Maxine Elliot Hicks.

Good programmer has Myers as a girl with a champagne appetite, who comes to the city to snare a wealthy husband. Living with her rich godmother, who agrees to help in this quest, she falls in love with a poor but handsome young man. Her godmother, however, also loves this fellow and fills Myers' head with lies about him. Out of anger and hurt, she decides to marry a millionaire who proposed earlier, but after being rescued from death she learns the truth about the lad and comes to the conclusion that the best things in life don't necessarily cost a fortune.

d, Rollin Sturgeon; w, Doris Schroeder (based on a story by Katherine L. Robbins, Lorne H. Fontaine).

Drama **(PR:A MPAA:NR)**

GILDED HIGHWAY, THE* (1926) 7 reels WB bw

Dorothy Devore *(Primrose Welby)*, John Harron *(Jack Welby)*, Maclyn Arbuckle *(Jonathan Welby)*, Myrna Loy *(Irene Quartz)*, Florence Turner *(Mrs. Welby)*, Sheldon Lewis *(Uncle Nicholas Welby)*, Andree Tourneur *(Amabel)*, Gardner James *(Hugo Blythe)*, Mathilde Comont *(Sarah)*, Thomas Mills *(Adolphus Faring)*.

Dated melodrama about a middle-class family that takes leave of its senses and becomes quite obnoxious after inheriting a fortune. The film ends with the family losing everything, but being accepted back by the people the family members once loved.

d, J. Stuart Blackton; w, Marian Constance (based on the novel *A Little More* by William Babington Maxwell); ph, Nicholas Musuraca.

Drama **(PR:A MPAA:NR)**

GILDED LILY, THE*** (1921) 7 reels FP/PAR bw

Mae Murray *(Lillian Drake)*, Lowell Sherman *(Creighton Howard)*, Jason Robards *(Frank Thompson)*, Charles Gerard *(John Stewart)*, Leonora Ottinger *(Mrs. Thompson)*.

One of Murray's best performances, and one which gave her the opportunity to show off numerous beautiful gowns, as well as her considerable dancing skill. She plays a cafe hostess who is sought after by playboy Sherman and country boy Robards (in his film debut). She marries Robards and retires from the fast life. Robards, however, becomes a hopeless drunk and forces her to return to the world of cafe society. Later, in a well-directed scene, Murray collapses on the dance floor but is rescued by Sherman, who asks her to be his wife.

d, Robert Z. Leonard; w, (based on a story by Clara Beranger); t, Tom McNamara; ph, Ernest Haller; art d, Robert M. Hass.

Drama **(PR:A MPAA:NR)**

GILDED SPIDER, THE** (1916) 5 reels BLUE bw

Louise Lovely *(Leonita/Elisa)*, Lon Chaney *(Giovanni)*, Lule Warenton *(Rosa)*, Gilmore Hammond *(Cyrus Kirkham)*, Marjorie Ellison *(Mrs. Kirkham)*, Hayward Mack *(Burton Armitage)*, Jay Belasco *(Paul Winston)*.

Depressing film about an American millionaire who abducts a Mediterranean dance girl (Lovely) and drives her to suicide. Some time later, her Italian husband comes to the U.S. with his daughter (Lovely, who plays both parts) to seek revenge. The libertine also lusts for the young girl, but dies of a heart attack, at which point the Italian takes his own life.

d, Joseph De Grasse; w, Ida May Park.

Drama **(PR:A MPAA:NR)**

GIMMIE*** (1923) 6 reels Goldwyn bw

Helene Chadwick *(Fanny Daniels)*, Gaston Glass *(Clinton Ferris)*, Kate Lester *(Mrs. Roland Ferris)*, Eleanor Boardman *(Clothilde Kingsley)*, David Imboden *(Claude Lambert)*, May Wallace *(Mrs. Cecily McGimsey)*, Georgia Woodthorpe *(Annabel Wainwright)*, H. B. Walthall *(John McGimsey)*, Jean Hope *(Lizzie)*.

Long before women's lib became a popular topic for theatrical and made-for-TV movies, this film told of a young woman (Chadwick) who borrows $500 from her employer to pay for the trousseau she intends to wear at her wedding to Glass. Later, when her boss asks to be repaid, she gives him a check written on her husband's account. This causes chauvinist Glass to blow his cork, and his bride to leave the love nest and return to the office. GIMMIE is an interesting and amusing movie, which ends with Glass begging forgiveness from his wife and agreeing to grant her complete equality.

d&w, Rupert Hughes (based on a story by Adelaide and Rupert Hughes); ph, John J. Mescall; art d, Cedric Gibbons.

Comedy/Drama **(PR:A MPAA:NR)**

GINSBERG THE GREAT** (1927) 6 reels WB bw

George Jessel *(Johnny Ginsberg)*, Audrey Ferris *(Mary)*, Gertrude Astor *(Sappho)*, Douglas Gerrard *(Sam Hubert)*, Jack Santoro *(Hawkins)*, Theodore Lorch *(Charles Wheeler)*, Jimmie Quinn *(A Crook)*, Stanley J. Sanford *(Hercules)*, Akka the Chimp.

Jessel made the career mistake of a lifetime when he turned down the lead in Warner's first talkie, THE JAZZ SINGER, and instead made this trifling little program comedy about a would-be carnival magician who saves a theatrical producer's jewels from being stolen.

d, Byron Haskin; w, Anthony Coldewey; ph, Conrad Wells; ed, Clarence Kolster.

Comedy **(PR:A MPAA:NR)**

GIRL FROM CHICAGO, THE* 1/2** (1927) 6 reels WB bw

Conrad Nagel *(Handsome Joe)*, Myrna Loy *(Mary Carlton)*, William Russell *("Big Steve" Drummond)*, Carroll Nye *(Bob Carlton)*, Paul Panzer *(Dopey)*, Erville Alderson *(Col. Carlton)*.

Southern girl Loy comes to New York to clear her brother who is accused of murder. Learning that he was framed by gangsters, she passes herself off as a Chicago gun moll and becomes the object of Nagel and Russell's desires. It turns out that Nagel is really an undercover cop, and when the mob discovers this, they set out to get him. In an ending worthy of D. W. Griffith, there is a terrific gun battle between the gangsters and Nagel, who is cornered at Loy's apartment. The couple manage to get word to the police, and a motorcycle squadron is sent to their rescue. The besieged pair fight a strategic retreat from room to room, with the blistering machinegun fire of the mobsters coming closer and closer to killing them. The director cuts effectively back and forth between this and the roaring motorcycle squad, until the men in blue arrive to rout the gangsters. With his last dying gasp, Russell clears Loy's brother, who, as it turns out, is on the verge of walking the last mile.

d, Ray Enright; w, Graham Baker (based on the story "Business is Best" by Arthur Somers Roche); ph, Hal Mohr.

Crime **(PR:A MPAA:NR)**

GIRL FROM DOWNING STREET, THE***
(1918, Brit.) 5 reels International Exclusives/But bw

Ena Beaumont *(Peggy Marsden)*, Sidney Paxton *(Capt. Paul Muller)*, William Stack *(Cyril Godfrey)*.

Good British wartime thriller about a girl who daringly steals the plans of the Hindenburg line and then is chased through Europe by a German spy. In the end all is well, as the agent turns out to be an English operative.

d&w, Geoffrey H. Malins (based on a story by Garth Grayson).

War **(PR:A MPAA:NR)**

GIRL FROM HIS TOWN, THE* (1915) 4 reels AM bw

Margarita Fischer *(Sarah Towney)*, C. Elliott Griffen *(Don Blair)*, Beatrice Van *(Duchess of Breakwater)*, Joseph Harris *(Prince Ponitowski)*, Joseph Singleton *(Lord Galory)*, Fred Gamble *(Joshua Ruggles)*, Robyn Adair *(Blair, the Elder)*, Carlton Elliott Griffin, Lucille Ward, Joseph Harris.

Routine programmer about a western girl with a good singing voice, who works at a soda fountain and is loved by the son of the town millionaire. She goes on the stage, and, when his father dies, the young man visits Singleton, an old family friend, in England. The vulnerable young fellow becomes engaged to an opportunistic British woman, but fortunately sees his American sweetheart, who is appearing in a London production, and the two return to the U.S. as husband and wife.

d, Harry Pollard; w, (based on the novel by Marie Van Vorst).

Drama **(PR:A MPAA:NR)**

GIRL FROM RIO, THE** (1927) 6 reels GOTH/LUM bw-c

Carmel Myers *(Lola)*, Walter Pidgeon *(Paul Sinclair)*, Richard Tucker *(Antonio Santos)*, Henry Herbert *(Farael Fuentes)*, Mildred Harris *(Helen Graham)*, Edouard Raquello *(Raoul, the Dancer)*.

The Technicolor opening is the only worthwhile aspect of this ponderous tale about an engaged English coffee buyer, who falls in love with cafe dancer Myers, the mistress of Rio de Janeiro's most powerful citizen. He manages to overcome both jealousy and an attempt to murder him by her dancing partner, before finally settling down with Myers.

p, Sam Bischoff; d, Tom Terriss; w, Pauline Forney, Terriss (based on a story by Norman Kellogg); t, Forney; ph, Ray June.

Drama **(PR:A MPAA:NR)**

GIRL FROM THE WEST** (1923) 5 reels Sam Warner/AY bw

Jack Richardson, Juanita Hansen, Edward Sutherland.

To win the love of an Eastern college girl with romantic notions about the West, a young man goes there, lands a job on a ranch, captures a gang of cattle rustlers, and proves himself the equal of any cowboy.

d, Wallace MacDonald; w, (based on a story by Carter De Haven).

Western/Drama **(PR:A MPAA:NR)**

GIRL IN EVERY PORT, A** 1/2 (1928) 6 reels FOX bw

Victor McLaglen *(Spike Madden)*, Maria Casajuana *(Chiquita)*, Natalie Joyce, Dorothy Mathews, Elena Jurado *(Girls in Panama)*, Louise Brooks *(Marie, Girl in France)*, Francis McDonald *(Gang Leader)*, Phalba Morgan *(Lena, Girl in Holland)*, Felix Valle *(Lena's Husband)*, Greta Yoltz *(Other Girl in Holland)*, Leila Hyams *(The Sailor's Wife)*, Robert Armstrong *(Salami)*, Sally Rand *(Girl in Bombay)*, Natalie Kingston *(Girl in South Sea Islands)*, Caryl Lincoln *(Girl from Liverpool)*.

Hawks directed this fairly entertaining, though chauvinistic "men's picture" about a couple of sailors starting out as rivals for the women they encounter on shore and becoming close friends after the usual bits of gobs-on-a-tear horseplay. The film ends with Armstrong convincing McLaglen to return to sea and not settle down with Brooks, a French gold digger. This film showed audiences that Brooks—whose mere presence on the screen exuded sex appeal—was a talent worthy of more than the routine flapper comedies in which she was usually cast. She would prove her wonderful abilities the following year in Germany where, under the direction of G. W. Pabst, she appeared in the critically acclaimed PANDORA'S BOX and DIARY OF A LOST GIRL.

d, Howard Hawks; w, Seton I. Miller, James K. McGuinness (based on a story by Hawks); t, Malcolm Stuart Boylan; ph, L. W. O'Connell, Rudolph Berquist; ed, Ralph Dixon.

Comedy **(PR:A MPAA:NR)**

GIRL IN THE DARK, THE*** (1918) 5 reels BLUE bw

Ashton Dearholt *(Brice Ferris)*, Carmel Myers *(Lois Fox)*, Frank Tokanaga *(Ming)*, Frank Deschon *(Lao Wing)*, Harry Carter *(Strang)*, Alfred Allen *(Struber)*, Betty Schade *(Sally)*.

Action-packed (to the point of resembling a serial) programmer, set in Chinatown, has a young couple pitted against an army of Chinese villains. There are secret passages, sliding panels, torture chambers, and plenty of death-defying escapes as the heroes outwit the bad guys, who are after the coveted green seal ring.

d, Stuart Paton; w, A. G. Kenyon (based on the novel *The Green Seal* by Charles Edmund Walk).

Crime/Adventure **(PR:A MPAA:NR)**

GIRL OF LONDON, A** (1925, Brit.) 7 reels STOLL bw

Genevieve Townsend *(Lil)*, Ian Hunter *(Peter Horniman)*, Harvey Braban *(George Duncan)*, G. H. Mulcaster *(Wilson)*, Nora Swinburne *(Vee-Vee)*, Edward Irwin *(Lionel Horniman)*, Bernard Dudley *(Lawton)*, Nell Emerald *(The Mother)*.

British thriller about the disowned son of a Parliament member who saves a girl from certain ruin at the hands of her stepfather, who is involved with a dope den, by marrying her.

d, Henry Edwards; w, (based on the novel by Douglas Walshe).

Crime **(PR:A MPAA:NR)**

GIRL OF MY HEART* (1920) 5 reels FOX bw

Shirley Mason, Raymond McKee, Martha Mattox, Calvin Weller, Cecil Van Auker, Alfred Fremont, Hooper Toler, Alfred Willer.

The last surviving member of an aristocratic Southern family of musicians is told by his doctor that, in order to live, he must give up his instrument and move West. He is about to shoot himself, when a girl who has run away from her cruel mistress intervenes. She conveys to him the meaning of "true love" and he adopts her, follows the sun, and they later marry.

d, Edward J. LeSaint; w, LeSaint (based on the novel *Joan of Rainbow Springs* by Frances Marion Mitchell); ph, Friend Baker.

Drama **(PR:A MPAA:NR)**

GIRL OF THE GOLDEN WEST, THE**** (1915) 5 reels LAS bw

Mabel Van Buren, House Peters, Theodore Roberts, Anita King, Sidney Deane, Billy Elmer, Jeanie Macpherson, Raymond Hatton, Dick La Strange, Tex Driscoll, James Griswald, Art Ortego, John Ortego, Ed Harley, Russell Simpson.

By 1915, westerns had become old hat. Then DeMille gave the movie-going public THE GIRL OF THE GOLDEN WEST—the story of a decent girl's love for a dashing outlaw, set against the California gold rush of 1849. The picture was so beautifully crafted that it started the genre all over again.

d, Cecil B. DeMille; w, DeMille (based on a play by David Belasco); ph, Alvin Wyckoff.

Western/Romance **(PR:A MPAA:NR)**

GIRL OF THE GOLDEN WEST, THE*** (1923) 7 reels AFN bw

Sylvia Breamer *(The Girl)*, J. Warren Kerrigan *(Ramerrez)*, Russell Simpson *(Jack Rance)*, Rosemary Theby *(Nina Micheltorena)*, Wilfred Lucas *(Ashby)*, Nelson McDowell *(Sonora Slim)*, Charles McHugh *(Trinidad Joe)*, Hector V. Sarno *(Castro)*, Jed Prouty *(Nick)*, Cecil Holland *(Antonio)*, Thomas Delmar *(Handsome Harry)*, Fred Warren *(Old Jed Hawkins)*, Sam Appel *(Pedro Micheltorena)*, Minnie Prevost *(The Squaw)*.

The second filming of this title fell short of the DeMille original, which practically revived the western genre single-handedly. Interestingly, by the time this one was shot, the horse opera had again passed out of favor and was just making a comeback following the release of the epic, THE COVERED WAGON. Actually, this was really a pretty good film and would no doubt be remembered with greater affection if it were not for the excellent first edition.

p, Robert North; d, Edwin Carewe; w, Adelaide Heilbron (based on the play by David Belasco); ph, Sol Polito, Thomas Storey; ed, Robert De Lacy; art d, Milton Menasco.

Western **(PR:A MPAA:NR)**

GIRL ON THE MOON, THE

(SEE: WOMAN ON THE MOON, THE, 1929, Ger.)

GIRL ON THE STAIRS, THE*** (1924) 7 reels Peninsula/PDC bw

Patsy Ruth Miller *(Dora Sinclair)*, Frances Raymond *(Agatha Sinclair)*, Arline Pretty *(Joan Wakefield)*, Shannon Day *(Manuela Sarmento)*, Niles Welch *(Frank Farrell)*, Freeman Wood *(Dick Wakefield)*, Bertram Grassby *(Jose Sarmento)*, Michael Dark *(Wilbur)*, George Periolat *(Dr. Bourget)*.

Good mystery about a girl who becomes engaged, on the rebound, to a young attorney, after discovering that the man she loves is married. To her dismay, the rotter refuses to return her love letters, and one night while sleepwalking she enters his house to retrieve them. The next morning she remembers none of this, but he is found murdered and the girl is accused. At the trial, her fiance, who is defending her, arranges to have her hypnotized. While in a trance, she recalls that a South American (who found his wife having an affair with the murdered man) committed the crime. The girl is exonerated, and finding herself truly in love, marries the brilliant young lawyer for all of the right reasons.

d, William Worthington; sup & w, Elmer Harris (based on the story by Winston Bouve); ph, Joseph Walker, Charles Kaufman.

Mystery **(PR:A MPAA:NR)**

GIRL SHY**** (1924) 8 reels Harold Lloyd/Pathe bw

Harold Lloyd *(Harold Meadows the Poor Boy)*, Jobyna Ralston *(Mary Buckingham the Rich Girl)*, Richard Daniels *(Jerry Meadows the Poor Man)*, Carlton Griffin *(Ronald DeVore the Rich Man)*.

Riotous Lloyd comedy about a painfully shy, stuttering tailor's apprentice, who comes to the city to sell a book he has written called "The Secrets of Making Love" (a premise which gave Lloyd the opportunity to present several comic fantasies, including one dealing with vampire women and another with flappers). On the train, he helps pretty Ralston hide her dog from the conductor and becomes smitten. However, after the publisher rejects his manuscript, Lloyd feels unworthy and decides not to see her again. Later, the publisher changes his mind and, equipped with his $3,000 advance, the athletic funny man—in one of his most inventive sequences—races by car, horse, trolley, and motorcycle to save Ralston at the very last second from marrying a bigamist.

d, Fred Newmeyer, Sam Taylor; w, (based on a story by Ted Wilde, Tim Whelan, Tommy Gray, Taylor); ph, Walter Lundin, Henry Kohler.

Comedy **(PR:A MPAA:NR)**

GIRL WHO DARED, THE** (1920) 5 reels REP bw

Edythe Sterling *(Barbara Hampton)*, Jack Carlyle *(Joe Knowles)*, Steve Clements *(Pedro Ramez)*, Yakima Canutt *(Bob Purdy)*, Gordon Sackville *(Judd Hampton)*.

Sterling, one of the most popular cowgirls of the 1920s, plays a female sheriff in this one, who brings a gang of Mexican rustlers and a crooked sheriff to justice.

d, Cliff Smith; w, Alvin J. Neitz.

Western **(PR:A MPAA:NR)**

GIRL WHO LOVES A SOLDIER, THE**

(1916, Brit.) 5 reels G. B. Samuelson/Moss bw

Vesta Tilley *(Vesta Beaumont)*, Sydney Folker *(Chris Barker)*, James Lindsay *(Lord Strathmore)*, Norman Cheyne *(Billy Williams)*, Rutland Barrington *(Mr. Beaumont)*.

In this British WW I romance, a young lady becomes a nurse and then passes herself off as a man in order to be near her wounded fiance.

d, Alexander Butler.

War **(PR:A MPAA:NR)**

GIRL WHO STAYED AT HOME, THE*** 1/2 (1919) 6 reels ART/PAR bw

Carol Dempster *(Atoline France)*, Adolphe Lestina *(Mons. France)*, Frances Parkes *(The Chum)*, Richard Barthelmess *(Ralph Grey)*, Robert Harron *(James Grey)*, Syn De Conde *(Count de Brissac)*, George Fawcett *(Edward Grey)*, Kate Bruce *(Mrs. Edward Grey)*, Edward Piel *(The Turnverein Terror)*, Clarine Seymour *(Cutie Beautiful)*, Tully Marshall, Adolph Lestina, David Butler.

This underrated Griffith film, about two brothers caught up in WW I, the women they love, and an unreconstructed old Confederate (living in France) who decides to reclaim his U.S. citizenship, is full of the master's magnificent touches. And it should be pointed out that Griffith again became the object of considerable public criticism (some four years after THE BIRTH OF A NATION) for producing a motion picture which many regarded as being far too tolerant of "the German race."

d, D. W. Griffith; w, S. V. E. Taylor, Griffith; ph, G. W. Bitzer; ed, James Smith.

War **(PR:A MPAA:NR)**

GIRL WHO TOOK THE WRONG TURNING, THE**

(1915, Brit.) 5 reels British Empire bw

Henry Lonsdale *(James Harcourt)*, Alice Belmore *(Sophie Coventry)*, Nina Lynn *(Vesta le Clere)*, Ronald Adair *(Willie Mason)*, Mercy Hatton *(Lucy Coventry)*, Wingold Lawrence *(Jack Fenton)*, Andrew Emm *(Johnny Walker)*, Sidney Sarl *(Bill Slater)*, Eva Dare *(Poppy Slater)*, C. F. Collings *(Richard Fenton)*.

In this early British thriller, an aristocrat's nephew leads his wife's sister into a life of vice, after framing his cousin for murder.

d, Leedham Bantock; w, (based on the play by Walter Melville).

Crime **(PR:A MPAA:NR)**

GIRL WHO WOULDN'T QUIT, THE** (1918) 5 reels UNIV bw

Louise Lovely *(Joan Tracy)*, Henry A. Barrows *(Roscoe Tracy)*, Mark Fenton *(Joshua Siddons)*, Charles H. Mailes *(Robert Carter)*, Gertrude Astor *(Stella Ramson)*, William Chester *(Joe Morgan)*, Philo McCullough *(Jim Younger)*, Clyde Benson.

In this standard melodrama with a western setting, Lovely plays a mine-owner's daughter who doesn't quit until she proves her wrongly accused father innocent of robbery.

d, Edgar Jones; w, Doris Schroeder (based on the story "The Quest of Joan" by James Oliver).

Drama **(PR:A MPAA:NR)**

GIRL WHO WOULDN'T WORK, THE* (1925) 6 reels SCHUL bw

Lionel Barrymore *(Gordon Kent)*, Marguerite De La Motte *(Mary Hale)*, Henry B. Walthall *(William Hale)*, Lilyan Tashman *(Greta Verlaine)*, Forrest Stanley *(William Norworth)*, Winter Hall *(The District Attorney)*, Thomas Ricketts *(A Rounder)*.

A splendid cast was completely wasted in this banana about a girl (De La Motte) who loses the job she hates after flirting with playboy-philanderer Barrymore. Infuriated by this turn of events, her straight-arrow father throws her out of the house, but Barrymore is decent enough to give her his apartment while he moves into his club. Tashman, Barrymore's former mistress, gets word of this and throws poor De La Motte out on her ear. De La Motte's father then (as if he hadn't done enough already) shows up, mistakes Tashman for Barrymore, and shoots her. Barrymore magnanimously takes the blame for this, but the old boy refuses this gesture and, instead, permits Barrymore to bankrupt himself by paying the legal fees which ultimately get him off the hook.

d, Marcel De Sano; w, Lois Hutchinson (based on the novel by Gertie Wentworth-James); ph, Allen Siegler.

Drama **(PR:A MPAA:NR)**

GIRL WITHOUT A SOUL, THE*** (1917) 5 reels Rolfe/Metro bw

Viola Dana *(Unity/Priscilla Beaumont)*, Robert Walker *(Hiram Miller)*, Fred Jones *(Ivor)*, Henry Hallam *(Dominic Beaumont)*, Margaret Seddon *(Henrietta Hateman)*, Margaret Vaughan *(Louise, a Victim)*.

Dana gives a fine dual performance as twin sisters. One of the girls, Priscilla, is an artistic type who becomes involved with a Russian musician, while the other loves the town smithy and church trustee. Through the evil influence of the Russian, Priscilla steals the church funds and her sister's young man is accused of the crime. There is a well-staged courtroom scene in which the truth is brought to light, and the family is reconciled.

d&w, John H. Collins.

Drama **(PR:A MPAA:NR)**

GIRLS DON'T GAMBLE** (1921) 5 reels D. N. Schwab/Jans bw

David Butler, Harry Todd, Elinor Field, Elsie Bishop, Rhea Haines, Alice Knowland, Margaret Joslin, Elmer Dewey, Rex Zane, Jack Cosgrave, Wilbur Higby.

Average independent production featuring Butler (the street cleaner in SEVENTH HEAVEN and later a top Hollywood director) as a mechanically inclined lad who leaves home and becomes a department store owner's chauffeur. He falls in love with the "right girl," is framed of committing a crime, and later saves the store from being robbed with an exciting and well-staged fight.

d, Fred J. Butler; w, (based on the *Saturday Evening Post* story "Girls Don't Gamble Anymore" by George Weston); ph, Robert Martin.

Comedy **(PR:A MPAA:NR)**

GIRL'S FOLLY, A*** (1917) 5 reels Paragon/WORLD bw

Robert Warwick, June Elvidge, Doris Kenyon, Chester Barnett, Jane Adair, Johnny Hines, Leatrice Joy.

When a motion picture company visits her rural area to shoot locations, a pretty country girl falls in love with the leading man. She runs away to become a star, but fails completely. Finally, the actor offers to provide her with all of the luxuries if she will become his mistress. She struggles with this but finally agrees, and he throws a party to celebrate the conquest to come. During the bash, her mother arrives from the hinterlands, causes him to realize the error of his desire, and the girl returns home with honor intact.

d, Maurice Tourneur; w, Tourneur, Frances Marion (based on the story "A Movie Romance" by Marion).

Comedy/Drama **(PR:A MPAA:NR)**

GIRLS GONE WILD*** (1929) 6 reels FOX bw

Sue Carol *(Babs Holworthy)*, Nick Stuart *(Buck Brown)*, William Russell *(Dan Brown)*, Roy D'Arcy *(Tony Morelli)*, Leslie Fenton *(Boots)*, Hedda Hopper *(Mrs. Holworthy)*, John Darrow *(Speed Wade)*, Matthew Betz *(Augie Sten)*, Edmund Breese *(Judge Elliot)*, Minna Ferry *(Grandma)*, Louis Natheaux *(Dilly)*, Lumsden Hare *(Tom Holworthy)*.

Carol falls out of love with Stuart when she discovers that his father, Russell, is the motorcycle cop who not only refused a bribe, but dragged her into court. While attending a dance in the tough part of town, the free-spirited Carol is taking a turn with a notorious bootlegger when rival gangsters gun him down. Fortunately, Stuart is in the neighborhood and manages to get her to his car. But before they can get away, the mobsters kidnap the couple and set out to "take 'em for a ride." This turns into a tire-screeching chase in which Stuart's father is shot from his bike and Stuart is thrown from the car. Grabbing his dad's pistol, the young man manages to get the upper hand on the killers, who throw down their weapons and surrender. Carol, needless to say, is impressed enough by all of this to forgive her boy friend and his father for their former lack of consideration.

d, Lewis Seiler; w, Beulah Marie Dix (based on a story by Bertram Millhauser); t, Malcolm Stuart Boylan; ph, Arthur Edeson, Irving Rosenberg.

Drama **(PR:A MPAA:NR)**

GIRLS WHO DARE* (1929) 6 reels Trinity bw

Rex Lease *(Chet Randolf)*, Priscilla Bonner *(Sally Casey)*, Rosemary Theby *("Alabam" Kenyon)*, Ben Wilson *(Robert Randolf)*, Steve Hall *(Dick Burke)*, Eddie Brownell *(Pat Moran)*, Sarah Roberts *(Mrs. Randolf)*, May Hotely *(Miss Casey)*, Hall Cline.

Awful movie, in every way, about a wealthy young man who overcomes his father's objection to marrying a chorus girl. Helping him in his argument is the fact that his father is himself carrying on with the nightclub hostess.

d, Frank S. Mattison; w, Cecil Burtis Hill (based on a story by Ben Hershfield, Mattison); t, Arthur Hotaling; ph, Jules Cronjager; ed, Minnie Steppler.

Drama **(PR:A MPAA:NR)**

GLADIOLA* (1915) 4 reels Edison bw

Viola Dana, Robert Conness, Pat O'Malley, Charles Sutton, Jessie Stevens, Eldean Steuart.

Innocent country girl falls for summer city person and goes to live with him in New York where she has his child. When his wife arrives on the scene, the girl, horrified by his betrayal, returns home where she is the object of community scorn. The wife later dies and the husband goes to the country girl to ask for her hand in marriage. She almost weakens when she sees her daughter standing next to him, but finally says, "No, never!" Then she marries the town's number one chump, who has been saving himself for her for four long reels.

d, John H. Collins; w, Mary Rider.

Drama **(PR:A MPAA:NR)**

GLEAM O'DAWN** (1922) 5 reels FOX bw

John Gilbert *(Gleam O'Dawn)*, Barbara Bedford *(Nini)*, James Farley *(Caleb Thomas)*, John Gough *(Gordon Thomas, His Son)*, Wilson Hummel *(Pierre)*, Edwin Booth Tilton *(Silas Huntworth)*.

Gilbert was on the threshold of super stardom when he made this North Woods drama of jealousy, love, and hate. The film was a modest programmer at best, but Gilbert's charm and sex appeal were very much in evidence.

d, Jack Dillon; w, Jules G. Furthman (based on the novel by Arthur Frederick Goodrich); ph, Don Short.

Drama **(PR:A MPAA:NR)**

GLORIOUS ADVENTURE, THE***
(1922, U.S./Brit.) 7 reels Blackton/Allied c

Diana Manners *(Lady Beatrice Fair)*, Gerald Lawrence *(Hugh Argyle)*, Cecil Humphreys *(Walter Roderick)*, Victor McLaglen *(Bullfinch)*, Alice Crawford *(Stephanie Dangerfield)*, Lois Sturt *(Nell Gwyn)*, William Luff *(King Charles II)*, Fred Wright *(Humpty)*, Flora Le Breton *(Rosemary)*, Haidee Wright *(Mrs. Bullfinch)*, Rudolf De Cordova *(Thomas Unwin)*, Lawford Davidson *(Lord Fitzroy)*, Rosalie Heath *(Queen Catherine)*, Gertrude Sterroll *(Duchess of Morland)*, Tom Heslewood *(Solomon Eagle)*, Marjorie Day *(Olivia)*, Geoffrey Clinton *(Charles Hart)*, Tom Coventry *(Lelerc)*, Jeff Barlow *(Valet)*, John East *(Major Domo)*, Violet Blackton *(Lady Beatrice as a Child)*, Lennox Pawle *(Samuel Pepys)*, Elizabeth Beerbohm *(Barbara Castlemaine)*.

This much better-than-average U.S.-British co-production, directed by film pioneer Blackton, and set against the great fire of London, was the first English feature shot in color. Lawrence is returning to England after years in the Indies and as the ship approaches land, his crew of cutthroats attempt to murder him so that their leader, Humphreys, can assume his identity. Stripped of all identification and believed to be dead, his body is thrown overboard and, after docking, Humphreys (posing as the nobleman) sets out to court the beautiful and influential Manners. Meanwhile, Lawrence, who has survived the ordeal, appears in disguise to thwart the evil scheme, and the film ends with a terrific chase and struggle between the hero and villain, who has abducted Manners in the crypt of St. Paul. The color process, although less than perfect, added greatly to the film's enjoyment, and audiences on both sides of the Atlantic approved.

p&d, J. Stuart Blackton; w, Felix Orman, Blackton; ph, William T. Crespinel (Prizma Color).

Costume Adventure **(PR:A MPAA:NR)**

GO WEST**** (1925) 7 reels Buster Keaton/Metro-Goldwyn bw

Buster Keaton *(Friendless)*, Brown Eyes the Cow, Howard Truesdale *(Ranch Owner)*, Kathleen Myers *(His Daughter)*, Ray Thompson *(The Foreman)*.

The most pathos-filled of all Keaton films has the comedian making his way westward and landing a job on a ranch. He befriends a cow named Brown Eyes and spends most of the film trying to save the creature from the slaughterhouse. Marvelous sight gags as Keaton satirizes Tom Mix, William S. Hart, and even D. W. Griffith in a poker game trying to win enough money to buy his pet. When he accuses a player of cheating, the westerner brandishes a shootin' iron and, quoting Owen Wister's THE VIRGINIAN, says "When you say that—smile!" The Great

Stoneface, of course, can't and resorts to forcing the expression with his fingers as Lillian Gish did in several famous moments from BROKEN BLOSSOMS. The film draws to an end with typical Keaton surrealism, as the comic leads a cattle drive right through the heart of the city, thus saving his boss from financial ruin. The grateful rancher then tells Keaton that he can have anything he desires and Keaton points behind saying "I want her." The viewer is led to believe the comedian has chosen the old fellow's pretty daughter, but The Great Stoneface has actually selected Brown Eyes, who is standing nearby. The fadeout comes as Keaton, Brown Eyes, the rancher and his daughter all drive off into the sunset in a battered and dusty convertible.

d, Buster Keaton; w, Raymond Cannon (based on a story by Keaton); ph, Elgin Lessley, Bert Haines.

Comedy **(PR:A MPAA:NR)**

GO WEST, YOUNG MAN*** (1919) 5 reels Goldwyn bw

Tom Moore *(Dick Latham)*, Ora Carew *(Rosa Crimmins)*, Melbourne MacDowell *(Amos Latham)*, Jack Richardson, Edward Coxen, Robert Chandler, Hector V. Sarno.

Good little drama has Moore, the lazy son of a millionaire, heading west after his father all but throws him out of the house. Once settled, he becomes a new man and is even elected sheriff. The many difficulties he encounters during this adjustment make up the bulk of this intelligent and realistically written film.

d, Harry Beaumont; w, (based on a story by Willard Mack); ph, George Webber.

Drama **(PR:A MPAA:NR)**

GOAT GETTER*** (1925) 5 reels Harry J. Brown/RAY bw

Billy Sullivan *(Billy Morris)*, Johnny Sinclair *(Pie-Eye Pickens)*, Kathleen Myers *(Virginia Avery)*, Virginia Vance *(Mamie Arthur)*, Eddie Diggins *(Lightning Bradley)*, William Buckley *(Carter Bond)*, Joe Moore *(Slug Geever)*.

Nonstop action is what makes this movie, starring stuntman Sullivan, fun. It all has to do with his desire to take on the lightweight champion of the world, who knocked him out in an earlier exhibition match. Sullivan follows him to Hollywood where the champ is making a picture, gets a part in the production, and their fight scene becomes the real thing. In the end, Sullivan wins the battle and the movie's leading lady.

d, Albert Rogell; w, Grover Jones; ph, Lee Garmes.

Adventure **(PR:A MPAA:NR)**

GOD AND THE MAN** (1918, Brit.) 7 reels ID bw

Langhorne Burton *(Christiansen)*, Joyce Carey *(Priscilla Sefton)*, Bert Wynne *(Richard Christiansen)*, Edith Craig *(Dame Christiansen)*, Sybil Arundale *(Kate Orchardson)*, Henry Vibart *(Mr. Sefton)*, Nelson Ramsey *(Squire Christiansen)*, E. Vivian Reynolds *(John Wesley)*.

In this British thriller about victims and vengeance, a Squire's son follows the man who seduced his sister to Labrador.

d, Edwin J. Collins; w, Eliot Stannard (based on the novel by Robert Buchanan).

Adventure **(PR:A MPAA:NR)**

GOD IN THE GARDEN, THE** (1921, Brit.) 6 reels Master/But bw

Edith Craig *(Miss Carroway)*, Arthur Pusey *(Rev. Mr. Hatch)*, Mabel Poulton *(Stella)*, Mabel Archdale *(Alicia Snitterfield)*, James English *(Mr. Snitterfield)*, Beatrice Grosvenor *(Jane Box)*, Cecil Morton York, A. Harding Steerman.

In this unpretentious little British romantic comedy, everyone who enters a spinster's garden is brought love by Cupid.

p, H. B. Parkinson; d&w, Edwin J. Collins (based on the novel by Keble Howard).

Comedy **(PR:A MPAA:NR)**

GOD'S HALF ACRE** (1916) 6 reels Rolfe/Metro bw

Mabel Taliaferro *(Blossom)*, J. W. Johnston *(Henry Norman)*, Helen Dahl *(Rose Norman)*, Lorraine Frost *(Bess Norman)*, Richard Neill *(Perry Westley)*, John Smiley *(Prof. Sterling)*, Daniel Jarrett *(Parker)*, Miriam Hutchins *(Lucy)*.

When Johnston, a married man, moves into an old folks home to gather material for a book he is writing, he falls in love with Taliaferro, a pretty young girl who works there. The situation is rather uncomfortable, to say the least, until Johnston's wife decides to run away with her husband's best friend and is killed in an automobile accident.

d, Edwin Carewe; w, June Mathis (based on a story by Shannon Fife).

Drama **(PR:A MPAA:NR)**

GOD'S OUTLAW* (1919) 5 reels Metro bw

Francis X. Bushman, Beverly Bayne, Helen Dunbar, Samuel Framer, Charles A. Fang, Belle Bruce, Valentine Mott, Emily Chichester.

Bushman's career had taken a nose dive (partly because of his marital problems) when someone got the idea of taking an earlier film which had been shelved and releasing it as a satire. The picture began with the title "This is a Drammer! Honest it is!" and from that point on, what was once a straight Bushman production became, through the use of gag titles, the object of ridicule. This was a devastatingly cruel embarrassment for America's one-time favorite movie star, and the gimmick served only to make a bad picture worse.

d&w, William Christy Cabanne; ph, William Fildew.

Drama/Satire **(PR:A MPAA:NR)**

GOING THE LIMIT*** (1925) 5 reels Paul Gerson bw

Richard Holt, Ruth Dwyer, Garry O'Dell, Miriam Fouche, Robert Cosgrif, Rupert Drum, George Kelly, Hal Stephens.

Shot some 43 years before Steve McQueen's BULLITT, this action-packed film about a young man's rescue of a millionaire's daughter, features a thrilling chase scene up and down the hills of San Francisco.

d, Duke Worne; w, Grover Jones; ph, Alfred Gosden.

Action/Drama **(PR:A MPAA:NR)**

GOLD AND THE GIRL** (1925) 5 reels FOX bw

Buck Jones *(Dan Prentiss)*, Elinor Fair *(Ann Donald)*, Bruce Gordon *(Bart Colton)*, Claude Peyton *(Rankin)*, Lucien Littlefield *(Weasel)*, Alphonz Ethier *(Sam Donald)*, Pal the Dog.

Below average Jones western has the great cowboy star playing an undercover agent for a mining company, who is sent to investigate a series of robberies. He falls for a girl, who happens to be the niece of the leader of the gang, but his solving the case does not get in the way of her feelings for him. Jones was always good, but this picture just didn't happen to be one of his best.

d, Edmund Mortimer; w, John Stone; ph, Allen Davey.

Western **(PR:A MPAA:NR)**

GOLD DIGGERS, THE*** (1923) 6 reels WB bw

Hope Hampton *(Jerry La Mar)*, Wyndham Standing *(Stephen Lee)*, Louise Fazenda *(Mabel Munroe)*, Gertrude Short *(Topsy St. John)*, Alec Francis *(James Blake)*, Jed Prouty *(Barney Barnett)*, Arita Gillman *(Eleanor Montgomery)*, Peggy Browne *(Trixie Andrews)*, Margaret Seddon *(Mrs. La Mar)*, Johnny Harron *(Wally Saunders)*, Anne Cornwall *(Violet Dayne)*, Louise Beaudet *(Cissie Gray)*, Edna Tichenor *(Dolly Baxter)*, Frances Ross *(Gypsy Montrose)*, Marie Prade *(Sadie)*.

This was the first offering in a three-picture deal which Belasco made with the Warner brothers. Based on a very popular Broadway show, it was about a chorus girl (Hampton) vamping stuffed shirt, Standing, in order to make her best friend, Cornwall (whom Standing refuses to allow his nephew to marry), look angelic by comparison. In the process, Standing loosens up, falls in love with Hampton, and gives his blessing to his nephew.

p, David Belasco; d, Harry Beaumont; w, Grant Carpenter (based on the play by Avery Hopwood); ed, Frank Dazey.

Comedy/Drama **(PR:A MPAA:NR)**

GOLD MADNESS*** (1923) 6 reels Perfect Principal bw

Guy Bates Post *(Jim Kendall/Calgarth)*, Cleo Madison *(Olga McGee)*, Mitchell Lewis *(Scotty McGee)*, Grace Darmond *(Hester Stanton)*.

Good direction and acting elevated this above-average programmer about a struggling miner who has his "gold mad" wife taken away by a swindler, only to see them arrested in the end after he has struck it rich.

d, Robert T. Thornby; w, Fred Kennedy Myton (based on the story "The Man from Ten Strike" by James Oliver Curwood).

Drama **(PR:A MPAA:NR)**

GOLD RUSH, THE***** (1925) 9 reels Charles Chaplin/UA bw

Charles Chaplin *(Lone Prospector)*, Georgia Hale *(Georgia)*, Mack Swain *(Big Jim McKay)*, Tom Murray *(Black Larson)*, Betty Morrissey, Kay Desleys, Joan Lowell *(Georgia's Friends)*, Malcolm Waite *(Jack Cameron)*, Henry Bergman *(Hank Curtis)*, John Rand, Heinie Conklin, Albert Austin, Allan Garcia, Tom Wood *(Prospectors)*, Stanley Sanford *(Barman)*, Barbara Pierce *(Manicurist)*, A. J. O'Connor, Art Walker *(Officers)*, "Daddy" Taylor *(Ancient Dancing Prospector)*, Margaret Martin, Princess Neela *(Squaws)*, Frank Aderias, Leona Aderias *(Eskimo Children)*, E. Espinosa, Ray Morris *(Eskimos)*, Fred Karno, Jr., Jack Adams, Sam Allen, Claude Anderson, Harry Arras, F. J. Beauregard, William Bell, Francis Bernhardt, E. Blumenthal, William Bradford, George Brock, William Butler, Pete Brogan, R. Campbell, Leland Carr, H. C. Chisolm, Harry Coleman, Harry De Mors, Jimmy Dime, W. S. Dobson, John Eagown, Aaron Edward, Elias Elizaroff, Leon Fary, Richard Foley, Charles Force, J. C. Fowler, Ray Grey, William Hackett, James Hammer, Ben Hart, R. Hausner, Tom Hawley, Jack Herrick, Jack Hoefer, George Holt, Tom Hutchinson, Carl Jenson, Harry Jones, Bob Kelly, John King, Bob Leonard, Francis Lowell, Clyde McAtee, John McGrath, Chris Martin, John Millerta, Mr. Myers, George Neely, H. C. Oliver, William Parmalee, Jack Phillips, Art Price, Frank Rice, E.M. Robb, C. F. Roarke, J. Ryan, J. J. Smith, Joe Smith, C. B. Steele, Armand Triller, John Tully, Jack Vedders, John Wallace, Sharkey Weimar, Ed Wilson, C. Whitecloud, H. Wolfinger, Dave Wright, Ah Yot, George Young, Ed Zimmer, Lillian Adrian, Rebecca Conroy, Donnabella Custer, Kay De Lay, Inez Gomez, Mildred Hall, Gypsy Hart, Helen Hayward, Josie Howard, Jean Huntley, Gladys Johnson, Helen Kassler, Geraldine Leslie, Joan Lowell, Ruth Milo, Marie Muggley, Florence Murth, Lillian Rossino, Edna Rowe, Jane Sherman, Nina Trask, Mary Williams, Marie Willis, Lillian Reschm, Nellie Noxon, Dolores Mendes, Cecile Cameron, Joan Lowell, Betty Pierce, Marta Belfort, Dorothy Crane, Bessie Eade, James Darby, Frank E. Stockdale, Freddie Lansit, George Leslie, P. Nagle, M. Farrell, S. Murphy *(People in Dance Hall)*.

The first of Chaplin's comedy epics, THE GOLD RUSH opens with a spectacular scene in the vicinity of Truckee, high in the Sierra Nevadas about 20 miles from Reno. Hundreds of prospectors trek up a mountain pass—Chaplin among them, slipping and sliding on the snow-covered terrain—on their gold-seeking quest through the icy pass. Unaware of a huge bear striding in his slippery tracks, Chaplin pauses to lean on his cane, which sinks to its handle in the deep snow, rendering him supine. Still followed by the bear, the unsuspecting prospector makes his way to the sheltering cabin of the villainous Murray who, taking rifle in hand, orders him to leave. With the best of intentions, Chaplin attempts to do so, but a raging wind keeps pushing him back into the cabin. The same ill wind blows another prospector—a luckier one, who has found a massive gold nugget—into the cabin, the enormous Swain, who is also ordered to depart instantly. Less courteous than his fellow guest, Swain grabs for the gun; he and Murray wrestle for its possession, their choreographed struggle resulting in the gun barrel constantly pointing at the ever-evasive Chaplin, who scurries to every conceivable hiding place. Swain wins possession of the weapon, and the foodless trio decide that one of their number must depart to find provisions lest they all perish. They cut cards to determine which of them shall be the traveler; Murray, the loser, leaves. Along his way, he runs into two policemen who have been on his trail and murders them both. In the cabin, the two remaining famished fortune-seekers prepare their Thanksgiving day dinner: one of Chaplin's boots, which he cooks with care in a huge pot. Serving the shoe, Chaplin severs the sole and sets it before his huge companion who, savoring the larger part, deftly reverses their plates so that he has the upper. No matter; Chaplin makes the most of his meal, plucking the shoenails as if boning a fish, coiling the laces expertly, spaghettilike, about his fork, smacking his lips appreciatively, gourmandizing his fantasy. Time passes; the two survivors again approach starvation. Chaplin offers his remaining boot as sustenance, but the proposed feast is refused with revulsion by his corpulent companion. Maddened by hunger, Swain begins to visualize the petite prospector as an enormous, succulent chicken; he chases Chaplin around the cabin, brandishing a huge knife. Unable to catch his supple prey, Swain goes for the gun and fires a blast, which temporarily restores him to reason. Chaplin takes the rifle and prudently buries it in the snow outside the cabin. Cut to a scene depicting the malevolent Murray, on his quest for food, stumbling upon Swain's gold strike. The following morning, Swain's delusion returns; he and Chaplin—again as a chicken—battle one another. Chaplin is blinded by a blanket that swathes his head and, grappling, believes he has hold of his fur-coated, maniacal friend; in fact, he has a death clutch on the bear, which has tracked him into the cabin. The bear flees as the desperate Chaplin finds the rifle and fires. Mortally wounded, the fallen ursine visitor resolves the food-shortage problem. Nourished again, Chaplin and Swain bid each other a friendly farewell. Swain proceeds to the site of his gold strike, where he finds the murderer, Murray. The two men fight for the mineral rights and Swain is struck on the head, rendering him an incoherent amnesiac. Swain wanders off in a daze; Murray, savoring his victory, is suddenly visited by snowy justice in the form of an avalanche, which buries him. Meanwhile, Chaplin arrives at a gold-boom town where he is suddenly smitten with the sight of a beautiful dance-hall girl, Hale. Spotting an acquaintance across the crowded saloon floor, Hale chants out, "Charlie!" Enraptured, Chaplin smiles his greeting, but she proceeds past him to her same-named acquaintance. Crestfallen, Chaplin finds a torn photograph of the beauty and pockets it. Moments later, his spirits soar again as Hale—to teach her boy friend, Waite, a lesson—selects the sorriest specimen in the saloon, Chaplin, as a dance partner. As the pair pirouette, Chaplin's baggy trousers begin to fall. Desperately, the tiny terpsichorean grabs a rope from the floor and ties it to his waist to keep his trousers up, little realizing that the opposite end serves as a collar for a colossal canine. The huge dog gives chase to a passing cat, which brings the dance to a disastrous end. Presented with a flower by the delightful dancing girl, Chaplin incurs the wrath of the jealous Waite, who pulls his derby down. Blinded, Chaplin stumbles into a post, causing a clock to fall on the head of his rival. Delighted by his victory, the little gladiator takes his leave, seeking food and shelter. Spotting Bergman through the window of a comfortable cabin, Chaplin lies supine in the snow outside, waiting for his prospective host to emerge. Bergman spots the fallen figure, apparently frozen, and carries Chaplin inside to thaw. Bergman recruits his new-found friend as caretaker when he departs to prospect. Hale and three other dance-hall girls, out for a walk, spot Chaplin on the doorstoop and fling snowballs at him. He invites them in for a visit; as he leaves to get more firewood, Hale discovers the torn picture of herself that Chaplin had retrieved. As they depart, Chaplin invites them to return again for dinner and festivities on New Year's Eve. The girls, giggling at the tiny terror's temerity, pretend to accept his proffered invitation and depart. Elated, Chaplin does a dance of joy, flinging a pillow about until it bursts, filling the cabin with feathers. Returning for her forgotten gloves, Hale finds Chaplin embarrassed by the simulated snow he has created. Needing funds to procure the provisions for his planned feast, Chaplin decides to shovel snow for his neighbors. Cleverly, he enhances business by shoveling snow from one doorway, only to pile it up on the adjacent one. New Year's Eve arrives and Chaplin awaits his guests, his preparations meticulously made. Hearing a noise at the cabin door, he flings it open, to be greeted only by Bergman's hungry mule, which he has forgotten to feed. His dilatory guests delayed, he waits again. Dissolve to the cabin at the height of the festivities, the gaily attired girls exclaiming over their party favors and requesting a speech from their gracious host. Chaplin offers to dance for them instead; spearing two dinner rolls with forks, he performs a dainty dance, a pastry ballet complete with high kicks, graceful *plies*, and sidewise shuffles. Enchanted by the *prima* performance, Hale kisses the balletomane of bread, causing him to swoon with joy. It was all a dream, of course; chastened, Chaplin awakens to the sound of gunfire. Midnight has arrived; Hale, in the saloon, has fired a brace of pistols in celebration. Suddenly remembering the invitation, Hale and the girls—with Waite in tow—decide to visit the "Little Fellow" after all. Arriving at the cabin, Hale is touched to see the party preparations. Again, she rebuffs Waite, Chaplin now her preference. Later, Swain turns up, his memory restored save only for the location of his gold strike. Spotting Chaplin in the saloon, he embraces his old friend, explaining that if they can find the old cabin, he will be able to find the gold, as well. The two set off and reach the cabin, where they spend the night. During the darkness, a savage storm blows the cabin to the brink of an enormous abyss. Rising, Chaplin walks about, causing the cabin to teeter dangerously, rocking back and forth with his transits as it sways on the cliff's edge. The waking Swain panics, but Chaplin reassures him, stating that the apparent swaying is simply the natural result of their previous night's partying. Unable to see through the frosted window, Chaplin opens the door to step outside. He finds himself hanging from the door, swinging in terror over the seemingly bottomless drop. Hauled back into the cabin by Swain, the friends find themselves at a precipitous angle, clambering over one another in their efforts to reach the landward door. Swain manages to make the door; dropping, he discovers the marker to his gold claim, and forgets his friend in the sliding cabin. At the last moment, Chaplin makes his escape and the cabin plunges into the precipice. Later, the gold mine having proved to be just that to the two friends, Chaplin and Swain—rich beyond the dreams of Croesus—are interviewed on board a ship by reporters. To reprise his history, Chaplin dons his old prospecting clothes. Tripping, he falls from the deck into the steerage section below, where he finds the homeward-bound Hale. As the disheveled little fellow is about to be clapped in irons as a stowaway, Hale protests that she will pay his fare. The captain and the reporters arrive to assure her that her charity case is a millionaire, and the lovers are happily reunited. THE GOLD RUSH was Chaplin's first starring vehicle for the new distributing company, United Artists, that he had co-founded with Douglas Fairbanks, Mary Pickford, and D.W. Griffith six years previously (he had directed, but not starred in, that company's release A WOMAN OF PARIS in 1923). Reportedly, Chaplin came up with the idea for the picture while breakfasting with his husband-and-wife partners, Fairbanks and Pickford, who had some stereograms depicting scenes from the Klondike gold rush. He also had become intensely interested in the fate of the fabled Donner party of 1846, whose tragic transcontinental trek had ended in death after their food ran out (and whose surviving members indulged in cannibalism to stay alive). Chaplin had read Charles Fayette McGlashan's *History of the Donner Party*, originally published in 1879. He also might have been partly influenced by documentary director Robert Flaherty's film NANOOK OF THE NORTH, released in 1922. That the Donner story could have evoked so hilariously funny a film should come as no surprise in an industry founded on pratfalls; Chaplin well knew that "tragedy stimulates the spirit of ridicule." He began preparations for the picture almost immediately after completing A WOMAN OF PARIS; his initial script, "The Lucky Strike," was copyrighted as "a play in two scenes" only two months after that picture's premiere in October, 1923. Meticulously planned as a comic epic, the film's cost was high, reportedly exceeding $900 thousand; hundreds of extras were transported to the remote Sierra Nevada location camp at $5 a day, and Chaplin's cinematographers shot at a 25-to-one ratio, retaking until their perfectionist director was satisfied. Chaplin's boots, which served as a meal for the protagonist and his pal Swain, were made of licorice (a natural laxative, as the already ailing Swain discovered; his revulsion to the offer of a second such meal was perfectly real), and 20 pairs were made to satisfy the outtake requirements of the picky Chaplin. The director was experiencing severe family problems during filming. He had only recently invited his mother, Hannah, to emigrate from England to live with him. Apparently senile, but with lucid moments, Hannah visited the set and saw her son illuminated by the bluish beams of Cooper-Hewitt vapor lamps in his none-too-natty working clothes. Said she, "I've got to get you a new suit—and you have a ghastly color. You ought to go out in the sunlight." But Hannah was the least of Chaplin's domestic problems. Chaplin had initially chosen a visitor to the set, the 16-year-old Lillita McMurray—who had worked with him as a child in THE KID in 1921 playing "The Angel of Temptation"—as his heroine. Chaplin changed her name to Lita Grey and signed her as his co-star at $75 weekly. The nubile adolescent proved to be an angel of temptation indeed; she got pregnant by Chaplin. Faced with her hysterical mother (to say nothing of a possible jail sentence for statutory rape), Chaplin quickly married the girl in Mexico. Some of his co-star's scenes had already been shot, but Chaplin realized that Grey's burgeoning belly (she was delivered of a child six months after the shotgun wedding) would rule his young bride out as the dance-hall girl if he was to keep to his planned schedule. Lita Grey Chaplin was replaced in the role by Hale, a one-time Miss America contestant, who had come to the attention of director Josef von Sternberg (she had the leading role in his first helming effort, THE SALVATION HUNTERS). Chaplin had screened von Sternberg's film and liked it. He met Hale at a later screening and asked her to take the co-starring role in his forthcoming picture. Hale had already been signed for a picture by Chaplin's good friend Fairbanks, but the latter released her from the commitment as a favor to his partner. The film turned out to be a marvel of comedy; years later, it was cited by the prestigious International Film Jury as the second greatest film of all time (THE BATTLESHIP POTEMKIN came first). Not all of the wildly funny sequences are entirely original (Roscoe "Fatty" Arbuckle had performed a dance using bread rolls in the 1918 film THE COOK), but never have they been performed with such grace and spirit. Chaplin himself later stated that this was the film by which he would most like to be remembered; to assure its continuation, he reissued a version in 1941 with music and his own spoken narrative. Curiously, through an oversight, the picture's copyright was not renewed when it lapsed in 1953. Perhaps the oversight was for the best; THE GOLD RUSH continues to be screened, free of royalty payments, delighting audiences all over the world.

p,d&w, Charles Chaplin; ph, Roland Totheroh; art d, Charles D. Hall.

Comedy **Cas.** **(PR:A MPAA:NR)**

GOLDEN BIRD, THE (SEE: LITTLE MISS HOOVER, 1918)

GOLDEN CHANCE, THE*** (1915) 5 reels LAS/PAR bw

Cleo Ridgley, Wallace Reid, Horace B. Carpenter, Edythe Chapman, Ernest Joy, Raymond Hatton.

When a judge's beautiful daugher, Ridgley, marries a small-time crook, she is forced from a life of luxury to one of drudgery as a seamstress. Later, one of her wealthy clients asks her to pose as an heiress in order to help her husband land a business deal with young millionaire Reid. On meeting her at the party, the young man falls desperately in love. Meanwhile, her crooked husband attempts to rob the house and is nearly captured. Believing his wife to be unfaithful, the burglar attempts to murder Reid, but is badly beaten in a fist fight. Later he is killed by the police, leaving the door open for Reid to marry the judge's sadder, but wiser daughter.

d, Cecil B. DeMille; w, Jeanie Macpherson; ph, Alvin Wyckoff.

Drama (PR:A MPAA:NR)

GOLDEN GIFT, THE** (1922) 5 reels Metro bw

Alice Lake *(Nita Gordon)*, John Bowers *(James Llewelyn)*, Harriet Hammond *(Edith Llewelyn)*, Joseph Swickard *(Leonati)*, Bridgetta Clark *(Rosana)*, Louis Dumar *(Malcolm Thorne)*, Geoffrey Webb *(Stephen Brand)*, Camilla Clark *(Joy Llewelyn)*.

Acceptable programmer, featuring former Mack Sennett comedienne Lake, about a singer who loses her voice after giving birth. This leads her free-loading husband to desert her, and the desperate young woman ultimately gives her child up for adoption and becomes a dancer in a Mexican nightclub. Then, while performing one night, her former vocal teacher discovers her and, convinced that her voice can be restored, takes her to Europe. Not only does the treatment work, but she soon finds herself performing as a star of the Metropolitan Opera, where she meets and falls in love with Bowers, the man who adopted her baby. He is of the firm position that no fit woman would ever abandon her child, so when the truth comes out he almost gives her the air. Fortunately, he thinks about this twice and, after evaluating the extenuating circumstances of the case, decides to marry the mother of the child he loves.

d, Maxwell Karger; w, Florence Hein (based on a story by June Mathis); ph, John Boyle; art d, Joseph Calder.

Drama (PR:A MPAA:NR)

GOLDFISH, THE*** (1924) 7 reels Constance Talmadge/AFN bw

Constance Talmadge *(Jennie Wetherby)*, Jack Mulhall *(Jimmy Wetherby)*, Frank Elliott *(Duke of Middlesex)*, Jean Hersholt *(Herman Krauss)*, ZaSu Pitts *(Amelia Pugsley)*, Edward Connelly *(Count Nevski)*, William Conklin *(J. Hamilton Powers)*, Leo White *(Casmir)*, Nellie Bly Baker *(Ellen)*, Kate Lester *(Mrs. Bellmore)*, Eric Mayne *(The Prince)*, William Wellesley *(Mr. Crane)*, Jacqueline Gadsden *(Helen Crane)*, Percy Williams *(Wilton)*, John Patrick *(Reporter)*.

Clever adaptation of the Broadway comedy about a young "modern" married couple who agree that if either should decide to end their arrangement, they will do so by presenting the other with a bowl of goldfish. Following an argument with her song-plugger husband, the ambitious girl gives her husband the goldfish and takes off on her own. She rapidly scales society's ladder through two marriages to extremely prominent men. She is about to announce her fourth marriage, this one to a duke, when her first spouse strikes it rich, and she enthusiastically decides to return to him, leaving the nobleman with a bowl of wriggling creatures to remember her by.

d, Jerome Storm; w, C. Gardner Sullivan (based on the play by Gladys Unger); ph, Ray Binger.

Comedy (PR:A MPAA:NR)

GOLEM: HOW HE CAME INTO THE WORLD, THE*½** (1920, Ger.) 6 reels UFA bw (DER GOLEM: WIE ER IN DE WELT)

Paul Wegener *(Golem)*, Albert Steinruck *(Rabbi Lowe)*, Ernst Deutsch, Lydia Salmonova, Hanns Strum, Otto Gebuhr, Lothar Muthel.

Wegener's second filming (he codirected with Henrik Galeen a version in 1914) of the Jewish folk legend about a Rabbi who creates a soulless monster out of clay, only to have it fall in love with his daughter. This film had an obvious influence on the American FRANKENSTEIN and, in a scene which James Whale would borrow from a little over a decade later, the creature loses his life when he befriends a child who offers him an apple and then removes the Star of David from his person.

d, Paul Wegener, Carl Boese; w, Wegener, Henrik Galeen (based on a story by Gustav Meyrink); ph, Karl Freund, Guido Seeber; art d, Hans Poelzig.

Fantasy/Horror Cas. (PR:C MPAA:NR)

GOOD AND NAUGHTY*** (1926) 6 reels FP/PAR bw

Pola Negri *(Germaine Morris)*, Tom Moore *(Gerald Gray)*, Ford Sterling *(Bunny West)*, Miss Du Pont *(Claire Fenton)*, Stuart Holmes *(Thomas Fenton)*, Marie Mosquini *(Chouchou Rouselle)*, Warner Richmond *("Bad News" Smith)*.

Fine vehicle for Negri, breezily directed by St. Clair, about a wealthy young woman who poses as a slob in order to be hired by the decorating firm (which has a policy *not* to employ pretty girls because they are potentially flirtatious) owned by a man she loves. There are a number of complications which Negri solves after becoming her true, beautiful self.

d, Malcolm St. Clair; w, Pierre Collings (based on the play "Naughty Cinderella" by Rene Peter, Henri Falk); ph, Bert Glennon.

Romance/Comedy (PR:A MPAA:NR)

GOOD BAD MAN, THE*** (1916) 5 reels FA/TRI bw

Douglas Fairbanks *("Passin' Through")*, Sam de Grasse *(Bud Fraser)*, Pomeroy Doc Cannon *(Bob Emmons)*, Joseph Singleton *(The Weazel)*, Bessie Love *(Amy)*, Mary Alden *(Jane Stuart)*, George Beranger *(Thomas Stuart)*, Fred Burns *(The Sheriff)*, Charles Stevens.

Fairbanks wrote and starred in this western about "Passin' Through," a man with a mission, who robs the rich to provide comfort for illegitimate children. Along the way his path crosses de Grasse, the outlaw who murdered his father when he was a small boy, and our hero gains his revenge with a well-placed slug from a 45. Many of Fairbanks' films dealt with lineage and legitimacy, not surprising since he personally experienced parental desertion.

d, Allan Dwan; w, Douglas Fairbanks; ph, Victor Fleming.

Western (PR:A MPAA:NR)

GOOD-BYE, BILL*** (1919) 5 reels PAR bw

Shirley Mason, Ernest Truex, Joseph Allen, Carl de Planta, Joseph Burke, H. E. Koser, J. Herbert Frank.

Interesting wartime comedy written by Loos, about the Kaiser bringing the inventor of a "mustache fixer" (and his pretty daughter) from Hoboken to Berlin. The Kaiser is sure that an army led by stiff-mustached officers will be invincible, but the daughter's sweetheart follows them, captures the German head of state, and cuts *his* mustache off.

d, John Emerson; w, Anita Loos, Emerson (based on the story "Gosh Darn the Kaiser" by Loos); ph, Jacques Monteran.

Political Comedy (PR:A MPAA:NR)

GOOD-BYE KISS, THE** (1928) 8 reels MS/FN bw

Johnny Burke *(Johnny)*, Sally Eilers *(Sally)*, Matty Kemp *(Bill Williams)*, Wheeler Oakman *(Sgt. Hoffman)*, Irving Bacon *(Col. von Stein)*, Lionel Belmore *(The General)*, Alma Bennett *("Toots")*, Carmelita Geraghty *(Mlle. Nannette)*, Eugene Pallette *(The Captain)*, Jean Laverty *(Mlle. Jeanne)*, Andy Clyde *(The Grandfather)*.

Sennett, whose metier was the two-reel comedy, stretched himself a bit thin in this fair comedy feature about a girl who follows her man to France during the war and transforms him from coward to hero. Strangely, the action scenes outshine the comedic ones.

d, Mack Sennett; w, Jefferson Moffitt, Sennett (based on a story by Moffitt, Phil Whitman, Carl Harbaugh); t, Harbaugh; ph, John Boyle; ed, William Hornbeck; syn sc; s eff.

Comedy/War (PR:A MPAA:NR)

GOOD-FOR-NOTHING, THE** (1914) 4 reels Essanay bw

G.M. Anderson, Victor Potel, Carl Stockdale, Lee Willard.

Anderson abandoned his "Broncho Billy" character to play the wastrel son of a stockbroker who is thrown out of the firm, moves west, befriends a dying Indian (who discloses the whereabouts of a gold mine) and returns home to bail his parents out of the workhouse.

Drama (PR:A MPAA:NR)

GOOD LITTLE DEVIL, A** (1914) 5 reels FP bw

Mary Pickford, William Norris, Ernest Truex, Wilda Bennett, David Belasco (In the Prologue).

Pickford and Belasco brought this popular stage presentation to the screen with limited success. Pickford as the little blind girl is wonderful, but the production, which closely followed the play in direction, is singularly uncinematic. It was, however, Pickford's natural and instinctive motion picture acting which caused the heads of Famous Players to rethink their "famous players in famous plays" approach to filmmaking. Before long they would be making pictures that moved, and Pickford would be their greatest star. Before taking to the stage to perform the role she recreated here, Pickford had to make the difficult decision to leave her mentor, D. W. Griffith. In accepting Belasco's offer, she explained that she wouldn't be able to begin rehearsing until she had first talked with Griffith. Leaving the New York theater where the play was being produced, she boarded a downtown-bound subway for the Biograph Studios on 14th Street. There she encountered Griffith in the middle of rehearsal and explained that she was leaving Biograph to return to stage work. The great director dismissed the cast and crew and is reputed to have simply said: "Be good. Be a good actress." What's more, when the play opened in Philadelphia, Griffith and the entire company were there in the audience.

d, Edwin S. Porter, J. Searle Dawley; sup, David Belasco; w, Austin Strong (based on the play by Maurice Rostand, Rosemonde Gerard); ph, Porter.

Drama (PR:A MPAA:NR)

GOOD NIGHT, PAUL*** (1918) 5 reels SEL bw

Constance Talmadge *(Matilda Landers)*, Norman Kerry *(Richard Landers)*, Harrison Ford *(Paul Boudeaux)*, John Steppling *(Batiste Boudeaux)*, Beatrice Van *(Rose)*, Rosita Marstini *(Mme. Julie)*, ZaSu Pitts.

Talmadge, one of the movies' best comediennes, is in top form as a girl who poses as the wife of a businessman to insure that his uncle (a maniac about marriage) will deliver the $50,000 necessary to keep his operation afloat. There are laughs-a-plenty when the uncle decides to remain on for a month, forcing Talmadge to deal with a triple whammy—the uncle's deception, a misogynistic business partner, and a very jealous husband.

d, Walter Edwards; w, Julia Crawford Ivers (based on the play by Roland Oliver, Charles Dickson); ph, James C. Van Trees.

Comedy (PR:A MPAA:NR)

GOOSE GIRL, THE*** (1915) 5 reels LAS bw

Marguerite Clarke *(Gretchen)*, Monroe Salisbury *(King Frederick)*, Sidney Deane *(Prince Regent of Jugendheit)*, Robert N. Dunbar *(Grand Duke of Ehrenstein)*, James Neill *(Count Von Herbeck)*, Larry Payton *(Von Wallenstein)*, Page E. Peters *(Carmichael)*, Horace B. Carpenter *(Torpete the Gypsy)*, Ernest Joy *(Hans)*, J. M. Cassidy *(Gottfried)*, Miss Johnson *(Princess Hildegarde)*, Jane Darwell *(Irma)*.

Set in one of those light operetta kingdoms, Clarke, a tender of geese, is actually the true princess who was abducted from the castle as an infant and replaced by the chancellor's daughter. The handsome prince, who refuses to marry the impostor sight unseen, deserts his duty and happens upon Clarke, with whom he falls madly in love. Of course the movie ends with the happy couple occupying their rightful throne. Clarke, who by 1918 would be second only to Mary Pickford in popularity, gave her usual distinctive and delightful performance.

d, Fred Thompson; w, William C. DeMille (based on the novel and play by Harold McGrath).

Drama **(PR:A MPAA:NR)**

GOOSE WOMAN, THE**** (1925) 7 reels UNIV bw

Louise Dresser *(Mary Holmes/Marie de Nardi)*, Jack Pickford *(Gerald Holmes)*, Constance Bennett *(Hazel Woods)*, James O. Barrows *(Jacob Riggs)*, George Cooper *(Reporter)*, Gustav von Seyffertitz *(Mr. Vogel)*, George Nichols *(Detective Lopez)*, Marc MacDermott *(Amos Ethridge)*.

Inspired by the sensational Rev. Hall-Eleanor Mills murder case of 1922, Clarence Brown's beautifully directed film tells of a world renowned opera singer (Dresser), who loses her voice and friends after giving birth to a bastard son. Embittered by the hand fate dealt her, she changes her name and dwells drunkenly in the past, eventually becoming a tender of geese and living in a broken down shack on the outskirts of town. When her son becomes engaged to an actress, out of cruel spite she informs him of his illegitimacy and then claims to have witnessed a headline-making murder (in order to once again experience the celebrity she craves, not realizing that this will implicate her offspring). Horrified by the result of her actions, she admits her lie and, for the first time, her true maternal feelings are allowed to surface. A good performance by Pickford and a triumph for Dresser in what is no doubt her greatest role.

d, Clarence Brown; w, Melville Brown (based on a story by Rex Beach); t, Dwinelle Benthall; ph, Milton Moore; ed, Ray Curtiss; art d, E. E. Sheeley, William R. Schmidt.

Drama **(PR:C MPAA:NR)**

GOVERNOR'S BOSS, THE*

(1915) 5 reels The Governors Boss Photoplay bw

William Sulzer *(Himself)*, Pauline Hall *(Mrs. Morton)*, Edward P. Sullivan *(The Boss)*, Anna Logan *(Ruth)*, Edward F. Roseman *(Fordyce Manville)*, Elsie Balfour *(Edith)*, Bert Tuey *(Archie Tally)*, Dorothy Kingdon *(Grace Ferguson)*, Rev. Madison C. Peters *(A Delegate)*, Frank Tinney *(Policy Seller)*.

Interesting film in which ex-Governor William Zulzer plays himself in the story of how political bosses allegedly framed and drove him out of office. The movie is set apart by lewd scenes of rape and depravity, terrible acting, and cinematography which is in focus only a small part of the time.

d, Charles E. Davenport.

Drama **(PR:A MPAA:NR)**

GRAIN OF DUST, THE*** (1928) 7 reels TS bw

Ricardo Cortez *(Fred Norman)*, Claire Windsor *(Josephine Burroughs)*, Alma Bennett *(Dorothea Hallowell)*, Richard Tucker *(George)*, John St. Polis *(Mr. Burroughs)*, Otto Hoffman *(Head Clerk)*.

All but forgotten now, second-string vamp Bennett has her moments as the secretary who lures Cortez from his wife, his best friend to suicide, and his business to ruin.

d, George Archainbaud; w, Frances Hyland, L. G. Rigby (based on the novel by David Graham Phillips); t, Paul Perez; ph, Ernest Miller; ed, Robert Kern; art d, Hervey Libbert; set d, George Sawley.

Drama **(PR:A MPAA:NR)**

GRAND DUCHESS AND THE WAITER, THE (1926) 7 reels FP/PAR bw

Adolphe Menjou *(Albert Durant)*, Florence Vidor *(Grand Duchess Zenia)*, Lawrence Grant *(Grand Duke Peter)*, Andre Beranger *(Grand Duke Paul)*, Dot Farley *(Prascovia)*, Barbara Pierce *(Henriette)*, Brandon Hurst *(Matard)*, William Courtright *(Blake)*.

St. Clair, who directed in the Ernst Lubitsch manner, did very well with this delightful comedy about a French millionaire (Menjou) who falls in love with a grand duchess and enters her service to win her heart—which, of course, he ultimately does.

d, Malcolm St. Clair; w, Pierre Collings, John Lynch (based on a play by Alfred Savoir); ph, Lee Garmes.

Comedy **(PR:A MPAA:NR)**

GRANDMA'S BOY**** (1922) 5 reels HR/AEX bw

Harold Lloyd *(The Boy/Grandfather in Flashback)*, Mildred Davis *(The Girl)*, Anna Townsend *(Grandma)*, Charles Stevenson *(The Bully)*, Noah Young *(The Sheriff)*, Dick Sutherland *(The Tramp)*, Gus Leonard, Wallace Howe, Sammy Brooks, William Gillespie.

Lloyd's first feature began as a 2-reeler, but the comedian insisted on developing his character regardless of length or expense, and it ended up costing over $100,000 to produce. It tells of a cowardly small-town boy who runs to his grandmother for comfort when he can't face the responsibility of participating in the manhunt for a killer. The wise old lady tells him the story of how his equally timid grandfather was made invincible when a haggish witch gave him the magic charm of the Zuni and because of this, singlehandedly captured invaluable Yankee plans during the war. The boy is spellbound by this tale, and when his grandmother gives him the amulet (actually the handle from one of her old umbrellas), the lad is instilled with such a blind sense of valor that to the astonishment of all he captures (in a beautifully executed fight scene) the brutish criminal alone.

d, Fred Newmeyer; w, Hal Roach, Sam Taylor, Jean Havez, Thomas J. Crizer, Harold Lloyd; t, H. M. Walker; ph, Walter Lundin.

Comedy **(PR:A MPAA:NR)**

GREAT ADVENTURE, THE** (1915, Brit.) 6 reels ID/Turner bw

Henry Ainley *(Liam Carve)*, Esme Hubbard *(Janet Cannott)*, Rutland Barrington *(Mr. Texel)*, E. H. Brooke *(Sampson Ebag)*, Amy Lorraine *(Mrs. Shawn)*, Arthur M. Cullin *(Albert Shawn)*, Hubert Harben *(Cyrus Carve)*, Dorothy Rowan *(Lady Alice Rowfant)*, Fred Rains *(Courier)*, Campbell Gullan *(Reporter)*.

Offbeat little British comedy about a wealthy artist who takes the identity of a dead valet, marries a poor woman, and then discovers his man-servant had a wife and children.

d, Larry Trimble; w, Benedict James (based on the play by Arnold Bennett).

Comedy **(PR:A MPAA:NR)**

GREAT ADVENTURE, THE** (1918) 5 reels Pathe bw

Bessie Love *("Rags")*, Flora Finch *(Her Aunt)*, Donald Hall *(Mr. Sheen)*, Chester Barnett *(Billy Blake)*, Florence Short *(Hazel Lee)*, Walter Craven, Jack Dunn.

Love plays a small-town girl who comes to New York to make it on "the great white way." While staying at her aunt's boarding house, she becomes romantically involved with Barnett, a chorus boy. It looks like wedding bells, until one night the leading lady fails to go on and Love takes her place. Overnight she is discovered, moves to Park Avenue, rides in a limo, and begins to keep company with Broadway's No. 1 matinee idol, Hall. This turn of events does little to enhance Barnett's disposition, but Love comes to her senses after a boating accident reveals Hall to be a sniveling coward, and Barnett saves her life. The one highlight of this film was the comeback appearance of former John Bunny costar, Finch.

d, Alice Guy-Blache; w, Agnes Christine Johnston (based on the novel *The Painted Scene* by Henry Kitchell Webster); ph, George K. Hollister, John G. Hass.

Drama **(PR:A MPAA:NR)**

GREAT EXPECTATIONS*** (1917) 5 reels FP/PAR bw

Louise Huff *(Estella)*, Jack Pickford *(Pip)*, Frank Losee *(Abel Magwitch, Alias Provis)*, W. W. Black *(Joe Gargery)*, Marcia Harris *(Mrs. Gargery)*, Grace Barton *(Miss Havisham)*, Herbert Prior *(Mr. Jaggers)*.

The atmosphere of 19th Century England is well depicted in this classic story about young Mr. Pip (Pickford) and his mysterious benefactor. Good acting by all except Pickford, who just didn't seem right for the central character. Fine direction was handled by Vignola throughout most of the film until he was taken ill and Kaufman was given the last few scenes.

d, Robert G. Vignola, Joseph Kaufman; w, Paul West (based on the novel by Charles Dickens); ph, William C. Marshall.

Drama **(PR:A MPAA:NR)**

GREAT GAME, THE* (1918, Brit.) 6 reels I.B. Davidson/Ruffells bw

Billy Wells *(John Cranston)*, A. E. Coleby, Ernest A. Douglas, Judd Green, H. Nicholls-Bates, Eve Marchew.

Typical British sporting film about a squire's son who must rally to win the big horse race to earn his fabulous fortune.

d&w, A. E. Coleby (based on the novel *The Straight Game* by Andrew Soutar).

Drama **(PR:A MPAA:NR)**

GREAT GATSBY, THE*** (1926) 8 reels FP/PAR bw

Warner Baxter *(Jay Gatsby)*, Lois Wilson *(Daisy Buchanan)*, Neil Hamilton *(Nick Carraway)*, Georgia Hale *(Myrtle Wilson)*, William Powell *(George Wilson)*, Hale Hamilton *(Tom Buchanan)*, George Nash *(Charles Wolf)*, Carmelita Geraghty *(Jordon Baker)*, Eric Blore *(Lord Digby)*, "Gunboat" Smith *(Bert)*, Claire Whitney *(Catherine)*.

First filming of the great Fitzgerald novel about the mysterious Jay Gatsby (Baxter) and his long-time love for Long Island socialite Daisy Buchanan (Wilson) was well-directed and acted. In many ways this production was superior to the 1949 and 1979 remakes.

d, Herbert Brenon; w, Becky Gardiner, Elizabeth Meehan (based on the novel by F. Scott Fitzgerald); ph, Leo Tover.

Drama **(PR:A MPAA:NR)**

GREAT K & A TRAIN ROBBERY, THE**** (1926) 5 reels FOX bw

Tom Mix *(Tom Gordon)*, Dorothy Dwan *(Madge Cullen)*, William Walling *(Eugene Cullen)*, Harry Grippe *(DeLuxe Harry)*, Carl Miller *(Burton)*, Edward Piel *(Leader of the Bandits)*, Curtin McHenry *(Cullen's Butler)*, Tony the Horse.

THE GREAT K & A TRAIN ROBBERY is one the fastest movies ever made and presents super cowboy star Mix at his best. Shot on location in Colorado, the scenery is almost as breathtaking as the action, with Mix playing a railroad detective sent from Texas to break up a gang of robbers. He poses as a masked outlaw and not only brings the desperadoes to justice, but wins the heart of the railroad president's daughter as well.

d, Lewis Seiler; w, John Stone (based on a novel by Paul Leicester Ford); ph, Dan Clark.

Western **(PR:A MPAA:NR)**

GREAT LEAP, THE** (1914) 4 reels Majestic/MUT bw

Mae Marsh, Robert Harron, Irene Hunt, Ralph Lewis, Raoul Walsh, Donald Crisp.

Cabanne directed the Griffith stock company with competence in this story of feuding mountain families and the love of a boy from one family for a girl from the other. In the end, their devotion overcomes the traditional hostilities.

d, W. Christy Cabanne; w, Anthony P. Kelly.

Drama **(PR:A MPAA:NR)**

GREAT LOVE, THE** ½** (1918) 7 reels ART/PAR bw

Robert Harron *(Jim Young)*, Henry B. Walthall *(Sir Roger Brighton)*, Gloria Hope *(Jessie Lovewell)*, Lillian Gish *(Suzie Broadplains)*, Maxfield Stanley *(John Broadplains)*, George Fawcett *(Rev. Josephus Broadplains)*, Rosemary Theby *(Mlle. Corintee)*, George Siegmann *(Mr. Seymour)*, Queen Alexandria, Lily Elsie, Lady Diana Manners, Mrs. John Lavery, Bettina Stuart-Wortley, Elizabeth Asquith, Violet Keppel, The Countess of Massarne, The Honorable Mrs. Montague, The Princess of Monaco, Lady Paget, Sir Frederick Theves, The Baroness Rothschild, Sir Henry Stanley *(Themselves)*.

Griffith not only had war footage left over from his production of HEARTS OF THE WORLD but, more importantly (because he was both Anglophile and snob), scenes of British aristocrats and titled personages doing their bit for the military effort. Therefore, S. E. V. Taylor and the director threw together this picture about an American idealist (Harron) who volunteers to fight with the Canadians and meets an equally moral-minded Australian girl (Gish) in England. Walthall, as a womanizing war profiteer, shows up along the way, and there are those shots of the "beautiful people" pitching in along with the common folk, but the picture never really rises above being more than just an entertaining programmer.

d, D. W. Griffith; w, Capt. Victor Marier [Griffith, S. E. V. Taylor]; ph, G. W. Bitzer; ed, James Smith.

Drama/War (PR:A MPAA:NR)

GREAT LOVE, THE*** (1925) 6 reels MGM bw

Robert Agnew *(Dr. Lawrence Tibbits)*, Viola Dana *(Minette Bunker)*, Frank Currier *(Mr. Bunker)*, ZaSu Pitts *(Nancy)*, Chester Conklin *(Perkins)*, Junior Coughlan *(Patrick)*, Malcolm Waite *(Tom Watson)*, Norma the Elephant.

Delightful Neilan-directed comedy about a small-town doctor who saves the life of a circus elephant and then can't get rid of the lovesick beast. When the doctor's girl friend is abducted, he manages to get her back with the help of the well-trained animal and some 2,000 Boy Scouts.

d, Marshall Neilan; w, Benjamin F. Glazer, Neilan.

Comedy (PR:A MPAA:NR)

GREAT MAIL ROBBERY, THE*** (1927) 7 reels R-C/FBO bw

Theodore von Eltz *(Lt. Donald Macready)*, Frank Nelson *(Sgt. Bill Smith)*, Jeanne Morgan *(Laura Phelps)*, Lee Shumway *(Philip Howard)*, De Witt Jennings *(Capt. Davis)*, Cora Williams *(Mrs. Davis)*, Nelson McDowell *(The Sheriff)*, Charles Hill Mailes *(Stephen Phelps)*, Yvonne Howell *(Sally)*.

Exciting movie about a Marine who infiltrates a gang of train robbers and then radios for help when they are about to make their big strike. Effective use of airplanes, machine guns, tear gas, and bombs as the corps delivers still another victory, made this film a winner.

d, George B. Seitz; w, Peter Milne; ph, Joe Walker.

Crime/Adventure (PR:A MPAA:NR)

GREAT NIGHT, THE*** (1922) 5 reels FOX bw

William Russell *(Larry Gilmore)*, Eva Novak *(Mollie Martin)*, Winifred Bryson *(Papita Gonzales)*, Henry Barrows *(Robert Gilmore)*, Wade Boteler *(Jack Denton)*, Harry Lonsdale *(Simpkins)*, Earl Metcalfe *(Green)*.

Good little comedy with the old plot line about the fellow who must marry by a certain date or lose his inheritance. When news of this reaches the papers, he is besieged by an army of wild-eyed females, but manages to go underground by becoming a uniformed policeman. In this capacity, Russell captures a gang of thieves (giving him the opportunity to show off his considerable athletic prowess) and meets the girl who loves him for himself. A few years later, Buster Keaton would use this same premise to create his comedic masterpiece SEVEN CHANCES.

d, Howard M. Mitchell; w, Joseph Franklin Poland; ph, David Abel.

Comedy/Adventure (PR:A MPAA:NR)

GREAT SHADOW, THE*** (1920) 6 reels Adanac/REP bw

Tyrone Power, Donald Hall, Dorothy Bernard, John Rutherford, Louis Stern, E. Emerson, Eugene Hornbostle.

Fascinating, blatantly propagandistic, lavishly produced, anti-Communist film was able to work up audiences in its day like teenagers at a pep rally. It all had to do with alien Soviet saboteurs blowing up U.S. factories, causing labor and capital to join forces in the common struggle against the Red menace.

d, Harley Knoles; w, Rudolph Berliner.

Drama (PR:A MPAA:NR)

GREATER LAW, THE* (1917) 5 reels BLUE bw

Myrtle Gonzalez *(Barbara Henderson)*, Gretchen Lederer *("Seattle" Lou)*, Maud Emory *(Anne Malone)*, G. M. Rickerts *(Jimmy Henderson)*, Lawrence Payton *(Cort Dorian)*, George Hernandez *(Tully Winkle)*, Jack Curtis *(Laberge)*, Jean Hersholt *(Basil Pelly)*.

Far-fetched frozen tundra tale about a girl who travels to the Klondike to avenge her brother's murder and falls in love with a handsome young fellow who teaches her to shoot. Later she is led to believe that her lover is the killer, and she challenges him to a duel in which he is badly wounded. The picture mercifully ends with the brother returning home with the town tart, with whom he eloped, and the boy friend bouncing back to health.

d&w, Lynn F. Reynolds (based on the story "The Code of the Klondike" by Charles J. Wilson, Jr.); ph, Clyde Cook.

Adventure/Romance (PR:A MPAA:NR)

GREATER NEED, THE** (1916, Brit.) 5 reels LFP/JUR bw

Milton Rosmer *(Bob Leroy)*, Gerald Ames *(Jack Leroy)*, Amy Brandon-Thomas *(Mary Firth)*, Philip Hewland *(Inspector)*, Gwynne Herbert, Mary Dilby, Hubert Willis.

This British drama made during WW I tells of a shiftless youth who enlists in the Army after his brother loses his arm in battle.

d, Ralph Dewsbury; w, Frank Fowell.

Drama (PR:A MPAA:NR)

GREATER THAN FAME* (1920) 5 reels SF/SEL bw

Elaine Hammerstein, Walter McGrail, W. H. Tooker, Julia Swayne Gordon, Cora Williams, John Walker, Arthur Donaldson, Florida Kingsley, Eugenie Woodward, James A. Furey, Albert Roccardi.

Hammerstein, a small-town girl with a singing talent, is sent by her parents to New York with an allowance of $20 a week to study voice. In the big city she overcomes numerous temptations before deciding to give up her career for the man she loves and secretly married a year earlier.

d, Alan Crosland; w, Katharine Reed (based on a play by S. Jay Kaufman); ph, Jules Cronjager.

Drama (PR:A MPAA:NR)

GREATEST QUESTION, THE** ½** (1920) 6 reels FN bw

Lillian Gish *(Nellie Jarvis)*, Robert Harron *(Jimmie Hilton)*, Ralph Graves *(John Hilton, Jr.)*, Eugenie Besserer *(Mrs. Hilton)*, George Fawcett *(John Hilton, Sr.)*, Tom Wilson *(Uncle Zeke)*, George Nichols *(Martin Cain)*, Josephine Crowell *(Mrs. Cain)*, Carl Stockdale.

Gish has written that Griffith produced THE GREATEST QUESTION quickly in California to partially fulfill his contractual obligation to First National, before moving to his own studio at Mamaroneck, New York. To be sure, this is not one of the great director's masterpieces, but it still contains scenes of tremendous beauty, power, and suspense. The film is a curious mixture of spiritual and melodramatic themes, and Gish, as the girl menaced by a married couple whom she saw commit murder years earlier, gives her usual sensational performance.

d, D. W. Griffith; w, S. E. V. Taylor (based on a story by William Hale); ph, G. W. Bitzer; ed, James Smith.

Drama (PR:A MPAA:NR)

GREATEST THING IN LIFE, THE**** (1918) 7 reels Griffith/ART bw

Lillian Gish *(Jeanette Peret)*, Robert Harron *(Edward Livingston)*, Adolphe Lestina *(Leo Peret)*, David Butler *(Mons. Le Bebe)*, Elmo Lincoln *(An American Soldier)*, Edward Piel *(The German Officer)*, Kate Bruce *(Jeanette's Aunt)*, Peaches Jackson *(Mlle. Peaches)*, Ernest Butterworth, Fred Malatesta, Lucille Younge, Carol Dempster.

One of the most sought after of all lost films is this war picture which Gish referred to in her autobiography as unquestionably a major Griffith work. It dealt with a prejudiced young Southerner who learns the true meaning of humanity in the trenches of France and at the close of the photoplay kisses a dying black soldier who confuses him for his mother. The titles read: "Mammy—Kiss me!" To dying ears, "Here—here's your mammy."

d, D. W. Griffith; w, Capt. Victor Marier [Griffith, S. E. V. Taylor]; ph, G. W. Bitzer; ed, James Smith.

Dramatic/War (PR:AAA MPAA:NR)

GREATEST WISH IN THE WORLD, THE*** (1918, Brit.) 6 reels International Exclusives bw

Bransby Williams *(Father O'Leary)*, Ordette Goimbault *(Peggy)*, Edward Combermere *(Stephen Gale)*, Ada King *(Mrs. Parfitt)*, Douglas Munro *(Pinches)*, Gwynne Herbert *(Mrs. Gooseberry)*, Jean Alwyn *(Mother Superior)*, Edward Arundell, Will Corri.

British drama in which a poor young girl is adopted by a kindly Irish priest. Later she is seduced and becomes pregnant. After struggling with her conscience, the girl gives up the child for adoption and becomes a nun.

d, Maurice Elvey; w, Bannister Merwin (based on the novel by E. Temple Thurston).

Drama (PR:A MPAA:NR)

GREED***** (1925) 10 reels Metro-Goldwyn bw

Gibson Gowland *(McTeague)*, ZaSu Pitts *(Trina)*, Jean Hersholt *(Marcus Schouler)*, Chester Conklin *(Mr. Sieppe)*, Sylvia Ashton *(Mrs. Sieppe)*, Oscar Gottell, Otto Gottell *(The Sieppe Twins)*, Frank Hayes *(Old Grannis)*, Jack Curtis *(McTeague's Father)*, Tempe Pigott *(McTeague's Mother)*, James F. Fulton *(Sheriff)*, Jack McDonald *(Gribbons)*, Lon Poff *(Lottery Agent)*, Max Tyron *(Mr. Oelberman)*, Erich von Ritzau *(Traveling Dentist)*, William Mollenheimer *(The Palmist)*, Hugh J. McCauley *(The Photographer)*, S. S. Simon *(Frena)*, William Barlow *(Minister)*, Mrs. E. Jones *(Mrs. Heise)*, Mrs. Reta Rebia *(Mrs. Ryer)*, J. Libbey *(Mr. Ryer)*, James Gibson *(Deputy)*, Dale Fuller *(Maria)*, Joan Standing *(Selina)*, Austin Jewel *(August Sieppe)*, Fanny Midgley *(Miss Baker)*, Hughie Mack *(Mr. Heise)*, Cesare Gravina *(Zerkow, a Junkman)*, Florence Gibson *(Hag)*.

Once von Stroheim decided to film Norris' novel, he was determined to shoot it page for page, paragraph for paragraph. This resulted in a film 42 reels in length which his old nemesis, Irving Thalberg (the boy wonder who had taken editing control away from von Stroheim on his 34-reel FOOLISH WIVES and fired him from MERRY-GO-ROUND at Universal), reduced to 10 when he became production head at Metro. When the blowup first occurred between Thalberg and the director, von Stroheim agreed to allow Rex Ingram, a filmmaker he greatly respected, to re-edit the picture. The Irishman cut it to 18 reels, but Thalberg brought in Mathis, who trimmed it to 10. However, screen credit for editing went to Farnham. But even in its truncated form, this film about the power of money to corrupt, is still a masterpiece. The director's images burn bright in the memory, and he stopped at nothing to achieve the effect he wanted—including the knocking out of walls so that his cameras might be placed at an angle to pick up cable cars through the open windows of real San Francisco buildings. And surely the last scene of GREED (shot on location in Death Valley) must rank among the greatest ever made, as Gowland kills his longtime rival, Hersholt, only to find that he is handcuffed to the corpse and will die an agonizing death under the sun, making the bag of gold by his side now as worthless as the sands which surround him. Kevin Brownlow, in his important book *Hollywood, the Pioneers*, quotes the great filmmaker on his art: "I was not going to compromise. I felt that after the last war, the motion picture-going public had tired of the cinematic 'chocolate eclairs' which had been stuffed down their throat. I felt they were ready for a large dose of plebeian but honest 'corned beef and cabbage.' I felt they had become weary of insipid pollyanna stories, with their doll-like heroines steeped in eternal virginity, and their hairless, flat-chested sterile heroes who were as lily-white as the heroines. I had graduated from the D. W. Griffith school of film-making and intended to go the Master one better as regards film realism. I knew that everything could be done with film, the only medium which could reproduce life as it really was."

p, Erich von Stroheim, Samuel Goldwyn; d, von Stroheim; w, von Stroheim, June Mathis (based on the novel *McTeague* by Frank Norris); t, von Stroheim, Mathis, Joseph Farnham; ph, William H. Daniels, Ben F. Reynolds, Ernest B. Schoedsack; m, James and Jack Brennan; ed, Frank Hull, Farnham; prod d, Capt. Richard Day, von Stroheim; art d, Louis Germonprez, Edward Sowders.

Drama **Cas.** **(PR:C MPAA:NR)**

GREEN CARAVAN, THE* (1922, Brit.) 6 reels Master/Granger bw

Catherine Calvert *(Gypsy)*, Gregory Scott *(Hugo Drummond)*, Valia *(Lilian Vesey)*, Ivo Dawson *(Lord Listane)*, Wallace Bosco *(Sir Simeon Marks)*, Sundae Wilshin *(Maisie Gay)*, Harry Newman *(Hiram J. Mutt)*.

Fairly well-acted but terribly written English film about a vindictive woman who finally tells the truth about the innocence of a lord's gypsy-wife in an affair, when the nomad cures her daughter of a deadly illness.

d&w, Edwin J. Collins (based on the novel by Oliver Sandys).

Drama **(PR:A MPAA:NR)**

GREEN FLAME, THE*** (1920) 5 reels Burton/Hodkinson bw

J. Warren Kerrigan, Fritzi Brunette, Jay Morley, Claire Du Brey, Miles McCarthy, Edwin Wallock, William Moran.

Well-acted and produced thriller about the theft of a crown jewel—a magnificent emerald—and its passage from one crooked hand to the next, until Kerrigan, a private cop employed by the Jewelers Protective Association, nabs the bad guys and returns the gem to its rightful owners.

d, Ernest C. Warde; w, Jack Cunningham (based on a story by Raymond G. Hill); ph, Arthur Todd.

Crime **(PR:A MPAA:NR)**

GRETCHEN, THE GREENHORN*** (1916) 5 reels FA/TRI bw

Dorothy Gish *(Gretchen)*, Ralph Lewis *(Jan Van Houck)*, Frank Bennett *(Pietro)*, Eugene Pallette *(Rogers)*, Kate Bruce *(Widow Garrity)*, George Stone, Violet Radcliffe, Carmen De Rue, Beulah Burns, Francis Carpenter, Tom Spencer *(The Garrity Kids)*.

An old Dutch engraver and his daughter (Gish) move into a melting pot neighborhood in New York, where she falls in love with an Italian-American. Counterfeiters execute a kidnaping in order to force the Dutchman to make their plates, but a group of Irish-American kids race to the rescue in this exciting, fast-paced drama.

d, Sidney A. Franklin, Chester M. Franklin; w, Bernard McConville (based on the story "Gretchen Blunders In" by McConville); ph, Frank Good.

Drama **(PR:A MPAA:NR)**

GREY DEVIL, THE** (1926) 5 reels George Blaisdell/RAY bw

Jack Perrin, Tom London, Lorraine Eason, Andy Waldron, Jerome La Grasse, Milburn Morante, Starlight *(Grey Devil the Horse)*.

Average Perrin B western about a cowboy who is fired after being suspected of stealing cattle, but goes on to track down the real rustler, who just happens to be a rival for his girl.

d, Bennett Cohn; w, Henry Ziegler; ph, William Thornley.

Western **(PR:A MPAA:NR)**

GREYHOUND, THE** (1914) 5 reels Life Photo Film bw

Elita Proctor Otis *(Deep Sea Kitty)*, William H. Tooker *(Louis Fellman the Greyhound)*, Catherine Carter *(Claire Fellman, His Wife)*, Harry Spingler *(Whispering Alex)*, George de Carlton *(The Pale Faced Kid)*, David Wall, Lillian Langdon, Victor Benoit, Rex Tompkins, Anna Laughlin.

Less-than-inspired film adaptation of a play co-authored by the great personality Mizner (longtime paramour of Anita Loos and manager of the legendary middleweight champion Stanley Ketchel) has to do with the exploits of a gambler named the Greyhound (Tooker), who gets his due in the end.

d, Lawrence McGill; w, Louis Reeves Harrison (based on a play by Wilson Mizner, Paul Armstrong).

Drama **(PR:A MPAA:NR)**

GRIM GAME, THE*** (1919) 5 reels PAR bw

Harry Houdini *(Harvey Hanford)*, Thomas Jefferson *(Cameron)*, Ann Forrest *(Mary Cameron)*, Augustus Phillips *(Clifton Allison)*, Tully Marshall *(Richard Raver)*, Arthur Hoyt *(Dr. Harvey Tyson)*, Mae Busch *(Ethel)*, Edward Martin *(Police Reporter)*, George Cowl.

This Houdini actioner, about a newspaper reporter who is wrongly accused of murdering his uncle, is full of stunts and escapes. The thing that set it apart was a real-life crash between two airplanes while the great magician was hanging from a rope ladder. Director Willat kept his cameras cranking and got a spectacular scene (miraculousy, no one was seriously hurt) and Jesse Lasky's billboard and newspaper advertising blitz assured the film's success.

d, Irvin V. Willat; w, Walter Woods (based on a story by Arthur B. Reeve, John W. Grey); ph, Frank Blount, J. O. Taylor.

Adventure **(PR:A MPAA:NR)**

GRIT* (1924) 6 reels Film Guild/Hodkinson bw

Glenn Hunter *("Kid" Hart)*, Clara Bow *(Orchid McGonigle)*, Helenka Adamowska *(Annie Hart)*, Roland Young *(Houdini Hart)*, Osgood Perkins *(Boris Giovanni Smith)*, Townsend Martin *(Flashy Joe)*, Dore Davidson *(Pop Finkle)*, Martin Broder *(Bennie Finkle)*, Joseph Depew *(Tony O'Cohen)*.

Hunter is born the night his father is murdered by an East Side gang. His mother dies of shock, and the child is raised by the gangster who did the deed. Growing up a tremendous coward, the boy is a slave of the mob until sassy little Bow instills in him the guts to get out. It is a tribute to the great Bow that in spite of the shoddiness of this production, her talent still managed to sparkle.

d, Frank Tuttle; w, James Ashmore Creelman (based on a story by F. Scott Fitzgerald); ph, Fred Waller; set d, Junius Crovins.

Crime **(PR:A MPAA:NR)**

GRIT OF A JEW, THE*** (1917, Brit.) 5 reels BUT bw

Augustus Yorke *(Moses Levi)*, Manora Thew *(Leah)*, Fred Groves *(Russell)*, Hayford Hobbs *(Ben Levi)*, Margaret Blanche *(Elsie Maudsley)*, Rachel de Solla *(Mrs. Levi)*, Cecil Mannering, Frank Stanmore, Fred Morgan, Will Asher, Inez Bensusan.

Interesting issue-oriented film about a Jewish man who discovers a loophole in the marriage contract with a money lender that allows his son to marry the Jewish girl he really loves.

p, F. W. Baker; d, Maurice Elvey; w, Kenelm Foss.

Drama **(PR:A MPAA:NR)**

GRIT WINS** (1929) 5 reels UNIV bw

Ted Wells *(Jack Deering)*, Kathleen Collins *(Nan Pickens)*, Al Ferguson *(Logan)*, Buck Connors *(Ted Pickens)*, Nelson McDowell *(John Deering)*, Edwin Moulton *(Jake)*.

Plenty of action, but no surprises, in this standard western about Wells clearing the man who is accused of murdering his father (to gain oil rights) and winning the pretty daughter along the way.

d, Joseph Levigard; sup, William Lord Wright; w, George Plympton; t, Val Cleveland; ph, William Adams; ed, Gene Havlick.

Western **(PR:A MPAA:NR)**

GUILE OF WOMEN**** (1921) 5 reels Goldwyn bw

Will Rogers *(Yal)*, Mary Warren *(Hulda)*, Bert Sprotte *(Skole)*, Lionel Belmore *(Armstrong)*, Charles A. Smiley *(Capt. Larsen)*, Nick Cogley *(Capt. Stahl)*, Doris Pawn *(Annie)*, John Lince *(The Butler)*, Jane Starr *(The Maid)*.

Rogers plays a Swedish sailor who comes to the U.S. and, after working hard, sends $1,000 to his sweetheart, Warren, to pay her fare to San Francisco. Five years pass and she fails to show up, so Rogers becomes involved with Pawn, for whom he buys a delicatessen. Smiley, the owner of the company for which Rogers works, offers a partnership in one of his ships, but Pawn refuses to sell the business which is necessary to provide the needed capital. And then, to make things worse, Rogers finds her making love to his best friend. The Swedish seaman has had more than his share of women's guile when he bumps into Warren, who, it turns out, never received the money he sent but came to the U.S. to find him and is now the adopted daughter of Smiley. Later, when the old fellow dies, she inherits the company and Rogers becomes her partner for life. Rogers was wonderful in this offbeat role and proved to be superb at portraying pathos.

d, Clarence Badger; w, Edfrid A. Bingham, Peter Clark MacFarlane; ph, Marcel Picard.

Comedy/Drama **(PR:A MPAA:NR)**

GUILTY OF LOVE* (1920) 5 reels PAR bw

Dorothy Dalton *(Thelma Miller)*, Julia Hurley *(Aunt Martha)*, Henry J. Carville *(Dr. Wentworth)*, Lawrence Johnston *(Bab Watkins)*, Ivy Ward *(Mary Watkins)*,Augusta Anderson *(Mrs. Helen Watkins)*, Edward Langford *(Norris Townsend)*, Charles Lane *(Goddard Townsend)*, Douglas Redmond *(David, Their Son)*.

This was the kind of title that drew the ladies into the theaters in 1920, but after they got there most of them must have been disappointed by this banana. It tells of a young girl who gives her love to a man who swears to do right by her. But the rotter later backs out, and the girl literally forces him to marry her. She then storms off, and after five years of living with his guilt, he finally manages to locate her and the child she had by their union, and the two find happiness in each others arms.

d, Harley Knoles; w, Rosina Henley (based on the play "This Woman—This Man" by Avery Hopwood); ph, Philip Hatkin.

Drama **(PR:C MPAA:NR)**

GUN LAW** (1929) 6 reels FBO/RKO bw

Tom Tyler *(Tom O'Brien)*, Barney Furey *(Cy Brown)*, Ethlyne Clair *(Nancy)*, Frankie Darro *(Buster Brown)*, Lew Meehan *(Big Bill Driscoll)*, Tom Brooker *(Surveyor)*, Harry Woods *(Bull Driscoll)*.

Tyler (who would go on to become the king of the talkie serials) wins the love of the girl who earlier rejected him after he out-races the heavy to get to the land office and claim some disputed ore-rich land in her name.

d, John Burch; w, Oliver Drake; t, Helen Gregg; ph, Nick Musuraca; ed, Jack Kitchen.

Western **(PR:A MPAA:NR)**

GUN RUNNER, THE*** (1928) 6 reels TS bw

Richardo Cortez *(Julio)*, Nora Lane *(Inez)*, Gino Corrado *(Garcia)*, John St. Polis *(The Presidente)*.

Cortez's popularity was on the wane by the time he made this pleasant little comedy-adventure about a South American officer who is ordered by his *presidente* to capture a bandit about to start a revolution. He accomplishes his mission, but, in doing so, falls in love with the desperado's beautiful sister. Having to choose between love and duty, Cortez elects to let the outlaw go, on the condition that he lay down his guns. For this treasonous act he is forced to face a firing squad, but manages to escape at the last minute with the girl of his dreams and the applause of his countrymen.

d, Edgar Lewis; w, J.F. Natteford (based on the novel by Arthur Stringer); t, Paul Perez; ph, Harry Jackson; ed, Ed Sherman Kell.

Comedy/Adventure **(PR:A MPAA:NR)**

GYPSY OF THE NORTH** (1928) 6 reels T/C/RAY bw

Georgia Hale *(Alice Culhane)*, Huntley Gordon *(Steve Farrell)*, Jack Dougherty *(Chappie Evans)*, William Quinn *(Baptiste)*, Hugh Saxon *(Davey)*, Henry Roquemore *(Theater Manager)*, Erin La Bissoniere *(Jane)*.

Hale's career really never took off after starring with Chaplin in THE GOLD RUSH, as illustrated by this Poverty Row feature in which she is once again cast as an Alaskan dance hall girl.

d, Scott Pembroke; w, Arthur Hoerl (based on a story by Howard Emmett Rogers); ph, Hap Depew; ed, Charles A. Post.

Drama **(PR:A MPAA:NR)**

HABIT OF HAPPINESS, THE*** (1916) 5 reels FA/TRI bw

Douglas Fairbanks *("Sunny" Wiggins)*, Dorothy West *(Elsie Pepper)*, George Fawcett *(Jonathan Pepper)*, George Backus *(Mr. Wiggins)*, Grace Rankin *(Clarice Wiggins)*, Macey Harlam *(Foster)*, William Jefferson *(Jones)*, Shannon Fife, Adolphe Menjou.

In this third film for Triangle, Fairbanks plays the son of a *nouveau riche* family snubbed by "society" who believes in laughter and brotherhood. One night he brings a group of derelicts home, and the next day they present themselves at the table, upsetting a party his sister had arranged to ingratiate herself with the uppity set. On the suggestion that he practice what he preaches, Fairbanks sets up a home on skid row where he not only feeds the down-and-outers, but teaches them to laugh as well. After a time, a doctor who donates a little of his time to the needy asks the young man to help a wealthy patient of his who is so gloomy that he plays funeral marches on the cello to unwind. Fairbanks agrees, accomplishes his mission, wins the gentlemen's daughter, and opens the door for his sister to become "socially" desirable.

d, Allan Dwan; w, Shannon Fife, Dwan (based on an idea by D. W. Griffith).

Comedy **(PR:A MPAA:NR)**

HAIR TRIGGER BAXTER** (1926) 5 reels IP/FBO bw

Bob Custer *(Baxter Brant)*, Eugenia Gilbert *(Rose Moss)*, Lew Meehan *(Mont Blake)*, Murdock MacQuarrie *(Joe Craddock)*, Jim Corey *(Jim Dodds)*, Fannie Midgley *(Mrs. Craddock)*, Ernie Adams *(Shorty Hillis)*, Hugh Saxon *(Silas Brant)*.

Average B western, with above-average B-western star Custer saving a girl from the clutches an evil saloon keeper and his father's ranch from the rustlers the bad man led.

p, Jesse J. Goldburg; d, Jack Nelson; w, Paul M. Bryan (based on a story by James Ormont); ph, Ernest Miller or Ernest Haller.

Western **(PR:A MPAA:NR)**

HAIRPINS*** (1920) 5 reels PAR bw

Enid Bennett *(Muriel Rossmore)*, Matt Moore *(Rex Rossmore)*, William Conklin *(Hal Gordon)*, Margaret Livingston *(Effie Wainright)*, Grace Morse *(Mrs. Kent)*, Al Filson *(John Burman)*, Aggie Herring *(The Maid)*.

A young housewife lets her appearance go while she devotes full time to running the house, only to find her husband looking elsewhere. At this point she starts dressing like a flapper and vamps some sense into his head.

d, Fred Niblo; sup,Thomas H. Ince; w, C. Gardner Sullivan; ph, George Barnes.

Drama **(PR:A MPAA:NR)**

HALDANE OF THE SECRET SERVICE**
(1923) 6 reels Houdini Picture/FBO bw

Harry Houdini *(Heath Haldane)*, Gladys Leslie *(Adele Ormsby)*, William Humphrey *(Edward Ormsby)*, Richard Carlyle *(Joe Ivor)*, Jane Jennings *(Mrs. Clara Usher)*, Charles Fang *(Ah Sing)*, Myrtle Morse *(Andrea Dayton)*, Irving Brooks *(Bruce Dayton)*, Edward Bouldin *(Raoul Usher)*.

Great escape artist Houdini works his magic in this film about a daring young man who tracks down the gang that killed his detective father, only to learn, to his horror, that it is led by the father of the girl he loves.

d, Harry Houdini; ph, Frank Zucker, Irving B. Rubenstein.

Crime/Drama **(PR:A MPAA:NR)**

HALF A BRIDE*** (1928) 7 reels PAR bw

Esther Ralston *(Patience Winslow)*, Cary Cooper *(Capt. Edmunds)*, William Worthington *(Mr. Winslow)*, Freeman Wood *(Jed Session)*, Mary Doran *(Betty Brewster)*, Guy Oliver *(Chief Engineer)*, Ray Gallagher *(2nd Engineer)*.

Inspired by a radio program, Ralston enters into a trial marriage against her father's will. Before it is consummated, the old boy kidnaps his daughter and takes her to sea on his yacht. When Ralston escapes, the captain (Cooper) jumps overboard and they are swept onto an island in a storm. Several weeks pass before the two are rescued, and Ralston's father is delighted to hear that they have fallen in love and that his daughter wants an annulment.

d, Gregory La Cava; w, Doris Anderson, Percy Heath (based on the story "White Hands" by Arthur Stringer); t, Julian Johnson; ph, Victor Milner; ed, Verna Willis.

Drama **(PR:A MPAA:NR)**

HALF A TRUTH** (1922, Brit.) 5 reels STOLL bw

Margaret Hope *(Virginia)*, Lawford Davidson *(Chris Kennaway)*, Miles Mander *(Marquis Sallast)*, Norma Whalley *(Lady Lucille Altamont)*, Irene Rooke *(Octavia Madison)*, Percy Standing *(Sir Richard Madison)*, Philip Simmons *(Barry Connell)*, Stella Wood-Sims *(Doreen Madison)*.

Average British mystery about a crooked noblewoman who tries to blackmail the daughter of a millionaire into marrying her accomplice in crime.

d, Sinclair Hill; w, Leslie Howard Gordon (based on the novel *Rita)*.

Crime **(PR:A MPAA:NR)**

HAM AND EGGS (SEE: HAM AND EGGS AT THE FRONT, 1927)

HAM AND EGGS AT THE FRONT***
(1927) 6 reels WB bw (AKA: HAM AND EGGS)

Tom Wilson *(Ham)*, Heinie Conklin *(Eggs)*, Myrna Loy *(Fifi)*, William J. Irving *(Von Frimil)*, Noah Young *(Sergeant)*, Cameo the Dog.

An example of how far the motion picture industry has really come regarding the use of black actors, may be seen in this black-face comedy about a couple of "colored" doughboys from a Negro regiment, who are vamped by a French waitress (Loy, also in burnt cork) out to learn military secrets. The boys turn the tables on her, however, and after a wild runaway balloon incident, capture the enemy general.

d, Roy Del Ruth; w, Robert Dillon, James A. Starr (based on a story by Darryl Francis Zanuck); ph, Charles Clarke.

Comedy **(PR:A MPAA:NR)**

HAMLET*** (1913, Brit.) 6 reels Hepworth/GAU bw

Johnston Forbes-Robertson *(Hamlet)*, Gertrude Elliot *(Ophelia)*, Walter Ringham *(Claudius)*, Adeleine Bourne *(Gertrude)*, J. H. Barnes *(Polonius)*, S. A. Cookson *(Horatio)*, Alex Scott-Gatty *(Laertes)*, Grendon Bentley *(Fortinbras)*, Montagu Rutherford (Rosencrantz), J. H. Ryley *(A Gravedigger)*, Percy Rhodes *(The Ghost)*, Robert Atkins *(The lst Player)*.

This ambitous early motion picture version of Shakespeare's immortal play about the prince who avenges his father's murder was surprisingly well crafted.

d, Hay Plumb; w, (based on the play by William Shakespeare).

Drama **(PR:A MPAA:NR)**

HANDLE WITH CARE*** (1922) 5 reels Rockett/AEX bw

Grace Darmond *(Jeanne Lee)*, Harry Myers *(Ned Picard)*, James Morrison *(Phil Burnham)*, Landers Stevens *(David Norris)*, William Austin *(Peter Carter)*, William Courtleigh *(MacCullough)*, Patsy Ruth Miller *(Marian)*.

Darmond is delightful as the beauty who chooses a husband from five enthusiastic suitors. After two years of marriage, however, her husband forgets their anniversary, and she becomes so angered that he agrees to enter into a most remarkable pact: he will give her a divorce in the event that she can induce any of her former boy friends to elope with her. There are plenty of laughs from this point on and, of course, she ends up with hubby after all.

p, Al Rockett, Ray Rockett; d, Philip E. Rosen; w, Will M. Ritchie (based on a story by Charles Belmont Davis); ph, Philip Hurn.

Comedy **(PR:A MPAA:NR)**

HANDS ACROSS THE BORDER*** (1926) 6 reels R-C/FBO bw

Fred Thompson *(Fred Drake)*, Tyrone Power, Sr. *(John Drake)*, Bess Flowers *(Ysabel Castro)*, William Courtwright *(Grimes)*, Clarence Geldert *(Don Castro)*, Tom Santschi *(Breen)*, Silver King the Horse.

Entertaining Thompson western about a millionaire's son who rescues a beautiful Mexican girl from kidnapers at a Los Angeles horse show. Later he goes to the border to investigate drug smuggling on his father's property, which is near the girl's ranch. Impersonating a smuggler, he infiltrates the gang, but is captured and held prisoner along with the girl and her father. It looks like all is lost until Thompson's famous horse, Silver King, arrives with both the U.S. and Mexican armies.

d, David Kirkland; w, William E. Wing (based on a story by Frank M. Clifton); t, Malcolm Stuart Boylan; ph, Ross Fisher.

Western **(PR:A MPAA:NR)**

HANDS UP**** (1926) 6 reels FP/PAR bw

Raymond Griffith *(Confederate Spy)*, Marion Nixon *(The Girl He Loves)*, Virginia Lee Corbin *(The Other Girl He Loves)*, Mack Swain *(Mineowner)*, Montagu Love *(Union General)*, George Billings *(Abe Lincoln)*, Noble Johnson *(Sitting Bull)*, Charles K. French *(Brigham Young)*.

Truly great Civil War comedy starring the terribly underrated Griffith as a Confederate spy out to stop a Yankee agent from acquiring gold for the Northern cause. One marvelous sight gag after another builds to the end, when Griffith must choose between the two equally beautiful girls who love him. Then, with a cinematic punch line equalled by Joe E. Brown's last line in SOME LIKE IT HOT, the spy takes off with both the lovelies in a coach marked "Salt Lake City".

d. Clarence Badger; w, Monty Brice, Lloyd Corrigan (based on a story by Reginald Morris); ph, H. Kinley Martin.

Comedy **(PR:A MPAA:NR)**

HANDSOME BRUTE, THE* (1925) 5 reels COL bw

William Fairbanks *(Larry O'Day)*, Virginia Lee Corbin *(Nelly Egan)*, Lee Shumway *(John Granger)*, Robert Bolder *(Thomas Egan)*, J. J. Bryson *(Captain)*, Daniel Belmont *(Watchman)*.

Laughable melodrama about a young cop who is removed from the force but wins his job back when he rounds up a gang of jewel thieves. The leader of the gang, believe it or not, turns out to be a detective called in to solve the case.

d, Robert Eddy; w, Lillian Taft Maize; ph, George Meehan.

Action **(PR:A MPAA:NR)**

HANDY ANDY** (1921, Brit.) 5 reels ID bw

Peter Coleman *(Handy Andy)*, Kathleen Vaughan *(Una O'Reilly)*, Warwick Ward *(Squire O'Grady)*, John Wyndham *(Michael Dwyer)*, Wally Bosco *(Murphy)*, May Price *(Ragged Nan)*, Hessel Crayne *(Dr. Browling)*.

This British comedy with a 19th-Century Irish setting tells of a stable boy who takes on the identity of a cousin in order to foil a kidnaping and, because of this subterfuge, is forced to marry his sister.

d, Bert Wynne; w, Elio Stannard (based on the novel by Samuel Lover).

Comedy (PR:A MPAA:NR)

HANGING JUDGE, THE** (1918, Brit.) 6 reels Hepworth/Moss bw

Henry Edwards *(Dick Veasey)*, Chrissie White *(Molly)*, Hamilton Stewart *(Sir John Veasey)*, Randle Ayrton *(Reginald Tamlyn)*, Gwynne Herbert *(Lady Veasey)*, A. V. Bramble *(Prosecution)*, John McAndrews *(Ned Blake)*.

In this British 6-reeler, a judge disowns his son, who becomes a crusading newspaperman and marries the daughter of the man his father wrongly convicted.

d&w, Henry Edwards (based on the play by Leon M. Lion and a story by Tom Gallon).

Drama (PR:A MPAA:NR)

HARD TIMES** (1915, Brit.) 4 reels TRA bw

Bransby Williams *(Gradgrind)*, Leon M. Lion *(Tom Gradgrind)*, Dorothy Bellew *(Louisa)*, Madge Tree *(Rachael)*, Mr. Forrest, *(Stephen Blackpool)*, F. Lymons *(Josiah Bounderby)*, Will Corrie *(Sleary)*, Clara Cooper *(Cissie Jupe)*, J. Wynn Slater *(James Harthouse)*.

A Dickens novel was the inspiration for this British film about a thief who robs the mill his brother-in-law owns and then frames a weaver for the crime.

d&w, Thomas Bentley (based on the novel by Charles Dickens).

Drama (PR:A MPAA:NR)

HARD WAY, THE** (1916, Brit.) 5 reels BRO/Walturdaw bw

Muriel Martin Harvey *(Lilah Chertsey)*, J. R. Tozer *(Noel Creighton)*, Thomas H. MacDonald *(Arnold Graves)*, Lily Saxby *(Clarice Creighton)*, George Bellamy *(Lepine)*, Owen Francis *(Martin Graves)*.

In this British drama set in Paris, a woman inadvertently commits bigamy and then finds herself the victim of a blackmailer, until she finally learns of the death of her artist husband.

p&d, Walter West; w, (based on the novel *A Peer)*.

Drama (PR:A MPAA:NR)

HARDBOILED* (1929) 7 reels FBO bw

Sally O'Neill *(Teena Johnson)*, Donald Reed *(Kyle Stannard)*, Lilyan Tashman *(Minnie)*, Bob Sinclair *(Scotty)*, Ole M. Ness *(Warren Kennedy)*, Tom O'Grady *(Jerry)*.

Tepid tale of a chorus girl who marries the son of a millionaire and refuses to be bought off by the father. After the old boy disinherits his son, the lad goes to work for the first time, and the bride returns to the chorus. After a while they separate, and he runs up a horrendous stack of debts. At this point, the father realizes the girl's worth, takes care of the money problems, and brings the kids together again.

d, Ralph Ince; w, Enid Hibbard; t, Ince; ph, Robert Martin.

Drama (PR:A MPAA:NR)

HAROLD TEEN*** (1928) 8 reels FN bw

Arthur Lake *(Harold Teen)*, Mary Brian *(Lillums Lovewell)*, Lucien Littlefield *(Dad Jenks)*, Jack Duffy *(Grandpop Teen)*, Alice White *(Giggles Dewberry)*, Jack Egan *(Horace Teen)*, Hedda Hopper *(Mrs. Hazzit)*, Ben Hall *(Goofy)*, William Bakewell *(Percival)*, Lincoln Stedman *(Beezie)*, Fred Kelsey *(Mr. Lovewell)*, Jane Keckley *(Mrs. Teen)*, Ed Brady *(Officer Axel Dewberry)*, Virginia Sale *(Mrs. Schmittenberger)*.

Lake, who would go on to world fame playing another comic strip character, Dagwood Bumstead, is fine as Carl Ed's creation, Harold Teen. Lake is a country boy who moves to the city and becomes extremely popular in high school. He talks his teacher into letting him direct a cowboy movie in place of a school play, and the amateur production (which is shown in the auditorium) provides plenty of laughs. There is one hitch, however, when the kids blow up a real dam by mistake. This causes Lake to go into hiding, but he makes it back in time to win the big football game.

p, Allan Dwan; d, Mervyn LeRoy; w&t, Tom J. Geraghty (based on the comic strip by Carl Ed); ph, Ernest Haller; ed, LeRoy Stone.

Comedy (PR:A MPAA:NR)

HARVEST OF HATE, THE** (1929) 5 reels UNIV bw

Rex the Wonder Horse, Jack Perrin *(Jack Merritt)*, Helen Foster *(Margie Smith)*, Tom London *(Martin Trask)*, Starlight the Horse.

Rex the Wonder Horse saves his mistress, a carnival trick-rider, from the rotter who bought the show. The beautiful creature then sees to it that she finds lasting happiness in the arms of handsome Perrin.

d, Henry MacRae; w, George H. Plympton (based on a story by William Lord Wright, Plympton); t, Gardner Bradford; ph, George Robinson; ed, Thomas Malloy.

Western (PR:A MPAA:NR)

HAS THE WORLD GONE MAD!**
(1923) 7 reels Daniel Carson Goodman/EPC bw

Robert Edeson *(Mr. Adams)*, Hedda Hopper *(Mrs. Adams)*, Vincent Coleman *(Their Son)*, Mary Alden *(Mrs. Bell)*, Charles Richman *(Mr. Bell)*, Elinor Fair *(Their Daughter)*, Lyda Lola *(Cabaret Dancer)*.

Unusual jazz-age drama about a mother (Hopper) who gets swept up in the rhythm of the "Roaring Twenties." She moves away from home and into her own flat, has an affair with the father of her son's girl friend, and then, realizing the error of her ways, returns to the nest.

d, J. Searle Dawley; w, Daniel Carson Goodman; ph, Ned Van Buren, Hal Sintzenich, Bert Dawley; set d, Tilford Cinema Studios.

Drama (PR:A MPAA:NR)

HATER OF MEN*** (1917) 5 reels KB/TRI bw

Bessie Barriscale *(Janice Salsbury)*, Charles K. French *(Phillips Hartley)*, Jack Gilbert *(Billy Williams)*.

Provocative Sullivan script about a girl reporter who, while covering a sensational divorce trial (involving a sugar daddy and his army of chorus girls), begins to doubt the wisdom of marriage. She returns her engagement ring to a fellow reporter and throws herself into living the bohemian life, acting like and being accepted as "one of the boys." There are plenty of laughs along the way before an older friend drums some sense into her head, and she decides that marriage is the right course, after all. An intriguing premise for 1917.

d, Charles Miller; w, C. Gardner Sullivan.

Comedy/Drama (PR:A MPAA:NR)

HAUNTED PAJAMAS*** (1917) 5 reels Yorke/Metro bw

Harold Lockwood *(Richard Hudson)*, Carmel Myers *(Frances Kirkland)*, Ed Sedgwick *(Jack Billings)*, Lester Cuneo *(Judge Billings)*, Paul Willis *(Francis Billings)*, Harry De Roy *(Jenkins)*, Helen Ware *(Elizabeth Billings)*, William De Vaull *(Col. Kirkland)*, Goro Kino.

Using the stage convention mastered by George M. Cohan, whereby the audience is let in on the secret while the characters grope about in the dark, this is a rollicking comedy from beginning to end. It has to do with a magic pair of pajamas which are sent to a wealthy young New Yorker from his friend in China. The magic consists of turning the wearer into the person who had them on last when a certain string is pulled. Thus, the characters in the film go about transforming themselves into various forms, from Chinese wise men, to hunted murderers until, at the end, the young man pulls his magic chord, and the girl he loves materializes before his very delighted eyes.

d&w, Fred J. Balshofer (based on the novel by Francis Perry Elliot); ph, Antonio Gaudio.

Comedy (PR:A MPAA:NR)

HAUNTED RANCH, THE (SEE: HAUNTED RANGE, THE, 1926)

HAUNTED RANGE, THE 1/2**
(1926) 5 reels Davis Distributing Division bw (AKA: THE HAUNTED RANCH)

Ken Maynard *(Terry Baldwin)*, Alma Rayford *(Judith Kellerd)*, Harry Moody *(Alex Forester)*, Al Hallett *(Executor)*, Fred Burns *(Charlie Titus)*, Bob Williamson *(Ralph Kellerd)*, Tarzan the Horse.

Maynard is given the opportunity to do plenty of riding, shooting, and fighting in this cowboy mystery about a young man who inherits a ranch on the condition that he solve a murder within six months. Maynard does it in five reels and wins a pretty girl as well.

d, Paul Hurst; w, Frank Howard Clark; ph, Frank Cotner.

Western (PR:A MPAA:NR)

HAWTHORNE OF THE U.S.A.*** (1919) 5 reels PAR bw

Wallace Reid *(Anthony Hamilton Hawthorne)*, Harrison Ford *(Rodney Blake)*, Lila Lee *(Princess Irma)*, Tully Marshall *(Nitchi)*, Charles Ogle *(Radulski)*, Guy Oliver *(Henloe)*, Edwin Stevens *(Vladimir)*, Clarence Burton *(Fredericks)*, Theodore Roberts *(Sen. Ballard)*, Ruth Renick *(Kate Ballard)*, Robert Brower *(King Augustus III)*, Frank Bonner.

In the role Douglas Fairbanks introduced on the stage, Reid plays an American who makes a killing at Monte Carolo and then journeys to a small European country which is threatened by a Communist takeover. Reid falls for the ruler's daughter and, using his Yankee know-how and grit, saves her father's government.

d, James Cruze; w, Walter Woods (based on the play by James B. Fagan); ph, Frank Urson.

Adventure/Comedy (PR:A MPAA:NR)

HAZARDOUS VALLEY* (1927) 6 reels Ellbee bw

Vincent Brownell, Virginia Brown Faire, Sheldon Lewis, Pat Harmon, David Torrence, Andrew Arbuckle, Burr McIntosh.

Poorly made movie about a young man (Brownell) who goes to his father's lumber camp to make sure that a vitally important shipment of logs is dispatched. He not only defeats his father's rival (Torrence), but wins the love of his daughter as well.

d, Alvin J. Neitz; w, A. B. Barringer; ph, Harold Wenstrom.

Adventure (PR:A MPAA:NR)

HE WHO GETS SLAPPED**** (1924) 7 reels MGM bw

Lon Chaney *(Paul Beaumont/"He Who Gets Slapped")*, Norma Shearer *(Consuelo)*, John Gilbert *(Bezano)*, Tully Marshall *(Count Mancini)*, Marc

MacDermott *(Baron Regnard)*, Ford Sterling *(Tricaud)*, Harvey Clarke *(Briquet)*, Paulette Duval *(Zinida)*, Ruth King *(Beaumont's Wife)*, Clyde Cook, Brandon Hurst, George Davis *(Clowns)*.

Studio executive Irving Thalberg and producer Mayer were determined to make their first MGM release an artistic as well as a commercial success, and they showed courage in selecting as their source a Russian play of literary merit, backed up, however, by the three biggest stars in their employ, Gilbert, Shearer, and Chaney. Seastrom, the brilliant Swedish director, was given the responsibility of taking an unpleasant story about a scientist, whose professional and domestic humiliations drive him to performing as a masochistic circus clown, and making it appeal to general audiences. He succeeded so well that the visual tapestry he painted in 1924 is as beautifully compelling today as it was on the night that this marvelous motion picture was premiered. This was Seastrom's second picture made in the U.S. under his loan agreement to MGM from Svensk Filmindustri, and was far worthier of his talents than his first picture, THE MASTER OF MEN, a story dealing with the mother-out-of-wedlock theme. HE WHO GETS SLAPPED was shot in one month at the ridiculously low cost of $140,000, and in one week at the Capitol Theater in New York City grossed more than $70,000. Chaney deeply impressed Seastrom. In a newspaper interview, Seastrom called him without question the finest actor in the history of the screen or the stage.

p, Louis B. Mayer; d, Victor Seastrom [Sjostrom]; w, Carey Wilson, Seastrom (based on the play "He, The One Who Gets Slapped" by Leonid Andreyev, translated by Gregory Zilboorg); ph, Milton Moore; ed, Hugh Wynn; set d, Cedric Gibbons.

Drama **(PR:A MPAA:NR)**

HEAD MAN, THE*** (1928) 7 reels FN bw

Charlie Murray *(Watts)*, Loretta Young *(Carol Watts)*, Larry Kent *(Billy Hurd)*, Lucien Littlefield *(Ed Barnes)*, E. J. Ratcliffe *(Wareham)*, Irving Bacon *(The Mayor)*, Harvey Clark *(McKugg)*, Sylvia Ashton *(Mrs. Briggs)*, Dot Farley *(Mrs. Denny)*, Martha Mattox, Rose Gore *(The Twins)*.

Comedian Murray is fine in this straight dramatic role about an ex-senator who is forced into obscurity when he refuses to become the lackey of a political boss. Finally he gets his dander up, runs for the office of mayor, and defeats the machine. A very early featured appearance on the screen for Young, who was then 15 years old.

d, Eddie Cline; w, Howard Green, Harvey Thew (based on a story by Harry Leon Wilson); t, Sidney Lazarus, Gerald Duffy; ph, Michael Joyce; ed, Terrell Morse.

Drama **(PR:A MPAA:NR)**

HEAD OF THE FAMILY, THE*** (1922, Brit.) 6 reels Artistic bw

Johnny Butt *(Green)*, Cynthia Murtagh *(Betty Foster)*, Charles Ashton *(Robert Letts)*, Daisy England *(Mrs. Green)*, Bertie White *(Henry Whidden)*, Moore Marriott *(Mate)*.

In this British comedy, a widow unknowingly marries a domineering husband and finds her life made miserable until she arranges for a tough sailor to pose as her long-lost son. It doesn't take long before the swabby has the old boy eating out of the little lady's hand.

p, George Redman; d, Manning Haynes; w, Lydia Hayward (based on the story by W.W. Jacobs).

Comedy **(PR:A MPAA:NR)**

HEAD OF THE FAMILY, THE*** (1928) 7 reels GOTH/LUM bw

William Russell *(The Plumber)*, Mickey Bennett *(His Assistant)*, Virginia Lee Corbin *(Alice Sullivan)*, Richard Walling *(Charley Sullivan)*, Alma Bennett *(Mabel Manning)*, William Welsh *(Daniel Sullivan)*, Aggie Herring *(Maggie Sullivan)*.

Nice comedy programmer has Welsh (a good man with a dreadful family) putting Russell, the plumber, in charge while he escapes to a health spa. When Welsh returns, he discovers, to his delight, that the young man has saved his son from a vamp, taught the lady of the house respect, and become engaged to his one-time flapper daughter.

d, Joseph C. Boyle; w, Peter Milne (based on a story by George Randolph Chester); t, Casey Robinson; ph, Charles Van Enger; ed, Donn Hayes.

Comedy **(PR:A MPAA:NR)**

HEADIN' SOUTH*** (1918) 5 reels Fairbanks/ART bw

Douglas Fairbanks *(Headin' South)*, Catherine MacDonald *(The Girl)*, Frank Campeau *(Spanish Joe)*, James Mason, Jack Holt, Majorie Daw, Alice Smith, Bob Emmons, Hoot Gibson, Art Acord, Edward Burns, Tommy Grimes, Johnny Judd.

Disguised as the mysterious outlaw "Headin' South", Fairbanks, an officer of the Northwest Mounted Police, infiltrates Campeau's gang and falls for a pretty girl who, along with her mother, is being held captive. Naturally, after a number of thrilling stunts, Fairbanks frees the captives and captures Campeau. Not quite as many acrobatics or laughs as usual, but still Fairbanks.

d, Arthur Rosson; sup&w, Allan Dwan; ph, Hugh C. McClung, Harry Thorpe.

Western **(PR:A MPAA:NR)**

HEADIN' WESTWARD** (1929) 5 reels ED/SYN bw

Bob Custer *(Oklahoma Adams)*, Mary Mayberry *(Mary Benson)*, John Lowell *(Ed Benson)*, J. P. McGowan *(Sneezer Clark)*, Charles Whittaker *(Buck McGrath)*, Mack V. Wright *(Slim McGee)*, Cliff Lyons *(Pat Carle)*, Dorothy Vernon *(Lizzie)*.

No subtle nuances nor surpise twists in this Custer oater, which has the cowboy star befriending a girl whose father is being ruined by rustlers. In the end, the bad hombre turns out to be— you guessed it—her dad's foreman.

d, J. P. McGowan; w, Sally Winters, Philip Schuyler; ph, Paul Allen.

Western **(PR:A MPAA:NR)**

HEADS UP 1/2** (1925) 6 reels Harry Garson/FBO bw

Maurice B. Flynn *(Breckenridge Gamble)*, Kathleen Myers *(Angela)*, Kalla Pasha *(Malofich)*, Jean Perry *(Cortez)*, Milton Ross *(Losada)*, Harry McCoy *(Biff)*, Hazel Rogers *(Anita)*, Ray Ripley *(Comandante)*, Robert Cautier *(Spy)*, Raymond Turner *(Zeke)*.

"Lefty" Flynn is bored by his millionaire's life in the U.S. and goes off to a South American republic to deliver a secret message. Once there, he breaks up a revolution, rescues the president, and wins the love of the chief-of-state's daughter. Lots of kid-pleasing stunts by Flynn, but the picture is stolen by the comic antics of Ripley, who plays a prison officer.

d, Harry Garson; w, Rob Wagner (based on a story by A. B. Barringer).

Adventure **(PR:A MPAA:NR)**

HEART OF A COWARD, THE** (1926) 5 reels Duke Worne/RAY bw

Billy Sullivan, Edith Yorke, Jack Richardson, Myles McCarthy.

In this comic book of a movie, Sullivan, a boy writer, is nearly swindled out of some oil property by a crook who claims to be acting for a publisher. Sullivan thwarts this plot and ends up winning the love of the publisher's daughter.

p, W. Ray Johnston; d, Duke Worne; ph, Ernest Smith.

Adventure **(PR:A MPAA:NR)**

HEART OF A FOLLIES GIRL, THE* (1928) 7 reels FN bw

Billie Dove *(Teddy O'Day)*, Larry Kent *(Derek Calhoun)*, Lowell Sherman *(Rogers Winthrop)*, Clarissa Selwynne *(Caroline Winthrop)*, Mildred Harris *(Florine)*.

Over 180 captions were used to tell this hokey, uncinematic story of a male secretary who commits forgery to buy a "Follies" girl an engagement ring. In the end—after a jail stretch—the two are reunited, but it really doesn't matter when you have titles such as, "A Follies girl is a chump in her heart and a dumbbell in her head."

p, Sam E. Rork; d, John Francis Dillon; w, Charles A. Logue, Gerald C. Duffy (based on a story by Adela Rogers St. Johns); t, Dwinelle Benthall, Rufus McCosh; ph, James Van Trees; ed, Harold Young.

Comedy **(PR:A MPAA:NR)**

HEART OF MARYLAND, THE*** (1921) 6 reels VIT bw

Catherine Calvert *(Maryland Calvert)*, Crane Wilbur *(Alan Kendrick)*, Felix Krembs *(Col. Fulton Thorpe)*, Ben Lyon *(Bob Telfair)*, William Collier, Jr. *(Lloyd Calvert)*, Warner Richmond *(Tom Boone)*, Bernard Siegel *(Provost-Sgt. Blount)*, Henry Hallam *(Gen. Kendrick)*, Victoria White *(Nanny McNair)*, Marguerite Sanchez *(Phoebe Yance)*, Jane Jennings *(Mrs. Claiborne)*.

Wilbur, a Southern-born officer, remains loyal to the Union when the Civil War breaks out. His sweetheart, Calvert, however, takes the side of the South. Later, when he is captured, she saves him from a rebel firing squad. Remade by Warner Bros. in 1927.

d, Tom Terriss; w, William B. Courtney (based on a play by David Belasco); ph, Tom Malloy.

Drama **(PR:A MPAA:NR)**

HEART OF THE BLUE RIDGE, THE*** (1915) 5 reels Shubert/WORLD bw

Clara Kimball Young *(Plutina)*, Chester Barnett *(Zeke)*, Robert Cummings *(Dan Hodges)*.

Young is a mountain girl who loves and is loved by her neighbor Barnett. Cummings, an outlaw who runs a still, lusts after Young, but before he can force himself upon her, Barnett kills him in a nicely staged fight on top of a mountain.

d, James Young; w, Travers Vale (based on a story by Waldon Bailey Aldrich).

Drama **(PR:A MPAA:NR)**

HEART RAIDER, THE*** (1923) 6 reels FP/PAR bw

Agnes Ayres *(Muriel Gray, a Speed Girl)*, Mahlon Hamilton *(John Dennis, a Bachelor)*, Charles Ruggles *(Gaspard McMahon, an Insurance Clerk)*, Frazer Coulter *(Reginald Gray, Muriel's Father)*, Marie Burke *(Mrs. Dennis, John's Mother)*, Charles Riegal *(Jeremiah Wiggins, Yacht Captain)*.

Wild comedy has Ayres out to get her man at any cost, including her poor father's mental health. The old boy takes out an insurance policy to cover any damage she might cause him as she stalks her prey with reckless abandon. And, indeed, nothing gets in her zany way as she races after her fellow by automobile and speedboat, until finally on their wedding day, a title card reads, "I wonder if I will have as much trouble holding you as I had in getting you."

d, Wesley Ruggles; w, Jack Cunningham (based on a story by Harold Riggs Durant, Julie Herne); ph, Charles E. Schoenbaum.

Comedy/Adventure **(PR:A MPAA:NR)**

HEART TROUBLE*** (1928) 6 reels Harry Langdon/FN bw

Harry Langdon *(Harry Van Housen)*, Doris Dawson *(The Girl)*, Lionel Belmore *(Adolph Van Housen)*, Madge Hunt *(Mrs. Adolph Van Housen)*, Bud Jamieson *(Contractor)*, Mark Hamilton, Nelson McDowell *(Conductors)*.

Perhaps the best of Langdon's late silent features. In this one he plays a German-American who desperately wants to join the service during WW I to prove his patriotism. After being turned down for unfitness, he accidentally stumbles upon a German base, frees a captured U.S. officer, takes the enemy troops prisoner, blows the facility up, and wins the love of the girl he so wished to impress.

d, Harry Langdon; w, Earle Rodney, Clarence Hennecke (based on a story by Arthur Ripley); t, Gardner Bradford; ph, Frank Evans, Dev Jennings; ed, Alfred De Gaetano.

Comedy **(PR:A MPAA:NR)**

HEARTS ADRIFT* (1914) 4 reels FP bw

Mary Pickford, Harold Lockwood.

It is incredible that Porter, the man who electrified the screen with his directorial tour de force THE GREAT TRAIN ROBBERY, would spend the rest of his years behind the megaphone producing barely adequate, uninspired motion pictures. Perhaps, as has been theorized, he was truly interested solely in the mechanical, invention-oriented aspects of the cinema. If so, this Pickford feature certainly bears that theory out. In fact, it is America's Sweetheart alone who brings anything worthwhile to this unoriginal melodrama, which concludes with a young mother leaping with her child into the mouth of a bubbling volcano.

d, Edwin S. Porter; w, Mary Pickford (based on the story "As the Sparks Fly Upward" by Cyrus Townsend Brady).

Drama **(PR:A MPAA:NR)**

HEARTS AND FISTS* (1926) 6 reels H.C. Weaver/AEX bw

John Bowers *(Larry Pond)*, Marguerite De La Motte *(Alexia Newton)*, Alan Hale *(Preston Tolley)*, Dan Mason *(Tacitus Hopper)*, Lois Ingraham *(Jean Carrol)*, Howard Russell *(Luther Newton)*, Jack Curtis *(Gus Brent)*, Kent Mead *(Egbert Head)*, Charles Mailes *(Bill Fawcett)*.

Good cast, but a poor film, in which a young man inherits a bankrupt lumber company from his father and sets out to make it solvent, with the help of his dad's loyal clerk and a college chum. A rival lumberman stops at nothing to prevent this but, by the last reel, loses the fight and his girl.

d, Lloyd Ingraham; w, Paul Schofield (based on a story by Clarence Buddington Kelland); ph, Abe Scholtz; ed, Peter L. Shamray.

Adventure **(PR:A MPAA:NR)**

HEARTS OF MEN*** (1919) 6 reels Abrams-Beban bw

George Beban *(Nicolo Rosetti)*, Sarah Kernen *(Marie Rossetti)*, George Beban, Jr. (Beppo), Mabel Van Buren *(Tina Ferronni)*, Harry Rattenberry *(Judge Newcomb)*, Leo Pierson *(Steve)*, Clarence Burton *(Buck Hughes)*, Hop Sing *(Himself)*.

The wonderful character actor George Beban also directed this touching film about an Italian immigrant who discovers his sick mother needs a change of climate and is taken in by a land swindler. He arrives in Arizona to discover that his property is little more than a stretch of desert, but a gang of construction workers nearby are charmed by his beautiful young son and help him build a house. They also convince him that his boy needs a mother, so he arranges to have a bride brought over from the old country. The woman, who turns out to be totally unworthy, takes the child and runs off with the picture's heavy. The film ends on a happy note, with the child being returned and the Italian finding oil on his property, which he gladly shares with his American friends.

d, George Beban; w, Harvey F. Thew (based on a story by William M. McCoy); ph, William McGann.

Drama **(PR:A MPAA:NR)**

HEARTS OF OAK*** (1924) 6 reels FOX bw

Hobart Bosworth *(Terry Dunnivan)*, Pauline Starke *(Chrystal)*, Theodore von Eltz *(Ned Fairweather)*, James Gordon *(John Owen)* Francis Powers *(Grandpa Dunnivan)*, Jennie Lee *(Grandma Dunnivan)*, Francis Ford.

John Ford followed his triumphant IRON HORSE with this drama about love and the sea. The story, dealing with an older seaman who sacrifices his life for the happiness of a couple in love, is pure hokum. But Ford's genius was such that he could make something of it anyway.

d, John Ford; w, Charles Kenyon (based on a play by James A. Herne); ph, George Schneiderman.

Drama **(PR:A MPAA:NR)**

HEARTS OF THE WORLD*** 1/2** (1918) 12 reels D.W. Griffith/ART bw

Adolphe Lestina *(The Grandfather)*, Josephine Crowell *(The Mother)*, Lillian Gish *(The Girl)*, Robert Harron *(The Boy)*, Jack Cosgrove *(The Boy's Father)*, Kate Bruce *(The Boy's Mother)*, Ben Alexander *(The Littlest Brother)*, Marion Emmons, Francis Marion *(The Boy's Other Brothers)*, Dorothy Gish *(The Little Disturber)*, Robert Anderson *(Mons. Cuckoo)*, George Fawcett *(The Village Carpenter)*, George Siegmann *(Von Strohm)*, Fay Holderness *(The Innkeeper)*, L. Lowry *(A Deaf and Blind Musician)*, Eugene Pouyet *(A Poilu)*, Anna May Walthall *(A French Peasant Girl)*, Yvette Duvosin *(A Refugee)*, Herbert Sutch *(A French Major)*, Alphonse Dufort *(A Poilu)*, Jean Dumercier *(A Poilu)*, Gaston Riviere, Jules Lemontier *(The Stretcher Bearers)*, George Loyer *(A Poilu)*, George Nicholls *(A German Sergeant)*, Mrs. Mary Gish *(A Refugee Mother)*, Mrs. Harron *(Woman with Daughter)*, Jessie Harron *(A Refugee)*, Johnny Harron *(Boy with Barrel)*, Mary Hay *(A Dancer)*, Noel Coward *(Boy with Wheelbarrow)*, Erich von Stroheim *(A German Soldier)*, William Elliott.

At the request of the British government (the U.S. had yet to enter the war), Griffith took his company to Europe to make this propaganda picture. Much of the film was shot on the battlefields of France and in England, but the project was completed in California, on the lot which housed the INTOLERANCE sets. Perhaps the film suffers somewhat in retrospect because of its black and white sterotypes, but there are passages of great power, such as the climactic scene where the hero and heroine are holding off the rape-oriented Siegmann, and Lillian Gish begs Harron to shoot her and be saved from a fate worse than death. Griffith's cross-cutting, at this point between the couple, the menacing Huns, the rescue-bound French troops, battle scenes, and Dorothy Gish—who is also attempting to intervene—is simply dazzling, as well as charming. In fact, Dorothy Gish, as the Little Disturber, with her provocative and flirtatious walk, predated the whole flapper trend—personified by Clara Bow—by nearly a decade.

d, D. W. Griffith; w, M. Gaston de Tolignac/Capt. Victor Marier [both pseudonyms for Griffith]; ph, Billy Bitzer, Hendrik Sartow; m, Carlie Elinor, Griffith; ed, James and Rose Smith.

War **Cas.** **(PR:A MPAA:NR)**

HEARTSTRINGS*** (1923, Brit.) 5 reels B&C bw

Gertrude McCoy *(Norah)*, Victor McLaglen *(Frank Wilson)*, Edith Bishop *(Alice Wilson)*, Russell Thorndike *(Tom Openshaw)*, Sydney Fairbrother *(Mrs. Chadwick)*, George Bishop *(Mr. Chadwick)*, Kate Gurney *(Mrs. Wilson)*.

This better-than-average English feature is a triumph for McLaglen. It's a variation on the Enoch Arden theme about a seaman lost at sea and believed dead, who returns home to find that his wife has married a prosperous merchant to provide a home for his crippled child. The couple also has a baby of their own and, after surveying the situation, McLaglen elects to commit suicide rather than stand in the way of the others' happiness.

p, Edward Godal; d, Edwin Greenwood; w, Eliot Stannard (based on the novel *A Manchester Marriage* by Elizabeth Cleghorn Gaskell).

Drama **(PR:A MPAA:NR)**

HEIR TO JENGHIZ KHAN, THE (SEE: STORM OVER ASIA, 1929, USSR)

HELD BY THE LAW*** (1927) 7 reels UNIV bw

Ralph Lewis *(George Travis)*, Johnnie Walker *(Tom Sinclair)*, Marguerite De La Motte *(Mary Travis)*, Robert Ober *(Boris Morton)*, Fred Kelsey *(Detective)*, Maude Wayne *(Ann)*, E. J. Ratcliffe *(Henry Sinclair)*.

De La Motte's father is wrongly accused of murdering Walker's father at their engagement party. Actually, Ober, the groom's cousin, did the deed to avoid being caught stealing a necklace. Later, the engaged couple conspire to have Ober accompany them to the scene of the crime, and when the killer attempts to retrieve a glove, the cops are there to nab him.

d, Edward Laemmle; w, Charles A. Logue (based on a story by Bayard Veiller); ph, Jackson Rose.

Crime **(PR:A MPAA:NR)**

HELD TO ANSWER*** (1923) 6 reels Metro bw

House Peters *(John Hampstead)*, Grace Carlyle *(Marian Dounay)*, John Sainpolis *(Hiram Burbeck)*, Lydia Knott *(Mrs. Burbeck)*, Evelyn Brent *(Bessie Burbeck)*, James Morrison *(Rollie Burbeck)*, Bull Montana *("Red" Lizard)*, Gale Henry *(The Maid)*, Thomas Guise *(The Judge)*, Robert Daly *(The Organist)*, Charles West *("Spider" Welch)*, Charles Mailes *(District Attorney Searle)*.

Nice inspirational programmer about an actor who becomes a minister and is wrongly accused of theft by his jealous former sweetheart Carlyle. The real thief is the brother of his fiancee, and just as it appears that the reverend will lose everything, the boy confesses.

d, Harold Shaw; w, Winifred Dunn (based on the novel by Peter Clark MacFarlane); ph, George Rizard.

Drama **(PR:A MPAA:NR)**

HELEN'S BABIES** (1924) 6 reels Principal bw

Baby Peggy *(Toddie)*, Clara Bow *(Alice Mayton)*, Jean Carpenter *(Budge)*, Edward Everett Horton *(Uncle Harry)*, Claire Adams *(Helen Lawrence)*, George Reed *(Rastus)*, Mattie Peters *(Housekeeper)*, Richard Tucker *(Tom Lawrence)*.

Custom-built Baby Peggy movie about a bachelor uncle who is writing a book on child raising, left with a couple of kids who nearly drive him crazy. A few laughs and an early look at the wonderful Bow.

p, Sol Lesser; d, William A. Seiter; w, Hope Loring, Louis D. Lighton (based on the novel by John Habberton); ph, William Daniels, Glen MacWilliams; ed, Owen Marks.

Comedy **(PR:A MPAA:NR)**

HELL-TO-PAY AUSTIN*** (1916) 5 reels FA/TRI bw

Wilfred Lucas *(Hell-to-Pay Austin)*, Bessie Love *(Briar Rose)*, Ralph Lewis *(Her Father)*, Mary Alden *(Doris Valentine)*, Eugene Pallette *(Harry Tracey)*, James O'Shea *(Jack Dale)*, Clyde Hopkins *(Daniel Marston)*, Marie Wilkson *(Old Sallie)*, A.D. Sears *(Fred, the Weak)*, William H. Brown *(Peter, the Kind)*, Tom Wilson *(Bill, the Bully)*, Monte Blue.

Good little lumber camp picture has Love's minister-father dying, due to alcoholism, and the woodsmen deciding that she must be taken care of. She goes with Lucas, and her goodness changes him from a hard-drinking, two-fisted fighting man, to a decent Christian—who marries the girl the second she comes of age.

d, Paul Powell; w, Mary H. O'Connor; ph, John W. Leezer.

Drama **(PR:A MPAA:NR)**

HELL'S HINGES***** (1916) 5 reels TRI bw

William S. Hart *(Blaze Tracy)*, Clara Williams *(Faith Henley)*, Jack Standing *(Rev. Robert Henley)*, Alfred Hollingsworth *(Silk Miller)*, Robert McKim *(Clergyman)*, J. Frank Burke *(Zeb Taylor)*, Louise Glaum *(Dolly)*, John Gilbert, Jean Hersholt, Robert Kortman, Leo Willis.

Hart's magnificent film about an eastern minister who is seduced by the town whore after he and his sister are assigned a parish in a town known as Hell's Hinges. The picture is full of beautiful imagery and symbolism as the reverend degenerates to the point where he leads the town's criminal element in the burning down of his own church. Then Hart, who plays a one-time gunfighter converted through love for the minister's sister, retaliates by systematically shooting out the saloon's overhead lanterns and, ultimately, turning the whole town into a flaming holocaust. The picture ends with Hart and the girl burying her brother and setting off together, leaving Hell's Hinges smouldering behind them. A western classic, Hart here achieves much more than a routine western sets out to do. The very idea of a minister in the Old West being anything but a paragon of civic pride is foreign to any concept in the genre. His photography of a rugged but poetic West is unique in raising his story almost to the lovel of American literature and providing highly charged drama rather than a straight action feature. And, finally, the town in flames and the mob scene that ensue are supremely vigorous filmic accounts of how it might have been then as Hart stands firm behind his two blazing six guns meting out justice to the good and vengeance to the bad.

d, William S. Hart, Charles Swickard; w, C. Gardner Sullivan; ph, Joseph August.

Western **Cas.** **(PR:A MPAA:NR)**

HELP WANTED—MALE!** (1920) 6 reels Pathe bw

Blanche Sweet *(Leona Stafford)*, Henry King *("Tubbs")*, Frank Leigh *(Clerk)*, Mayme Kelso *(Mrs. Dale)*, Thomas Jefferson *(Harris)*, Jay Belasco *(Lieutenant)*, Jean Acker *(Ethel)*, Kid *(Toodles the Dog)*.

Sweet, one of filmdom's most charming actesses, somehow manages to make this load of cinematic fluff work. She plays a telephone girl who inherits $1,000, half of which she spends on clothes and the other half on a summer vacation at a luxury hotel. She is almost taken in by a phony English fortune hunter (who falls for her wealthy disguise), but at the last minute is rescued by a good-looking American chap, who recognizes her to be the operator who once failed to get him his phone call. Of course, as these things usually go, he turns out to be a millionaire, and she then turns out to be his bride.

d, Henry King; w, George H. Plympton (based on the story "Leona Goes A-Hunting" by Edwina Levin); ph, Lucien Andriot.

Drama **(PR:A MPAA:NR)**

HE-MAN'S COUNTRY, A** (1926) 5 reels Ben Wilson/RAY bw

Dick Hatton.

Dick Hatton directed this off-the-wall western programmer about a cowboy who is given the assignment of cleaning up a gang of rustlers. To do this he disguises himself as a black man, captures the crooks, and wins the sheriff's daughter.

d, Dick Hatton.

Western **(PR:A MPAA:NR)**

HER BOY** (1915, Brit.) 5 reels Hepworth/Thanhouser bw

Stewart Rome *(Hugh Vane)*, Violet Hopson *(Nance)*, Lionelle Howard *(Eric)*, Chrissie White *(Isabelle)*.

In this British tear-jerker, a good-for-nothing gambler goes through his poor mother's savings, completely wipes out his wealthy wife, and then dies, regretting his sins.

d, Frank Wilson; w, Gertrude Allen.

Drama **(PR:A MPAA:NR)**

HER CONDONED SIN (SEE: JUDITH OF BETHULIA, 1914)

HER ELEPHANT MAN*** (1920) 5 reels FOX bw

Shirley Mason, Albert Roscoe, Henry J. Herbert, Ardiata Mellonino, Harry Todd, Dorothy Lee.

Mason plays the daughter of a missionary who dies of fever in the jungles of Africa, leaving word that the first white men who find her should deliver her to a bishop friend to be raised. She is discovered by a circus troupe who follow those instructions. However, when she is rudely treated by his man servant, she decides to join the show, becomes a bareback rider, and marries the elephant trainer.

d, Scott Dunlap; w, Isabelle Johnson (based on a story by Pearl Doles Bell).

Drama **(PR:A MPAA:NR)**

HER FATAL MILLIONS*** (1923) 6 reels Metro/AFN bw

Viola Dana *(Mary Bishop)*, Huntly Gordon *(Fred Garrison)*, Allan Forrest *(Lew Carmody)*, Peggy Browne *(Louise Carmody)*, Edward Connelly *(Amos Bishop)*, Kate Price *(Mary Applewin)*, Joy Winthrop *(The Landlady)*.

Dana is superb (she even does a Chaplin imitation) in this fast-moving comedy about a jewelry store salesgirl who "borrows" some expensive pieces to convince her former sweetheart—whom she believes is married to a society girl—that she is the wife of the town millionaire. Needless to say, it all works out for the two of them in this thoroughly charming little film.

d, William Beaudine; w, Arthur Slatter (based on a story by William Dudley Pelley); ph, John Arnold.

Comedy **(PR:A MPAA:NR)**

HER FIGHTING CHANCE*** (1917) 7 reels A. H. Jacobs/Frank G. Hall bw

Jane Grey *(Marie)*, Thomas Holding *(Jan Thoreau)*, Percy G. Standing *(Cpl. Blake)*, Edward Porter *(Sgt. Fitzgerald)*, Fred Jones *(Francois Breault)*, William Cohill *(Pastamoo)*.

Atmospheric north woods drama about a God-fearing woman (nicely played by Grey) who is willing to give herself to a brute to save her husband from being hanged. He does, however, escape the noose and, at the film's end, destroys the bad guy in a fist fight.

d, Edwin Carewe; w, (based on the novel *The Fiddling Man* by James Oliver Curwood); ph, Arthur Martinelli.

Drama/Adventure **(PR:A MPAA:NR)**

HER FIVE-FOOT HIGHNESS*** (1920) 5 reels UNIV bw

Edith Roberts *(Eleen)*, Virginia Ware *(Lady Harriet)*, Odgen Crane *(Wesley Saundres)*, Harold Miller *(Sir Gerald Knowlton)*, Stanhope Wheatcroft *(Lord Pomeroy)*, Kathleen Kirkham *(Lady Clara)*, Rudolph Christians *(Solicitor)*, Hugh Saxon *(Butler)*, Leota Lorraine *(Chorus Girl)*, Leonard Clapham *(Slim Higgins)*, Henry Woodward *(Williams)*.

Combination western and society drama works only because of good acting and direction. American girl Roberts becomes heir to the title and estate of her uncle, the Duke of Wilshire, upon his death, because her late father renounced the title earlier and moved to the U.S. Roberts' crooked lawyer sees the chance to pull one off and, having the documentation in his possession, hires a chorus girl to pose as the rightful heir. Roberts goes to England, exposes the plot, renounces the title herself and, taking advantage of leap year, proposes to her bashful cowboy admirer, Clapham.

d, Harry L. Franklin; w, Hal Hoadley (based on a story by Tarkington Baker); ph, Roy Klaffki.

Western/Drama **(PR:A MPAA:NR)**

HER GILDED CAGE*** (1922) 6 reels FP/PAR bw

Gloria Swanson *(Suzanne Ornoff)*, David Powell *(Arnold Pell, an American Artist)*, Harrison Ford *(Lawrence Pell, His Brother)*, Walter Hiers *(Bud Walton, Publicity Man)*, Anne Cornwall *(Jacqueline Ornoff)*, Charles A. Stevenson *(Gaston Petitfils)*.

This was the kind of Swanson film audiences of the 1920s loved. As sole support of an old uncle and a crippled sister, Swanson goes from teaching music in France to modeling for an American artist. After falling in love with him, she lands a job dancing in a cabaret where a press agent catches her act and turns her into a star by inventing the story that she is the "favorite" of King Fernando. Before long, Swanson comes to the U.S. to perform, encounters her artist (who was angered by the alleged affair), and he not only realizes the foolishness of his jealousy, but introduces his brother (an eminent physician) to the crippled sister. The picture ends with everybody declaring their love and the sister experiencing a complete cure.

d, Sam Wood; w, Elmer Harris, Percy Heath (based on the play by Anne Nichols); ph, Alfred Gilks.

Romance **(PR:A MPAA:NR)**

HER GREAT CHANCE*** (1918) 5 reels SEL bw

Alice Brady *(Lola Gray)*, David Powell *(Charles Cox)*, Nellie Parker Spaulding *(Mrs. Gray)*, Gloria Goodwin *(Ida Bell Gray)*, Gertrude Barry *(Genevieve)*, Hardee Kirkland *(Cox, Sr.)*, Ormi Hawley *(Kitty)*, C. A. de Lima *(A Lawyer)*, Jefferson de Angelis *(Bonifact)*.

Nice location shots of the Catskill Mountains, as well as the popular roadhouses outside New York, are a plus for this pleasant little programmer about a salesgirl who goes with a millionaire's son, but refuses to marry him as long as dad is paying the bills. However, when the old boy stops supporting him, she changes her mind and, of course, the young fellow makes good.

d&w, Charles Maigne (based on the novel *Golden Fleece* by Fannie Hurst); ph, Leo Rossi.

Drama **(PR:A MPAA:NR)**

HER HERITAGE** (1919, Brit.) 5 reels Ward's bw

Jack Buchanan *(Bob Hales)*, Phyllis Monkman *(Lady Mary Strode)*, E. Holman Clark *(Gerald Pridling)*, Edward O'Neill *(Lord Heston)*, Winifred Dennis *(Mrs. Wilter)*.

In this modest British thriller, a lady posing as a domestic servant enlists the aid of an artist to steal the letters her cousin has been using to blackmail her.

d, Bannister Merwin; w, (based on a story by Arthur Weigell).

Crime **(PR:A MPAA:NR)**

HER LONELY SOLDIER*** (1919, Brit.) 5 reels Barker/New Bio bw

Daphne Glenne *(Veronica)*, Dulcie Parsons *(Kitterkins de Vere)*, Eva Brooke, Suzanne Morris.

In this sweet little English romance, a spinster sends a picture of her sister to a soldier. Happiness triumphs when his buddy shows up, posing as him.

p, Jack W. Smith; d, Percy Nash; w, (based on a story by Irene Miller).

Love **(PR:A MPAA:NR)**

HER MAD BARGAIN* (1921) 6 reels Anita Stewart/AFN bw

Anita Stewart *(Alice Lambert)*, Arthur Edmund Carew *(Grant Lewis)*, Helen Raymond *(Mrs. Henry Beresford)*, Adele Farrington *(Mrs.Gordon Howe)*, Margaret McWade *(Mrs. Dunn)*, Percy Challenger *(Parsons)*, Walter McGrail *(David Leighton)*, Gertrude Astor *(Ruth Beresford)*, George B. Williams *(Mons. Armand)*, Ernest Butterworth *(Jerry Dunn, Jr.)*, Will Badger *(Jerry Dunn, Sr.)*.

Absurd movie about an artist who gives a girl $50,000 on the condition that within a year she must commit suicide so that he can collect $75,000 from her life insurance. During that time, however, he falls in love with her, and the deal is canceled.

d, Edwin Carewe; w, Josephine Quirk (based on a story by Florence Auer); ph, Robert B. Kurrle; art d, William Darling.

Drama **(PR:A MPAA:NR)**

HER MAN* (1924) 5 reels Phil Goldstone/REN bw

William Fairbanks, Tom McGuire, James Pierce, Frank Whitson, Margaret Landis.

Uneventful Fairbanks western in which the hero rescues the daughter of a millionaire who is the victim of a mock kidnaping. Her father and a fellow capitalist set up the gag to wager on the exact time of her return. Fairbanks, not knowing this, brings the girl home. When it is disclosed that he is the son of a wealthy meat packer, the green light is given for them to marry.

p, Phil Goldstone.

Western **(PR:A MPAA:NR)**

HER OWN FREE WILL* (1924) 6 reels Eastern/Hodkinson bw

Helene Chadwick *(Nan Everard)*, Holmes Herbert *(Peter Craddock)*, Allan Simpson *(Jerry Lister)*, George Backus *(Colonel Evarard)*, Violet Mersereau *(Mona Everard)*.

Chadwick (director William Wellman's first wife) contributed little more than her blonde beauty to this poor programmer about a woman who sacrifices her true love to marry a wealthy admirer, after discovering her father is broke.

d, Paul Scardon; w, Gerald C. Duffy (based on a story by Ethel May Dell); ph, J. Roy Hunt.

Drama **(PR:A MPAA:NR)**

HER SECRET*** (1919, Brit.) 5 reels Barker/Urban bw

Margaret Bannerman *(Margaret Henderson)*, Frederick Jensen *(Dr. Paul Henderson)*.

Tight British drama about a husband whose jealousy is such that it drives him from his wife. After a while, however, he realizes the foolishness of his ways and returns in time to save her life.

p, Jack W. Smith; d&w, Frederick S. Jensen.

Drama **(PR:A MPAA:NR)**

HER STORY** (1920, Brit.) 5 reels G.B. Samuelson/GEN bw

Madge Titheradge *(Betty Thorpe)*, Campbell Gullan *(Oscar Koplan)*, C. M. Hallard *(Ashelyn)*.

By the 1920s, British film companies were beginning to go on location more often. Butler brought his troupe to Hollywood to direct this rather stark drama about a Russian gambler who crashes out of jail and tries to kill his former wife, who married her employer.

d, Alexander Butler; w, William B. Laub (based on a story by Dion Titheradge).

Drama **(PR:A MPAA:NR)**

HER WINNING WAY*** (1921) 5 reels Realart/PAR bw

Mary Miles Minter *(Ann Annington)*, Gaston Glass *(Harold Hargrave)*, Carrie Clark Ward *(Nora)*, Fred Goodwins *(Sylvester Lloyd)*, Helen Dunbar *(Mrs. Hargrave)*, Grace Morse *(Evangeline)*, John Elliot *(Mallon)*, Omar Whitehead *(Dr. Claude Gravat)*.

Minter is a reporter out to get an interview with a writer of women's books who refuses to have anything to do with the press. Posing as a maid, she lands a job in his house, breaks up the engagement his mother arranged by planting bobby pins and female apparel in his room, and ends up winning the fellow for herself.

d, Joseph Henabery; w, Douglas Doty (based on the novel *Ann Annington* by Edgar Jepson and the play "Ann" by Lechemere Worrall); ph, Faxon Dean.

Comedy **(PR:A MPAA:NR)**

HERO, THE*** (1923) 7 reels PRE/Al Lichtman bw

Gaston Glass *(Oswald Lane)*, Barbara La Marr *(Hester Lane)*, John Sainpolis *(Andrew Lane)*, Martha Mattox *(Sarah Lane)*, Frankie Lee *(Andy Lane)*, David Butler *(Bill Walters)*, Doris Pawn *(Martha)*, Ethel Shannon *(Hilda Pierce)*, Cameo the Dog.

Glass is perfectly cast as the young man who returns home to his small town and beguiles everyone with his war stories. While staying with his rather dull brother, he makes hay with the Belgian maid and nearly seduces his sister-in-law. Later he steals the church funds, which were in his brother's care, and takes off. Before he leaves town, however, there is a fire at the school, and he becomes badly burned while saving a number of children, and thus becomes a real hero. His brother volunteers to participate in a skin graft, and the hero returns the money.

d, Louis J. Gasnier; w, Eve Unsell (based on the play by Gilbert Emery); ph, Karl Struss.

Drama **(PR:A MPAA:NR)**

HEROIC LOVER, THE* (1929) 6 reels Richard Talmadge/Parthenon bw

Leonard St. Leo, Barbara Bedford, Stuart Holmes, Ted Snell, Hugh Metcalf, William Franey.

A couple of salesmen inadvertently foil a train robbery and become the heroes of a small town. A lightweight comedy with lightweight directing and acting.

d, Noel Mason; w, Betty Moore; t, Al Martin; ph, Harry Cooper, William Wheeler; ed, Martin Obzina.

Comedy **(PR:A MPAA:NR)**

HE'S A PRINCE (SEE: REGULAR FELLOW, A, 1925)

HEY! HEY! COWBOY*** ½ (1927) 6 reels UNIV-Jewel bw

Hoot Gibson *(Jimmie Roberts)*, Nick Cogley *(Julius Decker)*, Kathleen Key *(Emily Decker)*, Wheeler Oakman *(John Evans)*, Clark Comstock *(Joe Billings)*, Monte Montague *(Hank Mander, Decker's Foreman)*, Milla Davenport *(Aunt Jane)*, Jim Corey *(Blake)*, Slim Summerville *(Spike Doolin)*.

This was action director-writer Reynolds' last film before his death. It came at a time when Gibson was threatening to quit the Universal studios because of his dissatisfaction with the scripts he was being given and surely must have encouraged the cowboy star to stay on. Gibson plays a detective hired to get the goods on a neighbor with whom his employer is carrying on a feud. Comedian Summerville is most effective as his counterpart, but it turns out that Oakman, a stranger from the city after both spreads, is the guilty party.

d&w, Lynn Reynolds; ph, Harry Neumann; art d, David S. Garber.

Western **(PR:A MPAA:NR)**

HEY RUBE!*** (1928) 7 reels FBO bw

Hugh Trevor *(String)*, Gertrude Olmstead *(Lutie)*, Ethlyne Clair *(Zelda)*, Bert Moorehouse *(Moffatt)*, Walter McGrail *(Duke)*, James Eagle *(Andy)*.

Carnival story has Clair, a fire diver, attempting to murder a woman reporter because of jealousy over a game operator she loves. Clair is killed after diving into an empty tank, and there is a thrilling rescue in which the hero swings by rope from the ferris wheel to snatch the reporter from the fiery diving platform. This is an atmospheric film, which gives the impression of being much more expensively produced than it was.

d, George B. Seitz; w, Wyndham Gittens (based on a story by Louis Sarecky, Gittens); t, Randolph Bartlett; ph, Robert Martin; ed, Ann McKnight.

Drama **(PR:A MPAA:NR)**

HIDDEN SCAR, THE*** (1916) 5 reels PEER/WORLD bw

Ethel Clayton *(Janet Hall)*, Holbrook Blinn *(Stuart Doane)*, Irving Cummings *(Dale Overton)*, Montagu Love *(Henry Dalton)*, Madge Evans *(Dot)*, Edward M. Kimball *(Rev. James Overton)*, Eugenie Woodward *(Mrs. Overton)*.

A once-fallen woman marries a minister without filling him in about her past. Then, when he learns the truth, all of the love and forgiveness he has been preaching goes right out the window. Finally a friend shows him the error of his ways and he makes it up to her. Better than one might think.

d, Barry O'Neil; w, Frances Marion (based on the story "The Scorching Way" by Mrs. Owen Bronson).

Drama **(PR:A MPAA:NR)**

HIGH AND HANDSOME*** (1925) 6 reels R-C/FBO bw

Maurice B. Flynn *(Joe Hanrahan)*, Ethel Shannon *(Marie Ducette)*, Tom Kennedy *(Bat Kennedy)*, Ralph McCullough *(Irving Ducette)*, Jean Perry *(Jim Burke)*, Marjorie Bonner *(Myrt Riley)*, John Gough *(Jimmy Le Doux)*, Lydia Knott *(Mrs. Hanrahan)*.

"Lefty" Flynn, the ex-Yale football star, was well suited for the role of Joe Hanrahan, a cop suspended from the force for refusing a boxing promoter's bribe to stay mum about a badly constructed balcony in his arena. Hanrahan is also the department heavyweight champ, so it seems perfectly logical that he could beat the promoter's top fighter, Kennedy (a former boxer in real life, and brother of comedian Edgar) at the film's end, while the balcony comes crashing down to provide his vindication.

d, Harry Garson; w, Rex Taylor (based on a story by Gerald Beaumont); ph, Ernest Hallor.

Drama **(PR:A MPAA:NR)**

HIGH HEELS** (1921) 5 reels UNIV bw

Gladys Walton *(Christine Trevor)*, Frederick Vogeding *(Dr. Paul Denton)*, William Worthington *(Joshua Barton)*, Freeman Wood *(Cortland Van Ness)*, George Hackathorne *(Laurie Trevor)*, Charles De Briac *(Daffy Trevor)*, Raymond De Briac *(Dilly Trevor)*, Milton Markwell *(Douglas Barton)*, Dwight Crittenden *(John Trevor)*, Robert Dunbar *(Robert Graves)*, Ola Norman *(Amelia)*, Leigh Wyant *(Jennie Chubb)*, Jean De Briac *(Armand)*, Hugh Saxon *(Mike)*.

Pampered young woman discovers, on her father's death, that he was on the verge of bankruptcy. She turns down a wealthy young man's proposal of marriage in order to help her younger brother and sister and ends up with the family doctor, after discovering that the other fellow was really a rotter.

d, Lee Kohlmar; w, Wallace Clifton (based on a story by Louise B. Clancy); ph, Earl Ellis.

Drama **(PR:A MPAA:NR)**

HIGH SPEED* (1917) 5 reels Butterfly bw

Jack Mulhall *(Speed Cannon)*, Fritzi Ridgeway *(Susan)*, Harry Rattenberry *(Father)*, Lydia Yeamans Titus *(Mother)*, Albert MacQuarrie *(Count Englantine)*, J. Morris Foster *(Count's Friend)*.

Slow-moving, overly padded, formula stuff about a socially ambitious mother's attempt to marry her daughter off to royalty. Her father, on the other hand, stands timidly behind his little girl's desire to wed the man she loves—square-jawed, all-American Speed Cannon (Mulhall). The film's only bright spot is when the young couple elope in a fast car and are nearly hit by an oncoming train as they race across the tracks.eb;just

d, Elmer Clifton, George L. Sargent; w, Tom Gibson, H. P. Pearson (based on a story by Helen Starr, Leo Sargent).

Romance/Adventure **(PR:A MPAA:NR)**

HILLS OF KENTUCKY*** (1927) 7 reels WB bw

Rin-Tin-Tin *(The Grey Ghost)*, Jason Robards *(Steve Harley)*, Dorothy Dwan *(Janet)*, Tom Santschi *(Ben Harley)*, Billy Kent Schaeffer *(Little Davey)*, Rin-Tin-Tin, Jr. *(The Puppy)*, Nanette *(Herself)*.

Perhaps the best of the Rin-Tin-Tin pictures, full of action and pathos, with a wonderful moral lesson for children. "Rinty" is one of many dogs let loose by their owners because of famine in the land. But, on his own, he protects the boy who befriended him from attack by a dog pack and saves the schoolteacher from certain death in an out-of-control canoe.

d, Howard Bretherton; w, Edward Clark (based on the story "The Untamed Heart" by Dorothy Yost); ph, Frank Kesson.

Adventure Cas. (PR:A MPAA:NR)

HILLS OF MISSING MEN*** (1922) 5 reels PG/AEX bw

J. P. McGowan *(The Dragon)*, Jean Perry *(Crando)*, James Wang *(Li Fung)*, Charles Brinley *(Bandini)*, Andrew Waldron *(Buck Allis)*, Florence Gilbert *(Hilma Allis)*, Helen Holmes *(Amy Allis)*.

Fast-moving B western about a criminal who forms an army out of disenchanted veterans and outlaws, with the intention of taking over lower California and setting himself up as king. He has heard of a famous desperado (McGowan) and welcomes him to join the company. It turns out, however, that McGowan is actually an undercover agent who, with the help of the American cavalry, foils the plot.

d&w, J. P. McGowan (based on a story by John B. Clymer); ph, Ben Bail.

Western (PR:A MPAA:NR)

HIS DARKER SELF*** (1924) 5 reels G. and H./W. W. Hodkinson bw

Lloyd Hamilton *(George Sappington)*, Tom Wilson *(Bill Jackson)*, Tom O'Malley *(Uncle Eph)*, Lucille La Verne *(Darktown's Cleopatra)*, Edna May Sperl *(Bill Jackson's Sweetheart)*, Sally Long *(Claude's Sweetheart)*, Kate Bruce *(Claude's Mother)*, Warren Cook *(The Governor)*.

Al Jolson was to have made this film for D. W. Griffith, but for some reason the deal fell through. Instead, Grey (Griffith's brother) produced it, replacing Jolson with comedian Hamilton and using Noble to direct. It was actually a good little action-comedy about a mystery writer who puts on burnt cork to infiltrate and capture a ring of black bootleggers.

p, Albert L. Grey; d, John W. Noble; w, Arthur Caesar; t, Ralph Spence.

Comedy (PR:A MPAA:NR)

HIS ENEMY'S DAUGHTER (SEE: MODERN MONTE CRISTO, A, 1917)

HIS FATHER'S SON*** (1917) 5 reels Rolfe/Metro bw

Lionel Barrymore *(J. Dabney Barron)*, Irene Howley *(Betty Arden)*, Frank Currier *(John Arden)*, Charles Eldridge *(Adam Barron)*, Charles A. Wright *(Perkins, Dabney's Valet)*, Phil Sanford, Walter Horton.

Neat little comedy about a wealthy father who throws his playboy son out of the house, penniless, with the bet that he will not be able to hold down a job for one month. The lad not only wins the wager but returns with a bride, who happens to be the half-owner of a fabulous jewel the old man has long coveted.

d, George D. Baker; w, June Mathis (based on a story by Channing Pollock, Rennold Wolf); ph, John Arnold.

Comedy/Drama (PR:A MPAA:NR)

HIS HOUR*** (1924) 7 reels Louis B. Mayer/MG bw

Aileen Pringle *(Tamara Loraine)*, John Gilbert *(Gritzko)*, Emily Fitzroy *(Princess Ardacheff)*, Lawrence Grant *(Stephen Strong)*, Dale Fuller *(Olga Gleboff)*, Mario Carillo *(Count Valonne)*, Jacqueline Gladson *(Tatiane Shebanoff)*, George Waggoner *(Sasha Basmanoff)*, Carrie Clark Ward *(Princess Murieska)*, Bertram Grassby *(Boris Varishkine)*, Jill Reties *(Sonia Zaieskine)*, Wilfred Gough *(Lord Courtney/Jack)*, Frederick Vroom *(British Minister)*, Mathilde Comont *(Fat Harem Lady)*, E. Eliazaroff *(Khedive)*, David Mir *(Serge Grekoff)*,Bert Sprotte *(Ivan)*.

Another commercial success by Glyn, the inventor of the term "It" to describe Clara Bow. This time the near-naughty theme has to do with an Englishwoman (Pringle) who is attracted to a Russian prince (Gilbert) with a reputation for lovemaking. In order to not become one of his statistics, she tries to remain aloof. One night, however, when a storm forces them to seek refuge in his lodge, she faints and awakens with her waist garment open. Believing herself violated, she consents to marry the fellow but soon discovers that they are truly in love.

d, King Vidor; sup&w, Elinor Glyn; t, Maude Fulton, Vidor; ph, John Mescall; art d, Cedric Gibbons.

Drama (PR:A MPAA:NR)

HIS HOUSE IN ORDER*** (1928, Brit.) 8 reels QTS/ID bw

Tallulah Bankhead *(Nina Graham)*, Ian Hunter *(Hilary Jesson)*, David Hawthorne *(Filmer Jesson)*, Eric Maturin *(Maj. Mauerwarde)*, Mary Dibley *(Geraldine)*, Windham Guise *(Sir Daniel Ridgeley)*, Nancy Price *(Lady Ridgeley)*, Claude Beerbohm *(Pryce Ridgeley)*, Sheila Courtney *(Annabel Jesson)*, Pat Courtney *(Derek Jesson)*.

Bankhead was the toast of London and the darling of the "bright young people," when she starred in this picture about a millionaire who finally breaks the feeling of worship he feels for his first wife upon discovering that his son is illegitimate.

p, Mayrick Milton; d, Randle Ayrton; w, Patrick L. Mannock (based on the play by Arthur Wing Pinero).

Drama (PR:A MPAA:NR)

HIS JAZZ BRIDE** (1926) 7 reels WB bw

Marie Prevost *(Gloria Gregory)*, Matt Moore *(Dick Gregory)*, Gayne Whitman, John Patrick, Mabel Julienne Scott, Stanley Wayburn, Don Alvarado, Helen Dunbar, George Irving, George Seddon.

A couple of young wives who want to enjoy the "jazz life" leave their strait-laced husbands at home and go for a cruise on a pleasure steamer. One of the husbands is a government inspector who, in order to pay for the extravagant behavior of his bride, accepted a bribe to overlook safety hazards aboard the ship. That night, the vessel sinks and the husbands race by speedboat to save their wives, barely making it in time. Needless to say in this 1926 production, after being pulled from the drink, the ladies were more than willing to return to the world of household duties.

d, Herman C. Raymaker; w, Charles A. Logue, Walter Morosco (based on the novel *The Flapper Wife* by Beatrice Burton); ph, David Abel; ed, Clarence Kolster.

Drama (PR:A MPAA:NR)

HIS LAST DOLLAR*** (1914) 4 reels FP/PAR bw

David Higgins *(Joe Braxton)*, Betty Gray *(Eleanor Downs)*, Hal Clarendon *(Linson)*, E. L. Davenport *(Col. Downs)*, Wellington Playter *(Broker)*, Jack Pickford *(Jones, the Jockey)*, Nat Deverich *(Ross, the Jockey)*.

Although no longer a kid (a reality the camera was unmerciful in pointing out), Higgins' wealthy westerner who comes to New York, is cleaned out by sharpies, but makes another fortune after winning the big race, was an entertaining and well-produced movie.

d, D. W. Griffith, or Frank Powell; w, (based on the play by David Higgins, Baldwin G. Cooke).

Drama (PR:A MPAA:NR)

HIS MAJESTY THE AMERICAN*** (1919) 8 reels Fairbanks/UA bw

Douglas Fairbanks *(William Brooks)*, Marjorie Daw *(Felice, Countess of Montenac)*, Lillian Langdon *(Marguerita)*, Frank Campeau *(Grand Duke)*, Sam Southern, Jay Dwiggins, Albert MacQuarrie, Karla Schramm, Boris Karloff.

In his first film for United Artists (a company he formed along with Mary Pickford, Charles Chaplin, and D. W. Griffith) Fairbanks produced what might be considered a "Fairbanksian" PRISONER OF ZENDA. He is a young man who receives a substantial allowance from an unknown source and is unaware of his heritage which, it turns out, places him in line for the throne of a small European kingdom. Of course he eventually goes there, discovers that conspirators are attempting to take over, and dispatches them in his own inimitable, athletic way. He also wins the hand of the most beautiful princess in the land in the process.

d, Joseph Henabery; w, Henabery, Elton Banks, Fairbanks; ph, Victor Fleming, Glen MacWilliams.

Comedy/Adventure Cas. (PR:A MPAA:NR)

HIS MASTER'S VOICE*** (1925) 6 reels GOTH/LUM bw

Thunder the Dog, George Hackathorne *(Bob Henley)*, Marjorie Daw *(Mary Blake)*, Mary Carr *(Mrs. Henley)*, Will Walling *(William Marshall)*, Brooks Benedict *(Jack Fenton)*, White Fawn *(The White Dog)*, Flash *("The Pup")*.

This entertaining children's film is told by a dog to his pups. It has to do with the adventures he shared with his master during WW I, whereby the small-town fellow overcomes his cowardice, emerges a hero, wins the heart of a Red Cross volunteer, returns home to thrash his long-time rival, and exposes him to be a crook.

p, Sam Sax; d, Renaud Hoffman; w, Henry McCarty, James J. Tynan (based on a story by Frank Foster Davis); ph, Jack MacKenzie; m, Joseph E. Zivelli; m/l, "His Master's Voice," Gus Edwards, Howard Johnson, Irving Bibo.

Adventure (PR:A MPAA:NR)

HIS ROBE OF HONOR*** (1918) 7 reels Paralta bw

Henry B. Walthall *(Julian Randolph)*, Mary Charleston *(Roxan Frisbee)*, Lois Wilson *(Laura Nelson)*, Noah Beery *("Boss" Nordhoff)*, Joseph J. Dowling *(Bruce Nelson)*, Ray Laidlow *(Robert Partland)*, Fred Montague *(Million Mulligan)*, Eugene Pallette *(Clifford Nordhoff)*, Guy Newhard *("Carrots")*.

Another fine performance by Walthall (the immortal "Little Colonel" of THE BIRTH OF A NATION) as a shyster lawyer who worms his way to the top of the political machine by getting gangster Beery's brother free from a murder charge. His payment is a seat on the supreme court, and he is more than willing to play ball with the forces of corruption until he falls for Beery's niece, a very proper young woman. Regenerated by her inspiration, he courageously comes down against a giant corporation the machine controls, thus winning both her admiration and love.

d, Rex Ingram; w, Julian L. Lamothe (based on a story by Ethel and James Dorrance); ph, Carl Widem.

Drama (PR:A MPAA:NR)

HIS SECRETARY*** (1925) 7 reels MGM bw

Norma Shearer *(Ruth Lawrence)*, Lew Cody *(David Coleman)*, Willard Louis *(John Sloden)*, Karl Dane *(Janitor)*, Gwen Lee *(Clara Bayne)*, Mabel Van Buren *(Mrs. Sloden)*, Estelle Clark *(Minnie)*, Ernest Gillen *(Head Clerk)*.

Shearer is excellent as the homely, bespectacled stenographer with a crush on her boss. After overhearing him tell his partner that he wouldn't kiss her for a thousand dollars, Shearer goes to a beautician and is transformed into a knockout. From that point on, both partners are in hot pursuit. At the end Shearer allows her heartthrob to give her a smack and, as a joke, has the janitor pose as her husband, catch them in the act, and demand a thousand bucks. After her boss' initial shock, Shearer tells him it was all in fun and announces her love for him.

d, Hobart Henley; w, Louis D. Lighton, Hope Loring (based on a story by Carey Wilson); t, Joseph W. Farnham; ph, Ben Reynolds; ed, Frank Davis; art d, Cedric Gibbons, Richard Day.

Comedy **(PR:A MPAA:NR)**

HOLD 'EM YALE!** (1928) 8 reels DM/Pathe bw (AKA: AT YALE)

Rod La Rocque *(Jamie Emmanuel Avlarado Montez)*, Jeanette Loff *(Helen)*, Joseph Cawthorn *(Professor)*, Tom Kennedy *(Detective)*, Jerry Mandy *(Valet)*, Hugh Allan *(Oscar)*.

Typical 1920s college story about the wise guy student who falls for a faculty member's daughter and manages to win the big football game at the last minute. Kennedy, as a comic cop, steals the show.

d, Edward H. Griffith; w, George Dromgold, Sanford Hewitt (based on the play "Life at Yale" by Owen Davis); t, John Krafft; ph, Arthur Miller; ed, Harold McLernon; art d, Anton Grot.

Drama **(PR:A MPAA:NR)**

HOLY ORDERS** (1917, Brit.) 5 reels I. B. Davidson/Ruffells bw

Malvina Longfellow *(Jacynth)*, A. E. Coleby *(Dan Kiernan)*, Arthur Rooke *(Rev. Richard Everton)*, Dorna Leigh *(Azalea Everton)*, Maud Yates *(Jenny Kiernan)*, Terence Boddy *(Lawrence)*, N. Watts-Phillips, Olive Bell.

Less-than-cheerful British saga about a mistress who causes the death of her alcoholic lover's wife, then manages to run over him. She later marries a millionaire, but receives her just due when she falls out of a hot air balloon.

d, A. E. Coleby, Arthur Rooke; w, Rowland Talbot (based on the novel by Marie Corelli).

Drama **(PR:A MPAA:NR)**

HOME*** (1916) 5 reels Kay-Bee/TRI bw

Bessie Barriscale *(Bessie Wheaton)*, Charles Ray *(Bob Wheaton)*, Clara Williams *(Inez Wheaton)*, George Fisher *(Allan Shelby)*, Agnes Herring *(Clara Wheaton)*, Thomas S. Guise *(Jerimah Wheaton)*, Louise Glaum *(Daisy Flores)*, Joseph J. Dowling *(Count d'Orr)*.

Barriscale delivers a fine performance as the little sister who makes her family realize how loathsome they have become since inheriting a fortune. Another excellent script by Sullivan.

d, Charles Miller; w, C. Gardner Sullivan.

Drama **(PR:A MPAA:NR)**

HOME STRUCK*** (1927) 6 reels R-C/FBO bw

Viola Dana *(Barbara Page)*, Alan Brooks *(Lyn Holmes)*, Tom Gallery *(Dick Cobb)*, Nigel Barrie *(Warren Townsend)*, George Irving *(President Wallace)*, Charles Howard *(Nick Cohen)*.

Better-than-average movie depiction of theater life has chorus girl Dana marrying bank clerk Gallery and retiring to become a homemaker. Gallery becomes addicted to wild parties and Dana reluctantly joins him, much to the regret of theatrical agent Brooks, who deeply loves her. Later, Barrie, a fellow clerk, encourages Gallery to "borrow" money from the bank then, because he lusts for Dana, blows the whistle on his associate. With Gallery a fugitive, Barrie now makes his move, telling Dana that he will help, if she gives herself to him. At this point, Brooks steps in, secures the role of a lifetime for the woman he loves, and makes her a star. Then, to completely guarantee her happiness, this selfless man of the theatrical world makes it possible for Dana and her husband (who has learned his lesson) to be together again.

d, Ralph Ince; w, Ewart Adamson (based on a story by Peter Milne); ph, Jules Cronjager.

Drama **(PR:A MPAA:NR)**

HOME STUFF** (1921) 6 reels Metro bw

Viola Dana *(Madge Joy)*, Tom Gallery *(Robert Deep)*, Josephine Crowell *("Ma" Deep)*, Nelson McDowell *("Pa" Deep)*, Priscilla Bonner *(Susan Deep)*, Robert Chandler *(Mr. "Pat")*, Aileen Manning *(Mrs. "Pat")*, Phillip Sleeman *(Jim Sackett)*.

Dana falls asleep in a haystack after her theatrical company replaces her with a stagestruck young girl who offers to cover the company's expenses. Discovered the next day, she passes herself off as a runaway orphan and is taken in by a family. Gallery, the lad who found her, is an aspiring playwright, and they hit it off right away. Before long, the stagestruck girl returns home and turns out to be the daughter of the farm family. Dana convinces the irate father to forgive the wayward one by threatening to run off with his son, and when later she becomes a big Broadway star, she sends for the boy and together they enjoy love and success.

d, Albert Kelley; w, Frank Dazey, Agnes Christine Johnston; ph, John Arnold; art d, A. F. Mantz.

Comedy **(PR:A MPAA:NR)**

HOME SWEET HOME** ½ (1914) 6 reels REL-Majestic/MUT bw

Henry B. Walthall *(John Howard Payne)*, Josephine Crowell *(His Mother)*, Lillian Gish *(His Sweetheart)*, Dorothy Gish *(His Sister)*, Fay Tincher *(The Woman of the World)*, Mae Marsh *(Apple Pie Mary)*, Spottiswoode Aitken *(Her Father)*, Robert Harron *(The Man from the East)*, Miriam Cooper *(His Fiancee)*, Mary Alden *(The Mother, from the 2nd Story)*, Donald Crisp, James Kirkwood, Jack Pickford *(Her Sons)*, Fred Burns *(The Sheriff)*, Courtenay Foote *(The Husband, from the 3rd Story)*, Blanche Sweet *(The Wife)*, Owen Moore *(The Tempter)*, Edward Dillon *(The Musician)*, Betty Marsh *(The Infant)*, W. H. Long, John Dillon, Earle Foxe, Teddy Sampson, F. A. Turner, W. E. Lawrence, George Siegmann, Ralph Lewis, Irene Hunt, Howard Gaye, Karl Brown, Betty George Berringer.

It can be argued that this film, inspired by the life of John Howard Payne who wrote the lyrics for the song "Home Sweet Home," was a trial run for Griffith's massive masterpiece INTOLERANCE, in that it told three separate stories interconnected by the influence that ballad had upon the picture's various characters. Griffith's use of symbolism, depicting greed, avarice, and lust as figures on the screen, may seem a bit heavy-handed by today's standards, but audiences (and they were the director's primary concern) in 1914 accepted them completely, and the film—although not a total critical success—made enough money so he could continue his preparations for the BIRTH OF A NATION, his next monumental film.

d, D. W. Griffith; w, H. E. Aitken, Griffith (based on the song "Home Sweet Home" by John Howard Payne); ph, Billy Bitzer; ed, James Smith, Rose Ritchel.

Drama **Cas.** **(PR:A MPAA:NR)**

HOMESICK** (1928) 6 reels FOX bw

Sammy Cohen *(Sammy Schnable)*, Harry Sweet *(Ambrose)*, Marjorie Bebe *(Babe)*, Henry Armetta *(Bicycle Rider)*, Pat Harmon *(Polish Bicycle Rider)*.

Fair comedy in which Cohen and Sweet participate in a cross-country bicycle race to win the hand of a domestic servant who placed a "husband wanted" ad in the paper. After a number of less-than-inspired sight gags, Cohen wins the day.

d, Henry Lehrman; w, John Stone; t, William Kernell; ph, Charles Van Enger; ed, Ralph Dixon.

Comedy **(PR:A MPAA:NR)**

HOMESPUN VAMP, A*** (1922) 5 reels Realart/PAR bw

May McAvoy *(Meg Mackenzie)*, Darrel Foss *(Stephen Ware)*, Lincoln Stedman *(Joe Dobbs)*, Josephine Crowell *(Mrs. Dobbs)*, Charles Ogle *(Donald Craig)*, Guy Oliver *(Duncan Craig)*, Helen Dunbar *(Mrs. Ware)*, Kathleen Kirkham *(Beatrice Carlisle)*.

McAvoy is an orphan who lives in the country with her two tight-fisted uncles. They plan on marrying her off to the son of the town's blacksmith, but then one day a writer arrives to finish his novel and catches the girl's eye. When a crime is committed, the stranger is suspected and, while fleeing a mob, is wounded. He collapses at McAvoy's door, and because her uncles are away she takes him in. The following day, the real crook is caught, but her uncles are so outraged that a man spent the night in her company that they demand a wedding. The young man goes along with this to protect McAvoy's honor and takes her to live in the home he shares with his mother, while awaiting the annulment. However, by the time the papers are processed, the two have truly fallen in love and a big church wedding is planned.

d, Frank O'Connor; w, Harvey Thew (based on a story by Hector Turnbull); ph, Hal Rosson.

Drama **(PR:A MPAA:NR)**

HONEYMOON*** (1929) 5 reels MGM bw

Polly Moran *(Polly)*, Harry Gribbon *(Harry)*, Bert Roach *(Bert)*, Flash the Dog.

Lots of laughs when Roach, a disappointed suitor, gives Moran and Gribbon a police dog on their wedding day. The dog has been trained to bite the head off anyone who so much as lays a finger on his mistress which, needless to say, is a source of profound frustration for Gribbon on his honeymoon. The picture has a great gag ending, with the dog—who has fallen for a little white cat—giving *his* sweetheart a great big smack.

d, Robert A. Golden; w, George O'Hara, Richard Schayer (based on a story by Lew Lipton); t, Robert Hopkins; ph, Maximilian Fabian; ed, Ben Lewis; art d, Cedric Gibbons.

Comedy **(PR:A MPAA:NR)**

HONEYMOON AHEAD***

(1927, Brit.) 7 reels BIP/Wardour bw (GB: ADAM'S APPLE)

Monty Banks *(Monty Adams)*, Gillian Dean *(Ruth Appleby)*, Lena Halliday *(Mrs. Appleby)*, Judy Kelly *(Vamp)*, Dino Galvani *(Crook)*, Colin Kenney *(Husband)*, Hal Gordon *(Drunk)*, Charles O'Shaughnessy *(Official)*.

The English, who were having a terrible time getting their motion picture industry off of the ground from an entertainment standpoint, hired U.S. director Whelan to help them out with this effort about a honeymooning Yank who arranges for underworld types to kidnap his mother-in-law.

d, Tim Whelan; w, (based on a story by Whelan, Rex Taylor).

Comedy **(PR:A MPAA:NR)**

HONEYMOON FLATS* (1928) 6 reels UNIV bw

George Lewis *(Jim Clayton)*, Dorothy Gulliver *(Lila Garland)*, Kathlyn Williams *(Mrs. Garland)*, Ward Crane *(Anthony Weir)*, Bryant Washburn *(Tom Twitchell)*, Phillips Smalley *(Mr. Garland)*, Jane Winton *(Jane Twitchell)*, Patricia Caron *(Mrs. French)*, Eddie Phillips *(Mr. French)*.

Williams tries hard to break up her daughter's marriage to an earnest young man of limited means. She fails, as does this early attempt at satirizing suburban living.

d, Millard Webb; w, Joseph Franklin Poland, Morton Blumenstock (based on a story by Earl Derr Biggers); t, Albert De Mond; ph, Ross Fisher; ed, Frank Hekinson.

Comedy **(PR:A MPAA:NR)**

HONOR SYSTEM, THE*** ½ (1917) 5 reels FOX bw

Milton Sills *(Joseph Stanton)*, Mrs. Cora Drew *(His Mother)*, James A. Marcus *(Gov. John Hunter)*, Arthur Mackley *(Steven Holt, the Sheriff)*, Miriam Cooper *(Edith, His Daughter)*, George Walsh *(Jack Taylor)*, Charles Clary *(Charles Harrington, a*

Lawyer), Gladys Brockwell *(Trixie Bennett)*, Roy Rice *("Three-Fingered" Louis)*, P. J. Cannon *(James Phelan, Warden)*, Johnny Reese *(Mugsey)*, Carrie Clark Ward, William Eagle Eye, Thomas X. Brian, Countess Du Cello.

Director Walsh checked himself into a state penitentiary and took Jack Pickford along for laughs in order to get the real feel of prison life for this excellent motion picture about a man who is wrongly sent away after killing a man in self-defense. This film made an eloquent and powerful appeal for the humane treatment of convicts some 25 years before Paul Muni was subjected to his ordeal in I AM A FUGITIVE FROM A CHAIN GANG.

d&w, Raoul A. Walsh (based on a story by Henry Christeen Warnack); ph, George S. Benoit.

Drama **(PR:A MPAA:NR)**

HOODLUM THE*** (1919) 6 reels Mary Pickford/FN bw

Mary Pickford *(Amy Burke)*, Ralph Lewis *(Alexander Guthrie)*, Kenneth Harlan *(John Graham)*, Melvin Messenger *(Dish Lowry)*, Dwight Crittenden *(John Burke)*, Aggie Herring *(Nora)*, Andrew Arbuckle *(Pat O'Shaughnessy)*, Max Davidson *(Abram Isaacs)*, Paul Mullen *(The Pugilist)*, B. A. Lewis, Nellie Anderson.

This Pickford showcase allowed her to portray the spoiled granddaughter of a millionaire, as well as a girl of the slums. As the latter she is at her comic best, dancing the shimmy, outracing a cop, and playing off a couple of stereotypical Irish and Jewish characters. She also falls for a fellow wrongly accused of committing a crime, clears his name, and persuades her grandfather to accept him. Although this picture was made for First National, 1919 was the year Pickford joined Charlie Chaplin, Douglas Fairbanks, and D. W. Griffith in forming the United Artists Corporation. It was also the year that she brought an end to her eight-year marriage to actor Owen Moore.

d, Sidney A. Franklin; w, Bernard McConville (based on the story "Burkeses Amy" by Julie M. Lippmann); ph, Charles Rosher.

Comedy/Drama **(PR:A MPAA:NR)**

HOOFBEATS OF VENGEANCE*** (1929) 5 reels UNIV bw

Rex the Wonder Horse, Jack Perrin *(Sgt. Jack Gordon)*, Helen Foster *(Mary Martin)*, Al Ferguson *(Jud Regan)*, Starlight the Horse, Markee the Horse.

Rex the Wonder Horse helps Perrin, of the Royal Canadian Mounted Police, capture the man who murdered his master and win for him the heart of the girl who was the villain's ward.

d, Henry MacRae; w, George Plympton (based on a story by William Lord Wright, Plympton); t, Gardner Bradford; ph, George Robinson; ed, Thomas Malloy.

Adventure **(PR:A MPAA:NR)**

HOOK AND LADDER*** (1924) 6 reels UNIV bw

Hoot Gibson *(Ace Cooper)*, Mildred June *(Sally Drennan)*, Frank Beal *(Capt. "Smoky Joe" Drennan)*, Edwards Davis *("Big Tom" O'Rourke)*, Philo McCullough *(Gus Henshaw)*.

Sedgwick combined two of the most popular kid movie genres—cowboy and fireman—to create this exciting Gibson feature, in which the appealing star brings a crooked politician to justice and saves the firechief's daughter from a not-so-towering inferno.

d, Edward Sedgwick; w, E. Richard Schayer (based on a story by Raymond L. Schrock, Sedgwick); ph, Virgil Miller.

Western **(PR:A MPAA:NR)**

HOOK AND LADDER NO. 9** (1927) 6 reels R-C/FBO bw

Cornelius Keefe *(Johnny Graham)*, Edward Hearn *(Dan Duffy)*, Lucy Beaumont *(Mother Smith)*, Dione Ellis *(Mary Smith)*, Thomas Brower *(Chief Finnerby)*, Johnny Gough *(Joker)*.

Firemen Keefe and Hearn are rivals for beautiful Ellis. Hearn is shy, Keefe outgoing and quick with the smile. Ellis marries Keefe, and Hearn becomes hateful toward them both. Later, Hearn saves the lives of Ellis and her baby in a terrible fire and is badly injured. The film's ending is rather ambiguous, and the audience is left wondering if he will survive.

d, F. Harmon Weight; w, Peter Milne; ph, H. Lyman Broening.

Drama **(PR:A MPAA:NR)**

HOOSIER SCHOOLMASTER*** (1914) 5 reels Alliance/Masterpiece bw

Max Figman, Lolita Robertson.

Figman was another of those early "legit" actors who willingly made the successful transition from stage to screen in the days when doing so was considered selling out to the devil. In this, the first release for Alliance, a charming and humorous rural atmosphere is quite skillfully re-created, and the film ends with an attempted lynching which provides a terrific wallop.

w, (based on the novel by Edward Eggleston).

Comedy/Drama **(PR:A MPAA:NR)**

HOP, THE DEVIL'S BREW*** (1916) 5 reels BLUE bw

Phillips Smalley *(Ward Jensen)*, Lois Weber *(Lydia Jensen)*, C. Norman Hammond *(William Waters)*, Juan De LaCrux *(Con Leech)*, Marie Walcamp *(Jane)*.

This intriguing Weber-Smalley film—made with the cooperation of the U.S. Customs Bureau—dealt with the evils of opium. Smalley is a government agent sent to investigate the manner in which dope is smuggled into the U.S. While he is gone, his wife becomes an addict, and on his return he not only manages to break up the gang, but sees her through the cure as well.

d, Lois Weber, Phillips Smalley; w, Weber (based on a story by Rufus Steele).

Crime **(PR:A MPAA:NR)**

HOT NEWS*** (1928) 7 reels PAR bw

Bebe Daniels *(Pat Clancy)*, Neil Hamilton *(Scoop Morgan)*, Paul Lukas *(James Clayton)*, Alfred Allen *(Michael Clancy)*, Spec O'Donnell *(Spec)*, Ben Hall *(Benny)*, Mario Carillo *(Maharajah)*, Maude Turner Gordon *(Mrs. Van Vleck)*.

Hamilton, the top cameraman on a local newspaper, quits when the publisher hires his daughter, Daniels, as a newsreel photographer. Hamilton, who refuses to work with anyone in a skirt, joins another paper and the two become bitter rivals. Then, while covering the theft of a precious gem, they are both captured and taken aboard the criminal's yacht. By the time help arrives, the two have discovered love and decide to pop their bulbs together for life.

d, Clarence Badger; w, Florence Ryerson, Lloyd Corrigan, Grover Jones (based on a story by Harlan Thompson, Monte Brice); ph, William Marshall; ed, Tay Malarkey.

Comedy/Drama **(PR:A MPAA:NR)**

HOT WATER*** (1924) 5 reels Harold Lloyd/Pathe bw

Harold Lloyd *(Hubby)*, Jobyna Ralston *(Wifey)*, Josephine Crowell *(Her Mother)*, Charles Stevenson *(Her Big Brother)*, Mickey McBan *(Her Little Brother)*, Pat Harmon *(Straphanger)*, Andy DeVilla *(A Cop)*, Genevieve *(The Turkey)*, Jack the Dog.

HOT WATER is actually three short comedies held together by a thin story line. The first has to do with Lloyd returning home on a trolley with a live turkey. The second finds him taking a spin in his new car with his wife and his obnoxious in-laws, and the film ends with a rather typical haunted house segment. This is not Lloyd's best film, but one could certainly make the point that it is as funny as any comedy made since the movies learned to talk.

d, Sam Taylor, Fred Newmeyer; w, Thomas J. Gray, Tim Whelan, John Grey, Taylor; ph, Walter Lundin; ed, Allen McNeil.

Comedy **(PR:A MPAA:NR)**

HOTEL MOUSE, THE** (1923, Brit.) 7 reels British Super/JUR bw

Lilian Hall Davis *(Mauricette)*, Campbell Gullan *(Marchant) Warwick Ward (Estaban)*, Josephine Earle *(Lola)*, Morgan Wallace *(Honorable Harry Hurlingham.)*

British thriller set in Nice, about a female crook who comes to the aid of an American, helping him retrieve some papers from a blackmailer, as well as his gambling losses.

p, G.B. Samuelson; d, Fred Paul; w, Walter Summers (based on the play by Gerbidon and Armat).

Crime **(PR:A MPAA:NR)**

HOUSE NEXT DOOR, THE* (1914) 5 reels Lubin bw

Gaston Bell, George Soule Spencer, Ethel Clayton, Edwin Barbour, Joseph Kaufman, George Trimble.

Poorly acted, directed, and photographed Lubin adaptation of a successful stage play which dealt with the hatred between a Gentile and a Jew. The film's only highlight is when one of them perishes in the collapse of a granite and mortar house.

d, Barry O'Neil; w, Clay M. Greene (based on a play by J. Hartley Manners).

Drama **(PR:A MPAA:NR)**

HOUSE OF TEMPERLEY, THE*** (1913, Brit.) 5 reels LONDON/JUR bw

Charles Maude *(Capt. Jack Temperley)*, Ben Webster *(Sir Charles Temperley)*, Lillian Logan *(Ethel Morley)*, Charles Rock *(Sir John Hawker)*, Edward O'Neill *(Jakes)*, Wyndham Guise *(Ginger Stubbs)*, Cecil Morton York *(Gentleman Jackson)*, Claire Pauncefoot *(Lady Temperley)*, Rex Davis *(Gloster Dick)*, John M. East *(Tom Cribb)*, Hubert Willis *(Shelton)*, F. Bennington *(Joe Berks)*, Yolande May *(Lucy)*.

This pioneering 1913 British feature about the adopted son of a blacksmith who is accused of murdering his gambler brother, was so popular that Jury Films revived it five years later.

d, Harold M. Shaw; w, (based on the novel *Rodney Stone* by Arthur Conan Doyle).

Drama **(PR:A MPAA:NR)**

HOUSE OF THE LOST CORD, THE*** (1915) 5 reels Edison bw

Gertrude McCoy *(Elinore Vane)*, Viola Dana *(Delores Edgerton)*, Mrs. Wallace Erskine *(Mrs. Edgerton)*, Helen Strickland *(Lady Rosamond)*, Robert Conness *(Sir Anthony Elliot)*, Duncan McRae *(Capt. Elliot)*, Sally Crute *(Nina Desmond)*, William West *(The Butler)*.

The Edison company made quite an impression on audiences and critics with its first long feature about good and evil brothers who become involved in seduction and murder. Dana would become a major star after the release of this picture.

d, Charles Brabin; w, (based on a novel by Mrs. C. N. Williamson).

Drama **(PR:A MPAA:NR)**

HOUSE OF YOUTH, THE*** (1924) 7 reels RF/PDC bw

Jacqueline Logan *(Corinna Endicott)*, Malcolm McGregor *(Spike Blaine)*, Vernon Steele *(Rhodes Winston)*, Gloria Grey *(Amy Marsden)*, Richard Travers *(Mitch Hardy)*, Lucilla Mendez *(Linda Richards)*, Edwin Booth Tilton *(Cornelius Endicott)*, Aileen Manning *(Aunt Maggie)*, Hugh Metcalf *(The Butler)*, Barbara Tennant *(Mrs. Mitch Hardy)*.

Fast-paced, jazz age movie with plenty of hot cars, flappers, and booze. Logan, a sassy but moral girl, is involved in a speakeasy raid. The newspapers ruin her reputation and her fiance, an English writer, drops her like a hot potato. In the end, she shows the world her true character by opening a fresh air farm for slum kids, at which point the Britisher attempts to win her back, but is turned down in favor of her old pal and fellow doer-of-good-deeds, McGregor.

d, Ralph Ince; w, C. Gardner Sullivan (based on the novel by Maude Radford Warren); ph, J. O. Taylor.

Drama **(PR:A MPAA:NR)**

HOUSE ON THE MARSH, THE** (1920, Brit.) 6 reels LONDON/JUR bw

Cecil Humphreys *(Gervas Rayner)*, Peggy Patterson *(Violet Christie)*, Harry Welchman *(Laurence Reed)*, Frank Stanmore *(Rev. Golightly)*, Madge Tree *(Sarah Gooch)*, Mary Godfrey *(Miss Rayner)*.

Tepid little British mystery about a governess who sleuths about and finally puts the finger on her employer, exposing him as the ringleader of a criminal gang.

d, Fred Paul; w, (based on the novel by Florence Warden).

Crime **(PR:A MPAA:NR)**

HOW MOLLY MADE GOOD***

(1915) 6 reels Kulee Features bw (AKA; HOW MOLLY MALONE MADE GOOD)

Marguerite Gale, William H. Tooker, Helen Hilton, W. A. Williams, Armand Cortes, James Bagley, Edward Sullivan, John Reeding, and, as themselves, Leo Ditrichstein, Cyril Scott, May Robson, Lulu Glaser, Julia Dean, Charles J. Ross, Mabel Fenton, Henry Kolker, Julian Eltinge, Henrietta Crosman, Robert Edeson, Mme. Fjorde.

In one of the earliest use of cameo appearances, this film dealt with an Irish immigrant girl who lands a job on a newspaper and is assigned to interview real-life celebrities. The movie also provided a thrill ending, with the girl flying from Wilton, Connecticut, to Park Row in New York to make her deadline.

d, Lawrence B. McGill; w, Burns Mantle.

Drama **(PR:A MPAA:NR)**

HOW MOLLY MALONE MADE GOOD

(SEE: HOW MOLLY MADE GOOD, 1915)

HUCK AND TOM*** (1918) 5 reels Morosco/PAR bw

Jack Pickford *(Tom Sawyer)*, Robert Gordon *(Huck Finn)*, George Hackathorne *(Sid)*, Alice Marvin *(Mary)*, Edythe Chapman *(Aunt Polly)*, Clara Horton *(Becky Thatcher)*, Helen Gilmore *(Widow Douglas)*, Antrim Short *(Joe Harper)*, Tom Bates *(Muff Potter)*, Jane Keckley *(Mrs. Judge Thatcher)*, Frank Lanning *(Injun Joe)*, John Burton *(Judge Thatcher)*.

Continuing their characterizations of Tom Sawyer and Huck Finn, Pickford and Gordon, under the skillful direction of Taylor, find themselves witnessing their arch enemy, Injun Joe (Lanning) commit a murder in a spooky midnight graveyard. The boys eventually bring Lanning to justice and discover buried treasure along the way.

d, William Desmond Taylor; w, Julia Crawford Ivers (based on the novels by Mark Twain); ph, Homer Scott.

Adventure **(PR:A MPAA:NR)**

HUCKLEBERRY FINN*** (1920) 7 reels PAR bw

Lewis Sargent *(Huck)*, Gordon Griffith *(Tom)*, Katherine Griffith *(Widow Douglas)*, Martha Mattox *(Miss Watson)*, Frank Lanning *(Huck's Father)*, Orral Humphrey *(The Duke)*, Tom D. Bates *(The King)*, Edythe Chapman *(Aunt Polly)*, Thelma Salter *(Becky Thatcher)*, George H. Reed *(Jim)*, L. M. Wells *(Judge Thatcher)*, Harry Rattenbury *(Uncle Harvey)*, Esther Ralston *(Mary Jane Wilks)*, Fay Lemport *(Johanna)*, Eunice Van Moore *(Mrs. Sally Phelps)*, Charles Edler *(Schoolteacher)*.

Director Taylor takes another crack at the Huck Finn saga, this time without Pickford as Tom Sawyer. Good production values, direction, and acting make this one a winner, too, and having an actor portray Mark Twain at the film's beginning and end is a nice touch.

d, William Desmond Taylor; w, Julia Crawford Ivers (based on the novel by Mark Twain); ph, Frank E. Garbutt.

Drama **(PR:A MPAA:NR)**

HUMAN DESIRES** (1924, Brit.) 7 reels Anglia/GAU/bw

Marjorie Daw *(Joan Thayer)*, Clive Brook *(George Gautier)*, Juliette Compton *(Andree de Vigne)*, Warwick Ward *(Pierre Brandon)*, Russell Thorndike *(Paul Perot)*, Jean di Limur *(Henri Regnier)*.

In this British love story, an actress finally divorces her jealous impresario husband and marries the police officer who at one time saved her life after a suicide attempt. Nice performances by Hollywood actress Daw and an outstanding English cast.

p, F. J. Nettlefold; d, Burton George; w, Louis Stevens (based an a story by George).

Drama **PR:A MPAA:NR)**

HUMAN STUFF** (1920) 5 reels UNIV bw

Harry Carey, Rudolph Christians, Charles Le Moyne, Joe Harris, Fontaine La Rue, Ruth Fuller Golden, Mary Charleson, Bobby Mack.

Average Carey oater about a wealthy young fellow who hates the family business so much that his father sets him up out West with a sheep farm. The usual complications arise, but when the head cattleman kidnaps Carey's Eastern bride, the city boy rises to the occasion and dispatches the bad hombre in a shootout.

d, Reeves Eason; w, Harry Carey, Eason (based on a story by Tarkington Baker); ph, Roy Klaffki.

Western **(PR:A MPAA:NR)**

HUN WITHIN, THE**** (1918) 5 reels PAR bw

George Fawcett *(Henry Wagner)*, Dorothy Gish *(Beth)*, Charles Gerard *(Karl Wagner)*, Douglas MacLean *(Frank Douglas)*, Herbert Sutch *(Krippen)*, Max Davidson *(Max)*, Lillian Clarke *(Leone)*, Robert Anderson *(Krug)*, Erich von Stroheim *(Von Bickel)*, Adolphe Lestina *(Beth's Father)*, Kate Bruce *(Frank's Mother)*.

D. W. Griffith, under his pseudonym of Granville Warwick, wrote this excellent wartime drama about a German immigrant who comes to the U.S. and makes a fortune. Then, prior to the European hostilities, he sends his son to the fatherland to study chemistry, and the boy becomes caught up in the wave of Teutonic nationalism which is sweeping that country. He returns home a committed agent of the Kaiser, bent on sabotaging the American war effort. There is a tremendously powerful scene where father and son encounter each other—the older man a patriot, the younger one a traitor—which ends shockingly with the fanatic shooting his father in cold blood. A love plot involving Gish (who gives a great performance) is also here, but not enough can be said in praise of Griffith, who depicted the elder German in this film as a good citizen and a decent human being at a time when hamburgers were being called "liberty sandwiches" and innocent little dachshund dogs were often abused by flag-waving, chauvinistic fools.

d, Chester Withey; w, Granville Warwick [D. W. Griffith]; ph, David Abel.

Drama/War **(PR:A MPAA:NR)**

HUNCH, THE*** (1921) 6 reels S-L/Metro bw

Gareth Hughes *(Jimmy)*, Ethel Grandin *(Barbara Thorndyke)*, John Steppling *(John C. Thorndyke)*, Edward Flanagan *(George Taylor)*, Harry Lorraine *(Sheriff Henry Clay Greene)*, Gale Henry *(Minnie Stubbs)*, William H. Brown *(Hodges)*.

Funny film has Hughes waking up in his bathtub after a night on the town, with the message "buy Jerusalem Steel" written on his shirt. He decides to play the hunch, borrows the money to buy 5,000 shares from his future father-in-law, and the stock flops. Then, when the old man demands immediate repayment, Hughes, with the help of his fiancee and a friend, fake his being murdered. Later, after being attacked by thieves, the young man finds himself accused of murder. When his girl friend's father arrives to set the record straight, it is revealed that Jerusalem Steel has gone over the top.

d, George D. Baker, w, (based on the story by Percival Wilde); ph, Rudolph Bergquist; art d, E. J. Shulter.

Comedy **(PR:A MPAA:NR)**

HUNCHBACK OF NOTRE DAME, THE****

(1923) 12 reels UNIV Super-Jewel bw

Lon Chaney *(Quasimodo)*, Ernest Torrence *(Clopin)*, Patsy Ruth Miller *(Esmeralda)*, Norman Kerry *(Phoebus)*, Kate Lester *(Mme. De Gondelaurier)*, Brandon Hurst *(Jehan)*, Raymond Hatton *(Gringoire)*, Tully Marshall *(Louis XI)*, Nigel De Brulier *(Dom Claude)*, Harry Van Meter *(Mons. Neufchatel)*, Gladys Brockwell *(Godule)*, Eulalie Jensen *(Marie)*, Winifred Bryson *(Fleur de Lys)*, Nick De Ruiz *(Mons. le Torteru)*, Edwin Wallock *(King's Chamberlain)*, W. Ray Meyers *(Charmolou's Assistant)*, William Parke, Sr. *(Josephus)*, John Cossar *(Judge of Court)*, Roy Laidlaw *(Charmolou)*, George MacQuarrie, Jay Hunt, Harry De Vere, Pearl Tupper, Eva Lewis, Jane Sherman, Helen Bruneau, Gladys Johnston, Cesare Gravina.

The distorted creature-servitor of the cruel Hurst—brother of De Brulier, the archdeacon of the famed cathedral—the monstrous-appearing Chaney is incited to an attack which brings the wrath of the law down on him. Saved through the help of a beautiful Gypsy girl, Miller, Chaney reciprocates when she herself is charged with stabbing Kerry, the officer she loves. Spirited to the high towers of the cathedral by the bell-ringing hunchback, she is rescued by Chaney, and then is defended against a nocturnal assault on the cathedral by Torrence's army of thieves and beggars. Ultimately, the hideous hunchback sacrifices his life to save the lovely gypsy girl who treated him with compassion. Chaney derived his characterization directly from Hugo's description of his deformed protagonist: a hideous lump, made from 40 pounds of rubber, covered his back (Charles Laughton's hump in his 1939 version, made of *papier mache*, weighed only two pounds). Coupled to the hump was a breastplate and harness made of leather that added another 30 pounds of weight and constrained his movements to a crouch. His teeth were jagged and misshapen; one sightless eye bulged grotesquely from its socket. His scurrying gait was knock-kneed and erratic. Over all but his outer garments, Chaney wore a tight suit of rubber covered with patches of animal hair. The truly hideous result considerably enhanced this saga of the beauty and the beast, one of many such that the actor was to play in. The secondary story of sociological stratification—royalty, the law, and the clergy on one hand and the thieves and beggars of Paris on the other—is brilliantly handled, with special honors attending the performance of Torrence, playing the king of the latter group contrapuntally to the royal presence of Marshall as King Louis XI. The sets are wonders, particularly the massive cathedral reconstruction and the "court of miracles": the cave of the beggars, assassins, and thieves where the mendicants heal themselves of their simulated maladies—the lame walk, the sightless see—under the provenance of their leader, the bethroned Torrence. The night assault on the cathedral, with its torch-bearing, howling mob, is a technical marvel that required Universal to borrow and beg every arc lamp and portable generator within 100 miles of the set. THE HUNCHBACK OF NOTRE DAME was Chaney's first high-budget starring picture, and it established his reputation once and for all as a major star. It also brought him into a close working relationship with the respected Irving Thalberg, then an executive at

Universal, who became the *wunderkind* at MGM responsible for much of that studio's best work. Carl Laemmle, Universal's head man, had refused to put Chaney under contract, preferring to employ him on a picture-by-picture basis. This film made the powerful Laemmle regret that decision. The "man of a thousand faces" did fine work for Universal again, but he did it on loan from MGM; Thalberg had signed him to a long-term contract. From this time on, Chaney received all the perquisites of a true Hollywood star; in every subsequent film, studio musicians Sam and Jack Feinberg were to play mood music for him on the set, a mark of arrival, a rite of passage. Director Worsley (one of his assistant directors was the 21-year-old William Wyler) has few directorial credits to his name; this is his only important picture. It is enough.

d, Wallace Worsley; w, Edward T. Lowe, Jr., Perley Poore Sheehan (based on the novel *Notre'Dame de Paris* by Victor Hugo); ph, Robert Newhard, Tony Kornman.

Drama **Cas.** **(PR:A MPAA:NR)**

HUNGRY HEARTS*** (1922) 7 reels Goldwyn bw

Bryant Washburn *(David Kaplan)*, Helen Ferguson *(Sara Levin)*, E. A. Warren *(Abraham Levin)*, Rosa Rosanova *(Hannah Levin)*, George Siegmann *(Rosenblatt)*, Otto Lederer *(Gedalyah Mindel)*, Millie Schottland *(Mishel Mindel)*, Bert Sprotte *(Cossack)*, A. Budin *(Sopkin)*, Edwin B. Tilton *(The Judge)*.

Rosanova and her family emigrate from Russia to America looking for a better life, but end up living in squalor. Then, when Siegmann, the landlord, raises their rent, Rosanova angrily damages his property. She is forced to stand trial for this, but is defended by Siegmann's nephew, Washburn, a successful lawyer who loves young Ferguson. Washburn wins the case, marries the girl, and takes the family out of the ghetto.

d, E. Mason Hopper, w, Julien Josephson (based on a novel by Anzia Yezierska); t, Montague Glass; ph, Robert Newhard.

Drama **(PR:A MPAA:NR)**

HUNTED MEN** (1930) Big/Syndicate Pictures bw

Bob Steele, Jean Reno, Lew Meehan, Mac V. Wright, Thomas G. Lingham, Clark Comstock.

Standard western formula about the good man saving the girl's ranch has only the presence of scrappy, little Steele to make it bearable.

d, J. P. McGowan; w, Sally Winters; ph, Herbert Kirkpatrick.

Western **(PR:A MPAA:NR)**

HUNTINGTOWER*** (1927, Brit.) 7 reels Walsh-Pearson-Elder/PAR bw

Sir Harry Lauder *(Dickson McCunn)*, Vera Veronia *(Princess Saskia)*, Pat Aherne *(Capt. John Heritage)*, Lilian Christine *(Mrs. McCunn)*, John Manners *(Prince Paul)*, Moore Marriott *(Speidel)*, Douglas Herald *(Leon)*, Suzanne Morris *(Mother)*, W. Cronin Wilson *(Dobson)*, Nancy Price *(Mrs. Moran)*, Jerrold Robertshaw *(Father)*, Harry Malonie *(Dougal)*.

The presence of Lauder, one of the world's greatest entertainers, made this British film about a retired Scottish grocer and a group of kids saving a Russian prince from Bolshevik agents a cut above that nation's usual product.

d, George Pearson; w, Charles Whittaker (based on the novel by John Buchan).

Action/Drama **(PR:A MPAA:NR)**

HUNTRESS, THE** (1923) 6 reels AFN bw

Colleen Moore *(Bela)*, Lloyd Hughes *(Sam Gladding)*, Russell Simpson *(Big Jack Skinner)*, Walter Long *(Joe Hagland)*, Charles Anderson *(Black Shand Frazer)*, Snitz Edwards *(Musq'oosis)*, Wilfrid North *(John Gladding)*, Helen Raymond *(Mrs. John Gladding)*, William Marion *(William Gladding)*, Lila Leslie *(Mrs William Gladding)*, Lawrence Steers *(Richard Gladding)*, Helen Walron *(Mrs. Richard Gladding)*, John Lince *(Butler)*, Lalo Encinas *(Beavertail)*, Chief Big Tree *(Otebaya)*.

Prospector Hughes decides to marry Moore, the white girl raised by native Americans after an Indian wise man makes him realize he really loves her. But first he must find her, for she has run away from the tribe to avoid marrying a brave. He does, and love wins out in the end.

d, Lynn Reynolds; w, Percy Heath (based on the novel by Hulbert Footner); ph, James C. Van Trees; art d, Milton Menasco.

Drama **(PR:A MPAA:NR)**

HURRICANE, THE* (1926) 5 reels TRU bw

Alice Lake *(The Wife)*, Stuart Holmes *(The Smuggler)*, Jack Richardson *(The Husband)*.

A stinker from start to finish. The nonsense all has to do with the dissatisfied wife of the U.S. revenue officer on the Canadian border who hates the great outdoors so much that she runs away to the city with a man who turns out to be a smuggler. At the film's end, she kills the naughty bloke and is forgiven by her husband.

d, Fred Caldwell.

Drama **(PR:A MPAA:NR)**

HURRICANE KID, THE*** (1925) 6 reels UNIV bw

Hoot Gibson *(The Hurricane Kid)*, Marion Nixon *(Joan Langdon)*, William A. Steele *Lafe Baxter)*, Arthur Machley *(Col. Langdon)*, Violet La Plante *(Joan's Friend)*, Harry Todd *(Hezekial Potts)*, Fred Humes *(Jed Hawks)*, Pal the Horse.

Gibson's flair for comedy and his rodeo skills are put to good use in this better-than-average western about a cowboy who tames a rival and a horse and then wins the big race for the girl he loves.

d, Edward Sedgwick; w, E. Richard Schayer, Raymond L. Schrock (based on a story by Will Lambert); ph, Virgil Miller; art d, Leo E. Kuter.

Western **(PR:A MPAA:NR)**

HUSBAND HUNTERS* 1/2** (1927) 6 reels TIF bw

Mae Busch *(Marie Devere)*, Charles Delaney *(Bob Garrett)*, Jean Arthur *(Letty Crane)*, Walter Hires *(Sylvester Jones)*, Duane Thompson *(Helen Gray)*, Mildred Harris *(Cynthia Kane)*, Robert Cain *(Bartley Mortimer)*, Jimmy Harrison *(Jimmy Wallace)*, Nigel Barrie *(Rex Holden)*, James Mack *(Mr. Casey)*, Marcin Asher *(Mr. Cohen)*, Fred Fisher *(Archibald Percival Springer)*.

Spicy (for its time) and highly entertaining story about a couple of wisecracking chorus girls who take in Arthur, a small town innocent with show business ambitions. The girl gets involved with a rotter, but after he is killed in a train accident she settles down with the fellow who was right for her all along. Great performances by dependable Busch and Arthur, who was on her way to stardom.

d, John G. Adolfi; w, Esther Shulkin (based on a story by Douglas Bronston); ph, Joseph A. Dubray, Steve Norton; ed, Harold Young; art d, Edwin B. Willis.

Comedy **(PR:A MPAA:NR)**

HUSBANDS AND LOVERS* (1924) 8 reels Louis B. Mayer/FN bw

Lewis S. Stone *(James Livingston)*, Florence Vidor *(Grace Livingston)*, Dale Fuller *(Marie)*, Winter Hall *(Robert Stanton)*, Edithe Yorke *(Mrs. Stanton)*.

Feeble programmer about a husband who chides his wife for letting herself go, which leads her to apply a little makeup and become a flapper. Her new appearance causes her husband's best friend to fall head over heels, and he proposes marriage. However, at the last minute, the husband wins her back, and the friend is left standing at the altar.

d, John M. Stahl; w, A. P. Younger (based on a story by Frances Irene Reels, Stahl); t, Madge Tyrone; ph, Antonio Gaudio; ed, Robert Kern, Margaret Booth; art d, Jack Holden.

Comedy/Drama **(PR:A MPAA:NR)**

HUSBANDS FOR RENT*** (1927) 6 reels WB bw

Owen Moore *(Herbert Willis)*, Helene Costello *(Molly Devoe)*, Kathryn Perry *(Doris Knight)*, John Miljan *(Hugh Frazer)*, Claude Gillingwater *(Sir Reginald Knight)*, Arthur Hoyt *(Waldo Squibbs)*, Helen Lynch *(A Maid)*, Hugh Herbert *(A Valet)*.

Gillingwater is pleased that his nephew Moore is about to announce his engagement to Perry, his ward. But then Perry falls for Miljan, and Moore gets hot under the collar for the beauteous Costello. The uncle persuades them to have a double wedding, but on the night before the service, Miljan and Costello, in a veritable explosion of passion, decide to elope. The uncle, who is stuck with all the food and wine, not to mention the band, talks Moore and Perry into getting married themselves, and strangely enough it all works out rather nicely after all.

d, Henry Lehrman; w, C. Graham Baker (based on a story by Edwin Justus Mayer); t, Joseph Jackson, James A. Starr; ph, Barney McGill; ed, Clarence Kolster.

Comedy/Romance **(PR:A MPAA:NR)**

HUSH MONEY** (1921) 5 reels REA/PAR bw

Alice Brady *(Evelyn Murray)*, George Fawcett *(Alexander Murray)*, Lawrence Wheat *(Bert Van Vliet)*, Harry Benham *(Bishop Deems)*, Jerry Devine *(Terry McGuire)*.

Fair little programmer has socialite Brady fleeing the scene after hitting a newsboy with her automobile. She was, however, observed by a garage attendant who forces her father to pay hush money. Later, when she meets the bishop of New York who is raising funds for a youth foundation, the young woman is conscience-stricken, visits the boy in the hospital, and against the wishes of her father and fiance, takes him under her wing.

d&w, Charles Maigne (based on a story by Samuel Merwin); ph, Gilbert Warrenton.

Drama **(PR:A MPAA:NR)**

HUTCH STIRS 'EM UP*** (1923, Brit.) 5 reels ID bw

Charles Hutchison *(Hurricane Hutch)*, Joan Barry *(Joan)*, Malcolm Tod *(Tom Grey)*, Gibson Gowland *(Sir Arthur Blackross)*, Sunday Wilshin *(Mrs. Grey)*, Aubrey Fitzgerald *(Cruddas)*, Violet Forbes *(Mrs. Cruddas)*.

Hutchison, the very popular U.S. star of action pictures and serials, was brought to England to headline in this curious film about a cowboy who saves a girl from a mad squire's chamber of tortures.

d, Frank H. Crane; w, Eliot Stannard (based on the novel *The Hawk of Rede* by Harry Harding).

Action **(PR:A MPAA:NR)**

HYPOCRITES*** (1914) 4 reels Bosworth bw

The screen's greatest woman director, Weber, scored an artistic triumph with this allegorical film which featured a lovely young naked lady set against nature's beauty. She represented the reincarnated spirit of a priest who was stoned to death earlier by a mob of hypocrites for erecting a beautiful statue. Weber, who was a devout Christian, presented this potentially shocking theme with great dignity and taste.

d&w, Lois Weber; ph, Dal Clawson.

Drama **(PR:A MPAA:NR)**

I

I LOVE YOU*** (1918) 7 reels Kay-Bee/TRI bw

Alma Rubens *(Felice)*, John Lince *(Ravello)*, Francis McDonald *(Jules Mardon)*, Wheeler Oakman *(Armande de Gautier)*, Frederick Vroom *(Prince del Chinay)*, Lillian Langdon, Peaches Jackson.

Rubens is well cast as the beautiful Italian peasant the villagers refer to as "The Passion Flower." A French artist passes through and begs to paint her. While this is being done they seem to fall in love, but without warning he moves on, leaving the girl brokenhearted. Sometime later, the painting becomes the sensation of Paris, and a young millionaire is completely taken by the image on the canvas. He asks the artist how to find her, seeks the girl out, and they marry. The union seems perfect until the painter arrives on the scene and attempts to seduce the girl who once loved him. The husband discovers them, thinks the worst, and orders his wife out of the house. Finally he comes to learn the truth, there is a reconciliation, and the artist gets what's coming to him.

d, Walter Edwards; w, Catherine Carr; ph, C. Gus Peterson.

Drama **(PR:A MPAA:NR)**

I WANT TO FORGET*** (1918) 5 reels FOX bw

Evelyn Nesbit *(Varda Deering)*, Russel Thaw *(Chauffeur's Son)*, Henry Clive *(Lieut. John Long)*, Alphonz Ethier *(August Von Grossman)*, William R. Dunn *(Helgar)*, Jane Jennings *(Cordelia Deering)*, Blanche Craig.

Nesbit (best remembered as the woman in the middle of the scandal in which her husband Harry K. Thaw shot famed architect Stanford White) is really quite good as the vamp who wraps men around her little finger. Then she meets and falls in love with handsome, decent, and square-jawed Clive. The war breaks out and Clive goes off to fight. Inspired by his patriotism, Nesbit joins the secret service and finds good use for her seductive talents when she goes to work on one of her old admirers, the nasty, guttural-voiced hun, Ethier. There is plenty of gunplay and lots of action in this thoroughly enjoyable picture, which really moves.

d&w, James Kirkwood (based on a story by Harry O. Hoyt, Hamilton Smith).

War **(PR:A MPAA:NR)**

IBANEZ' TORRENT (SEE: TORRENT, THE, 1926)

ICE FLOOD, THE*** (1926) 6 reels UNIV-Jewel bw

Kenneth Harlan *(Jack De Quincy)*, Viola Dana *(Marie O'Neill)*, Frank Hagney *(Dum-Dum Pete)*, Fred Kohler *("Cougar" Kid)*, De Witt Jennings *(James O'Neill)*, Kitty Barlow *(Cook)*, James Gordon *(Thomas De Quincy)*.

Good programmer about a young Oxford graduate who goes to his father's lumber camp using an assumed name to clean things up. Before the picture is over the lad, who happens to be the light heavyweight champion of his campus, rids the place of bootleggers and the thugs who have been trying to take over. He also wins the girl after saving her from the disaster referred to in the title. The ice floe scenes are a bit on the disappointing side, but then after WAY DOWN EAST what isn't?

d, George B. Seitz; w, James O. Spearing, Gladys Lehman, Seitz (based on the story "The Brute Breaker" by Johnston McCulley); ph, Merritt Gerstad.

(PR:A MPAA:NR)

ICEBOUND*** (1924) 7 reels FP/PAR bw

Richard Dix *(Ben Jordan)*, Lois Wilson *(Jane Crosby)*, Helen Du Bois *(Emma Jordan)*, Edna May Oliver *(Hannah)*, Vera Reynolds *(Nettie Moore)*, Mary Foy *(Sadie Fellowes)*, Joseph Depew *(Orin Fellowes)*, Ethel Wales *(Ella Jordan)*, Alice Chapin *(Mrs. Jordan)*, John Daly Murphy *(Henry Jordan)*, Frank Shannon *(Judge Bradford)*.

Based on a successful Broadway play, the movie follows closely the story of a young man (Dix) who runs away from his New England home after accidentally setting fire to the family barn. Upon his mother's death, he returns home to find that she left everything to Wilson, her ward. Wilson loves Dix and offers to give him work and pay the money necessary to keep him out of prison. She later decides to transfer the estate to his name and leave town, but then discovers him romancing his cousin Reynolds. At the last minute, however, Dix sees the light and asks Wilson to become his wife.

d, William De Mille; w, Clara Beranger (based on the play by Owen Davis); ph, Guy Wilky.

Drama **(PR:A MPAA:NR)**

ICED BULLET, THE*** (1917) 5 reels Kay-Bee/TRI bw

William Desmond *(Horace Lee)*, Robert McKim *(Donald Greene)*, J. Barney Sherry *(Richard Deering)*, Margaret Thompson *(Evelyn Deering)*, J.J. Dowling *(The Butler)*, Jerry Storm *(Butler's Son)*, Louis Durham *(Joe, Lee's Assistant)*, J. Frank Burke *(Specialist)*.

The presence of handsome, muscular (soon to be the king of the serials) Desmond, plus good direction by Barker and a clever script by Sullivan, made this detective film—with just the right amount of comedy and action—a winner.

d, Reginald Barker; w, C. Gardner Sullivan.

Mystery **(PR:A MPAA:NR)**

IDAHO RED** (1929) 6 reels FBO bw

Tom Tyler *(Andy Thornton)*, Patricia Caron *(Mary Regan)*, Frankie Darro *(Tadpole)*, Barney Furey *(Dave Lucas)*, Lew Meehan *(George Wilkins, Sheriff)*.

In this B western, ex-Marine Tyler befriends an orphaned boy and breaks up a counterfeit ring operating out of his ranch in Idaho. An exciting chase sequence has Tyler's horse outrunning an automobile, and Tyler leaping from the horse to the car to capture the beady-eyed villains.

d, Robert De Lacey; w, Frank Howard Clark; t, Helen Gregg; ph, Nick Musuraca; ed, Leona De Lacey.

Western **(PR:A MPAA:NR)**

IDLE HANDS** (1921) 6 reels Park-Whiteside/PIO bw

Gail Kane *(Gloria Travers)*, Thurston Hall *(Henry Livingston)*, J. Herbert Frank *(Adolph Pym)*, William Betchel *(Commissioner Deering)*, Norbert Wicki *(Mock Lee)*, Nellie Burt *(Marjorie Travers)*, Paul Lane *(Robert Deering)*.

Shortly after coming to New York to launch a business career, Burt is kidnaped while visiting Chinatown. Her older sister, Kane, appeals to the mayor for help and he puts the vice commissioner, Betchel, on the case. It turns out that Betchel is actually an underworld kingpin with a drug addict for a son. But Burt is rescued, the criminals arrested, and Kane receives a proposal of marriage from the mayor.

d, Frank Reicher; w, J. Clarkson Miller (based on a story by Willard King Bradley); ph, George Benoit.

Crime **(PR:A MPAA:NR)**

IDLE RICH, THE*** (1921) 5 reels Metro bw

Bert Lytel *(Samuel Weatherbee)*, Virginia Valli *(Mattie Walling)*, John Davidson *(Dillingham Coolidge)*, Joseph Harrington *(Judge O'Reilly)*, Thomas Jefferson *(Uncle Coolidge)*, Victory Bateman *(Mrs. O'Reilly)*, Leigh Wyant *(Jane Coolidge)*, Max Davidson *(The Taylor)*.

When a wealthy young man discovers that his fortune is gone, he goes into the junk business, makes another million, and marries the girl who stuck by him. At the finale he gives the raspberry to the one-time friends who dropped him like a hot potato.

d, Maxwell Karger; w, June Mathis (based on the story "Junk" by Kenneth Harris); ph, Arthur Martinelli; art d, Julian Garnsey.

Comedy **(PR:A MPAA:NR)**

IDOL DANCER, THE** (1920) 7 reels FN bw

Richard Barthelmess *(Dan McGuire, the Beachcomber)*, Clarine Seymour *(Mary/Wite ALMOND FLOWER)*, Creighton Hale *(Walter Kinkaid)*, George MacQuarrie *(Rev. Franklin Blythe)*, Kate Bruce *(Mrs. Blythe)*, Porter Strong *(Peter, a Native Man of the Cloth)*, Anders Randolf *(Blackbirder)*, Walter James *(Chief Wando)*, Thomas Carr *(Donald Blythe)*, Herbert Sutch *(Old Thomas)*, Adolphe Lestina *(Black Slave)*, Ben Grauer *(Native Boy)*, Walter Kolomoku *(Native Musician)*, Florence Short *(Pansy)*.

When D. W. Griffith and his party set sail from Florida for Nassau in 1919 to shoot exteriors for THE IDOL DANCER and THE LOVE FLOWER, they ran into a tremendous storm and wisely decided to dock at a friendly port. Their three-day disappearance made headlines all over the world, and there were cynics who accused the director of pulling off a sensational publicity stunt. If this is true, then it was a wise move on the master's part, as these are two of his weakest films. THE IDOL DANCER, with its story of the regeneration of a drunken American beachcomber, an attack by natives stirred up by a nasty white opportunist on a near-helpless mission, and ultimate conversion of the minister's adopted native daughter, is even suspected by some students of Griffith's work to have been, in reality, directed by one of his less-inspired assistants. There is nothing to substantiate this, save the quality of the picture itself, but one is hard-pressed to find anything to praise here except the performances of Barthelmess and Seymour who, if she had not died in 1920 at the age of 21, would have become one of the movies' brightest stars.

d, D. W. Griffith; w, S. E. V. Taylor (based on the story "Blood of the Covenanters" by Gordon Ray Young); ph, G. W. Bitzer; ed, James Smith.

Drama **(PR:A MPAA:NR)**

IDOL OF THE NORTH, THE*** (1921) 6 reels FP/PAR bw

Dorothy Dalton *(Colette Brissac)*, Edwin August *(Martin Bates)*, E. J. Ratcliffe *(Lucky Folsom)*, Riley Hatch *(Ham Devlin)*, Jules Cowles *(One-Eye Wallace)*, Florence St. Leonard *(A Soubrette)*, Jessie Arnold *(The Big Blond)*, Marguerite Marsh *(Gloria Waldron)*, Joe King *(Sgt. McNair)*.

Dalton plays a dancehall girl from the Canadian Northwest who spurns the advances of New Yorker Ratcliffe. This causes him to marry gold digger Marsh, who is really in love with engineer August. Subsequently August, who is hitting the bottle, staggers into town and is forced by the miners to marry Dalton. Later, when Marsh and Ratcliffe show up, the gold digger sets out to seduce the now sober engineer and is brought to her senses only after Dalton wings her husband with a "shootin' iron."

d, R. William Neill; w, Frank S. Beresford (based on a story by J. Clarkson Miller); t, Tom McNamara; ph, Lawrence E. Williams.

Adventure **(PR:A MPAA:NR)**

IDOL OF THE STAGE, THE** (1916) 5 reels GAU bw

Malcolm Williams, Charles W. Travis, John Mackin, Lucille Taft, Richard Garrick, James Levering, Helen Marten, Charles Winston, Harry Chira, James Arbuckle, Jr., Allan Robinson.

When his wife becomes ill, an actor takes a job with a distant stock company to cover the expenses. He gets into trouble with a young woman and is sent to prison. The wife recovers, goes to the town to await his release, but is taken away by an ex-convict. The husband, believing that she has been unfaithful, refuses to ever see her again. Years pass and the former actor, now a successful businessman, encounters a young newsboy and is drawn to him. When he realizes that this lad is his son and the truth about his wife is revealed, the family is reunited and the happiness which so long eluded them is now theirs in abundance.

d, Richard Garrick; w, Paul M. Bryan.

Drama **(PR:A MPAA:NR)**

IF*** (1916, Brit.) 5 reels FP/Fenning bw

Iris Delaney *(Madame X)*, Ernest Leicester *(Armstrong)*, Judd Green *(Count Hoffman)*.

Interesting British war film about a lady thief who aids a detective in stopping a German count from carrying out a plot to divert the weapons needed to defend London. They pull off this feat by employing bogus airships, while secret guns are positioned to destroy the city.

d, Stuart Kinder.

War **(PR:A MPAA:NR)**

IF FOUR WALLS TOLD** (1922, Brit.) 6 reels British Super/JUR bw

Lillian Hall Davis *(Martha Tregoning)*, Fred Paul *(Jan Rysling/Tom)*, Campbell Gullan *(David Rysling)*, John Stuart *(Ned Mason)*, Minna Grey *(Elizabeth Rysling)*, Enid King *(Clare Sturgis)*, Pollie Emery *(Mrs. Sturgis)*, Somers Bellamy (Toby Crouch), Marie Ault.

Set in Cornwall, this British drama tells of a man who adopts his brother's illegitimate son but is ultimately rewarded when a body containing a will is washed ashore.

p, G. B. Samuelson; d, Fred Paul; w, Walter Summers (based on the play by Edward Percy).

Drama **(PR:A MPAA:NR)**

IF I MARRY AGAIN** (1925) 8 reels FN bw

Doris Kenyon *(Jocelyn Margot)*, Lloyd Hughes *(Charlie Jordan)*, Frank Mayo *(Jeffrey Wingate)*, Hobart Bosworth *(John Jordan)*, Anna Q. Nilsson *(Alicia Wingate)*, Myrtle Stedman *(Mme. Margot)*, Dorothy Brock *(Sonny)*.

Socialite Hughes falls in love with and marries, against his father's will, Kenyon, the daughter of a notorious San Francisco madam. As punishment, Hughes is sent to manage one of the family's plantations in the tropics. They have a child and, after four years, the unrelenting old man sends Mayo, his personal manager, to buy Kenyon off. Mayo arrives shortly after Hughes' death by fever, and Kenyon vows that her son shall have what is due him as sole heir to her husband's name. Returning to San Francisco, she decides to reopen her mother's bordello and, as a means of humiliating and blackmailing her former father-in-law, plans to invite the cream of society. In the end she is unable to go through with the scheme, which causes the old boy to realize her true worth, and she and her son are welcomed into his life. Mayo, in the meantime, has fallen in love with her and at the film's end proposes marriage.

d, John Francis Dillon; sup, Earl Hudson; w, Kenneth B. Clarke (based on a story by Gilbert Frankau); ph, James C. Van Trees; ed, Marion Fairfax, LeRoy Stone; art d, Milton Menasco.

Drama **(PR:A MPAA:NR)**

IF I WERE QUEEN½** (1922) 6 reels R-C/FBO bw

Ethel Clayton *(Ruth Townley)*, Andree Lejon *(Oluf)*, Warner Baxter *(Valdemir)*, Victory Bateman *(Aunt Ollie)*, Murdock MacQuarrie *(Duke of Wortz)*, Genevieve Blinn *(Sister Ursula)*.

To cash in on the PRISONER OF ZENDA craze then sweeping the country, FBO produced this handsomely mounted story of an American heiress who is mistaken for a princess by the prince of one of those comic-opera Balkan kingdoms, and becomes his bride. Not only the kingdoms are imaginary in this clunker.

d, Wesley Ruggles; w, Carol Warren (based on "The Three Cornered Kingdom" by Du Vernet Rabell); ph, Joseph A. Dubray.

Romance **(PR:A MPAA:NR)**

IF I WERE SINGLE*** (1927) 7 reels WB bw

Conrad Nagel *(Ted Howard)*, May McAvoy *(May Howard)*, Myrna Loy *(Joan)*, Andre Beranger *(Claude)*.

Pleasant little diversion about a happily married man who, nonetheless, flirts with a pretty girl he meets on a golf outing. He also forgets his cigarette lighter, and when his wife later introduces him to her old school friend—the same lady—she returns his lighter. This causes their first spat and, to teach him a lesson, the wife inaugurates a flirtation with her music teacher. As luck would have it, the two couples find themselves in the same auto stranded in the middle of nowhere. It is then that they all make the decision to cut out the flirting and return to the norm.

d, Roy Del Ruth; w, Robert Lord; t, Joseph Jackson; ph, Ed Du Par; ed, Ralph Dawson.

Comedy **(PR:A MPAA:NR)**

IF ONLY JIM** (1921) 5 reels UNIV bw

Harry Carey *(Jim Golden)*, Carol Halloway *(Miss Amay Dot Denniham)*, Ruth Royce *(Miss Richards)*, Duke Lee *(Keno)*, Roy Coulson *(Henry)*, Charles Brinley *(Parky)*, George Bunny *(Uncle Johnny)*, Joseph Hazelton *(Bill Bones)*, Minnie Prevost *(A Squaw)*, Thomas Smith *(Kid)*, Pal the Dog.

Carey is a shiftless gold miner who finds an abandoned baby, and the responsibility changes his life. Through hard work his claim becomes a bonanza, which leads crooked Brinley to try to take it. Carey's guns have their say, however, and the mine is saved. Carey also wins the love of Halloway, the postmistress who turns out to be the perfect mother for the little one.

d, Jacques Jaccard; w, William C. Hull (based on the novel *Bruvver Jim's Baby* by Philip Verrill Mighels); ph, Harry Fowler.

Western **(PR:A MPAA:NR)**

IF THOU WERT BLIND** (1917, Brit.) 5 reels CL/New Bio bw

Ben Webster *(Hayden Strong)*, Evelyn Boucher *(Christine Leslie)*, Joan Legge *(Mary Barton)*, Minna Grey, Clifford Pembroke, Sydney Lewis Ransome, Harry Lorraine.

British love story about a woman who returns to the sculptor she has always loved after being told in a dream that his blindness would render him helpless.

d, F. Martin Thornton; w, Kenelm Foss.

Drama **(PR:A MPAA:NR)**

IF WOMEN ONLY KNEW*

(1921) 6 r eels J. N. Haulty-Gardner Hunting/R-C bw

Robert Gordon *(Maurice Travers)*, Blanche Davenport *(Mrs. Travers)*, Harold Vosburgh *(Prof. Storey)*, Frederick Burton *(Donna's Father)*, Charles Lane *(Dr. John Strong)*, Leon Gendron *(Billie Thorne)*, Madelyn Clare *(Madeline Marshall)*, Virginia Lee *(Donna Wayne)*, Lila Lee.

Through great personal sacrifice on the part of his mother, Gordon is able to attend college. He goofs off, however, and fails to graduate. Then he marries rich girl Lee and the two move to New York where their life becomes one big party. When his mother dies, Clare, an orphan who has been living with her, decides to remain on because of her secret love for Gordon. Growing bored with her husband (probably because of some latent streak of decency) Lee runs off with a wealthy admirer, and Gordon marries Clare as soon as his divorce is finalized.

d, E. H. Griffith; w, Gardner Hunting (based loosely on *La Physiologie du Mariage* by Honore de Balzac); ph, William McCoy; art d, David G. Flynn.

Drama **(PR:A MPAA:NR)**

IF YOU BELIEVE IT, IT'S SO*** (1922) 7 reels FP/PAR bw

Thomas Meighan *(Chick Harris)*, Pauline Starke *(Alvah Morley)*, Joseph Dowling *(Ezra Wood, a Patriarch)*, Theodore Roberts *(Sky Blue)*, Charles Ogle *(Col. Williams)*, Laura Anson *(Tessie Wyngate)*, Charles French *(Frank Tine, Realty Agent)*, Tom Kennedy *(Bartender)*, Ed Brady *(Constable)*.

Meighan is a big city crook out to swindle an elderly gentleman. Small town life—and especially one of its female citizens— completely regenerates him, however, and he even takes the money one of his crooked pals was going to use for a sting and uses it to build a church. Good performances all around, but Roberts steals the show as "Sky Blue," the confidence man.

d, Tom Forman; w, Waldemar Young (based on a story by Perley Poore Sheehan); ph, Harry Perry.

Crime/Drama **(PR:A MPAA:NR)**

IF YOUTH BUT KNEW** (1926, Brit.) 8 reels Reciprocity bw

Godfrey Tearle *(Dr. Martin Summers)*, Lilian Hall-Davis *(Dora/Doreen)*, Wyndham Standing *(Sir Ormsby Ledger)*, Mary Ordette *(Loanda)*, Mary Rorke *(Mrs. Romney)*, Patrick Waddington *(Arthur Noel-Vane)*, May Beamish *(Mrs. Sumner)*, Minnie Rayner *(Martha)*, Forrester Harvey *(Amos)*, Donald Walcott *(Aulole)*.

This British love story, set in Nigeria, tells of a doctor who has fallen in love with the beautiful daughter of an ex-sweetheart, but selflessly surrenders her to the younger chap she loves.

p, G. B. Samuelson; d, George A. Cooper; w, Harry Engholm (based on the play by K. C. Spiers).

Romance/Drama **(PR:A MPAA:NR)**

I'LL GET HIM YET**** (1919) 5 reels New Art/PAR bw

Dorothy Gish *(Susy Faraday, Alias Skinflint Jones)*, George Fawcett *(Bradford Warrington Jones)*, Richard Barthelmess *(Scoop McCreedy)*, Ralph Graves *(Harold Packard)*, Edward Pell *(Robert E. Hamilton)*, Porter Strong *(William R. Craig)*, Wilbur Higby.

Perfect property for Gish, one of the screen's greatest comediennes. She plays the daughter of a millionaire, out to land a dashing newspaper reporter who has a thing about being considered a fortune hunter, so Gish swears never to touch a penny of her father's money. What she doesn't tell hubby is that she is worth $5 million on her own. When the superintendent, attorney, and general manager of the railroad she owns show up at their suburban home, Gish's desperate attempt to keep her wealth a secret causes her husband to become jealous of her "male friends." This delicious comedic premise is played to perfection by Gish, and in the end her husband is so ashamed of his behavior that he consents to become the president of the railroad.

d, Elmer Clifton; w, (based on a story by Harry Carr); ph, Lee Garmes, John Leezer.

Comedy **(PR:A MPAA:NR)**

IMMEDIATE LEE*** (1916) 5 reels AM bw

Frank Borzage *(Immediate Lee)*, Anna Little *(Beulah)*, Jack Richardson *(Hurley)*, William Stowell, Charles Newton.

This above average western was directed by and featured Borzage, who would go on to become one of filmdom's greatest directors. Borzage convinces Little, the dancehall girl, to go straight. Then after being knifed by cattle rustler Richardson, he tracks the outlaw down, claims revenge with his gun, and captures the gang.

d, Frank Borzage; w, Kenneth B. Clarke.

Western **(PR:A MPAA:NR)**

IMMIGRANT, THE*** (1915) 5 reels LAS bw

Valeska Suratt *(Masha)*, Theodore Roberts *(J. J. Walton)*, Thomas Meighan *(David Harding)*, Jane Wolf *(Olga)*, Raymond Hatton *(Munsing)*, Ernest Joy *(Walton's Partner)*, Gertrude Keller *(Walton's Housekeeper)*.

Suratt (who would become a rival to fellow FOX actress Theda Bara in the vamp department) is a Russian girl wronged by a nasty construction company owner. After being raped, she consents to marry the man but falls in love with engineering competitor Meighan, who beats her husband out of a lucrative dam contract, inspiring the rotter to blow the facility up. In doing so, however, he is killed and Meighan is bankrupted. The picture ends with Suratt pledging her love, and the couple starting out fresh together.

d, George Melford; w, Marion Fairfax.

Drama **(PR:A MPAA:NR)**

IMMORTALS OF BONNIE SCOTLAND
(SEE: LIFE OF ROBERT BURNS, THE, 1926, Brit.)

IMPOSSIBLE CATHERINE*** (1919) 6 reels Virginia Pearson/Pathe bw

Virginia Pearson *(Catherine Kimberly)*, J. H. Gilmour *(Grant Kimberly)*, William B. Davidson *(John Henry Jackson)*, Ed Roseman *(Rosky)*, James Hill *(Kewpie the Camp Cook)*, Mabel McQuade *(Dorothy Kimberly)*, John Walker *(Herbert Drake)*, Sheldon Lewis *(White Cloud)*.

Modern version of William Shakespeare's *Taming of the Shrew* about the daughter of a multimillionaire who is impossible in every way, until she meets a wealthy young man who drags her off to his lumber camp and forces her to "act like a *woman*." After he is hurt in a fight protecting her honor, she realizes the "silliness" of her former attitude and allows herself to fall in love with him.

d, John B. O'Brien; w, Frank S. Beresford; ph, Lawrence E. Williams.

Comedy/Drama **(PR:A MPAA:NR)**

IMPOSSIBLE MRS. BELLEW, THE 1/2** (1922) 8 reels FP/LAS bw

Gloria Swanson *(Betty Bellew)*, Robert Cain *(Lance Bellew)*, Conrad Nagel *(John Helstan)*, Richard Wayne *(Jerry Woodruff)*, Frank Elliott *(Count Radisloff)*, Gertrude Astor *(Alice Granville)*, June Elvidge *(Naomi Templeton)*, Herbert Standing *(Rev. Dr. Helstan)*, Mickey Moore *(Lance Bellew, Jr., Age 4)*, Pat Moore *(Lance Bellew, Jr., Age 6)*, Helen Dunbar *(Aunt Agatha)*, Arthur Hull *(Attorney Potter)*, Clarence Burton *(Detective)*.

The only impressive thing about THE IMPOSSIBLE MRS. BELLEW is Swanson's elaborate wardrobe. The movie is about a playboy husband (Cain) who returns home after a night with his mistress and finds his wife, Swanson, innocently in the presence of a male neighbor. He flies into a rage, shoots the fellow, and is arrested. For the sake of her family, Swanson remains silent during the trial, causing the jury to decide that her husband was only guilty of practicing the unwritten law. For this, she loses her reputation and possession of their little boy. Crushed by this turn of events, Swanson sails to Europe where she eventually becomes part of a fast-living set, headed by a noted libertine (Elliott). The disillusioned and vulnerable lady is about to fall into his clutches when, at the suggestion of his aunt, the husband rushes to Europe, realizes his error, and brings his wife home.

d, Sam Wood; w, Percy Heath, Monte M. Katterjohn (based on the novel by David Lisle); ph, Alfred Gilks.

Drama **(PR:A MPAA:NR)**

IMPOSSIBLE WOMAN, THE*** (1919, Brit.) 5 reels ID bw

Constance Collier *(Mme. Kraska)*, Langhorne Burton *(Gregory Jardine)*, Christine Rayner *(Karen)*, Alan Byrne *(Edwin Drew)*, Edith Craig *(Mrs. Talcotte)*.

Peter Sellers, Alastair Sim, and Alec Guinness would carry on the British comedy tradition which was established in films like this one about an arty aunt and her poetry-writing boy friend, who create all kinds of difficulties when her ward marries a lawyer.

d, Meyrick Milton; w, (based on the play by Haddon Chambers and the novel *Tante* by Anne Sedgwick).

Comedy **(PR:A MPAA:NR)**

IMPOSTER, THE** (1918) 5 reels MUT bw

Ann Murdock, David Powell, Lionel Adams, Richie Ling, Charlotte Granville, Eleanor Seybolt, Edyth Latimer, Charles Mussette, Anita Rothe.

A girl living with her aunt in a small New England town sings in the church choir and is taken in by a phony music teacher, who claims he can make an opera star of her in six months. She goes to New York, finds his studio closed by the police and, before long, is destitute. At the invitation of a wealthy, older man, she innocently accompanies him to his apartment, where they encounter a friend of his wife. To cover the potential indiscretion, the older man introduces the girl as his sister-in-law. A family of social climbers overhears this and, because of the millionaire's clout, they pursue a friendship with the girl, which leads to her attending a lavish party at their summer home. There she meets a handsome and prosperous young man who falls madly in love with her.

d, Del Henderson; w, Anthony Kelly (based on a play by Michael Morton, Leonard Merrick).

Drama **(PR:A MPAA:NR)**

IMPULSE** (1922) 5 reels Berwilla/Arrow bw

Neva Gerber *(Julia Merrifield)*, Jack Dougherty *(Robert Addis)*, Goldie Madden *(Virginia Howard)*, Douglas Gerrard *(David Usher)*, Ashton Dearholt *(Count Sansone)*, Helen Gilmore *(Mrs. Cameron)*, Miss Grey *(Felicia)*.

Deserted by her husband, working girl Gerber spends two weeks at a luxury hotel posing as a society person. There she meets millionaire Dougherty and they fall in love. When returning home by train, there is a terrible wreck which separates the two, and Gerber returns to her tedious job. Later, to help a friend, she assumes the guilt for a crime, then runs off and takes a job as companion to the elderly Gilmore. It is then that her missing husband turns up plotting to rob the old lady. Gerber, of course, at the risk of her own imprisonment, prevents this from happening, and as fate usually had it in the world of B movies, Gilmore's nephew turns out to be none other than Dougherty, who forgives Gerber for her little fib, and they spend the rest of their lives basking in luxurious bliss.

p, Ben Wilson; d, Norval MacGregor; w, J. Grubb Alexander (based on the story "Her Unknown Knight" by Maude Woodruff Newell).

Drama **(PR:A MPAA:NR)**

IN AGAIN-OUT AGAIN*** (1917) 5 reels Fairbanks/ART bw

Douglas Fairbanks *(Teddy Rutherford)*, Arline Pretty *(Jane Smith)*, Walter Walker *(Her Father)*, Arnold Lucy *(Amos Jennings Ford)*, Helen Greene *(Pacifice)*, Albert Parker *(Jerry)*, Bull Montana *(The Burglar)*, Ada Gilman *(His Mother)*, Frank Lalor *(The Druggist)*, Betty Tyrel *(The Nurse)*, Spike Robinson *(The Trusty)*, Erich von Stroheim.

Biting and hilarious Loos script about a young man, Fairbanks, dedicated to military preparedness (this was filmed on the eve of our entrance into WW I), who breaks up with his pacifist fiancee. After tying one on, he lands in the pokey and falls madly in love with the jailor's daughter. He is released before his 30 day stretch is served, and Fairbanks' attempts to break *into* prison are among some of his funniest motion picture moments. There is also a development in the plot which calls for Fairbanks to escape a lynching party, and this provides the opportunity for plenty of action and stunts.

d, John Emerson; w, Anita Loos; ph, Victor Fleming; art d, Erich von Stroheim.

Comedy/Adventure **(PR:A MPAA:NR)**

IN BAD** (1918) 5 reels AM bw

William Russell, Francelia Billington, Bull Montana, Carl Stockdale, Lucille Ward, Harvey Clark, Fred Smith.

Typically entertaining Russell actioner about a man who proves his decency to his family and girl, after beating out—and up—a band of cutthroats for a fabulous buried treasure in the Yucatan.

d, Edward Sloman; w, (based on a story by Raymond L. Schrock).

Adventure **(PR:A MPAA:NR)**

IN BORROWED PLUMES* (1926) 6 reels Welcome Pictures/Arrow bw

Marjorie Daw *(Mildred Grantley/Countess D'Autreval)*, Niles Welch *(Philip Dean)*, Arnold Daly *(Sam Wassup)*, Louise Carter *(Clara Raymond)*, Peggy Kelly *(Mrs. Harrison)*, Wheeler Oakman *(Jack Raymond)*, Dagmar Godowski *(Clarice)*.

Daw, an impoverished girl from a society background with a yen for the stage, passes herself off as a countess and meets a very prominent family. Before long, she and one of the family (Welch) are madly in love, so it comes as somewhat of a shock when a woman claiming to be the real countess arrives on the scene and asks to be introduced to Welch's family. Welch's mother becomes suspicious on meeting her, hires a private detective, and it is discovered that the woman is actually an international jewel thief. Finally, the *true* countess does make her entrance, becomes enchanted by Daw, and is the very first to suggest that the sweethearts should marry.

d, Victor Hugo Halperin.

Drama **(PR:A MPAA:NR)**

IN EVERY WOMAN'S LIFE** (1924) 7 reels AFN bw

Virginia Vale *(Sara Langford)*, Lloyd Hughes *(Julian Greer)*, Marc MacDermott *(Count Coti Desanges)*, George Fawcett *(Douglas Greer)*, Vera Lewis *(Diana Lansdale)*, Ralph Lewis *(Captain)*, Stuart Holmes *(Charles Carleton)*, John Sainpolis *(Dr. Philip Logan)*.

Vale, a beautiful American girl living in Paris, is pursued by three men—an elderly count (MacDermott), a married man, and the man she loves (Hughes). The count proves his love for her by rescuing Hughes from the sea—an act of heroism which costs him his eyesight—and later shooting the married man when he tries to attack Vale.

p, M. C. Levee; d, Irving Cummings; w, Albert Shelby Le Vino (based on the novel *Belonging* by Olive Wadsley); ph, Arthur L. Todd; ed, Charles J. Hunt; art d, Jack Okey.

Drama **(PR:A MPAA:NR)**

IN FAST COMPANY 1/2** (1924) 6 reels Carlos/TRU bw

Richard Talmadge *(Perry Whitman, Jr.)*, Mildred Harris *(Barbara Belden)*, Sheldon Lewis *(Drexel Craig)*, Douglas Gerrard *(Reginald Chichester)*, Jack Herrick *(The "Bolivian Bull")*, Charles Clary *(Perry's Father)*, Snitz Edwards *(Mike Ricketts)*, Lydia Yeamans Titus *(Maid)*.

The plot never really mattered in a Talmadge movie—it was the thrills and stunts the audience paid to see, and in this case they were not disappointed. Talmadge is a college student who celebrates his expulsion from school by throwing a lavish party. His father disowns him, but after he saves a beautiful and wealthy girl from kidnapers, the father forgives the lad and offers his blessing to their marriage.

d, James W. Horne; w, Garrett Elsden Fort (based on a story by Alfred A. Cohn); ph, William Marshall.

Adventure **(PR:A MPAA:NR)**

IN FOLLY'S TRAIL*** (1920) 5 reels UNIV bw

Carmel Myers *(Lita O'Farrell)*, Charles Howard *(Thomas Holding)*, George B. Williams *(Max Goldberg)*, Arthur Clayton, Viola Lind, W. H. Bainbridge, Beth Ivins.

This film marked Myers' return to the screen after a successful run in musical comedy. She is radiant here as a show girl who almost marries millionaire Williams, known on Broadway as the "Prince of Hosts." At a beautifully filmed masked ball, she meets Howard, an artist in need of a divine spark of inspiration. Needless to say, he finds it in Myers—and Howard quickly changes her mind about becoming the "Princess of Hosts."

d, Rollin S. Sturgeon; w, Doris Schroeder (based on a story by Katherine L. Robbins); ph, Harry B. Harris.

Comedy/Drama **(PR:A MPAA:NR)**

IN FOR THIRTY DAYS*** (1919) 5 reels Metro/bw

May Allison *(Helen Corning)*, Robert Ellis *(Brett Page)*, Mayme Kelso *(Mrs. Corning)*, Rex Cherryman *(Count Dronsky)*, Jay Dwiggins *(Judge Carroll)*, George Berrell *(Homer Brown)*, Bull Montana *("Hot Stove" Kelly)*.

Delightful comedy featuring the charming Allison as a wealthy young girl caught speeding in one of those Southern towns where prisoners may be rented out during the day to perform chores. In this case, she is assigned to a handsome young author who not only uses her as the inspiration for his novel, but takes her to be his bride as well.

d, Webster Cullison; w, Tom J. Geraghty, George D. Baker (based on a story by Luther A. Reed); ph, William Fildew.

Comedy **(PR:A MPAA:NR)**

IN HIGH GEAR** (1924) 5 reels SUN/AY bw

Kenneth McDonald, Helen Lynch.

In this extremely improbable, low-budget affair, two wealthy and bored socialites each disguise themselves as poor folks and, by chance, happen to meet. She gets into a jam, is kidnaped, and is thrown into a Chinatown dungeon. He rescues her and they fall in love, admit their true identities, and marry.

d, Robert North Bradbury; w, Frank Howard Clark, Bradbury; ph, Bert Longenecker.

Adventure/Comedy **(PR:A MPAA:NR)**

IN HIS GRIP** (1921, Brit.) 6 reels GAU/British Screencraft bw

Cecil Morton York *(Sir Donald McVeigh)*, David Hawthorne *(James Rutledge)*, Netta Westcott *(Jessie Vicars)*, Cecil du Gue *(Benjamin Hart)*, George Bellamy *(Norman Vicars)*, Hugh Miller *(Alec Vicars)*, W. T. Ellwanger *(Izzy)*.

In this British drama, set in Glasgow, Scotland, a contractor attempts to steal the jewels owned by his ward, but runs into quite a surprise when he encounters the brother everyone believed dead out to snatch them himself.

d, C. C. Calvert; w, Paul Rooff (based on the novel by David Christie Murray).

Drama **(PR:A MPAA:NR)**

IN HOLLYWOOD WITH POTASH AND PERLMUTTER***
(1924) 7 reels Goldwyn/AFN bw

Alexander Carr *(Morris Perlmutter)*, George Sidney *(Abe Potash)*, Vera Gordon *(Rosie Potash)*, Betty Blythe *(Rita Sismondi)*, Belle Bennett *(Mrs. Perlmutter)*, Anders Randolph *(Blanchard)*, Peggy Shaw *(Irma Potash)*, Charles Meredith *(Sam Pemberton)*, Lillian Hackett *(Miss O'Ryan)*, David Butler *(Crabbe)*, Sidney Franklin, Joseph W. Girard *(Film Buyers)*, Constance Talmadge, Norma Talmadge.

Sidney took over the role of Abe Potash after the death of Barney Bernard. This time the boys abandon their textile business to become producers of motion pictures. Their first effort is a failure, but they manage to get a banker to finance their next production on the condition that they will obtain the services of Blythe, the famous vamp. The lady enters their lives—and nearly ruins their marriages—before the film is completed. It turns out to be a great success, however, and the fellows put their lives back together, while Blythe turns her attention to the director. This is an entertaining film, made all the more so because of cameo appearances by Norma and Constance Talmadge as auditioning actresses.

p, Samuel Goldwyn; d, Alfred E. Green; w, Frances Marion (based on the play "Business Before Pleasure" by Montague Glass, Jules Eckert Goodman); t, Glass; ph, Arthur Miller, Harry Hallenberger; ed, Stuart Heisler; art d, Ben Carre.

Comedy **(PR:A MPAA:NR)**

IN OLD KENTUCKY*** (1920) 7 reels Louis B. Mayer bw

Anita Stewart *(Madge Brierly)*, Mahlon Hamilton *(Frank Layson)*, Edward Coxen *(Joe Lorey)*, Charles Arling *(Horace Holten)*, Edward Connolly *(Col. Sandusky Doolittle)*, Adele Farrington *(Aunt Aleathea)*, Marcia Manon *(Barbara Holten)*, Frank Duffy *(Eddie Lennhardy)*, John Curry *(Uncle Neb)*.

Grand old melodramatic fare about a mountain girl who falls in love with the man whose life she saved. She follows him home and rescues the horse on which his future rests, snatches him from the clutches of a scheming woman, and—finally—rides his horse to triumph in the big race.

d, Marshall Neilan, Alfred E. Green; w, Thomas Geraghty (based on the play by Charles T. Dazey); ph, Tony Gaudio.

Drama **(PR:A MPAA:NR)**

IN OLD KENTUCKY 1/2** (1927) 7 reels MGM bw

James Murray *(Jimmy Brierly)*, Helene Costello *(Nancy Holden)*, Wesley Barry *("Skippy" Lowry)*, Dorothy Cumming *(Mrs. Brierly)*, Edward Martindel *(Mr. Brierly)*, Harvey Clark *(Dan Lowry)*, Stepin Fetchit *(Highpockets)*, Carolynne Snowden *(Lily May)*, Nick Cogley *(Uncle Bible)*.

Routine story about a young soldier who returns home from the war to find the family estate in near ruin but sets everything right by winning the derby. The great black character comedian, Fetchit, made his screen debut in this one.

d, John M. Stahl; w, A.P. Younger, Lew Lipton (based on the play by Charles T. Dazey); t, Marian Ainsley, Ruth Cummings; ph, Maximilian Fabian; ed, Basil Wrangell, Margaret Booth; set d, Cedric Gibbons, Ernst Fegte; cos, Gilbert Clark.

Drama **(PR:A MPAA:NR)**

IN SEARCH OF A SINNER*** (1920) 5 reels Constance Talmadge/FN bw

Constance Talmadge *(Georgianna Chadbourne)*, Rockcliffe Fellowes *(Jack Garrison)*, Corliss Giles *(Jeffry)*, William Rosselle *(Sam)*, Marjorie Milton *(Helen)*, Evelyn C. Carrington *(Katie)*, Lillian Worth *(Valeska)*, Arnold Lucy *(Henry)*, Charles Whittaker *(Roue)*, Ned Sparks *(Waiter)*, William Boshell *(Policeman)*, Ralph Bunker.

After her older husband—a "good man"—dies, Talmadge decides she's had enough virtue to last a lifetime and sets off for New York to find a "wild man." In Central Park she flirts with a fellow who later holds off a cop who tries to issue Talmadge a citation for picking flowers. After getting away she is sure she has found the guy for her. It turns out that this bohemian gent of her dreams is really a clean-living lad from California, who happens to be the best friend of her brother-in-law, with whom she is staying. The big laughs come with Talmadge's desperate attempt to corrupt the fellow enough to make him a suitable husband candidate. The snappy gag titles one expects from a Loos script are here in abundance, as the film gallops along to its happy and very funny conclusion.

d, David Kirkland; w, John Emerson, Anita Loos (based on a story by Charlotte Thompson); ph, Oliver Marsh.

Comedy **(PR:A MPAA:NR)**

IN SEARCH OF A THRILL** (1923) 5 reels Metro bw

Viola Dana *(Ann Clemance)*, Warner Baxter *(Adrian Torrens)*, Mabel Van Buren *(Lila Lavender)*, Templar Saxe *(Sir George Dumphy)*, Robert Schable *(Tommy Perkins)*, Walter Wills *(Rene de Farge)*, Rosemary Theby *(Jeanne)*, Billy Elmer *(Percy, the Valet)*, Leo White *(Dance Professor)*.

While visiting Paris, millionairess Dana is taken on a tour of the slums by social reformer Baxter. The experience moves her profoundly and, after marrying Baxter and adopting a child, she devotes the rest of her life to serving others.

d, Oscar Apfel; w, Basil Dickey, Winifred Dunn (based on the story "The Spirit of the Road" by Kate Jordan); ph, John Arnold.

Drama **(PR:A MPAA:NR)**

IN THE BALANCE*** (1917) 5 reels VIT bw

Earle Williams *(The Younger Brother)*, Grace Darmond *(Louise Maurel)*, Miriam Miles, Denton Vane, Robert Gaillard, Templar Saxe, Julia Swayne Gordon.

Better-than-average Vitagraph feature about an actress who is taken in to spend the night by a couple of rural brothers when her car breaks down. The younger man falls in love with her, not realizing that she was on her way to meet a prince with the reputation of being a libertine. He follows her when she leaves, but returns home brokenhearted after learning the truth. The film does end happily, however, when the actress comes to realize her *true* love and returns to the farm.

d, Paul Scardon; w, Garfield Thompson (based on the novel *The Hillman* by E. Phillips Oppenheim).

Drama **(PR:A MPAA:NR)**

IN THE BLOOD*** (1923, Brit.) 6 reels Walter West/But bw

Victor McLaglen *(Tony Crabtree)*, Lillian Douglas *(Marian)*, Cecil Morton York *(Sir James Crabtree)*, Valia *(Lady Crabtree)*, John Glidden *(Ralph Hardy)*, Arthur Walcott *(Osman Shebe)*, George Foley *(Flemming)*, Humbertson Wright *(Malcolm Jove)*, Judd Green *(Stoney Isaac)*, Adeline Hayden Coffin *(Lady Crabtree)*, Clifford McLaglen *(Kansas Cat)*, Kenneth McLaglen *(The Whaler)*.

Victor McLaglen, who fought for the heavyweight championship of the world and also won the Academy Award for his brilliant performance in THE INFORMER, added an extra dimension to this British drama about a lad who is framed by his stepmother, Valia, and then goes on to take the place of his father's champion boxer, who has been doped, and proceeds to win the big fight.

d, Walter West; w, J. Bertram Brown (based on the novel by Andrew Soutar).

Adventure/Drama **(PR:A MPAA:NR)**

IN THE DAYS OF SAINT PATRICK***
(1920, Brit.) 5 reels General Film Supply/Janion bw

Ira Allen *(St. Patrick)*, Vernon Whitten *(St. Patrick as a Child)*, Alice Cardinall *(Conchessa)*, Dermot McCarthy *(Calpurnius)*, J. B. Carrickford *(St. Martin)*, George Brame *(Pope Celestin)*, Ernest Matthewson *(Bishop Tassach)*, George Griffin *(King Laoghaire)*, Maude Hume *(Queen)*, Mary Murnane *(Foster Mother)*, Herbert Mayne *(Gornias)*, Eddie Lawless *(Milcho)*, O'Carroll Reynolds *(Niall)*, Jack McDermott *(Victor)*.

Handsomely mounted British film tells the inspiring saga of how St. Patrick brought Christianity to Ireland, his tribulations, and his ultimate triumph.

p&d, Norman Whitten; w, Mr. McGuinness.

History/Religion **(PR:A MPAA:NR)**

IN THE HANDS OF THE LONDON CROOKS (1913, Brit.) 5 reels Barker/City bw

Thomas H. MacDonald *(Frank Linley)*, Blanche Forsythe *(Hilda Linley)*, Fred Paul *(Capt. Bland)*, Roy Travers *(Harry Norman)*, Dora de Winton *(Delilah)*, J. Hastings Batson *(Sir James Linley)*.

In this early British feature film thriller, a gambler who has been framed for forgery, and subsequently disowned, redeems himself by becoming a hero in Afghanistan.

d, Alexander Butler; w, Rowland Talbot.

Crime **(PR:A MPAA:NR)**

IN THE NAME OF LOVE** (1925) 6 reels FP/PAR bw

Ricardo Cortez *(Raoul Melnotte)*, Greta Nissen *(Marie Dufrayne)*, Wallace Beery *(M. Glavis)*, Raymond Hatton *(Marquis de Beausant)*, Lillian Leighton *(Mother Dufrayne)*, Edythe Chapman *(Mother Melnotte)*, Richard Arlen *(Dumas Dufrayne)*.

After making a fortune in Chicago, Cortez returns to France to find his childhood sweetheart, Nissen. Unfortunately, Nissen has become a wealthy social climber and refuses to marry anyone untitled. Enlisting the aid of two men she recently rejected, Cortez poses as a prince, marries Nissen, and then discloses the truth. By the time the honeymoon is over, however, Nissen is willing to forget her former ambitions and settle down with a man she can really love.

d, Howard Higgin; w, Sada Cowan (based on the novel *The Lady of Lyons; or, Love and Pride* by Edward Bulwer-Lytton); ph, C. Edgar Schoenbaum.

Comedy/Romance **(PR:A MPAA:NR)**

IN THE STRETCH*** (1914) 4 reels Ramo bw

Phil Scovelle, Stuart Holmes, Courtney Collins, William S. Rising, Jack Hopkins.

Well-done story of doped horses, fixed contests, and a jockey who, after serving a stretch in the pen, rescues a girl. He also helps break up a gang of crooked gamblers and, in the end, wins the big race.

d, Phil Scovelle; w, Scovelle, Will S. Davis.

Drama **(PR:A MPAA:NR)**

IN WALKED MARY** 1/2** (1920) 5 reels Capellani/Pathe bw

June Caprice, Thomas Carrington, Stanley Walpole, Vivienne Osborne, Frances M. Grant.

Another sweet little Caprice film, this time about a Southern orphan who takes a Northern gentleman's offer to help so seriously that she follows him to the city and moves into his house. Caprice manages to create a great deal of mischief before saving her "benefactor" from a fortune-hunting female and turning her visit into a permanent situation.

d, George Archainbaud; w, George D. Proctor (based on the play "Liza-Ann" by Oliver D. Bailey); ph, Lucien Tainguy.

Comedy/Drama **(PR:A MPAA:NR)**

INCORRIGIBLE DUKANE, THE* (1915) 4 reels FP bw

John Barrymore *(James A. Dukane, Jr.)*, W. T. Carleton *(James A. Dukane, Sr.)*, Stuart Baird *(Corbettson)*, William Meech *(Lantry, Camp Bully)*, C. E. McDonald *(Crofton, Ranch Owner)*, Helen Weir *(Enid Crofton)*.

Poorly produced drama with dreadful special effects, has Barrymore, the son of a construction company owner discovering that some workmen are using shoddy materials in the building of a dam and pocketing the difference. He foils the plot, wins the girl, and completes the job. Throughout the film, Barrymore does a sort of Charlie Chaplin impression, which doesn't quite work but is, none-the-less, the picture's highlight.

d, James Durkin; w, (based on a play by George C. Shedd).

Drama **(PR:A MPAA:NR)**

INDIAN LOVE LYRICS, THE** (1923, Brit.) 7 reels STOLL bw

Catherine Calvert *(Queen Vashti)*, Owen Nares *(Prince Zahirudin)*, Malvina Longfellow *(Princess Nadira)*, Shayle Gardner *(Ahmed Kahn)*, Fred Raynham *(Ibrahim-beg-Ismael)*, Roy Travers *(Hassan Ali Khan)*, William Parry *(Mustapha Khan)*, Nelson Ramsey *(Sultan Abdul Rahin)*, Daisy Campbell *(Sjltana Manavour)*, Fred Rains *(Selim)*, Pino Conti *(Youssef)*, Arthur McLaglen *(Champion)*.

Terrible title for an equally unimpressive British romantic film, set in India, about a princess who attempts to escape her forced marriage to a prince by posing as a commoner.

d&w, Sinclair Hill (based on the poem "Garden of Karma" by Laurence Hope).

Drama **(PR:A MPAA:NR)**

INEZ FROM HOLLYWOOD** (1924) 7 reels Sam E. Rork/FN bw

Anna Q. Nilsson *(Inez Laranetta)*, Lewis S. Stone *(Stewart Culyer)*, Mary Astor *(Fay Bartholdi)*, Lawrence Wheat *(Pat Summerfield)*, Rose Dione *(Marie d'Albrecht)*, Snitz Edwards *(The Old Sport)*, Harry Depp *(Scoop Smith)*, Ray Haller *(Freddie)*, E. H. Calvert *(Gardner)*.

Nilsson is branded the "worst woman in Hollywood" because of clever press manipulation on the part of her manager and her notorious vampire movie roles. Actually, she is basically a decent woman, concerned primarily with protecting her sister Astor (who does not know of Nilsson's screen persona), from the lustful proclivities of men. When she learns that Stone, a wealthy New Yorker who once pursued her, is involved with Astor, she rushes to Gotham to break up the affair. Stone informs her that his intentions are strictly honorable, and that they plan to marry, but only on the condition that Nilsson (because of her terrible reputation) never see her sister again. Thinking only of Astor's happiness, Nilsson selflessly agrees to this demand and returns to Hollywood and her manager.

d, Alfred E. Green; w, J. G. Hawks (based on the story "The Worst Woman in Hollywood" by Adela Rogers St. John); ph, Arthur Edeson; ed, Dorothy Arzner; set d, Jack Okey.

Drama **(PR:A MPAA:NR)**

INFAMOUS MISS REVELL, THE** (1921) 6 reels Metro bw

Alice Lake *(Julien/Paula Revell)*, Cullen Landis *(Max Hildreth)*, Jackie Saunders *(Lillian Hildreth)*, Lydia Knott *(Mary Hildreth)*, Herbert Standing *(Samuel Pangborn)*, Alfred Hollingsworth *(Maxwell Putnam)*, Stanley Gothals, Francis Carpenter, May Giraci, Geraldine Condon *(The Revell Children)*.

Twins Julien and Paula Revell (both played by Lake), try desperately to support their younger brothers and sisters, but are unable to find bookings for their singing act. When a wealthy patron offers to provide the needed funds—and more—if one of the girls will act as a "companion" during his final days, Julien volunteers. A couple of years pass and the millionaire dies, leaving his fortune to Julien on the condition that she never marry. Then she falls in love with Landis, the children's tutor. He loves her, as well, but is reluctant to propose because of her scandalous past. Of course, as Hollywood would have it, the girl turns out to actually be *Paula*, who assumed her sister's identity for the children's sake, when Julien followed her sponsor in death.

d, Dallas M. Fitzgerald; w, Arthur J. Zellner; ph, Roy Klaffki; art d, Joseph Calder.

Drama **(PR:A MPAA:NR)**

INFATUATION** (1915) 4 reels AM bw

Margarita Fisher *(Phillis Ladd)*, Joseph E. Singleton *(Robert Ladd)*, Harry Pollard *(Cyril Adair)*, Lucille Ward.

A railroad president's daughter marries a traveling actor, and the angry father disowns her. Later, the actor loses his position with the troupe because of drunkenness and returns to New York, where he had at one time been a star. The old man uses his influence to deprive his hated son-in-law of work, but finally the player triumphs and is accepted as a member of the family.

w, Lloyd Osbourne.

Drama **(PR:A MPAA:NR)**

INFERIOR SEX, THE** (1920) 5 reels FN bw

Mildred Harris Chaplin *(Alisa Randall)*, Milton Sills *(Knox Randall)*, Mary Alden *(Clarissa Mott-Smith)*, John Steppling *(George Mott-Smith)*, Bertram Grassby *(Porter Maddox)*, James O. Barrows *(Capt. Andy Drake)*, Yvette Mitchell.

Good production values and direction almost save this bubble-headed movie about a bride who keeps calling her husband at the office to ask if he still loves her but, in the end, saves his sister from running off with a rotter, at the risk of endangering her own reputation.

d, Joseph Henabery; w, Waldemar Young (based on a play by Frank Stayton); ph, Tony Gaudio; art d, George Hopkins.

Comedy/Drama **(PR:A MPAA:NR)**

INFIDELITY*** (1917) 4 reels Erbograph/Art Dramas bw

Anna Q. Nilsson, Eugene Strong, Miriam Nesbitt, Fred F. Jones, Elizabeth Spencer, Arthur Morrison, Warren Cook.

Good little programmer about an artist who is wrongly sent to prison after the man he accused of having an affair with his wife is found murdered. On his release he refuses to see her, but when the daughter he did not know he had meets him at an exhibit of his paintings, a reconciliation takes place.

d, Ashley Miller.

Drama **(PR:A MPAA:NR)**

INNER CHAMBER, THE* (1921) 6 reels VIT bw

Alice Joyce *(Claire Robson)*, Jane Jennings *(Mrs. Robson)*, Pedro De Cordoba *(Dr. George Danilo)*, Holmes E. Herbert *(Edward J. Wellman)*, John Webb Dillon *(Sawyer Flint)*, Grace Barton *(Mrs. Sawyer Flint)*, Ida Waterman *(Mrs. Finch-Brown)*, Josephine Whittell *(Nellie McGuire)*, Mrs. De Wolf Hopper *(Mrs. Candor)*.

The great talent of Joyce is all but wasted in this hopelessly old-fashioned and badly directed Vitagraph potboiler. A girl marries out of gratitude, but ends up with the man she loves after her obliging husband commits suicide.

d, Edward Jose; w, C. Graham Baker.

Drama **(PR:A MPAA:NR)**

INNER MAN, THE** (1922) 5 reels Syracuse/PG bw

Wyndham Standing *(Thurlow Michael Barclay, Jr.)*, J. Barney Sherry *(Barclay, Sr.)*, Louis Pierce *(Old Man Wolf)*, Leslie Hunt *(Bob)*, Dorothy Mackaill *(Sally)*, Gustav von Seyffertitz *(Jud Benson)*, Arthur Dewey *(Randall)*, Martin Kinney *(Ned Sawyer)*, Kathryn Kingsley *(Margaret Barclay)*, Nellie Parker Spalding *(Mrs. Wolf)*, Arthur Caldwell, Jr. *(Ben Wolf)*.

At his father's command, Standing, a wimpish teacher of mathematics, travels to Kentucky to inspect the family mine. Along the way, he develops courage in his heart and dynamite in his fists, both of which enable him to save the mine from crooks, win the hand of the girl he loves, and earn the respect and blessing of his once scornful father.

d, Hamilton Smith; w, Charles Mackay; ph, Arthur A. Cadwell.

Comedy/Adventure **(PR:A MPAA:NR)**

INNOCENCE* (1923) 6 reels COL/C.B.C. Film Sales bw

Anna Q. Nilsson *(Fay Leslie)*, Freeman Wood *(Don Hampton)*, Earle Foxe *(Paul Atkins)*, Wilfred Lucas *(Collingwood)*, William Scott *(Publicity Agent)*, Marion Harlan *(Chorus Girl)*.

Nilsson's beauty is the only thing going for this Cohn potboiler about a millionaire who marries—against his parents' will—a show business dancer. Later the socialite wrongly accuses his bride of having an affair with her former dancing partner, but by the film's dreary conclusion he is proven wrong, and they get on with their marriage.

p, Harry Cohn; d, Edward J. Le Saint; w, Jack Strumwasser (based on the story "Circumstances Alter Divorce Cases" by Lewis Allen Browne).

Drama **(PR:A MPAA:NR)**

INNOCENCE OF RUTH, THE** (1916) 5 reels Edison bw

Viola Dana *(Ruth Travers)*, Edward Earle *(Mr. Carter)*, Augustus Phillips *(Mortimer Reynolds)*, Lena D'Arvil *(Edna Morris)*, T. Tamamoto *(Togo)*, Nellie Grant.

A rather ordinary film about a girl (Dana) who becomes the ward of a well-known bounder after her father's death. Her presence changes his outlook on life, and when another womanizer attempts to seduce her, the guardian steps in and the audience is left to believe that he intends to make her his wife.

d, John H. Collins; w, William Addison Lathrop.

Drama **(PR:A MPAA:NR)**

INNOCENT*** (1918) 5 reels Astra/Pathe bw

Fannie Ward *(Innocent)*, John Miltern *(John Wyndham)*, Armand Kaliz *(Louis Doucet)*, Frederick Perry *(Peter McCormack)*, Nathaniel Sack, Rae Allen.

Big-budgeted Ward feature is solid on all counts. She plays a girl raised in China by a drunken father who is virtually held prisoner and longs to possess the beautiful clothes she sees Western women wearing. When her father dies, she is made the ward of Miltern, who takes her to Paris and allows her to become self-indulgent in matters of apparel. After a while she falls into the seductive trap of a cad whom Miltern shoots. The girl is horrified but later comes to her senses and follows her guardian to China, where she declares her love for *him* and accepts his proposal of marriage.

d, George Fitzmaurice; w, (based on the play by George Broadhurst).

Drama **(PR:A MPAA:NR)**

INNOCENT** (1921, Brit.) 6 reels STOLL bw

Madge Stuart *(Innocence)*, Basil Rathbone *(Amadis de Jocelyn)*, Lawrence Anderson *(Robin)*, Edward O'Neill *(Hugo de Jocelyn)*, Frank Dane *(Ned Landon)*, W. Cronin Wilson *(Armitage)*, Ruth Mackay *(Lady Maude)*, Mme. d' Esterre *(Miss Leigh)*, Annie Esmond *(Housekeeper)*.

An orphaned girl dies in a storm after learning that the artist whom she loves betrayed her. The only thing of interest in this distasteful British drama is an early appearance by the magnificent Rathbone.

d, Maurice Elvey; w, William J. Elliott (based on the novel by Marie Corelli).

Drama **(PR:A MPAA:NR)**

INNOCENT LIE, THE*** (1916) 5 reels FP bw

Valentine Grant *(Nora O'Brien)*, Jack Clark *(Terry O'Brien)*, Morris Foster *(Pat O'Brien)*, Hunter Arden *(Nora Owen)*, Robert Cain *(Capt. Stewart)*, Helen Lindroth.

The picture opens in Ireland with Grant, an orphan, running the house for her two brothers. Foster, the youngest, sails for the U.S., and later Grant comes over to join him. Unfortunately they miss connections, and the lass finds herself on her own. After a number of adventures, she meets, falls in love with, and marries a wealthy American, who is in a fine position to open all of the right doors for her brothers.

d, Sidney Olcott; w, Lois Zellner; ph, Alfonso Liguori.

Drama **(PR:A MPAA:NR)**

INNOCENT MAGDALENE, AN*** (1916) 5 reels FA/TRI bw

Lillian Gish *(Dorothy Raleigh)*, Spottiswoode Aitken *(Col. Raleigh)*, Sam De Grasse *(Forbes Stewart)*, Mary Alden *(The Woman)*, Seymour Hastings *(The Preacher)*, Jennie Lee *(Mammy)*, William DeVaull *(Old Joe)*.

Griffith wrote the story in which Gish plays the daughter of a poor-but-proud Kentuckian who marries a gambling man from New York. For this, the old man enters her death in the family Bible, and before long, the husband is sent to jail for a term of one year. When Gish discovers she is pregnant she returns home, but her father will have nothing to do with her. The child is born in the black quarter of town, with the assistance of her former mammy. Some time later, another woman arrives on the scene and tells the little mother that she is married to the father of the child. Crushed, Gish remembers her father's words, "all things evil must die." She is about to take her own life when her husband shows up, explains the situation, and takes her in his arms. Another sensational performance by perhaps the silent screen's finest actress.

d, Allan Dwan; w, Roy Somerville (based on a story by Granville Warwick [D. W. Griffith).

Drama **(PR:A MPAA:NR)**

INNOCENT SINNER, THE*** (1917) 5 reels FOX bw

Miriam Cooper *(Mary Ellen Ellis)*, Charles Clary *(David Graham)*, Jack Standing *(Walter Benton)*, Jane Novak *(Jane Murray)*, Rosita Marstini *(Mme. De Coeur)*, William E. Parsons *("Bull" Clark)*, Johnny Reese *("The Weasel")*, Jennie Lee.

It is a tribute to Walsh's great directorial talent that he could take the tired old story of a virtuous country girl brought to the city to be seduced by a slicker, and breathe suspense into it. His use of extras—many of whom were actually people in or on the fringe of the underworld—gave this film a tremendous sense of authenticity, and there is a whale of a fist fight before the girl happily marries the rotter's wealthy brother.

d&w, Raoul A. Walsh (based on a story by Mary Synon).

Drama **(PR:A MPAA:NR)**

INSEPARABLES, THE** (1929, Brit.) 7 reels Whitehall/WB bw

Elissa Landi *(Velda)*, Pat Aherne *(Laurie Weston)*, Annette Benson *(Adrienne)*, Gabriel Gabrio *(Pietro)*, Jerrold Robertshaw *(Sir Reginal Farleigh)*, Fred Rains *(Alexander Figg)*.

In this British romantic film, which featured the talented and beautiful Landi, a smuggler falls madly in love with the gypsy girl he rescues from a storm off the coast of the Riviera, but alas, she is in love with her wounded companion.

p, Adelqui Millar; d, John Stafford, Millar; w, Stafford (based on a story by Guarino Glavany, Millar).

Romance **(PR:A MPAA:NR)**

INSIDE THE LINES*** (1918) 6 reels Pyramid/WORLD bw

Lewis S. Stone, Marguerite Clayton, Carl Herlinger, Nick Cogley, Ida Lewis, Arthur Allardt, Helen Dunbar, Joseph Singleton, George Field.

A great deal of effort was devoted to details in this wartime film, such as casting actors who looked like real German officers and British Tommies, and it paid off. The story has to do with an attempt, on the part of the bad Hun, to blow up Gibraltar and sink the Royal Navy stationed in that area. In the end, Stone, an officer in the service of his majesty the king, reigns supreme and saves the day for Old Britannia.

d, David M. Hartford; w, Monte M. Katterjohn (based on the play by Earl Derr Biggers).

War **(PR:A MPAA:NR)**

INTO NO MAN'S LAND*** (1928) 7 reels EXCEL bw

Tom Santschi *(Tom Blaisdell/Western Evans)*, Josephine Norman *(Florence Blaisdell)*, Jack Daugherty *(Clayton Taggart)*, Betty Blythe *(The Countess)*, Crauford Kent *(The Duke)*, Mary McAllister *(Katherine Taggart)*, Syd Crossley *(Happy)*.

Santschi is the head of a gang of "gentlemen crooks," a sideline his daughter Norman is not aware of. Daugherty, an ambitious young lawyer, investigates a jewel robbery he suspects Santschi of being involved in, and falls in love with Norman. When one of the gang—motivated by greed—threatens to kill him, Santschi responds in kind and flees to France as a member of the American Expeditionary Force. The war rages on, and in the trenches Daugherty and Santschi meet. The older man fully intends to kill the former investigator, until the lad sustains a wound and, in a state of delirium, whispers his daughter's name. The war ends and Norman and Daugherty marry; Santschi is thought dead, but actually has returned to America, where he wanders the country as a tramp. Years pass, and one night the dying and pathetic one-time big shot appears at his daughter's house claiming to be an old friend of her late father. The girl does not recognize his war-scarred face, but her husband does. To see his daughter one last time was his only wish and, having done so, crumbles slowly to his death with the suggestion of a smile on his lips.

p, Burton King; d, Cliff Wheeler, Arthur Guy Empey; w, Elsie Werner (based on the story "You're in the Army Now" by Bennett Southard, Werner); ph, Teddy Tetzlaff.

Drama **(PR:A MPAA:NR)**

INTO THE NIGHT** (1928) 6 reels Raleigh bw

Agnes Ayres *(Billie Mardon)*, Forrest Stanley *(Gavin Murdock)*, Robert Russell *(Walter Van Buren)*, Tom Lingham *(Howard K. Howard)*, Rhody Hathaway *(Jim Marden)*, Allan Sears *(John Harding)*, Corliss Palmer *(Mrs. Harding)*, Arthur Thalasso *(Pat Shannon)*.

The career of THE SHEIK star Ayres was on the decline when she made this Poverty Row programmer. She is a girl who becomes a thief to prove her father's innocence and wins the love of the district attorney along the way. The advent of sound destroyed her career the next year, and after that she appeared in only one more movie, in 1937, before she died at the age of 44.

d, Duke Worne; w, James Bronis (based on a story by George W. Pyper); t, Joe Traub; ph, Jack Jellet.

Crime **(PR:A MPAA:NR)**

INTOLERANCE**** (1916) 14 reels Wark bw

Lillian Gish *(The Woman Who Rocks the Cradle)*; Modern Story 1914: Mae Marsh *(The Dear One)*, Fred Turner *(Her Father)*, Robert Harron *(The Boy)*, Sam de Grasse *(Arthur Jenkins)*, Vera Lewis *(Mary T. Jenkins)*, Mary Alden, Pearl Elmore, Lucille Brown, Luray Huntley, Mrs. Arthur Mackley *(The "Uplifters")*, Miriam Cooper *(The Friendless One)*, Walter Long *(The Musketeer of the Slums)*, Tully Marshall *(A Friend of the Musketeer)*, Tom Wilson *(The Kindly Policeman)*, Ralph Lewis *(The Governor)*, Lloyd Ingraham *(The Judge)*, Barney Bernard *(Attorney for the Boy)*, Rev. A. W. McClure *(Father Farley)*, Max Davidson *(The Kindly Neighbor)*, Monte Blue *(A Striker)*, Marguerite Marsh *(A Debutante Guest at the Ball)*, Jennie Lee *(Woman at Jenkins' Employees' Dance)*, Tod Browning *(Owner of the Racing Car)*, Edward Dillon *(Chief Detective)*, Clyde Hopkins *(Jenkins' Secretary)*, William Brown *(The Warden)*, Alberta Lee *(Wife of the Kindly Neighbor)*; Judean Story A.D.27: Howard Gaye *(The Christ)*, Lillian Langdon *(Mary, the Mother)*, Olga Grey *(Mary Magdalene)*, Gunther von Ritzau, Erich von Stroheim

(Pharisees), Bessie Love *(The Bride of Cana)*, George Walsh *(The Bridegroom)*; French Story A.D.1572: Margery Wilson *(Brown Eyes)*, Eugene Pallette *(Prosper Latour)*, Spottiswoode Aitken *(Brown Eyes' Father)*, Ruth Handforth *(Brown Eyes' Mother)*, A.D. Sears *(The Mercenary)*, Frank Bennett *(Charles IX)*, Maxfield Stanley *(Mons. La France, Duc d'Anjou)*, Josephine Crowell *(Catherine de Medici)*, Georgia Pearce [Constance Talmadge] *(Marguerite de Valois)*, W. E. Lawrence *(Henry of Navarre)*, Joseph Henabery *(Adm. Coligny)*, Morris Levy *(Duc de Guise)*, Howard Gaye *(Cardinal Lorraine)*, Louis Romaine *(A Catholic Priest)*; Babylonian Story 539 B.C.: Constance Talmadge *(The Mountain Girl)*, Elmer Clifton *(The Rhapsode)*, Alfred Paget *(Belshazzar)*, Seena Owen *(Attarea, the Princess Beloved)*, Carl Stockdale *(King Nabonidus)*, Tully Marshall *(High Priest of Bel)*, George Siegmann *(Cyrus, the Persian)*, Elmo Lincoln *(The Mighty Man of Valor)*, George Fawcett *(A Babylonian Judge)*, Kate Bruce *(A Babylonian Mother)*, Ruth St. Denis *(Solo Dancer)*, Loyola O'Connor *(Attarea's Slave)*, James Curley *(The Charioteer of Cyrus)*, Howard Scott *(A Babylonian Dandy)*, Alma Rubens, Ruth Darling, Margaret Mooney *(Girls of the Marriage Market)*, Mildred Harris, Pauline Starke *(Favorites of the Harem)*, Winifred Westover *(The Favorite of Egibi)*, Grace Wilson *(The 1st Dancer of Tammuz)*, Lotta Clifton *(The 2nd Dancer of Tammuz)*, Ah Singh *(The 1st Priest of Nergel)*, Ranji Singh *(The 2nd Priest of Nergel)*, Ed Burns *(The 2nd Charioteer of the Priest of Bel)*, Martin Landry *(Auctioneer)*, Wallace Reid *(A Boy Killed in the Fighting)*, Charles Eagle Eye *(Barbarian Chieftain)*, Charles Van Courtlandt *(Gobyras, Lieutenant of Cyrus)*, Jack Cosgrove *(Chief Eunuch)*.

Smarting from what he considered to be intolerance on the part of the pressure groups which attempted to ban his masterpiece THE BIRTH OF A NATION, Griffith took a film he was working on with a contemporary theme (dealing with the struggle between capital and labor) called THE MOTHER AND THE LAW, and added three additional stories which traced the inhumanity of man through the ages. The result was a "cinematic fugue" which spectactularly depicted the fall of Belshazzar's Babylon, the Passion of Christ, and the Massacre of St. Bartholomew. The four stories were interconnected by the use of Walt Whitman's verse—"Out of the cradle endlessly rocking, Uniter of here and hereafter," with Gish rocking a symbolic cradle. Each of the episodes (with the possible exception of the Passion Play, which is a bit shorter) can stand as a masterwork on its own, but Griffith brings them crashing together in shorter and shorter intervals, as Babylon struggles under siege, the Savior is nailed to His cross, the Huguenots are slaughtered, and the Irish Catholic boy of the Modern Story walks innocently to the gallows stair. It is an overwhelming artistic accomplishment, and to quote Edward Wagenknecht from the book *The Films of D. W. Griffith*, which he wrote with Anthony Slide, "There are a good many of us who will never be convinced that INTOLERANCE is not the greatest of all motion pictures." INTOLERANCE is not, as some have contended, Griffith's absolution for the racial attitudes expressed in THE BIRTH OF A NATION. The director did not alter his antebellum, anti-reconstructionist views, which reflected his Southern upbringing. On the contrary, the film is a bitter defense of his right to self-expression, a right which had been threatened by censorship. The modern theme was the only one of the four parts of the picture that had been conventionally scripted; Griffith made up the others—and ordered his small army of technicians and designers to construct appropriate settings for them—as he went along. The modern segments had originally been a complete short feature-length film, completed even before work began on THE BIRTH OF A NATION, but never released. Griffith conceived this film on the basis of two major sources; a report from a Federal Industrial Commission which came into his hands, and newspaper reports detailing the Stielow case in New York. The Commission report detailed the acts of a hypocritical industrialist who flaunted his charitable philanthropies while simultaneously denying his own workers a living wage, employing corrupt police to break the resulting strike (19 strikers were shot to death). The New York case involved a condemned youth whose circumstances very much resembled those of his protagonist, played by Harron. Ordinarily meticulous in researching his subjects, Griffith pulled much of the rest of the picture from his own head, very closely skirting the same charges of racism that had stemmed from his earlier epic. According to a contemporary account, Griffith had his assistants scour a Jewish neighborhood for what he considered to be appropriately orthodox types for the crucifixion scenes. When the B'nai Brith heard of this, they commissioned a group of respected Jews (including Joseph Brandeis and Louis Marshall) to call on the director with proof that the Jews were not the ones who crucified Christ. They gave Griffith an ultimatum, promising him a concerted campaign of blacklisting unless he modified the film. The director caved in, burning the negative of scenes already shot, and re-shooting them with "Roman soldiers" replacing the Jews. Griffith also wanted elephants in his picture, so he used them in areas and historical periods where they had never existed. Considering the animals, the chariot charges, the spears and arrows, and the massive sets, surprisingly few human casualties resulted from the production. While about a hundred persons were injured, only one death occurred when a worker fell from some scaffolding. Due to the enormous financial success of Griffith's earlier epic, he found it easy to raise the money (reportedly five times as much money) to make the film. As in the earlier case, a separate corporation was set up to handle the production. Unlike its predecessor, INTOLERANCE lost money and the corporation went bankrupt. Griffith re-cut the negative into two shorter films, THE FALL OF BABYLON and THE MOTHER AND THE LAW. No complete copy of the film as originally released now exists, although the Film Library of The Museum of Modern Art has reconstructed a close approximation of it from a combination of negative and print stocks.

d&w, D. W. Griffith; ph, G. W. Bitzer, Karl Brown; m, Joseph Carl Breil, Griffith; ed, James and Rose Smith; set d, Frank "Huck" Wortman.

Drama **Cas.** **(PR:C MPAA:NR)**

INTRODUCE ME*** (1925) 7 reels Douglas MacLean/AEX bw

Douglas MacLean *(Jimmy Clark)*, Anne Cornwall *(Betty Perry)*, Robert Ober *(Algy Baker)*, E. J. Ratcliffe *(John Perry)*, Lee Shumway *(J. K. Roberts)*, Wade Boteler *(Bruno)*.

Funny comedy has MacLean allowing himself to be mistaken for a famous American mountain climber in order to impress a pretty young lady he meets at a Paris railroad station. After arriving in the Alps, the real climber shows up but is tickled to death to go along with the gag. MacLean's problem is that he's terrified of heights, so there are plenty of hilarious sight gags, culminating with his rolling down the side of the mountain, picking up snow as he bounces along, taking on the form of a huge snowball, and finally smashing into the girl, who is on the slopes, and together they continue the descent—legs, arms, and faces jutting from the icy sphere—until they finally crash. Good stuff from one of the movies' best light comedians.

d, George J. Crone; sup, Al Santell; w, Wade Boteler, Raymond Cannon; ph, Jack MacKenzie, Paul Perry.

Comedy **(PR:A MPAA:NR)**

INVADERS, THE** (1929) 7 reels Big Productions/SYN bw

Bob Steele, Edna Aslin, Thomas Lingham, J. P. McGowan, Celeste Rush, Tom Smith, Bud Osborne, Chief Yowlache.

A wagon train is attacked by Indians, and the sole survivors are two children, a brother and sister. The girl is taken by them and raised as "Black Fawn." The boy, however, is rescued by the cavalry and grows up to be a trooper himself. Eventually he is reunited with his sister after bravely fighting off another Indian attack.

d, J. P. McGowan; w, Walter Sterret (based on a story by Sally Winters); t, William Stratton; ph, Hap Depew; syn sc; s eff.

Western **(PR:A MPAA:NR)**

INVISIBLE FEAR, THE* (1921) 6 reels Anita Stewart/AFN bw

Anita Stewart *(Sylvia Langdon)*, Walter McGrail *(Arthur Comstock)*, Allan Forrest *(Bentley Arnold)*, Hamilton Morse *(Marshall Arnold)*, Estelle Evans *(Mrs. Marshall Arnold)*, George Kuwa *(Nagi)*, Edward Hunt *(The Butler)*, Ogden Crane *(John Randall)*.

A terrible mystery movie about a woman who believes she killed the man who tried to rape her, only to meet him years later at a party she is attending with her husband. The rotter hypnotizes her and wills her to open her safe while sleeping. In the end it is proved that he murdered the lawyer who drew up the papers which disinherited him, and set fire to the building in which the girl saw the body that led her to believe herself a killer.

d, Edwin Carewe; w, Madge Power (based on a story by Hampton Del Ruth); ph, Robert B. Kurrle; art d, John D. Schulze.

Mystery **(PR:A MPAA:NR)**

INVISIBLE POWER, THE*** (1921) 7 reels Goldwyn bw

House Peters *(Sid Chambers)*, Irene Rich *(Laura Chadwick)*, De Witt Jennings *(Mark Shadwell)*, Sydney Ainsworth *(Bob Drake)*, Jessie De Jainette *(Mrs. Shadwell)*, William Friend *(Mr. Miller)*, Gertrude Claire *(Mrs. Miller)*, Lydia Yeamans Titus *(The Giggling Neighbor)*.

Ex-convict Peters marries schoolteacher Rich and they move to the city. Then Jennings, the detective who sent him up, demands information about a former gang member. Peters refuses and is railroaded into another jail term. While he is in prison, Rich has a baby but gives it up for adoption, fearing it might develop criminal tendencies. When Peters gets out he vows to kill Jennings. Rich rushes to his home to warn him and discovers that the detective is raising her child. At this point there is an explosion of maternal emotion, and the sentimental policeman arranges for the family to be reunited.

p&d, Frank Lloyd; w, Charles Kenyon; ph, Norbert Brodin; art d, Cedric Gibbons.

Drama/Crime **(PR:A MPAA:NR)**

IRENE*** (1926) 9 reels FN bw-c

Colleen Moore *(Irene O'Dare)*, Lloyd Hughes *(Donald Marshall)*, George K. Arthur *(Mme. Lucy)*, Charles Murray *(Pa O'Dare)*, Kate Price *(Ma O'Dare)*, Ida Darling *(Mrs. Warren Marshall)*, Eva Novak *(Eleanor Hadley)*, Edward Earle *(Larry Hadley)*, Laurence Wheat *(Bob Harrison)*, Maryon Aye *(Helen Cheston)*, Bess Flowers *(Jane Gilmour)*, Lydia Yeamans Titus *(Mrs. Cheston)*, Cora Macey *(Mrs. Gilmour)*.

Delightful Moore movie version of the popular 1919 musical about the pretty Irish girl who meets a millionaire while job hunting and through him lands a job working at Madame Lucy's Fashion Salon. Mme. Lucy's homosexuality is played with such good humor and skill by Arthur, that he not only fails to offend, but nearly steals the show from Moore at her best. The Celtic lass eventually is given the chance to model (in a beautiful technicolor sequence) and becomes a sensation. There are the usual complications, whereby the wealthy mother disdains her son's interest in a commoner, but it is all resolved in the end.

p, John McCormick; d, Alfred E. Green; w, June Mathis, Rex Taylor, Mervyn LeRoy (based on the musical comedy "Irene" by James Montgomery); t, George Marion, Jr.; ph, T. D. McCord (Technicolor); m, Harry Tierney, Joseph McCarthy; ed, Edwin Robbins; art d, John D. Schulze.

Comedy/Romance **(PR:A MPAA:NR)**

IRIS** (1915, Brit.) 6 reels Hepworth/ID bw

Henry Ainley *(Maldonado)*, Alma Taylor *(Iris)*, Stewart Rome *(Laurence Trenwith)*.

The Pinero play about a wealthy widow who is forbidden to marry and therefore turns to a paramour did not make a successful transition to the screen in this British production.

d, Cecil M. Hepworth; w, (based on the play by Arthur Wing Pinero).

Drama **(PR:A MPAA:NR)**

IRISH DESTINY**
(1925, Brit.) 5 reels Eppel's European bw (AKA: AN IRISH MOTHER)

Denis O'Shea *(Denis O'Hara)*, Una Shiels *(Mona Barry)*, Daisy Campbell *(The Mother)*, Brian Magowan *(Beecher)*, Clifford Pembroke, Kit O'Malley, Pat O'Rourke.

In this British drama set in Ireland, a man is wounded while escaping from prison, but does manage to reach his sweetheart before she becomes the victim of a rape.

p, d&w, I. J. Eppel.

Crime **(PR:A MPAA:NR)**

IRISH HEARTS* (1927) 6 reels WB bw

May McAvoy *(Sheila)*, Jason Robards, Sr. *(Rory)*, Warner Richmond *(Emmett)*, Kathleen Key *(Clarice)*, Walter Perry *(Sheila's Father)*, Walter Rodgers *(Restaurant Owner)*, Les Bates *(Taxi Driver)*.

This film was a complete waste of the great McAvoy's bountiful talents. It had to do with Richmond, an Irish lad who sails for America, followed shortly thereafter by his fiancee, McAvoy. En route, the lass loses her lucky shamrock, and shortly after landing her sweetheart, who has become quickly Americanized, takes up with a flapper. Working as a waitress, poor little McAvoy makes the acquaintance of Robards, a former boxer who now works on the docks. She confides in him, and he is more than willing to provide the broad shoulder she needs to cry on. Robards finds her lucky flower and returns it just in time to watch the apple-of-his-eye disrupt Richmond's wedding by hurling bottomless barrels of rotten vegetables and fruit into the proceedings. This is not a movie one would want to book for the Hibernian Hall on the 17th of March.

d, Byron Haskin; w, Bess Meredyth, Graham Baker (based on a story by Melville Crossman); ph, Virgil Miller.

Drama/Comedy **(PR:A MPAA:NR)**

IRISH MOTHER, AN (SEE: IRISH DESTINY, 1925, Brit.)

IRON HORSE, THE**** (1924) 11 reels FOX bw

George O'Brien *(Davy Brandon)*, Madge Bellamy *(Miriam Marsh)*, Cyril Chadwick *(Peter Jesson)*, Fred Kohler *(Bauman)*, Gladys Hulette *(Ruby)*, James Marcus *(Judge Haller)*, Francis Powers *(Sgt. Slattery)*, J. Farrell MacDonald *(Cpl. Casey)*, James Welch *(Pvt. Schultz)*, Walter Rogers *(Gen. Dodge)*, George Wagner *(Buffalo Bill Cody)*, John Padjan *(Wild Bill Hickok)*, Charles O'Malley *(Maj. North)*, Charles Newton *(Collis P. Huntington)*, Charles Edward Bull *(Abraham Lincoln)*, Colin Chase *(Tony)*, Jack O'Brien *(Dinny)*, Delbert Mann *(Charles Crocker)*, Chief Big Tree *(Cheyenne Chief)*, Chief White Spear *(Sioux Chief)*, Edward Piel *(Old Chinaman)*, James Gordon *(David Brandon, Sr.)*, Winston Miller *(Davy as a Child)*, Peggy Cartwright *(Miriam as a Child)*, Thomas C. Durant *(Jack Ganzhorn)*, Stanhope Wheatcroft *(John Hay)*, Frances Teague *(Polka Dot)*, Will Walling *(Thomas Marsh)*, Dan Borzage, Clark Gable, Jupiter of the Central Pacific, 119 of the Union Pacific *(Railroad Locomotives)*, A Regiment of U.S. Army Troops and Cavalry, 3,000 Railway Workmen, 1,000 Chinese Laborers, 800 Pawnee, Sioux, and Cheyenne Indians, 2,800 Horses, 1,300 Buffalo, 10,000 Texas Steers.

Expansionist capitalists-versus-Indians is the theme of this first of director Ford's epics, a landmark film dealing with the construction of the first transcontinental railroad, culminating in the ceremony of the driving of a golden railroad spike as East meets West. Young Davy Brandon (Miller) accompanies his father, Gordon, as the latter confers with general contractor Walling. When Walling criticizes Gordon for his dream of the construction of a railroad joining both coasts, he is chastised by none other than the eavesdropping Abraham Lincoln (Bull), who points out that the future of the country lies in the minds of such visionaries. Gordon and his son attempt to survey an appropriate route through the mountains for the coming railroad (the site is director Ford's favorite Western location of Monument Valley, at a pass dividing enormous cliffs that was also used in his films STAGECOACH [1939] and STRAIGHT SHOOTING [1917]). As they find the pass, Gordon is murdered by "Indians" whose leader has only three fingers on one of his hands. The years pass, and Davy (now played by O'Brien) is a rider for the short-lived Pony Express (ironically, a victim of the very railroad represented in the film). To escape from attacking Indians, O'Brien abandons his winded steed and leaps aboard a fortuitously passing train traveling along the first section of the incipient transcontinental tracks. At the train's destination—where new track is being laid—O'Brien renews his acquaintance with Walling, now the railroad's chief contractor, and his daughter (grown into a lovely young woman), Bellamy. She is engaged to Chadwick, a surveyor who is ostensibly concerned with the very problem—finding an appropriate pass through the mountains—that O'Brien's father had resolved so many years previously. Chadwick is secretly in the employ of rancher Kohler, who wants the railroad to pass through his large tracts of land, knowing that he will thereby profit mightily. Unable to understand Chadwick's reluctance to accept his proffered solution to the problem of the pass, O'Brien ultimately discovers the plot when Chadwick makes an attempt on his life. The clues lead him to Kohler, the three-fingered man who killed O'Brien's father. After a rousing fight with the villain, O'Brien goes to work, helping to assure the success of the railroad, uniting with Bellamy as eastbound and westbound track sections are finally joined. Although the murder-mystery subplot tends to distract from the near-documentary parts of many segments of the picture, director Ford developed many of the elements here that he was to use in his later epics. The heavier parts of the film are leavened with humerous interactions among the laborers, notably the three Civil War veterans, played by Powers, MacDonald, and Welch (a Musketeers-like coterie which would appear in many other Ford opuses). This was the athletic O'Brien's first starring role. A long-time family friend of "The Well-dressed Cowboy," Tom Mix (whom Ford had directed in NORTH OF HUDSON BAY, released a year earlier), O'Brien and Ford were acquainted, and the director invited him to be one of the 80 or so actors to test for the leading role. O'Brien, who had done only small parts and stunts—in addition to filling in as an assistant on cinema crews—to that date (his first credited role, in WHITE HANDS in 1922, had required him to double as a shark, menacing the heroine with a fin strapped to his back) went on to become a staple in B westerns, the very genre from which Ford was to graduate with this majestic picture. Look for Clark Gable in a bit part in his first year in Hollywood.

d, John Ford; w, Charles Kenyon (based on a story by John Russell, Kenyon); t, Charles Darnton; ph, George Schneiderman, Burnett Guffey; m, Erno Rapee.

Western **Cas.** **(PR:A MPAA:NR)**

IRON JUSTICE**
(1915, Brit.) 4 reels Renaissance/Kinematograph Trading Company bw

Fanny Tittell-Brune *(Margaret Brand)*, Sydney Fairbrother *(Mrs. O'Connor)*, Julian Royce *(Martin Brand)*, Alfred Drayton *(Frank Deakin)*, Cecil Fletcher *(Ronald O'Connor)*, Marguerita Jesson *(Phyllis Brand)*, A. Harding Steerman *(Jabez Cole)*, Joan Morgan *(Phyllis as a Child)*, John M. Payne *(Footman)*.

This British feature, about a clerk who is sent to prison for committing fraud and then paces his cell while his former employer's wife turns his beloved daughter into a prostitute, was not exactly a Keystone comedy.

p, John M. Payne; d&w, Sidney Morgan.

Drama **(PR:C MPAA:NR)**

IRON MAN, THE**
(1925) 5 reels Whitman Bennett/CHAD bw (AKA: A MAN OF IRON)

Lionel Barrymore *(Philip Durban)*, Mildred Harris *(Claire Bowdoin)*, Winifred Barry *(Martha Durban)*, Dorothy Kingdon *(Edith Bowdoin)*, Alfred Mack *(Hugh Bowdoin)*, J. Moy Bennett *(Denis Callahan)*, Isobel De Leon *(Maybelle Callahan)*, Jean Del Val *(Prince Novakian)*.

Harris is jilted by the prince she is engaged to marry after her father, a chocolate magnate, buys him for his royalty-struck daughter. On the rebound, Harris marries Barrymore, a millionaire. In time she comes to love her husband, and discovers the prince was actually a phony.

d, William Bennett; w, Lawrence Marsten; ph, Edward Paul.

Drama **(PR:A MPAA:NR)**

IRON RING, THE* (1917) 5 reels PEER/WORLD bw

Edward Langford *(Aleck Hulette)*, Gerda Holmes *(Bess Hulette)*, Arthur Ashley *(Jack Delmore)*, Herbert Frank *(Ellery Leonard)*, George MacQuarrie *(Stephen Graves)*, George Cowl *(Charles Brown)*, Alexandria Carewe *(Mrs. Georgie Leonard)*, Gladys Thompson *(Dorothy Delmore)*, Victor Kennard *(Dr. Hogue)*, Richard Clarke *(Sloane)*, Katherine Johnston.

Heavy-handed and disjointed film which clearly sends the moral statement: Married women should never cheat! The picture follows three characters, two of whom fall just short of "doing it," and the third who does cross over the line, causing the suicide of her husband.

d, George Archainbaud; w, (based on the story "Partnership" by Horace Hazelton [Charles Stokes Wayne]); p, Philip Hatkin.

Drama **(PR:A MPAA:NR)**

IRRESISTIBLE LOVER, THE*** (1927) 7 reels UNIV-Jewel bw

Norman Kerry *(J. Harrison Gray)*, Lois Moran *(Betty Kennedy)*, Gertrude Astor *(Dolly Carleton)*, Lee Moran *(Lawyer)*, Myrtle Stedman *(Hortense Brown)*, Phillips Smalley *(Mr. Brown)*, Arthur Lake *(Jack Kennedy)*, Walter James *(Mr. Kennedy)*, George Pearce *(Smith)*.

This amusing farce leans too much on its titles to deliver the laughs, but is nonetheless worth watching because of Kerry and, especially, Moran. It all has to do with a romantically insatiable playboy who can't keep up with the women in his life, until he meets Moran after he is hit by a car.

d, William Beaudine; sup, Carl Laemmle; w, Beatrice Van, Edward Luddy, James J. Tynan (based on a story by Evelyn Campbell); t, Albert De Mond; ph, John Stumar.

Comedy/Romance **(PR:A MPAA:NR)**

IS DIVORCE A FAILURE?** (1923) 6 reels Arthur Beck/AEX bw

Leah Baird *(Carol Lockwood)*, Richard Tucker *(David Lockwood)*, Walter McGrail *(Kelcey Barton)*, Tom Santschi *(Smith)*, Alec B. Francis *(Philip Wilkinson)*, Pansy *(Pansy)*.

Baird decides to give her marriage to Tucker one last chance by taking an ocean voyage with him. However, McGrail, the man with whom she is infatuated, books passage on the same cruise, as does Santschi, who also loves her. When the ship sinks the four of them are cast up on a desert island. Life in the rough isn't easy for these city folks, especially after a volcano erupts and a tornado strikes. But, through it all, Tucker proves to be the better man, and this does not go unnoticed by his wife.

d, Wallace Worsley; w, Leah Baird (based on the play "All Mine" by Dorian Neve).

Drama/Adventure **(PR:A MPAA:NR)**

IS LOVE EVERYTHING?** (1924) 6 reels Garrson Enterprises/AEX bw

Alma Rubens *(Virginia Carter)*, Frank Mayo *(Robert Whitney)*, H. B. Warner *(Jordan Southwick)*, Walter McGrail *(Boyd Carter)*, Lilyan Tashman *(Edythe Stanley)*, Marie Schaefer *(Mrs. Carter)*, Irene Howley *(Mrs. Rowland)*.

Through parental pressure, Rubens marries millionaire Warner, but her love for Mayo remains constant. She is completely faithful to her husband, but he foolishly suspects her of having an affair with his former rival. As a test, he arranges a yachting party and invites Mayo to attend. The boat sinks and Warner is thought dead. When he finally does return, he sees Rubens in Mayo's arms and, realizing the truth, selflessly leaves them to their happiness and signs on with the captain who earlier rescued him.

d, William Christy Cabanne; w, Raymond S. Harris (based on a story by Cabanne); t, William B. Laub; ph, Walter Arthur, Philip Armand; ed, Laub.

Drama **(PR:A MPAA:NR)**

IS MONEY EVERYTHING?** (1923) 6 reels D. M. Film/Lee-Bradford bw

Norman Kerry *(John Brand)*, Miriam Cooper *(Mrs. Brand)*, Andrew Hicks (Sam Slack), John Sylvester *(Rev. John Brooks)*, Martha Mansfield *(Mrs. Justice Pelham)*, William Bailey *(Roy Pelham)*, Lawrence Brooke *(Phil Graham)*.

After becoming obsessed with making money, Kerry leaves his wife, Cooper, for the company of a married socialite. Realizing his dreams of grandeur are really a sickness, Cooper arranges his financial ruin, and the two return to the farm where they spend the rest of their lives enjoying the simple but "more important" things.

d&w, Glen Lyons; ph, Alvin Knechtel.

Drama **(PR:A MPAA:NR)**

IS THAT NICE?** (1926) 5 reels R-C/FBO bw

George O'Hara *(Ralph Tanner)*, Doris Hill *(Doris Leslie)*, Stanton Heck *(John Gorman)*, Charles Thurston *(Sherman Dyke)*, Roy Laidlaw *(Horace Wildert)*, Babe London *(Winnie Nash)*, "Red" Kirby *(Bill Schultz)*, Ethan Laidlaw *(O'Brien)*.

This action comedy, about a cub reporter who writes a blazing expose on a political boss, loses it, and then sets out to get the proof he needs to keep out of a nasty libel suit, is full of slapstick in the Mack Sennett style. It doesn't quite come off, but everyone tries hard, and at least they deliver entertainment.

d, Del Andrews; w, Paul Gangelin, Jack Collins (based on a story by Walter A. Sinclair); ph, Jules Cronjager.

Comedy/Adventure **(PR:A MPAA:NR)**

IS YOUR DAUGHTER SAFE?** (1927) 6 reels CHAD bw

Vivian Winston *(The Girl)*, Jerome Young *(The Boy)*, Henry Roquemore *(The Beast)*, Georgia O'Dell *(The Madam)*, Slim Mahoney *(The White Slaver)*, William Dennis *(The Deceiver)*, Bernice Breacher *(The Victim)*, Palmer Morrison *(The Doctor)*, Winfield Jones *(The Governor)*, Joe Bonner *(The Rounder)*, Hugh Saxon *(The Gambler)*, Hazel Jones *(The Maid)*, Vera White, Hortense Petra, Virginia Hobbs, Alta Faulkner, Dorothy Jay, June D'Eon, Mildred Northmore, Ann Porter, Geraldine Johnson, Mildred McClune *(Ladies of Leisure)*, Mayor William Hale Thompson, Chicago Vice Commission.

Exploitation film advertised as a means of warning the public about the dangers of venereal disease and to show how young girls could be protected from the clutches of white slavers. There is even a segment showing how children born of parents afflicted with venereal disease are affected by the scourge.

p, S. S. Millard; d, Louis King, Leon Lee; w, (based on a story by Max Abramson).

Drama **(PR:C MPAA:NR)**

IS ZAT SO?*** (1927) 7 reels FOX bw

George O'Brien *(Ed Chick Cowan)*, Edmund Lowe *(Hap Hurley)*, Kathryn Perry *(Marie Mestretti)*, Cyril Chadwick *(Robert Parker)*, Doris Lloyd *(Sue Parker)*, Dione Ellis *(Florence Hanley)*, Richard Maitland *(Maj. Fitz Stanley)*, Douglas Fairbanks, Jr. *(G. Clinton Blackburn)*, Philippe De Lacy *(Little Jimmy Parker)*, Jack Herrick *(Gas House Duffy)*.

On their way to the championship of the world, boxer O'Brien and his manager, Lowe, become friendly with millionaire Fairbanks and prevent his crooked brother-in-law from taking him to the cleaners. Top-rate cast in a snappy, well-produced farce.

d, Alfred E. Green; w, Philip Klein (based on the play by James Gleason, Richard Taber); ph, George Schneiderman.

Comedy **(PR:A MPAA:NR)**

ISLAND OF INTRIGUE, THE** (1919) 5 reels Metro bw

May Allison *(Maide Waring)*, Jack Mower *(Gilbert Spear)*, Frederick Vroom, *(Thomas Waring)*, Mrs. Lucille Ward *(Mrs. Julius Smith)*, Gordon Marr *(Alaric Smith)*, Lillian West *(Yorna Smith)*, Hector V. Sarno *(Count Pellessier)*, Tom Kennedy *(Jackson)*, Chance Ward *(Mr. Gobel)*, Edward Alexander *(Jones)*.

Well directed but somewhat padded melodrama about a millionaire's daughter who is kidnaped and held for ransom on a deserted island. A wealthy young man just happens to be camping there with his dog, however, and, of course, he rescues and wins the girl. Not as exciting a picture as it might have been with a more athletic hero.

d, Henry Otto; w, June Mathis, A. S. Le Vino (based on the novel by Isabelle Ostrander); ph, William Fildew.

Adventure **(PR:A MPAA:NR)**

ISLAND OF REGENERATION, THE*** (1915) 6 reels VIT bw

Edith Storey *(Katherine Brenton)*, Antonio Moreno *(The Nomad)*, Bobby Connelly *(The Boy)*, S. Rankin Drew, Leo Delaney, Naomi Childers, Jack Brawn, Lillian Herbert, Logan Paul.

Little Connelly all but stole the show from a fine cast in this entertaining movie about a group of people stranded on a desert island. The Vitagraph used Florida locations to very good effect, and the earthquake scene at the picture's end was particularly well done.

d, Harry Davenport; w, (based on a novel by Cyrus Townsend Brady).

Adventure **(PR:A MPAA:NR)**

ISLE OF CONQUEST*** (1919) 5 reels SEL bw

Norma Talmadge, Natalie Talmadge, Wyndham Standing, Charles Gerard, Hedda Hopper, Claire Whitney, Gareth Hughes, Joe Smiley, Mercita Esmonde, William Bailey.

Forced by her mother to marry a wealthy libertine, Talmadge grows to despise all men. When her ship is torpedoed by the Germans, she is rescued by a young stoker (a college man who hates women because of the shoddy way his fiancee treated him) who manages to get her to a deserted island. As time passes, they find true love with each other, and after her husband dies from a heart attack they are finally free to marry. A much better picture than is sounds, with fresh direction, a good script, and clever acting.

d, Edward Jose; w, John Emerson, Anita Loos (based on the story "By Right of Conquest" by Arthur Hornblow); ph, David Abel.

Drama **(PR:A MPAA:NR)**

ISLE OF FORGOTTEN WOMEN 1/2** (1927) 6 reels COL bw

Conway Tearle *(Bruce Paine)*, Dorothy Sebastian *(Marua)*, Gibson Gowland *(John Stort)*, Alice Calhoun *(Alice Burroughs)*, Harry Semels, William Welch, Eddie Harris.

Tearle confesses to a crime he believes his father committed and flees to a desert island where he encounters the despicable Gowland and his native mistress Sebastian. His fiancee, Calhoun, never loses faith in him and continues working back home to clear his name. One day, Tearle interferes with Gowland as he cruelly abuses Sebastian, and wins the love of the girl and the hatred of the man. The situation comes to a head when Gowland tries to kill Tearle with a speer, but Sebastian shields his body with her own and shoots her degenerate master. The beautiful native dies in his arms, and Tearle soon receives word from the mainland that his name has been cleared.

p, Harry Cohn; d, George B. Seitz; w, Norman Springer (based on a story by Louella Parsons); ph, Joseph Walker; makeup, Fred C. Ryle.

Drama **(PR:A MPAA:NR)**

ISLE OF HOPE, THE*** (1925) 6 reels Richard Talmadge/FBO bw

Richard Talmadge *(Bob Mackay)*, Helen Ferguson *(Dorothy Duffy)*, James Marcus *(Capt. Duffy)*, Bert Strong *(1st Mate)*, Howard Bell *(2nd Mate)*, Edward Gordon *(Chinese Cook)*, George Reed *(Negro Cook)*.

Talmadge, "the prince of pep," plays a wealthy sportsman who sets sail with Marcus to search for treasure on the Isle of Hope. The crew, actually a gang of thugs, mutinies and sets fire to the ship, but Talmadge and the captain's daughter (Ferguson) make it to a deserted island. The ruffians from the boat locate them, however, and capture Ferguson. Then Talmadge, using every stunt in the book, rescues her, captures them, and signals for his friends from the yachting club to come and pick them up.

d, Jack Nelson; w, James Bell Smith; ph, William Marshall, Jack Stevens.

Adventure **(PR:A MPAA:NR)**

ISLE OF LOST MEN** (1928) 6 reels T/C/RAY bw

Tom Santschi *(Capt. Jan Jodahl)*, James Marcus *(Malay Pete)*, Allen Connor *(David Carlisle)*, Patsy O'Leary *(Alma Fairfax)*, Paul Weigel *(Preacher Jason)*, Jules Cowles *(Ship's Cook)*, Maude George *(Kealani)*, Sailor Sharkey.

Shoestring production has Connor locating a fortune in rubies and rescuing a girl who had been kidnaped from Australia and brought to a place populated by desperate fugitives, known as the Isle of Lost Men. The "Lost Men", a lot of scumbags led by Santschi, almost find the vital chart which would lead Connor to the fortune, but in a thrilling climax Connor saves the day.

p, W. Ray Johnston; d, Duke Worne; w, George Pyper (based on a story by Frederick Nebel); t, Dudley Early; ph, Hap Depew; ed, John S. Harrington.

Adventure **(PR:A MPAA:NR)**

ISLE OF LOST SHIPS, THE* 1/2** (1923) 7 reels Tourneur/AFN bw

Anna Q. Nilsson *(Dorothy Fairfax)*, Milton Sills *(Frank Howard)*, Frank Campeau *(Detective Jackson)*, Walter Long *(Peter Forbes)*, Bert Woodruff *(Patrick Joyce)*, Aggie Herring *(Mother Joyce)*, Herschel Mayall *(Capt. Clark)*.

Tourneur, the great director who was also a fine painter, put that talent to good use in this chillingly atmospheric story about a man (Sills) wrongly accused of murder and a beautiful American girl (Nilsson) whose crippled and abandoned vessel drifts into the Sargasso Sea where 15 derelict ships, occupied by 50 strange people, form a lost colony ruled by the brutish Long. When he claims Nilsson to be his own, Sills, in a remarkably realistic fight scene, manages to whip Long and then, putting his mechanical experience to use, renders a submarine operational, and the two escape. Later they are picked up by a U.S. Navy gunboat and Sills eventually proves his innocence and marries his companion in danger.

p, Ned Marin; d, Maurice Tourneur; w, Charles Maigne (based on the novel *The Isle of Dead Ships* by Crittenden Marriott); ph, Arthur Todd; ed, Frank Lawrence; set d, Milton Menasco.

Fantasy/Drama **(PR:A MPAA:NR)**

ISLE OF RETRIBUTION, THE** (1926) 7 reels R-C/FBO bw

Lillian Rich *(Bess Gilbert)*, Robert Frazer *(Ned Cornet)*, Victor McLaglen *(Doomsdorf)*, Mildred Harris *(Lenore Hardenworth)*, Kathleen Kirkham *(Her Mother)*, David Torrence *(Godfrey Cornet) Inez Gomez (Sindy)*.

In an effort to make a man of him, playboy Frazer's millionaire father sends him to Alaska to manage some family holdings. Accompanying him is Rich, his private secretary. The ship sinks, and they make it to an island run by a crazed Russian (McLaglen). The Russian tries to kill Frazer and have his way with Rich, but the young man outwits his adversary and McLaglen is killed by an avalanche. Frazer and Rich then return home to his proud father— and wedding bells.

d, James P. Hogan; w, Fred Kennedy Myton (based on the novel by Edison Marshall); ph, Jules Cronjager; art d, Frank Ormston.

Adventure/Drama (PR:A MPAA:NR)

ISN'T LIFE WONDERFUL**** (1924) 9 reels UA bw

Carol Dempster *(Inga)*, Neil Hamilton *(Paul)*, Helen Lowell *(The Grandmother)*, Erville Alderson *(The Professor)*, Frank Puglia *(Theodor)*, Marcia Harris *(The Aunt)*, Lupino Lane *(Rudolf)*, Hans von Schlettow *(Leader of the Hungry Workers)*, Paul Rehkopf, Robert Scholz *(Hungry Workers)*, Walter Plimmer, Jr. *(The American)*.

Griffith traveled to Germany to make this film about the deplorable conditions which existed there following WW I. Feelings against the former enemy of the Allies were still running high, and it took a great deal of courage for the director to produce this picture, although he did fudge a bit by depicting the central characters as being Polish. This is another landmark achievement by Griffith, and one which certainly influenced the future of the Soviet and German cinemas and even anticipated Italian neo-realism by more than 40 years.

p,d&w, D. W. Griffith (based on a short story by Maj. Geoffrey Moss); ph, Hendrik Sartov, Hal Sintzenich; m, Louis Silvers, Caesare Sudero.

Drama Cas. (PR:A MPAA:NR)

ISOBEL* (1920) 6 reels George H. Davis bw

House Peters *(Sgt. Billy McVeigh)*, Jane Novak *(Isobel Deane)*, Edward J. Pell *(Scottie Deane)*, Tom Wilson *(Cpl. Bucky Smith)*, Bob Walker *(Thomas Pelliter)*, Richard Larned *(Jim Blake)*, Pearlie Norton *(Little Mystery)*, Dick La Reno, Horin Konishi, Hal Wilson.

Drawn out nonsense about a husband and wife who escape to an Eskimo village after killing a whaling captain who attempted to rape her. Later, Peters, of the mounted police, tracks them down and the girl convinces him that her husband is dead. While he is in hiding, the two fall in love, and it comes as no surprise that the people responsible for this dribble would have the husband conveniently expire in time for the last reel clinch.

d&w, Edwin Carewe (based on the novel *The Trails End* by James Oliver Curwood); ph, Robert B. Kurrle.

Drama (PR:A MPAA:NR)

IT** (1927) 7 reels FP/PAR bw

Clara Bow *(Betty Lou)*, Antonio Moreno *(Cyrus Waltham)*, William Austin *(Monty)*, Jacqueline Gadsdon *(Adela Van Norman)*, Gary Cooper *(Newspaper Reporter)*, Julia Swayne Gordon *(Mrs. Van Norman)*, Priscilla Bonner *(Molly)*, Eleanor Lawson *(1st Welfare Worker)*, Rose Tapley *(2nd Welfare Worker)*, Elinor Glyn *(Herself)*, Lloyd Corrigan *(Boat Steward)*.

Combining the title IT with the movie debut of the nationally renowned fiction writer who coined the term (Glyn), plus the presence of perhaps the screen's most saucy personality, Bow, made this one a box office bonanza. The picture, which deals with a shop girl who wins the heart of her department store owner, is predictible but entertaining. There is also a very young and handsome Cooper in the cast, but the thing which, above all else, gives this picture "It" is the presence of that delightfully naughty-but-nice queen of the flappers, Bow. Director Badger became ill during part of the filming of IT, thus von Sternberg is credited with directing several scenes.

d, Clarence Badger, Joseph von Sternberg; w, Hope Loring, Louis D. Lighton, Elinor Glyn (based on the story by Glyn); t, George Marion, Jr.; ph, Kinley Martin; ed, E. Lloyd Sheldon.

Comedy/Drama Cas. (PR:A MPAA:NR)

IT CAN BE DONE* (1921) 5 reels Earl Williams/VIT bw

Earl Williams *(Austin Crane)*, Elinor Fair *(Eve Standish)*, Henry Barrows *(Webb Standish)*, Jack Mathies *(Jasper Braden)*, Jack Carlisle *(Bill Donahue)*, Alfred Aldridge *(Spike Dawson)*, William McCall *(Byron Tingley)*, Florence Hart *(Mrs. Standish)*, Mary Huntress *(Mrs. Faire)*.

A writer is hired by a newspaper to expose three business profiteers but finds he can not do this to his sweetheart's father—who happens to be one—and reforms him instead. A poor picture with too many titles and too little plot.

d, David Smith; w, Frederick J. Jackson; ph, Jack MacKenzie.

Crime/Comedy (PR:A MPAA:NR)

IT IS THE LAW 1/2** (1924) 7 reels FOX bw

Arthur Hohl *(Albert Woodruff/"Sniffer")*, Herbert Heyes *(Justin Victor)*, Mimi Palmeri *(Ruth Allen)*, George Lessey *(Inspector Dolan)*, Robert Young *(Travers)*, Florence Dixon *(Lillian Allen)*, Byron Douglas *(Cummings)*, Olaf Hytten *(Bill Elliott)*, De Sacia Mooers *(Bernice)*, Guido Trento *(Manee)*, Byron Russell *(Harley)*.

Rejected by Palmeri, Hohl murders his double and pins the crime on Heyes, his victorious rival. Heyes is convicted and, years later after his release from prison, kills Hohl. In a nice pre-code twist, he is let off on the grounds that one can not be tried twice for the same crime.

d, J. Gordon Edwards; w, Curtis Benton (based on the play by Elmer Rice, Hayden Talbot); ph, George W. Lane.

Mystery (PR:A MPAA:NR)

IT MUST BE LOVE**** (1926) 7 reels John McCormick/FN bw

Colleen Moore *(Fernie Schmidt)*, Jean Hersholt *(Pop Schmidt)*, Malcolm McGregor *(Jack Dugan)*, Arthur Stone *(Peter Halitovsky)*, Bodil Rosing *(Mom Schmidt)*, Dorothy Seastrom *(Min)*, Cleve Moore *(Al)*, Mary O'Brien *(Lois)*, Ray Hallor *(Joe)*.

Moore lives with her family in the back of her father's German delicatessen and hates the sounds and the smells of the place. To make things worse, her father (Hersholt) has arranged for her to marry his sausage maker (Stone), who smells like a walking garlic clove. One night, against her father's wishes, she attends a dance and meets McGregor, a good looking man she assumes is in stocks. When she returns home, her father, believing that she is ashamed of her family and his business, orders her out of the house. Moore manages to land a job in a department store where she again runs into McGregor and her assumption was correct—he is in stocks. In fact, he's the head stock boy. They continue to see each other, and one night McGregor tells her that he's managed to save $5,000, has great plans for the future, and would like her to be his bride. Moore accepts, and the following week she is invited to dinner at her father's deli. All is forgiven and, in fact, Hersholt proudly informs her that he sold the business, bought a bungalow, and would like her to move in with him. Then the sausage man pops in to propose marriage, and before she can say no there is another knock on the door, and it turns out to be the new owner—McGregor! The world has gone full circle for love-struck Moore but, as the old saying goes, "when you're in love, the whole world is German."

p, John McCormick; d, Alfred E. Green; w, Julian Josephson (based on the story "Delicatessen" by Brooke Hanlon); ph, H. F. Koenekamp.

Comedy/Drama (PR:A MPAA:NR)

ITALIAN, THE* 1/2** (1915) 5 reels New York Motion Picture bw

George Beban *(The Italian)*, Clara Williams *(His Wife)*, Fanny Midgley, J. Frank Burke, Leo Willis.

The great character actor Beban is brilliant as an Italian immigrant who loses his only son because of the indifference of his ward boss. The Italian is sentenced to prison and, after his release, finds himself in a position to cause the death of the politician's child. At the last minute he is unable to go through with it, however, because the little one reminds him of his own baby. A notable early film of producer Ince's and most outstanding for its realistic study of how life was in the slums of New York City for those who came over from Europe in the early 1900s. Graphic as the setting was, it was all done on a set at the mouth of the Santa Ynez canyon, in a growing complex of stages that looked overall like a construction camp, and which would become known as "Inceville."

d, Reginald Barker; sup, Thomas H. Ince; w, C. Gardner Sullivan, Ince (based on a novel by Percy N. Williams).

Drama (PR:A MPAA:NR)

ITALIAN STRAW HAT, AN* 1/2** (1927, Fr.) 7 reels Albatross/Kamenka bw

Albert Prejean *(Ferdinand)*, Olga Tschekowa, Marise Maia, Alice Tissot, Yvonneck, Alex Bondi, Paul Olivier, Jim Gerald.

Clair was 30-years-old when he directed this wonderful comedy. A man must postpone his wedding in order to find a hat identical to the one a woman was wearing while on her way to a romantic rendezvous until his horse ate it. The critical acclaim the young French filmmaker earned for this effort elevated him to the top, and his contribution to the screen would be impressive for many years to come.

d&w, Rene Clair (based on the play by Eugene Labiche, Marc Michel); ph, Maurice Desfassiaux, Nicholas Roudakoff; ed, Henri Dobb; art d, Alexandre Kamenka, Georges Lacombe, Lily Jumel.

Comedy/Farce Cas. (PR:A MPAA:NR)

IT'S A BEAR*** (1919) 5 reels TRI bw

Taylor Holmes *(Orlando Winthrop)*, Vivian Reed *(School Teacher)*, Howard Davies *(William Gogney)*, Edna Holmes *(Belle Waylay)*, Bessie the Bear.

Holmes, who would become a top character actor in the talkies, made a career in the earlier days of playing a wimp. In this one he is a hopeless tenderfoot, sent to his father's ranch from the East to be turned into a man. He encounters plenty of cruelty from the hired hands before taking on the bully foreman and winning the pretty school marm.

d, Lawrence Windom; w, (based on a story by Nina Wilcox Putnam, Norman Jacobson); ph, Sam Landers.

Comedy/Drama (PR:A MPAA:NR)

IT'S HAPPINESS THAT COUNTS* (1918, Brit.) 5 reels BP/BUT bw

Queenie Thomas *(Prudence)*, Harry Drummond *(Richard Blair)*, Ralph Hollis *(Galahad Sanctuary)*.

British love story about a wealthy man who gives up everything in order to marry a free-spirited girl, whose father was destroyed by money.

p&d, Bertram Phillips.

Drama (PR:A MPAA:NR)

IT'S NO LAUGHING MATTER*** (1915) 4 reels Bosworth bw

Macklyn Arbuckle, Adele Farrington, Myrtle Stedman, Herbert Standing, Charles Marriot, Cora Drew.

Homey little rural drama about a poetry-writing postman who brings a husband and wife together again and then reunites them with her mother. The postman loses his job and house, and then when all seems hopeless the checks begin to arrive from the publisher who loved the verses his daughter secretly submitted.

d&w, Lois Weber (based on a story by Jack London).

Comedy/Drama **(PR:A MPAA:NR)**

IT'S THE OLD ARMY GAME* ** (1926) 7 reels FP/PAR bw

W.C. Fields *(Elmer Prettywillie)*, Louise Brooks *(Marilyn Sheridan)*, Blanche Ring *(Tessie Overholt)*, William Gaxton *(George Parker)*, Mary Foy *(Sarah Pancoast)*, Mickey Bennett *(Mickey)*, Josephine Dunn, Jack Luden *(Society Bathers)*, George Currie *(Artist)*, Elisa Cavanna *(Morning Stamp Customer)*, John Merton *(Fireman)*.

There are plenty of vintage Fields gags in this episodic feature, which really consists of three of the great Ziegfeld Follies sketches: "The Drug Store," "A Peaceful Morning," and "The Family Flivver." Brooks' totally natural sexuality nearly bursts from the screen, and the only thing that stands in the way of the fun is watching Ring, one of early vaudeville's greatest stars, reduced to playing a matronly flapper.

p&d, Edward Sutherland; w, Tom J. Geraghty, J. Clarkson Miller (based on the play by Joseph Patrick McEvoy; from sketches written by McEvoy, Fields); t, Ralph Spence, Fields; ph, Alvin Wychoff.

Comedy **(PR:A MPAA:NR)**

IVANHOE (SEE: REBECCA THE JEWESS, 1913, Brit.)

IVANHOE**** (1913) 4 reels IMP bw

King Baggot, Leah Baird, Evelyn Hope, Arthur Scott-Cravan, W. Calvert, Mr. Norman, Wallace Bosco, George Courtenay, Wallace Widdecombe, Jack Bates, A. J. Charlwood, Herbert Brenon, H. Holles, Helen Downing, W. Thomas.

In 1913, Brenon, the Dublin-born director who would go on to rival Griffith, traveled from the U.S. to Britain to film this impressive version of the Sir Walter Scott classic, where the knight of Ivanhoe (Baggot) is beloved by a beautiful Jewess and loves her in turn, but who decides to wed another because of the difference in their stations in life. A variety of action and an entourage of chivalric knights of their ladies, the pageantry of a tournament, and a great castle afire make this a fast-paced and exciting story.

d&w, Herbert Brenon (based on the novel by Sir Walter Scott); ph, E. G. Palmer, S. P. Kinder.

Historical **(PR:A MPAA:NR)**

IVORY SNUFF BOX, THE*** (1915) 5 reels Brady/WORLD bw

Holbrook Blinn, Alma Belwin, Norman Trevor, Robert Cummings.

Beautifully directed and photographed spy film about an American secret service agent who stops the Germans from capturing a snuff box with the secret plans which could lead to the defeat of France. Tourneur's torture chamber scene, where the agent's wife is forced to watch her husband being abused by ultra-violet rays, is masterful.

d, Maurice Tourneur; w, E. M. Ingleton (based on a novel by Frederic Arnold Kummer).

War **(PR:A MPAA:NR)**

J

JACK AND JILL*** (1917) 5 reels Morosco/PAR bw

Jack Pickford *(Jack Ranney)*, Louise Huff *(Mary Dwyer)*, Leo Houck *("Young" Kilroy)*, J. H. Holland *(Lopez Cabrillo)*, Hart Hoxie *("Cactus" Jim)*, Col. Lenone *(Senor Cabrillo)*, Beatrice Burnham *(Doria Cabrillo)*.

Taylor directed this picture about a boxer who heads west after killing an opponent in the ring and saves the ranch he's working on from Mexican bandits. Good performances by Pickford and Huff (as his Bowery sweetheart).

d, William Desmond Taylor; w, Gardner Hunting (based on a story by Margaret Turnbull).

Drama/Western **(PR:A MPAA:NR)**

JACK AND THE BEANSTALK* 1/2** (1917) 10 reels Standard/FOX bw

Francis Carpenter *(Francis/Jack)*, Virginia Lee Corbin *(Virginia/Princess Regina)*, Violet Radcliffe *(Prince Rudolpho)*, Carmen Fay DeRue *(King of Cornwall)*, Jim G. Tarver *(Blunderbore, the Giant)*, Vera Lewis *(The Giantess)*, Ralph Lewis *(Francis' Father)*, Eleanor Washington *(Francis' Mother)*, Ione Glennon *(Virginia's Mother)*, Buddy Messinger, Raymond Lee, Dorothy MacKaye.

A cast of cute children and some very clever sets make this tale of magic beans, hens with golden eggs, and a terrible giant excellent entertainment.

d, C. M. and S. A. Franklin; w, Mary Murillo; ph, Frank Good, Harry Gerstad.

Fantasy **(PR:A MPAA:NR)**

JACK KNIFE MAN, THE* 1/2** (1920) 5 reels King Vidor/FN bw

Fred Turner *(Peter Lane)*, Harry Todd *("Booge")*, Bobby Kelso *("Buddy")*, Willis Marks *(Rev. Resmer Briggles)*, Lillian Leighton *(Mrs. Potter)*, James Corrigan *(George Rapp)*, Claire McDowell *(Liza Merdin)*, Charles Arling *(The Doctor)*, Florence Vidor *(Mrs. Montgomery)*, Anna Dodge, Irene Yeager.

Heart-warming story of an old recluse living on a houseboat who takes in a little boy after his mother's death, and the adventures they share together. Vidor's direction is wonderful, as is the acting and the film's happy ending. Its intrinsic decency makes it a joy to watch over and over again.

d, King Vidor; w, William Parker, Vidor (based on a story by Ellis Parker Butler); ph, Ira H. Morgan.

Drama **Cas.** **(PR:A MPAA:NR)**

JACK O' CLUBS** (1924) 5 reels UNIV bw

Herbert Rawlinson *(John Francis Foley)*, Ruth Dwyer *(Tillie Miller)*, Eddie Gribbon *(Spike Kennedy)*, Esther Ralston *(Queenie Hatch)*, Joseph Girard *(Capt. Dennis Malloy)*, Florence D. Lee *(Mrs. Miller)*, John Fox, Jr. *(Toto)*, Noel Stewart *(Otto)*.

Thinking he shot his sweetheart, Dwyer, crack cop Rawlinson loses his nerve. But when he learns that gangster Gribbon actually fired the bullet, Rawlinson beats the thug to a pulp and restores order to the area.

d, Robert F. Hill; w, Rex Taylor, Raymond L. Schrock (based on a story by Gerald Beaumont); ph, William Thornley.

Drama **(PR:A MPAA:NR)**

JACK O'HEARTS*

(1926) 6 reels David Hartford/American Cinema bw (AKA: JACK OF HEARTS)

Cullen Landis *(Jack Farber)*, Gladys Hulette, Bert Cummings, Antrim Short, John T. Dwyer, John Prince, Vester Pegg.

Too many titles and far too little acting is the problem with this adaptation of a play about a young minister wrongfully sentenced to prison, whose faith eventually allows him to clear his name.

p&d, David Hartford; w, Frances Nordstrom (based on the play "Jack in the Pulpit" by Gordon Morris); ph, Walter Griffin.

Drama **(PR:A MPAA:NR)**

JACK OF HEARTS (SEE: JACK O'HEARTS, 1926)

JACK RIDER, THE** (1921) 5 reels Charles R. Seeling/AY bw

Guinn "Big Boy" Williams *(Frank Stevens)*, Thelma Worth *(Ruth Welsh)*, S. D. Wilcox *(John Welsh)*, J. Buckley Russell *(Howard Gribbon)*, Will Rogers, Jr. *(Little Buster)*.

In order to inherit his father's ranch, tenderfoot Williams must prove himself a man. This he does by laughing off a series of practical jokes pulled on him by the ranch hands, excelling in a rodeo competition and saving the banker's daughter from bandits.

d, Charles R. Seeling; w, Guinn Williams.

Western **(PR:A MPAA:NR)**

JACK, SAM AND PETE** (1919, Brit.) 5 reels Pollock-Daring bw

Percy Moran *(Jack)*, Eddie Willey *(Sam)*, Ernest A. Trimingham *(Pete)*, Manning Haynes *(Cyril Danvers)*, Enid Heather *(Violet Danvers)*, Capt. Jack Kelly *(The Scorpion)*, Garrick Aitken *(The Boy)*, Jack Harding *(The Ferret)*.

The U.S. influence on the British cinema was very much in evidence in this adventure film about a group of cowboys who rescue a child from a kidnap gang set on finding a hidden fortune.

p, Leon Pollock; d, Jack Daring [Percy Moran]; w, (based on the stories of S. Clarke-Hook).

Adventure **(PR:A MPAA:NR)**

JACK SPURLOCK, PRODIGAL*** (1918) 5 reels FOX bw

George Walsh *(Jack Spurlock)*, Dan Mason *(Spurlock, Sr.)*, Ruth Taylor *(Anita Grey)*, Robert Vivian *(Col. Jackson)*, Mike Donlin, Jack Goodman.

Solid comedy has college student Walsh being thrown out of school when his pet bear follows him into the classrooms. Later, he becomes involved with the Onion Workers Union in Newark—taking his father's business on and winning.

d, Carl Harbaugh; w, Ralph H. Spence (based on the novel by George Horace Lorimer); ph, Arthur Edeson.

Comedy **(PR:A MPAA:NR)**

JACK STRAW*** (1920) 5 reels PAR bw

Robert Warwick *(Archduke Sebastian of Pomerania/Jack Straw)*, Carrol McComas *(Ethel Parker Jennings)*, Sylvia Ashton, Charles Ogle, Helene Sullivan, Jean Monte Dumont, Frances Parks, Lucien Littlefield, Robert Brower, Mayme Kelso.

Long overshadowed by his brother Cecil, this is a fine example of William C. De Mille's fine directorial talent. Warwick is a nobleman who does not take himself at all seriously and enjoys working at a number of jobs, just to see how the rest of the world lives. While employed as a waiter in California, he is given the opportunity (as part of a practical joke) to impersonate a man of royal personage. He jumps at the chance because one of the targets of the gag is a newly rich young woman he has long admired from afar. The rib is executed perfectly, the girl falls in love with him and, to the delight of all, in the end he discloses the truth about his *real* lineage.

d, William C. DeMille; w, Olga Printzlau (based on the play by W. Somerset Maugham); ph, L. Guy Wilky.

Comedy/Drama **(PR:A MPAA:NR)**

JACK TAR*** (1915, Brit.) 5 reels Barker/ICC bw

Jack Tessier *(Lt. Jack Atherley)*, Edith Yates *(Mary Westwood)*, Eve Balfour *(Margherita)*, Thomas H. MacDonald *(Max Schultz)*, Harry Royston *(Dick Starling)*, J. Hastings Batson *(Sir Michael Westwood)*, Blanche Forsythe *(The Maid)*.

Based on a popular play, this English wartime thriller deals with the courageous daughter of a British admiral who poses as a Turk in order to save a lieutenant who was framed, and thus rescue the Smyrnan consulate from the nefarious ambitions of a German spy ring.

d, Bert Haldane; w, Rowland Talbot (based on the play by Arthur Shirley, Ben Landeck).

War **(PR:A MPAA:NR)**

JACQUELINE, OR BLAZING BARRIERS**

(1923) 7 reels Pine Tree/Arrow bw (AKA: BLAZING BARRIERS)

Marguerite Courtot *(Jacqueline Roland)*, Helen Rowland *(Jacqueline, as a Child)*, Gus Weinberg *(Her Father)*, Effie Shannon *(Her Mother)*, Lew Cody (Raoul Radon), Joseph Depew *(Raoul Radon, as a Child)*, Russell Griffin *(Little Peter)*, J. Barney Sherry *(His Father)*, Edmund Breese *(Edmund MacDonald)*, Edria Fisk *(His Daughter)*, Sheldon Lewis *(Henri Dubois)*, Charles Fang *(Li Chang)*, Paul Panzer *(Gambler)*, Taxi, the Dog.

North Woods programmer about a pretty girl, whom everybody from the lumber camp owner to the Chinese villain, covet. She ends up, or course, with the clean-cut hero, but only after a badly staged forest fire.

d, Dell Henderson; w, Thomas F. Fallon, Dorothy Farnum (based on the story by James Oliver Curwood); ph, George Peters, Charles Downs, Dan Maher.

Drama **(PR:A MPAA:NR)**

JAILBIRD, THE*** (1920) 5 reels PAR bw

Douglas MacLean *(Shakespeare Clancy)*, Doris May *(Alice Whitney)*, Lew Morrison *("Skeeter" Burns)*, William Courtright *(Noah Gibbs)*, Wilbur Higby *(Joel Harvey)*, Otto Hoffman *(Elkemah Pardee)*, Monty Collins *(Asa Grider)*, Bert Woodruff *(Grandpa Binney)*.

Pleasant comedy has MacLean this time playing a crook who escapes from prison six months early, and then inherits some property and a small-town newspaper in Kansas. There is an oil swindle which actually turns into a gusher, and in the end, everybody goes straight. MacLean made better pictures, but this one does not fail to entertain.

d, Lloyd Ingraham; sup, Thomas H. Ince; w, Julien Josephson; ph, Bert Cann.

Comedy **(PR:A MPAA:NR)**

JAKE THE PLUMBER* (1927) 6 reels R-C/FBO bw

Jess Devorska *(Jake)*, Sharon Lynn *(Sarah Levine)*, Rosa Rosanova *(Mrs. Levine)*, Ann Brody *(Mrs. Schwartz)*, Bud Jamison *(Fogarty)*, Carol Halloway *(Mrs. Levis)*, William H. Tooker *(Mr. Levis)*, Dolores Brinkman *(Sadrie Rosen)*, Eddie Harris *(Poppa Levine)*, Fanchon Frankel *(Rachael Rosenblatt)*.

The usual Jewish and Irish ethnic humor, with a touch of poor slapstick and forced pathos. FBO's attempt to make a feature film star out of the very plain Devorska was a complete failure—as was this picture.

d, Edward I. Luddy; w, James J. Tynan (based on a story by Luddy); ph, Phillip Tannura.

Comedy **(PR:A MPAA:NR)**

JAMESTOWN** (1923) 4 reels Chronicles of America/Pathe bw

Dolores Cassinelli *(Pocahontas)*, Robert Gaillard *(Sir Thomas Dale)*, Harry Kendall *(Capt. George Yeardley)*, Leslie Stowe *(The Reverend Richard Buck)*, Paul McAllister *(Don Diego de Molina)*, Leslie Austin *(John Rolfe)*.

Part of the Chronicles of America series for the Yale University Press, this historical re-creation deals with the struggle between the British settlers and their Spanish enemy, with the situation being saved by Indian intervention on the side of the English following the marriage of John Rolfe (Austin) to Pocahontas (Cassinelli).

d, Edwin L. Hollywood; w, Roswell Dague (based on *Pioneers of the Old South; A Chronicle of English Colonial Beginnings* by Mary Johnston).

Historical **(PR:A MPAA:NR)**

JANE EYRE**** (1921) 7 reels Hugo Ballin/Hodkinson bw

Norman Trevor *(Mr. Rochester)*, Mabel Ballin *(Jane Eyre)*, Crauford Kent *(St. John Rivers)*, Emily Fitzroy *(Grace Poole, a Servant)*, John Webb Dillon *(Mason, Rochester's Brother)*, Louis Grisel *(John Eyre, Jane's Uncle)*, Stephen Carr *(John Reed)*, Vernie Atherton *(Miss Fairfax)*, Elizabeth Aeriens *(Mrs. Rochester)*, Harlan Knight *(Mr. Breckelhurst)*, Helen Miles *(Burns)*, Julia Hurley *(Rivers' Maid)*, Sadie Mullen *(Miss Ingram)*, June Ellen Terry *(Adele, Mr. Rochester's Ward)*, Florence Flager *(Miss Mason)*, Bertha Kent *(Rochester's Maid)*, Marie Shaffer *(Mrs. Reed)*.

The moody, irascible Rochester (Trevor) takes grown-up orphan Jane Eyre (Ballin) into his home as companion to his young ward, Terry. Love blossoms, but on the day Ballin is to marry Trevor, it is revealed that his insane wife has long been isolated within his house. Ballin escapes the house and is consoled by clergyman Kent, who also comes to love her. Trevor's wife escapes her close confinement and sets his house afire, losing her life in the process, and causing his blindness. Balling returns to him; his sight is restored for a happy ending. Hugo Ballin's splendid sense of the pictorial, and Mabel Ballin's lovely performance, made this translation of the classic Bronte novel a near work of art.

p,d&w, Hugo Ballin (based on the novel by Charlotte Bronte); ph, James Diamond.

Drama **(PR:A MPAA:NR)**

JANE GOES A' WOOING* (1919) 5 reels PAR bw

Vivian Martin *(Jane Neill)*, Niles Welch *(Monty Lyman)*, Casson Ferguson *(Micky Donovan)*, Spottiswoode Aitken *(David Lyman)*, Helen Dunbar *(Mrs. Arliss)*, Byrdine Zuber *(Nita Arliss)*, Clyde Benson *(Harmon)*, McKenzie Twins *(The Kids)*, Herbert Standing *(Deronodo), Lila Lee*.

Martin, a winsome and prankishly endearing ingenue, made somewhat of a career out of Cinderella roles such as this one about a girl who raises her twin sisters and runs the family lunch wagon after her father dies. She arranges for Ferguson, a young man with a crush on her, to handle the business while she takes a job as secretary to a millionaire and his nephew, who is writing a play. When the old man dies he leaves everything to Martin, but the girl who thought she had a thing for the nephew comes to realize that the lad is a weakling, tears up the will, and returns to Ferguson. The couple do manage to live comfortably, however, because the profits from the play are assigned to Martin, and it turns out to be a blockbuster.

d, George Melford; w, Edith Kennedy; ph, Paul Perry.

Romance **(PR:A MPAA:NR)**

JANICE MEREDITH**** (1924) 11 reels COS/MG bw-c

Marion Davies *(Janice Meredith)*, Harrison Ford *(Charles Fownes)*, Holbrook Blinn *(Lord Clowes)*, Maclyn Arbuckle *(Squire Meredith)*, Hattie Delaro *(Mrs. Meredith)*, Joseph Kilgour *(George Washington)*, Mrs. Maclyn Arbuckle *(Martha Washington)*, George Nash *(Sir William Howe)*, [Frederick] Tyrone Power *(Lord Cornwallis)*, Robert Thorne *(Patrick Henry)*, Walter Law *(Gen. Charles Lee)*, Lionel Adams *(Thomas Jefferson)*, Nicolai Koesberg *(Lafayette)*, George Siegmann *(Col. Rahl)*, W. C. Fields *(British Sergeant)*, Edwin Argus *(Louis XVI)*, Princess De Bourbon *(Marie Antoinette)*, Wilfred Noy *(Dr. Joseph Warren)*, Ken Maynard *(Paul Revere)*, Helen Lee Worthing *(Mrs. Loring)*, Spencer Charters *(Squire Hennion)*, Olin Howland *(Philemon Hennion)*, May Vokes *(Susie)*, Douglas Stevenson *(Charles Mowbray)*, Harlan Knight *(Theodore Larkin)*, Mildred Arden *(Tabitha Larkin)*, Lee Beggs *(Benjamin Franklin)*, Joe Raleigh *(Arthur Lee)*, Wilson Reynolds *(Parson McClave)*, Jerry Peterson *(Cato)*, Isadore Marcel *(Inn-Keeper)*, Keane Waters *(Servant)*, Edgar Nelson *(Tailor)*, Byron Russell *(Capt. Parker)*, Colonel Patterson *(Maj. Pitcairn)*, George Cline *(Trooper Heirich Bruner)*, Burton McEvilly *(Alexander Hamilton)*.

It is said that William Randolph Hearst spent more than $1.5 million to have Davies and costar Ford (who plays a British aristocrat-turned-patriot) win the Revolutionary War for Washington. Along the way they created quite a picture, and some of the highlights—in addition to the love story—were lavish re-creations of Paul Revere's ride, the Boston Tea Party, Patrick Henry's "give me liberty, or give me death" speech, the winter at Valley Forge, Washington crossing the Delaware, the battles of Lexington and Trenton, and the surrender of Cornwallis at Yorktown.

d, E. Mason Hopper; w, Lillian Hayward (based on *Janice Meredith, a Story of the American Revolution* by Paul Leicester Ford); ph, Ira H. Morgan, George Barnes; m, Deems Taylor; ed, Walter Futter; set d. Joseph Urban; cos, Gretl Urban Thurlow.

Historical Drama **(PR:A MPAA:NR)**

JAVA HEAD*** (1923) 8 reels FP/PAR bw

Leatrice Joy *(Taou Yuen)*, Jacqueline Logan *(Nettie Vollar)*, Frederick Strong *(Jeremy Ammidon)*, Albert Roscoe *(Gerrit Ammidon)*, Arthur Stuart Hull *(William Ammidon)*, Rose Tapley *(Rhoda Ammidon)*, Violet Axzelle *(Laurel Ammidon)*, Audrey Berry *(Sidsall Ammidon)*, Polly Archer *(Camilla Ammidon)*, Betty Bronson *(Janet Ammidon)*, George Fawcett *(Barzil Dunsack)*, Raymond Hatton *(Edward Dunsack)*, Helen Lindroth *(Kate Vollar)*, Dan Pennell *(Broadrick)*, George Stevens *(Butler)*, Mimi Sherwood *(Maid)*, Frances Hatton *(Nurse)*.

Joy is splendid as the Chinese princess an American marries to save from being ritualistically killed. He brings her home to New England, even though he still desperately loves a home-town girl. Later, when the princess learns of her husband's feelings and the sacrifice he made on her behalf, she commits suicide by overdosing on opium.

d, George Melford; w, Waldemar Young (based on the novel by Joseph Hergesheimer); ph, Bert Glennon.

Drama **(PR:A MPAA:NR)**

JAWS OF STEEL*** (1927) 6 reels WB bw

Rin-Tin-Tin *(Rinty)*, Jason Robards *(John Warren)*, Helen Ferguson *(Mary Warren)*, Mary Louise Miller *(Baby Warren)*, Jack Curtis *(Thomas Grant Taylor)*, Robert Perry *(The Sheriff)*, George Connors *(Alkali Joe)*.

Another in the series of entertaining Rin-Tin-Tin pictures. This time the canine star is lost in the desert as a pup and grows up to be thought of as a wild killer. He is hunted throughout most of the film, narrowly avoiding capture, until he finally brings the bad guys to justice and proves his true identity to his delighted owners.

d, Ray Enright; w, Charles R. Condon (based on a story by Gregory Rogers); ph, Barney McGill.

Western **(PR:A MPAA:NR)**

JAZZ GIRL, THE** (1926) 6 reels Motion Picture Guild bw

Gaston Glass *(Rodney Blake)*, Edith Roberts *(Janet Marsh)*, Howard Truesdale *(John Marsh)*, Murdock MacQuarrie *(Henry Wade)*, Colt Albertson *(Frank Arnold)*, Ernie Adams *(Detective)*, Sabel Johnson *(Big Bertha)*, Dick Sutherland *(The Chef)*, Lea Delworth *(Sadie Soakum)*.

Contrary to the impression the title gives, this movie is not about a young lady who takes up the trombone after listening to Kid Ory. It's actually about an amateur girl detective, who falls in love with a newspaper reporter while breaking up a gang of rum runners.

d, Howard Mitchell; w, Bruce Truman; ph, Ernest Miller.

Crime/Romance **(PR:A MPAA:NR)**

JAZZ MAD** (1928) 7 reels UNIV-Jewel bw AKA: THE SYMPHONY

Jean Hersholt *(Franz Hausmann)*, Marion Nixon *(Elsa Hausmann)*, George Lewis *(Leopold Ostberg)*, Roscoe Karns *(Sol Levy)*, Torben Meyer *(Kline)*, Andrew Arbuckle *(Schmidt)*, Charles Clary *(Mr. Ostberg)*, Clarissa Selwynne *(Mrs. Ostberg)*, Patricia Caron *(Miss Ostberg)*, Alfred Hertz *(Conductor)*, The Hollywood Bowl Symphony Orchestra.

Hersholt, a serious composer who cannot sell his music, takes a job leading a vaudeville band so that his daughter Nixon will be in a position to marry Lewis, the son of a super snob. After catching Hersholt's act, Lewis' father is so impressed that he forbids his son to even talk to the composer's daughter on the telephone—a command which immediately plunges Hersholt into a paralytic state. The old boy does recover, however, and even manages to rush onto the stage and wave a baton when Nixon, with the help of a show biz agent, arranges for the Hollywood Bowl Orchestra to play his unpublished symphony. This was a cornball plot to be sure, but it did lend itself to the new technology of synchronized music. The studio, unfortunately, failed to take advantage of this opportunity.

d, F. Harmon Weight; w, Charles Kenyon (based on a story by Svend Gade); t, Walter Anthony; ph, Gilbert Warrenton; ed, Edward Cahn.

Drama **(PR:A MPAA:NR)**

JAZZLAND*** (1928) 6 reels A. Carlos/QDC bw

Bryant Washburn *(Ernest Hallam)*, Vera Reynolds *(Stella Baggott)*, Carroll Nye *(Homer Pew)*, Forrest Stanley *(Hamilton Pew)*, Virginia Lee Corbin *(Martha Baggott)*, Violet Bird *(Kitty Pew)*, Carl Stockdale *(Joe Bitner)*, Edward Cecil *(Wilbraham)*, George Raph *(Nedick)*, Nicholas Caruso *(Jackson)*, Florence Turner *(Mrs. Baggott)*, Richard Belfield *(Mr. Baggott)*.

In an attempt to prevent a big time nightclub from opening in their small New England town, a newspaper reporter and his brother seek out the identity of the owner. The brother is murdered at the club, and the leading lady's sister gets slapped around a bit but, in the end, the criminals get theirs.

d, Dallas M. Fitzgerald; w, Ada McQuillan (based on a story by Samuel Merwin); t, Tom Miranda; ph, Faxon Dean, Lauren A. Draper; ed, George McGuire.

Crime/Drama **(PR:A MPAA:NR)**

JAZZMANIA** (1923) 9 reels TIF/Metro bw

Mae Murray *(Ninon)*, Rod La Rocque *(Jerry Langdon)*, Robert Frazer *(Capt. Valmar)*, Edward Burns *(Sonny Daimler)*, Jean Hersholt *(Prince Otto of Como)*, Lionel Belmore *(Baron Bolo)*, Herbert Standing *(Josephus Ranson)*, Mrs. J. Farrell MacDonald *(Marline)*, Wilfred Lucas *(Julius Furman, American Capitalist)*, J. Herbert Frank *(Col. Kerr)*, Carl Harbaugh *(Gavona)*, Harry Northrup *(American Capitalist)*, Thomas Guise *(Gen. Muroff)*, Henry Barrows *(August Daimler)*.

This absurd script about the jazz-loving queen of a Balkan country who refuses to marry a prince, and he in turn starts a revolution, is really only an excuse for Murray to model dozens of beautiful costumes and perform a couple of dance numbers. The picture ends with Murray turning the kingdom into a republic and marrying her American sweetheart.

d, Robert Z. Leonard; w, Edmund Goulding; t, Alfred A. Cohn; ph, Oliver T. Marsh; set d, Cedric Gibbons.

Drama **(PR:A MPAA:NR)**

JEALOUS HUSBANDS** (1923) 7 reels Tourneur/AFN bw

Earle Williams *(Ramon Martinez)*, Jane Novak *(Alice Martinez)*, Ben Alexander *(Bobbie/Spud)*, Don Marion *(Sliver)*, George Siegmann *("Red" Lynch)*, Emily Fitzroy *(Amaryllis)*, Bull Montana *("Portland Kid")*, J. Gunnis Davis *("Sniffer Charlie")*, Carl Miller *(Harvey Clegg)*, Wedgewood Nowell *(George Conrad)*, Carmelita Geraghty *(Carmen Inez)*.

Williams believes that his wife, Novak, is cheating, so he gives their little boy Alexander to a band of traveling gypsies. Actually, Novak was covering for Williams' sister Geraghty. Later, the sister dies in a shipwreck, and Alexander (now known by his Gypsy name, Spud) returns home to reunite his parents. This was not the great Tourneur's finest moment.

d, Maurice Tourneur; w, Fred Kennedy Myton; ph, Scott R. Beal.

Drama **(PR:A MPAA:NR)**

JENNY BE GOOD** (1920) 6 reels REA bw

Mary Miles Minter *(Jenny Riano)*, Jay Belasco *(Royal Renshaw)*, Margaret Shelby *(Jolanda Van Mater)*, Frederick Stanton *(Aaron Shuttles)*, Sylvia Ashton *(Sophia Shuttles)*, Edwin Brown *(Prof. Gene Jiggs)*, Lillian Rambeau *(Mrs. Van Mater)*, Catherine Wallace, Fanny Cossar, Maggie Halloway Fisher, Grace Pike.

It is to their credit that Taylor and Minter could do anything with this truly terrible script about a family of social-climbing millionaires who kidnap their son and ship him off by yacht, while they arrange to have his marriage to a little orphan (Minter) annulled. On his return he is informed that she wanted the union terminated, so he rebounds by marrying an aristocratic dope fiend. Later, while taking his wife to a sanitarium for the cure, there is an automobile accident in which she is killed and he badly injured. Minter, by this time, has become an ace violinist, and on the night of her big debut at the opera house, a wire arrives telling of her former husband's hospitalization. Naturally, she leaves a couple of thousand patrons sitting on their hands, while she rushes off to be a part of his recovery— and forever his wife.

d, William Desmond Taylor; w, Julia Crawford Ivers (based on the novel by Wilbur Finley Fauley); ph, James C. Van Trees.

Drama **(PR:A MPAA:NR)**

JESSE JAMES*** (1927) 8 reels PAR bw

Fred Thomson *(Jesse James)*, Nora Lane *(Zerelda Mimms)*, Montagu Love *(Frederick Mimms)*, Mary Carr *(Mrs. Zerelda Samuels)*, James Pierce *(Frank James)*, Harry Woods *(Bob Ford)*, William Courtright *(Parson Bill)*, Silver King the Horse.

Thomson gave a certain heroically athletic dash to this telling of the legendary outlaw's life and death. His great love for a Yankee girl is the main departure here, and the film is well done, for the most part. As one of the first motion pictures to glorify a cold-blooded killer, it did, however, meet with a certain amount of controversy at the time of its release.

d, Lloyd Ingraham; sup, Alfred L. Werker; w, Frank M. Clifton, Jesse James, Jr.; ph, Allen Siegler.

Biography/Western **(PR:A MPAA:NR)**

JESSE JAMES AS THE OUTLAW*** (1921) Mesco bw

Jesse James, Jr. *(Himself/Jesse James)*, Diana Reed, Marguerite Hungerford.

In this sequel to JESSE JAMES UNDER THE BLACK FLAG, the eastern millionaire has finished reading the first volume on the life of Jesse James and informs the outlaw's son that he still wants to marry his daughter. But James insists that he read the second volume before proposing. The picture then flashes back to tell the familiar story, which concludes with the shooting of the man "society made a criminal." Then, when the film flashes forward, the easterner's love for James' daughter has only increased, which pleases her father very much.

d&w, Franklin B. Coates; set d, Edgar Kellar.

Biographical/Western **(PR:A MPAA:NR)**

JESSE JAMES UNDER THE BLACK FLAG*** (1921) 8 reels Mesco bw

Jesse James, Jr. *(Himself/Jesse James)*, Franklin B. Coates *(Himself)*, Diana Reed, Marguerite Hungerford.

Author Coates is going over his book on the life of Jesse James with the outlaw's son and granddaughter when a young eastern millionaire crash-lands his airplane nearby. The easterner is immediately attracted to the girl, but she refuses to tell him her last name. Finally he visits the famous bank robber's son and is given the Coates book to read. The film then flashes back to 1863 and chronicles James' involvement with Quantrill's Missouri Guerrillas. The narrative ends with the conclusion of the Civil War, and the picture flashes forward to the flier understanding the girl's reluctance to disclose her identity. In a sequel, JESSE JAMES AS THE OUTLAW, the story continues.

d&w, Franklin B. Coates; set d, Edgar Kellar.

Biographical/Western **(PR:A MPAA:NR)**

JEWELS OF DESIRE*** (1927) 6 reels Metropolitan/PDC bw

Priscilla Dean *(Margarita Solano)*, John Bowers *(Maclyn Mills)*, Walter Long *(Pedro)*, Luke Cosgrave *(Capt. Blunt)*, Syd Crossley *(Taxi Driver)*, Ernie Adams *(The Rat)*, Raymond Wells *(Spanish Joe)*, Marie Percivale *(Old Indian Woman)*.

When Dean inherits an old Spanish estate, she also uncovers a map detailing the location of buried treasure. With the help of a couple of male friends, she sets out to find it. They are forced along the way, however, to do battle with a gang of cutthroats (providing plenty of thrills in the tradition of Pearl White and Ruth Roland) before good triumphs over evil and, in the end, the wealth is delivered to the deserving.

d, Paul Powell; w, Anthony Coldewey (based on a short story by Agnes Parsons); ph, Georges Benoit; art d, Charles Cadwallader.

Adventure **(PR:A MPAA:NR)**

JILT, THE* (1922) 5 reels UNIV bw

Marguerite De La Motte *(Rose Trenton)*, Ralph Graves *(Sandy Sanderson)*, Matt Moore *(George Prothero)*, Ben Hewlett *(His Secretary)*, Harry De Vere *(Rose's Father)*, Eleanor Hancock *(Her Mother)*.

De La Motte nearly marries Moore, who was blinded in the Great War, but can't go through with it because of her love for Graves. Moore goes off to Europe and, after returning, takes a ride with his former rival. He comes back alone, and explains that they were attacked by thugs and, because he could not help in fighting them off, Graves was killed. The next day, De La Motte receives a letter informing her that Moore had some time ago had an operation which restored his sight. At that point, Graves, who is alive after all, rushes in and throws the rotter out.

d, Irving Cummings; w, Arthur Statter (based on a story by R. Ramsey); ph, William Marshall.

Drama **(PR:A MPAA:NR)**

JIM GRIMSBY'S BOY*** (1916) 5 reels Kay-Bee/TRI bw

Frank Keenan, Enid Markey, Fanny Midgley, J. P. Lockney.

The wonderful character actor, Keenan, plays a mountain man who just can't accept his wife presenting him with a daughter rather than a son. So he names the child "Bill" and proceeds to raise it as a boy. Those little feminine instincts begin to show through, though——so much so, in fact, that "Bill" ends up winning the heart of the much sought after, and very handsome, sheriff.

d, Reginald Barker; sup, Thomas Ince; w, Lanier Bartlett.

Drama/Comedy **(PR:A MPAA:NR)**

JIM THE CONQUEROR*** (1927) 6 reels Metropolitan/PDC bw

William Boyd *(Jim Burgess)*, Elinor Fair *(Polly Graydon)*, Walter Long *(Hank Milford)*, Tully Marshall *(Dave Mahler)*, Tom Santschi *(Sam Black)*, Marcelle Corday *(Judy)*.

Boyd admires a girl he sees while in Italy and New York and is surprised, upon returning home to the West during the cattle wars, that she is a local ranch owner. At first he is met by her hostility, but that soon turns to love after Boyd (in his pre-Hopalong Cassidy days) defeats the bad men and restores order to the territory. Unusually good cast for a Poverty Row western makes this one far above the average.

d, George B. Seitz; w, Will M. Ritchey (based on the novel by Peter Bernard Kyne); ph, Hal Rosson; art d, Charles Cadwallader.

Western **(PR:A MPAA:NR)**

JIM THE PENMAN** (1921) 6 reels Whitman Bennett/AFN bw

Lionel Barrymore *(James Ralston)*, Doris Rankin *(Nina Bronson)*, Anders Randolf *(Baron Hartfeld)*, Douglas MacPherson *(Louis Percival)*, Gladys Leslie *(Agnes Ralston)*, Charles Coghlan *(Capt. Redwood)*, James Laffey *(E. J. Smith)*, Ned Burton *(Enoch Bronson)*, Arthur Rankin *(Lord Drelincourt)*.

Barrymore programmer about a man who becomes embroiled in a life of crime in order to save the father of the woman he loves from financial ruin. Finally, guilt-ridden by his deeds, he sinks the yacht on which the mob has gathered, killing everyone—including himself.

p, Whitman Bennett; d, Kenneth Webb; w, Dorothy Farnum (based on the play by Charles Lawrence Young); ph, T. L. Griffith, Harry Stradling.

Crime **(PR:A MPAA:NR)**

JIMMIE'S MILLIONS**

(1925) 6 reels Carlos/FBO bw (AKA: JIMMY'S MILLIONS)

Richard Talmadge *(Jimmie Wicherly)*, Betty Francisco *(Susan Jane Montague)*, Charles Clary *(Luther Ball)*, Brinsley Shaw *(John Saunders)*, Dick Sutherland *(William Johnson)*, Ina Anson *(Patience Delavan)*, Lee Moran *(Speck Donnelly)*, Wade Boteler *(Mickey Flannagan)*.

Talmadge, an habitually tardy person, is left $1 million by his uncle, on the condition that he report to the old man's lawyer every day at a certain time for three months. The person to whom the fortune will go, in the event that Talmadge slips up, frames him for murder. But Talmadge gets out of jail, clears his name, inherits the cash, and marries his lawyer's ward.

d, James P. Hogan; w, Frank Howard Clark (based on a story by John Moroso); ph, William Marshall; ed, Doane Harrison.

Adventure **(PR:A MPAA:NR)**

JIMMY** (1916, Brit.) 4 reels B&C/GAU bw

John Astley *(Jimmy St. Quinton)*, George Tully *(Sir Phillip St. Quinton)*, Letty Paxton *(Marion Denbeigh)*, A. V. Bramble *(John Denbeigh)*, Phyllis Thatcher *(Ruth Denbeigh)*, M. Gray Murray *(Ferguson)*, Malcolm Keen *(Dr. Stoneham)*, Betty O'Neill *(Nurse Vivian)*, Brett Strange Winter *(Cook)*.

Shot during WW I, this morale-boosting British feature tells of the crooked son of a patriotic banker, who enlists in the service, is wounded while performing bravely under enemy fire, wins an honorary medal, and returns home a new man.

d, Elliot Stannard, A. V. Bramble; w, Stannard (based on the novel by John Strange Winter).

War **(PR:A MPAA:NR)**

JIMMY'S MILLIONS (SEE: JIMMIE'S MILLIONS, 1925)

JO THE CROSSING SWEEPER** (1918, Brit.) 5 reels Barker/Bolton bw

Unity Moore *(Jo)*, Dora de Winton *(Lady Dedlock)*, Andre Beaulieu *(Tulkinghorne)*, Connie Lever *(Esther)*, Rolf Leslie *(Bucket)*.

Based on a Dickens novel, this British drama deals with a woman who eventually dies from grief after she is accused of murdering the attorney who revealed the existence of a child by her former marriage.

d, Alexander Butler; w, Irene Miller (based on the novel *Bleak House* by Charles Dickens).

Drama **(PR:C MPAA:NR)**

JOAN OF PLATTSBURG*** (1918) 6 reels Goldwyn bw

Mabel Normand *(Joan)*, Robert Elliott *(Capt. Lane)*, William Fredericks *(Superintendent Fisher)*, Edward Elkas *(Silverstein)*, John W. Dillion *(Miggs)*, Willard Dashiell *(Colonel)*, Edith McAlpin *(Mrs. Lane)*, Isabel Vernon *(Mrs. Miggs)*, Joseph Smiley.

Living in an orphan asylum near the Army training camp at Plattsburg, Normand is given a copy of the life of Joan of Arc by one of the officers. The patriotic little orphan is inspired by this great story and dreams only of serving her country. One night, while sitting in the basement reading her book, she hears voices. At first, she believes them to be a figment of her very active imagination, but they turn out to actually belong to spies—which, of course, gives Normand the opportunity to bring them to justice, save her country, and be rather like the saintly lady of her book.

d, George Loane Tucker, William Humphrey; w, Tucker (based on the play by Porter Emerson Browne); ph, Oliver T. Marsh.

Comedy/War **(PR:A MPAA:NR)**

JOAN OF THE WOODS* (1918) 5 reels WORLD bw

June Elvidge *(Joan Travers)*, Walter Pratt Lewis *(Old Man Travers)*, Albert Hart *(Paul)*, George MacQuarrie *(Phillip Wentworth)*, Marguerite Gale *(Mrs. Dicks)*, John Bowers *(Norman Dicks)*, Henrietta Simpson *(Mrs. Morris)*, Dore Davison *(Pawnbroker)*, Mrs. Tansey *(Pawnbroker's Wife)*, Marie Pagano *(Mollie)*.

This shoddy melodrama tells of a lawyer who marries a mountain girl and brings her back to the city, where she is almost completely ignored. A daughter comes from this union, but the mother soon dies of a broken heart, and a pawnbroker takes the little girl in. The lawyer marries an old flame who has a son by a previous marriage, and the young man, while in college, hocks a few items at the pawn shop and meets the unfortunate girl. They are secretly married, and the young fellow, now in the Navy, ships out. Before leaving, however, he makes his bride swear that she will keep their wedding a secret. This she does, even after their child is born. The puritanical pawnbroker throws her out, and she is befriended by a prostitute. The baby dies, and the girl is accused of its murder. She is brought before the court, and the judge turns out to be her *father*! He is about to throw the book at her, when the sailor rushes in, identifies himself as her husband—and the picture mercifully ends.

d, Travers Vale; w, Louise Vale.

Drama **(PR:O MPAA:NR)**

JOAN THE WOMAN**** (1916) 10 reels LAS/Cardinal bw

Geraldine Farrar *(Joan of Arc)*, Raymond Hatton *(Charles VII)*, Hobart Bosworth *(Gen. La Hire)*, Theodore Roberts *(Cauchon)*, Wallace Reid *(Eric Trent)*, Charles Clary *(La Tremouille)*, James Neill *(Laxart)*, Tully Marshall *(L'Oiseleur)*, Lawrence Peyton *(Gaspard)*, Horace B. Carpenter *(Jacques d'Arc)*, Lillian Leighton *(Isambeau)*, Marjorie Daw *(Katherine)*, Stephen Gray *(Pierre)*, Ernest Joy *(Robert de Beaudricourt)*, John Oaker *(Jean de Metz)*, Hugo B. Kotch *(The Duke of Burgundy)*, William Conklin *(John of Luxembourg)*, Walter Long *(The Executioner)*, William Elmer *(Guy Townes)*, Emilius Jorgensen *(Michael)*, Cleo Ridgely, Ramon Samaniego [Novarro], Lucien Littlefield, Donald Crisp, James Young, George Melford, P. Perry, Clarence Geldert.

Director DeMille truly turned a corner in his career with this, the first of his many epic historical spectacles. In a trench in France during WW I, young English soldier Reid unearths an old, rusty sword dating back to the early part of the 15th century. As he muses over his find, he falls into a sleepy reverie which casts him as a soldier in the service of La Pucelle, the Maid of Orleans—Joan of Arc—the stocky peasant girl of 16 summers (played by Farrar) whose angel-inspired quest was to wrest the throne of France from the invading English forces and thrust it on a somewhat reluctant Dauphin, later Charles VII (played by Hatton). Farrar, prodded to her mission by voices only she can hear (voices visualized by the camera as the Angel Azael, marching to battle beside her as a ghostly shade in double exposure), having convinced the French courtiers of the truth of her assertions, leads her troops in the ultimately successful siege of Orleans. Tempted by the temporal, especially her handsome lieutenant, Reid, she battles both the English troops and her own hormones, lifting the spirits of citizenry and soldiery alike. Exhorting her forces by her own brave example, she breaches the walls of mighty La Tourelle, brandishing her broadsword with the best of the alternative gender. In the furious fighting—some of the best battle footage ever—the white-armored maiden beats back the Britons and their traitorous Burgundian allies, winning the honor of attending the majestic coronation of Hatton at the great cathedral at Rheims. Jealous of her popularity among the peasantry, the courtiers later conspire to undermine the Maid, and Farrar's logistics are curtailed severely. Her campaign falters. Finally, Farrar is captured by the turncoat Burgundians, who peddle her to the Britons. Uneasy about her because of her apparent spiritual support, the English defer her fate until such a time as she can be defamed; they turn her over to a French ecclesiastical court for trial. Pilloried by the clerics for failing to go through channels in her discourses with the deity, her inquisitors sentence her to burn at the stake. Fearful of the impending fire and wearied by the priestly prisonkeepers, Farrar recants; her death warrant is commuted to life imprisonment. Later, gaining fresh courage, she again avows her faith in her voices. The death sentence prevails; the weak-willed king, Hatton—her presumptive protector—is unable to save the Maid from the pyre. A city square glows in the first rays of dawn light, a centered stake its only occupant. A workman enters bearing bundles of faggots. He carefully positions the wood about the upright. Slowly the square fills with curious onlookers. The death procession arrives; Farrar is again offered an opportunity to disavow her voices. Refusing to recant, she is bound to the stake. The flames blaze up around her. Reid, in his contemporary uniform, awakens in his trench. Sparked by the example of the Maid of Orleans, he bravely sacrifices his own life in a dangerous night assault on a nearby German position. This sweeping epic, which allegorized by mixing the historical with the contemporary—a device DeMille was to employ frequently in years to come—is a remarkable production. The total budget for the film was over $300,000, a staggering cost for the time. The studio was becoming more cost-conscious; during filming, the Jesse L. Lasky Feature Play Company founded by DeMille, Lasky, and Samuel Goldfish (later Goldwyn) merged with the Famous Players Film Company headed by the tight-fisted Adolph Zukor. More than 1,400 armored extras were employed in the great panoramic battle scenes, the first of many such crowded choreographies DeMille was to film. For the first time in cinematic history, a director used telephone sets to communicate with his assistant directors during these massed field maneuvers, a device that saved an enormous amount of time. The great cathedral at Rheims, the mighty fortress of La Tourelle, and the other massive setpieces were constructed and filmed at Lasky's enormous ranch. Release prints were hand-tinted in delicate colors segment by segment to match the mood of each scene, blue for night shots, red during the rising flames of the condemned Joan's pyre. Night shots were actually filmed at night, necessitating the procurement of nearly every generator and lighting unit in the entire industry. The great panoramas were shot by cinematographer Wyckoff in deep focus, anticipating the technique used by Gregg Toland in Orson Welles' CITIZEN KANE by many years. Writer Macpherson stretched history a bit in her script; as the title suggests, the character of Joan was given a Hollywood treatment, her religious zeal and her ardor in battle seeming no more than sublimation of sexual desire. The real Joan—a stocky peasant androgyne—had all the sexuality of a stone, according to contemporary accounts. The character played by the dreaming Reid, Farrar's lieutenant, bears little resemblance to the real Joan's comrade-in-arms upon whom it was apparently patterned—Gilles de Rais, a brave soldier but a homosexual satanist child rapist and murderer, who decimated the youth in the areas adjacent to his mighty estates—a man at whom any woman was unlikely to cast a longing glance. DeMille had his doubts about casting one-time grand opera diva Farrar as Joan— doubts echoed by a critic after release, who thought her "too buxom, too knowing"—despite her success in three of his previous films, which had also co-starred Reid. The critic would have preferred the sylph-like Mae Marsh to Farrar, who had—like the real Joan—gotten plump, and who was also rather long in the tooth. Farrar did a fine job of acting in the film (DeMille cleverly presented her character as a lifelong pyrophobe, flinching at every campfire portending her impending immolation) despite adverse circumstances. Steaming in the weighty armor, bedecked with heavy weapons and a massive banner, and forced to ride a steed (the director's biographer Charles Higham states that Farrar was terrified of horses; that cowboy actor Jack Holt had to rescue her in a daring chase when her mount was spooked by a trumpet fanfare announcing the start of a take), the actress handled her job with her customary capability. The picture ran into problems with critics even before its release. It was savaged by a number of Catholic groups objecting to the presentation of the clerical inquisitors who tormented the sainted Joan. After a New York preview, Lasky and Zukor urged DeMille to trim the offending scenes; the director attempted to bargain with them, suggesting that the film be released in different edited versions for release in largely Catholic or largely Protestant areas of the country. DeMille's problems with his fellow cinemoguls—which ultimately led him to form his own production company—were exacerbated by what he considered to be their minimal efforts to promote the picture. JOAN THE WOMAN remains one of the director's finest works, a landmark film, a herald of epics yet to come.

d,Cecil B. DeMille; w, Jeanie Macpherson; ph, Alvin Wyckoff; art d, Wilfred Buckland.

Historical/Drama **(PR:C MPAA:NR)**

JOANNA** (1925) 8 reels Edwin Carewe/FN bw

Dorothy Mackaill *(Joanna Manners)*, Jack Mulhall *(John Wilmore)*, Paul Nicholson *(Frank Brandon)*, George Fawcett *(Anthony Eggleson)*, John T. Murray *(Lord Teddy Dorminster)*, Rita Carewe *(Georgie Leach)*, Dolores Del Rio *(Carlotta de Silva)*, Lillian Langdon *(Mrs. Roxanna Adams)*, Edwards Davis *(Grayson)*, Bob Hart *(The Chauffeur)*.

When Mackaill, a girl who works in an exclusive women's shop, inherits a million dollars, she is invited into the company of a fast-living crowd. She goes to Europe for a few months and comes back with a "reputation." Later, when she fights off the advances of one of her wealthy new friends, she is told that the inheritance was only a ruse to carry out a bet on her chastity. There is some consolation, however, in that one of the tycoons adopts her, and her former fiance has saved himself for her.

d, Edwin Carewe; w, Lois Leeson (based on the novel *Joanna, of the Skirts Too Short and the Lips Too Red and the Tongue Too Pert* by Henry Leyford Gates); ph, Robert B. Kurrle, Al M. Greene; ed, Edward McDermott; art d, John D. Schulze.

Drama **(PR:A MPAA:NR)**

JOHN BARLEYCORN*** (1914) 6 reels Bosworth bw

Matty Roubert *(Jack, Ist Period)*, Antrim Short *(Jack, 2nd Period)*, Elmer Clifton *(Jack, 3rd Period)*, Viola Barry *(Haydee)*, Hobart Bosworth.

Jack London's autobiographical account of his battle with alcoholism is re-created faithfully here, beginning with his drinking as a child, and following him up to his marriage to Haydee (Barry), the girl who helps him kick the habit.

d, Hobart Bosworth; w, Lois Weber (based on the novel by Jack London).

Biography **(PR:A MPAA:NR)**

JOHN GLAYDE'S HONOR*** (1915) 5 reels Frohman/Gold Rooster bw

C. Aubrey Smith, Mary Lawton, Richard Hatteras, Ida Waterman, Ben Hendricks, Charlie Butler, Jack Sherrill, Etta De Groff, Elaine Ivans, Sidney Mason.

It's the old "husband too caught up with his work to pay the proper attention to his wife, thus driving her into the arms of an artist" theme. This time with a twist, though. Although they come close several times throughout the picture, in this case the husband does *not* win her back in the end. A good performance by Smith, who would go on to become Hollywood's favorite professional Englishman.

d&w, Henry George Irving (based on a play by Alfred Sutro).

Drama **(PR:A MPAA:NR)**

JOHN HALIFAX, GENTLEMAN** (1915, Brit.) 6 reels G.B. Samuelson/Moss bw

Fred Paul *(John Halifax)*, Peggy Hyland *(Ursula March)*, Harry Paulo *(Abel Fletcher)*, Lafayette Ranney *(Phineas Fletcher)*, Charles Bennett *(John as a Child)*, Edna Maude *(Ursula, as a Child)*, Bertram Burleigh.

In this British drama dealing with class differential, an apprentice falls heir to his master's prosperous mill, marries a disowned heiress, but refuses to turn his back on or separate himself from his own people.

d, George Pearson; w, James L. Pollitt (based on the novel by Elizabeth Craik).

Drama **(PR:A MPAA:NR)**

JOHN HERIOT'S WIFE** (1920, Brit.) 6 reels AH/N bw

Mary Odette *(Camillia Heriot)*, Henry Victor *(John Heriot)*, Adelqui Migliar *(Eric Ashlynne)*, Anna Bosilova *(Sara Headcombe)*.

British crime picture about a moneylender who lets a woman off the hook once she delivers the financial secrets he seeks from the wife of a minister.

p, Maurits Binger; d&w, B. E. Doxat-Pratt (based on the novel by Claude and Alice Askew).

Crime **(PR:A MPAA:NR)**

JOHN NEEDHAM'S DOUBLE*** (1916) 5 reels BLUE bw

Tyrone Power, Marie Walcamp, Agnes Emerson, Frank Elliot, Walter Belasco, Frank Lanning, Buster Emmonds.

Tyrone Power, Sr. gave a fine performance in dual roles, and the double exposure photography was as good as anything done in the U.S. up until that time. The story, about a nobleman who squanders the fortune of his ward and then murders to keep his secret, was faithfully adapted from the great stage success which featured E. S. Willard.

d, Lois Weber, Phillips Smalley; w, Olga Printzlau (based on the play by Joseph Hatton).

Drama **(PR:A MPAA:NR)**

JOHN SMITH** (1922) 6 reels SF/SEL bw

Eugene O'Brien *(John Smith)*, Viva Ogden *(Cook)*, W. J. Ferguson *(Butler)*, Tammany Young *(Chauffeur)*, Estar Banks *(Mrs. Lang)*, Frankie Mann *(Maid)*, Mary Astor *(Irene Mason)*, George Fawcett *(Haynes)*, J. Barney Sherry *(Martin Lang)*, John Butler *(Crook)*, Walter Greene *(District Attorney)*, Warren Cook *(Doctor)*, Henry Sedley *(Lawyer)*, Daniel Haynes *(A Gangster)*.

Wrongly accused of a crime, O'Brien serves his time and changes his name after being released. He secures employment in the home of a wealthy family, and when some former acquaintances try to get him to pull an inside job, he refuses. There is a robbery and murder, and O'Brien refuses to talk. He is arrested, tried, and about to be sentenced, when his parole officer comes forward with the real criminals and, knowing that O'Brien has fallen in love with a household secretary, destroys all of his former records.

d, Victor Heerman; w, Lewis Allen Browne (based on a story by Heerman); ph, Jules Cronjager.

Crime **(PR:A MPAA:NR)**

JOHNNY GET YOUR GUN*** (1919) 5 reels ART/PAR bw

Fred Stone *(Johnny Wiggins, a Film Star)*, Mary Anderson *(Ruth Gordon)*, Casson Ferguson *(Bert Whitney)*, Dan Crimmins *(Pollitt, a Valet)*, James Cruze *(Count Bullion-nia, a Fortune Hunter)*, Sylvia Ashton *(Aunt Agatha)*, Nina Byron *(Janet Burnham, Bill's Sister)*, Maym Kelso *(Mrs. Tupper)*, Fred Huntley *(Jeune, a Butler)*, Raymond Hatton *(Milton C. Milton, a Broker)*, Noah Beery *(Town Marshall)*, Clarence Geldart *(The Director)*, Ernest Joy.

Stage star Stone rivaled Douglas Fairbanks when it came to performing stunts, and in this picture, playing a cowboy movie star who heads east to save a pal's sister from a fortune hunter, he had plenty of chances to do his stuff.

d, Donald Crisp; w, Gardner Hunting (based on the play by Edmund Lawrence Burke); ph, Henry Kotani.

Comedy/Adventure **(PR:A MPAA:NR)**

JOHNNY GET YOUR HAIR CUT** (1927) 7 reels MGM bw

Jackie Coogan *(Johnny O'Day)*, Mattie Witting *(Mother Slap)*, Maurice Costello *(Baxter Ryan)*, Pat Hartigan *(Jiggs Bradley)*, James Corrigan *(Pop Slocum)*, Bobby Doyle *(Bobby Dolin)*, Knute Erickson *(Whip Evans)*.

Outside of the haircut mentioned in the title and the big race at the end, there is very little to recommend about this weak Coogan entry of a kid who rides to victory and saves the day for a horse owner and his daughter.

d, B. Reaves Eason, Archie Mayo; sup, Jack Coogan, Sr.; w, Florence Ryerson (based on a story by Gerald Beaumont); t, Ralph Spence; ph, Frank Good; ed, Sam S. Zimbalist.

Drama/Comedy **(PR:A MPAA:NR)**

JOHNNY-ON-THE-SPOT** (1919) 5 reels Metro bw

Hale Hamilton *(Johnny Rutledge)*, Louise Lovely *(Anne Travers)*, Philo McCullough *(Arthur Abingon, Alias Cooley)*, Ruth Orlamond *(Mrs. Webster)*, Edward J. Connelly *(Judge Martin Crandall)*, Hardee Kirkland *(Dr. Barnabas Bunyon)*, Lilie Leslie *(Lillian Dupre)*, E. N. Wallack *(Jim Burton)*, Fred H. Warren *("Pipe" Brooks)*, Neal Hardin *("Buck" Bates)*, Orral Humphrey *("Cannary" Kelly)*.

Hamilton and Lovely are writers living in the same boarding house. He is working on a novel called *Taking It Easy or Everything Comes to Him Who Waits*, while she submits short stories which are never accepted. It happens that a great deal of money is left to her, on the condition that she is married without being told of her inheritance by a certain date. Of course the crooked ones move in and try to take advantage of this, but in the end she winds up with her fellow author.

d, Harry L. Franklin; w, June Mathis (based on a story by Shannon Fife.)

Comedy **(PR:A MPAA:NR)**

JOHNNY RING AND THE CAPTAIN'S SWORD*** (1921) 5 reels Temple bw

Ben Warren *(Russell H. Conwell)*, Frank Walker *(Johnny Ring)*.

Rumored to be the true life experience of a Philadelphia minister, the story tells of a Union officer (a confirmed atheist) and his orderly, Johnny Ring (Walker), a devout Christian who prays for his superior, even though he is refused permission to read the Bible. During a rebel attack, the orderly gives his life to save the officer's cherished sword, and some time later, when the captain is himself wounded, he prays that if he might be spared, he will do the Christian work of two—himself and Johnny Ring.

d, Norman L. Stevens; w, Russell H. Conwell; ph, Harry L. Keepers, Charles E. Gilson.

Religious **(PR:A MPAA:NR)**

JOHNSTOWN FLOOD, THE*** (1926) 6 reels FOX bw

George O'Brien *(Tom O'Day)*, Janet Gaynor *(Ann Burger)*, Florence Gilbert *(Gloria Hamilton)*, Anders Randolf *(John Hamilton)*, Paul Nicholson *(Peyton Ward)*, Paul Panzer *(Joe Burger)*, George Harris *(Sidney Mandel)*, Max Davidson *(David Mandel)*, Walter Perry *(Pat O'Day)*, Sid Jordan *(Mullins)*.

Randolph is the lumber baron whose logging operations threaten to weaken an enormous dam; O'Brien, a civil engineer (who is *particularly* civil to Randolph's lovely daughter Gilbert) asks him to desist. Randolph scoffs at the request, refusing to acknowledge the danger, and the resulting flood wipes out the town. Lower-class girl Gaynor dies while warning the endangered, but O'Brien and Gilbert escape the wall of water. Very good special effects and the pairing of Gaynor and O'Brien make for solid entertainment in this motion picture account of the famous Pennsylvania disaster.

d, Irving Cummings; w, Edfrid Bingham, Robert Lord; ph,George Schneiderman.

Historical **(PR:A MPAA:NR)**

JOLT, THE** (1921) 5 reels FOX bw

Edna Murphy *(Georgette)*, Johnnie Walker *(Johnnie Stanton)*, Raymond McKee *(Terrence Nolan)*, Albert Prisco *(Jerry Limur)*, Anderson Smith *(Col. Anderson)*, Wilson Hummell *(Georgette's Father)*, Lule Warrenton *(Georgette's Mother)*.

When private Walker comes marching home with his French bride, Murphy, he is unable to find work. Tempted to return to a life of crime by his one-time friends, the doughboy gives in but is saved at the last minute when the robbery he is about to commit is broken up. This gives Walker a second chance, and when a job comes his way, he makes the most of it.

d, George E. Marshall; w, Jack Strumwasser (based on a story by Marshall, Strumwasser); ph, Jack MacKenzie.

Drama **(PR:A MPAA:NR)**

JORDAN IS A HARD ROAD*** (1915) 5 reels FA/TRI bw

Dorothy Gish, Owen Moore, Frank Campeau, Sarah Truax, Ralph Lewis, Fred Burns, Mabel Wiles, Lester Perry, Jim Kid, Walter Long, Joseph Singleton.

Griffith supervised and Dwan directed this handsome film, set in the North Woods, about a notorious highwayman who devotes the latter part of his life to a daughter kept ignorant of his exploits. There are some wonderful crowd scenes, and the prolog depicting the throng walking to Jordan and judgment is quite effective.

d, Allan Dwan; sup, D. W. Griffith; w, Dwan (based on a novel by Sir Gilbert Parker).

Drama **(PR:A MPAA:NR)**

JOSSELYN'S WIFE** (1926) 6 reels TIF bw

Pauline Frederick *(Lillian Josselyn)*, Holmes Herbert *(Thomas Josselyn)*, Armond Kaliz *(Pierre Marchand)*, Josephine Hill *(Ellen Marchand)*, Carmelita Geraghty *(Flo)*, Freeman Wood *(Mr. Arthur)*, Pat Harmon *(Detective)*, Ivy Livingston *(Maid)*, W. A. Carroll *(Butler)*.

When artist Kaliz leaves her to marry another woman, Frederick finds true happiness married to Herbert. Kaliz and his new wife, Hill, return to the States and, while dining with Frederick and her husband, the painter becomes flirtatious towards his former love. Hill, who already suspects her husband of having an affair with vampish dancer Geraghty, throws herself at one of her husband's oldest friends. Then, for some reason (actually horrible script writing), Frederick agrees to poses for Kaliz at his studio, but leaves in a hurry when he makes a pass. The artist is later found murdered, and Frederick, believing herself guilty of the crime, confesses. At the trial, in a gallant effort to save her, Herbert also confesses, but the judge dismisses them both because Geraghty, the dancing tart, also confessed just before her death.

d, Richard Thorpe; w, Agnes Parsons (based on the Kathleen Norris novel); ph, Milton Moore, Mack Stengler; ed, Harold Young; art d, Edwin B. Willis.

Drama **(PR:A MPAA:NR)**

JOURNEY'S END*** (1918) 5 reels WORLD bw

Ethel Clayton *(Aline Marsden)*, John Bowers *(Phil Marsden)*, Louise Vale *(Bernice De Armond)*, Frank Mayo *(Wayne Annis)*, Victor Kennard *(H. E. Barnet)*, Jean Loew *(Bernice's Maid)*, Muriel Ostriche, Jack Drumier.

Thinly plotted but nonetheless breezy little comedy about a wife who, after discovering her husband in a tryst, forces him to sign a contract stipulating that each shall have complete freedom for three months. The lady heads for Palm Beach, with hubby in hot pursuit and her outrageous flirtations nearly drive him insane with jealousy. A good role for Clayton, and Bowers is fine as the gentleman who more than learns his lesson.

d, Travers Vale; w, Roy S. Sensabaugh; ph, Max Schneider.

Comedy **(PR:A MPAA:NR)**

JOURNEY'S END, THE*** (1921) 8 reels Hugo Ballin/Hodkinson bw

Mabel Ballin *(The Girl)*, George Bancroft *(The Ironworker)*, Wyndham Standing *(The Mill Owner)*, Georgette Bancroft *(The Child)*, Jack Dillon *(The Uncle)*.

This film, shot entirely without titles four years before F. W. Murnau's THE LAST LAUGH, tells of a convent-bred girl who goes to live with her uncle in a Pennsylvania mill town. On arriving, she is so depressed by the surroundings that she enters into a marriage with a worker she considers to be far below her station. They have a child, and after two years she meets and falls in love with the cultured owner of the mill. Afraid of yielding to temptation, she takes her baby and leaves. Her husband, a decent man, senses her feeling and switches identities with a worker killed in an accident, then retires to an Italian monastery. His wife marries the foundry owner and, while honeymooning in Italy, they happen to visit the monastery in which he is cloistered. There is a very moving scene in which he (unrecognizable because of his beard and hood) takes them on a tour of the shrine and then dies, leaving them to continue their lives in happiness.

p,d&w, Hugo Ballin; ph, James Diamond.

Drama **(PR:A MPAA:NR)**

JOY AND THE DRAGON*** (1916) 5 reels Balboa/Gold Rooster bw

Baby Marie Osborne, Henry King, Mollie McConnell, Cullen Landis.

Osborne is a sea waif who, after a series of adventures, meets the black sheep of a wealthy eastern family at a grubby mining camp. The beguiling tot casts her spell, completely regenerates the young man, and is rewarded by his taking her home to live in luxury.

d, Henry King; w, Will M. Ritchey.

Comedy/Drama **(PR:A MPAA:NR)**

JOY GIRL, THE*** (1927) 6 reels FOX bw-c

Olive Borden *(Jewel Courage)*, Neil Hamilton *(John Jeffrey Fleet)*, Marie Dressler *(Mrs. Heath)*, Mary Alden *(Mrs. Courage)*, William Norris *(Herbert Courage)*, Helen Chandler *(Flora)*, Jerry Miley *(Vicary)*, Frank Walsh *(Hugh Sandman)*, Clarence J. Elmer *(Valet)*, Peggy Kelly *(Isolde)*, Jimmy Grainger, Jr. *(Chauffeur)*.

Filmed partially in Palm Beach, Florida (with some very effective Technicolor scenes) the story deals with a girl who rejects the man she is sweet on, a chauffeur, to marry a millionaire. It turns out, however, that the millionaire is really a chauffeur, and that for a lark the two traded places. Inspired by this adversity, the young thing goes on to become a tremendously successful businesswoman; her marriage is annulled, and she ends up happily in the arms of the original fellow.

d, Allan Dwan; w, Frances Agnew, Adele Camondini (based on a story by May Edginton); t, Malcolm Stuart Boylan; ph, George Webber, William Miller (Technicolor).

Comedy **(PR:A MPAA:NR)**

JOY STREET** (1929) 7 reels FOX bw

Lois Moran *(Marie "Mimi" Colman)*, Nick Stuart *(Joe)*, Rex Bell *(Eddie)*, Jose Crespo *(Juan)*, Dorothy Ward *(Dot)*, Ada Williams *(Beverly)*, Maria Alba *(Agnes)*, Sally Phipps *(Mabel)*, Florence Allen *(Becky)*, Mabel Vail *(Dean of the Boarding School)*, Carol Wines *(Maid)*, John Breeden *(Tom)*, Marshall Ruth *(Dick)*, James Barnes *(Harry)*, Allen Dale *(Dizzy)*, Capt. Marco Elter *(Skiing Mailman)*, Destournelles De Constant *(Teacher)*.

After inheriting a fortune, Moran leaves her Swiss boarding school and returns to the U.S., where she becomes a jazz-happy, party-loving flapper. Stuart loves her, but his attempts to make her reform are ignored, until she has an automobile accident and comes to her senses.

d, Raymond Cannon; w, Charles Condon, Frank Gay (based on a story by Cannon); t, Malcolm Stuart Boylan; ph, Ernest Miller; syn sc; s eff.

Drama **(PR:A MPAA:NR)**

JOYOUS ADVENTURES OF ARISTIDE PUJOL, THE*** (1920, Brit.) 5 reels Foss/Phillips bw

Kenelm Foss *(Aristide Pujol)*, Pauline Peters *(Arlesienne/Euphemie)*, Barbara Everest *(Anne Honeywood)*, George Tawde *(Bondon)*, Irene Tripod *(Mme. Gougasse)*, Arthur Helmore *(Smith)*, Bryan Powley *(Bocardon)*, Douglas Heathcote *(Honorable Harry Ralston)*, Blanche Churms *(Christabel Smith)*.

Breezy British comic hijinx, set in France, about an eccentric chap who passes himself off as a baron, markets a cure for corns, adopts an adorable little child, brings a couple of quarreling lovers together again, and marries a wealthy spinster.

p, Kenelm Foss; d&w, Frank Miller (based on the novel by W. J. Locke).

Comedy **(PR:A MPAA:NR)**

JOYOUS LIAR, THE** (1919) 5 reels Brunton/Hodkinson bw

J. Warren Kerrigan, Lillian Walker, Joseph J. Dowling, Albert Cody, Pell Trenton, Alfred Hollingsworth.

Kerrigan, an artist looking for atmosphere, enters a deserted house and stumbles upon a girl being held captive by two thugs. He intervenes, is knocked out, and she escapes. When the police are notified, they find Kerrigan, mistake him for a criminal, and he's arrested. The girl's father, a noted criminologist, has him released to his custody (for research purposes), and the young man goes along with this to be near the girl, whom he eventually wins over and marries, once she realizes that he is just a "joyous liar."

d, Ernest C. Warde; w, (based on a story by Jack Cunningham; ph, Charles Kaufman.

Comedy/Adventure **(PR:A MPAA:NR)**

JOYOUS TROUBLEMAKERS, THE*** (1920) 6 reels FOX bw

William Farnum *(William Steele)*, Louise Lovely *(Beatrice Corlin)*, Henry J. Hebert, *(Joe Embry)*, Harry De Vere *(Richard Stanton)*, G. Raymond Nye *(Bill Rice)*, Clarence Morgan *(Turk Smith)*, George Nichols *(Cash Truit)*, Sedley Brown *(1st Miner)*, John Underhill *(Butler)*, Harry Archer *(Under Butler)*, Al Fremont, Earl Crain, Chiek Leyva *(Tough Guys)*, Pedro De Leon *(Hostler)*, Claire De Lorez *(Mrs. Denham)*, Molly Bishop *(Maid)*.

Entertaining satire of melodramas in which popular Farnum converts a spoiled, selfish little socialite into the sweet, submissive archetypical woman then in vogue. Hebert's delicious lampoon of the classic villain was perhaps the film's high point.

d, J. Gordon Edwards; w, Charles Kenyon (based on the story by Jackson Gregory); ph, John W. Boyle.

Satire **(PR:A MPAA:NR)**

JUBILO** (1919) 6 reels Goldwyn bw

Will Rogers, Josie Sedgwick, Charles French, Willard Louis, James Mason, Guinn Williams.

Rogers' second film for Sam Goldwyn was pretty much a disappointment. The only laughs (and there were few) came from the titles, and the plot seemed to drag on long beyond its 55 minutes.

d, Clarence D. Badger; w, Robert F. Hill (based on the story by Ben Ames Williams); ph, Marcel Le Picard.

Comedy **(PR:A MPAA:NR)**

JUDGE HER NOT** (1921) 5 reels Harmony/Sunnywest bw

Jack Livingston *(Ned Hayes)*, Pauline Curley *(May Harper)*.

When a producer refuses to pay them their salaries, actress Curley takes the chorus girls to live on her ranch. The foreman has discovered gold on the property and stops at nothing to force Curley to leave, including the spread of rotten rumors about the girl's morality. Finally, after a terrific fist fight, cowboy Livingston fells the foreman, tells Curley of the gold, and causes the townspeople to see the light.

d&w, George Edward Hall.

Western **(PR:A MPAA:NR)**

JUDGE NOT** (1920, Brit.) 4 reels LFP/JUR bw

Fay Compton *(Nelly)*, Fred Groves *(Burke)*, Chappell Dossett *(Frank Raymond)*, Eric Barclay *(Billy)*, Frank Stanmore, Mary Brough, Henry Vibart, George Bellamy, Wallace Bosco, Christine Silver.

In this British drama, which advocates understanding, a skid row missionary searches high and low for his lost daughter after trying to kill his wife, whom he suspected of having an affair.

d, Einar J. Bruun; w, Holger Madsen.

Drama **(PR:A MPAA:NR)**

JUDGE NOT OR THE WOMAN OF MONA DIGGINGS** (1915) 6 reels UNIV bw

Harry Carey, Harry Carter, Marc Robbins, Julia Dean, Kingsley Benedict, Joe Singleton, Paul Machette, Lydia Yeamans Titus, Walter Belasco.

A young lady who is tricked into a phony marriage with a Montana saloon owner befriends Carey, the son of a wealthy easterner, who is on the slide. She gives Carey some money and tells him to return to New York and make something of himself. This the lad does, eventually becoming a judge. Believing her husband killed when their casino burns down, the girl heads for Gotham, where she becomes part of the social whirl. Carey wishes to marry her, but his strait-laced father won't hear of it. Then, when her false husband shows up to cause trouble, the distraught girl kills him, and Carey successfully defends her in court. Now nothing can stop their wedding, and Carey quotes the biblical line to his father, "Judge not, lest ye be judged."

d, Robert Leonard; w, Harvey Gates, Leonard (based on the story "Renunciation" by Peter B. Kyne); ph, R. E. Irish; art d, Joseph D. Webster.

Drama **(PR:A MPAA:NR)**

JUDGMENT OF THE HILLS*** (1927) 6 reels R-C/FBO bw

Virginia Valli *(Margaret Dix)*, Frankie Darro *(Tad Dennison)*, Orville Caldwell *(Brant Dennison)*, Frank McGlynn, Jr. *(Jeb Marks)*, Johnny Gough *(Lige Turney)*.

Much better-than-average programmer has a drunken mountain man, possessed of great physical strength, allowing his kid brother (beautifully played by Darro) to attend school at the request of the pretty young teacher, Valli. When war breaks out, the big fellow, after having seen a crippled veteran, refuses to serve and is literally dragged off. He proves to be a hero, however, and the whole town turns out to celebrate his triumphant return. But when he steps off the train, the medal winner is drunk and can't wait to perform the acts of strength his good-ol'-boy pals have missed so much in his absence. It is only when his little brother, with tears streaming down his cheeks, berates him for his disgusting demeanor, that the doughboy swears to reform, leaving more than just the suggestion of romance for the future as Valli looks on understandingly.

d, James Leo Meehan; w, Dorothy Yost (based on the story by Larry Evans); ph, Allen Siegler.

Drama **(PR:A MPAA:NR)**

JUDGMENT OF THE STORM** (1924) 7 reels Palmer Photoplay/FBO bw

Lloyd Hughes *(John Trevor)*, Lucille Ricksen *(Mary Heath)*, George Hackathorne *(Bob Heath)*, Myrtle Stedman *(Mrs. Trevor)*, Claire McDowell *(Mrs. Heath)*, Philo McCullough *(Martin Freeland)*, Bruce Gordon *(Dave Heath)*, Frankie Darro, Fay McKenzie *(The Heath Twins)*.

On learning that his mother owns the gambling joint in which his sweetheart's brother—the family breadwinner—was accidentally killed, Hughes moves in and takes over. At first he is treated with scorn by the family, but eventually they grow to love him again.

d, Del Andrews; w, Ethel Styles Middleton; ph, Max Dupont, Henry Sharp.

Drama **(PR:A MPAA:NR)**

JUDITH OF BETHULIA* 1/2**
(1914) 4 reels American Biograph bw (AKA: HER CONDONED SIN)

Blanche Sweet *(Judith)*, Henry B. Walthall *(Holofernes)*, Mae Marsh *(Naomi)*, Robert Harron *(Nathan)*, Lillian Gish *(A Young Mother)*, Dorothy Gish *(The Crippled Beggar)*, Kate Bruce *(Judith's Maid)*, G. Jiguel Lanoe *(Holofernes' Eunuch Attendant)*, Harry Carey *(A Traitor)*, W. Chrystie Miller, Gertrude Robinson, Charles Hill Mailes, Eddie Dillon, Gertrude Bambrick, J. J. Lance.

The great Griffith's final film for Biograph, the studio that preyed on his talents for survival for so many years, whose executives refused to allow him to make the epics for which he became so rightly famed. Based on the Apocrypha, the story deals with wealthy but lonely young widow Judith (Sweet) whose fortress city lies in the path of Assyrians led by Holofernes (Walthall), their lusty, full-bearded captain, who are marching on nearby Jerusalem. Outside the thick walls of the city are the public wells, where lovely young Naomi (Marsh), with other women, draws water. Her sweetheart Harron joins her at the well, helping her raise her water jug and gazing upon her with longing. Walthall is seen leading his army to its attack across the open fields that front the city walls. At the wells, the women flee; the gates of the massive walls are secured, and the Assyrians butcher those left without. Marsh is captured and carried to the camp of Walthall. The mourning Sweet, in widow's isolation, watches from her window, anguished by the fate of her townspeople. The Assyrians storm the great walls for many days and nights, but are unable to breach the defenses. Frustrated, the Assyrians retire to their tents, consoling themselves with bacchanalian rites and assorted cruelties—Walthall has the traitorous Carey crucified—while they await the want of water within the walls to force the surrender of the Jews. The already mourning Sweet mourns yet more, this time for the agonies undergone by her compatriots, donning sackcloth and powdering herself with ashes. In contrast, wicked Walthall lounges languidly in his tent, gorging himself with all manner of luxuries (Walthall's was a relaxing role; the director had him perform almost constantly supine). Within the walls of her city, Sweet renounces sackcloth for finery; gowning herself in courtesan's clothing—and accompanied by her servant Bruce—she proceeds to the encampment of the cruel captain. Her plan, of course, is sweet revenge. Vamping Walthall with every wile she can muster, Sweet offers to betray Bethulia, assuring the opening of the heavily guarded gates to the onslaught of the Assyrians. Dazzled by her beauty, Walthall gives Sweet the run of the camp and offers her his heart. She finds herself strangely attracted to the autocratic captain, but remembering his cruelties, she hardens her heart against him. That night, she revels with the witless Walthall, getting him blind drunk. Thereupon, Sweet severs the head from her tyrant lover's body and takes it to Bethulia for display. The Assyrians panic upon seeing their fallen captain's visage glaring from the walls and retreat in disorder. Survivor Harron rescues his beloved, Marsh, from the burning enemy tent in which she has been bound. Director Griffith had helmed hundreds of one- and two-reelers for Biograph; with this film, his first epic, he broke the mold, against the wishes of the studio's executives. The moguls were busy in New York finishing construction of a new studio in the Bronx; the independent director was filming in far-off California, where he was able to exercise complete autonomy. JUDITH OF BETHULIA had been budgeted at $18 thousand—a massive cost for the studio's films of that period—but Griffith spent at least twice that much on the production. The huge partial set (built between rock massifs to save money and construction time) was four weeks in the making in Chatsworth Park in California's San Fernando Valley; the sets occupied 12 square miles. Griffith reportedly used an orchestra on the set to get his players—notably Sweet— in the appropriate mood, a first in the industry. Some historians suggest that Griffith's desire to make a lengthy spectacle stemmed from the recent release of the Italian epic QUO VADIS? (Griffith claimed never to have seen that antecedent, although film historian Kevin Brownlow quotes actress Sweet as stating that she and the director had seen it together in New York during a visit). The idea for the production had been generated years before, when young actor "Lawrence Griffith" was employed by actress Nance O'Neill in her touring theatrical company. O'Neill had commissioned author Aldrich to write his biblical drama and Griffith had rehearsed his role in the poem-play in Boston during a tour in 1906 (the tour ended and the play was never mounted there). Reasoning that the Holy Bible was, after all, in the public domain, the studio's story editor avoided paying royalties to Aldrich by commissioning a similar story from writer Pierce. The director returned to New York to shoot some few final scenes in the newly completed Bronx studio, where he revealed to the executives what he had wrought. They immediately asked him to cut the film into four separate one-reelers, informing him that although they *had* decided to crank out features, they planned to do so only through their design to film hit plays under an arrangement with the theatrical firm of Klaw and Erlanger. Griffith was told to stick to his old forte, the one- and two-reel low-budget quickie. That decision spelled the end of Griffith's long association with Biograph, which shortly afterward went belly-up. In the last years of the company's existence, it subsisted largely on reissues of Griffith's old shorts. With its dying gasp in 1917, Biograph reissued a modified version of the director's first feature film, calling it "D. W. Griffith's HER CONDONED SIN, founded on JUDITH OF BETHULIA." The reissue was half again as lengthy as the tightly cut Griffith original; the studio had added two reels of the director's outtakes.

d&w, D. W. Griffith (based on the story by Grace A. Pierce, and [uncredited] on the narrative verse play "Judith and Holofernes" by Thomas Bailey Aldrich, which was in turn based on the Book of Judith in the Old Testament); t, Frank Woods; ph, G. W. Bitzer; ed, James Smith.

Historical **Cas.** **(PR:C MPAA:NR)**

JUDITH OF THE CUMBERLANDS*** (1916) 5 reels Signal bw

Helen Holmes, Leo D. Maloney, Paul C. Hurst, Thomas G. Lingham, William Brunton, Clara Mosher, Harry Lloyd, Sam Morje, G.H. Wisschussen, Alma Reubens.

J. P. McGowan, who became perhaps the most prolific director of serials and B westerns in the 1920s and early 1930s, directed his wife, Holmes, in this movie about mountain folks who are taught the folly of "feudin' and shootin'" after an accidental near-lynching of one of their own.

d, J. P. McGowan; w, (based on a novel by Alice McGowan).

Drama **(PR:A MPAA:NR)**

JUDY FORGOT*** (1915) 5 reels UNIV bw

Marie Cahill, Samuel B. Hardy.

Cahill's stage hit "Judy Forgot" made the transition to the screen quite successfully. It had to do with a comic opera star whose wink drove men crazy and her husband insanely jealous. There is a mistaken-identity subplot and some most impressive European outdoor sets in this charmingly pleasing comedy.

d, T. Hayes Hunter; w, Raymond L. Schrock (based on the play by Avery Hopwood).

Comedy **(PR:A MPAA:NR)**

JUDY OF ROGUES' HARBOUR*** (1920) 6 reels REA bw

Mary Miles Minter *(Judy)*, Charles Meredith *(Lt. Teddy Kingsland)*, Herbert Standing *(Gov. Kingsland)*, Theodore Roberts *(Grandpop Ketchel)*, Claude King *(The Lady of the Roses)*, Fritzi Ridgeway *(Olive Ketchel)*, Allan Sears *(Jim Schuckles)*, Frankie Lee *(Denny)*, George Periolat *(Peter Kingsland)*.

Director Taylor and player Minter made an emotional success of this two-handkerchief drama about a group of orphaned children who finally escape the cruel exploitation of man posing as their grandfather.

d, William Desmond Taylor; w, Clara S. Beranger (based on the novel by Grace Miller White); ph, James C. Van Trees.

Drama **(PR:A MPAA:NR)**

JUGGERNAUT, THE** (1915) 5 reels VIT bw

Anita Stewart, Earle Williams, Julia Swayne Gordon, William Dunn, Eulalie Jensen, Frank Currier, Paul Scardon, Jack Brawn.

Vitagraph wrecked a real train in this drawn-out picture about a greedy railroad owner who places his customers in jeopardy by allowing his line to fall into disrepair. The movie's only punch comes when the old man races by auto to intercept the train he knows is headed for danger, and which he learns his daughter is on. A one-thrill film, which is at least two reels too long.

d, Ralph Ince; w, Donald I. Buchanan, Ince; ph, Jimmy French.

Drama **(PR:A MPAA:NR)**

JULES OF THE STRONG HEART*** (1918) 5 reels LAS/PAR bw

George Beban *(Jules Lemaire)*, Helen Eddy *(Joy Farnsworth)*, Charles Ogle *(Tom, Her Father)*, Raymond Hatton *(Ted Kendall)*, Guy Oliver *(Jim Burgess)*, Ernest Joy *(Jack Liggitt)*, H. B. Carpenter *(Louis, the "Red Fox")*, Edward Martin, James Neill.

Beban stars in the role of a French Canadian lumberman who cares for the motherless child of a friend and almost gives his life for the lumber camp owner and his daughter, who befriended him. Another good performance by Beban, and this time he even gets the girl.

d, Donald Crisp; ph, Harvey F. Thew, Frank X. Finnegan (based on a story by William Merriam Rouse).

Drama **(PR:A MPAA:NR)**

JUNE FRIDAY** (1915) 4 reels Edison bw

Gertrude McCoy, Robert Conness, Duncan McRea, Augustus Phillips.

Rather unpleasant film about a girl who enters into a mock marriage and later weds the man she really loves. When her common-law husband later shows up to blackmail her, the girl stabs him to death. Then her father commits suicide, leaving a note confessing to the killing. This opens the door for his daughter to continue her carefree and happy existence.

d, Duncan McRae; w, Lee Arthur.

Drama **(PR:A MPAA:NR)**

JUNE MADNESS** (1922) 6 reels Metro bw

Viola Dana *(Clytie Whitmore)*, Bryant Washburn *(Ken Pauling)*, Gerald Pring *(Cadbury Todd II)*, Leon Barry *(Hamilton Peeke)*, Eugenie Besserer *(Mrs. Whitmore)*, Snitz Edwards *(Pennetti)*, Anita Fraser *(Mamie O'Gallagher)*.

Unable to go through with her marriage to Pring, Dana rushes out of the church and into the passing car of jazz musician Washburn. Later, she escapes her locked room, goes to the roadhouse where Washburn is playing, dances in his act, and finally receives her family's permission to marry him.

d&w, Harry Beaumont (based on a story by Crosby George); ph, John Arnold; art d, J. J. Hughes.

Comedy **(PR:A MPAA:NR)**

JUNGLE, THE*** (1914) 5 reels All Star Features bw

George Nash, Gail Kane, Alice Marc, Robert Cummings, George Irving, W. Vermilyea, Julia R. Hurley, Clarence Handyside, R. Payton Gibbs, Maxine Hodges, May McCabe, Ernest Evers, Nickelas Sinnerella, Upton Sinclair.

From Lithuania to Packingtown, U.S.A.; from misery to perhaps even greater misery. This motion picture adaptation of Sinclair's scathing indictment of capitalism certainly pulled no punches. But it was just too depressing to be a commercial success, in spite of the presence of the author, playing himself.

d, Augustus Thomas; w, (based on the novel by Upton Sinclair).

Drama **(PR:A MPAA:NR)**

JUNGLE CHILD, THE*** (1916) 5 reels Kay-Bee/TRI bw

Dorothy Dalton, Howard Hickman, Gertrude Claire, Dorcas Matthews, Frederick Vroom, Elsa Lorrimer, Leo Willis.

When her family perishes in the South American jungle, a Spanish child is taken in by natives and grows up to become a beautiful Amazon. A shifty white man stumbles upon her village and, on going through her belongings, discovers that she is heir to millions in the U.S.. The rotter marries her, they move to New York, and with the fortune they begin living the high life. One night, during a drunken orgy, he boasts to his friends about the cleverness of his scheme, not knowing that his bride is within earshot. Infuriated, the girl rushes to her room, slips into her jungle outfit, and kills the opportunist with her bare hands.

d, Walter Edwards; w, Monte M. Katterjohn.

Drama **(PR:A MPAA:NR)**

JUNGLE TRAIL, THE*** (1919) 5 reels FOX bw

William Farnum *(Robert Morgan)*, Anna Luther *(Mary Lamar)*, Lester Chambers *(Philip Garson)*, Sara Alexander *(Mrs. Morgan)*, Anne Schaeffer *(Mrs. Lamar)*, Edward Roseman, Henry Armetta, G. Raymond Nye, Anna Lehr, George Stone, Marie Shaffer.

Sent on a wild-goose chase to the jungles of Africa by Chambers (who wants to make a move on his sweetheart), Farnum eludes the stooges who were sent to kill him, is made a god by the tribe which takes him in, and eventually makes it back to the States to see justice done. An elaborate production, and one of Farnum's better roles.

d, Richard Stanton; w, Adrian Johnson (based on a story by George V. Hobart); ph, Harry Plimpton.

Adventure **(PR:A MPAA:NR)**

JUNGLE WOMAN, THE** (1926, Brit.) 6 reels STOLL-Hurley bw

Eric Bransby Williams *(Martin South)*, Lillian Douglas *(Eleanor Mack)*, Jameson Thomas *(Stephen Mordyke)*, W. G. Saunders *(Peter Mack)*, Grace Savieri *(Hurana)*.

In this British adventure set in New Guinea, a man finally escapes from the natives and manages to prevent the young lady he loves from marrying his partner, who is not only a crook, but an out-and-out rotter.

p,d&w, Frank Hurley.

Adventure **(PR:A MPAA:NR)**

JUST A GIRL** (1916, Brit.) 7 reels Samuelson/Moss bw

Owen Nares *(Lord Trafford)*, Daisy Burrell *(Esmeralda)*, J. Hastings Batson *(The Duke)*, Minna Grey *(The Duchess)*, Paul England *(The Miner)*.

In another of those British social-class soap operas, an Australian heiress rejects an impoverished lord to marry the miner she really loves.

d, Alexander Butler; w, Harry Engholm (based on the novel by Charles Garvice).

Romance **(PR:A MPAA:NR)**

JUST A SONG AT TWILIGHT** (1922) Dixie/Producers Security bw

Richard Barthelmess *(George Turner)*, Pedro De Cordoba *(Carlysle Turner)*, Evelyn Greeley *(Lucy Winter/Lucy Lee)*, Charles Wellesley *(Stephen Winter)*, Nellie Grant *(Mrs. Lee)*, Frank A. Lyon *(A Fake Oil Lands Promoter)*.

Wealthy widower Wellesley refuses his daughter Greeley's request that she be allowed to marry humble gardener Barthelmess, plighting her troth to another. The defeated young gardener gives the girl a parting present—a necklace bequeathed to him by his late mother—which is recognized by Wellesley. In flashback, the latter relives a past misdeed in which he permitted De Cordoba—his rival in love—to go to jail for a crime he did not commit. De Cordoba had given the necklace to Wellesley's wife (also played by Greeley) in a reprise of more recent events. Waking from his reverie, Wellesley confesses to Barthelmess that the jailed man is the long-lost father. He obtains a pardon for De Cordoba; Greeley and Barthelmess are free to wed. Some confusion exists as to whether the picture was made in 1916 or six years later.

d, Carlton S. King; w, Henry Albert Phillips; ph, Harry L. Keepers.

Drama **(PR:A MPAA:NR)**

JUST A WOMAN*** (1925) 7 reels FN bw

Claire Windsor *(June Holton)*, Conway Tearle *(Robert Holton)*, Dorothy Brock *(Bobby Holton)*, Percy Marmont *(George Rand)*, Dorothy Revier *(Clarice Clement)*, George Cooper.

Marmont, who lives in the house of a married couple (Windsor and Tearle), has invented a new process for refinishing steel. Windsor sells the invention to the company for which they work, and everybody becomes filthy rich. The money goes to Tearle's head, and he begins seeing an old girl friend who convinces him that Rand and his wife are having an affair. Tearle files for divorce but ultimately comes to his senses, and the marriage is saved.

d, Irving Cummings; w, Jack Cunningham (based on the play by Eugene Walter); ph, Arthur L. Todd; ed, Charles J. Hunt; art d, Jack Okey.

Drama **(PR:A MPAA:NR)**

JUST AROUND THE CORNER** (1921) 7 reels COS/PAR bw

Margaret Seddon *(Ma Birdsong)*, Lewis Sargent *(Jimmie Birdsong)*, Sigrid Holmquist *(Essie Birdsong)*, Edward Phillips *(Joe Ullman)*, Fred Thomson *(The Real Man)*, Peggy Parr *(Lulu Pope)*, Mme. Rosa Rosanova *(Mrs. Finshreiber)*, William Nally *(Mr. Blatsky)*.

Holmquist, an East Side girl attracted to New York City's fast life, gets a job ushering in a second-rate theater and becomes engaged to hustler Phillips. Her mother, who is dying, asks only to meet the fiance, but Phillips can't be bothered. Finally the old lady suffers a heart attack and begs Holmquist to bring him. The girl tracks him down at a pool hall, but the little rat still refuses to put himself out. In desperation, Holmquist confides her sad story to a strange man who volunteers to impersonate Phillips. The mother is so impressed by the manner of the fellow she *thinks* is going to marry her daughter, that she dies happily, and Holmquist experiences true love for the first time.

d&w, Frances Marion (based on the story by Fannie Hurst); ph, Henry Cronjager; set d, Joseph Urban.

Drama **(PR:A MPAA:NR)**

JUST DECEPTION, A* (1917, Brit.) 6 reels I.B. Davidson-Tiger/Walturdaw bw

Agustus Yorke *(Aaron Cohen)*, Robert Leonard *(Moses Moss)*, Blanche Forsythe *(Mary Turner)*, Maud Yates *(Rachel)*.

There were not a lot of laughs in this heavy-handed British drama about a Jew who is bribed to make a switch between the illegitimate child of a Christian and the dead baby of his blind wife. Later, when the plot is discovered, he is completely ruined by the girl's irate father.

d, A. E. Coleby; w, (based on the novel *Aaron the Jew* by B. L. Farjeon.)

Drama **(PR:C MPAA:NR)**

JUST FOR TONIGHT*** (1918) 5 reels Goldwyn bw

Tom Moore *(Theodore Whitney, Jr.)*, Lucy Fox *(Betty Blake)*, Henry Sedley *(Crandall)*, Henry Hallam *(Maj. Blackburn)*, Robert Broderick *(Theodore Whitney, Sr.)*, Ethel Grey Terry *(Lady Roxenham)*, Edwin Sturgis *(Detective Chase)*, Phil Ryley *(Butler)*, Maude Turner Gordon *(Mrs. Blackburn)*.

Smitten by a pretty young woman who is suspected by an insurance company of stealing her uncle's jewels, Moore takes the place of a private detective, moves into the house where the crime was committed, and proves the butler and maid—both wanted criminals—to be the culprits.

d, Charles Giblyn; w, (based on a story by Charles A. Logue); ph, Lloyd Lewis.

Comedy/Mystery **(PR:A MPAA:NR)**

JUST JIM*** (1915) 4 reels UNIV bw

Harry Carey, Jean Taylor, Mr. Edmundsen, Olive Golden, William Crinley, Duke Worne, J. F. Abbott, Mr. Loraine.

Excellent performance by Carey as a New York burglar who happens upon a dying woman who begs him to deliver a package to her daughter out West. This Carey does, and after a number of interesting plot twists, the former crook proves to the law—and the girl—that he is truly a decent man.

d&w, Oscar A. C. Lund.

Western **(PR:A MPAA:NR)**

JUST LIKE A WOMAN** (1923) 5 reels Grace S. Haskins/Hodkinson bw

Marguerite De La Motte *(Peggy Dean)*, George Fawcett *(Judge Landon)*, Ralph Graves *(James Landon)*, Jane Keckley *(Abigail)*, Julia Calhoun *(Salina)*, J. Frank Glendon *(Peggy's Brother)*.

Harmless little comedy about a girl who leaves boarding school to live with her aunts, and assumes the role of a proper little missionary in order to offset their displeasure with her father marrying an actress. Later she drops the disguise to win handsome Graves, but her dishonesty only causes him to bolt. The movie ends with her chasing after him in a race car and convincing him that she is really a good girl, and definitely good for him.

d, Scott R. Beal, Hugh McClung; w, Hal Conklin (based on a story by Grace S. Haskins); ph, Chester Lyons, Reginald Lyons, John Leezer.

Comedy **(PR:A MPAA:NR)**

JUST MARRIED*** (1928) 6 reels PAR bw

James Hall *(Bob Adams)*, Lila Lee *(Victoire)*, Ruth Taylor *(Roberta)*, Harrison Ford *(Jack Stanley)*, William Austin *(Percy Jones)*, Ivy Harris *(Mrs. Jack Stanley)*, Tom Ricketts *(Makepeace Witter)*, Maude Turner Gordon *(Mrs. Witter)*, Arthur Hoyt *(Steward)*, Wade Boteler *(Purser)*, Mario Carillo *(Magnoir)*.

Good comedy programmer has Lee, a Paris model, booking passage on a ship bound for the U.S. to break up the engagement of her former heart throb, Austin, and an American beauty, Taylor. Hall spots Taylor boarding the ship, falls instantly in love, and also books passage. There are tons of tried-and-true gags as the ship crosses the Atlantic, and by the time it arrives in New York, Hall is engaged to Taylor and Lee to Austin.

d, Frank Strayer; w, Frank Butler, Gilbert Pratt (based on the play by Adelaide Matthews, Anne Nichols); t, George Marion; ph, Edward Cronjager; ed, B. F. Zeidman, William Shea.

Comedy **(PR:A MPAA:NR)**

JUST OFF BROADWAY** (1924) 6 reels FOX bw

John Gilbert *(Stephen Moore)*, Marian Nixon *(Jean Lawrence)*, Trilby Clark *(Nan Norton)*, Pierre Gendron *(Florelle)*, Ben Hendricks, Jr. *(Comfort)*.

Gilbert plays an amateur detective and millionaire who infiltrates and breaks up a gang of counterfeiters. At the same time he saves Nixon, a starving actress who fell under their evil influence when she was rescued from starvation by Clark, a gangland sweetheart who bore the poor woman little good.

w, Frederic Hatton, Fanny Hatton; ph, G. O. Post.

Crime **(PR:A MPAA:NR)**

JUST OFF BROADWAY** (1929) 7 reels CHES bw

Donald Keith *(Tom Fowler)*, Ann Christy *(Nan Morgan)*, Larry Steers *(Marty Kirkland)*, De Sacia Mooers *(Rene)*, Jack Tanner *(William Grady)*, Sid Saylor *(Bennie Barnett)*, Beryl Roberts *(Bessie)*, Albert Dresden *(Ed Fowler)*.

Low-budget affair has a young man dropping out of school for the night clubs of Broadway in search of the gangsters who murdered his racketeer brother. Along the way he meets a girl dancer and falls in love with her. The pair are set up by the racketeer murderer but outwit him in the end and the schoolboy marries the dancer.

d, Frank O'Connor; sup, Lon Young; w, Arthur Hoerl (based on a story by Fanny D'Morgal); t, Lon Young, Hoerl; ph, M. A. Anderson; ed, James Sweeney.

Crime **(PR:A MPAA:NR)**

JUST OUT OF COLLEGE*** (1921) 5 reels Goldwyn bw

Jack Pickford *(Ed Swinger)*, Molly Malone *(Caroline Pickering)*, George Hernandez *(Septimus Pickering)*, Edythe Chapman *(Mrs. Pickering)*, Otto Hoffman *(Prof. Bliss)*, Irene Rich *(Miss Jones)*, Maxfield Stanley *(Herbert Poole)*, Maurice B. Flynn *(Paul Greer)*, Loretta Blake *(Genevieve)*.

Wealthy businessman Hernandez is opposed to his daughter marrying Pickford, so he gives him $20,000 on the condition that unless he can double it in 60 days, he must never see the girl again. Pickford and a couple of pals go into the pickle business and are so successful that Hernandez (not knowing its ownership) buys the company for $100,000. Of course, Pickford wins the girl.

d, Alfred Green; w, Arthur F. Statter (based on the play by George Ade); ph, George Webber.

Comedy **(PR:A MPAA:NR)**

JUST SUPPOSE*** (1926) 7 reels INSP/FN bw

Richard Barthelmess *(Prince Rupert)*, Lois Moran *(Linda Lee Stafford)*, Geoffrey Kerr *(Count Anton Teschy)*, Henry Vibart *(Baron Karnaby)*, George Spelvin *(King)*, Harry Short *(Crown Prince)*, Bijou Fernandez *(Mrs. Stafford)*, Prince Rokneddine *(Private Secretary)*.

Prince Rupert of Koronia (Barthelmess) has had his fill of pomp and circumstance, so when he comes to America he takes the opportunity to live just like a "regular fellow." But no sooner does he fall in love with beautiful Moran than the crown prince suddenly dies, and he is called home. It almost looks as though Barthelmess will have to spend the rest of his life being the object of genuflection, when the widow of the crown prince gives birth—freeing Barthelmess to marry the woman he loves.

d, Kenneth Webb; w, Violet E. Powell, C. Graham Baker (based on the play by A. E. Thomas); ph, Stuart Kelson; ed, William Hamilton; set d, Tec-Art Studios.

Romance **(PR:A MPAA:NR)**

JUST SYLVIA** (1918) 5 reels WORLD bw

Barbara Castleton *(Sylvia)*, John Hines *(Henry)*, Jack Drumier *(Zebulon Hicks)*, Gertrude Berkeley *(Octavia Hicks)*, Franklyn Hanna *(J. Orlando Dell)*, Henry Warwick *(Danglar)*, Anthony Merlo *(Frank Hayward)*, Eloise Clement *(Annie)*, Theresa Maxwell Conover *(Mrs. Layton Du Roc)*.

Handsomely produced but garbled story about a rural couple who find millions in ore on their property, and the various characters who try to either exploit their wealth or steal their property. Hines, the underrated comic who would become a star in the 1920s, practically steals the whole show.

d, Travers Vale; w, Hamilton Smith (based on a story by Harry O. Hoyt); ph, Philip Hatkin.

Drama **(PR:A MPAA:NR)**

JUST TONY*** (1922) 5 reels FOX bw

Tony the Horse, Tom Mix *("Red" Ferris)*, Claire Adams *(Marianne Jordan)*, J.P. Lockney *(Oliver Jordan)*, Duke Lee *(Manuel Cordova)*, Frank Campeau *(Lew Hervey)*, Walt Robbins *("Shorty")*.

Mix western in which his marvelous horse, Tony, is actually the star. Throughout much of the film, Tony plays the leader of a wild herd of desert horses and is completely on his own as he seeks vengeance against the human beings who mistreated him. His actions are uncannily human, even to the point of rescuing Mix and his girl at the picture's end, after Mix has saved him from a beating. A beautiful study of a beast's capability of both rage and affection.

d&w, Lynn F. Reynolds (based on the novel *Alcatraz* by Max Brand); ph, Dan Clark.

Western **Cas.** **(PR:A MPAA:NR)**

JUSTICE** (1914, Brit.) 4 reels Hepworth/Renters bw

Alec Worcester *(Jack Raynor)*, Alma Taylor *(Nan Prescott)*, Stewart Rome *(Paul Meredith)*, Harry Royston *(Joe Prescott)*, Ruby Belasco *(Mrs. Prescott)*, Jamie Darling *(John Meredith)*, Marie de Solla *(Mrs. Meredith)*.

British thriller about a desperate man who hires an underworld character to murder his father, then changes his mind, betrays the would-be assassin, and kidnaps his daughter.

d, Frank Wilson.

Mystery **(PR:A MPAA:NR)**

JUSTICE OF THE FAR NORTH** (1925) 6 reels COL bw

Arthur Jasmine *(Umluk)*, Marcia Manon *(Wamba)*, Laska Winter *(Nootka)*, Chuck Reisner *(Mike Burke)*, Max Davidson *(Izzy Hawkins)*, George Fisher *(Dr. Wells)*, Katherine Dawn *(Lucy Parsons)*, Steve Murphy *(Broken Nose McGee)*, Ilak the Wolf Dog.

When his halfbreed bride-to-be and a former whaler who has been wooing her with trinkets kidnap his sister and take off, an Eskimo chief (Jasmine) follows them across the vast frozen tundra. After a number of setbacks, he catches up with the three and saves his sister, leaving the woman who betrayed him to an icy fate.

d&w, Norman Dawn; ph, Tony Mormann, George Madden.

Adventure **(PR:A MPAA:NR)**

K—THE UNKNOWN** (1924) 9 reels UNIV bw

Virginia Valli *(Sidney Page)*, Percy Marmont *("K" Le Moyne)*, Margarita Fisher *(Charlotte Harrison)*, Francis Feeney *(George "Slim" Benson)*, John Roche *(Dr. Max Wilson)*, Maurice Ryan *(Joe Drummond)*, Myrtle Vane *(Aunt Harriett Kennedy)*, William A. Carroll *(Dr. Ed Wilson)*.

Feeney and Ryan are rivals for the affection of Valli, but she is interested in surgeon Roche and also strangely attracted to a lodger in her house. When Feeney shoots Roche, thinking he has been with Valli, the lodger saves his life by operating and identifies himself as a famous surgeon in his own right.

d, Harry Pollard; w, Hope Loring, Raymond L. Schrock, Louis D. Lighton (based on the novel by Mary Roberts Rinehart); ph, Charles Stumar.

Drama **(PR:A MPAA:NR)**

KAISER, BEAST OF BERLIN, THE*** (1918) 7 reels Jewel bw

Rupert Julian *(The Kaiser)*, Allan Sears *(Capt. von Wohlbold)*, Nigel de Brulier *(Capt. von Neigel)*, Lon Chaney *(Von Bethmann Hollweg)*, Mark Fenton *(Adm. von Tirpitz)*, Jay Smith *(Field Marshal von Hindenburg)*, Harry Carter *(Gen. von Kluck)*, W.H. Bainbridge *(Col. Schmiedeke)*, Harry Van Meter *(Capt. von Hancke)*, Walter Belasco *(Adm. von Pliscott)*, Ed Clark *(Gen. Erich von Falkenhayn)*, K. Painter *(Gen. von Baeseler)*, W. Coburn *(Gen. von der Goltz)*, F. Beauregard *(Gen. von Weddingen)*, E. Corcoran *(Gen. von Hoetzendorf)*, Wadsworth Harris *(Gen. von Ruesselheim)*, Capt. Anderson *(Capt. Kovisch)*, Winter Hall *(Dr. von Gressler)*, Elmo Lincoln *(Marsas the Blacksmith)*, Orio Eastman *(The President)*, Joseph Gerard *(Ambassador Gerard)*, M. Alfred Allen *(Gen. Pershing)*, Harry Barrows *(Gen. Haig)*, Harry Holden *(Gen. Joffre)*, Pedro Soso *(Gen. Diax)*, Jack MacDonald *(King Albert)*, Master Georgie Hupp *(Little Jean)*, Master Frankie Lee *(Hansel)*, Ruth Clifford *(Gabrielle)*, Betty Carpenter *(New Bride)*, Ruby Layfayette *(Grandmother Marcas)*, Gretchen Lederer *(Bertha von Niegel)*, Mistress Zoe Rae *(Gretel)*, Lawrence Grant, George Huff.

Julian wrote, directed, and played the Kaiser in one of the most blatant propaganda films ever made. He didn't miss a trick in depicting the emperor as a bloodthirsty beast, obsessed with personal glory, who derived pleasure from the suffering of innocent people—especially women and children. There are some fine battle scenes, and the sets are exquisite, including the palace of Belgium's King Albert, where Julian optimistically decides to banish the Kaiser after the defeat of Germany, which would not occur in reality for months to come.

d, Rupert Julian; w, Elliott Clawson, Julian.

War **(PR:A MPAA:NR)**

KAISER'S FINISH, THE*** (1918) 8 reels WB bw

Earl Schenck, Claire Whitney, Percy Standing, Louis Dean, Vic DeLinsky, Jean Sunderland, Fred G. Hearn, Charles T. Parr, Philip Van Loan, Billie Wagner.

Actual newsreel footage of the Kaiser is incorporated with good effect into this entertaining story of his look-alike, illegitimate, American-born son, who volunteers to go to Germany as a spy and assassinate his father. A propaganda pipe dream, but interesting for the shots of war at that time.

d, John Joseph Harvey, Clifford P. Saum; ph, R. B. Schellinger.

War **(PR:A MPAA:NR)**

KAISER'S SHADOW, THE** (1918) 5 reels PAR bw

Dorothy Dalton *(Paula Harris)*, Thurston Hall *(Hugo Wagner)*, Edward Cecil Clement Boyd *(Inventor)*, Leota Lorraine *(Dorothy [Robinson] Boyd, His Wife)*, Otto Hoffman *(A German Chemist)*, Charles French *(William Kremlin, a German Spy)*.

Pretty standard wartime propaganda stuff which reflected its magazine serial origin. The Germans are after the plans to a new U.S. weapon, but are foiled by a male-female Secret Service team which infiltrates their ranks. This was one of several films capitalizing on WW I produced in quick succession by Thomas Ince.

d, R. William Neill; sup, Thomas H. Ince; w, J. G. Hawks (based on the magazine serial by Octavus Roy Cohen, J. H. Giesey); ph, John S. Stumar; art d, Harold Percival.

War **(PR:A MPAA:NR)**

KATHLEEN MAVOURNEEN** (1919) 5 reels FOX bw

Theda Bara *(Kathleen)*, Edward O'Connor *(Her Father)*, Jennie Dickerson *(Her Mother)*, Raymond McKee *(Terence O'Moore)*, Marc McDermott *(The Squire of Tralse)*, Marcia Harris *(Lady Clancarthy)*, Henry Hallam *(Sir John Clancarthy)*, Harry Gripp *(Denis O'Rourke)*, Morgan Thorpe *(Father O'Flynn)*.

In an attempt to escape being forever typecast as a vamp, Bara (not too successfully) took on the role of an Irish colleen nearly forced to give herself to the landlord to save her parents from eviction. There is, of course, a young man in her life who saves the day. The film was made from the graceful Irish lyrical poem by the great writer of poems and Irish folk tunes, Thomas Moore ("Believe Me, If All Those Endearing Young Charms"), a personal friend of Lord Byron. Bara, of course, known to her fans as "The Wickedest Woman in the World," was not well-received in this by her fans who preferred her with horns and hooves and a cigarette between her lips.

d&w, Charles J. Brabin (based on the poem by Thomas Moore and the play by Dion Boucicault); ph, George Lane.

Drama **(PR:A MPAA:NR)**

KEEP MOVING** (1915) 5 reels Kleine bw

Harry Watson, Jr. *(Musty Suffer)*, George Bickel *(Willie Work)*, Alma Hanlon *(The Queen)*, Tom Nawn *(The King)*, Dan Crimmons *(Burglar)*, Rose Gore *(Dippy Mary)*, Cissie Fitzgerald *(Cissie)*, Ruby Hoffman *(Governess)*, Frank Belcher *(Lord Chamberlain)*, Maxfield Moree *(Fairy Tramp)*, H. H. McCullum *(Tony)*, Snitz Edwards *(Hypo Jake)*.

Snappy little comedy featured a cast of vaudeville and musical comedy stars. The story of a little prince who is transformed into a tramp so that he might see the world left plenty of room for countless tried-and-true gags from the variety stage. All are carried along smartly until the little tramp returns to the castle and once again becomes the little prince.

d, George Kleine.

Comedy **(PR:A MPAA:NR)**

KEEP SMILING*** (1925) 6 reels Monty Banks/AEX bw

Monty Banks *(The Boy)*, Anne Cornwall *(Rose Ryan)*, Robert Edeson *(James P. Ryan)*, Stanhope Wheatcroft *(Gerald Deane)*, Glen Cavender *(Double-crosser)*, Donald Morelli *(Bordanni)*, Syd Crossley *(Ryan's Butler)*, Martha Franklin *(The Mother)*, Jack Huff *(The Child)*.

Daredevil comedian Banks invents an automatically inflatable life preserver. He saves the life of Cornwall, the daughter of a steamboat magnate (Edeson), and is rewarded with the chance to show his creation off. Edeson, however, mistakes Banks for a speedboat racer, and circumstances place the little comic behind the wheel of the hottest boat the world has ever known. There are plenty of thrills and a number of laughs as Banks manages to survive, sell his invention, and end up with the boss's daughter.

d, Gilbert W. Pratt, Albert Austin; w, (based on a story by Herman Raymaker, Clyde Bruckman, Banks); ph, James Diamond, Lee Garmes, Barney McGill.

Comedy **(PR:A MPAA:NR)**

KEEPER OF THE DOOR** (1919, Brit.) 6 reels STOLL bw

Basil Gill *(Max Wyndham)*, Peggy Carlisle *(Olga Ratcliffe)*, Hamilton Stewart *(Nick Ratcliffe)*, Marjorie Hume *(Violet Campion)*, George Harrington *(Dr. Ratcliffe)*, Ivo Dawson *(J. Hunt Goring)*.

This British tear-jerker really pours it on. It all has to do with a young woman who suffers amnesia after trying to poison a friend who has gone insane, but recovers her memory when she encounters the ex-boy friend who saved her brother's eyesight.

d, Maurice Elvey; w, R. Byron-Webber (based on the novel by Ethel M. Dell).

Drama **(PR:A MPAA:NR)**

KEEPING UP WITH LIZZIE** (1921) 6 reels Rockett/Hodkinson bw

Enid Bennett *(Lizzie Henshaw)*, Otis Harlan *(Sam Henshaw)*, Leo White *(Count Louis Roland)*, Victory Bateman *(Mrs. Henshaw)*, Landers Stevens *("Soc" Potter)*, Edward Hearn *(Dan Pettigrew)*, Harry Todd *(Mr. Pettigrew)*, Lila Leslie *(Mrs. Warburton)*.

Bennett is sent by her father to a finishing school to prevent her from marrying Hearn, the son of a business rival, while Hearn, in turn, is given a Harvard education. Shortly after, Bennett returns from Europe with a fortune-hunting count, and her father (who has bankrupted himself by maintaining this charade) is forced to visit a moneylender. The count, on hearing of this, demands a dowry. Hearn exposes him to be a phony, and the sweethearts are at last permitted to find happiness living together on a modest little farm.

d, Lloyd Ingraham; w, Will M. Ritchey (based on the novel by Irving Addison Bacheller); ph, Ross Fisher.

Drama/Comedy **(PR:A MPAA:NR)**

KENNEDY SQUARE 1/2** (1916) 5 reels VIT bw

Antonio Moreno, Charles Kent, Muriel Ostriche, Tom Brooke, Raymond Bloomer, Dan Jarrett, Hattie Delaro, Harold Foshay, Herbert Barry, Logan Paul, Katherine Lewis.

Set in the pre-Civil War South, a young man (Moreno) almost loses his lady friend because of his love for the grape. An elderly friend patches things up and at their engagement party another young fellow, who is intoxicated, forces his intentions on the girl. This leads to a duel, and after Moreno shoots the offender, his father disowns him, forcing Moreno to move into his older friend's house in the fashionable Kennedy Square section of New York. After a time, Moreno's father dies, leaving him just enough money to finance a trip to South America for ruby prospecting. He strikes it rich in no time, returns to the U.S., where he bails out the old gentleman who has fallen upon hard times, and marries the girl he never stopped loving for a minute.

d, Del Henderson; w, (based on a story by Elizabeth Frazer); ph, Arthur Quinn.

Drama **(PR:A MPAA:NR)**

KENT, THE FIGHTING MAN**
(1916, Brit.) 6 r eels I. B. Davidson-Tiger/GAU bw

"Bombardier" Billy Wells *(John Westerley)*, Hetty Payne *(Constance)*, A.E. Coleby *(Adams)*, Arthur Rooke *(Honorable Jimmy Greenback)*, Frank Dane *(Brother)*, Nelson Phillips *(Col. Rapton)*, Harry Lofting *(Jim Dace)*, Fred Drummond *(Button)*, Tom Coventry *(Clown)*, Charles Vane, Sidney Bland, Dick Webb, Judd Green, N. Watts-Phillips, Ernie Collins.

After being disowned, a gambler turns to his boxing skills and reaps revenge through the "sweet science" by bankrupting the gamblers (who treated him badly) when he defeats the pug they put up against him.

d, A. E. Coleby; w, Rowland Talbot (based on the novel by George Edgar).

Drama **(PR:A MPAA:NR)**

KENTUCKIANS, THE*** (1921) 6 reels FP/PAR bw

Monte Blue *(Boone Stallard)*, Wilfred Lytell *(Randolph Marshall)*, Diana Allen *(Anne Bruce)*, Frank Joyner *(Mace Keaton)*, J. H. Gilmour *(Governor)*, John Miltern *(Colton, a Newspaperman)*, Thomas S. Brown *(Jake Stallard)*, J. W. Johnston *(Boone's Brother)*, Russell Parker *(Constable)*, John Carr *(Young Keaton)*, Albert Hewitt *(Young Stallard)*, Eugenie Woodward *(Ma Stallard)*, Wesley Jenkins *(Uncle Cadmus)*, Grace Reals *(Mrs. Marshall)*.

Blue is very good as the Lincolnesque mountain man elected to the Kentucky Legislature, who incurs the wrath of rural aristocrat Lytell. When a shooting feud breaks out involving his family, Blue returns home and restores peace. Lytell is so impressed by the way his adversary handles matters that he arranges for Blue's brother's death sentence to be commuted and Blue, in return, realizing the differences in their backgrounds, elects not to ask the governor's daughter to marry him, thus leaving the path clear for Lytell.

d, Charles Maigne; w, Frank W. Tuttle (based on the novel by John William Fox); ph, Andre Barlatier.

Drama **(PR:A MPAA:NR)**

KENTUCKY CINDERELLA, A** (1917) 5 reels BLUE bw

Harry Carter *(Windfield Gordon/Henry Gordon)*, Rupert Julian *(John Silverwood)*, Ruth Clifford *(Nannie)*, Gretchen Lederer *(Mrs. Morgan)*, Myrtle Reeves *(Rachel Gordon)*, Aurora Pratt *(Mrs. Gordon)*, Emory Johnson *(Tom Boling)*, Eddie Polo *(Ed Long)*, Frank Lanning *(Frank Long)*, Lucretia Harris *(Aunt Chlorindy)*.

When Clifford's father dies working his mine in California, his partner sends her to live with her uncle in Kentucky. The uncle has married a widow with a very pampered daughter, and the ladies make life for Clifford very difficult. Then a clever black mammy arranges for the orphan to meet the handsome young man, whom the uncle's stepdaughter has her eye on. There is a Cinderella ending, and the happy young couple even get the fortune from Clifford's half of the mine, which has been piling up in a West Coast bank.

d, Rupert Julian; w, Elliot J. Clawson (based on the novel by F. Hopkinson Smith).

Drama **(PR:A MPAA:NR)**

KENTUCKY DAYS** (1923) 5 reels FOX bw

Dustin Farnum *(Don Buckner)*, Margaret Fielding *(Elizabeth Clayborne)*, Miss Woodthrop *(Margarite Buckner)*, Bruce Gordon *(Gordon Carter)*, William De Vaull *(Scipio)*.

Farnum goes to California in search of gold and is away so long that his wife questions whether he is alive or dead. A lustful cousin tries to kiss her, and when Farnum's mother sees this she thinks her daughter-in-law unfaithful and dies from a heart attack. Farnum returns, visits his mother's grave, believes the rumors he hears, and kills the cousin in a duel. He then burns his property to the ground, frees his slaves, and sets off for California alone. His wife follows behind, and when she gets lost in a sandstorm, Farnum realizes he still loves her and they continue on together.

d, David Soloman; w, Dorothy Yost (based on a story by John Lynch).

Western/Drama **(PR:A MPAA:NR)**

KENTUCKY DERBY, THE** (1922) 6 reels UNIV bw

Reginald Denny *(Donald Gordon)*, Lillian Rich *(Alice Brown)*, Emmett King *(Col. Moncrief Gordon)*, Walter McGrail *(Ralph Gordon)*, Gertrude Astor *(Helen Gordon)*, Lionel Belmore *(Col. Rome Woolrich)*, Kingsley Benedict *(Joe)*, Bert Woodruff *(Rance Newcombe)*, Bert Tracy *(Topper Tom)*, Harry Carter *(Bob Thurston)*, Wilfred Lucas *(Capt. Wolff)*, Pat Harmon *(Jensen)*, Anna Hernandez *(Mrs. Clancy)*, Verne Winter *(Timmy Clancy)*.

Denny is disowned by his wealthy father, a Kentucky colonel, when the old man finds out that his son is secretly married. This is revealed to him after a couple, posing as relatives to the colonel, come to his home and try to marry their daughter off to Denny in an attempt to get at the family fortune. The phony couple later have Denny framed on a theft charge. In the end, he brings the crooks to justice, saves the Kentucky Derby for his father, and is finally allowed to live openly with his wife.

d, King Baggot; w, George C. Hull (based on the play "The Suburban" by Charles T. Dazey); ph, Victor Milner.

Drama **(PR:A MPAA:NR)**

KENTUCKY HANDICAP* (1926) 6 reels HARRY J. BROWN/RAY bw

Reed Howes, Alice Calhoun, Robert McKim, Lydia Knott, Josef Swickard, James Bradbury, Jr..

Nothing unusual in this story about a Derby horse owner who is disbarred from the race. To get his horse off he overcomes several obvious adversities, wins the big race, and the pretty little girl as well.

d, Harry J. Brown; w, Henry Roberts Symonds.

Adventure **(PR:A MPAA:NR)**

KICK BACK, THE** (1922) 6 reels R-C/FBO bw

Harry Carey *(White Horse Harry)*, Henry B. Walthall *(Aaron Price)*, Charles J. Le Moyne *(Chalk Eye)*, Vester Pegg *(Ramon Pinellos)*, Mingenne *(Conchita Pinellos)*, Ethel Grey Terry *(Nellie)*.

In order to steal Carey's girl and ranch, Walthall hires him to buy horses in Mexico, but provides the cowboy with phony papers which lead to his arrest. With the help of a native girl Carey escapes, and he and the Texas Rangers bring the bad men to justice.

p, P. A. Powers; d, Val Paul; w, George Edwardes-Hall (based on a story by Harry Carey); ph, Robert Thornby, Robert De Grasse.

Western **(PR:A MPAA:NR)**

KICK IN*** (1917) 5 reels Astra/Gold Rooster bw

William Courtenay, Robert Clugston, Mollie King, Richard Taber, Suzanne Willa, John Boyle.

Woods produced both the stage and screen versions of Mack's saga of a couple of pals who grow from teenage street gang members to adult gangsters. In this case the motion picture version is superior.

p, A. H. Woods; d, George Fitzmaurice; w, (based on the play by Willard Mack).

Crime **(PR:A MPAA:NR)**

KICK IN*** (1922) 7 reels FP/PAR bw

Betty Compson *(Molly Brandon)*, Bert Lytell *(Chick Hewes)*, May McAvoy *(Myrtle)*, Gareth Hughes *(Benny)*, Kathleen Clifford *("Frou Frou")*, Maym Kelso *(Mrs. Brandon)*, John Miltern *(District Attorney Brandon)*, Walter Long *(Whip Fogarty)*, Robert Agnew *(Jerry Brandon)*, Jed Prouty *(Jimmy Monahan)*, Carlton King *(Diggs Murphy)*, Charles Ogle *(John Stephens)*, Charles Stevenson *(Handsome the Yegg)*.

Finding it difficult to go straight after getting out of prison because of police harassment, and especially after watching the district attorney's son cavalierly kill a slum child with his automobile, Lytell decides to pull one last job. Then, while burglarizing the D. A.'s home, he discovers the son in the process of robbing it himself. There is a struggle, which ends with the little rotter trying to pin his own crime on Lytell. But the daughter of the house (who is in love with him) intervenes, and the two are given the okay to head west where they will, of course, find happiness.

d, George Fitzmaurice; w, Ouida Bergère (based on the play by Willard Mack); ph, Arthur Miller.

Crime **(PR:A MPAA:NR)**

KICK-OFF, THE 1/2** (1926) 6 reels EXCEL bw

George Walsh *(Tom Stephens)*, Leila Hyams *(Marilyn Spencer)*, Bee Amann *(Ruth)*, Earle Larrimore *(Frank Preston)*, W. L. Thorne, Joseph Burke, Jane Jennings.

Clean-cut and athletic Walsh was a natural for this one. Here he is the shy country boy who overcomes the ridicule of his big college classmates and the dirty tricks of his No. 1 rival to finally win the big football game—and the campus beauty, Hyams.

d, Wesley Ruggles; w, (based on a story by H. H. Van Loan); t, Jack Conway; ph, Frank Zukor.

Drama **(PR:A MPAA:NR)**

KID, THE*** (1916) 6 reels VIT bw

Lillian Walker *(The Kid)*, Ned Finley *(Dunster)*, Eulalie Jensen *(Mare Paree)*, Robert Gaillard *(Joe Hazzard)*.

Walker is the kid born out of wedlock by a rotter (who is driven out of town by an irate citizenry when they learn of his dastardly seduction) and a naive immigrant girl. The kid is raised by newspaperman Gaillard, who is transferred to The New York Herald. On her 19th birthday, Gaillard tells her the truth and also arranges for his editor to read some examples of her writing. Walker is hired by the Herald and, as fate would have it, her first assignment is to cover a meat price-fixing story involving her father, who has since become the cattle king of Mexico. The big climactic scene comes when the old man (who was instantly regenerated on seeing his flesh and blood) pleads with his daughter to forgive his past sins and allow him to be her daddy. But the kid looks him square in the eye, says no thank you, and returns to New York to be with Gaillard, the only real father she has ever known.

d&w, Wilfred North.

Drama **(PR:A MPAA:NR)**

KID, THE***** (1921) 6 reels Charles Chaplin/AFN bw

Charles Chaplin *(Tramp)*, Edna Purviance *(Mother)*, Jackie Coogan *(The Kid)*, Baby Hathaway *(The Kid as a Baby)*, Carl Miller *(Artist)*, Granville Redmond *(His Friend)*, May White *(Policeman's Wife)*, Tom Wilson *(Policeman)*, Henry Bergman *(Night Shelter Keeper)*, Charles Riesner *(Bully)*, Raymond Lee *(His Kid Brother)*, Lillita McMurray [Lita Grey] *(Flirtatious Angel)*, Edith Wilson *(Lady with Pram)*, Baby Wilson *(Baby in Pram)*, Nellie Bly Baker *(Slum Nurse)*, Albert Austin *(Man in Shelter)*, Jack Coogan, Sr. *(Pickpocket/Guest/Devil)*, Edgar Sherrod *(Priest)*, Beulah Bains *(Bride)*, Robert Dunbar *(Bridegroom)*, Kitty Bradbury *(Bride's Mother)*, Rupert Franklin *(Bride's Father)*, Flora Howard *(Bridesmaid)*, Elsie Sindora *(Bridesmaid)*, Walter Lynch *(Tough Cop)*, Dan Dillon *(Bum)*, Jules Hanft *(Physician)*, Silas Wilcox *(Cop)*, Kathleen Kay *(Maid)*, Minnie Stearns *(Fierce Woman)*, Frank Campeau *(Welfare Officer)*, F. Blinn *(His Assistant)*, John McKinnon *(Chief of Police)*, Elsie Young, V. Madison, Evans Quirk, Bliss Chevalier, Grace Keller, Irene Jennings, Florette Faulkner, Martha Hall, Estelle Cook, J. B. Russell, Lillian Crane, Sarah Kernan, Philip D'Oench, Charles I. Pierce *(Extras in Wedding Scene)*, Elsie Codd, Mother Vinot, Louise Hathaway, Amada Yanez and Baby *(Extras in Alley Scene)*, Clyde McAtee, Frank Hale, Ed Hunt, Rupert Franklin, Frances Cochran, George Sheldon *(Extras in Reception Scene)*, Sadie Gordon, Laura Pollard, L. Parker, Ethel O'Neil, L. Jenks, Esther Ralston, Herny Roser *(Extras in Heaven Scene)*.

"A Picture With A Smile And Perhaps A Tear" read the opening title, but THE KID is much more than this sentimental opening implies. With this film, the first feature length work he wrote and directed, Chaplin more fully realized the intimations of pathos he had injected into such shorts as EASY STREET and THE IMMIGRANT (both 1917) without sacrificing humor in the least. The story opens with Purviance, an unwed mother, leaving the hospital with her newborn son. She passes the wedding of a young and clearly unhappy bride to an older, well-off man. A flower falls from the bride's bouquet and the groom, unknowingly, crushes it with his foot. Purviance realizes she can't give her child the care he needs, so she pins a note to him and places the infant in the back seat of a fancy car (in actuality the automobile used had been loaned to Chaplin by its owner, D. W. Griffith). A pair of thieves grab the car but soon discover the unwanted cargo. Rather than risk kidnaping charges, they stop the auto in nearby slums and leave the baby in a back alley. Along comes Chaplin out on a stroll, who finds the baby. At first he tries to place it in another baby carriage but after staving off blows from Wilson, Chaplin takes back the baby. He raises the eyebrows of a cop in his efforts to rid himself of the child but then finds the note and decides to raise the boy himself. Meanwhile, Purviance has had a change of heart but is shocked when she discovers the automobile stolen. Chaplin sets up his simple flat as a nursery, improvising a baby bottle with a coffee pot and nipple, while cutting out diapers from a sheet. Five years pass and the child (Coogan) has become a thriving partner in Chaplin's window repairing business. Coogan throws rocks through someone's window and Chaplin knocks on the door offering to repair the broken pane. In the meanwhile Purviance has become a well-known singer. She does volunteer work in the slums and one day meets Coogan, not realizing the youngster is her own child. After the boy gets into a fight, Purviance urges Chaplin, believing him to be Coogan's father, to have a doctor take a look at the child. The doctor, a complete incompetent, learns that Chaplin found the child in the streets and arranges for the proper authorities to take the boy away. As a tearful Coogan is driven away in a truck Chaplin gives a rooftop pursuit and catches up with the vehicle. They are reunited in an emotional embrace and seek refuge. Meanwhile, the doctor shows Purviance a note Chaplin gave him and the singer recognizes it as the note she had written five years ago. She puts an ad in the paper offering a reward for Coogan's return. Chaplin and Coogan attempt to hide out in a flophouse, but since the Tramp can only afford to pay for one of them, he sneaks Coogan in. The proprietor recognizes Coogan's description from the paper and takes the boy while Chaplin is sleeping. In the morning Chaplin is heartsick to find Coogan missing and begins a vain search for the boy. Worn out from his efforts, Chaplin falls asleep in a doorway and dreams of life in Heaven. He finds himself rudely awakened by a cop, but instead of arrest he is taken to Purviance's home. The boy leaps into the Tramp's arms and together they go into the house. Unlike the slapstick shorts, with their emphasis on slapstick for laughs, Chaplin here builds the humor on smaller moments of character and situation. What's more, each moment of comedy, such as Chaplin's attempts to get rid of the unwanted infant and the flophouse confrontations between Chaplin and a pickpocket, are funny bits built on genuinely serious premises. THE KID is not just a beautifully told dramatic comedy, it is a daring experiment in structure by Chaplin that succeeds on every level. It proved to be a turning point in his work and pointed Chaplin towards a continual exploration of the serious and the funny within his feature films. Chaplin had just completed SUNNYSIDE (1919), a two-reel comedy, and had gone into a depression following the death of his newborn son who had suffered from severe birth defects. He had been working on a comedy tenatively titled CHARLIE'S PICNIC when he took in an evening of vaudeville. Watching Jack Coogan, a comic dancer performing with his little boy, Chaplin was immediately taken with the son, Jackie. He saw enormous potential for this bright, talented boy and without signing him began planning a film around the child. His hopes were nearly dashed when he learned that Roscoe "Fatty" Arbuckle had signed Jack Coogan but was relieved to learn it was the father the rotund comedian had put under contract. The chemistry between Chaplin and Coogan is genuine on screen because it was merely an extension of their off-screen relationship. The man and boy became fast friends with a mutual respect that would last throughout their lives. Years later, when Chaplin returned to America after his exile in Switzerland, the two were reunited after a 50-year separation. Coogan, who then was best known as "Uncle Fester" on TV's "The Addams Family," met with Chaplin in a real-life tearful reunion. Chaplin took Coogan's wife aside and told her "You must never forget. Your husband is a genius." Chaplin was amazed at Coogan's abilities. For their emotional separation scene, Coogan's father attempted to induce tears in his son by threatening to send him off to a workhouse. A concerned Chaplin took Coogan aside after the shooting was over to assure the boy this would never happen, but through his tears the youngster surprised his older friend with a seasoned reply, "I knew Daddy was fooling." Appearing as a flirtatious angel who causes Chaplin some real trouble in the dream sequence was a 12-year-old actress named Lillita McMurray. Chaplin had been captivated by the girl's looks after being introduced to her by an assistant who was a neighbor of McMurray's mother. Four years later, under the name Lita Grey, this girl became Chaplin's second wife in what would prove to be a bitter union for both. Grey claimed to be the inspiration for the Heaven sequence though that point is debatable. This dream sequence remains one of the most charming moments Chaplin ever devised. The slum is transformed into a clean, happy place with the film's principals—including the local bully and Chaplin's nemisis, the cop—appearing as winged angels. Man and boy are reunited with all seemingly blissful until the Devil (played by Coogan's father) comes to upset things. He tempts Chaplin with a girl (McMurray) which raises the bully's ire since she's his girl friend. The bully shoots Chaplin, and Coogan, crying over his friend's body, tries to shake the Tramp awake. The scene dissolves into reality with the cop shaking the sleeping Chaplin from his slumber. Chaplin's vision of Heaven is not grandiose but a simple picture of a happier life for the poor man. The director showed a clear understanding of his character and his world, never straying beyond the hopes and needs of the Tramp. Getting THE KID edited proved to be quite a task. Chaplin's business associates at First National sided with his wife, Mildred Harris, in an ongoing divorce suit. Among Chaplin's assets the company wanted to control in this suit were included the film's negative. With the collaboration of his creative associates, Chaplin snuck the negative (some 400,000 feet in 12 crates) out of California to Salt Lake City. A cutting room was set up in Chaplin's hotel room despite the fire hazard the nitrate film posed. After a test showing, the film was taken to an empty New Jersey studio and under the guise "Blue Moon Film Company" the final editing took place. The results proved to be a resounding success for Chaplin and made Coogan the biggest child star of the 1920s. Though other short comedies followed, with THE KID Chaplin clearly established himself with both the public and filmmaking community as an artist who understood the delicate balance between comedy and drama.

p,d&w, Charles Chaplin; ph, Roland H. Totheroh.

Comedy/Drama **Cas.** **(PR:AA MPAA:NR)**

KID BOOTS* ½** (1926) 9 reels FP/PAR bw

Eddie Cantor *(Kid Boots)*, Clara Bow *(Jane Martin)*, Billie Dove *(Polly Pendleton)*, Lawrence Gray *(Tom Sterling)*, Natalie Kingston *(Carmen Mendoza)*, Malcolm Waite *(George Fitch)*, William Worthington *(Polly's Father)*, Harry von Meter *(Carmen's Lawyer)*, Fred Esmelton *(Tom's Lawyer)*.

Comic, singer Cantor made a howlingly successful transition from the musical stage to the silent screen in this very funny comedy in which he starred on the stage. The story is about a tailor's assistant who, along with Bow, prevents the gold-digging chorus girl who tricked his pal into marriage from getting the fortune he inherited.

d, Frank Tuttle; w, Tom Gibson, Luther Reed (based on the musical comedy by William Anthony McGuire, Otto Harbach, J. P. McCarthy); t, George Marion, Jr.; ph, Victor Milner.

Comedy **(PR:A MPAA:NR)**

KID BROTHER, THE**** (1927) 8 reels Harold Lloyd/PAR bw

Harold Lloyd *(Harold Hickory)*, Jobyna Ralston *(Mary Powers)*, Walter James *(Sheriff Jim Hickory)*, Leo Willis *(Leo Hickory)*, Olin Francis *(Olin Hickory)*, Constantine Romanoff *(Sardoni, the Crook)*, Eddie Boland *("Flash" Farrell)*, Frank Lanning *(Sam Hooper)*, Ralph Yearsley *(Hank Hooper)*, Gus Leonard.

Cinematically lovely film has Lloyd—the meek, cinderella-like son of a small town sheriff who raised his boys to be men—rising to the challenge and subduing a town brute. This exciting and hilarious pathos-filled movie is perhaps the comedian's best, because it contains the finest elements of his earlier films. The picture was another $2-million-plus grosser for Lloyd, and kept him the No. 1 box office attraction of 1927, a position he maintained in 1928 when his next film, SPEEDY, came out. The film took eight months in production, the longest of any Lloyd movie, and most of it was shot on Catalina Island and in around Placentia, California, and Santa Ana Canyon. It also is the one Lloyd picture that does not depend on daredevil stunts to keep up the excitement—that was done with the exquisite acting and story line themselves. A timeless work of art.

d, Ted Wilde, J. A. Howe, Lewis Milestone; w, John Grey, Tom Crizer, Lex Neal, Howard Green, Wilde; ph, Walter Lundin.

Comedy **(PR:A MPAA:NR)**

KID CANFIELD THE REFORM GAMBLER** (1922) 5 reels Canfield/Champion bw

Kid Canfield *(Himself)*, C. Williams, Mrs. Sharkey.

Criminals had become definite celebrities by the time the 1920s really began to roar, and Canfield (who claimed to be a notorious gambler) picked up a little pocket money showing this film and lecturing on the evils of wagering.

w&d, Kid Canfield.

Dramatic/Documentary **(PR:A MPAA:NR)**

KID SISTER, THE ½** (1927) 6 reels COL bw

Marguerite De La Motte *(Helen Hall)*, Ann Christy *(Mary Hall)*, Malcolm McGregor *(Thomas Webster)*, Brooks Benedict *(Ted Hunter)*, Tom Dugan *(Stage Manager)*, Sally Long *(Ann Howe)*, Barrett Greenwood *(Ann's Friend)*.

Christy leaves her quiet small town and comes to the city to be with her sister (De La Motte), a virtuous chorus girl. McGregor, a millionaire, loves De La Motte but is snubbed in return. Later, when Christy gets into a jam at a roadhouse while protecting her honor and is sent to jail, De La Motte goes to McGregor and promises him "anything" if he will come up with the $5,000 needed to spring her sister. McGregor agrees and takes De La Motte to his handsomely appointed home, leads her up the stairs to his bedroom, slowly opens the door—and introduces her to his mother. De La Motte and McGregor get married, and Christy—all the wiser now—returns home to her boy friend.

p, Harry Cohn; d, Ralph Graves; w, Harry O. Hoyt (based on the story "The Lost House" by Dorothy Howell); ph, J. O. Taylor.

Drama **(PR:A MPAA:NR)**

KIDNAPPED*** (1917) 5 reels Forum/Edison bw

Raymond McKee *(David Balfour)*, Joseph Burke *(Ebenezer Balfour)*, Robert Cain *(Alan Breck)*, William Wadsworth *(Angus Bankeillor)*, Ray Hallor *(Ransome, the Cabin Boy)*, Walter Craven *(Riach)*, John Nicholson *(Shuan)*, Franklin Hanna *(Capt. Hoseason)*, Sam Niblack *(Cluny McPherson)*, Horace Hain *(Conlin Campbell)*, James Levering.

Well-directed, acted, and produced telling of the often-filmed Stevenson 18th Century adventure. This one was much more faithful to the novel than all of the subsequent versions telling the adventures of young David Balfour and the Jacobite (Cain), who is considered one of Stevenson's best-drawn characters.

d, Allan Crosland; w, Sumner Williams (based on the novel by Robert Louis Stevenson).

Adventure **(PR:A MPAA:NR)**

KID'S CLEVER, THE** (1929) 6 reels UNIV bw

Glenn Tryon *(Bugs Raymond)*, Kathryn Crawford *(Ruth Decker)*, Russell Simpson *(John Decker)*, Lloyd Whitlock *(Ashton Steele)*, George Chandler *(Hank)*, Joan Standing *(A Girl)*, Max Asher *(Magician)*, Florence Turner *(Matron)*, Virginia Sale *(Secretary)*, Stepin Fetchit *(Negro Man)*.

Tryon, who invents an auto that runs without fuel, meets Crawford, the daughter of a wealthy car manufacturer, and she arranges a demonstration. A rival salesman sabotages the showing, but later Tryon and Crawford force her dad to take a ride, and he is sold.

d, William James Craft; sup, Harry Decker; w, Jack Foley (based on a story by Vin Moore); t, Albert De Mond; ph, Al Jones; ed, Charles Craft; art d, Charles D. Hall.

Comedy **(PR:A MPAA:NR)**

KIKI**** (1926) 9 reels Norma Talmadge/FN bw

Norma Talmadge *(Kiki)*, Ronald Colman *(Renal)*, Gertrude Astor *(Paulette)*, Marc MacDermott *(Baron Rapp)*, George K. Arthur *(Adolphe)*, William Orlamond *(Brule)*, Erwin Connelly *(Joly)*, Frankie Darro *(Pierre)*, Mack Swain *(Pastryman)*.

Producer Schenck spent a fortune producing this excellent movie about a Parisian gamin who adores a theatrical manager and is willing to take on the whole world, and especially his actress girl friend, in order to win his love. Her beauty and charm do eventually triumph, and Talmadge was given perhaps the ultimate compliment when, a few years later, Mary Pickford herself elected to remake the film.

p, Joseph M. Schenck; d, Clarence Brown; w, Hans Kraly (based on the play by Andre Picard); ph, Oliver Marsh.

Comedy/Drama **(PR:A MPAA:NR)**

KILDARE OF STORM** (1918) 5 reels Metro bw

Emily Stevens *(Mrs. Kildare)*, King Baggot, Crauford Kent, Florence Short, Edward David, Helen Lindroth, Maggie Breyer, Fred Warren.

Stevens, who has entered into a marriage of convenience, is attracted to a young doctor who practices in the area. Her husband, motivated by jealousy, goes to see him and is murdered. The doctor is sent to prison and is pardoned in five years, but refuses to see Stevens as long as the world thinks him a criminal. When a maid later confesses to actually doing the deed, the couple are united.

d, Harry L. Franklin; w, Jere Looney, June Mathis (based on the novel by Eleanor Mercein Kelly); ph, Arthur Martinelli.

Drama **(PR:A MPAA:NR)**

KILLER, THE**** (1921) 6 reels Benjamin B. Hampton/Pathe bw

Claire Adams *(Ruth Emory)*, Jack Conway *(William Sanborn)*, Frankie Lee *(Bobby Emory)*, Frank Campeau *(Henry Hooper)*, Tod Sloan *(Artie Brower)*, Edward Peil *(Ramon)*, Frank Hayes *(Windy Smith)*, Will Walling *(John Emory)*, Milton Ross *(Buck Johnson)*, Tom Ricketts *(Tim Westmore)*, Zack Williams *(Aloysius Jackson)*.

Beautifully directed, written, acted, and atmospherically photographed story of a man—he enjoys killing in general—who murders his partner and has his sights set on the dead man's children before a neighboring rancher intercedes and causes his death. The heavy in this film is so skillfully played against type that the picture—a modest success commercially—was a triumph of mood and suspense.

d, Howard Hickman; w, E. Richard Schayer (based on the novel by Stewart Edward White); ph, Harry Vallejo.

Mystery/Western **(PR:C MPAA:NR)**

KILMENY** (1915) Morosco bw

Leonore Ulrich *(Kilmeny)*, Herbert Standing *(Gypsy Chief)*, Howard Davies *(Barouche)*, Marshall Mackaye *(Pierre)*, Frederick Wilson *(Lord Leigh)*, Myrtle Stedman *(Lady Leigh)*, William Desmond *(Bob Meridith)*.

Standard gypsy stuff about a kidnaped child who, on becoming a young woman, runs away, senses rejection, and returns to the nomadic society. There she consents to marry but at the last moment is resuced by her father, who comes racing into the camp in his high-powered motor car.

d, Oscar Apfel; w, Louie R. Stanwood.

Drama **(PR:A MPAA:NR)**

KILTIES THREE** (1918, Brit.) 6 reels Gaiety/GAU bw

Bob Reed *(Kiltie)*, Rowland Hill *(Kiltie)*, Robert Vallis *(Kiltie)*, Ernest Esdaile *(Otto Klein)*, Gladys Foyle *(Mary Strong)*, Scott Layton *(Silas Strong)*, Phyllis Beadon *(Mrs. Strong)*.

British wartime film, set in Scotland, about the owner of a foundry who marries a patriotic nurse who, at one time, was married to a German spy.

p&d, Maurice Sandground; w, Bernard Merivale.

War **(PR:A MPAA:NR)**

KINDLED COURAGE*** (1923) 5 reels UNIV bw

Hoot Gibson *(Andy Walker)*, Beatrice Burnham *(Betty Paxton)*, Harold Goodwin *(Hugh Paxton)*, Harry Tenbrook *(Sid Garrett)*, James Gordon Russell *(Sheriff)*, J. Russell Powell *(Marshal)*, Albert Hart *(Overland Pete)*.

Driven out of town and branded a coward, Gibson hops a freight, and when the brakeman shoots a couple of mean hombres he is mistakenly considered a hero and made deputy sheriff. Later Gibson is sent to capture Hart's gang, and somehow manages to rise to the occasion and pull it off. He returns home with one of the outlaw's sisters as his bride and beats the devil out of the bully who made his life so miserable.

d, William Worthington; w, Raymond L. Schrock (based on a story by Leete Renick Brown); ph, Virgil Miller.

Western **(PR:A MPAA:NR)**

KINDLING*½** (1915) 5 reels LAS bw

Charlotte Walker *(Maggie Schultz)*, Thomas Meighan *(Henie Schultz)*, Raymond Hatton *(Steve, a Crook)*, Mrs. Lewis McCord *(Mrs. Bates)*, Billy Elmer *(Rafferty)*, Lillian Langdon *(Mrs. Burke-Smith)*, Florence Dagmar *(Alice)*, Tom Forman *(Doctor Taylor)*, Tex Driscoll.

Living in a Hell's Kitchen tenement where half the infant population dies before the age of one, Walker, the wife of a hard-working longshoreman, vows that her unborn child will be given a better break. She therefore agrees to assist a petty crook in robbing the one woman who had treated her kindly, in order to get the funds needed to move her family out West. She is caught by the police and double-crossed by her partner in the crime, but the eloquent appeal Walker makes for the infant she is carrying gets her off the hook and out of the neighborhood. DeMille's feeling for atmosphere and sense of outrage for the slum conditions of that time, make this modest (by his standards) production somewhat special.

d, Cecil B. DeMille; w, DeMille (based on the book by Charles A. Kenyon, Arthur Hornblow and the play by Kenyon); ph, Alvin Wyckoff.

Drama **(PR:A MPAA:NR)**

KINDRED OF THE DUST*** (1922) 8 reels R.A. Walsh/AFN bw

Miriam Cooper *(Nan of the Sawdust Pile)*, Ralph Graves *(Donald McKaye)*, Lionel Belmore *(The Laird of the Tyee)*, Eugenie Besserer *(Mrs. McKaye)*, Maryland Morne *(Jane McKaye)*, Elizabeth Walters *(Elizabeth McKaye)*, W.J. Ferguson *(Mr. Daney)*, Caroline Ranklin *(Mrs. Daney)*, Pat Rooney *("Dirty" Dan O'Leary)*, John Herdman *(Caleb Brent)*, Bruce Guerin *(Little Donald)*.

Cooper is shunned by everyone in her hometown—with the exception of her former sweetheart—when she returns with a child after discovering she was married to a bigamist. The young man's feelings for her lead to his disinheritance, but all is forgiven after she nurses him back from what appears to be a fatal illness.

d, R. A. Walsh; w, James T. O'Donohue (based on the novel by Peter Bernard Kyne); ph, Charles Van Enger, Lyman Broening; art d, William Cameron Menzies.

Drama **(PR:A MPAA:NR)**

KING CHARLES** (1913, Brit.) 4 reels CL bw

P. G. Ebbutt *(King Charles II)*, Dorothy Bellew *(Dulcia Beard)*.

This pioneering British feature film chronicles the escape of King Charles II to France following the Battle of Worcester in the 17th Century.

d, Wilfred Noy; w, Low Warren (based on the novel by Harrison Ainsworth).

Historical **(PR:A MPAA:NR)**

KING LEAR** (1916) Thanhouser/Gold Rooster bw

Frederick Warde, Ernest Warde, Ina Hammer, Edith Diestel, Charles Brooks, Lorraine Huling, J. H. Gilmour, Boyd Marshall, Hector Dion, Edwin Stanley, Robert Whittier, Wayne Arey.

Without inspired direction or photography, this straightforward silent interpretation of the Bard's work has little to recommend it. A lot of foot stomping, hand waving, and posturing fails to put across Lear's deep tragedy on being betrayed by two of his daughters, and seeing the third, who he learns truly loved him, hanged.

d, Ernest Warde; w, Philip Lonergan (based on the play by William Shakespeare); ph, William Zollinger.

Drama **(PR:A MPAA:NR)**

KING OF DIAMONDS, THE* (1918) 5 reels VIT bw

Harry Morey *(Oliver Bennett)*, Betty Blythe *(Mrs. Bennett)*, William Dennison *(Dr. Sanderson)*, Jean Paige, George Majeroni.

The old "murder the husband and nail the wife" plot, only this time the lustful rat is a doctor who keeps inoculating the husband of the woman he wants with leprosy germs. Somehow the man survives to see justice served in what can only be classified as a very bad movie.

d, Paul Scardon; w, Edward S. Ballou; ph, Robert Stuart.

Drama **(PR:A MPAA:NR)**

KING OF KINGS, THE***** (1927) 14 reels DM/PDC bw-c

H. B. Warner *(Jesus the Christ)*, Dorothy Cumming *(Mary the Mother)*, Ernest Torrence *(Peter)*, Joseph Schildkraut *(Judas)*, James Neill *(James)*, Joseph Striker *(John)*, Robert Edeson *(Matthew)*, Sidney D'Albrook *(Thomas)*, David Imboden *(Andrew)*, Charles Belcher *(Philip)*, Clayton Packard *(Bartholomew)*, Robert Ellsworth *(Simon)*, Charles Requa *(James, the Less)*, John T. Prince *(Thaddeus)*, Jacqueline Logan *(Mary Magdalene)*, Rudolph Schildkraut *(Caiaphas, High Priest of Israel)*, Sam De Grasse *(The Pharisee)*, Casson Ferguson *(The Scribe)*, Victor Varconi *(Pontius Pilate, Governor of Judea)*, Majel Coleman *(Proculla, Wife of Pilate)*, Montagu Love *(The Roman Centurion)*, William Boyd *(Simon of Cyrene)*, M. Moore *(Mark)*, Theodore Kosloff *(Malchus, Captain of the High Priest's Guard)*, George Siegmann *(Barabbas)*, Julia Faye *(Martha)*, Josephine Norman *(Mary of Bethany)*, Kenneth Thomson *(Lazarus)*, Alan Brooks *(Satan)*, Viola Louie *(The Woman Taken in Adultery)*, Muriel McCormac *(The Blind Girl)*, Clarence Burton *(Dysmas, the Repentant Thief)*, James Mason *(Gestas, the Unrepentant Thief)*, May Robson *(Mother of Gestas)*, Dot Farley *(Maid Servant of Caiaphas)*, Hector Sarno *(The Galilean Carpenter)*, Leon Holmes *(The Imbecile Boy)*, Jack Padgen *(Captain *of the Roman Guard)*, Robert St. Angelo, Redman Finely, James Dime, Richard Alexander, Budd Fine, William De Boar, Robert McKee, Tom London, Edward Schaeffer, Peter Norris, Dick Richards *(Soldiers of Rome)*, James Farley *(An Executioner)*, Otto Lederer *(Eber, a Pharisee)*, Bryant Washburn *(A Young Roman)*, Lionel Belmore *(A Roman Noble)*, Monte Collins *(A Rich Judean)*, Luca Flamma *(A Gallant of Galilee)*, Sojin *(A Prince of Persia)*, Andre Cheron *(A Wealthy Merchant)*, William Costello *(A Babylonian Noble)*, Sally Rand *(Slave to Mary Magdalene)*, Noble Johnson *(A Charioteer)*, Jere Austin, W. Azenberg, Fred Becker, Baldy Belmont, Ed Brady, Joe Bonomo, George Calliga, Fred Cavens, Colin Chase, Charles Clary, Denis D'Auburn, Victor De Linsky, Malcolm Denny, David Dunbar, Jack Fife, Sidney Franklin, Kurt Furberg, Bert Hadley, Edwin Hearn, Stanton Heck, Fred Huntley, Brandon Hurst, Otto Kottka, Edward Lackey, Theodore Lorch, Bertram Marburgh, James Marcus, George F. Marion, Earl Metcalf, Max Montor, Louis Natheaux, Richard Neill, Robert Ober, A. Palasthy, Louis Payne, Edward Piel, Albert Priscoe, Herbert Pryor, Warren Rodgers, Charles Sellon, Tom Shirley, Walter Shumway, Bernard Siegel, Phil Sleeman, Charles Stevens, Carl Stockdale, William Strauss, Mark Strong, Josef Swickard, Wilbert Wadleigh, Fred Walker, Will Walling, Paul Weigel, Charles West, Emily Barrye, Elaine Bennett, Lucille Brown, Kathleen Chambers, Edna Mae Cooper, Josephine Crowell, Frances Dale, Milla Davenport, Anna De Linsky, Lillian Elliott, Anielka Elter, Evelyn Francisco, Margaret Francisco, Dale Fuller, Natalie Galitzen, Inez Gomez, Edna Gordon, Julia Swayne Gordon, Winifred Greenwood, Eulalie Jensen, Kadja, Jane Keckley, Isabelle Keith, Nora Kildare, Lydia Knott, Alice Knowland, Celia Lapan, Alla Moskova, Gertrude Norman, Patricia Palmer, Gertrude Quality, Rae Randall, Hedwig Reicher, Reeka Roberts, Peggy Schaffer, Evelyn Selbie, Semone Sergis, Anne Teeman, Barbara Tennant, Mabel Van Buren, Stanhope Wheatcroft.

In his most important and beautiful film, DeMille tells the story of Christ's life, beginning with the redemption of Mary Magdalene and ending with His Crucifixion, Resurrection, and Ascension. It is a reverential masterwork which should be seen again and again by everyone interested in religious history or the cinema. A movie with such a subject could not help but create controversy, and KING OF KINGS did. Jewish organizations blasted it because they claimed it condemned them as the crucifiers of Christ. DeMille was called a man with "a warped sense of religion," and a propagandist for the Christian religion, a man of tremendous bad taste, and a panderer after the basest emotions of his audiences. On the other hand, to date KING OF KINGS is believed to have been seen by more than eight billion people worldwide, and thousands have given testimony of how the picture changed their lives. Its versimilitude is testified to by the fact that during the filming a Jesuit priest from the Federal Council of Churches was on hand with another clergyman, to ensure the film's proper attitude of belief and reverence to its subject. Further, Gabe Essoe and Raymond Lee say in their highly readable *De Mille: The Man and His Pictures:* "The first day of shooting started with the uttering of prayers by representatives of Protestant, Catholic, Jewish, Buddhist, and Moslem faiths." Further, "H. B. Warner in costume as Christ was spoken to by no one save the director..." and he was "also instructed not to be seen in public during production." He wore a black veil as he left his car for the set, and ate alone in a tent on location. For all of that travail, an old drinking problem was set off in the actor, a fact resolutely kept secret by DeMille. KING OF KINGS was reissued in 1931 with the addition of a synchronized musical score.

p&d, Cecil B. DeMille; w, Jeanie Macpherson; ph, Peverell Marley, Fred Westerberg, Jacob A. Badaracco (Technicolor); ed, Anne Bauchens, Harold McLernon, Clifford Howard; art d, Mitchell Leisen, Anton Grot.

Religious **Cas.** **(PR:AA MPAA:NR)**

KING OF THE CASTLE** (1925, Brit.) 7 reels STOLL bw

Marjorie Hume *(Lady Oxborrow)*, Brian Aherne *(Colin O'Farrell)*, Dawson Millward *(Chris Furlong)*, Prudence Vanbrugh *(Leslie Rain)*, Moore Marriott *(Peter Coffin)*, Albert E. Raynor *(Matlock)*, E. C. Matthews *(Ezekiel Squence)*.

British drama about a widow who learns to love the man she is forced to marry after he saves her child from death.

d, Henry Edwards; w, Alicia Ramsey (based on the play by Keble Howard).

Drama **(PR:A MPAA:NR)**

KING OF THE HERD* (1927) 6 reels Frank S. Mattison/AY bw

Raymond McKee *(Paul Garrison)*, Nola Luxford *(Nancy Dorrance)*, Bud Osborne *(Barry Kahn)*, Laura Miskin, Billy Franey, Evelyn Francisco, Fred Shanley, Arthur Hotaling, Eddie Harris, Hugh Saxon, White Star *(King the Horse)*.

There is hardly enough *real* action for the kids in this oater which had McKee capturing White Star, the stallion leader of a wild herd. Later they rescue Luxford and win the big Santa Barbara polo match, defeating super snob Osborne. There is a double happy ending, which finds McKee married to Luxford, and White Star near Luxford's little filly, whom he adores.

d, Frank S. Mattison; ph, Jack Fuqua.

Western **(PR:A MPAA:NR)**

KING OF THE RODEO*** (1929) 6 reels UNIV bw

Hoot Gibson *(Montana Kid)*, Kathryn Crawford *(Dulcie Harlan)*, Slim Summerville *(Slim)*, Charles K. French *(Chip, Sr.)*, Monty Montague *(Weasel)*, Joseph W. Girard *(Harlan)*, Jack Knapp *(Shorty)*, Harry Todd *(J. G.)*, Bodil Rosing *(Mother)*.

Gibson's farewell to the silent screen came with a bang, as he played a traveling rodeo rider who chases a robber through the traffic-jammed streets of Chicago. Exciting stuff—and a fitting sendoff to the talkies.

p, Hoot Gibson; d, Henry MacRae; w, George Morgan (based on a story by B. M. Bower); t, Harold Tarshis, Bower; ph, Harry Neumann; ed, Gilmore Walker; art d, David S. Garber.

Western **(PR:A MPAA:NR)**

KING OF THE SADDLE** (1926) 5 reels AEX bw

Bill Cody, Joan Meredith.

At the Kansas City stockyards, Cody and his friend discover, to their horror, that their stock is worth $3 instead of $300,000, due to the bankruptcy of a ranchowner. They go to a restaurant where the sympathetic countergirl provides them with a free meal and falls head-over-heals with the equally love-stunned Cody. Later she is shocked to see that the worthless stock certificate he holds bears the name of her long lost father. At this point, the improbable becomes even more so, as the script has the old man striking oil on his property. So Cody and his bride return west to live the luxurious life with her father, as well as Cody's not-so-funny comic sidekick-stock partner.

d, William J. Craft; w, (based on a story by Carl Krusada).

Western/Comedy Drama **(PR:A MPAA:NR)**

KING OF THE TURF, THE*** (1926) 7 reels FBO bw

George Irving *(Col. Fairfax)*, Patsy Ruth Miller *(Kate Fairfax)*, Kenneth Harlan *(John Doe Smith)*, Al Roscoe *(Tom Selsby)*, Kathleen Kirkham *(Letitia Selsby)*, Mary Carr *(Martha Fairfax)*, David Torrence *(Martyn Selsby)*, Dave Kirby *(Red Kelly)*, William Franey *(Soup Conley)*, Eddie Phillips *(Dude Morlanti)*.

Torrence frames his horse-breeding business partner, Irving, and the old boy is sent to prison. Later, overcome by guilt, Torrence draws up a confession but dies before the document reaches the right people. His wife secures the paper in her safe to avoid scandal, and Irving serves his time. When he gets out, he brings home a few of the friends he made in the pokey—Harlan, a horse trainer who made a little mistake, Kirby, Franey, and Phillips. Terrence's toady son Roscoe is in love with Irving's beautiful daughter Miller, and offers to produce his father's confession if she will marry him. Harlan overhears this and puts his comrades' talents to use by cracking the safe. Irving is then cleared and, to make sure that the movie ends on an exciting note, the family horse wins the coveted gold cup, and Harlan and Miller announce their intention to wed.

d, James P. Hogan; w, J. Grubb Alexander, John C. Brownell, Louis Joseph Vance; ph, Jules Cronjager.

Drama/Adventure **(PR:A MPAA:NR)**

KING OF THE WILD HORSES, THE*** (1924) 5 reels HR/Pathe bw

Rex *(The Black)*, Edna Murphy *(Mary Fielding)*, Leon Bary *(Billy Blair)*, Charles Parrott *(Boyd Fielding)*, Sidney De Gray *(John Fielding)*, Pat Hartigan *(Wade Galvin)*, Frank Butler, Sidney D'Albrook.

Good children's film about a beautiful wild horse that helps the man who mastered him win the girl and capture the rustlers. Rex establishes his rule over the herd with derring-do that captivates the audience. One minute he is outdistancing, with his fellows, pursuing cowboys, and another he is protecting his herd from the same cowboys with paws outspread and balancing high on his rear legs. In the end, though, he submits willingly after his capture, and becomes a pal of his captor and the girl his captor loves.

p, Hal Roach; d, Fred Jackman; w, Carl Himm (based on a story by Roach); ph, Floyd Jackman.

Western **(PR:A MPAA:NR)**

KING, QUEEN, JOKER*** (1921) 5 reels FP/PAR bw

Sydney Chaplin *(The King/The Joker)*, Lottie MacPherson *(The Queen/Chief Plotter)*.

One can only speculate as to how much influence this Chaplin dual-role comedy about a barber's assistant (the exact double of an unpopular king, who is placed on the throne of Coronia by revolutionists) had on his half-brother Charlie Chaplin's magnificent political satire THE GREAT DICTATOR. In any event, the barber's assistant has the time of his life impersonating the king until he is brought to his heels and the king to his social senses.

d&w, Sydney Chaplin; ph, Murphy Darling.

Comedy **(PR:A MPAA:NR)**

KING SPRUCE** (1920) 7 reels Dial/Hodkinson bw

Mitchell Lewis, Mignon Anderson, Melbourne McDowell, Arthur Millett, James O'Neill, Betty Wales, Joe Ray, Gus Saville, Frederick Herzog.

Fair programmer about a lumber king who returns to the forest where, 20 years earlier, he was responsible for fathering an illegitimate daughter. After he evicts a group of squatters (including his unknown daughter), the girl ties him to a tree and sets his timberland on fire. He is eventually saved, but not before acknowledging the obligation he owes his flesh and blood.

d, Roy Clements; w, (based on the novel by Holman F. Day); ph, Fred Hartman.

Drama **(PR:A MPAA:NR)**

KING TUT-ANKH-AMEN'S EIGHTH WIFE*

(1923) 5 reels Max Cohen bw (AKA: THE MYSTERY OF TUT-ANKH-AMEN'S EIGHTH WIFE)

The curse of King Tut's tomb was almost as sensational a curiosity in the 1920s as flying saucers were in the 1950s. This little quickie was produced to cash in on that interest which revolved around the idea that anybody who violated the tomb would be violated himself by the fates that be.

d, Andrew Remo; w, George M. Merrick, Max Cohen (based on a story by Remo); ph, John Bitzer.

Mystery (PR:A MPAA:NR)

KINGDOM OF LOVE, THE** (1918) 5 reels FOX bw

Jewel Carmen *(Violet Carson)*, Nancy Caswell *(Violet Carson as a Child)*, Genevieve Blinn *(Mrs. Agnes Carson)*, L. C. Shumway *(Rev. David Cromwell)*, Fred Milton *(Frank Carson)*, Ernest Wade *(Frank Carson as a Child)*, Joseph Manning *(Henry Carson)*, G. Raymond Nye *(Caribou Bill)*, Murdock MacQuarrie *(Buck, Dance Hall Owner)*, Richard La Reno.

After a divorce a brother and sister are separated when the father and the girl move to the Kondike. Time passes, the boy heads North, and, not knowing the girl's true background, falls in love with her. Later the sister offers her body to the highest bidder as a means of coming up with the money to send him back to the States so that he might be with their dying mother. A minister, who knows the whole story, pledges $6,000, discovers gold, and ultimately marries the grateful girl.

d&w, Frank Lloyd (based on a story by C. Doty Hobart).

North Woods/Drama (PR:A MPAA:NR)

KINGDOM WITHIN, THE** (1922) 7 reels Producers Security/Hodkinson bw

Russell Simpson *(Caleb Deming)*, Z. Wall Covington *(Danny West)*, Gaston Glass *(Amos)*, Pauline Starke *(Emily Preston)*, Hallam Cooley *(Will Preston)*, Ernest Torrence *(Krieg)*, Gordon Russell *(Dodd)*, Marion Feducha *(Connie)*.

Glass grows up with a profound spiritual sense because of a crippled arm and the abuse his blacksmith father heaps on him because of it. Later, when he comes to the aid of a girl who has shut herself off from the world (because of her brother's imprisonment), a miracle occurs, and his limb is made well.

d, Victor Schertzinger; w, Kenneth B. Clarke; ph, John S. Stumar.

Drama (PR:A MPAA:NR)

KINGFISHER'S ROOST, THE*** (1922) 5 reels Pinnacle bw

Neal Hart *(Barr Messenger)*, Yvette Mitchell *(Betty Brownlee)*, William Quinn *("Bull" Keeler)*, Ben Corbett *("Red" McGee)*, Chet Ryan *(Sheriff Breen)*, Jane Fosher *(Mrs. Brownlee)*, Floyd Anderson *(Dan McGee)*, W. S. Weatherwax *(Bill Jackson)*, John Judd *(Chief of the Rurales)*, Earl Simpson *(Pete, McGee's Henchman)*, Earl Dwyer *(Dave Butler the Grocer)*.

Entertaining B western has Hart clearing his name after being framed, breaking up an entire gang of outlaws, and winning the heart of a girl who had also been framed. Hart fans expected plenty of action from their hero, and they got it in this one.

d&w, Louis Chaudet, Paul Hurst.

Western (PR:A MPAA:NR)

KING'S CREEK LAW*** (1923) 5 reels William Steiner/Photo Drama bw

Leo Maloney *(Tom Hardy)*, Josephine Hill *(Milly Jameson)*, Milton Brown *(Saul Jameson)*, Horace Carpenter *(The Sheriff)*, Frank Ellis *(James Lawton)*, Chet Ryan *(Kirk Jameson)*, Bullet the Dog.

Maloney plays a Texas Ranger out to get his man, who wanders into the town of King's Creek, which is run by Brown, an old Confederate officer who never surrendered and (very much in the manner of Judge Roy Bean) considers himself the only law. When the old fellow's beloved son is suspected of murder, Brown vows to conduct the trial with complete impartiality but, to his great relief, Maloney captures the real killer. It is then that the old soldier agrees to pledge allegiance to the flag again, and is more than delighted that his surprisingly youthful daughter has fallen head-over-heals for the handsome and resourceful Ranger. Bullet plays the murdered man's dog which is later adopted by Maloney, according to the shooting script in the copyright files, although his presence in the film cannot be confirmed.

d, Leo Maloney, Bob Williamson; w, Frances and Ford Bebe; ph, Ben Bail.

Western (PR:A MPAA:NR)

KING'S DAUGHTER, THE** (1916, Brit.) 5 reels LFP/JUR bw

Gerald Ames *(Montrose)*, Janet Ross *(Helene)*, Edward O'Neill *(The King)*, Hayford Hobbs *(Dubois)*, Hubert Willis *(Chief of Police)*.

British thriller, based on a novel by Dumas, about an assassin's daughter who gives her life to save her king after discovering that she is, in actuality, his illegitimate daughter.

d, Maurice Elvey; w, (based on the novel *Une Fille de Regent* by Alexandre Dumas pere).

Drama (PR:A MPAA:NR)

KING'S GAME, THE** (1916) 5 reels Gold Rooster bw

Pearl White, George Probert, Sheldon Lewis, Nora Moore, George Parks.

White took time away from her serial activities to star in this confusing adventure about a Russian officer and his daughter, who are forced to flee the old country and fall in with a band of nihilists, dedicated to assassinating royal personages. They, of course, manage to avoid any involvement in the bloodshed and even participate in the downfall of the terrorists.

d, Ashley Miller; w, Arnold Daly, Miller (based on a play by George B. Seitz).

Adventure (PR:A MPAA:NR)

KINKAID, GAMBLER** (1916) 5 reels Red Feather bw

Ruth Stonehouse *(Nellie Gleason)*, R. A. Cavin *(Jim Kinkaid)*, Raymond Whittaker *(George Arnold)*, Noble Johnson *(Romero Valdez)*, Harry Mann *(Lefty Frank)*, Harry Griffith *(McPherson)*, J. H. Knowles *(Murphy)*, Cleo Loring *(Nochita)*, Jean Hersholt.

Stonehouse is a female detective sent to Mexico to nail Cavin, a man accused of stealing $10,000 and then slipping over the border to his gambling casino. When Stonehouse arrives, Cavin is immediately smitten and allows himself to be taken across the line, where the young lady has a certain park bench she loves to sit on. They do this until it becomes routine, but when the time comes to set up the arrest, she realizes that she loves the big lug. However, she also remembers a certain sacred oath she took before God and her government, and so, with tears pouring down her cheeks, she sets up his fall. Movie audiences expected a lot from their leading ladies in 1916, and certainly this would never do. So the director (in that happy time before the production code) simply provided Stonehouse with a change of heart, as well as a key to the calaboose, and the picture ends with the two of them crossing into the land of the enchilada, never to return again.

d, Raymond Wells; w, Fred Myton (based on a story by Wells).

Drama (PR:A MPAA:NR)

KIPPS*** (1921, Brit.) 6 reels STOLL bw

George K. Arthur *(Arthur Kipps)*, Edna Flugrath *(Ann Pornick)*, Christine Rayner *(Helen Walsingham)*, Teddy Arundell *(Chitterlow)*, Norman Thorpe *(Chester Coote)*, Arthur Helmore *(Shalford)*, John M. East *(Old Kipps)*, Miss Atterbury *(Mrs. Walsingham)*, Mr. Gerrard *(Young Walsingham)*, Mr. Barbour *(Old Pornick)*, Judd Green *(Senior Citizen)*.

Good British comedy, based on a novel by Wells, about a fellow who inherits 3,000 pounds a year, takes a whirl at high society living, and decides wisely to return to his former working-class world and the girl he left behind.

d, Harold Shaw, w, Frank Miller (based on the novel by H. G. Wells).

Comedy (PR:A MPAA:NR)

KISMET*1/2** (1920) 9 reels R-C bw

Otis Skinner *(Hajj)*, Herschell Mayall *(Sheikh Jawan)*, Nicholas Dunaew *(Guide Nasir)*, Leon Bary *(The Caliph Abdalla)*, Emmett C. King, *(The Wazir Abu Bakr)*, Hamilton Revelle *(The Wazir Mansur)*, Paul Weigel *(Afife)*, Elinor Fair *(Marsinah)*, Matilda Comont *(Marjis)*, Frederick Lancaster *(Zayd)*, Sam Kaufman *(Amru)*, Rosemary Theby *(Kut-al-Kulub)*, Cornelia Skinner *(Miskah)*, Sidney Smith *(Jester)*, James Adams *(Chamberlain)*, Thomas Kennedy, Fanny Ferrari, Emily Seville, Harry Lorraine, Robert Evans, Frederic Peters, C. E. Collins.

Skinner, who made something of a career portraying Hajj, the begger, on the stage, made his motion picture debut in a lavish and most satisfying production of the Edward Knoblock Arabian Nights fantasy, KISMET. The distinguished actor proved to be as effective before the camera as he was on the boards and starred in a talking version of this classic in 1931. KISMET was remade twice by director William Dieterle (1931 and 1944) and as a musical by Vincent Minnelli in 1955.

d, Louis Gasnier; w, Charles E. Whittaker (based on the play by Edward Knoblock); ph, Joseph A. Dubray, Tony Gaudio.

Costume/Romance (PR:A MPAA:NR)

KISS, THE*** (1916) 5 reels FP bw

Owen Moore *(Jean-Marie)*, Marguerite Courtot *(Louise D'Auvergne)*, Kate Lester *(Grandma Vanvechten)*, Virginia Hammond *(Mrs. Jack Vanvechten)*, Adolphe Menjou *(Pennington)*, Gus Weinberg *(Castaigne)*.

Moore is a wealthy young airman, flying for the French during WW I. When he comes home on furlough, he is instantly attracted to Courtot, his grandmother's secretary, but plans have already been made to throw a lavish party to which every eligible girl in town has been invited. At the soiree, where everyone attending is masked, he kisses Courtot (not knowing who she is) and decides right on the spot that this is the only girl in the world for him to marry. Then, to prove his point, he osculates—with dissapointing results—every female at the party. At the height of the festivities some valuable jewlery is stolen and, naturally, the lowly working girl is blamed. But she manages to escape, with the police in hot pursuit. Moore, who at this point still only thinks of her as a friend, takes off in a hydroplane and heads for the boat he somehow knows she is being chased on. Then, in a scene which can only be described as bizarre, he flies his machine next to her ship, and the girl hops into the drink. Moore fishes her out but, in doing so, bumps his head and is stunned. When Courtot gives him a little smooch to help his revival, the title flashes across the screen "AT LAST I HAVE FOUND THAT KISS!" In the meantime, the real crooks have also been found, and this silly little movie—which definately falls into the so-bad-it's-good class—comes to an end with, what else, a big wet one.

d, Del Henderson; w, (based on a story by Elizabeth Frazer).

Drama (PR:A MPAA:NR)

KISS, THE** (1929) 7 reels MGM bw

Greta Garbo *(Irene)*, Conrad Nagel *(Andre)*, Anders Randolf *(Guarry)*, Holmes Herbert *(Lassalle)*, Lew Ayres *(Pierre)*, George Davis *(Durant)*.

THE KISS, the last silent film made by both Garbo and MGM, was nothing memorable. Garbo's talents were certainly worthy of more than this dull script—a love triangle affair with the actress standing trial for the murder of her husband, Randolf, who suspected her of having an affair with young Ayres (in his film debut). To protect Ayres' honor, Garbo is almost convicted of the crime (which she *did* commit, but only to protect the lad) before her true love, attorney Nagel, saves her life, and then makes her his bride. There are good performances by all and some nice directorial touches by Belgium director Feyder, but that's about it.

d, Jacques Feyder; w, Hans Kraly (based on the story by George M. Saville); t, Marian Ainslee; ph, William Daniels; ed, Ben Lewis; art d, Cedric Gibbons; cos, Adrian; syn sc; s eff.

Drama (PR:A MPAA:NR)

KISS BARRIER, THE** (1925) 6 reels FOX bw

Edmund Lowe *(Richard March)*, Claire Adams *(Marion Weston)*, Diana Miller *(Suzette)*, Marion Harlan *(Connie)*, Thomas Mills *(O'Hara)*, Charles Clary *(Col. Hale)*, Grace Cunard *(Widow)*.

Lowe plays a matinee idol who becomes a flier during WW I. Nurse Adams comes to his rescue when he is shot down and he steals a kiss. After the armistice they meet again and have a romance, but when she suspects Lowe of having an affair with a cheap little flapper she drops him like a hot potato. This inspires Lowe to write and produce a play based on this experience which Adams later sees, loves, and then, of course, she understands him.

d, R. William Neill; w, E. Mangus Ingleton (based on a story by Frederick and Fannie Hatton).

Drama **(PR:A MPAA:NR)**

KISS FOR CINDERELLA, A*** (1926) 10 reels FP/PAR bw

Betty Bronson *(The Girl/Cinderella)*, Tom Moore *(The Bobby)*, Esther Ralston *(Fairy Godmother)*, Henry Vibart *(Richard Bodie)*, Dorothy Cumming *(The Queen)*, Ivan Simpson *(Mr. Cutaway)*, Dorothy Walters *(Mrs. Maloney)*, Flora Finch *(2nd Customer)*, Juliet Brenon *(3rd Customer)*, Marlyn McLain *(Gladys)*, Pattie Coakley *(Marie-Therese)*, Mary Christian *(Sally)*, Edna Hagen *(Gretchen)*.

Although skillfully directed and lavishly produced, this story of a little English cleaning girl who inadvertantly violates the air raid blackout code and attracts the attention, and later the love, of a kindhearted bobby is rather ponderous and slow-moving. But the dream sequence (with its pumpkins, fairies, and magical effects), which takes place after the girl falls asleep in the snow, is a complete delight. Stepping surely into the "classics" mold today, A KISS FOR CINDERELLA at the time of its release was pure old hat to an audience that was in the business of making a lot of money, drinking a lot of booze, and hollering it up on the dance floors of the nation. Barrie just wasn't in, too whimsical, went the typical audience reaction. However, looking at it today one can see the genius of all who were associated with it, and why, once a year at Eastman House in Rochester, it is screened along with PETER PAN to the delight of children of all ages. The film is a masterpiece pictorially, and the best director Brenon ever did. Bronson deservedly earned raves as the "three faces" of Cinderella—as the slavey, while waiting for the Fairy Godmother to appear, and finally, as Cinderella, but Ralston, the beautiful blonde labeled "The American Venus" in the 1920s, was absolute perfection as the Fairy Godmother, her head graced by a pretty crown and her long, magical wand held in her slender right hand. And Moore, as the London bobby, gives an unusually sensitive performance to a role where subtlety is not generally a part of the act. "Magic" is the word for this picture, and "stunning" is its effect on audiences even today.

d, Herbert Brenon; w, Willis Goldbeck, Townsend Martin (based on the play by James Matthew Barrie); ph, J. Roy Hunt; art d, Julian Boone Fleming.

Fantasy **(PR:A MPAA:NR)**

KISS FOR SUSIE, A** (1917) 5 reels Pallas/PAR bw

Vivian Martin *(Susie Nolan)*, Tom Forman *(Phil Burnham)*, John Burton *(Schwartz)* Jack Nelson *(Jim Nolan, Jr.)*, Pauline Perry *(Lizzie Nolan)*, Chris Lynton *(Jim Nolan, Sr.)*, Eleanor Hancock.

Predictable programmer has the millionaire heir to the family business taking a job as a laborer to learn the ropes. He falls for Martin, the daughter of one of his employees, and in the end after her family has invested and lost an inherited fortune, he steps forth, informs them that he handled their money himself, and they are really loaded. Then he discloses his true identity and proposes to the delighted Martin.

d, Robert Thornby; Harvey Thew (based on a story by Paul West).

Drama **(PR:A MPAA:NR)**

KISS IN THE DARK, A** (1925) 6 reels FP/PAR bw

Adolphe Menjou *(Walter Grenham)*, Aileen Pringle *(Janet Livingstone)*, Lillian Rich *(Betty King)*, Kenneth MacKenna *(Johnny King)*, Ann Pennington *(Dancer)*, Kitty Kelly *(Chorus Girl)*.

Disappointing movie adaptation of a popular play misfires on almost every level. Even Menjou, as the womanizer who reforms and then brings a quarreling young married couple together again, was off his mark.

d, Frank Tuttle; w, Townsend Martin (based on the play by Frederick Lonsdale); ph, Alvin Wyckoff; art d, Van Nest Polglase.

Comedy **(PR:A MPAA:NR)**

KISS IN TIME, A*** (1921) 5 reels REA bw

Wanda Hawley *(Shelia Athlone)*, T. Roy Barnes *(Brian Moore)*, Bertram Johns *(Robert Codman Ames)*, Walter Hiers *(Bertie Ballast)*, Margaret Loomis *(Nymph)*.

Snappy little comedy about a magazine artist who refuses to illustrate a particular story because she feels its premise—that a girl would allow herself to be kissed four hours after meeting a fellow—is ridiculous. The author, posing as a butcher boy, induces the girl to take a ride out into the country, and after he saves the life of a little boy, she rewards him with a kiss— just two minutes before the deadline.

d, Thomas N. Heffron; w, Douglas Doty (based on the story "From Four to Eleven-Three" by Royal Brown); ph, William E. Collins.

Comedy **(PR:A MPAA:NR)**

KISS ME AGAIN***** (1925) 7 reels WB bw

Marie Prevost *(Loulou Fleury)*, Monte Blue *(Gaston Fleury)*, John Roche *(Maurice Ferriere)*, Clara Bow *(Grizette, Dubois' Secretary)*, Willard Louis *(Avocat Dubois)*.

A superb film on every level, and perhaps Lubitsch's best silent. Prevost is a married woman who takes instrumental lessons to be near the musician she thinks she loves. When she asks her husband, Blue, for a divorce, he pretends to be delighted to comply, which, of course, causes her to reconsider everything. In the end she is directing all of her attention and passion his way. Saucy, sophisticated, cinematically stunning, and a virtual triumph for Bow in a supporting role.

d, Ernst Lubitsch; w, Hans Kraly (based on the play "Divorcons" by Victorien Sardou, Emile de Najac); ph, Charles Van Enger.

Comedy **(PR:A MPAA:NR)**

KISSED** (1922) 5 reels UNIV bw

Marie Prevost *(Constance Keener)*, Lloyd Whitlock *(Dr. Sherman Moss)*, Lillian Langdon *(Mrs. Keener)*, J. Frank Glendon *(Merton Torrey)*, Arthur Hoyt *(Horace Peabody)*, Percy Challenger *(Needham, the Editor)*, Harold Miller *(Bob Rennesdale)*, Marie Crisp *(Miss Smith)*, Harold Goodwin *(Jim Kernochan)*.

Absurd plot has Prevost telling her millionaire fiance, Glendon, that he fails to produce the kind of "romantic thrills" she craves. Later, at a masquerade ball which she attends alone, Prevost is grabbed and kissed by a masked stranger. Assuming the gent with the superior pucker is Whitlock, she elopes with him but realizes her mistake when, on the train, the good doctor gives her a kiss. Before long the train makes a routine stop and a masked bandit swaggers on board and carries the struggling Prevost away. The girl resists only until she is kissed by him, and then she realizes that he is the very one who won her heart at the ball. Imagine her surprise and delight when she removes the desperado's mask and discovers those passionate lips belong to none other than Glendon!

d, King Baggot; w, Doris Schroeder (based on a short story by Arthur Somers Roche); ph, Ben Bail.

Comedy **(PR:A MPAA:NR)**

KISSES*** (1922) 5 reels Metro bw

Alice Lake *(Betty Ellen Estabrook)*, Harry Myers *(Bill Bailey)*, Edward Connelly *(Thomas Estabrook)*, Edward Jobson *(John Maynard)*, Dana Todd *(Norman Maynard)*, Mignon Anderson *(Bessie Neldon)*, John MacKinnon *(Edward Neldon)*, Eugene Pouyet *(Gustave)*.

Entertaining comedy about a girl who sells everything she owns to pay off the creditors when her father dies. Her fiance deserts her at this point, but with the help of a couple of friends (including a fellow she recently met on a train), she turns her talent for baking candy kisses into a thriving business. She sells the company to her former sweetheart, leaving her with more than enough money to get life started with the man from the train, whom she marries.

d, Maxwell Karger; w, June Mathis (based on a story by May Tully); ph, Allan Siegler; art d, Joseph Calder.

Comedy **(PR:A MPAA:NR)**

KISSING CUP'S RACE** (1920, Brit.) 7 reels Hopson/BUT bw

Violet Hopson *(Constance Medley)*, Gregory Scott *(Lord Hilhoxton)*, Clive Brook *(Lord Rattlington)*, Arthur Walcott *(John Wood)*, Philip Hewland *(Vereker)*, Adeline Hayden Coffin *(Lady Corrington)*, Joe Plant *(Bob Doon)*.

Not a single novel touch was brought into play to help this weary old story of a British lord overcoming every scheme and trick of a rival to win the big race.

d, Walter West; w, J. Bertram Brown, Benedict James; w, (based on the poem by Campbell Rae Brown).

Adventure **(PR:A MPAA:NR)**

KIT CARSON** (1928) 8 reels FP/PAR bw

Fred Thomson *(Kit Carson)*, Nora Lane *(Josefa)*, Dorothy Janis *(Sings-in-the-Clouds)*, Raoul Paoli *(Shuman)*, William Courtright *(Old Bill Williams)*, Nelson McDowell *(Jim Bridger)*, Raymond Turner *(Smokey)*.

After stirring up something of a hornets' nest with his 1927 film, JESSE JAMES, which glorified the famed outlaw, Thomson (an ordained Presbyterian minister) was on safe ground again in this film which had Kit Carson bringing peace to the white man and the Indians by saving the life of a chief's daughter.

d, Alfred L. Werker, Lloyd Ingraham; w, Paul Powell (based on a story by Frank M. Clifton); t, Frederick Hatton; ph, Mack Stengler; ed, Duncan Mansfield.

Western **(PR:A MPAA:NR)**

KNAVE OF HEARTS, THE** (1919, Brit.) 6 reels H bw

James Knight *(Lord Hillsdown)*, Evelyn Boucher *(Peggy Malvern)*, H. Agar Lyons *(Earle of Brinmore)*, J. Edwards Barber *(Oliver Slade)*, Arthur J. Mayne *(Sir Guy)*, Lottie Blackford, Nessie Blackford, Adeline Hayden Coffin.

In this British love story, a lord is tricked into marrying the niece of a discharged worker, but later, without realizing their true identities, they fall in love for real.

d, F. Martin Thornton; w, Reuben Gillmer

Romance **(PR:A MPAA:NR)**

KNICKERBOCKER BUCKAROO, THE*** (1919) 5 reels Fairbanks/ART bw

Douglas Fairbanks *(Teddy Drake)*, Marjorie Daw *(Mercedes)*, William Wellman *(Her Brother)*, Edythe Chapman *(Her Mother)*, Frank Campeau *(Crooked Sheriff)*, Albert MacQuarrie *(Manuel Lopez, the Bandit)*, Ted Reed, Ernest Butterworth, James Mason.

Another Fairbanks comedy western. An Eastern playboy heads for the land of cactus—this time to save a young lady, her brother, and their fortune, from the greedy clutches of a band of outlaws. Great stunts, snappy titles, and the introduction to the screen of a young war hero Fairbanks once saw play scholastic hockey in Boston, named William Wellman, later to become the noted director.

d, Albert Parker; w, Douglas Fairbanks; ph, Hugh McClung, Glen MacWilliams.

Western/Comedy **(PR:A MPAA:NR)**

KNIFE, THE** (1918) 5 reels SEL bw

Alice Brady *(Kate Tarleton)*, Frank Morgan *(Robert Manning)*, Crauford Kent *(Billy Meredith)*, Helen Lackaye *(Louise Meredith)*, Paul Doucet *(Jimmy Bristol)*, Alice Hollister *(Stella Hill)*, Johnnie Walker *(Hampton Gray)*, Frank Evans *(Detective Ellis)*, Myra Brooks, Edwards Davis, Anne Cornwall.

Brady did some fine work as the sweet Southern girl who comes to New York, only to be drugged and taken advantage of. She ultimately does meet the right fellow, but the film lost some of the original raw power the play possessed.

d, Robert G. Vignola; w, Charles Maigne (based on the play by Eugene Walter); ph, H. Lewis Physioc.

Drama **(PR:A MPAA:NR)**

KNIGHT OF THE EUCHARIST** (1922) 7 reels Creston bw

James Flanagan.

Bitterly anti Ku-Klux-Klan film about a Catholic boy who gives his life defending the Holy Eucharist from a gang of hooded bullies. This picture was independently produced by Catholic laymen at a time when their church was at the top of the Klan's hate list.

Drama **(PR:A MPAA:NR)**

KNIGHT OF THE RANGE, A ***1/2 (1916) 5 reels Red Feather/UNIV bw

Harry Carey *(Cheyenne Harry)*, Olive Golden *(Bess Dawson)*, Hoot Gibson *(Bob Graham)*, William Canfield *(Gentleman Dick)*, Bud Osborne *(Sheriff)*, A. D. Blake *(Nick)*, Bill Gettinger *(Buck)*, Peggy Coudray *(Dolores)*.

This very good western opens with all of the characters riding full gallop up to the camera, wheeling about, and riding off. The story is equally strong, with Carey taking the blame for a stagecoach holdup to shield the fiance of the woman he loves; the title reads, "What I'm doing kid ain't for your sake, but for the little girl what believes in you." He does, of course, win the girl, but not before plenty of thrilling riding, fighting, and shooting.

d, Jacques Jaccard; w, Harry D. Carey.

Western **(PR:A MPAA:NR)**

KNIGHT OF THE WEST, A**
(1921) 5 reels W.B.M. Photoplays/C. O'D. Blanchfield bw

Olin Francis *(Jack "Zip" Garvin)*, Estelle Harrison *(Dora McKittrick)*, Billy Franey *("Mana Palover")*, Otto Nelson *(Daniel McKittrick)*, May Foster *(Mother McKittrick)*, Claude Peyton *(Ralph Barton)*, Fay McKenzie *(Fay Murten)*.

Francis, the most bashful cowboy in the history of the West, loves the daughter of a neighboring rancher but can't bring himself to tell her of his feelings. Actions speak louder than words, however, and after he rescues her from the clutches of a rustler, she shows him how she feels.

d, Robert McKenzie; w, (based on a story by Eva B. Heazlit); t, Reed Heustis; ph, Len Powers.

Western/Comedy **(PR:A MPAA:NR)**

KNOCK ON THE DOOR, THE* (1923) 5 reels Johnnie Walker bw

Eddie Polo.

Strongman Polo, the one-time serial king, was fast losing his popularity when he made this feature which used a dream sequence in order to justify his exaggerated athletics. This was the one-time "Hercules of the Screen's" last year in American films. He went on to Germany to make a picture in 1929, but the coming of sound ended his career except for rare bit roles subsequently.

p, Johnnie Walker; d, William Hughes Curran.

Adventure **(PR:A MPAA:NR)**

KNOCKNAGOW** (1918, Ireland) 8 reels Film Company of Ireland bw

Fred O'Donovan *(Arthur O'Connor)*, Kathleen Murphy *(Norah Laby)*, Brian Magowan *(Mat Donovan)*, Nora Clancy *(Mary Karney)*, Brenda Burke *(Honor Laby)*, Valentine Roberts *(Father O'Donnell)*, Moira Breggni *(Peg)*, Cyril Cusack *(Child)*.

Irish film set during the 1850s about an absentee landlord's local representative who tries to pin a crime on his rival and enemy. Look for a very young Cusack in his film debut.

d, Fred O'Donovan; w, N. F. Patton (based on the play "The Homes of Tipperary" by Charles Kikham).

Crime **(PR:A MPAA:NR)**

KNOCKOUT, THE** (1923, Brit.) 6 reels Napoleon/JUR bw

Lilian Hall Davis *(Polly Peach)*, Rex Davis *(Billy Berks)*, Josephine Earle *(Lady Clare)*, Tom Reynolds *(Manager)*, Julian Royce *(Guy Ballinger)*, Micky Brantford *(Scout)*.

In this rather ordinary British drama, a prizefighter is knocked unconscious, dreams that he becomes the owner of a racehorse, is later kidnaped, and remains helpless while his wife commits suicide.

p, G. B. Samuelson; d, Alexander Butler; w, (based on a story by Walter Summers).

Drama **(PR:A MPAA:NR)**

KNOCKOUT, THE*** (1925) 8 reels FN bw

Milton Sills *(Sandy Donlin)*, Lorna Duveen *(Jean Farot)*, John Philip Kolb *(Black Jack Ducane)*, Edward Lawrence *(Mike Leary)*, Harry Cording *(Steve McKenna)*, Frankie Evans *(Brown)*, Harlan Knight *(Farot)*, Jed Prouty *(Mac)*, Claude King *(Parker)*.

He-man Sills wins the light heavyweight championship of the world but hurts his right arm and is forced to retire. Accepting a job as foreman of a lumber camp, he learns that his boss is trying to take over the neighboring camp owned by the father of a girl with whom he has fallen in love. The bad guys dynamite the dam, making it impossible for the old man to sell his logs and make his bank payment. It looks like all is lost when Sills climbs back into the ring, wins the fight, saves the lumber camp, and retires from the world of boxing to marry and live the life of a logger.

d, Lambert Hillyer; sup, Earl Hudson; w, Joseph Poland, Earle Snell (based on the novel *The Come-Back* by Morris DeCamp Crawford); ph, Roy Carpenter; ed, Arthur Tavares; art d, Milton Menasco.

Adventure **(PR:A MPAA:NR)**

KNOCKOUT KID, THE** (1925) 5 reels Harry Webb/RAY bw

Jack Perrin *(Jack Lanning)*, Molly Malone *(Jenny Jenkins)*, Eva Thatcher *(Widow Jenkins)*, Bud Osborne *(Piute Sam)*, Martin Turner *(Snowball)*, Ed Burns *(Ranch Foreman)*, Jack Richardson *(Assistant Foreman)*, Starlight the Horse.

In this harmless little western comedy, Perrin wins a boxing match but is disinherited by his millionaire father, who loathes the "sweet science." The young man, accompanied by Martin, his black valet, heads for Texas where he is forced to dodge the amorous advance of widow Thatcher while, at the same time, falling for her beautiful niece. Later, when Perrin saves the payroll and captures the bandit leader, he also wins the heart of the pretty little girl.

d, Albert Rogell; w, Forrest Sheldon.

Western/Comedy **(PR:A MPAA:NR)**

KNOCKOUT REILLY*** (1927) 7 reels FP/PAR bw

Richard Dix *(Dundee Reilly)*, Mary Brian *(Mary Malone)*, Jack Renault *(Killer Agerra)*, Harry Gribbon *(Pat Malone)*, Osgood Perkins *(Spider Cross)*, Lucia Backus Seger *(Mrs. Reilly)*, Larry McGrath *(Kewpie Dugan)*, Myrtland La Varre *(Buck Lennard)*.

Steel worker Dix comes to the rescue of Brian, who is being hassled by a masher and, without realizing it, knocks out world champion boxer Renault. Brian's brother Gribbon, a former boxer, convinces Dix to take up the "sweet science," and after serving a short stretch on the rock pile for a crime he didn't commit, Dix emerges with the kind of strength that enables him (in a beautifully staged match) to win the crown. This one is a lot better than it sounds, due to St. Clair's skillful direction and a very good performance by the always reliable Dix, who actually fractured a number of ribs in the big fight scene.

d, Malcolm St. Clair; w, Pierre Collings, Kenneth Raisbeck; t, Jack W. Conway; ph, Edward Cronjager.

Drama **(PR:A MPAA:NR)**

KNOW YOUR MEN** (1921) 6 reels FOX bw

Pearl White *(Ellen Schuyler)*, Wilfred Lytell *(Roy Phelps)*, Downing Clarke *(Warren Schuyler)*, Harry C. Browne *(John Barrett)*, Byron Douglas *(Van Horn)*, Estar Banks *(Mrs. Barrett)*, William Eville *(Watson)*.

In this off-beat White vehicle, the serial queen plays a woman who marries out of gratitude, almost leaves her husband and child for a former sweetheart, but reconciles in the end. Another disaster for the queen of the serials, in her adamant drive to make Fox Film Corporation give her what she termed "real parts." Most of the 10 films she made in this spurt were filmed in Manhattan, at the Fox studio (new at that time) at 10th Avenue and 55th Street.

d, Charles Giblyn; w, Paul H. Sloane; ph, Joseph Ruttenberg.

Drama **(PR:A MPAA:NR)**

KRIEMHILDS RACHE (SEE: KRIEMHILD'S REVENGE, 1924, Ger.)

KRIEMHILD'S REVENGE****
(1924, Ger.) 12 reels UFA bw (KRIEMHILDS RACHE)

Margarethe Schon *(Kriemhild)*, Theodor Loos *(King Gunther)*, Hanna Ralph *(Brunhild)*, Georg John *(Blaodel)*, Hans Carl Muller *(Gerenot)*, Bernhard Goetzke *(Volker von Alzey)*, Hans Adalbert von Schlettow *(Hagen Tronje)*, Rudolf Rittner *(Markgraf Rudiger von Bechlarn)*, Fritz Alberti *(Dietrich von Bern)*, Georg August Koch *(Hildebrand)*, Rudolph Klein-Rogge *(King Etzel)*, Hubert Heinrich *(Werbel)*, Grete Berger *(A Hun)*, Rose Lichtenstein.

Part two of director Lang's epic saga DIE NIBELUNGEN (the first of the two-part series is SIEGFRIED, released the same year), filmed as a single entity over a 9-month period, continues the legend following the death of Siegfried. Reprising the final events of SIEGFRIED, the slain hero's widow, Kriemhild (played by Schon), standing at her late husband's bier, bitterly accuses von Schlettow—her sinister half-brother—of his murder. She urges her brother the king (Loos) to visit justice on the villain. At the urging of young courtier Muller, the weakling king elects to do nothing about the murder of Siegfried, averring that the family must stick together. Now realizing the king's complicity in the killing, which was to his personal advantage, Schon plots her vengeance against her own clan. Months pass, and a messenger, Rittner, arrives from the East bearing the marriage proposal of Klein-Rogge—playing Etzel, king of the Huns—to the widowed Schon. The dispirited king agrees to the marital alliance of his sister and the barbarian ruler, and the embittered Schon departs from the Burgundian palace, riding eastward with her retinue through the snow. Arriving at the spring—now frozen—where her beloved

Siegfried was slain, she dismounts to mourn her murdered love, and then resumes her journey. The life style of the troglodytic Huns, so at variance with the cultured Burgundians' elegance, distresses Schon, but she agrees to marry Klein-Rogge. She bears the ruler a son, the apple of his eye. Soon afterward, Schon invites her regal Burgundian relatives to a feast. The meeting proves pleasant enough for a time, but Schon has arranged that the vassals of the two groups—during a separate wild party in the caves that constitute the dwellings of the Huns—shall offend one another. The rioting Huns are incited to a bloodbath, finally storming from the caves to seek the regal Burgundians in the hall above. During the fracas, the wicked von Schlettow kills the child of Schon and Klein-Rogge. Enraged, the barbarian ruler vows vengeance. The surviving Burgundians manage to hold the hall and bar the door. Schon offers to release the trapped guests in return for the head of the hated von Schlettow, but the Burgundians turn the offer down. She sets the hall afire, killing most of those inside. Only von Schlettow survives, staggering outside to be slain by Schon with the magic sword that he had stolen from her heroic husband. Schon is herself then slain by Koch, a disgruntled barbarian. She falls, welcoming the surcease of death. Strongly redolent of the feast of blood in William Shakespeare's play "Titus Andronicus," and perhaps owing more to that work than to the Nordic legends from which the rest of the film springs, the slaughter scenes in the latter part of the picture stand in stark contrast to the slow pace of the somnolent early scenes. The pace quickens just as the widowed Schon reaches the domain of the Huns; spotted by tree-born sentries, her arrival is heralded by a wild gallop of hundreds of Hun horsemen in one of the very few location scenes in the largely studio shot picture. In a switch, these "Huns" were actually Russian cavalrymen who—as, in reality, they later did—invade Berlin. They did so at the invitation of Lang, who assembled them there for transport to the Rebergen, an arid plain not far away. A large camp city was set up to accommodate the Russian guests. Producer Pommer initially objected to the scene, citing its concomitant costs, but the ever-supportive producer ultimately decided the scene was important to the picture. Following the lengthy, mind-boggling two-part production, Lang took a brief vacation. UFA had just incorporated its U.S. subsidiary, so the director paid a celebratory visit to Hollywood, where he witnessed the technical work on the science-fiction film THE LOST WORLD with great interest. He had handled historical legend brilliantly; now he was to turn his attention to his coming futuristic masterpiece, METROPOLIS.

p, Erich Pommer; d, Fritz Lang; w, Thea von Harbou (based on the anonymous poem "Das Nibelungenlied" and various Nordic legends); ph, Carl Hoffmann, Gunther Rittau; art d, Otto Hunte, Eric Kettelhut, Karl Vollbrecht; cos, Paul Gerd Guderian, Anne Willkom; makeup, Otto Genath.

Spectacle **Cas.** **(PR:C MPAA:NR)**

L

LA POUPEE (1920, Brit.) 5 reels Meyrick Milton/Ward bw

Fred Wright *(Hilarius)*, Flora le Breton *(Alesia)*, Richard Scott *(Launcelot Chantrelle)*, William Farren *(Father Maxim)*, Gladys Vicat *(Mme. Hilarius)*.

Strange English comedy, set in France, about a monk who honors the conditions of a will by marrying a doll, only to discover to his amazement that the craftsman who made it actually put his daughter in its place.

d&w, Meyrick Milton (based on the play by Edmond Audran).

Comedy **(PR:A MPAA:NR)**

LABOUR LEADER, THE*** (1917, Brit.) 6 reels BA bw

Fred Groves *(John Webster)*, Fay Compton *(Diana Hazlitt)*, Owen Nares *(Gilbert Hazlitt)*, Christine Silver *(Nell Slade)*, Lauri De Frece *(Bert Slade)*, Fred Volpe *(Sir George Hazlitt)*, Mrs. Charles Macdona *(Mrs. Slade)*.

Interesting story about a socialist who marries a laundress expecting a baby, becomes actively involved in politics, and is the first member of the Labour Party elected to Parliament.

d, Thomas Bentley; w, Kenelm Foss.

Drama **(PR:A MPAA:NR)**

LADDIE BE GOOD** (1928) 4 reels Bill Cody/Pathe bw

Bill Cody *(Himself)*, Rose Blossom *(Ruth Jones)*, George Bunny *(Pierpont Jones)*, Henry Herbert *(John Norton)*, Fred Gambold *(Henry Cody)*.

Cowboy actor Cody took a shot at comedy in this folksy little film about a rancher who finally wins the acceptance of his sweetheart's father when he foils a criminal plot.

p, Bill Cody; d, Bennett Cohn; w, L. V. Jefferson (based on a story by Cody); t, Delos Sutherland; ed, Fred Burnworth.

Comedy **(PR:A MPAA:NR)**

LADIES AT EASE** (1927) 6 reels CHAD/FD bw

Pauline Garon *(Polly)*, Gertude Short *(Gert)*, Gardner James *(Bill Brewster)*, Raymond Glenn *(Buck Bevin)*, Lillian Hackett *(Mae Dotty)*, Jean Van Vliet *(June Dotty)*, William H. Strauss *(Abe Ginsberg)*, Charles Meakin *(John McMay)*, Henry Roquemore *(A Producer)*.

Second-string backstage comedy about a couple of underwear models who steal the boy friends of performing sisters. To get even, the sisters have the models fired. The models then lock the show biz pair in their apartment, cop their costumes and, for a lark, perform that night at the "Ziggy Foolies." Well the act is so bad that the girls have 'em rolling in the aisle, and they are offered a lucrative, long-running contract. The picture ends with the girls visiting their old place of employment and discovering, to their delight, the performing sisters now modelling underwear.

d, Jerome Storm; w, Rob Wagner (based on a story by Leon Lee); t, Jean La'Ple; ph, Ernest Miller; ed, Gene Milford.

Comedy **(PR:A MPAA:NR)**

LADIES AT PLAY*** (1926) 7 reels FN bw

Doris Kenyon *(Ann Harper)*, Lloyd Hughes *(Gil Barry)*, Louise Fazenda *(Aunt Katherine)*, Ethel Wales *(Aunt Sarah)*, Hallam Cooley *(Terry)*, John Patrick *(Andy)*, Virginia Lee Corbin *(Dotty)*, Philo McCullough *(Hotel Clerk)*, Tom Ricketts *(Deacon Ezra Boody)*.

Kenyon shines in this comedy-with-punch, about a young lady who must marry within three days in order to inherit $6 million. Half of this one's fun comes from the snappy, and often hilarious, titles by Marion.

d, Alfred E. Green; w, Carey Wilson (based on the play "Loose Ankles" by Sam Janney); t, George Marion, Jr.; ph, George Folsey.

Comedy **(PR:A MPAA:NR)**

LADIES MUST DRESS** (1927) 6 reels FOX bw

Virginia Valli *(Eve)*, Lawrence Gray *(Joe)*, Hallam Cooley *(Art)*, Nancy Carroll *(Mazie)*, Earle Foxe *(George Ward, Jr.)*, Wilson Hummell *(Office Manager)*, William Tooker *(Mr. Ward, Sr.)*.

Boylan's clever and funny titles carry this modest picture about a stenographer who finally wins the hand of the fellow she loves, when she takes the advice of her pal Carroll and starts to dress with a little flash. It's amazing how a change of outfit or the removal of eyeglasses can turn a Plain Jane into a movie star.

d, Victor Heerman; w, Reginald Morris (based on a story by Heerman); t, Malcolm Stuart Boylan; ph, Glen MacWilliams.

Comedy/Romance **(PR:A MPAA:NR)**

LADIES OF THE MOB*** (1928) 7 reels PAR bw

Clara Bow *(Yvonne)*, Richard Arlen *("Red")*, Helen Lynch *(Marie)*, Mary Alden *("Soft Annie")*, Carl Gerrard *(Joe)*, Bodil Rosing *(The Mother)*, Lorraine Rivero *(Little Yvonne)*, James Pierce *(The Officer)*.

When Bow's father dies in the electric chair, she takes up a life of crime until she falls in love with her partner, Arlen. To prevent him from following in her father's footsteps, she shoots him in the shoulder the night of a big caper. The wound shocks him to his senses, and they live happily forever after, following the straight and righteous path.

d, William Wellman; w, John Farrow, Oliver H. P. Garrett (based on the story by Ernest Booth); t, George Marion; ph, Henry Gerrard; ed, Alyson Shaffer.

Crime **(PR:A MPAA:NR)**

LADIES TO BOARD*** (1924) 6 reels FOX bw

Tom Mix *(Tom Faxton)*, Gertrude Olmstead *(Edith Oliver)*, Philo McCullough *(Evan Carmichael)*, Pee Wee Holmes *(Bunk McGinnis)*, Gertrude Claire *(Mrs. Carmichael)*, Dolores Rousse *(A Model)*.

Change-of-pace picture for Mix has the great cowboy star inheriting an old folks home from an elderly lady, whose life he saved earlier. There are a lot of human interest and a number of laughs along the way as Mix safeguards the well-being of the senior citizens and wins a pretty young girl.

d, John G. Blystone; w, Donald W. Lee (based on a story by William Dudley Pelley); ph, Daniel Clark.

Drama/Comedy **(PR:A MPAA:NR)**

LADY BE GOOD** (1928) 7 reels FN bw

Jack Mulhall *(Jack)*, Dorothy Mackaill *(Mary)*, John Miljan *(Murray)*, Nita Martin *(Madison)*, Dot Farley *(Texas West)*, James Finlayson *(Trelawney West)*, Aggie Herring *(Landlady)*, Jay Eaton, Eddie Clayton *(Dancers)*, Yola D'Avril *(Assistant)*.

After Mulhall and Mackaill, a couple of vaudeville magicians, break up, she takes a job as dancing partner to Miljan. The dancer makes a pass, and Mackaill leaves the act in a small town close to where Mulhall is performing. Seeing the bad shape the magician is in, Mackaill talks his assistant into letting her secretly take her place, and the delighted Mulhall proposes marriage.

p, Charles R. Rogers; d, Richard Wallace; w, Adelaide Heilbron, Jack Wagner (based on the show by Guy Bolton, Fred Thompson, George Gershwin); t, Gene Towne, Sidney Lazarus; ph, George Folsey; ed, Stuart Heisler.

Comedy/Romance **(PR:A MPAA:NR)**

LADY FROM HELL, THE** (1926) 6 reels Stuart Paton/AEX bw

Roy Stewart *(Sir Robin Carmichael)*, Blanche Sweet *(Lady Margaret Darnely)*, Ralph Lewis *(Earl of Kennet)*, Frank Elliot *(Sir Hugh Stafford)*, Edgar Norton *(Honorable Charles Darnely)*, Margaret Campbell *(Lady Darnely)*, Ruth King *(Lucy Wallace)*, Mickey Moore *(Billy Boy)*.

Stewart, a Scotch officer, comes to the U.S. and assuming a new name, lands a job as foreman on a western ranch. One night the owner, using Stewart's gun, kills his wife and is shot to death by his stepson. When the Scotsman returns home to marry Sweet, he is extradited to the U.S., tried for murder, and sentenced to hang. Just as the rope is around his neck and all seems lost, the courageous stepson comes forward and stops the execution. The title of this film comes from an expression the Germans used during the war when they encountered Scottish troops (in their feminine-appearing kilts) who fought bravely, even when facing the machine gun's carnage.

d, Stuart Paton; w, J. Grubb Alexander (based on the story "My Lord of the Double B" by Norton S. Parker); t&ed, John W. Krafft.

Western/Drama **(PR:A MPAA:NR)**

LADY IN LOVE, A** (1920) 5 reels PAR bw

Ethel Clayton *(Barbara)*, Harrison Ford *(Brent)*, Boyd Irwin *(Burton Sedgwick)*, Ernest Joy *(George Sedgwick)*, Elsa Lorimer *(Clara Sedgwick)*, C. H. Geldart *(Gilbert Rhodes)*, Ernee Goodleigh *(Anna)*, Frances Raymond *(Mrs. Sedgwick)*.

It's difficult to determine if the director and writer of this film, about a convent girl who marries a man only to discover that he already has a wife and child, were making a satire or just injected enough gag material (at the cost of melodramatic exposition) to create an unintentional comedy.

d, Walter Edwards; w, Alice Eyton (based on a story by Harriet Ford, Caroline Duer); ph, William Marshall.

Drama/Comedy **(PR:A MPAA:NR)**

LADY NOGGS-PEERESS** (1929, Brit.) 5 reels Progress/But bw

Joan Morgan *(Lady Noggs)*, George Bellamy *(Lord Errington)*, Yvonne Dulquette *(Mme. Karsovitch)*, Arthur Lennard *(Rev. Greig)*, James Prior *(Caldicott Beresford)*, Jenny Earle *(Miss Stetson)*.

British drama about an adopted child who saves a member of Parliament's grandson from the clutches of a European fortune hunter.

d&w, Sidney Morgan (based on the play by Cicely Harrington and the novel by Selwyn Jepson).

Drama **(PR:A MPAA:NR)**

LADY OF THE LAKE, THE*** (1928, Brit.) 5 reels Gainsborough/SEL bw

Percy Marmont *(James V)*, Benita Hume *(Ellen Douglas)*, Haddon Mason *(Malcolm Graeme)*, Lawson Butt *(Roderick Dhu)*, James Carew *(Moray)*, Douglas Payne *(Douglas)*, Leo Dryden *(Allen Bane)*, Hedda Bartlett *(Margaret)*, J. Nelson Ramsay *(Brian)*, Sara Francis *(Blanche of Devon)*, James Douglas *(Douglas)*.

This British adaptation of the Scott poem about an exiled girl who saves the king from bandits, was so popular that in 1931 a sound track was added and the film was reissued.

d, James A. Fitzpatrick; w, Angus Macphail, Fitzpatrick (based on the poem by Sir Walter Scott).

Costume Drama **(PR:A MPAA:NR)**

LADY OF THE NIGHT** (1925) 6 reels MGM bw

Norma Shearer *(Molly/Florence)*, Malcolm McGregor *(David)*, George K. Arthur *(Chunky)*, Fred Esmelton *(Judge Banning)*, Dale Fuller *(Miss Carr)*, Lew Harvey *(Chris)*, Betty Morrisey *(Gertie)*.

Shearer is the only winner in this glorified programmer in which she plays two lookalike characters. Molly is a kid of the slums, while Florence is the daughter of wealthy parents. McGregor likes Molly a lot, but falls in love with Florence when he meets her. That's all there is to it.

d, Monta Bell; w, Alice D. G. Miller (based on the story by Adela Rogers St. John); ph, Andre Barlatier; ed, Ralph Dawson; art d, Cedric Gibbons.

Drama **(PR:A MPAA:NR)**

LADY ROBINHOOD** 1/2 (1925) 6 reels R-C/FBO bw

Evelyn Brent *(Senorita Catalina/La Ortiga)*, Robert Ellis *(Hugh Winthrop)*, Boris Karloff *(Cabraza)*, William Humphrey *(Governor)*, D'Arcy Corrigan *(Padre)*, Robert Cauterio *(Raimundo)*.

Brent, the ward of a Spanish aristocrat, becomes fed up with the injustice afforded the peasants, disguises herself as a bandit, and sets out to do something about it. Eventually she rids the province of its evil governor and wins the love of an American mine owner.

d, Ralph Ince; w, Frederick Myton (based on a story by Clifford Howard, Burke Jenkins); ph, Silvano Balboni.

Adventure **(PR:A MPAA:NR)**

LADY WINDERMERE'S FAN**** (1925) 8 reels WB bw

Ronald Colman *(Lord Darlington)*, Irene Rich *(Mrs. Erlynne)*, May McAvoy *(Lady Windermere)*, Bert Lytell *(Lord Windermere)*, Edward Martindel *(Lord Augustus)*, Helen Dunbar, Carrie d'Aumery, Billie Bennett *(Gossipy Duchesses)*.

Lubitsch translated Wilde's epigrammatic wit (which one would think essential to the success of the play) to the visual medium of silent cinema so brilliantly that LADY WINDERMERE'S FAN made the 10 best picture list of 1925.

d, Ernst Lubitsch; w, Julien Josephson (based on the play by Oscar Wilde); ph, Charles Van Enger.

Comedy **Cas.** **(PR:A MPAA:NR)**

LADYBIRD, THE** (1927) 7 reels CHAD/FD bw

Betty Compson *(Diana Whyman)*, Malcolm McGregor *(Duncan Spencer)*, Sheldon Lewis *(Spider)*, Hank Mann *(The Brother)*, Leo White *(Phillipe)*, John Miljan *(Jules Ranier)*, Ruth Stonehouse *(Lucille)*, Joseph Girard *(Jacob Gale)*, Jean De Briac *(Jacques)*, Matthew Matron *(The Proprietor)*.

Society girl Compson falls in with a gang of crooks known as the Ladybirds during New Orleans Mardi gras and captures the leader with the use of jujitsu.

d, Walter Lang; w, John F. Natteford (based on a story by William Dudley Pelley); ph, Ernest Miller, Ted Tetzlaff.

Crime **(PR:A MPAA:NR)**

LAFFIN' FOOL, THE** (1927) 5 reels Morris R. Schlank/RAY bw

Jack Perrin.

Handsome Perrin rides to the rescue of a beautiful girl and saves her from marrying the money lender who has threatened to take her ranch.

d, Bennett Cohn; ph, William Hyer.

Western **(PR:A MPAA:NR)**

LAMB, THE** 1/2 (1915) 5 reels TRI/FA bw

Douglas Fairbanks *(Gerald)*, Seena Owen *(Mary)*, Lillian Langdon, Monroe Salisbury, Kate Toncray, Alfred Paget, William E. Lowery, Eagle Eye.

Fairbanks' first film is of primary interest today because, in spite of its flaws, it reveals the qualities (comic and athletic) which the Broadway star would put to use in becoming the movies' dominant male personality. The formula was there from the start: a wealthy young fop is spurned by his sweetheart when he proves to be a coward. The lad takes boxing and jujitsu lessons, heads west, is captured by Indians, and puts his acrobatic prowess to use, saving himself and his girl.

d, W. Christy Cabanne; sup, D. W. Griffith; w, Cabanne (based on the story "The Man and the Test" by Griffith); ph, William E. Fildew.

Adventure-Western/Comedy **(PR:A MPAA:NR)**

LAMPLIGHTER, THE* (1921) 6 reels FOX bw

Shirley Mason *(Gertie)*, Raymond McKee *(Willie Sillivan)*, Albert Knott *(The Lamplighter)*, Edwin Booth Tilton *(Malcolm Graham)*, Iris Ashton *(Emily Graham)*, Philo McCullough *(Philip Amory)*, Madge Hunt *(Housekeeper)*.

This tearjerker about an abandoned child who is taken in by an old lamplighter, might have worked had the mediocre acting been able to compensate for the terrible direction, script, sets, and cinematography.

d, Howard M. Mitchell; w, Robert Dillon (based on a story by Marie Susanna Cummins); ph, Glen MacWilliams.

Drama **(PR:A MPAA:NR)**

LAND OF HOPE AND GLORY* (1927, Brit.) 9 reels Glory/Napoleon bw

Ellaline Terriss *(Mrs. Whiteford)*, Lyn Harding *(Roger Whiteford)*, Robin Irvine *(Ben Whiteford)*, Ruby Miller *(Myra Almazov)*, Enid Stamp Taylor *(Jane)*, Arthur Pusey *(Matt Whiteford)*, Henry Vibart *(Sir John Maxeter)*, Lewin Mannering *(Boris Snide)*, Kenneth McLaglen *(Stan Whiteford)*.

Hopelessly dated nonsense about a girl saving her sweetheart's airplane stabilizer plans from spies, and his getting back to the family homestead in time to show his mother that he's a success on her 60th birthday. The old Biograph Studios were producing better pictures than this even before D. W. Griffith joined their ranks.

p, Samuel W. Smith; d, Harley Knoles; w, Adrian Brunel (based on a story by Valentine Williams).

Drama **(PR:A MPAA:NR)**

LARIAT KID, THE*** (1929) 6 reels UNIV bw

Hoot Gibson *(Tom Richards)*, Ann Christy *(Mary Lou)*, Cap Anderson *(Scar Hagerty)*, Mary Foy *(Aunt Bella)*, Walter Brennan *(Pat O'Shea)*, Andy Waldron *(George Carson)*, Bud Osborne *(Trigger Finger)*, Joe Bennett *(Pecos Kid)*, Jim Corey *(Jackknife)*, Francis Ford *(Cal Gregg)*, Joe Rickson *(Tony)*.

Gibson is at his best as a deputy who rides into Hell's Gulch to arrest the men who murdered his lawman father—and win pretty Christy.

d, Reaves Eason; w, Jacques Jaccard, Sylvia Bernstein Seid (based on a story by Buckleigh Fritz Oxford); t, Harold Tarshis; ph Harry Neumann; ed, Gilmore Walker.

Western **(PR:A MPAA:NR)**

LASH OF THE WHIP** (1924) 5 reels Ben Wilson/Arrow bw

Ashton Dearholt *("Pinto Pete")*, Harry Dunkinson *(His Servant)*, Florence Gilbert *(Florence)*, Francis Ford *("Hurricane" Smith)*, Frank Baker *(Frank Blake)*.

Dearholt, the original Lash LaRue, pops his whip on behalf of a young couple who are endangered by Ford and his band of toughs, out to stop the progress of the railroad.

p, Ben Wilson; d&w, Francis Ford.

Western **(PR:A MPAA:NR)**

LASS O' THE LOOMS, A**
(1919, Brit.) 5 reels Grenville-Taylor-Union Photoplays/Kilner bw

Stella Muir *(Nellie Hesketh)*, Henry Victor *(Jack Brown)*, Douglas Payne *(Foreman)*, Betty Hall *(Girl)*.

Lancaster is the setting for this British mystery film about a mill owner's son passing himself off as a worker in order to nail the foreman who has been robbing his father blind.

p, H. Grenville-Taylor; d, Jack Denton; w, Langford Reed.

Crime **(PR:A MPAA:NR)**

LAST ALARM, THE** (1926) 6 reels Paul Gerson/RAY bw

Rex Lease, Wanda Hawley, Maurice Costello *(Father of a Fireman)*, Florence Turner, Theodore von Eltz, Hazel Howell, Jimmy Aubrey.

A fireman has a fist fight with a rival for his girl and gives the fellow a good thrashing. Later, the beaten and bitter adversary steals the money from the firemen's ball, for which his opponent is responsible. The fireman, his girl, and a couple of friends locate the hidden cash, but the heavy sets the building on fire, and the four are saved at the last minute by the fireman's co-workers. The most interesting thing about this Poverty Row programmer is the presence of early superstars Costello and Turner in small supporting roles.

d, Oscar Apfel; w, John Francis Natteford.

Action/Drama **(PR:A MPAA:NR)**

LAST CHANCE, THE** (1921) 5 reels Selig Canyon bw

Franklyn Farnum *(Rance Sparr)*, Vester Pegg *(Black Sparr)*, Gertrude Hall *(Vivian Morrow)*, Churchill Scott *(Braden)*, David Mansfield *(Dynamite Dan)*.

Farnum, the son of a hard-drinking ranch owner, falls for his beautiful neighbor, Hall. She rejects him, however, in favor of Scott, a wealthy gent who offers her "the good life." Farnum then turns to drink and hits bottom, until a certain "gal of the town" straightens him out. When she is abducted by the meanest outlaw in the territory, Farnum rescues her and they fall in love and marry—while Hall, whose life with Scott is miserable at best, looks on with envy and despair.

p, Col. William N. Selig; d, Webster Cullison; w, (based on a story by William E. Wing).

Western **(PR:A MPAA:NR)**

LAST CHANCE, THE* (1926) 5 reels Sierra/CHES bw

Bill Patton.

Posing as a crook, post office inspector Patton infiltrates the mob and brings to justice a desperate gang of mail sack thieves.

d, H. B. Carpenter; ph, Paul Allen.

Western **(PR:A MPAA:NR)**

LAST CHAPTER, THE*** (1915) 5 reels Favorite Players bw

Carlyle Blackwell, Ruth Hartman, John Sheehan.

After becoming engaged, a young British explorer returns to Africa with a party which includes a man who loves his fiancee. In the jungle the jealous one convinces the natives to assist him in the murder of his rival. They attack the young fellow, steal his papers, and leave him for dead. Later, they are set upon by head-hunters and killed. A group of white men find the body of the rotter whom (because of the identification he bears) they think to be the explorer, bury his body, and notify London. Back home the fiancee's father forces his daughter to marry a man she doesn't love, and when the explorer finally comes home, he considers her to be unfaithful and returns unnoticed to the bush. The girl, who has taken as much as she can of her unhappy union, runs away to Africa to be near the grave of her loved one, whom she encounters upon her arrival, and they find happiness at last.

d, William D. Taylor; w, Richard Willis (based on the novelette *The Unfinished Story* by Richard Harding Davis).

Drama **(PR:A MPAA:NR)**

LAST COMMAND, THE**** (1928) 9 reels PAR bw

Emil Jannings *(Gen. Dolgorucki/Grand Duke Sergius Alexander)*, Evelyn Brent *(Natascha Dobrowa)*, William Powell *(Leo Andreiev)*, Nicholas Soussanin *(Adjutant)*, Michael Visaroff *(Serge, the Valet)*, Jack Raymond *(Assistant Director)*, Vaicheslav Savitsky *(A Private)*, Fritz Feld *(A Revolutionist)*, Harry Semels *(Soldier Extra)*, Alexander Ikonnikov, Nicholas Kobyliansky *(Drillmasters)*.

Jannings won the first Academy Award for acting (actually it was presented for this film and THE WAY OF ALL FLESH) with this portrayal of Sergius Alexander, a one-time commander of the Russian Army and a cousin to the Tzar, who has been reduced to seeking out a living working as a Hollywood extra. A top film director (Powell) selects him to play a Russian general in a big-budgeted production, and when the pathetically palsied Jannings dresses with the other "atmosphere" players, he applies a medal the Emperor gave him to the uniform Powell has made sure is perfect in every way. At this point the memories come rushing back, and we see Jannings as a dashing figure, strong, handsome—the one man capable of subduing the hostile forces of Germany. There is, however, unrest in the land, and a couple of actors suspected of subversive activities are arrested and brought before him. One is the beautiful Brent, and the other is Powell. When Powell's obstinate attitude angers the general, the officer strikes him with a whip and orders him to the dungeon. For Brent he has other plans, and the actress cleverly manipulates his emotions to the point where Jannings falls hopelessly in love. Later, after growing to understand him, she saves him from being torn apart by a mob of Bolsheviks and dies in a train wreck after making sure that he has jumped to safety. It is this sight which turned the general into the wretched figure we see once again, as the action returns to the present. It is no accident that Jannings has been selected to play this role. The director has waited many years to repay him for the sting of that whip—and now it is Powell who stands in command. The film's ending provides Jannings with the opportunity to do some of his best work. He is called upon to lead his troops into battle, and as the studio wind machines whirl into action and the lighting effects simulate the flashes of battle, the old officer begins to stand erect. Fantasy becomes reality, illusion, truth. Grabbing the flag of Russia with trembling hands, as the studio orchestra plays the national anthem of his native land, he charges into the imagined fray then, clutching his chest from a thunderbolt-like pain, staggers, spins, and collapses in death—the last soldier to fall for Mother Russia, and her Tzar.

p, B. P. Schulberg; d, Josef von Sternberg; sup, J. G. Bachmann; w, John F. Goodrich (based on a story by Lajos Biro); t, Herman J. Mankiewicz; ph, Bert Glennon; ed, William Shea; set d, Hans Dreier.

Drama **(PR:A MPAA:NR)**

LAST EDITION, THE** (1925) 7 reels Emory Johnson/FBO bw

Ralph Lewis *(Tom MacDonald)*, Lila Leslie *(Mary MacDonald)*, Ray Hallor *(Ray MacDonald)*, Frances Teague *(Polly MacDonald)*, Rex Lease *(Clarence Walker)*, Lou Payne *(George Hamilton)*, David Kirby *("Red" Moran)*, Wade Boteler *(Mike Fitzgerald)*, Cuyler Supplee *(Gerald Fuller)*, Leigh Willard *(Aaron Hoffman)*, Will Frank *(Sam Blotz)*, Ada Mae Vaughn *(Stenographer)*, William Bakewell *("Ink" Donovan)*.

Producer-director Johnson made a series of action programmers glorifying policemen, mail carriers, firemen, etc. This one had a newspaper theme mixed with bootleggers, and also made a substantial profit.

p&d, Emory Johnson; w, Emilie Johnson; ph, Gilbert Warrenton, Frank Evans.

Adventure **(PR:A MPAA:NR)**

LAST EGYPTIAN, THE*** (1914) 5 reels Oz bw

J. Farrell MacDonald, Vivian Reed, Mae Wells, Jane Urban, C. Charles Haydon.

Baum, best remembered for his *Wizard of Oz* stories, wrote and directed this interesting and action-filled film about the last descendant in a line of Egyptian kings, who is told on his grandmother's deathbed that an English nobleman violated his mother, and that the scoundrel's blood runs through his veins. After an exciting and complicated series of events, the Egyptian gets his revenge with the killing of the Britisher, but not until he perishes himself in the ancient tomb of his ancestors.

d&w, L. Frank Baum (based on his novel).

Drama **(PR:A MPAA:NR)**

LAST LAUGH, THE*****
(1924, Ger.) 7 reels UFA bw (DER LETZTE MANN)

Emil Jannings *(The Doorman)*, Mary Delschaft *(His Daughter)*, Kurt Hiller *(Her Fiance)*, Emelie Kurtz *(His Aunt)*, Hans Unterkirchen *(Hotel Manager)*, Olaf Strom *(Young Guest)*, Emma Wyda *(Thin Neighbor)*, Georg John *(Night Watchman)*.

This classic film about a proud Berlin doorman who is demoted to men's room attendant when he can no longer handle the heavy lifting his job requires, is perhaps the perfect example of pure cinema in that it tells its story completely in visual terms. Not a single title is used to relate the tale of his humiliation, rejection, and ultimate triumph after inheriting the fortune of a wealthy American who left his bundle to the last man who saw him alive. A triumph for Murnau, Mayer, Freund, and Jannings, and a work of art which changed the face of motion picture making forever.

p, Erich Pommer; d, F. W. Murnau; w, Carl Mayer; ph, Karl Freund; art d, Robert Herlth, Walter Rohrig.

Drama **Cas.** **(PR:A MPAA:NR)**

LAST OF THE INGRAHAMS, THE** (1917) 5 reels Kay-Bee/TRI bw

William Desmond *(Jules Ingraham)*, Margery Wilson *(Mercy Reed)*, Robert McKim *(Rufus Moore)*, Walt Whitman *(Israel Spence)*, Mary Armiyn *(Agnes Moore)*, Thelma Salter *(Ruth Moore)*.

Jules Ingraham (Desmond), last of an old New England puritan family, is drinking himself to death. After selling his possessions to buy booze, he is evicted from the family mansion by a nasty banker and taken in by a one-time sinner (Wilson) who is the object of the whole town's scorn. With her help, the old boy licks his drinking habit, learns that a parcel of family land out West produced a gusher, and the two depart as man and wife.

d, Walter Edwards; w, John Lynch.

Drama **(PR:A MPAA:NR)**

LAST OF THE MOHICANS, THE*** (1920) 6 reels Tourneur-AP bw

Wallace Beery *(Magua)*, Barbara Bedford *(Cora Munro)*, Albert Roscoe *(Uncas)*, Lillian Hall *(Alice Munro)*, Henry Woodward *(Maj. Heyward)*, James Gordon *(Col. Munro)*, George Hackathorne *(Capt. Randolph)*, Nelson McDowell *(David Gamut)*, Harry Lorraine *(Hawkeye)*, Theodore Lorch *(Chingachgook)*, Jack McDonald *(Tamenund)*, Sydney Deane *(Gen. Webb)*, Boris Karloff.

First-class adventure makes up what is often called the best filmed version of any of the James Fenimore Cooper stories. A visually beautiful work of art, the second of Cooper's *The Leatherstocking Tales*, tells the efforts of Alice and Cora Munro (Hall and Bedford), to join up with their father, the commander of the British-held Fort William Henry near Lake Champlain in New York state. A group of Huron Indians, led by the fierce Magua (Beery) and allied with the French against the British, block their way, but they are outwitted at every turn by the last of the Mohicans, Uncas (Roscoe), his father, Chingachgook (Lorch), and the famous fictional character Hawkeye (Lorraine). The cruel Huron's massacre at Fort Henry is savage and spectacular, as is the pursuit of Bedford by Beery, which ends on a high precipice and a stalking game by the Indian, who waits through the night for Bedford to fall asleep. When she does, momentarily, he is upon her, and in a rapid sequence of action the loyal Roscoe steals up to save her but the treacherous Beery forces her to fall from the rocky ledge to her death. It is powerful and most poignant stuff, with rarely a dull moment, and through it all the camera work is deft and sharp. Often called the best treatment of the many LAST OF THE MOHICAN film versions (the Germans tried one of their own and Hollywood made two talkie versions, the first in 1936 with Randolph Scott, Binnie Barnes, and Heather Angel, and in 1977 with Steve Forrest as Hawkeye), this one was directed by the great French director Tourneur, who arrived in the U.S. in 1914 and went on to spectacular success due to his highly developed esthetic sense, which demanded photography of beauty as well as narrative development. THE LAST OF THE MOHICANS is considered his best picture, in spite of the fact that it was marred by accidents. Chief of these was one that happened to the director. Suffering ptomaine poisoning and a bout of pleurisy, he fell off a parallel bar and went to bed for three months. Director Brown thereafter claimed that he helmed the greatest portion of the picture, but it is a fact that Tourneur saw all the rushes, gave the last word on retakes when they were needed, and directed almost all of the studio scenes.

d, Clarence Brown, Maurice Tourneur; w, Robert A. Dillon (based on the novel by James Fenimore Cooper); ph, Philip R. Dubois, Charles Van Enger.

Costume Drama **Cas.** **(PR:A MPAA:NR)**

LAST ROSE OF SUMMER, THE*
(1920, Brit.) 7 reels G. B. Samuelson/Granger bw

Daisy Burrell *(Lotus Devine)*, Owen Nares *(Oliver Selwyn)*, Minna Grey *(Amy Palliser)*, Tom Reynolds *(Mr. Palliser)*, Richard Barry *(Alf Purvis)*, John Phelps *(Percy Melville)*.

It's unlikely that this little English drama, about a *serious* collector who fakes being in love with a spinster just to get to her father's tea service, exactly knocked audiences out of their seats.

d, Albert Ward; w, Roland Pertwee (based on the novel by Hugh Conway).

Drama **(PR:A MPAA:NR)**

LAST ROUNDUP, THE** (1929) 5 reels J. P. McGowan/Syndicate bw

Bob Custer *(Denver Dixon)*, Hazel Mills *(Lucy Graves)*, Bud Osborne *(The Villain)*, Cliff Lyons, Hank Bell, J. P. McGowan, Adabelle Driver.

In one of the last silent westerns, director McGowan threw all of the ingredients into his cinematic stew: cattle rustling, an abducted school marm, a brush fire and, needless to say, plenty of fist fights.

d, J. P. McGowan; w&t, Sally Winters; ph, Hap Depew; syn sc.

Western **(PR:A MPAA:NR)**

LAST STRAW, THE*** (1920) 5 reels FOX bw

Buck Jones, Vivian Rich, Jane Talent, Colin Kenny, Charles Le Moyne, Bob Chandler, William Gillis, H. W. Padgett, Hank Bell, Zeib Morris, Lon Poff.

William Fox knew he had a potential star and a rival for the popularity Tom Mix enjoyed, when he featured Jones in this entertaining western about a cowboy who wins the heart of a party-loving city girl.

d&w, Dennison Clift, Charles Swickard (based on a story by Harold Titus); ph, Vernon Walker.

Western **(PR:A MPAA:NR)**

LAST TRAIL 1/2** (1921) 7 reels FOX bw

Maurice B. Flynn *(The Stranger)*, Eva Novak *(Winifred Samson)*, Wallace Beery *(William Kirk)*, Rosemary Theby *(Chiquita)*, Charles K. French *(Sheriff Nelson)*, Harry Springler *(Campbell)*, Harry Dunkinson *(Kenworth Samson)*.

When a stranger (Flynn) rides into town, he is thought to be the bandit known as "The Night Hawk," who has been plundering the territory. Novak, convinced of his innocence, hides him away, but dam engineer Beery, her fiance, blows the whistle. Later, Beery steals the company payroll and dynamites the dam, but the stranger, who is actually an undercover agent, prevents his escape.

d, Emmett J. Flynn; w, Jules Furthman, Paul Schofield (based on the novel by Zane Grey); ph, Lucien Andriot.

Western **(PR:A MPAA:NR)**

LAST TRAIL, THE* 1/2** (1927) 6 reels FOX bw

Tom Mix *(Tom Dane)*, Carmelita Geraghty *(Nita Carrol)*, William Davidson *(Morley)*, Frank Hagney *(Ben Ligget)*, Lee Shumway *(Joe Pascal)*, Robert Brower *(Pete)*, Jerry the Giant, *(Tom Dane Pascal)*, Oliver Eckhardt *(Carrol)*, Tony *(The Wonder Horse)*.

Loosely based on the 1921 production, this big-budgeted, action-packed Mix western added an Indian attack, as well as a spectacular stage-coach race which, in its own way, rivaled the chariot affair featured in BEN HUR, two years earlier.

d, Lewis Seiler; w, John Stone (based on the novel by Zane Grey); ph, Dan Clark.

Western **(PR:A MPAA:NR)**

LAST VOLUNTEER, THE** (1914) 5 reels ECL bw

Eleanor Woodruff, Paul Panzer, Robert Broderick, Irving Cummings.

Pro-German film, made before the U.S. entrance into WWI, tells of a young woman who volunteers to give her life (by raising the signal flags) to bring relief to the embattled prince, whom she loves.

d, Oscar Apfel.

War **(PR:A MPAA:NR)**

LAST WITNESS, THE** (1925, Brit.) 6 reels STOLL bw

Isobel Elsom *(Letitia Brand)*, Fred Paul *(Stephen Brand, King's Counsel)*, Stella Arbenina *(Mrs. Stapleton)*, Queenie Thomas *(Lady Somerville)*, John Hamilton *(Eric Norton)*, Tom Nesbitt *(Maurice Tregarthen)*, Aubrey Fitzgerald *(Lord Bunny Somerville)*.

British courtroom drama involves the prosecution, by a King's counsel, of his own wife, who is accused of murdering her Member of Parliament paramour.

d, Fred Paul; w, (based on the novel by F. Britten Austin).

Crime/Drama **(PR:A MPAA:NR)**

LATEST FROM PARIS, THE** (1928) 8 reels MGM bw

Norma Shearer *(Ann Dolan)*, George Sidney *(Sol Blogg)*, Ralph Forbes *(Joe Adams)*, Tenen Holtz *(Abe Littauer)*, William Blakewell *(Bud Dolan)*, Margaret Landis *(Louis Martin)*, Bert Roach *(Bert Blevins)*.

Shearer is given the chance to wear some snappy outfits as a traveling garment salesperson. Actually, in this only average programmer about love lost and won, she's pretty much the whole show.

d, Sam Wood; w, A. P. Younger; t, Joe Farnham; ph, William Daniels; ed, Basil Wrangell; set d, Cedric Gibbons, Arnold Gillespie.

Comedy/Romance **(PR:A MPAA:NR)**

LAUGH, CLOWN, LAUGH* 1/2** (1928) 8 reels MGM bw

Lon Chaney *(Tito Beppi)*, Bernard Siegel *(Simon)*, Loretta Young *(Simonette)*, Cissy Fitzgerald *(Giancinta)*, Nils Asther *(Count Luigi Ravelli)*, Gwen Lee *(Lucretia)*, Leo Feodoroff, Emmett King.

Superb performance by Chaney as a circus clown who falls in love with the girl he adopted and makes audiences laugh while his own heart is breaking. In the end, Chaney kills himself while performing his "slide of death" in order to free the girl to marry the young man she really loves.

d, Herbert Brenon; w, Elizabeth Meehan (based on the play by David Belasco, Tom Cushing); t, Joe Farnham; ph, James Wong Howe; ed, Marie Halvey; set d, Cedric Gibbons.

Drama **(PR:A MPAA:NR)**

LAUGHING AT DANGER*** (1924) 6 reels Carlos/FBO bw

Richard Talmadge *(Alan Remington)*, Joe Girard *(Cyrus Remington)*, Joe Harrington *(Prof. Leo Hollister)*, Eva Novak *(Carolyn Hollister)*, Stanhope Wheatcroft *(Darwin Kershaw)*.

Plenty of action in this Talmadge feature as "Mr. Pep" plays the son of a wealthy Washington politician. Talmadge prevents the agents of a foreign power from destroying the U.S. fleet and rescues Harrington (the inventor of a remarkable death ray) and his daughter from their sinister clutches.

d, James W. Horne; w, Frank Howard Clark; ph, William Marshall; stunts, Richard Talmadge.

Adventure **(PR:A MPAA:NR)**

LAUGHTER AND TEARS** (1921, Brit.) 6 reels Granger/Binger bw

Evelyn Brent *(Pierrette)*, Adelqui Millar *(Mario Mari)*, Dorothy Fane *(Countess Maltakoff)*, E. Story Gofton *(Adolpho)*, Maudie Dunham *(Zizi)*, Bert Darley *(Ferrado)*.

Evelyn Brent, the U.S. star, made several pictures in Britain, including this one about a Venice artist who becomes infatuated by a countess, but then comes to his senses and declares true love for his model.

d, B. E. Doxat-Pratt; w, Adelqui Millar.

Drama **(PR:A MPAA:NR)**

LAVENDER AND OLD LACE** (1921) 6 reels Renco/Hodkinson bw

Marguerite Snow *(Mary Ainslie)*, Seena Owen *(Ruth Thorne)*, Louis Bennison *(Capt. Charles Winfield/Carl Winfield)*, Victor Potel *(Joe Pendleton)*, Zella Ingraham *(Hepsey)*, Lillian Elliot *(Jane Hathaway)*, James Corrigan *(Jimmy Ball)*.

After waiting 30 years for her fiance (Bennison) to return, a young friend brings a Boston newspaperman to the home of elderly patient Snow. The old lady is startled by his resemblance to the man she loves, and when she finds out that he's the son of her sweetheart and that the captain is dead, the old lady loses her will to live and slips off.

d, Lloyd Ingraham; w, (based on the novel by Myrtle Reed); ph, Ross Fisher.

Drama **(PR:A MPAA:NR)**

LAVENDER BATH LADY, THE** (1922) 5 reels UNIV bw

Gladys Walton *(Mamie Conroy)*, Charlotte Pierce *(Jeanette Gregory)*, Edward Burns *(David Bruce)*, Tom Ricketts *(Simon Gregory)*, Lydia Yeamans Titus *(Maggie)*, Mary Winston *(Susanne)*, Al MacQuarrie *(Dorgan)*, Harry Lorraine *(Drake)*, Earl Crain *(Hallet)*.

Shopgirl Walton becomes friendly with millionairess Pierce and saves her from being kidnapped. For this Walton is welcomed into the Pierce home as a member of the family. Later she is accused of participating in a robbery but is cleared by Burns, the underground cop with whom she has fallen in love.

d, King Baggot; w, George Randolph Chester, Doris Schroeder (based on a story by Shannon Fife); ph, Victor Milner.

Comedy **(PR:A MPAA:NR)**

LAW FORBIDS, THE*** (1924) 6 reels UNIV-Jewel bw

Baby Peggy *(Peggy)*, Robert Ellis *(Paul Remsen)*, Elinor Fair *(Rhoda Remsen)*, Winifred Bryson *(Inez Lamont)*, James Corrigan *(John Martin)*, Anna Hernandez *(Martha Martin)*, Joseph Dowling *(The Judge)*, Ned Sharks *(Clyde Vernon)*, Eva Thatcher *(Mrs. Grimes)*, Victor Potel *(Joel Andrews)*, William E. Lawrence *(Monte Hanley)*, Hayden Stevenson *(Lawyer for the Defense)*, William Welch *(Lawyer for the Plaintiff)*, Bobby Bowes *(Theatrical Producer)*, Alexander *(Himself)*.

Engaging Baby Peggy programmer has the little charmer sneaking off from her mother's country retreat and returning home to the big city, where she is instrumental in repairing her parents' ruptured marriage.

d, Jesse Robbins; w, Lois Zellner, Ford I. Beebe (based on a story by Bernard McConville); ph, Charles Kaufman, Jack Stevens.

Drama **(PR:A MPAA:NR)**

LAW OF THE LAND, THE** (1917) 5 reels LAS/PAR bw

Olga Petrova *(Margaret Harding)*, Wyndham Standing *(Richard Harding)*, Mahlon Hamilton *(Geoffrey Morton)*, J. D. Haragan *(Brockland)*, Robert Vivian *(Chetwood)*, Riley Hatch *(Inspector Cochrane)*, William Conklin.

Petrova is quite good as the woman who is driven to kill her husband because of his brutality. Fortunately, the police inspector understands the situation and declares the death accidental, which gives the widow the opportunity to marry the decent man she really loves.

d, Maurice Tourneur; w, Charles Whittaker (based on the play by George Broadhurst).

Drama **(PR:A MPAA:NR)**

LAW OF THE LAWLESS, THE** (1923) 7 reels FP/PAR bw

Dorothy Dalton *(Sahande)*, Charles De Roche *(Costa)*, Theodore Kosloff *(Sender)*, Tully Marshall *(Ali Mechmet)*, Fred Huntley *(Osman)*, Margaret Loomis *(Fanutza)*.

De Roche, a gypsy chief, outbids and angers Kosloff by buying his sweetheart, Dalton, a Tartar slave. The girl feels only hatred for her master, but the gypsy gives her 10 days to change her mind, declaring that at the end of that time he will fight her lover. Kosloff and a small army capture De Roche and imprison him in a tower. When it catches on fire, however, the Tartar realizes she loves the gypsy after all and, at great personal risk, saves his life.

d, Victor Fleming; w, E. Lloyd Sheldon, Edfrid Bingham (based on a story by Konrad Bercovici); ph, George R. Meyer.

Drama **(PR:A MPAA:NR)**

LAW OF THE MOUNTED*** (1928) 5 reels ED/Syndicate bw

Bob Custer, J. P. McGowan, Sally Winters, Frank Ellis, Cliff Lyons, Mary Mayberry, Lynn Sanderson, Mack V. Wright, Bud Osborne.

Good Northwest actioner has mountie Custer breaking up a gang of fur smugglers and arresting McGowan, who is fine as an Erich von Stroheim-type heavy.

d, J. P. McGowan; w, Philip Schuyler (based on a story by Sally Winters), ph, Paul Allen.

Adventure **(PR:A MPAA:NR)**

LAW OF THE RANGE, THE½** (1928) 6 reels MGM bw

Tim McCoy *(Jim Lockheart)*, Joan Crawford *(Betty Dallas)*, Rex Lease *(The Solitaire Kid)*, Bodil Rosing *(Mother Lockheart)*, Tenen Holtz *(Cohen)*.

Two brothers are separated as children when their wagon is attacked by Indians. McCoy grows up to be a Texas Ranger, while his brother (Lease) becomes an outlaw known as the Solitaire Kid. When McCoy tracks Lease down, they become aware of their relationship due to matching tatoos. Then, when a terrible brush fire hits, Lease gives his life to save his brother.

d, William Nigh; w, Richard Schayer (based on a story by Norman Houston); t, Robert Hopkins; ph, Clyde De Vinna; ed, Dan Sharits.

Western **(PR:A MPAA:NR)**

LAW OF THE SNOW COUNTRY, THE* (1926) 5 reels Bud Barsky bw

Kenneth McDonald *(Sgt. Jimmy Burke)*, Jane Thomas *(Marie)*, Noble Johnson *(Martell)*, William Strauss *(Father Fajans)*, Hazel Howell *(The Blonde)*, Bud Osborne *(Pig Eye Perkins)*, Ben Corbett *(Jim Wolf)*, Billy Cinders *(Goofy Joe)*.

After surviving ambushes, fist fights, and a low budget disaster, mountie McDonald not only gets his man, but the best-looking woman in the frozen North, as well.

d, Paul Hurst.

Action **(PR:A MPAA:NR)**

LAWFUL CHEATERS*** (1925) 5 reels B. P. Schulberg bw

Clara Bow *(Molly Burns)*, David Kirby *(Noony)*, Raymond McKee *(Richard Steele)*, Edward Hearn *(Roy Burns)*, George Cooper *(Johnny Burns)*, Fred Kelsey *(Tom Horan)*, Gertrude Pedlar *(Mrs. Perry Steele)*, Jack Wise *("Graveyard" Lazardi)*, John T. Prince *("Silent" Sam Riley)*.

Director O'Connor captures the mood of New York at a time when gangsters and bootleggers roamed its streets at will. Bow is a standout as the girl who, after being sent to prison, persuades her friends to reform. She even does a sensational male impersonation.

d&w, Frank O'Connor.

Crime **(PR:A MPAA:NR)**

LAWFUL LARCENY*** (1923) 6 reels FP/PAR bw

Hope Hampton *(Marion Dorsey)*, Conrad Nagel *(Andrew Dorsey)*, Nita Naldi *(Vivian Hepburn)*, Lew Cody *(Guy Tarlow)*, Russell Griffin *(Sonny Dorsey)*, Yvonne Hughes *(Billie Van de Vere)*, Dolores Costello *(Nora, the Maid)*, Gilda Gray, Florence O'Denishawn, Alice Maison *(Dancers at the Rendez-vous)*.

Good cast, script, and direction make this movie, about a woman who vamps the owner of a crooked gambling casino in order to get back the check her husband drew against his company to cover his losses, a winner.

d, Allan Dwan; w, John Lynch (based on the play by Samuel Shipman); ph, Hal Rosson.

Drama **(PR:A MPAA:NR)**

LAWLESS LEGION, THE** (1929) 6 reels FN bw

Ken Maynard *(Cal Stanley)*, Nora Lane *(Mary Keiver)*, Paul Hurst *(Ramirez)*, J. P. McGowan *(Matson)*, Frank Rice *(Flapjack)*, Howard Truesdell *(Sheriff Keiver)*, Tarzan the Horse.

After being drugged by bandit Hurst and having the cattle he was responsible for stealing, Maynard poses as a beef buyer, rounds up the outlaws, returns the herd to its rightful owner, and wins the girl.

d, Harry J. Brown; w, Fred Allen, Bennett Cohn (based on a story by Cohn); t, Lesley Mason; ph, Frank Good; ed, Allen.

Western **(PR:A MPAA:NR)**

LAZY LIGHTNING** (1926) 5 reels BS/UNIV bw

Art Acord *(Lance Lighton)*, Fay Wray *(Lila Rogers)*, Bobby Gordon *(Dickie Rogers)*, Vin Moore *(Sheriff Dan Boyd)*, Arthur Morrison *(Henry S. Rogers)*, George K. French *(Dr. Hull)*, Rex De Roselli *(William Harvey)*.

Acord does some mighty fine riding through a terrific rainstorm to get the serum needed to save little Gordon's life. He also prevents a crooked uncle from taking over and wins the heart of the boy's sister, sweetly played by Wray.

d, William Wyler; w, Harrison Jacobs; ph, Eddie Linden.

Western **(PR:A MPAA:NR)**

LAZYBONES*** (1925) 8 reels FOX bw

Charles Jones *(Lazybones)*, Madge Bellamy *(Kit)*, Virginia Marshall *(Kit, as a Child)*, Edythe Chapman *(Mrs. Tuttle)*, Leslie Fenton *(Dick Ritchie)*, Jane Novak *(Agnes Fanning)*, Emily Fitzroy *(Mrs. Fanning)*, ZaSu Pitts *(Ruth Fanning)*, William Norton Bailey *(Elmer Ballister)*.

William Fox was grooming the great cowboy star "Buck" Jones for major stardom (billing him as Charles) in this dramatic picture about a small town fellow and his adventures with love and war. Fortunately, for just about every boy in the U.S., it wasn't long before "Buck" was in the saddle again.

d, Frank Borzage; w, Frances Marion (based on the novel by Owen Davis); ph, Glen MacWilliams, George Schneiderman.

Drama **(PR:A MPAA:NR)**

LEAD, KINDLY LIGHT** (1918, Brit.) 4 reels H. B. Parkinson/White bw

Dorothy Bellew, Manning Haynes, Gwen Williams.

In this British-made love story, a lowly flower girl climbs to stardom as an actress and later is reunited with the parson she once loved, whom she finds performing as a street musician.

d, Rex Wilson; w, H. B. Parkinson (based on a story by H. Hurlock).

Romance **(PR:A MPAA:NR)**

LEAP TO FAME** (1918) 5 reels WORLD bw

Carlyle Blackwell *(Charles Trevor)*, Evelyn Greely *(Dorothy)*, Muriel Ostriche *(Tootsie Brown)*, Alec B. Francis *(Judge Hendricks Trevor)*, Frank Beamish *(City Editor)*, Philip Van Loan *(Tony Figlio)*, Lionel Belmore *(Carl Hoffman)*, William Bailey *(Hoffman's Servant)*, Benny Nedell *(Oscar)*.

Breezy wartime entertainment about a playboy college student, who is thrown out of his millionaire father's house, becomes a cub reporter, saves the daughter of a weapons inventor (and his latest contraption) from German spies, and ends up marrying the girl, with his father's blessing.

d, Carlyle Blackwell; w, (based on a story by Raymond Schrock); ph, Lucien Tainguy.

Adventure **(PR:A MPAA:NR)**

LEARNING TO LOVE*** (1925) 7 reels Talmadge/FN bw

Constance Talmadge *(Patricia Stanhope)*, Antonio Moreno *(Scott Warner)*, Emily Fitzroy *(Aunt Virginia)*, Edythe Chapman *(Aunt Penelope)*, Johnny Harron *(Billy Carmichael)*, Ray Hallor *(Tom Morton)*, Wallace MacDonald *(Prof. Bonnard)*, Alf Goulding *(John, the Barber)*, Byron Munson *(Count Coo-Coo)*, Edgar Norton *(Butler)*.

Loos and Emerson produced the gags and Talmadge provided the zip for this delightfully funny movie about a natural born flirt who becomes involved in so many sensational affairs that her guardian (Moreno) orders her to marry the next man with whom her name becomes linked scandalously. Talmadge secretly spends the night in Moreno's apartment, tips off the newspapers, creates her "situation" and marries her guardian, who just happens to be the only man she truly loves anyway.

d, Sidney A. Franklin; w, Anita Loos, John Emerson; ph, Victor Milner.

Comedy **(PR:A MPAA:NR)**

LEECH, THE** (1921) 5 reels Selected/PIO bw

Ray Howard *(Teddy)*, Alex Hall *(Bill)*, Claire Whitney *(Dorothy)*, Katherine Leon *(Ruth)*, Ren Gennard *(Joe Turner)*.

Although released in 1921, this motivational film was most likely produced right after WW I. It has to do with two brothers who are wounded in France. The one, who lost a leg, takes a vocational course and lands a job, while the other one, whose leg wound is minor, stays home and sulks until he learns his lesson in a dream.

d, Herbert Hancock; ph, Alvin Knechtel.

Drama **(PR:A MPAA:NR)**

LEGALLY DEAD** (1923) 6 reels UNIV bw

Milton Sills *(Will Campbell)*, Margaret Campbell *(Mrs. Campbell)*, Claire Adams *(Minnie O'Reilly)*, Edwin Sturgis *(Jake Dorr)*, Faye O'Neill *(Jake's Sweetheart)*, Charles A. Stevenson *(Malcolm Steel)*, Joseph Girard *(District Attorney)*, Albert Prisco *(The Anarchist)*, Herbert Fortier *(The Judge)*, Charles Wellesley *(The Governor)*, Robert Homans *(Detective Powell)*, Brandon Hurst *(Dr. Gelzer)*.

Anti-capital punishment film has writer Sills getting himself arrested to prove that most executed convicts are actually innocent. Later, after his release, he breaks up a robbery in which a policeman is killed, but because he picked up the pistol, Sills is arrested, convicted, and ultimately hanged. He is declared dead, but when *his* innocence is substantiated, a doctor brings him back to life through the use of adrenaline.

d, William Parke; w, Harvey Gates (based on a story by Charles Furthman); ph, Richard Fryer.

Drama **(PR:A MPAA:NR)**

LEGEND OF HOLLYWOOD, THE*** (1924) 6 reels Charles R. Rogers/PDC bw

Percy Marmont *(John Smith)*, ZaSu Pitts *(Mary Brown)*, Alice Davenport *(Mrs. Rooney)*, Dorothy Dorr *("Blondie")*, Cameo *(Himself)*.

Unusual little drama about a writer (Marmont) who comes to Hollywood to make his mark and checks into a boarding house shared by a homely girl (interestingly played by Pitts) whose friends have cruelly encouraged to go into pictures. After his script is repeatedly rejected and Davenport the landlady gives him seven days notice, Marmont fatalistically pours seven glasses of wine, adds poison to one, then mixes the glasses up. Each day he drinks one and then, on the seventh morning, just after polishing off the fatal vessel, a letter containing a hefty check arrives informing him that his screenplay is a sensation. The poor devil staggers about his room clutching his throat and cursing fate, until he realizes that Pitts actually replaced the poisoned glass with another. From that day on she begins to look beautiful in *his* eyes.

d, Renaud Hoffman; w, Alfred A. Cohn (based on a story by Frank Condon); t, Cohn; ph, Karl Struss; ed, Glenn Wheeler.

Drama **(PR:A MPAA:NR)**

LEND ME YOUR HUSBAND** (1924) 6 reels C. C. Burr bw

Doris Kenyon *(Aline Stackton)*, David Powell *(Henry Seton)*, Dolores Cassinelli *(Mrs. Seton)*, J. Barney Sherry *(Burrows Stackton)*, Violet Mersereau *(Jenny MacDonald)*, Burr McIntosh *(Fergus MacDonald)*, Connie Keefe *(Robert Towers)*, Coit Albertson *(Count Ferrari)*, Helen D'Algy *(Countess Ferrari)*.

When Mersereau, the gardener's daughter, is discovered having an affair with rotter Powell, society girl Kenyon covers for her, in spite of the effect this has on *her* reputation. Later, the truth comes out and Kenyon marries wealthy Keefe.

d, William Christy Cabanne; w, Raymond S. Harris (based on a story by Marguerite Gove); ph, Jack Brown, Neil Sullivan.

Drama **(PR:A MPAA:NR)**

LEOPARD LADY, THE** (1928) 7 reels DM/Pathe bw

Jacqueline Logan *(Paula)*, Alan Hale *(Caesar)*, Robert Armstrong *(Chris)*, Hedwig Reicher *(Fran Holweg)*, James Bradbury, Sr. *(Herman Berlitz)*, Dick Alexander *(Hector, the Lion Tamer)*, William Burt *(Presner)*, Sylvia Ashton *(Mama Lolita)*, Kay Deslys, Willie May Carson *(Austrian Maids)*.

Leopard trainer Logan is hired by the police to join a circus which has left a wake of murders on its tour. She discovers that Hale, the ape trainer, is responsible and, though he once saved her life, she turns him over to the cops when the beast tries to kill her fiance.

p, Bertram Millhauser; d, Rupert Julian; w, Beulah Marie Dix (based on the play by Edward Childs Carpenter); ph, John Mescall; ed, Claude Berkeley.

Mystery **(PR:A MPAA:NR)**

LES MISERABLES*** (1918) 8 reels FOX bw

William Farnum *(Jean Valjean)*, George Moss *(The Bishop)*, Hardee Kirkland *(Javert)*, Sonia Markova *(Frantine)*, Kittens Reichert *(Cosette, at the Age of 8)*, Jewel Carmen *(Cosette, at the Age of 18)*, Harry Spingler *(Marius)*, Dorothy Bernard *(Eponine)*, Anthony Phillips *(Gavroche)*, Edward Elkas *(Thenardier)*, Mina Ross *(Mme. Thenardier)*, Gus Alexander, May De Lacy, Greta Hartman.

Lloyd, one of the movies' better directors, did very well with this first U.S. (France had produced one shortly before) feature film version of the classic Hugo novel about the reformed thief and his unrelenting policeman persecutor, but the casting of chunky Farnum was a complete mistake.

d, Frank Lloyd; w, Lloyd, Marc Robbins (based on the novel by Victor Hugo); ph, William C. Foster.

Drama **(PR:A MPAA:NR)**

LESSONS IN LOVE*** (1921) 6 reels Constance Talmadge/AFN bw

Constance Talmadge *(Leila Calthorpe)*, Kenneth Harlan *(John Warren)*, Flora Finch *(Agatha Calthorpe)*, James Harrison *(Robert Calthorpe)*, George Fawcett *(Hanover Priestley)*, Frank Webster *(Henry Winkley)*, Florence Short *(Ruth Warren)*.

Made-to-order story line for Talmadge has the talented comedienne posing as a maid to bug Harlan, who refuses to honor his uncle's suggestion that he marry her sight unseen. There are plenty of comic situations, of the mistaken identity kind, before he rescues her from a fire and comes to realize that he really loves her.

p, Joseph M. Schenck; d, Chet Withey; w, Grant Carpenter (based on the play "Perkins" by Douglas Murray); ph, Oliver T. Marsh.

Comedy **(PR:A MPAA:NR)**

LET 'ER BUCK*** (1925) 6 reels UNIV bw

Hoot Gibson *(Bob Carson)*, Marion Nixon *(Jacqueline McCall)*, Charles K. French *(Col. Jeff McCall)*, G. Raymond Nye *(James Ralston)*, William A. Steele *(Kent Crosby)*, Josie Sedgwick *(Miss Mabel Thompson)*, Fred Humes *(Sheriff)*.

Believing he killed the cousin of the girl he loves in a duel, Gibson flees to Pendleton, Oregon where their big round-up is going on. Shot on location there, this gave the real-life champion rodeo rider plenty of opportunity to show off his stuff. And, in the end, he is, of course, reunited with his sweetheart.

d, Edward Sedgwick; w, Sedgwick, Raymond L. Schrock; ph, Virgil Miller.

Western **(PR:A MPAA:NR)**

LET 'ER GO GALLEGHER** (1928) 6 reels DM/Pathe bw

Junior Coghlan *(Gallegher)*, Harrison Ford *(Callahan)*, Elinor Fair *(Clarissa)*, Wade Boteler *(McGinty)*, E. H. Calvert *(The City Editor)*, Ivan Lebedeff *(Four Fingers)*.

Newsboy Coghlan happens to see a murder committed by a well-known crook, Lebedeff, and gives the tip to his reporter friend Ford. The sudden fame this brings turns Ford into such a boastful bore that he loses both his job and his girl. Figuring the only way to win the two back is to capture Lebedeff, Coghlan and Ford track the killer down and bring him back alive.

d, Elmer Clifton; w, Elliott Clawson (based on "Gallegher: A Newspaper Story" by Richard Harding Davis); t, John Krafft; ph, Lucien Andriot; ed, Harold McLernon; art d, Stephen Goosson.

Crime **(PR:A MPAA:NR)**

LET IT RAIN*** (1927) 7 reels Douglas MacLean/PAR bw

Douglas MacLean *("Let-It-Rain" Riley)*, Shirley Mason *(The Girl)*, Wade Boteler *(Kelly, the Gob)*, James Bradbury, Jr. *(Butch)*, Lincoln Stedman *(Bugs)*, Lee Shumway *(Captain of the Marines)*, James Mason, Edwin Sturgis, Ernest Hilliarp *(The Crooks)*, Frank Campeau *(The Major of Marines)*.

Most of this entertaining comedy takes place on board a ship where the rivalry between leatherneck MacLean and the gob, Boteler, provides plenty of laughs. The competitiveness really heats up when they meet beautiful Mason and assume, because of the fancy address on her card, that she's loaded. It turns out she's actually a switchboard operator, and in their attempt to win her favor, the two men break up a robbery. Then, when the time comes to make her choice, the lucky fellow turns out to be the leatherneck, and the gob is more than pleased to act as best man.

d, Eddie Cline; w, Wade Boteler, George J. Crone, Earle Snell; ph, Jack MacKenzie.

Comedy **(PR:A MPAA:NR)**

LET'S GET MARRIED*½** (1926) 7 reels FP-LAS/PAR bw

Richard Dix *(Billie Dexter)*, Lois Wilson *(Mary Corbin, "the Only Girl")*, Nat Pendleton *(Jimmy, a Friend)*, Douglas MacPherson *(Tommy)*, Gunboat Smith *(Slattery, an Arm of the Law)*, Joseph Kilgour *(Billy's Father)*, Tom Findley *(Mary's Father)*, Edna May Oliver *(J. W. Smith)*.

By 1926, Dix was proving himself to be quite adept at handling comedy, especially when La Cava was directing him. In this funny farce, Dix plays a college football player, swept up in jazz-age zaniness, who becomes involved with a female Bible-selling dipsomaniac, and has a hilarious time trying to get his girl to the altar.

d, Gregory La Cava; w, J. Clarkson Miller, Luther Reed (based on the play "The Man from Mexico" by Harry A. Du Souchet); t, John Bishop; ph, Edward Cronjager.

Comedy **(PR:A MPAA:NR)**

LET'S MAKE WHOOPEE (SEE: RED WINE, 1928)

LIEUT. DANNY, U.S.A.*** (1916) 5 reels Kay-Bee/TRI bw

William Desmond *(Lt. Danny Ward)*, Enid Markey *(Ysobel)*, Gertrude Claire *(Senorita Marie Ventura)*, Thornton Edwards *(Don Mario Ventura)*, Robert Kortman *(Pedro Lopez, the Butcher)*.

Desmond plays a lieutenant, fresh from West Point, sent to the Mexican border to deal with the bandido problem. He falls in love with a beautiful senorita (Markey), and one day while visiting her, is captured by a loathsome hombre, very much in the mold of Pancho Villa. Desmond is lined up against the wall along with a number of others, but the bullet from the firing squad is deflected by a religious medal his sweetheart gave him. After recovering he kills the bandit, who is in the process of forcing his intentions on Markey, and brings her home at dawn, just as Old Glory is being hoisted proudly into the sky.

d, Walter Edwards; w, (based on a story by J. G. Hawks).

Adventure **(PR:A MPAA:NR)**

LIEUTENANT DARING RN AND THE WATER RATS
(1924, Brit.) 6 reels MacDowell bw

Percy Moran *(Lt. Jack Daring)*, Leila King *(Lola)*, George Fowley *(Fawcett)*, Muriel Gregory *(Fiancee)*, N. Watts Phillips *(The Crook)*.

One could call this one the Percy Moran show, as the popular Englishman wrote, starred in, and co-directed this thriller about a naval officer who saves his sweetheart from the clutches of dope smugglers.

p, J. B. MacDowell; d, Edward R. Gordon, James Youngdeer, Percy Moran; w, Youngdeer, Moran.

Crime **(PR:A MPAA:NR)**

LIFE** (1928, Brit.) 7 reels Whitehall/New Era bw

Adelqui Millar *(Juan Jose)*, Marie Ault *(Isidora)*, Manuela del Rio *(Rosa)*, Marcel Vibert *(Paco)*, Jose Lucio *(Andres)*, Denise Lorys *(Tournela)*.

British thriller, set in Spain, about a fired bricklayer who becomes involved in a crime because of his love for a dancer and later breaks out of jail to kill her when she becomes the paramour of his former boss.

p&d, Adelqui Millar; w, (based on the novel *Juan Jose* by Joacquim Dicenta).

Drama **(PR:A MPAA:NR)**

LIFE OF ROBERT BURNS, THE**
(1926, Brit.) 7 reels Scottish Film Academy bw (AKA: IMMORTALS OF BONNIE SCOTLAND)

Wal Croft *(Robert Burns)*, George Campbell.

Sandground directed and Croft played the part of Robert Burns in this biographical picture based on the life of the great Scottish poet.

d, Maurice Sandground.

Biographical **(PR:A MPAA:NR)**

LIFE WITHOUT SOUL*** (1916) 5 reels Ocean bw

William A. Cohill *(Victor Frawley, a Medical Student)*, Percy Darrell Standing *(His Creation)*, George De Carlton *(William Frawley, His Father)*, Jack Hopkins *(Richard Clerval, His Friend)*, Lucy Cotton *(Elizabeth Lavenza, Ward of William Frawley)*, Pauline Curley *(Claudia Frawley, His Sister)*, David McCauley *(Victor Frawley, as a Child)*, Violet De Biccari *(Elizabeth, as a Child)*.

This was the first feature length version of the Frankenstein saga (Edison made a one-reel version in 1910) and, for the most part, it was quite satisfactory—although one can only speculate about the work of art it might have become in the hands of D. W. Griffith.

d, Joseph W. Smiley; w, Jesse J. Goldberg (based on the novel *Frankenstein* by Mary Shelley).

Horror **(PR:A MPAA:NR)**

LIFE'S DARN FUNNY*** (1921) 6 reels Metro bw

Viola Dana *(Zoe Robert)*, Gareth Hughes *(Clay Warwick)*, Eva Gordon *(Miss Dellaroc)*, Kathleen O'Connor *(Gwendolyn Miles)*, Mark Fenton *(Prince Karamazov)*.

Violinist Dana has nothing to wear for her concert, so her friend, Hughes, whips up a gown from a couple of yards of brocade. The outfit is so highly praised that they decide to go into business by using the apartment and charge account of a friend who is out of town. They sell a number of frocks to wealthy customers, but when no one pays their bills, a collection agency comes and cleans out the flat. Finally they are saved when New York's foremost art critic buys a gown for his daughter.

d, Dallas M. Fitzgerald; w, Mary O'Hara, Arthur Ripley (based on the story "Caretakers Within" by Christine Jope Slade); ph, John Arnold.

Comedy **(PR:A MPAA:NR)**

LIFE'S WHIRLPOOL*** (1916) 5 reels Brady/WORLD bw

Walter Green *(Marcus Schuller)*, Phil Robson *(Mr. Sieppe)*, Fania Marinoff *(Trina Sieppe)*, Julia Stuart *(Mrs. Sieppe)*, Rosemary Dean *(Selina Sieppe)*, Elenore Blanchard *(Maria Cappa)*, Holbrook Blinn *(McTeague)*.

O'Neill made this motion picture adaptation of the Norris novel *McTeague* some seven years before Erich von Stroheim used the same source for his epic (though butchered) masterpiece GREED. The story lines are very similar, although needless to say O'Neill's is, by far, the more modest of the two—and one wonders if "the man you love to hate" may have taken a little peek at this less-expansive predecessor.

d&w, Barry O'Neill (based on the novel *McTeague* by Frank Norris).

Drama **(PR:A MPAA:NR)**

LIFE'S WHIRLPOOL* (1917) 5 reels Rolfe/Metro bw

Ethel Barrymore, Alan Hale, Paul Everton, Reginald Carrington, Ricca Allen, Frank Leigh, Walter Hiers, Leslie Hunt, Philip Robson.

Barrymore directed his sister Ethel in this routine programmer about an abusive land owner who mistreats his wife to the point of driving her into the arms of a former sweetheart, well played by Hollywood's greatest scene-stealer, Hale. It all ends most conveniently when one of the long-suffering tenants kills the husband and opens the door for Barrymore and Hale to finally get together.

d&w, Lionel Barrymore.

Drama **(PR:A MPAA:NR)**

LIFTING SHADOWS** (1920) 6 reels Perret/Pathe bw

Emmy Wehlen *(Vania)*, Stuart Holmes *(Clifford Howard)*, Wyndham Standing *(Hugh Mason)*, Julia Swayne Gordon *(Countess Lobanoff)*, F. French *(Gregory Lobanoff)*, Rafael Bongini *(Serge Ostrowski)*.

Wehlen was a musical comedy star who really never made the transition to pictures, although everybody certainly tried hard in this film about a political refugee who flees to the U.S., marries and later kills her drunkenly abusive husband, and then falls in love with a lawyer who rescues her from her old enemies, the "Ring of Death."

d&w, Leonce Perret (based on a play by Henri Ardel); ph, Alfred Ortlieb.

Drama/Adventure **(PR:A MPAA:NR)**

LIGHT AT DUSK, THE** (1916) 6 reels Lubin bw

Orrin Johnson *(Vladimir Krestovsky/Mr. Krest)*, Mary Kennevan Carr *(Nataska)*, Sally Crute *(Mrs. Krest)*, Hedda Kuszewski *(Olga)*, Robert W. Fraser *(Nicholas)*, Evelyn Terrill *(Frances Farrell)*.

Average Lubin feature about a Russian peasant who leaves his wife and child behind, while he sets out to make his fortune in the New World. Endowed with plenty of moxie, he rises to the top and eventually becomes the owner of a mighty steel company. He also lands a socially prominent American wife along the way and, when she dies, the tycoon goes through a prolonged period of mourning. It is during this time that Christ appears to him in a dream and demands kinder treatment of his pre-unionized employees. This he does, and as chance would have it (and often did in pictures of this sort), his Russian wife and child make their way from the old country and end up with jobs in his mill. Of course, at the picture's end, they are happily reunited.

d, Edgar Lewis; w, Anthony P. Kelly.

Drama **(PR:A MPAA:NR)**

LIGHT IN THE DARK, THE*** (1922) 8 reels Hope Hampton/AFN bw-c

Hope Hampton *(Bessie MacGregor)*, E. K. Lincoln *(J. Warburton Ashe)*, Lon Chaney *(Tony Pantelli)*, Theresa Maxwell Conover *(Mrs. Templeton Orrin)*, Dorothy Walters *(Mrs. Callerty)*, Charles Mussett *(Detective Braenders)*, Edgar Norton *(Peters)*, Dore Davidson *(Jerusalem Mike)*, Mr. McClune *(Socrates Stickles)*.

Chaney walked away with this spiritually moving film about a girl who is restored to health through the powers of the Holy Grail. Chaney, as a gangster, loses her in the end to the regenerated millionaire she really loves, in a most poignant scene. The whole picture was dyed using beautiful tints of blue, purple, and grey. The Holy Grail subplot, which took the form of a flashback, was actually shot in color. Brown's direction was topnotch throughout.

d, Clarence L. Brown; w, William Dudley Pelley, Brown (based on a story by Pelley); ph, Alfred Ortlieb, Ben Carre.

Drama **(PR:A MPAA:NR)**

LIGHT IN THE WINDOW, THE* (1927) 6 reels T/C/RAY bw

Henry B. Walthall *(Johann Graff)*, Patricia Avery *(Dorothy Graff)*, Erin La Bissoniere *(Maizie)*, Henry Sedley *(Peter Mayfield)*, Tom O'Grady *(Teddie Wales)*, Cornelius Keefe *(Bert Emmonds)*.

It took some really feeble direction to make Walthall deliver a bad performance, but that's exactly what Pembroke acomplished in this poor film about a protective father who nearly destroys his daughter's happiness.

d, Scott Pembroke; w, Leota Morgan (based on a story by Arthur Hoerl); ph, Ernest Depew.

Drama **(PR:A MPAA:NR)**

LIGHT OF VICTORY*** (1919) 5 reels BLUE/UNIV bw

Bob Edmonds *("Traction Jim" Cripps)*, Fred Wilson *(Lt. Kenwood Cripps)*, Monroe Salisbury *(Lt. George Benton)*, Fred Kelsey *(Capt. Eric Von Prohme)*, Betty Compson *(Jane Ravenslee)*, Beatrice Dominguez *(Luhua)*, Andrew Robson, George Nicholls.

In this highly unusual wartime film, Salisbury, a lieutenant of the U.S. Navy, becomes drunk instead of delivering important papers to the English naval department at the outbreak of hostilities. The documents are stolen by German agents, and his fellow officers conduct a private court-martial in which Salisbury is given the privilege of shooting himself. He refuses and is banished to a Pacific island, where he becomes involved in aiding the U-boats of the Central Powers. At the film's end, he is shot in the back by a German officer, and his very last gesture is to salute the U.S. flag.

d, William Wolbert; w, Waldemar Young (based on a story by George C. Hull); ph, Harry B. Harris.

War **(PR:A MPAA:NR)**

LIGHTHOUSE BY THE SEA, THE*** (1924) 7 reels WB bw

Rin-Tin-Tin *(Himself)*, William Collier, Jr. *(Albert Dorn)*, Louise Fazenda *(Flora Gale)*, Charles Hill Mailes *(Caleb Gale)*, Douglas Gerrard *(Edward Cavanna)*, Matthew Betz *(Joe Dagget)*.

Action-packed Rin-Tin-Tin adventure in which the great canine star and his shipwrecked master save the lives of a blinded lighthouse keeper and his pretty daughter (who has secretly been performing his duties) from a sinister band of rum runners.

d, Mal St. Clair; w, Darryl F. Zanuck (based on the play by Owen Davis); ph, Lyman Broening; ed, Howard Bretherton; art d, Lewis Geib, Esdras Hartley.

Adventure **(PR:A MPAA:NR)**

LIGHTNING CONDUCTOR, THE*** (1914) 6 reels Hefco/Sawyer bw

Dustin Farnum, Walter Hale, William Elliott.

Flimsy plot has an aristocratic Englishman becoming smitten by the wealthy daughter of a U.S. banker (who is touring Europe by motorcar with her aunt) finagling a job as chauffeur in order to be near her. It is all an excuse to show some breathtaking scenery (filmed on location in Italy), in what really amounts to a pleasant travelog.

d, Walter Hale; w, (based on the Williamson novel).

Romance **(PR:A MPAA:NR)**

LIGHTNING LARIATS** (1927) 5 reels R-C/FBO bw

Tom Tyler *(Tom Potter)*, Dorothy Dunbar *(Janet Holbrooke)*, Frankie Darro *(Alexis, King of Roxenburg)*, Ruby Blaine *(Cynthia Storne)*, Fred Holmes *(Henry Storne)*, Ervin Renard *(1st Officer)*, Carl Silvera *(2nd Officer)*, Leroy Scott *(Gus)*.

When the nation of Roxenburg falls to rebels, a young king (Darro) and his American governess flee to Arizona. Tyler takes them under his wing and thwarts the attempts of revolutionary officers to do them harm.

d, Robert De Lacey; w, F. A. E. Pine (based on a story by George Worthing); ph, Nicholas Musuraca.

Western **(PR:A MPAA:NR)**

LIGHTNING REPORTER* (1926) 6 reels Ellbee bw

Johnny Walker, Sylvia Breamer, Burr McIntosh, Lou Archer, Nelson McDowell, Joseph Girard, Mayme Kelso.

Modest independent B production has Walker landing a railroad president's daughter after helping the old fellow whip his financial arch rival in a stock market deal.

d&w, Jack Noble (based on a story by Tom Gibson); ph, Harry Davis.

Drama **(PR:A MPAA:NR)**

LIGHTNING ROMANCE** (1924) 5 reels Harry J. Brown/RAY bw

Reed Howes *(Jack Wade)*, Ethel Shannon *(Lila Grandon)*, Wilfred Lucas *(Richard Wade)*, David Kirby *(Red Taylor)*, Cuyler Supplee *(Arnold Stewart)*, Frank Hagney *(Arizona Joe)*, H. C. Hallett *(Butler)*, Rex *(Horse)*.

Rayart Pictures billed Howes as "the youngest, handsomest, peppiest fellow on the screen today." The original model for Arrow Collars, as well as Chesterfield Cigarettes and Stetson Hats, Howes made an appealing hero in this action programmer, about a young man whose craving for adventure forces his tycoon father to invent some for him.

d, Albert Rogell; w, Marion Jackson; ph, Ross Fisher.

Adventure **(PR:A MPAA:NR)**

LIGHTS OF NEW YORK, THE* (1916) 5 reels VIT bw

Leah Baird *(Yolande Cowles)*, Walter McGrail *(Hawk Chovinski)*, Arthur Cozine *(Skelly)*, Adele De Garde *(Poppy Brown)*, Leila Blow *(Mrs. Cowles)*, Agnes Wadleigh *(Mrs. Cropsey)*, Don Cameron *(Martin Drake)*, Edwina Robbins *(Mrs. Blossom)*.

Awful Vitagraph film which expected its audience to accept the premise that a petty pickpocket could hire a dancing master to coach him to pass for a European baron in three weeks. The titles were even worse than the plot, such as: "And the wolf slinks like a dark shadow along the great gulches of the dark street," and, "Oh! the will of a woman is woeful when she knows not the wiles of the wicked!"

d, Van Dyke Brooke; w, Charles L. Gaskill.

Drama **(PR:A MPAA:NR)**

LIGHTS OF THE DESERT*** (1922) 5 reels FOX bw

Shirley Mason *(Yvonne Laraby)*, Allan Forrest *(Clay Truxall)*, Edward Burns *(Andrew Reed)*, James Mason *(Slim Saunders)*, Andree Tourneur *(Marie Curtis)*, Josephine Crowell *(Ma Curtis)*, Lillian Langdon *(Susan Gallant)*.

Well-crafted modern western programmer about a stranded actress who stays on in a small Nevada town, after her fellow players return to San Francisco, to consider a proposal of marriage. Later she falls for an oil man and convinces her suitor to return to his better-suited former sweetheart.

d, Harry Beaumont; w, Paul Schofield (based on a story by Gladys E. Johnson); ph, Frank Good.

Western/Drama **(PR:A MPAA:NR)**

LIKENESS OF THE NIGHT, THE* (1921, Brit.) 6 reels Screen Plays/ British Exhibitors' bw

Renee Kelly *(Mary)*, Minna Grey *(Mildred)*, Harold Deacon *(Bernard Acherson)*, Florence Shee *(Lady Carruthers)*.

In this British drama, the unfaithful wife of a lawyer realizes the error of her ways, fakes suicide, and enters a convent in order to give her husband the freedom to marry his mistress.

d, Percy Nash; w, (based on the play by Mrs. W. K. Clifford).

Drama **(PR:A MPAA:NR)**

LILAC TIME* 1/2** (1928) 11 reels FN bw

Colleen Moore *(Jeannine Berthelot)*, Gary Cooper *(Capt. Philip Blythe)*, Burr McIntosh *(Gen. Blythe)*, George Cooper *(Mechanic's Helper)*, Cleve Moore *(Capt. Russell)*, Kathryn McGuire *(Lady Iris Rankin)*, Eugenie Besserer *(Mme. Berthelot)*, Emile Chautard *(Mayor)*, Jack Stone *(The Infant)*, Edward Dillon *(Mike, a Mechanic)*, Dick Grace, Stuart Knox, Harlan Hilton, Richard Jarvis, Jack Ponder, Dan Dowling *(Aviators)*.

LILAC TIME is rather a combination of WINGS and SEVENTH HEAVEN. It tells of the love between an English flyer and gentleman (Cooper) and a French farm girl (Moore) on whose land the Royal Flying Corps is billeted. The battle scenes fall short of the earlier WINGS, and the ending, where the lovers are at last reunited, does not pull at the heartstrings to the same degree as SEVENTH HEAVEN, but Moore is fine, Cooper good, and the film (in spite of its excessive length) is quite entertaining.

p, John McCormick; d, George Fitzmaurice; w, Carey Wilson, Willis Goldbeck (based on the play by Jane Cowl, Jane Murfin); ph, Sidney Hickox (aerial ph, Alvin Knechtel); m, Nathaniel Shilkret; ed, Al Hall; m/l, "Jeannine, I Dream of Lilac Time" by L. Wolf Gilbert; syn sc; s eff, Vitaphone; technical flight commander, Dick Grace; technical expert, Capt. L. J. S. Scott; French military advisor, Capt. Robert De Couedic; ordnance expert, Harry Redmond.

War/Romance **(PR:A MPAA:NR)**

LILY AND THE ROSE, THE*** (1915) 5 reels FA/TRI bw

Lillian Gish, Rozsika Dolly, Loyola O'Connor, Cora Drew, Wilfred Lucas, Mary Alden, Elmer Clifton, William Hinkley, Frank Mills, Alberta Lee.

Griffith supervised and provided the story for this Gish showcase about a wealthy cad who marries an innocent girl and then takes up with a dancer, driving the heartbroken girl out of his house and leading her to suicide. Granville Warwick, the pseudonym that Griffith used on the novel that served as the basis for this film, also appeared as his writing credit for his story for THE LAMB, directed by Christy Cabanne.

d, Paul Powell; sup, D. W. Griffith; w, Powell (based on the novel *Mrs. Billie* by Granville Warwick [D. W. Griffith].

Drama **(PR:A MPAA:NR)**

LILY OF THE ALLEY (1923, Brit.) 7 reels Hepworth bw

Henry Edwards *(Bill)*, Chrissie White *(Lily)*, Campbell Gullan *(Sharkey)*, Mary Brough *(Widow)*, Frank Stanmore *(Alf)*, Lionel d'Aragon *(Dad)*.

This British drama, about the wife of a coffee seller who dreams that her husband loses his sight and is then killed in a tragic fire, was completely shot without titles, two years before F. W. Murnau electrified the cinematic world by doing the same with his masterpiece THE LAST LAUGH.

d&w, Henry Edwards.

Drama **(PR:A MPAA:NR)**

LINDA*** (1929) 7 reels Mrs. Wallace Reid/Willis Kent bw

Warner Baxter *(Dr. Paul Randall)*, Helen Foster *(Linda)*, Noah Beery *(Decker)*, Mitchell Lewis *(Stillwater)*, Kate Price *(Nan)*, Allan Connor *(Kenneth Whittmore)*, Bess Flowers *(Annette Whittmore)*.

Well-made programmer about a dreamy North Woods girl who is forced by her brutal father to marry an older man. Her heart is with a young doctor, but because her husband is kind to her, she finally stays with him (after running away briefly) until his early death.

d, Mrs. Wallace Reid; w, Wilfred Noy, Maxine Alton, Frank O'Connor (based on the novel by Margaret Prescott Montague); t, Ruth Todd; ph, Henry Cronjager, Bert Baldridge, Ernest Laszlo; ed, Willis Kent; m/l, "Linda," Al Sherman, Charles Tobias, Harry Tobias; syn sc; s eff.

Drama **(PR:A MPAA:NR)**

LINGERIE 1/2** (1928) 6 reels TS bw

Alice White *(Angele Ree/"Lingerie")*, Malcolm McGregor *(Leroy Boyd)*, Mildred Harris *(Rosemary)*, Armand Kaliz *(Jack Van Cleve)*, Cornelia Kellog *(Rosemary's Mother)*, Kit Guard, Victor Potel *(Slim and Handsome, Leroy's Pals)*, Richard Carlyle *(Pembroke)*, Marcelle Corday *(Modiste)*.

When he discovers that his bride, Harris, is unfaithful, McGregor joins the Army to fight Germans. While in France he falls in love with a little native girl (White), and when he is seriously wounded and can neither hear nor speak, she follows him to the U.S. and gets a job working in his home. After White nurses McGregor back to health, he throws his treacherous wife out and devotes his full attention to the loyal little French lady.

d, George Melford; w, John Francis Natteford; t, Ben Grauman Kohn; ph, Jackson Rose; ed, Byron Robinson; art d, Hervey Libbert; set d, George Sawley.

Drama/War **(PR:A MPAA:NR)**

LION'S MOUSE, THE** (1922, Brit.) 6 reels Granger/Binger bw

Wyndham Standing *(Dick Sands)*, Mary Odette *(Mouse)*, Rex Davis *(Justin O'Reilly)*, Marguerite Marsh *(Olga Beverley)*.

Not particularly thrilling British thriller about a secret society kidnaping a man to force his sister to boost some valuable plans. Naturally, in the last reel, the bad blokes are brought to justice.

d, Oscar Apfel; w, (based on the novel by A. N. and A. M. Williamson).

Crime **(PR:A MPAA:NR)**

LITTLE ANGEL OF CANYON CREEK, THE*** (1914) 5 reels Broadway Star/VIT bw

Gertrude Short, George Stanley, Violet Malone, W. V. Ranous.

Good drama with a northwestern setting, about an orphaned child who completely regenerates a town of tough, sinnin' miners, and makes them realize that the "straight" course is best.

d, Rollin S. Sturgeon; w, Cyrus Townsend Brady.

Drama **(PR:A MPAA:NR)**

LITTLE ANNIE ROONEY*** (1925) 9 reels Mary Pickford/UA bw

Mary Pickford *(Little Annie Rooney)*, William Haines *(Joe Kelly)*, Walter James *(Officer Rooney)*, Gordon Griffith *(Tim Rooney)*, Carlo Schipa *(Tony)*, Spec O'Donnell *(Abie)*, Hugh Fay *(Spider)*, Vola Vale *(Mamie)*, Joe Butterworth *(Mickey)*, Eugene Jackson *(Humidor)*, Oscar Rudolph *(Athos)*.

When Pickford's policeman father is killed, her brother thinks Haines (Pickford's heartthrob) guilty and shoots him with his dad's service revolver. Pickford saves the young man with a blood transfusion and then, with the help of the neighborhood kids, captures the real killer. With films like Frances Marion's THE LOVE LIGHT (1921) and Ernst Lubitsch's ROSITA (1923), Pickford tried to break free of the innocent Cinderella roles that she had built her career upon, but the public continued to demand the kind of characters from her that they were used to and LITTLE ANNIE ROONEY is no exception. A year later she would work again with director Beaudine on the much superior SPARROWS. This may not be America's Sweetheart's best picture, but it's great fun anyway.

d, William Beaudine; w, Hope Loring, Louis D. Lighton (based on a story by Katherine Hennessey); t, Tom McNamara; ph, Charles Rosher, Hal Mohr; art d, John D. Schulze, Harry Oliver, Paul Youngblood.

Drama/Comedy **Cas.** **(PR:A MPAA:NR)**

LITTLE BIG HORN** (1927) 5 reels Oxford Exchange bw

John Beck *(Gen. George A. Custer)*, Roy Stewart *(Lem Hawks)*, Helen Lynch *(Betty Rossman)*, Edmund Cobb *(Capt. Page)*.

A thin story line was tacked on to add a little depth to this depiction of Custer's last stand, but the picture unfortunately fails to capture the tremendous drama of that occurrence in history, which took place on June 25, 1876.

d, Harry L. Frasier; w, Carrie E. Rawles.

Historical **(PR:A MPAA:NR)**

LITTLE BROTHER, THE*** (1917) 5 reels Kay-Bee/TRI bw

Enid Bennett *(Jerry Ross)*, William Garwood *(Frank Girard)*, Josephine Headley *(Janet Girard)*, Dorcas Matthews *(Dulcie Hapes)*, Carl Ullman *(Dillon)*.

Nice performance by Bennett as a street urchin who dresses in boys' clothes to better sell her newspapers. She is adopted by a kindhearted millionaire and sent away to school. When she returns as a beautiful young woman, her benefactor takes one look, falls in love, and asks her to be his wife. Really better than it sounds.

d, Charles Miller; w, Lois Zellner (based on a story by Lambert Hillyer).

Drama **(PR:A MPAA:NR)**

LITTLE CHURCH AROUND THE CORNER*** (1923) 6 reels WB bw

Kenneth Harlan *(David Graham)*, Claire Windsor *(Leila Morton)*, Hobart Bosworth *(Morton)*, Walter Long *(Hex)*, Pauline Starke *(Hetty)*, Alec Francis *(Rev. Bradley)*, Margaret Seddon *(Mrs. Graham)*, George Cooper *(Jude)*, Winter Hall *(Doc Graham)*, Cyril Chadwick *(Mark Hanford)*, Fred Stanton, Winston Miller, Mary Jane Irving.

Set in a mining town, this is the story of a deeply religious orphaned boy who is sent to divinity school by the mine owner. When he returns to live with his benefactor, he finds himself falling in love with the daughter of the house. Before long, a group of miners appear to plead for better safety. When they are denied this, the minister elects to join them and moves into their shanty town. On the day of his return, there is a cave-in, and the reverend leads the search for survivors. The climax comes when a vengeance-seeking mob confronts the owner and his daughter. The minister, however, turns them back by working a miracle in which a dumb girl is made to speak. This was the kind of solid programmer small town America loved.

d, William Seiter; w, Olga Printzlau (based on a play by Marion Russell); ph, Homer Scott, E. B. DuPar; ed, C. R. Wallace; set d, Lewis Geib.

Drama **(PR:A MPAA:NR)**

LITTLE CLOWN, THE** (1921) 5 reels Realart bw

Mary Miles Minter *(Pat)*, Jack Mulhall *(Dick Beverley)*, Winter Hall *(Col. Beverley)*, Helen Dunbar *(Mrs. Beverley)*, Cameron Coffey *(Roddy Beverley)*, Neely Edwards *(Toto)*, Wilton Taylor *(Jim Anderson)*, Lucien Littlefield *(Connie Potts)*, Zelma Maja *(Liz)*, Laura Anson *(Nellie Johnson)*.

Minter is orphaned and raised in the circus by a clown (Edwards). After she grows up and becomes part of the act, he dreams of marrying her, but Minter falls in love with Mulhall, a wealthy young southerner who joins the troupe as a trick rider after quarreling with his parents. The young couple marry and, after some tough sledding, Minter is welcomed into the family.

d, Thomas N. Heffron; w, Eugene B. Lewis (based on the play by Avery Hopwood); ph, Faxon M. Dean.

Comedy/Drama **(PR:A MPAA:NR)**

LITTLE COMRADE*** (1919) 5 reels PAR bw

Vivian Martin *(Genevieve)*, Niles Welch *(Bobbie Hubbard)*, Gertrude Claire *(Mother Hubbard)*, Richard Cummings *(Father Hubbard)*, Larry W. Steers *(Lt. Hubbard)*, Eleanor Hancock, Nancy Chase, Pearl Lovici.

Martin is charming as the girl who thinks only of the latest dance steps, until her sister and mother make her realize the importance of the war effort. Volunteering as a "farmerette," she puts every agricultural prop available to good comic use, and also falls in love with the handsome farmer's son, whom she helps mold into a good officer.

d, Chester Withey; w, Alice Eyton (based on the story "The Two Benjamins" by Juliet Wilbur Tompkins).

Comedy **(PR:A MPAA:NR)**

LITTLE DOOR INTO THE WORLD, THE**
(1923, Brit.) 5 reels Dewhurst-Thomson/Astra-N bw
(AKA: THE EVIL THAT MEN DO)

Lawford Davidson *(Lefarge)*, Nancy Beard *(Maria Jose/Celestine)*, Olaf Hytten *(Mountebank)*, Peggy Patterson *(Dancer)*, Victor Tandy *(Agent)*, Arthur Mayhew *(Troubadour)*, Robert Williamson *(Manager)*.

Dewhurst, who wrote, directed, and produced this British film (shot in Berlin) was a one-man depression platoon. The story had to do with a nun who saves a dancer from the libidinal clutches of a squire by pretending to seduce him and then revealing that she is, in actuality, his bastard daughter.

p,d&w, George Dewhurst.

Drama **(PR:A MPAA:NR)**

LITTLE EVA ASCENDS*** (1922) 5 reels S-L Pictures/Metro bw

Gareth Hughes *(Roy St. George/Little Eva)*, Eleanor Fields *(Mattie Moore)*, May Collins *(Priscilla Price)*, Unice Vin Moore *(Blanche St. George)*, Benjamin Haggerty *(John St. George/Uncle Tom)*, Edward Martindel *(Mr. Wilson)*, Harry Lorraine *(Junius Brutus)*, Mark Fenton *(Mr. Moore)*, John Prince *(Mr. Price)*, Fred Warren *(Montgomery Murphy)*, W. H. Brown *(Richard Bansfield/Aunt Chloe)*.

Nice little programmer about a traveling "Uncle Tom's Cabin" theater troupe, run by Vin Moore and her two very reluctant children (one of whom is forced to play Little Eva). The group stops at a village in Connecticut where they check into the hotel, run by Martindel. Vin Moore becomes furious when she discovers that he is the husband who left her, when the kids were infants, because of her theatrical obsession. At that night's performance, everything possible goes wrong, and when Little Eva (Hughes) finally makes her/his ascent, the crowd bursts into a deafening collection of boos and jeers. Hughes tears off his wig, throws it at the crowd, and escapes to his father's farm (he has since learned the truth), where Martindel arranges to buy Vin Moore her own theater in exchange for custody of the children.

d, George D. Baker; w, (based on a story by Thomas Beer); ph, Rudolph Berquist; art d, E. J. Shulter.

Comedy/Drama **(PR:A MPAA:NR)**

LITTLE 'FRAID LADY, THE** (1920) 6 reels R-C bw

Mae Marsh *(Cecilia)*, Tully Marshall *(Giron)*, Herbert Prior *(Judge Carteret)*, Charles Meredith *(Saxton Graves)*, Kathleen Kirkham *(Mrs. Helen Barrett)*, Gretchen Hartman *(Sirotta)*, George Bertholon, Jr., Jacques III, the Dog.

Marsh puts her extraordinary acting range to very good use, in what would otherwise be little more than a modest programmer about a young female artist who leaves the city heartbroken, but finds true love in the near wilderness.

d, John G. Adolfi; w, Joseph W. Farnham (based on the novel *The Girl Who Lived in the Woods* by Marjorie Benton Cooke); ph, Georges Benoit.

Drama **(PR:A MPAA:NR)**

LITTLE GRAY LADY, THE** (1914) 4 reels FP bw

Jane Gray *(Anna Grey)*, James Cooley *(Perry Carlyle)*, Jane Fearnley *(Ruth Jordon)*, Hal Clarendon *(Sam Meade)*, Julia Walcott *(Mrs. Jordon)*, Robert Cummings *(Richard Graham)*, Mathaleen Aamold *(Mrs. Graham)*, Edgar Davenport *(John Moore)*, Sue Balfour *(Mrs. Carlyle)*.

A country boy lands a job in the nation's capital, where he yields to the temptations of city life. His rural sweetheart, however, not only sticks by him, but rescues the boy from the sinful life and returns him to the green fields of virtue.

d, Francis Powers; w, Channing Pollock.

Drama **(PR:A MPAA:NR)**

LITTLE IRISH GIRL, THE** (1926) 7 reels WB bw

Dolores Costello *(Dot Walker)*, John Harron *(Johnny)*, Matthew Betz *(Jerry Crawford)*, Lee Moran *(Mr. Nelson)*, Gertrude Claire *(Granny)*, Joseph Dowling *(Capt. Dugan)*, Dot Farley *(Gertie)*, Henry Barrows *(Bankroll Charlie)*.

When Harron comes to town, he meets Costello, who is shilling for a gambling house. The kid loses all of his money and invites the sharps to return with him to make an offer for his hotel. When they get there, his nimble-witted granny takes *them* for all they're worth. Costello later reforms, and she and Harron turn the hotel into a gold mine.

d, Roy Del Ruth; w, Darryl Francis Zanuck (based on the story "The Grifters" by C. D. Lancaster); ph, Lyman Broening, Willard Van Enger; ed, Clarence Kolster.

Drama **(PR:A MPAA:NR)**

LITTLE JOURNEY, A*** (1927) 7 reels MGM bw

Claire Windsor *(Julia Rutherford)*, William Haines *(George Manning)*, Harry Carey *(Alexander Smith)*, Claire McDowell *(Aunt Louise)*, Lawford Davidson *(Alfred Demis)*.

Charming, underplayed comedy in which Windsor boards a train for San Francisco to marry old family friend Carey for the sake of her parents. When she loses her ticket, Haines gladly comes to her assistance and, as they travel across the country, true love develops. Then, when it seems the happy couple must separate, Carey sneaks on the train to surprise his bride-to-be, observes the situation, and gallantly bows out.

d, Robert Z. Leonard; w, Albert Lewin (based on the play by Rachel Crothers); t, George Marion, Jr.; ph, Ira Morgan; ed, William Le Vanway; set d, Cedric Gibbons, Park French.

Comedy **(PR:A MPAA:NR)**

LITTLE LIAR, THE*** (1916) 5 reels FA/TRI bw

Mae Marsh *(Maggie)*, Robert Harron *(Bobby)*, Olga Gray *(Fanny)*, Carl Stockdale *(Dick Slade)*, Jennie Lee *(Boardinghouse Keeper)*, Ruth Handforth *(Maggie's Mother)*, Tom Wilson *(Maggie's Father)*, Loyola O'Connor *(Matron of the Jail)*.

Strangely cynical film has Marsh as a slum girl with the kind of imagination that gets her into all kinds of trouble. In fact, she ends up in jail, where she writes her observations and sends them to the warden. He is so impressed with her talent that he shows her work to a reporter who says there's a slot for her on his paper. The two of them rush down to tell the girl the good news only to discover that she has killed herself.

d, Lloyd Ingraham; w, Anita Loos.

Drama **(PR:A MPAA:NR)**

LITTLE LORD FAUNTLEROY**
(1914, Brit.) 6 reels Natural Colour Kinematograph c

Gerald Royston *(Cedric Erroll)*, Jene Wells *("Dearest" Erroll)*, H. Agar Lyons *(Earl of Dorincourt)*, Bernard Vaughn *(Havisham)*, V. Osmond *(Minna Tipton)*, Frank Strather *(Ben Tipton)*, D. Callan *(Tommy Tipton)*, Harry Edwards *(Dick Tipton)*, Edward Viner *(Cedric)*, John M. East *(Thomas)*, Stella St. Audrie *(Bridget)*, F. Tomkins *(Silas Hobbs)*, Fred Eustace *(Bliss)*.

This first filmed version of the Burnett classic about an American heir to a British earldom, who reunites his grandfather with his widowed mother, was, unfortunately (with the exception of the kinemacolor process), pretty much of a bore.

d, F. Martin Thornton; w, (based on the novel by Frances Hodgson Burnett); ph, (Kinemacolor).

Drama **(PR:A MPAA:NR)**

LITTLE LORD FAUNTLEROY**** (1921) 10 reels Mary Pickford/UA bw

Mary Pickford *(Cedric, Little Lord Fauntleroy/Dearest, Cedric's Mother)*, Claude Gillingwater *(The Earl of Dorincourt)*, Joseph Dowling *(Haversham, the Earl's Counsel)*, James Marcus *(Hobbs, the Grocer)*, Kate Price *(Mrs. McGinty, the Applewoman)*, Fred Malatesta *(Dick, the Bootblack)*, Rose Dione *(Minna, the Adventuress)*, Frances Marion *(Her Son, the Pretender)*, Arthur Thalasso *(The Stranger, Her Husband)*, Colin Kenny *(Bevis, the Earl's Son)*, Emmett King *(Rev. Mordaunt, the Minister)*, Madame de Bodamere *(Mrs. Higgins, a Tenant)*.

Pickford is splendid in a double role—she plays the American widow of the youngest son of the Earl of Dorincourt (played by Gillingwater), as well as her young son Cedric. Gillingwater, who now is without an heir, sends his solicitor to New York to fetch Cedric, who lives in near poverty with his mother. Because Gillingwater believes the boy's mother married his son for money, he refuses to allow her to stay in the castle with her son. The child, however, charms everybody he encounters, and when a pretender attempts to usurp his title, a couple of American pals, Marcus and Price, arrive with proof which foils the plot. The delighted earl, realizing his error, welcomes his daughter-in-law into the family and there is a truly happy ending. The scenes where Pickford appears with herself are really astounding (she is three inches taller than the son), and the famous sequence where the two characters kiss took 15 hours to shoot and lasts only a couple of seconds.

d, Alfred E. Green, Jack Pickford; w, Bernard McConville (based on the novel by Frances Hodgson Burnett); ph, Charles Rosher; m, Louis F. Gottschalk.

Dramatic Comedy **(PR:A MPAA:NR)**

LITTLE MADEMOISELLE, THE** (1915) 5 reels Shubert/WORLD bw

Vivian Martin *(The French Girl)*, Arthur Ashley *(Jim Pemberton)*.

Martin is charming as a little French immigrant who becomes lost while on her way to join her guardians, by straying from her train's observation platform. While roaming in a small U.S. town, she is befriended by Ashley, a disinherited millionaire's son, with mechanical instincts. Later, he drives a racing car (which the uncle she was on her way to visit manufactured) to victory and, with the prize money, reunites the French cutie with her guardians. For all of this, Ashley is given a great job with the auto firm and, of course, there are wedding bells in the future.

d, Oscar Eagle; w, Mark Swan.

Drama **(PR:A MPAA:NR)**

LITTLE MISS BROWN** (1915) 5 reels Brady/WORLD bw

Vivian Martin *(Betty Brown)*, Julia Stuart *(Jane Glenton)*, Edward M. Kimball *(Justine Glenton)*, Crauford Kent *(Joseph Clews)*, Chester Barnett *(Robert Mason)*, Ethel Lloyd *(Mrs. Dennison)*, Charles Dickson *(Richard Dennison)*, W. J. Ferguson *(Mr. Burke, His Uncle)*, Alberta Gullatin *(Mrs. Burke)*, Ned A. Sparks *(Night Clerk)*, Jewel Hilburn *(Telephone Girl)*, John Hines *(Bellboy)*.

Set in a Hartford, Connecticut, hotel, this marital mixup farce was not exactly fresh, even back in 1915. There are a few laughs, however, with Martin and young Hines (as a comic bellboy) taking the honors.

d, James Young; w, (based on the play by Phillip Bartholomae).

Comedy **(PR:A MPAA:NR)**

LITTLE MISS HOOVER***

(1918) 5 reels PAR bw (AKA; THE GOLDEN BIRD)

Marguerite Clark *(Nancy Craddock)*, Eugene O'Brien *(Major Adam Baldwin)*, Alfred Hickman *(Matthew Berry)*, Forrest Robinson *(Col. William Craddock)*, Frances Kaye *(Polly Beardsley)*, John Tansey *(Bud)*, J. M. Mason *(Silas Beardsley)*, Dorothy Walters, Hal Reid, J. J. Williams.

Interesting propaganda film takes place at the end of WW I and was meant to encourage farmers to work harder and be more productive to meet the needs of starving Europeans. Mixed in throughout the entire film is an appealing love story between Clark and O'Brien.

d, John Stuart Robertson; w, Adrian Gil-Spear (based on the novel *The Golden Bird* by Maria Thompson Daviess); ph, William Marshall.

Drama **(PR:A MPAA:NR)**

LITTLE MISS REBELLION*** (1920) 5 reels New Art/PAR bw

Dorothy Gish *(Grand Duchess Marie)*, Ralph Graves *(Sgt. Richard Ellis)*, George Siegmann *(Col. Moro)*, Riley Hatch *(Stephen)*, Marie Burke *(Lady In Waiting)*, George Fawcett.

Gish comedy about a princess in one of those comic opera kingdoms, who sneaks out of the palace one day and falls for a doughboy who stayed on in Europe after the war. Later, the Bolsheviks revolt and the princess and her number one servant escape with the crown jewels to New York, where Gish lands a job in a restaurant. The Reds, who want the gems—and her scalp—trail them to Gotham, break into her tenement, and torture the faithful one to get information relating to both. Meanwhile, the doughboy, freshly discharged from the service, spots Gish at the eatery, follows her home, wipes up the floor with the commies, declares his love for the princess—in spite of her royal blood—and they settle down to live the life of good, albeit very rich, Americans.

d, George Fawcett; w, Wells Hastings (based on a story by Harry Carr); ph, Walter Hill.

Comedy/Adventure **(PR:A MPAA:NR)**

LITTLE MISS SMILES*** (1922) 5 reels FOX bw

Shirley Mason *(Ruth Aaronson)*, Gaston Glass *(Dr. Jack Washton)*, George Williams *(Papa Aaronson)*, Martha Franklin *(Mama Aaronson)*, Arthur Rankin *(Davie Aaronson)*, Alfred Testa *(Louis Aaronson)*, Richard Lapan *(Leon Aaronson)*, Sidney D'Albrook *("The Spider")*, Baby Blumfield *(Baby Aaronson)*.

With virtually nothing to work with, director Ford still managed to deliver an entertaining film about the tribulations of a poor Jewish family living in New York, whose prizefighter son gets into trouble with gangsters, and whose daughter ("Little Miss Smiles"), naturally ends up marrying a doctor.

d, Jack Ford; w, Jack Strumwasser, Dorothy Yost (based on the novel *Little Aliens* by Myra Kelly); ph, David Abel.

Drama **(PR:A MPAA:NR)**

LITTLE PAL** (1915) 5 reels FP bw

Mary Pickford *("Little Pal")*, Russell Bassett *(Sid Gerue, Her Father)*, George Anderson *(John Grandon)*, William Lloyd *("Pill Box" Andy)*, Joseph Manning *("Black Brand")*, Constance Johnson *(Frances Grandon)*, Bert Hadley *(The Servant)*, James Kirkwood, Marshall Neilan.

Pickford plays a girl who loves but lives platonically with Anderson, a prospector, in the North Woods. When his wife arrives on the scene, and the two decide to return to civilization, Pickford steals enough ore for them to make the trip and then, brokenheartedly, commits suicide. Pickford's famous blonde curls were hidden beneath a black wig that significantly altered her appearance in this, one of her lesser efforts. The ice cold setting of the picture is effectively conveyed by the snowy scenes that punctuate the proceedings.

d, James Kirkwood; w, Marshall Neilan, Frances Marion.

Drama **(PR:A MPAA:NR)**

LITTLE PATRIOT, A** (1917) 5 reels Diando/Pathe bw

Baby Marie Osborne *(The Little Patriot)*, Herbert Standing *(Her Grandfather)*, Marian Warner *(Her Mother)*, Jack Connolly, Frank Lanning, Madge Evans.

Full of the spirit of war (after her teacher reads the story of Joan of Arc) Osborne and her many little friends play soldier in an empty lot. The child becomes friendly with an old inventor, who has perfected an aerial torpedo, so when Osborne discovers that one of her mother's boarders is actually a German spy out to blow the old gent and his weapon up, she swings into action, rallies her children, and together they capture the murderous agent. Then, as fate would have it, the old boy turns out to be the grandfather who disinherited Osborne's mother when she married against his will, and the film concludes with the whole family, at the end of the war, living happily in his enormous mansion.

d, William Bertram; w, Lela Leibrand (based on the story by John W. Grey).

Comedy/Adventure/War **(PR:A MPAA:NR)**

LITTLE SAVAGE, THE* (1929) 5 reels FBO/RKO bw

Buzz Barton *(Red)*, Milburne Morante *(Hank)*, Willard Boelner *(Baby)*, Patricia Palmer *(Kitty)*, Sam Nelson *(Norton)*, Ethan Laidlaw *(Blake)*.

Slow-moving, predictable oater left little room for kid cowboy star Barton to do his trick riding stuff, which was the film's only attraction in the first place.

d, Louis King; w, Frank Howard Clark; t, Randolph Bartlett; ph, Virgil Miller; ed, George Marsh.

Western **(PR:A MPAA:NR)**

LITTLE SCHOOL MA'AM, THE** (1916) 5 reels FA/TRI bw

Dorothy Gish *(Nan)*, Elmer Clifton *(Wilbur Howard)*, George Pierce *(Squire Tolliver)*, Jack Brammall *(Jim Tolliver)*, Howard Gaye *(Old Man Tyler)*, Josephine Crowell *(Widow Larkin)*, Luray Huntley *(Sally)*, Millard Webb *(Jebb)*, Hal Wilson *(Washington)*, George Stone *(Billy)*, Violet Radcliffe, Carmen De Rue, Francis Carpenter.

Gish almost makes up for this cornball plot about a country schoolteacher who becomes the target of gossip but wins in the end by marrying the successful writer, who came to the village to gather local color.

d, C. M. and S. A. Franklin; w, Frank R. Woods, Bernard McConville; w, Frank Good.

Drama **(PR:A MPAA:NR)**

LITTLE WILD GIRL, THE** (1928) 6 reels Hercules/Trinity bw

Lila Lee *(Marie Cleste)*, Cullen Landis *(Jules Barbier)*, Frank Merrill *(Tavish McBride)*, Sheldon Lewis *(Wanakee)*, Boris Karloff *(Maurice Kent)*, Jimmy Aubrey *(Posty McKnuffle)*, Bud Shaw *(Oliver Hampton)*, Arthur Hotaling *(Duncan Cleste)*, Cyclone *(Momo, the Dog)*.

Lee is discovered in the North Woods by a playwright and song writer, both of whom fall madly in love with her. They take her back to New York when it is believed her father and her fiance were killed in a forest fire (actually her lover survived but is crippled). Soon Lee becomes a big Broadway star, but hastily returns home when she is wrongly implicated in a murder. The townsfolk receive her coolly, but Lee could care less after she is reunited with her fiance, who luckily inherited a fortune and regained the use of his legs.

d, Frank S. Mattison; w, Cecil Burtis Hill (based on a story by Putnam Hoover); t, Gordon Kalem; ph, Jules Cronjager; ed, Minnie Steppler.

Drama **(PR:A MPAA:NR)**

LITTLE WILDCAT* (1922) 5 reels VIT bw

Alice Calhoun *(Mag o' the Alley)*, Ramsey Wallace *(Judge Arnold)*, Herbert Fortier *(Robert Ware)*, Oliver Hardy *("Bull" Mulligan)*, Adele Farrington *(Mrs. Wilding)*, Arthur Hoyt *(Mr. Wilding)*, Frank Crane *(Jack Wilding)*, James Farley *(Pete)*, Henry Herbert *(Capt. Carl Herman)*, Maud Emery *(Babette)*.

Fortier tries to prove a social theory to his friend, Wallace, by taking in a ragged vagrant girl (Calhoun) and turning her into a proper young lady. Years pass, and during the war Wallace meets and falls in love with a beautiful nurse. She turns out to be none other than Calhoun, and Fortier wins his bet—much to his friend's delight.

d, David Divad; w, Bradley J. Smollen (based on a story by Gene Wright); ph, Stephen Smith, Jr.

Drama **(PR:A MPAA:NR)**

LIVE WIRES** 1/2** (1921) 5 reels FOX bw

Johnnie Walker *(Bob Harding)*, Edna Murphy *(Rena Austin)*, Alberta Lee *(Mrs. Harding)*, Frank Clark *(James Harding)*, Bob Klein *(Slade)*, Hayward Mack *(James Flannery)*, Wilbur Higby *(Austin/Melody)*, Lefty James *(The Coach)*.

Typical big football game college stuff in which the star player (Walker) is forced to miss the game. But at least this one provided an off-beat twist to the last minute gridiron heroics, when the young hero makes the big play after an airplane picks him up from the roof of a speeding train and delivers him to the stadium.

d, Edward Sedgwick; w, Jack Strumwasser (based on a story by Charles E. Cook, Sedgwick); ph, Victor Milner.

Adventure **(PR:A MPAA:NR)**

LIVINGSTONE*** (1925, Brit.) 10 reels Hero/BUT bw (AKA: STANLEY)

M. A. Wetherell *(David Livingstone)*, Molly Rogers *(Mary Moffatt)*, Henry Walton *(H. M. Stanley)*, Reginald Fox *(Gordon Bennett)*, Douglas Cator *(Robert Moffatt)*, Sir Simeon Stuart *(Neil Livingstone)*, Blanche Graham *(Queen Victoria)*, Douglas Pierce *(David as a Child)*.

This handsomely mounted British biography of the famous Scottish explorer was given a new title (STANLEY) and reissued in 1933 with a soundtrack added and, of course, remade with Spencer Tracy by MGM in 1939.

d&w, M. A. Wetherell.

Biography/Adventure **(PR:A MPAA:NR)**

LOADED DOOR, THE*** (1922) 5 reels UNIV bw

Hoot Gibson *(Bert Lyons)*, Gertrude Olmstead *(Molly Grainger)*, Bill Ryno *(Bud Grainger)*, Eddie Sutherland *(Joe Grainger)*, Noble Johnson *(Blackie Lopez)*, Joseph Harris *(Stan Calvert)*, Charles Newton *(Dad Stewart)*, Charles A. Smiley *(Purdy)*, Victor Potel *(Slim)*, C. L. Sherwood *(Fatty)*.

Good Gibson oater about a cowpoke who returns home to find his former boss murdered and the spread in the hands of dope dealer Harris, whose henchman, Johnson, kidnaps Olmstead, his boss' daughter. Gibson, in an action-packed series of scenes, rescues the girl and clears her brother (played by future director Sutherland) of a crime he didn't commit.

d, Harry A. Pollard; w, George Hively (based on the story "Cherub of Seven Bar" by Ralph Cummins); ph, Sol Polito.

Western **(PR:A MPAA:NR)**

LODGE IN THE WILDERNESS, THE½** (1926) 6 reels TIF bw

Anita Stewart *(Virginia Coulson)*, Edmund Burns *(Jim Wallace)*, Duane Thompson *(Dot Marshall)*, Lawrence Steers *(John Hammond)*, Victor Potel *(Goofus, the Half-Wit)*, Eddie Lyons *(Buddy O'Brien)*, James Farley *(Bill Duncan)*.

Engineer Burns falls in love with Stewart, owner of the lumber camp and earns the hatred of Steers, the operation's superintendent. When Steers is murdered, Burns is blamed and sent to prison. He later escapes in time to save Stewart from a well-filmed forest fire and prove that the crime was actually committed by the local half-wit.

d, Henry McCarthy; w, Wyndham Gittens (based on the story by Gilbert Parker); ph, Jack MacKenzie.

Drama **(PR:A MPAA:NR)**

LODGER, THE*½**

(1926, Brit.) 8 reels Gainsborough/W&F bw (AKA: THE CASE OF JONATHAN DREW; THE LODGER: A STORY OF THE LONDON FOG)

Ivor Novello *(The Lodger/Jonathan Drew)*, June *(Daisy Bunting)*, Marie Ault *(Mrs. Bunting, Her Mother)*, Arthur Chesney *(Mr. Bunting)*, Malcolm Keen *(Joe Betts, the Policeman and Daisy's Fiance)*.

Novello plays a quiet, unassuming boarder at a lodging house. Slowly the evidence mounts up against him until the audience is led to believe he is Jack the Ripper. An angry mob sets out to get him, but at the last moment it is discovered that he is innocent. In fact, his sister was one of the killer's victims and Novello is pursuing him as well. THE LODGER was considered the first *true* Hitchcock film. Here, for the first time, was presented a theme he would use in many of his later movies: a man wrongly accused of a crime attempting to escape his pursuers. Reviewers called THE LODGER the best British film ever made. This was no doubt due in part to the technical effects Hitchcock had added; in one scene, the landlady can hear Novello's footsteps and the audience is shown what she is thinking as she pictures him above her. This was done by shooting through a glass floor, although it appeared to be a double-exposure on the screen. Also the use of suggestive shadows created by lighting haunted the film throughout.

p, Michael Balcon; d, Alfred Hitchcock; w, Hitchcock, Eliot Stannard (based on the novel by Mrs. Belloc-Lowndes); t, Ivor Montagu; ph, Baron [Giovanni] Ventigmilia; ed, Montagu; art d, C. Wilfred Arnold, Bertram Evans; set d, Islington.

Crime/Suspense **(PR:A MPAA:NR)**

LODGER: A STORY OF THE LONDON FOG, THE

(SEE: LODGER, THE, 1926, Brit.)

LOLA*** (1914) 5 reels Shubert/WORLD bw (AKA: WITHOUT A SOUL)

Clara Kimball Young *(Lola)*, Frank Holland, Alec B. Francis, James Young.

Fascinating Jekyll and Hyde-like story has Lola (sensually played by Young) as a virtuous and dedicated daughter who attends to her widowed father—a scientist who invented a machine capable of restoring life several hours after a person's death. Lola is killed in an accident, and her desperate father tries his creation for the first time on her. It works, but the person who returns is not the sweet little girl he once loved, but rather an immoral sex pot, who thinks only of carnal pleasures. She rejects her former sweetheart and embarks upon several (very erotically filmed for the time) love affairs. Later, when Lola is again near death's door, she pleads with her father, whom she has completely neglected, to give her a second dose of his "life" medicine—but the old man, seeing the result of his invention writhing before his very eyes, grabs a hammer and smashes his machine to pieces. Reissued in 1916 under the title WITHOUT A SOUL.

d&w, James Young (based on the play by Owen Davis).

Drama **(PR:A MPAA:NR)**

LONDON** (1926, Brit.) 6 reels BN/PAR bw

Dorothy Gish *(Mavis Hogan)*, Adelqui Millar *(Paul Merlan)*, John Manners *(Geoffrey Malvern)*, Hubert Carter *(Charles Down)*, Gibb McLaughlin *(Ah Kwang)*, Margaret Yarde *(Eliza Critten)*, Elissa Landi *(Alice Cranston)*, Daisy Campbell *(Lady Arbourfield)*, Paul Whiteman and His Orchestra.

Typically bland British production, despite Gish's presence and a script by Burke, who also wrote the 1919 classic BROKEN BLOSSOMS. It has to do with a lady who adopts a slum girl (Gish) because she resembles her dead daughter, after seeing her likeness in a portrait. The girl runs away from her society surroundings, however, when another young lady lays claim on the nephew to whom she is attracted. In the end, the artist who painted her portrait seeks her out, declares his love, and they marry. An interesting sidelight to this film shows Whiteman's large orchestra crammed onto the tiny bandstand of London's famous Kit Cat Club. It seems that that U.S. band leader caused quite a stir in Old Blighty at that time by complaining openly about his working conditions.

p, J. D. Williams; d, Herbert Wilcox; w, Thomas Burke.

Romantic/Drama **(PR:A MPAA:NR)**

LONDON AFTER MIDNIGHT***

(1927) 7 reels MGM bw (AKA: THE HYPNOTIST)

Lon Chaney *(Burke)*, Marceline Day *(Lucille Balfour)*, Henry B. Walthall *(Sir James Hamlin)*, Percy Williams *(Butler)*, Conrad Nagel *(Arthur Hibbs)*, Polly Moran *(Miss Smithson)*, Edna Tichenor *(Bat Girl)*, Claude King *(The Stranger)*, Jules Cowles *(Gallagher)*, Andy McLennan *(Scotland Yard Detective)*.

Unconvinced, after five years, of the "suicide" death of a London man, Chaney, a Scotland Yard inspector-detective, continues his investigation. After gathering the various suspects together, Chaney uses hypnosis on them and recreates the crime. This plot convention gives "The Man of a Thousand Faces" the opportunity to present his second most horrifying makeup (exceeded only by that of Erik in THE PHANTOM OF THE OPERA)—a sharp-toothed, eye-bulging, cape-wielding vampire. Chaney successfully uses the disguise to elicit a confession from the killer.

p&d, Tod Browning; w, Browning, Waldemar Young (based on a story by Browning); t, Joe Farnham; ph, Merritt B. Gerstad; ed, Harry Reynolds; set d, Cedric Gibbons, Arnold Gillespie; cos, Lucia Coulter.

Mystery **(PR:A MPAA:NR)**

LONDON PRIDE** (1920, Brit.) 6 reels LFP/JUR bw

Edna Flugrath *(Cherry)*, Fred Groves *(Cuthbert Tunks)*, O. B. Clarence *(Mr. Tunks)*, Mary Brough *(Mrs. Tunks)*, Constance Backner *(Maude Murphy)*, Frank Stanmore *(Mooney)*, Douglas Munro *(Garlic)*, Mary Dibley *(Mrs. Topleigh-Trevor)*, Edward Arundell *(Bill Guppy)*, Cyril Percival *(Menzies)*.

British comedy set during WW I, about a simple little cockney greengrocer who wins the Victoria Cross after bumbling his way through military life, and even faking amnesia.

d, Harold Shaw; w, Bannister Merwin (based on the play by Arthur Lyons, Gladys Unger).

Comedy/War **(PR:A MPAA:NR)**

LONDON'S ENEMIES*** (1916, Brit.) 5 reels Phoenix-Couragio/Phillips bw

Percy Moran *(Lt. Jack Moran)*, Marietta de Leyse *(Zareda)*, Lionel d'Aragon *(Butler)*.

This British war thriller was an all-Moran show in which he portrays a two-fisted Allied officer who saves his sister from the clutches of a gang of German spies and then, to give his picture a little punch, blows up a U-boat belonging to the Central Powers.

d, Percy Moran.

War **(PR:A MPAA:NR)**

LONE EAGLE, THE½** (1927) 6 reels UNIV-Jewel bw

Raymond Keane *(Lt. William Holmes)*, Barbara Kent *(Mimi)*, Nigel Barrie *(Capt. Richardson)*, Jack Pennick *(Sven Linder)*, Donald Stuart *(Red McGibbons)*, Cuyler Supplee *(Lebrun)*, Frank Camphill *(Desk Lieutenant)*, Marcella Daly *(Nannette)*, Eugen Pouyet *(Innkeeper)*, Wilson Benge *(Truckdriver)*, Brent Overstreet, Lt. Egbert Cook *(Aviators)*, Trixie the Dog.

Some of the more spectacular combat footage is used several times and the miniatures are not altogether convincing, but this movie about a U.S. aviator, assigned to the Royal Flying Corps, who overcomes his initial cowardice to finally down a great German Ace—and win the love of Kent, the pretty French girl—is still entertaining.

d, Emory Johnson; w, John Clymer, Emilie Johnson (based on a story by Howard Blanchard); t, Tom Reed; ph, Arthur Todd.

Drama **(PR:A MPAA:NR)**

LONE HAND, THE** (1920) 5 reels Alexander bw

Roy Stewart, Josie Sedgwick, Harry Van Meter, William Higby.

Decent western with versatile Stewart as a cowpuncher who is framed by a bandit using his deputy's job as cover. The sheriff's daughter, who loves Stewart, springs him from the pokey, and the cowboy eventually gets the goods on the outlaw.

d, Cliff Smith; w, (based on a story by Alvin J. Neitz).

Western **(PR:A MPAA:NR)**

LONE HORSEMAN, THE** (1929) 5 reels J. P. McGowan Syndicate Pictures bw

Tom Tyler *(Jack Gardiner)*, J. P. McGowan, Black Jack, Mrs. B. Tanzey, Charlotte Winn, Tom Bay, Mack V. Wright.

Tyler gets out of the hospital to discover that his ranch has been sold out from under him to a widow and her niece. Tyler finally establishes his identity, gets back his spread (on which gold has been discovered), nails the crooks, and marries the niece.

d, J. P. McGowan; w, (based on a story by Sally Winters); ph, Hap Depew.

Western **(PR:A MPAA:NR)**

LONE WAGON, THE* (1924) 5 reels Sanford bw

Matty Mattison, Vivian Rich, Lafayette McKee, Earl Metcalf, Gene Crosby.

The great success of THE COVERED WAGON inspired a number of imitations, but none as bad as this one about a Southern family's journey west, following the Civil War. The hero is a Spaniard, whom the family barely tolerates until he saves them from a series of Indian attacks, at which point they gladly offer him their daughter's hand in marriage.

d&w, Frank S. Mattison; ph, Elmer G. Dyer.

Western **(PR:A MPAA:NR)**

LONELY ROAD, THE* (1923) 6 reels PRE/AFN bw

Katherine MacDonald *(Betty Austin)*, Orville Caldwell *(Warren Wade)*, Kathleen Kirkham *(Leila Mead)*, Eugenie Besserer *(Martha True)*, William Conklin *(Dr. Devereaux)*, James Neill *(Uncle Billy Austin)*, Frank Leigh *(Stewart Bartley)*, Charles French *(Hiram Wade)*, Stanley Goethals *(The Wade's Son)*.

Caldwell becomes a domineering bore after marrying MacDonald, so she visits her friend in the city and meets a charming doctor (Conklin). Deciding to give her husband another chance, MacDonald returns home and shortly thereafter their little boy is injured. Conklin cures the child, Caldwell becomes aware of his chauvinism and vows to change, and for the first time there is true happiness in their home.

d, Victor Schertzinger; w, Lois Zellner (based on a story by Charles Logue); ph, Joseph Brotherton; ed, Eve Unsell.

Drama **(PR:A MPAA:NR)**

LONG CHANCE, THE*** (1922) 5 reels UNIV bw

Henry B. Walthall *(Harley P. Hennage)*, Marjorie Daw *(Kate Corbaly/Dana Corbaly)*, Ralph Graves *(Bob McGraw)*, Jack Curtis *("Borax" O'Rourke)*, Leonard Clapham *(John Corbaly)*, Boyd Irwin *("Boston"/T. Morgan Carey)*, William Bertram *(Sam Singer)*, Grace Marvin *(Soft Wind)*, George A. Williams *(Dr. Taylor)*.

Good direction by Conway and a grand performance by Walthall make this programmer about a western gambler who takes in an orphaned girl and later saves the land her father left her from a ruthless capitalist, solid entertainment.

d, Jack Conway; w, Raymond Schrock (based on the novel by Peter Bernard Kyne); ph, Benjamin Reynolds.

Drama/Western **(PR:A MPAA:NR)**

LONG LIVE THE KING*** (1923) 10 reels Metro bw

Jackie Coogan *(Crown Prince Otto)*, Rosemary Theby *(Countess Olga)*, Ruth Renick *(Princess Hedwig)*, Vera Lewis *(Archduchess Annunciata)*, Alan Hale *(King Karl)*, Allan Forrest *(Nikky)*, Walt Whitman *(The Chancellor)*, Robert Brower *(The King)*, Raymond Lee *(Bobby, the American Boy)*, Monte Collins *(Adelbert)*, Sam Appel *(Black Humbert)*, Allan Sears *(Bobby's Father)*, Ruth Handforth *(Mrs. Braithwaite)*, Larry Fisher *(Herman Spier)*, Eddie Boland *(Chief Guard)*, Loretta McDermott *(Countess Olga's Maid)*, Henry Barrows *(The Bishop)*.

Coogan is in great form as Prince Otto, heir to the throne of Livonia, who wants only to be a normal boy. He runs away with an American youngster (played by future film author Lee) and for a while enjoys the pleasures of childhood. When the king dies, Coogan finally makes it back to the palace—with the swashbuckling aid of his protector, Forrest—after being abducted by conspirators, in time to quell a rebellion.

d, Victor Schertzinger; w, C. Gardner Sullivan, Eve Unsell (based on the novel by Mary Roberts Rinehart); ph, Frank B. Good.

Adventure **(PR:A MPAA:NR)**

LONG ODDS** (1922, Brit.) 6 reels STOLL bw

A. E. Coleby *(Gus Granville)*, Edith Bishop *(Sally Walters)*, Sam Marsh *(Jim Straker)*, Fred Paul *(Hastings Floyd)*, Sam Austin *(Tony Walters)*, H. Nicholls-Bates *(Sam Marshall)*, Frank Wilson *(Ned Boutler)*, Madge Royce *(Mrs. Granville)*, Harry Marsh *(Pat Malone)*.

British potboiler about a jockey who gets out of bed to win the big race after the original rider is thrown and injured.

d&w, A. E. Coleby.

Adventure **(PR:A MPAA:NR)**

LONG PANTS*** (1927) 6 reels Harry Langdon/FN bw

Harry Langdon *(The Boy)*, Gladys Brockwell *(His Mother)*, Alan Roscoe *(His Father)*, Alma Bennett *(The Vamp)*, Frankie Darro *(Harry, as a Small Boy)*, Priscilla Bonner *(Priscilla)*.

Langdon's last film with director Capra led to a bitter and vindictive parting of the ways. The director would, of course, go on to greatness, while the cherubic little comic (who rivaled Chaplin and Lloyd in popularity) would stumble into oblivion. The movie, about a boy coming of age when he falls for a vamp from the city but marries the "right" girl in the end, was full of wonderful gags, and still remains a unique and satisfying cinematic experience.

d, Frank Capra; w, Robert Eddy (based on a story by Arthur Ripley); ph, Elgin Lessley, Glenn Kershner.

Comedy **(PR:A MPAA:NR)**

LOOKING FOR TROUBLE** (1926) 5 reels BS/UNIV bw

Jack Hoxie *(Jack William Pepper)*, Marceline Day *(Tulip Hellier)*, J. Gordon Russell *(Jasper Murchison)*, Clark Comstock *(Jim Hellier)*, Edmund Cobb *(Phil Curtis)*, Bud Osborne *(Lou Burkhold)*, Peggy Montgomery *(Laura Burkhold)*, William Dyer *(Sheriff Tom Plump)*, Scout the Horse.

Routine stuff, except that there is less action than in the usual Hoxie western. In this one the popular cowboy breaks up a diamond-smuggling ring and wins the pretty girl.

d, Robert North Bradbury; w, George C. Hively (based on a story by Steven Chalmers); ph, William Nobles, Harry Mason.

Western **(PR:A MPAA:NR)**

LORD JIM*** (1925) 7 reels FP/PAR bw

Percy Marmont *(Lord Jim)*, Shirley Mason *(Jewel)*, Noah Beery *(Capt. Brown)*, Raymond Hatton *(Cornelius)*, Joseph Dowling *(Stein)*, George Magrill *(Dain Waris)*, Nick De Ruiz *(Sultan)*, J. Gunnis Davis *(Scoggins)*, Jules Cowles *(Yankee Joe)*, Duke Kahanamoku *(Tamb Itam)*.

Director Fleming did fairly well by the Conrad novel about the first mate (Marmont) who deserts his ship after an accident and ends up on the island of Patusan, where he makes a new life for himself, until his former shipmates show up, leading to his ultimate execution.

d, Victor Fleming; w, George C. Hull, John Russell (based on the novel by Joseph Conrad); ph, Faxon Dean.

Drama **(PR:A MPAA:NR)**

LORD LOVES THE IRISH, THE*** (1919) 5 reels Brunton/Hodkinson bw

J. Warren Kerrigan *(Miles Machree)*, Aggie Herring *(Mother Machree)*, Fritzi Brunette *(Sheila Lynch)*, James O. Barrows *(Timothy Lynch)*, William Ellingford *(Malachi Nolan)*, Wedgewood Nowell *(Allyn Dexter)*, Joseph J. Dowling *(Hugo Strauss)*.

At his uncle's behest, young Kerrigan prepares to depart the old sod for the New World, but before leaving he meets Brunette, an Irish-American lass, who treats him like an underripe spud. Kerrigan makes the voyage, during which he saves Brunette from a disastrous alliance. She sees the laughter in his eyes, listens to the lilt in his voice, and becomes more than willing to have her shamrock laddie after the vows are read by the priest.

d, Ernest C. Warde; w, (based on a story by Monte M. Katterjohn); ph, Arthur Todd.

Comedy/Adventure **(PR:A MPAA:NR)**

LORNA DOONE*** (1927) 7 reels THI/AFN bw

Madge Bellamy *(Lorna Doone)*, John Bowers *(John Ridd)*, Frank Keenan *(Sir Charles Ensor)*, Jack McDonald *("The Counsellor")*, Donald MacDonald *(Carver Doone)*, Norris Johnson *(Ruth)*, May Giraci *(Lorna, as a Child)*, Charles Hatton *(John, as a Child)*.

Tourneur's screen adaptation of this classic romance has the look of an oil painting from that period. And the telling of the tale about the aristocratic girl (Bellamy), captured and raised by bandits, who is later rescued and loved by the dashing John Ridd (Bowers), is good entertainment.

p&d, Maurice Tourneur; w, Katherine Reed, Cecil G. Mumford, Wyndham Gittens, Tourneur (based on the novel by Richard Doddridge Blackmore); ph, Henry Sharp; set d & cos, Milton Menasco.

Costume **Cas.** **(PR:A MPAA:NR)**

LOSER'S END, THE** 1/2 (1924) 5 reels William Steiner bw

Leo Maloney *(Bruce Mason)*, Roy Watson *(Capt. Harris)*, Tom London *(Barney Morris)*, Whitehorse *(John Kincaid)*, Josephine Hill *(Lois Kincaid)*, Bud Osborne *(Lucky Hamish)*, Barney Furey *(Simmie Busch)*, Wong Ti Set *(Cook)*, Bullet the Dog.

This Maloney cowboy programmer, in which the fast-riding, hard-fighting hero captures a dope smuggler and wins the pretty girl, accomplished exactly what it set out to do—entertain.

w, (based on a story by Ford Beebe); ph, Jacob A. Badaracco.

Western **(PR:A MPAA:NR)**

LOST BRIDEGROOM, THE* (1916) 5 reels FP bw

John Barrymore, Katherine Harris, Ida Darling, Jane Dale, Hardee Kirkland, Edward Sturgis, Jack Dillon, Tammany Young, William Sherwood.

Even the great Barrymore's presence couldn't help this stinker about a wealthy young man who loses his memory when some crooks hit him over the head the night before his wedding. The young man then becomes a thief himself, but regains his memory when his mob robs the home of his fiancee.

d, James Kirkwood; w, Willard Mack.

Drama **(PR:A MPAA:NR)**

LOST CHORD, THE* (1917, Brit.) 5 reels CL bw

Barbara Conrad *(Madeleine)*, Malcolm Keen *(David)*, Concordia Merrill *(Joan)*, Dorothy Bellew, Mary Ford, Manning Haynes.

Typical heavy-handed British nonsense about a musician falling in love with a married woman who responds by entering a convent. But, being a real glutton for punishment, the poor fool later turns around and falls in love with her daughter.

d, Wilfred Noy; w, Reuben Gillmer

Drama **(PR:A MPAA:NR)**

LOST LADY, A** (1924) 7 reels WB bw

Irene Rich *(Marian Forrester)*, Matt Moore *(Neil Herbert)*, June Marlowe *(Constance Ogden)*, John Roche *(Frank Ellinger)*, Victor Potel *(Ivy Peters)*, George Fawcett *(Capt. Forrester)*, Eva Gordon *(Bohemian Mary)*, Nanette Valone *(Gypsy Dancer)*.

Rich excels as a beautiful woman who makes her way through a number of men and always manages to marry the older, wealthy ones. Aside from Rich, the continuity is flawed, but the production good.

d, Harry Beaumont; w, Dorothy Farnum (based on the novel by Willa Cather); ph, David Abel.

Drama **(PR:A MPAA:NR)**

LOST LIMITED, THE* (1927) 6 reels Harry J. Brown/RAY bw

Reed Howes *(Leonard Hathaway)*, Ruth Dwyer *(Nora Murphy)*, Henry Barrows *(Silas Brownley)*, Billy Franey *(Rambling Red)*, J. P. McGowan *(Thomas Webber)*, George French, Dot Farley.

Director McGowan used stock footage of a train collision (apparently taken at a state fair) to give this movie, about a young man's attempt to win an ore-hauling contract, the only production value it had.

d, J. P. McGowan; w, Henry R. Symonds; ph, Walter Griffen.

Drama **(PR:A MPAA:NR)**

LOST PATROL, THE** (1929, Brit.) 8 reels BI/FOX bw

Cyril McLaglen *(The Sergeant)*, Sam Wilkinson *(Sanders)*, Terence Collier *(Cpl. Bell)*, Hamilton Keene *(Morelli)*, Fred Dyer *(Abelson)*, Charles Emerald *(Hale)*, Andrew McMaster *(Brown)*, James Watts *(Cook)*, John Valentine *(Mackay)*, Frederick Long *(Pearson)*.

Only fair original British filming of the story about an English patrol pinned down in a desert oasis by Arab snipers. Interestingly, the role of the sergeant was played by McLaglen, whose Hollywood actor-brother Victor McLaglen would play the same part in the much superior John Ford 1934 remake.

p, H. Bruce Woolfe; d&w, Walter Summers (based on the novel *Patrol* by Phillip Macdonald).

War **(PR:A MPAA:NR)**

LOST WORLD, THE*½** (1925) 10 reels FN bw

Bessie Love *(Paula White)*, Lloyd Hughes *(Edward J. Malone)*, Lewis Stone *(Sir John Roxton)*, Wallace Beery *(Prof. Challenger)*, Arthur Hoyt *(Prof. Summerlee)*, Margaret McWade *(Mrs. Challenger)*, Finch Smiles *(Austin, Challenger's Butler)*, Jules Cowles *(Zambo, Roxton's Servant)*, Bull Montana *(Apeman)*, George Bunny *(Colin McArdle)*, Charles Wellesley *(Maj. Hibbard)*, Alma Bennett *(Gladys Hungerford)*, Virginia Browne Faire *(Half-Caste Girl)*, Nelson MacDowell *(Attorney)*.

A film which stunned and amazed audiences in 1925, THE LOST WORLD was the first feature length film to indulge in a staggering symphony of special effects while telling an engrossing adventure story. After years of making short fantasy films, stop-motion animation genius Willis O'Brien was finally given the budget and facilities to create a state-of-the-art adventure film based on a novel by Doyle. The film opens in London, where a young reporter, Hughes, proposes to his sweetheart, Bennett. She coolly informs her suitor that she cannot possibly marry him until he has done something heroic and extraordinary. Determined to win her hand, Hughes joins an expedition into the Amazon led by Prof. Beery. The explorers intend to search for Love's father, a fellow scientist who was lost while trying to locate a legendary plateau where dinosaurs still exist. While hacking their way through the dense foliage, Hughes and Love grow fond of each other and the reporter begins to forget his fiancee back in London. Eventually the searchers reach the fabled plateaus and are greeted by a pterodactyl, a giant flying lizard that should have died out millions of years ago. The tiny group of explorers climb to the top of the plateau and cut down a tree to use as a bridge over a chasm. During this exercise an ape man (Montana) watches the explorers. The next prehistoric beast the group encounters is a huge brontosaurus, which pounds its way past them. The giant creature knocks the log bridge into the chasm below, stranding the explorers in this strange land. As they push on, the party sees dozens of other monsters, including several vicious meat-eating allosaurs, which kill and feed off other less fortunate beasts. When the brontosaurus is attacked by an allosaur, the huge beast tries to escape and falls off the plateau into the muck below. In a cave, the explorers find the skeletal remains of Love's father. Suddenly, there is a massive volcanic eruption which sends all species of dinosaur on a wild stampede to escape the lava. The search party uses a rope to climb down off the plateau, but the ape man reappears and tries to foil their escape. Forced to shoot the beast, the explorers manage to leave the prehistoric land in the nick of time. Below the plateau, they find the brontosaurus still alive and unharmed, but stuck in the mud. Beery becomes determined to bring the creature back to London alive. He does just that, but as the giant dinosaur is being unloaded, its cage is damaged and it manages to escape. The confused beast roams through the London streets destroying everything in its path. When it wanders onto the London Bridge, its massive weight collapses the structure and it swims off out to sea down the Thames. Meanwhile, Hughes has learned that his fiancee, Bennett, has married another, allowing him to court his new sweetheart, Love. It is difficult to describe the impact THE LOST WORLD had on audiences in 1925. Nothing like it had ever been seen before—not just on the movie screen, but anywhere. The effects were accomplished by animating 18-inch model dinosaurs constructed by O'Brien's assistant, Marcel Delgado. These models were placed within detailed miniature jungles and then moved only a fraction of an inch per film exposure. When the film was developed and projected, the models appeared to be alive. In 1922, when O'Brien was embroiled in shooting test footage of the dinosaurs, he sent a finished reel to author Doyle. Doyle was amazed at the footage and used it to stun a meeting of the Society of American Magicians in New York. The film showing made the front page of the *New York Times* the next morning with the reporter unsure as to whether or not the monsters he saw were real. Sensing that speculation was starting to snowball, Doyle explained the true nature of the film to Harry Houdini, who was the president of the Society of American Magicians, and to the newspapers. In 1924, after finally getting major studio backing from First National, THE LOST WORLD went into full-time production. After a year of shooting and special effects work at a staggering cost of $1 million, the film was released road-show style to amazed audiences. Though the human drama suffers from slow pacing and silly romantic subplots, the adventure footage all but makes up for it. O'Brien's monsters were a big hit in Hollywood and in the next few years several new projects were announced, including *Creation* for RKO. *Creation* and all of the other projects never came to fruition, but O'Brien's work for RKO led to the deal that would allow him to make his monumental masterpiece in 1933, KING KONG.

d, Harry O. Hoyt, William Dowling; sup, Earl Hudson; w, Marion Fairfax (based on the novel by Sir Arthur Conan Doyle); ph, Arthur Edeson; ed, George McGuire; set d, Milton Menasco; spec. eff, Willis H. O'Brien.

Adventure/Fantasy **Cas.** **(PR:A MPAA:NR)**

LOUISIANA* (1919) 5 reels PAR bw

Vivian Martin *(Louisiana Rogers)*, Robert Ellis *(Laurence Ferol)*, Noah Beery *(Lem Rogers)*, Arthur Allardt *(Cass Floyd)*, Lillian West *(Olivia Ferol)*, Lillian Leighton *(Aunt Casandry)*.

Martin rises above the banality of this script about a mountain girl who turns down her boy friend (who is really a rat anyway) in favor of the wealthy city playwright who came to the country to gather local color.

d, Robert G. Vignola; w, Alice Eyton (based on the novel by Frances Hodgson Burnett); ph, Frank E. Garbutt.

Drama **(PR:A MPAA:NR)**

LOVE** (1916, Brit.) 4 reels Eve Balfour/JTR bw (AKA: EVE'S DAUGHTER)

Eve Balfour *(Veronica Leigh)*, Frank Tennant *(Hubert Price)*, Agnes de Winton *(Lil Trancing)*, Arthur M. Cullin *(Roger Hoskin)*, Dora de Winton *(La Belle Lola)*, J. Hastings Batson.

In this British drama a man jumps in front of the bullet fired by an ex-mistress to save the life of his former wife, who has happily remarried.

d, L. C. MacBean; w, Rowland Talbot (based on the novel *When Love Dies* by Rathmell Wilson).

Drama **(PR:A MPAA:NR)**

LOVE** (1927) 8 reels MGM bw

Greta Garbo *(Anna Karenina)*, John Gilbert *(Vronsky)*, George Fawcett *(Grand Duke)*, Emily Fitzroy *(Grand Duchess)*, Brandon Hurst *(Karenin)*, Philippe De Lacy *(Serezha, the Child)*.

In order to follow the tremendous success of FLESH AND THE DEVIL (1926), Irving Thalberg teamed Garbo and Gilbert once again, after selecting what he thought to be a suitable script. The "Boy Wonder" had chosen the novel *Anna Karenina* without having read it and was horrified to discover that Tolstoy ended his work by having Anna throw herself under a train. This, of course, would never do, so MGM changed the title and the conclusion and, after suitable punishment for her affair, Garbo was permitted to become a widow, marry the dashing Gilbert, and spend the rest of her days in LOVE. Garbo denied MGM publicity which linked her romantically to Gilbert during the making of LOVE, but everyone on the set knew he was infatuated with the star and spent every offscreen moment in her dressing room. The actor's inability to adapt to sound films during the next several years turned him to heavy drinking, which may have led to his early death, less than 10 years later, at the age of 41.

p&d, Edmund Goulding; w, Frances Marion, Lorna Moon (based on the novel *Anna Karenina* by Leo Nikolayevich Tolstoy); t, Marian Ainslee, Ruth Cummings; ph, William Daniels; m, Ernst Luz; ed, Hugh Wynn; set d, Cedric Gibbons, Alexander Toluboff; m/l, "That Melody of Love," Howard Dietz, Walter Donaldson; syn sc.

Drama **PR:C MPAA:NR)**

LOVE AFLAME*** (1917) 5 reels Red Feather bw

Ruth Stonehouse *(Betty Mason)*, Jack Mulhall *(Jack Calvert)*, Jean Hersholt *(Reginald)*, Nita White *(Martha)*, Raymond Whittaker *(Mason)*, Fronzie Gunn *(King's Favorite)*, Noble Johnson *(Cannibal King)*, Dana Ong.

Mulhall is a young fellow making his way to Constantinople without a penny in his pocket to win a bet, and Stonehouse is a girl dressed in men's clothes, running away from a forced marriage. They meet, and the adventures they share before Mulhall discovers Stonehouse's gender and the feelings he has for her, make for a good little comedy.

d, Raymond Wells; w, Fred Myton (based on a story by Wells).

Comedy **(PR:A MPAA:NR)**

LOVE AND LEARN½** (1928) 6 reels PAR bw

Esther Ralston *(Nancy Blair)*, Lane Chandler *(Anthony Cowles)*, Hedda Hopper *(Mrs. Ann Blair)*, Claude King *(Robert Blair)*, Jack J. Clark *(Hansen)*, Jack Trent

(Jim Riley), Hal Craig *(Sgt. Flynn)*, Helen Lynch *(Rosie)*, Catherine Parrish *(Jail Matron)*, Martha Franklin *(Martha)*, Jerry Mandy *(Gardener)*, Dorothea Wolbert *(Maid)*, Johnny Morris *(Bum)*, Guy Oliver *(Detective)*.

Ralston is quite fetching in her scanties, as she places her reputation in jeopardy to save that of a political candidate the opposition is trying to frame by placing in a compromising position with a woman. Lots of bedroom laughs, which are so well-handled by director Tuttle that they never offend.

d, Frank Tuttle; w, Louise Long, Florence Ryerson (based on a story by Doris Anderson); t, Herman J. Mankiewicz; ph, Harry Fischbeck; ed, Verna Willis.

Comedy **(PR:A MPAA:NR)**

LOVE AND SACRIFICE (SEE: AMERICA, 1924)

LOVE AT THE WHEEL* (1921, Brit.) 6 reels Master/BUT bw

Victor Humfries *(Eric Gordon)*, Pauline Johnson *(Ruth Emerson)*, Leslie Steward *(Ned Wright)*, Annette Benson *(Helen Warwick)*, Arthur Claremont *(Enoch Emerson)*, Clare Greet *(Martha)*, A. Harding Steerman *(John Gordon)*, May Price *(Mrs. Gordon)*.

Pale British imitation of what had long been a cliched Hollywood formula for program films—that of a wrongly fired mechanic who builds his own car and wins the big race.

p, H. B. Parkinson; d, Bannister Merwin; w, Frank Miller.

Adventure **(PR:A MPAA:NR)**

LOVE AUCTION, THE* (1919) 5 reels FOX bw

Virginia Pearson *(Mrs. Vanderveer)*, Elizabeth Garrison *(Mrs. Sebastian)*, Gladys MacClure *(Jean Dale)*, Hugh Thompson *(Dorian Vanderveer)*, Edwin Stanley *(Jack Harley)*, Thurlow Bergen *(Dr. Charters)*, Charles Mason *(Mr. Sebastian)*.

Typical, though poorly produced, society tearjerker about a poor girl who marries a drunken millionaire to escape her misery, but instead finds complete unhappiness when he turns out to be a brute.

d, Edmund Lawrence; w, Julia Burnham, Lawrence (based on a story by May Edginton); ph, Al Leach.

Drama **(PR:A MPAA:NR)**

LOVE CHARM, THE ½** (1921) 5 reels REA/PAR bw

Wanda Hawley *(Ruth Sheldon)*, Mae Busch *(Hattie Nast)*, Sylvia Ashton *(Julia Nast)*, Warner Baxter *(Thomas Morgan)*, Carrie Clark Ward *(Housekeeper)*, Molly McGowan *(Maybelle Mooney)*.

Average-but-pleasing retelling of the Cinderella story has an orphaned girl (Hawley) going to live with her aunt and cousin and finding herself being treated like a slave. But, in the end, it is Hawley who wins the handsome Baxter, rather than her nasty cousin Busch.

d, Thomas N. Heffron; w, Percy Heath (based on a story by Harvey J. O'Higgins); ph, William E. Collins.

Dramatic Comedy **(PR:A MPAA:NR)**

LOVE FLOWER, THE ½** (1920) 7 reels UA bw

Carol Dempster *(Stella Bevan)*, Richard Barthelmess *(Jerry Trevethon)*, George MacQuarrie *(Thomas Bevan)*, Anders Randolf *(Matthew Crane)*, Florence Short *(Mrs. Bevan)*, Crauford Kent *(Mrs. Bevan's Paramour)*, Adolphe Lestina *(Bevan's Servant)*, William James, Jack Manning *(Crane's Assistants)*.

This melodrama about a man who kills the paramour of his second wife and then escapes with his daughter to a distant tropical island, is certainly below the Griffith standard, but it does maintain a certain interest and charm. There's a detective right out of *Les Miserables* who vows to follow the old boy to the end of the earth, and does catch up with him, thanks to a young adventurer (played nicely by Barthelmess) who, while tracing the footsteps of Robert Louis Stevenson, brings him to the island in his boat. Later, when the policeman and his prey engage in a beautifully filmed underwater struggle, the old man is believed killed, and the detective returns home, leaving the young couple to find happiness in each other's arms, and the father peace and serenity. (See THE IDOL DANCER.)

d&w, D. W. Griffith (based on the story "The Black Beach" by Ralph Stock); ph, Billy Bitzer; ed, James Smith.

Drama **(PR:A MPAA:NR)**

LOVE GAMBLER, THE*** (1922) 5 reels FOX bw

John Gilbert *(Dick Manners)*, Carmel Myers *(Jean McClelland)*, Bruce Gordon *(Joe McClelland)*, Cap Anderson *(Curt Evans)*, William Lawrence *(Tom Gould)*, James Gordon *(Col. Angus McClelland)*, Mrs. Cohen *(Mrs. McClelland)*, Barbara Tennant *(Kate)*, Edward Cecil *(Cameo Colby)*, Doreen Turner *(Ricardo, Kate's Child)*.

This 1922 update on a *Taming of the Shrew* theme has ranch hand Gilbert betting a pal that he can tame a wild horse and kiss the pretty daughter of his boss by whistling a certain tune. He accomplishes both.

d, Joseph Franz; w, Jules Furthman (based on the story "Where the Heart Lies" by Lillian Bennett-Thompson, George Hubbard); ph, Joe August.

Western/Drama **(PR:A MPAA:NR)**

LOVE GIRL, THE*** (1916) 5 reels BLUE bw

Ella Hall *(Ambrosia)*, Adele Farrington *(Her Aunt)*, Betty Schade *(Her Cousin)*, Harry Depp *(The Boy Next Door)*, Grace Marvin *(The Maid)*, Wadsworth Harris *(Swami)*, Kingsley Benedict.

Enjoyable programmer about an orphaned country girl who is sent to the city to live with her wealthy aunt and young cousin. At first the child is treated with cold indifference, but when she rescues her cousin from kidnapers, she is given all the love a little girl needs. Good performance by adorable Hall.

d&w, Robert Z. Leonard.

Drama/Comedy **(PR:A MPAA:NR)**

LOVE, HONOR AND OBEY* (1920) 5 reels Lubin/Metro bw

Wilda Bennett *(Conscience Williams)*, Claire Whitney *(Marion Holbury)*, Henry Harmon *(William Williams)*, Kenneth Harlan *(Stuart Emmett)*, George Cowl *(Eben Tollman)*, E. J. Radcliffe *(Jack Holbury)*.

The Buck novel on which this film was based sold more than 200,000 copies. The book—dealing with a Puritan's daughter who loves an author whose sexual views her father disapproves of, and is forced to marry an older, more acceptable man, only to eventually end up with the writer—was nothing to rave about, and the movie was not a whole lot better.

d, Leander de Cordova; w, Eugene Walter (based on the novel *The Tyranny of Weakness* by Charles Neville Buck); ph, Arthur Martinelli.

Drama **(PR:A MPAA:NR)**

LOVE IN A HURRY** (1919) 5 reels WORLD bw (AKA: ALLIES)

Carlyle Blackwell *(Charles Conant)*, Evelyn Greeley *(Lady Joan Templer)*, Isabel O'Madigan *(Lady Dartridge)*, George MacQuarrie *(George Templer)*, William Betchel *(John Murr)*, Kid Broad *(Shorty)*, Dick Collins *(Captain)*, Louis Grisel *(Gardner)*, Mr. Barrington, Mr. Dewey *(Secret Service Men)*, Albert Hart.

Blackwell takes a job on a ship, delivering horses to France, when his wealthy father threatens to cut him off after an argument. He jumps ship in England to visit his titled relatives and is taken for a German spy. Blackwell experiences a number of adventures, along with the beautiful Greeley, as he is, in reality, an agent for the U.S. Secret Service. Then, after doing his bit for the war cause, the two of them return to the U.S. as man and wife.

d, Dell Henderson; w, Wallace C. Clifton (based on the story "A Huge, Black, One-Eyed Man" by Kenyon Gambier [Lorin Andrews Lathrop]); ph, Lucien Tainguy.

Drama/Comedy **(PR:A MPAA:NR)**

LOVE IN A WOOD** (1915, Brit.) 5 reels London-Diploma/JUR bw

Elizabeth Risdon *(Rosiland)*, Gerald Ames *(Orlando)*, Vera Cunningham *(Celia)*, Frank Stanmore *(Touchstone)*, Kenelm Foss *(Oliver)*, Cyril Percival, Dolly Tree.

This British film, based on the Shakespearean play "As You Like It," was primarily of interest because it was done in modern dress.

d, Maurice Elvey; w, Kenelm Foss (based on the play "As You Like It" by William Shakespeare).

Comedy **(PR:A MPAA:NR)**

LOVE IS AN AWFUL THING*** (1922) 7 reels Owen Moore/Selznick bw

Owen Moore *(Anthony Churchill)*, Thomas Guise *(Judge Griggs)*, Marjorie Daw *(Helen Griggs)*, Kathryn Perry *(Ruth Allen)*, Arthur Hoyt *(Harold Wright)*, Douglas Carter *(Porter)*, Charlotte Mineau *(Marion)*, Snitz Edwards *(Superintendent)*, Alice Howell *(His Wife)*.

Good little farce has the old girl friend showing up just before Moore's wedding to Daw and threatening to sue for breach of promise. Moore claims to already be wed, and a number of solid laughs develop from this situation.

d&w, Victor Heerman; ph, Jules Cronjager.

Comedy **(PR:A MPAA:NR)**

LOVE LETTER, THE* (1923) 5 reels UNIV bw

Gladys Walton *(Mary Ann McKee)*, Fontaine La Rue *(Kate Smith)*, George Cooper *(Red Mike)*, Edward Hearne *(Bill Carter)*, Walt Whitman *(Rev. Halloway)*, Lucy Donohue *(Mrs. Carter)*, Alberta Lee *(Mrs. Halloway)*.

Walton works in a factory that manufactures overalls. As a lark, she slips lonely heart notes into some of them before they are shipped. Her boy friend, Cooper, involves her in a robbery, and she runs away to a town where a respondent to one of her dispatches lives. Later, Cooper locates Walton and goes to retrieve her, but when he sees how happy she and her husband are with their child, he changes his mind and lets them be.

d, King Baggot; w, Hugh Hoffman (based on a story by Bradley King); ph, Victor Milner.

Drama **(PR:A MPAA:NR)**

LOVE LIAR, THE** (1916) 5 reels Centaur bw

Crane Wilbur *(David McCare)*, Fred Goodwins, Lucy Payton, Mae Gaston, Nan Christy, Ella Golden, Gale Landon.

Wilbur plays a man the women love, and he goes through more than his share of them. He marries a pretty society girl, but she willingly gives him up when he becomes bored. Finally, Wilbur falls for a cabaret tramp who treats him as he treated others, and the picture ends with him shooting himself to death in a crowded restaurant.

d&w, Crane Wilbur.

Drama **(PR:A MPAA:NR)**

LOVE LIGHT, THE*** (1921) 8 reels Mary Pickford/UA bw

Mary Pickford *(Angela)*, Evelyn Dumo *(Maria)*, Fred Thomson *(Joseph)*, Edward Phillips *(Mario)*, Albert Prisco *(Pietro)*, Raymond Bloomer *(Giovanni)*, George Rigas *(Tony)*, Jean De Briac *(Antonio)*.

Audiences were disappointed in this "grown up" Pickford picture in which she plays a girl who tends a lighthouse in Italy while her brothers serve at the front. A German spy is washed ashore claiming to be a U.S. seaman, and the two fall in love, marry, and eventually Pickford becomes pregnant. After she helps the German escape and realizes he may have been responsible for the death of her brother, Pickford goes into shock. Later her husband dies, and she has a child which she gladly gives to Dumo, who recently lost her own baby. Then Pickford's former sweetheart, Bloomer, returns, blinded in the war. Dumo is killed in a storm, but Pickford manages to save the child, and the three find happiness and peace after all. WW I not only served as the backdrop for this picture, but was also responsible for bringing together three of the film's principals: Pickford and screenwriter-director Marion were visiting a wartime hospital and encountered then-chaplain Thomson, who was recovering from a broken leg. After the war Thomson and Marion dated and married in 1919. Leaving the cloth, he embarked on an acting career that began, interestingly enough, with THE LOVE LIGHT.

d&w, Frances Marion; ph, Charles Rosher, Henry Cronjager; art d, Stephen Goosson.

Drama **(PR:A MPAA:NR)**

LOVE MAKES 'EM WILD*** (1927) 6 reels FOX bw

Johnny Harron *(Willie Angle)*, Sally Phipps *(Mary O'Shane)*, Ben Bard *(Blankenship)*, Arthur Housman *(Charlie Austin)*, J. Farrell MacDonald *(W. Barden)*, Natalie Kingston *(Mamie)*, Albert Gran *(Green)*, Florence Gilbert *(Lulu)*, Earle Mohan *(Sam)*, Coy Watson, Jr. *(Jimmy)*, Noah Young *(Janitor)*, William B. Davidson *(Mamie's Ex-husband)*.

Harron (younger brother of the great Griffith star, Robert Harron) gives one of his best performances as a pantywaist who gets even with everyone who ever dumped on him when a doctor informs him that he only has six months to live. Of course, the diagnosis was wrong, and the bravery he exhibited wins him the heart of the beautiful girl he has always secretly worshiped.

d, Albert Ray; w, Harold Shumate (based on the story "Willie the Worm" by Florence Ryerson); ph, Chester Lyons.

Comedy **(PR:A MPAA:NR)**

LOVE ME AND THE WORLD IS MINE** (1928) 6 reels UNIV-Jewel bw

Mary Philbin *(Hannerl)*, Norman Kerry *(Von Vigilatti)*, Betty Compson *(Mitzel)*, Henry B. Walthall *(Van Denbosch)*, Mathilde Brundage *(Mrs. Van Denbosch)*, Charles Sellon *(Mr. Thule)*, Martha Mattox *(Mrs. Thule)*, George Siegmann *(Porter)*, Robert Anderson *(Orderly)*, Albert Conti *(Billie)*, Emily Fitzroy *(The Porter's Wife)*, Charles Puffy *(Coachman)*.

Philbin plays an Austrian girl who nearly marries a middle-aged man (Walthall) because she believes her true love, Kerry, has been unfaithful. She realizes her mistake at the altar and rushes to Kerry as he is leaving for the front. This was Dupont's first U.S. film and was pretty much of a disappointment after the German director's masterpiece, VARIETY.

d, E. A. Dupont; w, Paul Kohner, Edward Sloman, Edward J. Montagne, Dupont, Imre Fazekas (based on the novel *Die Geschichte von der Hannerl und ihren Liebhabern* by Rudolph Hans Bartsch); t, Albert De Mond, Walter Anthony; ph, Jackson J. Rose; ed, Edward Cahn, Daniel Mandell.

Drama **(PR:A MPAA:NR)**

LOVE SWINDLE* (1918) 5 reels BLUE bw

Edith Roberts, Emanuel Turner, Leo White, Clarissa Selwynne, Reggie Morris, F. A. Turner.

It's all about a filthy rich gal who can't stand her many wealthy suitors. While visiting her country estate (to get away from them) she is attacked by tramps, and an automobile salesman comes to her rescue. She is very taken by the young man, but he turns out to have socialistic leanings which, of course, precludes his becoming involved with a woman of means. Now here is where the love swindle comes in; she asks him to deliver some money to her impoverished sister, poses as same, and the young fellow, not realizing the rib, falls madly in love and proposes marriage. Not the worst movie ever made, but close to it.

d, Jack Dillon; w, Fred Myton (based on the story "The Doings of Diana" by Rex Taylor).

Drama **(PR:A MPAA:NR)**

LOVE TOY, THE*** (1926) 6 reels WB bw

Lowell Sherman *(Peter Remsen)*, Jane Winton *(The Bride)*, Willard Louis *(King Lavoris)*, Gayne Whitman *(Prime Minister)*, Ethel Grey Terry *(Queen Zita)*, Helene Costello *(Princess Patricia)*, Maude George *(Lady-in-Waiting)*.

Sherman, the screen's greatest sophisticated rotter, is given the chance to play the good guy in this amusing comedy about an American who takes over the Luzanian Army, saves that nation from invasion, and wins the hand of the princess, Costello.

d, Erle C. Kenton; w, (based on a story by Charles Logue); ph, John J. Mescall.

Comedy **(PR:A MPAA:NR)**

LOVELORN, THE* (1927) 7 reels COS/MGM bw

Sally O'Neil *(Georgie Hastings)*, Molly O'Day *(Ann Hastings)*, Larry Kent *(Bill Warren)*, James Murray *(Charlie)*, Charles Delaney *(Jimmy)*, George Cooper *(Joe Sprotte)*, Allan Forrest *(Ernest Brooks)*, Dorothy Cumming *(Beatrice Fairfax)*.

When O'Day falls in love with her sister's boy friend, Kent, she decides to get some quick advice from a newspaper lovelorn columnist. She and her sister, O'Neil, discover that Kent is only looking for money, so the girls turn to a couple of fellows who have been quietly waiting in the wings.

d, John P. McCarthy; w, Bradley King (based on a story by Beatrice Fairfax); t, Frederic Hatton; ph, Henry Sharp; ed, John W. English; set d, Cedric Gibbons, Alexander Toluboff.

Drama **(PR:A MPAA:NR)**

LOVER'S ISLAND 1/2** (1925) 5 reels Encore/AEX bw

Hope Hampton *(Clemmy Dawson)*, James Kirkwood *(Jack Avery)*, Louis Wolheim *(Capt. Joshua Dawson)*, Ivan Linow *(Sam Johnson)*, Flora Finch *(Amanda Dawson)*, Flora Le Breton *(Julia Daw)*, Jack Raymond *(Randy Phelps)*.

This Hampton programmer about a romance-struck girl who leaves her New England village and goes to Lover's Island—where she almost marries the wrong man but ends up with Mr. Right—is better than it sounds.

p&d, Henri Diamant-Berger; w, Arthur Hoerl (based on the story by T. Howard Kelly); ph, Alfred Ortlieb; ed, Marie St. Clair.

Romance **(PR:A MPAA:NR)**

LOVER'S LANE** (1924) 7 reels WB bw

Robert Ellis *(Dr. Tom Singleton)*, Gertrude Olmstead *(Mary Larkin)*, Crauford Kent *(Herbert Woodbridge)*, Kate Toncray *(Aunt Mattie)*, George Periolat *(Dr. Stone)*, Norval MacGregor *(Rev. Singleton)*, Frances Dale *(Mrs. Woodbridge)*, Bruce Guerin *(Dick Woodbridge)*, Ethel Wales *(Aunt Melissy)*, Maxine Elliott Hicks *(Simplicity)*, Charles A. Sellon *(Uncle Bill)*, Aileen Manning *(Miss Mealy)*, Dorothy Vernon *(Mrs. Stone)*.

Olmstead is about to break her engagement with Ellis, a small-town physician, in favor of the charismatic Kent, when she discovers the latter is married. Then, when Ellis cures Kent's son, Olmstead realizes the depth of her feeling for the doctor.

d, Phil Rosen; w, Dorothy Farnum (based on the play by Clyde Fitch); ph, Charles Van Enger.

Drama **(PR:A MPAA:NR)**

LOVER'S OATH, A** (1925) 6 reels Ferdinand P. Earle/Astor bw

Ramon Novarro *(Ben Ali)*, Kathleen Key *(Sherin)*, Edwin Stevens *(Hassen Ben Sabbath)*, Frederick Warde *(Omar Khayyam)*, Hedwig Reicher *(Hassan's Wife)*, Snitz Edwards *(Omar's Servant)*, Charles A. Post *(Commander of the Faithful)*, Arthur Edmund Carew *(Prince Yussuf)*, Paul Weigel *(Sheik Rustum)*, Philippe De Lacy *(His Son)*, Warren Rodgers *(Haja)*.

A great deal of money was spent on this minor league THIEF OF BAGDAD, but the only impressive aspect of the picture is its sets. Novarro looks great, but he is mostly limited to walking around reading lines with title cards like: "O moon of my delight! I will build for thee the alabaster palaces of my dreams—for thee, beloved, I will conquer the seven kingdoms of the earth."

d, Ferdinand P. Earle; w, (based on Edward Fitzgerald's translation of the poem "The Rubaiyat of Omar Khayyam"); ph, George Benoit; ed, Milton Sills.

Fantasy **(PR:A MPAA:NR)**

LOVE'S BLINDNESS*** (1926) 7 reels MGM bw

Pauline Starke *(Vanessa Levy)*, Antonio Moreno *(Hubert Culverdale, 8th Earl of St. Austel)*, Lilyan Tashman *(Alice, Duchess of Lincolnwood)*, Sam De Grasse *(Benjamin Levy)*, Douglas Gilmore *(Charles Langely)*, Kate Price *(Marchioness of Hurlshire)*, Tom Ricketts *(Marquis of Hurlshire)*, Earl Metcalf *(Col. Ralph Dangerfield)*, George Waggner *(Oscar Issacson)*, Rose Dione *(Mme. De Jainon)*, Ned Sparks *(Valet)*.

Glyn (famous for inventing the term "It" and inspiring the movie of the same title), adapted her own story about a nobleman who marries the daughter of a Jewish money lender to avoid ruin, but eventually grows to love her. MGM gave the film a slick production.

d, John Francis Dillon; w, Elinor Glyn; ph, John Arnold, Oliver Marsh; ed, Frank Sullivan; set d, Cedric Gibbons, James Basevi.

Drama **(PR:A MPAA:NR)**

LOVES OF RICARDO, THE*** (1926) 8 reels George Beban bw

George Beban *(Ricardo)*, Soliga Lee *(Annetta)*, Amille Milane *(Annetta, in the Live Sequence)*, Jack Singleton *(Steve)*, Monte Collins, Jr. *(Steve, in the Live Sequence)*, Albano Valerio *(Marco)*, Mika Aldrich *(Flora)*, Signor Frondi *(Tony)*, Giulio Cortesi *(Mike Ferrera)*, E. E. McLeod, Jr. *("Skeets")*, Norman Ives *("Hap")*, Helen Hunton *(Madge)*, Rosa Vega *(Rosetta)*, Estella De Barr, Jack Howard, Mrs. Giulio Cortesi, Maria Barbarita, Wenonah Forgay.

Character actor Beban (who specialized in playing Mediterranean types) loses Lee, the ward he has grown to love, to city slicker Singleton. On her wedding night the girl realizes she really loves Beban, who has gone off and made a killing with a Florida land deal. The Italian is kidnaped by bootleggers, but with the help of his pet parrot, manages to escape and is delighted to find Lee waiting for him. When this film opened at the Rivoli Theatre in New York, Beban wrote and appeared, along with Milane and Collins, in a 24-minute live dramatic sequence which was performed in the middle of the picture and carried the exposition along.

d&w, George Beban; ph, Allen Siegler.

Drama **(PR:A MPAA:NR)**

LOVE'S OLD SWEET SONG* (1917, Brit.) 4 reels CL/New Bio bw

Evelyn Boucher *(Ruth Mereton)*, Leo Belcher *(Dan Ash)*, Rita Ortway *(Muriel Mereton)*, Jeff Barlow *(Farmer Mereton)*, Clifford Pembroke *(Robert Ash)*.

The wife of a musician becomes a nun after shooting her lover, and later her daughter falls in love with the son of her former lover. It's no wonder that Griffith and DeMille never felt threatened by the British cinema.

d, F. Martin Thornton; w, Reuben Gillmer.

Drama **(PR:A MPAA:NR)**

LOVE'S PENALTY*** (1921) 5 reels Hope Hampton/AFN bw

Hope Hampton *(Janis Clayton)*, Irma Harrison *(Sally Clayton)*, Mrs. Phillip Landau *(Martha Clayton)*, Percy Marmont *(Steven Saunders)*, Jack O'Brien *(Bud Gordon)*, Virginia Valli *(Mrs. Steven Saunders)*, Douglas Redmond *("Little Jack")*, Charles Lane *(Rev. John Kirchway)*, Mrs. L. Faure *(Mme. Natalie)*.

Before Gilbert became America's number one heart throb, he wrote and directed this interesting film about a young woman (Hampton) who sets out to ruin the man (Marmont) who, in betraying her sister, caused her suicide and the subsequent death of her mother. Obtaining a job as his secretary, Hampton encourages Marmont's attentions to the point where he sends his wife to Europe on a ship he deliberately orders through hazardous waters. Later, when the rotter learns of Marmont's scheme, he attempts to kill her but is instead murdered by a grief-crazed man whose wife and child went down on the ship.

d&w, Jack Gilbert; ph, Alfred Ortlieb; t&ed, Katherine Hilliker.

Drama **(PR:A MPAA:NR)**

LOVE'S REDEMPTION*** (1921) 6 reels Norma Talmadge/FN bw

Norma Talmadge *(Jennie Dobson/Ginger)*, Harrison Ford *(Clifford Standish)*, Montagu Love *(Frederick Kent)*, H. Cooper Cliffe *(John Standish)*, Ida Waterman *(Mrs. Standish)*, Michael M. Barnes *(Capt. Bill Hennessey)*, E. L. Fernandez *(Overseer)*, Frazer Coulter *(Club Steward)*.

Talmadge plays an orphaned girl who was raised in Jamaica by an old salt, Barnes. She falls in love with an exiled Englishman, Ford, who has nearly hit bottom because of drink. Talmadge saves him from being murdered and then nurses him back to health. The grateful Ford marries her and then learns from his brother that he has inherited a fortune. The couple move to Britain, where Ford's drinking and his aristocratic family make life so miserable for Talmadge that she decides to return to the islands. It is then that the Englishman realizes the depth of his love, and they set sail together.

p, Joseph M. Schenck; d, Albert Parker; w, Anthony Paul Kelly (based on the story "On Principal" by Andrew Soutar); ph, J. Roy Hunt.

Drama **(PR:A MPAA:NR)**

LOVE'S TOLL* (1916) 5 reels Lubin bw

Rosetta Brice *(Marian Lane)*, Richard Buhler *(Dr. George Page)*, Crauford Kent *(Allen Craven)*, Inez Buck *(Lucy Mallory)*, Garda Dolotskova *(Sonia Crater)*, William H. Turner *(Mr. Lane)*, Clara Lambert *(Mrs. Lane)*, Mrs. Carr.

A girl from the country falls for a wealthy cad, becomes pregnant, is dropped like a sack of flour, and goes to the maternity hospital where her baby dies. Then she meets a prominent doctor who, assuming she is widowed, marries her. It turns out the cad is a friend of the doctor's, and when they meet, the girl breaks down and confesses everything. When a fight breaks out, the rotter's pistol discharges, killing him, but his mistress informs the police that it was suicide, which encourages the physician to welcome his bride back into his life.

d, John H. Pratt; w, (based on a Daniel Carson Goodman story).

Drama **(PR:A MPAA:NR)**

LOVE'S WILDERNESS*** (1924) 7 reels Corinne Griffith/FN bw

Corinne Griffith *(Linda Lou Heath)*, Holmes E. Herbert *(David Tennant)*, Ian Keith *(Paul L'Estrange)*, Maurice Cannon *(Pierre Bazin)*, Emily Fitzroy *(Matilda Heath)*, Anne Schaefer *(Prudence Heath)*, Bruce Covington *(Col. Heath)*, David Torrence *(The Governor)*, Frank Elliot *(Van Arsdale)*, Adolph Millar *(Capt. Moreau)*, Jim Blackwell *(Jubilo)*, W. H. Post *(Lamaire)*.

In a departure from her usual worldly roles, Griffith does very well as an aristocratic southern girl who marries Keith, a wanderer, when Herbert, the man she really loves, goes off to Africa to practice medicine. After her husband fakes being killed, Griffith weds her original love and moves with him to Devil's Island, where it turns out Keith is incarcerated. During a terrific storm, Keith escapes and goes to Griffith. When Herbert finds them together, he assumes they are still in love. Magnanimously, the doctor sets out to have the convict released, but Keith is murdered by a fellow prisoner and, to Herbert's great relief, Griffith explains her true feelings.

d, Robert Z. Leonard; w, Eve Unsell, Helen Klumph (based on the story "Wilderness" by Helen Campbell); ph, Oliver Marsh; art d, Milton Menasco.

Drama **(PR:A MPAA:NR)**

LOYAL LIVES* (1923) 6 reels Postman/VIT bw

Brandon Tynan *(Dan O'Brien)*, Mary Carr *(Mary O'Brien)*, Faire Binney *(Peggy)*, William Collier, Jr. *(Terrence)*, Charles McDonald *(Michael O'Hara)*, Blanche Craig *(Lizzie O'Hara)*, Chester Morris *(Tom O'Hara)*, Tom Blake *(Brady)*, John Hopkins *(Judkins)*, Mickey Bennett *(Terrence, as a Child)*, Blanche Davenport *(Mrs. Brady)*.

Not much to applaud in this low-budget programmer about a hard-working postman who raises a son who grows up to join the post office himself and, in a moment of glory, saves the mail from crooks.

p, Whitman Bennett; d, Charles Giblyn; w, (based on a story by Charles G. Rich, Dorothy Farnum); ph, Edward Paul.

Drama **(PR:A MPAA:NR)**

LUCK*** (1923) 7 reels C. C. Burr/Mastodon bw

Johnny Hines *(Robert Carter)*, Robert Edeson *(Judge Templeton)*, Edmund Breese *(Alan Crosby)*, Violet Mersereau *(Sylvia Templeton)*, Charles Murray *(The Plumber)*, Flora Finch *(His Wife)*, Warner Richmond *(Pollard)*, Polly Moran *(Fight Fan)*, Harry Fraser *(A Lawyer)*, Matthew Betts *(Fighting Miner)*.

Hines had some heavyweight comic support in this fast-moving and entertaining comedy about a fellow who wagers $100,000 that he can begin with nothing and make $10,000 within a year. He starts out wearing only a track suit, and along the way he also earns plenty of laughs with the help of such veterans as Murray, Moran, and Finch.

p, C. C. Burr; w, Doty Hobart; t, Ralph Spence; ph, Charles E. Gilson, Neil Sullivan.

Comedy **(PR:A MPAA:NR)**

LUCK AND PLUCK*** (1919) 5 reels FOX bw

George Walsh *(Joe Grim, Alias "Velvet")*, Virginia Lee *(Laura White)*, Joe Smiley *(Her Father)*, George Fisher *(Karl Richter)*, Corinne Uzzell *(Countess Briand)*, George Halpin *("Velvet's" Valet)*.

Action and fun-filled Walsh romp, in which he plays a burglar who is reformed after saving a pretty girl from a ring of German spies. He then turns them over to her father, who just happens to be the head of the Secret Service.

d, Edward Dillon; w, Raymond L. Schrock (based on a story by George Scarborough).

Adventure **(PR:A MPAA:NR)**

LUCKY HORSESHOE, THE**** (1925) 5 reels FOX bw

Tom Mix *(Tom Foster)*, Billie Dove *(Eleanor Hunt)*, Malcolm Waite *(Denman)*, J. Farrell MacDonald *(Mack)*, Clarissa Selwynne *(Aunt Ruth)*, Ann Pennington *(Dancer)*, J. Gunnis Davis *(Valet to Denman)*.

More than just the usual exciting Mix western, this one has a dream sequence in which the great cowboy star imagines himself to be Don Juan (giving Douglas Fairbanks a race for the money when it comes to sword play and stunts). There is, of course, a western plot where Mix wins the heart of the beautiful, but snooty, owner of the ranch on which he works (played by Dove who, interestingly, would star opposite Douglas Fairbanks in THE BLACK PIRATE a year later). This is Mix at his ridin', shootin', and fightin' best, and that's saying something.

d, J. G. Blystone; w, John Stone (based on a story by Robert Lord); ph, Dan Clark.

Western **(PR:A MPAA:NR)**

LULLABY, THE* (1924) 7 reels R-C/FBO bw

Jane Novak *(Felipa/Antoinette)*, Robert Anderson *(Tony)*, Fred Malatesta *(Pietro)*, Dorothy Brock *(The Baby)*, Cleo Madison *(Mrs. Marvin)*, Otis Harlan *(Thomas Elliott)*, Peter Burke *(Thomas, Jr.)*, Lydia Yeamans Titus *(Mary)*.

Unpleasant programmer has Anderson hanged for killing the man who seduced his bride, Novak, while she is sentenced to 20 years as an accomplice. She gives birth in prison, and at the age of three the child is adopted by the judge who sentenced her. Years later, when she is released from jail, the guardian (who is now governor) takes Novak in after she relinquishes all of her parental rights.

d, Chester Bennett; w, Hope Loring, Louis D. Lighton (based on a story by Lillian Ducey); ph, Jack MacKenzie.

Drama **(PR:A MPAA:NR)**

LURE, THE*** (1914) 5 reels Shubert bw

The original play about white slavery and life inside a sporting house, was closed down regularly by the New York Police Department, which no doubt encouraged the producers of the film to approach some of the more sensational scenes conservatively. The result was a rather tame product compared to the theatrical version but, nonetheless, a better-than-average movie melodrama.

p,d&w, Alice Blache (based on the play by George Scarborough).

Drama **(PR:A MPAA:NR)**

LURE OF GOLD** (1922) 5 reels William Steiner bw

Neal Hart *(Jack Austin)*, William Quinn *(Chuck Wallace)*, Ben Corbett *(Latigo Bob)*.

After striking it rich in gold, cowboy Hart moves to a small western town where he saves a lady opera singer from an attack by a wild bull. When a couple of outlaws attempt to rob him of his wealth, the lady singer spoils the plot and she and Hart find peace and happiness in one another's arms.

d&w, Neal Hart; ph, Jake Badaracco.

Western **(PR:A MPAA:NR)**

LURE OF LONDON, THE** (1914, Brit.) 6 reels Barker/Co-operative bw

Ivy Close *(Daisy Westbury)*, Edward Viner *(William Anderson)*, M. Gray Murray *(Charlie Brooks)*, William Harbord *(Sir John Westbury)*, Leal Douglas *(Lady Westbury)*, Gwenda Wren *(Olga Westbury)*, H. L. Pringle *(George Stanford)*.

In this British feature the daughter of a prominent surgeon becomes lost and is taken in by a drunken cockney. Years later, after becoming a dancer, she is run over. A doctor manages to save her life, and he turns out to be, in fact, her father.

d, Bert Haldane; w, Rowland Talbot (based on the play by Arthur Applin).

Drama **(PR:A MPAA:NR)**

LURE OF LOVE, THE* (1924) 5 reels Pictures in Motion/Ace-High bw

Zena Keefe, Edward Earle.

Exiled to the U.S. by an officer who lusts for his sister, a young Russian climbs to the top of a steel company, marries the boss' daughter, puts down labor unrest, and manages to bring his sister over.

d, Leon E. Dadmum.

Drama **(PR:A MPAA:NR)**

LURE OF THE WILD, THE** 1/2** (1925) 6 reels COL bw

Lightning *(Shep the Dog)*, Jane Novak *(Agnes Belmont)*, Alan Roscoe *(James Belmont)*, Billie Jean *(Baby Cuddles)*, Richard Tucker *(Gordon Daniels)*, Mario Carillo *(Poleon Dufresne)*, Pat Harmon *(Mike Murdock)*.

Cohn must have stewed as he watched the brothers Warner earn a fortune with their number one star, Rin-Tin-Tin. Enter Lightning, another well-trained dog, who in this picture, with a more adult theme, all but raises the child of a murdered man who took his daughter to the Canadian woods after suspecting his wife was unfaithful.

p, Harry Cohn; d, Frank R. Strayer; w, Tom J. Hopkins; ph, George Meehan; ed, Charles J. Hunt.

Adventure/Drama **(PR:A MPAA:NR)**

LURE OF THE YUKON** (1924) 6 reels Norman Dawn Alaskan/Lee-Bradford bw

Eva Novak *(Sue McCraig)*, Spottiswoode Aitken *(Sourdough McCraig)*, Kent Sanderson *(Bob Force)*, Arthur Jasmine *(Kuyak)*, Howard Webster *(Dan Baird)*, Katherine Dawn *(Ruth Baird)*, Eagle Eye *(Black Otter)*.

Formula Yukon story about an old sourdough, Aitken, who, along with his daughter Novak, take off for Alaska to find gold. When Aitken dies, Novak meets up with Sanderson, who also comes to her rescue when the villainous Webster captures her. In the end, it is Sanderson who captures the heart of Novak.

d&w, Norman Dawn; ph, George Madden.

Adventure **(PR:A MPAA:NR)**

LURE OF YOUTH, THE** (1921) 6 reels Metro bw

Cleo Madison *(Florentine Fair)*, William Conklin *(Morton Mortimer)*, Gareth Hughes *(Roger Dent)*, Lydia Knott *("Ma" Dent)*, William Courtwright *("Pa" Dent)*, Helen Weir *(Marjorie Farnol)*.

A Broadway star (Madison) becomes infatuated with a simple, aspiring young playwright (Hughes) and brings him to New York. Her fiance, Conklin, is madly jealous, but backs the play anyway because of its quality. Hughes becomes the toast of the theatrical world and proposes to Madison, who turns him down in favor of Conklin.

p, Bayard Veiller; d, Phillip E. Rosen; w, Luther Reed; ph, Robert Kurrle.

Drama **(PR:A MPAA:NR)**

LYING LIPS*** (1921) 7 reels THI/AP bw

House Peters *(Blair Cornwall)*, Florence Vidor *(Nancy Abbott)*, Joseph Kilgour *(William Chase)*, Margaret Livingston *(Lelia Dodson)*, Margaret Campbell *(Mrs. Abbott)*, Edith Yorke *(Mrs. Prospect)*, Calvert Carter *(Horace Prospect)*, Emmett C. King *(John Warren)*.

When wealthy Englishwoman Vidor falls in love with Canadian rancher Peters, she can't give up "the good life" and decides to stick with her British aristocrat fiance Kilgour. Later, the ship on which Vidor and Peters are both sailing sinks, and she admits her true feelings for him, but asks to be rescued alone when a boat arrives to save them. At her wedding, she collapses before the service is completed and then wisely sails with the man she really loves to happiness.

d, John Griffith Wray; sup, Thomas H. Ince; w, Bradley King (based on a story by May Edgington); ph, Charles Stumar, Henry Sharp.

Drama **(PR:A MPAA:NR)**

LYING TRUTH, THE** (1922) 6 reels EF/American bw

Pat O'Malley *(Bill O'Hara)*, Noah Beery *(Lawrence De Muidde)*, Marjorie Daw *(Sue De Muidde)*, Tully Marshall *(Horace Todd)*, Charles Mailes *(Sam Clairborne, Sr.)*, Claire McDowell *(Mrs. Sam Clairborne)*, Adele Watson *(Ellie Clairborne)*, George Dromgold *(Sam Clairborne, Jr)*, Robert Brauer *(Mose)*, Wade Boteler *(Bill O'Hara, Sr.)*, Pete Smith.

O'Malley, who was raised by a newspaper family after becoming orphaned, inherits his stepfather's business after the real son (Mailes) is disowned because he is a drug addict. To stimulate newspaper circulation, O'Malley creates a fake murder and offers a reward. Later, Mailes' body is found in a swamp and dope pusher Beery accuses O'Malley, whipping up the townspeople into a hateful uproar. The mob nearly lynches O'Malley, but his stepmother arrives in time with her son's suicide note to save her stepson's life. One of the unbilled actors here, playing a reporter, is none other than Pete Smith, the famous publicist who later created a series of classic comedy shorts for MGM.

d&w, Marion Fairfax; ph, René Guissart.

Drama **(PR:A MPAA:NR)**

M

MAD DANCER** (1925) 6 reels Jans bw

Ann Pennington *(Mimi)*, Johnny Walker *(Keith Arundel)*, Coit Albertson *(Serge Verlaine)*, John Woodward *(Robert Halleck)*, Frank Montgomery *(Jean Gaboule)*, Rica Allen *(Ada Halleck)*, William F. Haddock *(Elmer Halleck)*, John Costello *(John Arundel)*, Nellie Savage *(Princess Gibesco)*, Echlin Gayer *(Prince Carl)*, Clarence Sunshine *(Cupid Karsleed)*.

Fair programmer has Ziegfeld Follies star Pennington playing an American dancer in Paris, who poses nude for a famous sculptor and later suffers the consequences when she returns to the more puritanical climate of the U.S..

d, Burton King; w, William B. Laub (based on the story by Louise Winter); ed, Laub; set d, Tec-Art Studios.

Drama **(PR:A MPAA:NR)**

MAD MARRIAGE, THE* (1921) 5 reels UNIV bw

Carmel Myers *(Jane Judd)*, Truman Van Dyke *(Jerry Paxton)*, William Brunton *(Willie)*, Virginia Ware *(Mrs. Brendon)*, Margaret Cullington *(Harmonia)*, Jane Starr *(Althea)*, Arthur Carewe *(Christiansen)*, Nola Luxford *(Bob)*, Lydia Yeamans Titus *(Mrs. Boggs)*.

Ludicrous plot has Greenwich Village artist Van Dyke marrying fledgling playwright Myers and making her his slavey. When she secretly authors a play with Carewe which becomes a great success, Van Dyke turns into a raving maniac. Their marriage almost breaks up but is saved when the couple's baby becomes ill, and they are made aware of the true meaning of family.

d, Rollin Sturgeon; w, Marian Fairfax (based on the novel *Cinderella Jane* by Marjorie Benton Cooke); ph, Alfred Gosden.

Drama **(PR:A MPAA:NR)**

MADAME BUTTERFLY*½** (1915) 5 reels FP bw

Mary Pickford *(Choo-Choo-San, Madame Butterfly)*, Olive West *(Suzuki)*, Jane Hall *(Adelaide)*, Lawrence Wood *(Choo-Choo-San's Father)*, Caroline Harris *(Her Mother)*, M. W. Rale *(The Mikado)*, W. T. Carleton *(American Consul)*, David Burton *(The Prince)*, Frank Bekum *(Naval Officer)*, Marshall Neilan *(Lt. Pinkerton)*, Cesare Gravina *(The Soothsayer)*.

Critics who thought Pickford was a one-dimensional actress of light quality, were amazed by the sensitive performance she gave as the tragic Japanese maiden. Pickford, however, seemed to have been less than satisfied with the role of Choo-Choo-San. Disappointed by the picture's lack of action, she is said to have suggested that the film would have been more appropriately titled *Madame Snail*. The film is credited as being adapted from the novel by Long, rather than from the opera by Giacomo Puccini or the play by Long and David Belasco. This may explain Famous Player's unlikely casting of Pickford in the role instead of Geraldine Farrar, the renowned star of the Metropolitan Opera, who was also working for Adolph Zukor's company at the time.

d, Sidney Olcott; w, (based on the novel by John Luther Long); ph, Hal Young.

Drama **(PR:A MPAA:NR)**

MADAME DUBARRY (SEE: PASSION, 1920, Ger.)

MADAME POMPADOUR*** (1927, Brit.) 7 reels BN/PAR bw

Dorothy Gish *(Mme. Pompadour)*, Antonio Moreno *(Rene Laval)*, Nelson Keys *(Duc de Courcelette)*, Henri Bosc *(Louis XV)*, Gibb McLaglen *(Gogo)*, Marsa Beauplan *(Mme. Poisson)*, Marie Ault *(Belotte)*.

German director Dupont would never make another film to equal his masterpiece VARIETY, but he was involved (this time as producer) in a few good pictures made in England before setting out on what was basically a second-rate Hollywood career. This one, directed by the talented Irishman, Herbert Wilcox, dealt with Madame Pompadour's love affair with a prisoner.

p, E. A. Dupont; d, Herbert Wilcox; w, Frances Marion, Dupont (based on the play by Rudolph Schanzer, Ernst Wellish).

Costume **(PR:A MPAA:NR)**

MADAME SPY*** (1918) 5 reels Butterfly bw

Jack Mulhall *(Robert Wesley)*, Wadsworth Harris *(Adm. John Wesley)*, Jean Hersholt *(Count Von Ornstorff)*, Donna Drew *(Phyliss Covington)*, Claire Du Brey *(Baroness Von Hulda)*, Maude Emory, George Gebhart.

Good wartime programmer has a U.S. admiral's son (Mulhall), who just flunked out of the naval academy, discovering his father's butler passing secrets and preparing for the arrival of a German baroness. Mulhall captures the lady, does a terrific female impersonation, and smashes the spy ring. Needless to say, he is welcomed back to Annapolis with open arms.

d, Douglas Gerrard; w, Harvey Gates (based on a story by Lee Morrison).

Spy **(PR:A MPAA:NR)**

MADCAP BETTY*** (1915) 5 reels Bosworth bw

Elsie Janis *(Betty)*, Owen Moore *(Jim Denning)*, June Hastings *(Betty's Cousin)*, Herbert Standing *(Her Uncle)*, Vera Lewis *(Her Aunt)*, Harry Ham *(The Boarder)*, Roberta Hickman *(Mazie Follette)*.

The great vaudeville star, Janis, used all of her theatrical tricks (short of singing and doing impressions) in this comedy about a convent-reared girl who dreams about some secular adventures and awakens with the decision to marry her boy friend at once.

d, Phillip Smalley; w, Elsie Janis.

Comedy **(PR:A MPAA:NR)**

MADE IN HEAVEN** (1921) 5 reels Goldwyn bw

Tom Moore *(Bill Lowry)*, Helene Chadwick *(Claudia Royce)*, Molly Malone *(Elizabeth Royce)*, Kate Lester *(Mrs. Royce)*, Al Filson *(Mr. Royce)*, Freeman Wood *(Davidge)*, Charles Eldridge *(Lowry, Sr.)*, Renee Adoree *(Miss Lowry)*, Herbert Prior *(Leland)*, Fronzie Gunn *(Ethel Hadden)*, John Cossar *(Mr. Hadden)*.

After saving Chadwick from a burning building and learning that she is due to marry against her will, Irish immigrant Moore suggests that she enter into a phony marriage with him. Later, after almost marrying another undesirable, Chadwick comes to the realization that she actually loves Moore, and they tie the knot for real.

d, Victor Schertzinger; w, Arthur F. Statter (based on a story by William Hurlbut); ph, Ernest Miller; art d, Cedric Gibbons.

Comedy **(PR:A MPAA:NR)**

MADNESS OF YOUTH½** (1923) 5 reels FOX bw

John Gilbert *(Jaca Javalie)*, Billie Dove *(Nanette Banning)*, Donald Hatswell *(Peter Reynolds)*, George K. Arthur *(Ted Banning)*, Wilton Taylor *(Theodore P. Banning)*, Ruth Boyd *(Mme. Jeanne Banning)*, Luke Lucas *(Mason, the Butler)*, Julanne Johnston *(The Dancer)*.

Con man Gilbert poses as an evangelist who converts his victims and then takes off with their money. When he falls in love with the daughter of an intended target, he sees the light and becomes an advocate of his own message.

d, Jerome Storm; w, Joseph Franklin Poland (based on the story "Red Darkness" by George Frank Worts); ph, Joseph August.

Drama **(PR:A MPAA:NR)**

MADONNAS AND MEN½** (1920) 7 reels B. A. Rolfe/Jans bw

Edmund Lowe *(Gordion/Gordon Turner)*, Anders Randolf *(Emperor Turnerius/Marshall Turner)*, Gustav von Seyffertitz *(Grimaldo/John Grimm)*, Evan-Burrows Fontaine *(Nerissa/Minon)*, Raye Dean *(Laurentia/Laura)*, Faire Binney *(Patsy)*, Blanche Davenport *(Mrs. Grimm)*.

Obviously inspired by the work of D. W. Griffith, this film also deals with the intolerant proclivities of humankind. In this case, the producers tell two stories, with one set in ancient Rome and the other in the present, using the same actors in both. This, of course, opens the door to plenty of "feed the Christians to the lions" stuff, as well as a somewhat raunchy depiction of a jazz-age "midnight frolic." The picture's closing title, "Remember, a nation with unrestricted moral standards cannot endure; and no civilization is permanent which is founded on the debasing of womanhood" apparently is used to justify all earlier excesses.

d, B. A. Rolfe; w, Violet Clark (based on a story by Carey Wilson, Edmund Goulding); ph, Arthur Cadwell.

Costume/Drama **(PR:C MPAA:NR)**

MAGNIFICENT FLIRT, THE** (1928) 7 reels PAR/FP bw

Florence Vidor *(Mme. Florence Laverne)*, Albert Conti *(Count D'Estrange)*, Loretta Young *(Denise Laverne, the Daughter)*, Matty Kemp *(Hubert, the Count's Nephew)*, Marietta Millner *(Fifi, a Perfect Lady)*, Ned Sparks *(Tim, an American in Paris)*.

Gerrard's cinematography, lensed in the German style, is the only bright spot in this farce, set in Paris, about an aristocrat who suspects his son is being taken in by Vidor's daughter and tries to break up the relationship. The picture ends with *him* falling for Vidor and a Venetian double wedding.

d, Harry D' Abbadie D' Arrast; w, Jean De Limur, D' Arrast (based on the play "Maman" by Jose Germain Drouilly); t, Herman J. Mankiewicz; ph, Henry Gerrard; ed, Frances Marsh.

Comedy **(PR:A MPAA:NR)**

MAID OF THE WEST* (1921) 5 reels UNIV bw

Eileen Percy *(Betty)*, William Scott *(Bert Cragnair)*, Hattis Buskirk *(Mrs. Sedgwick)*, Charles Meakin *(Bruce)*, June La Vere *(Maid)*, Jack Brammall *(Butler)*, Frank Clark *(Amos Jansen)*.

A wealthy female Texan is sent to New York by her family to get her away from the aviator she loves. While there, her pearl necklace is stolen by crooks, but Scott, who happens to be on hand, saves the day. The best things about this stinker were the dated vaudeville gags, which were used in the titles to stretch the film's length, and some stock airplane footage.

d, Philo McCullough, C. R. Wallace; w, John Montague (based on a story by W.E. Spencer); ph, Otto Brautigan.

Drama **(PR:A MPAA:NR)**

MAILMAN, THE* (1923) 7 reels Emory Johnson/FBO bw

Ralph Lewis *(Bob Morley)*, Johnnie Walker *(Johnnie Morley)*, Martha Sleeper *(Betty)*, Virginia True Boardman *(Mrs. Morley)*, Dave Kirby *(Jack Morgan)*, Josephine Adair *(Virginia)*, Taylor Graves *(Harry)*, Hardee Kirkland *(Capt. Franz)*, Richard Morris *(Adm. Fleming)*, Rosemary Cooper *(Mrs. Thompson)*.

Postman Walker is given a job on a mail boat after being commended for doing his job well. Later, he is framed for stealing bonds and murdering the ship's officer but, of course, he is also cleared by the picture's end.

d, Emory Johnson; w, Emilie Johnson; ph, Ross Fisher.

Drama **(PR:A MPAA:NR)**

MAKING A MAN** (1922) 6 reels FP/PAR bw

Jack Holt *(Horace Winsby)*, J. P. Lockney *(Jim Owens)*, Eva Novak *(Patricia Owens)*, Bert Woodruff *(Henry Cattermole)*, Frank Nelson *(Shorty)*, Robert Dudley *(Bailey)*.

This comedy about a snobbish, unfeeling California millionaire (Holt), who would just as soon foreclose on a farmer's mortgage as pick an orange, starts off slowly but picks up momentum. When Holt arrives in New York, he has his wallet stolen and finds himself forced to live the life of a near-mendicant. Of course, this changes his outlook on life completely, turns him into a man of great compassion, and wins him the love of beautiful Novak.

d, Joseph Henabery; w, Albert Shelby Le Vino (based on the story "Humanizing Mr. Winsby" by Peter Bernard Kyne); ph, Faxon Dean.

Comedy **(PR:A MPAA:NR)**

MAKING GOOD (SEE: RIGHT WAY, THE, 1921)

MAKING THE GRADE**

(1921) David Butler/Western Pictures Exploitation bw

David Butler *(Eddie Ramson)*, Helen Ferguson *(Sophie Semenoff)*, William Walling *(Mr. Ramson)*, Lillian Lawrence *(Mrs. Ramson)*, Jack Cosgrove *(Capt. Carleton)*, Alice Wilson *(Mrs. Garnie Crest)*, Otto Lederer, Jack Rollins.

There were few films made in the U.S. about America's intervention into the Russian Civil War (Woodrow Wilson reluctantly sent an expeditionary force to Archangel), and unfortunately this one is only second rate. It's a comedy-adventure about a hard-drinking playboy soldier who marries a peasant girl and brings her home, much to the chagrin of his socialite parents. The bride is followed by Bolshevik agents who attempt a kidnaping, but the mother-in-law foils the plot, discovers that the undesirable one is in reality a princess, and from that time on, the welcome mat is at the door.

d, Fred J. Butler; w, A. P. Younger (based on the story "Sophie Semenoff" by Wallace Irwin); ph, Robert Newhard, Robert Martin.

Comedy/Adventure **(PR:A MPAA:NR)**

MAKING THE VARSITY* (1928) 7 reels EXCEL bw

Rex Lease *(Ed Ellsworth)*, Arthur Rankin *(Wally Ellsworth)*, Gladys Hulette *(Estelle Carter)*, Edith Yorke *(Mrs. Ellsworth)*, Florence Dudley *(Gladys Fogarty)*, Carl Miller *(Jerry Fogarty)*, James Latta *(Gridley)*.

Bottom-of-the-barrel college gridiron movie has an honor student punching his younger brother out when he learns the little rat is planning to throw the big game. Only the stock newsreel footage of a real game is of interest here.

d, Cliff Wheeler; w, Elsie Werner, Bennett Southard; t, Lee Anthony; ph, Edward Kull; ed, Anthony; football supervisor, Jeff Cravath.

College/Drama **(PR:A MPAA:NR)**

MALE AND FEMALE**** (1919) 9 reels PAR bw

Thomas Meighan *(Crichton)*, Gloria Swanson *(Lady Mary Lasenby)*, Lila Lee *(Tweeny)*, Theodore Roberts *(Lord Loam)*, Raymond Hatton *(Honorable Ernest Wolley)*, Mildred Reardon *(Agatha Lasenby)*,Bebe Daniels *(The King's Favorite)*, Robert Cain *(Lord Brockelhurst)*, Julia Faye *(Susan)*, Rhy Darby *(Lady Eileen Dun Craige)*, Maym Kelso *(Lady Brockelhurst)*, Edward Burns *(Treherne)*, Henry Woodward *(McGuire)*, Sidney Deane *(Thomas)*, Wesley Barry *("Buttons")*, Edna Mae Cooper *(Fisher)*, Lillian Leighton *(Mrs. Perkins)*, Guy Oliver *(Pilot of Lord Loam's Yacht)*, Clarence Burton *(Captain of Yacht)*, W. Lawson Butt, Kamuela Searle.

DeMille changed the title of Barrie's play "The Admirable Crichton" to MALE AND FEMALE because he was afraid U.S. audiences might think it was a naval story. It is, in fact, one of the flamboyant director's best efforts. The story satirizes the British class system by telling of a party of aristocrats who become stranded on an island and, in order to survive, find their roles reversed with Meighan, the butler, being forced to take charge. Lady Mary (beautifully played by Swanson) even falls madly in love with him during this time, but when they are rescued and return to England, the class business surfaces once again and she ends up marrying nobility.

d, Cecil B. DeMille; w, Jeanie Macpherson (based on the play "The Admirable Crichton" by Sir James M. Barrie); ph, Alvin Wyckoff.

Satire **(PR:A MPAA:NR)**

MAN ABOVE THE LAW** (1918) 5 reels TRI bw

Jack Richardson *(Duce Chalmers)*, Josie Sedgwick *(Esther Brown)*, Claire McDowell *(Natcha)*, May Giraci *(Tonah)*.

Programmer about an Eastern fugitive who sets up a saloon in a western territory inhabited by Mexicans and Indians. A schoolteacher arrives and convinces him to allow the child he has sired by an Indian woman to attend class. Then, realizing the harm his firewater has caused the community, the regenerated one smashes his booze, marries his squaw, and rides off into the sunset with his family.

d, Raymond Wells; w, (based on the novel by Lanier Bartlett); ph, Pliny Horne.

Western/Drama **(PR:A MPAA:NR)**

MAN AND HIS MATE, A** (1915) 4 reels Reliance bw

Henry Woodruff, Sam De Grasse, Gladys Brockwell.

Broadway actor Woodruff had this picture stolen from him by character player De Grasse, who portrays an Oriental competing against a white man (Woodruff) for the love of a young Wild West beauty.

d, John Adolfi; w, (based on the novel and play by H. R. Durant).

Western/Drama **(PR:A MPAA:NR)**

MAN AND HIS WOMAN** (1920) 6 reels Blackton/Pathe bw

Herbert Rawlinson *(Dr. John Worthing)*, Eulalie Jensen *(Clare Eaton)*, May McAvoy *(Eve Cartier)*, Warren Chandler *(Hugh Conway)*, Louis Dean *(Dr. Elliot)*, Charles Dean *(The Stranger)*, Charles Kent.

This Blackton production gave audiences a peek at the seamy side of life in telling the story of a doctor who hits rock bottom through alcohol and drug addiction, before being saved by a beautiful and dedicated nurse.

p&d, J. Stuart Blackton; w, Stanley Olmsted (based on a story by Shannon Fife); ph, William S. Adams.

Drama **(PR:C MPAA:NR)**

MAN AND MAID* (1925) 6 reels MG bw

Lew Cody *(Sir Nicholas Thormonde)*, Harriet Hammond *(Alathea Bulteel)*, René Adoré *(Suzette)*, Paulette Duval *(Coralie)*, Alec Francis *(Burton)*, Crauford Kent *(Col. George Harcourt)*, David Mir *(Maurice)*, Gerald Grove *(The Honorable Bobby Bulteel)*, Jacqueline Gadsden *(Lady Hilda Bulteel)*, Winston Miller *(Little Bobby)*, Jane Mercer *(Little Hilda)*, Irving Hartley *(Alwood Chester)*, Dagmar Desmond *(Odette)*, Leonie Lester *(Alice)*.

Farfetched Glyn nonsense about an English member of the Red Cross who saves the life of a British officer in France during WW I and unknowingly becomes his secretary after the armistice. There is a saucy little French girl who attracts his attention through part of the film, but in the end he falls in love with the former Red Crosser and rescues her aristocratic father from the poverty his gambling habit has driven him to.

d, Victor Schertzinger; w, Elinor Glyn; ph, Chet Lyons; art d, Cedric Gibbons.

Drama **(PR:A MPAA:NR)**

MAN AND THE MOMENT, THE**

(1918, Brit.) 6 reels Windsor/Walturdaw bw

Manora Thew *(Sabine Delburg)*, Hayford Hobbs *(Lord Michael Arranstoun)*, Charles Vane *(Lord Henry Fordyce)*, Maud Cressall *(Princess Moravia)*, Peggy Carlisle *(Miss Van Der Water)*, Jeff Barlow *(Armstrong)*, Kenelm Foss *(Prince Torniloni)*.

In order to honor the stipulation in a will, an American heiress marries a Scottish nobleman, and then takes off for Italy. She returns, however, after the tragic news of her child's death.

d, Arrigo Bocchi; w, Kenelm Foss (based on the novel by Elinor Glyn).

Drama **(PR:C MPAA:NR)**

MAN AND THE WOMAN, A*

(1917) 5 reels American Amusements/Art Dramas bw

Edith Hallor *(Agnes Van Suyden)*, Leslie Austen *(James Duncan)*, Kirke Browne *(Mr. Van Suyden)*, H. Bradley Barker *(Allen Crawford)*, Yolande Doquette *(Miss Perrier)*, Zadee Burbank *(Mrs. Van Suyden)*, Lorna Volare *(The Child)*.

Poor programmer about a wealthy woman who enters into a marriage of convenience with an impoverished young man to give her child a legitimate birth. In time, the husband grows to love the child and its mother, and tries to commit suicide when he is separated from them and her previous lover returns. The woman, however, soon realizes that she loves the young man, as well, rushes to the garret he formerly occupied, and prevents him from blowing his brains out at the last moment.

d&w, Mme. Blache [Alice Guy] (based on the novel *Nantas* by Emile Zola).

Drama **(PR:A MPAA:NR)**

MAN BAIT* (1926) 6 reels Metropolitan/PDC bw

Marie Prevost *(Madge Dreyer)*, Kenneth Thomson *(Gerald Sanford)*, Douglas Fairbanks, Jr. *(Jeff Sanford)*, Louis Natheaux *(Delancy Hasbrouck)*, Eddie Gribbon *(Red Welch)*, Betty Francisco *(Betty Gerber)*, Adda Gleason *(Florence Hasbrouck)*, Sally Rand *(Nancy)*, Fritzi Ridgeway *(Gloria)*.

Below-par hokum about a shopgirl (Prevost) who is fired from a department store for belting one of the owners, who made a pass. Later, while working as a "taxi-dancer" she becomes engaged to Fairbanks, who just happens to be the son of her ex-employer. At first the girl is snubbed by her future in-laws, but everything ends on a happy note when she and her fiance's brother Thomson fall in love for real, and young Fairbanks returns to his socially prominent former sweetheart.

d, Donald Crisp; w, Douglas Z. Doty (based on the story by Norman Houston); ph, Hal Rosson; art d, Charles Cadwallader.

Comedy/Romance **(PR:A MPAA:NR)**

MAN BEHIND THE DOOR, THE*** (1914) 4 reels VIT bw

Wally Van, Nitra Frazer, Cissy Fitzgerald, Louise Beaudet.

Good early comedy feature (Mack Sennett would make his first long comedy, TILLIE'S PUNCTURED ROMANCE, that same year) about a college oarsman's romantic adventures, leading up to the moment when he snares the girl he really loves, the daughter of the professor.

d, Wally Van; w, Archibald Clavering Gunter.

Comedy **(PR:A MPAA:NR)**

MAN CRAZY** (1927) 6 reels Charles R. Rogers/FN bw

Dorothy Mackaill *(Clarissa Janeway)*, Jack Mulhall *(Jeffery Pell)*, Edythe Chapman *(Grandmother Janeway)*, Phillips Smalley *(James Janeway)*, Walter McGrail *(Van Breamer)*, Ray Hallor *(Danny)*.

Upset by her free-wheeling lifestyle, Mackaill's parents try to marry her off to McGrail, another Mayflower descendant. Mackaill, however, loves truck driver Mulhall, and when she learns of a plot to hijack his vehicle, the two combine to break up a gang of bootleggers. Later it is revealed that Mulhall is actually a blueblood with democratic inclinations, which pleases everyone.

p, Charles R. Rogers; d, John Francis Dillon; w, Perry Nathan (based on the story *Clarissa and the Post Road* by Grace Sartwell Mason); t, Dwinelle Benthall, Rufus McCosh; ph, James Van Trees.

Comedy/Drama **(PR:A MPAA:NR)**

MAN FOUR-SQUARE, A** ½ (1926) 5 reels FOX bw (AKA: THE MAN FOUR-SQUARE)

Buck Jones *(Craig Norton)*, Marion Harlan *(Polly)*, Harry Woods *(Ben Taylor)*, William Lawrence *(Jim Clanton)*, Jay Hunt *(Polly's Father)*, Sidney Bracey *(Homer Webb)*, Florence Gilbert *(Bertie Roberts)*, Frank Beal *(Wallace Roberts)*.

Wealthy young rancher Jones returns home from the city to find himself suspected of cattle rustling by the sheriff, his foreman, and Harlan, the prettiest girl in the territory. Jones later proves himself innocent, rescues the foreman and the girl, and wins the heart of Harlan in the process.

d, R. William Neill; w, Charles Darnton, John Stone (based on the novel by William MacLeod Raine); ph, Reginald Lyons.

Western **(PR:A MPAA:NR)**

MAN FOUR-SQUARE, THE (SEE: MAN FOUR-SQUARE, A, 1926)

MAN FROM BEYOND, THE** (1922) 7 reels Houdini bw

Harry Houdini *(The Man from Beyond)*, Arthur Maude *(Dr. Gilbert Trent)*, Albert Tavernier *(Dr. Crawford Strange)*, Erwin Connelly *(Dr. Gregory Sinclair)*, Frank Montgomery *(Francois Duval)*, Luis Alberni *(Capt. of the Barkentine)*, Yale Benner *(Milt Norcross)*, Jane Connelly *(Felice Strange/Felice Norcross)*, Nita Naldi *(Marie Le Grande)*.

Bizarre, hokey, and great fun, best describes this Houdini thriller about a man (Houdini) who is revived by Arctic explorers after being frozen in a block of ice for 100 years. When brought back to New York, the first thing the human popsicle does is break up the wedding of Connelly, a girl who just happens to be the spitting image of her grandmother—the very person "the man from beyond" was once engaged to. The remainder of the film has to do with the rescue of Connelly's father from a gang of crooks, which provides the great escape artist with plenty of opportunity to show off his unique talents as he fights for justice. He rescues the girl he has fallen in love with (at second sight, as it were) from plunging over Niagara Falls, and the film ends pitching the possibility of reincarnation's existence.

d, Burton King; w, Coolidge Streeter (based on a story by Harry Houdini), ph, Frank Zuker, Irving B. Ruby, Harry A. Fischbeck, A. G. Penrod, Louis Dunmyre, L. D. Littlefield.

Adventure/Mystery **Cas.** **(PR:A MPAA:NR)**

MAN FROM HARDPAN, THE** ½ (1927) 6 reels Leo Maloney/Pathe bw

Leo Maloney *(Robert Alan)*, Eugenia Gilbert *(Elizabeth Warner)*, Rosa Gore *(Sarah Lackey)*, Murdock MacQuarrie *(Henry Hardy)*, Paul Hurst *(Larry Lackey)*, Ben Corbett *(Jack Burton)*, Albert Hart *(Sheriff)*.

Fairly sophisticated B western has Maloney being held up and his papers stolen while on his way to claim an inheritance of half a ranch. The outlaw who robbed him assumes Maloney's identity, and the real Maloney is jailed after being taken for the bad man. Later he escapes and sets the record straight.

d, Leo D. Maloney; w, Ford I. Beebe; ph, Vernon Walker.

Western **(PR:A MPAA:NR)**

MAN FROM HEADQUARTERS*** (1928) 6 reels T/C/RAY bw

Cornelius Keefe *(Yorke Norray)*, Edith Roberts *(Countess Jalna)*, Charles West *(No. 1)*, Lloyd Whitlock *(No. 2)*, Ludwig Lowry *(No. 3)*, Wilbert Emile *(No. 4)*, Dave Harlow *(No. 5)*, Fred Huston *(Duke Albert)*, Joseph Mack.

Solid mystery has U.S. Secret Service agent Keefe taking on a gang of foreign operatives out to steal valuable documents, and falling for the female member, Roberts, who really only wants to feed her nation's starving poor. There is lots of action and intrigue on a fast-moving train; in scenes which would become quite familiar to movie-goers with the advent of sound.

d, Duke Worne; w, Arthur Hoerl (based on the novel *The Black Book* by George Bronson Howard); ph, Hap Depew; ed, J. S. Harrington.

Mystery **(PR:A MPAA:NR)**

MAN FROM HOME, THE*** (1914) 5 reels LAS bw

Charles Richman *(Daniel Vorhees Pike)*, Theodore Roberts *(The Grand Duke)*, Fred Montague *(Earl of Hawcastle)*, Monroe Salisbury *(Honorable Almeric St. Aubyn)*, Horace B. Carpenter *(Ivanoff)*, Jode Mullally *(Horace Granger Simpson)*, Dick La Reno *(Old Man Simpson)*, Dorothy Quincy *(Ethel Granger Simpson)*, Miss Anita King *(Helen)*, James Neill, Jack W. Johnston, Florence Dagmar, Mabel Van Buren, Robert Fleming, Tex Driscoll.

DeMille took his company to northern California to shoot this enjoyable movie and convincingly created the impression that real locations, such as Russia and Italy, were used. The man from home (well played by stage star Richman) travels to Sorrento, where he prevents his ward from foolishly marrying the son of a British lord, saves an innocent escaped Russian prisoner from recapture, and wins the most beautiful girl for himself.

d, Cecil B. DeMille, Oscar Apfel; w, DeMille (based on the play by Booth Tarkington, Harry Leon Wilson); ph, Alvin Wyckoff.

Drama **(PR:A MPAA:NR)**

MAN FROM MONTANA, THE** ½ (1917) 5 reels UNIV bw

Neal Hart *(Duke Farley)*, George Berrell *(Dad Petzel)*, E. J. Peil *(Warren Summers)*, Betty Lamb *(Mrs. Summers)*, Willard Wayne *(Allen Spencer)*, Vivian Rich *(Meta Cooper)*, Miriam Shelby.

"America's Pal" Hart, clears himself of violating the Mann Act, and then triumphs over the crooks who stole his mine, in this off-beat, action-packed western.

d, George Marshall; w, Harvey Gates (based on a story by Marshall).

Western **(PR:A MPAA:NR)**

MAN FROM PAINTED POST, THE*** (1917) 5 reels Douglas Fairbanks/ART bw

Douglas Fairbanks *(Fancy Jim Sherwood)*, Eileen Percy *(Jane Forbes)*, Frank Campeau *(Bull Madden)*, Frank Clark *(Toby Madden)*, Herbert Standing *(Warren Bronson)*, William Lowery *(Charles Ross)*, Reah Haines *(Wah-na Madden)*, Charles Stevens *(Tony Lopez)*, Monte Blue *(Slim Carter)*.

Fairbanks foils a gang of rustlers and wins the prettiest girl in the West by dressing and behaving like a city dude, and then riding and fighting like blazes when the right time comes.

d, Joseph Henabery; w, Douglas Fairbanks (based on the story "Silver Slippers" by Jackson Gregory); ph, Victor Fleming, Harry Thorpe.

Western **Cas.** **(PR:A MPAA:NR)**

MAN FROM WYOMING, THE*** (1924) 5 reels UNIV bw

Jack Hoxie *(Ned Bannister)*, Lillian Rich *(Helen Messiter)*, William Welsh *(David Messiter)*, Claude Payton *(Jack Halloway)*, Ben Corbett *(Red)*, Lon Poff *(Jim McWilliams)*, George Kuwa *(Sing Lee Wah)*, James Corrigan *(Governor of Wyoming)*.

Better-than-average B western has sheepman Hoxie accused of murder by his greedy cattle-raising neighbor, but clearing his name in the end with his fists. Great riding and stunt work by the popular cowboy star and some sharp direction on the part of Bradbury.

d, Robert North Bradbury; w, Isadore Bernstein (based on the novel *Wyoming* by William MacLeod Raine); ph, Merritt Gerstad.

Western **(PR:A MPAA:NR)**

MAN GETTER, THE (SEE: TRAIL'S END, 1922)

MAN HATER, THE** (1917) 5 reels TRI bw

Winifred Allen *(Phemie Sanders)*, Jack Meredith *(Joe Stull)*, Harry Neville *(Phemie's Father)*, Jessie Shirley *(Phemie's Mother)*, Marguerite Gale *(Lucy Conyer)*, Robert Vivian *(The Doctor)*, Anna Lehr *(Phemie's Little Sister)*, Thomas Tracey.

Because of her father's boozing, pretty little Allen becomes a man hater. Later she marries Meredith, the village blacksmith, on the condition that the union exist sans sex. Meredith agrees to this, figuring that with a little patience, she'll eventually see the light. Well, after a year or so, he runs out of patience and begins to visit a widow lady who spent some time in the city and knows the score. This brings Allen to her senses, and the couple are reunited in more ways than one.

d, Albert Parker; sup, Allan Dwan; w, Mary Brecht Pulver (based on a story by James Oliver Curwood).

Drama **(PR:C MPAA:NR)**

MAN HUNT, THE** (1918) 5 reels WORLD bw

Ethel Clayton *(Betty Hammond)*, Rockliffe Fellowes *(James Ogden)*, Henry Warwick *(English Lord)*, John Ardizonia *(French Count)*, Herbert Barrington *(Russian Prince)*, Jack Drumier *(Parson Brown)*, Al Hart *(Bigfoot Ben)*, John Dungan *(Lemuel Thomas)*.

Poorly made programmer about a young American millionairess who visits Monte Carlo, is sought after by a trio of penniless noblemen, and ends up marrying the foreman of one of her own lumber mills.

d, Travers Vale; w, (based on the story "The Silver Linings" by Fred Jackson).

Drama **(PR:A MPAA:NR)**

MAN IN HOBBLES, THE** (1928) 6 reels TS bw

John Harron *(The Boy)*, Lila Lee *(The Girl)*, Lucien Littlefield, Sunshine Hart, Betty Egan, Eddie Nugent, William Anderson *(The Girl's Family)*, Vivian Oakland *(The Other Woman)*.

Comedy programmer about a young photographer who marries a girl and finds her whole family moving in with him. Later the lad goes to New York, makes good, and finally finds the gumption to toss everyone but his bride out.

d, George Archainbaud; w, J. F. Natteford (based on the story by Peter Bernard

Kyne); t, Frederick Hatton, Fanny Hatton; ph, Harry Jackson; ed, Desmond O'Brien; art d, Hervey Libbert; set d, George Sawley.

Comedy/Drama **(PR:A MPAA:NR)**

MAN IN THE OPEN, A*** (1919) 6 reels United Pictures Theatres bw

Dustin Farnum *(Sailor Jesse)*, Hershall Mayall *(Trevor)*, Lamar Johnstone *("Bull" Brookes)*, Joseph Dowling *(James Brown)*, Claire Du Brey *(Polly)*, Irene Rich *(Kate)*, Aggie Herring.

Farnum goes from sailor, to cowboy, to ranger in this fast-paced western, which is loaded with fist fights, gun play and women of virtue and shame. A well-written, directed, and acted cowboy thriller.

d, Ernest C. Warde; w, Fred Myton (based on a story by Roger Pocock); ph, Robert Newhard.

Western **(PR:A MPAA:NR)**

MAN IN THE ROUGH** (1928) 5 reels FBO bw

Bob Steele *(Bruce Sherwood)*, Marjorie King *(Tess Winters)*, Tom Lingham *(Cale Winters)*, William Norton Bailey *(Jim Kane)*, Jay Morley *(Buck Helm)*.

Steele disguises himself as the killer hired by a land speculator to steal the property of an old-timer and his daughter, and sets out to warn them. After being taken by the girl for a real outlaw, Steele convinces them of his honesty, foils the plot, and wins the daughter.

d, Wallace Fox; w, Frank Howard Clark (based on a story by W. C. Tuttle); t, Randolph Bartlett; ph, Phil Tannura; ed, Della M. King.

Western Drama **(PR:A MPAA:NR)**

MAN OF IRON, A (SEE: IRON MAN, THE, 1925)

MAN OF NERVE, A** (1925) 5 reels R-C/FBO bw

Bob Custer *(Hackamore Henderson)*, Jean Arthur *(Loria Gatlin)*, Leon Holmes *(Buddy Simms)*, David Dunbar *(Rangey Greer)*, Buck Moulton *(Bandit)*, Ralph McCullogh *(Art Gatlin)*.

Custer falls in love with millinery store owner Arthur, whom he meets while tracking down stray cows. Custer is framed for the murder of his boss but manages to escape a lynch mob, with Arthur's help, and captures the real killer.

d, Louis Chaudet; w, George Hively (based on a story by John Harold Hamlin); ph, Allen Davey.

Western **(PR:A MPAA:NR)**

MAN ON THE BOX, THE 1/2** (1925) 8 reels WB bw

Sydney Chaplin *(Bob Warburton)*, David Butler *(Bob's Brother-In-Law)*, Alice Calhoun *(Betty Annesly)*, Kathleen Calhoun *(Mrs. Lampton)*, Theodore Lorch *(Mr. Lampton)*, Helene Costello *(Bob's Sister)*, E. J. Ratcliffe *(Col. Annesly)*, Charles F. Reisner *(Badkoff)*, Charles Gerrard *(Count Karaloff)*, Henry Barrows *(Warburton, Sr.)*.

This one was geared to give Chaplin (Charlie's half brother) the chance to appear in drag and hopefully repeat the success he enjoyed in CHARLIE'S AUNT. Unfortunately, THE MAN ON THE BOX, scriptwise, just didn't have the heft—although Chaplin's impression of a maid determined to prevent foreign agents from stealing the plans for a helicopter which his/her girl friend's father invented, does have its moments.

d, Charles Reisner; w, Charles A. Logue (based on the novel by Harold MacGrath); ph, Nick Barrows.

Comedy **(PR:A MPAA:NR)**

MAN THE ARMY MADE, A ** (1917, Brit.) 4 reels Holmfirth bw

Queenie Thomas *(Queenie Clarke)*, Cpt. Paul R. Hall *(Dick Clarke)*, H. Agar Lyons *(Irwin Lockwood)*, Micky Brantford *(Derry Clarke)*.

Stiff-upper-lip British wartime drama about a boozer who enlists in the service, becomes a hero, and returns home just in time to save his wife from the clutches of a rotten slacker.

d, Bertram Phillips; w, F. Martin Thornton (based on a story by Capt. Cecil Shaw).

War **(PR:A MPAA:NR)**

MAN TO MAN*** (1922) 6 reels UNIV-Jewel bw

Harry Carey *(Steve Packard)*, Lillian Rich *(Terry Temple)*, Charles Le Moyne *(Joe Blenham)*, Harold Goodwin *(Slim Barbee)*, Willis Robards *(Bill Royce)*.

Good Carey western (his last for Universal) has the veteran actor playing a derelict on a South Sea island who gives up the drink when he receives word his father has died, left him the family ranch, and that the inheritance is in danger. Carey returns, outslugs and outsmarts the bad guys, and even wins the love of his pretty neighbor.

d, Stuart Paton; w, George C. Hull (based on the novel by Jackson Gregory); ph, William Thornley; art d, E. E. Sheeley.

Western **(PR:A MPAA:NR)**

MAN WHO, THE*** (1921) 6 reels Metro bw

Bert Lytell *(Bedford Mills)*, Lucy Cotton *(Helen Jessop)*, Virginia Valli *(Mary Turner)*, Frank Currier *(St. John Jessop)*, Tammany Young *("Shorty" Mulligan)*, Fred Warren *("Bud" Carter)*, Clarence Elmer *(Radford Haynes)*, William Roselle *("Bing" Horton)*, Mary Louise Beaton *(Sarah Butler)*, Frank Strayer *(Jack Hyde)*.

Good comedy has Lytell, a war hero, falling for a socialite who learns he is a lowly bank clerk and demands that he go out into the world and become a man of importance. Lytell decides that postwar shoes are entirely too expensive and inaugurates a campaign for shoelessness. This nonconformist attitude makes him a media sensation, and Lytell finds himself falling mutually in love with a pretty artist who accompanies him on his well-publicized strolls—despite the fact that her daddy is the president of the footwear trust.

d, Maxwell Karger; w, June Mathis, Arthur J. Zellner (based on a story by Lloyd Osbourne); ph, Arthur Martinelli.

Comedy **(PR:A MPAA:NR)**

MAN WHO CHANGED HIS NAME, THE** (1928, Brit.) 7 reels BL bw

Stewart Rome *(Selby Clive)*, Betty Faire *(Nita Clive)*, James Raglan *(Frank O'Ryan)*, Ben Field *(Sir Ralph Whitcombe)*, Wallace Bosco *(Jerry Muller)*, Douglas Payne *(Canadian)*.

Not-too-exciting British thriller about a woman who mistakes her husband of being a murderer while cheating on him.

d, A. V. Bramble; w, Kathleen Hayden (based on a play by Edgar Wallace).

Mystery **(PR:A MPAA:NR)**

MAN WHO COULD NOT LOSE, THE* (1914) 5 reels Favorite Players bw

Carlyle Blackwell *(Champneys Carter)*, Hal Clements *(Jackson Carter)*, William Branton *(Count Lecoff)*, James J. Sheehan *(Rev. Orlondo Stone)*, J. M. Strong *(Spink)*, Thomas Delmar *(Sol Burbank)*, Harry Keenan *(Herbert Ingram)*, Gypsie Abbott *(Mellissa)*, Ruth Hartman *(Dolly)*.

D. W. Griffith could probably have made this one work as a one reeler at Biograph. But this story, about a man who bets his last cent and hits it big on a horse race he saw the ending of in a dream, stretches awfully thin over five.

w, Robert A. Dillon (based on a story by Richard Harding Davis).

Drama **(PR:A MPAA:NR)**

MAN WHO FORGOT, THE* (1917) 5 reels Paragon/WORLD bw

Robert Warwick *(John Smith)*, Gerda Holmes *(Mary Leslie)*, Doris Kenyon *(Edith Mallon)*, Alex Shannon *(Al Simpson)*, Ralph Delmore *(Sen. Mallon)*, Frederick C. Truesdell *(Congressman Mannersley)*, J. Reinhart *(Charles Waller)*.

Pro-prohibition propaganda has a trio of Americans (two men and a woman) living in the Orient as opium addicts. Warwick decides to kick the habit and returns to Cincinnati, where he arrives a complete amnesic. In the slums he falls for a social worker who happens to be the daughter of a U.S. senator, whom the liquor lobby needs to control. In order to obtain this influence, the liquor trust later forces the girl who shared her pipe with Warwick in China to claim that she's his wife. Not being able to remember *anything* about those days, Warwick is unable to deny the accusation. But in the end, the wretched girl confesses the truth and is welcomed into the society of sober people.

d&w, Emile Chautard (based on a novel by James Hay, Jr.); ph, Philip Hatkin, Lucien Tainguy.

Drama **(PR:A MPAA:NR)**

MAN WHO LAUGHS, THE**** (1927) 10 reels UNIV bw

Conrad Veidt *(Gwynplaine)*, Mary Philbin *(Dea)*, Olga Baclanova *(Duchess Josiana)*, Josephine Crowell *(Queen Anne)*, George Siegmann *(Dr. Hardquannone)*, Brandon Hurst *(Barkilphedro, the Jester)*, Sam De Grasse *(King James II)*, Stuart Holmes *(Lord Dirry-Noir)*, Cesare Gravina *(Ursus)*, Nick De Ruiz *(Wapentake)*, Edgar Norton *(Lord High Chancellor)*, Torben Meyer *(The Spy)*, Julius Molnar, Jr. *(Gwynplaine, as a Child)*, Charles Puffy *(Innkeeper)*, Frank Puglia, Jack Goodrich *(Clowns)*, Carmen Costello *(Dea's Mother)*, Zimbo *(Homo, the Wolf)*, Lon Poff.

Wonderfully atmospheric film about a boy (Veidt) who has his expression surgically changed into a permanent smile by order of his father's political rival, James II. He is taken in by a traveling showman who exhibits him first as a freak and later as a clown, gaining Veidt fame as "The Man Who Laughs." In their company is a beautiful blind girl who loves the poor devil for what he is, and in the end the two are permitted to find happiness. This was Universal's first film with a recorded sound track, and although it would seem that Carl Laemmle intended this to be a vehicle for Lon Chaney (with whom he had such great success in THE HUNCHBACK OF NOTRE DAME and THE PHANTOM OF THE OPERA), Veidt gives a performance of great sensitivity and depth.

d, Paul Leni; w, J. Grubb Alexander, Charles Whittaker, Marion Ward, May McLean (based on the novel *L'Homme Qui Rit* by Victor Hugo); t, Walter Anthony; ph, Gilbert Warrenton; ed, Maurice Pivar, Edward Cahn; art d, Charles D. Hall, Joseph Wright, Thomas F. O'Neill; m/l, "When Love Comes Stealing," Walter Hirsch, Lew Pollack, Erno Rapee; syn sc; s eff.

Costume/Drama **(PR:C MPAA:NR)**

MAN WHO MADE GOOD, THE** (1917) 5 reels FA/TRI bw

Jack Devereaux *(Tom Burton)*, Winifred Allen *(Frances Clayton)*, Henry P. Dixon *(Flash Lewis)*, Barney Gilmore *(Josiah Whitney)*.

Dixon, the famous burlesque producer, appears as the heavy in this fair programmer about a country boy who makes the grade through perseverance and grit.

d, Arthur Rosson; sup, Allan Dwan; w, Robert Shirley; ph, Roy Overbaugh.

Drama **(PR:A MPAA:NR)**

MAN WHO PLAYED GOD, THE* 1/2** (1922) 6 reels DIST/UA bw

George Arliss *(John Arden)*, Ann Forrest *(Marjory Blaine)*, Ivan Simpson *(Carter)*, Edward Earle *(Philip Stevens)*, Effie Shannon *(Mildred Arden)*, Miriam Battista *(Little Girl)*, Mickey Bennett *(Little Boy)*, Mary Astor *(Young Woman)*, Pierre Gendron *(Young Man)*, Margaret Seddon *(Old Woman)*, J. D. Walsh *(Old Man)*.

Arliss gives a wonderful performance as a premier musician who loses his hearing. He becomes despondent and embittered and is about to commit suicide when he comes to realize the truly desperate plight of others. With this he turns to philanthropy and becomes a changed man, preserving his marriage in the process. Then a fall causes him to regain his hearing, and once again he shares his art with a grateful world. Arliss would play the same part in a remake of this picture as a talkie in 1932.

d, Harmon Weight; w, Forrest Halsey (based on the play "The Silent Voice" by Jules Eckert Goodman); ph, Harry A. Fischbeck; art d, Clark Robinson.

Drama (PR:A MPAA:NR)

MAN WHO SAW TOMORROW, THE** (1922) 7 reels FP/PAR bw

Thomas Meighan *(Burke Hammond)*, Theodore Roberts *(Capt. Morgan Pring)*, Leatrice Joy *(Rita Pring)*, Albert Roscoe *(Jim McLeod)*, Alec Francis *(Sir William De Vry)*, June Elvidge *(Lady Helen Deene)*, Eva Novak *(Vonia)*, Laurance Wheat *(Larry Camden)*, John Miltern (Prof. Jansen), Robert Brower *(Bishop)*, Edward Patrick *(Botsu)*, Jacqueline Dyris *(Maya)*.

Good performances, lavish settings, and fine photography don't quite make up for the weakness in this script about a young man, pursued by two women, who enters into a hypnotic trance and is able to see the future he would share with each. The first, a wealthy English lady, would guarantee him a life full of fortune and fame, but not true love. The second, a sea captain's daughter, would provide plenty of the latter and very little of the former. It is also suggested that a marriage to the second girl might end with his death by an assassin's bullet. None the less, he chooses the hometown lass and decides to take his chances.

d, Alfred E. Green; w, Will M. Ritchey, Frank Condon (based on a story by Perley Poore Sheehan, Condon); ph, Alvin Wyckoff.

Drama (PR:A MPAA:NR)

MAN WHO TURNED WHITE, THE*** (1919) 5 reels Superior bw

H. B. Warner *(Capt. Rand/Ali Zaman)*, Barbara Castleton *(Ethel Lambert)*, Wedgewood Nowell *(Capt. Beverly)*, Carmen Phillips *(Fanina)*, Manuel Ojeda *(Joudar)*, Jay Dwiggins *(M. Mirabeau)*, Walter Perry *(Watchman)*, Eugenie Forde.

After suffering a gross indignity by friends who believe they are protecting a woman, Warner leaves the British African Corps and takes on the guise of an Arab outlaw. There is a nice sense of atmosphere about this picture, which ends with the woman saving Warner's life and bringing him back to the world of "civilized man."

d, Park Frame; w, George Elwood Jenks (based on a story by F. McGrew Willis); ph, William Foster.

Costume Drama (PR:A MPAA:NR)

MAN WITHOUT DESIRE, THE*** (1923, Brit.) 7 reels Atlas Biocraft/Novello-Atlas bw

Ivor Novello *(Count Vittorio Donaldo)*, Nina Vanna *(Leonora/Genevia)*, Sergio Mari *(Almoro/Gordi)*, Chris Walker *(Roger/Mawdesley)*, Jane Dryden *(Luigia)*, Dorothy Warren *(Foscolnia)*, Adrian Brunel *(Reporter)*.

British fantasy, featuring the popular Novello and set in the Venice of 1723, has to do with a scientist who masters the art of suspending life and is reunited with the one he loves 200 years later.

p, Ivor Novello; d, Adrian Brunel; w, Frank Fowell, Monckton Hoffe.

Fantasy (PR:A MPAA:NR)

MAN WORTH WHILE, THE½** (1921) 5 reels Romaine Fielding/Hillfield bw

Joan Arliss *(Mary Alden)*, Lawrence Johnson *(The Child)*, Eugene Acker *(Herbert Loring)*, Margaret Seddon *(Mrs. Ward)*, Frederick Eckhart *(Andre)*, Peggy Parr *(Cecile)*, Vanda Tierendelli *(Miss Flo)*, Barney Gilmore *(The Judge)*, Natalie O'Brien *(The Dancer)*, "Tex" Cooper *(The Parson)*, Kid Broad *(A Lifer)*, Emile Le Croix *(The Doctor)*, Frank De Vernon *(Eddie Loring)*, Burt Hodkins *(Percy)*, Clarence Heritage *(The Sheriff)*, Ruth Buchanan *(The Operator)*, Tammany Young *("Useless")*, Billy Quirk *(Napoleon)*, Romaine Fielding *(Don Ward)*.

Tearjerker set in the Canadian North Woods has pretty Arliss being tricked into marrying De Vernon, the lumber camp owner's son. Before long, the rotter deserts her, not caring that she is pregnant. Then, Fielding, a ranger and the man Arliss really loves, sets out to kill him but is arrested before performing the deed. Years later, when the child asks about her daddy, Arliss goes to De Vernon's house to implore him to acknowledge her child's legitimacy, and is shocked to find that her husband has been murdered by a French Canadian who discovered him taking advantage of his daughter. In the end Arliss and Fielding are reunited, and the little one is provided with the perfect home.

d, Romaine Fielding; w, (based on a poem by Ella Wheeler Wilcox).

Drama (PR:A MPAA:NR)

MANCHESTER MAN, THE*½ (1920, Brit.) 5 reels ID bw

Hayford Hobbs *(Jabez Clegg)*, Aileen Bagot *(Augusta Ashton)*, Warwick Ward *(Capt. Aspinall)*, A. Harding Steerman *(Mr. Ashton)*, Dora de Winton *(Mrs. Ashton)*, Hubert Willis *(Simon Clegg)*, Joan Hestor *(Bess Clegg)*, William Burchill *(Rev. Jotty Brooks)*, Charles Pelly *(Kit)*, Cecil Calvert *(Man of Affairs)*.

Set in Lancaster in 1880, this British drama deals with a lowly clerk madly in love with the daughter of a wealthy merchant who decides to run off with a criminal.

d, Bert Wynne; w, Eliot Stannard (based on a novel by Mrs. Linnaeus Banks).

Drama (PR:A MPAA:NR)

MANHATTAN*** (1924) 7 reels FP/PAR bw

Richard Dix *(Peter Minuit)*, Jacqueline Logan *(Mary Malone)*, Gregory Kelly *(Spike, Her Brother)*, George Siegmann *(Bud McGinnis)*, Gunboat Smith *(Joe Madden)*, Oscar Brimberton Figman, Edna May Oliver *(The Trapes)*, Alice Chapin *(Housekeeper)*, James Bradbury *(Trainer)*.

Always reliable (in any genre) Dix is a millionaire member of New York's "400." Bored with his society life, Dix passes himself off as a safecracker named "Gentleman George," and becomes part of the Hell's Kitchen underworld. Later he saves a girl and her brother from a life of crime after falling in love with her. There are plenty of laughs, a terrific fist fight between Dix and gang leader Siegmann, and fine performances all around.

d, R. H. Burnside; w, Paul Sloan, Frank W. Tuttle (based on the novel *The Definite Object a Romance of New York* by Jeffery Farnol); ph, Hal Rosson.

Comedy/Drama (PR:A MPAA:NR)

MANHATTAN COWBOY** (1928) 5 reels ED/Syndicate Pictures bw

Bob Custer, Lafe McKee, Mary Mayberry, Charles Whitaker, John Lowell Russell, Lynn Sanderson, Mack V. Wright, Cliff Lyons, Dorothy Vernon.

After stealing a cab driver's coat, society playboy Custer is sent to a ranch out West to straighten out. He proves to be the best rider, shooter, and fighter on the spread and completely redeems himself after rescuing the foreman's daughter from kidnapers.

d, J. P. McGowan; w, Sally Winters, Ernest Vajda (based on a story by Winters); ph, Paul Stern.

Western (PR:A MPAA:NR)

MANHATTAN KNIGHTS*** (1928) 7 reels EXCEL bw

Barbara Bedford *(Margaret)*, Walter Miller *(Robert Ferris)*, Betty Worth *(Julia)*, Ray Hallor *(James Barton)*, Crauford Kent *(Henry Ryder)*, Eddie Boland *(Chick Watson)*, Noble Johnson *(Doc Mellis)*, Joseph Burke *(Barry)*, Leo White *(Giuseppi)*, Maude Truax.

A sister (well played by Bedford) sets out with her sweetheart (Miller) to get back the $50,000 post-dated check her naive brother gave to a group of card sharps. Director King packed this standard crime drama with plenty of action. Particularly effective is the scene where the good guys are rescued in the nick of time from a burning building by the Los Angeles fire department.

d, Burton King; w, Adeline Leitzback; ph, Edward Kull, Walter Haas; ed, De Leon Anthony.

Action/Drama (PR:A MPAA:NR)

MANHATTAN MADNESS**** (1916) 5 reels FA/TRI bw

Douglas Fairbanks *(Steve O'Dare)*, Jewel Carmen *(The Girl)*, George Beranger *(The Butler)*, Ruth Darling *(The Maid)*, Eugene Ormonde *(Count Marinoff)*, Macey Harlam *(The Villain)*, W. P. Richmond *(Jack Osborne)*, Albert MacQuarrie, Norman Kaiser [Norman Kerry], Adolphe Menjou, John Richmond.

Wonderful combination of laughter and thrills has Fairbanks playing an ex-New Yorker who returns from his ranch in the west with a shipment of cattle and horses. At his club he tells his city pals that, from his point of view, there is not a single thrill to be found in all of Gotham. His friends wager $5,000 that if he remains on for one week more, he will find the action he craves. Then they set about to stage a rib, the likes of which would do in anyone but the irrepressible Fairbanks. Of course he manages to outwit the actors who have been hired for the stunt, and even wins the actress who was central to the gag, in one of his very best noncostume pictures. While filming MANHATTAN MADNESS, Fairbanks traveled to the Fine Arts studio each morning by way of the Harlem and Hudson Rivers in the comfort of his yacht, which was harbored nearby. According to the star, "Why use an automobile, taxi or even a street car, when you can have a yacht?"

d, Allan Dwan; w, Charles T. Dazey (based on a story by E. V. Durling).

Comedy/Adventure (PR:A MPAA:NR)

MAN-MADE WOMEN* (1928) 6 reels DM/Pathe bw

Leatrice Joy *(Nan Payson)*, H. B. Warner *(Jules Moret)*, John Boles *(John Payson)*, Seena Owen *(Georgette)*, Jay Eaton *(Garth)*, Jeanette Loff *(Marjorie)*, Sidney Bracey *(Owens)*.

Joy, an actress of considerable beauty and charm, was given far too many turkeys during her career, including this one about a jazz-happy bride who leaves her husband because she considers his friends boring, but then comes to her senses and returns.

p, Ralph Block; d, Paul L. Stein; w, Alice D. G. Miller (based on a story by Ernest Pascal); t, Edwin Justus Mayer; ph, John Mescall; ed, Doane Harrison; art d, Stephen Goosson.

Drama/Comedy (PR:A MPAA:NR)

MANON LESCAUT* (1914) 4 reels PG bw

Lina Cavalieri, Lucien Muratore, Dorothy Arthur, W. L. Abingdon, Charles Hammond, Frank H. Westerton, Henry Weaver, Frank Hardy, H. L. Winslow, Walter Cecil.

The presence of famed European opera stars Cavalieri and Muratore did little to help this very uncinematic adaptation of Prevost's classic love story.

w, (based on the novel by Abbe Prevost).

Drama (PR:A MPAA:NR)

MAN'S HOME, A½** (1921) 6 reels SL/SEL bw

Harry T. Morey *(Frederick Osborn)*, Kathlyn Williams *(Frances Osborn)*, Faire Binney *(Lucy Osborne)*, Margaret Seddon *(Amanda Green)*, Grace Valentine *(Cordelia Wilson)*, Roland Bottomley *(Jack Wilson)*, Matt Moore *(Arthur Lynn)*.

Ince skillfully directed this tale of a woman's obsession with the fast life after her husband strikes it rich, and how she almost destroys her daughter's future happiness because of her actions. This was far better than most stage adaptations, and the acting and production values were equally fine.

d, Ralph Ince; w, Edward J. Montagne (based on the play by Anna Steese Richardson, Edmund Breese); ph, William J. Black.

Drama (PR:A MPAA:NR)

MAN'S LAW AND GOD'S* (1922) 5 reels Finis Fox/ARC bw

Jack Livingston *(Bruce MacDonald)*, Ethel Shannon *(Kitty Roshay)*, Kate Anderson *(Bruce's Mother)*, Bobby Mack *("Uncle Jimmie")*, Joy Winthrop *(Aunt Jenny)*, George Cummings *("Cameo" Brooks)*, Rosa Melville *(Helen DuBrose)*.

Shannon, a wealthy girl with a sense of fun, answers an ad in a matrimonial paper which was placed by Mack for (but without the knowledge of) police mountie Livingston. Later Livingston mistakes Shannon for a fugitive dance hall girl and, after nabbing the wrong girl, he discovers she is really the *right* girl for him. Then, to everyone's delight, Mack finds his long, lost love when he runs into Shannon's very available aunt, Winthrop.

d&w, Finis Fox.

Drama (PR:A MPAA:NR)

MAN'S MAN, A** (1929) 8 reels MGM bw

William Haines *(Mel)*, Josephine Dunn *(Peggy)*, Sam Hardy *(Charlie)*, Mae Busch *(Violet)*, John Gilbert *(Himself)*, Greta Garbo *(Herself)*, Gloria Davenport.

Farnham's funny titles are the only bright spot in this otherwise routine comedy drama about a girl who goes to Hollywood to break into the movies and ends up marrying a good-natured soda jerk. Guest appearances by Gilbert and Garbo also add a little interest.

d, James Cruze; w, Forrest Halsey (based on the novel by Patrick Kearney); t, Joe Farnham; ph, Merritt B. Gerstad; ed, George Hively; art d, Cedric Gibbons; m/l, "My Heart Is Bluer Than Your Eyes, Cherie," Al Bryan, Monte Wilhitt; syn sc; s eff.

Comedy/Drama (PR:A MPAA:NR)

MAN'S PREROGATIVE, A* (1915) 4 reels Mutual Masterpiece bw

Robert Edeson *(Oliver Rand)*, Mary Alden *(Elizabeth Town)*, Charles Cleary *(The Artist)*, Billie West *(The Model)*.

This feature about a man's infidelity after marriage would have made a much better one reeler. At four it drags considerably and lacks any cinematic punch.

d, George Nichols; w, Frank E. Woods.

Drama (PR:A MPAA:NR)

MAN'S SHADOW, A* (1920, Brit.) 6 reels Progress/But bw

Langhorne Burton *(Peter Beresford/Julian Grey)*, Violet Graham *(Vivian Beresford)*, Gladys Mason *(Yolande Hampden)*, J. Denton-Thompson *(Williams)*, Sydney Paxton *(Billings)*, Babs Ronald *(Helen Beresford)*, Warris Linden *(Simon Oppenheim)*.

Unpleasant British mystery about the look-alike of an impoverished down-and-outer, who murders a Jewish money lender but in the end is betrayed by his former paramour.

p, Frank E. Spring; d&w, Sidney Morgan (based on a play by Robert Buchanan).

Crime (PR:C MPAA:NR)

MANXMAN, THE½** (1929, Brit.) 8 reels British International/Ufa Eastman bw

Carl Brisson *(Pete Quilliam)*, Malcolm Keen *(Philip Christian)*, Anny Ondra *(Kate Cregeen)*, Randle Ayrton *(Her Father)*, Clare Greet *(Her Mother)*, Wilfred Shine *(Doctor)*, Kim Peacock *(Ross Christian)*, Harry Terry *(Man)*, Nellie Richards *(Wardress)*.

Hitchcock was very disappointed in his last silent film, THE MANXMAN. The audiences, however, loved it and one review referred to it as "a film of remarkable power and gripping interest." It told the story of two men, a fisherman and a lawyer, in love with the same woman. The fisherman (Brisson) asks the girl, Ondra, to marry him but her father forces her to decline because of his lowly background. Brisson leaves to find his fortune and when he is reported killed, Keen, the lawyer, begins to date Ondra. But Ondra continues to love Brisson and when he suddenly turns up alive, she marries him. Soon she gives birth to a child which turns out to be Keen's. The mood of the film darkens considerably and ends on an unhappy note with an attempted suicide once the truth is discovered.

p, John Maxwell; d, Alfred Hitchcock; w, Eliot Stannard (based on the novel by Sir Hall Caine); ph, Jack Cox; set d, Elstree.

Drama Cas. (PR:A MPAA:NR)

MARCH HARE, THE** (1919, Brit.) 6 reels Lucky Cat/ID bw

Godfrey Tearle *(Guy)*, Ivy Duke *(Ivy)*, Will Corrie, Philip Hewland, Lewis Gilbert, Douglas Heathcote, Percy Crawford, Peggy Maurice, John Miller.

British comedy about a man who comes to the assistance of a desperate gambler by pretending to be an escaped maniac who then robs his father.

d&w, Frank Miller (based on a story by Guy Newall).

Comedy (PR:A MPAA:NR)

MARE NOSTRUM**** (1926) 10 reels MGM bw

Uni Apollon *(The Triton)*, Alex Nova *(Don Estaban Ferragut)*, Kada-Abd-el-Kader *(His Son, Ulysses)*, Hughie Mack *(Caragol)*, Alice Terry *(Freya Talberg)*, Antonio Moreno *(Ulysses Ferragut)*, Mlle. Kithnou *(His Wife, Dona Cinta)*, Michael Brantford *(Their Son, Estaban)*, Rosita Ramirez *(Their Niece, Pepita)*, Frederick Mariotti *(Toni, the Mate)*, Mme. Paquerette *(Dr. Fedelmann)*, Fernand Mailly *(Count Kaledine)*, Andre von Engleman *(Submarine Commander)*.

Ingram directed this stunning film (shot entirely in Europe) about a female German agent who gives her life for the fatherland. Although lost, stills indicate that this picture may contain the greatest firing squad sequence ever shot (with the possible exception of PATHS OF GLORY). And, as an anti-war statement, MARE NOSTRUM made a wonderful follow-up to the earlier Ingram-Ibanez triumph, THE FOUR HORSEMEN OF THE APOCALYPSE.

p&d, Rex Ingram; w, Willis Goldbeck (based on the novel by Vicente Blasco-Ibanez); ph, John F. Seitz; ed, Grant Whytock; art d, Ben Carre.

War (PR:A MPAA:NR)

MARK OF ZORRO**** (1920) 8 reels Douglas Fairbanks/UA bw

Douglas Fairbanks *(Don Diego Vega/Zorro)*, Noah Beery *(Sgt. Gonzalez)*, Marguerite de la Motte *(Lolita)*, Robert McKim *(Capt. Juan Ramon)*, Charles Hill Mailes *(Don Carlos Pulido)*, Claire McDowell *(Dona Catalina, His Wife)*, George Periolat *(Gov. Alvarado)*, Walt Whitman *(Father Felipe)*, Sydney De Grey *(Don Alejandro)*, Albert MacQuarrie, Charles Stevens, Tote Du Crow, John Winn, Charles Belcher, Noah Beery, Jr., Gilbert Clayton, Snitz Edwards.

Fairbanks' first—and most famous—costume picture about the California fop who liberates his people from the clutches of tyranny by disguising himself as the athletic, swashbuckling Zorro. Nonstop action and some very clever comedy touches as well. MARK OF ZORRO is historic in that it was the picture that convinced Fairbanks that swashbuckling roles could not only be profitable at the box office, but fun for himself besides. Up to this picture, his featured roles had been as the American playboy or the six-shooting range rider in madcap adventures, and the idea of wearing a cloak and using a dueling sword left him very much up in the air as to how his audience would accept him. There was little worry—his vigor and sense of timing, the wonderful comic touches he was allowed to make as the fop, and the theme of the crusading fighter for the rights of Mexicans made the film tremendously popular and changed the course of his future, leading most spectacularly to ROBIN HOOD, the unsurpassable achievement of his career, in spite of its sometimes overbearing pretentiousness. There are some exciting duel sequences in the picture and Fairbanks' usual amazing acrobatics. In support, de la Motte does a fine job of despising Fairbanks the dandy but loving Fairbanks as Zorro (unaware that both are the same man), while being loved by McKim, the greasy Capt. Juan Ramon. Beery is a winning character in an offbeat role, that of an enemy of Zorro who is defeated by him so many times that in the end he gives up the battle, throws down his sword, and decides to be friends to the brilliant masked duelist.

p, Douglas Fairbanks; d, Fred Niblo; w, Elton Thomas [Douglas Fairbanks] (based on the story "The Curse of Capistrano" by Johnston McCulley); ph, William McGann, Harry Thorpe; m, William Perry; art d, Edward Langley.

Costume/Adventure Cas. (PR:A MPAA:NR)

MARKED MONEY** (1928) 6 reels Pathe bw

Junior Coghlan *(Boy)*, George Duryea *(Clyde)*, Tom Kennedy *(Bill Clemons)*, Bert Woodruff *(Capt. Fairchild)*, Virginia Bradford *(Grace Fairchild)*, Maurice Black *(Donovan)*, Jack Richardson *(Scudder)*.

Fair kids' film with Coghlan (who would go on to play Billy Batson in the Republic serial CAPTAIN MARVEL) as an orphaned boy living with a kindly captain, Woodruff. With the help of Woodruff's daughter and her Navy flier sweetheart, a couple of crooks are prevented from stealing Coghlan's $25,000 inheritance.

d, Spencer Gordon Bennett; w, George Dromgold, Sanford Hewitt (based on a story by Howard J. Green); t, John Krafft; ph, Edward Snyder; ed, Harold McLernon; md, Josiah Zuro; art d, Edward Jewell.

Adventure (PR:A MPAA:NR)

MARKET OF VAIN DESIRE, THE*** (1916) 5 reels Kay-Bee/TRI bw

H. B. Warner *(John Armstrong)*, Clara Williams *(Helen Badgley)*, Charles Miller *(Count Bernard d' Montaigne)*, Gertrude Claire *(Mrs. Badgley)*, Leona Hutton *(Belle)*.

Well-made movie with a moral has Warner as a minister (he would later play Christ in THE KING OF KINGS) who discovers that one of his parishioners, a beautiful young millionairess, is being forced to marry an impecunious nobleman by her title-hungry mother. The following Sunday, he hires a prostitute to attend services and, from the pulpit, points to the woman and draws the comparison between selling one's body for money and selling out for prestige. In so doing, he not only breaks up his parishioner's engagement, but wins her undying love as well.

d, Reginald Barker; w, C. Gardner Sullivan.

Drama (PR:A MPAA:NR)

MARRIAGE CIRCLE, THE**** (1924) 8 reels WB bw

Florence Vidor *(Charlotte Braun)*, Monte Blue *(Dr. Franz Braun)*, Marie Prevost *(Mizzie Stock)*, Creighton Hale *(Dr. Gustav Mueller)*, Adolphe Menjou *(Prof. Josef Stock)*, Harry Myers *(Private Detective)*, Dale Fuller *(Neurotic Patient)*, Esther Ralston.

Inspired by Charlie Chaplin's WOMAN OF PARIS, Lubitsch made this wonderfully sophisticated comedy of manners and thus became, next to D. W. Griffith, the most imitated director in the world. THE MARRIAGE CIRCLE was the favorite film of such giants of the cinema as Hitchcock, Kurosawa and Chaplin himself. And according to Herman G. Weinberg, who wrote the indispensable *Lubitsch Touch*, it was the director's as well.

d, Ernst Lubitsch; w, Paul Bern (based on the play "Only a Dream" by Lothar Schmidt [Goldschmidt]); ph, Charles Van Enger.

Comedy **(PR:A MPAA:NR)**

MARRIAGE CLAUSE, THE** (1926) 8 reels UNIV bw

Francis X. Bushman *(Barry Townsend)*, Billie Dove *(Sylvia Jordan)*, Warner Oland *(Max Ravenal)*, Henri La Garde *(Doctor)*, Grace Darmond *(Mildred Le Blanc)*, Caroline Snowden *(Pansy)*, Oscar Smith *(Sam)*, Andre Cheron *(Critic)*, Robert Dudley *(Secretary)*, Charles Meakin *(Stage Manager)*.

Broadway love story has small town girl Dove being molded into a theatrical star by director Bushman. They fall in love, but before their wedding producer Oland presents the actress with a three-year contract containing a no-marriage clause. Through a misunderstanding, Bushman leaves Dove and the theater. All of this has a negative effect on Dove's health, and on opening night she becomes dreadfully ill. Learning that Bushman is in attendance, the brave little trooper goes on, gives the performance of her life, and collapses at the final curtain. Later she recovers, and the director-actress team reunite to create personal and show business magic together.

d&w, Lois Weber (based on the story "Technic" by Dana Burnet); ph, Hal Mohr.

Drama **(PR:A MPAA:NR)**

'MARRIAGE LICENSE?'*** 1/2 (1926) 8 reels FOX bw

Alma Rubens *(Wanda Heriot)*, Walter McGrail *(Marcus Heriot)*, Richard Walling *(Robin)*, Walter Pidgeon *(Paul)*, Charles Lane *(Sir John)*, Emily Fitzroy *(Lady Heriot)*, Langhorne Burton *(Cheriton)*, Edgar Norton *(Beadon)*, George Cowl *(Abercrombie)*, Lon Poff *(Footman)*.

Rubens plays a Canadian woman who sacrifices happiness with the man she loves to go back to the English nobleman (who allowed his family to annul their marriage) in order to give her son legitimacy before he goes off to war. An extremely touching film with a fine performance by Rubens and skillful direction by Borzage.

d, Frank Borzage; w, Bradley King (based on a play "The Pelican" by F. Tennyson Jesse, Harold Marsh Harwood); t, Elizabeth Pickett; ph, Ernest Palmer.

Drama **(PR:A MPAA:NR)**

MARRIAGE OF KITTY, THE** 1/2 (1915) 5 reels LAS bw

Fanny Ward *(Katherine Silverton)*, Richard Morris *(John Travers)*, Jack Dean *(Lord Riginald Belsize)*, Cleo Ridgely *(Helen de Samiano)*, Tom Forman *(Jack Churchill)*, Mrs. Lewis McCord *(Annie)*, Theodore Roberts, Lucien Littlefield.

In this snappy little comedy set in England and Newport, a Lord, who is infatuated with a music hall entertainer, weds an impoverished girl for a fee in order to honor a provision in his inheritance forbidding his marrying an actress. The Lord later falls in love with his new wife when he realizes how beautiful she really is, and she proves the music hall entertainer to be a crook.

d, George Melford; w, Hector Turnbull (based on the play "La Passerelle" by F. de Croisset, Fred de Gressac and Cosmo Gordon Lennox's version of it).

Comedy **(PR:A MPAA:NR)**

MARRIAGE OF WILLIAM ASHE, THE ** (1921) 6 reels Metro bw

May Allison *(Kitty Bristol)*, Wyndham Standing *(William Ashe)*, Zeffie Tilbury *(Lady Tranmore)*, Frank Elliot *(Geoffrey Cliffe)*, Robert Bolder *(Lord Parham)*, Clarissa Selwynne *(Lady Mary Lyster)*, Lydia Yeamans Titus *(Lady Parham)*.

Adequate screen adaptation of the popular Ward novel and play about the French convent-trained girl who marries Britain's Secretary of House Affairs and, after being snubbed, scandalizes London society with her caricatures of Parliamentary members, and later attends a gala semi-nude.

d, Edward Sloman; sup, Bayard Veiller; w, Ruth Ann Baldwin (based on the novel by Mary Augusta Ward and the play by Margaret Mayo and Ward); ph, Jackson Rose; art d, John Holden.

Drama **(PR:A MPAA:NR)**

MARRIAGE PRICE* (1919) 5 reels ART bw

Elsie Ferguson *(Helen Tremaine)*, Wyndham Standing *(Frederick Lawton)*, Lionel Atwill *(Kenneth Gordon)*, Maud Hosford *(Amelia Lawton)*, Clariette Anthony, Robert Schable.

Ponderous drama about a pampered girl who is forced to get a job when her father dies and leaves her penniless. There are a couple of fellows who have always loved her, and she chooses the one who was her father's best friend.

d, Emile Chautard; w, Eve Unsell (based on the story "For Sale" by Griswold Wheeler); ph, Jacques Bizeul.

Drama **(PR:A MPAA:NR)**

MARRIED ALIVE** (1927) 5 reels FOX bw

Lou Tellegen *(James Duxbury)*, Margaret Livingston *(Amy Duxbury)*, Matt Moore *(Charles Orme)*, Claire Adams *(Viola Helmesley Duxbury)*, Gertrude Claire *(Lady Rockett)*, Marcella Daly *(Blanche Fountain Duxbury)*, Henry Sedley *(Max Ferbur)*, Eric Mayne *(Dr. McMaster)*, Charles Lane *(Mr. Fountain)*, Emily Fitzroy *(Mrs. Maggs Duxbury)*.

Strange combination of comedy and tragedy has a professor becoming involved with a polygamist (Tellegen), and marrying the fellow's aristocratic fourth "wife" himself. Pretty much a failure on every level.

d, Emmett Flynn; w, Gertrude Orr (based on a novel by Ralph Strauss); ph, Ernest Palmer.

Comedy/Drama **(PR:A MPAA:NR)**

MARRIED FLIRTS*** (1924) 7 reels MGM/MG bw

Pauline Frederick *(Nellie Wayne)*, Conrad Nagel *(Perley Rex)*, Mae Busch *(Jill Wetherell)*, Huntley Gordon *(Pendleton Wayne)*, Paul Nicholson *(Peter Granville)*, Patterson Dial *(Evelyn Draycup)*, Alice Hollister *(Mrs. Callender)*, John Gilbert, Hobart Henley, Robert Z. Leonard, May McAvoy, Mae Murray, Aileen Pringle, Norma Shearer.

Frederick loses her husband to Busch after neglecting him to concentrate on becoming a writer. Later she becomes the literary toast of Europe and encounters Busch, who is vacationing with her new lover, Nagel. To get even, Frederick seduces Nagel to the point of surrender and then discards him in favor of her husband, who is delighted to reconcile. A number of MGM luminaries, including Gilbert, Shearer, Murray, Pringle, Henley, McAvoy and Leonard, have cameo roles, appearing as the principals in a forthcoming motion picture based on one of Frederick's novels.

d, Robert G. Vignola; w, Julia Crawford Ivers (based on the novel *Mrs. Paramor* by Louis Joseph Vance); t, Frederic Hatton, Fanny Hatton; ph, Oliver Marsh; ed, Frank E. Hull; set d, Charles L. Cadwallader.

Drama **(PR:A MPAA:NR)**

MARRIED TO A MORMAN** (1922, Brit.) 6 reels Master/Astral bw

Evelyn Brent *(Beryl Fane)*, Clive Brook *(Lionel Daventry)*, George Wynn *(Philip Lorimer)*, Booth Conway *(Bigelow)*, Molly Adair.

In 1922 all ethnic and religious groups were fair game, and in this intolerant British drama a Mormon takes leave of his wealthy English wife to marry a second woman in Utah, but pays the price when he is murdered by his first wife's paramour.

p&d, H. B. Parkinson; w, Frank Miller.

Drama **(PR:A MPAA:NR)**

MARRY IN HASTE** (1924) 5 reels Phil Goldstone bw

William Fairbanks *(Wayne Sturgis)*, Dorothy Revier *(Joan Prescott)*, Alfred Hollingsworth *(Manager)*, Gladden James *(Monte Brett)*, William Dyer *(Champion)*, Al Kaufman *(Jack Dugan)*.

Not many laughs in this dramatic comedy about a young westerner (Fairbanks) who is disinherited by his wealthy father after marrying an art student (Revier). The couple struggle along on a small farm until the old boy decides to forgive them and issues an invitation to move to his ranch.

d, Duke Worne; w, Jean Duvane.

Western/Comedy **(PR:A MPAA:NR)**

MARRY THE GIRL* (1928) 6 reels STER bw

Barbara Bedford *(Elinor)*, Robert Ellis *(Harry Wayland)*, De Witt Jennings *(Martin Wayland)*, Freddie Frederick *(Sonny, the Child)*, Florence Turner *(Miss Lawson, the Housekeeper)*, Paul Weigel *(The Butler)*, Allan Roscoe *(Cliff Lawson, the Secretary)*.

In an attempt to swindle an old millionaire out of his fortune, a couple of crooked servants frame his son for theft and cause the lad to be driven from the house. They then bring in Bedford, a sweet, recently widowed mother, whom they pass off as the son's bride, after convincing the old man that his son was killed. Bedford believes that she has been hired to offer comfort to a lonely gentleman and therefore goes along with the scam in complete innocence. Fortunately, the son returns in time to expose the plot, and falls in love with Bedford and her child.

d, Philip Rosen; w, Frances Guihan (based on a story by Wyndham Gittens); t, Guihan; ph, Herbert Kirkpatrick; ed, Leotta Whytock.

Drama **(PR:A MPAA:NR)**

MARSHAL OF MONEYMINT, THE** (1922) 5 reels Ben Wilson/Arrow bw

Jack Hoxie *(Jack Logan)*, Jim Welch *(Jimsy MacTavish)*, James Rock *(Buck Lanning)*, William Lester *(Slick Boyle)*, Andree Tourneur *(Mollie Benton)*, Claude Payton *(Velvet Joe Sellers)*, Goldie Madden *(Mandie St. Claire)*.

When the gutless sheriff of Moneymint refuses to help the decent folks protect their mining claims from bad guy Payton, Hoxie gets himself appointed deputy, convinces Tourneur that he is not the villain, and brings the crooks to justice.

p, Ben Wilson; d&w, Roy Clements.

Western **(PR:A MPAA:NR)**

MARTHA'S VINDICATION*** (1916) 5 reels FA/TRI bw

Norma Talmadge *(Martha)*, Seena Owen *(Dorothea)*, Ralph Lewis *(Deacon Hunt)*, Tully Marshall *(Sell Hawkins)*, Josephine Crowell *(Jennie Hawkins)*, Charles West *(William Burton)*, William Hinckley *(John)*, Francis Carpenter *(Francis)*, George Stone *(George)*, Alice Knowland *(The Frump)*, Alberta Lee *(The Nurse)*, Edwin Harley *(Her Husband)*, George Pearce *(The Minister)*, Porter Strong *(Hotel Clerk)*, Lillian Langdon.

Talmadge heads a fine cast in this story about a girl accused of having an illegitimate child, who covers for her friend (the real mother whose lover was killed in an accident) when the girl marries and has another baby. In the end, Talmadge is cleared and accepts the proposal of the fellow who stood by her through the entire ordeal.

d, Sidney and Chester Franklin; w, Frank Woods (based on a story by Ella Carter Woods); ph, Frank Good.

Drama **(PR:A MPAA:NR)**

MARTYRS OF THE ALAMO, THE*** (1915) 5 reels FA/TRI bw

Sam De Grasse *(Silent Smith)*, Walter Long *(Santa Anna)*, Tom Wilson *(Sam Houston)*, A. D. Sears *(David Crockett)*, Alfred Paget *(James Bowie)*, Augustus Carney *(Old Soldier)*, John Dillon *(Col. Travis)*, Fred Burns *(Capt. Dickinson)*, Ora Carew *(Mrs. Dickinson)*, Juanita Hansen *(Old Soldier's Daughter)*.

Excellent combat scenes and a nice sense of detail make this exciting account of the legendary battle between a group of heroic Texans and the forces of Santa Anna, stand out. There is fine direction by Cabanne, but one wonders how much Griffith had to do with its more impressive moments.

d, W. Christy Cabanne; sup, D. W. Griffith; w, Cabanne (based on a story by Theodosia Harris).

Historical/War (PR:A MPAA:NR)

MARY LATIMER, NUN** (1920, Brit.) 5 reels Famous Pictures bw

Malvina Longfellow *(Mary Latimer)*, Warwick Ward *(Honorable Alfred Pierpoint)*, Ethel Fisher *(Clarice Pierpoint)*, George Foley *(Sam Tubbs)*, H. Agar Lyons *(Lord Pierpoint)*, Moore Marriott *(Dickey Stubbs)*, Laurence Tessier, Minnie Rayner.

In this British drama, an aristocrat marries a girl from the wrong side of the tracks and deserts her. She then goes on to become London's most celebrated music hall star.

d, Bert Haldane; w, R. Byron Webber (based on the novel by Eva Elwen and the play by Will H. Glaze).

Drama (PR:A MPAA:NR)

MASK, THE½** (1921) 7 reels Selig/EIFC bw

Jack Holt *(Kenneth Traynor/Handsome Jack)*, Hedda Nova *(Helen Traynor)*, Mickey Moore *(Mickey, Their Son)*, Fred Malatesta *(Senor Enrico Keralio)*, Harry Lonsdale *(Winthrop Parker)*, Byron Munson *(Arthur Steele)*, Janice Wilson *(Rae Madison)*, William Clifford *(Francois)*.

Entertaining programmer, despite some sloppy special effects, about a reformed man who breaks up a diamond robbery. And Holt, the star, was just on the threshold of much bigger things in his career.

d, Bertram Bracken; w, Arthur Lavon (based on a story by Arthur Hornblow); ph, Edwin Linden.

Mystery (PR:A MPAA:NR)

MASKED ANGEL* (1928) 6 reels CHAD/FD bw

Betty Compson *(Betty Carlisle)*, Erick Arnold *(Jimmy Pruett)*, Wheeler Oakman *(Luther Spence)*, Jocelyn Lee *(Lola Dugan)*, Grace Cunard *(Cactus Kate)*, Lincoln Plummer *(Wilbur Ridell)*, Robert Homans *(Detective Bives)*, Jane Keckley *(Nurse)*.

To escape the police for a crime she is falsely accused of committing, nightclub hostess Compson slips into a hosptial where she meets and falls in love with a blinded soldier. She ultimately nurses him back to health, and he ignores the stories a malicious rival tells him about her past.

p, I. E. Chadwick; d, Frank O'Connor; w, Maxine Alton (based on a story by Evelyn Campbell); t, Isadore Bernstein; ph, Ted Tetzlaff; ed, Gene Milford.

Drama (PR:A MPAA:NR)

MASKED AVENGER, THE*
(1922) 5 reels DOUB/Western Pictures Exploitation bw

Lester Cuneo *(Austin Patterson)*, Mrs. Wallace Reid *(Valerie Putnam)*, Billy Reid *(The School Boy)*, Claude Payton *(Bruno Douglas)*, William Donovan *(Sheriff Dan Dustin)*, Phil Gastrock *(Ebenezer Jones)*, Tempe Pigott *("Aunt Phoebe Dyer")*, Burt Maddock *("Lariat Bill Williams")*, Ah Wing *(Quong Lee)*.

Low-budget oater about a rancher (Cuneo) who draws the suspicion of his neighbors when he refuses to join them in trying to stop a band of rustlers. But then when his herd is hit, Cuneo sports a mask, waits in the darkness, and then mops up the gang.

d, Frank Fanning; sup, Charles W. Mack; w, Henry McCarthy, Leo Meehan.

Western (PR:A MPAA:NR)

MASKED EMOTIONS½** (1929) 6 reels FOX bw

George O'Brien *(Bramdlet Dickery)*, Nora Lane *(Emily Goodell)*, J. Farrell MacDonald *(Will Whitten)*, David Sharpe *(Thad Dickery)*, James Gordon *(Capt. Goodell)*, Edward Peil, Sr. *(Lee Wing)*, Frank Hagney *(Lagune)*.

Entertaining programmer has O'Brien at his most muscular, as he breaks up a gang which smuggles Chinese aliens into the U.S. Film is noteworthy for the early appearance of ace stunt man Sharpe, as O'Brien's younger brother.

d, David Butler, Kenneth Hawks; w, Harry Brand, Benjamin Markson (based on the story "A Son of Anak" by Ben Ames Williams); t, Douglas Z. Doty; ph, Sidney Wagner; syn sc; s eff.

Drama (PR:A MPAA:NR)

MASQUERADERS, THE½** (1915) 5 reels FP bw

Hazel Dawn *(Dulcie Larendie)*, Elliott Dexter *(David Remon)*, Frank Losee *(Sir Brice Skene)*, Norman Tharp *(Monte Lushington)*, Ida Darling *(Lady Crandover)*, Evelyn Farris *(Clarice)*, Nina Lindsey *(Helen Lardendie)*, Charles Bryant *(Eddie Remon)*, Russell Bassett *(Inn Proprietor)*.

Somewhat diverting story has an impoverished young Englishwoman turning down the man she really loves to marry millionaire Losee. Later she discovers him to be a drunkard, but before setting out to file for divorce, Losee is murdered by a blackmailer.

d, James Kirkwood; w, (based on the play by Henry Arthur Jones).

Drama (PR:A MPAA:NR)

MASTER CRACKSMAN, THE **½
(1914) 6 reels PROGRESSIVE MOTION PICTURE CORP bw

Harry Carey *(Gentleman Joe, the Cracksman)*, E. A. Lock *(The Uncle)*, Rexford Burnett *(Harold Martin)*, Fern Foster *(Harold's Sister)*, Marjorie Bonner *(Violet Dane)*.

Carey wrote, directed, and starred in this interesting film about a safecracker (with honest instincts) who saves an innocent boy from going to the electric chair, by cracking the case.

d&w, Harry Carey.

Crime (PR:A MPAA:NR)

MASTER MIND, THE* (1914) 5 reels LAS bw

Edmund Breese, Mabel Van Buren, Robert Edeson, Fred Montague, Jane Darwell, Monroe Salisbury, Billy Elmer.

Even by 1914, when this crime film was produced, the use of trap doors and secret compartments was old hat. So was this film about an ex-convict who seeks revenge on the district attorney who sent him up, but lets him off the hook to marry the girl he loves in the end. Breese had enjoyed some success with this old-timer on the stage, but the film misfires completely.

d, Oscar Apfel; sup, William C. DeMille; w, Clara Beranger (based on a play by Daniel D. Carter [David Daniel Cohen]).

Crime (PR:A MPAA:NR)

MASTER MIND, THE** (1920) 5 reels Whitman Bennett/FN bw

Lionel Barrymore *(Henry Allen)*, Gypsy O'Brien *(Maggie)*, Ralph Kellard *(Wainwright)*, Bradley Barker *(Creegan)*, Marie Shotwell *(Sadie)*, Bernard Randall *(Diamond Willie)*, Charles Edwards, Louis Stearns, Alma Aiken, Charles Brandt.

Fair programmer has Barrymore setting out to avenge his innocent brother's execution through the mistake of a judge. After pinning a crime on a young girl, he arranges for the magistrate to fall in love with her and then plans to inform the world of her "background" when his enemy runs for governor. In the end, Barrymore is unable to carry out his scheme, and the picture ends with the couple setting out along the road to happiness.

d&w, Kenneth Webb (based on a story by Daniel D. Carter [Daniel Cohen]); ph, Rial Schellinger, T. L. Griffith.

Drama (PR:A MPAA:NR)

MASTER OF CRAFT, A** (1922, Brit.) 5 reels ID bw

Fred Groves *(Capt. Flower)*, Mercy Hatton *(Matilda Tapping)*, Judd Green *(George)*, Arthur Cleave *(Joe)*, John Kelt *(Green)*, Roy Byford *(Pat)*, Pope Stamper *(Mate)*, Lilian Douglas, Jerrold Robertshaw, Eva Westlake, Ian Wilson.

In this British comedy, a sea captain pretends to have drowned in order to escape a clause in his uncle's will, which stipulates that he must marry.

d, Thomas Bentley; w, Eliot Stannard (based on a story by W. W. Jacobs).

Comedy (PR:A MPAA:NR)

MASTER STROKE, A* (1920) 5 reels VIT bw

Earle Williams *(Yale Durant)*, Vola Vale *(Minnie Patton)*, Lee Hill *(Jack Millington)*, Henry Barrows *(Sam Millington)*, John Elliott *(George Trevor)*, Ethel Shannon, Frank Crane, Paul Weigel, Rhea Haines.

Tiresome nonsense about a man who goes broke and tries to commit suicide, when a pal asks him to run his troubled business for a week. Of course our hero turns it into a roaring success, falls in love with his secretary, and even gets to have her in the last reel, when his fiancee runs off with another fellow.

d, Chester Bennett; w, Lucien Hubbard (based on a story by Frederic Van Rensselaer Dey).

Drama (PR:A MPAA:NR)

MATINEE IDOL, THE*** (1928) 6 reels COL bw

Bessie Love *(Ginger Bolivar)*, Johnnie Walker *(Don Wilson/Harry Mann)*, Lionel Belmore *(Col. Jaspar Bolivar)*, Ernest Hilliard *(Wingate)*, Sidney D'Albrook *(J. Madison Wilberforce)*, David Mir *(Eric Barrymaine)*.

Capra's second film for Cohn at Columbia was this little comedy gem, shot on a shoestring, about a rural stock company which is so bad that they create a comedy sensation while playing a straight Civil War drama on Broadway. In his excellent autobiography, *The Name Above the Title*, Capra wrote that it was in this film that he mastered the technique of blending a love theme with his broader comedic elements.

p, Harry Cohn; d, Frank Capra; w, Peter Milne, Elmer Harris (based on the story "Come Back to Aaron" by Robert Lord, Ernest Pagano); ph, Philip Tannura; ed, Arthur Roberts; art d, Robert E. Lee.

Comedy (PR:A MPAA:NR)

MATINEE LADIES** (1927) 7 reels WB bw

May McAvoy *(Sallie Smith)*, Malcolm McGregor *(Bob Ward)*, Hedda Hopper *(Mrs. Aldrich)*, Margaret Seddon *(Mrs. Smith)*, Richard Tucker *(Tom Mannion)*, Jean Lefferty *(Maizie Blossom)*, Cissy Fitzgerald *(Mme. Leonine)*, William Demarest *(Man-About-Town)*.

McGregor, who is working his way through college by dancing with bored society wives at a roadhouse, falls for McAvoy, the cigarette girl. She is lured, under false pretenses, to the yacht of wealthy rotter Tucker, but fortunately a storm saves her from suffering a fate worse than death. When McGregor rescues her from nearly drowning, they vow to dry off and set the date.

d, Byron Haskin; w, Graham Baker (based on a story by Albert S. Howson, Sidney R. Buckman); ph, Frank Kesson.

Drama **(PR:A MPAA:NR)**

MATING OF MARCUS, THE** (1924, Brit.) 6 reels STOLL bw

Dollie *(Vivi Chester)*, Billie *(Naomi Chester)*, David Hawthorne *(Marcus Netherby)*, George Bellamy *(Mr. Chester)*, Molly Johnson *(Valerie Westmacott)*, W. G. Saunders.

A man overcomes the taunting attitude of his fellow townsfolk to rescue a couple of girls from a flood and win the heart of the most desirable one.

d, W. P. Kellino; w, (based on a novel by Mabel Barnes Grundy).

Romantic Drama **(PR:A MPAA:NR)**

MATRIMANIAC, THE*** (1916) 5 reels FA/TRI bw

Douglas Fairbanks *(Jimmy Conroy)*, Constance Talmadge *(Marna Lewis)*, Wilbur Higby *(Theo. Lewis)*, Clyde Hopkins *(G. Walter Henderson)*, Fred Warren *(Rev. Tobias Tubbs)*, Winifred Westover *(The Maid)*, Carmel Myers.

Plenty of action and laughs as Fairbanks, who has been separated from his sweetheart by a disapproving daddy, races by auto, train, and even a wheelbarrow to be by her side. The film's bizarre ending has Fairbanks walking across a maze of telephone wires and arranging for a lineman, who acts as a witness, to connect him to the room where his lady friend is secluded, while a minister, who has been patched in, performs a marriage service.

d, Paul Powell; w, Anita Loos, John Emerson (based on a story by Octavus Roy Cohen, James Giesy).

Comedy/Adventure **(PR:A MPAA:NR)**

MAY BLOSSOM*** (1915) 4 reels FP bw

Gertrude Robinson *(May Blossom)*, Russell Bassett *(Tom Blossom)*, Marshall Neilan *(Richard Ashcroft)*, Donald Crisp *(Steve Harland)*, Gertrude Norman *(Aunt Deborah)*.

Satisfying adaptation of a Belasco play about a man's regeneration on the Confederate battlefield, and the woman who learns to love him because of it. Nicely directed, acted, and photographed.

d, Allan Dwan; w, (based on the play by David Belasco).

War/Drama **(PR:A MPAA:NR)**

MEASURE OF A MAN, THE** (1916) 5 reels BLUE bw

Louise Lovely *(Pattie Batch)*, Katherine Campbell *(Jenny Hendy)*, J. Warren Kerrigan *(John Fairmeadow)*, Ivor MacFadden *(Billy)*, Marion Emmons *(Donnie)*, Harry Carter *(Jack Flack)*, Marc Robbins *(Tom Hendy)*.

Predictable, but nonetheless diverting tale of a lumberjack preacher who gets his message across to the woodsmen because he's as good with his fists as he is with his sermons. He also wins the heart of the pretty Lovely, who, for some reason, was given top billing in this picture.

d, Jack Conway; w, Maude Grange (based on the novel by Norman Duncan).

Adventure **(PR:A MPAA:NR)**

MEASURE OF A MAN, THE* (1924) 5 reels UNIV bw

William Desmond *(John Fairmeadow)*, Albert J. Smith *(Jack Flack)*, Francis Ford *("Pale" Peter)*, Marin Sais *(Clare, His Wife)*, William J. Dyer *(Billy the Beast)*, Bobby Gordon *("Pale" Peter's Son)*, Harry Tenbrook *(Charley, the Bartender)*, Zala Davis *(Jenny Hitch)*, William Turner *(Tom Hitch)*, Mary McAllister *(Pattie Batch)*.

Reformed drunk Desmond lifts himself out of a Bowery gutter, heads west disguised as a minister, cleans up a logging town, and marries the orphaned girl he protected from the community meany.

d, Arthur Rosson; w, Wyndham Gittens, Isadore Bernstein (based on the novel by Norman Duncan); ph, Jackson Rose.

Drama **(PR:A MPAA:NR)**

MEDDLER, THE** (1925) 5 reels UNIV bw

William Desmond *(Richard Gilmore)*, Dolores Rousse *(Gloria Canfield)*, Claire Anderson *(Dorothy Parkhurst)*, Albert J. Smith *(Bud Meyers)*, Jack Daugherty *(Jesse Canfield)*, C.L. Sherwood *(Sheriff)*, Kate Lester *(Mrs. Gilmore)*, Georgie Grandee *(Secretary)*, Donald Hatswell *(Capt. Forsythe)*.

Desmond, a Wall Street broker, heads west after being jilted by his sweetie, to prove himself a man. He becomes a road agent known as "The Meddler," who always returns everything he robs, save for worthless mementos. During one of the holdups he falls in love with beautiful Rousse, whom he eventually marries and settles down with in the great open spaces.

d, Arthur Rosson; w, W. Scott Darling (based on a story by Miles Overholt); ph, Gilbert Warrenton.

Western **(PR:A MPAA:NR)**

MEDIATOR, THE** (1916) 5 reels FOX bw

George Walsh *(Lish Henley)*, Juanita Hansen *(Maggie)*, James Marcus *(Big Bill)*, Lee Willard *(Bill Higgins)*, Pearl Elmore *(Martha Higgins)*, Sedley Brown *(Channel Smith)*, J. Gordon Russell.

Fox cast Walsh in the William S. Hart mold in this feature about a decent man who licks a drunk in a fist fight and then discovers the fellow is a family man, down on his luck, who owns a boarding house in the toughest town in the West. Walsh cleans up the town, reunites the family, and ends up with the reformed drunk's daughter. A somewhat appealing action player, Walsh was; William S. Hart, he definitely was not.

d, Otis Turner; w, Ethel Webber, Turner (based on the novel by Roy Norton).

Western **(PR:A MPAA:NR)**

MEG** (1926, Brit.) 5 reels Walter Shaw/Wardour bw

Mabel Armatage *(Meg)*, Noel Greenwood *(Jack Horton)*, Ruth Kalinsky *(Constance Hope)*.

Producer-director Shaw used the British setting of Drewsbury to tell this story of a girl-on-the-run who nurses the injured son of a mine owner, who it turns out is engaged to her sister.

p&d, Walter Shaw; w, Arnold Tolson.

Drama **(PR:A MPAA:NR)**

MEMORY LANE** (1926) 8 reels John M. Stahl/FN bw

Eleanor Boardman *(Mary)*, Conrad Nagel *(Jimmy Holt)*, William Haines *(Joe Field)*, John Steppling *(Mary's Father)*, Eugenie Ford *(Mary's Mother)*, Frankie Darro *(Urchin)*, Dot Farley, Joan Standing *(Maids)*, Kate Price *(Telephone Booth Patron)*, Florence Midgley, Dale Fuller, Billie Bennett.

Boardman loves hard working but poor, Haines. When he leaves town to make his fortune, Boardman marries Nagel, the son of the town millionaire. Haines returns home, kidnaps Boardman and then, guilt-ridden, lets her go. Now Boardman realizes that her love for Nagel is real, and later, when Haines is invited to dinner, he pretends to be uncouth to remove any doubts from the mind of the girl he adores.

d, John M. Stahl; w, Benjamin Glazer, Stahl; ph, Percy Hilburn; ed, Margaret Booth; set d, Cedric Gibbons.

Drama **(PR:A MPAA:NR)**

MEN SHE MARRIED, THE ½** (1916) 5 reels PEER/WORLD bw

Gail Kane *(Beatrice Raymond)*, Arthur Ashley *(Ralph Semple)*, Montagu Love *(Jerry Trainer)*, Louise M. Bates *(Ada Semple)*, Muriel Ostriche *(Edith Trainer)*.

Director Vale does surprisingly well with this potboiler about a girl (Kane) who innocently marries a man who already has a wife. The rotter steals her jewelry, takes off for South America, and is then reported dead. Later, Kane meets and marries "Mr. Right," a widower with a young daughter. The rat soon returns from south of the boarder, blackmails Kane, and convinces her stepdaughter to run away with him. Kane rushes to his room to prevent this and is discovered by her husband who suspects the worst. But a logical explanation finally sets everything straight and sends "Mr. Wrong" to the pokey.

d, Travers Vale; w, (based on a story by Harold Vickers).

Drama **(PR:A MPAA:NR)**

MERCHANT OF VENICE, THE* (1916, Brit.) 6 reels BRO bw

Matheson Lang *(Shylock)*, Nellie Hutin Britton *(Portia)*, J. R. Tozer *(Bassanio)*, George Skillan *(Antonio)*, Kathleen Hazel Jones *(Jessica)*, Ernest Caselli *(Lorenzo)*, Marguerite Westlake *(Nerissa)*, Terence O'Brien *(Tubal)*, George Morgan *(Lancelot)*.

Tepid early British filmed version of the bard's immortal play about Shylock and the "pound of flesh."

p&d, Walter West; w, (based on the play by William Shakespeare).

Drama **(PR:A MPAA:NR)**

MERRY-GO-ROUND*** (1923) 10 reels UNIV bw

Norman Kerry *(Count Franz Maxmillian von Hohenegg)*, Mary Philbin *(Agnes Urban)*, Cesare Gravina *(Sylvester Urban)*, Edith Yorke *(Ursula Urban)*, George Hackathorne *(Bartholomew Gruber)*, George Siegmann *(Shani Huber)*, Dale Fuller *(Mariana Huber)*, Lillian Sylvester *(Mrs. Aurora Rossreiter)*, Spottiswoode Aitken *(Minister of War/Gisella's Father)*, Dorothy Wallace *(Komtasse Gisella von Steinbrueck)*, Al Edmundsen *(Nepomuck Navrital)*, Albert Conti *(Rudi/Baron von Leightsinn)*, Charles L. King *(Nicki/Baron von Nubenmuth)*, Fenwick Oliver *(Eitel/Prince Eitel Hogemut)*, Sidney Bracey *(Gisella's Groom)*, Anton Vaverka *(Emperor Franz Josef)*, Maude George *(Mme. Elvira)*, Helen Broneau *(Jane)*, Jane Sherman *(Marie)*.

Kerry plays a handsome count employed as the personal aide to the emperor of Austria during the reign of Franz Josef. His plans to marry Wallace, the daughter of the minister of war, are interrupted when he mets and falls in love with Philbin, an organ grinder for a merry-go-round. Kerry, who is posing as a necktie salesman while courting Philbin, decides to break off his engagement with Wallace, but the wedding somehow proceeds. Philbin and her father, Gravina, are embittered when they discover the truth about the necktie-selling impostor, but secretly Philbin continues to love Kerry. During the war Kerry finds Gravina lying near death on the battlefield, and the man delivers a stinging denunciation before passing on. By the time Kerry returns home after the war, he has been stripped of his rank and finds himself a widower. He pays a visit to Philbin, who believing Kerry was killed in the war, has now promised herself to Hackathorne, a hunchback circus performer who loves her dearly. In the end, however, Hackathorne leaves the scene, and allows the two lovers to finally be united. After their bitter combat while making FOOLISH WIVES, Thalberg and Von Stroheim nearly came to blows again while the director was involved in creating MERRY-GO-ROUND. It was rumored that the extravagant genius had ordered the underwear used by the military extras to be embroidered with the royal Austrian coat of arms; also that Von Stroheim was fond of spending hours marching and drilling his "soldiers." At any rate—much to the chagrin of the cast and crew, who truly loved him—the flamboyant Austrian was replaced by a journeyman director named Rupert Julian. It is said that the newcomer destroyed most of his predecessor's footage and began practically from scratch. This seems highly unlikely since so many brilliant sequences were left in this story that Von Stroheim's spirit seems present almost until the end. Certainly the sets and props are most lavish (the coach was actually the one belonging to the Austrian emperor) and it is great fun to watch the picture and single out the work of the master. But even with Julian's more sentimental direction, the picture is good. Still one can't help regretting that what was a very good film, could have been a masterpiece.

p, Irving Thalberg; d, Rupert Julian, Erich von Stroheim; w, Finis Fox, uncredited (based on a story by Harvey Gates); t, Mary O'Hara; ph, Charles Kaufman, William Daniels; m, Ben Reynolds; ed, Maurice Pivar, James McKay; art d, E. E. Sheeley; set d, Richard Day; cos, Von Stroheim, Day.

Drama **(PR:A MPAA:NR)**

MERRY WIDOW, THE**** (1925) 10 reels MGM bw/c

Mae Murray *(Sally O'Hara)*, John Gilbert *(Prince Danilo)*, Roy D'Arcy *(Prince Mirko)*, Tully Marshall *(Baron Sadoja)*, Josephine Crowell *(Queen Milena)*, George Fawcett *(King Nikita)*, Albert Conti *(Danilo's Adjutant)*, Wilhelm von Brincken *(Danilo's Aide-de-camp)*, Sidney Bracey *(Danilo's Footman)*, Don Ryan *(Mirko's Adjutant)*, Hughie Mack *(Innkeeper)*, Ida Moore *(Innkeeper's Wife)*, Lucille von Lent *(Innkeeper's Daughter)*, Charles Margelis *(Flo Epstein)*, Harvey Karels *(Jimmy Watson)*, Edna Tichenor *(Dopey Marie)*, Gertrude Bennett *(Hard Boiled Virginia)*, Zalla Zorana *(Frenchie Christine)*, Jacqueline Gadsdon *(Madonna)*, Estelle Clark *(French Barber)*, D'Arcy Corrigan *(Horatio)*, Clara Wallucks, Frances Primm *(Hansen Sisters)*, Zack Williams *(George Washington White)*, Eugene Pouget *(Francois)*, Edward Connelly *(Ambassador)*, Meriwyn Thayer *(Ambassador's Wife)*, George Nichols *(Doorman at Francois')*, Dale Fuller *(Sally's Maid)*, Lon Poff *(Sadoja's Lackey)*, Anielka Elter *(Blindfolded Musician)*, Carolynne Snowden *(Black Dancer)*, Louise Hughes, Anna Maynard, Helen Howard Beaumont, Beatrice O'Brien *(Chorus Girls)*.

By the time Von Stroheim was ready to begin work on THE MERRY WIDOW, Samuel Goldwyn had become part of the MGM merger, and the director found himself working at the Culver City plant. One of the studio's biggest stars was Murray (a former Ziegfeld dancer) and she demanded this plum. Von Stroheim had never worked with a "movie queen" and wanted no part of her—preferring instead to use an unknown whom he could develop and mold himself. But Louis B. Mayer, who knew that the director had not received a penny in salary for nearly a year, persuaded him to accept Murray by offering him an advance of $30,000. With Thalberg (Von Stroheim's constant nemesis), an attempt was made to encourage a reasonable shooting schedule by offering the following bonus incentives: If the director could bring the picture in in three weeks, he would be given a bonus of $10,000. This dropped to $7,500 for seven weeks and $5,000 for eight (he would accomplish the task in four months and three weeks). To assist him with the shooting script, MGM hired the Belfast-born Benjamin Glazer (who would go on to script SEVENTH HEAVEN and FLESH AND THE DEVIL). Von Stroheim had never worked with a collaborator before, and Glazer was smart enough to stay pretty much out of his way. In the souvenir book for the film's release the cowriter did, however, offer this insight regarding the great director's genius: "Modest little ideas grew into sturdy episodes and expanded into sequences of epochal length. A slender, seemingly artificial musical comedy plot took root in reality and blossomed into a sturdy drama. Heaps upon heaps of manuscript accumulated. Scenes multiplied into thousands. Secretaries almost fainted from exhaustion. And art directors' eyes gave out. But Von Stroheim worked on, energetic as an ant, tireless as a horse...When you see THE MERRY WIDOW on the screen you will notice episode after episode done swiftly, briefly, impressionistically. But don't be deceived. Beneath what is there accomplished in a few significant vignettes and a few phantom-like dissolves, lies a solid and elaborate scaffolding. When Von Stroheim has chosen to show you merely a muffled drum you may be sure that first he planned and painstakingly worked out the entire funeral procession which it symbolizes. He refuses every short cut. He leaves nothing to chance. Though open-minded as a child in a discussion of general ideas of plot structure and character development, he is pedantic as a professor when it comes to detail. This is his own particular responsibility, and he regards it with all solemnity. He literally directs his pictures as he writes them." Von Stroheim's script completely departs from the saccharine musical comedy, and tells the story of an army out on maneuvers in one of those Ruritanian kingdoms. The officers are billeting at the local inn when Murray, the principal dancer of the Manhattan Follies, and her company arrive. When she lifts her skirt to examine a run in her stocking, the young American inspires the admiration of every officer present, including the cousins Prince Danilo (John Gilbert) and Prince Mirko (Roy D'Arcy) the heir to the throne. Although Gilbert enjoys a good tryst now and again, he is basically a decent fellow. But, D'Arcy is a libertine without conscience. He is a rank, immoral bounder who was equalled in his loathsomeness only by Von Stroheim himself in the role of Karamzin, in FOOLISH WIVES. A rivalry between the cousins begins almost at once, when they all dine together (the director injects a nice light touch here when the princes end up playing footsie with each other, thinking they are getting the attention of the beautiful American). But a third rival appears in the presence of the wonderful Tully Marshall, who plays Baron Sadoja, the true power behind the crown. They are all present at Murray's performance, and as she dances Von Stroheim's camera examines the reactions of the three. Gilbert concentrates on her face, which indicates his sense of actual love, while D'Arcy's eyes lustfully explore her hips and breasts, and Marshall, who plays a cripple with a foot fetish, explores her nimbly moving slippers. The director would continue to dwell upon Murray's feet throughout the film. (Kevin Brownlow, in his landmark book *The Parades Gone By*, relates this tale—which may or may not be apocryphal, "A story told at MGM describes Thalberg's reaction as he watched some rushes on THE MERRY WIDOW—long, long scenes in which Von Stroheim had shot the contents of a baron's wardrobe—boots, shoes, slippers, shoe trees . . . 'What the hell is all this about?' asked Thalberg. 'I wanted to establish that this man is a foot fetishist,' explained Von Stroheim. Thalberg was nearly apoplectic. 'You,' he said, 'are a footage fetishist!' ") The Baron invites the dancer out after the performance, but is refused. Later, she accepts Gilbert's invitation to dine at an apartment of pleasure, where they sit at a beautiful candlelit table, while a couple of practically nude, blindfolded female musicians, accompany their repast. This romantic (if somewhat offbeat) scene is then contrasted with Marshall who is having his own party in the same building, attended by teenagers gilded in gold. At the same time, D'Arcy is throwing an orgy which seems to be populated by the entire headquarters staff. This scene gives Von Stroheim the chance to establish Mirko as an expert shot, when, during his bacchanal, he shoots the eyes out of a statue. At one point, Gilbert spills some soup on Murray's dress and she is forced to change into a robe. Then, when it seems as if the young lady is about to give in to his affections, D'Arcy and his drunken horde come crashing into their apartment. The libertine quickly accuses his cousin of being a fornicator, but Gilbert gallantly defends the honor of his companion by stating that they plan to be married. D'Arcy storms out, and vents his anger on a crippled doorman, whom he beats unmercifully. Needless to say, the King and Queen (Fawcett and Crowell) will not accept a commoner into the family. So the rejected Murray is susceptible to a proposal of marriage when it comes from Marshall, with the promise that his power and wealth will put her in the position to exact a little revenge. On their wedding night, the nauseated Murray has all she can do to hold down her dinner, as the truly repulsive Marshall throws caution to the winds and acts out all of his erotic fantasies with her feet. But then, to her relief, and horror, he suffers a seizure and help must be summoned. Months pass as he lies paralyzed in bed. Then one day, he gets another of his urges. Slowly he drags himself from under the covers and crawls across the floor and over to Murray's closet, where he expires and collapses upon a mountain of his wife's shoes. At this point, the story begins to resemble the musical. Gilbert and Murray encounter one another in Paris but the dashing officer has been drinking and when he expresses his love she believes that he is interested only in her money, and shuts him off by claiming to be in love with his cousin. Later, the antagonists fight a duel. Gilbert, devastated by his loss, fires his pistol into the air, and Murray arrives just in time to see him fall wounded to the ground. D'Arcy returns to his homeland following the death of Fawcett, and as he marches in the funeral procession, the crippled doorman, whom he so often abused, leaps out from the crowd and assassinates him. The scene then switches to Gilbert's apartment in the palace, where he is making a gradual recovery. He is in the process of telling Murray that her fortune presents a barrier which no honorable man can overcome, when word arrives that he has become the new king. The film ends with a technicolor sequence showing Gilbert and his lady marching in their coronation. It's a big scene with plenty of troops, representing scores of nations, and as the American Marines lower Old Glory to salute the new queen, their one-time countryman kisses it. She does the same for her new land, and the picture draws to a spectacular conclusion. It is said that Von Stroheim hated this typically Hollywood happy ending, although it does exist in his original shooting script. But according to an article by Thomas Quinn Curtiss in "Film Culture" magazine, during a 1955 screening of the film at the Palais des Beaux Arts in Brussels, "he went so far as to order the house lights turned up just after the duel scene. 'That's where my story ended, but they insisted on the ending you see now'." THE MERRY WIDOW was a great success and enhanced the careers of both the director and Murray, in spite of the fact that they hated each other and fought nonstop from the first foot of film. When the anticipated waltz number came up—this was to be the star's big moment and about the only one which slightly resembled the story line she had expected—she was ready to do her thing. To be her most radiant. To show the world her dancing skills. To radiate like an MGM *star*. In an interview with the director's widow, Richard Koszarsky, in his excellent biography *The Man You Love To Hate*, she tells him, "With 350 extras finally in position, filming on the dance was about to begin when Von Stroheim went up to Mae Murray and 'showed her how to do the step'. This was the last straw. 'You dirty Hun,' she screamed. 'You think you know everything!' She threw her peacock headdress to the ground and began stamping her feet. Erich and Valerie (his wife) turned quickly, left the stage, and went home." Thalberg was not well, so Mayer handled the situation personally by firing the director and replacing him with Monta Bell. But in spite of his autocratic manner, the cast and crew were loyal to their director, and the whole production became bogged down. A few days later, Von Stroheim and Mayer managed to call a truce and the picture was completed. But the bitterness remained, and in spite of the film's success, the director and his studio went their separate ways. For the first time since 1918, when he walked into Carl Laemmle's office and talked him into producing a picture called BLIND HUSBANDS, one of the motion pictures' true geniuses was out of work.

p, Irving Talberg; d, Erich von Stroheim; w,von Stroheim, Benjamin Glazer (based on the operetta by Victor Leon, Leo Stein, music by Franz Lehar); t, Marian Ainslee; ph, Oliver Marsh, William Daniels, Ben Reynolds; m, David Mendoza, William Axt; ed, Frank Hull; prod d, Cedric Gibbons; cos, Richard Day, Von Stroheim; technicolor sequence, Ray Rennahan.

Drama **(PR:C MPAA:NR)**

MERTON OF THE MOVIES**** (1924) 8 reels FP/PAR bw

Glenn Hunter *(Merton Gill)*, Viola Dana *(Sally Montague, "Flips")*, Charles Sellon *(Pete Gashwiler)*, Sadie Gordon *(Mrs. Gashwiler)*, Gale Henry *(Tessie Kearns)*, Luke Cosgrave *(Lowell Hardy)*, De Witt Jennings *(Jeff Baird)*, Elliott Roth *(Harold Parmalee)*, Charles Ogle *(Mr. Montague)*, Frank Jonasson *(Henshaw)*, Eleanor Lawson *(Mrs. Patterson)*.

One of the all-time best movies-about-movies, has small town clerk Hunter going to Hollywood to make his mark and, after a number of misadventures, becoming a star of slapstick comedies. It was remade in 1932 as MAKE ME A STAR with Stuart Erwin, and again in 1947 with Red Skelton.

p&d, James Cruze; w, Walter Woods (based on the novel by Harry Leon Wilson and the play by George S. Kaufman, Marc Connelly); ph, Karl Brown.

Comedy **(PR:A MPAA:NR)**

MESSAGE FROM MARS, A** (1913, Brit.) 4 reels United Kingdom bw

Charles Hawtrey *(Horace Parker)*, E. Holman Clark *(Ramiel)*, Crissie Bell *(Minnie)*, Frank Hector *(Arthur Dicey)*, Hubert Willis *(Tramp)*, Kate Tyndale *(Aunt Martha)*, Evelyn Beaumont *(Bella)*, Eileen Temple *(Mrs. Clarence)*, R. Crompton *(God of Mars)*, B. Stanmore *(Wounded Man)*, Tonie Reith *(His Wife)*.

This early British fantasy, about a Martian who visits Earth to transform a particularly selfish man into a decent chap, was a very successful stage play, but the film is static and dull.

p, Nicholson Ormsby-Scott; d&w, J. Wallett Waller (based on the play by Richard Ganthony).

Fantasy **(PR:A MPAA:NR)**

METROPOLIS**** (1927, Ger.) 6 reels UFA bw

Alfred Abel *(Joh Fredersen)*, Gustav Frolich *(Freder)*, Rudolf Klein-Rogge *(Rotwang)*, Brigitte Helm *(Maria/Robot)*, Fritz Rasp *(Slim)*, Theodor Loos *(Josaphat/Joseph)*, Erwin Biswanger *(Georg, No. 11811)*, Heinrich George *(Grot, the Foreman)*, Olaf Storm *(Jan)*, Hans Leo Reich *(Marinus)*, Heinrich Gotho *(Master of Ceremonies)*, Margarete Lanner *(Woman in Car/Woman in Eternal Garden)*, Max Dietze, Georg John, Walter Kuhle, Arthur Reinhard, Erwin Vater *(Workers)*, Grete Berger, Olly Boheim, Ellen Frey, Lisa Gray, Rose Lichtenstein, Helene Weigel *(Female Workers)*, Beatrice Garga, Anny Hintze, Helen von Munchhofen, Hilde Woitscheff *(Women in Eternal Garden)*, Fritz Alberti *(Robot)*, 750 Bit Players, 30,000 (Plus) Extras.

Fritz Lang was inspired to make METROPOLIS while visiting New York when he first saw the vast and seemingly endless peaks and canyons of skyscrapers from the deck of his ship. His wife, Thea von Harbou, at his suggestion, wrote a futuristic novel (some historians believe the screenplay came first) and the director, using all of his considerable skills, eventually put it on film. It became the biggest production of the silent era (surpassing even the mighty INTOLERANCE and ROBIN HOOD, as well as Lang's earlier "Nibelungen" sagas, SIEGFRIED and KRIEMHILD'S REVENGE). Approximately two million feet of film were shot, and 25,000 actors, 11,000 actresses and 750 children were part of the project. (Forrest J. Ackerman told this author that a reunion of these children was held in Germany in the early 1980s). The special effects astound to this day, and much of the credit for this must go to Eugen Shuftan, who invented the "Shuftan Process"—an ingenious mirror device which gave miniatures the appearance of looking like enormous buildings, and could be combined with real people. (Shuftan later won an Oscar for his cinematography on THE HUSTLER). The story is set in the year 2000, and tells of a mighty city which is ruled by Joh Fredersen (Abel), a heartless capitalist, whose only son Freder (Gustav Frolich) lives an idyllic life, enjoying the beautifully sculptured gardens, which are his birthright. Then one day he meets Maria (Helm), a saintly figure who cares for the children of the slaves who toil in the workers' city below to keep the wheels of industry rolling. Frolich follows her and is appalled to see the conditions that exist there. Returning to the surface, he confronts his father, and when he's told that that's the way things are, he decides to desert his class and become one with his downtrodden brethren. Before long, Frolich is invited to attend a meeting where the Christ-like Maria is addressing the workers and imploring them to reject the use of violence to improve their lot, and to think in terms of love and the savior who will some day come in the form of a mediator. But even this minor act of defiance is too much for Abel, who has observed the speech in the company of Rotwang (brilliantly played by Klein-Rogge) his mad scientist hireling. Given the green light to do his worst, Klein-Rogge abducts Helm, creates a robot in her image, and programs it to return and lead the workers in a revolt. Then follows some truly spectacular footage in which the lower city is flooded as a means of making the "subhuman" populace who dwell there forever subservient. Frolich, however, rescues the real Maria, and together they manage to save the children. Then, fearing that his own son may have been killed in the madness, Abel surveys the ruins and comes to the realization that Helm was right, and that love is the most important of human emotions. The picture ends with Klein-Rogge's death and the capitalist shaking the hand of the representative of labor. The story line may at times seem a bit silly, but this is a visual work of art and the narrative is really only an excuse for Lang to overwhelm us with his masses of humanity forming incredible geometric patterns, his expressionistic moods, and his art nouveau sets and futuristic creations which leave the viewer stunned. And to all of these, of course, are added enough pure, melodramatic thrills to satisfy any devotee of the Saturday afternoon western, or for that matter, the serial genre. In the early thirties, Lang was summoned before Dr. Josef Goebbels (the propagandist had seen METROPOLIS with Adolf Hitler when it was first released) and was offered the position of head of the entire German film industry. The director told the Nazi that he was "tickled pink," honored beyond words, in fact. Then he took his leave, packed everything of value he could find, and grabbed a plane for Paris. His wife, writer von Harbou, remained behind and became a Nazi. Critics of the time (and, later, historians) widely condemned the picture becaues of its socio-political content. English writer H. G. Wells (no slouch at futuristic themes himself) was offended by the message he saw in the film that machines might make slaves of people. Quite the reverse, he averred. Others objected to the suggestion that the differences between capital and labor could be resolved through charity (the head and the hands need the heart as mediator). Lang himself escaped most such criticism; people were eager to place the blame for the picture's message on von Harbou, whose sloppily sentimental novelization was published after the film's release. Perhaps the picture appeared in the wrong temporal context: its socio-political content would have seemed relevant to the Luddites of the early 19th century, who had smashed the machines that displaced their labor in the English textile mills, machines that condemned them not to the slavery of endless toil, but to that of poverty and purposelessness. Nor would the message have seemed so unlikely at a later time, when the governments of great nations deliberately avoided automating some industries in order to give their people useful work to do (overpopulated India had an oil refinery redesigned after purchasing it from the U.S.; the refinery had not required enough human hands for its operation). Endless toil was not the problem in Depression-ridden Germany during the 1920s; finding something at which to toil was the problem. METROPOLIS, two years in the making, did its part to help; Land hired 1,000 unemployed men who were willing to have their heads shaved for the tower of Babel scene, and wanted to hire 5,000 more (this striking segment, like the rest of the film, was shot at the aptly named Neubabelsberg studio of UFA). The monumental picture no longer exists in its original 17-reel form; even on its initial English release, it was severely edited, whole sub-plots being excised for fear of censorship. In 1984, Giorgio Morodor re-released METROPOLIS with new tintings, new title cards, and a repulsive rock score (Pat Benatar, Loverboy, and Queen, the latter of which also ruined the 1980 version of FLASH GORDON). Morodor must be given credit for bringing added life to this classic and initiating a new audience of teenagers to the film, but he should have stuck with his own synthesized score.

d, Fritz Lang; w, Lang, Thea von Harbou (based on her novel); t, (English) Channing Pollock; ph, Karl Freund, Gunther Rittau; art d, Otto Hunte, Erich Kettlehut, Karl Vollbrecht; spec eff, Eugen Schufftan [Eugene Shuftan]; cos, Ann Willkomm.

Fantasy **Cas.** **(PR:A MPAA:NR)**

MICE AND MEN** (1916) 5 reels FP bw

Marguerite Clark *(Peggy)*, Marshall Neilan *(Capt. Lovell)*, Charles Waldron *(Mark Embury)*, Clarence Handysides *(Roger Goodlake)*, Maggie Halloway Fisher *(Mrs. Deborrah)*, Helen Dahl *(Joanna)*, Robert Conville *(Minister Goodlake/Goodlake's Servant)*, William McKey *(Embury's Servant)*, Ada Deaves *(Matron)*, Francesca Warde *(Colored Mammy)*.

Totally predictable and overly padded nonsense about a wealthy bachelor who adopts an orphan in order to "train" her to be the perfect bride. But in the end, it is his career officer nephew who gives her a military wedding.

d, J. Searle Dawley; w, (based on the play by Madeline Lucette Ryley).

Drama **(PR:A MPAA:NR)**

MICHIGAN KID, THE** 1/2** (1928) 6 reels UNIV bw

Conrad Nagel *(Jimmy Cowan)*, Renee Adoree *(Rose Morris)*, Fred Esmelton *(Hiram Morris)*, Virginia Grey *(Rose, as a Child)*, Maurice Murphy *(Jimmy as a Child)*, Adolph Milar *(Shorty)*, Lloyd Whitlock *(Frank Hayward)*, Donald House *(Frank Hayward, as a Child)*.

Nagel gives a good performance in this standard North Woods drama about two boys who become rivals for the same girl. But the real star of the picture is Stumar, the cinematographer who created a splendid forest fire sequence.

d, Irvin Willat; w, Peter Milne, J. Grubb Alexander, J. G. Hawks, Charles Logue, Willat (based on the story by Rex Beach); t, Walter Anthony; ph, Charles Stumar; ed, Harry Marker.

Drama **(PR:A MPAA:NR)**

MICKEY* 1/2** (1919) 7 reels Mabel Normand/MS bw

Mabel Normand, Lew Cody, Minta Durfee, Wheeler Oakman, Tom Kennedy, George Nichols, Laura La Varnie, Minnie Ha Ha.

Enormously popular film which became known around the Sennett lot as "the mortgage lifter." Normand is a Western girl sent East to live with her relatives, but is turned into a domestic when they discover she has no money. This is Normand at her best, in a picture which is as much melodrama as comedy and provides almost as many thrills as laughs.

d, F. Richard Jones; sup, Mack Sennett; w, J. G. Hawks; ph, Frank Williams.

Comedy **Cas.** **(PR:A MPAA:NR)**

MIDNIGHT EXPRESS, THE*** (1924) 6 reels COL/C.B.C. Film Sales bw

Elaine Hammerstein *(Mary Travers)*, William Haines *(Jack Oakes)*, George Nichols *(John Oakes)*, Lloyd Whitlock *(Joseph Davies)*, Edwin Booth Tilton *(James Travers)*, Pat Harmon *(Silent Bill Brachley)*, Bertram Grassby *(Arthur Bleydon)*, Phyllis Haver *(Jessie Sybil)*, Roscoe Karns *(Switch Hogan)*, Jack Richardson *(Detective Collins)*, Noble Johnson *(Deputy Sheriff)*, Dan Crimmins, George Meadows *(Railroad Operators)*.

Superior programmer, based on a grand old stage melodrama about a railroad president's son (Haines), who gives up the playboy life to become a train engineer. He then captures a dangerous criminal, saves the Midnight Express from a disastrous crash, and wins the love of a fellow engineer's daughter.

d&w, George W. Hill; w, (based on a popular melodrama).

Drama **(PR:A MPAA:NR)**

MIDNIGHT LIFE** 1/2** (1928) 5 reels GOTH/LUM bw

Francis X. Bushman *(Jim Logan)*, Gertrude Olmstead *(Betty Brown)*, Eddie Buzzell *(Eddie Delaney)*, Monte Carter *(Steve Saros)*, Cosmo Kyrle Bellew *(Harlan Phillips)*, Carlton King.

Considering this gangster programmer was shot in only six days, it really isn't bad. Bushman is fine as the hot-shot police detective who avenges the murder of a pal, and the nightclub atmosphere, for the most part, rings true.

d, Scott R. Dunlap; sup, Harold Shumate; w, Adele Buddington, Arthur Statter (based on the novel *The Spider's Web* by Reginald Wright Kauffman); t, Delos Sutherland; ph, Ray June; ed, Dunlap, Ray Snyder.

Crime (PR:A MPAA:NR)

MIDNIGHT MADNESS***** (1928) 6 reels DM/Pathe bw

Jacqueline Logan *(Norma Forbes)*, Clive Brook *(Michael Bream)*, Walter McGrail *(Childers)*, James Bradbury *(John Forbes)*, Oscar Smith *(Manubo)*, Vadim Uraneff *(Joe)*, Louis Natheaux *(Masher)*, Clarence Burton *(A Sailor)*, Virginia Sale *(The Gargoyle)*, Frank Hagney *(Harris)*, Emmett King *(Robert Strong)*.

Brook, a millionaire gold miner, proposes to Logan, a shooting gallery opertor, and then comes to realize the girl is a fortune hunter. Determined to teach her a lesson, Brook subjects her to practically every hardship Africa has to offer, and the education makes Logan realize that she loves Brook for himself. Better than it sounds.

d, F. Harmon Weight; w, Robert N. Lee (based on the play "The Lion Trap" by Daniel Nathan Rubin); ph, David Abel; ed, Harold McLernon; art d, Stephen Goosson.

Drama (PR:A MPAA:NR)

MIDNIGHT MESSAGE, THE* (1926) 5 reels Goodwill bw

Wanda Hawley *(Mary Macy)*, Mary Carr *(Widow Malone)*, John Fox, Jr. *(The Boy)*, Stuart Holmes *("Red" Fagan)*, Creighton Hale *(Billy Dodd)*, Mathilda Brundage *(Mrs. Richard Macy)*, Otis Harlan *(Richard Macy)*, Earl Metcalf *("Burl")*, Karl Silvera *("Thin")*, Wilson Benge *(The Butler)*.

Poverty Row programmer has a Western Union messenger boy delivering a telegram late at night to the home of a millionaire. There he breaks up a robbery, and uses the reward money to buy his weary old mother, Carr (OVER THE HILL TO THE POORHOUSE), a new sewing machine that she might work her fingers a little less to the bone.

d, Paul Hurst; w, H. H. Van Loan.

Drama (PR:A MPAA:NR)

MIDNIGHT PATROL, THE*** (1918) 5 reels THI/SEL bw

Thurston Hall *(Officer Terrence Shannon)*, Rosemary Theby *(Patsy O'Connell)*, Goro Kino *(Wu Fang)*, Charles French *(Jim Murdock)*, Marjorie Bennett *(Minnie)*, Harold Holland *(Officer Michael O'Shea)*, William Musgrave *("Chink" Ross)*, Togo Yamamoto *(Sing Bok)*, Harold Johnstone *(Sgt. Joe Duncan)*.

Exciting Ince-produced police story about the Los Angeles Flying Squadron, led by Hall, and its triumphant battle with opium smugglers in Chinatown.

d, Irvin Willat; sup, Thomas H. Ince; w, Julien Josephson, Dennison Clift; ph, Dwight Warren.

Crime (PR:A MPAA:NR)

MIDNIGHT ROMANCE, A*** (1919) 6 reels Mayer/FN bw

Anita Stewart *(Marie)*, Jack Holt *(Roger Sloan)*, Edward Tilton *(His Father)*, Elinor Hancock *(His Mother)*, Helen Yoder *(His Sister)* Juanita Hansen *(Blondie Mazie)*, Jean Montague Dumont *(Blinkey Deal)*.

Nicely directed Weber romance about a princess who is torpedoed by the Germans while crossing the Atlantic, takes a job at a seaside resort, meets a wealthy young man at a ball, and renounces her title for love.

d&w, Lois Weber (based on a story by Marion Orth); ph, Dal Clawson.

Romance (PR:A MPAA:NR)

MIDNIGHT WATCH, THE** (1927) 6 reels T/C/RAY bw

Roy Stewart *(Bob Breemer)*, Mary McAllister *(Rose Denton)*, David Torrence *(Chief Callahan)*, Ernest Hilliard, Marcella Daly.

Fair mystery film about a college student working as a detective (Stewart) who is given the midnight shift by his chief because of his cockey attitude. Stewart manages to clear his girl friend of stealing a necklace, and brings the real crook—a society member—to justice.

p, W. Ray Johnston; d, Charles Hunt; w, (based on a story by Trem Carr); ph, Harold Wenstrom.

Mystery (PR:A MPAA:NR)

MIDSUMMER MADNESS*** (1920) 6 reels PAR bw

Jack Holt *(Bob Meredith)*, Conrad Nagel *(Julian Osborn)*, Lois Wilson *(Margaret Meredith)*, Lila Lee *(Daisy Osborn)*, Betty Francisco *(Mary Miller)*, Claire McDowell *(Mrs. Osborn)*, Charlotte Jackson *(Peggy Meredith)*, Ethel Wales *(Mrs. Hicks)*, Charles Ogle *(Caretaker)*, Lillian Leighton *(Caretaker's Wife)*, George Kuwa *(Servant)*.

De Mille directed this picture about a neglected woman who turns to another man and then, with skill and grace, decides that infidelity is not for her. The "message" this film delivers—advocating the sanctity of the marriage vow—never seems to preach, and there is a splendid performance by Nagel, as the spouse who learns his lesson.

d, William C. De Mille; w, Olga Printzlau (based on the novel *His Friend and His Wife* by Cosmo Hamilton); ph, L. Guy Wilky.

Drama (PR:C MPAA:NR)

MIKE*** (1926) 7 reels MGM bw

Sally O'Neil *(Mike)*, William Haines *(Harlan)*, Charlie Murray *(Father)*, Ned Sparks *(Slinky)*, Ford Sterling *(Tad)*, Frankie Darro *(Boy)*, Junior Coughlan *(Boy)*, Muriel Frances Dana *(Girl)*, Sam De Grasse *(Brush)*.

Murray and Sterling, the veteran comedians of the Keystone school, steal the show in this satisfying film with a railroad theme. Besides the laughs the boys provide, the movie's punch comes when two squadrons of army airplanes foil a train robbery with bombs and parachute troops.

d, Marshall Neilan; w, Marion Jackson (based on a story by Neilan); ph, David Kesson.

Drama (PR:A MPAA:NR)

MILLION DOLLAR ROBBERY, THE** (1914) 4 reels Solax bw

Claire Whitney, Vinnie Barnes, Fraunie Fraunholz, James O'Neill, Harris Gordon, Edwin Brandt, Jack Burns, J. W. Conway, Harrish Ingraham, Frank Cooke, Harry Mack.

Barely average little four-reeler dealing with hypnotism and somnambulism has one of the characters revealing the truth about a robbery after being put in a trance on the witness stand.

Crime (PR:A MPAA:NR)

MILLION FOR LOVE, A** (1928) 6 reels STER bw

Reed Howes *(Danny Eagan)*, Josephine Dunn *(Mary Norfleet)*, Lee Shumway *(D.A. Norfleet)*, Mary Carr *(Mrs. Eagan)*, Lewis Sargent *(Jimmy Eagan)*, Jack Rich *(Slim)*, Frank Baker *(Pete)*, Alfred Fisher *(Judge)*.

Routine courtroom programmer has Howes refusing to defend himself at his trial for the murder of a gang leader, so as to protect the girl he loves. Finally the district attorney's daughter (Dunn) comes forth, confesses her love for Howes, and swears that she was with him the night of the killing.

d, Robert F. Hill; w, Frances Guihan (based on a story by Peggy Gaddis); t, Guihan; ph, Herbert Kirkpatrick; ed, Leotta Whytock.

Drama/Crime (PR:A MPAA:NR)

MILLIONAIRE, THE** (1921) 5 reels UNIV bw

Herbert Rawlinson *(Jack Norman)*, Bert Roach *(Bobo Harmsworth)*, William Courtwright *(Simon Fisher)*, Verne Winter *(Jimmy)*, Lillian Rich *(Kate Blair)*, Margaret Mann *(Grandmother)*, Fred Vroom *(Delmar)*, Mary Huntress *(Mrs. Clever)*, Doris Pawn *(Marion Culbreth)*, E. A. Warren *(Evers)*.

Director Conway does what he can with this hokum about an out-of-work young fellow (Rawlinson) who inherits $80 million from a murdered man who once loved his mother. There is a lot of secret panel and sliding door stuff, which takes place in an old mansion, as the killers later try to knock off Rawlinson. But the hero solves the case and delivers the wrongdoers to the police.

d, Jack Conway; w, Wallace Clifton (based on a story by Hulbert Footner); ph, E. J. Vallejo.

Suspense/Drama (PR:A MPAA:NR)

MIND OVER MOTOR* 1/2 (1923) 5 reels Ward Lascelle/Principal bw

Trixie Friganza *(Tish)*, Ralph Graves *(Jasper McCutcheon)*, Clara Horton *(Bettina Bailey)*, Lucy Handforth *(Lizzie)*, Caroline Rankin *(Aggie)*, Grace Gordon *(Marie)*, Pietro Sosso *(Officer)*, George Guyton *(Gardiner)*, Mrs. Lee *(Mother)*, Larry Steers *(Ellis)*, Edward Hearne *(Starter)*.

This below-average comedy sees Friganza, a car enthusiast, talked into financing a big race. At the last minute, her friend Graves, who is expected to win the meet, is prevented from competing by crooks. The sheriff then informs Friganza that she will be arrested for conspiracy if someone outside of the competitors doesn't win. At that point she jumps into a racecar and goes on to capture first place.

p&d, Ward Lascelle; w, H. Landers Jackson (based on the story by Mary Roberts Rinehart); t, Bennet Cohen, Jackson.

Comedy (PR:A MPAA:NR)

MIRACLE MAKERS, THE* (1923) 6 reels Leah Baird/AEX bw

Leah Baird *(Doris Mansfield)*, George Walsh *(Fred Norton)*, Edith Yorke *(Mrs. Emma Norton)*, George Nichols *(Capt. Joe Mansfield)*, Edythe Chapman *(Mrs. Martha Mansfield)*, Richard Headrick *(The Boy)*, Mitchell Lewis *(Bill Bruce)*.

Even a director with Van Dyke's talent had trouble making anything out of this script. It tells the story of a girl (Baird) who is forced into marrying a man who smuggled Chinese aliens. In the meantime, the man Baird was engaged to, air coast patrolman Walsh, thinks she no longer loves him and goes to serve overseas. Not until several years later, when Baird's brutish spouse dies by falling down a well, is she reunited with the doughboy of her dreams.

d, W. S. Van Dyke; w, (based on a story by Leah Baird); ph, Andre Barlatier.

Drama (PR:A MPAA:NR)

MIRACLE MAN, THE* 1/2** (1919) 8 reels Mayflower/PAR bw

Thomas Meighan *(Tom Burke)*, Betty Compson *(Rose)*, Lon Chaney *(The Frog)*, Jean M. Dumont *(The Dope)*, W. Lawson Butt *(Richard King)*, Elinor Fair *(Claire King)*, Joseph J. Dowling *(The Patriarch)*, F. A. Turner, Lucille Hutton, T. Dwight Crittenden, Tula Belle, Frankie Lee, Ruby Lafayette.

A trio of con artists, who set out to make a fortune running a faith-healing scam, end up participating in a real miracle. Meighan, Compson, and Chaney all emerged from this very popular movie as major stars.

d&w, George Loane Tucker (based on the story by Frank L. Packard and the play be George M. Cohan); ph, Philip Rosen, Ernest Palmer.

Drama (PR:A MPAA:NR)

MIRAGE, THE** (1920, Brit.) 6 reels George Clarke/STOLL bw

Edward O'Neill *(Viscount Guescin)*, Dorothy Holmes-Gore *(Rozanne)*, Douglas Munro *(Courtot)*, Geoffrey Kerr *(Richard Dalziell)*, William Parry *(Somerset)*, Blanche Stanley *(Mrs. Bulpitt)*.

British love story about an impoverished viscount who makes the sacrifice of leaving the woman he loves to a younger rival when the fortune he was expecting to inherit falls through.

d, Arthur Rooke; w, Guy Newall (based on a novel by E. Temple Thurston).

Romance **(PR:A MPAA:NR)**

MIRIAM ROZELLA** (1924, Brit.) 8 reels ASTRA-N bw

Moyna McGill *(Miriam Rozella)*, Owen Nares *(Rudolph)*, Gertrude McCoy *(Lura Wood)*, Ben Webster *(Lord Laverock)*, Nina Boucicault *(Mrs. Rozella)*, Russell Thorndike *(Crewe Slevens)*, Mary Brough *(Housekeeper)*, Henrietta Watson *(Lady Laverock)*, Gordon Craig *(Cecil Rozella)*, Sydney Paxton *(Priest)*.

After her father commits suicide, a woman becomes the mistress of a debauched millionaire who sees the moral light when his sister catches him in the middle of one of his orgies.

d&w, Sidney Morgan (based on a novel by B. J. Farjeon).

Drama **(PR:C MPAA:NR)**

MISCHIEF MAKER, THE** (1916) 5 reels FOX bw

June Caprice *(Effie Marchand)*, Harry Benham *(Al Tournay)*, John Reinhardt *(Jules Gerard)*, Margaret Fielding *(May Muprey)*, Inez Marcel *(Mme. Briand)*, Minnie Milne *(Her Sister)*, Tom Brooks *(Henry Tournay)*, Nellie Slattery *(Mrs. Marchand)*.

Ordinary Caprice vehicle about the parents of a girl in boarding school and a boy in college who decide that their children (they haven't met) should be married. The young folks rebel and, while escaping their fate, accidentally meet, fall in love, and elope.

d&w, John G. Adolfi (based on a story by Alfred Solman); ph, Rial Schellinger.

Romance **(PR:A MPAA:NR)**

MISS BLUEBEARD*** (1925) 7 reels FP/PAR bw

Bebe Daniels *(Colette Girard)*, Robert Frazer *(Larry Charters)*, Kenneth MacKenna *(Bob Hawley)*, Raymond Griffith *(The Honorable Bertie Bird)*, Martha Madison *(Lulu)*, Diana Kane *(Gloria Harding)*, Lawrence D'Orsay *(Col. Harding)*, Florence Billings *(Eva)*, Ivan Simpson *(Bounds)*.

This successful stage comedy, about mistaken identities and marriage in name only, was first made popular by the great Broadway entertainer, Irene Bordoni. The film, however, required a lot of adaptation to suit the screen personality of its star, Daniels. But in the end, it was that most underrated of all movie comedians, Griffith, who completely walked away with the show.

d, Frank Tuttle; w, Townsend Martin (based on the play by Avery Hopwood); ph, J. Roy Hunt.

Comedy **(PR:A MPAA:NR)**

MISS BREWSTER'S MILLIONS*** 1/2 (1926) 7 reels FP/PAR bw

Bebe Daniels *(Polly Brewster)*, Warner Baxter *(Thomas B. Hancock, Jr.)*, Ford Sterling *(Ned Brewster)*, Andre de Beranger *(Mr. Brent)*, Miss Beresford *(Landlady)*.

Very funny adaptation of the popular novel, play and movie BREWSTER'S MILLIONS, this time sees a female movie extra (Daniels) being put to the task of spending a million dollars in order to inherit five. After plenty of laughs, the picture ends with the disclosure that her uncle is actually broke. But Daniels' investment in a motion picture company makes her wealthy anyway, and she ends up with Baxter to boot.

d, Clarence Badger; w, Lloyd Corrigan, Harold Shumate, Monty Brice (based on the novel *Brewster's Millions* by George Barr McCutcheon and the play by Winchell Smith, Byron Ongley); ph, H. Kinley Martin.

Comedy **(PR:A MPAA:NR)**

MISS CRUSOE*** (1919) 5 reels WORLD bw

Virginia Hammond *(Dorothy Evans)*, Rod La Rocque *(Harold Vance)*, Nora Cecil *(Miss Meeker)*, Irving Brooks *(Jeb Mills)*, Albert Hart *("Curley" Kidd)*, Edwin Sturgis *("Red")*, W. R. Randall *("Chuck")*, Richard Taber *("The Dog")*.

Nifty little comedy-adventure has a couple of young women vacationing on an island in Chesapeake Bay and becoming involved with a gang of crooks. Also on the scene appears a dashing fellow they believe to be an escaped convict. He actually turns out to be a famous detective and, while rescuing them from the bad guys, wins the heart of the prettiest.

d, Frank Crane; w, J. Clarkson Miller (based on a story by Roy S. Sensabaugh); ph, Jacob A. Badaracco.

Comedy/Crime **(PR:A MPAA:NR)**

MISS DULCIE FROM DIXIE** 1/2 (1919) 5 reels VIT bw

Gladys Leslie *(Dulcie)*, Charles Kent *(Col. Culpepper)*, Arthur Donaldson *(Uncle John)*, Julia Swayne Gordon *(Aunt Joan)*, James Morrison *(Orrin Castleton)*, Agnes Ayres.

Pretty fair programmer has Leslie, a Southern belle traveling north to put an end to the feud which exists between her father and uncle. Her uncle's sister, fearing that the girl is after an inheritance, throws up a few roadblocks, but Leslie and her son fall in love and all ends well.

d, Joseph Gleason; w, G. Marion Burton (based on the novel by Lulah Ragsdale); ph, Jules Cronjager.

Drama **(PR:A MPAA:NR)**

MISS HOBBS** (1920) 5 reels Realart bw

Wanda Hawley *(Miss Hobbs)*, Harrison Ford *(Wolff Kingsearl)*, Helen Jerome Eddy *(Beulah Hackett)*, Walter Hiers *(George Jessup)*, Julanne Johnston *(Millicent Farey)*, Emily Chichester *(Alice Joy)*, Frances Raymond *(Mrs. Kingsearl)*, Jack Mulhall.

Paramount star Hawley went to Realart to make this so-so comedy about a cult-prone, man-hating young woman who persuades her two best friends to leave the men in their lives. All three see the light, however, when Ford arrives on the scene and makes a "woman" out of Hawley.

d, Donald Crisp; w, Elmer Harris (based on the play by Jerome K. Jerome); ph, C. Edgar Schoenbaum.

Comedy **(PR:A MPAA:NR)**

MISS NOBODY*** (1926) 7 reels FN bw

Anna Q. Nilsson *(Barbara Brown)*, Walter Pidgeon *(Bravo)*, Louise Fazenda *(Mazie Raleigh)*, Mitchell Lewis *(Harmony)*, Clyde Cook *(Bertie)*, Arthur Stone *(Happy)*, Anders Randolph *(J.B. Hardiman)*, Claire Du Brey *(Ann Adams)*, Jed Prouty *(The Farmer)*, Caroline Rankin *(His Wife)*, George Nichols *(The Sheriff)*, Oleta Otis *(Miriam Arnold)*, James Gordon *(Police Sergeant)*, Fred Warren *(Sideshow Barker)*.

Nice little comedy has socialite Nilsson visiting California and discovering that her father died in New York, leaving her without a cent. In desperation, she accepts the invitation of a wealthy rotter to attend a fashionable masquerade party and goes dressed as a boy. When the masher makes a pass, Nilsson escapes and falls into the company of a group of hoboes led by Pidgeon. They set out to ride the rails together, but Pidgeon isn't fooled by her disguise for a second. After a number of comic adventures, the band is arrested by the police, and Pidgeon reveals himself to actually be a famous and rich writer traveling the country looking for literary ideas. The couple and their pals make the rest of the trip to New York by Pullman—on the Honeymoon Express.

d, Lambert Hillyer; w, Wid Gunning (based on the story "Shebo" by Tiffany Wells); t, George Marion, Jr.; ph, John Boyle; ed, Al Hall; art d, E. J. Shulter.

Comedy **(PR:A MPAA:NR)**

MISSING MILLIONS*** (1922) 6 reels FP/PAR bw

Alice Brady *(Mary Dawson)*, David Powell *(Boston Blackie)*, Frank Losee *(Jim Franklin)*, Riley Hatch *(John Webb, Detective)*, John B. Cooke *(Handsome Harry Hawks)*, William B. Mack *(Thomas Dawson, Mary's Father)*, George Le Guere *(Daniel Regan, Ship's Purser)*, Alice May *(Mrs. Regan, His Mother)*, H. Cooper Cliffe *(Sir Arthur Cumberland, A Thief)*, Sydney Deane *(Donald Gordon, Secretary)*, Beverly Travers *(Claire Dupont, Passenger)*, Sidney Herbert *(Frank Garber, Criminal Lawyer)*.

Good Boston Blackie mystery has society crook Brady enlisting the help of Blackie (Powell) to get even with Losee, the man responsible for sending her father to the penitentiary. The two intercept a shipment of gold which was to be used by Losee to cover money owed his "creditors," and the yellow rat takes the easy way out by committing suicide.

d, Joseph Henabery; w, Albert Shelby Le Vino (based on the story "A Problem in Grand Larceny" by Jack Boyle); ph, Gilbert Warrenton.

Mystery **(PR:A MPAA:NR)**

MISSING THE TIDE** (1918, Brit.) 5 reels BRO bw

Violet Hopson *(Margaret Carson)*, Basil Gill *(Sir Felix Faber)*, Ivy Close *(Letty Fairfax)*, Gerald Ames *(Capt. Harry Wyndham)*, James Lindsay *(Carson)*, Nicholas Hopson Worcester *(The Child)*.

In this British drama a woman delays too long before leaving the husband who has mistreated her, and discovers that her lover is now married to a nurse.

d, Walter West; w, R. Byron-Webber (based on the novel by Alfred Turner).

Drama **(PR:C MPAA:NR)**

MR. BARNES OF NEW YORK* (1914) 6 reels Broadway Star/VIT bw

Maurice Costello *(Mr. Barnes)*, Mary Charleson *(Marina Paoli)*, Charles Kent, William Humphrey, Darwin Karr, Donald Hall, S. Rankin Drew, Naomi Childers, Alberta Gallatin, Adele De Garde, Robert Gaillord, Albert Roccardi.

The Costello name was about the only thing this disjointed and overly long feature, about an American who travels abroad and becomes involved in various adventures (including the bombardment of an Egyptian city), had going for it.

d, Maurice Costello, Robert Gaillord; sup, J. Stuart Blackton; w, Eugene Mullin (based on the novel and play by Archibald Clavering Gunter).

Drama **(PR:A MPAA:NR)**

MR. BILLINGS SPENDS HIS DIME** 1/2 (1923) 6 reels FP/PAR bw

Walter Hiers *(John Percival Billings)*, Jacqueline Logan *(Suzanna Juarez)*, George Fawcett *(Gen. Pablo Blanco)*, Robert McKim *(Capt. Gomez)*, Patricia Palmer *(Priscilla Parker)*, Josef Swickard *(Estaban Juarez)*, Guy Oliver *(John D. Starbock)*, Edward Patrick *(White)*, Clarence Burton *(Diego)*, George Field *(Manuel)*, Lucien Littlefield (Martin Green).

Hiers falls in love with the girl (Logan) whose picture is on a cigar band, journeys to the South American country where her father (Swickard) is president, prevents some revolutionists from toppling his government, and wins the heart of the grateful beauty.

d, Wesley Ruggles; w, Albert Shelby Le Vino (based on a story by Dana Burnet); ph, Charles E. Schoenbaum.

Comedy **(PR:A MPAA:NR)**

MR. FIX-IT*** (1918) 5 reels Douglas Fairbanks/ART bw

Douglas Fairbanks *(Mr. Fix-It)*, Wanda Hawley *(Mary)*, Marjorie Daw *(Olive)*, Katherine MacDonald *(Georgina Burroughs)*, Frank Campeau *(Uncle "Hen")*, Leslie Stuart, Ida Waterman, Alice Smith, Mrs. H. R. Hancock, Mr. Russell, Fred Goodwin, Margaret Landis, Joe Brooks.

Fairbanks is a student in England, whose U.S. roommate is summoned home to marry a wealthy girl he hasn't seen since childhood. Because the fellow is in love with a British lass, Fairbanks volunteers to take his place. Of course there is the usual assortment of laughter and thrills before the picture's inevitable, happy conclusion.

d&w, Allan Dwan (based on a story by Ernest Butterworth); ph, Hugh McClung.

Comedy **(PR:A MPAA:NR)**

MR. JUSTICE RAFFLES** (1921, Brit.) 6 reels Hepworth bw

Gerald Ames *(A. J. Raffles)*, Eileen Dennes *(Camilla Belsize)*, James Carew *(Dan Levy)*, Hugh Clifton *(Teddy Garland)*, Lyonel Watts *(Bunny)*, Gwynne Herbert *(Lady Laura Belsize)*, Henry Vibart *(Mr. Garland)*, Peggy Patterson *(Dolly Fairfield)*, Pino Conti *(Foreigner)*, Townsend Whitling *(Tough)*.

Produced at a time when stereotypes were still, for the most part, acceptable, this British mystery deals with a gentleman thief who comes to the aid of a pal and helps his fiancee escape the clutches of a Jewish money lender.

d, Gerald Ames, Gaston Quiribet; w, Blanche McIntosh (based on a novel by E. W. Hornung).

Crime **(PR:A MPAA:NR)**

MR. NOBODY** (1927, Brit.) 5 reels British Screen Classics/FOX bw

Frank Stanmore *(Mr. Nobody)*, Pauline Johnson *(Alice Meadows)*, Pat Whitcombe *(Geoffrey Forbes)*, Cameron Carr, James Knight, George Bellamy, Wyndham Guise.

British drama about a student who is kicked out of school, travels abroad, and returns home to claim his inheritance just in the nick of time.

d&w, Frank Miller; w, (based on a story by Eric Strang).

Drama **(PR:A MPAA:NR)**

MR. WU*** (1919, Brit.) 5 reels STOLL bw

Matheson Lang *(Mr. Wu)*, Lillah McCarthy *(Mrs. Gregory)*, Meggie Albanesi *(Nang Ping)*, Roy Royston *(Basil Gregory)*, Teddy Arundell *(Mr. Gregory)*.

This British mystery, about a Chinaman who kills his daughter and then captures the man who seduced her, demanding his mother as the currency of his exchange, was good enough to inspire the great Lon Chaney to make his own version some eight years later.

d, Maurice Elvey; w, Frederick Blatchford (based on the play by Harry Maurice Vernon, Harold Owen).

Mystery **(PR:A MPAA:NR)**

MR. WU*** (1927) 8 reels MGM bw

Lon Chaney *(Mr. Wu/Mr. Wu's Grandfather)*, Louise Dresser *(Mrs. Gregory)*, Renee Adoree *(Nang Ping)*, Holmes Herbert *(Mr. Gregory)*, Ralph Forbes *(Basil Gregory)*, Gertrude Olmstead *(Hilda Gregory)*, Mrs. Wong Wing *(Ah Wong)*, Claude King *(Mr. Muir)*, Sonny Loy *(Little Wu)*, Anna May Wong *(Loo Song)*.

Chaney was partial to playing Orientals and portrayed two of them (grandfather and grandson) in this interesting film about a Chinaman who kills his own daughter when he discovers her involvement with Forbes, a British aristocrat. Attempting to wreak revenge on the Englishman's family, he is ultimately stabbed to death by Forbes' mother.

d, William Nigh; w, Lorna Moon (based on the play by Harry Maurice Vernon, Harold Owen); t, Lotta Woods; ph, John Arnold; ed, Ben Lewis; set d, Cedric Gibbons, Richard Day.

Drama **(PR:C MPAA:NR)**

MRS. BLACK IS BACK*** (1914) 4 reels FP bw

May Irwin *(Mrs. Black)*, Charles Lane *(Prof. Newton Black)*, Wellington A. Playter *(Tom Larkey)*, Clara Blandick *(Emily Mason)*, Elmer Booth *(Jack Dangerfield)*, James Herter *(Maj. Thorne)*, Cyril Chadwick *(Bramley Bush)*, Marie Pavis *(Priscila Black)*, Howard Missimer.

Irwin brought her successful stage comedy to the screen here with the story of a widow who lies about her age—claiming to be 29—when she marries a professor. The fun begins when her grown son shows up and happens to be in love with his stepfather's daughter.

d, J. Searle Dawley; w, (based on the play by George V. Hobart).

Comedy **(PR:A MPAA:NR)**

MRS. SLACKER** (1918) 5 reels Astra/Pathe bw

Gladys Hulette *(Susie Simpkins)*, Creighton Hale *(Robert Gibbs)*, Paul Clerget *(His Father)*.

To avoid being drafted, wealthy pantywaist Hale marries washergirl Hulette. But when Hulette discovers his true motive, she leaves him flat, refusing to be a "Mrs. Slacker." Later, she foils a plot to blow up a nearby dam, which inspires Hale to enlist, and thereby provides the audience with a happy, and patriotic, ending.

d, Hobart Henley; w, Agnes C. Johnston.

War **(PR:A MPAA:NR)**

MRS. THOMPSON** (1919, Brit.) 5 reels G. B. Samuelson/GEN bw

Minna Grey *(Mrs. Thompson)*, C. M. Hallard *(Prentice)*, Isobel Elsom *(Enid Thompson)*, Bertram Burleigh *(Dickey Marsden)*, Tom Reynolds *(Archibald Bence)*, James Lindsay *(Charles Kennion)*, Marie Wright *(Yates)*, Wyndham Guise *(Mears)*.

British drama about the daughter of a hard-working shopkeeper who marries a rotter and then watches her family business go right down the tubes.

d, Rex Wilson; w, (based on the novel by W. B. Maxwell).

Drama **(PR:A MPAA:NR)**

MISTRESS NELL** 1/2 (1915) 5 reels FP bw

Mary Pickford *(Mistress Nell)*, Owen Moore *(Charles II, King of England)*, Arthur Hoops *(Duke of Buckingham)*, Ruby Hoffman *(Louise, Duchess of Portsmouth)*, Amelia Rose *(Orange Moll)*, Hayward Mack, Nathanael Sack.

Pickford's great popularity made this rather ordinary film adaptation of the stage play—about the flower girl who wins the heart of England's king—a hit. Pickford discovers that duchess Hoffman and duke Hoops are working as secret agents for the King of France, attempting to overthrow English king Moore's reign. Disguising herself, Pickford gets the goods on the traitors and saves the day. Moore, who played King Charles II, was Pickford's first husband and often acted opposite her on both stage and screen.

d, James Kirkwood; w, Frances Marion (based on the play "Nell Gwynn" by George C. Hazelton, Jr.).

Drama **(PR:A MPAA:NR)**

MISTRESS OF SHENSTONE, THE** (1921) 6 reels R-C bw

Pauline Frederick *(Lady Myra Ingleby)*, Roy Stewart *(Jim Airth)*, Emmett C. King *(Sir Deryck Brand)*, Arthur Clayton *(Ronald Ingram)*, John Willink *(Billy Cathcart)*, Helen Wright *(Margaret O'Mara)*, Rosa Gore *(Amelia Murgatroyd)*, Helen Muir *(Eliza Murgatroyd)*, Lydia Yeamans Titus *(Susannah Murgatroyd)*.

Ace director King did what he could with this banal story about an Englishwoman (Frederick) who escapes to the beach resort of Cornwall to mourn the accidental death of her husband in the war. At Cornwall, she meets and falls in love with Stewart after he saves her life on the beach. When she finds he is the same man responsible for the death of her husband, she quickly departs. In the end, however, Frederick puts the past behind her and returns to Stewart's waiting arms.

d, Henry King; w, Florence L. Barclay; ph, J. D. Jennings.

Drama **(PR:A MPAA:NR)**

MIXED FACES** (1922) 5 reels FOX bw

William Russell *(Judge J. Woodworth Granger/Jimmy Gallop)*, Renee Adoree *(Mary Allen Sayre)*, De Witt Jennings *(Murray McGuire)*, Elizabeth Garrison *(Mrs. Sayre)*, Charles French *(Mr. Sayre)*, Aileen Manning *(Mrs. Molly Crutcher)*, Harvey Clarke *(William Haskins)*.

Double role stuff has Russell playing both the part of a judge who is running for mayor and a wisecracking salesman who wanders into town. Political enemies capture the judge and hire the salesman to impersonate him and sabotage the campaign. But instead of following their scheme, the young fellow puts his charm to work, gets his look alike elected, and wins the love of the girl who was once part of the conspiracy.

d, Rowland V. Lee; w, Paul Schofield (based on the novel by Roy Norton); ph, David Abel.

Drama/Comedy **(PR:A MPAA:NR)**

M'LISS*** 1/2 (1918) 5 reels ART bw

Mary Pickford *(M'liss)*, Theodore Roberts *("Bummer" Smith)*, Thomas Meighan *(Charles Gray)*, Charles Ogle *(Yuba Bill)*, Tully Marshall *(Judge McSnagley)*, Monte Blue *(Mexican Joe)*, Helen Kelly *(Clytemnestra Vernonica McSnagley)*, Winifred Greenwood *(Clara Parker)*, Val Paul *(Jim Peterson)*, William H. Brown *(Sheriff Sandy Waddles)*, John Burton *(Parson Bean)*, Bud Post *(Butch Saunders)*, Guy Oliver *(Snakebit Saunders)*, Harry Rattenberry.

Pickford's screen persona was perfectly suited to play the role of Harte's M'liss, the untamed child of Red Gulch who can swear like a sailor but break your heart at the same time. Fine direction by Neilan, good performances by all (particularly by the bewhiskered Theodore Roberts), and a handsome production by Artcraft. The director of some of Pickford's most successful films, the handsome Neilan, a D. W. Griffith protege, also acted with her in a number of films before stepping behind the camera.

d, Marshall Neilan; w, Frances Marion (based on the story by Bret Harte and the play by Clay M. Greene); ph, Walter Stradling.

Drama **(PR:A MPAA:NR)**

MOCKERY*** (1927) 7 reels MGM bw

Lon Chaney *(Sergei)*, Ricardo Cortez *(Dimitri)*, Barbara Bedford *(Tatiana)*, Mack Swain *(Mr. Gaidaroff)*, Emily Fitzroy *(Mrs. Gaidaroff)*, Charles Puffy *(Ivan)*, Kai Schmidt *(Butler)*.

Another fascinating performance by Chaney, this time as a dimwitted Russian peasant who is given food and a job in return for guiding a countess (Bedford) from Siberia to her home in Novokursk. There he turns into a revolutionary and becomes hateful towards the countess and everything she stands for. During a peasant uprising, Chaney attacks Bedford, who later shields him from arrest by claiming he was trying to protect her. There is then another uprising and Chaney actually does protect the countess and, in so doing, gives up his own life.

d, Benjamin Christensen; w, Bradley King, Christensen (based on a story by Stig Esbern); t, Joe Farnham; ph, Merritt B. Gerstad; ed, John W. English; set d, Cedric Gibbons, Alexander Toluboff.

Drama **(PR:C MPAA:NR)**

MODERN CINDERELLA, A 1/2** (1917) 5 reels FOX bw

June Caprice *(Joyce)*, Frank Morgan *(Tom)*, Betty Prendergast *(Polly)*, Stanhope Wheatcroft *(Harry)*, Grace Stevens *(Mother)*, Tom Brooke *(Father)*, William B. Davidson.

Caprice stars as a girl from a middle class family who has a crush on one of her older sister's boy friends. One night she puts on some makeup, dresses up in a lovely gown, and sneaks off to the big dance. There she fascinates the man of her desires and later rushes home, leaving one of her slippers behind. The rest of the story is obvious, but well done.

d, John G. Adolfi; w, Florence Auer (based on her own story); ph, Rial Schellinger.

Comedy/Drama **(PR:A MPAA:NR)**

MODERN MARRIAGE** (1923) 7 reels F.X.B./American Releasing bw

Francis X. Bushman *(Hugh Varley)*, Beverly Bayne *(Denise Varley)*, Roland Bottomley *(Frank Despard)*, Ernest Hilliard *(Cort Maitland)*, Zita Moulton *(Nita Blake)*, Frankie Evans *(Hugh, Jr.)*, Arnold Lucy *(Elihu Simpson)*, Pauline Dempsey *(Mammy)*, Blanche Craig *(Blossom Young)*.

Most of the magic Bushman and Bayne once generated was gone by the time they got around to making this programmer. It tells of a neglectful husband (Bushman) whose unfaithful wife (Bayne) becomes implicated in the murder of her lover. The real killer then tries to blackmail her but accidentally shoots himself and confesses to the crime before dying.

d, Lawrence C. Windom; sup, Whitman Bennett; w, Dorothy Farnum (based on the story "Lady Varley" by Derek Vane); ph, Edward Paul; art d, Elsa Lopez.

Drama **(PR:A MPAA:NR)**

MODERN MONTE CRISTO, A***

(1917) 5 reels Thanhouser/Gold Rooster bw (AKA: HIS ENEMY'S DAUGHTER)

Vincent Serrano *(Dr. Emerson)*, Thomas A. Curran *(William Deane)*, Helen Badgley *(Virginia Deane)*, Boyd Marshall *(Tom Bemberton)*, Gladys Dore.

After being ruined by Curran, a rival for the woman he loves, Serrano vanishes for years. He returns, fabulously wealthy and bent on revenge. Luring Curran to a ship he owns, Serrano locks himself in a cabin with his enemy and, to the horror of his foe, it becomes obvious that the vessel is slowly sinking. The film daringly, for that day, left audiences pondering the possible outcome of this situation.

d, Eugene Moore; w, Lloyd Lonergan.

Drama **(PR:A MPAA:NR)**

MODERN MUSKETEER, A* 1/2** (1917) 5 reels Douglas Fairbanks/ART bw

Douglas Fairbanks *(Ned Thacker)*, Marjorie Daw *(Dorothy Moran)*, Kathleen Kirkham *(Mrs. Moran)*, Tully Marshall *(Phillip Marden)*, Frank Campeau *(Indian Guide)*, Eugene Ormonde *(Raymond Vandeteer)*, ZaSu Pitts.

Born during a Kansas cyclone to a mother who constantly reads *The Three Musketeers*, Fairbanks grows up committed to the performance of chivalrous acts. Unfortunately, his daring deeds invariably backfire, until he heads west and meets the girl he is destined to rescue and wed. There are plenty of stunts and laughs in this snappy five-reeler, and a dream sequence, in which he satirizes the character of D'Artagnan, is a delightful prevue of things to come.

d&w, Allan Dwan (based on the story "D'Artagnan of Kansas" by Eugene P. Lyle, Jr.); ph, Harry Thorpe, Victor Fleming.

Western/Comedy **(PR:A MPAA:NR)**

MODERN SALOME, A** (1920) 5 reels Hope Hampton/Metro bw

Hope Hampton, Sidney L. Mason, Percy Standing, Arthur Donaldson, Wyndham Standing, Agnes Ayres.

Hampton went on to become a star of some stature, as well as a major figure in New York society, after making her screen debut in this adaptation of a Wilde poem about a self-centered woman who sacrifices a man for her own convenience, but finds redemption in the end.

d, Leonce Perret; w, Nora Jansen, Perret (based on the poem "Salome" by Oscar Wilde); ph, Harry Harde, Alfred Ortlieb.

Drama **(PR:C MPAA:NR)**

MOLLY BAWN* (1916, Brit.) 5 reels Hepworth bw

Alma Taylor *(Eleanor Massareene)*, Stewart Rome *(Tedcastle Luttrell)*, Violet Hopson *(Marcia Amherst)*, Lionelle Howard *(Philip Shadwell)*, Fred Wright *(Mr. Amherst)*, Chrissie White *(Lady Cecil Stafford)*, John MacAndrews *(John Massareene)*, Henry Vibart *(Marigny)*, Valerie McLintock *(Letitia Massareene)*, Percy Manton *(Plantaganet Potts)*.

Set in the British occupied Ireland of 1850, this is the story of a couple who desperately try to win back the approval of their grandfather.

d, Cecil M. Hepworth; w, Blanche McIntosh (based on the novel by Mrs. Hungerford).

Drama **(PR:A MPAA:NR)**

MOLLY ENTANGLED 1/2** (1917) 5 reels Pallas/PAR bw

Vivian Martin *(Molly Shawn)*, Harrison Ford *(Barney Malone)*, Noah Beery *(Shawn)*, G. S. Spaulding *(Jim Barry)*, Helen Dunbar *(Mrs. Barry)*, C. H. Gowland *(O'Marra)*, W. A. Carroll *(Leary)*, Jane Keckley.

Sweet little family entertainment has Martin marrying Spaulding on his deathbed to save his fortune for the family who helped hers out years before. Martin is really in love with Ford, so when Spaulding recovers, the little darlin's heart is after breakin' but—saints preserve us—the priest who did the splicin' turns out to be an impostor, and sure ain't the world a grand place after all!

d, Robert Thornby; w, (based on a story by Edith Kennedy).

Comedy/Romance **(PR:A MPAA:NR)**

MOLLY O'*** (1921) 8 reels MS-Mabel Normand/AFN bw

Mabel Normand *(Molly O')*, George Nichols *(Tim O'Dair)*, Anna Hernandez *(Mrs. Tim O'Dair)*, Albert Hackett *(Billy O'Dair)*, Eddie Gribbon *(Jim Smith)*, Jack Mulhall *(Dr. John S. Bryant)*, Lowell Sherman *(Fred Manchester)*, Jacqueline Logan *(Miriam Manchester)*, Ben Deely *(Albert Faulkner)*, Gloria Davenport *(Mrs. James W. Robbins)*, Carl Stockdale *(The Silhouette Man)*, Eugenie Besserer *(Antonia Bacigalupi)*.

Somewhat disappointing after her triumphant feature MICKEY, this Normand comedy is a Cinderella story about the daughter of an Irish ditchdigger who falls in love with a prominent doctor on seeing his picture in a newspaper. Of course after a number of funny and pathos-tinged experiences, she ultimately marries him. In spite of its shortcomings, MOLLY O' is still quite special because of the delightfully wistful presence of its star.

d, F. Richard Jones; sup, Mack Sennett; w, Mary Hunt, Fred Stowers (based on a story by Sennett); t, John Grey; ph, Fred Jackman; ed, Allen McNeil; art d, Sanford D. Barnes; spec eff, Paul Guerin.

Comedy **(PR:A MPAA:NR)**

MOLLY OF THE FOLLIES*** (1919) 5 reels AM bw

Margarita Fischer *(Molly Malone)*, Jack Mower *(Joe Holmquist, the Human Submarine)*, Lulu Warrenton *(Kate Malone)*, Millard L. Webb *(Milton Wallace)*, J. Farrell MacDonald *(Swannick)*, Mary Lee Wise *(Emily Ewing)*.

Fischer plays a side show dancer who loves an acrobat (Mower) who bills himself as "The Human Submarine." However, Fischer's fortune-telling mother also has eyes for the acrobat. A lot of the interest this little comedy generated was from the location shots at Coney Island's Luna Park.

d, Edward Sloman; w, (based on a story by Peter Clark MacFarlane).

Comedy **(PR:A MPAA:NR)**

MOLLYCODDLE, THE* 1/2** (1920) 6 reels Douglas Fairbanks/UA bw

Douglas Fairbanks *(Richard Marshall)*, Ruth Renick *(Virginia Hale)*, Betty Boulton *(Molly Warren)*, Wallace Beery *(Henry Von Holkar)*, George Stewart *(Ole Olsen)*, Albert MacQuarrie *(Desert Yacht Driver)*, Charles Stevens *(Yellow Horse)*, Paul Burns *(Samuel Levinski)*, Morris Hughes *(Patrick O'Flannigan)*, Adele Farrington *(Mrs. Warren)*, Lewis Hippe *(First Mate)*.

Fairbanks, at his funniest and most athletic, plays a British-educated American whom everyone regards as a mollycoddle until he brings a smuggler (well-played by Beery) to justice in the wilds of Arizona.

d, Victor Fleming; w, Tom J. Geraghty, Fairbanks (based on a story by Harold McGrath); ph, William McGann, Harry Thorpe.

Adventure/Western **Cas.** **(PR:A MPAA:NR)**

MONEY CORRAL, THE*** (1919) 5 reels WSHP/ART bw

William S. Hart *(Lem Beason)*, Jane Novak *(Rose)*, Herschel Mayall *(Carl)*, Winter Hall *(Gregory Collins)*, Rhea Mitchell *(Janet, His Daughter)*, Patricia Palmer *(Chicago Kate)*.

Enjoyable Hart feature has the great cowboy star playing a rodeo champion who is hired by a Chicago banker to protect his vaults from a gang of crooks. Hart does his job, arrests the gangsters, and wins the beautiful Novak, as well.

d&w, William S. Hart, Lambert Hillyer (based on the story "Somebody's Fool" by Hart); ph, Joseph August.

Western/Crime **(PR:A MPAA:NR)**

MONEY HABIT, THE** (1924, Brit.) 7 reels COM/Granger bw

Clive Brook *(Noel Jason)*, Nina Vanna *(Cecile d'Arcy)*, Warwick Ward *(Varian)*, Fred Rains *(Marley)*, Eva Westlake *(Duchess)*, Philip Hewland *(Mr. Hastings)*, Muriel Gregory *(Typist)*, Kate Gurney *(Mrs. Hastings)*, Annette Benson *(Diana Hastings)*.

Before establishing himself as a Hollywood star, Brook gave many competent performances in British films, including this one dealing with a sharpie who gets his mistress to use her charms to convince a man of means to buy a phony oil well.

d, Walter Niebuhr; w, Alicia Ramsey (based on a novel by Paul Potter).

Mystery **(PR:A MPAA:NR)**

MONEY ISN'T EVERYTHING** (1925, Brit.) 5 reels STOLL bw

Olive Sloane *(Elizabeth Tuter)*, Arthur Burne *(James Rodgers)*, Gladys Hamer *(Adele Rockwell)*, John Hamilton *(William Channon)*, Lewis Gilbert, Gladys Crebbin.

British love story about a clerk who suddenly becomes wealthy when he wins the sweepstakes and then marries an office girl who has an affair with her former boss.

d, Thomas Bentley; w, Isobel Johnstone (based on a novel by Sophie Cole).

Romantic Drama **(PR:A MPAA:NR)**

MONEY MAGIC* (1917) 5 reels VIT bw

Laura Winston *(Mrs. Gilman)*, Edith Storey *(Bertha)*, William Duncan *(Marshall Haney)*, Antonio Moreno *(Ben Fordyce)*, Florence Dye *(Alice Heath)*.

The Vitagraph company certainly didn't have comedy on their mind when they produced this little charmer about a girl who, out of pity, marries a Western millionaire left wheelchair bound by a gunshot wound. Shortly thereafter, an impoverished Eastern lawyer comes to the wide open spaces with his fiancee, who is dying of tuberculosis, and the joyful foursome meet. Between coughs, the consumptive lass convinces her paraplegic friend that they are standing (or, in his case, sitting) in the way of their loved ones' happiness. So she breaks her engagement and returns to the drafty dampness of the East, and her comrade-in-pain (who has been told by his doctor to avoid altitude, due to a weak heart) rolls his way to the peak of the nearest mountain and grits his teeth in grim anticipation.

d, William Wolbert; w, A. Van Buren Powell (based on a novel by Hamlin Garland).

Drama **(PR:A MPAA:NR)**

MONEY! MONEY! MONEY!* (1923) 6 reels PRE/AFN bw

Katherine MacDonald *(Priscilla Hobbs)*, Carl Stockdale *(George C. Hobbs)*, Frances Raymond *(Mrs. Hobbs)*, Paul Willis *(Lennie Hobbs)*, Herschel Mayall *(Mr. Carter)*, Brenda Fowler *(Mrs. Carter)*, Margaret Loomis *(Caroline Carter)*, Charles Clary *(J. J. Grey)*, Jack Dougherty *(Reggie Grey)*.

While social climber MacDonald and her mother await an expected inheritance, they talk her father into borrowing money from wealthy Mayall. Later Dougherty, who is in love with MacDonald, discovers that the opportunistic Mayall only lent out the money to MacDonald and her family as a way of later taking over the factory her father owns. To prevent this, Dougherty secretly buys a partnership in the factory when their family inheritance proves to be less than anticipated. This one did not have the audiences sitting on the edge of their seats.

d, Tom Forman; w, Hope Loring (based on a story by Larry Evans); ph, Joseph Brotherton.

Drama **(PR:A MPAA:NR)**

MONKEY TALKS, THE*½** (1927) 6 reels FOX bw

Olive Borden *(Olivette)*, Jacques Lerner *(Jocko Lerner/Fano)*, Don Alvarado *(Sam Wick/Pierre)*, Malcolm Waite *(Bergerin)*, Raymond Hitchcock *(Lorenzo)*, Ted McNamara *(Firmin)*, Jane Winton *(Maisie)*, August Tollaire *(Mata)*.

This most interesting Walsh drama of circus life has three members of a traveling show stranded in the French provinces making a living by dressing Lerner, the handyman, in the costume of a monkey and passing him off as a talking animal. Lerner brings prosperity and fame to everyone with his wonderful act, but then Alvarado, his oldest and best friend, falls in love with Borden, the high wire artist, whom Lerner also loves. In an ending worthy of Lon Chaney, the little man sacrifices his own life to save the wire walker from an attack by a wild beast, thus freeing her to marry the man of her choice.

d, Raoul Walsh; w, L. G. Rigby (based on a play by Rene Fauchois); ph, L. William O'Connell.

Drama **(PR:A MPAA:NR)**

MONKEY'S PAW, THE** (1923, Brit.) 6 reels Artistic bw

Moore Marriott *(John White)*, Marie Ault *(Mrs. White)*, Charles Ashton *(Herbert White)*, Johnny Butt *(Sgt. Tom Morris)*, Tom Coventry *(Engine Driver)*, A. B. Imeson, George Wynn.

British fantasy about a couple who dream that they are reunited with their deceased son through the magic of an animal's paw.

p, George Redman; d, Manning Haynes; w, Lydia Hayward (based on a play by W. W. Jacobs).

Fantasy **(PR:A MPAA:NR)**

MONSIEUR BEAUCAIRE½** (1924) 10 reels FP/PAR bw

Rudolph Valentino *(Duke de Chartres/Beaucaire)*, Bebe Daniels *(Princess Henriette)*, Lois Wilson *(Queen Marie of France)*, Doris Kenyon *(Lady Mary)*, Lowell Sherman *(King Louis XV)*, Paulette Duval *(Mme. Pompadour)*, John Davidson *(Richelieu)*, Louis Waller *(Francois)*, Ian MacLaren *(Duke of Winterset)*, Frank Shannon *(Badger)*, Templar Powell *(Molyneux)*, H. Cooper Cliffe *(Beau Nash)*, Downing Clarke *(Lord Chesterfield)*, Yvonne Hughes *(Duchesse de Flauhault)*, Harry Lee *(Voltaire)*, Florence O'Denishawn *(Colombine)*, Oswald York *(Miropoix)*, Flora Finch *(Duchesse de Montmorency)*.

Although an ideal property for the considerable talent of its star, Valentino, this famous motion picture—about the Duke of Chartres escaping France disguised as a barber and then infiltrating the British court as the dashing Beaucaire—is actually pretty much a bore. There are some wonderful sets and an all-star cast, but the film never quite takes off, and it seems much longer than its 100 minutes.

p, Sidney Olcott; w, Forrest Halsey (based on the novel by Booth Tarkington and the play by Evelyn Greenleaf Sutherland, Tarkington); ph, Harry Fischbeck; ed, Patricia Rooney; art d, Natacha Rambova.

Costume Drama **Cas.** **(PR:A MPAA:NR)**

MONSTER, THE*** (1925) 7 reels MG bw

Lon Chaney *(Dr. Ziska)*, Gertrude Olmsted *(Betty Watson)*, Hallam Cooley *(Watson's Head Clerk)*, Johnny Arthur *(The Under Clerk)*, Charles A. Sellon *(The Constable)*, Walter James *(Caliban)*, Knute Erickson *(Daffy Dan)*, George Austin *(Rigo)*, Edward McWade *(Luke Watson)*, Ethel Wales *(Mrs. Watson)*.

Greatly imitated horror film has Chaney as a mad doctor who abducts passing motorists for experimental purposes. All the atmospheric ingredients are here—from laboratory to dungeon—and then there's the girl's last minute rescue, which would become a necessary part of the genre. There's plenty of slapstick comedy relief, as well, in the form of an asylum full of lunatics.

d, Roland West; w, Williard Mack, Albert Kenyon (based on the play by Crane Wilbur); t, C. Gardner Sullivan; ph, Hal Mohr; ed, A. Carle Palm.

Horror **(PR:A MPAA:NR)**

MONTY WORKS THE WIRES** (1921, Brit.) 5 reels Artistic bw

Manning Haynes *(The Man)*, Mildred Evelyn *(The Girl)*, Eva Westlake *(The Auntie)*, Charles Ashton *(The Brother-in-law)*, Gladys Hamer *(The Maid)*, Thomas Canning *(The Doctor)*.

British comedy has a man's dog tell his puppy just how his owner courted and married a woman who was the owner of a Pekingese.

p, George Redman; d, Challis Sanderson, Manning Haynes; w, Lydia Hayward, Haynes.

Comedy **(PR:A MPAA:NR)**

MOON MADNESS* (1920) 5 reels Haworth/R-C bw

Edith Storey *(Valerie/Zora)*, Sam De Grasse *(Adrien)*, Josef Swickard *(Latour)*, Wallace MacDonald *(Jan)*, Irene Hunt *(Badoura)*, William Courtleigh *(Raoul)*, Frankie Lee *(The Child)*, Frederick Starr *(Arab Chief)*.

A French girl living in Africa is raised by Arabs when she wanders into their camp after her mother, who was running away with a paramour, is killed. The chief's son falls in love with the girl, but she becomes smitten with an artist and follows him to Paris. Later in the film, the painter, who it turns out is the very same fellow who earlier betrayed her mother, tries to have his way with her. But somehow the girl's father shows up, kills the painter, and reunites his little girl with the prince who, all of a sudden, looks pretty darn good in his European-tailored evening clothes.

d, Colin Campbell; w, J. Grubb Alexander; ph, Fred Schoedsack.

Drama **(PR:C MPAA:NR)**

MOONSHINE VALLEY** (1922) 6 reels FOX bw

William Farnum *(Ned Connors)*, Sadie Mullen *(His Wife)*, Holmes Herbert *(Dr. Martin)*, Dawn O'Day *(Nancy, the Child)*, Jean Bronte *(Jeane, the Dog)*.

Farnum turns to alcohol when his wife leaves him and marries Herbert, a doctor. Then Farnum finds a little lost girl and straightens out for her sake. Sometime later, the tot is taken ill and as a last resort Farnum arranges for her to be examined by his enemy. Herbert recognizes the girl as his daughter, attempts to kidnap her, and is killed by Farnum. The picture ends with Farnum and his former wife being brought together again through mutual love for the adorable moppet.

d, Herbert Brenon; w, Mary Murillo, Brenon (based on a story by Lenora Asereth, Murillo); ph, Tom Malloy.

Western/Drama **(PR:A MPAA:NR)**

MORAL FIBRE* (1921) 6 reels VIT bw

Corinne Griffith *(Marion Wolcott)*, Catherine Calvert *(Grace Elmore)*, William Parke, Jr. *(Jared Wolcott)*, Harry C. Browne *(George Elmore)*, Joe King *(John Corliss)*, Alice Concord *(Nancy Bartley)*.

When small-town storekeeper Parke commits suicide after discovering that Calvert, the city woman with whom he is in love, is actually married, his younger sister Griffith vows revenge. Later the girl becomes a successful illustrator in New York and lands a job doing the art work for a novel by Calvert's husband. Griffith almost breaks up their marriage by giving the impression that she is having an affair with the writer, but backs down at the last moment after discovering that King, the man *she* secretly loves, is the brother of Calvert. All ends well, however, when King follows Griffith to her home town and pops the question.

d, Webster Campbell; w, William B. Courtney (based on a story by William Harrison Goadby).

Drama **(PR:A MPAA:NR)**

MORALS**** (1921) 5 reels REA/PAR bw

May McAvoy *(Carlotta)*, William P. Carleton *(Sir Marcus Ordeyne)*, Marian Skinner *(Mrs. McMurray)*, Nicholas De Ruiz *(Hamdi)*, Starke Patterson *(Harry)*, William Lawrence *(Sebastian Pasquale)*, Kathlyn Williams *(Judith Mainwaring)*, Bridgetta Clark *(Antoinette)*, Sidney Bracey *(Stinson)*.

Director Taylor built his great reputation on sensitively filmed and acted pictures such as this one, about a girl (McAvoy) who escapes a Turkish harem and is taken under the protective wing of a British aristocrat (Carleton). There are, of course, complications which separate the two, all of which work themselves out in the end. An excellent performance is given by that most neglected of all female silent stars, McAvoy.

d, William Desmond Taylor; w, Julia Crawford Ivers (based on the play "The Morals of Marcus Ordeyne" by William J. Locke); ph, James C. Van Trees.

Drama **(PR:A MPAA:NR)**

MORAN OF THE LADY LETTY*** (1922) 7 reels FP/PAR bw

Dorothy Dalton *(Moran/Letty Sternersen)*, Rudolph Valentino *(Ramon Laredo)*, Charles Brinley *(Capt. Sternersen)*, Walter Long *(Capt. Kitchell)*, Emil Jorgenson *(Nels)*, Maude Wayne *(Josephine Herrick)*, Cecil Holland *(Bill Trim)*, George Kuwa *("Chopstick" Charlie)*, Charles K. French *(Tavern Owner)*.

Solid adventure film has Valentino as a Spanish aristocrat, shanghaied in San Francisco by a gang of smugglers (led by super villain Long) and taken aboard a ship headed for Mexico. At sea they encounter the vessel Lady Letty in flames and rescue the only survivor, the beautiful Dalton (whom Valentino was attracted to earlier), dressed as a man. The Spaniard keeps her identity as long as he can, but after a number of exciting developments, Long comes to realize the truth and the inevitable showdown occurs. In a sensationally staged fight, which takes place all over the ship's deck and up into the rigging and mast, Valentino amazed both his critics and fans with his athletic prowess and, of course, no one was surprised when the totally offensive Long plunged to his death.

d, George Melford; w, Monte M. Katterjohn (based on the novel by Frank Norris); ph, William Marshall.

Adventure **(PR:A MPAA:NR)**

MORE TROUBLE** (1918) 5 reels Astra/Pathe bw

Frank Keenan *(Lemuel Deering)*, John Gilbert *(Harvey Deering)*, Ida Lewis *(Mrs. Deering)*, Roberta Wilson *(Miriam Deering)*, Joseph J. Dowling *(Cecil Morrowton)*, Jack Rollins *(Harold Morrowton)*, Helen Dunbar *(Mrs. Morton Wells)*, Al Ray, Clyde Benson, Aggie Herring.

Gilbert graduates at the top of his class, neither smokes nor drinks, and goes into business with his justifiably proud father (courageously played by Keenan). Before long, enormous expenditures attributed to the lad (although he denies being responsible) drive Keenan to the brink of financial ruin. There is an explanation for all of this, of course. The son's former fraternity brother and pal, Rollins, has been forging his name on bank drafts since falling out with his millionaire father. But in the end, the money is replaced, and the wheels of commerce grind on.

d, Ernest C. Warde; w, Ouida Bergere (based on a story by Edgar Franklin).

Farce **(PR:A MPAA:NR)**

MORGAN'S LAST RAID** (1929) 6 reels MGM bw

Tim McCoy *(Capt. Daniel Clairbourne)*, Dorothy Sebastian *(Judith Rogers)*, Wheeler Oakman *(John Bland)*, Allan Garcia *(Morgan)*, Hank Mann *(Tex)*, Montague Shaw *(Gen. Rogers)*.

Veteran comedian Mann pulled off a few laughs in this Civil War yarn which has McCoy refusing to fight against his native state of Tennessee, and being branded a coward by his lady friend. She changes her mind when later, as a member of Morgan's Confederate raiders, he saves her life.

d, Nick Grinde; w, Bradley King (based on a story by Madeleine Ruthven, Ross B. Wills); t, Harry Braxton; ph, Arthur Reed; ed, William Le Vanway.

Historical/Adventure **(PR:A MPAA:NR)**

MORIARTY (SEE: SHERLOCK HOLMES, 1922)

MORMON PERIL, THE (SEE: TRAPPED BY MORMONS, 1922, Brit.)

MOTH AND THE FLAME, THE**½ (1915) 5 reels FP/PAR bw

Stewart Baird *(Edward Fletcher)*, Edwin Mordant *(Mr. Dawson)*, Bradley Barker *(Douglas Rhodes)*, Arthur Donaldson *(Mr. Walton)*, Adele Ray *(Marion Walton)*, Dora M. Adams *(Mrs. Walton)*, Irene Howley *(Jeanette Graham)*, Maurice Stewart *(Jeanette's Boy)*.

Talented pioneer filmmaker Olcott was able to make something of this old warhorse about a girl, seduced and scorned, who breaks up the wedding of the man who did her dirt.

d, Sidney Olcott; w, (based on the play by Clyde Fitch).

Drama **(PR:A MPAA:NR)**

MOTHER**½ (1914) 4 reels WORLD bw

Emma Dunn, Edwin Baker, Henri Desforges, Lillian Cook, Priscilla Dean, Belle Adair.

The popular Dunn, under the sensitive direction of Tourneur, successfully brought her stage role, about a widow's struggle to raise a large family, to the screen.

d&w, Maurice Tourneur (based on a play by Jules Eckert Goodman); ph, John van den Broek.

Drama **(PR:A MPAA:NR)**

MOTHERHOOD* (1915, Brit.) 5 reels B&C-PM/GAU bw

Lilian Braithwaite *(Lady Cadby)*, Fay Temple *(Gwen)*, A. V. Bramble *(Sir Thomas Cadby)*, A. Caton Woodville *(Hal Carruthers)*, Laura Leycester *(Mrs. Preece)*, Victor Boggetti *(Agent)*.

Not too many laughs in this British drama about a Tory millionaire who forbids his ward to marry a young Socialist until he discovers that the lad is actually his illegitimate son.

d&w, Harold Weston.

Drama **(PR:C MPAA:NR)**

MOTHERS-IN-LAW** (1923) 7 reels SCHUL/PRE bw

Ruth Clifford *(Vianna Courtleigh)*, Gaston Glass *(David Wingate)*, Vola Vale *(Ina Phillips)*, Crauford Kent *(Alden Van Buren)*, Josef Swickard *(Newton Wingate)*, Edith Yorke *("Mom" Wingate)*, Doris Stone *(Tessie Clark)*.

The marital strain between fast-living Clifford and stay-at-home Glass is resolved when Glass' mother kidnaps her granddaughter and holds the child captive until the jazz hound learns her lesson and straightens out.

d, Louis Gasnier; w, Olga Printzlau (based on a story by Frank Dazey, Agnes Christine Johnston); ph, Karl Struss.

Drama **(PR:A MPAA:NR)**

MOTORING** (1927, Brit.) 6 reels Inter-Cine bw

Harry Tate *(Harry)*, Violet Ellison *(Mary Flint)*, Henry Latimer *(Basil Love)*, Roy Travers *(Sir Stone Flint)*, Ronnie Tate *(The Boy)*, Alice O'Day.

Screenwriter Stannard elaborated on the popular sketch of British music hall comedian Tate to create this motion picture property for the entertainer. It had to do with a motorist who comes to the assistance of a knight's ward and arranges for an elopement.

d, George Dewhurst; w, Eliot Stannard (based on the music hall sketch by Harry Tate).

Comedy **(PR:A MPAA:NR)**

MOULIN ROUGE*** (1928, Brit.) 90m BIP/Wardour bw

Olga Tschechowa *(Parysia)*, Eve Gray *(Camille)*, Jean Bradin *(Andre)*, Georges Treville *(Father)*, Marcel Vibert *(Marquis)*, Blanche Bernis *(Wardrobe Mistress)*, Ellen Pollock *(Girl)*.

Dupont, who dazzled audiences with VARIETY (1926), his masterpiece about circus life, also wrote, produced, and directed this better-than-average British backstage film about a young man who falls in love with his sweetheart's mother, the dance star of the Moulin Rouge.

p,d&w, E. A. Dupont.

Drama **(PR:C MPAA:NR)**

MOUNTAIN EAGLE, THE (SEE: FEAR O' GOD, 1926, Brit.)

MOUNTAIN RAT, THE** (1914) 4 reels Reliance bw

Dorothy Gish *(The Girl)*, Henry B. Walthall *(The Drinking Man)*, Irene Hunt, Donald Crisp, James Kirkwood.

Gish gives a good performance as a dance hall girl who nurses a wealthy drunkard from the East (Walthall) back to health and marries him in the end. The picture, however, just fails to click.

d, James Kirkwood; w, Frank Woods (based on a story by Mary Rider Mechtold).

Western/Drama **(PR:A MPAA:NR)**

MUMSIE**½ (1927, Brit.) 7 reels Herbert Wilcox/W&F bw

Pauline Frederick *(Mumsie)*, Nelson Keys *(Spud Murphy)*, Herbert Marshall *(Col. Armytage)*, Frank Stanmore *(Nobby Clarke)*, Donald McCardle *(Noel Symonds)*, Irene Russell *(Louise Symonds)*, Rolf Leslie *(Edgar Symonds)*, A. Barry *(Carl Kessler)*, Frank Perfitt *(Maj. Bowen)*, Patrick Susands, Tom Coventry.

U.S. actress Frederick journeyed to England to star in this curious war story about a pacifist with a gambling habit who becomes a spy, and then passes on the plans of his father's poison gas factory to the other side.

d, Herbert Wilcox; w, (based on the play by Edward Knoblock).

War **(PR:A MPAA:NR)**

MUNITION GIRL'S ROMANCE, A** (1917, Brit.) 5 reels BRO bw

Violet Hopson *(Jenny Jones)*, Gregory Scott *(George Brandon)*, George Foley *(Sir Harrison)*, Tom Beaumont *(Heckman)*, H. Sykes *(Pilot)*.

British wartime adventure about a young girl who saves the plans for a secret weapon from the clutches of a spying foreman while doing her part for Old Blighty, working as a munitionette.

p, Walter West; d, Frank Wilson; w, Charles Barnett.

Mystery/War **(PR:A MPAA:NR)**

MUTINY** (1925, Brit.) 4 reels George Clark/Ducal bw

Nigel Barrie *(John England)*, Doris Lytton *(Diana)*, Walter Tennyson, Clifton Boyne, Donald Searle.

In this British actioner, a man framed by a lord breaks out of jail and signs on the yacht owned by his persecutor, then later shows his true metal by rescuing the man's daughter from a shipwreck.

d, F. Martin Thornton; w, (based on a novel by Ben Bolt).

Adventure **(PR:A MPAA:NR)**

MY AMERICAN WIFE*** (1923) 6 reels FP/PAR bw

Gloria Swanson *(Natalie Chester)*, Antonio Moreno *(Manuel La Tassa)*, Josef Swickard *(Don Fernando De Contas)*, Eric Mayne *(Carlos De Grossa)*, Gino Corrado *(Pedro De Grossa)*, Edythe Chapman *(Donna Isabella La Tassa)*, Aileen Pringle *(Hortensia De Varela)*, Walter Long *(Gomez)*, F. R. Butler *(Horace Beresford)*, Jacques D'Auray *(Gaston Navarre)*, Loyal Underwood *(Danny O'Hara)*, Mary Land *(Maid)*.

Entertaining love story-horse racing combination, set in Argentina, has Kentucky beauty Swanson finding romance in the arms of aristocrat Moreno, who fights a duel for her honor. Wood's direction kept everything moving right along with this fine cast.

d, Sam Wood; w, Monte M. Katterjohn (based on the novel by Hector Turnbull); ph, Alfred Gilks.

Drama **(PR:A MPAA:NR)**

MY BEST GIRL**** (1927) 8 reels Mary Pickford/UA bw

Mary Pickford *(Maggie Johnson)*, Charles Rogers *(Joe Grant)*, Sunshine Hart *(Ma Johnson)*, Lucien Littlefield *(Pa Johnson)*, Carmelita Geraghty *(Liz Johnson)*, Hobart Bosworth *(Mr. Merrill)*, Evelyn Hall *(Mrs. Merrill)*, Avonne Taylor *(Millicent Rogers)*, Mack Swain *(The Judge)*, Frank Finch Smiles *(Butler)*, William Courtwright

(Stock Clerk), John Junior *(Nick Powell)*, Harry Walker *(Floorwalker)*, Sidney Bracey *(Butler)*.

Fine Pickford film (co-star Rogers would eventually become her third husband) about a dime-store sales girl who unselfishly keeps her amiable family above water and ends up marrying her boss' son. Littlefield, her father, is a postman; mother Hart has a predilection for funerals; and Geraghty, her sister, is a woman of questionable morals—all are more or less dependent on the plucky Pickford. The owner's son is engaged to a society miss, but he pops the question to Pickford. When the lad's dad finds out, he tries to bribe Pickford into calling the whole thing off, but when she demonstrates that she has her price, the entrepreneur decides that she has plenty of good sense and gives his blessing. Beautifully directed by Taylor, Pickford leads a splendid cast in a movie full of laughter and tears. This was Pickford's last silent picture and the first she did with Taylor, who directed the remainder of her screen efforts with the exception of SECRETS.

d, Sam Taylor; w, Hope Loring, Allen McNeil, Tim Whelan (based on a story by Kathleen Norris); ph, Charles Rosher, David Kesson; art d, Jack Schulze.

Comedy/Romance Cas. (PR:A MPAA:NR)

MY BOY*** (1922) 5 reels Jackie Coogan/AFN bw

Jackie Coogan *(Jackie Blair)*, Claude Gillingwater *(Captain Bill)*, Mathilde Brundage *(Mrs. Blair)*, Patsy Marks *(Little Girl)*.

Heart-warming and funny Coogan film about an orphaned immigrant (his mother died on the trip over) who escapes the Ellis Island authorities that wish to deport him. Coogan then adopts a sickly, old, impoverished sea captain, Gillingwater, who loves the boy. Later Coogan's wealthy American grandmother takes him home, but not before the kid gives the old sea dog a new lease on life, as well as a swell place to live. Austin, who co-directed this film, came over from England with Charlie Chaplin in the Fred Karno comedy troupe and appeared in many of the Little Fellow's films.

p, Sol Lesser; d, Victor Heerman, Albert Austin; sup, Jack Coogan, Sr.; t, Shirley Vance Martin, Max Abramson; ph, Glen MacWilliams, Robert Martin; ed, Irene Morra.

Dramatic Comedy (PR:A MPAA:NR)

MY COUSIN** (1918) 5 reels ART bw

Enrico Caruso *(Mario Nanni/Cesare Carulli)*, Henry Leone *(Robert Bombardi)*, Caroline White *(Rea Ventura)*, Joseph Riccardi *(Pietro Ventura)*, A. G. Corbelle *(Luigi Veddi)*, Bruno Zirato *(Secretary)*, Master William Bray *(Ludovico)*.

Adolph Zukor was still thinking in terms of "great players in great plays" when he hired the magnificent Caruso to appear in two films. In this, his first, the opera star showed a real talent for comedy, but the picture did so poorly at the box office that the second, THE SPLENDID ROMANCE, was never released.

d, Edward Jose; w, Margaret Turnbull; ph, Hal Young.

Comedy (PR:A MPAA:NR)

MY DAD* (1922) 6 reels R-C/FBO bw

Johnnie Walker *(Tom O'Day)*, Wilbur Higby *(Barry O'Day)*, Mary Redmond *(Mrs. O'Day)*, Ruth Clifford *(Dawn)*, Les Bates *(La Due)*, Harry von Meter *(The Factor)*, Rin-Tin-Tin *(Himself)*.

Inferior frozen north drama about a young man who clears his father of a murder charge, nails the guilty party, and wins the girl. Of interest only because of an early appearance by Rin-Tin-Tin.

p&d, Cliff Smith; w, E. Richard Schayer (based on a story by Walter Richard Hall); ph, John Thompson.

Adventure (PR:A MPAA:NR)

MY FOUR YEARS IN GERMANY**
(1918) 9 reels My Four Years in Germany Inc. bw

Halbert Brown *(Ambassador Gerard)*, Williard Dashiell *(British Ambassador)*, Louis Dean *(Kaiser)*, Earl Schenck *(Crown Prince)*, George Riddell *(Von Hindenburg)*, Frank Stone *(Prince Henry of Prussia)*, Karl Dane *(Bethmann-Hollweg)*, Fred Hearn *(Von Jagow)*, Percy Standing *(Zimmerman)*, William Bittner *(Von Tirpitz)*, Arthur C. Duvel *(Von Falkenhayn)*, Ann Dearing *(Miss Delaporte)*, Eugene Acker.

Gerard, the one-time U.S. Ambassador to Germany, wrote the book and had complete control over this incendiary screen adaptation, purporting to tell the inside story about the development of Teutonic militarism. Regarded, at the time, as "Truth Not Fiction," as its titles repetitiously stated, MY FOUR YEARS IN GERMANY was, in fact, stereotypical chauvinism of the most blatant kind.

d, William Nigh; w, Charles A. Logue (based on the book by James W. Gerard); ph, Rial B. Schellinger; art d, John D. Schulze.

Historical Drama (PR:A MPAA:NR)

MY HOME TOWN** (1928) 6 reels T/C/RAY bw

Gladys Brockwell *(Mae Andrews)*, Gaston Glass *(David Warren)*, Violet La Plante *(Priscilla)*, Carl Stockdale *(The Evangelist)*, Henry Sedley *(Denver Eddy)*, William Quinn *(Joey)*, Ruth Cherrington *(The Mother)*, Frank Clark *(The Father)*.

Glass, a small town fellow, escapes to the city after accidentally causing the death of a policeman. He becomes involved with a gang of crooks and falls in love with Brockwell, a female member. Brockwell loves him also, but pretends to make love to another fellow to prevent Glass from becoming snared in a life of crime. The young man returns home crushed, but when he learns of her sacrifice, they are reunited.

d, Scott Pembroke; w, Arthur Hoerl; ph, Hap Depew; ed, Charles A. Post.

Drama/Crime (PR:A MPAA:NR)

MY HUSBAND'S WIVES*½ (1924) 5 reels FOX bw

Shirley Mason *(Vale Harvey)*, Bryant Washburn *(William Harvey)*, Evelyn Brent *(Marie Wynn)*, Paulette Duval *(Mme. Corregio)*.

The best thing about this Fox programmer—in which Mason invites an old school chum to visit, not knowing that the lady was once married to (and is interested in winning back) her husband—is the suggestive title. Naturally, everything works out in Mason's favor by the end of the fifth reel.

d, Maurice Elvey; w, Dorothy Yost (based on a story by Barbara La Marr); ph, Joseph Valentine.

Drama (PR:A MPAA:NR)

MY LADY INCOG** (1916) 5 reels FP/PAR bw

Hazel Dawn *(Nell Carroll)*, George Majeroni *(Rene Lidal)*, Robert Cain *(Teddy De Veaux)*, Dora Mills Adams *(Mrs. De Veaux)*, Franklyn Hanna *(Chief of Police)*, Frank Wunderlee *(Bull Rice)*.

Dawn inherits her father's mansion upon his death. There is, however, a large mortgage which the penniless girl is unable to pay. Her lawyer arranges for her to earn that sum if she does a little undercover detective work in a wealthy section of Florida which has been troubled by a rash of burglaries. Not only does little Dawn break up the gang—she also wins the heart of a young man whose family owns the bank which holds the mortgage on her late father's home.

d, Sidney Olcott; w, William Clifford

Drama (PR:A MPAA:NR)

MY LORD THE CHAUFFEUR*½
(1927, Brit.) 6 reels British Screen Classics bw

Kim Peacock *(Philip Parr)*, Pauline Johnson *(Margaret)*, Sydney Fairbrother *(Lady Parr)*, Jerrold Robertshaw *(Lord Parr)*, Jack Hellier *(Thunder)*, Gladys Hamer *(Mrs. Thunder)*, Diana Dare *(The Girl)*.

Zany British comedy has an aristocrat's nephew going off his nut, becoming a bus driver, and joining a group called the "Frothblowers."

d, B. E. Doxat-Pratt; w, Jack Hellier.

Comedy (PR:A MPAA:NR)

MY OLD DUTCH** (1915, Brit.) 6 reels Turner/ID bw

Albert Chevalier *(Joe Brown)*, Florence Turner *(Sal Gray)*, Henry Edwards *(Herbert Brown)*, Harry Brett *(Erb Uggins)*, Arthur Shirley *(Doctor)*, Richard Cotter *(Nipper)*, Amy Lorraine, Minnie Rayner.

U.S. actress Turner enjoyed great success in Britain with films such as this one, under her own banner, about a man who rushes back from the colonies just in time to rescue his cockney parents.

d, Larry Trimble; w, Albert Chevalier, Arthur Shirley.

Drama (PR:A MPAA:NR)

MY SON*** (1925) 7 reels FN bw

Nazimova *(Ana Silva)*, Jack Pickford *(Tony, Her Son)*, Hobart Bosworth *(Ellery Parker, the Sheriff)*, Ian Keith *(Felipe Vargas, a Fisherman)*, Mary Akin *(Rosa Pina)*, Charles Murray *(Capt. Joe Bamby)*, Constance Bennett *(Betty Smith)*, Dot Farley *(Hattie Smith)*.

Good film adaptation of a successful play about a Portuguese boy in a New England fishing town who falls under the spell of a wealthy vacationing flapper and almost loses the love of his sweetheart and mother because of his actions. Pickford and Bennett shine in their subtle and complicated roles.

d, Edwin Carewe; w, Finis Fox (based on the play by Martha M. Stanley); ph, L. W. O'Connell; ed, Laurence Croutz; art d, John D. Schulze.

Drama (PR:A MPAA:NR)

MYSTERIOUS LADY, THE½** (1928) 9 reels MGM bw

Greta Garbo *(Tania)*, Conrad Nagel *(Karl von Heinersdorff)*, Gustav von Seyffertitz *(Gen. Alexandroff)*, Albert Pollet *(Max)*, Edward Connelly *(Col. von Raden)*, Richard Alexander *(Aide to the General)*.

In spite of the money spent on extras and sets, this film about a beautiful female Russian spy (Garbo) who falls for her Austrian enemy (Nagel) and opts for love rather than country, has little to recommend it except the presence of the exceptional Garbo.

d, Fred Niblo; w, Bess Meredyth (based on the novel *Der Krieg im Dunkel* by Ludwig Wolff); t, Marian Ainslee, Ruth Cummings; ph, William Daniels; ed, Margaret Booth; set d, Cedric Gibbons.

Drama/Romance (PR:A MPAA:NR)

MYSTERIOUS WITNESS, THE** (1923) 5 reels R-C/FBO bw

Robert Gordon *(Johnny Brant)*, Elinor Fair *(Ruth Garland)*, Nanine Wright *(Mrs. John Brant)*, Jack Connolly *(Ed Carney)*, J. Wharton James *(Jim Garland)*.

The cowboys all consider Gordon a miser, not knowing that he sends his paychecks home to his mother. When the foreman frames Gordon for the murder of the ranch owner, he sends for the lad's mother and tries to steal her cash. The scheme is exposed by young Gordon, who also wins the heart of the late boss' daughter.

d, Seymour Zeliff; w, (based on the novel *The Stepsons of Light* by Eugene Manlove Rhodes.

Western/Drama (PR:A MPAA:NR)

MYSTERY OF MR. BERNARD BROWN* 1/2

(1921, Brit.) 6 reels STOLL bw

Ruby Miller *(Helen Thirwell)*, Pardoe Woodman *(Bernard Brown)*, Clifford Heatherley *(Sir Alan Beaumerville)*, Annie Esmond *(Lady Thirwell)*, Ivy King *(Rachel Kynaston)*, Lewis Dayton *(Sir Geoffrey Kynaston)*, Frank E. Petley *(Benjamin Levy)*, Teddy Arundell *(Guy Thirwell)*, Norma Whalley *(Mrs. Martival)*.

In this British mystery, a novelist is forced to prove his innocence after being accused of murdering a man who was engaged to a squire's daughter.

d, Sinclair Hill; w, Mrs. Sydney Groome (based on a novel by E. Phillips Oppenheim).

Mystery **(PR:A MPAA:NR)**

MYSTERY OF THE POISON POOL, THE 1/2**

(1914) 5 reels Picture Playhouse bw

James Gordon, E. A. Turner, Betty Harte.

An African adventurer has his life saved from cannibals by a British trooper. Years later, the two men, not recognizing each other, both fall in love with a missionary girl. The adventurer was somewhat of a rough sort, whom the religious lass regenerated, so when a murder occurs, he is the first one to be suspected. Fearing a lynching, he takes off, with the trooper in hot pursuit. The chase ends with a terrific struggle, and the trooper is beaten into a comatose state. It is then that the adventurer recognizes his former rescuer, due to a locket the injured man is wearing, and endangers his own life to carry the unconscious man back to the village. The movie ends with a snappy, last-minute rescue as the missionary girl rides like blazes with a note from the trooper (who has regained his faculties) just in time to save the adventurer from a necktie party.

w, J. Searle Dawley; ph, Charles Rosher.

Adventure/Romance **(PR:A MPAA:NR)**

MYSTERY OF TUT-ANK-AMEN'S EIGHTH WIFE, THE

(SEE: KING TUT-ANK-AMEN'S EIGHTH WIFE, 1923)

N

NAKED HEARTS* (1916) 5 reels BLUE bw

Rupert Julian *(Cecil, 2nd Period)*, Francelia Billington *(Maud, 2nd Period)*, Gordon Griffith *(Cecil, 1st Period)*, Douglas Gerrard *(Lord Lovelace)*, George Hupp *(Howard, 1st Period)*, Jack Holt *(Howard, 2nd Period)*, Benjamin Horning *(Maud's Father)*, Paul Weigel *(Cecil's Father)*, Nanine Wright *(Cecil's Mother)*, Zoe Beck [Zoe Rae].

Director-writer-actor Julian (who would go on to direct PHANTOM OF THE OPERA in 1925) missed the mark with this romance about a group of children who grow up in Colonial America. A boy and girl from neighboring families fall in love, but a duel between the brother of the girl and her sweetheart brings a sudden end to the romance. When the Revolution breaks out, the brother is killed and the former lover is reported missing. Heartbroken, the young lady enters a nunnery, but her fiance, who managed to survive, tracks her down and, standing below the convent window, sings a song imploring her to return.

d, Rupert Julian; w, Olga Printzlau, Julian (based on the poem "Maud" by Alfred Lord Tennyson).

Romance **(PR:A MPAA:NR)**

NAKED TRUTH, THE (SEE: PERFECT LOVER, THE, 1919)

NAME THE WOMAN* (1928) 6 reels COL bw

Anita Stewart *(Florence)*, Huntly Gordon *(Marshall)*, Gaston Glass *(Joe Arnold)*, Chappell Dossett *(Judge)*, Julanne Johnston *(Nina Palmer)*, Jed Prouty *(Sam Palmer)*.

Glass is finally acquitted during his murder trial when a mysterious masked woman (who turns out to be the wife of the prosecutor) admits being with him at the time of the crime.

p, Harry Cohn; d&w, Erle C. Kenton, Peter Milne, Elmer Harris; ph, Ben Reynolds; ed, Ben Pivar; art d, Joseph Wright.

Drama **(PR:A MPAA:NR)**

NAMELESS MEN*** (1928) 6 reels TS bw

Claire Windsor *(Mary)*, Antonio Moreno *(Bob)*, Eddie Gribbon *(Blackie)*, Ray Hallor *(Hughie)*, Charles Clary *(Mac)*, Carolynne Snowden *(Maid)*, Sally Rand, Stepin Fetchet.

Good programmer has a detective going to jail to find out from a youth where the money from a robbery is hidden. He discovers that the brain behind the caper—the one who didn't get caught—is the man who knows. Later, after getting out, the policeman falls in love with the kid's sister and shoots it out with the criminal who, in the end, is betrayed by the reformed youngster.

d, Christy Cabanne; w, John Francis Natterford (based on a story by E. Morton Hough); t, Viola Brothers Shore, Harry Braxton; ph, Chester Lyons; ed, Martin G. Cohn; set d, Burgess Beal.

Crime **(PR:A MPAA:NR)**

NAN OF MUSIC MOUNTAIN*** (1917) 5 reels LAS/PAR bw

Wallace Reid *(Henry deSpain)*, Ann Little *(Nan Morgan)*, Theodore Roberts *(Duke Morgan)*, James Cruze *(Gale Morgan)*, Charles Ogle *(Sasson)*, Raymond Hatton, Hart Hoxie [Jack Hoxie], Guy Oliver, James P. Mason, Henry Woodward, Ernest Joy, Alice Marc, Horace B. Carpenter, Charlie McHugh.

A tremendous blizzard is the highlight of this first-class western, which has Reid taking a job as manager of a stage line in an outlaw-infested territory to avenge the death of his father. He cleans up the gang and also wins the love of the girl whose family had been harboring the desperados. It is rumored that Cecil B. DeMille actually shot the storm sequence, but this has yet to be proven.

d, George H. Melford; w, Beulah Marie Dix (based on the novel by Frank H. Spearman); ph, Paul Perry.

Western/Drama **(PR:A MPAA:NR)**

NANCY COMES HOME*** (1918) 5 reels TRI bw

Myrtle Lind *(Nancy Worthing)*, Jack Gilbert *(Phil Ballou)*, George Pearce *(Mr. Mortimer Worthing)*, Myrtle Rishell *(Mrs. Mortimer Worthing)*, Eugene Burr *(Clavering Hayes)*, Anna Dodge *(Mrs. Jerry Ballou)*, Percy Challenger *(Mr. Jerry Ballou)*, J. P. Wild *(Stillson)*.

Pretty good programmer has Lind, a neglected daughter who is shuffled off to boarding school, returning home on vacation to find her parents entirely too busy to bother. Lind pawns one of her mother's fur coats, buys an evening gown, hires a chauffeur (who happens to be the son of equally wealthy, self-absorbed parents) and visits a notorious nightclub. That night there's a shooting and the young fellow is arrested for the crime. Lind and both sets of parents step forward, straighten the matter out, and the picture ends with everyone vowing to correct their shortcomings.

d, Jack Dillon; w, Robert F. Hill (based on a story by B. D. Carber); ph, Steve Norton.

Drama **(PR:A MPAA:NR)**

NANCY FROM NOWHERE 1/2** (1922) 5 reels REA/PAR bw

Bebe Daniels *(Nancy)*, Edward Sutherland *(Jack Halliday)*, Vera Lewis *(Mrs. Kelly)*, James Gordon *(Mr. Kelly)*, Myrtle Stedman *(Mrs. Halliday)*, Albert Lee *(Martha)*, Helen Holly *(Elizabeth Doane)*, Dorothy Hagan *(Mrs. Doane)*.

Daniels is the adopted daughter of very abusive parents. When Sutherland vacations nearby, the girl makes his acquaintance, then hides in the trunk of his car and is driven to his home in the city. Sutherland provides Daniels with a beautiful wardrobe, but Holly, his jealous fiancee, and Sutherland's parents convince her that she is wrong for the boy, and she returns to her unhappy dwelling place in her original rags. No sooner is she gone, however, than Sutherland realizes his love for her and rushes to her side just in time to rescue her from a beating.

d, Chester M. Franklin; w, Douglas Doty (based on the story "Spring Fever" by Grace Drew Brown, Katherine Pinkerton); ph, George Folsey.

Dramatic Comedy **(PR:A MPAA:NR)**

NANCY'S BIRTHRIGHT* (1916) 5 reels Signal/MUT bw

Murdock MacQuarrie *(John Martingale)*, Edythe Sterling *(Nancy Levine, Daughter/Nancy Levine, Granddaughter)*, Norbert A. Myles *(Leslie Warner)*, Millard K. Wilson *(William Preston)*, V. T. Henderson.

Tired potboiler about a poor little girl who is badly mistreated by a brutish father after her mother dies in childbirth, only to discover that she is actually the descendant of a terribly wealthy family. They see to it that her happiness is assured—and that her father's is not.

d, Murdock MacQuarrie; w, Clarice Manning MacQuarrie

Drama **(PR:A MPAA:NR)**

NANETTE OF THE WILDS* (1916) 5 reels FP bw

Pauline Frederick *(Nanette Gautier)*, Willard Mack *(Constable Thomas O'Brien)*, Charles Brandt *(Joe Gautier)*, Frank Joyner *(Andy Joyce)*, Wallace MacDonald *(Harry Jennings)*, Macey Harlem *(Baptiste Flammant)*, Daniel Pennell *(Sgt. Maj. O'Hara)*, Jean Stewart *(Marie Beaudeaut)*, Robert Conville *(Constable Jeune)*.

It was rumored that director Kaufman had so much trouble with writer-star Mack that he requested his name be removed from the credits of this stinker, which was all about murdering smugglers who slip U.S. whiskey across the border to Canadian lumberjacks.

d, Joseph Kaufman; w, Willard Mack.

Adventure **(PR:A MPAA:NR)**

NAPOLEON***** (1927, Fr.) 17 reels Gaumont/Metro-Goldwyn bw-c

Albert Dieudonne *(Napoleon Bonaparte)*, Wladimir Roudenko *(Bonaparte as a Child)*, Gina Manes *(Josephine de Beauharnais)*, Nicolas Koline *(Tristan Fleuri)*, Suzanne Charpentier [Annabella] *(Violine Fleuri)*, Serge Freddykarll *(Marcellin Fleuri)*, Edmond Van Daele *(Maximilien Robespierre)*, Alexandre Koubitzky *(Danton)*, Antonin Artaud *(Marat)*, Abel Gance *(Saint-Just)*, Max Maxudian *(Barras)*, Philippe Heriat *(Salicetti)*, Acho Chakatouny *(Pozzo di Borgo)*, Eugenie Buffet *(Laetizia Bonaparte)*, Yvette Dieudonne *(Elisa Bonaparte)*, Georges Lampin *(Joseph Bonaparte)*, Sylvio Cavicchia *(Lucien Bonaparte)*, Simone Genevois *(Pauline Bonaparte)*, Louis Sance *(Louis XVI)*, Suzanne Bianchetti *(Marie-Antoinette)*, Pierre Batcheff *(Gen. Lazare Hoche)*, Philippe Rolla *(Massena)*, Alexandre Bernard *(Dugommier)*, W. Percy Day *(Adm. Hood)*, Genica Missirio *(Capt. Joachim Murat)*, Robert de Ansorena *(Capt. Desaix)*, Harry-Krimer *(Rouget de l'Ilse)*, Marguerite Gance *(Charlotte Corday)*, Roger Blum *(Talma)*, Jean Henry *(Sgt. Andoche Junot)*, Maryse Damia *(La Marseillaise)*, Henri Baudin *(Santo-Ricci)*, Georges Henin *(Eugene de Beauharnais)*, Roblin *(Picot De Peccaduc)*, Vidal *(Phelippeaux)*, Robert Vidalin *(Camille Desmoulins)*, Mlle. Carvalho *(Fortune-Teller)*, Maurice Schutz *(Pasquale Paoli)*, Leon Courtois *(Gen. Carteaux)*, Daniel Burret *(Augustin Robespierre)*, M. Caillard *(Thomas Gasparin)*, Pierre de Canolle *(Capt. August Marmont)*, Pierre Danis *(Col. Muiron)*, M. Dacheux *(Gen. Du Teil)*, Jack Rye *(Gen. O'Hara)*, Henry Krauss *("Moustache")*, M'Viguier *(Couthon)*, Francine Mussey *(Lucille Desmoulins)*, Georges Cahuzac *(Vicomte De Beauharnais)*, Jean d'Yd *(La Bussiere, Eater of Documents)*, Boris Fastovich *(L'oeil-Vert, Executions Office Overseer)*, Jean Gaudray *(Jean Lambert Tallien)*, M. Mathillon *(Gen. Scherer)*, M. Faviere *(Joseph Fouche)*, Andree Standard *(Therese Tallien)*, Suzy Vernon *(Mme. Recamier)*, Janine Pen *(Hortense De Beauharnais)*.

A true legend in the history of motion pictures, Abel Gance's amazing epic NAPOLEON has been shown in no less than 19 versions since its premiere at the Theatre National de l'Opera in Paris in 1927. Filled with stunning technical innovations, the highlight of which sees the frame explode into three screens of visual imagery that at times meld into one giant shot (called a triptych), NAPOLEON was distributed in several truncated versions throughout the world with or without the triptych. A few years later NAPOLEON disappeared entirely. Gance remade another version with sound in 1934, but his original masterpiece seemed lost forever—lost, that is, until a young British film aficionado named Kevin Brownlow began to unearth segments of the film being sold for viewing on home movie projectors. The all-too-brief sequences he was able to find filled the schoolboy with an obsession to resurrect Gance's masterpiece intact. Finally, in 1980, after years of research, digging, and recovery, Abel Gance's NAPOLEON was given triumphant showings in the U.S. and Europe accompanied by a full orchestra playing a score composed and conducted by Carmine Coppola (his son, Francis Ford Coppola, provided much needed financial support for the project). The film begins with young Napoleon (Roudenko) embroiled in a military-style snowball fight while away at school. Roudenko shows his leadership and strategic skills during the battle and his teachers know that he will make something of himself some day. Unfortunately, his fellow students do not think so highly of Roudenko and the boy consoles himself in the company of a pet eagle. Even this simple pleasure is denied the boy, for his classmates free the pet. Roudenko angrily tries to fight all his enemies, but the monks who run the school throw him out into the snow to cool off. As the boy leans against a cannon and cries, the eagle returns and sits perched on the weapon. Years later, France is in the throes of revolution. Napoleon (now played by Dieudonne) is now a young lieutenant in the army. On a visit to his native Corsica, Dieudonne decides that his homeland must also join the revolution. There is resistance, however, and Dieudonne is forced to flee on a small boat, using the French tricolor flag as a sail. As he is tossed and turned during a violent storm, another squall is brewing in the halls of the revolution. Dieudonne returns to France and proves himself a brilliant strategist on the battlefield. Now a captain, he is given permission to attack the British forces. The battle is fought during a vicious storm, but Dieudonne and his men force the British to retreat. Dieudonne returns to Paris only to discover that the Reign of Terror has seized the revolution. The Committee of Public Safety tests Dieudonne's loyalty by offering him the command of Paris. The soldier declines, not wanting to defend the culprits of the Terror against the people. For this he is imprisoned. There he meets Josephine (Manes), who has also been accused of disloyalty. Luckily, before either meets the guillotine, Saint-Juce (played by director Gance) manages to end the Terror. When given the opportunity to fight the Royalists, Dieudonne once again refuses a commission, stating that he'd rather fight foreign invaders than his fellow Frenchmen. To discipline the soldier, Dieudonne is sent to the Office of Topography. Bored, he makes plans for the invasion of Italy. His brilliant work is rejected by dimwitted superiors who don't even understand his plan. Eventually the Royalists gain enough strength to threaten the revolutionary government. Dieudonne accepts the challenge and defeats the uprising in the streets of Paris. Now a hero, Dieudonne finds himself invited to dozens of wild parties thrown to celebrate the survival of the revolution. During one party Dieudonne and Manes meet again, and this time she is very intrigued by the sullen soldier. Dieudonne falls in love with the beautiful woman and they make plans to marry. Using her influence, Manes has Dieudonne appointed commander of the Army of the Alps. Excited by this promise of military glory, Dieudonne immediately begins to revise his plans for the invasion of Italy. Unfortunately, he becomes so embroiled in his work that he forgets to attend his own wedding. When he arrives, hours late, he hurries the judge through the service. Shortly after the wedding, Dieudonne leaves his bride to conquer Italy. Before departing France, Dieudonne visits the empty convention hall of the revolution. There the ghosts of Jean-Paul Marat, Louis-Antoine-Leon de Saint Just, Maximilien Robespierre, Georges-Jacques Danton, and Georges Couthon materialize and ask Dieudonne to be the new leader of the revolution. Dieudonne accepts the challenge and declares that he soon will end all war. Arriving in the Alps, he is dismayed to find his troops in disarray. Undisciplined, starving, and cold from lack of proper clothing, the morale of the soldiers is at the lowest since the revolution began. Impatient with his generals, Dieudonne announces that the army will now take the offensive in the battle. He then orders a review of the troops. At this point in the film the curtains open to reveal two more screens and the first image is a panoramic, wide-screen shot of the army camp. When the tired army sees Dieudonne ride up, the soldiers gather themselves together and rise. The charismatic commander infuses each man with a renewed sense of purpose and the revitalized army marches into Italy. The climax of NAPOLEON is a wonderful spectacle which sees the triptych change from one panoramic shot into three separate images, and then back again for more stunning, wide-screen views. As the army marches into Italy, the three screens are tinted blue, white, and red, making a giant tricolor out of the screen. It is a breathtaking moment in cinema history, but NAPOLEON is filled with breathtaking moments. The opening snowball fight is literally a blizzard of motion. Gance had his cinematographer, Kruger, put the camera on a sled that was pushed into the flurry of boys throwing snowballs so that the audience would feel they were part of the action. To enhance the effect, Kruger's assistants threw snowballs at the boys from behind the camera, so that it appeared that the viewer was throwing snowballs back at the attackers. Aside from the closing triptych, the most memorable sequence in NAPOLEON is the "Double Tempest," which sees Napoleon sailing back to France through a storm, while a political hurricane is blowing in the Paris Convention Hall. While Napoleon battles the waves, the hall seems to sway and shift as if on the sea. The effect was achieved by putting the camera on a giant pendulum which swung towards and then away from the frantically gesturing actors. Three pendulums of different sizes were built, but only the footage from the highest one was used. Gance's triptych sequences, predating CinemaScope by 25 years, were shot by a specially built camera system which mounted three cameras on one tripod. These cameras were driven by a single motor which ensured that all three pictures would be synchronous when played back. Not only does Gance use the triptych for sweeping panoramas, but he also uses the three scenes to create an on-screen montage of pictures that audiences can view simultaneously. The effect is almost overwhelming. Gance was convinced that the triptych would revolutionize the motion picture industry forever. Unfortunately, sound arrived soon after NAPOLEON's release and caused such a sensation that Gance's film, also burdened with distribution problems, sank into obscurity. Luckily, through the dedicated efforts of Kevin Brownlow, Gance's masterpiece was resurrected nearly intact and he was able to show the restored film to its elderly 89-year-old creator at the Telluride Film Festival in Colorado. The screening was held outdoors because Telluride had no theater big enough to show the massive film. Gance watched from his hotel room window, and when the climactic triptych sequence that ends the film was over (at 3 a.m.) the stunned audience burst into wildly enthusiastic applause and hailed the old man in the window. After an absence of 50 years, NAPOLEON had returned to the acclaim it deserved.

p,d&w, Abel Gance; ph, Jules Kruger, Leonce-Henry Burel; m, Arthur Honegger (1927), Carmine Coppola (1980); ed, Marguerite Beauge, Henriette Pinson; art d, Alexandre Benois, Pierre Schildknecht, Lochavoff, Jacouty, Meinhardt, Eugene Lourie; cos, Charmy, Sauvageau, Mme. Augris, Jeanne Lanvin.

Historical Biography **Cas.** **(PR:A MPAA:NR)**

NARROW PATH, THE* (1918) 5 reels Astra/Pathe bw

Fannie Ward *(Marion Clark)*, W. E. Lawrence *(Dick Strong)*, Irene Aldwyn *(Gladys Strong)*, Sam De Grasse *(Malcolm Dunn)*, Antrim Short *(Jimmy Glidden)*, Mary Alden.

Inferior in every way (although Ward does try hard), an old-hat melodrama, dealing with the heroine's assumption of guilt in order to protect her wrongly accused newspaper-man brother.

d, George Fitzmaurice; w, Ouida Bergere, Jack Cunningham (based on a stage play); ph, Arthur Miller, Percy Hilburn.

Drama **(PR:A MPAA:NR)**

NARROW STREET, THE*** (1924) 7 reels WB bw

Matt Moore *(Simon Haldane)*, Dorothy Devore *(Doris)*, David Butler *(Ray Wyeth)*, George Pearce *(Edgar Deems)*, Russell Simpson *(Garvey)*, Gertrude Short *(Nell Mangan)*, Joe Butterworth *(Office Boy)*, Kate Toncray *(Aunt Albina)*, Tempe Pigott *(Aunt Agnes)*, Mme. Sul-Te-Wan *(Easter)*.

Wonderful performance by Moore and clever direction by the underrated Beaudine make this delightful comedy a winner. It's all about a pantywaist, raised by old maid aunts, who becomes a man when his small-town neighbors wrongly assume he married the boss' daughter. In 1930 Warner Brothers made a second version of this film with the title WIDE OPEN, starring Edward Everett Horton.

d, William Beaudine; w, Julien Josephson (based on the novel by Edwin Bateman Morris); ph, Ray June.

Comedy **(PR:A MPAA:NR)**

NARROW VALLEY, THE** (1921, Brit.) 6 reels Hepworth bw

Alma Taylor *(Victoria)*, George Dewhurst *(Jerry Hawkins)*, James Carew *(Eli Jones)*, Hugh Clifton *(Richard Jones)*, Gwynne Herbert *(Ursula Jones)*, Lottie Blackford *(Miss Pine)*, Nessie Blackford *(Miss Pine)*, Gordon Holloway *(Mr. Pine)*.

British love story about a domestic servant who overcomes the persecution of the town fathers and marries the son of a poacher.

d, Cecil M. Hepworth; w, George W. Dewhurst.

Romance **(PR:A MPAA:NR)**

NATION'S PERIL, THE 1/2** (1915) 5 reels Lubin bw

Ormi Hawley *(Ruth Lyons)*, William H. Turner *(Adm. Lyons)*, Earl Metcalf *(Lt. Sawyer)*, Eleanor Barry *(Mrs. Sawyer)*, Arthur Matthews *(Oswald Dudley)*, Herbert Fortier *(Bertold Henchman)*.

Pop Lubin's "preparedness" offering has a young woman with strong pacifist leanings rejecting her sweetheart, who invented an aerial torpedo, and becoming engaged to a foreign spy who claims to be equally opposed to war. The agent induces the girl to steal her boy friend's plans, and when she realizes his motive, a struggle ensues and she runs him through with a sword. Shortly thereafter, the enemy attack and capture an American city, but the U.S. Navy (which apparently cooperated in the production of this film) arrives off the coast and bombards them into submission.

d, George W. Terwilliger; w, Harry Chandlee, Terwilliger.

War **(PR:A MPAA:NR)**

NATURE OF THE BEAST, THE** (1919, Brit.) 6 reels Hepworth/But bw

Alma Taylor *(Anna de Berghem)*, Gerald Ames *(John Ingledew)*, James Carew *(Kleinenberger)*, Gwynne Herbert *(Mrs. de Berghem)*, Stephen Ewart *(Sir James Standish)*, Mary Dibley *(Lady Standish)*, Victor Prout *(Mr. de Berghem)*, Christine Rayner *(Guest)*, John McAndrews *(Friend)*.

British wartime thriller about a Belgian refugee who marries a prominent manufacturer of military materials and is blackmailed by the German agent who raped her.

d, Cecil M. Hepworth; w, E. Temple Thurston.

War **(PR:A MPAA:NR)**

NAUGHTY BABY*** (1929) 7 reels FN bw

Alice White *(Rosie McGill)*, Jack Mulhall *(Terry Vandeveer)*, Thelma Todd *(Bonnie Le Vonne)*, Doris Dawson *(Polly)* James Ford *(Terry's Friend)*, Natalie Joyce *(Goldie Torres)*, Frances Hamilton *(Bonnie's Friend)*, Fred Kelsey *(Dugan)*, Rose Dione *(Mme. Fleurette)*, Fanny Midgley *(Mary Ellen Toolen)*, Georgie Stone *(Tony Caponi)*, Benny Rubin *(Benny Cohen)*, Andy Devine *(Joe Cassidy)*, Larry Banthim *(Toolen)*.

Lightweight but entertaining flapper comedy about a hat check girl who sets out to save a Boston millionaire from the clutches of a tall, blonde gold digger and ends up landing him herself. Alice White (First National's answer to Clara Bow) is competent in the role of Rosie McGill, but it's the little Jewish vaudevillian Bennie Rubin and the comedic Miss Thelma Todd who walk away with the picture.

d, Mervyn LeRoy; w, Tom Geraghty (based on a story by Charles Beahan, Garrett Fort); t, Tom and Gerald Geraghty; ph, Ernest Haller; ed, Leroy Stone; syn s; s eff.

Comedy **(PR:A MPAA:NR)**

NAUGHTY NANETTE* (1927) 5 reels R-C/FBO bw

Viola Dana *(Nanette Pearson)*, Patricia Palmer *(Lola Leeds)*, Edward Brownell *(Bob Dennison)*, Helen Foster *(Lucy Dennison)*, Joe Young *(Bill Simmons)*, Sidney De Gray *(Grandfather Dennison)*, Alphonse Martel *(Carlton)*, Mary Gordon *(Mrs. Rooney)*, Florence Wix *(Mrs. Trainor)*, Barbara Clayton *(Dorothy Trainor)*.

Second-rate version of KIKI has lovely Dana struggling to overcome a bad script, direction, and production values as a movie extra who befriends a disinherited and sickly girl (Foster) and reunites her with her grandfather. Of course, Dana wins her fellow by the picture's end, as well.

d, James Leo Meehan; w, Doris Schroeder (based on a story by Charles H. Smith); ph, Allen Siegler.

Dramatic Comedy **(PR:A MPAA:NR)**

NAUGHTY, NAUGHTY!** (1918) 5 reels PAR bw

Enid Bennett *(The Girl)*, Earl Rodney, Gloria Hope, Marjorie Bennett, Andrew Arbuckle.

Screenwriter Sullivan had one of his rare misses in this preposterous comedy about a country girl who returns home after spending four months in the city, and shocks her community by the level of her sophistication. A good cast, however, almost makes it work.

d, Jerome Storm; sup, Thomas H. Ince; w, C. Gardner Sullivan; ph, John Stumar.

Comedy **(PR:A MPAA:NR)**

NAULAHKA, THE*** (1918) 6 reels Astra/Pathe bw

Antonio Moreno *(Nicholas Tarvin)*, Mlle. Doraldina *(Sitahbal)*, Helene Chadwick *(Kate Sheriff)*, Warner Oland *(Maharajah)*, Mary Alden *(Prince's Mother)*, J. H. Gilmour *(Mutrie)*, Edna Hunter.

Ambitious programmer about a female doctor who sets off for India to minister to the needy. Her fiance, who is against this, journeys to that exotic land as well, but his motive is to secure a valuable piece of jewelry in the possession of the royal family. The young couple prevent the rightful prince from having his kingdom stolen, expose the potentate's wife (actually a gypsy) for the conniver she is, and return to the good old U.S. to become husband and wife.

d, George Fitzmaurice; w, George B. Seitz (based on a story by Rudyard Kipling, Wolcott Balestier; ph; Arthur Miller.

Drama **(PR:A MPAA:NR)**

NAVIGATOR, THE**** (1924) 6 reels Buster Keaton/MGM bw

Buster Keaton *(Rollo Treadway)*, Kathryn McGuire *(The Girl)*, Frederick Vroom *(The Girl's Father)*, Noble Johnson *(Cannibal Chief)*, Clarence Burton, H. M. Clugston.

When Keaton learned that a 500-foot ocean liner called the *S.S. Buford* was headed for the scrap heap, he bought it at once. Here was the ultimate prop and Keaton took full advantage, stringing together so many ingenious gags that THE NAVIGATOR became his biggest moneymaker, grossing over $2 million in its initial release—nearly 10 times what it cost to make. It also elevated him to the position of rivaling Charlie Chaplin and Harold Lloyd. The premise has Keaton, a completely helpless millionaire, deciding to marry McGuire, an equally pampered socialite, being rejected, and then finding himself alone with her on an abandoned ocean liner which has been cast adrift to sink. It is impossible to imagine any sight gag which was overlooked here, in what is perhaps the great comedian's funniest overall work. Included are a number of thrills, which come as the couple drift onto a cannibal-inhabited island and Keaton rescues the girl from the savages, emerging from the water in a diving suit, giving the impression he's an ocean monster. Just before this (in a scene suggested by an accident which actually took place on the set) Keaton is shown with a cigarette hanging out of his mouth as McGuire screws the diving helmet on. The blank expression on his face becomes one of panic when we next view him through a smoke-filled helmet window. An underwater sequence supplies some wonderfully crafted gags, with Keaton plodding about the ocean floor, fighting off swordfish and an octopus. The film ends with Keaton and McGuire returning to civilization on a submarine, which fortunately is under the command of a real seaman.

p, Joseph M. Schenck; d, Donald Crisp, Buster Keaton; w&t, Clyde Bruckman, Joseph Mitchell, Jean Havez; ph, Elgin Lesley, Byron Houck.

Comedy **(PR:A MPAA:NR)**

NEAR LADY, THE** (1923) 5 reels UNIV bw

Gladys Walton *(Nora Schultz)*, Jerry Gendron *(Basil Van Bibber)*, Hank Mann *(Lodger)*, Kate Price *(Bridget Schultz)*, Otis Harlan *(Herman Schultz)*, Florence Drew *(Aunt Maggie Mahaffey)*, Emmett King *(Stuyvesant Van Bibber)*, Henrietta Floyd *(Mrs. S. Van Bibber)*.

Hokey nonsense has a family becoming wealthy when the father (Harlan) invents a sausage-making machine. They are quickly tossed into the social whirl with a prominent local family whose business is greatly benefited by the invention. For the sake of their parents, Walton and Gendron pretend to be romantically interested in one another, but the game becomes real by the end of the fifth reel.

d, Herbert Blache; w, Hugh Hoffman (based on a story by Frank R. Adams); ph, William Thornley.

Comedy **(PR:A MPAA:NR)**

NEARLY A KING*** (1916) 5 reels FP bw

John Barrymore, Katherine Harris, Russell Bassett, Adolphe Menjou.

Good Barrymore feature has the Great Profile playing an actor who reads a movie script which soon dissolves into one of those PRISONER OF ZENDA stories, about a young actor and the adventure he experiences due to his resemblance to the monarch of a musical comedy kingdom. The picture is loaded with action and comedy, Barrymore shines in his dual role, and the double-exposure photography is outstanding.

d, Frederick Thompson; w, William H. Clifford

Fantasy-Adventure/Comedy **(PR:A MPAA:NR)**

NEARLY A LADY** (1915) 5 reels Bosworth/PAR bw

Elsie Janis, Myrtle Stedman, Owen Moore, Frank Elliott, Harry Ham, Roberta Hickman.

The great vaudeville star, Janis, really wasn't right for the movies, but she did all right in this one about a wealthy Western girl who nearly marries a monocle-wearing Britisher, travels to New York where she becomes the darling of society, but returns in the end to the West with the cowboy she always loved.

d, William Desmond Taylor; w, Julia Crawford Ivors (based on a story by Elsie Janis).

Comedy **(PR:A MPAA:NR)**

NECESSARY EVIL, THE** (1925) 7 reels FN bw

Ben Lyon *(Frank Jerome)*, Viola Dana *(Shirley Holmes)*, Frank Mayo *(Dick Jerome)*, Thomas Holding *(David Devanant)*, Gladys Brockwell *(Frances Jerome)*, Mary Thurman *(Hattie)*, Betty Jewel *(Belle)*, Martha Madison *(Esther)*, Arthur Housman *(Pug)*, Beach Cooke *(Reggie)*.

Wealthy Holding promises a dying woman that he will become guardian to her son Lyon. The boy grows up to be a hell-raising, hooch-drinking terror who ends up marrying a saucy little gold digger while on a drunken binge. The little tart informs Holding that she will give the lad a divorce only when a substantial sum crosses her palm. The old boy refuses, and the girl steals a few bonds, leaving the impression that Lyon committed the crime. Holding pretends to accept the guilt of his young charge as an excuse to have the lad sent off to a South Sea island where he can dry out and contemplate the future. After some time the regenerated youth returns home and is shocked to discover that Holding is about to marry his other ward, Dana, whom Lyon also loves. There is an exchange of words, whereby the whole purpose of the tropical hiatus is explained. Then the kindly Holding clutches his chest, expires dramatically, and thoughtfully leaves his youthful sparrows to pursue the course of mutual pleasure.

d, George Archainbaud; w, Eve Unsell (based on the story "Uriah's Son" by Stephen Vincent Benet); ph, George Folsey; ed, Arthur Tavares; art d, Milton Menasco.

Drama **(PR:A MPAA:NR)**

NED MCCOBB'S DAUGHTER* 1/2** (1929) 7 reels Pathe bw

Irene Rich *(Carrie)*, Theodore Roberts *(Ned McCobb)*, Robert Armstrong *(Babe Callahan)*, George Barraud *(George Callahan)*, Edward Hearn *(Butterworth)*, Carole Lombard *(Jennie)*, Louis Natheaux *(Kelly)*.

Fine later silent feature has Armstrong, a rumrunner, staying behind to protect the wife and children of his rat of a brother Barraud, who deserts them when Prohibition officers begin to close in. Great feeling of atmosphere and suspense, plus fine performances, put this one over. And there's a happy ending, with Armstrong saving the kids' lives and vowing to return to their mother (he is arrested while attempting to stop Barraud, who is trying to escape) when he finishes serving his time.

d, William J. Cowen; w, Beulah Marie Dix (based on the play by Sidney Howard); t, Edwin Justus Mayer; ph, David Abel; ed, Anne Bauchens; art d, Edward Jewell; syn sc; s eff.

Drama **(PR:A MPAA:NR)**

NE'ER-DO-WELL, THE 1/2** (1916) 10 reels Selig bw

Wheeler Oakman *(Kirk Anthony)*, Kathlyn Williams *(Mrs. Edith Cortland)*, Harry Lonsdale *(Stephen Cortland)*, Frank Clark *(Darwin K. Anthony)*, Norma Nichols *(Chiquita Garavel)*, Will Machin *(Weller/Locke)*, Jack MacDonald *(Allan Allan)*, Sidney Smith *(Ramon Alfarez)*, Fred Huntly *(Andres Garavel)*, Lamar Johnstone *(Runnels)*, Harry De Vere *(Detective Williams)*.

As a follow-up to their very successful production of THE SPOILERS, Selig selected this Beach novel about a shiftless playboy who is thrown unconscious and penniless aboard a ship bound for Panama. The film deals with his regeneration—after being wrongly accused of murdering the husband of the woman who put him back on his feet—but the picture's real high points are the wonderful scenes of the canal before and after its completion.

d, Colin Campbell; w, (based on the novel by Rex Beach).

Drama **(PR:A MPAA:NR)**

NEGLECTED WIVES* (1920) 5 reels WI bw

Anne Luther *(The Wife)*, E. J. Radcliffe *(The Husband)*, Al Hart *(The Political Boss)*, Ivy Ward, Claire Whitney, Charles Gerard, J. W. Johnston.

A few lavish sets are the only things to praise in this tired old melodrama about the neglected wife who is almost compromised by a ruthless political boss. Of course the picture ends with her husband coming to the realization that he has placed far too much emphasis on business and not enough on marriage. Then the heavy withdraws from the woman's life with the title, "You win. I know when I'm beaten."

d, Burton King; w, Lloyd Lonergan; ph, Ernest Haller.

Drama **(PR:A MPAA:NR)**

NEIGHBORS*** (1918) 5 reels WORLD bw

Madge Evans *(Clarissa Leigh)*, Violet Palmer *(Ruth Leigh)*, J. A. Furey *(Grandpa Leigh)*, Johnny Hines *(Paul Harding)*, Maxine Elliott Hicks *(Effie Harding)*, Mathilde Brundage *(Mrs. William Harding)*, Kitty Johnson *(Edith Norris)*, Frank Beamish *(Lucien Adamson)*, Charles Hartley *(Ebenezer Hicks)*, Ray Howard, Ivy Ward, Herbert Pattee.

Entertaining children's picture with a rural setting has Evans playing a mischievous 9-year-old female counterpart to PECK'S BAD BOY. A great deal of credit must be given to director Crane, who depicted his kids as natural little human beings. And comedian Hines, playing a college student, was finally given the opportunity to show what he could do.

d, Frank H. Crane; w, Hamilton Smith, Harry O. Hoyt (based on a story by Maravene Thompson); ph, Jacques Monteran.

Children's Comedy (PR:A MPAA:NR)

NELL GWYNNE* (1914) 4 reels Sawyer's bw

Nellie Stuart.

This saga of an actress who wins the heart of a king had enjoyed a successful stage run shortly before this picture was made. The director (whose name has been lost) elected to transfer the theatrical presentation to the screen, resulting in a static and completely uncinematic piece of work. It would be 12 years before Dorothy Gish would breathe real life into the character of Nell, creating one of England's finest silent features.

Biographical (PR:A MPAA:NR)

NELL GWYNNE*½** (1926, Brit.) 8 reels W.M.-BN/FN bw

Dorothy Gish *(Nell Gwynne)*, Randle Ayrton *(Charles II)*, Juliette Compton *(Lady Castlemaine)*, Sydney Fairbrother *(Mrs. Gwynne)*, Donald McCardle *(Duke of Monmouth)*, Johnny Butt *(Samuel Pepys)*, Gibb McLaughlin *(Duke of York)*, Judd Green *(Toby Clinker)*, Edward Sorley *(Dickon)*, Forrester Harvey *(Charles Hart)*, Fred Rains *(Earl of Shaftesbury)*, Rolf Leslie *(Evelyn)*, Aubrey Fitzgerald *(Tom Killigrew)*, Tom Coventry *(Innkeeper)*, Booth Conway *(Messenger)*, Dorinea Shirley *(Maid)*.

Splendid performance by Gish as the street gamin who rose to stardom on the London stage, defeated Lady Castlemaine for the affection of King Charles, and died being faithful to her monarch and her class. With this superb production, Irish-born producer-director-writer Wilcox showed the world that the British cinema did not have to be forever pedestrian and boring.

p,d&w, Herbert Wilcox (based on a novel by Marjorie Bowen).

Historical/Drama (PR:A MPAA:NR)

NELL OF THE CIRCUS** (1914) 4 reels Sawyer bw

Cecil Spooner.

A circus girl is kept from knowing about her aristocratic background by a most nasty villain in this entertaining film (despite its low production expenditure), written by and featuring Spooner.

w, Cecil Spooner.

Drama (PR:A MPAA:NR)

NELLIE, THE BEAUTIFUL CLOAK MODEL*
(1924) 7 reels Goldwyn/Goldwyn-COS bw

Claire Windsor *(Nellie)*, Betsy Ann Hisle *(Nellie, at 5 Years)*, Edmund Lowe *(Jack Carroll)*, Mae Busch *(Polly Joy)*, Raymond Griffith *(Shorty Burchell)*, Lew Cody *(Walter Peck)*, Hobart Bosworth *(Thomas Lipton/Robert Horton)*, Lilyan Tashman *(Nita)*, Dorothy Cumming *(Mrs. Horton)*, Will Walling *(Blizzard Dugan)*, Mayme Kelso *(Miss Drake)*, William Orlamond *(Mosely)*, Arthur Houseman, David Kirby *(Gangsters)*.

An excellent cast is wasted in this hopelessly dated melodrama about a rich girl (Windsor) who is mistreated by her father, raised in poverty, becomes a fashion model (the picture made a big point of showing the latest frocks), and is ultimately terrorized by her mother's rotten nephew, who is determined to prevent her from discovering her true identity. The movie ends, believe it or not, with the hero rescuing Windsor from an onrushing train as she lies helplessly tied to the railroad track.

d, Emmett Flynn; w, H. H. Van Loan (based on the play by Owen Davis); ph, Lucien Andriot.

Drama (PR:A MPAA:NR)

NELSON** (1918, Brit.) 7 reels Master-International Exclusives/Apex bw

Donald Calthrop *(Horatio Nelson)*, Malvina Longfellow *(Lady Hamilton)*, Ivy Close *(Mrs. Nesbit)*, Ernest Thesiger *(William Pitt)*, Allan Jeayes *(Sir William Hamilton)*, Edward O'Neill *(King of Naples)*, Teddy Arundell *(Capt. Berry)*, Eric Barker *(Nelson, as a Child)*, Judd Green, Sir Edmund Freemantle.

Full-blown, but rather boring chronicle of Lord Nelson's life between 1794 and 1805, dealing with his scandalous affair with Lady Hamilton, his naval triumphs, and his ultimate death.

p, Low Warren; d, Maurice Elvey; w, Eliot Stannard (based on the book *The Life of Nelson* by Robert Southey).

Biographical (PR:A MPAA:NR)

NELSON*** (1926, Brit.) 8 reels BI/New Era bw

Cedric Hardwicke *(Horatio Nelson)*, Gertrude McCoy *(Lady Hamilton)*, Frank Perfitt *(Capt. Hardy)*, Frank Arlton *(Governor)*, Pat Courtney *(Nelson, as a Child)*, Gladys Harvey, Johnny Butt.

The British cinema celebrated the life of its great naval hero, Horatio Nelson, often. This silent version, dealing with his sensational affair with Lady Hamilton, featured Hardwicke, that wonderful actor who would go on to Hollywood stardom, as well as knighthood in his native land.

p, H. Bruce Woolfe; d&w, Walter Summers (based on the book *The Life of Nelson* by Robert Southey).

Biographical Drama (PR:A MPAA:NR)

NEPTUNE'S DAUGHTER*½** (1914) 7 reels UNIV bw

Annette Kellermann, William E. Shay, William Welsh, Leah Baird, Mrs. Allen Walker, Herbert Brenon, Edward Mortimer, Lewis Hooper, Millie Liston, Katherine Lee, Edward Boring.

Great swimming star and physical culture advocate Kellermann, under the skillful direction of Brenon, provided audiences in 1914 a motion picture filled with wonder and enchantment. It was a fairy tale of underwater kingdoms, evil witches with magic spells, and the armies of righteousness, locked in battle with the advocates of darkness. And the beautiful Kellermann, outfitted in a full length body stocking covered by her flowing long hair, gave the feeling of nudity without offending even the children who flocked to see this most engrossing film.

d, Herbert Brenon, Otis Turner; w, Leslie T. Peacocke.

Fantasy (PR:A MPAA:NR)

NERO*½** (1922, U.S./Ital.) 12 reels FOX bw

Jacques Gretillat *(Nero)*, Alexander Salvini *(Horatius)*, Guido Trento *(Tullius)*, Enzo De Felice *(Otho)*, Nero Bernardi *(The Apostle)*, Adolfo Trouche *(Hercules)*, Nello Carolenuto *(Galba)*, Americo De Giorgio *(Gracchus)*, Alfredo Galaor *(Garth)*, Ernando Cecilia *(Roman General)*, Enrico Kant *(Roman Captain)*, Paulette Duval *(Poppaea)*, Edy Darclea *(Acte)*, Violet Mersereau *(Marcia)*, Lina Talba *(Julia)*, Lydia Yaguinto *(1st Handmaiden)*, Maria Marchiali *(2nd Handmaiden)*.

Filmed in Italy at tremendous expense, director Edwards presented a fascinating look at the Roman Empire during the time of Nero's reign. The tyrant's life (portrayed by Gretillat)) was traced from the beginning of his rise to power, showing his abortive love for Marcia (Mersereau), the beautiful young Christian woman, and culminating in his death through the manipulation of his consort, the Empress Poppaea (Duval). Released three full years before MGM's BEN HUR, this mighty motion picture, with its lavish depictions of Christian martyrdom, chariot races at the Circus Maximus, and the spectacular burning of Rome, left audiences breathless.

d, J. Gordon Edwards; w, Virginia Tracy, Charles Sarver; ph, Harry Plimpton; ed, Hettie Grey Baker; art d, John D. Braddon.

Biographical (PR:A MPAA:NR)

NERVOUS WRECK, THE*** (1926) 7 reels Christie/PDC bw

Harrison Ford *(Henry Williams)*, Phyllis Haver *(Sally Morgan)*, Chester Conklin *(Mort)*, Mack Swain *(Jerome Underwood)*, Hobart Bosworth *(Jud Morgan)*, Paul Nicholson *(Bob Wells)*, Vera Steadman *(Harriet Underwood)*, Charles Gerrard *(Reggie De Vere)*, Clarence Burton *(Andy McNab)*.

Ford is a Pittsburgh man who believes he is dying from a terminal disease and decides to head west. In Arizona he meets Haver and her father, who provide him with a meal. Haver is engaged to the sheriff, and Ford volunteers to drive her across the desert. This is where the fun begins—the couple are suspected of eloping, and Ford holds up a man with a wrench in order to get gas, takes a job as a waiter at the ranch owned by the man he robbed, and finally, after a mad chase in which their car cascades down the side of a mountain, comes to the conclusion that he's going to live after all. He also decides that Haver is the girl for him, and they elope for real.

d, Scott Sidney; w, F. McGrew Willis (based on the play by Owen Davis); ph, Alec Phillips.

Comedy Cas. (PR:A MPAA:NR)

NEST, THE** (1927) 8 reels EXCEL bw

Pauline Frederick *(Mrs. Hamilton)*, Holmes Herbert *(Richard Elliott)*, Thomas Holding *(Archer Hamilton)*, Ruth Dwyer *(Susan Hamilton)*, Reginald Sheffield *(Martin Hamilton)*, Rolland Flander *(Monroe)*, Jean Acker *(Belle Madison)*, Wilfred Lucas *(Howard Hardy)*.

This 1927 soap opera has a widow (Frederick) losing control of her daughter, who marries a snob, and her son, who becomes involved with the underworld. The widow goes off to Paris, returns as a beautiful and desirable flapper, and marries the executor of her husband's estate (Herbert), who straightens the children out.

d, William Nigh; w, Charles E. Whittaker (based on the play "Les Noces d'Argent" by Paul Geraldy); ph, Jack Brown, Harry Stradling.

Drama (PR:A MPAA:NR)

NET, THE* (1916) 5 reels Thanhouser bw

Bert Delaney *(The Fisherman)*, Marian Swayne *(His Sweetheart)*, Inda Palmer *(His Mother)*, Ethel Jewett *(Mysterious Girl)*, Arthur Bauer *(Her Former Employer)*, Morgan Jones *(The Detective)*.

Terrible nonsense about a young Florida fisherman who saves the lives of two girls (one of whom is a crook) and becomes engaged to both. When it is revealed that the lad is actually heir to a million, the crooked Jane goes after him, but a mysterious stranger blows the plot and the lad marries the decent one.

d, George Foster Platt; w, (based on a story by Lloyd Lonergan).

Crime (PR:A MPAA:NR)

NET, THE** (1923) 7 reels FOX bw

Barbara Castleton *(Allayne Norman)*, Raymond Bloomer *(Bruce Norman)*, Albert Roscoe *(The Man)*, Peggy Davis *(The Model)*, William H. Tooker *(Mr. Royce)*, Helen Tracy *(The Nurse)*, Eliah Nadel *(The Boy)*, Claire De Lorez *(The Vamp)*, Arthur Gordini *(The Artist)*, Alexander Gaden *(The Inspector)*, Byron Douglas *(The Doctor)*.

Bloomer, a hard-drinking gambler, kills his wife's artist cousin during an argument and switches identities with a poor devil suffering from amnesia who just happens to stagger into the studio and pass out. The wife, Castleton, goes along with the deception for the sake of her little boy, but is guilt-ridden until her husband dies. Then the innocent one regains his memory, clears himself, and marries Castleton.

d, J. Gordon Edwards; w, Olga Linek Schnoll, Virginia Tracy (based on the novel *The Woman's Law* by Maravene Thompson); ph, Bennie Miggins.

Drama (PR:A MPAA:NR)

NETS OF DESTINY** (1924, Brit.) 6 reels I. B. Davidson/But bw

Stewart Rome *(Lawrence Averil)*, Mary Odette *(Marion Graham)*, Gertrude McCoy *(Constance)*, Cameron Carr *(Reingold)*, Judd Green *(Capt. Menzies)*, Reginald Fox *(Pat Dwyer)*, Benson Kleve *(Jock Menzies)*, James English *(Maj. Graham)*, George Turner *(Jerry Fisher)*, Laura Walker *(Mrs. Jardine)*, Eddie Dolly Dance Troupe.

After his father takes his own life, a young man lands a job as a deckhand and falls madly in love with the daughter of a man his father drove to ruin.

d, Arthur Rooke; w, Eliot Stannard (based on the novel *The Salving of a Derelict* by Maurice Drake).

Drama (PR:A MPAA:NR)

NEVADA*** (1927) 7 reels PAR bw

Gary Cooper *(Nevada)*, Thelma Todd *(Hettie Ide)*, William Powell *(Clan Dillon)*, Philip Strange *(Ben Ide)*, Ernie S. Adams *(Cash Burridge)*, Christian J. Frank *(Sheriff of Winthrop)*, Ivan Christy *(Cawthorne)*, Guy Oliver *(Sheriff of Lineville)*.

Standard formula western, about the good gunslinger (Cooper), the rancher's daughter (Todd) who falls in love with him, and the struggle against cattle rustlers, is elevated a notch or two by the presence of an outstanding cast and some truly beautiful cinematography.

d, John Waters; w, John Stone, L. G. Rigby (based on the novel by Zane Grey); t, Jack Conway; ph, C. Edgar Schoenbaum.

Western (PR:A MPAA:NR)

NEVER SAY DIE*** (1924) 6 reels Douglas MacLean/AEX bw

Douglas MacLean *(Jack Woodbury)*, Lillian Rich *(Violet Stevenson)*, Helen Ferguson *(La Cigale)*, Hallam Cooley *(Hector Walters)*, Lucien Littlefield *(Griggs)*, Tom O'Brien *(Gun Murray)*, Andre Lanoy *(Verchesi)*, Wade Boteler *(Dr. Fraser)*, Eric Mayne *(Dr. Galesby)*, William Conklin *(Dr. Gerhardt)*, George Cooper *(Gaston Gibbs)*.

Funny MacLean comedy has the popular star mistakenly diagnosed as only having a few months to live. His best friend sets out to arrange a marriage which will land him MacLean's considerable fortune. Of course the girl ends up falling for her victim, and the pal is left standing in the cold. There is a thrill sequence in this picture where MacLean wanders blindfolded onto the ledge of a skyscraper, rivaling Harold Lloyd's best stuff.

d, George J. Crone; w, Raymond Cannon (based on a story by Raymond Griffith, Wade Boteler and from a short story by William H. Post, William Collier); ph, Jack MacKenzie.

Comedy (PR:A MPAA:NR)

NEVER SAY QUIT** (1919) 5 reels FOX bw

George Walsh, Florence Dixon, Henry Hallam, William Frederick, Frank Jacobs, Joe Smiley, Jean Acker, Joseph Mack.

Typical Walsh comedy-adventure has the action star playing a young man plagued with bad luck from the day of his birth on Friday the 13th. Throughout the entire picture, one disaster after another befalls him until he breaks the spell by cleaning up a gang of crooks intent on holding a millionaire and his daughter hostage on their yacht.

d, Edward Dillon; w, Raymond L. Schrock; ph, R. B. Schellinger.

Adventure/Comedy (PR:A MPAA:NR)

NEVER THE TWAIN SHALL MEET 1/2** (1925) 8 reels COS/MG bw

Anita Stewart *(Tamea)*, Bert Lytell *(Dan Prichard)*, Huntley Gordon *(Mark Mellenger)*, Justine Johnstone *(Maise Morrison)*, George Siegmann *(James Muggridge)*, Lionel Belmore *(Gaston Larrieau)*, William Norris *(Squibbs)*, Emily Fitzroy *(Mrs. Pippy)*, Princess Marie de Bourbon *(Miss Smith)*, Florence Turner *(Julia)*, James Wang *(Sooey Wan)*, Ben Deeley *(Doctor)*, Roy Coulson *(Assistant Doctor)*, Thomas Ricketts *(Andrew J. Carson)*, Ernest Butterworth *(Capt. Hackett)*.

The daughter of a South Sea island queen and a French sea captain is taken in by wealthy Lytell when her father learns he has leprosy and kills himself. Before long, Lytell falls in love with the exotic young creature (Stewart) and when he goes bankrupt, a concerned newspaper reporter, Gordon, arranges for the couple to return to the island, where they are married. Later Lytell is stricken with jungle fever, and Gordon sails over to assist his friend. When he is strong enough, Gordon organizes Lytell's return to the U.S. and, being no dummy, remains on to offer comfort and love to the lonely princess.

d, Maurice Tourneur; w, Peter B. Kyne, Eugene Mullin (based on a novel by Kyne); t, Kyne; ph, Ira H. Morgan, J. B. Shackelford; ed, Donn Hayes; set d, Joseph Urban.

Drama (PR:A MPAA:NR)

NEW BROOMS 1/2** (1925) 6 reels FP/PAR bw

Neil Hamilton *(Thomas Bates, Jr.)*, Bessie Love *(Geraldine Marsh)*, Phyllis Haver *(Florence Levering)*, Robert McWade *(Thomas Bates, Sr.)*, Fred Walton *(Williams)*, Josephine Crowell *(Margaret)*, Larry Steers *(George Morrow)*, James Neill *(Kneeland)*.

Based on a moderately successful play, and somewhat of an improvement, this movie tells about a young fellow who is given the responsibility of running his father's business and household for a year in order to make a man out of him. Love sparkles as the servant who wins him away from the snooty girl for whom he was intended.

d, William DeMille; w, Clara Beranger (based on the play by Frank Craven); ph, L. Guy Wilky.

Comedy (PR:A MPAA:NR)

NEW CHAMPION** (1925) 5 reels Perfection/COL bw

William Fairbanks *(Bob Nichols)*, Edith Roberts *(Polly Rand)*, Lotus Thompson *(Lucy Nichols)*, Lloyd Whitlock *(Jack Melville)*, Frank Hagney *(Knockout Riley)*, Al Kaufman *(Fight Promoter)*, Marion Court *(Mrs. Nichols)*, Bert Apling *(Blacksmith)*.

Prizefighter Hagney hurts his hand while training at the home of Fairbanks, a small town blacksmith. Fairbanks takes his place in the ring, however, and after a seesaw battle, manages to win the bout.

d, Reeves Eason; w, Dorothy Howell; ph, George Meehan.

Adventure (PR:A MPAA:NR)

NEW CLOWN, THE** (1916, Brit.) 5 reels ID bw

James Welch *(Lord Cyril Garston)*, Manora Thew *(Rosie Dixon)*, Richard Lindsay *(Capt. Trent)*, Tom Coventry *(Tom Baker)*, Brian Daly *(Pennyquick)*, E. C. Arundell *(Strong Man)*, Kathleen Blake *(Maud Chesterton)*, Marjory Day *(Winnie Chesterton)*, Edward Sass *(Showman)*, Arthur Milton *(Innkeeper)*.

Believing that he was responsible for a man's death, a British lord joins a traveling circus and becomes a clown.

d, Fred Paul; w, Benedict James (based on a play by H. M. Paull).

Comedy (PR:A MPAA:NR)

NEW COMMANDMENT, THE*** (1925) 7 reels FN bw

Blanche Sweet *(Renee Darcourt)*, Ben Lyon *(Billy Morrow)*, Holbrook Blinn *(William Morrow)*, Clare Eames *(Mrs. Parr)*, Effie Shannon *(Marquise de la Salle)*, Dorothy Cumming *(Countess Stoll)*, Pedro De Cordoba *(Picard)*, George Cooper *(Red)*, Diana Kane *(Ethel)*, Lucius Henderson *(Henri Darcourt)*, Betty Jewel.

When Lyon learns that he is sailing with the stepdaughter of socialite Eames for the purpose of arranging a marriage, he jumps ship and ends up in Paris. There he falls madly in love with Sweet, an artist's model, and there are some pretty steamy love scenes along the way. But fearing she really cares for painter De Cordoba, Lyon joins the Foreign Legion at the outbreak of the German war. The youthful Yank fights bravely, is wounded in action, and when he regains consciousness, Sweet, who is acting as a volunteer, is by his side.

d, Howard Higgin; w, Sada Cowan, Higgin (based on the novel *Invisible Wounds* by Frederick Palmer); ph, Ernest Haller; ed, Paul F. Maschke; art d, Robert M. Hass.

Drama/War (PR:A MPAA:NR)

NEW DISCIPLE, THE** (1921) 6 reels Federation bw

Pell Trenton *(John McPherson)*, Alfred Allen *(Peter Fanning)*, Norris Johnson *(Mary Fanning)*, Margaret Mann *(Marion Fanning)*, Walt Whitman *(Sandy McPherson)*, Alice H. Smith *(Mother McPherson)*, Arthur Stuart Hull *(Frederick Wharton)*, Walter Perkins *(Daddy Whipple)*, Charles Prindley *(Jennings)*.

War profiteer Allen goes broke when a bitter strike prevents him from meeting his obligations. His workers form a coalition with farm laborers and together they buy the factories and fulfill the American dream.

d, Ollie Sellers; w, William Pigott (based on a story by John Arthur Nelson).

Drama (PR:A MPAA:NR)

NEW KLONDIKE, THE*** (1926) 8 reels FP/PAR bw

Thomas Meighan *(Tom Kelly)*, Lila Lee *(Evelyn Lane)*, Paul Kelly *(Bing Allen)*, Hallie Manning *(Flamingo Applegate)*, Robert Craig *(Morgan West)*, George De Carlton *(Owen)*, J. W. Johnston *(Joe Cooley)*, Brenda Lane *(Bird Dog)*, Tefft Johnson *(Col. Dwyer)*, Danny Hayes *(The Spieler)*.

Land swindling was a big story at the time, and it helped keep this pleasant little comedy—shot on location in Florida— breezing right along. The story has to do with a star player, Meighan, who is fired from the team by a jealous manager, but goes on to make a killing in property speculation for himself and his fellow athletes. At the picture's end, he cleans up a gang of real estate con men, obtains the managerial position, and wins the heart of pretty Lee. Nice performance by Meighan, but young Kelly steals the show as the baseball ace who doesn't know how to forget a pal.

d, Lewis Milestone; w, Thomas J. Geraghty (based on a story by Ring Lardner); ph, Alvin Wyckoff; art d, Walter E. Keller.

Drama/Comedy (PR:A MPAA:NR)

NEW LIVES FOR OLD** (1925) 7 reels FP/PAR bw

Betty Compson *(Olympe)*, Wallace MacDonald *(Hugh Warren)*, Theodore Kosloff *(De Montinbard)*, Sheldon Lewis *(Pugin)*, Jack Joyce *(Jean Bertaut)*, Margaret Seddon *(Widow Turrene)*, Joseph Dowling *(Sen. Warren)*, Helen Dunbar *(Mrs. Warren)*, Gale Henry *(Berthe)*, Marvel Quivey *(Nancy)*, Ed Faust *(Cafe Manager)*.

While on vacation Compson, a French nightclub dancer, becomes engaged to a wealthy U.S. soldier who believes her to be an innocent peasant. He goes off to the front, and she answers her country's call by becoming a spy and using her charms to nail a traitor in the service of France. At war's end, she marries her young man and moves to the U.S. The German agent shows up, however, and Compson unselfishly steps forward and puts the finger on him. He strikes back by telling her in-laws (who were not too crazy about her humble background to begin with) that their daughter-in-law is, in reality, a notorious cabaret cutie. All ends well, however, when high-ranking representatives of the French government turn up to deliver their most coveted decoration to their most courageous heroine.

d, Clarence Badger; w, Adelaide Heilbron; ph, Guy Wilky.

Spy/Drama **(PR:A MPAA:NR)**

NEW LOVE FOR OLD** (1918) 5 reels UNIV bw

Emory Johnson *(Kenneth Scott)*, Ella Hall *(Daphne Sawyer)*, Gretchen Lederer *(Marie Beauchamp)*, Winter Hall *(Ben Sawyer)*, Harry Holden *("Doc" Padden)*, E. A. Warren *(Louis Bracchi)*.

When a young man is rejected by his girl friend he sets off for the country to leave the bad memories behind. There he falls in love with another young lady, who just happens to be the sister of the girl who threw him over. Things begin to get a bit tricky when the original sweetheart decides to open a roadhouse in the area, but our hero makes the right decision and elects to marry the girl with the farm.

d, Elsie Jane Wilson; w, Waldemar Young.

Drama **(PR:A MPAA:NR)**

NEW MOON, THE** (1919) 6 reels Norma Talmadge/SEL bw

Norma Talmadge *(Princess Marie Pavloyna/Sonia Sazonoff)*, Charles Gerard *(Theo Kameneff)*, Stuart Holmes *(Orel Kosloff)*, Marc MacDermott *(Vasili Lazoff)*, Ethel Kaye *(Masha Lazoff)*, Harry Sothern *(Leo Pushkin)*, Marguerite Clayton *(Nadia Kameneff)*, Pedro de Cordoba *(Prince Michail Koloyar)*, Mathilde Brundage.

Some beautifully staged mob scenes and exquisite photography greatly enhance this otherwise pedestrian melodrama about the escape of a beautiful princess and her fiance from a Russia occupied by blood-crazed Bolsheviks.

d&w, Chester Withey (based on a story by H. H. Van Loan); ph, David Abel.

Drama **(PR:A MPAA:NR)**

NEW TEACHER, THE** (1922) 5 reels FOX bw

Shirley Mason *(Constance Bailey)*, Allan Forrest *(Bruce Van Griff)*, Earl Metcalf *(Edward Hurley)*, Otto Hoffman *(Joseph Hurley)*, Ola Norman *(Mrs. Brissell)*, Pat Moore *(George Brissell)*, Kate Price *(Mrs. Brennan)*.

Society girl Mason refuses to marry Forrest because she wants to "do something" with her life. Then, when their private plane makes a forced landing on New York's Lower East Side, and she sees the deplorable conditions which exist there, the decision is made to become a teacher and work with the children of the slums. Forrest, in order to keep an eye on her, joins the police force and is stationed right around the corner from his sweetheart's schoolhouse. After saving Mason from a number of scrapes, the couple decide to finally tie the knot—secure in the knowledge that they have done their bit for humankind.

d, Joseph Franz; w, Dorothy Yost (based on the novel *The Island of Faith* by Margaret Elizabeth Sangster); ph, Frank B. Good.

Romance/Drama **(PR:A MPAA:NR)**

NEW YEAR'S EVE** 1/2 (1929) 7 reels FOX bw

Mary Astor *(Marjorie Ware)*, Charles Morton *(Edward Warren)*, Earle Foxe *(Barry Harmon)*, Florence Lake *(Pearl)*, Arthur Stone *(Steve)*, Helen Ware *(Landlady)*, Freddie Frederick *(Little Brother)*, Jane La Verne *(Little Girl)*, Sumner Getchell *(Edward's Friend)*, Stuart Erwin *(Landlady's Son)*, Virginia Vance *(Little Girl's Mother)*.

Less-than-cheerful programmer with Astor, unemployed and without means to support her young brother, forced to pay a visit to a gambler she knows desires her body. The gambler is murdered during the time Astor is on the scene, so the police charge her with the crime. Later, the real killer dies in an accident, and Astor is cleared. At this point, her old gentleman friend (Warren) shows up to steal her heart.

d, Henry Lehrman; sup, Kenneth Hawks; w, Dwight Cummins (based on the story "$100.00" by Richard Connell); t, William Kernell; ph, Conrad Wells; m, S. L. Rothafel; syn sc; s eff.

Drama **(PR:A MPAA:NR)**

NEW YORK*** (1916) 5 reels Gold Rooster bw

Florence Reed, Fania Marinoff, John Miltern, Jessie Ralph, Forrest Winant.

Well-directed, acted, and produced showbiz story of life on The Great White Way had all of the stereotypes and cliches long before Busby Berkeley got around to perfecting them.

d, George Fitzmaurice; w, Ouida Bergere (based on the play by William Hurlbut); ph, Arthur Miller.

Drama **(PR:A MPAA:NR)**

NEW YORK** (1927) 7 reels FP/PAR bw

Ricardo Cortez *(Michael Angelo Cassidy)*, Lois Wilson *(Marjorie Church)*, Estelle Taylor *(Angie Miller)*, William Powell *(Trent Regan)*, Norman Trevor *(Randolph Church)*, Richard "Skeets" Gallagher *(Buck)*, Margaret Quimby *(Helena Matthews)*, Lester Schariff *(Izzy Blumenstein)*, Charles Byer *(Jimmie Wharton)*.

When four pals from the Bowery decide to go their separate ways, one of them, Powell, becomes a gangster. His girl friend, Taylor, was once crazy about Cortez, a member of the foursome, and upon hearing that he is about to wed, she pays him a visit to congratulate him. Powell, thinking his girl unfaithful, accidentally shoots her, and Cortez is charged with murder. All works out in the end, however, when another group member uncovers the truth. Many of the scenes here were shot on the streets of Manhattan.

d, Luther Reed; w, Forrest Halsey (based on a story by Becky Gardiner, Barbara Chambers); ph, J. Roy Hunt.

Drama **(PR:A MPAA:NR)**

NEW YORK IDEA, THE*** (1920) 5 reels REA bw

Alice Brady, Lowell Sherman, Hedda Hopper, George Howell, Lionel Pape, Margaret Linden, Edwards Davis, Harry Hocky, Nina Herbert, Emily Fitzroy, Julia Hurley.

Subtle and funny satire of New York's society set and its cavalier attitude towards marriage and divorce is contrasted with a wealthy couple who actually strive to make their union work. Sherman is grand in his first sympathetic role, after creating the movie's greatest all time rat in WAY DOWN EAST.

d, Herbert Blache; w, Mary Murillo (based on the play by Langdon Mitchell); ph, Jacques Bizuel.

Satire **(PR:A MPAA:NR)**

NEW YORK NIGHTS (SEE: NEW YORK NIGHTS, 1929, Vol. VI)

NEW YORK PEACOCK, THE*** (1917) 5 reels FOX bw

Valeska Suratt *(Zena)*, Harry Hilliard *(Billy)*, Eric Mayne *(Martin)*, Alice Gale *(Mrs. Martin)*, Claire Whitney, W. W. Black, John Mackin, Frank Goldsmith.

Suratt, an all-but-forgotten movie vamp, was at her best in this picture about a woman who lures businessmen into turning their factories over to a munitions cartel. She sets out to seduce a young man representing his father's firm who has come to the city, but falls in love with him against her will. Part of the scheme is to place the lad in the debt of a ruthless gambler, and having accomplished this, she must now act quickly to save his life. Suratt decides to take the next wealthy man she meets to the cleaners, but as luck would have it, the patsy turns out to be the boy's father. To make things worse, the old boy has gone completely nuts over the saucy temptress. The film ends with the three confronting each other in her suite. There the father and son console one another and then leave arm in arm to catch their train as the incomparable Suratt turns to her friend, the gambler, and says (in one of the whippiest title cards in all of silent cinema), "Ah, hell, let's go and get something to eat."

d, Kenean Buel; w, Mary Murillo.

Crime/Drama **(PR:A MPAA:NR)**

NEWS PARADE, THE** 1/2 (1928) 7 reels FOX bw

Nick Stuart *("Newsreel Nick" Naylor)*, Sally Phipps *(Sally Wellington)*, Brandon Hurst *(A. K. Wellington)*, Cyril Ring *(Prince Oscar)*, Earle Foxe *(Ivan Vodkoff, the Mysterious Stranger)*, Franklin Underwood *(Bill Walpole)*, Truman Talley *(Director-in-Chief Talley)*.

One of the first movies to glorify the daredevil cameramen who shot the newsreels. This fair comedy has a character (Stuart) appropriately named "Newsreel Nick," given the assignment to cover a millionaire with an obsession for privacy. Stuart follows the gentleman and his beautiful daughter halfway across the U.S. and on to Cuba, where he prevents them from being kidnaped and gets some swell footage while he's at it.

d, David Butler; w, Burnett Hershey (based on a story by William M. Conselman, Butler); t, Malcolm Stuart Boylan; ph, Sidney Wagner, Joseph A. Valentine; ed, Irene Morra.

Comedy **(PR:A MPAA:NR)**

NICE PEOPLE*** (1922) 7 reels FP/PAR bw

Bebe Daniels *(Theodora "Teddy" Gloucester)*, Wallace Reid *(Billy Wade)*, Conrad Nagel *(Scotty Wilbur)*, Julia Faye *(Hallie Livingston)*, Claire McDowell *(Margaret Rainsford)*, Edward Martindel *(Hubert Gloucester)*, Eve Southern *(Eileen Baxter-Jones)*, Bertram Jones *(Trever Leeds)*, William Boyd *(Oliver Comstock)*, Ethel Wales *(Mrs. Heyfer)*.

Lavish DeMille jazz-age entertainment about a flapper (Daniels) who, after being chastised by her father for innocently staying out all night with a boy (Nagel) who had too much to drink, changes her ways and becomes an old-fashioned wife to Reid, the man who saved her honor on that occasion.

d, William DeMille; w, Clara Beranger (based on the play by Rachel Crothers); ph, Guy Wilky.

Drama **(PR:A MPAA:NR)**

NIGHT BRIDE, THE** 1/2 (1927) 6 reels Metropolitan/PDC bw

Marie Prevost *(Cynthia Stockton)*, Harrison Ford *(Stanley Warrington)*, Franklin Pangborn *(John Stockton)*, Robert Edeson *(Adolphe Biggles)*, Constance Howard *(Renee Stockton)*, Richard Crawford *(Addison Walsh)*, George Kuwa *(Japanese Gardener)*.

Perky Prevost has an automobile accident with woman-hating author Ford. They engage in a whale of a fight, and then Prevost flees in a milk truck, returns home, and finds her fiance smooching with her sister. Horrified, she takes off into the night, unknowingly stumbles upon Ford's home, and beds down in one of his spare rooms. Later, when her furious father finds them together, Prevost explains the situation by claiming to be married. The delighted father provides them with the gift of an ocean voyage, and before the vessel reaches its destination the formerly misogynous Ford arranges for the captain to make the situation legitimate.

d, E. Mason Hopper; sup, F. McGrew Willis; w, Fred Stanley, Zelda Sears (based on a story by Frederick Chapin); ph, Dewey Wrigley.

Comedy **(PR:A MPAA:NR)**

NIGHT CLUB, THE*** (1925) 6 reels FP/PAR bw

Raymond Griffith *(Robert White)*, Vera Reynolds *(Grace Henderson)*, Wallace Beery *(Diablo)*, Louise Fazenda *(Carmen)*.

Confirmed bachelor Griffith is told that he will inherit a million dollars if he marries Reynolds. When they meet, Griffith falls in love with her without realizing who she is, but Reynolds is convinced he is only after the money. Then, when he finds out that the money will go to her upon his death, the dapper comedian tries to kill himself in a number of comic ways. All of this effort and pain convinces Reynolds that his feelings are sincere, and they marry in the end. This is not a great comedy, but there is just enough of Griffith's special magic to make it more than worthwhile.

d, Frank Urson, Paul Iribe; w, Keene Thompson, Walter Woods (based on the play "After Five" by William C. and Cecil B. DeMille); ph, Peverell Marley.

Comedy **(PR:A MPAA:NR)**

NIGHT CRY, THE*** (1926) 7 reels WB bw

Rin-Tin-Tin *(Himself)*, John Harron *(John Martin)*, June Marlowe *(Mrs. John Martin)*, Gayne Whitman *(Miguel Hernandez)*, Heinie Conklin *(Tony)*, Don Alvarado *(Pedro)*, Mary Louise Miller *(The Martin Baby)*.

Perhaps the most important star under contract to the brothers Warner at this time was Rin-Tin-Tin. In this picture he is wrongly accused of killing sheep and sentenced to death under the law of the range. But when a giant condor captures the daughter of Rinty's master, the heroic canine kills the creature and exonerates himself.

d, Herman C. Raymaker; w, Ewart Adamson (based on a story by Paul Klein, Edward Meagher); ph, Ed Du Par, Walter Robinson; ed, Clarence Kolster.

Adventure **(PR:A MPAA:NR)**

NIGHT FLYER, THE** (1928) 7 reels James Cruze/Pathe bw

William Boyd *(Jimmy Bradley)*, Jobyna Ralston *(Kate Murphy)*, Philo McCullough *(Bat Mullins)*, Ann Schaeffer *(Mrs. Murphy)*, DeWitt Jennings *(Bucks)*, John Milerta *(Tony)*, Robert Dudley *(Freddy)*.

Boyd, a fireman on the old locomotive No. 99, is rejected by Ralston because he tied one on at her birthday party. His main rival, McCullough, is the engineer on the new train hired to deliver the mail. But when McCullough's machine overturns, Boyd delivers the goods, wins the government contract, and rekindles the love of Ralston as well.

p, James Cruze; d, Walter Lang; w, Walter Woods (based on the story "Held for Orders" by Frank Hamilton Spearman); ph, Ernest Miller; ed, Mildred Johnson; art d, Charles Cadwallader.

Drama **(PR:A MPAA:NR)**

NIGHT HORSEMAN, THE*** (1921) 5 reels FOX bw

Tom Mix *(Whistling Dan)*, May Hopkins *(Kate Cumberland)*, Harry Lonsdale *(Old Joe Cumberland)*, Joseph Bennett *(Dr. Byrne)*, Sid Jordan *(Buck Daniels)*, Bert Sprotte *(Mac Strann)*, Cap Anderson *(Jerry Strann)*, Lon Poff *(Haw Haw)*, Charles K. French *(Marshall)*.

Good Mix western about a man who chooses not to kill the man who tried to gun him down and finally comes to realize that marriage to the right woman is preferable to his earlier inclination of following the call of the wild geese.

d&w, Lynn F. Reynolds (based on the novel by Max Brand); ph, Ben Kline.

Western **(PR:A MPAA:NR)**

NIGHT LIFE½** (1927) 7 reels TIF bw

Alice Day *(Anna)*, Johnny Harron *(Max)*, Eddie Gribbon *(Nick)*, Walter Hiers *(Manager)*, Lionel Braham *(War Profiteer)*, Kitty Barlow *(His Wife)*, Dawn O'Day, Jane Irving, Audrey Sewell *(His Daughters)*, Earl Metcalf *(Amorous Swain)*, Patricia Avery *(Amorous Maid)*, Leopold Archduke of Austria *(Chief of Detectives)*, Snitz Edwards *(Merry-go-round Manager)*, Violet Palmer *(Beer Garden Waitress)*, Lydia Yeamans Titus *(Landlady)*.

Harron and Gribbon return to Vienna after the war and are forced by poverty to become pickpockets. Before long they are prospering, and Harron finds himself the victim of an attempted snatch on the part of Day, a pretty young woman who is also driven to crime out of desperation. Harron takes her to an amusement park, buys her dinner, and they fall in love. Day becomes a beer garden waitress and one night happens to see her sweetheart stealing a diamond brooch. When she confronts him with this and demands that he return it, Gribbon, who has been seething with jealousy, informs the police that it was Day who stole the valuable piece. But the spirit of true friendship and love prevails, and Gribbon assumes the blame for the crime himself, leaving the happy couple to fulfill their destiny alone.

d, George Archainbaud; w, Gertrude Orr (based on a story by Albert S. Le Vino); t, Viola Brothers Shore, Harry Braxton; ph, Chester Lyons; ed, Desmond O'Brien; set d, Burgess Beall.

Drama **(PR:A MPAA:NR)**

NIGHT LIFE IN HOLLYWOOD** (1922) 6 reels A. B. Maescher/Arrow bw

J. Frank Glendon *(Joe)*, Josephine Hill *(Leonore Baxter, a Movie Star)*, Gale Henry *(Carrie)*, J. L. McComas *(Pa Powell)*, Elizabeth Rhodes *(Ma Powell)*, Jack Connolly *(Elkins, a Movie Actor)*, Delores Hall *(Amy, Joe's Childhood Sweetheart)*, Wallace Reid and Family *(Themselves)*, Theodore Roberts *(Himself)*, Sessue Hayakawa and Wife *(Themselves)*, Tsuru Aoki *(Himself)*, William Desmond *(Himself)*, Bryant Washburn and Family *(Themselves)*, Bessie Love *(Herself)*, J. Warren Kerrigan and Mother *(Themselves)*, Johnny Jones *(Himself)*, Denishawn Dancers.

Glendon and Henry play a couple of Arkansas yokels who head for Hollywood in search of titilation and thrills only to discover that the stars are folks just like everybody else. A somewhat sensational title is all this one had going for it.

d&w, Fred Caldwell.

Drama **(PR:A MPAA:NR)**

NIGHT LIFE OF NEW YORK*** (1925) 8 reels FP/PAR bw

Rod La Rocque *(Ronald Bentley)*, Ernest Torrence *(John Bentley)*, Dorothy Gish *(Meg)*, Helen Lee Worthing *(Carrie Reed)*, George Hackathorne *(Jimmy)*, Arthur Housman *(Jerry)*, Riley Hatch *(William Workman)*.

Pleasant hokum with La Rocque as an Iowa boy moving to New York against his father's will. It seems his father (skillfully played by Torrence) had an unhappy romance in Gotham and never forgave the city. La Rocque arrives, not knowing that his dad has arranged with a business associate to make things so hectic and scary that he'll gladly hop aboard the next train headed west. Instead he meets Gish, becomes involved in a real crime by protecting her kid brother who pulled a heist, and ends up in the pokey. Gish clears things up, however, and his father comes barreling into town, takes a good look around, and decides to stay in the Big Apple permanently.

d, Allan Dwan; w, Paul Schofield (based on a story by Edgar Selwyn); ph, George Webber.

Comedy **(PR:A MPAA:NR)**

NIGHT OF LOVE, THE*** (1927) 8 reels Goldwyn/UA bw

Ronald Colman *(Montero)*, Vilma Banky *(Princess Marie)*, Montagu Love *(Duke de la Garda)*, Natalie Kingston *(Donna Beatriz)*, John George *(Jester)*, B. Hyman, Gibson Gowland *(Bandits)*, Laska Winters *(The Gypsy Bride)*, Sally Rand *(A Gypsy Dancer)*, William Tooker *(Spanish Ambassador)*, Charles Holt *(Grandee)*, Marion Morgan Dancers.

Handsomely mounted costumer has Colman as the son of a gypsy king, watching helplessly as his bride is taken away on their wedding night by a nefarious duke (Love) who feels he is entitled by law to have his royal way with her. The girl chooses death instead, and sometime later at the marriage feast of the nobleman, Colman and his outlaw band capture the duke's royal bride (Banky) and spirit her away. During the time of her imprisonment, Banky falls in love with the handsome gypsy, but the duke discovers the hideout, captures Colman and arranges for a public execution. As he stands, tied to the stake, Colman's eloquence stirs the masses and they rise up to overthrow their cruel oppressor. Colman and Banky were the Garbo and Gilbert of the Goldwyn studio, and this picture proved to be quite successful.

d, George Fitzmaurice; w, Lenore J. Coffee (based on the writing of Pedro Calderon de la Barca); ph, George Barnes, Thomas Brannigan; ed, Viola Lawrence; art d, Karl Oscar Borg.

Costume **(PR:A MPAA:NR)**

NIGHT OF MYSTERY, A* (1928) 6 reels PAR bw

Adolphe Menjou *(Capt. Ferreol)*, Evelyn Brent *(Gilberte Boismartel)*, Nora Lane *(Therese D'Egremont)*, William Collier, Jr. *(Jerome D'Egremont)*, Raoul Paoli *(Marcasse)*, Claude King *(Marquis Boismartel)*, Frank Leigh *(Rochemore)*, Margaret Burt *(Rochemore's Secretary)*.

Slow-moving mystery has Menjou witnessing a murder while visiting the apartment of a former paramour. The killer threatens to tell the woman's husband if Menjou talks, so the Frenchman packs his evening clothes and sails for Africa. Later, when he discovers that his sweetheart's brother has been accused of the crime, Menjou returns and confesses to performing the deed himself. An error in his statement clears him, however, and the young chap gets off the hook as well.

d, Lothar Mendes; w, Ernest Vajda (based on the novel *Ferreol* by Victorien Sardou); t, Herman J. Mankiewicz; ph, Harry Fischbeck; ed, Frances Marsh.

Mystery **(PR:A MPAA:NR)**

NIGHT OUT, A*** (1916) 5 reels VIT bw

May Robson *(Granmum)*, Flora Finch *(Mrs. Haslem)*, Kate Price *(Mrs. Duncan)*, Charles Brown *(Jonas Deacon)*, George Cooper *(Waldo Deacon)*, Hughie Mack *(Jeff Dorgan)*, Belle Bruce *(Grace)*, Ethel Corcoran *(Betty)*, Arthur Cozine *(Paul)*, Jack Storey *(Jack)*, Frank Bunny *(Reporter)*, Eva Taylor, William Shea.

The wonderful Robson, who would become one of Hollywood's top character actresses (and be nominated for an Oscar for her portrayal of Apple Annie in Capra's LADY FOR A DAY), is perfection in this screen adaptation of her own hit play about a woman who has the time of her life when a couple of grandsons take her out for a night on the town.

d, George D. Baker; w, May Robson, Charles T. Dazey.

Comedy/Drama **(PR:A MPAA:NR)**

NIGHT OWL, THE* (1926) 5 reels Harry J. Brown/ RAY bw

Reed Howes *(Larry Armitage)*, Gladys Hulette *(Mary Jackson)*, Harold Austin *(Jimmy Jackson)*, Joseph W. Girard *(William Armitage)*, Dave Kirby *(Harlem Red)*, James Mason *(Gentleman Joe)*.

Bottom-of-the-barrel stuff about a cigarette girl who betrays the gang she's involved with to help the man she loves thwart the abduction of his wealthy father.

d, Harry J. Brown; w, Henry Roberts Symonds; ph, William Tuers.

Action/Drama **(PR:A MPAA:NR)**

NIGHT PATROL, THE½** (1926) 6 reels Richard Talmadge-Carlos/FBO bw

Richard Talmadge *(Tom Collins)*, Rose Blossom *(Louise Hollister)*, Mary Carr *(Mrs. Hollister)*, Gardner James *(Roy Hollister, the Boy)*, Josef Swickard *(John*

Pendleton), Grace Darmond *(Goldie Ferguson)*, Victor Dillingham *(Chuck Wolcott)*, Arthur Conrad *(Terry the Rat)*.

Talmadge is an Irish cop who arrests his sweetheart's brother for murder. Convinced the lad is innocent, Talmadge disguises himself as the "Frisco Kid" and worms his way into the confidence of the real killers. After a series of spectacular stunts, he brings the bad guys to justice and manages to save the kid from the electric chair at the last minute.

p, Richard Talmadge; d, Noel Mason Smith; w, Frank Howard Clark; ph, Jack Stevens, Charles Lang; ed, Doane Harrison.

Crime/Adventure **(PR:A MPAA:NR)**

NIGHT SHIP, THE* 1/2 (1925) 6 reels GOTH/LUM bw

Mary Carr *(Martha Randall)*, Tom Santschi *(Capt. Jed Hobbs)*, Robert Gordon *(Bob Randall)*, Margaret Fielding *(Elizabeth Hobbs)*, Charles A. Sellon *(Jimson Weed)*, Willis Marks *(David Brooks)*, Charles W. Mack *(Eli Stubbs)*, Mary McLane *(Janet Hobbs)*, L. J. O'Connor *(Cassidy)*, Julian Rivero *(Pedro Lopez)*.

Gordon returns home after being shipwrecked for six years to find his sweetheart married to Santschi, the rat who dispossessed Gordon's mother of her home and caused her death. Determined to get revenge, Gordon discovers that Santschi is the leader of a gun-running gang and during a terrific scene on board a ship loaded with arms, an explosion kills Santschi. Gotham's use of Carr's name to sell this film is rather outrageous as her onscreen time is so brief that it must have required one day of shooting.

d&w, Henry McCarthy; ph, Jack McKenzie.

Adventure **(PR:A MPAA:NR)**

NIGHT WATCH, THE* (1926) 5 reels TRU bw

Mary Carr *(Mrs. Blackwell)*, Jack Richardson *(Mr. Powell)*, Charles Delaney *(George Blackwell)*, Gloria Grey *(Nellie Powell)*, Muriel Reynolds, Raymond Rousenville, Ethel Schram, Charles W. Mack, Fred Caldwell.

It's the old story about a couple of lovers who are kept apart because their mountain families are engaged in a feud. There's a pro-prohibition twist to this one, however, when the sweethearts are finally allowed to find their happiness once the good revenue officers close down the stills.

d, Fred Caldwell.

Drama/Romance **(PR:A MPAA:NR)**

NIGHT WATCH, THE 1/2** (1928) 7 reels FN bw

Billie Dove *(Yvonne)*, Paul Lukas *(Capt. Corlaix)*, Donald Reed *(D'Artelle)*, Nicholas Soussanin *(Brambourg)*, Nicholas Bela *(Leduc)*, George Periolat *(Fargasson)*, William Tooker *(Mobrayne)*, Gus Partos *(Dagorne)*, Anita Garvin *(Ann)*.

Ponderous direction by Korda is the main weakness in this otherwise interesting wartime picture about a woman who steps forward at a military trial to admit an indiscretion and clear her husband, who is being court-martialed for neglect of duty. Good performance by Dove.

d, Alexander Korda; sup, Ned Marin; w, Lajos Biro (based on the play "In the Night Watch" by Michael Morton); t, Dwinelle Benthall, Rufus McCosh; ph, Karl Struss; ed, George McGuire; syn s; s eff.

Drama **(PR:C MPAA:NR)**

NIGHT WORKERS, THE** (1917) 5 reels Essanay bw

Marguerite Clayton *(Ethel Carver)*, Jack Gardner *(Clyde Manning)*, Julien Barton *(Mitchell)*, Mabel Bardine *(Mrs. Mitchell)*, Arthur W. Bates *(The Artist)*.

Gardner escapes from an orphanage and lands a job doing odd chores on a small town newspaper. As he grows up, the lad becomes a pretty good reporter and graduates to a big city daily, where he develops into the hotshot man-on-the-beat. Then the bottle takes control, and he hits the skids hard. Fortunately, there's a young woman on the paper who loves him, and when she inherits her grandfather's country paper, the two go there to run it. Of course, to *nobody's* surprise, it turns out to be the very same journal he worked on as a boy. And the girl who saved his life and picked him up from the gutter is none other than the freckle-faced little kid with ink stains on her cheeks, whom he used to take such great delight in teasing.

d, J. Charles Haydon; w, J. Bradley Smollen.

Drama **(PR:A MPAA:NR)**

NIGHTINGALE, THE*** (1914) 5 reels All Star bw

Ethel Barrymore, William Courtleigh, Jr., Frank Andrews, Conway Tearle, Charles Stevenson, Irving Brooks, Mario Majeroni, Philip Hahn, Ida Darling.

Barrymore made her motion picture debut in this screen adaptation of one of her earlier stage successes. The transition was nothing short of a triumph, and there were a number of prominent reviewers who even admitted to preferring the shadow play version.

d&w, Augustus Thomas.

Drama **(PR:A MPAA:NR)**

NINA, THE FLOWER GIRL** (1917) 5 reels FA/TRI bw

Bessie Love *(Nina)*, Elmer Clifton *(Jimmie)*, Bert Hadley *(Fred Townsend)*, Loyola O'Connor *(Mrs. Townsend)*, Alfred Paget *(Archie Dean)*, Fred Warren *(Dr. Fletcher)*, Adele Clifton *(Fifi Chandler)*, Rhea Haines *(Lotta, Her Chum)*, Jennie Lee *(Nina's Grandmother)*, Mrs. Higby.

Love is a blind flower girl (the similarity to CITY LIGHTS ends here) who loves a hunchbacked newspaper peddler, whom she sees in her mind's eye as dashing and handsome. When a kindly family arranges for an operation which restores her sight, her friend decides to leap in front of a fast-moving train. But, at the last second, the doctor who restored Love's visual capacity (and is now in love with her) stops the suicide, makes the newsie normal with another of his sensational operations, and then steps back to allow the sweethearts to marry.

d, Lloyd Ingraham; w, (based on a story by Mary H. O'Connor); ph, Frank Urson.

Drama **(PR:A MPAA:NR)**

NINE AND THREE-FIFTHS SECONDS** (1925) 6 reels A. G. Steen bw

Charles Paddock *(Charles Raymond)*, Helen Ferguson *(Mary Bowser)*, George Fawcett *(Jasper Raymond)*, Jack Giddings *(Walter Raymond)*, Peggy Schaffer *(Lucille Pringle)*, G. Raymond Nye *(Link Edwards)*, Otis Harlan *(Motherbund)*.

Unbelievable programmer has college athlete Paddock heading west after being disowned by his father. There he falls in love with a rancher's daughter, Ferguson, and makes an impression on her by outrunning her favorite horse. Later, when she is kidnaped by a somewhat envious suitor, Paddock chases them down on foot and gives the poor devil a tremendous thrashing. As if all of this were not enough, the movie ends with young Paddock competing in the Olympics, establishing a new record for the sprint, and marrying Ferguson, who has some honeymoon to look forward to.

d, Lloyd B. Carleton; w, Roy Clements; ph, Edward Henderson, Gordon Pollock.

Adventure/Western **(PR:A MPAA:NR)**

NINE O'CLOCK TOWN, A*** (1918) 5 reels PAR bw

Charles Ray *(David Clary)*, Jane Novak *(Katherine)*, Otto Hoffman *(John Clary)*, Gertrude Claire *(Mrs. Clary)*, Catherine Young *(The Dame)*, Dorcas Matthews *(The Model)*, Caroline Rankin.

Ray is the son of a small town department store owner, who heads for New York to make his mark after his dad rejects his ideas for modern sales techniques. While in the Big Apple, Ray fails completely and even has his watch stolen by a female con artist. When Ray returns home, his father puts him in charge of the business for six months while he takes a much-needed rest. A burlesque show arrives for a one nighter, and in the company is the same girl who stole his ticker in New York. She claims to have taken it for safe keeping and asks Ray to pick it up that evening at her hotel. The youth innocently complies, only to have the woman's husband burst into the room and threaten to blackmail Ray unless he gives them a $5,000 payoff. The next day, Ray conducts the sale of sales, using his own innovative concepts. The female crook, who had been wronged by her husband after Ray's departure, confesses the truth, while the owner of a multi-million dollar chain of department stores happens to pass by and offers the enterprising young chap $75,000 for the purchase of his business. Of course he accepts, remains on to manage the enterprise, and marries the local girl who has always worshiped him.

d, Victor L. Schertzinger; sup, Thomas H. Ince; w, Schertzinger.

Comedy/Drama **(PR:A MPAA:NR)**

NINETEEN AND PHYLLIS*** (1920) Charles Ray/FN bw

Charles Ray *(Andrew Jackson Cavanaugh)*, George Nichols *(His Uncle, Daniel Cavanaugh)*, Cora Drew *(Mrs. Daniel Cavanaugh)*, Clara Horton *(Phyllis Laurin)*, Frank Norcross *(Judge Lee Laurin)*, Lincoln Stedman *(Jimmy Long)*, DeWitt Jennings.

Possessing the slimmest of plots, this homespun story about a poor Southern boy who beats out the son of the town's wealthiest family for the hand of a judge's granddaughter is nonetheless the perfect showcase for the unique and considerable charm of its star, Ray.

d, Joseph De Grasse; w, Bernard McConville, Isabel Johnston (based on a story by Frederick Stowers); ph, Chester Lyons.

Comedy/Drama **(PR:A MPAA:NR)**

NINETY AND NINE, THE 1/2** (1922) 7 reels VIT bw

Warner Baxter *(Tom Silverton/Phil Bradbury)*, Colleen Moore *(Ruth Blake)*, Lloyd Whitlock *(Mark Leveridge)*, Gertrude Astor *(Kate Van Dyke)*, Robert Dudley *(Abner Blake)*, Mary Young *(Rachel)*, Arthur Jasmine *(Bud Bryson)*, Ernest Butterworth *(Reddy)*, Aggie Herring *(Mrs. Dougherty)*, Dorothea Wolbert *(Mrs. Markham)*, Rex Hammel *(Eric Van Dyke)*, Charles Moore *(Sam Grant)*.

Old-fashioned melodrama has Baxter being framed for murder, moving to a new town under a different name, and saving the lives of hundreds by driving his locomotive through a forest fire. In the end he also clears his name, nails the real killer, and wins the hand of the girl he loves.

d, David Smith; w, C. Graham Baker (based on a story by Ramsay Morris); ph, Steve Smith, Jr.

Drama **(PR:A MPAA:NR)**

NIOBE*** (1915) 5 reels FP bw

Hazel Dawn, Charles Abbe.

Clever comedy inspired by the Greek legend of Niobe, wife of King Amphion of Thebes, who was turned to stone by the gods because of her boastfulness. In this picture, an insurance man who has covered the shipment of a statue of Niobe for $400,000, falls asleep and dreams about the figure coming to life. There are a number of laughs and some very clever business when Niobe escapes into the park and becomes involved with a number of her fellow statues, including Hercules. The harassed fellow of course wakes up to discover everything in order, but not before a delightful early example of cinematic narrative was given the opportunity to unfold.

w, Harry Paulton, Edward A. Paulton.

Comedy **(PR:A MPAA:NR)**

NO BABIES WANTED** $^{1}/_{2}$ (1928) 6 reels Plaza bw (AKA: THE BABY MOTHER)

Priscilla Moran *(Patsy O'Day)*, William V. Mong *(Michael O'Day)*, Dorothy Devore *(Martha Whitney)*, Emily Fitzroy *("Old Ironsides," the Landlady)*, Cissy Fitzgerald *(The Orphanage Woman)*, John Richard Becker *(The Baby)*, Dinty *(Himself)*.

Moran, an 8-year-old, finds an abandoned baby while her grandfather is in the hospital, and the remainder of the picture deals with her attempt to keep the little nipper out of the clutches of a nasty landlady and the authorities from the orphanage. Better than it sounds.

d, John Harvey; w, Harriet Hinsdale, H. T. Crist; t, Harry Chandlee; ph, L. William O'Connell; ed, Chandlee.

Drama **(PR:A MPAA:NR)**

NO CONTROL** (1927) 6 reels Metropolitan/PDC bw

Harrison Ford *(John Douglas, Jr.)*, Phyllis Haver *(Nancy Flood)*, Jack Duffy *(Noah Flood)*, Tom Wilson *(Asthma)*, Toby Claude *(Mrs. Douglas)*, E. J. Ratcliffe *(John Douglas)*, Larry Steers *(Kid Dugan)*.

Fair comedy has a young businessman saving the one-ring circus of the girl he loves by entering a dancing horse in the big race. Knowing that the nag is terrified of lions, they attach earphones to its head and use an appropriate sound effect to spur him across the finish line first.

d, Scott Sidney, E. J. Babille; w, Zelda Sears, Tay Garnett (based on the story "Speed But No Control" by Frank Condon); ph, Georges Benoit; art d, Charles Cadwallader.

Comedy **(PR:A MPAA:NR)**

NO MAN'S GOLD*** (1926) 6 reels FOX bw

Tom Mix *(Tom Stone)*, Eva Novak *(Jane Rogers)*, Frank Campeau *(Frank Healy)*, Forrest Taylor *(Wat Lyman)*, Harry Grippe *(Lefty Logan)*, Malcolm Waite *(Pete Krell)*, Mickey Moore *(Jimmy)*, Tom Santschi *(An Outlaw)*, Tony the Horse.

The usual good production values enhance this Mix western, which has the great cowboy star finding a man dying from gunshot wounds, who has torn into parts a map revealing the location of his mine. Mix is given part of the puzzle, as well as the man's little boy to care for. Later, at a rodeo, Mix protects a pretty young woman from the advances of an hombre who turns out to be one of the killers. The rest of the picture is crammed with action and stunts (some of which Tony the horse participates in) as Mix locates the mine and delivers justice to the murderers.

d, Lewis Seiler; w, John Stone (based on the novel *Dead Man's Gold* by J. Allen Dunn); ph, Dan Clark.

Western **(PR:A MPAA:NR)**

NO MAN'S LAND (SEE: NO MAN'S LAW, 1927)

NO MAN'S LAW*** (1927) 7 reels HR/Pathe bw (AKA: NO MAN'S LAND)

Rex the Wonder Horse, Barbara Kent *(Toby Belcher)*, Jimmy Finlayson *(Jack Belcher)*, Theodore von Eltz *(Spider O'Day)*, Oliver Hardy *(Sharkey Nye)*.

A wild horse protects the mine of an old sourdough and his foster daughter from the nasty Hardy, who is out to get it. Interesting western featured Hal Roach's famous wonder horse, Rex, with two of his truly wonderful comedians, Finlayson and Hardy.

d, Fred Jackman; w, Frank Butler (based on a story by F. Richard Jones); ph, Floyd Jackman, George Stevens.

Western **Cas.** **(PR:A MPAA:NR)**

NO MAN'S WOMAN*** (1921) 5 reels Helen Gibson/Associated-Photoplays bw

Helen Gibson *(The Girl)*, Edwin Coxen *(The Man)*, Leo Maloney *(Cullen)*.

Serious western has a man searching for his wife and child, who were abducted by gambler Maloney. After a time, his path crosses that of the young woman who tried in vain to save his wife's life, and has been caring for his child ever since. But when the man discovers she's a woman of the dance halls, he berates her terribly. At this point, Maloney shows up and is killed in a whale of a fight. And the man, now realizing the goodness of this victim of circumstances, asks her to become the permanent mother of his child.

d, Wayne Mack, Leo Maloney; w, Ford I. Bebe (based on a story by L. V. Jefferson).

Western/Drama **(PR:A MPAA:NR)**

NO MORE WOMEN** $^{1}/_{2}$ (1924) 6 reels Associated Authors/Allied bw

Matt Moore *(Peter Maddox)*, Madge Bellamy *(Peggy Van Dyke)*, Kathleen Clifford, *(Daisy Crenshaw)*, Clarence Burton *("Beef" Hogan)*, George Cooper *(Tex)*, H. Reeves-Smith *(Howard Van Dyke)*, Stanhope Wheatcroft *(Randolph Parker)*, Don the Dog.

Pleasant little comedy, well acted by Moore and Bellamy, about an oil millionaire's daughter who wins the love of a confirmed bachelor doing geological work in the area.

p, Elmer Harris; d, Lloyd Ingraham; w, Harris.

Comedy **(PR:A MPAA:NR)**

NO MOTHER TO GUIDE HER* (1923) 7 reels FOX bw

Genevieve Tobin *(Mary Boyd, as an Adult)*, John Webb Dillon *(Charles Pearson)*, Lolita Robertson *(His Wife)*, Katherine Downer *(Kathleen, Their Daughter)*, Dolores Rousse *(Kathleen, Grown Up)*, Frank Wunderlee *(Jim Boyd)*, Maude Hill *(His Wife)*, Ruth Sullivan *(Mary, His Daughter)*, J. D. Walsh *(The Grandfather)*, Jack Richardson *(James Walling)*, George Dewey *(Donald, His Son)*, Jack McLean *(Donald, Grown Up)*, Lillian Lee *(Walling's Sister)*, Marion Stevenson *(Widow Mills)*, William Quinn *(Billy, Her Son)*, Irving Hartley *(Billy, Grown Up)*.

Tricked into a mock marriage, Rousse flees to Europe with her friend, Tobin, when she learns the truth. They return with a baby and Tobin claims to be the mother to protect Rousse. Later, the rat who pulled the dastardly deed is killed in an automobile accident, the marriage is revealed to be legitimate after all, and Tobin accepts the proposal of the terribly decent chap who stuck by her through thick and thin.

d, Charles Horan; w, Michael O'Connor (based on the play by Lillian Mortimer); ph, Thomas Malloy.

Drama **(PR:C MPAA:NR)**

NO OTHER WOMAN** $^{1}/_{2}$ (1928) 6 reels FOX bw

Dolores Del Rio *(Carmelita Desano)*, Don Alvarado *(Maurice)*, Ben Bard *(Albert)*, Paulette Duval *(Mafalda)*, Rosita Marstini *(Carmelita's Aunt)*, Andre Lanoy *(Grand Duke Sergey)*.

Actor Lou Tellegen, who appeared opposite Sara Bernhardt in 1912, took a crack at directing in this picture and did rather well. It's all about a Frenchman who loses his South American sweetheart to a fortune-hunting rotter, but later wins her back after most of her fortune is dissipated.

d, Lou Tellegen; w, Jessie Burns, Bernard Vorhaus (based on a story by Polan Banks); t, Katherine Hilliker, H. H. Caldwell; ph, Ernest Palmer, Paul Ivano; ed, Edwin Robbins.

Drama **(PR:A MPAA:NR)**

NO TRESPASSING** (1922) 7 reels Holtre/Hodkinson bw

Irene Castle *(Mabel Colton)*, Howard Truesdale *(James Colton)*, Emily Fitzroy *(Mrs. James Colton)*, Ward Crane *(Roscoe Paine)*, Eleanor Barry *(Mrs. Paine)*, Blanche Frederici *(Dorinda)*, Charles Eldridge *(Lute)*, Leslie Stowe *(Capt. Dean)*, Betty Bouton *(Nellie Dean)*, Al Roscoe *(Victor Carver)*, Harry Fisher *(Simeon Eldridge)*, George Pauncefort *(George Davis)*.

Offbeat role for the sophisticated Castle finds the great dancing star playing a small town New England girl who wins the love of a kindly man of property, after his lands are saved from the clutches of an unscrupulous rotter.

d, Edwin L. Hollywood; w, Howard Irving Young (based on the novel *The Rise of Roscoe Paine* by Joseph Crosby Lincoln); ph, Robert A. Stuart; art d, E. Douglas Bingham.

Drama **(PR:A MPAA:NR)**

NO WOMAN KNOWS*** (1921) 7 reels UNIV bw

Mabel Julienne Scott *(Fanny Brandeis)*, Bernice Radom *(Fanny, as a Child)*, Earl Schenck *(Clarence Hyle)*, Stuart Holmes *(Michael Fenger)*, Max Davidson *(Ferdinand Brandeis)*, Snitz Edwards *(Herr Bauer)*, Grace Marvin *(Molly Brandeis)*, Danny Hoy *(Aloysius)*, E. A. Warren *(Rabbi Thalman)*, Raymond Lee *(Little Theodore Brandeis)*, Joseph Swickard *(The Great Schabelitz)*, Richard Cummings *(Father Fitzpatrick)*, Joseph Sterns *(Little Clarence Hyle)*, John Davidson *(Theodore Brandeis)*.

Ferber's novel, about a girl who sacrifices everything for her brother's European musical education, only to see him marry a German chorus girl and cause his mother's death from a broken heart, was well translated to the screen by Browning. The girl goes to Chicago, becomes a powerful businesswoman, and almost decides to live as the paramour of a millionaire, until her childhood sweetheart makes her realize the importance of spiritual matters.

d, Tod Browning; w, George Yohalem, Browning (based on the novel *Fanny Herself* by Edna Ferber); ph, William Fildew.

Drama **(PR:A MPAA:NR)**

NOBODY** (1921) 7 reels Roland West/AFN bw

Jewel Carmen *(Little Mrs. Smith)*, William Davidson *(John Rossmore)*, Kenneth Harlan *(Tom Smith)*, Florence Billings *(Mrs. Fallon)*, J. Herbert Frank *(Hedges)*, Grace Studiford *(Mrs. Rossmore)*, George Fawcett *(Hiram Swanzey)*, Lionel Pape *(Noron Ailsworth)*, Henry Sedley *(Rossmore's Secretary)*, Ida Darling *(Mrs. Van Cleek)*, Charles Wellesley *(Clyde Durand)*, William De Grasse *(Rossmore's Skipper)*, Riley Hatch *(The "Grouch" Juror)*.

Modest programmer has a jury deciding to let a man charged for murder go after they discover that a woman who was drugged, seduced, and blackmailed, actually did the killing. The jurors also swear to remain silent for the sake of the woman's husband and child.

p&d, Roland West; w, Charles H. Smith, West (based on a story by West); ph, Harry Fischbeck.

Mystery **(PR:A MPAA:NR)**

NOBODY HOME (SEE: OUT OF LUCK, 1919)

NOBODY'S BRIDE** (1923) 5 reels UNIV bw

Herbert Rawlinson *(Jimmy Nevins)*, Edna Murphy *(Doris Standish)*, Alice Lake *(Mary Butler)*, Harry Van Meter *(Morgan)*, Frank Brownlee *(Vesher Charley)*, Sidney Bracey *(Smithy, the Dip)*, Phillips Smalley *(Cyrus W. Hopkins)*, Robert Dudley *(Uncle Peter Standish)*, Lillian Langdon *(Mrs. Myrtle Standish)*.

After losing his fortune, Rawlinson falls in with a gang of crooks led by Lake. They trick him into driving the getaway car while they rob the home of his former fiancee, Murphy, during her wedding. But the bride gets cold feet, runs into Rawlinson, and begs him to take her away. The furious mobsters track them down and hold Murphy for ransom, but Lake, who has fallen in love with Rawlinson, intervenes and takes the fall.

d, Herbert Blache; w, Albert Kenyon (based on a story by Evelyn Campbell); ph, Virgil Miller.

Crime (PR:A MPAA:NR)

NOBODY'S CHILD** (1919, Brit.) 5 reels B&C/BUT bw

Jose Collins *(Francesca Samarjo)*, Godfrey Tearle *(Ernest d'Alvard)*, Ben Webster *(Joseph Samarjo)*, Christine Maitland *(Countess Althea)*, J. Fisher White *(Baron Troeffer)*, Saba Raleigh *(Baroness d'Alvard)*, Pardoe Woodman *(Antoine)*, Frances Wetherall *(Nita Samarjo)*.

In this British romance set in Corsica, a frustrated and lonely wife becomes a celebrated opera star when her husband leaves her alone while he cares for his sick mother.

p, Edward Godal; d, George Edwardes Hall; w, (based on Hall's play "The Whirlpool").

Romance (PR:A MPAA:NR)

NOBODY'S FOOL** 1/2 (1921) 5 reels UNIV bw

Marie Prevost *(Polly Gordon)*, Helen Harris *(Mary Hardy)*, Vernon Snively *(Vincent DePuyster)*, R. Henry Guy *(Dr. Hardy)*, Percy Challenger *(Joshua Alger)*, Harry Myers *(Artemis Alger)*, George Kuwa *(Ah Gone)*, Lucretia Harris *(Melinda)*, Lydia Titus *(Housekeeper)*.

Myers is very good as the misogynist author who writes a book proclaiming that women are unnecessary. Later he meets plain-Jane Prevost, who has blossomed into a knockout after inheriting half a million dollars. The presence of a handsome young suitor only primes his interest in the girl, and the picture ends with the unlikely couple locked in each other's arms.

d, King Baggot; w, Doris Schroeder (based on a story by Roy Clements); ph, Bert Glennon.

Comedy (PR:A MPAA:NR)

NOBODY'S KID** (1921) 5 reels R-C bw

Mae Marsh *(Mary Cary)*, Kathleen Kirkham *(Katherine Trent)*, Anne Schaefer *(Miss Bray)*, Maxine Elliott Hicks *(Pinky Moore)*, John Steppling *(Dr. Rudd)*, Paul Willis *(John Maxwell)*.

Pathos-filled little programmer about a girl's mistreatment in an orphanage and her ultimate triumph when she learns of her aristocratic British background. Marsh deserved much better.

d, Howard Hickman; w, Catherine Carr, Hickman (based on the story "Frequently Martha" by Kate Langley Bosher); ph, Robert Newhard.

Dramatic Comedy (PR:A MPAA:NR)

NOBODY'S MONEY*** (1923) 6 reels FP/PAR bw

Jack Holt *(John Webster)*, Wanda Hawley *(Grace Kendall)*, Harry Depp *(Eddie Maloney)*, Robert Schable *(Carl Russell)*, Walter McGrail *(Frank Carey)*, Josephine Crowell *(Mrs. Judson)*, Julia Faye *(Annette)*, Charles Clary *(Gov. Kendall)*, Will R. Walling *(Briscoe)*, Clarence Burton *(Kelly)*, Aileen Manning *(Prue Kimball)*, James Neill *(Miller)*.

In his first comedy role, Holt is fine as a lumber camp owner who poses as a book agent, falls in love with the governor's daughter, manages her father's re-election, and foils an attempt to politically railroad him.

d, Wallace Worsley; w, Beulah Marie Dix (based on the play by William Le Baron); ph, Charles E. Schoenbaum.

Drama/Comedy (PR:A MPAA:NR)

NOBODY'S WIDOW*** (1927) 7 reels DM/PDC bw

Leatrice Joy *(Roxanna Smith)*, Charles Ray *(Honorable John Clayton)*, Phyllis Haver *(Betty Jackson)*, David Butler *(Ned Stevens)*, Dot Farley *(Roxanna's Maid)*, Fritzi Ridgeway *(Mlle. Renee)*, Charles West *(Valet)*.

Joy marries a flirtatious English aristocrat (Ray) while traveling abroad. But when she discovers him kissing another girl on their wedding night, she heads for the U.S. and tells everyone that her husband is dead. Her friend (nicely played by Haver) arranges a meeting between them at her house, and the Britisher convinces Joy that his love is true.

d, Donald Crisp; w, Clara Beranger, Douglas Doty (based on the play by Avery Hopwood); ph, Arthur Miller.

Farce (PR:A MPAA:NR)

NOBODY'S WIFE** (1918) 5 reels UNIV bw

Louise Lovely *(Hope Ross)*, Hart Hoxie *(Jack Darling)*, Betty Schade *(Dancing Pete)*, A. G. Kenyon *(Tom Smythe)*, Grace McLean *(Betty Smythe)*.

Hoxie is a mounted policeman who sets out to get his man, and after learning he's the sheriff of a frozen tundra town, plots a robbery with him, and thereby exposes and arrests the varmint.

d, Edward J. Le Saint; w, Charles Kenyon (based on a story by F. Clark, R. N. Bradbury).

Adventure (PR:A MPAA:NR)

NO-GUN MAN, THE** 1/2 (1924) 5 reels Harry Garson/FBO bw

Lefty Flynn *(Robert Jerome Vincent)*, William Jack Quinn *(Bill Kilgore)*, Gloria Grey *(Carmen Harroway)*, Raymond Turner *(Obediah Abraham Lincoln Brown)*, Bob Reeves *(Oklahoma George)*, Harry McCabe *(Snooper)*, James Gordon Russell *(Tom West)*.

Pretty good western has Flynn, the former Yale football star, playing the president of a bank who infiltrates an outlaw gang to apprehend the men who robbed him earlier. He also wins the girl along the way.

d, Harry Garson; w, Dorothy Arzner, Paul Gangelin; ph, Louis W. Physioc.

Western (PR:A MPAA:NR)

NOISE IN NEWBORO, A** (1923) 6 reels Metro bw

Viola Dana *(Martha Mason)*, David Butler *(Ben Colwell)*, Eva Novak *(Anne Paisley)*, Allan Forest *(Buddy Wayne)*, Betty Francisco *(Leila Wayne)*, Alfred Allen *(Eben Paisley)*, Malcolm McGregor *(Harry Dixon)*, Joan Standing *(Dorothy Mason)*, Bert Woodruff *("Dad" Mason)*, Hank Mann.

Homely Dana leaves her small town and its derisive citizenry and moves to New York where she blossoms into a successful and attractive artist. Some time later, she returns to expose the corrupt practices of the man (Butler) who once treated her like dirt, and at the same time provide her former neighbors with a well-deserved raspberry.

d, Harry Beaumont; w, Rex Taylor (based on a story by Edgar Franklin); ph, John Arnold.

Drama/Comedy (PR:A MPAA:NR)

NOMADS OF THE NORTH*** (1920) 6 reels James Oliver Curwood/AFN bw

Betty Blythe *(Nanette Roland)*, Lon Chaney *(Raoul Challoner)*, Lewis Stone *(Cpl. O'Conner)*, Francis J. McDonald *(Buck McDougall)*, Melbourne McDowell *(Duncan McDougall)*, Spottiswoode Aitken *(Old Roland)*, Gordon Mullen.

Good programmer for kids, set in the North Woods, has a couple of adorable wild animals, a well-directed forest fire, and a mounted policeman allowing a man wrongly sought after by the law to share his freedom with the woman he secretly loves.

d, David M. Hartford; w, Hartford, James Oliver Curwood (based on a novel by Curwood); ph, Walter Griffin.

North Woods Cas. (PR:A MPAA:NR)

NONE BUT THE BRAVE** (1928) 6 reels FOX bw-c

Charles Morton *(Charles Stanton)*, Sally Phipps *(Mary)*, Sharon Lynn *(Paula)*, J. Farrell MacDonald *(John Craig)*, Tom Kennedy *(Noah)*, Billy Butts *(Freckles)*, Alice Adair *(Mary's Cook)*, Tyler Brooke *(Hotel Clerk)*, Earle Foxe, Gertrude Short.

A beauty pageant shot in technicolor is the one highlight of this otherwise routine comedy, about a college man (Morton) who becomes a lifeguard and falls in love with a pretty girl who runs a concession. Unconfirmed sources state that actress Dorothy Knapp was also part of the cast.

d, Albert Ray; w, Dwight Cummins, Frances Agnew (based on a story by Fred Stanley, James Gruen); t, Norman McLeod; ph, Charles Van Enger, Edward Estabrook (Technicolor); ed, Alex Troffey.

Comedy (PR:A MPAA:NR)

NONENTITY, THE* (1922, Brit.) 5 reels STOLL bw

Annette Benson *(Beryl Danvers)*, Hugh Buckler *(Lord Ronald Prior)*, Gordon Rickarts *(Maj. Fletcher)*. Daisy Campbell *(Mrs. Ellis)*, Bryan Powley *(Robert Ellis)*.

British empire saga set in India has a lord taking on the identity of a native in order to rescue a wealthy widow from the unscrupulous intentions of a gambling-addicted officer.

d&w, Sinclair Hill.

Drama (PR:A MPAA:NR)

NON-STOP FLIGHT, THE** (1926) 6 reels Emory Johnson/FBO bw

Knute Erickson *(Lars Larson)*, Marcella Daly *(Anna Larson)*, Virginia Fry *(Marie Larson)*, C. Ogden *(Jack Nevers)*, Frank Hemphill *(Jan Johnson)*, David Dunbar *(Capt. Holm)*, Peggy O'Neil *(Olga Nelson)*, Bob Anderson *(Eric Swanson)*, Otis Stantz, Skiles Ralph Pope *(Pilots)*.

This melodramatic chop suey—dealing with an abandoned Swedish sea captain, a shipwrecked maiden, Oriental lust for white womanhood, and red-blooded Americans to the rescue—was thrown together by Johnson to capitalize on the historic and headline-making non-stop flight of a group of U.S. Naval pilots made between San Francisco and Hawaii.

d, Emory Johnson; w, Emilie Johnson; ph, Gilbert Warrenton.

Adventure (PR:A MPAA:NR)

NOOSE, THE*** (1928) 8 reels FN bw

Richard Barthelmess *(Nickie Elkins)*, Montagu Love *(Buck Gordon)*, Robert E. O'Connor *(Jim Conley)*, Jay Eaton *(Tommy)*, Lina Basquette *(Dot)*, Thelma Todd *(Phyllis)*, Ed Brady *(Seth McMillan)*, Fred Warren *(Dave)*, Charles Giblyn *(Bill Chase)*, Alice Joyce *(Mrs. Bancroft)*, William Walling *(Warden)*, Robert T. Haines *(Governor)*, Ernest Hilliard *(Craig)*, Emile Chautard *(Priest)*, Romaine Fielding *(Judge)*, Yola D'Avril, Corliss Palmer, Kay English, Cecil Brunner, Janice Peters, Ruth Lord, May Atwood *(Cabaret Girls)*.

A top-notch cast supports Barthelmess in this tough and suspense-filled picture about a young hijacker who kills his father to prevent him from blackmailing his mother, who is now the wife of the governor. Great ending as Barthelmess walks the last mile, while his mother agonizes over whether to tell her husband the truth and beg for her son's life to be spared.

p, Henry Hobart; d, John Frances Dillon; w, H. H. Van Loan, Willard Mack, James

T. O'Donohoe (based on the play by Mack and the story by Van Loan); t, Garrett Graham; ph, James C. Van Trees; ed, Jack Dennis.

Drama/Crime **(PR:C MPAA:NR)**

NORTH OF HUDSON BAY*** (1923) 5 reels FOX bw

Tom Mix *(Michael Dane)*, Kathleen Key *(Estelle McDonald)*, Jennie Lee *(Dane's Mother)*, Frank Campeau *(Cameron McDonald)*, Eugene Pallette *(Peter Dane)*, Will Walling *(Angus McKenzie)*, Frank Leigh *(Jeffrey Clough)*, Fred Kohler *(Armond LeMoir)*.

On his way to northern Canada to join his brother Pallette, who has discovered gold, Mix falls in love with Key. They arrive to learn that Pallette has been murdered and that his partner, Walling, has been found guilty and is being punished in the local manner, which means a forced march across the tundra by armed guards until you die of hunger, thirst, or exhaustion. When Mix determines that Walling is innocent, he comes to his aid, is captured, and then subjected to the same ordeal himself. Of course he escapes, and after a terrific fight with a pack of wolves, chases the real killer (who turns out to be Key's uncle) down a rampaging river until the villain plunges to his death over a waterfall.

d, Jack Ford; w, Jules Furthman; ph, Don Clark.

Adventure **(PR:A MPAA:NR)**

NORTH OF NEVADA** (1924) 5 reels MON/FBO bw

Fred Thomson *(Tom Taylor)*, Hazel Keener *(Marion Ridgeway)*, Josef Swickard *(Mark Ridgeway)*, Joe Butterworth *(Red O'Shay)*, Chester Conklin *(Lem Williams)*, Taylor Graves *(Reginald Ridgeway)*, George Magrill *(Joe Deerfoot)*, Wilfred Lucas *(C. Hanaford)*, Silver King the Horse.

Below-average Thomson western has the popular cowboy star saving a ranch and the pretty girl who owns it from the clutches of a "college-educated, bad Indian." The best thing about this picture is the acting of Thomson's wonder horse, Silver King.

p, Harry J. Brown; d, Albert Rogell; w, Marion Jackson; ph, Ross Fisher.

Western **(PR:A MPAA:NR)**

NORTH OF THE RIO GRANDE*** (1922) 5 reels FP-LAS/PAR bw

Jack Holt *(Bob Haddington)*, Bebe Daniels *(Val Hannon)*, Charles Ogle *(Col. Haddington, Bob's Father)*, Alec B. Francis *(Father Hillaire)*, Will R. Walling *(John Hannon, Val's Father)*, Jack Carlyle *(Brideman, a Gambler)*, Fred Huntley *(Briston)*, Shannon Day *(Lola Sanchez)*, Edyth Chapman *(Belle Hannon)*, George Field *(Paul Perez)*, W. B. Clarke *(Clendenning)*.

Well-produced western has Holt, the son of a wealthy rancher, becoming a vigilante after his father is killed. He falls in love with Daniels (the actress put her real equestrian skills to good use in this picture), who saves him from being hanged at the last minute, after her dying father confesses to the crimes for which Holt has been blamed.

d, Joseph Henabery; w, William M. Ritchie (based on the novel *Val of Paradise* by Vingie E. Roe); ph, Faxon M. Dean.

Western **(PR:A MPAA:NR)**

NORTH OF 36**** (1924) 8 reels FP-LAS/PAR bw

Jack Holt *(Don McMasters)*, Ernest Torrence *(Jim Nabours)*, Lois Wilson *(Taisie Lockheart)*, Noah Beery *(Slim Rudabaugh)*, David Dunbar *(Dell Williams)*, Stephen Carr *(Cinquo Centavos)*, Guy Oliver *(Maj. McCoyne)*, William Carroll *(Sanchez)*, Clarence Geldert *(Col. Griswold)*, George Irving *(Pattison)*, Ella Miller *(Milly)*.

This big-budgeted western is worthy of comparison to the earlier classic, COVERED WAGON. The picture has everything—from the long, white parade of prairie schooners, to a large-scale Indian attack, as well as one of the best cattle drives and stampedes ever filmed.

d, Irvin Willat; w, James Shelley Hamilton (based on the novel by Emerson Hough); ph, Alfred Gilks.

Western **(PR:A MPAA:NR)**

NORTH WIND'S MALICE, THE* (1920) 6 reels Rex Beach/Goldwyn bw

Tom Santschi *(Roger)*, Joe King *(Carter)*, Henry West *(Harkness)*, William H. Strauss *(Abe)*, Vera Gordon *(Rachel)*, Walter Abell *(Tom)*, Edna Murphy *(Dorothy)*, Dorothy Wheeler *(Malice)*, Jack Crosby, Julia Stuart.

A lot of characters come and go in this confusing film about a frozen tundra couple who argue, separate, and then get together after the birth of their child. The picture's only bright spots are an early movie appearance by Abell, and some clever comedy in the presence of Gordon and Strauss as a Jewish couple who overcome some pretty heavy odds.

d, Carl Harbaugh, Paul Bern; w, (based on a story by Rex Beach); ph, Lucien Tainguy.

North Woods **(PR:A MPAA:NR)**

NORTHERN CODE** (1925) 6 reels GOTH/LUM bw

Robert Ellis *(Louis Le Blanc)*, Eva Novak *(Marie La Fane)*, Francis McDonald *(Raoul La Fane)*, Josef Swickard *(Pere Le Blanc)*, Jack Kenney *(Pierre De Val)*, Claire De Lorez *(Senorita Mendez)*, Raye Hampton *(Mama Le Blanc)*.

Frozen tundra programmer has Novak heading north after believing she killed her abusive husband. Before long she meets and marries nice guy Ellis, who understandably tosses her original hubby, McDonald, over a cliff when he tracks her down and attempts to muck things up.

d, Leon De La Mothe; w, Everett C. Maxwell; ph, Donald Parker.

North Woods **(PR:A MPAA:NR)**

NOSFERATU, A SYMPHONY OF HORROR

(SEE: NOSFERATU, THE VAMPIRE, 1922, Ger.)

NOSFERATU, A SYMPHONY OF TERROR

(SEE: NOSFERATU, THE VAMPIRE, 1922, Ger.)

NOSFURATU, EINE SYMPHONIE DES GRAUENS

(SEE: NOSFERATU, THE VAMPIRE, 1922, Ger.)

NOSFERATU, THE VAMPIRE****

(1922, Ger.) 5 reels Prana Co. bw (NOSFERATU, EINE SYMPHONIE DES GRAUENS; AKA: NOSFERATU, A SYMPHONY OF TERROR; NOSFERATU, A SYMPHONY OF HORROR)

Max Schreck *(Graf Orlok, Nosferatu)*, Alexander Granach *(Knock, an Estate Agent)*, Gustav von Wangenheim *(Hutter, His Employee)*, Greta Schroeder *(Ellen, His Wife)*, G. H. Schnell *(Harding, Shipowner)*, Ruth Landshoff *(Annie, His Wife)*, John Gottowt *(Prof. Bulwer)*, Gustav Botz *(Prof. Sievers)*, Max Nemetz *(Captain of the "Demeter")*, Wolfgang Heinz, Albert Venohr *(Seamen)*, Guido Herzfeld *(Innkeeper)*, Hardy von Francois *(Doctor)*.

The first Dracula (the title was changed to avoid copyright problems) is a wonderfully atmospheric work, made more eerie because of its authentic location shooting. The story tells of Von Wangenheim, a real estate clerk in the city of Bremen, who leaves his bride to conduct a little business in the distant Carpathian mountains with an "eccentric" client named Orlok (Schreck). The journey is a long one and the closer he gets the more frightening the people he encounters become. There are rumors of foul things which occur in and around the castle of Schreck and, towards the end of his trip, the coachman drops him off in the middle of nowhere, and vanishes. Another coach arrives, one that moves at great speed and should present a warning to the ambitious young man, because director Murnau shot it on negative stock. At last they reach the castle, and with the director's splendid sense of composition a mood of ghoulish neoreality is presented, which is guaranteed to make the skin of the most devoted horror fan crawl. A lot of credit for this must go to Schreck, who is no doubt the most loathsome-looking character in the history of cinema. As the young man enjoys a little repast while discussing the property his host is interested in purchasing in Bremen, he cuts his thumb while slicing some bread. The hideous one is up like a flash sucking on the startled traveler's thumb. But somehow Von Wangenheim overlooks this little quirk, bids his client a weary good night, and retires to his room. After a few evenings of blood-letting, the lad begins to get the picture. He discovers the coffin of Schreck and, though weakened, manages to escape. But the vampire, determined to reach Germany, has his casket checked aboard a Bremen-bound ship, and as the craft slowly makes its way the entire crew is stricken with the pestilence the evil one is carrying. All except the captain, whom the vampire desires to have for dinner. There is a scene here (where Schreck rises straight up from his coffin) which is unparalleled in the annals of movie horror. Schreck reaches the city on the ship of death, carries his casket to his new home, and there follows an epidemic in which people begin to die like flies. Von Wangenheim's wife (whose neck the vampire had earlier admired from a locket), however, saves Bremen, and perhaps the rest of the world as well, by giving herself to the monster, delaying him long enough for the sun's rays to destroy him. Compared to this remarkable version of the Dracula saga, the Tod Browning-Bela Lugosi 1931 adaptation is like watching Walt Disney.

d, F. W. Murnau; w, Henrik Galeen (based on the novel *Dracula* by Bram Stoker); t, Ben de Casseres; ph, Fritz Arno Wagner; set d, Albin Grau.

Horror **Cas.** **(PR:C MPAA:NR)**

NOT FOR SALE** (1924, Brit.) 7 reels STOLL bw

Mary Odette *(Annie Armstrong)*, Ian Hunter *(Martin Dering)*, Gladys Hamer *(Florrie)*, Mary Brough *(Mrs. Keane)*, Lionelle Howard *(Bertie Strangeways)*, Phyllis Lytton *(Virginia Strangeways)*, Edward O'Neill *(Earl of Rathbury)*, Mickey Brantford *(John Armstrong)*, Julie Kean *(Tibbles Armstrong)*, W. G. Saunders *(Sunny Jim)*, Jack Trevor *(Desmond North)*, Maud Gill *(Miss Carter)*, Minna Leslie *(Mrs. Lovell)*, Robert Vallis *(Roberts)*, Moore Marriott *(Solicitor)*, George Bellamy *(Boarder)*.

Ambitious, but typically dull British offering, about the disgraced son of an earl who takes a job as a chauffeur and then is sentenced to prison after being caught in a robbery he participated in to win the favor of the landlady with whom he has fallen in love.

d, W. P. Kellino; w, Lydia Hayward (based on a novel by Monica Ewer).

Drama **(PR:A MPAA:NR)**

NOT GUILTY** (1919, Brit.) 6 reels Windsor/Walturdaw bw

Kenelm Foss *(Sir Graham Carfax)*, Charles Vane *(Andrew McTaggart)*, Hayford Hobbs *(Donald McTaggart)*, Olive Atkinson *(Minnie Day)*, Barbara Everest *(Hetty Challis)*, Bert Wynne *(Tom Dent)*, Evelyn Harding *(Matron)*, Philip Hewland *(Dillingham)*.

British comedy about a lawyer who tricks a mean and miserly millionaire into making a substantial charitable donation, and then defends himself successfully at the ensuing trial.

d, Arrigo Bocchi; w, Kenelm Foss.

Comedy **(PR:A MPAA:NR)**

NOT GUILTY* (1921) 7 reels Whitman Bennett/AFN bw

Sylvia Breamer *(Elsa Chetwood)*, Richard Dix *(Paul Ellison/Arthur Ellison)*, Molly Malone *(Margy Ellison)*, Elinor Hancock *(Mrs. Ellison)*, Herbert Prior *(Newell Craig)*, Lloyd Whitlock *(Frank Mallow)*, Alberta Lee *(Martha, the Chaperon)*, Charles West *(Herbert Welch)*, Alice Forbes *(Virginia Caldwell)*.

Confusing mystery has Dix changing identities with his twin brother (whom he feels he let down, leading him to commit a murder) after falling in love with the beautiful Breamer. Dix assumes the guilt for this, and five years later, when Breamer meets Dix's twin, she believes him to be Dix and the couple become engaged. At the same time, Dix is spotted by Prior, who decides to turn him over to the police and collect reward money to cover his gambling debts. The picture comes to less than a crashing conclusion when Prior confesses to being the real killer on his deathbed. A nice performance by Dix is the film's only bright spot.

d, Sidney A. Franklin; w, J. Grubb Alexander, Edwin Bower Hesser (based on the novel *Parrot and Company* by Harold MacGrath).

Drama/Mystery **(PR:A MPAA:NR)**

NOT MY SISTER*** (1916) 5 reels Kay-Bee/TRI bw

Bessie Barriscale *(Grace Tyler)*, William Desmond *(Michael Arnold)*, Franklin Ritchie *(John Marshall)*, Alice Taaffe *(Ruth Tyler)*, Louise Brownell *(Mrs. Tyler)*.

Good Sullivan-Montgomery script has Barriscale, a well-bred young girl, becoming an artist's model when her family fortune is lost. She is seduced and becomes pregnant by a sculptor who flees to Europe, forcing her to marry a man she doesn't love. Years later, the artist returns and begins the same routine all over again with his victim's younger sister. Barriscale rushes to his studio to prevent a second tragedy, followed closely by her husband who has become suspicious. A fight ensues in which Barriscale kills her betrayer, but her husband is accused of the crime. At his trial, the sisters relate the true facts, the innocent man is exonerated, and Barriscale becomes aware of the love she feels for her husband for the first time.

d, Charles Giblyn; w, James Montgomery, C. Gardner Sullivan.

Drama **(PR:A MPAA:NR)**

NOT QUITE A LADY** (1928, Brit.) 7 reels BIP/Wardour bw

Mabel Poulton *(Ethel Borridge)*, Janet Alexander *(Mrs. Cassilis)*, Barbara Gott *(Mrs. Borridge)*, Maurice Braddell *(Geoffrey Cassilis)*, Dorothy Bartlam *(Mabel Marchmont)*, George Bellamy *(Maj. Warrington)*, Gibb McLaughlin *(Vicar)*, Sam Wilkinson *(Mr. Borridge)*.

British comedy about an aristocratic woman who attempts to discourage a working class girl from marrying her son by throwing the most boring house party imaginable.

d, Thomas Bentley; w, Eliott Stannard (based on the play "The Cassilis Engagement" by St. John Hankin).

Comedy **(PR:A MPAA:NR)**

NOT SO LONG AGO*** (1925) 7 reels FP-LAS/PAR bw

Betty Bronson *(Betty Dover)*, Ricardo Cortez *(Billy Ballard)*, Edwards Davis *(Jerry Flint)*, Julia Swayne Gordon *(Mrs. Ballard)*, Laurence Wheat *(Sam Robinson)*, Jacquelin Gadsdon *(Ursula Kent)*, Dan Crimmins *(Michael Dover)*.

Turn-of-the-century romance has the starry-eyed daughter of a struggling inventor taking a job in the home of a wealthy widow, falling in love with her son and winning his heart, after her father's horseless carriage explodes on its trial run. Director Olcott manages to instill a nice sense of nostalgia into this gentle comedy, and Bronson delivers her usual fine performance.

d, Sidney Olcott; w, Violet Clark (based on the play by Arthur Richman); ph, James Wong Howe.

Comedy/Romance **(PR:A MPAA:NR)**

NOTHING BUT THE TRUTH* (1920) 6 reels Taylor Holmes/Metro bw

Taylor Holmes *(Robert Bennett)*, Elsie Mackaye *(Gwendolyn Gerald)*, Ned A. Sparks *(The Monocle Man)*, Marcelle Carroll *(Dolly)*, Ben Hendricks *(Commodore Dan)*, Edna Phillips *(Mrs. Commodore Dan)*, Radcliffe Steele *(The Hammer-Thrower)*, Elizabeth Garrison *(Mrs. Clarence)*, Charles Craig *(Mr. Clarence)*, Colin Campbell *(Dickie)*, Beth Franklyn.

This popular stage success lost most of its appeal and almost all of its laughs in transition to the screen. And, as such, it exists only as a vehicle for Holmes that, unfortunately, just failed to work.

d, David Kirkland; w, Katherine Speer, Kirkland (based on a story by Frederick S. Isham and the play by James Montgomery); ph, Jacob Badaracco.

Comedy **(PR:A MPAA:NR)**

NOTHING TO WEAR*** (1928) 6 reels COL bw

Jacqueline Logan *(Jackie Standish)*, Theodore Von Eltz *(Phil Standish)*, Bryant Washburn *(Tommy Butler)*, Jane Winton *(Irene Hawley)*, William Irving *(Detective)*, Edythe Flynn *(Maid)*.

Logan goes to see her former boy friend, Washburn, after her husband refuses to buy her a fur coat. When he changes his mind and picks out a beauty, Von Eltz sends it to his bride and she wrongly assumes it to be a gift from Washburn. Afraid her husband will find out, Logan has it delivered to her old flame, whose present lady friend thinks it's a token for her. Everybody ends up at the station house where the situation is finally worked out to the satisfaction of all.

p, Jack Cohn; d, Erle C. Kenton; w, Peter Milne; ph, Joseph Walker; ed, Ben Pivar; art d, Harrison Wiley.

Comedy **(PR:A MPAA:NR)**

NOTORIETY***

(1922) 8 reels L. Lawrence Weber-Bobby North/Apollo Trading bw

Maurine Powers *("Pigeon" Deering)*, Mary Alden *(Ann Boland)*, Rod La Rocque *(Arthur Beal)*, George Hackathorne *("Batty")*, Richard Travers *(Tom Robbins)*, J. Barney Sherry *(Horace Wedderburn)*, Mona Lisa *(Dorothy Wedderburn)*, Anders Randolf *(The Theatrical Agent)*, John Goldsworthy *(Van Dyke Gibson)*, Ida Watterman *(Mrs. Beal)*, William Gudgeon *(The Hired Man)*.

Director-writer Nigh enjoyed a long track record of successful programmers, including this one in which slum girl Powers witnesses a society murder and then confesses to the crime for the attention it will bring her. At the trial, La Rocque, a prominent lawyer, "clears her name." Later, she decides on a theatrical career against his advice and La Rocque tricks her into visiting his country home on the pretense that auditions are to be held there. Upon arriving, she is "attacked" by a hired man who claims to be attracted by her celebrity status. Her benefactor quickly comes to her rescue, however, after which Powers decides to trade in the bright lights of Broadway for the role of counselor's wife.

d&w, William Nigh; ph, James Diamond.

Drama **(PR:A MPAA:NR)**

NOTORIOUS LADY, THE** (1927) 7 reels Sam E. Rork/FN bw

Lewis Stone *(Patrick Marlowe/John Carew)*, Barbara Bedford *(Mary Marlowe/Mary Brownlee)*, Ann Rork *(Kameela)*, Earl Metcalfe *(Anthony Walford)*, Francis McDonald *(Manuela Silvera)*, Grace Carlyle *(Marcia Rivers)*, E. J. Ratcliffe *(Dr. Digby Grant)*, J. Gunnis Davis *(William)*.

Average programmer has Stone killing a man he suspects is having an affair with his wife, Bedford. She lies about the romance in order to save her husband, and Stone takes off for the diamond fields of Africa. When word reaches England that her spouse has been killed, Bedford sets off for the Dark Continent to learn the truth. On the voyage she meets Metcalfe, who falls madly in love with her. Later, Stone shows up alive and circumstances throw the rivals together. But during a native attack, Metcalfe demands that Stone escape, while he covers him with his weapon. The Englishman returns just in time to save the hero and finally comes to realize the depth of his wife's love, bringing about a reconciliation.

d, King Baggot; w, Jane Murfin (based on the play "The River" by Patrick Hastings); ph, Tonio Gaudio.

Drama **(PR:A MPAA:NR)**

NOTORIOUS MISS LISLE, THE***

(1920) 5 reels Katherine MacDonald/FN bw

Katherine MacDonald *(Gaenor Lisle)*, Nigel Barrie *(Peter Garstin)*, Margaret Campbell *(Mrs. Lisle)*, Ernest Joy *(Maj. Lisle)*, William Clifford *(Craven)*, Dorothy Cumming *(Mrs. Lyons)*.

MacDonald, who was known as "America's Beauty," was often accused of being all looks and no talent. But she proved her critics wrong (as Mary Pickford did in STELLA MARIS) in this film about a woman wrongly named correspondent in a sensational London divorce case, who marries for love in Brittany and then leaves her husband to save his honor. After her flight, she is seriously injured in an accident, and the husband, who never lost faith, returns to London, vindicates her good name, and finally provides his wife with a life of happiness.

d&w, James Young (based on the novel by Mrs. Baillie Reynolds); ph, Joseph Brotherton; art d, Milton Menasco.

Drama **(PR:A MPAA:NR)**

NOTORIOUS MRS. CARRICK, THE** (1924, Brit.) 6 reels STOLL bw

Disa *(Sybil Tregarthen)*, Cameron Carr *(David Carrick)*, A. B. Imeson *(Tony Tregarthen)*, Sydney Folker *(David Arman)*, Gordon Hopkirk *(Gerald Rosario)*, Jack Denton *(Allen Richards)*, Peggy Lynn *(Honor Tregarthen)*, Basil Saunders *(Inspector Samson)*, Arthur Lumley *(Owen Lawson)*.

In this British mystery, a woman who has remarried well finds herself in the awkward position of being blackmailed by her former husband, who threatens to reveal the truth about her murdering an ex-lover.

d, George Ridgwell; w, (based on the novel *Pools of the Past* by Charles Proctor).

Mystery **(PR:A MPAA:NR)**

NOTORIOUS MRS. SANDS, THE* (1920) 5 reels R-C bw

Bessie Barriscale *(Mary Ware)*, Forrest Stanley *(Ronald Cliffe)*, Dorothy Cumming *(Dulcie Charrerts)*, Harry Myers *(Grey Sands)*, Ben Alexander *(The Child)*.

Routine society drama about an impoverished woman of former means who desires to marry her daughter off to a millionaire. The girl, however, is in love with an earnest, hard-working young fellow who, by the final reel, makes his own fortune and returns his mother-in-law to the lifestyle she once enjoyed.

d, William Christy Cabanne; w, (based on a story by M. B. Havey).

Drama **(PR:A MPAA:NR)**

NOW WE'RE IN THE AIR* 1/2** (1927) 6 reels PAR bw

Wallace Beery *(Wally)*, Raymond Hatton *(Ray)*, Russell Simpson *(Lord Abercrombie McTavish)*, Louise Brooks *(Grisette Chelaine)*, Emile Chautard *(Mons. Chelaine)*, Malcolm Waite *(Prof. Saenger)*, Duke Martin *(Top Sergeant)*.

Beery and Hatton score again in this very funny film which has the boys joining the U.S. Flying Corps (in one of the first films to use extensive aerial gags) as a means of nailing their Scotch grandfather's fortune. During the course of the action, they blow over to the German lines in a circus balloon and are mistakenly regarded by the enemy as war heros. They are sent back to spy on the U.S. side, where they are captured and nearly shot, but in the end manage to work everything out. A definitely happy addition to this most entertaining motion picture is the presence of the incomparable Brooks, of whom Variety wrote, "Louise Brooks has an altogether pale and negative part, but this snappy young brunette justifies herself by just being present in any visible capacity."

d, Frank Strayer; w, Tom J. Geraghty (based on a story by Monte Brice, Keene Thompson); t, George Marion, Jr.; ph, Harry Perry.

Comedy **(PR:A MPAA:NR)**

NTH COMMANDMENT, THE*** (1923) 8 reels COS/PAR bw

Colleen Moore *(Sara Juke)*, James Morrison *(Harry Smith)*, Eddie Phillips *(Jimmie Fitzgibbons)*, Charlotte Merriam *(Angine Sprunt)*, George Cooper *(Max Plute)*.

Moore is a department store clerk who marries Morrison, a young man with consumption, in spite of her attraction to a handsome and successful writer. The couple struggle against the disease and poverty and manage to defeat both in the end.

d, Frank Borzage; sup&w, Frances Marion (based on the story by Fannie Hurst); ph, Chester Lyons.

Drama **(PR:A MPAA:NR)**

NUGGET NELL*** (1919) 5 reels New Art/PAR bw

Dorothy Gish *(Nugget Nell)*, David Butler *(Big-Hearted Jim)*, Raymond Cannon *(The City Chap)*, Regina Sarle *(Chield)*, James Farley *(1st Badman)*, Bob Fleming *(2nd Ditto)*, Wilbur Higby *(Nell's Uncle)*, Emily Chichester *(The Ingenue)*.

NUGGET NELL gives Gish, one of the screen's most gifted comediennes, the opportunity to lampoon the western film genre. She is quite wonderful as the gun-toting cafe owner who falls for an Easterner, but then drops him for the cowboy who really loves her when she spots the yellow streak running down his back. There are some weak spots in the script, but Gish and director Clifton almost make you overlook them.

d, Elmer Clifton; w, Hugh R. Osborne (based on a story by John R. Cornish); ph, John Leezer.

Comedy/Western **(PR:A MPAA:NR)**

NO. 5 JOHN STREET** (1921, Brit.) 6 reels Astra bw

Zena Dare *(Tilda)*, Mary Odette *(Celia Ridler)*, Lionelle Howard *(Seaton Ridler)*, Randle Ayrton *(I. Azreal)*, Roy Travers *(Sir Charles Pounds)*, Charles Danvers *(Sir Marmaduke Ridler)*, James McWilliams *(Stubbs)*, Peggy Bayfield *(Nance)*.

British drama about a young man who poses as a worker at the soap factory he has inherited and decides that the appalling conditions must be changed. Later a flower girl saves him from an anarchist, and he rewards her by making her his wife.

p, H. W. Thompson; d&w, Kenelm Foss (based on a novel by Richard Whiteing).

Drama **(PR:A MPAA:NR)**

NUMBER 17*** (1920) 5 reels FOX bw

George Walsh, Mildred Reardon, Charles Mussett, Lillian Beck, Louis Wolheim, Harold Thomas, Charles Slattery, Jack Newton, Spencer Charters, Lillian Griffith.

Walsh is a newspaper reporter who infiltrates the underworld and saves a girl and her father from the wrath of several tong organizations, which the old boy antagonized in China. There are some great gang war sequences, with Walsh, of course, beating everyone involved.

d, George A. Beranger; w, (based on a story by Louis Tracy); ph, Charles Gilson.

Adventure **(PR:A MPAA:NR)**

NURSE MARJORIE* 1/2 (1920) 5 reels Realart bw

Mary Miles Minter *(Nurse Marjorie)*, Clyde Fillmore *(John Danbury)*, George Periolat *(Mr. Danbury, Sr.)*, Mollie McConnell *(Mrs. Danbury)*, Frank Leigh *(Lord Douglas Fitztrevor)*, Vera Lewis *(Duchess of Donegal)*, Arthur Hoyt *(Duke of Donegal)*, Frankie Lee *(Dick)*, Lydia Yeamans Titus *(Biddy O'Mulligan)*.

Minter turns in a good performance and does quite well with her comedy touches in this otherwise stuffy and boring picture about an aristocratic nurse who falls in love with and marries a parliamentary leader of the Labor Party, to the great chagrin of her family.

d, William Desmond Taylor; w, Julia Crawford Ivers (based on the play by Israel Zangwill); ph, J. C. Van Trees.

Drama **(PR:A MPAA:NR)**

NUT, THE* 1/2** (1921) 6 reels Douglas Fairbanks/UA bw

Douglas Fairbanks *(Charlie Jackson)*, Marguerite De La Motte *(Estrell Wynn)*, William Lowery *(Philip Feeney)*, Gerald Pring *(Gentleman George)*, Morris Hughes *(Pernelius Vanderbrook, Jr.)*, Barbara La Marr *(Claudine Dupree)*, Charles Chaplin *(Himself)*.

Fairbanks' last contemporary comedy before entering exclusively into the world of costume fantasy is a wonderful combination of camera trickery, illusion, and inspired comedic imagery. He plays a wealthy, happy-go-lucky inventor type, who falls in love with De La Motte, a society girl dedicated to the thought that underprivileged children can become outstanding citizens if allowed to spend time in the homes of the affluent. Naturally Fairbanks sets out to assist her through his personal contacts and limitless energy, but one thing after another goes wrong, which provides the star the opportunity to put into play a number of bizarre comedy situations. One of these has Fairbanks throwing a party for a bunch of swells, where he entertains the crowd with his impersonations of a series of historical figures, ending with Charlie Chaplin. The changes are executed with breathtaking speed, though none of them is in the least believable, including the latter, and the punch line is that they have all actually been performed by Chaplin himself in a cameo appearance. The entire picture has this surrealistic feeling about it, and is a delight to view over and over again. Of course it also has its sense of melodrama, whereby Fairbanks is given the chance to put his athletic talents to use by saving the heroine from the clutches of the villainous Lowery in the end.

p, Douglas Fairbanks; d, Theodore Reed; w, William Parker, Elton Thomas [Fairbanks], Lotta Woods (based on a story by Kenneth Davenport); ph, William McGann, Harry Thorpe.

Comedy **Cas.** **(PR:A MPAA:NR)**

NUT-CRACKER, THE** (1926) 6 reels Samuel S. Hutchinson/AEX bw

Edward Everett Horton *(Horatio Slipaway)*, Mae Busch *(Martha Slipaway)*, Harry Myers *(Oscar Briggs)*, Thomas Ricketts *(Isaac Totten)*, Martha Mattox *(Julia Trotten)*, George Kuwa *(Saki)*, Katherine Lewis *(Hortense)*, Albert Priscoe *(Senor Gonzales)*, George Periolat *(Senor Gomez)*.

Horton is so henpecked that when a streetcar hits him, he fakes amnesia and invests the $500 insurance settlement in the market, making a killing. He then takes on the identity of a South American millionaire, and when his wife, who hears about her missing husband's Latin lookalike, fixes herself up and sets out to meet him, Horton takes one look at what a knockout she's become, quickly regains his memory, and their marriage takes on new life.

d, Lloyd Ingraham; w, Madge Myton (based on the novel by Frederick Stewart Isham); ph, Jack MacKenzie.

Comedy **(PR:A MPAA:NR)**

OAKDALE AFFAIR, THE** (1919) 5 reels WORLD bw

Evelyn Greeley, Corene Uzzell, Charles Mackay, Reginald Denny, Maude Turner Gordon, Ben Johnson, Eric Dalton, Albert Hart, Eric Mayne, Mona Kingsley, Frank Joyner, Eddie Sturgis, Frank Nelson, Edward Elkas.

Predictable story of a girl who runs away from her prosperous home dressed as a boy, rather than marry the wimp her parents have selected for her. She experiences plenty of adventures and joins up with a poet-tramp, who is actually a world famous novelist doing a little research. Of course the writer falls in love with his little friend after seeing her in a dress, and the picture's final two titles read, "Life is the road to anywhere; will you take it with me?"—her answer, "I'll take the road to anywhere anytime with you."

d, Oscar Apfel; w, (based on a story by Edgar Rice Burroughs); ph, Alfred Gondolfi.

Drama **(PR:A MPAA:NR)**

OATH-BOUND** (1922) 5 reels FOX bw

Dustin Farnum *(Lawrence Bradbury)*, Ethel Grey Terry *(Constance Hastings)*, Fred Thomson *(Jim Bradbury)*, Maurice B. Flynn *(Ned Hastings)*, Norman Selby *(Hicks)*, Aileen Pringle *(Alice)*, Bob Perry *(Gang Leader)*, Herschel Mayall *(Capt. Steele)*.

Nothing special about this B feature which has Farnum, the wealthy owner of a shipping company, attempting to break up a gang of silk smugglers who are using his boats, and, to his shock, discovering that the ringleader is his brother.

d, Bernard J. Durning; w, Jack Strumwasser, Edward J. Le Saint (based on a story by Le Saint); ph, Don Short.

Mystery **(PR:A MPAA:NR)**

OBEY YOUR HUSBAND** (1928) 6 reels Morris R. Schlank/ANCH bw

Gaston Glass *(Arthur Reade)*, Dorothy Dawn *(Joyce Kennedy)*, Alice Lake *(Belle)*, Henry Sedley *(Leland Houghton)*, Robert Homans *(Stephens)*, Robert Elliott *(Mr. Kennedy)*, Jack Johnston *(District Attorney)*, Joseph Burke *(Jim)*.

Director Hunt kept this predictable programmer—all about a young bride who takes marriage lightly until she learns her lesson by becoming implicated in the murder of a gambler—moving right along. Nothing to rave about, but nonetheless an acceptable diversion.

d, Charles J. Hunt; w, Arthur Hoerl; ph, Robert E. Cline; ed, William Holmes.

Drama **(PR:A MPAA:NR)**

OBJECT—ALIMONY*** (1929) 7 reels COL bw

Lois Wilson *(Ruth Rutledge)*, Hugh Allan *(Jimmy Rutledge)*, Ethel Grey Terry *(Mrs. Carrie Rutledge)*, Douglas Gilmore *(Renaud Graham)*, Roscoe Karns *(Al Bryant)*, Carmelita Geraghty *(Mabel)*, Dickie Moore *(Jimmy Rutledge, Jr.)*, Jane Keckley *(Boardinghouse Owner)*, Thomas Curran *(Philip Stone)*.

Nicely crafted little drama about a poor girl (Wilson) who marries her boss (Allan) against his mother's will, becomes pregnant, and is wrongly accused of being unfaithful. Driven from her husband's home, she takes a room in a boardinghouse, becomes friendly with an aspiring writer (Gilmore) and relates her tale of woe. The talented scribe turns the story into a best-selling novel, as well as a hit play, and Allan, repentant after reading and seeing both, goes to the little mother and begs to be taken back.

p, Jack Cohn; d, Scott R. Dunlap; w, Peter Milne, Sig Herzig (based on a story by Elmer Harris); ph, Joseph Walker; ed, Ben Pivar; art d, Harrison Wiley.

Drama **(PR:A MPAA:NR)**

OCCASIONALLY YOURS** (1920) 5 reels Gasnier/R-C bw

Lew Cody *(Bruce Sands)*, Betty Blythe *(Bunny Winston)*, Elinor Fair *(Audrey Woodward)*, J. Barney Sherry *(John Woodward)*, Lloyd Hamilton *(Bob Hale)*, Lillian Rambeau *(Mrs. Lydia Parsons)*, Gertrude Astor *(Mona)*, Yvonne Gardelle *(Model)*, William Quinn *(Parker)*, Cleo Ridgely *(Gossip)*, Dorothy Wallace, Boots the Dog, Julius the Mouse.

Handsome Cody deserved much better material than the Robertson-Cole people gave him in productions such as this one about a "lady killer" who promises a girl on her deathbed that he will marry her, only to have the delighted female survive.

d, James W. Horne; w, H. Tipton Steck (based on a story by Elmer Forst); ph, J. A. Du Bray.

Comedy/Drama **(PR:A MPAA:NR)**

OCTOBER (SEE: TEN DAYS THAT SHOOK THE WORLD, 1927, USSR)

ODDS AGAINST HER, THE** (1919, Brit.) 6 reels Barker/JUR bw

Milton Rosmer *(Leo Strathmore)*, Edmee Dormeuil *(Nanette)*, Lorna Della *(Lolita Rios)*, George Foley *(The Baron)*, Thomas H. MacDonald, Nancy Benyon, Vernon Davidson, Andre Randall.

British thriller has an orphaned girl, who grows up to become a successful dancer, preventing a Spanish golddigger and a German baron from pulling a fast deal on her guardian.

p, Jack W. Smith; d, Alexander Butler.

Drama **(PR:A MPAA:NR)**

ODYSSEY OF THE NORTH, AN*½ (1914) 6 reels Bosworth bw

Hobart Bosworth *(Nass)*, Rhea Haines *(Unga)*, Gordon Sackville *(Axel Bunderson)*.

Bosworth took his company on location to shoot this Klondike saga of three people who face the treacheries of the North with only one (Bosworth) returning to tell the tale. Even though it is based on a well-known story by London, the picture's narrative is difficult to follow and definitely does not hold up on its own.

d, Hobart Bosworth; w, (based on a story by Jack London).

North Woods **(PR:A MPAA:NR)**

OFF THE HIGHWAY*** (1925) 8 reels Hunt Stromberg/PDC bw

William V. Mong *(Caleb Frey/Tatterly)*, Marguerite De La Motte *(Ella Tarrant)*, John Bowers *(Donald Brett)*, Charles Gerard *(Hector Kindon)*, Gino Corrado *(Rabbitt)*, Buddy Post *(Grizzly Bear)*, Joseph Swickard *(Master)*, Smoke Turner *(Student)*.

Good comedy programmer about a man who disinherits his nephew (Bowers) because the lad chooses to be an artist rather than a businessman. Then, when his butler (who is the spitting image of him) drops dead, the millionaire assumes his identity, watches another nephew squander a portion of the fortune, moves in with the artist, and in short order sees to it that the lad with the brushes gets the money. He also wins the girl, nicely played by De La Motte.

d, Tom Forman; sup, Hunt Stromberg; w, Dorothy Farnum (based on the novel *Tatterly, the Story of a Dead Man* by Thomas Gallon).

Comedy **(PR:A MPAA:NR)**

OFFENDERS, THE* (1924) 5 reels Margery Wilson/IP bw

Margery Wilson, Percy Helton.

Shot on location in Vermont, this low-budget film about a girl wrongly accused of murder who is cleared when a half-wit who witnessed the crime is cured, looks as if it was produced using a cast of local amateurs.

d, Fenwicke L. Holmes; w, (based on a story by Katherine Holmes).

Drama **(PR:A MPAA:NR)**

OFFICER JIM* (1926) 5 reels Mrs. Frank J. Hart/Lee-Bradford bw

Joseph Swickard, Gloria Grey, Roy Hughes.

This simple programmer—about a cop who foils a bank robbery, eventually nails the gang, and is rewarded by the love of the banker's beautiful daughter—is proof that *anybody* with the money can produce a motion picture.

d, Wilbur McGaugh.

Crime **(PR:A MPAA:NR)**

OFF-SHORE PIRATE, THE*½ (1921) 6 reels Metro bw

Viola Dana *(Ardita Farnam)*, Jack Mulhall *(Toby Moreland)*, Edward Jobson *(Uncle John Farnam)*, Edward Cecil *(Ivan Nevkova)*.

It took a lot of padding to produce a feature film from this Fitzgerald short story about a girl (Dana) who is tricked by her uncle into falling in love with a "real" American (Mulhall), in order to save her from the clutches of a fortune-hunting Russian.

d, Dallas M. Fitzgerald; w, Waldemar Young (based on the short story by F. Scott Fitzgerald); ph, John Arnold, Lt. Joseph Waddell; art d, A. F. Mantz.

Comedy/Drama **(PR:A MPAA:NR)**

OH, BOY!½** (1919) 6 reels A. Capellani/Pathe bw

June Caprice *(Lou Ellen Carter)*, Creighton Hale *(George Budd)*, Zena Keefe *(Jackie Sampson)*, Flora Finch *(Miss Penelope Budd)*, W. H. Thompson *(Judge Daniel Carter)*, Grace Reals *(Mrs. Carter)*, Joseph Conyers *(Constable Simms)*, J. K. Murray *(Dean of Richguys College)*, Maurice Bennett "Lefty" Flynn, Ben Taggart, Charles Hartley, Irene Tams.

Decent comedy has a young couple getting married—to the great chagrin of her parents and his aunt, who are teetotalers—because the lad has been known to drink a little. A friend of the girl, who is quite an actress, induces the bride's father to try some spirits, and the picture ends with all of the objecting parties (including the aunt) tying one on, while the kids slip away to their own pleasures.

d&w, Albert Capellani (based on the play by P. G. Wodehouse, Guy Bolton); ph, Lucien Andriot.

Comedy **(PR:A MPAA:NR)**

OH, DOCTOR*** (1924) 7 reels UNIV bw

Reginald Denny *(Rufus Billups, Jr.)*, Mary Astor *(Dolores Hicks)*, Otis Harlan *(Mr. Clinch)*, William V. Mong *(Mr. McIntosh)*, Tom Ricketts *(Mr. Peck)*, Lucille Ward *(Aunt Beulah Rush)*, Mike Donlin *(Buzz Titus)*, Clarence Geldert *(Dr. Seaver)*, Blanche Payson *(Osteopath)*, George Kuwa *(Chang)*, Martha Mattox *("Death Watch" Mary Schulta)*, Helen Lynch *(Maid)*.

Top-notch comedy has a penniless hypochondriac (wonderfully played by Denny), who will inherit a fortune in three years, striking up a deal with a group of wealthy old codgers to front the money for a California sanitarium stay on the condition that his eventual windfall will go to them. To make sure that Denny lasts that long, the old boys plant a beautiful nurse (Astor) on the scene, and he falls for her like a ton of bricks. He then sets out to impress the lady by performing a series of hair-raising stunts, which not only win Astor's heart, but prove without a doubt that he's fit as a fiddle—and ready for love.

d, Harry A. Pollard; w, Harvey Thew (based on the novel by Harry Leon Wilson); ph, Gilbert Warrenton.

Comedy **(PR:A MPAA:NR)**

OH, JOHNNY*** (1919) 5 reels Betzwood/Goldwyn bw

Louis Bennison *(Johnny Burke)*, Alphonse Ethier *(John Bryson)*, Edward Roseman *(Charlie Romero)*, John Daly Murphy *(Van Pelt Butler)*, Frank Goldsmith *(Earl of Barncastle)*, Virginia Lee *(Adele Butler)*, Anita Cortez *(Dolores)*, Louise Brownell *(Mrs. Van Pelt Butler)*, Frank Evans, Ralph Nairn.

Bennison is one of those intriguing figures who made a splash on Broadway when he appeared in the play on which this picture is based. At the time, he gave every indication of having all the requirements needed to become a major movie star (Variety described him as a combination of Douglas Fairbanks and Charles Chaplin), but then he just seemed to vanish. Here he plays a man of the West who heads East to save his mine, becomes the darling of society, and fights his way to a just conclusion.

d, Ira M. Lowry; w, (based on the play by Wilson Bayley); ph, David Calcagni.

Comedy/Adventure **(PR:A MPAA:NR)**

OH, KAY*** (1928) 7 reels FN bw

Colleen Moore *(Lady Kay Rutfield)*, Lawrence Gray *(Jimmy Winter)*, Alan Hale *(Jansen)*, Ford Sterling *(Shorty McGee)*, Claude Gillingwater *(Judge Appleton)*, Julanne Johnston *(Constance Appleton)*, Claude King *(The Earl of Rutfield)*, Edgar Norton *(Lord Braggot)*, Percy Williams *(The Butler)*, Fred O'Beck *(Capt. Hornsby)*.

Depressed at the thought of marrying a dreadful lord, Moore takes a little sail on her sloop, is blown out to sea in a storm, rescued by rum-runners, and escapes to find shelter in an unoccupied mansion owned by Gray. That night Gray shows up and Moore convinces him to let her pose as his wife, in order to fool a detective who suspects her of being a bootlegger. Actually the house *is* being used as a storehouse for liquor, and one of the bootleggers (nicely played by veteran comic Sterling) pretends to be a butler to protect his stock. Naturally, the picture ends with Moore and her handsome host falling in love, and Sterling (to the delight of everyone who resented the Volstead Act) making a clean break with his load of illegal spirits. Based on a popular musical, this may have been a "lesser" Moore effort, but still an entertaining and very amusing motion picture.

d, Mervyn LeRoy; w, Carey Wilson, Elsie Janis (based on the musical by Guy Bolton, Pelham Grenville Wodehouse); t, Wodehouse; ph, Sid Hickox; ed, Paul Weatherwax.

Comedy **(PR:A MPAA:NR)**

OH, LADY, LADY** (1920) 5 reels REA bw

Bebe Daniels *(May Barber)*, Harrison Ford *(Hale Underwood)*, Walter Hiers *(Willoughby Finch)*, Charlotte Woods *(Molly Farrington)*, Lillian Langdon *(Mrs. Farrington)*, Jack Doud *(Alec Smart)*.

This motion picture adaptation of the popular musical about an actress and a press agent who attempt to separate a romantic couple lacks the sparkle of the original and, unfortunately, the laughs as well.

d, Maurice Campbell; w, Edith Kennedy (based on the musical comedy by Guy Bolton, P. G. Wodehouse); ph, H. Kinley Martin; art d, Una Nixon Hopkins.

Comedy **(PR:A MPAA:NR)**

OH, WHAT A NIGHT!*** (1926) 5 reels STER bw

Raymond McKee *(Bob Brady)*, Edna Murphy *(June Craig)*, Charles K. French *(John Craig)*, Ned Sparks *("Slicky")*, Jackie Coombs *(Baby)*, Hilliard Karr *(Fat Man)*, Frank Alexander *(Another Fat Man)*.

Inspired by George M. Cohan's SEVEN KEYS TO BALDPATE, this is the story of a playwright (McKee) who sets out for his producer's apartment to rewrite the last act of his show, due to open the following night. Along the way he becomes involved in a robbery, encounters a number of shady characters, and is suspected by a fascinating blonde of being a crook. But McKee works the whole thing out in the end, using these experiences to give his play the punch it was missing.

d, Lloyd Ingraham; w, Colin Clements (based on a story by Florence Ryerson); ph, Herbert Kirkpatrick.

Comedy/Mystery **(PR:A MPAA:NR)**

OH, WHAT A NURSE!*** (1926) 7 reels WB bw

Sydney Chaplin *(Jerry Clark)*, Patsy Ruth Miller *(June Harrison)*, Gayne Whitman *(Clive Hunt)*, Matthew Betz *(Capt. Ladye Kirby)*, Edith Yorke *(Mrs. Clark)*, David Torrence *(Big Tim Harrison)*, Edgar Kennedy *(Eric Johnson)*, Raymond Wells *(Mate)*, Henry Barrows *(Newspaper Editor)*.

Sydney Chaplin's follow-up to his very popular feature, CHARLIE'S AUNT, had the underrated comedian again doing his female impersonator routine. This time, as a newspaper reporter, he impersonates an influential lovelorn columnist, prevents a wealthy young girl from marrying a fortune hunter, and wins the girl for himself. The gags are plentiful, and the production is tops.

d, Charles Reisner; w, Darryl Francis Zanuck (based on the novel by Robert Emmett Sherwood, Bertram Bloch); ph, John Mescall, Nelson Larabee.

Comedy **(PR:A MPAA:NR)**

OH, YOU TONY!*** (1924) 7 reels FOX bw

Tom Mix *(Tom Masters)*, Claire Adams *(Betty Faine)*, Dick La Reno *(Mark Langdon)*, Earle Foxe *(Jim Overton)*, Dolores Rousse *(The Countess)*, Charles K. French *(Blakely)*, Pat Chrisman *(The Chief)*, Miles McCarthy *(Senator from Arizona)*, Mathilda Brundage *(Senator's Wife)*, May Wallace *(Etiquette Instructor)*, Tony the Horse.

Mix delivers plenty of laughs in this one. It's all about a cowboy who heads for Washington, has his ranch stolen by a crooked lobbyist, but wins it all back with the help of a pretty little miss (Adams) and his great horse, Tony, who wins the big race. Another good Mix entertainment.

d, J. G. Blystone; w, Donald W. Lee; ph, Daniel Clark.

Western/Comedy **(PR:A MPAA:NR)**

OKLAHOMA KID, THE*½ (1929) 5 reels J. P. McGowan/SYN bw

Bob Custer *(The Kid)*, Henry Roquemore, Vivian Ray, Tommy Bay, J. P. McGowan, Walter Patterson.

The prolific McGowan produced and directed this low-budget Custer film, about an Oklahoma cowboy who sets off for New Mexico on a cattle deal and is waylaid by outlaws who take his name. He eventually breaks up the gang and proves his identity by flashing a map of his native state, which is tattooed on his body. He also manages to win the girl before the film's end.

p&d, J. P. McGowan; w, Walter Sterret (based on a story by Sally Winters); t, William Stratton; ph, Hap Depew.

Western **(PR:A MPAA:NR)**

OKLAHOMA SHERIFF, THE** (1930) 5 reels Big Productions/SYN bw

Bob Steele, Jean Reno, Perry Murdock, Cliff Lyons, Mac V. Wright, Thomas G. Lingham, Clark Comstock.

Scrappy little cowboy star Steele enhanced this modest oater with his own special sense of film presence. It's all about a young man who exposes the crooked deputy of his sweetheart's sheriff father, and manages to win the old boy over by his actions.

d, J. P. McGowan; w, Sally Winters; ph, Herbert Kirkpatrick.

Western **(PR:A MPAA:NR)**

OLD AGE HANDICAP½** (1928) 6 reels Trinity bw

Alberta Vaughn, Gareth Hughes, Vivian Rich, Olaf Hytten, Mavis Villiers, Bud Shaw, Jimmy Humes, Carolyn Wethall, Robert Rodman, Frank Mattison, Jr., Ford Jessen, Hall Cline, Edna Hearne, Arthur Hotaling, White Star.

Movie with a moral has roadhouse dancer Vaughn saving the sister of the man she loves (Hughes) from seduction by the town rat, though it costs her much in the way of her reputation. Vaughn then defies the odds by riding her family horse to victory in a rigged race with a $5,000 purse.

d, Frank Mattison; w, Charles A. Taylor, Cecil Burtis Hill (based on a story by Tod Underwood); t, Putnam Hoover; ph, Jules Cronjager; ed, Minnie Steppler.

Drama **(PR:A MPAA:NR)**

OLD ARM CHAIR, THE** (1920, Brit.) 6 reels Screen Plays/BEF bw

Manora Thew *(Mrs. Soper)*, Cecil Mannering *(Arthur Bentley)*, Joan Ritz *(Kate)*, Frank Tennant *(Samuel Soper)*, Ida Fayne *(Miss Soper)*, Pat Royale *(Sammy Soper)*.

Set in 1840, this British crime drama tells the saga of a crooked moneylender who frames a clerk for a crime he didn't commit. The twist comes when the innocent man ends up adopting the real thief's son.

d, Percy Nash; w, George Pickett (based on a novel by Mrs. O. F. Walton).

Mystery/Crime **(PR:A MPAA:NR)**

OLD BILL THROUGH THE AGES*** (1924, Brit.) 8 reels ID bw

Syd Walker *(Old Bill)*, Arthur Cleave *(Bert)*, Jack Denton *(Alf)*, Gladys Ffolliott *(Queen Elizabeth)*, Austin Leigh *(William Shakespeare)*, Franzi Carlos *(Ann Hathaway)*, William Pardue *(The Redskin)*, Douglas Payne, Cecil Morton York, Clive Currie, Wally Bosco, Cyril Dane, Bruce Bairnsfather.

There is a spirit of fun in this British fantasy about an enlisted soldier who dreams that he participated in great historical events, fought beside William the Conquerer, and took part in the Boston Tea Party.

d, Thomas Bentley; w, (based on cartoons by Bruce Bairnsfather).

Fantasy **(PR:A MPAA:NR)**

OLD CLOTHES½** (1925) 6 reels Jackie Coogan/MG bw

Jackie Coogan *(Tim Kelly)*, Max Davidson *(Max Ginsberg)*, Joan Crawford *(Mary Riley)*, Allan Forrest *(Nathan Burke)*, Lillian Elliott *(Mrs. Burke)*, James Mason *(Dapper Dan)*, Stanton Heck *(The Adjuster)*, Dynamite the Horse.

Strangely cast movie has young Coogan playing an adultlike Irishman who, along with his partner, Davidson, loses the fortune they have made on rags by investing in a copper company. Crawford (playing the female lead in only her second film) is a poor girl whom they take in as a boarder. She soon falls in love with wealthy Forrest, whose family does not approve of her until Coogan announces that their copper investment is the hottest stock on the market, making everyone very wealthy. Director Cline injected some nice touches, but little Coogan is somewhat disturbing, parading about in adult clothes, wearing a derby hat, and acting very much like a Wall Street Republican.

d, Edward Cline; w, Willard Mack; t, Robert Hopkins; ph, Frank B. Good, Harry Davis.

Comedy/Drama **(PR:A MPAA:NR)**

OLD CODE, THE* (1928) 6 reels Morris R. Schlank/ANCH bw

Walter McGrail *(Pierre Belleu)*, Lillian Rich *(Marie d'Arcy)*, Cliff Lyons *(Jacques de Long)*, Melbourne MacDowell *(Steve MacGregor)*, J. P. McGowan *(Raoul de Valle)*,

Neva Gerber *(Lola)*, Ervin Renard *(Henri Langlois)*, Mary Gordon *(Mary MacGregor)*, Rhody Hathaway *(Father Le Fane)*, John Rainbow.

Northwest hokum of the worst sort, badly written, directed, acted, and photographed. The overly long, boring titles are the picture's best feature, and one really doesn't care if the half-breed heavy gets what's coming to him because the hero and heroine merely take up space on the screen.

d, Benjamin Franklin Wilson; w, E. C. Maxwell (based on a story by James Oliver Curwood); ph, Frank Cotner, Jack Jackson; ed, Earl C. Turner.

North Woods **(PR:A MPAA:NR)**

OLD COUNTRY, THE*** (1921, Brit.) 5 reels ID bw

Gerald McCarthy *(James Fountain)*, Kathleen Vaughan *(Mary Lorimer)*, Haidee Wright *(Mrs. Fountain)*, George Bellamy *(Squire)*, Ethel Newman *(Annette Alborough)*, Stanley Roberts *(Austin Wells)*, Sydney Paxton *(Steward)*.

Interesting British drama about a self-made U.S. millionaire who buys a squire's great home, brings his once-impoverished mother back to live there, and then discovers he is the son of the man from whom he bought the property.

d, A. V. Bramble; w, Eliot Stannard (based on a play by Dion Clayton Calthrop).

Drama **(PR:A MPAA:NR)**

OLD CURIOSITY SHOP, THE** (1913, Brit.) 6 reels Hepworth/Renters bw

Mai Deacon *(Little Nell)*, Warwick Buckland *(Grandfather Trent)*, E. Felton *(Quilp)*, Alma Taylor *(Mrs. Quilp)*, Jamie Darling *(The Single Gentleman)*, Willie West *(Dick Swiveller)*, Billy Rex *(Tom Codlin)*, S. May *(Sampson Brass)*, Bert Stowe *(Short)*, Sydney Locklynne *(Jerry)*, Moya Nigent *(Marchioness)*, R. Phillips *(Mrs. Jarley)*.

Ambitious (for its time) British film version of the lesser Dickens novel about the adventures of Little Nell, her grandfather, Mr. and Mrs. Quilp, and the money-lending dwarf who comes to their aid.

d&w, Thomas Bentley (based on the novel by Charles Dickens).

Drama **(PR:A MPAA:NR)**

OLD CURIOSITY SHOP, THE** (1921, Brit.) 7 reels Welsh-Pearson/JUR bw

Mabel Poulton *(Little Nell)*, William Lugg *(Grandfather)*, Hugh E. Wright *(Tom Codlin)*, Pino Conti *(Daniel Quilp)*, Bryan Powley *(Single Gentleman)*, Barry Livesey *(Tom Scott)*, Cecil Bevan *(Sampson Brass)*, Beatie Olna Travers *(Sally Brass)*, Minnie Rayner *(Mrs. Jarley)*, Dennis Harvey *(Short Trotters)*, Dezma DuMay *(Mrs. Quilp)*, Colin Craig *(Dick Swiveller)*, Fairy Emlyn *(Marchioness)*, A. Harding Steerman *(Mr. Marton)*.

British drama has a money-lending dwarf coming to the aid of a granddaughter, as well as a down-and-out gambler, and hiding them from the clutches of a nasty millionaire.

p, George Pearson; d, Thomas Bentley; w, J. A. Atkinson (based on a novel by Charles Dickens).

Drama **(PR:A MPAA:NR)**

OLD FASHIONED BOY, AN*** (1920) 5 reels PAR bw

Charles Ray *(David Warrington)*, Ethel Shannon *(Betty Graves)*, Alfred Allen *(Dr. Graves)*, Wade Boteler *(Herbert)*, Grace Morse *(Sybil)*, Gloria Joy *(Violet)*, Frankie Lee *(Herbie)*, Hal Cooley *(Ferdie)*, Virginia Brown *(The Baby)*.

Ray charmer about a bachelor who buys and furnishes a house without informing his sweetheart. She becomes so angered by his presumptuousness that she breaks their engagement and Ray has to win her all over again. There are numerous complications and laughs as he sets out on, executes, and accomplishes his mission.

d, Jerome Storm; sup, Thomas H. Ince; w, Agnes Christine Johnston; ph, Chester Lyons.

Comedy **(PR:A MPAA:NR)**

OLD FOLKS AT HOME, THE*** (1916) FA/TRI bw

Sir Herbert Beerbohm Tree *(John Coburn)*, Josephine Crowell *(Mrs. Coburn)*, Elmer Clifton *(Steve Coburn)*, Mildred Harris *(Marjorie)*, Lucille Younge *(Lucia Medina)*, W. E. Lawrence *(Stanley)*, Spottiswoode Aitken *(The Judge)*, Charles Lee, Alfred Paget, Wilbur Higby.

The great Shakespearean actor, Tree, who learned the art of eloquent silence by studying Lillian Gish at work, is quite good as the state senator who defends his son against a murder charge in a court of law. The picture's big punch comes when the boy's mother stands up before the judge and jury and pleads, "I want my boy!" Of course she gets him back, and the film ends on a satisfying, if improbable, happy note.

d, Chester Withey; w, (based on the story by Rupert Hughes).

Drama **(PR:A MPAA:NR)**

OLD HOME WEEK*** (1925) 7 reels FP-LAS/PAR bw

Thomas Meighan *(Tom Clark)*, Lila Lee *(Ethel Harmon)*, Charles Dow Clark *(Marshall Coleman)*, Max Figman *(Townsend Barton)*, Charles Sellon *(Uncle Henry)*, Selma Tiden *(Mary Clark)*, Sidney Paxton *(Judge Harmon)*, Joseph Smiley *(Jim Ferguson)*, Jack Terry *(Frikkle)*, Leslie Hunt *(Otey Jinks)*, Isabel West *(Mrs. Clark)*, Clayton Frye *(Congressman Brady)*.

Returning home for a town reunion, Meighan, owner of a failing gas station, passes himself off as an oil millionaire. He becomes involved with Clark and Figman, a couple of con men who have sold the town a phony oil well. Catching on to the scheme before it's too late, however, the young fellow connects the well to the town's water supply, fakes a gusher, sells the property back to the crooks at an enormous profit, and wins the love of the prettiest and richest girl in the county.

d, Victor Heerman; w, Thomas J. Geraghty (based on the story by George Ade); ph, Alvin Wyckoff; art d, Walter E. Keller.

Comedy **(PR:A MPAA:NR)**

OLD IRONSIDES* 1/2** (1926) 11 reels PAR bw

Esther Ralston *(Esther)*, Wallace Beery *(Bos'n)*, George Bancroft *(Gunner)*, Charles Farrell *(The Commodore)*, Johnny Walker *(Lt. Stephen Decatur)*, George Godfrey *(Cook)*, Guy Oliver *(1st Mate)*, Eddie Fetherston *(Lt. Somers)*, Effie Ellsler *(Esther's Mother)*, William Conklin *(Esther's Father)*, Fred Kohler *(2nd Mate)*, Charles Hill Mailes *(Commodore Preble)*, Nick De Ruiz *(The Bashaw)*, Mitchell Lewis *(Pirate Chief)*, Frank Jonasson, Frank Bonner, Duke Kahanamoku *(Pirate Captains)*, Arthur Ludwig *(2nd Mate)*, Spec O'Donnell *(Cabin Boy)*, Boris Karloff *(A Saracen Guard)*, Tetsu Komai.

Great direction and a fine cast combine to make this epic of America's merchant seamen and their defeat of the pirates on the shores of Tripoli grand entertainment. A small fortune was lavished on this production and it shows, especially in the Magnascope sequence, just before the first intermission, where the screen opens up to almost three times its normal size and the mighty Constitution is pictured racing directly towards the audience. After its world premiere in 1926, more than two reels were cut out of the film to give a more action-packed version in its general release 15 months later.

d, James Cruze; sup, B. P. Schulberg; w, Dorthy Arzner, Walter Woods, Harry Carr (based on a story by Laurence Stallings); t, Rupert Hughes; ph, Alfred Gilks, Charles Boyle; spec eff, Roy Pomeroy.

Historical **(PR:A MPAA:NR)**

OLD LOVES AND NEW*** (1926) 8 reels Sam E. Rork/FN bw

Lewis Stone *(Gervas Carew)*, Barbara Bedford *(Marny)*, Walter Pidgeon *(Clyde Lord Geradine)*, Katherine MacDonald *(Lady Elinor Carew)*, Tully Marshall *(Hosein)*, Ann Rork *(Kitty)*, Arthur Rankin *(Denny O'Meara)*, Albert Conti *(Dr. Chalmers)*.

Tourneur's wonderful sense of atmosphere and Stone's feeling for understatement made something of this story about a betrayed British aristocrat (Stone) who goes to Algeria to live with and minister to needy Arab tribesmen. During the course of the film, his faithless wife gets what's coming to her, the friend who had the affair with her is killed by an elephant, and the woman who was once married to the rotter falls madly in love with the dashing "White Man of the Desert."

d, Maurice Tourneur; w, Marion Fairfax (based on the novel *The Desert Healer* by Edith Maude Hull); ph, Henry Cronjager; ed, Patricia Rooney; art d, Jack Okey.

Costume/Romance **(PR:A MPAA:NR)**

OLD MAID'S BABY, THE 1/2** (1919) 5 reels Diando/Pathe bw

Baby Marie Osborne *(Tiny)*, Jack Richardson *(Her Father)*, Marion Warner *(Her Mother)*, Jack Connelly *(Frank Dodge)*, Claire Du Brey *(Sylvia Deane)*, William Quinn *(Prof. Caldwell)*, Georgia Woodthorpe *(Mrs. Caldwell)*, Little Sambo *(Joffre Pershing Johnson)*.

This Osborne tearjerker has the child adopted by her old maid aunt when her parents are killed in a parachute fall. The kid does have a way of playing on the heart-strings, especially in the scene where she tries to commit suicide by walking into the ocean (in the Norman Mayne manner), but is saved when her lame dog brings help. Osborne ultimately finds happiness in the home of her mother's sister, and the old girl does all right as well by winning the love of a kindly college professor.

d, William Bertram; w, (based on a story by Agnes Christine Johnston); ph, Tom Middleton.

Drama **(PR:A MPAA:NR)**

OLD SAN FRANCISCO*** (1927) 8 reels WB bw-c

Dolores Costello *(Dolores Vasquez)*, Warner Oland *(Chris Buckwell)*, Charles Emmett Mack *(Terrence O'Shaughnessy)*, Josef Swickard *(Don Hernandez Vasquez)*, John Miljan *(Don Luis)*, Anders Randolf *(Michael Brandon)*, Sojin *(Lu Fong)*, Angelo Rossitto *(Dwarf)*, Anna May Wong *(Chinese Girl)*.

Costello is ravishing, and the earthquake and fire sequences (enhanced by color and Vitaphone sound effects) most impressive; but the melodramatic story line dealing with Oland, the king of Chinatown's underworld, and his attempt to take the estate of wealthy Swickard, is pretty routine stuff.

d, Alan Crosland; w, Anthony Coldewey (based on a story by Darryl Francis Zanuck); t, Jack Jarmuth; ph, Hal Mohr; m, Hugo Riesenfeld; syn sc; s eff.

Costume/Drama **(PR:A MPAA:NR)**

OLD SHOES*** (1927) 7 reels PEER/Hollywood bw

Johnny Harron *(The Boy)*, Noah Beery *(The Stepfather)*, Viora Daniels, Ethel Grey Terry, ZaSu Pitts, Russell Simpson, Snitz Edwards.

No doubt inspired by TOL'ABLE DAVID, this better-than-average programmer tells of a mild-mannered country boy (Harron) who works up the courage to stand up to his abusive stepfather and defeat him in a rough-and-tumble fist fight. Harron was no Dick Barthelmess, and Stowers was certainly no Henry King, but they both did very well with this one.

d&w, Frederick Stowers.

Drama **(PR:A MPAA:NR)**

OLD SOAK, THE*** (1926) 8 reels UNIV bw

Jean Hersholt *(Clement Hawley, Sr.)*, George Lewis *(Clemmy Hawley)*, June Marlowe *(Ina Heath)*, William V. Mong *(Cousin Webster)*, Gertrude Astor *(Sylvia De Costa)*, Louise Fazenda *(Annie)*, Lucy Beaumont *(Mrs. Hawley)*, Adda Gleason *(Lucy)*, Tom Ricketts *(Roue)*, George Siegmann *(Al)*, Arnold Gregg *(Shelly Hawley)*.

By electing to drop the comedy aspects (which made the original play such a success) and strive for straight melodrama, Universal weakened this otherwise charming rural drama. Hersholt is splendid, however, as the retired garage owner with a distinct leaning for bootleg whiskey, who takes the blame for a crime he didn't commit in order to protect his son who loves a showgirl with social aspirations. Everything somehow works out in the end, but one has the feeling that the opportunity to produce a truly fine film was lost along the way.

d, Edward Sloman; w, Charles Kenyon (based on the play by Don Marquis); ph, Jackson Rose.

Drama **(PR:A MPAA:NR)**

OLD SWIMMIN' HOLE, THE 1/2** (1921) 5 reels Charles Ray/AFN bw

Charles Ray *(Ezra)*, James Gordon *(His Pa)*, Laura La Plante *(His Ma)*, Blanche Rose *(Myrtle)*, Marjorie Prevost *(Esther)*, Lincoln Stedman *(Skinny)*, Lon Poff *(Schoolmaster)*.

Early attempt to shoot a feature film without the use of titles is less than impressive because the picture has very little story line. For the most part, it relates the activities of love-sick rural boy Ray, who does everything in his power to get the attention of Rose, but only manages to get himself into trouble. Then, during an innocent lunch along the riverfront with Prevost, he discovers true love with the girl who has always admired him from afar.

d, Joseph De Grasse; w, Bernard McConville (based on the poem by James Whitcomb Riley); ph, George Rizard; ed, Larry L. Decker.

Comedy **(PR:A MPAA:NR)**

OLD WIVES FOR NEW**** (1918) 6 reels ART bw

Elliott Dexter *(Charles Murdock)*, Sylvia Ashton *(Sophy Murdock)*, Wanda Hawley *(Sophy, in the Prologue)*, Florence Vidor *(Juliet Raeburn)*, Theodore Roberts *(Berkeley)*, Helen Jerome Eddy *(Norma Murdock)*, Marcia Manon *(Viola)*, Julia Faye *(Jessie)*, J. Parks Jones *(Charley Murdock)*, Edna Mae Cooper *(Bertha)*, Gustav von Seyffertitz *(Biagden)*, Tully Marshall *(Simcox)*, Lillian Leighton, Mayme Kelso, William Boyd, Alice Taaffe, Irene Rich.

Crafty showman DeMille had already sensed the subtle transition of moral standards in the U.S. when he beautifully directed this film about a man who marries young, has a couple of children, and then watches as his wife grows repulsive and fat. He takes a trip north and falls in love with a local beauty who spurns his attentions after he tells her of his marital status. The film ends with the gentleman following the woman he loves to Italy, informing her of his divorce, and making her his second wife. Audiences were either deeply moved or greatly shocked by what they saw on the screen, but they waited in line to do so.

d, Cecil B. DeMille; w, Jeanie Macpherson (based on the novel by David Graham Phillips); ph, Alvin Wyckoff.

Drama **(PR:C MPAA:NR)**

OLD WIVES' TALE, THE** (1921, Brit.) 5 reels ID bw

Fay Compton *(Sophie Barnes)*, Florence Turner *(Constance Barnes)*, Henry Victor *(Gerald Scales)*, Francis Lister *(Cyril Povey)*, Mary Brough *(Mrs. Barnes)*, J. R. Tozer *(Chirac)*, Norman Page *(Samuel Povey)*, Drusilla Wills *(Maggie)*, Tamara Karsavina *(Dancer)*.

British drama with a WW I setting about a woman who leaves her husband to run a boardinghouse in Paris, and after the confusion and heartbreak of the struggle, is reunited with her beloved sister when the war ends.

d&w, Denison Clift (based on a novel by Arnold Bennett).

Drama **(PR:A MPAA:NR)**

OLDEST LAW, THE* (1918) 5 reels WORLD bw

June Elvidge *(Jennie Cox)*, Captain Charles *(Daddy Cox)*, John Bowers *(Billy West)*, Eloise Clement *(Cora West)*, Frank Andrews *(Rolfe)*, Frank Norcross *(Henry Walker)*.

Elvidge, a girl from the mountains, comes to New York, loses her job as a typist, and spends her last $3 at a fancy restaurant, where she meets a dashing man of means who is in the process of getting a divorce. The young chap offers her a position, which includes running his household and acting as hostess at his society parties. Later, when he gets into a scrape over some unpaid gambling debts, Elvidge (who has maintained a platonic relationship with her boss) offers to give herself to his creditor if he will let the man she has grown to love off the hook. But fortunately his ex-wife, who has opened her own sporting den (with the generous alimony payments she has been provided) covers the debt, leaving the young folks free to marry.

d, Harry Knoles; w, Virginia Tyler Hudson (based on the story "The Price She Did Not Pay" by Romena Rue); ph, J. Monteran.

Drama **(PR:C MPAA:NR)**

OLIVER TWIST* 1/2** (1916) 5 reels LAS bw

Marie Doro *(Oliver Twist)*, Hobart Bosworth *(Bill Sykes)*, Tully Marshall *(Fagin)*, Raymond Hatton *(The Artful Dodger)*, James Neill, Elsie Jane Wilson, Harry Rattenberry, Carl Stockdale, W. S. Van Dyke, Jack Sacker, Robert McKenzie.

Doro, who played Oliver very successfully on the stage, is equally impressive in this motion picture version. Her supporting players, particularly Bosworth as Bill Sykes and Marshall as Fagin, the crafty teacher of thieves, are standouts. A fine film on every level, which Jackie Coogan would remake some six years later.

d&w, James Young (based on the novel by Charles Dickens).

Drama **(PR:A MPAA:NR)**

OLIVER TWIST* 1/2** (1922) 8 reels Jackie Coogan/AFN bw

Jackie Coogan *(Oliver Twist)*, Lon Chaney *(Fagin)*, Gladys Brockwell *(Nancy Sikes)*, George Siegmann *(Bill Sikes)*, Edouard Trebaol *(Artful Dodger)*, Lionel Belmore *(Mr. Brownlow)*, Carl Stockdale *(Monks)*, Eddie Boland *(Toby Crackit)*, Taylor Graves *(Charlie Bates)*, Lewis Sargent *(Noah Claypool)*, James Marcus *(Bumble the Beadle)*, Aggie Herring *(Mrs. Corney)*, Joan Standing *(Charlotte)*, Esther Ralston *(Rose Maylie)*, Florence Hale *(Mrs. Bedwin)*, Nelson McDowell *(Sowerberry)*, Joseph Hazelton *(Mr. Grimwig)*, Gertrude Claire *(Mrs. Maylie)*.

Director Lloyd virtually makes the pages of Dickens' great novel come to life in retelling the story of the orphaned Oliver (Coogan) who becomes an apprentice to an undertaker, learns the art of pickpocketing, and is kidnaped before finally being rescued and receiving the inheritance due him. If Coogan seems a bit young for the part, his charm and acting skill more than make up for it. The rest of the cast are equally splendid, with a special round of applause due Chaney for his restrained portrayal of the infamous Mr. Fagin.

d, Frank Lloyd; sup, Jack Coogan, Sr.; w, Harry Weil, Lloyd (based on the novel by Charles Dickens); t, Walter Anthony; ph, Glen MacWilliams, Robert Martin; ed, Irene Morra; art d, Stephen Goosson; cos, Walter J. Israel.

Costume Drama **Cas.** **(PR:A MPAA:NR)**

OLIVER TWIST, JR.* (1921) 5 reels FOX bw

Harold Goodwin *(Oliver Twist, Jr.)*, Lillian Hall *(Ruth Norris)*, George Nichols *(Schoolmaster)*, Harold Esboldt *(Dick)*, Scott McKee *(Artful Dodger)*, Wilson Hummell *(Fagin)*, G. Raymond Nye *(Bill Sykes)*, Hayward Mack *(Monks)*, Pearl Lowe *(Mrs. Morris)*, George Clair *(James Harrison)*, Fred Kirby *(Judson)*, Irene Hunt *(Nancy)*.

It didn't take a lot of imagination or talent to borrow Dickens' classic work and give it a contemporary American setting. The result was what one might expect in the familiar story which sees the orphaned Oliver (Goodwin) joining up with a gang of thieves, getting shot in a robbery attempt and befriended by the woman (Hall) who finds him, and finally learning his true identity.

d, Millard Webb; w, F. McGrew Willis (based on the novel by Charles Dickens); ph, William C. Foster.

Drama **(PR:A MPAA:NR)**

OLYMPIC HERO, THE*

(1928) 5 reels James P. Lyons/Zakaro-Supreme bw (AKA: THE ALL AMERICAN)

Charles Paddock *(Charlie Patterson)*, Julanne Johnston *(Mary Brown)*, Donald Stuart *(Assistant Coach)*, Harvey Clark *(Coach Regan)*, Crauford Kent *(Man-about-town)*, Jack Selwyn *(Harold Fellows)*, Emile Chautard *(Grandpa Brown)*, Richard Pennell *(Professor)*, Aileen Manning *(P. T. Instructress)*, Bob Maxwell *(Balfor Champ)*, Raoul Paoli *(French Champ)*.

Olympic sprinter Paddock enjoyed a popularity in his day which rivaled Babe Ruth, Jack Dempsey, and other sports luminaries. To capitalize on this, the producers of this film concocted a paper-thin collegiate plot and threw in a lot of racing footage from the 1924 Olympic Games, featuring the great runner.

d, R. William Neill; w, Ronald De Gastro; t, Walter Weems; ph, Faxon Dean; ed, Henry Weber.

Sports **(PR:A MPAA:NR)**

O'MALLEY OF THE MOUNTED*** (1921) 6 reels WSHP/PAR bw

William S. Hart *(O'Malley)*, Eva Novak *(Rose Lanier)*, Leo Willis *(Red Jaeger)*, Alfred Allen *(Big Judson)*, Bert Sprotte *(The Sheriff)*, Antrim Short *(Bud Lanier)*.

Not quite up to the Hart standard, this one has the great cowboy star playing a mountie who crosses over the border to track down a killer. He assumes the role of badman, wins the love of a girl, brings the outlaws to justice, and clears his sweetheart's brother, who committed his crime to protect her honor.

d, Lambert Hillyer; w, William S. Hart; ph, Joe August; art d, J. C. Hoffner.

Western **(PR:A MPAA:NR)**

ON HER WEDDING NIGHT** (1915) 4 reels VIT bw

Edith Storey *(Helen Carter, Society Girl)*, Antonio Moreno *(Henry Hallem, Clubman)*, Carolyn Birch *(The Woman)*, Charles Kent *(Helen's Father)*, Louise Beaudet *(Jessica Carter, Her Mother)*, William Dunn *(Carlo Picalli, Immigrant)*, Denton Vane *(John Klendon, Helen's Fiance)*.

Far-fetched melodrama has a bridegroom shot to death while talking on the phone to his fiancee on their wedding day. A man who saw the murder is hit by a car and loses his memory. The groom's best friend takes the poor soul in and decides to devote the rest of his life to his chum's sweetheart. Eventually the witness snaps out of it and fingers the woman who committed the killing. She then takes her own life after being identified, and the faithful pal proposes to the little lady he has grown to love.

d, William Humphrey; w, Eugene Mullin.

Crime/Drama **(PR:A MPAA:NR)**

ON LEAVE** (1918, Brit.) 5 reels Barker/Anglo bw

Daphne Glenne *(Claude Carewe)*, George Foley *(Col. Carewe)*, Aubrey Fitzmaurice *(Lt. Jack Fordyce)*, Rolf Leslie *(Burglar)*, Judd Green, Nita Russell.

British wartime diversion has a young army lieutenant on leave assuming the blame for a shop girl's suspected theft, only to discover to his great surprise that she's married to his commanding officer.

d, Alexander Butler; w, (based on a story by Irene Miller).

Drama **(PR:A MPAA:NR)**

ON PROBATION* (1924) 5 reels William Steiner bw

Edith Thornton *(Mary Forrest)*, Robert Ellis *(Bruce Winter)*, Joseph Kilgour *(Judge Winter)*, Wilfred Lucas *(Detective Reilly)*, Helen Lynch *(Nan Miller)*, Eddie Phillips *(Phil Coleman)*, Betty Francisco *(Dolores Coleman)*, Lincoln Stedman *(Ralph Norton)*.

This potboiler—about a society flapper, Thornton, whose snooty friends turn their backs on her when she's caught speeding, only to have a kindly judge take her under his protective wing and even allow his son, Ellis, to marry her—is very short on fizz.

d, Charles Hutchinson; w, J. F. Natteford; ph, Ernest Miller.

Drama **(PR:A MPAA:NR)**

ON RECORD½** (1917) 5 reels LAS/PAR bw

Mae Murray *(Helen Wayne)*, Tom Forman *(Rand Calder)*, Henry A. Barrows *(Martin Ingleton)*, Charles Ogle *(Frederick Manson)*, Louis Morrison *(Detective Dunne)*, Bliss Chevalier *(Mrs. Calder)*, Gertrude Maitland, Jane Wolf, Mrs. Lewis McCord, Lucien Littlefield.

Hopelessly padded saga of a girl who is wrongly accused of a crime and fingerprinted. She falls in love with an inventor, whose rival for a hot new idea finds out about her "past" and has the poor lady dragged into court. The judge listens to her story, tears her fingerprints to shreds, throws the heavy's lawyer out of court—then suggests that the couple participate in a little marriage ceremony.

d, Robert Z. Leonard; w, Beulah Marie Dix, George Dubois Proctor (based on a story by John B. Clymer, Paul West); ph, Charles Rosher.

Drama **(PR:A MPAA:NR)**

ON THE BANKS OF ALLAN WATER** (1916, Brit.) 4 reels CL/Lacoque bw

Basil Gill *(Richard Warden)*, Violet Leicester *(Elsie)*, J. Hastings Batson, F. G. Clifton, Roy Byford, Grania Gray.

Still another of those British class-getting-in-the-way-of-love stories. This time, using a Scottish setting, the miller's daughter nearly commits suicide when her aristocratic sweetheart's family attempts to break them up.

d, Wilfred Noy; w, Reuben Gilmer.

Drama **(PR:A MPAA:NR)**

ON THE BANKS OF THE WABASH* (1923) 7 reels VIT bw

Mary Carr *(Anne Bixler)*, Burr McIntosh *("Cap" Hammond)*, James Morrison *(David)*, Lumsden Hare *(Paul Bixler)*, Mary MacLaren *(Yvonne)*, Madge Evans *(Lisbeth)*, George Neville *(Sash Brown)*, Marcia Harris *(Tilda Spiffen)*, Ed Roseman *(Westerley Spiffen)*.

Blackton needed a good title for this mediocre movie, so he used the great Dresser tune, which had absolutely nothing to do with the picture's story line. Actually, it tells of a young inventor (Morrison) who goes off to the city to sell his gadget, completely forgetting about Evans, the girl back home who loves him. The memory is rekindled, however, when he returns for a visit, has his life saved by the young lady, and rewards her with a proposal of marriage.

d, J. Stuart Blackton; w, Elaine Sterne (based on the song "On the Banks of the Wabash Far Away" by Paul Dresser); ph, Nicholas Musuraca; art d, Joseph Clement.

Drama **(PR:A MPAA:NR)**

ON THE DIVIDE** (1928) 5 reels ED/SYN bw

Bob Custer *(Jim Carson)*, Peggy Montgomery *(Sally Martin)*, Lafe McKee, Bud Osborne, J. P. McGowan.

Director-actor McGowan always delivered action in his pictures, and this one—featuring Custer as the cowboy who saves a ranch from claim-grabbers and wins the daughter of the house—was no exception.

d, J. P. McGowan; sup, J. Charles Davis; w, Sally Winters; ph, Paul Allen.

Western **(PR:A MPAA:NR)**

ON THE GO½** (1925) 5 reels Action/Weiss Brothers Artclass bw

Buffalo Bill, Jr. *(Bill Drake)*, Helen Foster *(Nell Hall)*, Lafe McKee *(Mr. Hall)*, Nelson McDowell *(Philip Graves)*, Raye Hampton *(Matilda Graves)*, Charles Whitaker *(Tom Evans)*, Louis Fitzroy *(Mr. Evans)*, George F. Marion *(Eb Moots)*, Alfred Hewston *(Snoopy O'Sullivan)*, Morgan Davis *(Sheriff)*, Pietro Sosso *(City Specialist)*.

Buffalo Bill, Jr. saves a disoriented girl who has fainted and arranges for her to stay with his friend. Later, he brings Whitaker, the outlaw son of his former boss, to justice and prevents the young lady, who is being spirited away by her wealthy father, from leaving the territory by chasing the train on horseback, bounding through the window, and proposing marriage.

d, Richard Thorpe; w, Frank L. Inghram; ph, Ray Ries.

Western **(PR:A MPAA:NR)**

ON THE HIGH SEAS*** (1922) 6 reels FP-LAS/PAR bw

Dorothy Dalton *(Leone Deveraux)*, Jack Holt *(Jim Dorn, a Stoker)*, Mitchell Lewis *(Joe Polack, a Ruffian)*, Winter Hall *(John Deveraux)*, Michael Dark *(Harold Van Allen)*, Otto Brower *(Lt. Gray, U.S.N.)*, William Boyd *(Dick Deveraux)*, James Gordon *(Captain of S.S. Andren)*, Alice Knowland *(Aunt Emily)*, Vernon Tremaine *(Maid)*.

Good miniatures and a script which doesn't take itself too seriously make this melodrama—about a couple (Dalton and Holt) who survive a shipwreck, abduction of the young lady, and life on a plague-infested derelict tanker—a better-than-average romantic adventure.

d, Irvin Willat; w, E. Mangus Ingleton (based on a story by Edward Brewster Sheldon); ph, Charles Edgar Schoenbaum.

Adventure/Romance **(PR:A MPAA:NR)**

ON THE QUIET*** (1918) 5 reels PAR bw

John Barrymore *(Robert Ridgeway)*, Frank Losee *(Judge Ridgeway, His Father)*, Lois Meredith *(Agnes Colt)*, Al Hickman *(Hix, a Reporter)*, Helen Greene *(Ethel Colt)*, Cyril Chadwick *(Duke of Carbondale)*, Frank H. Belcher *(McGeachy, A Bookmaker)*, Nan Christy, Dell Boone *(Chorus Girls)*, Dan Mason *(Clerk)*, Frank Hilton *(Secretary)*, Otto Okuga *(Valet)*, Louise Lee *(Maid)*, J. W. Johnston.

Wonderful farce, which could have been written for Douglas Fairbanks but is splendidly played by Barrymore, has the "Great Profile" stopping at nothing to triumph at business or win the hand of his lady fair. He performs some truly remarkable stunts in bringing this character to life, and the result is completely satisfying.

d, Chester Withey; w, Charles E. Whittaker (based on the play by Augustus Thomas).

Comedy **(PR:A MPAA:NR)**

ON THE STROKE OF THREE* (1924) 7 reels Associated Arts/FBO bw

Kenneth Harlan *(Judson Forrest)*, Madge Bellamy *(Mary Jordon)*, Mary Carr *("Ma" Forrest)*, John Miljan *(Henry Mogridge)*, Robert Dudley *(Jasper Saddler)*, Leonore Matre *(Lillian Haskins)*, Edwards Davis *(Lafayette Jordon)*, Edward Phillips *(Austin Dudley)*, Dorothy Dahm *(Emily Jordon)*.

Overly used story line about the young man (Harlan) who must raise money and then race like crazy to reach the old homestead in time to prevent foreclosure. Of course he does, and also marries Bellamy, the girl he earlier believed betrayed him.

d, F. Harmon Weight; w, O. E. Goebel, Philip Lonergan (based on the novel *The Man From Ashaluna* by Henry Payson Dowst); ph, Victor Milner, Paul Perry.

Drama **(PR:A MPAA:NR)**

ON THIN ICE ** (1925) 7 reels WB bw

Tom Moore *(Charles White)*, Edith Roberts *(Rose Lore)*, William Russell *(Dapper Crawford)*, Theodore Von Eltz *(Dr. Paul Jackson)*, Wilfred North *(Harrison Breen)*, Gertrude Robinson *(Forger)*, Texas Kid, Jimmy Quinn *(Gangsters)*.

Suspected of being involved in a bank robbery, Roberts is trailed by mobsters and police, both out to find the missing loot. Moore, a smalltime operator, is hired by the mob to impersonate her long-lost brother, but he falls in love with Roberts and vows to go straight. In the end, the gang leader is shot but clears Roberts before dying, leaving the *almost* brother and sister the option of becoming man and wife.

d, Mal St. Clair; w, Darryl Francis Zanuck (based on the novel *The Dear Pretender* by Alice Ross Colver); ph, Byron Haskins; ed, Clarence Kolster.

Crime **(PR:A MPAA:NR)**

ON TIME*** (1924) 6 reels Carlos/TRU bw

Richard Talmadge *(Harry Willis)*, Billie Dove *(Helen Hendon)*, Stuart Holmes *(Richard Drake)*, George Siegmann *(Wang Wu)*, Tom Wilson *(Casanova Clay)*, Charles Clary *(Horance Hendon)*, Douglas Gerard *(Mr. Black)*, Fred Kirby *(Dr. Spinks)*, Frankie Mann *(Mrs. Spinks)*.

Lots of fun in this Talmadge action-packed thriller, which has the superlative stunt actor taking on most of the Chinese population of Los Angeles in an unbelievable fist fight, tangling with an army of men at a costume ball, and even pitting himself against a mad doctor who desires to transplant an ape's brain into his. It all turns out to be a secret testing procedure on the part of a Hollywood studio to see if he qualifies for potential stardom. Of course he does, and gets the girl as well.

d, Henry Lehrman; w, Garrett Fort (based on a story by Al Cohn); t, Ralph Spence; ph, William Marshall; ed, Spence.

Adventure **(PR:A MPAA:NR)**

ON TO RENO*** (1928) 6 reels James Cruze/Pathe bw

Marie Prevost *(Vera)*, Cullen Landis *(Bud)*, Ethel Wales *(Mrs. Holmes)*, Ned Sparks *(Herbert Holmes)*, Jane Keckley *(The Housekeeper)*.

After a series of expensive road show productions, including COVERED WAGON in 1924, Cruze directed this entertaining little comedy which has Prevost, a happily married but financially pressed young bride, accepting a job impersonating millionairess Wales in order to fulfill her three-month residency requirement for divorce. The fun really gets under way when both husbands show up to try to stop the proceeding. Of course it all ends well, with Wales and her spouse reunited, and Prevost's husband winning a big contract from the gent with whom he shared the laughs and confusion.

d, James Cruze; w, Walter Woods (based on a story by Joseph Jackson); t, John Krafft, Woods; ph, Ernest Miller; ed, Mildred Johnson; art d, Charles Cadwallader.

Comedy **(PR:A MPAA:NR)**

ON TRIAL** (1917) 7 reels Essanay bw

Sidney Ainsworth *(Robert Strickland)*, Barbara Castleton *(Mrs. Robert Strickland)*, Mary McAllister *(Doris Strickland)*, James Young *(Gerald Trask)*, Corene Uzzell *(Mrs. Gerald Trask)*, Patrick Calhoun *(Glover)*, Doris Kenyon.

Based on a popular play, this courtroom drama is only average as a film. It is interesting that the stage production (which was equally mediocre) owed its success to the fact that it used the motion picture technique of the flashback to impress audiences. In 1917 there were few examples of the screen imitating the stage imitating the screen.

d&w, James Young (based on the play by Elmer L. Reisenstein [Elmer Rice]).

Drama **(PR:A MPAA:NR)**

ON WITH THE DANCE*** (1920) 6 reels PAR bw

Mae Murray *(Sonia Varinoff)*, David Powell *(Peter Derwynt)*, Alma Tell *(Lady Loane Tremelyn)*, John Miltern *(Schuyler Van Vechtan)*, Robert Schable *(Jimmie Sutherland)*, Ida Waterman *(Countess of Raystone)*, Zola Talma *(Fay Desmond)*, James A. Furey, Pete Raymond.

Slick Paramount production values and good direction by Fitzmaurice make this story of a little Russian dancer (Murray) who mistakenly weds the secretary of a millionaire, gets mixed up with another married man, survives a murder and trial and finally ends up with the right fellow, better than average.

d, George Fitzmaurice; w, Ouida Bergere (based on the play by Michael Morton); ph, Arthur Miller.

Drama **(PR:A MPAA:NR)**

ON ZE BOULEVARD* 1/2** (1927) 6 reels MGM bw

Lew Cody *(Gaston Pasqual)*, Rene Adoree *(Musette)*, Anton Vaverka *(Ribot)*, Dorothy Sebastian *(Gaby de Sylva)*, Roy D'Arcy *(Count de Guissac)*.

Top comedy has French waiter Cody winning a fortune in a gambling pool and going completely off his nut. A couple of crooks try to take him to the cleaners, but the young fellow's thrifty and cunning girl friend, Adoree, saves the day—as well as his bankroll.

d, Harry Millarde; w, Richard Schayer, Scott Darling (based on a story by F. Hugh Herbert, Florence Ryerson); t, Joe Farnham, Earl Baldwin; ph, Andre Barlatier, William Daniels; ed, George Hively; art d, Cedric Gibbons, Frederic Hope.

Comedy **(PR:A MPAA:NR)**

ONCE A PLUMBER 1/2** (1920) 5 reels UNIV bw

Eddie Lyons, Lee Moran, George B. Williams, Sidney Dean, Jeff Osborne, Lillian Hackett, Edna Mae Wilson, Jane Elliott, Ethel Ritchie, Lew Short, Harry Archer, Walter "Doc" Butell, Frederick Peters.

The popular comedy team of Lyons and Moran, who starred in numerous two-reelers, were about to part company when they made this feature about a couple of plumbers who are conned into taking over a phony company, take on social airs, and exonerate themselves in the end. Certainly not Laurel and Hardy, but still good for a few laughs.

d, Eddie Lyons, Lee Moran; w, C. B. Hoadley (based on a story by Edgar Franklin).

Comedy **(PR:A MPAA:NR)**

ONCE ABOARD THE LUGGER**

(1920, Brit.) 6 reels Hepworth/Imperial bw

E. Holman Clarke *(Mr. Marrapit)*, Eileen Dennes *(Mary Humfray)*, Evan Thomas *(George)*, Denis Cowles *(Bill Wyvern)*, Reginald Bach *(Bob Chater)*, Gwynne Herbert *(Mrs. Major)*, John MacAndrews *(Fletcher)*, Winifred Sadler *(Mrs. Chater)*, Fred Lewis *(Vyvian Howard)*.

Boys will be boys in this British comedy of college life which has a fun-loving student abducting his uncle's cat and holding it for ransom.

d, Gerald Ames, Gaston Quiribet; w, Blanche McIntosh (based on the novel by A.S.M. Hutchinson).

Comedy **(PR:A MPAA:NR)**

ONCE UPON A TIME** (1918, Brit.) 7 reels BA/STOLL bw

Lauri de Frece *(Sam Dunn)*, Manora Thew *(Sally Drury)*, Dorothy Minto *(Lottie Price)*, Nelson Keys *(Harry Gwynne)*, Joan Legge *(Mary Gwynne)*, A. E. Matthews *(Guy Travers)*, Fred Volpe *(Mr. Goodheart)*, Charles Macdona *(Dr. Brown)*, Adelaide Grace *(Mrs. Gwynne)*, Jeff Barlow *(Ned Drury)*, Kenelm Foss *(Charles Dickens)*, Noel Fisher *(Eustace Travers)*.

In this British love story with a circus background, the daughter of a clown does everything she can to avoid marrying a comedian, much to the great displeasure of her adoptive parents. Of course, in the end, it all works out.

d, Thomas Bentley; w, (based on a story by Kenelm Foss).

Romance **(PR:A MPAA:NR)**

ONCE UPON A TIME* (1922) 5 reels Henry Bollman bw

Ruth Bryan Owen, The Community Players of Cocoanut Grove.

Off-the-wall movie, featuring Florida's Community Players of Cocoanut Grove and someone named Ruth Bryan Owen, about an Indian Shah who returns from exile to save an Eastern beauty from the filthy intentions of an odious sex maniac who delights in exploring the really weird.

d&w, Ruth Bryan Owen; ph, Dudley Read.

Fantasy **(PR:A MPAA:NR)**

ONE A MINUTE*** (1921) 5 reels THI/PAR bw

Douglas MacLean *(Jimmy Knight)*, Marian De Beck *(Miriam Rogers)*, Victor Potel *(Jingo Pitts)*, Frances Raymond *(Grandma Knight)*, Andrew Robson *(Silas P. Rogers)*, Graham Pettie *(Martin Duffey)*.

When a super capitalist offers to buy out his family drugstore, MacLean falls in love with the tycoon's daughter (De Beck) and sets out to make his own fortune by selling his father's patent medicine. There are plenty of laughs leading up to MacLean's trial for violating the Pure Food and Drug Act. But when he cures the judge of a gastritis attack, the court rules him innocent, the millionaire's daughter declares her adoration, and the town elects him mayor.

d, Jack Nelson; sup, Thomas H. Ince; w, Joseph Franklin Poland (based on the play by Fred Jackson); ph, Bert Cann.

Comedy **(PR:A MPAA:NR)**

ONE ARABIAN NIGHT* 1/2**

(1921, Ger.) 6 reels Decla-Bioskop/FN bw (SUMURUN)

Ernst Lubitsch *(Yeggar, the Hunchback Clown)*, Pola Negri *(Yannaia, a Dancer)*, Paul Wegener *(The Sheik)*, Jenny Hasselquist *(Zuleika, the Sheik's Favorite)*, Aud Egede Nissen *(Haidee, Her Maid)*, Harry Liedtke *(Nur-al-Djin, a Merchant)*, Carl Clewing *(The Sheik's Son)*, Margarete Kupfer *(The Old Woman)*, Jakob Tiedtke *(Head Eunuch of the Sheik's Harem)*, Max Kronert *(Muffti, 1st Servant of Nur-al-Djin)*, Paul Biensfeldt *(Slave Dealer)*, Paul Graetz *(Pufti, 2nd Servant of Nur-al-Djin)*.

Lubitsch not only directs but plays the part of a dwarf comedian who travels with a troupe of entertainers, including Negri, a beautiful dancer, a juggler, and an old lady who charms snakes. When they reach an Arab town controlled by Wegener, an old sheik who suspects his favorite wife of being unfaithful, the trouble begins. Hearing of the beauty of the dancer, Wegener demands that she be brought to his harem to act as a replacement. The dwarf, who has always loved Negri from afar, follows her and arrives just in time to see the potentate kill the young woman for being attracted to his son. Lubitsch, horror-stricken and brokenhearted, avenges his love by in turn murdering the sheik. This is a beautifully crafted film and one which had much to do with the German director's invitation to later join the Hollywood colony.

d, Ernst Lubitsch; w, Hans Kraly, Lubitsch (based on the stage pantomime "The Arabian Nights" by Friedrich Freska, Victor Hollander); ph, Theodor Sparkuhl; m, Hollander; set d, Kurt Ritcher, Erno Metzner; cos, Ali Hubert.

Drama **(PR:A MPAA:NR)**

ONE CHANCE IN A MILLION** (1927) 5 reels GOTH/LUM bw

William Fairbanks *(Jerry Blaine)*, Viora Daniels *(Ruth Torrence)*, Charles K. French *(Richard Torrence)*, Henry Herbert *(Robert Weston)*, Eddie Borden *(Horace Featherby)*, Duke Martin *(Pat Drogan)*.

More than enough action to satisfy the kids in this Fairbanks programmer in which the actor plays a Secret Service agent who infiltrates a gang of jewel thieves, prevents a theft, saves Daniels, the daughter of a millionaire, from marrying the wrong fellow, and wins her for himself.

d, Noel Mason Smith; w, L. V. Jefferson; ph, James Brown.

Action **(PR:A MPAA:NR)**

ONE CLEAR CALL*** (1922) 8 reels Louis B. Mayer/AFN bw

Milton Sills *(Dr. Alan Hamilton)*, Claire Windsor *(Faith)*, Henry B. Walthall *(Henry Garnett)*, Irene Rich *(Maggie Thornton)*, Stanley Goethals *(Sonny Thornton)*, William Marion *(Tom Thornton)*, Joseph Dowling *(Col. Garnett)*, Edith Yorke *(Mother Garnett)*, Doris Pawn *(Phyllis Howard)*, Donald MacDonald *(Dr. Bailey)*, Shannon Day *(Jim Ware's Daughter)*, Annette De Foe *(Yetta)*, Fred Kelsey *(Starnes)*, Albert MacQuarrie *(Jim Holbrook)*, Nick Cogley *(Toby)*.

Good weeper sees Sills as a Southern doctor who falls in love with Windsor, a husbandless mother who has just arrived in town. When she rejects him because of her shameful past, the good doctor takes to drinking. In the meantime, his best friend, a well-bred gambler (beautifully played by Walthall), has only a short time to live and desires to make up for past wrongs. Just before his death, Walthall confesses to his friend that Windsor was his wife in name only, leaving Sills and his lady love free to pursue their lives in happiness.

d, John M. Stahl; w, Bess Meredyth (based on the novel by Frances Nimmo Green); ph, Ernest G. Palmer; ed, Madge Tyrone.

Drama **(PR:A MPAA:NR)**

ONE COLUMBO NIGHT** (1926, Brit.) 5 reels STOLL bw

Godfrey Tearle *(Jim Farnell)*, Marjorie Hume *(Rosemary Thurman)*, Nora Swinburne *(Jeane Caldicott)*, James Carew *(Richard Baker)*, J. Fisher White *(Father Anthony)*, William Pardue *(Pabu)*, Julie Suedo *(Lalla)*, Dawson Millward *(Governor)*, Annie Esmond *(Wife)*.

British love story set in Ceylon has a bankrupted plantation owner traveling to Australia where he makes a second fortune and returns home just in time to save the girl he loves from entering a convent.

d, Henry Edwards; w, Alicia Ramsey (based on a novel by Austin Phillips).

Romance **(PR:A MPAA:NR)**

ONE DAY*** (1916) 5 reels B. S. Moss bw

Victor Sutherland *(Paul)*, Jeanne Iver *(Opal)*, Barklay Barker *(Paul Verdayne)*, John Webb Dillon *(Pavlovitch)*, Robert Broderick *(Dimitri)*, Arthur Evers *(Stefan)*, Hal Clarendon *(Prince Ronneaus)*, Walter D. Nealand *(Romeau)*, Frank Whitson *(Accomplice)*, William Bechtel *(Prime Minister)*, Master Richard Ross *(Master Paul)*.

In novelist Glyn's sequel to THREE WEEKS, Iver plays the daughter of the man who stole the throne of Veseria. Although in love with the young prince (Sutherland) to whom the kingdom belonged, she has been forced into an engagement with a wealthy rotter. Fate, however, brings Ivers and Sutherland together when they meet in France and are forced, because of a terrible storm, to spend the night together in a deserted hunting lodge. Eventually the people of Veseria rise up and kill the wicked ruler, which allows the film to end with a well-produced epilogue, in which the lovers are united in marriage and Sutherland assumes his rightful position.

d, Hal Clarendon; w, (based on a novel by Elinor Glyn); ph, Ernest Powell.

Drama **(PR:A MPAA:NR)**

ONE EXCITING NIGHT* (1922) 11 reels D. W. Griffith/UA bw

Carol Dempster *(Agnes Harrington)*, Henry Hull *(John Fairfax)*, Porter Strong *(Romeo Washington)*, Morgan Wallace *(J. Wilson Rockmaine)*, C. H. Crocker-King *(The Neighbor)*, Margaret Dale *(Mrs. Harrington)*, Frank Sheridan *(The Detective)*, Frank Wunderlee *(Samuel Jones)*, Grace Griswold *(Auntie Fairfax)*, Irma Harrison *(The Maid)*, Herbert Sutch *(Clary Johnson)*, Percy Carr *(The Butler)*, Charles E. Mack *(A Guest)*.

Griffith may have created the spooky-house mystery genre with this film, but that's the only positive thing one can say about it. The picture is a dismal combination of comedy (there are a couple of "feets git movin'" characters in blackface) and murder, with a gang of bootleggers thrown in for good measure. The story begins in Africa, where a group of white hunters and their wives are on a safari through the jungle when one of the women dies in childbirth. The baby girl is brought to the U.S. where she is adopted by Dale, who is overbearing and unaffectionate towards the child. Years pass and the girl, now a young woman (Dempster), is a guest at the home of Hull, where bootleggers are secretly trying to uncover a large sum of hidden money, while conniving Dale is attempting to trap wealthy Wallace into a marriage with her unconsenting daughter. A couple of murders then take place and Dempster and Hull are prime suspects. By the last reel Dempster not only discovers the real killer, but her true identity as the daughter of a very wealthy man, and she and Hull decide to tie the knot. Outside of the happy ending, there was very little to smile about in this disappointing Griffith production.

d, D. W. Griffith; w, Griffith (based on his own story "The Haunted Grange" which was copywritten under the pseudonym Irene Sinclair); ph, Hendrik Sartov, Irving B. Ruby; set d, Charles M. Kirk; spec eff, Edward Scholl.

Mystery/Comedy **(PR:A MPAA:NR)**

ONE GLORIOUS SCRAP* (1927) 5 reels UNIV bw

Fred Humes *(Larry Day)*, Dorothy Gulliver *(Joan Curtis)*, Robert McKenzie *(Prof. Parkinson)*, Francis Ford *(Ralph Curtis)*, George French *(Ezra Kramer)*, Cuyler Supplee *(Carl Kramer)*, Benny Corbett *(Benny)*, Gilbert "Pee Wee" Holmes *(Pee Wee)*, Dick L'Estrange *(Lazy)*, Scotty Mattraw *(Scotty)*.

Cliche-ridden B western about the bad guys trying to control the water supply and buy up all of the good guys' ranches. But Humes and his riders from the Bar None prevent this, and Humes wins the hand of pretty Gulliver as well. The most incredible part of it all is that it took three people to write this one.

d, Edgar Lewis; w, George H. Plympton, George Morgan (based on a story by Leigh Jacobson); t, Gardner Bradford; ph, Eddie Linden; art d, David S. Garber.

Western **(PR:A MPAA:NR)**

ONE HOUR OF LOVE ½** (1927) 7 reels TIF bw

Jacqueline Logan *("Jerry" McKay)*, Robert Frazer *(James Warren)*, Montagu Love *(J. W. McKay)*, Taylor Holmes *(Joe Monahan)*, Duane Thompson *(Neely)*, Mildred Harris *(Gwen)*, Hazel Keener *(Vi)*, William Austin *(Louis Carruthers)*, Henry Sedley *(Tom Webb)*, Billy Bletcher *("Half Pint" Walker)*.

Fair romantic fluff about a society girl (Logan) who goes west with her father to inspect some property, has a run-in with a strong-willed young engineer (Frazer) and bets that she can get him to propose within a week. He does, and to her delight, she discovers that they really are in love.

d, Robert Florey; w, Sarah Y. Mason (based on the novel *The Broken Gate* by Emerson Hough); ph, Milton Moore, Jack Stengler; ed, James McKay; art d, Edwin B. Willis.

Romance **(PR:A MPAA:NR)**

ONE LAW FOR BOTH** (1917) 8 reels IV bw

Rita Jolivet *(Elga Pulaski)*, Leah Baird *(Helen Hutchinson)*, Margaret Greene *(Renee Doucet)*, James Morrison *(Ossip Pulaski)*, Helen Arnold *(Magda Strunski)*, Vincent Serrano *(Norman Hutchinson)*, Pedro De Cordoba *(Count de Fernac)*, Paul Capellani *(Baron Jan Slazek)*, Anders Randolf *(Sergeious Gourko)*, Hassan Mussali *(Feodor Wolski)*, Walter Gould *(Henri)*.

Overly long, but courageous for its time, motion picture which took the position that infidelity is as wrong for a man as it is for a woman. The point is made by contrasting two married couples, but the message gets all but washed out in the tedium.

d&w, Ivan Abramson; ph, Marcel Le Picard.

Drama **(PR:A MPAA:NR)**

ONE LAW FOR THE WOMAN* (1924) 6 reels Charles E. Blaney/VIT bw

Cullen Landis *(Ben Martin)*, Mildred Harris *(Polly Barnes)*, Cecil Spooner *(Phillis Dair)*, Stanton Heck *(Brennan)*, Otis Harlan *(Judge Blake)*, Bertram Grassby *(Bartlett)*, Charlotte Stevens *(Nellie)*.

There is not an awful lot to recommend in this programmer about Landis being sold a phony mine lease but going on to hit a bonanza, marry Harris (Charlie Chaplin's ex-wife), and bring the crooks to justice.

p, Charles E. Blaney; d, Del Henderson; w, Harry Chandlee (based on a story by Blaney).

Western **(PR:A MPAA:NR)**

ONE MAN DOG, THE** (1929) 6 reels FBO/RKO bw

Ranger *(Grit, the Dog)*, Sam Nelson *(Larry)*, Edward Hearne *(Pierre)*, Virginia Bradford *(Babette)*, William Patton *(Gadsky)*, Art Robbins *(Trapper)*.

When Nelson is falsely accused of murder, Ranger, his dog, tracks down the real killer, forces him to his death over a cliff, and clears his master's name.

d, Leon D'Usseau; w, Frank Howard Clark; t, Helen Gregg; ph, Robert De Grasse; ed, Tod Chessman.

North Woods **(PR:A MPAA:NR)**

ONE MILLION DOLLARS ½** (1915) 5 reels Rolfe/Metro bw

William Faversham *(Richard Duvall, a Criminologist)*, Henry Bergman *(Count Raoul D'Este)*, George LeGuere *(Emile, His Nephew)*, Mayme Kelso *(Countess D'Este)*, Carlotta De Felice *(Grace Ellicott, Her Niece)*, Arthur Morrison *(Purtab Gar, an Indian Servant)*, Charles Graham *(Chief of Police)*, Camilla Dahlberg *(Mrs. Cooke, the Count's Housekeeper)*.

Good direction and acting, as well as some nicely constructed sets, make up for a dime novel script about a criminologist who saves the life of a Buddhist priest and the fortune of a young girl who almost has it stolen by the Count who married her aunt. The movie is supposed to take place in India and carries off the illusion quite well.

d, John W. Noble; w, Arnold Fredericks.

Mystery **(PR:A MPAA:NR)**

ONE MILLION IN JEWELS* ½
(1923) 5 reels William B. Brush/American Releasing bw

Helen Holmes *(Helen Morgan)*, J. P. McGowan *(Burke)*, Elinor Fair *(Sylvia Ellis)*, Nellie Parker Spaulding *(Jane Angle)*, Charles Craig *(George Beresford)*, Leslie Casey *(William Abbott)*, Herbert Pattee *(Morgan)*.

Secret Service agent McGowan marries Fair after she helps him break up a gang of jewel thieves led by Holmes—a woman secretly in love with him—who is killed during the caper.

d&w, J. P. McGowan; ph, William Tuers.

Crime **(PR:A MPAA:NR)**

ONE MINUTE TO PLAY ½** (1926) 8 reels R-C/FBO bw

Red Grange *(Red Wade)*, Mary McAllister *(Sally Rogers)*, Charles Ogle *(John Wade)*, George Wilson *(Player "33")*, Ben Hendricks, Jr. *("Biff" Wheeler)*, Lee Shumway *(Tex Rogers)*, Al Cooke *(Brakeman)*, Kit Guard *(Train Worker)*, Lincoln Stedman *(Toodles)*, Jay Hunt *(President Todd)*, Edythe Chapman *(Mrs. Wade)*, King Tut the Dog.

To the U.S. movie-going public of 1926, Red Grange *was* football, and he does rather well as the young college student who overcomes some really nonsensical obstacles before getting out there in the last quarter and winning the big game.

d, Sam Wood; w, Byron Morgan; ph, Charles Clarke.

Sports **(PR:A MPAA:NR)**

ONE MORE AMERICAN*** (1918) 5 reels LAS/PAR bw

George Beban *(Luigi Riccardo)*, Camille Ankewitch *(Maria)*, May Giraci *(Tessa)*, Helen Jerome Eddy *(Lucia)*, Raymond Hatton *(Bump Rundle)*, Jack Holt *(Sam Potts)*, H. B. Carpenter *(Boss Regan)*, Hector Dion *(Dr. Ross)*, May Palmer *(Mrs. Ross)*, Ernest Joy *(Mr. Fearing)*, Signor Buzzi *(Musician)*, Marcia Manon.

Beban brings his popular Italian character to the screen again. This time he's a citizen loved by the community and feared by the local political wardheeler. In order to keep the little immigrant in line, the boss arranges to have his family detained at Ellis Island, and even threatens their deportation to the old country. A crusading newspaper reporter intervenes, however, and with Beban's help, the family is reunited and the crooked politician exposed.

d, William C. De Mille; w, Olga Printzlau (based on the play "The Land of the Free" by De Mille); ph, Charles Rosher.

Drama **(PR:A MPAA:NR)**

ONE OF MANY* ½ (1917) 5 reels COL/Metro bw

Frances Nelson *(Shirley Bryson)*, Niles Welch *(Harold Templeton)*, Mary Mersch *(Emma Bryson)*, Caroline Harris *(Mrs. Bryson)*, Harold Entwistle *(Wilfred Templeton)*, Richard Dix *(James Lowery)*, Walter Worden *(Policeman)*, Adella Barker *(Landlady)*, Shirley Bryson.

This probability-stretcher has a poor girl selling herself to a millionaire to pay for her mother's medical expenses. When the rat throws her out, she becomes a nightclub dancer, then nurses a young drunkard back to healthy sobriety and marries him. The lad turns out to be the son of her former sponsor, and when the old boy shows up and announces this, the kid also gives her the boot. Later, he comes to realize that his bride was the victim of circumstances and takes her back. Not a pretty story.

d&w, William Christy Cabanne; ph, William C. Fildew.

Drama **(PR:C MPAA:NR)**

ONE OF OUR GIRLS*** (1914) 4 reels FP bw

Hazel Dawn *(Miss Shipley)*, William Roselle, Hal Clarendon, Lionel Adams, Fania Marinoff, Camilla Dahlberg, Charles Krauss, David Powell, George Backus, Clarence Handyside, Rolinda Bainbridge.

Musical comedy star Dawn made her screen debut in this romance about a British officer who falls in love with and fights a duel for the hand of a beautiful American girl. The film was set in France, and Famous Players did a nice job of disguising the fact that it was actually shot in New Jersey.

d, Thomas N. Heffron; w, Eve Unsell (based on the play by Bronson Howard).

Drama **(PR:A MPAA:NR)**

ONE OF THE BEST** (1927, Brit.) 8 reels Gainsborough-Piccadilly/W&F bw

Carlyle Blackwell *(Philip Ellsworth)*, Walter Butler *(Lt. Dudley Keppel)*, Eve Gray *(Mary Penrose)*, Randle Ayrton *(Gen. Gregg)*, James Carew *(Col. Gentry)*, Julie Suedo *(Claire Melville)*, James Lindsay *(Maurice de Gruchy)*, Pauline Johnson *(Esther)*, Elsa Lanchester *(Kitty)*, Charles Emerald *(Pvt. Jupp)*, Cecil Barry *(Lt. Wynne)*, Sir Simeon Stuart *(Squire Penrose)*, Harold Huth *(Adjutant)*.

English mystery set in 1820 deals with an officer who implicates an acquaintance when a criminal attempts to force him to steal valuable secrets.

p, Michael Balcon; d, T. Hayes Hunter; w, Patrick L. Mannock (based on the play by Seymour Hicks, George Edwardes.

Mystery **(PR:A MPAA:NR)**

ONE OF THE BRAVEST** 1/2** (1925) 6 reels GOTH/LUM bw

Ralph Lewis *(John Kelly)*, Edward Hearn *(Dan Kelly)*, Sidney Franklin *(Morris Levin)*, Pat Somerset *("Satin" Sanderson)*, Claire McDowell *(Mrs. Kelly)*, Marion Mack *(Sarah Levin)*.

Here the ABIE'S IRISH ROSE theme is given a few added thrills as an Irish firefighter (Hearn) falls in love with a Jewish girl (Mack). When the funds for the Fireman's Ball are discovered missing, Hearn—a coward in his fireman father's eyes because of his fear of fire—is accused of the theft and Mack's father lends him the funds to cover it. Later a big blaze breaks out and Hearn saves the day by rescuing his father and the real crook (after beating the tar out of the rat), and he and his Jewish sweetheart become engaged.

d, Frank O'Connor; sup, Renaud Hoffman; w, Henry McCarty (based on a story by James J. Tynan); ph, Ray June; ed, Irene Morra.

Adventure **(PR:A MPAA:NR)**

ONE PUNCH O'DAY* (1926) 5 reels Harry J. Brown/RAY bw

Billy Sullivan *(Jimmy O'Day)*, Charlotte Merriam *(Alice Felton)*, Jack Herrick *(Joe Hemmingway)*, William Malan *(Elwood Felton)*, J. C. Fowler *(Charles Hargreaves)*, Eddie Diggins *(Kid Martin)*.

Minor B effort has a prizefighter putting on a bout to win the cash needed to buy back the oil lease his sweetheart's father (using the whole town's funds) was swindled out of. The boxer also knocks out the crooks before the movie's end.

d, Harry J. Brown; w, Henry R. Symonds.

Drama **(PR:A MPAA:NR)**

ONE-ROUND HOGAN** 1/2** (1927) 7 reels WB bw

Monte Blue *(Robert Emmett Hogan)*, Leila Hyams *(Helen Davis)*, James J. Jeffries *(Tim Hogan)*, Frank Hagney *("Big Joe" Morgan)*, Tom Gallery *(Ed Davis)*, Texas Kid *(Himself)*, Abdul the Turk *(Sniffy)*.

Standard boxing film with Blue making a convincing appearance as the fighting son of a former pugilist, played surprisingly well by former heavyweight champion of the world Jeffries. There are the usual complications, ending with Blue winning the big match—and the love of the girl who always opposed the sport.

d, Howard Bretherton; w, Charles R. Condon (based on a story by F. L. Giffen, George Godfrey); ph, Norbert Brodin.

Sport/Drama **(PR:A MPAA:NR)**

ONE SHOT ROSS*** (1917) 5 reels TRI bw

Roy Stewart *(One Shot Ross)*, Josie Sedgwick *(Nan Sheridan)*, Jack Richardson *(Jim Butler)*, Louis Durham *("Shorty")*, William Ellingford *(Mr. Sheridan)*, Leo Willis *(Briggs)*.

Hillyer, who directed some of William S. Hart's best films, scripted this western about a man (Stewart) so good with his shootin' irons that he's known as One Shot. Deciding to give up the gunfighting life, he's caught without his pistols while leaving the territory and almost beaten to death. He falls in love with the daughter of the rancher who nurses him back to health, and straps on his guns one more time to save them from the band of outlaws who earlier attacked him.

d, Cliff Smith; w, Lambert Hillyer.

Western **(PR:A MPAA:NR)**

ONE SPLENDID HOUR* (1929) 6 reels EXCEL bw

Viola Dana *(Bobbie Walsh)*, George Periolat *(Sen. Walsh)*, Allan Simpson *(Dr. Thornton)*, Lewis Sargent *(Jimmy O'Shea)*, Jack Richardson *(Peter Hoag)*, Lucy Beaumont *(Mother Kelly)*, Florice Cooper *(Rose Kelly)*, Ernie S. Adams *(Solly)*, Hugh Saxon *(The Roue)*, Charles Hickman *(Police Captain)*.

Looking for kicks, Dana, a socialite with a sense of adventure, drops in at a skid row cafe and is strongly attracted to Simpson, a neighborhood settlement doctor. When she returns the following night, a couple of tough lugs make a pass, and Simpson knocks them cold. Everyone ends up in night court where Dana reveals her true identity, and from then on she and the good doctor begin to keep steady company.

d, Burton King; w, Sylvia Bernstein, Jacques Jaccard, Isadore Bernstein (based on a story by Adeline Leitzbach); ph, William Miller, Walter Hass; ed, Betty Davis.

Drama **(PR:A MPAA:NR)**

ONE STOLEN NIGHT* (1923) 5 reels VIT bw

Alice Calhoun *(Diantha Ebberly)*, Herbert Heyes *(Herbert Medford)*, Otto Hoffman *(Horace Ebberly)*, Adele Farrington *(Mrs. Ebberly)*, Russ Powell, Oliver Hardy.

Blatant ripoff of THE SHEIK has a young English girl (Calhoun) traveling to the Sahara to meet her fiance for the first time, becoming involved with a dashing Arab who saves her life, and in the end discovering to her delight that *he* is her betrothed. Remade in 1929 by Warner Brothers under the same title.

d, Robert Ensminger; w, Bradley J. Smollen (based on the story "The Arab" by D. D. Calhoun); ph, Steve Smith, Jr.

Romance **(PR:A MPAA:NR)**

ONE SUMMER'S DAY** (1917, Brit.) 4 reels BA bw

Fay Compton *(Maisie)*, Owen Nares *(Capt. Dick Rudyard)*, Sam Livesey *(Philip Marsden)*, Eva Westlake *(Chiara)*, A. G. Poulton, Caleb Porter, Roy Royston, Gwendoline Jesson.

The intrigue gets pretty thick in this British drama about a captain who adopts the daughter of a gypsy, only to later find himself the victim of blackmail. Features Compton, one of England's more appealing actresses.

d, Frank G. Bayley; w, H. V. Esmond (based on a play by Esmond).

Drama **(PR:A MPAA:NR)**

$1,000 REWARD* (1923) 5 reels Charles R. Seeling/AY bw

Big Boy Williams.

Low-budget Williams film has the cowboy wrongly accused of a murder, escaping to become deputy sheriff in another town, and there arresting the hombre who framed him in the first place.

d, Charles R. Seeling.

Western **(PR:A MPAA:NR)**

ONE WEEK OF LOVE*** (1922) 7 reels SF bw

Elaine Hammerstein *(Beth Wynn)*, Conway Tearle *(Buck Fearnley)*, Kate Lester *(Mrs. Wynn, Beth's Aunt)*, Hallam Cooley *(Francis Fraser)*.

Hammerstein agrees to marry wealthy Cooley if he can defeat her in an airplane race. When her plane crashes into a Mexican mountainside, she is rescued by Tearle, a renegade, whom Hammerstein manages to reform after a week. Tearle then returns the young lady to Cooley, but there's a flood, followed by a train wreck in which the millionaire is killed. Fortunately Tearle gets there in time to rescue Hammerstein and win her love. Tearle shines in this offbeat role.

p, Myron Selznick; d, George Archainbaud; w, (based on a story by Edward J. Montgue Archainbaud); ph, Jules Cronjager; ed, H. P. Bretherton, Harold McCord.

Drama **(PR:A MPAA:NR)**

ONE WILD WEEK* (1921) 5 reels REA bw

Bebe Daniels *(Pauline Hathaway)*, Frank Kingsley *(Bruce Reynolds)*, Mayme Kelso *(Emma Jessop)*, Frances Raymond *(Mrs. Brewster)*, Herbert Standing *(Judge Bancroft)*, Edwin Stevens *(Oliver Tobin)*, Edythe Chapman *(Mrs. Dorn)*, Carrie Clark Ward *(Cook)*, Bull Montana *(Red Mike)*.

In what would seem an attempt to capitalize on the publicity Daniels received for her real life trip to jail for speeding violations, her studio came up with this terrible flapper comedy about a girl who is wrongly arrested for picking a pocket and is forced to then experience a number of not-very-funny escapades in order to protect her considerable inheritance.

d, Maurice Campbell; w, Percy Heath (based on a story by Frances Harmer); ph, H. Kinley Martin.

Comedy **(PR:A MPAA:NR)**

ONE WOMAN TO ANOTHER** 1/2** (1927) 5 reels FP/PAR bw

Florence Vidor *(Rita Farrell)*, Theodore Von Eltz *(John Bruce)*, Marie Shotwell *(Mrs. Gray)*, Hedda Hopper *(Olive Grenshaw)*, Roy Stewart *(Rev. Robert Farrell)*, Joyce Coad *(The Niece)*, Jimsy Boudwin *(The Nephew)*.

Marion's titles are the best thing this bedroom farce has going for it. The picture has to do with a young couple, Vidor and Von Eltz, who are having one whale of a time getting married. And then, to make things worse, the lad is not allowed to see his fiancee because the children she is caring for have developed a disease and are under quarantine for what seems like an eternity. It's then that a hot little cutie sets out to vamp the lad, which drives his sweetheart to pull a little trick of her own, and the couple finally get it together.

d, Frank Tuttle; w, J. L. Campbell (based on the play "The Ruined Lady" by Frances Nordstrom); t, George Marion, Jr.; ph, L. Guy Wilky.

Comedy **(PR:A MPAA:NR)**

ONE YEAR TO LIVE** (1925) 7 reels FN bw

Aileen Pringle *(Elsie Duchanier)*, Dorothy Mackaill *(Marthe)*, Sam De Grasse *(Dr. Lucien La Pierre)*, Rosemary Theby *(Lolette)*, Leo White *(Stage Manager)*, Joseph Kilgour *(Maurice Brunel)*, Antonio Moreno *(Capt. Tom Kendrick)*, Rose Dione *(Nanette)*, Chester Conklin *(Froquin)*.

Pretty hokey stuff about Pringle, the maid to a French dancing star, who is told that she has only a year to live. Consequently, she agrees to give herself to Paris theatrical producer Kilgour if he can make her a star during her lifetime. He does, but Pringle doesn't fulfill her promise to him because Moreno, the U.S. officer she has worshipped from a distance, returns to France, saves her from a fate almost worse than death, proves that the doctor's prognosis was a lie, and then asks the lady to be his, which she happily agrees to.

d, Irving Cummings; w, J. G. Hawks (based on a newspaper series by John Hunter); t, Robert Hopkins; ph, Arthur L. Todd; ed, Charles J. Hunt; art d, Jack Okey.

Drama **(PR:A MPAA:NR)**

ONLY A MILL GIRL* (1919, Brit.) 5 reels Foxwell/ID bw

Harry Foxwell *(John Raymond)*, Betty Farquhar *(Mary)*, Arthur Condy *(Jack Ainsleigh)*, Ida Lambert *(Constance Darville)*, Frank Lovett *(George Thornton)*.

This British melodrama about the daughter of a foreman who prevents a woman with plenty of money, but no scruples, from stealing an inventor's plans, doesn't exactly keep the audience riveted to their seats.

p, Harry Foxwell; d, Lewis Willoughby (based on a play by Sheila Walsh).

Drama **(PR:A MPAA:NR)**

ONLY A SHOP GIRL½** (1922) 7 reels C.B.C. Film Sales bw

Estelle Taylor *(Mame Mulvey)*, Mae Busch *(Josie Jerome)*, Wallace Beery *(Jim Brennan)*, William Scott *(Danny Mulvey)*, James Morrison *(Charles Black)*, Josephine Adair *(Angelina Jerome)*, Willard Louis *(James Watkins)*, Claire Du Brey *(Mrs. Watkins)*, Tully Marshall *(Manager of Watkins' Store)*.

Cohn built his Columbia Studio by cranking out acceptable programmers such as this one about an ex-con (Scott) who takes the blame for a murder he believes his sweetheart (Busch) committed. Of course the real killer makes a deathbed confession, after being saved from an adequately filmed fire sequence.

p, Harry Cohn; d&w, Edward J. Le Saint.

Drama **(PR:A MPAA:NR)**

ONLY SON, THE* (1914) 5 reels LAS bw

Thomas W. Ross, Jane Darwell, James Blackwell, Merta Carpenter, M. MacMillan, John P. Wild, Fred Starr, Milton Brown.

Ross brought his breezy comic characterization from the stage to screen but failed to make it work. In fact the picture fell down on every level, including the big scene, which went for the heartstrings, as the only son of the family sticks by his mother when she is cast aside by his father. Jesse Lasky was shooting for another BREWSTER'S MILLIONS with this one and ended up with small change.

d, Thomas N. Heffron; sup, William C. DeMille; w, Clara Beranger (based on the play by Winchell Smith).

Comedy/Drama **(PR:A MPAA:NR)**

ONLY 38*** (1923) 7 reels FP-LAS/PAR bw

May McAvoy *(Lucy Stanley)*, Lois Wilson *(Mrs. Stanley)*, Elliott Dexter *(Prof. Charles Giddings)*, George Fawcett *(Hiram Sanborn)*, Robert Agnew *(Bob Stanley)*, Jane Keckley *(Mrs. Newcomb)*, Lillian Leighton *(Mrs. Peters)*, Taylor Graves *(Sydney Johnson)*, Anne Cornwall *(Mary Hedley)*.

Well-done DeMille-McAvoy picture about the mother of teenage twins who drops her dowdy ways when her minister husband dies, falls in love with a college instructor but gives him up when her selfish children fail to approve. Later they come to understand the situation, and the wonderful McAvoy is allowed the happiness she deserves.

d, William C. De Mille; w, Clara Beranger (based on the play by A. E. Thomas); ph, Guy Wilky.

Dramatic/Comedy **(PR:A MPAA:NR)**

ONLY WAY, THE*** (1926, Brit.) 10 reels Herbert Wilcox/FN bw

John Martin Harvey *(Sidney Carton)*, Madge Stuart *(Mimi)*, Betty Faire *(Lucy Manette)*, Ben Webster *(Marquis St. Evremonde)*, J. Fisher White *(Dr. Manette)*, Frederick Cooper *(Charles Darnay)*, Mary Brough *(Miss Pross)*, Frank Stanmore *(Jarvis Lorry)*, Gibb McLaughlin *(Barsad)*, Gordon McLeod *(Ernest Defarge)*, Jean Jay *(Jeanne Defarge)*, Margaret Yarde *(The Vengeance)*, Judd Green *(Prosecution)*, Fred Rains *(President)*, Jack Raymond *(Jacques)*, Michael Martin Harvey *(No. 46)*.

Inspired by the great Dickens novel, this lavishly produced British film told of a down-and-out English aristocrat who volunteers to go to the guillotine in place of his double during the French reign of terror. Nicely directed by the Irish-born Wilcox, this was one of Britain's better silent efforts.

p,d&w, Herbert Wilcox (based on the novel *A Tale of Two Cities* by Charles Dickens, and the play by Freeman Wills, Frederick Longbridge).

Costume **(PR:A MPAA:NR)**

ONLY WOMAN, THE*** (1924) 7 reels Norma Talmadge/FN bw

Norma Talmadge *(Helen Brinsley)*, Eugene O'Brien *(Rex Herrington)*, Edwards Davis *("Fighting Jerry" Herrington, Rex's Father)*, Winter Hall *(William Brinsley)*, Matthew Betz *(Ole Hanson)*, E. H. Calvert *(Rodney Blake)*, Stella Di Lanti *(Bingo)*, Murdock MacQuarrie *(Yacht Captain)*, Rev. Neal Dodd *(A Minister)*, Brooks Benedict *(1st Officer)*, Charles O'Malley *(Steward)*.

First National invested a lot of money, and Olcott and Talmadge combined their talents to make this predictable story much more than just an average programmer. It's all about a ruthless millionaire, Davis, who blackmails Talmadge into marrying his drunken son O'Brien in hopes that she can make a *real* man out of him. Before the film's end, Davis proves his true mettle to her, and Talmadge discovers she has fallen in love with her husband. Dodd, who plays the part of a clergyman, was actually the popular minister of Hollywood's Little Church Around the Corner.

d, Sidney Olcott; w, (based on a story by C. Gardner Sullivan); ph, Tony Gaudio.

Drama **(PR:A MPAA:NR)**

ONWARD CHRISTIAN SOLDIERS***

(1918, Brit.) 5 reels G. B. Samuelson bw

Isobel Elsom *(The Girl)*, Owen Nares *(The Soldier)*, Minna Grey *(The Sister)*, Tom Reynolds *(The Man)*.

British wartime tearjerker about a homely girl who sends the picture of her pretty sister to a soldier at the front and then marries him after he is blinded in battle.

d, Rex Wilson.

War/Romance **(PR:A MPAA:NR)**

OPEN ALL NIGHT*** (1924) 6 reels FP-LAS/PAR bw

Viola Dana *(Therese Duverne)*, Jetta Goudal *(Lea)*, Adolphe Menjou *(Edmund Duverne)*, Raymond Griffith *(Igor)*, Maurice B. Flynn *(Petit Mathieu)*, Gale Henry *(Isabelle Fevre)*, Jack Giddings *(Von De Hoven)*, Charles Puffy *(Bibendum)*.

Sophisticated comedy has Dana, a woman who craves to be dominated by a man, becoming involved with famous bicyclist Flynn, while her easygoing husband, Menjou, falls under the spell of vampish beauty Goudal. There is a hilarious six-day race which takes place before the married couple come to realize that they are ideally suited for one another.

d, Paul Bern; w, Willis Goldbeck (based on a story by Paul Morand); ph, Bert Glennon.

Comedy **(PR:A MPAA:NR)**

OPEN COUNTRY* (1922, Brit.) 5 reels STOLL bw

Dorinea Shirley *(Sanchia Percival)*, David Hawthorne *(Neville Ingram)*, Bertram Burleigh *(Jack Senhouse)*, George Bellamy *(Mr. Percival)*, Norma Whalley *(Mrs. Percival)*, Miles Mander *(Honorable William Chevenix)*, Bryan Powley *(Roger Charnock)*, Isobel Lee *(Vicky Percival)*, Rosina Wright *(Mrs. Percival)*.

British drama about a millionaire who gives up everything to take on the life of a strolling artist. During his travels he meets and falls in love with a beautiful girl, but as fate would have it (and usually did in these less-than-brilliant English things), she has given her heart to a married man.

d&w, Sinclair Hill (based on a novel by Maurice Hewlett).

Drama **(PR:C MPAA:NR)**

OPEN YOUR EYES* (1919) 7 reels WB bw

Faire Binney, Gaston Glass, Mrs. Joupert, Jack Hopkins, Halbert Brown, Eddie Beryll, Emily Marceau, Viola Allen, Ben Lyon, Jack Warner.

This exploitation film opens with a medical convention where statistics concerning the dangers of syphilis are discussed. The picture then fades to the story of a well-bred girl who falls in love with a young man who has tasted the "delights" of Broadway and contracted the sexual disease. At their wedding, a suburban girl, whom the groom seduced, infected, and then set up in a love nest, steps forward and blows the whistle. The producers claimed that the picture was made to alert the public to the dangers of the dreaded disease and to warn them to stay away from quacks who claimed to possess miracle cures. The fact that the Brothers Warner made a few dollars along the way, however, was no mere coincidence.

d, Gilbert P. Hamilton; w, Saul L. Warner, C. B. Mintz.

Exploitation **(PR:C MPAA:NR)**

OPENED SHUTTERS, THE*** (1914) 4 reels Gold Seal bw

Anna Little, Herbert Rawlinson, Betty Schade, William Worthington, Cora Drew, Frank Lloyd.

Provocative Weber script has a young girl, who is thought ill of by her strict New England aunt and uncle, taken in by a dear man who treats her with kindness and brings out her inner beauty. An heiress later takes an interest in the child and sponsors her education as an artist. A few years pass, and when the girl becomes successful she falls in love with a millionaire who buys her an old mill for use as a studio. At the end of the picture, all of the characters are assembled, and, in a nice Weberian touch, the blinds are lifted and for the first time they are seen in their true light.

d, Otis Turner; w, Lois Weber (based on a novel by Clara Louise Burnham).

Drama **(PR:A MPAA:NR)**

ORA PRO NOBIS (1917, Brit.) 5 reels Windsor/Walturdaw bw

Henry Victor *(Lord Osborne)*, Harding Thomas *(The Organist)*.

British drama has a musician falling asleep and dreaming that he murders the nobleman who ran off and married his adopted daughter.

p, Arrigo Bocchi; d, Rex Wilson; w, (based on a story by Rowland Talbot).

Drama **(PR:A MPAA:NR)**

ORDEAL, THE*** (1914) 5 reels Life Photo bw

William H. Tooker *(The General)*, George De Carlton *(The Father)*, Harry Spingler *(The Patriot)*, Anna Laughlin *(The Patriot's Sweetheart)*, Margot Williams *(His Sister)*, Mrs. Balfour *(His Mother)*.

This blatantly anti-German, pro-Allied motion picture caused quite a stir when it was released in 1914. The German government issued a formal complaint to Washington, and German-American societies were outraged. They had good reason to be; in the picture a French youth (using a dream sequence) is captured by the "Bosch" and the interrogating general, who is the spitting image of the Kaiser, proceeds to have the lad's entire family single-handedly marched before a Teutonic firing squad in an attempt to make the young patriot give away the position of his men. The youth refuses and the slaughter continues until he is awakened from the nightmare. Needless to say the protestations of the Central Powers fell on deaf ears, but it only took a few years for the message of this film to accomplish its goal.

w, Edward M. Roskam (based on the poem "The Ballad of Splendid Silence" by E. Nesbitt).

War **(PR:C MPAA:NR)**

ORDEAL, THE** (1922) 5 reels FP-LAS/PAR bw

Clarence Burton *(George Bruce)*, Agnes Ayres *(Sybil Bruce)*, Conrad Nagel *(Dr. Robert Acton)*, Edna Murphy *(Helen Crayshaw)*, Anne Schaefer *(Minnie)*, Eugene Corey *(Gene)*, Adele Farrington *(Mme. St. Levis)*, Edward Martindel *(Sir Francis Maynard)*, Shannon Day *(Kitty)*, Claire Du Brey *(Elise)*.

Ayres marries a man 20 years her senior in order to provide for her brother and sister. When her husband dies, it is suspected that she killed him by withholding his medication because she has fallen in love with Nagel. A provision of the old boy's will forbids her to remarry, and Nagel refuses to entertain a *real* love affair unless the act is sanctioned by God. Later the maid confesses to the killing, Ayres renounces her fortune, and the long-suffering lady is rewarded by a good (and consecrated) romance .

d, Paul Powell; w, Buelah Marie Dix (based on a story by W. Somerset Maugham); ph, Harry Perry.

Drama **(PR:C MPAA:NR)**

ORPHAN OF THE SAGE** 1/2** (1928) 6 reels FBO bw

Buzz Barton *(David "Red" Hepner)*, Frank Rice *(Hank Robbins)*, Tom Lingham *(Jeff Perkins)*, Annabelle Magnus *(Mary Jane Perkins)*, Bill Patton *(Nevada Naldene)*.

Action-packed film produced for the kids' market had Barton, the boy cowboy, riding like blazes to bring back the army to rescue a wagon train under Indian attack. Nothing new in this oater, but then nothing new was expected—or desired.

d, Louis King; w, Oliver Drake; t, Helen Gregg; ph, Nick Musuraca; ed, Jack Kitchen, Della King.

Western **(PR:A MPAA:NR)**

ORPHANS OF THE STORM**** (1922) 12 reels D. W. Griffith/UA bw

Lillian Gish *(Henriette Girard)*, Dorothy Gish *(Louise)*, Joseph Schildkraut *(Chevalier de Vaudrey)*, Frank Losee *(Count de Linieres)*, Katherine Emmett *(Countess de Linieres)*, Morgan Wallace *(Marquis de Praille)*, Lucille La Verne *(Mother Frochard)*, Sheldon Lewis *(Jacques Frochard)*, Frank Puglia *(Pierre Frochard)*, Creighton Hale *(Picard)*, Leslie King *(Jacques-Forget-Not)*, Monte Blue *(Danton)*, Sidney Herbert *(Robespierre)*, Lee Kohlmar *(King Louis XVI)*, Adolphe Lestina *(Doctor)*, Kate Bruce *(Sister Genevieve)*, Flora Finch *(Starving Peasant)*, Louis Wolheim *(Executioner)*, Kenny Delmar *(The Chevalier, as a Boy)*, Herbert Sutch *(Meat-Carver at Fete)*, James Smith, Rose Smith *(Dancers)*.

When Lillian Gish suggested to D. W. Griffith that he film the old melodrama "The Two Orphans," the director replied, "You only want me to make that story because there's a part in it for Dorothy." The actress defended her position by pointing out that the play had been successful in 40 languages and that in New York alone, during the 1920s, it had played Chinese, German, and Yiddish theaters and at that very moment was playing an Italian theater. The couple decided to see the play for themselves, and although he understood not a word of the language, Griffith was so impressed by the performance of Frank Puglia that when he decided to make the film he hired the actor to repeat his role of Pierre, the cripple. Griffith sensed that the little play lacked the scope for a major motion picture, so he changed the period to the time leading up to the French Revolution, which gave him all the latitude in the world. The film opens with the slaying of a commoner, who married a daughter of the powerful de Vaudrey family, by her irate relatives. Her infant daughter is taken from her and placed on the steps of Notre Dame with a large purse and a note reading: "Her name is Louise. Save her." An impoverished man, who has brought his own child to the cathedral in the hopes of finding her a home, is so touched by the sight of the deserted baby that he is moved to return home with both of them. The money is substantial and allows him to raise both girls in comfortable provincial surroundings. While they are in their teens a terrible plague strikes the countryside, killing both parents and leaving one of the girls, Dorothy Gish, blinded. The story really gets underway now as Lillian Gish takes her "sister" to Paris in hopes of finding a doctor who can restore her sight. Along the way they encounter a villainous nobleman, Wallace, who later abducts Lillian when the girls arrive in Paris. Poor Dorothy, now unaided, almost falls into the Seine River, but she is rescued by Puglia, the crippled and abused son of an old hag, La Verne, and her other son Lewis. Lillian, meanwhile, is taken to a fete which is attended by the dashing Chevalier de Vaudrey (Schildkraut) who feels a sense of empathy for the downtrodden and is the nephew of Dorothy's real mother, Emmett, now the wife of a count (Losee), the prefect of the Paris police, from whom she has kept her past a secret. At this beautifully staged bacchanal, Lillian becomes the victim of the aristocrats' cruelty, but Schildkraut comes to her defense, wounds Wallace in a duel, and they escape. When Schildkraut attempts to secure the prefect's aid in finding Dorothy, the official, angered by the youth's earlier behavior, refuses. But his aunt, wishing to help, goes to visit Lillian in her apartment. In the meantime, the young lady has attracted the attention of Danton (Blue), much to the chagrin of his associate, the woman-hating Robespierre (Herbert). Griffith, as always, keeps the interest perking right along by switching to the plight of Dorothy, who is completely at the mercy of old hag La Verne, and Lewis, who has been prevented from having his way with the girl only through the intervention of his brother Puglia. The evil mother and older son are intent on turning the blind beauty into a street singer, and after stalwartly refusing, Dorothy finally succumbs when she is thrown into a rat-infested cellar. Then, in a truly memorable scene, Lillian is shown conversing with the countess when she hears Dorothy singing in the street below. She rushes to the window, catches a glimpse of her and then bolts towards the door. But before she can reach her sister, the prefect arrives and places Lillian under arrest. So powerful is this scene, that audiences over the years have sworn they could actually hear Dorothy's voice. But Lillian is not the only victim. Schildkraut is also apprehended and placed in confinement just outside of Paris. Then the revolution erupts, the Bastille is stormed and Lillian is set free. The young lady makes her way through the madly celebrating mobs and wanders into the dwelling place of La Verne. Spotting her sister's scarf, Lillian is told that the girl is dead. Meanwhile, Schildkraut escapes and takes refuge in Lillian's room. A former enemy observes this, notifies the revolutionary guards, and the couple are taken to the courtroom where their fate under the reign of terror is all but assured. In the court Blue sees them being carted off and makes a stirring speech before the body, pleading for moderation. Puglia, meanwhile, finds the courage to take on his formidable older brother and kills him in a knife fight. By this time Blue has won the crowd over to his side, but Lillian and Schildkraut are already on the way to the guillotine. So still another of Griffith's hair-raising, splendidly edited chases is committed to film. Lillian is already on the block, head in place, when Puglia leaps up on the stand and stabs the executioner before he can cause the blade to fall. The picture ends with Emmett telling her husband the truth about her past—about which he is sympathetic—Lillian marrying Schildkraut, Dorothy having her sight restored, and the countess taking Puglia in for saving her daughter. This was the last picture the Gish sisters would make together and the last one Lillian Gish would make for Griffith. In a moving portion of her autobiography, she writes of their separation and tells how the great director called her to his office: "'You know as much about the high cost of making pictures as I do,' he said. 'With all the expenses I have, I can't afford to pay you what you're worth.' I read his mind in an instant, remembering Mary Pickford, Blanche Sweet, Mae Marsh—all the stars he had created and then sent on their way. 'You should go out on your own. Your name is of as much value as mine with the public, and I think in your own interest you should capitalize on it while you can.'" That was truly the end of an era. And it surely says something about the man who made her a star. When she wrote her book *The Movies, Mr. Griffith, and Me* some 49 years later, she gave herself third billing.

p&d, D. W. Griffith; w, Gaston de Tolignac [Griffith] (based on the play "The Two Orphans" by Adolphe Philippe Dennery, Eugene Cormon and material inspired by *A Tale of Two Cities* by Charles Dickens and *The French Revolution* by Thomas Carlyle.); ph, Hendrik Sartov, Paul Allen, G. W. Bitzer; ed, James and Rose Smith; art d, Charles M. Kirk; set d, Edward Scholl.

Historical Drama **Cas.** **(PR:A MPAA:NR)**

OTHER KIND OF LOVE, THE** (1924) 5 reels Phil Goldstone bw

William Fairbanks *(Adam Benton)*, Dorothy Revier *(Elsie Brent)*, Edith Yorke *(Mary Benton)*, Robert Keith *(George Benton)*, Rhea Mitchell *(The Chorus Girl)*.

Fairbanks proved here that he could, when the occasion arose, handle dramatic as well as action roles. In the story he gives his live savings to his wastrel college student-brother, Keith, to keep the bum out of jail. At the same time, Fairbanks' sweetheart, Revier (who is attracted to men with "book learnin'"), has a fling with Keith and marries him. Before long it's revealed that Keith already has a little woman, after the girl just happens to drop over to say hello. Her arrival sparks a terrific fist fight between the brothers, which culminates in Keith's regeneration. Then Revier realizes that Fairbanks is the better catch after all—a development which is uncomplicated by the fact that the bride and groom never got around to consummating their arrangement.

d, Duke Worne; w, Jefferson Moffitt (based on the story "Thicker Than Water" by Buckleigh Fritz Oxford); ph, Roland Price.

Drama **(PR:A MPAA:NR)**

OTHER MAN, THE*** (1918) 5 reels VIT bw

Harry Morey *(John Stedman/Martin West)*, Grace Darmond *(Dorothy Harmon)*, Florence Deshon *(Lucia)*, Frank Norcross *(The Political Boss)*, Jessie Stevens *(Mrs. Holohan)*, Stanley Walpole, Mrs. Chapin.

Nicely done melodrama has a doctor hitting the skids when his wife leaves him for another man. He becomes a surgeon to gangsters who sober him up when one of their boys takes a slug. Society girl Darmond bets her chums $10,000 that she can live in the slums for a month on $5. During that time, she meets the doctor and on his recommendation is given a job at a boardinghouse. They fall in love, and after she wins her bet Darmond arranges for the money to be used for his regeneration. At this point, fate intervenes and the lovers are separated. But, some time later when he is once again at the top of his profession, the doctor is summoned to a swanky hotel to perform an emergency operation, finds the woman for whom he has been searching, and they are united forever.

d, Paul Scardon; w, Fred Buckley (based on a story by Rex Taylor, Irma Whelpley Taylor).

Drama **(PR:A MPAA:NR)**

OTHER MAN'S WIFE, THE* (1919) 5 reels WB bw

Ellen Cassity *(Mrs. Fred Hartley)*, Stuart Holmes *(J. Douglas Kerr)*, Ned Hay *(Fred Hartley)*, Olive Trevor *(Elsie Drummond)*, Halbert Brown *(Bruce Drummond)*, Mrs. Garrison *(Mrs. Bruce Drummond)*, Lesley Casey *(Wilbur Drummond)*, Danny Sullivan *(Jimmy Moore)*, Regina Quinn *(Betty Moore)*, Laura Newman *(Mrs. Moore)*, George Jessel *(Davy Simon)*, Evelyn Brent *(Becky Simon)*, Tom Cameron.

Another of the old husband-works-too-hard, ignores-the-needs-of-his-wife-but-sees-the-light-in-the-end stories—is not helped very much even by the inclusion of German spies and scenes of labor unrest.

d, Carl Harbaugh; w, Mary Murillo; ph, William Crowley.

Drama **(PR:A MPAA:NR)**

OTHER MEN'S DAUGHTERS** (1918) 5 reels FOX bw

Peggy Hyland *(Shirley Reynolds)*, Eric Mayne *(Shirley's Father)*, Elizabeth Garrison *(Shirley's Mother)*, Regina Quinn *(Lola Wayne)*, Riley Hatch *(Lola's Father)*, Frank Goldsmith *(Trask)*, Robert Middlemass *(Richard Ormsby)*.

Unpleasant little melodrama has Hyland, the only daughter of a millionaire who is having an affair with a young rural girl turned dancer, attempting to prevent her parents from divorcing. Meanwhile, the father of the girl involved in the affair, gets wind of what is going on and comes to New York to try and drag Hyland down to his own child's level. Good performances all around, but not exactly a barrel of laughs.

d, Carl Harbaugh; w, (based on a story by E. Lloyd Sheldon).

Drama **(PR:A MPAA:NR)**

OTHER PERSON, THE** (1921, Brit.) 6 reels Granger-Binger bw

Zoe Palmer *(Alice Dene)*, Adelqui Migliar *(Andrew Grain)*, Arthur Pusey *(Chris Larcher)*, E. Story-Gofton *(Dr. Pess)*, William Huntre *(Amos Larcher)*, Ivo Dawson *(Squire Grain)*, Nora Hayden *(Dolly Banks)*, Arthur Walcott *(Rev. Augustus Dene)*.

British mystery-fantasy in which it is shown at a seance that a spiritualist was forced to commit a murder at the bidding of a ghost.

d, B. E. Doxat-Pratt; w, Benedict James (based on a novel by Fergus Hume).

Fantasy **(PR:A MPAA:NR)**

OUR DANCING DAUGHTERS*** (1928) 9 reels COS/MGM bw

Joan Crawford *(Diana Medford)*, John Mack Brown *(Ben Blaine)*, Nils Asther *(Norman)*, Dorothy Sebastian *(Beatrice)*, Anita Page *(Ann)*, Kathlyn Williams *(Ann's Mother)*, Edward Nugent *(Freddie)*, Dorothy Cumming *(Diana's Mother)*, Huntley Gordon *(Diana's Father)*, Evelyn Hall *(Freddie's Mother)*, Sam De Grasse *(Freddie's Father)*.

It was this film which soared Crawford to superstardom. In it she plays a saucy, gin-drinking, fast-stepping flapper in love with millionaire Brown, who is deeply hurt when he marries Page. The marriage turns out to have been an arrangement which the bride, a heavy drinker, was forced into by her mother. In the end Page is killed in a fall and Brown turns to Crawford for comfort and true love.

p, Hunt Stromberg; d, Harry Beaumont; w, Josephine Lovett; t, Marian Ainslee, Ruth Cummings; ph, George Barnes; ed, William Hamilton; set d, Cedric Gibbons; cos, David Cox; song, "I Loved You Then As I Love You Now" by Ballard MacDonald, William Axt, David Mendoza; syn sc; s eff.

Romance **(PR:A MPAA:NR)**

OUR HOSPITALITY**** (1923) 7 reels Joseph M. Schenk/Metro bw

Buster Keaton *(William McKay)*, Natalie Talmadge *(Virginia Canfield)*, Buster Keaton, Jr. *(The Baby)*, Joseph Keaton *(Lem Doolittle)*, Kitty Bradbury *(Aunt Mary)*, Joe Roberts *(Joseph Canfield)*, Leonard Clapham *(James Canfield)*, Craig Ward *(Lee Canfield)*, Ralph Bushman *(Clayton Canfield)*, Edward Coxen *(John McKay)*, Jean Dumas *(Mrs. McKay)*, Monte Collins *(Rev. Benjamin Dorsey)*, James Duffy *(Sam Gardner)*.

One of Keaton's very best, OUR HOSPITALITY has everything— nostalgia (it's set in the American South of 1831), thrills, plenty of laughs, and a great story line. In it Keaton heads South to claim his family inheritance. Entertaining a vision of the ante-bellum land of Dixie, so often illustrated on calendars, he makes the journey on the funniest little railroad train ever filmed. (The comedian was fascinated by all things mechanical and selected the Stephenson Rocket for this film because it was the oddest looking of all the vintage trains. Keaton had it duplicated—down to the tiniest detail—and when the project was completed, donated it to the Smithsonian Institute). On board he meets Talmadge (Keaton's real-life wife) who invites him to dinner. While eating, Keaton learns that he's the last survivor of the family with which his hosts have had a long and very deadly feud, and that they intend to shoot him. The only thing stopping them is Southern hospitality—it just wouldn't do to kill a guest in one's own home. The Yankee therefore pulls every gag in the book to avoid leaving and finally makes his escape dressed as a woman. He races for the river, with the girl's family in hot pursuit, followed by Talmadge, who wishes to save him. The girl falls into the water and Keaton, in one of his most spectacular sequences, saves her from falling over a waterfall by swinging from a rope on a ledge and catching her as she topples into his arms. This act of bravery endears him to her family, and the age-old rivalry is brought to an end. The last stunt proved a very difficult one to execute and caused the comedian a great deal of pain. A number of takes were of course necessary, and on one occasion the wire which was used for support purposes snapped, and Keaton plunged head first into the water below, nearly drowning, and had to be taken to a hospital. Then, in an earlier sequence which had him rushing down the river grasping a 16 foot-long log, the wire also broke and he was nearly battered to death in the rapids. The camera of course kept grinding, capturing the moment where Keaton barely saves himself by grabbing some overhead branches, and the incredible scene was included in the finished print.

d, Buster Keaton, John Blystone; w&t, Jean Havez, Joseph Mitchell, Clyde Bruckman; ph, Elgin Lessley, Gordon Jennings; art d, Fred Gabourie.

Comedy **(PR:A MPAA:NR)**

OUR LEADING CITIZEN*** (1922) 7 reels FP-LAS/PAR bw

Thomas Meighan *(Thomas Bentley, Lawyer)*, Lois Wilson *(Katherine Fendle, His Fiancee)*, William P. Carleton *(Oglesby Fendle, a Capitalist)*, Theodore Roberts *(Col. Sam De Mott, a Politician)*, Guy Oliver *(Cale Higginson, Dan's Friend)*, Laurence Wheat *(J. Sylvester Dubley, a Law Student)*, Charles Ogle *(The Judge)*, Tom Kennedy *(Boots)*, Sylvia Ashton *(Mrs. Brazey)*, Ethel Wales *(Eudora Mawdle)*, James Neill *(Honorable Cyrus Blagdon, Congressman)*, Lucien Littlefield *(The Editor)*.

Entertaining film about a small town lawyer (well played by Meighan) who goes off to war, returns a hero, is persuaded to run for congress by Wilson, a Red Cross girl he met in France, and wins the election in spite of his refusal to cooperate with the machine.

d, Alfred E. Green; w, Waldemar Young (based on a story by George Ade); ph, L. Guy Wilky, William Marshall.

Drama/Comedy **(PR:A MPAA:NR)**

OUR LITTLE WIFE*** (1918) 6 reels Goldwyn bw

Madge Kennedy *(Dodo)*, George Forth *(Herb)*, William Davidson *(Dr. Elliott)*, Wray Page *(Mrs. Elliott)*, Kempton Greene *(Tommy)*, Walter Hiers *(Bobo)*, Marguerite Marsh *(Angie)*, Gladys Fairbanks.

Well-paced farce has Kennedy (she excels at this sort of material) returning from her European honeymoon with three former suitors. There is a very funny confused-identities scene where Kennedy intervenes to prevent her girl friend from getting involved in what she believes to be a romantic encounter. And in the end, of course, her husband understands and accepts everything. Such is the charm the delightful Kennedy possesses.

d, Edward Dillon; w, Roy Somerville (based on a play by Avery Hopwood).

Comedy **(PR:A MPAA:NR)**

OUR MRS. McCHESNEY*** (1918) 5 reels Metro bw

Ethel Barrymore *(Emma McChesney)*, Huntley Gordon *(T. A. Buck, Jr.)*, Wilfred Lytell *(Jack McChesney)*, Lucille Lee Stewart *(Veva Sherwood)*, William H. St. James *(Ed Myers)*, Walter Percival *("Beauty" Blair)*, Ricca Allen *(Hattie Stitch)*, George Trimble *(Joe Greenbaum)*, Sammy Cooper *(Issy Greenbaum)*, Fred Walters *(Sam Harrison)*, John Daly Murphy.

Barrymore brings her stage success to the screen with equally satisfying results. She plays a department store buyer who designs a new dress style. Meanwhile, her son (who is somewhat of a goofball) marries a chorus girl, and the kindly Barrymore arranges for him to be brought into the firm and the girl to go to finishing school. At one point the lad is falsely accused of stealing company funds, but the movie's big punch comes when the model who is set to show Barrymore's design collapses, and her daughter-in-law takes over. The garment is a sensation, Barrymore marries her boss, and the two couples set off on a mutual honeymoon.

d, Ralph Ince; w, (based on the "Emma McChesney" stories by Edna Ferber).

Comedy/Drama **(PR:A MPAA:NR)**

OUR MODERN MAIDENS*** (1929) 8 reels MGM bw

Joan Crawford *(Billie)*, Rod La Rocque *(Abbott)*, Douglas Fairbanks, Jr. *(Gil)*, Anita Page *(Kentucky)*, Edward Nugent *(Reg)*, Josephine Dunn *(Ginger)*, Albert Gran *(B. Bickering Brown)*.

Crawford had already become America's quintessential flapper (with all of Louis B. Mayer's power behind her) when she made this picture with husband-to-be Fairbanks. In the film she marries him, endures his infidelity as long as she can, and after her divorce falls madly in love with La Rocque, the man who had once been her friend and confidant.

d, Jack Conway; w, Josephine Lovett; t, Marian Ainslee, Ruth Cummings; ph, Oliver Marsh; m, William Axt; ed, Sam S. Zimbalist; art d, Cedric Gibbons; ch, George Cunningham; syn sc; s eff.

Drama **(PR:A MPAA:NR)**

OUT ALL NIGHT*** (1927) 6 reels UNIV-Jewell bw

Reginald Denny *(John Graham)*, Marian Nixon *(Molly O'Day)*, Wheeler Oakman *(Kerrigan)*, Dorothy Earle *(Rose)*, Dan Mason *(Uncle)*, Alfred Allen *(Captain)*, Robert Seiter *(Purser)*, Ben Hendricks, Jr. *(Dr. Allen)*, Billy Franey *(Taxi Driver)*, Harry Tracey *(Valet)*, Lionel Braham *(Officer)*.

Plenty of punch in this Denny picture, which has the light comedian becoming stuck in an elevator overnight with musical comedy star Nixon. The two fall in love and head for the marriage bureau the very next morning. Then, when Nixon discovers that her job contract calls for a cut in salary in the event of her marrying, the couple decides to keep the union a secret. The laughs come fast and heavy as Nixon sails with her company for Europe, and Denny signs on as ship's doctor. It all works out in the end, of course, and the movie is a total delight all the way.

d, William A. Seiter; w, Harvey Thew, Marcel Perez, Charles Diltz (based on a story by Gladys Lehman); ph, Arthur Todd.

Comedy **(PR:A MPAA:NR)**

OUT OF A CLEAR SKY* (1918) 5 reels PAR bw

Marguerite Clark *(Countess Celeste de Bersek)*, Thomas Meighan *(Robert Lawrence)*, E. J. Radcliffe *(Uncle Dryek)*, Raymond Bloomer *(Crown Prince)*, Bobby Connelly *(Boy)*, Robert Dudley *(Father)*, W. P. Lewis *(Steve)*, Maggie Halloway Fisher *(Granny White)*, Helen Montrose *(Governess)*, Robert Vivian *(Valet)*, Nell Clark Keller *(Mamie)*, Mercedes de Cordoba, Walter Abel.

Good cast and a wonderful director are wasted on this nonsense about a Belgian countess who runs away to Tennessee to escape marrying a German prince. She falls in love with an American, barely escapes being hit by lightning, but because some of her personal possessions are discovered in the demolished shack, is assumed dead by her family. They return to Europe and leave the young lovers to find their own happiness. It would seem that the great Neilan considered this one to be such a stinker from the start, that he just went through the motions with his camera and cast.

d, Marshall Neilan; w, Charles Maigne (based on a story by Maria Thompson Davies); ph, Walter Stradling.

Drama **(PR:A MPAA:NR)**

OUT OF LUCK*** (1919) 5 reels New Art/PAR bw (AKA: NOBODY HOME)

Dorothy Gish *(Fran Wadsworth)*, Ralph Graves *(Malcolm Dale)*, Raymond Cannon *(Crandall Park)*, Vera McGinnis *(Mollie Rourke)*, George Fawcett *(Rockaway Smith)*, Emily Chichester *(Sally Smith)*, Rudolph Valentino *(Maurice Rennard)*, Norman McNeill *(Rosebud Miller)*, Porter Strong *(Eddie the Pup)*, Kate V. Toncray *(The Strong Minded Aunt)*, Vivian Montrose *(Florence Wellington)*.

Gish feature about the most superstitious girl in the world gives the great comedienne plenty of opportunity to display the genius of her craft as she meddles in the lives of everyone she knows, convinced that the signs and omens which surround her are no laughing matter. Of course they are, and it all results in a highly entertaining and original piece of work.

d, Elmer Clifton; w, Lois Zellner.

Comedy **(PR:A MPAA:NR)**

OUT OF LUCK*** (1923) 6 reels UNIV bw

Hoot Gibson *(Sam Pertune)*, Laura La Plante *(Mae Day)*, Howard Truesdell *(Ezra Day)*, Elinor Hancock *(Aunt Edith Bristol)*, De Witt Jennings *(Capt. Bristol)*, Freeman Wood *(Cyril La Mount)*, Jay Morley *(Boggs)*, Kansas Moehring *("Kid" Hogan)*, John Judd *("Pig" Hurley)*.

Unusual Gibson comedy-adventure has the popular star joining the Navy when he thinks he has killed a fellow. Then, when he realizes it was all a mistake, the laughs come fast as the former cowboy pulls every trick in the book to get out. In the end he saves Jennings from a lunatic and wins the love of his beautiful niece.

d, Edward Sedgwick; w, George C. Hull, Raymond L. Schrock (based on a story by Sedgwick); ph, Virgil Miller.

Comedy/Adventure **(PR:A MPAA:NR)**

OUT OF THE DRIFTS*1/2 (1916) 5 reels FP bw

Marguerite Clark *(Elsie)*, J. W. Johnston *(Rudolph)*, Albert Gran *(Father Benedict)*, William Courtleigh, Jr. *(George Van Rensselear)*, Ivan Simpson *(Martin)*, Kitty Brown *(Cleo)*, Florence Johns *(Trixie)*, DeWitt Lillibridge *(Reggie Featherstone)*, Robert Conville.

An alcoholic London playboy, in Switzerland drying out, tries to seduce an innocent mountain girl while the two are trapped by a well-filmed avalanche. He then returns home and turns over a new leaf, leaving the girl in the Alps, where she slowly begins to die of a broken heart. A guide who rescued the pair and secretly loves her, spots a large check that the Englishman sent to the local monastery and decides the fellow isn't so bad after all. So he goes to England and describes the young lady's deteriorating condition to the reformed rotter, who quickly rushes to her side.

d, J. Searle Dawley; w, William H. Clifford.

Drama **(PR:A MPAA:NR)**

OUT OF THE DUST1/2** (1920) 6 reels J. P. McCARTHY bw

Russell Simpson, Robert McKim, Dorcas Matthews, Francis Powers, Eunice Woodruff.

Good direction, photography, and a feeling for the history of its setting, cause this western to ring true. It's all about a bored housewife and mother who runs away with a handsome trapper, only to find him a disgusting drunk. The woman (who was never intimate with her companion) becomes a dance hall singer and is ultimately reunited with her husband and child.

d&w, John P. McCarthy; ph, Victor Milner.

Western/Drama **(PR:C MPAA:NR)**

OUT OF THE PAST* (1927) 6 reels Dallas M. Fitzgerald/PEER bw

Robert Frazer *(Beverly Carpenter)*, Mildred Harris *(Dora Prentiss()*, Ernest Wood *(Harold Nesbitt)*, Rose Tapley *(Mrs. Prentiss)*, Mario Marano *(Juan Sorrano)*, Joyzelle Joyner *(Saida)*, Harold Miller *(Capt. John Barrister)*, Byron Sage *(Beverly Carpenter, Jr.)*, William Clifford.

When her lover dies in the war, Harris marries on the emotional rebound. The union is a disaster and the fellow takes off for the South Seas, where he enjoys the carnal pleasures of countless native girls. Meanwhile, her old flame returns, bringing obvious joy to his original love. The husband then also comes back, but when he sees the happy relationship his wife is involved in, he decides to do the decent thing and returns to his native companions. This was a bad picture on every level, made even worse by titles such as "Fate's Grim Jest," and "Thus was Wrought a Miracle."

d, Dallas M. Fitzgerald; w, H. Tipton Steck (based on a story by John S. Lopez); ph, Milton Moore.

Drama **(PR:C MPAA:NR)**

OUT OF THE SHADOW* (1919) 5 reels PAR bw

Pauline Frederick *(Ruth Minchin)*, Wyndham Standing *(Richard Steel)*, Ronald Byram *(Edward Langholm)*, William Gross *(Rev. Woodgate)*, Emma Campbell *(Mrs. Woodgate)*, Nancy Hathaway *(Mrs. Vanables)*, Agnes Wakefield, Jack W. Johnson, Syn De Conde, William T. Hayes.

Hornung (author of RAFFLES) was a topflight writer of mystery novels, and the one on which this film is based was no exception. Unfortunately, all of the original story's suspense was eliminated in the transition, and the whole cast gives the impression of merely going through the motions.

d, Emile Chautard; w, Eve Unsell (based on the novel *The Shadow of the Rope* by Ernest William Hornung); ph, Jacques Bizeul.

Mystery **(PR:A MPAA:NR)**

OUT OF THE SILENT NORTH** (1922) 5 reels UNIV bw

Frank Mayo *(Pierre Baptiste)*, Barbara Bedford *(Marcette Vallois)*, Frank Leigh *(Ashleigh Nefferton)*, Harris Gordon *(Reginald Stannard)*, Christian J. Frank *(Pete Bellew)*, Frank Lanning *(Jean Cour)*, Louis Rivera *(Mattigami)*, Dick La Reno *("Lazy" Lester)*.

Routine frozen North programmer has a decent French Canadian (Mayo) keeping the love of the storekeeper's daughter (Bedford) in spite of the competition provided by an English prospector (Gordon). In the end the local boy strikes it rich and saves his claim from the clutches of a ruthless crook.

d, William Worthington; w, Wallace Clifton, George Hull (based on a story by Harry Sinclair Drago, Joseph Noel); ph, Art Reeves.

Romance **(PR:A MPAA:NR)**

OUT OF THE STORM***

(1920) 6 reels G. Atherton/Goldwyn bw (AKA: TOWER OF IVORY)

Barbara Castleton *(Margaret Hill)*, John Bowers *(John Ordham)*, Sidney Ainsworth *(Al Levering)*, Doris Pawn *(Mabel Cutting)*, Elinor Hancock *(Mrs. Cutting)*, W. Lawson Butt *(Lord Bridgeminister)*, Edythe Chapman *(Lady Bridgeminister)*, Ashton Dearholt *(Walter Driscombe)*, Carrie Clark Ward *(Teddy)*, Lincoln Stedman *(Sir Reggie Blanchard)*, Clarissa Selwynne *(Lady Rosamond)*, J. Ray Avery.

Good melodrama has an orphaned girl being taken in by a Barbary Coast saloonkeeper and given a job singing. A patron discovers her, is impressed and arranges for her to study voice. The Good Samaritan is later arrested for embezzlement, and his protege promises to marry him on his release from prison. The girl's talent, however, takes her to Europe and after a well-filmed shipwreck, she and a British aristocrat fall madly in love. Some time passes and her sponsor escapes from jail and heads for London, where the woman he loves has become a great opera star. The girl unselfishly agrees to honor her commitment, but in the last reel, the American is shot to death. There are a couple of directorial flaws, such as placing automobiles on the wrong side of London's streets, and having the British police carrying pistols, but none of this distracts from an otherwise entertaining programmer.

d, William Parke; w, J. E. Nash (based on the novel *The Tower of Ivory* by Gertrude Atherton); ph, Andre Barlatier.

Drama/Crime **(PR:A MPAA:NR)**

OUT OF THE WEST1/2** (1926) 5 reels R-C/FBO bw

Tom Tyler *(Tom Hanley)*, Bernice Welch *(Bernice O'Connor)*, L. J. O'Connor *(Jim Rollins)*, Ethan Laidlaw *(Bide Goodrich)*, Alfred Hewston *(John O'Connor)*, Frankie Darro *(Frankie)*, Gertrude Claire *("Grannie" Hanley)*, Barney Furey *(A Scout)*.

Entertaining combination of western and baseball genres has Tyler, a good cowpuncher but a great pitcher, taking a job on a ranch whose owner lives only for the 4th of July baseball game with his rival spread. Just before the big contest, Tyler is captured by his fellow employee Laidlaw (who loves the boss' daughter, Welch, and has been throwing the previous games), but with the help of little Darro, Tyler escapes, hits the game-winning home run, beats the tar out of his enemy, turns down an offer to play in the big leagues, and marries Welch. It could only happen in America.

d, Robert De Lacy; w, Wyndham Gittens (based on a story by Frederick Arthur Mindlin); ph, John Leezer.

Western **(PR:A MPAA:NR)**

OUT TO WIN** (1923, Brit.) 6 reels ID bw

Catherine Calvert *(Auriole Craven)*, Clive Brook *(Barraclough/Altar)*, Irene Norman *(Isobel)*, Cameron Carr *(Harrison Smith)*, A. B. Imeson *(Ezra Phipps)*, Ivo Dawson *(Lawrence)*, Olaf Hytten *(Cumberston)*, Norman Page *(Van Diet)*, Robert English *(Lord Almont Frayne)*, Ernest A. Douglas *(Hilbert Torrington)*, James McWilliams *(Doran)*, Daisy Campbell *(Mrs. Barraclough)*, Ernest Dagnall *(Sydney)*.

British mystery has a poor soul, down on his luck completely, hired to obtain the radium concession owned by a Balkan state by passing himself off as a respected financier.

d&w, Denison Clift (based on the play by Dion Clayton Calthrop, Roland Pertwee).

Mystery **(PR:A MPAA:NR)**

OUT WITH THE TIDE** (1928) 6 reels PEER bw

Cullen Landis *(John Templeton)*, Dorothy Dawn *(Joan Renshaw)*, Crauford Kent *(Ralph Kennedy)*, Mitchell Lewis *(Capt. Lund)*, Ernest Hilliard *(Snake Doyle)*, Sojin *(Chee Chee)*, James Aubrey *(Jimmy)*, Arthur Thalasso *(Clancey)*, Etta Lee, Harry Semels, Charles Alexandra.

Before starring in the first all-talking picture, THE LIGHTS OF NEW YORK, in the same year, Landis made this low-budget film with Dawn about a newspaper reporter wrongly accused of murdering a banker, who along with his sweetheart (the victim's daughter), tracks the real killer down in Shanghai.

d, Charles Hutchison; w, Elaine Towne (based on a story by John C. Brownell, G. Marion Burton); t, Paul Perez; ph, Leon Shamroy; ed, Perez.

Mystery **(PR:A MPAA:NR)**

OUT YONDER*** (1920) 5 reels SF/SEL bw

Olive Thomas *(Flotsam)*, Huntley Gordon *(Edward Elmer)*, Mary Cloverdale *(Mrs. Elmer)*, Louise Prussing *(Clarice Stapleton)*, John Smiley *(Amos Bart)*, Cyril Chadwick *(Reggie Hughes)*, Edward Ellis *(Joey Clark)*.

This gripping melodrama has a yachting party docking by a lighthouse and a young society fellow falling in love with the keeper's daughter. A jealous suitor accuses the keeper of having murdered his father, and tells the society chap that the girl is a waif the old man took in. The father goes along with the lie for the sake of his daughter's happiness, but when she learns the truth, the girl slips away from the ship and returns to her dad. When a terrible storm breaks out and the yacht returns to find her, the girl braves the elements—lantern in hand because the beacon has lost its power—and guides the craft to safety. There is, of course, a happy ending and plenty of well-staged thrills.

d, Ralph Ince; w, Edward R. Montagne (based on the play "The Girl from Out Yonder" by Pauline Phelps, Marion Short); ph, Hal Sintzenich.

Drama **(PR:A MPAA:NR)**

OUTCAST*** (1928) 8 reels FN bw

Corinne Griffith *(Miriam)*, James Ford *(Tony)*, Edmund Lowe *(Geoffrey)*, Huntley Gordon *(Hugh)*, Kathryn Carver *(Valentine)*, Louise Fazenda *(Mable)*, Claude King *(Moreland)*, Sam Hardy *(Jack)*, Patsy O'Byrne *(Mrs. O'Brien)*, Lee Moran *(Fred)*.

Interesting drama about Griffith, a down-and-out prostitute, who is taken in and cared for by Lowe, a hard-drinking society chap, rebounding from a broken love affair. The poor devil even takes Griffith to watch his one-time sweetheart's marriage. This encourages the streetwalker to fall madly in love with this gentle man, and she vows to devote her life to him. Later, the former fiancee decides to win Lowe back, but Griffith cleverly proves who the *real* tart is, and love wins out. OUTCAST was a remake of a 1922 production under the same name, directed by Chet Withey and starring Elsie Ferguson.

d, William A. Seiter; w, Agnes Christine Johnston (based on the play by Hubert Henry Davies); t, Forrest Halsey, Gene Towne; ph, John Seitz; ed, Hugh Bennett; syn sc; s eff.

Drama **(PR:C MPAA:NR)**

OUTCASTS OF POKER FLAT, THE* 1/2** (1919) 6 reels UNIV bw

Harry Carey *(The Man/John Oakhurst)*, Cullen Landis *(Billy Gentry/Oakhurst's Adopted Son)*, Gloria Hope *(Ruth Watson/The Girl)*, Joseph Harris *(Ned Stratton)*, J. Farrell MacDonald, Charles Hill Mailes, Victor Potel, Louise Lester, Virginia Chester, Duke Lee, Vester Pegg.

Superior western blends two of author Harte's most popular works, using the story-within-a-story technique. The film opens with two men in love with the same girl, but because Landis is the younger and handsomer of the two, Carey assumes that the young lady prefers him. Then Carey reads "Outcasts of Poker Flat," and the tale unfolds using the same actors. The Harte classic, of course, ends with the more mature westerner sacrificing his life for the others, but the film ends with Carey back in the present expressing the opinion, "The fella in the book was a durn fool." He then proposes to the young lady, is accepted, and the movie ends with a smile. Fine performances, and some truly inventive direction by Ford, make this one a winner.

d, Jack Ford; w, H. Tipton Steck (based on the stories "The Luck of Roaring Camp" and "Outcasts of Poker Flat" by Bret Harte); ph, John W. Brown.

Western **(PR:A MPAA:NR)**

OUTLAW DOG, THE** (1927) 5 reels R-C/FBO bw

Ranger the Dog, Helen Foster *(Helen Meadows)*, Rex Lease *(Bill Brady)*, Alfred Allen *(Henry Jordan)*, Harry Tenbrook *(Mike)*, Bruce Gordon *(Ed)*, Spencer Bell *("Snowball" Black)*, Vic Allen *(Sheriff)*.

Ranger (one of the great Rin-Tin-Tin's lesser rivals) goes it alone after being accused of turning on his master and rendering him speechless. On his travels, he becomes friendly with Lease, the operator of a remote telegraph station, and his sweetheart, Foster. Then, when a couple of outlaws attempt to heist the payroll and blow up a railroad bridge, Ranger subdues them and flags down an oncoming train just in the nick of time. As a wedding present, the couple are given the dog as a gift from his former owner who, somewhere along the line, regained his voice.

d, J. P. McGowan; w, F. A. E. Pine (based on a story by Ewart Adamson); ph, Joe Walker.

Adventure **(PR:A MPAA:NR)**

OUTLAW REFORMS, THE 1/2** (1914) 4 reels WORLD bw

Charles Gebhart, Jeanie Macpherson.

The producers couldn't have crammed much more action then they did into this 4-reeler about a boy who grows up to become a bandit after his claim is stolen and his father murdered. In the end, after Indian battles, fist fights, and lavish shoot-outs, he sees justice done and is "reformed" by the sheriff's beautiful sister.

Western **(PR:A MPAA:NR)**

OUTLAWED 1/2** (1929) 7 reels FBO bw

Tom Mix *(Tom Manning)*, Sally Blane *(Anne)*, Frank M. Clark *(Seth)*, Al Smith *(Dervish)*, Ethan Laidlaw *(McCasky)*, Barney Furey *(Sagebrush)*, Al Ferguson *(Sheriff)*.

The great Mix had left Fox and was beginning his decline when this picture was made for the second string FBO studio. It's pretty routine stuff, with Mix being falsely accused of a train robbery, escaping the hangman's noose, bringing the real bad men to justice, and winning the love of Loretta Young's lovely sister Blane in the end.

d, Eugene Forde; w, George W. Pyper; t, Helen Gregg; ph, Norman Devol; ed, Henry Webber.

Western **(PR:A MPAA:NR)**

OUTLAW'S DAUGHTER, THE*** (1925) 5 reels UNIV bw

Josie Sedgwick *(Flora Dale)*, Edward Hearne *(Jim King)*, Robert Walker *(Slim Cole)*, Jack Gavin *(Stephen Dale)*, Harry Todd *(Bookkeeper)*, Ben Corbett *(Bill)*, Bob Burns *(Sheriff)*.

Sedgwick, one of the truly believable female western stars, is at her best as a girl who is taken in by Hearne, a mine manager, after being shot. In the end she saves her benefactor's life by causing the bad hombre to fall to his death from an aerial gondola.

d, John B. O'Brien; w, Harold Shumate; ph, Ben Kline.

Western **(PR:A MPAA:NR)**

OUTLAWS OF RED RIVER* 1/2** (1927) 6 reels FOX bw

Tom Mix *(Tom Morley)*, Marjorie Daw *(Mary Torrence)*, Arthur Clayton *(Sam Hardwick)*, Lee Shumway *(Mr. Torrence)*, Ellen Woonston *(Mrs. Torrence)*, Jimmy Downs *(Tom Morley)*, Virginia Marshall *(Mary, as a Child)*, William Conklin *(Capt. Dunning)*, Duke Lee *(Dick Williams)*, Frances McDonald *(Ben Tanner)*.

Great Mix western has the popular star playing a Texas Ranger out to find the bandits who killed his parents when he was a child. He finally infiltrates their ranks and, with the help of an army of fellow Rangers equipped with an armored coach, destroys the outlaw fortress and rescues Daw, a young lady who lost her parents in the same manner as Mix.

d, Lewis Seiler; w, Harold Shumate (based on a story by Gerald Beaumont); t, Malcolm Stuart Boylan; ph, Dan Clark.

Western **(PR:A MPAA:NR)**

OUTLAWS OF THE SEA** (1923) 5 reels John Brunton/American Releasing bw

Pierre Gendron *(Robert Graham)*, Marguerite Courtot *(Polly Grimshaw)*, Gordon Standing *(Leonard Craven)*, Herbert Pattee *(Capt. Abel Grimshaw)*.

Potboiler about Courtot and her sea captain father, Pattee, who get caught up in a rum-running operation and are arrested by the young lady's revenue commander boy friend, Gendron. At the trial, the old salt is cleared and the couple make their wedding plans.

d&w, Jack Okey; t, William B. Laub; ph, Paul Allen.

Crime **(PR:A MPAA:NR)**

OUTSIDE THE LAW* 1/2** (1921) 8 reels UNIV bw

Priscilla Dean *(Molly Madden/Silky Moll)*, Ralph Lewis *("Silent" Madden)*, Lon Chaney *("Black Mike" Sylva/Ah Wing/Guess Who)*, Wheeler Oakman *("Dapper Bill" Ballard)*, E. A. Warren *(Chang Lo)*, Stanley Goethals *("That Kid")*, Melbourne MacDowell *(Morgan Spencer)*, Wilton Taylor *(Inspector)*.

Nifty underworld picture has Chaney playing three roles in his second film for Browning. After deciding to go straight, at the behest of Warren, a crook, Lewis, is framed by Chaney and sent to jail. Unaware of Chaney's role in this, Lewis' daughter, Dean, joins the gang and with her sweetheart, Oakman, pulls off a big society jewel caper. Eventually the couple have a showdown with Chaney and the gangster is killed. Dean and Oakman are sent to prison, but the highly respected Warren secures their release when the gems are returned.

d, Tod Browning; w, Lucien Hubbard, Browning (based on a story by Browning); ph, William Fildew.

Crime **Cas.** **(PR:A MPAA:NR)**

OUTSIDE WOMAN, THE* (1921) 5 reels REA bw

Wanda Hawley *(Dorothy Ralston)*, Clyde Fillmore *(Dr. Frederick Ralston)*, Sidney Bracey *(Mr. Cambridge)*, Rosita Marstini *(Mrs. Cambridge)*, Misao Seki *(Togo)*, Thena Jasper *(Gussie)*, Mary Winston *(Mrs. Trent)*, Jacob Abrams *(Curator)*.

The laughs are few and far between (which may explain why the director took no screen credit) in this programmer about a newlywed who trades her husband's priceless Aztec idol for a silk shawl. The remainder of the picture deals with her escapades in getting it back, and nothing quite works.

w, Douglas Bronston (based on the play "All Night Long" by Philip Bartholomae, Paul B. Sipe); ph, Paul Perry.

Comedy **(PR:A MPAA:NR)**

OUTSIDER, THE*** (1926) 6 reels FOX bw

Jacqueline Logan *(Leontine Sturdee)*, Lou Tellegen *(Anton Ragatzy)*, Walter Pidgeon *(Basil Owen)*, Roy Atwell *(Jerry Sidon)*, Charles Lane *(Sir Jasper Sturdee)*, Joan Standing *(Pritchard)*, Gibson Gowland *(Shadow)*, Bertram Marburgh *(Dr. Talley)*, Crauford Kent *(Dr. Ladd)*, Louis Payne *(Dr. Helmore)*.

When Logan, a British dancer, journeys to Hungary to learn a few native steps, she suffers a terrible accident which leaves her crippled. On hand is Tellegen, a famous and mystical faith healer, whom she regards to be a charlatan and therefore refuses his help. but Tellegen, who now loves the girl, follows her to England and begs to minister to her. At first she refuses, but then she comes to realize that her feelings for him are more than platonic as well. The picture ends with her dramatically rising from her chair and walking towards his outstretched arms.

d, Rowland V. Lee; w, Robert N. Lee (based on the play by Dorothy Brandon); ph, G. O. Post.

Drama **(PR:A MPAA:NR)**

OUTWITTED* 1/2 (1917) 5 reels Metro bw

Emily Stevens, Frank Currier, Earle Foxe, Ricca Allen, Paul Everton, Frank Joyner, Fred Truesdell, Joseph Burke.

Familiar family triangle situation which reaches its conclusion with somewhat of a surprise ending is badly directed and photographed and well below the Metro standard.

d, George D. Baker; sup, Maxwell Karger; w, Mary Murillo (based on a story by Charles A. Logue).

Drama **(PR:A MPAA:NR)**

OUTWITTED** (1925) 5 reels Independent Pictures bw

Helen Holmes *(Helen Kinney)*, William Desmond *(Jack Blaisdel)*, J. P. McGowan *(Tiger McGuire)*, Grace Cunard *(Lucy Carlisle)*, Alec Francis *(John Kinney)*, Emily Fitzroy *(Meg)*.

That most prolific writer and director of action programmers, McGowan, brought serial stars Holmes and Desmond together to star in this tale of counterfeiters, Treasury agents, and a damsel in distress. All of the old cliffhanger thrills are here, which makes for grand fun in spite of the many plot deficiencies.

d&w, J. P. McGowan; ph, Walter Griffin; ed, Betty Davis.

Adventure **(PR:A MPAA:NR)**

OVAL DIAMOND, THE** (1916) 5 reels Thanhouser bw

Harris Gordon *(Robert Ledyard)*, Barbara Gilroy *(Sylvia Daunt)*, Arthur Bauer *(Her Father)*.

After discovering a huge diamond, a miner and his daughter are forced to flee Africa because a gang of crooks, led by the man's brother-in-law, are out to steal it. After arriving in the U.S., the miner is killed and the girl kept prisoner, until an alert and brave young man comes to her rescue—and wins her love.

d, W. Eugene Moore; w, (based on a novel by David S. Foster).

Mystery **(PR:A MPAA:NR)**

OVER THE BORDER*** (1922) 7 reels FP-LAS bw

Betty Compson *(Jen Galbraith)*, Tom Moore *(Sgt. Flaherty)*, J. Farrell MacDonald *(Peter Galbraith)*, Casson Ferguson *(Val Galbraith)*, Sidney D'Albrook *(Snow Devil)*, L. C. Shumway *(Cpl. Bying)*, Jean De Briac *(Pretty Pierre)*, Edward J. Brady *(Inspector Jules)*, Joe Ray *(Borden)*.

Above-average, well-produced and -acted frozen tundra story about Mountie Moore's love for Compson, the daughter of a notorious rumrunner. The lawman does his duty, clears the old man of murder, and gets the girl, who was really honest from the start. A terrific storm sequence is just one of the film's better touches.

d, Penrhyn Stanlaws; w, Albert Shelby Le Vino (based on the story "She of the Triple Chevron" by Gilbert Parker); ph, Paul Perry.

North Woods **(PR:A MPAA:NR)**

OVER THE HILL (SEE: OVER THE HILL TO THE POOR HOUSE, 1920)

OVER THE HILL TO THE POORHOUSE***
(1920) 11 reels FOX bw (AKA: OVER THE HILL)

Mary Carr *(Ma Benton)*, Johnny Walker *(Johnny, as an Adult)*, William Welch *(Dad Benton)*, Noel Tearle *(Issac, as an Adult)*, Wallace Ray *(Charles, as an Adult)*, Phyllis Diller *(Rebecca, as an Adult)*, Louella Carr *(Susan, as an Adult)*, Vivienne Osborne *(Isabella Strong)*, Dorothy Allen *(Agulutia, Issac's Wife)*, Edna Murphy *(Lucy, Charles' Wife)*, Sheridan Tansey *(Issac, as a Child)*, Stephen Carr *(Thomas, as a Child)*, John Dwyer *(Thomas, as an Adult)*, Jerry Devine *(Johnny, as a Child)*, James Sheldon *(Charles, as a Child)*, Rosemary Carr *(Rebecca, as a Child)*, May Beth Carr *(Susan, as a Child)*, Marion Ross [Marion Roland], Frances Victory, Joe Donohue.

The quintessential mother-love movie (it would be remade in 1931, with James Dunn) which established Mary Carr as the very essence of all things maternal. The story goes for the heartstrings and succeeds in spades. A young man (Walker) who seems to always be in trouble, but is truly a decent lad, heads west to earn a living for his mother's sake when his father dies. He sends the money home regularly to Tearle, his pious, bible-quoting older brother, to see to his mother's needs, but the rotter pockets the cash and the old lady ends up scrubbing floors in the poorhouse. The ending, when Walker returns to discover the truth and drags Tearle through the streets to apologize to the kindly soul who gave them both life, is guaranteed to bring tears to the eyes of anyone capable of feeling human emotions.

d, Harry Millarde; w, Paul H. Sloane (based on the poems "Over the Hill to the Poorhouse" and "Over the Hill from the Poorhouse" by Will Carleton); ph, Arthur H. C. Sintzenich.

Drama **(PR:A MPAA:NR)**

OVER THE STICKS* (1929, Brit.) 4 reels Cinema Exclusives/FOX bw

Tom Shelton *(Lord Burton)*, Molly Wright, Billy Phelps.

British drama about an aristocratic horse breeder who, after being blackmailed, fakes his own death and then makes a second fortune as a bookmaker.

p, Frank Wheatcroft; d, G. B. Samuelson, A. E. Coleby; w, Samuelson.

Drama **(PR:A MPAA:NR)**

OVERALLS** (1916) 5 reels AM bw

William Stowell *(Herbert Drew)*, Warren Ellsworth *(Walter Daniels)*, Rhea Mitchell *(Bettina Warren)*, Perry Banks *(Harrison Warren)*, Sylvia Ashton *(Widow Malone)*, Estelle Allen *(Peggy Malone)*, George Ahren *(Flap-Jack)*, Jack Prescott *(Buck Finnegan)*, George Bailey *(Casey)*.

Only fair North Woods film has Stowell (a second-string Broncho Billy Anderson) saving a girl's lumber camp from being stolen by a gang of hard-drinking thugs led by a crooked lawyer.

d, Jack Halloway; w, (based on a story by L. V. Jefferson).

Adventure **(PR:A MPAA:NR)**

OVERLAND LIMITED, THE*** (1925) 6 reels GOTH/LUM bw

Malcolm McGregor *(David Barton)*, Olive Borden *(Ruth Dent)*, Alice Lake *(Violet Colton)*, Ethel Wales *(Mrs. Barton)*, Ralph Lewis *(Ed Barton)*, John Miljan *(Brice Miller)*, Roscoe Karns *(Pat Madden)*, Emmett King *(Carson North)*, Charles Hill Mailes *(Schuyler Dent)*, Charles West *(Bitterroot Jackson)*, Charles "Buddy" Post *("One Round" Farrell)*, Evelyn Jennings *(Agnes Jennings)*.

Superior independent has McGregor designing a railroad bridge across a mountain gorge, which is tampered with by Miljan, his rival for the affection of the locomotive driver's daughter, Borden. There is a wreck which kills Borden's mother, but after Miljan confesses to his wrongdoing, her father negotiates his big baby safely over the construction, and McGregor is absolved of all blame.

d, Frank O'Neill; sup, Renaud Hoffman; w, (based on a story by James J. Tynan); ph, Jack MacKenzie.

Drama **(PR:A MPAA:NR)**

OVERLAND RED*** (1920) 6 reels UNIV bw

Harry Carey *(Overland Red)*, Vola Vale *(Louise Alacarme)*, Charles Le Moyne *(Silent Saunders)*, David B. Gally *(Billy Winthrop)*, C. Anderson *(Boggs)*, Joe Harris *(Sago)*, Morris Foster, Harold Goodwin.

Always a pleasure to watch, Carey scores again in this budget-minded western about a hobo who takes on a gang of tough hombres to save the gold mine he discovered. Lots of hard riding, gunplay, and fist fights in this entertaining oater.

d&w, Lynn F. Reynolds (based on a story by Henry Herbert Knibbs); ph, Hugh McClung.

Western **(PR:A MPAA:NR)**

OVERLAND TELEGRAPH, THE** (1929) 6 reels MGM bw

Tim McCoy *(Capt. Allen)*, Dorothy Janis *(Dorothy)*, Frank Rice *(Easy)*, Lawford Davidson *(Briggs)*, Clarence Geldert *(Maj. Hammond)*, Chief Big Tree *(Medicine Man)*.

The breathtaking beauty of Glacier National Park, where most of this film was shot, is about the only bright spot in an otherwise tedious movie about an army officer who thwarts an Indian attack at the outbreak of the Civil War. The other highlight is when McCoy proposes marriage to Janis over the telegraph, and she accepts.

d, John Waters; w, George C. Hull, Edward Meagher (based on a story by Ward Wing); t, Harry Sinclair Drago; ph, Arthur Reed; ed, William Le Vanway; cos, Lucia Coulter.

Western **(PR:A MPAA:NR)**

OWD BOB** (1924, Brit.) 7 reels Atlantic Union/Novello-Atlas bw

J. Fisher White *(Adam McAdam)*, Ralph Forbes *(Davie McAdam)*, James Carew *(James Moore)*, Yvonne Thomas *(Maggie Moore)*, Frank Stanmore *(Jim Burton)*, Grace Lane *(Mrs. Moore)*, Robert English *(Squire)*.

British tearjerker has an old and pathetic farmer's pet dog being saved from a bullet to the brain when it is proven that another dog is actually the sheep killer.

d, Henry Edwards; w, Hugh Maclean (based on a novel by Alfred Olivant).

Drama **(PR:C MPAA:NR)**

P

PACE THAT THRILLS, THE* (1925) 7 reels FN bw

Ben Lyon *(Danny Wade)*, Mary Astor *(Doris)*, Charles Beyer *(Duke)*, Tully Marshall *(Hezekiah Sims)*, Wheeler Oakman *(Director)*, Thomas Holding *(John Van Loren)*, Evelyn Walsh Hall *(Mrs. Van Loren)*, Warner Richmond *(Jack Van Loren)*, Fritzi Brunette *(Paula)*, Paul Ellis *(Toreador)*.

Lots of hokum in this one about a mother (Brunette) who is wrongly sentenced to life in prison after killing her husband, who was pulling a drunken prank, in order to protect her baby. The child grows up to become a movie star (played by Lyon) and spends every cent he makes trying to get the woman out of prison. When the lad is reluctant, under the circumstances, to perform his own death-defying stunts, he is labeled a coward by the press. To prove them wrong, Lyon enters himself in the world's most dangerous automobile race. He loses the contest but does manage to win his manhood back and get his mother out of the penitentiary in the process.

d, Webster Campbell; w, (based on a story by Byron Morgan); t, John Krafft; ph, T. D. McCord; ed, Krafft.

Drama/Adventure **(PR:A MPAA:NR)**

PADDY, THE NEXT BEST THING*** (1923, Brit.) 7 reels Graham/Wilcox bw

Mae Marsh *(Paddy Adair)*, Darby Foster *(Lawrence Blake)*, Lilian Douglas *(Eileen Adair)*, George K. Arthur *(Jack O'Hara)*, Nina Boucicault *(Mrs. Blake)*, Haidee Wright *(Jane O'Hara)*, Marie Wright *(Mary O'Hara)*, Marie Ault *(Mrs. Adair)*, Sir Simeon Stuart *(Gen. Adair)*, Mildred Evelyn *(Doreen Blake)*, Tom Coventry *(Mickey Doolan)*.

One of the better British silents, featuring Marsh in fine form, has the young woman saved from drowning by handsome Foster, whom she decides to dislike. This feeling is intensified when she learns that her sister, Douglas, is strongly attracted to the young gentleman, and that he in return is nuts about Marsh. Meanwhile, Arthur, who worships Douglas, sets off to make his fortune, then comes back a millionaire and is more than accepted by the object of his ambition and desire. In the midst of all this, Marsh has returned to the old sod and gotten herself lost in the hills. When word of her danger reaches home, Foster dashes off to her successful rescue, and the two become aware of their mutual love.

p, Herbert Wilcox; d, Graham Cutts; w, Wilcox, Eliot Stannard (based on a novel by Gertrude Page); ph, Rene Guissart.

Love **(PR:A MPAA:NR)**

PAGES OF LIFE*½ (1922, Brit.) 6 reels Adelqui Millar/BUT bw

Evelyn Brent *(Mitzi/Dolores)*, Luis Hildago *(Walter Swinburne)*, Richard Turner *(Valerius)*, Jack Trevor *(Lord Mainwaring)*, Bardo da Mart *(Count Boris Malinski)*, Sundae Wilshin *(Phyllis Mainwaring)*.

American film star Brent brought a little substance to this British drama about the neighbor of a composer who rescues a down-and-out girl from sexual seduction, only to discover that she's his long lost daughter.

d&w, Adelqui Millar.

Drama **(PR:A MPAA:NR)**

PAID BACK** (1922) 5 reels UNIV bw

Gladys Brockwell *(Carol Gordon)*, Mahlon Hamilton *(David Hardy)*, Stuart Holmes *(Jack Gregory)*, Lillian West *(Dorothy Britton)*, Kate Price *(Carol's Servant)*, Edna Murphy *(Eloise Hardy)*, Arthur Stuart Hull *(Jason Lockhart)*, Wilfred Lucas *(Ship Captain)*.

Routine programmer has wealthy orphan Brockwell marrying the executor of her estate against her will, being blackmailed for an affair she never had, luring the rotter to an island in the South Seas (where he gets his), and then marrying the provincial superintendent when her husband dies.

d, Irving Cummings; w, Hope Loring (based on a story by Louis Duryea Lighton); ph, William Fildew, Jackson Rose.

Drama **(PR:A MPAA:NR)**

PAINTED FLAPPER, THE*½ (1924) 6 reels CHAD bw

James Kirkwood *(Richard Whitney)*, Pauline Garon *(Arline Whitney)*, Claire Adams *(Eunice Whitney)*, Hal Cooley *(Danny Lawrence)*, John Harron *(Jimmy Arnold)*, Maine Geary *(Lester Howe)*, Anita Simons *(Lucy May)*, Al Roscoe *(Lord Raynesford)*, Carlton Griffin *(Lord Coventry)*, Pauline French *(Leita Stokes)*, Crauford Kent *(Egbert Van Alyn)*, Kathlyn Williams *(Isabel Whitney)*.

The Chadwick studio certainly did not shoot for originality with this jazz-age drama about a flapper (Garon) who prevents her sister (Adams) from marrying a crook posing as a society member and then reunites her separated parents.

d, John Gorman; ph, Andre Barlatier.

Drama **(PR:A MPAA:NR)**

PAINTED PEOPLE½** (1924) 7 reels AFN bw

Colleen Moore *(Ellie Byrne)*, Ben Lyon *(Don Lane)*, Charlotte Merriam *(Stephanie Parrish)*, Joseph Striker *(Preston Dutton)*, Charles Murray *(Tom Byrne)*, Russell Simpson *(Fred Lane)*, Mary Alden *(Mrs. Byrne)*, Mary Carr *(Mrs. Lane)*, Sam De Grasse *(Henry Parrish)*, June Elvidge *(Mrs. Dutton)*, Anna Q. Nilsson *(Leslie Carter)*, Bull Montana *(Ed Decker)*.

The attractive pairing of Moore and Lyon is really the only thing that makes this movie work. They portray a couple of slum kids who see their dreams come true—she as an actress, he as a writer—and in the end realize their love for each other and reject the hometown untouchables who flamed their earlier desires.

d, Clarence Badger; w, Edward J. Montagne (based on the story *The Swamp Angel* by Richard Connell); ed, Marion Fairfax, George McQuire; art d, Milton Menasco.

Drama/Comedy **(PR:A MPAA:NR)**

PAINTED PICTURES** (1930, Brit.) 6 reels Bernard Smith/FOX bw

Haddon Mason *(John Marsh)*, Evelyn Spillsbury *(The Girl)*, Winifred Evans *(The Flirt)*.

British drama in which an artist finds himself with the power to reform the various faults his friends possess when he paints their portraits.

d&w, Charles Barnett.

Drama **(PR:A MPAA:NR)**

PAINTED PONIES*** (1927) 6 reels UNIV bw

Hoot Gibson *(Bucky Simms)*, William Dunn *(Pinto Pete)*, Charles Sellon *(Mr. Blenning)*, Otto Hoffman *(Jim)*, Ethlyne Clair *(Pony Blenning)*, Slim Summerville *(Beanpole)*, Chief White Spear, Black Hawk, Chief Big Tree, Mary Lopez.

Gibson participates in a small town rodeo where he meets and is attracted to a girl, who, along with her father, operates a merry-go-round. He also encounters roughneck Dunn, who covets the young lady. There is a whale of a fist fight in which Dunn is badly beaten and humiliated. Later, while Gibson is showing off with his six-shooter, Dunn kills the girl's father and pins the blame on him. Gibson vindicates himself and in a terrific battle on a runaway canoe, Dunn is taken prisoner. The picture ends with the amiable cowpoke settling down to help his bride tend to her "painted ponies."

d, Reeves Eason; w, Arthur Statter, Frank Beresford (based on the story by John Harold Hamlin); t, Tom Reed, ph, Harry Neumann; art d, David S. Garber.

Western **(PR:A MPAA:NR)**

PAINTED SOUL, THE*½** (1915) 5 reels MUT bw

Bessie Barriscale *(Woman of the Streets)*, Charles Ray *(The Painter)*, Truly Shattuck *(The Mother)*, Milton Ross, Tully Marshall.

Excellent drama has artist Ray, who has created a masterpiece called "The Painted Soul," going to night court to find the inspiration for another work he intends to do called "The Fallen Woman." There he meets Barriscale, a prostitute, whom he hires to be his model, and during the course of the project they fall in love. The girl becomes so completely regenerated that when Ray's mother pleads with her to leave the painter because marriage will destroy his career, Barriscale goes out, deliberately has herself arrested for solicitation, and sees to it that her fiance is present when she pleads guilty. The picture ends movingly, with the talented Barriscale returning to his studio that night to look at his masterpiece.

d, Scott Sidney; w, C. Gardner Sullivan.

Drama **(PR:C MPAA:NR)**

PAINTING THE TOWN*** (1927) 6 reels UNIV bw

Glenn Tryon *(Hector Whitmore)*, Patsy Ruth Miller *(Patsy Deveau)*, Charles Gerrard *(Raymond Tyson)*, George Fawcett *(Fire Commissioner)*, Sidney Bracey *(Secretary)*, Max Ascher *(Wilson)*, Monte Collins *(Justice of the Peace)*.

Well-constructed picture has two-reel comedian Tryon graduating to features and doing fine as a country boy inventor who takes seriously Miller's self-amusing flirtation (going on as her escort is paying a speeding ticket) and follows her to New York. His invention, which allows an automobile to do 150 miles per hour and stop on a dime, is a natural for the fire and police departments. Tryon sells it to a city official when he takes the poor devil on a truly hair-raising and hilarious ride. He also manages to win the hand of Miller.

d, William James Craft; w, Harry O. Hoyt, Vin Moore (based on a story by Hoyt); t, Albert De Mond; ph, Al Jones.

Comedy **(PR:A MPAA:NR)**

PAIR OF CUPIDS, A½** (1918) 5 reels Metro bw

Francis X. Bushman *(Peter Warburton)*, Beverly Bayne *(Virginia Parke)*, Charles Sutton *(Henry Burgess)*, Gerald Griffin *(Michael McGroghan)*, Jessie Stevens *(Bridget McGroghan)*, Edgar Norton *(Martin)*, Lou Gorey *(Marie)*, Mrs. Turner *(Lizette)*, Thomas Blake *(Bat Small)*, Louis R. Wolheim *(Dirk Thomas)*, John Judge *(John Henry)*, Elwell Judge *(Mary Ann)*.

Pleasing drawing room comedy has the popular romantic team of Bushman and Bayne being brought together in a most unusual way. Bushman is a stockbroker with no other thought but his business. His uncle, who is the guardian of Bayne (a girl concerned only with her Pomeranian puppy), decides to do a little matchmaking and hires the twin children of his cleaning lady. He leaves one on each of the self-absorbed young folks' doorsteps—which, needless to say, gives them something else to think about—brings them together, and encourages the creation of a family of their own.

d, Charles Brabin; w, (based on a story by Luther A. Reed); ph, R. J. Bergquist.

Comedy **(PR:A MPAA:NR)**

PAIR OF SILK STOCKINGS, A½** (1918) 5 reels SEL bw

Constance Talmadge *(Mrs. Mollie Thornhill)*, Harrison Ford *(Sam Thornhill)*, Wanda Hawley *(Pamela Bristowe)*, Vera Doria *(Irene Maitland)*, Florence Carpenter

(Maudie Plantagent), Thomas Persse *(Sir John Gower)*, Louis Willoughby *(Capt. Jack Bangal)*, Helen Haskell *(Angela)*, L. W. Steers *(McIntyre)*, Robert Gordon *(Brook)*, Sylvia Ashton.

Talmadge gives her usual good comic performance as the married woman who always seems to become involved in compromising situations. But the rest of the cast seems awfully American in what is supposed to be a very British setting.

d, Walter Edwards; w, Edith M. Kennedy (based on the play by Cyril Harcourt); ph, James C. Van Trees.

Comedy **(PR:A MPAA:NR)**

PAIR OF SIXES, A*** (1918) 5 reels Essanay bw

Taylor Holmes *(T. Boggs Johns)*, Robert Conness *(George Nettleton)*, Alice Mann *(Florence Cole)*, Edna Phillips Holmes *(Mrs. Nettleton)*, Cecil Owen *(Thomas J. Vanderholt)*, Maude Eburne *(Coddles)*, Charles E. Ashley *(Krome)*, John Cossar *(Applegate)*, Byron Aldenn *(Tony Toler)*, Virginia Bowker *(Sally Parker)*, Tommy Carey *(Jimmie)*.

Good comedy programmer has a couple of pharmaceutical tycoons, unable to get along with each other, using a game of cards to settle their bickering. The winner is to have complete control of the business for one year, and the loser is to act as the other's butler for the same period of time. The comic complications are plentiful, and the film quite satisfying.

d, L. C. Windom; w, Charles McGuirk (based on the play by Edward Peple).

Comedy **(PR:A MPAA:NR)**

PAJAMAS*** (1927) 6 reels FOX bw

Olive Borden *(Angela Wade)*, John J. Clark *(Daniel Wade)*, Lawrence Gray *(John Weston)*, Jerry Miley *(Russell Forrest)*.

The Fox studio's use of actual on-location footage of the Canadian Rockies enhanced this pleasant comic romance. Borden plays a wealthy girl who replaces her father's personal pilot, crashes in the wilderness and falls in love while wading through the wilds.

d, J. G. Blystone; w, William Conselman; t, Malcolm Stuart Boylan; ph, Glen MacWilliams.

Comedy/Romance **(PR:A MPAA:NR)**

PALAIS DE DANSE (1928, Brit.) 8 reels GAU bw

Mabel Poulton *(No. 16)*, John Longden *(No. 1)*, Robin Irvine *(Tony King)*, Hilda Moore *(Lady King)*, Chili Bouchier *(No. 2)*, Jerrold Robertshaw *(Sir William King)*.

Director Elvey, a competent craftsman, delivers another British drama which amounts to little more than a fair programmer. It's actually rather a complicated affair dealing with blackmail, professional dancers, and a gigolo who possesses a somewhat incriminating photograph.

p, V. Gareth Gundrey, Maurice Elvey; d, Elvey; w, John Longden (based on a story by Jean Jay).

Drama **(PR:A MPAA:NR)**

PALS OF THE PRAIRIE* 1/2 (1929) 5 reels FBO bw

Buzz Barton *(Red Hepner)*, Frank Rice *(Hank Robbins)*, Tom Lingham *(Don Jose Valencia)*, Duncan Renaldo *(Francisco)*, Milburn Morante *(Pedro Terrazzes)*, Natalie Joyce *(Dolores)*, Bill Patton *(Pete Sanger)*.

A music and sound effects track does little to help this Barton western which has the cowboy kid helping to rid a Mexican town of its hated oppressor. He also gets to act the part of Cupid by arranging a marriage between the mayor's beautiful daughter and a U.S. resident.

d, Louis King; w, Frank Howard Clark (based on a story by Oliver Drake); t, Helen Gregg; ph, Virgil Miller; ed, George Marsh; syn sc; s eff.

Western **(PR:A MPAA:NR)**

PANDORA'S BOX* 1/2**

(1929, Ger.) 9 reels Nero/Moviegraphs bw (DIE BUECHSE DER PANDORA)

Louise Brooks *(Lulu)*, Fritz Kortner *(Dr. Peter Schon)*, Franz Lederer *(Alwa Schon, His Son)*, Carl Gotz *(Schigolch/Papa Brommer)*, Alice Roberts *(Countess Anna Geschwitz)*, Daisy d'Ora *(Marie de Zarniko)*, Krafft Raschig *(Rodrigo Quast)*, Michael von Newlinsky *(Marquis Casti-Piani)*, Siegfried Arno *(The Stage Manager)*, Gustav Diessl *(Jack the Ripper)*.

Brooks is brilliant in her portrayal of Lulu, the sexually insatiable, totally amoral creature, who uses human beings for her erotic pleasures and purposes, then discards them when they are of no further use to her. She is the mistress of Kortner, a wealthy doctor, whom she forces into marriage. But the marriage lasts only a day, for Brooks ends up killing him when he becomes jealous of her infatuation with his son Lederer. The son follows the lady when she sails to London after fleeing her trial. There the couple live in poverty and Brooks turns to prostitution. The film's conclusion is a shocker. Brooks becomes strangely attracted to a man she passes in the streets on Christmas Eve. When he confesses that he has no money, she answers, "Come on—I like you." She then takes him to her room, and as she performs a little dance for her own delight as much as his, the stranger catches the gleam of a knife's blade in the candlelight. The man (Diessl) is the infamous Jack the Ripper, and Brooks is to be his next victim. The blade slips into her gut as she embraces him, and she dies as she lived—in the midst of an erotic experience. When the great German director Pabst decided to film PANDORA'S BOX he had one great obstacle to overcome; he could not find the right actress to play his central character, Lulu. Pabst sent his assistant, Paul Falkenberg, everywhere to round up girls to be interviewed. He found them in shops and cafes, at bus stops and on subways, but no one was right for the part. Then the director saw a U.S. film in which an actress named Louise Brooks had a secondary part. This was the girl he'd been searching for. This was his Lulu. Pabst immediately contacted Paramount to secure Brooks' services, but his dispatch was ignored. At the same time, Brooks was called to the front office and told that her new contract would call for a cut in salary. (Sound had given the studios a golden opportunity to use a little leverage on their contract players, and it was either play it their way or walk.) Brooks decided to quit, but before she got to the door, B. P. Schulberg had the decency to tell her of the German offer. The young lady soon set sail for Germany to make a movie she really didn't care about, directed by a man of whom she had never heard. It's a good thing she did not hesitate because, as she relates in her book *Lulu in Hollywood*, "If I had not acted at once I would have lost the part of Lulu. At that very hour in Berlin, Marlene Dietrich was waiting with Pabst in his office. Pabst later said, "Dietrich was too old and too obvious—one sexy look and the picture would become a burlesque. But I gave her a deadline, and the contract was about to be signed when Paramount cabled saying I could have Louise Brooks." Pabst's instinct regarding Brooks was right on the money. The actress was the most naturally sensual personality in the history of the movies, and it's as if the part were written for her. In what is perhaps the film's most famous sequence Brooks dances with a lesbian at her wedding party. Again, quoting her book, Brooks gives an interesting insight into the working methods of her director: "Then Mr. Pabst began explaining the action of the scene in which she (the Belgian actress Alice Roberts) was to dance the tango with me. Suddenly, she understood that she was to touch, to embrace, to make love to another woman. Her blue eyes bulged and her hands trembled. Anticipating the moment of explosion, Mr. Pabst, who proscribed unscripted emotional outbursts, caught her arm and sped her away out of sight behind the set. A half hour later, when they returned, he was hissing soothingly to her in French and she was smiling like the star of the picture—which she was in all her scenes with me. I was just there obstructing the view. Both in two shots and in her closeups photographed over my shoulder, she cheated her look past me to Mr. Pabst, who was making love to her off camera. Out of the funny complexity of this design, Mr. Pabst extracted his tense portrait of sterile lesbian passion, and Mme. Roberts satisfactorily preserved her reputation."

p, George C. Horsetzky; d, G. W. Pabst; w, Ladislaus Vajda (based on the plays "Erdgeist" and "Die Buechse der Pandora" by Frank Wedekind); t, Joseph R. Fliesler; ph, Gunther Krampf; ed, Fleisler; art d, Andrei Andreiev; cos, Gottlieb Hesch.

Drama **Cas.** **(PR:C MPAA:NR)**

PARADISE*** (1926) 8 reels Ray Rockett/FN bw

Milton Sills *(Tony)*, Betty Bronson *(Chrissie)*, Noah Beery *(Quex)*, Lloyd Whitlock *(Teddy)*, Kate Price *(Lady George)*, Charlie Murray *(Lord Lumley)*, Claude King *(Pollock)*, Charles Brook *(Perkins)*, Ashley Cooper *(McCoustie)*.

A good cast—headed by two-fisted Sills—plus well-executed action and exotic settings, made this a fun film. Sills plays a society stunt pilot who is given an island paradise for a wedding present. After arriving on the South Seas island, however, Sills and his bride, Bronson, are appalled to find that its caretaker, Beery, is brutally mistreating the natives. In the exciting climax the islanders take out their revenge on Sills, while Beery recognizes his wrongdoing, rescues Sills and Bronson, then commits suicide.

d, Irvin Willat; w, Paul Schofield (based on the novel by Cosmo Hamilton, John Russell); t, Frances Agnew, Morton Barnard; ph, Charles Van Enger.

Adventure **(PR:A MPAA:NR)**

PARADISE** (1928, Brit.) 7 reels BIP/Wardour bw

Bettly Balfour *(Kitty Cranston)*, Joseph Striker *(Dr. John Halliday)*, Alexander d'Arcy *(Spirdoff)*, Winter Hall *(Rev. Cranston)*, Barbara Gott *(Lady Liverage)*, Dino Galvani *(Manager)*, Boris Ranevsky *(Commissionaire)*, Albert Brouett *(Detective)* Ena se la Haye *(Douchka)*.

The setting of this film is the Riviera, where a doctor boosts the winnings of a working girl to prevent her from falling into the clutches of a gigolo. The lovely presence of Britain's most appealing cinema star, Balfour, makes this drama not only bearable, but almost good.

d, Denison Clift; w, Violet Powell (based on the novel *The Crossword Puzzle* by Phillip Gibbs).

Drama **(PR:A MPAA:NR)**

PARADISE ALLEY* (1931, Brit.) 5 reels Argyle Art Pictures bw

John Argyle *(Joe)*, Margaret Delane *(Claire Stellar)*.

Argyle is literally the whole show in this British thriller about an altruistic miner who assumes his brother's guilt after the lad holds up and shoots a man.

p, d&w, John Argyle.

Mystery **(PR:A MPAA:NR)**

PARADISE GARDEN** (1917) 6 reels Yorke/Metro bw

Harold Lockwood *(Jerry Benham)*, Vera Sisson *(Una Habberton)*, Virginia Rappe *(Marcia Van Wyck)*, William Clifford *(Roger Canby)*, Lester Cuneo *(Jack Ballard)*, G. Sprotte *(Henry Ballard)*, Catherine Henry, Olive Bruce, Harry DeRoy, George Hupp.

An interesting film only in the sense that it features a young actress named Virginia Rappe playing a flirtatious vamp who seduces a wealthy young man into throwing a number of wild parties at his newly inherited estate. The youth ultimately is made aware of her trampish ways and orders her out of his life rather spectacularly, tearing the back of her dress from her sensuous body. History remembers Rappe as the girl who died in the tragic Fatty Arbuckle rape case. His audience certainly did not forgive, and his career and life were subsequently destroyed.

d, Fred J. Balshofer; w, Balshofer, Richard V. Spencer (based on a novel by George Gibbs); ph, Tony Gaudio.

Drama **(PR:C MPAA:NR)**

PARDON MY NERVE!*** (1922) 5 reels FOX bw

Charles Jones *(Racey Dawson)*, Eileen Percy *(Molly Dale)*, Mae Busch *(Marie)*, G. Raymond Nye *(Bill McFluke)*, Joe Harris *(Jack Harpe)*, Otto Hoffman *(Luke Tweezy)*, William Steele *(Nebraska Jones)*, Robert Daly *(Henry Dale)*.

Above-average western drama has Jones, an ace gunman, wrongly accused of killing the man who tried to steal his sweetheart's ranch. The dog belonging to a dance hall girl he befriended, however, delivers the murder weapon, clearing Jones and making it possible for the two-fisted hero to marry Percy, the girl he loves and settle down.

d, Reaves Eason; w, Jack Strumwasser (based on the novel *The Heart of the Range* by William Patterson White); ph, George Schneiderman.

Western **(PR:A MPAA:NR)**

PARIS GREEN*** (1920) 5 reels PAR bw

Charles Ray *(Luther Green)*, Ann May *(Ninon Robinet)*, Bert Woodruff *(Mathew Green)*, Gertrude Claire *(Sarah Green)*, Donald MacDonald *(Jules Benoit)*, Gordon Douglas Mullen *("Hairpin" Petrie)*, Norris Johnson *(Edith Gleason)*, William Courtright, Ida Lewis *(Mrs. Miller)*, Otto Hoffman *(Andre Robinet)*, Aggie Herring.

Entertaining Ray comedy has the likable star taking a whirlwind tour of Paris before leaving for home following the war. Upon returning, the girl who promised to wait breaks off their engagement, but a pretty little French girl he met in Paris arrives on the scene, and she and Ray fall in love. There are lots of laughs and even a few thrills along the way.

d, Jerome Storm; sup, Thomas H. Ince; w, (based on a story by Julien Josephson); ph, Chester Lyons.

Comedy **(PR:A MPAA:NR)**

PARSON OF PANAMINT, THE*** (1916) 5 reels Pallas bw

Dustin Farnum *(Phillip Pharo)*, Winifred Kingston *("Buckskin Liz")*, "Doc" Pomeroy Cannon *("Chuckawalla Bill")*, Howard Davies *(Bud Deming)*, Colin Chase *("Chappie" Ellerton)*, Ogden Crane *(Absalom Randall)*, Jane Keckley *(Arabella Randall)*, Tom Bates *("Grabapple" Thompson)*.

Interesting western has oldtimer Cannon sitting on the ruins of what was once a thriving mining town and telling (through the use of flashbacks) the community's history. From this point on, Farnum takes over as the fighting parson who is brought in from San Francisco, builds the church, rids the place of its bad element, and finally gives his life to save an enemy in a fire. Good atmosphere, acting, and an unusual script, make this one a winner.

d, William Desmond Taylor; w, Julia Crawford Ivers (based on a novel by Peter B. Kyne).

Western/Drama **(PR:A MPAA:NR)**

PARTNERS AGAIN*** (1926) 6 reels Goldwyn/UA bw

George Sidney *(Abe Potash)*, Alexander Carr *(Mawruss Perlmutter)*, *Betty Jewel (Hattie Potash)*, Allan Forrest *(Dan)*, Robert Schable *(Schenckmann)*, *Lillian Elliott (Rosie Potash)*, Earl Metcalf *(Aviator)*, Lew Brice *(Pazinsky)*, Gilbert Clayton *(Sammett)*, Anna Gilbert *(Mrs. Sammett)*.

Director King proves to be as adept at comedy as he is with the serious material in this delightful film, chronicling the further adventures of Abe Potash and Mawruss Perlmutter. In this case, the boys (played by Sidney and Carr) go into the automobile business. An argument naturally ensues, breaking up the partnership, and Abe is put in the position of taking the fall for a couple of swindlers. Mawruss, as always, comes to his old friend's aid, helping him escape to Canada, and after a number of very funny developments, the crooks are exposed and the lovable duo are reunited to continue their endless squabbling.

d, Henry King; w, Frances Marion (based on the play by Montague Glass, Jules Eckert Goodman); t, Glass; ph, Arthur Edeson.

Comedy **(PR:A MPAA:NR)**

PARTNERS IN CRIME* 1/2** (1928) 7 reels PAR bw

Wallace Beery *(Mike Doolin, the Detective)*, Raymond Hatton *("Scoop" McGee, the Reporter)*, Raymond Hatton *("Knife" Reagan, Terror of the Underworld)*, Mary Brian *(Marie Burke, the Cigarette Girl)*, William Powell *(Smith)*, Jack Luden *(Richard Deming, Assistant District Attorney)*, Arthur Housman *(Barton)*, Albert Roccardi *(Kanelli, the Restaurant Owner)*, *Joseph W. Girard (Chief of Police)*, George Irving *(B. R. Cornwall)*, Bruce Gordon *(Dodo)*, *Jack Richardson (Jake)*.

Superior Beery-Hatton comedy in which the boys satirize the underworld movie genre. The result is wonderful because everything feels so right. The gangsters are almost played straight (according to type), while Beery, as a half-witted private eye, and Hatton as a not-very-bright, wise-cracking reporter, fumble about the picture, become involved in the criminal world, and then quite by accident deliver the crooks to the cops.

d, Frank Strayer; w, Grover Jones, Gilbert Pratt; t, George Marion, Jr.; ph, William Marshall; ed, William Shea.

Comedy/Crime **(PR:A MPAA:NR)**

PARTNERS OF THE NIGHT 1/2** (1920) 5 reels Goldwyn bw

William B. Davidson, Pinna Nesbit, William Ingersoll, Emmett Corrigan, Mario Majeroni, Vincent Coleman, Frank Kingdon, Tenny Wright, Louis O'Connor.

Interesting crime drama about a detective who is as concerned with seeing potential criminals go straight as he is in making his arrest quota. He meets a girl, turns her life around, and together they get the goods on the crooked chief of police.

d, Paul Scardon; w, Leroy Scott, Charles Whittaker (based on a story by Scott); ph, A. A. Calder.

Crime **(PR:A MPAA:NR)**

PARTNERS OF THE TIDE 1/2** (1921) 7 reels Irvin V. Willat/Hodkinson bw

Jack Perrin *(Bradley Nickerson)*, Marion Faducha *(Bradley, as a Boy)*, Gordon Mullen *(Sam Hammond)*, Daisy Robinson *(Augusta Baker)*, Gertrude Norman *(Grandma Baker)*, L. P. Lockney *(Capt. Ezra Titcomb)*, *Joe Miller (Carl Swenson)*, Bert Hadley *(James Williams)*, Fred Kohler *(1st Mate)*, *Florence Midgley (Temperance Allen)*, Ashley Cooper *(Seth Rogers)*.

Perrin, in a non-cowboy role, does well in this effective little drama about an orphan who grows up to become an insurance investigator and nails the crooks who sabotaged a ship. There are some good underwater diving sequences which add suspense, and the shipwreck is particularly well executed for a low-budget production.

p, Irvin V. Willat; d, L. V. Jefferson; w, Willat (based on the novel by Joseph Crosby Lincoln); ph, Paul Eagler.

Drama **(PR:A MPAA:NR)**

PASSING OF MR. QUIN, THE* (1928, Brit.) 9 reels Strand-Cecil Cattermoul/Argosy bw

Stewart Rome *(Dr. Alec Portal)*, Trilby Clark *(Eleanor Appleby)*, Ursula Jeans *(Vera)*, Clifford Heatherley *(Prof. Appleby)*, Mary Brough *(Cook)*, Vivian Baron *(Derek Cappel)*, Kate Gurney *(Landlady)*.

There is a fairly interesting courtroom scene in which the witnesses are shown double exposed with the accused. That, and the name of Agatha Christie, is all this picture has going for it. There are three suspects involved in the murder of a cad, and after nearly nine reels, when the killer turns out to be a neighbor, nobody really gives a hoot.

p, Julius Hagen; d&w, Leslie Hiscott (based on the novel by Agatha Christie).

Mystery **(PR:A MPAA:NR)**

PASSION**** (1920, Ger.) 6 reels Union-UFA/FN bw (MADAME DUBARRY)

Pola Negri *(Jeanette Becu/Mme. Dubarry)*, Emil Jannings *(Louis XV)*, Harry Liedtke *(Armand de Foix)*, Eduard von Winterstein *(Jean Dubarry)*, Reinhold Schunzel *(Duc de Choiseul)*, Elsa Berna *(Duchesse de Grammont)*, Frederich Immler *(Duc de Richelieu)*, Gustave Czimeg *(Duc d'Aiguillon)*, Carl Platen *(Guillaume Dubarry)*, Bernhard Goetzke, Magnus Stifter, Paul Biensfeldt, Willy Kaiser, Alexander Ekert, Robert Sortsch-Pla, Marga Kohler.

Lubitsch, whom biographer Herman Weinberg rightfully referred to as the "humanizer of history" directed this magnificent 18th Century spectacle about the milliner (Negri) who became the mistress of France's King Louis XV (Jannings) and was tragically beheaded in the end. This was the film which opened the American market to Germany and established UFA as the leading studio outside of Hollywood. It also made Negri a star and established Lubitsch as one of the world's greatest directors.

d, Ernst Lubitsch; w, Fred Orbing, Hans Kraly; t, Katherine Hillaker; ph, Theodore Sparkuhl; m, David Mendoza, William Axt; set d, Karl Machus, Kurt Richter; cos, Ali Hubert.

Historical Drama **Cas.** **(PR:A MPAA:NR)**

PASSION ISLAND* (1927, Brit.) 8 reels Film Manufacturing bw

Lillian Oldland *(Josettes Bernatti)*, Moore Marriott *(Beppo)*, Randle Ayrton *(Paolo Bernatti)*, Walter Butler *(Tony)*, Dacia Deane *(Santa)*, Gladys Hamer *(Clare)*, Leal Douglas *(Desiree)*, Johnny Butt *(Tomasco)*.

Boring, overlong British production is at least 10 years out of date. And the story line, dealing with revenge in Corsica, completely lacks interest. Bad direction, acting, sets, and script make this one a near zero.

p, G. A. Atkinson; d, Manning Haynes; w, Lydia Hayward (based on a novel by W. W. Jacobs).

Drama **(PR:A MPAA:NR)**

PASSION OF JOAN OF ARC, THE***** (1928, Fr.) 10 reels Societe Generale Des Films bw

Renee (Marie) Falconetti *(Joan of Arc)*, Eugene Silvain *(Bishop Pierre Cauchon)*, Maurice Schultz *(Nicholas Loyseleur)*, Michel Simon *(Jean Lemaitre)*, Antonin Artraud *(Jean Massieu)*, Louis Ravet *(Jean Beaupere)*, Andre Berley *(Jean d'Estivet)*, Jean d'Yd *(Guillaume Erard)*.

On the strength of the popularity in France of his film THOU SHALT HONOR THY WIFE, Danish director Carl Theodor Dreyer was offered a contract by the Societe Generale des Films to direct a motion picture devoted to a great French historical figure. Dreyer selected Joan of Arc, who had been canonized in 1920, because, as he wrote, "I wanted to interpret a hymn to the triumph of the soul over life." At the time, Joseph Delteil's novel *Vie de Jeanne d'Arc* was highly revered, so he was hired to write the screenplay. Dreyer was not pleased with the result, however, and although Delteil was given credit the Dane created his own script using Pierre Champion's 1921 text of the actual trial. The story has Joan (Falconetti), a girl of 19, at the Palace of Justice, where she is about to be tried for heresy and witchcraft. Her real crime, however, was successfuly leading an army against the British forces occupying France. Her military victories were breathtaking, but the Burgundian allies of the English captured her and turned her over to the court of ecclesiastics, who were in reality under the thumb of the Earl of Warwick. When she is brought before her judges, she is denounced for wearing men's attire, and claiming to be conversant with St. Michael. But she refuses to buckle under and tells her tormentors that she will eventually be released from prison "by means of a great victory." She is later ordered to renounce her visions and is shown the instruments of torture, which are so skillfully depicted by Dreyer that the viewer can almost feel the agony they are capable of inflicting. Falconetti passes out and is returned to her cell. She awakens, stricken with fever and weakened by having been bled. She is told that if she signs the confession her reward will be the body and blood of Christ, and she is shown the Eucharist. Again she denounces her accusers. She is placed on a stretcher and carried to the churchyard where the pyre awaits her, and this time she gives in. They return her to her place of confinement to have her head shaved. But as she undergoes this humiliation she sees a pile of straw which resembles the Crown of Thorns, and fearfully demands that the punishment be carried out. Her agony at the stake is so skillfully handled by Dreyer and Falconetti that it is almost unbearable to watch. And as it takes place the crowd begins to turn against the executioners. Falconetti *has* left the prison "victorious"—and . . . the victory is her martyrdom. There are few films as powerful as THE PASSION OF JOAN OF ARC. Dreyer, with his constant use of the subjective camera (mostly in closeup and executed from dazzling angles), his skillful exploitation of montage, and the rhythm of his images, all combine to give his audience a sense of participating in the passion. In fact, the film is so effective that it was banned in England until 1930. But unquestionably its greatest asset is the performance of Falconetti (Dreyer had considered Lillian Gish for the part), a boulevard comedienne in whom the director saw the quality he wanted. She is sheer perfection in this film (many consider it the greatest performance in all of cinema), and although it's the only motion picture she ever made, it earned her immortality.

d&w, Carl Theodor Dreyer (screenplay credit was also given to Joseph Delteil but his material was not used); ph, Rudolph Mate; ed, Dreyer; m, Victor Alix, Leo Pouget.

Drama **Cas.** **(PR:A MPAA:NR)**

PASSIONATE ADVENTURE, THE***
(1924, Brit.) 8 reels Gainsborough/GAU bw

Alice Joyce *(Drusilla Sinclair)*, Marjorie Daw *(Vickey)*, Clive Brook *(Adrien St. Clair)*, Lilian Hall Davis *(Pamela)*, Victor McLaglen *(Herb Harris)*, J. R. Tozer *(Inspector Stewart Sladen)*, Mary Brough *(Lady Rolls)*, John Hamilton *(Bill)*.

Hitchcock scripted the screen version of this British novel—enhanced by a mostly U.S. cast—about a fellow who is married to a sexually frigid society lady and returns from the war to find her still cold. He then comes to the rescue of a battered slum girl, Daw, who convinces Joyce, his wife, of her shortcomings, and the picture ends on a happy note. The presence of Hitchcock, as well as the first-rate cast, make this one of the few English imports which can hold its own alongside the best U.S. programmers.

p, Michael Balcon; d, Graham Cutts; w, Alfred Hitchcock (based on a novel by Frank Stayton).

Drama **(PR:C MPAA:NR)**

PASSIONATE FRIENDS, THE* (1922, Brit.) 7 reels STOLL bw

Milton Rosmer *(Steven Stratton)*, Valia *(Lady Mary Christian)*, Fred Raynham *(Harrison Justin)*, Madge Stuart *(Rachel Moore)*, Lawford Davidson *(Guy Ladislaw)*, Ralph Forster *(Philip Evesham)*, Teddy Arundell *(Edward Stratton)*, Annie Esmond *(Maid)*.

Improbable plot has a gentleman marrying on the rebound a woman who adores him, while continuing to carry the torch for his first sweetheart. The bride understands the situation, and the groom begins to fall for her as well. The husband of the first lady is not as liberal in his thinking, however, and threatens divorce, naming the other fellow as correspondent. Then, the first woman commits suicide to protect the career of the man she initially spurned. Not a pretty picture—or a very good one, at that.

d, Maurice Elvey; w, Leslie Howard Gordon (based on the novel by H. G. Wells).

Drama **(PR:A MPAA:NR)**

PASSIONATE YOUTH* (1925) 6 reels TRU bw

Beverly Bayne *(Mary Rand)*, Frank Mayo *(John Rand)*, Pauline Garon *(Henrietta Rand)*, Bryant Washburn *(Corbin)*, Carmelita Geraghty *(Peggy)*, Ralph McCullough *(Matt Rutherford)*, Ernest Wood *(Jimmy Wellington)*, Lawrence Underwood *(Prosecuting Attorney)*, Jack Fowler *(District Attorney)*, Walter Deming *(Harry Perrin)*, James McElhern *(Deacon Collins)*, William McIllwain *(Judge Ford)*.

Ambitious Bayne divorces her minister husband and joins a high-powered law firm. Before long she falls in love with their ace attorney, Washburn. The problem is that he is attracted to Bayne's daughter Garon, and when Washburn is found murdered, the girl is accused and put on trial. Fortunately, her father was a good lawyer in his own right before deciding to turn his collar around, and he brilliantly defends and exonerates his little girl, in a poorly filmed courtroom scene. Bayne, who has been watching the whole thing with slack-jawed amazement, begs to be taken back, and her former husband, who is above all else a good Christian, agrees.

d, Dallas M. Fitzgerald; w, J. Grubb Alexander; t, Ben Allah; ph, Milton Moore; ed, Jean Spencer Ware.

Drama **(PR:A MPAA:NR)**

PATCHWORK GIRL OF OZ, THE*** (1914) 5 reels Oz bw

Violet MacMillan *(Ojo, Munchkin Boy)*, Frank Moore *(Unc Nunkie, Guardian)*, Fred Woodward *(The Woozy/Mewel, the Waif)*, Raymond Russell *(Dr. Pipt, the Crooked Magician)*, Leontine Dranet *(Marglotte, the Wife)*, Bobby Gould *(Jesseva, the Daughter)*, Dick Rosson *(Danx, the Munchkin Boy)*, Jessie May Walsh *(Ozma, Ruler of Oz)*, Frank Bristol *(Soldier with the Green Whiskers)*, Pierre Couderc *(The Patchwork Girl)*, Marie Wayne *(Jinjur)*, Lon Musgrave, William Cook, Ben Deeley, Todd Wright, Herbert Glennon, Al Roach, Andy Anderson.

Baum's story comes to life in this entertaining movie which has an old man, a boy, and the Patchwork Girl (Couderc), created by the conniving Dr. Pipt (Russell), captured by the Queen of Oz (Walsh), and ultimately finding the ingredients necessary to bring life back to their friends, who have been turned to stone.

d, J. Farrell MacDonald; w, L. Frank Baum; ph, James A. Crosby.

Fantasy **(PR:A MPAA:NR)**

PATHS TO PARADISE**** (1925) 7 reels FP/PAR bw

Betty Compson *(Molly)*, Raymond Griffith *(The Dude from Duluth)*, Tom Santschi *(Callahan)*, Bert Woodruff *(Bride's Father)*, Fred Kelsey *(Confederate)*.

One of the great comedies of all time had Griffith playing a con man who boosts a queen crook (Compson) of all the money she just fleeced from a number of victims in Chinatown. Later they meet again at a millionaire's mansion—she dressed as a maid, he as a detective—both pursuing a fabulous necklace. At this point the two team up and steal the necklace with little difficulty. What follows is perhaps the funniest chase scene ever filmed. The sight gags are brilliant and seemingly endless as the two shady characters race for the Mexican border with what seems like every motorcycle cop in America on their tail. Of course Griffith and Compson finally make it, and of course they fall in love along the way, and of course they decide to go straight, get married, and return the necklace in the end. Griffith had a speech impediment which prevented him from speaking above a whisper, so he never made the transition to talkies. He did, however, enjoy a successful career as a producer, and his last screen appearance, ironically, is better remembered than this near masterpiece. In it Griffith played a small part as the dying French soldier in the trench with Lew Ayres, who grunts the request that the German lad contact his family, in ALL QUIET ON THE WESTERN FRONT (1930).

d, Clarence Badger; w, Keene Thompson (based on the play "The Heart of a Thief" by Paul Armstrong); ph, H. Kinley Martin.

Comedy **Cas.** **(PR:A MPAA:NR)**

PATRICIA BRENT, SPINSTER** (1919, Brit.) 6 reels Garrick bw

Ena Beaumont *(Patricia Brent)*, Laurence Leyton *(Lord Peter Bowen)*, Victor Robson *(The MP)*, Nessie Blackford *(Miss Wangle)*, Bruce Winston *(Bolton)*, Pollie Emery *(Lodger)*.

Lightweight British comedy about the adventures of a spinster, who finally has the last laugh after she cons a man into posing as her fiance.

d, Geoffrey H. Malins; w, Eliot Stannard (based on a novel by Herbert Jenkins).

Comedy **(PR:A MPAA:NR)**

PATRIOT, THE*** (1916) 5 reels KayBee/TRI bw

William S. Hart *(Bob Wiley)*, George Stone *(Little Bobs)*, Joe Goodboy *(Himself)*, Roy Laidlaw *(Pancho Zapilla)*, Francis Carpenter *(Billy Allen)*, Milton Ross *(Denman Hammond)*, P. D. Tabler *(Jordan Mason)*, Charles K. French *(Col. Bracken)*, Rags.

When his mine is stolen by an Eastern swindler, Spanish-American War vet Hart goes to Washington to plead his case and is ignored. Then, when he returns home to discover his little boy dead, Hart nearly goes crazy with grief, joins a band of Mexican bandits, and participates in the attack on a U.S. settlement. During the height of the battle, Hart happens upon an orphaned boy—the same age his son would have been—comes to his senses, and turns the struggle in favor of his own people. The picture ends touchingly with the great western star, once more filled with pride for his country, heading home with the little boy in his arms.

d, William S. Hart; w, Monte M. Katterjohn; ph, Joseph August; art d, Robert Brunton.

Western **(PR:A MPAA:NR)**

PATSY½** (1921) 5 reels Fred Swanton/TRU bw

ZaSu Pitts *(Patsy)*, John MacFarlane *(Pops)*, Tom Gallery *(Bob Brooks)*, Marjorie Daw *(Margaret Vincent)*, Fannie Midgley *(Mrs. Vincent)*, Wallace Beery *(Gustave Ludermann)*, Harry Todd *(Tramp)*, Milla Davenport *(Matron)*, Henry Fortson *(Bones)*.

Pitts steals the whole show with Beery handling his role as heavy well, in this dramatic comedy about an orphan who runs away, crosses the country, and is taken in by a kindly scientist who thinks she's a boy. Pitts demonstrates the kind of grit which gets her elected head of the kids' gang and saves her benefactor from a crooked conspiracy. In the end she reunites him with his daughter.

d&w, John McDermott (based on the play by Er Lawshe).

Dramatic Comedy **(PR:A MPAA:NR)**

PAULA** (1915, Brit.) 6 reels Holmfirth/Initial bw

Hettie Payne *(Paula)*, Frank McClellan *(Vincent Hallam)*.

British tearjerker about a devoted woman who uproots her life in England to follow the man she loves to Italy and is rewarded by expiring after giving blood in an attempt to save his life.

d, Cecil Birch; w, (based on a novel by Victoria Cross).

Drama **(PR:A MPAA:NR)**

PAWN TICKET 210** (1922) 5 reels FOX bw

Shirley Mason *(Meg)*, Robert Agnew *(Chick Saxe)*, Irene Hunt *(Ruth Sternhold)*, Jacob Abrams *(Abe Levi)*, Dorothy Manners *(Mrs. Levi)*, Fred Warren *(Harris Levi)*.

No comparison to ABIE'S IRISH ROSE is this drama about a girl (Mason) who is left in the Levi's pawn shop, and raised by them. Eventually the father (Abrams) places her in the custody of his wealthy friend in order that she be given the "proper" social exposure. Later, Mason's mother returns to claim her child, and in an emotional scene is reunited with her daughter's charge, who it turns out is the girl's actual father. The picture is given a double happy ending, as Mason is now allowed to be with her sweetheart, Agnew.

d, Scott Dunlap, w, Jules Furthman (based on the play by David Belasco, Clay M. Greene); ph, George Schneiderman.

Drama **(PR:A MPAA:NR)**

PAWS OF THE BEAR*½ (1917) 5 reels KayBee/TRI bw

William Desmond *(Ray Bourke)*, Clara Williams *(Olga Raminoff)*, Robert McKim *(Boris Drakoff)*, Wallace Worsley *(Curt Schrieber)*, Charles French *(Gen. von Mittendorf)*.

Weak programmer has Desmond an American student in Belgium at the outbreak of WW I, becoming involved with a female Russian agent and deciding to do his bit for the victims of oppression.

d, Reginald Barker; w, J. G. Hawks.

War **(PR:A MPAA:NR)**

PAYING THE LIMIT* (1924) 5 reels Paul Gerson bw

Ora Carew *(Raffles)*, Helen Nowell *(Joan Lowden)*, Eddie O'Brien *(Thunder Lowden)*, Arthur Wellington *(Jerry Davis)*, Jay Morley *(Tom Dover)*, Stanley J. Sanford *(Ole)*, Dick Stevens *(Baptiste Tudor)*.

Bottom-of-the-barrel programmer has Carew, a recently released girl convict, landing a job as a maid for a rich family, saving her employer's daughter from marrying a crook she recognizes, and almost being blamed for stealing some cash that the girl actually took at his bidding. The picture ends with everybody declaring that Carew is the salt of the earth, and the company foreman begging her to become his wife.

d&w, Tom Gibson; ph, George Crocker.

Drama **(PR:A MPAA:NR)**

PEACEFUL PETERS* (1922) 5 reels Ben Wilson/Arrow bw

William Fairbanks *("Peaceful Peters")*, Harry La Mont *(Jim Blalock)*, W. L. Lynch *(Peter Hunter)*, Evelyn Nelson *(Mary Langdon)*, Wilbur McGaugh *("Sad" Simpson)*, Monte Montague *("Cactus" Collins)*.

Dreadful Fairbanks potboiler has the cowboy star finding a dying miner whose claim has been stolen by outlaws. Fairbanks brings the killers to justice after a few reels and saves nice girl Nelson, who answered an ad as dance teacher at the local saloon, from becoming a pleasure object. When the picture finally ends, it comes as no great surprise that the dance instructor is in reality the late miner's niece.

d, Lewis King; w, Daniel Whitcomb (based on the story "Peaceful" by Wilbur C. Tuttle); ph, Jack Fuqua; ed, Earl C. Turner.

Western **(PR:A MPAA:NR)**

PEACOCK ALLEY*** (1922) 8 reels TIF/Metro bw

Mae Murray *(Cleo of Paris)*, Monte Blue *(Elmer Harmon)*, Edmund Lowe *(Phil Garrison)*, W. J. Ferguson *(Alex Smith)*, Anders Randolph *(Hugo Fenton)*, William Tooker *(Joseph Carleton)*, Howard Lang *(Abner Harmon)*, William Frederic *(Mayor of Harmontown)*, M. Durant *(Mons. Dubois)*, Jeffrys Lewis *(Toto)*, Napoleon the Dog.

One of Murray's best has the star playing a dancer in Paris who marries Blue, a U.S. businessman, and returns to his Pennsylvania home where she's the object of local scorn. When her husband goes broke, forges his uncle's signature to a check and is arrested in New York, Murray returns to the stage, becomes a sensation, and bails Blue out of trouble. There is a misunderstanding on his part regarding her relationship with a theatrical friend, but in the end everything is resolved. Remade by Murray in 1930 with dialog, color sequences, and a very different story line.

d&sup, Robert Z. Leonard; w, Edmund Goulding (based on a story by Ouida Bergere); t, Frederic and Fanny Hatton; ph, Oliver Marsh; set d, Charles Cadwallader.

Drama **(PR:A MPAA:NR)**

PEACOCK FAN*** (1929) 6 reels CHES bw

Lotus Long *(Feliti)*, Fujii Kishii *(Okuri)*, Wong Foo *(Men Ching)*, Lucien Prival *(Dr. Chang Dorfman)*, Dorothy Dwan *(Peggy Kendall)*, Tom O'Brien *(Sgt. O'Brien)*, Rosemary Theby *(Mrs. Rossmore)*, Carlton King *(Mr. Rossmore)*, Gladden James *(Bertram Leslie)*, David Findlay *(Jerry Carlyle)*, James Wilcox *(Bob Kendall)*, Fred Malatesta *(Thomas Elton)*, Alice True *(Lily)*, Spencer Bell *(Arthur)*, John Fowler *(Dr. Whalen)*.

Good mystery begins with a prolog about the tragic history of a priceless Chinese peacock fan and its effect on its owners. The picture then moves to the present and the murder of its latest collector. Prival enters the case, and after investigating a number of suspects, solves the crime.

p, Lon Young; d, Phil Rosen; w, Arthur Hoerl (based on a story by Adeline Leitzbach); t, Lee Authmar; ph, M. A. Anderson; ed, James Sweeney.

Mystery **Cas.** **(PR:A MPAA:NR)**

PEARL OF THE SOUTH SEAS** (1927, Brit.) 5 reels STOLL/Hurley bw

Eric Bransby Williams *(John Strong)*, Lillian Douglas *(Marjorie Jones)*, Jameson Thomas *(John Darley)*, W. G. Saunders *(Cockeye Jones)*, Mollie Johnson *(Lady Cynthia)*, Dallas Cairns *(Mr. Bullyer)*.

Hurley came on like Orson Welles or Charles Chaplin, writing, producing, and directing this British South Seas adventure of pearl divers, natives, and attempted murder. The comparison ends there, however, with the quality of his work showing little resemblance.

p,d&w; Frank Hurley.

Adventure **(PR:A MPAA:NR)**

PECK'S BAD BOY*** (1921) 5 reels Irving M. Lesser/AFN bw

Jackie Coogan *(Peck's Bad Boy)*, Wheeler Oakman *(The Doctor)*, Doris May *(His Sister)*, James Corrigan *(His Father)*, Raymond Hatton *(The Grocer)*, Lillian Leighton *(Ma Peck)*, Charles Hatton *(Jackie's Pal)*, Gloria Wood *(His Girlfriend)*, Queenie the Dog.

Coogan is the whole show here, performing his charming, amusing, and touching bits of business at a circus, church, home, and railroad station. There is a love interest involving his older sister, and pathos (although rather forced) when his dog is nearly taken to the pound. But what we basically have in this picture is a great star almost elevating a mediocre movie to something more by his very presence.

d&w, Sam Wood (based on the stories of George Wilbur Peck); t, Irvin S. Cobb; ph, Alfred Gilks, Harry Hallenberger.

Comedy **Cas.** **(PR:A MPAA:NR)**

PECK'S BAD GIRL*½** (1918) 5 reels Goldwyn bw

Mabel Normand *(Minnie Peck)*, Earle Foxe *(Dick)*, Corinne Barker *(Hortense Martinot)*, Blanche Davenport *(Miss Olivia)*, Leslie Hunt *(Adam Raskell)*, E. M. Favor *(Peck)*, Edwin Sturgis *(Pearson)*, Joseph Granby *(Walker)*, F. G. Patton, Auge Becker, Riley Hatch.

Normand is at her best as Minnie Peck, the town cutup. She pulls off so many pranks (one causes a run on the bank) that the powers-to-be decide to send her to a reformatory. She is spared this fate, however, when a kindly soul arranges for her to be given a job modeling clothes. There are plenty of great sight gags here, and when Normand breaks up a bank robbery, she not only becomes a heroine to her fellow citizens, but the fiancee of the detective who had been trailing the crooks all along.

d, Charles Giblyn; w, (based on a story by Tex Charwate); ph, Louis Physioc.

Comedy **(PR:A MPAA:NR)**

PEEP BEHIND THE SCENES, A* (1918, Brit.) 5 reels Master/New Bio bw

Ivy Close *(Norah Joyce)*, Gerald Ames *(Augustus Joyce)*, Gertrude Bain *(Lucy Leslie)*, Vera Bryer *(Rosalie Joyce)*, Kenneth Gore *(Toby Charlton)*, E. Blackton *(Mother Manikin)*.

U.S. filmmakers felt little threat from British films such as this dark one about a young woman who dies when the actor she ran off with deserts her, leaving their child to wander through the countryside until she reaches her aunt.

p, Low Warren; d, Geoffrey H. Malins, Kenelm Foss; w, Foss (based on a novel by Mrs. O. F. Walton).

Drama **(PR:A MPAA:NR)**

PEEP BEHIND THE SCENES, A**
(1929, Brit.) 8 reels British & Dominions/Woolf & Freedman bw

Frances Cuyler *(Rosalie Joyce)*, Haddon Mason *(Toby Charlton)*, H. Saxon-Snell *(Augustus Joyce)*, Vera Stanton *(Gypsy Belle)*, Johnny Butt *(Jim)*, Renee Macready *(Norah Joyce)*, Ethel Irving *(Lucy Leslie)*, Clarence Blakiston *(Henry Leslie)*, Shirley Whyte *(Mother Manikin)*.

British drama about a female circus performer who, after years of mistreatment on the part of her father, runs away to her aunt when her mother passes away. The old man follows, but all works out in the end.

p, Herbert Wilcox; d, Jack Raymond; w, Lydia Hayward (based on a novel by Mrs. O. F. Walton).

Drama **(PR:A MPAA:NR)**

PEG OF THE PIRATES* (1918) 5 reels FOX bw

Peggy Hyland *(Peg)*, Sidney Mason, Carleton Macy, Frank Evans, James Davis, Louis Wolheim, Ajax Carroll, Eric Mayne.

The creators of this picture couldn't seem to make up their minds as to whether they wanted a comedy or adventure film. The result is one of the worst movies of 1918. There is, in fact, absolutely nothing to redeem it except for the few chuckles, which are completely accidental.

d&w, O. A. C. Lund (based on a story by W. L. Randall); ph, Joseph Ruttenberg.

Comedy/Adventure **(PR:A MPAA:NR)**

PEGGY*** (1916) 7 reels Kay-Bee/TRI

Billie Burke *(Peggy Cameron)*, William H. Thompson *(Andrew Cameron)*, William Desmond *(Rev. Donald Bruce)*, Charles Ray *(Colin Cameron)*, Nona Thomas *(Janet McLeod)*, Gertrude Claire *(Mrs. Cameron)*, Truly Shattuck *(Mrs. Van Allyn)*, Claire Du Brey.

The delightful Burke made her screen debut in this entertaining comedy about a hoydenish free-spirit who is whisked away from New York's social whirl to join her puritanical guardian in Scotland. The town is never the same after Burke's arrival, and she even ends up marrying the handsome young minister.

d, Charles Giblyn; w, C. Gardner Sullivan.

Comedy **(PR:A MPAA:NR)**

PELL STREET MYSTERY, THE* (1924) 5 reels Robert J. Horner/RAY bw

George Larkin, Carl Silvera.

Kiddie favorite Larkin is surrounded by cheap sets and some really off-the-wall stereotypes, in this action programmer about a reporter who infiltrates and breaks up a gang in Chinatown and finds himself rewarded by the love of a beautiful blonde, as well as a scoop for his paper.

d, Joseph Franz; w, Jeanne Poe, George Larkin.

Adventure **(PR:A MPAA:NR)**

PENALTY, THE*** (1920) 6 reels Gouverneur Morris/Goldwyn bw

Lon Chaney *(Blizzard)*, Claire Adams *(Barbara)*, Kenneth Harlan *(Wilmot)*, Charles Clary *(Doctor)*, Ethel Grey Terry *(Rose)*, Edouard Trebaol *(Bubble)*, Milton Ross *(Lichtenstein)*, James Mason *(Pete)*, Doris Pawn *(Barbary Nell)*, Lee Phelps *(cop)*, Wilson Hummel, Montgomery Carlyle, Madalaine Travers.

There are flaws in this fascinating film, but Chaney's impression of a legless madman (his limbs were amputated below the knees by mistake when he was a child) who sets out to reap revenge on the doctor, his family, and society in general, is incomparable. The actor is in constant pain as he bounds about the sets with his legs lashed behind him, and it is impossible to watch this film without sharing the discomfort with him. Director Worsley also contributes some wonderful images, especially in the scenes where Chaney's army of illegal aliens attacks the financial district of San Francisco. And even the titles, with a few exceptions, are topnotch, such as the one where one of Chaney's henchmen shoots the master criminal and the title card reads, "I am interested in death."

d, Wallace Worsley; w, Charles Kenyon, Philip Lonegran (based on the story by Gouverneur Morris); ph, Don Short.

Mystery **(PR:A MPAA:NR)**

PENITENTES, THE*** 1/2** (1915) 5 reels FA/TRI bw

Orin Johnson *(Manuel)*, Seena Owen *(Dolores)*, Paul Gilmore *(Col. Juan Raca)*, Irene Hunt *(Senorita Carmella)*, Josephine Crowell *(Her Mother)*, F. A. Turner *(Father Rossi)*, Charles Clary *(Father David)*, A.D. Sears *(The Chief Brother)*, Dark Cloud *(Indian Chief)*.

Strange, weird, and certainly off-beat, is this thriller set in 17th Century Mexico, which tells the fictional story of a fanatical splinter group of the Roman Catholic Church which enjoyed the practice of real crucifixions every Good Friday. Needless to say the neighbors suffered pangs of nervousness annually until the cult was finally stamped out. Great direction by Conway, especially in the eerie depiction of the Night Riders silhouetted against the moonlight, very much in the style D. W. Griffith used for his famous rescue by the Klan in THE BIRTH OF A NATION (1915). In fact it is rumored that the master may have supervised Conway, his one-time assistant, in the shooting of these remarkable sequences.

d, Jack Conway; w, Mary H. O'Connor (based on a novel by Robert Ellis Wales).

Drama **(PR:A MPAA:NR)**

PENNILESS MILLIONAIRE, THE* 1/2
(1921, Brit.) 5 reels BRO/Walturdaw bw

Stewart Rome *(Bernard Jarrold)*, Fabienne Fabreges *(Angela Jarrold)*, Gregory Scott *(Belthorp)*, Cameron Carr *(Tim Dolan)*, George Foley *(Martin Stornaway)*.

The British cinema was almost developing a feeling for action pictures when this film was made. Set in China, it tells about an aristocrat's black sheep son who battles bandits and exposes the scheme of a female crook to seize power.

p, Walter West; d, Einar J. Bruun; w, Frank Fowell (based on the novel by David Christie Murray). .

Adventure **(PR:A MPAA:NR)**

PENNINGTON'S CHOICE*** (1915) 5 reels Quality/Metro bw

Francis X. Bushman *(Robert Pennington, Wealthy Young New Yorker)*, Beverly Bayne *(Eugenia Blondeau/Marie, Her Pretend Twin)*, Wellington Playter *(Jules Bondeau, Her Father)*, H. O'Dell, William Farris *(Her Brothers)*, Helen Dunbar *(Mrs. Allison, Her Aunt)*, Lester Cuneo *(Jean, Leader of the Conspirators)*, Morris Cytron *(Pierre, a Guide)*, Jim Jeffries *(Himself)*.

Snappy comedy has Bushman playing a society chap who falls for Bayne when she drops down from Canada to visit her aunt in New York. Bayne explains to Bushman that he must win her father's approval before she can even *consider* becoming his wife, so the lad grabs a train and heads north. When he finally gets there, Bayne is waiting at her father's cabin, where she pretends to be her own twin sister, and performs a series of hilarious outdoor feats which would make even the athletic Pearl White green with envy. She also pretends to make a play for the visitor from Gotham, but the lad remains steadfastly true to her alter ego. Later, a couple of resentful lumberjacks give the tenderfoot a terrific shellacking, which encourages Bushman to look up his old pal, Jeffries, the former heavyweight champion of the world (playing himself), who just happens to be training nearby. Then with the champ's help, Bushman returns to the lumber camp, gives the bullies the beating of *their* lives, makes an even greater impression on Bayne, and wins the enthusiastic approval of her father.

d, William J. Bowman; w, John C. Culley.

Comedy/Adventure **(PR:A MPAA:NR)**

PENROD*** 1/2** (1922) 8 reels Marshall Neilan/AFN bw

Wesley Barry *(Penrod)*, Tully Marshall *(Mr. Schofield)*, Claire McDowell *(Mrs. Schofield)*, John Harron *(Robert Williams)*, Gordon Griffith *(Sam Williams)*, Newton Hall *(George Bassett)*, Harry Griffith *(Foster)*, Cecil Holland *(John Barrett)*, Sunshine Morrison *(Herman)*, Florence Morrison *(Verman)*, Marjorie Daw *(Margaret)*, Clara Horton *(Marjorie Jones)*, Peggy Jane *(Baby Rennsdale)*, Wheeler Dryden, Mayme Kelso, Grace Green, Earl Crain, Fred Thomson, Theodore Chapin, Junior Alden, Winston Radom, Adelaide Baxter, Francis Plottner, Charles Meakin, Harry Todd, Lina Basquette, Julian Lenne, Bernice Radom, George Dromgold, Virginia True Boardman, Charles Arling, Noah Beery, Jr., Bennie Billings, Jack Condon, Peggy Cartwright, Bradford Ralston, Stephen Welz, Billie Bennett, May Baxter, Kenneth Green, Carrie Clark Ward, R. D. Saunders, Blanche Light, Eugenie Besserer.

Perhaps a bit on the long side, but vastly superior to Coogan's PECK'S BAD BOY, is director Neilan's look at the mischievous antics of Tarkington's all-American boy. There are plenty of laughs which result from Penrod's various pranks, but when he's directly responsible for the capture of a couple of crooks, the freckle-faced lad becomes the hero of his town. Barry delivers a delightful performance as the boy the whole world grew to love.

d&sup, Marshall Neilan; w, Lucita Squier (based on the play by Booth Tarkington); ph, David Kesson, Ray June; ed, Daniel J. Gray.

Dramatic Comedy **(PR:A MPAA:NR)**

PENROD AND SAM*** (1923) 7 reels J.K. McDonald/AFN bw

Ben Alexander *(Penrod Schofield)*, Joe Butterworth *(Sam Williams)*, Buddy Messinger *(Rodney Bitts)*, Newton Hall *(Georgie Bassett)*, Gertrude Messinger *(Marjorie Jones, Penrod's Girl Friend)*, Joe McGray *(Herman)*, Eugene Jackson *(Verman)*, Rockliffe Fellowes *(Mr. Schofield)*, Gareth Hughes *(Robert Williams, Margaret's Sweetheart)*, William V. Mong *(Deacon Bitts)*, Martha Mattox *(Miss Spence, Schoolteacher)*, Vic Potel *(Town Drunk)*, Bobby Gordon *(Maurice Levy)*, Gladys Brockwell *(Mrs. Schofield)*, Mary Philbin *(Margaret Schofield)*, Cameo *(Duke, Penrod's Dog)*.

Here we have the further adventures of Tarkington's all-American boy. This time Penrod (Alexander) and his pal Sam (Butterworth) refuse to let a couple of snooty kids join their club. But to Penrod's horror, his dad sells the land on which their clubhouse is located to the father of the chief pantywaist, who delights in turning the tables on the boys. Then, when Mr. Schofield (Fellowes) realizes how broken up his boy is (Penrod's recently departed dog is buried there), he purchases the property back and the boys have the last laugh.

d, William Beaudine; w, Hope Loring, Louis D. Leighton (based on the novel by Booth Tarkington); ph, Ray June, Edward Ulman; ed, Edward McDermott.

Comedy/Drama **(PR:A MPAA:NR)**

PERFECT CRIME, A*** (1921) 5 reels Allan Dwan/AP bw

Monte Blue *(Wally Griggs)*, Jacqueline Logan *(Mary Oliver)*, Stanton Heck *("Big Bill" Thaine)*, Hardee Kirkland *(Halliday)*.

Entertaining Dwan-directed drama has Blue living by day as a mild-mannered bank teller, but at night taking on the identity of a dashing sport who fascinates everyone (including the president of his bank and the lovely Logan) with his fictional accounts of worldwide adventures. He becomes involved in a real life intrigue when he saves Logan's fortune from being stolen and then gives up his career behind the cage to become a best-selling author.

d, Allan Dwan; w, (based on a story by Carl Clausen); ph, Lyman Broening.

Drama **(PR:A MPAA:NR)**

PERFECT LADY, A*** (1918) 5 reels Goldwyn bw

Madge Kennedy *(Lucille Le Jambon/Lucy Higgins)*, Jere Austin *(Rev. David Grayling)*, Walter Law *(John Griswald)*, Rod La Rocque *(Bob Griswald)*, Ben Hendricks, Sr. *(Sam Lipman)*, Harry Spingler *(Bert Snyder)*, Agnes Marc *(Flossie Day)*, May McAvoy *(Claire Higgins)*.

Entertaining Kennedy comedy has the star playing a burlesque queen who has been tramping the boards in order to send her sister through school. When the sheriff of a small town orders the show closed, Kennedy decides to open an ice cream parlour, much to the chagrin of a puritanical deacon who advocates driving the "sinner" from his community. Later, however, pictures of the deacon sitting on a Chicago chorus girl's lap surface, and Kennedy has the last laugh when she marries the handsome young minister.

d, Clarence G. Badger; w, (based on the play by Rennold Wolf, Channing Pollock); ph, Marcel Le Picard.

Comedy/Drama **(PR:A MPAA:NR)**

PERFECT LOVER, THE**
(1919) 5 reels SF/SEL bw (AKA: THE NAKED TRUTH)

Eugene O'Brien *(Brian Lazar)*, Lucille Lee Stewart *(Mrs. Byfield)*, Marguerite Courtot *(Eileen Hawthorn)*, Mary Boland *(Mrs. Whitney)*, Martha Mansfield *(Marvis Morgan)*, Carl McRayne *(Prof. Hawthorn)*, Ann Brody, Mercita Esmonde.

A handsome young artist comes to New York and quickly becomes the darling of the female society set. When he finally grows weary of the endless parties, he goes home, marries his childhood sweetheart, and returns with her to conquer the Big Apple. But finding himself no longer "in demand," the painter sinks to the bottom. Out of desperation he borrows a ring from a former "acquaintance," planning to pawn the gem only long enough to tide him over. But the lady, eager for revenge, summons the police and brings them to the artist's garret to have him arrested for theft. She changes her mind when he leads her down the long hallway and introduces her to his wife and newly born baby.

d, Ralph Ince; w, Edmund Goulding (based on the story "The Naked Truth" by Leila Burton Wells).

Drama **(PR:C MPAA:NR)**

PERILS OF THE COAST GUARD* (1926) 5 reels Gerson/RAY bw

Cullen Landis *(Capt. Tom Norris)*, Dorothy Dawn *(Natalie)*.

Coast Guard captain Norris is not accepted by his bride's socially prominent uncle, until he breaks up a gang of oyster pirates and saves the old boy from drowning.

d, Oscar Apfel.

Adventure (PR:A MPAA:NR)

PERSUASIVE PEGGY½** (1917) 6 reels Mayfair bw

Peggy Hyland *(Peggy Patton)*, William B. Davidson *(Ed Towbridge)*, Mary Cecil Parker *(Belle Newell)*, Gertrude Norman *(Peggy's Mother)*, Charles Sutton *(Peggy's Father)*, Jules Cowles *(Head Farmhand)*, Arthur Housman *(Percy Pipp)*.

When pretty and perky Hyland marries her gentleman farmer it has been decided the couple will honeymoon at Niagara Falls. The man of the house turns chauvinist, however, and makes plans to attend the state fair instead. So, when he awakens on the morning following their nuptials, he finds a note, but no wife. The young lass has shuffled off to Buffalo alone. The husband, of course, follows, and the film ends with the couple deciding that marriage is a two-way street.

d&w, Charles J. Brabin (based on a story by Maravene Thompson).

Comedy/Drama (PR:A MPAA:NR)

PEST, THE*** (1919) 5 reels Goldwyn bw

Mabel Normand *(Jiggs)*, John Bowers *(Gene Giles)*, Charles Gerard *(John Harland)*, Alec B. Francis *(Judge Fisher)*, Leota Lorraine *(Blanche Fisher)*, Jack Curtis *(Asher Blodgett)*, Pearl Elmore *(Amy Blodgett)*, James Bradbury *("Noisy" Wilson)*.

Normand is more dramatic than comedic (although she still manages to deliver lots of laughs) in this well-constructed film dealing with the mix-up of babies in a hospital nursery. In the end, Normand saves the life of her millionaire father, whose supposed child had tried to make her life miserable. The lovely star, of course, finds herself sitting on top of the world, but not at the expense of those she loves.

d, W. Christy Cabanne; w, Melville W. Brown; ph, Percy Hilburn.

Comedy/Drama (PR:A MPAA:NR)

PETAL ON THE CURRENT, THE*½ (1919) 6 reels UNIV bw

Mary MacLaren *(Stella)*, Gertrude Claire *(Her Mother)*, Fritzi Ridgeway *(Cora)*, Robert Anderson *(The Man)*, Beatrice Burnham *(Gertie Cobb)*, Victor Potel *(Skinny Flint)*, David Butler *(Ed Kenealy)*, Yvette Mitchell, Janet Sully.

Poor MacLaren is a sweet girl who accepts an invitation to attend a wild party, then gets drunk, is arrested and thrown into jail for 10 days. The shock and shame kills her mother, and when the brokenhearted little lass is released, only the intervention of a good man (who later makes her his wife) saves the girl from becoming a lady of the night.

d, Tod Browning; w, Waldemar Young (based on a story by Fannie Hurst); ph, William Fildew.

Drama (PR:C MPAA:NR)

PETER PAN*** (1924) 10 reels FP/PAR bw

Betty Bronson *(Peter Pan)*, Ernest Torrence *(Capt. Hook)*, Cyril Chadwick *(Mr. Darling)*, Virginia Brown Faire *(Tinker Bell)*, Anna May Wong *(Tiger Lily)*, Esther Ralston *(Mrs. Darling)*, George Ali *(Nana the Dog)*, Mary Brian *(Wendy)*, Philippe De Lacey *(Michael)*, Jack Murphy *(John)*.

The cast assembled for this James Barrie classic is quite wonderful, and the familiar story of the Darling family children, who encounter the boy who never grew up and follow him to never-never land, where they experience countless adventures with Tinker Bell, Capt. Hook, and the other wondrous characters—-is sure-fire. But Brenon's direction is a bit on the stagey side, and in spite of the many, many things this film has going for it (Howe's photography and Pomeroy's special effects dazzle the eye) the picture seems to drag, and sadly, never quite lives up to its potential. At 10 reels, the effort is a long film but Bronson is absolutely delicious in the way she catches the spirit of Peter Pan. She was strongly endorsed by the author himself (English music hall tradition has it that Peter Pan is always played by a girl). Her appeal was so great in this picture, in fact, that for a while it was believed that her popularity might surpass that of Mary Pickford (who at one point visited her on the set and wished her well in the role). Brian is her usual winning self as Wendy, and lovely Ralston is beautifully gracious as Wendy's mother. The biggest scene stealer in the entire picture, though, was vigorous Torrence, as Capt. Hook, and he had his way on the set with his scene stealing gestures, as none of the cast cared to compete with him. PETER PAN, along with LAUGH CLOWN LAUGH, is considered one of director Brenon's most notable films.

d, Herbert Brenon; w, Willis Goldbeck (based on the novel by James M. Barrie); ph, James Howe; spec eff, Roy Pomeroy.

Fantasy (PR:A MPAA:NR)

PHANTOM OF THE NORTH* (1929) 5 reels All-Star/Biltmore bw

Edith Roberts *(Doris Rayburn)*, Donald Keith *(Bob Donald)*, Kathleen Key *(Colette)*, Boris Karloff *(Jules Gregg)*, Joe Bonomo *(Pierre Blanc)*, Josef Swickard *(Col. Rayburn)*, Muro *(Himself)*, Arab *(Himself)*.

Far North nonsense has a fur trapper wrongly accused of killing a fellow outdoorsman after his pelts are stolen. In the end he proves his innocence and is responsible for the death of the real killer. A dog and horse were added to the cast in a vain attempt to convince the kiddies that they might be watching Rex and Rinty.

d, Harry Webb; w, George Hull, Carl Krusada (based on a story by Flora E. Douglas); ph, Arthur Reeves, William Thornley; ed, Fred Bain.

North Adventure (PR:A MPAA:NR)

PHANTOM OF THE OPERA, THE*½** (1925) 9 reels UNIV bw/c

Lon Chaney *(Erik/The Phantom)*, Mary Philbin *(Christine Daae)*, Norman Kerry *(Raoul de Chagny)*, Snitz Edwards *(Florine Papillon)*, Gibson Gowland *(Simon)*, John Sainpolis *(Philippe de Chagny)*, Virginia Pearson *(Carlotta)*, Arthur Edmund Carewe *(Ledoux)*, Edith Yorke *(Mama Valerius)*, Anton Vaverka *(Prompter)*, Bernard Siegel *(Joseph Buguet)*, Olive Ann Alcorn *(La Sorelli)*, Cesare Gravina *(Manager)*, George B. Williams *(M. Ricard)*, Bruce Covington *(M. Moncharmin)*, Edward Cecil *(Faust)*, John Miljan *(Valentin)*, Alexander Bevani *(Mephistopheles)*, Grace Marvin *(Martha)*, Ward Crane *(Count Ruboff)*, Chester Conklin *(Orderly)*, William Tryoler *(Director of Opera Orchestra)*.

In what is probably his most famous picture, and certainly his most horrifying makeup disguise, Chaney is magnificent as the disfigured maniac composer who takes an interest in Philbin, an understudy at the Paris Opera. From behind secret passages he coaches and perfects her art until she is a star. He then forces the leading soprano to step down by unleashing a series of terrors, including the spectacular scene (one of filmdom's most famous) where he sends an enormous chandelier crashing down on the audience during Philbin's Wagnerian performance. Eventually the Phantom lures Philbin to his subterranean apartment deep below the opera house, where he professes his love for her. He also agrees to let her return to the stage once again on the condition that she break off her relationship with Kerry. Philbin agrees, but once she is free rushes to her lover and they make plans to flee to England following her performance. Chaney overhears this, however, and kidnaps Philbin while she is singing. Kerry and a Secret Service agent set out to capture him, as does an enraged mob led by the brother of one of Chaney's victims. With torches alight (a scene, like so many others in this picture, which Universal would put to use during their long cycle of horror films), the mob slosh their way through the underground rivers and lakes in pursuit of the Phantom, who has removed his mask (another legendary scene) revealing his grotesque face. Through the streets of Paris the madman runs (past the expensive Notre Dame set), chased by what seems like a thousand extras. At one point he commandeers a stagecoach, with Philbin by his side—an unwilling hostage—-but the coach overturns and the young lady is thrown clear. The madman runs until he reaches the banks of the Seine and can go no further. Then, in a wonderful closing scene as the mob rushes him from the right, Chaney reaches into his cloak and cocks his arm back as if he's about to throw something. The mob halts, frozen in fear. He then does the same to those pursuing him from the left, and the result is the same. For a moment there is a stalemate. Then, laughing at them all, Chaney slowly opens his hand to reveal an empty palm. It is only then that the throng finds the courage to beat him to death and hurl him into the water. From the point of view of Universal Studio's management, THE PHANTOM OF THE OPERA was a horror show in more ways than one. The film was originally made in 1923, but did not reach the theaters for two years. When it was originally previewed in California, the critics were brought in and told Carl Laemmle that he had a turkey on his hands unless he offset the scary aspects with plenty of comedy relief. So Laemmle brought in Conklin from the Sennett lot and a lot of additional footage was shot. Then they discovered that these additions necessitated a whole new set of titles, and the expensive Walter Anthony was hired to provide them. With what they hoped would be a prestige production (at that time Universal was almost exclusively involved in the making of potboilers) THE PHANTOM OF THE OPERA was screened in San Francisco, and this time the consensus of opinion was that the picture had some wonderful moments but failed to make sense. So the whole thing was turned over to a new staff of title writers and editors, who really tore it apart. Out came the comedy, as well as a whole subplot which involved Crane and dealt with a lot of sword play, until finally the studio felt they had their "big picture." THE HUNCHBACK OF NOTRE DAME had been a smash in England, so James Bryson, Universal's foreign representative, saw the opportunity to really ballyhoo this Chaney blockbuster. He arranged for a military escort to safeguard him and his print from the Port of Southampton to London. It was a great stunt, but the British press chose to regard it as an insult to His Majesty's sacred uniform, and much of Britain elected to boycott the picture. It all worked out in the end, however. Universal made a bundle, Chaney went on to super-stardom at MGM, and best of all, the rest of the world had the definitive PHANTOM.

d, Rupert Julian; w, Raymond Schrock, Elliott J. Clawson (based on the novel by Gaston Leroux); t, Tom Reed; ph, Virgil Miller, Milton Bridenbecker, Charles J. Van Enger (Technicolor sequences); ed, Maurice Pivar; art d, Charles D. Hall.

Horror Cas. (PR:A MPAA:NR)

PHANTOM OF THE RANGE½** (1928) 5 reels FBO bw

Tom Tyler *(Duke Carlton)*, Charles McHugh *(Tim O'Brien)*, Duane Thompson *(Patsy O'Brien)*, Frankie Darro *(Spuds O'Brien)*, James Pierce *("Flash" Corbin)*, Marjorie Zier *(Vera Van Swank)*, Beans the Dog.

Off-beat western has Tyler playing a cowboy-turned-actor who becomes stranded in a western town when the theatrical manager takes off with the payroll. Tyler administers a good beating to a real estate swindler who is trying to make a move on pretty Thompson and as a reward is given a job on her father's ranch. There Tyler manages not only to prevent the ranch from being stolen by his adversary, but marries the boss' daughter as well. There is a subplot in which an actress shows up claiming to be the hero's husband, which doesn't make a great deal of sense, but as stated earlier, this is an off-beat western.

d, James Dugan; w, Frank Howard Clark (based on a story by Oliver Drake); t, Randolph Bartlett; ph, Nick Musuraca; ed, Pandro S. Berman.

Western (PR:A MPAA:NR)

PHANTOM PICTURE, THE* (1916, Brit.) 6 reels British Empire bw

Henry Lonsdale *(John Gordon)*, Violet Campbell *(Pauline Mainwaring)*, Arthur Poole *(Lionel Carruthers)*, Ivan Berlyn *(Issac Bernstein)*.

There is more than just a hint of anti-Semitism in this British mystery about a Jewish art lover who is exposed as the murderer of a wealthy collector when an artist's model poses in the real life picture.

d&w, Albert Ward (based on a play by Harold Simpson).

Mystery **(PR:A MPAA:NR)**

PHANTOM RIDER, THE* (1929) 5 reels SYN bw

Tom Tyler *(Dick Cartwright)*, Lotus Thompson *(Grace Darling)*, J. P. McGowan, Harry Woods.

Weak western has Tyler getting together with Thompson, the girl he loves (even though their families are involved in a feud) when the Phantom Rider, who started the trouble by committing a couple of murders, gets his.

d, J. P. McGowan; ph, Frank Cotner.

Western **(PR:A MPAA:NR)**

PHYLLIS OF THE FOLLIES*1/2 (1928) 6 reels UNIV bw

Alice Day *(Phyllis Sherwood)*, Matt Moore *(Howard Decker)*, Edmund Burns *(Clyde Thompson)*, Lilyan Tashman *(Mrs. Dexter)*, Duane Thompson *(Mabel Lancing)*.

Hokey backstage comedy has follies girl Day helping her married friend, Tashman (a former chorus girl), play a trick on one of her husband's law clients—a man attracted only to married women. Day pretends to be Tashman and the gentleman goes bonkers over her. When the truth is revealed, the delighted couple set the wedding date.

d, Ernst Laemmle; w, John B. Clymer (based on a story by Arthur Gregor); t, Albert De Mond; ph, George Robinson.

Comedy **(PR:A MPAA:NR)**

PHYSICIAN, THE* (1928, Brit.) 8 reels GAU bw

Miles Mander *(Walter Amphiel)*, Elga Brink *(Edana Hinde)*, Ian Hunter *(Dr. Carey)*, Lissi Arna *(Jessie Gurdon)*, Humberston Wright *(Stephen Gurdon)*, Julie Suedo *(Lady Valerie Camille)*, Mary Brough *(Landlady)*, Henry Vibart *(Rev. Peregrine Hinde)*, Johnny Ashby *(Jessie's Son)*.

There is a definite shortage of bellylaughs in this heavy-handed British saga of a temperance lecturer whose fiance discovers he has a bastard son running about, and that when her back is turned he drinks everything but her fingernail polish remover.

p, Maurice Elvey, Gareth Gundrey; d, George Jacoby; w, Edwin Greenwood (based on a play by Henry Arthur Jones); ph, Baron Ventimiglia.

Drama **(PR:C MPAA:NR)**

PICTURE OF DORIAN GRAY, THE*
(1916, Brit.) 6 reels Barker-Neptune/Browne bw

Henry Victor *(Dorian Gray)*, Pat O'Malley *(Sybil Vane)*, Jack Jordan *(Lord Henry Wootton)*, Sydney Bland *(Basil Hallward)*, A.B. Imeson *(Satan)*, Douglas Cox *(James Vane)*, Dorothy Fane *(Lady Marchmont)*, Miriam Ferris.

Oscar Wilde's classic novel about a libertine who remains perpetually young while his portrait's features register the excesses of his lifestyle, is not done justice in this stodgy, early British version. The flamboyant Irish author would no doubt have been much more pleased with the Hollywood version of 1944.

d, Fred W. Durrant; w, Rowland Talbot (based on the novel by Oscar Wilde).

Horror **(PR:C MPAA:NR)**

PIERRE OF THE PLAINS*1/2 (1914) 5 reels All Star bw

Edgar Selwyn, William Conklin, Joseph Rieder, William Riley Hatch, Sydney Seward, Dorothy Dalton.

Selwyn assumed the lead in this motion picture version of his own play, which dealt with the trials, tribulations, and dangers of life in the American West. But for the most part, it turned out a rather dull and uneventful affair.

w, (based on the story by Sir Lewis Parker and the play by Edgar Selwyn).

Western **(PR:A MPAA:NR)**

PILGRIM, THE*1/2** (1923) 4 reels Charlie Chaplin/AFN bw

Charles Chaplin *(The Pilgrim)*, Edna Purviance *(The Girl)*, Kitty Bradbury *(Her Mother)*, Mack Swain *(The Deacon)*, Loyal Underwood *(The Elder)*, Dinky Dean *(The Boy)*, Mai Wells *(His Mother)*, Sydney Chaplin *(Her Husband)*, Chuck Reisner *(The Crook)*, Tom Murray *(The Sheriff)*, Monta Bell *(Policeman)*, Henry Bergman *(The Traveler)*, Raymond Lee *(The Real Pastor)*, Edith Bostwick, Phyllis Allen, Florence Latimer *(Ladies of the Parish)*.

Escaping from prison, Chaplin steals a minister's clothes and is welcomed at the railroad station by his new congregation. Aware that the real reverend has been delayed, Chaplin goes along with the ruse and—in one of his most famous scenes—pantomimes the story of David and Goliath from the pulpit. Later the little fellow prevents a crook he knew in jail from stealing his landlady's mortgage money. By this time his true identity is revealed and the film ends with the sheriff taking Chaplin to the Mexican border and telling him to pick some flowers on the other side. Innocently he reaches down and grabs a bunch in front of him. But the lawman rejects the bouquet, kicks his prisoner across the boundary and rides off, leaving Chaplin alone with a couple of bandits who are taking pot shots at one another. Then—in what is almost a parody of his earlier Essanay endings, where the tramp walks down the dusty road away from the camera—Chaplin brings his association with First National to a conclusion by racing off towards the horizon with one leg on each side of the border. The artist had not been happy with this studio, and he demanded that they consider THE PILGRIM to be two films and thus terminate his contractual arrangement. He would now be free to join his friends Mary Pickford and Douglas Fairbanks at United Artists, the studio they founded together. But more importantly, he would now be free to produce the kind of pictures he wanted.

d&w, Charles Chaplin; ph, Rollie Totheroh.

Comedy **Cas.** **(PR:A MPAA:NR)**

PINCH HITTER, THE*** (1917) 5 reels Kay-Bee/TRI bw

Charles Ray *(Joel Parker)*, Sylvia Breamer *(Abbie Nettleton)*, Joseph J. Dowling *(Obadiah Parker)*, Jerome Storm *(Jimmie Slater)*, Darrel Foss *(Alexis Thompson)*, Louis Durham *(Coach Nolan)*.

Ray is a bashful country boy who is sent to college only because of a deathbed promise his father made his mother. At school his cloddish ways make him the butt of countless student pranks, and only the girl who works in the soda shop shows him any kindness. Ray is made the baseball team's mascot because the coach believes the presence of a complete boob might bring the squad some degree of luck. When Ray hits the winning home run, however, he earns the love of the girl, as well as the respect of the whole student body. One wonders if Harold Lloyd ever saw this picture.

d, Victor Schertzinger; w, C. Gardner Sullivan.

Comedy/Drama **(PR:A MPAA:NR)**

PINK TIGHTS* (1920) 5 reels UNIV bw

Jack Perrin *(Rev. Jonathon Meek)*, Gladys Walton *(Mazie Darton)*, David De Winter *(Jerry McKeon)*, Reeves Eason, Jr. *(Johnny Bump)*, Stanton Heck, Dan Crimmins, Rose Gore, Dorothea Wolbert, Martin Neilan.

In this inept attempt to cash in on the popularity by POLLY OF THE CIRCUS the Big Top is stranded in a small town where everybody snubs the show folks except a nice-looking young minister. There is a disappointing end to this version, however, when the circus girl's old boy friend shows up to claim her in the last reel instead of the personable clergyman.

d, Reeves Eason; w, Philip Hurn (based on a story by J. U. Giesy); ph, Virgil Miller.

Drama **(PR:A MPAA:NR)**

PIONEER SCOUT, THE*** (1928) 7 reels PAR bw

Fred Thomson *(Fred)*, Nora Lane *(Mary Baxter)*, William Courtright *(Old Bill)*, Tom Wilson *(Handy Anderson)*.

The popular Thomson was at the top of his riding, fighting, and shooting form in this western which had the cowboy star helping Lane and her father make their way across the desert by covered wagon. There's a bad hombre with a hook for a hand, and outlaws who disguise themselves as Indians, but none of them are a match for Thomson.

d, Lloyd Ingraham, Alfred L. Werker; w, Frank M. Clifton; t, Garrett Graham; ph, Mack Stengler; ed, Duncan Mansfield.

Western **(PR:A MPAA:NR)**

PIPES OF PAN, THE*1/2 (1923, Brit.) 6 reels Hepworth bw

Alma Taylor *(Polly Bunning)*, G.H. Mulcaster *(Irwin Farman)*, Eileen Dennes *(Enid Markham)*, Hugh Clifton *(Cyril Farman)*, John McAndrews *(Miles Bunning)*, Buena Bent *(Aunt Maggie)*, Lawrence Hanray *(James Flaxman)*, Leslie Attwood *(Derek Hulme)*, James Annand *(Irwin Farman)*.

Good photography and pleasant scenery are the best things about this British romance(?) in which a tinker's daughter falls in love with a reclusive widower after his little boy wanders into the woods and the three meet. The tinker invents a metal polish, becomes wealthy, and enters the lower strata of English society. Later, however, his company is stolen from him and the old boy and his daughter return to the forest, and with what can only be interpreted as Hepworth's feeble stab at a happy ending, the young couple are reunited when the little boy dies.

d, Cecil M. Hepworth; w, (based on a story by George Dewhurst).

Drama/Romance **(PR:C MPAA:NR)**

PIRATES OF THE SKY** (1927) 5 reels Hurricane/Pathe bw

Charles Hutchison *(Bob Manning)*, Wanda Hawley *(Doris Reed)*, Crauford Kent *(Bruce Mitchell)*, Jimmy Aubrey *(Jeff Oldring)*, Ben Walker *(Stone)*.

A little less action than usual in this Hutchison adventure, but still enough to keep the kids sitting on the edge of their seats. Hutchison is asked by the Secret Service to locate a missing mail plane, and with his athletic prowess and terrific talent for stunt flying, gets the job done.

d, Charles Andrews; w, Elaine Wilmont; ph, Leon Shamroy.

Adventure **(PR:A MPAA:NR)**

PLACE IN THE SUN, A* (1916, Brit.) 5 reels Turner/BUT bw

Reginald Owen *(Stuart Capel)*, Margaret Blanche *(Rosie Blair)*, Malcolm Cherry *(Dick Blair)*, Lydia Bilbrooke *(Marjorie Capel)*, Campbell Gullan *(Arthur Blagden)*, Lyston Lyle *(Sir John Capel)*, Frances Wetherall *(Mrs. Moultrie)*, John MacAndrews *(Ben Goodge)*.

Unpleasant British class-conflict nonsense in which a young man is forbidden by his aristocrat father to marry his pregnant peasant girl friend. To get back at the father, the boy's sister becomes romantically involved with the farm girl's brother.

d&w, Larry Trimble (based on a play by Cyril Harcourt).

Drama **(PR:C MPAA:NR)**

PLACE OF HONOUR, THE** (1921, Brit.) 5 reels STOLL bw

Hugh Buckler *(Maj. Eustace Tudor)*, Madge White *(Mrs. Tudor)*, Pardoe Woodman *(Lt. Philip Trevor)*, Luther Miles *(Lt. Devereaux)*, M. Gray Murray *(Capt. Raleigh)*, Ruth Mackay *(Mrs. Raleigh)*, Bob Vallis *(Pvt. Archie Smith)*.

Stiff-upper-lip British colonial drama, set in India, about a man who saves his wife's lover by taking his place when the natives cause an uprising.

d, Sinclair Hill; w, William J. Elliott (based on a novel by Ethel M. Dell).

Drama/Adventure **(PR:A MPAA:NR)**

PLASTIC AGE, THE*** (1925) 7 reels SCHUL bw

Donald Keith *(Hugh Carver)*, Clara Bow *(Cynthia Day)*, Mary Alden *(Mrs. Carver)*, Henry B. Walthall *(Henry Carver)*, Gilbert Roland *(Carl Peters)*, J. Gordon Edwards, Jr. *(Norrie Parks)*, Felix Valle *(Merton Billings)*, David Butler *(Coach Henry)*.

Bow is a knockout as the college girl who toys with the emotions of a young athlete (Keith) and causes him to fail at all of his endeavors. Realizing the effect her flirtatious manner is having on him, Bow decides to stop pulling his string, which of course straightens Keith out completely. When he later wins the big football game, Bow decides she really does love him, and they finish the semester happily united.

d, Wesley Ruggles; w, Eve Unsell, Frederica Sagor (based on the novel by Percy Marks); ph, Gilbert Warrenton, Allen Siegler.

Drama/Comedy **(PR:A MPAA:NR)**

PLAY GIRL, THE** (1928) 6 reels FOX bw

Madge Bellamy *(Madge Norton)*, Johnny Mack Brown *(Bradley Lane)*, Walter McGrail *(David Courtney)*, Lionel Belmore *(The Greek Florist)*, Anita Garvin *(Millie)*, Thelma Hill *(The Salesgirl)*, Harry Tenbrook *(The Chauffeur)*.

Bellamy deserved better than this flimsy comedy about a girl who loses her job in a hotel florist shop, then takes a shot at being a "good-time Jane" but finds her morals getting in the way. She finally ends up marrying "Mr. Right" (Brown), but not before being given the opportunity to bounce about in some very sexy undergarments.

d, Arthur Rosson; w, John Stone; t, Norman Z. McLeod; ph, Rudolph Berquist; ed, Ralph Dietrich.

Comedy **(PR:A MPAA:NR)**

PLAY SAFE*** (1927) 5 reels Monty Banks/Pathe bw

Monty Banks *(The Boy)*, Virginia Lee Corbin *(Virginia Craig)*, Charles Mailes *(Silas Scott, Crooked Trustee)*, Charles Gerard *(His Son)*, Bud Jamieson *(Big Bill)*, Rosa Gore, Syd Crossley, Max Ascher, Fatty Alexander.

PLAY SAFE is a little more than a 2-reeler padded to include a story line about an heiress and some nasty characters out to steal her estate. The picture's real value rests in an incredible stunt sequence (shot without trick effects), taking place on a fast-moving freight train, in which Banks risks his life repeatedly in scenes rivaling anything Harold Lloyd *ever* did.

d, Joseph Henabery; sup, Howard Estabrook; w, Charles Horan, Harry Sweet (based on a story by Banks); ph, Blake Wagner.

Comedy **(PR:A MPAA:NR)**

PLAYING DOUBLE* (1923) 5 reels Western Pictures Exploitation bw

Dick Hatton, Ethel Shannon.

This one looks like it was made up as they went along. The production values are nonexistent—only one shabby interior set used and completely uninspired outdoor locations. It all has to do with a cowboy rescuing a girl from kidnapers and, even though unarmed, beating them into submission just in time for the sheriff's posse to cart the varmints off to jail. Hatton, the male star, would make a few more westerns and die at age 40, just as the talkies had completely entrenched themselves. Shannon's career, however, was a bit brighter; she played opposite Syd Chaplin in CHARLEY'S AUNT, and made a series of programmers before descending to the life of a Hollywood extra.

d, Dick Rush; w, J. Stewart Woodhouse.

Western **(PR:A MPAA:NR)**

PLAYING IT WILD*** (1923) 6 reels VIT bw

William Duncan *(Jerry Hoskins)*, Edith Johnson *(Beth Webb)*, Francis Powers *(Old Man Webb)*, Dick La Reno *(Sheriff Gideon)*, Edmund Cobb *(Chris Gideon, His Son)*, Frank Beal *(Wetherby, a Painter)*, Frank Weed *(Bill Rucker)*.

Good western, boosted by effective comedy relief, features serial star Duncan (along with his real life wife Johnson) as a stranger who wins a newspaper in a poker game, disguises himself as an outlaw, and embarrasses the crooked sheriff out of his job.

d, William Duncan; w, C. Graham Baker; ph, George Robinson.

Western/Comedy **(PR:A MPAA:NR)**

PLAYING THE GAME*** (1918) 5 reels PAR bw

Charles Ray *(Larry Prentiss)*, Doris Lee *(Moya Shannon)*, Harry Rattenberry *(Matt Shannon)*, Robert McKim *("Flash" Purdy)*, Billy Elmer *(Hodges)*, Leota Lorraine *(Babe Fleur de Lis)*, Charles Perley *(Hickey Trent)*, Melbourne MacDowell.

Predictably enjoyable movie has wealthy young souse Ray heading West to take a job as a cowboy. Of course he falls in love with the pretty girl of the ranch and later proves his manhood in a nicely staged fight scene with one of the silent cinema's premier villains, McKim.

d, Victor L. Schertzinger; sup, Thomas H. Ince; w, R. Cecil Smith (based on a story by Julien Josephson); ph, Chester L. Lyons.

Western **(PR:A MPAA:NR)**

PLAYTHINGS OF DESIRE** (1924) 7 reels Jans bw

Estelle Taylor *(Gloria Dawn)*, Mahlon Hamilton *(Pierre du Charme)*, Dagmar Godowsky *(Renee Grant)*, Mary Thurman *(Anne Cabbot)*, Lawrence Davidson *(James Malvern)*, Walter Miller *(Brom Jones)*, Edmund Breese *(Gov. Cabbot)*, Bradley Barker *(Wheeler Johnson)*, Ida Pardee *(Gloria's Mother)*, Lee Beggs *(Caretaker)*.

Mediocre melodrama has Taylor (in what was likely her first film after becoming Mrs. Jack Dempsey) a Broadway star marrying Davidson, a no good society playboy. While honeymooning in Canada, Hamilton, the caretaker for the Davidson's estate, saves Taylor's life. The grateful actress later becomes attracted to Hamilton when she discovers her husband cheating. After returning to New York, Davidson is murdered and Hamilton (who followed them south) is accused, put on trial, and sentenced to die in the electric chair. But before the switch is thrown, the clever Taylor proves that the actual killer is Barker, a ticked-off theatrical agent. Hamilton is set free and the young couple returns to the romantic environment of the Canadian woods.

d, Burton King; w, William B. Laub (based on the novel by Wesley J. Putnam).

Drama **(PR:A MPAA:NR)**

PLAYTHINGS OF DESTINY 1/2** (1921) 7 reels Anita Stewart/AFN bw

Anita Stewart *(Julie Leneau)*, Herbert Rawlinson *(Geoffrey Arnold)*, Walter McGrail *(Hubert Randolph)*, Grace Morse *(Claire)*, William V. Mong *(Conklin)*, Richard Headrick *(Julie's Child)*.

Stewart marries Rawlinson in Canada only to be devastated when told by Morse that her husband is a bigamist. Escaping, she becomes snowbound with McGrail, a government official. Together they travel to Jamaica where Stewart marries the chap to give her child a name. Later, Rawlinson shows up, proves that Morse was lying, and McGrail gallantly departs, allowing the true tide of love to flow freely.

d, Edwin Carewe; w, Anthony Paul Kelly (based on the play by Jane Murfin); ph, Robert Kurrle.

Drama **(PR:A MPAA:NR)**

PLEASURE GARDEN, THE 1/2**
(1925, Brit./Ger.) 7 reels Gainsborough-Emelka/Amyon Independent bw

Virginia Valli *(Patsy Brand)*, Carmelita Geraghty *(Jill Cheyne)*, Miles Mander *(Levett)*, John Stuart *(Hugh Fielding)*, Nita Naldi *(Native Girl)*, George Schnell *(Oscar Hamilton)*, C. Falkenberg *(Prince Ivan)*, Ferdinand Martini *(Mr. Sidey)*, Florence Helminger *(Mrs. Sidey)*.

Hitchcock's first complete directorial assignment was shot in Munich through his studio's arrangement with the great German producer, Erich Pommer. The story deals with good and bad chorus girls, Valli and Geraghty (the two American actresses were hired to encourage distribution to the U.S.), who are employed by a theater known as the Pleasure Garden. Valli marries Mander, a friend of Geraghty's fiance, Stuart, and after a honeymoon her husband leaves for the colonial tropics. Valli returns home to find her evil counterpart carrying on with other men. When she later goes to join her husband in the islands, she is shocked to find him in the arms of a native woman, Naldi (who would become the lead in Hitchcock's next film, FEAR O' GOD), and announces that she is leaving him. In the end Mander goes mad and kills Naldi, in what is made to look like a suicide, then tries to kill Valli, but is shot down by a local doctor. Valli at last finds solace in the arms of Stuart, who was abandoned by Geraghty. Hitchcock had to pinch pennies all the way through the making of THE PLEASURE GARDEN, though he never let on to Valli and Geraghty, who came to Europe with loads of luggage expecting the big-star treatment. His suggestion that the actresses stay at a modest but comfortable hotel was brushed off by Valli, one of Hollywood's hottest stars at the time, who insisted that they spend the night in more luxurious accommodations. Only Alma Reville, Hitchcock's assistant director and fiancee, knew the difficulties he faced in making THE PLEASURE GARDEN, as well as his lack of confidence in his directorial abilities. Though the film's plot was predictable and typically British, there was a quality about Hitchcock which would catch the fancy of reviewers the world over. It was said that he handled his material and actors like an American—no doubt the influence of his apprenticeship at Famous Players-Lasky. The picture's ending did not sit well with the German producer, however, who jumped up during the final scene at the first screening and shouted "It's impossible! You can't show a scene like this!" It seems Hitchcock had read a theory that, when near death, the insane return momentarily to normalcy, and incorporated this into the ending for effect. Thus, at the moment Mander is shot, he simply looks up and says matter-of-factly, "Oh, hello, doctor," then notices that he is bleeding and suddenly collapses and dies. Pommer thought the scene was "too brutal," yet Hitchcock left it in exactly that way and would use the same effect brilliantly nine years later in THE MAN WHO KNEW TOO MUCH.

p, Michael Balcon; d, Alfred Hitchcock; w, Eliot Stannard (based on the novel by Oliver Sandys); ph, Baron [Giovanni] Ventigmilia; set d, Emelka.

Drama **(PR:A MPAA:NR)**

PLEASURE MAD** (1923) 8 reels Louis B. Mayer/Metro bw

Huntley Gordon *(Hugh Benton)*, Mary Alden *(Marjorie Benton)*, Norma Shearer *(Elinor Benton)*, William Collier, Jr. *(Howard Benton)*, Winifred Bryson *(Geraldine de Lacy)*, Ward Crane *(David Templeton)*, Frederick Truesdell *(John Hammond)*, John Standing *(Hulda)*.

Just another of those jazz-age society dramas in which a suburban man (Gordon) strikes it rich, moves his family to Park Avenue, is seduced by a vamp, obtains a divorce, but then, upon seeing his daughter being lured into the same pleasure pattern, delivers a thrashing to the lounge lizard, learns his lesson, and returns happily to his family.

d, Reginald Barker; w, A. P. Younger (based on the novel *The Valley of Content* by Blanche Upright); ph, Norbert Brodine, Alvin Wyckoff.

Drama **(PR:C MPAA:NR)**

PLEASURES OF THE RICH** (1926) 7 reels TIF/REN bw

Helene Chadwick *(Mary Wilson)*, Mary Carr *(Kate Wilson)*, Marcin Asher *(Henry "Pushcart" Wilson)*, Jack Mulhall *(Frank Clayton)*, Lillian Langdon *(Mrs. Clayton)*, Dorothea Wolbert *(Maggie, the Maid)*, Hedda Hopper *(Mona Vincent)*, Julanne Johnston *(Phyliss Worthing)*, Katherine Scott *(Mrs. Worthing)*.

Even a good cast barely gets this one over. Asher plays a self-made man of wealth who becomes infatuated with Hopper, an attractive divorcee. His daughter Chadwick is in love with Mulhall, the young man for whom Hopper lusts, and the shady lady tells Chadwick she will let her dad off of the string if she gives Mulhall the air. Depressed by the whole business, Chadwick tries to drown herself, which brings her father to his senses— and Mulhall to her side.

d, Louis Gasnier.

Drama **(PR:A MPAA:NR)**

PLEYDELL MYSTERY, THE** (1916, Brit.) 5 reels British Empire bw

Cecil Humphreys *(John Pleydell)*, Christine Silver *(Felicity Harwood)*, Richard Lindsay *(Tony Masters)*, Mrs. Bennett *(Rosa Latimer)*, Frank Randall.

In this British mystery a rotter deserts his wife but returns when she comes into a small fortune, and then tries to frame her for poisoning his mistress.

d&w, Albert Ward (based on the novel *Poison* by Claude and Alice Askew).

Mystery **(PR:A MPAA:NR)**

PLOW GIRL, THE** ½ (1916) 5 reels LAS bw

Mae Murray *(Margot)*, Elliott Dexter *(John Stoddard)*, Charles Gerard *(Lord Percy)*, Edythe Chapman *(Lady Brentwood)*, Horace B. Carpenter *(M. Pantani)*, Lillian Leighton, William Elmer, Jane Wolff, Theodore Roberts.

When Chapman's son and daughter-in-law are killed in South America, she tries desperately to locate the grandaughter who survived. A scheming relative, with the help of an impoverished lawyer, purchase a peasant girl and pass her off as the missing relation. They return to England, and before long the young woman (nicely played by Murray) completely steals the heart of the lonely aristocrat. Before long, however, the girl and the lawyer become guilt ridden and make a complete confession. But, as motion pictures would have such things, Murray turns out to be the real heiress after all, and she marries the attorney who has made so many valuable contacts that a successful career is all but guaranteed.

d, Robert Z. Leonard; w, Harvey Thew (based on a story by Edward Morris); ph, Charles Rosher.

Drama **(PR:A MPAA:NR)**

PLUNDERER, THE** ½ (1915) 5 reels FOX bw

William Farnum, Harry Springler, William Gross, William Riley Hatch, Claire Whitney, Flavia Arcaro.

Director Lewis took his company to a real mining camp in Georgia to achieve the realistic feeling this picture enjoys. The script is pretty typical, dealing with a man who has to fight in order to protect his claim. Of course the part was made to order for Farnum.

d, Edgar Lewis; w, Garfield Thompson, Louise Keller (based on a novel by Roy Norton).

Adventure **(PR:A MPAA:NR)**

PLUNGING HOOFS** (1929) 5 reels UNIV bw

Rex and Starlight *(Themselves)*, Jack Perrin *(Parson Jed Campbell)*, Barbara Worth *(Nanette)*, J. P. McGowan *(Jim Wales)*, David Dunbar *("Squint" Jones)*.

Rex the Wonder Horse and his pal Starlight (the almost wonder horse) wait patiently until the end of the picture to knock off McGowan, the cruel saloon owner who has designs on Worth, his clean-cut dance hall employee. This opens the way for Perrin (cast out of character as a preacher), who takes the opportunity to marry the girl and move her to a healthier environment.

d, Henry MacRae, w, George Morgan (based on a story by Basil Dickey, William Lord Wright); t, Gardner Bradford; ph, George Robinson; ed, Thomas Malloy.

Western **(PR:A MPAA:NR)**

POINTING FINGER, THE** (1922, Brit.) 6 reels STOLL bw

Milton Rosmer *(Lord Rollestone/Earl Edensore)*, Madge Stuart *(Lady Susan Silchester)*, J. R. Tozer *(Capt. Jasper Mallory)*, Teddy Arundell *(Danny O'Shea)*, Irene Rooke *(Lady Anne Silchester)*, James English *(Earl of Edensore)*, Norma Whalley *(Mrs. Ebury)*, Gibb McLaughlin *(The Monk)*.

Rosmer plays a double role in this British thriller about a captain who abducts a half brother in an attempt to seize an earldom.

d, George Ridgwell; w, Paul Rooff (based on the novel *Rita)*.

Adventure **(PR:A MPAA:NR)**

POINTS WEST*** (1929) 6 reels UNIV bw

Hoot Gibson *(Cole Lawson, Jr.)*, Alberta Vaughn *(Dorothy)*, Frank Campeau *(McQuade)*, Jack Raymond *(His Nibs)*, Martha Franklin *(The Mother)*, Milt Brown *(Parsons)*, Jim Corey *(Steve)*.

Good western has Gibson infiltrating a gang led by Campeau, the man who murdered his father. He also wins the love of Vaughn, a girl who works at the mountain retreat where the gang is hiding out, and whom Campeau intends to marry. With Vaughn's assistance Gibson obtains his revenge in the end and holds onto the girl who helped him do it.

d, Arthur Rosson; w, Rowland Brown (based on the novel by B. M. Bower); t, Harold Tarshis; ph, Harry Neumann.

Western **(PR:A MPAA:NR)**

POISON** ½ (1924) 5 reels William Steiner/New-Cal bw

Charles Hutchison *(Bob Marston)*, Edith Thornton *(Doris Townsend)*, Otto Lederer *(Gale Preston)*, John Henry *(Rog Harvey)*, Ethel Stairt *(Grace Elliston)*, Frank Hagney *(Joe Tracey)*, Jack Mathis *(Gordon)*, Police Chief John O'Brien *(Himself)*.

There is plenty of good old-fashioned action in this entertaining programmer, which has serial star Hutchison playing a San Francisco society chap whose hobby is solving crimes. Hutchison is approached by Police Chief O'Brien (played by the real life figure whose fame was surpassed only by his movie star son George) to help break up a gang of bootleggers who are flooding the "City by the Bay" with bad liquor. The lad gladly accepts the invitation, and after a number of hair-raising, stunt-filled adventures, brings the bunch—some of whom are society folk—to justice.

p, William Steiner; d, James Chapin; w, Charles Hutchison; ph, Ernest Miller

Crime **(PR:A MPAA:NR)**

POLAR STAR, THE* (1919, Brit.) 5 reels Windsor/Walturdaw bw

Manora Thew, Hayford Hobbs, Peggy Patterson, Bert Wynne, Charles Vane.

British film, set in Italy, deals with the mystery of a prominent London lawyer's ultimate disgrace and death.

d, Arrigo Bocchi; w, Leslie Stiles.

Mystery **(PR:A MPAA:NR)**

POLICE PATROL, THE*** (1925) 6 reels GOTH/LUM bw

James Kirkwood *(Officer Jim Ryan)*, Edna Murphy *(Alice Bennett/Dorothy Stone)*, Edmund Breese *(Tony Rocco)*, Bradley Barker *(Maurice Ramon)*, Frankie Evans *(Buddy Bennett)*, Joseph Smiley *(Lt. Burke)*, Blanche Craig *(Nora Mullen)*, Edward Roseman *("Chicago" Charley)*, Tammany Young *("The Crasher")*, Charles Craig *(Perkins)*, James Laffey *(Inspector Regan)*, Monya Andree *(Mlle. Semonoff)*.

Nifty little programmer has officer Kirkwood in love with dressmaker Murphy, who happens to be the spitting image of an ace crook. When Kirkwood is ordered to bring his sweetheart in, he argues vainly on her behalf, quits the force and, with Murphy posing as her double, manages—after a terrific speedboat chase—to nail the real gang and its leader. A fun film from start to finish.

d, Burton King; sup, Lon Young; w, Victoria Moore (based on a story by A. Y. Pearson); ph, C. J. Davis, Jack Brown.

Crime **(PR:A MPAA:NR)**

POLLY OF THE CIRCUS*** (1917) 8 reels Goldwyn bw

Mae Marsh *(Polly)*, Vernon Steele *(John Douglas, the Minister)*, Charles Eldridge *(Toby, the Clown)*, Wellington Playter *(Big Jim, Boss Canvasman)*, George Trimble *(Barker and Owner of the Show)*, Lucille La Verne *(Mandy)*, Dick Lee *(Hasty, Her Lesser Half)*, Charles Riegel *(Deacon Strong)*, Lucille Slatherwaite *(His Daughter)*, J. B. Hollis *(Deacon Elverson)*, Helen Sallinger *(Mrs. Elverson)*, Isabel Vernon *(Sallie)*, Viola Compton *(Jane, the Widow)*, John Carr *(Jim)*, Stephen Carr *(John)*, Mildred Call *(Little Polly)*, Maury Stewart, Jr., Louis R. Grisel, Bingo and the Rest of the Beasts *(Themselves)*.

Samuel Goldwyn's first film under his own banner was this very popular Marsh circus story about a bareback rider who has a terrible accident, wins the big horse race, and finally marries the handsome young minister. It was a picture full of atmosphere, drama, and plenty of tears.

d, Charles Thomas Horan, Edwin L. Hollywood; w, Adrian Gil-Spear, Emmett Campbell Hall (based on the play by Margaret Mayo); ph, George W. Hill; art d, Everett Shinn, Herbert Messmore.

Drama **(PR:A MPAA:NR)**

POLLY OF THE STORM COUNTRY** (1920) 5 reels Louis B. Mayer/FN bw

Mildred Harris Chaplin *(Polly Hopkins)*, Emory Johnson *(Robert Robertson)*, Charlotte Burton *(Evelyn Robertson)*, Harry Northrup *(Marcus MacKenzie)*, Ruby Lafayette *(Granny Hope)*, Maurice Valentin *(Jeremiah Hopkins)*, Charles West *(Oscar Bennett)*, Mickey Moore *(Wee Jerry)*, Fred Kohler, Cora Drew, Cameron Coffey, Dick Rosson.

Chaplin plays a poor girl living in slum conditions who, along with her impoverished neighbors, are being driven out by nasty Northrup. He has hired Johnson to help him accomplish this task, but the young man falls in love with Chaplin and switches his allegiance to the oppressed. Their romance is disrupted, however, when Chaplin is nearly forced to marry another man to save her father from a trumped up criminal charge. But justice triumphs in the last reel, Johnson marries his girl, and living conditions improve dramatically for the former victims of the spiteful Northrup.

d, Arthur H. Rosson; w, Frank M. Dazey (based on the novel by Grace Miller White); ph, Harold Rosson.

Drama **(PR:A MPAA:NR)**

POLLYANNA**** (1920) 6 reels Mary Pickford/UA bw

Mary Pickford *(Pollyanna)*, J. Wharton James *(Rev. Whittier)*, Katherine Griffith *(Aunt Polly Harrington)*, Herbert Prior *(Dr. Chilton)*, William Courtleigh *(John Pendleton)*, Helen Jerome Eddy *(Nancy)*, George Berrell *(Tom)*, Howard Ralston *(Jimmie Bean)*, Frederic Peters, Gordon Sackville, Doc Crane, Dorothy Rosher.

Pickford is wonderful as Pollyanna, the daughter of a missionary who taught her to be "glad" because things can always be worse. When he dies, the girl is taken in by her aunt, Griffith, a resentful and embittered woman who never got over her breakup with Prior, a wealthy local doctor. Despite the cold treatment Pickford receives from her aunt, the little girl manages to win the love of the whole town with her optimistic attitude. She even convinces the man who once loved her mother to adopt her little pal, Ralston. Later, when Pickford is struck by an automobile while rescuing a child, Griffith finally realizes her true feelings for her ward. She sends for a specialist who sadly announces that the little girl will never walk again. Pickford pleads with her aunt to allow her doctor friend, Prior, to examine her, and not only does he provide a cure but a reconciliation transpires between the former sweethearts. There are more than a few tears in this kindhearted motion picture, as well as plenty of laughs. And the ending, where Pickford is seen playing "family" with her little boy friend, Ralston, and they take their pretend children for a free ride on an imaginary trolley car, is guaranteed to make the world seem like a better place.

d, Paul Powell; w, Frances Marion (based on the novel by Eleanor H. Porter and the play by Catherine Chisholm Cushing); ph, Charles Rosher.

Comedy/Drama **Cas.** **(PR:A MPAA:NR)**

PONY EXPRESS, THE ** ½ (1925) 10 reels FP-LAS/PAR bw

Betty Compson *(Molly Jones)*, Ricardo Cortez *(Jack Weston)*, Ernest Torrence *("Ascension" Jones)*, Wallace Beery *("Rhode Island" Red)*, George Bancroft *(Jack Slade)*, Frank Lackteen *(Charlie Bent)*, John Fox, Jr. *(Billy Cody)*, William Turner *(William Russell)*, Al Hart *(Sen. Glen)*, Charles Gerson *(Sam Clemens)*, Rose Tapley *(Aunt)*, Vondell Darr *(Baby)*, Hank Bell *(Townsman)*, Ernie Adams *(Shorty)*, Toby Wing *(Girl)*.

Paramount spent a lot of money attempting to come up with another COVERED WAGON, but this picture is little more than a melodrama about a power-hungry senator (Hart) who tries to anex California, steal a little more of Mexico, and establish his own empire. His evil scheme is thwarted by gambler-turned-pony-express-rider Cortez, but what real vitality the movie has is provided by Beery and Torrence.

d, James Cruze; w, Walter Woods (based on a novel by Henry James Forman and Woods written for the film and issued in conjunction with its release); ph, Karl Brown; m, Hugo Riesenfeld.

Western **(PR:A MPAA:NR)**

PONY EXPRESS RIDER* (1926) 5 reels Robert H. Horner/AY bw

Kit Carson, Pauline Curley.

Very inexpensively produced cowboy picture about an outlaw who goes straight, becomes a pony express rider, saves the mail from Indians and road agents, and, in the end, wins the love of Curley.

d, Robert J. Horner; ph, Lauren A. Draper.

Western **(PR:A MPAA:NR)**

POOR LITTLE RICH GIRL, A**** (1917) 6 reels ART bw

Mary Pickford *(Gwendolyn)*, Madeline Traverse *(Her Mother)*, Charles Wellesley *(Her Father)*, Gladys Fairbanks *(Jane, the Nurse)*, Frank McGlynn *(The Plumber)*, Emile La Croix *(The Organ Grinder)*, Marcia Harris *(Miss Royle, the Governess)*, Charles Craig *(Thomas, the Footman)*, Frank Andrews *(Potter, the Butler)*, Herbert Prior *(The Doctor)*, George Gernon *(Johnny Blake)*, Maxine Hicks *(Susie May Squoggs)*.

Directed by Tourneur, Mary Pickford's first film portraying a child was filled with pathos, wonderful gags, and a nightmare sequence that has never been equalled. When the film was completed, everyone thought they had a flop on their hands, and the star even thought her career might be over. Then the reviews came out and audiences began to pack the theaters. Miss Pickford's little girl character was a sensation, and her adoring public would insist that she play it until the actress was well into her thirties. Pickford was 20 years old when she was playing 11-year-old "Gwen" in A POOR LITTLE RICH GIRL, and she carried it off without effort not only through her mischievous quality and director Tourneur's refined pictorial sense, but with a little level-headedness as well. One morning while preparing to go on the set, she noticed her mirror lying at an angle which caught the early morning light and shone onto her face. She thought the angle made her look younger, so she promptly told Tourneur about it on the set, asking if she could have a light on her placed low. They tried it and the director saw it was effective, so it was thereafter used and called the "baby spot."

d, Maurice Tourneur; w, Frances Marion, Ralph Spence (based on the novel and play by Eleanor Gates); ph, Lucien Andriot, John van der Broek.

Comedy/Drama **Cas.** **(PR:A MPAA:NR)**

POOR MEN'S WIVES*** (1923) 7 reels PRE/Al Lichtman bw

Barbara La Marr *(Laura Maberne)*, David Butler *(Jim Maberne)*, Betty Francisco *(Claribel)*, Richard Tucker *(Richard Smith-Blanton)*, ZaSu Pitts *(Apple Annie)*, Muriel McCormac, Mickey McBan *(The Twins)*.

Superior direction by Gasnier and photography by German master Struss, plus fine acting all around, really make something of this programmer. La Marr plays a working class mother who borrows a gown on approval to wear to a wealthy friend's ball. Later she steals money from her husband's savings to pay for the dress, which her children ruined the following day. The husband, Butler, throws her out of the house, but all is forgiven when he later finds his wife fighting off the advances of her friend's millionaire husband. There is a wonderful scene in this picture, shot at an amusement park, where Struss mounts his camera in front of a rollercoaster and shoots La Marr and Butler as they actually experience the terror and pleasures of a hair-raising ride.

d, Louis J. Gasnier; w, Agnes Christine Johnston, Frank Dazey; t, Eve Unsell; ph, Karl Struss.

Drama **(PR:A MPAA:NR)**

POOR RELATIONS** (1919) 5 reels Brentwood/R-C bw

Florence Vidor *(Dorothy Perkins)*, Lillian Leighton *(Ma Perkins)*, William De Vaull *(Pa Perkins)*, Roscoe Karns *(Henry Hubbard)*, ZaSu Pitts *(Daisy Perkins)*, Charles Meredith *(Monte Rhodes)*.

Vidor wrote the story and directed his wife in this familiar tale about a country girl who marries a city millionaire, is opposed and driven away by his domineering mother, and then reunited in the end. The story may have been ordinary, but Vidor's sense of cinema was not.

d&w, King Vidor (based on his play "Caste"); ph, Ira Morgan.

Drama **(PR:A MPAA:NR)**

POPPIES OF FLANDERS** (1927, Brit.) 9 reels BIP/Wardour bw

Jameson Thomas *(Jim Brown)*, Eve Gray *(Beryl Kingwood)*, Malcolm Todd *(Bob Standish)*, Gibb McLaughlin *(Shorty Bill)*, Henry Vibart *(Earl of Strangeways)*, Daisy Campbell *(Countess)*, Cameron Carr *(Merrick)*, Vivienne Whittaker *(Mrs. Merrick)*, Tubby Phillips *(Fat Man)*.

Some pretty heavy stuff in this British drama about an earl's son who returns from wartorn France in 1914, discovers that the woman he loves is involved with another man and, after contemplating murder, gives his own life to save his rival.

d, Arthur Maude; w, Violet Powell (based on the story "Sapper" by H. C. McNeile).

War/Drama **(PR:A MPAA:NR)**

POPPY GIRL'S HUSBAND, THE*** (1919) 5 reels WSHP/ART bw

William S. Hart *(Hairpin Harry Dutton)*, Juanita Hansen *(Polly, the Poppy Girl)*, Fred Starr *(Big Mike McCafferty)*, David Kirby *(Montana Kid)*, Georgie Stone, Leo Pierson.

Hart is wonderful in this non-western role as a man who is paroled from prison to discover that his wife has divorced him and married the detective who framed him. But his hatred is tempered when he meets his little boy, and without disclosing his true identity, develops a loving relationship. Later Hart is told that the detective and his ex-wife are planning to set him up again. Nearly crazy with anger Hart heads for her house, determined to disfigure her beautiful but treacherous face. Before he has a chance to do this, though, the voice of his son crying from another room brings him to his senses. He sweeps the child up in his arms, and together they head westward to begin a new and rewarding life.

d, William S. Hart, Lambert Hillyer; sup, Thomas H. Ince; w, C. Gardner Sullivan (based on a story by Jack Boyle); ph, Joseph August.

Drama/Crime **(PR:A MPAA:NR)**

PORT OF MISSING MEN** (1914) 5 reels FP bw

Arnold Daly *(John Armitage)*, Marguerite Skirvin *(Shirley Clairborn)*, Minna Gale Haines, Mortimer Martini, Frederick Bock, Augustus Balfour, Dave Wall.

Broadway star Daly (who would go on to support Pearl White in a group of serials) registers well in this otherwise weak picture about a dashing American who outsmarts and fights off an army of European rotters, determined to steal the throne from its rightful heir. He also turns down the proposal of a royal beauty in order to marry the American girl he meets while performing his heroics.

w, (based on a novel by Meredith Nicholson).

Adventure **(PR:A MPAA:NR)**

PORTS OF CALL*** (1925) 6 reels FOX bw

Edmund Lowe *(Kirk Rainsford)*, Hazel Keener *(Marjorie Vail)*, William Davidson *(Randolph Sherman)*, William Conklin *(Archer Rainsford)*, Bobby Mack *(Sly)*, Lilyan Tashman *(Lillie)*, Alice Ward *(Mrs. Rainsford)*, Mary McLean *(Peggy)*.

Good program feature has Lowe disowned by his father and spurned by Keener, the girl he loves, when he behaves cowardly during a fire. Lowe becomes a derelict and ends up in Manila, where he is almost killed protecting Tashman, a female drifter, from thugs. The girl nurses him back to health, causes his regeneration, and they take jobs on a plantation owned by Davidson, the man who married Lowe's sweetheart, Keener. Before long, there is a native uprising in which Davidson is killed, but Lowe saves Keener and restores order. The grateful girl confesses to still being in love with him and begs for a reconciliation, but Lowe gently tells her no and departs with the woman he has truly come to worship.

d, Denison Clift; w, Edfrid Bingham (based on a story by Garrett Elsden Fort).

Drama **(PR:A MPAA:NR)**

POSSESSION* ½ (1919, Brit.) 5 reels Hepworth/BUT bw

Henry Edwards *(Blaise Barewsky)*, Chrissie White *(Valerie Sarton)*, Gerald Ames *(Richard Staire)*, Gwynne Herbert *(Tante)*, Stephen Ewart *(John Sarton)*, Annie Esmond *(Marquise)*, Bubbles Brown *(Valerie, as a Child)*.

In this depressing British film the secret wife of a Russian is forced to marry her own cousin in order to give her unwanted baby a name.

d, Henry Edwards; w, (based on a novel by Olive Wadsley).

Drama **(PR:A MPAA:NR)**

POTEMKIN (SEE: BATTLESHIP POTEMKIN, THE, 1925, USSR)

POTTERS, THE*** (1927) 7 reels FP-LAS/PAR bw

W. C. Fields *(Pa Potter)*, Mary Alden *(Ma Potter)*, Ivy Harris *(Minnie)*, Jack Egan *(Bill)*, Richard "Skeets" Gallagher *(Red Miller)*, Joseph Smiley *(H. B. Rankin)*, Bradley Barker *(Eagle)*.

Fields really comes into his own (after some satisfactory earlier work) in this very funny movie about a lowly office worker who takes his family savings and invests in bogus oil well shares. Of course he ends up owning the land, in which a gusher erupts, much to the relief of his sour-faced, dominating wife, Alden. The formula the great comedian would use over and over again in his talkies is here, as is that wonderful sense of pantomime which made him a Ziegfeld star and which, unfortunately, he chose to call upon less frequently in later years.

d, Fred Newmeyer; w, J. Clarkson Miller, Sam Mintz, Ray Harris (based on the play "The Potters: An American Comedy" by Joseph Patrick McEvoy); ph, Paul Vogel.

Comedy **(PR:A MPAA:NR)**

POTTER'S CLAY* (1922, Brit.) 6 reels Big Four Famous/ANCH bw

Ellen Terry *(Lady Merrall)*, Dick Webb *(Clifford Merrall)*, Peggy Hathaway *(Hypatia Dalroy)*, Douglas Payne *(Henry J. Smith)*, W. Bosco *(Louis)*, Henry Doughty *(Mr. Dalroy)*.

This film, about an actress who is hired by an underworld figure to seduce a young man into giving her his father's pottery secret, did not elicit much excitement from cinema patrons.

d, H. Grenville Taylor, Douglas Payne; w, Langford Reed, Hetty Spiers.

Mystery **(PR:A MPAA:NR)**

POVERTY OF RICHES, THE*** (1921) 6 reels Goldwyn bw

Richard Dix *(John Colby)*, Leatrice Joy *(Katherine Colby)*, John Bowers *(Tom Donaldson)*, Louise Lovely *(Grace Donaldson)*, Irene Rich *(Mrs. Holt)*, De Witt Jennings *(Lyons)*, David Winter *(Stephen Phillips)*, Frankie Lee *(John, in Prolog)*, Dorothy Hughes *(Katherine, in Prolog)*, Roy Laidlaw *(Hendron)*, John Cossar *(Edward Phillips, Sr.)*.

Interesting and daring film about a man (Dix) who refuses to give his wife (Joy) children until he reaches a certain plateau of success and wealth. Eventually his professional life becomes a triumph, but he still refuses his wife her only wish. After a time he comes to realize his selfishness, but before he can fulfill his wife's great desire, a terrible automobile accident renders the poor woman sterile for life. Strong and mature motion picture—well written, directed, and acted.

d, Reginald Barker; w, Arthur F. Statter (based on the short story "The Mother" by Leroy Scott); ph, Percy Hilburn.

Drama **(PR:A MPAA:NR)**

POWDER MY BACK* (1928) 7 reels WB bw

Irene Rich *(Fritzi Foy)*, Audrey Ferris *(Ruth Stevens)*, Andre Beranger *(Claude)*, Anders Randolf *(Rex Hale)*, Carroll Nye *(Jack Hale)*.

When her slightly naughty show is closed by Randolf, a reform-oriented mayor, Rich, the leading lady, fakes an accident which gets her access to this home. She then has her press agent, who is posing as a doctor, prescribe bed rest for several days. During this time the mayor's son Nye falls madly in love with Rich, but the actress sends him back to his brokenhearted fiancee and marries the equally smitten father.

d, Roy Del Ruth; w, Robert Lord, Joseph Jackson (based on a story by Jerome Kingston); t, Jack Jarmuth; ph, Frank Kesson; ed, Owen Marks.

Drama **(PR:A MPAA:NR)**

POWER OF DECISION, THE** (1917) 5 reels Rolfe/Metro bw

Frances Nelson *(Margaret)*, Richard Tucker *(Austin Bland)*, John Davidson *(Duhanel)*, Sally Crute *(Mrs. Duhanel)*, Mary Asquith *(Mrs. Hall)*, Fuller Mellish *(The Old Artist)*, Hugh Jeffrey.

Nelson becomes the model and wife of a successful artist who fails to inform her that he is already married. When she finally learns the truth, she leaves brokenhearted and takes a job posing for a female painter of miniatures. Time passes and she meets a well-known author, whom she marries. One day her husband, whom she respects greatly, asks her to pose for the pictures which are to be used in his latest book. Of course she agrees, but is shocked to discover that the illustrator is none other than the man for whom she still secretly lusts. During the sittings, the artist declares his love for her and attempts a second seduction, but rather than surrender, Nelson recalls the lessons of fidelity her husband's books advocate, and this gives her the strength to resist.

d, John W. Noble; w, June Mathis (based on a story by George W. Gunn); ph, Herbert O. Carleton.

Drama **(PR:A MPAA:NR)**

POWER OF RIGHT, THE** (1919, Brit.) 5 reels H bw

James Knight *(Gerald Stafford)*, Evelyn Boucher *(Elsie Vigor)*, Frank E. Petley *(Danvers)*, Leslie Reardon *(Leslie Stafford)*, Prince of Wales *(Himself)*, Marjorie Villis, Adeline Hayden Coffin, Sidney Grant, Clifford Pembroke, John Gliddon.

Wartime British drama in which the Prince of Wales made a cameo appearance, deals with an escaped German prisoner who provides a threat to the Empire until a high-ranking officer's cadet son kills him.

d, F. Martin Thornton; w, (based on a story by Reuben Gilmer).

War **(PR:A MPAA:NR)**

POWER OF THE PRESS, THE*** (1928) 7 reels COL bw

Douglas Fairbanks, Jr. *(Clem Rogers)*, Jobyna Ralston *(Jane Atwill)*, Mildred Harris *(Marie)*, Philo McCullough *(Blake)*, Wheeler Oakman *(Van)*, Robert Edeson *(City Editor)*, Edwards Davis *(Mr. Atwill)*, Del Henderson *(Johnson)*, Charles Clary *(District Attorney)*.

The Capra touch is very much in evidence in this nicely crafted picture in which Fairbanks, a cub reporter, breaks a story implicating Ralston, the daughter of a man running for mayor, in a murder. After being let out on bail, Ralston convinces the newspaper-man of her innocence, and together they bring the real killer (her father's political opponent) to justice. Good performances by Fairbanks and Ralston.

p, Jack Cohn; d, Frank Capra; w, Frederick A. Thompson, Sonya Levien (based on a story by Thompson); ph, Chet Lyons, Ted Tetzlaff; ed, Frank Atkinson; art d, Harrison Wiley.

Crime/Drama **(PR:A MPAA:NR)**

POWER OF THE WEAK, THE** (1926) 7 reels CHAD/IP bw

Arnold Gregg *(The Man)*, Alice Calhoun *(Myra)*, Carl Miller *(Raymond)*, Spottiswoode Aitken *(The Father)*, Marguerite Clayton, Jack Fowler.

A city girl inherits a lumber camp and rejects the advances of a woodsman. Out of spite he sets out to ruin her business, but a young chap who has wandered north to forget that his father disinherited him (for popping about with a chorus girl) intervenes. The fellow, in fact, gives the rotter a good thrashing, makes the enterprise a winner and marries its owner.

d, William J. Craft; w, Wyndham Gittens, Craft; ph, Arthur Reeves.

North Woods/Adventure **(PR:A MPAA:NR)**

POWER OVER MEN** (1929, Brit.) 7 reels British Filmcraft/PAR bw

Isabel Jeans *(Marion Delacour)*, Jameson Thomas *(Phillipe Garnier)*, Wyndham Standing *(Emile Delacour)*, Gibb McLaughlin *(Alexandre Billot)*, Jerrold Robertshaw *(Fournier)*, James Knight *(Cesa)*, Franklyn Bellamy *(Bottomley)*, Gabrielle Morton *(Maid)*, Judd Green, Hugh Crumplin.

British mystery about the wife of a diplomat who takes the blame for the murder of her husband because she thinks her lover did it. But in the end it turns out a spy was actually responsible for the deed.

p, d&w, George J. Banfield (based on a story by Denison Clift).

Mystery **(PR:A MPAA:NR)**

PRAIRIE WIFE, THE*** ½** (1925) 7 reels Eastern/MG bw

Dorothy Devore *(Chaddie Green)*, Herbert Rawlinson *(Duncan MacKail)*, Gibson Gowland *(Ollie)*, Leslie Stuart *(Percy)*, Frances Prim *(Olga)*, Boris Karloff *(Diego)*, Erich von Ritzau *(Doctor)*, Rupert Franklin *(Rufus Green)*.

Very good programmer—no doubt inspired by SECRETS (1924)—has Devore, an impoverished society girl, returning from Europe and marrying Rawlinson, who takes her West to develop some property he has inherited. The hiring of Gowland, a mentally deranged caretaker, and the presence of Stuart, a sickly English neighbor whom Devore nurses back to health (creating a jealousy factor), provide some roadblocks along the way, but in the end everything works out and the couple find the happiness and security they craved from the beginning. Here is an independent production which can hold its own with the best of the major studios.

d&w, Hugo Ballin (based on a story by Arthur Stringer); t, Katherine Hilliker, H. H. Caldwell; ph, James Diamond; ed, Hilliker, Caldwell.

Western/Drama **(PR:A MPAA:NR)**

PRAISE AGENT, THE*** (1919) 5 reels WORLD bw

Arthur Ashley *(Jack Bartling)*, Dorothy Green *(Nell Eubanks)*, Jack Drumier *(Sen. Eubanks)*, Lucille La Verne *(Mrs. Eubanks)*, J. W. Johnston *(Stanley Adams)*, Lola Frink *(Marjorie Lorraine)*, Mrs. Priestly Morrison *(Miss Pettigrew)*.

Amusing little comedy has publicist Ashley in love with the daughter of Drumier, a senator who owns the Floating Lily Soap Company. An avid anti-suffragette, Drumier convinces his wife, who happens to be a leader in the women's movement, that if she can get her army of ladies to collect and hold on to the Lily rebate coupons, victory may be within their grasp. Therefore, when the chits are hoarded to the amount of $650,000, the senator is faced with the obligation of paying out all of that money at once. Rather than face financial ruin, he opts to cast his all-important vote in favor of equality.

d, Frank Crane; w, Clara Beranger (based on a story by Earle Mitchell); ph, Max Schneider.

Comedy **(PR:A MPAA:NR)**

PREHISTORIC MAN, THE** ½** (1924, Brit.) 5 reels STOLL bw

George Robey *(He-of-the-Beetle-Brow)*, Marie Blanche *(She-of-the-Permanent-Wave)*, H. Agar Lyons *(He-of-the-Clutching-Hand)*, W. G. Saunders *(He-of-the-Knotty-Joints)*, Johnny Butt *(He-of-the-O-Cedar-Mop)*, Elsie Marriot-Watson *(She-of-the-Tireless-Tongue)*, Laurie Leslie *(He-of-the-Matted-Beaver)*.

Truly zany British comedy has a caveman eloping in a "borrowed" auto and then winning the approval of his hostile father-in-law after saving him from being abducted.

d, A. E. Coleby; w, Sinclair Hill (based on a story by George Robey).

Comedy **(PR:A MPAA:NR)**

PREP AND PEP*** (1928) 6 reels FOX bw

David Rollins *(Cyril Reade)*, Nancy Drexel *(Dorothy Marsh)*, John Darrow *(Flash Wells)*, E. H. Calvert *(Col. Marsh)*, Frank Albertson *(Bunk Hill)*, Robert Peck *(Coach)*.

Using a lot of footage shot at Indiana's famed Culver Military Academy, director Butler put together a good juvenile story in which Rollins plays the son of the school's all-time greatest athlete, who tries to follow in his father's footsteps and turns out to be a complete flop. Later, after hard work and determination, he breaks an unmanageable horse, becomes a member of the prestigious Black Horse Troop, and saves the commandant's daughter from a fire.

d, David Butler; w, John Stone; t, Malcolm Boylan; ph, Sidney Wagner, Joseph Valentine; ed, Irene Morra; syn sc; s eff.

Drama/Comedy **(PR:A MPAA:NR)**

PREPARED TO DIE* (1923) 5 reels Johnnie Walker bw

Eddie Polo *(John Pendleton Smythe)*, Ena Gregory *(Vivienne Van de Vere)*, James McElhern *(Storekeeper)*.

Polo, the strongman king of the serials, is completely miscast as a society wimp who attempts to commit suicide when his girl leaves him by getting himself involved in a hillbilly feud. Actually, fate turns him into a *real* man, and he wins the local lovely by beating the tar out of the resident bully.

d, William Hughes Curran; w, Keene Thompson.

Adventure/Drama **(PR:A MPAA:NR)**

PRESUMPTION OF STANLEY HAY, MP, THE** (1925, Brit.) 5 reels STOLL bw

David Hawthorne *(Stanley Hay)*, Betty Faire *(Princess Berenice)*, Fred Raynham *(Baron Hertzog)*, Eric Bransby Williams *(Honorable Bertie Sellinger)*, Kinsey Peile *(The King)*, Nelson Ramsey *(The Spy)*, Dora de Winton *(Lady Barmouth)*, Mme. d'Esterre *(Mme. de Vere)*.

British adventure has a dashing member of Parliament (Hawthorne) getting himself involved in the kind of intrigue which can only take place in one of those comic opera kingdoms. He does manage to throw himself square in the middle of it all and marries the princess who was the object of a kidnaping plot.

d, Sinclair Hill; w, Alicia Ramsey (based on a novel by Nowell Kaye).

Adventure **(PR:A MPAA:NR)**

PRETENDERS, THE*** (1916) 5 reels Rolfe/Metro bw

Emmy Wehlen *(Helen Pettingill)*, Paul Gordon *(Hubert Stanwood)*, Charles Eldridge *(Silas T. Pettingill)*, Kate Blancke *(Maria Pettingill)*, Edwin Holt *(Inspector Burke)*, William Davidson *(Macklin Thurston)*, Howard Truesdell *(John Stafford)*, Jerome Wilson *(Joseph Bailey)*, Ilean Hume *(Rita)*, Harry Neville *(Dugan)*, Hugh Jeffrey.

Better-than-it-sounds movie has a nice old farmer striking oil and moving to Park Avenue with his socially ambitious wife and daughter. One night the old boy ties one on and brings his chauffeur home for the evening. To cover the situation with his wife, the driver is passed off as being a European count. There are, of course, the usual con men about—one of whom is posing as royalty—but dad and his pal straighten everything out. In the end the chauffeur turns out to be a *real* count, who took his menial job to learn the secret of becoming a true American.

d, George D. Baker; w, (based on the play by Rennold Wolf, Channing Pollock); ph, William Wagner.

Comedy **(PR:A MPAA:NR)**

PRETTY CLOTHES*** (1927) 6 reels STER bw

Jobyna Ralston *(Marian Dunbar)*, Gertrude Astor *(Rose Dunbar)*, Johnny Walker *(Russell Thorpe)*, Lloyd Whitlock *(Philip Bennett)*, Charles Clary *(Thorpe, Sr.)*, Jack Mower *(Albert Moore)*, Lydia Knott *(Mrs. Dunbar)*.

Kirkpatrick's outstanding photography is the highlight of this otherwise satisfying programmer about a young girl (Ralston) who unwittingly finds herself compromised when she accepts a lovely gown from the man instructed by her sweetheart's father to break up their romance. At her mother's deathbed, however, the lad comes to realize that Ralston committed no sin, nor violated any law to obtain the garment, and the lovers are reunited.

d, Phil Rosen; sup, Joe Rock; w, Frances Guihan, Edwin Myers (based on a story by Peggy Gaddis); t, Wyndham Gittens; ph, Herbert Kirkpatrick.

Drama **(PR:A MPAA:NR)**

PRETTY LADIES*** (1925) 6 reels MG bw

ZaSu Pitts *(Maggie Keenan)*, Tom Moore *(Al Cassidy)*, Ann Pennington *(Herself)*, Lilyan Tashman *(Selma Larson)*, Bernard Randall *(Aaron Savage)*, Helen D'Algy *(Adrienne)*, Conrad Nagel *(Maggie's Dream Lover)*, Norma Shearer *(Frances White)*, George K. Arthur *(Roger Van Horn)*, Lucille Le Sueur [Joan Crawford] *(Bobby)*, Paul Ellis *(Warren Hadley)*, Roy D'Arcy *(Paul Thompson)*, Gwen Lee *(Fay)*, Dorothy Seastrom *(Diamond Tights)*, Lew Harvey *(Will Rogers)*, Chad Huber *(Frisco)*, Walter Shumway *(Mr. Gallagher)*, Dan Crimmins *(Mr. Shean)*, Jimmie Quinn (Eddie Cantor).

Pitts is quite wonderful as a comedienne who marries Moore, a musician, and almost has her heart broken when he enters into an affair with a Follies beauty. This is a fascinating Hollywood recreation of Florenz Ziegfeld's empire, with many of his biggest stars portrayed quite interestingly by actors, including Crawford in her film debut. In the end, of course, Pitts and Moore do manage to work everything out.

d, Monta Bell; w, Alice D. G. Miller (based on the story by Adela Rogers St. John); ph, Ira H. Morgan.

Dramatic Comedy **(PR:A MPAA:NR)**

PRETTY MRS. SMITH*** (1915) 5 reels Bosworth/PAR bw

Fritzi Scheff *(Drucilla)*, Owen Moore *(Mr. Smith No. 3)*, Forrest Stanley *(Mr. Smith No.2)*, Louis Bennison *(Mr. Smith No.1)*, Leila Bliss *(Letitia Proudfoot)*.

Scheff, the Viennese star of Broadway musicals, re-creates her stage success in this better-than-average comedy about the complications a beautiful young woman encounters when her three husbands show up at the same time.

d, Hobart Bosworth; w, (based on the play by Oliver Morosco, Elmer Harris).

Comedy **(PR:A MPAA:NR)**

PRETTY SISTER OF JOSE½** (1915) 5 reels FP bw

Marguerite Clark, Jack Pickford, Rupert Julian, Edith Chapman, William Lloyd, Teddy Sampson, Dick Rosson, Gertrude Norman.

Clark gives her usual topflight performance as a young woman who is alienated towards all men because her womanizing father deserted the family. The Spanish settings register well in this picture, as does Pickford as the young man who teaches her how to love again.

d, Allan Dwan; w, (based on the play version of a story by Frances Hodgson Burnett).

Drama **(PR:A MPAA:NR)**

PRICE FOR FOLLY, A** (1915) 5 reels VIT bw

Edith Storey *(Mlle. Dorothea Jardeu)*, Antonio Moreno *(Jean de Segni)*, Harry T. Morey *(Henri Landon)*, Charles Kent *(Duke de Segni)*, Louise Beaudet *(Duchess de Segni)*, Ethel Corcoran, T. Wain-Cogan Draper, Helen Pillsbury, John Hines, Arthur Cozine.

After a day of drinking at his club, a young playboy dreams that his father murders his mother from his deathbed, rather than leave her in the care of a chorus girl-chasing libertine. He of course awakens a regenerated man, and even turns down an invitation extended by a beautiful actress he had his eye on. Good direction and cast can't make up for a skin-and-bones script.

d, George D. Baker; w, George P. Dillenback.

Drama **(PR:A MPAA:NR)**

PRICE MARK, THE½** (1917) 6 reels PAR bw

Dorothy Dalton *(Paula Lee)*, William Conklin *(Fielding Powell)*, Thurston Hall *(Dr. D. Melfi)*, Adele Farrington *(Marie)*, Dorcas Matthews *(Nakhia)*, Edwin Wallock *(Hassan)*, Clio Ayres *(Belle de Farge)*.

Impoverished Dalton moves to the city and is forced to become the mistress of libertine Conklin. It doesn't take long for the rotter to discover that Dalton possesses very special qualities, and he leaves town with the words, "If I return, it will be to ask you to become my wife." Meanwhile, Dalton falls in love with young Hall, a doctor with whom she is doing volunteer work amongst the poor. Years before, Hall saved Conklin's life along the banks of the Nile, but nonetheless, when the rotter returns and discovers the budding romance, he decides to reveal the sordid past of the sweet little girl he forced into bondage. Fortunately, one of his servants, an Egyptian whose sister Conklin earlier deflowered, stabs him to death before he has a chance to tell his dirty little tale. This, of course, leaves the young couple free to marry without Dalton's embarrassing background coming to the forefront.

d, Roy William Neill; sup, Thomas H. Ince; w, John B. Ritchie.

Drama **(PR:A MPAA:NR)**

PRICE OF A PARTY, THE** (1924) 6 reels Howard Estabrook/AEX bw

Hope Hampton *(Grace Barrows)*, Harrison Ford *(Robert Casson)*, Arthur Carew *(Kenneth Bellwood)*, Mary Astor *(Alice Barrows)*, Dagmar Godowsky *(Evelyn Dolores)*, Fred Hadley *(Stephen Darrell)*, Edna Richmond *(Evelyn's Maid)*, Donald Lashey *(Hall Boy)*, Florence Richardson *(Jazz Queen)*, Edward Lawrence *(Officer)*.

Hampton walks through this slow-moving film about a nightclub dancer who reluctantly agrees (in order to pay her mother's medical expenses) to vamp businessman Ford as a means of stopping him from going to Brazil and renewing a valuable mineral option. When her kid sister, Astor, arrives in New York and is attracted to Carew, the crook behind the scheme, Hampton and the rotter's former mistress visit his apartment and the ex-paramour kills him. Astor is accused of the crime and put on trial, but a suicide note left by the real killer gets her off the hook. After learning the whole story, Ford asks Hampton to marry him, and the little sister returns home where plenty of *decent* men are available.

d, Charles Giblyn; w, Charles F. Roebuck (based on the novel by William Briggs MacHarg); ph, John Seitz.

Drama **(PR:A MPAA:NR)**

PRICE OF SILENCE, THE½**
(1920, Brit.) 6 reels G.B. Samuelson/Sunrise bw (GB: AT THE MERCY OF TIBERIUS)

Peggy Hyland *(Byrle Brentano)*, Campbell Gullan *(Col. Luke Darrington)*, Tom Chatterton *(Lennox Dunbar)*, Van Dycke *(Frank Darrington)*, Dorothy Gordon *(Mrs. Brentano)*.

Filmed in Hollywood, this better-than-average British production has a girl being saved from a murder charge when the face of her grandfather's real killer is imprinted on a window by lightning.

d, Fred Leroy Granville; w, (based on a novel by Augusta Wilson).

Mystery **(PR:A MPAA:NR)**

PRIDE OF DONEGAL, THE** (1929, Brit.) 7 reels H.B. Parkinson/FOX bw

Rex Sherren *(Roland Terrence)*, Robina Maugham *(Molly Cross)*, Syd Crossley *(Mike O'Flanagan)*, Graeme Low *(Blarney Stone)*.

British film set in the Emerald Isle has a young groom saving a horse who has been badly mistreated and then riding him to victory in the Grand National. Nothing original, but pleasant enough.

d, J. Steven Edwards; w, Norman Lee.

Drama **(PR:A MPAA:NR)**

PRIDE OF JENNICO, THE** (1914) 4 reels FP bw

House Peters *(Basil Jennico)*, Hal Clarendon, Marie Leonhard, Betty Harte, Wellington Playter, Peter Lang, Cecilia Loftus.

This motion picture version of the very popular Hackett play gets off to a slow start, but when the prince (nicely played on the screen by Peters) finally gets into the swashbuckling business of saving his royal sweetheart, the wait is worthwhile. Some beautiful shots taken on location in Cuba are also a plus.

d, J. Searle Dawley; w, Abby Sage Richardson, Grace Livingston Furniss (based on a play by James K. Hackett).

Drama **(PR:A MPAA:NR)**

PRIDE OF PALOMAR, THE*** (1922) 8 reels COS/PAR bw

Forrest Stanley *(Don Mike Farrell)*, Marjorie Daw *(Kay Parker)*, Tote Du Crow *(Pablo)*, James Barrows *(Father Dominic)*, Joseph Dowling *(Don Miguel)*, Alfred Allen *(John Parker)*, George Nichols *(Conway)*, Warner Oland *(Okada)*, Mrs. Jessie Hebbard *(Mrs. Parker)*, Percy Williams *(Butler)*, Mrs. George Hernandez *(Caroline)*, Edward Brady *(Lostolet)*, Carmen Arselle *(Mrs. Supaldio)*, Eagle Eye *(Nogi)*, Most Mattoe *(Alexandria)*.

William Randolph Hearst managed to slip in a plug for his "Yellow Peril" theory in this melodrama which has Stanley returning home from the service to discover that his father is dead and that an unscrupulous caretaker is about to turn his ranch land over to a Japanese potato baron for the purpose of Oriental colonization. Of course the Yankee Doodle boy smashes the scheme and even manages to win the heart of the operator's daughter Daw, who is not only beautiful but a darn good American as well.

d, Frank Borzage; w, Grant Carpenter, John Lynch (based on the novel by Peter Bernard Kyne); ph, Chester A. Lyons.

Drama **(PR:A MPAA:NR)**

PRIDE OF SUNSHINE ALLEY** (1924) 5 reels Bud Barsky/SUN bw

Kenneth McDonald *(Tim)*, Monte Collins *(Pat)*, Violet Schram *(Mary O'Neill)*, Eddie O'Brien, William Gould, Phil Ford, Edith Yorke, Charles K. French.

Fair "sidewalks of New York" programmer has McDonald, a young Irish cop, falling in love with Schram, whose brother is mixed up with a gang of automobile thieves. When the leader of the mob (who is also in love with Schram) takes a pasting from McDonald, he gets even by framing the policeman's father, Collins. The young Irishman takes the blame and while out on bail is informed by Schram's brother that the whole thing was the gang leader's doing. McDonald then sets everything straight, sends the crook to jail, marries Schram, and sees to it that his brother-in-law follows the straight and narrow path.

d, William J. Craft; sup, Bud Barskey; w, Samuel M. Pyke; ph, Arthur Reeves.

Drama **(PR:A MPAA:NR)**

PRIDE OF THE CLAN, THE*** (1917) 7 reels ART bw

Mary Pickford *(Marget MacTavish, the Pride of the Clan)*, Matt Moore *(Jamie Campbell)*, Warren Cook *(Robert)*, Kathryn Browne Decker *(The Countess of Dunstable)*, Edward Roseman *(Pitcairn)*, Joel Day *(The Dominie)*, Leatrice Joy.

Director Tourneur's artist's eye created a completely believable Scottish atmosphere for this engaging Pickford feature, which has the star playing the daughter of a captain lost at sea. The girl moves into her father's fishing boat just offshore, along with the barnyard animals, who have become her friends. Pickford falls in love with a local fisher lad, Moore (her real-life brother-in-law), but when it's discovered that he's the heir to a title, his parents separate the couple. Later Pickford's ship is in the process of sinking when Moore's yacht approaches, and the young man saves her life. It is then that he makes the decision to dispense with royalty and ask the girl he adores to be his wife. While filming this picture, the ship the studio was using for dressing rooms actually did sink, and Tourneur led Pickford to safety at the very last moment. No doubt the experience helped her performance when it came to shooting the big thrill scene.

d, Maurice Tourneur; w, Elaine Sterne, Charles E. Whittaker; ph, Lucien Androit, John van der Broek.

Drama **Cas.** **(PR:A MPAA:NR)**

PRIDE OF THE FANCY, THE***
(1920, Brit.) 6 reels G. B. Samuelson/GEN bw

Rex Davis *(Phil Moran)*, Daisy Burrell *(Kitty Ruston)*, Tom Reynolds *(Prof. Ruston)*, Fred Morgan *(Ireton)*, Dorothy Fane *(Hilda Douglas)*, Wyndham Guise *(Sir Rufus Douglas)*, Pope Stamper *(Oswald Gordon)*, Kid Gordon *(James Croon)*.

Good British sporting drama has Davis, a prizefighter, falling in love with Burrell, a show girl, and winning the title after a letter written by the manager of the champ (who openly lusts for Burrell), implicating the girl in a scandal, is proven to be false.

d, Albert Ward; w, (based on a novel by George Edgar).

Drama **(PR:A MPAA:NR)**

PRIDE OF THE FORCE, THE* (1925) 5 reels RAY bw

Tom Santschi *(Officer Moore)*, Edythe Chapman *(Mother Moore)*, Gladys Hulette *(Mary Moore)*, James Morrison *(Jimmy Moore)*, Francis X. Bushman, Jr. *(Jack Griffen)*, Crauford Kent *(Charley Weldon)*, Joseph Girard *(Police Captain)*.

This picture strives for tears, thrills, and suspense, but only seems to generate laughs. It all begins with officer Santschi being refused a promotion for allowing a couple of crooks to get away because he stopped to aid a crippled child. Later, when he breaks up a robbery at the bank belonging to his friend, Bushman, the poor devil is forced to arrest his own daughter Hulette, who appears to be implicated. Finally Bushman, who is in love with Hulette, steps forward and proves the girl's innocence. Thus Santschi is finally promoted to sergeant—which brings the biggest howl of all.

d, Duke Worne; w, Arthur Hoerl.

Crime/Drama **(PR:A MPAA:NR)**

PRIDE OF THE NORTH, THE**
(1920, Brit.) 5 reels I. B. Davidson/Ruffells bw

Cecil Humphreys *(John Hargreaves)*, Nora Roylance *(Rose Eva)*, Richard Buttery *(Jack Hargreaves)*, James English *(Bill Webster)*, Blanche Kellino *(Mother)*, H. Nicholls-Bates *(Father)*, Eva Llewellyn, Eve Marchew.

When his greyhound wins the prized Waterloo Cup, a son is reunited with his mine-owner father. About average for a British production of this time.

d&w, A. E. Coleby.

Drama **(PR:A MPAA:NR)**

PRIMAL LURE, THE** (1916) 5 reels Kay-Bee/TRI bw

William S. Hart, Margery Wilson, Robert McKim, Jerome Storm, Joe Goodboy.

Disappointing Hart feature has the star playing the manager of a far north trading company. He's discharged and replaced by a chap who proves to be a coward when the settlement comes under Indian attack. Hart, of course, saves the day and also wins the love of the girl.

d, William S. Hart; w, J. G. Hawks (based on a story by Vingie E. Roe); ph, Joseph August.

North Woods Adventure **(PR:A MPAA:NR)**

PRINCE AND THE BEGGARMAID, THE** (1921, Brit.) 5 reels ID bw

Henry Ainley *(Prince Olaf)*, Kathleen Vaughn *(Princess Monika)*, Harvey Braban *(King Hildred)*, Sam Wilkinson *(Prince Michael)*, Sydney Paxton *(Chief of State)*, John Wyndham *(Capt. Karsburg)*, Laurence Forster *(Gen. Erlenberg)*, Francis Duguid *(Capt. Schwartz)*, Frank Woolf *(Capt. Hector)*.

This British charmer is set in Ruritania and deals with a king who gets his country involved in a war in order to force a neighboring princess to marry his ugly little hunchbacked brother.

d, A. V. Bramble; w, Eliot Stannard (based on a play by Walter Howard).

Drama **(PR:C MPAA:NR)**

PRINCE AND THE PAUPER, THE*** (1915) 5 reels FP bw

Marguerite Clark *(Prince of Wales/Tom Canty, the Pauper)*, William Burrows *(Earl of Hertford)*, William Sorelle *(Miles Hendon)*, William Frederick *(Tom's Father)*, Alfred Fisher *(Father Andrew)*, Robert Broderick, Ed Mordant.

Clark is fine playing a double role as the English prince who changes places with a beggar lad in this Mark Twain classic set during the reign of Henry VIII. Some excellent double exposure photography and impressive sets add to the film's overall ability to please.

d&w, Edwin S. Porter, Hugh Ford (based on the novel by Mark Twain).

Costume Drama **(PR:A MPAA:NR)**

PRINCE IN A PAWNSHOP, A*** (1916) 5 reels VIT bw

Barney Bernard *(David Solomon)*, Garry McGarry *(Maurice)*, Bobby Connelly *(Bobby)*, Charlotte Ives *(Ethel)*, Edna Hunter *(Mary Brown)*, Brinsley Shaw *(Thomas W. Stevens)*, Lester Bernard *(Abe Goldstein)*.

Story of a Jewish banker who exacts 10 percent interest from his wealthy clients and secretly runs a pawn shop in the slums where he passes these profits on to the needy. This could have been a great film but falters in script and direction. There is a moving subplot in which the girl who had a child by the banker's son is discovered 10 years later and rescued from poverty by the old Hebrew.

d, Paul Scardon; w, Garfield Thompson (based on a play by Marie De Sarlabous, Andre de Segurola).

Drama **(PR:A MPAA:NR)**

PRINCE OF AVENUE A., THE*** (1920) 5 reels UNIV bw

James J. "Gentleman Jim" Corbett *(Barry O'Conner)*, Mary Warren *(Mary Tompkins)*, Harry Northrup *(Edgar Jones)*, Cora Drew *(Mary O'Conner)*, Richard Cummings *(Patrick O'Conner)*, Frederick Vroom *(William Tompkins)*, Mark Fenton *(Father O'Toole)*, George Vanderlip *(Reggie Vanderlip)*, Johnny Cooke *(Butler)*, Lydia Yeamans Titus *(Housekeeper)*, George Fisher.

Ford directed this well-crafted picture and got a good performance from the former world heavyweight champ, "Gentleman" Jim Corbett, as a young fellow from the old neighborhood who climbs to the top of the political world—without forgetting his roots—and ends up winning the heart of a millionaire's daughter.

d, Jack Ford; w, Charles J. Wilson, Jr. (based on a story by Charles T. Dazey, Frank M. Dazey); ph, John W. Brown.

Drama **(PR:A MPAA:NR)**

PRINCE OF INDIA, A*** (1914) 4 reels Wharton/ECL bw

Thurlow Bergen, William Riley Hatch, Elsie Esmonde, Billy Mason, M. O. Penn.

Four-reel feature crammed with action and laughs has a young reporter battling a trio of crooks–one of them a girl who seduced an Oriental prince's son into stealing his father's priceless gem–and returning the jewel to its rightful owner after a terrific fist fight on a runaway trolley car.

d, Leopold Wharton; w, Lew Wallace.

Crime/Adventure **(PR:A MPAA:NR)**

PRINCE OF PILSEN, THE*** (1926) 7 reels Belasco/PDC bw

George Sidney *(Hans Wagner)*, Anita Stewart *(Nellie, His Daughter)*, Allan Forrest *(Frederick, Prince of Pilsen)*, Myrtle Stedman *(Princess Bertha of Thorwald)*, Otis Harlan *(Bandit Chief)*, Rose Tapley *(Lady in Waiting)*, William Von Brincken *(Captain of the Guard)*, William von Hardenburg *(Court Physician)*.

Sidney is terrific as a Dutch brewer who returns to the old country and at a banquet is mistaken, due to his lodge uniform, for the Prince of Pilsen. It seems the real prince (Forrest) is due to marry a princess of a neighboring state, and the little Dutchman goes along with the whole affair, assuming it's part of his club's initiation rights. The movie is full of clever little touches and plenty of big laughs, and ends with the true prince marrying Sidney's daughter, nicely played by Stewart.

d, Paul Powell; w, Anthony Coldewey (based on the musical comedy by Frank Pixley, Gustav Luders); ph, James C. Van Trees; art d, Charles Cadwallader.

Comedy **(PR:A MPAA:NR)**

PRINCE THERE WAS, A** (1921) 6 reels FP-LAS/PAR bw

Thomas Meighan *(Charles Edward Martin)*, Mildred Harris *(Katherine Woods)*, Charlotte Jackson *(Comfort Brown)*, Nigel Barrie *(Jack Carruthers)*, Gul Oliver *(Bland)*, Arthur Hull *(J. J. Stratton)*, Sylvia Ashton *(Mrs. Prouty)*, Fred Huntley *(Mr. Cricket)*.

The greatly talented Cohan wrote and starred on Broadway in this play about a young millionaire who passes himself off as an assistant editor and moves into the boardinghouse occupied by a young, aspiring female writer, whom he loves. Eventually the gentleman buys a popular magazine and publishes all of the stories written by the girl who becomes his wife. Unfortunately, the special magic that Cohan brought to his theatrical production is missing here, and the motion picture is only second rate.

d, Tom Forman; sup, Frank E. Woods; w, Waldemar Young (based on the play by George M. Cohan); ph, Harry Perry.

Comedy/Drama **(PR:A MPAA:NR)**

PRINCESS FROM HOBOKEN, THE*** (1927) 6 reels TIF bw

Edmund Burns *(Terrence O'Brien)*, Blanche Mehaffey *(Sheila O'Toole)*, Ethel Clayton *(Mrs. O'Brien)*, Lou Tellegen *(Prince Anton Balakrieff)*, Babe London *(Princess Sonia Alexanderovna Karpoff)*, Will R. Walling *(Mr. O'Brien)*, Charles McHugh *(Pa O'Toole)*, Aggie Herring *(Ma O'Toole)*, Charles Crockett *(Whiskers)*, Robert Homans *(McCoy)*, Harry Bailey *(Cohen)*, Sidney D'Albrook *(Tony)*, Broderick O'Farrell *(Immigration Officer)*, Boris Karloff *(Pavel)*.

Better-than-average Tiffany production has the owners of O'Tooles restaurant in Hoboken changing the name of their business to the Russian Inn in order to cash in on the publicity a Russian princess living in Chicago has been receiving. On opening night, Mehaffey, the owner's dauger, poses as the famous expatriate and is approached by Burns, a hopeless romantic, and Tellegen, a refugee and con artist posing as a prince. The real fun begins when the authentic princess shows up, and after a number of amusing situations, Tellegen is exposed and Mehaffey ends up in Burns' arms.

d, Allan Dale; w, Sonya Levien; ph, Robert Martin, Joseph Dubray; ed, James C. McKay; art d, Edwin B. Willis.

Comedy **(PR:A MPAA:NR)**

PRINCESS OF HAPPY CHANCE, THE**
(1916, Brit.) 5 reels London/JUR bw

Elizabeth Risdon *(Princess Felicia/Lucidora Eden)*, Gerald Ames *(Prince Jocelyn)*, Hayford Hobbs *(Harvey Royle)*, Dallas Cairns *(Prince)*, Douglas Munro, Gwynne Herbert, Edna Maude, Cyril Percival, Janet Ross, Beatrix Templeton.

In the less-than-subtle imitation of THE PRISONER OF ZENDA, a princess from one of those comic-opera nations escapes a forced marriage by changing places with her perfect double.

d, Maurice Elvey; w, (based on the novel by Tom Gallon).

Adventure/Romance **(PR:A MPAA:NR)**

PRISONER, THE** (1923) 5 reels UNIV bw

Herbert Rawlinson *(Philip Quentin)*, Eileen Percy *(Dorothy Garrison)*, George Cowl *(Lord Bob)*, June Elvidge *(Lady Francis)*, Lincoln Stedman *(Dickey Savage)*, Gertrude Short *(Lady Jane)*, Bertram Grassby *(Prince Ugo Ravorelli)*, Mario Carillo *(Count Sallonica)*, Hayford Hobbs *(Duke Laselli)*, Lillian Langdon *(Mrs. Garrison)*, *Bert Sprotte (Courant)*, Boris Karloff *(Prince Kapolski)*, Esther Ralston *(Marie)*, J. P. Lockney *(Father Bivot)*.

Rawlinson, an American traveling in Europe, runs into his former hometown sweetheart, Percy, and saves her from marrying a bogus prince whom he recognizes as a man wanted for murder in Brazil. Universal threw in a few expensive sets to make this pot-boiler resemble a first-class production. If they had only approached the material with a tongue-in-cheek attitude, it may have worked.

d, Jack Conway; w, Edward T. Loew, Jr. (based on the novel *Castle Craneycrow* by George Barr McCutcheon); ph, Benjamin Reynolds.

Adventure **(PR:A MPAA:NR)**

PRISONER OF THE PINES* (1918) 5 reels Paralta bw

J. Warren Kerrigan *(Hillaire Latour)*, Lois Wilson *(Rosalie Dufrense)*, Walter Perry *("Spud" Lafferty)*, Claire Du Brey *(Louise)*.

Far-fetched plot has Kerrigan going off to a lumber camp to support his bride and new baby. After a year he returns home with his savings, stops at a saloon, is suckered by a lady-of-the-night into losing all of his cash in a card game, and returns to the woods to start all over again. Another year passes and he returns to the same saloon, encounters the same woman, is hit over the head, has his poke stolen and returns to the forest a third time. Still another year goes by and this time he heads for the cabaret determined to reap a little revenge. When Kerrigan finds the saloon girl, he strangles her until she returns the proper amount of cash, and his wife and child show up just in time to provide the required happy ending.

d, Ernest C. Warde; w, (based on a story by Kenneth B. Clarke); ph, Charles Stumar.

North Woods/Adventure **(PR:A MPAA:NR)**

PRISONER OF ZENDA, THE*** (1915, Brit.) 6 reels LON/JUR bw

Henry Ainley *(Rudolph Rassendyl)*, Jane Gail *(Princess Flavia)*, Gerald Ames *(Rupert)*, Arthur Holmes-Gore *(Duke Michael)*, Charles Rock *(Col. Sapt)*, George Bellamy *(Capt. Reichenheim)*, Norman Yates *(Fritz von Tarlenheim)*, Marie Anita Bozzi *(Antoinette)*.

This was the first major motion picture adaption of Anthony Hope's classic Ruritanian adventure (there had been an earlier non-feature version) about a British tourist who assumes the identity of his royal double to prevent the overthrow of his kingdom. Well done indeed, with plenty of action and impressive production values.

d, George Loane Tucker; w, William Courtenay Rowden (based on the novel by Anthony Hope and the play by Edward Rose).

Adventure **(PR:A MPAA:NR)**

PRISONER OF ZENDA, THE**** (1922) 10 reels Metro bw

Lewis Stone *(Rudolf Rassendyll/King Rudolf)*, Alice Terry *(Princess Flavia)*, Robert Edeson *(Col. Sapt)*, Stuart Holmes *(Duke "Black" Michael)*, Ramon Samaniegos [Novarro] *(Rupert of Hentzau)*, Barbara La Marr *(Antoinette de Mauban)*, Malcolm McGregor *(Count von Tarlenheim)*, Edward Connelly *(Marshal von Strakencz)*, Lois Lee *(Countess Helga)*.

Another of director Ingram's smash hits of the 1920s (following THE FOUR HORSEMEN OF THE APOCALYPSE) is the sentimental, often sweetly so, story about an Englishman on vacation in Ruritania who runs into the country's politics and in the end saves the kingdom. While the sodden king of the country awaits his coronation, he is drugged by his brother, Samaniegos (Ramon Novarro's early movie name), who is hoping to complete a coup d'etat. His plans go haywire when the king's double (Stone in a dual role) is substituted at the coronation. "Black" Michael (Holmes) discovers the deception and kidnaps the real king, holding him captive in the castle of Zenda. Stone helps rescue the king and, scorning the love for him profferred by Terry, he returns to England. Though it may seem old-fashioned today, the picture caused a sensation when it came out, and much of the credit for that should go to Novarro, who, before he became the super-star rival to Rudolph Valentino, was engaging and refreshing. But it was Ingram who really held the pulse of the public, as he evidenced in THE FOUR HORSEMEN, when he had Valentino slouch around with a cigarette dangling from his mouth and having him dance the tango with all of his natural Mexican grace.

p&d, Rex Ingram; w, Mary O'Hara (based on the play by Edward E. Rose and the novel by Anthony Hope); ph, John F. Seitz.

Costume Adventure **(PR:A MPAA:NR)**

PRISONERS OF LOVE 1/2** (1921) 6 reels Betty Compson/Goldwyn bw

Betty Compson *(Blanche Davis)*, Ralph Lewis *(Her Father)*, Claire McDowell *(Her Mother)*, Clara Horton *(Her Sister)*, Emory Johnson *(James Randolph)*, Kate Toncray *(His Mother)*, Roy Stewart *(Martin Blair)*.

Compson's first starring role after the sensation she caused in THE MIRACLE MAN, has the actress leaving home and moving to San Francisco when she discovers that her father, Lewis, is a woman chaser. Taking a job with a law firm, she becomes involved with Johnson, one of the attorneys, and lives with him as his mistress. Her father later comes to town with the youngest daughter, buys off Compson's paramour, and the former actress marries a partner in the law firm.

d, Arthur Rossen; w, Catherine Henry; ph, Ernest G. Palmer, Ross Fisher.

Drama **(PR:C MPAA:NR)**

PRIVATE IZZY MURPHY** (1926) 8 reels WB bw

George Jessel *(Izzy Murphy)*, Patsy Ruth Miller *(Eileen Cohannigan)*, Vera Gordon *(Sara Goldberg)*, Nat Carr *(The Shadchen, Moe Ginsburg)*, William Strauss *(Jacob Goldberg)*, Spec O'Donnell *(The Monohan Kid)*, Gustav von Seyffertitz *(Cohannigan), Douglas Gerrard (Robert O'Malley)*, Tom Murray *(The Attorney)*.

Jessel, who one year later would turn down the lead (and screen immortality) in THE JAZZ SINGER, plays a prosperous Jewish merchant, in love with Miller, an Irish girl. Jessel goes to France as a member of the famed Celtic regiment, the Fighting 69th. He returns a hero, but Miller's father will have nothing to do with him when he learns of his Jewish faith. Finally Jessel's buddies talk some sense into the old boy and the couple go off to be married. Just another variation on the ABIE'S IRISH ROSE theme, but this time it fails because the "religious problem" is handled seriously and strives for pathos instead of the gentle humor which made the original such a great success.

d, Lloyd Bacon; w, Philip Lonergan (based on a story by Raymond L. Schrock, Edward Clark); ph, Virgil Miller.

Comedy/Drama **(PR:A MPAA:NR)**

PRIVATE PEAT** ½** (1918) 5 reels PAR bw

Harold R. Peat *(Himself)*, Miriam Fouche *(Mrs. Peat/Mary)*, William T. Sorelle *(Old Bill)*, Edwin Grant.

Interesting propaganda film, directed towards the encouragement of army enlistment and war-related volunteer work, follows the military career of Harold R. Peat, his combat experiences and subsequent battlefield wounds. The picture makes a big point of the fact that 22 percent of the Civil War wounded died while only 2 ½ percent of those involved in WW I. The film ends with a speech by President Wilson. Newsreel footage is used very effectively throughout.

d, Edward Jose; w, Charles Whittaker (based on the story by Harold Reginald Peat); ph, Hal Young.

War **(PR:A MPAA:NR)**

PRIVATE SCANDAL, A*** (1921) 5 reels Realart bw

May McAvoy *(Jeanne Millet)*, Bruce Gordon *(Jerry Hayes)*, Ralph Lewis *(Phillip Lawton)*, Kathlyn Williams *(Carol Lawton)*, Lloyd Whitlock *(Alec Crosby)*, Gladys Fox *(Betty Lawton)*.

One of the cinema's most underrated actresses, McAvoy, gives another splendid performance here as a French war orphan adopted and raised by a California couple. McAvoy falls for Gordon, a horsetrainer, but when her adoptive father, Lewis, returns from an extended business trip and hears rumors that his wife is having an affair with Whitlock, McAvoy tries to take the fall, claiming that Whitlock is *her* lover. A terrific fist fight takes place between the two men, but later the misunderstanding is cleared up and the picture ends on a happy note for everyone, save perhaps Whitlock.

d, Chester M. Franklin; w, Eve Unsell (based on a story by Hector Turnbull); ph, J. O. Taylor.

Drama **(PR:A MPAA:NR)**

PRODIGAL SON, THE**** (1923, Brit.) 17 reels STOLL bw

Stewart Rome *(Magnus Stephenson)*, Henry Victor *(Oscar Stephenson)*, Edith Bishop *(Helga Neilson)*, Colette Brettelle *(Thora Neilson/Elin)*, Adeline Hayden Coffin *(Anna Stephenson)*, Henry Nicholls-Bates *(Oscar Neilson)*, Louise Conti *(Aunt Margaret)*, Peter Upcher *(Nils Finsen)*, Sam Austin *(Captain)*, Frank Wilson *(Stephen Stephenson)*.

The longest British silent film ever made was this completely faithful adaption of Sir Hall Caine's novel, shot in 17 reels (two years before von Stroheim attempted the same thing with GREED) and released in two parts–the second titled THE RETURN OF THE PRODIGAL. It was exceptionally good for a British production, with fine acting and direction throughout. And the story–beginning in the hostile environment of Iceland where a young man steals the woman his brother loves, deserts her when she dies in childbirth, and then sets off for Nice, where he seduces her sister–never loses the interest of the audience. In fact, the scenes of debauchery and carnal obsessiveness are almost worthy of the Austrian genius, von Stroheim, as are the concluding moments when the reformed scoundrel returns home, desperately seeking atonement–very much a compliment to the cinematic sense of morality embraced by the father of motion picture art, D. W. Griffith.

d&w, A. E. Coleby (based on the novel by Hall Caine).

Drama **(PR:A MPAA:NR)**

PRODIGAL WIFE, THE** (1918) 5 reels Screencraft bw

Mary Boland *(Marion Farnham)*, Lucy Cotton *(Marna, Her Daughter)*, Raymond Bloomer *(Dr. Frederick Farnham)*, Alfred Keppler *(Thomas Byrne)*, Harris Gordon *(Dallas Harvey)*, Vincent Coleman *(Victor Middleton)*, Mrs. Stuart Robson *(Mrs. Dovey)*.

Boland gives a splendid performance in this otherwise mediocre film about a woman who leaves her neglectful husband and child, then turns to prostitution when her paramour walks out on her and she is wrongly informed that her daughter is dead. Later Boland encounters her child and reveals the truth about her past in order to prevent the girl from making the kind of mistake which ruined her life.

d, Frank Reicher; w, Eve Unsel (based on the story "Flaming Ramparts" by Edith Barnard Delano); ph, Ira B. Schwartz.

Drama **(PR:C MPAA:NR)**

PROFIT AND THE LOSS** (1917, Brit.) 6 reels ID bw

James Carew *(Dicky Bransome)*, Randle Ayrton *(Jenkins)*, Margaret Halstan, Saba Raleigh.

British drama has a tenant farmer facing the various adversities until finally, when his friends abandon him, the man begins to make money.

d, A.V. Bramble, Eliot Stannard; w, Stannard (based on a play by H. F. Maltby).

Drama **(PR:A MPAA:NR)**

PROFLIGATE, THE** (1917, Brit.) 4 reels Milton/Walturdaw bw

Ben Webster *(Dunstan Renshaw)*, Dorothy Bellew *(Leslie Brundenall)*, Langhorne Burton *(Hugh Murray)*, Cecil Humphreys *(Lord Danvers)*, Amy Brandon Thomas *(Irene Stonehay)*, Geoffrey Kerr *(Wilfred)*, Isabel Jeans *(Janet Preece)*, Fred Volpe *(Mr. Cheal)*, Edith Mellor *(Mrs. Stonehay)*, Isobel Foster *(Miss Grieves)*.

Rather heavy-handed British screen adaptation of the Pinero play set in Italy, about an aristocrat who marries a student from the convent while his brother hires and falls in love with the young woman he earlier seduced.

d&w, Meyrick Milton (based on the play by Arthur Wing Pinero).

Drama **(PR:C MPAA:NR)**

PROHIBITION* (1915) 5 reels Prohibition/Photodrama bw

Thurlow Bergen, David Wall, Charles Trowbridge, Charles Dow Clark, Maude Westbrook.

Produced by various prohibition pressure groups, and featuring a prologue which introduces such anti-drink figures as William Jennings Bryan, Richard Pearse Hobson, and Josephus Daniels, this blatant propaganda film is actually laughable. The featured story has a fellow getting even with the brother who won the love of his sweetheart by slipping alcohol into everything the poor devil consumes. Because drunkenness runs in the family, the lad becomes a roaring dipsomaniacal fiend who kills his tormentor. The picture ends with all of the various characters straightening out their acts and becoming happy soldiers in the war to advocate teetotalism.

w, Hal Reid.

Drama **(PR:C MPAA:NR)**

PROTECTION** (1929) 6 reels FOX bw

Robert Elliott *(Wallace Crockett)*, Paul Page *(Chick Slater)*, Dorothy Burgess *(Myrtle Hines)*, Ben Hewlitt *(James Rollans)*, Dorothy Ward *(Judy Revis)*, Joe Brown *(Joe)*, Roy Stewart *(Ollie Bogardt)*, William H. Tooker *(Harry Lamson)*, Arthur Hoyt *(Society Editor)*.

Acceptable newspaper story has ace reporter Page discovering that certain high city officials are providing protection for the king of the bootleggers. After the influential politicians kill the story, Page quits, joins a smaller, independent outfit, and brings the group to justice with his exposé.

d, Benjamin Stoloff; w, Frederick Hazlitt Brennan (based on a story by J. Clarkson Miller); ph, Joseph Valentine.

Drama/Crime **(PR:A MPAA:NR)**

PROUD FLESH*** (1925) 7 reels MG bw

Eleanor Boardman *(Fernanda)*, Pat O'Malley *(Her Contractor)*, Harrison Ford *(Don Jaime)*, Trixie Friganza *(Mrs. McKee)*, William J. Kelly *(Mr. McKee)*, Rosita Marstini *(Vincente)*, Sojin *(Wong)*, Evelyn Sherman *(Spanish Aunt)*, George Nichols *(Spanish Uncle)*, Margaret Seddon *(Mrs. O'Malley)*, Lillian Elliott *(Mrs. Casey)*, Priscilla Bonner *(San Francisco Girl)*.

Deft direction and acting—especially Ford's marvelous tongue-in-cheek portrayal of a Latin lover—make this sophisticated comedy really work. The story is about an aristocratic San Francisco earthquake survivor, Boardman, who is raised in Spain and then returns to the U.S. where she falls in love with O'Malley, a plumbing contractor. Director Vidor fills the film with his special little touches, including the plumber's mother taking the position that Boardman simply "isn't good enough!" for *her* son. And in the end, in spite of Ford's attempts to woo Boardman back, the couple are ultimately united.

d, King Vidor; w, Harry Behn, Agnes Christine Johnston (based on the novel by Lawrence Rising); ph, John Arnold.

Comedy **(PR:A MPAA:NR)**

PROWLERS OF THE NIGHT* ½ (1926) 5 reels UNIV bw

Fred Humes *(Jack Morton)*, Barbara Kent *(Anita Parsons)*, Slim Cole *(Al Parsons)*, John T. Prince *(George Moulton)*, Joseph Belmont *(Sheriff Brandon)*, Walter Maly *(Bell)*.

Humes, a lesser light in Universal's cowboy stable, is a sheriff wounded by bandits and nursed back to health by Kent, the daughter of their leader. Humes falls madly in love, finds himself torn between duty and emotion, and choses the former. Kent's father is killed in the final shootout but forgives the lawman and becomes his wife.

d, Ernst Laemmle; w, Emil Forst (based on a story by Laemmle); ph, Edward Ulman.

Western **(PR:A MPAA:NR)**

PRUDES FALL, THE** (1924, Brit.) 6 reels Gainsborough/Woolf & Freedman bw

Jane Novak *(Beatrice Audley)*, Julanne Johnson *(Sonia Roubetsky)*, Warwick Ward *(Andre le Briquet)*, Hugh Miller *(Marquis de Rocqueville)*, Gladys Jennings *(Laura Westonry)*, *Miles Mander (Sir Neville Moreton)*, Henry Vibart *(Dean Carey)*, Marie Ault *(Mrs. Masters)*.

Alfred Hitchcock wrote the screen adaption of this play about a French captain who, in order to test the true love of his sweetheart, proposes that she become his mistress.

p, Michael Balcon; d, Graham Cutts; w, Alfred Hitchcock (based on a play by Rudolf Besier, May Edginton).

Romance **(PR:A MPAA:NR)**

PRUNELLA**** (1918) 5 reels PAR bw

Marguerite Clark *(Prunella)*, Jules Raycourt *(Pierrot)*, Harry Leone *(Scarame)*, Marcia Harris, Isabel Berwin, Nora Cecil *(The Aunts)*, William J. Gross, A. Voorhes Wood, Charles Hartley *(The Gardeners)*, Arthur Kennedy, Edward Elkas.

One of Tourneur's most beautiful and poetically conceived motion pictures. It is, in fact, almost the perfect example of what can be accomplished artistically within the controlled environment of the studio. And Clark, who also played Prunella on the stage, is wonderful as the girl who dreams of romance, runs away with a strolling player, has her heart broken, but is happily reunited with him in the end.

d, Maurice Tourneur; w, Charles Maigne (based on a play by Granville Barker, Laurence Housman); ph, John van der Broek; art d, Ben Carre.

Drama **(PR:A MPAA:NR)**

PUPPET CROWN, THE*½ (1915) 5 reels LAS bw

Ina Claire *(Alexia, Princess of Olsa)*, Carlyle Blackwell *(Bob Carewe)*, Christian Lynton *(King Leopold of Olsa)*, Cleo Ridgley *(Duchess Sylvia of Olsa)*, Horace Carpenter *(Count Mallendorf)*, John Abraham *(Marshal Kampf)*, George Gebhardt *(Col. Beauvals)*, Tom Forman *(Lt. Von Mitter)*, Marjorie Daw *(Countess Elsa)*.

Stage star Claire (who would later marry screen idol John Gilbert) is a bit too theatrical in this, one of her few early movie efforts. The picture deals with a European princess who comes to the U.S. to learn the art of Yankee love-making, which she has read about in books. Shortly after this mediocre offering, Claire returned to her successful stage life, but did enjoy a future film career with the advent of talkies.

d, George Melford; w, Harold McGrath, William DeMille.

Drama **(PR:A MPAA:NR)**

PUPPET MAN, THE***

(1921, Brit.) 6 reels B&C/FBO bw (AKA: PUPPETS OF FATE)

Hugh Miller *(Alcide le Beau)*, Molly Adair *(Jenny Rose)*, Hilda Anthony *(Lilla Lotti)*, Marie Belocci *(Little Bimbo)*, Harry Paulo *(Joe)*, Leo Fisher *(Bimbo)*, Johnny Reid *(Bobby)*.

Stark British drama, set in Austria, about a man who is horribly disfigured, becomes a circus puppeteer, and seeks to destroy the love a young girl feels for him. The film was reissued in 1930 as PUPPETS OF FATE.

p, Edward Godal; d, Frank H. Crane; w, (based on the novel by Cosmo Gordon Lennox).

Drama **(PR:C MPAA:NR)**

PUPPETS* (1926) 8 reels Al Rockett/FN bw

Milton Sills *(Nicki)*, Gertrude Olmstead *(Angela)*, Francis McDonald *(Bruno)*, Mathilde Comont *(Rosa)*, Lucien Prival *(Frank)*, William Ricciardi *(Sandro)*, Nick Thompson *(Joe)*.

Poor melodrama has an Italian-American puppeteer (Sills) falling in love with Olmstead, a girl he sees in the audience. Sills goes off to war, loses his hearing, and returns to find his sweetheart engaged to McDonald, his former wardrobe master. There is a badly staged fire sequence in which McDonald proves to be a coward; Sills saves McDonald, however, and as Olmstead redeclares her devotion for him, the delighted puppet master regains his hearing.

d, George Archainbaud; w, John F. Goodrich (based on the play by Frances Lightner); ph, Charles Van Enger; ed, Arthur Tavares; art d, Milton Menasco.

Drama **(PR:A MPAA:NR)**

PUPPETS OF FATE (SEE: PUPPET MAN, THE, 1921, Brit.)

PURE GRIT* (1923) 5 reels UNIV bw

Roy Stewart *(Bob Evans)*, Esther Ralston *(Stella Bolling)*, Jere Austin *(Jim Kemp)*, Jack Mower *(Frank Bolling)*, Verne Winter *(Buddy Clark)*.

Super low-budget picture has Texas Ranger Stewart tracking an escaped convict and posing as Ralston's long lost brother on their way to the Mexican border. There he nails a gang of cattle rustlers and saves the girl from the heavy's libidinous intentions.

d, Nat Ross; w, Isadore Bernstein (based on the novel *The Lone Ranger* by William MacLeod Raine); ph, Ben Kline.

Western **(PR:A MPAA:NR)**

PURPLE CIPHER, THE*** (1920) 5 reels VIT bw

Earle Williams, Vola Vale, Ernest Shields, Allan Forrest, Henry A. Barrows, Goro Kino, Frank Seki, Arthur Redden.

This Williams action movie, set in Chinatown and dealing with a Tong leader's lustful desire for the heroine, has the feeling of those great old serials. The submarine sequence, in which the villains are dispatched to their watery grave, is particularly effective and the film is very well mounted for a programmer.

d, Chester Bennett; w, J. Grubb Alexander (based on a story by Will F. Jenkins): ph, Jack MacKenzie.

Adventure **(PR:A MPAA:NR)**

PURSUING VENGEANCE, THE*** (1916) 5 reels Unity Sales bw

Sheldon Lewis *(Crochard)*, Jane Meredith *(Mimi)*, Henry Mortimer *(Godfrey)*, Henry Cargill *(Lester)*, Grace Hampton *(Countess Simone)*, Ernest Cossar *(Vantine)*, William Frederic *(Simmons)*, Fred Annerly *(Pigot)*, Alfred Hese *(Drouet)*,Emil Hoch *(Morrell)*, John Gray, Margaret Forrest, Margaret Woodburn, Frederick Rogers.

Lots of action, murders, fights, and thrills in this mystery which has Lewis, an "invincible" crook, finally brought to justice by the forces of law and order. Well done on every level and delivers the kind of fun which was so special to the silent serials.

d, Martin Sabine; w, (based on the novel *The Mystery of the Boulle Cabinet* by Burton E. Stevenson).

Mystery **(PR:A MPAA:NR)**

PURSUIT OF PAMELA, THE** (1920, Brit.) 5 reels London/JUR bw

Edna Flugrath *(Pamela Dodder)*, Templar Powell *(Alan Graeme)*, Douglas Munro *(John Dodder)*, Ada Palmer *(Miss Astley)*, Hubert Willis *(Peter Dodder)*, Windham Guise *(Scot McVelie)*, Ma Fue *(Fah Nin)*.

British drama, set in China, has an heiress running away from her husband, then posing as a widow and marrying her paramour, after her servant infects the pursuing husband with a rare disease.

d, Harold Shaw; w, Bannister Merwin (based on a play by C. B. Fernald).

Drama **(PR:C MPAA:NR)**

PURSUIT OF THE PHANTOM, THE* (1914) 5 reels BOSWORTH bw

Hobart Bosworth, Courtenay Foote.

Bosworth wrote, directed, and starred in this poor offering about a father's conflict with his son, who has fallen in love with the daughter of the woman the father once loved and lost. It's all very melodramatic—and very, very tedious.

d&w, Hobart Bosworth.

Drama **(PR:A MPAA:NR)**

PUTTING IT OVER*** (1919) 5 reels PAR bw

Bryant Washburn *(Buddy Marsh)*, Shirley Mason *(Mary)*, Winnifred Greenwood *(Jane Pelly)*, Adele Farrington *(Mrs. Pelly)*, Clarence Geldart *(Mr. Hard)*, Edward Alexander *(George Montagu)*, Robert Dunbar, Guy Oliver, Casson Ferguson, Edna Mae Cooper.

Washburn plays a $12-a-week soda clerk who meets and falls in love with Mason at the Drug Clerks' Ball. He tries to give her the impression that he's a big shot, but being wise to him (and also in love) she secretly takes a job so they can afford to marry. Washburn is about to be fired when he learns what Mason has done, and this gives him the moxie to present his big money-making scheme to his boss. It turns out to be a success, and he's rewarded with an executive position.

d, Donald Crisp; w, Marion Fairfax (based on the story "The Village Cut-Up" by George Weston).

Comedy **(PR:A MPAA:NR)**

PUTTING IT OVER½** (1922) 5 reels Phil Goldstone bw

Richard Talmadge *(Bob Merritt)*, Doris Pawn *(Barbara Norton)*, Thomas Ricketts *(Arnold Norton)*, Harry Van Meter *(Mark Durkham)*, Henry Barrows *(James Merritt)*, Victor Metzetti *(Tate Busby)*, William Horne *(George Norton)*, Earl Schaeffer *("Porky" Donovan)*, Andrew Waldron *(Lem Kendall)*.

Phil Goldstone pinched his pennies in the production of this Talmadge movie in which the actor plays the son of a political leader. Talmadge switches sides when he realizes that not only has he fallen in love with Pawn, the daughter of the man his dad selected him to run against, but that his father's camp has been using some "dirty tricks." There are the usual breathtaking acrobatics expected of Talmadge, as well as decent comic touches. And in spite of the many shortcomings usually found in a Goldstone motion picture, the whole thing is still great fun because of the presence of its irrepressible star.

d&w, Grover Jones.

Comedy/Adventure **(PR:A MPAA:NR)**

QUALIFIED ADVENTURER, THE** ½** (1925, Brit.) 7 reels STOLL bw

Matheson Lang *(Peter Duff)*, Genevieve Townsend *(Jimmy Fellowes)*, Fred Raynham *(Northcote)*, Kyoshi Tekase *(Yen San)*, Cameron Carr *(Weames)*, Nelson Ramsey *(McNab)*, Moore Marriott *(Bosun)*, Windham Guise *(Capt. Fellowes)*, Dave O'Toole *(Evans)*.

In this British adventure film, set in the South Seas, a dashing author puts down a mutiny involving a gang of cutthroats with the help of a Chinese cook, who turns out in the end to actually be a Manchurian prince.

d&w, Sinclair Hill (based on a novel by Selwyn Jepson).

Adventure (PR:A MPAA:NR)

QUALITY STREET****** (1927) 8 reels COS/MGM bw

Marion Davies *(Phoebe Throssel)*, Conrad Nagel *(Dr. Valentine Brown)*, Helen Jerome Eddy *(Susan Throssel)*, Flora Finch *(Mary Willoughby)*, Margaret Seddon *(Nancy Willoughby)*, Marcelle Corday *(Henrietta Turnbull)*, Kate Price *(Patty)*.

Davies is very good as the spinster who passes herself off as her own niece because she's afraid her suitor will think her old after returning from a 10-year absence in the military. There are many very funny bits of business in this delightfully filmed version of the Barrie play. Of course the picture ends with the officer (nicely played by Nagel) loving Davies for herself.

d, Sidney Franklin; w, Hans Kraly, Albert Lewin (based on the play by James M. Barrie); t, Marian Ainslee, Ruth Cummings; ph, Hendrik Sartov; ed, Ben Lewis; set d, Cedric Gibbons, Allen Ruoff.

Comedy/Drama (PR:A MPAA:NR)

QUARTERBACK, THE***** (1926) 8 reels FP/PAR bw

Richard Dix *(Jack Stone)*, Esther Ralston *(Louise Mason)*, Harry Beresford *(Elmer Stone)*, David Butler *("Lumpy" Goggins)*, Robert Craig *(Denny Walters)*, Mona Palma *(Nellie Webster)*.

Intelligent football comedy rings true thanks to fine performances by Dix and Ralston, plus a supporting company without that "Hollywood" look, and sensitive direction on the part of Newmeyer. Beresford plays the captain of the 1899 Colton College pigskin squad who vows to remain on until his team defeats its arch rival, State University. He does so—even after his wife's death—but his son Dix follows in his footsteps and completes the deed. There are some wonderfully executed comedic moments, as well as a touching love story and some great gridiron action.

p, Ralph Block; d, Fred Newmeyer; football sup, Fielding "Hurry Up" Yost; w, Ray Harris (based on a story by William Slavens McNutt, William O. McGeehan; ph, Edward Cronjager.

Comedy/Romance (PR:A MPAA:NR)

QUEEN ELIZABETH**** (1912, Fr.) 3 reels Film d'Art/FP bw

Sarah Bernhardt *(Elizabeth)*, Lou Tellegen *(Essex)*, Members of the Comedie Francaise.

QUEEN ELIZABETH has long been thought of as the feature film which launched Adolph Zukor's Famous Players company when he began showcasing the film in America in 1912. Actually it is only a three-reeler and the mogul falsely advertised it as being four reels in length. It was, however, indeed responsible for the birth of Paramount, as well as the acceptance of longer films (along with Italian imports) in the U.S. And because it featured the divine Sarah Bernhardt in an adaptation of her popular play, other theatrical stars such as James O'Neill, Minnie Maddern Fiske, James Hackett, and Lily Langtry were encouraged to drop their prejudices against the "flickers" and allow themselves to be recorded for the ages.

p, Louis Mercanton; d, Mercanton, Henri Desfontaines.

Drama Cas. (PR:A MPAA:NR)

QUEEN KELLY*** ½** (1929) 8 reels Gloria Productions/UA bw

Gloria Swanson *(Queen Kelly, an Orphan)*, Walter Byron *(Prince "Wild" Wolfram von Hohenberg Falsenstein)*, Seena Owen *(Queen Regina, His Cousin and Fiancee)*, Wilhelm von Brincken *(Prince's Adjutant)*, Madge Hunt *(Mother Superior)*, Wilson Benge *(Valet)*, Sidney Bracey *(Prince Wolfram's Valet)*, Lucille van Lent *(Maid to Prince Wolfram)*, Ann Morgan *(Nun)*, Tully Marshall *(Jan Bloehm Vryheid)*, Florence Gibson *(Kelly's Aunt)*, Mme. Sul Te Wan *(Kali)*, Ray Gaggett *(Coughdrops)*, Sylvia Ashton *(Kelly's Aunt)*.

When Gloria Swanson left Paramount to form her own production company (releasing her product through United Artists) her first film was pretty much a flop. Then, quite daringly, she elected to change her whole screen persona, and made the realistic and saucy SADIE THOMPSON. That picture was a smash and encouraged her to continue experimenting with the off-beat. The actress had in the meantime discovered that the business end of independence was not to her liking, so she brought in as her associate an easterner with administrative skills, Joseph P. Kennedy, who was doing very well producing programmers and westerns. Without getting into their personal lives, of which enough has been written, it should be pointed out that Kennedy had ambitions to produce films of real quality, and was interested in placing Swanson in a picture he felt would endure throughout the ages. Enter Erich von Stroheim—the Teutonic genius had just experienced a falling out with Paramount, as he had done earlier with Universal and MGM. But his latest film, THE WEDDING MARCH, was being highly acclaimed before its release, so Kennedy arranged a meeting with the Austrian, Miss Swanson, and himself. The director overwhelmed them as he acted out his latest creation, a film he swore he had written just for her, called THE SWAMP. Kennedy, who by now was also managing the star, began to think of the project as his own, and went about securing Stroheim's release from Pat Powers, with whom the director was under contract. The Austrian wasted little time, however, in getting things going by using a surrogate, Wilhelm von Brinken (a Stroheim clone, best remembered for his overacted role of Von Richter in HELL'S ANGELS) to research costumes and hire a number of authentic cavalrymen. Then, when the director was free of his contractual obligations and after the usual numerous delays which accompanied any von Stroheim production, the picture finally got under way. There seems to have been bitter arguments between the director and star from the beginning, and the picture was stopped and started on a number of occasions. To further exacerbate matters, Kennedy completely lost interest in the whole matter, became involved in the creation of RKO, and handed the supervision of QUEEN KELLY (as it had now become known) to William Le Baron and Benjamin Glazer, who pretty much left von Stroheim to his own devices. The story has Kitty Kelly (Swanson) an American girl attending a European convent school, making the acquaintance of Prince Wolfram (Byron) while she and her classmates are walking along a country lane and her pantaloons fall down—just as the prince and his men ride by. The nobleman is quite taken by her and she with him, but when she returns to the convent the mother superior orders her to go without dinner and pray for forgiveness. She does pray, but it's to see the prince again. Meanwhile, Wolfram is attending a dinner thrown by the queen (sadistically played by Owen) and he is horrified by her announcement that they will be married the following day. Determined to have one last night of pleasure, the prince goes to the convent, lights a harmless fire to cause a diversion, and steals Miss Swanson away in the turmoil. They return to his apartment, where a romantic candlelit dinner is prepared. Swanson's innocence is about to be stripped away when the scene changes to Owen who is bathing in a great sunken tub. She arises, and, naked except for a white cat which she strategically clutches to her bosom, puts on a robe and wanders over to the rooms occupied by her fiance. Finding him with Swanson, she grabs one of the whips in her collection and begins to flail the startled girl down the length of the palace. Swanson cries out in a title card, "He's going to marry you?" Then the reply, "No—I'm going to marry him." Swanson, humiliated and repentent, makes her way to a bridge, where she begs the forgiveness of God and commits suicide by jumping in the river. In Stroheim's original conception she would be saved and would return to the convent where she would receive a telegram from her dying aunt and benefactor summoning her to journey to East Africa. Swanson would go there, only to discover that the old lady is the proprietor of a loathesome brothel. Before long, she would be forced to marry a degenerate, crippled millionaire (played, as he did in THE MERRY WIDOW, by Tully Marshall) and the wedding would take place in the whorehouse, with the aunt on her death bed, while a black priest reads the vows in the presence of the collected prostitutes who make up the bridal party. To cap off the story, Stroheim planned to have the prince stationed in Africa where he rekindles his love for Kitty. *Her* husband was to die, *his* wife was to do the same, and the prince was to return to Europe and assume his throne on the condition that Swanson could accompany him to become his real life queen Kelly. Only a few of the African scenes were actually shot, and the movie star-producer reached the end of her rope, when during the marriage sequence a large quantity of Marshall's tobacco-drenched spittle dripped on her hand. Swanson blew her top and when Marshall told her that he was following von Stroheim's instructions, she was on the phone to Kennedy, demanding that the "madman" be fired. A number of attempts were made to save the picture, which included adding some dialog and musical numbers. And thought was even given to turning the picture into a kind of operetta (Miss Swanson possessed a fine singing voice) but all of this came to naught. In 1931, however, Swanson hired Gregg Toland to shoot some additional footage which has the prince going to the convent where Kitty Kelly's drowned body was laid out, and committing suicide himself. There was now a finished version of the picture, but the advent of the talkies made it impossible to market it except in Europe, where it was released in 1932 to generally favorable reviews. In 1985 a "restored" version, using stills to fill in the narrative gaps, was brought out, and in spite of the obvious limitations even this version possesses the result is nonetheless a fascinating cinematic experience.

p, Joseph P. Kennedy; d&w, Erich von Stroheim; t, Marian Ainslee; ph, Paul Ivano, Gordon Pollock, Ben Reynolds, additional ph, Gregg Toland; m, Adolf Tandler; ed, Viola Lawrence; art d, Robert Day, Stroheim, Harold Miles; cos, Max Ree.

Drama Cas. (PR:A MPAA:NR)

QUEEN MOTHER, THE* ½** (1916, Brit.) 5 reels CL bw

Owen Roughwood *(The Duke)*, Gladys Mason *(Princess of Saxonia)*, Barbara Rutland *(Duchess Miramar)*, Sydney Lewis Ransome *(Prince Ludwig)*, Ronald Hammond *(Osric)*, M. Mills *(King of Montania)*.

Ruritanian adventure has an endangered queen being saved by her dashing ex-lover from the villainous prince who murdered her father, and seeks the power of the throne.

d, Wilfred Noy; w, (based on the play by J. A. Campbell).

Adventure (PR:A MPAA:NR)

QUEEN O' DIAMONDS**** (1926) 6 reels R-C/FBO bw

Evelyn Brent *(Jeanette Durant/Jerry Lyon)*, Elsa Lorimer *(Mrs. Ramsey)*, Phillips Smalley *(Mr. Ramsey)*, William N. Bailey *(LeRoy Phillips)*, Theodore von Eltz *(Daniel Hammon)*.

Before starring in Josef von Sternberg's UNDERWORLD and LAST COMMAND, Brent made this programmer about a chorus girl who passes herself off as a lookalike Broadway actress, becomes involved with a gang of crooks led by the real star's husband, and is suspected of murder before proving herself innocent.

d, Chet Withey; w, Fred Myton; Roy Klaffki.

Crime (PR:A MPAA:NR)

QUEEN OF MY HEART** (1917, Brit.) 5 reels CL/Globe bw

Hayden Coffin *(The Singer)*, Christine Rayner *(Dorothy Lethridge)*, Charles Vane *(Joseph Hawks)*, Alfred Lugg *(Jack Lethridge)*, Jack Wilcocks *(Mr. Lethridge)*.

British mystery has a really low-life criminal framing his cousin for a crime *he* committed and then seducing the poor fellow's wife.

d, Albert Ward; w, Reuben Gillmer (based on a story by Hetty Langford Reed).

Mystery (PR:C MPAA:NR)

QUEEN OF SHEBA, THE*** (1921) 9 reels FOX bw

Betty Blythe *(Queen of Sheba)*, Fritz Leiber *(King Solomon)*, Claire De Lorez *(Queen Amrath, Wife of Solomon)*, George Siegmann *(King Armud of Sheba)*, Herbert Heyes *(Tamaran, Courtier of Sheba)*, Herschel Mayall *(Menton, Sheba's Minister of State)*, G. Raymond Nye *(Adonijah, Brother of Solomon)*, George Nichols *(King David)*, Genevieve Blinn *(Beth-Sheba)*, Pat Moore *(Sheba's Son, Aged 4)*, Joan Gordon *(Nomis, Sheba's Sister)*, William Hardy *(Olos, Sheba's Giant Slave)*, Paul Cazeneuve *(The Envoy of the Pharaoh)*, John Cosgrove *(King of Tyre)*, Nell Craig *(The Princess of Vashti)*, Al Fremont *(A Captain of Adonijah's Army)*, Earl Crain *(Joab, a Soldier)*.

Tom Mix directed the spectacular chariot race, which is just one of the outstanding sequences in this big-budgeted film inspired by the legendary Queen of Sheba. There are also some beautifully staged battles as the forces of Solomon clash with those of the jealous Adonijah.

d, J. Gordon Edwards (chariot race directed by Tom Mix); w, Virginia Tracy; ph, John W. Boyle.

Historical Drama (PR:C MPAA:NR)

QUEEN OF THE WICKED** (1916, Brit.) 6 reels British Empire bw

Henry Lonsdale *(Lucien La Verne)*, Nina Lynn *(Ligeah Dupont)*, Janet Alexander *(Lady Doris Manners)*.

In this British mystery a one-time dancer drugs and strangles her husband, cleans out the safe, and frames a lord for the whole affair.

d&w, Albert Ward (based on a play by Ronald Grahame).

Mystery (PR:A MPAA:NR)

QUEENIE** (1921) 6 reels FOX bw

Shirley Mason *(Queenie Gurkin)*, George O'Hara *(Vivian Van Winkle)*, Wilson Hummell *(Simon Pepper/Abner Quigley)*, Aggie Herring *(Pansy Pooley)*, Lydia Titus *(Mrs. Mulliken)*, Adolphe Menjou *(Count Michael)*, Clarissa Selwynne *(Mrs. Torrence)*, Pal the Dog.

Below-average melodrama has Mason leaving her girl's school to work as a domestic, and after surviving an attempt to steal her reclusive employer's fortune, marries O'Hara, a wealthy young fellow with ambitions to be a poet.

d, Howard M. Mitchell; w, Dorothy Yost (based on the novel by Wilbur Finley Fauley); ph, George Schneiderman.

Drama (PR:A MPAA:NR)

QUEEN'S EVIDENCE** (1919, Brit.) 5 reels B&C/Moss bw

Godfrey Tearle *(Adam Pascall)*, Unity More *(Eve Pascall)*, Janet Alexander *(Joan Hocking)*, Lauderdale Maitland *(Jerrem)*, Edward Sorley *(Jonathan)*, Bruce Winston *(Job)*, Pardoe Woodman *(Reuben May)*, Ada King.

British movie of smuggling and sibling rivalry has a criminal blaming his brother when his real enemy alerts the coast guard to his whereabouts.

p, Edward Godal; d, James McKay; w, George Edwardes Hall (based on the play "Adam and Eve" by Louisa Parr, C. E. Munro).

Adventure (PR:A MPAA:NR)

QUEST OF LIFE, THE* (1916) 5 reels FP bw

Maurice Walton *(Maurice Bretton)*, Florence Walton *(Ellen Young)*, Julien L'Estrange *(Alec Mapleton)*, Royal Byron *(Percy)*, Daniel Burke *(Baronti)*, Russell Bassett *(Ellen's Father)*, Mrs. William Betchel *(Ellen's Mother)*, Robert Brower.

Poorly produced and somewhat morbid film, featuring the popular dance team of Maurice and Florence Walton, has the latter leaving her job in a butcher shop and going into show business by forming an act with Maurice. Before long Florence is told by her doctor that she has only one year to live, so they put together a little act called "The Dance of Death." The couple are a sensation, and when Florence becomes smitten by a stagedoor-Johnnie, a somewhat miffed Maurice carts her off to a sanitarium where the prescription for good health is hope. Of course the young lady is cured, and when the time comes to choose between the playboy and her partner, Florence decides to dance, dance, DANCE!

d, Ashley Miller; w, (based on the play "Ellen Young" by Edmund Goulding and Gabriel Enthoven).

Drama (PR:A MPAA:NR)

QUESTION, THE½** (1916) 5 reels EQ/WORLD bw

Marguerite Leslie *(Grace Hamilton)*, Marie Benton *(Mrs. Hamilton)*, Lorell Gibson *(Mrs. Ray)*, Louise Evans *(Mrs. Hildred)*, Clara Whipple *(Anna Lee)*, George Anderson *(Ralph Tudor)*, Bernard Randall *(Eric Lee)*.

Interesting film dealing with the sensitive subject of abortion has a society wife refusing to sacrifice the season by having a baby and paying a doctor $500 to terminate her pregnancy. This drives the husband to drink and into an affair with his pretty little stenographer, who is soon carrying his child. Her boss, who is sailing for Brazil, instructs his clerk to deposit $2,000 in her account. On his way to deliver the funds, however, the fellow is robbed and killed, and the young woman dies giving birth. Later the guilt-ridden wife adopts the child, and a note revealing the infant's true parentage provides the film with a strained, but none-the-less happy, ending.

d, Harry Handworth; w, Roy L. McCardell.

Drama (PR:C MPAA:NR)

QUESTION OF HONOR, A** (1922) 7 reels Anita Stewart/AFN bw

Anita Stewart *(Anne Wilmot)*, Edward Hearn *(Bill Shannon)*, Arthur Stuart Hull *(Leon Morse)*, Walt Whitman *(Sheb)*, Bert Sprotte *(Charles Burkthaler)*, Frank Beal *(Stephen Douglas)*, Adele Farrington *(Mrs. Katherine Wilmot)*, Mary Land *(Mrs. Elton, Morse's Sister)*, Ed Brady *(John Bretton)*, Doc Bytell *(Parsons)*.

Hull comes to the Sierras with his fiancee, Stewart, to try and con engineer Hearn into turning the property for a dam he's constructing over to his railroad interests. During the course of the movie Stewart falls for Hearn and prevents his project from being dynamited at the last second. Of course Hearn sees to it that Hull gets what's coming to him, and his men save Stewart from being buried alive. Only a fair programmer at best.

d, Edwin Carewe; w, Josephine Quirk (based on the story by Ruth Cross); ph, Robert B. Kurrle; set d, William Darling.

Adventure (PR:A MPAA:NR)

QUESTION OF TRUST, A** (1920, Brit.) 5 reels STOLL bw

Madge Stuart *(Stephanie)*, Harvey Braban *(Pierre Dumaresque)*, Teddy Arundell *(Jouvain)*, C. H. Croker-King *(Governor of Maritas)*, Kitty Fielder *(Anita)*.

British adventure set in one of those comic-opera kingdoms has an aristocratic rebel saving the beautiful daughter of the governor from his fellow revolutionists and making a woman of her aboard his ship.

d, Maurice Elvey; w, Sinclair Hill (based on a novel by Ethel M. Dell).

Adventure/Romance (PR:A MPAA:NR)

QUICKER'N LIGHTNIN'** (1925) 5 reels Action/Weiss Brothers-Artclass bw

Buffalo Bill, Jr. *(Quicker'n Lightnin')*, B. F. Blinn *(John Harlow)*, Dorothy Dorr *(Helen Harlow)*, Harry Todd *(Al McNutt)*, J. Gordon Russell *(Mowii)*, Raye Hampton *(Squaw)*, Lucille Young *(Morella)*, Charles Roberts *(Truxillo)*.

Buffalo Bill, Jr. is given plenty of opportunity to show off his riding and fighting skills in this western about a cowboy who saves a girl whose father was murdered by Indians from becoming a victim of a human sacrifice.

d, Richard Thorpe; w, Betty Burbridge (based on a story by Reginald C. Barker).

Western (PR:A MPAA:NR)

QUICKSANDS*** (1918) 5 reels PAR bw

Dorothy Dalton *(Mary Bowen)*, Ed Coxen *(Jim Bowen)*, Philo McCullough *(Allan Perry)*, Henry A. Barrows *(John Boland)*, Frankie Lee *(Frankie Bowen)*.

When Dalton's husband is wrongly convicted of forgery, she becomes a nightclub singer and plays the two men who can prove his innocence against one another. This results in her husband's exoneration and the imprisonment of the real crook.

d, Victor Schertzinger; sup, Thomas H. Ince; w, R. Cecil Smith, J. G. Hawks (based on a story by John Lynch); ph, John Stumar.

Drama (PR:A MPAA:NR)

QUO VADIS?*** (1913, Ital.) 8 reels Cines/Kleine bw

Amleto Novelli, Gustavo Serena, Lea Gunghi, Amelia Cattaneo, Bruto Castellani, Giovanni Gizzi, Leo Orlandini, Mrs. O Brandini.

The landmark Italian historical spectacle that sparked a revolution in the movie business. Closely following Nobel Prize-winning author Sienkiewicz's world-famous novel, the film details the rise and fall of the decadent Roman emperor, Nero, in the first century A.D. The lustful emperor covets the body of the fair Christian maiden Lygia. The lecherous lyre player strums madly as two-thirds of Rome goes up in flames, blaming the tragedy on the Christian consorts of Paul, who are sacrificed to ravenous lions in the Circus Maximus arena. At the picture's climax, the beauteous Lygia is lashed to the back of a raging bull, to be saved by the neck-twisting giant, Castellani. Divided into three acts, the picture was a product of a burgeoning independent Italian industry schooled in the popular open-air live theatrical spectacles native to the country. Italy's Cines company had already made a name for itself with briefer pictures based on history; with three open-air studios (the Rome facility comprised 128,000 square feet), and with a fine group of set designers and technicians, the company was well equipped to make this marvelous movie which played for more than two hours. Entrepreneur George Kleine acquired the American distribution rights to this first real feature film to be screened in the U.S. at a time when the movies were one- and two-reelers, playing in arcades at a going rate of 15 cents per ticket. QUO VADIS? opened at a "legitimate" theater—the Astor, in New York City—with a price 10 times as high as the cinema-going public was accustomed to pay. A huge success, the picture played in major theaters all over the country. By the end of June, Kleine had 22 road companies covering the U.S. and Canada screening prints of the picture, which earned $150,000 in North America alone. The success of the film was said to have been the catalyst behind the decision of D. W. Griffith to make the first American historical epic, JUDITH OF BETHULIA, (Griffith claimed not to have seen this Continental precursor of his great works, but actress Blanche Sweet, in a conversation with film historian Kevin Brownlow, said that she and Griffith had seen the picture together.) America was not the only land of opportunity for the Italian filmmakers; QUO VADIS? was screened successfully at London's 20,000-seat Albert Hall, and King George V and Queen Mary were reported to have enjoyed it immensely. Promoters in the different countries in which it played made independent arrangements for musical accompaniment for the film. At the New York premiere, composer Frank Byng's score was rendered by means of a huge pipe organ which had been especially installed for the purpose, replacing the conventional orchestra in the Astor Theatre. The French promoters were even more musically ambitious; the score they commissioned from composer Jean Nogues reportedly called for a 150-voice massed choir. Critics of the time praised not only the massive, historically accurate sets and the well-choreographed crowd scenes, but also the acting. (One nationalistic American critic averred that he recognized at least one experienced U.S. film actress on the screen.) The picture was originally to have been helmed by director Mario Caserini, who had already achieved some fame with his earlier THE THREE MUSKETEERS for the same studio, but Caserini resigned and was replaced by Guazzoni. Truly a trust-busting project, this is the picture that sounded the death knell for the titans of the time, the studios that chose to remain with one- and two-reelers such as American Biograph, and opened the way to the type of cinema we know today. The picture was remade by the same studio (released in the U.S. in 1925) with an international cast that included Emil Jannings.

d&w, Enrico Guazzoni (based on the novel by Henryk Sienkiewicz).

Historical Epic **(PR:A MPAA:NR)**

RACE, THE* (1916) 5 reels LAS bw

Robert Bradbury *(James Grayson, Sr.)*, Victor Moore *(Grayson, Jr.)*, William Dale *(Andrew Van Dyke)*, Anita King *(Grace Van Dyke)*, Mrs. Lewis McCord *(Mrs. Jefferson)*, Ernest Joy *(Mr. Anderson)*, Horace B. Carpenter *(Mechanic)*, Jane Wolf, Jimmy Carter.

There are enough directorial errors in this uninspired effort to make up a blooper reel. It all has to do with the disinherited son of a millionaire who takes a job as a chauffeur, meets a female conterpart, and then wins the big cross-country race, which returns him into favor and keeps his sweetheart's father from going to prison. Among the picture's other shortcomings is the unfortunate miscasting of the gifted Moore.

d, George Melford; w, Hector Turnbull, Clinton H. Stagg.

Comedy/Drama **(PR:A MPAA:NR)**

RACING FOR LIFE** (1924) 5 reels COL/C.B.C. bw

Eva Novak *(Grace Danton)*, William Fairbanks *(Jack Grant)*, Philo McCullough *(Carl Grant)*, Wilfred Lucas *(Hudford)*, Ralph De Palma *(The Champion)*, Lydia Knott *(Mrs. Grant)*, Frankie Darro *(Jimmy Danton)*, Edwin Booth Tilton *(David Danton)*, Frank Whitson *(Hudford's Partner)*, Harley Moore *(Murray)*, Larry La Verne *(Diggett)*, George Atkinson *(Jackson Heath)*, Paul J. Derkum *(Race Starter)*, Ed Kennedy *(Tom Grady)*.

Novak's sweetheart, Fairbanks, agrees to drive her father's car in the big race if the old man promises not to press charges against his brother for stealing company cash. Before the day of the contest, however, Fairbanks is kidnaped by his brother, but manages to escape and reach the track just in time to score a victory—and the hand of Dalton.

d, Henry MacRae; w, Wildred Lucas; ph, Allan Thompson.

Adventure **(PR:A MPAA:NR)**

RACING HEARTS*** (1923) 6 reels FP/PAR bw

Agnes Ayres *(Virginia Kent)*, Richard Dix *(Roddy Smith)*, Theodore Roberts *(John Kent)*, Robert Cain *(Fred Claxton)*, Warren Rogers *(Jimmy Britt)*, J. Farrell MacDonald *(Silas Martin)*, Edwin J. Brady *(Pete Delaney)*, Fred J. Butler *(Burton Smith)*, Robert Brower *(Horatio Whipple)*, Kalla Pasha *(Mechanic)*, James A. Murphy, Johnny Wonderlich, Eddie Hefferman *(Racing Drivers)*.

Ayres' father, the owner of an automobile manufacturing company, refuses to advertise, so when the old boy is in Europe she has a race car built as a publicity stunt. Meanwhile, Dix, the son of a rival manufacturer, infiltrates the operation and falls in love with Ayres. When the big race arrives there is the usual plot to prevent Ayres (who is driving the car with her company's colors) from winning, but a nudge from Dix in the car behind bumps her over the finishing line first, and the picture ends with a merger between the competitors through marriage.

d, Paul Powell; w, Will M. Ritchey (based on a story by Bryon Morgan); ph, Bert Baldridge.

Comedy/Adventure **(PR:A MPAA:NR)**

RACING ROMANCE** (1926) 5 reels Harry J. Brown/RAY bw

Reed Howes, Virginia Brown Faire, Harry S. Northrup, Mathilda Brundage, Victor Potel, Ethan Laidlaw.

It's the same old story—save the Kentucky homestead from the clutches of a ruthless mortgage holder. Only this time the hero returns from the north, escapes a criminal frame-up, and saves the day by riding the family pride to victory in the big race.

d, Harry J. Brown; w, Henry Roberts Symonds; ph, William Tuers.

Drama **(PR:A MPAA:NR)**

RACING ROMEO 1/2** (1927) 7 reels R-C/FBO bw

Harold "Red" Grange *(Red Walden)*, Jobyna Ralston *(Sally)*, Trixie Friganza *(Aunt Hattie)*, Walter Hiers *(Sparks)*, Ben Hendricks, Jr. *(Rube Oldham)*, Warren Rogers *(Silas, the Chauffeur)*, Ashton Dearholt *(Movie Director)*, Jerry Zier *(Movie Star)*.

Football star Red Grange delivers a credible performance in his second feature film. This time he's a young mechanic with a weakness for auto racing who, of course, wins the big competition and the pretty girl, played by Ralston. Some exciting action footage and more than a few laughs keep this one speeding right along.

d, Sam Wood; w, Byron Morgan; ph, Charles G. Clarke.

Adventure/Comedy **(PR:A MPAA:NR)**

RACKET, THE* 1/2** (1928) 8 reels Caddo/PAR bw

Thomas Meighan *(Capt. McQuigg)*, Marie Prevost *(Helen Hayes, an Entertainer)*, Louis Wolheim *(Nick Scarsi)*, George Stone *(His Brother)*, John Darrow *(Ames, Cub Reporter)*, Skeets Gallagher *(Miller, a Reporter)*, Lee Moran *(Pratt, a Reporter)*, Lucien Prival *(Chick, a Gangster)*, Tony Marlo *(Chick's Chauffeur)*, Henry Sedly *(Corcan, a Bootlegger)*, Sam De Grasse *(District Attorney)*, Burr McIntosh *("The Old Man")*, G. Pat Collins *(Johnson, a Patrolman)*.

Terrific gangster movie with all the classic touches—the clatter of tommyguns, the roar of bootleg liquor trucks, and crooked politicians practicing their power. In the end the gang leader (wonderfully played by Wolheim) is riddled by bullets after murdering a patrolman. This was one of the earliest films in which a young Howard Hughes invested his money and talents as a producer. The film was based on a play about author Bartlett Cormack's real life experiences as a Chicago newspaperman, and gave such a harsh portrayal of that town's criminal and corrupt political element that it was banned there as a play and ran into censorship difficulties as a film.

p, Howard Hughes; d, Lewis Milestone; w, Harry Behn, Del Andrews, Bartlett Cormack (based on the play by Cormack); t, Eddie Adams; ph, Tony Gaudio; ed, Tom Miranda.

Crime **(PR:A MPAA:NR)**

RAFFLES, THE AMATEUR CRACKSMAN 1/2** (1925) 6 reels UNIV bw

House Peters *(Raffles)*, Miss Du Pont *(Gwendolyn Amersteth)*, Hedda Hopper *(Mrs. Clarice Vidal)*, Frederick Esmelton *(Capt. Bedford)*, Walter Long *(Crawshay)*, Winter Hall *(Lord Amersteth)*, Kate Lester *(Lady Amersteth)*, Freeman Wood *(Bunny Manners)*, Rolland Bottomley *(Lord Crowley)*, Lillian Langdon *(Mrs. Tilliston)*, Robert Bolder *(Mr. Tilliston)*.

Here the further adventures of Raffles has the society thief embarrassing a noted British criminologist by stealing (and later returning) a certain string of pearls he boasted was beyond reach, escaping a plot to nab him, and sailing for the U.S. with the lovely Du Pont, whom he takes to be his bride. Excessive titles, a mediocre performance by Du Pont, and overpadding prevent this film from being really topnotch.

d, King Baggot; w, Harvey Thew (based on the play "Raffles; Further Adventures of the Amateur Cracksman" by Ernest William Hornung); ph, Charles Stumar.

Crime/Drama **(PR:A MPAA:NR)**

RAG MAN, THE*** (1925) 6 reels MG bw

Jackie Coogan *(Tim Kelly)*, Max Davidson *(Max Ginsberg)*, Lydia Yeamans Titus *(Mrs. Mallory)*, Robert Edeson *(Mr. Bernard)*, William Conklin *(Mr. Kemper)*, Dynamite the Horse.

When his orphanage burns down, little Timothy Michael Patrick Aloysius Kelly (Coogan) is taken in by kindly Jewish junk dealer Davidson. The kid is taught all the tricks of the trade, becomes an incredible little businessman, and eventually wins back the patent (worth a fortune) which his mentor had stolen from him. The picture ends delightfully with the partners—now New York's most prominent antique brokers—playing golf at their country club. Coogan is just about to make a shot when someone behind him shouts "Fore," to which the kid responds, "Not a penny more than $3.98!"

d, Eddie Cline; sup, Jackie Coogan, Sr.; w, Willard Mack; ph, Frank Good, Robert Martin; ed, Irene Morra.

Comedy **(PR:A MPAA:NR)**

RAGE OF PARIS, THE** (1921) 5 reels UNIV bw

Miss Du Pont *(Joan Coolidge)*, Elinor Hancock *(Mrs. Coolidge)*, Jack Perrin *(Gordon Talbut)*, Leo White *(Jean Marot)*, Ramsey Wallace *(Mortimer Handley)*, Freeman Wood *(Jimmy Allen)*, Eve Southern *(Mignonne Le Place)*, Mathilde Brundage *(Mme. Courtigny)*, J. J. Lanoe *(Mons. Dubet)*.

DuPont, whose first name was Patricia, made her film debut in this modest programmer about a young woman who escapes the abusive husband she was forced to marry and runs away to Europe, where her talent for dancing makes her the rage of Paris. When her former sweetheart tracks her down through a portrait she posed for, the couple journey to Arabia where he works as a civil engineer. The husband locates her whereabouts and follows on the next boat, but before he can destroy their happiness a sandstorm causes his death.

d, Jack Conway; w, Lucien Hubbard (based on the story "The White Peacock Feathers" by Du Vernet Rabell); ph, Harry Vallejo.

Drama **(PR:A MPAA:NR)**

RAGGED EDGE, THE*** (1923) 7 reels DIST/Goldwyn-COS bw

Alfred Lunt *(Howard Spurlock)*, Mimi Palmeri *(Ruth Endicott)*, Charles Fang *(Ah Cum)*, Wallace Erskine *(The Doctor)*, George MacQuarrie *(McClintock)*, Charles Slattery *(O'Higgins)*, Christian Frank *(The Wastrel)*, Grace Griswold *(Prudence Jedson)*, Alice May *(Angelina Jedson)*, Percy Carr *(Hotel Manager)*, Marie Day *(The Aunt)*, Charles Kent *(Rev. Luther Enschede)*, Sidney Drew *(Rev. Dalby)*, Hattie Delaro *(Mrs. Dalby)*.

Agreeable drama with some nice comedy touches has Lunt, a young society fellow, escaping to China because he wrongly believes he committed a crime. In the Orient, after a number of adventures, he meets and falls in love with Palmeri, the daughter of a missionary, and together they journey to the South Seas. When a detective hired by his friends in the U.S. shows up to tell him that he has been exonerated of the deed which instigated his flight, Lunt finally feels worthy to marry his sweetheart—and does.

d, Harmon Weight; w, Forrest Halsey (based on the novel by Harold MacGrath).

Drama **(PR:A MPAA:NR)**

RAGGED HEIRESS, THE* 1/2 (1922) 5 reels FOX bw

Shirley Mason *(Lucia Moreton)*, John Harron *(Glen Wharton)*, Edwin Stevens *(Sam Moreton)*, Cecil Van Auker *(James Moreton)*, Claire McDowell *(Sylvia Moreton)*, Aggie Herring *(Nora Burke)*, Eileen O'Malley *(Lucia, Age 3)*.

Mason's performance nearly makes up for the shortcomings of this hard-to-swallow plot, which has her escaping the cruel relatives her father placed her with before going to prison. Several years pass, and Mason, now a young woman, changes her name and takes a job as a housemaid in the home of her relatives, though neither party recognizes the other. When word comes that the father is being released from jail, the relatives beg their "maid" to pose as their ward. Naturally, Mason is reunited with her dad in the end, shares in his considerable wealth, and marries the young man she had her eye on.

d, Harry Beaumont; w, Jules Furthman; ph, Lucien Andriot.

Drama **(PR:A MPAA:NR)**

RAGGED MESSENGER, THE* (1917, Brit.) 5 reels BRO bw

Violet Hopson *(Mary Ainslee)*, Gerald Ames *(Walter Bowman)*, Basil Gill *(Rev. John Morton)*, George Foley *(Henry Vavasour)*, Harry Gilbey, Ruby Belasco, John McAndrews, Marjorie West.

Cheerful little British entertainment about the paralyzed son of a millionaire who goes completely insane when he discovers that the woman he married is actually his father's mistress.

p, Walter West; d, Frank Wilson; w, (based on a novel by W. B. Maxwell).

Drama **(PR:C MPAA:NR)**

RAGS*½** (1915) 5 reels FP bw

Mary Pickford *("Rags"/Alice McCloud)*, Marshall Neilan *(Keith Duncan)*, Joseph Manning *(John Hardesty)*, J. Farrell MacDonald *(Paul Ferguson)*.

Pickford plays both mother and daughter in this fine film about a young woman who falls in love with a bank clerk who attempts to rob his employer, her guardian. The banker lets the criminal go for the sake of his ward, and the couple head west to a mining camp, where they marry and the woman dies in childbirth. At this point, the picture fades forward to the future and we see America's Sweetheart as a lovable tomboy who manages to endure, through laughter, the humiliation of being the town drunk's daughter. She also becomes quite smitten by a handsome engineer (well played by her future director, Marshall Neilan) and arranges a special dinner party for him, which she manages to put together through tremendous personal sacrifice. On the big day, while Pickford steps out for a moment, her father and his cronies stagger into the little shack and wolf down nearly everything in sight. Horrified to find the feast gone, Pickford arranges the few remaining scraps on Neilan's plate, and upon his arrival, tries bravely to cover her embarrassment with this title card, "I was so hungry I jes' couldn't wait for you." This is a scene of tremendous poignancy, which surely must have influenced Charles Chaplin's famous New Year's Eve sequence in THE GOLD RUSH. Later in the film, Pickford overhears her father plotting to rob the engineer and his partner's payroll, and she manages to reach the sheriff in time to save the day. In the ensuing gun battle, however, her father is killed and the girl is sent back east to live with her mother's guardian. There is a happy ending as Neilan, it turns out, is an employee of the kindly old gentleman, and the young couple are reunited in marriage as well as friendship.

d, James Kirkwood; w, Frances Marion, Mary Pickford (based on a story by Edith Barnard Delano).

Drama/Comedy **(PR:A MPAA:NR)**

RAGS TO RICHES*** (1922) 7 reels WB bw (AKA: FROM RAGS TO RICHES)

Wesley Barry *(Marmaduke Clarke)*, Niles Welch *(Dumbbell/Ralph Connor)*, Ruth Renick *(Mary, an Orphan)*, Russell Simpson *(The Sheriff)*, Minna Redman *(The Sheriff's Wife)*, Richard Tucker *(Blackwell Clarke)*, Eulalie Jensen *(Mrs. Blackwell Clarke)*, Jane Keckley *(Marmaduke's Governess)*, Sam Kaufman *(Tony, the "Wop")*, Dick Sutherland *(Bull)*, Jimmy Quinn *(Louis, the Dope)*, Snitz Edwards, Aileen Manning *(Members of the Purists' League)*.

This truly entertaining kids' feature starred Barry in his first film for Warner Brothers. Not only did RAGS TO RICHES help to launch young Barry's career, but he became the biggest draw the studio had seen since Rin Tin Tin. In it Barry plays the pampered son of a millionaire. He isn't allowed to have any fun, so when a gang of crooks robs his house, the kid does everything he can to help. Later he runs away and becomes friendly with Welch, a member of the same gang. But when his new pal discovers that there is a plot to hold Barry for ransom and murder him if the cash is not delivered, the two escape and find jobs on a farm. To the sheltered Barry it's more like an amusement park than work, while Welch, in the meantime, falls in love with Renick, the farmer's orphaned ward. Time passes, and Welch becomes the victim of the local legion of puritans. By then the crooks show up, as do Barry's parents, but Welch—who it turns out is really a member of the Secret Service—manages to get everything and everyone under control.

p, Harry Rapf; d, Wallace Worsley; w, Walter De Leon, William Nigh (based on a story by Grace Miller White); ed, Clarence Kolster.

Comedy/Adventure **(PR:A MPAA:NR)**

RAGTIME* (1927) 7 reels James Ormont/FD bw

John Bowers *(Ted Mason)*, Marguerite De La Motte *(Beth Barton)*, Robert Ellis *(Steve "Slick" Martin)*, Rose Dione *(Yvonne "Goldie" Martin)*, William H. Strauss *(Max Ginsberg)*, Kate Bruce *(Mrs. Mason)*, Bernard Siegel.

Hokey programmer has Bowers a writer of popular songs, creating a love tune for society girl De La Motte. When Dione steals the music from the piano and gives it to her tap dancer husband, Ellis, who publishes it under his own name, the song becomes a big hit. This somehow leads to De La Motte being drummed out of the social register, but Bowers writes her another ditty—closer to the classical tradition—exposes Ellis, and all ends harmoniously.

d, Scott Pembroke; w, George Dromgold, Jean Plannette (based on a story by Joseph Mitchell); t, Dromgold; ph, Ted Tetzlaff, Ernest Miller.

Drama **(PR:A MPAA:NR)**

RAIDERS, THE* (1921) 5 reels William N. Selig/Canyon bw

Franklyn Farnum *(Pvt. Fitzgerald of the Royal Mounted Police)*, Bud Osborne *(Pvt. Herrick)*, Vester Pegg *(Bob Thiele)*, Claire Windsor *("Honey" Moore)*, Frederick Soult *("Big" Moore)*, H. Abbott *(Oscar Nelson)*, J. K. Van Buren *(Dave Moore)*, John Hatfield *(Hank Nelson)*.

Terrible frozen tundra nonsense has mountie Farnum, hot on the trail of a gang of bootleggers, stopping at a farm where he falls in love with Windsor, the pretty daughter of the house. It turns out that her boy friend is the leader of the smugglers, and when the hero and villain engage in the inevitable last reel fist fight—to the horror of every kid in the audience—the mountie is knocked cold. God intervenes, however, by sending down a bolt of lightning which does the whiskey runner in before he can kill the lawman. Nature takes care of the rest and Farnum rides off with Windsor, one of Hollywood's great beauties.

d, Nate Watt; w, William E. Wing (based on the story "The Whiskey Runners" by Bertrand W. Sinclair).

Adventure **(PR:A MPAA:NR)**

RAILROADED* (1923) 5 reels UNIV bw

Herbert Rawlinson *(Richard Ragland)*, Esther Ralston *(Joan Dunster)*, Alfred Fisher *(Hugh Dunster)*, David Torrence *(Judge Garbin)*, Lionel Belmore *(Foster)*, Mike Donlin *(Corton)*, Herbert Fortier *(Bishop Selby)*.

Skimpy Universal production has Rawlinson, the son of one of Britain's most prominent judges, thrown into prison on trumped-up-charges. He manages to escape and his father secretly arranges for him to serve out the rest of his sentence on the estate of a family friend. There he meets and falls in love with Ralston, the daughter of the house, who prevents Rawlinson from carrying out his revenge on Donlin, the man who framed him. Instead the young couple marry and sail for Africa.

d, Edmund Mortimer; w, Charles Kenyon (based on the novel *Richard* by Marguerite Bryant); ph, Allen Davey.

Drama **(PR:A MPAA:NR)**

RAINBOW** (1921) 5 reels VIT bw

Alice Calhoun *(Rainbow Halliday)*, Jack Roach *(George Standish)*, William Gross *(Shang Jordan)*, Charles Kent *(Andy MacTavish)*, Tom O'Malley *(Denny Farrell)*, George Lessey *(Rufus Halliday)*, Cecil Kern *(Estelle Jackson)*, Tammany Young *(Kid Short)*, Ivan Christie *(Joe Sheady)*.

Unpretentious little programmer tells of an orphaned girl, Calhoun, who is raised by three middle-aged men who work at the mine she inherited from her father. Roach, a young man from Chicago, arrives on the scene and claims that the mine is rightfully his. He later saves her from the advances of Christie, and after a number of complications, the couple fall in love and marry. Of course the property, to the relief of everyone involved, becomes jointly owned.

d, Edward Jose; w, C. Graham Baker (based on a story by Harry Dittmar).

Drama **(PR:A MPAA:NR)**

RAINBOW PRINCESS, THE*** (1916) 5 reels FP bw

Ann Pennington *(Hope Daingerfield)*, William Courtleigh, Jr. *(Warren Reynolds)*, Augusta Anderson *(Edithe Worthington)*, Grant Stewart *(Judge Daingerfield)*, Charles Sutton *(Pop Blodgett)*, Harry Lee *(Dave, His Son)*, Edwin Sturgis *(Joe, His Son)*, Clifford Gray *(George Waters)*, Herbert Rice *(Mons. Paul)*, Queen Pearl *(Mlle. Fifi)*, Amy Manning *(Rose, the Circus Fat Lady)*, Carl Gordon *(Simon, the Human Skeleton)*, Walter D. Mealand.

Famous Players hired a real circus to provide just the right flavor for this story of the big top, starring Ziegfeld Follies sensation Pennington. She plays the dancing featured attraction of the show, known as the Rainbow Princess, who is tricked by the owner to pose as the long-lost granddaughter of a small-town millionaire. When Pennington learns the truth, the horrified girl runs away, only to be brought back by the old boy's adopted son, who begs her to be his wife. The picture's highlight is the actual hula number Pennington performed in the Follies, backed by the original supporting beauties.

d, J. Searle Dawley; w, Shannon Fife; ph, Lyman Broening.

Drama **(PR:A MPAA:NR)**

RAINBOW RANGERS** (1924) 5 reels William Steiner/New-Cal bw

Pete Morrison *(Buck Adams)*, Peggy Montgomery *(Rose Warner)*, Lew Meehan *(Manual Lopez)*, Eddie Dennis *(Anteater Jake)*, Nelson McDowell *(Deacon Slim)*, Milburn Morante *(English Charlie)*, Martin Turner *(Barbecue Sam)*, Lafe McKee *(Luke Warner)*, Victor Allen *(Frank Owens)*, Raye Hampton *(Tilly)*.

This western comedy, which provided more thrills than laughs, sees a band of wandering rangers, led by Morrison, saving a girl (played by one-time child star "Baby Peggy" Montgomery) from the clutches of an outlaw gang.

d&w, Forrest Sheldon; ph, Ross Fisher.

Western/Comedy **(PR:A MPAA:NR)**

RAINBOW TRAIL, THE*** (1925) 6 reels FOX bw

Tom Mix *(John Shefford/Lassiter)*, Anne Cornwall *(Fay Larkin)*, George Bancroft *(Jake Willets)*, Lucien Littlefield *(Joe Lake)*, Mark Hamilton *(Beasley Willets)*, Vivian Oakland *(Bessie Erne)*, Thomas Delmar *(Venters)*, Fred De Silva *(Shadd)*, Steve Clements *(Nas Ta Bega)*, Doc Roberts *(Lassiter)*, Carol Halloway *(Jane)*, Diana Miller *(Anne)*.

Mix is at his athletic best in this western which has the great cowboy star thwarting an Indian attack on a wagon, saving a squaw from the unwanted attention of a half-breed, rescuing a girl from a forced marriage, and liberating his uncle and his lady friend from an outlaw gang. The action is non-stop from beginning to end, and the production is topnotch on every level.

d&w, Lynn Reynolds (based on the novel by Zane Grey); ph, Daniel Clark.

Western **(PR:A MPAA:NR)**

RAINMAKER, THE*** (1926) 7 reels FP/PAR bw

William Collier, Jr. *(Bobby Roberston)*, Georgia Hale *(Nell Wendell)*, Ernest Torrence *(Mike)*, Brandon Hurst *(Doyle)*, Joseph Dowling *(Father Murphy)*, Tom Wilson *(Chocolate)*, Martha Mattox *(Head Nurse)*, Charles K. French *(Hospital Doctor)*, Jack Richardson *(Western Doctor)*, Melbourne MacDowell *(Benson)*.

Interesting drama about a jockey (Collier) who, because of a war wound, is able to predict rain. He uses this to personal advantage, both selling his information to owners of horses that run well in the mud, and placing bets himself. When Collier is hurt in a race, he falls in love with a nurse, Hale, a former dance hall girl. Hale is later fired from the hospital, and out of desperation takes a job working for an old friend who has opened a saloon on the border. The jockey finally tracks her down and discovers that the town is suffering from a plague which is the result of a terrible drought. An enemy of Hale's boss has prevented medical supplies from getting through, so Collier saves the day—experiences his own regeneration—by falling to his knees and actually *praying* for relief. His appeal is answered and a torrential downpour rescues the community. The couple marry, and with an inheritance left to Hale by her boss, a victim of the epidemic, the road to happiness is assured.

d, Clarence Badger; w, Hope Loring, Louis Duryea Lighton (based on the story "Heavenbent" by Gerald Beaumont); ph, H. Kinley Martin.

Drama **(PR:A MPAA:NR)**

RAJAH'S AMULET, THE (SEE: EACH TO HIS KIND, 1917)

RAMONA*** (1916) 10 and 12 reels Clune bw

Adda Gleason, Monroe Salisbury, Richard Sterling, Mabel Van Buren, H.M. Best, Lurline Lyons, Red Wing, Alice Morten Otten, Anna Lehr, Nigel de Brulier, E. Valencia, Mrs. Davenport, James Needham [Donald Crisp], Baby Ann Lehr [Ann Dvorak], Harry Tavares.

Donald Crisp, a disciple of D. W. Griffith, did very well by the master in this mammoth production (in California it ran a full 12 reels), which explored the delicate subject of the American Indian's abuse at the hands of the white man. In the Crisp version, 36 years of character development are covered, whereas Griffith, who originally filmed the Helen Hunt Jackson novel in 1910, made his film in one reel.

d, Donald Crisp; w, Lloyd Brown (based on the novel by Helen Hunt Jackson); ph, Enrico Vallejo, Bert Glennon.

Drama **(PR:A MPAA:NR)**

RAMONA 1/2** (1928) 8 reels INSP/UA bw

Dolores Del Rio *(Ramona)*, Warner Baxter *(Alessandro)*, Roland Drew *(Felipe)*, Vera Lewis *(Senora Moreno)*, Michael Visaroff *(Juan Canito)*, John T. Prince *(Father Salvierderra)*, Mathilde Comont *(Marda)*, Carlos Amor *(Sheepherder)*, Jess Cavin *(Bandit Leader)*, Rita Carewe *(Baby)*, Jean the Dog.

Ramona (Del Rio) discovers that she is actually a half-breed after years of abusive treatment from her guardian (Lewis), a wealthy Spanish sheep rancher. The girl disobeys Lewis by running off and marrying an Indian chief, although she deeply regrets leaving the woman's son, Drew, with whom she has become good friends. Del Rio's misfortune continues, however; she loses her daughter after an outlaw raid, and her husband is wrongly hanged for horse stealing. This all leads the poor girl to suffer a breakdown, which results in amnesia. Then after wandering aimlessly throughout the countryside, Drew finds her and restores the girl's memory by having her listen to the melody of a song she loved as a child.

d, Edwin Carewe; w, Finis Fox (based on the novel by Helen Hunt Jackson); t, Fox; ph, Robert B. Kurrle, Al M. Green; ed, Jeanne Spencer; art d, Al D'Agostino; m/l, "Ramona," Mabel Wayne, L. Wolf Gilbert.

Drama **(PR:A MPAA:NR)**

RAMSHACKLE HOUSE** (1924) 6 reels Tilford Cinema/PDC bw

Betty Compson *(Pen Broome)*, Robert Lowing *(Don Counsell)*, John Davidson *(Ernest Riever)*, Henry James *(Pendleton Broome)*, William Black *(Keesing)*, Duke Pelzer *(Spike Talley)*, Josephine Norman *(Blanche Paglar)*, Joey Joey *(Alligator Wrestler)*.

Fair programmer set in southern Florida has Lowing, a camper, suspected of killing his business partner. He is saved by Compson, a beautiful local girl, when she exposes the real culprit by tricking the triggerman into fingering him with the belief that he has been double-crossed.

d, Harmon Weight; w, Coolidge Streeter (based on the novel by Hulbert Footner); ph, Larry Williams, Bert Wilson.

Drama **(PR:A MPAA:NR)**

RANGE RIDERS, THE* 1/2 (1927) 5 reels Ben Wilson/RAY bw

Ben Wilson *(Shannon)*, Neva Gerber *(Betty Grannan)*, Al Ferguson *("Sundown" Sykes)*, Ed La Niece *(Henry Fellows)*, Earl C. Turner *(Capt. Lane)*, Fang *(Pard, the Dog)*.

A range rider falls in love with the sister of one of the outlaws he brings to justice and provides her with a happy, law-abiding life.

d, Ben Wilson; w, Robert Dillon; t, Earl C. Turner; ph, Eddie Linden; ed, Turner.

Western **(PR:A MPAA:NR)**

RANGER OF THE BIG PINES** (1925) 7 reels VIT bw

Kenneth Harlan *(Ross Cavanagh)*, Helene Costello *(Virginia Weatherford)*, Eulalie Jensen *(Lize Weatherford)*, Will Walling *(Sam Gregg)*, Lew Harvey *(Joe Gregg)*, Robert Graves *(Redfield)*.

Forest ranger Harlan brings a band of cattlemen under control who have refused to pay a government grazing tax. He also falls in love with Costello, a student home from college, and rescues the girl and her mother from having to run a boarding-house occupied by toughs when he marries her and moves his new family East.

d, William S. Van Dyke; w, Hope Loring, Louis D. Lighton (based on the novel *Cavanagh, Forest Ranger; A Romance of the Mountain West* by Hamlin Garland); ph, Allan Thompson.

Western **(PR:A MPAA:NR)**

RANGER OF THE NORTH** (1927) 5 reels FBO bw

Ranger the Dog *(Himself)*, Hugh Trevor *(Bob Fleming)*, Lina Basquette *(Felice MacLean)*, Bernard Siegel *(Bruce MacLean/Eagle Claw)*, Jules Rancourt *(Louis Dubois)*, William Van Vleck *(Haggerty)*.

Easterner Trevor removes a porcupine quill from the paw of Ranger, a wild dog. From that day the animal becomes his protector, helping him discover a lost mine, win the pretty girl, and drive the villains to their watery grave.

d, Jerome Storm; w, Leon D'Usseau (based on a story by Ewart Adamson); ph, Charles Boyle.

Adventure **(PR:A MPAA:NR)**

RANK OUTSIDER 1/2** (1920, Brit.) 4 reels BRO/Walturdaw bw

Gwen Stratford *(Myra Wynchmore)*, Cameron Stratford *(Capt. Ferndale)*, Lewis Dayton *(Guy Selby)*, John Gliddon *(Ralph Wynchmore)*, Luther Miles, Martita Hunt.

Better-than-average British sporting film has a man returning home from Australia after being framed for murder, locating the champion racehorse some crooks stole from his sister, and then winning the big race.

p, Walter West; d, Richard Garrick; w, Patrick L. Mannock (based on a novel by Nat Gould).

Drama **(PR:A MPAA:NR)**

RANSOM, THE*** (1916) 5 reels Triumph Equitable bw

Julia Dean *(Janet Osborne)*, Louise Huff *(Marcia Osborne)*, James Hall *(Mark Osborne)*, Ethel Lloyd *(Sarah Osborne)*, Willard Case *(Ellis Raymond)*, Kenneth Hunter *(Geoffrey Allen)*.

Eve Unsell may have owed a slight debt to *Madame X* and *East Lynne*, but she still came up with a heart-rending screenplay. It is the story of a woman who deserts her husband and child in search of a theatrical life, only to sink eventually to the gutter and despair. She finally lands a job working anonymously as a maid for her daughter, who has become a Broadway star. The film's big punch comes when she kills the man who ruined her—only to protect her child from a similar fate—and then dies herself, a lonely heroine, unrecognized by the person for whom she finally gave all.

d, Edmund Lawrence; w, Eve Unsell (based on her play "The Marionettes").

Drama **(PR:A MPAA:NR)**

RANSOM** (1928) 6 reels COL bw

Lois Wilson *(Lois Brewster)*, Edmund Burns *(Burton Meredith)*, William V. Mong *(Wu Fang)*, Blue Washington *(Oliver)*, James B. Leong *(Scarface)*, Jackie Coombs *(Bobby)*.

Chemist Burns invents a deadly gas which Mong, the leader of Chinatown's underworld, is determined to steal. Mong kidnaps Burns' sweetheart's little boy, Coombs, and later captures his girl as well. But the chemist rescues them both—with a little help from the police department—and Burns and his love decide to tie the knot.

p, Harry Cohn; d, George B. Seitz; w, Dorothy Howell, Elmer Harris (based on a story by Seitz); ph, Joseph Walker; art d, Joseph Wright.

Adventure **(PR:A MPAA:NR)**

RANSON'S FOLLY** (1915) 4 reels Edison bw

Marc MacDermott, Mabel Trunnelle, Marjorie Ellison, Edward Earle, Joseph Bingham, Gladys Leslie, Jessie Stevens, James Harris, George A. Wright.

A New York saloon owner's daughter attends a convent school where the student body snubs her because of her father's profession. The two head west, where the father lands a job at an army post. When a young lieutenant arrives, fresh from campaigning in the Philippines, he falls in love with the pretty young lady, but a series of holdups performed by a bandit known as the "Red Rider" makes him a prime suspect. Realizing his daughter's feelings for the young officer, the former saloon owner commits suicide and leaves a note confessing to be the daring outlaw, which clears the way for the couple to marry. In the hands of a more skilled director, this motion picture, featuring MacDermott, one of the silent cinema's finest actors, might have been quite good. But as it stands, the film is only fair.

d&w, Richard Ridgely (based on a novel by Richard Harding Davis).

Western/Drama **(PR:A MPAA:NR)**

RANSON'S FOLLY 1/2** (1926) 8 reels INSP/FN bw

Richard Barthelmess *(Lt. Ranson)*, Dorothy Mackaill *(Mary Cahill)*, Anders Randolf *(The Post Trader)*, Pat Hartigan *(Sgt. Clancy)*, Brooks Benedict *(Lt. Curtis)*, William

Norton Bailey *(Lt. Crosby)*, Col. C. C. Smith, *(Col. Bolland)*, Pauline Neff *(Mrs. Bolland)*, Billie Bennett *(Mrs. Trusedale)*, Frank Coffyn *(Post Adjutant)*, Capt. John S. Peters *(Judge Advocate)*, Taylor Duncan *(Capt. Car)*, Jack Fowler *(Col. Patten)*, E. W. Corman *(Pop Henderson)*, Bud Pope *(Abe Fisher)*, Forrest Seabury *(Drummer)*, Chief Eagle Wing *(Indian Pete)*, Chief Big Tree *(Chief Standing Bear)*.

Barthelmess swashes his buckle in this adaptation of the popular Richard Harding Davis novel about a bored army officer who bets his friends he can hold up a stagecoach with a pair of scissors while impersonating a notorious outlaw. Later, when the paymaster is killed, Barthelmess is accused of the crime and arrested. He gallantly confesses in order to save his sweetheart's father (whom he believes is involved), but in the end the real bandit is captured, and the film comes to a happy conclusion for everyone.

d, Sidney Olcott; w, Lillie Hayward (based on the novel by Richard Harding Davis); ph, David W. Gobbett.

Drama **(PR:A MPAA:NR)**

RAT, THE*** (1925, Brit.) 8 reels Gainsborough/W&F bw

Ivor Novello *(Pierre Boucheron)*, Mae Marsh *(Odile Etrange)*, Isobel Jeans *(Zelie de Chaumet)*, Robert Scholtz *(Hermann Stetz)*, James Lindsay *(Inspector Caillard)*, Marie Ault *(Mere Colline)*, Julie Suedo *(Mou-Mou)*, Hugh Brook *(Paul)*, Esme Fitzgibbons *(Madeleine)*, Lambart Glasby *(An American)*, Iris Grey *(Rose)*.

Set in Paris, an Apache is attracted to a wealthy seductress, despite his love for the virginal Marsh. One of the worldy woman's friends tries to force himself on Marsh, however, and the Apache kills him. Marsh's love for her sweetheart is such that she makes everyone believe she is the murderer. But a sympathetic court releases her and Marsh is reunited with the man she adores.

p, Michael Balcon; d&w, Graham Cutts (based on the play by Ivor Novello, Constance Collier).

Drama **(PR:A MPAA:NR)**

RAWHIDE KID, THE*** (1928) 6 reels UNIV bw

Hoot Gibson *(Dennis O'Hara)*, Georgia Hale *(Jessica Silverberg)*, William H. Strauss *(Simon Silverberg)*, Frank Hagney *(J. Francis Jackson)*, Tom Lingham *(Deputy)*, Harry Todd *(Comic)*.

Unusual western has Gibson playing an Irishman who befriends an old Jewish peddler and his daughter. The cowboy later wins the big race, beating the villain who stole his horse and causing the peddler to make a fortune on his wisely placed wager. The film naturally ends with the daughter in Gibson's arms, and the old man operating a topnotch business. This film theme was popular in 1928, and would be made a classic by ABIE'S IRISH ROSE the following year.

d, Del Andrews; w, Arthur Statter, Isadore Bernstein (based on a story by Peter B. Kyne); t, Tom Reed; ph, Harry Neumann; ed, Rodney Hickok; art d, David S. Garber.

Western/Drama **(PR:A MPAA:NR)**

REACHING FOR THE MOON*** (1917) 5 reels Douglas Fairbanks/ART bw

Douglas Fairbanks *(Alexis Caesar Napoleon Brown)*, Eileen Percy *(Elsie)*, Richard Cummings *(Old Bingham)*, Millard Webb *(Mr. Mann)*, Eugene Ormonde *(Minister of Vulgaria)*, Frank Campeau *(Black Boris)*, Jim Hogan, Keene Thompson, Joe Brooks, Charles Stevens, Erich von Stroheim.

In this one Fairbanks plays a clerk in a button company who knows that his mother, of royal Vulgarian blood, ran away with his commoner father and died in childbirth. Trying to catch a glimpse of the prime minister (Ormonde) of Vulgaria who is visiting New York, Fairbanks takes too long a lunch break and is fired. Returning home, he falls asleep and dreams that the prime minister comes to his digs, informs him that he is the last of the royal line and must return to the place of his mother's birth to prevent the villainous Campeau from seizing the throne. From this point on, the star is given plenty of opportunity to put his athletic prowess to use as he dodges countless attempts to take his life. And there are lots of laughs as well, as author Loos slings her shots at comic opera kingdoms and aristocratic protocol. But the picture ends on a rather disturbing note, with the awakened Fairbanks depicted dwelling in a typical little suburban home with a regulation little suburban family. It would be the only time this greatest of stars would place his much bigger-than-life motion picture persona in such mundane surroundings.

d, John Emerson; w, Anita Loos, Emerson; ph, Harry Thorpe, Victor Fleming.

Adventure/Comedy **(PR:A MPAA:NR)**

READY MONEY*** (1914) 5 reels LAS bw

Edward Abeles *(Steve Baird)*, Monroe Salisbury *(Sidney Rosenthal)*, Jode Mullally *(John H. Tyler)*, Jane Darwell *(Mrs. Tyler)*, Bessie Barriscale *(Grace Tyler)*, Florence Dagmar *(Ida Tyler)*, Fred Montague *(James R. Morgan)*, James Neill *(Jackson Ives)*, Theodore Roberts *(Mike Reardon)*, Billy Elmer *(Jim Dolan)*, Sydney Deane *(Owner of Skyrocket)*, Dick La Reno *(Capt. West, Secret Service)*, Howard Hickman.

Cecil B. DeMille's screenplay (taken from a popular play) moves right along as it tells the story of a westerner, Abeles, who comes to New York to finance his mine, is almost arrested for counterfeiting, but triumphs in business and love by the end of reel 5. Some skillfully handled comedy relief also helps to make this one a winner.

d, Oscar Apfel; w, Cecil B. DeMille (based on a play by James Montgomery).

Drama **(PR:A MPAA:NR)**

REAL ADVENTURE, THE* 1/2**

(1922) 5 reels Florence Vidor-Cameo/AEX bw

Florence Vidor *(Rose Stanton)*, Clyde Fillmore *(Rodney Aldrich, Her Husband)*, Nellie Peck Saunders *(Mrs. Stanton)*, Lilyan McCarthy *(Portia)*, Philip Ryder *(John Walbraith)*.

Sensative King Vidor film has Florence Vidor seeking her personal identity in marriage and being forced by a condescending husband to strike out on her own. Vidor's ambition is to practice law, but circumstances force her to rely on her physical beauty, and she takes a job working in a Broadway chorus line. It doesn't take long, however, before the young lady puts her true talent to use, and after much hard work and perseverance, she becomes head of the most exclusive clothing salon in New York. Her husband, in the meantime, comes to his senses, recognizes her intellect, and pleads with Vidor to again enter into marriage—this time as an equal partner.

p, Arthur S. Kane; d, King Vidor; w, Mildred Considine (based on the novel by Henry Kitchell Webster); ph, George Barnes.

Drama **(PR:A MPAA:NR)**

REAL FOLKS 1/2** (1918) 5 reels TRI bw

Francis McDonald *(Jimmie Dugan)*, Alberta Lee *(Mrs. Dugan)*, J. Barney Sherry *(Mr. Dugan)*, Fritzi Ridgeway *(Joyce Clifton)*, Marion Skinner *(Lady Blessington)*, Betty Pearce *(Margaret Van Arsden)*, George Pearce *(Van Arsden)*.

The Triangle Studio and *Photoplay* magazine conducted a contest for best amateur scenario and Kate Corbaley won with this homey little programmer about a rural family that strikes it rich when oil is discovered on their farm. The father develops social ambitions, but after learning the hard way who the "real folks" are, gladly returns to his former way of life.

d, Walter Edwards; w, Jack Cunningham (based on the story by Kate Corbaley); ph, C. O. Peterson.

Drama **(PR:A MPAA:NR)**

REBECCA OF SUNNYBROOK FARM**** (1917) 6 reels ART bw

Mary Pickford *(Rebecca Randall)*, Eugene O'Brien *(Adam Ladd)*, Helen Jerome Eddy *(Hannah Randall)*, Charles Ogle *(Mr. Cobb)*, Marjorie Daw *(Emma Jane Perkins)*, Mayme Kelso *(Jane Sawyer)*, Jane Wolff *(Mrs. Randall)*, Josephine Crowell *(Aunt Miranda)*, Jack MacDonald *(Rev. Jonathan Smellie)*, Violet Wilkey *(Minnie Smellie)*, Frank Turner *(Mr. Simpson)*, Kate Toncray *(Mrs. Simpson)*, Emma Gordes *(Clara Belle Simpson)*, ZaSu Pitts.

One of Pickford's best (and that's saying something) has the star once again playing a child. This time she's sent to live with her strict aunt, Crowell, in a small New England town, because her mother can no longer afford to care for her large family. Pickford is wonderful as she blends comedy (some of the sight gags equal Keaton's and Chaplin's best) with pathos under Neilan's inspired direction. The film ends happily with the little "troublemaker" growing up to snare O'Brien, the town's most eligible bachelor. Wiggin, the author of the novel and co-writer of the play that provided the basis for the film, was apparently not a great fan of the picture. It may have been that, like some of the critics, she thought the impact of the novel was dissipated by the changes to the story line and the addition of comic antics.

d, Marshall Neilan; w, Frances Marion (based on the novel by Kate Douglas Wiggin and the play by Wiggin, Charlotte Thompson); ph, Walter Stradling.

Comedy/Drama **Cas.** **(PR:A MPAA:NR)**

REBECCA THE JEWESS

(1913, Brit.) 6 reels Zenith/Big A bw (GB: IVANHOE)

Lauderdale Maitland *(Ivanhoe)*, Edith Bracewell *(Rebecca)*, Nancy Bevington *(Lady Rowena)*, Hubert Carter *(Isaac)*, Henry Lonsdale *(Sir Brian)*, Austin Milroy *(Front de Boeuf)*.

In this British period film, taken from a play based loosely on the classic Sir Walter Scott novel, a discredited knight defends a Jewish woman charged with practicing witchcraft.

d&w, Leedham Bantock (based on a play by Walter and Frederick Melville).

Drama **(PR:C MPAA:NR)**

RECKLESS AGE, THE*** (1924) 7 reels UNIV-Jewel bw

Reginald Denny *(Dick Minot)*, Ruth Dwyer *(Cythia Meyrick)*, John Steppling *(Spencer Meyrick)*, May Wallace *(Auntie Meyrick)*, William Austin *(Lord Harrowby)*, Tom McGuire *(Martin Wall)*, Fred Malatesta *(Manuel Gonzales)*, Henry A. Barrows *(John Thacker)*, Frederick Vroom *(Owen Jephson)*, William E. Lawrence *(John Paddock)*, Hayden Stevenson *(Henry Trimmer)*, Frank Leigh *(George Jenkins)*.

Denny establishes himself as a light comedian of the first order in this breezy entertainment about the adventures of an insurance agent sent to usher at the wedding of a client who has just purchased a huge policy protecting him in the event of the loss of his young millionairess bride. After a number of mixups and complications, Denny wins the girl for himself and saves his company a bundle.

d, Harry Pollard; w, Rex Taylor (based on the story "Love Insurance" by Earl Derr Biggers); ph, William Fildew.

Comedy **(PR:A MPAA:NR)**

RECKLESS CHANCES 1/2** (5 reels) 1922 Herald/PG bw

J. P. McGowan *(Terry Nolan)*, Dorothy Wood *(Nora Murphy)*, Andrew Waldron *(Dan Murphy)*, Robert Walker *(Harry Allen)*.

Good programmer featuring prolific writer-director-actor McGowan as a railroad stationmaster who is wrongly accused of stealing metal ore. McGowan changes his identity, rescues the railroad president's daughter from the real crooks, and is rewarded by her hand in marriage.

d&w, J. P. McGowan (based on a story by Anthony Coldewey); ph, Chuck Welty.

Adventure **(PR:A MPAA:NR)**

RECKLESS LADY, THE* ** (1926) 8 reels FN bw

Belle Bennett *(Mrs. Fleming)*, Lois Moran *(Sylvia Fleming)*, James Kirkwood *(Col. Fleming)*, Lowell Sherman *(Feodor)*, Ben Lyon *(Ralph Hillier)*, Marcia Harris *(Sophie)*, Charlie Murray *(Gendarme)*.

Bennett and Moran, who teamed up in STELLA DALLAS the year before, are again cast as mother and daughter, but this time in a story dealing with Bennett's addiction to gambling. She is forced into having an affair with a Russian aristocrat in order to cover her debts, and when her husband learns of this, he files for divorce. Bennett takes Moran to Monte Carlo and manages to eke out a living by approaching the table conservatively. The Russian appears on the scene, is attracted to Moran, and begins subtly to make his move. The mother pleads with him to leave her daughter alone, but he orders her to keep out and threatens to tell Moran about their past relationship. In desperation, Bennett tries to raise the money needed to escape by gambling, and ends up losing everything. She is about to commit suicide when her former husband arrives and rescues her in the nick of time. The film ends on a happy note—the parents reconcile (after Bennett confesses everything to her daughter), the Russian is sent packing, and Moran finds true romance with a suitable young man.

d, Howard Higgin; w, Sada Cowan (based on the novel by Phillip Hamilton Gibbs); ph, Ernest Haller; ed, Paul F. Maschke; art d, Robert M. Hass.

Drama **(PR:C MPAA:NR)**

RECKLESS ROMANCE* ** (1924) 6 reels Christie/PDC bw

T. Roy Barnes *(Jerry Warner)*, Harry Myers *(Christopher Skinner)*, Sylvia Breamer *(Edith Somers)*, Wanda Hawley *(Beatrice Skinner)*, Tully Marshall *(Judge Somers)*, Jack Duffy *(Grandpa)*, Lincoln Plumer *(Uncle Bellamy)*, Morgan Wallace *(Harold Shrewsbury, Oil Stock Salesman)*, George French *(Lyman Webster)*.

Breamer's father disapproves of her sweetheart, Barnes, so the young man borrows $10,000 from an uncle to make a proposition. Her father, Marshall, will allow Barnes to marry his daughter if he is able to hold onto the cash for 30 days. Barnes immediately invests half the money in some bad stock and then loans the rest to a pal. As the deadline draws near, Barnes desperately accepts an assignment from his friends—a married couple—to act as corespondent in a brief divorce which is necessary to save an inheritance. A number of well-executed comedic situations end with the couple remaining married, Barnes' stock going through the ceiling, and Breamer's father gladly permitting his daughter to wed.

d, Scott Sidney; w, Walter Woods, F. McGrew Willis (based on the play "What's Your Wife Doing?" by Herbert Hall Winslow, Emil Nyitray); t, Joseph W. Farnham; ph, Gus Peterson, Paul Garnett.

Comedy **(PR:A MPAA:NR)**

RECKLESS SEX, THE* ** (1925) 6 reels Phil Goldstone/TRU bw

Madge Bellamy *(Mary Hamilton)*, William Collier, Jr. *(Juan)*, Johnnie Walker *(Robert Lanning, Jr.)*, Wyndham Standing *(Carter Trevor)*, Claire McDowell *(Concha)*, Gertrude Astor *(Lucile Dupre)*, Alec B. Francis *(Emanuel Garcia)*, Gladys Brockwell *(Mrs. Garcia)*, David Torrence *(Robert Lanning)*, Helen Dunbar, Walter Long.

Superior independent programmer with an impressive cast has Walker, a young Bostonian, going to check on his father's New Mexico estate, from where it is suspected guns are being smuggled into Mexico. Along the way he finds Bellamy, a stranded actress who played Little Eva in an Uncle Tom company. Thinking her a child, he takes her to the family ranch. Meanwhile, his suspicions turn out to be correct, and young Walker wipes out the gang. He then discovers Bellamy's real age and ends up making her his bride.

d, Alvin J. Neitz; w, (based on a story by Travers Wells); ph, Bert Baldridge, Edgar Lyons.

Adventure **(PR:A MPAA:NR)**

RECKLESS YOUTH 1/2** (1922) 6 reels SF/SEL bw

Elaine Hammerstein *(Alice Schuyler)*, Niles Welch *(John Carmen)*, Myrtle Stedman *(Mrs. Schuyler-Foster)*, Robert Lee Keeling *(Mr. Schuyler-Foster)*, Huntley Gordon *(Harrison Thornby)*, Louise Prussing *(Mrs. Dahlgren)*, Frank Currier *(Cumberland Whipple)*, Kate Cherry *(Martha Whipple)*, Constance Bennett *(Chorus Girl)*.

Hammerstein is expelled from her convent school and is forced to live with her equally strict grandparents while her mother is off honeymooning. The rebellious young lady runs away and marries Welch, a lodge-keeper, and moves to New York where she becomes the fast-living darling of society. When Welch finds her at a dance with playboy Gordon, he orders her home. But Hammerstein refuses, runs off with the millionaire, and is seriously injured in an automobile accident. While unconscious, she dreams that Gordon forces her to board his yacht, where he almost has his way with her until a steamer crashes into their craft. It is then that the young woman awakens, realizes her husband's true worth, and returns to him. Hammerstein delivers her usual good performance, but the picture is all but stolen by Bennett, in her film debut, playing the small role of a wisecracking chorus girl.

d, Ralph Ince; w, Edward Montagne (based on the novel by Cosmo Hamilton); ph, Jules Cronjager, Jack Brown.

Drama **(PR:A MPAA:NR)**

RECOIL, THE* 1/2 (1924) 7 reels Goldwyn/MG bw (AKA: RECOIL)

Betty Blythe *(Norma Selbee)*, Mahlon Hamilton *(Gordon Kent)*, Clive Brook *(Marchmont)*, Fred Paul *(William Southern)*, Ernest Hilliard *(Jim Selbee)*.

Barely acceptable programmer has Hamilton and a detective hounding Blythe, the wife who deserted him, and her paramour, Brook, and discovering not only the man's criminal background, but that Blythe is a bigamist. Hamilton is about to bid farewell to bad rubbish when the woman saves him from a blackmail plot, then begs his forgiveness and (for reasons known only to Rex Beach) is taken back.

d, T. Hayes Hunter; w, Gerald C. Duffy (based on a story by Rex Beach); ph, Rene Guissart; ed, Alex Troffey; art d, Henri Menessier.

Drama **(PR:C MPAA:NR)**

RECOMPENSE 1/2** (1925) 7 reels WB bw

Marie Prevost *(Julie Gamelyn)*, Monte Blue *(Peter Graham)*, John Roche *(Dr. Sampson)*, George Siegmann *(Stenhouse)*, Charles Stevens *(Mosheshoe)*, Virginia Brown Faire *(Angelica)*, William B. Davidson *(Col. Donovan)*, Katherine Lewis *(Mrs. Donovan)*.

Protestant minister Blue leaves the clergy to become a doctor during the war and falls in love with nurse Prevost while serving on the South African front. When peace comes, Prevost takes a position with a hospital in Cape Town, while Blue finds work in the interior. After he is shot in a drunken brawl, Prevost nurses him back to health and he journeys to London to establish a mission. There he encounters Faire, a woman with whom he once had an affair and who is now destitute and pregnant. Blue takes the poor creature in and offers to marry her, but when she dies in childbirth, he slips the ring on the finger of Prevost, who conveniently blew in from Africa to assist in the operation.

d, Harry Beaumont; w, Dorothy Farnum (based on the novel *Recompense* by Robert Keable); ph, David Abel.

Drama **(PR:C MPAA:NR)**

RECKONING DAY, THE* ** (1918) 5 reels TRI bw

Belle Bennett *(Jane Whiting)*, Jack Richardson *(Kube)*, J. Barney Sherry *(Senator)*, Tom Buckingham *(Frank Wheeler)*, Lenore Fair *(Lola Schram)*, Louise Lester *(Mrs. Schram)*, Lee Phelps *(Jimmy Ware)*, Lucile Desmond *(Tilly Ware)*, Sidney De Grey *(District Attorney)*.

Good wartime thriller has Bennett, a woman lawyer, accepting the assignment of exposing a gang of German spies by posing as chairperson for a war relief charity. Fair, whose mother is an enemy agent, is seeing Buckingham, the son of a prominent senator whom Bennett is in love with. Richardson, the head of the ring, lusts for Fair, but when he realizes that she's about to blow the whistle, he kills her. At first Buckingham is wrongly accused, but Bennett cleverly exposes the Germans and clears the name of her future son-in-law.

d, Harry Pollard; w, (based on a story by Robert F. Hill); ph, Sol Polito, Roy E. Irish.

War **(PR:A MPAA:NR)**

RED DICE* 1/2** (1926) 7 reels DM/PDC bw

Rod La Rocque *(Alan Beckwith)*, Marguerite De La Motte *(Beverly Vane)*, Ray Hallor *(Johnny Vane)*, Gustav von Seyffertitz *(Andrew North)*, George Cooper *(Squint Scoggins)*, Walter Long *(Nick Webb)*, Edithe Yorke *(Mrs. Garrison)*, Clarence Burton *(Butler)*, Charles Clary *(District Attorney)*, Alan Brooks *(Conroy)*.

Fine production on every level has La Rocque, who is down on his luck, agreeing to insure his life at $100,000 and naming a notorious bootlegger as beneficiary in return for a loan of $300. To make it look good, La Rocque also agrees to marry the sister of a gang member. There is plenty of suspense (the contract calls for the murder to take place within a period of one year) and a number of laughs along the way, all ending on a happy note with La Rocque falling in love with the girl and the hit man turning out to be an undercover agent.

d, William K. Howard; w, Jeanie Macpherson, Douglas Doty (based on the novel *The Iron Chalice* by Octavus Roy Cohen); ph, Lucien Androit; ed, Macpherson; art d, Max Parker.

Drama **(PR:A MPAA:NR)**

RED HAIR* ** (1928) 7 reels PAR bw-c

Clara Bow *("Bubbles" McCoy)*, Lane Chandler *(Robert Lennon)*, William Austin *(Dr. Eustace Gill)*, Jacqueline Gadsdon *(Minnie Luther)*, Lawrence Grant *(Judge Rufus Lennon)*, Claude King *(Thomas L. Burke)*, William Irving *("Demmy")*.

Producer B. P. Schulberg and director Clarence Badger combined their talents once again and brought about another box office success for Paramount as they had a year earlier with IT, also starring Bow. Again they used a novel by Elinor Glyn as the basis of the script, in which Bow is delightfully cast as a gold-digging manicurist who captures the attention of wealthy young Chandler, but accepts expensive gifts from his three wards. There's a great scene where Bow throws a temper tantrum at her engagement party when Chandler's friends give her the air, rips off every article of clothing save her lingerie, and jumps into the swimming pool. The beginning of the film sees the title effectively illustrated in a short technicolor sequence.

p, B. P. Schulberg; d, Clarence Badger; w, Agnes Brand Leahy, Percy Heath, Lloyd Corrigan (based on the novel *The Vicissitudes of Evangeline* by Elinor Glyn); t, George Marion, Jr.; ph, Alfred Gilks; ed, Doris Drought.

Comedy **(PR:A MPAA:NR)**

RED HOT DOLLARS* ** (1920) 5 reels PAR bw

Charles Ray *(Tod Burke)*, Gladys George *(Janet Muir)*, Charles Mailes *(Angus Muir)*, William Conklin *(Peter Garton)*, Mollie McConnell *(Cornelia Garton)*.

Ray is employed by and loves the granddaughter of a sour-faced old Scotsman who owns a small foundry and refuses to sell out to his millionaire competitor. As fate would have it, Ray saves the rival tycoon's life, is badly injured in the process, and taken in to the metal magnate's home to live as his son. This infuriates the Scot, and Ray is forbidden to see his sweetheart again. But of course the picture ends with the lovers united and the rivals merging their businesses to everyone's advantage. A charming motion picture which delivers a few tears along with its many laughs.

d, Jerome Storm; sup, Thomas H. Ince; w, Julien Josephson; ph, Chester Lyons.

Comedy/Drama (PR:A MPAA:NR)

RED HOT ROMANCE** (1922) 6 reels John Emerson-Anita Loos/AFN bw

Basil Sydney *(Rowland Stone)*, Henry Warwick *(Lord Howe-Greene)*, Frank Lalor *(King Caramba XIII)*, Carl Stockdale *(Gen. de Castanet)*, Olive Valerie *(Mme. Puloff de Plotz)*, Edward Connelly *(Col. Cassius Byrd)*, May Collins *(Anna Mae Byrd)*, Roy Atwell *(Jim Conwell)*, Tom Wilson *(Thomas Snow)*, Lillian Leighton *(Mammy)*, Snitz Edwards *(Signor Frijole)*.

When Sydney discovers that an expected inheritance is nothing more than a job with his father's insurance company, he visits the country of Bunkonia, where he finds himself in the middle of a royal conspiracy. In the end he manages to save the crown and win the heart of Collins, the girl he loved all along. Anita Loos and John Emerson went all out in satirizing a popular Hollywood genre—the comic opera kingdom—but sadly this picture misses the mark.

d, Victor Fleming; w, Anita Loos, John Emerson; ph, Ernest G. Palmer, Oliver T. Marsh.

Satire (PR:A MPAA:NR)

RED KIMONO** 1/2 (1925) 7 reels Mrs. Wallace Reid/Vital Exchanges bw

Priscilla Bonner *(Gabrielle Darley)*, Theodore von Eltz [Frederick], Tyrone Power, Mary Carr, Virginia Pearson, Mrs. Wallace Reid.

White slavery exposé has young Bonner seduced into prostitution by the town shark, who turns her into his personal meal ticket. Things are bad enough, but when Bonner discovers that the rat plans to marry another, she shoots him to death. Bonner is tried and acquitted and later taken in by a publicity-seeking society woman until the novelty wears off and Bonner once again finds herself back on the streets. She is about to return to the sinful life when the chauffeur of her former "protectress" comes to the rescue and proclaims his love. The film ends with the young man marching off to war, and the newly cleansed Bonner waiting faithfully for his return.

d, Walter Lang; w, Dorothy Arzner (based on a story by Adela Rogers St. Johns); ph, James Diamond.

Drama Cas. (PR:A MPAA:NR)

RED LANE, THE* 1/2 (1920) 5 reels UNIV bw

Frank Mayo *(Norman Aldrich)*, Lillian Rich *(Marie Beaulieus)*, Jean Hersholt *(Vetal Beaulieus)*, James Mason *(Dave Roi)*, James O'Neill *(The Half-wit)*, Frank Thorne *(Louis Blais)*, Paul Weigel *(Father Le Claire)*, Karl Formes *(Henri)*, Fred Herzog *(Andre, the Plowman)*, Margaret Mann, Milla Davenport, Harry Lamont.

Universal cut a lot of financial corners in this heavily padded, mostly outdoor adventure about a New England revenue agent (Mayo) who breaks up a gang of smugglers, wins the girl, and is elected to the legislature.

d, Lynn Reynolds; w, Violet Clark, Reynolds (based on the novel by Holman Day); ph, Ben Kline.

Adventure (PR:A MPAA:NR)

RED LIGHTS** 1/2 (1923) 7 reels Goldwyn/Goldwyn-COS bw

Marie Prevost *(Ruth Carson)*, Raymond Griffith *(Sheridan Scott)*, Johnnie Walker *(John Blake)*, Alice Lake *(Norah O'Neill)*, Dagmar Godowsky *(Roxy)*, William Worthington *(Luke Carson)*, Frank Elliott *(Kirk Allen)*, Lionel Belmore *(Alden Murray)*, Jean Hersholt *(Ezra Carson)*, George Reed *(Porter)*, Charles B. Murphy *(The Henchman)*, Charles West *(The Conductor)*.

Routine melodrama has the life of Prevost, a railroad president's daughter, threatened by mysterious forces until "crime deflector" Griffith is put on the payroll. Griffith (who plays the part wonderfully for laughs) breaks the case wide open and sees to it that the wrongdoers get what's coming to them.

d, Clarence G. Badger; w, Carey Wilson, Alice D. G. Miller (based on the play "The Rear Car" by Edward E. Rose); ph, Rudolph Berquist.

Mystery (PR:A MPAA:NR)

RED LIPS** (1928) 7 reels UNIV bw (AKA: CREAM OF THE EARTH)

Charles Buddy Rogers *(Hugh Carver)*, Marion Nixon *(Cynthia Day)*, Stanley Taylor *(Stewart Freeman)*, Hayden Stevenson *("Pop" Moultin)*, Andy Devine *(A Sophomore)*, Robert Seiter *(Roache)*, Hugh Trevor *("Spike" Blair)*, Earl McCarthy *(Upper-classman)*.

Rogers is expelled from the track team after Nixon is innocently discovered in his dorm. For a while the dejected lad behaves recklessly, but Nixon straightens him out, gets him reinstated on the squad, and the happy youth goes out and breaks the world record at the big meet.

d, Melville Brown; w, Edward J. Montagne, James T. O'Donohue, Brown (based on the novel *The Plastic Age* by Percy Marks); t, Tom Reed; ph, John Stumar; ed, Ray Curtiss.

Drama (PR:A MPAA:NR)

RED MARK, THE*** (1928) 8 reels James Cruze/Pathe bw

Gaston Glass *(Bibi-Ri)*, Nina Quartaro *(Zelie)*, Gustav von Seyffertitz *(De Nou)*, Rose Dione *(Mother Caron)*, Luke Cosgrave *(Papa Caron)*, Eugene Pallette *(Sergeo)*, Jack Roper *(Bombiste)*, Charles Dervis *(Crippled Priest)*.

Great atmosphere and wonderful images provided by director James Cruze make up for a somewhat confusing story line in which von Seyffertitz, a penal colony executioner, is about to have Glass, a young pickpocket—and his rival for the affections of the beautiful Quartaro—beheaded at the guillotine. Seconds before the execution can take place, however, von Seyffertitz recognizes a red birth mark on Glass' neck, identifying him as his long lost son, and sets the youth free to find happiness with Quartaro.

d, James Cruze; w, Julien Josephson (based on a story by John Russell); ph, Ira Morgan; ed, Mildred Johnson; art d, Charles Cadwallader.

Drama (PR:A MPAA:NR)

RED MILL, THE** (1927) 7 reels COS/MGM bw

Marion Davies *(Tina)*, Owen Moore *(Dennis)*, Louise Fazenda *(Gretchen)*, George Siegmann *(Willem)*, Karl Dane *(Capt. Jacob Edam)*, J. Russell Powell *(Burgomaster)*, Snitz Edwards *(Caesar)*, William Orlamond *(Governor)*, Fred Gambold *(Innkeeper)*, Sunshine Hart, Ignatz the Mouse.

W. R. Hearst, who had much to do with the destruction of Fatty Arbuckle's career by constantly sensationalizing the Arbuckle rape-murder trial in his newspapers, allowed his mistress, Marion Davies, to hire the comedian to direct (under the name of William Goodrich) this little costume picture of skating and romance. For the production, Hearst constructed a complete Dutch village on the Metro lot, and added a complicated piping system to freeze the canal with ammonia gas. The effect was quite wonderful—the movie was not. It is the simplistic story of drudges, courtship, and haunted houses, as Davies, a slavey at a Dutch inn who often is the object of the unfair wrath of her boss, Siegmann, falls in love with a newcomer to the Netherlands, Moore. Meanwhile, Fazenda, the burgomaster's daughter, is in love with Dane but is betrothed to the elderly Orlamond. Davies masquerades as Fazenda to help thwart the forced marriage, and when she gets herself locked in a haunted mill, she is rescued by Moore, thus ending this nepotistic mess, another film underwirtten by Davies' boy friend, Hearst, for his lady love. Getting Arbuckle to direct the film put him in an embarrassing position, and Davies knew this. Buster Keaton had approached her and asked her to hire Arbuckle as director, under the name Keaton had given him, "Goodrich." Keaton explained that Arbuckle was broke after his legal fight, was in bad shape emotionally, and he thought that perhaps one directing job might get him back on his feet, explaining that if he gave the man a job Arbuckle would construe it as charity because they were friends. In the end Arbuckle took the assignment because he did not dare to miss out on helming an expensive picture.

d, William Goodrich [Fatty Arbuckle]; w, Frances Marion (based on the musical by Victor Herbert, Henry Martyn Blossom); t, Joe Farnham; ph, Hendrik Sartov; ed, Daniel J. Gray; set d, Cedric Gibbons; cos, Andre-ani.

Comedy/Drama (PR:A MPAA:NR)

RED PEARLS** (1930, Brit.) 7 reels Nettlefold/But bw

Lillian Rich *(Sylvia Radshaw)*, Frank Perfitt *(Gregory Marston)*, Arthur Pusey *(Paul Gordon)*, Frank Stanmore *(Martin Radshaw)*, *Kyoshi Tekase (Tamira)*.

With her career in decline, Rich left Hollywood and returned to her native England to appear in this mystery about a Japanese businessman who drives a murderer completely insane by sending him letters forged in the hand of the man he killed.

p, Archibald Nettleford; d, Walter Forde; w, H. Fowler Mear (based on the novel *Nearer! Nearer!* by J. Randolph James).

Mystery (PR:A MPAA:NR)

RED POTTAGE** (1918, Brit.) 5 reels ID bw

C. Aubrey Smith *(Lord Newhaven)*, Mary Dibley *(Lady Newhaven)*, Gerald Ames *(Hugh Scarlett)*, E. Holman Clark *(The Bishop)*, Marjorie Hume *(Rachel West)*.

Eliot Stannard's script generates a degree of suspense in this British drama about a husband gambling with his wife's lover to see which of them will commit suicide.

d, Meyrick Milton; w, Eliot Stannard (based on the novel by Mary Cholmondeley).

Drama (PR:A MPAA:NR)

RED, RED HEART, THE*** (1918) 5 reels BLUE bw

Monroe Salisbury *(Kut-Lee)*, Ruth Clifford *(Rhoda Tuttle)*, Val Paul *(Jack Newman)*, Gretchen Lederer *(Katherine Newman)*, Allan Sears *(John Dewitt)*, Monte Blue *(Billy Porter)*, Princess Neola *(Molly)*.

Salisbury plays a college-educated American Indian who returns to his native desert to work on an irrigation project for a wealthy family. One day their niece, Clifford, who is suffering from a nervous disorder brought about by an accident, comes to visit. The Indian saves her life following a tarantula bite and is invited to her relatives' home for dinner. There is a strong attraction between Salisbury and the girl, but when the Indian suggests that Clifford join him in the desert and allow the wonders of nature to work their cure, she refuses the offer with a cruel and sarcastic "no!" It is then that Salisbury returns to the dress of his people and abducts the girl. A series of exciting chase sequences follow, which terminate with the girl realizing that she has not only been cured, but has fallen in love with her handsome captor as well. The film ends with the couple being married in a desert church and riding off to spend the rest of their lives in the beauty of his beloved homeland.

d, Wilfred Lucas; w, Bess Meredyth (based on the novel *The Heart of the Desert* by Honore Wilsie); ph, Dal Clawson, Alan Siegler.

Western Drama (PR:A MPAA:NR)

RED WIDOW, THE*** (1916) 4 reels FP bw

John Barrymore *(Cicero Hannibal Butts)*, Flora Zabelle *(Anna Varvara)*, John Hendricks *(Baron)*, George E. Mack *(Popova)*, Eugene Redding *(Ivan Scorpinoff)*, Millard Benson *(Basil Ramanoff)*, Lillian Tucker *(Mrs. Butts)*, John W. Goldsworthy.

Barrymore surely must have enjoyed making this slapstick comedy about a young man's honeymoon adventures. The Great Profile used more "low gags" and old-fashioned "shtick" than any of the clowns out at Mack Sennett's Keystone lot and delivered them with relish. A different, but most delightful Barrymore, indeed.d, James Durkin; w, (based on the play by Channing Pollock, Rennold Wolf).

Comedy **(PR:A MPAA:NR)**

RED WINE** ½** (1928) 7 reels FOX bw (AKA: LET'S MAKE WHOOPEE)

Conrad Nagel *(Charles H. Cook)*, June Collyer *(Alice Cook)*, Arthur Stone *(Jack Brown)*, Sharon Lynn *(Miss Scott)*, E. Alyn Warren *(Jack's lst Pal)*, Ernest Hilliard *(2nd Pal)*, Ernest Wood *(3rd Pal)*, Marshall Ruth *(4th Pal)*, Dixie Gay *(Stenographer)*, Margaret La Marr *(Spanish Cigarette Girl)*, Bo Ling *(Chinese Dancer)*, Dolores Johnson *(Mrs. Brown)*, Michael Tellegen *(Headwaiter)*, Betty Lorraine *(Slinky)*, Lialani Deas *(Hawaiian Dancer)*.

Nagel is the whole show in this heavily padded feature which would have made a dandy two-reeler. The story has Nagel playing a straight-laced fellow persuaded by some pals to visit a nightclub where he gets bombed, passes out, and is tricked into thinking he has had an affair. The next day is his wedding aniversary, and his wife, Collyer, insists that they celebrate at a popular night spot—the same one Nagel secretly attended the evening before. From this point on are all the expected complications, but not nearly the number of laughs one might have desired.

d, Raymond Cannon; w, Andrew W. Bennison, Charles Condon (based on a story by Cannon); t, Garrett Graham; ph, Daniel Clark; cos, Sophie Wachner; syn sc; s eff.

Comedy **(PR:A MPAA:NR)**

REDEEMING SIN, THE*** (1925) 7 reels VIT bw

Nazimova *(Joan)*, Lou Tellegen *(Lupin)*, Carl Miller *(Paul Dubois)*, Otis Harlan *(Papa Chuchu)*, Rosita Marstini *(Mere Michi)*, William Dunn *(Gaston)*, Rose Tapley *(Marquise)*.

Solid direction by Blackton and a good performance by Nazimova make something of this tired story about a Parisian apache dancer who falls in love with a society artist, wrongly suspects him of being unfaithful, and then after striking out at him—having her former lover steal the jewels from the sculptor's mother—repents and begs his forgiveness.

d, J. Stuart Blackton; w, Marian Constance (based on the novel by L. V. Jefferson); ph, L. W. O'Connell.

Drama **(PR:A MPAA:NR)**

REDHEADS PREFERRED*** (1926) 6 reels TIF bw

Raymond Hitchcock *(Henry Carter)*, Marjorie Daw *(Angela Morgan)*, Theodore von Eltz *(John Morgan)*, Cissy Fitzgerald *(Mrs. Henry Carter)*, Vivian Oakland *(Mrs. Bill Williams)*, Charles A. Post *(Bill Williams)*, Leon Homes *(Office Boy)*, Geraldine Leslie *(Miss Crisp)*.

More than a few laughs in this better-than-average independent programmer which has straight-laced businessman von Eltz agreeing to take a red-headed lady to a costume ball to help land a business deal with a client. Daw, his wife, finds out about her husband's scheme and dons a red wig and mask and accompanies her unsuspecting husband to the dance. Not only does Daw completely pull the masquerade off, she also manages to win the business contract for her husband.

d, Allan Dale; w, Douglas Bronston; ph, Milton Moore, Joseph A. Dubray; ed, Malcolm Knight; art d, Edwin B. Willis.

Comedy **(PR:A MPAA:NR)**

REFEREE, THE*** (1922) 5 reels SF/SEL bw

Conway Tearle *(John McArdle)*, Gladys Hulette *(Janie Roberts)*, Anders Randolf *(Steve Roberts)*, Gus Platz, Frank Ryan *(Fighters)*, Joe Humphries *(Announcer)*, Patsy Haley *(Referee)*.

Tearle delivers a strong performance, and director Ince captures the color and feeling of the boxing world, in this entertaining story of a fighter, Tearle, who is forced to relinquish his title after suffering a severe automobile accident. Tearle opens a billiard parlor and falls in love with Hulette, but her father refuses to allow her to see the pugilist. Tearle finally wins the old man over by stopping a championship bout in progress after realizing it's been fixed.

d, Ralph Ince; w, Lewis Allen Browne (based on the story "John McCardle, Referee" by Gerald Beaumont); ph, William Wagner.

Drama **(PR:A MPAA:NR)**

REGGIE MIXES IN*** (1916) 5 reels FA/TRI bw

Douglas Fairbanks *(Reggie Morton)*, Bessie Love *(Agnes, the Girl of the Slums)*, Joseph Singleton *(Morton's Valet)*, W. E. Lowery *(Tony Bernard)*, Wilbur Higby *(The Saloon Proprietor)*, Frank Bennett *(His Right Hand Man)*, A. D. Sears *(An Admirer of Miss Fleming)*, Alam Rubens, Lillian Langdon, Alberta Lee, Tom Wilson.

Millionaire Fairbanks takes a job as bouncer in a tough saloon after wiping up the floor with a bully and falling for Love, who is forced to work there in order to support her mother. Later, in a beautifully staged fight, he also licks the leader of a gang of toughs (who outweighs him by 50 pounds), sees to it that Love inherits $100,000, which she is led to believe has come from a long lost relative, and then, after she accepts his proposal, discloses the truth about his social stature. Love had entered pictures only one year before REGGIE MIXES IN when she came to Fine Arts to apply for a job in the summer while on vacation from school. During the making of the film, Fairbanks insisted on using professional fighters, despite objections by D. W. Griffith, who feared the star would be badly injured. Fairbanks wanted to make the scene as realistic as possible, though admittedly he got a bit "gouged up."

d, William Christy Cabanne; w, Roy Somerville (based on a story by Robert M. Baker); ph, William Fildew.

Adventure/Comedy **(PR:A MPAA:NR)**

REGULAR FELLOW, A***

(1925) 5 reels FP/PAR bw (AKA: HE'S A PRINCE)

Raymond Griffith *(The Prince)*, Mary Brian *(The Girl)*, [Frederick] Tyrone Power *(The King)*, Edgar Norton *(Valet)*, Nigel De Brulier *(Revolutionist)*, Gustav von Seyffertitz *(The Prime Minister)*, Kathleen Kirkham *(Girl's Companion)*, Carl Stockdale, Michael Dark *(Royal Aides)*, Lincoln Plummer *(Tourist Guide)*, Jacqueline Gadsden *(The Princess)*, Jerry Austin *(Lover)*.

Lots of beautifully executed gags here as the great Griffith lampoons the manner in which Britain once used the Prince of Wales as a public relations tool. To avoid offending English viewers, however, the original title HE'S A PRINCE was dropped, and the setting was shifted to the Balkans. But the laughs are nonstop as *this* prince flits from one ceremonial function to another (so many, in fact, that he's forced to change uniforms in a speeding limousine in order to be properly attired) until fate throws him in the path of a beautiful tourist with whom he falls madly in love. The prince does manage to escape his duties briefly to spend time with the lovely lady, but with his father's death he scurries back to reality and barely manages to make it in time for his own coronation. It doesn't take long for the new monarch to work out the problem of marrying a commoner (which plagued England's Edward before his abdication); Griffith merely hires a band of anarchists to overthrow his government, establishes free elections, and ends up in the last reel a very happily wedded President.

d, Edward Sutherland; w, Keene Thompson (based on a story by Reginald Morris, Joseph Mitchell); ph, Charles Boyle.

Comedy **(PR:A MPAA:NR)**

REGULAR SCOUT, A*** (1926) 6 reels R-C/FBO bw

Fred Thomson *(Fred Blake)*, Olive Hasbrouck *(Olive Monroe)*, William Courtright *(Luke Baxter)*, T. Roy Barnes *(Steve Baxter)*, Margaret Seddon *(Mrs. Monroe)*, Buck Black *(Buddy Monroe)*, Robert McKim *(Ed Powell)*, Harry Woods *(Scar Stevens)*, Silver *(Silver King, Fred's Horse)*.

Superior Thomson western has the idol of America's youth setting out to avenge his mother's death by getting even with the family of the man who was partly responsible. But after discovering that they are really decent folk, Thomson saves them in the end from a band of outlaws with the help of a Boy Scout troop.

d&w, David Kirkland (based on a story by Buckleigh F. Oxford); ph, Ross Fisher.

Western **(PR:A MPAA:NR)**

REJECTED WOMAN, THE** (1924) 8 reels DIST/Goldwyn-COS bw

Alma Rubens *(Diane Du Prez)*, Bela Lugosi *(Jean Gagnon)*, George MacQuarrie *(Samuel Du Prez)*, Conrad Nagel *(John Leslie)*, Frederick Burton *(Leyton Carter)*, Antonio D'Algy *(Craig Burnett)*, Aubrey Smith *(Peter Leslie)*, Wyndham Standing *(James Dunbar)*, Juliet La Violette *(Aunt Rose)*, Leonora Hughes *(Lucille Van Tuyl)*.

Even the presence of a good cast doesn't do much to help this programmer about a North Woods girl (Rubens) who falls in love with a New York socialite (Nagel) after his plane crash-lands in her backyard tundra. When Nagel receives word of his father's sudden death, he returns home and is followed to the big city by Rubens. There she suffers much ridicule because of her mountain apparel and rough mannerisms and is persuaded by Nagel's business manager (who is in a position to have Nagel's inheritance revert to him if the young man marries unwisely) to sail for Europe for a crash course in social demeanor. When Rubens returns, a few more complications surface, but she eventually wins her man, and the heavy is given the thrashing he so well deserves.

d, Albert Parker; w, John Lynch; ph, Roy Hunt; art d, Clark Robinson.

Drama **(PR:A MPAA:NR)**

RENDEZVOUS, THE*** (1923) 8 reels Goldwyn/Goldwyn-COS bw

Conrad Nagel *(Walter Stanford)*, Lucille Ricksen *(Vera)*, Richard Travers *(Prince Sergei)*, Kathleen Key *(Varvara)*, Emmett Corrigan *(Vassily)*, Elmo Lincoln *(Godunoff)*, Sydney Chaplin *(Winkie)*, Kate Lester *(Mrs. Stanford)*, Cecil Holland *(Nichi)*, Lucien Littlefield, Max Davidson *(Commissars)*, Eugenie Besserer *(Nini)*, R. O. Pennell *(Czar)*.

It's a tribute to Marshall Neilan's considerable talents that he was able to take this shallow story and turn it into a good entertainment. It's all about an orphaned and abandoned Russian princess, Ricksen, who is forced to marry a brutish Cossack leader while in Siberia during WW I. When the Cossack is accidentally killed, Ricksen happily unites with Nagel, an American soldier who once saved her life. Chaplin is good here as a comic cockney soldier, and Lincoln gives the performance of his life playing the heavy.

d, Marshall Neilan; w, Josephine Lovett (based on a story by Madeline Ruthven); ph, David Kesson.

Drama **(PR:A MPAA:NR)**

RENO* ½ (1923) 7 reels Goldwyn/Goldwyn-COS bw

Helene Chadwick *(Mrs. Emily Dysart Tappan)*, George Walsh *(Walter Heath)*, Lew Cody *(Roy Tappan)*, Carmel Myers *(Mrs. Dora Carson Tappan)*, Dale Fuller *(Aunt Alida Kane)*, Hedda Hopper *(Mrs. Kate Norton Tappan)*, Kathleen Key *(Yvette, the Governess)*, Rush Hughes *(Jerry Dysart, Emily's Brother)*, Marjorie Bonner *(Marjory Towne)*, Robert De Vilbiss *(Paul Tappan, Emily's Son)*, Virginia Loomis *(Ivy Tappan, Emily's Daughter)*, Richard Wayne *(Arthur Clayton)*, Hughie Mack *(The Justice of the Peace)*, Boyce Combe *(Hal Carson)*, Victor Potel *(McRae, Detective)*, Percy Hemus *(Lemile Hake)*, Maxine Elliott Hicks *(Mattie Hake)*, Billy Eugene *(Tod Hake)*, Adele Watson *(Mrs. Tod Hake)*, Evelyn Sherman *(Mrs. Towne)*, Jack Curtis *(Hod Stoat)*, Patterson Dial *(Mrs. Hod Stoat)*.

Cody divorces his wife, Chadwick, and leaves his two children to marry Myers, a woman he believes is wealthy. Chadwick then marries her former sweetheart,

Walsh, but to their horror the newlyweds discover that her divorce is not valid in their state. Meanwhile Cody kidnaps his children and delivers them to his aunt who has offered to pay a tidy sum for their possession. Chadwick and Walsh track them down, snatch the tots back, and move to Yellowstone National Park, one of the areas where their marriage is considered valid. Cody follows and is killed in a fight with Walsh when a geyser erupts and turns him into an unguided missile. Goldwyn supposedly set out to make a statement about the inequity which existed due to the conflicting divorce laws at the time in the 48 states, but all he really accomplished was the production of a below-par melodrama.

d&w, Rupert Hughes; ph, John J. Mescall.

Drama **(PR:A MPAA:NR)**

REPENTANCE** (1922, Brit.) 6 reels B&Z/Renters bw

Peggy Hathaway *(Queenie Creedon)*, Roy Haymond *(Frank Hepburn)*, Geoffrey Benstead *(Toby)*, Ray Lankester *(Dr. Smith)*, Ward McAllister, Fabbie Benstead.

Hokum abounds in this British melodrama about an abused girl who wins the heart of an aristocrat. When the girl becomes ill, the gentleman arranges for her to stay at his summer home, but his mother finds out, assumes they are having an affair, and disinherits him, telling the lad that he was actually adopted. Later the girl's brutish father makes a deathbed confession, and it's revealed that his daughter is actually the child of the titled lady. The girl is welcomed home and marries the man who would otherwise have been her brother. One wonders if her mother and his mother-in-law ever got this situation straight.

p, Geoffrey Benstead; d&w, Edward R. Gordon.

Drama **(PR:A MPAA:NR)**

REPORTED MISSING*** (1922) 7 reels Owen Moore/SF bw

Owen Moore *(Richard Boyd)*, Pauline Garon *(Pauline Blake)*, Tom Wilson *(Sam)*, Togo Yamamoto *(J. Young)*, Frank Wunderlee *(Capt. Ferguson)*, Robert Cain *(Andrew Dunn)*, Nita Naldi *(Nita)*, Micky Bennett *(A Kid)*.

Henry "Pathe" Lehrman put his close association as comic and director for Mack Sennett to good use in this funny and exciting comedy-drama about a sneaky, unscrupulous Japanese shipping tycoon who tries to steal the merchant fleet that Moore has inherited. There are plenty of thrills (in the serial tradition) as his evil scheme is completely thwarted, and the studio enlisted the services of popular newspaper wags H. I. Phillips, John Medbury, and Will Johnson to add some additional punch to the titles.

d, Henry Lehrman; sup, Myron Selznick; w, Lewis Allen Browne (based on a story by Owen Moore, Lehrman); t, H. I. Phillips, John Medbury, Will B. Johnson, E. V. Durling, Tom Bret; ph, Jules Cronjager; ed, George M. Arthur.

Comedy/Adventure **(PR:A MPAA:NR)**

REPUTATION*** (1921) 7 reels UNIV-Jewel bw

Priscilla Dean *(Fay McMillan/Laura Figlan/Pauline Stevens)*, Harry Van Meter *(Monty Edwards)*, May Giraci *(Pauline Stevens, as a Child)*, Harry Carter *(Dan Frawley)*, Niles Welch *(Jimmie Dorn)*, William Welsh *(Max Gossman)*, Spottiswoode Aitken *(Karl)*, Rex De Roselli *(Theater Owner)*, William Archibald *(Photographer)*, Harry Webb *(His Assistant)*, Madge Hunt *(Matron)*; Stage Sequence: Allan Garcia *(Leading Man)*, James McLaughlin *(Heavy Man)*, Kathleen Myers, Joey McCreery *(Ingenues)*, Alice H. Smith *(Charwoman)*, Francois Dumas *(Charman)*, Joe Ray *(Stage Manager)*.

Tour-de-force performance by Dean (in a dual role as mother and daughter), despite Stuart Patton's poor directing, makes this one worth viewing. It's the story of an actress-mother who misses her Broadway opening because she's become a drug addict in Paris, and the abandoned daughter who takes her name and place and scores a triumph in the production. Later, the furious mother returns to New York, commits a murder, and arranges for her alter ego to take the fall. But when the pathetic actress comes to realize that the girl she framed is actually her own daughter, she writes a confession and then destroys herself.

d, Stuart Patton; w, Doris Schroeder, Lucien Hubbard (based on the story "False Colors" by Edwina Levin); ph, Harold Janes; m, Hugo Riesenfeld.

Drama **(PR:A MPAA:NR)**

RESCUE, THE*** (1917) 5 reels BLUE bw

Dorothy Phillips *(Anne Wetherall)*, Gretchen Lederer *(Nell Jerrold)*, William Stowell *(Kent Wetherall)*, Lon Chaney *(Thomas Holland)*, Molly Malone *(Betty Jerrold)*, Claire Du Brey *(Henriette)*, Gertrude Astor *(Mrs. Hendricks)*.

As a means of preventing a young woman from making the mistake of marrying the man she just divorced, Phillips performs the ultimate sacrifice and marries him again. Shortly thereafter she discovers that the light of love is still burning, and that the courtship she tried in vain to sabotage was all contrived to bring about the reconciliation.

d&w, Ida May Park (based on a story by Hugh Kahler); ph, King Gray.

Drama **(PR:A MPAA:NR)**

RESCUE, THE*** (1929) 9 reels Goldwyn/UA bw

Ronald Colman *(Tom Lingard)*, Lily Damita *(Lady Edith Travers)*, Alfred Hickman *(Mr. Travers)*, Theodore Von Eltz *(Carter)*, John Davidson *(Hassim)*, Philip Strange *(D'Alacer)*, Bernard Siegel *(Jorgensen)*, Sojin *(Daman)*, Harry Cording *(Belarab)*, Laska Winters *(Immada)*, Duke Kahanamoku *(Jaffir)*, Louis Morrison *(Shaw)*, George Rigas *(Wasub)*, Christopher Martin *(Tenga)*.

Herbert Brenon's large and skillfully directed film based on Joseph Conrad's novel is solid cinema on every level. In it Colman plays a British adventurer who gives refuge to an island prince and his sister who have been driven from their village by rebellious natives. As Colman prepares to assist the prince in getting back his island, he is sidetracked by a wealthy English couple who are traveling in the area on their yacht. The wife, Damita, is attracted to Colman and the two have an affair. Later, when natives overtake her husband's ship, Damita goes to summon Colman, but in a moment of passion, they never reach their destination. When they discover afterwards that the ship was dynamited and all aboard, including her husband, have been killed, Colman sends Damita away and lives out his life in seclusion.

d, Herbert Brenon; w, Elzabeth Meehan (based on the novel by Joseph Conrad); t, Katherine Hilliker, H. H. Caldwell; ph, George Barnes; m, Hugo Riesenfeld; ed, Marie Halvey, Hilliker, Caldwell; art d, William Cameron Menzies; syn sc; s eff.

Drama **(PR:A MPAA:NR)**

REST CURE, THE** (1923, Brit.) 5 reels STOLL bw

George Robey *(George)*, Sydney Fairbrother *(Mrs. George)*, Gladys Hamer *(The Maid)*, Bertie White *(The Idiot)*, Harry Preston *(The Squire)*, Bob Reed *(The Vicar)*, Mickey Brantford *(The Boy)*, Joan Whalley *(The Girl)*, Minna Leslie *(The Friend)*, George Bishop *(The Cabman)*, Raymond Ellis *(The Landlord)*.

Popular British entertainer Robey wrote the novel and then played his own character in this comedy about a man from the city who decides to take a rest in the country but runs into so many incredible and unsettling complications that he returns to the peace and quiet of urban life.

d&w, A. E. Coleby (based on the novel by George Robey).

Comedy **(PR:A MPAA:NR)**

RETURN OF PETER GRIMM, THE* 1/2** (1926) 7 reels FOX bw

Alec B. Francis *(Peter Grimm)*, John Roche *(Frederick Grimm)*, Janet Gaynor *(Catherine)*, Richard Walling *(James Hartman)*, John St. Polis *(Andrew MacPherson)*, Lionel Belmore *(Rev. Bartholomey)*, Elizabeth Patterson *(Mrs. Bartholomey)*, Bodil Rosing *(Marta)*, Mickey McBan *(William)*, Florence Gilbert *(Annamarie)*, Sammy Cohen *(The Clown)*.

Gaynor was well on her way to stardom when she delivered this sensitive performance as the young girl who swears to marry her dying guardian's nephew and afterwards discovers he has fathered another woman's child. The old man returns from the grave (in one of director Schertzinger's creative double exposure sequences), enters his delirious nephew's mind, and turns him into a decent human being. A very kind-spirited motion picture, loaded with laughter as well as tears.

d, Victor Schertzinger; w, Bradley King (based on the play by David Belasco); ph, Glen MacWilliams.

Drama **(PR:A MPAA:NR)**

RETURN OF THE PRODIGAL, THE
(SEE: PRODIGAL SON, THE, 1923, Brit.)

REVELATION* (1924) 9 reels MG bw

Viola Dana *(Joline Hofer)*, Monte Blue *(Paul Granville)*, Marjorie Daw *(Mlle. Brevoort)*, Lew Cody *(Count de Roche)*, Frank Currier *(Prior)*, Edward Connelly *(Augustin)*, Kathleen Key *(Madonna)*, Ethel Wales *(Mme. Hofer)*, George Siegmann *(Hofer)*, Otto Matiesen *(Du Clos)*, Bruce Guerin *(Jean Hofer)*.

Hokum-a-plenty in this poorly produced drama about a girl, Dana, who is thrown out of the house by her father, abandons her baby, and moves to Paris to live the fast life. She becomes an artist's model and falls in love with Blue, a young American painter who refuses to let her pose for his portrait of the Virgin Mary. The girl insists, however, and during the sitting she experiences a complete regeneration. The picture ends with her married to the artist, who has become rich and famous, and reunited with her father and child.

d&w, George D. Baker (based on the novel *The Rosebush of a Thousand Years* by Mabel Wagnalls); ph, John Arnold; ed, Grant Wytock, Lew Ostrow; art d, John J. Hughes.

Drama **(PR:A MPAA:NR)**

REWARD, THE*** (1915) 4 reels Reliance bw

Bessie Barriscale *(Jane Wallace)*, Authur Maude *(Dan Colby)*, Louise Glaum *(Trixie)*, Margaret Thompson *(Pinkie)*.

Backstage drama has chorus girl Barriscale, known to all as the "Iceberg" because of her refusal to live the wild life, almost yielding to the seductive suggestions of a millionaire. She changes her mind, however, when on her way to his apartment she is called upon to assist in an emergency childbirth. The young man who witnesses the scene is so taken by her kindness and natural maternal instincts that he proposes—and she gladly gives up the theater.

d, Reginald Barker; w, C. Gardner Sullivan, Thomas H. Ince.

Drama **(PR:A MPAA:NR)**

RICH MEN'S WIVES** (1922) 7 reels PRE/Al Lichtman bw

House Peters *(John Masters)*, Claire Windsor *(Gay Davenport)*, Rosemary Theby *(Mrs. Lindley-Blair)*, Gaston Glass *(Juan Camillo)*, Myrtle Stedman *(Mrs. Davenport)*, Richard Headrick *(Jackie)*, Mildred June *(Estelle Davenport)*, Charles Clary *(Mr. Davenport)*, Carol Holloway *(Maid)*, Martha Mattox *(Nurse)*, William Austin *(Reggie)*.

It's the old society drama formula about the wife wrongly accused of cheating, losing her baby (and visitation rights) in the divorce, and the husband yielding in her absence to the temptation of debauchery. One night the mother, Windsor, slips into the family home to catch a glimpse of her child, only to find a whale of a party in progress, and the baby being used by the revelers to portray Cupid. Maternal instinct overcomes caution, and Windsor rushes over and snatches the child from the circle of drunks. Her ex-husband, Peters, is touched by this action and, realizing his own error, sobers up and begs his wife to take him back.

d, Louis J. Gasnier; sup, B. P. Schulberg; w, Lois Zellner (based on a story by Frank Dazey, Agnes Christine Johnston); ph, Karl Struss.

Drama **(PR:A MPAA:NR)**

RIDDLE: WOMAN, THE* 1/2 (1920) 6 reels AEX/Pathe bw

Geraldine Farrar *(Lilla)*, Montagu Love *(Larz Orlik)*, Adele Blood *(Kristine)*, William T. Carleton *(Eric Helsingor)*, Frank Losee *(Sigurd Gravert)*, Madge Bellamy *(Marie Meyer)*, Louis Stern *(Isaac Meyer)*.

Disappointing film adaptation of an interesting play completely abandons the psychological motivations which made the stage version work. Farrar does what she can with the role, which has her spurning her seducer, but it is Love, as the dedicated libertine, who brings this picture its only spark.

d, Edward Jose; w, John B. Clymer (based on the play by Carl Jacoby); ph, Max Schneider.

Drama **(PR:A MPAA:NR)**

RIDE FOR YOUR LIFE 1/2** (1924) 6 reels UNIV bw

Hoot Gibson *(Bud Watkins)*, Laura La Plante *(Betsy Burke)*, Harry Todd *("Plug" Hanks)*, Robert McKim *("Gentleman Jim" Slade)*, Howard Truesdell *(Dan Burke)*, Fred Humes *(The Cocopah Kid)*, Clark Comstock *(Tim Murphy)*, Mrs. George Hernandez *(Mrs. Donnegan)*, William Robert Daly *(Dan Donnegan)*.

After taking the identity of a notorious outlaw who died in his presence, Gibson sets out to retrieve the ranch which gambler McKim cheated him out of. In the course of doing so he also wins the love of La Plante, the sheriff's daughter, and brings the entire gang of outlaws to justice.

d, Edward Sedgwick; w, Raymond L. Schrock, E. Richard Schayer (based on a story by Johnston McCulley); ph, Virgil Miller.

Western **(PR:A MPAA:NR)**

RIDERS OF MYSTERY** (1925) 5 reels IP bw

Bill Cody *(Bob Merriwell)*, Frank Rice *(Jerry Jones)*, Tom Lingham *(John Arliss)*, Peggy O'Dare *(Helen Arliss)*, Mack V. Wright *(Dan Blair)*.

Accused of being the leader of a gang known as the Phantom Bandits, Cody saves the life of a wounded stagecoach driver, rescues the driver's daughter from the real Phantom Bandit, Wright, and brings the outlaws to justice.

d, Robert North Bradbury; sup, Jesse J. Goldburg; w, George W. Pyper; ph, Bert Longenecker.

Western **(PR:A MPAA:NR)**

RIDERS OF THE DAWN** (1920) 6 reels Hampton/Hodkinson bw

Roy Stewart *(Kurt Dorn)*, Claire Adams *(Lenore Anderson)*, Marc Robbins *(Chris Dorn)*, Joseph J. Dowling *(Tom Anderson)*, Robert McKim *(Henry Neuman)*, Frederick Starr *(Nash)*, Violet Schram *(Olga)*, Frank Brownlee *(Glidden)*, Marie Messenger *(Kathleen)*, Arthur Morrison, Nelson McDowell, Charles Murphy.

A couple of big scenes are about the only things this western, about a man who returns from the service to battle an outlaw gang intent on stealing all of the wheat land, has to offer. There were supposed to be some veiled references to an early labor movement known as the Industrial Workers of the World, but apparently the producers figured that was a hot potato, and dropped them.

d, Jack Conway; w, William H. Clifford, L. V. Jefferson (based on the novel *The Desert of Wheat* by Zane Grey); ph, Harry Vallejo.

Western **(PR:A MPAA:NR)**

RIDERS OF THE PURPLE SAGE*** (1925) 6 reels FOX bw

Tom Mix *(Jim Lassiter)*, Beatrice Burnham *(Millie Erne)*, Arthur Morrison *(Frank Erne)*, Seesel Ann Johnson *(Bess Erne, as a Child)*, Warner Oland *(Lew Walters/Judge Dyer)*, Fred Kohler *(Metzger)*, Charles Newton *(Herd)*, Joe Rickson *(Slack)*, Mabel Ballin *(Jane Withersteen)*, Charles Le Moyne *(Richard Tull)*, Harold Goodwin *(Bern Venters)*, Marion Nixon *(Bess Erne)*, Dawn O'Day [Anne Shirley], *(Fay Larkin)*, Wilfred Lucas *(Oldring)*.

When his sister and her daughter are abducted by Oland, a vengeful lawyer, Texas Ranger Mix devotes his life to finding them. During the search he takes a job on a ranch owned by Ballin, and the two fall in love. Ballin informs Mix that the man he's looking for has become a judge and is living under an assumed name, at which point Mix confronts the skunk and shoots him dead. A posse is quickly formed, and Mix and his sweetheart escape to a plateau which can only be reached through steps carved in the side of the rock. Mix drops a boulder which destroys these steps, and the young lovers decide to spend the rest of their days in blissful seclusion.

d, Lynn Reynolds; w, Edfrid Bingham (based on the novel by Zane Grey); ph, Dan Clark.

Western **(PR:A MPAA:NR)**

RIDERS OF THE RIO GRANDE* (1929) 5 reels J. P. McGowan/SYN bw

Bob Custer *(Jack Beresford)*, Edna Aslin *(Barbara Steelman)*, H. B. Carpenter *(Dan Steelman)*, Kip Cooper *(John Steelman)*, Bob Erickson *(Pinto Quantrell)*, Martin Cichy *("Snakey" Smiley)*, Merrill McCormick *("Tough" Hawkins)*.

Substandard B western offers no suspense, few thrills, and the usual story of the hero rescuing a kidnaped girl and bringing the outlaws to justice.

d, J. P. McGowan; w&t, Sally Winters; ph, Hap Depew; syn sc.

Western **(PR:A MPAA:NR)**

RIDERS OF VENGEANCE*** (1919) 6 reels UNIV bw

Harry Carey *(Cheyenne Harry)*, J. Farrell MacDonald *(Buell)*, Seena Owen *(Lola Madison)*, Joseph Harris *(Gale Thurman)*, Glita Lee *(Virginia)*, Alfred Allen, Jennie Lee, Betty Schade, Clita Gale, Vester Pegg, M.K. Wilson.

Carey, who barely escapes when his entire family is gunned down by a gang, hides low for a while and then returns to kill the murderers one by one. Along the way he saves Owen from an Apache raid and falls in love with her, even though she's engaged to sheriff Harris, one of the men on Carey's death list. Toward the film's end, Carey comes to Harris' aid when he is attacked by Indians, and in a running gunfight (which director Ford would use again and again over the years) the two manage to escape. But the sheriff, who it turns out was not involved in the slaughter of Carey's family, dies of his wounds, leaving the door open for the hero to take Owen as his wife.

p, A. Powers; d, Jack [John] Ford; w, Eugene B. Lewis (based on a story by Harry Carey, Ford); ph, John W. Brown.

Western **(PR:A MPAA:NR)**

RIDGEWAY OF MONTANA** (1924) 5 reels UNIV bw

Jack Hoxie *(Buck Ridgeway)*, Olive Hasbrouck *(Aline Hanley)*, Herbert Fortier *(Simon Hanley)*, Lew Meehan *(Steve Pelton)*, Charles Thurston *(Rev. McNabb)*, Pat Harmon *(Pete Shagmire)*, Lyndon Hobart *(Pierre Gendron)*.

Hoxie captures a gang of rustlers, but their leader, Meehan, gets away. Later, while taking his cattle to market, Hoxie becomes involved with Hasbrouck, a flapper who toys with him and becomes infuriated when he doesn't fall head over heels. When they are forced to spend the night at his lodge, however, due to a blizzard, Hoxie does fall hard, and subsequently rescues the young lady from the foul advances of Meehan. The couple then vow their love for one another and decide to tie the knot.

d, Clifford S. Smith; w, E. Richard Schayer, Isadore Bernstein, Raymond L. Schrock (based on the novel *A Sacrifice to Mammon* by William MacLeod Raine); ph, Harry Neumann.

Western **(PR:A MPAA:NR)**

RIDIN' MAD 1/2** (1924) 5 reels Ben Wilson/Arrow bw

Yakima Canutt *(Steve Carlson)*, Lorraine Eason *(Marion Putman)*, Wilbur McGaugh *(Allen Walker)*, Helen Rosson *(Ruth Carlson)*, Annabelle Lee *(Beth Carlson)*, Dick La Reno *(Thornton Hawks)*.

Ace stuntman and champion rodeo cowboy Canutt puts his considerable skills to good use in this little western about a man who clears his name by escaping from jail and nails the crook who murdered his sweetheart's father.

d&w, Jacques Jaccard.

Western **(PR:A MPAA:NR)**

RIDIN' THE WIND*** (1925) 6 reels MON/FBO bw

Fred Thomson *(Jim Harkness)*, Jacqueline Gadsdon *(May Lacy)*, Lewis Sargent *(Dick Harkness)*, David Dunbar *(Black Hat Gangleader)*, Betty Scott *(Dolly Dutton)*, David Kirby *(Sheriff Lacy)*, Silver King the Horse.

After sacrificing everything to send his young brother to college, Thomson breaks up a train robbery and captures one of the bandits. The outlaw turns out to be his brother, so Thomson returns the stolen loot, straightens the kid out, brings the gang to justice and, as a reward, marries Gadsdon, the sheriff's beautiful schoolteacher daughter.

d, Del Andrews, Al Werker; w, Marion Jackson (based on a story by Frank M. Clifton); ph, Ross Fisher.

Western **(PR:A MPAA:NR)**

RIDIN' WILD 1/2** (1922) 5 reels UNIV bw

Hoot Gibson *(Cyril Henderson)*, Edna Murphy *(Grace Nolan)*, Wade Boteler *(Art Jordan)*, Jack Walker *(George Berge)*, Otto Hoffman *(Andrew McBride)*, Wilton Taylor *(Sheriff Nolan)*, Bert Wilson *(Alfred Clark)*, Gertrude Claire *(Mrs. Henderson)*, William Welsh *(John Henderson)*.

Raised as a Quaker, Gibson, because of his gentle ways, is the butt of much laughter on the part of the town's menfolk. But when his father is accused of murder, Gibson swings into action, gives the real killer a good pasting, rescues Murphy, the girl he loves, and slips a ring on her finger.

d, Nat Ross; w, Roy Myers, Edward T. Lowe, Jr. (based on a story by Myers); ph, Virgil Miller.

Western **(PR:A MPAA:NR)**

RIDING WITH DEATH 1/2** (1921) 5 reels FOX bw

Charles "Buck" Jones *(Dynamite Steve Dorsey)*, Betty Francisco *(Anita Calhoun)*, Jack Mower *(Val Nelson)*, J. Farrell MacDonald *(Sheriff Pat Garrity)*, H. von Sickle *(Col. Lee Calhoun)*, William Steele *(Chick Dillon)*, William Gettinger *(Garrity's Friend)*, Bill Gillis *(Capt. Jack Hughes)*, Artie Ortega *(Tony Carilla)*, Tina Medotti *(Rosa Carilla)*.

Texas Ranger Jones takes on sheriff MacDonald and his men after the crooked lawman oversees the death of Jones' best friend. Jones is thrown into jail but manages to get word to the Rangers, who sweep into town and defeat the outlaws. Once freed, Jones rides to the rescue of Francisco, the girl MacDonald kidnaped, and in a final showdown sends the crooked sheriff off to meet his maker.

d, Jacques Jaccard; w, Agnes Parsons (based on a story by Jaccard); ph, Frank B. Good.

Western **(PR:A MPAA:NR)**

RIGHT THAT FAILED, THE*** (1922) 5 reels Metro bw

Bert Lytell *(Johnny Duffey)*, Virginia Valli *(Constance Talbot)*, De Witt Jennings *(Mr. Talbot)*, Philo McCullough *(Roy Van Twiller)*, Otis Harlan *(Mr. Duffey)*, Max Davidson *(Michael Callahan)*.

Diverting comedy has Lytell playing the part of a lightweight boxing champion who breaks his hand in a fight and takes off for a fashionable resort to rest. There he wins the love of Valli, a pretty little society girl, but to his chagrin discovers that she is engaged to stuffed shirt McCullough. Valli's father, who has no use for his prospective son-in-law, takes an immediate shine to Lytell. McCullough, who recognizes the champ and feels threatened by him, wires Lytell's father, manager, and top challenger to come to the resort where he plans to reveal to Valli his rival's true identity. Her father, however, gets wind of the plot, lets the visitors in on the scheme, and they make a complete fool of McCullough by denying everything. Lytell then breaks his hand on the rotter's jaw, tells Valli the whole story, and is enthusiastically welcomed into the family.

d, Bayard Veiller; w, Lenore Coffee (based on a story by John Phillips Marquand); ph, Arthur Martinelli.

Comedy **(PR:A MPAA:NR)**

RIGHT TO LIE, THE** (1919) 7 reels Capellani/Pathe bw

Dolores Cassinelli *(Carlotta)*, Frank Mills *(Curtis Austin)*, Joseph King *(Crosby Dana)*, Warren Cook *(J. Winthrop Drake)*, Grace Reals *(Mrs. Drake)*, George Deneubourg *(Signor Riccardo Novelli)*, Claire Grenville *(Signora Dolores)*, Violet Reed *(Edith Austin)*, Rae Allen.

Old-fashioned hokum about a married couple who are separated, with each believing the other to be dead. When the woman is actually on her deathbed, her husband arrives in time to discover that they have a daughter. The man takes the child home, where she is badly mistreated by her stepmother. Later, the woman becomes involved with another man, whom the husband shoots. When he learns at the trial that his wife compromised herself to save him, he forgives her deed and the family is reunited. The daughter, who has found the perfect young man, closes the film in a montage of wedding bells.

d, Edwin Carewe; w, Jane Murfin; ph, Lucien Andriot.

Drama **(PR:A MPAA:NR)**

RIGHT WAY, THE***

(1921) 7 reels Thomas Mott Osborne/Producers Security-Standard bw (AKA: WITHIN PRISON WALLS; MAKING GOOD)

Edwards Davis *(The Father)*, Helen Lindroth *(The Mother)*, Joseph Marquis *(The Rich Boy)*, Vivienne Osborne *(The Sweetheart)*, Sidney D'Albrook *(The Poor Boy)*, Annie Ecleston *(His Mother)*, Helen Ferguson *(His Sweetheart)*, Elsie McLeod *(His Sister)*, Tammany Young *(The Smiler)*, Thomas Brooks *(The New Warden)*.

Interesting film produced by Thomas Mott Osborne, former warden of Sing Sing Prison and leader of the Mutual Welfare League (a group dedicated to penal reform and advocates of the honor system), which spoke out in favor of humane methods of incarceration. The picture is not weighted down with propaganda, however, and very subtly communicates its point. It tells the story (nicely directed by Sidney Olcott) of two convicts, one poor and a victim of the sadistic old methods, and the other, a rich man's son convicted of forgery, who experiences the more "enlightened" process of incarceration. The two become friends and are eventually paroled after being regenerated, but not before an innocent man is sent to the chair.

d, Sidney Olcott; w, Basil Dickey.

Drama **(PR:A MPAA:NR)**

RILEY THE COP*** (1928) 6 reels FOX bw

J. Farrell MacDonald *(James Riley)*, Louise Fazenda *(Lena Krausmeyer)*, Nancy Drexel *(Mary Coronelli)*, David Rollins *(Joe Smith)*, Harry Schultz *(Hans Krausmeyer)*, Mildred Boyd *(Caroline)*, Ferdinand Schumann-Heink *(Julius Kuchendorf)*, Del Henderson *(Judge Coronelli)*, Mike Donlin *(Crook)*, Russell Powell *(Mr. Kuchendorf)*, Tom Wilson *(Sergeant)*, Billy Bevan *(Paris Cab Driver)*, Otto Fries *(Munich Cab Driver)*, Robert Parrish.

Enjoyable John Ford comedy has officer MacDonald, an easygoing cop, loved by everyone he knows except for Schultz, the policeman on the next beat and his lifelong rival. MacDonald is sent to Europe to bring back Rollins, a neighborhood lad who has followed his sweetheart abroad after her snooty aunt breaks up their marriage and he is falsely accused of stealing funds from his employer. While in Europe, MacDonald has the time of his life and places Rollins on the honor system, giving the lad plenty of opportunity to continue his romance. Riley, who plans to establish Rollins' innocence once they return, has, in the meantime, discovered romance himself. The lifelong bachelor falls head-over-heels-in-love with an engaging lady he meets at a beer garden. The two declare their undying affection for one another and, in a scene which could take place only in the movies, MacDonald is dumfounded to discover his sweetheart is none other than the sister of his arch rival, Schultz. But, alas, all ends on a happy note.

d, John Ford; w, Fred Stanley, James Gruen; ph, Charles Clarke; ed, Alex Troffey; syn sc; s eff.

Comedy/Drama **(PR:A MPAA:NR)**

RING, THE*** (1927, Brit.) 9 reels BIP/Wolfe and Freedman bw

Carl Brisson *(Jack Sander, the "Round One")*, Lilian Hall-Davis *(Nelly)*, Ian Hunter *(Bob Corby)*, Forrester Harvey *(Harry, the Traveling Showman of the Ring)*, Gordon Harker *(George)*, Harry Terry *(Barker)*, Billy Wells *(Boxer)*, Charles Farrell *(Second)*, Clare Greet *(Gypsy)*.

Hitchcock's second best silent film after THE LODGER (1926) has a young man falling for a girl who works the pay box for a boxer who takes on all comers at the circus (more than a suggestion of Dupont's VARIETY [1926] here). The lad marries the girl, turns pro, but loses her affections to the champion. Later, during the big fight, she shows up to jeer her husband, but when she sees the beating he's taking, she rushes to the corner and gives him the boost he needs to win the big match. There are some excellent directorial touches and photographic effects (in the German tradition) in this picture. Though the script is really pretty hokey, the film stands out most vividly when compared to the rest of Britain's dismal output at that time.

p, John Maxwell; d, Alfred Hitchcock; w, Hitchcock, Alma Reville (based on a story by Hitchcock); ph, John J. Cox; set d, Elstree.

Drama **(PR:A MPAA:NR)**

RING AND THE MAN, THE 1/2** (1914) 4 reels FP bw

Bruce McRae *(George Fordyce)*, Helen Aubrey *(Mrs. Jim Martin)*, Wellington A. Player *(Haldane)*, Robert Broderick *(Big Jim Martin)*, Violet Horner, Charles Douglas.

McRae, an appealing actor who, strangely, never gained film stardom, is cast as a westerner who takes the blame for a woman who kills her abusive husband while trying to escape. Later, McRae changes his name and heads East, where he becomes a millionaire and defeats a crooked politician out to gain control of the traction trust.

d, Francis Powers; w, Cyrus Townsend Brady.

Drama **(PR:A MPAA:NR)**

RINGER, THE** (1928, Brit.) 7 reels BL/ID bw

Leslie Faber *(Dr. Lomond)*, Annette Benson *(Cora Ann Milton)*, Lawson Butt *(Maurice Meister)*, Nigel Barrie *(Inspector Wembury)*, Hayford Hobbs *(Inspector Bliss)*, John Hamilton *(John Lenley)*, Charles Emerald *(Sam Hackett)*, Esther Rhodes *(Gwenda Milton)*, Muriel Angelus *(Mary Lenley)*.

The Edgar Wallace mystery play, so popular in Europe and England, fails to generate much excitement on the screen. It all has to do with trying to figure out the identity of a master criminal known as The Ringer, but beyond that the thrills are few and far between.

d, Arthur Maude; w, Edgar Wallace (based on his own play).

Mystery **(PR:A MPAA:NR)**

RIP-TIDE, THE* (1923) 6 reels A.B. Maescher/Arrow bw

J. Frank Glendon *(Prince Tagor)*, Dick Sutherland *(The lst Man)*, George Rigas *(The Philosopher)*, Diana Alden *(Princess Indora)*, Stuart Holmes *(Count Boris Voronsky)*, Russell Simpson *(The Maharajah)*, Rosemary Theby *(Countess Dagmar)*.

Feeble programmer has Glendon, India's envoy to England, converting to the Anglican faith and becoming a minister. When Glendon returns to his native land to convert his people and wed his fiancee, Alden, he discovers that his sweetheart is engaged to Holmes, a Russian count, and that they desire him to perform the nuptials. The honeymoon is still in progress when a countess, Theby, blows the whistle on Holmes and announces that he is her husband. To fulfill his father's sense of honor, Glendon challenges the Russian to a duel but does not kill him for the sake of the woman he still loves. Alden, however, sees her husband for what he is and begs the gentle man-of-God to forgive her.

d, Jack Pratt; w, J. Grubb Alexander; ph, Harry Keepers.

Drama **(PR:A MPAA:NR)**

RIP VAN WINKLE*** (1914) Rolfe Photoplays/Alco bw

Thomas Jefferson *(Rip Van Winkle)*, Clariet Claire, H. B. Blackmore.

Nicely done film version of Washington Irving's classic novel, although the picture probably owes more to the popular stage play by Thomas Jefferson's father, Joseph Jefferson. It's the well-known story of the kindly fellow who enjoys his drink, and after being driven from his home by a shrewish wife, goes to the mountains where he sleeps for 20 years. Everything has changed when he awakens, but his daughter, now a lovely young lady, is saved from marrying the town meanie, and Rip Van Winkle (Jefferson) is invited to live happily with her and the sailor she really loves and later marries. RIP VAN WINKLE was so well received, that Jefferson repeated his starring role in another version in 1921, the same year this 1914 version was reissued.

w, Edwin Middleton (based on the play by Joseph Jefferson, Dion Boucicault, from the novel by Washington Irving).

Fantasy **(PR:A MPAA:NR)**

RIP VAN WINKLE** (1921) 7 reels Ward Lascelle/Hodkinson bw

Thomas Jefferson *(Rip Van Winkle)*, Milla Davenport *(Gretchen Van Winkle)*, Daisy Robinson *(Meenie Van Winkle)*, Gertrude Messinger *(Meenie Van Winkle, 20 Years Later)*, Pietro Sosso *(Derrick Van Beekman)*, Max Asher *(Nick Vedder)*, Francis Carpenter *(Hendrick Vedder)*.

Thomas Jefferson, whose father Joseph Jefferson was so closely associated with the character of Rip Van Winkle on the stage that many people assumed he wrote the book, plays the part for the second time in his film career. (He made a film of the same title in 1914, which was reissued in 1921.) The story is the same—the old reprobate who falls asleep for 20 years after tying one on—and though an enjoyable diversion, it should have been much more.

p&d, Ward Lascelle; w, Agnes Parsons (based on the play by Joseph Jefferson, Dion Boucicault and the novel by Washington Irving); ph, David Abel, George Larson.

Drama/Fantasy **(PR:A MPAA:NR)**

RISE OF JENNIE CUSHING, THE*** (1917) 5 reels ART bw

Elsie Ferguson *(Jennie Cushing)*, Elliott Dexter *(Donelson Meigs)*, Fania Marinoff *(Marie)*, Frank Goldsmith *(Mr. Harrish)*, Callie Delatorre *(Edith Gerrard)*, Mae Bates

(Granny), Edith McAlpin *(Mrs. Meigs)*, Isabel Vernon *(Aunt Carrie)*, Blanche Craig, James Cogan, Marie Burke.

Ferguson gives a good performance and Tourneur's direction is splendid in this story of a slum girl who spends a few years in a reformatory and then becomes the common-law wife of an artist. When her past catches up with her, she runs away to spare her lover any humiliation, but he follows her and eventually the couple marry. There are many beautiful moments in this picture, but the most shocking is when the painter first proposes and she replies, "No, I won't marry you—but I'll live with you." To which he cavalierly responds, "You're on."

d, Maurice Tourneur; w, Charles Maigne (based on the novel by Mary S. Watts).

Drama **(PR:C MPAA:NR)**

RISKY ROAD, THE** (1918) 5 reels UNIV bw

Dorothy Phillips *(Marjorie Helmer)*, William Stowell *(Melville Kingston)*, George Chesebro *(Robert Grant)*, Edward Cecil *(Miles Kingston)*, Joseph Girard *(Van Belt)*, Juanita Hansen *(Lottie Bangor)*, Claire Du Brey *(Mrs. Miles Kingston)*, Sally Starr *(Myrtle)*.

Second-rate programmer has a down-on-her-luck stenographer allowing herself to be "kept" in a swanky aprartment by her former boss. There is no hanky-panky involved in this arrangement, but when her country boy friend comes to town, assumes the worst, and tries to make a pass, she sends him packing. The picture of course ends with the little stenographer marrying the fellow with the funds.

d&w, Ida May Park (based on the story "Her Fling" by Katherine Lazer Robbins).

Drama **(PR:A MPAA:NR)**

ROAD HOUSE** 1/2** (1928) 5 reels FOX bw

Maria Alba *(Spanish Marla)*, Warren Burke *(Larry Grayson)*, Lionel Barrymore *(Henry Grayson)*, Julia Swayne Gordon *(Mrs. Henry Grayson)*, Tempe Piggott *(Grandma Grayson)*, Eddie Clayton *(Jim, Larry's Pal)*, Jack Oakie *(Sam)*, Jane Keckley *(Maid)*, Joe Brown *(Himself)*, Kay Bryant *(Mary, Larry's Girl)*.

Fox was able to sneak in plenty of wild parties, hip flask stuff, sexy Charleston dancing, roadhouse vamps, as well as an underworld theme, in this jazz-age "expose" which used as its justification the message that lenient parents are often responsible for the misdeeds of their sons and daughters.

d, Richard Rosson; w, John Stone (based on a story by Philip Hurn); ph, George Schneiderman.

Drama **(PR:A MPAA:NR)**

ROAD TO LONDON, THE*** (1921, Brit.) 5 reels Screenplays/AEX bw

Bryant Washburn *(Rex Rowland)*, Joan Morgan *(Lady Emily)*, George Folsey *(Mr. Rowland)*, Gibb McLaughlin *(The Count)*, Saba Raleigh *(Duchess)*, Rev. Dr. Batchelor *(Vicar)*, Mabel Washburn *(Maid)*, Sir Bertran Hays *(Captain of H.M.S. Olympic)*.

Good British mixture of comedy and adventure has Washburn, an American tourist, saving Morgan, a young titled lady, from a forced marriage. The film is almost one long chase sequence, with the couple fleeing through some of England's most historic and scenic locations while Morgan's aunt and the nasty fiance's gang follow in hot pursuit. The picture ends with the couple falling in love and sailing in style for the good old U.S.

d, Eugene Mullen; w, Dwight Cleveland (based on a novel by David Skaats Foster); ph, Charles Davis.

Adventure/Comedy **(PR:A MPAA:NR)**

ROAD TO MANDALAY, THE*** (1926) 7 reels MGM bw

Lon Chaney *(Singapore Joe)*, Lois Moran *(Joe's Daughter)*, Owen Moore *(The Admiral)*, Henry B. Walthall *(Father James)*, Kamiyama Sojin *(English Charlie Wing)*, Rose Langdon *(Pansy)*, John George *(Servant)*.

Chaney plays the operator of a Singapore dive who sent his daughter to be raised in a Mandalay convent after his wife died in childbirth, and has kept his relationship to her a secret. Later his associate, a shady character known as The Admiral (Moore) falls in love with the girl, now grown up (Moran), and completely reforms. When Chaney learns that they plan to marry, he abducts Moore and takes him to his brothel. Moran follows them, and while the former friends are engaged in a struggle to the death, she stabs her father in the back. Mortally wounded, Chaney forces himself to stay alive long enough to allow the couple to escape from a villainous Chinaman, skillfully played by the always excellent Sojin. For this characterization of Singapore Joe, Chaney created one of his most famous makeup disguises—that of a man with a badly scarred face and a white cataract-like eye, which he apparently achieved by using the skin from the interior of an egg shell.

d, Tod Browning; w, Elliott Clawson (based on a story by Herman Mankiewicz, Browning); t, Joe Farnham; ph, Merritt Gerstad; ed, Errol Taggart; art d, Cedric Gibbons, Arnold Gillespie.

Drama **(PR:C MPAA:NR)**

ROAD TO RUIN, THE** (1913, Brit.) 4 reels Barker/New Era bw

George Gray *(George Wyndham)*, G. Somerset *(Lucy Probyn)*, Harry W. Scadden *(Jack Probyn)*, Thomas H. MacDonald *(Lord Layton)*, Val Gurney *(Dick Hinton)*, E. Vaudray *(Mrs. Wyndham)*, Mary Smithers *(Katy Probyn)*.

After a terrifying nightmare, in which he witnesses his own doom, a hard-drinking gambler awakens a reformed man.

d, George Gray, Bert Haldane; w, (based on a play by George Gray).

Drama **(PR:A MPAA:NR)**

ROARING RAILS*** (1924) 6 reels Stellar/PDC bw

Harry Carey *(Big Bill Benson)*, Frankie Darro *(Little Bill)*, Edith Roberts *(Nora Burke)*, Wallace MacDonald *(Malcolm Gregory)*, Frank Hagney *(Red Burley)*.

Good action drama has Carey serving in WW I, adopting Darro, a French orphan, and bringing him back to the U.S., where Carey resumes his position as a railroad engineer. Due to an error on his part, there is a terrible accident which leaves the boy blinded. Carey then loses his job and cannot afford the needed operation, so he agrees to help his boss' son escape a murder rap in exchange for the cash to cover young Darro's medical expenses. The killer gets away as planned but fails to live up to his end of the bargain, so Carey and his little friend wander the countryside picking up whatever work they can. Eventually the ex-marine lands a job laying track and falls in love with Roberts, the foreman's lovely daughter. Fate, then provides him with the opportunity for redemption as a forest fire erupts nearby. Carey drives a locomotive through the middle of it, saving Roberts, the boy, and the railroad company from ruin. As a reward, he is given a job driving the big ones. To add to Carey's joy, little Darro has his sight restored, and the foreman's daughter becomes his bride. A well-directed and -acted picture with some great special effects and beautiful location settings in Klamath Falls, Oregon.

d, Tom Forman; sup, Hunt Stromberg; w, Doris Dorn, Stromberg; ph, Sol Polito.

Drama/Adventure **(PR:A MPAA:NR)**

ROARING ROAD, THE** 1/2** (1919) 5 reels PAR bw

Wallace Reid *(Toodles Waldron)*, Ann Little *(The Chub, His Sweetheart)*, Theodore Roberts *(J. D. Ward)*, Guy Oliver *(Tom Darby)*, C. H. Geldart *(Wheeler)*.

Entertaining comedy has Reid playing an automobile salesman who works for a crusty old capitalist (well played by the great character actor Roberts) referred to as The Bear. Reid has only two ambitions in life: to marry the boss' daughter and to participate in an auto race which pits a car against a train from San Francisco to Los Angeles. Naturally Reid wins both in the end.

d, James Cruze; w, Marion Fairfax (based on a collection of stories by Byron Morgan); ph, Frank Urson.

Comedy **(PR:A MPAA:NR)**

ROB ROY** 1/2** (1922, Brit.) 6 reels GAU/WEST bw

David Hawthorne *(Rob Roy MacGregor)*, Gladys Jennings *(Helen Campbell)*, Sir Simeon Stuart *(Duke of Montrose)*, Wallace Bosco *(James Grahame)*, Alec Hunter *(The Dougal Creatur)*, Tom Morris *(Sandy the Biter)*, Eva Llewellyn *(Mother MacGregor)*, Roy Kellino *(Ronald MacGregor)*.

Hawthorne turns outlaw after his lands are stolen and his clan is persecuted by a duke (Stuart). This has come about because Jennings prefers the handsome Hawthorne, but in the end his clan rallies, defeats the forces of the duke, and peace is restored to the land. Not a bad costume film, but the action sequences are unconvincing, and compared to the work of Douglas Fairbanks, really come up short.

d, W. P. Kellino; w, (based on a story by Alicia Ramsey).

Costume **(PR:A MPAA:NR)**

ROBIN HOOD****

(1922) 11 reels Douglas Fairbanks/UA bw (AKA: DOUGLAS FAIRBANKS IN ROBIN HOOD)

Douglas Fairbanks *(The Earl of Huntington/Robin Hood)*, Wallace Beery *(Richard the Lion-Hearted)*, Sam De Grasse *(Prince John)*, Enid Bennett *(Lady Marian Fitzwalter)*, Paul Dickey *(Sir Guy of Gisbourne)*, William Lowery *(The High Sheriff of Nottingham)*, Roy Coulson *(The King's Jester)*, Billie Bennett *(Lady Marian's Serving Woman)*, Merrill McCormick, Wilson Benge *(Henchmen to Prince John)*, Willard Louis *(Friar Tuck)*, Alan Hale *(Little John)*, Maine Geary *(Will Scarlett)*, Lloyd Talman *(Alan-a-Dale)*, Rita Gillman.

Fairbanks was enthusiastic about filming the story of Robin Hood right from the start. According to Robert Florey, head of foreign publicity for the Fairbanks-(Mary) Pickford partnership, the actor was pounding his fist on a small table as he excitedly announced, "We'll build the sets right here in Hollywood and call it 'The Spirit of Chivalry.' Mary and I are going to have to buy a new studio, where we can all work together. I'm thinking of the old Jesse Hampton studio in Santa Monica. There's nothing but fields around there, and we can put up some really big sets—Nottingham in the 12th Century, Richard the Lion Heart's castle, a town in Palestine, Sherwood Forest and the outlaw's lair. There's a big field to the south where we can set up the Crusaders camp in France. We'll have several thousand costumes designed from contemporary documents, we'll order shields, lances, and swords by the thousand, we'll stage a tournament. . ." At this point, John Fairbanks, the actor's brother and company treasurer, interrupted to inquire about the expenses. "That's not the point," the star answered, "These things have to be done properly, or not at all." Fairbanks and Pickford (his wife then) left for New York on business, and while they were gone the production team went to work. 500 laborers and craftsmen erected the sets (the castle designed by Buckland was the largest ever built, surpassing even the Babylon structure of INTOLERANCE), designed the costumes, and produced the props. When the job was completed, this 12th-Century world could be seen for miles away. Some of the interiors were too large to be lighted with electricity, so they were assembled as outdoor sets, painted to provide the right atmospheric shadows, with enormous reflectors to get the desired effects from the sun. The entire undertaking was so stupendous that by the time Fairbanks arrived at the Pasadena station, a throng was there to greet him; they couldn't wait to catch his reaction. He showed great interest, especially since the industry was in a slump, and he was forced to put $1 million of his own money into the production. As he toured the sight, Fairbanks was delighted and amazed and then, according to director Dwan, he suddenly became depressed. "I can't compete with that, "

Fairbanks told Dwan. "My work is intimate. People know me as an intimate actor. I can't work in a vast thing like that. What could I do in there?" The director pleaded with him to cheer up and then asked him to return in a couple of days. Quoting Dwan again: "I then took him onto the set. About 40 feet up, there was a balcony. I'd hung a big drape from the ceiling, sweeping down across that balcony to the ground. Now, I said, 'you get into a sword fight with the knights and they chase you up the stairs, battling all the way. You fight like mad and you succeed in getting away, but as you run out onto the balcony, some more knights rush out of the door at the end and you're caught between them. You haven't a chance so you jump on the balustrade and you're fighting them—'" At this point Fairbanks, a bit impatient, wanted to know what he could possibly do next. Dwan went on, "I showed him. I climbed onto the balustrade and jumped into this drape. I had a slide—a kid's slide—hidden inside it and I slid right down that curtain to the ground with a gesture like he used to make, and I ran through the arch to freedom. He bought it like that. 'I'll do it!' he shouted. He immediately sent out for some people, ran up to the balcony and explained it to them, then jumped in the drape and slid down. He did it a thousand times—like a kid." The picture *was* made (*without* a change in the original story title), and opened with the shot of the enormous drawbridge lowering right into the camera, followed by squires and knights and two-column long pennants waving in the breeze. Then came a long tracking shot showing King Richard (Beery) and the final tournament which is to be held before he takes his mighty army to do battle in the Crusades. Here we are also introduced to Fairbanks in his role as the Earl of Huntington. He is about to joust with the villainous Sir Guy (Dickey), who has strapped himself onto his horse. But in spite of this trickery, Fairbanks is victorious and the king makes him his second in command. They go off to fight the "heathen," but when Fairbanks receives word that Prince John (De Grasse) has attempted to overtake the throne, he returns to England, and assumes the guise of Robin Hood. From this point on, the action is practically nonstop as the Prince of Thieves does in the usurpers, rescues Maid Marian (Bennett), and restores Richard (Beery) to the throne. ROBIN HOOD was a great artistic as well as financial success, and for the first time Fairbanks owed almost as much to his production values and sets as he did his own persona. Chaplin, in his autobiography, tells a charming story regarding his friend's creation of early Britain: "He built a 16-acre set for ROBIN HOOD—a castle with enormous ramparts and drawbridges, far bigger than any castle that ever existed. With great pride Douglas showed me the huge drawbridge. 'Magnificent,' I said. 'What a wonderful opening for one of my comedies: the drawbridge comes down, and I put out the cat and take in the milk.'"

p, Douglas Fairbanks; d, Allan Dwan; w, Lotta Woods (based on a story by Elton Thomas [Fairbanks]); ph, Arthur Edeson; ed, William Nolan; art d, Wilfred Buckland, Irvin J. Martin, Edward M. Langley; cos, Mitchell Leisen; spec eff, Paul Eagler.

Costume Adventure **Cas.** **(PR:A MPAA:NR)**

ROBINSON CRUSOE** ½ (1927, Brit.) 7 reels Epic bw

M. A. Wetherell (*Robinson Crusoe*), Fay Compton (*Sophie*), Herbert Waithe (*Friday*), Reginald Fox.

Acceptable British version of the famous Daniel Defoe novel about the adventures of a shipwrecked man. The film was reissued in 1932, with a soundtrack, which added little.

p,d&w, M. A. Wetherell (based on the novel by Daniel Defoe).

Adventure **(PR:A MPAA:NR)**

ROGUE IN LOVE, A*** (1922, Brit.) 6 reels Diamond Super/Globe bw

Frank Stanmore (*Frank Badgery*), Ann Trevor (*Pattie Keable*), Gregory Scott (*Joe Bradwick*), Fred Raines (*Joseph Keable*), Lawford Davidson (*Ray Carrell*), Betty Farquhar (*Eudocia*), Kate Gurney (*Landlady*).

Nice little British drama about an old man who, expecting a fortune from his brother, has lied to his daughter (a boarding school student) about the state of his finances. An ex-convict shows up to tell the old boy that a friend of his actually killed the brother and spent the money, but can't bring himself to do so when he sees the situation. There is also a crooked lawyer who covets the daughter, and after finding himself rejected, exposes the whole matter. The ending, which reveals the brother to actually be alive, is rather improbable. Beyond that, this is a most satisfying feature.

d, Albert Brouett; w, Harry Hughes (based on a novel by Tom Gallon).

Drama **(PR:A MPAA:NR)**

ROGUES OF LONDON, THE** (1915, Brit.) 5 reels Barker/Ashley bw

Blanche Forsythe (*Ruth Davies*), Fred Paul (*Ralph Munt*), Maud Yates (*Vera Verez*), Roy Travers.

In this British thriller a clergyman's son prevents a maid from committing suicide, and she returns the favor later by clearing his name when he's framed for murdering the mistress of a crook.

d, Bert Haldane; w, (based on a story by Rowland Talbot).

Mystery **(PR:A MPAA:NR)**

ROLLED STOCKINGS*** (1927) 7 reels PAR bw

James Hall (*Jim Treadway*), Louise Brooks (*Carol Fleming*), Richard Arlen (*Ralph Treadway*), Nancy Phillips (*The Vamp*), El Brendel (*Rudolph*), David Torrence (*Mr. Treadway*), Chance Ward (*Coach*).

Superior film depicting college life in 1927 has two brothers in love with the same girl, Brooks. The elder fellow, Hall, is an irresponsible, party-loving type who lets his father down by not making the rowing team, while his studious younger brother Arlen does. On the night before the big race, Hall takes Brooks to the school dance, which so infuriates his jealous brother, that he violates curfew by picking up a blonde flapper and escorting her to a roadhouse which is strictly off limits. Hall follows his brother, takes him on in a fist fight, then smuggles him out of the club and assumes responsibility for being with the girl. The next day, Arlen wins the rowing competition and clears the air by confessing that he's responsible for the jam his brother is in. The picture ends with Brooks rewarding the older man with her love—which beats winning a trophy any day of the week.

p, B.P. Schulberg; d, Richard Rosson; w, Percy Heath (based on a story by Frederica Sagor); t, Julian Johnson; ph, Victor Milner; ed, Johnson.

Drama **(PR:A MPAA:NR)**

ROLLING HOME*** (1926) 7 reels UNIV bw

Reginald Denny (*Nat Alden*), Marion Nixon (*Phyllis*), E.J. Ratcliffe (*Mr. Grubbell*), Ben Hendricks, Jr. (*Dan Mason*), Margaret Seddon (*Mrs. Alden*), George Nichols (*Col. Lowe*), Alfred Allen (*Gen. Wade*), C.E. Thurston (*Sheriff*), George F. Marion (*Selectman No. 1*), Alfred Knott (*Selectman No. 2*), Anton Vaverka (*Pemberton*), Howard Enstedt (*Office Boy*), Adele Watson (*Aunt*).

Clever Denny comedy has the likable star being fired as a promoter by the high-powered Ratcliffe when his various ventures fail. On his way out, he talks his old army pal, who happens to be Ratcliffe's chauffeur, into giving him a ride home. When they arrive, the townsfolk, who think Denny is a roaring success, greet him with a brass band and the county fire engine. After taking one look at the Rolls-Royce, of course, they assume that Denny is even more of a winner than they suspected. Out of embarrassment and desperation Denny pulls one last deal and purchases the local power company and a nearby waterfall. Meanwhile, Ratcliffe arrives on the scene, denounces Denny, takes a look at the electrical works which his one-time employee put together, and buys the company. Our hero puts the money in the bank and marries Nixon, the town's most beautiful girl, who would have no part of him when she thought he was a millionaire.

d, William A. Seiter; w, Rex Taylor, John McDermott (based on the play by John Hunter Booth); ph, Arthur Todd.

Comedy **(PR:A MPAA:NR)**

ROMANCE AND ARABELLA** (1919) 5 reels SEL bw

Constance Talmadge (*Arabella Cadenhouse*), Harrison Ford (*Bill*), Gertrude Claire (*Aunt Effie*), Monte Blue (*Harry Atteridge*), Arthur Edmund Carew (*Claude Easterbrooke*), Antrim Short (*Peter Harper*), James Neill (*Dr. Henry*).

Talmadge tries hard in this comedy about a young widow, who after her experiences with a stodgy old man, sets out to discover a little romance in life. She becomes involved with four fellows, all of whom are wrong for her, but in the final reel ends up with the conservative lad who kept her from straying and loves her madly. There is a lot of padding in this one, which unfortunately depends heavily on its titles to keep things together.

d, Walter Edwards; w, Edith Kennedy (based on a play by William J. Hurlbut); ph, James C. Van Trees.

Comedy **(PR:A MPAA:NR)**

ROMANCE LAND*** (1923) 5 reels FOX bw

Tom Mix (*"Pep" Hawkins*), Barbara Bedford (*Nan Harvess*), Frank Brownlee (*"Scrub" Hazen*), George Webb (*Counterfeit Bill*), Pat Chrisman (*White Eagle*), Wynn Mace (*Sheriff*).

Tongue-in-cheek Mix western with plenty of laughs has the great cowboy star sporting a suit of armor because of his love for romantic tales of knighthood and maidens fair. He saves the life of Bedford, a beautiful rancher's daughter who is also romantically inclined, but is disappointed to discover that she has been promised by her father to his foreman. Therefore a full-fledged medieval tournament is arranged between the two which culminates in a thrilling chariot race. Mix, of course, wins the competition and the girl, then rescues his sweetheart from the sore loser who abducted her.

d, Edward Sedgwick; w, Joseph Franklin Poland (based on the novel *The Gun Fanner* by Kenneth Perkins); ph, Dan Clark.

Western/Comedy **(PR:A MPAA:NR)**

ROMANCE OF HAPPY VALLEY, A*** ½ (1919) 6 reels D.W. Griffith/PAR-ART bw

Robert Harron (*John L. Logan, Jr.*), Lillian Gish (*Jennie Timberlake*), Lydia Yeamans Titus (*Auntie Smiles*), Kate Bruce (*Mrs. Logan*), George Fawcett (*John L. Logan, Sr.*), George Nicholls (*Gish's Father*), Adolphe Lestina (*Jim Darkly*), Bertram Grassby (*Judas, the City Man*), Porter Strong (*The Funny Waiter*), Andrew Arbuckle (*The Minister*), Frances Sparks (*Topsy*), Carol Dempster (*A Girl John Logan Meets in the City*).

Another of Griffith's beautiful "little" pictures. This time set in the director's native Kentucky, the story tells of an ambitious farm boy, Harron, who, much to the chagrin of his God-fearing neighbors—especially Gish, who loves him—sets off for the sinful city of New York to make his fortune. It takes seven years, but Harron returns home in time to marry Gish and save the family farm after striking it rich with the invention of a toy frog. There is a bit of melodramatic, confused identity hokum at the end, which is the only flaw that places this beautifully acted and atmospheric production a peg below the similar TRUE HEART SUSIE made the same year.

d, D.W. Griffith; w, Capt. Victor Marier [Griffith], S. E. V. Taylor (based on a story by Mary Castleman); ph, Billy Bitzer; ed, James Smith.

Drama **(PR:A MPAA:NR)**

ROMANCE OF TARZAN, THE** ½ (1918) 7 reels National Film/FN bw

Elmo Lincoln (*Tarzan*), Enid Markey (*Jane Porter*), Cleo Madison (*The Vamp*), Thomas Jefferson (*Prof. Porter*), Colin Kenny, Monte Blue, Nigel de Brulier, Clyde

Benson, Phil Dunham, John Cook, True Boardman, Bessie Toner, Geroge French, Gordon Griffith, Kathleen Kirkham.

Interesting, though somewhat disappointing sequel to TARZAN OF THE APES, also released the same year. This time the jungle king (again played by the mighty Lincoln) heads to the U.S., where he spends most of his time in black tie and becomes the target of a most attractive female vampire, to the chagrin of Jane (portrayed for the second time by Markey).

d, Wilfred Lucas; w, Bess Meredyth (based on the novel *Tarzan of the Apes* by Edgar Rice Burroughs); ph, Harry Vallejo.

Adventure (PR:A MPAA:NR)

ROMANCE OF THE AIR, A*** (1919) 7 reels En L'Air/Crest bw

Bert Hall *(Lt. Bert Hall)*, Edith Day *(Edith Day)*, Florence Billings *(Countess of Moravia)*, Stuart Holmes *(Archduke of Moravia)*, Brian Darley *(Gen. Montaigne)*, Thomas Burrows *(Gen. DuBois)*, Herbert Standing *(Maj. William Thaw)*, Joseph Lertora *(Lt. Le Roy)*, Franklin B. Coates *(Herbert Stair)*, Emma Campbell *(Mme. Dumont)*, Emil Hoch *(Gen. von Hoch)*, Warner Richmond.

Lt. Bert Hall, an ace flyer with the famed Lafayette Escadrille, plays himself in this fast-paced war drama. Shot down behind enemy lines, Hall changes into a German uniform and meets his U.S. sweetheart, Day, who, visiting Europe at the outbreak of the war, is unable to get out. They plan an escape by air, taking with them Day's friend, the Countess of Moravia (Billings). After landing safely in France, Billings turns out to be an agent for the Central Powers, and Hall is accused of being an accomplice. The flyer is put on trail, where his splendid war record is revealed, and released in time to—with the help of Day—destroy the network of spies. Lt. Hall traveled with this film delivering a lecture. One of his anecdotes told of being decorated by the Czar of Russia four days before the revolution toppled him from power.

d, Harry Revier; w, Franklin B. Coates (based on the book *In the Air* by Lt. Bert Hall); ph, John K. Holbrook, Al Ligouri.

War (PR:A MPAA:NR)

ROMANCE OF THE REDWOODS, A* 1/2** (1917) 8 reels ART bw

Mary Pickford *(Jenny Lawrence)*, Elliott Dexter *("Black" Brown)*, Charles Ogle *(Jim Lyn)*, Tully Marshall *(Sam Sparks)*, Raymond Hatton *(Dick Roland)*, Walter Long *(The Sheriff)*, Winter Hall *(John Lawrence)*.

Director De Mille and Pickford argued throughout the making of this entertaining western, much of which was shot in northern California. But in spite of this, they produced a meritorious film dealing with the 1849 gold rush. Pickford plays a young lady whose father is killed in an Indian attack and later falls in love with Dexter, a dashing outlaw, whom she helps free after his capture by claiming to be pregnant by him and showing the sheriff dolls' clothes as proof. In reviewing this picture for the *New Republic*, the noted poet, Vachel Lindsay wrote, "To reject this girl in haste is high treason to the American heart."

d, Cecil B. De Mille; w, Jeanie Macpherson, De Mille; ph, Alvin Wyckoff.

Western (PR:A MPAA:NR)

ROMANCE RANCH** (1924) 5 reels FOX bw

John Gilbert *(Carlos Brent)*, Virginia Brown Faire *(Carmen Hendley)*, John Miljan *(Clifton Venable)*, Bernard Seigel *(Felipe Varillo)*, Evelyn Selbie *(Tessa)*.

Superstardom was within Gilbert's grasp at the time he made this mediocre programmer in which he plays a man who inherits the family ranch but is reluctant to evict the people living there because he loves Faire, the daughter of the house. Gilbert finally resolves the problem by abducting and marrying the girl, thus becoming the legal owner of the homestead.

d, Howard M. Mitchell; w, Dorothy Yost (based on a story by Jessie Maude Wybro); ph, Bert Baldridge.

Drama (PR:A MPAA:NR)

ROMANCE ROAD*** (1925) 5 reels Granada/TRU bw

Raymond McKee *(Patrick O'Brien)*, Billy Bletcher *(Buddy)*, Marjorie Meadows *(Mary Van Tassler)*, Dick Gordon *(Arthur Waddington Watts)*, Gertrude Claire *(Ma O'Brien)*, Billy Fletcher *(Pat's Pal)*, Hash the Dog.

Unpretentious, but most pleasing comedy about a penniless doughboy, McKee, who returns to his upstate New York home, begins to romance Meadows, a socialite who has been promised to another by her snooty aunt, but wins her in the end when his automotive invention makes him a millionaire.

d, Fred Windemere; ph, Lenwood Abbott.

Comedy (PR:A MPAA:NR)

ROMEO AND JULIET 1/2** (1916) 7 reels FOX bw

Theda Bara *(Juliet)*, Harry Hilliard *(Romeo)*, Glen White *(Mercutio)*, Walter Law *(Friar Laurence)*, John Webb Dillon *(Tybalt)*, Einar Linden *(Paris)*, Elwin Eaton *(Montague)*, Alice Gale *(Nurse)*, Helen Tracy *(Lady Capulet)*, Victory Bateman *(Lady Montague)*, Jane Lee, Katherine Lee, May De Lacy, Edwin Holt *(Capulet)*.

Director J. Gordon Edwards wisely kept his camera centered on Bara (Fox's number one star at the time) in this version of the Shakespearian classic, which never lost sight of the audience it intended to reach. Although Bara may not have been born to play this part, she did look exotic in the skimpy nightgowns the wardrobe department provided her with.

d, J. Gordon Edwards; w, Adrian Johnson (based on the play by William Shakespeare); ph, Phil Rosen.

Drama (PR:A MPAA:NR)

ROMOLA*** (1925) 12 reels INSP/MG bw

Lillian Gish *(Romola)*, Dorothy Gish *(Tessa)*, William H. Powell *(Tito Melema)*, Ronald Colman *(Carlo Buccellini)*, Charles Lane *(Baldassarre Calvo)*, Herbert Grimwood *(Savonarola)*, Bonaventure Ibanez *(Bardo Bardi)*, Frank Puglia *(Adolpo Spini)*, Amelia Summerville *(Brigida)*, Angelo Scatigna *(Bratti)*, Edulilo Mucci *(Nello)*, Tina Rinaldi *(Monna Ghita)*, Alfredo Bertone, Alfredo Martinelli, Ugo Ucellini, Thelma Raye.

When they are attacked by pirates, Baldassarre Calvo, a Greek scholar (Lane), gives his jewelry and identification card to his adopted son, Tito Melema (Powell) and orders him to jump overboard, sell the gems, and pay his ransom. Instead Powell uses the cash to finance a trip to Florence, where he marries Romola (Lillian Gish), the daughter of a blind intellectual. The unscrupulous Powell then makes the acquaintance of another rogue, Puglia, and with his evil assistance rises to the position of chief magistrate. Powell's abuses are many and include a mock marriage to a beautiful peasant girl, Dorothy Gish, whom he impregnates and deserts, as well as executing a popular priest and champion of the people, Grimwood. This last outrage leads to an uprising and Powell is ultimately drowned by his father who has returned in time to gain that satisfaction. The film ends with Lillian Gish marrying Colman, a young artist who never stopped loving her, and the two of them and Gish's child make up for the unhappiness her late and unlamented husband caused them. Although handsomely produced (the picture cost $2 million to produce) and shot on location, there were so many modern incongruous intrusions in the way, such as street car tracks and telephone poles, that it was necessary to build a number of sets and thus recreate the splendor of Florence within the city itself. And although there are good performances by everyone involved (especially Powell, who is marvelously villainous), the picture has a tendency to drag. Lillian Gish, in her autobiography, tells an interesting story about how, in a scene where Powell attempts to drown her in the Arno River, the actress was unable to sink. They would push her down in the polluted waterway, and she'd just keep popping up again. Finally, Lillian herself shot the scene in Mamaroneck, by giving her sister, Dorothy, a strong belt of booze and then using a diver to pull her under. The temperature was close to zero, and the actress (in the tradition of her sister's WAY DOWN EAST experience, nearly froze to death). They just don't make actresses like that any more. Colman arranged a bit part for his then wife, Raye, in the film; they were divorced in 1925.

d, Henry King; w, Will M. Ritchey (based on the novel by George Eliot); art d, Robert M. Hass.

Drama (PR:A MPAA:NR)

ROOKIE'S RETURN, THE 1/2** (1921) 5 reels THI/PAR bw

Douglas MacLean *(James Stewart Lee)*, Doris May *(Alicia)*, Frank Currier *(Dad)*, Leo White *(Henri)*, Kathleen Key *(Gloria)*, Elinor Hancock *(Mrs. Radcliffe)*, William Courtright *(Gregg)*, Frank Clark *(Tubbs)*, Aggie Herring *(Mrs. Perkins)*, Wallace Beery *(Francois Dupont)*.

Somewhat disappointing sequal to 23 1/2 HOURS LEAVE (1919), has MacLean inheriting a fortune from his aunt shortly after his return from the war. There is a stipulation in the old gal's will, however, which provides that if any of her servants are fired, he will only get $5,000. MacLean's lawyer, who, unknown to him is also the father of the girl he loves, handles the domestic problems, and then arranges for his client's fake kidnaping to bring about a marriage between his daughter and the heir.

d, Jack Nelson; sup, Thomas H. Ince; w, Archer McMackin; ph, Bert Cann.

Comedy (PR:A MPAA:NR)

ROSE OF PARIS, THE* 1/2 (1924) 7 reels UNIV bw

Mary Philbin *(Mitsi)*, Robert Cain *(Christian)*, John Sainpolis *(Andre du Vallois)*, Rose Dione *(Mme. Bolomoff)*, Dorothy Revier *(Florine du Vallois)*, Gino Corrado *(Paul Maran)*, Doreen Turner *(Yvette)*, Edwin J. Brady *(Jules)*, Charles Puffy *(Victor)*, Carrie Daumery *(Mother Superior)*, Cesare Gravain *(George)*, Alice H. Smith *(Governess)*, Frank Currier *(George Der Vroo)*, D.J. Mitsoras *(Majordomo)*.

Less-than-inspired production has Philbin, a convent-reared orphan, brought to a Paris nightclub where an attempt is made to exploit her inheritance. She manages to escape the plotters, however, and secures employment as a domestic in the home of her grandfather. In the end her true identity is discovered, and she marries Cain, the aristocrat with whom she has fallen in love.

d, Irving Cummings; w, Melville Brown, Edward T. Lowe, Jr., Lenore J. Coffee, Bernard McConville (based on the French novel *Mitsi* by Delly); ph, Charles Stumar.

Drama (PR:A MPAA:NR)

ROSE OF THE RANCHO 1/2** (1914) 5 reels LAS bw

Bessie Barriscale *(Juanita)*, Jane Darwell *(Senora Castro-Kenton)*, Dick La Reno *(Ezra Kinkaid)*, J.W. Johnston *(Kearney)*, Monroe Salisbury *(Don Luis)*, James Neill *(Padre Antonio)*, Sidney Deane *(Senor Espinoza)*, Jeanie Macpherson *(Isabelita)*, William Elmer *(Half Breed)*, Lee Pate, Mary Wilkinson, William C. DeMille.

When William DeMille joined his brother Cecil in the West, the latter was shooting this competent film about claim jumpers in the early days of California's annexation. There is ample outdoor action and a good performance by Barriscale, but for the most part this was not one of the director's better efforts.

d, Cecil B. DeMille, Oscar Apfel; w, DeMille (based on a play by David Belasco, Richard Walton Tully); ph, Alvin Wyckoff.

Western (PR:A MPAA:NR)

ROSE OF THE WORLD*** (1918) 5 reels ART bw

Elsie Ferguson *(Rosamond English)*, Wyndham Standing *(Capt. Harry English)*,

Percy Marmont *(Lt. Bethune)*, Ethel Martin *(Lady Cunningham)*, Clarence Handysides *(Sir Gerardine)*, June Sloane *(His Niece)*, Marie Benedetta *(Jani)*, Gertrude Le Brandt *(Mary)*, Sloane De Masber *(Dr. Chatelard)*.

After Ferguson's officer husband is killed putting down a native insurrection in India, she marries Handysides, the governor of the province, and returns with him to England. Shortly thereafter, Marmont who has been commissioned by the Crown to write the story of her late husband's exploits, arrives to request her cooperation. Ferguson agrees and when she rereads his letter, becomes aware of a burning love which still exists. So much so, that she approaches her Indian maid and implores the woman to call upon the Eastern gods to return her late husband in spiritual form. He does come back—but in the flesh. It seems he survived the battle and took a job (heavily disguised) as a servant to her present husband and was reluctant to step forward if Ferguson was really in love with the governor.

d, Maurice Tourneur; w, Charles Maigne (based on the novel by Agnes and Egerton Castle).

Drama **(PR:A MPAA:NR)**

ROSE OF THE WORLD***　(1925) 8 reels WB bw

Patsy Ruth Miller *(Rose Kirby)*, Allan Forrest *(Jack Talbot)*, Pauline Garon *(Edith Rogers)*, Rockliffe Fellowes *(Clyde Bainbridge)*, Barbara Luddy *(Cecilia Kirby)*, Alec Francis *("Gramp" Tallifer)*, Helen Dunbar *(Mrs. John Talbot)*, Lydia Knott *(Mrs. Kirby)*, Edward Peil, Jr. *(The Boy)*, Carrie Clark Ward *(Sally Towsey)*.

Nicely done programmer in which Forrest fails to marry Miller, the girl he loves, because his wealthy family considers her to be his social inferior. He does provide for her in his will, however, and later, after each has experienced an unfortunate marriage, they finally put the pieces together and find the happiness they were meant to have.

d, Harry Beaumont; w, Julien Josephson, Dorothy Farnum (based on the novel by Kathleen Norris); ph, David Abel.

Drama **(PR:A MPAA:NR)**

ROSES OF PICARDY**　(1927, Brit.) 9 reels GAU bw

Lilian Hall-Davis *(Madeleine Vanderlynden)*, John Stuart *(Lt. Skene)*, Humbertson Wright *(Jerome Vanderlynden)*, Jameson Thomas *(Georges d'Archeville)*, Marie Ault *(Baroness d'Archeville)*, A. Bromley Davenport *(Baron d'Archeville)*, Clifford Heatherley *(Uncle)*.

Ponderous, heavily padded British film, with only the title going for it, tells of two soldiers—one English and one French—in love with the same Flemish girl. There are some routine battle scenes, which just seem to be there, and the movie ends on the same kind of boring note on which it began.

p, Maurice Elvey, Victor Saville; d, Elvey; w, V. Gareth Gundrey (based on "Spanish Farm and Sixty-Four, Ninety-Four" by R.H. Mottram).

War **(PR:A MPAA:NR)**

ROSITA* 1/2**　(1923) 9 reels Mary Pickford/UA bw

Mary Pickford *(Rosita, a Street Singer)*, Holbrook Blinn *(The King)*, Irene Rich *(The Queen)*, George Walsh *(Don Diego)*, Charles Belcher *(Prime Minister)*, Frank Leigh *(Prison Commandant)*, Mathilde Comont *(Rosita's Mother)*, George Periolat *(Rosita's Father)*, Bert Sprotte *(Jailer)*, Snitz Edwards *(Little Jailer)*, Mme. de Bodamere *(Servant)*, Phillipe de Lacey, Donald McAlpin *(Brothers of Rosita)*, Mario Carillo *(Majordomo)*, Doreen Turner *(Rosita's Sister)*, Charles Farrell, Marion Nixon.

Ernst Lubitsch was brought to Hollywood from Germany by Mary Pickford, who desperately wanted to break away from playing children, to direct her in DOROTHY VERNON OF HADDON HALL. After arriving, Lubitsch refused to make the picture, and they finally settled on an adaptation of the novel *Don Cesar de Bazan* (which, interestingly enough, Pola Negri, the director's top star, also made an American version of in that same year, called THE SPANISH DANCER). These two great artists clashed from the start, and Pickford always regarded the product of their collaboration to be her worst film. The story tells about a Spanish street singer, Pickford, who is loved by the King of Spain, while she herself is in love with a penniless nobleman, Walsh. Walsh defends her when she is arrested for singing a song lampooning the king, and both are imprisoned; Walsh sentenced to death, and Pickford sentenced to seduction by the king, who tempts her with gifts of clothing and a beautiful home. Diabolically, the king arranges a wedding between Pickford and her lover—with both of them blindfolded—in order to make her a countess before she becomes a widow. Walsh's life is saved by the queen, who puts blank cartridges in the executioners' guns. In a stunning finale, Walsh, feigning death, is brought to Pickford's house and he leaps up to save the king just as the sorrowing Pickford raises a knife to stab him. Walsh wins a pardon—and Pickford—at the curtain. As for the quibbling on the set, Pickford never got over it. She is quoted as saying that not only was this her worst film, thanks to Lubitsch, whom she claimed could only direct men, but it was a costly experience for her as well. She never forgave what she termed his Teutonic arrogance, and refused to see anything he ever made after ROSITA.

d, Ernst Lubitsch; w, Edward Knoblock, Norbert Falk, Hans Kraly (based on the play "Don Cesar de Bazan" by Adolphe Philippe Dennery, Philippe Francois Pinel); ph, Charles Rosher; m, Louis F. Gottschalk; art d, William Cameron Menzies; set d, Svend Gade.

Costume Drama **(PR:A MPAA:NR)**

ROUGH AND READY**　(1918) 6 reels FOX bw

William Farnum *(Bill Stratton)*, Violet Palmer *(Evelyn Durant)*, Alphonse Ethier *(Jack Belmont)*, Jessie Arnold *(Estelle Darrow)*, David Higgins *(Matthew Durant)*, Frank Newton *(Ed Brown)*, Mabel Bardine *(Bess Brown)*, Franklyn McGlynn *(The Siwash)*.

Outdoor saga has Farnum breaking up with his fiancee and heading for the Klondike, where he becomes the big man about town. Farnum untimately reunites his sweetheart with her one-time mine owner father, who is now down on his luck, and the picture ends happily. A couple of good fights and a lot of snow are about all this one has to offer.

d, Richard Stanton; w, Stanton, Edward Sedgwick.

North Woods Adventure **(PR:A MPAA:NR)**

ROUGH HOUSE ROSIE***　(1927) 6 reels PAR bw

Clara Bow *(Rosie O'Reilly)*, Reed Howes *(Joe Hennessey)*, Arthur Housman *(Kid Farrell)*, Doris Hill *(Ruth)*, Douglas Gilmore *(Arthur Russell)*, John Miljan *(Lew McKay)*, Henry Kolker *(W.S. Davids)*.

Clever titles by George Marion, Jr., good direction by Frank Strayer, and the presence of lovely Bow, make this film solid entertainment. In it Bow plays a girl with show business aspirations and a hankering for society life, who decides to give it all up for the love of her prizefighter sweetheart, Howes, whom she helps to win the championship bout by distracting his opponent in the ring.

p, B.P. Schulberg; d, Frank Strayer; w, Louise Long, Ethel Doherty, Max Marcin (based on a story by Nunnally Johnson); t, George Marion, Jr.; ph, James Murray, Hal Rosson.

Comedy **(PR:A MPAA:NR)**

ROUGH LOVER, THE**　(1918) 5 reels BLUE bw

Franklyn Farnum *(Richard/Spike)*, Juanita Hansen *(Helen)*, Martha Mattox *(Aunt Mary)*, Catherine Henry *(Countess Wintershin)*, Fred Montague *(Count Wintershin)*.

Mistaken identity comedy has Hansen rejecting bookworm Richard (Farnum) because of his lack of athletic ability. Henry, however, can't resist the boy, who pretends to be dead after a swimming accident in order to escape her. In the meantime, Hansen meets Spike (Farnum), his perfect double and the lighweight boxing champion of the world. There is a lot of comic business which just fails to come off, including a seance sequence in which Spike/Farnum (who has returned to gather his look alike's clothes) is taken for a ghost. While he's there, however, the champ does have the opportunity to put his fists to good use, which ultimately secures Hansen's love for his double.

d, Joseph De Grasse; w, Charles A. Kenyon (based on a story by Joseph E. Poland).

Comedy **(PR:A MPAA:NR)**

ROUGH RIDERS, THE***　(1927) 10 reels PAR-LAS bw

Charles Farrell *(Stewart Van Brunt)*, Noah Beery *(Hell's Bells)*, George Bancroft *(Happy Joe)*, Charles Emmett Mack *(Bert Henley)*, Mary Astor *(Dolly)*, Frank Hopper *(Theodore Roosevelt)*, Col. Fred Lindsay *(Leonard Wood)*, Fred Kohler *(Sgt. Stanton)*.

Before producer B.P. Schulberg even saw OLD IRONSIDES released in 1926, he was so sure of its success that he began working on THE ROUGH RIDERS, another big, action-filled "special." Paramount spared no expenses on this one, as well, and even though OLD IRONSIDES turned out to be a box office disappointment, they went ahead with a big publicity hype, even giving THE ROUGH RIDERS extended runs at gala openings with increased admission prices. Well, it never became the box office smash Paramount had hoped for, but nevertheless director Victor Fleming cleverly mixed comedy, drama, and action in this somewhat glamorized account of Teddy Roosevelt's famous Rough Riders. There is a romantic subplot which does not get in the way, and West Coast book agent Frank Hopper bears an astonishing resemblance to the quintessential American hero. There are some sensational battle scenes, beautifully photographed by James Howe, and the edited insertions of Hopper into actual footage of President Roosevelt's inauguration is most effective. It is interesting to note that Farrell, who plays the romantic lead in both this and OLD IRONSIDES, was afterwards labeled a "jinx" at Paramount and subsequently dropped from their roster. Fox, however, was quick to sign him, and as film history would show, he went on to even greater fame by joining Janet Gaynor to form one of the greatest screen teams known to Hollywood.

p, B.P. Schulberg; d, Victor Fleming; w, Robert N. Lee, Keene Thompson, John F. Goodrich (based on a story by Hermann Hagedorn); t, George Marion, Jr.; ph, James Howe.

Historical Drama **(PR:A MPAA:NR)**

ROUGH SHOD**　(1925) 5 reels FOX bw

Charles "Buck" Jones *("Steel" Brannon)*, Helen Ferguson *(Betty Lawson)*, Ruth Renick *(Josephine Hamilton)*, Maurice B. Flynn *("Satan" Latimer)*, Jack Rollins *(Les Artwell)*, Charles Le Moyne *("Denver")*.

Only the presence of Jones makes this predictable western work. In it he plays a foreman on a ranch owned by Ferguson, his fiancee. When Easterner Renick comes to the ranch for a visit she enables Jones to discover the identity of the man who murdered his father. Jones then gives the rat a push which sends him flying off the edge of a cliff to his death.

d, Reaves Eason; w, Jack Strumwasser (based on the novel *West* by Charles Alden Seltzer); ph, Lucien Andriot.

Western **(PR:A MPAA:NR)**

ROUGHNECK, THE***　(1924) 8 reels FOX bw

George O'Brien *(Jerry Delaney)*, Billie Dove *(Felicity Arden)*, Harry T. Morey *(Mad McCara)*, Cleo Madison *(Anne Delaney)*, Charles A. Sellen *(Sam Meldon)*, Anne Cornwall *(Zelle)*, Harvey Clark *(Fight Manager)*, Maryon Aye *(Marrat's Girl)*, Edna Eichor *(Zamina)*, Buddy Smith *(Jerry Delaney, Age 3)*.

Better-than-average programmer has O'Brien escaping to a South Seas island after mistakenly believing he killed a man in the boxing ring. In this tropical paradise he is reunited with his mother, who was lured there years earlier by the villainous Morey after he told her that her little boy had died in an accident. The boxer also saves lovely Dove, with whom he fell in love onboard his ship, from Morey's libidinous clutches and destroys the rotter in a nicely staged fight. The picture ends with everyone returning to San Francisco and the couple getting married as soon as O'Brien discovers that he's not guilty of manslaughter.

d, Jack Conway; w, Charles Kenyon (based on the novel by Robert William Service); ph, George Schneiderman.

Adventure **(PR:A MPAA:NR)**

ROULETTE* (1924) 5 reels Aetna/SF bw

Edith Roberts *(Lois Carrington)*, Norman Trevor *(John Tralee)*, Maurice Costello *(Ben Corcoran)*, Mary Carr *(Mrs. Harris)*, Walter Booth *(Peter Marineaux)*, Effie Shannon *(Mrs. Marineaux)*, Montagu Love *(Dan Carrington)*, Henry Hull *(Jimmy Moore)*, Flora Finch *(Mrs. Smith-Jones)*, Jack Raymond *(Hastings)*, Diana Allen *(Mrs. Hastings)*, Dagmar Godowsky *(Rita)*.

As the ward of gambler Trevor, Roberts is used as bait for his gambling house. One of the players, Booth, suspects her of cheating, so Roberts offers herself as the payoff in a game between the handsome young sportsman and her guardian. Actually, Roberts is in love with the fellow and secretly fixes the wheel to spin in his favor. The two are later married. Not a great film.

d, S.E.V. Taylor; w, Gerald C. Duffy, Lewis Allen Browne (based on a story by William Briggs MacHarg).

Drama **(PR:A MPAA:NR)**

ROUND UP, THE** (1920) 5 reels PAR bw

Roscoe "Fatty" Arbuckle *(Slim Hoover)*, Irving Cummings *(Dick Lane)*, Mabel Julienne Scott *(Echo Allen)*, Tom Forman *(Jack Payson)*, Jean Acker *(Polly Hope)*, Guy Oliver *(Uncle Jim)*, Lucien Littlefield *(Parenthesis)*, Wallace Beery *(Buck McKee)*, Fred Huntley *(Sagebrush Charlie)*, Jane Wolfe *(Josephine)*, George Kuwa *(Chinese Boy)*, Edward Sutherland *(Bud Lane)*.

Arbuckle's first 5-reel feature is a strange departure for the great comedian, in that he plays basically the straight role of sheriff in what is at best a routine western. There are so many subplots that Arbuckle is seen in less than half the picture, and even then the big boy is hardly in evidence. There are few laughs in this picture and only one big action scene towards the end when the outlaws are forced to surrender to the U.S. Cavalry. Even the ending (which was meant to deliver pathos)—where all of the main characters from the subplots go into a clinch, leaving Arbuckle alone, leaning against a fence exclaiming, "Nobody loves a fat man"—doesn't quite come off.

d, George Melford; w, Tom Forman (based on the play by Edmund Day); ph, Paul Perry.

Comedy/Western **(PR:A MPAA:NR)**

ROWDY, THE*** (1921) 5 reels UNIV bw

Gladys Walton *(Kit Purcell)*, Rex Roselli *(Capt. Dan Purcell)*, Anna Hernandez *(Mrs. Purcell)*, C.B. Murphy *(Pete Curry)*, Jack Mower *(Burt Kincaid)*, Frances Hatton *(Mrs. Curry)*, Bert Roach *(Howard Morse)*, Alida B. Jones *(Beatrice Hampton)*, Countess De Cella *(Clarissa Hampton)*.

Intelligent melodrama with plenty of laughs has little Walton taken in by a retired New England sea captain when she is lost during a storm. She grows up to be a salty young lady who wins the heart of Mower, a ship's captain. Later it's learned that Walton is really the daughter of a wealthy family, and she is forced to move into their mansion. Walton hates her new life, so it comes as a great relief when it is subsequently disclosed that she is actually the child of a one-time servant of the family, and the girl is free to return to the waiting arms of her seafaring sweetheart.

d, David Kirkland; w, Doris Schroeder (based on the story "The Ark Angel" by Hamilton Thompson); ph, Earl Ellis.

Drama **(PR:A MPAA:NR)**

ROYAL FAMILY, A** (1915) 5 reels COL/Metro bw

Ann Murdock, Lila Barclay, Montagu Love, Mathilde Brundage, Fuller Mellish, W.J. Draper, Edwin Mordant, Niles Welch, Albert Lewis, J.D. Cowles, Charles Prince, William Nigh, Grace Atwell.

To prevent war with a neighboring kingdom whose princess has refused the cardinal's suggestion that she form an alliance through marriage, the prince of that state crosses her border incognito and the two meet and fall in love. The scenes in which an army insurrection is put down are rather skimpy in their production values. There is a subplot dealing with the abduction of a child who is heir to the throne and his return as a young adult.

d, William Nigh; w, Charles Frohman; ph, A.A. Cadwell.

Drama **(PR:A MPAA:NR)**

ROYAL OAK, THE*** (1923, Brit.) 6 reels STOLL bw

Betty Compson *(Lady Mildred)*, Henry Ainley *(Oliver Cromwell)*, Henry Victor *(Charles I/Charles II)*, Thurston Hall *(Col. Ancketell)*, Clive Brook *(Dorian Clavering)*, Bertie Wright *(Dearlove)*, Peter Dear *(Lord Cholmondeley)*, Dallas Cairns *(Pendrel)*, Blanche Walker *(Parry)*, Rolf Leslie *(Melchizedeck)*.

With Oliver Cromwell (Ainley) and his Roundheads hot on the trail of King Charles (Victor), a young man sacrifices his life to protect him, and the lad's sister (interestingly played by U.S. actress Compson) poses as the monarch to buy him the time needed to escape. The young lady is captured and sentenced to death, but at the last minute, Cromwell changes his mind and allows her to return to Hollywood. Good all-around production, marred only by an overly sympathetic depiction of Cromwell, one of history's authentic monsters.

d, Maurice Elvey; w, Lucita Squier (based on a play by Henry Hamilton, Augustus Harris).

Costume **(PR:A MPAA:NR)**

ROYAL RIDER, THE*** (1929) 7 reels FN bw

Ken Maynard *(Dick Scott)*, Olive Hasbrouck *(Ruth Elliott)*, Philippe De Lacey *(King Michael XI)*, Theodore Lorch *(Prime Minister)*, Joseph Burke *(King's Tutor)*, Harry Semels *(Parvene)*, William Franey, Frank Rice, Bobby Dunn, Johnny Sinclair, Benny Corbett *(Members of the Wild West Show)*, Tarzan the Horse.

Offbeat Maynard vehicle has the cowboy star taking his Wild West show to the Balkan kingdom of Alvania, where the king is so impressed with the troupe that he hires them to act as his palace guard. Later, Maynard and his boys crush an attempted revolt, and the westerner wins the hand of Hasbrouck, the royal governess. A good action picture played mostly for laughs.

d, Harry J. Brown; w, Jacques Jaccard, Sylvia Bernstein Seid (based on a story by Nate Gatzert); t, Lesley Mason; ph, Ted McCord; ed, Fred Allen.

Adventure/Comedy **(PR:A MPAA:NR)**

RUBBER TIRES** (1927) 7 reels DM/PDC bw

Bessie Love *(Mary Ellen Stack)*, Erwin Connelly *(Pat Stack)*, Junior Coghlan *(Charley Stack)*, May Robson *(Mrs. Stack)*, Harrison Ford *(Bill James)*, John Patrick *(Adolph Messer)*, Clarence Burton *(The Mexican)*.

Alan Hale directed this acceptable comedy about the misadventures of a family who sell everything to buy an automobile and make the long trip west to California. There are a number of predicatable complications along the way, but they reach their destination, receive a reward from a car manufacturer, and the daughter, Love, marries her nice young man.

d, Alan Hale; sup, A.H. Sebastian; w, Zelda Sears, Tay Garnett (based on a story by Frank Condon); ph, Robert Newhard.

Comedy **(PR:A MPAA:NR)**

RUGGED WATER** (1925) 6 reels FP/PAR bw

Lois Wilson *(Norma Bartlett)*, Wallace Beery *(Capt. Bartlett)*, Warner Baxter *(Calvin Homer)*, Phyllis Haver *(Myra Fuller)*, Dot Farley *(Mrs. Fuller)*, L.P. Lockney *(Superintendent Lockney)*, James Mason *(Wally Oakes)*, Willard Cooley *(Sam Bearse)*, Walter Ackerman *(Cook)*, Knute Erickson *(Jarvis)*, Thomas Delmar *(Gammon)*, Jack Byron *(Orrin Hendricks)*, Walter Rodgers *(Bloomer)*, Warren Rodgers *(Josh Phinney)*.

A couple of good storm rescue sequences and an outstanding cast are about all this film has going for it. The story dealing with nautical life at Cape Cod, a religious fanatic (Beery) in charge of water safety, and the troubled romance between his daughter, Wilson, and Baxter, the man who should have been given his job, is stretched pretty thin. In the end Baxter takes over in an emergency for Beery (who proves to be a coward) and, when the old man dies in a storm, marries his daughter. Wilson played the part of the daughter nicely, and director Willat did his best, but the material just wasn't there.

d, Irvin Willat; w, James Shelley Hamilton (based on the novel by Joseph Crosby Lincoln); ph, Alfred Gilks.

Drama **(PR:A MPAA:NR)**

RUGGLES OF RED GAP**** (1923) 8 reels FP/PAR bw

Edward Horton *(Ruggles)*, Ernest Torrence *(Cousin Egbert Floud)*, Lois Wilson *(Kate Kenner)*, Fritzi Ridgeway *(Emily Judson)*, Charles Ogle *(Jeff Tuttle)*, Louise Dresser *(Mrs. Effie Floud)*, Anna Lehr *(Mrs. Belknap-Pettingill)*, Thomas Holding *(Earl of Brinstead)*, Frank Elliott *(Honorable George)*, Kalla Pasha *(Herr Schwitz)*, Sidney Bracey *(Sam Henshaw)*, Milt Brown *(Sen. Pettingill)*, Guy Oliver *(Judge Ballard)*, Mister Barker the Dog.

RUGGLES OF RED GAP, a personal triumph for director James Cruze, is a delight on every level. It is the charming tale of Ruggles (Horton), a British valet who is won in a poker game by a nouveaux rich westerner (wonderfully played by Torrence) while on a vacation in Europe. When Torrence returns to his backwoods hometown of Red Gap, he introduces Horton to everyone as a colonel and he is treated with great honor. When the British gentleman who formerly employed Horton stops by Red Gap for a visit, he falls in love with Wilson, one of its residents. Later, the Englishman's brother arrives on the scene to break up the mismatch and ends up marrying Wilson himself. In the meantime, Horton becomes the owner of a successful restaurant and marries lovely Ridgeway.

d, James Cruze; w, Walter Woods, Anthony Coldeway (based on the novel by Harry Leon Wilson); ph, Karl Brown.

Drama **(PR:A MPAA:NR)**

RULING PASSION, THE ½** (1922) 7 reels DIST/UA bw

George Arliss *(James Alden)*, Doris Kenyon *(Angie Alden)*, Edward Burns *(Bill Merrick)*, Ida Darling *(Mrs. Alden)*, J.W. Johnston *(Peterson)*, Ernest Hilliard *(Carter Andrews)*, Harold Waldridge *("Al")*, Brian Darley *(Dr. Stillings)*.

Uneven production, in spite of a fine performance by Arliss, about a man who becomes a millionaire through the invention of an automobile engine. Told by his doctor to retire, Arliss secretly goes into the garage business with Burns, an enterprising young man. The filling station becomes a great success, hard work makes Arliss fit as a fiddle again, and his daughter Kenyon marries his associate.

d, Harmon Weight; w, Forrest Halsey (based on the story by Earl Derr Biggers); ph, Harry A. Fischbeck; art d, Clark Robinson.

Comedy/Drama **(PR:A MPAA:NR)**

RUNAWAY, THE ½** (1926) 7 reels FP/PAR bw

Clara Bow *(Cynthia Meade)*, Warner Baxter *(Wade Murrell)*, William Powell *(Jack Harrison)*, George Bancroft *(Lesher Skidmore)*, Edythe Chapman *(Wade's Mother)*.

Believing she has killed her fiance Powell in an accidental shooting while filming a movie in Tennessee, actress Bow flees the scene and is helped by mountainman Baxter, who takes her to his home in Kentucky. There is the usual feuding clan business, and when Bow senses that Baxter is falling in love with her, she decides to leave. It is then that Powell, completely recovered, shows up and saves Baxter's life from a family enemy. Powell then asks Bow to return with him and become his wife. She declines, preferring to remain on with her protector. This was Bow's first starring role, and an unusually serious part for her. Both she and Powell were stars whose careers would soon skyrocket. Within a year, in fact, Bow would zoom to superstardom with the box office smash IT.

d, William C. DeMille; w, Albert Shelby Le Vino (based on the novel *The Flight to the Hills* by Charles Neville Buck); ph, Charles Boyle.

Drama **(PR:A MPAA:NR)**

RUNAWAY GIRLS * ½ (1928) 6 reels COL bw

Shirely Mason *(Sue Hartley)*, Arthur Rankin *(Jim Grey)*, Hedda Hopper *(Mrs. Hartley)*, Alice Lake *(Agnes Brady)*, George Irving *(John Hartley)*, Edward Earle *(Varden)*.

This low-budget, sensation-oriented picture has Mason leaving home when her parents separate, taking a job as a model, and almost being dragged into a life of white slavery. Mason is saved at the last minute, however, when her sweetheart, Rankin, crashes into the villain's apartment just as the rat is shot to death. At first, Rankin is suspected of the killing, but a father, whose daughter was ruined by the rotter, confesses to the deed. The picture ends with the sweethearts getting married and the bride's parents working out their domestic problems.

p, Harry Cohn; d, Mark Sandrich; w, Dorothy Howell (based on a story by Lillie Hayward); t, Morton Blumenstock; ph, Harry Davis; ed, Frank Atkinson; art d, Harrison Wiley.

Drama **(PR:A MPAA:NR)**

RUNNING FIGHT, THE*** (1915) 5 reels Pre-Eminent/PAR bw

Robert Cummings *(The Banker)*, Violet Heming *(His Daughter)*, Robert Cain *(The District Attorney)*, Thurlow Bergen *(The Young Lawyer)*.

Above-par melodrama has a banker destroying his own institution in order to abscond with a fortune in deposits. There are some wonderful crowd scenes showing the customers in a state of panic, and a moment where the tycoon's paramour goes insane as she tries to kill her lover, only to have his secretary leap in front of the bullet. The banker has a daughter who is worshipped by both the district attorney and a young lawyer, and after some tightly knit narrative, the innocent man who was sent up for the earlier killing is cleared, the banker is brought to justice, and his daughter marries the young counselor who has just been elected governor.

w, William Hamilton Osborne.

Drama **(PR:A MPAA:NR)**

RUNNING WATER* (1922, Brit.) 6 reels STOLL bw

Madge Stuart *(Sylvia Skinner)*, Lawford Davidson *(Capt. Hilary Cheyne)*, Julian Royce *(Garrett Skinner)*, A. Bromley Davenport *(Capt. Barstow)*, Irene Rooke *(Mrs. Thesiger)*, George Turner *(Wallie Hine)*, E. Lewis Waller *(Archie Parminter)*, George Harrington *(Michel)*.

When young Turner, an illiterate mountain fellow, accidently inherits a fortune, a good portion of the cast sets out to separate him from it. Fortunately, Stuart, with thehelp of Davidson, manages to prevent her father, Royce, from doing him in. The Alpine scenery is the only thing positive about this one.

d, Maurice Elvey; w, Kinchen Wood (based on the novel by A.E.W. Mason).

Drama **(PR:A MPAA:NR)**

RUPERT OF HENTZAU** (1915, Brit.) 6 reels London/JUR bw

Henry Ainley *(Rudolph Rassendyl)*, Jane Gail *(Queen Flavia)*, Gerald Ames *(Rupert)*, Charles Rock *(Col. Sapt)*, George Bellamy *(Count Reichenheim)*, Warwick Wellington *(Lt. Berenstein)*, Douglas Munro *(Bauer)*, Stella St. Audrie *(Chancellor's Wife)*, Jeff Barlow, Eva Westlake.

Early British version (it would be filmed and televised many more times) of Anthony Hope's popular novel *The Prisoner of Zenda*—the story of an Englishman on vacation in Ruritania, who changes places with the endangered king, who happens to be his perfect look alike.

d, George Loane Tucker; w, William Courtenay Rowden (based on the novel *The Prisoner of Zenda* by Anthony Hope).

Adventure **(PR:A MPAA:NR)**

RUPERT OF HENTZAU ½** (1923) 9 reels SF bw

Elaine Hammerstein *(Queen Flavia)*, Bert Lytell *(King of Ruritania/Rudolph Rassendyll)*, Lew Cody *(Rupert of Hentzau)*, Claire Windsor *(Countess Helga)*, Hobard Bosworth *(Col. Sapt)*, Bryant Washburn *(Count Fritz)*, Marjorie Daw *(Rosa Holf)*, Mitchell Lewis *(Bauer)*, Adolphe Menjou *(Count Rischenheim)*, Elmo Lincoln *(Simon, the King's Forester)*, Irving Cummings *(Von Bernenstein)*, Josephine Crowell *(Mother Holf)*, Nigel De Brulier *(Herbert)*, Gertrude Astor *(Paula)*.

Inferior sequel to THE PRISONER OF ZENDA (1922) sorely misses the presence of that film's director, Rex Ingram, and its stars, Lewis Stone and Ramon Novarro. But once again the villainous Rupert (Cody) is out to steal the throne of Ruritania, and once more he is defeated by the dashing English look alike for the king, Rudolph Rassendyll (Lytell). Good production values and a well-staged duel help to make up for the poor casting and sluggish direction.

d, Victor Herman; sup, Myron Selznick; w, Edward J. Montagne (based on the novel by Anthony Hope); ph, Glen MacWilliams, Harry Thorpe.

Costume Adventure **(PR:A MPAA:NR)**

RUSH HOUR, THE* ½ (1927) 6 reels DM/Pathe bw

Marie Prevost *(Margie Dolan)*, Harrison Ford *(Dan Morely)*, Seena Owen *(Yvonne Doree)*, David Butler *(William Finch)*, Ward Crane *(Dunrock)*.

Perky Prevost does what she can to bring a little sparkle to this inferior comedy, which has a working girl, fed up with morning rush hours and a parsimonious fiance, stowing away on a ship bound for France. She gets caught and goes through the predictable "work-for-your-fare" seasick gags. On the Riviera she becomes involved with a couple of confidence operators who use her as bait to snare an oil millionaire. In the end, of course, the crooks are caught, and Prevost marries her sweetheart, Ford, who has learned to loosen his purse strings. This picture's only other bright spot is a nifty performance by David Butler, as the oil tycoon.

d, E. Mason Hopper; sup, F. McGrew Willis; w, Fred Stanley, Zelda Sears (based on the story "The Azure Shore" by Frederic and Fanny Hatton); t, Lesley Mason; ph, Dewey Wrigley; ed, Donn Hayes; art d, Charles Cadwallader.

Comedy **(PR:A MPAA:NR)**

RUSTLER'S RANCH** (1926) 5 reels UNIV bw

Art Acord *(Lee Crush)*, Olive Hasbrouck *(Lois Shawn)*, Duke R. Lee *(Boggs)*, George Chesebro *(Bud Harvey)*, Edith Yorke *(Mary Shawn)*, Matty Kemp *(Clem Allen)*, Stanton Heck *(Bull Dozier)*, Lillian Worth *(Tessie)*, Ned Bassett *(Sheriff Collins)*.

Not much action in this Acord western, which has the cowboy believing he killed a man in a fair fight and taking a job at the ranch of widow Hasbrouck. There he falls in love with the owner's daughter, Yorke, and saves the spread from the clutches of a crook. Acord then marries the girl after learning that the fellow he punched out is actually alive and well.

d, Clifford S. Smith; w, Harrison Jacobs, E. Richard Schayer (based on a story by W.C. Tuttle); ph, Eddie Linden.

Western **(PR:A MPAA:NR)**

S

SABLE LORCHA, THE*** (1915) 5 reels FA/TRI bw

Tully Marshall *(Soy)*, Thomas Jefferson *(His Enemy)*, Charles Lee, Loretta Blake, George Pearce, Hal Wilson, Raymond Wells, Kura Kotanio.

Marshall gives his usual fine performance as Soy, a Chinese Tong leader, who out of revenge murders the U.S. businessman responsible for the deaths of his entire family while trying to smuggle them out of China and into slavery. Having accomplished his mission—after a number of atmospheric Chinatown situations—there follows an exciting police chase which culminates with the oriental man taking his own life before the Statue of the Seven Heads.

d, Lloyd Ingraham; w, Cecil B. Clapp (based on a novel by Horace Hazeltine [Charles Stokes Wayne]); ph, Hugh C. McClung.

Crime **(PR:A MPAA:NR)**

SACRED SILENCE** (1919) 6 reels FOX bw

William Russell *(Capt. Craig)*, Agnes Ayres *(Madge Summers)*, James Morrison *(Lt. Harrison)*, George McQuarrie *(Maj. Carson)*, Mabel Julienne Scott, Tom Brooke, Riza Royce.

Russell deserts his army post to save the reputation of his foster brother who, while having an affair with a major's wife, was killed by the irate husband. Having assumed the blame, Russell is tracked down and thrown into the stockade. Afterwards the guilt-ridden major, who has had the truth presented to him by girl detective Ayres, strangles his wife to death, clears Russell, and makes possible a happy ending to the film.

d, Harry Millarde; w, Roy Somerville, Thomas F. Fallon, Howard I. Young (based on the play "The Deserter" by Anna Alice Chapin, Robert Peyton Carter); ph, George Lane.

Drama **(PR:A MPAA:NR)**

SADIE THOMPSON* 1/2** (1928) 9 reels Gloria Swanson/UA bw

Gloria Swanson *(Sadie Thompson)*, Lionel Barrymore *(Alfred Atkinson)*, Raoul Walsh *(Sgt. Tim O'Hara)*, Blanche Frederici *(Mrs. Atkinson)*, Charles Lane *(Dr. McPhail)*, Florence Midgley *(Mrs. McPhail)*, James A. Marcus *(Joe Horn, the Trader)*, Sophia Artega *(Ameena)*, Will Stanton *(Quartermaster Bates)*.

Swanson managed to get around the moral objections of the Hays Office by convincing Will Hays that dropping the title "Rain" (the name of the steamy and extremely popular play which inspired the film) and transforming one of the leading characters, a lecherous clergyman, into a religious fanatic, would make the plot acceptable. Hays agreed, and the film, which won Swanson an academy award nomination for best actress, is for the most part an outstanding work. In it Swanson Garbo plays a wayward woman trying to hide her identity in the South Seas when she falls in love with Walsh, a marine, and the two decide to marry. The zealot (beautifully played by Barrymore) threatens to expose her to local authorities unless she quits her "immoral" ways. When Swanson reforms, the obsessed Barrymore seduces her and then commits suicide. Walsh and Swanson are then reunited and set sail for Australia. The New York Times, when reviewing the film, pointed out that audiences exiting the theater were surprised to find themselves walking into a beautiful sunny day—so successful was the picture at creating a South Seas atmosphere, with its obsessive rain, humidity, and sense of eroticism.

d&w, Raoul Walsh (based on the story "Miss Thompson" by William Somerset Maugham and the play "Rain" by John Colton, Clemence Randolph); t, C. Gardner Sullivan; ph, Oliver Marsh, George Barnes, Robert Kurrle; ed, Sullivan; art d, William Cameron Menzies.

Drama **(PR:C MPAA:NR)**

SAFETY FIRST** (1926, Brit.) 7 reels STOLL bw

Brian Aherne *(Hippocrates Rayne)*, Queenie Thomas *(Nanda MacDonald)*, Mary Brough *(Caroline Lowecraft)*, Patrick Susands *(Birdie Nightingale)*, Doreen Banks *(Angela St. Jacques)*, Humberston Wright *(Butler)*.

Before achieving Hollywood stardom, handsome Aherne made a number of British films, including this comedy about a chap who persuades his friends to pose as inmates from a lunatic asylum in order to manipulate his wealthy aunt.

d, Fred Paul; w, Geoffrey H. Malins (based on a novel by Margot Neville).

Comedy **(PR:A MPAA:NR)**

SAFETY LAST**** (1923) 5 reels HR/Pathe Exchange bw

Harold Lloyd *(The Boy)*, Mildred Davis *(The Girl)*, Bill Strother *(The Pal)*, Noah Young *(The Law)*, Westcott B. Clarke *(The Floorwalker)*, Mickey Daniels *(The Kid)*, Anna Townsend *(The Grandma)*, Charles Stevenson, Gus Leonard, Helen Gilmore.

SAFETY LAST was most certainly Lloyd's most famous film. Even people who have never seen a single movie with the comedian are familiar with the image of a man hanging from a clock, high above the streets of downtown Los Angeles. But there are plenty of laughs in this wonderful film even before he gets that far. Full of ambition and armed with the knowledge that his girl, Davis, will drop him like a lump of coal if he doesn't make good, the boy sets out to earn his fortune in the big city. He is only able to land a job clerking in a department store, but he writes home telling his sweetheart how well he's doing and skips a lot of lunches in order to send her some expensive gifts. Lloyd's ruse is so convincing that Davis' mother suggests it might be wise to go to him before something—or someone—separates him from that small fortune he is apparently amassing. When she arrives, Lloyd, who is at his station in the store, cleverly manages to give her the impression he's actually the manager, and then sets about the task of pulling off a miracle. Lloyd's roommate is a "human fly," so when the young man overhears his boss say that he would pay $1,000 for a good publicity stunt, Lloyd talks him into hiring the daredevil to climb the side of his building. He then makes a deal with his pal to perform the stunt and split the cash. But on the big day, a cop who had a run-in with "the fly" earlier shows up to make a pinch, and the clerk is forced to climb the 12 stories himself. What takes place is a comedy masterpiece as one obstacle after another is hurled in Lloyd's way while he inches his way upward. The suspense is as unbearable as the belly laughs are abundant. Of course he does reach the top and he also wins the hand of Davis, who now considers her man a real hero. Lloyd did it all himself (except for the very long shots where Strother doubled), and in spite of some false building facades which were put into use and a safety platform a full three stories below, the star subjected himself to a great deal of danger while making this exceptional film. His accomplishment was all the more remarkable when it is taken into consideration that he had earlier lost the thumb and forefinger on his right hand after a prop bomb he was holding exploded. As a result the artist was forced to go through the rest of his career wearing a special glove.

d, Fred Newmeyer, Sam Taylor; w, Hal Roach, Tim Whelan, Taylor; ph, Walter Lundin; ed, Fred L. Guiol; art d, Guiol.

Comedy **Cas.** **(PR:A MPAA:NR)**

SAHARA*** (1919) 5 reels Hodkinson/Pathe bw

Louise Glaum *(Mignon)*, Matt Moore *(John Stanley)*, Edwin Stevens *(Baron Alexis)*, Pat Moore *(The Boy)*, Nigel de Brulier *(Mustapha)*, Ernest Pasque.

A popular Parisian actress marries a U.S. engineer and joins him in the Sahara, where he is assigned. Before long the dreadful desert conditions nearly drive her insane, and she leaves her husband and child to be kept by a Russian millionaire in an Egyptian palace. Time passes and one day she discovers her husband (who has become a drug addict) and little boy begging in the streets of Cairo. Guilt-ridden, she takes them home to be cared for. This so angers the Russian that he attempts to strangle his paramour, but the husband intervenes and kills the brute. At this point, the family is reunited, the husband kicks his habit, and the three depart the wretched land of sand forever.

d, Arthur Rosson; sup, Allan Dwan; w, C. Gardner Sullivan; ph, Charles Stumar.

Drama **(PR:C MPAA:NR)**

SAILOR IZZY MURPHY** (1927) 7 reels WB bw

George Jessel *(Izzy Goldberg)*, Audrey Ferris *(Marie)*, Warner Oland *(Mons. Jules de Gondelaurier)*, John Miljan *(Orchid Joe)*, Otto Lederer *(Jake)*, Theodore Lorch *(1st Mate), Clara Horton (Cecile)*.

Jessel's second feature has the comedian once again playing the character of Izzy Goldberg. This time he's in the perfume business and takes the name of "Muscle-Bound Murphy" to save the owner of a multimillion-dollar cosmetics firm and his daughter, Ferris, from a band of escaped maniacs led by a screwball who is out to kill anyone who harms flowers. Jessel's reward is a fat contract for his firm, and best of all, the love of the tycoon's daughter.

d, Henry Lehrman; w, Edward T. Lowe, Jr.; ph, Frank Kesson.

Comedy **(PR:A MPAA:NR)**

SAILOR-MADE MAN, A*** (1921) 4 reels AEX/Pathe bw

Harold Lloyd *(The Boy)*, Mildred Davis *(The Girl)*, Noah Young *(The Rowdy Element)*, Dick Sutherland *(Maharajah)*, Gus Leonard *(Lawyer)*, Charles Stevenson *(Recruiting Officer)*, Leo Willis *(Recruiting Officer)*, Fred Guiol *(Enlistee)*.

Lloyd's first feature actually began as a two-reeler and was going so well that it was decided to keep the cameras rolling. The film tends to be a bit episodic but the laughs and the stunt thrills, which had become the comedian's trademark, more than make up for that. Lloyd plays a wealthy idler who is informed by the father of Davis, the girl he loves, that if he has any idea of winning her hand in marriage he'd better make something of himself. Lloyd joins the navy and after setting shore in Khairpura-Bhandanna, he's given his chance by rescuing Davis, whose yacht has also arrived there, from the forces of a villainous maharajah (Sutherland) and his army of sword-wielding warriors.

d, Fred Newmeyer; w, Hal Roach, Sam Taylor, Jean Havez; t, H. M. Walker; ph, Walter Lundin.

Comedy **(PR:A MPAA:NR)**

SAILOR'S SWEETHEART, A*** (1927) 6 reels WB bw

Louise Fazenda *(Cynthia Botts)*, Clyde Cook *(Sandy MacTavish)*, Myrna Loy *(Claudette Ralston)*, William Demarest *(Detective)*, John Miljan *(Mark Krisel)*, Dorothea Wolbert *(Lena Svenson)*, Tom Ricketts *(Prof. Meekham)*.

The engaging Fazenda, with good support from Cook, makes what would have only scored as a two-reeler a most enjoyable feature. In it Fazenda plays a spinster schoolteacher who inherits a fortune, sails for Hawaii to land a husband, and is tricked into marrying Miljan, who turns out to be a bigamist. She later runs into

Cook, a scrappy little Scotch sailor, and the two are abducted by rum-runners. Theysoon realize their love for one another, and after escaping from their predicament, are married.

d, Lloyd Bacon; w, Harvey Gates (based on a story by George Godfrey); ph, Frank Kesson.

Comedy **(PR:A MPAA:NR)**

ST. ELMO zero (1923, Brit.) 6 reels R.W. Syndicate/CAP bw

Shayle Gardner *(St. Elmo Murray)*, Gabrielle Gilroy *(Agnes Powell)*, Madge Tree *(Mrs. Murray)*, Harding Thomas *(Rev. Hammond)*.

The U.S. version of the popular novel by Evans-Wilson, about a man who becomes a minister after killing a rival in a duel, was poor. This British adaptation of the same story makes the Yankee production look like THE BIRTH OF A NATION.

d&w, Rex Wilson (based on the novel by Augusta J. Evans-Wilson).

Drama **(PR:A MPAA:NR)**

ST. ELMO* (1923) 6 reels FOX bw

John Gilbert *(St. Elmo Thornton)*, Barbara La Marr *(Agnes Hunt)*, Bessie Love *(Edna Earle)*, Warner Baxter *(Murray Hammond)*, Nigel De Brulier *(Rev. Alan Hammond)*, Lydia Knott *(Mrs. Thornton)*.

A great cast is completely wasted in this poorly scripted and directed screen version of the popular novel (and later theatrical stock company perennial) about a man (Gilbert) who kills his sweetheart's (La Marr's) paramour, travels the world as a devout misogynist, but returns home to discover *true* love with the blacksmith's daughter (Love) and becomes a minister through her influence.

d, Jerome Storm; w, Jules G. Furthman (based on the novel by Augusta Jane Evans-Wilson); ph, Joe August.

Drama **(PR:A MPAA:NR)**

SAINTED DEVIL, A*** (1924) 9 reels FP/PAR bw

Rudolph Valentino *(Don Alonzo Castro)*, Nita Naldi *(Carlotta)*, Helen D'Algy *(Julietta)*, George Siegmann *(El Tigre)*, Dagmar Godowsky *(Dona Florencia)*, Jean Del Val *(Casimiro)*, Antonio D'Algy *(Don Luis)*, Rogers Lytton *(Don Baltasar)*, Isabel West *(Dona Encarnacion)*, Louise Lagrange *(Carmelita)*, Rafael Bongini *(Congo)*, Frank Montgomery *(Indian Spy)*, William Betts *(Priest)*, Edward Elkas *(Notary)*, A. De Rosa *(Jefe Politico)*, Ann Brody *(Duenna)*, Evelyn Axzell *(Guadalupe)*, Marie Diller *(Irala)*.

Good performance by Valentino as an Argentinean aristocrat whose bride, Helen D'Algy, is abducted on their wedding night by the ruthless Siegmann. When Valentino sets out to track them down, he finds a woman wearing his bride's wedding veil making love to the ruffian. He retreats in horror and develops a hatred for all womankind. Later the two men meet again, engage in a beautifully staged fist fight, and Siegmann is killed by Antonio D'Algy, another of his enemies. It is then that Valentino learns that the woman he saw in Siegmann's arms was actually his former girl friend, Naldi, and that his true love had safely hidden in a convent.

d, Joseph Henabery; w, Forrest Halsey (based on the story "Rope's End" by Rex Beach); ph, Harry Fischbeck; art d, Lawrence Hitt.

Drama **(PR:A MPAA:NR)**

SALAMANDER, THE*** (1915) 5 reels B.S. Moss bw

Ruth Findlay *(Dore Dexter)*, Iva Shepard *(Beatrice Snyder)*, John F. Sainpolis *(Albert Sassoon)*, J. F. Glendon *(Garry Lindaberry)*, Edgar J. L. Davenport *(Phillip Massingale)*, J. Albert Hall *(Harrigan Blood)*, H. H. Pattee *(Samuel Ludlow)*, Dan Baker *(Count De Joncy)*, Mabel Trinnear *(Ida Summers)*, Beatrice James *(Winona)*, Rita Allen *(Miss Pim)*, Violet Davis *(Baby Betty)*.

Outright melodrama about a young lady who goes to the city and brings to justice the man who stole her parents' fortune, caused their deaths, and later tried to obtain her valuable upstate property. Along the way she finds the time to win the love of a millionaire, in what is really a much better picture than it sounds.

d, Arthur Donaldson; w, (based on a novel by Owen Johnson).

Adventure **(PR:A MPAA:NR)**

SALLY*** (1925) 9 reels FN bw

Colleen Moore *(Sally)*, Lloyd Hughes *(Blair Farquar)*, Leon Errol *(Duke of Checkergovinia)*, Dan Mason *(Pops Shendorf)*, John T. Murray *(Otis Hooper)*, Eva Novak *(Rosie Lafferty)*, Ray Hallor *(Jimmy Spelvin)*, Carlo Schipa *(Sascha Commuski)*, Myrtle Stedman *(Mrs. Ten Brock)*, Capt. E. H. Calvert *(Richard Farquar)*, Louise Beaudet *(Mme. Julie Du Fay)*.

Wonderful vehicle for the talents of Moore has the actress playing an orphan who is adopted by kindly dance teacher Beaudet. When the instructor's studio goes bankrupt, Moore takes a job as a dishwasher in a restaurant owned by Mason. There she becomes acquainted with Hughes, a handsome young millionaire to whom she becomes greatly attracted. At a lavish society party given by Hughes' mother, a renowned Russian dancer who is to be the guest performer fails to show up and Moore is hired to impersonate her. Moore's routine is a sensation, but Mason, who has followed her from the restaurant, exposes her as a fraud to the guests. She is immediately ordered from Hughes' home (giving Moore the opportunity to inject a little pathos). All ends happily, however, when word comes that Florenz Ziegfeld was present at the party and wants her to star in his Follies. She follows up on the offer—as well as a proposal of marriage from the apologetic Hughes.

d, Alfred E. Green; w, June Mathis (based on the play by Guy Bolton, Clifford Grey); ph, T. D. McCord; ed, George McGuire; art d, E. J. Shulter.

Comedy **(PR:A MPAA:NR)**

SALLY IN OUR ALLEY* (1927) 6 reels COL bw

Shirley Mason *(Sally Williams)*, Richard Arlen *(Jimmie Adams)*, Alec B. Francis *(Sandy Mack)*, Paul Panzer *(Tony Garibaldi)*, William H. Strauss *(Abraham Lapidowitz)*, Kathlyn Williams *(Mrs. Gordon Mansfield)*, Florence Turner *(Mrs. Williams)*, Harry Crocker *(Chester Drake)*.

Blatantly banal attempt at comedy has Mason, an orphan, being adopted by three older men—a Jew, an Italian, and a Scot. She is also loved by Arlen, the plumber, and everything is just great in their working class neighborhood. Then Mason is discovered by her millionaire aunt and taken away to live with the upper crust. On her 18th birthday her foster parents and former boy friend attend a party at the mansion, and their table manners are so poor that the girl cannot hide her embarrassment. Dejected, the four return to their own world, and Arlen arranges to sign on with a merchant ship. In the end though, the girl comes to her senses, rejects the life of riches, and returns to her real home and the young fellow she truly loves.

p, Harry Cohn; d, Walter Lang; w, Dorothy Howell (based on a story by Edward Clark); ph, J. O. Taylor; art d, Robert E. Lee.

Comedy/Drama **(PR:A MPAA:NR)**

SALLY OF THE SAWDUST*** (1925) 10 reels D. W. Griffith/UA bw

Carol Dempster *(Sally)*, W. C. Fields *(Prof. Eustace P. McGargle)*, Alfred Lunt *(Peyton Lennox)*, Erville Alderson *(Judge Henry L. Foster)*, Effie Shannon *(Mrs. Foster)*, Charles Hammond *(Lennox, Sr.)*, Roy Applegate *(Detective)*, Florence Fair *(Miss Vinton)*, Marie Shotwell *(Society Woman)*, Glenn Anders *(Leon the Acrobat)*, Tammany Young *(Yokel in the Old Army Game)*, William "Shorty" Blanche *(Stooge)*.

Dempster is raised by circus juggler and sharpster Fields when her mother, who was disowned by her parents for marrying a bigtop performer, dies. Now that Dempster is becoming a young lady, Fields sets out to find her grandparents. Fate brings them to the very town they're looking for when Fields lands a job with a carnival. Lunt, a wealthy young friend of Dempster's family, falls in love with the girl, but his parents despise entertainers. After a number of complications, Dempster is arrested for assisting her guardian in a con game and dragged off to jail. Fields, who managed to evade the police, hears of this, steals a car, and in a completely untypical Griffith chase, makes it to the courthouse in time to inform her grandfather—who turns out to be the judge—of her true parentage. Naturally, in the end, all is forgiven; the grandparents embrace their lost darling, Lunt proposes marriage, and Fields is persuaded to remain on and become a real estate agent. This was Griffith's only comedy of feature length, and of course it's often compared unfavorably with his major works. But the film is not without its charm, and Fields, who is actually doing a lot of his own material, is fascinating to watch. (Remade as POPPY in 1936).

d, D. W. Griffith; w, Forrest Halsey (based on the play "Poppy" by Dorothy Donnelly); ph, Harry Fischbeck, Hal Sintzenich; ed, James Smith; art d, Charles M. Kirk.

Comedy **Cas.** **(PR:A MPAA:NR)**

SALLY OF THE SCANDALS*½ (1928) 7 reels FBO bw

Bessie Love *(Sally Rand)*, Irene Lambert *(Mary)*, Allan Forrest *(Steve Sinclair)*, Margaret Quimby *(Marian Duval)*, Jimmy Phillips *(Kelly)*, Jack Raymond *(Bennie)*, Jerry Miley *(Bill Reilly)*.

Even Love looks bad in this backstage flop which has her becoming a chorus girl to support her crippled sister, Lambert. After turning down Forrest, a producer, because she suspects his intentions, Love almost ends up marrying a gangster (who has passed himself off as being legit) when he volunteers to come up with the money for Lambert's operation. In the end Love is cleared of stealing some jewelry, planted on her by a jealous actress, and realizes that Forrest's intentions were actually honorable. She then becomes his bride—as well as Broadway's biggest star.

d, Lynn Shores; w, Enid Hibbard; t, Randolph Bartlett, Jack Conway; ph, Philip Tannura; ed, Archie Marshek.

Drama **(PR:A MPAA:NR)**

SALOME½** (1922) 6 reels Nazimova/Allied Producers and Distributors bw

Nazimova *(Salome)*, Rose Dione *(Herodias)*, Mitchell Lewis *(Herod)*, Nigel De Brulier *(Jokaanan)*, Earl Schenck *(Young Syrian)*, Arthur Jasmine *(Page)*, Frederick Peters *(Naaman, the Executioner)*, Louis Dumar *(Tigellinus)*.

Well-intended, highly stylized, loosely adapted film version of the Oscar Wilde work, with interesting sets by Rudolph Valentino's wife Natacha Rambova (designed in black, white, and gold) based on the original illustrations of Aubrey Beardsley. A film which disappoints and fascinates at the same time.

d, Charles Bryant; w, Peter M. Winters (based on the work by Oscar Wilde); ph, Charles Van Enger; art d, set d & cos, Natacha Rambova.

Drama **Cas.** **(PR:A MPAA:NR)**

SALOMY JANE*** (1914) 6 reels California Motion Picture bw

Beatriz Michelena *(Salomy Jane)*, House Peters *(Madison Clay)*, Andrew Robson, William Nigh, Forrest Halsey, Mabel Hilliard, Jack Holt.

Good western set during the gold rush days of 1849 is loaded with hard-riding gunplay and well-staged fist fights. And with the exception of some minor liberties taken by the directors, the production remains faithful to Harte's original story. Holt makes his film debut here in a bit part and also does some stunt work.

d, J. Searle Dawley, Alex E. Beyfuss; w, (based on the story "Salomy Jane's Kiss" by Bret Harte and the play by Paul Armstrong).

Western **(PR:A MPAA:NR)**

SALOMY JANE*** (1923) 7 reels FP/PAR bw

Jacqueline Logan *(Salomy Jane)*, George Fawcett *(Yuba Bill)*, Maurice B. Flynn *(The Man)*, William Davidson *(The Gambler)*, Charles Ogle *(Madison Clay)*, William Quirk *(Col. Starbottle)*, G. Raymond Nye *(Red Pete)*, Louise Dresser *(Mrs. Pete)*,

James Neill *(Larabee)*, Tom Carrigan *(Rufe Waters)*, Clarence Burton *(Baldwin)*, Barbara Brower *(Mary Ann)*, Milton Ross *(Steve Low)*.

Good programmer has Salomy Jane (Logan) instigating the escape of a stranger about to be lynched by a band of vigilantes by giving him a farewell kiss. Logan later marries the fellow after both he and her father are exonerated of the killing of a long-time family enemy.

d, George Melford; w, Waldemar Young (based on the story "Salomy Jane's Kiss" by Bret Harte); ph, Bert Glennon.

Western **(PR:A MPAA:NR)**

SALVAGE** (1921) 6 reels R-C bw

Pauline Frederick *(Bernice Ridgeway/Kate Martin)*, Ralph Lewis *(Cyrus Ridgeway)*, Milton Sills *(Fred Martin)*, Helen Stone *(Ruth Martin)*, Rose Cade *(Tessie)*, Raymond Hatton *(The Cripple)*, Hobart Kelly *(The Baby)*.

A lot of hokum in this overly padded tearjerker, which has a millionaire, Lewis, telling his wife that their baby died in childbirth, when it was actually born crippled and he decided to send it away. The wife (Frederick) leaves her husband and moves into a tenement, where she becomes the friend of a mother who is struggling because her spouse was sent to jail for a minor offense. When the woman commits suicide, Frederick takes her name and sets about raising the child properly. The convict (Sills) returns from prison, keeps the secret, and falls in love with his wife's replacement. The picture ends with Frederick's husband making a deathbed confession that the child she is raising is really hers (cured after an operation) and that all of his money is to go to her—giving a much deserved break to Frederick, the child, and Sills—who immediately pops the question.

d, Henry King; w, (based on a story by Daniel F. Whitcomb); ph, J. D. Jennings.

Drama **(PR:A MPAA:NR)**

SALVATION HUNTERS, THE** (1925) 6 reels Academy Photoplays/UA bw

George K. Arthur *(The Boy)*, Georgia Hale *(The Girl)*, Bruce Guerin *(The Child)*, Otto Matiesen *(The Man)*, Nellie Bly Baker *(The Woman)*, Olaf Hytten *(The Brute)*, Stuart Holmes *(The Gentleman)*.

Pretentious, self-indulgent little film shot on a shoestring was praised by Chaplin (although it is rumored he did so as a joke to test the artistic gullibility of certain people in the industry), an endorsement which opened the door to director von Sternberg's better work that lay ahead. THE SALVATION HUNTERS dealt with a boy, a girl, and a child (played by Arthur, Hale, and Guerin, respectively) who leave a rotten life behind and make their way to the city. There they overcome corruption as well as adversity before moving along to what von Sternberg indicates, in his final title, is a better lot..."It isn't conditions, nor is it environment—it is faith that controls our lives."

d&w, Josef von Sternberg; ph, Edward Gheller.

Drama **(PR:A MPAA:NR)**

SALVATION JANE* (1927) 6 reels R-C/FBO bw

Viola Dana *(Salvation Jane)*, J. Parkes Jones *(Jerry O'Day)*, Fay Holderness *(Capt. Carrie Brown)*, Erville Alderson *(Gramp)*.

Below-par programmer has slum girl Dana donning a Salvation Army uniform to part an out-of-towner of his cash, then repenting and returning the money when the man tries to commit suicide. She also manages to reform the young crook who had blackmailed her into helping him by offering to pay her grandfather's medical bills. In the end Dana discovers, to her pleasant surprise, that grandpa has stored away a small fortune.

d, Phil Rosen; w, Doris Schroeder (based on the story by Maude Fulton); ph, Lyman Broening.

Drama **(PR:A MPAA:NR)**

SALVATION NELL*** (1921) 7 reels Whitman Bennett/AFN bw

Pauline Starke *(Nell Sanders)*, Joseph King *(Jim Platt)*, Gypsy O'Brien *(Myrtle Hawes)*, Edward Langford *(Maj. Williams)*, Evelyn C. Carrington *(Hallelujah Maggie)*, Charles McDonald *(Sid McGovern)*, Matthew Betz *(Al McGovern)*, Marie Haynes *(Hash House Sal), A. Earl (Giffen)*, William Nally *(Callahan)*, Lawrence Johnson *(Jimmie)*.

Solid drama has Starke, a slum girl, forced to work as a scrubwoman in McDonald's lower East Side saloon. When his brother tries to force himself on her, Starke's sweetheart, King, kills him in a fist fight and is sent to prison for manslaughter. Sometime later, Starke has a child and becomes a member of the Salvation Army, where she distinguishes herself as a speaker. Langford, her commanding officer, falls in love with the bright young convert and asks her to be his wife. About the same time, King returns and does the same. Starke struggles with the decision, until the dilemma resolves itself after King volunteers to forget his past ways and lead a Christian life.

d, Kenneth Webb; sup, Whitman Bennett; w, Dorothy Farnum (based on the play by Edward Brewster Sheldon); ph, Ernest Haller; art d, Roy Webb, Al D'Agostino.

Drama **(PR:A MPAA:NR)**

SAMSON** (1914) 6 reels UNIV bw

J. Warren Kerrigan *(Samson)*, Kathleen Kerrigan *(Delilah)*, Mayme Kelso, Harold Lloyd, Hal Roach *(Extras)*.

A lot of money was spent on this picture, which virtually covered the entire legend of Samson, including his famous haircut and the strong man's ultimate death while destroying the temple of the Phillistines. J. Warren Kerrigan was too small for the part, however, and at least one wag at the film's opening suggested that he should have switched roles with his larger sister, who did not make an altogether convincing Delilah. Working in the film as extras were Roach and Lloyd, a couple of fellows who were destined to make more than a little film history.

d, Lorimer Johnston, G. P. Hamilton; w, Johnston.

Costume **(PR:A MPAA:NR)**

SANCTUARY* (1916, Brit.) 4 reels Claude Harris/Davison Film Sales Agency bw

Sylvia Cavalho *(Mrs. Carlton)*, Clifford Pembroke *(Ned Ferrers)*.

British thriller about an artist who puts away his brushes long enough to come to the assistance of the wife of a member of parliament who shot her blackmailer. It is not geared to keep the audience sitting on the edge of their seats.

p&d, Claude Harris; w, Sylvia Chavalho (based on the play by Malcolm Watson).

Mystery **(PR:A MPAA:NR)**

SAND 1/2** (1920) 5 reels WSHP/PAR bw

William S. Hart *(Dan Kurrie)*, Mary Thurman *(Margaret Young)*, G. Raymond Nye *(Joseph Garber)*, Patricia Palmer *(Josie Kirkwood)*, William Patton *(Pete Beckett)*, Lon Poff *(Jim Kirkwood)*, Hugh Saxon *(Pop Young)*.

Pretty fair Hart western has the star losing his job on the railroad because the heavy, who owns stock in the company, covets his sweetheart. The villain and his gang are later caught by Hart attempting to rob a train, and the hero gets his job back, as well as the hand of the girl he loves.

d, Lambert Hillyer; w, William S. Hart, Hillyer (based on the story "Dan Kurrie's Inning" by Russell A. Boggs); ph, Joseph August, Dwight Warren; art d, Thomas A. Brierley.

Western **(PR:A MPAA:NR)**

SANDY*** (1926) 8 reels FOX bw

Madge Bellamy *(Sandy McNeil)*, Leslie Fenton *(Douglas Keith)*, Harrison Ford *(Ramon Worth)*, Gloria Hope *(Judith Moore)*, Bardson Bard *(Ben Murillo)*, David Torrence *(Angus McNeil)*, Lillian Leighton *(Isabel McNeil)*, Charles Farrell *(Timmy)*, Charles Coleman *(Bob McNeil)*, Joan Standing *(Alice McNeil)*.

Good direction by Harry Beaumont and a fine performance by Bellamy make this jazz-age tragedy a first-rate hearttugger. Bellamy plays a flapper who reluctantly marries a wealthy man her father has chosen. His cruelty leads to the death of their child, and Bellamy leaves her husband and falls in love with Ford, an architect she meets. But Ford's former lover returns on the scene, causing heartbroken Bellamy to flee to her cousin's home. To complicate her life even more, Bellamy then falls in love with her cousin's sweetheart, Fenton. Ford, however, returns to claim Bellamy and ends up shooting her and then killing himself. Fenton, out of love for Bellamy, takes the rap and is tried for murder. But Bellamy recovers just in time to vindicate him and the two are united.

d, Harry Beaumont; w, Eve Unsell (based on the story by Elenore Meherin); ph, Rudolph Bergquist.

Drama **(PR:A MPAA:NR)**

SAPHEAD, THE*** (1921) 7 reels Metro bw

William H. Crane *(Nicholas Van Alstyne)*, Buster Keaton *(Bertie Van Alstyne, His Son)*, Carol Holloway *(Rose Turner)*, Edward Connelly *(Musgrave)*, Irving Cummings *(Mark Turner)*, Edward Jobson *(Rev. Murray Hilton)*, Jack Livingston *(Dr. George Wainwright)*, Jeffrey Williams *(Hutchins)*, Beulah Booker *(Agnes Gates)*, Henry Clauss *(The Waiter)*, Odette Tylor *(Mrs. Cornelia Opdyke)*, Edward Alexander *(Watson Flint)*, Katherine Albert *(Hattie)*, Helen Holte *(Henrietta Reynolds)*, Alfred Hollingsworth *(Hathaway)*.

Keaton has said that Douglas Fairbanks, who played the role of Bertie in the play "The Henrietta" on Broadway, suggested him for that part in the movie version, which underwent a title change to THE SAPHEAD. It was a very wise choice, and Keaton is wonderful as the dimwitted son of a Wall Street tycoon, who rallies in the end to save his father from bankruptcy, in a terrific scene which takes place on the floor of the stock market. In this film, Keaton left behind the broad slapstick parts he had played as Fatty Arbuckle's second banana and emerged as a tuxedo-clad, wealthy idler. It was a character he would use again in several of his best features. THE SAPHEAD is an interesting film and has more than its share of sparkling moments, but Keaton's true genius was about to be exposed to the world in his series of two-reel masterpieces which lay ahead.

p, John L. Golden, Winchell Smith, Marcus Loew; d, Herbert Blache; sup, Smith; w, June Mathis (based on the play "The New Henrietta" by Smith, Victor Mapes, which was in turn based on the play "The Henrietta" by Bronson Howard); ph, Harold Wenstrom.

Comedy **(PR:A MPAA:NR)**

SATAN'S SISTER*** (1925, Brit.) 8 reels BWP/W & F bw

Betty Balfour *(Jude Tyler)*, Guy Phillips *(Satan Tyler)*, Phillip Stevens *(Bobbie Ratcliffe)*, James Carew *(Tyler)*, Frank Stanmore *(Cleary)*, Caleb Porter *(Carquinez)*, Frank Perfitt *(Sellers)*, Jeff Barlow *(Bones)*.

Better-than-average British feature, filmed on location in Jamaica, has Balfour, a man-hating, tomboyish daughter-of-the-sea, setting out with her brother to locate buried treasure. They have a run-in with pirates, Balfour meets the right chap, and all ends well.

p, George Pearson, Betty Balfour; d&w, Pearson (based on the novel *Satan* by H. DeVere Stacpoole).

Adventure **(PR:A MPAA:NR)**

SATURDAY NIGHT** (1922) 9 reels FP/PAR bw

Leatrice Joy *(Iris Van Suydam, Society Girl)*, Conrad Nagel *(Richard Wynbrook*

Prentiss, Her Fiance), Edith Roberts *(Shamrock O'Day, Laundress)*, Jack Mower *(Tom McGuire, Chauffeur)*, Julia Faye *(Elsie, Richard's Sister)*, Edythe Chapman *(Mrs. Prentiss)*, Theodore Roberts *(Van Suydan)*, John Davidson *(The Count Demitry Scardoff)*, James Neill *(Tompkins, Butler)*, Winter Hall *(The Professor)*, Sylvia Ashton *(Mrs. O'Day, Washerwoman)*, Lillian Leighton *(Mrs. Ferguson)*.

Society drama has Joy and Nagel, an uppercrust couple, breaking off their engagement to marry the working-class boy and girl each has become attracted to. In the end, however, nobody can make the adjustment, leaving the blue-collar couple to find love with one another, while the blue *bloods* put the pieces back together again. Cecil B. DeMille was never happy with this picture, and it's easy to see why.

d, Cecil B. DeMille; w, Jeanie Macpherson; ph, Alvin Wyckoff, Karl Struss.

Drama **(PR:A MPAA:NR)**

SAVING THE FAMILY NAME*** (1916) 5 reels BLUE bw

Mary MacLaren *(Estelle Ryan)*, Gerard Alexander *(Mrs. Winthrop)*, Carl Von Schiller *(Wally Dreislin)*, Jack Holt *(Jansen Winthrop)*, Phillips Smalley *(Robert Winthrop)*, Harry Depp *(Billie Schram)*.

A snobbish family talk their young socialite son out of marrying the chorus girl he has proposed to and the youth commits suicide. The dancer is then swept to stardom on the strength of the publicity given the story by the tabloids, and a second young millionaire falls in love with her. His family also objects, but this time a slightly older bachelor brother takes it upon himself to kidnap the girl and seclude her in the family lodge. Time passes quickly, the couple fall in love, and a blow is struck for democracy when they decide to marry. The story is rather ordinary, but Weber's direction is not.

d, Lois Weber, Phillips Smalley; w, Weber (based on a story by Evelyn Heath); ph, Allen Siegler.

Drama **(PR:A MPAA:NR)**

SAWDUST** (1923) 5 reels UNIV bw

Gladys Walton *(Nita Moore)*, Niles Welch *(Phillip Lessoway)*, Edith Yorke *(Mrs. Nancy Wentworth)*, Herbert Standing *(Ethelbert Wentworth)*, Matthew Betz *(Runner Bayne)*, Frank Brownlee *("Pop" Gifford)*, William Robert Daly *("Speck" Dawson)*, Mattie Peters *(Tressie)*, Mike *(Sawdust, the Dog)*.

Even Jack Conway's skillful direction failed to pump any life into this average programmer in which Walton, a circus girl, escapes her cruel ringmaster stepfather and convinces an elderly couple that she's their long-missing daughter. The family lawyer, Welch, exposes the lie, saves the young thing from committing suicide, and then asks Walton's hand in marriage when he realizes he loves her.

d, Jack Conway; w, Doris Schroeder, Harvey Gates (based on a story by Courtney Ryley Cooper); ph, Allan Davey.

Drama **(PR:A MPAA:NR)**

SAWDUST TRAIL*** (1924) 6 reels UNIV bw

Hoot Gibson *(Clarence Elwood Butts)*, Josie Sedgwick *("Calamity" Jane Webster)*, David Torrence *(Jonathan Butts)*, Charles K. French *(Square Deal McKenzie)*, Harry Todd *(Quid Jackson)*, G. Raymond Nye *(Gorilla Lawson)*, Pat Harmon *(Ranch Foreman)*, Taylor Carroll *(Lafe Webster)*, W. T. McCulley *(Red McLaren)*.

Clever combination of western thrills and sight gags has Gibson playing an eastern college man who pretends to be a wimp and joins a Wild West show. He plays endless practical jokes on Sedgwick, the man-hating star of the troupe, but manages to win her love and respect in the end.

d, Edward Sedgwick; w, E. Richard Schayer, Raymond L. Schrock (based on a story by Dudley Pelley); ph, Virgil Miller.

Western/Comedy **(PR:A MPAA:NR)**

SAY! YOUNG FELLOW*** (1918) 5 reels Douglas Fairbanks/ART bw

Douglas Fairbanks *(Cub Reporter)*, Marjorie Daw *(The Girl)*, Frank Campeau *(The Villain)*, Edythe Chapman, James Neill, Ernest Butterworth.

Fairbanks is a cub reporter who takes over when the newspaper's ace fails to get an interview with a man who made a million dollars in one day. Of course Fairbanks does not approach his assignment in the traditional manner. He leaps, climbs, bounds, and hurls himself into the man's bedroom, where at gunpoint he secures the "yarn." Along the way he wins the love of lovely Daw, turns down a position from the impressed tycoon, and ends up bringing a gang of crooks to justice.

d&w, Joseph Henabery; ph, Hugh McClung, Glen MacWilliams.

Comedy/Adventure **(PR:A MPAA:NR)**

SCALES OF JUSTICE, THE** (1914) 5 reels FP bw

Jane Fearnly *(Edith Russell Dexter)*, Hal Clarendon *(Walter Elliott)*, Mark Price *(The Grandfather)*, Paul McAllister, Harold Lockwood, Mrs. Leslie Carter, Viola Allen, Katherine Lee, Daniel Jarrett, Mary Blackburn, Beatrice Moreland.

A lot of melodramatics in this one about a district attorney who refuses to prosecute the woman he loves for the murder of her grandfather and quits his post until the real killer is exposed. There is also a secondary plot in which the granddaughter is disinherited for marrying a man who turns out to be a drunkard and is killed by a speeding automobile, as well as a sweet little girl whom the director and scriptwriter use shamelessly to evoke tears.

d&w, Thomas N. Heffron (based on a play by John Reinhart).

Drama **(PR:A MPAA:NR)**

SCANDAL* 1/2** (1915) 5 reels UNIV bw

Lois Weber, Phillips Smalley, Rupert Julian, Adele Farrington, Abe Mundon, Alice Thomson.

Directors Weber and Smalley make a wonderfully cinematic indictment of gossip in this picture, which depicts three deaths and two divorces, as well as a generally unhappy ending for all concerned, due to a false accusation which gets out of control.

d, Lois Weber, Phillips Smalley; w, Weber.

Drama **(PR:A MPAA:NR)**

SCANDAL, THE** (1923, Brit.) 7 reels I.B. Davidson/Granger bw

Hilda Bayley *(Charlotte Ferrioul)*, Henry Victor *(Artenezzo)*, Edward O'Neill *(Jeannetier)*, Vanni Marcoux *(Maurice Ferrioul)*, Mme. de la Croix *(Mme. Ferrioul)*.

Set in Italy, this British mystery has to do with a handsome singer who is accused of stealing the valuable jewels a married woman loaned him to cover gambling expenses.

d, Arthur Rooke; w, Kinchen Wood (based on a play by Henri Battaille).

Crime **(PR:A MPAA:NR)**

SCARAB RING, THE*** (1921) 6 reels VIT bw

Alice Joyce *(Constance Randall)*, Maude Malcolm *(Muriel Randall)*, Joe King *(Ward Locke)*, Edward Phillips *(Burton Temple)*, Fuller Mellish *(John Randall)*, Claude King *(Hugh Martin)*, Joseph Smiley *(James Locke)*, Jack Hopkins *(Mr. Kheres)*, Armand Cortez *(Kennedy)*.

One of Vitagraph's better efforts has Joyce promising her dying father that she will not reveal to her sister Malcolm the knowledge of his being blackmailed for a crime he once committed. Later Claude King unearths the incriminating evidence and threatens to go public with it unless Joyce agrees to persuade her sister to marry him. On the day he was to break the story, however, King is discovered dead and Joyce's scarab ring is found next to his body. At a trial she is released as a suspect for lack of sufficient proof, but in the end Joyce confesses to her sweetheart, Joe King, that she did indeed kill the rotter when he tried to force himself upon her.

d, Edward Jose; w, C. Graham Baker (based on the story "The Desperate Heritage" by Harriet Gaylord); ph, Joe Shelderfer.

Mystery **(PR:A MPAA:NR)**

SCARAMOUCHE**** (1923) 10 reels Metro bw

Ramon Novarro *(Andre-Louis Moreau)*, Alice Terry *(Aline de Kercadiou)*, Lewis Stone *(The Marquis de la Tour d'Azyr)*, Lloyd Ingraham *(Quintin de Kercadiou)*, Julia Swayne Gordon *(The Countess Therese de Plougastel)*, William Humphrey *(The Chevalier de Chabrillane)*, Otto Matiesen *(Philippe de Vilmorin)*, George Siegmann *(George Jacques Danton)*, Bowditch Turner *(Le Chapelier)*, James Marcus *(Challefau Binet)*, Edith Allen *(Climene Binet)*, Lydia Yeamans Titus *(Mme. Binet)*, John George *(Polinchinelle)*, Nelson McDowell *(Rhodomont)*, De Garcia Fuerburg *(Maximilien Robespierre)*, Roy Coulson *(Jean Paul Marat)*, Edwin Argus *(Louis XVI)*, Clotilde Delano *(Marie Antoinette)*, Willard Lee Hall *(The King's Lieutenant)*, Slavko Vorkapitch *(Napoleon Bonaparte)*, Lorimer Johnston *(Count Dupuye)*, Edward Connelly *(Minister to the King)*, Howard Gaye *(Viscount d'Albert)*, J. Edwin Brown *(Mons. Benoit)*, Carrie Clark Ward *(Mme. Benoit)*, Edward Coxen *(Jacques)*, William Dyer *(The Gamekeeper)*, Rose Dione *(La Revolte)*, Arthur Jasmine *(Student of Rennes)*, Tom Kennedy *(A Dragoon)*, Kalla Pasha *(Keeper of the Paris Gate)*, B. Hyman, Louis Carver *(Extras)*.

Another Ingram-directed film of great power and beauty, with inspired photography by John F. Seitz. The story has a young law student, Novarro, joining French revolutionaries when his best friend is unfairly killed in a duel by ruthless aristocrat Stone. He joins a band of strolling players and becomes a Robin Hood figure, disguised as Scaramouche the clown. Novarro is in love with Terry, his godfather's daughter, but she is attracted to Stone. On the rebound, Novarro becomes engaged to Allen, a fellow actress, who, he later discovers, is Stone's mistress. Before long Terry discovers this fact as well and is awakened to her true feelings towards the dashing Novarro. When the revolution erupts, Novarro helps the aristocratic Allen and her aunt escape, and Stone is killed by the mob—but not before boasting that he is Novarro's true father in the end. Novarro was discovered by Ingram after the director had an argument with Rudolph Valentino. As a result Novarro went on to subsequent stardom. SCARAMOUCHE was lavishly produced, and the depiction of France in turmoil in many ways equalled D. W. Griffith's ORPHANS OF THE STORM.

d&sup, Rex Ingram; w, Willis Goldbeck (based on the novel by Rafael Sabatini); ph, John F. Seitz; ed, Grant Whytock; cos, O'Kane Cornwell, Eve Roth, Van Horn.

Historical/Adventure **(PR:A MPAA:NR)**

SCARLET CAR, THE** (1923) 5 reels UNIV bw

Herbert Rawlinson *(Billy Winthrop)*, Claire Adams *(Beatrice Forbes)*, Edward Cecil *(Ernest Peabody)*, Norris Johnson *(Violet Gayner)*, Tom McGuire *(Jim Winthrop)*, Marc Robbins *(Jerry Gayner)*, Tom O'Brien *(Mitt Deagon)*.

Fair programmer has Rawlinson exposing crooked political candidate Cecil, who is backed by his father and engaged to Adams, the woman he loves. The lady, of course, jumps on Rawlinson's bandwagon when she discovers the truth.

d, Stuart Paton; w, George Randolph Chester (based on the story by Richard Harding Davis); ph, Virgil Miller.

Drama **(PR:A MPAA:NR)**

SCARLET DAYS* 1/2 (1919) 7 reels D.W. Griffith/PAR-ART bw

Richard Barthelmess *(Alvarez, a Bandit)*, Eugenie Besserer *(Rosie Nell)*, Carol Dempster *(Lady Fair, Her Daughter)*, Clarine Seymour *(Chiquita, a Mexican Dance-Hall Girl)*, Ralph Graves *(Randolph, a Virginia Gentleman)*, George Fawcett *(The Sheriff)*, Walter Long *(King Bagley, the Dance-Hall Proprietor)*, Kate Bruce *(An Aunt)*, Rhea Haines *(Spasm Sal)*, Adolphe Lestina *(Randolph's Partner)*, Herbert Sutch *(The Marshal)*, J. Wesley Warner *(Alvarez's Man)*.

Besserer (who would earn film immortality as Al Jolson's mother in THE JAZZ SINGER) runs a California dance hall during the gold rush days of 1849. She has kept her daughter Dempster in an Eastern school, ignorant of her mother's way of life. Then the bottom falls out of Besserer's world and she's nearly lynched on a trumped-up murder charge. Fortunately, she is saved by Barthelmess, a bandit (a character based on the real-life Joaquin Murietta, who was a Robin Hood-like figure). Later Besserer's cabin is attacked by the forces of her enemy and she and Dempster, who has come to join her, are nearly killed. The scene is very reminiscent of situations used by director Griffith in his earlier films, THE BATTLE AT ELDERBUSH GULCH (a 1914 two-reeler) and THE BIRTH OF A NATION (1915). Once again Barthelmess rides to the rescue. This time the old woman is killed, however, and the bandit is captured by the sheriff. When his sweetheart, Seymour, comes to plead for his life, the couple manage to escape and the audience is led to believe that happiness will indeed be theirs. When this film was in the planning stages, Dorothy Gish pleaded with Griffith to use the relatively unknown Rudolph Valentino for the lead and the great director turned her down, with the explanation that the actor's foreign looks would not appeal to American women.

d, D. W. Griffith; w, S. E. V. Taylor; ph, G. W. "Billy" Bitzer; ed, James Smith.

Western **(PR:A MPAA:NR)**

SCARLET DOVE, THE* (1928) 6 reels TS bw

Lowell Sherman *(Ivan Orloff)*, Josephine Borio *(Mara)*, Margaret Livingston *(Olga)*, Robert Frazer *(Alexis Petroff)*, Shirley Palmer *(Eve)*, Carlos Durand *(Gregory)*, Julia Swayne Gordon *(The Aunt)*.

Poor programmer has Borio, a wealthy Russian convent girl, forced into a marriage with officer Sherman, a man she doesn't love, who is only interested in her fortune. On their wedding night she escapes with Frazer, an officer under his command, and is believed killed in a sleigh accident. Later her lover is accused of her murder, but Borio shows up at the trial to clear him. Mortified by this, Sherman challenges Frazer to a duel on the frozen river, but is killed when he falls through the ice.

d&w, Arthur Gregor; w, John Francis Natteford; t, Harry Braxton, Viola Brothers Shore; ph, Ernest Miller; ed, Martin G. Cohn; art d, Hervey Libbert.

Drama **(PR:A MPAA:NR)**

SCARLET LADY, THE 1/2** (1928) 7 reels COL bw

Lya De Putti *(Lya)*, Don Alvarado *(Prince Nicholas)*, Warner Oland *(Zaneriff)*, Otto Matiesen *(Valet)*, John Peters *(Captain)*, Valentina Zimina *(A Revolutionist)*.

Sensual Putti is a Russian revolutionist who falls in love with prince Alvarado and is later spurned by him when the nobleman discovers she was once the paramour of the dreaded Red assassin, Oland. Towards the film's end Oland is popping aristocrats off like clay pigeons and hands his pistol to Putti that she may kill Alvarado, his most prominent target. Instead she shoots her former lover and with the prince escapes over the border to safety and happiness.

p, Harry Cohn; d, Alan Crosland; w, (based on a story by Bess Meredyth); ph, James Van Trees; ed, Frank Atkinson; art d, Harrison Wiley; m/l, "My Heart Belongs to You" by Lou Herscher.

Drama **(PR:A MPAA:NR)**

SCARLET LETTER, THE**** (1926) 9 reels MGM bw

Lillian Gish *(Hester Prynne)*, Lars Hanson *(The Rev. Arthur Dimmesdale)*, Henry B. Walthall *(Roger Prynne)*, Karl Dane *(Giles)*, William H. Tooker *(The Governor)*, Marcelle Corday *(Mistress Hibbins)*, Fred Herzog *(The Jailer)*, Jules Cowles *(The Beadle)*, Mary Hawes *(Patience)*, Joyce Coad *(Pearl)*, James A. Marcus *(A Sea Captain)*, Chief Yowlachie *(Indian)*, Polly Moran *(Townswoman)*.

Gish personally guaranteed that Hawthorne's novel could be brought to the screen without being offensive, and women and church groups all over the country agreed not to boycott it because of the actress' flawless reputation. Louis B. Mayer suggested Hanson for the part of Dimmesdale, Hester Prynne's clergyman and partner in adultery, and the Swedish actor sailed for the U.S. and stardom at MGM. Seastrom directed brilliantly and the film, like the novel, is an American classic, sometimes called the best novel ever written by an American. Simply told, it is the story of the wife of a doctor who has disappeared. She falls in love with the village pastor and bears his child, both keeping it secret since it would impair his spiritual leadership of the village. The husband returns and the pastor, tortured by a guilty conscience, confesses his "sin" publicly and dies in front of his congregation. The puritan ethic, so illustrated, won a huge audience when it was published and subsequently three movie versions were made of it, none better than the 1926 version. Strangely, it took a Swedish director and a Swedish male star, Hanson, to help put it across, although it is true that Gish herself was a star of worldwide fame at the time. But the director, Seastrom (often spelled Sjostrom), brought with him to the picture the Scandinavian talent for "darkness," the stark tragedy of the story, the grim settings, the pastoral elements that helped make the picture so elemental. A cold, organized hand was surely at the helm, and that was Seastrom, with his third U.S. film since being brought to the U.S. in 1923 under a unique "loan" deal Metro Goldwyn made with Svensk Filmindustri in Stockholm, which wanted the sole distribution rights to Metro pictures. The "deal" hinged on them being granted those rights. Gish liked the Swedish director immensely, and they became lifelong friends. Insightfully, she said (quoted in her biography by Albert Bigelow Paine), "I knew that we must have a Swedish director. The Swedish people are closer to what our Pilgrims were...than we present day Americans....He got the spirit of the story exactly...I never worked with anybody I liked better than Seastrom."

d, Victor Seastrom [Sjostrom]; w, Frances Marion (based on the novel by Nathaniel Hawthorne); t, Marion; ph, Hendrick Sartov; ed, Hugh Wynn; set d, Cedric Gibbons, Sidney Ullman; cos, Max Ree.

Drama **(PR:A MPAA:NR)**

SCARLET LILY, THE*** (1923) 6 reels PRE/AFN bw

Katherine MacDonald *(Dora Mason)*, Orville Caldwell *(Lawson Dean)*, Stuart Holmes *(Jessup Barnes)*, Edith Lyle *(Mrs. Barnes)*, Adele Farrington *(Trixie Montresse)*, Gordon Russell *(Laurence Peyton)*, Grace Morse *(Beatrice Milo)*, Jane Miskimin *(Little Mollie)*, Lincoln Stedman *(John Rankin)*, Gertrude Quality *(Mrs. Rosetta Bowen)*.

Deftly directed drama has MacDonald accepting an offer to use Holmes' apartment, while he's abroad, to care for her dying sister. The gentleman's wife appears on the scene, however, misinterprets the situation, and names MacDonald corespondent in a divorce action. Escaping to a country hideaway, she falls in love with Caldwell, a young lawyer who is recuperating from an eye problem. Later, after her sister's death, she marries the attorney and he runs against Holmes for the office of D.A., at which point MacDonald's "past" becomes an embarrassment. But the lady toughs it out, proves her innocence, and forces Holmes to throw in the towel.

d, Victor Schertzinger; w, Lois Zellner, Florence Hein (based on a story by Fred Sittenham); ph, Joseph Brotherton; ed, Eve Unsell.

Drama **(PR:A MPAA:NR)**

SCARLET ROAD, THE* (1916) 5 reels Kleine bw

Malcolm Duncan *(Harry Tremain)*, Anna Q. Nilsson *(Betty Belgrave)*, Della Connor *(Alice Holbrook)*, Iva Shepard *(Mrs. Holbrook)*, John Jarrott *(Lorimer Wilbur)*.

Inferior programmer has the young inventor of an airplane motor inheriting $200,000 and yielding to the lure of the bright lights, where a Broadway vamp takes him for everything he has. Disgusted with himself, the poor devil sets out to commit suicide, but instead saves a millionaire's daughter from drowning and is rewarded with the capital to make his invention a success.

d, Bruno Lessing, Clarkson Miller (based on a story by Mrs. Wilson Woodrow); ph, Jugo Johnson.

Drama **(PR:A MPAA:NR)**

SCARLET SEAS 1/2** (1929) 7 reels FN bw

Richard Barthelmess *(Steve Donkin)*, Betty Compson *(Rose McRay)*, Loretta Young *(Margaret Barbour)*, James Bradbury, Jr. *(Johnson)*, Jack Curtis *(Toomey)*, Knute Erickson *(Capt. Barbour)*.

Richard Barthelmess is a free-spirited sea captain who takes prostitute Compson on board when she's thrown out of Shanghai. Their ship sinks, and after floating about on a lifeboat they encounter a craft which has been seized by mutineers. The tough band of cutthroats is no match for the dashing Barthelmess, who brings them under control and saves the captain and his daughter, Young.

d, John Francis Dillon; w, Bradley King (based on a story by W. Scott Darling); t, Louis Stevens; ph, Sol Polito; ed, Edward Schroeder, Jack Gardner; syn sc; s eff.

Drama **(PR:A MPAA:NR)**

SCARLET SIN, THE 1/2** (1915) 4 reels UNIV bw

Hobart Bosworth *(The Minister)*, Jane Novak *(His Wife)*, Hart Hoxie, Grace Thompson, Frank Elliott, Ed Brown, Wadsworth Harris, Helen Wright.

Bosworth impresses as the minister who cleans up a mining town with his fists, and then—even though his heart is breaking from within—stoically bids farewell to the wife who betrayed him.

d, Otis Turner, Hobart Bosworth; w, James Dayton (based on a story by Olga Printzlau Clark).

Drama **(PR:A MPAA:NR)**

SCARS OF JEALOUSY** (1923) 7 reels THI/AFN bw

Frank Keenan *(Col. Newland)*, Edward Burns *(Jeff Newland)*, Lloyd Hughes *(Coddy Jakes)*, Marguerite De La Motte *(Helen Meanix)*, James Neill *(Col. Meanix)*, Walter Lynch *(Pere Jakes)*, James Mason *(Zeke Jakes)*, Mattie Peters *(Mandy)*, George Reed *(Mose)*.

After disinheriting his prankster son Burns, colonel Keenan finds a Cajun lad from the Alabama hills, brings him home to be educated, and makes him his heir. Later the young man, Hughes, is suspected of murder and escapes to the hills where he meets the regenerated Burns, who molds him into a real man. With the help of De La Motte, who loves the Cajun, Burns goes on to help Hughes escape a lynching party, rescues his father from a forest fire, and is welcomed back into the family fold.

d&w, Lambert Hillyer (based on a story by Anthony H. Rudd); ph, J. O. Taylor; m, Sol Cohen.

Drama **(PR:A MPAA:NR)**

SCHOOL DAYS*** (1921) 7 reels Harry Rapf/WB bw

Wesley Barry *(Speck Brown)*, George Lessey *(His Guardian, the Deacon)*, Nellie P. Spaulding *(His Friend's Wife)*, Margaret Seddon *(His Teacher)*, Arline Blackburn *(His Sweetheart)*, J. H. Gilmore *(The Stranger)*, John Galsworthy *(Mr. Hadley, His New Friend)*, Jerome Patrick *(Mr. Wallace, Attorney)*, Evelyn Sherman *(His Sister)*, Arnold Lucy *(The Valet)*, Hippy the Dog.

Inspired by the famous Gus Edwards song, SCHOOL DAYS is a warm-hearted and often funny look at a rural America, which was beginning to pass from the scene, and especially that hallowed institution known as the one-room schoolhouse. Barry is excellent as the country boy who is given the chance to receive a New York education, becomes involved with a couple of crooks, and in the end chooses to return to his small town, where the people are real and life is decent.

p, Harry Rapf; d, William Nigh; w, Walter De Leon, Nigh; t, Hoey Lawlor; ph, Jack Brown, Sidney Hickox; set d, Tilford Studios.

Comedy/Drama **(PR:A MPAA:NR)**

SCRAPPER, THE** (1922) 5 reels UNIV bw

Herbert Rawlinson *(Malloy)*, Gertrude Olmstead *(Eileen McCarthy)*, William Welsh *(Dan McCarthy)*, Frankie Lee *(The Kid)*, Hal Craig *(Policeman)*, George McDaniels *(McGuirk)*, Fred Kohler *(Oleson)*, Edward Jobson *(Riley)*, Al MacQuarrie *(Simms)*, Walter Perry *(Rapport)*.

Modest production has handsome young Irishman Rawlinson graduating from engineering college, taking over the construction of a skyscraper, falling in love with the boss' daughter, Olmstead, whipping a big Swede who tries to sabotage the project, and convincing Olmstead to be his wife.

d, Hobart Henley; w, E. T. Lowe, Jr. (based on the story "Malloy Campeador" by Ralph G. Kirk); ph, Virgil Miller.

Drama **(PR:A MPAA:NR)**

SEA BEAST, THE*** ½ (1926) 10 reels WB bw

John Barrymore *(Ahab Ceeley)*, Dolores Costello *(Esther Harper)*, George O'Hara *(Derek Ceeley)*, Mike Donlin *(Flask)*, Sam Baker *(Queequeg)*, George Burrell *(Perth)*, Sam Allen *(Sea Captain)*, Frank Nelson *(Stubbs)*, Mathilde Comont *(Mula)*, James Barrows *(Rev. Harper)*, Vadim Uraneff *(Pip)*, Sojin *(Fedallah)*, Frank Hagney *(Daggoo)*.

One of Barrymore's most popular films was loosely based on the Melville classic about a man who is crippled by and becomes obsessed with the desire to kill Moby Dick, the great white whale. In true Hollywood tradition, the studio provided a happy ending, with Barrymore, in the role of Ahab, settling down to marry Costello following his spectacular duel with the mighty mammal. Less happy was actress Priscilla Bonner, whom "The Great Profile" had fired in favor of the beautiful unknown. Bonner sued Warner's and the brothers settled out of court for a tidy sum.

d, Millard Webb; w, Bess Meredyth (based on the novel *Moby Dick* by Herman Melville); ph, Byron Haskins, Frank Kesson.

Drama **(PR:A MPAA:NR)**

SEA HORSES*** (1926) 7 reels FP/PAR bw

Jack Holt *(George Glanville)*, Florence Vidor *(Helen Salvia)*, William Powell *(Lorenzo Salvia)*, George Bancroft *(Cochran)*, Mack Swain *(Bimbo-Bomba)*, Frank Campeau *(Senor Cordoza)*, Allan Simpson *(Harvey)*, George Nichols *(Marx)*, Mary Dow *(Cina Salvia)*, Dick La Reno *(Henry)*, Frank Austin *(Cheadle)*.

Great cast in a well-directed melodrama has Vidor sailing with her 4-year-old daughter to an African port to find Powell, the husband who deserted her some time earlier. On board, two of the crew, Bancroft and Simpson, become quite smitten with Vidor, while the captain, Holt, maintains his distance. At the movie's end, however, after a well-filmed storm sequence, Holt saves the lady from Powell—who has become a drunken beast—with the help of Bancroft, who sacrifices his life. The couple then sail home to England—and happiness.

d, Allan Dwan; w, James Shelley Hamilton, Becky Gardiner (based on the novel by Francis Brett Young); ph, James Howe.

Drama **(PR:A MPAA:NR)**

SEA LION, THE** (1921) 5 reels BOSWORTH/AP bw

Hobart Bosworth *(Nels Nelson)*, Emory Johnson *(Tom Walton)*, Bessie Love *(Nymph)*, Carol Holloway *(Dolly May)*, Florence Carpenter *(Florence)*, Charles Clary *(Green)*, Jack Curtis *(Bentley)*, Richard Morris *(Billy)*, J. Gordon Russell *(Simmons)*.

Bosworth (in what appears to be a sequel to his earlier film THE SEA WOLF) is a captain who has dedicated his life to being mean ever since his wife deserted him. When Bosworth's ship is low on water, young Johnson is sent to locate some on an island where he runs into an old man and a beautiful young woman (Love). Johnson brings them back to the ship, and Bosworth takes all of his hatred out on the poor girl. Finally, Johnson and Love escape in a small boat just as an enormous storm is coming up. Bosworth turns his ship in the other direction, but then happens to find the girl's Bible, in which it is written that she is actually *his* child and that his wife was really abducted. Bosworth reverses his course and rescues them in time to prevent tragedy.

d, Rowland V. Lee; w, Joseph Franklin Poland (based on a story by Emilie Johnson); ph, J. O. Taylor.

Drama **Cas.** **(PR:A MPAA:NR)**

SEA TIGER, THE** (1927) 6 reels FN bw

Milton Sills *(Justin Ramos)*, Mary Astor *(Amy)*, Larry Kent *(Charles Ramos)*, Alice White *(Manuella)*, Kate Price *(Bridget)*, Arthur Stone *(Enos)*, Emily Fitzroy *(Mrs. Enos)*, Joe Bonomo *(Sebastiano)*.

Barely adequate low-budget programmer has Sills playing a Canary Islands fisherman who is overly protective of Kent, the younger brother left in his care. Kent begins making advances toward Astor, an aristocrat's daughter, but Sills proves his brother's dishonorable intentions and wins the love of the girl he always secretly adored.

p, Carey Wilson; d, John Francis Dillon; w, Wilson (based on the story "A Runaway Enchantress" by Mary Heaton Vorse); ph, Charles Van Enger.

Drama **(PR:A MPAA:NR)**

SEA-WOLF, THE** (1913) 7 reels Bosworth bw

Hobart Bosworth *(Wolf Larsen)*, Viola Barry *(Miss Brewster)*, Herbert Rawlinson *(Van Weyden)*, J. Charles Hayden *(Cook)*.

Fairly good adaptation of London's classic novel about a nasty sea captain (Bosworth) contains a number of exciting moments, including the sadist going blind, his attempt to have his way with the beautiful Barry, and his ultimate death at the hands of Rawlinson.

d, Hobart Bosworth; w, (based on the novel by Jack London).

Drama **(PR:A MPAA:NR)**

SEALED LIPS*** (1915) 5 reels EQ/WORLD bw

William Courtenay *(Henry Everard)*, Arthur Ashley *(Cyril Maitland)*, Mary Charleson *(Alma Lee)*, Adele Ray *(Lillian Maitland)*, Marie E. Wells *(Marian Everard)*.

Good screen adaptation of the popular Gray novel about a minister who seduced a girl while he was a deacon, caused the death of her father, allowed his best friend to take the blame, and 20 years later publicly repents when the innocent fellow returns, not for revenge, but in the spirit of Christian forgiveness.

d, John Ince; w, Frank Condon (based on the story "The Silence of Dean Maitland" by Maxwell Gray).

Drama **(PR:A MPAA:NR)**

SEALED VALLEY, THE***(1915) 5 reels Metro bw (AKA: SEALED VALLEY)

Dorothy Donnelly *(Nahnya Crossfox)*, J. W. Johnson *(Dr. Cowdray)*, Kitty Sholto *(Rene Ditling)*.

Interesting film about an Indian girl who leaves her sacred and mineral-rich land to fetch a doctor to attend to her wounded mother. During their return journey the physician falls in love with her, but when a white woman enters the picture, the maiden decides to remain with her own people and blows up the valuable mine on her property to prevent Caucasian opportunists from exploiting it.

d, Lawrence McGill; w, Hulbert Footner; ph, W. C. Thompson.

Drama **(PR:A MPAA:NR)**

SEATS OF THE MIGHTY, THE** (1914) 6 reels Colonial/WORLD bw

Lionel Barrymore, Millicent Evans, Lois Meredith, Thomas Jefferson, Glen White, Clinton Preston, Marjorie Bonner, Grace Leigh, Harold Hartsell.

Although this filmed adaptation of Parker's novel about colonial Quebec is elaborately produced and for the most part well acted, the scenario is cluttered and hard to follow. The depiction of DuBarry's Court and the battle which brings this film to its conclusion do, however, impress.

d, T. Hayes Hunter; w, (based on the novel by Sir Gilbert Parker).

Historical **(PR:A MPAA:NR)**

SECOND FIDDLE*** (1923) 6 reels Film Guild/W.W. Hodkinson bw

Glenn Hunter *(Jim Bradley)*, Mary Astor *(Polly Crawford)*, Townsend Martin *(Herbert Bradley)*, Mary Foy *(Mrs. Bradley)*, Helenka Adamowska *(Cragg's Daughter)*, Otto Lang *(Dr. Crawford)*, William Nally *(Cragg)*, Leslie Stowe *(George Bradley)*, Osgood Perkins.

Well-directed, - acted, and -written melodrama dealing with sibling rivalry has young Hunter trying to prove he is his brother's equal by holding off a killer with an unloaded pistol. When Hunter realizes the pistol was empty, he faints and becomes the butt of his brother Martin's cruel sense of humor. But he later proves his true mettle when the opportunity arises to rescue his sweetheart, Astor, after the murderer escapes from prison. In the end, Hunter is declared a hero by all, his brother returns to college, and Astor sees her boy friend in a new light.

d, Frank Tuttle; w, James Ashmore Creelman, Tuttle; ph, Fred Waller, Jr.

Drama **(PR:A MPAA:NR)**

SECOND HAND LOVE** (1923) 5 reels FOX bw

Charles Jones *(Andy Hanks)*, Ruth Dwyer *(Angela Trent)*, Charles Coleman *("Dugg"/Johnny Walker)*, Harvey Clark *(The Detective, "Scratch")*, Frank Weed *(Deacon Seth Poggins)*, James Quinn *(Dugg's Partner)*, Gus Leonard *(The Constable)*.

William Fox saw general box office appeal in his cowboy star Buck Jones, so he started billing him as Charles and put him in this inferior production about a decent small-town fellow who saves Dwyer, the girl he loves, from her bootlegger husband and later from Weed, the county skinflint and Jones' rival for Dwyer's affections.

d, William Wellman; w, Charles Kenyon (based on a story by Shannon Fife); ph, Don Short.

Drama **(PR:A MPAA:NR)**

SECOND HAND ROSE*** (1922) 5 reels UNIV bw

Gladys Walton *(Rose O'Grady)*, George B. Williams *(Isaac Rosenstein)*, Eddie Sutherland *(Nat Rosenstein)*, Wade Boteler *(Frankie "Bull" Thompson)*, Max Davidson *(Abe Rosenstein)*, Virginia Adair *(Rebecca Rosenstein)*, Alice Belcher *(Rachel Rosenstein)*, Jack Dougherty *(Terry O'Brien)*, Walter Perry *(Tim McCarthy)*, Bennett Southard *(Hawkins)*, Camilla Clark *(Little Rosie)*, Marion Faducha *(Little Nat)*.

Still another variation on the ABIE'S IRISH ROSE (1929) theme— this time with some melodrama crime thrown in—has Celtic girl Rose O'Grady (Walton) adopted by a Jewish family that operates a New York City pawn shop. When Sutherland, her brother, is accused of stealing from his boss, Perry (an older man who has a crush on Walton), the girl offers to marry him providing he drops the charges. Later, Sutherland arranges for the real crooks to get nailed, and the kindly Perry releases Walton from her promise, realizing she could never be happy with a "second hand" husband when she really loves young Dougherty.

d, Lloyd Ingraham; w, A. P. Younger (based on the song by Grant Clarke, James F. Hanley); ph, Bert Cann.

Drama (PR:A MPAA:NR)

SECOND IN COMMAND, THE** (1915) 5 reels Quality/Metro bw

Francis X. Bushman *(Lt. Col. Miles Anstruther)*, Marguerite Snow *(Muriel Mannering)*, William Clifford *(Maj. Bingham)*, Lester Cuneo *(Lt. Sir Walter Mannering)*, Helen Dunbar *(Lady Sarah Harburgh)*, Paul Byron *(Honorable Bertie Carstairs)*, Evelyn Greeley *(Maid)*, Marcia Moore *(Nora Vining)*.

Bushman's first film for Metro is a rather tired affair dealing with two British officers during the Boer War who are in love with the same girl. In the middle of a well-staged battle scene, Clifford admits that he used some sneaky tactics in separating Bushman from the young lady, and vows to bow out when things calm down.

d, William J. Bowman; w, Clyde Fitch; ph, William F. Adler.

Drama (PR:A MPAA:NR)

SECOND YOUTH** (1924) 6 reels DIST/Goldwyn-COS bw

Alfred Lunt *(Roland Farwell Francis)*, Dorothy Allen *(Polly, the Maid)*, Lynne Fontanne *(Rose Raynor)*, Walter Catlett *(John McNab)*, Herbert Corthell *(George Whiggam)*, Margaret Dale *(Mrs. Twombly)*, Mini Palmeri *(Ann Winton)*, Winifred Allen *(Phoebe Barney)*, Charles Lane *(Weeks Twombley)*, Lumsden Hare *(James Remmick)*, Mickey Bennett *(Willie, Mrs. Benson's Son)*, Faire Binney *(Lucy Remmick)*, Hugh Huntley *(Harley Forbes)*, Jobyna Howland *(Mrs. Benson)*.

Good performance by Lunt in an otherwise average comedy about a mild-mannered silk salesman who, on a bet with her brother, becomes the object of Palmeri's affection. Lunt is dragged into a world of wild parties and Greenwich Village escapades, which turn him into a human dynamo. The change is noticed by all and he soon finds himself promoted to the position of assistant buyer and wins the heart of Palmeri for real.

d, Albert Parker; w, John Lynch (based on the novel by Allan Eugene Updegraff); ph, J. Roy Hunt; art d, Clark Robinson.

Comedy (PR:A MPAA:NR)

SECRET GAME, THE*** (1917) 5 reels PAR bw

Sessue Hayakawa *(Nara-Nara)*, Jack Holt *(Maj. Northfield)*, Florence Vidor *(Kitty Little)*, Mayme Kelso *(Miss Loring)*, Charles Ogle *(Dr. Ebell Smith)*, Raymond Hatton *(Mrs. Harris)*.

Director De Mille keeps the action moving right along in this fascinating wartime thriller which has German spies attempting to determine the movement of U.S. troop ships bound for Russia. The convoy is to be escorted by Japanese gunboats (an interesting twist in lieu of WW II alliances and the "Yellow Peril" obsessions of the time) and Hayakawa, a secret service agent from the Land of the Rising Sun, arrives on the scene to help the U.S. effort. Both Hayakawa and a major (nicely played by Holt) fall in love with Vidor, an American girl being used by the Germans. But the plot to sabotage the expedition is exposed, the Japanese bravely sacrifices his own life, and Vidor helps Holt as he routs the ring of ruthless Huns.

d, William C. De Mille; w, Marion Fairfax; ph, Charles Rosher.

War (PR:A MPAA:NR)

SECRET HOUR, THE*** (1928) 8 reels PAR bw

Pola Negri *(Amy)*, Jean Hersholt *(Tony)*, Kenneth Thomson *(Joe)*, Christian J. Frank *(Sam)*, George Kuwa *(Ah Gee)*, George Periolat *(Doctor)*.

Paramount tried unsuccessfully to revitalize Negri's sagging screen career with this intelligently handled film adaptation of a steamy stage play in which old and lonely Italian orange grower Hersholt meets and falls in love with Negri, a waitress in San Francisco. The old man returns home, writes her a letter proposing marriage, and includes a snapshot of his handsome foreman, Thomson, which he claims to be himself. Before Negri's arrival Hersholt breaks both of his legs in an accident and is bedridden. Naturally Negri and the foreman fall in love and then marry in secret. Several months pass and Hersholt, on his feet again, plans a big wedding. It is then that the couple make their confession, and the old man, though furious at first, realizes that he too is to blame and invites Thomson to remain on with his bride. Despite a strong performance by Negri, she was never able to regain the popularity she enjoyed for several years in Hollywood and left for Europe the following year when the advent of sound offered the thickly accented actress very little hope of continued success in this country. She returned to the German cinema, where she originally made her name, and managed to star in several films during the 1930s (she was suspected of being Jewish, but disproved the rumors and later was even said to be romantically linked with Adolf Hitler). After the outbreak of WW II, Negri returned to the U.S. once again and played character parts in two more films.

d&w, Rowland V. Lee (based on the play "They Knew What They Wanted" by Sidney Howard); t, Julian Johnson; ph, Harry Fischbeck; ed, Robert Bassler.

Drama (PR:A MPAA:NR)

SECRET LOVE*** (1916) 6 reels BLUE bw

Helen Ware *(Joan Lowrie)*, Jack Curtis *(Don Lowrie)*, Dixie Carr *(Liz)*, Harry Carey *(Fergus Derrick)*, Harry Carter *(Ralph Lansdale)*, Marc Robbins *(The Rector)*, Harry Southard *(Paul Grace)*, Warren Elsworth *(Mine Foreman)*, Ella Hall *(Annice)*, Willis Marks *(Craddock)*, Lule Warrenton *(Mother)*.

Stage star Ware is most impressive in this well-directed and beautifully photographed drama about an English girl from Lancaster whose coal-miner father is the hard-drinking, quick-fisted terror of the town. His intemperance eventually leads to his death, which clears the way for Ware to marry the local boy she has always secretly loved.

d&w, Robert Leonard (based on the novel *That Lass o' Lowries* by Frances Hodgson Burnett).

Drama (PR:A MPAA:NR)

SECRET OF THE HILLS, THE** (1921) 5 reels VIT bw

Antonio Moreno *(Guy Fenton)*, Lillian Hall *(Marion)*, Kingsley Benedict *(Lincoln Drew)*, George Clair *(Francis Freeland)*, Walter Rodgers *(Benjamin Miltimore)*, Oleta Otis *(Mrs. Miltimore)*, J. Gunnis Davis *(Richards)*, Frank Thorne *(De Vrillefort)*, Arthur Sharpe *(Sidney Coleridge)*.

Plenty of action in the old serial tradition has Moreno, U.S. newspaperman in London, getting involved with mystery and murder when he accidentally exchanges overcoats with the guardian of a beautiful young woman. A map is found in the coat, which eventually leads the two-fisted Yank to the treasure of King James III and the love of Hall, the lovely lady, whom he rescues after clearing his name from a frame-up.

d, Chester Bennett; w, E. Magnus Ingleton (based on a novel by William Garrett); ph, Jack MacKenzie.

Mystery (PR:A MPAA:NR)

SECRET ORCHARD* (1915) 5 reels LAS bw

Blanche Sweet *(Diane)*, Cleo Ridgley *(Cora May)*, Edward Mackaye *(Duke of Cluny)*, Gertrude Keller *(Duchess)*, Carlyle Blackwell *(Lt. Dodd, U.S.N.)*, Theodore Roberts *(Facereau)*, Cynthia Williams *(Diane, Age 1)*, Marjorie Daw *(Diane, Age 17)*, Loyola O'Connor *(Nanette's Mother)*, Sydney Deane *(Nanette's Father)*, Mrs. Lewis McCord.

Overly long, tedious nonsense about a girl who is seduced by a British nobleman, falls in love with a U.S. naval officer who overlooks her indiscretion, and marries the Yank after he kills the rotter in a duel.

d, Frank Reicher; w, William C. De Mille (based on the play by Channing Pollock and the novel by Agnes and Egerton Castle).

Drama (PR:A MPAA:NR)

SECRETS OF PARIS, THE*** (1922) 7 reels Whitman Bennett-HV/Mastodon bw

Lew Cody *(King Rudolph)*, Gladys Hulette *(Mayflower)*, Effie Shannon *(Mme. Ferrand)*, Montagu Love *(The Schoolmaster)*, Harry Sothern *(Hoppy)*, Rose Coghlan *(Owl)*, William "Buster" Collier, Jr. *(Francois)*, J. Barney Sherry *(Chancellor)*, Dolores Cassinelli *(Lola)*, Bradley Barker *(The Hindoo)*, Walter James *(The Strangler)*, Jane Thomas *(Margot)*.

Good old-fashioned melodrama, replete with secret passages, subterranean chambers, and all the other sure-fire crowd-pleasers, has a king, Cody, traveling to Paris to find the daughter of a peasant girl he once loved. He becomes attracted to Hulette, whose best friend and constant companion is Collier, leader of the French underground. After many adventures, Collier gives his life to save Cody and the girl from a flooding dungeon. Only then does Cody realize that Hulette is the girl for whom he has been searching, and the two, who have fallen in love, return to his kingdom.

p, Whitman Bennett; d, Kenneth Webb; w, Dorothy Farnum (based on the novel *Mysteres de Paris* by Eugene Sue); ph, Edward Paul, Harry Stradling; art d, Elsa Lopez.

Adventure (PR:A MPAA:NR)

SEEING'S BELIEVING** (1922) 5 reels Metro bw

Viola Dana *(Dianna Webster)*, Allan Forrest *(Bruce Terring)*, Gertrude Astor *(Aunt Sue)*, Philo McCullough *(Jimmy Harrison)*, Harold Goodwin *(Hack Webster)*, Edward Connelly *(Henry Scribbins)*, Josephine Crowell *(Martha Scribbins)*, Colin Kenny *(Mr. Reed)*, Grace Morse *(Mrs. Reed)*, J. P. Lockney *(Sheriff)*.

Modest but entertaining comedy has Dana suspected of being naughty when a storm forces her to spend the night in a country hotel with her aunt's fiance, McCullough. In the end, however, she proves her virtue to Forrest, the fellow she really loves, and demonstrates that seeing does not necessarily deserve believing.

d, Harry Beaumont; w, Edith Kennedy (based on a story by Rex Taylor); ph, John Arnold; art d, A. F. Mantz.

Comedy (PR:A MPAA:NR)

SENATOR, THE*** (1915) 5 reels Triumph-EQ bw

Charles J. Ross *(Sen. Rivers)*, Joseph Burke *(Sen. Keene)*, Ben Graham *(Silas Denman)*, Thomas Tracy *(Secretary Armstrong)*, Phillip Hahn *(Count Ernest von Strahl)*, Dixie Compton *(Mrs. Hillary)*, Constance Molineux *(Mabel)*, Gene Luneska *(Mrs. Armstrong)*.

Nice little programmer about a freshman senator from the Midwest who goes to bat for an old man whose family had never been compensated by the government for the use of a ship during the Revolutionary War. The young fellow not only wins the case, but the elderly gentleman's lovely daughter as well.

d, Joseph Golden; w, Sydney Rosenfeld.

Drama (PR:A MPAA:NR)

SENSATION SEEKERS*** (1927) 7 reels UNIV bw

Billie Dove *("Egypt" Hagen)*, Huntley Gordon *(Ray Sturgis)*, Raymond Bloomer *(Rev. Lodge)*, Peggy Montgomery *(Margaret Todd)*, Will Gregory *(Col. Todd)*, Helen Gilmore *(Mrs. Todd)*, Edith Yorke *(Mrs. Hagen)*, Phillips Smalley *(Mr. Hagen)*, Cora Williams *(Mrs. W. Symme)*, Sidney Arundel *(Deacon W. Symme)*, Clarence Thompson *(Rabbitt Smythe)*, Nora Cecil *(Mrs. Lodge)*, Frances Dale *(Tottie)*, Lillian Lawrence, Fanchon Frankel *(Tibbett Sisters)*, Hazel Howell *(Guest)*.

Splendidly directed Lois Weber film about a jazz baby (Love) who falls for a young minister (Bloomer), but turns him down when she comes to realize that her reputation will be a source of embarrassment. She does become his bride after all when Gordon, playboy gentleman friend with whom she eloped, is killed in a spectacularly filmed shipwreck. Good performances by all in a most thoughtful picture.

d&w, Lois Weber (based on the story "Egypt" by Ernest Pascal); ph, Ben Kline.

Drama **(PR:A MPAA:NR)**

SENTIMENTAL LADY, THE* (1915) 5 reels Kleine bw

Irene Fenwick *(Amy Cary)*, Frank Belcher *(Peter Cary)*, John Davidson *(Norman Van Aulsten)*, Thomas McGrath *(Van Aulsten, Sr.)*, Jack Devereaux *(Bob Nelson)*, Richie Ling *(Johnson)*, Anna Reader *(His Daughter)*, Lila Barclay *(Helen Nelson)*, Della Connor *(Florence Russell)*, Ben L. Taggart *(Tom Woodbury)*.

Inferior low-budget picture about a girl who has her money invested in utility stocks and a fiance whose father is out to unload a lot of bad paper he possesses on that company. A dedicated young attorney, hired by the minority shareholders, disrupts this scheme, however, and is rewarded by winning the girl's love.

d, Sidney Olcott; w, (based on a play by Owen Davis).

Drama **(PR:A MPAA:NR)**

SERPENT, THE*** (1916) 6 reels FOX bw

Theda Bara *(Vania Lazar)*, James Marcus *(Ivan Lazar)*, Lillian Hathaway *(Martsa Lazar)*, Charles Craig *(Grand Duke Valanoff)*, Carl Harbaugh *(Prince Valanoff)*, George Walsh *(Andrey Sobi)*, Nan Carter *(Erna Lachno)*, Marcel Morhange *(Gregoire)*.

Under Walsh's direction, Bara exhibits a virtuoso performance playing a Russian peasant girl who is assaulted by a duke, watches her sweetheart murdered by him, and leaves the country with the hush money provided. In London Bara becomes a famous vamp and ultimately the toast of the British stage. One night the duke sees her perform, becomes infatuated without recognizing her, and while visiting her apartment receives word that his son has been wounded in action. The aristocrat, visibly shaken, declares, "If anything should happen to my boy, I think it would kill me." This is all Bara needs to hear. She enlists in the Red Cross, connives her way to the front, and seeks out the now one-armed, paralyzed lad. Before long the young officer is vamped into submission, and Bara says to him, "Tell me about the battle of Ancourt." This gives director Walsh the opportunity to hurl some terrific battle footage on the screen, and when the picture returns to the present, the crippled young man and his nurse are being married. They return to Russia where the wily Bara manages to seduce the duke just at the moment her husband enters the room. The poor devil just hobbles out into the courtyard and blows his brains out. It is then that Bara discloses her true identity to the horrified nobleman: "I am Vania, the peasant girl. Three years ago I swore to repay you and I've done it." With that the world's most famous vamp falls out of bed and the whole affair turns out to be a dream.

d, Raoul Walsh; w, Raoul Walsh, George Walsh (based on the story "The Wolf's Claw" by Philip Bartholomae); ph, George Benoit.

Drama **(PR:C MPAA:NR)**

SEVEN CHANCES**** (1925) 6 reels Buster Keaton/MG bw-c

Buster Keaton *(Jimmie Shannon)*, T. Roy Barnes *(Billy Meekin)*, Snitz Edwards *(Lawyer)*, Ruth Dwyer *(Mary Jones)*, Frankie Raymond *(Her Mother)*, Jules Cowles *(Hired Man)*, Erwin Connelly *(Clergyman)*, Jean Havez *(Man on the Landing)*, Loro Bara, Marion Harlan, Hazel Deane, Pauline Toler, Judy King, Eugenie Burkette, Edna Hammon, Barbara Pierce, Jean Arthur, Connie Evans, Rosalind Mooney.

Keaton was against making this picture, probably because his brother-in-law, producer Joseph Schenck, bought the rights without telling him, and the comedian felt it was better suited for comic Harold Lloyd. But before SEVEN CHANCES was finished, Keaton made it his very own. The story has him playing a young lawyer who discovers that if he is married by seven o'clock that night, he'll inherit $7 million. He's turned down by his own girl, Dwyer, when he bungles the proposal, and is consequently rejected by everyone else he meets, including a Scotsman and a female impersonator. His pal, Barnes, comes up with the idea to advertise for a bride in the paper and states the time and church address. Exhausted, Keaton arrives early and falls asleep in the first pew. There is a wonderful scene where he wakes up to find what looks like a thousand women jammed into the building. They are of every age, race, and national origin, and most of them wearing bridal gowns and veils made up of countless improvised materials. Keaton manages to escape and runs into his sweetheart's servant, who hands him a note saying she forgives him. Keaton is on his way to her house when the "brides" pick up his scent. What follows is one of the wildest chase sequences ever filmed, with the ladies pursuing him from one end of town to the other and then out into the country. When Keaton prevued this film, he noticed that the audience got a big charge out of one part in the chase, where he dislodges a few small rocks which bounced behind him down a long incline. This was the topper he needed, so the comedian gathered his company together again and reshot the entire scene, using what seems to be thousands of boulders, some as large as eight feet in diameter. The result was unforgettable as well as hilarious, and more than delivered the big punch Keaton wanted before showing the happy ending, which has him marrying Dwyer just in time to earn the fortune. Re-released in the 1960s in France with a score by jazz musician Claude Bolling.

d, Buster Keaton; w, Jean Halvez, Clyde Bruckman, Joseph Mitchell (based on the comedy in three acts by Roi Cooper Megrue); ph, Elgin Lessley, Byron Houck (Technicolor); art d, Fred Gabourie.

Comedy **(PR:A MPAA:NR)**

SEVEN SISTERS, THE*** (1915) 5 reels FP bw

Madge Evans *(Clara)*, Dorothea Camden *(Liza)*, Georgia Furnstman *(Perka)*, Marguerite Clark *(Mica)*, Jean Stewart *(Ella)*, I. Feder *(Sari)*, Conway Tearle *(Horkoy)*, Lola Barclay *(Katinka)*, Georges Renavent *(Toni)*, Mayme Lynton *(Gilda)*, Sydney Mason *(Sandorffy)*, Charles Krauf *(Inn Keeper)*, Madam Dalburg *(Mother)*, Marjori Nelson *(Bertha)*, Edwin Mordant *(Baron Radviny)*, Dick Lee *(Servant)*, Lizzie Goods *(Inn Keeper's Wife)*.

Clark is charming as the hoydenish girl in a Hungarian family of seven daughters, where it is believed that if a younger sister marries first, then the older ones will be doomed to a life of spinsterhood. Her sister Evans has a great time pulling pranks which discourage a number of potential suitors, and for this she is sent away to a convent school. There she meets another mischievous student, and the two go over the wall to attend a masked ball. Evans meets a dashing count, Tearle, who falls madly in love with her, and after a number of entertaining occurrences, manages to marry all of her sisters off to splendid young men and then claim the delighted Evans as his very own.

d, Sidney Olcott; w, Edith Ellis Furness (based on a Hungarian story).

Comedy **(PR:A MPAA:NR)**

SEVENTH DAY, THE** (1922) 6 reels INSP/AFN bw

Richard Barthelmess *(John Alden, Jr.)*, Frank Losee *(Uncle Jim Alden)*, Leslie Stowe *(Uncle Ned)*, Tammany Young *(Donald Peabody)*, George Stewart *(Reggie Van Zandt)*, Alfred Schmid *(Monty Pell)*, Grace Barton *(Aunt Abigail)*, Anne Cornwall *(Betty Alden)*, Patterson Dial *(Katinka)*, Teddie Gerard *("Billie" Blair)*, Louise Huff *(Patricia Vane)*.

The team of Barthelmess and King followed up their wonderful TOL'ABLE DAVID (1921) with this disappointment. In fact, there is a lot of hokum in this story of a society couple, Stewart and Huff, who set out to mock a simple New England fisherman, Barthelmess, and his sister Cornwall, and end up falling in love with them instead.

d, Henry King; w, Edmund Goulding (based on a story by Porter Emerson Browne); ph, Henry Cronjager; ed, Duncan Mansfield.

Drama **(PR:A MPAA:NR)**

SEVENTH HEAVEN*½** (1927) 12 reels FOX bw

Janet Gaynor *(Diane)*, Charles Farrell *(Chico)*, Ben Bard *(Col. Brissac)*, David Butler *(Gobin)*, Marie Mosquini *(Mme. Gobin)*, Albert Gran *(Boul)*, Gladys Brockwell *(Nana)*, Emile Chautard *(Père Chevillon)*, George Stone *(Sewer Rat)*, Jessie Haslett *(Aunt Valentine)*, Brandon Hurst *(Uncle George)*, Lillian West *(Arlette)*, Henry Armetta.

Farrell plays a Paris sewer worker who dreams of someday being elevated to the position of street cleaner. At night he lights candles and prays God will find him a blonde wife and is disappointed when his request is not answered. Then one day he runs into Gaynor, whom he is able to save from the police by claiming she is his wife. The two fall deeply in love and marry, but war soon breaks out and Farrell is called to duty. When Gaynor later receives word that Farrell has been killed in battle she becomes terribly distraught and loses her faith in God. Farrell, however, returns in the end, blinded, to an overjoyed Gaynor who renews her faith in God and love. No doubt the most popular love story ever filmed, SEVENTH HEAVEN goes right for the heart and hits the mark. The sentimentality is blatant and the schmaltz is as thick as pea soup, but it doesn't matter. The characters of Diane (Gaynor won the first Academy Award ever for her performance) and Chico, "that remarkable fellow" (played by Farrell) grab the soul. Their struggle against adversity, in that garret so many floors up that one can almost touch the stars, completely captivates. Much of the credit must go to Borzage, who also won an Academy Award for his directing of SEVENTH HEAVEN. The Paris he creates is, to be sure, made of plaster and canvas, but it looks so right. It is Paris as Paris *should* be, and as any honest tourist will tell you isn't. And his battle scenes surely must have made an impression on director Stanley Kubrick, because the ones he painted in his classic PATHS OF GLORY (1957) have much the same feel. Sure the corn abounds when Farrell, who was reported killed in action, fights his way, blinded by his wounds, through the streets crowded with people celebrating the Armistice and grapples his way up the endless stairs to reach Gaynor until he finally throws open the door and she rushes into his arms—but so what? This was pure Hollywood—the kind which had magic and emotion and decency! And the millions who sat spellbound, sometimes for two and three showings, to share in the lives of Chico and Diane never forgot the experience.

p, William Fox; d, Frank Borzage; w, Benjamin Glazer (based on the play by Austin Strong); t, Katherine Hilliker, H. H. Caldwell; ph, Ernest Palmer; ed, Hilliker, Caldwell; set d, Harry Oliver; m/l, Erno Rapee, Lew Pollack.

Romance **(PR:A MPAA:NR)**

SEVENTH SHERIFF, THE* (1923) 5 reels Wild West/Arrow bw

Neva Gerber *(Mary Tweedy)*, Richard Hatton *(Jack Rockwell)*.

Paper-thin plot has adventurous stranger taking the job of sheriff in a town where law enforcement officers are used for target practice. The adventurer not only rids the town of its crooks, but claims pretty Gerber for his reward.

d&w, Richard Hatton.

Western Drama **(PR:A MPAA:NR)**

SEX½** (1920) 7 reels J. Parker Read, Jr./Hodkinson bw

Louise Glaum *(Adrienne)*, Peggy Pearce *(Daisy)*, Irving Cummings *(Dick Wallace)*, Myrtle Stedman *(Mrs. Morgan)*, William Conklin *(Edward Morgan)*.

The title is the most provocative thing about this picture, which has an actress, Glaum, deliberately breaking up a happy marriage and then cruelly ridiculing the wife, who comes to beg for the return of her husband. Later, Glaum falls madly in love and has the same thing happen to her. The film ends with the actress sailing for Europe, brokenhearted and very much alone.

d, Fred Niblo; w, (based on a story by C. Gardner Sullivan); ph, Charles Stumar.

Drama **(PR:A MPAA:NR)**

SHACKLES OF GOLD*** (1922) 6 reels FOX bw

William Farnum *(John Gibbs)*, Myrtle Bonillas *(Marie Van Dusen)*, Al Loring *(Charles Van Dusen)*, Marie Shotwell *(Mrs. Van Dusen)*, Wallace Ray *(Harry, Their Son)*, C. Elliott Griffin *(Donald Valentine)*, Ellen Cassity *(Elsie Chandler)*, Henry Carvill *(William Hoyt)*.

Good direction by Brenon makes something of this Farnum drama about a man who rises from dock laborer to a position of power in the stock market. Bonillas, an impoverished socialite, marries him for his money and later goes out with his lifelong enemy, Griffin, who insults her. When Farnum learns of this, he destroys the rotter in the market, even though it means his own financial ruin. It is then that Bonillas comes to realize she actually *loves* her husband, and the two begin their marriage anew.

d, Herbert Brenon; w, Paul H. Sloane (based on the novel *Samson* by Henri Bernstein); ph, Tom Malloy.

Drama **(PR:A MPAA:NR)**

SHADOW OF EGYPT, THE** (1924, Brit.) 8 reels Astra-N bw

Carlyle Blackwell *(Sheik Hanan)*, Alma Taylor *(Lilian Westcott)*, Milton Rosmer *(Harold Westcott)*, Joan Morgan *(Moonface)*, John Hamilton *(Apollo)*, Arthur Walcott *(Abdullah)*, Charles Levey *(Yusef)*.

The Valentino influence stretched all the way across the Atlantic Ocean to inspire this British romantic adventure, set in Egypt, about a sheik who loves the wife of an artist, but is killed in a political uprising.

d&w, Sidney Morgan (based on a novel by Nora Lorimer).

Adventure **(PR:A MPAA:NR)**

SHADOWS** (1922) 7 reels PRE/Al Lichtman bw

Lon Chaney *(Yen Sin, "The Heathen")*, Maurguerite De La Motte *(Sympathy Gibbs)*, Harrison Ford *(John Malden)*, John Sainpolis *(Nate Snow)*, Walter Long *(Daniel Gibbs)*, Buddy Messenger *("Mister Bad Boy")*, Priscilla Bonner *(Mary Brent)*, Frances Raymond *(Emsy Nickerson)*.

Chaney's exquisite performance barely compensates for this sluggish production about a dying Chinaman (Chaney) who converts to Christianity to prevent his friend, Ford, a Protestant minister, from being blackmailed.

d, Tom Forman; w, Eve Unsell, Hope Loring (based on the story "Ching, Ching, Chinaman" by Wilbur Daniel Steele); ph, Harry Perry.

Drama **Cas.** **(PR:A MPAA:NR)**

SHADOWS OF CONSCIENCE* (1921) 7 reels Russell bw

Russell Simpson *(Jim Logan)*, Landers Stevens *(Wade Curry)*, Barbara Tennant *(Alice)*, W. Bradley Ward *(Pedro, the Halfbreed)*, Nelson McDowell *(Wesley Coburn)*, Ashley Cooper *(Judson Craft)*, Ida McKenzie *(Winnie Coburn)*, Fred Burns *(Sheriff Bowers)*, Gertrude Olmstead *(Winifred Coburn)*.

Boring programmer has Simpson clashing with Stevens, the sneak who tricked his sister into a mock marriage and then caused her death. Ther hero takes McKenzie, the daughter of Stevens' murdered partner, and rides off. Years later they meet again and Stevens is attracted to the girl who has grown into splendid womanhood. He tries to pin the murder of McKenzie's father on Simpson, but the plan backfires and it's revealed that Stevens actually killed his partner.

d, John P. McCarthy; w, Francis Powers, McCarthy; t, H. Landers Jackson; ph, Victor Milner; ed, Fred Allen; art d, Louis E. Myers.

Western/Drama **(PR:A MPAA:NR)**

SHADOWS OF THE NIGHT½** (1928) 7 reels MGM bw

Flash the Dog *(Himself)*, Warner Richmond *(Feagan)*, Tom Dugan *(Connelly)*, Alphonse Ethier *(O'Flaherty)*, Polly Moran *(Entertainer)*, Lawrence Gray *(Jimmy Sherwood)*, Louise Lorraine *(Molly)*.

Entertaining kids' movie, featuring the popular dog Flash, is different because it's set in the city rather than the open spaces of the West. The predictable story sees the canine and his human companion saving the girl and mopping up the mob.

d&w, D. Ross Lederman (based on a story by Ted Shane); t, Robert Hopkins; ph, Maximilian Fabian; ed, Dan Sharits.

Adventure/Crime **(PR:A MPAA:NR)**

SHADOWS OF THE SEA*** (1922) 5 reels SF/SEL bw

Conway Tearle *(Capt. Dick Carson)*, Jack Drumier *(Shivering Sam)*, Crauford Kent *(Andrews)*, Arthur Houseman *(Ralph Dean)*, J. Barney Sherry *(Dr. Jordan)*, Doris Kenyon *(Dorothy Jordan)*, Frankie Mann *(Molly)*, Harry J. Lane *("Red")*, William Nally *(Capt. Hobbs)*.

Implausible but highly entertaining movie has Tearle playing a seafaring adventurer who finds his thrills at ports around the world. He finally decides to settle down, however, after falling in love with Kenyon, the widow of a doctor who treated him for a bullet wound. But first he beats the tar out of Houseman, the scoundrel who tried to have his way with the lady after murdering her husband.

d, Alan Crosland; w, Lewis Allen Browne (based on a story by Frank Dazey); ph, Jules Cronjager, Jacob A. Badaracco.

Adventure **(PR:A MPAA:NR)**

SHAM*** (1921) 5 reels FP/PAR bw

Ethel Clayton *(Katherine Van Riper)*, Clyde Fillmore *(Tom Jaffrey)*, Walter Hiers *(Monte Buck)*, Theodore Roberts *(Jeriamiah Buck)*, Sylvia Ashton *(Aunt Bella)*, Helen Dunbar *(Aunt Louisa)*, Arthur Carewe *(Bolton)*, Thomas Ricketts *(Uncle James)*, Blanche Gray *(Clementine Vickers)*, Eunice Burnham *(Maud Buck)*, Carrie Clark Ward *(Rosie)*.

Underplayed and engaging comedy has socialite Clayton discovering there is nothing left in her father's estate due to his extravagance. The family is pressuring her to marry dreadful Hiers, son of an oil millionaire, but by using her wits Clayton not only saves the family honor, but ends up with Fillmore, the man she really loves.

d, Thomas N. Heffron; w, Douglas Doty (based on the play by Elmer Harris, Geraldine Bonner); ph, Charles Edgar Schoenbaum.

Comedy **(PR:A MPAA:NR)**

SHAME** (1921) 9 reels FOX bw

John Gilbert *(William Fielding/David Fielding, His Son)*, Mickey Moore *(David, at 5)*, Frankie Lee *(David, at 10)*, George Siegmann *(Foo Chang)*, William V. Mong *(Li Clung)*, George Nichols *(Jonathan Fielding)*, Anna May Wong *(The Lotus Blossom)*, Rosemary Theby *(The Weaver of Dreams)*, Doris Pawn *(Winifred Wellington)*, "Red" Kirby *("Once-over" Jake)*.

After Gilbert is murdered in Shanghai, his 5-year-old son is taken to San Francisco to live with his grandfather. As a young man (played by Gilbert in a dual role), he inherits the family shipping business and marries well. His father's Oriental killer (Siegmann) shows up and tries to blackmail Gilbert into smuggling opium by threatening to expose the lad as being a half-caste. Devastated by the lie, Gilbert flees to Alaska with his infant son, but his wife and a faithful Oriental servant, Mong, soon track him down. Mong ultimately kills the villainous Siegmann and relieves Gilbert of the "shame" imposed on him by the slandering murderer. A pretty good performance by Gilbert in what is otherwise a rather distasteful motion picture.

d, Emmett J. Flynn; w, Bernard McConville, Flynn (based on the story "Clung" by Max Brand); ph, Lucien Andriot.

Drama **(PR:A MPAA:NR)**

SHAMS OF SOCIETY*½ (1921) 6 reels Walsh-Fielding/R-C bw

Barbara Castleton *(Helen Porter)*, Montagu Love *(Herbert Porter)*, Macey Harlam *(Milton Howard)*, Julia Swayne Gordon *(Mrs. Crest)*, Ann Brody *("Mama" Manning)*, Gladys Feldman, Sallie Tysha *(Manning Sisters)*, Lucille Lee Stewart *(Lucille Lee)*, Edwards Davis *(Judge Harrington)*, Victor Gilbert *(Reggie Frothingham)*.

Pretentious nonsense, denouncing the values of society life, has Castleton, the wife of skinflint millionaire Love, almost being driven into the arms of another man before her husband learns his lesson and comes to realize the real values in life.

d, Thomas B. Walsh; w, Mary Murillo, Kenneth O'Hara (based on the story "Shams" by Walter McNamara); ph, John S. Stumar, Charles Stumar.

Drama **(PR:A MPAA:NR)**

SHARK MASTER, THE* (1921) 5 reels UNIV bw

Frank Mayo *(McLeod Dean)*, Dorris Deane *(June Marston)*, Herbert Fortier *(Capt. Marston)*, Oliver Cross *(Donaldson)*, May Collins *(Flame Flower)*, "Smoke" Turner *(Native Priest)*, Nick De Ruiz *(Native Chief)*, Carl Silvera *(Moto)*.

Laughable low-budget South Seas feature has Mayo shipwrecked on an island where he encounters a beautiful white girl (Collins) called Flame Flower. They have a child together, and when Mayo's society fiancee, Deane, tracks him down, there are a few uncomfortable moments. Deane elects to return to civilization, but Collins, thinking she has lost Mayo, tries to drown herself. Mayo rescues her by diving into the ocean, and the couple return to their island paradise, where they never have to worry about being subjected to movies like this.

d, Fred Leroy Granville; w, George C. Hull (based on a story by Granville); ph, Leland Lancaster.

Adventure **(PR:A MPAA:NR)**

SHARP SHOOTERS*** (1928) 6 reels FOX bw

George O'Brien *(George)*, Lois Moran *(Lorette)*, Noah Young *(Tom)*, Tom Dugan *(Jerry)*, William Demarest *("Hi Jack" Murdock)*, Gwen Lee *(Flossy)*, Josef Swickard *(Grandpère)*.

Good comedy programmer has O'Brien, a sailor with a girl at every port, sweeping Moran, a French dancer, off her feet in Morocco. She is taken in by his sweet talk and follows him to the U.S., where he does everything he can to avoid her. In the end his two pals throw the couple together, and for O'Brien it's love at second sight.

d, J. G. Blystone; w, Marion Orth (based on a story by Randall H. Faye); t, Malcolm Stuart Boylan; ph, Charles Clarke.

Comedy **(PR:A MPAA:NR)**

SHATTERED IDOLS*** (1922) 6 reels J.L. Frothingham/AFN bw

Marguerite De La Motte *(Sarasvati)*, William V. Mong *(Rama Pal)*, James Morrison *(Lt. Walter Hurst/David Hurst)*, Frankie Lee *(David Hurst, the Child)*, Ethel Grey Terry *(Jean Hurst)*, Alfred Allen *(The Judge)*, Louise Lovely *(Diana Chichester)*, Harvey Clark *(Col. Chichester)*, Josephine Crowell *(Mrs. Chichester)*, Robert Littlefield *(Dick Hathaway)*, Mary Wynn *(Ethel Hathaway)*, George Periolat *(The High Priest)*, Thomas Ricketts *(The Rev. Dr. Romney)*.

Solid motion picture has Morrison, the son of a British officer who was killed subjugating Indian freedom fighters, returning to the land of his father's death after being educated in England. He is considered somewhat of a coward by his friends and even his mother until one day he rescues De La Motte, a beautiful native girl, from being sacrificed before an idol. Then to everyone's horror, he marries the woman and returns to London where he is elected to Parliament. Life in England is difficult for the Indian beauty, however, and she flees to her native land. Morrison follows and arrives just in time to become involved in another uprising. The fighting is ferocious, and as Morrison attempts to rescue his bride from the thick of it, De La Motte sacrifices her life to save his. It took courage for the producers to make this film with its unhappy ending, especially since it dealt with positive ethnic relations, and did so quite well.

d, Edward Sloman; w, William V. Mong (based on the novel *The Daughter of Brahma* by Ida Alexa Wylie); ph, Tony Gaudio.

Drama **(PR:A MPAA:NR)**

SHATTERED REPUTATIONS zero (1923) 5 reels Lee-Bradford bw

Johnnie Walker *(Henry Wainright)*, Jackie Saunders *(Sis Hoskins/Mul)*, John Mordaunt *(Dave Hoskins)*, Alfred Lewis *(Joe Hoskins)*, Fred Stonehouse *(Charles Osborne)*, Arthur Bowan *(Stephen Wainright)*, Helen Grant *(Fannie Wainright)*, Torrance Burton *(Vasco da Gama Byles)*.

Horrible hokum about a girl (Saunders) who tries to save her father from having his heart broken by his errant son (Lewis). In the end the situation is saved by a young millionaire who the girl thought was a chauffeur.

Drama **(PR:A MPAA:NR)**

SHE LOVES AND LIES*** (1920) 5 reels SEL bw

Norma Talmadge *(Marie Callender)*, Conway Tearle *(Ernest Lismore)*, Octavia Broske *(Polly Poplar)*, Phillips Tead *(Bob Brummell)*, Ida Darling.

Clever Talmadge comedy has the talented star playing an actress who is engaged to a millionaire but falls for Tearle when he saves her from a fire. She inherits her former fiance's estate, poses as an old woman, and enters into a marriage of convenience with Conway to save his endangered fortune. Later, she poses as a Greenwich bombshell, vamps Tearle into submission, and surprises him with her true identity.

d, Chester Withey; w, Withey, Grant Carpenter (based on a short story by Wilkie Collins); ph, David Abel.

Comedy **(PR:A MPAA:NR)**

SHEER BLUFF** (1921) 5 reels Granger/Binger bw

Henry Victor *(Maurice Hardacre)*, Maudie Dunham *(Esther)*, Percy Standing *(Jasper Hardacre)*, Nico de Jong *(Stokes)*, William Hunter, Julie Ruston, Lilian Ruston.

In this British drama, a millionaire uses all of the power at his disposal to bankrupt his main adversary's nephew as a means of testing the lad's mettle before enthusiastically permitting him to marry his beloved daughter.

p, Maurits Binger; d, Frankland A. Richardson; w, Benedict James.

Drama **(PR:A MPAA:NR)**

SHEFFIELD BLADE, A** (1918, Brit.) 5 reels British Pictures bw

George Foley *(Billy Baxter)*, Jill Willis *(Ruth Roland)*.

Modest little British drama has an upper-class factory owner's son discovering what the real world is like by assuming the role of a working stiff. He not only makes the mark, but invents a rustproof blade in the process.

d, Harry Roberts, Joseph Jay Bamberger; w, Bamberger (based on a story by A. G. Hales).

Drama **(PR:A MPAA:NR)**

SHEIK, THE 1/2** (1921) 7 reels FP/PAR bw

Agnes Ayres *(Diana Mayo)*, Rudolph Valentino *(Sheik Ahmed Ben Hassan)*, Adolphe Menjou *(Raoul de Saint Hubert)*, Walter Long *(Omair)*, Lucien Littlefield *(Gaston)*, George Waggner *(Youssef)*, Patsy Ruth Miller *(Slave Girl)*, F. R. Butler *(Sir Aubrey Mayo)*.

After his success as the tango-dancing Julio in THE FOUR HORSEMEN OF THE APOCALYPSE the same year, Paramount put Valentino under contract and produced this modest film, giving him second billing under Ayres, who plays an English beauty abducted by a desert prince (Valentino) and taken to his camp. Ayres refuses to surrender to his will and is later captured by the truly sinister Omair (played by veteran D. W. Griffith heavy Long), who is quite willing to offer her a fate worse than death. The prince and his men arrive in time, however, to prevent Ayres from committing suicide, but Valentino is nearly killed in the struggle. As Ayres nurses him back to health, she realizes that she loves him and the picture ends with the couple becoming husband and wife. The top brass at Paramount thought they had a real turkey with this one, but millions of women felt otherwise (many fainted at the exhibition showing), and Valentino ushered in a new term for male sex appeal, along with his superstardom.

d, George Melford; w, Monte M. Katterjohn (based on the novel by Edith Maude Hull); ph, William Marshall.

Costume/Adventure Romance **(PR:A MPAA:NR)**

SHERLOCK BROWN** (1921) 5 reels Metro bw

Bert Lytell *(William Brown)*, Ora Carew *(Barbara Musgrave)*, Sylvia Breamer *(Hilda)*, De Witt Jennings *(J. J. Wallace)*, Theodore Von Eltz *(Frank Morton)*, Wilton Taylor *(Chief Bard)*, Hardee Kirkland *(Gen. Bostwick)*, George Barnum *(Henry Stark)*, George Kuwa *(Sato)*.

Lytell does as well as can be expected with this featherweight script about a bumbling fool who takes a mail order course on the science of crime detection, foils a plot to steal a secret formula belonging to the government, and somehow wins the love and respect of Carew in the end.

d, Bayard Veiller; w, Lenore J. Coffee (based on a story by Veiller); ph, Arthur Martinelli; art d, A. F. Mantz.

Comedy **(PR:A MPAA:NR)**

SHERLOCK HOLMES 1/2** (1922) 9 reels Goldwyn bw

John Barrymore *(Sherlock Holmes)*, Roland Young *(Dr. Watson)*, Carol Dempster *(Alice Faulkner)*, Gustav von Seyffertitz *(Prof. Moriarty)*, Louis Wolheim *(Craigin)*, Percy Knight *(Sid Jones)*, William H. Powell *(Forman Wells)*, Hedda Hopper *(Madge Larrabee)*, Peggy Bayfield *(Rose Faulkner)*, Margaret Kemp *(Therese)*, Anders Randolf *(James Larrabee)*, Robert Schable *(Alf Bassick)*, Reginald Denny *(Prince Alexis)*, David Torrence *(Count Von Stalburg)*, Robert Fischer *(Otto)*, Lumsden Hare *(Dr. Leighton)*, Jerry Devine *(Billy)*, John Willard *(Inspector Gregson)*.

Location shooting in London and Switzerland helps this picture (which owes more to the Gillette play than the Doyle stories) and Barrymore makes an interesting Sherlock, in spite of the fact that he was really concentrating on playing Hamlet in a stage production at the time, and was also drinking heavily. But it is that splendid German actor, von Seyffertitz, in the role of the villain, who walks away with the picture. The story has the master detective clearing the name of a prince (Denny), bringing the evil professor and his gang to justice, and finding the love of D. W. Griffith's leading lady, Dempster.

p, F. J. Godsol; d, Albert Parker; w, Marion Fairfax, Earle Browne (based on the play by William Gillette, based on Sir Arthur Conan Doyle's stories); ph, J. Roy Hunt; art d, Charles Cadwallader, John Barrymore.

Mystery **(PR:A MPAA:NR)**

SHERLOCK, JR.**** (1924) 5 reels Buster Keaton/Metro bw

Buster Keaton *(Sherlock, Jr.)*, Kathryn McGuire *(The Girl)*, Ward Crane *(The Rival)*, Joseph Keaton *(The Father)*, Erwin Connolly *(Villain's Henchman)*, Horace Morgan, Jane Connelly, Ford West, George Davis, John Patrick, Ruth Holley.

One of Keaton's most innovative films (he truly indulged his mechanical and editing proclivities in this one) has the star playing a small-town movie projectionist and floor sweeper who has taken a correspondence course in crime detection. Buster buys his girl, McGuire, a $1.00 box of chocolates (which he alters to read $4.00) while his rival, the slimy Crane, steals her father's watch, hocks it, and buys the girl a more expensive gift. Crane then plants the pawn ticket on Keaton's person and sees to it that it's discovered. Keaton is ordered out of the house, but putting his sleuthing skills to work, he follows the villain until it's time to report to the theater. Exhausted, he falls asleep while the movie HEARTS AND PEARLS, OR THE LOUNGE LIZARD'S LOST LOVE is being projected. At this point Keaton steps out of his body and studies the film. All of a sudden the actors on the screen are the real people he was with earlier, only now everyone is dressed in the manner of an Adolphe Menjou picture. The plot with which they are concerned also deals with a stolen article of jewelry, in this case an expensive necklace. Keaton goes down to the theater and attempts to enter the movie, but as he does a series of quick film edits plays havoc with him. First he's thrown into a lion's den and after escaping finds himself in the middle of a desert, where from nowhere a train almost runs him over. Following this, Keaton sits on a cactus, but the picture turns into an island. Keaton attempts to jump into the water but another cut finds him diving into a mountain of snow. Then, finally, he makes his way into the picture through the mansion door. Only now he too is dressed in a tuxedo. The projectionist has in fact become a part of the photoplay. McGuire's father announces that he has sent for the famous detective, Sherlock, Jr., and that the master criminologist will certainly locate the necklace. The rest of the film involves a series of highly inventive chase gags, which culminates with the detective's car crashing into the river and Keaton waking up. Standing next to him is the real life McGuire, who has come to beg his forgiveness. The flustered fellow doesn't know what to do or say, but he sneaks a look at the screen, where the movie's leading man has turned his costar towards him and pats her head. Keaton does the same. The man on the screen gives his leading lady a soulful kiss, and Keaton gives McGuire a tiny peck. The matinee idol presents his fair lady with a ring, and the comedian follows suit. Then Keaton looks at the screen again and the actors are shown playing with three babies. At this point, the "Great Stone Face" scratches his head, and the picture comes to a most satisfying conclusion.

d, Buster Keaton; w, Clyde Bruckman, Jean Havez, Joseph Mitchell; ph, Byron Houck, Elgin Lessley; art d, Fred Gabourie; cos, Clare West.

Comedy **(PR:A MPAA:NR)**

SHE'S A SHEIK*** (1927) 6 reels PAR bw

Bebe Daniels *(Zaida)*, Richard Arlen *(Capt. Colton)*, William Powell *(Kada)*, Josephine Dunn *(Wanda Fowler)*, James Bradbury, Jr. *(Jerry)*, Billy Franey *(Joe)*, Paul McAllister *(Sheik Yusiff ben Hamad)*, Al Fremont *(The Major)*.

Clever Daniels comedy has the star playing the daughter of a Spanish mother and an Arab sheik. She insists on marrying a Christian (even though a fierce desert warrior [Powell] lusts for her) and falls head-over-heels for Arlen, a captain of the French garrison. When Arlen fails to return her attentions, Daniels has him abducted a la Valentino style and held captive in her desert digs. The officer eventually succumbs to her charms, and there is a most innovative punch line to the picture when an Arab attack on the poorly fortified fort is driven back by a couple of U.S. showmen who project footage of an advancing army across the desert with their portable projector (the unique film-within-a-film sequence was taken from Paramount's BEAU SABREUR released a year later).

d, Clarence Badger; w, Lloyd Corrigan, Grover Jones (based on a story by John McDermott); t, George Marion, Jr.; ph, J. Roy Hunt.

Comedy **(PR:A MPAA:NR)**

SHIELD OF HONOR, THE*** (1927) 6 reels UNIV bw

Neil Hamilton *(Jack MacDowell)*, Dorothy Gulliver *(Gwen O'Day)*, Ralph Lewis *(Dan MacDowell)*, Nigel Barrie *(Robert Chandler)*, Claire McDowell *(Mrs. MacDowell)*, Fred Esmelton *(Howard O'Day)*, Harry Northrup *(A.E. Blair)*, Thelma Todd *(Rose Fisher)*, David Kirby *(Red)*, Joseph Girard *(Chief of Police)*, William Bakewell *(Jerry MacDowell)*, Hank the Dog.

This one, intended purely for entertainment, delivered that and more. Hamilton plays the first pilot in the Los Angeles Police Department, and he and Gulliver, a young socialite, fall instantly in love at the ceremony she attends to christen his airplane. Her father is the victim of a series of jewel robberies and Hamilton and *his* father, a retired officer, are pressed into action and heroically bring the criminals to justice following a thrilling night air battle between two planes.

d, Emory Johnson; w, Leigh Jacobson, Gladys Lehman (based on a story by Emilie Johnson); t, Viola Brothers Shore; ph, Ross Fisher.

Adventure/Crime (PR:A MPAA:NR)

SHIPS THAT PASS IN THE NIGHT**

(1921, Brit.) 5 reels Screen Plays/BEF bw

Filippi Dowson *(Bernadine Holme)*, Francis Roberts *(Robert Allitsen)*, Daisy Markham *(Winifred Reffold)*, Arthur Vezin *(Mr. Reffold)*, Irene Rookee *(Esther Allitsen)*.

British romance has an architect meeting a staunch and one-time man-hating women's liberationist at a tuberculosis hospital in Switzerland, where they fall in love and eventually marry.

d&w, Percy Nash (based on the novel by Beatrice Marraden).

Drama/Romance (PR:A MPAA:NR)

SHIRLEY OF THE CIRCUS* 1/2 (1922) 5 reels FOX bw

Shirley Mason *(Nita)*, George O'Hara *(Pierre)*, Crauford Kent *(James Blackthorne)*, Alan Hale *(Max)*, Lule Warrenton *(Blanquette)*, Maude Wayne *(Susan Van Der Pyle)*, Mathilde Brundage *(Mrs. Van Der Pyle)*.

Paper-thin plot has Mason, a French circus performer, taken under the wing of an American artist who sends her to school. After a few years the girl follows him to the U.S. and is disappointed to discover that he's engaged to be married. Fortunately Mason encounters her old circus pals who are on tour and is reunited with her original love.

d, Rowland V. Lee; w, Robert N. Lee; ph, G. O. Post.

Drama (PR:A MPAA:NR)

SHOCK, THE 1/2** (1923) 7 reels UNIV bw

Lon Chaney *(Wilse Dilling)*, Virginia Valli *(Gertrude Hadley)*, Jack Mower *(Jack Cooper)*, William Welsh *(Mischa Hadley)*, Henry Barrows *(John Cooper, Sr.)*, Christine Mayo *(Anne Vincent/"Queen Anne")*, Harry Devere *(Olaf Wismer)*, John Beck *(Bill)*, Walter Long *(The Captain)*.

Chaney plays a crippled criminal who is sent to San Francisco to expose a banker his gang has been blackmailing. There he falls in love with the man's daughter, Valli, and experiences a regeneration. He then destroys the evidence, and after the great earthquake, finds himself able to walk again. This was certainly not one of Chaney's better efforts (he was overly made up to the point of looking almost ridiculous) and the use of phony models for the unconvincing earthquake scene didn't help. Still anything with the fascinating Chaney is always of value.

d, Lambert Hillyer; w, Arthur Statter (based on a story by William Dudley Pelley); ph, Dwight Warren.

Crime/Drama Cas. (PR:A MPAA:NR)

SHOCKING NIGHT, A** (1921) 5 reels UNIV bw

Eddie Lyons *(Richard Thayer)*, Lee Moran *(William Harcourt)*, Alta Allen *(Bessie Lane)*, Lillian Hall *(Maude Harcourt)*, Lionel Belmore *(Bill Bradford)*, Clark Comstock *(Jack Lane)*, Florence Mayon *(Cook)*, Charles McHugh *(Butler)*.

In this familiar but diverting farce, Lyons and his fiancee, Allen, pose as servants to help married friends who recently went broke and want to impress a visiting millionaire. The ruse works, their friends, Moran and Hall, manage to land a big contract with the tycoon, and there are even a few laughs along the way.

d, Eddie Lyons, Lee Moran; w, C. B. Hoadley (based on a story by Edgar Franklin); ph, Alfred Gosden.

Comedy (PR:A MPAA:NR)

SHOEBLACK OF PICCADILLY, THE*

(1920, Brit.) 5 reels Academy Photoplays bw

Eileen Magrath *(Cherry)*, Daisy Cordell, Victor Humfrey, Ernest A. Douglas, Eric Gray.

Inept British slush about a girl of the slums who is shown a little kindness by a wealthy gentleman, and is given the opportunity to repay him by saving the chap's son from schemers.

d, L. Stuart Greening.

Drama (PR:A MPAA:NR)

SHOOTIN' FOR LOVE*** (1923) 5 reels UNIV bw

Hoot Gibson *(Duke Travis)*, Laura La Plante *(Mary Randolph)*, Alfred Allen *(Jim Travis)*, William Welsh *(Bill Randolph)*, William Steele *(Dan Hobson)*, Arthur Mackley *(Sheriff Bludsoe)*, W. T. McCulley *(Sandy)*, Kansas Moehring *(Tex Carson)*.

Director Sedgwick and cowboy star Gibson made a number of clever and superior programmers, including this one about a shell-shocked young vet who, on returning from the service by train, falls in love with the daughter of the man his father is feuding with over water rights. When the movie's villain blows up the dam, the jolt cures Gibson of his fear of action, and he proves his mettle by giving the bad guy a terrific pasting and reuniting the families through marriage.

d, Edward Sedgwick; w, Albert Kenyon, Raymond L. Schrock (based on a story by Schrock, Sedgwick); ph, Virgil Miller.

Western (PR:A MPAA:NR)

SHOOTIN' IRONS** (1927) 6 reels PAR bw

Jack Luden *(Pan Smith)*, Sally Blane *(Lucy Blake)*, Fred Kohler *(Dick Hardman)*, Richard Carlyle *(Jim Blake)*, Loyal Underwood *(Blinky)*, Guy Oliver *(Judge Mathews)*, Scott McGee *(Cook)*, Arthur Millett *(Sheriff)*.

This Paramount production is no better than most of the B westerns made by popular outdoor stars like Buck Jones, Tim McCoy, and Hoot Gibson. There is sufficient action, and the plot, which has the hero clearing the father of the girl he loves, is, to say the least, familiar. Good performance, though, by Kohler, one of the cinema's all-time great heavies.

p, B. P. Schulberg; d, Richard Rosson; w, J. Walter Ruben, Sam Mintz (based on the story by Richard Allen Gates); ph, Henry Gerrard.

Western (PR:A MPAA:NR)

SHOOTING OF DAN MCGREW, THE**

(1915) 5 reels Popular Plays and Players/Metro bw

Edmund Breese *(Jim)*, Katheryn Adams *(Lou)*, Audrine Stark *(Jim's Daughter)*, Betty Riggs [Evelyn Brent] *(Nell, at Age 12)*, Wallace Stopp *(Nell's Husband)*, William A. Morse *(Dan McGrew)*.

A lot of padding was needed to turn this poem into a feature film. The ending was changed to allow the piano playing hero to shoot Morse and then escape across the frozen tundra with Adams.

d, Herbert Blache; w, (based on the poem by Robert W. Service); ph, Alfred Ortlieb.

Northwoods Adventure (PR:A MPAA:NR)

SHOPSOILED GIRL, THE* 1/2 (1915, Brit.) 4 reels British Empire bw

Henry Lonsdale *(Mark Faulkner)*, Alice Belmore *(Jessie Brown)*, Nina Lynn *(Flossie de Vigne)*, Frank Randall *(Joe Kelly)*, Gladys Williams *(Vera Thurston)*.

There is a whale of a lot of intrigue going on in this British mystery. A rotter assists his mistress in the murder of her husband, and then attempts to pass the blame on to the husband of her stepdaughter.

d, Leedham Bantock; w, (based on the play by Walter Melville).

Mystery (PR:A MPAA:NR)

SHORE LEAVE*** (1925) 7 reels INSP/FN bw

Richard Barthelmess *("Bilge" Smith)*, Dorothy Mackaill *(Connie Martin)*, Ted McNamara *("Bat" Smith)*, Nick Long *(Capt. Bimby Martin)*, Marie Shotwell *(Mrs. Schuyler-Payne)*, Arthur Metcalfe *(Mr. Schuyler-Payne)*, Warren Cook *(Adm. Smith)*, Samuel Hines *(Chief Petty Officer)*.

Implausible but entertaining story about a sailor, Barthelmess, who wins the heart of Mackaill, whose late father was a sea captain. The gob sails off and forgets the pretty little thing, but she goes through a great deal of trouble to have her dad's old ship completely overhauled and made seaworthy for the man she loves. There are the expected complications, like Barthelmess assuming the lady is rich and refusing to marry into wealth. But before the sailor allows his enlistment to expire, he decides to sail through life on the vessel of love.

d, John S. Robertson; w, Josephine Lovett (based on the play by Hubert Osborne); t, Agnes Smith; ph, Roy Overbaugh, Stewart Nelson; ed, William Hamilton; set d, Tec-Art Studios.

Comedy Cas. (PR:A MPAA:NR)

SHOULD A WIFE FORGIVE?** (1915) 5 reels EQ/WORLD bw

Lillian Lorraine *(La Belle Rose)*, Mabel Van Buren *(Mary Holmes)*, Henry King *(Jack Holmes)*, Lewis Cody *(Alfred Bedford)*, William Lampe *(Dr. Charles Hoffman)*, Mollie McConnell *(Mrs. Forrester)*.

Follies star Lorraine, one of the best dressed women of her day, stars in her first feature film playing a vamp who lures a married man away from his wife and child. The man blows his family fortune on a show for his paramour, which is a miserable flop. All the while Lorraine is secretly being kept by a millionaire, and when the two men meet, a fight breaks out and Lorraine is shot to death. A letter surfaces, however, written by the seductress, in which she expresses her intention to commit suicide, so charges are never pressed. Later, the married gentleman tries for a reconciliation, but his wife will have none of it, leaving the picture hanging with this title: "Should a Wife Forgive?"

w, Joseph E. Howard.

Drama (PR:A MPAA:NR)

SHOULD A WIFE WORK?* 1/2 (1922) 7 reels J.W. Film bw

Edith Stockton *(Betty Evans)*, Alice Lowe *(Nina Starr)*, Stuart Robson *(Ed Barnes)*, Louis Kimball *(David Locke)*, Elinor Curtis *(Mme. Theodora)*, Walter McEwen *(Jim Paget)*, Harry Mowbray *(Larry Grant)*.

The title is the most sensational thing about this movie which has two young women seeking different rewards in life. Stockton chooses a career and Lowe marriage, but their destinies intertwine throughout the film and the audience is left to make its own decision regarding the provocative question the title poses.

d, Horace G. Plympton; w, Lois Zellner.

Drama **(PR:A MPAA:NR)**

SHOULD A WOMAN DIVORCE? zero (1914) 5 reels IV bw

Lea Leland *(The Woman)*, Leonid Samoloff *(Her Husband)*.

This stinker never answers the provocative question posed in its title, but it does tell the story of a woman who walks out on her midwestern husband and child to live with an eminent New York physician. Later, when the kid is seriously ill, her husband comes to the doctor for help, encounters his wife and begs her to return to him. The medicine man becomes so obsessed with the fear that his woman might leave that he drinks himself to death. And the object of all this activity merely packs her trunks and departs the scene.

d, Ivan Abramson.

Drama **(PR:A MPAA:NR)**

SHOULD A WOMAN TELL?* (1920) 6 reels Screen Classics/Metro bw

Alice Lake *(Meta Maxon)*, Jack Mulhall *(Albert Tuley)*, Frank Currier *(Mr. Maxon)*, Relyea Anderson *(Mrs. Maxon)*, Lydia Knott *(Clarissa Sedgwick)*, Don Bailey *(The Doctor)*, Richard Headrick *(The Maxon Boy)*, Carol Jackson *(The Maxon Girl)*, Jack Gilbert.

Highly improbable and unpleasant melodrama has a young woman assaulted by the nephew of her benefactress. Later, before she is about to marry, the girl sends a letter to her fiance telling him of the episode, but he never receives the note. The couple are happily married for some time when she makes the mistake of bringing the subject up. Her husband flies into a rage, leaves her flat, and encourages her to consider him dead. At this point, she marries the rotter who wronged her, and (to really put a strain on the law of credibility) the original husband returns, beats his replacement to death, and the two survivors live joyously forever more.

d, John E. Ince; w, Finis Fox; ph, Sol Polito.

Drama **(PR:C MPAA:NR)**

SHOW GIRL, THE** (1927) 6 reels T/C/RAY bw

Mildred Harris *(Maizie Udell)*, Gaston Glass *(Billy Barton)*, Mary Carr *(Mrs. Udell)*, Robert McKim *(Edward Hayden)*, Eddie Borden *("Breezy" Ayres)*, William Strauss *(Moe Kenner)*, Sam Sidman *(Heinie)*, Aryel Darma *(Alma Dakin)*.

Thanks to some clever publicity, a nightclub owned by Harris and Glass soon begins attracting a higher class of patrons, one of whom, theatrical producer Strauss, is impressed by the talents of Harris. At the same time, Harris becomes attracted to lecherous McKim, and when Glass finds her in his arms, he swears he is through with Harris for good. Sometime later, Harris prepares for her opening night performance but loses her nerve at the last minute. Her former partner, who just happens to be there, stands up in the box and begins singing. The audience assumes it's all part of the show, and when Harris joins in she is a hit. Harris becomes the toast of Broadway, and the two are reunited for keeps after the rotter who tried to move in is murdered by a woman he formerly treated like dirt.

p, Trem Carr; d, Charles J. Hunt; w, H. H. Van Loan.

Drama **(PR:A MPAA:NR)**

SHOW PEOPLE**** (1928) 9 reels MGM bw

Marion Davies *(Peggy Pepper)*, William Haines *(Billy Boone)*, Dell Henderson *(Col. Pepper)*, Paul Ralli *(André)*, Tenen Holtz *(Casting Director)*, Harry Gribbon *(Comedy Director)*, Sidney Bracy *(Dramatic Director)*, Polly Moran *(Maid)*, Albert Conti *(Producer)*, John Gilbert, Mae Murray, Charles Chaplin, Douglas Fairbanks, Elinor Glyn, Renee Adoree, George K. Arthur, Karl Dane, William S. Hart, Leatrice Joy, Rod la Rocque, Louella Parsons, Aileen Pringle, Dorothy Sebastian, Norma Talmadge, Estelle Taylor, Claire Windsor *(Themselves)*.

Vidor directed this wonderful salute to a Hollywood genre—the slapstick two-reeler—which was about to pass. He even took over the old Mack Sennett studio when "The King of Comedy" moved his operation to Burbank, California, where he would go bankrupt within a couple of years. SHOW PEOPLE had Davies playing a Southern girl who comes to Hollywood to be a serious actress and ends up at a company (much like Keystone) involved in turning out knockabout shorts. She falls in love with the studio's top comic (beautifully played by Haines) but drops him like a hot potato when she wins stardom at a major studio, where the famous leading man makes a play for her. By the picture's end, Davies realizes her error and is reunited with Haines, but not before some truly wonderful cinema is unfolded. It is said that this film was inspired by the career of Gloria Swanson, who made her way from comedy foil with Sennett to superstardom with Cecil B. DeMille. The movie's most famous sequence is the one at the MGM commissary, where Chaplin, Fairbanks (he is seen wearing a black arm band, mourning the recent death of his brother), Gilbert, Glyn (the creator of IT), and Murray are shown laughing and clowning before the camera.

d, King Vidor; w, Wanda Tuchock, Agnes Christine Johnson, Laurence Stallings; t, Ralph Spence; ph, John Arnold; ed, Hugh Wynn; set d, Cedric Gibbons; m/l, "Crossroads," by William Axt, David Mendoza; syn sc; s eff.

Comedy **(PR:A MPAA:NR)**

SIBERIA** (1926) 7 reels FOX bw

Alma Rubens *(Sonia Vronsky)*, Edmund Lowe *(Leonid Petroff)*, Lou Tellegen *(Egor Kaplan)*, Tom Santschi *(Alexis Vetkin)*, Paul Panzer *(Commandant)*, Vadim Uraneff *(Kyrill [Cyril] Vronsky)*, Lilyan Tashman *(Beautiful Blonde)*, Helen D'Algy *(Beautiful Brunette)*, James Marcus *(Andrei Vronsky)*, Daniel Makarenko *(Governor)*, Harry Gripp *(Ivan the Nameless)*, Samuel Blum *(Feodor)*.

Disappointing film, in spite of a good cast and director, has beautiful Russian schoolteacher Rubens siding with the cause of Lenin and being sent to Siberia where Lowe, the officer who loves her, is later transferred. When the revolution erupts, Rubens helps her sweetheart escape the Red mob, and they successfully flee across the frozen tundra on a sleigh, pursued by wolves, as well as the movie's main heavy, Tellegen.

d, Victor Schertzinger; w, Eve Unsell, Nicholas A. Dunaev (based on the play by Bartley Campbell); ph, Glen MacWilliams, Robert Martin.

Drama **(PR:A MPAA:NR)**

SIDESHOW OF LIFE, THE* ½** (1924) 8 reels FP/PAR bw

Ernest Torrence *(Andrew Lackaday)*, Anna Q. Nilsson *(Lady Auriol Dayne)*, Louise Lagrange *(Elodie)*, Maurice Cannon *(Horatio Bakkus)*, Neil Hamilton *(Charles Verity-Stewart)*, William Ricciardi *(Mignon)*, Mrs. Pozzi *(Ernestine)*, Lawrence D'Orsay *(Sir Julius Verity-Stewart)*, Effie Shannon *(Lady Verity-Stewart)*, Katherine Lee *(Evadne)*.

Superb performance by Torrence as a French-reared English circus clown who enlists at the outbreak of WW I and rises to the rank of brigadier general. When the last shot is fired, Torrence returns to his former circus world where he discovers he has lost his skill as a juggler. He eventually finds happiness through the love of a British noblewoman, Nilsson. The scene where Torrence's little dog is run over and the subsequent burial is a real tearjerker.

p&d, Herbert Brenon; w, Willis Goldbeck, Julie Herne (based on the novel *The Mountebank* by William John Locke and the play by Ernest Denny); ph, James Howe.

Drama **(PR:A MPAA:NR)**

SIEGFRIED****

(1924, Ger.) 11 reels UFA bw (SIEGFRIEDS TOD; AKA: SIEGFRIED'S DEATH)

Paul Richter *(Siegfried)*, Margarethe Schon *(Kriemhild)*, Theodor Loos *(King Gunther)*, Hanna Ralph *(Brunhild)*, Georg John *(Mime the Smith/Alberich)*, Gertrud Arnold *(Queen Ute)*, Hans Carl Muller *(Gerenot)*, Erwin Biswanger *(Giselher)*, Bernhard Goetzke *(Volker von Alzey)*, Hans Adalbert von Schlettow *(Hagen Tronje)*, Hardy von Francois *(Dankwart)*, Hubert Heinrich *(Werbel)*, Frida Richard *(Lecturer)*, Georg Jurowski *(Priest)*, Iris Roberts *(Page)*.

In the court of the Burgundians, lute-strumming minnesinger Goetzke chants of the adventures of Siegfried (played by blond-wigged Richter) and the saga itself unfolds in flashback. (A cut-down release of 1933 has a Wagnerian score and a narration in modern German of the first few stanzas of the 12th-century poem "Die Niebelungenlied" added as a prolog. This version was not approved by director Lang, who despised Richard Wagner's music.) The son of a Norse king, Richter has been apprenticed to blacksmith—and master swordmaker—Mime (John, in one of his two roles; he plays yet a third part in the sequel, KRIEMHILD'S REVENGE). Having learned all his master knows about the trade, Richter ventures forth to make his name and his fortune, and to seek the hand of Kriemhild (Schon), the most beautiful maiden in the known world. On a white horse, bearing the magic sword he has forged, Richter is led by his retainers—all nobles—through a forest, where he meets a fierce dragon. Richter manages to pierce the fire-breathing beast's thick hide. Told that he will become invulnerable to weapons if he bathes in the dragon's blood, Richter does just that. As he laves himself in the crimson fluid, he fails to notice that a falling leaf has landed on his back, shielding a small part of his body from the gore. The procession continues through the forest, where the little band chances on the realm of the Nibelungs, ruled by the gnarled dwarf Alberich (John in his second role). The dwarf is the possessor of wondrous things, including casket upon casket of treasure and a magic helmet which can render the one who wears it invisible. The dwarf displays these marvels to Richter, whom he plans to kill, but Richter outwits the diminutive demon and slays him instead. As he dies screaming a curse to the new keeper of the treasure, John and his followers turn to stone. Bearing the riches of the Nibelung, Richter's group continues its journey, arriving at the Burgundian court of King Gunther (Loos), who welcomes the travelers. There he falls in love with the beauteous Schon, sister of the king, and asks for her hand in marriage. The price of the king's consent is assistance with his own amorous pursuit: Richter must help the king to marry the Amazonian queen of Iceland, Brunhild (played by Ralph), who boasts that no man may share her bed without first besting her in single combat. Using the helmet of invisibility, Richter assures Loos' victory in the fight, and the vanquished queen returns with them to Burgundy, where the two couples are wed in a wondrous ceremony. Ralph, however, refuses to consummate the union until she is once again tricked by Richter, who wrests from her the bracelet that signifies her virginity. When Schon discovers the bracelet in Richter's possession, he is forced to reveal what he has done, including the story of his leaf-shielded laving in dragon's blood. Richter's ascendancy at the court has earned him the jealousy of the king's half-brother, the wrathful von Schlettow, who—on the pretense of protecting the hero—has tricked Schon into revealing her husband's weakness. Schon has had a dream of foreboding in which a white dove is downed by two black falcons (a wonderful piece of animation by the talented Ruttmann) and so has sought von Schlettow's assistance. The warrior woman, Ralph, learning of the duplicity that resulted in her marriage to Loos, has told her husband—falsely—that she has made love to Richter, whom she adores, in fact. Loos thus agrees to give his blessing to von Schlettow's plot to kill Richter during a hunt. The ebullient Richter takes leave of his bride under a flowering tree and goes off to join the hunting party. Schon then sees the tree shed its flowers and assume the form of a skull. During the hunt, as Richter stoops to drink from a spring, von Schlettow's spear pierces his vulnerable spot and passes through his body. Richter's corpse is carried back to the castle, where blood again spurts from his wound, signifying that his murderer is among the assembled mourners. Initially jubilant about the death of her adversary, Ralph, realizing that she loved the fallen Richter, kills herself beside his bier, her crumpled body framing the entrance of the bereft Schon, who kneels before her fallen husband's form. This first episode of director Lang's great two-part picture DIE NIBELUNGEN (on initial release the second part, KRIEMHILD'S REVENGE, was screened on the following day) was director Lang's first venture into big-budget magnificence; he had previously helmed many action-oriented adventure films with exotic settings, but none had approached the scope—or the cost—of this epic. The wonderfully composed visuals, rivaling anything done by D. W. Griffith or Cecil B. DeMille, filled with pomp and pageantry and processions (especially in the Burgundian court), with extras and actors used architecturally (when Brunhild's ship docks, she crosses a bridge with pillars formed by a legion of helmeted knights) in perfect balance with the massive set constructions and background dioramas, brought some contemporary criticism. One viewer held that the film was "like a succession of pictures in a museum. . . . Had Lang only made the film work as cinema, it would have been beautiful." The sets were real constructions; Lang and his crew had not yet joined forces with Eugen Schufftan, the special-effects expert who was to prove so useful to his next major project (which used many miniatures), METROPOLIS. Visiting the Neubabelsberg UFA studio, a young Alfred Hitchcock viewed and described one of the giant outdoor stages, 200 feet wide, 400 feet long, flanked by scaffolding 100 feet in height with 12-foot-wide multiple platforms. All of the special effects were realized the hard way—in the camera—the film being rolled back as necessary for superimpositions, footage and frame counts being meticulously recorded, and actors being required to hold positions for lengthy periods of time. The great trees of the fog-shrouded "forest" scenes were crafted of cement, formed over wooden armatures (Lang averred that had the Black Forest grown American Redwoods, his crew could have been spared a lot of work). Since shooting the two parts of the saga took nine months—compassing three seasons—real flowers, real snow, and real ice could be used; apart from the actors, these were virtually the only natural elements in the mise en scene. The dragon was a mechanical marvel, a veritable Trojan dragon operated by 17 technicians riding inside the massive plaster-and-rubber skin (their training at the controls required several months). The writhing, menacing "beast" could also drink, drool, belch fire and smoke, and spurt "blood" when mortally wounded. Extensive rehearsals resulted in all movements being choreographed with the precision and timing of a ballet. Based largely on "Das Nibelungenlied," an anonymous poem dating from about 1200 A.D., some film historians have suggested that scripter von Harbou—the director's wife, as well as his frequent collaborator—borrowed heavily from the play (a trilogy) "Die Nibelungen" written in 1862 by Friedrich Hebbel. Von Harbou certainly knew of the play; she had once acted in it, starring in the part of Kriemhild. She herself asserted that the script was derived from many sources, stating "...there are more [versions of the story] than most people think." SIEGFRIED, with its sequel, was the favorite cinema of Adolf Hitler and his propaganda minister, Josef Goebbels. Certainly the blond, blue-eyed hero, Richter, might have served as the ideal Third Reich specimen. Historian Siegfried Kracauer carries the analogy a step further, averring that anti-semitism is expressed in the "Jewish" features of John in his role as Alberich (the character who, to strengthen the similarity, guards a hoard of gold and jewels, thus fulfilling the "banker" stereotype), but Lang's biographer Lotte Eisner points out that the director and makeup artist Genath were probably influenced by the character makeup used by the Russian-Jewish Habimah theater company then performing in Berlin. Scripter von Harbou *did* become a valued Nazi later—unlike her director husband—but Hitler's partisanship probably lies in the legend itself (he also liked Richard Wagner's Ring Cycle operas) rather than in Lang's marvelous realization of it. The picture had many advocates of many differing political perspectives, including Serge Eisenstein; many of the latter's films, such as ALEXANDER NEVSKI and the IVAN THE TERRIBLE histories, attest to the influence of SIEGFRIED and its sequel.

p, Erich Pommer; d, Fritz Lang; w, Thea von Harbou (based on the anonymous poem "Das Nibelungenlied" and various traditional Nordic legends); ph, Carl Hoffmann, Gunther Rittau; art d, Otto Hunte, Eric Kettelhut, Karl Vollbrecht; cos, Paul Gerd Guderian, Anne Willkom; makeup, Otto Genath; animation, Walther Ruttman.

Spectacle **Cas.** **(PR:C MPAA:NR)**

SIEGFRIED'S DEATH (SEE: SIEGFRIED, 1924, Ger.)

SIEGFRIEDS TOD (SEE: SIEGFRIED, 1924, Ger.)

SIGN OF THE ROSE, THE*** (1922) 6 reels George Beban/American Releasing bw

Helene Sullivan *(Lillian Griswold)*, Charles Edler *(William Griswold)*, Jeanne Carpenter *(Dorothy Griswold)*, Gene Cameron *(Philip Griswold)*, Louise Calmenti *(Rosa)*, Stanhope Wheatcroft *(Cecil Robbins)*, Arthur Thalasso *(Detective Lynch)*, George Beban *(Pietro Balletti)*, Dorothy Giraci *(Rosina Balletti)*, M. Solomon *(Moses Erbstein)*.

Beban, the popular dialect actor and comedian, presented a live playlet about halfway through the projection of this film (using a set identical to the one in the picture), which ran about 18 minutes. Then the lights dimmed and the picture was started again. The story tells of a kindly Italian (Beban) who is falsely accused of a kidnaping and later sees his own child run over. He finds some happiness in the end, however, when he is vindicated and reunited with his wife, whom he thought dead.

d, Harry Garson; sup, George Beban; w, J. A. Brocklehurst, Carroll Owen (based on the play by Beban, Charles T. Dazey); t, Coral Burnette; ph, Sam Landers; ed, Violet Blair; art d, Floyd Mueller.

Drama **(PR:A MPAA:NR)**

SIGNAL TOWER, THE*** (1924) 7 reels UNIV bw

Virginia Valli *(Sally Tolliver)*, Rockliffe Fellowes *(Dave Tolliver)*, Frankie Darro *(Sonny Tolliver)*, Wallace Beery *(Joe Standish)*, James O. Barrows *(Old Bill)*, J. Farrell MacDonald *(Pete)*, Dot Farley *(Gertie)*, Clarence Brown *(Switch Man)*, Jitney *(The Dog)*.

Director Clarence Brown keeps the action speeding right along in this exciting melodrama which harkens back to the days of D. W. Griffith's Biograph Company. In this case Fellowes, a railroad signalman, takes his assistant, Beery, in as a boarder. Then, while Fellowes is risking his life to control a runaway freight train during a storm one night, the drunken Beery attempts to attack Fellowes' wife, Valli, who fights him off from room to room. Naturally, Fellowes returns in time to save the day in a thrill-packed ending. Strong performance by Beery, good special effects, and the train footage is a wow.

d, Clarence L. Brown; w, James O. Spearing (based on the story by Wadsworth Camp); ph, Ben Reynolds.

Adventure **(PR:A MPAA:NR)**

SILENT CALL, THE ** 1/2 (1921) 7 reels H.O. Davis/AFN bw

Strongheart *(Flash)*, John Bowers *(Clark Moran)*, Kathryn McGuire *(Betty Houston)*, William Dyer *(Ash Brent)*, James Mason *(Luther Nash)*, Nelson McDowell *(Dad Kinney)*, Edwin J. Brady *(Jimmy the Dude)*, Robert Bolder *(James Houston)*.

Strongheart, Rin-Tin-Tin's chief competitor, is half dog and half wolf, but human enough in this engaging programmer to save McGuire, the heroine, clear her father's name, and drive Dyer, the villain, to his watery grave. In the last reel McGuire, Flash, and his owner, Bowers, are united for a happy ending.

d, Lawrence Trimble; w, Jane Murfin (based on the novel *The Cross Pull* by Hal G. Evarts); ph, Charles Dreyer, Glen Gano.

Adventure **(PR:A MPAA:NR)**

SILENT COMMAND, THE*** (1923) 8 reels FOX bw

Edmund Lowe *(Capt. Richard Decatur)*, Bela Lugosi *(Hisston)*, Carl Harbaugh *(Menchen)*, Martin Faust *(Cordoba)*, Gordon McEdward *(Gridley)*, Byron Douglas *(Adm. Nevins)*, Theodore Babcock *(Adm. Meade)*, George Lessey *(Mr. Collins)*, Warren Cook *(Ambassador Mendizabal)*, Henry Armetta *(Pedro)*, Rogers Keene *(Jack Decatur)*, J. W. Jenkins *(The Butler)*, Alma Tell *(Mrs. Richard Decatur)*, Martha Mansfield *(Peg Williams, the Vamp)*, Florence Martin *(Her Maid)*, Betty Jewel *(Dolores)*, Kate Blancke *(Mrs. Nevins)*, Elizabeth Foley *(Jill Decatur)*.

Plenty of good old-fashioned flag waving in this military picture which blatantly encouraged viewers to join the U.S. Navy. It's all about a band of sinister enemy agents out to blow up the Panama Canal. The man with the know-how is Lowe, a young captain whom the spies sic the sultry vamp, Mansfield, on. Lowe, who pretends to go along, actually works with the Secret Service. In an exciting conclusion, the wrongdoers are crushed, like tropical bugs, while Lowe, who suffered the disgrace of being drummed out of the service, is given a hero's tribute.

d, J. Gordon Edwards; w, Anthony Paul Kelly (based on a story by Rufus King); ph, George W. Lane.

Adventure **(PR:A MPAA:NR)**

SILENT EVIDENCE** (1922, Brit.) 6 reels GAU/British Screencraft bw

David Hawthorne *(Mark Stanton)*, Marjorie Hume *(Rosamund)*, Frank Dane *(Raoul de Merincourt)*, H. R. Hignett *(Charles)*, Cecil du Gue *(Dr. Hickson)*, Winifred Nelson *(Fiancee)*.

British combination of fantasy and mystery genre has an inventor using his television-like device to spy on his wife, whom he suspects of having an affair with a Frenchman, and uncovering a jewel thief in the process.

d, C. C. Calvert; w, Alicia Ramsey.

Mystery/Fantasy **(PR:A MPAA:NR)**

SILENT LOVER, THE 1/2** (1926) 7 reels FN bw

Milton Sills *(Count Pierre Tornai)*, Natalie Kingston *(Vera Sherman)*, William Humphrey *(Cornelius Sherman)*, Arthur Edmund Carewe *(Capt. Herault)*, William V. Mong *(Kobol)*, Viola Dana *(Scadsza)*, Claude King *(Contarini)*, Charlie Murray *(O'Reilly)*, Arthur Stone *(Greenbaum)*, Alma Bennett *(Haldee)*, Montagu Love *(Ben Achmed)*.

Slightly better-than-average picture about a French aristocrat (Sills) who joins the Foreign Legion after squandering his fortune, falls in love with a wealthy American girl (Kingston), is worshiped by the lost daughter of a Bedouin chief, and saves the garrison from being slaughtered by the chief's forces when he reunites father and daughter.

d, George Archainbaud; w, Carey Wilson (based on the play "Der Legioner" by Lajos Biro).

Adventure/Romance **(PR:A MPAA:NR)**

SILENT PARTNER, THE*** (1923) 6 reels FP/PAR bw

Leatrice Joy *(Lisa Coburn)*, Owen Moore *(George Coburn)*, Robert Edeson *(Ralph Coombes)*, Robert Schable *(Harvey Dredge)*, Patterson Dial *(Cora Dredge)*, E. H. Calvert *(Jim Harker)*, Maude Wayne *(Gertie Page)*, Bess Flowers *(Mrs. Nesbit)*, Laura Anson *(Mrs. Harker)*, Bert Woodruff *(Owens)*, Robert Grey *(Charles Nesbit)*.

Well-acted drama with some deft comedy touches has Joy saving the money and gifts her stockbroker husband, Moore, lavishes on her, only to use them to rescue Moore from financial ruin when he loses everything on the market.

d, Charles Maigne; w, Sada Cowan (based on the story by Maximilian Foster); ph, Walter Griffin.

Drama **(PR:A MPAA:NR)**

SILENT POWER, THE*** (1926) 6 reels GOTH/LUM bw

Ralph Lewis *(John Rollins)*, Ethel Shannon *(Olive Spencer)*, Charles Delaney *(Rob Rollins)*, Vadim Uraneff *(Jerry Spencer)*, Robert E. Homans *(David Webster)*.

This Poverty Row production goes out on a limb to make a rather powerful anti-capital punishment statement. It has to do with a father (Lewis) having to pull the switch which will electrocute his own son (Delaney) for murder. He goes through with the deed, then passes out, only to learn on coming to that the wires were cut by the real killer (the crazed brother of Delaney's sweetheart) who is killed in the process, while Delaney's life is saved.

d, Frank O'Connor; sup, Renaud Hoffman; w, James Bell Smith (based on a story by James J. Tynan); ph, Ray June.

Drama (PR:A MPAA:NR)

SILENT VOICE, THE** (1915) 6 reels Quality/Metro bw

Francis X. Bushman, Marguerite Snow, Lester Cuneo, Helen Dunbar, Ann Drew, Miss C. Henry, Frank Bacon, William Clifford.

There is not much to praise about this Bushman drama which has the matinee idol playing a great violinist who loses his hearing. The fellow becomes a blasphemer and drives his wife out of the house. But later a miraculous operation restores his sense of hearing, and the little woman returns to be by his side.

d, William Bowman, Fred Balshofer; w, Bowman (based on the play by Jules Eckert Goodman).

Drama (PR:A MPAA:NR)

SILENT VOW, THE* 1/2 (1922) 5 reels VIT bw

William Duncan *(Richard Stratton/"Dick" Stratton)*, Edith Johnson *(Anne)*, Dorothy Dwan *(Ethel)*, Maud Emery *(Elizabeth Stratton)*, J. Morris Foster *("Doug" Gorson)*, Henry Hebert *("Jim" Gorson)*, Fred Burley *("Bill" Gorson)*, Jack Curtis *("Sledge" Morton)*, Charles Dudley *(The Professor)*.

Duncan directed and plays a double role (father and son) in this potboiler about a Mountie who tracks down the man who ran away with his mother years earlier, encounters his half brothers, who turn out to be pretty decent fellows, and with their help rescues a couple of kidnaped girls and bring the territorial bad men to justice.

d, William Duncan; w, Bradley J. Smollen; ph, George Robinson.

Adventure (PR:A MPAA:NR)

SILK LEGS** (1927) 6 reels FOX bw

Madge Bellamy *(Ruth Stevens)*, James Hall *(Phil Barker)*, Joseph Cawthorn *(Ezra Fulton)*, Maude Fulton *(Mary McGuire)*, Margaret Seddon *(Mrs. Fulton)*.

Bellamy is given the opportunity to wear a lot of lingerie in this inoffensive little comedy about a couple of rival hosiery sales people, who forget the competition and tie the knot in the end.

d, Arthur Rosson; sup, William Conselman; w, Frances Agnew (based on a story by Frederica Sagor); t, Delos Sutherland; ph, Rudolph Bergquist.

Comedy (PR:A MPAA:NR)

SILKS AND SADDLES***
(1929) 6 reels UNIV bw (AKA: THOROUGHBREDS)

Richard Walling *(Johnny Spencer)*, Marion Nixon *(Lucy Calhoun)*, Sam De Grasse *(William Morrissey)*, Montagu Love *(Walter Sinclair)*, Mary Nolan *(Sybil Morrissey)*, Otis Harlan *(Jimmy McKee)*, David Torrence *(Judge Clifford)*, Claire McDowell *(Mrs. Calhoun)*, John Fox, Jr. *(Ellis)*, Hayden Stevenson *(Trainer)*.

Pretty good racetrack drama has Walling, a jockey, throwing a race because of his interest in vamp Nolan, but then making it up to his former boss (and Nixon, her daughter, who never stopped loving him) by taking over the high-spirited horse his replacement can't handle and winning the big competition.

d, Robert F. Hill; w, J. G. Hawks, Paul Gangelin, Faith Thomas, Edward Clark, James Gruen (based on a story by Gerald Beaumont); t, Albert De Mond; ph, Joseph Brotherton; ed, Daniel Mandell.

Drama (PR:A MPAA:NR)

SILVER CAR, THE*** (1921) 6 reels VIT bw

Earle Williams (Anthony Trent), Kathryn Adams *(Daphne Grenvil)*, Geoffrey Webb *(Arthur Grenvil)*, Eric Mayne *(Count Michael Temesvar)*, Emmett King *(Earl of Rosecarrel)*, Mona Lisa *(Pauline)*, John Steppling *(Vicar)*, Max Asher *(Hentzi)*, Walter Rodgers *(Col. Langley)*.

Better-than-average Vitagraph offering has Williams playing an international thief who comes to the aid of a retired British colonel by using his talent as a safecracker to obtain and then destroy evidence being used by Mayne, a Croatian count, to blackmail him. For this considerable effort, Williams is given a few thousand acres of land in Australia to share with the lovely Adams, who assisted him along the way.

d, David Smith; w, Wyndham Martin; ph, Jack MacKenzie.

Adventure (PR:A MPAA:NR)

SILVER COMES THROUGH* 1/2
(1927) 6 reels R-C/FBO bw (AKA: SILVER COMES THRU; SILVER KING COMES THRU)

Fred Thomson *(Fred)*, Edna Murphy *(Lucindy)*, William Courtright *(Zeke, Ranchowner)*, Harry Woods *(Stanton)*, Mathilde Brundage *(Mrs. Bryce-Collins)*, Silver King the Horse.

They weren't giving Thomson the scripts or the production values he once enjoyed when he made this below-average actioner. In it he plays a ranch hand who falls in love with Murphy, his boss' daughter, after rescuing her from a runaway horse. Later, at a party given by Murphy, Thomson becomes jealous by the attentions shown her by neighboring rancher Woods, whose men secretly plot to steal Silver King, Murphy's horse, before a big race. Of course Thomson saves the day and wins the steeplechase and the hand of Murphy.

d&w, Lloyd Ingraham (based on a story by Frank M. Clifton); ph, Mack Stengler.

Western (PR:A MPAA:NR)

SILVER COMES THRU (SEE: SILVER COMES THROUGH, 1927)

SILVER KING COMES THRU (SEE: SILVER COMES THROUGH, 1927)

SILVER LINING, THE*** (1921) 6 reels Iroquois/Metro bw

Jewel Carmen *("The Angel")*, Leslie Austen *(Robert Ellington)*, Coit Albertson *(George Johnson)*, Virginia Valli *(Evelyn Schofield)*, Julia Swayne Gordon *("Gentle Annie")*, J. Herbert Frank *("Big Joe")*, Edwards Davis *(George Schofield)*, Marie Coverdale *(Mrs. George Schofield)*, Gladden James *(Billy Dean)*, Theodore Babcock *(Eugene Narcom)*, Charles Wellesley *(Burton Hardy)*, Henry Sedley *(Mr. Baxter)*, Jule Powers *(Mrs. Baxter)*, Arthur Donaldson *(Friend of the Baxters)*, Paul Everton *(A Detective)*, Carl Hyson, Dorothy Dickson *(The Dancers)*.

Interesting programmer has Albertson, a Secret Service agent, telling some friends a story (through the use of flashbacks) of two sisters—Valli, adopted by high society folk, and Carmen, by crooks—who lead differing lives and prove conclusively that a criminal disposition is *not* hereditary. A fine performance by Carmen as the disadvantaged one, who turns out in the end to be "on the square."

p&d, Roland West; w, D. J. Buchanan, Charles H. Smith, West; ph, Edward Wynard, Frank Zucker; set d, Charles O. Seessel.

Drama (PR:A MPAA:NR)

SILVER SLAVE, THE*** (1927) 7 reels WB bw

Irene Rich *(Bernice Randall)*, Audrey Ferris *(Janet Randall)*, Holmes Herbert *(Tom Richards)*, John Miljan *(Philip Caldwell)*, Carroll Nye *(Larry Martin)*.

Solid performance by Rich as a woman who turns down the man she loves and marries for money. After her husband's death, Rich's daughter, for whom she has sacrificed everything, becomes infatuated with a cad, whom Rich nearly seduces to prove his villainy to her child. The scheme works, the daughter sees the light and finds happiness with Nye, her adoring, lifelong friend.

d, Howard Bretherton; w, Peter Milne, Anthony Coldewey (based on a story by Howard Smith); ph, Frank Kesson.

Drama (PR:A MPAA:NR)

SILVER THREADS AMONG THE GOLD** (1915) 6 reels K&R bw

Richard J. Jose, Dora Dean, Mrs. R. E. French, Guy D'Ennery.

After he is framed for stealing a purse at a barn dance and denounced by his father, a young country boy heads for the big city and hits the skids. Eventually an old family friend straightens him out, and the lad becomes a successful businessman. The film ends with his return home on a snowy Christmas Eve, where he is warmly welcomed by both his father and the girl who saved herself for him.

d, Pierce Kingsley.

Drama (PR:A MPAA:NR)

SILVER VALLEY* 1/2** (1927) 5 reels FOX bw

Tom Mix *(Tom Tracey)*, Dorothy Dwan *(Sheila Blaine)*, Philo McCullough *(Black Jack Lundy)*, Jocky Hoefli *(Silent Kid)*, Tom Kennedy *(Hayfever Hawkins)*, Lon Poff *(Slim Snitzer)*, Harry Dunkinson *(Mike McCool)*, Clark Comstock *(Wash Taylor)*.

Mix plays a cowboy with a love for airplanes—one of which refuses to get off the ground and wrecks city girl Dwan's auto and costs Mix his job. Finding work as a sheriff in a town where lawmen don't last long, Mix eventually brings an outlaw gang to their flaming doom, after rescuing Dwan from their volcanic hideout in his plane and escaping seconds before the mountain erupts.

d, Ben Stoloff; w, Harold B. Lipsitz (based on a story by Harry Sinclair Drago); t, Malcolm Stuart Boylan; ph, Dan Clark.

Western (PR:A MPAA:NR)

SILVER WINGS** (1922) 9 reels FOX bw

Mary Carr *(Anna Webb)*, Lynn Hammond *(John Webb, Her Husband)*, Knox Kincaid *(John)*, Joseph Monahan *(Harry)*, Maybeth Carr *(Ruth)*, Claude Brook *(Uncle Andrews)*, Robert Hazelton *(The Minister)*, Florence Short *(Widow Martin)*, May Kaiser *(Her Child)*, Percy Helton *(John)*, Joseph Striker *(Harry)*, Jane Thomas *(Ruth)*, Roy Gordon *(George Mills)*, Florence Haas *(Little Anna)*, Roger Lytton *(Bank President)*, Ernest Hilliard *(Jerry Gibbs)*.

Banal movie places Mary Carr in the role of still another long-suffering mother. This time her wealthy inventor husband dies, Monahan, her son, squanders the fortune, Kincaid, covering for his brother, skips town when an embezzlement is discovered, and Maybeth Carr, her daughter, elopes. The poor mother hits the bottom like a depth charge, but when a human interest-oriented magazine article appears describing her plight, the whole family rushes to rescue her from her wretched cold water flat, including the new son-in-law (who just happens to be a darned nice guy) and her adorable little grandchild. Famed director John Ford handled only the film's prolog.

d, Edwin Carewe, Jack [John] Ford; w, Paul H. Sloane; ph, Robert Kurrle, Joseph Ruttenberg.

Drama (PR:A MPAA:NR)

SIMON THE JESTER 1/2** (1915) 5 reels Gold Rooster bw

Edwin Arden *(Simon de Gex)*, Edgar L. Davenport *(His Brother)*, Irene Warfield *(The Cat Queen)*, Alma Tell, Crauford Kent.

Unusual and convoluted story has a cynical, aristocratic member of the British Parliament becoming a new man after learning that he has only a few months to live. He quits his post and becomes involved in a number of bizarre experiences, including the murder by a crazed dwarf of the man whose widow marries his secretary, a life-saving operation, which occurs after he has given away his fortune, and in the end, marriage to a music hall animal-trainer known as "The Cat Queen," who accepts his proposal only after the dwarf escapes from his insane asylum and blinds her with a toy pistol.

d, Edward Jose; w, (based on the novel by William J. Locke).

Drama **(PR:C MPAA:NR)**

SIN*** (1915) 5 reels FOX bw

Theda Bara *(Rosa)*, Warner Oland *(Pietro)*, William E. Shay *(Luigi)*, Louise Real *(Maria)*, Henri Leone *(Giovanni)*.

Bara plays an Italian peasant who falls in love with Oland, a gang leader visiting from the U.S. She leaves with him for New York and is followed by her former sweetheart, who presents her with jewels from the Madonna (which he stole during a religious festival) to demonstrate the depth of his love. When Bara shows up at her paramour's place sporting the gems, Oland, who is religious in his own way, blows his top and orders her out into the street, where a mob of worshipers tear her to shreds with their bare hands. The picture ends with Bara's repentant former sweetheart committing suicide before the Madonna, whose sacred countenance he had earlier desecrated.

d&w, Herbert Brenon.

Drama **(PR:C MPAA:NR)**

SIN OF MARTHA QUEED, THE*** (1921) 6 reels Mayflower Photoplay/AEX bw

Mary Thurman *(Martha Queed)*, Joseph J. Dowling *(Marvin Queed)*, Eugenie Besserer *(Alicia Queed)*, Frankie Lee *(Georgie Queed)*, Niles Welch *(Arnold Barry)*, George Hackathorne *(Atlas)*, Frank Campeau *(David Boyd)*, Gertrude Claire *(Grandmother)*.

When Thurman visits her sweetheart Welch's cabin in the mountains, a nasty relative informs her father, and he forces his daughter to marry Welch. The next day the relative is discovered murdered and Welch is accused of the crime. Thurman, in a state of shock, wanders into a swamp where she contracts a fever and is cared for by Hackathorne, a strange and deformed boy. Welch is convicted and sentenced to die, and when word of this reaches Hackathorne, the boy rushes to town and confesses to committing the crime himself, allowing the picture to end with Thurman marrying the man she truly loves.

d&w, Allan Dwan; ph, Tony Gaudio.

Drama **(PR:A MPAA:NR)**

SIN SISTER, THE* (1929) 7 reels FOX bw

Nancy Carroll *(Pearl)*, Lawrence Gray *(Peter Van Dykeman)*, Josephine Dunn *(Ethelyn Horn)*, Myrtle Stedman *(Sister Burton)*, Anders Randolf *(Joseph Horn)*, Richard Alexander *(Bob Newton)*, George Davis, David Callis, Frederick Graham.

Confusing combination of melodrama and slapstick comedy has a family stranded on the frozen tundra with a villainous fur trader and a crazed Eskimo. Into the midst of all this comes vaudeville hoofer Carroll, who saves the day with a blazing six-shooter and elopes by dog sled with the family's male secretary.

d, Charles Klein; w, Harry Behn, Andrew Bennison (based on a story by Frederick Hazlitt Brennan, Becky Gardiner); t, William Kernell; ph, Charles Clarke, George Eastman.

Drama/Comedy **(PR:A MPAA:NR)**

SIN THAT WAS HIS, THE** (1920) 6 reels SF bw

William Faversham *(Raymond Chapelle)*, Lucy Cotton *(Malerie Lafeur)*, Pedro de Cordoba *(Father Aubert)*, Miss Sherman *(Mme. Lafeur)*, Lulu Warrenton *(Mme. Blondin)*, Robert Conville *(Blondin)*, John Burton *(Bishop)*, Bobby Connelly, Miriam Battista, Robert Agnew.

Straightforward but depressing tale (by the author of THE MIRACLE MAN) in which a gambler, Faversham, who once studied for the priesthood, sets out to deliver the money a dying friend left his mother. When he arrives at her house another son tries to steal the cash, and the mother shoots her boy by mistake. Faversham then assumes the identity of a priest who lost his memory in an accident, not realizing that the clergyman would be accused of the crime. But in the end the old woman confesses to the killing, and the picture draws to a logical, if less than joyous, conclusion.

d, Hobart Henley; w, Edmund Goulding (based on the novel by Frank Lucius Packard); ph, Ned Van Buren.

Drama **(PR:C MPAA:NR)**

SINGED* (1927) 6 reels FOX bw

Blanche Sweet *(Dolly Wall)*, Warner Baxter *(Royce Wingate)*, James Wang *(Wong)*, Alfred Allen *(Jim)*, Clark Comstock *(Wes Adams)*, Howard Truesdale *(Indian Agent)*, Claude King *(Ben Grimes)*, Ida Darling *(Mrs. Eleanor Cardigan)*, Mary McAllister *(Amy Cardigan)*, Edwards Davis *(Howard Halliday)*, Edgar Norton *(Ernie Whitehead)*.

Even the wonderful Sweet could not do anything with this hokey story in which she plays a dance hall girl who invests in an oil well and makes Baxter, her wastrel sweetheart, a millioniare. When Baxter later rises to the heights of New York society, Sweet is condemned for her past and he decides to marry high class McAllister. In a jealous rage Sweet threatens to splash acid into Baxter's face, but he shoots at the bottle, accidentally wounding Sweet. Thinking he has killed her, the old boy realizes his love for Sweet and the two are reunited in the end.

d, John Griffith Wray; w, Gertrude Orr (based on the story "Love o' Women" by Adela Rogers St. Johns); ph, Charles Clarke.

Drama **(PR:A MPAA:NR)**

SINGED WINGS*** (1922) 8 reels FP/PAR bw

Bebe Daniels *(Bonita Della Guerda)*, Conrad Nagel *(Peter Gordon)*, Adolphe Menjou *(Bliss Gordon)*, Robert Brower *(Don Jose Della Guerda)*, Ernest Torrence *(Emilio, a Clown)*, Mabel Trunnelle *(Eve Gordon)*.

Daniels is quite good as the impoverished descendant of Spanish aristocrats who is forced to dance in a San Francisco cabaret to support her grandfather. She tells the old man about a nightmare she has in which she sees herself killed by a court jester after declaring her love for a handsome prince. Her grandfather tells the startled girl that this is the family curse and will be her destiny. Daniels becomes reluctant to allow herself to fall in love with the handsome young man (Nagel) who frequents her club and seems to be most attracted to her. Instead she takes solace in the attentions bestowed upon her by the lad's uncle (well played by Menjou). This angers not only the nephew but also Torrence, the half-witted clown who secured her the dancing job and thinks of himself as her protector. Feeling betrayed, Torrence attempts to kill Daniels, but ends up shooting Menjou's wife, who has taken Daniels' place in the show that night. After this tragic incident, Daniels realizes that the family "curse" is only superstition and allows herself to fall in love with the man of her real dreams.

d, Penrhyn Stanlaws; w, Ewart Adamson, Edfrid A. Bingham (based on the story by Katharine Newlin Burt); ph, Paul Perry.

Drama **(PR:A MPAA:NR)**

SINGER JIM MCKEE* 1/2 (1924) 7 reels WSHP/PAR bw

William S. Hart *("Singer" Jim McKee)*, Phyllis Haver *(Mary Holden)*, Gordon Russell *(Buck Holden)*, Bert Sprotte *(Dan Gleason)*, Patsy Ruth Miller *(Betty Gleason)*, Edward Coxen *(Hamlin Glass, Jr.)*, William Dyer *(Hamlin Glass)*, George Siegmann *("Brute" Bernstein)*, Baby Turner *(Mary Holden, as a Baby)*.

Unfortunately this Hart film borders on the ludicrous as he plays a character who bursts into song every time he feels the tinge of an emotion. It might have been worse as a talkie (or singie), but in the silent medium Hart is—to be kind—rather embarrassing. The story sees the westerner raising Haver, the daughter of his late mining partner, and then going to prison after committing a holdup to provide the girl with the clothes she needs to be accepted by the genteel society into which he desires to place her. The movie ends on another unintentional laugh when Haver, now a woman, tracks Hart down after hearing his pet parrot impersonating its master rendering one of his favorite songs. At this point she declares her love (though according to the film's time lapse, Hart would be over twice her age), and the three ride off to lead full, happy, and musical lives. At the time SINGER JIM MCKEE was made, Hart's popularity was fading fast and he was nearing the end of his career. This 28th film with Paramount would be his last with them after moving there from Triangle when that company collapsed in 1918.

d, Clifford S. Smith; w, J. G. Hawks (based on a story by Hart); ph, Dwight Warren; ed, William Shea.

Western **(PR:A MPAA:NR)**

SINGING RIVER** (1921) 5 reels FOX bw

William Russell *(Lang Rush)*, Vola Vale *(Alice Thornton)*, Clark Comstock *(John Thornton)*, Jack Roseleigh *(Lew Bransom)*, Arthur Morrison *(Sam Hemp)*, Jack McDonald *(Bert Condon)*, Jack Hull *(Freud)*, Louis King *(Kane)*, Charles L. King *(Grimes)*.

Adequate B western has Russell striking it rich with a silver mine, clearing his name of murder, bringing the real killers to justice, and winning Vale, the daughter of the one man who believed in him.

d, Charles Giblyn; w, Jules Furthman (based on a story by Robert J. Horton); ph, George Schneiderman.

Western **(PR:A MPAA:NR)**

SINGLE MAN, THE** (1919, Brit.) 5 reels BL/ID bw

Cecil Mannering *(Maj. Henry Worthington)*, Doris Lytton *(Mrs. Worthington)*, George Mallett *(Robert Worthington)*, Alice de Winton *(Louise Parker)*, Irene Drew *(Miss Hesletine)*.

British comedy about the amorous adventures of a crusty old chap who chases a saucy flapper, is himself chased by a love-hungry old maid, and finally settles down with his secretary.

p, David Falcke; d, A. V. Bramble; w, (based on a play by Hubert H. Davis).

Comedy **(PR:A MPAA:NR)**

SINGLE MAN, A*** (1929) 7 reels MGM bw

Lew Cody *(Robin Worthington)*, Aileen Pringle *(Mary Hazeltine)*, Marceline Day *(Maggie)*, Edward Nugent *(Dickie)*, Kathlyn Williams *(Mrs. Cottrell)*, Aileen Manning *(Mrs. Farley)*.

Diverting entertainment in which Cody, a middle-aged fellow, falls for a saucy flapper and becomes involved in a number of comic situations by trying to look and act half his age, but ends up *really* falling for his long-time secretary, Pringle, who fixes herself up and proves to be the true beauty. This would be the last movie in which Cody and Pringle would star together, after a successful teaming in several earlier films.

d, Harry Beaumont; w, F. Hugh Herbert, George O'Hara (based on the play by Hubert Henry Davies); t, Joe Fanham, Lucille Newmark; ph, Andre Barlatier; ed, Ben Lewis; set d, Cedric Gibbons; gowns, Adrian.

Comedy **(PR:A MPAA:NR)**

SINGLE STANDARD, THE** (1929) 8 reels MGM bw

Greta Garbo *(Arden Stuart)*, Nils Asther *(Packy Cannon)*, John Mack Brown *(Tommy Hewlett)*, Dorothy Sebastian *(Mercedes)*, Lane Chandler *(Ding Stuart)*, Robert Castle *(Anthony Kendall)*, Mahlon Hamilton *(Mr. Glendenning)*, Kathlyn Williams *(Mrs. Glendenning)*, Zeffie Tilbury *(Mrs. Handley)*.

THE SINGLE STANDARD attempted to address the then-controversial subject of the film's title by having the free-thinking Garbo turn down a proposal of marriage by millionaire Brown to embark on a little fling with Castle, the family chauffeur. After that poor devil commits suicide, the lady becomes involved with Asther, a prizefighter-turned-artist, and the couple sail lustfully away to the tropics on his yacht. This relationship is also destined to fail, and Garbo returns to marry Brown and have his child in time for the close of the last reel. Garbo would make only one more silent film, THE KISS, before moving on to her first sound picture, ANNA CHRISTIE the following year.

d, John S. Robertson; w, Josephine Lovett (based on the story by Adela Rogers St. Johns); t, Marion Ainslee; ph, Oliver Marsh; m, William Axt; ed, Blanche Sewell; art d, Cedric Gibbons; syn sc; s eff.

Drama **(PR:A MPAA:NR)**

SINGLE TRACK, THE ½** (1921) 5 reels VIT bw

Corinne Griffith *(Janetta Gildersleeve)*, Richard Travers *(Barney Hoyt)*, Charles Kent *(Andrew Geddes)*, Sidney Herbert *(Peddar)*, Jessie Stevens *(Ma Heaney)*, Edward Norton *(Roland Winfield)*, Matthew Betts *(Mallison)*, Fuller Mellish *(Jud Pettinger)*.

Griffith was on the road to major stardom when she made this programmer about an heiress who loses everything from her father's estate except a western mine which needs a single-track railroad in order to survive. Griffith heads west, disguises herself as a waitress, and, with the help of a two-fisted young man (Travers), prevents her enemy from stealing her claim. Griffith is radiant in this picture and performs a very steamy dance.

d, Webster Campbell; w, C. Graham Baker, Harry Dittmar (based on a story by Douglas Grant); ph, Charles Davis.

Drama **(PR:A MPAA:NR)**

SINNERS IN HEAVEN** (1924) 7 reels FP/PAR bw

Bebe Daniels *(Barbara Stockley)*, Richard Dix *(Alan Croft)*, Holmes Herbert *(Hugh Rochedale)*, Florence Billings *(Mrs. Madge Fields)*, Betty Hilburn *(Native Girl)*, Montagu Love *(Native Chief)*, Effie Shannon *(Mrs. Stockley)*, Marcia Harris *(Barbara's Aunt)*.

Hard-to-swallow South Seas romantic adventure has pilot Dix and his strictly raised British passenger, Daniels, crash-landing on a desolate beach. At first they are taken for gods, but then a native girl, who has a thing for Dix and is jealous of Daniels, notices that he nicked himself shaving and the divinity ruse is over. The couple are about to be devoured by cannibals when a rescue plane shows up and whisks Daniels off to Old Blighty, where she is treated like dirt for having lived with a man out of wedlock. Dix, who was left behind, somehow manages to escape and bounds over to Daniels' estate, where the two bind their union legally.

d, Alan Crosland; w, James Ashmore Creelman (based on the novel by Clive Arden); ph, Henry Cronjager.

Romantic Adventure **(PR:A MPAA:NR)**

SINNERS IN LOVE* ½ (1928) 6 reels FBO bw

Olive Borden *(Ann Hardy)*, Huntley Gordon *(Ted Wells)*, Seena Owen *(Yvonne D'Orsy)*, Ernest Hilliard *(Silk Oliver)*, Daphne Pollard *(Mabel)*, Phillips Smalley *(Spencer)*.

Marginal programmer has Borden heading for the Big Apple, where she lands a job as a roulette girl. When she discovers that the games are rigged, the little lady quits, much to the chagrin of gambler Gordon, who has fallen in love with her. Meanwhile, Owen, his former paramour, tries to get even by sending Borden to the apartment of Hilliard, New York's biggest lout. Hilliard tries to have his way with her, and Borden drills him full of holes. In the end Borden is found innocent, Gordon vows to go straight, and the two start a fresh, new life together as man and wife.

d, George Melford; w, J. Clarkson Miler; t, Randolph Bartlett; ph, Paul Perry; ed, Archie Marshek; cos, Walter Plunkett.

Drama **(PR:A MPAA:NR)**

SINNER'S PARADE** (1928) 6 reels COL bw

Victor Varconi *(Al Morton)*, Dorothy Revier *(Mary Tracy)*, John Patrick *(Bill Adams)*, Edna Marion *(Connie Adams)*, Marjorie Bonner *(Sadie)*, Clarissa Selwynne *(Mrs. Adams)*, Jack Mower *(Chauffeur)*.

Schoolteacher Revier moonlights as a dancer at Varconi's nightclub to help support her sister and little niece. When she becomes attracted to Patrick, whose mother is a leader of an anti-vice organization, the gallant little lady quits her nighttime job. But Varconi, who loves Revier, holds her to her contract, and before it has time to expire the police raid the joint, Revier makes the front page of the paper, and the school board gives the teacher her walking papers. Meanwhile, Varconi discovers that Patrick is actually the leader of a crime ring and threatens to blow the whistle. Word of this reaches Patrick, however, and he and his boys decide to take the former cabaret owner for a little ride. At about this point, the disenchanted Revier has come to realize that she actually loves Varconi, not Patrick, and calls the police. Finally the *real* threat to society is put behind bars, and Revier agrees to become the wife of Varconi.

p, Harry Cohn; d, John G. Adolfi; w, Beatrice Van (based on a story by David Lewis); ph, James Van Trees; ed, Ben Pivar; art d, Harrison Wiley.

Drama/Crime **(PR:A MPAA:NR)**

SINS OF ROZANNE*** (1920) 5 reels PAR bw

Ethel Clayton *(Rozanne)*, Jack Holt *(Sir Dennis Harlenden)*, Fontaine La Rue *(Rachel Bangat)*, Mabel Van Buren *(Mrs. Ozanne)*, Fred Malatesta *(Syke Ravenal)*, Grace Morse *(Kitty Drummond)*, C. H. Geldart *(Leonard Drummond)*, Dorothy Messenger *(Precious Drummond)*, James Smith *(Hiangeli)*, Guy Oliver *(Hiangeli's Father)*.

In the diamond-rich area of South Africa, a Malay nurse offers to save a dying girl through witchcraft, providing she may have the child for two years. The girl does survive, but grows up with occult powers and unknowingly assists in the smuggling of nuggets for a gang of crooks, of which the mysterious woman is a member. In the end the girl is set free when Holt brings the wrongdoers to justice, and the evil nurse is killed.

d, Tom Forman; w, Mary O'Connor (based on the story "Rozanne Ozanne" by Cynthia Stockley); ph, Alfred Gilks, Harry Perry.

Mystery **(PR:A MPAA:NR)**

SINS OF SOCIETY** (1915) 5 reels Brady/WORLD bw

Robert Warwick *(Capt. Dorian March)*, Alice B. Francis *(Noel Ferrers)*, Ralph Delmore *(Robert Morris)*, Royal Byron *(Henty Hogg)*, George Ingleton *(Detective Parker)*, Robert B. Mantell, Jr. *(Jim Baines)*, Harry Weir *(Col. Gretton)*, Dorothy Fairchild *(Marian Beaumont)*, Frances Nelson *(Gwendolin Beaumont)*, Lila Hayward Chester *(Mme. D'Orrville)*, Mildred Havens *(Mary)*.

Fair programmer has a couple of orphaned girls inheriting their father's weakness for gambling along with his bankrupt estate. They try desperately to maintain their social status in spite of all this, and after a number of adventures succeed.

d, Oscar Eagle; w, Cecil Raleigh, Henry Hamilton; ph, Sol Polito.

Drama **(PR:A MPAA:NR)**

SINS OF THE MOTHERS** (1915) 5 reels VIT bw

Julia Swayne Gordon *(Mrs. Raymond)*, Anita Stewart *(Her Daughter)*, Earle Williams, Lucille Lee Stewart, Mary Maurice, Paul Scardon.

This muckraker, advertised by Vitagraph as "A pulsating, throbbing, alluring five-part drama of the curse of heredity," took a shot at society's underworld. It told the story of a girl who inherits her mother's weakness for gambling, and after marrying a young district attorney, is killed during a raid her husband pulls on a gambling house. There are some well-staged scenes, but not enough to overcome the film's obvious sensational content.

d, Ralph Ince; w, Elaine Sterne, Donald Buchanan.

Drama **(PR:A MPAA:NR)**

SIOUX BLOOD*** (1929) 6 reels MGM bw

Tim McCoy *(Flood)*, Robert Frazer *(Lone Eagle)*, Marian Douglas *(Barbara Ingram)*, Clarence Geldert *(Miles Ingram)*, Chief Big Tree *(Crazy Wolf)*, Sidney Bracy *(Cheyenne Jones)*.

Interesting and well-done McCoy western about two boys who are separated during an Indian raid. McCoy, who is raised by whites, grows up to become an Indian scout, while Frazer grows up with Indians and becomes a courageous brave. The two meet in combat when McCoy sets out with Douglas, the girl he loves, to save her father who is a prisoner of the Indians, and during a struggle they recognize one another. In the end, the one who has been reared in the ways of the red man elects to become a part of his brother's world again.

d, John Waters; w, George C. Hull, Houston Branch (based on a story by Harry Sinclair Drago); t, Lucille Newmark; ph, Arthur Reed; ed, William Le Vanway.

Western **(PR:A MPAA:NR)**

SIREN CALL, THE** (1922) 6 reels FP/PAR bw

Dorothy Dalton *(Charlotte Woods, a Dancer)*, David Powell *(Ralph Stevens, a Prospector)*, Mitchell Lewis *(Beauregard, a Trapper)*, Edward J. Brady *(Edward Brent, a Gambler)*, Will Walling *(Gore)*, Leigh Wyant *(Eleanor Du Bois)*, Lucien Littlefield *(Irishman)*, George B. Williams *(Judge Green)*.

In this Northwest frozen tundra drama, dance hall girl Dalton adopts a baby, kills the man who is forced upon her by her no-good husband, then marries Powell, the good-looking prospector who loves her for what she really is, after her spouse is devoured by wolves.

d, Irvin Willat; w, J. E. Nash, Phillip Hurn, Victor Irvin; ph, Charles Edgar Schoenbaum.

Adventure **(PR:A MPAA:NR)**

SISTER TO ASSIST 'ER, A* (1922, Brit.) 5 reels Baron/GAU bw

Mary Brough *(Mrs. Millie May)*, Pollie Emery *(Mrs. Mull)*, Muriel Aked *(Mrs. Crawley)*, Cecil Morton York, John McAndrews, Billy Baron.

This little British comedy about an impoverished woman who disguises herself to be her own millionairess twin sister in order to get back at her nasty landlady, is not calculated to keep 'em rollin' in the aisle.

p, John L. Baron; d&w, George Dewhurst (based on the play by John le Breton).

Comedy **(PR:A MPAA:NR)**

SISTER TO ASSIST 'ER, A* 1/2 (1927, Brit.) 6 reels GAU bw

Mary Brough *(Mrs. May)*, Pollie Emery *(Mrs. Mull)*, Humberston Wright *(Mr. Mull)*, A. Bromley Davenport *(Jim Harris)*, Alf Goddard *(Sailor)*, Jack Harris *(Alf)*.

The translation to the silent screen of this comedy about an impoverished woman who poses as a rich twin in order to get even with a nasty landlady, just fails to make it. Brough, however, does deliver a performance which surpasses her material.

p, Maurice Elvey, Victor Saville, Gareth Gundrey; d&w, George Dewhurst (based on a play by John le Breton).

Comedy **(PR:A MPAA:NR)**

SISTERS*** (1922) 7 reels International Film Service/American Releasing bw

Seena Owen *(Alix Strickland)*, Gladys Leslie *(Cherry Strickland)*, Mildred Arden *(Anna Little)*, Matt Moore *(Peter Joyce)*, Joe King *(Martin Lloyd)*, Tom Guise *(Dr. Strickland)*, Robert Schable *(Justin Little)*, Frances Grant *(Colored Mammy)*, Fred Miller *(Colored Servant)*.

Brokenhearted because Leslie, the girl he adores, has married another man, Moore sets off on a world cruise. He returns to find that Leslie's father has passed on, and out of pity decides to wed Owen, the remaining daughter. Leslie's life with her husband, King, soon hits the skids and she moves in with her sister. Before long, however, the old feelings return and Moore and Leslie decide to run away together. Owen discovers the plot and delivers a blistering tongue-lashing to the potential adulterers. Then King is injured in a logging accident, which causes Leslie to realize she still loves him, and the repentant young lady rushes to her husband's side. Owen later tells Moore that she will try to forgive and forget, and the two begin their marriage anew.

d, Albert Capellani; w, E. Lloyd Sheldon (based on the novel by Kathleen Norris); ph, Chester Lyons; set d, Joseph Urban.

Drama **(PR:C MPAA:NR)**

SIX DAYS 1/2** (1923) 9 reels Goldwyn/Goldwyn-COS bw

Corinne Griffith *(Laline Kingston)*, Frank Mayo *(Dion Leslie)*, Myrtle Stedman *(Olive Kingston)*, Claude King *(Lord Charles Chetwyn)*, Maude George *(Clara Leslie/Gilda Lindo)*, Spottiswoode Aitken *(Père Jerome)*, Charles Clary *(Richard Kingston)*, Evelyn Walsh Hall *(Honorable Emily Tarrant-Chetwyn)*, Paul Cazeneuve *(Chef)*, Jack Herbert *(Guide)*, Robert De Vilbiss *(Dion Leslie, as a Child of 6)*.

The sexual innuendo which Elinor Glyn (creative genius of the smash-hit IT, 1927) delivered in her novel is completely missing from this movie about a couple (Griffith and Mayo) who become trapped for six days in an old German underground barrack. After a number of well-filmed and thrilling experiences, they finally manage to escape, but not before a priest who was their guide marries them and then dies in a cave-in. Fine performance by Griffith.

d, Charles Brabin; w, Ouida Bergere (based on the novel by Elinor Glyn); ph, John Mescall.

Drama **(PR:A MPAA:NR)**

SIXTY CENTS AN HOUR*** (1923) 6 reels FP/PAR bw

Walter Hiers *(Jimmy Kirk, a Soda-Jerker)*, Jacqueline Logan *(Mamie Smith, His Sweetheart)*, Ricardo Cortez *(William Davis, Jimmy's Rival)*, Charles Ogle *(James Smith, a Banker)*, Lucille Ward *(Mrs. Smith, Mamie's Mother)*, Robert Dudley *(Storekeeper)*, Clarence Burton, Guy Oliver, Cullen Tate *(Three Crooks)*.

Good comedy has fat funny-man Hiers playing a California soda jerk in love with Logan, the banker's daughter. When he finds a substantial sum of money belonging to the bank, his rival, Ogle, tries to stop him from collecting the reward. But Hiers reveals that the bank actually encroaches on a four-foot piece of property he owns, and the big fellow ends up not only with the cash he has coming, but the girl as well.

d, Joseph Henabery; w, Grant Carpenter (based on a story by Frank Condon); ph, Faxon M. Dean.

Comedy **(PR:A MPAA:NR)**

SKID PROOF*** (1923) 6 reels FOX bw

Charles Jones *(Jack Darwin)*, Laura Anson *(Nadine)*, Fred Eric *(Dutton Hardmere)*, Jacqueline Gadsden *(Lorraine Hardmere)*, Peggy Shaw *(Marie Hardmere)*, Earl Metcalf *(Rufus Tyler)*, Claude Peyton *(Masters)*, Harry Tracey *(Dancing Joe)*.

Jones is fine as an auto racing ace who is forced to give up the game when a rival shoots him from a plane during a transcontinental competition. His heroics, however, bring him to the attention of a Hollywood producer and Jones becomes a movie star. He falls in love with a beautiful actress, Anson, and finally returns to win the really big race.

d, Scott Dunlap; w, Harvey Gates (based on a story by Byron Morgan); ph, Don Short.

Adventure **(PR:A MPAA:NR)**

SKINNER'S BIG IDEA 1/2** (1928) 7 reels FBO bw

Bryant Washburn *(Skinner)*, William Orlamond *(Hemingway)*, James Bradbury, Sr. *(Carlton)*, Robert Dudley *(Gibbs)*, Ole M. Ness *(Perkins)*, Charles Wellesley *(McLaughlin)*, Martha Sleeper *(Dorothy)*, Hugh Trevor *(Jack McLaughlin)*, Ethel Grey Terry *(Mrs. Skinner)*.

Washburn, who starred as the original Skinner in a series of films made in 1917, is back in what turns out to be a slightly disappointing sequel. This time the young man, now a partner in the firm, is ordered to fire the three old-timers who always stood behind him, while the two senior partners are on vacation. Skinner/Washburn decides to rejuvenate the old codgers by hiring a young cutie to work in the office. The little charmer, Sleeper, not only encourages them to spruce up by wearing hair pieces and bouncing about the place like Douglas Fairbanks, but also convinces them to take up the game of golf, and they land a stupendous contract on the fairway. This secures them in their jobs forever, and Washburn breathes a sigh of relief.

d, Lynn Shores; w, Matt Taylor (based on the novel *Skinner's Big Idea* by Henry Irving Dodge); t, Randolph Bartlett; ph, Phil Tannura; ed, Archie Marshek.

Comedy **(PR:A MPAA:NR)**

SKINNER'S DRESS SUIT*** (1917) 5 reels Essanay bw

Bryant Washburn *(Skinner)*, Hazel Daly *(Mrs. Skinner)*, Harry Dunkinson, James C. Carroll, U. K. Haupt, Florence Oberle, Frances Raymond, Marion Skinner.

Delightful Washburn comedy about a timid office worker, who, after being badgered by his wife to demand a raise, finally lies and says he got one. She immediately buys a dress suit and gown and the two are a social sensation. Skinner of course is now in the position to land the big deal and ends up a partner in the firm.

d, Harry Beaumont; w, Charles J. McQuirk (based on the novel by Henry Irving Dodge); ph, Jackson Rose.

Comedy **(PR:A MPAA:NR)**

SKINNER'S DRESS SUIT*** (1926) 7 reels UNIV bw

Reginald Denny *(Skinner)*, Laura La Plante *(Honey)*, Ben Hendricks, Jr. *(Perkins)*, E. J. Ratcliffe *(McLaughlin)*, Arthur Lake *(Tommy)*, Hedda Hopper *(Mrs. Colby)*, Lionel Braham *(Jackson)*, Henry Barrows *(Mr. Colby)*, Frona Hale *(Mrs. McLaughlin)*, William H. Strauss *(Tailor)*, Betty Morrisey *(Miss Smith)*, Lucille De Nevers *(Mrs. Crawford)*, Lucille Ward *(Mrs. Jackson)*, Lila Leslie *(Mrs. Wilton)*, Broderick O'Farrell *(Mr. Wilton)*, Grady Sutton *(Dance Extra)*.

This Denny remake of the 1917 hit is even better than the original. The plot is updated, giving the star the opportunity to throw in a teriffic Charleston. La Plante is delightful as his ambitious wife, and thanks to the sharp directing skills of her real-life husband, Seiters, the sight gags pay off plenty.

d, William A. Seiter; w, Rex Taylor (based on the novel by Henry Irving Dodge); ph, Arthur Todd; art d, Leo E. Kutler.

Comedy **(PR:A MPAA:NR)**

SKIPPER'S WOOING, THE*** (1922, Brit.) 5 reels Artistic bw

Gordon Hopkirk *(The Skipper)*, Cynthia Murtagh *(Annie Getting)*, Johnny Butt *(Sam)*, Thomas Marriott *(Dick)*, Bobbie Rudd *(The Child)*, Jeff Barlow *(Mr. Dunn)*.

Unassuming little British comedy has a crafty schoolteacher sending a couple, who have protested just a bit *too* loudly about hating each other, off on a bogus mission. They are to find a father who is supposedly hiding out from a murder rap, but the real accomplishment is that they will return as sweethearts.

p, George Redman; d, Manning Haynes; w, Lydia Hayward (based on a novel by W. W. Jacobs).

Comedy **(PR:A MPAA:NR)**

SKY HIGH* 1/2** (1922) 5 reels FOX bw

Tom Mix *(Grant Newburg)*, J. Farrell MacDonald *(Jim Halloway)*, Eva Novak *(Estelle, His Daughter)*, Sid Jordan *(Bates)*, William Buckley *(Victor Castle)*, Adele Warner *(Marguerite)*, Wynn Mace *(Patterson)*, Pat Chrisman *(Pasquale)*.

Topnotch Mix western has the great cowboy star playing an immigration officer who breaks up a gang involved in smuggling Chinese laborers over the Mexican border. There are some truly sensational thrills involving an airplane and mountaintop battles as Mix brings the culprits to justice and rescues Novak, the daughter of the gang's leader. Snappy direction and some beautiful photography, shot on location at the Grand Canyon, also help to make this one a winner.

d&w, Lynn Reynolds; ph, Ben Kline.

Western **(PR:A MPAA:NR)**

SKY-HIGH SAUNDERS* 1/2 (1927) 5 reels UNIV bw

Al Wilson *("Sky-High" Saunders/Michael Saunders)*, Elsie Tarron *(Helen Leland)*, Frank Rice *("Whispering" Hicks)*, Bud Osborne *(George Delatour)*.

Stunt pilot Wilson plays twin brothers in this low-budget feature which has the ace flyer assuming the identity of his smuggler brother after mistakenly shooting him down and watching the lad die in his arms. Wilson blows up the gang's mountain hideout, using dynamite for bombs. Some fine stunt work is all but canceled out by some very bad comedy relief.

d&w, Bruce Mitchell; t, Gardner Bradford; ph, William S. Adams.

Adventure **(PR:A MPAA:NR)**

SKY PILOT, THE* 1/2** (1921) 7 reels Cathrine Curtis/AFN bw

John Bowers *(The Sky Pilot)*, Colleen Moore *(Gwen)*, David Butler *(Bill Hendricks)*, Harry Todd *(The Old Timer)*, James Corrigan *(Honorable Ashley)*, Donald MacDonald *(The Duke)*, Kathleen Kirkham *(Lady Charlotte)*.

Well-done King Vidor western has Bowers, a young minister, accepting an assignment in the Canadian Northwest, where he is met with derision by the cowboys. But after acquitting himself well in a fist fight with ranch foreman Butler, he is accepted by the townsfolk, who nickname him "Sky Pilot," and he builds his church. Later the clergyman saves Butler's sweetheart, Moore, from a cattle stampede, but the girl is left crippled. Angered by this, Moore's father and a gang of rustlers burn the church to the ground. But the girl, forgetting her disability, enters the flaming structure and drags the Sky Pilot out, and in so doing regains the use of her legs. The film ends with the minister converting Moore's father and then officiating at the marriage of his two friends.

p, Cathrine Curtis; d, King Vidor; w, John McDermott, Faith Green (based on the novel by Ralph Connor); ph, Gus Peterson.

Drama **(PR:A MPAA:NR)**

SKY RIDER, THE* (1928) 5 reels CHES bw

Alfred Heuston, Gareth Hughes, Josephine Hill, J. P. Lockney, John Tansey, Edward Cecil, Lew Meehan, Sheldon Lewis, Champion the Dog.

When a nasty young chap is disinherited, he attempts to get even by blowing his cousin up in his airplane. Later, he hires a gang of thugs to abduct his wealthy uncle, but the plot is thwarted by the cousin who survived and his dog, Champion.

d&w, Alvin J. Neitz; ph, M. A. Anderson; ed, Neitz; syn sc.

Adventure **(PR:A MPAA:NR)**

SKY SKIDDER, THE** (1929) 5 reels UNIV bw

Al Wilson *(Al Simpkins)*, Helen Foster *(Stella Hearns)*, Wilbur McGaugh *(Silas Smythe)*, Pee Wee Holmes *(Bert Beatle)*.

Some good thrills by ace stunt flyer Wilson save this paper-thin story about a pilot who invents a fuel able to deliver a thousand miles to the pint, and the villain who tries to steal it. Exciting air footage includes scenes in which Wilson rescues the heroine (Foster) from a speeding car by the use of a rope ladder dropped from his plane, and another in which he leaps from the wing of his aircraft onto another plane to do battle with bad guy McGaugh.

d, Bruce Mitchell; w, Val Cleveland; t, Gardner Bradford; ph, William Adams; ed, Harry Marker.

Adventure **(PR:A MPAA:NR)**

SKYROCKET, THE*** (1926) 8 reels Celebrity/AEX bw

Gladys Brockwell *(Rose Kimm)*, Charles West *(Edward Kimm)*, Muriel McCormac *(Sharon Kimm, as a Child)*, Junior Coughlan *(Mickey Reid, as a Child)*, Peggy Hopkins Joyce *(Sharon Kimm, as an Adult)*, Owen Moore *(Mickey Reid, as an Adult)*, Gladys Hulette *(Lucia Morgan)*, Paulette Duval *(Mildred Rideout)*, Lilyan Tashman *(Ruby Wright)*, Earle Williams *(William Dvorak)*, Bernard Randall *(Sam Hertzfelt)*, Sammy Cohen *(Morris Pincus)*, Bull Montana *(Film Comedian)*, Arnold Gregg *(Stanley Craig)*, Ben Hall *(Peter Stanton)*, Nick Dandau *(Vladmir Strogin)*, Eddie Dillon *(Comedy Director)*, Hank Mann *(Comedy Producer)*, Joan Standing *(Sharon's Secretary)*, Eugenie Besserer *(Wardrobe Mistress)*.

Joyce, the sensational darling of the tabloids, makes her motion picture debut as a poor young woman who fights her way to movie stardom, becomes an egomaniac, and sabotages her own career because of her arrogance. After hitting the skids, she returns to her wonderful old self and falls in love with the fellow who was pictured with her as a child in a prolog dealing with tenement life. There is a bit of a surprise ending when it's revealed that her sweetheart was the author of the screenplay which skyrocketed Joyce to fortune and fame.

d, Marshall Neilan; w, Benjamin Glazer (based on the novel by Adela Rogers St. Johns); ph, David Kesson.

Drama **(PR:A MPAA:NR)**

SLANDER THE WOMAN* (1923) 7 reels Allen Holubar/AFN bw

Dorothy Phillips *(Yvonne Desmarest)*, Lewis Dayton *(Mons. Duroacher)*, Robert Anderson *(Dr. Emile Molleur)*, Mayme Kelso *(Nanette)*, George Siegmann *(Scarborough)*, Ynez Seabury *(Indian Girl)*, Herbert Fortier *(Father Machette)*, Geno Corrado *(Tetreau, the Guide)*, William Orlamond *(The Stranger)*, Robert Schable *(Mons. Redoux)*, Rosemary Theby *(Mme. Redoux)*, Irene Haisman *(Marie Desplanes)*, Cyril Chadwick *(Mons. Lemond)*.

Substandard programmer has Phillips, a woman wrongly accused of being involved in a murder case, escaping to the North Woods. She is followed there by Dayton, the judge who presided over the case, who now realizes he treated her badly. After a number of complications, during which the judge becomes the suspect in a killing, everything finally works out, and the couple are married.

d, Allen Holubar; w, Violet Clark (based on the story "The White Frontier" by Jeffrey Deprend); ph, Byron Haskin; ed, Frank Lawrence.

Drama **(PR:A MPAA:NR)**

SLAVE OF DESIRE*** (1923) 7 reels Goldwyn/Goldwyn-COS bw

Goerge Walsh *(Raphael Valentin)*, Bessie Love *(Pauline Gaudin)*, Carmel Myers *(Countess Fedora)*, Wally Van *(Restignac)*, Edward Connelly *(The Antiquarian)*, Eulalie Jensen *(Mrs. Gaudin)*, Herbert Prior *(Mr. Gaudin)*, William Orlamond *(Champrose)*, Nicholas De Ruiz *(Tallifer)*, William von Hardenburg *(The General)*, Harmon MacGregor *(Emile)*, George Periolat *(The Duke)*, Harry Lorraine *(Finot)*, Calvert Carter *(The Major Domo)*.

Sam Goldwyn took a lot of liberties with this Honore de Balzac story, but the saga of a poet who is driven to despair by the notorious Countess Fedora, and is then given the skin of an ass, which has the power to grant his every wish, is rather well done. With every wish however, the skin grows smaller and will eventually lead to the death of its possessor. But because the poet uses his power to strip the countess of her influence over men, and then again on behalf of the poor girl he once knew in his garret days, the spell is broken, and he lives on to find love with the girl.

d, George D. Baker; w, Charles E. Whittaker , Alice D. G. Miller (based on the story "La Peau de Chagrin" by Honore de Balzac); ph, John Boyle.

Drama **(PR:A MPAA:NR)**

SLAVES OF BEAUTY*** (1927) 6 reels FOX bw

Olive Tell *(Anastasia Jones)*, Holmes Herbert *(Leonard Jones)*, Earle Foxe *(Paul Perry)*, Margaret Livingston, *(Goldie)*, Sue Carol *(Dorothy Jones)*, Richard Walling *(Robert)*, Mary Foy *(Irishwoman)*, Mickey Bennett.

Pretty good picture with more than a dash of irony has Herbert, an uncomely inventor, creating a youth-rejuvenating facial clay. This improves the appearance of his wife who, tired of her husband's looks, has a fling with Foxe, the handsome, young manager of her beauty shop. Herbert, in the meantime, opens his own salon, all but destroys the business of his ungrateful spouse, and finally accepts her back after giving her former boy friend a shiner.

d, J. G. Blystone; w, William M. Conselman (based on the story "The Grandflapper" by Nina Wilcox Putnam); t, James K. McGuinness; ph, William O'Connell; ed, Margaret V. Clancey.

Dramatic Comedy **(PR:A MPAA:NR)**

SLAVES OF DESTINY** (1924, Brit.) 5 reels STOLL bw

Matheson Lang *(Luke Charnock)*, Valia *(Miranda Warriner)*, Henry Victor *(Ralph Warriner)*, Humberston Wright *(Hassan)*, H. Agar Lyons *(Wilbrahim)*.

British drama set in Africa deals with the trials and tribulations of an Englishman who is sold into slavery, but finally earns freedom and marries the woman he loves after her nasty husband is killed by a blind beggar.

d, Maurice Elvey; w, (based on the novel *Miranda of the Balcony* by A. E. W. Mason).

Drama **(PR:A MPAA:NR)**

SLEEPWALKER, THE* (1922) 5 reels Realart/PAR bw

Constance Binney *(Doris Dumond)*, Jack Mulhall *(Phillip Carruthers)*, Edythe Chapman *(Sister Ursula)*, Florence Roberts *(Mrs. Fabian Dumond)*, Bertram Grassby *(Ambrose Hammond)*, Cleo Ridgely *(Mrs. Langley)*, Winifred Edwards *(Mary Langley)*.

Incredulous nonsense about a sleepwalking girl, Binney, entering the apartment of a jewelry dealer who is going to have her mother arrested for selling some gems before fully paying for them. The jeweler detains the young lady, notifies her mother, her sweetheart, Mulhall, and the house detective, but none of them believe her story until the following night when she takes another nocturnal stroll and saves a baby from falling over a ledge in her building. It all ends well with Mulhall paying off the mother's debt and then proposing to monitor the young lady's sleeping habits personally.

d, Edward Le Saint; w, Wells Hastings (based on a story by Aubrey Stauffer); ph, H. Kinley Martin.

Drama **(PR:A MPAA:NR)**

SLIDE, KELLY, SLIDE**** (1927) 8 reels MGM bw

William Haines *(Jim Kelly)*, Sally O'Neil *(Mary Munson)*, Harry Carey *(Tom Munson)*, Junior Coghlan *(Mickey Martin)*, Warner Richmond *(Cliff Macklin)*, Paul Kelly *(Fresbie)*, Karl Dane *(Swede Hansen)*, Guinn Williams *(McLean)*, Mike Donlin, Irish Meusel, Bob Meusel, Tony Lazzeri *(Themselves)*.

Although the subject of baseball usually spelled poison at the box office, this film proved just the opposite and became a smash hit. It was one of Haines' best efforts, in which he plays a bush-league pitcher who joins the New York Yankees, becomes a sensation, but then develops a swelled head and quits the team during the World Series after an argument with his manager. When little Coughlan, the team mascot, is brought to the ballpark in a wheel chair after an accident, Haines comes through just in time to win the game. Later, after accepting the forgiveness of his teammates, Haines claims the love of O'Neil, his manager's daughter.

d, Edward Sedgwick; w, A. P. Younger; t, Joe Farnham; ph, Henry Sharp; ed, Frank Sullivan; set d, Cedric Gibbons, David Townsend.

Comedy/Drama **(PR:A MPAA:NR)**

SLIGHTLY USED 1/2** (1927) 7 reels WB bw

May McAvoy *(Cynthia Martin)*, Conrad Nagel *(Maj. John Smith)*, Robert Agnew *(Donald Woodward)*, Audrey Ferris *(Helen Martin)*, Anders Randolf *(Mr. Martin)*, Eugenie Besserer *(Aunt Lydia)*, Arthur Rankin *(Gerald)*, Davir Mir *(Horace)*, Sally Eilers *(Grace Martin)*, Jack Santoro *(Harold)*.

In spite of a fine cast, good direction, and better-than-average photography, this one just doesn't quite make it. After being teased by her younger sisters, who accuse her of being an old maid, McAvoy claims to have married a major who was then forced to rejoin his regiment in Nicaragua. Later she becomes attracted to young Woodward and "kills" her so-called husband off by having his death notice printed in all of the New York papers. The real major, Nagel, reads these and visits the home of the "widow," claiming to be her late husband's best friend. The expected complications result, but all resolve themselves in the end when the couple fall in love and tie the knot for real.

d, Archie L. Mayo; w, C. Graham Baker (based on a story by Melville Crossman [Darryl Zanuck]); t, Jack Jarmuth; ph, Hal Mohr.

Comedy **(PR:A MPAA:NR)**

SLIM FINGERS* (1929) 5 reels UNIV bw

Bill Cody *(Al Wellsley)*, Duane Thompson *(Kate)*, Wilbur Mack *(Dan Donovan)*, Monte Montague *(Valet)*, Arthur Morrison *(Riley)*, Charles L. King *(Morgan)*.

Dreadful, low-budget Cody film has the hero forced at gunpoint to take lovely Thompson to her apartment after she and Mack steal a valuable painting. The police then believe that Cody is involved and a chase ensues in which he gives them the slip. Cody later whips the tar out of Mack, reforms Thompson and asks for her hand in marriage.

d, Josef Levigard; w, William Lester; t, Val Cleveland; ph, Charles Stumar; ed, Harry Marker.

Mystery **(PR:A MPAA:NR)**

SLIM PRINCESS, THE** (1915) 4 reels Essanay bw

Francis X. Bushman *(The American Millionaire)*, Ruth Stonehouse *(The Slim Princess)*, Harry Dunkinson *(Her Father)*, Wallace Beery, Bryant Washburn.

Acceptable comedy has U.S. millionaire Bushman visiting Turkey and falling in love with a slim and beautiful princess (Stonehouse). She is the younger of two sisters, much to the relief of her whole family since in that country only rotund women are desirable, and native law dictates that the younger sister must marry first.

d, E. H. Calvert; w, Edward T. Lowe (based on a story by George Ade); ph, Jackson Rose.

Comedy **(PR:A MPAA:NR)**

SLIM SHOULDERS** (1922) 6 reels Tilford/W. W. Hodkinson bw

Irene Castle *(Naomi Warren)*, Rod La Rocque *(Richard Langden)*, Anders Randolph *(Edward Langden)*, Warren Cook *(John Clinton Warren)*, Mario Carillo *(Count Guilo Morranni)*, Marie Burke *(Mrs. Warren)*.

Castle was never more beautiful than in this below-par programmer where she plays a society girl fighting to prevent her father from going to prison. The movie does, however, provide Castle with the opportunity to do a little dancing, model some breathtaking clothes, ride horseback, take the wheel of a high-powered speed boat, and wear men's clothing. Outside of a decent script, who could ask for more?

d, Alan Crosland; w, Lawrence McCloskey (based on a story by Charles K. Harris); ph, George Falsey.

Adventure/Drama **(PR:A MPAA:NR)**

SLIPPY MCGEE zero (1923) 7 reels Oliver Morosco/AFN bw

Wheeler Oakman *(Slippy McGee)*, Colleen Moore *(Mary Virginia)*, Sam De Grasse *(Father De Rance)*, Edmund Stevens *(George Inglesby)*, Edith Yorke *(Mme. De Rance)*, Lloyd Whitlock *(Howard Hunter)*, Pat O'Malley *(Lawrence Mayne)*.

Oakman and Moore gave good performances, but they struggled against insurmountable odds here and just weren't able to save this inferior production. Oakman plays a safecracker who loses his leg in a train accident while escaping the police, and is nursed back to health by a priest and his pretty female volunteer, Moore. He falls in love with the girl, and when a rotter attempts to blackmail her into marrying him, Oakman pulls one more job and destroys the incriminating evidence. The movie just ends here. There is no real conclusion, but at this point no one really cares.

d, Wesley Ruggles; w, Marie Conway Oemler.

Drama **(PR:A MPAA:NR)**

SMALL TOWN IDOL, A*** (1921) 7 reels MS/AP bw

Ben Turpin *(Sam Smith/Samuel X. Smythe)*, James Finlayson *(J. Wellington Jones)*, Phyllis Haver *(Mary Brown)*, Bert Roach *(Martin Brown)*, Al Cooke *(Joe Barnum)*, Charles Murray *(Sheriff Sparks)*, Marie Prevost *(Marcelle Mansfield)*, Dot Farley *(Mrs. Smith)*, Eddie Gribbon *(Bandit Chief)*, Kalla Pasha *(Bandit Chief's Rival)*, Billy Bevan *(Director)*, George O'Hara *(Cameraman)*.

Wonderful slapstick comedian Turpin, whose crossed eyes became his trademark (he even had them insured against uncrossing with Lloyds of London), is supported here by a cast of Mack Sennett zanies, making for nonstop fun all the way. It's all about a small town boy who is wrongly accused of stealing and heads for Hollywood, where he doubles for a reluctant actor and zooms to movie stardom. In the end the lad returns home to vindicate himself and marry the girl he left behind.

d, Erle Kenton; sup&w, Mack Sennett; ph, Perry Evans, J. R. Lockwood, Fred Jackman.

Comedy **(PR:A MPAA:NR)**

SMART SET, THE*** (1928) 7 reels MGM bw

William Haines *(Tommy)*, Jack Holt *(Nelson)*, Alice Day *(Polly)*, Hobart Bosworth *(Durant)*, Coy Watson, Jr. *(Sammy)*, Constance Howard *(Cynthia)*, Paul Nicholson *(Mr. Van Buren)*, Julia Swayne Gordon *(Mrs. Van Buren)*.

Haines' patented characterization of the brash, egocentrical, fun-loving youth is put to good use once again in this movie about a polo player who is expelled from the U.S. team because of his insistence on hogging the game. But when his rival for Day is injured, he's accepted back on the squad just in time to defeat the British—and win the girl.

d, Jack Conway; w, Byron Morgan, Ann Price (based on a story by Morgan); t, Robert Hopkins; ph, Oliver Marsh; ed, Sam S. Zimbalist; set d, Cecric Gibbons, Merrill Pye.

Comedy/Drama **(PR:A MPAA:NR)**

SMASHING THROUGH* 1/2 (1928, Brit.) 7 reels GAU bw

John Stuart *(Richard Bristol)*, Alf Goddard *(Alf)*, Eve Gray *(Kitty Masters)*, Hayford Hobbs *(James Masters)*, Julie Suedo *(Miss Duprez)*, Gladys Hamer *(Ethyl)*, Charles Ashton *(Westlake)*, Mike Johnson *(Mate)*, H. Saxon-Snell *(Driver)*.

More on the old auto racing theme, this time using the inventor of a supercharger who's convinced by a vamp to compete against a pal to create suspense in the film. Unfortunately, this picture was not in the least exciting, and proved vastly inferior to even the most budget-minded U.S. programmer of the same variety.

p, Maurice Elvey, V. Garuth Gundrey; d, W. P. Kellino; w, L'Estrange Fawcett (based on a story by William Lees, John Hunter).

Adventure/Mystery **(PR:A MPAA:NR)**

SMILE, BROTHER, SMILE*** (1927) 7 reels Charles R. Rogers/FN bw

Jack Mulhall *(Jack Lowery)*, Dorothy Mackaill *(Mildred Marvin)*, Philo McCullough *(Harvey Renrod)*, E. J. Ratcliffe *(Fred Bowers)*, Harry Dunkinson *(Mr. Potter)*, Ernest Hilliard *(Mr. Saunders)*, Charles Clary *(Mr. Markel)*, Jack Dillon *(Mr. Kline)*, Yola D'Avril *(Daisy)*, Hank Mann *(The Collector)*, T. Roy Barnes, Jed Prouty, Sam Blum *(Three High-powered Salesmen)*.

Dependable Mulhall and lovely Mackaill are both good as the new salesman and clever secretary of a cosmetic company who expose their manager as being in the employ of a competitor. The two then go on to land a huge deal when Mackaill transforms herself from homely girl to raving beauty in the presence of the world's biggest wholesaler.

p, Charles R. Rogers; d, John Francis Dillon; w, Rex Taylor (based on a story by Al Boasberg); t, Dwinelle Benthall, Rufus McCosh; ph, Charles Van Enger.

Comedy/Drama **(PR:A MPAA:NR)**

SMILES ARE TRUMPS 1/2** (1922) 5 reels FOX bw

Maurice B. Flynn *(Jimmy Carson)*, Ora Carew *(Marjorie Manning)*, Myles McCarthy *(John Slevin)*, Herschel Mayall *(James Manning)*, Kirke Lucas *(Enrico)*, C. Norman Hammond *(Martino)*.

Yale football star "Lefty" Flynn handles himself well in this programmer about a railroad employee who, after being wrongly accused of stealing, fights his way to vindication and then rescues the kidnaped daughter of the line's president in a thrilling locomotive chase.

d, George E. Marshall; w, Delbert F. Davenport (based on the story "The Iron Rider" by Frank L. Packard); ph, Frank B. Good.

Adventure **(PR:A MPAA:NR)**

SMILIN' AT TROUBLE 1/2**
(1925) 6 reels Harry Garson/FBO bw (AKA: SMILING AT TROUBLE)

Maurice B. Flynn *(Jerry Foster)*, Helen Lynch *(Alice Arnold)*, Ray Ripley *(Lafayette Van Renselaer)*, Lee Shumway *(Swazey)*, Charles McHugh *(Clancey O'Toole)*, Hal Wilson *(Michael Arnold)*, Kathleen Myers *(Kathleen O'Toole)*, Raymond Turner *(Colored Boy)*, Joe O'Brien *(Tom)*.

"Lefty" Flynn does not disappoint his army of kid fans in this action-packed adventure which has the hero playing an engineer who exposes a crooked construction foreman on a dam-building project. There is a well-staged flood sequence where the villain gets his just deserts in a watery grave, while Flynn saves Lynch, his boss' daughter, and wins her love.

d, Harry Garson; w, Gertrude Orr, A. B. Barringer (based on a story by Rob Wagner); ph, Gilbert Warrenton.

Adventure **(PR:A MPAA:NR)**

SMILING AT TROUBLE (SEE: SMILIN' AT TROUBLE, 1925)

SMOKE BELLEW* (1929) 7 reels Big 4/FD bw

Conway Tearle *(Kit "Smoke" Bellew)*, Barbara Bedford *(Joy Gastrell)*, Mark Hamilton *(Shorty)*, Alphonse Ethier *(Harry Sprague)*, William Scott *(Stine)*, Alaska Jack, J. P. Lockney.

Dismal frozen tundra stuff about a man who comes to Alaska to forget his past, falls in love with a sourdough's daughter, and helps them strike it rich. An embarrassment for one-time leading players Tearle and Bedford.

d, Scott Dunlap; sup, David Thomas; w, Fred Myton (based on the story by Jack London); t, Myton; ph, J. O. Taylor, Joseph Walters; ed, Charles Hunt.

Drama **(PR:A MPAA:NR)**

SNARE, THE* (1918, Brit.) 6 reels BRO bw

Violet Hopson *(Diana)*, George Foley *(Lord Marston)*, Trever Bland *(Hugh)*, James Lindsay *(Carlton Flint)*.

British love story about a highborn woman who catches a millionaire poaching on her land, finds herself in the position where she has to marry him, and then, to her great delight, discovers that she has actually fallen in love with the assassin of little creatures.

p, Walter West; d, Frank Wilson.

Romance **(PR:A MPAA:NR)**

SNOB, THE*** (1924) 7 reels MGM bw

John Gilbert *(Eugene Curry)*, Norma Shearer *(Nancy Claxton)*, Conrad Nagel *(Herrick Appleton)*, Phyllis Haver *(Dorothy Rensheimer)*, Hedda Hopper *(Mrs. Leiter)*, Margaret Seddon *(Mrs. Curry)*, Aileen Manning *(Lottie)*, Hazel Kennedy *(Florence)*, Gordon Sackville *(Sherwood Claxton)*, Roy Laidlaw *(Doctor)*, Nellie Bly Baker *(Maid)*.

Interesting film with an all-star cast and top MGM production values has socially ambitious schoolteacher Gilbert marrying Shearer, not knowing she's an heiress. Gilbert continues his affair with wealthy but shallow Haver because of his snobbish obsession with wealth, and when Shearer's child is delivered stillborn, she blames it on her husband's affair. It is then that she tells Gilbert of her own considerable fortune, and leaves him pleading for forgiveness while she goes off to marry Nagel, a childhood sweetheart.

d&w, Monta Bell (based on the novel by Helen Reimensyder Martin); ph, Andre Barlatier; ed, Ralph Lawson; set d, Cedric Gibbons; cos, Sophie Wachner.

Drama **(PR:A MPAA:NR)**

SNOBS*** (1915) LAS bw

Victor Moore *(Charles Disney)*, Anita King *(Ethel Hamilton)*, Ernest Joy *(Mr. Phipps)*, Constance Johnson *(Laura Phipps)*.

Moore is fine as a milkman who inherits $20 million, along with a title, and is immediately welcomed into high society, where an army of eligible young ladies is thrown his way. After a while, Moore comes to realize that he is really an object of scorn on the part of his new acquaintances, and in a very moving scene during the annual ball, proceeds to tell them exactly how he feels. When his old sweetheart refuses to have anything to do with him because of the airs he briefly adopted, Moore decides to turn down the fortune and return to his milk route. The girl wisely talks him out of that move, however, and consents to share his good fortune with him for life.

d, Oscar Apfel; w, Cecil B. DeMille (based on a play by George Bronston Howard).

Comedy/Drama (PR:A MPAA:NR)

SNOWBLIND*** (1921) 6 reels Goldwyn bw

Russell Simpson *(Hugh Garth)*, Mary Alden *(Bella)*, Cullen Landis *(Pete Garth)*, Pauline Starke *(Sylvia Dooner)*.

Good programmer has Simpson, a British fugitive who escaped to the Canadian Northwest, taking in and falling in love with Starke, a stranded actress who has become blind. Later the girl regains her sight and loses her heart to the Englishman's handsome younger brother Landis. The film ends untypically with Simpson taking Alden, the woman who has stuck by him through everything, away with him, and leaving the youngsters to find their own happiness.

d, Reginald Barker; w, J. G. Hawks (based on the story by Katharine Newlin Burt); ph, Percy Hilburn.

Drama (PR:A MPAA:NR)

SO BIG* 1/2** (1924) 9 reels FN bw

Colleen Moore *(Selina Peake)*, Joseph De Grasse *(Simeon Peake)*, John Bowers *(Pervus DeJong)*, Ben Lyon *(Dirk DeJong)*, Wallace Beery *(Klass Poole)*, Gladys Brockwell *(Maartje Poole)*, Jean Hersholt *(Aug Hempel)*, Charlotte Merriam *(Julie Hempel)*, Dot Farley *(Widow Paarlenburg)*, Ford Sterling *(Jacob Hoogenduck)*, Frankie Darrow *(Dirk DeJong as a Boy)*, Henry Herbert *(William Storm)*, Dorothy Brock *(Dirk DeJong as a Baby)*, Rosemary Theby *(Paula Storm)*, Phyllis Haver *(Dallas O'Meara)*.

Moore had become a big enough star through her flapper roles (which made her First National's top moneymaker) to be in a position to demand and get a part with some dramatic substance. Her studio had just purchased the rights to the Ferber novel *So Big*, and in this screen incarnation Moore plays a wealthy girl reduced to poverty when her father dies, after losing his fortune gambling. Forced to take a job teaching school in a puritanical Dutch community near Chicago, Moore eventually marries a parsimonious farmer (Bowers) and has a son by him and from this point on knows only hard work and austerity. When her husband dies, Moore tries to make a living by selling vegetables door to door and encounters an old school chum who arranges for her to borrow enough money to make her land turn a profit. Time passes (the actress ages about 40 years in this picture), Moore sends her son Lyon through college, and then, in a beautifully played scene, intervenes on his behalf when he becomes involved in a messy affair with a married woman. The film ends pleasantly (much to the horror of its authoress, who resented the happy Hollywood conclusion and blamed Moore) with the old lady—content because of her son's success as an architect—settling down to run her very profitable agricultural business. Years later Moore encountered Ferber at a social occasion and was reluctant to approach her. But Ferber, who had since viewed a number of versions of her story and realized Moore was not responsible for changes made in the first film, grabbed her by the hand and exclaimed, "Oh my dear, how nice to see you. Of all the women who've played Selina in *So Big*, you're the only one who gave a true performance." This was also Moore's favorite personal performance, and probably her best.

d, Charles Brabin; sup, Earl Hudson; w, Adelaide Heilbron, Hudson (based on the novel by Edna Ferber); ph, T. D. McCord; ed, Arthur Tavares; art d, Milton Menasco.

Drama (PR:A MPAA:NR)

SO THIS IS ARIZONA zero (1922) 6 reels William M. Smith/Merit bw

Franklyn Farnum *(Norman Russell)*, Francis Ford *(Ned Kendall)*, "Shorty" Hamilton *(Art Pulvers)*, Al Hart *(Buck Saunders)*, Genevieve Bert *(Peggy Newton)*, Art Phillips *(Bob Thompson)*.

Poor western tries to make up for its deficiencies by throwing in some slapstick comedy which also fails to work. The story has to do with New Yorker Farnum finding a woman's purse on a bridle path, setting off for Arizona to return it to her, being taken for a crook, trapped by outlaws in a cave, and finally rescued by the sheriff and his men who were summoned by the young lady.

d, Francis Ford; w, (based on the story by Marie Schrader, C. C. Wadde); ph, Reginald Lyons.

Western (PR:A MPAA:NR)

SO THIS IS LOVE*** (1928) 6 reels COL bw

Shirley Mason *(Hilda Jensen)*, William Collier, Jr. *(Jerry McGuire)*, Johnnie Walker *("Spike" Mullins)*, Ernie Adams *("Flash" Tracy)*, Carl Gerard *(Otto)*, William H. Strauss *("Maison" Katz)*, Jean Laverty *(Mary Malone)*.

Pleasant little Capra-directed comedy about a dress designer who takes boxing lessons, whips the Greenwich Village champ, and wins the heart of a counter girl who loves the "sweet science." This was only the second film Capra worked on with producer Cohn, but their association marked a turning point in Capra's career. Prior to this he had experienced several flops in Hollywood and was on a meager $75-a-week salary (down from $600) writing 2-reeler comedies for Mack Sennett. Then Cohn asked him to sign on as a director for Columbia Pictures, a move which would zoom Columbia to the height of a major studio and prove Capra to be one of Hollywood's leading directors, earning him three Academy Awards in just five years (IT HAPPENED ONE NIGHT, 1934; MR. DEEDS GOES TO TOWN, 1936; YOU CAN'T TAKE IT WITH YOU, 1938).

p, Harry Cohn; d, Frank Capra; w, Rex Taylor, Elmer Harris (based on a story by Norman Springer); ph, Ray June; ed, Arthur Roberts; art d, Robert E. Lee.

Comedy (PR:A MPAA:NR)

SO THIS IS PARIS**** (1926) 7 reels WB bw

Monte Blue *(Dr. Giraud)*, Patsy Ruth Miller *(Suzanne Giraud)*, Lilyan Tashman *(Georgette Lalle)*, Andre de Beranger *(Mons. Lalle)*, Myrna Loy *(The Maid)*, Sidney D'Albrook *(The Cop)*.

The famed Lubitsch touch is very much in evidence in this charmer (rated one of the 10 best pictures of 1926 by the *New York Times*) about a flirtatious dance team, Tashman and De Beranger, who become involved in harmless little affairs to keep the spark going in *their* relationship. They enter into a double tryst with a married couple, Blue and Miller, which produces plenty of laughs as the parties desperately try to keep the situation a secret. But in the end it all works out to the satisfaction of everyone concerned. The film's highlight is the grand ball sequence where Lubitsch's camera seems to move everywhere—amounting to a cinematic symphony—with a goodly share of jazz thrown in to make it even spicier.

d, Ernst Lubitsch; w, Hans Kraly (based on the play "Le Reveillon" by Henri Meilhac, Ludovic Halevy); ph, John Mescall.

Comedy (PR:A MPAA:NR)

SOCIAL CELEBRITY, A**** (1926) 6 reels FP/PAR bw

Adolphe Menjou *(Max Haber)*, Louise Brooks *(Kitty Laverne)*, Elsie Lawson *(April King)*, Roger Davis *(Tenny)*, Hugh Huntley *(Forrest Abbott)*, Chester Conklin *(Johann Haber)*, Freeman Wood *(Gifford Jones)*, Josephine Drake *(Mrs. Jackson-Greer)*, Ida Waterman *(Mrs. Winifred King)*.

St. Clair, one of the few true rivals of director Ernst Lubitsch, made this delightful picture with great skill. In it barber Menjou is bobbing female hair in his father's small-town barbershop when he is spotted by New York socialite Drake, who persuades him to come to the Big Apple and open a salon. Menjou agrees because he's in love with his manicurist, Brooks, who moved there to become a dancer. But life in New York is not as easy as Menjou anticipated, and he's forced to accept work in a busy hotel tonsorial parlor. One of the guests there is quite taken by Menjou's good looks and bearing and asks him to pose as a French nobleman who has cancelled his plans to attend a huge society party. Decked out in a fur coat, high hat, and tails, the barber becomes the toast of New York's "upper strata." In the end the bubble bursts and Menjou decides to return to the sanity and stability of his hometown—an idea which also appeals to Brooks. This is topnotch entertainment on every level, with special attention due slapstick comedian Conklin, who turns in a lovely and pathos-tinged performance as Menjou's whimsical father.

d, Malcolm St. Clair; w, Pierre Collings (based on a story by Monte M. Katterjohn); ph, Lee Garmes.

Dramatic Comedy (PR:A MPAA:NR)

SOCIAL CODE, THE* (1923) 5 reels Metro bw

Viola Dana *(Babs Van Buren)*, Malcolm McGregor *(Dean Cardigan)*, Edna Flugrath *(Connie Grant)*, Huntley Gordon *(Judge Evans Grant)*, Cyril Chadwick *(Colby Dickinson)*, William Humphrey *(District Attorney)*, John Sainpolis *(Attorney for the Defense)*.

Tepid little programmer about a flapper who prevents her sweetheart from going to the electric chair by appearing at the trial and clearing his name, while refusing to implicate a certain woman in his testimony.

d, Oscar Apfel; w, Rex Taylor (based on the story "To Whom It May Concern" by Rita Weiman); ph, John Arnold.

Drama (PR:A MPAA:NR)

SOCIAL HIGHWAYMAN, THE** (1926) 7 reels WB bw

John Patrick *(Jay Walker)*, Dorothy Devore *(Elsie Van Tyler)*, Montagu Love *(Ducket Nelson)*, Russell Simpson *(The Mayor's Partner)*, George Pearce *(Old Van Tyler)*, Lynn Cowan *(Bobbie)*, James Gordon *(Editor)*, Frank Brownlee *(Simpson)*, Fred Kelsey *(Chief of Police)*, Charles Hill Mailes *(The Mayor)*.

Beaudine's direction is the only thing noteworthy in this less-than-inspired comedy about a cub reporter's various misadventures while capturing a notorious crook. With title cards like, "Evening came because afternoon had gone and morning was not due until dawn," it's no wonder this one was a box-office failure.

d, William Beaudine; w, Edward T. Loew, Jr., Philip Klein (based on a story by Darryl Francis Zanuck); ph, John Mescall.

Comedy/Adventure (PR:A MPAA:NR)

SOCIAL SECRETARY, THE*** (1916) 5 reels FA/TRI bw

Norma Talmadge *(Mayme)*, Kate Lester *(Mrs. Van Puyster)*, Helen Weir *(Elsie Van Puyster)*, Gladden James *(Jimmie Van Puyster)*, Herbert Frank *(The Count)*, Eric von Stroheim *(The Buzzard)*, Nathaniel Sack, Vivian Ogden.

Nice little Talmadge comedy has the star taking a job as a social secretary to a wealthy woman after discovering that the work world is loaded with libidinous employers. In order to land the job, however, Talmadge makes herself over to look very plain. But before long she has the young man of the house eating out of her hand, saves his sister from the clutches of a villainous count, and thus wins the approval of her boss to marry into the family. Shortly after the release of THE SOCIAL SECRETARY, Talmadge left the Fine Arts Film Company and organized her own studio. Only months earlier she was hosting afternoon teas at Hamburger's Cafe Beautiful in downtown Los Angeles to promote her films. Publicized by *The Moving Picture World* as "a fad which promises to be popular," every woman who attended the Majestic Theatre, where the Fine Arts films were being offered, was invited to the teas afterward.

d, John Emerson; w, Anita Loos.

Comedy **Cas.** **(PR:A MPAA:NR)**

SOCIETY SCANDAL, A*** (1924) 7 reels FP/PAR bw

Gloria Swanson *(Marjorie Colbert)*, Rod La Rocque *(Daniel Farr)*, Ricardo Cortez *(Harrison Peters)*, Allan Simpson *(Hector Colbert)*, Ida Waterman *(Mrs. Maturin Colbert)*, Thelma Converse *(Mrs. Hamilton Pennfield)*, Fraser Coalter *(Schuyler Burr)*, Catherine Proctor *(Mrs. Burr)*, Wilfred Donovan *(Hamilton Pennfield)*, Yvonne Hughes *(Patricia De Voe)*, Catherine Coleburn, Marie Shelton, Dorothy Stokes, Cornelius Keefe *(Friends of Marjorie)*.

Director Dwan captures a true society feeling and Swanson delivers a fine performance (no doubt enjoying the opportunity to wear countless gowns) in this script about a married woman who is deliberately compromised and has her reputation badly damaged through the efforts of a high-powered attorney hired by her husband. Later in the same lawyer's office Swanson tears her clothes, musses her own hair, and accuses the counselor of attacking her. The lawyer, La Rocque, is then forced to endure the same embarrassment he inflicted upon her. In the end the two realize they have fallen in love with one another. Good production values and performances all around.

p&d, Allan Dwan; w, Forrest Halsey (based on the play "The Laughing Lady" by Alfred Sutro); ph, Hall Rosson.

Drama **(PR:A MPAA:NR)**

SOCIETY SNOBS* (1921) 5 reels SF/SEL bw

Conway Tearle *(Lorenzo Carilo/Duke d'Amunzi)*, Vivian Forrester *(Martha Mansfield)*, Ida Darling *(Mrs. Forrester)*, Jack McLean *(Ned Forrester)*, Huntley Gordon *(Duane Thornton)*.

Ludicrous Tearle drama about a man rejected by a socially ambitious woman (Forrester). He then introduces her to an Italian waiter (Tearle) whom he passes off as a duke. The girl and her mother encourage a courtship and the couple are soon married. On his wedding night, the guilt-ridden Tearle discloses the truth, and plans are immediately made for an annulment. The film ends with Tearle actually turning out to be an engineer who is assigned a position in South America. Before he leaves, his bride comes to realize she loves him for what he is, and begs to be taken back.

d, Hobart Henley; w, Lewis Allen Browne (based on a story by Tearle); ph, Jack Brown.

Drama **(PR:A MPAA:NR)**

SOFT CUSHIONS*** (1927) 7 reels PAR bw

Douglas MacLean *(The Young Thief)*, Sue Carol *(The Girl)*, Richard Carle *(The Slave Dealer)*, Russell Powell *(The Fat Thief)*, Frank Leigh *(The Lean Thief)*, Wade Boteler *(The Police Judge)*, Nigel De Brulier *(The Notary)*, Albert Prisco *(The Wazir)*, Boris Karloff *(The Chief Conspirator)*, Albert Gran *(The Sultan)*, Fred Kelsey *(The Police)*, Harry Jones *(The Citizen)*, Noble Johnson *(The Captain of the Guard)*.

MacLean, as an Arabian thief, comes off more like a modern man (the titles use contemporary slang, and he pulls a number of 1920s gags) romping about in Douglas Fairbanks' Bagdad. He's in love with slave girl Carol, who at one point manages to dance the Black Bottom, and after a number of amusing adventures (in which MacLean barely avoids decapitation), the thief finally wins her. An offbeat comedy which wears well and delights more with each screening.

d, Edward F. Cline; w, Wade Boteler, Frederic Chapin (based on a story by George Randolph Chester); ph, Jack MacKenzie; set d, Ben Carre.

Comedy **(PR:A MPAA:NR)**

SOIL (SEE: EARTH, 1930, USSR)

SOLD* (1915) 5 reels FP bw

Pauline Frederick, Thomas Holding, Julian L'Estrange, Lowell Sherman, Russell Bassett.

Poor programmer has Frederick trying to get her artist husband out of debt by posing for his more successful rival for a fee of $5,000. When her impoverished spouse hears of this, he rushes to his former friend's studio, starts a fight, and accidentally shoots Frederick. A series of titles uncinematically explain that everything works out in the end, but the picture completely fails to satisfy.

d, Edwin S. Porter, Hugh Ford; w, Ford (based on George Erastov's adaptation of the play "Le Secret" by Henri Bernstein).

Drama **(PR:A MPAA:NR)**

SOLD AT AUCTION* (1917) 5 reels Balboa/Gold Rooster bw

Lois Meredith *(Nan)*, William Conklin *(Richard Stanley)*, Marguerite Nichols *(Helen)*, Frank Mayo *(Hal Norris)*, Charles Dudley *(William Raynor)*, Lucy Blake *(Raynor's Sister)*.

Ugly little programmer has Conklin sending his daughter, Meredith, to live with a cruel foster mother when he learns of his wife's infidelity. In time Conklin becomes quite wealthy and provides the woman with a handsome salary. Meredith, meanwhile, has fallen in love, and to prevent her marriage and the subsequent termination of funds, the foster mother tells the girl that her father is a mulatto. Horrified by this revelation, Meredith runs away and falls into the clutches of a notorious madame who auctions her off at a party attended by a group of drunken, degenerate capitalists. To make the unpleasant film even more so, the highest bidder turns out to be the poor soul's father. But fortunately, the boy she loves arrives just in the nick of time and brings this disturbing film to its conclusion.

d, Sherwood McDonald; w, Daniel Whitcomb.

Drama **(PR:O MPAA:NR)**

SOLDIER AND A MAN, A** (1916, Brit.) 4 reels B&C/Kin-Ex bw

George Keene *(Harold Sinclair)*, Minna Grey *(Rose Melbury)*, A. V. Bramble *(Hubert Walepole)*, Charles Vane *(Gen. Sinclair)*, M. Gray Murray *(David Melbury)*, Arthur Walcott.

British wartime thriller has an English general's son framed as a crooked gambler by a spy, and then enlisting as a private in the army, where he not only saves his father from being captured by the enemy, but his sweetheart as well.

d, Dave Aylott; w, Eliot Stannard (based on a play by Ben Landeck).

Drama/War **(PR:A MPAA:NR)**

SOMEHOW GOOD* (1927, Brit.) 8 reels Film Manufacturing/Pathe bw

Fay Compton *(Rosalind Nightingale)*, Stewart Rome *(Jerry Harrison)*, Dorothy Boyd *(Sally)*, Frank Perfitt *(Dederich)*, Colin Keith-Johnson *(Doctor)*, J. Fisher White *(Old Fossil)*.

Heavy-handed British programmer has a man who suffers from amnesia marrying the woman he earlier spurned after she was attacked in a lowly brothel. Not much to applaud here.

p, John Sloane; d, Jack Raymond; w, Lydia Hayward (based on the novel by William de Morgan).

Drama **(PR:A MPAA:NR)**

SOMETHING TO THINK ABOUT** (1920) 7 reels PAR bw

Elliott Dexter *(David Markley)*, Gloria Swanson *(Ruth Anderson)*, Theodore Roberts *(Luke Anderson)*, Monte Blue *(Jim Dirk)*, Mickey Moore *(Danny)*, Julia Faye *(The Banker's Daughter)*, James Mason *(A Country Masher)*, Togo Yamamoto *(A Servant)*, Theodore Kosloff *(A Clown)*, Claire McDowell *(A Housekeeper)*.

Cecil B. DeMille's first film with a religious theme has Swanson, a blacksmith's daughter, engaged to Dexter, a wealthy cripple, but running away to marry handsome Blue. When Blue is killed on the job, she returns home with child, completely broke, to discover that her father has gone blind and is living in the poorhouse because he's too proud to seek the help of her former fiance. Swanson attempts to commit suicide, but the man who once loved her intervenes and marries her on the condition that the arrangement remain platonic. Years pass, and Swanson grows to love Dexter, but he continues to keep his distance until their housekeeper, a deeply religious woman, conducts a seance which leads to the husband being cured, the father forgiving Swanson, and the marriage finally getting consummated.

d, Cecil B. DeMille; w, Jeanie Macpherson; ph, Alvin Wyckoff, Karl Struss.

Drama **(PR:A MPAA:NR)**

SOMEWHERE IN SONORA*** (1927) 6 reels Charles R. Rogers/FN bw

Ken Maynard *(Bob Bishop)*, Kathleen Collins *(Mary Burton)*, Frank Leigh *(Monte Black)*, Joe Bennett *(Bart Leadley)*, Charles Hill Mailes *(Mexicali Burton)*, Carl Stockdale *(Bob Leadley)*, Yvonne Howell *(Patsy)*, Richard Neill *(Ramón Bistula)*, Ben Corbett *("Sockeye" Kelly)*, Monte Montague *("Kettle Belly" Simpson)*, Tarzan the Horse.

Better-than-average production values for a Maynard picture, and a plot which gives the cowboy star plenty of opportunity to show off his horse Tarzan's trick abilities. It made this western, about a man who saves a pal's son from becoming an outlaw, while at the same time rescuing a pretty young lady from the gang, good entertainment for kids and adults alike.

d, Albert Rogell; sup, Harry J. Brown; w, Marion Jackson (based on the novel *Somewhere South in Sonora* by Will Levington Comfort); ph, Sol Polito.

Western **(PR:A MPAA:NR)**

SOMME, THE*** (1927, Brit.) 8 reels New Era bw

Interesting recreation of the battles fought at the Somme mixes live action with newsreel footage to good effect. There is no attempt to introduce a plot, which makes the picture all the more important as a historical document.

p, Gordon Craig; d, M. A. Wetherell; w, Geoffrey Barkas (based on a story by Boyd Cable.)

Historical/War **(PR:A MPAA:NR)**

SON OF THE SHEIK*** 1/2** (1926) 7 reels Feature/UA bw

Rudolph Valentino *(Ahmed/The Sheik)*, Vilma Banky *(Yasmin)*, George Fawcett *(André)*, Montagu Love *(Ghabah)*, Karl Dane *(Ramadan)*, Bull Montana *(Ali)*, B. Hyman *(Pincher)*, Agnes Ayres *(Diana)*, Charles Requa, William Donovan, Erwin Connelly.

Valentino's last and best film is rather a tongue-in-cheek examination of his own bigger-than-life screen persona, with the actor playing the double role of father and son. Valentino (the son) falls in love with Banky, a beautiful dancer. Later, when he is captured and held for ransom by her roguish father's thieves, Valentino holds the beautiful young woman responsible. He soon escapes, however, and carries the girl off to have his way with her. When the sheik (Valentino) intervenes, and it is discovered that Banky is innocent of betrayal, the young Arab follows her to a cafe where he outswashbuckles the evil ones and dispatches them all to Allah. This fast-paced film has lost none of its charm with the passage of time and proves over and over again that Rudolph Valentino was without question the least understood and most maligned of all of Hollywood's great stars. SON OF THE SHEIK, shot in Yuma, Arizona (where BEAU GESTE would be filmed the following year), shimmers with beautiful landscapes, and the photography of George Barnes extracts from the desert hues of richness and luxury no resident, or tourist, for that matter, has ever seen. It was the picture Valentino hoped would give his career a possible boost after a string of what he believed were unsatisfactory stories. And perhaps it might have. The film is full-blooded and romantic to the nth degree, containing exciting desert chases and climactic rescues, stunts, and wonderful fights. In any event, it is revived constantly in both movie houses and on TV, the quintessential piece of popular entertainment.

p, John W. Considine, Jr.; d, George Fitzmaurice; w, Frances Marion, Fred De Gresac (based on the novel *The Sons of the Sheik* by Edith Maude Hull); t, George Marion, Jr.; ph, George Barnes; art d, William Cameron Menzies.

Adventure **Cas.** **(PR:A MPAA:NR)**

SON OF THE WOLF, THE** (1922) 5 reels R-C bw

Wheeler Oakman *(Scruff Mackenzie)*, Edith Roberts *(Chook-Ra)*, Sam Allen *(Father Roubeau)*, Ashley Cooper *(Ben Harrington)*, Fred Kohler *(Malemute Kid)*, Thomas Jefferson *(Chief Thling Tinner)*, Fred Stanton *(The Bear)*, Arthur Jasmine *(The Fox)*, William Eagle Eye *(Shaman)*.

Fair North Woods drama has Oakman falling in love with an Indian girl (Roberts). The priest who is her ward informs him that he must wait for the arrival of Roberts' real father before permission for marriage can be granted. In the meantime, Oakman goes off to town to purchase some gifts for his intended, and falls under the spell of a dance hall girl. Deeply hurt, Roberts secretly takes dancing lessons and manages to win him back at the annual ball, only to lose him again when her father shows up and drags her off to live with her own people. Oakman follows them to the Indian lands, however, and fights an epic battle with the brave to whom she has been promised. He kills the warrior, claims Roberts for his very own, and brings her back with him to be married.

d, Norman Dawn; w, W. Heywood (based on the story by Jack London).

Drama **(PR:A MPAA:NR)**

SONG OF HATE, THE*½** (1915) 6 reels FOX bw

Betty Nansen *(Flora Tosca)*, Arthur Hoops *(Baron Scarpia)*, Dorothy Bernard, Claire Whitney.

One suspects that the great Irish-born director, Ingram, who wrote the screenplay for this beautifully produced motion picture version of "La Tosca," may have had a little something to do with the direction of this film, as much of it certainly bears the stamp of his genius.

d, J. Gordon Edwards; w, Rex Ingram (based on the play "La Tosca" by Victorien Sardou).

Drama **(PR:A MPAA:NR)**

SONG OF LIFE, THE** (1922) 7 reels Louis B. Mayer/AFN bw

Gaston Glass *(David Tilden)*, Grace Darmond *(Aline Tilden)*, Georgia Woodthorpe *(Mary Tilden)*, Richard Headrick *(Neighbor's Boy)*, Arthur Stuart Hull *(District Attorney)*, Wedgewood Nowell *(Richard Henderson)*, Edward Peil *(Amos Tilden)*, Fred Kelsey *(Police Inspector)*, Claude Payton *(Central Office Man)*.

No longer able to bear the drudgery of marriage to a railroad foreman and their life in the desert, Woodthorpe deserts her husband and child and moves to the city. She gets a job washing dishes and continues there for the next 25 years until one day she gives up entirely on life and attempts suicide. A young writer, Glass, saves her just in time and takes her into his home to relieve his wife from household duties so that she may resume her singing career. Glass later discovers his wife is having an affair and he shoots her lover. In the meantime, Woodthorpe has since discovered that Glass is her son, but does not disclose this to him until she finds out about the murder. Both are implicated until the good news comes that the man shot has survived the bullet. In the end, of course, she and her husband and son are reunited as a family.

d, John M. Stahl; w, Bess Meredyth (based on a story by Frances Irene Reels); ph, Ernest Palmer.

Drama **(PR:A MPAA:NR)**

SONG OF LOVE, THE*** (1923) 8 reels Norma Talmadge/AFN bw

Norma Talmadge *(Noorma-hal)*, Joseph Schildkraut *(Raymon Valverde)*, Arthur Edmund Carew *(Ramlika)*, Laurence Wheat *(Dick Jones)*, Maude Wayne *(Maureen Desmard)*, Earl Schenck *(Commissionaire Desmard)*, Hector V. Sarno *(Chandra-lal)*, Albert Prisco *(Chamba)*, Mario Carillo *(Capt. Fregonne)*, James Cooley *(Dr. Humbert)*.

This desert drama allowed Talmadge the opportunity to perform a rather sensational Oriental dance in a scene where she is playing up to the lustful desires of an Arab chieftain (Carew), although she secretly desires French spy Schildkraut. In the end Schildkraut puts down a revolt lead by Carew, who is killed in the process, and Talmadge gets her man. Talmadge is the whole show here and that in itself is enough.

d, Chester Franklin, Frances Marion; w, Marion (based on the novel *Dust of Desire* by Margaret Peterson); ph, Antonio Gaudio.

Adventure **(PR:A MPAA:NR)**

SONG OF THE WAGE SLAVE, THE***
(1915) 5 reels Popular Plays and Players/Metro bw

Edmund Breese *(Ned Lane)*, Helen Martin *(Mildred Hale)*, J. Byrnes *(Andrew Hale)*, Fraunie Fraunholz *(Frank Dawson)*, Albert Vroom *(Edwin Dawson)*, George MacIntyre *(Rev. Francis Pettibone)*, Wallace Scott *(Talck)*, Mabel Wright *(Mrs. Talck)*, Claire Hillier *(Meda)*, Kitty Reichert *(Alice)*, William Morse *(Sims)*.

When Martin is made pregnant by Fraunholz, the paper mill owner's son, the young man offers to do the right thing, but is forbidden by his father who sends the boy away. Unknown to Fraunholz, Martin then marries Breese, a working stiff, who offers to give her child a name. Sometime later, Fraunholz' father dies, and the son writes a letter to Martin's father explaining that he intends to finally return and make things right. Breese, who finds the note, leaves town after scribbling a message to his wife saying he won't stand in the way of her happiness. The poor man then goes through an incredible series of hard times, and shortly thereafter word reaches the mill that he was killed in a gambling argument. It is only then that Martin consents to marry Fraunholz. The report was wrong, however, and Breese returns to become the leader of a labor union which has taken on Fraunholz and his capitalists. This of course places Martin in an awkward situation, which is resolved when Breese sacrifices his life to save Fraunholz from a bomb planted in mill headquarters by an overzealous supporter. Breese' gallant death is not completely in vain, since the gesture causes Fraunholz to look at the workers' side, and adjustments are soon made to benefit them.

d, Herbert Clache; w, Aaron Hoffman (based on a poem by Robert W. Service).

Drama **(PR:C MPAA:NR)**

SONNY*½** (1922) 7 reels INSP/AFN bw

Richard Barthelmess *(Sonny/Charles Crosby/Joe)*, Margaret Seddon *(Mrs. Crosby)*, Pauline Garon *(Florence Crosby)*, Lucy Fox *(Madge Craig)*, Herbert Grimwood *(Harper Craig)*, Patterson Dial *(Alicia)*, Fred Nicholls *(Summers)*, James Terbell *(James)*, Margaret Elizabeth Falconer, Virginia Magee *(Crosby Twins)*.

The teaming of Barthelmess and director King help to overcome the somewhat hokey aspects of this story in which Barthelmess plays look-alike Army buddies (Sonny, a rich fellow with a blind mother, and Joe, a pool hall operator) who enter into a pact moments before one dies of a gunshot. The two agree that Joe should impersonate his pal in order to spare the feelings of the sightless mother. He manages to pull it off, too, in spite of the fact that he's fallen for his friend's kid sister, until the mother "sees" the truth in a dream and truly welcomes the good-hearted young man to become part of her family.

p&d, Henry King; w, Frances Marion, King (based on the play by George V. Hobart, Raymond Hubbell); ph, Henry Cronjager; ed, Duncan Mansfield; art d, Charles Osborne Seessel.

Drama **(PR:A MPAA:NR)**

SONORA KID, THE*** (1927) 5 reels R-C/FBO bw

Tom Tyler *(Tom MacReady)*, Peggy Montgomery *(Phyllis Butterworth)*, Billie Bennett *(Aunt Marie)*, Mark Hamilton *(Chuck Saunders)*, Jack Richardson *(Arthur Butterworth)*, Ethan Laidlaw *(Tough Ryder)*, Bruce Gordon *(James Poindexter)*, Barney Furey *(Doc Knight)*, Vic Allen *(Sheriff)*, Beans, a Dog.

Tyler saves Montgomery, the daughter of the rancher who fired him, from the clutches of the man her father favored. After exposing the potential son-in-law for the rat he really is, Tyler is given his job back, as well as the hand of the pretty girl. Nice little western with some well-executed comic touches.windshield

d, Robert De Lacy; w, Percy Heath, J. G. Hawks (based on the story "A Knight of the Range" by William Wallace Cook); ph, Nick Musuraca.

Western **(PR:A MPAA:NR)**

SORROWS OF SATAN*** (1926) 9 reels FP/PAR bw

Adolphe Menjou *(Prince Lucio de Rimanez)*, Ricardo Cortez *(Geoffrey Tempest)*, Lya De Putti *(Princess Olga)*, Carol Dempster *(Mavis Claire)*, Ivan Lebedeff *(Amiel)*, Marcia Harris *(The Landlady)*, Lawrence D'Orsay *(Lord Elton)*, Nellie Savage *(Dancing Girl)*, Dorothy Hughes *(Mavis' Chum)*, Josephine Dunn, Dorothy Nourse, Jeanne Morgan, Raymond Griffith, Owen Nares.

Cecil B. De Mille was slated to direct this picture, but when he struck out on his own, Paramount assigned the property to Griffith, who hated the popular novel on which it was based. None-the-less, the father of American cinema—armed with a number of pre-production changes—set out to do his best. The story has to do with a couple of struggling London writers, Dempster and Cortez, who love each other and live in the same boarding house. When his poverty and constant publisher rejections finally drive him to the point of desperation, Cortez curses God. It is then that Satan (Menjou), in the guise of a suave prince, appears to inform the writer that he has inherited a fortune, which will be his only if he places himself in the nobleman's hands. Cortez is then introduced to London society, where his constant companion is an earl (D'Orsay) and his Russian niece, a princess (sensously played by De Putti). Before long, Menjou commands the writer to marry De Putti, and although he still loves Dempster, his greed wins out and he obeys the Devil's decree. Soon he realizes that De Putti married him for his money—and to be near Menjou, whom she is obsessed with. Cortez leaves the fortune hunter, who kills herself, and returns to the woman he has never stopped loving—but not before Menjou reveals his true, satanic self. The film ends with the lovers reunited and the Devil driven from their presence because of the lady's unswerving faith in God. Over the years, this film has been the subject of considerable criticism. Actually many of the scenes are brilliant (especially when Satan pursues Cortez in the form of a shadowy bat, and the prologue which depicts Lucifer's ejection from heaven). And it was this picture, Dempster's last, which proved once and for all that she *can* act.

d, D. W. Griffith; w, Forrest Halsey, John Russell, George Hull (based on the novel *The Sorrows of Satan; or the Strange Experience of One Geoffrey Tempest, Millionaire* by Marie Corelli); t, Julian Johnson; ph, Harry Fischbeck, Arthur De Titta; ed, Johnson; art d, Charles Kirk.

Drama **(PR:A MPAA:NR)**

SO'S YOUR OLD MAN* 1/2** (1926) 7 reels FP/PAR bw

W. C. Fields *(Samuel Bisbee)*, Alice Joyce *(Princess Lescaboura)*, Charles Rogers *(Kenneth Murchison)*, Kittens Reichert *(Alice Bisbee)*, Marcia Harris *(Mrs. Bisbee)*, Julia Ralph *(Mrs. Murchison)*, Frank Montgomery *(Jeff)*, Jerry Sinclair *(Al)*, Charles Beyer *(Prince Lescaboura)*, William "Shorty" Blanche *(Caddy)*.

Superior Fields comedy, deftly directed by La Cava, has the comedian playing the would-be inventor of a break-proof automobile windshield glass, who, of course, enjoys his booze. When the wealthy future mother-in-law of his daughter Reichert visits their ramshackled home for the first time, Fields, who has had more than a few, appears and ruins it for the girl. Determined to make amends, he sets off for Washington to demonstrate his invention before a convention of car manufacturers, but his machine is moved while he's in his hotel, and Fields performs his demonstration on another. The result is disastrous and while returning home on the train, the poor devil decides to end his life by taking poison. His bottle is broken, however, and when the train makes a sudden lurch, Fields is hurled into the compartment of a Spanish princess, Joyce, whom the comedian also believes is plotting self-destruction because of the iodine bottle in front of her. The lady does not disclose her royal background, and is quite moved by his attempt to disuade her from the act through the elaborate use of pantomime. Also on the train, however, are two of the town's biggest gossips, and within minutes after his return word has spread far and wide about his "adventure" in the compartment. Afraid to return home, Fields goes on a three day binge. The princess, in the meantime, arranges to visit his home town. This, of course, is the greatest moment in that community's history and the society folk pull out all of the stops to welcome her. So when the lady of the blood asks to see her very good friend, Fields is not only welcomed into their company, but also invited to whack the first golf ball at the new country club (La Cava wisely encouraged his star to use a number of his tried-and-true stage bits, including this famous golf routine). Then, to make the ending completely joyous, the chairman of the auto manufacturer's association shows up to tell the delighted comic that the real car had been found and tested, and that he was making an offer of $1 million for the right to use his invention.

p&d, Gregory La Cava; w, J. Clarkson Miller, Howard Emmett Rogers, Tom J. Geraghty (based on the story "Mr. Bisbee's Princess" by Julian Leonard Street); t, Julian Johnson; ph, George Webber; ed, Johnson; art d, John Held, Jr.

Comedy **(PR:A MPAA:NR)**

SOUL MATES* 1/2 (1925) 6 reels MGM bw

Aileen Pringle *(Velma)*, Edmund Lowe *(Lord Tancred)*, Phillips Smalley *(Markrute)*, Antonio D'Algy *(Velma's Brother)*, Edythe Chapman *(Tancred's Mother)*, Mary Hawes *(Velma's Maid)*, Catherine Bennett *(Dolly)*, Lucien Littlefield *(Stevens)*, Ned Sparks *(Tancred's Chauffeur)*.

Boring story, adapted from Elinor Glyn's 1911 novel, has Pringle refusing to marry the nobleman her uncle, Smalley, has selected for her as a means of paying off the mortgage on their estate. Instead she falls in love with Lowe, unaware that he is the very same man her uncle had in mind. Pringle later weds Lowe, but believing he has only married her to fulfill her uncle's plan, it is a marriage "in name only." When she later discovers that Lowe paid off the mortgage to Smalley's home *before* the wedding, she realizes he really loves her and their arrangement is consummated .

d, Jack Conway; w, Carey Wilson (based on the novel *The Reason Why* by Elinor Glyn); t, Joe Farnham; ph, Oliver Marsh; ed, James McKay; set d, Cedric Gibbons, James Basevi.

Drama **(PR:A MPAA:NR)**

SOUL OF BROADWAY, THE*** (1915) 5 reels FOX bw (AKA: SOUL OF BROADWAY)

Valeska Suratt *(Grace Leonard)*, William E. Shay, George Middleton, Jane Lee, Gertrude Berkeley, Sheridan Block, Mabel Allen.

Vaudeville star Suratt was hired by Fox to become their backup vamp to Theda Bara, and she made a good one. In this Brenon-directed feature, the sensuous lady seduces a young man while being kept by an older millionaire. The young fellow goes to prison when he accidentally shoots her, and three years later Suratt makes a love slave of the lad's father-in-law, shortly after the boy's release and marriage. She also murders her original sugar daddy, threatens to expose her former boy friend's prison background, performs her popular variety act on the screen, and dies after a well-played insanity scene.

d&w, Herbert Brenon; ph, Philip Rosen.

Drama **(PR:A MPAA:NR)**

SOUL OF THE BEAST*** (1923) 5 reels THI/Metro bw

Madge Bellamy *(Ruth Lorrimore)*, Oscar the Elephant, Cullen Landis *(Paul Nadeau)*, Noah Beery *(Caesar Durand)*, Vola Vale *(Jacqueline)*, Bert Sprotte *(Silas Hamm)*, Harry Rattenberry *(Père Boussut)*, Carrie Clark Ward *(Mrs. Boussut)*, Lincoln Stedman *(Henri)*, Larry Steers *(Policeman)*, Vernon Dent *(The Boob)*.

Bellamy is abused by her circus-owner stepfather, who forces her to play the role of a wild woman, wearing horns and eating raw meat. During a big-top fire, her elephant friend, Oscar, bends the bars and carries Bellamy off and she escapes to the Canadian woods. There she meets and marries Landis, a crippled musician, but not before Oscar mightily disposes of all those deserving his wrath.

d, John Griffith Wray; w, Ralph H. Dixon (based on a story by C. Gardner Sullivan); ph, Henry Sharp.

Drama **(PR:A MPAA:NR)**

SOUL OF YOUTH, THE*** (1920) 5 reels REA bw

Lewis Sargent *(The Boy)*, Ernest Butterworth *(Mike)*, Clyde Fillmore *(Mr. Hamilton)*, Grace Morse *(Mrs. Hamilton)*, Lila Lee *(Vera Hamilton)*, William Collier, Jr. *(Dick Armstrong)*, Elizabeth Janes *(Ruth Hamilton)*, Claude Peyton *(Pete Moran)*, Betty Schade *(Maggie)*, Fred Huntley *(Mr. Hodge)*, Sylvia Ashton *(Mrs. Hodge)*, Russ Powell *(Patrolman Jones)*, Judge Ben Lindsey *(Himself)*, Mrs. Ben Lindsey *(Herself)*, Jane Keckley *(Matron)*, Eunice Moore *(Cook)*, Barbara Gurney *(Baby's Mother)*.

Ben Lindsey, a Denver judge famous for his work with wayward children, appears as himself in this well-directed and acted story of a kid from the streets who is arrested, sent to children's court, and given a second chance in life.

d, William Desmond Taylor; w, Julia Crawford Ivers; ph, J. C. Van Trees.

Drama **(PR:A MPAA:NR)**

SOULS AFLAME*** (1928) 7 reels Furst Wells/FD bw

Gardner James, Grace Lord, Buddy Barton, Raymond Wells, Edward Lackey, Gael Kelton.

On-location filming in the Ozarks, plus a cast of native mountain folk, give this well-made picture an almost documentary feeling. The story deals with two feuding families who have been fighting for years over the murder of a member of one of them. In the end the guilty family is wiped out after a blazing battle which finally brings peace to the land.

p, James Ormont; d&w, Raymond Wells; t, Jack Kelly; ph, Jack Fuqua; ed, Earl Turner.

Drama **(PR:A MPAA:NR)**

SOULS FOR SALE* 1/2** (1923) 8 reels Goldwyn bw

Eleanor Boardman *(Remember Steddon)*, Mae Busch *(Robina Teele)*, Barbara La Marr *(Leva Lemaire)*, Richard Dix *(Frank Claymore)*, Frank Mayo *(Tom Holby)*, Lew Cody *(Owen Scudder)*, Arthur Hoyt *(Jimmy Leland)*, David Imboden *(Caxton)*, Roy Atwell *(Arthur Tirrey)*, William Orlamond *(Lord Fryingham)*, Forrest Robinson *(Rev. John Steddon)*, Edith Yorke *(Mrs. Steddon)*, Dale Fuller *(Abigail Tweedy)*, Snitz Edwards *(Hank Kale)*, Jack Richardson *(Motion Picture Heavy)*, Aileen Pringle *(Lady Jane)*, Eve Southern *(Velma Slade)*, May Milloy *(Mrs. Sturges)*, Sylvia Ashton *(Mrs. Kale)*, Margaret Bourne *(Leva Lemaire's Mother)*, Fred Kelsey *(Quinn)*, Jed Prouty *(Magnus)*, Yale Boss *(Prop Man)*, William Haines *(Pinkey)*, George Morgan *(Spofford)*, Auld Thomas *(Assistant Cameraman)*, Leo Willis *(Electrician)*, Walter Perry *(Grip)*, Sam Damen *(Violin Player)*, R. H. Johnson *(Melodeon Player)*, Rush Hughes *(2nd Cameraman)*, L. J. O'Connor *(Doyle)*, Charles Murphy *(Boss Canvasman)*, Hugo Ballin, Mabel Ballin, T. Roy Barnes, Barbara Bedford, Hobart Bosworth, Charles Chaplin, Chester Conklin, William H. Crane, Elliott Dexter, Robert Edeson, Claude Gillingwater, Dagmar Godowsky, Raymond Griffith, Elaine Hammerstein, Jean Haskell, K. C. B., Alice Lake, Bessie Love, June Mathis, Patsy Ruth Miller, Marshall Neilan, Fred Niblo, Anna Q. Nilsson, ZaSu Pitts, John Sainpolis, Milton Sills, Anita Stewart, Erich von Stroheim, Blanche Sweet, Florence Vidor, King Vidor, Johnny Walker, George Walsh, Kathlyn Williams, Claire Windsor.

SOULS FOR SALE gave not only a fascinating inside look at the movie business, but positive propaganda for an industry which had been hit hard by a number of scandals. Boardman plays a girl escaping from the husband she mistrusts while the two are at a railroad desert watering stop. In time she's rescued by a movie company on location and taken back to Hollywood by actor Mayo and director Dix. Her beauty and spunk would make the girl a potential natural for pictures, but she refuses her protector's invitation to take a screen test because of the negative things she's heard about the film colony. To open her eyes, Boardman's friends take her on a tour of the various studios (a plot development which opens the door to feature many real-life actors, writers, and directors in cameo appearances, like Erich von Stroheim, shown actually directing his masterpiece GREED). Boardman is impressed by what she sees and decides to give acting a try. After much effort the young lady makes the grade and eventually becomes a star. It's then that her husband—who it turns out makes a living marrying women for their money and then murdering them—shows up to get his piece of the pie. At picture's end the rotter is killed by a studio wind machine during a fight with Dix, and the actress decides to marry her hero.

p,d&w, Rupert Hughes; ph, John Mescall.

Drama **(PR:A MPAA:NR)**

SOUTH OF NORTHERN LIGHTS** (1922) 5 reels William Steiner bw

Neal Hart *(Jack Hampton)*, James McLaughlin *(Cpl. McAllister)*, Ben Corbett *(Chick Rawlins)*, Hazel Deane *(Jane Wilson)*.

Hart plays a cowboy who slips across the Canadian border after being framed by a gang of crooks trying to steal his land for its gold. He is chased by the Mounties, a U.S. sheriff, as well as pretty Canadian spy Deane. In the end Hart manages to escape the men, rescue Deane and wring a confession from the real killer just before he dies.

d&w, Neal Hart; ph, William Steiner, Jr., Jacob A. Badaracco.

Adventure **(PR:A MPAA:NR)**

SOUTH OF SUVA*** (1922) 5 reels REA/PAR bw

Mary Miles Minter *(Phyllis Latimer)*, Winifred Bryson *(Pauline Leonard)*, Walter Long *(Sydney Latimer)*, John Bowers *(John Webster)*, Roy Atwell *(Marmaduke Grubb)*, Fred Kelsey *(Karl Swartz)*, Lawrence Steers *(Alfred Bowman)*.

Entertaining adventure has Minter sailing to the Fiji Islands to rejoin her husband and finds him in a drunken stupor with a harem of native girls swarming around him. Repulsed, she escapes to another island and passes herself off as the ward that Bowers is waiting to meet. Later Minter's husband abducts her and turns her over to his savages to be used for a human sacrifice. But Bowers and the police arrive in time, and the rotter is killed. When Bowers finally realizes Minter's true identity, he proposes and she accepts.

d, Frank Urson; w, Fred Myton (based on a story by Ewart Adamson); ph, Allen Davey.

Adventure **(PR:A MPAA:NR)**

SOUTH SEA LOVE* (1923) 5 reels FOX bw

Shirley Mason *(Dolores Medina)*, J. Frank Glendon *(Gerald Wilton)*, Francis McDonald *(Manuel Salarno)*, Lillian Nicholson *(Maria)*, Charles A. Sellon *(Captain)*, Fred Lancaster *(Innkeeper)*, Robert Conville *(Stubbs)*.

South Seas potboiler has Mason falling in love with Glendon, the man who became her guardian upon her father's death, and then becoming disillusioned when she discovers that he's married. Mason runs away to become a dancer in one of those steamy nightclubs and must fight off the libidinous overtures of her boss. She then saves Glendon from a mob who is horsewhipping him, and learning he is now a widower, commits herself to him for life.

d, David Soloman; w, Harrison Josephs (based on the story "With the Tide" by Frederick and Fanny Hatton).

Adventure **(PR:A MPAA:NR)**

SOUTHERN LOVE (SEE: WOMAN'S SECRET, A, 1924, Brit.)

SPARROWS****** (1926) 9 reels Mary Pickford/UA bw

Mary Pickford *(Mama Mollie)*, Gustav von Seyffertitz *(Grimes)*, Roy Stewart *(Richard Wayne)*, Mary Louise Miller *(Doris Wayne)*, Charlotte Mineau *(Mrs. Grimes)*, Spec O'Donnell *(Ambrose Grimes)*, Lloyd Whitlock *(Bailey)*, A. L. Schaeffer *(His Confederate)*, Mark Hamilton *(Hog Buyer)*, Monty O'Grady *(Splutters)*, Muriel McCormac, Billy "Red" Jones, Cammilla Johnson, Mary McLane, Billy Butts, Jack Lavine, Florence Rogan, Seesel Ann Johnson, Sylvia Bernard *(The Sparrows)*.

This wonderful picture opens with a landscape setting (actually a brilliantly crafted miniature) so loathesome and forbidding that one feels uneasy just at the sight of it. It is a swampland with twisted trees growing out of its muddy soil like so many fingers reaching up out of Hades. And then the opening title explains what our eyes have questioned. "The Devil's share in the world's creation was a Southern swampland—a masterpiece of horror. And the Lord, appreciating a good job, let it stand." Then the twisted figure of a menacing creature enters the picture and makes his way along the winding trail which leads to a farmhouse, and a second title dissolves in, "Then the Devil went himself one better and had Mr. Grimes live in the swamp." At this point we are shown Grimes, played by the completely unhuman, totally debased, probably inbred, monsterous appearing, Gustav von Seyffertitz (one of the most abominable villains in the movies). Grimes runs a baby farm, a place where mothers who can't afford to raise their children send them to be well cared for and educated. Whenever possible, they also send little gifts, and on this occasion a doll has been included with the mail he picks up as he reaches the gate to the stockade wall. He pockets the money which came in the envelope and then crushes the doll with one hand, tosses it into the quicksand, and smirks as it slowly bubbles and sinks into the quagmire. In contrast we are shown Pickford, who as the eldest and leader-protector of the children (they call her Mama Molly) is attempting to fly a homemade kite out of the compound, with a note attached begging for help. The kite crashes and the children begin to wonder if perhaps they are not the "Sparrows" God forgot. Life on the farm is terribly hard on the children as they work long hours in the fields and are fed a diet of potatoes. But there are a couple of scenes in this film which possess great beauty (and prove emphatically what a truly underrated director William Beaudine is). The first comes when one of the boys, O'Grady, fails to get back to the barn where the kids are billeted, and is discovered by a hog farmer who is there to do a little business with Von Seyffertitz. When he's spotted, the men make a deal and the child is sold. As the wagon slowly pulls out, O'Grady, putting up a brave front when they pass the barn, tries to smile, and limply waves goodbye. And through the cracks in the wall of the barn, one hand, followed by another and then another, juts out, like so many birds' wings, to bid farewell to their departing friend. In another scene, Pickford is holding a dying baby in her lap when she falls asleep. At that point, the figure of Christ steps in from the field beyond the building and claims the soul of the child. The Lord then walks away and Mary wakes up to discover the cold, lifeless body in her arms. But in a moment, beautifully underplayed, she merely looks up and nods her head, indicating that she understands. The villain has a stepson (Spec O'Donnell) who is a chip off the old block, and after they accept the kidnaped child of a millionaire and the cops look like they might be moving in, O'Donnell brags to Pickford that his father is going to probably deep six the kid that night. It's then that Pickford and the children plan their escape. This is accomplished by throwing bales of hay and boxes on the quicksand which surrounds their barn and then making their way over these and through the alligator-infested swamp, in a tension-filled collection of scenes. The flight takes up almost the entire second part of the film, and has rarely been equaled for thrills and suspense. There are a number of comic moments in this picture, and of course Von Seyffertitz gets his, in the very quicksand which earlier served his evil purpose. And there is a happy ending, which, though cleverly constructed, some have found a bit too convenient. But this is a Mary Pickford movie. There should have been enough horror and depression earlier in the film to satisfy even the most ardent advocates of directors like Sam Peckinpah and Brian De Palma. But what this picture exudes, and what the followers of those latter-day filmmakers should understand, is that there is more to the motion picture experience then basking in blood, pain, and horror—and among those things are love and kindness and yes, even an occasional—happy ending.

d, William Beaudine; w, C. Gardner Sullivan (based on a story by Winifred Dunn); t, George Marion, Jr.; ph, Charles Rosher, Karl Struss, Hal Mohr; art d, Harry Oliver.

Drama/Horror **Cas.** **(PR:C MPAA:NR)**

SPAWN OF THE DESERT* (1923) 5 reels Berwilla/Arrow bw

William Fairbanks *(Duke Steele)*, Florence Gilbert *(Nola "Luck" Sleed)*, Dempsey Tabler *(Silver Sleed)*, Al Hart *(Sam Le Saint)*.

Lower end of the spectrum western has Fairbanks setting out to help an old man who saved his life locate the hombre who ran off with his wife and child years before. Of course the villain, Tabler, turns out to be the owner of the town saloon, whom Fairbanks takes to the cleaners in a poker game, then kills in a fair fight, and reunites father and daughter.

p&d, Ben Wilson; w, Daniel F. Whitcomb (based on the story by W. C. Tuttle).

Western **(PR:A MPAA:NR)**

SPECIAL DELIVERY*½ (1927) 6 reels FP/PAR bw

Eddie Cantor *(Eddie)*, Jobyna Ralston *(Madge)*, William Powell *(Harold Jones)*, Donald Keith *(Harrigan)*, Jack Dougherty *(Flannigan)*, Victor Potel *(Nip)*, Paul Kelly *(Tuck)*, Mary Carr *(The Mother)*.

Disjointed plot, dated gags, and a disappointing performance by Cantor, all contribute to the failure of this comedy about a boobish mailman who exposes a crooked scheme and wins the girl of his dreams because of it. Unfortunately, Roscoe "Fatty" Arbuckle, who directed this film under the pseudonym of William Goodrich (following his blacklisting after the scandalous manslaughter trial in 1921) failed to instill the sense of comic genious which had served theater-goers of the world so well before Hollywood decided to crucify him.

p, B. P. Schulberg; d, William Goodrich; w, John Goodrich (based on a story by Eddie Cantor); t, George Marion, Jr.; ph, Henry Hallenberger.

Comedy **(PR:A MPAA:NR)**

SPEED COP*½ (1926) 5 reels Duke Worne/RAY bw

Billy Sullivan *(The Speed Cop)*, Rose Blossom *(The Girl)*, Francis Ford *(The Gentleman Crook)*.

Speed cop Sullivan gives a ticket to Blossom, a judge's daughter, and the pretty young lady falls for him at first sight. Later she arranges a banquet to which the officer is summoned in such a manner that he believes he's to be fired. But no sooner is the joke revealed, than Sullivan spots society crook Ford, makes the arrest, and gladly accepts the love of his hostess.

d, Duke Worn; w, Grover Jones; ph, Ernest Smith.

Adventure **(PR:A MPAA:NR)**

SPEED CRAZED*½ (1926) 5 reels Duke Worne/RAY bw

Billy Sullivan *(Billy Meeks)*, Andrée Tourneur *(Eloise Harfer)*, Joseph W. Girard *(Maclyn Harfer)*, Harry Maynard *(Mr. Payton)*, Albert J. Smith *(Dave Marker)*.

Sullivan is abducted by a gang of crooks and forced to drive the getaway car used in a holdup. The leader gets away, but Sullivan is captured and sent to jail. He later escapes, hops a freight, and ends up in a town where he lands a job driving a kindly old man's racing car. The gangster who originally kidnaped him does so again because he has big money bet against the elderly gent's machine. Sullivan once again manages to free himself and makes it to the big race (mostly made up of stock newsreel footage) in time to win the contest, see to it that the villain is arrested, and steal the heart of his boss' daughter.

d, Duke Worne; w, Grover Jones (based on a story by Suzanne Avery); ph, King Grey.

Adventure **(PR:A MPAA:NR)**

SPEED GIRL, THE zero (1921) 5 reels REA/PAR bw

Bebe Daniels *(Betty Lee)*, Theodore von Eltz *(Tom Manley)*, Frank Elliott *(Carl D'Arcy)*, Walter Hiers *(Soapy Taylor)*, Norris Johnson *(Hilda)*, Truly Shattuck *(Mrs. Lee)*, William Courtright *(Judge Ketcham)*, Barbara Maier *(Little Girl)*.

Inept and confusing motion picture, inspired by the tremendous publicity Daniels received in real life when she was arrested for speeding and sentenced to several days in jail. The film, in which a movie star experiences a similar fate, has so many disjointed plot lines that it's almost impossible to synopsize. An exploitation completely unworthy of Daniels' considerable gifts, with little to redeem it except the star herself.

d, Maurice Campbell; w, Douglas Doty (based on a story by Elmer Harris); ph, H. Kinley Martin.

Comedy **(PR:A MPAA:NR)**

SPEED KING*** (1923) 5 reels Phil Goldstone bw

Richard Talmadge *(Jimmy Martin/King Charles)*, Virginia Warwick *(Princess Margaret)*, Mark Fenton *(Gen. Mendell)*, Harry Van Meter *(Rodolph D'Henri)*.

Talmadge pays a motorcycle driver who visits the Kingdom of Mandavia for a competition and is talked into impersonating the king by a villain who desires to take over. He soon falls in love with Warwick, the princess of Alvernia, and quickly discovers the truth. From this point on Talmadge leaps, bounds, swings, climbs, flips, and fights until justice is done. Nobody could handle these little entertainments like Talmadge, "The Prince of Pep," who is certainly at his best here.

d, Grover Jones; ph, Arthur Todd.

Adventure **(PR:A MPAA:NR)**

SPEED MAD* (1925) 5 reels Perfection/COL bw

William Fairbanks *(Bill Sanford)*, Edith Roberts *(Betty Hampton)*, Lloyd Whitlock *(Alan Lawton)*, Melbourne MacDowell *(John Sanford)*, John Fox, Jr. *(Freckles Smithers)*, Florence Lee *(Grandma Smithers)*, Charles K. French *(Charles Hampton)*, Buddy the Dog.

Fairbanks, a speed-crazy youth who loves to outrace motorcycle cops, is evicted from his father's house, but finally settles down to win the big $5,000 race. This enables him to save his sweetheart, Roberts', home from foreclosure. He also foils a villain's plot to steal the property and wins back the respect of his father as well.

d, Jay Marchant; w, Dorothy Howell; t, Malcolm Stuart Boylan; ph, George Meehan; ed, Charles J. Hunt.

Drama **(PR:A MPAA:NR)**

SPEEDY* 1/2** (1928) 8 reels Harold Lloyd/PAR bw

Harold Lloyd *(Harold "Speedy" Swift)*, Ann Christy *(Jane Dillon)*, Bert Woodruff *(Pop Dillon)*, Brooks Benedict *(Steven Carter)*, George Herman "Babe" Ruth *(Himself)*, Dan Wolheim *(Motorcycle Cop)*, Byron Douglas *(W. S. Wilton)*, Hank Knight *(Bit)*, Walter Hiers *(The Cook)*, Herbert Evans *(Store Manager)*, Ernie S. Adams *(Baseball Fan)*, Gus Leonard *(Civil War Vet)*, Bobby Dunn, James Dime *(Goons)*, Josephine Crowell *(Lady in a Car)*, James Bradbury, Jr. *(Chauffeur)*, Jack Hill, Sam Lufkin *(Extras)*, King Tut *(A Dog)*.

"Just step right up and call me Speedy!" That line was a running gag in the FRESHMAN (1925), as well as Lloyd's real life nickname. SPEEDY was the comedian's last silent film and the only one shot in New York. It's a funny as well as heartwarming story in which Lloyd plays a baseball-crazy young fellow who falls in love with a pretty young lady (Christy) and ultimately saves her grandfather's business—the last horse-drawn trolly line in the city—from being stolen. Lloyd rallies all of the old-timers in the neighborhood to fight off the goons sent by the traction magnates to disrupt things. And then, in one of his most hair-raising sequences, Lloyd rides the abducted trolly through the streets of the Big Apple, managing to arrive just in time for the daily run. Director Wilde was nominated for an Academy Award for this effort, and Lloyd said farewell to the silent cinema with style. Look for the delightful cameo appearance of baseball great "Babe" Ruth.

d, Ted Wilde; w, John Grey, Lex Neal, Howard Emmett Rogers, Jay Howe; t, Albert De Mond; ph, Walter Lundin; m/l, "Speedy Boy," Ray Klages, Jesse Greer.

Comedy **(PR:A MPAA:NR)**

SPENDTHRIFT, THE** (1915) 6 reels George Kleine bw

Irene Fenwick, Mattie Ferguson, Cyril Keightley, Malcolm Duncan, John Nicholson, Roy Pilcher, Viola Savoy.

Implausible story has a young wife mismanaging the family money to the point that her stockbroker husband is nearly bankrupted. She encounters a former gentleman friend who, with no strings attached, loans her the money to get her spouse back on his feet. But when the broker sees them together, he thinks the worst and orders her out of the house. The poor creature barely survives by working in a sweatshop, but eventually her husband comes to his senses, seeks her out, and there is a happy reconciliation.

d, Walter Edwin; w, (based on the play by Porter Emerson Browne).

Drama **(PR:A MPAA:NR)**

SPIDER, THE** (1916) 5 reels FP bw

Pauline Frederic *(Valerie St. Cyr/Joan Marche)*, Thomas Holding *(Julian St. Saens)*, Frank Losee *(Count Du Poissy)*, Helen Lindroth.

Frederick, playing two roles, tries hard to breathe some life into this acceptable melodrama about a mother who deserts her husband and daughter, flees to Paris, where she becomes mistress to a count, and later finds herself attracted to her daughter's artist boy friend. The daughter, meanwhile, catches the count's eye and is forced to stab him to death when he tries to have his way with her. Realizing that the lovely young girl is actually her flesh and blood, the mother assumes the guilt for her paramour's murder and is guillotined in the end.

d, Robert Vignola; w, William H. Clifford.

Drama **(PR:C MPAA:NR)**

SPIDER AND THE ROSE, THE* 1/2 (1923) 7 reels B. F. Ziedman/Principal bw

Alice Lake *(Paula)*, Richard Headrick *(Don Marcello, as a Child)*, Gaston Glass *(Don Marcello)*, Joseph J. Dowling *(The Governor)*, Robert McKim *(Mendozza)*, Noah Beery *(Maître Renaud)*, Otis Harlan *(The Secretary)*, Frank Campeau *(Don Fernando)*, Andrew Arbuckle *(The Priest)*, Alec Francis *(Good Padre)*, Edwin Stevens *(Bishop Oliveros)*, Louise Fazenda *(Dolores)*.

Less-than-inspiring film about the son of a southern California governor during the days of Mexican rule, who returns home to discover that his father's tyrannical secretary has taken over, and joins the people in overthrowing his cruel regime. Actors McKim and Beery, who appeared in Douglas Fairbanks' original MARK OF ZORRO, must have squirmed while they made this one.

d, John McDermott; w, Gerald C. Duffy; ph, Charles Richardson, Glen MacWilliams.

Adventure **(PR:A MPAA:NR)**

SPIDER WEBS* (1927) 6 reels Artlee bw

Niles Welch *(Bert Grantland)*, Alice Lake *(Flora Benham)*, J. Barney Sherry *(Chester Sanfrew)*, Martin Faust *(Joe Dickson)*, Bert Harvey *(Nick Sinclair)*, Maurice Costello *(Jeffrey Stanton)*, Edna Richmond *(Mrs. Stanton)*.

Some nice location shots of Times Square, Penn Station, Park Avenue, and other New York locations, are about all that can be said in favor of this primitive melodrama about a young woman who is used to obtain incriminating letters and then falsely accused of murder. Fortunately, there is a hero here with the grit to clear her name and nail the real crooks.

d, Wilfred Noy; w, Charles Horan (based on the story "The Fast Pace" by H. G. Logalton); ph, Roy Hunt, Alvin Wyckoff.

Mystery **(PR:A MPAA:NR)**

SPIES**** (1929, Ger.) 5 reels UFA/MGM bw (SPIONE; AKA: THE SPY)

Rudolf Klein-Rogge *(Haghai)*, Gerda Maurus *(Sonia)*, Willy Fritsch *(The Detective, Agent 326)*, Lupu Pick *(Masimoto)*, Fritz Rasp *(Ivan Stepanov)*, Lien Deyers *(Kitty)*, Craighall Sherry *(Burton Jason)*, Julius Falkenstein *(Hotel Manager)*, Georg John *(Train Conductor)*, Paul Rehkopf *(Strotch)*, Paul Horbiger *(Valet)*, Louis Ralph *(Hans Morriera)*, Hermann Valentin, Greta Berger, Hertha von Walther.

The first of two thrillers made by director Lang after his completion of METROPOLIS finds him sailing into safe harbor after that visually astonishing, architecturally amazing *avante garde* film. Lang's first production, also, as an independent, SPIES was made by Fritz Lang-Film after Lang established his own company. It is a thrilling story based on reports of Soviet spy activity in London, and, tightly edited, economically produced, rapid-paced, and exciting in execution, is much preferred by many people over his slower moving productions. With his headquarters in a large European bank, Klein-Rogge directs an international spy ring that specializes in the theft of government documents. Murder, blackmail, and sabotage are used willy-nilly by Klein-Rogge to achieve his nefarious ends, and at his wit's end the head of the secret service assigns his best agent, Agent 326 (Fritsch) to the case, aided by a Russian *emigre*, Maurus, who once worked with Klein-Rogge but has turned into his opponent. Fritsch is successful in trapping the spy but rather than be captured, Klein-Rogge, disguised as a clown, shoots himself on the stage of the music hall to the wild applause of the audience, which believes his death is part of the performance. A "thriller" to its core, SPIES was a melange of work already done in the genre, and Lang pilfered from all he knew. There are chase scenes, secret papers, a smashup of the European Express, and the wonderful finale when the clown shoots himself to roaring applause. Maurus is a fetchingly beautiful European woman and Pick gives an admirable performance as a Japanese envoy.

p&d, Fritz Lang; w, Thea von Harbou, Lang; ph, Fritz Arno Wagner; m, Werner R. Heymann; art d, Otto Hunte, Karl Vollbrecht.

Suspense **Cas.** **(PR:A MPAA:NR)**

SPINDLE OF LIFE, THE 1/2** (1917) 5 reels Butterfly bw

Neva Gerber *(Gladsome)*, Jessie Pratt *(Mrs. Harrison)*, Ed Brady *(Jason)*, Richard La Reno *("Hooky")*, Winter Hall *(James Bradshaw)*, Hayward Mack *(Vincent Bradshaw)*, Ben Wilson *("Alphabet" Carter)*, A. E. Witting, Willard Wayne.

Pleasant little dramatic comedy has Gerber playing an attractive tomboy who spends most of her time with the village fisherman. Meanwhile, the bankrupt manager of her widowed mother's estate plots to win the wealthy girl for his son. But the plan is foiled when Gerber falls in love with and marries a vacationing stockbroker.

d, George Cochrane; w, Karl Coolidge (based on the novel *Gladsome* by Sidney Robinson); ph, Pliny Horne.

Comedy/Drama **(PR:A MPAA:NR)**

SPITE MARRIAGE*** (1929) 9 reels Joseph M. Schenck/MGM bw

Buster Keaton *(Elmer)*, Dorothy Sebastian *(Trilby Drew)*, Edward Earle *(Lionel Denmore)*, Leila Hyams *(Ethyle Norcrosse)*, William Bechtel *(Nussbaum)*, John Byron *(Giovanni Scarzi)*, Hank Mann.

Keaton's last silent film, and his second for MGM, is much better than many have claimed (although not up to his earlier efforts when he had complete autonomy). The story has the comic playing a pants presser who falls in love with a stage actress, Sebastian, and attends her every performance. When the lady is jilted by Earle, her leading man, she marries Keaton out of spite. On their wedding night, Sebastian becomes drunk and passes out. This provides the comedian with one of his greatest bits as he tries every method imaginable to get the lady into bed without waking her up (Keaton would use this routine while playing vaudeville in Europe during the 1950s with his third wife, Eleanor Norris). When he learns the truth about his marriage, the poor fellow leaves and takes a job as a sailor on a rum-running boat, which in the end provides Keaton with the opportunity to save the woman he loves from a gangster (in a fight scene rivaling the one in BATTLING BUTLER, 1926) and actually win her love. There is a marvelous chemistry between Sebastian and the comic (prior to this film all of his leading ladies had been mere props), which may be attributed to the fact that they were involved in a torrid affair at the time. SPITE MARRIAGE may not be Keaton at his best, but since this film was made—with the exception of Chaplin, Hardy, and Laurel—no one's been better when it comes to the execution of sight gags.

d, Edward Sedgwick; sup, Larry Weingarten; w, Richard Schayer, Ernest S. Pagano (based on a story by Lew Lipton); t, Robert Hopkins; ph, Reggie Lanning; ed, Frank Sullivan; art d, Cedric Gibbons.

Comedy **(PR:A MPAA:NR)**

SPITFIRE, THE*** (1924) 7 reels Murray W. Garsson/AEX bw

Betty Blythe *(Jean Bronson)*, Lowell Sherman *(Horace Fleming)*, Elliott Dexter *(Douglas Kenyon)*, Robert Warwick *(Oliver Blair)*, Pauline Garon *(Marcia Walsh)*, Burr McIntosh *(Joshua Carrington)*, Jack Donovan *(Abel Carrington)*, Ray Allen *(Henry Hammil)*.

D. W. Griffith alumnus, Cabanne, keeps a tight rein on this engrossing drama in which Dexter loses his position at his sweetheart's bank when he innocently allows a show girl he "won" at an all night bash to sleep on his couch. After their separation, his fiancee, Blythe, becomes an actress and the young man wins her back when he delivers a terrific beating to Sherman, a theatrical producer who attempts to dishonor her.

d, William Christy Cabanne; w, Raymond S. Harris (based on the novel *Plaster Saints* by Frederick Arnold Kummer); ph, Walter Arthur, Jack Brown.

Drama **(PR:A MPAA:NR)**

SPITFIRE OF SEVILLE, THE 1/2** (1919) 6 reels UNIV bw

Hedda Nova *(Carmelita)*, Thurston Hall *(Kent Staunton)*, Claire Anderson *(Alice Foster)*, Marion Skinner *(Her Mother)*, Carl Stockdale *(Don Salvador)*, Leo Maloney *(Pedro)*, Edgar Allen *(Romero)*, Robert Bray.

Lots of action in this six-reeler set in Mexico which has Nova being pursued by Allen and Maloney, falling in love with Hall and upsetting Anderson, his American lady friend, before finally landing the fellow she wants.

d, George Siegmann; w, Waldemar Young (based on a story by Joseph Franklin Poland); ph, Alfred Gosden.

Adventure/Romance **(PR:A MPAA:NR)**

SPLENDID LIE, THE*** (1922) 6 reels J. G. Pictures/Arrow bw

Grace Davison *(Dorris Delafield)*, Jack Drumier *(David Delafield)*, Noel Tearle *(Crafton Wolcott)*, J. Thornton Baston *(Dean De Witt)*, Mabel Baudine *(Goldie)*, Jere Austin *(James Holden)*, Emily Fitzroy *(Mrs. Wolcott Delafield)*.

Better-than-average programmer has hard-working Davison rewarded with a vacation to Hot Springs, Arkansas, and taking her sickly grandfather along. There she encounters Baston, a married man claiming to be a bachelor, who proposes to her. But Baston's wife discovers them together and has Davison and her grandfather thrown out of the resort. Word of the "scandal" reaches home, causing her to lose her job, but fortunately she meets Austin, who hires her to act as his mother's secretary. Although Baston continues to harass the poor girl, Austin will have no part of it, and proposes marriage himself.

d&w, Charles Horan.

Drama **(PR:A MPAA:NR)**

SPLENDID ROAD, THE* 1/2 (1925) 8 reels Frank Lloyd/FN bw

Anna Q. Nilsson *(Sandra De Hault)*, Robert Frazer *(Stanton Halliday)*, Lionel Barrymore *(Dan Clehollis)*, Edwards Davis *(Banker John Grey)*, Roy Laidlaw *(Capt. Sutter)*, De Witt Jennings *(Capt. Bashford)*, Russell Simpson *(Capt. Lightfoot)*, George Bancroft *(Buck Lockwell)*, Gladys Brockwell *(Satan's Sister)*, Pauline Garon *(Angel Allie)*, Marceline Day *(Lilian Grey)*, Mary Jane Irving *(Hester Gephart)*, Mickey McBan *(Billy Gephart)*, Edward Earle *(Dr. Bidwell)*.

This western about a young woman who adopts three children on her way to the California Gold Rush and then avoids the man she loves for "the sake of his career," never quite gets off the ground. And even the big flood scene, which literally throws the couple together at the end, seems flat. Below Lloyd's usual directorial standard.

d, Frank Lloyd; w, J. G. Hawks (based on the novel by Vingie E. Roe); ph, Norbert F. Brodin.

Western/Drama **(PR:A MPAA:NR)**

SPLENDID SIN, THE ** (1919) 5 reels FOX bw

Madlaine Traverse *(Lady Marion Chatham)*, Charles Clary *(Sir Charles Chatham)*, Jeanne Calhoun *(Gertrude)*, Wheeler Oakman *(Stephen Hartley)*, Elinor Hancock *(The Dowager Lady St. Aubrey)*, George Hackathorne *(The Honorable George Granville)*, Edwin Booth Tilton *(Dr. Kent)*, Ruth Royce.

When her sister has a baby out of wedlock, Traverse, the childless U.S. wife of a British government official stationed abroad, adopts it and passes the infant off as her own. At first the husband is delighted, but then jealousy and suspicions arise, which are of course resolved by the end of the fifth reel.

d, Howard M. Mitchell; w, Dennison Clift (based on a story by E. Forst); ph, Walter Williams.

Drama **(PR:C MPAA:NR)**

SPLITTING THE BREEZE*** (1927) 5 reels R-C/FBO bw

Tom Tyler *(Death Valley Drake)*, Harry Woods *(Dave Matlock)*, Barney Furey *(Rev. Otis Briggs)*, Tom Lingham *(Tom Rand)*, Peggy Montgomery *(Janet Rand)*, Red Lennox *(Red)*, Alfred Heuston *(Hank Robbins)*, Barbara Starr *(Lois Cortez)*.

Good western has Tyler joining saloon owner Woods' gang after he is wrongly accused of shooting the sheriff. Working from the inside, Tyler clears his name, kills Woods in a fight, and claims the love of Montgomery, the lawman's daughter.

d, Robert De Lacey; w, Frank Howard Clark; ph, Nick Musuraca.

Western **(PR:A MPAA:NR)**

SPOILERS, THE** (1914) 9 reels SELIG bw

William Farnum *(Glennister)*, Thomas Santschi *(McNamara)*, Kathlyn Williams *(Cherry Marlotte)*, Bessie Eyton *(Helen Chester)*, Frank Clark *(Dextry)*, Wheeler Oakman *(Broncho Kid)*, Marshall Farnum *(Lawyer Wheaton)*, N. MacGregory *(Judge Stillman)*, W. H. Ryno *(Struve)*, Jack McDonald *(Slap-Jack)*.

The first important filming of the Rex Beach novel about adventure in the gold fields and frontier towns of Alaska deserves its place in history, if for no other reason than its sheer ambition. In 1914, nine reels was a lot of film. But the picture with its muddy, unglamorized look does move along, and there is a feeling of authenticity that all of the later incarnations lost sight of. The fight scene in which it was rumored that Santschi and Farnum went at it for real and nearly killed each other, is, however, most disappointing. Compared to the contemporary work of Ince and Griffith, this production of Colonel Selig's is downright primitive, but it did enthrall the masses and it made him a fortune. Filmgoers today, though, probably have not been able to see the picture, and thus its legends grow without the counterbalancing factor of evidence to corroborate or disprove. The fight scene is a case in point. Though it still packs a wallop, it hardly stands up to fight scenes in today's movies, with their breakaway furniture, doubles, and other points of deception which make belief out of make believe. One of THE SPOILERS biggest virtues, in fact, is just that: everything was low key and unpolished, not stagey, which certainly enhances the excitement of watching the story unroll. For the first colorful adventure given seven reel treatment, this was a surprisingly good production by an almost amateur company, and no doubt set the stage for thousands of brawling adventure films to follow.

d, Colin Campbell; w, Campbell (based on the novel by Rex Beach and the play by Beach, James MacArthur).

Adventure **Cas.** **(PR:A MPAA:NR)**

SPOOK RANCH** (1925) 6 reels UNIV bw

Hoot Gibson *(Bill Bangs)*, Ed Cowles *(George Washington Black)*, Tote Du Crow *(Navarro)*, Helen Ferguson *(Elvira)*, Robert McKim *(Don Ramies)*, Frank Rice *(Sheriff)*.

Typical haunted house antics, this time set out West, has Gibson and his black valet, Cowles, being ordered by a sheriff (after breaking a plate over a Chinese cook's head) to investigate a mysterious "spook ranch." Naturally it turns out to be an outlaw's hideout, and a mineral-rich rancher's daughter is being held captive there. Gibson, in his very best fashion, brings them all under submission, but not until the audience has been treated to an abundance of "feet's git movin'" comedy, broadly supplied by Cowles.

d, Edward Laemmle; w, Raymond L. Schrock (based on a story by Schrock, Edward Sedgwick); ph, Harry Neumann.

Western **(PR:A MPAA:NR)**

SPORT OF KINGS, THE* 1/2 (1921, Brit.) 5 reels I. B. Davidson/Granger bw

Victor McLaglen *(Frank Rosedale)*, Phyllis Shannaw *(Elaine Winter)*, Cyril Percival *(Harry Lawson)*, Douglas Munro *(James Winter)*.

A man finances a wealthy young woman's work amongst the poor by winning the big race on his ex-fiancee's horse. Only the presence of Academy Award winner McLaglen makes this predictable story bearable.

d&w, Arthur Rooke.

Adventure **(PR:A MPAA:NR)**

SPORTING GOODS*** (1928) 6 reels PAR bw

Richard Dix *(Richard Shelby)*, Ford Sterling *(Mr. Jordan)*, Gertrude Olmstead *(Alice Elliott)*, Philip Strange *(Henry Thorpe)*, Myrtle Stedman *(Mrs. Elliott)*, Wade Boteler *(Regan)*, Claude King *(Timothy Stanfield)*, Maude Turner Gordon *(Mrs. Stanfield)*.

Clever direction by St. Clair, snappy titles by Marion, and good performances by everyone involved, make this comedy a winner. Dix is the inventor and sole salesman of the "Elasto-Tweed" golf suit, and while on the road with it, he meets the beautiful Olmstead, who takes him for millionaire King. Not wishing to disappoint her, Dix goes along with the ruse and finds himself registered in a $60-a-day hotel suite. Unfortunately, the good-natured but ambitious lad only has $4 to his name, which he hands out to the bellboys. After a number of very funny complications, involving Sterling, the owner of a department store chain, the suits prove to be a sensation, Dix is made rich, and Olmstead becomes his.

d, Malcolm St. Clair; w, Ray Harris, Tom Crizer; t, George Marion; ph, Edward Cronjager; ed, Otto Levering.

Comedy **(PR:A MPAA:NR)**

SPREADING DAWN, THE* 1/2** (1917) 6 reels Goldwyn bw

Jane Cowl *(Patricia Mercer Vanderpyl)*, Orme Caldara *(Anthony Vanderpyl)*, Harry Springer *(Bentley Vanderpyl)*, Florence Billings *(Mrs. Cornelia LeRoy)*, Henry Stephenson *(LeRoy)*, Alice Chapin *(Mrs. Mercer)*, Helen Blair *(Young Lizzie)*, Cecil Owen *(Col. Lee)*, Mabel Ballin *(Georgina Vanderpyl)*, Edmund Lowe *(Capt. Lewis Nugent)*, Edith McAlpin *(Old Lizzie)*, Charles Hammond, Lettie Ford, Marion Knapp, Antoinette Erwin.

Bitterly disappointed in love, Cowl forbids her niece to marry a young man who is about to leave for France and the war. To make her point, Cowl presents her diary and insists the girl read it. The film flashes back to Civil War days and shows the aunt's husband visiting a married woman with whom his brother has been having an affair. Her husband, thinking the visitor to be the guilty party, aims his pistol and fires a fatal shot, leaving Cowl to assume he was caught committing adultery. For this reason she refuses to accept the existence of romantic love and desperately desires to save her niece from experiencing the pain she has suffered. But the girl discovers a letter the man wrote before dying (which the aunt has never opened), explaining everything and ending with the pledge that he will someday meet her at the "spreading dawn." The joy of reading this is too much for the old woman, and she clutches at her breast, falls across the table, and spiritually joins the only man she ever loved— forever.

d, Larry Trimble; w, (based on a story by Basil King); ph, Philip Rosen.

Drama **(PR:A MPAA:NR)**

SPRINGTIME** (1915) 5 reels Life Photo Film/Alco bw

Florence Nash *(Madeline De Valette)*, William H. Tooker *(Val De Valette)*, Adele Ray *(L'Acadienne)*, Frank Holland *(Raoul De Villette)*, Charles Travis *(Richard*

Steel), E. F. Flannigan *(Father O'Mara)*, Bert Gardner *(Gilbert Steel)*, Edward F. Roseman *(Wolf)*, Warner P. Richmond *(Crawley)*, Sue Balfour *(Marguerite)*, Arim Tooker *(Louise)*.

Director Roskam took his company to New Orleans and St. Augustine to shoot this Tarkington story about a pretty young girl who breaks up with the cousin she was instructed to marry and weds instead the son of the man who had been trying to ruin her father, thus providing a happy ending for all concerned.

d, Edwin Roskam; w, (based on a story by Booth Tarkington).

Drama **(PR:A MPAA:NR)**

SPUDS** (1927) 5 reels Larry Semon/Pathe Exchange bw

Larry Semon *("Spuds")*, Dorothy Dwan *(Madelon)*, Edward Hearn *(Captain/Arthur)*, Kewpie Morgan *(Sergeant)*, Robert Graves *(General)*, Hazel Howell *(Bertha)*, Hugh Fay *(Spy)*.

Semon never made the successful transition to features which comedians Chaplin, Keaton, and Lloyd enjoyed, and the laughs are sparse in this comedy about a doughboy who returns the payroll car his friend had stolen from him by driving it across a battlefield under heavy fire.

d&w, Larry Semon; ph, H. F. Koenekamp, James Brown.

Comedy/War **(PR:A MPAA:NR)**

SQUAW MAN, THE**** (1914) 6 reels LAS bw

Dustin Farnum *(Capt. James Wyngate)*, Winifred Kingston *(Diana, Countess of Kerhill)*, Redwing *(Nat-U-Rich)*, Monroe Salisbury *(Henry, Earl of Kerhill)*, Billy Elmer *(Cash Hawkins)*, Dick La Strange *(Grouchy)*, Foster Knox *(Sir John)*, Joe E. Singleton *(Tabywana)*, Dick La Reno *(Big Bill)*, Fred Montague *(Mr. Petrie)*, Baby de Rue *(Hal)*, Mrs. A. W. Filson *(The Dowager Lady Kerhill)*, Haidee Fuller *(Lady Mabel Wyngate)*, Art Acord, Utahna La Reno.

DeMille faced numerous challenges in making (with Apfel) his first motion picture THE SQUAW MAN. Actually he put his life on the line to see the film through to its conclusion. At one point, while directing the scene where an abandoned schooner burns, 100 sulphur pots had to be ignited for a final explosion. When no one else offered to do the lighting, DeMille himself set about the task. But something went wrong and suddenly there was a great explosion, which sent the director hurtling into the sea. He was dragged out unconscious and suffered minor burns as a result. The next day he was on the set again—this time with the Los Angeles Fire Department on hand—and the scene was shot perfectly. But more trouble was ahead. One morning DeMille discovered a pile of film negatives from THE SQUAW MAN heaped on the floor all trampled on, making it completely unusable. From then on, DeMille slept right in the laboratory with a gun at his side. But the problems did not end there. Near the end of the shooting, DeMille rented a small house in the country. The roads leading to the studio were so bad that the director rode a horse to work. One day a shot rang out, causing his horse to buck dangerously. The same thing occurred in nearly the same spot a few days later. Each time DeMille pulled his gun, but could find no one around. At the same time he was receiving death threats in letters demanding that he quit filming THE SQUAW MAN at once—or else. But DeMille persisted and finally completed his historical—in every sense of the word—motion picture version of the Royle play. It told the story of an English nobleman (Farnum) who takes the blame for a theft in order to protect the woman he loves (Kingston) who is married to the guilty party. Fleeing to America, he makes his way west to Wyoming and incurs the hostility of the local bad man, Elmer. Farnum saves Redwing, a beautiful Indian maiden, from Elmer's lustful clutches, and she in turn saves the Englishman's life and nurses him back to health. Eventually Redwing becomes pregnant by him and when he marries her, Farnum is turned into a social outcast known as "The Squaw Man." Sometime later, Kingston arrives on the scene with the news that her husband confessed to the crime before his death and that Farnum has been made the Earl of Kerhill. In the end Redwing takes her own life to avoid arrest for the murder of Elmer, freeing the Briton to return home with his child and the woman he has always loved. Things did not work out quite so well for DeMille and his associates. When the film opened in New York and Los Angeles, the picture jumped about on the screen so badly that it was totally unwatchable. Sam Goldfish (later known as Goldwyn), one of the film's investors, suggested that they take the negative and a print to "Pop" Lubin, who owned the Lubin Motion Picture Company of Philadelphia, and knew more about the mechanics of the cinema than anyone. The kindly old gentleman checked their materials, determined that sprocket adjustments would solve the problem, and the rest is history. DeMille's first film was a tremendous hit, and he would continue turning them out for the next three decades.

p,d&w, Cecil B. DeMille, Oscar Apfel (based on the play by Edwin Milton Royle); ph, Alfred Gandolfi; ed, Mamie Wagner.

Western **(PR:A MPAA:NR)**

SQUIBS*** (1921, Brit.) 6 reels Welsh-Pearson/JUR bw

Betty Balfour *(Squibs Hopkins)*, Hugh E. Wright *(Sam Hopkins)*, Fred Groves *(PC Charlie Lee)*, Mary Brough *(Mrs. Lee)*, Cronin Wilson *(Bully Dawson)*, Annette Benson *(Ivy Hopkins)*, Ambrose Manning *(Inspector Robert Lee)*, Tom Morriss *(Gus Holly)*, William Matthews *(Peters)*.

In 1921, director Pearson cast the delightful Balfour in the role of a flower girl named Squibs, who overcomes a number of comic complications while carrying on a romance with her policeman boy friend. The movie was such a hit with Balfour's British public that they demanded additional features dealing with the appealing character, and they were granted their wish.

d, George Pearson; w, Pearson, Eliot Stannard (based on a music hall sketch by Clifford Seyler).

Comedy **(PR:A MPAA:NR)**

SQUIBS' HONEYMOON*** (1926, Brit.) 6 reels Welsh-Pearson/GAU bw

Betty Balfour *(Squibs)*, Hugh E. Wright *(Sam Hopkins)*, Fred Groves *(Charlie Lee)*, Frank Stanmore *(Horace Honeybunn)*, Irene Tripod *(Euphemia Fitzbulge)*, Robert Vallis *(Bob)*, Maurice Redmund *(Jean)*.

The emphasis in this Squibs picture is on laughs, with the popular Balfour honeymooning in Paris and then having to disguise herself as a man in order to escape a band of apaches.

d, George Pearson; w, Pearson, Betty Balfour, T. A. Welsh.

Comedy **(PR:A MPAA:NR)**

SQUIBS, MP*** (1923, Brit.) 6 reels Welsh-Pearson/GAU bw

Betty Balfour *(Squibs Hopkins)*, Hugh E. Wright *(Sam Hopkins)*, Fred Groves *(PC Charlie Lee)*, Irene Tripod *(Euphemia Fitzbulge)*, Frank Stanmore *(Horace Honeybunn)*, Odette Myrtil *(Dancer)*.

The delightful Balfour is at her charming best in this movie about a flower girl who runs for Parliament when her sweetheart is accused of taking a bribe. Another in the highly popular Squibs series.

p&d, George Pearson; w, Pearson, Leslie Hiscott, Will Dyson.

Comedy **(PR:A MPAA:NR)**

SQUIBS WINS THE CALCUTTA SWEEP***

(1922, Brit.) 5 reels Welsh-Pearson/JUR bw

Betty Balfour *(Squibs Hopkins)*, Fred Groves *(PC Charlie Lee)*, Hugh E. Wright *(Sam Hopkins)*, Bertram Burleigh *(The Weasel)*, Annette Benson *(Ivy Hopkins)*, Mary Brough *(Mrs. Lee)*, Hal Martin *(Detective Reeve)*, Donald Searle *(Reporter)*, Tom Morris *(Bob)*, Sam Lewis *(Nosey)*.

Squibs Hopkins (Balfour) comes to the rescue again in this entertaining addition to the popular series. This time the flower girl takes her entire family to Paris after winning 60,000 pounds, in order to rescue her sister from her brutish brother-in-law. This Squibs entry was played for thrills more than laughs, but delivered both.

d&w, George Pearson.

Drama **(PR:A MPAA:NR)**

STAGE KISSES** (1927) 6 reels COL bw

Kenneth Harlan *(Donald Hampton)*, Helene Chadwick *(Fay Leslie)*, John Patrick *(Keith Carlin)*, Phillips Smalley *(John Clarke)*, Ethel Wales *(Mrs. John Clarke)*, Frances Raymond *(Mrs. Hampton)*.

Average "women's picture" about a chorus girl, Chadwick, who causes her husband to be disinherited by his wealthy parents when she marries him. Later Chadwick is set up to look like an adultress, but she turns the table on the perpetrator and compromises *him*. The film ends as one would expect, with the young man's family welcoming the little hoofer into their midst.

p, Harry Cohn; d, Albert Kelly; w, Dorothy Howell; ph, Joseph Walker; art d, Robert E. Lee.

Drama **(PR:A MPAA:NR)**

STAGE MADNESS*** (1927) 6 reels FOX bw

Virginia Valli *(Mme. Lamphier)*, Tullio Carminati *(Andrew Marlowe)*, Virginia Bradford *(Dora Anderson)*, Lou Tellegen *(Pierre Doumier)*, Richard Walling *(Jimmy Mason)*, Tyler Brooke *(H. H. Bragg)*, Lillian Knight *(French Maid)*, Bodil Rosing *(Maid)*.

Valli, under Schertzinger's direction, delivers a most moving performance as a mother who yearns for the bright lights and resumes her career as a ballet dancer. Her angry husband abducts their daughter, Bradford, and years later, when Valli is lying close to death, she discovers to her great joy that the dancer who has been hired to replace her is in actuality her daughter.

d, Victor Schertzinger; w, Randall H. Faye (based on a story by Polan Banks); ph, Glen MacWilliams.

Drama **(PR:A MPAA:NR)**

STAIN, THE** (1914) 6 reels ECL bw

Edward Jose, Thurlow Bergen, Virginia Pearson, Eleanor Woodruff, Samuel Ryan, Theodosia De Coppett [Theda Bara].

Unabashed melodrama has a young bank clerk passing the bar examination, embezzling funds, deserting his wife and daughter, and moving to New York where he becomes connected with the political machine and is eventually appointed judge. Years pass and his daughter becomes the secretary and sweetheart of a crusading young attorney. At a trial presided over by the despicable judge, his wife is called upon to appear as a witness and recognizes the man in robes to be the person who deserted her, and denounces him before the entire courtroom. The judge rises to his feet, admits his guilt, clutches his chest, and falls over dead.

d, Frank Powell; w, (based on a novel by Forrest Halsey, Robert H. Davis).

Drama **(PR:A MPAA:NR)**

STAIRS OF SAND** 1/2 (1929) 6 reels PAR bw

Wallace Beery *(Guerd Larey)*, Jean Arthur *(Ruth Hutt)*, Phillips R. Holmes *(Adam Wansfell)*, Fred Kohler *(Boss Stone)*, Chester Conklin *(Tim)*, Guy Oliver *(Sheriff Collishaw)*, Lillian Worth *(Babe)*, Frank Rice *(Stage Driver)*, Clarence L. Sherwood *(Waiter)*.

Beery delivers his usual fine performance (in the type of role he would survey so many times in upcoming talking films) as an outlaw with a heart of gold who sacrifices his own love for the happiness of a young couple.

d, Otto Brower; w, Agnes Brand Leahy, Sam Mintz, J. Walter Ruben (based on the novel by Zane Grey); t, Ben Grauman Kohn; ph, Rex Wimpy; ed, Frances Marsh.

Western **(PR:A MPAA:NR)**

STAND AND DELIVER** (1928) 6 reels De Mille/Pathe Exchange bw

Rod La Rocque *(Roger Norman)*, Lupe Velez *(Jania)*, Warner Oland *(Chika)*, Louis Natheaux *(Capt. Dargis)*, James Dime (Patch Eye), A. Palasthy *(Muja)*, Frank Lanning *(Pietro)*, Bernard Siegel *(Blind Operator)*, Clarence Burton *(Commanding Officer)*, Charles Stevens *(Krim)*, Donald Crisp *(London Club Member)*.

Fair adventure movie has British WW I veteran La Rocque joining the Greek Army in search of adventure, falling for Velez, being captured by a notorious band of bandits, and pretending to join their ranks. In the end he captures their leader, is welcomed back into the service, and marries Velez.

p&d, Donald Crisp; w, Sada Cowan; t, John Krafft; ph, David Abel; art d, Anton Grot; cos, Adrian.

Adventure **(PR:A MPAA:NR)**

STANLEY (SEE: LIVINGSTONE, 1925, Brit.)

STAR DUST (SEE: STARDUST, 1921)

STARDUST** (1921) 6 reels Hobart Henley/AFN bw (AKA: STAR DUST)

Hope Hampton, Edna Ross *(Lily Becker)*, Thomas Maguire *(Henry Becker)*, Mary Foy *(Mrs. Becker)*, Charles Mussett *(Jethro Penny)*, Vivia Ogden *(Mrs. Penny)*, Ashley Buck, Noel Tearle *(Albert Penny)*, George Humbert *(Antonio Marvelli)*, Gladys Wilson *(Daisy Cameron)*, Charles Wellesley *(Bruce Visigoth)*, James Rennie *(Thomas Clemons)*.

Authoress Hurst made much ado about how her novel's integrity was destroyed in this motion picture adaptation. Actually, the story of a mistreated wife who flees to New York, falls in love with a struggling composer, is given free voice lessons by a maestro who believes in her talent, becomes an opera star, and is liberated to marry the man of her choice when her husband is killed in a train wreck, is pretty banal stuff to begin with. In fact, the train crash, which is magnificently filmed, far exceeds Hurst's original description of the event in prose form.

d, Hobart Henley; w, Anthony Paul Kelly (based on the novel by Fannie Hurst); ph, Alfred Ortlieb.

Drama **(PR:A MPAA:NR)**

STARTING POINT, THE* (1919, Brit.) 5 reels BL/But bw

Constance Worth *(Nancy)*, Evan Thomas *(Lawrence Murray)*, Marjorie Villis *(Camille)*, Henry Thompson *(Mayne)*, Whimsical Walker *(Mr. Murray)*.

Drippy little British love story has a working stiff winning a fortune but then pretending to be broke in order to test the true feelings of a self-consumed society girl. Realizing that she's a phony, he then marries the fishergirl who was right for him in the first place.

p, David Falcke; d, Edwin J. Collins; w, Elliot Stannard.

Drama **(PR:A MPAA:NR)**

STEADFAST HEART, THE** (1923) 7 reels DIST/Goldwyn bw

Marguerite Courtot *(Lydia Canfield)*, Miriam Battista *(Lydia Canfield, as a Child)*, Joseph Striker *(Angus Burke)*, Joseph Depew *(Angus Burke, as a Child)*, Hugh Huntley *(Malcolm Crane)*, Jerry Devine *(Malcolm Crane, as a Child)*, William B. Mack *(Crane)*, Sherry Tansey *(Biswang)*, Mary Alden *(Mrs. Burke)*, William Black *(Henry Woodhouse)*, Mario Majeroni *(David Wilkins)*, Harlan Knight *(Jake Bicknell)*, Walter Lewis *(Titus Burke)*, Louis Pierce *(Trueman)*, Mildred Ardin *(Mary)*, Helen Strickland *(Mrs. Canfield)*, Leslie Hunt *(Craig Browning)*.

Ordinary programmer deals with the intolerance of a small town's populace towards a young man after he accidentally shoots the sheriff who has come to arrest his father. He is hounded from his job on a newspaper, but returns years later to buy the journal and save the townsfolk from a crooked scheme.

d, Sheridan Hall; w, Philip Lonergan (based on the novel by Clarence Budington Kelland).

Drama **(PR:A MPAA:NR)**

STEAMBOAT BILL, JR.**** (1928) 7 reels Buster Keaton/UA bw

Buster Keaton *(Steamboat Bill, Jr.)*, Ernest Torrence *(Steamboat Bill)*, Tom Lewis *(His 1st Mate)*, Tom McGuire *(John James King, His Rival)*, Marion Byron *(Mary King, His Daughter)*, Joe Keaton *(Barber)*.

Torrence gives another of his outstanding performances as Steamboat Bill, the big riverboat captain who is on the verge of losing his ship to a rival, McGuire, the town tycoon. Torrence's only hope is his son (Keaton), whom he hasn't seen in years and is returning from college. But to the old man's horror, the lad turns out to be a little beret-wearing, ukelele-playing wimp, who sports a disgusting mustache to boot. Torrence takes his boy to the barbershop for a shave, where Keaton runs into his college chum, Byron, who is having her hair bobbed and just happens to be McGuire's daughter. Then Torrence takes his son to a clothing store where he orders his boy to pick out some *men's* duds. There is a wonderful scene here, where left alone, Keaton tries on one hat after another, and then in a beautifully understated moment puts on the pork pie style, which was his trademark, scrutinizes it carefully, and then rejects it. To his father's total chagrin, Keaton emerges from the store dressed in a yachting outfit. Meanwhile, McGuire manages to have Torrence's boat condemned, and when the captain flattens him he ends up in jail. Keaton attempts to spring his dad by delivering a huge loaf of bread with a file in it, but is discovered by the sheriff. Keaton tries to escape and is sent to the hospital when an automobile hits him. Then follows one of the artist's greatest and most surreal sequences. As he lays in his infirmary bed, a cyclone hits, lifts him out of the building, and hurls the comedian into a series of brightly executed sight gags, the most celebrated of which is the shot where, standing in the street, a three-story building comes crashing down on him and he is saved only because the third floor window is open. Keaton literally risked his life for that shot, as the opening left only a three-inch clearance over his head and around his shoulders and the set weighed over a ton. Then the tree he's using for shelter is uprooted, and Keaton is deposited in the river next to his father's boat. He climbs on board and spots the girl floating by on the rooftop of a house. Keaton leaps back into the water and saves her. No sooner is this done than her father is washed by and the comic rescues him as well. Then for an inspired closing gag, Keaton leaps into the water one more time and emerges with a minister to perform the marriage and thus unite the families.

d, Charles E. Reisner; w&t, Carl Harbaugh; ph, Dev Jennings, Bert Haines; ed, Sherman Kell.

Comedy **Cas.** **(PR:A MPAA:NR)**

STEELHEART** (1921) 6 reels VIT bw

William Duncan *(Frank Worthing)*, Edith Johnson *(Ethel Kendall)*, Jack Curtis *("Butch" Dorgan)*, Walter Rodgers *(Steve)*, Euna Luckey *(Mrs. Freeman)*, Ardeta Malino *(Vera)*, Earl Crain *(Dick Colter)*, Charles Dudley *("Old Tom" Shelley)*.

Nothing earthshaking about this western (except for a poorly filmed mine cave-in) which has Duncan taking an Eastern gal Johnson under his wing while they search for her husband. The fellow turns out to be an outlaw and is later killed in a gun battle, opening the door of romance for Duncan and his "purty little filly."

d, William Duncan; w, Bradley J. Smollen; ph, George Robinson.

Western **(PR:A MPAA:NR)**

STELLA DALLAS**** (1925) 11 reels Goldwyn/UA bw

Ronald Colman *(Stephen Dallas)*, Belle Bennett *(Stella Dallas)*, Alice Joyce *(Helen Morrison)*, Jean Hersholt *(Ed Munn)*, Beatrix Pryor *(Mrs. Grovesnor)*, Lois Moran *(Laurel Dallas)*, Douglas Fairbanks, Jr. *(Richard Grovesnor)*, Vera Lewis *(Miss Tibbets)*, Maurice Murphy, Jack Murphy, Newton Hall *(Morrison Children)*, Charles Hatten, Robert Gillette, Winston Miller *(Morrison Children 10 Years Later)*.

Wonderful heart-tugger has Stella Dallas (Bennett) marrying a wealthy young man (Colman) who visits her little town to get away after his father's suicide. The two have nothing in common and he soon leaves her to return to New York, while she remains at home to care for their daughter, Moran. When the child grows up, Bennett, realizing that she can't afford to do what's right by her, agrees to a divorce, and against Moran's wishes, sends her off to live in the big city with her father and his new bride, Joyce. In time, Moran becomes engaged to Fairbanks, Jr. and, not wishing to embarrass her daughter in front of her new society friends, the uneducated, poorly dressed mother watches the wedding from the street through the window of a Park Avenue mansion, while the rain drips down upon her angelic face and becomes mixed with the salt of her tears. It is a scene which because of the artistry of King and Bennett, remains in the mind forever. What paid off for STELLA DALLAS was what director King brought to the screen. In a story essentially a tearjerker, big, glossy, and polished, he bathed it in warmth and humanity in spite of prosaic camera approaches. Like TOL'ABLE DAVID, another pathos-drenched story elevated to greatness by King's uniquely sensitive approach to American themes, the deeply emotional STELLA DALLAS was as real as the cop who, at the end, while Bennett is observing her daughter's happiness, tells her to "move along." The fine cast was abetted by Colman's sterling performance, and another by Hersholt, who at the time was specializing in playing cads long before he became the warm-hearted "Dr. Christian" of movie and radio fame, as a coarse riding master. Moran, of course, was exceptional. An 11-year-old girl in real life, she convinced Sam Goldwyn and director King that she could play the role of the daughter all the way up to her marriage to Fairbanks, Jr., which she did, with exemplary style. And Fairbanks, Jr. was entirely winning with the little mustache King gave him, which was frowned upon by his father, Fairbanks, Sr., because it made him look older than he was (and, thus, was a tidy reminder to the vain actor that he was growing older, too).

d, Henry King; w, Frances Marion (based on the novel by Olive Higgins Prouty); ph, Arthur Edeson; ed, Stuart Heisler; art d, Ben Carre.

Drama **(PR:A MPAA:NR)**

STELLA MARIS**** (1918) 5 reels ART bw

Mary Pickford *(Stella Maris/Unity Blake)*, Conway Tearle *(John Risca)*, Camille Ankewich *(Louise Risca)*, Ida Waterman *(Lady Blount)*, Herbert Standing *(Sir Blount)*, Josephine Crowell, Mrs. Coonleu, Teddy *(The Sennett Dog)*.

Under Neilan's inspired direction, Pickford delivers what is possibly her greatest performance—or perhaps we should say performances because the actress plays two parts here. As Stella Maris, Pickford portrays a beautiful young cripple whose millionaire parents died and left her in the care of an aunt and uncle, with the provision that she should be raised like a princess—shut completely away from the depressing realities of the world. Pickford also plays Unity Blake, a homely little slavey whom Tearle's alcoholic wife, Ankewich, adopts to be her servant and punching bag when he leaves her. Tearle and Stella are in love, and when Unity is taken in by him after Ankewich is sent to prison for badly beating the poor child, she falls in love with him as well. In fact, the degree of her love is such that the poor girl murders Ankewich when she returns from jail and threatens to destroy the happiness of Stella and her beloved, before taking her own life. Neilan skillfully avoids leaving the audience with a downer, however, by showing Stella (who has regained the use of her legs) and Tearle together on the grounds of her family estate. He closes the picture with a beautiful dolly shot in which the camera pulls away slowly and finally fades to black. In her autobiography, Pickford tells an interesting story about Adolph Zukor visiting the set while she was in her Unity Blake character, and almost suffering a heart attack when he took a look at his very expensive star.

According to "America's Sweetheart," the studio mogul was most relieved when he discovered that she was about to be killed off.

d, Marshall Neilan; w, Frances Marion (based on the novel by William J. Locke); ph, Walter Stradling.

Drama **(PR:A MPAA:NR)**

STELLA MARIS* 1/2 (1925) 7 reels UNIV bw

Mary Philbin *(Stella Maris/Unity Blake)*, Elliott Dexter *(John Risca)*, Gladys Brockwell *(Louisa Risca)*, Jason Robards *(Walter Herold)*, Phillips Smalley *(Sir Oliver Blount)*, Lillian Lawrence *(Lady Blount)*, Robert Bolder *(Dr. Haynes)*, Aileen Manning *(Mary Heaton)*.

Inferior remake of a motion picture classic suffers without Mary Pickford in the lead or Mickey Neilan behind the megaphone. The story was even changed to permit a young leading man to win Stella's (Philbin's) love after an operation restores her ability to walk, rather than the dedicated friend in the original version. Excellent double-exposure photography by Moore is the only real bright spot in this otherwise disappointing film.

d, Charles J. Brabin; w, Brabin, Mary Alice Scully (based on the novel by William John Locke); ph, Milton Moore.

Drama **(PR:A MPAA:NR)**

STEP ON IT!* ** (1922) 5 reels UNIV bw

Hoot Gibson *(Vic Collins)*, Edith Yorke *(Mrs. Collins)*, Frank Lanning *(Pidge Walters)*, Barbara Bedford *(Lorraine Leighton)*, Vic Potel *(Noisy Johnson)*, Gloria Davenport *(Letty Mather)*, Joe Girard *(Lafe Brownell)*, L. C. Shumway *(Bowman)*.

Plenty of riding and gunplay in this western which has Gibson, Bedford, and Girard putting their heads together to bring to justice the gang of rustlers who were responsible for sending the young lady's brother to prison.

d, Jack Conway; w, Arthur F. Statter (based on the story "The Land of the Lost" by Courtney Ryley Cooper); ph, Charles Kaufman.

Western **(PR:A MPAA:NR)**

STEPHEN STEPS OUT* ** (1923) 6 reels FP/PAR bw

Douglas Fairbanks, Jr. *(Stephen Harlow, Jr.)*, Theodore Roberts *(Stephen Harlow, Sr.)*, Noah Beery *(Muley Pasha)*, Harry Myers *(Harry Stetson)*, Frank Currier *(Dr. Lyman Black)*, James O. Barrows *(Prof. Gilman)*, Fannie Midgley *(Mrs. Gilman)*, Bertram Johns *(Virgil Smythe)*, George Field *(Osman)*, Maurice Freeman *(Rustem)*, Fred Warren *(The Sultan)*, Pat Moore *(The Sultan's Son)*, Jack Herbert *(Secretary)*, Frank Nelson *(Hotel Proprietor)*.

A 13-year-old Douglas Fairbanks, Jr. makes his screen debut here starring as a student who flunks a course in Turkish history and is sent by his father to that country to learn the culture firsthand. After becoming involved in a number of adventures, Fairbanks saves the sultan's son and returns to school an expert on the subject which originally gave him so much trouble. Douglas Fairbanks Sr. was strongly opposed to his son's entrance into films, arguing that Paramount was exploiting his name. Outside of this he showed little interest in the boy, who was raised by his mother, Anna Beth Sully (Fairbanks' first wife) from the age of 9, and even once confessed that he had "no more paternal feelings than a tiger in the jungle for his cub." During the 1930s, however, father and son did grow to become good friends.

d, Joseph Henabery; w, Edfrid Bingham (based on the story "The Grand Cross of the Desert" by Richard Harding Davis); ph, Faxon Dean.

Comedy/Adventure **(PR:A MPAA:NR)**

STEPPING ALONG** (1926) 7 reels B&H Enterprises/FN bw

Johnny Hines *(Johnny Rooney)*, Mary Brian *(Molly Taylor)*, William Gaxton *(Frank Moreland)*, Ruth Dwyer *(Fay Allen)*, Edmund Breese *(Prince Ferdinand Darowitsky)*, Dan Mason *(Mike)*, Lee Beggs *(Boss O'Brien)*.

Too much padding completely throws off the timing on what could have been a funny comedy about a newspaper vendor (Hines) who overcomes numerous obstacles to win an election as an East Side New York assemblyman. The film's highlights are actually a couple of excellent dance numbers performed by Hines.

d, Charles Hines; w, (based on the story "The Knickerbocker Kid" by Matt Taylor); ph, George Peters;, Albert Wetzel, Albert Wilson.

Comedy **(PR:A MPAA:NR)**

STEPPING FAST* ** (1923) 5 reels FOX bw

Tom Mix *(Grant Malvern)*, Claire Adams *(Helen Durant)*, Donald MacDonald *(Fabian)*, Hector Sarno *(Martinez)*, Edward Peil *(Sun Yat)*. George Siegmann *("Red" Pollock)*, Tom S. Guise *(Quentin Durant)*, Edward Jobson *(Commodore Simpson)*, Ethel Wales *(Miss Higgins)*, Minna Redman *(Mrs. Malvern)*, Tony the Horse.

There's a little of everything for action fans in this Mix adventure. In it the hero is attacked by a gang of crooks in Chinatown because he possesses a map and ring (clues to a hidden treasure) given him by a dying old scientist who made the cowboy pledge to deliver them to his daughter. Mix escapes only to later discover, to his horror, that the villains have caused the deaths of his mother and dog. Mix is really motivated to track them down now, but is once again overpowered and this time thrown into the San Francisco Bay, where he is believed drowned. A tramp steamer picks him up, however, and the cowboy works his way to China, stoking coal. The crooks arrive in the Orient on another ship and abduct the scientist's daughter, whom they hold in a torture den. But Mix is soon on the scene, and with the help of a bunch of U.S. sailors, liberates the young lady. The race is then on to cross the Pacific and get through the U.S. desert to reach the treasure first. Mix and the girl are successful, the cutthroats are killed in a fight, and the young couple decide to marry and share the wealth.

d, Joseph J. Franz; w, Bernard McConville; ph, Dan Clark.

Adventure **(PR:A MPAA:NR)**

STILL WATERS* ** (1915) 5 reels FP bw

Marguerite Clark *(Nesta)*, Robert Broderick *(Joe Martin)*, Robert Vaughn *(John Ramsey, M.D.)*, Arthur Evers *(Ring Master)*, Ottola Nesmith *(Drassa La Rue)*, Phillip Tonge *(Jed Perkins)*, Robert Conville *(Mike)*, Harry La Pearl *(Bounding Bonnell)*.

Clark, the granddaughter of a canal boat captain, expresses a desire to attend a circus which is playing a town downstream. The old gent refuses and relates the story of how her mother ran away to marry a member of the big top and of how he later raised Clark when she and her mother became accidentally separated. There is plenty of authentic circus atmosphere from this point on, as Clark sets out and locates her lost parent. But the picture ends with the girl deciding to marry a young doctor rather than follow the sawdust trail. Another winning performance by the star and nice direction on the part of Dawley.

d, J. Searle Dawley; w, Hugh Ford (based on a story by Edith Barnard Delano); ph, Henry Broening.

Drama **(PR:A MPAA:NR)**

STILL WATERS RUN DEEP* 1/2 (1916, Brit.) 5 reels ID bw

Lady Tree *(Mrs. Sternhold)*, Milton Rosmer *(John Mildmay)*, Rutland Barrington *(Mr. Potter)*, Sydney Lewis Ransome *(Capt. Hawksley)*, Hilda Bruce-Potter *(Mrs. Mildmay)*, E. H. Brooke.

Tepid British mystery drama about an unscrupulous captain who worms his way into the home of a wealthy family. He then attempts to blackmail one of his hosts with some incriminating letters before getting his just desserts.

d, Fred Paul, w, Dane Stanton (based on the play by Tom Taylor).

Mystery **(PR:A MPAA:NR)**

STING OF THE LASH** (1921) 6 reels R-C bw

Pauline Frederick *(Dorothy Keith)*, Clyde Fillmore *(Joel Gant)*, Lawson Butt *(Rhodes)*, Lionel Belmore *(Ben Ames)*, Jack Richardson *(Seeley)*, Edwin Stevens *(Daniel Keith)*, Betty Hall *(Crissy, Aged 6)*, Evelyn McCoy *(Crissy, Aged 10)*, Percy Challenger *(Rorke)*.

After Frederick marries miner Fillmore, the young man's claim is confiscated by her cousin, Belmore, for a development company. The couple sink into poverty and Frederick takes in laundry, while Fillmore turns to bootlegging and heavy drinking. One night, while on a bender, he threatens to beat their little niece, but an infuriated Frederick ties her husband up and gives him a terrible whipping. Later she accepts a job with the mining company, Fillmore reforms, and the couple are reunited.

d, Henry King; w, H. Tipton Steck (based on a story by Harvey Gates); ph, Dev Jennings.

Drama **(PR:A MPAA:NR)**

STING OF THE SCORPION, THE*

(1923) 5 reels Ashton Dearholt/Arrow bw

Edmund Cobb, Ashton Dearholt, Helene Rosson, Joseph Girard, Arthur Morrison, Harry Dunkinson.

Below-par B western has a young man winning the friendship of an Indian gold mine owner. The saloon keeper, who is after the treasure as well as the rancher's pretty daughter, frames the hero for murdering his native American friend, but the young fellow clears himself, wins the girl, brings the crook to justice, and inherits the mine.

d, Richard Hatton; w, Daniel F. Whitcomb.

Western **(PR:A MPAA:NR)**

STOCKS AND BLONDES* 1/2 (1928) 6 reels FBO bw

Gertrude Astor *(Goldie)*, Jacqueline Logan *(Patsy)*, Richard "Skeets" Gallagher *(Tom Greene)*, Albert Conti *(Powers)*.

Inept little programmer has Gallagher, a wisecracking stock broker, losing his job just as he and his nightclub dancer sweetheart, Logan, are about to make the first down payment on their honeymoon cottage. Over cocktails, Logan is able to get the inside lowdown on the market from Gallagher's former boss, and using a phony name, places a couple of big orders through her boy friend. Gallagher makes a killing because of these and develops into an arrogant pain-in-the-neck. Then when he spots Logan and his former boss consulting, he blows his top and accuses his girl of cheating on him. To put him in his place, Logan then arranges for Gallagher to lose everything. Not until he has returned to his old self again does she forgive him, and the two are reunited.

d&w, Dudley Murphy; sup, Louis Sarecky; t, Jack Conway, Randolph Bartlett; ph, Virgil Miller; ed, Pandro S. Berman.

Comedy/Drama **(PR:A MPAA:NR)**

STOLEN BRIDE, THE** (1927) 8 reels FN bw

Billie Dove *(Sari, Countess Thurzo)*, Lloyd Hughes *(Franz Pless)*, Armand Kaliz *(Captain, the Baron von Heimberg)*, Frank Beal *(Count Thurzo)*, Lilyan Tashman *(Ilona Taznadi)*, Cleve Moore *(Lt. Kiss)*, Otto Hoffman *(Papa Pless)*, Charles Wellesley *(The Regiment Pater)*, Bert Sprotte *(The Sergeant)*.

Dull picture recounts the love of a Hungarian countess for a U.S. reared commoner who is drafted into her army during WW I. Although handsomely mounted, the story is so sluggish that by the end, when the lovers escape to the U.S., it really doesn't seem to matter much. This was the first film effort of Hungarian director

Korda, who would zoom to the top several years later in Britain, where he would produce a string of successes and found London Films.

p, Carey Wilson; d, Alexander Korda; w, Wilson; ph, Robert Kurrle; cos, Max Ree.

Drama **(PR:A MPAA:NR)**

STOLEN PLEASURES* (1927) 6 reels COL bw

Helene Chadwick *(Doris Manning)*, Gayne Whitman *(John Manning)*, Dorothy Revier *(Clara Bradley)*, Ray Ripley *(Herbert Bradley)*, Harlan Tucker *(Guy Summers)*.

Following an argument, two married couples separate from their spouses. Later, one of the husbands, Ripley, sees the other's wife, Chadwick, walking and offers her a ride home. She accepts, but a storm arises and the two are forced to seek shelter at a nearby roadhouse. While this is going on, a flirtatious young fellow takes Ripley's unsuspecting wife, Revier, to the same club and tries to make a pass at her. When a fire breaks out, everyone escapes (Chadwick running out in her underwear is the only bright spot in the movie), and Ripley is accused of having an affair with Chadwick when her husband sees them together. At this point, Revier comes forth to prove Chadwick's innocence, and the picture ends with a reconciliation.

d, Philip E. Rosen; sup, Harry Cohn; w, Leah Baird; ph, J. O. Taylor.

Drama **(PR:A MPAA:NR)**

STOLEN VOICE*** (1915) 5 reels Brady/WORLD bw

Robert Warwick, Frances Nelson.

Warwick is an opera singer making $2,000 a week in vaudeville, adored by a little shop girl who gives him a dandelion at the stage door, and coveted by an adventuress who sends him a rose. The mysterious lady's lover is a doctor of some sort, who out of jealousy causes the singer to lose his voice through hypnotic suggestion. Warwick journeys to Europe in search of a cure, and failing that, returns to the U.S. where he is given the cold shoulder by all of his former friends. The poor devil is at rope's end when he encounters a fellow entertainer he once helped out, who is now a successful movie director. Anxious to repay the kindness, he gives the former singer a job acting in silent pictures, where he becomes a star of adventure films. At this point a movie within a movie is cleverly presented at a New York theater, which is attended by the fortune hunter and her paramour. Seeing his rival on the screen is too much for the evil doctor and he dies of a heart attack. There is another nice, if not quite plausible, touch in this engaging entertainment, which has the director meeting the shop girl pictured earlier in the stage door sequence, noticing a quality about her eyes, and making her Warwick's co-star. The film ends delightfully with the singer regaining his voice and proposing marriage over the telephone to the girl who has always adored him.

w, Frank H. Crane (based on a story by Paul McAllister).

Drama **(PR:A MPAA:NR)**

STOP THAT MAN*** (1928) 6 reels UNIV bw

Arthur Lake *(Tommy O'Brien)*, Barbara Kent *(Muriel Crawford)*, Eddie Gribbon *(Bill O'Brien)*, Warner Richmond *(Jim O'Brien)*, Walter McGrail *("Slippery Dick" Sylvaine)*, George Siegmann *("Butch" Barker)*, Joseph W. Girard *(Capt. Ryan)*.

Lake, best known for his portrayal of comic strip characters Harold Teen and Dagwood Bumstead, delivers more than a few laughs in this pleasing comedy. In it he plays the younger brother of two burly Irish cops who puts on a policeman's uniform one day and unknowingly helps a notorious crook pull off a job. Later he makes it up to the family and the girl he was trying to impress when he captures the crook and delivers him to the police station in an old streetcar.

d, Nat Ross; w, Joseph Franklin Poland, Harry O. Hoyt, Dick Smith (based on a story by George V. Hobart); t, Tom Reed; ph, George Robinson; ed, Robert Jahns.

Comedy **(PR:A MPAA:NR)**

STOP THIEF*** (1920) 5 reels Goldwyn bw

Tom Moore *(Jack Dougan)*, Hazel Daly *(Snatcher Nell)*, Irene Rich *(Madge Carr)*, Kate Lester *(Mrs. Carr)*, Molly Malone *(Joan Carr)*, Edward McWade *(Mr. Carr)*, Raymond Hatton *(James Cluney)*, Harris Gordon *(Dr. Willoughby)*, Henry Ralston *(Rev. Dr. Spelvin)*, John Lince *(Detective Thompson)*, Maurice B. Flynn *(Police Sergeant)*, Otto Hoffman, Andrew Robson, James Neill.

Slick and effective comedy about a man and woman who sneak into a mansion to commit a robbery, become involved with their "hosts," and end up marrying and going straight. Fine performance by Moore, but Daly, as the girl burglar, almost steals the show.

d, Harry Beaumont; w, Charles Kenyon (based on the play by Carlyle Moore); ph, Norbert Brodine.

Comedy/Mystery **(PR:A MPAA:NR)**

STORK'S NEST, THE***

(1915) 5 reels COL/Rolfe-Metro bw (AKA: EMMY OF STORK'S NEST)

Mary Miles Minter *(Emmy Garrett)*, Niles Welch *(Benton Cabot)*, Mr. Bresee *(Hiram Garrett)*, Charles Prince *(Bije Stork)*, William Cowper *(Si Stork)*, Mathilda Brundage *(Crishy Stork)*, Martin Faust *(Jim Whitlicks)*, Jules Cowles *(Hicky Price)*.

It was because of films like this one—about a backwoods tomboy who grows into beautiful young womanhood—that Minter developed into Mary Pickford's closest rival.

d, William Nigh; w, (based on a novel by J. Breckenridge Ellis).

Drama **(PR:A MPAA:NR)**

STORM, THE*** (1922) 8 reels UNIV bw

Matt Moore *(Dave Stewart)*, House Peters *(Burr Winton)*, Josef Swickard *(Jacques Fachard)*, Virginia Valli *(Manette Fachard)*, Frank Lanning *(Manteeka)*, Gordon McGee *(Northwest Mounted Police Sergeant)*.

Good special effects enhance this frozen tundra drama about a couple of army pals who vie for the love of a girl whose dying father placed her in their charge. Of course one of the men (Moore) finally makes the sacrifice which enables the others to find happiness—but not before a spectacularly filmed, color-tinted forest fire is thrown in, to keep the audience on the edge of their seats.

d, Reginald Barker; w, J. G. Hawks (based on a play by Langdon McCormick); ph, Percy Hilburn.

Drama **(PR:A MPAA:NR)**

STORM DAUGHTER, THE*** (1924) 6 reels UNIV bw

Priscilla Dean *(Kate Masterson)*, Tom Santschi *("Brute" Morgan)*, William B. Davidson *(Rennert)*, J. Farrell MacDonald *(Con Mullaney)*, Cyril Chadwick *(The Duke)*, Bert Roach *(Olaf Swensen)*, Alfred Fisher *(Hoskins)*, George Kuwa *(Ah Sin)*, Harry Mann *(Izzy)*.

Thanks to a realistic setting (most of the picture was filmed on board a tramp schooner), this minor-league effort turned out most enjoyable. The Eugene O'Neill-like script, with all of the familiar ethnic and salt sea types, deals with a ruthless captain (splendidly played by long-time heavy, Santschi) who overpowers Dean's sailboat and enslaves her crew. In time his captives mutiny and Santschi is put in irons. He's later released, however, to take over the helm when a terrific storm blows up. After some great disaster footage, which ends with the deaths of everyone but Santschi and Dean, the two make their way to a deserted island, where the one-time brute reveals his complete regeneration.

d, George Archainbaud; w, Edward J. Montagne (based on a story by Leete Renick Brown); ph, Jules Cronjager.

Drama **(PR:A MPAA:NR)**

STORM OVER ASIA****

(1929, USSR) 6 reels Mejrabpomfilm/Amkino bw (AKA: THE HEIR TO JENGHIZ KHAN)

V. Inkizhinov *(The Son)*, A. Tchistiakov *(Rebel Leader)*, L. Dediseff *(Commander)*, L. Belinskaya *(His Wife)*, A. Sudkaveich *(Their Daughter)*.

Set during the Russian Revolution of 1918, this magnificent film has a Mongolian trapper bringing his pelts to be sold in a bustling, mud-ridden frontier town, which is in the control of the Whites and under the military protection of their British allies. In his collection is a particularly rare and valuable skin. But when he is cheated by an arrogant merchant, the angered trapper decides to join the forces of the Reds. Later, the Mongol is captured and casually ordered to be shot. While they are marching him to his doom, a professor, while examining his belongings, discovers that he is a descendant of the mighty Genghis Khan. "Stop the execution!" the order goes out. Here is a man who can be of use to the forces of imperialism. What better man to be placed in a position as puppet leader to his people then a man with that lineage. Troopers are dispatched to fetch their prize, but it's too late. The Mongol has been shot. But still breathing, they carry him back, and with the best possible medical care he slowly recovers. Finally, the time comes for the British and their Loyalist friends to dress their strangely unresponsive lackey in evening dress, so that he might attend a fine dinner for their amusement. But then something happens. As if the spirit of the real Genghis Khan himself enters the trapper's body, the passive Mongolian suddenly goes insane. He begins to tear the building apart, and escapes into the night, where, in an explosive conclusion, he leads an army of Oriental horsemen against the oppressors of his people. Pudovkin's use of montage and cinematic imagery is unparalleled, but he differs from his chief Soviet rival, Sergei Eisenstein, in that this film also leans heavily on narrative and employs a central character, brilliantly played by the Mongolian actor V. Inkizhinov. Pudovkin's attraction to a strong story line (of all the Russians, he was the one who leaned most heavily on this convention) can perhaps be best understood by quoting him from a 1929 New York Times interview: "About that time I happened to see Griffith's great film, INTOLERANCE. In that wonderful work I saw for the first time the possibilities of the epic picture. Yes, Griffith was really my teacher. Later I saw BROKEN BLOSSOMS, and I fell more and more under the spell of Griffith. My first three pictures, therefore, were really influenced by this great American director."

d, V. I. Pudovkin; w, O. Brik (based on a story by Novokshenov); ph, A. N. Golovnia; set d, S. V. Koslovski, Aronson.

Drama **Cas.** **(PR:A MPAA:NR)**

STORMSWEPT* 1/2 (1923) 5 reels Robert Thornby/FBO bw

Wallace Beery *(William McCabe)*, Noah Beery *(Shark Moran)*, Virginia Browne Faire *(Ann Reynolds)*, Arline Pretty *(Helda McCabe)*, Jack Carlyle *(Snape)*.

Less-than-satisfying programmer (despite the presence of both Wallace and Noah Beery) has Wallace Beery attempting suicide when he discovers that his wife has been unfaithful, but saving the life of seaman Noah Beery instead. He is then given a job working on the seaman's ship and before long, falls madly in love with Faire, the daughter of his supply boat's captain. Later the seaman rescues Wallace Beery's wife in a storm, makes a pass, and becomes involved in an argument with his pal. In the end all is forgiven, however, and the unfaithful wife promises to give her husband the divorce he seeks.

p&d, Robert Thornby; w, Winifred Dunn (based on a story by H. H. Van Loan); ph, Ben Reynolds.

Drama **(PR:A MPAA:NR)**

STORMY SEAS** (1923) 5 reels Continental Pictures/AEX bw

J. P. McGowan *(Capt. Morgan)*, Helen Holmes *(Mary Weems)*, Leslie Casey *(George Tracey)*, Harry Dalroy *(Angus McBride)*, Francis Seymour *("Storm" Weems)*, Gordon Knapp *("Shorty" the Steward)*.

Action director McGowan gives one of his better acting performances in this programmer about an alcoholic sea captain who steps out of the picture to allow the young man who rescued him to find happiness with the woman they both love.

d, J. P. McGowan; w, Arthur W. Donaldson.

Drama **(PR:A MPAA:NR)**

STORMY WATERS** (1928) 6 reels TS bw

Eve Southern *(Lola)*, Malcolm McGregor *(David Steele)*, Roy Stewart *(Capt. Angus Steele)*, Shirley Palmer *(Mary)*, Olin Francis *(Bos'n)*, Norbert Myles *(1st Mate)*, Bert Apling *(2nd Mate)*.

Nothing out of the ordinary in this seafaring saga of a prostitute (Southern) who is taken on board a ship when she claims to be married to crewman McGregor, the younger brother of the captain. McGregor is smitten by the scarlet woman, but when she tries to seduce everyone on board, they put her in a lifeboat near shore, and the young man returns to the "nice girl" who has been waiting for him back home.

d, Edgar Lewis; sup, Roy Fitzroy; w, Harry Dittmar (based on the story "Yellow Handkerchief" by Jack London); t, Leslie Mason; ph, Ernest Miller; ed, Martin G. Cohn; art d, Hervey Libbert; set d, George Sawley.

Drama **(PR:A MPAA:NR)**

STRAIGHT IS THE WAY** 1/2 (1921) 5 reels COS/PAR bw

Matt Moore *("Cat" Carter)*, Mabel Bert *(Aunt Mehitabel)*, Gladys Leslie *(Dorcas)*, George Parsons *("Loot" Follett)*, Henry Sedley *(Jonathan Squoggs)*, Van Dyke Brooks *(Constable Whipple)*, Emily Fitzroy *(Mrs. Crabtree)*, Peggy Parr *(Bobby)*.

Pleasant little comedy has a couple of crooks (Moore and Parsons) coming to the aid of elderly Bert and her niece, Leslie, by saving their mortgage from an unscrupulous loan shark. After the good deed, the boys reform and Parsons marries the girl.

d, Robert G. Vignola; w, Frances Marion (based on the story "The Manifestations of Henry Ort" by Ethel Watts Mumford); ph, Al Ligouri.

Comedy **(PR:A MPAA:NR)**

STRAIGHT ROAD, THE*** (1914) 4 reels FP bw

Gladys Hanson *(Mary O'Hara)*, William Russell *(Bill Hubbell)*, Iva Shepard *(Lazy Liz)*, Arthur Hoops *(Douglas Aines)*. Lorraine Huling *(Ruth Thompson)*.

Director Dwan remains quite faithful to the Fitch play about a little girl (Hanson) who struggles from the tenement where she is orphaned to a life of happiness with the man she loves. There is a beautifully staged prizefight sequence, which takes place in the back room of a very real looking East Side New York saloon.

d, Allan Dwan; w, (based on the play by Clyde Fitch).

Drama **(PR:A MPAA:NR)**

STRANDED** (1927) 6 reels STER bw

Shirley Mason *(Sally Simpson)*, William Collier, Jr. *(Johnny Nash)*, John Miljan *(Grant Payne)*, Florence Turner *(Mrs. Simpson)*, Gale Henry *(Lucille Lareaux)*, Shannon Day *(Betty)*, Lucy Beaumont *(Grandmother)*, Rosa Gore *(Landlady)*.

Fairly good production values barely save this story Anita Loos must have whipped up between phone calls about an Iowa girl, Mason, who fails to make it in the movies and almost gives herself to a cad to obtain the $500 needed for her mother's operation. Fortunately her boy friend from back home arrives in time to knock the rotter's block off and bring his sweetheart back to the real world.

d, Phil Rosen; sup, Joe Rock; w, Frances Guihan (based on a story by Anita Loos); t, Wyndham Gittens; ph, Herbert Kirkpatrick; ed, Leotta Whytock.

Drama **(PR:A MPAA:NR)**

STRANGER, THE*** (1924) 7 reels FP/PAR bw

Betty Compson *(Peggy Bowlin)*, Richard Dix *(Larry Darrant)*, Lewis Stone *(Keith Darrant)*, Tully Marshall *(The Stranger)*, Robert Schable *(Jim Walenn)*, Mary Jane Irving *(Maizie Darrant)*, Frank Nelson *(Jackal/Bill Cutts)*, Marian Skinner *(Landlady)*.

Well-acted film adaptation of Galsworthy's novel about a poor London pub scrubman who takes the blame when a man is murdered while attacking a barmaid. Actually the real killer is Dix, the fiance of barmaid Compson, and he is about to step forward and confess when the scrubman suddenly dies of a heart attack just before being hung from the gallows. Of course this saves Dix's family name from scandal, and he and Compson are happily married. Although Henabery's direction is a bit stiff on occasion, he has really captured British author Galsworthy's concern for his nation's tradition of class discrimination. The outdoor sets could have looked a bit more English, but for the most part THE STRANGER is an intelligent and engrossing motion picture.

d, Joseph Henabery; w, Edfrid Bingham (based on the novel *The First and the Last* by John Galsworthy); ph, Faxon M. Dean, L. Guy Wilky.

Drama **(PR:A MPAA:NR)**

STRANGER THAN FICTION** 1/2 (1921) 6 reels Katherine MacDonald/AFN bw

Katherine MacDonald *(Diane Drexel)*, Dave Winter *(Dick Mason)*, Wesley Barry *(Freckles)*, Wade Boteler *(The Black Heart)*, Jean Dumont *(The Shadow)*, Harry O'Connor *(The Croaker)*, Evelyn Burns *(Diane's Aunt)*, Tom McGuire *(Police Commissioner)*.

This curiosity, which uses a movie within a movie, can't quite decide whether to go for satire or drama. Socialite MacDonald throws a party to screen her homemade version of CARMEN, featuring all of her guests. Instead they are shown a melodrama full of action, airplane chases, and a hooded villain. When the show ends, the lights go on and MacDonald smugly points out that this is the way pictures *should* be made. The rest of us are left to wonder what CARMEN might have been like.

d, J. A. Barry; w, Charles Richman, Albert Shelby Le Vino; t, Ralph Spence; ph, Joseph Brotherton; ed, Spence; art d, A. Douda.

Adventure **(PR:A MPAA:NR)**

STRANGER'S BANQUET*** 1/2 (1922) 7 reels Marshall Neilan/Goldwyn bw

Hobart Bosworth *(Shane Keogh)*, Claire Windsor *(Derith Keogh)*, Rockliffe Fellowes *(Angus Campbell)*, Ford Sterling *(Al Norton)*, Eleanor Boardman *(Jean McPherson)*, Thomas Holding *(John Trevelyan)*, Eugenie Besserer *(Mrs. McPherson)*, Nigel Barrie *(John Keogh)*, Stuart Holmes *(Prince)*, Claude Gillingwater *(Uncle Sam)*, Margaret Loomis *(Bride)*, Tom Guise *(Bride's Father)*, Lillian Langdon *(Bride's Mother)*, William Humphrey *(Groom's Friend)*, Edward McWade *(Harriman)*, Lorimer Johnson *(Ross)*, James Marcus *(Braithwaite)*, Edward W. Borman *(Dolan)*, Jack Curtis *(McKinstry)*, Brinsley Shaw *(Krischenko)*, Arthur Hoyt *(Morel)*, Aileen Pringle *(Mrs. Schuyler-Peabody)*, Virginia Ruggles *(Olive Stockton)*, Cyril Chadwick *(Bond)*, Philo McCullough *(Britton)*, Jean Hersholt *(Fiend)*, Lucille Ricksen *(Flapper)*, Dagmar Godowsky *(Spanish Señorita)*, Hayford Hobbs *(Toreador)*, Violet Joy *(Cabaret Girl)*.

Director Neilan's brilliance is very much in evidence in this big picture which takes a number of subplots and ties them neatly together to tell the main story. In it we see Windsor inheriting her father's shipyard and falling in love with its supervisor, Fellowes, who refuses to declare his mutual feelings lest he be thought of as a "climber." Windsor faces up to a group of dissatisfied workers led by Holding, who has turned fanatical and become the tool of Red agitators after learning of his bastard birth. The big strike is ultimately prevented when Fellowes and Windsor convince Holding of his true worth, and the labor boss (after taking a bullet meant for Fellowes) persuades his men that a fair deal can be achieved through peaceful arbitration. Neilan's images are dazzling throughout, and he ends the picture with Fellowes accepting the proposal of marriage issued by his employer.

d, Marshall Neilan; w, Neilan, Frank Urson (based on the novel by Brian Oswald Donn-Byrne; ph, David Kesson, Max Fabian.

Drama **(PR:A MPAA:NR)**

STRANGERS OF THE NIGHT*** (1923) 8 reels Louis B. Mayer/Metro bw

Matt Moore *(Ambrose Applejohn)*, Enid Bennett *(Poppy Faire)*, Barbara La Marr *(Anna Valeska)*, Robert McKim *(Borolsky)*, Mathilde Brundage *(Mrs. Whatacombe)*, Emily Fitzroy *(Mrs. Pengard)*, Otto Hoffman *(Horace Pengard)*, Thomas Ricketts *(Lush)*.

Winning combination of laughter and thrills in this Moore feature about a British gentleman who dreams of his dashing sea captain ancestor and awakens to thwart a gang of crooks out to steal the old boy's hidden treasure. He also wins the love of a very surprised and delighted Bennett.

p&d, Fred Niblo; w, Bess Meredyth, C. Gardner Sullivan (based on the play "Captain Applejack" by Walter Hackett); t, Renaud; ph, Alvin Wyckoff.

Comedy/Adventure **(PR:A MPAA:NR)**

STREET OF SIN, THE** (1928) 7 reels PAR bw

Emil Jannings *("Basher" Bill)*, Fay Wray *(Elizabeth)*, Olga Baclanova *(Annie)*, Ernest W. Johnson *(Mr. Smith)*, George Kotsonaros *("Iron Mike")*, John Gough, Johnnie Morris *(Cronies of "Basher Bill")*, John Burdette *(Proprietor of Pub)*.

A poor outing for supersilent star Jannings and one of Europe's greatest directors, Mauritz Stiller, the discoverer of Greta Garbo. A retired prizefighter turned criminal, Jannings pretends to reform by joining a Salvation Army shelter in London. Wray, a pious, wraith-like creature, runs the shelter and Jannings is drawn to her, although he already has a girl friend named Annie (Baclanova), a "street girl." Under Wray's influence, Jannings confesses to a bank robbery and attempts to go straight, but he is turned in by his jilted "street girl." Jannings escapes, but his gang member ex-pals use the nursery children as hostages against the police. Jannings then sacrifices his life to save the children and the nursery. A bleak and dismal motion picture, its director was a broken and humiliated man when he bagan this film. Although given a big budget, a well-balanced script, and a natural setting, Stiller got involved in a row with the studio heads in mid-production and quit the picture, forcing the director and scriptwriter, Von Sternberg, to finish it. Stiller returned to Stockholm where he began his career, and a few months after THE STREET OF SIN opened he died of a respiratory illness at the age of 45.

d, Mauritz Stiller, Josef von Sternberg; w, Chandler Sprague (based on a story by Von Sternberg, Benjamin Glazer); t, Julian Johnson; ph, Bert Glennon; ed, George Nichols, Jr.; set d, Hans Dreier.

Drama **(PR:A MPAA:NR)**

STREETS OF NEW YORK, THE* 1/2 (1922) 7 reels State/Arrow bw

Anders Randolf *(Gideon Bloodgood)*, Leslie King *(Badger)*, Barbara Castleton *(Lucy Bloodgood)*, Edward Earle *(Paul Fairweather)*, Dorothy Mackaill *(Sally Ann)*, Kate Blanke *(Jennie)*.

The only thing this low-budget yawner actually has to do with the Big Apple are a number of disjointed newsreel clips showing various landmarks. The rest of the picture is a poorly directed and dated melodrama, with the usual blackmail and love triangle stuff, culminating in a moderately well-staged storm sequence which claims the life of the heavy and allows the young lovers to unite at last.

d, Burton King; w, (based on the play by Leota Morgan); ph, Alfred Ortlieb.

Drama (PR:A MPAA:NR)

STRIVING FOR FORTUNE** (1926) 6 reels EXCEL bw

George Walsh *(Tom Sheridan)*, Beryl Roberts *(Hope Loring)*, Tefft Johnson, Joseph Burke, Louise Carter, Dexter McReynolds.

Average programmer, enhanced by on-location shooting in the New York shipyards, has Walsh, an employee of a steamship company, preventing the hireling of a rival firm from sabotaging his company's new vessel. He then convinces his boss to purchase his sweetheart's father's nautical invention, and wins a big promotion for his efforts.

d, Nat Ross; w, Merle Johnson.

Adventure (PR:A MPAA:NR)

STRONG BOY*** (1929) 6 reels FOX bw

Victor McLaglen *(Strong Boy)*, Leatrice Joy *(Mary McGregor)*, J. Farrell MacDonald *(Angus McGregor)*, Clyde Cook *(Pete)*, Kent Sanderson *(Wilbur Watkins)*, Douglas Scott *(Wobby)*, Slim Summerville *(Slim)*, Tom Wilson *(Baggage Master)*, Eulalie Jensen *(Queen of Lisonia)*, David Torrence *(President of the Railroad)*, Dolores Johnson *(Prima Donna)*, Robert Ryan, Jack Pennick *(Baggage Men)*.

McLaglen and director Ford seemed to have a good time putting together this ordinary screenplay about a giant of a baggage handler, who goes about doing good deeds, earning promotions, and in the end breaks up a train robbery. Joy, as the newsstand girl he loves, doesn't have very much to do except to realize that her boy will never graduate to a white collar position. But McLaglen's characterization of the not-too-bright mountainous fellow, and Ford's affectionate handling of him, make for the most interesting forerunner to their Academy Award-winning collaboration, THE INFORMER (1935).

d, John Ford; w, James Kevin McGuinness, Andrew Bennison, John McLain (based on a story by Frederick Hazlitt Brennan); t, Malcolm Stuart Boylan; ph, Joseph August; syn sc; s eff.

Comedy/Drama (PR:A MPAA:NR)

STRONG MAN, THE*½** (1926) 7 reels Harry Langdon/FN bw

Harry Langdon *(Paul Bergot)*, Priscilla Bonner *(Mary Brown)*, Gertrude Astor *(Gold Tooth)*, William V. Mong *(Parson Brown)*, Robert McKim *(Roy McDevitt)*, Arthur Thalasso *(Zandow the Great)*.

Langdon's most satisfying feature has the comic playing a Belgian soldier who falls in love with his American pen pal, Bonner. Langdon comes to the U.S. after the war with Thalasso, a German circus performer he met while a prisoner, and begins searching for the girl of his dreams. They finally meet when his show plays a little town which has been taken over by bootleggers. And because she turns out to be blind, he is allowed to win her love by being himself. (Chaplin would later use the blind girl angle in his 1931 masterpiece CITY LIGHTS and approach it from the directly opposite direction.) Langdon even wins the respect of Bonner's show business-hating father when in some beautifully staged and very funny sequences he subdues a gang of crooks who have terrorized the community. This would be Langdon's last film with Frank Capra, the man most responsible for his success. They had fought during most of the production, and now they were to go their separate ways. The great Italian-American director to the top, and the strangest of all film comedians to oblivion.

d, Frank Capra; w, Arthur Ripley, Capra; ph, Elgin Lessley, Glenn Kershner.

Comedy (PR:A MPAA:NR)

STRUGGLE, THE** (1921) 5 reels William N. Selig/Canyon bw

Franklyn Farnum *(Dick Storm)*, Genevieve Bert *(Norma Day)*, Edwin Wallock *(Hayes Storm)*, Karl Formes *(Dr. Beer)*, Vester Pegg *(Diamond Joe)*, Bud Osborne *(Sheriff)*, George Washington Jones *(Pumpkins)*.

Plenty of action in this unpretentious little western about a hard-fighting army vet who heads West to join an outlaw gang but is reformed instead by the love of a good woman.

d, Otto Lederer; w, William E. Wing.

Western (PR:A MPAA:NR)

STUDENT OF PRAGUE, THE****

(1927, Ger.) 5 reels Sokal bw (DER STUDENT VON PRAG; AKA: THE MAN WHO CHEATED LIFE)

Conrad Veidt *(Baldwin)*, Werner Krauss *(Scapinelli)*, Agnes Esterhazy, Elizza La Porte, Ferdinand von Alten.

The second version of the famous story by Hanns Heinz Ewers (who later gained notoriety for becoming the official chronicler of Nazi hero Horst Wessel) that owes its debt to the Germanic legend of Faust. A 1913 original was directed by Stellan Rye, and a 1936 production starred Anton Walbrook, but this version is historic because it practically closed out Germany's romantic Gothic cinema period and therefore contains both wild expressionist sets, stylishness, and elements of the oncoming naturalism. Veidt gives a brilliant portrayal of a student who sells his reflection in the mirror to the eccentric Scapinelli (Krauss) in exchange for riches and the woman he loves. The reflection then becomes a Doppleganger which haunts him until he finally commits suicide. One of the few standout directorial efforts by Galeen, he brings beautiful poetic atmosphere to haunt the story and nurtures the deep psychology of its theme, with Veidt performing the role with an ability he never showed again. A superb film showing the inner conflicts of the student, the changing atmosphere of its time, with sorrow and human weakness rendered with compassion and skill. THE STUDENT OF PRAGUE is one of the best movies of the school of filmmaking which it helped ring the knell to.

d&w, Henrik Galeen (based on a novel by Hanns Heinz Ewers from the story "William Wilson" by Edgar Allan Poe); ph, Gunther Krampf, Erich Nitzschmann; set d, Hermann Warm.

Drama Cas. (PR:A MPAA:NR)

SUBMARINE PIRATE, A*** (1915) Keystone/TRI bw

Sydney Chaplin, Wesley Ruggles, Glen Cavender, Phyllis Allen, Virginia Fox, Edgar Kennedy, Heinie Conklin.

Good mixture of laughter and thrills has Chaplin (Charlie's half brother) playing a waiter who overhears a gang of pirates plotting their next job, and then foiling the caper by taking over the submarine they use for the deed.

d, Charles Avery, Sydney Chaplin; sup&w, Mack Sennett.

Comedy (PR:A MPAA:NR)

SUBURBAN, THE** (1915) 4 reels Imp bw

King Baggot *(Don Gordon)*, William Bailey *(His Pal)*, Iva Shepard *(His Bride)*, Brinsley Shaw *(Ralph Fisher)*, Helen Malone *(Fisher's Sister)*, Frank Smith *(Don's Father)*, Ned Reardon.

When Baggot marries secretly, he is disinherited by his father who had chosen the daughter of his former business partner for him. Then, to really rub it in, the old boy appoints the girl's brother his sole heir. Setting off to make his way in the world, Baggot is shanghaied and then shipwrecked in the South Seas. He returns after two years, just in time to see his father's horse win the famed Suburban Handicap and to receive forgiveness when it's disclosed that the little sneak who replaced him in his father's esteem tried to fix the race in his own favor.

d, George A. Lessey; w, James Dayton (based on a story by Charles T. Dazy).

Drama (PR:A MPAA:NR)

SUCCESS*** (1923) 7 reels Murray W. Garsson/Metro bw

Brandon Tynan *(Barry Carleton)*, Naomi Childers *(Jane Randolph)*, Mary Astor *(Rose Randolph)*, Dore Davidson *(Sam Lewis)*, Lionel Adams *(Willis Potter)*, Stanley Ridges *(Gilbert Gordon)*, Robert Lee Keeling *(Henry Briggs)*, Billy Quirk *(Nick Walker)*, Helen Macks *(Ruth)*, Gaylord Pendleton *(Joe)*, John Woodford *(Treadwell)*.

Well-done tear-jerker has Tynan as a great Shakesperean actor who becomes a hopeless drunk, hits bottom, and vanishes into the anonymous mass of skid row citizenry. His wife tells their little girl, Astor, that "daddy is dead," but years later the all-but-forgotten old trooper straightens out and auditions for the part of Lear in the company in which his daughter is now appearing. He is only able to land a job dressing the star of the play (who is madly in love with Astor), but when the actor learns his valet's true identity, *he* goes off on a bender and Tynan goes on in his place. The performance causes a sensation, and after an abundance of tears and smeared grease paint, the family is reunited once again.

d, Ralph Ince; w, Theodore A. Liebler, Jr., Adeline Leitzbach (based on their own play); t, George V. Hobart; ph, William J. Black; set d, Tec-Art Studios.

Drama (PR:A MPAA:NR)

SUCH A LITTLE QUEEN** (1914) 5 reels FP bw

Mary Pickford *(Queen Anna Victoria)*, Carlyle Blackwell *(King Stephen)*, Harold Lockwood *(Robert Trainor)*, Russell Bassett *(The Prime Minister)*, Arthur Hoops *(Prince Eugene)*.

Lesser Pickford effort (under the uninspired direction of Porter and Ford) has America's Sweetheart playing the queen of a comic-opera nation. At the urging of her prime minister she consents to marry Blackwell, the king of a neighboring country, who, like Pickford, has reluctantly agreed to his political advisor's request for a wedding that will bring the two nations closer together for their mutual good. In the middle of the nuptials, Hoops, a rejected former suitor, is anything but able to forever hold his peace, and not only disrupts the ceremony, but also engineers a revolution that sends the regents scurrying off to the U.S. There are a few nice comic touches as the aristocrats attempt to survive in the Big Apple, but the picture ends rather tediously with their return to Europe when cooler heads prevail in their homelands. By the time Pickford sank her teeth into the role of Queen Anna Victoria it had already been essayed by Elsie Ferguson in a stage comedy and Mizzi Hajos in an operetta entitled "Her Little Highness."

d, Edwin S. Porter, Hugh Ford; w, Ford (based on the play by Channing Pollock).

Drama/Comedy (PR:A MPAA:NR)

SUCH A LITTLE QUEEN *** (1921) 5 reels REA bw

Constance Binney *(Anne Victoria of Gzbfernigambia)*, Vincent Coleman *(Stephen of Hetland)*, J. H. Gilmour *(Baron Cosaco)*, Roy Fernandez *(Bob Trainor)*, Frank Losee *(Adolph Lawton)*, Betty Carpenter *(Elizabeth Lawton)*, Jessie Ralph *(Mary)*, Henry Leone *(Boris)*.

Remake of the Mary Pickford hit of 1914, this is actually the better picture because of Fawcett's superior direction, and although she is up against the toughest of all actresses to be compared with, Binney makes a most appealing Anne Victoria. In the story the queen leaves her fiance, Coleman, the king of Hetland, and flees the country with a baron. The two come to the U.S. where they make friends with office worker Fernandez, whose wealthy boss, Losee, finds them an apartment. Losee's daughter, Carpenter, is in love with Fernandez, but believes he has eyes for the queen. In the end, Coleman arrives on the scene, revives the romance with Binney, and Carpenter is offered a proposal of marriage from the man of her dreams.

d, George Fawcett; w, J. Clarkson Miller, Lawrence McCloskey (based on the play by Channing Pollock); ph, Ernest Haller.

Comedy/Drama (PR:A MPAA:NR)

SUDS**** (1920) 5 reels Mary Pickford/UA bw

Mary Pickford *(Amanda Afflick)*, William Austin *(Horace Greensmith)*, Harold Goodwin *(Benjamin Pillsbury Jones)*, Rose Dione *(Mme. Jeanne Gallisilet Didier)*, Theodore Roberts, Taylor Duncan, Hal Wilson, Lavendor *(The Horse)*.

Mary Pickford delivers a wonderful performance, full of laughter and pathos, as a homely little slavey in a cheap London laundry. In STELLA MARIS, by playing a double role, the actress was able to create the unforgettable Unity Blake—ugly and pathetic—and still satisfy her public by giving them the Mary they loved. But here, the film ends with the central character very much alone, her heart broken, her future doomed. It took great courage to make this picture—and it paid off—artistically.

d, Jack Dillon; w, Waldemar Young (based on the play "Op o' Me Thumb" by Frederick Fenn, Richard Pryce); ph, Charles Rosher.

Drama **(PR:A MPAA:NR)**

SUMMER BACHELORS*** (1926) 6 reels FOX bw

Madge Bellamy *(Derry Thomas)*, Allan Forrest *(Tony Landor)*, Matt Moore *(Walter Blakely)*, Hale Hamilton *(Beverly Greenway)*, Leila Hyams *(Willowdean French)*, Charles Winninger *(Preston Smith)*, Clifford Holland *(Martin Cole)*, Olive Tell *(Mrs. Preston Smith)*, Walter Catlett *(Bachelor No. 1)*, James F. Cullen *(Bachelor No. 2)*, Cosmo Kyrle Bellew *(Bachelor No. 3)*, Charles Esdale *(Bachelor No. 4)*.

There is just a hint of naughtiness in this delightful Dwan-directed comedy, which has Bellamy playing a girl adverse to marriage because of her sisters' bad experiences, who opens a club for the enjoyment of men whose wives have fled New York's oppressive summer heat. At a department store she meets Forrest, a wealthy man she assumes to be married, and invites him to join her club. Later, while under a hypnotic trance at a party, she admits she's in love with him. That's all that Forrest , who is actually single, needs to hear, and in the wink of an eye he calls upon a fellow, who happens to be a judge, to marry them.

d, Allan Dwan; w, James Shelly Hamilton (based on the novel *Summer Widowers* by Warner Fabian); ph, Joseph Ruttenberg; art d, Sam Corso; set d, Al Panci, Miss S. Baxter.

Comedy **(PR:A MPAA:NR)**

SUMURUN (SEE: ONE ARABIAN NIGHT, 1921, Ger.)

SUNRISE—A SONG OF TWO HUMANS***** (1927) 9 reels FOX bw (AKA: SUNRISE)

George O'Brien *(The Man)*, Janet Gaynor *(The Wife)*, Bodil Rosing *(Maid)*, Margaret Livingston *(Woman from the City)*, J. Farrell MacDonald *(Photographer)*, Ralph Sipperly *(Barber)*, Jane Winton *(Manicure Girl)*, Arthur Housman *(The Obtrusive Gentleman)*, Eddie Boland *(The Obliging Gentleman)*, Sally Eilers, Gino Corrado, Barry Norton, Robert Kortman, Sidney Bracey.

On the strength of his two great German films, FAUST and THE LAST LAUGH, William Fox brought director Murnau to Hollywood and gave him a completely free reign. The result, SUNRISE—A SONG OF TWO HUMANS, was one of the most beautiful films ever made. The story is a simple one, dealing with a handsome country boy (O'Brien) who is seduced by an earthy woman of the city (Livingston). The vamp then convinces O'Brien to kill his wife Gaynor, sell his farm, and join her where the bright lights shine. O'Brien plans to dispose of Gaynor by drowning her, and claim that there was a boating accident. But when the time comes and they reach the middle of the lake, he gets up to do the deed and her screams seem to break the spell. Guilt ridden, O'Brien rows like a man possessed until he reaches the far shore, where his terrified wife scrambles to get away and boards a trolley. (From this point on nothing seems quite real, and the film takes on that stylized look which distinguished much of the German cinema). The trolley makes its way through its fantasy rural world with O'Brien, who got on at the last second, begging for forgiveness. They finally reach the city—a truly wondrous set with everything blown out of proportion and scale to create the impression of what it would be through the eyes of these simple folk who had never seen its likes before. There O'Brien takes Gaynor into a restaurant, where he buys her cakes and tries to obtain her absolution (much of Murnau's work uses Catholic symbology) and slowly she begins to yield. Then they set out on a series of adventures, which include a visit to a barbershop (again bigger then life), a photographer's studio, a church where they eavesdrop on a wedding and renew their own vows, and finally to an amusement park. Through it all Murnau's camera moves constantly, and we feel ourselves being sucked right into the middle of the drama as only the silent cinema is capable of doing. When the time comes for them to return home and they make their way across the water, the couple are more in love than at any time in their lives. It is the most idyllic of scenes until suddenly the thunder begins to roar and the lightning cracks across the heavens (the musical score and moderately used sound effects do much to enhance here) and the waves begin to toss the tiny boat about like a leaf in the wind. O'Brien quickly gives his wife the bulrushes he had planned to use earlier to assure his own survival, and the craft capsizes. The young man somehow makes it to shore and the storm leaves as quickly as it arrived. But there is no sign of the girl. Grief-stricken, O'Brien is led back to his farmhouse by his neighbors while the fishing ships cast off to search for the worst. Livingston, believing that this is all part of her paramour's act, comes to him in the night. When O'Brien sees her he goes insane and chases her through the swamp, intent on destroying her. Livingston stumbles and O'Brien is on top of her, squeezing her throat with all of his force, when he hears his mother's joyous cry announcing that his wife has been found alive. O'Brien releases his grip and leaves to join the woman he loves. The next morning, Livingston boards the boat which will take her back to the city. Gaynor's performance here and in SEVENTH HEAVEN, made the same year, won her the first Academy Award ever given for best actress. Everything about this film is exquisite, including the cinematography, which also won Academy Awards for Rosher and Struss.

d, F. W. Murnau; w, Carl Mayer (based on the novel *Die Reise nach Tilsit* by Hermann Sudermann); t, Katherine Hilliker, H. H. Caldwell; ph, Charles Rosher, Karl Struss; m, Hugo Riesenfeld; ed, Hilliker, Caldwell; prod d, Rochus Gliese; art d, Edgar Ulmer; syn sc; s eff.

Drama **(PR:A MPAA:NR)**

SUNSET DERBY, THE** (1927) 6 reels FN bw

Mary Astor *(Molly Gibson)*, William Collier, Jr. *(Jimmy Burke)*, Ralph Lewis *(Sam Gibson)*, David Kirby *(Mike Donovan)*, Lionel Belmore *(Jock McTeague)*, Burt Ross *(Bobby McTeague)*, Henry Barrows *("Lucky" Davis)*, Bobby Doyle *(Skeeter Donohue)*, Michael Visaroff *(Peddler)*.

Just another racehorse movie, this time dealing with a jockey, Collier, who loses his nerve after a riding fall, but regains it just in time to win the all-important competition, as well as the love of beautiful Astor.

p, Charles R. Rogers; d, Albert Rogell; w, Curtis Benton (based on the story by William Dudley Pelley); t, Mort Blumenstock; ph, Ross Fisher.

Drama **(PR:A MPAA:NR)**

SUNSET LEGION, THE*** (1928) 7 reels PAR bw

Fred Thomson *(Black-Robed Stranger/Whittling Cowboy)*, William Courtright *(Old Bill)*, Edna Murphy *(Susan)*, Harry Woods *(Honest John)*, Silver King *(The Horse)*.

Popular Thomson plays a dual role in this entertaining western about a Texas Ranger who rides into an outlaw-infested town and passes himself off as a timid salesman of firearms. Before long he falls in love with Murphy, a miner's daughter, but she's attracted to the dashing "Black-Robed Stranger," a Zorro-like figure whom Thomson becomes in order to bring the gang and its saloon owning leader, Woods, to justice. After a number of thrilling sequences, many of which feature Thomson's magnificant horse, Silver King (who also sports a black costume), the hero gets the job done, reveals his true identity, and wins the love of the woman he adores.

d, Lloyd Ingraham, Alfred L. Werker; w, Frank M. Clifton; t, Garrett Graham; ph, Mack Stengler; ed, Duncan Mansfield.

Western **(PR:A MPAA:NR)**

SUNSET PASS** 1/2** (1929) 6 reels PAR bw

Jack Holt *(Jack Rock)*, Nora Lane *(Leatrice Preston)*, John Loder *(Ashleigh Preston)*, Christian J. Frank *(Chuck)*, Pee Wee Holmes *(Shorty)*, Chester Conklin *(Windy)*, Pat Harmon *(Clink Peeples)*, Alfred Allen *(Amos Dabb)*, Guy Oliver *(Clark)*, James Mason.

Holt plays a marshal working undercover as a cowpuncher on a ranch owned by Englishman Loder, whom he suspects is a cattle rustler. His suspicions prove correct, but Holt, who has fallen in love with Loder's sister Lane, gives the crook a chance to reform. Loder refuses and in a final showdown is killed by Holt. After Holt's contract with Paramount had lapsed, that studio resourcefully used footage from the actor's high-budget silents and melded them into low-budget sound films as a means of saving money during the Depression era. In the 1933 remake of SUNSET PASS starring Randolph Scott, a new cast was dressed in the same costumes used in the silent version to match the footage showing long shots of Holt (who went uncredited).

d, Otto Brower; w, J. Walter Ruben, Ray Harris (based on the story by Zane Grey); t, Harris; ph, Roy Clark; ed, Jane Loring.

Western **(PR:A MPAA:NR)**

SUNSHINE TRAIL THE*** (1923) 5 reels THI/AFN bw

Douglas MacLean *(James Henry MacTavish)*, Edith Roberts *(June Carpenter)*, Muriel Frances Dana *(Algernon Aloysius Fitzmaurice Bangs)*, Rex Cherryman *(Willis Duckworth)*, Josephine Sedgwick *(Woman Crook)*, Albert Hart *(Col. Duckworth)*, Barney Furey *(Man Crook)*, William Courtright *(Mystery Man)*.

Engaging satirical farce in which MacLean decides his mission in life is to "scatter seeds of kindness" as he makes his way back home to the East. Along the way, the good soul encounters numerous complications, which include being robbed of his money and clothes, inadvertently helping a couple of crooks escape the law, and finally being jailed for impersonating himself in order to inherit a fortune. But when word reaches his hometown that MacLean *wasn't* killed in the war, the lad is set free, given a hero's welcome, and also catches the attention of Roberts, the girl he's loved since they both were kids.

d, James W. Horne; w, Bradley King (based on a story by William Wallace Cook); ph, Henry Sharp.

Comedy/Western **(PR:A MPAA:NR)**

SUPER-SEX, THE*** (1922) 6 reels Frank R. Adams/American Releasing bw

Robert Gordon *(Miles Brewster Higgins)*, Charlotte Pierce *(Irene Hayes)*, Tully Marshall *(Mr. Higgins)*, Lydia Knott *(Mrs. Higgins)*, Gertrude Claire *(Grandma Brewster)*, Albert MacQuarrie *(Cousin Roy)*, Louis Natheaux *(J. Gordon Davis)*, George Bunny *(Mr. Hayes)*, Evelyn Burns *(Mrs. Hayes)*.

Well-directed and acted comedy, in the Charles Ray tradition, has Gordon, a shy small-town youth, standing by in silence as his girl friend, Pierce, becomes smitten by the flashy attentions of a newly arrived, slick-talking auto salesman. When Gordon strikes it rich through a lucky stock investment, he decides to use his newly acquired wealth to lure the traitor back and then get even by dumping her. But his grandmother quickly informs the town grapevine that he actually lost his shirt in the market, and Pierce declares her love for him anyway, bringing the film to a happy and most satisfying conclusion.

p, P. H. Burke; d&w, Lambert Hillyer; ph, John S. Stumar.

Comedy **(PR:A MPAA:NR)**

SUPREME TEST, THE zero (1923) 6 reels Cosmosart bw

Johnny Harron, Gloria Grey, Minna Redman, Eugene Beaudino, Dorothy Revier, Ernest Shields, Geraldine Powell, Gene Walsh.

Hopeless, inept, and banal melodrama about a man wrongly accused of a crime, who clears himself in time to marry the blind girl he loves, just before she has her sight restored in the last 400 feet of the film.

p, J. E. Bowan; d&w, W. P. MacNamara.

Drama (PR:A MPAA:NR)

SURE FIRE FLINT*** (1922) 7 reels Mastadon bw

Johnny Hines *(Sure Fire Flint)*, Edmund Breese *(Johnny Jetts)*, Robert Edeson *(Anthony De Lanni)*, Effie Shannon *(Mrs. De Lanni)*, Barney Sherry *(The Proud Father)*, Doris Kenyon *(June De Lanni)*, Charles Gerard *(Dipley Poole)*.

Good Hines vehicle gives the comedian plenty of room for stunt work playing a WW I vet who is fired from a number of jobs before finally landing a managerial position as a reward for returning the plant owner's lost cash. In the end, he saves Kenyon, the boss's daughter, whom he loves, from a safe in which the villain locked her.

p, C. C. Burr; d, Del Henderson; w, Gerald C. Duffy; t, Ralph Spence; ph, Billy Bitzer, Charles Gibson, Neil Sullivan.

Comedy/Adventure (PR:A MPAA:NR)

SURGING SEAS** (1924) 5 reels Hurricane/New-Cal bw

Charles Hutchison *(Bob Sinclair)*, Edith Thornton *(Edith Stafford)*, George Hackathorne *(Charles Stafford)*, David Torrence *(Lionel Sinclair)*, Earl Metcalfe *(Edwin Sinclair)*, Charles Force *(Capt. Regan)*, Pat Harmon *(Mate Hansen)*.

Hutchison, the popular serial star better known as "Hurricane Hutch," delivers the expected number of daredevil stunts in this feature, in which he clears himself of an attempted murder charge, beats the real villain into submission, and wins back the heart of Thornton, the girl he loves.

p, William Steiner; d, James Chapin; w, J. F. Natteford; ph, Ernest Miller.

Adventure (PR:A MPAA:NR)

SUZANNA 1/2** (1922) 8 reels MS/Allied bw

Mabel Normand *(Suzanna)*, George Nichols *(Don Fernando)*, Walter McGrail *(Ramon)*, Evelyn Sherman *(Dona Isabella)*, Leon Bary *(Pancho)*, Eric Mayne *(Don Diego)*, Winifred Bryson *(Dolores)*, Carl Stockdale *(Ruiz)*, Lon Poff *(Alvarez)*, George Cooper *(Miguel)*, Indian Minnie *(Herself)*, Black Hawk *(Himself)*.

This modestly produced tale of old California was a tame comedy by Sennett standards, but still delivered a number of laughs. Normand gives a pleasing performance as the peasant girl who is loved by an aristocrat, McGrail, while Bryson, the daughter of wealthy rancher Mayne, adores a bullfighter. In the end, however, everything works out when it is revealed that Normand was kidnaped as a child and is the true daughter of Mayne. Both young women are finally free to marry the men they really love, leaving both sets of parents equally happy.

d, F. Richard Jones; sup&w, Mack Sennett (based on the story by Linton Wells); ph, Homer Scott, Fred W. Jackman, Robert Walters; ed, Allen McNeil; art d, Sanford D. Barnes; cos, Mme. Violet.

Comedy/Drama (PR:A MPAA:NR)

SWAMP, THE*** (1921) 6 reels Hayakawa/R-C bw

Sessue Hayakawa *(Wang)*, Bessie Love *(Mary)*, Janice Wilson *(Norma)*, Frankie Lee *(Buster)*, Lillian Langdon *(Mrs. Biddle)*, Harland Tucker *(Spencer Wellington)*, Ralph McCullough *(Johnnie Rand)*.

There is a lot of kindness in this drama which has Hayakawa playing a Chinese vegetable peddler who befriends a boy and his deserted mother. When their rent is due, the Chinaman sells his horse to prevent their eviction, and discovers the new landlord to be an old sweetheart of the mother. Then, with the boy acting as his assistant, Hayakawa develops a successful mind-reading act, which is booked to play at the bigamous wedding of the child's father. Using his routine, Hayakawa exposes the cad for what he is, opens the door for his friend to marry the landlord, buys back his horse, and returns to the Orient to marry the girl who has saved herself for him.

d, Colin Campbell; w, J. Grubb Alexander (based on a story by Sessue Hayakawa); ph, Frank D. Williams; art d, W. L. Heywood.

Drama (PR:A MPAA:NR)

SWEET ADELINE*** (1926) 7 reels CHAD bw

Charles Ray *(Ben Wilson)*, Gertrude Olmstead *(Adeline)*, Jack Clifford *(Bill Wilson)*, John P. Lockney *(Pa Wilson)*, Sibyl Johnston *(Fat Lady)*, Gertrude Short *(Cabaret Dancer)*, Ida Lewis *(Ma Wilson)*.

Entertaining Ray feature has the actor again playing a small-town youth. This time he's constantly harassed by an oafish older brother who also competes with him for the affection of Adeline (Olmstead), the prettiest girl in the county. Possessing a good singing voice, Ray takes off for Chicago to forge a theatrical career and lands a job performing in a nightclub. His hick-like demeanor causes the audience to laugh him right off the stage. But the gritty lad returns, tears off his jacket, steps back into the spotlight, and brings down the house with a beautiful rendition of "Sweet Adeline." There is of course an impresario present who knows a *real* voice when he hears one, thus assuring Ray a bright future in the world of music, as well as the love of the girl back home.

d, Jerome Storm; w, Charles E. Banks (based on the song "Sweet Adeline" by Richard H. Gerrard, Harry Armstrong); ph, Philip Tannura.

Comedy/Drama (PR:A MPAA:NR)

SWEET SIXTEEN* (1928) 6 reels T/C/Ray bw

Helen Foster *(Cynthia Perry)*, Gertrude Olmstead *(Patricia Perry)*, Gladden James *(Howard De Hart)*, Lydia Yeamans Titus *(Grandma Perry)*, Reginald Sheffield *(Tommy Lowell)*, William H. Tooker *(Patrick Perry)*, Harry Allen, Carolynne Snowden.

Foster does as well as can be expected in this low-budget picture about a teenaged girl who falls under the spell of an older man. But Foster's virtue is saved by her older sister, Olmstead, who risks *her* reputation by going to the rotter's appartment and showing him up for what he really is.

d, Scott Pembroke; w, Arthur Hoerl (based on a story by Phyllis Duganne); ph, Walter Griffin; ed, J. S. Harrington.

Drama (PR:A MPAA:NR)

SWELL-HEAD, THE 1/2** (1927) 6 reels COL bw

Ralph Graves *(Lefty Malone)*, Johnnie Walker *(Bill O'Rourke)*, Eugenia Gilbert *(Molly O'Rourke)*, Mildred Harris *(Kitty)*, Mary Carr *(Mother Malone)*, Tom Dugan.

Acceptable prizefight programmer has Graves going into the ring to make the money needed for his crippled mother's operation. The promoters build him up with a couple of setups, and the kid develops a head the size of the Statue of Liberty. Before long, he's hanging around with a vampish flapper, drinking great quantities of liquor, and completely ignoring the girl from the old neighborhood who loves him. Then they put him into the ring with a contender who knocks his block off. The excitement somehow causes his mother to regain the use of her legs, Graves learns his lesson, and his sweetheart completely forgives him.

p, Harry Cohn; d, Ralph Graves; w, Robert Lord; ph, Conrad Wells.

Drama (PR:A MPAA:NR)

SWORD OF VALOR, THE* (1924) 5 reels Phil Goldstone bw

Rex "Snowy" Baker, Dorothy Revier, Percy Challenger, Eloise Hess, Stella De Lanti, Otto Lederer, Fred Kavens, Armando Pasquali, Edward Cecil.

The daughter of a Spanish don falls in love with an American captain the moment she sees him. Her father takes the girl to the Riviera, where she is promised to a wealthy cad, but the captain arrives in time to rescue her from him as well as a crazed gypsy who has abducted her.

d, Duke Worne; w, Jefferson Moffitt (based on a story by Julio Sabello); ph, Roland Price.

Adventure (PR:A MPAA:NR)

SYLVIA GRAYzero (1914) 4 reels Broadway Star/VIT bw

Helen Gardner, Charles Kent, Mary Charleson, Gladden James, Charles Dietz, Evelyn Dumo.

Perfectly dreadful picture has a playwright and his wife and child living on the edge of poverty. Everything depends on him selling his latest work, so when a rejection letter arrives, his wife takes off, leaving him with the kids. Then another producer comes forward and pays him $5,000 for the rights, and the playwright hides the bills in his wall. It is then that he discovers his wife has flown the coop with another man and his reaction is a perfectly normal one—he loses his memory and his mind and vanishes from the scene. Years pass, and the child grows up to be an artist's model. As fate would have it, all of the characters who have appeared up to this point return to the little village at the same time, and there is a lot nonsense involving a search for the hidden $5,000. It all works out in the end of course, but the movie is so ludicrous, and unintentionally hilarious, that after the first reel nobody really cares.

d&w, Charles L. Gaskill.

Mystery (PR:A MPAA:NR)

SYMPHONY, THE (SEE: JAZZ MAD, 1928)

SYNCOPATING SUE*** (1926) 7 reels Corinne Griffith/FN bw

Corinne Griffith *(Susan Adams)*, Tom Moore *(Eddie Murphy)*, Rockliffe Fellowes *(Arthur Bennett)*, Lee Moran *(Joe Horn)*, Joyce Compton *(Marge Adams)*, Sunshine Hart *(Landlady)*, Marjorie Rambeau *(Herself)*.

Stylish comedy has Griffith, an aspiring actress, and Moore, a jazz drummer, overcome a number of obstacles to be united in one of Hollywood's zaniest denouements. After a misunderstanding, Moore sets sail to play on a cruise as Griffith chases him to the end of the pier and shouts her love for him. The fellow then jumps overboard, the girl leaps from the dock, and they end up in each other's arms, floating on the big bass drum that a pal threw over the side.

d, Richard Wallace; w, Adelaide Heilbron, Jack Wagner (based on the play by Reginald Butler Goode); ph, Harold Wenstrom.

Comedy Romance (PR:A MPAA:NR)

T

TABU**** (1931) 6 reels F. W. Murnau-Robert J. Flaherty/PAR bw

Anna Chevalier *(Reri, the Young Girl)*, Matahi *(The Young Man)*, Hitu *(Chief)*, Jean *(Police Agent)*, Jules *(Captain)*, Kong Ah *(Chinese Tradesman)*.

Following the difficulties director Murnau had with Fox while making CITY GIRL (aka: OUR DAILY BREAD), the director met with another Hollywood maverick, Robert (NANOOK OF THE NORTH) Flaherty. The documentary filmmaker told the German a story he had heard in the South Seas about a pearl diver, and Murnau could hardly contain his enthusiasm. Here was an opportunity to leave the politics of the studio system behind and collaborate with a fellow artist on the business of creating beauty. The cinema giants had little trouble convincing an independent company, called Colorart, to put up the money, and Flaherty left to get things under way. Murnau set sail on his new yacht *The Bali* for a leisurely trip to Tahiti, where he joined his friend. To his horror the German discovered that the company had gone broke, Flaherty was all but bankrupt, and shooting had come to a halt. Murnau was determined to finish his film, however, and began paying for the production out of his own pocket. But the project almost seemed to be cursed, and over the next 18 months the company was faced with bad weather, numerous accidents, illness on the part of cast and crew, and growing strife between the codirectors. Flaherty decided to drop out, and the two parted amicably. So what we have in this film, which Murnau did manage to complete, is a romantic and poetic work of art rather than the realistic documentary, which would have been more in evidence had Flaherty played a bigger part. The story is about a beautiful native girl who has been consecrated to the gods by her people, and because of this is forbidden to fall in love with or marry a mortal. She does, however, fall in love, and to prevent her from consummating the emotion the island's holy man has the girl snatched from the arms of her lover and taken away on his ship. The young man,heartbroken, attempts to swim after them, but eventually becomes exhausted and perishes in the water. It is a beautiful, highly stylized work of art and, fortunately, Flaherty was able to make a deal with Paramount to provide the funds for its completion, commission an original score, and handle distribution. But Paramount went one better and offered Murnau a 10-year contract. The director returned triumphantly to Hollywood and then made plans to sail for Europe to visit his mother. A fortune teller he was in the habit of consulting told the director that he would be with his mother on April 5, a date which was not in keeping with his plans. Shortly thereafter, the artist (who, by the way, was shot down a number of times while serving his country in WW I and was the only member of his squadron to survive) was thrown from his automobile and killed on the outskirts of Los Angeles. His remains were shipped back to Germany where they arrived on the fourth of April, and were claimed by the woman who gave him life on the fifth.

p, F. W. Murnau, Robert Flaherty, David Flaherty; d, Murnau; w, Murnau, Robert Flaherty; ph, Floyd Crosby; m, Hugo Riesenfeld; syn sc; s eff.

Drama **(PR:A MPAA:NR)**

TAILOR MADE MAN, A*** (1922) 9 reels Charles Ray/UA bw

Charles Ray *(John Paul Bart)*, Thomas Ricketts *(Anton Huber)*, Ethel Grandin *(Tanya Huber)*, Victor Potel *(Peter)*, Stanton Heck *(Abraham Nathan)*, Edythe Chapman *(Mrs. Nathan)*, Irene Lentz *(Miss Nathan)*, Frederick Thompson *(Mr. Stanlaw)*, Kate Lester *(Mrs. Stanlaw)*, Jacqueline Logan *(Corinne Stanlaw)*, Frank Butler *(Theodore Jellicot)*, Douglas Gerrard *(Gustavus Sonntag)*, Nellie Peck Saunders *(Kitty Dupuy)*, Charlotte Pierce *(Bessie Dupuy)*, Thomas Jefferson *(Gerald Whitcomb)*, Henry Barrows *(Hobart Sears)*, Eddie Gribbon *(Russell)*, Michael Dark *(Cecil Armstrong)*, Isabelle Vernon *(Mrs. Fitzmorris)*, Aileen Manning *(Miss Shayn), John McCallum (Butler)*, William Parke *(Rowlands)*, Frederick Vroom *(Harvey Benton)*, Harold Howard *(Arthur Arbuthnot)*, S. J. Bingham *(Cain)*, Fred Sullivan *(Flynn)*.

Ray, the all-American boy, is at his best in this comedy-adventure about a pants-presser who borrows an expensive suit, crashes a society party, and lands a job managing labor relations for a big shipping company. Before long, however, the lad is exposed by his rival, Gerrard, and forced to return to his former position in the tailor shop. But when word reaches him that there is trouble at the shipyard, he fights his way (in the grandest Douglas Fairbanks tradition) through an army of agitators, and reaches the docks in time to prevent a strike. For this Ray is given an executive appointment and asks the tailor's daughter to join him at the top of the ladder.

d, Joseph De Grasse; w, Albert Ray (based on the play by Harry James Smith); ph, George Rizard, George Meehan; ed, Harry L. Decker; art d, Robert Ellis.

Comedy/Adventure **(PR:A MPAA:NR)**

TAILOR OF BOND STREET, THE** (1916, Brit.) 5 reels Barker/Gerrard bw

Augustus Yorke *(Marcovitch Einstein)*, Robert Leonard *(Lew Mendel)*, Peggy Richards *(Esther)*, Kenneth Barker *(Reggie as a Child)*, Thomas H. MacDonald *(Reggie Einstein)*.

This British drama pulls at the heartstrings in telling the story of an ambitious young Jew who changes his name and identity to succeed—even denying his father's existence—until the last reel, when the oldtimer dies in his arms.

Drama **(PR:A MPAA:NR)**

TAKE IT FROM ME*** (1926) 7 reels UNIV-Jewel bw

Reginald Denny *(Tom Eggett)*, Blanche Mehaffey *(Grace Gordon)*, Ben Hendricks, Jr. *(Dick)*, Lee Moran *(Van)*, Lucien Littlefield *(Cyrus Crabb)*, Ethel Wales *(Miss Abbott)*, Bertram Johns *(Percy)*, Jean Tolley *(Gwen Forsythe)*, Tom O'Brien *(Taxi Driver)*, Vera Lewis *(Mrs. Forsythe)*.

Lots of belly laughs in this breezy Denny comedy which has a bankrupt young man inheriting his uncle's floundering department store, providing he can run it at a profit for three months. Denny turns the place into an amusement park, with sales clerks on roller skates, mannequins dressed in Paris gowns, and countless other innovations. Of course the go-getter pulls it off, foils the plot of his uncle's manager to ruin him, and finds love with the lovely secretary who helped him make the grade.

d, William A. Seiter; w, Harvey Thew (based on the play by William B. Johnstone, Will R. Anderson); ph, Arthur Todd.

Comedy **(PR:A MPAA:NR)**

TAKE ME HOME 1/2** (1928) 6 reels PAR bw

Bebe Daniels *(Peggy Lane)*, Neil Hamilton *(David North)*, Lilyan Tashman *(Derelys Devore)*, Doris Hill *(Alice Moore)*, Joe E. Brown *(Bunny)*, Ernie Wood *(Al Marks)*, Marcia Harris *(Landlady)*, Yvonne Howell *(Elsie)*, Janet MacLeod *(Betty)*, J. W. Johnston *(The Producer)*.

The great director, Neilan, was already at the beginning of his tragic decline (he had taken on Louis B. Mayer—and the bottle— one too many times) when he made this adequate backstage dramatic comedy about a chorus girl (Daniels) who loves stage-struck country boy Hamilton, gives a licking to Tashman, the vampish star who tries to seduce him, and then makes her go on stage disheveled and bruised. Daniels then performs, creates a sensation, but decides to settle down on the farm with Hamilton.

d, Marshall Neilan; w, Ethel Doherty (based on a story by Harlan Thompson); t, Herman Mankiewicz; ph, J. Roy Hunt; ed, Otho Lovering.

Dramatic Comedy **(PR:A MPAA:NR**

TAKING CHANCES 1/2** (1922) 5 reels Phil Goldstone bw

Richard Talmadge *(Himself)*, Zella Gray *(Mildred Arlington)*, Elmer Dewey *(Jose Borquez)*, Percy Challenger *(James Arlington)*.

Talmadge is given plenty of opportunity to display his amazing acrobatic skills in this adventure about a young man who lands a job as secretary to a tycoon, saves his company from a Mexican crook, and wins the man's daughter for his efforts. The stunt work is overdone, but in a Talmadge movie that's most of the fun.

d, Grover Jones; w, (based on the story "Vim, Vigor, and Vitality", anon); ph, Harry Fowler.

Adventure **(PR:A MPAA:NR**

TALE OF TWO CITIES, A* 1/2** (1917) 7 reels FOX bw

William Farnum *(Charles Darnay/Sidney Carton)*, Jewel Carmen *(Lucie Manette)*, Charles Clary *(Marquis St. Evremonde)*, Herschel Mayall *(Jacques De Farge)*, Rosita Marstini *(Mme. De Farge)*, Josef Swickard *(Dr. Alexandre Manette)*, Ralph Lewis *(Roger Cly)*, William Clifford *(Gabelle)*, Marc Robbins *(Mr. Jarvis Lorry)*, Willard Louis *(Mr. Stryver)*, Olive White, Harry De Vere, Florence Vidor, James Morrison.

Beautifully directed, acted, and photographed motion picture. The double-exposure shots showing Darnay and Carton (both played by Farnum) together are perhaps the best ever executed up to this point. Based on the classic Dickens novel, set during the French Reign of Terror, it retells the story of a man who sacrifices his life to the guillotine in order that his rival, and the woman they both love, might find happiness.

d&w, Frank Lloyd (based on the novel by Charles Dickens); ph, William C. Foster

Costume Drama **(PR:A MPAA:NR**

TALE OF TWO WORLDS, A*** (1921) 6 reels Goldwyn bw

J. Frank Glendon *(Newcombe)*, Leatrice Joy *(Sui Sen)*, Wallace Beery *(Ling Jo)*, E. A. Warren *(Ah Wing)*, Margaret McWade *(Attendant)*, Togo Yamamoto *(One Eye)*, Jack Abbe *(The Worm)*, Louie Cheung *(Chinaman)*, Chow Young *(Slave Girl)*, Etta Lee *(Ah Fah)*, Ah Wing *(Servant Spy)*, Goro Kino *(Windlass Man)*, Arthur Soames *(Dr. Newcombe)*, Edythe Chapman *(Mrs. Newcombe)*, Dwight Crittenden *(Mr. Carmichael)*, Irene Rich *(Mrs. Carmichael)*.

When her parents are killed during the Boxer Rebellion, Joy is taken in by a faithful servant and raised as her own child in San Francisco's Chinatown. Years later, a nasty Boxer leader (played quite believably by Beery) abducts the girl, but she's saved by the wealthy American who loves her, and Beery is killed by the trap he himself set for the Yank.

d, Frank Lloyd; w, J. E. Nash (based on a story by Gouverneur Morris); ph, Norbert Brodine.

Drama **(PR:A MPAA:NR**

TANGLE, THE* 1/2 (1914) 4 reels Broadway Star/VIT bw

Darwin Karr *(Lt. Jack Bradley)*, Naomi Childers *(His Sweetheart)*.

When Karr's sweetheart, Childers, finds a picture of his sister in his pocket, she jumps to the wrong conclusion, flies into a rage, and marries his commanding officer. Later she realizes her mistake and tries to make it up to Karr—which throws her husband into a tiff. Along comes the Spanish American War; they all go off to fight and when the colonel is mortally wounded after learning the truth, he orders Karr to marry his widow when things calm down.

d, Harry Lambart; w, Jasper Ewing Brady.

Drama **(PR:A MPAA:NR)**

TANGLED FATES** (1916) 5 reels PEER/WORLD bw

Alice Brady *(Jane Lawson)*, Arthur Ashley *(George Blake)*, Helen Weir *(Ruth Lawson)*, George Morgan *(Will Rogers)*, Edward Kimball.

Brady is thrown out of her New England home after covering for her sister, who innocently spent the evening with a traveling salesman. She heads for New York, lands a job in a department store (where the salesman is now working), and eventually marries the boss' son. The young fellow turns out to be a drunkard and thief, whom the salesman stakes to an Alaskan regeneration trip. There the lad strikes it rich, takes a mistress, and is lynched after shooting a man in the back. Brady is shocked to learn of her husband's behavior, but finds comfort when the salesman proposes marriage, confessing that he has loved her from the start. Brady managed to obtain half of her late spouse's fortune before he departed the scene, which she will now happily share with a man *deserving* of her love.

d, Travers Vale; w, Frances Marion (based on the story "The Grubstaker" by William Anthony McGuire).

Drama **(PR:A MPAA:NR)**

TAR HEEL WARRIOR, THE** (1917) 5 reels TRI bw

Walt Whitman *(Col. Dabney Mills)*, Ann Kroman [Ann Forrest] *(Betty Malroy)*, William Shaw *(Paul Darrell)*, James W. McLaughlin *(James Adams)*, Dorcas Matthews *(Anna Belle Adams)*, George West *(Uncle Tobe)*, Wilbur Higby *(John Mason)*, John P. Lockney *(Lemuel L. Burke)*, Thomas S. Guise *(Maj. Amos)*.

Average programmer has Whitman, a gentleman of the Old South, heading for New York to seek the help of his granddaughter's stockbroker husband, because he's about to lose the family plantation. Unfortunately, the younger man's capital is tied up in a big deal, and Whitman takes $5,000, which is given him by a junior partner to deliver, and blows it in a "sure-fire" deal. Shamed by his actions, the old boy leaves his relatives a note informing them of his intention to return to the plantation and commit suicide. The youngsters rush off to prevent this (secure in the knowledge that the grandson-in-law's project has made them filthy rich) and arrive just in the nick of time. The film ends with Whitman remarking, "Well now that you are here, let's have a drink."

d, E. Mason Hopper; w, J. G. Hawks.

Drama **(PR:A MPAA:NR)**

TARGET, THE* 1/2 (1916) 5 reels Red Feather bw

Hobart Bosworth *(Big Bill Brent)*, Anna Lehr *(His Mother)*, Ronald Bradbury *(Jack Taylor)*, Jane Novak *(Nita)*, A. Kanmeyer *(Walter Peyton)*, Dick La Reno *(George Harris)*, Albert MacQuarrie *(James Fowler)*, Maude George.

Syrupy melodrama has a young lawyer marrying a fast woman and hitting the bottle when she cleans him out. He is sentenced to 15 years for killing a man in a drunken brawl and becomes friendly with a fellow convict who is serving time for a crime he didn't commit. Together they escape to Alaska and rescue a beautiful young woman from a shipwreck. Before long, both men fall in love with her, but the lawyer soon realizes that the girl feels deeply about his pal, and he elects to return home and serve out his sentence. He later ends up in the company of, as a title describes it, "His only true friend, his mother."

d, Norval MacGregor; w, Ronald Bradbury.

Drama **(PR:A MPAA:NR)**

TARTUFFE** (1927, Ger.) 4 reels UFA bw

Emil Jannings *(Tartuffe)*, Werner Krauss *(Orgon)*, Lil Dagover *(Elmire)*.

The French comic dramatist, Moliere, might have gotten a deep sarcastic laugh from this production of his satirical comedy about the religious hypocrite who worms his way into the heart of an old man and gets him to deed all of his property to him, which the old man (Krauss) does in the belief that Tartuffe (Jannings), will marry his daughter. Notwithstanding the fact that the sets are inventive and well lighted, rare for that time, the story's point manages to get lost in the telling. Beginning as a movie within a movie, a repulsive old woman is shown trying to wheedle a fortune from an old man. The elderly man's grandson brings in a movie of "Tartuffe" to show him, hoping to expose the woman, which he does. And the woman, like Tartuffe in the play, is thrown out of the house. On the stage, Tartuffe succeeds in winning the old man's fortune and when he is exposed and ordered from the house, he turns the tables and evicts the family, since he is now possessor of the deed. Only an edict from the king finally saves the foolish old man, and brings Tartuffe his just deserts. As a preachment against hypocrisy, TARTUFFE hardly works; it is slick and pretentious in design and some would say self-conscious in its camera work, with contrasting styles for the modern sequences, and a diffuse style for the film-within-a film sequences. Essentially, it manages to flatter an audience which much prefers the idea of "theater" to what ideas are being presented there.

d, F. W. Murnau; w, Carl Mayer; ph, Karl Freund; set d, Walter Rohrig, Robert Herlth.

Drama **(PR:A MPAA:NR)**

TARZAN OF THE APES*** (1918) 8 reels National Film Corp. of America bw

Elmo Lincoln *(Tarzan)*, Enid Markey *(Jane Porter)*, Gordon Griffith *(Tarzan as a Child)*, True Boardman *(Lord Greystoke)*, Kathleen Kirkham *(Lady Greystoke)*, George B. French *(Binns)*, Colin Kenny *(The Greystoke Nephew)*, Thomas Jefferson *(Prof. Porter)*, Bessie Toner, Fred Wilson, Eugene Pallette, Rex Ingram.

When Winslow Wilson, the actor hired to play the ape man, walked away from immortality on the Louisiana location to join the Army when America joined the war, he was replaced by the mighty Elmo Lincoln (he stood 5-foot 11 1/2 inches and weighed over 200 pounds) who had appeared in a number of D. W. Griffith films. This picture follows the Burroughs novel a lot closer than later versions, telling the story of how British subjects Lord and Lady Greystoke were marooned on the coast of Africa and of how, when they were killed, their son was taken and raised by Kala, a female ape. The boy grows up a part of the jungle, educates himself through his father's books, and eventually meets a British seaman. Before long, the Englishman discovers that Tarzan is the Greystoke heir, goes to his homeland, and returns with a rescue party. In the group is Jane (Enid Markey) and when she takes a look at Elmo's chest, it's love at first sight. The picture ends with the sweethearts returning to civilization together, but not before the film's big "thrill." One of the movie's "highlights" was when Lincoln was attacked by an ancient lion and was forced to actually kill the poor beast with his knife. Its hide was placed on display at the various first- run engagements of TARZAN OF THE APES, and helped to make its investors a fortune. This first TARZAN picture was also one of the first six American films to gross more than $1 million.

d, Scott Sidney; w, William E. Wing (based on the novel by Edgar Rice Burroughs); ph, Harry M. Fowler, Harry Vallejo.

Adventure **Cas.** **(PR:A MPAA:NR)**

TATTERLY** (1919, Brit.) 6 reels Locoque/Artistic bw

Cecil Mannering *(Donald Brett)*, Mercy Hatton *(Ellen Tarrant)*, Charles Rock *(Caleb Fry)*, George Foley *(Hector Kindon)*, Harry Lofting *(Morton Tarrant)*, Madge Tree.

In this British drama, a nasty old man undergoes a change of heart and assumes the identity of his dead servant in order to rescue the young couple he earlier ruined.

d, H. Lisle Lucoque; w, Nellie E. Lucoque (based on a novel by Tom Gallon).

Drama **(PR:A MPAA:NR)**

TAXI DANCER, THE** (1927) 7 reels MGM bw

Joan Crawford *(Joslyn Poe)*, Owen Moore *(Lee Rogers)*, Marc MacDermott *(Henry Brierhalter)*, Gertrude Astor *(Kitty Lane)*, Rockliffe Fellowes *(Stephen Bates)*, Douglas Gilmore *(James Kelvin)*, William Orlamond *(Doc Ganz)*, Claire McDowell *(Aunt Mary)*, Bert Roach *(Charlie Cook)*.

Compelled to leave her impoverished Virginia plantation, Crawford heads for New York where she hopes to make it as a show business dancer. She takes a room in a boarding house, meets Moore, a cardsharp who becomes her protector, and is finally forced to accept work as a 10-cents-a-dance girl. Through a wise-cracking fellow employee, Crawford meets Gilmore, a successful but caddish Broadway hoofer, and falls for him. Later, when the rotter accidentally kills a man, Crawford is almost forced to compromise her virtue to save Gilmore's skin, but fortunately before that happens, he is himself killed, and Crawford comes to realize that it's actually Moore whom she loves.

d, Harry Millarde; w, A. P. Younger (based on the novel by Robert Terry Shannon); t, Ralph Spence; ph, Ira Morgan; ed, George Hively; set d, Cedric Gibbons, David Townsend.

Drama **(PR:A MPAA:NR)**

TAXI MYSTERY, THE* (1926) 6 reels BAN/Henry Ginsberg bw

Edith Roberts *(Nancy Cornell/Vera Norris)*, Robert Agnew *(Harry Canby)*, Virginia Pearson *(Mrs. Blaine Jameson)*, Phillips Smalley *(Willoughby Thomson)*, Bertram Grassby *(Fred Norris)*.

Completely unsuspenseful mystery about a young fellow (Agnew) who comes to the aid of a young lady by rescuing her from a gang of toughs through the use of an abandoned taxicab. The rest of the picture has to do with his trying to learn her identity (which shouldn't have been that hard seeing she's a Broadway star) and getting there just in time to save her from a murderous understudy. Roberts, in a dual role, does remarkably well considering what she has to work with.

d, Fred Windermere; w, Tom J. Hopkins.

Mystery **(PR:A MPAA:NR)**

TAXI! TAXI! 1/2** (1927) 7 reels UNIV-Jewel bw

Edward Everett Horton *(Peter Whitby)*, Marian Nixon *(Rose Zimmerman)*, Burr McIntosh *(Grant Zimmerman)*, Edward Martindel *(David Parmalee)*, William V. Mong *(Nosey Ricketts)*, Lucien Littlefield *(Billy Wallace)*, Freeman Wood *(Jersey)*.

While following an assignment to escort his boss' niece around town, Horton and Nixon fall in love. Then one night while visiting a notorious roadhouse Nixon was forbidden by her uncle to enter, they encounter the old boy himself entertaining a client. Taking off in a hurry, the couple commandeer an abandoned taxicab which, it turns out, was used in a murder. The two are spotted by Horton's employer and this leads to the young man being fired and the girl grounded. But the couple had already set a date with the minister, and it's here that the movie finally comes to life. Nixon sneaks out of the house with her uncle hot on her heels, and while racing for the church, the cops spot the supicious cab and join in the chase. Then, in a clever bit of business, the couple, followed by the throng, dash about the church with the reverend shouting a portion of the vows at every pass until the sacrament is completed. The bride and groom are, of course, cleared of the crime and forgiven by the uncle, who rewards Horton with a nice promotion.

d, Melville W. Brown; w, Brown, Raymond Cannon (based on the story by George Weston); ph, Gilbert Warrenton.

Comedy **(PR:A MPAA:NR)**

TEA FOR THREE*½ (1927) 7 reels MGM bw

Lew Cody *(Carter Langford)*, Aileen Pringle *(Doris Langford)*, Owen Moore *(Philip Collamore)*, Phillips Smalley *(Harrington)*, Dorothy Sebastian *(Annette)*, Edward Thomas *(Austin, the Butler)*.

Following the highly successful teaming of Pringle and Cody in ADAM AND EVIL (1927), MGM quickly paired them up again, along with director Leonard, but the result was a disappointment. A mechanical comedy with the laughs few and far between, TEA FOR THREE has Cody playing a man whose jealousy for his wife, Pringle, leads to his cutting cards with his imagined rival, Moore, and the loser agreeing to commit suicide. After some heavily padded and uninspired business aboard an ocean liner, the situation mercifully works itself out in the end.

d, Robert Z. Leonard; w, F. Hugh Herbert, Roi Cooper Megrue (based on the play by Karl Sloboda); t, Garrett Graham, Lucille Newmark; ph, Andre Barlatier; ed, William Le Vanway; set d, Cedric Gibbons, Richard Day.

Comedy **(PR:A MPAA:NR)**

TELEPHONE GIRL, THE*½ (1927) 6 reels FP-LAS bw

Madge Bellamy *(Kitty O'Brien)*, Holbrook Blinn *(Jim Blake)*, Warner Baxter *(Matthew Standish)*, May Allison *(Grace Robinson)*, Lawrence Gray *(Tom Blake)*, Hale Hamilton *(Mark)*, Hamilton Revelle *(Van Dyke)*, W. E. Shay *(Detective)*, Karen Hansen *(Mrs. Standish)*.

Predictable and disappointing film, considering the impressive director and cast involved, has Bellamy, a telephone operator, preventing political boss Blinn from destroying the reputation of his party's opponent for governor and then marrying Gray, the winner's son, after his father is vindicated.

p&d, Herbert Brenon; w, Elizabeth Meehan (based on the play by William Churchill De Mille); ph, Leo Tover.

Drama **(PR:A MPAA:NR)**

TELL IT TO THE MARINES**** (1926) 9 reels MGM bw

Lon Chaney *(Sgt. O'Hara)*, William Haines *(Private "Skeet" Burns)*, Eleanor Boardman *(Norma Dale)*, Eddie Gribbon *(Cpl. Madden)*, Carmel Myers *(Zaya)*, Warner Oland *(Chinese Bandit Leader)*, Mitchell Lewis *(Native)*, Frank Currier *(Gen. Wilcox)*, Maurice E. Kains *(Harry)*.

This was, next to FLESH AND THE DEVIL, MGM's biggest box office picture of 1926—and what a movie it was! Chaney, without makeup here, is perfection as the hardboiled Marine sergeant who carefully hides his heart of gold. Haines, as the wise guy whom the corps turns into a man, became a major star on the strength of his performance here. There are plenty of laughs, action, and romance, as well as a splendidly directed sequence in which the leathernecks rescue a beleaguered party of whites, including Navy nurse Boardman, from Chinese bandits. The film ends with Boardman and Haines coming to realize their love for one another, and Chaney, who worshipped the girl from a distance, remaining at his post to train future heroes for his country.

d, George Hill; w, E. Richard Schayer; t, Joe Farnham; ph, Ira Morgan; ed, Blanche Sewell; set d, Cedric Gibbons, Arnold Gillespie.

Drama **(PR:A MPAA:NR)**

TELLING THE WORLD*** (1928) 8 reels MGM bw

William Haines *(Don Davis)*, Anita Page *(Chrystal Malone)*, Eileen Percy *(Maizie)*, Frank Currier *(Don's Father)*, Polly Moran *(Landlady)*, Bert Roach *(Lane)*, William V. Mong *(City Editor)*, Matthew Betz *(The Killer)*.

Entertaining combination of comedy and adventure has America's most self-assured citizen, Haines, applying for a job as newspaper reporter when his millionaire father disinherits him. He's given the job and his first assignment is to interview his dad. Later, as a gag, his fellow scribes send him to a nightclub to cover a murder. Then, not only does one occur, but Haines nabs the killer and meets the girl of his dreams as well. When her theatrical troupe sails for China to entertain U.S. servicemen, Haines follows her, becomes involved in a revolution, and with the help of the marines rescues his sweetheart from the executioner's axe. Director Wood keeps the action moving right along, and the performances are most engaging on everyone's part. Farnham's snappy title writing for this film and two other MGM productions won him an Oscar in 1928, the year the Academy of Motion Picture Arts and Sciences staged their first award ceremony. The subtitle category was dropped the following year.

d, Sam Wood; w, Raymond L. Schrock (based on a story by Dale Van Every); t, Joe Farnham; ph, William Daniels; ed, Margaret Booth, John Colton; art d, Cedric Gibbons.

Comedy Adventure **(PR:A MPAA:NR)**

TEMPEST*½** (1928) 10 reels Joseph M. Schenck/UA bw

John Barrymore *(Sgt. Ivan Markov)*, Camilla Horn *(Princess Tamara)*, Louis Wolheim *(Sgt. Bulba)*, Boris De Fas *(Peddler)*, George Fawcett *(General)*, Ullrich Haupt *(Captain)*, Michael Visaroff *(Guard)*, Lena Malena, Albert Conti.

Beautifully directed, acted, photographed, and written love story, set against the background of the Russian Revolution, has Barrymore, an officer in the czar's army, falling in love with a princess (Horn, the star of Murnau's FAUST, in her U.S. film debut) who rejects him because of his peasant background. Horn then has the soldier stripped of his rank and thrown in prison. Time passes and when the revolution explodes, Barrymore becomes a leader of the Red Army and rescues his beloved by killing his villainous superior officer. The two then escape to another land and happiness. The "Great Profile" was 46 when this film was made, but Rosher's use of his own Kino Portrait soft-focus lens made the actor appear most convincingly as a man in his 20s.

p, John W. Considine; d, Sam Taylor; w, C. Gardner Sullivan; ph, Charles Rosher; m, Hugo Riesenfeld; art d, William Cameron Menzies; cos, Alice O'Neill.

Drama **Cas.** **(PR:A MPAA:NR)**

TEMPORARY MARRIAGE*** (1923) 7 reels Sacramento/Principal bw

Kenneth Harlan *(Robert Belmar)*, Mildred Davis *(Hazel Manners)*, Myrtle Stedman *(Mrs. Hugh Manners)*, Tully Marshall *(Hugh Manners)*, Maude George *(Olga Kazonoff)*, Stuart Holmes *(Preston Ducayne)*, Edward Coxen *(Prosecuting Attorney)*.

Director-writer Hillyer really makes something of what might have been just another potboiler. It all has to do with Stedman, a woman in her 40s, who tires of Marshall, her stodgy lawyer husband, throws a divorce ball, and becomes "involved" with a gambler and his mistress. When the fellow is murdered, Stedman is accused of the crime, but in a beautifully executed courtroom sequence, Marshall clears his wife and forces the victim's paramour to confess.

d, Lambert Hillyer; w, Hillyer, Gilbert Patton; ph, John Stumar.

Drama **(PR:A MPAA:NR)**

TEMPORARY VAGABOND, A** (1920, Brit.) 5 reels Hepworth/But bw

Henry Edwards *(Dick Derelict)*, Chrissie White *(Peggie Hurst)*, Stephen Ewart *(James Hurst)*, Gwynne Herbert *(Emma)*, Douglas Munro *(Mike)*, John McAndrews *(Davis)*.

There is much rejoicing when the son of the world's meanest squire comes to town to write a novel and improves the life of every citizen. Director-writer Edwards provided himself with a juicy part, but that certainly didn't do much to effect the needed laughs.

d&w, Henry Edwards (based on a story by Stuart Woodley).

Comedy **(PR:A MPAA:NR)**

TEMPTATION** (1915) 5 reels LAS-PAR bw

Geraldine Farrar *(Renee Dupree)*, Pedro de Cordoba *(Julian)*, Theodore Roberts *(Otto Muller)*, Elsie Jane Wilson *(Mme. Maroff)*, Raymond Hatton *(Baron Chevrial)*, Anita King, Jessie Arnold, Ernest Joy, Sessue Hayakawa, Tex Driscoll, Lucien Littlefield.

Lesser DeMille effort has the great opera star, Farrar, playing (not too convincingly) a gifted soprano who is discharged by a lecherous impresario because she refuses to yield to his sexual demands. The singer's sweetheart, a brilliant composer, suffers the same fate, but everything works out in the end, when the nasty one (well played by Roberts) is stabbed to death by his jealous mistress.

d, Cecil B. DeMille; w, Hector Turnbull; ph, Alvin Wyckoff.

Drama **(PR:A MPAA:NR)**

TEMPTATION½** (1923) 7 reels CBC bw

Bryant Washburn *(Jack Baldwin)*, Eva Novak *(Marjorie Baldwin)*, June Elvidge *(Mrs. Martin)*, Phillips Smalley *(Frederick Arnold)*, Vernon Steele *(John Hope)*.

Diverting programmer with an interesting angle has stockbroker Smalley setting out to prove that any woman can be corrupted by wealth. He manipulates the market to make Novak (for whom he lusts) and her husband, Washburn, overnight millionaires. The money does go to Novak's head, and before long she starts hanging around the hedonistic social set. Smalley then sets out to ruin Washburn, who has also begun to travel in the fast lane, but fails in his attempt. The police then raid a roadhouse where the married couple are both in attendance, causing the two to come to their senses and return to the real world.

d&w, Edward J. LeSaint (based on a story by Lenore Coffee); ph, King Gray.

Drama **(PR:A MPAA:NR)**

TEMPTRESS, THE*** (1926) 9 reels COS/MGM bw

Greta Garbo *(Elena)*, Antonio Moreno *(Robledo)*, Roy D'Arcy *(Manos Duros)*, Marc MacDermott *(Mons. Fontenoy)*, Lionel Barrymore *(Canterac)*, Virginia Brown Faire *(Celinda)*, Armand Kaliz *(Torre De Bianca)*, Alys Murrell *(Josephine)*, Robert Anderson *(Pirovani)*, Francis McDonald *(Timoteo)*, Hector V. Sarno *(Rojas)*, Inez Gomez *(Sebastiana)*, Steve Clemento *(Salvadore)*, Roy Coulson *(Trinidad)*.

Mauritz Stiller, Garbo's mentor, wrote the original screenplay for this picture and was given the assignment of directing it under his three-year contract with MGM. The script department, to his horror, completely butchered his work and within 10 days studio executive Irving Thalberg, who regarded Stiller as another trouble maker in the mold of Erich von Stroheim, replaced the Scandinavian genius with Niblo, who just completed directing BEN HUR. The result was a Hollywood production loaded with hokum, in which Garbo becomes the mistress of MacDermott, a wealthy banker, while she is married to Kaliz. When her husband's Argentine friend, Moreno, comes to Paris to visit them, Garbo is immediately attracted to the handsome South American. MacDermott becomes quite jealous and scolds Garbo, who later ends their relationship when she finds he is bankrupt. As a result, MacDermott commits suicide and Garbo's husband, who is embarrassed by the scandalous situation, travels to Argentina where Moreno is overseeing the building of a dam. Moreno tries to steer clear of Garbo, but ends up in a quarrel over her with D'Arcy, a local hoodlum, and a murder results. D'Arcy then blows up the dam, causing a dangerous flood. Moreno hunts for Garbo, intending to kill her, but ends up succumbing to her seductive charms. She leaves him and returns to Paris, where years later Moreno, accompanied by his new wife, encounters Garbo drinking in a bar and calls her name. She does not recognize him and for a split second his bearded face appears to be that of Christ judging her for all the evil she has caused. During this incredible scene Garbo removes a ruby ring from her finger and gives it to him, saying "You died for love." Garbo then awakens from the momentary vision and sees Moreno standing before her. This was Garbo's second

U.S. film (curiously, she played Latins in both) and in spite of its many weaknesses, her performance is so magnificant that nothing else really seems to matter. THE TEMPTRESS received good reviews, the public loved it (although the actress never stopped apologizing for her performance), and one of the motion picture's greatest legends was about to be born.

d, Fred Niblo (Mauritz Stiller, uncredited); w, Dorothy Farnum (Stiller, uncredited) (based on the novel *La Tierra de Todos* by Vicente Blasco-Ibanez, translated as *The Temptress* by Leo Ongley); t, Marian Ainslee; ph, Gaetano Gaudio, William Daniels; ed, Lloyd Nosler; set d, Cedric Gibbons, James Basevi.

Drama **(PR:A MPAA:NR)**

TEN COMMANDMENTS, THE*** (1923) 13 reels FP-LAS/PAR bw-c

Theodore Roberts *(Moses)*, Charles de Roche *(Rameses)*, Estelle Taylor *(Miriam)*, Julia Faye *(Pharaoh's Wife)*, Terrence Moore *(Pharaoh's Son)*, James Neill *(Aaron)*, Lawson Butt *(Dathan)*, Clarence Burton *(The Taskmaster)*, Noble Johnson *(The Bronze Man)*, Edythe Chapman *(Mrs. Martha McTavish)*, Richard Dix *(John McTavish)*, Rod La Rocque *(Dan McTavish)*, Leatrice Joy *(Mary Leigh)*, Nita Naldi *(Sally Lung)*, Robert Edeson *(Redding, an Inspector)*, Charles Ogle *(The Doctor)*, Agnes Ayres *(The Outcast)*, Viscount Glerawly.

DeMille almost came to blows with the New York office over the money he was spending on the preparation of this film, and even offered to buy it from Adolph Zukor for $1 million in cash (the mogul wisely refused). The total cost of the production came to $1.2 million, a figure which understandably rattled financier Zukor, especially in view of the failure of DeMille's previous picture, ADAM'S RIB. The arguments raised during this production ultimately led to renegotiation of the director's deal with the studio (and his departure from it); DeMille got 50 percent of the *gross* profits (not the actual profits) at this time. Reportedly, DeMille donated all his income from this film—and from his other great Biblical epic, THE KING OF KINGS (1927)—to charity. C. B. did, however, back down on taking his company to the Middle East to shoot at the actual biblical locations, and settled instead for central California. But DeMille continued his lavish expenditures and gave Paul Iribe the nod to construct sets which were 2,500 feet long and 300 feet high. He also sent his assistant, Mrs. Florence Meehan, on a 20,000-mile journey to acquire props, costumes, and jewels. By the time he was ready to begin shooting, the director had built a city in the desert, with a network of electrical generators, 200 camels, a commissary which prepared 7,500 sandwiches a day to feed 2,500 actors. There were 4,500 additional animals, a complete hospital, 500 carpenters, 380 decorators, 400 painters, and an army of other workers, which brought his payroll to $40,000 a day. The purpose of all this was to film the 2-color Technicolor prolog which recreated the stories of the Old Testament Book of Exodus. As in the director's other films of good versus evil, goodness does not triumph until plenty of interesting evil has been displayed; lovely, lightly-clad Taylor gets a great deal of exposure during the orgy sequence as the Golden Calf is adored, a circumstance that probably accounts for the picture's good reception by the public despite generally poor reviews. The original Calf was demolished by wrath-of-God-simulating dynamite blasts, and had to be replaced by a stand-in. As was the case with many of the director's high-budget films, such accidents resulted in many other injuries to cast, crew, and animals; at one point, men and mounts of the 11th U.S. Cavalry, costumed as the pursuing troops of the Pharaoh, inadvertently charged into the 30-piece orchestra DeMille had employed to play during filming. THE TEN COMMANDMENTS marked the end of DeMille's long association with actor-turned-cinematographer Alvin Wyckoff. At the outset of production planning, the director and his cameraman quarreled over technique; DeMille wanted his spectacular and costly sets to be revealed in all their glorious detail, while Wyckoff favored the low-key lighting that had characterized many of their previous successes. Wyckoff was also becoming an activist on behalf of the new cinematographers' trade union; a capitalist to the core, DeMille was extremely resentful of what he considered to be disloyalty. He recruited a number of other cinematographers for this production, notably Marley, with whom he continued a long association. But in spite of the spectacular aspects, direction is really rather sluggish, and in retrospect the picture is vastly inferior to D. W. Griffith's INTOLERANCE. Even the famous parting of the Red Sea sequence is little more than an acceptable special effect. The second part of the film has a modern setting and is straight melodrama, dealing with a bible-toting mother who raises two sons, one (Richard Dix) who honors the Commandments and another (La Rocque) who breaks them every chance he gets. The boys both love Leatrice Joy, but she chooses La Rocque, who makes a fortune as a building contractor by using inferior materials and greasing some political palms. In the end, the sinner gets his (in the meantime a cathedral he constructed collapses on his mother in another big scene) when he murders his Oriental mistress who is blackmailing him, discovers that he's contracted leprosy, becomes falling-down drunk, and is killed when his boat is dashed against some rocks. DeMille had guaranteed Zukor a commercial ending and he delivered one by having Miss Joy discover that she loves Mr. Dix after all.

p&d, Cecil B. DeMille; w, Jeanie Macpherson; ph, Bert Glennon, J. Peverell Marley, Edward S. Curtis, Fred Westerberg, Donald Biddle Keyes, Archibald Stout, Ray Rennahan (part Technicolor); ed, Anne Bauchens; art d, Paul Iribe; cos, Claire West; tech d, Roy Pomeroy.

Biblical **(PR:A MPAA:NR)**

TEN DAYS THAT SHOOK THE WORLD****
(1927, USSR) 7 reels Sovkino/bw (AKA:OCTOBER)

Nikandrof *(Lenin)*, N. Popov *(Kerensky)*, Boris Livanov *(Minister of Terechtichenko)*, Eduard Tisse *(A German)*, Thousands of Extras.

Eisenstein was commissioned by the Soviet government to make a film celebrating the 10 days of a decade earlier when the Kerensky regime was overthrown by the Bolsheviks. Although flawed (more about that later), this is still a near masterwork, loaded with the director's spellbinding use of montage and visual symbols. And because the government cooperated completely, the many historical re-creations are given a sense of spectacle equaled by only the largest Hollywood productions. For example, during the attack on the Winter Palace, 11,000 soldiers and workers were provided, along with weapons and blank ammunition. For the night scenes, there was not enough electricity to light the actual buildings, bridges, and other structures, so the whole city of Leningrad was plunged into darkness in order to provide the needed current. In many ways, the director even exceeded his earlier triumph BATTLESHIP POTEMKIN . . . But alas the picture was not allowed to be shown. One of the main characters in the historical epoch Eisenstein had so skillfully re-created was Leon Trotsky, and by the time this film was completed, there had been the schism which pitted him against the Communist party. The director was forced to spend the next five months removing any mention or sight of that "enemy" of the state from the completed film. One can only imagine the frustration he felt, but some time later Eisenstein had occasion to meet another great director, Frank Capra, while Capra was visiting the Soviet Union. The American recalls the encounter in his autobiography: "We asked about Eisenstein and, as in Moscow, we got the vague answers: 'He is in the Crimea . . . in Kiev . . . He's not well . . . Nobody has seen him.' " Capra and his touring party returned to Moscow and found a message from the great Russian director with a phone number, to be called at a certain hour of the day. Capra made the call and Eisenstein answered. "Fronk," he said cautiously, "you vant to see me? Vy?" Capra told him how disappointed he would be to return home without paying his respects to one of the great artists of film (they had met earlier in Hollywood). Flattered, the Russian gave him an address to give a taxi driver, and said that if he could shake his government tail to come at once. Capra again: "We found the great Eisenstein sitting alone in a broken-down booth of a broken-down Georgian cafe in one of Moscow's broken-down sections. Making sure we were alone, he asked us to sit down and have a hot glass of tea with melting butter floating in it. He looked drawn and depressed. 'Fronk, Bub,' he said smiling wryly, 'I am in the dog house.' We laughed at his American slang. 'I can make no pictures. I can no go in studios, no movie workers can talk to me. I am in the dog house.' Then he explained. The Kremlin had asked him to make a film trilogy on the life of Ivan the Terrible. 'I make Part One; the Kremlin bosses see it—they give me big medal. Good. Soviet hero! I make Part Two; big shots see it—they take back my medal. Stalin say no Part Three, no more films; say I make big political mistake. Soviet bum! Three months now I'm in the dog house. You like?' " Frank Capra did not. Nor did anyone else in the world—who respected and loved the art of cinema.

d, Sergei M. Eisenstein; w, Eisenstein, Grigori Alexandrov; ph, Eduard Tisse, V. Popov.

Historical **Cas.** **(PR:A MPAA:NR)**

TEN DOLLAR RAISE, THE*** (1921) 6 reels J. L. Frothingham/AP bw

William V. Mong *(Wilkins)*, Marguerite De La Motte *(Dorothy)*, Pat O'Malley *(Jimmy)*, Helen Jerome Eddy *(Emily)*, Hal Cooley *(Don)*, Lincoln Plumer *(Bates)*, Charles Hill Mailes *(Stryker)*.

The American dream comes true in this pleasant programmer which has Mong toiling for 20 years as a bookkeeper, but being unable to marry De La Motte, a stenographer, because his Scrooge-like boss keeps denying him a raise. In the end, however, Mong purchases some seemingly worthless property, which turns out to be loaded with oil, enabling him to buy out his flabbergasted employer, marry De La Motte, and take care of his old friends.

p, J. L. Frothingham; d, Edward Sloman; w, Albert S. Le Vino (based on the story by Peter Bernard Kyne); ph, Tony Gaudio.

Drama **(PR:A MPAA:NR)**

TENDER HOUR, THE ** (1927) 8 reels John McCormick/FN bw

Billie Dove *(Marcia Kane)*, Ben Lyon *(Wally McKenzie)*, Montagu Love *(Grand Duke Sergei)*, Alec B. Francis *(Francis Chinilly)*, Constantine Romanoff *(Gorki)*, Laska Winter *(Tana)*, T. Roy Barnes *(Tough-House Higgins)*, George Kotsonaros *(The Wrestler)*, Charles A. Post *(Pussy-Finger)*, Anders Randolph *(Leader of Pageant)*, Frank Elliott, Lionel Belmore, Lon Poff *(Guests at Party)*, August Tollaire *(Prefect of Police)*, Yola D'Avril *(Cabaret Girl)*.

Dove is lovely, Lyon athletically unconvincing, and Love deliciously villainous, while Fitzmaurice moves his camera constantly through sets of great opulence. That's about all that can be said for this expensively padded production, which has American go-getter Lyon saving Dove, the girl he adores, from Love, the expatriate Russian grand duke, whom she was tricked into marrying.

d, George Fitzmaurice; w, Winifred Dunn (based on a story by Carey Wilson); ph, Robert Kurrle.

Drama/Adventure **(PR:A MPAA:NR)**

TENNESSEE'S PARDNER*** (1916) 5 reels LAS bw

Fannie Ward *(Tennessee)*, Jack Dean *(Jack Hunter)*, Charles Clary *(Romaine)*, Jessie Mae Arnold *(Kate Kent)*, William Bradbury *(Bill Kent)*, Raymond Hatton *(Gewilliker Hay)*, James Neill *(The Padre)*, Lee Pate.

A little girl is placed in a convent school by Dean, who wishes to honor a last request made by her father before dying of a gunshot wound inflicted by Clary, the man who ran off with his wife. Years pass and the girl, now a young woman (played by Ward), has graduated and decided to head West to meet Dean, whom she believes is her father. On the way, however, the stagecoach is held up by Clary, who abducts Ward and decides to take the lovely young thing to be his bride. He then introduces her to his mistress, who has no idea the girl is really her daughter. In the end, Dean and an army of peace officers track the road agent down, throw a little necktie party, and mother and daughter are reunited. The ending also leads one to strongly suspect that a romantic alliance between Ward and Dean is more than just a possibility.

d, George Melford; w, Marion Fairfax (based on the play by Scott Marble, inspired by the story by Bret Harte).

Western (PR:A MPAA:NR)

TERROR OF BAR X, THE** (1927) 5 reels Bob Custer/FBO bw

Bob Custer *(Bob Willis)*, Ruby Blaine *(Dorothy Hunter)*, William Rhine *(Ross Hunter)*, Jack Castle *(Reginald Brooks)*, Duke R. Lee *(Jim Ashland)*, Walter Maly *(Hoke Channing)*, Roy Bassett *(Sheriff)*.

Unusual B western pays almost as much attention to the love story as it does the action. Custer is a ranch foreman who borrows a large sum of money from a wealthy Indian friend to prevent his sweetheart's crippled father from having his ranch confiscated by Lee, a gambler who desires the girl. Lee then frames Custer for a stage robbery and abducts the young lady. But the cowboy breaks out of jail, leads the sheriff and his men to the real road agent, and saves his darling from suffering a fate worse than death.

d, Scott Pembroke; w, George M. Merrick (based on the story "Stan Willis, Cowboy" by George M. Johnson); t, Ruth Todd; ph, Ernest Miller.

Western (PR:A MPAA:NR)

TESS OF THE D'URBERVILLES**** (1924) 8 reels MG bw

Blanche Sweet *(Tess)*, Conrad Nagel *(Angel Clare)*, Stuart Holmes *(Alec D'Urberville)*, George Fawcett *(John Durbeyfield)*, Victory Bateman *(Joan Durbeyfield)*, Courtenay Foote *(Dick)*, Joseph J. Dowling *(The Priest)*.

Director Neilan and his wife, Sweet, traveled to England to get the atmospheric footage they wanted to bring this Thomas Hardy classic to the screen. The result is an uncompromising work of great beauty and emotional power. Sweet, the film's heroine, plays a girl who is seduced by her employer, loses her child to death, and is deserted by the man she loves when that fellow learns the truth about her past. Neilan throws all commercial caution to the wind by having the heroine executed at the end. The scene where Sweet is forced to kill her tormentor and Neilan's camera moves in closer and closer to the terrified girl's face until practically the entire screen is filled with the expression of her horror, is unforgettable.

d, Marshall Neilan; w, Dorothy Farnum (based on the novel by Thomas Hardy); ph, David Kesson.

Drama (PR:A MPAA:NR)

TESS OF THE STORM COUNTRY*** (1914) 5 reels FP bw

Mary Pickford, W. R. Walters, Olive Fuller Golden, David Hartford, Harold Lockwood, Lorraine Thompson, Louise Dunlap, Richard Garrick, Jack Henry, H. R. Macy, Eugene Walter, H. L. Griffith.

This was the film which made Pickford a star of the first magnitude—in spite of Porter's sluggish direction and refusal to use a single close-up. America's Sweetheart overcame those shortcomings through the sheer magic of her artistry, and scenes such as her stealing a Bible, after falling in love with a divinity student, and memorizing its contents; or taking his pregnant sister into her little shack and assuming guilt for the child's birth in order to spare him shame; and then when the baby is dying and the minister refuses to baptize a "creature of sin," Pickford storms into the church and administers the sacrament herself. These scenes moved audiences as they had never been moved before. This is the only film Pickford ever chose to remake, and the second version, directed by John S. Robertson in 1922, more than justified this decision. There was a happy conclusion to each film with Pickford being asked by her young man to become his wife, and of course accepting.

d&w, Edwin S. Porter (based on the novel by Grace Miller White).

Drama (PR:A MPAA:NR)

TESS OF THE STORM COUNTRY*½** (1922) 10 reels Mary Pickford/UA bw

Mary Pickford *(Tessibel Skinner)*, Lloyd Hughes *(Frederick Graves)*, Gloria Hope *(Teola Graves)*, David Torrence *(Elias Graves)*, Forrest Robinson *(Daddy Skinner)*, Jean Hersholt *(Ben Letts)*, Danny Hoy *(Ezra Longman)*, Robert Russell *(Dan Jordan)*, Gus Saville *(Old Man Longman)*, Madame De Bodamere *(Mrs. Longman)*.

A story Pickford felt was so good that she remade it, the only one of her films she ever thought that much of. And well she should have, since the 1914 version, together with HEARTS ADRIFT, were the two movies that announced to the world that an actress of the first magnitude had arrived on the screen. As in the 1914 version, Pickford is the innocent and completely captivating squatter girl in a great number of outrageous and endearing situations as her lover's sister bears a baby out of wedlock to her lover's best friend. Pickford not only takes in both mother and child but protects the mother by saying the child is hers, thereby losing her lover. All works out in the end, however, when the sister reveals the baby as her own and Tess is reunited with her lover. The 1914 version of the film had a great deal going against it, in spite of its power in shooting Pickford to the top. The direction was desultory, to say the least, and there was not a single close-up in the film. The 1922 version was immeasurably better, and credit for that is due director Robertson.

d, John S. Robertson, w, Elmer Harris (based on the novel by Grace Miller White); ph, Charles Rosher, Paul Eagler; art d, Frank Ormston.

Drama (PR:A MPAA:NR)

TESTING BLOCK, THE*½** (1920) 6 reels WSHP/PAR bw

William S. Hart *("Sierra" Bill)*, Eva Novak *(Nellie Gray)*, Florence Carpenter *(Rosita)*, Richard Headrick *(Sonny)*, Ira McFadden *(Slim)*, Gordon Russell.

Another strong Hart western. This time the good-bad man is the leader of an outlaw band in the Sierras who is regenerated by Novak, a violinist in a traveling theatrical company. There are some fine action sequences, but the primary emphasis in this production involves character development, an area in which both of the leading players score heavily.

d&w, Lambert Hillyer (based on a story by William S. Hart); ph, Joseph August; art d, J. C. Hoffner.

Western (PR:A MPAA:NR)

TEXAS STEER, A*** (1927) 8 reels Sam E. Rork/FN bw

Will Rogers *(Maverick Brander)*, Louise Fazenda *(Mrs. Ma Brander)*, Sam Hardy *(Brassy Gall)*, Ann Rork *(Bossy Brander)*, Douglas Fairbanks, Jr. *(Fairleigh Bright)*, Lilyan Tashman *(Dixie Style)*, George Marion, Sr. *(Fishback)*, Bud Jamieson *(Othello)*, Arthur Hoyt *(Knott Innitt)*, Mack Swain *(Bragg)*, William Orlamond *(Blow)*, Lucien Littlefield *(Yell)*.

Rogers co-wrote the snappy and topical titles for this engaging comedy in which he plays a Texas rancher unknowingly elected to Congress through the efforts of his ambitious wife (Fazenda), romantic daughter (Rork), and a trio of political bosses (Swain, Orlamond, and Littlefield), referred to as Bragg, Blow, and Yell, who need him to vote for the passage of a particular bill. Opponents of the legislation kidnap Rogers, lock him in a boardinghouse and steal his clothes. But the Texan manages to escape, and after a number of well-executed sight gags, reaches the capitol in time to cast his opposing vote and expose the crooks.

d, Richard Wallace; w, Bernard McConville, Paul Schofield (based on the musical play by Charles Hale Hoyt); t, Will Rogers, Garrett Graham; ph, Jack MacKenzie; ed, Frank Lawrence.

Comedy (PR:A MPAA:NR)

THAIS* (1914) 4 reels Loftus/Sawyer bw

Arthur Maude, Constance Crawley, George Gebhardt.

Poorly produced, acted, written, and photographed feature was reviewed in the *Harvard Lampoon* as follows: "Thais Lady, Morals Shady; Holy Prophet, Preaches Tophet, Lady Bawls; Prophet Falls. She Repents. Love Prevents. He Invades Cloister Shades. She Devout, Passes Out. Pangs Acute, Follows Suit."

d, Arthur Maude, Constance Crawley; w, Maude (based on the novel by Anatole France).

Drama (PR:C MPAA:NR)

THANKS FOR THE BUGGY RIDE½** (1928) 6 reels UNIV bw

Laura La Plante *(Jenny)*, Glenn Tryon *(Joe Hall)*, Richard Tucker *(Mr. McBride)*, Lee Moran *(Bill Barton)*, David Rollins *(Harold McBride)*, Kate Price *(Mrs. Crogan)*, Jack Raymond *(Mr. Belkoff)*, Trixie Friganza *(Actress)*.

Decent comedy-romance has entertainer La Plante falling in love with song-plugger Tryon, unknowingly insulting his publishing boss at a nightclub and losing the chance to audition her sweetheart's tune "Thanks for the Buggy Ride" for the old boy. To make it up, La Plante disguises herself, crashes a fancy bash attended by vaudeville performers looking for material, and puts the number over so well that Friganza (playing herself) buys the song and provides the youngsters with enough cash to purchase the little cottage of their dreams. Nice directing touch by La Plante's real-life husband, Seiter.

d, William A. Seiter; w, Beatrice Van (based on a story by Byron Morgan); t, Tom Reed; ph, Arthur Todd; ed, Joseph Franklin Poland, Edward McDermott.

Comedy (PR:A MPAA:NR)

"THAT ROYLE GIRL"*½

(1925) 10 reels FP/PAR bw (AKA: D. W. GRIFFITH'S "THAT ROYLE GIRL")

Carol Dempster *(Joan Daisy Royle/The Royle Girl)*, W. C. Fields *(Her Father)*, James Kirkwood *(Calvin Clarke/Deputy District Attorney)*, Harrison Ford *(Fred Ketlar/King of Jazz)*, Marie Chambers *(Adele Ketlar)*, Paul Everton *(George Baretta)*, George Rigas *(His Henchman)*, Florence Auer *(Baretta's "Girl")*, Ida Waterman *(Mrs. Clarke)*, Alice Laidley *(Clarke's Fiancee)*, Dorothea Love *(Lola Neeson)*, Dore Davidson *(Elman)*, Frank Allworth *(Oliver)*, Bobby Watson *(Hofer)*, William "Shorty" Blanche *(Bit)*.

Griffith, in his second Paramount production, was forced to take on a film which other contract directors had already turned down. The inferior melodrama had Dempster playing an idealistic young woman (she worships the statue of Lincoln in a Chicago park) who becomes a model and gets involved with the nightclub crowd. She soon falls for orchestra leader Ford, whose former wife is the paramour of Everton, a notorious gangster. When the woman is murdered, Ford is convicted of the crime, but Dempster, with the help of a crusading district attorney, Kirkwood, proves that the mobster was the real killer, and they manage to reach the governor just in time to prevent the musician's execution. Griffith was embarrassed by this clunker, which completely wasted the talents of W. C. Fields (as Dempster's drunken con-man father) and he's quoted by Anthony Slide in his book *The Films of D. W. Griffith* as having told an interviewer, "He (the director) may indulge his art visions and his creative dreams and his vistas of the golden glow of humanity if he wants to—as I did once in BROKEN BLOSSOMS, the most artistic picture I ever produced. But he has to square up at the box office on his batting average now and again."

p&d, D. W. Griffith; w, Paul Schofield (based on the novel by Edwin Balmer); ph, Harry Fischbeck, Hal Sintzenich; ed, James Smith; art d, Charles M. Kirk.

Crime (PR:A MPAA:NR)

THAT'S MY BABY*** (1926) 7 reels FP/PAR bw

Douglas MacLean *(Alan Boyd)*, Margaret Morris *(Helen Raynor)*, Claude Gillingwater *(John Raynor)*, Eugenie Forde *(Mrs. John Raynor)*, Wade Boteler *(Dave Barton)*, Richard Tucker *(Schuyler Van Loon)*, Fred Kelsey *(Murphy)*, Harry Earles *(The Baby)*, William Orlamond *(Drug Clerk)*.

Director Beaudine skillfully sets up his comedic premise in which MacLean, a young man jilted at the altar, swears off women for life and then falls madly in love with the daughter of his business competitor. To this merriment add Earles (the midget from Lon Chaney's UNHOLY THREE, 1925) playing a baby suddenly left in MacLean's care. A number of side-splitting situations evolve and culminate with the tot sitting on the tip of an airplane wing, laughing and pointing to the scenery far below, as MacLean musters up the courage to climb out on the wing and rescue him. When he does, little Earles pulls the ripcord and the two of them float to earth, where MacLean finally finds happiness through love and success.

d, William Beaudine; w, Joseph Franklin Poland (based on a story by George J. Crone, Wade Boteler); ph, Jack MacKenzie.

Comedy **(PR:A MPAA:NR)**

THELMA*½ (1922) 6 reels Chester Bennett/FBO bw

Jane Novak *(Thelma Guildmar)*, Barbara Tennant *(Britta)*, Gordon Mullen *(Lovissa)*, Bert Sprotte *(Olaf Guildmar)*, Vernon Steel *(Sir Phillip Errington)*, Peter Burke *(Lorimer)*, Jack Rollens *(Sigund)*, Harvey Clark *(Dyceworthy)*, June Elvidge *(Lady Clara Winsleigh)*, Wedgewood Nowell *(Lennox)*, Virginia Novak *(Little Thelma)*, Harry Lonsdale *(Neville)*.

Ponderous programmer has a beautiful Norwegian girl (Novak) wedding an English aristocrat (Steel) and moving to London, where his "friends" plot to break up their marriage. Tricked into thinking him unfaithful, the mistaken bride returns to her native land, but the Britisher follows and convinces her of the truth.

d, Chester Bennett; w, Thomas Dixon, Jr. (based on the novel by Marie Corelli); ph, Jack MacKenzie.

Drama **(PR:A MPAA:NR)**

THIEF, THE* (1915) 5 reels Box Office Attractions/FOX bw

Dorothy Donnelly *(The Wife)*, Richard Buhler *(Her Husband)*, E. L. Davenport, Ivy Shepard, Harry Spingler, George De Carlton.

Primitive, by 1915 standards, is this domestic melodrama about a woman who steals her friend's household allowance and then must face her husband's wrath when the deed is exposed.

d&w, Edgar Lewis (based on the play by Henri Bernstein).

Drama **(PR:A MPAA:NR)**

THIEF OF BAGDAD, THE**** (1924) 12 reels Douglas Fairbanks/UA bw

Douglas Fairbanks *(The Thief of Bagdad)*, Snitz Edwards *(His Evil Associate)*, Charles Belcher *(The Holy Man)*, Julanne Johnston *(The Princess)*, Anna May Wong *(The Mongol Slave)*, Winter Blossom *(The Slave of the Lute)*, Etta Lee *(The Slave of the Sand Board)*, Brandon Hurst *(The Caliph)*, Tote Du Crow *(The Soothsayer)*, Sojin *(The Mongol Prince)*, K. Nambu *(His Counselor)*, Sadakichi Hartmann *(His Court Magician)*, Noble Johnson *(The Indian Prince)*, Mathilde Comont *(The Persian Prince)*, Charles Stevens *(His Awaker)*, Sam Baker *(The Sworder)*, Jess Weldon, Scotty Mattraw, Charles Sylvester *(Eunuchs)*, Jesse Fuller.

Watching THE THIEF OF BAGDAD is a truly wondrous experience. The incredible sets by Menzies, the lavish and authentic costumes of Leisen, Walsh's inspired direction, and a cast of thousands, led by Fairbanks at his athletic best, combine to make this motion picture a timeless masterpiece. The story has a crafty thief (Fairbanks) sneaking into the palace, where, passing himself off as a nobleman, he falls in love with the beautiful princess, Johnston. Fairbanks is caught and severely punished, but Johnston saves his life, professes her love, and gives him a ring. A test is then devised to select the proper husband from her various suitors: "Send them to distant lands to seek some rare treasure. At the Seventh Moon let them return. Who brings the rarest treasure I will wed." The evil Mongol, Cham Shang, King of Ho Sho, Governor of Wah Hoo and the Island of Wak (played to perfection by the Japanese actor, Sojin) greatly desires the beautiful flower of Bagdad, not to mention the tremendous wealth which is hers, and he sets out on the quest, using all of the resources at his royal command. Meanwhile, the thief goes to a mosque to beg forgiveness and seek the advice of a holy man, and is told, "Allah hath made thy soul to yearn for happiness, but thou must earn it." Fairbanks then sets out on a series of adventures, the likes of which the screen had never seen (*The New York Times* in its review wrote, "There are some wonderfully well worked out double-exposure photographic effects, and even to the experienced eye the illusion is in nearly every instance kept up to a state of perfection") as he matches his agility and brains against the various obstacles he meets during the incomparable sequences of the Seven Moons. In these, he travels many miles (through the wondrous constructions of William Cameron Menzies), fights various monsters, including an enormous sea creature which he slays in an eye-popping underwater scene, accomplished through the use of glass and slow motion. There are additional thrills as the hero wanders into the "Cavern of the Enchanted Trees," meets the "Old Man of the Midnight Sea," and makes his way to the "Abode of the Winged Horse." But the picture's real punch comes when Fairbanks races home to defeat the evil Mongol who has captured Bagdad with 20,000 troops by hurling magic seeds to the ground, which explode into billows of smoke and conjure up soldiers of his own. Fairbanks pulls this off with the precision of a surgical bombing strike, until he has raised his own army of 100,000 men. (In his autobiography, Raoul Walsh wrote of getting these extras by sending buses and trucks to Los Angeles' Mexican section with signs which read in Spanish, "Free Ride! See Douglas Fairbanks in person making THE THIEF OF BAGDAD!" So many people accepted the offer that he had to turn hundreds away.) Fairbanks then revives the princess who had been poisoned, and the picture ends with him claiming his prize and the sweethearts sailing over the city in one of the suitor's magic carpets. To accomplish this effect, Walsh used a crane with wires painted white attached to the carpet, which was reinforced by a steel frame. in his autobiography, the director explained the procedure. "When the drum winch began to turn, the whole thing with Fairbanks and Miss Johnston sitting cross-legged on it rose before the eyes of the suitably astonished spectators and thin wires pulled it toward the window." Mr. Walsh goes on, "To strengthen the illusion of flying, I made two low-angle shots, added cut-ins of the people staring up from the streets—obtained by perching cameramen and myself on a platform at the top boom and shooting down—then resumed the slow pan showing the travelers on their way." It is said that this was the first $2 million movie. It looks it, and the picture certainly has the power to entertain and amaze as much today as it did in 1924.

d, Raoul Walsh; w, Lotta Woods (based on a story by Elton Thomas [Douglas Fairbanks]; ph, Arthur Edeson; m, Mortimer Wilson; ed, William Nolan; art d, William Cameron Menzies; cos, Mitchell Leisen.

Fantasy **Cas.** **(PR:A MPAA:NR)**

THIRD ALARM, THE** (1922) 7 reels Emory Johnson/FBO bw

Ralph Lewis *(Dan McDowell)*, Johnnie Walker *(Johnny McDowell)*, Ella Hall *(June Rutherford)*, Virginia True Boardman *(Mother McDowell)*, Richard Morris *(Dr. Rutherford)*, Josephine Adair *(Alice McDowell)*, Frankie Lee *(Little Jimmie)*, Bullet the Horse.

Walker is forced to drop out of medical school and join the fire department when his father, Lewis, is dismissed for not being able to handle the new equipment. To make things worse, the old fellow is forced to sell his horse, and when the faithful beast returns, Lewis is wrongly accused of stealing it. Then, when his sweetheart's house catches on fire, Walker and his company rush to the scene, where he and the girl become trapped under a safe, with the flames inching ever closer. The brave fire fighters can't budge them and all seems lost, until Lewis and his steed arrive on the scene and drag the couple to safety. The picture, which does offer a number of honest thrills, ends with Walker practicing medicine, and his father assigned the pleasurable task of tending to the department's retired livestock.

p&d, Emory Johnson; w, Emilie Johnson; ph, Henry Sharp.

Adventure **(PR:A MPAA:NR)**

THIRD DEGREE, THE*** (1926) 8 reels WB bw

Dolores Costello *(Annie Daly)*, Louise Dresser *(Alicia Daly)*, Rockliffe Fellowes *(Underwood)*, Jason Robards *(Howard Jeffries, Jr.)*, Kate Price *(Mrs. Chubb)*, Tom Santschi *("Daredevil Daly")*, Harry Todd *(Mr. Chubb)*, Mary Louise Miller *(Annie as a Baby)*, Michael Vavitch *(Clinton)*, David Torrence *(Howard Jeffries, Sr.)*, Fred Kelsey *(Assistant Chief of Detectives)*.

Hungarian-born director Curtiz' first U.S. film is full of the imagery and moving camera techniques so popular in the German cinema. Using a Coney Island circus setting as his background, Curtiz skillfully presented a story dealing with desertion, murder, unselfish bogus confessions, and the ultimate happiness of the young lovers in the end. Curtiz' talent would soon make him Warner Brothers' number one director, and he would go on to make such noted films as CASABLANCA (1942), for which he won an Academy Award.

d, Michael Curtiz; w, Graham Baker (based on the play "The Music Master" by Charles Klein); ph, Hal Mohr; ed, Clarence Kolster.

Drama/Mystery **(PR:A MPAA:NR)**

13 WASHINGTON SQUARE*** (1928) 6 reels UNIV bw

Jean Hersholt *("Deacon" Pyecroft)*, Alice Joyce *(Mrs. De Peyster)*, George Lewis *(Jack De Peyster)*, ZaSu Pitts *(Mathilde)*, Helen Foster *(Mary Morgan)*, Helen Jerome Eddy *(Olivetta)*, Julia Swayne Gordon *(Mrs. Allistair)*, Jack McDonald *(Mayfair)*, Jerry Gamble *(Sparks)*.

Intelligent comedy has socialite Joyce canceling her European vacation to break up a romance between her son and a working girl. Her scheme involves posing as a resident at her cousin's boardinghouse, where she meets gentleman thief Hersholt and learns of his plans to "knock over" her fashionable Washington Square residence. Rushing home, along with her also-disguised maid (wonderfully played by Pitts), Joyce finds it swarming with people, including the young couple who dropped by to pick up a few things, the robber, and a small army of reporters and police. In the midst of all this confusion—and to avoid any hint of scandal—the mother gives her blessing to the kids, and introduces Hersholt to the throng as her "art broker."

d, Melville W. Brown; w, Harry O. Hoyt (based on the play by Leroy Scott); t, Walter Anthony ; ph, John Stumar, ed, Ray Curtiss.

Comedy **(PR:A MPAA:NR)**

THIRTY DAYS** (1922) 5 reels FP/PAR bw

Wallace Reid *(John Floyd)*, Wanda Hawley *(Lucille Ledyard)*, Charles Ogle *(Judge Hooker)*, Cyril Chadwick *(Huntley Palmer)*, Herschel Mayall *(Giacomo Polenta)*, Helen Dunbar *(Mrs. Floyd)*, Carmen Phillips *(Carlotta)*, Kalla Pasha *(Warden)*, Robert Brower *(Prof. Huxley)*.

This Cruze-Reid comedy delivers some laughs, but should have been better. The story has to do with Reid becoming innocently involved with the wife of a madly jealous Italian. Reid has himself thrown into jail to escape the fellow's wrath, and then discovers that the Latin has also been incarcerated. The complications abound until Reid ultimately straightens things out with his fiancee, and the husband is put on a boat for a cooling off period. THIRTY DAYS was Reid's final film before his tragic death in 1923 as a result of drug addiction. The actor had suffered a head injury in a train wreck on the way to a movie location in 1919 and was given morphine to ease the pain. His resulting addiction to the drug was aggravated by heavy drinking and the popular star was placed in a sanitarium where he suffered an agonizing death.

d, James Cruze; w, Walter Woods (based on the play by A. E. Thomas, Clayton Hamilton); ph, Karl Brown.

Comedy **(PR:A MPAA:NR)**

THIS HERO STUFF** (1919) 5 reels Russell/AM bw

William Russell *(Capt. November Jones)*, Winifred Westover *(Nedra Joseph)*, J. Barney Sherry *(Jackson J. Joseph)*, Charles K. French *(Samuel Barnes)*, Mary Thurman *(Teddy Craig)*, Harvey Clark *(Jonathan Pillsbury)*, J. Farrell MacDonald *(Softnose Smith)*.

Made-to-order movie for action star Russell, about a modest war hero who returns home and tries so hard to avoid the adulation of his neighbors that the town grows to regard him a coward. Aware of this, he swings into action, and after a score of breathtaking stunts, brings a crooked broker to justice and the town beauty into his arms.

d, Henry King; w, Stephen Fox; ph, George Rizard.

Adventure **(PR:A MPAA:NR)**

THIS MARRIAGE BUSINESS* (1927, Brit.) 6 reels FBO bw

Estelle Brody *(Annette)*, Owen Nares *(Robert)*, Marjorie Hume *(Pat)*, Jack Rutherford *(Duncan)*, Jeff Barlow *(Perkins)*, Polly Ward *(Maid)*.

Long before the British film industry was producing comedic gems like those starring Alec Guinness, Terry-Thomas, and Alastair Sim, this little picture about a newlywed who breaks into his wife's bedroom disguised as a burglar to make his wife more attentive, was thrust upon the English public.

p, F. A. Enders; d&w, Leslie Hiscott.

Comedy **(PR:A MPAA:NR)**

THORNS AND ORANGE BLOSSOMS** (1922) 7 reels PRE/Al Lichtman bw

Estelle Taylor *(Rosita Mendez)*, Kenneth Harlan *(Alan Randolph)*, Arthur Hull *(Barnes Ramsey)*, Edith Roberts *(Violet Beaton)*, Carl Stockdale *(Col. Beaton)*, John Cossar *(Pio Guerra)*, Evelyn Selbie *(Fallie)*.

Average programmer has Harlan, a California businessman, visiting New Orleans, where he falls in love with a Spanish opera singer (nicely played by Taylor). But then remembering the girl back home, to whom he's engaged, Harlan breaks off the affair and returns to do "the right thing." The hot-blooded singer follows Harlan, however, and in a scuffle stabs herself with her own knife. At the trial, the singer lies about the confrontation and Harlan is sentenced to hard labor. In the end he's set free when Taylor learns that his wife is expecting, and steps forward to tell the truth.

d, Louis J. Gasnier; w, Hope Loring (based on the novel by Bertha M. Clay); ph, Karl Struss; ed, Eve Unsell.

Drama **(PR:A MPAA:NR)**

THOROUGHBREDS (SEE: SILKS AND SADDLES, 1929)

THOSE WITHOUT SIN*1/2** (1917) 5 reels LAS/PAR bw

Blanche Sweet *(Melanie Landry)*, Tom Forman *(Bob Wallace)*, C. H. Geldert *(Richard Landry)*, Guy Oliver *(Henry Mellon)*, James Neill *(Dr. Wallace)*, Charles Ogle *(Col. Dackins)*, George Beranger *(Chester Wallace)*, Mabel Van Buren, Dorothy Abril, Edna Wilson, Little Billy Jacobs, Mayme Kelso, Jane Wolff, Mrs. Smith, Mrs. Lewis McCord.

At a time when partriotism was at its zenith, this well directed and acted picture caused more than a little stir. It depicted a U.S. officer as a drunken brute, willing to kill a Southern girl who almost sacrificed herself for her Confederate sweetheart. In a more objective era, this film would have been judged a mutual triumph for Sweet and director Neilan.

d, Marshall Neilan; w, Harvey F. Thew (based on a story by George Dubois Proctor, Thomas Geraghty).

Drama **(PR:A MPAA:NR)**

THOU ART THE MAN*1/2 (1920) 5 reels PAR bw

Robert Warwick *(Myles Calthorpe)*, Lois Wilson *(Joan Farrant)*, J. M. Dumont *(Henry Farrant)*, Clarence Burton *(Matt Solomon)*, Clarence H. Geldert *(Brummage)*, Harry Carter *(Mr. Prescott)*, Dorothy Rosher *(Ellie Prescott)*, Viora Daniel *(Fannie Dering)*, Richard Wayne *(Tom Dering)*, Lorenza Lazzarini *(Lucille)*, Lillian Leighton *(Cook)*, Sylvia Ashton, Henry Hicks, Jane Wolfe.

When this picture was released a great deal was made of director Heffron's method of allowing his actors the freedom to perform pretty much on their own. It's a theory that has never worked, and this completely uninspired film set in the diamond fields of Africa, about a man who goes to prison to protect the reputation of a woman, is proof of that.

d, Thomas Heffron; w, Margaret Turnbull (based on the novel *Myles Calthorpe, I.D.B.* by F. E. Mills Young); ph, Victor Ackland.

Drama **(PR:A MPAA:NR)**

THOU FOOL (1926, Brit.) 5 reels STOLL/EB bw

Stewart Rome *(Robert Barker)*, Marjorie Hume *(Elsie Glen)*, Mary Rorke *(Lady MacDonald)*, J. Fisher White *(James Scobie)*, Windham Guise *(Duncan Glen)*, Mickey Brantford *(Robert, as a Child)*, Darby Foster *(Harry Clement)*, Pat Aherne.

In this British drama, a Scotsman sets out to destroy his former boss when that fellow's daughter weds the man who became a millionaire at his own father's expense.

d, Fred Paul; w, (based on a novel by J. J. Bell).

Drama **(PR:A MPAA:NR)**

THOU SHALT NOT** (1914) 4 reels University/Ramos bw

Stuart Holmes, Edith Hallor, Harry Collier.

Four action-packed reels in this frozen tundra saga about a man who, during a fair fight, kills the rotter who ran off with his wife, then watches as she dies of a fever. But life is renewed for him when he falls in love with the sister of his "victim," and with her help escapes the mounties and settles down with her in another town.

d&w, Will H. Davis.

North Woods Drama **(PR:A MPAA:NR)**

THOU SHALT NOT KILL (SEE: AVENGING CONSCIENCE, THE, 1914)

THREE AGES, THE*** (1923) 6 reels Keaton-Schenck/Metro bw

Buster Keaton *(The Young Man)*, Wallace Beery *(The Rival)*, Margaret Leahy *(The Girl)*, Joe Roberts *(The Girl's Father)*, Lilian Lawrence *(The Girl's Mother)*, Horace Morgan *(The Emperor)*, Oliver Hardy, Blanche Payson.

Keaton's first feature film, a parody of D. W. Griffith's masterpiece INTOLERANCE (1913), has three parallel stories (rather than Griffith's four). In an opening sequence, the major characters are introduced: the beauty, Leahy; her suitor-selecting parents, Roberts and Lawrence; the worshiper of beauty, Keaton; and the favored rival, Beery. Segue to prehistoric times, with the parents evaluating the rivals—who arrive astride a mastodon and a dinosaur, respectively—by thumping them with clubs to ascertain their hardiness (the stoical Beery withstands the onslaught; Keaton collapses at the merest tap). Transportation plays a premier part in the alternative ages. In the Roman segments, the rivals race their respective chariots to win the girl (as in the 1913 Italian epic QUO VADIS, and the 1907 BEN HUR), but the race occurs during a raging snowstorm. Beery's beautiful chariot and his team of noble steeds contrast strangely with Keaton's makeshift affair with four mismatched equines, which include a mule and a burro. Keaton outwits his rival by strapping sledge runners to his conveyance and replacing the equines with canines, mushing them to victory (when one of the dogs suffers an injury, Keaton rushes to the rear of his makeshift sled to fetch a spare pooch). In the modern segment, the race is between Beery's classy custom roadster and Keaton's Model T Ford; at the photo finish, the latter hits a bump and collapses. In another episode, the rivals attempt to evoke the jealousy of the girl they both favor by various schemes. Caveman Keaton attempts to drag the pulchritudinous Payson off to his lair by her hair, but fails; when she stands, he discovers that Payson (a one-time policewoman) is taller than he by a foot and a half. The Romanesque Keaton has a similar misfortune, selecting an Amazonian female gladiator to make his point. In the contemporary segment, Keaton inadvertently imbibes bootleg gin from a water flask at a restaurant and makes a play for a lady at an adjacent table, only to be confronted by her enormous escort. The climactic scenes in which Keaton finally gets the girl are— in each of the three ages—drawn-out, action-filled chases, the sort at which Keaton excelled, proceeding from one zany resolution to another. The three-tiered epilog reflects the altering birth rate of each of the ages; the cave man and his wife have a veritable army of cave children pattering after them; the Roman pair have five; the contemporary couple possess only a puppy. As was the case with Charlie Chaplin's THE GOLD RUSH, the episodic layout of the film was basically in the form of three two-reelers; the untrusting moviemaker apparently considered the possibility of re-editing to convert to the shorter format if the feature-length film failed to make its mark.

p, Joseph M. Schenck; d, Buster Keaton, Eddie Cline; w, Clyde Bruckman, Jean Havez, Joseph Mitchell; ph, William McGann, Elgin Lessley; prod d, Fred Gabourie.

Comedy **Cas.** **(PR:A MPAA:NR)**

THREE MUSKETEERS, THE**** (1921) 12 reels Douglas Fairbanks/UA bw

Douglas Fairbanks *(D'Artagnan)*, Leon Barry *(Athos)*, George Siegmann *(Porthos)*, Eugene Pallette *(Aramis)*, Boyd Irwin *(De Rocheford)*, Thomas Holding *(George Villiers, Duke of Buckingham)*, Sidney Franklin *(Bonacieux)*, Charles Stevens *(Planchet, D'Artagnan's Lackey)*, Nigel De Brulier *(Cardinal Richelieu)*, Willis Robards *(Capt. de Treville)*, Lon Poff *(Father Joseph)*, Mary MacLaren *(Queen/Anne of Austria)*, Marguerite De La Motte *(Constance Bonacieux)*, Barbara La Marr *(Milady de Winter)*, Walt Whitman *(D'Artagnan's Father)*, Adolphe Menjou *(Louis XIII, King of France)*, Charles Belcher *(Bernajoux)*.

In writing his review of this film for *Life* magazine, Robert E. Sherwood noted, "When Alexander Dumas sat down at his desk, smoothed his hair back, chewed the end of his quill pen, and said to himself, 'Well, I guess I might as well write a book called *The Three Musketeers*,' he doubtless had but one object in view: to provide a suitable story for Douglas Fairbanks to act in the movies." This was Fairbanks' first full-fledged historical adventure. Earlier he had approached THE MARK OF ZORRO (1920) at the suggestion of his wife, Mary Pickford, with some caution, and the production values were rather conservative. But in THE THREE MUSKETEERS he used lavish sets, a huge cast of characters and extras, and magnificant costumes. And Sherwood was perfectly correct—Fairbanks *was* D'Artagnan. The story begins with a young provincial lad who comes to Paris with the ambition of becoming a Musketeer. By proving his skill with a sword, he wins the friendship of the king's Three Musketeers (Barry, Siegmann, and Pallette) and eventual membership in their company. Then, when Cardinal Richelieu (De Brulier) attempts a coup by threatening to expose the queen's love for the Duke of Buckingham (Holding), Fairbanks embarks on a very dangerous journey to England to retrieve a diamond brooch—a gift of the king—which was given to the Englishman as a love token. After a number of swashbuckling adventures, the gallant Musketeer steals it back and returns to defeat De Brulier's further plans. He also wins the love of the beautiful Constance (De La Motte), who, to please the censors, was transformed from a married woman—and the hero's mistress—to a virginal servant of the queen, and is rescued from the death she suffered in the novel. But Fairbanks would later subject her to this fate, as he would himself (for the first and last time), in his extremely moving farewell to the silent screen—THE IRON MASK (a 1929 film made with a talking sequence).

d, Fred Niblo; w, Edward Knoblock, Lotta Woods (based on the novel by Alexandre Dumas Pere); ph, Arthur Edeson; m, Louis F. Gottschalk; ed, Nellie Mason; art d, Edward M. Langley; cos, Paul Burns.

Historical Romance **Cas.** **(PR:A MPAA:NR)**

THREE SINNERS**½** (1928) 8 reels PAR bw

Pola Negri *(Baroness Gerda Wallentin)*, Warner Baxter *(James Harris)*, Paul Lukas *(Count Dietrich Wallentin)*, Anders Randolph *(Count Hellemuth Wallentin)*, Tullo Carminati *(Raoul Stanislav)*, Anton Vaverka *(Valet to Dietrich)*, Ivy Harris *(Countess Lilli)*, William von Hardenburg *(Prince von Scherson)*, Olga Baclanova *(Baroness Hilda Brings)*.

On becoming aware that her husband, Lukas, is seeing another woman, Negri, a countess, takes a train trip to Vienna. On board she meets world famous musician Carminati, and agrees to spend time with him at his village which is enroute. After they depart the train, there is a terrible accident and Negri is reported killed. Feeling guilty over her affair, Negri chooses not to face her husband, then bleaches her hair and lands a job as hostess in a gambling casino. Years later, her husband visits the establishment and is attracted to the lady because of her resemblance to his late wife. Negri is pleased by this, but when she discovers that the count is still involved with his paramour, she reveals the truth, puts him in his place, and sails for the U.S. to start a whole new life. This highly incredulous motion picture posseses some fine production values, but its primary source of interest is seeing the striking Negri conduct herself as a blonde.

d, Rowland V. Lee; w, Doris Anderson, Jean De Limur (based on the play "Das Zweite Leben" by Bernauer Osterreicher; t, Julian Johnson; ph, Victor Milner; ed, Robert Brassler.

Drama **(PR:C MPAA:NR)**

THREE WISE FOOLS*½** (1923) 7 reels Goldwyn bw

Claude Gillingwater *(Theodore Findley)*, Eleanor Boardman *(Rena Fairchild/ Sydney Fairchild)*, William H. Crane *(Honorable James Trumbull)*, Alec B. Francis *(Dr. Richard Gaunt)*, John Sainpolis *(John Crawshay)*, Brinsley Shaw *(Benny)*, Fred Esmelton *(Gray)*, William Haines *(Gordon Schuyler)*, Lucien Littlefield *(Douglas)*, ZaSu Pitts *(Mickey)*, Martha Mattox *(Saunders)*, Fred J. Butler *(Poole)*, Charles Hickman *(Clancy)*, Craig Biddle, Jr. *(Young Findley)*, Creighton Hale *(Young Trumbull)*, Raymond Hatton *(Young Gaunt)*.

Director Vidor is at his best in this touching domestic comedy about a girl who is taken in by three wealthy bachelors, wins their hearts, and changes their stodgy ways for the better. There is a subplot in which the young lady is accused of a crime, as well as a romantic angle, but the relationship between Boardman and her three devoted guardians is what makes this charming motion picture really sparkle.

d, King Vidor; w, Vidor, June Mathis, John McDermott, James O'Hanlon (based on the play by Austin Strong, Winchell Smith); ph, Charles Van Enger.

Comedy/Drama **(PR:A MPAA:NR)**

THREE'S A CROWD½** (1927) 6 reels Harry Langdon/FN bw

Harry Langdon *(The Odd Fellow)*, Gladys McConnell *(The Girl)*, Cornelius Keefe *(The Man)*, Henry Barrows, Frances Raymond, Agnes Steele, Brooks Benedict, Bobby Young, Julia Brown, Joe Butterworth, Fred Warren, John Kolb, Arthur Thalasso.

Langdon's greatest career mistake was firing Frank Capra and deciding to direct his own films. The little man was funny and popular, but totally lacked the genius, or for that matter the introspection regarding his own persona, to perform as auteur in the manner of Chaplin and Keaton. The film deals with a lonely fellow who takes a pregnant woman in from the cold, and then after she gives birth, breaks his back to provide for his "pretend family." There are amusing moments, but it is inevitable that she will eventually return to her husband, and that the comedian will have his heart shattered. The problem is that it's all presented in a heavy-handed manner, and as one watches the comedy and tries to relate to the pathos, there exists a feeling of discomfort—or perhaps it's really embarrassment for the artist that might have been.

d, Harry Langdon; w, James Langdon, Robert Eddy (based on a story by Arthur Ripley); ph, Elgin Lessley, Frank Evans; m/l, "Body and Soul," John W. Green.

Comedy/Drama **(PR:A MPAA:NR)**

THUMBS DOWN*½ (1927) 5 reels BAN/STER bw

Creighton Hale *(Richard Hale)*, Lois Boyd *(Helen Stanton)*, Wyndham Standing *(James Breen)*, Helen Lee Worthing *(Marion Ames)*, Vera Lewis *(Mrs. Hale)*, Scott Seaton *(Mr. Stanton)*.

Feeble programmer has society chap Hale marrying stenographer Boyd against his mother's wishes. The mother then convinces Hale that his bride is having an affair, but fortunately he realizes in time that the man she visits is helping her secure a release for her wrongly imprisoned father. Of course there are apologies galore and plenty of rejoicing when the old-timer steps out into the sunshine once again.

d, Phil Rosen; w, Frances Guihan (based on a story by Gladys E. Johnson); ph, Herbert Kirkpatrick.

Drama **(PR:A MPAA:NR)**

THUNDER** (1929) 9 reels MGM bw

Lon Chaney *(Grumpy Anderson)*, Phyllis Haver *(Zella)*, George Duryea *(Jim)*, James Murray *(Tommy)*, Frances Norris *(Molly)*, Wally Albright, Jr. *(Davey)*.

Despite a good performance by Chaney, THUNDER, his last silent film, is pretty much of a disappointment. There is a sound effects only track which was used to "enhance" the theater orchestras or organs, but the synchronization was so poor that it merely served as a distraction. The story itself is pure melodrama and, except for a few special effects, could have been shot 15 years earlier. It all has to do with a railroad engineer (Chaney) so obsessed with making his train run on time that he causes several tragedies which separate him from his family. In the end, of course, Chaney wins them back by racing a Red Cross train through flood waters which treaten the lives of countless citizens, including his estranged son and Haver, a nightclub singer who shows him sympathy.

d, William Nigh; sup, Hunt Stromberg; w, Byron Morgan, Ann Price (based on a story by Morgan); t, Joe Farnham; ph, Henry Sharp; ed, Ben Lewis; ch, George Cunningham; syn sc; s eff.

Drama **(PR:A MPAA:NR)**

TIDES OF FATE*** (1917) 5 reels WORLD bw

Alexandra Carlisle *(Fanny Lawson)*, Frank Holland *(John Cross)*, William A. Sheer *(Stephen King)*, Charles Graham *(Fergus McManus)*, Jane Kent *(Claudia Nelson)*, Walter Ryder *(Azray Heath)*.

Unaware that he is wanted for counterfeiting, Carlisle marries Sheer after he saves her from drowning. Holland, a Canadian Mountie who is vacationing nearby (and secretly loves Carlisle), leaves when he hears the news. Before long, Sheer begins to badly mistreat his bride, and when the authorities arrive on the scene, the fugitive escapes and Carlisle is accused of possessing bogus money. Meanwhile, Holland, who has lost his nerve, is dismissed from the Mounted Police. To prove his manhood, he joins the U.S. Army and goes off to fight the Moro uprising in the Phillipines. Carlisle then escapes from prison and heads for New York, where she runs into her husband, who tries to blackmail her, as well as Holland, who is recovering from wounds suffered on the field of battle. There is of course the inevitable showdown, in which Sheer is killed. But in a last-breath confession, he clears Carlisle, the Canadian is reinstated by the Mounted Police, and the couple find happiness in each other's arms.

d, George Cowl; w, (based on the story "Creeping Tides" by Kate Jordan).

Crime **(PR:A MPAA:NR)**

TIE THAT BINDS, THE*½ (1923) Jacob Wilk/WB bw

Walter Miller *(David Winthrop)*, Barbara Bedford *(Mary Ellen Gray)*, Raymond Hatton *(Hiram Foster)*, William P. Carleton *(Daniel Kenyon)*, Robert Edeson *(Charles Dodge)*, Julia Swayne Gordon *(Leila Brant)*, Marian Swayne *(Flora Foster)*, Effie Shannon *(Mrs. Mills)*.

Predictable programmer has Bedford marrying a co-worker, to the chagrin of her lustful boss, Carleton. Then, when her husband is fired and Bedford is forced to return to the office, she is placed in the position of having to fight off her employer's unwanted attentions. The rotter is later found dead, and Bedford is the number one suspect, but her husband gallantly confesses to the crime. Things work out in the end—as they always do in pictures of this sort—when the night watchman steps forward and confesses to murdering the man who wronged his daughter.

d, Joseph Levering, w, Paul Keating (based on the story by Peter Bernard Kyne); ph, George Robinson.

Drama **(PR:A MPAA:NR)**

TIGER WOMAN, THE*** (1917) 6 reels FOX bw

Theda Bara *(Princess Petrovitch)*, E. F. Roseman *(Prince Petrovitch)*, Louis Dean *(The Baron)*, Emil De Varny *(The Count)*, John Webb Dillon *(Stevan)*, Glenn White *(Edwin Harris)*, Mary Martin *(Mrs. Edwin Harris)*, Herbert Heyes *(Mark Harris)*, Kittens Reichert *(Their Child)*, Edward Holt *(Harris Boy's Father)*, Florence Martin *(Marion Harding)*, George Clarke *(Marion's Father)*, Kate Blancke *(Marion's Mother)*, Charles McCann.

There is almost nonstop vamping in this Bara saga about a wicked woman who ruins the life of an ambassador, destroys a family by causing a son to kill his father, and then breaks up his brother's marriage by latching on to the lad. It all comes to an end when a Russian valet (whom Bara caused to be imprisoned) makes the sensuous one stab herself, and is followed by the title, "The Wages of Sin is Death."

d, J. Gordon Edwards; w, Adrian Johnson (based on a story by James W. Adams); ph, Phillip E. Rosen.

Drama **(PR:A MPAA:NR)**

TIGER'S CLAW, THE½** (1923) 6 reels FP/PAR bw

Jack Holt *(Sam Sandell)*, Eva Novak *(Harriet Halehurst)*, George Periolat *(Henry Frazer Halehurst)*, Bertram Grassby *(Raj Singh)*, Aileen Pringle *(Chameli Brentwood)*, Carl Stockdale *(Sathoo Ram)*, Frank Butler *(George Malvin)*, George Field *(Prince)*, Evelyn Selbie *(Azun)*, Frederick Vroom *(Col. Byng)*, Lucien Littlefield *(Goyrem)*, Robert Cain *(Sothern)*, Robert Dudley, Robin Hood *(A Horse)*.

A couple of pretty good thrills enhance this jungle drama which has Holt playing a U.S. engineer saved from a tiger by a beautiful halfcaste (Pringle), whom he marries. Later the girl is killed by a bullet meant for Holt when her uncle and a former lover plot to kill him and blow up his dam. This time Holt is rescued by his former British sweetheart, Novak, and the two find happiness in each other's arms.

d, Joseph Henabery; w, Jack Cunningham; ph, Faxon M. Dean.

Adventure **(PR:A MPAA:NR)**

TIGRESS, THE*** (1914) 4 reels Popular Plays and Players/Alco bw

Olga Petrova *(Stella)*.

When Petrova repulses the advances of the Eutrurian governor, he has her husband shot by a firing squad and her child abducted. She is thrown into prison but escapes by exchanging places with a dead nurse. Devastated by these experiences, Petrova seeks revenge against all of mankind by joining a gang of international spies. Later she learns that her child was adopted by a kindly American diplomat, so when her comrades steal the plans to a number of vital U.S. fortifications, she risks her life by retrieving them and directs the big guns to blow the spy ship out of the water. Good performance by Petrova, as well as screenplay by Blache and Hoffman.

w, Alice Blache, Aaron Hoffman (based on a play by Ramsey Morris).

War **(PR:A MPAA:NR)**

TILLIE** (1922) 5 reels REA/PAR bw (AKA: TILLIE, A MENNONITE MAID)

Mary Miles Minter *(Tillie Getz)*, Noah Beery *(Jacob Getz)*, Allan Forrest *(Jack Fairchild)*, Lucien Littlefield *(Doc Weaver)*, Lillian Leighton *(Sarah Oberholtzer)*, Marie Treboul *(Sallie Getz)*, Virginia Adair *(Louisa)*, Robert Anderson *(Absalom Puntz)*, Ashley Cooper *(Lawyer)*.

Less-than-inspired Minter rural drama about the daughter of a Pennsylvania Dutch farmer whose brutal father keeps her as a slave and withholds news of a considerable inheritance she is to receive on the condition that she become a Mennonite. Minter attempts suicide but fails and is taken in under the wing of young Forrest, who not only sees to it that she gets her due, but makes her his wife as well.

d, Frank Urson; w, Alice Eyton (based on the play "Tillie, a Mennonite Maid" by Frank Howe, Jr.); ph, Allen Davey.

Drama **(PR:A MPAA:NR)**

TILLIE THE TOILER** 1/2 (1927) 6 reels COS/MGM bw

Marion Davies *(Tillie Jones)*, Matt Moore *(Mac)*, Harry Crocker *(Pennington Fish)*, George Fawcett *(Mr. Simpkins)*, George K. Arthur *(Mr. Whipple)*, Estelle Clark *(Sadie)*, Bert Roach *(Bill)*, Gertrude Short *(Bubbles)*, Claire McDowell *(Maude Jones)*, Arthur Hoyt *(Mr. Smythe)*.

Davies looks wonderful and manages to deliver more than a few laughs as a dumb stenographer who wins the heart of millionaire Crocker, but at the last minute decides to marry office clerk Moore, whose love for Davies gives him the gumption to land a big job. This is a fairly entertaining little comedy, but the picture's real star is Spence, the title writer.

d, Hobart Henley; w, A. P. Younger (based on a story by Agnes Christine Johnston, Edward T. Lowe, Jr., and the comic strip by Russ Westover); t, Ralph Spence; ph, William Daniels; ed, Daniel J. Gray; art d, Cedric Gibbons, David Townsend.

Comedy **(PR:A MPAA:NR)**

TILLIE WAKES UP** 1/2 (1917) 5 reels PEER/WORLD bw

Marie Dressler *(Tillie Tinklepaw)*, Johnny Hines *(Mr. Pipkins)*, Frank Beamish *(Henry Tinklepaw)*, Rubye de Remer *(Mrs. Luella Pipkins)*, Ruth Barrett *(Mrs. Nosey)*, Jack Brown *(Mr. Nosey)*, May De Lacy.

Better than TILLIE'S TOMATO SURPRISE (1915), but not nearly as good as the original TILLIE'S PUNCTURED ROMANCE (1914), the third entry in the series is little more than a padded two reeler. Set amongst the novelty devices and rides of Coney Island, this story of a dominated wife who has "a little fun" with her neighbor's husband, does have its moments, and the presence of young Hines is a definite plus. Included are some very interesting shots of New York's fabled amusement park.

d, Harry Davenport; w, Frances Marion (based on a story by Mark Swan).

Comedy **(PR:A MPAA:NR)**

TILLIE'S PUNCTURED ROMANCE*** (1914) 6 reels Keystone bw

Marie Dressler, Charles Chaplin, Mable Normand, Charles Bennett, Mack Swain, Joe Bordeaux, Chester Conklin, Edgar Kennedy, Charles Chase, Charles Murray, Minta Durfee, Gordon Griffith, Phyllis Allen, Alice Davenport, Harry McCoy, Alice Howell, Wallace MacDonald, Hank Mann, Slim Summerville, Al St. John, Billy Bennett, Eddie Sutherland, G. G. Ligon.

Historically important as the first feature length comedy (it was released a year before THE BIRTH OF A NATION) and esthetically pleasing because it's a funny movie. Sennett pulled out all the stops for this one and put practically everyone he had under contract before the camera. The story has con man Chaplin sweet-talking country girl Dressler into stealing her father's money and running away with him to the city, where he loses her to continue his romance with pretty Normand. Dressler gets a job in a restaurant and when Chaplin hears that she inherited a fortune from her millionaire uncle, he asks her to become his wife. The couple throw a wedding party at Dressler's mansion, where they perform an hilarious tango. But the mood changes when Dressler discovers Chaplin kissing Normand, who is working as a maid. After some slapstick mayhem which includes the firing of a number of pistol shots and the tossing of numerous pies, the uncle (who is quite alive) returns in time to save Chaplin from being strangled to death. He escapes, followed by Dressler, Normand, and the Keystone Kops. The whole party goes flying over a pier and into the drink, and when they emerge the girls decide to leave Chaplin to his misery. "He ain't no good to neither of us," the title card says.

d, Mack Sennett; w, Hampton Del Ruth (based on the play "Tillie's Nightmare" by Edgar Smith); ph, Frank D. Williams.

Comedy **Cas.** **(PR:A MPAA:NR)**

TILLIE'S PUNCTURED ROMANCE** 1/2 (1928) 6 reels CC/PAR bw

W. C. Fields *(Ringmaster)*, Chester Conklin *(Haratio Q. Frisbee)*, Louise Fazenda *(Tillie)*, Mack Swain *(Tillie's Old Man/Gen. Pilsner)*, Doris Hill *(The Girl Trapezist)*, Grant Withers *(The Boy Trapezist/Wireless Operator)*, Tom Kennedy *(The Villain)*, Babe London *(The Strong Woman)*, Kalla Pasha *(The Axe Thrower)*, William Platt *(The Midget)*, Mickey Bennett *(The Bad Boy)*, Mike Rafetto *(The Lion Tamer)*, Baron von Dobeneck *(The German Officer)*.

There are laughs in this comedy—which bears absolutely no resemblance to the original Mack Sennett classic—but somehow the movie just fails to click. The principals are all good, and the business where the circus travels to France to entertain the doughboys, gets caught in a storm, and the players end up serving in the German Army, is satisfying. But in spite of clever direction by Sutherland and some hefty production values, the whole thing falls just a bit short.

d, Edward Sutherland; w, Monte Brice, Keene Thompson (based on the play "Tillie's Nightmare" by Edgar Smith); ph, Charles Boyle, William Wheeler, ed, Arthur Huffsmith.

Comedy **(PR:A MPAA:NR)**

TILLIE'S TOMATO SURPRISE* (1915) 5 reels Lubin bw

Marie Dressler *(Tillie)*, Tom McNaughton *(Percy Jitney)*, Colin Campbell, Sarah McVickar, Eleanor Fairbanks, James the Monkey.

Dressler's sequel to her own landmark TILLIE'S PUNCTURED ROMANCE (the first comedy feature, released a year earlier, by Mack Sennett) lacked all of the charm and humor of the original. This one is slapstick for its own sake, and the absence of Charles Chaplin, Mabel Normand, and the other Keystone zanies is sorely felt. The script was written by long-time *New York Evening Sun* drama critic, Davies, and the numerous actors, directors, and playwrights he dragged over the coals throughout his career must surely have relished this embarrassment.

d, Howell Hansel; w, Acton Davies; ph, George Webber.

Comedy **(PR:A MPAA:NR)**

TIME TO LOVE** 1/2 (1927) 5 reels PAR bw

Raymond Griffith *(Alfred Sava-Goiu)*, William Powell *(Prince Alado)*, Vera Voronina *(Countess Elvire)*, Josef Swickard *(Elvire's Father)*, Mario Carillo *(1st Duelist)*, Pierre De Ramey *(2nd Duelist)*, Helene Giere *(Elvire's Guardian)* Alfred Sabato *(Hindu Mystic)*.

Griffith does as well as can be expected with the spotty material he's provided with here. The comedian plays a brokenhearted Frenchman who, while trying to commit suicide, accidentaly jumps into Voronina's boat, falls madly in love with the lady, and saves her from going over the side of a waterfall. He then becomes involved with Powell, a prince engaged to Voronina, who challenges Griffith to a duel. At the picture's end, Griffith abducts his sweetheart from her forced wedding, escapes in a balloon which is to be used for anti-aircraft target practice, and parachutes right into his darling's domicile, where a nearsighted clergyman pronounces them man and wife.

p, B. P. Schulberg; d, Frank Tuttle; w, Pierre Collings (based on a story by Alfred Savoir); ph, William Marshall.

Comedy **(PR:A MPAA:NR)**

TIMOTHY'S QUEST*** (1922) 7 reels Dirigo/American Releasing bw

Joseph Depew *(Timothy)*, Baby Helen Rowland *("Lady Gay")*, Marie Day *(Miss Avilda Cummins)*, Margaret Seddon *(Samantha Ann Ripley)*, Bertram Marburgh *(Jabe Slocum)*, Vivia Ogden *(Hitty Tarbox)*, Gladys Leslie *(Miss Dora)*, William F. Haddock *(Dave Milliken)*, Rags the Dog.

Nice, sentimental little movie has Depew, an orphan boy, and Rowland, the tot he protects, leaving their New York slum when they learn they are about to be institutionalized. The two wind up in a small New England town, where they are taken in by a couple of spinsters. Before long they win the ladies' love, and it's discovered that the boy is really the nephew of one of the women. Director Olcott obtained remarkable performances from the children, and the result was a truly heartwarming film.

d, Sidney Olcott; w, Katherine Stuart (based on the novel by Kate Douglas Wiggin); ph, Al Ligouri, Eugene French; set d, Tec-Art Studios.

Drama **(PR:A MPAA:NR)**

TIN GODS* 1/2 (1926) 9 reels FP/PAR bw

Thomas Meighan *(Roger Drake)*, Renee Adoree *(Carita)*, Aileen Pringle *(Janet Stone)*, William Powell *(Tony Santelli)*, Hale Hamilton *(Dr. McCoy)*, John Harrington *(Dougherty)*, Joe King *(1st Foreman)*, Robert E. O'Connor *(2nd Foreman)*, Delbert Emory Whitten, Jr. *(Billy)*.

A lot of talent is wasted in this potboiler about an engineer, Meighan, who separates from his politically ambitious wife, Pringle, after their child is killed in an accident. The fellow hits the skids and ends up in South America, where he's hired to construct a bridge. There he's stricken by jungle fever, and Adoree, a beautiful native dancer, nurses him back to health and falls desperately in love with the good-looking Yank. Later, when Adoree fears her man is planning to return to his wife, she commits suicide by jumping from the structure he has built. Deeply moved by this, Meighan erects a church in her honor, and returns every year to pray for the deliverance of her almighty soul.

p, William Le Baron; d, Allan Dwan; w, James Shelley Hamilton, Paul Dickey, Howard Emmett Rogers (based on the play by William Anthony McGuire); ph, Alvin Wyckoff.

Drama **(PR:A MPAA:NR)**

TIPPED OFF* 1/2 (1923) 5 reels Harry A. McKenzie/PG bw

Arline Pretty *(Mildred Garson)*, Harold Miller *(Anthony Moore)*, Tom Santschi *("The Fox," Dan Grogan)*, Noah Berry *(Chang Wo)*, Stuart Holmes *(Sidney Matthews)*, Zella Gray *(Rita Garson)*, Tom O'Brien *(Jim "Pug" Murphy)*, Bessie Wong *(Chinese Maid)*, James Alamo *(Chuck Morrison)*, Jimmie Truax *(Baldy Bates)*, Si Wilcox *(The Detective Sergeant)*, James Wang *(Chan Wo's Major-Domo)*, Scotty MacGregor *(The Stage Director)*.

The hokum comes pretty thick in this melodrama about a playwright's fiancee (Pretty) who involves her brother and sister in a fake robbery in order to prove she is the right person to play the lead in his new mystery. Of course a gang of real crooks show up at the same time, but they are subdued and the lady wins her part.

p, William Matthews; d, Finis Fox; w, Frederick Reel, Jr.; ph, Harry Fowler.

Mystery **(PR:A MPAA:NR)**

TO HAVE AND TO HOLD*** (1922) 8 reels FP/PAR bw

Betty Compson *(Lady Jocelyn Leigh)*, Bert Lytell *(Capt. Ralph Percy)*, Theodore Kosloff *(Lord Carnal)*, W. J. Ferguson *(Jeremy Sparrow)*, Raymond Hatton *(King James I)*, Claire Du Brey *(Patience Worth)*, Walter Long *(Red Gill)*, Anne Cornwall *(Lady Jane Carr)*, Fred Huntley *(Paradise)*, Arthur Rankin *(Lord Cecil)*, Lucien Littlefield *(Duke of Buckingham)*.

Compsom escapes marriage to the hated Kosloff, a favorite lord of England's king, by joining her maid on a ship of women bound for Jamestown, where nuptial arrangements with that colony's male settlers has been planned. In the New World she is taken under the protective wing of Lytell, a captain whom she falls in love with and marries. Kosloff, in the meantime, arrives, abducts Compson, and has Lytell imprisoned. The gallant captain escapes, however, rescues his bride from the departing ship, and forces Kosloff to board his small boat as a hostage. Before long a terrible storm blows them into a pirate's den, but through Lytell's wit and courage they escape and manage to make their way back to England. Once home, the despicable nobleman has his rival thrown into a dungeon, and prepares the lavish wedding with Compson, for whom he has so long craved. But Lytell escapes and with the assistance of a sympathetic lord, forces his enemy into a duel. Then, in a well-staged encounter, the dashing captain kills the man who had once enjoyed a reputation as England's most skilled blade, and this handsomely mounted and most absorbing picture concludes with the lovers reunited at last.

d, George Fitzmaurice; w, Ouida Bergere (based on the novel by Mary Johnston); ph, Arthur Miller.

Costume Adventure/Romance **(PR:A MPAA:NR)**

TO THE LAST MAN 1/2** (1923) 7 reels FP/PAR bw

Richard Dix *(Jean Isbel)*, Lois Wilson *(Ellen Jorth)*, Noah Beery *(Colter)*, Robert Edeson *(Gaston Isbel)*, Frank Campeau *(Blue)*, Fred Huntley *(Lee Jorth)*, Edward Brady *(Daggs)*, Eugene Pallette *(Simm Bruce)*, Leonard Clapham *(Guy)*, Guy Oliver *(Bill)*, Winifred Greenwood *(Mrs. Guy)*.

The action is practically nonstop in this well-directed western dealing with feuding cattle ranchers and sheep raisers. The picture ends with only one son and daughter of the rival clans surviving, and their somehow managing to find love together in spite of all the bloodshed and hatred.

d, Victor Fleming; w, Doris Schroeder (based on the novel by Zane Grey); ph, James Howe, Bert Baldridge.

Western **(PR:A MPAA:NR)**

TODAY*** (1917) 5 reels Harry Rapf/Pathe bw

Florence Reed *(Lilly Morton)*, Gus Weinberg *(Henry Morton)*, Frank Mills *(Fred Morton)*, Alice Gale *(Emma Morton)*, Leonore Harris *(Marion Garland)*, Harry Lambert *(Richard Hewlett)*, Kate Lester *(Mrs. Farrington)*.

Satisfying motion picture adaptation of the very popular play (it ran for over a year on Broadway and had six road companies) about a woman who sacrifices her family's love for the material "rewards" of the fast life, only to awaken relieved to discover it was all a nightmare.

d, Ralph Ince; w, Frederic Chapin (based on the play by George Broadhurst, Abraham Schomer).

Drama **(PR:A MPAA:NR)**

TOILERS, THE*** (1928) 8 reels TS bw

Douglas Fairbanks, Jr. *(Steve)*, Jobyna Ralston *(Mary)*, Harvey Clark *(Joe)*, Wade Boteler *(Toby)*, Robert Ryan *(Butch)*.

Beginning as a study of the lives of three coal-miner buddies, this develops into the suspenseful story of a mine disaster. One of the miners, Fairbanks, rescues Ralston from a storm, and they fall in love. But on the day they are to marry, Fairbanks is one of 12 miners trapped in the shaft when a fire breaks out. A rescue crew struggles to dig them out, and some 36 hours later they do. This early sound picture did not include any dialog, rather it used the R.C.A. Photophone process for sound effects and musical accompaniment, which included three choruses of a miner's doggeral.

d, Reginald Barker; w, L. G. Rigby; t, Harry Braxton; ph, Ernest Miller; ed, Robert J. Kern; md, Joseph Littau; art d, Hervey Libbert; set d, George Sawley; syn sc; s eff.

Drama **(PR:A MPAA:NR)**

TOL'ABLE DAVID**** (1921) 7 reels INSP/AFN bw

Richard Barthelmess *(David Kinemon)*, Gladys Hulette *(Esther Hatburn)*, Walter P. Lewis *(Iscah Hatburn)*, Ernest Torrence *(Luke Hatburn)*, Ralph Yearsley *(Luke's Brother)*, Forrest Robinson *(Grandpaw Hatburn)*, Laurence Eddinger *(Sen. Gault)*, Edmund Gurney *(David's Father)*, Warner Richmond *(David's Brother, Allen)*, Marion Abbott *(David's Mother)*, Henry Hallam *(The Doctor)*, Patterson Dial *(Rose Allen's Wife)*, Lassie The Dog.

This timeless slice of rural Americana is director King's masterwork and a wonderful vehicle for the entire cast, especially Torrence, who delivers perhaps the greatest interpretation of villainy in the history of the motion picture. It is nothing short of a revelation to watch his portrayal of an inbred, foul-toothed, degenerate. The story is eloquently simple, telling of the three Hatburns (Torrence, Lewis, and Yearsley), fugitives who invade the peaceful Virginia countryside and force themselves upon their kindly and honest cousin, Robinson, who is the grandfather of Barthelmess' sweetheart, Hulette. The Hatburn boys lack any redeeming attributes and before long begin their reign of terror. Barthelmess worships his older brother Richmond, who drives the town mail wagon, and when Torrence cripples him with a blow to the head following the killing of the family dog, Barthelmess swears vengeance. His father, however, suffers a fatal stroke and Barthelmess' mother pleads with the boy not to throw his life away for he is now needed to run the farm and care for his crippled brother. Barthelmess is branded a coward by a number of the townsfolk until one day the opportunity comes for him to drive the mail cart. The clash with the Hatburn boys is inevitable, and it comes when the trio attempt to hold up the wagon. What follows is one of the truly greatest fight scenes ever filmed, during which young Barthelmess kills Torrence, then, wounded and half beaten to death, brings the mail through. This remarkable picture was once the property of D. W. Griffith, who began the adaptation, and part of the treatment may well be his. It is doubtful, however, that even the master could have improved on this extraordinary work. There is an interesting bit of background to the making of TOL'ABLE DAVID. One of King's partners wanted to shoot the picture in Pennsylvania, but the director, a Southerner, insisted that it be made in his native Virginia. He sent his assistant there and told him the most important thing to look for was the presence of rail fences. A short time later the fellow telephoned and told the director that he had looked out from the top of a hill and located everything that they had discussed. King then took his company to the sight and made his greatest movie less than eight miles from the place of his birth.

d, Henry King; w, Edmund Goulding, King (based on the story by Joseph Hergesheimer); ph, Henry Cronjager; ed, Duncan Mansfield.

Drama **Cas.** **(PR:A MPAA:NR)**

TOLL GATE, THE* 1/2** (1920) 6 reels WSHP/PAR bw

William S. Hart *(Black Deering)*, Anna Q. Nilsson *(Mary Brown)*, Jack Richardson *(The Sheriff)*, Joseph Singleton *(Jordan)*, Master Richard Headrick *("The Little Feller")*, Leo Willis, Fritz The Horse.

Hart's first film after breaking up with Thomas Ince and starting his own company, is also one of his best. The star once again plays an outlaw regenerated by his love for a good woman (Nilsson), as well as her little boy. There is plenty of suspense in this one, right up to the very end when Hart takes on her brutish husband and kills him by throwing him over a cliff. Earlier, the reformed bad man had earned the respect of the territorial peacekeepers and they offered him amnesty. Miss Nilsson pleads for him to stay, her child does the same, but Hart, feeling that a better man will come along for her, rides off alone.

d, Lambert Hillyer; w, Hillyer, William S. Hart (based on the story "By Their Fruits Ye Shall Know Them" by Hart); ph, Joe August.

Western **Cas.** **(PR:A MPAA:NR)**

TOLL OF MAMON zero (1914) 4 reels Excelsior bw

Octavia Handworth, Gordon De Maine, Tom Tempest, William A. Williams.

This immoral and totally reprehensible exploitation film, which claimed to provide the only cure for consumption, was aimed at the poor, on whom the disease took its greatest toll. The recommendation of fresh air, dairy products, and plenty of rest was hardly a revelation.

d&w, Harry Handworth.

Drama **(PR:A MPAA:NR)**

TOM AND HIS PALS** (1926) 5 reels R-C/FBO bw

Tom Tyler *(Tom Duffy)*, Doris Hill *(Mary Smith)*, Frankie Darro *(Frankie Smith)*, Dicky Brandon *(Junior Carroll)*, LeRoy Mason *(Courtney)*, Helen Lynch *(Pandora Golden)*, Beans The Dog, Sitting Bull.

Kid star Darro is the best thing about this low-budget oater, which has a movie company using Tyler's ranch for location shooting. Mason, the sleazy leading man, tries to move in on Tyler's sweetheart, Hill, while Tyler becomes infatuated with the picture's female star. But the cowboy comes to his senses in time to rescue Hill from the clutches of the villain, who has dragged her away on a fast-moving train. The fight scene is most unconvincing, but the behind-the-scenes movie business is of interest.

d, Robert De Lacy; w, F. A. E. Pine (based on a story by Frederick Arthur Mindlin); ph, John Leezer, Gilbert Warrenton.

Western **(PR:A MPAA:NR)**

TONGUES OF MEN, THE 1/2** (1916) 5 reels Morosco/PAR bw

Constance Collier *(Jane Bartlett)*, Forrest Stanley *(Rev. Sturgis)*, Herbert Standing *(Rev. Dr. Darigal)*, Elizabeth Burbridge *(Georgine)*, Helen Eddy *(Winifred Leeds)*, Lamar Johnstone *(Dr. Lyn Fanshawe)*, Lydia Yeamans Titus *(Mrs. Kearsley)*, Miss Marlborough *(Mme. Sternberg-Reese)*, Charles Marriot *(Mr. Goadby)*, John McKinnon *(Mr. Loughram)*.

Early performance by Collier has that fine actress doing very well indeed as a singer who is openly condemmed from the pulpit by a fire-and-brimstone minister, and then after making him fall in love with her—much to the horror of his parishioners—lets him down gently.

d, Frank Lloyd; w, (based on the play by Edward Childs Carpenter); ph, Fred Dobson.

Drama **(PR:A MPAA:NR)**

TONY RUNS WILD*** (1926) 6 reels FOX bw

Tom Mix *(Tom Trent)*, Tony *(The Horse)*, Jacqueline Logan *(Grace Percival)*, Lawford Davidson *(Slade)*, Duke Lee *(Bender)*, Vivian Oakland *(Mrs. Johnson)*, Edward Martindel *(Mr. Johnson)*, Marion Harlan *(Ethel Johnson)*, Raymond Wells *(Sheriff)*, Richard Carter *(Ranch Foreman)*, Arthur Morrison *(Auto Stage Driver)*, Lucien Littlefield *(Red)*, Jack Padjan *(Deputy Sheriff)*.

Mix saves Logan from a stampeding herd of wild horses and is challenged by the girl to tame its leader, Tony, before the film's villain, Slade, can get the job done. Mix, of course, pulls this off, shows the barely interested young lady the various tricks he taught the beautiful animal, and then sets it free. Later, when Slade and his gang capture Logan, the badly outnumbered Mix does his best to fight them off, but it is Tony, at the head of his wild herd, who routes the outlaws and nudges Logan into Mix's waiting harms.

d, Thomas Buckingham; w, Edfrid Bingham, Robert Lord (based on a story by Henry Herbert Knibbs); ph, Daniel Clark.

Western **(PR:A MPAA:NR)**

TOO MUCH BUSINESS*** (1922) 7 reels VIT bw

Edward Horton *(John Henry Jackson)*, Ethel Grey Terry *(Myra Dalton)*, Tully Marshall *(Amos Comby)*, John Steppling *(Simon Stecker)*, Carl Gerard *(Ray Gorham)*, Elsa Lorimer *(Mrs. Comby)*, Helen Gilmore *(The Head Nurse)*, Mark Fenton *(Robert Gray)*, Tom Murray *(Officer 16)*.

Engaging comedy has Horton in love with Terry, his boss' private secretary, and persuading the girl to marry him on the condition that he will double his salary within 30 days. When the boss (beautifully played by Marshall) fires Horton, the young go-getter hurls himself into the baby sitting business on a grand scale. Later, when a competitor seeks to merge with Marshall's firm on the stipulation that Horton be made manager, the old boy tries to lure his former employee back and is flatly turned down. Through underhanded play, Horton's nurses are encouraged to strike and an army of children go on a rampage. This not only provides the film an ending loaded with sight gags, but places Horton in the position of running his old company.

d, Jess Robbins; w, Ford I. Beebe (based on the story "John Henry and the Restless Sex" by Earl Derr Biggers); ph, Irving Reis.

Comedy **(PR:A MPAA:NR)**

TOO MUCH SPEED*** (1921) 5 reels FP/PAR bw

Wallace Reid *(Dusty Rhoades)*, Agnes Ayres *(Virginia MacMurran)*, Theodore Roberts *(Pat MacMurran)*, Jack Richardson *(Tyler Hellis)*, Lucien Littlefield *(Jimmy Rodman)*, Guy Oliver *("Howdy" Zeeker)*, Henry Johnson *(Billy Dawson)*, Jack Herbert *(Hawks)*.

Reid was perhaps the most popular male star in the U.S. when he made this fast-paced film in which a young fellow wins over the auto manufacturing father of the girl he eloped with by driving the old gent's car in the big race and securing for him a huge South American order.

d, Frank Urson; w, Byron Morgan; ph, Charles E. Schoenbaum.

Adventure **(PR:A MPAA:NR)**

TOP OF NEW YORK, THE* (1925) 5 reels REA/PAR bw

May McAvoy *(Hilda O'Shaunnessey)*, Walter McGrail *(Emery Gray)*, Pat Moore *(Micky O'Shaunnessey)*, Edward Cecil *(Gregory Stearns)*, Charles Bennett *(Mr. Isaacson)*, Mary Jane Irving *(Susan Gray)*, Carrie Clark Ward *(Mrs. Brady)*, Arthur Hoyt *(Mr. Brady)*.

McAvoy, one of the great actresses of the screen, is completely wasted in this banal load of hokum about a decent Irish working girl who accepts and hocks an expensive gift from her lecherous boss to pay for her crippled brother's operation. The guilt-ridden girl then tries to commit suicide, but is saved by McGrail, the very fellow who had his wife stolen by her employer. The picture ends with McAvoy marrying her protector and enjoying their future all the more, content in the knowledge that her little brother's operation was a success, and now the lad is in a position to explore the challenging hobby of tap dancing.

d, William Desmond Taylor; w, George Hopkins (based on a story by Sonya Levien); ph, James Van Trees.

Drama **(PR:A MPAA:NR)**

TORMENT** (1924) 6 reels Tourneur/AFN bw

Owen Moore *(Hansen)*, Bessie Love *(Marie)*, Jean Hersholt *(Boris)*, Joseph Kilgour *(Charles G. Hammond)*, Maude George *(Mrs. Hammond)*, Morgan Wallace *(Jules Carstock)*, George Cooper *(Chick Fogarty)*.

Lesser Tourneur-directed effort has Moore playing a crook who reforms when he meets the beautiful Love, helps foil an attempt to steal the jewels which a defecting Russian count (Hersholt) plans to sell in order to feed his displaced countrymen, and becomes involved in a Japanese earthquake. During the disaster Hersholt is killed, but Love and Moore carry on his humanitarian mission as man and wife.

d, Maurice Tourneur; w, Fred Myton (based on the story by William Dudley Pelley); t, Marion Fairfax; ph, Arthur L. Todd; ed, Frank Lawrence; set d, Jack Okey.

Mystery **(PR:A MPAA:NR)**

TORRENT, THE* (1921) 5 reels UNIV bw

Eva Novak *(Velma Patton)*, Oleta Ottis *(Anne Mayhew)*, Jack Perrin *(Lt. Paul Mack)*, L. C. Shumway *(Sam Patton)*, Jack Curtis *(Red Galvin)*, Harry Carter *(Jud Rossen)*, Bert Alpino *(1st Mate)*.

In a script which could have been written by the Women's Christian Temperance Union, Novak finds herself married to Shumway, a rotter so tacky that he invites his mistress to join them on a little sail. On board, the scoundrel—much to Novak's horror—tries to force her to take a *cocktail*, and then, as if God were making a statement, Shumway suffers a paralytic stroke, which his bride interprets as being terminal. At this point a storm comes up, and Novak finds herself washed up on a nearby island. Before long, her loneliness is disrupted by the arrival of airman Perrin, whose hydroplane ran out of gas, necessitating a forced landing. In time the couple fall in love, but their happiness is disrupted by a gang of *bootleggers* who take them captive. There are a few rough days before they escape and head for Novak's house, where, to everybody's shock, her husband is still alive. This puts a whole new light on things, and Novak, compelled to do the "right thing," resigns herself to spending the rest of her days sitting by the man's wheelchair, answering his every loathsome request. But it turns out that Shumway does possess a modicum of decency after all, for when Novak is looking the other way, he takes his own life by ingesting a shot of *whiskey*!

d, Stuart Paton; w, Philip Hurn, Wallace Clifton (based on the story "Out of the Sunset" by George Rix); ph, Bert Glennon, Roland Price.

Drama/Adventure **(PR:A MPAA:NR)**

TORRENT, THE½** (1926) 7 reels COS/MGM bw (AKA: IBANEZ' TORRENT)

Ricardo Cortez *(Don Rafael Brull)*, Greta Garbo *(Leonora)*, Gertrude Olmsted *(Remedios)*, Edward Connelly *(Pedro Moreno)*, Lucien Littlefield *(Cupido)*, Martha Mattox *(Dona Bernarda Brull)*, Lucy Beaumont *(Dona Pepa)*, Tully Marshall *(Don Andreas)*, Mack Swain *(Don Mattias)*, Arthur Edmund Carew *(Salvatti)*, Lillian Leighton *(Isabella)*, Mario Carillo *(King of Spain)*.

In her first U.S. film, Garbo plays a Spanish peasant who is dispossessed from her land when Cortez, the landlord's son, falls in love with her. The young lady makes her way to Paris, where she eventually becomes an opera star, and Cortez remains at home to climb the ladder of political success. When she returns on a visit, her former sweetheart saves her from a flood, and there is a reawakening of their romance. The picture, which no doubt would have been infinitely superior had her mentor, the brilliant Mauritz Stiller, been allowed to direct it, ends with the couple going their separate ways. Garbo is, as always, quite wonderful, and only her presence makes this film really worthwhile.

d, Monta Bell; w, Dorothy Farnum (based on the novel *Entre Naranjos* by Vicente Blasco-Ibanez); t, Katherine Hilliker, H. H. Caldwell; ph, William Daniels; ed, Frank Sullivan; set d, Cedric Gibbons, Merrill Pye.

Drama **(PR:A MPAA:NR)**

TOWER OF IVORY (SEE: OUT OF THE STORM, 1920)

TOWER OF LIES, THE** (1925) 7 reels MGM bw

Norma Shearer *(Glory)*, Lon Chaney *(Jan)*, Ian Keith *(Lars)*, Claire McDowell *(Katrina)*, William Haines *(August)*, David Torrence *(Eric)*.

Following the 1924 success of HE WHO GETS SLAPPED (MGM's first film), the studio reunited Shearer, Chaney, and Seastrom to produce this uninspired Swedish drama in which a hard-working farmer (Chaney, in one of his worst performances) finally finds a little joy in life when he fathers a daughter. Years pass and the family land is about to be foreclosed upon by Keith—the mentally unstable holder of the deed—when the daughter, Shearer, heads for the city in an attempt to raise the needed money. Shearer manages to earn the cash but is forced (rather unconvincingly) to turn to prostitution. Later she returns home and is met with the wrath of her puritanical neighbors and then watches helplessly as the landlord is killed in a fall. Chaney tries to follow his daughter, who has fled the scene, but topples over the side of the dock and drowns. After all of this, the film still ends happily, with Shearer marrying her childhood sweetheart, Haines.

d, Victor Seastrom; w, Agnes Christine Johnston, Max Marcin (based on the novel *Kejsarn av Portugallien; en Varmlandsberattelse* by Selma Ottiliana Lovisa Lagerlof); t, Marian Ainslee, Ruth Cummings; ph, Percy Hilburn; set d, Cedric Gibbons, James Basevi.

Drama **(PR:C MPAA:NR)**

TOWN SCANDAL, THE*** (1923) 5 reels UNIV bw

Gladys Walton *(Jean Crosby)*, Edward Hearne *(Toby Caswell)*, Edward McWade *(Avery Crawford)*, Charles Hill Mailes *(Bill Ramsey)*, William Welsh *(Samuel Grimes)*, William Franey *(Lysander Sprowl)*, Anna Hernandez *(Mrs. Crawford)*, Virginia Boardman *(Mrs. Sprowl)*, Rosa Gore *(Effie Strong)*, Nadine Beresford *(Mrs. Grimes)*, Louise Reming Barnes *(Mrs. Ramsey)*, Margaret Morris *(Trixie)*.

Enjoyable little comedy programmer has Broadway chorus girl Walton returning home to find that her brother-in-law, Franey, has squandered all of the money she forwarded to him. Now the town fathers, who fawned over her in New York, treat her like a professional harlot. To get even, the young lady, with the help of Hearne, a newspaper reporter, prints her memoirs, refuses the bribe money which is offered her, and returns triumphantly to the Big Apple with her new love, after getting the men in power to relax their blue laws.

d, King Baggot; w, Hugh Hoffman (based on the story by Frederic Arnold Kummer); ph, Victor Milner.

Drama/Comedy **(PR:A MPAA:NR)**

TRACKED TO EARTH*** (1922) 5 reels UNIV bw

Frank Mayo *(Charles Cranner)*, Virginia Valli *(Anna Jones)*, Harold Goodwin *(Dick Jones)*, Duke R. Lee *(Stub Lou Tate)*, Buck Connors *(Shorty Fuller)*, Arthur Millett *("Big Bill" Angus)*, Lon Poff *(Meenie Wade)*, Percy Challenger *(Zed White)*.

Good western programmer has Mayo, an undercover railroad agent, finding true love when Valli senses his innocence and protects him from the law when he's wrongly accused of horse stealing. He later clears his name, rounds up the crooks he was sent to find, and returns to the loyal lady.

d, William Worthington; w, Wallace Clifton (based on the story by William J. Neidig); ph, Leland Lancaster.

Western **(PR:A MPAA:NR)**

TRAFFIC COP, THE** (1916) 5 reels Thanhouser bw

Howard M. Mitchell *(Casey of Traffic "C")*, Gladys Hulette *(His Sweetheart)*, Ernest Howard *(The Banker)*, Theodore Von Eltz, Burnett Parker.

New York's police commissioner cooperated in the making of this picture, which used the slim story of a traffic cop saving the fortune belonging to a bank president's ward and ultimately winning her heart, to show the department in action. No great shakes, but interesting.

d, Howard M. Mitchell; w, (based on a story by Lloyd Lonergan).

Crime/Romance **(PR:A MPAA:NR)**

TRAFFIC IN SOULS*** (1913) 6 reels Imp bw

Matt Moore, Jane Gail, William Welsh, Howard Crampton, Ethel Grandin, William Turner, William Cavanaugh, Arthur Hunter, William Burbridge, Laura Huntley, Irene Wallace, William Powers, Mrs. Hudson Lyston, Walter Long.

Landmark motion picture about the horrors of white slavery has a rather thin plot line involving a young Irish cop and a young girl who works in a candy store. But the film's real punch comes with sequences showing female emigrants stalked and abducted, and young ladies from the country being sweet-talked at railroad stations and lured into bondage. There is also a good deal of footage devoted to the inside workings of brothel life, as well as some of the poor creatures attempting to escape. The movie ends melodramatically with the police raiding a vice den and the villains being brought to justice amid a hail of bullets. TRAFFIC IN SOULS packed them in for years and quite rightfully can be referred to as the movie which first proved that sex on the screen sells.

d, George Loane Tucker; w, Walter McNamara, Tucker.

Drama **(PR:A MPAA:NR)**

TRAGEDY OF YOUTH, THE*** (1928) 7 reels TS bw

Patsy Ruth Miller *(Paula Wayne)*, Warner Baxter *(Frank Gordon)*, William Collier, Jr. *(Dick Wayne)*, Claire McDowell *(Mother)*, Harvey Clarke *(Father)*, Margaret Quimby *(Diana)*, Billie Bennett *(Landlady)*, Stepin Fetchit *(Porter)*.

Superior production values and cast for a Tiffany-Stahl picture are reflected favorably here in this domestic drama about a neglected woman (Miller) who finds true romance with another (Baxter), returns to her husband after he attempts to commit suicide, but elects to start life all over again with the man she really loves in the end.

d, George Archainbaud; w, Olga Printzlau (based on a story by Albert Shelby Le Vino); t, Frederick Hatton, Fanny Hatton; ph, Faxon Dean; ed, Robert J. Kern; set d, Burgess Beall.

Drama **(PR:A MPAA:NR)**

TRAIL OF '98, THE**** (1929) 10 reels MGM

Dolores Del Rio *(Berna)*, Ralph Forbes *(Larry)*, Karl Dane *(Lars Peterson)*, Harry Carey *(Jack Locasto)*, Tully Marshall *(Salvation Jim)*, George Cooper *(Samuel Foote)*, Russell Simpson *(Old Swede)*, Emily Fitzroy *(Mrs. Bulkey)*, Tenen Holtz *(Mr. Bulkey)*, Cesare Gravina *(Berna's Grandfather)*, E. Alyn Warren *(Engineer)*, John Down *(Mother's Boy)*, Ray Gallagher, Doris Lloyd.

The story line in this $1 million production is secondary to the truly epic qualities which director Brown handles so deftly. The picture tells of gold and greed and the men and women who became caught up in it—often tragically—during the great Alaskan gold rush. The visuals are dazzling and a process called the Phantom Screen is put to marvelous use for those scenes which deliver the big outdoor visual punch. The system works this way: set on rollers, the screen moves forward towards the proscenium using a wide-angle lens which doubles the size of the image. Then, when it's appropriate to return to the conventional size for narrative purposes, the screen rolls back, and the effect is executed with great smoothness because it is done during titles. There are many stories within this remarkable film, but it is the love theme which grips and disturbs. The hero (Forbes) returns, victorious in his quest, after undergoing tremendous hardships, to find the girl he loves (Del Rio) in gaudy clothes, smothered with lipstick, existing as a prostitute under the influence of a claim-jumping, murdering rat (played nicely against character by Carey). Forbes kills the villain in a saloon brawl, while flames nearly engulf them both, and the picture then comes to an end with those few principals who have survived seemingly alone in the vastness of a hostile land. And one wonders if they truly *did* endure or if perhaps they may have indeed lost something not even a mountain of gold can buy—namely their immortal souls.

d, Clarence Brown; w, Benjamin Glazer, Waldemar Young (based on the novel by Robert W. Service); t, Joe Farnham; ph, John Seitz; m, David Mendoza, William Axt; ed, George Hively; art d, Cedric Gibbons, Merrill Pye; m/l, "I Found Gold When I Found You," Hazel Mooney, Evelyn Lyn, Axt; syn sc; s eff.

Drama **(PR:A MPAA:NR)**

TRAIL OF THE AXE, THE**

(1922) 5 reels Dustin Farnum/American Releasing bw

Dustin Farnum *(Dave Malkern)*, Winifred Kingston *(Betty Somers)*, George Fisher *(Jim Malkern)*, Joseph J. Dowling *(Dr. Somers)*.

Average Farnum outdoor adventure has the actor playing a lumber camp foreman who protects his drunken brother Fisher for the sake of Kingston, the girl they both love. Finally the lad goes too far and is fired. Seeking revenge, he goes on an alcoholic spree and blows up the sawmill, nearly killing Farnum. In one last act of charity, Farnum allows his brother to escape the wrath of his fellow lumbermen, and accepts the love of the pretty young lady.

d, Ernest C. Warde; w, Ridgwell Cullum; ph, Robert Newhard.

Adventure **(PR:A MPAA:NR)**

TRAIL OF THE SHADOW, THE½** (1917) 5 reels Rolfe/Metro bw

Emmy Wehlen *(Sylvia Mason)*, Eugene Strong *(Henry Hilliard)*, Harry S. Northrup *(Jack Leslie/The Shadow)*, Frank Currier *(Mr. Mason)*, Fuller Mellish *(Padre Constantine)*, Kate Blancke *(Mrs. Hilliard)*, Alice MacChesney *(Clara Hilliard)*, De Jalma West *(Sgt. Kent)*.

Entertaining but completely absurd programmer has a society girl heading west to make beads for the tourists, when her father is ruined and driven to an early death by his shady male secretary. A young Eastern playboy, who has partied himself sick, ends up in the same area to dry out and they fall in love. But before long, the lad's mother orders him home to marry the debutante of her choice, and he returns to explain the situation. Meanwhile, the very same man who destroyed her father turns up. The rotter is on the run and forces his way into the cabin of the young lady, who takes one look at him and faints straight away. Then, because he has always lusted for her, the outlaw leaves a note claiming that he performed the unspeakable upon her unconscious person, and will return to stake his claim at the first opportunity. In the wink of an eye, the young playboy has returned to ask her hand, but of course she refuses because of her great shame. The true-blue chap explains that it doesn't matter and that he's quite willing to walk down the aisle with her anyway. But this all becomes unnecessary in the end when the outlaw is shot by the Texas Rangers and with his dying breath clears the bead-maker's good name.

d, Edwin Carewe; w, June Mathis (based on a story by Oscar A. C. Lund); ph, Arthur Martinelli.

Western **(PR:C MPAA:NR)**

TRAIL'S END*

(1922) 5 reels William M. Smith/Merit bw (AKA: THE MAN GETTER)

Franklyn Farnum *(Wilder Armstrong)*, Peggy O'Day *(Edith Kilgallen)*, George Reehm *(Frayne)*, Al Hart *(Stanley)*, Shorty Hamilton *(Cahoots)*, Genevieve Bert *(Molly)*.

Low-budget Farnum western has the one-time matinee idol playing a rancher who protects his friend and a young lady, both of whom are rightful heirs to a fortune, from a crook who is out to steal their estates. The hero is then rewarded with the love of the girl.

d, Francis Ford; w, Arthur Somers Roche.

Western **(PR:A MPAA:NR)**

TRAMP, TRAMP, TRAMP*½** (1926) 6 reels Harry Langdon/FN bw

Harry Langdon *(Harry)*, Joan Crawford *(Betty Burton)*, Edwards Davis *(John Burton)*, Carlton Griffin *(Roger Caldwell)*, Alec B. Francis *(Harry's Father)*, Brooks Benedict *(Taxidriver)*, Tom Murray *(The Argentine)*.

Plenty of laughs in this Harry Langdon feature (his first) which has the little comic competing in a cross-country walking race sponsored by Burton Shoes. Burton's daughter is played by Joan Crawford and her face adorns enormous posters the contestants see as they make their way along the route. Naturally, Langdon falls in love with her, and after a series of terrific sight gags, which include his throwing rocks at a tornado, becoming part of a chain gang, and being chased by a herd of sheep, he leaps over a cliff where the only thing which keeps him from falling hundreds of feet to his death is a nail on which his coat is snared. The little man is not aware of this and he tries to do everything within his power to free himself. Then he looks down, and this is when the fun really begins. There is another wonderful bit where Crawford drives up next to him, parks her car, and says, "Hello champ." The poster girl, the woman of his dreams, has come to life. Langdon is beside himself with joy, and according to Capra in his autobiography the actress was so broken up by his antics that they had to do take after take, because of her uncontrollable laughter—and finally settled on shooting Joan from behind and taking her closeups the next day when Harry was not around. The picture ends improbably with the couple becoming married. A year or so later they are shown looking out of their window and calling to their baby. It turns out to be Harry in a huge crib, dressed in an infant's outfit, clutching a toy, with everything built to scale, and he was perfect for the part.

d, Harry Edwards; w, Frank Capra, Tim Whelan, Han Conklin, J. Frank Holliday, Gerald Duffy, Murray Roth; ph, Elgin Lessley.

Comedy **(PR:A MPAA:NR)**

TRAP, THE** (1922) 6 reels UNIV bw

Lon Chaney *(Gaspard)*, Alan Hale *(Benson)*, Dagmar Godowsky *(Thalie)*, Stanley Goethals *(The Boy)*, Irene Rich *(The Teacher)*, Spottiswoode Aitken *(The Factor)*, Herbert Standing *(The Priest)*, Frank Campeau *(The Police Sergeant)*.

Somewhat tedious North Woods melodrama has Chaney losing his sweetheart to Hale, then framing him for a shooting and taking his son for the purpose of revenge after Hale's wife dies. Chaney grows to love the boy, however, and when Hale is released from prison, rather than lose the child Chaney prepares a hideous ambush using a half-starved wolf. But, as fate would have it, the boy enters the trap instead, and Chaney saves his life by fighting the beast (the Man-of-a-thousand-faces actually wrestled a wolf bare-handed in this scene), and he and Hale are reconciled in the end.

d, Robert Thornby; w, George C. Hull; ph, Virgil Miller.

Drama **Cas.** **(PR:A MPAA:NR)**

TRAPPED BY THE LONDON SHARKS**

(1916, Brit.) 5 reels Barker/Magnet bw

Humbertson Wright *(John Manton)*, Blanche Forsythe *(Hilda Manton)*, Bertram Burleigh *(Inspector James Graham)*, Maud Yates *(Countess Zena)*, High Nicholson *(Baron Slomann)*.

In 1916, comedy king Mack Sennett had little to fear from British imports such as this one, which has gangsters gassing a tipsy bank employee to lead him to believe that he murdered his wife, and thus assist them in holding up his own institution.

d, L. C. MacBean.

Comedy **(PR:A MPAA:NR)**

TRAPPED BY THE MORMONS** (1922, Brit.) 6 reels Master/White bw (AKA: THE MORMON PERIL)

Evelyn Brent *(Nora Prescott)*, Lewis Willoughby *(Isoldi Keene)*, Ward McAllister *(Elder Kuyler)*, Olaf Hytten *(Elder Marz)*, Olive Sloane *(Sadie Keene)*, George Wynn *(Jim Foster)*, Cecil Morton York *(Mr. Prescott)*.

British thriller about a girl from Manchester who is coerced into joining a "secret society," but by film's end is liberated by the police. Interesting early performance by U.S. actress Brent. Reissued in 1928 under the title THE MORMON PERIL.

p&d, H. B. Parkinson; w, Frank Miller (based on the novel *The Love Story of a Mormon* by Winifred Graham).

Drama **(PR:C MPAA:NR)**

TRAVELIN' ON** ½** (1922) 7 reels WSHP/PAR-ART bw

William S. Hart *(J. B. The Stranger)*, James Farley *(Dandy Dan McGee)*, Ethel Grey Terry *(Susan Morton)*, Brinsley Shaw *(Hi Morton)*, Mary Jane Irving *(Mary Jane Morton)*, Robert Kortman *(Gila)*, Willis Marks *("Know-it-All" Haskins)*, Jacko the Monk *(Himself)*.

More than a few eyebrows were raised in the Protestant community by this well-meaning Hart western which has a crook-turned-preacher becoming a road agent to raise funds to build his church. When the "sky pilot" is caught, Hart, who loves the "preacher's" wife, Terry, prevents his lynching and takes the blame himself. He then escapes and rides off alone, no doubt to receive his eventual reward from a Higher Source.

d&w, Lambert Hillyer (based on the story "J. B. the Unbeliever" by William S. Hart); ph, Joe August; art d, J. C. Hoffner.

Western **(PR:A MPAA:NR)**

TREASURE ISLAND*** ½** (1920) 6 reels PAR bw

Shirley Mason *(Jim Hawkins)*, Josie Melville (Mrs. Hawkins), Al Filson *(Bill Jones)*, Wilton Taylor *(Black Dog)*, Lon Chaney *(Pew/Merry)*, Charles Ogle *(Long John Silver)*, Joseph Singleton *(Israel Hands)*, Bull Montana *(Morgan)*, Harry Holden *(Capt. Smollett)*, Sidney Dean *(Squire Trelawney)*, Charles Hill Mailes *(Dr. Livesey)*.

This most popular of director Tourneur's 56 U.S. films made between 1914 and 1926 combines his wonderful sense of artistic composition with a thrilling classic story of buried treasure, pirates, and mutiny, and some truly offbeat casting which had Mason playing young Jim Hawkins and Chaney surveying two roles, Merry and Pew. It would not be until six years later, with Douglas Fairbank Sr's BLACK PIRATE, that the world of bucaneers would be so satisfactorily depicted. A wonderful film on every level.

d, Maurice Tourneur; w, Stephen Fox [Jules Furthman] (based on the novel by Robert Louis Stevenson); ph, Rene Guissart.

Adventure **(PR:A MPAA:NR)**

TRILBY** (1915) 5 reels EQ/WORLD bw

Clara Kimball Young *(Trilby)*, Wilton Lackaye *(Svengali)*, Paul McAllister *(Gecko)*, Chester Barnett *(Little Billy)*, Phyllis Neilsson Terry, James Young.

Acceptable screening of the Svengali tale is highlighted by a good performance on the part of Young, but there are a number of production errors (such as a Paris policeman dressed in the uniform of an English Bobby) which should never have been allowed to make it through the final stages of production.

d, Maurice Tourneur; w, I. M. Ingleton (based on the novel by George du Maurier).

Drama **Cas.** **(PR:A MPAA:NR)**

TROUBLE*** (1922) 5 reels Jackie Coogan/AFN bw

Jackie Coogan *(Danny)*, Wallace Beery *(Ed Lee)*, Gloria Hope *(Mrs. Lee)*, Queenie the Dog.

Inexpensively produced, but delightful combination of pathos and comedy—which make the Coogan pictures so special—has an orphaned kid being placed in the home of a cruel, wife-beating, child-hating plumber (played to perfection by Beery). After a number of misadventures, Beery, with Coogan's help, is given a terrific pasting by a policeman who has befriended the child. The bully is sent to prison, and Coogan and his foster mother finally find happiness on her parent's farm. This was the Chaplin protege's third starring film, and little Coogan proved that he had what it took—and more.

p, Jack Coogan, Sr.; d, Albert Austin; t, Max Abramson; ph, Glen MacWilliams, Robert Martin; ed, Irene Morra.

Comedy/Drama **(PR:A MPAA:NR)**

TRUE HEART SUSIE**** (1919) 6 reels D.W. Griffith/ART bw

Lillian Gish *(Susie May Trueheart)*, Loyala O'Connor *(Her Aunt)*, Robert Harron *(William Jenkins, a Minister)*, Walter Higby *(His Father)*, Clarine Seymour *(Betty Hopkins, a Girl Wife)*, Kate Bruce *(Her Aunt)*, Raymond Cannon *(Sporty Malone)*.

Country girl Lillian Gish loves Robert Harron with all her heart, but he is blind to this fact. The young man's ambition is to become a minister and Gish, without his knowledge, raises the tuition by selling her prize cow. When Harron returns, she is pleased and proud to see him preach his first sermon, but then the lad falls under the spell of Seymour (a girl of questionable character) and makes her his wife. Gish is broken-hearted but she hides this, even as she shields Harron from the knowledge that his bride has become involved in a number of affairs. Then, while returning from one of her trysts, Seymour is caught in a tremendous storm, contracts pneumonia, and dies. Even now, Gish keeps her secret. But not the hussy's aunt (Kate Bruce) who not only spills the beans but straightens the young clergyman out as to how he got his degree. Harron's eyes are at last opened. He realizes his love for Gish and she is finally rewarded with the happiness she deserves. This is one of D. W. Griffith's most modest yet beautiful films. In it he captured an American era which was already beginning to disappear, and thanks to his supreme genius will now live on forever.

d, D. W. Griffith; w, Marion Freemont; ph, Billy Bitzer; ed, James Smith.

Drama **Cas.** **(PR:A MPAA:NR)**

TRUE TILDA* ½ (1920, Brit.) 5 reels JUR/LFP bw

Edna Flugrath *(Tilda)*, Teddy Gordon Craig *(Arthur)*, Edward O'Neill *(Dr. Purdie J. Gasson)*, Sir Simeon Stuart, Douglas Munro, George Bellamy.

After being injured, a girl from the circus helps a boy escape from a cruel orphanage, and is richly rewarded when it's revealed that he is actually the lost son of a lord.

d, Harold Shaw; w, Bannister Merwin (based on the novel by Arthur Quiller-Couch.

Drama **(PR:A MPAA:NR)**

TRUTH, THE** ½** (1920) 5 reels Goldwyn bw

Madge Kennedy *(Becky Warder)*, Tom Carrigan *(Tom Warder)*, Helene Greene *(Eve Linden)*, Kenneth Hill *(Fred Linden)*, Frank Doane *(Roland)*, Zelda Sears *(Mrs. Genevieve Crespigny)*, Horace Haine *(Jenks)*.

Kennedy is quite charming as the wide-eyed innocent girl who tries to bring a couple on the brink of divorce together again and finds herself being named corespondent. Naturally the situation is cleared up in the end, and although the picture is most acceptable, that crisp and witty dialog which made the Fitch play such a popular and aesthetic success, is sadly missed.

d, Lawrence C. Windom; w, A. F. Statter (based on the play by Clyde Fitch); ph, J. Roy Hunt.

Comedy/Drama **(PR:A MPAA:NR)**

TRUTH WAGON, THE** ½** (1914) 5 reels Masterpiece bw

Max Figman *(John Ross)*, Lolita Robertson *(Miss Deane)*, Al Filson, H. A. Livingston.

Entertaining, if not masterful, feature, directed by and starring Broadway luminary Figman, has to do with a lazy young playboy giving up the fast life, taking over the management of a newspaper, winning the war with a rival daily, and getting the girl in the end.

d, Max Figman; w, Elliott J. Clawson (based on the play by Hayden Talbot); ph, George Rizard.

Drama **(PR:A MPAA:NR)**

TRUTHFUL TULLIVER*** ½** (1917) 5 reels Kay-Bee/TRI bw

William S. Hart *("Truthful" Tulliver)*, Alma Rubens *(Grace Burton)*, Norbert A. Myles *(York Cantrell)*, Nina Byron *(Daisy Burton)*, Walter Perry *("Silver Lode" Thompson)*, Milton Ross *("Deacon" Doyle)*.

Hart is a straight shooter who takes on the town's villainous saloon owner, Ross. When Ross skips town after wronging the girl Hart loves, the great cowboy star chases down his train on horseback, snatches the rat, and brings him back to make restitution. Hart's ultimate, though dubious, reward comes in learning that it was actually his sweetheart's *sister* who was the victim. Another top-flight western by the master of that genre.

d, William S. Hart; sup, Thomas H. Ince; w, J. G. Hawks; ph, Joe August; art d, Robert Brunton.

Western **(PR:A MPAA:NR)**

TUMBLEWEEDS*** ½** (1925) 7 reels WSHP/UA bw

William S. Hart *(Don Carver)*, Barbara Bedford *(Molly Lassiter)*, Lucien Littlefield *("Kentucky Rose")*, J. Gordon Russell *(Noll Lassiter)*, Richard R. Neill *(Bill Freel)*, Jack Murphy *(Bart Lassiter)*, Lillian Leighton *(Mrs. Riley)*, Gertrude Claire *(Old Woman)*, George F. Marion *(Old Man)*, Capt. T. E. Duncan *(Major of Cavalry)*, James Gordon *(Hinman of Box K Ranch)*, Fred Gamble *(Hotel Proprietor)*, Turner Savage *(Riley Boy)*, Monte Collins *(Hicks)*.

Following the release of SINGER JIM MC KEE (Hart's worst film) the Paramount moguls considered him washed up. He was the most stubborn and uncompromising of actors, an artist determined to present the West in realistic terms while jazz-age audiences preferred the fancy costumes, thrilling stunts, and unabashed showmanship of Tom Mix and his army of impersonators. So the old man decided to retire (he had done so once before, in 1918 when the star was framed on a paternity suit). But then United Artists offered him a comeback picture. The studio's owners, Mary Pickford, Douglas Fairbanks, and Charles Chaplin, were feuding, so it was actually Joseph Schenck who handled the details. Hart was elated. This was to be his biggest picture yet, budgeted at $312,000. An epoch which appropriately would deal with the opening of the Cherokee Strip to homesteaders, the very historical act which brought an end to an American era the great star so revered. His only compromise to what the studio chiefs believed was now necessary for a commercial cowboy picture was the inclusion of Lucien Littlefield as a comic sidekick. Beyond that, the film was vintage Hart, opening with a scene showing the rancher and his hands on their final cattle drive. They look off into the distance, where change has already begun, and he solemnly exclaims, "Boys, it's the last of the West." The men all take their hats off, out of respect for the life they love and are about to lose. It's a beautifully filmed moment. As the story progresses, Hart falls in love with Bedford, one of the settlers, and protects her kid brother from a beating their villainous half brother, Russell, is dishing out. Hart decides to sign up for the rush, hoping to claim the water rich land where his ranch is located. But, smarting from his earlier humiliation, Russell and his partner in crime, Neill, have Hart arrested as a "sooner" after he enters the strip to round up a few cattle. With Hart in the stockade, the rush is about to begin. And, as the clock nears twelve, the directors (and one must truly believe that the film's star had as much to do with its direction as Baggot) deliver the cinematic payoff, when the title flashes on the screen, "Ready for the signal for the maddest stampede in American history." At this point, with mathematical precision, 684 frames are divided up into 25 separate shots. The homesteaders are contrasted with the troopers. Hart's horse is shown, tied to a tree alone, and when the cannon fires the shot to start the race, the great beast breaks free. This and the stampede which follows are an editing tour de force. And interestingly TUMBLEWEEDS was released in the same year and rivals the cutting of the supposedly trend-setting Sergei Eisenstein masterpiece POTEMKIN. Hart pole-vaults his way to freedom, mounts his faithful horse, and, in a dazzling riding display, gallops to victory. He also wins the girl and sees to it that the badmen are arrested. For some reason, Schenck decided not to push this film, and in spite of its merits it was not a big success. The great star retired for the last time and made only one more screen appearance. That was an eight-minute speech, shot on location at his ranch, for the prolog of a 1939 revival of this western for Grand National. In his deep Shakespearian-trained voice, one of the movies' most illustrious personalities told of the joys of filmmaking, and he thanked his countless fans for having given him the opportunity to do so. It a most moving moment.

d, King Baggot, and probably William S. Hart; w, C. Gardner Sullivan (based on a story by Hal G. Evarts); ph, Joseph August.

Western **Cas.** **(PR:A MPAA:NR)**

TUMBLING RIVER** (1927) 5 reels FOX bw

Tom Mix *(Tom Gier)*, Dorothy Dwan *(Edna Barton)*, William Conklin *(Jim Barton)*, Stella Essex *(Eileen Barton)*, Elmo Billings *(Kit Mason)*, Edward Peil, Sr. *(Roan Tibbets)*, Wallace MacDonald *(Keechie)*, Buster Gardner *(Cory)*, Harry Gripp *(Titus)*, Tony the Wonder Horse, Buster the Horse.

Fox decided to throw a couple of kid actors into this oater, probably to enhance the moppet box-office receipts. It turned out to be a big mistake because all they really managed to do was get in the way of the star, his horse, and their usual breathtaking stunt work. This is a below-average Mix entry, but it still has its moments. He plays a rancher whose horses are stolen by rustlers while he is away. During his search for them, he comes upon Dwan, whose ranch has also been raided by the outlaw gang. In the end, Mix escapes an ambush, saves Dwan from the rapids, and captures the rustlers.

d, Lewis Seiler; w, Jack Jungmeyer (based on the novel *The Scourge of the Little C* by Jesse Edward Grinstead); ph, Dan Clark.

Western **(PR:A MPAA:NR)**

TWELVE MILES OUT*** ½ (1927) 8 reels MGM bw

John Gilbert *(Jerry Fay)*, Ernest Torrence *(Red McCue)*, Joan Crawford *(Jane)*, Eileen Percy *(Maizie)*, Paulette Duval *(Trini)*, Dorothy Sebastian *(Chiquita)*, Gwen Lee *(Hulda)*, Edward Earle *(John Burton)*, Bert Roach *(Luke)*, Tom O'Brien *(Irish)*.

Gilbert and Torrence are sensational as the hard-drinking, adventure-loving rivals who engage in numerous hijinx during their frequent encounters around the world and end up in New York, competing as bootleggers. During a caper, Gilbert hides out in the seaside mansion occupied by Crawford, and when she threatens to blow the whistle, he forces her aboard his ship. Then, posing as revenue agents, Torrence and his mob seize their craft, and the old adversaries sit down to one last Olympian drinking bout. They had done this countless times in the past, and usually there was a woman to be won in the end by the victor. But this time things are different. Crawford is no common chippie. So when the boys go at it now, it is with a hungry vengeance. Rarely on the screen in these times had a gun battle been depicted with such bloody realism. In a powerfully shocking, wonderfully directed sequence, director Conway pits the antagonists against each other—guns spitting fire—until Torrence finally falls. The picture ends with Gilbert's regeneration as he surrenders to the Coast Guard. But in this case the denouement seems quite natural and not at all contrived; perhaps because it is apparent that the breathtakingly beautiful Crawford has promised to wait for her man.

d, Jack Conway; w, A. P. Younger (based on the play by William Anthony McGuire); t, Joe Farnham; ph, Ira Morgan; ed, Basil Wrangell; set d, Cedric Gibbons, Eugene Hornbostel; cos, Rene Hubert.

Crime Drama **(PR:A MPAA:NR)**

12-10** ½ (1919, Brit.) 5 reels B&C/WORLD bw

Marie Doro *(Marie Fernando)*, Ben Webster *(Lord Chatterton)*, Geoffrey Kerr *(Geoffrey Brooke)*, James Carew *(Arthur Newton)*, Fred Kerr *(Dr. Wrightman)*.

Doro, who won fame for her theater and 1916 film portrayals of Oliver Twist, lends a little substance to this modest British mystery, adequately handled by U.S. director Brenon. It all had to do with a lord who takes a life-suspending drug in order to prevent an adopted child from being murdered by a Spanish secretary.

p, Edward Godal; d, Herbert Brenon; w, George Edwardes Hall (based on a story by Earle Carroll).

Mystery **(PR:A MPAA:NR)**

20,000 LEAGUES UNDER THE SEA*** ½ (1916) 8 reels UNIV bw

Matt Moore *(Lt. Bond)*, Allen Holubar *(Capt. Nemo)*, June Gail *(Princess Dasker)*, William Welsh *(Charles Denver)*, Curtis Benton *(Ned Land)*, Dan Hamlon *(Professor Aronnax)*, Edna Pendleton *(Miss Aronnax)*, Howard Crampton *(Cyrus Harding)*, Wallace Clark *(Pencroft)*, Martin Murphy *(Herbert Brown)*, Leviticus Jones *(Neb)*, Lois Alexander *(Prince Dasker's Daughter)*, Joseph W. Girard.

The Williamson brothers built a special camera exclusively for 20,000 LEAGUES UNDER THE SEA, which enabled director Paton to film underwater, and the results were spectacular. The picture, a combination of two Jules Verne classics, *20,000 Leagues Under the Sea* and *The Mysterious Island*, delivered plenty of punch. Shot on location in the Bahamas, the story tells of Captain Nemo (Holubar), his submarine *Nautilus*, and the Americans on board who follow their adventures from the ocean's depth to a tropical island, where they carry out the rescue of Nemo's long-lost daughter. Audiences of the day were thrilled—especially during the famous octopus fight—and the production cost Universal studio head Carl Laemmle a fortune. Unfortunately, by the time the Williamson boys were through engineering their new underwater camera—without which the film would not have been nearly as impressive—the production budget had become so inflated that Laemmle did not make nearly what he hoped for.

d&w, Stuart Paton (based on the novels *20,000 Leagues Under the Sea* and *The Mysterious Island* by Jules Verne); ph, Eugene Gaudio, J. Ernest Williamson, George M. Williamson.

Adventure **(PR:A MPAA:NR)**

TWIN BEDS*** (1920) 6 reels De Haven/FN bw

Carter De Haven *(Signor Monti)*, Mrs. Carter De Haven *(Blanche Hawkins)*, Helen Raymond *(Signora Monti)*, William Desmond *(Harry Hawkins)*, Katherine Lewis *(Amanda Tate)*, William J. Irving *(Andrew Larkin)*, Lottie Williams *(Nora)*, Montgomery Carlyle, Eugene Pallette.

Adapted from a somewhat naughty theatrical bedroom farce, Carter De Haven went to great pains to provide a clean entertainment here. Although playing a tipsy musical comedy star, he still allows himself plenty of laughs by wandering into the private chambers of his real-life wife, and creating the usual complications with her husband, his wife, and everybody else concerned.

d, Lloyd Ingraham; w, Rex Taylor, Robert McGowan (based on the play by Margaret Mayo, Salisbury Field); ph, Ross Fisher.

Comedy **(PR:A MPAA:NR)**

TWINKLETOES** (1926) 8 reels John McCormick/FN bw

Colleen Moore *(Twinkletoes)*, Kenneth Harlan *(Chuck Lightfoot)*, Tully Marshall *(Dad Minasi)*, Gladys Brockwell *(Cissie)*, Lucien Littlefield *(Hank)*, Warner Oland *(Roseleaf)*, John Philip Kolb *(Bill Carsides)*, Julanne Johnston *(Lilac)*, William McDonald *(Inspector Territon)*.

Moore delivers a good performance and is given the opportunity to appear as a blonde in this adaptation of Burke's sordid novel about life in London's Chinatown. That's about all this picture about a slum girl with a talent for dancing, who finally finds comfort and love with a prizefighter who saves her from suicide, has going for it. Perhaps the most interesting thing about this film is that director Brabin, an Englishman, never really convinces us that it's actually Limehouse we are watching on the screen, whereas D. W. Griffith, the U.S. genius who directed another Burke novel, BROKEN BLOSSOMS nearly 10 years earlier, was able to provide his audience with a depiction of that notorious community so vividly that one could almost smell the fog and taste the stench.

d, Charles Brabin; w, Winifred Dunn (based on the novel by Thomas Burke); ph, James C. Van Trees.

Drama **(PR:A MPAA:NR)**

TWO-EDGED SWORD, THE* ½ (1916) 5 reels VIT bw

Edith Storey, Evart Overton, Josephine Earle, Robert Gaillard, Logan Paul, Marion Henry, Nellie Anderson.

Mediocre programmer has a young country girl taking a job with an author and then reaping revenge upon his wife, who once had an affair with the girl's brother, which led to his suicide when he learned she was married. The girl secretly plants a letter intimating that the woman's author-husband is having a tryst with his pretty employee. When the wife challenges him on this matter, the writer confesses that he does indeed love the girl. But later, when the hated woman is seriously hurt in an automobile accident, the good soul returns to her rural home—in spite of the fact that she, too, feels deeply for her employer—thus concluding the picture on an unsatisfactory note for all concerned.

d, George D. Baker; w, E. V. Brewster, L. Case Russell; ph, Joseph Shelderfer.

Drama **(PR:A MPAA:NR)**

TWO FLAMING YOUTHS*** (1927) 6 reels PAR-Famous Lasky bw

W. C. Fields *(Gabby Gilfoil)*, Chester Conklin *(Sheriff Ben Holden)*, Mary Brian *(Mary Gilfoil)*, Jack Luden *(Tony Holden)*, George Irving *(Simeon Trott)*, Cissy Fitzgerald *(Madge Malarkey)*, Jimmy Quinn *(Slippery Sawtelle)*, John Aasen *(The Giant)*, Anna Magruder *(The Fat Lady)*, William Platt *(The Dwarf)*, Chester Moorten *(The Human Pin Cushion)*, Lee W. Parker *(The Tattooed Man)*, John Seresheff *(The Strong Man)*, Jack Delaney *(Himself, a Boxing Kangaroo)*, Beery & Hatton, Clark & McCullough, Duncan Sisters, Kolb & Dill, Moran & Mack, Weber & Fields, Savoy & Brennan, Baker & Silvers, Benny & McNulty, Pearl & Bard *(Comedy Teams)*.

Phineas Barnum was a piker compared to the shilling going on in this crazy, mixed up movie that seems just made for the dizzy antics of Fields. A financially embarrassed circus showman with a hungry troupe of freaks screaming for food and salaries, Fields arrives in Sheriff Conklin's territory and the trouble starts immediately. In between shell games, tricky juggling events, and cigar box tricks, he views his new surroundings with one thought in mind: get the cash and run. However, at the hotel where the troupe is staying, the hotel owner, Madge Malarkey (Fitzgerald), takes a liking to the suave circus owner, even though she is being pursued by Conklin. Complications arise when Conklin suspects Fields of being a wanted criminal with a reward of $1,500 on his head; at the same time, two sheriffs from rival counties also claim the reward for bringing in the real criminal, Slippery Sawtelle (Quinn). Zany antics on the way to a resolution include a hilarious scene when Conklin is catapulted into a dugout containing a kangaroo and cannot get out. Fields, quickly seizing the opportunity, begins hawking tickets to the boxing match which is sure to follow, and packs in the house. He makes enough money to feed his troupe. In the end, a wealthy man of town, Irving, marries Fitzgerald, losing her pocketbook for both Fields and Conklin, who wind up friends. In the last scene, Conklin plays a shell game with Irving and wins a tidy sum, which he splits with Fields. Fields' many tricks in TWO FLAMING YOUTHS are his own and he makes the most of them through almost perfect pantomiming, at which he is a master. His funniness stems not from speech but from mannerisms, all somehow expressing suavity and an inner nastiness. In TWO FLAMING YOUTHS his genius, shorn of the spoken word, becomes manifest in his wild, never-ending acts of comedy and cruelty, essentially vulgar and crude, but nevertheless hilariously funny. For those who believe there is no Fields without the wheezing pretensions to literacy he came to be known for once talkies came into being, in the silents titles managed to convey a portion of this aspect of the versatile comedian.

d, John Waters; sup, Louis D. Lighton; w, Percy Heath, Donald Davis (based on a story by Percy Heath); t, Jack Conway, Herman J. Mankiewicz; ph, H. Kinley Martin; songs, "A Musical Bouquet," "Treasure Ships," "Mandalay."

Comedy **(PR:A MPAA:NR)**

TWO LOVERS*** (1928) 9 reels Goldwyn/UA bw

Ronald Colman *(Mark Van Rycke)*, Vilma Banky *(Donna Leonora de Vargas)*, Noah Beery *(The Duke of Azar)*, Nigel De Brulier *(The Prince of Orange)*, Virginia Bradford *(Grete)*, Helen Jerome Eddy *(Inez)*, Eugenie Besserer *(Mme. Van Rycke)*, Paul Lukas *(Ramon de Linea)*, Fred Esmelton *(Meinherr Van Rycke)*, Harry Allen *(Jean)*, Marcella Daly *(Marda)*, Scotty Mattraw *(Dandermonde Innkeeper)*, Lydia Yeamans Titus *(Innkeeper's Wife)*.

Samuel Goldwyn assured the success of this picture by ballyhooing it as being the very last time one of the world's favorite romantic movie couples, Banky and Colman, would ever appear together again. And then he went on to provide his audiences with a swashbuckling love story, dealing with the struggle of the Flemish people to overthrow their Spanish oppressors. It was loaded with swordplay, candlelight encounters, thunder and lightning backgrounds, and plenty of love scenes which sizzled like a projectionist's arc lamp, just for a little insurance. The parting of ways had a mixed effect on the successful team of Colman and Banky. For him it marked the beginning of even greater stardom in the upcoming sound films, while to Banky's career it proved disastrous and only four additional films, two of them talkies, were added to her credits.

d, Fred Niblo; w, Alice D. G. Miller (based on the novel *Leatherface* by Emmuska Orczy); t, John Colton; ph, George Barnes; m, Hugo Riesenfeld; ed, Viola Lawrence; art d, Carl Oscar Borg; m/l, "Grieving," Wayland Axtell, "Leonora," Abner Silver; syn sc; s eff.

Costume Romance **(PR:A MPAA:NR)**

TWO MINUTES TO GO*** (1921) 6 reels Charles Ray/AFN bw

Charles Ray *(Chester Burnett)*, Mary Anderson *(Ruth Turner)*, Lionel Belmore *(Her Father)*, Lincoln Stedman *("Fatty")*, Truman Van Dyke *("Angel")*, Gus Leonard *(Butler)*, Tom Wilson *(Football Coach)*, Bert Woodruff *(Janitor)*, Francois Dumas *(Dean of Baker University)*, Phillip Dunham *(Professor of Spanish)*.

Typical college football heroics, together with Ray's boyish charm, make this a diverting, if less than original, feature. Ray has incurred the wrath of his school's entire student body—with the exception of the chief cheerleader, Anderson—by quitting the squad and causing his team to suffer a losing season. Actually, his father's business went bust, and he's forced to deliver milk in order to pay the tuition. Anderson catches him making his rounds, berates him for being ashamed of "honest labor," and convinces him to suit up for the last big game against their archrival. Ray's team is trailing by three points with two minutes to play when the lad receives a telegram from his father informing him that the business has been saved. That's the news that does the trick and young Ray scores the winning points, is cheered once again by the throng, and accepts a big smooch from the young lady who never stopped rooting in his behalf.

d, Charles Ray; w, Richard Andres; ph, George Rizard.

Dramatic Comedy **(PR:A MPAA:NR)**

TYPHOON, THE*** (1914) 5 reels New York Motion Picture bw

Sessue Hayakawa, Tsuru Aoki, Charles French, Herschal Mayall, Gladys Brockwell, Frank Borzage, Leona Hutton, Henry Kotani.

Hayakawa's first film, which also featured his wife, Aoki, is an interesting and well-directed courtroom drama dealing with the trial of a man who murdered his mistress.

d, Reginald Barker; sup, Thomas H. Ince; w, Charles Swickard (based on the play by Melchior Lengyel).

Drama **(PR:A MPAA:NR)**

UNCHASTENED WOMAN** (1925) 7 reels CHAD bw

Theda Bara *(Caroline Knollys)*, Wyndham Standing *(Hubert Knollys)*, Dale Fuller *(Hildegarde Sanbury)*, John Miljan *(Lawrence Sanbury)*, Harry Northrup *(Michael Krellin)*, Eileen Percy *(Emily Madden)*, Mayme Kelso *(Susan Ambie)*.

Bara, moviedom's first vamp and the star who put Fox Studio on the map, had been out of vogue for more than five years when she made this comeback picture for the lowly, independent Chadwick company. The story has to do with a woman who is about to tell her husband, Wyndham, of her pregnancy, when she discovers he's having an affair with his secretary. Angered and hurt, Bara sails for Europe, where she becomes a woman of great "notoriety." Then, when she returns home with a handsome young fellow, her husband is almost driven mad with jealousy. Then he meets his child for the first time, his hostility turns to love, and the couple are reunited. In spite of a good performance by the one-time star, the picture flopped, and Bara made only one more film, a Hal Roach two-reel comedy in which she spoofed herself.

d, James Young; w, Douglas Doty (based on the play by Louis Kaufman Anspacher); ph, William O'Connell.

Drama **(PR:A MPAA:NR)**

UNCLE TOM'S CABIN** (1914) 5 reels WORLD bw

Mary Eline *(Little Eva)*, Irving Cummings *(Harris)*, Sam Lucas, Teresa Michelena, Roy Applegate, Paul Scardon, Boots Wall, Fern Andra.

Harriet Beecher Stowe's classic American anti-slavery novel had been filmed five times—once in 1903, twice in 1910, and twice in 1913—before this competent, though unextraordinary feature-length version was made.

d, William Robert Daly; w, Edward McWade (based on the novel by Harriet Beecher Stowe).

Drama **(PR:A MPAA:NR)**

UNDER FIRE** (1926) 5 reels Clifford S. Elfelt/Davis bw

Bill Patton, Jean Arthur, Cathleen Calhoun, Norbert Myles, William Bertram, Harry Moody, W. Cassel, H. Renard.

Routine B western has an army officer cashiered from the service when he is wrongly accused of cowardice while under an Indian attack. Then, after hooking up with an old prospector, he regains his honor and wins back the love of his sweetheart by riding like blazes to save the troops from another Indian raid.

p, Albert I. Smith; d, Clifford S. Elfelt; w, Frank Howard Clark (based on the novel by Capt. Charles King).

Western **(PR:A MPAA:NR)**

UNDER SUSPICION** (1919, Brit.) 5 reels BRO/Moss bw

Horace Hunter *(Maj. Paul Holt)*, Hilda Bayley *(Countess Nadia)*, Jack Jarman *(Her Brother)*, Cameron Carr *(Count Vasiloff)*, Arthur Walcott *(Peter Kharolff)*, Dorothy Warren *(Marie Petrovsky)*, Henry Latimer *(Gen. Noivard)*.

Offbeat British adventure is set in Russia and deals with the exploits of a dashing U.S. officer whose love for a countess drives him to fight a duel with the chief of police to save not only her brother, but her husband as well.

p&d, Walter West; w, Kenelm Foss, Benedict James (based on a play by Horace Hunter).

Adventure **(PR:A MPAA:NR)**

UNDER THE RED ROBE** (1923) 10 reels COS/Goldwyn-COS bw

Robert B. Mantell *(Cardinal Richelieu)*, John Charles Thomas *(Gil de Bérault)*, Alma Rubens *(Renée de Cocheforet)*, Otto Kruger *(Henri de Cocheforet)*, William H. Powell *(Duke of Orléans)*, Ian MacLaren *(King Louis XIII)*, Genevieve Hamper *(Duchess de Chevreuse)*, Mary MacLaren *(Anne of Austria)*, Rose Coghlan *(Marie de Medici)*, Gustav von Seyffertitz *(Clon)*, Sidney Herbert *(Father Joseph)*, Arthur Houseman *(Capt. La Rolle)*, Paul Panzer *(Lieutenant in the French Army)*, Charles Judels *(Antoine)*, George Nash *(Jules)*, Evelyn Gosnell *(Mme. de Cocheforet)*.

The costumes and sets almost put this rather sluggish romance of old France over. The story has to do with Louis XIII (MacLaren) and the enemies of his country who plot to have Cardinal Richelieu (Mantell) removed from his seat of power. There is also an abundance of beautiful scenery (portions of the film were shot in New England), but what the picture lacks is a Fairbanks or a Barrymore, or at least *someone* capable of really swashing his buckle.

d, Alan Crosland; w, Bayard Veiller (based on the novel by Stanley J. Weyman); ph, Harold Wenstrom, Gilbert Warrenton; m, William Frederick Peters; set d, Joseph Urban; cos, Gretl Urban.

Costume Adventure **(PR:A MPAA:NR)**

UNDERWORLD**** ½** (1927) 8 reels PAR bw

George Bancroft *("Bull" Weed)*, Clive Brook *("Rolls Royce")*, Evelyn Brent *("Feathers")*, Larry Semon *("Slippy" Lewis)*, Fred Kohler *("Buck" Mulligan)*, Helen Lynch *(Mulligan's Girl)*, Jerry Mandy *(Paloma)*, Karl Morse *("High Collar" Sam)*.

Gangster films were nothing new (Griffith had explored them as early as 1912 in his one-reeler MUSKETEERS OF PIG ALLEY, and in the modern segment of INTOLERANCE (1916) but von Sternberg, inspired by a story written by Chicago newspaperman Ben Hecht, took the concept and created a genre. It's all here in this 1927 production. Fast cars, flashing machine guns, molls with flasks, wise guys and cops—and even the plot line has all of the ingredients. Bull Weed (Bancroft) is a bank robber who befriends Brook, a sidewalk bum, while escaping from a job. Brook turns out to be a one-time gentleman with plenty of brains and he puts his intellectual abilities to work for Bancroft, making the crook an underworld king. Brook and Bancroft's girl, Feathers (Evelyn Brent) fall in love, but restrain themselves out of affection for "the big guy." When Bancroft is convicted of killing a rival mobster (following a powerful scene, shot in a flower shop and inspired by Al Capone's assassination of his North Side Chicago arch-enemy Charles Dion ("Deanie") O'Bannion), Brooks tries to spring him but fails. Bancroft mistakenly assumes that his best friend and girl have betrayed him. He breaks out of jail and then discovers otherwise in the movie's big shootout (James Cagney, Humphrey Bogart, George Raft, and Paul Muni would repeat this scene countless times) when Brook takes a slug to save his pal. Touched and ashamed, Bancroft surrenders to the coppers, and when he's told that he merely postponed the inevitable, he responds, "That hour was worth more to me than my whole life."

p, Hector Turnbull; d, Josef von Sternberg; w, Robert N. Lee, Charles Furthman (based on a story by Ben Hecht); t, George Marion, Jr.; ph, Bert Glennon; art d & set d, Hans Dreier.

Gangster **(PR:A MPAA:NR)**

UNGUARDED HOUR, THE** (1925) 7 reels FN bw

Milton Sills *(Andrea)*, Doris Kenyon *(Virginia Gilbert)*, Claude King *(Bryce Gilbert)*, Dolores Cassinelli *(Duchess Bianca)*, Cornelius Keefe *(Russell Van Alstyne)*, Jed Prouty *(Gus O'Rorick)*, Tammany Young *(Another Yeggman)*, Charles Beyer *(Stelio)*, Lorna Duveen *(Elena)*, Vivia Ogden *(Annie)*, J. Moy Bennett *(Butler)*.

Kenyon is sent to Europe to stay with her father's fiancee, Cassinelli, as a means of separating her from her boy friend. The girl's plane crashes into a radio tower belonging to Cassinelli's nephew, Sills, and before long the two are attracted to each other. Things become complicated, however, when Sills' sister Duveen begs Kenyon to intervene on her behalf with a count who refuses to marry her. So when Kenyon is discovered in the scoundrel's room, the worst is assumed and she refuses to reveal the truth in order to protect the sister of the man she loves. But Duveen has reached the end of her rope and commits suicide, leaving a note which explains everything, and the vengeful Sills kills the rotter in a fairly well-staged fight.

d, Lambert Hillyer; w, Joseph Poland (based on a story by Margaretta Tuttle); t, John Krafft; ph, Roy Carpenter; ed, Arthur Tavares; art d, Milton Menasco.

Drama **(PR:A MPAA:NR)**

UNHOLY THREE, THE*** ½** (1925) 7 reels MGM bw

Lon Chaney, Sr. *(Professor Echo/Granny O'Grady)*, Harry Earles *(Tweedledee)*, Victor McLaglen *(Hercules)*, Mae Busch *(Rosie O'Grady)*, Matt Moore *(Hector McDonald)*, Matthew Betz *(Regan)*, William Humphreys *(Defense Attorney)*, Walter Perry *(Dime Museum Announcer)*, John Merkyl *(Jeweler)*, Violet Cane *(Arlington Baby)*, Marjorie Morton *(Mrs. Arlington)*, Charles Wellesley *(John Arlington)*, Percy Williams *(Butler)*, Edward Connelly *(Judge)*, E. Allyn Warren *(Prosecuting Attorney)*, Alice Julian *(The Fat Lady)*, Peter Kortos *(Sword Swallower)*, Walter P. Cole *(The Human Skeleton)*, John Millerta *(Wild Man from Borneo)*, Vera Vance *(Dancer)*, Harvey Parry *(Stuntman)*, Mickey McBan.

Top Chaney-Browning collaboration has the "Man of a Thousand Faces" playing a sideshow ventriloquist who devises, together with his friend McLaglen, a strong man, Earles, a midget, and Busch, a pickpocket, a scheme to make a fortune. Posing as an old lady, Chaney opens up a parrot shop, throws his voice to convince wealthy customers that his birds have the gift of gab, and then when they fail to deliver personally visits the homes of his dissatisfied clients, pushing Earles (disguised as an infant) in a baby carriage, to case the layouts. Later they hire Moore, a simpish clerk, and for some reason the female member of the gang falls for him. Then, when McLaglen and Earles pull a job against the boss' wishes and the victim is killed, Moore is set up to take the rap. At their mountain hideout, Busch pleads with Chaney to save the innocent fellow and promises to marry him if he does. Chaney, in a cleverly directed scene, goes to the courtroom, and, using his ventriloquist talent, gets the wrongly accused man off the hook. The strong man and midget pay their debt to society when an ape kills them, and Chaney, now regenerated, frees the woman he loves to be with Moore. The picture ends as it began, with the ventriloquist working a dime museum, his dummy on his knee, telling the crowd, through a title card, "That's all there is to life folks; just a little laugh, just a little tear."

d, Tod Browning; w, Waldemar Young (based on the novel by Clarence Aaron Robbins); ph, David Kesson; ed, Daniel J. Gray; set d, Cedric Gibbons, Joseph Wright.

Crime/Drama **(PR:A MPAA:NR)**

UNINVITED GUEST, THE* ½** (1923, Brit.) 5 reels Dewhurst/Walker bw

Stewart Rome *(Philip Orme)*, Madge Stuart *(Mavis Steele)*, Cameron Carr *(Denton)*, Arthur Walcott *(Spaling)*, Cecil Morton York *(Felix Steele)*, Linda Moore *(Hilda)*, Leal Douglas *(Baines)*.

Producer-director-writer Dewhurst took his company to Berlin to shoot this drama about a capitalist, down on his luck, who hires a crook to assume the identity of a missing heir. In the end, to everyone's delight, it turns out that the chap is the real McCoy.

p,d&w, George Dewhurst.

Drama **(PR:A MPAA:NR)**

UNKNOWN, THE 1/2** (1921) 5 reels Phil Goldstone bw

Richard Talmadge *(Dick Talmadge/The Unknown)*, Andrée Tourneur *(Sylvia Sweet)*, Mark Fenton *(Parker Talmadge)*, J. W. Early *(J. Malcolm Sweet)*.

The plot really didn't matter much in a Talmadge movie. All the audience expected was nonstop action and the kind of stunt work for which he had no peer. In this one, Talmadge plays a foppish character who turns into a masked crusader known as The Unknown—a man dedicated to fighting a group of capitalists intent on forcing the common people to pay higher prices for their food. By the end of the fifth exciting reel, Talmadge knocks the stuffing out of the bad guys, stabilizes prices, and wins the love of Tourneur, who is amazed to learn his true identity when he's unmasked.

d, Grover Jones; ph, Harry Fowler.

Adventure **(PR:A MPAA:NR)**

UNKNOWN, THE* 1/2** (1927) 6 reels MGM bw

Lon Chaney *(Alonzo)*, Norman Kerry *(Malabor)*, Joan Crawford *(Estrellita)*, Nick De Ruiz *(Zanzi)*, John George *(Cojo)*, Frank Lanning *(Costra)*, Billy Seay *(The Little Wolf)*, John St. Polis.

Escaping from the law, Chaney (who is inflicted with a double thumb) joins a Spanish circus, and by having his limbs strapped to his side poses as an armless wonder. His act consists of trick shooting and knife throwing, assisted by Joan Crawford, who acts as the human target. Because the young lady resents being "pawed" by most of the men in the company, Chaney wrongly believes that his "condition" makes him attractive to her. Later, he murders the circus manager after being subjected to a cruel beating but Crawford catches a glimpse of the crime and notices that the killer has a double thumb. It is then that Chaney decides to have his arms amputated. It's an operation he endures for two reasons—the love of the girl, and the knowledge that she must never see his infirmity. When he returns to the big top, he is horrified to discover that the woman for whom he has sacrificed so much has pledged herself to Kerry, the circus strong man. Obsessed, Lon attempts to destroy his rival by having him torn in two by the horses Kerry chains himself to during his act, but the plot fails, and in the end, Chaney himself is killed. This is one of the great star's most morbid, unusual (the things he is able to do with his toes have to be seen to be believed), and satisfying performances, and everything else about the picture is topnotch, as well.

d, Tod Browning; w, Waldemar Young (based on a story by Browning); t, Joe Farnham; ph, Merritt Gestard; ed, Harry Reynolds, Errol Taggart; art d, Cedric Gibbons; cos, Lucia Coulter.

Drama **(PR:C MPAA:NR)**

UNKNOWN CAVALIER, THE 1/2** (1926) 7 reels Charles R. Rogers/FN bw

Ken Maynard *(Tom Drury)*, Kathleen Collins *(Ruth Gaunt)*, David Torrence *(Peter Gaunt)*, T. Roy Barnes *(Clout Pettingill)*, James Mason *(Henry Suggs)*, Otis Harlan *(Judge Blowfly Jones)*, Joseph Swickard *(Lingo)*, Bruce Gordon *(Bob Webb)*, Fred Burns *(Sheriff)*, Jimsy Boudwin *(Billy Gaunt)*, Pat Harmon, Frank Lackteen, Raymond Wells *(The Three Bad Men)*, Tarzan the Horse.

Maynard is at his very best in this hard-riding western, which has the cowboy saving the wonder horse, Tarzan, from destruction, and winning the girl, Collins, by bringing to justice a pillar of the community who secretly led a gang of crooks by using a disguise.

d, Albert Rogell; w, Marion Jackson (based on the novel *Ride Him Cowboy* by Kenneth Perkins); t, Don Ryan; ph, Sol Polito.

Western **(PR:A MPAA:NR)**

UNREST* (1920, Brit.) 6 reels Cairns Torquay/Allied Exporters bw

Dallas Cairns *(Martin Frensham)*, Mary Dibley *(Nella Frensham)*, Maud Yates *(Judith Ruddinger)*, Edward O'Neill, George Harrington, Marjorie Hoare.

Uninspired British drama has a writer dropping his wife to take off with a wealthy, fun-loving widow, but returning to the old homestead when he discovers that the woman he's betraying has given birth to his son.

p&d, Dallas Cairns; w, R. Byron-Webber (based on a novel by Warwick Deeping).

Drama **(PR:A MPAA:NR)**

UNTAMED LADY, THE* 1/2 (1926) 7 reels FP/PAR bw

Gloria Swanson *(St. Clair Van Tassel)*, Lawrence Gray *(Larry Gastlen)*, Joseph Smiley *(Uncle George)*, Charles Graham *(Shorty)*.

Swanson made a number of films like this one in which she plays a millionairesse (a role providing plenty of opportunity to show off her extensive wardrobe), who is spoiled and insufferable until the last reel, when she is tamed by, and falls madly in love with, a handsome young society chap (Gray).

d, Frank Tuttle; w, James Ashmore Creelman (based on the story by Fannie Hurst); ph, George Webber.

Drama **(PR:A MPAA:NR)**

UNWANTED, THE** (1924, Brit.) 7 reels Napoleon bw

C. Aubrey Smith *(Col. Carrington)*, Lilian Hall-Davis *(Marianne Dearsley)*, Nora Swinburne *(Joyce Mannering)*, Francis Lister *(John Dearsley)*, Walter Sondes *(Kenneth Carrington)*, Mary Dibley *(Genevieve)*.

Smith, that great master of "stiff-upper-lip" portrayals, plays another of his military roles in this British drama, which has the illegitimate son of a colonel convincing the world that his brother, a hopeless coward, died heroically.

p, G. B. Samuelson; d&w, Walter Summers.

Drama **(PR:A MPAA:NR)**

VALLEY OF BRAVERY, THE** (1926) 5 reels IP/FBO bw

Bob Custer *(Steve Tucker)*, Tom Bay *(Jim Saunders)*, Eugenia Gilbert *(Helen Coburn)*, William Gillespie *(Percy Winthrop)*, Ernie Adams *(Valet)*, Art Artego *(Joe)*, Nelson McDowell *(Missouri)*.

Custer, a wounded war vet, goes to Montana to be near Gilbert, the nurse who saved his life, and the little French orphan she adopted. A crook posing as a millionaire shows up and tries to steal Gilbert's shipment of ore. During the struggle, the villain kidnaps the girl, but Custer rides to the rescue, saves the day, and proves his manhood again.

p, Jesse J. Goldburg; d, Jack Nelson; w, Carl Krusada, James Ormont (based on a story by E. Lanning Masters); ph, Ernest Miller.

Western **(PR:A MPAA:NR)**

VALLEY OF SILENT MEN, THE** (1922) 7 reels COS/PAR bw

Alma Rubens *(Marette Radison)*, Lew Cody *(Cpl. James Kent of the Royal Northwest Mounted)*, Joseph King *("Buck" O'Connor)*, Mario Majeroni *(Pierre Radison)*, George Nash *(Inspector Kedsty, of the Mounted)*, J. W. Johnston *(Jacques Radison)*.

Some spectacular scenery and Rubens in a snug-fitting riding outfit are about all this Northwest drama has going for it. The story is all about a Mountie (Cody) who thinks he's dying from a gunshot wound and takes the blame for a couple of murders to save his friend, who's been wrongly accused. Cody survives, however, and is on hand when the real killer makes a deathbed confession.

d, Frank Borzage; w, John Lynch (based on the novel by James Oliver Curwood); ph, Chester Lyons.

Adventure **(PR:A MPAA:NR)**

VAMPING VENUS** (1928) 7 reels FN bw

Charlie Murray *(Michael Cassidy/King Cassidy of Ireland)*, Louise Fazenda *(Maggie Cassidy/Circe)*, Thelma Todd *(Mme. Vanezlos/Venus)*, Russ Powell *(Pete Papaglos/Bacchus)*, Joe Bonomo *(Simonides/Hercules)*, Big Boy Williams *(Mars)*, Spec O'Donnell *(Western Union Boy/Mercury)*, Fred O'Beck *(Vulcan)*, Gustav von Seyffertitz *(Jupiter)*, Gus Partos *(Shopkeeper)*, Janet MacLeod *(Juno)*, Yola D'Avril *(Stenographer)*.

In spite of a good comedy director, a topflight cast, and an interesting premise, this motion picture just fails to make it. The story has Murray, an Irish-American vaudeville performer, attending an annual party for entertainers, where he is accidentally knocked unconscious by a professional strongman and dreams he's the king of ancient Ireland. Somehow he finds himself in Greece, falls in love with Venus (Todd), becomes involved with various mythological characters (all played by people from his real life), and puts down a revolution using modern inventions, including machine guns and tanks. When Murray wakes up and he realizes that it was all a fantasy.

d, Eddie Cline; w, Howard J. Green, Bernard McConville; t, Ralph Spence; ph, Dev Jennings; ed, Paul Weatherwax.

Comedy **(PR:A MPAA:NR)**

VANISHING HOOFS** (1926) 5 reels Action/Weiss Brothers Artclass bw

Wally Wales *(Wally Marsh)*, Alma Rayford *(Lucy Bowers)*, William Ryno *(Col. Bowers)*, Hazel Keener *(Edith Marsh)*, Frank Ellis *(Jack Warren)*, William Dunn *(Jack Slade)*, Jane Sherman *(Kate)*, Charles Whittaker *(The Doctor)*, W. J. Willett *(The Sheriff)*.

Poverty Row oater stars Wales as a shell-shocked vet who overcomes his infirmity just in time to round up a gang of rustlers, save his pal from being lynched, and win the pretty girl.

d, John P. McCarthy; w, Betty Burbridge (based on a story by L. V. Jefferson).

Western **(PR:A MPAA:NR)**

VANITY* (1927) 6 reels DM/PDC bw

Leatrice Joy *(Barbara Fiske)*, Charles Ray *(Lloyd Van Courtland)*, Alan Hale *(Dan Morgan)*, Mayme Kelso *(Mrs. Fiske)*, Noble Johnson *(The Ship's Cook)*, Helen Lee Worthing *(Tess Ramsay)*, Louis Payne *(Butler)*.

Dismal film in every respect has bored society girl Joy putting on her best jewels and visiting Hale, the brutish captain of a tramp steamer, the day before her wedding to Ray. Johnson, a tattooed giant who works as ship's cook, is so overt in his lustful interest in the lady, that Hale attacks him and is killed. Joy in turn shoots Johnson to death, and after her pulse rate returns to normal, gladly marries the less exotic, but very wealthy, Ray. An embarrassment all around.

d, Donald Crisp; sup, C. Gardner Sullivan; w, Douglas Doty; t, John Krafft; ph, Arthur Miller; ed, Barbara Hunter; art d, Anton Grot; cos, Adrian.

Drama **(PR:A MPAA:NR)**

VARIETY**** ½** (1925, Ger.) 7 reels UFA/FP bw

Emil Jannings *(Boss)*, Maly Delschaft *(His Wife)*, Lya De Putti *(The Girl)*, Warwick Ward *(Artinelli)*, Alex Hyde and his Original New York Jazz Orchestra.

Wonderful German film has convict boss Huller (Jannings) appearing before the warden of the prison where he has long been incarcerated, and telling the story of his crime. As the picture flashes back, we see Jannings operating a shabby concession at a second rate amusement park. He's a bitter man who once knew glory as a trapeze artist, an art he had to give up after suffering an accident. One day a sailor brings him a sensuous young girl (Lya De Putti) and Jannings puts her on the payroll. Before long he is completely enslaved by her erotic nature, and they run away, leaving his wife to fend for herself. Jannings and De Putti put together an aerial act and begin playing the small-time carnival circuit. While they are performing at a Berlin fair, he is approached by the manager of the Wintergarden, who introduces him to the world-renowned acrobat Artinelli (superbly played by Ward) who has lost his brother in an accident and needs a catcher. The star has doubts about using a common carnival performer, but he changes his mind when he spots the lovely De Putti. At first, Jannings is not interested in the offer. He's comfortable the way things are, but De Putti toys with his ego, casts her sexual spell, and persuades him to join the act which will become known as *The Three Artinellis*. Before long, Ward seduces his partner, and they begin to carry on a torrid affair. Jannings learns of this when he accidently sees a cartoon a fellow performer has drawn on a restaurant table cloth depicting De Putti and Ward together and himself sketched as a goat. The big fellow flies into a rage, and later we are shown a remarkable scene where the catcher deliberately drops his partner during a triple summersault. But this turns out to be an act created by his imagination. Jannings is too much of a professional to do that. After the show, he goes to the apartment of his cuckholder, stabs him to death, and washes the blood from his hands before De Putti's horrified eyes in their suite which is just down the hall. Jannings is trance-like as he turns to leave, but the woman who betrayed him chases after, clutching his leg, and she apparently breaks her neck as he drags her down the flights of stairs which lead to the lobby. Jannings is oblivious to all of this as he climbs into a taxi and asks to be taken to the nearest police station. The picture then fades to the present, where Jannings is told by the sympathetic warden that he has suffered enough. The film ends with the prison gates symbolically opening. VARIETY is a visual tour de force, with Karl Freund's camera constantly moving and seeking out unusual camera angles (the cinematographer said he often had no choice, as the Wintergarden location provided little room for natural camera placement). Some of the action is seen in the reflections from eyeglasses, through binoculars, between the blades of a whirling electric fan, and often from the point of view of the characters themselves. VARIETY was the most successful German film to play the U.S. up to that time, and its two stars, Jannings and De Putti, as well as director Dupont, were offered work in Hollywood. (As part of Jannings' publicity buildup the story was invented that he was born in Brooklyn and moved to the Fatherland as a small boy. Actually, the place of his birth was Rorschach, Switzerland.) De Putti made a few American films (including BUCK PRIVATER and THE SORROWS OF SATAN) but died in 1932 at the age of 30. Dupont was never able to equal his success with this film and made only one American picture before going to England where he made five features, including ATLANTIC, the first complete English talking picture. He later returned to America where he directed a series of cheapies in the 1950s. Only Jannings became triumphant in the States, but he returned to Germany when sound came in and Paramount felt that his Teutonic accent would not be acceptable.

d&w, E. A. Dupont (based on the German novel *The Oath of Stephen Huller* by Hollaender); ph, Karl Freund.

Drama **Cas.** **(PR:C MPAA:NR)**

VEILED WOMAN, THE* ½ (1917, Brit.) 5 reels British Empire bw

Cecil Humphreys *(Gascoigne Devine)*, Gladys Mason *(Coralie Travers)*, Frank Randell *(Robert Travers)*, Marjorie Chard *(Naomi Sinclair)*.

The laws of probability are stretched a bit thin in this British mystery about a gambler's paramour assuming the identity of the married society woman, whom her man is blackmailing into becoming his lover.

d, Leedham Bantock; w, (based on a play by Harold Simpson).

Mystery **(PR:A MPAA:NR)**

VIRGINIAN, THE* ½** (1914) 5 reels LAS bw

Dustin Farnum *(The Virginian)*, Winifred Kingston *(Molly Wood)*, J. W. Johnston *(Steve)*, Billy Elmer *(Trampas)*, Sydney Deane *(Uncle Hughey)*, Horace B. Carpenter *(Spanish Ed)*, James Griswold *(Stage Driver)*, Tex Driscoll *(Shorty)*, Monroe Salisbury, Anita King, Dick La Reno, Hosea Steelman, Mrs. Lewis McCord.

Any doubt that certain properties were better suited for the screen rather than the stage were dispelled by this excellent DeMille adaptation of Wister's classic novel about a Virginian who falls in love with a schoolteacher, takes on a gang of cattle rustlers, is forced to hang his oldest friend, and then kills the colorful Elmer in a beautifully staged pistol duel. Wyckoff's camera work rivals that of the great Billy Bitzer, particularly in the use of shadows to depict the lynching, and with a specially coated lens he invented for the purpose of shooting directly into the sun—a technique which would become as common as the double exposure.

d&w, Cecil B. DeMille (based on the novel by Owen Wister and the play by Kirk La Shelle); ph, Alvin Wyckoff.

Western **(PR:A MPAA:NR)**

VIRGINIAN, THE** (1923) 8 reels SCHUL/PRE bw

Kenneth Harlan *(The Virginian)*, Florence Vidor *(Molly Woods)*, Russell Simpson *(Trampas)*, Pat O'Malley *(Steve)*, Raymond Hatton *(Shorty)*, Milton Ross *(Judge Henry)*, Sam Allen *(Uncle Hughey)*, Bert Hadley *(Spanish Ed)*, Fred Gambold *(Fat Drummer)*.

The second filming of Wister's western classic had its moments, but was inferior to Cecil B. De Mille's 1914 version and Victor Fleming's 1929 talkie with Gary Cooper. It did, however, more than hold its own with the lackluster 1945 remake starring

Joel McCrea. Harlan played the lead in this version about a Virginia cowboy who falls in love with a New England schoolteacher, but loses her affections when she discovers he is responsible for the hanging of his childhood friend. Actually Harlan was just doing his duty; he had been leading a posse which hunted down a gang of cattle rustlers, of which his old clum had been a part of. Later, when Harlan gets wounded, he is rescued by his sweetheart and the two are reunited.

d, Tom Forman; w, Hope Loring, Louis D. Lighton (based on the novel by Owen Wister and the play by Kirk La Shelle); ph, Harry Perry.

Western **(PR:A MPAA:NR)**

VIRGINIA'S HUSBAND** (1928, Brit.) 7 reels Nettlefold/BUT bw

Mabel Poulton *(Joyce)*, Lillian Oldland *(Virginia Trevor)*, Pat Aherne *(Bill Hemingway)*, Marie Ault *(Aunt Janet)*, Fewlass Llewellyn *(Uncle Donald)*, Ena Grossmith *(Elizabeth)*, Charles Dormer *(Freddy Parkinson)*.

Love conquers all in this little British comedy which has a pretty girl paying a former Army officer to assume the role of her husband in order to fool her wealthy relatives.

p, Archibald Nettlefold; d, Harry Hughes; w, H. Fowler Mear (based on a play by Florence Kilpatrick).

Comedy **(PR:A MPAA:NR)**

VOICE IN THE DARK** (1921) 5 reels Goldwyn bw

Ramsey Wallace *(Harlan Day)*, Irene Rich *(Blanche Walton)*, Alec Francis *(Joseph Crampton)*, Alan Hale *(Dr. Hugh Sainsbury)*, Ora Carew *(Adele Walton)*, William Scott *(Chester Thomas)*, Richard Tucker *(Lt. Patrick Cloyd)*, Alice Hollister *(Amelia Ellingham)*, Gertrude Norman *(Mrs. Lydiard)*, James Neill *(Edward Small)*.

The premise which has a blind person testifying at a murder trial, telling what he heard, and a deaf woman recounting what she saw, created a riviting effect on the stage. But the translation to the silent screen leaves something to be desired, although director Lloyd does present some compelling images, as well as good performances from his entire cast.

d, Frank Lloyd; Arthur E. Statter (based on the play by Ralph E. Dyar).

Mystery **(PR:A MPAA:NR)**

VOLCANO** (1926) 6 reels FP/PAR bw

Bebe Daniels *(Zabette de Chauvalons)*, Ricardo Cortez *(Stephane Sequineau)*, Wallace Beery *(Quembo)*, Arthur Edmund Carew *(Maurice Sequineau)*, Dale Fuller *(Cedrien)*, Eulalie Jensen *(Mme. de Chauvalons)*, Brandon Hurst *(Andre de Chauvalons)*, Marjorie Gay *(Marie de Chauvalons)*, Robert Perry *(Père Benedict)*, Snitz Edwards *(Auctioneer)*, Emily Barrye *(Azaline)*, Bowditch Turner *(Cafe Manager)*, Edith Yorke *(Mother Superior)*, Mathilde Comont *(Mme. Timbuctoo)*.

Some spectacular special effects redeem this otherwise intolerant film which has Daniels leaving a Brussels convent to visit her father in Martinique. Upon arriving, however, she discovers that he has died and is forced by his widow, the head of the French community, to move to the mulatto quarter as it is believed Daniels is the product of her father's affair with a native woman. The girl barely survives in the poor neighborhood and sells off her Paris frocks to get by. She does, however, arouse the interest of Beery, the mulatto villain, as well as Cortez, a French aristocrat "who loves her anyway." The picture ends with the well-filmed disaster promised by its title, and Daniels and Cortez sailing for Europe as man and wife—content in the knowledge that she is of *pure* French heritage.

d, William K. Howard; w, Bernard McConville (based on the play "Martinique" by Laurence Eyre); ph, Lucien Androit.

Drama **(PR:A MPAA:NR)**

VOLGA BOATMAN, THE*** (1926) 11 reels DM/PDC bw

William Boyd *(Feodor)*, Elinor Fair *(Vera)*, Robert Edeson *(Prince Nikita)*, Victor Varconi *(Prince Dimitri)*, Julia Faye *(Mariusha)*, Theodore Kosloff *(Stephan)*, Arthur Rankin *(Vasili)*.

More than a few generations of Americans have delighted in singing (usually in an exaggerated bass voice) the Russian folk song "Yo Heave Ho," which was the recurring theme played by orchestras, pianists, and organ players in theaters throughout the land when this portrait of the Soviet Revolution, as seen through the eyes of Cecil B. De Mille, was shown. Actually, it is a beautifully crafted and slickly produced melodrama, which has Boyd (a serf who agonizes his way through several reels, tugging on the rope which slowly propels boats along the Volga river) winning the love of a princess and eventually saving her from the wrath of a group of vengeful Reds, of which he is now the leader. And then in the end, in a thrilling chase scene, he escapes with her from the forces of the unbelievably cruel White Army. Like the melody, this was a picture which stirred the soul, and children who once sat spellbound watching the action and Boyd's glistening muscularity never quite forgot the images—or the tune.

d, Cecil B. DeMille; w, Lenore J. Coffee (based on the novel by Konrad Bercovici); ph, Arthur Miller, Peverell Marley, Fred Westerberg; ed, Anne Bauchens; art d, Max Parker, Mitchell Leisen, Anton Grot; cos, Adrian.

Drama **(PR:A MPAA:NR)**

VORTEX, THE* (1927, Brit.) 6 reels Gainsborough/Woolf and Freedman bw

Ivor Novello *(Nicky Lancaster)*, Wilette Kershaw *(Florence Lancaster)*, Frances Doble *(Bunty Mainwaring)*, Alan Hollis *(Tom Veryan)*, Sir Simeon Stuart *(David Lancaster)*, Kinsey Peile *(Pauncefort Qeuntin)*, Julie Suedo *(Anna Volloff)*, Dorothy Fane *(Helen Saville)*.

Poorly directed, watered-down adaptation of the cynical Coward play about a composer who falls in love with a lady writer and then discovers that his mother is having an affair with her former lover. Later, at his country estate, the composerdiscovers his sweetheart in the fellow's arms and all hell breaks loose. The mother swears to drop the younger chap and mature naturally, and the producers bring the picture to a happy and completely unsatisfactory conclusion.

p, Michael Balcon; d, Adrian Brunel; w, Eliot Stannard (based on the play by Noel Coward).

Drama **(PR:A MPAA:NR)**

WAGES FOR WIVES½** (1925) 7 reels FOX bw

Jacqueline Logan *(Nell Bailey)*, Creighton Hale *(Danny Kester)*, Earle Foxe *(Hughie Logan)*, ZaSu Pitts *(Luella Logan)*, Claude Gillingwater *(Jim Bailey)*, David Butler *(Chester Logan)*, Margaret Seddon *(Annie Bailey)*, Margaret Livingston *(Carol Bixby)*, Dan Mason *(Mr. Tevis)*, Tom Ricketts *(Judge McLean)*.

Pretty good comedy has Logan agreeing to marry Hale on the condition that he split his salary evenly with her. After the wedding, however, Hale reneges and Logan goes on strike, joined by her mother and sister in a show of solidarity. The laughs keep coming as their three deserted spouses attempt to fend for themselves—a situation which is complicated by the entrance of a saucy flapper. But Hale, with the enthusiastic agreement of his pals, finally surrenders, and the picture ends on a happy, if not hilarious note.

d, Frank Borzage; w, Kenneth B. Clarke (based on the play "Chicken Feed; or Wages for Wives" by Guy Bolton, Winchell Smith); ph, Ernest G. Palmer.

Comedy **(PR:A MPAA:NR)**

WALKING BACK*** (1928) 6 reels DM/Pathe bw

Sue Carol *(Patsy Schuyler)*, Richard Walling *(Smoke Thatcher)*, Ivan Lebedeff *(Beaut Thibaut)*, Robert Edeson *(Mr. Thatcher, Sr.)*, Jane Keckley *(Mrs. Thatcher)*, Florence Turner *(Mrs. Schuyler)*, James Bradbury, Sr., *(Gyp)*, Arthur Rankin *(Pet Masters)*, Billy Sullivan, George Stone *(Crooks)*.

Jazz-age, flaming-youth film has young Walling "borrowing" a neighbor's car to take Carol to a dance when his father grounds him for low grades. The crowd later becomes involved in an auto duel, and Walling's machine is all but destroyed. He takes it to a garage for repairs and the shop turns out to be a front for hot cars used to pull holdups. Walling and Carol are tricked into participating in a heist on the promise that they will be given another roadster, but it turns out to be Walling's father's company which is hit. His dad is then shot while trying to defend his property and the crooks point a gun to the back of the horrified youth's head and command him to drive the getaway car at a normal rate of speed so as not to draw the attention of the law. Instead the kid puts the pedal to the floor and finally screeches to a halt right inside of police headquarters. The picture ends with Walling receiving a fat reward, the forgiveness of his slightly wounded father, and the love of the perky and most appealing Carol.

d, Rupert Julian; w, Monte Katterjohn (based on the story "A Ride in the Country" by George Kibbe Turner); ph, John Mescall; ed, Claude Berkeley; art d, Anton Grot; cos, Adrian.

Drama **(PR:A MPAA:NR)**

WALL FLOWER, THE*** (1922) 6 reels Goldwyn bw

Colleen Moore *(Idalene Nobbin)*, Richard Dix *(Walt Breen)*, Gertrude Astor *(Pamela Shiel)*, Laura La Plante *(Prue Nickerson)*, Tom Gallery *(Roy Duncan)*, Rush Hughes *(Phin Larrabee)*, Dana Todd *(Allen Lansing)*, Fanny Stockbridge *(Mrs. Nobbin)*, Emily Rait *(Mrs. Nickerson)*.

Touching Hughes production has the talanted Moore playing a homely girl who attempts to commit suicide after being the butt of a group of cruel pranksters at a dance. She is taken in by socialite Astor, who nurses her back to health and teaches her the secrets of proper dress, makeup, and social demeanor. This results in Moore blooming into a creature of great beauty and charm, who later has the satisfaction of snubbing her former detractors and marrying Dix, a handsome young man of substantial means.

d&w, Rupert Hughes; ph, John J. Mescall.

Drama **(PR:A MPAA:NR)**

WALLFLOWER, THE (SEE: WALL FLOWER, THE, 1922)

WALLOP, THE*** (1921) 5 reels UNIV bw

Harry Carey *(John Wesley Pringle)*, Mignonne Golden *(Stella Vorhis)*, William Gettinger *(Christopher Foy)*, Charles Le Moyne *(Matt Lisner)*, Joe Harris *(Barela)*, C. E. Anderson *(Applegate)*, J. Farrell MacDonald *(Neuces River)*, Mark Fenton *(Maj. Vorhis)*, Noble Johnson *(Espinol)*.

Director Ford has cowboy star Carey striking it rich and returning home to discover that Golden, the girl he secretly loves, is engaged to his best pal, a candidate for the office of sheriff. The incumbent frames his rival on a murder charge, but Carey clears his friend, nails the villain, and returns to his mine—leaving the young couple to find their happiness.

d, Jack Ford; w, George C. Hull (based on the story "The Girl He Left Behind Him" by Eugene Manlove Rhodes); ph, Harry Fowler.

Western Drama **(PR:A MPAA:NR)**

WALLOPING WALLACE**
(1924) 5 reels Approved/Weiss Brothers Artclass bw

Buddy Roosevelt *(Buddy Wallace)*, Violet La Plante *(Carol Grey)*, Lew Meehan *(Squinty Burnt)*, N. E. Hendrix *(Shorty)*, Lillian Gale *(Ma Fagin)*, Terry Myles *(Spud)*, Olin Francis *(Sheriff)*, Dick Bodkins *(Cattle Buyer)*.

When La Plante is kidnaped by the varmint who wants to steal her ranch, her foreman, Roosevelt, springs into action, gives the crook the beating of his life, and wins the love of his grateful employer.

p, Lester F. Scott, Jr.; d, Richard Thorpe; w, Norbert Myles.

Western **(PR:A MPAA:NR)**

WALLS OF PREJUDICE*½ (1920, Brit.) 5 reels GAU/British Screencraft bw

Josephine Earle *(Margaret Benson)*, Dallas Anderson *(Patrick Benson)*, Pat Somerset *(Townsend)*, Zoe Palmer *(Madge Benson)*, Humberston Wright *(Bigton)*, Cyril Smith *(Karpat)*.

There is a happy if somewhat strained ending to this British drama about a hard-working man who is about to lose his garment business due to the dirty work of a dishonest wholesaler, when his wife comes to the rescue and reveals that she has been secretly operating a thriving dress shop.

d, C. C. Calvert; w, (based on the play "Break Down the Walls" by Mrs. Alexander Grossman).

Drama **(PR:A MPAA:NR)**

WANDERING GIRLS½** (1927) 6 reels COL bw

Dorothy Revier *(Peggy Marston)*, Eugenie Besserer *(Peggy's Mother)*, Frances Raymond *(Mrs. Arnold)*, Robert Agnew *(Jerry Arnold)*, William Welsh *(James Marston)*, Armand Kaliz *(Maurice Dumond)*, Mildred Harris *(Maxine)*.

Just another youth-on-a-tear movie, this time about a girl (Revier) who runs away from home to escape her strict father and becomes involved with a male-female burglar duo, who use a ballroom dance act to set up their heists. Later, Revier is wrongly accused of stealing jewels when the lady crook, Harris, switches suitcases with her. Revier's wealthy boy friend pays her bond, however, and Harris finally clears her name in a deathbed confession after an auto accident. Revier, having learned her lesson, returns home to be near her father and husband-to-be. This otherwise average movie was given a bit of sparkle by the performances of Revier and Harris.

d, Ralph Ince; sup, Harry Cohn; w, Harry O. Hoyt (based on a story by Dorothy Howell); ph, J. O. Taylor.

Drama **(PR:A MPAA:NR)**

WANING SEX, THE*** (1926) 7 reels MGM bw

Norma Shearer *(Nina Duane)*, Conrad Nagel *(Philip Barry)*, George K. Arthur *(Hamilton Day)*, Mary McAllister *(Mary Booth)*, Charles McHugh *(J. J. Flannigan)*, Tiny Ward *(J. J. Murphy)*, Martha Mattox *(Ellen B. Armstrong)*.

Shearer is at her most charming, and is even given the opportunity to wear a swimsuit, in this delighful comedy—reminiscent of the later Hepburn-Tracy comedies—about a liberated female lawyer who openly competes with a chauvinistic male district attorney. Finally, after a number of hi-jinks, the two decide to follow the merger route. Top direction by Leonard, script by Herbert, and titles by Farnham, also helped make this one a winner.

d, Robert Z. Leonard; w, F. Hugh Herbert (based on the play by Raymond and Fanny Hatton); t, Joe Farnham; ph, Ben Reynolds; ed, William Le Vanway; set d, Cedric Gibbons, Paul Youngblood.

Comedy **(PR:A MPAA:NR)**

WANTED—A COWARD½** (1927) 6 reels BAN/STER bw

Lillian Rich *(Isabell Purviance)*, Robert Frazer *(Rupert Garland)*, Frank Brownlee *(Adrian Purviance)*, James Gordon *(Bull Harper)*, Frank Cooley *(Bates)*, Harry S. Northrup *(Ortegas)*, Fred O'Beck *(Stamboff)*, William Bertram *(Slim Ellis)*.

This is the kind of film that only a Douglas Fairbanks—in his pre-swashbuckling, light comedy period—could really have pulled off. It all has to do with an adventurer (Frazer) who announces to his fellow club members that all men, including himself, are actually cowards. When the boys advertise for a coward, Frazer responds, and they set up a series of adventures to prove him a hero. Along the way, the man of derring-do also captures the heart of the actress (Rich) who was in on the gag from the start.

p&d, Roy Clements; w, Vincent Starrett.

Comedy/Adventure **(PR:A MPAA:NR)**

WANTED FOR MURDER½** (1919) 5 reels Harry Rapf/Chatham bw

Elaine Hammerstein *(Corrine)*, Mrs. Walker *(Mme. Fernard)*, Lillian Hall *(Annette)*, Charles Raven *(Dick)*, Irene Franklin, Burton Green *(Overseas Entertainers)*, Cpl. Darby Holmes *(Himself)*, Mrs. Eggleston.

Director Crane successfully uses newsreel footage to provide depth for this wartime propaganda film about a brave French girl who escapes the clutches of a lustful Hun and finds happiness in the arms of an American soldier.

d, Frank H. Crane; w, Collidge Streeter (based on a story by S. Jay Kaufman); ph, George Peters.

War **(PR:A MPAA:NR)**

WANTED FOR MURDER, OR BRIDE OF HATE
(SEE: BRIDE OF HATE, THE, 1917)

WANTERS, THE*½ (1923) 7 reels Louis B. Mayer/AFN bw

Marie Prevost *(Myra Hastings)*, Robert Ellis *(Elliot Worthington)*, Norma Shearer *(Marjorie)*, Gertrude Astor *(Mrs. Van Pelt)*, Huntley Gordon *(Theodore Van Pelt)*, Lincoln Stedman *(Bobby)*, Lillian Langdon *(Mrs. Worthington)*, Louise Fazenda *(Mary)*, Hank Mann *(The Star Boarder)*, Lydia Yeamans Titus *(The Landlady)*, Vernon Steele *(Tom Armstrong)*, Harold Goodwin *(Chauffeur)*, William Buckley *(Butler)*.

Prevost heads a good cast in what is otherwise a rather ordinary society drama about a house maid who marries a wealthy young man and is so upset by his family's snobbish attitude towards her that she runs away. There is nothing original in this picture, including the ending, which has the hero saving his bride from an onrushing train at the last second. With such Mack Sennett veterans as Fazenda, Mann, and Prevost herself in this production, it's no wonder this was a drama impossible to take seriously.

d, John M. Stahl; w, J. G. Hawks, Paul Bern (based on a story by Leila Burton Wells); ph, Ernest G. Palmer.

Drama **(PR:A MPAA:NR)**

WAR HORSE, THE*** (1927) 5 reels FOX bw

Buck Jones *(Buck Thomas)*, Lola Todd *(Audrey Evans)*, Lloyd Whitlock *(Capt. Collins)*, Stanley Taylor *(Lt. Caldwell)*, Yola D'Avril *(Yvonne)*, James Gordon *(Gen. Evans)*.

Lots of action, as well as good production values, in this unusual and well-directed Jones feature, which has the cowboy enlisting in the Army to be near his beloved horse, which was pressed into service. In France, Jones saves his men from the slaughter of a German ambush, and steals the heart of Todd, a pretty little nurse.

d&w, Lambert Hillyer (based on a story by Buck Jones, Hillyer); ph, Reginald Lyons.

War **(PR:A MPAA:NR)**

WAR PAINT*** (1926) 6 reels MGM bw

Tim McCoy *(Lt. Tim Marshall)*, Pauline Starke *(Polly Hopkins)*, Charles French *(Maj. Hopkins)*, Chief Yowlache *(Iron Eyes)*, Chief Whitehorse *(White Hawk)*, Karl Dane *(Petersen)*.

MGM's first western picture assured McCoy's place among the popular cowboy stars of the late silent era. Actually, he had been around since 1923, when he worked as an adviser on THE COVERED WAGON. In this picture, dealing with the U.S. Cavalry, McCoy put his knowledge of the real West to good use by using authentic Indian sign language. His real Army experience came in handy too; McCoy was a colonel who served in both World Wars and won the Bronze Star in WW II. WAR PAINT has to do with an "unfriendly" Indian, who swears to kill all whites after McCoy humiliates him in a knife fight. The Indian escapes from the stockade, but has his ambition thwarted by McCoy, with the timely help of his good friend, Chief Whitehorse, and his loyal braves. Director "Woody" Van Dyke was a new name on the MGM roster when he made WAR PAINT. He had originally started at age 17 as assistant to D. W. Griffith in the making of INTOLERANCE in 1916. He would go on to develop into one of MGM's most successful directors.

d, W. S. Van Dyke; w, Charles Maigne (based on a story by Peter B. Kyne); t, Joe Farnum; ph, Clyde De Vinna.

Western **(PR:A MPAA:NR)**

WARE CASE, THE** (1917, Brit.) 6 reels BRO/FBO bw

Matheson Lang *(Sir Hubert Ware)*, Violet Hopson *(Lady Magdalen Ware)*, Ivy Close *(Marian Scales)*, Gregory Scott *(Michael Ayde)*, George Foley *(Sir Henry Egerton)*.

The laughs are sparce in the British drama based upon a popular play about a nobleman who kills himself by ingesting poison after confessing that he murdered his hated brother-in-law.

p&d, Walter West; w, J. Bertram Brown (based on a play by George Pleydell Bancroft).

Mystery **(PR:A MPAA:NR)**

WARMING UP*1/2 (1928) 8 reels PAR bw

Richard Dix *(Bert Tulliver)*, Jean Arthur *(Mary Post)*, Claude King *(Mr. Post)*, Philo McCullough *(McRae)*, Billy Kent Schaefer *(Edsel)*, Roscoe Karns *(Hippo)*, James Dugan *(Brill)*, Mike Donlin *(Veteran)*, Mike Ready, Chet Thomas, Joe Pirrone, Wally Hood, Bob Murray, Truck Hannah *(Themselves)*.

Dix and Arthur worked beautifully together, yet their chemistry couldn't overcome this silly script. In it, Dix plays a baseball pitcher who loves his team owner's daughter, Arthur, but thinks his slugger-rival, McCullough, has a jinx on him. In the World Series, Dix deliberately walks his nemesis and is pulled out of the game. But naturally he comes back in the last inning of the final game to strike McCullough out, and is rewarded by Arthur's hand in marriage.

d, Fred Newmeyer; w, Ray Harris (based on a story by Sam Mintz); t, George Marion; ph, Edward Cronjager; ed, Otto Lovering; m/l, "Out of the Dawn," Walter Donaldson; syn sc; s eff.

Dramatic Comedy **(PR:A MPAA:NR)**

WARNING, THE*** (1927) 6 reels COL bw

Jack Holt *(Tom Fellows/Col. Robert Wellsley)*, Dorothy Revier *(Mary Blake)*, Frank Lackteen *(Tso Lin)*, Pat Harmon *(London Charlie)*, Eugene Strong *(No. 24)*. George Kuwa *(Ah Sung)*, Norman Trevor *(Sir James Gordon)*.

While in Shanghai, opium smuggler, Holt rescues secret agent 63, Revier, from the clutches of London's infamous Harmon. Later, Revier is captured again while trying to arrest the drug czar and is taken to his subterranean hideout. Holt saves her a second time and in a sensational, machine gun-blazing battle, routs the gangster's forces and indentifies himself as being chief of British Intelligence in China. Director Seitz kept the action moving at a terrific pace in a thrill-packed picture from start to finish.

p, Harry Cohn; d&w, George B. Seitz (based on a story by Lillian Ducey, H. Milner Kitchin); ph, Ray June; art d, Robert E. Lee.

Adventure **(PR:A MPAA:NR)**

WARRENS OF VIRGINIA, THE*** (1915) 5 reels LAS bw

Blanche Sweet *(Agatha Warren)*, James Neill *(Gen. Warren)*, House Peters *(Ned Burton)*, Page Peters *(Authur Warren)*, Mabel Van Buren *(Mrs. Warren)*, Dick La Reno *(Gen. Griffen)*, Sidney Dean *(Gen. Harding)*, Raymond Hatton *(Blake)*, Milton Brown *(Zeke Biggs)*, Dick La Strange *(Bill Peavey)*, Lucien Littlefield *(Tom Dabney)*, Gerald Ward *(Bob Warren)*, Mildred Harris *(Betty Warren)*, Mrs. Lewis McCord *(Sapho)*, Marguerite House, DeWitt Jennings.

Cecil B. DeMille directed a fine motion picture adaptation of his brother's play of the same title in which Mary Pickford had a prominent role. It's all about a Union officer in love with a Southern girl who learns, to her horror, that he's a spy. There is a wonderfully filmed ambush sequence, and after a great deal of suspense, the picture ends happily with the young people overcoming the hatred of war, and getting together.

d, Cecil B. DeMille; w, William B. DeMille (from his own play); ph, Alvin Wyckoff.

War/Romance **(PR:A MPAA:NR)**

WARRENS OF VIRGINIA, THE** (1924) 7 reels FOX bw

George Backus *(Gen. Warren)*, Rosemary Hill *(Betty Warren)*, Martha Mansfield *(Agatha Warren)*, Robert Andrews *(Arthur Warren)*, Wilfred Lytell *(Lt. Burton)*, Harlan Knight *("Pap")*, James Turfler *("Danny")*, Helen Ray Kyle *("The Little Reb")*, Lt. Wilbur J. Fox *(Gen. Grant)*, J. Barney Sherry *(Gen. Lee)*, Frank Andrews *(Gen. Griffin)*.

Director Clifton's remake of Cecil B. DeMille's pioneer motion picture is little more than an average Civil War programmer. The acting is also uninspired, which contributes to the whole production lacking snap. Its leading lady, Mansfield (who in 1920 played opposite John Barrymore in DR. JEKYLL AND MR. HYDE), was killed when her dress ignited during a fire sequence in this picture. It was a double tragedy because she was one of the film's few bright spots and showed promise.

d, Elmer Clifton; w, William C. DeMille (based on his own motion picture and play).

War/Romance **(PR:A MPAA:NR)**

WAS IT BIGAMY?* (1925) 5 reels William Steiner bw

Edith Thornton *(Ruth Steele)*, Earle Williams *(Carleton)*, Thomas Ricketts *(Judge Gaynor)*, Charles Cruz *(Harvey Gaynor)*, Wilfred Lucas *(Attorney)*, Natalie Warfield.

Horrible hokum has Thornton marrying for love and then committing bigamy with a wealthy rotter in order to aid her impoverished guardian. Everything about this film is substandard, including the South American set which is used as an excuse to have a jealous native kill her second "husband," and thus provide the expected B movie happy ending.

d, Charles Hutchinson; w, John Francis Natteford (based on a story by Forrest Sheldon); ph, Ernest Miller.

Drama **(PR:A MPAA:NR)**

WASHINGTON AT VALLEY FORGE*** (1914) 4 reels UNIV bw

Francis Ford *(George Washington)*, Grace Cunard *(Betty)*.

Francis Ford (John's older brother) wrote, directed, and played the father of his country in this interesting mini-spectacular which depicts the Minutemen, Paul Revere's ride, Lafayette's arrival, plenty of military encounters, and an innkeeper's daughter giving her life by switching rooms to take the knife the British intended for General Washington.

d&w, Francis Ford, Grace Cunard.

Historical **(PR:A MPAA:NR)**

WASTED LIVES* (1925) 6 reels BAN/Ginsberg bw

Elliott Dexter *(Harold Graypon)*, Edith Roberts *(Tommy Carlton)*, Cullen Landis, Betty Francisco, Henry Hull.

Wealthy Dexter takes the pretty but tomboyish Roberts under his wing after her brother's tragic death. At a society bash, the nonconforming girl completely outrages the guests by arriving in overalls, and is ordered to leave. Roberts moves to a shack in the mountains, becomes a successful maker of rustic furniture, and ultimately wins the love of Dexter.

p, George H. Davis, Samuel J. Briskin; d, John Gorman; w, Van A. James, Maude P. Kelso.

Drama **(PR:A MPAA:NR)**

WATCH HIM STEP** (1922) 5 reels Phil Goldstone bw

Richard Talmadge *(Dick Underwood)*, Ethel Shannon *(Dorothy Travers)*, Al Filson *(John Travers)*, Nellie Peck Saunders *(Mrs. John Travers)*, Colin Kenny *(Jack Allen)*, Hugh Saxon *(The Uncle)*.

Frugal production values, poor direction and scripting, as well as the inclusion of forced slapstick comedy bits, greatly hamper this Talmadge feature which has the hero proving his rival to be a crook, and overcoming the objections of his future father-in-law. Talmadge of course dazzles with his stunt work, and that's the real reason for watching the movie anyway.

d, Jack Nelson; w, W. Scott Darling; ph, Hal Mohr.

Adventure/Romance **(PR:A MPAA:NR)**

WATCH YOUR STEP*** (1922) 5 reels Goldwyn bw

Cullen Landis *(Elmer Slocum)*, Patsy Ruth Miller *(Margaret Andrews)*, Bert Woodruff *(Russ Weaver)*, George Pierce *(Lark Andrews)*, Raymond Cannon *(Lon Kimball)*, Gus Leonard *(Jennifer Kimball)*, Henry Rattenbury *(Constable)*, Joel Day *(Ky Wilson)*, L. J. O'Connor *(Detective Ryan)*, John Cossar *(Henry Slocum)*, Lillian

Sylvester *(Mrs. Spivey)*, L. H. King *(Lote Spivey)*, Cordelia Callahan *(Mrs. Andrews)*, Alberta Lee *(Mrs. Weaver)*.

Well-acted and-directed dramatic comedy has wealthy Landis believing he has killed a motorcop after knocking him down while speeding to get a doctor to an emergency. Landis escapes to a small town where he settles down and falls in love with Miller. Cannon, a rival for the affections of the young lady, becomes suspicious of the newcomer, and is more than a little happy when a private detective hired by his father is able to trace Landis' connection to the hit-and-run incident. In the end it is revealed that the policeman was not seriously injured, and Landis wins the love of Miller, as well as her hand in marriage.

d, William Beaudine; w, Julien Josephson; ph, John J. Mescall.

Comedy/Drama **(PR:A MPAA:NR)**

WATCH YOUR WIFE** (1926) 7 reels UNIV bw

Virginia Valli *(Claudia Langham)*, Pat O'Malley *(James Langham)*, Nat Carr *(Benjamin Harris)*, Helen Lee Worthing *(Gladys Moon)*, Albert Conti *(Alphonse Marsac)*, Aggie Herring *(Mme. Buff)*, Nora Hayden *(Maid)*.

Domestic comedy has writer O'Malley divorcing wealthy Valli, and hiring a "wife" (played by Ziegfeld beauty Worthing) to do his housework and cooking. When Valli sees them together, she assumes the worst and accepts the proposal of fortune hunter Conti. O'Malley learns of this, abducts Valli from a fast-moving train, tells her that his love has never ceased, and the couple decide to start all over again. This picture is diverting and even has its moments. The problem is there just aren't enough of them.

d, Svend Gade; w, Charles E. Whittaker, Gade (based on a story by Gosta Segercrantz); ph, Arthur L. Todd.

Dramatic Comedy **(PR:A MPAA:NR)**

WATCHING EYES* (1921) 5 reels Frazer/Arrow bw

Kiki the Dog, Edna Beaumont *(Evelyn Selby)*, Geoffrey H. Mallins *(Adam Dewey)*, John Wickens *(Clayton Miles)*.

Strange movie featuring a canine is not geared, as one would expect, to the kid's market—a la Rin-Tin-Tin and Strongheart—but plays instead to an adult audience. The story has Kiki, a trained Pomeranian, preventing its mistress from running off with a man who is after her fortune, and then bringing her to the realization that her original suitor is really the fellow for her.

w, Robert Blaine.

Drama **(PR:A MPAA:NR)**

WAY DOWN EAST**** (1920) 13 reels D.W. Griffith/UA bw

Lillian Gish *(Anna More)*, Mrs. David Landau *(Her Mother)*, Josephine Bernard *(Mrs. Tremont)*, Mrs. Morgan Belmont *(Diana Tremont)*, Patricia Fruen *(Her Sister)*, Florence Short *(The Eccentric Aunt)*, Lowell Sherman *(Lennox Sanderson)*, Burr McIntosh *(Squire Bartlett)*, Kate Bruce *(Mrs. Bartlett)*, Richard Barthelmess *(David Bartlett)*, Vivia Ogden *(Martha Perkins)*, Porter Strong *(Seth Holcomb)*, George Neville *(Reuben Whipple)*, Edgar Nelson *(Hi Holler)*, Mary Hay *(Kate Brewster)*, Creighton Hale *(Prof. Sterling)*, Emily Fitzroy *(Maria Poole)*, Una Merkel, Norma Shearer *(Extra)*.

WAY DOWN EAST, D.W. Griffith's second biggest money maker next to THE BIRTH OF A NATION, is remarkable for a number of reasons. The director shocked the industry by paying a record $175,000 (twice the cost of BIRTH OF A NATION) for the rights to this ancient Lottie Blair Parker melodrama which was first presented on the stage in 1898, and then hired Anthony Paul Kelly, for an additonal $3,000, to adapt it. This was, incidentally, the first time Griffith ever worked with a scenario. He also broke new ground for the industry by taking out insurance policies on the cast and weather. Gish passed with flying colors, but Barthelmess was discovered to possess a sinus condition, and Clarine Seymour was diagnosed as having "a problem." She would tragically die of intestinal complications during the shooting, and Hay, a dancer who resembled the actress, took her place. (She and Barthelmess were later married.) To be sure, the story did creak loudly, but Griffith took the nostalgia it possessed, obtained masterful performances from his principal players, turned the shortcomings of plot to his advantage, and created a motion picture of unparalleled beauty. The story had to do with a lovely but unworldly girl (Gish), who is tricked into a mock marriage by a wealthy playboy (portrayed by Sherman, in his finest performance). Time passes, Sherman grows bored with his little toy, and when he's told that she's pregnant, the cad simply deserts her by returning to the city. This leads to one of Gish's most moving moments before the camera. She is baptizing her dreadfully ill baby, clinging to the hope that it will survive. Then she is told that the infant is dead. She just stares straight ahead, rocking back and forth, moving her head slowly from left to right. Suddenly she goes into what can best be described as a catatonic seizure. It is an experience of extraordinary power, and one which could only have been created by an actress and a director who possessed an almost mystical artistic rapport. Having overcome this tragedy, Gish moves on and finds work on a farm owned by Barthelmess' family, who come to regard her with kindly affection. But things become complicated for the hapless Gish once again, when it turns out that the neighboring estate is owned by the family of Sherman, who is interested in Gish's employer's niece, Hay, and begins to spend a lot of time on the farm. Meanwhile, Barthelmess has fallen in love with Gish, but feeling unworthy of him she refuses to make a commitment. Then all hell breaks loose. Fitzroy, Gish's former landlady, arrives in town for a visit, spots the girl doing her shopping, and quickly spreads the story of how the girl had a baby and "there weren't no father!" At the big barn dance, Barthelmess' father, McIntosh, is told this gossip, and makes a visit to Fitzroy. He returns with his puritanical blood boiling, and orders Gish out of the house. Before leaving the girl condemns Sherman, who happens to be a guest, and then disappears into a blizzard. Barthelmess lunges at Sherman and throws him out of the house as well. What then follows are the film's most celebrated scenes as the dazed and disoriented Gish wanders through the storm, her eyes almost frozen shut until she collapses onto the frozen river, just as the ice is starting to break up. Searching for her is Barthelmess, lantern in hand. But already the poor young woman is unconscious on a slab of ice, which is slowly beginning to make its way towards the waterfalls. The young man spots her, however, and in one of the most thrilling scenes ever, Barthelmess leaps from one ice block to the next, often stumbling until he reaches Gish and pulls her to safety just before her own cake goes flying over the falls. With the truth finally out, McIntosh begs Gish's forgiveness and there is a wedding, but not before Barthelmess gives Sherman the beating he deserves. The blizzard was shot in March near Griffith's studio at Orienta Point in Mamaroneck, New York, after waiting all winter for it to arrive, and most of the ice footage was shot in zero weather at River Junction, Vermont, where Barthelmess and Gish literally put their lives on the line. That last great moment, where the resuce is executed was filmed, however, in the summer at Farmington, Connecticut, where Griffith skillfully used wooden blocks, painted to look like ice. There have been those who have, in the past, judged this film to be little more than slick melodrama. It is actually rather like a Currier and Ives painting come to life. And with the exception of some embarrassing comedy touches (this was always Griffith's weak suit) the film can—and does—hold its own with any.

p&d, D. W. Griffith; w, Anthony Paul Kelly, Griffith (based on the play by Lottie Blair Parker, Joseph R. Grismer); ph, G. W. Bitzer, Hendrik Sartov; m, Louis Silvers, William F. Peters; ed, James and Rose Smith; art d, Charles O. Seessel, Clifford Pember; cos, Lady Duff Gordon, O'Kane Cromwell.

Drama **Cas.** **(PR:A MPAA:NR)**

WAY OF A MAID, THE** ½ (1921) 5 reels SF/SEL bw

Elaine Hammerstein *(Naida Castleton)*, Niles Welch *(Thomas Lawlor)*, Diana Allen *(Dorothy Graham)*, Charles D. Brown *(Gordon Witherspoon)*, George Fawcett *(David Lawlor)*, Arthur Housman *(Jimmy Van Trent)*, Helen Lindroth *(Mrs. Lawlor)*.

Far-fetched but agreeable programmer has wealthy Hammerstein winning first prize at a costume party dressed as a maid. That night at a girl friend's apartment, Welch, a young candy manufacturing millionaire from Peoria, thinks her to be a domestic and asks for some towels, as well as her phone number. In the spirit of fun, she delivers both. A short time later, he moves to New York with his socially ambitious mother and calls Hammerstein and offers her the positon of companion to the woman. Because her family recently lost everything, she accepts the offer and finds herself working at Welch's old ancestral estate on Long Island. Naturally, before long, Welch discovers the young lady's true identity and it's wedding bells for the young couple, and a satisfactory conclusion for everyone else involved.

d, William P. S. Earle; w, Lewis Allen Browne (based on a story by Rex Taylor); ph, William Wagner.

Dramatic Comedy **(PR:A MPAA:NR)**

WAY OF A WOMAN*** (1919) 5 reels Norma Talmadge/SEL bw

Norma Talmadge *(Nancy Lee)*, Conway Tearle *(Anthony Weir)*, Gertrude Berkeley *(Mrs. Lee)*, May McAvoy *(Grace Lee)*, Frank De Vernon *(Mr. Lee)*, Stuart Holmes *(George Trevor)*, Jobyna Howland *(Mollie Wise)*, Hassard Short *(Johnnie Flinch)*, George Trevor), Jobyna Howland *(Mollie Wide)*, Hassard Short *(Johnnie Flinch)*, George Le Guere *(Douglas Weir)*, William Humphrey *(Nathan Casper)*.

Handsomely produced, well-directed and-acted dramatic comedy has Talmadge playing an impoverished Southern girl who comes to New York in order to support her family back home. She marries a millionaire instead of the fellow she really loves, and after the old boy dies, the fun starts as Talmadge tries every trick in the book to win her man back—and of course does.

d, Robert Z. Leonard; w, (based on the play "Nancy Lee" by Eugene Walter); ph, David Abel.

Drama/Comedy **(PR:A MPAA:NR)**

WAY OF ALL FLESH, THE**** (1927) 9 reels PAR bw

Emil Jannings *(August Schiller)*, Belle Bennett *(Mrs. Schiller)*, Phyllis Haver *(Mayme)*, Donald Keith *(August, Junior)*, Fred Kohler *(The Tough)*, Philippe De Lacey *(August, as a Child)*, Mickey McBan *(Evald)*, Betsy Ann Lisle *(Charlotte)*, Carmencita Johnson *(Elizabeth)*, Gordon Thorpe *(Karl)*, Jackie Coombs *(Heinrich)*, Dean Harrell, Anne Sheridan, Dorothy Kitchen.

Under Victor Fleming's sensitive direction, Jannings' first American film was a commercial and artistic triumph (he won the first Academy Award, for this and his performance in THE LAST COMMAND). It's the story of a Milwaukee bank clerk—a devoted husband and father—who leaves home for the first time since his honeymoon, to deliver a packet of bonds to Chicago. On the train he encounters Haver, a saucy flapper who gets him drunk and steals the packet. When she brings her boy friend in to apply a little muscle, Jannings struggles with the goon, who is killed by an onrushing train. The banker changes clothes with the crook and his family's honor is protected when the authorities report his heroic death. Years pass, and the poor devil sinks lower and lower, until he ends up a pathetic derelict. Then one day he discovers that his oldest son has become a world renowned classical violinist, and he panhandles enough to buy a ticket in the gallery to listen to him perform. Curiously, the great German actor's initial American success, the UFA production of THE LAST LAUGH, was not allowed to end on a sad note (because the producers believed it would turn off audiences on this side of the ocean), whereas this film's denouement shows the pathetic figure of the once proud man sneaking a look at his beloved family through the window of the house he once owned on a blustery Christmas day.

d, Victor Fleming; w, Jules Furthman, Lajos Biro (based on the story by Perley Poore Sheehan); t, Julian Johnson; ph, Victor Milner.

Drama **(PR:A MPAA:NR)**

WAY OF AN EAGLE, THE** (1918, Brit.) 7 reels G.B. Samuelson/Sun bw

Isobel Elsom *(Muriel Roscoe)*, Andre Beaulieu *(Nick Ratcliffe)*, Odette Goimbault *(Olga)*, Mary Dibley *(Daisy Musgrave)*, Annie Esmond *(Lady Barrett)*.

British wartime adventure set in occupied India has a younger soldier saving the garrison from attack, winning the respect of the colonel, and being rewarded by his lovely daughter's hand in marriage.

d, G. B. Samuelson; w, (based on the novel by Ethel M. Dell).

War **(PR:A MPAA:NR)**

WAY OF THE STRONG, THE*** (1928) 6 reels COL bw

Mitchell Lewis *(Handsome Williams)*, Alice Day *(Nora)*, Margaret Livingston *(Marie)*, Theodore von Eltz *(Dan)*, William Norton Bailey *(Tiger Louie)*.

The brilliant comedy director, Capra, was just beginning to experiment with serious themes (he had contracted with Harry Cohn's lowly Columbia Studio after being given the boot by Harry Langdon at First National) when he made this satisfactory melodrama. It told of an ugly racketeer (Lewis) who sacrifices his life in order that the blind girl he loves (Day) might find happiness with the piano player to whom she is attracted. The Capra touch is evident even in ths low-budget affair.

p, Harry Cohn; d, Frank Capra; w, Peter Milne (based on a story by William Conselman); ph, Ben Reynolds.

Crime/Drama **(PR:A MPAA:NR)**

WEALTH** (1921) 5 reels FP/PAR bw

Ethel Clayton *(Mary McLeod)*, Herbert Rawlinson *(Phillip Dominick)*, J. M. Dumont *(Gordon Townsend)*, Lawrence Steers *(Oliver Marshall)*, George Periolat *(Irving Seaton)*, Claire McDowell *(Mrs. Dominick)*, Jean Acker *(Estelle Rolland)*, Richard Wayne *(Dr. Howard)*.

Good production values fail to elevate this tear-jerker beyond the programmer class. Rawlinson plays a wealthy young man who falls in love with and marries Clayton, a struggling artist, and incurs the wrath of his snobbish mother, McDowell, who wanted him to marry a socialite. He remains financially dependent on her until the death of the couple's baby, at which point Rawlinson sets out with his bride to make it on his own.

d, William Desmond Taylor; w, Julia Crawford Ivers (based on a story by Cosmo Hamilton); ph, James C. Van Trees.

Drama **(PR:A MPAA:NR)**

WEAVERS OF FORTUNE* ½ (1922, Brit.) 6 reels I.B. Davidson/Granger bw

Henry Vibart *(Jackson)*, Dacia *(Minna Vandyck)*, Derek Glynne *(Tom Winter)*, Myrtle Vibart *(Molly Jackson)*.

It's the old win-the-big-race-in-the-last-reel formula, only this time the story involves a young chap who is thrown out of school, buys a nag, goes into the cartage business, and then trains his animal to pull off the expected miracle.

d, Arthur Rooke; w, Kinchen Wood.

Adventure **(PR:A MPAA:NR)**

WEB OF FATE** (1927) 6 reels Dallas M. Fitzgerald/PEER bw

Lillian Rich *(Gloria Gunther/Beverly Townsend)*, Henry Sedley *(Linton)*, Eugene Strong *(Don Eddington)*, John Cossar *(Carlton Townsend)*, Frances Raymond *(Mrs. Townsend)*, Edwin Coxen.

Rich does well in a double role as a nasty actress and the sweet small-town girl who substitutes for her when she is badly scarred in a fire. The film's villain is murdered and the "good kid" is blamed, but fortunately the actress confesses to the crime in the last reel and her look-alike is free to marry the millionaire she loves.

d, Dallas M. Fitzgerald; w, Gladys Gordon, Ada McQuillan (based on a story by Willard King Bradley); t, Gardner Bradford; ph, Milton Moore; ed, Desmond O'Brien.

Drama **(PR:A MPAA:NR)**

WEB OF THE LAW, THE* ½
(1923) 5 reels Gibson-Dyer Ranger/American Releasing bw

Ranger Bill Miller *(Bill Barton)*, Patricia Palmer *(Mollie Barbee)*, George Sherwood *("Wolf" Blake)*, Harry Belmour *(Buck Barbee)*, Alfred Heuston *(Jasper Leveen)*, Jean Walsh *("Slim" Easton)*, Barry Jackson *("Sundown" Brown)*, Frank Cutter *("Squint" Castile)*.

Real-life Texas Ranger Miller is featured in this low-budget film about a lawman who takes an undercover job with a rancher who has been victimized by rustlers. Before long, Miller falls in love with the old gent's daughter, rescues her from the outlaws who abducted her, and brings the gang to justice before they can reach the Mexican border.

d, Tom Gibson; w, Victor Gibson; ph, Elmer G. Dyer.

Western **(PR:A MPAA:NR)**

WEDDING BILL$*** ½ (1927) 6 reels PAR bw

Raymond Griffith *(Algernon Schuyler Van Twidder)*, Anne Sheridan *(Miss Bruce)*, Hallam Cooley *(Tom Milbank)*, Iris Stuart *(Miss Markham)*, Vivian Oakland *(Mlle. Mimi de Lyle)*, Tom S. Guise *(Mr. Markham)*, Louis Stern *(Judson)*, Edgar Kennedy *(Detective)*, John Steppling *(District Attorney)*.

Griffith combines his suave persona with the type of stunt comedy which "human fly" Harold Lloyd made famous in SAFETY LAST (1923), and the result is hilarious. As a perpetual best man, Griffith comes to the rescue of a pal whose former paramour, a Russian dancer, threatens to produce some steamy love letters on the day of his wedding unless a certain necklace worth $20,000 is produced. By arranging with the jeweler to take the piece out on approval, Griffith plans to give it to the vamp and then steal it back in time for its 5 p.m. return. But through happenstance, the gem ends up around the neck of one of the ceremonial pigeons, which then escapes and becomes the object of a very cleverly conceived series of chase sequences. Griffith follows the bird in his auto up narrow, winding mountain roads, through traffic-cluttered city streets, and finally to the top of several mile-high buildings, where after plenty of breathtaking experiences, the comedian not only manages to get the necklace back, but at last finds *himself* in the position of becoming a future groom.

p, B. P. Schulberg; d, Erle Kenton; w, Grover Jones, Keene Thompson, Lloyd Corrigan; t, George Marion, Jr.; ph, William Marshall.

Comedy **(PR:A MPAA:NR)**

WEDDING MARCH, THE**** (1927) 11 reels PAR bw-c

Erich von Stroheim *(Prince Nikki/Von Wildiebe-Rauffenburg)*, Fay Wray *(Mitzi Schrammell)*, ZaSu Pitts *(Cecelia Schweisser)*, Matthew Betz *(Schani Eberle)*, George Fawcett *(Prince von Wildliebe-Rauffenburg)*, Maude George *(Princess Maria Immaculata)*, George Nichols *(Fortunat Schweisser)*, Dale Fuller *(Katerina, Mitzi's Mother)*, Cesare Gravina *(Martin Schrammel, Mitzi's Father)*, Hughie Mack *(Schani's Father)*, Lucille van Lent *(Maid to Prince Nikki)*, Lurie Weiss *(Maid to Cecelia)*, Anton Vaverka *(Emperor Franz Joseph)*, Sidney Bracey *(Navratil, Nikki's Valet)*, Don Ryan *(Archduke Leopold Salvator)*, Carolynne Snowden *(Black Servant at Brothel)*, Danny Hoy *(Mountain Idiot)*, Lulee Wilson *(Servant)*, Capt. John Peters, Capt. Peter von Hartman, Carey Harrison, Mme. Ernestine Schumann-Heink, Harry Rinehardt, Albert Conti, Wilhelm von Brincken *(Officers of the Imperial Guard)*.

Fed up with the major studios which constantly tampered with his work, Von Stroheim was tempted to accept an offer to direct a film starring Peggy Hopkins Joyce, the lady friend of successful independent film producer Pat Powers. Before long, however, the director had talked the Irishman into producing instead a picture dealing with Vienna in the glorious days of the Empire. He would now make the picture he intended MERRY-GO-ROUND to be, before Irving Thalberg took it out of his hands and turned it over to the "hack" Rupert Julien. Von Stroheim, who had an affinity for Irishmen (almost all of his close friends were Celts) was delighted with the arrangement, and he went immediately to work on the script with his collaborator, Harry Carr. An interesting insight into the working methods of the Austrian genius can be found in an excerpt from an article Carr wrote for *Photoplay* magazine in 1928: "In the story there was to be a motherless girl. Von said he couldn't write about a motherless girl—unless he knew what her mother was like. So we had to sit down and spend days manufacturing the life story of a woman who was never intended to appear in the story. We told how she fell in love with her husband; their early struggles together; the coming of wealth; his temptations; and her sorrow. Finally her illness and death. Actually, Von made me invent a placard to be placed outside her house when she was dying: 'Please walk your horses quietly through the street: serious illness within.' And he translated it into German. And—mind you—this woman was never to appear in the story. 'Now,' said Von, when we properly killed the lady off, 'I know what the girl is like.' " With the script completed (in a record few weeks) the production got under way, and the film opens in the manner of many of the director's works, with Prince Nikki (Von Stroheim) getting out of bed ("So you'll know what he is when you see him on the throne") to prepare to ride in the feast of Corpus Christi, as a guard to the emperor. Before embarking, he tries to put the touch on his parents, but their response is "Blow your brains out—or marry money." Later, while lining up for the procession in front of St. Stephen's Cathedral, he sees the beautiful Mitzi (Wray) in the crowd. She is with her parents and Betz, a sadistic butcher. There is an immediate attraction between the nobleman and the peasant girl. (A development which does not go unnoticed by the aristocracy-hating Betz, who is in love with Wray.) Then, in a remarkable sequence using 200 shots, Von Stroheim establishes the mutual feelings they sense for each other (without once placing them in the same frame) which culminates in Wray placing a small bouquet in the prince's boot. At this point his horse rears up and comes crashing down upon the girl's foot. Betz angrily lunges for Von Stroheim, but is arrested as Wray is taken to the hospital. The procession then gets under way and, with the director's meticulous sense of detail, all of the pomp and circumstance which existed in Von Stroheim's mind's eye was filmed in technicolor. The next day, Von Stroheim calls upon Wray at the infirmary but hides his royal identity. "Lets make it plain—Nikki," the title reads. After her release, he calls on her at the wine garden run by her parents, and where Wray plays the harp. The couple then go to the Danube, where she tells him about the Iron Man and Danube maids, which symbolize evil and good. The scene ends at the apple bower, where Von Stroheim closes the sequence with his most tenderly romantic moment, as white blossoms fall upon the sweethearts. He then spends most of his time at a brothel catering to the wealthy but leaves early one night to be with Wray. Here the director brilliantly cross cuts between images of the lovers and the whorehouse, where Von Stroheim's father (Fawcett) drunkenly cuts a deal to have his son marry the crippled daughter (Pitts) of a social-climbing, corn-plaster magnate. When their orgy reaches the point where they begin to perform a slobbering parody of the wedding procession, Von Stroheim cuts back to Wray, who sees the specter of the Iron Man and its warning of doom. A dog sees it as well, and his barking awakens Betz, who has been released from jail. In a rage, he attacks Von Stroheim but is thrown into a pig sty. Wray goes to the cathedral to confess her seduction, and Von Stroheim depicts her absolution through a series of beautifully executed cinematic images. Meanwhile, the marriage between Von Stroheim and Pitts takes place, and Betz swears to kill the prince unless Wray will agree to marry him. She does, but at their service, Wray faints, which causes the butcher to take off for Von Stroheim's honeymoon lodge to finish him off for good. Wray arrives in time to warn Von Stroheim, yet it is the lame bride who jumps in front of the bullet. Betz is once again taken in custody, and Pitts, who survives, is told that she must remain absolutely still if she wishes to recover.

However, the gentle soul is aware of her husband's love for Wray, and she drags herself over to a giant crucifix, where she expires. Von Stroheim then returns to Vienna, but when he finds the wine garden closed he spends a great deal of time at the brothel. When war is declared, he joins the army and is attached to a patrol which is put in charge of destroying a gang of renegades who are terrorizing the Serbian border. Wray has entered the convent of the Sisters of the Bleeding Heart, and when they are attacked by the bandits (one of whom is Betz), Von Stroheim arrives in time to save his sweetheart from Betz' lust. They are married at the altar of the convent and, as Von Stroheim rides off at the head of his troops he yells, "Nobody can say—we didn't have a lot of music—such as it was." Von Stroheim had wanted to release this as a two-part picture, THE WEDDING MARCH and THE HONEYMOON—but Powers had run out of patience, and Paramount, who had become involved, decided to call it quits. The Austrain agreed to cut the film and deliver his feature with what footage he had, so, along with Frank Hull, he spent seven months editing the material. In 1928, Von Stroheim had this to say in the *Exhibitors Herald-World:* "On October 8, however, I was suddently taken off the film. B. P. Schulberg announced that he was suddenly turning the editing of the picture over to Josef von Sternberg, who, he stated, would edit the picture in two weeks time. Instead, Von Sternberg spent several weeks on the editing and then his version proved so unsatisfactory to Paramount that they took the picture away from him and turned it over to Julian Johnston for a new editing." The film, still very much a Von Stroheim work, opened to some success in New York (a truncated version of THE HONEYMOON, played in Europe but was never shown commercially in the U.S.) but the highly sophisticated and ribald content of THE WEDDING MARCH, combined with the new craze for talking pictures, doomed Von Stroheim's salute to old Vienna to failure in the provinces. It's a shame, because the director and his dream deserved much better.

p, P. A. Powers; d, Erich von Stroheim; w, Von Stroheim, Harry Carr; ph, Hal Mohr, Ben Reynolds, Bill McGann, Harry Thorpe, Roy Klaffki; m, J. S. Zamecnik, Louis de Francesco; ed, Frank Hull, Josef von Sternberg, Julian Johnston; art d, Richard Day, Von Stroheim; cos, Max Ree; m/l, "Paradise" by Harry D. Kerr, Zamecnik; syn sc; s eff.

Drama (PR:A MPAA:NR)

WEDDING SONG, THE*** (1925) 7 reels Cinema Corp. of America/PDC bw

Leatrice Joy *(Beatrice Glynn)*, Robert Ames *(Hayes Hallan)*, Charles Gerard *(Paul Glynn)*, Ruby Lafayette *("Mother")*, Rosa Rudami *(Ethea)*, Gertrude Claire *(Grandma)*, Ethel Wales *(Auntie)*, Gladden James *(Jeffrey King)*, Casson Ferguson *(Madison Melliah)*, Jack Curtis, Clarence Burton.

All around superior programmer has Joy (in fine form) playing a confidence woman who marries Ames, the owner of a tropical island rich in offshore pearls. The couple move to the island, along with her partners, who pass themselves off as a "family." The group is caught by Ames as they try to rob his safe, and all are ordered to leave. Joy, however, learns that a bomb has been placed under her husband's house, and at the risk of her own life, throws it over the side of a cliff at the last moment. The avalanche caused by the explosion kills the departing crooks, while the grateful owner of the island, realizing that his wife *does* love him, welcomes her back home.

d, Alan Hale; sup, Cecil B. DeMille; w, Charles E. Whittaker, Douglas Doty (based on the novel by Ethel Watts Mumford); t, George Marion, Jr.

Drama (PR:A MPAA:NR)

WEEKEND WIVES* (1928, Brit.) 7 reels BIP/Wardour bw

Monty Banks *(Amman)*, Jameson Thomas *(Henri Monard)*, Estelle Brody *(Gaby le Grand)*, Annette Benson *(Helene Monard)*, George Gee *(Mons le Grand)*, Ernest Thesiger *(Bertram)* Bebe Brune-Taylor *(Yvette)*.

Banks was capable of delivering laughs under the right direction, and made a couple of funny films in the U.S., but this Lachman-directed creaker about a divorce-bound couple who inadvertently spend the weekend at the same resort with their "lovers" and then go through a series of changes to avoid the detection of this, falls completely flat.

d, Harry Lachman; w, Victor Kendall, Rex Taylor (based on a story by Kendall); syn sc.

Comedy (PR:A MPAA:NR)

WELCOME CHILDREN* (1921) 5 reels Drascena/National Exchanges bw

Elsie Albert *(Mary Ellen Martin)*, Graham Griffiths *(Joey Martin)*, Doughboy *(Doughboy Martin)*, Dumplings *(Dumplings Martin)*, Sidney Franklin *(Isaac Cohen)*, Orpha Alba *(Rebecca Cohen)*, George Sherwood *(Dr. Randall)*.

When their farm is stolen after her mother's death, Albert moves her brood of brothers and sisters to the city. Unable to find an apartment because "children ain't allowed," the young lady sneaks them into a flat, where they find themselves involved in a robbery attempt. Albert's group helps to save the day, and all ends well when one of their neighbors, a medical doctor, asks her to become his bride and bring the crowd along on the honeymoon.

d, Harry C. Mathews.

Drama (PR:A MPAA:NR)

WELCOME STRANGER*½** (1924) 7 reels Belasco/PDC bw

Dore Davidson *(Isadore Solomon)*, Florence Vidor *(Mary Clark)*, Virginia Brown Faire *(Essie Solomon)*, Noah Beery *(Icabod Whitson)*, Lloyd Hughes *(Ned Tyler)*, Robert Edeson *(Eb Hooker)*, William V. Mong *(Clem Beemis)*, Otis Harlan *(Seth Trimble)*, Fred J. Butler *(Gideon Tyler)*, Pat Hartigan *(Detective)*.

Gratifying production on every level has Davidson, a Jew, being driven out of a small New England town when he attempts to open a store there. He and Vidor, another less-than-welcome newcomer, are befriended by Mong, a local handyman and inventor, who convinces them to invest in a project he is working on. This results in the village getting its first electrical power and trolley car system, and Davidson and Vidor are later honored by the townspeople. Vidor then accepts the marriage proposal of Hughes, the banker's fine son, who did his part from the beginning.

d, James Young; w, Willard Mack, Young (based on the play by Aaron Hoffman); t, Katherine Hilliker, H. H. Caldwell; ph, George Benoit.

Dramatic Comedy (PR:A MPAA:NR)

WE'RE ALL GAMBLERS* (1927) 7 reels PAR bw

Thomas Meighan *(Lucky Sam McCarver)*, Mariette Millner *(Carlotta Asche)*, Cullen Landis *(Georgie McCarver)*, Philo McCullough *(Monty Garside)*, Gertrude Claire *(Mrs. McCarver)*, Gunboat Smith *(Gunboat)*, Spec O'Donnell *(Spec)*.

Inferior script (showing little resemblance to the original play) and surprisingly poor direction by Cruze, make it impossible for the cast to do anything with this banal nonsense about a prizefighter (Meighan) who falls in love with a society girl (Millner), opens a nighclub where he plays sentimental songs for her on the piano, and finally wins her devotion by taking the blame for her on a murder charge. It all works out in the end, and the couple manage to get together—but it hardly seems to matter at this point.

d, James Cruze; sup, Lucien Hubbard; w, Hope Loring (based on the play "Lucky Sam McCarver, Four Episodes in the Life of a New Yorker" by Sidney Howard); t, Jack Conway; ph, Bert Glennon.

Drama (PR:A MPAA:NR)

WELSH SINGER, A* (1915, Brit.) 5 reels Turner/BUT bw

Florence Turner *(Mifanwy)*, Henry Edwards *(Leuan)*, Campbell Gullan *(Tom Pomfrey)*, Malcolm Cherry *(John Powys)*, Una Venning *(Laissabeth Powys)*, Fred Raines *(Music Master)*, Edith Evans *(Mrs. Pomfrey)*.

U.S. film star Turner may have given second thoughts to making pictures in England when she first set eyes on this script, which takes place in Wales and tells the story of a shepherd who becomes a world famous sculptor and a shepherdess who sings her way to fame in the opera.

d, Henry Edwards; w, Larry Trimble, Edwards (based on a novel by Allen Raine).

Drama (PR:A MPAA:NR)

WEST OF CHICAGO*** (1922) 5 reels FOX bw

Charles Jones *(Conroy Daly)*, Renee Adoree *(Della Moore)*, Philo McCullough *(John Hampton)*, Sidney D'Albrook *(English Kid)*, Charles French *(Judson Malone)*, Marcella Daly *(Patricia Daly)*, Kathleen Key *(Señorita Gonzales)*.

Good "Buck" Jones feature has the cowboy star playing a young Eastern cutup, who because of his numerous pranks is sent West to become a man. Upon reaching his uncle's ranch, he's told that the old boy has been murdered, so Jones sets out to solve the mystery. In the end, he not only brings the villain who was out to steal the spread to justice, but wins the love of the wrongly accused fellow's sister, and then—to the delight of all—discovers that his uncle is still alive.

d, Scott Dunlap, C. R. Wallace; w, Paul Schofield (based on a story by George Scarborough); ph, Lucien Androit.

Western Drama (PR:A MPAA:NR)

WEST OF SANTA FE*½ (1928) 5 reels ED/Syndicate Pictures bw

Bob Custer *(Jack)*, Peggy Montgomery *(Helen)*, Mack V. Wright, J. P. McGowan, Bud Osborne.

Penny-pinching western production has Custer preventing a gang from cheating a female rancher (Montgomery) out of her horses by posing as an army-purchasing detachment. After some little action, Custer also rescues the real major, who has been held captive, rounds up the bad guys, and wins the grateful love of the girl.

d, J. P. McGowan; w, Mack V. Wright (based on a story by Brysis Coleman); ph, Paul Allen.

Western (PR:A MPAA:NR)

WEST OF THE LAW*½ (1926) 5 reels Ben Wilson/RAY bw

Ben Wilson *(John Adams)*, Neva Gerber *(Alice Armstrong)*, Ashton Dearholt *(Frank Armstrong)*, Hal Walters *(Dick Walton)*, Cliff Lyons *(Sheriff)*, Lafe McKee *(Jim Armstrong)*, Al Ferguson *(Surly Dorgan)*, Myrna Thompson *(Phyllis Parker)*, Fang the Dog.

Wilson saves Gerber, the girl he loves, from death, covers her brother Dearholt's gambling debts, and snares a gang of rustlers who have framed him. Then he unselfishly rides off into the sunset with his dog, Fang, when he comes to realize that Gerber really cares for a young fellow from the East. What a man!

d, Ben Wilson.

Western (PR:A MPAA:NR)

WEST OF THE RAINBOW'S END** (1926) 5 reels George Blaisdell/RAY bw

Jack Perrin *(Don Brandon)*, Pauline Curley *(Daisy Kent)*, Billy Lamar *(Red)*, Tom London *(Harry Palmer)*, James Welch *(Abe Brandon)*, Milburn Morante *(Tim)*, Whitehorse *(Tom Palmer)*, Starlight the Horse, Rex the Dog.

Perrin returns from WW I to find his father murdered and his ranch stolen. For the next four reels he sets about getting it back—with the help of Morante, his comic sidekick, and little freckle-faced Lamar—and by the end not only brings the villain to justice, but wins the love of the pretty young lady who was forced to be the killer's ward.

p, Harry Webb; d, Bennett Cohn; w, Daisy Kent (based on a story by Victor Rousseau); ph, William Thornley.

Western (PR:A MPAA:NR)

WEST OF ZANZIBAR*** (1928) 7 reels MGM bw

Lon Chaney *(Flint)*, Lionel Barrymore *(Crane)*, Warner Baxter *(Doc)*, Mary Nolan *(Maizie)*, Jane Daly *(Anna)*, Roscoe Ward *(Tiny)*, Kalla Pasha *(Babe)*, Curtis Nero *(Bumbo)*, Jacquelin Gadsdon *(Anna)*.

Chaney is unforgettable as the crippled jungle lord, dragging himself throughout the atmospheric sets, dreaming only of revenge and getting it by turning Nolan, the daughter of the man who wronged him earlier, into a prostitute. In the end Chaney learns that the girl he has ruined is actually *his* own daughter, and sacrifices his life that she may escape the jungle and begin a new life with the doctor who loves her. This interesting film has flaws, but the "Man of a Thousand Faces" is not one of them.

d, Tod Browning; w, Elliott Clawson, Waldemar Young (based on a story by Chester De Vonde, Kilbourne Gordon); t, Joe Farnharm; ph, Percy Hilburn; ed, Harry Reynolds; set d, Cedric Gibbons; syn sc; s eff.

Drama (PR:A MPAA:NR)

WEST POINT*** (1928) 9 reels MGM bw

William Haines *(Brice Wayne)*, Joan Crawford *(Betty Channing)*, William Bakewell *("Tex" McNeil)*, Neil Neely *(Bob Sperry)*, Ralph Emerson *(Bob Chase)*, Leon Kellar *(Capt. Munson)*, Maj. Raymond G. Moses *(Coach Towers)*.

Director Sedgwick captures plenty of West Point atmosphere here through the use of on-location footage. And Haines plays basically the same wise-guy character who learns his lesson in the end which he popularized in SLIDE KELLY SLIDE (1927) and BROWN OF HARVARD (1926). In fact, in this film he also jettisons his obnoxious personality, quits the team, and then returns at game's end to single-handedly defeat a tough Navy football squad.

d, Edward Sedgwick; w, Raymond L. Schrock; t, Joe Farnham; ph, Ira Morgan; ed, Frank Sullivan; advisor, Maj. Raymond G. Moses, United States Military Academy.

Dramatic Comedy (PR:A MPAA:NR)

WESTBOUND* (1924) 5 reels SUN/AY bw

J.B. Warner *(Bob Lanier)*, Molly Malone *(Evelyn Vaughn)*, Mathilde Brundage *(Aunt Abigail)*, Theodore Lorch, Luis Barnes, Harry Fraser.

Warner's 10-gallon hat is the best thing about this Poverty Row oater, which was so cheaply produced that no director or writer credits were flashed on the title card. It tells of a cowboy who stages a fake robbery and kidnaping to impress an eastern girl and her aunt, but really gets the chance to score some points when the older woman is abducted and he rescues her for real.

Western (PR:A MPAA:NR)

WESTERN COURAGE*½ (1927) 5 reels Ben Wilson/RAY bw

Dick Hatton, Elsa Benham, Robert Walker, Ed La Niece, Al Ferguson.

Hatton defeats an outlaw gang to save Benham, the girl he loves, from being taken advantage of by a sharpster with whom she is smitten. Of course when the truth is revealed, the young lady realizes her error and pledges herself completely to the care of Hatton.

d, Ben Wilson; w, Leslie Curtis; ph, Eddie Linden.

Western (PR:A MPAA:NR)

WESTERN DEMON, A½** (1922) 5 reels Western Feature bw

William Fairbanks *(Ned Underwood)*, Marilyn Mills *(Rose Dale)*, Monte Montague *(Joe Dalton)*, Murray Miller *(The Bandit)*, Billy Franey *(The Cook)*.

Lots of action in this Fairbanks western, which has the hero taking an undercover job as a dishwasher at the ranch of a young lady, Mills, whose cattle are being stolen. The heavy turns out to be the foreman, and the movie ends with Fairbanks throwing him from a high-flying airplane after rescuing Mills from a bear who was locked in a cabin with her by the villain.

d, Robert McKenzie; ph, Edgar Lyons.

Western (PR:A MPAA:NR)

WESTERN FATE*½ (1924) 5 reels Wild West/Arrow bw

Dick Hatton, Neva Gerber.

Hatton had a habit of assisting eastern girls in his little low-budget westerns. In this case, the young lady is Gerber, and Hatton bruises a few knuckles while tracking down the murderer of her brother.

d, George Holt; w, George H. Plympton.

Western (PR:A MPAA:NR)

WESTERN FIREBRANDS** (1921) 5 reels Charles R. Seeling/AY bw

Big Boy Williams *(Billy Fargo)*, Virginia Adair *(Mildred Stanton)*, J. Conrad Needham *(Tom Fargo)*, William Horne *(Richard Stanton)*, Jack Pitcairn *(Victor Lanning)*, Bert Apling *(Pete Carson)*, Helen Yoder *(Red Feather)*.

Williams' likable, boyish personality is the best thing going for this modest B western, which has the big fellow winning the love of Adair, an eastern girl whose businessman father is trying to steal his lumber company. He later saves her from her dad's henchman, and after a knockdown and drag-out fight, the young lady is *sure* that he's the man for her.

d, Charles R. Seeling.

Western (PR:A MPAA:NR)

WESTERN HEARTS½** (1921) 5 reels Cliff Smith/Associated Photoplays bw

Josie Sedgwick *(Edith Caldwell)*, Art Straton *(Jack Manning)*, Floyd Taliaferro *(Pete Marcel)*, Hazel Hart *(Grace Adams)*, Edward Moncrief *(George Adams)*, Bert Wilson *(Robert Caldwell)*.

Noticeably less riding and shooting in this western drama which has Hart, a jealous cowgirl, devising a scheme to end the romance going on between Straton, a ranch hand whom she secretly loves, and an eastern girl whose father is about to take over her spread. Hart has Taliaferro, a hired hand, intercept letters exchanged between the couple, causing Straton to believe his sweetheart, Sedgwick, no longer loves him. When Sedgwick and her father arrive on the scene, they discover evidence of cattle rustling and call upon Straton's aid. He not only captures the outlaw, who turns out to be Taliaferro, but straightens everything out with Sedgwick by the end of the fifth reel.

d, Cliff Smith; w, Alvin J. Neitz, Smith; ph, Frank Cotner.

Western (PR:A MPAA:NR)

WESTERN LUCK*** (1924) 5 reels FOX bw

Charles Jones *(Larry Campbell)*, Beatrice Burnham *(Betty Gray)*, Pat Hartigan *(James Evart)*, Tom Lingham *(Lem Pearson)*, J. Farrell MacDonald *("Chuck" Campbell)*, Edith Kennick *(Mrs. Pearson)*, Bruce Gordon *(Leonard Pearson)*.

Interesting premise has two brothers separated as babies—the one being raised by his New York banker father to become a dishonest capitalist, while the other (Jones) is raised out West by a rancher. Years later, when the banker's son tries to pull a fast one and steal Jones' spread, the cowboy straightens him out and teaches him how to think like a human being, allowing for a rather touching reunion at the end.

d, George Andre Beranger; w, Robert N. Lee; ph, Joseph Brotherton.

Western Drama (PR:A MPAA:NR)

WESTERN MUSKETEER, THE**

(1922) 5 reels Long Beach Motion Pictures/TRU bw

Leo Maloney *(Ranger)*, Dixie Lamont, Gus Suvall *(Tom Wilkes)*.

The plot in this Maloney western is right off the rack, but there are a number of thrills. It all has to do with ranger Maloney protecting the girl he loves, a miner's daughter, from the lecherous advances of a villainous storekeeper who later commits a murder and is brought to justice by the ranger. But the big kick comes when Maloney saves his sweetheart from plunging to her death down what seems like an endless log chute.

d&w, William Bertram.

Western (PR:A MPAA:NR)

WESTERN ROVER, THE*½ (1927) 5 reels UNIV bw

Art Acord *(Art Hayes)*, Ena Gregory *(Millie Donlin)*, Charles Avery *(Hinkey Hall)*, William Welch *(Alexander Seaton)*, Raven the Horse, Rex the Dog.

Acord, who becomes a circus performer after a disagreement with his father, is forced to look for new work when the show closes. The ace rider lands a job on a ranch through the recommendation of Gregory, owner of the adjoining spread. Here Acord is quick to prevent the cattle from being rustled by his foreman and ushers the villain off to jail. He also manages to send the beef to market in Chicago in time to prevent the ranch owner's bankruptcy. Then, as fate would have it, the owner of the ranch turns out to be his very own father, who happily gives his blessing to a union between Gregory and his long missing son.

d, Albert Rogell; w, George C. Hively; ph, Edwin Linden; art d, David S. Garber.

Western (PR:A MPAA:NR)

WESTERN VENGEANCE* (1924) 5 reels IP bw

Franklyn Farnum *(Jack Caldwell)*, Doreen Turner *(Helen Caldwell)*, Marie Walcamp *(Mary Sterling)*, Jim Corey *(Santag)*, Martin Turner *(Luke Mosby)*, Mack V. Wright *(Dick Sterling)*, Pete the Dog.

Decidedly inferior western has mine owner Farnum fighting to protect his claim from a band of marauders and coming to the distressing realization that its leader is the brother of the woman he loves. Screenwriter Ormont provides a convenient solution to this sticky little problem, however, by having the errant lad commit suicide in the last reel.

d, J. P. McGowan; w, James Ormont; ph, Walter Griffin.

Western (PR:A MPAA:NR)

WESTERN WHIRLWIND, THE*½ (1927) 5 reels UNIV bw

Jack Hoxie *(Jack Howard)*, Margaret Quimby *(Molly Turner)*, Claude Payton *(Jeff Taylor)*, Billy Engle *("Beans" Baker)*, Edith Yorke *(Mrs. Martha Howard)*, Jack Pratt *(Jim Blake)*, Scout the Horse.

Hoxie returns home from WW I to discover that his sheriff father has been murdered by an outlaw band. He takes over the law enforcement position, but inexplicably allows his gray-haired mother, who fears for his safety, to dissuade him from encountering wrongdoers. The outraged townsfolk—especially pretty Quimby—naturally come to regard the lad as being a coward. But when his mother's house is robbed, Hoxie is infuriated enough to strike back and subdues the gang, forcing a confession about his father's murder from the leader. He also wins the respect of Quimby, after rescuing her along the way.

d, Albert Rogell; w, Harrison Jacobs (based on a story by Rogell); ph, William Nobles; art d, David S. Garber.

Western (PR:A MPAA:NR)

WET GOLD*** (1921) 6 reels Submarine/Goldwyn bw

Ralph Ince *(John Cromwell)*, Aleen Burr *(Grace Hamilton)*, Alicia Turner *(Susan)*, Harry McNaughton *('Arry)*, Thomas Megraine *(Col. Hamilton)*, John Butler *(Chubby Madison)*, Charles McNaughton *(James Chipman)*.

Underrated adventure film, chock full of atmosphere and thrills, has director-star Ince escaping from a band of thieves and encountering Megraine and his daughter Burr in Cuba. Ince has a map showing the location of sunken treasure, and when they set out to claim it, the trio is attacked by the group of cutthroats. In some wonderful underwater scenes using a submarine, Ince routs the villains and sends them to their watery, shark-infested graves.

p, J. Ernest Williamson; d, Ralph Ince; w, Williamson; ph, William J. Black, Jay Rescher.

Adventure **(PR:A MPAA:NR)**

WET PAINT*½** (1926) 6 reels FP/PAR bw

Raymond Griffith *(He)*, Helene Costello *(She)*, Bryant Washburn *(Her Brother)*, Natalie Kingston *(A Beautiful Woman)*, Henry Kolker *(A Husband)*.

When Griffith's girl friend, Costello, collects the bets of a number of chums who had been hiding as he proposed marriage, the heartbroken young man breaks off with her and vows to marry the first woman he meets. Unfortunately, that woman turns out to be married, and he becomes embroiled with her husband, Kolker, who discovers the couple in a "compromising" position. This results in one of the screen's longest and most amusing drunk sequences, involving a fire engine, runaway auto, steam bath, gullible cops, and much more. The movie ends as its audience wants, with Griffith finally marrying Costello, the girl who caused the mirth to begin with. Perhaps this was not the great comedian's best, but it certainly ranked above most of the laugh-oriented features which followed in its wake.

d, Arthur Rosson; w, Lloyd Corrigan (based on a story by Reginald Morris); ph, William Marshall.

Comedy **(PR:A MPAA:NR)**

WHAT A NIGHT!*** (1928) 6 reels PAR bw

Bebe Daniels *(Dorothy Winston)*, Neil Hamilton *(Joe Madison)*, William Austin *(Percy Penfield)*, Wheeler Oakman *(Mike Corney)*, Charles Sellon *(Editor Madison)*, Charles Hill Mailes *(Patterson)*, Ernie Adams *(Snarky)*.

Daniels is in top comic form as a society girl-turned-reporter who bumbles her way (after a series of inspired sight gags) into breaking the story of a decade, which exposes a gang leader. She is rewarded by the love of Hamilton, her mentor and the son of a very delighted city editor. Director Sutherland handled this clever script with consummate skill, and Mankiewicz' titles punctuated this fast-moving film.

d, Edward Sutherland; w, Louis Long (based on a story by Grover Jones, Lloyd Corrigan); t, Herman J. Mankiewicz; ph, Edward Cronjager; ed, Doris Drought.

Comedy **(PR:A MPAA:NR)**

WHAT DO MEN WANT?*** (1921) 6 reels Lois Weber/Wid Gunning bw

Claire Windsor *(Hallie)*, J. Frank Glendon *(Frank)*, George Hackathorne *(Arthur)*, Hallam Cooley *(Yost)*, Edith Kessler *(Bertha)*.

Weber, the highest-paid Hollywood female director of her day, often used social themes in her films and frequently portrayed the concerns of women in modern society. Here her directorial skill, and ability to obtain fine performances from her actors, took a somewhat preachy story and turned it into a good motion picture. In it Glendon plays a self-made man who becomes bored with family life and deserts his loved ones. His brother, Hackathorne, follows suit and leaves Kessler, a poor seamstress, only to find upon returning that she has drowned herself. Glendon, in the meantime, becomes jealous when he suspects his wife, Windsor, of having an affair. Realizing he was wrong to leave her, he shamefully returns to begin a new life with her.

p,d&w, Lois Weber; ph, Dal Clawson.

Drama **(PR:A MPAA:NR)**

WHAT EVERY GIRL SHOULD KNOW* (1927) 7 reels WB bw

Patsy Ruth Miller *(Mary Sullivan)*, Ian Keith *(Arthur Graham)*, Carroll Nye *(Dave Sullivan)*, Mickey McBan *(Bobby Sullivan)*, Lillian Langdon *(Mrs. Randolph)*, Hazel Howell *(Estelle Randolph)*, Carmelita Geraghty *(Mme. Le Fleur)*.

Poorly directed and written exercise in banality has Miller (completely unconvincing as a 17-year-old) and McBan, her little brother, being placed in an orphange when their older brother is wrongly arrested and sent to jail for hauling liquor. Keith, a young philanthropic bachelor who is on the institution's board, adopts the children, but the woman of his house makes their lives so miserable that they run away. A short time later, Miller somehow develops a talent for tennis, and turns pro. Then at a tournament (Miller, an avid tennis player, actually competed here with Hollywood champion Geraghty), her former benefactor sees her in action, proposes marriage, and uses his political pull to get her brother released.

d, Charles F. Reisner; w, Lois Jackson (based on a story by Jack Wagner); ph, David Abel.

Drama **(PR:A MPAA:NR)**

WHAT EVERY WOMAN KNOWS*½

(1917, Brit.) 5 reels Barker-Neptune/Lucoque bw

Hilda Trevelyan *(Maggie Wylie)*, Maud Yates *(The Comtesse)*, A. B. Imeson.

This British screen version of the popular Barrie play about a porter who is educated as payment for marrying a wealthy man's daughter, rises to a parliamentary office and then discovers he loves his wife after all, is vastly inferior to the 1921 U.S. version, directed by William C. DeMille.

d, Fred W. Durrant; w, (based on the play by James M. Barrie).

Drama **(PR:A MPAA:NR)**

WHAT EVERY WOMAN KNOWS*** (1921) 7 reels FP/PAR bw

Lois Wilson *(Maggie Wylie)*, Conrad Nagel *(John Shand)*, Charles Ogle *(Alick Wylie)*, Fred Huntly *(David Wylie)*, Guy Oliver *(James Wylie)*, Winter Hall *(Charles Venables)*, Lillian Tucker *(Sybil Tenterden)*, Claire McDowell *(Comtesse de la Brière)*, Robert Brower *(Scotch Lawyer)*.

Well-directed, -scripted, and -acted screen adaptation of the popular Barrie play (a triumph for the great stage actress Maude Adams) about a railroad porter (Nagel) who rises to political heights after being educated by a millionaire on the condition that he marry the daughter (Wilson) he fears is doomed to spinsterhood. Time passes and Nagel rises to great political heights, without realizing that it is actually the wit and wisdom of his wife's speech writing which has earned him his success. Then, from his lofty and arrogant pedestal, the ingrate sets out to have an affair with alluring socialite Tucker. But fortunately the fellow comes to realize the depth of his love for Wilson in time, and their union is saved.

d, William C. DeMille; w, Olga Printzlau (based on the play by James Matthew Barrie); ph, L. Guy Wilky.

Comedy/Drama **(PR:A MPAA:NR)**

WHAT FOOLS MEN** (1925) 8 reels FN bw

Lewis Stone *(Joseph Greer)*, Shirley Mason *(Beatrice Greer)*, Ethel Grey Terry *(Violet Williamson)*, Barbara Bedford *(Jenny McFarlan)*, John Patrick *(Lancing Ware)*, Hugh Allan *(Burns)*, David Torrence *(Williamson)*, Lewis Dayton *(Henry Craven)*, Joyce Compton *(Dorothy)*.

Barely acceptable drama has Stone, who is separated from his wife, trying to deal with his snooty daughter Mason, who takes a train from California and shows up on his Chicago doorstep. In order to open the gates of society for her, Stone sells one of his inventions to a millionaire, whose wife has eyes for him. The lady even makes a pass, and when the inventor spurns her advances, she sets out to have her husband destroy the poor devil. Meanwhile, his daughter has become humanized, is now married, and with her husband sets out to find her neglected father. They locate him living on skid row, sopping up huge quantities of liquor and deliberately trying to destroy himself. Films of this sort are compelled to have a happy ending, and in this case it comes with the daughter and her husband taking the all-but-beaten Stone into their little home, where he is given the complete run of their basement and encouraged to begin his tinkering all over again.

d, George Archainbaud; w, Eve Unsell (based on the novel *Joseph Greer and His Daughter* by Henry Kitchell Webster); ph, Norbert Brodin; ed, Bert Moore; art d, E. J. Shulter.

Drama **(PR:A MPAA:NR)**

WHAT FOOLS MEN ARE* (1922) 6 reels Pyramid/American Releasing bw

Faire Binney *(Peggy Kendricks)*, Lucy Fox *(Ola)*, Joseph Striker *(Ralph Demarest)*, Huntley Gordon *(Bartley Claybourne)*, Florence Billings *(Kate Claybourne)*, J. Barney Sherry *(Horace Demarest)*, Templar Saxe *(Bayard Thomas)*, Harry Clay Blaney *(Steve O'Malley)*.

There is little to recommend in this dreadful domestic drama about a neglected husband who has an affair with his wife's jazz-loving sister, is rejected by her after his divorce, and then disinherited by his wealthy father. But by the sixth reel there is a reconciliation when everybody but the flapper admits that they were wrong. Even the title to this one could have been improved upon.

d, George Terwilliger; w, Peter Milne (based on the play "The Flapper" by Eugene Walter); ph, Rudolph Mariner; art d, Ben Carre.

Drama **(PR:A MPAA:NR)**

WHAT HAPPENED TO FATHER*½ (1927) 6 reels WB bw

Warner Oland *(W. Bradberry)*, Flobelle Fairbanks *(Betty Bradberry)*, William Demarest *(Dibbin)*, Vera Lewis *(Mrs. Bradberry)*, John Miljan *(Victor Smith)*, Hugh Allan *(Tommy Dawson)*, Cathleen Calhoun *(Violet)*, Jean Lefferty *(Gloria)*.

Rinehart must have written this one while waiting for an elevator. It all has to do with a henpecked Egyptologist (Oland) who secretly writes a musical comedy and later asserts himself enough to stop his socially ambitious wife from separating their daughter, Fairbanks, from the boy she loves by marrying her off to the millionaire who just happens to be the backer of his show.

d, John G. Adolfi; w, Charles R. Condon (based on the story by Mary Roberts Rinehart); ph, Willard Van Enger.

Comedy **(PR:A MPAA:NR)**

WHAT HAPPENED TO JONES*** (1926) 7 reels UNIV bw

Reginald Denny *(Tom Jones)*, Marian Nixon *(Lucille Bigbee)*, Melbourne MacDowell *(Mr. Bigbee)*, Frances Raymond *(Mrs. Bigbee)*, Otis Harlan *(Ebenezer Goodly)*, Emily Fitzroy *(Mrs. Goodly)*, Margaret Quimby *(Marjorie Goodly)*, Ben Hendricks, Jr. *(Richard)*, William Austin *(Henry Fuller)*, Nina Romano *(Minerva Starlight)*, ZaSu Pitts *(Hilda)*, John Elliott *(The Bishop)*, Edward Cecil *(Smith)*, Broderick O'Farrell *(Rector)*.

Nonstop laughs in this Denny comedy which has the breezy lad escaping a poker party he attends on the night before his wedding, when it is raided by the cops. Denny and his pal, Harlan (who nearly steals the show as a henpecked husband) dodge into a ladies' turkish bath where, after causing a little stir, they exit safely, dressed in women's clothing. The boys then return to Harlan's house, where Denny puts on clerical garb and passes himself off as Harlan's brother, a bishop who is due to arrive at any time. The movie ends with the whole crowd again eluding the police, and the real bishop marrying Denny and his sweetheart in a speeding getaway car.

d, William A. Seiter; w, Melville W. Brown (based on the play by George H. Broadhurst); ph, Arthur Todd; art d, Leo E. Kuter.

Comedy **(PR:A MPAA:NR)**

WHAT HAPPENED TO ROSA?*** (1921) 5 reels Goldwyn bw

Mabel Normand *(Mayme Ladd)*, Hugh Thompson *(Dr. Drew)*, Doris Pawn *(Gwendolyn)*, Tully Marshall *(Peacock)*, Eugenie Besserer *(Mme. O'Donnelly)*, Buster Trow *(Jim)*.

Fine performance by Normand as a whimsical shopgirl whose late mother was a Spanish dancer in vaudeville. When Normand visits a fortuneteller who cons her into believing that she is the reincarnation of a Castilian noblewoman, the girl puts on her mother's gown and attends a shipboard dance, where she completely captivates a socially prominent doctor, Thompson, whom she has long loved from a distance. When a fight breaks out, Normand slips out of her costume rather than have her true identity revealed, jumps over the side of the boat and swims home. The doctor, believing her dead, takes the gown to his office, where it's displayed as a reminder of the love he was never able to fulfill. Meanwhile, Normand, dressed as a boy, goes through a number of comic attemptes to kill herself, culminating in her being hit and knocked unconscious by an Italian fruit peddler's cart. After being taken to the office of her beloved, Normand spots her gown and puts it on before Thompson returns to his examining room. The physician is, needless to say, delighted to find the woman of his dreams alive and well, and the film ends with the expected embrace.

d, Victor Schertzinger; w, Gerald C. Duffy (based on a story by Pearl Lenore Curran); ph, George F. Webber.

Comedy **(PR:A MPAA:NR)**

WHAT NO MAN KNOWS* (1921) 6 reels Harry Garson/EPC bw

Clara Kimball Young *(Norma Harvey)*, Lowell Sherman *(Craig Dunlap)*, Dorothy Wallace *(Bertha Dunlap)*, William P. Carleton *(Drake Blackly)*, Jeanne Carpenter *(Mazie)*, Dulcie Cooper.

Maudlin programmer has newspaper reporter Young devoting her life to working with the underprivileged. When her childhood sweetheart, Sherman, is disbarred for trying to bribe a witness to cover his wife's kleptomania, he hits the bottle and ends up on skid row. There Young finds him and takes him to her house, along with Carpenter, a little blind girl. On Young's recommendation, Sherman attempts a reconciliation, but is so disgusted by his wife's freewheeling lifestyle, that he drops her like a hot potato. He then returns to Young, just in time to save the child from being taken away because authorities believed she and Sherman had been living together "out of wedlock"—a situation he gladly rectifies the moment his divorce is finalized.

d, Harry Garson; w, Sada Cowan; ph, Sam Landers.

Drama **(PR:A MPAA:NR)**

WHAT PRICE GLORY* 1/2** (1926) 12 reels FOX bw

Victor McLaglen *(Capt. Flagg)*, Edmund Lowe *(Sgt. Quirk)*, Dolores Del Rio *(Charmaine)*, William V. Mong *(Cognac Pete)*, Phyllis Haver *(Hilda of China)*, Elena Jurado *(Carmen)*, Leslie Fenton *(Lt. Moore)*, August Tollaire *(French Mayor)*, Barry Norton *(Pvt. Lewisohn)*, Sammy Cohen *(Pvt. Lipinsky)*, Ted McNamara *(Pvt. Kiper)*, Mathilde Comont *(Camille, the Cook)*, Pat Rooney *(Mulcahy)*.

Voted one of the 10 best films of 1926 by the *New York Times*, director Walsh almost achieved the impossible when he took a very popular stage play—which depended principally on dialog to make its anti-war statement—and turned it into an even more popular silent film. Although, in all due respect to Walsh, who makes a great deal in his autobiography of how he managed to produce a film with a pacifist message, the film leaves anything but that impression. The story deals with a captain, McLaglen, and a sergeant, Lowe, two tough-as-nails marines who would rather do battle with each other than the Germans. But the main source of their rivalry here, is the saucy a little French girl (Del Rio) who gives her love to both of them. Towards the picture's end, McLaglen wins Del Rio in a wager, but decides not to collect when he realizes that she really loves Lowe. The film ends with McLaglen, while still on leave, heading back to the front. Lowe, wounded, yells for him to stop. Then, slapping a helmet on his head, he throws an arm around his long-time adversary and the two march off to war together. While the night battle scenes were being shot (a period of about two weeks) windows all over Beverly Hills were blown out. Walsh went through a series of assistant directors during that time; the police would show up and ask, "Who's in charge here?" Then one of the underlings would answer, "I am," and off he'd go to the pokey. The trench warfare sequences were extremely effective, but they did not come cheap. There were a number of casualties, and one man lost his life. Yet the film was so popular that it generated three sequels: THIS COCKEYED WORLD, WOMEN OF ALL NATIONS, and the disappointing John Ford remake of 1952. There was, however, another ingredient which led to this film's great success, and that was foul language so obvious that it did not require a skilled lip-reader to decipher the words. In fact, a running gag along Broadway when WHAT PRICE GLORY was in its first run was "Let's go to the Roxy and watch Captain Flagg call Sergeant Quirt a son of a bitch."

d, Raoul Walsh; w, James T. O'Donohoe (based on the play by Laurence Stallings, Maxwell Anderson); t, Malcolm Stuart Boylan; ph, Barney McGill, John Marta, John Smith; m, Erno Rapee.

War **(PR:A MPAA:NR)**

WHAT WIVES WANT* (1923) 5 reels UNIV bw

Ethel Grey Terry *(Claire Howard)*, Vernon Steele *(Austin Howard)*, Ramsey Wallace *(John Reeves)*, Niles Welsh *(David Loring)*, Margaret Landis *(Alice Loring)*, Lila Leslie *(Mrs. Van Dusen)*, Harry A. Burrows *(Newhart)*.

This low-budget Universal film has Landis, the sister of a woman ignored by her husband and involved in an affair, taking the blame when *her* husband discovers them all together. The outraged fellow demands a divorce, but his sister-in-law, Terry, confesses to *her* husband, who promises to be more attentive, and the film ends on a harmonious, if improbable note.

d, Jack Conway; w, Edward T. Lowe, Jr., Perry N. Vekroff (based on a story by Lowe); ph, Charles Kaufman.

Drama **(PR:A MPAA:NR)**

WHAT WOMEN WILL DO** (1921) 6 reels AEX/Pathe bw

Anna Q. Nilsson *(Lily Gibbs)*, Earl Metcalfe *(Jim Coring)*, Allan Forrest *(Arthur Brent)*, George Majeroni *(Dr. Joe)*, Jane Jennings *(Mrs. Wade)*, Riley Hatch *(Stryker)*.

Somewhat diverting programmer has Nilsson, along with a gentleman friend and another crook, conning a wealthy widow into believing (through the use of a phony seance) that she is the wife of the woman's recently departed son. After being welcomed into the lady's home, Nilsson falls in love with a well-healed family friend and discovers, to her horror, that her partners murdered the man whose wife she is pretending to be. Then, to no one's surprise, Nilsson's accomplices are killed off in the last reel, the young lady makes her confession and is forgiven, and the old lady, who never had a daughter of her own, begins making plans for a big wedding.

d, Edward Jose; w, Charles E. Whittaker (based on a story by Charles A. Logue); ph, J. Roy Hunt.

Crime/Drama **(PR:A MPAA:NR)**

WHATEVER SHE WANTS* (1921) 5 reels FOX bw

Eileen Percy *(Enid North)*, Herbert Fortier *(Henry North)*, Richard Wayne *(John Barr)*, Otto Hoffman *(Amos Lott)*.

Featherweight comedy has Percy secretly taking a job with a company belonging to her fiance, Wayne. Thinking her sweetheart is being unfaithful to her, Percy becomes involved with a co-worker who turns out to be married. Everything gets straightened out in the end, of course, and Percy quits her job to become the boss' wife.

d, C. R. Wallace; w, (based on a story by Edgar Franklin); ph, Otto Brautigan.

Dramatic Comedy **(PR:A MPAA:NR)**

WHAT'S A WIFE WORTH?** (1921) 6 reels R-C bw

Casson Ferguson *(Bruce Morrison)*, Ruth Renick *(Rose Kendall)*, Cora Drew *(Her Aunt)*, Virginia Caldwell *(Jane Penfield)*, Alec Francis *(James Morrison)*, Howard Gaye *(Henry Burton)*, Lillian Langdon *(Mrs. Penfield)*, Maxfield Stanley *(Murray Penfield)*, Charles Wyngate *(Dr. Durant)*, Helen Lynch *(Girl in the Retrospect)*.

Cabanne's direction just barely manages to overcome a maudlin screenplay, which, oddly enough, he wrote himself, about a good woman who allows her child to be given to the wealthy former husband who can provide it with all life's advantages. Actually the husband, Ferguson, was tricked into divorcing the child's mother, Renick, as part of a scheme which later caused him to marry Caldwell, the woman his father had chosen for him. In the end the couple are reunited when Ferguson discovers that his second wife is unworthy and the first is a saint.

d&w, William Christy Cabanne; ph, Georges Benoit.

Drama **(PR:A MPAA:NR)**

WHAT'S YOUR HURRY?*** (1920) 5 reels PAR bw

Wallace Reid *(Dusty Rhodes)*, Lois Wilson *(Virginia MacMurran)*, Charles Ogle *(Patrick MacMurran)*, Clarence Burton *(Brenton Harding)*, Ernest Butterworth *(Office Boy)*, Ernest Joy, Jack Young.

There are plenty of thrills in this nicely directed Wood production about a racing car driver (Reid) in love with the daughter of a truck manufacturer. The old man refuses to allow his daughter to marry a "speed freak" until Reid navigates one of the big machines through a driving storm over impossible terrain to set the dynamite charge which saves the lives of countless people living in the valley when the dam bursts.

d, Sam Wood; w, Byron Morgan (based on his story "The Hippopotamus Parade"); ph, Alfred Gilks.

Adventure **(PR:A MPAA:NR)**

WHEEL OF DESTINY, THE** (1927) 6 reels Duke Worne/RAY bw

Forrest Stanley, Georgia Hale, Percy Challenger, Miss Du Pont, Ernest Hilliard, Sammy Blum, B. Hyman, Jack Herrick.

Average low-budget Worne film has a scientist (Stanley) walking in a daze after being rejected by his snobbish sweetheart (Du Pont) and suffering amnesia due to a fall. He then meets a beautiful amusement park performer (Hale) who gets him a job with the show, wins his love, and helps him regain his memory. The couple eventually return to his hometown, where he is given a hero's welcome because of his discovery of a miracle serum. The fellow is also provided the opportunity to snub his former lady friend before marrying the new love in his life.

d, Duke Worne; w, George W. Pyper (based on the story "The Man Without a Past" by Joseph Anthony); ph, Walter Griffen.

Drama **(PR:A MPAA:NR)**

WHEELS OF JUSTICE* (1915) 4 reels VIT bw

George Cooper *(Red)*, Anders Randolf *(Tug)*, James Morrison *(Ralph Brooks)*,

Louise Beaudet *(Rita Reynolds)*, Dorothy Kelly *(Julia Dean)*, Eulalie Jensen, Charles Eldridge.

Poorly made Vitagraph drama deals with a female adventuress, a duped young man, murder, blackmail, a prison break, and justice in the end. Nothing original, nothing new, and absolutely nothing well done.

d, Theodore Marston; w, Edward J. Montagne.

Crime **(PR:A MPAA:NR)**

WHEN A WOMAN SINS½** (1918) 6 reels FOX bw

Theda Bara *(Lillian Marchard/Poppea)*, Joseph Swickard *(Mortimer West)*, Albert Roscoe *(Michael West)*, Alfred Fremont *(Augustus Van Brooks)*, Jack Rollens *(Reggie West)*, Genevieve Blinn *(Mrs. West)*, Ogden Crane.

Bara is almost virginal in this picture which has the legendary star playing a nurse, actress, and semi-vamp (she does cause a young man to blow his brains out) before being regenerated and marrying an Episcopal priest.

d, J. Gordon Edwards; w, E. Lloyd Sheldon (based on the story "The Message of the Lilies" by Beta Breuil); ph, John W. Boyle.

Drama **(PR:A MPAA:NR)**

WHEN BOYS LEAVE HOME**
(1928, Brit.) 8 reels Gainsborough/World Wide bw (GB: DOWNHILL)

Ivor Novello *(Roddy Berwick)*, Robin Irvine *(Tim Wakely)*, Lillian Braithwaite *(Lady Berwick)*, Isabel Jeans *(Julia)*, Ian Hunter *(Archie)*, Ben Webster *(Dr. Dowson)*, Sybil Rhoda *(Sybil Wakely)*, Violet Farebrother *(The Poetess)*, Norman McKinnel *(Sir Thomas Berwick)*, Jerrold Robertshaw *(Rev. Henry Wakely)*, Annette Benson *(Mabel)*, Barbara Gott *(Mme. Michet)*, Alfred Goddard *(The Swede)*, Hannah Jones, J. Nelson.

WHEN BOYS LEAVE HOME was co-written by its star, Novello, and told the story of a boy wrongly accused of stealing at school and expelled as a result. When his father turns on him in outrage, the dejected boy leaves home. He travels to Paris where he becomes romantically involved with an actress and has a series of downhill (the film's British title) experiences. His parents, in the meantime, discover that their son was innocent, and when he finally returns home they are remorseful and welcome him back. Hitchcock shot the dream sequences using superimpositions and blurred images, techniques which, although not new (Rene Clair and Abel Gance had used them in earlier films), were not in use by other directors of that time. In scenes where Novello's health is failing and he is delirious, Hitchcock instructed the lab technicians during editing to tint the scenes pale green—a technique he had seen effectively used in stage plays where green lighting created the appearance of ghosts and fantasy.

p, Michael Balcon; d, Alfred Hitchcock; w, Eliot Stannard (based on the play by Ivor Novello, Constance Collier, written under the pseudonym David Lestrange); ph, Claude McDonnell; ed, Ivor Montagu; set d, Islington.

Drama **(PR:A MPAA:NR)**

WHEN BROADWAY WAS A TRAIL*** (1914) 5 reels Shubert/WORLD bw

Barbara Tennant *(Priscilla Elliott)*, O. A. C. Lund *(Henry Minuet)*, Edward Roseman *(Peter Minuet)*, Lindsay J. Hall *(Salvation Kibbens)*, Alec B. Francis *(Standish Hope)*, Mary Nevarro *(Mistress Hibbens)*.

Director-actor Lund opens with a shot of the romantic principals standing on a skyscraper in modern Manhattan. Then he fades to the past and tells an engrossing story, set at the time of Dutch colonial rule, in which Peter Minuet's son (Lund) travels to Salem, Massachusetts, where he falls in love with a beautiful young woman who has been accused of practicing witchcraft. After a number of complications, he marries her in the safety of his more enlightend homeland. The picture then fades to the future and ends dramatically with the couple silhouetted against the bustling background of Times Square.

d&w, O.A.C. Lund.

Costume Drama **(PR:A MPAA:NR)**

WHEN DO WE EAT?*** (1918) 5 reels PAR bw

Enid Bennett *(Nora)*, Al Ray *(James Watterson Forbes)*, Jack Nelson *("Soup" McCool)*, Robert McKim, Frank Hayes, Caroline Rankin, Gertrude Claire.

Good little comedy has Bennett ending up in a small town after the Uncle Tom production, in which she played Little Eva, folds. There Bennett is taken in by the kindly owner of a boarding house, breaks up a bank robbery by posing as a female accomplice, and marries a fellow who works for the institution.

d, Fred Niblo; sup, Thomas H. Ince; w, C. Gardner Sullivan; ph, Robert Newhard.

Comedy **(PR:A MPAA:NR)**

WHEN EAST COMES WEST*½ (1922) 5 reels Phil Goldstone bw

Franklyn Farnum *(Jones)*, Andrew Waldron *(The Chinaman)*.

Farnum and his Chinese friend (played by Waldron) are U.S. marshals in disguise, who infiltrate a ranch owned by a pretty young woman and bring to justice the foreman and his gang, who have been running guns.

d, B. Reeves Eason; w, Anthony Coldeway.

Western **(PR:A MPAA:NR)**

WHEN GREEK MEETS GREEK** (1922, Brit.) 6 reels Walter West/BUT bw

Violet Hopson *(Christine Ward)*, Stewart Rome *(Cyrus Warner)*, Lillian Douglas *(Julia Warner)*, Lewis Gilbert *(Robert Craven)*, Arthur Walcott *(Strike Leader)*, Marjorie Benson *(Miss Lockwood)*, Tom Beaumont *(Robertson)*, Bert Darley *(Heller)*.

The international labor struggle was the inspiration for this pro-management British melodrama which has a two-fisted U.S. capitalist saving an English heiress from a mob of crazed workers, and then accepting her love as a reward.

d, Walter West; w, (based on a novel by Paul Trent).

Drama **(PR:A MPAA:NR)**

WHEN KNIGHTHOOD WAS IN FLOWER*** (1922) 12 reels COS/PAR bw

Marion Davies *(Princess Mary Tudor)*, Forrest Stanley *(Charles Brandon)*, Lyn Harding *(King Henry VIII)*, Theresa Maxwell Conover *(Queen Catherine)*, Pedro De Cordoba *(Duke of Buckingham)*, Ruth Shepley *(Lady Jane Bolingbroke)*, Ernest Glendenning *(Sir Edwin Caskoden)*, Arthur Forrest *(Cardinal Wolsey)*, Johnny Dooley *(Will Somers)*, William Kent *(The King's Tailor)*, Charles Gerrard *(Sir Adam Judson)*, Arthur Donaldson *(Sir Henry Brandon)*, Downing Clarke *(Lord Chamberlain)*, William Norris *(Louis XII of France)*, Macey Harlam *(Duc de Longueville)*, William H. Powell *(Francis I)*, George Nash *(Capt. Bradhurst)*, Gustav von Seyffertitz *(Grammont)*, Paul Panzer *(Captain of the Guard)*, Guy Coombes *(Follower of Buckingham)*, Flora Finch *(French Countess)*, Mortimer Snow, George Ogle, Red Wing, Black Diamond, Winchester *(Horses)*.

Tremendous production values, excellent direction, a good script, and an outstanding cast, headed by Marion Davies, combine to bring this saga of Mary Tudor to life. The story has Davies running away with commoner Charles Brandon (Stanley) rather than obey her brother Henry VIII's order that she marry the King of France (Norris). The lovers are captured, and in order to save her sweetheart from Henry's active axe, she agrees to wed the French monarch, on the condition that she and Brandon may be reunited after the death of her royal husband. Norris does indeed die shortly after the vows, and Marion and Stanley are allowed to live out their lives together (in spite of an attempt on the part of King Francis I—Powell—to have her) in this lavishly presented bit of historical fiction. Lavish is perhaps an understatement. Hearst spent $1,500,000 on this film, and, according to his biographer, W. A. Swanberg, when a friend once told the newspaper tycoon that there was money in pictures, he answered, "Yes I know—mine."

d, Robert G. Vignola; w, Luther Reed (based on the novel by Charles Major); ph, Ira Morgan, Harold Wenstrom; m, William Frederick Peters; set d, Joseph Urban; cos, Gretl Urban Thurlow; fencing sup, James Murray.

Historical Romance **(PR:A MPAA:NR)**

WHEN LIGHTS ARE LOW (SEE: WHERE LIGHTS ARE LOW, 1921)

WHEN ODDS ARE EVEN*½ (1923) 5 reels FOX bw

William Russell *(Jack Arnold)*, Dorothy Devore *(Caroline Peyton)*, Lloyd Whitlock *(Neal Travis)*, Frank Beal *(Clive Langdon)*, Allan Cavan *(British Consul)*.

Russell is all but wasted in this predictable South Seas programmer which has the hero competing for the love of Devore, as well as an opal mine on Pago Tai, and winning both.

d, James Flood; w, Dorothy Yost; ph, Joseph Brotherton.

Adventure **(PR:A MPAA:NR)**

WHEN ROME RULED** (1914) 5 reels ECL bw

Mabel Taliaferro *(Nydia)*, Ernest Truex *(Caius)*, Paul Panzer.

Decidedly inferior imitation of the Italian blockbusters which were making an impact on the U.S. market at the time. Nothing quite comes off in this recreation of ancient Rome, including the lions who are too old to be the slightest bit interested in chewing on Taliaferro's delectable body.

w, George Fitzmaurice.

Costume **(PR:A MPAA:NR)**

WHEN SCOUTING WON* (1930, Brit.) 5 reels J. H. Martin Cross bw

Cyril Chant *(Scout)*, Frankie Purnell *(Cub)*.

Even in England the talkies had proven that they were here to stay when this well-meaning little children's adventure, about a Boy Scout who saves his Cub Scout chum from a band of gypsies, was produced.

d&w, J. H. Martin Cross.

Adventure **(PR:A MPAA:NR)**

WHEN SECONDS COUNT*½ (1927) 5 reels Duke Worne/RAY bw

Billy Sullivan *(Billy Mathewson)*, Mildred June *(Elinor)*, Rose Kimman *(Mimi)*, Jerome La Grasse *(George Milburn)*, Marie Messenger *(Toots Sweet)*, James Aubrey *(Dizzy Durby)*, Earl Wayland Bowman *(Dave Streater)*, Joseph Girard *(James Mathewson)*.

After incurring his wealthy father's anger by becoming engaged to a gum-chewing chorus girl, Sullivan redeems himself by traveling to the small town where his dad is building a dam. There he not only nails a crook who is trying to make a killing on the project, but wins the love of June, the most beautiful and socially prominent girl in the village.

d, Oscar Apfel; w, Suzanne Avery; ph, Ernest Smith.

Drama **(PR:A MPAA:NR)**

WHEN THE CLOUDS ROLL BY****
(1920) 6 reels Douglas Fairbanks/UA bw

Douglas Fairbanks *(Daniel Boon Brown)*, Herbert Grimwood *(Dr. Metz)*, Kathleen Clifford *(Lucette Bancroft)*, Frank Campeau *(Mark Drake)*, Ralph Lewis *(Curtis Brown)*, Daisy Robinson *(Bobbie De Vere)*, Albert MacQuarrie *(Hobson)*.

Most of Fairbanks' earlier films dealt with a bit of satire, but in this one he pulls out all the stops. The picture opens with the title, "Guinea pigs and rabbits are often sacrificed for scientific purposes. But here is a new one." The character of Dr. Metz, a psychiatrist, (Grimwood) is then introduced. He is lecturing before a strange convention, and he goes on to say: "The power of suggestion can destroy both mind and body. But first I weaken the power of resistance in my subject by implanting psychic germs of fear, worry, superstition, and kindred annoyances." The object of his experiment is one Daniel Boon Brown (Fairbanks), America's most superstitous human being—and the doctor and his agents become a part of the unsuspecting fellow's everyday life in an insidious attempt to drive him to insanity and suicide. When Fairbanks needs a servant, one of the doctor's henchmen applies for the job and thus worms his way inside the victim's household. One of the blackguard's first actions is to get his boss to consume enormous quantities of Welsh rarebit, mince pie, lobster, and onions just before retiring. Naturally Fairbanks begins to dream, and this results in a horrifying nightmare: There is a shot of all the food tumbling around in his stomach, and then he discovers that a bizarre, elongated figure is in bed beside him. He pushes it over the side, where it becomes a cutout figure and then bounces up again. Great white hands snatch at him, and he leaps through the wall and right into a meeting of ladies. His pajamas are beginning to fall down, so he jumps into a still life painting of a seascape, passes right through it and ends up in a pool of water. He pulls himself out of the water and all of a sudden the food he ate earlier begins to chase him, only now the items are bigger than human size. The poor devil is running with all his might, but the picture turns to slow motion. He leaps fences, rolls in front of a moving truck, hops on a horse, and crashes through another wall. Now he's in a strange house and as he starts to explore it he walks up a wall, runs across the ceiling, and down another wall. The door opens and the food comes pouring in. Gripping the banister, he manages to escape the room. Then we see him again racing directly towards us—once again in slow motion. He manages to make it to a chimney and leaps in. Falling down a long shaft, he finally lands on a huge drum, and there are people all about him beating on it. At this point, he is awakened by another of the doctor's minions knocking at his door. The time has come for Grimwood to begin playing on his superstitions. Mirrors break, umbrellas are opened in his apartment. Then the crazed doctor frames Fairbanks of stealing some oil property that his sweetheart's father owns—causing both of them to turn their backs on him. When it looks like things just can't get any worse, the cops show up (actually men in the employ of the doctor) and chase Fairbanks all over the house. He stumbles into a closet where the camera shows the inside of his head. Located there are the figures of "Reason" sitting on a throne, and a couple of other characters called "Discord" and "Worry," who grab "Reason" and spirit her away from the figure "Sense of Humor," who is kneeling at the base of her throne. Fairbanks staggers out of the closet and fails to notice the revolver which Grimwood has placed in his pocket. He wanders off and is about to do himself in when he spots the attendents from the insane asylum grabbing Grimwood and carring him away. At last "Reason" is back on her throne, and it's time to make it up to his girl. If there was ever a film which did not need a topper, this was it. But Fairbanks gives us one anyway. A hurricane, followed by a flood, suddenly erupts, and he performs some more outstanding gymnastics. As he saves his girl, they are sitting on a rooftop when a preacher comes floating by on top of another home, and at the couple's request marries them. This was one of Fairbanks' last lighthearted comedies, although Lord knows it has its dark side. But a wonderful era was about to end, because waiting down the road were D'Artagnan, Zorro, Robin Hood, and a thief from Bagdad, who would perform a number of dazzling magical effects like the ones exhibited here, only this touch would not be quite carefree, nor would it seem to possess the same sense of personal delight.

d, Victor Fleming; w, Fairbanks, Tom Geraghty; ph, William McGann, Harry Thorpe.

Comedy/Adventure **Cas.** **(PR:A MPAA:NR)**

WHEN THE DEVIL DRIVES* (1922) 5 reels Leah Baird/AEX bw

Leah Baird *(Blanche Mansfield)*, Arline Pretty *(Grace Eldridge)*, Richard Tucker *(John Graham)*, Vernon Steel *(Robert Taylor)*, Katherine Lewis *(Nanette Henley)*.

When Steel tells his lover, Baird, that he has become engaged to another woman, she goes into a rage and wounds him with a knife. Pretty, his fiancee, then leaves him flat, moves away and changes her name. Meanwhile, Baird also leaves town and assumes a new identity, and the two women, not knowing each other's true identity, become best friends. The past soon catches up, however, and Pretty shoots Baird when she discovers the truth. Fortunately the lady recovers, earns her friend's forgiveness, and marries Tucker, the man she loved all along. Pretty is then reunited with Steel, making for a happy ending all around.

p, Arthur F. Beck; d, Paul Scardon; w, Leah Baird; ph, Charles Stumar.

Drama **(PR:A MPAA:NR)**

WHEN THE WIFE'S AWAY*** (1926) 6 reels COL bw

George K. Arthur *(Billy Winthrop)*, Dorothy Revier *(Ethel Winthrop)*, Thomas Ricketts *(Uncle Hiram)*, Ina Rorke *(Aunt Minerva)*, Ned Sparks *(Chicago Dan)*, Harry Depp *(Joe Carter)*, Lincoln Plummer, Bobby Dunn *(Detectives)*.

One of Columbia's best efforts to date is this fast-paced comedy which has Arthur and Revier renting a fancy apartment to impress his uncle, who is committed to distribute the inheritance of his grandfather's estate—providing the lad has "made good." Of course a host of complications arise, which include Arthur impersonating a butler and then dressing in drag (to the delight of the old boy, who finds him most attractive), as well as discovering themselves sharing the flat with a couple of crooks (one of whom is also impersonating a female), who are using the place as a hideout. The cops finally come crashing in on the scene, and when Arthur threatens to expose his uncle's flirtation with the "little lady," the inheritance becomes his.

d, Frank R. Strayer; sup, Harry Cohn; w, Douglas Bronston.

Comedy **(PR:A MPAA:NR)**

WHERE EAST IS EAST½** (1929) 7 reels MGM bw

Lon Chaney *(Tiger Haynes)*, Lupe Velez *(Toyo)*, Estelle Taylor *(Mme. de Sylva)*, Lloyd Hughes *(Bobby Bailey)*, Louis Stern *(Father Angelo)*, Mrs. Wong Wing *(Ming)*, Duke Kahanamoku *(Wild Animal Trainer)*, Richard R. Neill.

Chaney's makeup is the best thing about this rather contrived film set in the jungles of Indochina. The "Man of a Thousand Faces" plays a badly scarred trapper who sells wild animals to circuses and lives only for his daughter, Velez. The plot thickens when Velez falls in love with Hughes, the son of a big top owner, and Chaney's runaway wife, Taylor, returns and attempts to seduce the young man. Chaney kills his wife by releasing a wild gorilla and is himself mauled and dies shortly thereafter, but not before seeing his daughter marry Hughes.

d, Tod Browning; w, Richard Schayer, Waldemar Young (based on a story by Harry Sinclair Drago, Browning); t, Joe Farnham; ph, Henry Sharp; ed, Harry Reynolds; art d, Cedric Gibbons; cos, David Cox.

Drama **(PR:A MPAA:NR)**

WHERE LIGHTS ARE LOW***

(1921) 6 reels Hayakawa Feature Play/R-C bw (AKA: WHEN LIGHTS ARE LOW)

Sessue Hayakawa *(T'Su Wong Shih)*, Togo Yamamoto *(Chang Bong Lo)*, Goro Kino *(Tuang Fang)*, Gloria Payton *(Quan Yin)*, Kiyosho Satow *(Lang See Bow)*, Misao Seki *(Chung Wo Ho Kee)*, Toyo Fujita *(Wung)*, Jay Eaton *("Spud" Malone)*, Harold Holland *(Sgt. McConigle)*.

Excessive titles are one of the few drawbacks regarding this well-acted melodrama about a Chinese prince (Hayakawa) who comes to the U.S. to further his education, and later finds the girl he loved in the old country placed on auction in San Francisco's Chinatown. The prince bids a small fortune for her in competition with a notorious underworld figure, wins her freedom, and then sets about trying to earn the money to pay his debt. The auctioneer gives the young man an extension, but the furious gangster abducts the young lady. The film comes to an exciting climax with Hayakawa killing his enemy in a well-choreographed fight scene.

d, Colin Campbell; w, Jack Cunningham (based on the story "East is East" by Lloyd Osbourne); ph, Frank D. Williams.

Drama **(PR:A MPAA:NR)**

WHERE MEN ARE MEN*** (1921) 5 reels VIT bw

William Duncan *(Vic Foster)*, Edith Johnson *(Eileen, "Princess")*, George Stanley *(Frank Valone)*, Tom Wilson *("Dutch" Monahan)*, Gertrude Wilson *(Laura Valone)*, Harry Lonsdale *(R. C. Cavendish)*, George Kunkel *(Sheriff Grimes)*, William McCall *(Mike Regan)*, Charles Dudley *(Monty Green)*.

As much a mystery as a western, this Duncan-directed and acted feature holds one's interest from beginning to end. It tells the story of a down-and-out miner who escapes from Death Valley and encounters dance hall singer Johnson. While the girl asks Duncan if he knows a man named Waldron, the bar owner secretly drugs him and robs his claim deed. When Duncan comes to, he's informed that the sheriff is after him for the murder of his partner. Duncan escapes to the city, but when he learns that the lawman is still hounding him, he decides to return to the wilds and clear his name. Along the way he comes into the possession of a letter addressed to Waldron whom, it seems, was the father of Johnson. The letter's contents clear Duncan, convict the real killer, and disclose the location of a lost mine—which Duncan and Johnson decide to share as husband and wife.

d, William Duncan; w, Thomas Dixon, Jr. (based on the story "The Princess of the Desert Dream" by Ralph Cummins); ph, George Robinson.

Western/Mystery **(PR:A MPAA:NR)**

WHERE THE TRAIL DIVIDES* (1914) 5 reels LAS bw

Robert Edeson *(The Indian Boy)*, Winifred Kingston *(The White Girl)*, Theodore Roberts, Jack W. Johnston, James Neill, Constance Adams, Fred Montague, Antrim Short, Mary Jane Highbee, Merta Carpenter.

Disjointed, poorly directed and acted western about the love affair between an orphaned white girl and an Indian boy, the social pressures they endure, and how they finally find happiness together.

d, James Neill; w, (based on the novel and play by W. Lillibridge).

Western/Drama **(PR:A MPAA:NR)**

WHILE NEW YORK SLEEPS**** (1920) 8 reels FOX bw

"Out of the Night": Estelle Taylor *(The Wife)*, William Locke *(The Husband)*, Marc MacDermott *(The Strange Visitor)*, Harry Southern *(A Burglar)*; "The Gay White Way": Estelle Taylor *(The Vamp)*, Marc MacDermott *(The Man)*, Harry Southern *(Their-Friend)*; "A Tragedy of the East Side": Marc MacDermott *(The Paralytic)*, Estelle Taylor *(The Girl)*, Harry Southern *(The Son)*, Earl Metcalfe *(The Gangster)*, Harry Locke *(The Policeman)*.

In this most unusual motion picture, the same players are used in three separate stories, titled "Out of the Night," "The Gay White Way," and "A Tragedy of the East Side." The last one packs the real wallop. MacDermott is magnificent in it as the speechless paraplegic who can communicate only through the use of facial expressions and the batting of his eyelids. Living in a Lower East Side tenement, he watches as his son is murdered by his daughter-in-law and her hoodlum lover. The body is then dropped through a trap door into the East River, and when the police arrive to report the accident, MacDermott tries desperately to "tell" them what he has seen. It is a tour de force performance as ever so slowly the old man makes his point and the killers are finally given their just deserts through a hail of police gun bullets.

d, Charles J. Brabin; w, Brabin, Thomas F. Fallon; ph, George Lane.

Drama **(PR:A MPAA:NR)**

WHILE SATAN SLEEPS* (1922) 7 reels FP/PAR bw

Jack Holt *(Phil)*, Wade Boteler *(Red Barton)*, Mabel Van Buren *(Sunflower Sadie)*, Fritzi Brunette *(Salome Deming)*, Will R. Walling *(Bud Deming)*, J. P. Lockney *(Chuckkawalla Bill)*, Fred Huntley *(Absolom Randall)*, Bobby Mack *(Bones)*, Sylvia Ashton *(Mrs. Bones)*, Herbert Standing *(Bishop)*.

Sentimental but moving drama has the errant son of an Anglican bishop (beautifully played by Holt) escaping from prison, assuming the disguise of an Episcopalian clergyman, and heading west. He lands in a wide open frontier town with a large population desperately seeking to civilize itself, and takes the position of "Sky Pilot." His fists bring a number of converts, and with what seems like the perfect cover, he and his partner, Boteler, prepare to knock off the local bank. But along the way Holt falls in love with a woman who believes him, is completely regenerated, and risks his life to prevent the holdup. Then in a stirring, if somewhat manipulative scene, he goes before his entire congregation, confesses his past, and announces his intention to return to jail and finish his time. The film ends with a well-directed scene showing the penitentiary gates swinging open as his father and the woman he loves stand waiting in the wings, leaving no doubt that the church he helped found is anxiously anticipating his return.

d, Joseph Henabery; w, Albert S. Le Vino (based on the story "The Parson of Panamint" by Peter Bernard Kyne); ph, Faxon M. Dean.

Western (PR:A MPAA:NR)

WHILE THE CITY SLEEPS** (1928) 9 reels MGM bw

Lon Chaney *(Dan)*, Anita Page *(Myrtle)*, Carroll Nye *(Marty)*, Wheeler Oakman *(Skeeter)*, Mae Busch *(Bessie)*, Polly Moran *(Mrs. McGinnis)*, Lydia Yeamans Titus *(Mrs. Sullivan)*, William Orlamond *(Dwiggins)*, Richard Carle *(Wally)*.

Machine guns rattle and squad cars scream in this sound-synchronized gangster film, which has flapper Page learning too much about the operation of Oakman's crime ring and going to police veteran Chaney for help. Chaney (who is pretty much the whole show) puts her up at his boarding house, and eventually falls in love with the girl. At the picture's end, he brings the bad guys to justice in a hail of bullets, realizes that Anita loves Nye, a dapper ex-gangster trying to trod the straight and narrow, and reunites them, while resigning himself to a lifetime of soaking his feet, alone.

d, Jack Conway; w, A. P. Younger; t, Joseph Farnham; ph, Henry Sharp; ed, Sam S. Zimbalist; set d, Cedric Gibbons; cos, Gilbert Clark; syn sc; s eff.

Crime (PR:A MPAA:NR)

WHIP WOMAN, THE zero (1928) 5 reels Allan Dwan/FN bw

Estelle Taylor *(Sari)*, Antonio Moreno *(Count Michael Ferenzi)*, Lowell Sherman *(The Baron)*, Hedda Hopper *(Countess Ferenzi)*, Julanne Johnston *(Miss Haldane)*, Loretta Young *(The Girl)*.

It's hard to believe that the great Dwan had *anything* to do with producing this stinker about a whip-popping Hungarian peasant who saves a nobleman from suicide, and finally marries him after his snobbish mother throws a few obstacles in their way.

p, Allan Dwan; d, Joseph C. Boyle; w, Earle Roebuck (based on a story by Forrest Halsey, Leland Hayward); t, Edwin Justus Mayer; ph, Ernest Hallor; ed, Terrell Morse.

Drama (PR:A MPAA:NR)

WHISPERING SMITH* (1926) 7 reels Metropolitan/PDC bw

H. B. Warner *("Whispering Smith")*, Lillian Rich *(Dicksie Dunning)*, John Bowers *(McCloud)*, Lilyan Tashman *(Marion Sinclair)*, Eugene Pallette *(Bill Dancing)*, Richard Neill *(Lance Dunning)*, James Mason *(Du Sang)*, Warren Rogers *(Karg)*, Nelson McDowell *(Seagrue)*, Robert Edeson *(J. S. Bucks), Will Walling (Murray Sinclair)*.

Good combination of railroad and western genres has Warner playing an undercover railroad cop who falls in love with Tashman, the ex-wife of the bandit he's been hired to nail. In this well-directed and acted adventure, the action moves along at a rapid clip and culminates with Warner winning his woman, after his buddy, Pallette, kills her former husband in a shootout.

d, George Melford; w, Elliott J. Clawson, Will M. Ritchey (based on the novel by Frank Hamilton Spearman); ph, Charles G. Clarke, Joe La Shelle; art d, Charles Cadwallader.

Western (PR:A MPAA:NR)

WHISPERS* (1920) 5 reels SF bw

Elaine Hammerstein, Matt Moore, Charles Gerard, Phillips Tead, Ida Darling, Bernard Randall, Warren Cook, Maud Hill, Templar Saxe, Dorothy Worth, George Stevens, Edgar Hudson, Bertram Marbaugh.

Acceptable programmer with some pretty good production values and a number of interesting location shots of Washington D.C., has nice girl Hammerstein finding herself romantically linked with a married millionaire in a scandal sheet. She leaves New York to avoid being named co-respondent and, coincidentally, so does the gentleman in question. Hot on their trail—in fact, on the same train—is a young reporter who has had this nasty assignment forced upon him. But when everybody arrives in the small Maryland town where Hammerstein's father runs the local newspaper, the whole matter is straightened out and the writer remains on to help put the journal in the black and marry the publisher's daughter.

d, William P. S. Earle; w, George Proctor (based on a story by Marc C. Connelly); ph, William Wagner.

Drama (PR:A MPAA:NR)

WHITE AND UNMARRIED* (1921) 5 reels FP/PAR bw

Thomas Meighan *(Billy Kane)*, Jacqueline Logan *(Andrée Duphot)*, Grace Darmond *(Dorothea Welter)*, Walter Long *(Chicoq)*, Lloyd Whitlock *(Marechal)*, Fred Vroom *(Mr. Welter)*, Marian Skinner *(Mrs. Welter)*, Georgie Stone *(Victor)*, Jack Herbert *(Jacques)*.

Meighan sparkles in this pleasing comedy about a burglar who goes straight when he inherits a bundle and then tours France to celebrate his good fortune. In Paris he falls for Logan, a dancer, but a jealous Apache kidnaps the girl, giving young Meighan the opportunity to top off the laughs with a thrilling fight sequence.

d, Tom Forman; w, William M. Ritchey (based on the story "Billy Kane, White and Unmarried" by John D. Swain); ph, Harry Perry.

Comedy/Adventure (PR:A MPAA:NR)

WHITE BLACK SHEEP, THE** (1926) 7 reels INSP/FN bw

Richard Barthelmess *(Robert Kincairn)*, Patsy Ruth Miller *(Zelie)*, Constance Howard *(Enid Gower)*, Erville Alderson *(Yasuf)*, William H. Tooker *(Col. Kincairn)*, Gino Corrado *(El Rahib)*, Albert Prisco *(Kadir)*, Sam Appel *(Dimos)*, Col. G. L. McDonnell *(Col. Nicholson)*, Templar Saxe *(Stanley Fielding)*.

It's the old British-colonials-versus-the-ungrateful-Arabs story all over again—only this is far from the best version of that tired yarn. Barthelmess, the playboy son of an English colonel, has lost a bundle gambling, and takes the blame for a theft committed by his fiancee. Disgraced, he changes his name, joins the Army, and ends up being stationed in Palestine. There he falls in love with a Greek dancer (Miller) and gains the enmity of Corrado, an Arab traitor now employed by the British, when he saves the girl from his unwanted attentions. Later Barthelmess disguises himself as a mute native, infiltrates his enemy's camp, and discovers that an attack is about to be launched on the British garrison. He is then captured, put through the complete bag of Arab torture tricks, but escapes in time to ride like the devil and save the day. And, as fate would have it, his commanding officer has been replaced by his very own father, who has received word that Barthelmess' former sweetheart confessed to the crime. This, of course, opens the door for Barthelmess to marry Miller, who looks about as Greek in this movie as Sonja Henie.

d, Sidney Olcott; w, Jerome N. Wilson, Agnes Pat McKenna (based on a story by Violet E. Powell); ph, David W. Gobbett.

Adventure (PR:A MPAA:NR)

WHITE FLANNELS* (1927) 7 reels WB bw

Louise Dresser *(Mrs. Jacob Politz)*, Jason Robards *(Frank Politz)*, Virginia Brown Faire *(Anne)*, Warner Richmond *(Ed)*, George Nichols *(Jacob Politz)*, Brooks Benedict *(Paul)*, Rose Blossom *(Berenice Nolden)*, Rosemary Cooper *(Paul's Sister)*.

Blatantly maudlin dribble about a mother from a coal mining town who sacrifices everything to send her son to college, where he becomes a football star and darling of the rich set, only to have them turn against him when they learn of his humble origins. The film is embarrassing in its obvious attempt to constantly manipulate the emotions of its audience. The fact that Dresser was still able to deliver a subtle and convincing performance in spite of everything was a tribute to her artistry.

d, Lloyd Bacon; w, C. Graham Baker (based on the story by Lucian Cary); ph, Ed Du Par.

Drama (PR:A MPAA:NR)

WHITE FLOWER, THE** (1923) 6 reels FP/PAR bw

Betty Compson *(Konia Markham)*, Edmund Lowe *(Bob Rutherford)*, Edward Martindel *(John Markham)*, Arline Pretty *(Ethel Granville)*, Sylvia Ashton *(Mrs. Gregory Bolton)*, Arthur Hoyt *(Gregory Bolton)*, Leon Barry *(David Panuahi)*, Lily Philips *(Bernice Martin)*, Reginald Carter *(Edward Graeme)*, Maui Kaito *(Kahuna)*, A Native Hawaiian *(The Sorceress)*.

Compson does better than can be expected with this South Seas drama, partly shot on location in Hawaii, about a half-breed girl who is told by a sorceress that the man of her dreams will soon appear, bearing a perfect white flower. Before long a handsome American, Lowe, arrives on the scene and gives her a lovely gardenia at a social function. This (for some reason known only to director-writer Ivers) causes Compton's jealous native admirer (Barry) to persuade the object of his affection to have a curse put on Lowe's fiancee, Pretty. Later, when Compson sees Lowe's sweet, attentive manner towards Pretty as she slowly slips away, she has a change of heart, has the spell discontinued, then tries to do herself in by leaping into a volcano. Fortunately Lowe reaches her before it's too late, declares his love, and informs her that his engagement has been terminated. He then asks her to be his very own beautiful, white flower.

d&w, Julia Crawford Ivers; ph, James Van Trees.

Drama (PR:A MPAA:NR)

WHITE GOLD* (1927) 7 reels PDC bw

Jetta Goudal *(Dolores Carson)*, Kenneth Thomson *(Alec Carson)*, George Bancroft *(Sam Randall)*, George Nichols *(Carson, Alex's Father)*, Robert Perry *(Bucky O'Neil)*, Clyde Cook *(Homer)*.

A strange western, stuffy and sometimes smothering, WHITE GOLD nevertheless joins remarkable little known pictures such as STARK LOVE and CHANG as films that stand out among the common run of movies made at the time. Thomson is the son of a bitter old man, a sheepherder in Arizona, who marries a Mexican woman and brings her back with him to the ranch. Immediately, the old man, Nichols, takes a dislike to her and begins to undermine his son's faith in her fidelity. The wife, Goudal, is shaken by this turn of events. An itinerant sheepherder, Bancroft, comes to the ranch looking for work and is hired when the old man notices him flirting with Goudal. That night the husband and wife quarrel and end up with Thomson sleeping away from his wife in the bunkhouse. Bancroft, seeing his chance, slips into Goudal's bedroom and is found dead of a gunshot wound the next morning. Nichols tells his son he killed the cowboy because he caught the couple cuckolding him. Goudal refuses to explain what happened to Thomson because of his lack of faith in her, and, at the finale, she walks away to freedom, discarding the gun with which she killed Bancroft when he entered her bedroom. A complete washout at the box office when it first came out, WHITE GOLD has gone through a reassessment with time and was even planned for a remake with Charles Laughton at one point, but no print of the original could be found. A dark, dense story of sex and jealousy, the picture seems to go out of its way to be oppressive, and yet a deep psychology was achieved in this film that few others could boast. Director Howard paid more attention to atmosphere than to character, and to indirection, rather than direct story telling— as in one scene when, instead of a crowded dance hall, only shadows were shown. Known as an "open air" director, or as one of the pioneers in natural settings for his films, it is odd that in WHITE GOLD the sense of fresh air and freedom that the locale suggested resulted in claustrophobia. That it was an important picture to Howard is made clear by the fact that after retiring from the movies in the mid-1940s, when he was finding assignments more and more difficult to come by, he had just rewritten the script of WHITE GOLD for a proposed remake in 1954 when he died, not having made a film for eight years.

d, William K. Howard; sup, C. Gardner Sullivan; w, Garrett Fort, Marion Orth, Tay Garnett (based on a play by J. Palmer Parsons); t, John Krafft, John Farrow; ph, Lucien Andriot; ed, Jack Dennis; art d, Anton Grot.

Western **(PR:A MPAA:NR)**

WHITE HANDS*** (1922) 6 reels Graf/Wid Gunning bw

Hobart Bosworth *("Hurricane" Hardy)*, Robert McKim *(Leon Roche)*, Freeman Wood *(Ralph Alden)*, Al Kaufman *("Grouch" Murphy)*, Muriel Frances Dana *(Peroxide)*, Elinor Fair *(Helen Maitland)*, George O'Brien *(Sailor)*.

A good script by Sullivan, professional direction by Hillyer, and fine performances all around, really make something of this low-budget drama about a hard-boiled sea captain (Bosworth) who experiences a regeneration because of his love for a missionary woman and the purity of a child's touch. The writer and director had the courage to provide a semi-happy ending, which shows Bosworth going off and leaving the missionary free to care for a handsome young man, whom she helped to overcome drug and alcohol addiction.

p, Max Graf; d&w, Lambert Hillyer (based on a story by C. Gardner Sullivan).

Drama **(PR:A MPAA:NR)**

WHITE OAK*** (1921) 7 reels WSHP/PAR-ART bw

William S. Hart *(Oak Miller)*, Vola Vale *(Barbara)*, Alexander Gaden *(Mark Granger)*, Robert Walker *(Harry)*, Bert Sprotte *(Eliphalet Moss)*, Helen Holly *(Rose Miller)*, Chief Standing Bear *(Long Knife)*.

Action-packed western has Hart playing a gambler out to get Gaden, the man who seduced and ultimately caused the death of his sister. His pursuit places him in the position to save a wagon train from Chief Standing Bear and his braves who, through Gaden's instigation, have mounted an attack. But fate does not provide the gambler with the opportunity to kill the villain himself—that pleasure is given to Standing Bear, whose daughter was also ruined by the blackguard.

d, Lambert Hillyer; w, Bennet Musson (based on a story "Single Handed" by William S. Hart); ph, Joe August; ed, William O'Shea; art d, J. C. Hoffner.

Western **(PR:A MPAA:NR)**

WHITE OUTLAW, THE** (1925) 5 reels UNIV bw

Jack Hoxie *(Jack Lupton)*, Marceline Day *(Mary Gale)*, William Welsh *(Malcolm Gale)*, Duke Lee *(James Hill)*, Floyd Shackelford *(Cook)*, Charles Brinley *(Sheriff)*, Scout the Horse.

Hoxie's horse, Scout, is the real star of this modest B western. The animal plays a wild steed whom Hoxie captures and tames. He does such a good job of this, in fact, that when a rival for his master's sweetheart, Day, mistreats him, Scout escapes. He then gallops through the countryside and, with his knack for opening gates and barn doors, allows nearly the entire equestrian population in the area to exit their confinement. There's plenty of fancy riding as Hoxie, who has been wrongly accused (by the villain) of being a horse thief, rounds them up, saves his beloved from a stampede, and sees to it that the real culprit is put behind bars.

d, Clifford Smith; w, Isadore Bernstein; ph, William Nobles.

Western **(PR:A MPAA:NR)**

WHITE PANTS WILLIE*** (1927) 7 reels B&H Enterprises/FN bw

Johnny Hines *(Willie Bascom)*, Leila Hyams *(Helen Charters)*, Henry Barrows *(Philip Charters)*, Ruth Dwyer *(Judy)*, Walter Long *(Mock Epply)*, Margaret Seddon *(Winifred Barnes)*, George Kuwa *(Wong Lee)*, Bozo *(Peaches, an Educated Goose)*.

Entertaining comedy has Hines, a garage mechanic and inventor, meeting up with society girl Hyams and her father. Later, while delivering an automobile he repaired, Hines, along with his Chinese laundryman, Kuwa, bluff their way into a fancy country club (actually, his white pants do the trick), where Hyams and her father are staying. Through some nicely delivered and funny exposition, the lad wins a big polo match, sells his auto invention, and lands the girl as well.

d, Charles Hines; w, Howard J. Green (based on the story by Elmer Holmes Davis); ph, James Diamond.

Comedy **(PR:A MPAA:NR)**

WHITE ROSE, THE**** (1923) 12 reels D. W. Griffith/UA bw

Mae Marsh *(Bessie Williams, Known as "Teazie")*, Carol Dempster *(Marie Carrington)*, Ivor Novello *(Joseph Beaugarde)*, Neil Hamilton *(John White)*, Lucille La Verne *("Auntie" Easter)*, Porter Strong *(Apollo, a Servant)*, Jane Thomas *(A Cigarstand Girl)*, Kate Bruce *(An Aunt)*, Erville Alderson *(A Man of the World)*, Herbert Sutch *(The Bishop)*, Joseph Burke *(The Landlord)*, Mary Foy *(The Landlady)*, Charles Emmett Mack *(Guest at Inn)*, Uncle Tom Jenkins *(An Old Negro)*.

Novello, a Louisiana aristocrat, graduates from the seminary and decides to travel a bit to become acquainted with the worldly side of life with which, as a minister, he plans to do battle. At a hotel near New Orleans he meets Marsh, a sweet young girl who is pretending to be a flapper with "experience." They have an affair, and the guilt-ridden Ivor returns home to do penance and marry Dempster, a woman of his own class. Haunted by his fall from grace, he preaches from the pulpit against the sins of the flesh, while the object of his pleasure, ill, pregnant, and fired from her job as a cigar counter clerk, is taken in by kindly blacks. Marsh survives and appears before her former love, babe in arms. The clergyman realizes his love for the girl, confesses to God, and asks her to be his wife. Dempster in the meantime discovers that she is attracted to Hamilton, who has become a wealthy businessman, and they also decide to marry. Shot mostly on location in Louisiana, this is one of Griffith's last great films, and the final time he was to direct Marsh. She would never again give a performance of this remarkable range, and that is the world's loss.

d, D. W. Griffith; w, Irene Sinclair [Griffith]; ph, G. W. Bitzer, Hendrik Sartov, Hal Sintzenich; set d, Charles M. Kirk; spec eff, Edward Scholl.

Drama **(PR:A MPAA:NR)**

WHITE SISTER, THE* 1/2** (1923) 12 reels INSP/Metro bw

Lillian Gish *(Angela Chiaromonte)*, Ronald Colman *(Capt. Giovanni Severini)*, Gail Kane *(Marchesa de Mola)*, J. Barney Sherry *(Monsignor Saracinesca)*, Charles Lane *(Prince Chiaromonte)*, Juliette La Violette *(Mme. Bernard)*, Signor Serena *(Prof. Ugo Severini)*, Alfredo Bertone *(Filmore Durand)*, Roman Ibanez *(Count del Ferice)*, Alfredo Martinelli *(Alfredo del Ferice)*, Carloni Talli *(Mother Superior)*, Giovanni Viccola *(Gen. Mazzini)*, Antonio Barda *(Alfredo's Tutor)*, Giacomo D'Attino *(Solicitor to the Prince)*, Michele Gualdi *(Solicitor to the Count)*, Giuseppe Pavoni *(Archbishop)*, Francesco Socinus *(Prof. Torricelli)*, Sheik Mahomet *(Bedouin Chief)*, James Abbe *(Lt. Rossini)*, Ducan Mansfield *(Comdr. Donato)*.

In 1923, films dealing with historical religious themes were considered quite acceptable to the moguls, but the industry regarded contemporary religious stories to be box office poison. In fact, Inspiration Pictures couldn't even land a distributor for THE WHITE SISTER until it received rave reviews and solid audience response on its New York opening at the Capital Theatre on April 20, 1924. The story has Gish playing an Italian aristocrat, who, following her father's death, is driven out of her home by a nasty sister, who also destroys the will which provided her with half the estate. Gish is in love with an Italian army officer (Colman) and when he is reported killed in the war the broken-hearted girl decides to become a nun. On the ship crossing over to Europe—the entire film was shot on location in Italy, for $300,000—director King met the Papal delegate to Washington, who expressed his concern about filming the assumption of the veil. King, who later became a Catholic convert, asked if he might be given an advisor and his request was granted. When they were ready shoot the scene, a fat little priest arrived carrying a very thick script—it was the whole ceremony. The clergyman could speak no English, but King communicated that he should go ahead and stage it for the company. It took from eight in the morning until seven at night. Then, with the event fresh in his mind, King produced this beautiful and highly moving scene. Later, the director thanked the archbishop and told him that the little priest was one of the greatest directors he had ever seen. The prelate smiled and pointed out that actually he did have a good deal of experience. The priest was in fact, the head ceremonial director for the Vatican. The report of Colman's death was erroneous, and when the soldier returns home he pleads with his love to renounce her vocation. He even tricks her into leaving the convent, and tries to have her sign a petition to the Pope asking to be released from her vows. Gish again refuses him, and at this point Vesuvius erupts, causing flooding and storms. The dashing officer manages to save Gish, but her sister, who is not so lucky, dies in her arms after receiving her forgiveness. Colman then sets off to warn the villagers but is drowned in doing so—leaving the pious Gish to dedicate the rest of her life to serving God. Colman, whom King and Gish discovered in a Broadway play, had appeared in a number of films (THE TOILERS, 1919, HANDCUFFS OR KISSES, 1920, and THE ETERNAL CITY, 1921) but this was the picture that made him a star. And in that time, before his magnificent voice could be heard, his swarthy good looks led many to refer to him as "another Valentino."

d, Henry King; w, George V. Hobart, Charles E. Whittaker (based on the novel by Francis Marion Crawford); t, Will M. Ritchey, Don Bartlett; ph, Roy Overbaugh; m, Joseph Carl Brill; ed, Duncan Mansfield; art d, Robert Haas.

Drama **(PR:A MPAA:NR)**

WHITE YOUTH** (1920) 5 reels UNIV bw

Edith Roberts *(Aline Ann Belame)*, Alfred Hollingsworth *(Gen. Belame)*, Thomas Jefferson *(Francois Cayetane)*, Arnold Gregg *(Burton Striker)*, Hattie Peters *(Catalou)*, Lucas C. Luke *(Butler)*, Joseph Belmont *(Mons. Le Moyne)*, Phyllis Allen *(Mme. Le Moyne)*, Olga De Mojean *(Mme. La Roche)*, Sam Konnella *(Pierre)*, Alida D. Jones *(Mme. Martin)*, Gertrude Pedlar *(Mother Superior)*.

Routine programmer set in Louisiana has an orphaned girl being forced by her grandfather to marry one of his elderly friends. The old gent is actually getting back at his son for selecting a bride he did not approve of. Fortunately, in the end, a good looking Yankee sweeps the girl off her feet and saves her from a fate almost as bad as death.

d, Norman Dawn; w, George Hull (based on a story by Clara Beranger, Forrest Halsey); ph, Thomas Rae.

Drama **(PR:A MPAA:NR)**

WHY BE GOOD?** (1929) 8 reels FN bw

Colleen Moore *(Pert)*, Neil Hamilton *(Peabody, Jr.)*, Bodil Rosing *(Ma Kelly)*, John Sainpolis *(Pa Kelly)*, Edward Martindel *(Peabody, Sr.)*, Eddie Clayton *(Tom)*, Lincoln Stedman *(Jerry)*, Louis Natheaux *(Jimmy)*, Collette Merton *(Julie)*, Dixie Gay *(Susie)*.

Uninspired Moore comedy has the star playing the familiar role of a salesgirl in love with a millionaire's son. In this case, the old boy also happens to own the store where she works, and he accepts her into the family only after his son, Hamilton, proves her virtue by "testing" her at a notorious roadhouse. This one is below Moore's usual standard, but the little charmer does her best and manages to save the picture from being a complete failure.

d, William A. Seiter; w, Carey Wilson; t, Paul Perez; ph, Sidney Hickox; ed, Terry Morse; m/l, "I'm Thirsty for Kisses," Lou Davis, J. Fred Coots; syn sc.

Comedy **(PR:A MPAA:NR)**

WHY WORRY**** (1923) 6 reels HR/Pathe bw

Harold Lloyd *(Harold Van Pelham)*, Jobyna Ralston *(The Nurse)*, John Aasen *(Colosso)*, Leo White *(Herculeo)*, James Mason *(Jim Blake)*, Wallace Howe *(Mr. Pipps)*, Mark Jones, Charles Stevenson, Sam Lufkin, Lee Phelps, William Gillespie, Gaylord Lloyd.

One of Lloyd's funniest and most gag-packed films has the star playing a millionaire hypochondriac who sets out with his private nurse (Ralston, who replaced Mildred Davis when she retired to become the comedian's wife) for a South American island paradise in order to improve his health. Once there, he finds himself in the middle of a desperate revolution, which Lloyd assumes is being staged especially for his amusement. But when he's thrown into prison with a toothache-suffering giant, the pill-popping Yank discovers otherwise. After helping his very large friend extract his molar, the unlikely pair, through a series of hilarious sight gags, rescue Ralston, crush the rebellion, and provide the American renegade who is responsible for mischief with his just punishment. All of this excitement, of course, cures Harold of his imagined maladies, and he returns home to make his nurse his wife and pull the strings necessary to land his enormous pal a job directing traffic in downtown Los Angeles. This would be Lloyd's last film in conjunction with Hal Roach. The comedian had become a star of the first magnitude, and now it was time to open his own studio and continue to go about the business of making the world laugh on his own.

d, Fred Newmeyer, Sam Taylor; w, Taylor; ph, Walter Lundin; ed, Thomas J. Crizer.

Comedy **Cas.** **(PR:A MPAA:NR)**

WIDE-OPEN TOWN, A 1/2** (1922) 5 reels SF/SEL bw

Conway Tearle *(Billy Clifford)*, Faire Binney *(Helen Morely)*, James Seeley *(Mayor Morely)*, Harry Tighe *(Tug Wilson)*, Claude Brooks *(Fred Tatum)*, Ned Sparks *(Si Ryan)*, Danny Hayes *(Rufe Nimbo)*, John P. Wade *(Gov. Talbot)*, Alice May *(Mrs. Tatum)*, Bobby Connelly *(Gov. Talbot as a Boy)*, Jerry Devine *(Billy Clifford as a Boy)*.

Skillful direction by Ince elevates this potboiler in which Tearle, a gambling establishment owner, falls in love with Binney, the town mayor's daughter. Tearle's business partner discovers that the mayor is planning to raid their establishment so he kidnaps Binney to use as a bargaining chip. But before police arrive on the scene, Tearle rescues his sweetheart, killing his partner in the process. The young lady's reputation is spared but Tearle is sent to jail for life. The situation is rectified, however, when the governor, who happens to be the boyhood pal for whom the gambler once took a reform school rap, intervenes. After his release, he vows to go straight, and marriage to the mayor's lovely daughter is all the incentive he needs.

d, Ralph Ince; w, Edward J. Montagne (based on a story by Earle Mitchell); ph, William Wagner.

Crime/Drama **(PR:A MPAA:NR)**

WIE ER IN DE WELT

(SEE: GOLEM: HOW HE CAME INTO THE WORLD, THE, 1920, Ger.)

WIFE AGAINST WIFE** (1921) 6 reels Whitman Bennett/AFN bw

Pauline Starke *(Gabrielle Gautier)*, Percy Marmont *(Stannard Dole)*, Edward Langford *(Dr. Ethan Bristol)*, Emily Fitzroy *(Mrs. Dole)*, Ottola Nesmith *(Florence Bromley)*.

Starke, a Paris model, falls in love with Marmont, an American sculptor for whom she is posing. He leaves before the work is completed and when she later meets him in New York, Starke is shocked to discover that he is married. Marmont explains that his wife will not grant him a divorce, then he convinces Starke to help him finish the work they began in Paris. She does and after the piece is completed, the artist, who it turns out has been ill for some time, dies. Starke is comforted by Percy's best friend, Langford. The plot thickens when the couple are married and the sculptor's first wife, out of spite, threatens to destroy the union by informing Langford of his bride's former affair with Marmont. Their first child is soon born, however, and creates a family bond too strong to disrupt.

d, Whitman Bennett; w, Dorothy Farnum (based on the story "The Price" by George H. Broadhurst); ph, Ernest Haller.

Drama **(PR:A MPAA:NR)**

WIFE SAVERS*** (1928) 6 reels PAR bw

Wallace Beery *(Louis Hozenozzle)*, Raymond Hatton *(Rodney Ramsbottom)*, ZaSu Pitts *(Germaine)*, Sally Blane *(Colette)*, Tom Kennedy *(Gen. Lavoris)*, Ford Sterling *(The Tavern Keeper)*, George Y. Harvey *(The Major)*, August Tollaire *(The Mayor)*.

Though not quite up to their earlier efforts, Beery and Hatton still manage to pull in a number of laughs playing doughboys stationed in Switzerland at the end of WW I. Hatton falls in love with Blane, a local girl, but has a formidable rival in Kennedy, a Swiss general. Then, when Hatton is ordered home, he in turn orders Beery to become Blane's protector. With Hatton out of the way, the general passes a law stipulating that all single women must immediately get married, and Beery weds Blane just to save her from falling into the clutches of the "big hunk of cheese." Infuriated by this, Hatton crosses the ocean again and challenges Beery to a duel. Plenty of laughs here are interrupted only when Blane steps forward to explain the situation, revealing that she has been granted a divorce and plans to marry a handsome young major.

p, James Cruze; d, Ralph Cedar; w, Tom J. Geraghty, Grover Jones (based on the play "Louie the Fourteenth" by Paul Frank Wilhelm, Julius Wilhelm, Arthur Wimperis); t, George Marion, Jr.; ph, Alfred Gilks, H. Kinley Martin; ed, George Nichols, Jr.

Comedy **(PR:A MPAA:NR)**

WIFE'S AWAKENING, A zero (1921) 6 reels R-C bw

William P. Carleton *(Howard)*, Fritzi Brunette *(Florence Otis)*, Sam De Grasse *(George Otis)*, Beverly Travers *(Grace)*, Edythe Chapman *(Mrs. Kelcey)*.

Bottom-of-the-barrel programmer about a woman who finally comes to realize that the sharpster who married her for her money is no longer worthy of her company and leaves him to be with the nice young chap she always loved, anyway. This one shot for the lowest possible level and made it in spades.

d, Louis Gasnier; w, Joseph Dubray (based on a story by Jack Cunningham); ph, Dubray.

Drama **(PR:A MPAA:NR)**

WILD AND WOOLLY* 1/2** (1917) 5 reels Douglas Fairbanks/ART bw

Douglas Fairbanks *(Jeff Hillington)*, Eileen Percy *(Nell)*, Sam De Grasse *(Steve)*, Walter Bytell *(His Father)*, Joseph Singleton *(His Butler)*, Calvert Carter *(Hotel-keeper)*, Forest Seabury *(Banker)*, J. W. Jones *(Lawyer)*, Charles Stevens *(Pedro)*, Tom Wilson *(Engineer)*, Monte Blue, Bull Montana.

Lots of fun in this Fairbanks romp about the eastern son of a railroad president, who is obsessed by the Wild West he's read about in dime novels. To his delight, his dad sends him to Arizona to check out a town which can possibly be used as a spur. Discovering the young New Yorker's "idealized" attitudes, the whole town—in hopes of striking a deal—performs an elaborate hoax by setting up the atmosphere they know he wants. Loading his six guns and cartidge belt with blanks, Fairbanks is exposed to every action cliche he could hope for. Then a *real* gang of crooks takes advantage of the charade, and the happy New Yorker is given the chance to do some heroics on the square. The action in this Fairbanks five-reeler is practically nonstop, as are the laughs.

d, John Emerson; w, Anita Loos (based on a story by Horace B. Carpenter); ph, Victor Fleming.

Western/Comedy **Cas.** **(PR:A MPAA:NR)**

WILD BLOOD 1/2** (1929) 5 reels UNIV bw

Rex the Horse *(himself)*, Jack Perrin *(Jack Crosby)*, Ethlyne Clair *(Mary Ellis)*, Theodore Lorch *(Luke Conner)*, Nelson McDowell *(John Ellis)*, Starlight the Horse.

Pretty good kids' movie has cowboy star Perrin falling in love with Clair, owner of Rex the Wonder Horse. Lorch, proprietor of a saloon and the film's villain, tries to steal the steed and force his attentions on Clair. Perrin saves her from this fate worse than death, while Rex takes care of Lorch by pushing him over the side of a cliff.

d, Henry MacRae; w, George Morgan; t, Gardner Bradford; ph, George Robinson; ed, Thomas Malloy.

Western **(PR:A MPAA:NR)**

WILD GIRL, THE* (1925) 5 reels TRU bw

Louise Lorraine *(Pattie)*, Art Acord *(Billy Woodruff)*, Andrew Waldron *(Grandpapa Toto)*, Rex the Dog, Black Beauty the Horse.

Lorraine plays a beautiful wild girl of the woods who meets Acord (her husband in real life) while he is on a photographic excursion, and the sparks begin to fly. Later, when the villain of the forest frames her grandfather for murder and tries to have his way with her, Lorraine's dog, Rex, races to get Acord, and the young man arrives in time to beat the tar out of the degenerate. He also forces a confession out of him, which gets the old man released from jail, and then Acord marries his grateful sweetheart.

d, William Bletcher.

Adventure **(PR:A MPAA:NR)**

WILD GOOSE, THE* (1921) 7 reels COS/FP bw

Mary MacLaren *(Diana Manners)*, Holmes E. Herbert *(Frank Manners)*, Dorothy Bernard *(Mrs. Hastings)*, Joseph Smiley *(Mr. Hastings)*, Norman Kerry *(Ogden Fenn)*, Rita Rogan *(Tam Manners)*, Lucia Backus Seger *(Nou Nou)*.

Neglected by her husband, Herbert, who thinks only of business and travels constantly, MacLaren has an affair with handsome Kerry. Her husband returns early from a trip to San Francisco, learns the truth, and immediately thinks in terms of divorce. Bernard, who is madly in love with Herbert, though married to Smiley, persuades him to abandon this action for the sake of the his child. Smiley then learns of his own wife's scarlet activities and goes to the love nest, where he abducts Kerry and deliberately drives his car over the side of a cliff. Bernard then brings the couple together again when she approaches MacLaren and selflessly delivers this bit of banal dialog, via a title card: "You have wrecked your own and your husband's life and sent one good man and a scoundrel to destruction, but nothing counts except the child." And so it ends.

d, Albert Capellani; w, Gouverneur Morris; ph, Harold Wenstrom.

Drama (PR:A MPAA:NR)

WILD GOOSE CHASE, THE** (1915) 5 reels LAS bw

Ina Claire *(Betty Wright)*, Tom Forman *(Bob Randall)*, Lucien Littlefield *("Grind")*, Helen Marlborough *(Mrs. Wright)*, Raymond Hatton *(Mr. Wright)*, Ernest Joy *(Mr. Randall)*, Theodore Roberts *(Horatio Brutus Bangs)*, Florence Smythe *(Mrs. Randall)*, Tex Driscoll, Mrs. Lewis McCord, Jane Wolff.

It's the old story of an arranged marriage—rejected by both principals—where both run away, join the same traveling theatrical company, fall in love, discover each other's true identities, and marry in the last reel to everyone's delight. A lesser Cecil and William DeMille effort, of interest mainly because it introduced the wonderful Claire to the screen.

d, Cecil B. DeMille; w, William C. DeMille (based on his own play); ph, Alvin Wyckoff.

Comedy (PR:A MPAA:NR)

WILD HONEY*** (1919) 6 reels De Luxe/Sherry Service bw

Doris Kenyon *(Mrs. Holbrook/Wild Honey)*, Frank Mills *(Pastor Holbrook)*, Edgar Jones *(Dick Hadding)*, Howard Kyle *("Doc" Bliss)*, John Hopkins *(Joe Stacey)*, Joseph W. Mack *(Jim Belcher)*, Henry J. Herbert *(Ed Southern)*, Herbert Standing *(Rev. Davis Warwick)*, Vinnie Burns *(Trixianita)*, Ruth Taylor *(Gold Hill Ida)*, Mildred Leary *(Letty Noon)*, Nellie King.

When a young minister and his actress sweetheart visit Mills to discuss the problems they believe might occur if they should marry, the old pastor tells them the story of a fire-and-brimstone cleric who journeyed west at the time of the gold rush. Intent on saving numerous souls, the youthful zealot found his services being attended regularly by a dance hall girl (Kenyon) known as Wild Honey. Although the minister would berate the young woman week after week from his pulpit, she continued to return. Not only that, she also prevented the town toughs from riding the "sky pilot" out on a rail. In the end the saloon woman caught a bullet in the head for her trouble. The story made its point, with the young man of God and his lady deciding right then and there that nothing would stand in the way of their finding happiness through holy matrimony. Then the parson, quite pleased with himself, suggests, "Allow me to escort you to my living quarters, as I should like to introduce you to Mrs. Holbrook." And when he slides open the doors leading to the parlor, sitting on the other side, knitting in hand, is the woman who earlier was known as Wild Honey.

d, Francis J. Grandon; w, Louis Joseph Vance; ph, Ned Van Buren.

Drama (PR:A MPAA:NR)

WILD HONEY 1/2** (1922) 7 reels UNIV bw

Priscilla Dean *(Lady Vivienne)*, Noah Beery *(Henry Porthen)*, Lloyd Whitlock *("Freddy" Sutherland)*, Raymond Blathwayt *(Sir Hugh)*, Percy Challenger *(Ebenezer Leamish)*, Helen Raymond *(Joan Rudd)*, Landers Stevens *(Wolf Montague)*, Robert Ellis *(Kerry Burgess)*, Wallace Beery *("Buck" Roper)*, Carl Stockdale *(Liverpool Blondie)*, Christian J. Frank *(Repington)*, Harry De Roy *(Koos)*.

Dean's splendid screen persona makes something of this average programmer, which has her playing a young British noblewoman who lands in South Africa after indirectly being targeted as the cause of a suitor's murder. While making her way through the bush, Dean is rescued from bandits by Ellis, with whom she falls in love. Dean later runs into Whitlock, who was a witness at the murder and fled England because he was afraid of being implicated, and lifts the coward out of the gutter. In the movie's big thrill ending, she reaches the settlers of an outpost in time to warn them that Stevens, another fellow she spurned along the way, is about to blow up the dam. This gives Ellis a second opportunity to save her life, and one is left hoping that at last the lovely Universal star will be given the chance to enjoy a little peace and quiet.

d, Wesley Ruggles; w, Lucien Hubbard (based on the story by Cynthia Stockley); ph, Harry Thorpe.

Adventure/Drama (PR:A MPAA:NR)

WILD OATS LANE* 1/2** (1926) Marshall Neilan/PDC bw

Viola Dana *(The Girl/Marie)*, Robert Agnew *(The Boy)*, John MacSweeney *(The Priest)*, Margaret Seddon *(The Mother)*, George Barnum *(The Father)*, Jerry Miley *(The Dude)*, Scott Welch *(The Detective)*, Robert Brower *(The Kleptomaniac)*, Eddie James *(The Gangster)*, Mitchell Lewis *(The Bum)*.

Film scholars and critics have either neglected or all but forgotten this hard-hitting and heart-warming, skillfully directed Neilan picture about a kindly Irish priest who has dedicated his life to saving the dregs of society. In this case he brings a young Pennsylvania couple, who lost each other in New York and were forced into lives of prostitution and crime, together again. He saves them, as well as their souls, and personally performs the marriage. Neilan's commitment to detail pays off from beginning to end, and his depiction of gangsters and cops is the equal of, and perhaps even the inspiration for, the later work of Josef von Sternberg (UNDERWORLD, 1927) and the whole cycle of Warner Brothers crime films which followed half a decade later.

d, Marshall Neilan; w, Benjamin Glazer (based on the play by George H. Broadhurst); ph, David Kesson, Donald Keyes; ed, Helen Warne; art d, Harold Grieve.

Drama/Crime (PR:A MPAA:NR)

WILD ORCHIDS*** (1929) 11 reels MGM bw

Greta Garbo *(Lili Sterling)*, Lewis Stone *(John Sterling)*, Nils Asther *(Prince De Gace)*.

Garbo and her neglectful husband, Stone, meet a Javanese prince (Asther) while sailing to that land on a business trip. She and the wealthy prince come close to having an encounter on board, and when Garbo and her husband are later invited to visit his estate, it seems likely the sparks are going to fly. This plot development gives director Franklin the opportunity to dress the beautiful actress in several exotic Oriental gowns (actually, the outfits are Thai rather than Javanese). This brings the triangle to an exciting, if rather disappointing climax, whereby the now suspicious Stone resolves to kill the prince on a tiger hunt by unloading his rifle. When Asther is slightly wounded and Stone decides to leave his wife, Garbo declares her love for her husband and they sail home together. Art director Gibbons created a wonderful sense of Oriental atmosphere, and Asther and Garbo generate a lot of heat on their own—so much so that one wishes her final decision might have been otherwise.

d, Sidney Franklin; w, Hans Kraly, Richard Schayer, Willis Goldbeck (based on the story "Hunt" by John Colton); t, Marian Ainslee, Ruth Cummings; ph, William Daniels; ed, Conrad A. Nervig; art d, Cedric Gibbons; cos, Adrian; syn sc; s eff.

Drama Cas. (PR:A MPAA:NR)

WILDERNESS WOMAN, THE*** (1926) 8 reels Robert Kane/FN bw

Aileen Pringle *(Juneau MacLean/Junie)*, Lowell Sherman *(Alan Burkett)*, Chester Conklin *(Kodiak MacLean)*, Henry Vibart *(The Colonel)*, Robert Cain *(His Confederate)*, Harriet Sterling *(Squaw)*, Burr McIntosh *(The Judge)*.

Conklin is wonderful as an Alaskan miner who makes a million and heads for New York with his whiskey-drinking, hard-punching daughter, Pringle. On the train they encounter a couple of con men, posing as father and son, who attempt to sell the old-timer a subway station, though he doubts a train can really run under the river. But after Pringle becomes beautified at a fancy salon and wins the love of a young engineer (Sherman), the crooks are disposed of—the young one by Pringle's devastating right cross when he tries to make a pass—and Gotham becomes their oyster.

d, Howard Higgin; w, (based on the story by Arthur Stringer); t, Don Bartlett; ph, Ernest Haller; ed, Paul F. Maschke; art d, Robert M. Hass.

Comedy (PR:A MPAA:NR)

WINDING STAIR, THE*** (1925) 6 reels FOX bw

Alma Rubens *(Marguerite)*, Edmund Lowe *(Paul)*, Warner Oland *(Petras)*, Mahlon Hamilton *(Gerard)*, Emily Fitzroy *(Mme. Muller)*, Chester Conklin *(Onery)*, Frank Leigh *(Andrea)*.

Lowe, an officer in the French Foreign Legion, is ordered to put down a distant Arab uprising and discovers that it's really a trick to leave the city unprotected. When his superiors refuse to believe him, Lowe, dressed like a native, manages to save Rubens (his cabaret dancer-sweetheart), as well as the entire Christian community. The Legion, however, brands him a coward for deserting and he is drummed out of the corps. Later, when WW I breaks out, Lowe puts together a regiment of loyal subjects, and under an assumed name helps France win the Battle of Flanders. He is seriously wounded, decorated, exonerated, and finally reunited with Rubens, who has also committed herself well on the field of honor as a nurse. No masterpiece by any means, but lots of fun nonetheless.

d, John Griffith Wray; w, Julian La Mothe (based on the novel by Alfred Edward Woodley Mason); ph, Karl Struss.

War/Romance (PR:A MPAA:NR)

WING TOY* 1/2 (1921) 6 reels FOX bw

Shirley Mason *(Wing Toy)*, Raymond McKee *(Bob Harris)*, Edward McWade *(Wong)*, Harry S. Northrup *(Yen Low)*, Betty Schade *(White Lily)*, Scott McKee *(The Mole)*.

Featherweight hokum has Mason playing an orphaned "half-breed" girl who is raised by a kindly laundryman and then sold to Chinatown's leading underworld figure (Northrup) because he's in a position to "makee life better." Mason manages to escape his lustful clutches when Schade, his jealous Caucasian wife, does him in. This frees Mason to marry the newspaper reporter she loves, and then to everyone's delight it's discovered that she is actually the kidnaped daughter of New York's crusading district attorney.

d, Howard M. Mitchell; w, Thomas Dixon, Jr. (based on a story by Pearl Doles Bell); ph, Glen MacWilliams.

Drama (PR:A MPAA:NR)

WINGS** 1/2** (1927) 13 reels PAR bw

Clara Bow *(Mary Preston)*, Charles "Buddy" Rogers *(Jack Powell)*, Richard Arlen *(David Armstrong)*, Jobyna Ralston *(Sylvia Lewis)*, Gary Cooper *(Cadet White)*, El Brendel *(Herman Schwimpf)*, Arlette Marchal *(Celeste)*, Gunboat Smith *(Sergeant)*, Richard Tucker *(Air Commander)*, Julia Swayne Gordon *(Mrs. Armstrong)*, Henry B. Walthall *(Mr. Armstrong)*, George Irving *(Mr. Powell)*, Hedda Hopper *(Mrs. Powell)*, Roscoe Karns *(Lt. Cameron)*, Nigel De Brulier *(Peasant)*, James Pierce *(MP)*, Carl von Hartmann *(German Officer)*, William Wellman *(A Doughboy)*, Dick Grace, Rod Rogers, Tommy Carr *(Aviators)*, Charles Barton *(Doughboy Hit by Ambulance)*, Margery Chapin Wellman *(Peasant Woman)*, Gloria Wellman *(Peasant Child)*.

The tremendous popularity of THE BIG PARADE brought war pictures back into vogue, and Paramount was anxious to get on the bandwagon. Therefore, when John Monk Saunders, a former combat pilot, presented Jesse Lasky with a story dealing with the battle of the skies, the mogul was enthused. The studio was able to obtain the cooperation of the U.S. War Department on condition that the studio carry a $10,000 insurance policy on every man involved, arrange the shooting so that it would also serve training purposes, and agree not to release the film without government approval. Paramount was more than pleased to go along, and in return received thousands of soldiers, numerous tanks, tons of artillery, as well as other heavy equipment, and practically every pursuit plane the Army possessed (a number of flyers who participated in the making of WINGS went on to enjoy illustrious careers in the Air Force, including generals Hoyt Vanderberg and Frank Andrews). The location chosen for shooting the picture was the San Antonio area, where Kelly Field was available. And the 2nd Infantry Division's Army Engineers were used to create (at a cost to Paramount of a quarter of a million dollars) a replica of the battlefield of St. Mihiel. To direct the epochal film, the studio took a risk in hiring William Wellman, a young man with only one solid hit behind him. But "Wild Bill" (as he would become known) was the only director in Hollywood who had experience in aerial warfare, having served in the Lafayette Escadrille Flying Corps. In his autobiography, *A Short Time for Insanity*, Wellman describes the cool reception he received because of his youthful appearance (he was a young-looking 28) when he met the Army officers who would be technically under his command. It was at a dinner party, and the top general was curt to the point of rudeness. Naturally, the officers and their wives, all of whom were under him, followed suit. The director knew he had to do something, and his course of action went as follows: "The introductions over and everyone seated, Mr. Biggest General reached for his fruit cocktail, as did everyone else. This was the time. I bowed my head and mouthed a silent grace. It caught everybody by surprise. Saunders damn near slid under the table, Hubbard stared at me unbelievingly, and the fruit cocktails remained untouched. I held it long enough for all to see, finished my prayer, and started on my dinner as if nothing had happened, but I saw that it hit home with a few of the ladies. Some of them kept looking at me for an added moment; two or three whispered to their husbands. At least I had some of them going in a different direction." When the time came for the speeches to be made, Wellman got up and told the assemblage that the proper thing to say would be that he was happy and honored to be there, but that would not be the truth because he knew that they resented his ability because of age. The director then went on to confess that he was really only seven years old, but that for one so young he had lived quite an interesting life. He had been married not once, but twice. Had been in two armies, including the Foreign Legion, had been a successful combat flyer, directed a few movies, and even knew Clara Bow. Wellman ended his address on this note, 'Perhaps the most prosperous producing company in the motion picture business is the Paramount Pictures Corporation. The idiots have been so successful in the development of a multimillion-dollar industry that they have appointed a seven-year-old to guide the destiny of their most important project. Quite naturally, one so young must be considered in the category of genius and because of his infancy must be given unending help and encouragement. I stand before you as that young prodigy and in all humility request the decency and the support that is due him;' and I sat down." After a pause, the general's wife began to applaud, followed by her husband, and then everybody in the room, including the serving staff. Wild Bill had won the day, and as the party was leaving, the lady who had become his ally quietly approached to ask if he had really been saying grace, and the director looked her straight in the eye and answered, "No." The story line of this first picture to win an Academy Award is pretty straightforward, dealing with a couple of small-town, middle-class fellows, Rogers and Arlen, who love the same girl, Ralston. Bow is Buddy's neighbor and has a terrific crush on him, but Rogers thinks of her as just one of the guys. The war has broken out and the two join the air service where their rivalry eventually turns to friendship. At the training camp, they are placed in the same tent with a veteran flier. To them, this is a man who knows the score, and, in a wonderful scene, he takes a bite from a candy bar Arlen offers him, shows the boys his lucky charm, and then tells them, "When your time comes, you're going to get it." The airman is then called to duty, and after leaving with a friendly salute, the rookies notice that he's left behind his good luck piece. The flier is killed, but in their enthusiasm the reality of war's horror fails to strike home—that will come later. (The young veteran was played by Gary Cooper, whom Paramount was grooming for stardom, and his performance here was so engaging that thousands of letters were addressed to the studio demanding to see more of him.) The boys finish their training and head for the front, where some of the greatest air combat footage ever shot takes place. In this film, nothing was faked. There are no process shots. The cameras were placed on gun mounts, and live photographers were positioned in scores of planes to achieve a sense of realism which has never been equaled. And then, to add even more punch, the Magnascope Process—where the screen opens up to enormous proportions—was used in many of the first-run screenings. But, back to the story. While the fellows have distinguished themselves in the air, Bow arrives on the scene as an ambulance driver. Later, she is given the chance to show off her sex appeal when she poses as a saucy French girl to rescue Rogers from the clutches of a couple of tarts who are about to put him in the position of being court-martialed. Bow is sent back to the States in disgrace, and the boys go back to the war. When they are called upon to take out a couple of German observation balloons, Arlen is shot down behind enemy lines and after an eternity of waiting, Rogers receives word that his pal has been killed. Crazy with anger and grief, the lad takes off and attacks everything he can find in a German uniform. Meanwhile, Arlen manages to steal a Fokker and, though wounded, heads for home. Naturally, their paths cross and Rogers moves in for the kill. Arlen spots the shooting star emblem on the side of his friend's biplane and tries to signal him, but it's no use and, riddled with bullets, the American crashes to the ground. Rogers lands his craft, to cut the German insignia from the plane of his fallen foe, and realizes what he has done. There is a moving scene where his comrade dies in his arms and the flier unashamedly kisses him good-bye. WINGS is full of unforgettable scenes such as this, including some of the best infantry battle material ever committed to film, as the engagement at St. Mihiel is faithfully re-created. Not to mention the tremendously touching moment when Rogers returns home a hero, but breaks away from his welcoming parade to pay his respects to and receive the forgiveness of the parents of the man he mistakenly killed. There is some pretty grim and heavy stuff in this extraordinary motion picture, so when Bow finally ends up with her man it's a welcome relief rather than a convenient ending. For the director, there was also a moment of relief, but in his case, it was merciful. He had shot the big infantry scene from on top of a high tower and at a crucial moment someone interrupted his concentration, causing Wellman to set off the wrong charge. It could have been fatal, but wasn't. "Get out of here you son of a bitch" the director shouted, and continued with the five-minute battle which had been timed to perfection. He knew he had gotten what he wanted. But he also wanted the right cloud formations for an aerial sequence he needed, and the money men had lost their patience. Worst of all, they were in San Antonio to tell him so. Wellman did what any good Irishman would do under the circumstances. He went back to his room and poured himself a drink. And then he poured himself another. And then he took a shower which was interrupted by a loud knocking. Again, from the director's autobiography, "I opened the door and there they stood: the unholy three. I asked them in and poured them a drink. I did not take one myself. They sat down, all but Mr. [Otto] Kahn. He started to pace the room and I knew I was in for it, but what a hell of a way to go out. I had just shown them five minutes of unbroken madness, and I don't think they would ever forget it as long as they lived. I sat down and waited for the ultimatum. It came fast and concise. Mr. Kahn: 'Wellman, we like you'—I goddamned near passed out—'and furthermore, you stay here as long as you think is necessary to get what you believe is best for the picture. We have complete confidence in you, and the picture is in your young capable hands.' I excused myself and went into the bathroom to vomit." Then as the director knelt there, almost overcome by relief and joy, there was still another knock. It was the banker, Otto Kahn, asking if he was alright. Quoting Wellman again, "Yes sir, all right and getting sober," and then Kahn continued, 'I was that goddamned idiot who opened his big mouth at the wrong time. I am terribly sorry, and I apologize.' I heard them go out and the door close. I lay down on the floor and cried."

p, Lucien Hubbard; d, William Wellman; w, Hope Loring, Louis D. Lighton (based on a story by John Monk Saunders); t, Julian Johnson; ph, Harry Perry, E. Burton Steene, Cliff Blackston, Russell Harland, Bert Baldridge, Frank Cotner, Foxon M. Dean, Ray Olsen, Herman Schoop, L. Guy Wilky, Al Williams; m, J. S. Zamecnik; ed, Hubbard; art d, Laurence Hitt; cos, Edith Head; m/l, "Wings," Zamecnik, Ballard MacDonald; stunts, Dick Grace; flying sequences sup, S. C. Campbell, Ted Parson, Carl von Hartmann, James A. Healy.

War Cas. (PR:A MPAA:NR)

WINGS OF THE STORM*** (1926) 6 reels FOX bw

Thunder the Dog, Virginia Brown Faire *(Anita Baker)*, Reed Howes *(Allen Gregory)*, William Russell *(Bill Martin)*, Hank Mann *(Red Jones)*.

Good kids' movie has Thunder, the runt of a German shepherd litter, growing up to be a cowardly adult dog. He becomes separated from his mistress, who is visiting the lumber camp she owns to check on stealing, and is taken in by forest ranger Howes. The ranger teaches the canine his values, and the animal learns so well that he performs a number of heroic deeds before finally saving his mistress and Howes from the villainous camp superintendent who tries to kill them by unleashing an avalanche of logs. Thunder gives the great Rin-Tin-Tin a run for his money here, and the picture is done well enough to appeal to grownups as well as moppets.

d, J. G. Blystone; w, Dorothy Yost, L. G. Rigby (based on the story by Lawrence Williams Pedrose); t, Elizabeth Pickett; ph, Robert Kurrle.

Adventure (PR:A MPAA:NR)

WINNING GOAL, THE** (1929, Brit.) 5 reels G. B. Samuelson/GEN bw

Harold Walden *(Jack Metherill)*, Maudie Dunham *(Elsie Witworth)*, Tom Reynolds *(Uncle Edmund)*, Haidee Wright *(Mrs. Witworth)*, Jack Cock.

The popular soccer player, Jack Cock, and a number of other athletic stars appear in this predictable sports film which has a player (Walden) being traded to his long-time rival club. He then shows his stuff by winning the big game in spite of a broken arm.

d, G. B. Samuelson; w, (based on the play by Harold Brighouse).

Adventure (PR:A MPAA:NR)

WINNING OF BARBARA WORTH, THE* 1/2**

(1926) 9 reels Goldwyn/UA bw

Ronald Colman *(Willard Holmes)*, Vilma Banky *(Barbara Worth)*, Charles Lane *(Jefferson Worth)*, Paul McAllister *(The Seer)*, E. J. Ratcliffe *(James Greenfield)*, Gary Cooper *(Abe Lee)*, Clyde Cook *(Tex)*, Erwin Connelly *(Pat)*, Sam Blum *(Blanton)*.

Colman and Banky, Hollywood's most popular romantic couple of the day, were teamed once again for this Sam Goldwyn western (the producer almost lost the property to an independent and was forced to outbid them for it by $125,000), but the actor who really made the sparks fly in this picture was a young man from Montana who had only made a few small film appearances, Gary Cooper. Actually, his role as Ace Lee had been assigned to cowboy actor Harold Goodwin, but when Goodwin got hung up in another production, director King recalled the lanky fellow he had used in an earlier bit part, and whose screen test he had seen and was impressed by. The story has a child orphaned when her parents make their way westward being adopted by Lane when his party of settlers discover her. The little girl grows up to be Banky and she shares the dream of her foster father to reclaim the desert lands by using the Colorado River for irrigation purposes. Lane borrows the money from Ratcliffe, a crooked New York banker, who arrives with his engineer stepson, Colman. As the project develops, a town grows up, which the old boy calls "Barbara Worth," in honor of his darling. A rivalry develops between Colman and Cooper (who is also an engineer) for the love of Banky. But when Ratcliffe tries to pull a double cross, Lane orders him and his stepson, whom he assumes is involved in the scheme, from his land, and sets out to complete the project himself. Before long, however, Lane runs out of cash and Ratcliffe incites the workers to riot for their pay. It is then that the one-time rivals, Colman and Cooper, set out on an arduous all-day ride to come up with the needed money. On their way back, they are ambushed and Cooper is seriously wounded. Knowing that Banky is really in love with the easterner, he urges him to ride on alone, and the star gets back just in time to prevent a mob from lynching his future father-in-law. The big scene comes when the inferior materials used by Ratcliffe cause the dam to burst and a spectacular flood wipes out his town. The picture, of course, ends with Colman and Banky tying the knot and everybody pitching in to make the original dream a reality. For his part in this film, Cooper was paid $65 a week. Now, Goldwyn knew that the actor had something, especially when the reviews started to come in (Louella Parsons was quite taken with the westerner), but he thought that Cooper was under contract to Henry King, and he let him get away to Paramount. Years later when Gary was one of Hollywood's biggest stars and had made a series of expensive pictures for his former employer, his salary demands must surely have been the inspiration for at least one or two classic "Goldwynisms."

d, Henry King; w, Frances Marion (based on the novel by Harold Bell Wright); ph, George Barnes; art d, Karl Oscar Borg.

Western **(PR:A MPAA:NR)**

WINNING STROKE, THE** (1919) 5 reels FOX bw

George Walsh *(Buck Simmons)*, Jane McAlpine *(Aida Courtland)*, John Leslie *(Paul Browning)*, William Hayes *(Burton Hampden)*, Louis Este *("Crickett" Perry)*, William Woodford *(The Dean)*, Sidney Marion *("Chub" Winters)*, Byron Douglas *(Head Coach)*, Julien Beaubien.

Fair programmer has Walsh doing his athletic stuff as a collegiate boatman who overcomes a plot on the part of gamblers and a jealous freshman to have him lose the big competition.

d, Edward Dillon; w, Raymond Schrock, Edward Sedgwick (based on a story by Sedgwick); ph, Al Leach.

Adventure **(PR:A MPAA:NR)**

WISE FOOL, A* 1/2 (1921) 5 reels FP/PAR bw

James Kirkwood *(Jean Jacques Barbille)*, Alice Hollister *(Carmen Dolores)*, Ann Forrest *(Zoe Barbille)*, Alan Hale *(George Masson)*, Fred Huntley *(Sebastian Dolores)*, William Boyd *(Gerard Fynes)*, Truly Shattuck *(Virginia Poucette)*, Harry Duffield *(Fille)*, Charles Ogle *(Judge Carcasson)*, John Herdman *(The Curate)*, Mabel Van Buren *(Mme. Langlois)*.

Parker adapted his own novel to the screen and this was a big mistake on the part of Famous Players-Lasky, because the result is a confusing and uneven domestic melodrama. The story has to do with a wealthy French Canadian (Kirkwood) who falls in love with Hollister, the daughter of a Spanish adventurer, while crossing the Atlantic. They marry and have a daughter (later played by Forrest), but before long Kirkwood's indifference drives his wife into the arms of Hale. Aware that he is actually to blame, Kirkwood decides to spare Hale's life, but Hollister departs for Montreal, where she places her daughter in a convent school and lands a job performing as a chorus girl. Time passes, and in defiance of her father, Forrest marries Boyd and the couple head west to make their fortune. The picture ends on a most contrived and unsatisfactory note, with Kirkwood losing everything in a fire but finding himself reunited with his wife, daughter, and son-in-law. One has the feeling that Parker is trying to make a statement, and completely fails to do so.

d, George Melford; w, Gilbert Parker (based on his novel *The Money Master)*; ph, William Marshall.

Drama **(PR:A MPAA:NR)**

WISE HUSBANDS zero 6 reels PIO bw

Gail Kane, J. Herbert Frank, Gladden James, Arthur Donaldson, Lillian Worth.

Terrible low-budget production has a young millionaire falling in love with a Red Cross worker, of whom his snooty mother does not approve. His father thinks the world of her, however, and arranges for a friend to assume the role of a debauched artist and attempt to seduce his own wife, just to make the point that the girl—who is quite virtuous—will make a good daughter-in-law. The scheme works. The picture does not.

d, Frank Reicher; w, J. Clarkson Miller (based on a story by Charles D. Isaacson).

Drama **(PR:A MPAA:NR)**

WISHING RING, THE*** (1914) 5 reels Shubert/WORLD bw

Vivian Martin *(Sally)*, Alec B. Francis *(Earl of Bateson)*, Chester Barnett *(Giles)*, Simeon Wiltsie *(The Parson)*, Walter Morton *(Mr. Annesley)*, Johnny Hines, James Young, Holbrook Blinn.

Tourneur used his painter's eye to produce this lovely romantic story, set in Old England, about the handsome son of an earl who, after being expelled from college, is ordered to earn half a crown before being accepted back into the family. He takes a job gardening at the home of a country minister, falls in love with the daughter of the house, and through her sweet grace is once again embraced by his father.

d&w, Maurice Tourneur (based on a play by Owen Davis); ph, John van den Broek; art d, Ben Carre.

Romance **(PR:A MPAA:NR)**

WITCHING HOUR, THE* (1921) 7 reels FP/PAR bw

Elliott Dexter *(Jack Brookfield)*, Winter Hall *(Judge Prentice)*, Ruth Renick *(Viola Campbell)*, Robert Cain *(Frank Hardmuth)*, Edward Sutherland *(Clay Whipple)*, Mary Alden *(Helen Whipple)*, Fred Turner *(Lew Ellinger)*, Genevieve Blinn *(Mrs. Campbell)*, Charles West *(Tom Denning)*, L. M. Wells *(Judge Henderson)*, Clarence Geldert *(Col. Bailey)*, Jim Blackwell *(Harvey)*.

The original Thomas play had little going for it and this Taylor motion picture has even less. Loaded with titles and poor-taste "darkie" comedy relief, the absurd plot has to do with a superstitious young fellow (poorly played by Sutherland), who has an obsessive fear of cat's-eye jewelry and is goaded into killing West, when the latter taunts him with a scarf pin during a card game. The owner of the gambling house, Dexter, pulls some strings with a judge, gets the lad a second trail, and then through mental telepathy foils the villain of the film—ambitious politican Cain—from killing him. The youth is acquitted and asks for the hand of Dexter's niece, which mercifully brings the production to its unsatisfactory conclusion.

d, William Desmond Taylor; w, Julia Crawford Ivers (based on the play by Augustus Thomas); ph, James Van Trees.

Drama **(PR:A MPAA:NR)**

WITHIN PRISON WALLS (SEE: RIGHT WAY, THE, 1921)

WITHOUT A SOUL (SEE: LOLA, 1914)

WITHOUT FEAR* 1/2 (1922) 5 reels FOX bw

Pearl White *(Ruth Hamilton)*, Robert Elliott *(John Miles)*, Charles Mackay *(Warren Hamilton)*, Marie Burke *(Mrs. Hamilton)*, Robert Agnew *(Walter Hamilton)*, Macey Harlam *(Bill Barton)*.

Anyone looking for thrills in this feature, made by serial queen White, will be disappointed. It's really a lackluster domestic drama in which she plays a socialite (giving White plenty of opportunity to wear riding outfits, dresses, and gowns) who falls for Elliott, a fellow below her stature. White defies her father by continuing to see him, and then when she is spotted entering his home, is given a parental order to tie the knot. The rebellious White steadfastly refuses until she learns the extent of her man's devotion, and then smilingly agrees.

d, Kenneth Webb; w, Paul H. Sloane; ph, Tom Malloy.

Drama **(PR:A MPAA:NR)**

WITHOUT HOPE* (1914) 4 reels Flamingo bw

Harry Kendall *(The Playwright)*, Marguerite Loveridge *(Hope)*, Caroline Rankin, Kathleen Hammond *(The Alstyn Sisters)*, Mary Charleston, William Mandeville, Catherine Proctor, Gertrude Barrett, David Andrada, Johnny Doyle.

Hopeless script has a playwright posing as a waiter to unearth material for his latest work, and breaking up a plot to steal the formula for noiseless gunpowder.

d, Fred Mace; w, Elaine Sterne.

Mystery **(PR:A MPAA:NR)**

WITHOUT LIMIT* 1/2 (1921) 7 reels S-L Pictures/Metro bw

Anna Q. Nilsson *(Ember Edwards)*, Robert Frazer *(David Marlowe)*, Frank Currier *(The Reverend Marlowe)*, Kate Blancke *(Mrs. Marlowe)*, Charles Lane *(Clement Palter)*, Robert Schable *(Bunny Fish)*, Thomas W. Ross *(Charley)*, Nellie Anderson *(The Landlady)*.

The moral lesson this picture sets out to make falls short of being realized, in spite of the fact that the story line is really quite fundamental. It has to do with a minister's son, Frazer, who is talked into marrying Nilsson while on a drunken spree, and then loses his shirt at a gambling emporium. The repentant youth later explains his situation to Lane, the club owner, who happens to be a pretty good skate. Lane intervenes with the reverend on his behalf, and fortunately that great character builder, WW I, comes along. Frazer goes off to fight and in the trenches becomes a man and returns to find happiness with the woman he has grown to love.

d&w, George D. Baker (based on the story "Temple Dusk" by Calvin Johnston); ph, Andre Barlatier; set d, M. P. Staulcup.

Drama **(PR:A MPAA:NR)**

WIZARD OF OZ, THE 1/2** (1925) 7 reels CHAD bw

Larry Semon *(Scarecrow)*, Bryant Washburn *(Prince Kynde)*, Dorothy Dwan *(Dorothy)*, Virginia Pearson *(Countess Vishuss)*, Charles Murray *(The Wizard)*, Oliver Hardy *(The Tin Woodsman)*, Josef Swickard *(The Prime Minister)*, Mary Carr *(Dorothy's Mother)*, G. Howe Black *(Rastus)*, Otto Lederer, Frank Alexander.

Good children's movie (Larry Semon's frantic slapstick approach to his character is difficult for an adult audience to deal with) has Dorothy Dwan on her 18th birthday being swept away (in the company of her uncle and a couple of hired hands) by a cyclone to the magical land of Oz, where they experience the familiar adventures created by L. Frank Baum. It all turns out to be a dream, of course, and if one does not compare it with the definitive Judy Garland version of 1939, the film is quite acceptable.

d, Larry Semon; w, Lyman Frank Baum, Jr., Leon Lee, Semon (based on the works of Baum); t, Lee; ph, H. F. Koenekamp, Frank Good, Leonard Smith; ed, Sam S. Zimbalist; art d, Robert Stevens.

Fantasy **(PR:A MPAA:NR)**

WOLF LAW*** (1922) 5 reels UNIV bw

Frank Mayo *(Jefferson De Croteau)*, Sylvia Breamer *(Francine Redney)*, Tom Guise *(Etienne De Croteau)*, Dick Cummings *(Enoch Lascar)*, William Quinn *(Simon Santey)*, Nick De Ruiz *(Samson Bender)*, Harry Carter *("Dandy" Dawson)*, Paul Wismer *(Mountaineer)*.

The action is almost nonstop in this Mayo adventure, which has the star shooting a man who insulted him after losing a horse race, skipping over the border where he joins an outlaw band, and then becoming regenerated by a judge and his daughter, who are the objects of the gang's harassment. Mayo saves the pair and brings them home, where he discovers the man he shot was only wounded, and then proposes to the girl after clearing himself of a crime of which he was wrongly accused.

d, Stuart Paton; w, Charles Sarver (based on the story by Hugh Pendexter); ph, Benjamin Kline.

Adventure **(PR:A MPAA:NR)**

WOLF PACK zero (1922) 5 reels WORLD/Rialto bw

Joe Moore *(Joe Hammond)*, Eileen Sedgwick *(Jeanne Lamont)*, S.W. Williams *(Henry Lamont/Stephen Lamont)*, Robert Kortman *(The Wolf)*.

This film was so budget-minded that the cast of eight—including extras—was expanded to nine by having Williams play brothers. The rest was just routine stuff—probably shot outdoors in a day-and-a-half—dealing with a mountie, a girl, and the outlaws he subdues. What director-writer Craft lacks in exposition, he tries to make up for in action, and the fights pop up so frequently that it all seems entirely ludicrous.

d&w, William J. Craft.

Adventure **(PR:A MPAA:NR)**

WOLF'S CLOTHING*** (1927) 8 reels WB bw

Monte Blue *(Barry Baline)*, Patsy Ruth Miller *(Minnie Humphrey)*, John Miljan *(Johnson Craigie)*, Douglas Gerrard *(Herbert Candish)*, Lew Harvey *(Vanelli)*, Ethan Laidlaw *(Vanelli's Pal)*, J. C. Fowler *(Hotel Manager)*, Walter Rodgers *(Hotel Doctor)*, Arthur Millet *(Hotel Detective)*, John Webb Dillon *(Crook "Doctor")*, Lee Moran *(Millionaire)*, Paul Panzer, Charles Haefeli, Jack Cooper *(Toughs)*, Kalla Pasha *(Ship Captain)*, Jack Curtis, Edwin Sturgis *(Sailors)*.

Blue starred in seven pictures for Warner Brothers in 1927, the same year that studio made a record 43 films. This topnotch comedy has him playing a beleaguered New York City subway guard being hit on New Year's Eve by an escaped lunatic's speeding car. The madman, Miljan, changes clothes with his victim, and from that point on Blue finds himself hurled into a series of bizarre adventures, which include being taken for the millionaire maniac and attending a grand ball where he's drugged and abducted by a couple of blackmailers. The two spirit him off to a waterfront dive and order that he return a large bundle of cash, while they hold Miller, a maid, hostage. Blue goes through a number of additionally hilarious situations before getting the money from Miljan and capturing the crooks. He then escapes New York's finest, who also believe that he's the screwball, and in a beautifully executed scene saves a runaway subway train loaded with passengers from the inexhaustible Miljan, who is at the throttle. At this point Blue wakes up in a hospital bed to find it was all a terrible nightmare, but one that has its reward since the nurse holding his hand is Miller herself.

d, Roy Del Ruth; w, Darryl Francis Zanuck (based on the story by Arthur Somers Roche); ph, Byron Haskins.

Comedy **(PR:A MPAA:NR)**

WOLVERINE, THE* 1/2 (1921) 5 reels Spencer/Associated Photoplays bw

Helen Gibson *(Billy Louise)*, Jack Connolly *(Ward Warren)*, Leo Maloney *(Charlie Fox)*, Ivor McFadden *(Buck Olney)*, Anne Schaefer *(Martha Meilke)*, Gus Saville *(Jase Meilke)*.

Below-par programmer has Connolly returning home after wrongly serving a term in prison and settling on a ranch run by Gibson (a real-life Hollywood daredevil stuntwoman), whose parents died and left the spread to the 18-year-old. Connolly not only brings a gang of cattle rustlers to justice, but manages to clear his name and find love with his pretty young employer.

d, William Bertram; w, Helen Van Upp (based on the novel *The Ranch at the Wolverine* by B. M. Bower); ph, Steve Norton.

Western **(PR:A MPAA:NR)**

WOMAN, THE* 1/2** (1915) 5 reels LAS/Belasco bw

Lois Meredith, Theodore Roberts, James Neill, Mabel Van Buren, Ernest Joy, Raymond Hatton, Tom Forman, Helen Hill, Horace B. Carpenter, William Elmer, Dorothy Beitel.

Superior film version of a popular play has a political boss setting out to destroy his reform-minded rival by exposing an affair the young man is engaged in. In the end he discovers, to his horror, that the woman involved is his own daughter.

d, George Melford; w, William C. De Mille (based on the play by Henry C. De Mille, David Belasco).

Drama **(PR:A MPAA:NR)**

WOMAN AND WINE** (1915) 5 reels Brady/WORLD bw

William Elliott, Cynthia Day, Alec B. Francis, Dorothy Green, Henry Leone, Mrs. Moussel.

Familiar story has a young man inheriting a fortune from his aunt, then being taken for a ride by a gold digger and her paramour and deserting his loved ones in the process. This causes his father to go blind (though the old boy later regains his sight through an operation), but when the adventuress is killed, the son finally marries the pretty little family ward.

d, Arthur Shirley.

Drama **(PR:A MPAA:NR)**

WOMAN GOD CHANGED, THE*** (1921) 7 reels COS/PAR bw

Seena Owen *(Anna Janssen)*, E.K. Lincoln *(Thomas McCarthy)*, Henry Sedley *(Alastair De Vries)*, Lillian Walker *(Lilly)*, H. Cooper Cliffe *(Donogan)*, Paul Nicholson *(District Attorney)*, Joseph Smiley *(Police Commissioner)*, Templar Saxe *(French Commissionaire)*.

By using a series of flashbacks as witnesses testify at a trial, this film pieces together the story of how Owen, a promising dancer, gives up her career to become the mistress of Sedley, a wealthy bounder, and murders him when he takes up with another woman. Owen escapes to Tahiti where, a couple of years later, detective Lincoln (not to be confused with Elmo Lincoln, who played the first Tarzan) tracks her down, makes his arrest, and books passage back to the U.S. In a terrible storm their ship sinks and the couple are washed up on a desert island. Two additional years pass, and amidst the tropical splendor they fall in love and pledge their marriage vows to each other in the presence of God. All of this has a profound effect on Owen, and when a ship is finally spotted, she signals for it against her beloved's will. The film then flashes forward to the trial and a courtroom full of people who have been very moved by the various versions of the story they have just heard. The judge finally decides to release the defendant into the custody of her husband, and there is jubilation on the part of all.

d, Robert G. Vignola; w, Doty Hobart (based on the story by Brian Oswald Donn-Byrne); ph, Al Ligouri; set d, Joseph Urban.

Drama **(PR:A MPAA:NR)**

WOMAN OF AFFAIRS, A** (1928) 9 reels MGM bw

Greta Garbo *(Diana)*, John Gilbert *(Neville)*, Lewis Stone *(Hugh)*, John Mack Brown *(David)*, Douglas Fairbanks, Jr. *(Jeffrey)*, Hobart Bosworth *(Sir Morton)*, Dorothy Sebastian *(Constance)*.

When Gilbert's strict father puts an end to the marriage plans between his son and Garbo, the willful and impetuous British girl becomes involved in a number of romantic escapades. She is finally charmed into marriage by a man who is actually a thief, and when Garbo discovers the truth he commits suicide. Gilbert, who has since married, returns to the only woman he has ever loved, but Garbo sends him away when she realizes how destructive their affair would be to his life. Thinking of their ill-fated romance, the disheartened young woman drives off and is killed after crashing her car into the tree she sat under with Gilbert when he first declared his love for her. Based on *The Green Hat*, a popular "adult" novel of the day, the motion picture version was watered down to such an extent to get it past the Hays Office that the whole affair is, at best, tedious. This was the first time Gilbert received second billing to Garbo (actually he was given little to do beyond acting as her foil), and in spite of the usual splendid MGM production values and professional direction by Brown, the great Garbo is the only satisfying thing about this movie.

d, Clarence Brown; w, Bess Meredyth (based on the novel *The Green Hat* by Michael Arlen); t, Marian Ainslee, Ruth Cummings; ph, William Daniels; ed, Hugh Wynn; art d, Cedric Gibbons; m/l, "Love's First Kiss," William Axt, David Mendoza; syn sc; s eff.

Drama **(PR:A MPAA:NR)**

WOMAN OF MYSTERY, THE zero (1914) 4 reels Blache bw

Claire Whitney, Vinnie Burns, Fraunie Fraunholz.

The biggest mystery about this little programmer, which has an Oriental princess murdering an actress by sending her a box of poison snakes and then taking over the mind of a detective, is the motivation for these deeds. Nothing is explained, things just happen, and then the picture ends.

d&w, Alice Blache.

Mystery **(PR:A MPAA:NR)**

WOMAN OF PARIS, A**** (1923) 8 reels UA bw

Edna Purviance *(Marie St. Clair)*, Adolphe Menjou *(Pierre Revel)*, Carl Miller *(Jean Millet)*, Lydia Knott *(His Mother)*, Charles French *(His Father)*, Clarence Geldert *(Marie's Father)*, Betty Morrissey *(Fifi, Marie's Friend)*, Malvina Polo *(Paulette, Marie's Friend)*, Karl Gutman *(The Orchestra Conductor)*, Nellie Bly Baker *(Masseuse)*, Henry Bergman *(Maitre d'Hôtel)*, Harry Northrup *(Valet)*, Charles Chaplin *(Station Porter)*.

Marie St. Clair (Edna Purviance), a French country girl, is in love with Jean Millet (Carl Miller), a youthful art student. They are about to run away to Paris when Miller returns home to pick up a few things he forgot. While there his father dies. Purviance assumes he changed his mind and boards the train. In Paris, she becomes the mistress of Menjou, a wealthy bounder, but some time later she encounters Miller, who has come to the city with his mother, to study art. Purviance hires him to paint her portrait, the sparks begin to fly again, and the young man proposes marriage. She accepts and breaks off her relationship with Menjou, who has in turn become engaged to a socialite. But then, fearing that Miller asked her to be his wife out of compassion (he knew of her affair), Purviance decides to let him off the hook and turns him down. This act of charity leads to the young man's suicide and his mother's desire to destroy the woman who caused it. But when she approaches Purviance and realizes the depth of her grief, the two become friends and decide to return to their country home where they will perform good works in the memory of the person they both loved. The film ends on a wonderfully ironic note. Purviance, back in the country, is riding on a hay wagon when Menjou in a high-powered automobile passes her by. Neither party notices the other and Menjou's friend asks, "By the way, whatever became of Marie St. Clair?" The suave bounder merely shrugs and the car drives on. Chaplin in his autobiography had this to say about his landmark film: "Some critics declared that psychology could not be expressed on the silent screen, that obvious action, such as heroes bending ladies over tree trunks and breathing fervently down their tonsils, or chair-swinging rough stuff, was its only means of expression. A WOMAN OF PARIS was a challenge. I intended to convey psychology by subtle action. For example, Edna plays a *demimondaine*; her girl friend enters and shows her a society magazine which announces the marriage of Edna's lover. Edna nonchalantly takes the magazine, looks at it, then quickly casts it aside, acting with indifference, and lights a cigarette. But the audience can see that she has been shocked. After smilingly bidding her friend adieu at the door, she quickly goes back to the magazine and reads it with dramatic intensity. The film was full of subtle suggestion. In a scene in Edna's bedroom, a maid opens a chest of drawers and a man's collar accidentally falls to the floor, which reveals her relationship with the leading man (Menjou). The film was a great success with discriminating audiences. It was the first of the silent pictures to articulate irony and psychology. Other films of the same nature followed, including Ernst Lubitsch's THE MARRIAGE CIRCLE, with Menjou playing almost the same character again." After waiting four years for Chaplin to free himself of contractual obligations, his partners at United Artists, Mary Pickford and Douglas Fairbanks, were not exactly ecstatic over his choice of this film (he only played a bit part) to be their first Chaplin release. But the comedian felt a tremendous sense of loyalty to his leading lady of many years, Purviance. In this film, he attempted to launch a new career for her in serious films. The gesture unfortunately failed, but Chaplin paid the actress her full salary until the day she died in 1958.

p,d&w, Charles Chaplin; ph, Rollie Totheroh, Jack Wilson; ed, Monta Bell; art d, Arthur Stibolt.

Drama **Cas.** **(PR:C MPAA:NR)**

WOMAN ON THE MOON, THE***
(1929, Ger.) 12 reels UFA bw (FRAU IM MOND; AKA: THE GIRL ON THE MOON)

Gerda Maurus *(Frieda Venton)*, Willy Fritsch *(Prof. Helius)*, Fritz Rasp *(Walt Turner)*, Gustav von Wangenheim *(Hans Windegger)*, Klaus Pohl *(Prof. Manfeldt)*, Max Maximilian, Margarete Kupfer, Tilla Durieux, Heinrich Gothe, Gustl Stark-Gstettenbauer.

The special effects are the whole show here, as director Lang carefully created the scientific reality of space travel. (This was the first time the subject had been tackled seriously). The story is far less satisfying, dealing with a small party, including a beautiful woman, who blast off in search of lunar gold. For advisors, the director used Willy Ley, who later became an important part of the U.S. space program, as well as Hermann Oberth, who did the same for the Nazis and later participated in George Pal's 1950 production DESTINATION MOON. When THE WOMAN ON THE MOON was released, it scared the devil out of the British and the French, and shortly thereafter Hitler recalled the film and had the model used in its production destroyed. It too closely resembled a couple of weapons the Fuhrer already had on the drawing board and which would some day become known as the V1 and V2 bombs.

p&d, Fritz Lang; w, Thea Von Harbou; ph, Curt Courant, Oskar Fischinger, Otto Kanturek; art d, Otto Hunte, Emil Hasler, Karl Vollbrecht; spec eff, Konstantin Tschetwerikoff, Oskar Fischinger.

Fantasy **Cas.** **(PR:A MPAA:NR)**

WOMAN ON TRIAL, THE*½ (1927) 6 reels PAR bw

Pola Negri *(Julie)*, Einar Hanson *(Pierre Bouton)*, Arnold Kent *(Gaston Napier)*, André Sarti *(John Morland)*, Baby Dorothy Brock *(Paul)*, Valentina Zimina *(Henrietta)*, Sidney Bracey *(Brideaux)*, Bertram Marburgh *(Morland's Lawyer)*, Gayne Whitman *(Julie's Lawyer)*.

Stiller, the brilliant Danish director who brought his protege, Greta Garbo, to Hollywood with him (against the wishes of Louis B. Mayer, who thought she was too fat), was at the end of his rope when he made this box office failure. Stiller had been treated horribly by MGM and was the classic example of an artist who is refused the opportunity to practice his art. Erich Pommer, the great German producer and admirer who had plenty of clout at Paramount, brought Stiller to that studio, where he created the impressive, but money-losing, HOTEL IMPERIAL the same year. This courtroom drama—a popular convention of the day—told in flashbacks the story of a woman who murders a man who has it coming and is ultimately, to the cheers of the spectators, acquitted. The picture, which may very well have been a last-ditch attempt to win an American audience, failed on almost every level, and the broken-hearted Stiller made one last film, THE STREET OF SIN (1928), which he quit in mid-production after a quarrel with the studio, and Josef von Sternberg completed. The director then returned to his native land, where he died the same year.

p, B. P. Schulberg; d, Mauritz Stiller; w, Elsie von Koczain, Hope Loring (based on the play "Confession" by Erno Vajda); t, Julian Johnson; ph, Bert Glennon.

Drama **(PR:A MPAA:NR)**

WOMAN TEMPTED, THE* (1928, Brit.) 8 reels ME/Wardour bw

Juliette Compton *(Louise Harding)*, Warwick Ward (Jimmy Davier), Nina Vanna *(Maud Edworth)*, Malcolm Tod *(Basil Gilmore)*, Joan Morgan *(Sybil Helmsley)*, Adeline Hayden Coffin *(Mrs. Edworth)*, Judd Green.

This less than mediocre British drama has a woman who married for convenience turning into a vamp while involving herself in charity work. She destroys one man and is prevented from doing the same to another when the fiancee of the first victim kills her and then enters a convent. Ward, who was so fine as the heavy in VARIETY, is completely wasted in this one.

p, John Maxwell, Maurice Elvey; d, Elvey; w, Sidney Morgan (based on a novel by Countess Vera Cathcart).

Drama **(PR:A MPAA:NR)**

WOMAN WHO DID NOT CARE, THE*** (1927) 6 reels GOTH/LUM bw

Lilyan Tashman *(Iris Carroll)*, Edward Martindel *(Franklin Payne)*, Arthur Rankin *(Jeffrey Payne)*, Philo McCullough *(Gregory Payne)*, Olive Hasbrouck *(Diana Payne)*, Sarah Padden *(Mrs. Carroll)*, Guinn Williams *(Lars)*.

Well directed and acted programmer has the man-hating Tashman closing the boardinghouse, where she has been the victim of numerous male indignities, when her mother dies. The young lady then buys a swell wardrobe and sets out to exploit the opposite gender. Transformed into a beauty, she finds herself pursued by both a millionaire father *and* his son, who propose marriage. Alarmed by this, the daughter of the house turns to her misogynous sea captain-uncle, McCullough, to save the day. There are a number of amusing incidents before the two discover that they are actually in love, and the picture ends with the sweethearts deciding to sail off to paradise on his ship.

d, Phil Rosen; sup, Carrol Sax, Sam Bischoff; w, Marion Orth (based on the story by Rida Johnson Young); ph, Ray June.

Dramatic Comedy **(PR:A MPAA:NR)**

WOMAN WHO FOOLED HERSELF, THE½**
(1922) 6 reels Edward A. MacManus/AEX bw

Mary Allison *(Eva Lee)*, Robert Ellis *(Fernando Pennington)*, Frank Currier *(Don Fernando Casablanca)*, Bessie Wharton *(Doña Marie Pennington)*, Robert Schable *(Cameron Camden)*, Louis Dean *(Eban Burnham)*, Rafael Arcos *(The Padre)*.

Location shooting in Puerto Rico greatly enhanced this melodrama which had Allison taking a dancing job in South America to assist a couple of crooks who steal the land of Ellis' grandfather. The girl ultimately falls in love with her mark, however, and together they foil the plot.

d, Charles A. Logue, Robert Ellis; w, Logue; ph, A. Fried, Eugene O'Donnell.

Drama **(PR:A MPAA:NR)**

WOMAN WHO SINNED, A zero (1925) R-C/FBO bw

Morgan Wallace *(George Ransdell)*, Irene Rich *(Mrs. Ransdell)*, Lucien Littlefield *(Rev. Hillburn)*, Mae Busch *(Mrs. Hillburn)*, Dicky Brandon *(Her Son, as a Boy)*, Rex Lease *(Her Son, Grown)*, Ethel Teare *(Mitzi)*, Cissy Fitzgerald *(Burlesque Queen)*, Hank Mann *(Tattu)*, Snitz Edwards *(Grabini)*, Bobby Mack *(Sailor)*, Carlos and Jeanette *(Apache Dancers)*.

Terribly dated tripe in which a minister's wife, Rich, has an affair on a bounder's yacht and then leaves home to become his mistress. The man is actually a Wall Street sharpie, and eventually Rich turns the rotter in and sees to it that he's sent up the river. A reel or so grinds on, in which it's impossible to feel much sympathy for the woman (mainly because of Fox's banal direction and script) until her son, who has become an evangelist, bursts upon the scene and referring to the scriptures, manages to reunite his family.

d&w, Finis Fox; ph, Hal Mohr, Jean Smith.

Drama **(PR:A MPAA:NR)**

WOMAN WHO WALKED ALONE, THE** (1922) 6 reels FP/PAR bw

Dorothy Dalton *(The Honorable Iris Champneys)*, Milton Sills *(Clement Gaunt)*, E. J. Radcliffe *(Earl of Lemister)*, Wanda Hawley *(Muriel Champneys)*, Frederick Vroom *(Marquis of Champneys)*, Maym Kelso *(Marchioness of Champneys)*, John Davidson *(Otis Yeardley)*, Harris Gordon *(Sir Basil Deere)*, Charles Ogle *(Schriemann)*, Mabel Van Buren *(Hannah Shriemann)*, Maurice B. Flynn *(Jock MacKinney)*, Cecil Holland *(Mombo)*, John MacKinnon *(Lemister's Butler)*.

Credibility strainer has Dalton playing a British noblewoman, wrongly accused (by the husband she was forced to marry) of committing adultery when she tries to rescue her sister's compromising love letters. Meanwhile, Sills, the one-time employee of her husband and the man she really loves, has gone to South America and landed a job on a ranch, where the boss' wife has designs on more than just his saddle. The woman later shoots her husband and pins the blame on Sills, who rejected her advances. The English cowboy manages to escape the authorities, and some years later, runs into Dalton, who coincidentally just happens to be operating a saloon south-of-the-border. Hearing of his plight, Dalton rides to the ranch and informs the woman of the house that the former object of her affections has been executed. Then she arranges for Sills to make a surprise appearance, and the superstitious Latin—thinking she has encountered a ghost—confesses to her husband's murder.

d, George Melford; w, Will M. Ritchey (based on the story "The Cat That Walked Alone" by John Colton); ph, Bert Glennon.

Drama **(PR:A MPAA:NR)**

WOMAN WISE** (1928) 5 reels FOX bw

William Russell *(Ne'er-Do-Well)*, June Collyer *(Millie Baxter)*, Walter Pidgeon *(The U.S. Consul)*, Theodore Kosloff *(Abdul Mustapha)*, Ernie Shields *(Valet)*, Raoul Paoli *(Khurd Chief)*, Duke Kahanamoku *(Guard)*, Josephine Borio, Carmen Castillo *(Native Girls)*.

There are some laughs, as well as a few thrills, in this Fox programmer about a couple of Americans stationed in Persia who are rivals for Collyer, a pretty Yankee secretary, but join forces to prevent a lustful ruling pasha from stealing her away for himself. The young lady eventually casts her lot with Pidgeon, who impresses as the U.S. consul.

d, Albert Ray; w, Randall H. Fay, Andrew Bennison (based on a story by Donald McGibney, James Kevin McGuinness); t, Malcolm Boylan; ph, Sidney Wagner; ed, Ralph Dixon.

Comedy/Adventure **(PR:A MPAA:NR)**

WOMANHANDLED*½** (1925) 7 reels FP/PAR bw

Richard Dix *(Bill Dana)*, Esther Ralston *(Mollie)*, Cora Williams *(Aunt Abby)*, Olive Tell *(Gwen)*, Eli Nadel *(The Kid)*, Edmund Breese *(Uncle Les)*, Margaret Morris *(Lucille)*, Ivan Simpson *(Butler)*, Edgar Nelson *(Pinky)*.

Wonderful La Cava-directed comedy has society playboy Dix saving Ralston's obnoxious little nephew from "drowning" in Central Park's toy boat pond. The couple fall in love and Dix passes himself off as a westerner when he realizes that the cowboy type is her ideal. He then heads west to his uncle's ranch to make a man of himself, only to discover that all of the punchers are making movies, and when they do round up the herd it's from behind the wheel of their flivvers. To Dix's horror, the wide open spaces are full of tennis courts, swimming pools, and golf courses, and the ranch and bunkhouses have more convenieces than his Park Avenue apartment. The film is great up to this point, but the laughs really start to pile up when Dix receives a cable informing him that the girl of his dreams is on her way to visit his spread, and the poor devil nearly goes out of his mind trying to transform everything into the real McCoy before her arrival. Overnight he accomplishes the impossible, and when Ralston steps out of the coach, it's as if she has entered into a Tom Mix picture set. Even the black servants, dressed like Indians, are not offensive in La Cava's skillfuly directed hands. And the satire of America's favorite genre is as affectionate as it is devastating, with one cliche after another broadly lampooned. Of course the couple do end up as man and wife—in Manhattan, where the real West is no further away then the nearest movie palace.

d, Gregory La Cava; w, Luther Reed (based on the story "Woman-handled" by Arthur Stringer); ph, Edward Cronjager; ed, Ernest Fegte.

Comedy/Satire **(PR:A MPAA:NR)**

WOMANPOWER** 1/2** (1926) 7 reels FOX bw

Ralph Graves *(Johnny White Bromley)*, Kathryn Perry *(Jenny Killian)*, Margaret Livingston *(Dot)*, Ralph Sipperly *(Gimp Conway)*, William Walling *(Jake Killian)*, David Butler *(Mallory)*, Lou Tellegen *(The Broker)*, Anders Randolf *(Bromley, Sr.)*, Robert Ryan *(Sands)*, Frankie Grandetta *(Sheik)*.

When Tellegen slaps him around a little and his girl, Livingston, calls him a coward, playboy Graves visits a boxers' training camp to build himself up. There he falls in love with Perry, the owner's daughter, polishes up his pugilistic skills, and returns home to tell Livingston off and give Tellegen a good pasting. He also wins the respect of his father for the first time, and sets the date to marry Perry.

d, Harry Beaumont, w, Kenneth B. Clarke (based on the story "You Can't Always Tell" by Harold MacGrath); ph, Rudolph Berquist.

Drama/Comedy **(PR:A MPAA:NR)**

WOMAN'S BUSINESS, A zero (1920) 5 reels Jans bw

Olive Tell, Edmund Lowe, Lucille Lee Stewart, Donald Hall, Warner Richmond, Stanley Walpole, Annette Bade.

Tell is badly miscast in this pathetic domestic drama about a woman who sets out to find herself, divorces her husband, but then realizes her "mistake" and returns to him in the end.

d, B. A. Rolfe; w, Violet T. Clark, Carey Wilson (based on the novel *Nothing a Year* by Charles Belmont Davis); ph, A. A. Caldwell.

Drama **(PR:A MPAA:NR)**

WOMAN'S MAN* (1920) 5 reels Arrow bw

Romaine Fielding, Mary Graham, William Tooker, Velvet Beban, Walter Neeland, Emile La Croix, Julia Hurley.

In 1913 Fielding was voted the most popular movie actor in the U.S. But the star was over the hill (except for supporting roles) by the time he made this embarrassment about a man who almost loses his fortune, and his sweetheart, to a slick-talking millionaire.

d, Warren Gordon; w, Jerome N. Wilson (based on a story by Ruth Buchanan Sacks); ph, Harry Fishbeck.

Western/Drama **(PR:A MPAA:NR)**

WOMAN'S PLACE*** (1921) 6 reels Joseph M. Schenck/AFN bw

Constance Talmadge *(Josephine Gerson)*, Kenneth Harlan *(Jim Bradley)*, Hassard Short *(Freddy Bleeker)*, Florence Short *(Amy Bleeker)*, Ina Rorke *(Mrs. Margaret Belknap)*, Marguerite Linden *(Miss Jane Wilson)*, Jack Connolly *(Dan Dowd)*.

Amusing Loos and Emerson script, clever direction by Fleming, and a fine performance by Talmadge, combine to put this political satire over. It all has to do with Talmadge becoming the Women's League candidate and running against her fiance, Harlan, who has aligned himself with the political machine. After a number of funny situations, Talmadge manages to sweep the male vote, but her opponent wins by a slight margin by gaining the support of the League. The film ends with the ladies being appointed to most of the important posts, Harlan splitting with the organization, and Talmadge deciding to forgo personal ambition in favor of marriage.

d, Victor Fleming; w, John Emerson, Anita Loos; ph, Oliver Marsh, J. Roy Hunt.

Comedy/Satire **(PR:A MPAA:NR)**

WOMAN'S SECRET, A**

(1924, Brit.) 8 reels Graham-Wilcox bw (GB: SOUTHERN LOVE)

Betty Blythe *(Dolores)*, Herbert Langley *(Pedro)*, Randle Ayrton *(Count de Silva)*, Warwick Ward *(Dick Tennant)*, Liane Haid *(Countess de Silva)*, Hal Martin *(Gipsy)*.

Irish-born director Wilcox took a better-than-average British company to Vienna to shoot this acceptable film, set in Spain, about a band of gypsies who save a beautiful dancer from a life behind prison walls when the man who loves her kills the nobleman who tried to ruin her.

p,d&w, Herbert Wilcox (based on the poem "The Spanish Student" by Henry Longfellow).

Drama **(PR:A MPAA:NR)**

WON BY A HEAD* (1920, Brit.) 5 reels STER/BEF bw

Rex Davis *(Chester Lawton)*, Frank Tennant *(Milton Bell)*, Vera Cornish *(Phyllis Reid)*, Wallace Bosco *(Jim Kort)*, Douglas Payne, J. Edwards Barber, Madge Tree.

This British adventure film combined two sports genres to provide twice as many cliches in a story about a prizefighter who escapes from prison, proves he didn't murder his father, and then in the last reel wins the big race.

d, Percy Nash; w, (based on the novel by John Gabriel).

Adventure **(PR:A MPAA:NR)**

WONDERFUL WIFE, A** (1922) 5 reels UNIV bw

Miss Du Pont *(Chum)*, Vernon Steele *(Alaric Lewin)*, Landers Stevens *(Gregory)*, Charles Arling *(Halton)*, Ethel Ritchie *(Diana)*, Harris Gordon *(Nugent)*, Nick De Ruiz *(Native Groom)*.

Du Pont and her husband, Steele, are sent to an African island where he is to serve directly under Stevens, the hard-boiled commissioner of the British foreign service. Du Pont and Stevens have a bit of a fling, but when she learns that her paramour has sent her husband on a jungle mission which means certain death, she forces the commissioner, at gunpoint, to undertake his rescue. During a native attack, Stevens is killed, Steele is saved, and his marriage to Du Pont continues as if nothing has ever taken place.

d, Paul Scardon; w, Arthur F. Statter (based on the novel *The Rat Trap* by Dolf Wyllarde); ph, Ben Reynolds.

Drama **(PR:A MPAA:NR)**

WOODEN SHOES** (1917) 5 reels KB/TRI bw

Bessie Barriscale *(Pampy)*, Jack Livingston *(Donald Luther)*, J. J. Dowling *(Kaptain Hendrik von der Bloom)*, Thomas S. Guise *(Rufus Smith)*, Howard Hickman *(Jack Smith)*, Don Likes *(Hans Dunkleberger)*, Will H. Bray *(Dr. Blaisdell)*, J. Frank Burke *(Father Nepomuk)*, Gertrude Claire *(The Mevrouw)*, J. H. Gotch *(Jacob Hauptmann)*, Margaret Thompson *(Gertruida van Hoosen)*, George Cowl.

Nothing special about this one, which has Barriscale playing an orphaned Dutch girl who comes to the U.S. to find her millionaire grandfather. The old boy, it turns out, has also sent for her, but the letter was intercepted in Europe and a ringer was substituted. It all ends happily, however, when a group from the old country holds a reunion at an East Side travern and an artist, who had fallen in love with Barriscale, recognizes her as the girl he once painted in Holland.

d, Raymond West; w, J. G. Hawks.

Drama **(PR:A MPAA:NR)**

WORLDLINGS, THE* (1920, Brit.) 6 reels General Attractions-Globe bw

Basil Gill *(Maurice Blake/Philip Jardine)*, Ivy Close *(Lady Helen Cleve)*, Margaret Halstan *(Rosa Fleming)*, Edward O'Neill *(Sir Noel Jardine)*.

British social-strata nonsense has an aristocratically born lady remaining with her husband even *after* his former mistress exposes him to be a mere commoner.

d&w, Eric Harrison (based on a novel by Leonard Merrick).

Drama **(PR:A MPAA:NR)**

WORLD'S CHAMPION, THE*** (1922) 5 reels FP/PAR bw

Wallace Reid *(William Burroughs)*, Lois Wilson *(Lady Elizabeth)*, Lionel Belmore *(John Burroughs)*, Henry Miller, Jr. *(George Burroughs)*, Helen Dunbar *(Mrs. Burroughs)*, Leslie Casey *(Rev. David Burroughs)*, Stanley J. Sandford *(Lord Bockington)*, W. J. Ferguson *(Butler)*, Guy Oliver *(Mooney)*.

Agreeable Reid comedy has the star playing the son of a wealthy Englishman who is given a beating by a lord (Sanford) when he tries to rise above his station and make a play for Wilson, a woman of nobility. Disowned by his father, Reid stows away on a ship bound for the U.S., where he makes the acquaintance of a boxing trainer. Reid eventually becomes the middleweight champion of the world, earns a bundle, and becomes a celebrity. Then, on returning to England, he is shocked and delighted to find Wilson working for his father as a social secretary, due to family financial reverses. At first everyone is quite put off by Reid's occupation, but they come around when various royal personages seek the famous lad out. And the lovely Wilson even accepts his proposal of marriage after Reid gives Sanford a good pasting and announces that he intends to retire from the ring and take up the practice of law.

d, Philip E. Rosen; sup, Thompson Buchanan; w, J. E. Nash, Albert Shelby Le Vino (based on the play by Thomas Louden, A. E. Thomas); ph, Charles Edgar Schoenbaum.

Comedy **(PR:A MPAA:NR)**

WRATH OF THE GODS, THE or THE DESTRUCTION OF SAKURA JIMA**

(1914) 5 reels KB bw

Sessue Hayakawa, Tsuru Aoki, Frank Borzage, Herschal Mayall, Gladys Brockwell, Henry Kotani.

Early disaster film based on a Japanese legend has some pretty good special effects, including a volcanic eruption and a typhoon. But there isn't enough narrative exposition to raise it above the ordinary.

d, Reginald Barker; sup, Thomas H. Ince; w, C. Gardener Sullivan, William H. Clifford (based on a Japanese legend).

Drama/Adventure **(PR:A MPAA:NR)**

YANKEE CLIPPER, THE**½ (1927) 8 reels DM/PDC bw

William Boyd *(Hal Winslow)*, Elinor Fair *(Jocelyn Huntington)*, Junior Coghlan *(Mickey)*, John Miljan *(Richard)*, Walter Long *(Portuguese Joe)*, Louis Payne *(Huntington)*, Burr McIntosh *(Mr. Winslow)*, George Ovey *(Alf)*, Zack Williams *(Ham)*, William Blaisdell *(Ike)*, Clarence Burton *(Capt. McIntosh)*, Stanton Heck *(American Mate)*, Julia Faye *(Queen Victoria)*, Harry Holden *(Zachary Taylor)*, W. Sousania *(Prince Consort)*, James Wang *(Chinese Merchant)*.

There are a few thrills—a number of which are created through the use of miniatures—in this somewhat tedious film. In it Boyd, the son of a Boston shipbuilder, outraces a British vessel to win China's tea trade for America. He also manages to win the love of Fair (Boyd's real-life wife), the English girl whose father captains the opposing ship. Boyd, whose popularity diminished in 1931 when a stage actor also named William Boyd was linked in a gambling and liquor scandal, would go on to even greater heights in his career starring in the Hop-a-Long Cassidy series in 1935. (The hypens were later dropped and he became plain "Hopalong".)

d, Rupert Julian; sup, C. Gardner Sullivan; w, Garrett Fort, Garnett Weston (based on a story by Denison Clift); ph, John Mescall; art d, John Hughes.

Historical **Cas.** **(PR:A MPAA:NR)**

YANKEE SENOR, THE*** (1926) 5 reels FOX bw bw/c

Tom Mix *(Paul Wharton)*, Olive Borden *(Manuelita)*, Tom Kennedy *(Luke Martin)*, Francis McDonald *(Juan Gutiérrez)*, Margaret Livingston *(Flora)*, Alec B. Francis *(Don Fernando)*, Kathryn Hill *(Doris Mayne)*, Martha Mattox *(Aunt Abagail)*, Raymond Wells *(Ranch Foreman)*, Tony *(Paul's Horse)*.

Color sequences, especially those of a fiesta, greatly enhance this already superior south-of-the-border western, which has Mix playing the lost grandson of a Mexican aristocrat, returning to the family ranch. The old man, who disinherited his daughter when she married an American adventurer, is dying and wishes to make things right for Mix, but his adopted son has other ideas. There is plenty of action as the great cowboy fights the villain and his henchmen—along with the help of his horse, Tony, who takes part in several thrilling rescues—defeats them handily, and wins the love of the beautiful Borden, who is breathtaking in the color footage playing a lovely senorita.

d, Emmett Flynn; w, Eve Unsel (based on the novel *Conquistador* by Katherine Fullerton Gerould); ph, Daniel Clark.

Western **(PR:A MPAA:NR)**

YE BANKS AND BRAES* (1919, Brit.) 5 reels RF bw

Ethel Douglas Ross *(Jean)*, John Jenson *(Angus MacDonald)*, Daisy Jackson *(The Wife)*.

Dismal British picture about a Scottish girl who loses her heart to a nobleman, follows him to London—where to her chagrin she discovers that he's married—and then returns home to the people who really love her.

d, Tom Watts.

Drama **(PR:A MPAA:NR)**

YELLOW BACK, THE** (1926) 5 reels UNIV bw

Fred Humes *(Andy Hubbard)*, Lotus Thompson *(Anne Pendleton)*, Claude Payton *(Bruce Condon)*, Buck Connors *(John Pendleton)*, Willie Fung *(Chinese)*.

Humes, who has a fear of horses due to a childhood trauma, is fired by rancher Payton and hired by Connors when he saves his daugher Thompson from drowning in quicksand. Payton controls the water rights and is trying to force Connors, who can't afford to dig a well, off of his land. The picture's big punch comes toward the end, when Humes, because of his love for Thompson, musters up the courage to win the big race and save the day.

d&w, Del Andrews; ph, Al Jones.

Western **(PR:A MPAA:NR)**

YELLOW FINGERS**½ (1926) 6 reels FOX bw

Olive Borden *(Saina)*, Ralph Ince *(Brute Shane)*, Claire Adams *(Nona Deering)*, Edward Piel *(Kwong Li)*, Otto Matieson *(Kario)*, Nigel De Brulier *(Rajah Jagore)*, Armand Kaliz *(De Vries)*, Josephine Crowell *(Mrs. Van Kronk)*, May Foster *(Toinette)*, John Wallace *(Pegleg LaForge)*, Charles Newton *(Higgins)*.

Ince put down his director's megaphone long enough to deliver a good performance as a South Seas trader who adopts Borden, a native girl who adores him. Later, when Ince's men save Adams, an English girl, from the clutches of a Chinese opium den proprietor, and deliver her to his care, the jealous Borden plots with the oriental to have her snatched. In the end, however, Borden's basic decency overcomes her sense of rejection, and she leads her beloved to the rescue of Adams. The picture concludes in the grand tradition of happy Hollywood endings—with Ince marrying Adams, and Borden discovering that she is actually the granddaughter of a rajah and next in line to inherit his throne.

d, Emmett Flynn; w, Eve Unsell (based on the novel by Gene Wright); ph, Ernest G. Palmer, Paul Ivano.

Drama/Adventure **(PR:A MPAA:NR)**

YELLOW STAIN, THE** (1922) 5 reels FOX bw

John Gilbert *(Donald Keith)*, Claire Anderson *(Thora Erickson)*, John P. Lockney *(Quartus Hembly)*, Mark Fenton *(Olaf Erickson)*, Herschel Mayall *(Dr. Brown)*, Robert Daly *(Daniel Kersten)*, Mace Robinson *(Lyman Rochester)*, James McElhern *(Clerk)*, Frank Hemphill *(Pete Borg)*, May Alexander *(Mrs. Borg)*.

There is nothing original about this budget-minded drama with a North Woods setting, which has young, idealistic lawyer Gilbert coming to town and eventually causing the downfall of the ruthless capitalist, Lockney, who has terrorized the citizenry and established himself as emperor. The film suffers from the lack of wooded exterior needed to produce a true lumber camp feeling, but Gilbert does rather well considering what he has to work with.

d, Jack Dillon; w, Jules Furthman; ph, Don Short.

Drama **(PP:A MPAA:NR)**

YESTERDAY'S WIFE** (1923) 6 reels COL/CBC Film Sales bw

Irene Rich *(Megan Daye)*, Eileen Percy *(Viola Armes)*, Lottie Williams *(Sophia)*, Josephine Crowell *(Mrs. Harbours)*, Lewis Dayton *(Gilbert Armes)*, Philo McCullough *(Victor Fleming)*, William Scott *(Jeo Coombs)*.

Rich, a former real estate agent-turned-actress who had her first part as a bit player in Mary Pickford's STELLA MARRIS (1918), teams up with Dayton has a happily married couple who divorce after a little squabble. Rich then becomes the companion of a wealthy dowager, while Dayton marries gum-chewing switchboard operator Percy, and they all end up staying at the same resort. There are a couple of laughs before Percy is killed in a boating accident. This jolts Dayton and Rich and the couple conclude that they overreacted earlier and decide to tie the knot for a second time.

d, Edward J. Le Saint.

Comedy/Drama **(PR:A MPAA:NR)**

YOUNG WHIRLWIND** (1928) 5 reels FBO bw

Buzz Barton *(David "Red" Hepner)*, Edmund Cobb *(Jack)*, Frank Rice *(Hank)*, Alma Rayford *(Molly)*, Tom Lingham *(Sheriff)*, Eddie Chandler *(Johnson)*, Bill Patton *(Bart)*, Tex Phelps *(Bandit)*.

Barton, the kid cowboy star, rides like the devil and saves the airmail by knocking out a couple of bandits with his slingshot, and then leads the remainder of the gang right into the sheriff's arms. Nothing more than a clean entertainment for youngsters, which is all it intended to be.

p, William Le Baron; d, Louis King; w, Ethel Hill (based on a story by H. C. Schmidt); t, Helen Gregg; ph, Virgil Miller; ed, George Marsh.

Western **(PR:A MPAA:NR)**

YOUR WIFE AND MINE* (1927) 6 reels EXCEL bw

Phyllis Haver *(Phyliss Warren)*, Stuart Holmes *(Charlie Martin)*, Wallace MacDonald *(Robert Warren)*, Barbara Tennant *(Prisoner)*, Katherine Lewis *(Winifred Martin)*, Blance Upright *(Mrs. Coy)*, June Lufboro *(Tabitha Tubbs)*, Jay Emmett *(Antonio Tubbs)*.

The laughs fail to materialize in this farce, which has a younger lawyer and his socially prominent client breaking an attractive young lady out of jail to retrieve a fortune in stolen money. The gentlemen hide her out in a hotel, and the complications develop when their suspicious wives arrive on the scene. Haver, one of Hollywood's most popular sex queens, deserved better. The former Mack Sennett Bathing Beauty would quit making movies two years later to marry a Manhattan millionaire, whom she divorced after 16 years. She never returned to films, however, and was found dead at the age of 61 of barbituate poisoning, later ruled suicide.

d, Frank O'Connor; t, Marc Edmund Jones; ph, Andre Barlatier.

Comedy **(PR:A MPAA:NR)**

YOUTH FOR SALE*½ (1924) 6 reels C. C. Burr bw

Mary Allison *(Molly Malloy)*, Sigrid Holmquist *(Connie Sutton)*, Richard Bennett *(Montgomery Breck)*, Charles Emmett Mack *(Tom Powers)*, Alice Chapin *(Mrs. Malloy)*, Tom Blake *(Bill Brophy)*, Dorothy Allen *(Pansy Mears)*, Charles Beyer *(George Archibald)*, Harold Foshay *(Edward Higgins)*.

Bennett (the father of actresses Barbara, Constance, and Joan Bennett) all but walks away with this picture as the dapper gentleman with a roving eye. The story itself offers nothing out of the ordinary and tells of a girl (Allison) who becomes blinded by her first drink of bootleg liquor and her best friend (Holmquist), who almost marries a millionaire to help her through the ordeal. The dilemma is conveniently resolved, however, when the girl sails to Europe with her new husband and has her sight restored by a medical breakthrough.

d, William Christy Cabanne; w, Raymond S. Harris (based on the story "The Gray Path" by Izola Forrester); t, Harris; ph, Jack Brown.

Drama **(PR:A MPAA:NR)**

YOUTH TO YOUTH* (1922) 6 reels Metro bw

Bille Dove *(Eve Allinson)*, Edythe Chapman *(Mrs. Cora Knittson)*, Hardee Kirkland *(Taylor)*, Sylvia Ashton *(Mrs. Jolley)*, Jack Gardner *(Maurice Gibbon)*, Cullen Landis *(Page Brookins)*, Mabel Van Buren *(Mrs. Brookins)*, Tom O'Brien *(Ralph Horry)*, Paul Jeffrey *(Everett Clough)*, Carl Gerard *(Howe Snedecor)*, ZaSu Pitts *(Emily)*, Lincoln Stedman *(Orlando Jolley)*, Gertrude Short *(Luella)*, Noah Beery *(Brutus Tawney)*.

Absurd screenplay has Dove, a Broadway star with small-town roots, taking off and changing her identity when it is rumored that she has become the mistress of Beery, a big shot on the Great White Way. Dove joins a traveling show and falls in love with Landis, a farm boy who believes deeply in his fiancee's talent and writes to his old acquaintance, Beery, who consents to travel to the hinterland and catch her act. Then come the expected complications, which leads to Landis doubting Dove's virtue and almost driving her into the arms of the man she gave up everything to get away from in the first place. Fortunately, the young hothead realizes his mistake in time and the picture is permitted a happy, if completely improbable, ending.

p&d, Emile Chautard; w, Edith Kennedy (based on a story by Hulbert Footner); ph, Arthur Martinelli, art d, J. J. Hughes.

Drama **(PR:A MPAA:NR)**

Z

ZANDER THE GREAT*** (1925) 8 reels COS/MGM bw

Marion Davies *(Mamie Smith)*, Holbrook Blinn *(Juan Fernández)*, Harrison Ford *(Dan Murchison)*, Harry Watson *(Good News)*, Harry Myers *(Texas)*, George Siegmann *(Black Bart)*, Emily Fitzroy *(The Matron)*, Hobart Bosworth *(The Sheriff)*, Richard Carle *(Mr. Pepper)*, Hedda Hopper *(Mrs. Caldwell)*, Master Jack Huff *(Zander)*, Olin Howland *(Elmer Lovejoy)*.

Davies, one of the screen's most underrated comediennes, is fine as an orphan girl who is taken in by kindly Hopper and then assumes the responsibility of raising her son Huff when the lady dies. Davies and the boy head for Arizona in a little Ford, and when they get there, Davies, who has become transformed into her usual beautiful self, straightens out a bunch of lovable western characters involved in the moonshine trade, assists in the capture of an outlaw, and wins herself a husband. A nice combination of western thrills and comedy, plus some truly touching moments of pathos on the part of the star. Cosmopolitan—the studio created by William Randolph Hearst especially as a vehicle for producing Davies' films—joined with MGM shortly before the making of ZANDER THE GREAT. Louis B. Mayer decided it would be a wise business move to merge with the wealthy Hearst, whose new papers could provide plenty of free publicity, so he offered Davies a $10,000-a-week salary as part of the deal. Davies' starring roles became scant with the advent of sound, due to her tendency to stutter, and Hearst broke off from MGM in 1934, blaming production executive Irving Thalberg for using his wife, Norma Shearer, in lead parts he felt should have been given to Davies.

d, George Hill; w, Frances Marion (based on the play by Edward Salisbury Field); ph, Goerge Barnes, Harold Wenstrom; ed, James McKay; set d, Joseph Urban; Gretl Urban.

Western/Comedy Drama **(PR:A MPAA:NR)**

ZEMLYA (SEE: EARTH, 1930, USSR)

ZERO zero (1928, Brit.) 8 reels FILM MANUFACTURING/FN-Pathe bw

Stewart Rome *(John Garth)*, Fay Compton *(Mrs. Garth)*, Jeanne de Casalis *(Julia Norton)*, Sam Livesey *(Monty Sterling)*, Dorinea Shirely *(Veronica Sterling)*, J. R. Tozer *(Maj. Potterton)*, Lewis Shaw *(Victor Garth)*.

This British programmer has a writer faking his own death in order to share a little ecstasy with his paramour. Afterwards he regains his decency and returns to his wife when the woman becomes deperately ill.

p, James Sloan; d, Jack Raymond; w, Lydia Hayward (based on the novel by Colinson Owen).

Drama **(PR:C MPAA:NR)**

MISCELLANEOUS SILENTS

The following A-Z miscellaneous compilation of silent films include *all* feature-length films not covered in the preceding major entries. Approximately 10,000 films are herein listed, and, coupled to the major entries in this volume, 3500 in number, make up the world's most complete and comprehensive single-volume encyclopedia of silent film. Feature length, theatrically released films have been determined as any film exceeding a 50-minute running time, translated from approximately four reels or the equivalent footage. Those titles where (? r.) appears signifies that feature length is assumed but exact footage is undetermined. Throughout this volume running time has been given in reels as the best approximation of length. Number of reels listed are those of the original release. Minimum length is 3,000 feet which is 50 minutes at 16 fps, 16 frames per foot (35mm film); 16 frames per second (standard silent projection speed). Assuming approximately 870 feet per reel, 3,000 feet = 3 1/2 reels, which we round off to 4 reels. Entries are listed thusly: Title, (Year, Country), (Reels), Director or Producer (if possible), lead players (4 names if possible).

NOTE: Some foreign silents are dated as late as 1936.

A LA GARE (1925, Fr.)
(? r.) d, Robert Saidreau

A L'HORIZON DU SUD (1924, Fr.)
(? r.) d, Marco de Gastyne

A L'OMBRE DE VATICAN (1922, Fr.)
(? r.) d, Gaston Ravel

A L'OMBRE DES TOMBEAUX (1927, Fr.)
(? r.) d, Andre Hugon

ABC OF LOVE, THE (1919)
(6 r.) d, Leonce Perret; lp, Mae Murray, Holmes E. Herbert, Dorothy Green, Arthur Donaldson

ABANDONMENT, THE (1916)
(5 r.) d, Donald MacDonald; lp, E. Forrest Taylor, Helene Rosson, Harry Von Meter

ABORTION (1924, USSR)
(6 r.) d, Grigori Lemberg; lp, Liliveva

ABOUT TRIAL MARRIAGE
(SEE: TRIAL MARRIAGE, 1928)

ABOVE ALL LAW
(SEE: MYSTERIES OF INDIA, 1922, Ger.)

ABSINTHE (1914)
(4 r.) d, Herbert Brenon; lp, King Baggot, Leah Baird, Glenn White

ACCIDENTAL HONEYMOON, THE (1918)
(5 r.) d, Leonce Perret; lp, Robert Warwick, Elaine Hammerstein, Frank McGlynn, Frank Norcross

ACCOMPLICE, THE (1917)
(5 r.) d, Ralph Dean; lp, Dorothy Bernard, Jack Sherrill, Florence Hamilton, W.J. Brady

ACCUSED (1925)
(5 r.) d, Dell Henderson; lp, Dorothy Drew, Eric Mayne, Charles Delaney, Charles Gerrard

ACE HIGH (1918)
(5 r.) d, Lynn Reynolds; lp, Tom Mix, Kathleen O'Connor, Lloyd Perl, Louis Sargent

ACE OF CACTUS RANGE (1924)
(5 r.) d, Denver Dixon, Malon Andrus; lp, Art Mix, Virginia Warwick, Clifford Davidson, Harvey Stafford

ACE OF CLUBS, THE (1926)
(5 r.) d, J.P. McGowan; lp, Al Hoxie, Minna Redman, Andrew Waldron, Peggy Montgomery

ACE OF THE SADDLE (1919)
(6 r.) d, Jack [John] Ford; lp, Harry Carey, Peggy Pearce, Joe Harris, Duke R. Lee

ACROSS THE ATLANTIC (1928)
(7 r.) d, Howard Bretherton; lp, Monte Blue, Edna Murphy, Burr McIntosh, Robert Ober

ACROSS THE BORDER (1922)
(5 r.) d, Charles R. Seeling; lp, Big Boy Williams, Patricia Palmer, William McCall, Chet Ryan

ACROSS THE CONTINENT (1913)
(4 r.)

ACROSS THE DIVIDE (1921)
(6 r.) d, John Holloway; lp, Rex Ballard, Rosemary Theby, Ralph Fee McCullough, Thomas Delmar

ACROSS THE GREAT DIVIDE (1921)
(SEE: ACROSS THE DIVIDE, 1921)

ACROSS THE PACIFIC (1914)
(5 r.) d, Edwin Carewe; lp, Robert Warwick, Barbara Tennant

ACROSS THE PLAINS (1928)
(5 r.) d, Robert J. Horner; lp, Pawnee Bill, Jr., Ione Reed, Jack Richardson, Martha Barclay

ACTION (1921)
(5 r.) d, Jack [John] Ford; lp, Hoot Gibson, Francis Ford, J. Farrell MacDonald, Buck Connors

ADORABLE SAVAGE, THE (1920)
(5 r.) d, Norman Dawn; lp, Edith Roberts, Jack Perrin, Dick Cummings, Noble Johnson

ADVENTURE MAD (1928, Ger.)
(6 r.) d, Lothar Mendes

ADVENTURER, THE (1917)
(5 r.) d, Herbert Blache and/or Alice Blache lp, Marian Swayne, Pell Trenton, Kirke Brown, Charles Halton.

ADVENTURER, THE (1920)
(6 r.) d, J. Gordon Edwards; lp, William Farnum, Estelle Taylor, Paul Cazeneuve, Kenneth Casey

ADVENTURER, THE
(SEE: MICHAEL STROGOFF, 1926)

ADVENTURES OF A BOY SCOUT, THE (1915)
(5 r.)

ADVENTURES OF A MADCAP (1915)
(4 r.) lp, Jackie Saunders

ADVENTURES OF AN OCTOBERITE, THE (1924, USSR)
(4 r.) d, Grigori Kozintzen, Leonid Trauberg; lp, Z. Tarkhovskaya, Sergei Martinson

ADVENTURES OF BUFFALO BILL (1917)
(5 r.)

ADVENTURES OF PRINCE ACHMED, THE (1926, Ger.)
(4 r.) d, Lotte Reiniger (animated)

AELITA (1929, USSR)
(6 r.) d, Yakov A. Protazanov; lp, Nikolai M. Zeretelli, J. Solnzeva, Igor Ilinski, Konstantin Eggert

AFFAIR OF THREE NATIONS, AN (1915)
(5 r.) d, Arnold Daly, Ashley Miller; lp, Arnold Daly, Sheldon Lewis, William Harrigan, Charles Laite

AFFINITIES (1922)
(6 r.) d, Ward Lascelle; lp, John Bowers, Colleen Moore, Joe Bonner, Grace Gordon

AFGANISTAN (1929, USSR)
(7 r.) d, Vladimir Yerofeyev

AFTER DARK (1915, Brit.)
(4 r.) d, Warwick Buckland; lp, Flora Morris, Harry Royston, Harry Gilbey, Beatrice Read

AFTER DARK (1915)
(5 r.) d, Frederick Thompson; lp, Alec B. Francis, Dorothy Green, Eric Maxon, Melville Stewart

AFTER DARK (1923)
(5 r.)

AFTER HIS OWN HEART (1919)
(5 r.) d, Harry L. Franklin; lp, Hale Hamilton, Naomi Childers, Mrs. Louis, Frank Hayes.

AFTER SIX DAYS (1922)
(10 r.) d, Armando Vay, Piero Antonio Gariazzo

AFTER THE BALL (1914)
(6 r.) d, Pierce Kingsley; lp, Herbert Kelcey, Effie Shannon

AFTER THE WAR (1918)
(5 r.) d, Joseph De Grasse; lp, Grace Cunard, Edward Cecil, Herbert Prior, Dora Rogers

AFTER YOUR OWN HEART (1921)
(5 r.) d, George E. Marshall; lp, Tom Mix, Ora Carew, George Hernandez, William Buckley

AFTERGLOW (1923, Brit.)
(7 r.) d, G.B. Samuelson, Walter Summers; lp, Lilian Hall-Davis, Fred Hearne, James Lindsay, Minna Grey

AFTERMATH (1914)
(4 r.) lp, Virginia Pearson, Owen Moore

AGE OF DESIRE, THE (1923)
(6 r.) d, Frank Borzage; lp, Joseph Swickard, William Collier, Jr, Frank Truesdell, Mary Philbin

AGE OF INNOCENCE, THE (1924)
(7 r.) d, Wesley Ruggles; lp, Edith Roberts, Elliott Dexter, Willard Louis, Fred Huntley

AIN EL GHEZAL
(SEE: GIRL FROM CARTHAGE, THE, 1924)

AL CHRISTIE'S "MADAME BEHAVE"
(SEE: MADAME BEHAVE, 1925)

ALABASTER BOX, AN (1917)
(5 r.) d, Chester Withey

ALADDIN AND THE WONDERFUL LAMP (1917)
(8 r.) d, C.M. & S.A. Franklin lp, Francis Carpenter, Virginia Lee Corbin, Violet Radcliffe, Gertrude Messinger

ALARM, THE (1917, USSR)
(7 r.) d, Yevgeni Bauer; lp, Nikolai Radin, Vera Coralli, M. Narokov, V. Svoboda

ALGOL (1920, Ger.)
(? r.) d, Hans Werkmeister; lp, Emil Jannings, John Gottowt, Kathe Haack, Hanna Ralph

ALIAS JIMMY VALENTINE (1915)
(6 r.) d, Maurice Tourneur; lp, Robert Warwick, Ruth Shepley, John Hines, Alec B. Francis.

ALIAS LADYFINGERS
(SEE: LADYFINGERS, 1921)

ALIAS MARY FLYNN (1925)
(6 r.) d, Ralph Ince; lp, Evelyn Brent, Malcolm McGregor, William V. Mong, Gladden James

ALIAS MISS DODD (1920)
(5 r.) d, Harry L. Franklin lp, Edith Roberts, Walter Richardson, Johnnie Cooke, Harry Van Meter

ALIAS PHIL KENNEDY (1922)
(5 r.) d, William Bertram; lp, William Patton, Dixie Lamont

ALIBI, THE (1916)
(5 r.) d, Paul Scardon; lp, Betty Howe, James Morrison, Paul Scardon, Robert Whitworth

ALICE IN WONDERLAND (1916)
(6 r.) d, W.W. Young; lp, Viola Savoy

ALICE THROUGH A LOOKING GLASS (1928)
(4 r.) d, Walter Lang

ALICIA OF THE ORPHANS
(SEE: RAGGED PRINCESS, THE, 1916)

ALIEN BLOOD (1917)
(4 r.)

ALIENS
(SEE: UNWRITTEN CODE, THE, 1919)

ALL AROUND FRYING PAN (1925)
(6 r.) d, David Kirkland; lp, Fred Thompson, James Marcus, William Courtright, John Lince.

ALL AT SEA (1929)
(6 r.) d, Alf Goulding; lp, Karl Dane, George K. Arthur, Josephine Dunn, Herbert Prior.

ALL FOR A HUSBAND (1917)
(6 r.) d, Carl Harbaugh; lp, Virginia Pearson, Herbert Evans, Dorothy Quincy, Gladys Kelly

ALL FOR A WOMAN (1921, Ger.)
(? r.) d, Dimitri Buchowetski; lp, Emil Jannings, Werner Krauss, Conrad Veidt, Maly Delschaft

ALL NIGHT (1918)
(5 r.) lp, Carmel Myers, M. Rodolpho de Valentina

ALL OF A SUDDEN PEGGY (1920)
(5 r.) d, Walter Edwards; lp, Marguerite Clark, Jack Mulhall, Lillian Leighton, Maggie Holloway Fischer

ALMA, WHERE DO YOU LIVE? (1917)
(6 r.) d, Hal Clarendon; lp, Ruth MacTammany, George Larkin, Jack Newton, John Webb Dillon

ALMIGHTY DOLLAR, THE (1916)
(5 r.) d, Robert Thornby; lp, Frances Nelson, E.K. Lincoln, June Elvidge, George Anderson

ALMOST HUMAN (1927)
(6 r.) d, Frank Urson; lp, Vera Reynolds, Kenneth Thomson, Majel Coleman, Claire McDowell

ALOHA OE (1915)
(5 r.) d, G.P. Hamilton; lp, Willard Mack, Enid Markey, Margaret Thompson, Frank Borzage

ALONE IN NEW YORK (1914)
(5 r.) lp, Mr. Standing

ALSACE (1916, FR.)
(? r.) d, Henri Pouctal; lp, Rejane

ALTEMER LE CYNIQUE (1924, Fr.)
(? r.) d, Georges Monca

ALWAYS IN THE WAY (1915)
(5 r.) d, J. Searle Dawley; lp, Mary Miles Minter, Ethelmary Oakland, Lowell Sherman, Edna M. Holland

ALWAYS RIDIN' TO WIN (1925)
(5 r.) d, Forrest Sheldon; lp, Pete Morrison

AMATEUR ORPHAN, AN (1917)
(5 r.) d, Van Dyke Brooke; lp, Gladys Leslie, Isabel Vernon, Thomas A. Curran, Jean Armour

AMBUSHED (1926)
(5 r.) lp, Bob Reeves.

AME D'ARTISTE (1925, Fr.)
(? r.) d, Germaine Dulac; lp, Mabel Poulton, Nicolas Koline, Ivan Petrovich, Yvette Andreyor

AMERICAN BEAUTY, THE (1916)
(5 r.) d, William D. Taylor; lp, Myrtle Stedman, Elliott Dexter, Howard Davies, Jack Livingston

AMERICAN CITIZEN, AN (1914)
(4 r.) d, J. Searle Dawley;

AMERICAN GENTLEMAN, AN (1915)
(5 r.) lp, William Bonelli, Charles C. Graham, Wilbur Hudson, Virginia Fairfax

AMERICAN PLUCK (1925)
(6 r.) d, Richard Stanton; lp, George Walsh, Wanda Hawley, Sidney De Grey, Frank Leigh

AMERICA - THAT'S ALL (1917)
(5 r.) d, Arthur Rosson; lp, Jack Devereaux, Winifred Allen, Walter Walker, Blanche Davenport

AMES D'ENFANTS (1929, Fr.)
(? r.) d, Marie Epstein, Jean Benoit-Levy

AMES D'ORIENT (1919, Fr.)
(? r.) d, Leon Poirier

AMONG THE RUINS (1923, Jap.)
(? r.) d, Kenji Mizoguchi

AMOURS, DELICES ET ORGUES (1925, Fr.)
(? r.) d, Gaston Ravel

AND THE LAW SAYS (1916)
(5 r.) lp, Richard Bennett, George Periolat, Adrienne Morrison, Allan Forrest

ANDRE CORNELIS (1918, Fr.)
(? r.) d, Jean Kemm

ANDRE CORNELIS (1927, Fr.)
(? r.) d, Jean Kemm

ANDREI KOZHUKHOV (1917, USSR)
(7 r.) d, Yakov Protazanov; lp, Ivan Mozhukhin, Georgi Azagarov, Vera Orlova, Nikolai Rimsky

ANGEL CITIZENS (1922)
(5 r.) d, Francis Ford; lp, Franklyn Farnum, Al Hart, "Shorty" Hamilton, Peggy O'Day

ANGEL FACTORY, THE (1917)
(5 r.) d, Lawrence McGill; lp, Antonio Moreno, Helene Chadwick, Laura West, Margaret Greene

ANGEL OF THE WARD, THE (1915, Brit.)
(4 r.) d, Tom Watts; lp, Evelyn Cecil, Arthur Chisholm, Herbert Trumper

ANGOISSE (1917, Fr.)
(? r.) d, Andre Hugon

ANNA KARENINA (1914, USSR)
(? r.) d, Vladimir Gardin; lp, Maria Germanova, Vladimir Shaternikov, M. Tamarov, Zoya Barantsevich

ANNA KARENINA (1914)
d, J. Gordon Edwards; lp, Betty Nansen

ANNIE LAURIE (1916, Brit.)
(4 r.) d, Cecil M. Hepworth; lp, Alma Taylor, Stewart Rome, Lionelle Howard, Gwynne Herbert

ANNIE-FOR-SPITE (1917)
(5 r.) d, James Kirkwood; lp, Mary Miles Minter, George Fisher, Eugenie Forde, Gertrude Le Brandt

ANOTHER MAN'S SHOES (1922)
(5 r.) d, Jack Conway; lp, Herbert Rawlinson, Barbara Bedford, Una Trevelyn, Nick De Ruiz

ANSWER THE CALL (1915, Brit.)
(4 r.) d, L.C. MacBean; lp, Herbert Sydney, R.D. Nicholson

ANTIQUE DEALER, THE (1915)
(5 r.) d, Harley Knoles; lp, Cyril Maude, Lois Meredith, Montagu Love, Margot Williams

ANTOINETTE SABRIER (1927, Fr.)
(? r.) d, Germaine Dulac; lp, Gabriel Gabrio, Eve Francis, Yvette Armel

ANY NIGHT (1922)
(5 r.) d, Martin Beck; lp, Tully Marshall, Robert Edeson, Lila Leslie, Gordon Sackville

ANY WOMAN'S MAN
(SEE: WOMEN MEN LIKE, 1928)

ANYBODY HERE SEEN KELLY? (1928)
(7 r.) d, William Wyler; lp, Bessie Love, Tom Moore, Kate Price, Addie McPhail

APACHE DANCER, THE (1923)
(5 r.) d, Charles R. Seeling; lp, George Larkin, Ollie Kirby

APACHES OF PARIS, THE (1915)
(4 r.) d, Robert Ellis; lp, Robert Ellis, Marion Whitney, Edna Hibbard, Arthur Housman

APACHES OF PARIS (1928, Fr.)
(7 r.) d, Nicholas Malikoff

APPASSIONATA (1929, Fr.)
(7 r.) d, Leon Mathot; lp, Leon Mathot, Therese Kolb, Renee Heribel, Ruth Weyher

APPLE-TREE GIRL, THE (1917)
(5 r.) d, Alan Crosland; lp, Shirley Mason, Joyce Fair, Jessie Stevens, Paul Perez

APRIL (1916)
(5 r.) d, Donald MacDonald; lp, Helene Rosson, E. Forrest Taylor; Harry Von Meter, Louise Lester.

APRIL FOLLY (1920)
(5 r.) d, Robert Z. Leonard

ARABIA (1922)
(5 r.) d, Lynn Reynolds; lp, Tom Mix, Barbara Bedford, George Hernandez, Norman Selby

ARCTIC ADVENTURE (1922)
(5 r.) d, Chester Withey lp, William V. Mong, Alice Knowland, Charles Puffy, Jack Fuqua

ARGONAUTS OF CALIFORNIA (1916)
(10 r.) d, Henry Kabierske

ARISTOCRACY (1914)
(4 r.) d, Thomas Heffron; lp, Tyrone Power, Marguerite Skirvin, Edna Mayo, Arthur Hoops

ARIZONA (1913)
(6 r.) d, Lawrence B. McGill; lp, Gertrude Shipman, Cyril Scott, Gail Kane, Alma Bradley

ARIZONA NIGHTS (1927)
(7 r.) d, Lloyd Ingraham; lp, Fred Thompson, Nora Lane, J.P. McGowan, William Courtright

ARIZONA SPEED (1928)
(5 r.) d, Robert J. Horner; lp, Pawnee Bill, Jr.

ARIZONA STREAK, THE (1926)
(5 r.) d, Robert De Lacy; lp, Tom Tyler, Alfred Hewston, Ada Mae Vaughn, Frankie Darro

ARIZONA WHIRLWIND, THE (1927)
(5 r.) d, William J. Craft; lp, Bill Cody, Margaret Hampton, David Dunbar, Hughie Mack

ARREST NORMA MACGREGOR (1921)
(5 r.) lp, Joe Moore, Eileen Sedgwick

ART OF LOVE, THE (1928, Ger.)
(? r.) d, Robert Land; lp, Hermann Bottcher, Walter Rilla, Georg Alexander, Carmen Boni

AS A MAN THINKS (1919)
(4 r.) d, George Irving; lp, Leah Baird, Warburton Gamble, Betty Howe, Charles C. Brandt

AS MAN MADE HER (1917)
(5 r.) d, George Archainbaud; lp, Gail Kane, Frank Mills, Gerda Holmes, Edward Langford

AS NO MAN HAS LOVED
(SEE: MAN WITHOUT A COUNTRY, 1925)

AS THE SUN WENT DOWN (1915, Brit.)
(4 r.) d, Frank Wilson; lp, Stewart Rome, Chrissie White, Lionelle Howard, Gwynne Herbert

AS THE WORLD ROLLS ON (1921)
(7 r.) lp, Jack Johnson, Blanche Thompson

AS YE REPENT
(SEE: REDEEMED, 1915, Brit.)

ASHES (1922)
(5 r.) d, G.M. Anderson; lp, William Courtleigh, Leona Anderson, Margaret Landis, Myrtle Stedman

ASHES OF DESIRE (1919)
(6 r.) d, Frank Borzage; lp, Tsuru Aoki

ASHES OF REVENGE, THE (1915, Brit.)
(4 r.) d, Harold Shaw; lp, Edna Flugrath, Philip Hewland, Gwynne Herbert

ASIAN SUN, THE (1921, Ger.)
(7 r.) d, Edmund Heuberger; lp, Irena Marga, Paul Otto, Henry Size, Wladimir Agajeff

AT BAY (1915)
(5 r.) d, George Fitzmaurice; lp, Florence Reed, Frank Sheridan, Charles Waldron, Lester Chambers

AT FIRST SIGHT (1917)
(5 r.) d, Robert Leonard; lp, Mae Murray, Sam T. Hardy, Jules Raucourt, Julia Bruns

AT PINEY RIDGE (1916)
(5 r.) d, William Robert Daly; lp, Fritzi Brunette, Al W. Filson, Leo Pierson, Ed J. Peil

AT THE CROSSROADS (1922)
(6 r.) lp, Seena Owen

AT THE EDGE OF THE WORLD (1929, Ger.)
(7 r.) d, Karl Grune; lp, Albert Steinrueck, Wilhelm Dieterle, Imre Raday, Brigitte Helm

AT THE END OF THE WORLD (1921)
(6 r.) d, Penrhyn Stanlaws; lp, Betty Compson, Milton Sills, Mitchell Lewis, Casson Ferguson

AT THE GREY HOUSE
(SEE: CHRONICLES OF THE GREY HOUSE, THE, 1925, Ger.)

AT THE MERCY OF MEN (1918)
(5 r.) d, Charles Miller; lp, Alice Brady, Frank Morgan, Jack W. Johnson, Robert Walker

AT THE OLD CROSSED ROADS (1914)
(5 r.) d, Frank L. Dear; lp, Esta Williams, Mrs. Stuart Robson, Rae Ford, Arthur Morrison

AT THE SIGN OF THE JACK O'LANTERN (1922)
(6 r.) d, Lloyd Ingraham; lp, Betty Ross Clark, Earl Schenck, Wade Boteler, Victor Potel

AT THE TORRENT'S MERCY (1915, Brit.)
(4 r.) d, H.O. Martinek; lp, Percy Moran, Ivy Montford, A.V. Bramble, Jack Jarman

AT 3:25
(SEE: PARIS QUI DORT, 1924)

ATLANTIS (1913, Ger./Den.)
(? r.) d, August Blom; lp, Ida Orlov, Olaf Fonss, Michael Curtiz

ATONEMENT (1920)
(5 r.) d, William Humphrey; lp, Conway Tearle, Grace Davison, Huntley Gordon, Sally Crute

ATONEMENT OF GOSTA BERLING, THE
(SEE: LEGEND OF GOSTA BERLING, 1928, Swed.)

AU BONHEUR DES DAMES (1929, Fr.)
(? r.) d, Julien Duvivier; lp, Dito Parlo, Armand Bour, Pierre de Guingand, Germaine Rouer

AUCTION OF SOULS (1922)
(8 r.) d, Oscar Apfel; lp, Aurora Mardiganian, Anna Q. Nilsson, Eugenie Besserer, Lillian West

AU DELA DES LOIS HUMAINES (1920, Fr.)
(? r.) d, Gaston Roudes

AU PARADIS DES ENFANTS (1918, Fr.)
(? r.) d, Charles Burguet

AU SEUIL DU HAREM (1922, Fr.)
(? r.) d, Luitz-Morat

AUCTION OF VIRTUE, THE (1917)
(5 r.) d, Herbert Blache; lp, Naomi Childers, Leslie Austen, Kirke Brown, Wyndham Standing

AULD ROBIN GRAY (1917, Brit.)
(5 r.) d, Meyrick Milton; lp, Langhorne Burton, Miss June, R.A. Roberts

AUNTIE'S ANTICS (1929, Brit.)
(5 r.) d, Wilf Gannon; lp, Wilf Gannon, Hilda Sayer

AURORA LEIGH (1915)
(5 r.)

AUTOUR DU MYSTERE (1920, Fr.)
(? r.) d, Henri Desfontaines

AUTOUR D'UN BERCEAU (1925, Fr.)
(? r.) d, Georges Monca

AUTUMN (1916)
(5 r.) d, O.A.C. Lund

AUX JARDINS DE MURCIE (1923, Fr.)
(? r.) d, Rene Hervil, Louis Mercanton

AVALANCHE, THE (1915)
(5 r.) d, Will S. Davis; lp, Catherine Countiss, William H. Tooker, Violet Mersereau, Sue Balfour

AVENGING HAND, THE (1915, Brit.)
(4 r.) d, Charles Calvert; lp, Dorothy Bellew, Sydney Vautier, Douglas Payne

AVIATOR SPY, THE (1914, Brit.)
(4 r.) d, Charles Calvert; lp, Douglas Payne, Norman Howard

AWAKENING OF BESS MORTON, THE (1916)
(5 r.) d, Otis Thayer; lp, Gertrude Bondhill

AWAKENING OF HELENA RICHIE, THE (1916)
(5 r.) d, John W. Noble; lp, Ethel Barrymore, Robert Cummings, Frank Montgomery, J.A. Furey

AWAKENING OF RUTH, THE (1917)
(5 r.) d, Edward H. Griffith; lp, Shirley Mason, Donald MacClennan, Joseph Burke, William Hayes

AWAY IN THE LEAD (1925)
(5 r.) lp, Francis X. Bushman, Jr.

BAB THE FIXER (1917)
(5 r.) d, Sherwood MacDonald; lp, Jackie Saunders, Leslie T. Peacocke, Mollie McConnell, Ruth Lackaye

BABES IN THE WOODS (1917)
(6 r.) d, C.M. & S.A. Franklin; lp, Francis Carpenter, Virginia Lee Corbin, Violet Radcliffe, Carmen De Rue

BABETTE (1917)
(5 r.) d, Charles Brabin; lp, Marc MacDermott, Peggy Hyland, Templar Saxe, William Dunn

BABETTE OF THE BALLY HOO (1916)
(5 r.)

BAB'S MATINEE IDOL (1917)
(5 r.) d, J. Searle Dawley; lp, Marguerite Clark, Helen Greene, Nigel Barrie, Isabel O'Madigan

BABY CYCLONE, THE (1928)
(7 r.) d, Edward Sutherland; lp, Lew Cody, Aileen Pringle, Robert Armstrong, Gwen Lee

BACHELOR APARTMENTS (1920)
(5 r.) d, Johnny Walker; lp, Georgia Hopkins, George Dupree

BACHELOR BRIDES (1926)
(6 r.) d, William K. Howard; lp, Rod La Rocque, Eulalie Jensen, Elinor Fair, George Nichols

BACHELOR DADDY, THE (1922)
(7 r.) d, Alfred Green; lp, Thomas Meighan, Leatrice Joy, Maude Wayne, Adele Farrington

BACHELOR HUSBAND, A (1920 Brit.)
(5 r.) d, Kenelm Foss; lp, Lyn Harding, Renee Mayer, Hayford Hobbs, Irene Rooke

BACHELOR'S BABY, A (1922, Brit.)
(6 r.) d, Arthur Rooke; lp, Constance Woth, Malcolm Tod, Tom Reynolds, Haidee Wright

BACHELOR'S CHILDREN, A (1918)
(5 r.) d, Paul Scardon; lp, Harry Morey, Florence Deshon, Denton Vane, Alice Terry

BACHELOR'S CLUB, THE (1929)
(6 r.) d, Noel Mason; lp, Richard Talmadge, Barbara Worth, Edna Murphy, Edna Ellsmere

BACHELOR'S ROMANCE, THE (1915)
(4 r.) lp, John Emerson, Lorraine Huling, Maggie Fisher, George LeGuere

BACHELOR'S WIFE, A (1919)
(5 r.) d, Emmett J. Flynn; lp, Mary Miles Minter, Allan Forrest, Myrtle Reeves, Lydia Knott

BACK FROM SHANGHAI (1929)
(5 r.) d, Noel Mason; lp, Leonard St. Leo, Vera Reynolds, Sojin, Joseph W. Girard

BACK OF THE MAN (1917)
(5 r.) d, Reginald Barker; lp, Dorothy Dalton, Charles Ray, J. Barney Sherry, Margaret Thompson

BACK PAY (1922)
(7 r.) d, Frank Borzage; lp, Seena Owen, Matt Moore, J. Barney Sherry, Ethel Duray

BACK TO GOD'S COUNTRY (1919 US/Can.)
(6 r.) d, David M. Hartford; lp, Nell Shipman, Wheeler Oakman, Wellington Playter, Ralph Laidlow

BACK TO GOD'S COUNTRY (1927)
(6 r.) d, Irvin Willat; lp, Renee Adoree, Robert Frazer, Walter Long, Mitchell Lewis

BACK TO LIBERTY (1927)
(6 r.) d, Bernard McEveety; lp, Jean Del Val, George Walsh, Edmund Breese, De Sacia Mooers

BACK TO LIFE (1925)
(6 r.) d, Whitman Bennett; lp, Patsy Ruth Miller, David Powell, Lawford Davidson, Mary Thurman

BACK TO OLD VIRGINIA (1923)
(5 r.) lp, Judith Jordan

BACK TO THE WOODS (1918)
(5 r.) d, George Irving; lp, Mabel Normand, Herbert Rawlinson, T. Henderson Murray, Arthur Housman

BACK TO YELLOW JACKET (1922)
(6 r.) d, Ben Wilson; lp, Roy Stewart, Kathleen Kirkham, Earl Metcalfe, Jack Pratt

BACKBONE (1923)
(7 r.) d, Edward Sloman; lp, Edith Roberts, Alfred Lunt, William B. Mack, Frankie Evans

BACKSTAIRS (1921, Ger.)
(4 r.) d, Leopold Jessner, Paul Leni; lp, Henny Porten, Wilhelm Dieterle, Fritz Kortner

BAD BOYS (1917)
(5 r.) d, Chester Withey; lp, Robert Harron, Richard Cummings, Josephine Cromwell, Mildred Harris

BAD COMPANY (1925)
(6 r.) d, E.H. Griffith; lp, Madge Kennedy, Bigelow Cooper, Conway Tearle, Lucille Lee Stewart

BAD LANDS, THE (1925)
(6 r.) d, Dell Henderson; lp, Harry Carey, Wilfred Lucas, Lee Shumway, Gaston Glass

BAD MAN, THE (1923)
(7 r.) d, Edwin Carewe; lp, Holbrook Blinn, Jack Mulhall, Walter McGrail, Enid Bennett

BAD MAN FROM BODIE (1925)
(5 r.) lp, Big Boy Williams

BAD MAN'S BLUFF (1926)
(5 r.) d, Alvin J. Neitz; lp, Buffalo Bill, Jr., Molly Malone, Frank Whitson, Robert McKenzie

BAD MAN'S MONEY
(SEE: BAD MEN'S MONEY, 1929)

BAD MEN'S MONEY (1929)
(5 r.) d, J.P. McGowan; lp, Yakima Canutt, Peggy Montgomery, John Lowell, J.P. McGowan

BAG AND BAGGAGE (1923)
(6 r.) d, Finis Fox; lp, Gloria Grey, John Roche, Carmelita Geraghty, Paul Weigel

BAIT, THE (1916)
(5 r.) d, William J. Bowman; lp, Betty Harte, William Clifford, Margaret Gibson, Oliver C. Allen

BAITED TRAP (1926)
(5 r.) d, Stuart Paton; lp, Ben Wilson, Neva Gerber, Al Ferguson, Monty O'Grady

BALACLAVA
(SEE: JAWS OF HELL, 1928, Brit.)

BALL OF FORTUNE, THE (1926, Brit.)
(7 r.) d, Hugh Croise; lp, Billy Meredith, James Knight, Mabel Poulton, Geoffrey B. Partridge

BALLYHOO BUSTER, THE (1928)
(5 r.) d, Richard Thorpe; lp, Buffalo Bill, Jr., Peggy Shaw, Nancy Nash, Albert Hart

BANDBOX, THE (1919)
(7 r.) d, Roy William Neill; lp, Doris Kenyon, Alexander Gaden, Walter McEwen, Edward Keppler

BANDIT BUSTER, THE (1926)
(5 r.) d, Richard Thorpe; lp, Buddy Roosevelt, Molly Malone, Lafe McKee, Winifred Landis

BANDIT TAMER, THE (1925)
(5 r.) lp, Franklyn Farnum

BANDIT'S BABY, THE (1925)
(5 r.) d, James P. Hogan; lp, Fred Thompson, Helen Foster, Harry Woods, Mary Louise Miller

BANDIT'S DOUBLE, THE (1917)
(5 r.)

BANDITS OF THE AIR (1925)
(5 r.) lp, Melbourne MacDowell, Jane Starr

BANDOLERO, THE (1924)
(8 r.) d, Tom Terriss; lp, Pedro De Coroba, Gustav von Seyffertitz, Manuel Granado, Gordon Begg

BANKER'S DAUGHTER, THE (1914)
(5 r.) d, Edward M. Roskam, William Haddock; lp, Katherine La Salle, David Wall, William H. Tooker, William Bailey

BARB WIRE (1922)
(5 r.) d, Frank Grandon; lp, Jack Hoxie, Jean Porter, Olah Norman, William Lester

BARBARA FRIETCHIE (1915)
(5 r.) d, Clarence J. Harris; lp, Mary Miles Minter, Mrs. Thomas W. Whiffen, Guy Coombs, Fraunie Fraunholz

BARBARA FRIETCHIE (1924)
(8 r.) d, Lambert Hillyer; lp, Florence Vidor, Edmund Lowe, Emmett King, Joe Bennett

BARBARIAN, THE (1921)
(6 r.) d, Donald Crisp; lp, Monroe Salisbury, George Burrell, Barney Sherry, Elinor Hancock

BARBARY SHEEP (1917)
(6 r.) d, Maurice Tourneur; lp, Elsie Ferguson, Pedro de Cordoba, Lumsden Hare, Macey Harlam

BARBED WIRE
(SEE: BARB WIRE, 1922)

BAR-C MYSTERY, THE (1926)
(5 r.) d, Robert F. Hill; lp, Dorothy Phillips, Wallace MacDonald, Ethel Clayton, Philo McCullough

BARDELYS THE MAGNIFICENT (1926)
(9 r.) d, King Vidor; lp, John Gilbert, Eleanor Boardman, Roy D'Arcy, Lionel Belmore

BARE FISTS (1919)
(6 r.) d, Jack [John] Ford; lp, Harry Carey, Betty Schade, Joe Harris, Vester Pegg

BARE KNEES (1928)
(6 r.) d, Erle C. Kenton; lp, Virginia Lee Corbin, Donald Keith, Jane Winton, Johnnie Walker

BARE KNUCKLES (1921)
(5 r.) d, James P. Hogan; lp, William Russell, Mary Thurman, Correan Kirkham, George Fisher

BAREE, SON OF KAZAN (1918)
(5 r.) d, David Smith; lp, Nell Shipman, Alfred Whitman, Al Garcia, Joe Rickson

BAREE, SON OF KAZAN (1925)
(7 r.) d, David Smith; lp, Anita Stewart, Donald Keith, Jack Curtis, Joe Rickson

BARE-FISTED GALLAGHER (1919)
(5 r.) d, Joseph J. Franz; lp, William Desmond, Agnes Vernon, Arthur Milett, Frank Lanning

BAREFOOT BOY, THE (1923)
(6 r.) d, David Kirkland; lp, John Bowers, Marjorie Daw, Sylvia Breamer, George McDaniel

BARGAIN, THE (1914)
(7 r.) d, Reginald Barker; lp, William S. Hart, J. Frank Burke, Clara Williams, J. Barney Sherry

BARGAIN, THE (1921, Brit.)
(6 r.) d, Henry Edwards; lp, Henry Edwards, Chrissie White, Rex McDougall, Mary Dibley

BARGAINS (1923)
(6 r.)

BARKER, THE (1917)
(5 r.) d, J.A. Richmond; lp, Lew Fields, Amy Dennis, James Harris, A. Francis Lenz

BARKER, THE (1928)
(8 r.) d, George Fitzmaurice; lp, Milton Sills, Douglas Fairbanks Jr., George Cooper, John Erwin

BARNABY (1919, Brit.)
(5 r.) d, Jack Denton; lp, Dick Webb, Cyril Vaughan, Athalie Davis, Dorothy Fane

BARNABY RUDGE (1915)
(6 r.) d, Thomas Bentley; lp, Tom Powers, Violet Hopson, Stewart Rome, Chrissie White

BARNSTORMER, THE (1922)
(6 r.) d, Charles Ray; lp, Charles Ray, Wilfred Lucas, Florence Oberle, Lionel Belmore

BARNSTORMERS, THE (1915)
(4 r.) d, James W. Horne; lp, Myrtle Tannehill, William H. West, William Brunton

BAROCCO (1925, Fr.)
(? r.) d, Charles Burguet

BARRICADE, THE (1917)
(5 r.) d, Edwin Carewe;

BARRICADE, THE (1921)
(6 r.) d, William Christy Cabanne; lp, William H. Strauss, Katherine Spencer, Kenneth Harlan, Eugene Borden

BARRIERS BURNED AWAY (1925)
(7 r.) d, W.S. Van Dyke; lp, Mabel Ballin, Eric Mayne, Frank Mayo, Wanda Hawley

BARRIERS OF FOLLY (1922)
(5 r.) d, Edward Kull; lp, George Larkin, Eva Novak, Wilfred Lucas, Lillian West

BARRIERS OF SOCIETY (1916)
(5 r.) d, Lloyd B. Carleton; lp, Dorothy Davenport, Emory Johnson, Richard Morris, Alfred Allen

BARS OF IRON (1920, Brit.)
(6 r.) d, F. Martin Thornton; lp, Madge White, Roland Myles, J.R. Tozer, Leopold McLaglen

BARTON MYSTERY, THE (1920, Brit.)
(6 r.) d, Harry Roberts; lp, Lyn Harding, Hilda Bayley, Vernon Jones, Maud Cressall

BATTLE CRY, THE
(SEE: HER MAN, 1918)

BATTLE OF BALLOTS, THE (1915)
(6 r.) d, Frank B. Coigne; lp, Mayre Hall, William Wells, Dorothy Van Raven, Robert Web Lawrence

BATTLE OF HEARTS (1916)
(5 r.) d, Oscar Apfel; lp, William Farnum, Elda Furry [Hedda Hopper], Wheeler Oakman, Willard Louis

BATTLE OF MONS (1929)
(6 r.) d, Walter Summers

BATTLE OF SHILOH, THE (1914)
(4 r.) d, John Ince

BATTLE OF WATERLOO, THE (1913, Brit.)
(5 r.) d, Charles Weston; lp, Ernest G. Batley, George Foley, Vivian Ross

BATTLER, THE (1919)
(6 r.) d, Frank Reicher; lp, Earl Metcalfe, Virginia Hammond, Harry C. Brown, Edwin Dennison

BATTLER, THE (1925)
(5 r.) d, Robert N. Bradbury; lp, Kenneth McDonald

BATTLIN' BILL (1927)
(5 r.) lp, Dick Carter, Gene Crosby

BATTLIN' BUCKAROO (1924)
(5 r.) lp, Bill Patton, Peggy O'Day

BATTLING BATES (1923)
(5 r.) d, Webster Cullison; lp, Edmund Cobb

BATTLING BOOKWORM (1928)
(5 r.) lp, William Barrymore

BATTLING BUDDY (1924)
(5 r.) d, Richard Thorpe; lp, Buddy Roosevelt, Violet La Plante, William Lowery, Kewpie King

BATTLING BUNYON (1925)
(5 r.) d, Paul Hurst; lp, Wesley Barry, Molly Malone, Frank Campeau, Harry Mann

BATTLING BURKE (1928)
(5 r.) lp, Al Hoxie

BATTLING FOOL, THE (1924)
(5 r.) d, W.S. Van Dyke; lp, William Fairbanks, Eva Novak, Fred J. Butler, Laura Winston

BATTLING JANE (1918)
(5 r.) d, Elmer Clifton; lp, Dorothy Gish, George Nicholls, May Hall, Katherine MacDonald

BATTLING KID (1926)
(5 r.) d, Paul Hurst; lp, Al Hoxie

BATTLING KING (1922)
(5 r.) d, P. D. Sargent; lp, William J. Otts, Nevada Grey

BATTLING MASON (1924)
(5 r.) d, Jack Nelson, William James Craft; lp, Frank Merrill, Eva Novak, Billy Elmer, Dick Sutherland

BATTLING ORIOLES, THE (1924)
(6 r.) d, Ted Wilde, Fred Guiol; lp, Glenn Tryon, Blanche Mehaffey, John T. Prince, Noah Young

BAVU (1923)
(8 r.) d, Stuart Paton; lp, Wallace Beery, Estelle Taylor, Forrest Stanley, Sylvia Breamer

BAWBS O' BLUE RIDGE (1916)
(5 r.) d, Charles Miller; lp, Bessie Barriscale, Arthur Shirley, Joe Dowling, Frank Burke

BE A LITTLE SPORT (1919)
(5 r.) d, Scott Dunlap; lp, Albert Ray, Elinor Fair, Lule Warrenton, George Hernandez

BE MY WIFE (1921)
(5 r.) d, Max Linder; lp, Alta Allen, Caroline Rankin, Lincoln Stedman, Rose Dione

BEACH COMBER, THE
(SEE: UNDER CRIMSON SKIES, 1920)

BEACH OF DREAMS (1921)
(5 r.) d, William Parke; lp, Edith Storey, Noah Beery, Sr., Sidney Payne, Jack Curtis

BEANS (1918)
(5 r.) d, Jack Dillon; lp, Edith Roberts, William E. Lawrence; Charles Gerrard, Harry Carter

BEARCAT, THE (1922)
(5 r.) d, Edward Sedgwick; lp, Hoot Gibson, Lillian Rich, Charles French, Joe Harris

BEAR'S WEDDING, THE (1926, USSR)
(7 r.) d, Vladimir Gardin, Konstantin Eggert; lp, Konstantin Eggert, Vera Malinovskava, Natalya Rosenel, Yuri Zavadsdky

BEAST, THE (1916)
(5 r.) d, Richard Stanton; lp, George Walsh, Anna Luther, Gretchen Hartman, Alan Hale

BEATEN (1924)
(5 r.) d, H.G. Moody; lp, Jack Livingston

BEATING THE ODDS (1919)
(5 r.) d, Paul Scardon; lp, Harry T. Morey, Betty Blythe, Jean Paige, George Majeroni

BEAU BROADWAY (1928)
(7 r.) d, Malcolm St. Clair; lp, Lew Cody, Aileen Pringle, Sue Carol, Hugh Trevor

BEAU BROCADE (1916, Brit.)
(6 r.) d, Thomas Bentley; lp, Mercy Hatton, Charles Rock, Austin Leigh, Cecil Mannering

BEAUTE FATALE (1916, Fr.)
(? r.) d, Andre Hugon

BEAUTE QUI MEURT (1917, Fr.)
(? r.) d, George Lacroix

BEAUTIFUL ADVENTURE, THE (1917)
(5 r.) d, Dell Henderson; lp, Ann Murdock, Ada Boshell, Edward Fielding, David Powell

BEAUTIFUL CITY, THE (1925)
(7 r.) d, Kenneth Webb; lp, Richard Barthelmess, Dorothy Gish, William Powell, Frank Puglia

BEAUTIFUL JIM
(SEE: PRICE OF JUSTICE, THE, 1914, Brit.)

BEAUTIFUL LIE, THE (1917)
(5 r.) d, John W. Noble; lp, Frances Nelson, Harry S. Northrup, Edward Earle, Elsie McLeod

BEAUTIFUL MRS. REYNOLDS, THE (1918)
(5 r.) d, Arthur Ashley; lp, Arthur Ashley, Carlyle Blackwell, June Elvidge, Evelyn Greeley

BEAUTIFUL SINNER, THE (1924)
(5 r.) d, W.S. Van Dyke; lp, William Fairbanks, Eva Novak, George Nichols, Kate Lester

BEAUTIFULLY TRIMMED (1920)
(5 r.) d, Marcel De Sano; lp, Carmel Myers, Pell Trenton, Irving Cummings, Alfred Fisher

BEAUTY AND THE BAD MAN (1925)
(6 r.) d, William Worthington; lp, Mabel Ballin, Forrest Stanley, Russell Simpson, Andre de Baranger

BEAUTY AND THE BOLSHEVIK (1923, USSR)
(6 r.) d, Alexander Razumni; lp, Leontiev, Olga Tretyakov, Maria Blumenthal-Tamarina, N. Belayev

BEAUTY AND THE ROGUE (1918)
(5 r.) d, Henry King; lp, Mary Miles Minter, Allan Forrest, Orral Humphrey, George Periolat

BEAUTY FROM NIVERNAISE, THE
(SEE: LA BELLE NIVERNAISE, 1923, Fr.)

BEAUTY IN CHAINS (1918)
(5 r.) d, Elsie Jane Wilson; lp, Ella Hall, Emory Johnson, Ruby Lafayette, Winter Hall

BEAUTY MARKET, THE (1920)
(5 r.) d, Colin Campbell; lp, Katherine MacDonald, Roy Stewart, Kathleen Kirkham, Wedgewood Nowell

BEAUTY PRIZE, THE (1924)
(6 r.) d, Lloyd Ingrham; lp, Viola Dana, Pat O'Malley, Eddie Phillips, Eunice Vin Moore

BEAUTY PROOF (1919)
(5 r.) d, Paul Scardon; lp, Harry T. Morey, Betty Blythe, George Majeroni, Denton Vane

BEAUTY SHOP, THE (1922)
(7 r.) d, Edward Dillon; lp, Raymond Hitchcock, Billy B. Van, James J. Corbett, Louise Fazenda

BEAUTY SHOPPERS (1927)
(6 r.) d, Louis J. Gasnier; lp, Mae Busch, Doris Hill, Ward Crane, Thomas Haines

BEAUTY'S SORROWS (1931, Jap.)
(? r.) d, Yasujiro Ozu

BEAUTY'S WORTH (1922)
(7 r.) d, Robert G. Vignola; lp, Marion Davies, Forrest Stanley, June Elvidge, Truly Shattuck

BECAUSE (1918, Brit.)
(5 r.) d, Sidney Morgan; lp, Lilian Braithwaite, Ben Webster, George Webster, George Foley

BECAUSE (1921, Brit.)
(5 r.) d, Albert G. Frenguelli, Edith Mellor; lp, Margaret Campbell, Geoffrey Wilmer, Ida Fane, John Glidden

BECAUSE OF THE WOMAN (1917)
(5 r.) d, Jack Conway; lp, Belle Bennett, Jack Livingston, George Chesebro, Louella Maxam

BECKET (1923, Brit.)
(7 r.) d, George Ridgwell; lp, Sir Frank Benson, Gladys Jennings, Mary Clare, A.V. Bramble

BECKONING FLAME, THE (1916)
(5 r.) d, Walter Edwards; lp, Henry Woodruff, Tsuru Aoki, Rhea Mitchell, T. Frank Burke

BECKONING ROADS (1920)
(5 r.) d, Howard Hickman; lp, Bessie Barriscale, Niles Welch, George Periolat, Joseph J. Dowling

BECKONING TRAIL, THE (1916)
(5 r.) d, Jack Conway; lp, J. Warren Kerrigan, Lois Wilson, Maud George, Harry Carter

BECKY (1927)
(7 r.) d, John P. McCarthy; lp, Sally O'Neil, Owen Moore, Harry Crocker, Gertrude Olmstead

BED AND SOFA (1926, USSR)
(6 r.) d, Abram Room; lp, Nikolai Batalov, Ludmilla Semenova, Vladimir Fogel

BEETLE, THE (1919, Brit.)
(6 r.) d, Alexander Butler; lp, Maude Dunham, Hebden Foster, Fred Morgan, Nancy Benyon

BEFORE MIDNIGHT (1925)
(5 r.) d, John Adolfi; lp, William Russell, Barbara Bedford, Brinsley Shaw, Alan Roscoe

BEFORE THE WHITE MAN CAME (1920)
(6 r.) d, John E. Maple

BEGGAR GIRL'S WEDDING, THE (1915, Brit.)
(5 r.) d, Leedham Bantock; lp, Henry Lonsdale, Ethel Bracewell, Lauderdale Maitland, Nina Lynn

BEGGAR IN PURPLE, A (1920)
(6 r.) d, Edgar Lewis; lp, Leonard C. Shumway, Ruth King, Charles Arling, Stanhope Wheatcroft

BEGGAR OF CAWNPORE, THE (1916)
(5 r.) d, Charles Swickard; lp, H.B. Warner, Lola May, Wyndham Standing, H.E. Entwistle

BEGGAR PRINCE, THE (1920)
(5 r.) d, William Worthington; lp, Sessue Hayakawa, Beatrice La Plante, Thelma Percy, Bert Hadley

BEHIND CLOSED DOORS (1929)
(6 r.) d, R. William Neill; lp, Virginia Valli, Gaston Glass, Otto Matiesen, Andre De Segurola

BEHIND MASKS (1921)
(5 r.) d, Frank Reicher; lp, Dorothy Dalton, Frederick Vogeding, William P. Carleton, Julia Swayne

BEHIND THE ALTAR (1929, Ger.)
(6 r.) d, Wilheilm [William] Dieterle; lp, Wilheilm [William] Dieterle

BEHIND THE CURTAIN (1924)
(5 r.) d, Chester M. Franklin; lp, Lucille Ricksen, Johnny Harron, Winifred Bryson, Charles Clary

BEHIND THE DOOR (1920)
(6 r.) d, Irvin Willat; lp, Hobart Bosworth, Jane Novak, Wallace Beery, James Gordon

BEHIND THE LINES (1916)
(5 r.) d, Henry McRae; lp, Harry Carey, Edith Johnson, Ruth Clifford, Miriam Shelby

BEHIND THE MASK (1917)
(5 r.) d, Alice Blache; lp, Catherine Calvert, Richard Tucker, Kirke Brown, Charles Dungan

BEHIND THE SCENES (1914)
(5 r.) d, James Kirkwood; lp, Mary Pickford, Russell Bassett, James Kirkwood, Lowell Sherman

BEHIND TWO GUNS (1924)
(5 r.) d, Robert N. Bradbury; lp, J.B. Warner, Hazel Newman, Marin Sais, Jay Morley

BEHOLD MY WIFE! (1920)
(6 r.) d, George Melford; lp, Mabel Julienne Scott, Milton Sills, Winter Hall, Elliott Dexter

BEHOLD THE MAN (1921, US/Fr.)
(6 r.) d, Spencer Gordon Bennett; lp, H.O. Pettibone, Sybil Sheridan, Monsieur Moreau, Madame Moreau

BEHOLD THIS WOMAN (1924)
(7 r.) d, J. Stuart Blackton; lp, Irene Rich, Marguerite De La Motte, Charles A. Post, Harry Myers

BEILIS CASE, THE (1917, USSR)
(6 r.) d, Josef Soifer; lp, Y. Yakovlev, Malkevich-Khodakovskaya, S. Kuznetsov

BEING RESPECTABLE (1924)
(8 r.) d, Philip Rosen; lp, Marie Prevost, Monte Blue, Louise Fazenda, Irene Rich

BELGIAN, THE (1917)
(6 r.) d, Sidney Olcott; lp, Walker Whiteside, Valentine Grant, Georgio Majeroni, Anders Randolf

BELIEVE ME, XANTIPPE (1918)
(5 r.) d, Donald Crisp; lp, Wallace Reid, Ann Little, Ernest Joy, Henry Woodward

BELL BOY 13 (1923)
(5 r.) d, William Seiter; lp, Douglas MacLean, Margaret Loomis, John Steppling, Jean Walsh

BELLA DONNA (1915)
(5 r.) d, Edwin S. Porter, Hugh Ford; lp, Pauline Frederick, Thomas Holding, Julian L'Estrange, Eugene Ormonde

BELLA DONNA (1923)
(8 r.) d, George Fitzmaurice; lp, Pola Negri, Conway Tearle, Conrad Nagel, Adolphe Menjou

BELLE OF ALASKA (1922)
(5 r.) d, Chester Bennett; lp, J. Frank Glendon, Jane Novak, Noah Beery, Florence Carpenter

BELLE OF BROADWAY, THE (1926)
(6 r.) d, Harry O. Hoyt; lp, Betty Compson, Herbert Rawlinson, Edith Yorke, Armand Kaliz

BELLE OF NEW YORK, THE (1919)
(5 r.) d, Julius Steger; lp, Marion Davies, Raymond Bloomer, L. Rogers Lytton, Christian Rub

BELLE OF THE SEASON, THE (1919)
(5 r.) d, S. Rankin Drew; lp, Emmy Wehlen, S. Rankin Drew, Louis Wolheim

BELLS, THE (1914)
(4 r.)

BELLS, THE (1918)
(5 r.) d, Ernest C. Warde; lp, Frank Keenan, Lois Wilson, Joseph J. Dowling, Ida Lewis

BELLS, THE (1926)
(7 r.) d, James Young; lp, Lionel Barrymore, Fred Warren, Boris Karloff, Gustav von Seyffertitz

BELLS OF ST. MARY'S, THE (1928, Brit.)
(6 r.) d, Herbert "Red" Davis; lp, Tubby Phillips, Barbara Hood, Tom Gibson, Hal Martin

BELLS OF SAN JUAN (1922)
(5 r.) d, Scott Dunlap; lp, Charles Jones, Fritzi Brunette, Claude Peyton, Harry Todd

BELONGING (1922, Brit.)
(5 r.) d, F. Martin Thornton; lp, Barbara Hoffe, Hugh Buckler, William Lenders, Cecil A. Barry

BELOVED ADVENTURESS, THE (1917)
(5 r.) d, George Cowl; lp, Kitty Gordon, Jack Drumier, Inez Shannon, Madge Evans

BELOVED BLACKMAILER, THE (1918)
(5 r.) d, Del Henderson; lp, Carlyle Blackwell, Evelyn Greeley, W.T. Carleton, Isabelle Berwin

BELOVED BRUTE, THE (1924)
(7 r.) d, J. Stuart Blackton; lp, Marguerite De La Motte, Victor McLaglen, William Russell, Stuart Holmes

BELOVED CHEATER, THE (1920)
(5 r.) d, William Christy Cabanne; lp, Lew Cody, Eileen Percy, Doris Pawn, Jack Mower

BELOVED IMPOSTER, THE (1918)
(5 r.) d, Joseph Gleason; lp, Gladys Leslie, Huntley Gordon, Denton Vane, Mrs. Hurley

BELOVED JIM (1917)
(5 r.) d, Stuart Paton; lp, Harry Carter, Priscilla Dean, Joseph Girard, J. Morris Foster

BELOVED ROGUES (1917)
(5 r.) d, Al Santell; lp, Clarence William Kolb, Max M. Dill, May Cloy, Thomas Chatterton

BELOVED TRAITOR, THE (1918)
(6 r.) d, William Worthington; lp, Mae Marsh, E.K. Lincoln, George Fawcett, Hedda Hopper

BELOVED VAGABOND, THE (1916)
(6 r.) d, Edward Jose; lp, Edwin Arden, Kathryn Brown-Decker, Bliss Milford, Eric Mayne

BELOVED VAGABOND, THE (1923, Brit.)
(10 r.) d, Fred Leroy Granville; lp, Carlyle Blackwell, Madge Stuart, Phylis Titmuss, Sydney Fairbrother

BELOW THE DEAD LINE (1921)
(5 r.) d, J.P. McGowan; lp, H.B. Warner, Lillian Biron, Bert Sprotte, Robert Anderson

BELOW THE DEADLINE (1929)
(6 r.) d, J.P. McGowan; lp, Frank Leigh, Barbara Worth, Arthur Rankin, Walter Merrill

BELOW THE RIO GRANDE (1923)
(5 r.) d, Neal Hart; lp, Neal Hart

BELOW THE SURFACE (1920)
(6 r.) d, Irvin Willat; lp, Hobart Bosworth, Grace Darmond, Lloyd Hughes, George Webb

BELPHEGOR THE MOUNTEBANK (1921, Brit.)
(6 r.) d, Bert Wynne; lp, Milton Rosmer, Kathleen Vaughn, Warwick Ward, Nancy Price

BEN BLAIR (1916)
(5 r.) d, William D. Taylor; lp, Dustin Farnum, Winifred Kingston, Herbert Standing, Lamar Johnstone

BENEATH THE CZAR (1914)
(4 r.) d, Alice Blache; lp, Claire Whitney, Fraunie Fraunholz

BENNIE THE HOWL (1927, USSR)
(7 r.) d, Vladimir Vilner; lp, M. Lerorov, Yu. Shumski, A.D. Goricheva, A. Vabnik

BENTLEY'S CONSCIENCE (1922, Brit.)
(4 r.) d, Denison Clift; lp, Robert Loraine, Betty Faire, Henry Victor, Harvey Braban

BERLIN AFTER DARK (1929, Ger.)
(7 r.) d, Constantin J. David; lp, Kurt Gerron, Ernst Stahl-Nachbauer, Fritz Kampers, Grita Ley

BERLIN VIA AMERICA (1918)
(6 r.) d, Francis Ford; lp, Francis Ford, Edna Emerson, Jack Newton, George Henry

BESIDE THE BONNIE BRIER BUSH
(BONNIE BRIAR BUSH, THE, 1921, Brit.)

BEST BAD MAN, THE (1925)
(5 r.) d, J.G. Blystone; lp, Tom Mix, Buster Gardner, Cyril Chadwick, Clara Bow

BEST MAN, THE (1917)
(4 r.) d, Bertram Bracken; lp, Margaret Landis, William Ehfe, Gordon Sackville, Captain Nicholson

BEST MAN, THE (1919)
(5 r.) d, Thomas Heffron; lp, J. Warren Kerrigan, Lois Wilson, Alfred Whitman, Frances Raymond

BEST OF LUCK, THE (1920)
(6 r.) d, Ray C. Smallwood; lp, Kathryn Adams, Jack Holt, Lilie Leslie, Fred Malatesta

BEST PEOPLE, THE (1925)
(6 r.) d, Sidney Olcott; lp, Warner Baxter, Esther Ralston, Kathlyn Williams, Edwards Davis

BETES...COMES LES HOMMES (1923, Fr.)
(? r.) d, Alfred Machin, Henry Wuhlschleger

BETRAYAL, THE (1929)
(7 r.) d, Walter Summers; lp, Elissa Landi, Jerold Robertshaw, Gerald Pring, Charles Emerald

BETRAYAL (1929)
(8 r.) d, Lewis Milestone; lp, Emil Jannings, Esther Ralston, Gary Cooper, Jada Weller

BETRAYED! (1916)
(5 r.) d, Howard M. Mitchell; lp, Grace De Carlton, Robert Whittier, Roy Pilcher, Gladys Leslie

BETRAYED (1917)
(5 r.) d, R.A.(Raoul) Walsh; lp, Miriam Cooper, James Marcus, Hobart Bosworth, Monte Blue

BETSY ROSS (1917)
(5 r.) d, Travers Vale, George Cowl; lp, Alice Brady, John Bowers, Lillian Cook, Eugenie Woodward

BETSY'S BURGLAR (1917)
(5 r.) d, Paul Powell; lp, Constance Talmadge, Kenneth Harlan, Josephine Crowell, Kate Bruce

BETTA THE GYPSY (1918, Brit.)
(4 r.) d, Charles Raymond; lp, Marga la Rubia, Malvina Longfellow, George Foley, Edward Combermere

BETTER DAYS (1927)
(7 r.) d, Frank S. Mattison; lp, Dorothy Devore, Mary Carr, Gareth Hughes, Gaston Glass

BETTER HALF, THE (1918)
(5 r.) d, John S. Robertson; lp, Alice Brady, David Powell, Crauford Kent, W.T. Carleton

BETTER MAN, THE (1914)
(4 r.) d, Mr. Powers; lp, William Courtleigh, Robert Broderick, Alice Claire Elliott

BETTER MAN, THE (1915)
(5 r.) d, John W. Noble; lp, Henry Kolker, Elsie Balfour, Orlando Daly, Renee Kelly

BETTER MAN, THE (1921)
(5 r.) d, Wilfred Lucas; lp, Snowy Baker, Brownie Vernon, Charles Villiers, Wilfred Lucas

BETTER MAN, THE (1926)
(5 r.) d, Scott R. Dunlap; lp, Richard Talmadge, Ena Gregory, John Steppling, Margaret Campbell

BETTER MAN WINS, THE (1922)
(5 r.) d, Marcel Perez, Frank S. Mattison; lp, Pete Morrison, Dorothy Woods, E.L. Van Sickle, Jack Walters

BETTER TIMES (1919)
(5 r.) d, King W. Vidor; lp, Zasu Pitts, David Butler, Jack MacDonald, William De Vaull

BETTER WAY, THE (1926)
(6 r.) d, Ralph Ince; lp, Dorothy Revier, Ralph Ince, Eugene Strong, Armand Kaliz

BETTER WIFE, THE (1919)
(5 r.) d, William P.S. Earle; lp, Clara Kimball Young, Edward M. Kimball, Nigel Barrie, Kathlyn Williams

BETTER WOMAN, THE (1915)
(5 r.) d, Joseph A. Golden; lp, Lenore Ulrich, Edith Thornton, Lowell Sherman, Ben Graham

BETTINA LOVED A SOLDIER (1916)
(5 r.) d, Rupert Julian; lp, Louise Lovely, Rupert Julian, George Berrill, Francelia Billington

BETTY AND THE BUCCANEERS (1917)
(5 r.) d, Rollin S. Sturgeon; lp, Juliette Day, Charles Marriott, Joe King, Tote Du Crow

BETTY BE GOOD (1917)
(5 r.) d, Sherwood MacDonald; lp, Jackie Saunders, Arthur Shirley, Leslie T. Peacocke, Mollie McConnell

BETTY OF GRAYSTONE (1916)
(5 r.) d, Allan Dwan; lp, Dorothy Gish, Owen Moore, Kate Bruce, Albert Tavernier

BETTY TAKES A HAND (1918)
(5 r.) d, Jack Dillon; lp, Olive Thomas, Frederick Vroom, Bliss Chevalier, Mary Warren

BETTY TO THE RESCUE (1917)
(5 r.) d, Frank Reicher; lp, Fannie Ward, Jack Dean, Lillian Leighton, James Neill

BETWEEN DANGERS (1927)
(5 r.) d, Richard Thorpe; lp, Buddy Roosevelt, Alma Rayford, Rennie Young, Al Taylor

BETWEEN FRIENDS (1924)
(7 r.) d, J. Stuart Blackton; lp, Lou Tellegen, Anna Q. Nilsson, Norman Kerry, Alice Calhoun

BETWEEN MEN (1916)
(5 r.) d, William S. Hart; lp, William S. Hart, House Peters, Enid Markey, J. Barney Sherry

BETWEEN TWO HUSBANDS (1922)
(5 r.) lp, Jean Gabriel, Arline Pretty

BETWEEN TWO WORLDS
(SEE: DESTINY, 1921, Ger.)

BEULAH (1915)
(6 r.) lp, Henry B. Walthall, Joyce Moore

BEWARE (1919)
(5 r.) d, William Nigh; lp, Maurine Powers, Frank Norcross, Julia Hurley

BEWARE OF BLONDES (1928)
(6 r.) d, George B. Seitz; lp, Dorothy Revier, Matt Moore, Roy D'Arcy, Robert Edeson

BEWARE OF MARRIED MEN (1928)
(6 r.) d, Archie L. Mayo; lp, Irene Rich, Clyde Cook, Audrey Ferries, Myrna Loy

BEWARE OF STRANGERS (1918)
(8 r.) d, Colin Campbell; lp, Thomas Santschi, Fritzi Brunette, Bessie Eyton, Edward Coxen

BEWARE OF THE BRIDE (1920)
(5 r.) d, Howard M. Mitchell; lp, Eileen Percy, Walter McGrail, Hallam Cooley, Harry Dunkinson

BEWARE OF THE LAW (1922)
(5 r.) d, W.A. Douglas; lp, Marjorie Payne, William Coughey, Henry Van Bousen, Ann Deering

BEWARE OF WINDOWS (1927)
(6 r.) d, Wesley Ruggles; lp, Laura La Plante, Bryant Washburn, Paulette Duval, Walter Hiers

BEYOND ALL ODDS (1926)
(5 r.) d, Alvin J. Neitz; lp, Eileen Sedwick, Carlos Silvera, Ray Childs, Theodore Henderson

BEYOND LONDON LIGHTS (1928)
(6 r.) d, Tom Terriss; lp, Adrienne Dore, Lee Shumway, Gordon Elliott, Herbert Evans

BEYOND THE BORDER (1925)
(5 r.) d, Scott R. Dunlap; lp, Harry Carey, Mildred Harris, Tom Santschi, Jack Richardson

BEYOND THE CROSSROADS (1922)
(5 r.) d, Lloyd Carleton; lp, Ora Carew, Lawson Butt, Melbourne MacDowell, Stuart Morris

BEYOND THE DREAMS OF AVARICE (1920, Brit.)
(6 r.) d, Thomas Bentley; lp, Henry Victor, Joyce Dearsley, Alban Atwood, Frank Stanmore

BEYOND THE LAW (1918)
(6 r.) d, Theodore Marston; lp, Emmett Dalton, Virginia Lee, Bobby Connelly, Harris Gordon

BEYOND THE RAINBOW (1922)
(6 r.) d, William Christy Cabanne; lp, Harry Morey, Billie Dove, Virginia Lee, Diana Allen

BEYOND THE RIVER (1922, Ger.)
(4 r.) d, Ludwig Czerny; lp, Walter Janssen, Ada Svedin, Ilka Gruning, Lyda Salmonova

BEYOND THE ROCKIES (1926)
(5 r.) d, Jack Nelson; lp, Bob Custer, Eugenie Gilbert, David Dunbar, Bruce Gordon

BEYOND THE SHADOWS (1918)
(5 r.) d, J. W. McLaughlin; lp, William Desmond, Josie Sedwick, Graham Pette, Ed Brady

BEYOND THE SIERRAS (1928)
(6 r.) d, Nick Grinde; lp, Tim McCoy, Sylvia Beecher, Roy D'Arcy, Polly Moran

BEYOND THE TRAIL (1926)
(5 r.) d, Al Herman; lp, Bill Patton, Eric Mayne, Janet Dawn, Sheldon Lewis

BEYOND THE VEIL (1925, Brit.)
(6 r.) d, Sinclair Hill; lp, Matheson Lang, Stella Arbenia, Eric Bransby Williams, Genevieve Townsend

BEYOND THE WALL
(SEE: DESTINY, 1921, Ger.)

BIFF BANG BUDDY (1924)
(5 r.) d, Frank L. Inghram; lp, Buddy Roosevelt, Jean Arthur, Buck Conners, Robert Fleming

BIG ADVENTURE, THE (1921)
(5 r.) d, Reeves Eason; lp, Breezy Eason, Jr., Fred Herzog, Lee Shumway, Molly Shafer

BIG BROTHER (1923)
(7 r.) d, Allan Dwan; lp, Tom Moore, Edith Roberts, Raymond Hatton, Joe King

BIG DAN (1923)
(6 r.) d, William A. Wellman; lp, Charles Jones, Marian Nixon, Ben Hendricks, Trilby Clark

BIG DIAMOND ROBBERY, THE (1929)
(7 r.) d, Eugene Forde; lp, Tom Mix, Kathryn McGuire, Frank Beal, Martha Mattox

BIG DRIVE, THE (1928)
(7 r.) lp, Jack Harris

BIG HAPPINESS (1920)
(6 r.) d, Colin Campbell; lp, Dustin Farnum, Kathryn Adams, Fred Malatesta, Violet Schram

BIG HOP, THE (1928)
(7 r.) d, James W. Horne; lp, Buck Jones, Jobyna Ralston, Ernest Hilliard, Charles K. French

BIG JIM GARRITY (1916)
(5 r.) d, George Fitzmaurice; lp, Robert Edeson, Eleanor Woodruff, Carl Harbaugh, Lester Chambers

BIG KILLING, THE (1928)
(6 r.) d, F. Richard Jones; lp, Wallace Beery, Raymond Hatton, Anders Randolph, Mary Brian

BIG LITTLE PERSON, THE (1919)
(6 r.) d, Robert Z. Leonard; lp, Mae Murray, Clarissa Selwynne, Rudolph Valentino, Allan Sears

BIG MONEY (1918, Brit.)
(5 r.) d, Harry Lorraine; lp, Rose Manners, James Knight, Charles Rock, Edward O'Neill

BIG NOISE, THE (1928)
(8 r.) d, Allan Dwan; lp, Chester Conklin, Alice White, Bodil Rosing, Sam Hardy

BIG SHOW, THE (1926)
(6 r.) d, George Terwilliger; lp, John Lowell, Evangeline Russell, F. Serrano Keating, Jane Thomas

BIG SISTER, THE (1916)
(5 r.) d, John B. O'Brien; lp, Mae Murray, Matty Roubert, Armand Cortes, Harry C. Browne

BIG STAKES (1922)
(5 r.) d, Clifford S. Elfelt; lp, J.B. Warner, Elinor Fair, Les Bates, Willie May Carson

BIG STUNT (1925)
(5 r.) lp, Big Boy Williams

BIG TIMBER (1917)
(5 r.) d, William D. Taylor; lp, Kathlyn Williams, Wallace Reid, John Burton, Alfred Paget

BIG TIMBER (1924)
(5 r.) d, William J. Craft; lp, William Desmond, Olive Hasbrouck, Betty Francisco, Ivor McFadden

BIG TOWN ROUND-UP (1921)
(5 r.) d, Lynn Reynolds; lp, Tom Mix, Gilbert Holmes, Ora Carew, Harry Dunkinson

BIGAMIST, THE (1916)
(4 r.) lp, Arthur Wontner, Ethel Warwick, Dorothy Fayne, Hayden Coffin

BIGGER MAN, THE
(SEE: BETTER MAN, THE, 1915)

BIGGER THAN BARNUM'S (1926)
(6 r.) d, Ralph Ince; lp, Ralph Lewis, George O'Hara, Viola Dana, Ralph Ince

BIGGEST SHOW ON EARTH, THE (1918)
(5 r.) d, Jerome Storm; lp, Enid Bennett, Earl Rodney, Ethel Lynne, Bliss Chevalier

BILL APPERSON'S BOY (1919)
(6 r.) d, James Kirkwood; lp, Jack Pickford, Gloria Hope, Russell Simpson, George Nichols

BILL FOR DIVORCEMENT, A (1922)
(6 r.) d, Denison Clift; lp, Constance Binney, Fay Compton, Malcolm Keen, Henry Victor

BILL HENRY (1919)
(5 r.) d, Jerome Storm; lp, Charles Ray, Edith Roberts, William Carroll, Bert Woodruff

BILLIONS (1920)
(6 r.) d, Ray C. Smallwood; lp, Alla Nazimova, Charles Bryant, William J. Irving, Victor Potel

BILLY AND THE BIG STICK (1917)
(4 r.) d, Edward H. Griffith; lp, Raymond McKee, Yona Landowska, William Wadsworth, Jessie Stevens

BILLY'S SPANISH LOVE SPASM (1915, Brit.)
(4 r.) d, W.P. Kellino; lp, Billy Merson, Teddie Gerrard, Blanche Bella, F. Fullbrook

BING BANG BOOM (1922)
(5 r.) d, Fred J. Butler; lp, David Butler, Doris Pawn, Edwin Wallock, Kate Toncray

BIRD OF PREY, A (1916)
(5 r.) d, Eugene Nowland; lp, Kathryn Adams, John Lehnberg, Madeline Fairbanks, Robert Whittier

BIRD OF PREY, THE (1918)
(5 r.) d, Edward J. LeSaint; lp, Gladys Brockwell, Herbert Heyes, L.C. Shumway, Willard Louis

BIRDS OF PREY (1927)
(6 r.) d, William James Craft; lp, Priscilla Dean, Hugh Allan, Gustav von Seyffertitz, Ben Hendricks, Jr.

BIRDS' CHRISTMAS CAROL, THE (1917)
(5 r.) d, Lule Warrenton; lp, Little Mary Louise, Harold Skinner, Ella Gilbert, Donald Watson

BIRTH CONTROL (1917)
(5 r.) lp, Margaret Sanger

BIRTH OF A MAN, THE (1916)
(5 r.) lp, Henry B. Walthall

BIRTH OF A RACE (1919)
(6 r.) d, John W. Noble; lp, Jane Grey, George Le Guere, Ben Hendricks, Alice Gale

BIRTH OF A SOUL, THE (1920)
(5 r.) d, Edwin L. Hollywood; lp, Harry T. Morey, Jean Paige, Charles Eldridge, George Cooper

BIRTH OF CHARACTER, THE (1916)
(5 r.) d, E. Mason Hopper; lp, Muriel Ostrich

BIRTH OF PATRIOTISM, THE (1917)
(5 r.) d, E. Magnus Ingleton; lp, Irene Hunt, Ann Kroman [Ann Forrest], Leo Pierson, Ernie Shields

BIRTHRIGHT (1924)
(10 r.) lp, J. Homer Tutt, Evelyn Preer, Salem Tutt Whitney, Lawrence Chenault

BISHOP OF THE OZARKS, THE (1923)
(6 r.) d, Finis Fox; lp, Milford W. Howard, Derelys Perdue, Cecil Holland, William Kenton

BISHOP'S EMERALDS, THE (1919)
(6 r.) d, John B. O'Brien; lp, Virginia Pearson, Sheldon Lewis, Robert Broderick, Frank Kingsley

BISHOP'S SECRET, THE (1916)
(4 r.)

BIT O'HEAVEN, A
(SEE: BIRDS' CHRISTMAS CAROL, THE, 1917)

BIT OF HEAVEN, A (1928)
(7 r.) d, Cliff Wheeler; lp, Bryant Washburn, Lila Lee, Martha Mattox, Lucy Beaumont

BIT OF JADE, A (1918)
(5 r.) d, Edward S. Sloman; lp, Mary Miles Minter, Alan Forrest, David Howard, Vera Lewis

BIT OF KINDLING, A (1917)
(5 r.) d, Sherwood MacDonald; lp, Jackie Saunders, Arthur Shirley, J.P. Wade, Charles Dudley

BITS OF LIFE (1921)
(6 r.) d, Marshall Neilan; lp, Wesley Barry, Rockliffe Fellowes, Lon Chaney, Noah Beery

BITTER APPLES (1927)
(6 r.) d, Harry O. Hoyt; lp, Monte Blue, Myrna Loy, Paul Ellis, Charles Hill Mailes

BITTER SWEETS (1928)
(6 r.) d, Charles Hutchison; lp, Barbara Bedford, Ralph Graves, Crauford Kent, Joy McKnight

BITTER TRUTH (1917)
(6 r.) d, Kenean Buel; lp, Virginia Pearson, Jack Hopkins, William H. Tooker, Alice May

BLACK ACE, THE (1928)
(6 r.) d, Leo D. Maloney; lp, Don Coleman, Jeanette Loff, Billy Butts, J.P. McGowan

BLACK BAG, THE (1922)
(5 r.) d, Stuart Paton; lp, Herbert Rawlinson, Virginia Valli, Bert Roach, Clara Beyers

BLACK BOOMERANG, THE (1925)
(?) d, William H. Clifford

BLACK BUTTERFLIES (1928)
(7 r.) d, James W. Horne; lp, Jobyna Ralston, Mae Busch, Robert Frazer, Lila Lee

BLACK BUTTERFLY, THE (1916)
(5 r.) d, Burton L. King; lp, Mme. Petrova, Mahlon Hamilton, Anthony Merlo, Count Lewenhaupt

BLACK CARGOES OF THE SOUTH SEAS (1929)
(7 r.) d, Norman Dawn; lp, Susan Dennis, Walter Long, Jack Gavin, Jessica Harcourt

BLACK CIRCLE, THE (1919)
(5 r.) d, Frank Reicher; lp, Creighton Hale, Virginia Valli, Jack Drumier, Walter Horton

BLACK CROOK, THE (1916)
(5 r.) d, Robert Vignola; lp, E.P. Sullivan, Mae Thompson, Henry Hallam, Charles De Forrest

BLACK DIAMOND EXPRESS, THE (1927)
(6 r.) d, Howard Bretherton; lp, Monte Blue, Edna Murphy, Myrtle Stedman, Claire McDowell

BLACK FEAR (1915)
(5 r.) d, John W. Noble; lp, Grace Elliston, Edward Brennan, Grace Valentine, Paul Everton

BLACK FEATHER (1928)
(6 r.) d, John E. Ince; lp, Sally Rand, Allan Forrest, Maurice Costello, Wheeler Oakman

BLACK FRIDAY (1916)
(5 r.) d, Lloyd B. Carleton; lp, Dorothy Davenport, Emory Johnson, Richard Morris, Wilfred Roger

BLACK GATE, THE (1919)
(5 r.) d, Theodore Marston; lp, Earle Williams, Ruth Clifford;

BLACK GOLD (1924)
(5 r.) d, Forrest Sheldon; lp, Pete Morrison

BLACK GOLD (1928)
(6 r.) lp, Lawrence Corman, Kathryn Boyd

BLACK HEART, THE (1915)
(6 r.) lp, Miss E.O. Lindblom

BLACK HILLS (1929)
(5 r.) d, Norman Dawn; lp, Susan Dennis, George Chandler, George Fisher, Bob Webster

BLACK IS WHITE (1920)
(6 r.) d, Charles Giblyn; lp, Dorothy Dalton, Claire Mersereau, Lillian Lawrence, Holmes Herbert

BLACK JACK (1927)
(5 r.) d, Orville O. Dull; lp, Buck Jones, Barbara Bennett, Theodore Lorch, George Berrell

BLACK LIGHTING (1924)
(6 r.) d, James P. Hogan; lp, Clara Bow, Harold Austin, Eddie Philips, Joe Butterworth

BLACK MAGIC (1929)
(7 r.) d, George B. Seitz; lp, Josephine Dunn, Earle Foxe, John Holland, Henry B. Walthall

BLACK NIGHT, THE (1916, Brit.)
(4 r.) d, Harold Weston; lp, Gregory Scott, J.R.Tozer

BLACK ORCHIDS (1917)
(5 r.) d, Rex Ingram; lp, Cleo Madison, Richard La Reno, Francis McDonald, Wedgewood Nowell

BLACK OXEN (1924)
(8 r.) d, Frank Lloyd; lp, Corinne Griffith, Conway Tearle, Thomas Ricketts, Thomas Guise

BLACK PANTHER'S CUB, THE (1921)
(7 r.) d, Emile Chautard; lp, Florence Reed, Norman Trevor, Henry Stephenson, Paul Ducet

BLACK PARADISE (1926)
(5 r.) d, R. William Neill; lp, Leslie Fenton, Madge Bellamy, Edmund Lowe, Edward Piel

BLACK PEARL, THE (1928)
(6 r.) d, Scott Pembroke; lp, Lila Lee, Ray Hallor, Carlton Stockdale, Howard Lorenz

BLACK ROSES (1921)
(6 r.) d, Colin Campbell; lp, Sessue Hayakawa, Myrtle Stedman, Tsura Aoki, Andrew Robson

BLACK SAIL, THE (1929, USSR)
(6 r.) d, Sergei Yutkevitch; lp, Nina Shaternikova

BLACK SHADOWS (1920)
(5 r.) d, Howard M. Mitchell; lp, Peggy Hyland, Albert Roscoe, Correan Kirkham, Henry J. Hebert

BLACK SHEEP, A (1915)
(5 r.) d, T.N. Heffron; lp, Otis Harlan, James Bradbury, Grace Darmond, Rita Gould

BLACK SHEEP, THE (1920, Brit.)
(5 r.) d, Sidney Morgan; lp, Marguerite Blanche, George Keene, Eve Balfour, George Bellamy

BLACK SHEEP (1921)
(5 r.) d, Paul Hurst; lp, Neal Hart, Ted Brooks, George A. Williams, Frona Hale

BLACK SHEEP OF THE FAMILY, THE (1916)
(5 r.) d, Jay Hunt; lp, Francelia Billington, Jack Holt, Gilmore Hammond, Paul Byron

BLACK SPIDER, THE (1920, Brit.)
(6 r.) d, William J. Humphrey; lp, Lydia Kyasht, Bertram Burleigh, Sam Livesey, Ronald Colman

BLACK STORK, THE (1917)
(5 r.) lp, Dr. Harry J. Haiseld, Hamilton Revelle, Elsie Esmond, Henry Bergman

BLACK TEARS (1927)
(6 r.) d, John Gorman; lp, Bryant Washburn, Vola Vale, Jack Richardson, Hedda Hooper

BLACK THUNDERBOLT, THE (1922)
(7 r.) lp, Jack Johnson

BLACK TULIP, THE (1921, Brit.)
(5 r.) d, Frankland A. Richardson; lp, Zoe Palmer, Gerald McCarthy, Frank Dane, Harry Walter

BLACK WOLF, THE (1917)
(5 r.) d, Frank Reicher; lp, Lou Tellegen, Nell Shipman, H.J. Hebert, James Neill

BLACKBIRDS (1920)
(6 r.) d, Jack Dillon; lp, Justine Johnstone, William Boyd, Charles Gerrard, Jessie Arnold

BLACKIE'S REDEMPTION (1919)
(5 r.) d, John Ince; lp, Bert Lytell, Alice Lake, Henry Kolker, Bernard Durning

BLACKLIST (1916)
(5 r.) d, William C. DeMille; lp, Blance Sweet, Charles Clary, Ernest Joy, Billy Elmer

BLACKMAIL (1920)
(6 r.) d, Dallas M. Fitzgerald; lp, Viola Dana, Alfred Allen, Wyndham Standing, Edward Cecil

BLACKMAILERS, THE (1915, Brit.)
(4 r.) d, A.E. Coleby; lp, Arthur Rooke, Joan Legge

BLADE O' GRASS (1915)
(4 r.) d, Burton George; lp, Leonie Flugrath, Pat O'Malley, Eldean Stewart, Charles Sutton

BLADYS OF THE STEWPONY (1919, Brit.)
(5 r.) d, L.C. MacBean; lp, Marguerite Fox, Arthur Chishlom, Windham Guise, Harry J. Worth

BLANCHETTE (1921, Fr.)
(? r.) d, Rene Hervil; lp, Maurice de Feraudy, Leon Mathot, Pauline Johnson, Therese Kolb

BLARNEY (1926)
(6 r.) d, Marcel De Sano; lp, Renee Adoree, Ralph Graves, Paulette Duval, Malcolm Waite

BLASPHEMER, THE (1921)
(7 r.) d, O.E. Goebel

BLASTED HOPES (1924)
(5 r.) d, Arthur Rosson; lp, Edmund Cobb

BLAZE AWAY (1922)
(5 r.) d, W. Hughes Curran; lp, Guinn "Big Boy" Williams, Molly Malone, Hal Wilson, Ed Burns

BLAZING ARROWS (1922)
(5 r.) d, Henry McCarty; lp, Lester Cuneo, Francelia Billington; Clark Comstock, Laura Howard

BLAZING LOVE (1916)
(5 r.) d, Kenean Buel; lp, Virginia Pearson, Louise Huff

BLEAK HOUSE (1920, Brit.)
(6 r.) d, Maurice Elvey; lp, Constance Collier, Berta Gellardi, E. Vivian Reynolds, Norman Page

BLEAK HOUSE (1922, Brit.)
(4 r.) d, H.B. Parkinson; lp, Sybil Thorndike, Betty Doyle, Stacey Gaunt, Harry J. Worth

BLESSURE D'AMOUR (1916, Fr.)
(? r.) d, Georges Monca

BLIGHTY (1927, Brit.)
(8 r.) d, Adrian Brunel; lp, Ellaline Terriss, Lilian Hall Davis, Jameson Thomas, Nadia Sibirskaia

BLIND ADVENTURE, THE (1918)
(5 r.) d, Wesley H. Ruggles; lp, Edward Earle, Betty Howe, Frank Norcross, William Bailey

BLIND CIRCUMSTANCES (1922)
(5 r.) d, Milburn Morante; lp, George Chesebro, Alfred Hewston, Harry Arras, Vivian Rich

BLIND JUSTICE (1917)
(5 r.)

BLIND LOVE, THE (1920)
(6 r.) d, Oliver Bailey; lp, Lucy Cotton, George Le Guere, Thurlow Bergen, Frank O'Connor

BLIND MAN'S EYES (1919)
(5 r.) d, John Ince; lp, Bert Lytell, Naomi Childers, Frank Currier, Joseph Kilgour

BLIND MAN'S HOLIDAY (1917)
(4 r.) d, Martin Justice; lp, Jean Paige, Carlton King, John Costello, Aida Horton

BLIND MAN'S LUCK (1917)
(5 r.) d, George Fitzmaurice; lp, Mollie King, Earle Foxe, William Riley Hatch, Jessie Tilbury

BLIND TRAIL (1926)
(5 r.) d, Leo Maloney; lp, Leo Maloney, Josephine Hill, Nelson McDowell, Bud Osborne

BLIND WIVES (1920)
(9 r.) d, Charles Brabin; lp, Marc MacDermott, Estelle Taylor, Harry Sothern, Sally Crute

BLIND YOUTH (1920)
(6 r.) d, Edward Sloman; lp, Walter McGrail, Leatrice Joy, Ora Carew, Claire McDowell

BLINDFOLD (1928)
(6 r.) d, Charles Klein; lp, Lois Moran, George O'Brien, Maria Alba, Earle Foxe

BLINDFOLDED (1918)
(5 r.) d, Raymond B. West; lp, Bessie Barriscale, Joseph J. Dowling, Patrick Calhoun, David Kirby

BLINDING TRAIL, THE (1919)
(6 r.) d, Paul Powell; lp, Monroe Salisbury, Claire Anderson, Helen Jerome Eddy, Arthur Maude

BLINDNESS OF DEVOTION (1915)
(5 r.) d, J. Gordon Edwards; lp, Robert Mantell, Genevieve Hamper, Stuart Holmes

BLINDNESS OF DIVORCE, THE (1918)
(7 r.) d, Frank Lloyd; lp, Bertha Mann, Charles Clary, Fred Church, Rhea Mitchell

BLINDNESS OF LOVE, THE (1916)
(5 r.) d, Charles Horan; lp, Julius Steger, George Le Guere, Grace Valentine, Edgar L. Davenport

BLINDNESS OF VIRTUE, THE (1915)
(6 r.) d, Joseph Byron Totten; lp, Edna Mayo, Bryant Washburn, Thomas McLarnie, Harry Dunkinson

BLINKEYES (192?)
(7 r.) d, George Pearson; lp, Betty Balfour, Tom Douglas, Frank Stanmore, Pat Aherne

BLINKY (1923)
(6 r.) d, Edward Sedgwick; lp, Hoot Gibson, Esther Ralston, Mathilde Brundage, De Witt Jennings

BLIZZARD, THE (1924, Swed.)
(7 r.) d, Mauritz Stiller

BLOCK SIGNAL, THE (1926)
(6 r.) d, Frank O'Connor; lp, Ralph Lewis, Jean Arthur, Hugh Allan, George Chesebro

BLONDE FOR A NIGHT, A (1928)
(6 r.) d, E. Mason Hopper; lp, Marie Prevost, Franklin Pangborn, Harrison Ford, T. Roy Barnes

BLONDE OR BRUNETTE (1927)
(6 r.) d, Richard Rosson; lp, Adolphe Menjou, Greta Nissen, Arlette Marchal, Mary Carr

BLONDE SAINT, THE (1926)
(7 r.) d, Svend Gade; lp, Lewis Stone, Doris Kenyon, Ann Rork, Gilbert Roland

BLONDE VAMPIRE, THE (1922)
(6 r.) d, Wray Physioc; lp, De Sacia Mooers, Joseph Smiley, Charles Craig, Miriam Battista

BLONDES BY CHOICE (1927)
(7 r.) d, Hampton Del Ruth; lp, Claire Windsor, Allan Simpson, Walter Hiers, Bodil Rosing

BLOOD AND SOUL (1923, Jap.)
(? r.) d, Kenji Mizoguchi

BLOOD AND STEEL (1925)
(5 r.) d, J.P. McGowan; lp, Helen Holmes, William Desmond, Robert Edeson, Mack V. Wright

BLOOD BARRIER, THE (1920)
(6 r.) d, J. Stuart Blackton; lp, Sylvia Breamer, Robert Gordon, William R. Dunn, Eddie Dunn

BLOOD BOND, THE (1925)
(5 r.) lp, Leo Maloney, Josephine Hill

BLOOD MONEY (1921, Brit.)
(5 r.) d, Fred Goodwins; lp, Adelqui Migliar, Dorothy Fane, Frank Dane, Arthur Cullin

BLOOD NEED NOT BE SPILLED (1917, USSR)
(5 r.) d, Yakov Protazanov; lp, Olga Gzovskaya, Nikolai Panov, Vladamie Gaidarov

BLOOD OF HIS FATHERS (1917)
(5 r.) d, Harrish Ingraham; lp, Crane Wilbur

BLOOD OF THE TREVORS
(SEE: HEREDITY, 1918)

BLOOD SHIP, THE (1927)
(7 r.) d, George B. Seitz; lp, Hobart Bosworth, Jacqueline Logan, Richard Arlen, Walter James

BLOOD TEST (1923)
(5 r.) d, Don Marquis; lp, Dick Hatton, Nelson McDowell, William Moran, Lafayette McKee

BLOOD WILL TELL (1917)
(5 r.) lp, William Desmond, Enid Markey, David M. Hartford, Howard Hickman

BLOOD WILL TELL (1927)
(5 r.) d, Ray Flynn; lp, Buck Jones, Kathryn Perry, Lawford Davidson, Robert Kortman

BLOODHOUND, THE (1925)
(5 r.) d, William James Craft; lp, Bob Custer, David Dunbar, Ralph McCullough, Mary Beth Milford

BLOODY EAST, THE (1915, USSR)
(6 r.) d, Alexander Arkatov; lp, N. Chernobayeva, M. Tarov, I. Talanov

BLOOMING ANGEL, THE (1920)
(5 r.) d, Victor Schertzinger; lp, Madge Kennedy, Pat O'Malley, Margery Wilson, Arthur Housman

BLOW YOUR OWN HORN (1923)
(6 r.) d, James W. Horne; lp, Warner Baxter, Ralph Lewis, Derelys Perdue, Eugene Acker

BLUE BANDANNA, THE (1919)
(5 r.) d, Joseph J. Franz; lp, William Desmond, Jean Acker, Russell Simpson, Frank Lanning

BLUE BLAZES (1922)
(5 r.) d, Robert Kelly, Charles W. Mack; lp, Lester Cuneo, Francelia Billington, Fannie Midgley, Bert Sprotte

BLUE BLAZES (1926)
(5 r.) d, Joseph Franz; lp, Pete Morrison, Jim Welsh, Barbara Starr, Dick La Reno, Jr.

BLUE BLAZES RAWDEN (1918)
(5 r.) d, William S. Hart; lp, William S. Hart, Maude George, Gertrude Claire, Hart Hoxie

BLUE BLOOD (1922)
(6 r.) lp, Alice Calhoun

BLUE BLOOD AND RED (1916)
(5 r.) d, Raoul Walsh; lp, George Walsh, Doris Pawn, Vester Pegg, James A. Marcus

BLUE BONNET, THE (1920)
(6 r.) d, Louis Chaudet; lp, Billie Rhodes, Ben Wilson, Irene Rich, Stanhope Wheatcroft

BLUE DANUBE, THE (1928)
(7 r.) d, Paul Sloane; lp, Leatrice Joy, Joseph Schildkraut, Nils Asther, Seena Owen

BLUE EAGLE, THE (1926)
(7 r.) d, John Ford; lp, George O'Brien, Janet Gaynor, William Russell, Robert Edeson

BLUE ENVELOPE MYSTERY, THE (1916)
(5 r.) d, Wilfred North; lp, Lillian Walker, John D. Bennett, Bob Hay, Charles Kent

BLUE EXPRESS (1929, USSR)
(6 r.) d, Ilya Trauberg; lp, Sun Bo-yang, Chou Hsi-fan, Chang Kai, Sergei Minin

BLUE JEANS (1917)
(7 r.) d, John H. Collins; lp, Viola Dana, Robert Walker, Sally Crute, Clifford Bruce

BLUE MOON, THE (1920)
(6 r.) d, George L. Cox; lp, Pell Trenton, Elinor Field, Harry Northrup, Herbert Standing

BLUE MOUNTAIN MYSTERY, THE (1922)
(5 r.) d, Raymond Longford; lp, John Faulkner, Marjorie Osborne, Bernice Ware, Billy Williams

BLUE PEARL, THE (1920)
(6 r.) d, George Irving; lp, Edith Hallor, Faire Binney, Lumsden Hare, Florence Billings

BLUE PETER, THE (1928, Brit.)
(8 r.) d, Arthur Rooke; lp, Matheson Lang, Gladys Frazin, Mary Dibley, A. Bromley Davenport

BLUE SKIES (1929)
(6 r.) d, Alfred L. Werker; lp, Ethel Wales, Helen Twelvetrees, Frank Albertson, Rosa Gore

BLUE STREAK, THE (1917)
(5 r.) d, William Nigh; lp, William Nigh, Violet Palmer, Ruth Thorp, Martin Faust

BLUE STREAK MCCOY (1920)
(5 r.) d, Reeves Eason; lp, Harry Carey, Charles Arling, Lile Leslie, Breezy Eason, Jr.

BLUE STREAK O'NEIL (1926)
(5 r.) d, Paul Hurst; lp, Al Hoxie

BLUEBEARD, JR. (1922)
(5 r.) d, Scott Dunlap; lp, Mary Anderson, Jack Connolly, George Hernandez, Laura Anson

BLUEBEARD'S 8TH WIFE (1923)
(6 r.) d, Sam Wood; lp, Gloria Swanson, Huntley Gordon, Charles Green, Lianne Salvor

BLUEBIRD, THE (1918)
(5 r.) d, Maurice Tourneur; lp, Robin Macdougall, Tula Belle, Edwin E. Reed, Emma Lowry

BLUE-EYED MARY (1918)
(5 r.) d, Harry Millarde; lp, June Caprice, Bernard Randall, Helen Tracy, Blanche Hines

BLUFF (1916)
(5 r.) lp, C. William Kolb, Max M. Dill, May Cloy, Thomas Chatterton

BLUFF (1921, Brit.)
(6 r.) d, Geoffrey H. Malins; lp, Lewis Willoughby, Marorie Hume, Lawrence Anderson, Sydney Paxton

BLUFFER, THE (1919)
(5 r.) d, Travers Vale; lp, June Elvidge, Irving Cummings, Frank Mayo, George MacQuarrie

BOADICEA (1926, Brit.)
(8 r.) d, Sinclair Hill; lp, Phyllis Neilson-Terry, Lilian Hall-Davis, Clifford Heatherley, Humberston Wright

BOASTER, THE (1926)
(5 r.) d, Duke Worne; lp, Richard Holt, Gloria Grey

BOBBED HAIR (1922)
(5 r.) d, Thomas N. Heffron; lp, Wanda Hawley, William Boyd, Adele Farrington, Leigh Wyant

BOBBED HAIR (1925)
(6 r.) d, Alan Crosland; lp, Marie Prevost, Kenneth Harlan, Louise Fazenda, John Roche

BOBBIE OF THE BALLET (1916)
(5 r.) d, Joseph De Grasse; lp, Louise Lovely, Lon Chaney, Jay Belasco, Jean Hathaway

BODEN'S BOY (1923, Brit.)
(6 r.) d, Henry Edwards; lp, Henry Edwards, Chrissie White, Francis Lister, Henry Vibart

BODY AND SOUL (1920)
(6 r.) d, Charles Swickard; lp, Alice Lake, William Lawrence, Stuart Holmes, Carl Gerard

BODY AND SOUL (1925)
(5 r.) lp, Paul Robeson, Julia Theresa Russell, Mercedes Gilbert

BODY AND SOUL (1927)
(6 r.) d, Reginald Barker; lp, Aileen Pringle, Norman Kerry, Lionel Barrymore, T. Roy Barnes

BODY BEAUTIFUL (1928, Jap.)
(? r.) d, Yasujiro Ozu

BODY PUNCH, THE (1929)
(5 r.) d, Leigh Jason; lp, Jack Daugherty, Virginia Browne Faire, George Kotsonaros, Wilbur Mack

BOER WAR, THE (1914)
(5 r.) d, George Melford; lp, Carlyle Blackwell

BOHEMIAN DANCER (1929)
(6 r.) d, Frederick Zelnik; lp, Lya Mara, Harry Leitke

BOHEMIAN GIRL, THE (1922, Brit.)
(8 r.) d, Harley Knoles; lp, Gladys Cooper, Ivor Novello, C. Aubrey Smith, Ellen Terry

BOLD ADVENTURESS, A (1915, Brit.)
(4 r.) d, Walter West; lp, Nell Emerald, Walter West

BOLD EMMETT, IRELAND'S MARTYR (1915)
(4 r.) d, Sidney Olcott; lp, Sidney Olcott, Valentine Grant, Laurene Santley, P.H. O'Malley

BOLSHEVISM ON TRIAL (1919)
(5 r.) d, Harley Knoles; lp, Robert Frazer, Leslie Stowe, Howard Truesdell, Jim Savage

BOLTED DOOR, THE (1923)
(5 r.) d, William Worthington; lp, Frank Mayo, Charles A. Stevenson, Phyllis Haver, Nigel Barrie

BONANZA BUCKAROO, THE (1926)
(5 r.) d, Richard Thorpe; lp, Buffalo Bill, Jr., Harry Todd, Judy King, Lafe McKee

BOND BETWEEN, THE (1917)
(5 r.) d, Donald Crisp; lp, George Beban, John Burton, Nigel de Brulier, Paul Weigel

BOND BOY, THE (1922)
(7 r.) d, Henry King; lp, Richard Barthelmess, Charles Hill Mailes, Ned Sparks, Lawrence D'Orsay

BOND OF FEAR, THE (1917)
(5 r.) d, Jack Conway; lp, Belle Bennett, Roy Stewart, Melbourne McDowell, George Webb

BOND WITHIN, THE (1916)
(4 r.) d, Edward Sloman; lp, George Routh, Adda Gleason, Henry Russell, Joyce Wardlow

BONDAGE (1917)
(5 r.) d, Ida May Park [Mrs. Joseph De Grasse]; lp, Dorothy Phillips, Gretchen Lederer, Gertrude Astor, William Stowell

BONDAGE OF BARBARA, THE (1919)
(5 r.) d, Emmett J. Flynn; lp, Mae Marsh, Matt Moore, Arthur Housman, Jack McLean

BONDAGE OF FEAR, THE (1917)
(5 r.) d, Travers Vale; lp, Ethel Clayton, Rockliffe Fellowes, Arthur Ashley, John Bowers

BONDED WOMAN, THE (1922)
(6 r.) d, Philip E. Rosen; lp, Betty Compson, John Bowers, Richard Dix, J. Farrell MacDonald

BONDMAN, THE (1916)
(5 r.) d, Edgar Lewis; lp, William Farnum, Harry Spingler, Carey Lee

BONDMAN, THE (1929, Brit.)
(9 r.) d, Herbert Wilcox; lp, Norman Kerry, Frances Cuyler, Donald McCardle, Henry Vibart

BONDS OF HONOR (1919)
(5 r.) d, William Worthington; lp, Sessue Hayakawa, Tsuru Aoki, Marin Sais, Dagmar Godowsky

BONDS OF LOVE (1919)
(5 r.) d, Reginald Barker; lp, Pauline Frederick, Percy Standing, Frankie Lee, Betty Schade

BONDWOMEN (1915)
(5 r.) lp, Maude Fealy, Iva Shepard, Mildred Gregory, John Sainpolis

BONHOMME DE NEIGE (1917, Fr.)
(? r.) d, Georges Monca

BONNIE ANNIE LAURIE (1918)
(5 r.) d, Harry Millarde; lp, Peggy Hyland, William Bailey, Henry Hallam, Sidney Mason

BONNIE, BONNIE LASSIE (1919)
(6 r.) d, Tod Browning; lp, Mary MacLaren, David Butler, Arthur Carew, Spottiswoode Aitken

BONNIE BRIER BRUSH, THE (1921, Brit.)
(5 r.) d, Donald Crisp; lp, Donald Crisp, Mary Glynne, Alec Fraser, Dorothy Fane

BONNIE MARY (1918, Brit.)
(5 r.) d, A.V. Bramble; lp, Miriam Ferris, Leon Belcher, Arthur Cullin, Jeff Barlow

BONNIE MAY (1920)
(5 r.) d, Joseph De Grasse, Ida May Park; lp, Bessie Love, William Bainbridge, Charles Gordon, Lon Poff

BONNIE PRINCE CHARLIE (1923, Brit.)
(7 r.) d, C.C. Calvert; lp, Gladys Cooper, Ivor Novello, Hugh Miller, A.B. Imeson

BOOB, THE (1926)
(6 r.) d, William Wellman; lp, Gertrude Olmsted, George K. Arthur, Joan Crawford, Charles Murray

BOOK AGENT, THE (1917)
(5 r.) d, Otis Turner; lp, George Walsh, Doris Pawn, William Burress, Velma Whitman

BOOMERANG, THE (1919)
(7 r.) d, Bertram Bracken; lp, Henry B. Walthall, Melbourne McDowell, Helen Jerome Eddy, Nina Byron

BOOMERANG, THE (1925)
(7 r.) d, Louis Gasnier; lp, Anita Stewart, Bert Lytell, Donald Keith, Mary McAllister

BOOMERANG BILL (1922)
(6 r.) d, Tom Terriss; lp, Lionel Barrymore, Marguerite Marsh, Margaret Seddon, Frank Shannon

BOOMERANG JUSTICE (1922)
(5 r.) d, Edward Sedgwick; lp, George Larkin, Fritzi Ridgeway

BOOTLEGGERS, THE (1922)
(6 r.) d, Roy Sheldon; lp, Walter Miller, Paul Panzer, Jules Cowles, Hazel Flint

BOOTLEGGER'S DAUGHTER, THE (1922)
(5 r.) d, Victor Schertzinger; lp, Enid Bennett, Fred Niblo, Donald McDonald, Melbourne MacDowell

BOOTLE'S BABY (1914, Brit.)
(4 r.) d, Harold Shaw; lp, Ben Webster, Edna Flugrath, Langhorne Burton, Lewis Gilbert

BOOTS (1919)
(5 r.) d, Elmer Clifton; lp, Dorothy Gish, Richard Barthelmess, Fontaine La Rue, Edward Peil

BOOTS AND SADDLES (1916)
(5 r.) lp, R. Henry Grey, Robyn Adair, Norman Luke, Charles Dudley

BORDER BLACKBIRDS (1927)
(6 r.) d, Leo Maloney; lp, Leo Maloney, Eugenia Gilbert, Nelson McDowell, Joseph Rickson

BORDER CAVALIER, THE (1927)
(5 r.) d, William Wyler; lp, Fred Humes, Evelyn Pierce, C.E. "Captain" Anderson, Boris Bullock

BORDER INTRIGUE (1925)
(5 r.) d, J.P. McGowan; lp, Franklyn Farnum, Jack Vernon, Mathilda Brundage, Dorothy Wood

BORDER JUSTICE (1925)
(5 r.) d, Reeves Eason; lp, Bill Cody, John Gough, Robert Homans, Nola Luxford

BORDER LEGION, THE (1919)
(6 r.) lp, Hobart Bosworth, Blanche Bates, Eugene Strong, Horace Morgan

BORDER LEGION, THE (1924)
(7 r.) d, William K. Howard; lp, Antonio Moreno, Helene Chadwick, Rockliffe Fellowes, Gibson Gowland

BORDER PATROL, THE (1928)
(5 r.) d, James P. Hogan; lp, Harry Carey, Kathleen Collins, Phillips Smalley, Richard Tucker

BORDER RAIDERS, THE (1918)
(5 r.) d, Stuart Paton; lp, Betty Compson, George Larkin, Frank Deshon, Horace Carpernter

BORDER RAIDERS, THE (1921)
(5 r.) lp, Ben Hill, Walter Lynch

BORDER RIDER, THE (1924)
(5 r.) d, Frederick Reel, Jr. lp, Al Richmond, Lorraine Eason

BORDER SCOUTS, THE (1922)
(? r.) d, Bert Hall

BORDER SHERIFF, THE (1926)
(5 r.) d, Robert North Bradbury; lp, Jack Hoxie, Olive Hasbrouck, S.E.Jennings, Gilbert Holmes

BORDER VENGENCE (1925)
(5 r.) d, Harry Webb; lp, Jack Perrin, Minna Redman, Vondell Darr, Jack Richardson

BORDER WHIRLWIND, THE (1926)
(5 r.) d, John P. McCarthy; lp, Bob Custer, Sally Long, Josef Swickard, Wilbur Higby

BORDER WILDCAT, THE (1929)
(5 r.) d, Ray Taylor; lp, Ted Wells, Kathryn McGuire, Tom London, William Malan

BORDER WIRELESS, THE (1918)
(5 r.) d, William S. Hart; lp, William S. Hart, Wanda Hawley, Charles Arling, James Mason

BORDERLAND (1922)
(6 r.) d, Paul Powell; lp, Agnes Ayres, Milton Sills, Fred Huntley, Bertram Grassby

BORN RICH (1924)
(8 r.) d, Will Nigh; lp, Claire Windsor, Bert Lytell, Cullen Landis, Doris Kenyon

BORN TO BATTLE (1926)
(5 r.) d, Robert De Lacy; lp, Tom Tyler, Jean Arthur, Ray Childs, Fred Gambold

BORN TO BATTLE (1927)
(5 r.) d, Alvin J. Neitz; lp, Bill Cody

BORN TO THE SADDLE (1929)
(5 r.) d, Josef Levigard; lp, Ted Wells, Duane Thompson, Leo White, Byron Douglas

BORN TO THE WEST (1926)
(6 r.) d, John Waters; lp, Jack Holt, Margaret Morris, Raymond Hatton, Arlette Marchal

BORROWED CLOTHES (1918)
(6 r.) d, Lois Weber, Phillips Smalley; lp, Mildred Harris, Lewis J. Cody, Edward J. Peil, Helen Rosson

BORROWED HUSBANDS (1924)
(7 r.) d, David Smith; lp, Florence Vidor, Rockliffe Fellowes, Earle Williams, Robert Gordon

BORROWED PLUMAGE (1917)
(5 r.) d, Raymond B. West; lp, Bessie Barriscale, Arthur Maude, Doreas Matthews, J. Barney Sherry

BOSS, THE (1915)
(5 r.) d, Emile Chautard; lp, Holbrook Blinn, Alice Brady, William Marion, Julia Stuart

BOSS OF CAMP 4, THE (1922)
(5 r.) d, W.S. Van Dyke; lp, Charles Jones, Fritzi Brunette, G. Raymond Nye, Francis Ford

BOSS OF RUSTLER'S ROOST, THE (1928)
(5 r.) d, Leo Maloney; lp, Don Coleman, Ben Corbett, Tom London, Albert Hart

BOSS OF THE LAZY Y, THE (1918)
(5 r.) d, Cliff Smith; lp, Roy Stewart, Josie Sedgwick, Graham Pette, Frank McQuarrie

BOSTON BLACKIE (1923)
(5 r.) d, Scott Dunlap; lp, William Russell, Eva Novak, Frank Brownlee, Otto Matieson

BOSTON BLACKIE'S LITTLE PAL (1918)
(5 r.) d, E. Mason Hopper; lp, Bert Lytell, Rhea Mitchell, Joey Jacobs, Howard Davies

BOTTLE, THE (1915, Brit.)
(4 r.) d, Cecil M. Hepworth; lp, Albert Chevalier, Ivy Millais, Harry Brett, Stewart Rome

BOTTLE IMP, THE (1917)
(5 r.) d, Marshall Neilan; lp, Sessue Hayakawa, Margaret Loomis, George Kuwa, Guy Oliver

BOTTOM OF THE WELL (1917)
(5 r.) d, John Robertson; lp, Evart Overton, Agnes Ayres, Adele De Garde, Ned Finley

BOUCLETTE (1918, Fr.)
(? r.) d, Rene Hervil, Louis Mercanton; lp, Gaby Deslys

BOUGHT AND PAID FOR (1916)
(5 r.) d, Harley Knoles; lp, Alice Brady, Montagu Love, Frank Conlan, Josephine Drake

BOUGHT AND PAID FOR (1922)
(6 r.) d, William C. De Mille; lp, Agnes Ayres, Jack Holt, Walter Hiers, Leigh Wyant

BOUND IN MOROCCO (1918)
(4 r.) d, Allan Dwan; lp, Douglas Fairbanks, Pauline Curley, Edythe Chapman, Tully Marshall

BOUNDARY HOUSE (1918, Brit.)
(5 r.) d, Cecil M. Hepworth; lp, Alma Taylor, Gerald Ames, William Felton, Victor Prout

BOWERY BISHOP, THE (1924)
(6 r.) d, Colin Campbell; lp, Henry B. Walthall, Leota Lorraine, George Fisher, Lee Shumway

BOY CRAZY (1922)
(5 r.) d, William A. Seiter; lp, Doris May, Fred Gambold, Jean Hathaway, Frank Kingsley

BOY FRIEND, THE (1926)
(6 r.) d, Monta Bell; lp, Marceline Day, John Harron, George K. Arthur, Ward Crane

BOY GIRL, THE (1917)
(5 r.) d, Edwin Stevens; lp, Violet Mersereau, Florida Kingsley, Caroline Harris, Maud Cooling

BOY OF FLANDERS, A (1924)
(7 r.) d, Victor Schertzinger; lp, Jackie Coogan, Nigel De Brulier, Lionel Belmore, Nell Craig

BOY OF THE STREETS, A (1927)
(6 r.) d, Charles J. Hunt; lp, Johnny Walker, Mickey Bennett, Henry Sedley, Betty Francisco

BOY WOODBURN (1922, Brit.)
(7 r.) d, Guy Newall; lp, Guy Newall, Ivy Duke, A. Bromley Davenport, Mary Rorke

BOYS OF THE OLD BRIGADE, THE (1916, Brit.)
(5 r.) d, Ernest G. Batley; lp, George Leyton, Lettie Paxton, Stella Brereton, Charles Vane

BOYS OF THE OTTER PATROL (1918, Brit.)
(5 r.) d, Percy Nash; lp, Alfred Harding, Dorothy Mason, Edward Dryhurst Roberts, Sir Robert Baden-Powell

BOYS WILL BE BOYS (1921)
(5 r.) d, Clarence G. Badger; lp, Will Rogers, Irene Rich, C.E. Mason, Sydney Ainsworth

BRACE UP (1918)
(5 r.) d, Elmer Clifton; lp, Herbert Rawlinson, Claire Du Brey, Alfred Allen

BRAMBLE BUSH, THE (1919)
(5 r.) d, Tom Terriss; lp, Corinne Griffith, Frank Mills, Julia Swayne Gordon, Constance Deumar

BRAND (1915, USSR)
(4 r.) d, Pavel Orlenev; lp, Orlenev, V. Popova, G. Gnesin, Orlov

BRAND, THE (1919)
(7 r.) d, Reginald Barker; lp, Kay Laurell, Russell Simpson, Robert McKim, Robert Kunkel

BRAND OF COWARDICE (1925)
(5 r.) d, John P. McCarthy; lp, Bruce Gordon, Carmelita Geraghty, Cuyler Supplee, Ligio De Colconda

BRAND OF LOPEZ, THE (1920)
(5 r.) d, Joseph De Grasse; lp, Sessue Hayakawa, Florence Turner, Sidney Payne, Evelyn Ward

BRAND OF SATAN, THE (1917)
(5 r.) d, George Archainbaud; lp, Gerda Holmes, Montagu Love, Nat Gross, J. Herbert Frank

BRANDED (1920, Brit.)
(6 r.) d, C.C. Calvert; lp, Josephine Earle, Dallas Anderson, Nora Swinburne, Francis Lister

BRANDED A THIEF (1924)
(5 r.) d, Neal Hart; lp, Neal Hart

BRANDED MAN (1922)
(5 r.) lp, George Waggoner, Fritzi Ridgeway

BRANDED MAN (1928)
(6 r.) d, Scott Pembroke; lp, Charles Delaney, June Marlowe, Gordon Griffith, George Riley

BRANDED SOMBRERO, THE (1928)
(5 r.) d, Lambert Hillyer; lp, Buck Jones, Leila Hyams, Jack Baston, Francis Ford

BRANDED SOUL, A (1917)
(5 r.) d, Bertram Bracken; lp, Gladys Brockwell, Lewis J. Cody, Colin Chase, Vivian Rich

BRANDED SOUL, THE (1920, Brit.)
(6 r.) d, F. Martin Thornton; lp, Reginald Fox, Madge Stuart, Frank Petley, H. Agar Lyons

BRANDING FIRE (1930)
(5 r.) lp, Cheyenne Bill

BRAND'S DAUGHTER (1917)
(4 r.) d, Harry Harvey; lp, Daniel Gilfether, Julian Beaubien, Gloria Payton, R. Henry Grey

BRASA DORMIDA (1928, Braz.)
(? r.) d, Humberto Mauro; lp, Nita Rey, Luiz Sorace, Maximo Serrano

BRASS (1923)
(9 r.) d, Sidney A. Franklin; lp, Monte Blue, Marie Prevost, Harry Myers, Irene Rich

BRASS BOTTLE, THE (1914, Brit.)
(4 r.) d, Sidney Morgan; lp, Holman Clark, Alfred Bishop, Doris Lytton, Lawrence Grossmith

BRASS BOTTLE, THE (1923)
(6 r.) d, Maurice Tourner; lp, Harry Myers, Ernest Torrence, Tully Marshall, Clarissa Selwyn

BRASS BOWL, THE (1924)
(6 r.) d, Jerome Storm; lp, Edmund Lowe, Claire Adams, Jack Duffy, J. Farrell MacDonald

BRASS BUTTONS (1919)
(5 r.) d, Henry King; lp, William Russell, Eileen Percy, Frank Brownlee, Helen Howard

BRASS CHECK, THE (1918)
(7 r.) d, William S. Davis; lp, Francis X. Bushman, Beverly Bayne, Augustus Phillips, Frank Currier

BRASS COMMANDMENTS (1923)
(5 r.) d, Lynn F. Reynolds; lp, William Farnum, Wanda Hawley, Tom Santschi, Claire Adams

BRASS KNUCKLES (1927)
(7 r.) d, Lloyd Bacon; lp, Monte Blue, Betty Bronson, William Russell, Georgie Stone

BRAVEHEART (1925)
(7 r.) d, Alan Hale; lp, Rod La Rocque, Lillian Rich, Robert Edeson, Arthur Housman

BRAWN OF THE NORTH (1922)
(8 r.) d, Laurence Trimble; lp, Irene Rich, Lee Shumway, Joseph Barrell, Roger James Manning

BREAD (1918, USSR)
(4 r.) d, Boris Sushkevich, Richard Boleslawski; lp, Leonid Leonidov, Olga Baklanova, Yevgeni Vakhtangov

BREAD (1924)
(7 r.) d, Victor Schertzinger; lp, Mae Busch, Robert Frazer, Pat O'Malley, Wanda Hawley

BREAK THE NEWS TO MOTHER (1919)
(6 r.) lp, Pearl Shepard, Raymond Bloomer, Gertrude Berkeley, Alice Gerard

BREAKERS AHEAD (1918)
(5 r.) d, Charles J. Brabin; lp, Viola Dana, Clifford Bruce, Russell Simpson, Eugene Pallette

BREAKFAST AT SUNRISE (1927)
(7 r.) d, Malcolm St. Clair; lp, Constance Talmadge, Alice White, Bryant Washburn, Paulette Duval

BREAKING HOME TIES (1922)
(6 r.) d, Frank N. Seltzer; lp, Lee Kohlmar, Rebecca Weintraub, Richard Farrell, Arthur Ashley

BREAKING INTO SOCIETY (1923)
(5 r.) d, Hunt Stromberg; lp, Carrie Clark Ward, Bull Montana, Kalla Pasha, Francis Trebaol

BREAK-UP, THE (1930, USSR)
(5 r.) d, L. Zamkovoy; lp, M.C. Norakov, A.I. Bourkova, Lydia Koubkova, A.D. Smiranin

BREATH OF SCANDAL, THE (1924)
(7 r.) d, Louis Gasnier; lp, Betty Blythe, Patsy Ruth Miller, Jack Mulhall, Myrtle Stedman

BREATH OF THE GODS, THE (1920)
(6 r.) d, Rollin S. Sturgeon; lp, Tsuru Aoki, Stanhope Wheatcroft, Arthur Edmund Carew, Pat O'Malley

BREATHLESS MOMENT, THE (1924)
(6 r.) d, Robert F. Hill; lp, William Desmond, Charlotte Merriam, Alfred Fisher, Robert E. Homans

BRED IN OLD KENTUCKY (1926)
(6 r.) d, Eddie Dillon; lp, Viola Dana, Jerry Miley, Jed Prouty, James Mason

BRED IN THE BONE (1915)
(4 r.) d, Paul Powell; lp, Dorothy Gish, George A. Beranger, Margie Wilson, Alberta Lee

BREED OF COURAGE (1927)
(5 r.) d, Howard Mitchell; lp, Sam Nelson, Jeanne Morgan, Stanton Heck, Ethan Laidlaw

BREED OF THE BORDER, THE (1924)
(5 r.) d, Harry Garson; lp, Lefty Flynn, Dorothy Dwan, Louise Carver, Milton Ross

BREED OF THE SEA (1926)
(6 r.) d, Ralph Ince; lp, Ralph Ince, Margaret Livingston, Pat Harmon, Alphonz Ethier

BREED OF THE TRESHAMS, THE (1920, Brit.)
(6 r.) d, Kenelm Foss; lp, Martin Harvey, Mary Odette, Hayford Hobbs, A.B. Imeson

BREEZY BILL (1930)
(5 r.) d, J.P. McGowan; lp, Bob Steele, Alfred Hewston, George Hewston, Edna Aslin

BREEZY JIM (1919)
(5 r.) d, Lorimer Johnson; lp, Crane Wilbur, Juanita Hansen

BRIDE OF GLOMDAL, THE (1925, Nor.)
(? r.) d, Carl-Theodor Dreyer; lp, Stub Wiberg, Tove Tellback, Harald Stormeon, Einar Sissener

BRIDE OF VENGEANCE (1923)
(5 r.) lp, Ellen Richter

BRIDE'S CONFESSION, THE (1921)
(? r.) d, Ivan Abramson; lp, Leah Baird, Rita Jolivet

BRIDE'S PLAY, THE (1922)
(7 r.) d, George W. Terwilliger; lp, Marion Davies, Jack O'Brien, Wyndham Standing, Carlton Miller

BRIDGE OF SIGHS, THE (1915)
(4 r.) lp, Jeff Davis, Dorothy Welsh, Richard Carlyle, Stephen Reardon

BRIDGE OF SIGHS, THE (1922, Ital.)
(9 r.) lp, Sansonia

BRIDGE OF SIGHS, THE (1925)
(7 r.) d, Phil Rosen; lp, Dorothy Mackaill, Creighton Hale, Richard Tucker, Alec B. Francis

BRIDGES BURNED (1917)
(5 r.) d, Perry Vekroff; lp, Mahlon Hamilton, Arthur Hoops, Maury Steuart, Mme Petrova

BRIGADIER GERARD (1915, Brit.)
(5 r.) d, Bert Haldane; lp, Lewis Waller, Madge Titheradge, A.E. George, Blanche Forsythe

BRIGHT LIGHTS OF BROADWAY (1923)
(7 r.) d, Webster Cambell; lp, Doris Kenyon, Harrison Ford, Edmund Breese, Claire De Lorez

BRIGHT SHAWL, THE (1923)
(8 r.) d, John S. Robertson; lp, Richard Barthelmess, Andre Beranger, Edward G. Robinson, Mary Astor

BRIGHT SKIES (1920)
(5 r.) d, Henry Kolker; lp, ZaSu Pitts, Tom Gallery, Jack Pratt, Kate Price

BRINGIN' HOME THE BACON (1924)
(5 r.) d, Richard Thorpe; lp, Buffalo Bill, Jr., Jean Arthur; Bert Lindley, Lafe McKee

BRINGING HOME FATHER (1917)
(5 r.) d, William Worthington; lp, Franklyn Farnum, Agnes "Brownie" Vernon, Arthur Hoyt, Florence Mayon

BRINGING UP BETTY (1919)
(5 r.) d, Oscar Apfel; lp, Evelyn Greeley, Lester Chambers, Reginald Denny, Ben Johnson

BRINGING UP FATHER (1928)
(7 r.) d, Jack Conway; lp, J. Farrell MacDonald, Jules Cowles, Polly Moran, Marie Dressler

BRINK, THE (1915)
(4 r.) d, Walter Edwards; lp, Forest Winant, Rhea Mitchell, Arthur Maude, Joseph Dowling

BRITTON OF THE SEVENTH (1916)
(5 r.) d, Lionel Belmore; lp, Darwin Karr, Charles Kent, Bobby Connelly, Eleanor Woodruff

BROAD DAYLIGHT (1922)
(5 r.) d, Irving Cummings; lp, Lois Wilson, Jack Mulhall, Ralph Lewis, Kenneth Gibson

BROAD ROAD, THE (1923)
(6 r.) d, Edmund Mortimer; lp, Richard C. Travers, May Allison, Ben Hendricks, Jr., D.J. Flanagan

BROADWAY AFTER MIDNIGHT (1927)
(7 r.) d, Fred Windermere; lp, Matthew Betz, Priscilla Bonner, Cullen Landis, Gareth Hughes

BROADWAY AND HOME (1920)
(5 r.) d, Alan Crosland; lp, Eugene O'Brien, Elinor Fair, Warren Cook, Ellen Cassity

BROADWAY ARIZONA (1917)
(5 r.) d, Lynn F. Reynolds; lp, Olive Thomas, George Chesebro, George Hernandez, Jack Curtis

BROADWAY BILL (1918)
(5 r.) d, Fred J. Balshofer; lp, Harold Lockwood, Martha Mansfield, Cornish Beck, Raymond C. Hadley

BROADWAY BOOB, THE (1926)
(6 r.) d, Joseph Henabery; lp, Glenn Hunter, Mildred Ryan, Antrim Short, Beryl Halley

BROADWAY BROKE (1923)
(6 r.) d, J. Searle Dawley; lp, Mary Carr, Percy Marmont, Gladys Leslie, Dore Davidson

BROADWAY BUBBLE, THE (1920)
(5 r.) d, George L. Sargent; lp, Corinne Griffith, Joseph King, Stanley Wamerton, Robert Gaillard

BROADWAY BUCKAROO (1921)
(5 r.) lp, William Fairbanks

BROADWAY BUTTERFLY, A (1925)
(7 r.) d, William Beaudine; lp, Dorothy Devore, Louise Fazenda, Willard Louis, John Roche

BROADWAY COWBOY, THE (1920)
(5 r.) d, Joseph J. Franz; lp, William Desmond, Betty Francisco, Thomas Delmar, J.P. Lockney

BROADWAY DADDIES (1928)
(6 r.) d, Fred Windermere; lp, Jacqueline Logan, Alec B. Francis, Rex Lease, Phillips Smalley

BROADWAY DRIFTER, THE (1927)
(6 r.) d, Bernard McEveety; lp, George Walsh, Dorothy Hall, Bigelow Cooper, Arthur Donaldson

BROADWAY FEVER (1929)
(6 r.) d, Edward Cline; lp, Sally O'Neil, Roland Drew, Corliss Palmer, Calvert Carter

BROADWAY GALLANT, THE (1926)
(6 r.) d, Noel Mason; lp, Richard Talmadge, Clara Horton, Joe Harrington, Jack Richardson

BROADWAY GOLD (1923)
(7 r.) d, Edward Dillon; lp, Elaine Hammerstein, Eloise Goodale, Richard Wayne, Harold Goodwin

BROADWAY JONES (1917)
(6 r.) d, Joseph Kaufman; lp, George M. Cohan, Marguerite Snow, Russell Bassett, Crauford Kent

BROADWAY LADY (1925)
(6 r.) d, Wesley Ruggles; lp, Evelyn Brent, Marjorie Bonner, Theodore von Eltz, Joyce Compton

BROADWAY LOVE (1918)
(5 r.) d, Ida May Park; lp, Dorothy Phillips; lp, Dorothy Phillips, William Stowell, Lon Chaney, Juanita Hansen

BROADWAY MADNESS (1927)
(7 r.) d, Burton King; lp, Marguerite De La Motte, Donald Keith, Betty Hilburn, Margaret Cloud

BROADWAY MADONNA, THE (1922)
(6 r.) d, Harry Revier; lp, Dorothy Revier, Jack Connolly, Harry Van Meter, Eugene Burr

BROADWAY NIGHTS (1927)
(7 r.) d, Joseph C. Boyle; lp, Lois Wilson, Sam Hardy, Louis John Bartels, Philip Strange

BROADWAY OR BUST (1924)
(6 r.) d, Edward Sedgwick; lp, Hoot Gibson, Ruth Dwyer, King Zany, Gertrude Astor

BROADWAY PEACOCK, THE (1922)
(5 r.) d, Charles W. Lane; lp, Pearl White, Joseph Striker, Doris Eaton, Harry Southard

BROADWAY SAINT, A (1919)
(5 r.) d, Harry O. Hoyt; lp, Montagu Love, George Bunny, Helen Weer [Weir], Emile La Croix

BROADWAY SPORT, THE (1917)
(5 r.) d, Carl Harbaugh; lp, Stuart Holmes, Wanda Petit, Dan Mason, W.B. Green

BROKEN BARRIER
(SEE: QUICKSANDS, 1917, Brit.)

BROKEN BARRIERS (1919)
(5 r.) d, Charles E. Davenport; lp, Philip Sanford

BROKEN BARRIERS (1924)
(6 r.) d, Reginald Barker; lp, James Kirkwood, Norma Shearer, Adolphe Menjou, Mae Busch

BROKEN BARRIERS (1928)
(6 r.) d, Burton King; lp, Helene Costello, Gaston Glass, Joseph Girard, Frank Beal

BROKEN BUTTERFLY, THE (1919)
(5 r.) d, Maurice Tourneur; lp, Lew Cody, Mary Alden, Pauline Starke

BROKEN CHAINS (1922)
(7 r.) d, Allen Holubar; lp, Malcolm McGregor, Colleen Moore, Ernest Torrence, Claire Windsor

BROKEN CHAINS (1925, USSR)
(6 r.) d, Yakov Protazanov; lp, Anatoli Ktorov, V. Popova, Maria Blumenthal-Tamarina

BROKEN COMMANDMENTS (1919)
(5 r.) d, Frank Beal; lp, Gladys Brockwell, William Scott, Thomas Santschi, G. Raymond Nye

BROKEN FETTERS (1916)
(5 r.) d, Rex Ingram; lp, Violet Mersereau, William Garwood, Kittens Reichert, Charles Francis

BROKEN GATE, THE (1920)
(6 r.) d, Paul Scardon; lp, Bessie Barriscale, Joseph Kilgour, Marguerite de la Motte, Sam De Grasse

BROKEN GATE, THE (1927)
(6 r.) d, James C. McKay; lp, Dorothy Phillips, William Collier, Jr., Florence Turner, Jean Arthur

BROKEN HEARTS OF BROADWAY, THE (1923)
(7 r.) d, Irving Cummings; lp, Colleen Moore, Johnnie Walker, Alice Lake, Tully Marshall

BROKEN HOMES (1926)
(6 r.) d, Hugh Dierker; lp, Gaston Glass, Alice Lake, J. Barney Sherry, Jane Jennings

BROKEN LAW, THE (1915)
(5 r.) d, Oscar Apfel; lp, William Farnum, Dorothy Bernard

BROKEN LAW, THE (1924)
(5 r.) d, Bernard D. Russell;

BROKEN LAW, THE (1926)
(5 r.) lp, Jack Meehan

BROKEN LAWS (1924)
(7 r.) d, R. William Neill; lp, Mrs. Wallace Reid, Percy Marmont, Ramsey Wallace, Jacqueline Saunders

BROKEN MASK, THE (1928)
(6 r.) d, James P. Hogan; lp, Cullen Landis, Barbara Bedford, William V. Mong, Wheeler Oakman

BROKEN MELODY, THE (1916, Brit.)
(5 r.) d, Cavendish Morton; lp, Martin Harvey, Hilda Moore, Manora Thew, Courtice Pounds

BROKEN MELODY, THE (1920)
(5 r.) d, William P.S. Earle; lp, Eugene O'Brien, Lucy Cotton, Corinne Barker, Donald Hall

BROKEN ROAD, THE (1921, Brit.)
(5 r.) d, Rene Plaissetty; lp, Harry Ham, Mary Massart, Tony Fraser, June Putnam

BROKEN SHADOWS (1922)
(5 r.) d, Albert Ward

BROKEN SILENCE, THE (1922)
(6 r.) d, Del Henderson; lp, Zena Keefe, Robert Elliott, J. Barney Sherry, Jack Hopkins

BROKEN SPUR, THE (1921)
(5 r.) d, Ben Wilson; lp, Jack Hoxie, Evelyn Nelson, Jim Welch, Wilbur McGaugh

BROKEN THREADS (1917, Brit.)
(5 r.) d, Henry Edwards; lp, Henry Edwards, Chrissie White, A.V. Bramble, Harry Gilbey

BROKEN THREADS (1919)
(5 r.) lp, Bessie Barriscale

BROKEN TIES (1918)
(5 r.) d, Arthur Ashley; lp, June Elvidge, Montagu Love, Arthur Ashley, Pinna Nesbit

BROKEN VIOLIN, THE (1923)
(6 r.) d, Jack Dillon; lp, Joseph Blake, Warren Cook, Henry Sedley, Sydney Deane

BROKEN VIOLIN, THE (1927)
(7 r.) lp, J. Homer Tutt, Ardelle Dabney, Alice B. Russell, Ike Paul

BROKEN WING, THE (1923)
(6 r.) d, Tom Forman; lp, Kenneth Harlan, Miriam Cooper, Walter Long, Miss Du Pont

BROMLEY CASE, THE (1920)
(5 r.) d, Tom Collins; lp, Glenn White, Joseph Striker, Ethel Russell, Clarence Heritage

BRONC BUSTER, THE
(SEE: BRONC STOMPER, THE, 1928)

BRONC STOMPER, THE (1928)
(6 r.) d, Leo D. Maloney; lp, Don Coleman, Ben Corbett, Tom London, Bud Osborne

BRONCHO BUSTER, THE (1927)
(5 r.) d, Ernst Laemmle; lp, Fred Humes, Gloria Grey, George Connors, Charles Lee Quinn

BRONZE BRIDE, THE (1917)
(5 r.) d, Henry McRae; lp, Claire McDowell, Frank Mayo, Charles Hill Mailes, Eddie Polo

BROODING EYES (1926)
(6 r.) d, Edward J. Le Saint; lp, Lionel Barrymore, Ruth Clifford, Robert Ellis, Montagu Love

BROTH FOR SUPPER (1919)
(5 r.) d, Thomas [Tom] Ricketts; lp, Bert Sprotte, May Cloy, John Miltern, Lucia Backus Seger

BROTHERS (1929)
(6 r.) d, Scott Pembroke; lp, Cornelius Keefe, Arthur Rankin, Barbara Bedford, Richard Carle

BROTHERS DIVIDED (1919)
(5 r.) d, Frank Keenan; lp, Frank Keenan, Wallace MacDonald, Ruth Langston, Russ Powell

BROTHERS UNDER THE SKIN (1922)
(6 r.) d, E. Mason Hopper; lp, Pat O'Malley, Helene Chadwick, Mae Busch, Norman Kerry

BROWN DERBY, THE (1926)
(7 r.) d, Charles Hines; lp, Johnny Hines, Diana Kane, Ruth Dwyer, Flora Finch

BROWN OF HARVARD (1917)
(6 r.) d, Harry Beaumont; lp, Tom Moore, Hazel Daly, Warner Richmond, Kempton Greene

BROWN SUGAR (1922, Brit.)
(6 r.) d, Fred Paul; lp, Owen Nares, Lilian Hall-Davis, Eric Lewis, Henrietta Watson

BRUISED BY THE STORMS OF LIFE (1918, USSR)
(5 r.) d, Josef Soifer; lp, M. Zhdanova, Grigori Khmara, A. Gromov

BRUISER, THE (1916)
(5 r.) d, Charles Bartlett; lp, William Russell, Charlotte Burton, George Ferguson, Lizette Thorne

BRUTE, THE (1925)
(7 r.) lp, Evelyn Preer, Lawrence Chenault

BRUTE BREAKER, THE (1919)
(5 r.) d, Lynn F. Reynolds; lp, Frank Mayo, Kathryn Adams, Harry Northrup, Burwell Hamrick

BRUTE MASTER, THE (1920)
(5 r.) d, Charles H. Kyson; lp, Hobart Bosworth, Anna Q. Nilsson, William Conklin, Margaret Livingston

BUBBLES (1920)
(5 r.) d, Wayne Mack; lp, Jack Connolly, Mary Anderson, Jack Mower

BUCHANAN'S WIFE (1918)
(5 r.) d, Charles J. Brabin; lp, Virginia Pearson, Marc McDermott, Victor Sutherland, Ned Finley

BUCK PRIVATES (1928)
(7 r.) d, Melville Brown; lp, Lya De Putti, Malcolm McGregor, ZaSu Pitts, James Marcus

BUCKAROO KID, THE (1926)
(6 r.) d, Lynn Reynolds; lp, Hoot Gibson, Ethel Shannon, Burr McIntosh, Harry Todd

BUCKIN' THE WEST (1924)
(5 r.) lp, Pete Morrison

BUCKING BROADWAY (1918)
(5 r.) d, Jack [John] Ford; lp, Harry Carey, Molly Malone, L.M. Wells, Vester Pegg

BUCKING THE BARRIER (1923)
(5 r.) d, Colin Campbell; lp, Dustin Farnum, Arline Pretty, Leon Bary, Colin Chase

BUCKING THE LINE (1921)
(5 r.) d, Carl Harbaugh; lp, Maurice B. Flynn, Molly Malone, Norman Selby, Edwin B. Tilton

BUCKING THE TIGER (1921)
(6 r.) d, Henry Kolker; lp, Conway Tearle, Winifred Westover, Gladden James, Helene Montrose

BUCKSHOT JOHN (1915)
(4 r.) d, Hobart Bosworth; lp, Hobart Bosworth, Courtenay Foote, Helen Wolcott, Oscar Linkenhelt

BUFFALO BILL ON THE U.P. TRAIL (1926)
(6 r.) d, Frank S. Mattison; lp, Roy Stewart, Kathryn McGuire, Cullen Landis, Sheldon Lewis

BUGLE CALL, THE (1916)
(5 r.) d, Reginald Barker; lp, William Collier, Jr., Wyndham Standing, Anna Lehr, Thomas Guise

BUGLE CALL, THE (1927)
(6 r.) d, Edward Sedgwick; lp, Jackie Coogan, Claire Windsor, Herbert Rawlinson, Tom O'Brien

BUGLER OF ALGIERS, THE (1916)
(5 r.) d, Rupert Julian; lp, Ella Hall, Rupert Julian, Kingsley Benedict, Zoe Rae

BUILD THY HOUSE (1920, Brit.)
(5 r.) d, Fred Goodwins; lp, Henry Ainley, Ann Trevor, Reginald Bach, Warwick Ward

BUILDERS OF CASTLES (1917)
(5 r.) d, Ben Turbett; lp, Marc MacDermott, Miriam Nesbitt, William Wadsworth, Robert Brower

BUILT FOR RUNNING (1924)
(5 r.) lp, Leo Maloney

BULL DODGER, THE (1922)
(5 r.) lp, Bill Pickett

BULLDOGS OF THE TRAIL, THE (1915)
(4 r.) d, Kenneth MacDougall; lp, Kenneth MacDougall, Sydney Shields, Wynne Davidson, Hamilton Crane

BULLET-PROOF (1920)
(5 r.) d, Lynn F. Reynolds; lp, Harry Carey, William Ryno, Fred Gamble, Kathleen O'Connor

BULLETS AND BROWN EYES (1916)
(5 r.) d, Scott Sidney; lp, William Desmond, Bessie Barriscale, Wyndham Standing, J.J. Dowling

BULLETS AND JUSTICE (1929)
(5 r.) lp, Art Acord, Carol Lane

BUNCH OF KEYS, A (1915)
(5 r.) d, Richard Foster Baker; lp, Johnny Slavin, William Burress, June Keith, William Castelet

BUNCH OF VIOLETS, A (1916, Brit.)
(4 r.) d, Frank Wilson; lp, Chrissie White, Gerald Lawrence, Violet Hopson, Lionelle Howard

BURDEN OF PROOF, THE (1918)
(5 r.) d, Julius Steger; lp, Marion Davies, John Merkyl, Mary Richards, Eloise Clement

BURDEN OF RACE, THE (1921)
(6 r.) lp, Percy Verwayen, Edna Morton, Lawrence Chenault, Elizabeth Williams

BURGLAR, THE (1917)
(5 r.) d, Harley Knoles; lp, Carlyle Blackwell, Madge Evans, Evelyn Greeley, Victor Kennard

BURGLAR AND THE LADY, THE (1914)
(6 r.) d, Herbert Blache; lp, James J. Corbett, Claire Whitney, Fraunie Fraunholz

BURGLAR BY PROXY (1919)
(5 r.) d, Jack Dillon; lp, Jack Pickford, Gloria Hope, Jack Dillon, Robert Walker

BURGLAR-PROOF (1920)
(5 r.) d, Maurice Campbell; lp, Bryant Washburn, Lois Wilson, Grace Morse, Emily Chichester

BURGOMASTER OF STILEMONDE, THE (1928, Brit.)
(8 r.) d, George J. Banfield; lp, Sir John Martin Harvey, Fern Andra, Robert Andrews, John Hamilton

BURIDAN, LE HEROS DE LA TOUR DE NESLE (1924, Fr.)
(? r.) d, Pierre Marodon

BURIED GOLD (1926)
(5 r.) d, J.P. McGowan; lp, Al Hoxie

BURNING BRIDGES (1928)
(6 r.) d, James P. Hogan; lp, Harry Carey, Kathleen Collins, William N. Bailey, Dave Kirby

BURNING DAYLIGHT (1914)
(5 r.) d, Hobart Bosworth; lp, Hobart Bosworth

BURNING DAYLIGHT (1920)
(6 r.) d, Edward Sloman; lp, Mitchell Lewis, Helen Ferguson, William V. Mong, Alfred Allen

BURNING DAYLIGHT (1928)
(7 r.) d, Charles J. Brabin; lp, Milton Sills, Doris Kenyon, Arthur Stone, Big Boy Williams

BURNING GOLD (1927)
(6 r.) d, Jack Noble; lp, Herbert Rawlinson, Shirley Palmer, Sheldon Lewis, Nils Keith

BURNING QUESTION, THE (1919)
(8 r.) lp, Ida Edgington, Gilbert Rooney, Inez Marcel, May Kitson

BURNING THE CANDLE (1917)
(5 r.) d, Harry Beaumont; lp, Henry B. Walthall, Mary Charlson, Julien Barton, Frankie Raymond

BURNING THE WIND (1929)
(6 r.) d, Henry MacRae, Herbert Blache; lp, Hoot Gibson, Virginia Brown Faire, Cesare Gravina, Boris Karloff

BURNING TRAIL, THE (1925)
(5 r.) d, Arthur Rosson; lp, William Desmond, Albert J. Smith, Mary McIvor, James Corey

BURNING UP BROADWAY (1928)
(6 r.) d, Phil Rosen; lp, Helene Costello, Robert Frazer, Sam Hardy, Ernest Hilliard

BURNING WORDS (1923)
(5 r.) d, Stuart Paton; lp, Roy Stewart, Laura La Plante, Harold Goodwin, Edith Yorke

BURNT FINGERS (1927)
(6 r.) d, Maurice Campbell; lp, Eileen Percy, Ivan Doline, Edna Murphy, Wilfred Lucas

BURNT IN (1920, Brit.)
(5 r.) d, Duncan MacRae; lp, Gertrude McCoy, Bertram Burleigh, Sam Livesey, Henry Vibart

BURNT WINGS (1916, Brit.)
(4 r.) d, Walter West; lp, Eve Balfour, J.R. Tozer, Tom H. MacDonald, Lily Saxby

BURNT WINGS (1920)
(5 r.) d, Christy Cabanne; lp, Frank Mayo, Josephine Hill, Betty Blythe, Rudolph Christians

BUSH LEAGUER, THE (1927)
(7 r.) d, Howard Bretherton; lp, Monte Blue, Clyde Cook, Leila Hyams, William Demarest

BUSHER, THE (1919)
(5 r.) d, Jerome Storm; lp, Charles Ray, Colleen Moore, Margaret Livingston, Jack Gilbert

BUSHRANGER, THE (1928)
(7 r.) d, Chet [Chester] Withey; lp, Tim McCoy, Marian Douglas, Russell Simpson, Arthur Lubin

BUSINESS IS BUSINESS (1915)
(6 r.) d, Otis Turner; lp, Nat C. Goodwin, Maude George, Gretchen Lederer, Marc Robbins

BUSINESS OF LIFE, THE (1918)
(5 r.) d, Tom Terriss; lp, Alice Joyce, Walter McGrail, Betty Blythe, Percy Standing

BUSINESS OF LOVE, THE (1925)
(6 r.) d, Irving Reis, Jesse Robbins; lp, Edward Everett Horton, Barbara Bedford, ZaSu Pitts, Tom Ricketts

BUSTER, THE (1923)
(5 r.) d, Colin Campbell; lp, Dustin Farnum, Doris Pawn, Francis McDonald, Gilbert Holmes

BUSTIN' THRU (1925)
(5 r.) d, Clifford S. Smith; lp, Jack Hoxie, Helen Lynch, William Norton Bailey, Alfred Allen

BUTTER AND EGG MAN, THE (1928)
(7 r.) d, Richard Wallace; lp, Jack Mulhall, Greta Nissen, Sam Hardy, William Demarest

BUTTERFLIES IN THE RAIN (1926)
(8 r.) d, Edward Sloan; lp, Laura La Plante, James Kirkwood, Robert Ober, Dorothy Cumming

BUTTERFLY, THE (1915)
(5 r.) lp, Howard Estabrook, Barbara Tennant, Jessie Lewis, Julia Stuart

BUTTERFLY (1924)
(8 r.) d, Clarence Brown; lp, Laura La Plante, Ruth Clifford, Kenneth Harlan, Norman Kerry

BUTTERFLY GIRL, THE (1917)
(5 r.) d, Henry Otto; lp, Margarita Fischer, Jack Mower, John Steppling, Joseph Harris

BUTTERFLY GIRL, THE (1921)
(5 r.) d, John Gorman; lp, Marjorie Daw, Fritzi Brunette, King Baggot, Jean De Briac

BUTTERFLY RANCH
(SEE: BUTTERFLY RANGE, 1922)

BUTTERFLY RANGE (1922)
(5 r.) d, Neal Hart; lp, Neal Hart, Hazel Deane

BUTTONS (1927)
(7 r.) d, George Hill; lp, Jackie Coogan, Lars Hanson, Gertrude Olmstead, Paul Hurst

BUZZARD'S SHADOW, THE (1915)
(5 r.) d, Thomas Rickett's; lp, Harold Lockwood, May Allison, William Stowell, Harry Van Meter

BY BERWIN BANKS (1920, Brit.)
(5 r.) d, Sidney Morgan; lp, Langhorne Burton, Eileen Magrath, J. Denton-Thompson, C.W. Somerset

BY DIVINE RIGHT (1924)
(7 r.) d, R. William Neill; lp, Mildred Harris, Anders Randolf, Elliott Dexter, Sidney Bracey

BY HOOK OR CROOK (1918)
(5 r.) d, Dell Henderson; lp, Carlyle Blackwell, Evelyn Greeley, Jack Drumier, Jennie Ellison

BY RIGHT OF BIRTH (1921)
(6 r.) lp, Clarence Brooks, Anita Thompson

BY RIGHT OF PURCHASE (1918)
(6 r.) d, Charles Miller; lp, Norma Talmadge, Eugene O'Brien, Ida Darling, William Courtleigh, Jr.

BY THE LAW (1926, USSR)
(5 r.) d, Lev Kuleshov; lp, Alexandra Khokhlova, Sergei Komarov, Vladimir Fogel, Pyotr Galadzhev

BY THE SHORTEST OF HEADS (1915, Brit.)
(4 r.) d, Bert Haldane; lp, George Formby Jr., Jack Tessier, Moore Marriott, Jack Hulcup

C.O.D. (1915)
(4 r.) d, Tefft Johnson; lp, Harry Davenport, Hughie Mack, Charles Brawn, William Shea

CABARET (1927)
(7 r.) d, Robert G. Vignola; lp, Gilda Gray, Tom Moore, Chester Conklin, Mona Palma

CACTUS CRANDALL (1918)
(5 r.) d, Cliff Smith; lp, Roy Stewart, Marion Marvin, Pete Morrison, William Ellingford

CACTUS CURE, THE (1925)
(5 r.) d, Ward Hayes; lp, Dick Hatton, Yakima Canutt, Wilbur McGaugh, Marilyn Mills

CACTUS TRAILS (1925)
(5 r.) d, Harry Webb; lp, Jack Perrin

CACTUS TRAILS (1927)
(5 r.) d, Harry P. Crist; lp, Bob Custer, Marjorie Zier, Lew Meehan, Roy Watson

CAFE ELECTRIC (1927, Aust.)
(? r.) d, Gustav Ucicky; lp, Fritz Alberti, Marlene Dietrich, Anny Coty, Willi Forst

CAFE IN CAIRO, A (1924)
(6 r.) d, Chester [Chet] Withey; lp, Priscilla Dean, Robert Ellis, Carl Stockdale, Evelyn Selbie

CAGLIOSTRO (1920, Ger.)
(? r.) d, Reinhold Schunzel; lp, Conrad Veidt, Anita Berber, Reinhold Schunzel, Karl Gotz

CAGLIOSTRO (1928, Fr.)
(? r.) d, Richard Oswald; lp, Alfred Abel, Hans Stuwe, Rene Heribel, George Dullin

CAILLAUX CASE, THE (1918)
(6 r.) d, Richard Stanton; lp, Madlaine Travers, Henry Warwick, George Majeroni, Eugene Ormonde

CALEB PIPER'S GIRL (1919)
(5 r.) d, Ernest Traxler; lp, Helen Chadwick, Spottiswoode Aitken, William A. Lawrence

CALENDER GIRL, THE (1917)
(5 r.) d, Rollin S. Sturgeon; lp, Juliette Day, Ashton Dearholt, Clarissa Selwynne, Lamar Johnston

CALGARY STAMPEDE, THE (1925)
(6 r.) d, Herbert Blache; lp, Hoot Gibson, Virginia Brown Faire, Clark Comstock, Ynez Seabury

CALIBRE 45 (1924)
(5 r.) d, J.P. McGowan; lp, Franklyn Farnum, Dorothy Wood, Cathleen Calhoun

CALIBRE 38 (1919)
(6 r.) d, Edgar Lewis; lp, Mitchell Lewis, Hedda Nova, Sola Panzdrovna, Edward Roseman

CALIFORNIA IN '49 (1924)
(6 r.) d, Jacques Jaccard; lp, Edmund Cobb, Neva Gerber, Charles Brinley, Ruth Royce

CALIFORNIA MAIL, THE (1929)
(6 r.) d, Albert Rogell; lp, Ken Maynard, Dorothy Dwan, Lafe McKee, Paul Hurst

CALIFORNIA STRAIGHT AHEAD (1925)
(8 r.) d, Harry Pollard; lp, Reginald Denny, Gertrude Olmsted, Tom Wilson, Charles Gerrard

CALL OF COURAGE, THE (1925)
(5 r.) d, Clifford S. Smith; lp, Art Acord, Olive Hasbrouck, Duke Lee, Frank Rice

CALL OF HER PEOPLE, THE (1917)
(7 r.) d, John W. Noble; lp, Ethel Barrymore, Robert Whittier, William B. Davidson, William Mandeville

CALL OF HIS PEOPLE, THE (1922)
(6 r.) lp, George Edward Brown, Edna Morton, Mae Kemp, James Steven

CALL OF HOME, THE (1922)
(6 r.) d, Louis J. Gasnier; lp, Leon Barry, Irene Rich, Ramsey Wallace, Margaret Mann

CALL OF THE CANYON, THE (1923)
(7 r.) d, Victor Fleming; lp, Richard Dix, Lois Wilson, Marjorie Daw, Noah Beery

CALL OF THE CUMBERLANDS, THE (1915)
(5 r.) d, Frank Lloyd; lp, Dustin Farnum, Myrtle Stedman, Winifred Kingston, Herbert Standing

CALL OF THE DANCE, THE (1915)
(4 r.) d, George L. Sargent; lp, Yancsi Dolly, George E. Romain, Guy Coombs, E.T. Rosemon

CALL OF THE DESERT (1930)
(5 r.) d, J.P. McGowan; lp, Tom Tyler, Sheila Le Gay, Bud Osborne, Cliff Lyons

CALL OF THE EAST, THE (1917)
(5 r.) d, George H. Melford; lp, Sessue Hayakawa, Tsuru Aoki, Jack Holt, Margaret Loomis

CALL OF THE HEART (1928)
(5 r.) d, Francis Ford; lp, Dynamite (a dog), Joan Alden, Edmund Cobb, William A. Steele

CALL OF THE HILLS, THE (1923)
(5 r.) d, Fred Hornby; lp, Robert Broderick, Sally Edwards, Maude Malcolm, Louis J. O'Connor

CALL OF THE KLONDIKE, THE (1926)
(6 r.) d, Oscar Apfel; lp, Gaston Glass, Dorothy Dwan, Earl Metcalfe, Sam Allen

CALL OF THE MATE (1924)
(5 r.) d, Alvin J. Neitz; lp, William Fairbanks, Dorothy Revier, Milton Ross, Billie Bennett

CALL OF THE NIGHT (1926)
(5 r.)

CALL OF THE NORTH, THE (1921)
(5 r.) d, Joseph Henabery; lp, Jack Holt, Madge Bellamy, Noah Beery, Francis McDonald

CALL OF THE PIPES, THE (1917, Brit.)
(5 r.) d, Tom Watts; lp, Ernest A. Douglas

CALL OF THE ROAD, THE (1920, Brit.)
(6 r.) d, A.E. Coleby; lp, Victor McLaglen, Phyllis Shannaw, Warwick Ward, Philip Williams

CALL OF THE SEA, THE (1915)
(4 r.) d, Joseph Byron Totten; lp, Darwin Karr, Howard Lang, Betty Brown, Thomas Harper

CALL OF THE SEA, THE (1919, Brit.)
(5 r.) lp, Stella Muir, Henry Victor, Booth Conway

CALL OF THE SOUL, THE (1919)
(5 r.) d, Edward J. LeSaint; lp, Gladys Brockwell, William Scott, Charles Clary, Lydia Yeamans Titus

CALL OF THE WILD, THE (1914)
(5 r.)

CALL OF THE WILDERNESS, THE (1926)
(5 r.) d, Jack Nelson; lp, Sandow (a dog), Lewis Sargent, Edna Marion, Sydney D. Grey

CALL OF YOUTH, THE (1921, Brit.)
(4 r.) d, Hugh Ford; lp, Mary Glynne, Majorie Hume, Jack Hobbs, Malcolm Cherry

CALLED BACK (1914, Brit.)
(4 r.) d, George L. Tucker; lp, Henry Ainley, Jane Gail, Charles Rock, George Bellamy

CALLED BACK (1914)
(4 r.) d, Otis Turner; lp, Herbert Rawlinson, Anna Little, William Worthington, William J. Quinn

CALVAIRE D'AMOUR (1923, Fr.)
(? r.) d, Viatcheslaw Tourjansky

CALVARY (1920, Brit.)
(5 r.) d, Edwin J. Collins; lp, Malvina Longfellow, Henry Victor, Charles Vane, Dorothy Moody

CALVERT'S VALLEY (1922)
(5 r.) d, Jack Dillon; lp, Jack [John] Gilbert, Sylvia Breamer, Philo McCullough, Herschel Mayall

CAMBRIC MASK, THE (1919)
(5 r.) d, Tom Terriss; lp, Alice Joyce, Maurice Costello, Herbert Pattee, Roy Applegate

CAMEO KIRBY (1923)
(7 r.) d, John Ford; lp, John Gilbert, Gertrude Olmstead, Alan Hale, Eric Mayne

CAMILLE (1916)
(5 r.) d, Albert Capellani; lp, Clara Kimball Young, Paul Capellani, Lillian Cook, Robert Cummings

CAMILLE (1917)
(6 r.) d, J. Gordon Edwards; lp, Theda Bara, Albert Roscoe, Walter Law, Alice Gale

CAMILLE (1921)
(6 r.) d, Ray C. Smallwood; lp, Alla Nazimova, Rudolph Valentino, Arthur Hoyt, Zeffie Tilbury

CAMILLE OF THE BARBARY COAST (1925)
(6 r.) d, Hugh Dierker; lp, Mae Busch, Owen Moore, Fritzi Brunette, Burr McIntosh

CAMOUFLAGE KISS, A (1918)
(5 r.) d, Harry Millarde; lp, June Caprice, Bernard Thornton, Pell Trenton, George Bunny

CAN A WOMAN LOVE TWICE? (1923)
(7 r.) d, James W. Horne; lp, Ethel Clayton, Muriel Dana, Kate Lester, Fred Esmelton

CANADIAN, THE (1926)
(8 r.) d, William Beaudine; lp, Thomas Meighan, Mona Palma, Wyndham Standing, Dale Fuller

CANCELLED DEBT, THE (1927)
(6 r.) d, Phil Rosen; lp, Rex Lease, Charlotte Stevens, Florence Turner, Billy Sullivan

CANDY GIRL, THE (1917)
(5 r.) d, W. Eugene Moore; lp, Gladys Hulette, Helen Badgley, William Parke, Jr., J.H. Gilmour

CANDY KID, THE (1928)
(7 r.) d, David Kirkland; lp, Rex Lease, Pauline Garon, Frank Campeau, Harry Woods

CANDYTUFT, I MEAN VERONICA (1921, Brit.)
(5 r.) d, Frank Richardson; lp, Mary Glynne, Leslie Faber, George Relph, Ena Grossmith

CANTOR'S DAUGHTER, THE (1913, USSR)
(4 r.) d, Avrom Yitskhok Kaminsky; lp, Shmuel Landau, Regina Kaminska, Sonia Shlosberg, Lea Kompaniejec

CANVAS KISSER, THE (1925)
(5 r.) d, Duke Worne; lp, Richard Holt, Ruth Dwyer, Garry O'Dell, Cecil Edwards

CANYON OF ADVENTURE, THE (1928)
(6 r.) d, Albert Rogell; lp, Ken Maynard, Virginia Brown Faire, Eric Mayne, Theodore Lorch

CANYON OF LIGHT, THE (1926)
(6 r.) d, Benjamin Stoloff; lp, Tom Mix, Dorothy Dwan, Carl Miller, Ralph Sipperly

CANYON OF MISSING MEN, THE (1930)
(5 r.) d, J.P. McGowan; lp, Tom Tyler, Shelia Le Gay, Tom Forman, Bud Osborne

CANYON OF THE FOOLS (1923)
(6 r.) d, Val Paul; lp, Harry Carey, Marguerite Clayton, Fred Stanton, Joseph Harris

CANYON RUSTLERS (1925)
(5 r.) d, Harry Webb; lp, Jack Perrin

CAPITAL PUNISHMENT (1925)
(6 r.) d, James P. Hogan; lp, Eddie Phillips, Alec B. Francis, Elliott Dexter, George Hackathorne

CAPITOL, THE (1920)
(5 r.) d, George Irving; lp, Leah Baird, Robert T. Haines, Alexander Gaden, William B. Davidson

CAPRICE (1913)
(4 r.) d, J. Searle Dawley; lp, Mary Pickford, Ernest Truex, Owen Moore, James Gordon

CAPTAIN ALVAREZ (1914)
(6 r.) d, Rollin S. Sturgeon; lp, Edith Storey, Myrtle Gonzales, William D. Taylor, George Holt

CAPTAIN BLOOD (1924)
(11 r.) d, David Smith; lp, J. Warren Kerrigan, Jean Paige, Charlotte Merriam, James Morrison

CAPTAIN COWBOY (1929)
(5 r.) d, J.P. McGowan; lp, Yakima Canutt, Ione Reed, Charles Whittaker, John Lowell

CAPTAIN FLY-BY-NIGHT (1922)
(5 r.) d, William K. Howard; lp, Johnnie Walker, Francis McDonald, Shannon Day, Edward Gribbon

CAPTAIN JINKS OF THE HORSE MARINES (1916)
(5 r.) d, Fred E. Wright; lp, Richard C. Travers, Ann Murdock, John Junior, Edmund F. Cobb

CAPTAIN KIDD, JR. (1919)
(5 r.) d, William Desmond Taylor; lp, Mary Pickford, Douglas MacLean, Spottiswoode Aitken, Robert Gordon

CAPTAIN KIDDO (1917)
(5 r.) d, W. Eugene Moore; lp, Marie Osborne, Marion Warner, Philo McCullough, Harry Van Meter

CAPTAIN MACKLIN (1915)
(4 r.) d, John O'Brien, Jack Conway; lp, Jack Conway, Lillian Gish, Spottiswoode Aitken, Erich von Stroheim

CAPTAIN OF HIS SOUL (1918)
(5 r.) d, G.P. Hamilton; lp, William Desmond, Claire McDowell, Walt Whitman, Jules Friquet

CAPTAIN SWAGGER (1928)
(7 r.) d, Edward H. Griffith; lp, Rod La Rocque, Sue Carol, Richard Tucker, Victor Potel

CAPTAIN SWIFT (1920)
(5 r.) d, Tom Terriss; lp, Earle Williams, Alice Calhoun, Florence Dixon, Edward Clarke

CAR OF CHANCE, THE (1917)
(5 r.) d, William Worthington; lp, Franklyn Farnum, Brownie Vernon, Helen Wright, Molly Malone

CARD, THE (1922, Brit.)
(5 r.) d, A.V. Bramble; lp, Laddie Cliff, Hilda Cowley, Joan Barry, Mary Dibley

CARDBOARD LOVER, THE (1928)
(8 r.) d, Robert Z. Leonard; lp, Marion Davies, Jetta Gouldal, Nils Asther, Andres DeSegurola

CARDINAL RICHELIEU'S WARD (1914)
(6 r.) lp, James Cruz, Florence LaBadie, Morris Foster, Lila Chester

CAREER OF KATHERINE BUSH, THE (1919)
(5 r.) d, Roy William Neill; lp, Catherine Calvert, John Goldsworthy, Crauford Kent, Mathilda Brundage

CARELESS WOMAN, THE (1922)
(5 r.)

CARMEN (1915)
(6 r.) d, Raoul Walsh; lp, Theda Bara, Einar Linden, Carl Harbaugh, James A. Marcus

CARMEN (1916)
(4 r.) d, Charles Chaplin; lp, Charles Chaplin, Edna Purviance, John Rand, Leo White

CARMEN (1917, Ital.)
(? r.) lp, Marguerite Sylva

CARMEN
(SEE: GYPSY BLOOD, 1921)

CARMEN (1928, Fr.)
(9 r.) d, Jacques Feyder; lp, Racquel Meller, Louis Lerch, Gaston Modot, Victor Vina

CARMEN OF THE NORTH (1920)
(5 r.) d, Maurtis H. Binger; lp, Anna Bos

CARNIVAL (1921, Brit.)
(8 r.) d, Harley Knoles; lp, Matheson Lang, Hilda Bayley, Ivor Novello, Clifford Grey

CARNIVAL OF CRIME (1929, Ger.)
(6 r.) d, Willy Wolff; lp, Ellen Richter, Bruno Kaster, Henry Schroth, Evi Eva

CARROTS (1917, Brit.)
(4 r.) d, Frank Wilson; lp, Chrissie White, Lionelle Howard, Gerald Lawrence, W.G. Saunders

CARRY ON! (1927, Brit.)
(7 r.) d, Dinah Shurey, Victor Peers; lp, Moore Marriott, Trilby Clark, Alf Goodard, Johnny Butt

CASANOVA (1927, Fr.)
(? r.) d, Alexandre Volkoff; lp, Ivan Mosjoukine, Olga Day, Rina de Liguoro, Suzanne Bianchetti

CASE AT LAW, A (1917)
(5 r.) d, Arthur Rosson; lp, Riley Hatch, Pauline Curley, Dick Rosson, Jack Dillon

CASE OF BECKY, THE (1921)
(6 r.) d, Chester M. Franklin; lp, Constance Binney, Glenn Hunter, Frank McCormack, Montague Love

CASE OF LADY CAMBER, THE (1920, Brit.)
(6 r.) d, Walter West; lp, Violet Hopson, Stewart Rome, Gregory Scott, Mercy Hatton

CASE OF LENA SMITH, THE (1929)
(8 r.) d, Josef von Sternberg; lp, Esther Ralston, James Hall, Gustav von Seyffertitz, Emily Fitzroy

CASEY AT THE BAT (1916)
(5 r.) d, Lloyd Ingraham; lp, De Wolf Hopper, Kate Toncray, May Garcia, Carl Stockdale

CASEY JONES (1927)
(7 r.) d, Charles J. Hunt; lp, Ralph Lewis, Kate Price, Al St. John, Jason Robards

CASEY'S MILLIONS (1922, Brit.)
(5 r.) d, John MacDonagh; lp, Jimmy O'Dea, Kathleen Drago, Fred Jeffs, Chris Sylvester

CASTLE (1917, Brit.)
(5 r.) d, Larry Trimble; lp, Sir John Hare, Peggy Hyland, Mary Porke, Campbell Gullan

CASTLE OF DREAMS (1919, Brit.)
(5 r.) d, Wilfred Noy; lp, Mary Odette, Fred Groves, Gertrude McCoy, A.E. Matthews

CASTLES FOR TWO (1917)
(5 r.) d, Frank Reicher; lp, Marie Doro, Elliott Dexter, Mayme Kelso, Jane Wolff

CASTLES IN SPAIN (1920, Brit.)
(5 r.) d, H. Lisle Lucoque; lp, C. Aubrey Smith, Lilian Braithwaite, Bertie Gordon, Hayford Hobbs

CASTLES IN THE AIR (1919)
(5 r.) d, George D. Baker; lp, May Allison, Ben Wilson, Clarence Burton, Walter E. Percival

CASTLES IN THE AIR (1923, Brit.)
(5 r.) d, Fred Paul; lp, Nelson Keys, Lilian Hall-Davies, Campbell Gullan, Mary Rorke

CATCH MY SMOKE (1922)
(5 r.) d, William Beaudine; lp, Tom Mix, Lillian Rich, Claude Peyton, Gordon Griffith

CATHERINE (1924, Fr.)
(6 r.) d, Albert Dieudonne; lp, Catherine Hessling, Albert Dieudonne, Pierre Philippe, Champagne

CATSPAW, THE (1916)
(5 r.) d, George A. Wright; lp, Miriam Nesbitt, Marc MacDermott, William Wadsworth, Yale Benner

CAUGHT BLUFFING (1922)
(5 r.) d, Lambert Hillyer; lp, Frank Mayo, Edna Murphy, Wallace MacDonald, Jack Curtis

CAUGHT IN THE ACT (1918)
(5 r.) d, Harry Millarde; lp, Peggy Hyland, Leslie Austen, George Bunny, Carlotta Coer

CAUSE FOR DIVORCE (1923)
(7 r.) d, Hugh Dierker; lp, Fritzi Brunette, David Butler, Charles Clary, Helen Lynch

CAVALIER, THE (1928)
(7 r.) d, Irvin Willat; lp, Richard Talmadge, Barbara Bedford, Nora Cecil, David Torrence

CAVANAUGH OF THE FOREST RANGERS (1918)
(5 r.) d, William Wolbert; lp, Alfred Whitman, Nell Shipman, Otto Lederer, Laura Winston

CAVE GIRL, THE (1921)
(5 r.) d, Joseph J. Franz; lp, Teddie Gerard, Charles Meredith, Wilton Taylor, Eleanor Hancock

CAVELL CASE, THE
(SEE: WOMAN THE GERMANS SHOT, 1918)

CAVEMAN, THE (1915)
(5 r.) d, Theodore Marston; lp, Robert Edeson, Fay Wallace, Lillian Burns, George De Beck

CE COCHON DE MORIN (1924, Fr.)
(? r.) d, Viatcheslaw Tourjansky; lp, Nicolas Rimsky

CE PAUVRE CHERI (1923, Fr.)
(? r.) d, Jean Kemm

CECILIA OF THE PINK ROSES (1918)
(5 r.) d, Julius Steger; lp, Marion Davies, Harry Benham, Edward O'Connor, Willette Kershaw

CECROPIA MOTH, THE (1916)
(4 r.)

CELEBRATED SCANDAL, A (1915)
(5 r.) d, J. Gordon Edwards

CELEBRITY (1928)
(7 r.) d, Tay Garnett; lp, Robert Armstrong, Clyde Cook,

CELESTE OF THE AMBULANCE CORPS (1916)
(4 r.) d, Burton George; lp, Leonie Flugrath [Shirley Mason], Pat O'Malley, Charles Sutton

CELESTIAL CITY, THE (1929, Brit.)
(9 r.) d, John Orton; lp, Norah Baring, Cecil Fearnley, Lewis Dayton, Malvina Longfellow

CELLAR OF DEATH, THE (1914)
(4 r.)

CERTAIN RICH MAN, A (1921)
(6 r.) d, Howard Hickman; lp, Carl Gantvoort, Claire Adams, Robert McKim, Jean Hersholt

CERTAIN YOUNG MAN, A (1928)
(6 r.) d, Hobart Henley; lp, Ramon Novarro, Marceline Day, Renee Adoree, Carmel Myers

CHACALS (1918, Fr.)
(? r.) d, Andre Hugon

CHAIN INVISIBLE, THE (1916)
(5 r.) d, Frank E. Powell; lp, Bruce McRae, Gerda Holmes, Alfred Hickman, Tom McGrath

CHAIN LIGHTING (1927)
(6 r.) d, Lambert Hillyer; lp, Buck Jones, Dione Ellis, Ted McNamara, Jack Baston

CHAINED (1927, Ger.)
(4 r.) d, Carl-Theodor Dreyer; lp, Benjamin Christensen, Walter Slezak, Nora Gregor, Robert Garrison

CHAINS OF BONDAGE (1916, Brit.)
(4 r.) d, A.E. Coleby; lp, Basil Gill, Evelyn Millard, Arthur Rooke, Dora de Winton

CHAINS OF EVIDENCE (1920)
(5 r.) d, Dallas M. Fitzgerald; lp, Edmund Breese, Marie Shotwell, Anna Lehr, James F. Cullen

CHALICE OF COURAGE, THE (1915)

(6 r.) d, Rollin S. Sturgeon;
lp, Myrtle Gonzales, William Duncan, George Holt, W.V. Ranous

CHALICE OF SORROW, THE (1916)
(5 r.) d, Rex Ingram; lp, Cleo Madison, Blanche White, Charles Cumming, John McDermott

CHALK MARKS (1924)
(7 r.) d, John G. Adolfi; lp, Marguerite Snow, Ramsey Wallace, June Elvidge, Lydia Knott

CHALLENGE, THE (1916)
(5 r.) d, Donald Mackenzie; lp, Charles Gotthold, Montagu Love, Helene Chadwick

CHALLENGE, THE (1922)
(5 r.) d, Tom Terriss; lp, Rod La Rocque, Dolores Cassinelli, Warner Richmond, De Sacia Mooers

CHALLENGE OF THE LAW, THE (1920)
(5 r.) d, Scott Dunlap; lp, William Russell, Helen Ferguson, Arthur Morrison, James Farley

CHAMBER OF MYSTERY, THE (1920)
(5 r.) d, Abraham Schomer; lp, Claire Whitney, Earl Metcalfe, Sam Edwards, Robert Lee Allen

CHAMBER OF HORRORS (1929, Brit.)
(5 r.) d, Walter Summers; lp, Frank Stanmore, Elizabeth Hempel, Joan Maude, Leslie Holland

CHAMPI TORTU (1921, Fr.)
(? r.) d, Jacques de Baroncelli

CHANCE OF A LIFETIME, THE (1916, Brit.)
(5 r.) d, Bertram Phillips; lp, Queenie Thomas, Austin Camp, Fay Temple, H. Agar Lyons

CHANGING HUSBANDS (1924)
(7 r.) d, Frank Urson, Paul Iribe; lp, Leatrice Joy, Victor Varconi, Raymond Griffith, Julia Faye

CHANGING WOMAN, THE (1918)
(5 r.) d, David Smith;

CHANNING OF THE NORTHWEST (1922)
(5 r.) d, Ralph Ince; lp, Eugene O'Brien, Gladden James, Norma Shearer, James Seeley

CHANNINGS, THE (1920, Brit.)
(5 r.) d, H.B. Parkinson; lp, Lionelle Howard, Dick Webb, Dorothy Moody, Cowley Wright

CHANSON FILMEES (1918, Fr.)
(? r.) d, Roger Lion

CHANTE-LOUVE (1921, Fr.)
(? r.) d, Georges Monca

CHAPERON, THE (1916)
(5 r.) d, Arthur Berthelet; lp, Edna Mayo, Eugene O'Brien, Sydney Ainsworth, Frankie Raymond

CHAPPY - THAT'S ALL (1924, Brit.)
(5 r.) d, Thomas Bentley; lp, Joyce Dearsley, Gertrude McCoy, Francis Lister, Lewis Gilbert

CHAPTER IN HER LIFE, A (1923)
(6 r.) d, Lois Weber; lp, Claude Gillingwater, Jane Mercer, Jacqueline Gadsen, Frances Raymond

CHARGE IT TO ME (1919)
(5 r.) d, Roy William Neill; lp, Margarita Fisher, Emory Johnson, Augustus Phillips, L.S. McKee

CHARGE OF THE GAUCHOS, THE (1928)
(6 r.) d, Albert Kelly; lp, Francis X. Bushman, Jacqueline Logan, Guido Trento, Paul Ellis

CHARITY
(SEE: SOME ARTIST, 1919, Brit.)

CHARITY ANN (1915, Brit.)
(4 r.) d, Maurice Elvey; lp, Elizabeth Risdon, Fred Groves, Chappell Dossett, Winifred Sadler

CHARITY CASTLE (1917)
(5 r.) d, Lloyd Ingraham;

Clifford Calis, Eugenie Forde

CHARLATAN, THE (1916, Brit.)
(4 r.) d, Sidney Morgan; lp, Ellie Norwood, Violet Graham, Anna Mather, Frederick de Lara

CHARLES XII, PARTS 1 & 2 (1927, Swed.)
(24 r.) d, John W. Brunius; lp, Gosta Ekman, Bengt Djurberg, Augusta Lindberg, Mona Martenson

CHARLEY'S AUNT (1925)
(8 r.) d, Scott Sidney; lp, Sydney Chaplin, Ethel Shannon, James E. Page, Lucien Littlefield

CHARLOTTE (1917)
(6 r.) d, Oscar Eagle; lp, Charlotte

CHARMER, THE (1917)
(5 r.) d, Jack Conway; lp, Ella Hall, Belle Bennett, Martha Mattox, James McCandlas

CHARMING DECEIVER, THE (1921)
(5 r.) d, George L. Sargent; lp, Alice Calhoun, Jack McLean, Charles Kent, Eugene Acker

CHASE ME CHARLIE (1918, Brit.)
(7 r.) d, Langford Reed; lp, Graham Douglas

CHASING RAINBOWS (1919)
(5 r.) d, Frank Beal; lp, Gladys Brockwell, William Scott, Richard Rosson, Harry Dunkinson

CHASING TROUBLE (1926)
(1926) d, Milburn Morante; lp, Pete Morrison, Ione Reed, Tom London, Roy Watson

CHASTITY (1923)
(6 r.) d, Victor Schertzinger; lp, Katherine MacDonald, J. Gunnis Davis, J. Gordon Russell, Huntley Gordon

CHATEAU HISTORIQUE (1923, Fr.)
(? r.) d, Henri Desfontaines

CHATTEL, THE (1916)
(6 r.) d, Fred Thompson; lp, E.H. Sothern, Peggy Hyland, Rose E. Tapley, Charles Kent

CHEAP KISSES (1924)
(7 r.) d, John Ince; lp, Lillian Rich, Cullen Landis, Vera Reynolds, Phillips Smalley

CHEAPER TO MARRY (1925)
(7 r.) d, Robert Z. Leonard; lp, Conrad Nagel, Lewis S. Stone, Paulette Duval, Marguerite De La Motte

CHEAT, THE (1915)
(5 r.) d, Cecil B. DeMille; lp, Fannie Ward, Sessue Hayakawa, Jack Dean, James Neill

CHEAT, THE (1923)
(8 r.) d, George Fitzmaurice; lp, Pola Negri, Jack Holt, Charles De Roche, Dorothy Cumming

CHEATED LOVE (1921)
(5 r.) d, King Baggot; lp, Carmel Myers, George B. Williams, Allan Forrest, John Davidison

CHEATER, THE (1920)
(6 r.) d, Henry Otto; lp, May Allison, King Baggot, Frank Currier, Harry Van Meter

CHEATING CHEATERS (1919)
(5 r.) d, Allan Dwan; lp, Clara Kimball Young, Anna Q. Nilsson, Jack Holt, Nicholas Dunaew

CHEATING HERSELF (1919)
(5 r.) d, Edmund Lawrence; lp, Peggy Hyland, Harry Hilliard, Molly McConnell, William Elmer

CHEATING THE PUBLIC (1918)
(7 r.) d, Richard Stanton; lp, Ralph Lewis, Enid Markey, Bertram Gassby, Tom Wilson

CHECHAHCOS, THE (1924)
(8 r.) d, Lewis H. Moomaw; lp, William Dills, Albert Van Antwerp, Eva Gordon, Howard Webster

CHECKERED FLAG, THE (1926)
(6 r.) d, John G. Adolfi; lp, Elaine Hammerstein, Wallace MacDonald, Lionel Belmore, Robert Ober

CHECKERS (1919)
(6 r.) d, Richard Stanton; lp, Thomas J. Carrigan, Jean Acker, Ellen Cassity, Robert Elliott

CHECKMATE, THE (1917)
(5 r.) d, Sherwood MacDonald; lp, Jackie Saunders, Frank Mayo, Daniel Gilfether, Mollie McConnell

CHEER LEADER, THE (1928)
(6 r.) d, Alvin J. Neitz; lp, Ralph Graves, Gertrude Olmstead, Shirley Palmer, Ralph Emerson

CHEERFUL FRAUD, THE (1927)
(7 r.) d, William A. Seiter; lp, Reginald Denny, Gertrude Olmstead, Otis Harlan, Emily Fitzroy

CHEERFUL GIVERS (1917)
(5 r.) d, Paul Powell; lp, Bessie Love, Kenneth Harlan, Spottiswoode Aitken, Pauline Starke

CHEROKEE KID, THE (1927)
(5 r.) d, Robert De Lacy; lp, Tom Tyler, Sharon Lynn, Jerry Pembroke, Robert Burns

CHEROKEE STRIP, THE (1925)
(6 r.) lp, Herbert Bethew, Lucille Mulhall

CHERRY RIPE (1921, Brit.)
(5 r.) d, Kenelm Foss; lp, Mary Odette, Lionelle Howard, Roy Travers, Peggy Bayfield

CHESS PLAYER, THE (1930, Fr.)
(4 r.) d, Henri Dupuy-Mazuel; lp, Edithe Jehanne, Pierre Blanchar, Pierre Batchoff, Charles Dullin

CHEYENNE (1929)
(6 r.) d, Albert Rogell; lp, Ken Maynard, Gladys McConnell, James Bradbury, Jr., William Franey

CHEYENNE TRAILS (1928)
(5 r.) d, Robert J. Horner; lp, Pawnee Bill Jr., Bud Osborne, Bill Nestel

CHICHINETTE ET CLE (1921, Fr.)
(? r.) d, Henri Desfontaines

CHICK (1928, Brit.)
(7 r.) d, A.V. Bramble; lp, Bramwell Fletcher, Trilby Clark, Chili Bouchier, Rex Maurice

CHICKEN A LA KING (1928)
(7 r.) d, Henry Lehrman; lp, Nancy Carroll, George Meeker, Arthur Stone, Ford Sterling

CHICKEN IN THE CASE, THE (1921)
(5 r.) d, Victor Heerman; lp, Owen Moore, Vivian Ogden, Teddy Sampson, Edgar Nelson

CHICKIE (1925)
(8 r.) d, John Francis Dillon; lp, Dorothy Mackaill, John Bowers, Hobart Bosworth, Gladys Brockwell

CHIGNON D'OR (1916, Fr.)
(? r.) d, Andre Hugon; lp, Mistinguett

CHILD IN JUDGEMENT, A (1915)
(4 r.) d, Carlton King; lp, Mary Elizabeth Forbes, Richard Tucker, Augustus Phillips, Maurice Steuart

CHILD IN PAWN, A (1921)
(? r.)

CHILD OF DESTINY, THE (1916)
(5 r.) d, William Nigh; lp, Irene Fenwick, Gana Walska, Robert Ellis, Roy Applegate

CHILD OF GOD, A (1915)
(4 r.) d, John Adolfi; lp, Sam De Grasse, Francelia Billington

CHILD OF MYSTERY, A (1916)
(5 r.) d, Hobart Henley; lp, Hobart Henley, Gertrude Selby, Thomas Jefferson, Paul Byron

CHILD OF THE BIG CITY (1914, USSR)
(4 r.) d, Yevgeni Bauer; lp, Y. Smirnova, M. Salarov, A. Bibikov, Emma Bauer

CHILD OF THE PARIS STREETS, A (1916)
(5 r.) d, Lloyd Ingraham; lp, Mae Marsh, Robert Harron, Tully Marshall, Jennie Lee

CHILD OF THE PRAIRIE, A (1925)
(5 r.) d, Tom Mix; lp, Tom Mix, Rose Bronson, Ed Brady, Mort Thompson

CHILD OF THE WILD, A (1917)
(5 r.) d, John G. Adolfi; lp, June Caprice, Frank Morgan, Tom Cameron, Tom Brooks

CHILD THOU GAVEST ME, THE (1921)
(6 r.) d, John M. Stahl; lp, Barbara Castleton, Adele Farrington, Winter Hall, Lewis Stone

CHILDREN -- FLOWERS OF LIFE (1919, USSR)
(4 r.) d, Yuri Zheliabuzhsky; lp, V. Osvetsinsky, Anna Dmokhovskaya, A. Nelidov

CHILDREN IN THE HOUSE, THE (1916)
(5 r.) d, Sidney & Chester Franklin; lp, Norma Talmadge, Alice Rae, Jewel Carmen, William Hinckley

CHILDREN NOT WANTED (1920)
(6 r.) d, Paul Scardon; lp, Edith Day, Ruth Sullivan, Joe King, Lumsden Hare

CHILDREN OF BANISHMENT (1919)
(5 r.) d, Norval MacGregor; lp, Mitchell Lewis, Bessie Eyton, Herbert Heyes, Arthur Morrison

CHILDREN OF COURAGE (1921, Brit.)
(5 r.) d, A.E. Coleby; lp, Maurice Thompson, Stephen Frayne, Henry Doyle, Mrs. Watts-Phillips

CHILDREN OF DESTINY (1920)
(6 r.) d, George Irving; lp, Edith Hallor, Arthur Edmund Carew

CHILDREN OF DUST (1923)
(7 r.) d, Frank Borzage; lp, Bert Woodruff, Johnnie Walker, Frankie Lee, Pauline Garon

CHILDREN OF EVE, THE (1915)
(5 r.) lp, Viola Dana, Robert Conness, Thomas Blake, Nellie Grant

CHILDREN OF FATE (1926)
(7 r.) lp, Joseph Shoengold, Betty Hilburn

CHILDREN OF FATE (1928)
(8 r.) lp, Harry Henderson, Shingzie Howard, Lawrence Chenault, Arline Mickey

CHILDREN OF GIBEON, THE (1920, Brit.)
(5 r.) d, Sidney Morgan; lp, Joan Morgan, Langhorne Burton, Eileen Magrath, Sydney Fairbrother

CHILDREN OF JAZZ (1923)
(6 r.) d, Jerome Storm; lp, Theodore Kosloff, Ricardo Cortez, Robert Cain, Eileen Percy

CHILDREN OF STORM (1926, USSR)
(5 r.) d, Eduard Johanson, Friedrich Ermler; lp, Yakov Gudkin, Valeri Solovtsov, Mili Taut-Korso, Veronika Buzhinskava

CHILDREN OF THE FEUD (1916)
(5 r.) d, Joseph Henabery; lp, Dorothy Gish, Charles Gorman, Violet Radcliffe, Beulah Burns

CHILDREN OF THE GHETTO, THE (1915)
(5 r.) d, Frank Powell; lp, Wilton Lackaye, Ethel Kaufman, Ruby Hoffman, David Bruce

CHILDREN OF THE NEW DAY (1930, USSR)
(4 r.) d, Vladimir Petrov; lp, Fatima Giliadova, Boris Litkin, E.P. Lorchagima-Alexandrovskaya

CHILDREN OF THE RITZ (1929)
(7 r.) d, John Francis Dillon; lp, Dorothy Mackaill, Jack Mulhall, James Ford, Richard Carlyle

CHILDREN OF THE SEA (1926, Jap.)
(? r.) d, Kenji Mizoguchi

CHILDREN OF THE WHIRLWIND (1925)
(7 r.) d, Whitman Bennett; lp, Lionel Barrymore, Johnny Walker, Marguerite De La Motte, J.R. Roser

CHILDREN PAY, THE (1916)
(5 r.) d, Lloyd Ingraham; lp, Lillian Gish, Violet Wilkie, Keith Armour, Ralph Lewis

CHIMES, THE (1914)
(5 r.) d, Tom Terriss; lp, Fay Cusic, Alfred Hemming, Clarence Harvey, Milly Terris

CHINA BOUND (1929)
(7 r.) d, Charles F. Reisner; lp, Karl Dane, George K. Arthur, Josephine Dunn, Polly Moran

CHINA SLAVER (1929)
(6 r.) d, Frank S. Mattison; lp, Sojin, Albert Valentino, Iris Yamoaka, Ben Wilson

CHINATOWN CHARLIE (1928)
(7 r.) d, Charles Hines; lp, Johnny Hines, Louise Lorraine, Harry Gribbon, Fred Kohler

CHINESE BUNGALOW, THE (1926, Brit.)
(7 r.) d, Sinclair Hill; lp, Matheson Lang, Genevieve Townsend, Juliette Compton, Shayle Gardner

CHINESE PARROT, THE (1927)
(7 r.) d, Paul Leni; lp, Marian Nixon, Florence Turner, Hobart Bosworth, Edward Burns

CHINESE PUZZLE, THE (1919, Brit.)
(5 r.) d, Fred Goodwins; lp, Leon M. Lion, Lilian Braithwaite, Milton Rosmer, Sybil Arundale

CHIP OF THE FLYING U (1914)
(4 r.) d, Colin Campbell; lp, Kathlyn Williams, Tom Mix, Frank Clark, Fred Huntly

CHIP OF THE FLYING U (1926)
(7 r.) d, Lynn Reynolds; lp, Hoot Gibson, Virginia Browne Faire, Philo McCullough, Nora Cecil

CHIVALROUS CHARLEY (1921)
(5 r.) d, Robert Ellis; lp, Eugene O'Brien, George Fawcett, Nancy Deaver, D.J. Flanagan

CHOCOLATE SOLDIER, THE (1915)
(5 r.) d, Walter Morton;

CHORUS KID, THE (1928)
(6 r.) d, Howard Bretherton; lp, Virginia Browne Faire, Bryant Washburn, Thelma Hill, Hedda Hopper

CHORUS LADY, THE (1924)
(7 r.) d, Ralph Ince; lp, Margaret Livingston, Alan Roscoe, Virginia Lee Corbin, Lillian Elliott

CHORUS OF TOKYO (1931, Jap.)
(? r.) d, Yasujiro Ozu; lp, Kenji Oyama, Tokihiko Okada, Tatsuo Saito

CHOUCHOU POIDS PLUME (1925, Fr.)
(? r.) d, Gaston Ravel

CHOUQUETTE ET SON AS (1920, Fr.)
(? r.) d, Georges Monca

CHRISTIAN, THE (1915, Brit.)
(9 r.) d, George Loane Tucker; lp, Derwent Hall Caine, Elizabeth Risdon, Gerald Ames, Mary Dibley

CHRISTIAN, THE (1923)
(8 r.) d, Maurice Tourneur; lp, Richard Dix, Mae Busch, Gareth Hughes, Phyllis Haver

CHRISTIE JOHNSTONE (1921, Brit.)
(5 r.) d, Norman Macdonald; lp, Gertrude McCoy, Stewart Rome, Clive Brook, Mercy Hatton

CHRISTINE OF THE BIG TOPS (1926)
(6 r.) d, Archie Mayo; lp, Pauline Garon, Cullen Landis, Otto Matiesen, Robert Graves

CHRISTINE OF THE HUNGRY HEART (1924)
(8 r.) d, George Archainbaud; lp, Florence Vidor, Clive Brook, Ian Keith, Warner Baxter

CHRISTMAS EVE (1913, USSR)
(4 r.) d, Wladyslaw Starewicz; lp, Ivan Mozhukhin, Olga Obolenskaya, L. Tridenskaya, P. Lopukhin

CHRISTOPHE COLOMB (1919, Fr.)
(? r.) d, Gerard Bourgeois

CHRISTUS (1917, Ital.)
(8 r.) d, Gulio Antamoro

CHRONICLE OF THE MAY RAIN (1924, Jap.)
(? r.) d, Kenji Mizoguchi

CHRONICLES OF THE GRAY HOUSE, THE (1925, Ger.)
(? r.) d, Arthur von Gerlach; lp, Paul Hartmann, Lil Dagover, Arthur Kraussneck, Rudolph Rittner

CHRYSANTHEMUMS (1914, USSR)
(4 r.) d, Pyotr Chardynin; lp, Vera Coralli, Ivan Mozhukhin, R. Reisen

CHU CHIN CHOW (1923, Brit.)
(12 r.) d, Herbert Wilcox; lp, Betty Blythe, Herbert Langley, Randle Ayrton, Eva Moore

CIGARETTE GIRL, THE (1917)
(5 r.) d, William Parke; lp, Gladys Hulette, William Parke, Jr., Florence Hamilton, Warner Oland

CIGARETTE GIRL FROM MOSSELPROM (1924, USSR)
(8 r.) d, Yuri Zhelyabuzhsky; lp, Yulia Solntseva, Igor Ilinsky, Anna Dmokhovskaya, Nikolai Tseretelli

CIGARETTE MAKER'S ROMANCE, A (1920, Brit.)
(5 r.) d, Tom Watts; lp, Henderson Bland, Dorothy Vernon, William Parry, Tom Conventry

CINDERELLA (1926, Ger.)
(? r.) d, Ludwig Berger; lp, Helga Thomas, Frieda Richard, Paul Hartman, Herman Thimig

CINDERELLA AND THE MAGIC SLIPPER (1917)
(4 r.)

CINDERELLA MAN, THE (1918)
(6 r.) d, George Loane Tucker; lp, Tom Moore, Mae Marsh, Alec B. Francis, George Fawcett

CINDERELLA OF THE HILLS (1921)
(5 r.) d, Howard M. Mitchell; lp, Barbara Bedford, Carl Miller, Cecil Van Auker, Wilson Hummel

CINDERELLA'S TWIN (1920)
(6 r.) d, Dallas M. Fitzgerald; lp, Viola Dana, Edward Cecil, Edward Connelly, Irene Hunt

CINDERS (1926, Brit.)
(7 r.) d, Louis Mercanton; lp, Betty Balfour, Fred Wright, Andre Reanne, Louis Baron

CINEMA GIRL'S ROMANCE, A (1915, Brit.)
(4 r.) d, George Pearson; lp, Agnes Glynne, Fred Paul, Alice de Winton, Bernard Vaughan

CINEMA MURDER, THE (1920)
(5 r.) d, George D. Baker; lp, Marion Davies, Nigel Barrie, Anders Randolf, Reginald Barlow

CIPHER KEY, THE (1915)
(4 r.) d, George Terwilliger; lp, Earl Metcalfe, Kempton Greene, Mary Keane, Herbert Fortier

CIRCE THE ENCHANTRESS (1924)
(7 r.) d, Robert Z. Leonard; lp, Mae Murray, James Kirkwood, Tom Ricketts, Charles Gerard

CIRCLE, THE (1925)
(6 r.) d, Frank Borzage; lp, Eleanor Boardman, Malcolm McGregor, Alec Francis, Eugenie Besserer

CIRCULAR STAIRCASE, THE (1915)
(5 r.) d, Edward J. LeSaint; lp, Eugenie Besserer, Stella Razetto, Guy Oliver, Edith Johnson

CIRCUMSTANTIAL EVIDENCE (1920)
(5 r.) d, Tom Collins; lp, Glenn White, Leo Delaney, Jane McAlpine, Alfred Warman

CIRCUMSTANTIAL EVIDENCE (1929)
(7 r.) d, Wilfred Noy; lp, Cornelius Keefe, Helen Foster, Alice Lake, Charles Gerrard

CIRCUS COWBOY, THE (1924)
(5 r.) d, William A. Wellman; lp, Charles Jones, Marian Nixon, Jack McDonald, Ray Hallor

CIRCUS CYCLONE, THE (1925)
(5 r.) d, Albert Rogell; lp, Art Acord, Moe McCrea, Nancy Deaver, Cesare Gravina

CIRCUS JIM (1921, Brit.)
(5 r.) d, B.E. Doxat-Pratt; lp, Adelqui Migliar, Evelyn Brent, Norman Doxat-Pratt

CIRCUS JOYS (1923)
(5 r.) lp, Gloria Joy

CIRCUS LURE (1924)
(5 r.) d, Frank S. Mattison; lp, Matty Mattison, Lorraine Eason

CIRCUS OF LIFE, THE (1917)
(5 r.) d, Rupert Julian; lp, Zoe Rae, Mignon Anderson, Emory Johnson, Harry Carter

CIRCUS ROMANCE, A (1916)
(5 r.) d, Charles M. Seay; lp, Muriel Ostriche, Edward Davis, Jack Hopkins, Catherine Calhoun

CIRCUS ROOKIES (1928)
(6 r.) d, Edward Sedgwick; lp, Karl Dane, George K. Arthur, Louise Lorraine, Sidney Jarvis

CITIES AND YEARS (1931, USSR)
(5 r.) d, Evgeni Cherviakov; lp, Ivan Schuveler, G. Michurin, Bernard Goetzke, Sophie Magarill

CITY, THE (1916)
(5 r.) d, Theodore Wharton; lp, Thurlow Bergen, William Riley Hatch, Richard Stewart, Elsie Esmond

CITY, THE (1926)
(6 r.) d, Roy William Neill; lp, Nancy Nash, Robert Frazer, George Irving, Lillian Elliott

CITY DESTROYED, A (1922, Fr.)
(4 r.)

CITY OF BEAUTIFUL NONSENSE, THE (1919)
(6 r.) d, Henry Edwards; lp, Henry Edwards, Chrissie White, James Lindsay, Henry Vibart

CITY OF COMRADES, THE (1919)
(5 r.) d, Harry Beaumont; lp, Tom Moore, Seena Owen, Otto Hoffman, Albert Roscoe

CITY OF DIM FACES, THE (1918)
(5 r.) d, George Melford; lp, Sessue Hayakawa, Doris Pawn, Marin Sais, James Cruze

CITY OF FAILING LIGHT, THE (1916)
(4 r.) d, George W. Terwilliger; lp, Herbert Fortier, Leslie Auten, Octavia Handworth, William H. Turner

CITY OF ILLUSION, THE (1916)
(6 r.) d, Ivan Abramson; lp, Mignon Anderson, Paula Shay, Carleton Macey, Bradley Barker

CITY OF MASKS, THE (1920)
(5 r.) d, Thomas N. Heffron; lp, Robert Warwick, Lois Wilson, Theodore Kosloff, Edward Jobson

CITY OF PURPLE DREAMS (1928)
(6 r.) d, Duke Worne; lp, Barbara Bedford, Robert Frazer, David Torrence, Jacqueline Gadsdon

CITY OF SHADOWS (1929, Brit.)
(4 r.) d, Norman Lee; lp, Elizabeth Baxter

CITY OF TEARS, THE (1918)
(5 r.) d, Elsie Jane Wilson; lp, Carmel Myers, Edwin August, Earl Rodney, Leatrice Joy

CITY OF TEMPTATION (1929, Brit.)
(4 r.) d, Walter Niebuhr; lp, Olga Chekova, Julianne Johnson, Julius Klein, Hugh Miller

CITY OF YOUTH, THE (1928, Brit.)
(? r.) d, C.C. Calvert; lp, Betty Faire, Lillian Oldland, H. Fisher White, Desmond Roberts

CITY SPARROW, THE (1920)
(5 r.) d, Sam Wood; lp, Ethel Clayton, Walter Hiers, Clyde Fillmore, Lillian Leighton

CITY THAT NEVER SLEEPS, THE (1924)
(6 r.) d, James Cruze; lp, Louise Dresser, Ricardo Cortez, Kathlyn Williams, Virginia Lee Corbin

CIVILIAN CLOTHES (1920)
(6 r.) d, Hugh Ford; lp, Thomas Meighan, Martha Mansfield, Maude Turner Gordon, Alfred Hickman

CIVILIZATION'S CHILD (1916)
(5 r.) d, Charles Giblyn; lp, William H. Thompson, Anna Lehr, Jack Standing, Dorothy Dalton

CLAIM, THE (1918)
(5 r.) d, Frank Reicher; lp, Edith Storey, Wheeler Oakman, Mignon Anderson, Marion Skinner

CLARENCE (1922)
(7 r.) d, William C. De Mille; lp, Wallace Reid, Agnes Ayres, May McAvoy, Kathlyn Williams

CLARISSA
(SEE: GAMBLER'S ADVOCATE, 1915)

CLASH OF THE WOLVES (1925)
(7 r.) d, Noel Mason Smith; lp, Rin-Tin-Tin, June Marlowe, Charles Farrell, Heinie Conklin

CLASS AND NO CLASS (1921, Brit.)
(6 r.) d, W.P. Kellino; lp, Judd Green, Pauline Johnson, David Hawthorne, Marie Ault

CLASSIFIED (1925)
(7 r.) d, Alfred Santell; lp, Corinne Griffith, Jack Mulhall, Ward Crane, Carroll Nye

CLAUDE DUVAL (1924, Brit.)
(9 r.) d, George A. Cooper; lp, Nigel Barrie, Fay Compton, Hugh Miller, A.B. Imeson

CLAW, THE (1918)
(5 r.) d, Robert G. Vignola; lp, Clara Kimball Young, Milton Sills, Edward Kimball, Marcia Manon

CLAW, THE (1927)
(6 r.) d, Sidney Olcott; lp, Norman Kerry, Claire Windsor, Arthur Edmund Carewe, Tom Guise

CLAWS OF THE HUN, THE (1918)
(5 r.) d, Victor L. Schertzinger; lp, Charles Ray, Jane Novak, Robert McKim, Melbourne McDowell

CLEAN GUN, THE (1917)
(4 r.) d, Harry Harvey; lp, Stanley J. Preston, Edward Jobson, Kathleen Kirkham, Robert Weycross

CLEAN HEART, THE (1924)
(8 r.) d, J. Stuart Blackton; lp, Percy Marmont, Otis Harlan, Marguerite De La Motte, Andrew Arbuckle

CLEAN UP, THE (1922)
(5 r.) lp, William Fairbanks

CLEAN-UP, THE (1917)
(5 r.) d, William Worthington; lp, Franklyn Farnum, Brownie Vernon, Mary Talbot, Martha Mattox

CLEAN-UP, THE (1929)
(6 r.) d, Bernard F. McEveety; lp, Charles Delaney, Betty Blake, Bruce Gordon, Lewis Sargent

CLEAN-UP MAN, THE (1928)
(5 r.) d, Ray Taylor; lp, Ted Wells, Peggy O'Day, Henry Herbert, George Reed

CLEAR THE DECKS (1929)
(6 r.) d, Joseph E. Henabery; lp, Reginald Denny, Olive Hasbrouck, Otis Harlan, Lucien Litttlefield

CLEOPATRA (1913)
(6 r.) d, Charles L. Gaskill; lp, Helen Gardner, Robert Gaillord, Harley Knowles

CLEOPATRA (1917)
(10 r.) d, J. Gordon Edwards; lp, Theda Bara, Fritz Leiber, Thurston Hall, Herschal Mayall

CLICKING HOOFS (1926)
(5 r.)

CLIMBER, THE (1917)
(4 r.) d, Henry King; lp, Henry King, Jack McLaughlin, T.H. Gibson Gowland, Bert Ensminger

CLIMBERS, THE (1927)
(7 r.) d, Paul L. Stein; lp, Irene Rich, Clyde Cook, Forrest Stanley, Flobelle Fairbanks

CLINGING VINE, THE (1926)
(7 r.) d, Paul Sloane; lp, Leatrice Joy, Tom Moore, Toby Claude, Robert Edeson

CLOAK, THE (1926, USSR)
(6 r.) d, Grigori Kozintsev; lp, Andrei Kostrichkin, Sergei Gerasimov, Anna Zheimo

CLOCK, THE (1917)
(5 r.) d, William Worthington; lp, Franklyn Farnum, Agnes Vernon, Frank Whitson, Mark Fenton

CLODHOPPER, THE (1917)
(5 r.) d, Victor Schertzinger; lp, Charles Ray, Margery Wilson, Charles French, Lydia Knott

CLOISTER AND THE HEARTH, THE (1913, Brit.)
(5 r.) d, Hay Plumb; lp, Alec Worcester, Alma Taylor, Hay Plumb, Jamie Darling

CLOSE TO NATURE (1917)
(5 r.)

CLOSED DOORS (1921)
(5 r.) d, G.V. Seyffertitz; lp, Alice Calhoun, Harry C. Browne, Bernard Randall, A.J. Herbert.

CLOSED GATES (1927)
(6 r.) d, Phil Rosen; lp, Johnny Harron, Jane Novak, Lucy Beaumont, Sidney De Grey

CLOSED ROAD, THE (1916)
(5 r.) d, Maurice Tourneur; lp, House Peters, Barbara Tennant, Lionel Adams, Leslie Stowe

CLOSIN' IN (1918)
(5 r.) d, J. W. McLaughlin; lp, William Desmond, Maude Wayne, George Pearce, Darrel Foss

CLOSING NET, THE (1915)
(5 r.) d, Edward Jose; lp, Howard Estabrook, Bliss Milford, Kathryn Browne-Decker, Madeline Traverse

CLOTHES (1920)
(6 r.) d, Fred Sittenham; lp, Olive Tell, Crauford Kent, Cyril Chadwick, Zeffie Tilbury

CLOTHES (1924)
(4 r.) lp, James O'Leary, Doris C. Mallory

CLOTHES MAKE THE WOMAN (1928)
(6 r.) d, Tom Terriss; lp, Eve Southern, Walter Pidgeon, Charles Byer, George E. Stone

CLOUD DODGER, THE (1928)
(5 r.) d, Bruce Mitchell; lp, Al Wilson, Gloria Grey, Joe O'Brien, Julia Griffith

CLOUD RIDER, THE (1925)
(5 r.) d, Bruce Mitchell; lp, Al Wilson, Virginia Lee Corbin, Harry von Meter, Helen Ferguson

CLOUDBURST (1922)
(5 r.) lp, Billy Wells

CLOUDED MIND, A
(SEE: A CLOUDED NAME, 1923)

CLOUDED NAME, THE (1919)
(5 r.) d, Caryl S. Fleming; lp, John Lowell, Edgar Keller, Corene Uzzell, Charles Edwards

CLOUDED NAME, A (1923)
(5 r.) d, Austin O. Huhn; lp, Norma Shearer, Gladden James, Yvonne Logan, Richard Neill

CLOVER'S REBELLION (1917)
(5 r.) d, Wilfred North; lp, Anita Stewart, Rudolph Cameron, Brinsley Shaw, Eulalie Jensen

CLOWN, THE (1916)
(5 r.) d, William C. De Mille; lp, Victor Moore, Thomas Meighan, Florence Dagmar, Billy Jacobs

CLOWN, THE (1927, Swed.)
(SEE, GOLDEN CLOWN, THE, 1927, Swed.)

CLUB OF THE BIG DEED, THE (1927, USSR)
(7 r.) d, Grigori Kozintsev, Leonid Trauberg; lp, Pyotr Sobolevsky, Sergei Gerasimov, Sophie Magarill, Andrei Kostrichkin

CLUE, THE (1915)
(5 r.) d, James Neill; lp, Blanche Sweet, Gertrude Keller, Edward Mackaye, Sessue Hayakawa

CLUE OF THE CIGAR BAND, THE (1915, Brit.)
(4 r.) d, H.O. Martinek; lp, H.O. Martinek, Ivy Montford

CLUE OF THE NEW PIN, THE (1929, Brit.)
(7 r.) d, Arthur Maude; lp, Benita Hume, Kim Peacock, Donald Calthrop, [Sir] John Gielgud

CLUTCH OF CIRCUMSTANCE, THE (1918)
(5 r.) d, Henri Houry; lp, Corinne Griffith, Robert Gaillard, David Herblin, Florence Deshon

COAL KING, THE (1915, Brit.)
(4 r.) d, Percy Nash; lp, Douglas Cox, May Lynn, Frank Tennant, Daisy Cordell

COALS OF FIRE (1918)
(5 r.) d, Victor L. Schertzinger; lp, Enid Bennett, Fred Niblo, Melbourne McDowell, Billy Elmer

COAST GUARD PATROL, THE (1919)
(7 r.)

COAST OF FOLLY, THE (1925)
(7 r.) d, Allan Dwan; lp, Gloria Swanson, Anthony Jowitt, Alec Francis, Dorothy Cumming

COAST OF OPPORTUNITY, THE (1920)
(5 r.) d, Ernest C. Warde; lp, J. Warren Kerrigan, Fritzi Brunette, Herschel Mayall, Eddie Hearn

COAST PATROL, THE (1925)
(5 r.) d, Bud Barsky; lp, Kenneth McDonald, Claire De Lorez, Fay Wray, Spottiswoode Aitken

COAX ME (1919)
(5 r.) d, Gilbert P. Hamilton; lp, June Elvidge, Earl Metcalfe, Arthur Donaldson, Lola Humphrey

COBBLER, THE
(SEE: FIGHTING COBBLER, THE, 1915, Brit.)

COBWEB, THE (1917, Brit.)
(6 r.) d, Cecil M. Hepworth; lp, Henry Edwards, Alma Taylor, Stewart Rome, Violet Hopson

COCAINE
(SEE: WHILE LONDON SLEEPS, 1922, Brit.)

COCKTAILS (1928, Brit.)
(6 r.) d, Monty Banks; lp, Patachon, Enid Stamp-Taylor, Tony Wylde, Nigel Barrie

CODE OF HONOR
(SEE: HER CODE OF HONOR, 1919)

CODE OF THE AIR (1928)
(6 r.) d, James P. Hogan; lp, Kenneth Harlan, June Marlowe, Arthur Rankin, William V. Mong

CODE OF THE COW COUNTRY (1927)
(5 r.) d, Oscar Apfel; lp, Buddy Roosevelt, Hank Bell, Elsa Benham, Melbourne MacDowell

CODE OF THE NORTHWEST (1926)
(4 r.) d, Frank S. Mattison; lp, Sandow (a dog), Richard Lang, Tom London, Frank Austin

CODE OF THE SCARLET, THE (1928)
(6 r.) d, Harry J. Brown; lp, Ken Maynard, Gladys McConnell, Ed Brady, J.P. McGowan

CODE OF THE WEST (1925)
(7 r.) d, William K. Howard; lp, Owen Moore, Constance Bennett, Mabel Ballin, Charles Ogle

CODE OF THE WEST (1929)
(5 r.) d, J.P. McGowan; lp, Bob Custer, Vivian Bay, Bobby Dunn, Martin Cichy

CODE OF THE WILDERNESS (1924)
(7 r.) d, David Smith; lp, John Bowers, Alice Calhoun, Alan Hale, Charlotte Merriam

CODE OF THE YUKON (1919)
(5 r.) d, Bertram Bracken; lp, Mitchell Lewis, Tom Santschi, Vivian Rich, Arthur Morrison

COEUR DE TITI (1924, Fr.)
(? r.) d, Henri Etievant

COEUR FIDELE (1923, Fr.)
(6 r.) d, Jean Epstein; lp, Leon Mathot, Gina Manes, Edmond van Daele, Benedict

COEUR LEGER (1923, Fr.)
(? r.) d, Robert Saidreau

COEURS FAROUCHES (1923, Fr.)
(? r.) d, Julien Duvivier

COHEN'S LUCK (1915)
(4 r.) d, John H. Collins; lp, Viola Dana, William Wadsworth

COINCIDENCE (1921)
(5 r.) d, Chet Withey; lp, Robert Harron, June Walker, Bradley Barker, William Frederic

COLD DECK, THE (1917)
(5 r.) d, William S. Hart; lp, William S. Hart, Alma Rubens, Mildred Harris, Sylvia Breamer

COLD FURY (1925)
(5 r.) lp, Jack Richardson, Ora Carew

COLD NERVE (1925)
(5 r.) d, J.P. McGowan; lp, Bill Cody, Ena Gregory, Joe Bennett, Arthur Morrison

COLD STEEL
(SEE: TRAIL TO RED DOG, THE, 1921)

COLLEEN (1927)
(6 r.) d, Frank O'Connor; lp, Madge Bellamy, Charles Morton, J. Farrell MacDonald, Tom Maguire

COLLEEN OF THE PINES (1922)
(5 r.) d, Chester Bennett; lp, Jane Novak, Edward Hearn, Alfred Allen, J. Gordon Russell

COLLEGE BOOB, THE (1926)
(6 r.) d, Harry Garson; lp, Lefty Flynn, Jean Arthur, Jimmy Anderson, Bob Bradbury, Jr.

COLLEGE HERO, THE (1927)
(6 r.) d, Walter Lang; lp, Bobby Angew, Pauline Garon, Ben Turpin, Rex Lease

COLLEGE IS A NICE PLACE (1936, Jap.)
(? r.) d, Yasujiro Ozu; lp, Chishu Ryu

COLLEGE ORPHAN, THE (1915)
(6 r.) d, William Dowlin; lp, Carter De Haven, Flora Parker De Haven, Louis Morrison, Gloria Fonda

COLLEGE WIDOW, THE (1915)
(5 r.) d, Barry O'Neil; lp, Ethel Clayton, George Soule Spencer, Rosetta Brice, Edith Ritchie

COLLEGE WIDOW, THE (1927)
(7 r.) d, Archie L. Mayo; lp, Dolores Costello, William Collier, Jr., Douglas Gerrard, Anders Randolf

COLLEGIATE (1926)
(5 r.) d, Del Andrews; lp, Alberta Vaughn, Donald Keith, John Steppling, Alys Murrell

COLONEL NEWCOME THE PERFECT GENTLEMAN (1920, Brit.)
(6 r.) d, Fred Goodwins; lp, Milton Rosmer, Joyce Carey, Temple Bell, Lewis Willoughby

COLORADO (1915)
(5 r.) d, Norval MacGregor; lp, Hobart Bosworth, Carl von Schiller, Albert MacQuarrie, Edward Brown

COLORADO (1921)
(5 r.) d, Reaves Eason; lp, Frank Mayo, Charles Newton, Gloria Hope, Lillian West

COLORADO PLUCK (1921)
(5 r.) d, Jules G. Furthman; lp, William Russell, Margaret Livingston, William Buckley, George Fisher

COLUMBUS (1923)
(5 r.) d, Edwin L. Hollywood; lp, Fred Eric, Paul McAllister, Howard Truesdell, Leslie Stowe

COMBAT, THE (1916)
(6 r.) d, Ralph Ince; lp, Anita Stewart, John Robertson, Richard Turner, Virginia Norden

COMBAT, THE (1926)
(7 r.) d, Lynn Reynolds; lp, House Peters, Wanda Hawley, Walter McGrail, C.E. Anderson

COMBAT (1927)
(6 r.) d, Albert Hiatt; lp, George Walsh, Bradley Barker, Claire Adams, Gladys Hulette

COME AGAIN SMITH (1919)
(5 r.) d, E. Mason Hopper; lp, J. Warren Kerrigan, Lois Wilson, Henry A. Barrows, William Conklin

COME AND GET IT (1929)
(6 r.) d, Wallace Fox; lp, Bob Steele, Jimmy Quinn, Betty Welsh, Jay Morley

COME ON COWBOYS! (1924)
(5 r.) d, Ward Hayes; lp, Dick Hatton, Marilyn Mills, Harry Fenwick, Philip Sleeman

COME ON IN (1918)
(5 r.) d, John Emerson; lp, Shirley Mason, Ernest Truex, Charles De Planta, Joseph Burke

COME OUT OF THE KITCHEN (1919)
(5 r.) d, John S. Robertson; lp, Marguerite Clark, Eugene O'Brien, Frances Kaye, Bradley Barker

COME THROUGH (1917)
(7 r.) d, Jack Conway; lp, Herbert Rawlinson, Alice Lake, George Webb, Jean Hathaway

COME TO MY HOUSE (1927)
(6 r.) d, Alfred E. Green; lp, Olive Borden, Antonio Moreno, Ben Bard, Cornelius Keefe

COME-BACK, THE (1916)
(5 r.) d, Fred J. Balshofer; lp, Harold Lockwood, May Allsion, George Henry, Howard Truesdell

COMIN' THRO' THE RYE (1916, Brit.)
(6 r.) d, Cecil M. Hepworth; lp, Alma Taylor, Stewart Rome, Margaret Blanche, Campbell Gullan

COMIN' THRO' THE RYE (1923, Brit.)
(8 r.) d, Cecil M. Hepworth; lp, Alma Taylor, Shayle Gardner, Eileen Dennes, Ralph Forbes

COMING OF THE LAW, THE (1919)
(5 r.) d, Lynn F. Reynolds; lp, Tom Mix, Jane Novak, George Nicholls, Jack Curtis

COMING POWER, THE (1914)
(4 r.) d, Edward Mackey; lp, Lionel Adams, Edith Luckett, William Crimmins, Anna Rose

COMING THROUGH (1925)
(7 r.) d, Edward Sutherland; lp, Thomas Meighan, Lila Lee, John Miltern, Wallace Beery

COMMON CAUSE, THE (1918)
(7 r.) d, J. Stuart Blackton; lp, Herbert Rawlinson, Sylvia Breamer [Bremer], Huntley Gordon, Lawrence Grossmith

COMMON CLAY (1919)
(7 r.) d, George Fitzmaurice; lp, Fannie Ward, William E. Lawrence, Fred Goodwins, Easter Walters

COMMON GROUND (1916)
(5 r.) d, William C. De Mille; lp, Marie Doro, Thomas Meighan, Theodore Roberts, Mary Mersch

COMMON LEVEL, A (1920)
(5 r.) d, Burton King; lp, Edmund Breese, Claire Whitney, Sidney Grattan

COMMON PROPERTY (1919)
(6 r.) d, Paul Powell & William C. Dowlan; lp, Nell Craig, Robert Anderson, Colleen Moore, Johnnie Cooke

COMMON SENSE (1920)
(5 r.) d, Louis William Chaudet; lp, Vola Vale, Ralph Lewis

COMMON SENSE BRACKETT (1916)
(6 r.) lp, William Frederick, William J. Sorelle, John E. Mackin, Barbara Gilroy

COMMON SIN, THE (1920)
(6 r.) d, Burton King; lp, Grace Darling, Rod La Rocque, Anders Randolf, Virginia Valli

COMMUTORS, THE (1915)
(5 r.) d, George Fitzmaurice; lp, Irene Fenwick, Charles Judels, George Le Guere, Della Connor

COMPANIONATE MARRIAGE, THE (1928)
(7 r.) d, Erle C. Kenton; lp, Betty Bronson, Alec B. Francis, William Welsh, Edward Martindel

COMPASSION (1927)
(6 r.) d, Victor Adamson; lp, Gaston Glass, Alma Bennett, Josef Swickard, J. Frank Glendon

COMRADE JOHN (1915)
(5 r.) d, T. Hayes Hunter; lp, William Elliott, Ruth Roland, Lewis [Lew] J. Cody

COMRADES (1928)
(6 r.) d, Cliff Wheeler; lp, Donald Keith, Helene Costello, Gareth Hughes, Lucy Beaumont

COMRADESHIP (1919, Brit.)
(6 r.) d, Maurice Elvey; lp, Lily Elsie, Gerald Ames, Guy Newall, Dallas Cairns

CONCEALED TRUTH, THE (1915)
(5 r.) d, Ivan Abramson; lp, Gertrude Robinson, James Cooley, Frank de Vernon, Sue Balfour

CONCEIT (1921)
(5 r.) d, Burton George; lp, William B. Davidson, Hedda Hopper, Charles Gerard, Betty Hilburn

CONCERT, THE (1921)
(6 r.) d, Victor Schertzinger; lp, Lewis S. Stone, Myrtle Stedman, Raymond Hatton, Julienne Scott

CONDEMNED (1923)
(6 r.) d, Arthur Rosson; lp, Mildred Davis, Carl Miller

CONDUCTOR 1492 (1924)
(7 r.) d, Charles Hines, Frank Griffin; lp, Johnny Hines, Doris May, Dan Mason, Ruth Renick

CONEY ISLAND (1928)
(7 r.) d, Ralph Ince; lp, Lois Wilson, Lucilla Mendez, Eugene Strong, Rudolph Cameron

CONEY ISLAND PRINCESS, A (1916)
(5 r.) d, Dell Henderson; lp, Irene Fenwick, Owen Moore, Eva Francis, Clifford B. Gray

CONFESSION (1918)
(5 r.) d, S.A. Franklin; lp, Jewel Carmen, Fred Warren, L.C. Shumway, Jack Bramall

CONFESSION, THE (1920)
(7 r.) d, Bertram Bracken; lp, Henry B. Walthall, Francis McDonald, William Clifford, Margaret McWade

CONFESSIONS (1925, Brit.)
(6 r.) d, W.P. Kellino; lp, Ian Hunter, Joan Lockton, Eric Bransby Williams, Fred Raynham

CONFESSIONS OF A QUEEN (1925)
(7 r.) d, Victor Seastrom; lp, Alice Terry, Lewis Stone, John Bowers, Eugenie Besserer

CONFESSIONS OF A WIFE (1928)
(6 r.) d, Albert Kelly; lp, Helene Chadwick, Arthur Clayton, Ethel Grey Terry, Walter McGrail

CONFETTI (1927, Brit.)
(6 r.) d, Graham Cutts; lp, Jack Buchanan, Annette Benson, Sydney Fairbrother, Robin Irvine

CONFIDENCE (1922)
(5 r.) d, Harry Pollard; lp, Herbert Rawlinson, Harriet Hammond, Lincoln Plummer, William A. Carroll

CONFIDENCE MAN, THE (1924)
(8 r.) d, Victor Heerman; lp, Thomas Meighan, Virginia Valli, Laurence Wheat, Charles Dow Clark

CONFLICT, THE (1916)
(5 r.) d, Ralph Ince; lp, Lucille Lee Stewart, Jane Mortimer, Huntley Gordon, William Lytell, Jr.

CONGESTION (1918, USSR)
(5 r.) d, Alexander Panteleyev; lp, I. Lersky, Dmitri Leshchenko

CONJURE WOMAN, THE (1926)
(? r.) Evelyn Preer, Percy Verwayen

CONQUERING THE WOMAN (1922)
(6 r.) d, King Vidor; lp, Florence Vidor, Bert Sprotte, Mathilde Brundage, David Butler

CONQUEROR, THE (1916)
(5 r.) d, Reginald Barker; lp, Willard Mack, Enid Markey, J. Barney Sherry, Louise Brownell

CONQUEROR, THE (1917)
(10 r.) d, R.(Raoul) A. Walsh; lp, William Farnum, Jewel Carmen, Charles Clary, James A. Marcus

CONQUEST OF CANAAN, THE (1921)
(7 r.) d, Roy William Neill; lp, Thomas Meighan, Doris Kenyon, Diana Allen, Ann Egleston

CONQUEST OF THE CAUCASUS (1913, USSR)
(8 r.) d, L. Chorny, S. Esadze; lp, V. Guniya, N. Eristov, D. Chavchavadze

CONRAD IN QUEST OF HIS YOUTH (1920)
(5 r.) d, William C. De Mille; lp, Thomas Meighan, Kathlyn Williams, Mabel Van Buren, Mayme Kelso

CONSCIENCE (1915)
(4 r.) d, Stuart Paton; lp, Allen Holubar, Frances Nelson, William Welsh, William Bailey

CONSCIENCE (1917)
(6 r.) d, Bertram Bracken; lp, Gladys Brockwell, Marjorie Daw, Eugenie Forde, Eve Southern

CONSCIENCE OF JOHN DAVID, THE (1916)
(5 r.) lp, Crane Wilbur, Alice Rinaldo, Frederick Montague, John Oaker

CONSTANT NYMPH, THE (1928, Brit.)
(11 r.) d, Adrian Brunel; lp, Ivor Novello, Mabel Poulton, Frances Doble, Mary Clare

CONTINENTAL GIRL, A (1915)
(5 r.) d, Joseph Adelman; lp, May Ward, George Harcourt, William Sorell, Olaf Skavlan

CONTRABAND (1925)
(7 r.) d, Alan Crosland; lp, Lois Wilson, Noah Beery, Raymond Hatton, Raymond McKee

CONVICT KING, THE (1915)
(4 r.) d, Edward Sloman; lp, Melvin Mayo, Jay Morley, George Routh, L.C. Shumway

CONVICT 993 (1918)
(5 r.) d, William Parke; lp, Irene Castle, Harry Benham, Warner Oland, J.H. Gilmour

CONVICT 99 (1919, Brit.)
(6 r.) d, G.B. Samuelson; lp, Daisy Burrell, Wee Georgie Wood, Ernest A. Graham, Wyndham Guise

COOK OF CANYON CAMP, THE (1917)
(5 r.) d, Donald Crisp; lp, George Beban, Florence Vidor, Monroe Salisbury, Helen Jerome Eddy

COP, THE (1928)
(8 r.) d, Donald Crisp; lp, William Boyd, Alan Hale, Jacqueline Logan, Robert Armstrong

COPPERHEAD, THE (1920)
(7 r.) d, Charles Maigne; lp, Lionel Barrymore, Doris Rankin, William T. Carleton, Frank Joyner

COQUETTE, THE (1915)
(4 r.) lp, Rhea Martin, Henry Hallam, James Cooley, Joseph Sullivan

CORA (1915)
(5 r.) d, Edwin Carewe; lp, Emily Stevens

CORAL (1915)
(4 r.) d, Henry McRae; lp, Marie Walcamp, Wellington Playter

CORDELIA THE MAGNIFICENT (1923)
(7 r.) d, George Archainbaud; lp, Clara Kimball Young, Huntley Gordon, Carol Halloway, Lloyd Whitlock

CO-RESPONDENT, THE (1917)
(6 r.) d, Ralph Ince; lp, Elaine Hammerstein, Wilfred Lucas, George Anderson, Robert Cain

CORINTHIAN JACK (1921, Brit.)
(5 r.) d, Walter Courtenay Rowden; lp, Victor McLaglen, Kathleen Vaughn, Warwick Ward, Dorothy Fane

CORNER, THE (1916)
(5 r.) d, Walter Edwards; lp, Willard Mack, George Fawcett, Clara Williams, Louise Brownell

CORNER GROCER, THE (1917)
(5 r.) d, George Cowl; lp, Lew Fields, Madge Evans, Lillian Cook, Nick Long, Jr.

CORNER IN COTTON, A (1916)
(5 r.) d, Fred J. Balshofer, Howard Truesdell lp, Marguerite Snow, Frank Dayton, Zella Call, Howard Truesdell

CORNER MAN, THE (1921, Brit.)
(5 r.) d, Einar J. Bruun; lp, Ida Lambert, Eric Barclay, Sidney Folker, A. Harding Steerman

CORNERED (1924)
(7 r.) d, William Beaudine; lp, Marie Prevost, Rockliffe Fellowes, Raymond Hatton, John Roche

CORRUPTION (1917)
(6 r.) d, Jack Gorman;

CORSAIR, THE (1914)
(4 r.) d, Edward Jose; lp, Crane Wilbur

CORSICAN BROTHERS, THE (1920)
(6 r.) d, Colin Campbell; lp, Dustin Farnum, Wedgewood Nowell, Winifred Kingston, Will Machin

COSSACK WHIP, THE (1916)
(5 r.) d, John H. Collins; lp, Viola Dana, Richard Tucker, Grace Williams, Robert Walker

COSSACKS, THE (1928)
(10 r.) d, George Hill; lp, John Gilbert, Renee Adoree, Ernest Torrence, Nils Asther

COST OF BEAUTY, THE (1924, Brit.)
(6 r.) d, Walter Summers; lp, Betty Ross Clarke, Lewis Dayton, James Lindsay, Tom Reynolds

COST OF HATRED, THE (1917)
(5 r.) d, George Melford; lp, Kathlyn Williams, Tom Forman, Theodore Roberts, Jack W. Johnson

COTTON AND CATTLE (1921)
(5 r.) d, Leonard Franchon; lp, Al Hart, Jack Mower, Robert Conville, Edna Davies

COUNSEL FOR THE DEFENSE (1925)
(7 r.) d, Burton King; lp, Jay Hunt, Betty Compson, House Peters, Rockliffe Fellowes

COUNT OF LUXEMBOURG, THE (1926)
(7 r.) d, Arthur Gregor; lp, George Walsh, Helen Lee Worthing, Michael Dark, Charles Requa

COUNT OF MONTE CRISTO, THE (1913)
(5 r.) d, Edwin S. Porter, Joseph Golden; lp, James O'Neill, Murdock McQuarrie, Nance O'Neill

COUNT OF TEN, THE (1928)
(6 r.) d, James Flood; lp, Charles Ray, James Gleason, Jobyna Ralston, Edythe Chapman

COUNTERFEIT LOVE (1923)
(6 r.) d, Roy Sheldon, Ralph Ince; lp, Joe King, Marian Swayne, Norma Lee, Jack Richardson

COUNTESS CHARMING, THE (1917)
(5 r.) d, Donald Crisp; lp, Julian Eltinge, Florence Vidor, Edythe Chapman, Billy Elmer

COUNTRY BEYOND, THE (1926)
(6 r.) d, Irving Cummings; lp, Olive Borden, Ralph Graves, Gertrude Astor, J. Farrell MacDonald

COUNTRY BOY, THE (1915)
(5 r.) d, Frederick Thomson; lp, Marshall Neilan, Florence Dagmar, Dorothy Green, Loyola O'Connor

COUNTRY COUSIN, THE (1919)
(5 r.) d, Alan Crosland; lp, Elaine Hammerstein, Lumsden Hare, Bigelow Cooper, Walter McGrail

COUNTRY DOCTOR, THE (1927)
(8 r.) d, Rupert Julian; lp, Rudolph Schildkraut, Junior Coghlan, Sam De Grasse, Virginia Bradford

COUNTRY FLAPPER, THE (1922)
(5 r.) d, F. Richard Jones; lp, Dorothy Gish, Glenn Hunter, Mildred Marsh, Harlan Knight

COUNTRY THAT GOD FORGOT, THE (1916)
(5 r.) d, Marshall Neilan; lp, Thomas Santschi, Mary Charleson, George Fawcett, Will Machin

COUNTY FAIR, THE (1920)
(5 r.) d, Maurice Tourner, Edmund Mortimer; lp, Edythe Chapman, David Butler, Wesley Barry, Helen Jerome Eddy

COUPLE OF DOWN AND OUTS, A (1923, Brit.)
(6 r.) d, G.B. Samuelson; lp, Rex Davis, Edna Best, George Foley, Philip Hewland

COUPLE ON THE MOVE, A (1928, Jap.)
(? r.) d, Yasujiro Ozu

COURAGE (1924)
(5 r.) d, J.P. McGowan; lp, Franklyn Farnum, Dorothy Wood

COURAGE AND THE MAN (1915)
(4 r.) d, Edgar Jones; lp, Edgar Jones, Justina Huff, Arthur Mathews, Louis Mortelle

COURAGE FOR TWO (1919)
(5 r.) d, Dell Henderson; lp, Carlyle Blackwell, Evelyn Greeley, Rosina Henley, Henry West

COURAGE OF MARGE O'DOONE, THE (1920)
(7 r.) d, David Smith; lp, Pauline Starke, Niles Welch, George Stanley, Jack Curtis

COURAGE OF SILENCE, THE (1917)
(5 r.) d, William P.S. Earle; lp, Alice Joyce, Harry T. Morey, Willie Johnson, Mildred May

COURAGE OF THE COMMONPLACE (1917)
(5 r.) d, Ben Turbett; lp, Leslie Austin, William Calhoun, Mildred Havens, Lucia Moore

COURAGE OF WOLFHEART (1925)
(5 r.) lp, Big Boy Williams, Wolfheart (a dog)

COURAGEOUS COWARD, THE (1919)
(5 r.) d, William Worthington; lp, Sessue Hayakawa, Tsuru Aoki, Toyo Fujita, George Hernandez

COURAGEOUS COWARD, THE (1924)
(5 r.) d, Paul Hurst; lp, Jack Meehan, Jackie Saunders, Mary MacLaren, Earl Metcalf

COURAGEOUS FOOL (1925)
(5 r.) lp, Reed Howes

COURTESAN, THE (1916)
(5 r.) d, Arthur Maude; lp, Eugenie Forde, Hal Cooley, Al Fordyce, Nell Franzen

COURT-MARTIAL (1928)
(7 r.) d, George B. Seitz; lp, Jack Holt, Betty Compson, Pat Harmon, Doris Hill

COURT-MARTIALED (1915)
(4 r.) d, Stuart Paton; lp, Al Holubar, Frances Nelson, Hobart Henley, Lydia Knott

COUSIN KATE (1921)
(5 r.) d, Mrs. Sidney Drew; lp, Alice Joyce, Gilbert Emery, Beth Martin, Inez Shannon

COUSIN PONS (1924, Fr.)
(? r.) d, Jacques Robert

COUSINE DE FRANCE (1927, Fr.)
(? r.) d, Gaston Roudes

COVE OF MISSING MEN (1918)
(5 r.) d, Frederick Sullivan; lp, Edward Cecil, Boris Korlin, Leo Pierson, J. Frank Glendon

COVERED WAGON TRAILS (1930)
(5 r.) d, J.P. McGowan; lp, Bob Custer, Phyllis Bainbride, Perry Murdock, Charles Brinley

COWARD, THE (1914, USSR)
(5 r.) d, R. Ungern, Boris Glagolin; lp, I. Uralov, Glagolin, Y. Timme

COWARD, THE (1915)
(6 r.) d, Reginald Barker; lp, Frank Keenan, Charles Ray, Gertrude Claire, Margaret Gibson

COWARDICE COURT (1919)
(5 r.) d, William C. Dowlan; lp, Peggy Hyland, Jack Livingston, Arthur Hoyt, Kathryn Adams

COWBOY ACE, A (1921)
(5 r.) d, Leonard Franchon; lp, Al Hart, Jack Mower, Robert Conville, Ethel Dwyer

COWBOY AND THE COUNTESS, THE (1926)
(6 r.) d, Roy William Neill; lp, Buck Jones, Helen D'Algy, Diana Miller, Harvey Clark

COWBOY AND THE FLAPPER, THE (1924)
(5 r.) d, Alvin J. Neitz; lp, William Fairbanks, Dorothy Revier, Jack Richardson, Milton Ross

COWBOY AND THE LADY, THE (1915)
(5 r.)

COWBOY AND THE LADY, THE (1922)
(5 r.) d, Charles Maigne; lp, Mary Miles Minter, Tom Moore, Viora Daniels, Patricia Palmer

COWBOY AND THE OUTLAW, THE (1929)
(5 r.) d, J.P. McGowan; lp, Bob Steele, Edna Aslin, Bud Osborne, Thomas G. Lingham

COWBOY CAVALIER, THE (1928)
(5 r.) d, Richard Thorpe; lp, Buddy Roosevelt, Olive Hasbrouck, Charles K. French, Fannie Midgley

COWBOY CAVALIER (1929)
(5 r.) lp, Montana Bill

COWBOY COP, THE (1926)
(5 r.) d, Robert De Lacy; lp, Tom Tyler, Jean Arthur, Irvin Renard, Frankie Darro

COWBOY COURAGE (1925)
(5 r.) d, Robert J. Horner; lp, Kit Carson, Pauline Curley, Gordon Sackville

COWBOY GRIT (1925)
(5 r.) lp, Pete Morrison

COWBOY KID, THE (1928)
(5 r.) d, Clyde Carruth; lp, Rex Bell, Mary Jane Temple, Brooks Benedict, Alice Belcher

COWBOY KING, THE (1922)
(5 r.) d, Charles R. Seeling; lp, Big Boy Williams, Patricia Palmer, Elizabeth De Witt, William Austin

COWBOY MUSKETEER, THE (1925)
(5 r.) d, Robert De Lacy; lp, Tom Tyler, Jim London, Frances Dare, David Dunbar

COWBOY PRINCE, THE (1924)
(5 r.) d, Francis Ford; lp, Ashton Dearholt

COWBOY PRINCE, THE (1930)
(5 r.) lp, Cheyenne Bill

COYOTE FANGS (1924)
(5 r.) d, Harry Webb; lp, Jack Perrin, Josephine Hill

CRACK O'DAWN (1925)
(5 r.) d, Albert Rogell; lp, Reed Howes, J.P. McGowan, Ruth Dwyer, Henry A. Barrows

CRACKERJACK, THE (1925)
(7 r.) d, Charles Hines; lp, Johnny Hines, Sigrid Holmquist, Henry West, Bradley Barker

CRADLE OF COURAGE, THE (1920)
(5 r.) d, Lambert Hillyer; lp, William S. Hart, Ann Little, Thomas Santschi, Gertrude Claire

CRADLE OF THE WASHINGTONS, THE (1922)
(4 r.)

CRADLE SNATCHERS, THE (1927)
(7 r.) d, Howard Hawks; lp, Louise Fazenda, J. Farrell MacDonald, Ethel Wales, Franklin Pangborn

CRAINQUEBILLE (1922, Fr.)
(6 r.) d, Jacques Feyder; lp, Maurice de Feraudy, Jean Forest, Felix Oudart, Jeanne Cheiral

CRASH, THE (1928)
(8 r.) d, Eddie Cline; lp, Milton Sills, Thelma Todd, Wade Boteler, William Demarest

CRASHIN' THROUGH (1924)
(5 r.) d, Alvin J. Neitz; lp, Jack Perrin, Jack Richardson, Steve Clements, Dick La Reno

CRASHING COURAGE (1923)
(5 r.) d, Harry Moody; lp, Edith Hall, Jack Livingston

CRASHING THROUGH (1928)
(5 r.) d, Thomas Buckingham; lp, Jack Padjan, Sally Rand, William Eugene, Buster Gardner

CRAVING, THE (1916)
(5 r.) d, Charles Bartlett; lp, William Russell, Charlotte Burton, Helene Rosson, Rea Berger

CRAZY PAGE, A (1926, Jap.)
(4 r.) d, Teinosuke Kinguasa; lp, Masao Inoue, Yoshie Nakagawa, Ayako Iijima, Hiroshi Nemoto

CRAZY RAY, THE
(SEE: PARIS QUI DORT, 1924)

CREAKING STAIRS (1919)
(6 r.) d, Rupert Julian; lp, Mary MacLaren, Herbert Prior, Jack Mulhall, Clarissa Selwynne

CREPUSCULE D'EPOUVANTE (1921, Fr.)
(? r.) d, Henri Etievant

CRICKET, THE (1917)
(5 r.) d, Elsie Jane Wilson; lp, Zoe Rae, Rena Rogers, Fred Ward, Harry Holden

CRICKET ON THE HEARTH, THE (1923)
(7 r.) d, Lorimer Johnston; lp, Josef Swickward, Fritzi Ridgeway, Paul Gerson, Virginia Brown Faire

CRIME AND PUNISHMENT (1913, USSR)
(? r.) d, I. Vronsky; lp, Pavel Orlenev, Vronsky, M. Nesterova, V. Zimovoy

CRIME AND PUNISHMENT (1929, Ger.)
(6 r.) d, Robert Weine; lp, Gregor Chmara, Michael Tarshanoff, Maria Germanova, Maria Kryshanovskia

CRIME AND THE PENALTY (1916, Brit.)
(4 r.) d, R. Harley West; lp, Alesia Leon, Jack Lovatt, Louis Nanten

CRIME OF THE HOUR (1918)
(7 r.) d, Thomas H. Ricketts; lp, Edward Coxen, Vivian Rich

CRIMINAL, THE (1916)
(5 r.) d, Reginald Barker; lp, Clara Williams, William Desmond, Enid Willis, Joseph J. Dowling

CRIMSON CANYON, THE (1928)
(5 r.) d, Ray Taylor; lp, Ted Wells, Lotus Thompson, Wilbur Mack, Buck Connors

CRIMSON CIRCLE, THE (1922, Brit.)
(5 r.) d, George Ridgwell; lp, Madge Stuart, Rex Davis, Fred Groves, Clifton Boyne

CRIMSON CLUE (1922)
(5 r.) lp, Jack Richardson, Josephine Sedgwick

CRIMSON CROSS, THE (1921)
(5 r.) d, George Everett; lp, Van Dyke Brooks, Edward Langford, Marian Swayne, Eulalie Jensen

CRIMSON GARDENIA, THE (1919)
(6 r.) d, Reginald Barker; lp, Owen Moore, Hedda Nova, Tully Marshall, Hector V. Sarno

CRIMSON GOLD (1923)
(5 r.) d, Clifford S. Elfelt; lp, J.B. Warner, Edith Sterling, Martha McKay, George Burrell

CRIMSON SHOALS (1919)
(5 r.) d, Francis Ford; lp, Francis Ford, Pete Gerald, Eda Emerson, Martha Dean

CRIMSON SKULL, THE (1921)
(6 r.) lp, Anita Bush, Lawrence Chenault, Bill Pickett, Steve Reynolds

CRIMSON WING, THE (1915)
(6 r.) d, E.H. Calvert; lp, E.H. Calvert, Ruth Stonehouse, Beverly Bayne, Bryant Washburn

CRIPPLED HAND, THE (1916)
(5 r.) d, Robert Leonard, David Kirkland; lp, Robert Leonard, Ella Hall, Marc Robbins, Gladys Brockwell

CRISIS, THE (1915)
(12 r.) d, Colin Campbell; lp, Tom Santschi, Bessie Eyton, Sam Drane

CROOK OF DREAMS (1919)
(5 r.) d, Oscar Apfel; lp, Louise Huff, Frank Mayo, Virginia Hammond, Florence Billings

CROOKED ALLEY (1923)
(5 r.) d, Robert F. Hill; lp, Thomas Carrigan, Laura La Plante, Tom S. Guise, Owen Gorine

CROOKED ROMANCE, A (1917)
(5 r.) d, William Parke; lp, Gladys Hulette, Paul Clerget, J.H. Gilmour, William Parke, Jr.

CROOKED STRAIGHT (1919)
(5 r.) d, Jerome Storm; lp, Charles Ray, Margery Wilson, Wade Boteler, Gordon Mullen

CROOKS CAN'T WIN (1928)
(7 r.) d, George M. Arthur; lp, Ralph Lewis, Thelma Hill, Sam Nelson, Joe Brown

CROOK'S ROMANCE, A (1921)
(5 r.) lp, Helen Holmes, J.P. McGowan

CROOKY (1915)
(5 r.) d, C. Jay Williams; lp, Frank Daniels, Evart Overton, Harry T. Morey, Anna Laughlin

CROSS BEARER, THE (1918)
(8 r.) d, George Archainbaud; lp, Montagu Love, Jeanne Eagels, Anthony Merlo, George Morgan

CROSS CURRENTS (1916)
(5 r.) d, Francis Grandon; lp, Helen Ware, Teddy Sampson, Courtenay Foote, Sam De Grasse

CROSS ROADS (1922)
(5 r.) d, Francis Ford; lp, Franklyn Farnum, Shorty Hamilton, Al Hart, Genevieve Bert

CROSSED SIGNALS (1926)
(5 r.) d, J.P. McGowan; lp, Helen Holmes, Henry Victor, Georgie Chapman, William Lowery

CROSSED TRAILS (1924)
(5 r.) d, J.P. McGowan; lp, Franklyn Farnum, William Buehler, V.L. Barnes, Mack V. Wright

CROSSED WIRES (1923)
(5 r.) d, King Baggot; lp, Gladys Walton, George Stewart, Tom S. Guise, Lillian Langdon

CROSSROADS
(SEE: CROSSWAYS, 1928, Jap.)

CROSSROADS OF NEW YORK, THE (1922)
(6 r.) d, F. Richard Jones; lp, George O'Hara, Noah Beery, Ethel Grey Terry, Ben Deely

CROSSWAYS (1928, Jap.)
(6 r.) d, Teinosuke Kingugasa; lp, Junosuke Bando, Akiko Chihaya, Yukiko Ogawa, J. Soma

CROQUETTE (1927, Fr.)
(? r.) d, Louis Mercanton

CROWDED HOUR, THE (1925)
(7 r.) d, E. Mason Hopper; lp, Bebe Daniels, Kenneth Harlan, T. Roy Barnes, Frank Morgan

CROWN JEWELS (1918)
(5 r.) d, Roy Clements; lp, Claire Anderson, Joe Bennett, Lillian Langdon, Frank Lee

CROWN OF LIES, THE (1926)
(5 r.) d, Dimitri Buchowetski; lp, Pola Negri, Noah Berry, Robert Ames, Charles A. Post

CROWN OF THORNS (1934, Ger.)
(6 r.) d, Robert Wiene; lp, Gregori Chimara, Henny Porten, Asta Nielsen, Werner Krauss

CROWN PRINCE'S DOUBLE, THE (1916)
(5 r.) d, Van Dyke Brooke; lp, Maurice Costello, Norma Talmadge, Howard Hall, Anders Randolf

CROW'S NEST, THE (1922)
(5 r.) d, Paul Hurst; lp, Jack Hoxie, Ruddel Weatherwax, Evelyn Nelson, Tom Lingham

CROXLEY MASTER, THE (1921, Brit.)
(4 r.) d, Percy Nash; lp, Dick Webb, Dora Lennox, Jack Stanley, Joan Ritz

CRUCIAL TEST, THE (1916)
(5 r.) d, Robert Thornby, John Ince; lp, Kitty Gordon, Niles Welch, J. Herbert Frank, William Cohill

CRUCIBLE, THE (1914)
(5 r.) d, Edwin S. Porter, Hugh Ford; lp, Marguerite Clark, Harold Lockwood, Justine Johnston, Lucy Parker

CRUCIBLE OF LIFE, THE (1918)
(7 r.) d, Harry Lambart; lp, Grace Darmond, Frank O'Connor, Jack Sherill, Winifred Harris

CRUCIFIX OF DESTINY, THE (1920)
(6 r.) d, R. Dale Armstrong;

CRUEL TRUTH, THE (1927)
(6 r.) d, Phil Rosen; lp, Hedda Hooper, Constance Howard, Hugh Allan, Frances Raymond

CRUISE OF THE HELLION, THE (1927)
(7 r.) d, Duke Worne; lp, Donald Keith, Edna Murphy, Tom Santschi, Sheldon Lewis

CRUISE OF THE JASPER B, THE (1926)
(6 r.) d, James W. Horne; lp, Rod La Rocque, Mildred Harris, Jack Ackroyd, Snitz Edwards

CRUISE OF THE MAKE-BELIEVES, THE (1918)
(5 r.) d, George Melford; lp, Lila Lee, Harrison Ford, Raymond Hatton, William Brunton

CRUISKEEN LAWN (1922, Brit.)
(5 r.) d, John MacDonagh; lp, Tom Moran, Kathleen Armstrong, Jimmy O'Dea, Fred Jeffs

CRUSADE OF THE INNOCENT (1922)
(5 r.)

CRUSADER, THE (1922)
(5 r.) d, Howard M. Mitchell; lp, William Rusell, Gertrude Claire, Helen Ferguson, Fritzi Brunette

CRUSADERS OF THE WEST (1930)
(5 r.) lp, Cliff [Tex] Lyons

CRY FOR JUSTICE, THE (1919, Brit.)
(5 r.) d, A.G. Frenguelli; lp, Amy Brandon Thomas, Norman Page, Mary Glynne, Geoffrey Wilmer

CRY OF THE WEAK, THE (1919)
(5 r.) d, George Fitzmaurice; lp, Fannie Ward, Frank Elliott, Walt Whitman, Paul Willis

CRYSTAL GAZER, THE (1917)
(5 r.) d, George Melford; lp, Fannie Ward, Jack Dean, Winnifred Greenwood, Harrison Ford

CUP OF FURY, THE (1920)
(5 r.) d, T. Hayes Hunter; lp, Helene Chadwick, Rockcliffe Fellowes, Frank Leigh, Clarissa Selwynne

CUP OF LIFE, THE (1915)
(5 r.) d, Raymond B. West; lp, Bessie Barriscale, Enid Markey, Charles Ray, Frank Borzage

CUP OF LIFE, THE (1921)
(6 r.) d, Rowland V. Lee; lp, Hobart Bosworth, Madge Bellamy, Niles Welch, Tully Marshall

CUPID FORECLOSES (1919)
(5 r.) d, David Smith; lp, Bessie Love, Wallace McDonald, Frank Hayes, Dorothea Wolbert

CUPID IN CLOVER (1929, Brit.)
(6 r.) d, Frank Miller; lp, Betty Siddons, Eric Findon, Herbert Langley, Charles Garry

CUPID, THE COWPUNCHER (1920)
(5 r.) d, Clarence G. Badger; lp, Will Rogers, Helene Chadwick, Andrew Robson, Lloyd Whitlock

CUPID'S BRAND (1921)
(6 r.) d, Rowland V. Lee; lp, Jack Hoxie, Wilbur McGaugh, Charles Force, Mignon Anderson

CUPID'S FIREMAN (1923)
(5 r.) d, William A. Wellman; lp, Charles Jones, Marian Nixon, Brooks Benedict, Eileen O'Malley

CUPID'S KNOCKOUT (1926)
(5 r.) d, Bruce Mitchell; lp, Frank Merrill, Andree Tourneur, Donald Fullen, Marco Charles

CUPID'S ROUND-UP (1918)
(5 r.) d, Edward J. LeSaint; lp, Tom Mix, Wanda Petit, E.B. Tilton, Roy Watson

CUPID'S RUSTLER (1924)
(5 r.) d, Francis Ford; lp, Edmund Cobb, Florence Gilbert, Clark Coffey, Ashton Dearholt

CURIOUS CONDUCT OF JUDGE LEGARDE, THE (1915)
(5 r.) d, Will Davis; lp, Lionel Barrymore, Edna Pendelton, William H. Tooker, Arthur Morrison

CURLYTOP (1924)
(6 r.) d, Maurice Elvey; lp, Shirley Mason, Wallace MacDonald, Warner Oland, Diana Miller

CURSE OF EVE, THE (1917)
(7 r.) d, Frank Beal; lp, Enid Markey, Ed Coxen, Jack Standing, Grace Thompson

CURSE OF GREED, THE (1914, Fr.)
(4 r.) d, Georges Melies

CURSE OF IKU, THE (1918)
(7 r.) d, Frank Borzage; lp, Frank Borzage, Tsuru Aoki, Thomas Kurihara

CURSED MILLIONS (1917, USSR)
(8 r.) d, Yakov Protazanov; lp, A. Gribunina, Nikolai Rimsky, V. Charova, Z. Valevskaya

CURTAIN (1920)
(5 r.) d, James Young; lp, Katherine MacDonald, Edwin B. Tilton, Earl Whitlock, Charles Richman

CUSTARD CUP, THE (1923)
(7 r.) d, Herbert Brenon; lp, Mary Carr, Myrta Bonillas, Miriam Battista, Jerry Devine

CUSTER'S LAST FIGHT (1925)
(5 r.) p, Thomas H. Ince

CUSTOMARY TWO WEEKS, THE (1917)
(4 r.) d, Saul Harrison; lp, Craig Ward, Herbert Evans, Robert Ellis, Joseph Burke

CY WHITTAKER'S WARD (1917)
(5 r.) d, Ben Turbett; lp, Shirley Mason, William Wadsworth, William Burton, Carter Harkness

CYCLE OF FATE, THE (1916)
(5 r.) d, Marshall Neilan; lp, Bessie Eyton, Wheeler Oakman, Edith Johnson, Frank Clark

CYCLONE BLISS (1921)
(5 r.) d, Francis Ford; lp, Jack Hoxie, Frederick Moore, Evelyn Nelson, Fred Kohler

CYCLONE BOB (1926)
(5 r.) d, J.P. McGowan; lp, Bob Reeves, Tex Starr, D. Maley, Alma Rayford

CYCLONE BUDDY (1924)
(5 r.) d, Alvin J. Neitz; lp, Buddy Roosevelt, Norma Conterno, Alfred Hewston, Bud Osborne

CYCLONE CAVALIER (1925)
(5 r.) d, Albert Rogell; lp, Reed Howes, Carmelita Geraghty, Wilfred Lucas, Eric Mayne

CYCLONE COWBOY, THE (1927)
(5 r.) d, Richard Thorpe; lp, Wally Wales, Violet Bird, Raye Hampton, Richard Lee

CYCLONE HIGGINS, D.D. (1918)
(5 r.) d, W. Christy Cabanne; lp, Francis X. Bushman, Beverly Bane, Baby Ivy Ward, Charles Fang

CYCLONE JONES (1923)
(5 r.) d, Charles R. Seeling; lp, Big Boy Williams, Bill Patton, J.P. McKee, Kathleen Collins

CYCLONE RIDER, THE (1924)
(7 r.) d, Thomas Buckingham; lp, Reed Howes, Alma Bennett, William Bailey, Margaret McWade

CYNTHIA IN THE WILDERNESS (1916, Brit.)
(4 r.) d, Harold Weston; lp, Eve Balfour, Ben Webster, Milton Webster, Milton Rosmer

CYNTHIA-OF-THE-MINUTE (1920)
(6 r.) d, Perry Vekroff; lp, Leah Baird, Hugh Thompson, Burr McIntosh, Alexander Gaden

CYTHEREA (1924)
(? r.) d, George Fitzmaurice; lp, Lewis Stone, Constance Bennett, Irene Rich, Alma Rubens

DADDIES (1924)
(7 r.) d, William A. Seiter; lp, Mae Marsh, Harry Myers, Claude Gillingwater, Craufurd Kent

DADDY (1917, Brit.)
(5 r.) d, Thomas Bentley; lp, Langhorne Burton, Peggy Kurton, William Lugg, M.R. Morand

DADDY'S GIRL (1918)
(5 r.) d, William Bertram; lp, Marie Osborne, Marion Warner, Lewis J. Cody, Katherine McLaren

DADDY'S GONE A-HUNTING (1925)
(6 r.) d, Frank Borzage; lp, Alice Joyce, Percy Marmont, Virginia Marshall, Helena D'Algy

DADDY'S LOVE (1922)
(? r.)

DAD'S GIRL (1919)
(5 r.) d, David G. Fischer; lp, Jackie Saunders, Dixie Lee

DAMAGED GOODS (1917)
(7 r.) lp, Richard Bennett

DAMAGED GOODS (1919, Brit.)
(5 r.) d, Alexander Butler; lp, Campbell Gullan, Marjorie Day, J. Fisher White, James Lindsay

DAMAGED HEARTS (1924)
(6 r.) d, T. Hayes Hunter; lp, Mary Carr, Jerry Devine, Helen Rowland, Tyrone Power [Sr.]

DANCE MADNESS (1926)
(7 r.) d, Robert Z. Leonard; lp, Conrad Nagel, Claire Windsor, Douglas Gilmore, Hedda Hopper

DANCE MAGIC (1927)
(7 r.) d, Victor Halperin; lp, Pauline Starke, Ben Lyon, Louis Jordan Bartels, Isabel Elson

DANCER AND THE KING, THE (1914)
(5 r.) d, E. Artaud; lp, Victor Sutherland, Howard Dwight, Marguerita Dwight

DANCER OF BARCELONA (1929, Ger.)
(7 r.) d, Robert Wiene

DANCER OF PARIS, THE (1926)
(7 r.) d, Alfred Santell; lp, Conway Tearle, Dorothy Mackaill, Robert Cain, Henry Vibart

DANCER OF THE NILE, THE (1923)
(6 r.) d, William P.S. Earle; lp, Carmel Myers, Malcolm McGregor, Sam De Grasse, Bertram Grassby

DANCERS, THE (1925)
(7 r.) d, Emmett J. Flynn; lp, George O'Brien, Alma Rubens, Madge Bellamy, Templar Saxe

DANCIN' FOOL, THE (1920)
(5 r.) d, Sam Wood; lp, Wallace Reid, Bebe Daniels, Raymond Hatton, Willis Marks

DANCING CHEAT, THE (1924)
(5 r.) d, Irving Cummings; lp, Herbert Rawlinson, Alice Lake, Robert Walker, Jim Blackwell

DANCING DAYS (1926)
(6 r.) d, Albert Kelley; lp, Helene Chadwick, Forrest Stanley, Gloria Gordon, Lillian Rich

DANCING GIRL, THE (1915)
(5 r.) d, Allan Dwan; lp, Florence Reed, Fuller Mellish, Lorraine Huling, Malcolm Williams

DANGER (1923)
(6 r.) d, Clifford S. Elfelt; lp, J.B. Warner, Lillian Hackett, June La Vere, Edith Sterling

DANGER AHEAD (1921)
(5 r.) d, Rollin Sturgeon; lp, Mary Philbin, James Morrison, Jack Mower, Minna Redman

DANGER AHEAD (1923)
(5 r.) d, William K. Howard; lp, Richard Talmadge, Helen Rosson, J.P. Lockney, David Kirby

DANGER GAME, THE (1918)
(6 r.) d, Harry Pollard; lp, Madge Kennedy, Tom Moore, Paul Doucet, Ned Burton

DANGER GIRL, THE (1926)
(6 r.) d, Edward Dillon; lp, Priscilla Dean, John Bowers, Gustav von Seyffertitz, Cissy Fitzgerald

DANGER, GO SLOW (1918)
(6 r.) d, Robert Z. Leonard; lp, Mae Murray, Jack Mulhall, Lydia Knott, Joseph Girard

DANGER LINE, THE (1924)
(6 r.) d, E.E. Violet; lp, Sessue Hayakawa, Tsuru Aoki, Gina Palerme, Cady Winter

DANGER MAN, THE (1930)
(6 r.) d, Bud Pollard; lp, Charles Hutchinson, Edith Thornton, Virginia Pearson, Sheldon Lewis

DANGER PATH, THE
(SEE: NARROW PATH, THE, 1916)

DANGER PATROL (1928)
(6 r.) d, Duke Worne; lp, William Russell, Virginia Browne Faire, Wheeler Oakman, Rhea Mitchell

DANGER RIDER (1925)
(5 r.) lp, Tom Mix

DANGER QUEST (1926)
(5 r.) d, Harry J. Brown; lp, Reed Howes, Ethel Shannon, J.P. McGowan, David Kirby

DANGER RIDER (1925)
(5 r.) lp, Tom Mix

DANGER RIDER, THE (1928)
(6 r.) d, Henry MacRae; lp, Hoot Gibson, Eugenia Gilbert, Reeves Eason, Monty Montague

DANGER SIGNAL, THE (1925)
(6 r.) d, Erle C. Kenton; lp, Jane Novak, Dorothy Revier, Robert Edeson, Gaston Glass

DANGER SIGNALS (1917)
(7 r.)

DANGER STREET (1928)
(6 r.) d, Ralph Ince; lp, Warner Baxter, Martha Sleeper, Duke Martin, Frank Mills

DANGER TRAIL, THE (1917)
(5 r.) d, Frederick A. Thompson; lp, H.B. Warner, Violet Heming, W. Lawson Butt, Arthur Donaldson

DANGER TRAIL (1928)
(6 r.) d, Noel Mason; lp, Barbara Bedford, Stuart Holmes

DANGER WITHIN (1918)
(5 r.) d, Rea Berger; lp, Zoe Rae, True Boardman, William Carroll, Winnifred Greenwood

DANGER ZONE, THE (1918)
(5 r.) d, Frank Beal; lp, Madlaine Traverse, Thomas Holding, Fritzi Ridgeway, Edward Cecil

DANGER ZONE, THE (1925)
(5 r.) d, Robert N. Bradbury; lp, Kenneth McDonald, Frances Dair, Hal Waters, Bruce Gordon

DANGERS OF THE ENGAGEMENT PERIOD (1929, Ger.)
(? r.) d, Fred Sauer; lp, Willi Forst, Marlene Dietrich, Lotte Lorring, Elza Temary

DANGEROUS ADVENTURE, A (1922)
(7 r.) d, Sam Warner, Jack Warner; lp, Philo McCullough, Grace Darmond, Derelys Perdue, Robert Agnew

DANGEROUS AFFAIR, A (1919)
(5 r.) d, Charles Miller; lp, Herbert Rawlinson, Florence Billings, Stuart Holmes, Maude Hill

DANGEROUS BLONDE, THE (1924)
(5 r.) d, Robert F. Hill; lp, Laura La Plante, Edward Hearn, Arthur Hoyt, Philo McCullough

DANGEROUS BUSINESS (1920)
(5 r.) d, Roy William Neill; lp, Constance Talmadge, Kenneth Harlan, George Fawcett, Mathilde Brundage

DANGEROUS COWARD, THE (1924)
(5 r.) d, Albert Rogell; lp, Fred Thomson, Hazel Keener, Frank Hagney, Andrew Arbuckle

DANGEROUS CURVE AHEAD (1921)
(6 r.) d, E. Mason Hopper; lp, Helene Chadwick, Richard Dix, Maurice B. Flynn, James Neill

DANGEROUS DAYS (1920)
(7 r.) d, Reginald Barker; lp, W. Lawson Butt, Clarissa Selwynne, Rowland Lee, Barbara Castleton

DANGEROUS DUB, THE (1926)
(5 r.) d, Richard Thorpe; lp, Buddy Roosevelt, Peggy Montgomery, Joseph Girard, Fanny Midgley

DANGEROUS DUDE, THE (1926)
(5 r.) d, Harry J. Brown; lp, Reed Howes, Bruce Gordon, Dorothy Dwan, Billy Franey

DANGEROUS FISTS (1925)
(5 r.) lp, Jack Perrin

DANGEROUS FLIRT, THE (1924)
(6 r.) d, Tod Browning; lp, Evelyn Brent, Edward Earle, Sheldon Lewis, Clarissa Selwynne

DANGEROUS FRIENDS (1926)
(6 r.) d, Finis Fox; lp, T. Roy Barnes, Marjorie Gay, Arthur Hoyt, Gertrude Short

DANGEROUS GAME, A (1922)
(5 r.) d, King Baggot; lp, Gladys Walton, Spottiswoode Aitken, Otto Hoffman, Rosa Gore

DANGEROUS HOURS (1920)
(6 r.) d, Fred Niblo; lp, Lloyd Hughes, Barbara Castleton, Claire Du Brey, Jack Richardson

DANGEROUS INNOCENCE (1925)
(7 r.) d, William A. Seiter; lp, Laura La Plante, Eugene O'Brien, Jean Hersholt, Alfred Allen

DANGEROUS LIES (1921, Brit.)
(7 r.) d, Paul Powell; lp, David Powell, Mary Glynne, Minna Gray, Warburton Gamble

DANGEROUS LITTLE DEMON, THE (1922)
(5 r.) d, Clarence G. Badger; lp, Marie Prevost, Jack Perrin, Robert Ellis, Anderson Smith

DANGEROUS MAID, THE (1923)
(8 r.) d, Victor Heerman; lp, Constance Talmadge, Conway Tearle, Morgan Wallace, Charles Gerrard

DANGEROUS MOMENT, THE (1921)
(5 r.) d, Marcel De Sano; lp, Carmel Myers, Lule Warrenton, George Rigas, W.T. Fellows

DANGEROUS MONEY (1924)
(? r.) d, Frank Tuttle; lp, Bebe Daniels, Tom Moore, William Powell, Dolores Cassinelli

DANGEROUS ODDS (1925)
(5 r.) lp, Bill Cody

DANGEROUS PARADISE, THE (1920)
(5 r.) d, William P.S. Earle; lp, Louise Huff, Harry Benham, Templer Saxe

DANGEROUS PASTIME (1922)
(5 r.) d, James W. Horne; lp, Lew Cody, Cleo Ridgely, Elinor Fair, Mrs. Irving Cummings

DANGEROUS PATHS (1921)
(5 r.) d, Duke Worne; lp, Neva Gerber, Ben Wilson, Edith Stayart, Joseph W. Girard

DANGEROUS PLEASURE (1925)
(6 r.) d, Harry Revier; lp, Niles Welch, Dorothy Revier

DANGEROUS TALENT, THE (1920)
(6 r.) d, George L. Cox; lp, Margarita Fischer, Harry Hilliard, Beatrice Van, Harvey Clark

DANGEROUS TOYS (1921)
(7 r.) d, Samuel Bradley; lp, Frank Losee, Marion Elmore, Marguerite Clayton, William Desmond

DANGEROUS TRAFFIC (1926)
(5 r.) d, Bennett Cohn; lp, Francis X. Bushman, Jr., Jack Perrin, Mildred Harris, Tom London

DANGEROUS TRAILS (1923)
(6 r.) d, Alvin J. Neitz; lp, Irene Rich, Tully Marshall, Noah Beery, Allan Penrose

DANGEROUS WATERS (1919)
(5 r.) d, Joseph J. Franz; lp, William Desmond, Marguerite de la Motte, Walter Perry, Ida Lewis

DANIEL BOONE THRU THE WILDERNESS (1926)
(6 r.) d, Frank S. Mattison, Robert N. Bradbury; lp, Roy Stewart, Kathleen Collins

DANIEL DERONDA (1921, Brit.)
(6 r.) d, W.C. Rowden; lp, Reginald Fox, Ann Trevor, Clive Brook, Dorothy Fane

DANS LA RAFALE (1916, Fr.)
(? r.) d, George Lacroix

DANTON
(SEE: ALL FOR A WOMAN, 1921, Ger.)

DARBY AND JOAN (1919, Brit.)
(7 r.) d, Percy Nash; lp, Derwent Hall Caine, Ivy Close, Meggie Albanesi, George Wynne

DAREDEVIL, THE (1918)
(5 r.) d, Francis J. Grandon; lp, Gail Kane, Norman Trevor, W.W. Crimans, Roy Applegate

DAREDEVIL (1919, USSR)
(4 r.) d, M. Narokov, Nikandr Turkin; lp, M. Narokov, Alperov

DAREDEVIL, THE (1920)
(5 r.) d, Tom Mix; lp, Tom Mix, Eva Novak, Charles K. French, L.C. Shumway

DAREDEVIL KATE (1916)
(5 r.) d, Kenean J. Buel; lp, Virginia Pearson, Mary Martin, Kenneth Hunter, Leighton Stark

DARING DANGER (1922)
(5 r.) d, Cliff Smith; lp, Pete Morrison, Esther Ralston, Bill Ryno, Lew Meehan

DARING DAYS (1925)
(5 r.) d, John B. O'Brien; lp, Josie Sedgwick, Edward Hearne, Frederick Cole, Zama Zamoria

DARING DEEDS (1927)
(5 r.) d, Duke Worne; lp, Billy Sullivan, Molly Malone, Earl Metcalfe, Thomas Lingham

DARING HEARTS (1919)
(6 r.) d, Henry Houry; lp, Francis X. Bushman, Beverly Bayne, Arthur Donaldson, Jean Paige

DARING LOVE (1924)
(6 r.) d, Roland G. Edwards; lp, Elaine Hammerstein, Huntly Gordon, Walter Long, Gertrude Astor

DARING OF DIANA, THE (1916)
(5 r.) d, S. Rankin Drew; lp, Anita Stewart, Charles Wellesley, Francis [Frank] Morgan, Anders Randolf

DARING YEARS, THE (1923)
(7 r.) d, Kenneth Webb; lp, Mildred Harris, Charles Emmett Mack, Clara Bow, Mary Carr

DARK ANGEL, THE (1925)
(? r.) d, George Fitzmaurice; lp, Vilma Banky, Ronald Colman, Helen Jerome Eddy, Wyndham Standing

DARK CASTLE, THE (1915, Ger.)
(4 r.) d, Willy Zehn; lp, Eugen Burg, Friedrich Zellnik, Friedrich Kuhne, Hanni Weisse

DARK LANTERN, A (1920)
(5 r.) d, John S. Robertson; lp, Alice Brady, James L. Crane, Reginald Denny, Brandon Hurst

DARK SECRETS (1923)
(6 r.) d, Victor Fleming; lp, Dorothy Dalton, Robert Ellis, Jose Ruben, Ellen Cassidy

DARK SILENCE, THE (1916)
(5 r.) d, Albert Capellani; lp, Clara Kimball Young, Edward T. Langford, Paul Capellani, Barbara Gilroy

DARK STAR, THE (1919)
(6 r.) d, Allan Dwan; lp, Marion Davies, Norman Kerry, Matt Moore, Dorothy Green

DARK SWAN, THE (1924)
(7 r.) d, Millard Webb; lp, Marie Prevost, Monte Blue, Helene Chadwick, John Patrick

DARKENING TRAIL, THE (1915)
(4 r.) d, William S. Hart, Clifford Smith; lp, William S. Hart, Enid Markey, George Fisher, Nona Thomas

DARKEST HOUR, THE (1920)
(5 r.) d, Paul Scardon; lp, Harry T. Morey, Anna Lehr, Jean Paige, George Howard

DARKEST RUSSIA (1917)
(5 r.) d, Travers Vale; lp, Alice Brady, John Bowers, J. Herbert Frank, Norbert Wicki

DARKNESS AND DAYLIGHT (1923)
(? r.) d, Albert Plummer

DARKNESS BEFORE DAWN, THE (1915)
(4 r.) lp, Ethel Clayton, Joseph Kaufman, Earl Matcalfe, William H. Turner

DARLING OF NEW YORK, THE (1923)
(6 r.) d, King Baggot; lp, Baby Peggy Montgomery, Sheldon Lewis, Gladys Brockwell, Pat Hartigan

D'ARTAGNAN (1916)
(5 r.) d, Charles Swickard; lp, Orin Johnson, Dorothy Dalton, Louise Glaum, Rhea Mitchell

DARWIN WAS RIGHT (1924)
(5 r.) d, Lewis Seiler; lp, Nell Brantley, George O'Hara, Stanley Blystone, Dan Mason

DASHING THRU (1925)
(5 r.) lp, Frank Merrill, Kathryn McGuire, James Mason, Emily Gerdes

DAUGHTER ANGELE (1918)
(5 r.) d, William Dowlan; lp, Pauline Starke, Walt Whitman, Myrtle Rishell, Philo McCullough

DAUGHTER OF DAWN, THE (1920)
(6 r.) d, Norbert Myles

DAUGHTER OF DAWN, THE (1924)
(5 r.)

DAUGHTER OF DESTINY (1917)
(6 r.) d, George Irving; lp, Olga Petrova, Thomas Holding, Anders Randolf, Robert Broderick

DAUGHTER OF DEVIL DAN (1921)
(? r.) lp, Irma Harrison, Kempton Greene

DAUGHTER OF ENGLAND, A (1915, Brit.)
(4 r.) d, Leedham Bantock; lp, Marga Rubia Levy, Frank Randall, Frank H. Dane, George Barran

DAUGHTER OF EVE, A (1919, Brit.)
(5 r.) d, Walter West; lp, Violet Hopson, Stewart Rome, Cameron Carr, Ralph Forster

DAUGHTER OF FRANCE, A (1918)
(5 r.) d, Edmund Lawrence; lp, Virginia Pearson, Hugh Thompson, Herbert Evans, George Moss

DAUGHTER OF LUXURY, A (1922)
(5 r.) d, Paul Powell; lp, Agnes Ayres, Tom Gallery, Edith Yorke, Howard Ralston

DAUGHTER OF MACGREGOR, A (1916)
(5 r.) d, Sidney Olcott; lp, Valentine Grant, Sidney Mason, Helen Lindroth, Arda La Croix

DAUGHTER OF MARYLAND, A (1917)
(5 r.) d, John B. O'Brien; lp, Edna Goodrich, William T. Carleton, Helen Strickland, Carl Brickett

DAUGHTER OF THE CITY, A (1915)
(5 r.) d, E.H. Calvert; lp, Marguerite Clayton, E.H. Calvert, John Junior, Camille D'Arcy

DAUGHTER OF THE DON, THE (1917)
(6 r.) d, Henry Kabierske; lp, Hal Cooley, Marie McKeen, V.O. Whitehead, William Ramon Ehfe

DAUGHTER OF THE DON, THE (1918)
(5 r.) lp, Shorty Hamilton

DAUGHTER OF THE GODS, A (1916)
(10 r.) d, Herbert Brenon; lp, Annette Kellermann, Stuart Holmes, Jane Lee, Katherine Lee

DAUGHTER OF THE LAW, A (1921)
(5 r.) d, Jack Conway; lp, Carmel Myers, Jack O'Brien, Fred Kohler, Jack Walters

DAUGHTER OF THE OLD SOUTH, A (1918)
(5 r.) d, Emile Chautard; lp, Pauline Frederick, Pedro De Cordova, Vera Beresford, Rex McDougall

DAUGHTER OF THE PEOPLE, A (1915)
(5 r.) d, J. Searle Dawley; lp, Laura Sawyer, Frederick de Belleville, Robert Broderick

DAUGHTER OF THE POOR, A (1917)
(5 r.) d, Edward Dillon; lp, Bessie Love, Roy Stewart, Max Davidson, Carl Stockdale

DAUGHTER OF THE SIOUX, A (1925)
(5 r.) d, Ben Wilson; lp, Ben Wilson, Neva Gerber, Robert Walker, Fay Adams

DAUGHTER OF THE WEST, A (1918)
(5 r.) d, William Bertram; lp, Marie Osborne, Frank Whitson, Marion Warner, Leota Lorraine

DAUGHTER OF THE WILDS (1917, Brit.)
(4 r.) d, Frank Wilson; lp, Chrissie White

DAUGHTER OF THE WOLF, A (1919)
(5 r.) d, Irvin Willat; lp, Lila Lee, Elliott Dexter, Clarence Geldart, Raymond Hatton

DAUGHTER OF TWO WORLDS, A (1920)
(6 r.) d, James Young; lp, Norma Talmadge, Frank Sheridan, Jack Crosby, William Shea

DAUGHTER OF WAR, A (1917)
(5 r.)

DAUGHTERS OF DESIRE (1929)
(6 r.) d, Burton King; lp, Irene Rich, Richard Tucker, June Nash, Julius Molnar, Jr.

DAUGHTERS OF PLEASURE (1924)
(6 r.) d, William Beaudine; lp, Marie Prevost, Monte Blue, Clara Bow, Edythe Chapman

DAUGHTERS OF THE NIGHT (1924)
(6 r.) d, Elmer Clifton; lp, Orville Caldwell, Alyce Mills, Warner Richmond, Bobbie Perkins

DAUGHTERS OF THE RICH (1923)
(6 r.) d, Louis Gasnier; lp, Miriam Cooper, Gaston Glass, Ethel Shannon, Ruth Clifford

DAVID COPPERFIELD (1913, Brit.)
(8 r.) d, Thomas Bentley; lp, Kenneth Ware, Eric Desmond, Len Bethel, Alma Taylor

DAVID GARRICK (1913, Brit.)
(4 r.) d, Hay Plumb; lp, Charles Wyndham, Mary Moore, Louis Calvert, Chrissie White

DAVID GARRICK (1916)
(5 r.) d, Frank Lloyd; lp, Dustin Farnum, Winifred Kingston, Herbert Standing, Frank Bonn

DAVY CROCKETT (1916)
(5 r.) d, William Desmond Taylor; lp, Dustin Farnum, Winifred Kingston, Harry De Vere, Herbert Standing

DAVY CROCKETT AT THE FALL OF THE ALAMO (1926)
(6 r.) d, Robert North Bradbury; lp, Cullen Landis, Kathryn McGuire, Joe Rickson, Bob Fleming

DAWN (1919)
(6 r.) d, J. Stuart Blackton; lp, Sylvia Breamer, Robert Gordon, Harry Davenport, James Furey

DAWN MAKER, THE (1916)
(5 r.) d, William S. Hart; lp, William S. Hart, Blanche White, William Desmond, J. Frank Burke

DAWN OF A TOMORROW, THE (1924)
(6 r.) d, George Melford; lp, Jacqueline Logan, David Torrence, Raymond Griffith, Roland Bottomley

DAWN OF FREEDOM, THE (1916)
(5 r.) d, Paul Scardon, Theodore Marston; lp, Charles Richman, Arline Pretty, James Morrison, Thomas R. Mills

DAWN OF LOVE, THE (1916)
(5 r.) d, Edwin Carewe; lp, Mabel Taliaferro, Robert W. Frazer, Leslie M. Stowe, Peter Lang

DAWN OF REVENGE (1922)
(5 r.) d, Bernard Sievel; lp, Richard C. Travers, Muriel Kingston, Charles Graham, Florence Foster

DAWN OF THE TRUTH, THE (1920, Brit.)
(5 r.) d, L.C. MacBean; lp, John Gliddon, Helga Jerome, Frederick Sargent, Bernard Vaughn

DAWN OF UNDERSTANDING, THE (1918)
(5 r.) d, David Smith; lp, Bessie Love, Jack Gilbert, Frank Glendon, George A. Williams

DAY DREAMS (1919)
(5 r.) d, Clarence G. Badger; lp, Madge Kennedy, John Bowers, Jere Austin, Alec B. Francis

DAY OF FAITH, THE (1923)
(7 r.) d, Tod Browning; lp, Eleanor Boardman, [Frederick] Tyrone Power, Sr., Raymond Griffith, Wallace MacDonald

DAY SHE PAID, THE (1919)
(5 r.) d, Rex Ingram; lp, Francelia Billington, Charles Clary, Harry Van Meter, Lillian Rich

DAYBREAK (1918)
(6 r.) d, Albert Capellani; lp, Emily Stevens, Julien L'Estrange, Augustus Phillips, Herman Lieb

DAYS OF OUR LIFE (1914, USSR)
(5 r.) d, Vladimir Gardin; lp, M. Tamarov, B. Orlitsky, Y. Butkova, L. Sychova

DAYTIME WIVES (1923)
(7 r.) d, Emile Chautard; lp, Derelys Perdue, Wyndham Standing, Grace Darmond, William Conklin

DAZZLING MISS DAVISON, THE (1917)
(5 r.) d, Frank Powell; lp, Marjorie Rambeau, Fred Williams, Aubrey Beattie, Agnes Eyre [Ayres]

DEAD ALIVE, THE (1916)
(5 r.) d, Henry J. Vernot; lp, Marguerite Courtot, Sidney Mason, Henry W. Pemberton, James Levering

DEAD GAME (1923)
(5 r.) d, Edward Sedgwick; lp, Ed [Hoot] Gibson, Robert McKim, Harry Carter, Laura La Plante

DEAD HEART, THE (1914, Brit.)
(4 r.) d, Hay Plumb; lp, Alice de Winton, Lionelle Howard, Harry Gilbey, Edward Lingard

DEAD LINE, THE (1920)
(5 r.) d, Dell Henderson; lp, George Walsh, Irene Boyle, Anita Lopez, Joseph Hanaway

DEAD LINE, THE (1926)
(5 r.) d, Jack Nelson; lp, Bob Custer, Nita Cavalier, Robert McKim, Tom Bay

DEAD MAN, THE (1914, USSR)
(4 r.) d, Alexander Tairov; lp, Izvolsky, Catherine Devilliers, G. Voskresensky

DEAD MEN TELL NO TALES (1920)
(7 r.) d, Tom Terriss; lp, Catherine Calvert, Percy Marmont, Holmes Herbert, Gustav von Seyffertitz

DEAD OR ALIVE (1921)
(5 r.) d, Dell Henderson; lp, Jack Hoxie, Joseph Girard, Marin Sais, C. Ray Florhe

DEAD SOUL, THE (1915)
(4 r.) lp, George Routh, L.C. Shumway, Eleanor Blevins

DEADLIER SEX, THE (1920)
(6 r.) d, Robert Thornby; lp, Blanche Sweet, Mahlon Hamilton, Winter Hall, Roy Laidlaw

DEADLINE AT ELEVEN (1920)
(5 r.) d, George Fawcett; lp, Corinne Griffith, Frank Thomas, Webster Campbell, Alice Calhoun

DEAD-SHOT BAKER (1917)
(5 r.) d, William Duncan lp, William Duncan, Carol Holloway, J.W. Ryan, S.E. Jennings

DEADSHOT CASEY (1928)
(5 r.) lp, Al Hoxie, Al Richmond, Chris Allen, Berth Rae

DEADWOOD COACH, THE (1924)
(7 r.) d, Lynn Reynolds; lp, Tom Mix, George Bancroft, Frank Coffyn, Jane Keckley

DEAR FOOL, A (1921, Brit.)
(6 r.) d, Harold Shaw; lp, George K. Arthur, Edna Flugrath, Edward O'Neill, Bertie Wright

DEARIE (1927)
(6 r.) d, Archie Mayo; lp, Irene Rich, William Collier, Jr., Edna Murphy, Anders Randolf

DEATH AT DAWN (1924, Jap.)
(? r.) d, Kenji Mizoguchi

DEATH BAY (1926, USSR)
(7 r.) d, Abram Room; lp, Nikolai Saltikov, Alexei Kharlamov, Nikolai Okhlopkov, Andrei Fait

DEATH DANCE, THE (1918)
(5 r.) d, J. Searle Dawley; lp, Alice Brady, Mahlon Hamilton, Holmes E. Herbert, Helen Montrose

DEATH OF THE GODS (1917, USSR)
(5 r.) d, Vladimir Kasyanov; lp, Illarion Pevtsov, V. Gradov, Margerita Froman

DEATH RAY, THE (1925, USSR)
(10 r.) d, Lev Kuleshov; lp, Sergei Komarov, Porfiri Podobed, Vladimir Fogel, Khokhlova

DEATH VALLEY (1927)
(6 r.) d, Paul Powell; lp, Carroll Nye, Rada Rae, Sam Allen, Raymond Wells

DEATHLOCK, THE (1915)
(5 r.) lp, Fred J. Butler, Wilma Wilkie, David W. Butler, Patrick Dempsey

DEBT, THE (1917)
(5 r.) d, Frank Powell; lp, Marjorie Rambeau, T. Jerome Lawlor, Agnes Eyre [Ayres], Paul Everton

DEBT, THE
(SEE: HIS DEBT, 1919)

DEBT OF HONOR, A (1916)
(5 r.) d, William Nigh

DEBT OF HONOR, THE (1918)
(5 r.) d, O.A.C. Lund; lp, Peggy Hyland, Irving Cummings, Frank Goldsmith, Hazel Adams

DEBTOR TO THE LAW, A (1924)
(6 r.) lp, Henry Starr

DECEIT (1923)
(6 r.) lp, Evelyn Preer, William E. Fontaine, George Lucas, Narmon Johnston

DECEIVER, THE (1920)
(5 r.) d, Jean Hersholt, Lewis H. Moomaw; lp, Jean Hersholt, Carol Holloway, Lee Hill, Bert Sprotte

DECEMBRISTS (1927, USSR)
(7 r.) d, Alexander Ivanovsky; lp, S. Shishko, Gennadi Michurin, Boris Tamarin, V. Maximov

DECEPTION (1918, Brit.)
(6 r.) d, A.C. Hunter; lp, James Knight, Rose Manners, Charles Rock, Frank Gerrard

DECEPTION (1921, Ger.)
(8 r.) d, Ernest Lubitsch

DECIDING KISS, THE (1918)
(5 r.) d, Tod Browing; lp, Edith Roberts, Winnifred Greenwood, Hal Cooley, Thornton Church

DECLASSEE (1925)
(8 r.) d, Robert Vignola; lp, Lloyd Hughes, Corinne Griffith, Clive Brook, Rockcliffe Fellowes

DECOY, THE (1916)
(5 r.) d, George W. Lederer; lp, Frances Nelson, Gladden James, Leonore Harris, Robert W. Frazer

DEEDS OF DARING (1924)
(5 r.) d, Charles R. Seeling; lp, George Larkin

DEEMSTER, THE (1917)
(9 r.) d, Howell Hansel; lp, Derwent Hall Caine, Marian Swayne, Sidney Bracey, Albert Froom

DEEP PURPLE, THE (1915)
(5 r.) d, James Young; lp, Clara Kimball Young, Milton Sills, Edward M. Kimball, W.J. Ferguson

DEEP PURPLE, THE (1920)
(6 r.) d, Raoul Walsh; lp, Miriam Cooper, Helen Ware, Vincent Serrano, W.J. Ferguson

DEEP WATERS (1920)
(5 r.) d, Maurice Tourneur; lp, Jack Gilbert, Broeken Christians, Barbara Bedford, Florence Deshon

DEERSLAYER, THE (1923)
(5 r.)

DEFEAT OF THE CITY, THE (1917)
(4 r.) d, Thomas R. Mills; lp, J. Frank Glendon, Agnes Eyre [Ayres], Frank Chapman, Frank Heath

DEFENCE OF SEVASTOPOL (1911, USSR)
(6 r.) d, Vasili Goncharov, Alexander Khanzhonkov; lp, A. Gromov, N. Semyonov, P. Biryukov, Ivan Mozhukhin

DEFEND YOURSELF (1925)
(5 r.) d, Dell Henderson; lp, Dorothy Drew, Miss Du Pont, Robert Ellis, Sheldon Lewis

DEFINITE OBJECT, THE (1920, Brit.)
(4 r.) d, Countess Bubna; lp, Ann Elliott, Peter Upcher, Lionel Scott, Charles Stafford-Dickens

DEFYING DESTINY (1923)
(6 r.) d, Louis Chaudet; lp, Monte Blue, Irene Rich, Tully Marshall, Jackie Saunders

DEFYING THE LAW (1922)
(5 r.) d, Robert J. Horner; lp, Monte Montague, Ena Gregory

DEFYING THE LAW (1924)
(5 r.) d, Bertram Bracken; lp, Lew Cody, Renee Adoree, Josef Swickard, Charles "Buddy" Post

DELICIOUS LITTLE DEVIL, THE (1919)
(6 r.) d, Robert Z. Leonard; lp, Mae Murray, Harry Rattenbury, Richard Cummings, Rudolph Valentino

DELIVERANCE (1928)
(6 r.) d, B.K. Blake

DELUGE, THE (1925, USSR)
(8 r.) d, Yevgeni Ivanov-Barkov, Boris Vershilov, Ivan Pyriev

DELUXE ANNIE (1918)
(6 r.) d, Roland West; lp, Norma Talmadge, Eugene O'Brien, Frank Mills, Edward S. Davis

DEMI-BRIDE, THE (1927)
(7 r.) d, Robert Z. Leonard; lp, Norma Shearer, Lew Cody, Lionel Belmore, Tenen Holtz

DEMOCRACY (1920)
(7 r.) d, William Nigh; lp, J.H. Gilmore, William Nigh, Leslie Austin, Maurine Powers

DEMON, THE (1918)
(5 r.) d, George D. Baker; lp, Edith Storey, Lewis Cody, Charles Gerrard, Virginia Chester

DEMON, THE (1926)
(5 r.) d, Cliff Smith; lp, Jack Hoxie, Lola Todd, William Welsh, Jere Austin

DEMON RIDER, THE (1925)
(5 r.) d, Paul Hurst; lp, Ken Maynard, Alma Rayford, Fred Burns, Tom London

DEMOS
(SEE: WHY MEN FORGET, 1921, Brit.)

DENIAL, THE (1925)
(5 r.) d, Hobart Henley; lp, Claire Windsor, Bert Roach, William Haines, Lucille Rickson

DENNY FROM IRELAND (1918)
(5 r.) d, W.H. Clifford, Bob Gray; lp, Shorty Hamilton, Ellen Terry, Florence Drew, Andrew Arbuckle

DENVER DUDE, THE (1927)
(6 r.) d, B. Reeves Eason; lp, Hoot Gibson, Blanche Mehaffey, Robert McKim, George Summerville

DER MUDE TOD
(SEE: DESTINY, 1921, Ger.)

DER VERLORENE SCHATTEN
(SEE: LOST SHADOW, THE, 1921)

DERBY WINNER, THE (1915, Brit.)
(5 r.) d, Harold Shaw; lp, Augustus Harris, Edna Flugrath, Gerald Ames, Mary Dibley

DERELICT, THE (1917)
(5 r.) d, Carl Harbaugh; lp, Stuart Holmes, Mary Martin, June Daye, Carl Eckstrom

DERELICTS (1917, Brit.)
(5 r.) d, Sidney Morgan; lp, Violet Graham, Sydney Vautier, Julian Royce, Mona K. Harrison

DES VOLKES HELDENGANG
(SEE: GREAT WAR, THE, 1927, Ger.)

DESERT BRIDE, THE (1928)
(6 r.) d, Walter Lang; lp, Betty Compson, Allan Forrest, Edward Martindel, Otto Matiesen

DESERT BRIDEGROOM, A (1922)
(5 r.) d, Roy Clements; lp, Jack Hoxie, Evelyn Nelson

DESERT DEMON, THE (1925)
(5 r.) d, Richard Thorpe; lp, Buffalo Bill, Jr., Betty Morrissey, Frank Ellis, Harry Todd

DESERT DRIVEN (1923)
(6 r.) d, Val Paul; lp, Harry Carey, Marguerite, George Waggner, Charles J. Le Moyne

DESERT DUST (1917)
(5 r.)

DESERT DUST (1927)
(5 r.) d, William Wyler; lp, Ted Wells, Lotus Thompson, Bruce Gordon, Jimmy Phillips

DESERT GOLD (1919)
(6 r.) d, T. Hayes Hunter; lp, E.K. Lincoln, Margery Wilson, Eileen Percy, W. Lawson Butt

DESERT GOLD (1926)
(7 r.) d, George B. Seitz; lp, Neil Hamilton, Shirley Mason, Robert Frazer, William Powell

DESERT GREED (1926)
(5 r.) d, Jacques Jaccard; lp, Yakima Canutt

DESERT HAWK, THE (1924)
(5 r.) d, Leon De La Mothe; lp, Ben Wilson, Mildred Harris, William Bailey, Louise Lester

DESERT HONEYMOON, A (1915)
(4 r.) lp, Romaine Fielding, Vinnie Burns, Jack Lawton, Violet Malone

DESERT LAW (1918)
(5 r.) d, Jack Conway; lp, Jack Richardson, George Pearce, Al Whitman, Leota Lorraine

DESERT LOVE (1920)
(5 r.) d, Jacques Jaccard; lp, Tom Mix, Francelia Billington, Eva Novak, Lester Cuneo

DESERT MADNESS (1925)
(5 r.) d, Harry Webb; lp, Jack Perrin

DESERT MAN, THE (1917)
(5 r.) d, William S. Hart; lp, William S. Hartman, Margery Wilson, Walter Whitman, Jack Livingston

DESERT NIGHTS (1929)
(7 r.) d, William Nigh; lp, John Gilbert, Ernest Torrence, Mary Nolan

DESERT OF THE LOST, THE (1927)
(5 r.) d, Richard Thorpe; lp, Wally Wales, Peggy Montgomery, William J. Dyer, Edward Cecil

DESERT OUTLAW, THE (1924)
(6 r.) d, Edmund Mortimer; lp, Buck Jones, Evelyn Brent, DeWitt Jennings, William Haynes

DESERT RIDER (1923)
(5 r.) d, Robert North Bradbury; lp, Jack Hoxie, Frank Rice, Evelyn Nelson, Claude Peyton

DESERT SCORPION, THE (1920)
(5 r.) d, Otis B. Thayer; lp, Edmund F. Cobb, Claire Hatton, Vida Johnson, Otis Thayer

DESERT SECRET, THE (1924)
(5 r.) d, Frederick Reel, Jr.; lp, Bill Patton

DESERT SHEIK, THE (1924)
(6 r.) d, Tom Terriss; lp, Wanda Hawley, Nigel Barrie, Pedro De Cordoba, Edith Craig

DESERT VALLEY (1926)
(5 r.) d, Scott R. Dunlap; lp, Buck Jones, Virginia Brown Faire, Malcolm Waite, J.W. Johnston

DESERT VULTURES (1930)
(5 r.) lp, Art Mix

DESERT WOOING, A (1918)
(5 r.) d, Jerome Storm; lp, Enid Bennett, Jack Holt, Donald MacDonald, John P. Lockney

DESERTER, THE (1916)
(5 r.) d, Walter Edwards; lp, Charles Ray, Rita Stanwood, Wedgewood Nowell, Hazel Bedford

DESERTEUSE (1917, Fr.)
(? r.) d, Louis Feuillade

DESERT'S CRUCIBLE, THE (1922)
(5 r.) d, Roy Clements; lp, Jack Hoxie, Claude Payton, Andree Tourneur

DESIRE
(SEE: MAGIC SKIN, THE, 1920, Brit.)

DESIRE (1923)
(7 r.) d, Rowland V. Lee; lp, Marguerite De La Motte, John Bowers, Estelle Taylor, David Butler

DESIRE OF THE MOTH, THE (1917)
(5 r.) d, Rupert Julian; lp, Ruth Clifford, Rupert Julian, Monore Salisbury, William Herbert Bainbridge

DESIRED WOMAN, THE (1927)
(7 r.) d, Michael Curtiz; lp, Irene Rich, William Russell, William Collier, Jr., Douglas Gerrard

DESPERATE ADVENTURE, A (1924)
(5 r.) d, J.P. McGowan; lp, Franklyn Farnum, Marie Walcamp, Priscilla Bonner

DESPERATE CHANCE (1926)
(5 r.) d, J.P. McGowan; lp, Bob Reeves, Ione Reed, Leon De La Mothe, Charles Whittaker

DESPERATE COURAGE (1928)
(5 r.) d, Richard Thorpe; lp, Wally Wales, Olive Hasbrouck, Tom Bay, Lafe McKee

DESPERATE GAME, THE (1926)
(5 r.) d, Joseph Franz; lp, Pete Morrison, Dolores Gardner, James Welsh, Jere Austin

DESPERATE HERO, THE (1920)
(5 r.) d, Welsey Ruggles; lp, Owen Moore, Gloria Hope, Nell Craig, Henry Miller, Jr.

DESPERATE MOMENT, A (1926)
(6 r.) d, Jack Dawn; lp, Wanda Hawley, Theodore von Eltz, Sheldon Lewis, Leo White

DESPERATE ODDS (1925)
(5 r.) d, Horace B. Carpenter; lp, Bob Burns, Dorothy Donald

DESPERATE TRAILS (1921)
(5 r.) d, Jack [John] Ford; lp, Harry Carey, Irene Rich, Georgie Stone, Helen Field

DESPERATE YOUTH (1921)
(5 r.) d, Harry B. Harris; lp, Gladys Walton, J. Farrell MacDonald, Lewis Willoughby, Muriel Godfrey Turner

DESPERATION (1916, Brit.)
(5 r.) d, Maurice Elvey; lp, Elizabeth Risdon, Fred Groves, Guy Newall, Henrietta Watson

DESTIN (1927, Fr.)
(? r.) d, Dimitri Kirsanoff;

DESTINEE (1926, Fr.)
(? r.) d, Henry Roussel

DESTINY
(SEE: SOUL OF A WOMAN, THE, 1915)

DESTINY (1919)
(6 r.) d, Rollin S. Sturgeon; lp, Dorothy Phillips, William Stowell, Stanhope Wheatcroft, Antrim Short

DESTINY (1921, Ger.)
(8 r.) d, Fritz Lang; lp, Bernard Goetzke, Lil Dagover, Walther Janssen, Rudolph Klein-Rogge

DESTINY'S SKEIN (1915)
(4 r.) d, George Terwilliger; lp, Earl Metcalfe, Ormi Hawley, Kempton Greene, Hazel Hubbard

DESTINY'S TOY (1916)
(5 r.) d, John B. O'Brien; lp, Louise Huff, J.W. Johnston, John Bowers, Harry Lee

DESTROYERS, THE (1916)
(5 r.) d, Ralph Ince; lp, Lucille Lee Stewart, Huntley Gordon, John Robertson, Richard Turner

DESTROYING ANGEL, THE (1915)
(5 r.) d, Richard Ridgely; lp, Mabel Trunnelle, Marc MacDermott, Walter Craven

DESTROYING ANGEL, THE (1923)
(6 r.) d, W.S. Van Dyke; lp, Leah Baird, John Bowers, Noah Beery, Ford Sterling

DETECTIVE CRAIG'S COUP (1914)
(5 r.) d, Donald Mackenzie

DETECTIVES (1928)
(7 r.) d, Chester M. Franklin; lp, Karl Dane, George K. Arthur, Marceline Day, Tenen Holtz

DETERMINATION (1920)
(10 r.) d, Frederic F. Stoll; lp, B.W. Maynard, Todd Sloan, Philip Sanford, Dora Adams

DETERMINATION (1922)
(10 r.) d, Joseph Levering; lp, Alpheus Lincoln, Corinne Uzzell, Irene Tams, Maurice Costello

DEUCE DUNCAN (1918)
(5 r.) d, Thomas Heffron; lp, William Desmond, Louella Maxam, Ed Brady, George Field

DEUCE HIGH (1926)
(5 r.) d, Richard Thorpe; lp, Buffalo Bill, Jr., Alma Rayford, Robert Walker, J.P. Lockney

DEUCE OF SPADES, THE (1922)
(5 r.) d, Charles Ray; lp, Charles Ray, Marjorie Maurice, Lincoln Plumer, Phillip Dunham

DEVIL, THE (1921)
(6 r.) d, James Young; lp, George Arliss, Sylvia Breamer, Lucy Cotton, Edmund Lowe

DEVIL AT HIS ELBOW, THE (1916)
(5 r.) d, Burton L. King; lp, Clifford Bruce, Dorothy Green, J.K. Roberts, Frank McDonald

DEVIL DANCER, THE (1927)
(8 r.) d, Fred Niblo, Jr.; lp, Gilda Gray, Clive Brook, Anna May Wong, Serge Temoff

DEVIL DOG DAWSON (1921)
(5 r.) lp, Jack Hoxie, Helen Rosson, Evelyn Selbie, Wilbur McGaugh

DEVIL HORSE, THE (1926)
(6 r.) d, Fred Jackman; lp, Rex (a horse), The Killer (a horse), Lady (a horse), Yakima Canutt

DEVIL MCCARE (1919)
(5 r.) d, Lorimer Johnson; lp, Crane Wilbur

DEVIL STONE, THE (1917)
(6 r.) d, Cecil B. DeMille; lp, Geraldine Farrar, Wallace Reid, Hobart Bosworth, Tully Marshall

DEVIL, THE SERVANT AND THE MAN, THE (1916)
(4 r.) d, Frank Beal; lp, Kathlyn Williams, Guy Oliver, Jean Fraser, Lillian Hayward

DEVIL WITHIN, THE (1921)
(6 r.) d, Bernard J. Durning; lp, Dustin Farnum, Virginia Valli, Nigel De Brulier, Bernard Durning

DEVIL'S ANGEL, THE (1920)
(5 r.) d, Lejaren a'Hiller; lp, Helen Gardner, Templer Saxe, Peggy O'Neil, C.D. Williams

DEVIL'S ASSISTANT, THE (1917)
(5 r.) d, Harry Pollard; lp, Margarita Fischer, Monroe Salisbury, Kathleen Kirkham, Jack Mower

DEVIL'S BAIT, THE (1917)
(4 r.) d, Harry Harvey; lp, Ruth Roland, William Conklin, Edward J. Brady, Henry King

DEVIL'S BOND WOMAN, THE (1916)
(5 r.) d, Lloyd B. Carleton; lp, Dorothy Davenport, Emory Johnson, Richard Morris, Adele Farrington

DEVIL'S BONDMAN, THE
(SEE: SCORPION'S STING, THE, 1916, Brit.)

DEVIL'S BOWL, THE (1923)
(5 r.) d, Neal Hart; lp, Catherine Bennett, Fonda Holt, John Beck, William McLaughlin

DEVIL'S CAGE, THE (1928)
(6 r.) d, Wilfred Noy; lp, Pauline Garon, Ruth Stonehouse, Donald Keith, Armand Kaliz

DEVIL'S CIRCUS, THE (1926)
(7 r.) d, Benjamin Christensen; lp, Norma Shearer, Charles Emmett Mack, Carmel Myers, John Miljan

DEVIL'S CLAIM, THE (1920)
(5 r.) d, Charles Swickard; lp, Sessue Hayakawa, Rhea Mitchell, Colleen Moore, William Buckley

DEVIL'S CONFESSION, THE (1921)
(5 r.) d, John S. Lopez; lp, Frank Williams, Lillian Ward, Mary Eberle, Louise Lee

DEVIL'S DAUGHTER, THE (1915)
(5 r.) d, Frank Powell; lp, Theda Bara, Paul Doucet, Victor Benoit, Robert Wayne

DEVIL'S DICE (1926)
(6 r.) d, Tom Forman; lp, Barbara Bedford, Robert Ellis, Josef Swickard, Tom Forman

DEVIL'S DISCIPLE, THE (1926)
(? r.) lp, Evelyn Preer, Lawrence Chenault

DEVIL'S DOORYARD, THE (1923)
(5 r.) d, Lewis King; lp, William Fairbanks, Ena Gregory, Joseph Girard, Bob McKenzie

DEVIL'S DOUBLE , THE (1916)
(5 r.) d, William S. Hart; lp, William S. Hart, Enid Markey, Robert McKim, Thomas Kurihara

DEVIL'S GARDEN, THE (1920)
(6 r.) d, Kenneth Webb; lp, Lionel Barrymore, May McAvoy, Doris Rankin, Henry Cooper Cliffe

DEVIL'S GHOST, THE (1922)
(5 r.)

DEVIL'S GULCH, THE (1926)
(5 r.) d, Jack Nelson; lp, Bob Custer, Hazel Deane, Charles Belcher, Pat Beggs

DEVIL'S ISLAND (1926)
(7 r.) d, Frank O'Connor; lp, Pauline Frederick, Marion Nixon, George Lewis, Richard Tucker

DEVIL'S MATCH, THE (1923)
(5 r.)

DEVIL'S NEEDLE, THE (1916)
(5 r.) d, Chester Withey; lp, Norma Talmadge, Tully Marshall, Marguerite Marsh, F.A. Turner

DEVIL'S PAWN, THE (1922, Ger.)
(5 r.) d, Paul Ludwig Stein; lp, Pola Negri, Adolf Edgar Licho, Harry Liedtke, Werner Bernhardl

DEVIL'S PAY DAY, THE (1917)
(5 r.) d, William Worthington; lp, Franklyn Farnum, Leah Baird, Gertrude Astor, Charles Perley

DEVIL'S PIT, THE (1930)
(6 r.) d, Lew Collins; lp, Patiti Warbrick, Watarina Mitchell, Hoana Keeha, Ani Warbrick

DEVIL'S PRAYER-BOOK, THE (1916)
(5 r.) lp, Arthur Hoops, Alma Hanlon, Frank Belcher, Ruby Hoffman

DEVIL'S PRIZE, THE (1916)
(5 r.) d, Marguerite Bertsch; lp, Antonio Moreno, Naomi Childers, Albert S. Howson, Clio Ayres

DEVIL'S PROFESSION, THE (1915, Brit.)
(4 r.) d, F.C.S. Tudor; lp, Rohan Clensy, Alesia Leon, Sidney Strong, May Lynn

DEVIL'S RIDDLE, THE (1920)
(5 r.) d, Frank Beal; lp, Gladys Brockwell, William Scott, Richard Cummings, Claire McDowell

DEVIL'S SADDLE, THE (1927)
(6 r.) d, Albert Rogell; lp, Ken Maynard, Kathleen Collins, Francis Ford, Will Walling

DEVIL'S SKIPPER, THE (1928)
(6 r.) d, John G. Adolfi; lp, Belle Bennett, Montagu Love, Gino Corrado, Mary McAllister

DEVIL'S TOY, THE (1916)
(5 r.) d, Harley Knoles; lp, Edwin Stevens, Adele Blood, Montagu Love, Jack Halliday

DEVIL'S TRADEMARK, THE (1928)
(6 r.) d, Leo Meehan; lp, Belle Bennett, William V. Mong, Marian Douglas, William Bakewell

DEVIL'S TWIN, THE (1927)
(6 r.) d, Leo Maloney; lp, Leo Maloney, Josephine Hill, Don Coleman, Albert Hart

DEVIL'S WHEEL, THE (1918)
(5 r.) d, Edward J. LeSaint; lp, Gladys Brockwell, William Scott, Bertram Grassby, Lucille Young

DEVIL'S WHEEL, THE (1926, USSR)
(9 r.) d, Grigori Kozintsev; lp, Ludmila Semyonova, N. Foregger, Pyotr Sobolevsky, Sergei Gerasimov

DEVOTION (1921)
(6 r.) d, Burton George; lp, Hazel Dawn, E.K. Lincoln, Violet Palmer, Renita Randolph

DIAMANT NOIR (1922, Fr.)
(? r.) d, Andre Hugon; lp, Jean Toulout, Claude Merelle

DIAMOND BANDIT, THE (1924)
(5 r.) d, Francis Ford; lp, Arthur George, Florence Gilbert, Frank Baker, Robert McGowan

DIAMOND CARLISLE (1922)
(5 r.) d, Milburn Morante; lp, George Chesebro, Iva Brown, Virginia Morante, Alfred Hewston

DIAMOND HANDCUFFS (1928)
(7 r.) d, John P. McCarthy; lp, Lena Malena, Charles Stevens, Gwen Lee, Conrad Nagel

DIAMOND MAN, THE (1924, Brit.)
(6 r.) d, Arthur Rooke; lp, Arthur Wontner, Mary Odette, Reginald Fox, Gertrude McCoy

DIAMOND RUNNERS, THE (1916)
(5 r.) d, J.P. McGowan; lp, Helen Holmes, Paul C. Hurst, Leo D. Maloney, Thomas Lingham

DIAMONDS AND PEARLS (1918)
(5 r.) d, George Archainbaud; lp, Kitty Gordon, Milton Sills, Curtis Cooksey, George MacQuarrie

DIANA AND DESTINY (1916, Brit.)
(5 r.) d, F. Martin Thornton; lp, Evelyn Boucher, Wyndham Guise, Roy Travers, Frank E. Petley

DIANA OF DOBSON'S (1917, Brit.)
(5 r.) lp, Cecilia Loftus, A.B. Imeson, Rachel de Solla

DIANA OF THE CROSSWAYS (1922, Brit.)
(5 r.) d, Denison Clift; lp, Fay Compton, Henry Victor, J.R. Tozer, A. Harding Steerman

DIANA OF THE FOLLIES (1916)
(5 r.) d, W. Christy Cabanne; lp, Lillian Gish, Sam De Grasse, Howard Gaye, Lillian Langdon

DIANE OF THE GREEN VAN (1919)
(5 r.) d, Wallace Worsley; lp, Alma Rubens, Nigel Barrie, Lamar Johnstone, Josephine Crowell

DIARY OF A LOST GIRL (1929, Ger.)
(9 r.) d, G.W. Pabst; lp, Louise Brooks, Edith Meinhardt, Vera Pawlowa, Josef Rovensky

DICE OF DESTINY (1920)
(5 r.) d, Henry King; lp, H.B. Warner, Lillian Rich, Rosemary Theby, Howard Davies

DICE WOMAN, THE (1927)
(6 r.) d, Edward Dillon; lp, Priscilla Dean, John Bowers, Gustav von Seyffertitz, Lionel Belmore

DICK CARSON WINS THROUGH (1917, Brit.)
(4 r.) d, Henry Edwards; lp, Henry Edwards, Chrissie White, Lionelle Howard, Fred Johnson

DICK TURPIN'S RIDE TO YORK (1922, Brit.)
(8 r.) d, Maurice Elvey; lp, Matheson Lang, Isobel Elsom, Cecil Humphreys, Norman Page

DICK'S FAIRY (1921, Brit.)
(5 r.) d, Bert Wynne; lp, Joan Griffiths, Hargrave Mansell, Albert Brantford, Eva Westlake

DICKY MONTEITH (1922, Brit.)
(5 r.) d, Kenelm Foss; lp, Stewart Rome, Joan Morgan, Jack Minster, Douglas Munro

DIE GEHEIMNISSE EINER SEELE
(SEE: SECRETS OF A SOUL, 1928, Ger.)

DIPLOMACY (1916)
(5 r.) d, Sidney Olcott; lp, Marie Doro, Elliott Dexter, Frank Losee, Russell Bassett

DIPLOMACY (1926)
(7 r.) d, Marshall Neilan; lp, Blanche Sweet, Neil Hamilton, Arlette Marchal, Matt Moore

DIPLOMATIC MISSION, A (1918)
(5 r.) d, Jack Conway; lp, Earle Williams, Grace Darmond, Leslie Stuart, Kathleen Kirkham

DISAPPEARANCE OF THE JUDGE, THE (1919, Brit.)
(5 r.) d, Alexander Butler; lp, James Lindsay, Florence Nelson, Mark Melford, Joan Lockton

DISCARD, THE (1916)
(5 r.) d, Lawrence Windom; lp, Virginia Hammond, Ernest Maupain, Harry Beaumont, Betty Brown

DISCARDED WOMAN, THE (1920)
(6 r.) d, Burton L. King; lp, Grace Darling, James Cooley, Rod La Rocque, Madeline [Madelyn] Clare

DISCIPLE, THE (1915)
(5 r.) d, William S. Hart, Clifford Smith; lp, William S. Hart, Dorothy Dalton, Wedgewood Nowell, Charles K. French

DISCONTENTED HUSBANDS (1924)
(6 r.) d, Edward J. Le Saint; lp, James Kirkwood, Cleo Madison, Grace Darmond, Arthur Rankin

DISCONTENTED WIVES (1921)
(5 r.) d, J.P. McGowan; lp, J.P. McGowan, Fritzi Brunette, Jean Perry, Andy Waldron

DISRAELI (1916, Brit.)
(7 r.) d, Percy Nash, Charles Calvert; lp, Dennis Eadie, Mary Jerold, Cyril Raymond, Dorothy Bellew

DISRAELI (1921)
(7 r.) d, Henry Kolker; lp, George Arliss, Margaret Dale, Florence Arliss, Margaret Dale

DISTRICT ATTORNEY, THE (1915)
(5 r.) d, Barry O'Neil; lp, A.H. Van Buren, Dorothy Bernard, George Soule Spencer, Peter Lang

DIVINE GIFT, THE (1918, Brit.)
(5 r.) d, Thomas Bentley; lp, Joyce Dearsley, Jack Livesey, George Tully, Henrietta Watson

DIVINE SACRIFICE, THE (1918)
(5 r.) d, George Archainbaud; lp, Kitty Gordon, Jean Angelo, Celene Johnson, Frank Goldsmith

DIVINE SINNER (1928)
(6 r.) d, Scott Pembroke; lp, Vera Reynolds, Nigel De Brulier, Bernard Seigel, Ernest Hilliard

DIVORCE AND THE DAUGHTER (1916)
(5 r.) d, Frederick Sullivan; lp, Florence LaBadie, Edwin Stanley, Sam Niblack, Kathryn Adams

DIVORCE COUPONS (1922)
(5 r.) d, Webster Campbell; lp, Corinne Griffith, Holmes E. Herbert, Mona Lisa, Diana Allen

DIVORCE OF CONVENIENCE, A (1921)
(5 r.) d, Robert Ellis; lp, Owen Moore, Katherine Perry, George Lessey, Nita Naldi

DIVORCED (1915)
(5 r.) d, Joseph A. Golden; lp, Hilda Spong, Fred Eric, Charles Hutchinson, Lester Chambers

DIVORCEE, THE (1917)
(5 r.) d, William Wolbert; lp, Mary Anderson, Alfred Vosburgh, Pliny Goodfriend, Jean Hathaway

DIVORCEE, THE (1919)
(5 r.) d, Herbert Blache; lp, Ethel Barrymore, H.E. Herbert, E.J. Radcliffe, Naomi Childers

DIVORCONS (1915)
(4 r.) lp, Del Henderson, Gertrude Bambrick, Dave Morris, Florence Lee

DIXIE HANDICAP, THE (1925)
(7 r.) d, Reginald Barker; lp, Claire Windsor, Frank Keenan, Lloyd Hughes, John Sainpolis

DIXIE MERCHANT, THE (1926)
(6 r.) d, Frank Borzage; lp, J. Farrell MacDonald, Madge Bellamy, Jack Mulhall, Claire McDowell

DIZZY LIMIT, THE (1930, Brit.)
(6 r.) d, Edward Dryhurst; lp, Jasper Maskeleyne, Joy Windsor, Wallace Bosco, Dino Galvani

DO IT NOW (1924)
(6 r.) d, Duke Worne; lp, William Fairbanks, Alec B. Francis, Madge Bellamy, Arthur Hoyt

DO THE DEAD TALK? (1920)
(5 r.) d, Jack MacDonald; lp, Hermain France, Willard Burt, Grant Foreman, Elizabeth Yach

DO UNTO OTHERS (1915, Brit.)
(4 r.) d, Bert Haldane; lp, Tom H. MacDonald, Peggy Richards, Patrick J. Noonan, Pippin Barker

DOC (1914)
(4 r.) lp, Sydney Seaword

DOCKS OF NEW YORK, THE (1928)
(8 r.) d, Josef Von Sternberg; lp, George Bancroft, Betty Compson, Baclanova, Clyde Cook

DOCTOR AND THE BRICKLAYER, THE (1918)
(4 r.) d, Edward Jose; lp, Frank Belcher, Edithe Yorke

DOCTOR AND THE WOMAN, THE (1918)
(7 r.) d, Lois Weber, Phillips Smalley; lp, Mildred Harris, True Boardman, Albert Roscoe, Zella Caull

DR. MABUSE, DER SPIELER
(SEE: DR. MABUSE, THE GAMBLER, 1922, Ger.)

DR. MABUSE, THE GAMBLER (1922, Ger.)
(12 r.) d, Fritz Lang; lp, Rudolf Klein-Rogge, Alfred Abel, Aud Egede Nissen, Gertrude Welcker

DR. MACDONALD'S SANATORIUM (1920, Ger.)
(5 r.) d, Willy Zehn

DR. NEIGHBOR (1916)
(5 r.) d, L.B. Carleton; lp, Hobart Bosworth, Dorothy Davenport, Gretchen Lederer, Emory Johnson

DR. RAMEAU (1915)
(6 r.) d, Will S. Davis; lp, Frederick Perry, Jean Southern, Dorothy Bernard, Stuart Holmes

DR. WAKE'S PATIENT (1916, Brit.)
(4 r.) d, Fred Paul; lp, Phyllis Dare, Gerald McCarthy, James Lindsay, Mary Rorke

DOCTOR'S WOMEN, THE (1929, Ger.)
(4 r.) d, Gustav Molander

DOCUMENT SECRET (1916, Fr.)
(? r.) d, Gaston Ravel

DODGING A MILLION (1918)
(6 r.) d, George Loane Tucker; lp, Mabel Normand, Tom Moore, J. Herbert Frank, Shirley Aubert

DOES IT PAY? (1923)
(7 r.) d, Charles Horan; lp, Hope Hampton, Robert T. Haines, Florence Short, Walter Petri

DOG JUSTICE (1928)
(6 r.) d, Jerome Storm; lp, Ranger (a dog), Edward Hearn, Nita Martan, James Welsh

DOLLAR AND THE LAW, THE (1916)
(5 r.) d, Wilfred North; lp, Lillian Walker, Edward Elkas, Walter McGrail, Thomas R. Mills

DOLLAR DOWN (1925)
(6 r.) d, Tod Browning; lp, Ruth Roland, Henry B. Walthall, Maym Kelso, Earl Schenck

DOLLAR FOR DOLLAR (1920)
(5 r.) d, Frank Keenan; lp, Frank Keenan, Kathleen Kirkham, Kate Van Buren, Harry Van Meter

DOLLAR-A-YEAR MAN, THE (1921)
(5 r.) d, James Cruze; lp, Roscoe "Fatty" Arbuckle, Lila Lee, Winifred Greenwood, J.M. Dumont

DOLLARS AND THE WOMAN (1916)
(5 r.) d, Joseph Kaufman; lp, Ethel Clayton, Tom Moore, Crauford Kent, Bartley McCullum

DOLLARS AND THE WOMAN (1920)
(6 r.) d, George Terwilliger; lp, Alice Joyce, Robert Gordon, Crauford Kent, Jessie Stevens

DOLLARS IN SURREY (1921, Brit.)
(5 r.) d, George Dewhurst, Anson Dyer; lp, Alma Taylor, James Carew, Hugh Clifton, Gwynne Herbert

DOLL'S HOUSE, A (1917)
(5 r.) d, Joseph De Grasse; lp, Dorothy Phillips, William Stowell, Lon Chaney [Sr.], Sidney Dean

DOLL'S HOUSE, A (1922)
(7 r.) d, Charles Bryant; lp, Alan Hale, Alla Nazimova, Nigel De Brulier, Elinor Oliver

DOLLY (1929, Fr.)
(? r.) d, Pierre Colombier

DOLLY DOES HER BIT (1918)
(5 r.) d, William Bertram; lp, Marie Osborne, Alice Saunders, Louis Hahn

DOLORES (1928, Brit.)
(7 r.) d, Michael Balcon; lp, Benita Hume, C.M. Hallard, Gerald Ames, Betty Carter

DOMBEY AND SON (1917, Brit.)
(7 r.) d, Maurice Elvey; lp, Norman McKinnel, Lilian Braithwaite, Hayford Hobbs, Odette Goimbault

DOMESTIC MEDDLERS (1928)
(6 r.) d, James Flood; lp, Claire Windsor, Lawrence Gray, Roy D'Arcy, Jed Prouty

DOMESTIC RELATIONS (1922)
(6 r.) d, Chet [Chester] Withey; lp, Katherine MacDonald, William P. Carleton, Frank Leigh, Barbara La Marr

DOMESTIC TROUBLES (1928)
(6 r.) d, Ray Enright; lp, Clyde Cook, Louise Fazenda, Betty Blythe, Jean Laverty

DOMESTIC-AGITATOR (1920, USSR)
(4 r.) d, Yuri Zheliabuzhsky; lp, G. Burdzhalov, N. Kostromsky, Nikolai Khmelyov, N. Dobronravov

DON CAESAR DE BAZAN (1915)
(4 r.) d, Robert Vignola; lp, W. Lawson Butt, Alice Hollister, Harry Millarde, Robert D. Walker

DON DARE DEVIL (1925)
(5 r.) d, Clifford S. Smith; lp, Jack Hoxie, Cathleen Calhoun, Duke Lee, William Welch

DON DESPERADO (1927)
(6 r.) d, Leo Maloney; lp, Leo Maloney, Eugenia Gilbert, Frederick Dana, Charles Bartlett

DON JUAN ET FAUST (1923, Fr.)
(? r.) d, Marcel L'Herbier; lp, Jaque Catelain, Vanni Marcoux, Marcelle Pradot, Philippe Heriat

DON JUAN OF THE WEST (1928)
(5 r.) lp, Cheyenne Bill

DON JUAN'S THREE NIGHTS (1926)
(7 r.) d, John Francis Dillon; lp, Lewis Stone, Shirley Mason, Malcolm McGregor, Myrtle Stedman

DON QUICKSHOT OF THE RIO GRANDE (1923)
(5 r.) d, George E. Marshall; lp, Jack Hoxie, Emmett King, Elinor Field, Fred C. Jones

DON QUIXOTE (1916)
(5 r.) d, Edward Dillon; lp, De Wolf Hopper, Fay Tincher, Max Davidson, Rhea Mitchell

DON'T (1925)
(6 r.) d, Alf Goulding; lp, Sally O'Neil, John Patrick, Bert Roach, James Morrison

DON'T BLAME YOUR CHILDREN (1922, Brit.)
(6 r.) p, George Ridgwell

DON'T BUILD YOUR HAPPINESS ON YOUR WIFE AND CHILD (1917, USSR)
(5 r.) d, Josef Soifer; lp, M. Zhdanova, Grigori Khmara

DON'T CALL IT LOVE (1924)
(7 r.) d, William C. De Mille; lp, Agnes Ayres, Jack Holt, Nita Naldi, Theodore Kosloff

DON'T CHANGE YOUR HUSBAND (1919)
(6 r.) d, Cecil B. DeMille; lp, Elliott Dexter, Gloria Swanson, Lew Cody, Sylvia Ashton

DON'T DOUBT YOUR HUSBAND (1924)
(6 r.) d, Harry Beaumont; lp, Viola Dana, Allan Forrest, Winifred Bryson, John Patrick

DON'T DOUBT YOUR WIFE (1922)
(5 r.) d, James W. Horne; lp, Leah Baird, Edward Peil, Emory Johnson, Mathilde Brundage

DON'T EVER MARRY (1920)
(5 r.) d, Marshall Neilan, Victor Heerman; lp, Matt Moore, Marjorie Daw, Tom Guise, Adele Farrington

DON'T LEAVE YOUR HUSBAND
(SEE: DANGEROUS TOYS, 1921)

DON'T NEGLECT YOUR WIFE (1921)
(6 r.) d, Wallace Worsley; lp, Mabel Julienne Scott, Lewis S. Stone, Charles Clary, Kate Lester

DON'T SHOOT (1922)
(6 r.) d, Jack Conway; lp, Herbert Rawlinson, William Dyer, Harvey Clarke, Wade Boteler

DON'T TELL THE WIFE (1927)
(7 r.) d, Paul Stein; lp, Irene Rich, Huntly Gordon, Lilyan Tashman, Otis Harlan

DON'T WRITE LETTERS (1922)
(5 r.) d, George D. Baker; lp, Gareth Hughes, Bartine Burkett, Herbert Hayes, Harry Lorraine

DOOMSDAY (1928)
(6 r.) d, Rowland V. Lee; lp, Florence Vidor, Gary Cooper, Lawrence Grant, Charles A. Stevenson

DOOR BETWEEN, THE (1917)
(5 r.) d, Rupert Julian; lp, Ruth Clifford, Monroe Salisbury, George A. McDaniels, W.H. Bainbridge

DOOR THAT HAS NO KEY, THE (1921, Brit.)
(5 r.) d, Frank H. Crane; lp, George Relph, Betty Faire, Evelyn Brent, Wilfred Seagram

DOP DOCTOR, THE
(SEE: THE LOVE TRAIL, 1916, Brit.)

DORA THORNE (1915)
(4 r.) d, Lawrence Marston; lp, Lionel Barrymore, William Russell, Millicent Evans, Thomas Jefferson

DORIAN'S DIVORCE (1916)
(5 r.) d, O.A.C. Lund; lp, Lionel Barrymore, Grace Valentine, Edgar L. Davenport, Lindsay Hall

DORMANT POWER, THE (1917)
(5 r.) d, Travers Vale; lp, Ethel Clayton, Montagu Love, Joseph Herbert, Edward Langford

DOROTHY VERNON OF HADDON HALL (1924)
(10 r.) d, Marshall Neilan; lp, Mary Pickford, Anders Randolph, Marc MacDermott, Carrie Daumery

DOTTED LINE, THE
(SEE: LET WOMEN ALONE, 1925)

DOUBLE, THE (1916, USSR)
(5 r.) d, V. Demert; lp, N. Chernova, Oleg Froelich

DOUBLE ACTION DANIELS (1925)
(5 r.) d, Richard Thorpe; lp, Buffalo Bill, Jr., Lorna Palmer, Edna Hall, J.P. Lockney

DOUBLE CROSSED (1917)
(5 r.) d, Robert G. Vignola; lp, Pauline Frederick, Riley Hatch, Harris Gordon, Crauford Kent

DOUBLE DARING (1926)
(5 r.) d, Richard Thorpe; lp, Wally Wales, J.P. Lockney, Jean Arthur, Hank Bell

DOUBLE DEALING (1923)
(5 r.) d, Henry Lehrman; lp, Hoot Gibson, Helen Ferguson, Betty Francisco, Eddie Gribbon

DOUBLE EVENT, THE (1921, Brit.)
(5 r.) d, Kenelm Foss; lp, Mary Odette, Roy Travers, Lionelle Howard, Tom Coventry

DOUBLE FISTED (1925)
(5 r.) d, Harry Webb; lp, Jack Perrin

DOUBLE O, THE (1921)
(5 r.) d, Roy Clements; lp, Jack Hoxie, Steve Clemento, William Lester, Ed La Niece

DOUBLE SPEED (1920)
(5 r.) d, Sam Wood; lp, Wallace Reid, Wanda Hawley, Theodore Roberts, Tully Marshall

DOUBLE STANDARD, THE (1917)
(5 r.) d, Phillips Smalley; lp, Roy Stewart, Joseph Girard, Clarrisa Selwynne, Frank Brownlee

DOUBLE TROUBLE (1915)
(5 r.) d, W. Christy Cabanne; lp, Douglas Fairbanks, Margery Wilson, Richard Cummings, Olga Grey

DOUBLE-BARRELED JUSTICE (1925)
(5 r.) lp, Franklyn Farnum

DOUBLE-DYED DECEIVER, A (1920)
(5 r.) d, Alfred Green; lp, Jack Pickford, Marie Dunn, James Neill, Edythe Chapman

DOUBLE-ROOM MYSTERY, THE (1917)
(5 r.) d, Hobart Henley; lp, Hayward Mack, Edward Hearn, Edward Brady, Gertrude Selby

DOVE, THE (1927)
(9 r.) d, Roland West; lp, Norma Talmadge, Noah Beery, Gilbert Roland, Eddie Borden

DOWN CHANNEL (1929, Brit.)
(? r.) d, Michael Barringer; lp, Henry Victor, Alf Goddard, Christopher Anthony, Roy Travers

DOWN HOME (1920)
(7 r.) d, Irvin V. Willat; lp, James O. Barrows, Edward Hearn, Aggie Herring, Leatrice Joy

DOWN ON THE FARM (1920)
(5 r.) d, Erle C. Kenton, Ray Gray; lp, Louise Fazenda, Bert Roach, Harry Gribbon, Marie Prevost

DOWN UNDER DONOVAN (1922, Brit.)
(6 r.) d, Harry Lambart; lp, Cora Goffin, W.H. Benham, Bertram Parnell, William Lugg

DOWNHILL
(SEE: WHEN THE BOYS LEAVE HOME, 1928, Brit.)

DOWNSTREAM (1929, Brit.)
(6 r.) d, Guarino G. Glavany; lp, Chili Bouchier, Harold Huth, Marie Ault, David Dunbar

DRAFT 258 (1917)
(7 r.) d, William Christy Cabanne; lp, Mabel Taliaferro, Walter Miller, Earle Brunswick, Eugene Borden

DRAG HARLAN (1920)
(6 r.) d, J. Gordon Edwards; lp, William Farnum, Jackie Saunders, Arthur Millett, G. Raymond Nye

DRAGON, THE (1916)
(5 r.) d, Harry Pollard; lp, Margarita Fischer, Katherine Calhoun, Bennett Southhard, Joseph Harris

DRAGON HORSE, THE
(SEE: SILK BOUQUET, THE, 1926)

DRAGON PAINTER, THE (1919)
(5 r.) d, William Worthington; lp, Sessue Hayakawa, Tsuru Aoki, Toyo Fujita, Edward Peil

DREAM CHEATER, THE (1920)
(5 r.) d, Ernest C. Warde; lp, J. Warren Kerrigan, Sam Sothern, Wedgewood Nowell, Alice Wilson

DREAM DOLL, THE (1917)
(5 r.) d, Howard S. Moss; lp, Marguerite Clayton, John Cossar, Bobby Bolder, Rod La Rocque

DREAM GIRL, THE (1916)
(5 r.) d, Cecil B. DeMille; lp, Mae Murray, Theodore Roberts, Charles West, James Neill

DREAM LADY, THE (1918)
(5 r.) d, Elsie Jane Wilson; lp, Carmel Myers, Thomas Holding, Kathleen Emerson, Harry Van Meter

DREAM OF LOVE (1928)
(6 r.) d, Fred Niblo; lp, Nils Asther, Joan Crawford, Aileen Pringle, Warner Oland

DREAM OR TWO AGO, A (1916)
(5 r.) d, James Kirkwood; lp, Mary Miles Minter, Lizette Thorne, Clarence Burton, John Gough

DREAM WOMAN, THE (1914)
(4 r.) d, Alice Blache; lp, Claire Whitney, Fraunie Fraunholz

DREAMS OF YOUTH (1923, Jap.)
(? r.) d, Kenji Mizoguchi

DREAMS OF YOUTH (1928, Jap.)
(? r.) d, Yasujiro Ozu

DREARY HOUSE (1928)
(8 r.)

DRESSED TO KILL (1928)
(7 r.) d, Irving Cummings; lp, Edmund Lowe, Mary Astor, Ben Bard, Robert Perry

DRESSMAKER FROM PARIS, THE (1925)
(8 r.) d, Paul Bern; lp, Leatrice Joy, Ernest Torrence, Allan Forrest, Mildred Harris

DRIFTER, THE (1929)
(6 r.) d, Robert De Lacy; lp, Tom Mix, Dorothy Dwan, Barney Furey, Al Smith

DRIFTERS, THE (1919)
(5 r.) d, Jesse D. Hampton; lp, J. Warren Kerrigan, Lois Wilson, William Conklin, Casson Ferguson

DRIFTIN' THRU (1926)
(5 r.) d, Scott R. Dunlap; lp, Harry Carey, Stanton Heck, Ruth King, G. Raymond Nye

DRIFTING (1923)
(7 r.) d, Tod Browning; lp, Priscilla Dean, Matt Moore, Wallace Beery, J. Farrell MacDonald

DRIFTING KID, THE (1928)
(5 r.) lp, Tex Maynard, Betty Caldwell

DRIFTING ON (1927)
(5 r.) lp, Tom Bay

DRIFTWOOD (1916)
(5 r.) d, Marshall Farnum; lp, Vera Michelena, Clarissa Selwynne, Dora Heritage, Harry Spingler

DRIFTWOOD (1924)
(5 r.) lp, Al Ferguson, Virginia Abbot

DRIFTWOOD (1928)
(7 r.) d, Christy Cabanne; lp, Don Alvarado, Marceline Day, Alan Roscoe, J.W. Johnston

DRINK (1917, Brit.)
(6 r.) d, Sidney Morgan; lp, Fred Groves, Irene Browne, Alice O'Brien, George Foley

DRIVEN
(SEE: DESPERATION, 1916, Brit.)

DRIVEN (1923)
(6 r.) d, Charles J. Brabin; lp, Emily Fitzroy, Burr McIntosh, Charles Emmett Mack, George Bancroft

DRIVIN' FOOL, THE (1923)
(6 r.) d, Robert T. Thornby; lp, Alec B. Francis, Patsy Ruth Miller, Wilton Taylor, Wally Van

DRUG MONSTER, THE (1923)
(5 r.)

DRUG STORE COWBOY (1925)
(5 r.) d, Park Frame; lp, Franklyn Farnum, Robert Walker, Jean Arthur, Malcolm Denny

DRUGGED WATERS (1916)
(5 r.) d, William C. Dowlan; lp, Gloria Fonda, William C. Dowlan, E.P. Evers, George Berrell

DRUMS OF FATE (1923)
(6 r.) d, Charles Maigne; lp, Mary Miles Minter, Maurice B. Flynn, George Fawcett, Robert Cain

DRUMS OF JEOPARDY, THE (1923)
(7 r.) d, Edward Dillon; lp, Elaine Hammerstein, Jack Mulhall, Wallace Beery, David Torrence

DRUMS OF LOVE (1928)
(9 r.) d, D.W. Griffith; lp, Mary Philbin, Lionel Barrymore, Don Alvarado, Tully Marshall

DRUMS OF THE DESERT (1927)
(6 r.) d, John Waters; lp, Warner Baxter, Marietta Millner, Ford Sterling, Wallace MacDonald

DRUNKENNESS AND ITS CONSEQUENCES (1913, USSR)
(4 r.) d, A. Dvoretsky; lp, Ivan Mozhukhin

DRUSILLA WITH A MILLION (1925)
(7 r.) d, F. Harmon Weight; lp, Mary Carr, Priscilla Bonner, Kenneth Harlan, Henry Barrows

DRY MARTINI (1928)
(7 r.) d, H.D'Abbadie; lp, Mary Astor, Matt Moore, Jocelyn Lee, Sally Eilers

DRY VALLEY JOHNSON (1917)
(4 r.)

DU RIRE AUX LARMES (1917, Fr.)
(? r.) d, Gaston Ravel

DU SOLLIST NICHT EHEBRECHEN
(SEE: THERESE RAQUIN, 1928)

DUB, THE (1919)
(5 r.) d, James Cruze; lp, Wallace Reid, Nina Byron, Charles Ogle, Ralph Lewis

DUBARRY (1915)
(6 r.) d, George Kleine; lp, Richard Thornton, Campbell Gollan, Hamilton Revelle, Louis Payne

DUCHESS OF BUFFALO, THE (1926)
(7 r.) d, Sidney Franklin; lp, Constance Talmadge, Tullio Carminati, Edward Martindel, Rose Dione

DUCHESS OF DOUBT, THE (1917)
(5 r.) d, George D. Baker; lp, Emmy Wehlen, George Stuart Christie, Frank Currier, Peggy Parr

DUCHESS OF SEVEN DIALS, THE (1920)
(5 r.) d, Fred Paul; lp, Cecil Mannering, Marjorie Hume, Adelaide Grace, Daisy Elliston

DUDS (1920)
(5 r.) d, Thomas R. Mills; lp, Tom Moore, Naomi Childers, Christine Mayo, Edwin Stevens

DUEL (1928, Fr.)
(? r.) d, Jacques de Baroncelli

DUGAN OF THE DUGOUTS (1928)
(6 r.) d, Robert Ray; lp, Pauline Garon, Danny O'Shea, Ernest Hilliard, J.P. McGowan

DUKE OF CHIMNEY BUTTE, THE (1921)
(5 r.) d, Frank Borzage; lp, Fred Stone, Vola Vale, Josie Sedgwick, Chick Morrison

DUKE'S SON
(SEE: SQUANDERED LIVES, 1920, Brit.)

DULCIE'S ADVENTURE (1916)
(5 r.) d, James Kirkwood; lp, Mary Miles Minter, Allan Forrest, Bessie Banks, Marie Van Tassell

DUMMY, THE (1917)
(5 r.) d, Francis Grandon; lp, Jack Pickford, Frank Losee, Edwin Stanley, Helen Greene

DUNGEON, THE (1922)
(7 r.) lp, William E. Fountaine, Shingzie Howard, J. Kenneth Goodman, W.B.F. Crowell

DUNGEON OF DEATH, THE (1915, Brit.)
(4 r.) d, Charles Weston; lp, George Keen, Alice Inward, Lily Saxby, James Lindsay

DUPED (1925)
(5 r.) d, J.P. McGowan; lp, William Desmond, Helen Holmes, J.P. McGowan, Dorothea Wolbert

DUPLICITY OF HARGRAVES, THE (1917)
(4 r.) d, Thomas R. Mills; lp, Charles Kent, J. Frank Glendon, Myrtis Coney, Mrs. Fisher

DURAND OF THE BAD LANDS (1917)
(5 r.) d, Richard Stanton; lp, Dustin Farnum, Winifred Kingston, Tom Mix, Babe Cressman

DURAND OF THE BAD LANDS (1925)
(6 r.) d, Lynn Reynolds; lp, Buck Jones, Marion Nixon, Malcolm Waite, Fred De Silva

DUSK TO DAWN (1922)
(6 r.) d, King Vidor; lp, Florence Vidor, Jack Mulhall, Truman Van Dyke, James Neill

DUST (1916)
(5 r.) d, Edward Sloman; lp, Franklyn Ritchie, Winnifred Greenwood, Harry Von Meter, William Marshall

DUST OF EGYPT, THE (1915)
(5 r.) d, George D. Baker; lp, Antonio Moreno, Edith Storey, Hughie Mack, Charles Brown

DUTY FIRST (1922)
(5 r.) d, Marcel Perez; lp, Pete Morrison

DUTY'S REWARD (1927)
(6 r.) d, Bertram Bracken; lp, Allan Roscoe, Eva Novak, Lou Archer, Edward Brownell

DWELLING PLACE OF LIGHT, THE (1920)
(6 r.) d, Jack Conway; lp, Claire Adams, King Baggot, Robert McKim, Ogden Crane

DYNAMITE ALLEN (1921)
(5 r.) d, Del Henderson; lp, George Walsh, Edna Murphy, Dorothy Allen, Carola Parsons

DYNAMITE SMITH (1924)
(7 r.) d, Ralph Ince; lp, Charles Ray, Jacqueline Logan, Bessie Love, Wallace Beery

EAGLE OF THE SEA, THE (1926)
(8 r.) d, Frank Lloyd; lp, Florence Vidor, Ricardo Cortez, Sam De Grasse, Andre de Beranger

EAGLE'S NEST (1915)
(8 r.) d, Romaine Fielding; lp, Edwin Arden, Romaine Fielding, Harry Kenneth, Clark Comstock

EAGLE'S WINGS, THE (1916)
(5 r.) d, Robert Leonard; lp, Herbert Rawlinson, Grace Carlyle, Vola Smith [Vola Vale], Charles Hill

EARLY BIRDS (1923, Brit.)
(4 r.) d, Lucien Egrot; lp, Harry Wright, Fred Karno, Katherine Kilfoyle, J. Edwards Barber

EARTH WOMAN, THE (1926)
(6 r.) d, Walter Lang; lp, Mary Alden, Priscilla Bonner, Russell Simpson, Carroll Nye

EARTHBOUND (1920)
(7 r.) d, T.Hayes Hunter; lp, Wyndham Standing, Naomi Childers, Billie Cotton, Mahlon Hamilton

EARTHQUAKE MOTOR, THE (1917, Ger.)
(5 r.) d, Karl Heinz Wolff; lp, Hugo Flink

EASIEST WAY, THE (1917)
(7 r.) d, Albert Capellani; lp, Clara Kimball Young, Louise Bates, Joseph Kilgour, Rockliffe Fellowes

EAST LYNNE (1921)
(7 r.) d, Hugo Ballin; lp, Edward Earle, Mabel Ballin, Gladys Coburn, Gilbert Rooney

EAST LYNNE (1925)
(9 r.) d, Emmett J. Flynn; lp, Alma Rubens, Edmund Lowe, Lou Tellegen, Frank Keenan

EAST SIDE, WEST SIDE (1927)
(9 r.) d, Allan Dwan; lp, George O'Brien, Virginia Valli, J. Farrell MacDonald, Dore Davidson

EASTWARD HO! (1919)
(6 r.) d, Emmett J. Flynn; lp, William Russell, Lucille Lee Stewart, Mary Hay, Johnny Hines

EASY GOING (1926)
(5 r.) d, Richard Thorpe; lp, Buddy Roosevelt

EASY MONEY (1917)
(5 r.) d, Travers Vale; lp, Ethel Clayton, John Bowers, Frank Mayo, Louise Vale

EASY MONEY (1922)
(6 r.) lp, Edna Morton, H.L. Pryor, Inez Clough, Sherman H. Dudley, Jr.

ECHO OF YOUTH, THE (1919)
(6 r.) d, Ivan Abramson; lp, Charles Richman, Leah Baird, Pearl Shepard, Marie Shotwell

EDEN AND RETURN (1921)
(5 r.) d, William A. Seiter; lp, Doris May, Emmett King, Margaret Livingston, Earl Metcalfe

EDGE OF THE LAW (1917)
(5 r.) d, L.W. Chaudet; lp, Ruth Stonehouse, Lloyd Whitlock, Lydia Yeamans Titus, M.W. Testa

EDGE OF YOUTH, THE (1920, Brit.)
(6 r.) d, C.C. Calvert; lp, Josephine Earle, Dallas Anderson, Dick Webb, Violet Elliott

EDMUND KEAN--PRINCE AMONG LOVERS
(SEE: KEAN, 1924, Fr.)

EDUCATION DE PRINCE (1927, Fr.)
(? r.) d, Henri Diamant-Berger; lp, Edna Purviance

EGG CRATE WALLOP, THE (1919)
(5 r.) d, Jerome Storm; lp, Charles Ray, Colleen Moore, Jack Connelly, John P. Lockney

EIGHT BELLS (1916)
(5 r.) d, John F. Byrne; lp, Andrew Byrne, John Kearney, Dorothy Graham, Mabel Paige

"813" (1920)
(6 r.) d, Scott Sidney; lp, Wedgewood Nowell, Kathryn Adams, Laura La Plante, Ralph Lewis

1812 (1912, USSR)
(4 r.) d, Vasili Goncharov, Kai Hansen, A. Uralsky; lp, V, Seryozhinikov, P. Knorr

EILEEN OF THE TREES
(SEE: GLORIOUS YOUTH, 1928, Brit.)

EINE DU BARRY VON HEUTE
(SEE: MODERN DU BARRY, A, 1928, Ger.)

EL RELICARIO (1926)
(7 r.) lp, Miguel C. Torres, Sally Rand, Judy King

ELDER MISS BLOSSOM, THE
(SEE: WANTED A WIFE, 1918, Brit.)

ELDER VASILI GRYAZNOV (1924, USSR)
(8 r.) d, Cheslav Sabinsky; lp, Pytor Starkovsky, Y. Kaverina, Max Tereshkovich, Maria Babanova

ELDORADO (1921, Fr.)
(6 r.) d, Marcel L'Herbier; lp, Eve Francis, Jaque Catelain, Marcelle Pradot, Philippe Heriat

ELEVENTH [YEAR], THE (1928, USSR)
(5 r.) d, Dziga Vertov

ELIANE (1919, Fr.)
(? r.) d, Camille de Morlhon

ELISO (1928, USSR)
(8 r.) d, Nikolai Shengelaya; lp, I. Mamporiya, Kira Andronikashvili, Kokta Karalashvili

EMBERS (1916)
(5 r.) d, Arthur Maude; lp, Constance Crawley, Arthur Maude, Nell Franzen, William Carroll

EMBLEMS OF LOVE (1924)
(7 r.) lp, Jack Drumier, Jane Jennings, Charles Delaney, Grace Cunard

EMBODIED THOUGHT, THE (1916)
(4 r.) d, Edward Sloman; lp, Edward Sloman, Hazel Neice, Adelaide Bronti, Melvin Mayo

EMPIRE BUILDERS (1924)
(5 r.) lp, Snowy Baker

EMPIRE OF DIAMONDS, THE (1920)
(6 r.) d, Leonce Perret; lp, Robert Elliott, Lucy Fox, Henry G. Sell, Leon Mathot

EMPRESS, THE (1917)
(5 r.) d Mme. Blache [Alice Guy]; lp, Holbrook Blinn, Doris Kenyon, William Morse, Lyn Donaldson

EMPTY ARMS (1920)
(5 r.) d, Frank Reicher; lp, Gail Kane, Thurston Hall, J. Herbert Frank, Irene Blackwell

EMPTY CAB, THE (1918)
(5 r.) d, Douglas Gerrard; lp, Franklyn Farnum, Eileen Percy, Harry De Moore, Frank Brownlee

EMPTY CRADLE, THE (1923)
(7 r.) d, Burton King; lp, Mary Alden, Harry T. Morey, Mickey Bennett, Edward Quinn

EMPTY HEARTS (1924)
(6 r.) d, Al Santell; lp, John Bowers, Charles Murray, John Miljan, Clara Bow

EMPTY POCKETS (1918)
(6 r.) d, Herbert Brenon; lp, Ketty Galanta, Barbara Castleton, Bert Lytell, Malcolm Williams

EMPTY SADDLE, THE (1925)
(5 r.) d, Harry S. Webb; lp, Peter Morrison, Betty Goodwin

EN PLONGEE (1927, Fr.)
(? r.) d, Jacques Robert

EN RADE (1927, Fr.)
(6 r.) d, Alberto Cavalcanti; lp, Catherine Hessling, Nathalie Lissenko, Geores Charlia, Tommy Bourdel

EN RAEDSOM NAT (1914, Den.)
(5 r.) lp, Emilie Sannon

ENCHANTED BARN, THE (1919)
(? r.) d, David Smith

END OF ST. PETERSBURG, THE (1927, USSR)
(8 r.) d, Vsevolod Pudovkin; lp, A.P. Chistyakov, Vera Baranovskaya, Ivan Chuvelov, V. Chuvelov

END OF THE RAINBOW, THE (1916)
(5 r.) d, Lynn Reynolds; Myrtle Gonzales, George Hernandez, Val Paul, Jack Curtis

END OF THE ROAD, THE (1915)
(5 r.) d, Thomas Ricketts; lp, Harold Lockwood, May Allison, Helene Rosson, William Stowell

END OF THE ROAD, THE (1923)
(7 r.)

END OF THE ROPE (1923)
(5 r.) d, Charles R. Seeling; lp, Big Boy Williams

END OF THE TOUR, THE (1917)
(5 r.) d, George D. Baker; lp, Lionel Barrymore, Ethel Dayton [Ethel Corcoran], Frank Currier, Walter Hiers

ENEMY, THE (1916)
(7 r.) d, Paul Scardon; lp, Evart Overton, Peggy Hyland, Charles Kent, Julia Swayne

ENEMY TO SOCIETY, AN (1915)
(5 r.) d, Edgar Jones; lp, Hamilton Revelle, Lois Meredith, H. Cooper Cliffe, Henry Bergman

ENEMY TO THE KING, AN (1916)
(6 r.) d, Frederick Thomson; lp, E.H. Sothern, Edith Storey, John Robertson, Fred Lewis

ENERGETIC EVA (1916)
(5 r.) lp, Eva Tanguay

ENGINEER PRITE'S PROJECT (1918, USSR)
(4 r.) d, Lev Kuleshov; lp, L. Polevoy, Boris Kuleshov, E. Komarova, Ernest Kulganin

ENGLISHMAN'S HONOUR, AN (1915, Brit.)
(4 r.)

ENOCH ARDEN (1914, Brit.)
(4 r.) d, Percy Nash; lp, Gerald Lawrence, Fay Davis, Ben Webster, May Whitty

ENOCH ARDEN (1915)
(4 r.) d, W. Christy Cabanne; lp, Lillian Gish, Alfred Paget, Wallace Reid, Mildred Harris

ENLIGHTEN THY DAUGHTER (1917)
(7 r.) d, Ivan Abramson; lp, Frank Sheridan, Katharine Kaelred, Zena Keefe, Arthur Donaldson

ENTICEMENT (1925)
(7 r.) d, George Archainbaud; lp, Mary Astor, Clive Brook, Ian Keith, Vera Lewis

ENVIRONMENT (1917)
(5 r.) d, James Kirwood; lp, Mary Miles Minter, George Fisher, Harvey Clark, George Periolat

ENVOY EXTRAORDINARY, THE (1914)
(5 r.) d, Lorimer Johnston

ERMINE AND RHINESTONES (1925)
(6 r.) d, Burton King; lp, Edna Murphy, Niles Welch, Ruth Stonehouse, Coit Albertson

ERNEST MALTRAVERS (1920, Brit.)
(5 r.) d, Jack Denton; lp, Cowley Wright, Lilian Hall Davis, Hubert Gordon Hopkirk, Norman Partridge

EROTIKON (1920, Swed.)
(6 r.) d, Mauritz Stiller; lp, Anders de Wahl, Tora Teje, Karin Molander, Elin Lagergren

EROTIKON (1929, Czech.)
(7 r.) d, Gustav Machaty; lp, Ita Rina, Karel Schleichert, Olaf Fjord, Theo Pistek

ESCAPE, THE (1926)
(5 r.) d, Milburn Morante; lp, Pete Morrison, Barbara Starr, Frank Norcross, Bruce Gordon

ESCAPED CONVICT, THE (1927)
(6 r.) lp, Broncho Billy Anderson

ESSANAY-CHAPLIN REVUE OF 1916, THE (1916)
(5 r.) d, Charlie Chaplin; lp, Charlie Chaplin, Edna Purviance

ESSENTIAL SPARK OF JEWISHNESS, THE (1912, USSR)
(4 r.) d, A. Slavinsky

ESTHER REDEEMED (1915, Brit.)
(4 r.) d, Sidney Morgan; lp, Fanny Tittell-Brune, Julian Royce, Cecil Fletcher, William Brandon

ETERNAL CITY, THE (1923)
(8 r.) d, George Fitzmaurice; lp, Barbara La Marr, Bert Lytell, Lionel Barrymore, Richard Bennett

ETERNAL FLAME, THE (1922)
(8 r.) d, Frank Lloyd; lp, Norma Talmadge, Adolphe Menjou, Wedgewood Nowell, Conway Tearle

ETERNAL LIGHT, THE (1919)
(8 r.) d, O.E. Goebel, Conde B. Pallen;

ETERNAL MOTHER, THE (1917)
(5 r.) d, Frank Reicher; lp, Ethel Barrymore, Frank Mills, J.W. Johnston, Charles W. Sutton

ETERNAL MOTHER, THE (1921)
(? r.) d, William Davis; lp, Florence Reed

ETERNAL PEACE (1922)
(6 r.) lp, Betty Harte

ETERNAL QUESTION, THE (1916)
(5 r.) d, Burton L. King; lp, Olga Petrova, Mahlon Hamilton, Arthur Hoops, Warner Oland

ETERNAL TRIANGLE, THE (1917, Brit.)
(5 r.) d, Frank Wilson; lp, Chrissie White, Stewart Rome, Violet Hopson, Lionelle Howard

ETRE AIME POUR SOI-MEME (1920, Fr.)
(? r.) d, Henri Etievant

ETRE OU NE PAS ETRE (1922, Fr.)
(? r.) d, Rene Leprince

EUGENE ARAM (1924, Brit.)
(8 r.) d, Arthur Rooke; lp, Arthur Wontner, Barbara Hoffe, Mary Odette, James Carew

EVA (1918, USSR)
(5 r.) d, Ivan Perestiani; lp, Zoya Karabanova, Amo Bek-Nazarov, Ivan Perestiani

EVANGELINE (1914, Can.)
(5 r.) d, E.P. Sullivan, W.H. Cavanaugh

EVANGELINE (1919)
(5 r.) d, Raoul Walsh; lp, Miriam Cooper, Albert Roscoe, Spottiswoode Aitken, James Marcus

EVANGELIST, THE (1915)
(4 r.) d, Barry O'Neil; lp, Gladys Hanson, George Soule Spencer, Edith Ritchie, Jack Standing

EVE IN EXILE (1919)
(6 r.) d, Burton George; lp, Charlotte Walker, Thomas Santschi, Wheeler Oakman, Melbourne McDowell

EVEN AS EVE (1920)
(6 r.) d, B.A. Rolfe, Chester De Vonde; lp, Grace Darling, Ramsaye Wallace, E.J. Radcliffe, Sally Crute

EVEN BREAK, AN (1917)
(5 r.) d, Lambert Hillyer; lp, Olive Thomas, Charles Gunn, Margaret Thompson, Darrel Foss

EVER SINCE EVE (1921)
(5 r.) d, Howard M. Mitchell; lp, Shirley Mason, Herbert Heyes, Eva Gordon, Charles Spere

EVERLASTING WHISPER, THE (1925)
(6 r.) d, J.G. Blystone; lp, Tom Mix, Alice Calhoun, Robert Cain, George Berrell

EVERY GIRL'S DREAM (1917)
(5 r.) d, Harry Millarde; lp, June Caprice, Kittens Reichert, Harry Hilliard, Margaret Fielding

EVERY MOTHER'S SON (1919)
(5 r.) d, Raoul Walsh; lp, Charlotte Walker, Percy Standing, Edwin Stanley, [Charles] Ray Howard

EVERYBODY'S ACTING (1926)
(7 r.) d, Marshall Neilan; lp, Betty Bronson, Ford Sterling, Louise Dresser, Lawrence Gray

EVERYTHING BUT THE TRUTH (1920)
(5 r.) d, Eddie Lyons, Lee Moran; lp, Eddie Lyons, Lee Moran, Katherine Lewis, Anne Cornwall

EVERYTHING FOR SALE (1921)
(5 r.) d, Frank O'Connor; lp, May McAvoy, Eddie Sutherland, Kathlyn Williams, Edwin Stevens

EVERYWOMAN (1919)
(8 r.) d, George Melford; lp, Violet Heming, Monte Blue, Wanda Hawley, Irving Cummings

EVERYWOMAN'S HUSBAND (1918)
(5 r.) d, Gilbert P. Hamilton; lp, Gloria Swanson, Joe King, Lillian Langdon, George Pearce

EVE'S LEAVES (1926)
(7 r.) d, Paul Sloane; lp, Leatrice Joy, William Boyd, Robert Edeson, Walter Long

EVIDENCE (1922)
(5 r.) d, George Archainbaud; lp, Elaine Hammerstein, Niles Welsh, Holmes Herbert, Constance Bennett

EVIL EYE, THE (1917)
(5 r.) d, George Melford; lp, Blanche Sweet, Tom Forman, Webster Campbell, J. Parks Jones

EVIL THEREOF, THE (1916)
(5 r.) d, Robert Vignola; lp, Frank Losee, Grace Valentine, Crauford Kent

EVIL WOMEN DO, THE (1916)
(5 r.) d, Rupert Julian; lp, Elsie Jane Wilson, Francelia Billington, Rupert Julian, Hobart Henley

EXCHANGE OF WIVES (1925)
(7 r.) d, Hobart Henley; lp, Eleanor Boardman, Lew Cody, Renee Adoree, Creighton Hale

EXCLUSIVE RIGHTS (1926)
(6 r.) d, Frank O'Connor; lp, Gayne Whitman, Lillian Rich, Gloria Gordon, Raymond McKee

EXCUSE ME (1916)
(5 r.) d, Henry W. Savage; lp, George F. Marion, Robert Fischer, Harrison Ford, Vivian Blackburn

EXCUSE ME (1925)
(6 r.) d, Alf Goulding; lp, Norma Shearer, Conrad Nagel, Renee Adoree, Walter Hiers

EXILE (1917)
(5 r.) d, Maurice Tourner; lp, Olga Petrova, Wyndham Standing, Mahlon Hamilton, Warren Cook

EXPERIENCE (1921)
(7 r.) d, George Fitzmaurice; lp, Richard Barthelmess, John Miltern, Marjorie Daw, E.J. Radcliffe

EXPERIMENTAL MARRIAGE (1919)
(5 r.) d, Robert G. Vignola; lp, Constance Talmadge, Harrison Ford, Walter Hiers, Vera Sisson

EXPIATION (1918, Fr.)
(? r.) d, Camille de Morlhon

EXPIATION (1922, Brit.)
(6 r.) d, Sinclair Hill; lp, Ivy Close, Fred Raynham, Lionelle Howard, Malcolm Tod

EXQUISIT THIEF, THE (1919)
(6 r.) d, Tod Browning; lp, Priscilla Dean, J. Milton Ross, Sam De Grasse, Thurston Hall

EXTRA! EXTRA! (1922)
(5 r.) d, William K. Howard; lp, Edna Murphy, Johnnie Walker, Herschel Mayall, Wilson Hummell

EXTRAORDINARY ADVENTURES OF MR. WEST IN THE LAND OF THE BOLSHEVIKS (1924, USSR)
(8 r.) d, Lev Kuleshov; lp, Podobed, Valya Lopatina, Boris Barnet, Pytor Galadzhev

EXTRAVAGANCE (1916)
(5 r.) d, Burton L. King; lp, Olga Petrova, H. Cooper Cliffe, Mahlon Hamilton, Arthur Hoops

EXTRAVAGANCE (1921)
(6 r.) d, Philip E. Rosen; lp, Mary Allison, Robert Edeson, Theodore von Eltz, William Courtwright

EYE FOR AN EYE, AN (1915)
(4 r.) d, William D. Taylor; lp, Neva Gerber

EYE OF ENVY, THE (1917)
(5 r.) d, Harrish Ingraham; lp, Crane Wilbur, F.A. Thompson, Julia Jackson, Lillian Webster

EYE OF GOD, THE (1916)
(5 r.) d, Lois Weber, Phillips Smalley; lp, Tyrone Power, Lois Weber, Ethel Weber, Charles Gunn

EYES OF HOLLYWOOD (1925)
(5 r.) lp, Ward Wing, Priscilla Bonner

EYES OF MYSTERY, THE (1918)
(5 r.) d, Tod Browning; lp, Edith Storey, Bradley Barker, Harry S. Northrup, Frank Andrews

EYES OF THE DESERT (1926)
(5 r.) d, Frederick Reel, Jr.; lp, Al Richmond, Dorothy Donald

EYES OF THE FOREST (1923)
(5 r.) d, Lambert Hillyer; lp, Tom Mix, Pauline Starke, Sid Jordan, Buster Gardner

EYES OF THE SOUL (1919)
(5 r.) d, Emile Chautard; lp, Elsie Ferguson, Wyndham Standing, J. Flannigan, George Backus

EYES OF THE TOTEM (1927)
(7 r.) d, W.S. Van Dyke; lp, Wanda Hawley, Tom Santschi, Anne Cornwall, Gareth Hughes

EYES OF THE WORLD, THE (1917)
(10 r.) d, Donald Crisp; lp, Jane Novak, Jack Livingston, Kathleen Kirkham, Monroe Salisbury

EYES OF YOUTH (1919)
(7 r.) d, Albert Parker; lp, Clara Kimball Young, Milton Sills, Vincent Serrano, Pauline Starke

FABIENNE (1920, Fr.)
(? r.) d, Camille de Morlhon

FABIOLA (1923, Ital.)
(8 r.) lp, Elaine di Sangro, Adelaide Poletti, S. Sanfilippo, Anthony Novelli

FACE A L'OCEAN (1920, Fr.)
(? r.) d, Rene Leprince

FACE AT YOUR WINDOW, THE (1920)
(6 r.) d, Richard Stanton; lp, Gina Reilly, Earl Metcalfe, Robert Cummings, Edward Roseman

FACE BETWEEN, THE (1922)
(5 r.) d, Bayard Veiller; lp, Bert Lytell, Andree Tourneur, Sylvia Breamer, Hardee Kirkland

FACE IN THE DARK, THE (1918)
(6 r.) d, Hobart Henley; lp, Mae Marsh, Niles Welch, Alec B. Francis, Harry C. Myers

FACE IN THE FOG, THE (1922)
(7 r.) d, Alan Crosland; lp, Lionel Barrymore, Seena Owen, Lowell Sherman, George Nash

FACE OF THE WORLD (1921)
(6 r.) d, Irvin V. Willat; lp, Edward Hearn, Barbara Bedford, Harry Duffield, Lloyd Whitlock

FACE ON THE BARROOM FLOOR, THE (1923)
(6 r.) d, Jack [John] Ford; lp, Henry B. Walthall, Ruth Clifford, Walter Emerson, Frederick Sullivan

FACE TO FACE (1920)
(5 r.) d, Harry Grossman; lp, Marguerite Marsh, Edna Holman, Richard Stewart, Coit Albertson

FACE VALUE (1918)
(5 r.) d, Robert Z. Leonard; lp, Mae Murray, Clarissa Selwynne, Florence Carpenter, Wheeler Oakman

FACE VALUE (1927)
(5 r.) d, Robert Florey; lp, Fritzi Ridgeway, Gene Gowing, Betty Baker, Paddy O'Flynn

FACES OF CHILDREN
(SEE: VISAGE D'EFANTS, 1926)

FADED FLOWER, THE (1916)
(6 r.) d, Ivan Abramson; lp, Marguerite Snow, Arthur Donaldson, Rose Coghlan, Alma Hanlon

FAGASA (1928)
(6 r.) d, Raymond Wells; lp, George Kelley, Grace Lord, Gael Kelton, Raymond Wells

FAILURE, THE (1915)
(4 r.) d, Christy Cabanne; lp, John Emerson, Wahnetta Hanson, A.D. Sears, Olga Gray

FAILURE, THE
(SEE: DICK CARSON WINS THROUGH, 1917, Brit.)

FAINT PERFUME (1925)
(6 r.) d, Louis Gasnier; lp, Seena Owen, William Powell, Alyce Mills, Mary Alden

FAIR AND WARMER (1919)
(7 r.) d, Henry Otto; lp, May Allison, Pell Trenton, Eugene Pallette, Christine Mayo

FAIR BARBARIAN, THE (1917)
(5 r.) d, Robert Thornby; lp, Vivian Martin, Charles H. Geldert, Douglas MacLean, Jane Wolff

FAIR CHEAT, THE (1923)
(6 r.) d, Burton King; lp, Edmund Breese, Wilfred Lytell, Dorothy Mackaill, Marie White

FAIR IMPOSTER, A (1916, Brit.)
(5 r.) d, Alexander Butler; lp, Madge Titheradge, Gerald McCarthy, Charles Rock, Alice de Winton

FAIR LADY (1922)
(7 r.) d, Kenneth Webb; lp, Betty Blythe, Thurston Hall, Robert Elliott, Gladys Hulette

FAIR MAID OF PERTH, THE (1923, Brit.)
(6 r.) d, Edwin Greenwood; lp, Russell Thorndike, Sylvia Caine, Lionel d'Aragon, Tristram Rawson

FAIR WEEK (1924)
(5 r.) d, Rob Wagner; lp, Walter Hiers, Constance Wilson, Carmen Phillips, J. Farrell MacDonald

FAIRY AND THE WAIF, THE (1915)
(5 r.) d, Mary Hubert Frohman, George Irving; lp, Mary Miles Minter, Percy Halton, Will Archie, William Carleton

FAITH (1916)
(5 r.) d, James Kirkwood; lp, Mary Miles Minter, Clarence Burton, Lizette Thorne, Margaret Shelby

FAITH
(SEE: IN BONDAGE, 1919, Brit.)

FAITH (1919)
(5 r.) d, Charles Swickard; lp, Bert Lytell, Rosemary Theby, Edythe Chapman, Edwin Stevens

FAITH AND ENDURIN' (1918)
(5 r.) d, Cliff Smith; lp, Roy Stewart, Fritzi Ridgeway, W.A. Jeffries, Joe Bennett

FAITH AND FORTUNE (1915)
(4 r.) d, Frank McGlynn; lp, Grace Williams, Curtis Cooksey, Yale Benner, James Harris

FAITH FOR GOLD (1930)
(9 r.)

FAITH OF A CHILD, THE (1915, Brit.)
(4 r.) d, F. Martin Thornton; lp, Evelyn Boucher, Rolfe Leslie, Bert Grahame

FAITH OF THE STRONG, THE (1919)
(5 r.) d, Robert North Bradbury; lp, Mitchell Lewis, Gloria Payton, Patricia Palmer, Frank Whitson

FAITHFUL HEART, THE (1922, Brit.)
(6 r.) d, G.B. Samuelson; lp, Owen Nares, Lillian Hall Davies, Cathleen Nesbitt, A.B. Imeson

FAITHFUL HEART, THE
(SEE: COEUR FIDELE, 1923)

FAITHFUL WIVES (1926)
(6 r.) d, Norbert Myles; lp, Wallace MacDonald, Edythe Chapman, Doris May, Niles Welch

FAITHLESS LOVER (1928)
(6 r.) d, Lawrence Windom; lp, Eugene O'Brien, Gladys Hulette, Raymond Hackett, Jane Jennings

FAITHLESS SEX, THE (1922)
(5 r.) d, Henry J. Napier; lp, Frances Nelson, Leonore Harris, Gladden James, Robert Frazer

FAKER, THE (1929)
(6 r.) d, Phil Rosen; lp, Jacqueline Logan, Charles Delaney, Warner Oland, Charles Hill Mailes

FALL OF A NATION, THE (1916)
(7 r.) d, Bartley Cushing; lp, Arthur Shirley, Lorraine Huling, Flora MacDonald, Percy Standing

FALL OF A SAINT, THE (1920, Brit.)
(6 r.) d, W.P. Kellino; lp, Josephine Earle, Gerald Lawrence, W.T. Ellwanger, Dallas Anderson

FALL OF THE HOUSE OF USHER, THE (1928, Fr.)
(? r.) d, Jean Epstein; lp, Marguerite Gance, Jean Debucourt, Charles Lamy, Pierre Hot

FALL OF THE ROMANOFFS, THE (1917)
(8 r.) d, Herbert Brenon; lp, Iiodor, Nance O'Neil, Ketty Galanta, Alfred Hickman

FALLEN ANGEL, THE (1918)
(5 r.) d, Robert Thornby; lp, Jewel Carmen, L.C. Shumway, Charles Clary, Herbert Heyes

FALLEN ANGELS
(SEE: MAN, WOMAN, AND WIFE, 1929)

FALLEN IDOL, A (1919)
(5 r.) d, Kenean Buel; lp, Evelyn Nesbit, Lillian Lawrence, Sidney Mason, Lester Chambers

FALLEN STAR, A (1916, Brit.)
(5 r.) d, Cecil M. Hepworth; lp, Albert Chevalier, Harry Brett, Janet Alexander

FALSE ALARM, THE (1926)
(6 r.) d, Frank O'Connor; lp, Ralph Lewis, Dorothy Revier, John Harron, Mary Carr

FALSE AMBITION (1918)
(5 r.) d, Gilbert P. Hamilton; lp, Alma Rubens, Peggy Pearce, Lee Hill, Alberta Lee

FALSE CODE, THE (1919)
(5 r.) d, Ernest C. Warde; lp, Frank Keenan, Myles McCarthy, Joseph J. Dowling, Clyde Benson

FALSE FRIENDS (1926)
(5 r.) d, Francis Ford; lp, Jack Mower, Florence Ulrich

FALSE FRONTS (1922)
(5 r.) d, Samuel R. Bradley; lp, Edward Earle, Madelyn Clare, Frank Losee, Barbara Castleton

FALSE GODS (1919)
(5 r.) d, Wally Van; lp, Grace Darling, Hugh Thompson, Harry Mestayer, Florence Billings

FALSE KISSES (1921)
(5 r.) d, Paul Scardon; lp, Miss Du Pont, Pat O'Malley, Lloyd Whitlock, Camilla Clark

FALSE MAGISTRATE, THE (1914, Fr.)
(6 r.)

FALSE MORALS (1927)
(6 r.) lp, Gaston Glass, Joseph Swickard, Duane Thompson, Mary Carr

FALSE PLAY
(SEE: LONE HAND, THE, 1922)

FALSE PRIDE (1926)
(6 r.) d, Hugh Dierker; lp, Owen Moore

FALSE ROAD, THE (1920)
(5 r.) d, Fred Niblo; lp, Enid Bennett, Lloyd Hughes, Wade Boteler, Lucille Young

FALSE SHAME
(SEE: FOOLS OF PASSION, 1926, Ger.)

FALSE TRAILS (1924)
(5 r.) lp, Pete Morrison

FALSE WIRELESS, THE (1914, Brit.)
(4 r.) d, H.O. Martinek; lp, H.O. Martinek, Ivy Montford

FALSE WOMEN (1921)
(5 r.) d, R. Dale Armstrong; lp, Sheldon Smith, Audrey Chapman, Catherine Bradley, Antonio Corsi

FAMILY CLOSET, THE (1921)
(6 r.) d, John B. O'Brien; lp, Holmes Herbert, Alice Mann, Kempton Greene, Byron Russell

FAMILY HONOR, THE (1917)
(5 r.) d, Emile Chautard; lp, Robert Warwick, June Elvidge, Alec B. Francis, Henry Hull

FAMILY HONOR, THE (1920)
(5 r.) d, King Vidor; lp, Florence Vidor, Charles Meredith, Roscoe Karns, Ben Alexander

FAMILY STAIN, THE (1915)
(6 r.) d, Will S. Davis; lp, Frederick Perry, Walter Miller

FAMILY UPSTAIRS, THE (1926)
(6 r.) d, J.G. Blystone; lp, Virginia Valli, Allan Simpson, J. Farrell MacDonald, Lillian Elliott

FAMOUS MRS. FAIR, THE (1923)
(8 r.) d, Fred Niblo; lp, Myrtle Stedman, Huntly Gordon, Marguerite De La Motte, Cullen Landis

FAN FAN (1918)
(5 r.) d, C.M. & S.A. Franklin; lp, Virginia Lee Corbin, Francis Carpenter, Carmen De Rue, Violet Radcliffe

FANATICS (1917)
(5 r.) d, Raymond Wells; lp, Adda Gleason, J. Barney Sherry, William V. Mong, Donald Fuller

FANGS OF DESTINY (1927)
(5 r.) d, Stuart Paton; lp, Dynamite (a dog), Edmund Cobb, Betty Caldwell, George Periolat

FANGS OF FATE (1925)
(5 r.) d, Horace B. Carpenter; lp, Bill Patton, Dorothy Donald, Ivor McFadden, Beatrice Allen

FANGS OF FATE (1928)
(5 r.) d, Noel Mason Smith; lp, Arnold Gray, Henry Hebert, Robert Reault, Kathleen Collins

FANGS OF THE WOLF (1924)
(5 r.) d, Harry O. Hoyt, Joseph A. Golden; lp, Charles Hutchison

FANGS OF WOLFHEART (1925)
(5 r.) lp, Big Boy Williams, Wolfheart (a dog)

FANNY HAWTHORNE (1927, Brit.)
(9 r.) d, Maurice Elvey, Victor Saville; lp, Estelle Brody, John Stuart, Norman McKinnel, Marie Ault

FANTAISIE DE MILLARDAIRE (1919, Fr.)
(? r.) d, Edouard Violet

FANTASMA (1914)
(5 r.) d, Charles M. Seay; lp, George Hanlon, Jr., W.T. Carleton, William Ruge, George Schrode

FANTOMAS, THE CROOK DETECTIVE (1914, Fr.)
(6 r.)

FANTOMAS, THE FALSE MAGISTRATE
(SEE: FALSE MAGISTRATE, THE, 1914, Fr.)

FAR WESTERN TRAILS (1929)
(5 r.) d, Robert J. Horner; lp, Ted Thompson, Bud Osborne, Lew Ames, Betty O'Doan

FARMER'S DAUGHTER, THE (1928)
(6 r.) d, Norman Taurog, Arthur Rosson; lp, Marjorie Beebe, Frank Albertson, Arthur Stone, Lincoln Stedman

FASCINATING YOUTH (1926)
(7 r.) d, Sam Wood; lp, Charles Rogers, Ivy Harris, Jack Luden, Walter Goss

FASCINATION (1922)
(8 r.) d, Robert Z. Leonard; lp, Mae Murray, Creighton Hale, Charles Lane, Emily Fitzroy

FASHION MADNESS (1928)
(6 r.) d, Louis J. Gasnier; lp, Claire Windsor, Reed Howes, Laska Winters, Donald McNamee

FASHION ROW (1923)
(7 r.) d, Robert Z. Leonard; lp, Mae Murray, Earle Foxe, Freeman Wood, Mathilde Brundage

FASHIONABLE FAKERS (1923)
(5 r.) d, William Worthington; lp, Johnnie Walker, Mildred June, George Cowl, J. Farrell MacDonald

FASHIONS FOR WOMEN (1927)
(7 r.) d, Dorothy Arzner; lp, Esther Ralston, Raymond Hatton, Einar Hanson, Edward Martindel

FAST AND FEARLESS (1924)
(5 r.) d, Richard Thorpe; lp, Buffalo Bill, Jr., Jean Arthur, William Turner, George Magrill

FAST AND FURIOUS (1927)
(6 r.) d, Melville W. Brown; lp, Reginald Denny, Barbara Worth, Claude Gillingwater, Armand Kaliz

FAST COMPANY (1918)
(5 r.) d, Lynn F. Reynolds; lp, Franklyn Farnum, Juanita Hansen, Fred Montague, Katherine Griffith

FAST FIGHTIN' (1925)
(5 r.) d, Richard Thorpe; lp, Buddy Roosevelt, Nell Brantley, Joe Rickson, Emily Barrye

FAST MAIL, THE (1922)
(6 r.) d, Bernard J. Durning; lp, Charles Jones, Eileen Percy, James Mason, William Steele

FAST SET, THE (1924)
(8 r.) d, William De Mille; lp, Betty Compson, Adolphe Menjou, Elliott Dexter, ZaSu Pitts

FAST WORKER, THE (1924)
(7 r.) d, William Seiter; lp, Reginald Denny, Laura La Plante, Ethel Grey Terry, Muriel Frances Dana

FATAL HOUR, THE (1920)
(6 r.) d, George W. Terwilliger; lp, Thomas W. Ross, Wilfred Lytell, Francis X. Conlan, Lionel Pape

FATAL MARRIAGE, THE
(SEE: ENOCH ARDEN, 1915)

FATAL MISTAKE, THE (1924)
(5 r.) d, Scott Dunlap; lp, William Fairbanks, Eva Novak, Wilfred Lucas, Dot Farley

FATAL NIGHT, THE (1915)
(4 r.) lp, Constance Crawley, Arthur Maude

FATAL PLUNGE, THE (1924)
(5 r.) d, Harry O. Hoyt; lp, Charles Hutchinson, Ann Luther, Laura La Plante

FATAL 30, THE (1921)
(5 r.) d, John J. Hayes; lp, John J. Hayes, Fritzi Ridgeway, Lillian West, Carl Stockdale

FATALNA KLATWA (1913, Pol.)
(5 r.) d, Avrom Yitskhok Kaminsky; lp, Regina Kaminska, Gershon Weissman, Isaac Samberg, Mordkhe Fiszelewicz

FATE (1921)
(8 r.) lp, John Ince, Clara Smith Hamon

FATE AND THE CHILD (1917)
(4 r.) d, Edward Sloman; lp, William Russell, Charlotte Burton, William Tedmarsh, Rhea Mitchell

FATE OF A FLIRT, THE (1925)
(6 r.) d, Frank R. Strayer; lp, Dorothy Revier, Forrest Stanley, Thomas Ricketts, Phillips Smalley

FATE'S BOOMERANG (1916)
(5 r.) d, Frank Hall Crane; lp, Mollie King, Charles Gotthold, June Elvidge, Frank Goldsmith

FATHER AND SON (1916)
(5 r.) lp, Henry E. Dixey, Millicent Evans, Gladden James, Mabel Montgomery

FATHER AND THE BOYS (1915)
(5 r.) d, Joseph De Grasse; lp, Digby Bell, Harry Ham, Colin "Bud" Chase, Hayward Mack

FATHER FROST (1924, USSR)
(5 r.) d, Yuri Zheliabuzhsky; lp, Klavidya Yelanskaya, Varvara Massalitinova, Vasili Toporkov, Boris Livanov

FATHER SERGIUS (1918, USSR)
(6 r.) d, Yakov Protazanov; lp, Ivan Mozhukhin, V. Dzheneyeva, Vladimir Gaidrov, Natalia Lisenko

FATHER TOM (1921)
(5 r.) d, John B. O'Brien; lp, Tom Wise, James Hill, May Kitson, Myra Brooks

FATHERHOOD (1915)
(4 r.) d, Hobart Bosworth; lp, Hobart Bosworth, Joseph Flores, Hart Hoxie, Helen Wolcott

FATHERS OF MEN (1916)
(5 r.) d, William Humphrey; lp, Robert Edeson, Naomi Childers, William Humphrey, Bobby Connelly

FAUBOURG MONTMARTE (1924, Fr.)
(? r.) d, Charles Burguet

FAUST (1922, Fr.)
(? r.) d, Gerard Bourgeois

FAVOR TO A FRIEND, A (1919)
(5 r.) d, John Ince; lp, Emmy Wehlen, Jack Mulhall, Hugh Fay, Joseph Kilgour

FAZIL (1928)
(7 r.) d, Howard Hawks; Charles Farrell, Greta Nissen, Mae Busch, Vadim Uraneff

FEAR FIGHTER, THE (1925)
(5 r.) d, Albert Rogell; lp, Billy Sullivan, Ruth Dwyer, J.P. McGowan, "Gunboat" Smith

FEAR MARKET, THE (1920)
(5 r.) d, Kenneth Webb; lp, Alice Brady, Frank Losee, Henry Mortimer, Richard Hatteras

FEAR NOT (1917)
(5 r.) d, Allen Holubar; lp, Brownie Vernon, Murdock MacQuarrie, Myles McCarthy, Joseph Girard

FEAR O'GOD (1926, Brit.)
(8 r.) d, Alfred Hitchcock; lp, Nita Naldi, Malcolm Keen, John Hamilton, Bernhard Goetzke

FEAR WOMAN, THE (1919)
(5 r.) d, John A. Barry; lp, Pauline Frederick, Milton Sills, Walter Hiers, Emmett King

FEAR-BOUND (1925)
(6 r.) d, Will Nigh; lp, Marjorie Daw, Will Nigh, Niles Welch, Louise Mackintosh

FEARLESS DICK (1922)
(5 r.) lp, Dick Hatton

FEARLESS RIDER, THE (1928)
(5 r.) d, Edgar Lewis; lp, Fred Humes, Barbara Worth, Ben Corbett, Pee Wee Holmes

FEAST OF LIFE, THE (1916)
(5 r.) d, Albert Capellan; lp, Clara Kimball Young, E.M. Kimball, Pauline Kimball, Paul Capellani

FEATHERTOP (1916)
(5 r.) d, Henry J. Vernot; lp, Marguerite Courtot, James Levering, Gerald Griffin, Mathilde Baring

FECONDITE (1929, Fr.)
(? r.) d, Henri Etievant

FEDORA (1918)
(5 r.) d, Edward Jose; lp, Pauline Frederick, Alfred Hickman, Wilmuth Merkyl, Jere Austin

FEEL MY PULSE (1928)
(6 r.) d, Gregory La Cava; lp, Bebe Daniels, Melbourne MacDowell, George Irving, Charles Sellon

FEET OF CLAY (1917)
(4 r.) d, Harry Harvey; lp, Barney Furey, R. Henry Grey, Margaret Landis, Tom Morgan

FEET OF CLAY (1924)
(10 r.) d, Cecil B. De Mille; lp, Vera Reynolds, Rod La Rocque, Richardo Cortez, Robert Edeson

FELIANA L'ESPIONNE (1924, Fr.)
(? r.) d, Gaston Roudes

FELIX O'DAY (1920)
(5 r.) d, Robert Thornby; lp, H.B. Warner, Marguerite Snow, Lillian Rich, Ray Ripley

FEMALE, THE (1924)
(7 r.) d, Sam Wood; lp, Betty Compson, Warner Baxter, Noah Beery, Dorothy Cummings

FEMALE SWINDLER, THE (1916, Brit.)
(6 r.) d, Albert Ward; lp, Henry Lonsdale, Alice Belmore, Arthur Poole, Maud Olmar

FERRAGUS (1923, Fr.)
(? r.) d, Gaston Ravel

FETTERED (1919, Brit.)
(5 r.) d, Arrigo Bocchi; lp, Manora Thew, Hayford Hobbs, Fred Morgan, Charles Vane

FETTERED WOMAN, THE (1917)
(5 r.) d, Tom Terriss; lp, Alice Joyce, Webster Campbell, Donald McBride, Lionel Grey

FEU (1927, Fr.)
(? r.) d, Jacques de Baroncelli

FEU MATHIAS PASCAL
(SEE: LATE MATTHEW PASCAL, THE, 1927)

FEUD, THE (1919)
(6 r.) d, Edward J. LeSaint; lp, Tom Mix, Eva Novak, Claire McDowell, J. Arthur Mackley

FEUD GIRL, THE (1916)
(5 r.) d, Fred Thompson; lp, Hazel Dawn, Irving Cummings, Arthur Morrison, George Majeroni

FEUD WOMAN, THE (1926)
(6 r.) d, R.E. Williamson

FIANCAILLES (1926, Fr.)
(? r.) d, Roger Lion

FIBBERS, THE (1917)
(4 r.) d, Fred E. Wright; lp, Bryant Washburn, Virginia Valli, John Cossar, Mark Elliston

FIDELITE (1924, Fr.)
(? r.) d, Roger Lion

FIELD OF HONOR, THE (1917)
(5 r.) d, Allen Holubar; lp, Allen Holubar, Louise Lovely, Millard K. Wilson, Sidney Dean

FIELDS OF HONOR (1918)
(6 r.) d, Ralph Ince; lp, Mae Marsh, Marguerite Marsh, George Cooper, John Wessell

FIENDS OF HELL, THE (1914, Brit.)
(4 r.) d, Charles Calvert; lp, Douglas Payne, Norman Howard, Dr. Nikola Hamilton

FIEVRE (1921, Fr.)
(4 r.) d, Louis Delluc; lp, Elena Sagrary, Van Daele, Eve Francis, Gaston Modot

FIFTH AVENUE (1926)
(6 r.) d, Robert G. Vignola; lp, Marguerite De La Motte, Allan Forrest, Louise Dresser, William V. Mong

FIFTH AVENUE MODELS (1925)
(7 r.) d, Svend Gade; lp, Mary Philbin, Norman Kerry, Josef Swickard, William Conklin

FIFTH COMMANDMENT, THE (1915)
(5 r.) lp, Julius Steger, Forrest Robinson, Kathryn Brown Decker, Edith Thornton

FIFTH COMMANDMENT, THE (1927)
(6 r.) lp, Miss Dubinsky

FIFTH FORM AT ST. DOMINIC'S, THE (1921, Brit.)
(7 r.) d, A.E. Coleby; lp, Ralph Forbes, Maurice Thompson, Humberston Wright, Phyllis Shannaw

FIFTH HORSEMAN, THE (1924)
(7 r.) d, E.M. McMahon; lp, Cornelius Keefe, Una Merkel, Joseph Depew, Charles Brook

FIFTH MAN, THE (1914)
(4 r.) d, F.J. Grandon; lp, Bessie Eyton, Charles Clary, Lafayette McKee, Roy Watson

FIFTY-FIFTY (1916)
(5 r.) d, Allan Dwan; lp, Norma Talmadge, J.W. Johnston, Marie Chambers, Ruth Darling

FIFTY-FIFTY (1925)
(5 r.) d, Henri Diamant Berger; lp, Hope Hampton, Lionel Barrymore, Louise Glaum, J. Moy Bennett

$50,000 Reward (1924)
(5 r.) d, Clifford S. Elfelt; lp, Ken Maynard, Esther Ralston, Bert Lindley, Edward Peil

FIG LEAVES (1926)
(7 r.) d, Howard Hawks; lp, George O'Brien, Olive Borden, Phyllis Haver, Andre de Beranger

FIGARO (1929, Fr.)
(? r.) d, Gaston Ravel

FIGHT, THE (1915)
(5 r.) d, George W. Lederer; lp, Margaret Wycherly, John E. Kellerd, Katherine La Salle, Charles Trowbridge

FIGHT FOR FREEDOM, A OR EXILED TO SIBERIA (1914)
(4 r.) d, Herbert Blache

FIGHT FOR HONOR, A (1924)
(5 r.) d, Henry MacRae; lp, Eva Novak, William Fairbanks, Claire McDowell, Jack Byron

FIGHT FOR LOVE, A (1919)
(6 r.) d, Jack [John] Ford; lp, Harry Carey, Neva Gerber, Joe Harris, Mark Fenton

FIGHT FOR MILLIONS, THE (1913)
(4 r.) d, Herbert Blache; lp, Barney Gilmore, Darwin Karr, Marian Swayne, Joseph Levering

FIGHT FOR THE 'ULTIMATUM' FACTORY (1923, USSR)
(6 r.) d, Dmitri Bassaligo; lp, Olga Tretyakova, Tsekhanskaya, M. Lenin, Vladimir Karin

FIGHT TO THE FINISH, A (1925)
(5 r.) d, Reeves Eason; lp, William Fairbanks, Phyllis Haver, Tom Ricketts, Pat Harmon

FIGHTERS IN THE SADDLE
(SEE: FIGHTERS OF THE SADDLE, 1929)

FIGHTERS OF THE SADDLE (1929)
(5 r.) lp, Art Acord, John Lowell, Tom Bay, Peggy Montgomery

FIGHTIN' COMEBACK, THE (1927)
(5 r.) d, Tenny Wright; lp, Buddy Roosevelt, Clara Horton, Sidney M. Goldin, Richard Neill

FIGHTIN' DEVIL (1922)
(5 r.) d, Robert McKenzie; lp, Olin Francis

FIGHTIN' MAD (1921)
(6 r.) d, Joseph J. Franz; lp, William Desmond, Virginia Brown Faire, Doris Pawn, Rosemary Theby

FIGHTIN' ODDS (1925)
(5 r.) d, Bennett Cohn; lp, Bill Patton, Doris Dare, Jack House, Jack Ganzhorn

FIGHTIN' REDHEAD, THE (1928)
(5 r.) d, Louis King; lp, Buzz Barton, Duane Thompson, Milburn Morante, Bob Fleming

FIGHTIN' THRU (1924)
(5 r.) d, Roy M. Hughes; lp, Bill Patton, Donna Hale

FIGHTING ACE, THE
(SEE: FLYING ACE, 1928)

FIGHTING BACK (1917)
(5 r.) d, Raymond B. Wells; lp, William Desmond, Claire McDowell, Jack Richardson, Curley Baldwin

FIGHTING BLADE, THE (1923)
(9 r.) d, John S. Robertson; lp, Richard Barthelmess, Lee Baker, Morgan Wallace, Bradley Barker

FIGHTING BUCKAROO, THE (1926)
(5 r.) d, R. William Neill; lp, Buck Jones, Sally Long, Lloyd Whitlock, Frank Butler

FIGHTING CHANCE, THE (1920)
(6 r.) d, Charles Maigne; lp, Anna Q. Nilsson, Conrad Nagel, Clarence Burton, Dorothy Davenport

FIGHTING COBBLER, THE (1915, Brit.)
(4 r.) d, A.E. Coleby; lp, A.E. Coleby, Marjorie Villis, Arthur Rooke, N. Watts-Phillips

FIGHTING COLLEEN, A (1919)
(5 r.) d, David Smith; lp, Bessie Love, Anne Schaefer, Charles Spere, Jay Morley

FIGHTING COURAGE (1925)
(5 r.) d, Clifford S. Elfelt; lp, Ken Maynard, Peggy Montgomery, Melbourne MacDowell, Frank Whitson

FIGHTING COWBOY (1930)
(5 r.) lp, Al Hoxie

FIGHTING CRESSY (1919)
(6 r.) d, Robert T. Thornby; lp, Blanche Sweet, Russell Simpson, Edward Peil, Pell Trenton

FIGHTING DEATH (1914)
(4 r.) d, Herbert Blanche; lp, Constance Bennett, Rodman Law

FIGHTING DEMON, THE (1925)
(6 r.) d, Arthur Rosson; lp, Richard Talmadge, Lorraine Eason, Dick Sutherland, Peggy Shaw

FIGHTING DESTINY (1919)
(5 r.) d, Paul Scardon; lp, Harry T. Morey, Betty Blythe, Arthur Donaldson, George Majeroni

FIGHTING DOCTOR, THE (1926)
(5 r.) d, Robert North Bradbury; lp, Frank Merrill

FIGHTING EAGLE, THE (1927)
(8 r.) d, Donald Crisp; lp, Rod La Rocque, Phyllis Haver, Sam De Grasse, Max Barwyn

FIGHTING EDGE, THE (1926)
(7 r.) d, Henry Lehrman; lp, Kenneth Harlan, Patsy Ruth Miller, David Kirby, Charles Conklin

FIGHTING FAILURE, THE (1926)
(6 r.) d, E.G. Boyle; lp, Cullen Landis, Peggy Montgomery, Lucy Beaumont, Sidney Franklin

FIGHTING FATE (1925)
(5 r.) d, Albert Rogell; lp, Billy Sullivan, Johnny Sinclair, Nancy Deaver, Tom McGuire

FIGHTING FOR GOLD (1919)
(5 r.) d, Edward J. LeSaint; lp, Tom Mix, Teddy Sampson, Sid Jordan, Jack Nelson

FIGHTING FOR JUSTICE (1924)
(5 r.) d, Walter De Courcy; lp, Art Acord, Vane Truant, Paul Weigel

FIGHTING FURY (1924)
(5 r.) d, Clifford S. Smith; lp, Jack Hoxie, Helen Holmes, Fred Kohler, Duke R. Lee

FIGHTING GOB, THE (1926)
(5 r.) d, Harry L. Frazer; lp, Gordon Clifford, Charlotte Pierce

FIGHTING GRIN, THE (1918)
(5 r.) d, Joseph De Grasse; lp, Franklyn Farnum, Edith Johnson, J. Morris Foster, Charles H. Mailes

FIGHTING GRINGO, THE (1917)
(5 r.) d, Fred A. Kelsey; lp, Harry Carey, Claire Du Brey, George Webb, Bill Gettinger

FIGHTING GUIDE, THE (1922)
(5 r.) d, William Duncan, Don Clark; lp, William Duncan, Edith Johnson, Harry Lonsdale, William McCall

FIGHTING HEART, A (1924)
(6 r.) d, Jack Nelson; lp, Frank Merrill, Margaret Landis, Milburn Morante, May Sherman

FIGHTING HEART, THE (1925)
(7 r.) d, John Ford; lp, George O'Brien, Billie Dove, J. Farrell MacDonald, Victor McLaglen

FIGHTING HEARTS (1922)
(5 r.) lp, William Fairbanks;

FIGHTING HOMBRE, THE (1927)
(5 r.) d, Jack Nelson; lp, Bob Custer, Mary O'Day, Bert Sprotte, David Dunbar

FIGHTING HOPE, THE (1915)
(5 r.) d, George Melford; lp, Laura Hope Crews, George Gebhardt, Gerald Ward, Thomas Meighan

FIGHTING JACK (1926)
(4 r.) d, Louis Chaudet; lp, Bill Bailey, Hazel Deane, Frona Hale, John Byron

FIGHTING JIM GRANT (1923)
(5 r.) d, W. Adcook; lp, Lester Cuneo, Alma Deer

FIGHTING KENTUCKIANS, THE (1920)
(5 r.) d, J. Harrison Edwards; lp, Thornton Baston, Irma Harrison, Myra Brooks, Tom Burroughs

FIGHTING KID, THE (1922)
(5 r.)

FIGHTING LOVE (1927)
(7 r.) d, Nils Olaf Chrisander; lp, Jetta Goudal, Victor Varconi, Henry B. Walthall, Louis Natheaux

FIGHTING LOVER, THE (1921)
(5 r.) d, Fred Leroy Granville; lp, Frank Mayo, Elinor Hancock, Gertrude Olmsted, Jackson Read

FIGHTING LUCK (1926)
(5 r.) d, J.P. McGowan; lp, Bob Reeves, Ione Reed, Bill Ryno, Lew Meehan

FIGHTING MAD (1917)
(5 r.) d, Edward J. LeSaint; lp, William Stowell, Helen Gibson, Hector Dion, Betty Schade

FIGHTING MARINE, THE (1926)
(7 r.) d, Spencer Gordon Bennett; lp, Gene Tunney, Marjorie Gay, Walter Miller, Virginia Vance

FIGHTING PEACEMAKER, THE (1926)
(5 r.) d, Clifford S. Smith; lp, Jack Hoxie, Lola Todd, Ted Oliver, William A. Steele

FIGHTING RANGER, THE (1922)
(5 r.) lp, Bill Miller, May Carson

FIGHTING RANGER (1926)
(5 r.) d, Paul Hurst; lp, Al Hoxie

FIGHTING ROMEO, THE (1925)
(5 r.) d, Al Ferguson; lp, Al Ferguson, Elaine Eastman, Paul Emery, George Routh

FIGHTING SAP, THE (1924)
(6 r.) d, Albert Rogell; lp, Fred Thompson, Hazel Keener, Wilfred Lucas, George Williams

FIGHTING SHEPHERDESS, THE (1920)
(5 r.) d, Edward Jose; lp, Anita Stewart, Wallace MacDonald, Noah Beery, Walter Long

FIGHTING SHERIFF, THE (1925)
(5 r.) d, J.P. McGowan; lp, Bill Cody, Frank Ellis, Walter Shumway, Hazel Holt

FIGHTING STALLION, THE (1926)
(5 r.) d, Ben F. Wilson; lp, Yakima Canutt

FIGHTING STRAIN, THE (1923)
(5 r.) d, Neal Hart; lp, Neal Hart, Beth Mitchell, William Quinn, Bert Wilson

FIGHTING STRANGER, THE (1921)
(5 r.) d, Webster Cullison; lp, Franklyn Farnum, Flora Hollister, W.A. Alleman, Vester Pegg

FIGHTING STREAK, THE (1922)
(5 r.) d, Arthur Rosson; lp, Tom Mix, Patsy Ruth Miller, Gerald Pring, Al Fremont

FIGHTING THE FLAMES (1925)
(6 r.) d, Reeves Eason; lp, William Haines, Dorothy Devore, Frankie Darro, David Torrence

FIGHTING THOROBREDS (1926)
(5 r.) d, Harry J. Brown; lp, Billy Sullivan

FIGHTING THREE, THE (1927)
(5 r.) d, Albert Rogell; lp, Jack Hoxie, Olive Hasbrouck, Marin Sais, Fanny Warren

FIGHTING YOUTH (1925)
(5 r.) d, Reeves Eason; lp, William Fairbanks, Pauline Garon, George Periolat, William Norton Bailey

FIGUREHEAD, THE (1920)
(5 r.) d, Robert Ellis; lp, Eugene O'Brien, Anna Q. Nilsson, Ora Carew, Joseph Girard

FIGURES DON'T LIE (1927)
(6 r.) d, Edward Sutherland; lp, Esther Ralston, Richard Arlen, Ford Sterling, Doris Hill

FILLE D'ARTISTE (1916, Fr.)
(? r.) d, Camille de Morlhon

FILLE DE RIEN (1921, Fr.)
(? r.) d, Andre Hugon

FILLING HIS OWN SHOES (1917)
(5 r.) d, Harry Beaumont; lp, Bryant Washburn, Hazel Daly, Roderick La Rocque, Lyda Dalzell

FINAL EXTRA, THE (1927)
(6 r.) d, James P. Hogan; lp, Marguerite De La Motte, Grant Withers, John Miljan, Frank Beal

FINAL CLOSEUP, THE (1919)
(5 r.) d, Walter C. Edwards; lp, Shirley Mason, Francis McDonald, James Gordon, Betty Bouton

FINAL JUDGEMENT, THE (1915)
(5 r.) d, Edwin Carewe; lp, Ethel Barrymore, H. Cooper Cliffe, Beatrice Maude, Mahlon Hamilton

FINAL PAYMENT, THE (1917)
(5 r.) d, Frank Powell; lp, Nance O'Neil, Clifford Bruce, Alfred Hickman

FIND THE WOMAN (1918)
(5 r.) d, Tom Terriss; lp, Alice Joyce, Walter McGrail, Arthur Donaldson, Jessie Stevens

FIND THE WOMAN (1922)
(6 r.) d, Tom Terriss; lp, Alma Rubens, Eileen Huban, Harrison Ford, George MacQuarrie

FIND YOUR MAN (1924)
(7 r.) d, Mal St. Clair; lp, Rin-Tin-Tin, June Marlowe, Eric St. Clair, Charles Mailes

FINDERS KEEPERS (1921)
(6 r.) d, Otis B. Thayer; lp, Violet Mersereau, Edmund Cobb, Dorothy Simpson, Verne Layton

FINDERS KEEPERS (1928)
(6 r.) d, Wesley Ruggles; lp, Laura La Plante, John Harron, Edmund Breese, William Gorman

FINE CLOTHES (1925)
(8 r.) d, John M. Stahl; lp, Lewis Stone, Percy Marmont, Alma Rubens, Raymond Griffith

FINE FEATHERS (1915, Brit.)
(4 r.) d, Maurice Elvey; lp, Elizabeth Risdon, Fred Groves, Douglas Payne, Daisy Cordell

FINGER PRINTS (1927)
(7 r.) d, Lloyd Bacon; lp, Louise Fazenda, John T. Murray, Helene Costello, Myrna Loy

FINNIS TERRAE (1929, Fr.)
(? r.) d, Jean Epstein; lp, Bannec, Balanec & d'Ouessant islanders, "Pompero" & "Hermine" crewmen

FIRE AND STEEL (1927)
(6 r.) d, Bertram Bracken; lp, Jack Perrin, Philo McCullough, Mary McAllister, Burr McIntosh

FIRE BRIDE, THE (1922)
(5 r.) d, Arthur Rosson; lp, Ruth Renick, Edward Hearn, Walt Whitman, Fred Stanton

FIRE BRIGADE, THE (1926)
(9 r.) d, William Nigh; lp, May McAvoy, Charles Ray, Holmes Herbert, Tom O'Brien

FIRE CAT, THE (1921)
(5 r.) d, Norman Dawn; lp, Edith Roberts, Walter Long, William Eagle Eye, Olga D. Mojean

FIRE EATER, THE (1921)
(5 r.) d, Reaves Eason; lp, Hoot Gibson, Louise Lorraine, Walter Perry, Tom Lingham

FIRE FLINGERS, THE (1919)
(6 r.) d, Rupert Julian; lp, Rupert Julian, Jane Novak, E.A. Warren, Clyde Fillmore

FIRE PATROL, THE (1924)
(7 r.) d, Hunt Stromberg; lp, Anna Q. Nilsson, William Jeffries, Spottiswoode Aitken, Jack Richardson

FIREBRAND, THE (1918)
(5 r.) d, Edmund Lawrence; lp, Virginia Pearson, Victor Sutherland, Carleton Macy, Herbert Evans

FIREBRAND, THE (1922)
(5 r.) d, Alvin J. Neitz; lp, Franklyn Farnum, Ruth Langdon, Fred Gamble, Pat Harmon

FIREBRAND TREVISON (1920)
(5 r.) d, Thomas N. Heffron; lp, Buck Jones, Winifred Westover, Martha Mattox, Stanton Heck

FIREFLY OF FRANCE, THE (1918)
(5 r.) d, Donald Crisp; lp, Wallace Reid, Ann Little, Charles Ogle, Raymond Hatton

FIREFLY OF TOUGH LUCK, THE (1917)
(5 r.) d, E. Mason Hopper; lp, Alma Ruebens, Charles Gunn, Walt Whitman, Darrel Foss

FIRES OF REBELLION (1917)
(5 r.) d, Ida May Park; lp, Dorothy Phillips, William Stowell, Lon Chaney [Sr.], Belle Bennett

FIRES OF YOUTH (1917)
(5 r.) d, Emile Chautard; lp, Frederick Warde, Jeanne Eagles, Helen Badgley, Ernest Howard

FIRES OF YOUTH (1918)
(5 r.) d, Rupert Julian; lp, Ruth Clifford, Ralph Lewis, George Fisher

FIRES OF YOUTH (1924)
(5 r.) lp, Ted Edwards, Billie Rhodes

FIRING LINE, THE (1919)
(5 r.) d, Charles Maigne; lp, Irene Castle, David Powell, Irene West, May Kitson

FIRST AUTO, THE (1927)
(7 r.) d, Roy Del Ruth; lp, Barney Oldfield, Patsy Ruth Miller, Charles Emmett Mack, Russell Simpson

FIRST BORN, THE (1921)
(6 r.) d, Colin Campbell; lp, Sessue Hayakawa, Helen Jerome Eddy, "Sonny Boy" Warde, Goro Kino

FIRST BORN, THE (1928, Brit.)
(8 r.) d, Miles Mander; lp, Miles Mander, Madeleine Carroll, John Loder, Ella Atherton

FIRST DEGREE, THE (1923)
(5 r.) d, Edward Sedgwick; lp, Frank Mayo, Sylvia Breamer, Philo McCullough, George A. Williams

FIRST KISS, THE (1928)
(6 r.) d, Rowland V. Lee; lp, Fay Wray, Gary Cooper, Lane Chandler, Leslie Fenton

FIRST LAW, THE (1918)
(5 r.) d, Lawrence McGill; lp, Irene Castle, Antonio Moreno, Marguerite Snow, J.H. Gilmour [Gilmore]

FIRST LOVE (1921)
(5 r.) d, Maurice Campbell; Constance Binney, Warner Baxter, George Webb, Betty Schade

FIRST MEN IN THE MOON, THE (1919, Brit.)
(5 r.) d, J.L.V. Leigh; lp, Bruce Gordon, Heather Thatcher, Hector Abbas, Lionel d'Aragon

FIRST NIGHT, THE (1927)
(6 r.) d, Richard Thorpe; lp, Bert Lytell, Dorothy Devore, Harry Myers, Frederic Kovert

FIRST WOMAN, THE (1922)
(5 r.) d, Glen Lyons; lp, Percy Marmont, Lloyd Hammond, Donald Blakemore, Oliver La Baddie

FIVE AND TEN CENT ANNIE (1928)
(5 r.) d, Roy Del Ruth; lp, Louise Fazenda, Clyde Cook, William Demarest, Gertrude Astor

FIVE DAYS TO LIVE (1922)
(6 r.) d, Norman Dawn; lp, Sessue Hayakawa, Tsuru Aoki, Goro Kino, Misao Seki

FIVE DOLLAR BABY, THE (1922)
(6 r.) d, Harry Beaumont; lp, Viola Dana, Ralph Lewis, Otto Hoffman, John Harron

FIVE FAULTS OF FLO, THE (1916)
(5 r.) d, George Foster Platt; lp, Florence LaBadie, Harris Gordon, Samuel Niblack, Ernest Howard

FIVE NIGHTS (1915, Brit.)
(6 r.) d, Bert Haldane; lp, Eve Balfour, Thos H. MacDonald, Sybil de Bray, Tom Coventry

FIVE SINISTER STORIES (1919, Ger.)
(? r.) d, Richard Oswald; lp, Conrad Veidt, Reinhold Schunzel, Anita Berber, Georg John

FIVE THOUSAND AN HOUR (1918)
(5 r.) d, Ralph Ince; lp, Hale Hamilton, Lucille Lee Stewart, Florence Short, Gilbert Douglas

$5,000 REWARD (1918)
(5 r.) d, Douglas Gerrard; lp, Franklyn Farnum, Gloria Hope, William Lloyd, J. Farrell MacDonald

FIXED BY GEORGE (1920)
(5 r.) d, Eddie Lyons, Lee Moran; lp, Eddie Lyons, Lee Moran, Beatrice La Plante, Hazel Howell

FIXER, THE
(SEE: HELLO BILL!, 1915)

FLAME, THE (1920, Brit.)
(6 r.) d, F. Martin Thornton; lp, Evelyn Boucher, Reginald Fox, Dora de Winton, Fred Thatcher

FLAME OF HELLGATE, THE (1920)
(5 r.) d, George Middleton; lp, Beatriz Michelena, Jeff Williams, Albert Morrison, William Pike

FLAME OF LIFE, THE (1923)
(7 r.) d, Hobart Henley; lp, Priscilla Dean, Robert Ellis, Kathryn McGuire, Wallace Beery

FLAME OF PASSION, THE (1915)
(5 r.) d, Tom Terriss; lp, Tom Terriss, Lionel Pape, Rienzi de Cordova, Alfred Hemming

FLAME OF THE ARGENTINE (1926)
(5 r.) d, Edward Dillon; lp, Evelyn Brent, Orville Caldwell, Frank Leigh, Dan Makarenko

FLAME OF THE DESERT (1919)
(5 r.) d, Reginald Barker; lp, Geraldine Farrar, Lou Tellegen, Alec B. Francis, Edythe Chapman

FLAME OF THE YUKON, THE (1917)
(5 r.) d, Charles Miller; lp, Dorothy Dalton, Melbourne McDowell, Kenneth Harlan, Margaret Thompson

FLAME OF THE YUKON, THE (1926)
(6 r.) d, George Melford; lp, Seena Owen, Arnold Gray, Matthew Betz, Jack McDonald

FLAME OF YOUTH, THE (1917)
(5 r.) d, Elmer Clifton; lp, Jack Mulhall, Ann Croman, Donna Moon [Donna Drew], Hayward Mack

FLAME OF YOUTH (1920)
(5 r.) d, Howard M. Mitchell; lp, Shirley Mason, Raymond McKee, Philo McCullough, Cecil Van Auker

FLAMENCA LA GITANE (1928, Fr.)
(? r.) d, Henri Andreani

FLAMES (1926)
(6 r.) d, Lewis H. Moomaw; lp, Eugene O'Brien, Virginia Valli, Jean Hersholt, Bryant Washburn

FLAMES OF DESIRE (1924)
(6 r.) d, Denison Clift; lp, Wyndham Standing, Diana Miller, Richard Thorpe, Frank Leigh

FLAMES OF JOHANNIS, THE (1916)
(5 r.) d, Edgar Lewis; lp, Nance O'Neil, George Clarke, Eleanor Barry, Ethel Tully

FLAMES OF PASSION (1923)
(5 r.) d, H.G. Moody; lp, Frank Whitson, Al Ferguson, George Larkin, Frank Whitlock

FLAMES OF WRATH (1923)
(5 r.) lp, Roxie Mankins, John Burton, Charles Pearson, Anna Kelson

FLAMING CLUE, THE (1920)
(5 r.) d, Edwin L. Hollywood; lp, Harry T. Morey, Lucy Fox, Sidney D'Albrook, Eleanor Barry

FLAMING CRISIS, THE (1924)
(6 r.) lp, Calvin Nicholson, Dorothy Dunbar

FLAMING FOREST, THE (1926)
(7 r.) d, Reginald Barker; lp, Antonio Moreno, Renee Adoree, Gardner James, William Austin

FLAMING FORTIES, THE (1924)
(6 r.) d, Tom Forman; lp, Harry Carey, William Norton Bailey, Jacqueline Gadsdon, James Mason

FLAMING FRONTIER, THE (1926)
(9 r.) d, Edward Sedgwick; lp, Hoot Gibson, Anne Cornwall Dustin Farnum, Ward Crane

FLAMING FURY (1926)
(5 r.) d, James P. Hogan; lp, Ranger (a dog), Charles Delaney, Betty May, Boris Karloff

FLAMING HEARTS (1922)
(5 r.) d, Clifford S. Elfelt; lp, J.B. Warner, Kathleen Myers, Alma Bennett, George Hernandez

FLAMING HOUR, THE (1922)
(5 r.) d, Edward Sedgwick; lp, Frank Mayo, Helen Ferguson, Melbourne MacDowell, Charles Clary

FLAMING OMEN, THE (1917)
(5 r.) d, William Wolbert; lp, Alfred Whitman [Alfred Vosburgh], Mary Anderson, Otto Lederer

FLAMING PASSION
(SEE: LUCRETIA LOMBARD, 1923)

FLAMING SWORD (1915)
(5 r.)

FLAMING YOUTH (1923)
(9 r.) d, John Francis Dillon; lp, Colleen Moore, Milton Sills, Elliott Dexter, Sylvia Breamer

FLATTERY (1925)
(6 r.) d, Tom Forman; lp, John Bowers, Marguerite De La Motte, Alan Hale, Grace Darmond

FLAPPER WIVES (1924)
(7 r.) d, Jane Murfin, Justin H. McCloskey; lp, May Allison, Rockcliffe Fellowes, Vera Reynolds, Edward Horton

FLARE-UP SAL (1918)
(5 r.) d, Roy William Neill; lp, Dorothy Dalton, Thurston Hall, William Conklin, J.P. Lockney

FLASH, THE (1923)
(5 r.) d, William J. Craft; lp, George Larkin, Ruth Stonehouse

FLASH OF FATE, THE (1918)
(5 r.) d, Elmer Clifton; lp, Herbert Rawlinson, Mary MacDonald, Dana Ong, Madge Kirby

FLASH OF THE FOREST (1928)
(5 r.) lp, Braveheart (a dog)

FLASH O'LIGHTING (1925)
(5 r.) d, Leo Maloney; lp, Leo Maloney, Josephine Hill, Evelyn Thatcher, Whitehorse

FLASHING FANGS (1926)
(5 r.) d, Henry McCarthy; lp, Ranger (a dog), Robert Ramsey, Lotus Thompson, Eddie Chandler

FLASHING HOOFS (1928)
(5 r.) lp, Cliff "Tex" Lyons

FLASHING SPURS (1924)
(5 r.) d, Reeves Eason; lp, Bob Custer, Edward Coxen, Marguerite Clayton, Joe Bennett

FLASHING STEEDS (1925)
(5 r.) d, H.B. Carpernter; lp, Bill Patton, Dorothy Donald, Merrill McCormick, Ethel Childers

FLEET'S IN, THE (1928)
(8 r.) d, Malcolm St. Clair; lp, Clara Bow, James Hall, Jack Oakie, Bodil Rosing

FLEETWING (1928)
(5 r.) d, Lambert Hillyer; lp, Barry Norton, Dorothy Janis, Ben Bard, Robert Kortman

FLESH AND BLOOD (1922)
(6 r.) d, Irving Cummings; lp, Lon Chaney, Edith Roberts, De Witt Jennings, Noah Beery

FLESH AND SPIRIT (1922)
(6 r.) d, Joseph Levering; lp, Belle Bennett, Walter Ringham, Denton Vane, James McDuff

FLEUR D'AMOUR (1927, Fr.)
(? r.) d, Marcel Vandal

FLEUR DE PARIS (1916, Fr.)
(? r.) d, Andre Hugon; lp, Mistinquett

FLIGHT COMMANDER, THE (1927)
(8 r.) d, Maurice Elvey; lp, Sir Alan Cobham, Estelle Brody, John Stuart, Humberston Wright

FLIGHT OF THE DUCHESS, THE (1916)
(5 r.) d, Eugene Nowland; lp, Gladys Hulette, Wayne Arey, Robert Gray, Burnett Parker

FLIPOTTE (1920, Fr.)
(? r.) d, Jacques de Baroncelli

FLIRT, THE (1916)
(5 r.) d, Lois Weber, Phillips Smalley lp, Marie Walcamp, Grace Benham, Antrim Short, Juan de la Cruz

FLIRTING WITH DEATH (1917)
(5 r.) d, Elmer Clifton; lp, Brownie Vernon, Herbert Rawlinson, Frank McQuarrie, Mark Fenton

FLIRTING WITH LOVE (1924)
(7 r.) d, John Francis Dillon; lp, Colleen Moore, Conway Tearle, Winifred Bryson, Frances Raymond

FLOOD (1915, USSR)
(8 r.) d, Pyotr Chardynin; lp, A. Virubov, Ivan Mozhukhin, Pytor Starkovsky, A. Kheruvimov

FLOODGATES (1924)
(7 r.) d, George Irving; lp, John Lowell, Evangeline Russell, Jane Thomas, Baby Ivy Ward

FLOOR BELOW, THE (1918)
(6 r.) d, Clarence Badger; lp, Mabel Normand, Tom Moore, Helen Dahl, Wallace McCutcheon

FLORENCE NIGHTINGALE (1915, Brit.)
(4 r.) d, Maurice Elvey; lp, Elizabeth Risdon, Fred Groves, A.V. Bramble, M. Gray Murray

FLORINE LA FLEUR DU VALOIS (1926, Fr.)
(? r.) d, Donatien

FLOTSAM (1921)
(5 r.) d, Edmund Blake; lp, Marjorie Battress, Jack Warboys, Dorothy Warboys

FLOWER OF DOOM, THE (1917)
(5 r.) d, Rex Ingram; lp, Wedgewood Nowell, Gypsy Hart, Yvette Mitchell, Nicholas Dunaew

FLOWER OF FAITH, THE (1916)
(5 r.) d, Burton L. King; lp, Jane Grey, Frank Mills, Albert Tavernier, Percy Helton

FLOWER OF NIGHT (1925)
(7 r.) d, Paul Bern; lp, Pola Negri, Joseph Dowling, Youcca Troubetzkoy, Warner Oland

FLOWER OF NO MAN'S LAND, THE (1916)
(5 r.) d, John H. Collins; lp, Viola Dana, Duncan McRae, Harry C. Brown, Mitchell Lewis

FLOWER OF THE DUSK (1918)
(5 r.) d, John H. Collins; lp, Viola Dana, Guy Coombs, Jack McGowan, Howard Hall

FLOWER OF THE NORTH (1921)
(7 r.) d, David Smith; lp, Henry B. Walthall, Pauline Starke, Harry Northrup, Joe Rickson

FLOWERS ARE LATE, THE (1917, USSR)
(4 r.) d, Boris Sushkevich; lp, Olga Baklanova, Alexander Geirot, Boris Sushkevich, Maria Uspenskaya

FLOWING GOLD (1921)
(5 r.) d, Leonard Franchon; lp, Al Hart, Jack Mower, Robert Conville

FLYIN' COWBOY, THE (1928)
(6 r.) d, Reaves Eason; lp, Hoot Gibson, Olive Hasbrouck, Harry Todd, William Bailey

FLYIN' THRU (1925)
(6 r.) d, Bruce Mitchell; lp, Al Wilson, Elinor Fair, George French, James McElhern

FLYING ACE (1928)
(6 r.) lp, Lawrence Corman, Kathryn Boyd, J. Lawrence Criner

FLYING BUCKAROO, THE (1928)
(5 r.) d, Richard Thorpe; lp, Wally Wales, Jack D'Oise, J.P. Lockney, Fanny Midgley

FLYING COLORS (1917)
(5 r.) d, Frank Borzage; lp, William Desmond, Golda Madden, Jack Livingston, Laura Sears

FLYING DUTCHMAN, THE (1923)
(6 r.) d, Lloyd B. Carleton; lp, Lawson Butt, Nola Luxford, Ella Hall, Edward Coxen

FLYING FOOL (1925)
(5 r.) d, Frank S. Mattison; lp, Gaston Glass, Dick Grace, Wanda Hawley, Mary Land

FLYING HIGH (1926)
(5 r.) d, Charles Hutchinson; lp, William Fairbanks, Alice Calhoun, Frank Rice, LeRoy Mason

FLYING HOOFS (1925)
(5 r.) d, Clifford S. Smith; lp, Jack Hoxie, Bartlett A. Carre, William Welsh, Gordon Russell

FLYING HORSEMAN, THE (1926)
(5 r.) d, Orville O. Dull; lp, Buck Jones, Gladys McConnell, Bruce Covington, Walter Percival

FLYING LUCK (1927)
(7 r.) d, Herman C. Raymaker; lp, Monty Banks, Jean Arthur, J.W. Johnston, Kewpie Morgan

FLYING MAIL, THE (1926)
(5 r.) d, Noel Mason; lp, Al Wilson, Joseph W. Girard, Kathleen Myers, Carmelita Geraghty

FLYING SQUAD, THE (1929)
(8 r.) d, Arthur Maude; lp, Wyndham Standing, Dorothy Bartlam, John Longden, Donald Calthrop

FLYING TWINS, THE (1915)
(4 r.) lp, Madeline & Marion Fairbanks

FLYING U RANCH, THE (1927)
(5 r.) d, Robert De Lacy; lp, Tom Tyler, Nora Lane, Bert Hadley, Grace Woods

FOG BOUND (1923)
(6 r.) d, Irvin Willat; lp, Dorothy Dalton, David Powell, Martha Mansfield, Maurice Costello

FOGGY HARBOR (1923, Jap.)
(? r.) d, Kenji Mizoguchi

FOLKS FROM WAY DOWN EAST (1924)
(5 r.) d, Lee Beggs lp, Violet Horner, Robert Vaughn Robert Lawrence, Marie Trado

FOLLOW THE GIRL (1917)
(5 r.) d, L.W. Chaudet; lp, Ruth Stonehouse, Roy Stewart, Jack Dill, Claire Du Brey

FOLLY OF DESIRE, THE OR THE SHULAMITE (1916)
(5 r.) d, George Loane Tucker; lp, Manora Thew, Gerald Ames, Norman McKinnel, Lewis Gilbert

FOLLY OF REVENGE, THE (1916)
(5 r.) lp, Warren E. Lyle

FOLLY OF VANITY, THE (1924)
(6 r.) d, Maurice Elvey, Henry Otto; lp, Billie Dove, Jack Mulhall, Consuelo, Jean La Motte

FOLLY OF YOUTH (1925)
(5 r.)

FOOD GAMBLERS, THE (1917)
(5 r.) d, Albert Parker; lp, Wilfred Lucas, Elda Millar [Hedda Hopper], Mac Barnes, Russell Simpson

FOOL, THE (1925)
(10 r.) d, Harry Millarde; lp, Edmund Lowe, Raymond Bloomer, Henry Sedley, Paul Panzer

FOOL AND HIS MONEY, A (1920)
(5 r.) d, Robert Ellis; lp, Eugene O'Brien, Rubye De Remer, Arthur Housman, Emile La Croix

FOOL AND HIS MONEY, A (1925)
(6 r.) d, Erle C. Kenton; lp, Madge Bellamy, William Haines, Stuart Holmes, Alma Bennett

FOOL THERE WAS, A (1922)
(7 r.) d, Emmett J. Flynn; lp, Estelle Taylor, Lewis Stone, Irene Rich, Muriel Dana

FOOLISH AGE, THE (1921)
(5 r.) d, William A. Seiter; lp, Doris May, Hallam Cooley, Otis Harlan, Arthur Hoyt

FOOLISH LIVES (1922)
(? r.) lp, Frank Chatman, Henry Harris, Frank Carter, Jewell Cox

FOOLISH MATRONS, THE (1921)
(7 r.) d, Maurice Tourneur; lp, Hobart Bosworth, Doris May, Mildred Manning, Kathleen Kirkham

FOOLISH MEN AND SMART WOMEN (1924)
(5 r.) d, Fred Newmeyer

FOOLISH MONTE CARLO (1922)
(5 r.) d, William Humphrey; lp, Mary Clare, Sam Livesey, Robert Corbins, Betty Hall

FOOLISH MOTHERS (1923)
(6 r.) lp, Edward Coxen, Enid Markey

FOOLISH TWINS, THE (1923)
(5 r.) lp, Terry Twins

FOOLISH VIRGIN, THE (1917)
(5 r.) d, Albert Capellani; lp, Clara Kimball Young, Conway Tearle, Catherine Proctor, Sheridan Tansey

FOOLISH VIRGIN, THE (1924)
(6 r.) d, George W. Hill; lp, Elaine Hammerstein, Robert Frazer, Gladys Brockwell, Phyllis Haver

FOOLS AND RICHES (1923)
(5 r.) d, Herbert Blache; lp, Herbert Rawlinson, Katherine Perry, Tully Marshall, Doris Pawn

FOOLS AND THEIR MONEY (1919)
(5 r.) d, Herbert Blache; lp, Emmy Wehlen, Jack Mulhall, Emmett King, Millie McConnell

FOOL'S AWAKENING, A (1924)
(6 r.) d, Harold Shaw; lp, Harrison Ford, Enid Bennett, Alec Francis, Mary Alden

FOOLS FIRST (1922)
(6 r.) d, Marshall Neilan; lp, Richard Dix, Claire Windsor, Claude Gillingwater, Raymond Griffith

FOOLS FOR LUCK (1917)
(5 r.) d, Lawrence C. Windom; lp, Taylor Holmes, Helen Ferguson, Bobbie Bolder, Frankie Raymond

FOOLS FOR LUCK (1928)
(6 r.) d, Charles Reisner; lp, W.C. Fields, Chester Conklin, Sally Blane, Jack Luden

FOOL'S GOLD (1919)
(6 r.) d, Lawrence Trimble; lp, Mitchell Lewis, Florence Turner, Wellington Playter, Evelyn Brent

FOOLS' HIGHWAY (1924)
(7 r.) d, Irving Cummings; lp, Mary Philbin, Pat O'Malley, William Collier, Jr., Lincoln Plummer

FOOLS IN THE DARK (1924)
(8 r.) d, Al Santell; lp, Patsy Ruth Miller, Matt Moore, Bertram Grassby, Charles Belcher

FOOLS OF FASHION (1926)
(7 r.) d, James C. McKay; lp, Mae Busch, Marceline Day, Theodore von Eltz, Robert Ober

FOOL'S PARADISE (1921)
(9 r.) d, Cecil B. De Mille; lp, Dorothy Dalton, Mildred Harris, Conrad Nagel, Theodore Kosloff

FOOLS OF PASSION (1926, Ger.)
(6 r.) d, Rudolph Biebrach

FOOL'S PROMISE, A (1921)
(? r.)

FOOL'S REVENGE, THE (1916)
(6 r.) d, Will S. Davis; lp, William H. Tooker, Maude Gilbert, Ruth Findlay, Richard Neill

FOOT STEPS OF CAPTAIN KIDD, THE (1917)
(6 r.)

FOOTFALLS (1921)
(8 r.) d, Charles J. Brabin; lp, [Frederick] Tyrone Power, Tom Douglas, Estelle Taylor, Gladden James

FOOTLIGHT RANGER, THE (1923)
(5 r.) d, Scott Dunlap; lp, Charles Jones, Fritzi Brunette, James Mason, Lillian Langdon

FOOTLIGHTS (1921)
(7 r.) d, John S. Robertson; lp, Elsie Ferguson, Reginald Denny, Marc MacDermott, Octavia Handworth

FOOTLIGHTS AND SHADOWS (1920)
(5 r.) d, John W. Noble; lp, Olive Thomas, Alex Onslow, Ivo Dawson, E. Van Bousen

FOOTLIGHTS OF FATE, THE (1916)
(5 r.) d, William Humphrey; lp, Naomi Childers, Marc MacDermott, Templer Saxe, William Shea

FOOTLOOSE WIDOWS (1926)
(7 r.) d, Roy Del Ruth; lp, Louise Fazenda, Jacqueline Logan, Jason Robards [Sr.], Arthur Hoyt

FOR A WOMAN'S FAIR NAME (1916)
(5 r.) d, Harry Davenport; lp, Robert Edeson, Eulalie Jensen; Belle Bruce, Harry Morey

FOR ALIMONY ONLY (1926)
(6 r.) d, William De Mille; lp, Leatrice Joy, Clive Brook, Lilyan Tashman, Casson Ferguson

FOR ALL ETERNITY (1917, Brit.)
(5 r.) d, A.E. Coleby, Arthur Rooke; lp, Malvine Longfellow, A.E. Coleby, Arthur Rooke, Janet Alexander

FOR ANOTHER WOMAN (1924)
(6 r.) d, David Kirkland; lp, Kenneth Harlan, Florence Billings, Henry Sedley, Mary Thurman

FOR BETTER, FOR WORSE (1919)
(7 r.) d, Cecil B. De Mille; lp, Elliott Dexter, Gloria Swanson, Tom Forman, Sylvia Ashton

FOR BIG STAKES (1922)
(5 r.) d, Lynn Reynolds; lp, Tom Mix, Patsy Ruth Miller, Sid Jordan, Bert Sprotte

FOR FIVE THOUSAND DOLLARS A YEAR (1915)
(5 r.) lp, Louise Huff

FOR FRANCE (1917)
(5 r.) d, Wesley Ruggles; lp, Edward Earle, Betty Howe, Arthur Donaldson, Mary Maurice

FOR FREEDOM (1919)
(5 r.) d, Frank Lloyd; lp, William Farnum, Rubye De Remer, Coit Albertson, Anna Lehr

FOR HER FATHER'S SAKE (1921, Brit.)
(5 r.) d, Alexander Butler; lp, Owen Nares, Isobel Elsom, James Lindsay, Tom Reynolds

FOR HER PEOPLE (1914, Brit.)
(4 r.) d, Larry Trimble; lp, Florence Turner, Clifford Pembroke, Rex Davis, Franklyn Bellamy

FOR HIS MOTHER'S SAKE (1922)
(6 r.) lp, Jack Johnson, Mattie Wilkes

FOR HIS SAKE (1922)
(5 r.) d, John S. Lawrence; lp, John Dillon, Hilda Nord, Charles Jackson, Jane Jennis

FOR HUSBANDS ONLY (1918)
(6 r.) d, Lois Weber, Phillips Smalley; lp, Mildred Harris, Lewis J. Cody, Fred Goodwins, Kathleen Kirkham

FOR KING AND COUNTRY (1914, Ital.)
(6 r.)

FOR LADIES ONLY (1927)
(6 r.) d, Scott Pembroke; lp, John Bowers, Jacqueline Logan, Edna Marion, Ben Hall

FOR LIBERTY (1918)
(5 r.) d, Bertram Bracken; lp, Gladys Brockwell, Charles Clary, Bertram Grassby, Willard Louis

FOR LOVE OF SERVICE (1922)
(5 r.) lp, George Chesebro

FOR SALE (1918)
(5 r.) d, Fred Wright; lp, Gladys Hulette, Creighton Hale, Lionel Atwill

FOR SALE (1924)
(8 r.) d, George Archainbaud; lp, Claire Windsor, Adolphe Menjou, Robert Ellis, Mary Carr

FOR THE DEFENCE (1916)
(5 r.) d, Frank Reicher; lp, Fannie Ward, Jack Dean, Camille Astor, Horace B. Carpenter

FOR THE DEFENSE (1922)
(5 r.) d, Paul Powell; lp, Ethel Clayton, Vernon Steele, ZaSu Pitts, Bertram Grassby

FOR THE FREEDOM OF IRELAND (1920)
(6 r.) lp, Vincent Coleman, Lawrence Fisher, Robert Klugston

FOR THE FREEDOM OF THE EAST (1918)
(7 r.) d, Ira M. Lowry; lp, Lady Tsen Mei, Robert Elliott, Lai Mon Kim, Herbert Horton Pattee

FOR THE FREEDOM OF THE WORLD (1917)
(8 r.) d, Ira M. Lowry, F.J. Carroll; lp, E.K. Lincoln, Barbara Castleton, Romaine Fielding, Neil Moran

FOR THE LOVE OF MIKE (1927)
(7 r.) d, Frank Capra; lp, Claudette Colbert, Ben Lyon, George Sidney, Ford Sterling

FOR THE SOUL OF RAFAEL (1920)
(6 r.) d, Harry Garson; lp, Clara Kimball Young, J. Frank Glendon, Bertram Grassby, Eugenie Besserer

FOR THOSE WE LOVE (1921)
(6 r.) d, Arthur Rosson; lp, Betty Compson, Richard Rosson, Camille Astor, Bert Woodruff

FOR VALOUR (1917)
(5 r.) d, Albert Parker; lp, Winifred Allen, Richard Barthelmess, Henry Weaver, Mabel Ballin

FOR VALOUR (1928, Brit.)
(6 r.) d, G.B. Samuelson; lp, Dallas Cairns, Marjorie Stallor, Roy Travers, Mary Rorke

FOR WIVES ONLY (1926)
(6 r.) d, Victor Heerman; lp, Marie Prevost, Victor Varconi, Charles Gerrard, Arthur Hoyt

FOR WOMAN'S FAVOR (1924)
(6 r.) d, Oscar Lund; lp, Seena Owen, Elliott Dexter, Wilton Lackaye, Irma Harrison

FOR YOU MY BOY (1923)
(6 r.) d, William L. Roubert; lp, Ben Lewin, Louis Dean, Matty Roubert, Schuyler White

FOR YOUR DAUGHTER'S SAKE
(SEE: COMMON SIN, THE, 1920)

FORBIDDEN (1919)
(6 r.) d, Lois Weber, Phillips Smalley; lp, Mildred Harris, Henry Woodward, Fred Goodwins

FORBIDDEN CARGO (1925)
(5 r.) d, Thomas Buckingham; lp, Evelyn Brent, Robert Ellis, Boris Karloff

FORBIDDEN CITY, THE (1918)
(5 r.) d, Sidney A. Franklin; lp, Norma Talmadge, Thomas Meighan, E.A. Warren, L. Rogers Lytton

FORBIDDEN FIRE (1919)
(7 r.) d, Arthur Rosson; lp, Louise Glaum, Matt Moore, Edwin Stevens, Nigel de Brulier

FORBIDDEN FRUIT (1916)
(5 r.) d, Ivan Abramson; lp, James H. Lewis, Paula Shay, James Cooley, Kittens Reichert

FORBIDDEN FRUIT (1921)
(8 r.) d, Cecil B. De Mille; lp, Agnes Ayres, Clarence Burton, Theodore Roberts, Kathlyn Williams

FORBIDDEN GRASS (1928)
(5 r.) d, E.M. Eldridge; lp, William Anderson, Evelyn Nicholas, Jack Padjan, Otto Meek

FORBIDDEN HOURS (1928)
(6 r.) d, Harry Beaumont; lp, Ramon Novarro, Renee Adoree, Dorothy Cumming, Edward Connelly

FORBIDDEN LOVE (1921)
(6 r.) d, Philip Van Loan; lp, Creighton Hale, George MacQuarrie, Marguerite Clayton, Thomas Cameron

FORBIDDEN LOVE (1927, Brit.)
(7 r.) d, Graham Cutts; lp, Lili Damita, Paul Richter, Harry Leichke, Rosa Richards

FORBIDDEN LOVER (1923)
(5 r.) d, Nat Deverich; lp, Noah Beery, Barbara Bedford, Elliott Sparling

FORBIDDEN PARADISE (1922, Ital.)
(6 r.) d, Herbert Brennon

FORBIDDEN PATH, THE (1918)
(6 r.) d, J. Gordon Edwards; lp, Theda Bara, Hugh Thompson, Sidney Mason, Walter Law

FORBIDDEN PATHS (1917)
(5 r.) d, Robert S. Thornby; lp, Vivian Martin, Sessue Hayakawa, Tom Forman, Carmen Phillips

FORBIDDEN RANGE, THE (1923)
(5 r.) d, Neal Hart; lp, Neal Hart, Yakima Canutt

FORBIDDEN ROOM, THE (1914)
(? r.) d, Allan Dwan; lp, Lon Chaney Sr., Mudock MacQuarrie, Pauline Bush

FORBIDDEN ROOM, THE (1919)
(5 r.) d, Lynn F. Reynolds; lp, Gladys Brockwell, William Scott, J. Barney Sherry, Harry Dunkinson

FORBIDDEN THING, THE (1920)
(7 r.) d, Allan Dwan; lp, James Kirkwood, Helen Jerome Eddy, Marcia Manon, King Baggot

FORBIDDEN TRAIL, THE (1923)
(5 r.) d, Robert North Bradbury; lp, Jack Hoxie, Evelyn Nelson, Frank Rice, William Lester

FORBIDDEN TRAILS (1920)
(5 r.) d, Scott Dunlap; lp, Buck Jones, Winifred Westover, Stanton Heck, William Elmer

FORBIDDEN TRAILS (1928)
(5 r.) d, Robert J. Horner; lp, Kit Carosn, Pawnee Bill, Jr., Bud Osborne

FORBIDDEN VALLEY (1920)
(5 r.) d, J. Stuart Blackton; lp, May McAvoy, Bruce Gordon, William R. Dunn, Charles Kent

FORBIDDEN WATERS (1926)
(6 r.) d, Alan Hale; lp, Priscilla Dean, Walter McGrail, Dan Mason, Casson Ferguson

FORBIDDEN WOMAN, THE (1927)
(7 r.) d, William C. De Mille; lp, Jetta Goufal, Ivan Lebedeff, Leonid Snegoff, Josephine Norman

FORCE DE LA VIE (1920, Fr.)
(? r.) d, Rene Leprince

FORDINGTON TWINS, THE (1920, Brit.)
(7 r.) d, W.P. Kellino; lp, The Terry Twins, Dallas Anderson, Mary Brough, Nita Russell

FOREIGN LEGION, THE (1928)
(8 r.) d, Edward Sloman; lp, Norman Kerry, Lewis Stone, Crauford Kent, Mary Nolan

FOREMAN OF BAR Z RANCH, THE (1924)
(5 r.) lp, Tom Mix

FOREST HAVOC (1926)
(6 r.) d, Stuart Paton; lp, Forrest Stanley, Peggy Montgomery, Martha Mattox, Ernest Hilliard

FOREST KING, THE (1922)
(5 r.) d, F.G. Hartman; lp, L.M. Wells, Virginia Ware, Reed Chapman, Dahlia Pears

FOREST ON THE HILL, THE (1919, Brit)
(6 r.) d, Cecil M. Hepworth; lp, Alma Taylor, James Carew, Gerald Ames, Lionelle Howard

FOREST RIVALS (1919)
(5 r.) d, Harry O. Hoyt; lp, Dorothy Green, Arthur Ashley, Jack Drumier, Kempton Greene

FOREVER (1921)
(7 r.) d, George Fitzmaurice; lp, Wallace Reid, Elsie Ferguson, Montagu Love, George Fawcett

FORFEIT, THE (1919)
(5 r.) d, Frank Powell; lp, House Peters, Jane Miller, William Human, Hector V. Sarno

FORGED BRIDE, THE (1920)
(5 r.) d, Douglas Gerrard; lp, Mary MacLaren, Thomas Jefferson, Dagmar Godowsky, J. Barney Sherry

FORGER, THE (1928, Brit.)
(7 r.) d, G.B. Samuelson; lp, Lillian Rich, James Raglan, Nigel Barrie, Winter Hall

FORGET-ME-NOT (1922)
(7 r.) d, W.S. Van Dyke; lp, Irene Hunt, William Machin, Bessie Love, Gareth Hughes

FORGET-ME-NOTS (1917)
(5 r.) d, Emile Chautard; lp, Kitty Gordon, Montagu Love, Alec B. Francis, George MacQuarrie

FORGIVE AND FORGET (1923)
(6 r.) d, Howard M. Mitchell; lp, Estelle Taylor, Pauline Garon, Philo McCullough, Josef Swickard

FORGIVE US OUR TRESPASSES (1919, Brit.)
(6 r.) d, L.C. MacBean; lp, Mary Marsh Allen, George Bellamy, H.R. Hignett, Booth Conway

FORGOTTEN, THE (1912, USSR)
(4 r.) d, Avrom Yitskhok Kaminsky

FORGOTTEN (1914, Brit.)
(4 r.) d, Stuart Kinder; lp, Fred Storey, Ella Brandon, Martin Stuart, Maitland Stapley

FORGOTTEN FACES (1928)
(8 r.) d, Victor Schertzinger; lp, Clive Brook, Mary Brian, Baclanova, William Powell

FORGOTTEN LAW, THE (1922)
(7 r.) d, James W. Horne; lp, Milton Sills, Jack Mulhall, Cleo Ridgely, Alec B. Francis

FORGOTTEN WOMAN (1921)
(5 r.) d, Park Frame; lp, Pauline Starke, J. Frank Glendon, Allan Forrest, Laura Winston

FORLORN RIVER (1926)
(6 r.) d, John Waters; lp, Jack Holt, Raymond Hatton, Arlette Marchal, Edmund Burns

FORSAKING ALL OTHERS (1922)
(5 r.) d, Emile Chautard; lp, Colleen Moore, Cullen Landis, Sam De Grasse, June Elvidge

FORT FRAYNE (1926)
(5 r.) d, Ben Wilson; lp, Ben Wilson, Neva Gerber, Ruth Royce, Bill Patton

40TH DOOR, THE (1924)
(6 r.) d, George B. Seitz; lp, Allene Ray, Bruce Gordon, David Dunbar, Anna May Wong

FORTUNATE YOUTH, THE (1916)
(5 r.) lp, Wilmuth Merkyl, William Cohill, John A. Smiley, G. Davidson Clark

FORTUNE AT STAKE, A (1918, Brit.)
(7 r.) d, Walter West; lp, Violet Hopson, Gerald Ames, Edward O'Neill, James Lindsay

FORTUNE HUNTER, THE (1920)
(7 r.) d, Tom Terriss; lp, Earle Williams, Jean Paige, Van Dyke Brooke, Nancy Lee

FORTUNE HUNTERS, THE (1914)
(4 r.)

FORTUNE OF CHRISTINA MCNAB, THE (1921, Brit.)
(6 r.) d, W.P. Kellino; lp, Nora Swinburne, David Hawthorne, Francis Lister, Sara Sample

FORTUNE TELLER, THE (1920)
(5 r.) d, Albert Capellani; lp, Marjorie Rambeau, Frederick Burton, E. Fernandez, Raymond McKee

FORTUNE'S FOOL (1922, Brit.)
(7 r.) d, Geoffrey H. Malins; lp, Madge Stuart, J.R. Tozer, William Stack, Sir Simeon Stuart

FORTUNE'S MASK (1922)
(5 r.) d, Robert Ensiminger; lp, Earle Williams, Patsy Ruth Miller, Henry Hebert, Milton Ross

FORTUNES OF FIFI, THE (1917)
(5 r.) d, Robert G. Vignola; lp, Marguerite Clark, William Sorelle, John Sainpolis, Yvonne Chevalier

48, AVENUE DE L'OPERA (1917, Fr.)
(? r.) d, Dominique Bernard-Deschamps

.45 CALIBRE WAR (1929)
(5 r.) d, Leo Maloney; lp, Don Coleman, Ben Corbett, Al Hart, Edward Jones

45 MINUTES FROM BROADWAY (1920)
(6 r.) d, Joseph De Grasse; lp, Charles Ray, Dorothy Devore, Hazel Howell, Eugenie Besserer

FORTY-FIRST, THE (1927, USSR)
(6 r.) d, Yakov Protazanov; lp, Ada Voisik, Ivan Koval-Samborsky, I. Strauch

40-HORSE HAWKINS (1924)
(6 r.) d, Edward Sedgwick; lp, Hoot Gibson, Anne Cornwall, Richard Tucker, Helen Holmes

'49 - '17 (1917)
(5 r.) d, Ruth Ann Baldwin; lp, Joseph Girard, Donna Drew, Leo Pierson, Harry Rattenberry

FOUL PLAY (1920, Brit.)
(5 r.) lp, Renee Kelly, Henry Hallett, Randolph McLeod, Cecil Morton York

FOUND GUILTY (1922)
(5 r.) lp, Tom Santschi

FOUNDLING, THE (1916)
(5 r.) d, John B. O'Brien; lp, Mary Pickford, Edward Martindel, Maggie Weston, Mildred Morris

FOUR AROUND THE WOMAN (1921, Ger.)
(? r.) d, Fritz Lang; lp, Carola Trolle, Ludwig Hartau, Anton Edthofer, Rudolf Klein-Rogge

FOUR FEATHERS, THE (1921, Brit.)
(6 r.) d, Rene Plaissetty; lp, Harry Ham, Mary Massart, Cyril Percival, Henry Vibart

FOUR FLUSHER, THE (1919)
(5 r.) d, Harry L. Franklin; lp, Hale Hamilton, Ruth Stonehouse, Harry Holden, Ralph Bell

FOUR FROM NOWHERE, THE (1925)
(5 r.) d, Francis Ford; lp, Francis Ford, Peggy O'Day, Phil Ford, Billie Ford

FOUR HEARTS (1922)
(5 r.) d, Leonard Wheeler; lp, Dick Hatton, Nell Spaugh, Carmen Arselle, Bud Geary

FOUR JUST MEN, THE (1921, Brit.)
(5 r.) d, George Ridgwell; lp, Cecil Humphreys, Teddy Arundell, C.H. Croker-King, C. Tilson-Chowne

FOURFLUSHER, THE
(SEE: FOUR FLUSHER, THE, 1919)

FOURFLUSHER, THE (1928)
(6 r.) d, Wesley Ruggles; lp, George Lewis, Marion Nixon, Eddie Philips, Churchill Ross

FOUR-FOOTED RANGER, THE (1928)
(5 r.) d, Stuart Paton; lp, Dynamite (a dog), Edmund Cobb, Marjorie Bonner, Pearl Sindelar

FOURTEENTH LOVER, THE (1922)
(5 r.) d, Harry Beaumont; lp, Viola Dana, Jack Mulhall, Theodore von Eltz, Kate Lester

FOURTEENTH MAN, THE (1920)
(6 r.) d, Joseph Henabery; lp, Robert Warwick, Bebe Daniels, Walter Hiers, Robert Milash

FOURTH COMMANDMENT, THE (1927)
(7 r.) d, Emory Johnson; lp, Henry Victor, June Marlowe, Belle Bennett, Leigh Willard

FOURTH ESTATE, THE (1916)
(5 r.) d, Frank Powell; lp, Ruth Blair, Clifford Bruce, Victor Benoit, Alfred Hickman

FOURTH MARRIAGE OF DAME MARGARET
(SEE: PARSON'S WIDOW, THE, 1920, Den.)

FOURTH MUSKETEER, THE (1923)
(6 r.) d, William K. Howard; lp, Johnnie Walker, Eileen Percy, Eddie Gribbon, William Scott

FOX, THE (1921)
(7 r.) d, Robert Thornby; lp, Harry Carey, George Nichols, Gertrude Olmsted, Betty Ross Clark

FOX WOMAN, THE (1915)
(4 r.) lp, Teddy Sampson, Signe Auen, Elmer Clifton

FRAGMENT OF AN EMPIRE (1930, USSR)
(7 r.) d, Friedrich Ermler; lp, Fyodor Nikitin, Yakov Gudkin, Ludmila Semyonova, Valeri Solovtsov

FRAME-UP, THE (1915)
(5 r.) d, Otis Turner; lp, George Fawcett, Maude George, Harry Carter, Albert MacQuarrie

FRAMEUP, THE (1916)
(5 r.)

FRAME-UP, THE
(SEE: HIGH GEAR JEFFREY, 1921)

FRAME UP, THE (1923)
(5 r.) d, Harry Moody; lp, Jack Livingston

FRAMED (1927)
(6 r.) d, Charles J. Brabin; lp, Milton Sills, Natalie Kingston, E.J. Radcliffe, Charles Gerrard

FRAMING FRAMERS (1918)
(5 r.) d, Philip Hurn, Ferris Hartman; lp, Charles Gunn, Laura Sears, George Pearce, Mildred Delfino

FRECKLES (1917)
(5 r.) d, Marshall Neilan; lp, Jack Pickford, Louise Huff, Hobart Bosworth, Lillian Leighton

FRECKLES (1928)
(7 r.) d, Leo Meehan; lp, John Fox, Jr., Gene Stratton Porter, Hobart Bosworth, Eulalie Jensen

FREE AIR (1922)
(6 r.) d, E.H. Griffith; lp, Tom Douglas, Marjorie Seaman, George Pauncefort, Henry G. Sell

FREE AND EQUAL (1924)
(7 r.)

FREE KISSES (1926)
(6 r.) d, William Nye; lp, Maurine Powers, Fred Parke

FREE TO LOVE (1925)
(5 r.) d, Frank O'Connor; lp, Clara Bow, Donald Keith, Raymond McKee, Hallam Cooley

FREEZE OUT, THE (1921)
(5 r.) d, Jack [John] Ford; lp, Harry Carey, Helen Ferguson, Joe Harris, Charles Le Moyne

FREIBURG PASSION PLAY (1924)
(7 r.)

FRENCH HEELS (1922)
(7 r.) d, Edwin L. Hollywood; lp, Irene Castle, Ward Crane, Charles Gerard, Howard Truesdale

FRENZIED FLAMES (1926)
(6 r.) d, Stuart Paton; lp, Cullen Landis, Virginia Browne Faire, Mary Carr, Charles K. French

FRESH EVERY HOUR
(SEE: HOW TO HANDLE WOMEN, 1928)

FRIEND HUSBAND (1918)
(5 r.) d, Clarence G. Badger; lp, Madge Kennedy, Rockliffe Fellowes, George Bunny, Paul Everton

FRIEND WILSON'S DAUGHTER (1915)
(4 r.) d, Langdon West; lp, Gertrude McCoy, Robert Brower, Lillian Devere, Lawrence White

FRIENDLY ENEMIES (1925)
(7 r.) d, George Melford; lp, Lew Fields, Joe Weber, Virginia Brown Faire, Jack Mulhall

FRINGE OF SOCIETY, THE (1918)
(7 r.) d, Robert Ellis; lp, Ruth Roland, Milton Sills, George Larkin, Leah Baird

FRISCO SALLY LEVY (1927)
(7 r.) d, William Beaudine; lp, Tenen Holtz, Kate Price, Sally O'Neil, Leon Holmes

FRISKY MRS. JOHNSON, THE (1920)
(5 r.) d, Edward Dillon; lp, Billie Burke, Ward Crane, Huntley Gordon, Lumsden Hare

FRIVOLOUS SAL (1925)
(8 r.) d, Victor Schertzinger; lp, Eugene O'Brien, Mae Busch, Ben Alexander, Tom Santschi

FRIVOLOUS WIVES (1920)
(6 r.) d, Joseph Maxwell; lp, Vera Sisson, Kathleen Kirkham, Edward Jobson, Frank Newburg

FROGGY'S LITTLE BROTHER
(SEE: CHILDREN OF COURAGE, 1921, Brit.)

FROM A BROADWAY TO A THRONE (1916)
(5 r.) d, William Bowman; lp, Carter De Haven, Walter Belasco, Duke Worne, Yona Landowska

FROM HEADQUARTERS (1919)
(5 r.) d, Ralph Ince; lp, Anita Stewart, Earle Williams, Anders Randolf

FROM NOW ON (1920)
(6 r.) d, Raoul Walsh; lp, George Walsh, Regina Quinn, Mario Majeroni, Paul Everton

FROM SHOPGIRL TO DUCHESS (1915, Brit.)
(4 r.) d, Maurice Elvey; lp, Elizabeth Risdon, Fred Groves, A.V. Bramble, Hilda Sims

FROM SPARKS--FLAMES (1924, USSR)
(30 r.) d, Dmitri Bassaligo; lp, Olga Tretyakova, G. Levkoyev

FROM THE VALLEY OF THE MISSING (1915)
(5 r.) d, Frank Powell

FROM THE WEST (1920)
(5 r.)

FROM TWO TO SIX (1918)
(5 r.) d, Albert Parker; lp, Winifred Allen, Earle Foxe, Forrest Robinson, Robert Fischer

FROMONT JEUNNE ET RISLER AINE (1921, Fr.)
(? r.) d, Henry Krauss

FRONTIER OF THE STARS, THE (1921)
(6 r.) d, Charles Maigne; lp, Thomas Meighan, Faire Binney, Alphonz Ethier, Edward Ellis

FRONTIER TRAIL, THE (1926)
(6 r.) d, Scott R. Dunlap; lp, Harry Carey, Mabel Julienne Scott, Ernest Hilliard, Frank Campeau

FRONTIERSMAN, THE (1927)
(5 r.) d, Reginald Barker; lp, Tim McCoy, Claire Windsor, Tom O'Brien, Russell Simpson

FROU FROU (1914)
(4 r.) lp, Maude Fealy, Harry Benham, James Cruze, Phyllis Bostwick

FROZEN FATE (1929, Brit.)
(5 r.) d, Ben R. Hart, St. John L. Clowes

FROZEN WARNING, THE (1918)
(6 r.) d, Oscar Eagle; lp, Charlotte, Jack Meredith, Seymour Rose, Ralph Johnson

FRUIT OF DIVORCE, THE
(SEE: SAN FRANCISCO NIGHTS, 1928)

FRUITFUL VINE, THE (1921, Brit.)
(7 r.) d, Maurice Elvey; lp, Basil Rathbone, Valia, Robert English, Mary Dibley

FRUITS OF PASSION (1919)
(5 r.) d, George Ridgwell; lp, Alice Mann, Frances Mann, Emile J. de Varney, Colin Campbell

FUEL OF LIFE (1917)
(5 r.) d, Walter Edwards; lp, Belle Bennett, Frank H. Newburg, J. Barney Sherry, Texas Guinan

FUGITIVE, THE (1916)
(5 r.) d, Frederick Sullivan; lp, Florence LaBadie, Ethyle Cooke, George Marlo, Dorothy Benham

FUGITIVE, THE (1925)
(5 r.) d, Ben Wilson; lp, Ruth Stonehouse, Wilbur McGaugh, Ben Wilson, Natalie La Supervia

FUGITIVE FROM MATRIMONY (1919)
(5 r.) d, Henry King; lp, H.B. Warner, Seena Owen, Walter Perry, Adele Farrington

FULL HOUSE, A (1920)
(4 r.) d, James Cruze; lp, Bryant Washburn, Lois Wilson, Guy Milham, Hazel Howell

FULL OF PEP (1919)
(5 r.) d, Harry L. Franklin; lp, Hale Hamilton, Alice Lake, Alice Knowland, Fred Malatesta

FULL SPEED (1925)
(5 r.) d, Richard Thorpe; lp, Buffalo Bill, Jr.

FUN ON THE FARM (1926)
(5 r.) lp, Sammy Burns

FURNANCE, THE (1920)
(6 r.) d, William D. Taylor; lp, Agnes Ayres, Milton Sills, Jerome Patrick, Betty Francisco

FURTHER EXPLOITS OF SEXTON BLAKE, THE - MYSTERY OF THE S.S. OLYMPIC, THE (1919, Brit.) (5 r.) d, Harry Lorraine; lp, Douglas Payne, Marjorie Villis, Jeff Barlow, Frank Dane

FURY (1922)
(9 r.) d, Henry King; lp, Richard Barthelmess, [Frederick] Tyrone Power, Pat Hartigan, Barry Macollum

FURY OF THE WILD (1929)
(5 r.) d, Leon D'Usseau; lp, Ranger (a dog), Barbara Worth, Robert Homans, Pat O'Brien

FUSS AND FEATHERS (1918)
(5 r.) d, Fred Niblo; lp, Enid Bennett, Douglas MacLean, John P. Lockney, Charles French

GAIETY GIRL, THE (1924)
(8 r.) d, King Baggot; lp, Mary Philbin, Joseph J. Dowling, William Haines, James O. Barrows

GALLEY SLAVE, THE (1915)
(5 r.) d, J. Gordon Edwards; lp, Theda Bara, Stuart Holmes, Claire Whitney, Jane Lee

GALLOPER, THE (1915)
(5 r.) d, Donald Mackenzie; lp, Clifton Crawford, Melville Stewart, Fania Marinoff, Rhys Alexander

GALLOPING COWBOY, THE (1926)
(5 r.) d, William J. Craft; lp, Bill Cody, Alex Hart, Edmund Cobb, Barney Gilmore

GALLOPING DEVIL, THE
(SEE: GALLOPING DEVILS, 1920)

GALLOPING DEVILS (1920)
(5 r.) d, Nate Watt; lp, Franklyn Farnum, Vester Pegg

GALLOPING DUDE
(SEE: GALLOPING DEVILS, 1920)

GALLOPING FISH (1924)
(6 r.) d, Del Andrews; lp, Louise Fazenda, Sydney Chaplin, Ford Sterling, Chester Conklin

GALLOPING FURY (1927)
(6 r.) d, Reaves Eason; lp, Hoot Gibson, Otis Harlan, Sally Rand, Frank Beal

GALLOPING JINX (1925)
(5 r.) d, Robert Eddy; lp, Buddy Roosevelt, Gloria Heller, J. Gordon Russell, Ralph Whiting

GALLOPING LOVER, THE (1929)
(5 r.) lp, Cliff "Tex" Lyons

GALLOPING ON (1925)
(5 r.) d, Richard Thorpe; lp, Wally Wales, Jessie Cruzon, Louise Lester, Charles Whitaker

GALLOPING THUNDER (1927)
(5 r.) d, Scott Pembroke; lp, Bob Custer, Anne Sheridan, J.P. Lockney, Richard R. Neill

GALLOPING VENGEANCE (1925)
(5 r.) d, William James Craft; lp, Bob Custer, Mary Beth Milford, Ralph McCullough, Dorothy Ponedel

GAMBLE FOR LOVE, A (1917, Brit.)
(6 r.) d, Frank Wilson; lp, Violet Hopson, Gerald Ames, James Lindsay, George Foley

GAMBLE IN LIVES, A (1920, Brit.)
(5 r.) d, George Ridgwell; lp, Malvina Longfellow, Norman McKinnel, Alec Fraser, John Reed

GAMBLE IN SOULS, A (1916)
(5 r.) d, Walter Edwards; lp, William Desmond, Dorothy Dalton, Dempsey Tabler, Charles K. French

GAMBLER OF THE WEST, THE (1915)
(4 r.) lp, William J. Butler, Violet Reid, George Pearce, Charles Perley

GAMBLERS, THE (1914)
(5 r.) d, Barry O'Neill; lp, Gaston Bell, George Soule Spencer, Ethel Clayton, Earl Metcalfe

GAMBLERS, THE (1919)
(5 r.) d, Paul Scardon; lp, Harry T. Morey, Agnes Ayres, Charles Kent, Helen Ferguson

GAMBLER'S ADVOCATE (1915)
(4 r.) lp, Hazel Dawn, James Kirkwood, Fuller Mellish, Robert Broderick

GAMBLERS ALL (1919, Brit.)
(6 r.) d, Dave Aylott; lp, Madge Titheradge, Owen Nares, Ruby Miller, C.M. Hallard

GAMBLING FOOL, THE (1925)
(5 r.) d, J.P. McGowan; lp, Franklyn Farnum, Otto Myers, Fred Holmes, Harry Northrup

GAME CHICKEN, THE (1922)
(5 r.) d, Chester M. Franklin; lp, Bebe Daniels, Pat O'Malley, James Gordon, Martha Mattox

GAME FIGHTER, A (1924)
(5 r.) d, Tom Gibson; lp, Bill Patton

GAME OF LIBERTY, THE
(SEE: UNDER SUSPICION, 1916, Brit.)

GAME OF WITS, A (1917)
(5 r.) d, Henry King; lp, Gail Kane, George Periolat, Spottiswoode Aitken, Lewis J. Cody

GAME WITH FATE, A (1918)
(5 r.) d, Paul Scardon; lp, Harry Morey, Betty Blythe, Denton Vane, Percy Standing

GAME'S UP, THE (1919)
(5 r.) d, Elsie Jane Wilson; lp, Ruth Clifford, Al Ray, Mildred Lee, Harry Holden

GAMESTERS, THE (1920)
(6 r.) d, George L. Cox; lp, Margarita Fischer, Hayward Mack, L.C. Shumway, P. Dempsey Tabler

GANGSTERS, THE (1914)
(4 r.)

GARDEN OF ALLAH, THE (1916)
(9 r.) d, Colin Campbell; lp, Helen Ware, Thomas Santschi, Al W. Filson, Eugenie Besserer

GARDEN OF ALLAH, THE (1927)
(9 r.) d, Rex Ingram; lp, Alice Terry, Ivan Petrovich, Marcel Vibert, H.H. Wright

GARDEN OF EDEN, THE (1928)
(8 r.) d, Lewis Milestone; lp, Corinne Griffith, Louise Dresser, Lowell Sherman, Maude George

GARDEN OF LIES, THE (1915)
(5 r.) d, Augustus Thomas; lp, Jane Cowl, Violet Horner, William Russell, Philip Hahn

GARDEN OF WEEDS, THE (1924)
(6 r.) d, James Cruze; lp, Betty Compson, Rockliffe Fellowes, Warner Baxter, Charles Ogle

GARDIENS DE PHARE (1929, Fr.)
(7 r.) d, Jean Gremillon; lp, Geymond Vital, Fromet, Genica Athanasiou, Gabrielle Fontan

GARMENTS OF TRUTH (1921)
(5 r.) d, George D. Baker; lp, Gareth Hughes, Ethel Grandin, John Steppling, Frances Raymond

GARROWEN (1920, Brit.)
(6 r.) d, George Pearson; lp, Fred Groves, Hugh E. Wright, Moyna McGill, Bertram Burleigh

GARTER GIRL, THE (1920)
(5 r.) d, Edward H. Griffith; lp, Corinne Griffith, Sally Crute, Earl Metcalfe, Rod La Rocque

GAS, OIL AND WATER (1922)
(5 r.) d, Charles Ray; lp, Charles Ray, Otto Hoffman, Charlotte Pierce, Robert Grey

GASOLINE COWBOY (1926)
(5 r.) d, Frederick Reel, Jr. lp, Al Richmond

GATES OF BRASS (1919)
(5 r.) d, Ernest C. Warde; lp, Frank Keenan, Lois Wilson, George Fisher, Clyde Benson

GATES OF DOOM, THE (1917)
(5 r.) d, Charles Swickard; lp, Claire McDowell, L.C. Shumway, Jack Connolly, Mark Fenton

GATES OF DUTY (1919, Brit.)
(5 r.) d, Randle Ayrton; lp, James Knight, Mary Mayfren, Bertram Burleigh, Evelyn Trevor

GATES OF EDEN, THE (1916)
(5 r.) d, John H. Collins; lp, Viola Dana, Augustus Phillips, Robert Walker, Edward Earle

GATES OF GLADNESS (1918)
(5 r.) d, Harley Knoles; lp, Madge Evans, George MacQuarrie, Niles Welch, Rosina Henley

GAUNTLET, THE (1920)
(5 r.) d, Edwin L. Hollywood; lp, Harry T. Morey, Louiszita Valentine, Frank Hagney, Walter Horton

GAY DECEIVER, THE (1926)
(7 r.) d, John M. Stahl; lp, Lew Cody, Malcolm McGregor, Marceline Day, Carmel Myers

GAY DEFENDER, THE (1927)
(7 r.) d, Gregory La Cava; lp, Richard Dix, Thelma Todd, Fred Kohler, Jerry Mandy

GAY LORD QUEX, THE (1920)
(5 r.) d, Harry Beamont; lp, Tom Moore, Gloria Hope, Naomi Childers, Hazel Daly

GAY LORD WARING, THE (1916)
(5 r.) d, Otis Turner; lp, J. Warren Kerrigan, Lois Wilson, Bertram Grassby, Maude George

GAY OLD DOG, THE (1919)
(5 r.) d, Hobart Henley; lp, John Cumberland, Mary Chambers, Emily Lorraine, Inez Marcel

GAYEST OF THE GAY, THE (1924, Brit.)
(5 r.) d, Bertram Philips; lp, Queenie Thomas, John Stuart, Cecil Humphreys, Juliette Compton

GENERAL CUSTER AT LITTLE BIG HORN (1926)
(6 r.) d, Harry L. Fraser; lp, Roy Stewart, Helen Lynch, John Beck, Edmund Cobb

GENEVIEVE (1923, Fr.)
(? r.) d, Leon Poirier; lp, Mlle. Myrga

GENTLE CYCLONE, THE (1926)
(5 r.) d, William S. Van Dyke; lp, Buck Jones, Rose Blossom, Will Walling, Reed Howes

GENTLE INTRUDER, THE (1917)
(5 r.) d, James Kirkwood; lp, Mary Miles Minter, George Fisher, Eugenie Forde, Harvey Clark

GENTLEMAN FROM AMERICA, THE (1923)
(5 r.) d, Edward Sedgwick; lp, Ed "Hoot" Gibson, Tom O'Brien, Louise Lorraine, Carmen Phillips

GENTLEMAN FROM INDIANA, A (1915)
(5 r.) d, Frank Lloyd; lp, Dustin Farnum, Winifred Kingston, Herbert Standing, Joe Ray

GENTLEMEN IN BLUE, THE (1917, Brit.)
(4 r.)

GENTLEMAN OF FRANCE, A (1921, Brit.)
(6 r.) d, Maurice Elvey; lp, Ellie Norwood, Madge Stuart, Hugh Buckler, Sydney Seaward

GENTLEMAN OF PARIS, A (1927)
(6 r.) d, Harry D'Abbadie D'Arrast; lp, Adolphe Menjou, Shirley O'Hara, Arlette Marchal, Ivy Harris

GENTLEMAN OF QUALITY, A (1919)
(5 r.) d, James Young; lp, Earle Williams, Katherine Adams, Joyce Moore, James Carpenter

GENTLEMAN PREFFERED, A (1928)
(5 r.) d, Arthur Hotaling; lp, Gaston Glass, Jimmy Aubrey, Kathleen Myers, Jerome La Grasse

GENTLEMAN RIDER, THE
(SEE: HEARTS AND SADDLES, 1919, Brit.)

GENTLEMAN ROUGHNECK, A (1925)
(5 r.) d, Grover Jones; lp, Frank Merrill, William Conklin, Jack Richardson, Virginia Warwick

GENTLEMAN UNAFRAID (1923)
(5 r.) lp, George Larkin, Ollie Kirby

GENTLEMAN'S AGREEMENT, A (1918)
(5 r.) d, David Smith; lp, Alfred Whitman, Nell Shipman, Juan de la Cruz, Jack Abraham

GENUINE (1920, Ger.)
(? r.) d, Robert Wiene; lp, Fern Andra, Harald Paulsen Hans Heinrich Von Twardowski

GEO, LE MYSTERIEUX (1917, Fr.)
(? r.) d, Germaine Dulac

GEORGE WASHINGTON COHEN (1928)
(6 r.) d, George Archainbaud; lp, George Jessel, Robert Edeson, Corliss Palmer, Lawford Davidson

GEORGE WASHINGTON, JR. (1924)
(6 r.) d, Mal St. Clair; lp, Wesley Barry, Gertrude Olmstead, Leon Barry, Charles Conklin

GERALD CRANSTON'S LADY (1924)
(7 r.) d, Emmett J. Flynn; lp, James Kirkwood, Alma Rubens, Walter McGrail, J. Farrell McDonald

GERM, THE (1923)
(? r.) d, P.S. McGreeney;

GET YOUR MAN (1927)
(6 r.) d, Dorothy Arzner; lp, Clara Bow, Charles "Buddy" Rogers, Josef Swickard, Josephine Dunn

GET-RICH-QUICK WALLINGFORD (1921)
(7 r.) d, Frank Borzage; lp, Sam Hardy, Norman Kerry, Doris Kenyon, Diana Allen

GETTING 'EM RIGHT (1925)
(5 r.) lp, George Larkin, Jane Thomas

GETTING GERTIE'S GARTER (1927)
(7 r.) d, E. Mason Hopper; lp, Marie Prevost, Charles Ray, Harry Myers, Sally Rand

GETTING HER MAN (1924)
(5 r.) lp, Ora Carew, Jay Morley, Hal Stephens

GHETTO SHAMROCK, THE (1926)
(5 r.) d, Francis Ford; lp, Jack Mower, Gloria Gray

GHOST BREAKER (1914)
(4 r.) d, H.B. Warner, Rita Sanwood, Betty Johnson, Theodore Roberts

GHOST BREAKER, THE (1922)
(5 r.) d, Alfred E. Green; lp, Wallace Reid, Lila Lee, Walter Hiers, Arthur Carewe

GHOST CITY (1921)
(5 r.) d, William Bertram; lp, Helen Holmes, Ann Schaeffer, Leo Maloney, Leonard Clapham

GHOST CLUB, THE (1914)
(6 r.)

GHOST FLOWER, THE (1918)
(5 r.) d, Frank Borzage; lp, Alma Rubens, Charles West, Francis McDonald, Dick Rosson

GHOST HOUSE, THE (1917)
(5 r.) d, William C. De Mille; lp, Jack Pickford, Louise Huff, Olga Grey, James Neill

GHOST IN THE GARRET, THE (1921)
(5 r.) d, F. Richard Jones; lp, Dorothy Gish, Downing Clarke, William Parke, Jr., Ray Grey

GHOST OF OLD MORRO, THE (1917)
(5 r.) d, Richard Ridgley; lp, Herbert Prior, Robert Conness, Helen Strickland, Bigelow Cooper

GHOST OF ROSY TAYLOR, THE (1918)
(5 r.) d, Edward Sloman; lp, Mary Miles Minter, Alan Forrest, George Periolat, Helen Howard

GHOST OF THE RANCHO, THE (1918)
(5 r.) d, William Worthington; lp, Bryant Washburn, Rhea Mitchell

GHOST OF TOLSTON'S MANOR, THE (1923)
(? r.)

GHOST PATROL, THE (1923)
(5 r.) d, Nat Ross; lp, Ralph Graves, Bessie Love, George Nichols, George B. Williams

GHOST RIDER, THE (1925)
(5 r.) lp, Pete Morrison, Martin Turner

GHOST THAT NEVER RETURNS, THE (1930, USSR)
(8 r.) d, Abram Room; lp, O. Jisneva, M. Shtraukh

GHOST THAT WILL NOT RETURN, THE
(SEE: GHOST THAT NEVER RETURNS, THE, 1930, USSR)

GHOST TRAIN, THE (1927, Brit.)
(7 r.) d, Geza M. Bolvary; lp, Guy Newall, Ilse Bois, Louis Ralph, Anna Jennings

GHOSTS (1915, USSR)
(4 r.) d, Vladimir Gardin; lp, Pavel Orlenev

GHOSTS (1915)
(5 r.) d, John Emerson, George Nicholls; lp, Henry B. Walthall, Mary Alden, Nigel De Brulier, Juanita Archer

GHOSTS OF YESTERDAY (1918)
(6 r.) d, Charles Miller; lp, Norma Talmadge, Eugene O'Brien, Stuart Holmes, John Daly Murphy

GIANT OF HIS RACE, A (1921)
(7 r.) lp, Mabel Holmes, Walter Holeby, Walter Long, Ruth Freeman

GIFT, THE
(SEE: KISSING CUP, 1913, Brit.)

GIFT GIRL, THE (1917)
(5 r.) d, Rupert Julian; lp, Louise Lovely, Emory Johnson, Rupert Julian, Wadsworth Harris

GIFT O' GAB (1917)
(5 r.) d, W.S. Van Dyke; lp, Jack Gardner, Helen Freguson, Frank Morris, John Cossar

GIFT SUPREME, THE (1920)
(6 r.) d, Ollie L. Sellers; lp, Bernard Durning, Melbourne McDowell, Eugenie Besserer, Seena Owen

GIGOLETTE (1920, Fr.)
(? r.) d, Henri Pouctal

GIGOLO (1926)
(8 r.) d, William K. Howard; lp, Rod La Rocque, Jobyna Ralston, Louise Dresser, Cyril Chadwick

GILDED FOOL, THE (1915)
(5 r.) lp, William Farnum

GILDED LIES (1921)
(5 r.) d, William P.S. Earle; lp, Eugene O'Brien, Martha Mansfield, Frank Whitson, George Stewart

GILDED YOUTH, A (1917)
(5 r.) d, George L. Sargent; lp, Richard Bennett, Rhea Mitchell

GINGER (1919)
(5 r.) d, Burton George; lp, Violet Palmer, Raymond Hackett, Gareth Hughes, Paul Everton

GINGHAM GIRL, THE (1927)
(7 r.) d, David Kirkland; lp, Lois Wilson, George K. Arthur, Charles Crockett, Hazel Keener

GIPSY CAVALIER, A (1922, Brit.)
(7 r.) d, J. Stuart Blackton; lp, Georges Carpenter, Flora le Breton, Rex McDougall, Mary Clare

GIRL ALASKA, THE (1919)
(5 r.) d, Albert I. Smith; lp, Lottie Kruse [Cruze], Henry Bolton, C. Edward Cone

GIRL AND THE CRISIS, THE (1917)
(5 r.) d, William V. Mong; lp, Dorothy Davenport, Charles Perley, Harry Holden, William V. Mong

GIRL AND THE JUDGE, THE (1918)
(5 r.) d, John B. O'Brien; lp, Olive Tell, David Powell, Charlotte Granville, Eric Mayne

GIRL ANGLE, THE (1917)
(5 r.) d, Edgar Jones; lp, Anita King, Joseph Ryan, Daniel Gilfether, Mollie McConnell

GIRL AT BAY, A (1919)
(5 r.) d, Tom Mills; lp, Corinne Griffith, Walter Miller, Harry Davenport, Denton Vane

GIRL AT HOME, THE (1917)
(5 r.) d, Marshall Neilan; lp, Vivian Martin, Jack Pickford, James Neill, Olga Grey

GIRL BY THE ROADSIDE, THE (1918)
(5 r.) d, Theodore Marston; lp, Violet Mersereau, Cecil Owen, Ann Andrews, Allen Edwards

GIRL DODGER, THE (1919)
(5 r.) d, Jerome Storm; lp, Charles Ray, Doris Lee [Doris May], Hal [Hallam] Cooley, Jack Nelson

GIRL FROM BEYOND, THE (1918)
(5 r.) d, William Wolbert; lp, Nell Shipman, Alfred Whitman, Bob Burns, Hattie Buskirk

GIRL FROM BOHEMIA, THE (1918)
(5 r.) d, Lawrence McGill; lp, Irene Castle, Edward Cecil, Violet Axzelle

GIRL FROM CARTHAGE, THE (1924, Tunisia)
(? r.) d, Scemana Chikly; lp, Hayde Chikly, Ahmed Dziri, Abdelgassen Ben Taleb, Hadj Hadi Dehali

GIRL FROM CONEY ISLAND, THE
(SEE: JUST ANOTHER BLONDE, 1926)

GIRL FROM GAY PAREE, THE (1927)
(6 r.) d, Phil Stone; lp, Lowell Sherman, Barbara Bedford, Malcolm McGregor, Betty Blythe

GIRL FROM GOD'S COUNTRY, THE (1921)
(7 r.) d, Nell Shipman; lp, Nell Shipman, Edward Burns, Al Filson, George Berrell

GIRL FROM MONTMARTRE, THE (1926)
(6 r.) d, Alfred E. Green; lp, Barbara La Marr, Lewis Stone, Robert Ellis, William Eugene

GIRL FROM NOWHERE, THE (1919)
(5 r.) d, Wilfred Lucas, Bess Meredyth; lp, Cleo Madison, Wilfred Lucas

GIRL FROM NOWHERE, THE (1921)
(5 r.) d, George Archainbaud; lp, Elaine Hammerstein, William B. Davidson, Huntley Gordon, Louise Prussing

GIRL FROM PORCUPINE, THE (1921)
(6 r.) d, Dell Henderson; lp, Faire Binney, William "Buster" Collier, Jr., Jack Drumier, James Milady

GIRL FROM RECTOR'S, THE (1917)
(5 r.) lp, Ruth MacTammany, Lillian Concord

GIRL FROM ROCKY POINT, THE (1922)
(5 r.) d, Fred G. Becker; lp, Milton Ross, Ora Carew, Gloria Joy, Charles Spere

GIRL FROM THE OUTSIDE, THE (1919)
(7 r.) d, Reginald Barker; lp, Clara Horton, Cullen Landis, Wilton Taylor, Hallam Cooley

GIRL GLORY, THE (1917)
(5 r.) d, R. William Neill; lp, Enid Bennett, Walt Whitman, William Warters, Margery Bennett

GIRL HE DIDN'T BUY, THE (1928)
(6 r.) d, Dallas M. Fitzgerald; lp, Pauline Garon, Allan Simpson, William Eugene, Gladden James

GIRL I LEFT BEHIND ME, THE (1915)
(5 r.) d, Lloyd B. Carleton; lp, Robert Edeson, Claire Whitney, Stuart Holmes, Walter Hitchcock

GIRL I LOVED, THE (1923)
(8 r.) d, Joseph De Grasse; lp, Charles Ray, Patsy Ruth Miller, Ramsey Wallace, Edythe Chapman

GIRL IN BOHEMIA, A (1919)
(5 r.) d, Howard M. Mitchell; lp, Peggy Hyland, Joseph Swickard, L.C. Shumway, Betty Schade

GIRL IN HIS HOUSE, THE (1918)
(5 r.) d, Tom Mills; lp, Earle Williams, Grace Desmond, Jake Abraham, Irene Rich

GIRL IN HIS ROOM, THE (1922)
(5 r.) d, Edward Jose; lp, Alice Calhoun, Warner Baxter, Robert Anderson, Faye O'Neill

GIRL IN NUMBER 29, THE (1920)
(5 r.) d, Jack [John] Ford; lp, Frank Mayo, Elinor Fair, Claire Anderson, Harry Hilliard

GIRL IN THE CHECKERED COAT, THE (1917)
(5 r.) d, Joseph De Grasse; lp, Dorothy Phillips, Lon Chaney, William Stowell, Jane Bernoudy

GIRL IN THE LIMOUSINE, THE (1924)
(6 r.) d, Larry Sermon; lp, Larry Semon, Claire Adams, Charles Murray, Lucille Ward

GIRL IN THE PULLMAN, THE (1927)
(6 r.) d, Erle Kenton; lp, Marie Prevost, Harrison Ford, Franklin Pangborn, Kathryn McGuire

GIRL IN THE RAIN, THE (1920)
(5 r.) d, Rollin S. Sturgeon; lp, Lloyd Bacon, Anne Cornwall, Jessalyn Van Trump, James Farley

GIRL IN THE RAIN (1927)
(5 r.) lp, David Butler, Claribel Campbell, Hale Hamilton

GIRL IN THE TAXI, THE (1921)
(6 r.) d, Lloyd Ingraham; lp, Carter De Haven, Mrs. Carter De Haven, King Baggot, Grace Cunard

GIRL IN THE WEB, THE (1920)
(6 r.) d, Robert Thornby; lp, Blanche Sweet, Nigel Barrie, Thomas Jefferson, Jr., Adele Farrington

GIRL LIKE THAT, A (1917)
(5 r.) d, Del Henderson; lp, Irene Fenwick, Owen Moore, Tom O'Keefe, Edwin Sturgis

GIRL NAMED MARY, A (1920)
(5 r.) d, Walter Edwards; lp, Marguerite Clark, Kathlyn Williams, Wallace McDonald, Aggie Herring

GIRL O'DREAMS, THE (1918)
(5 r.)

GIRL OF GOLD, THE (1925)
(6 r.) d, John Ince; lp, Florence Vidor, Malcolm McGregor, Alan Roscoe, Bessie Eyton

GIRL OF LOST LAKE, THE (1916)
(5 r.) d, Lynn Reynolds; lp, Myrtle Gonzales, Mary Du Cello, Ruby Cox, Val Paul

GIRL OF MY DREAMS, THE (1918)
(5 r.) d, Louis William Chaudet; lp, Billie Rhodes, Leo Pierson, Frank McQuarrie, Lamar Johnstone

GIRL OF THE GYPSY CAMP, THE (1915)
(4 r.) d, Langdon West; lp, Bessie Learn, Carlton King, Charles Sutton, Frank McGlynn

GIRL OF THE LIMBERLOST, A (1924)
(6 r.) d, James Leo Meehan; lp, Gloria Grey, Emily Fitzroy, Arthur Currier, Raymond McKee

GIRL OF THE SEA (1920)
(6 r.) d, J. Winthrop Kelley; lp, Betty Hilburn, Chester Barnett, Kathryn Lean, Alex Shannon

GIRL OF THE SUNNY SOUTH, THE (1913)
(4 r.)

GIRL OF THE TIMBER CLAIMS, THE (1917)
(5 r.) d, Paul Powell; lp, Constrance Talmadge, A.D. Sears, Clyde Hopkins, Beau Byrd

GIRL OF THE WEST (1925)
(5 r.) d, Alvin J. Neitz; lp, Eileen Sedgwick

GIRL OF TODAY, THE (1918)
(5 r.) d, John S. Robertson; lp, Corinne Griffith, Webster Campbell, Marc McDermott, Charles A. Stevenson

GIRL PHILIPPA, THE (1917)
(8 r.) d, S. Ranklin Drew; lp, Anita Stewart, Sidney Rankin Drew, Frank Morgan, Anders Randolf

GIRL PROBLEM, THE (1919)
(5 r.) d, Kenneth Webb; lp, Corinne Griffith, Walter McGrail, Agnes Ayres, William David

GIRL WHO CAME BACK, THE (1918)
(5 r.) d, Robert G. Vignola; lp, Ethel Clayton, Elliott Dexter, Theodore Roberts, James Neill

GIRL WHO CAME BACK, THE (1923)
(6 r.) d, Tom Forman; lp, Miriam Cooper, Gaston Glass, Kenneth Harlan, Fred Malatesta

GIRL WHO COULDN'T GROW UP, THE (1917)
(5 r.) d, Harry A. Pollard; lp, Margarita Fischer, John Steppling, Jean Hathaway, Jack Mower

GIRL WHO DARED, THE
(SEE: PAID IN ADVANCE, 1919)

GIRL WHO DID NOT CARE, THE
(SEE: SEX LURE, THE, 1916)

GIRL WHO DIDN'T THINK, THE (1917)
(6 r.) d, William Haddock; lp, Jane Gail, Stanley Walpole, May Simon, Agnes Neilsen

GIRL WHO DOESN'T KNOW, THE (1917)
(5 r.) d, Charles Earl Bartlett; lp, Marie Empress, R. Henry Grey, Zada Marlow, Henry Stanley

GIRL WHO RAN WILD, THE (1922)
(5 r.) d, Rupert Julian; lp, Gladys Walton, Marc Robbins, Vernon Steele, Joseph Dowling

GIRL WHO WON OUT, THE (1917)
(5 r.) d, Eugene Moore; lp, Violet MacMillan, Barbara Conley, P.L. Pembroke, Charles Hill Mailes

GIRL WHO WRECKED HIS HOME, THE (1916, Brit.)
(5 r.) d, Albert Ward; lp, Henry Lonsdale, Alice Belmore, Arthur Poole, Maud Olmar

GIRL WITH A JAZZ HEART, THE (1920)
(5 r.) d, Lawrence C. Windom; lp, Madge Kennedy, Joe King, Leon Guerre Gendron, William Walcott

GIRL WITH NO REGRETS, THE (1919)
(5 r.) d, Harry Millarde; lp, Peggy Hyland, Charles Clary, Gene Burr, Betty Schade

GIRL WITH THE CHAMPAGNE EYES, THE (1918)
(5 r.) d, C.M. Franklin; lp, Jewel Carmen, L.C. Shumway, Charles Edler, G. Raymond Nye

GIRL WITH THE GREEN EYES, THE (1916)
(5 r.) d, Herbert Blache, Alice Guy; lp, Katharine Kaelred, Julian L'Estrange, Edith Lyle, Lucile Watson

GIRL WITH THE HAT-BOX (1927, USSR)
(5 r.) d, Boris Barnet; lp, Anna Sten, Ivan Koval-Samborsky, Vladimir Fogel, Sefafima Birman

GIRL WITH THE JAZZ HEART, THE (1920)
(5 r.) d, Lawrence C. Windom; lp, Madge Kennedy, Joe King, Leon Pierre Gendron, William Walcott

GIRL WOMAN, THE (1919)
(5 r.) d, Thomas R. Mills; lp, Gladys Leslie, Maurice Costello, Priestley Morrison, William E. Lawrence

GIRLS (1919)
(5 r.) d, Walter Edwards; lp, Marguerite Clark, Harrison Ford, Helene Chadwick, Lee Hill

GIRL'S DESIRE, A (1922)
(5 r.) d, David Divad; lp, Alice Calhoun, Warner Baxter, Frank Crane, Lillian Lawrence

GIRLS MEN FORGET (1924)
(6 r.) d, Maurice Campbell; lp, Johnnie Walker, Patsy Ruth Miller, Alan Hale, Mayme Kelso

GIRL-SHY COWBOY, THE (1928)
(5 r.) d, R. Lee Hough; lp, Rex Bell, George Meeker, Patsy O'Leary, Donald Stuart

GITANELLA (1924, Fr.)
(? r.) d, Andre Hugon

GIULLI (1927, USSR)
(7 r.) d, L. Push; lp, Nata Vachnadze, M. Vardeshvili

GIVE US THIS DAY (1913, Swed.)
(7 r.) d, Victor Sjostrom; lp, Hilda Borgstrom, Eric Lindholm, William Larsson

GIVING BECKY A CHANCE (1917)
(5 r.) d, Howard Estabrook; lp, Vivian Martin, Jack Holt, Jack Richardson, P.H. Sosso

GLAD EYE, THE (1920, Brit.)
(6 r.) d, Kenelm Foss; lp, James Reardon, Dorothy Minto, Hayford Hobbs, Pauline Peters

GLAD EYE, THE (1927, Brit.)
(8 r.) d, Maurice Elvey; lp, Estelle Brody, Hal Sherman, John Stuart, Mabel Poulton

GLASS HOUSES (1922)
(6 r.) d, Harry Beaumont; lp, Viola Dana, Gaston Glass, Maym Kelso, Helen Lynch

GLENISTER OF THE MOUNTED (1926)
(6 r.) d, Harry Garson; lp, Lefty Flynn, Bess Flowers, Lee Shumway, Walter James

GLIMPSES OF THE MOON, THE (1923)
(7 r.) d, Allan Dwan; lp, Bebe Daniels, Nita Naldi, David Powell, Maurice Costello

GLOIRE ROUGE (1923, Fr.)
(? r.) d, Albert Dieudonne

GLORIANA (1916)
(5 r.) d, E. Mason Hopper; lp, Zoe Rae, Virginia Foltz, William Canfield, Clarrisa Selwynne

GLORIOUS ADVENTURE, THE (1918)
(5 r.) d, Hobart Henley; lp, Mae Marsh, Wyndham Standing, Paul Stanton, Alec B. Francis

GLORIOUS FOOL, THE (1922)
(6 r.) d, E. Mason Hooper; lp, Helene Chadwick, Richard Dix, Vera Lewis, Kate Lester

GLORIOUS LADY, THE (1919)
(5 r.) d, George Irving; lp, Olive Thomas, Matt Moore, Evelyn Brent, Robert Taylor

GLORIOUS TRAIL, THE (1928)
(6 r.) d, Albert Rogell; lp, Ken Maynard, Gladys McConnell, Frank Hagney, Les Bates

GLORIOUS YOUTH (1928, Brit.)
(7 r.) d, Graham Cutts; lp, Anny Ondra, William Freshman, Randle Ayrton, Gibb McLaughlin

GLORY (1917)
(6 r.) d, Burton King, Francis Grandon; lp, Juanita Hansen, C. William Kolb [Clarence Kolb], Max Dill, Frank Mayo

GLORY OF CLEMENTINA, THE (1922)
(6 r.) d, Emile Chautard; lp, Pauline Frederick, Edward Martindel, George Cowl, Lincoln Plummer

GLORY OF LOVE, THE
(SEE: WHILE PARIS SLEEPS, 1923)

GLORY OF YOLANDA, THE (1917)
(5 r.) d, Marguerite Bertsch; lp, Anita Stewart, John Ardizonia, Denton Vane, Evart Overton

GLOW OF LIFE, THE (1918, Jap.)
(4 r.) d, Norimasa Kaeriyama; lp, Minoru Murata

GO AND GET IT (1920)
(7 r.) d, Marshall Neilan, Henry Symons; lp, Pat O'Malley, Agnes Ayres, Wesley Barry, J. Barney Sherry

GO GET 'EM GARRINGER (1919)
(5 r.) d, Ernest Traxler; lp, Franklyn Farnum, Helene Chadwick, Joseph Rickson, Dick La Reno

GO GET HIM (1921)
(5 r.) lp, William Fairbanks

GO STRAIGHT (1921)
(5 r.) d, William Worthington; lp, Frank Mayo, Cora Drew, Harry Carter, Lillian Rich

GO STRAIGHT (1925)
(6 r.) d, Frank O'Connor; lp, Owen Moore, Mary Carr, George Fawcett, Ethel Wales

GOAT, THE (1918)
(5 r.) d, Donald Crisp; lp, Fred Stone, Rhea Mitchell, Fannie Midgley, Charles McHugh

GOD BLESS OUR RED, WHITE AND BLUE (1918, Brit.)
(5 r.) d, Rex Wilson; lp, Isobel Elsom, Owen Nares, Madge Titherage, J. Fisher White

GOD GAVE ME TWENTY CENTS (1926)
(7 r.) d, Herbert Brenon; lp, Lois Moran, Lya De Putti, Jack Mulhall, William Collier, Jr.

GOD OF LITTLE CHILDREN (1917)
(5 r.) d, Richard Ridgley; lp, Alma Hanlon, Bigelow Cooper, Charles Hutchinson, William Hartman

GOD OF MANKIND (1928)
(5 r.) d, Grover Jones; lp, Emmett King, Eulalie Jensen, Jimmy Fulton, Ralph Faulkner

GOD OF VENGEANCE, THE (1914)
(4 r.)

GODDESS OF LOST LAKE, THE (1918)
(5 r.) d, Wallace Worsley; lp, Louise Glaum, W. Lawson Butt, Hayward Mack, Joseph J. Dowling

GODLESS MEN (1921)
(7 r.) d, Reginald Barker; lp, Russell Simpson, James Mason, Helene Chadwick, John Bowers

GOD'S CLAY (1919, Brit.)
(5 r.) d, Arthur Rooke; lp, Janet Alexander, Humberston Wright, Arthur Rooke, Maud Yates

GOD'S CLAY (1928, Brit.)
(6 r.) d, Graham Cutts; lp, Anny Ondra, Trilby Clark, Franklyn Bellamy, Haddon Mason

GOD'S COUNTRY AND THE LAW (1921)
(6 r.) d, Sidney Olcott; lp, Fred C. Jones, Gladys Leslie, William H. Tooker, Cesare Gravina

GOD'S COUNTRY AND THE WOMAN (1916)
(8 r.) d, Rollin S. Sturgeon; lp, William Duncan, Nell Shipman, George Holt, William Bainbridge

GOD'S CRUCIBLE (1917)
(5 r.) d, Lynn Reynolds; lp, George Hernandez, Val Paul, Frederick Montague, Myrtle Gonzalez

GOD'S CRUCIBLE (1921)
(7 r.) d, Henry MacRae; lp, Gaston Glass, Gladys Coburn, Wilton Lackaye, Edna Shipman

GOD'S GOLD (1921)
(5 r.) d, Webster Cullison; lp, Neal Hart, Audrey Chapman, James McLaughlin, Al Kaufman

GOD'S GOOD MAN (1921, Brit.)
(6 r.) d, Maurice Elvey; lp, Basil Gill, Peggy Carlisle, Barry Bernard, Hugh Dabernon-Stoke

GOD'S GREAT WILDERNESS (1927)
(6 r.) d, David M. Hartford; lp, Lillian Rich, Joseph Bennett, Russell Simpson, Mary Carr

GOD'S LAW AND MAN'S (1917)
(5 r.) d, John H. Collins; lp, Viola Dana, Robert Walker, Augustus Phillips, Henry Hallam

GOD'S MAN (1917)
(9 r.) d, George Irving; lp, H.B. Warner, Kate Lester, Albert Tavernier, Stanhope Wheatcroft

GODS OF FATE, THE (1916)
(5 r.) d, Jack Pratt; lp, Richard Buhler, Rosetta Brice, Thomas Koil, Rita Toofy

GOD'S PRODIGAL (1923, Brit.)
(5 r.) d, Bert Wynne, Edward Jose; lp, Gerald Ames, Flora le Breton, Frank Stanmore, Ada Ford

GOD'S WITNESS (1915)
(4 r.) lp, Florence LaBadie, Harris Gordon, Arthur Bauer, Morris Foster

GOING CROOKED (1926)
(6 r.) d, George Melford; lp, Bessie Love, Oscar Shaw, Gustav von Seyffertitz, Ed Kennedy

GOING SOME (1920)
(6 r.) d, Harry Beaumont; lp, Cullen Landis, Helen Ferguson, Lillian Hall, Lillian Langdon

GOING STRAIGHT (1916)
(5 r.) d, Sidney & Chester Franklin; lp, Norma Talmadge, Ralph Lewis, Ninon Fovieri, Francis Carpenter

GOING THE LIMIT (1926)
(5 r.) d, Chet Withey; lp, George O'Hara, Sally Long, Brooks Benedict, Tom Ricketts

GOING UP (1923)
(6 r.) d, Lloyd Ingraham; lp, Douglas MacLean, Hallam Cooley, Arthur Stuart Hull, Francis McDonald

GO-GETTER, THE (1923)
(8 r.) d, E.H. Griffith; lp, T. Roy Barnes, Seena Owen, William Norris, Tom Lewis

GOLD AND GRIT (1925)
(5 r.) d, Richard Thorpe; lp, Buddy Roosevelt, Ann McKay, William H. Turner, L.J. O'Connor

GOLD AND THE WOMAN (1916)
(6 r.) d, James Vincent; lp, Theda Bara, Henry Cooper Cliffe, Alma Hanlon, Harry Hilliard

GOLD CURE, THE (1919)
(5 r.) d, John H. Collins; lp, Viola Dana, John McGowan, William B. Davidson, Howard Hall

GOLD CURE, THE (1925)
(6 r.) d, W.P. Kellino; lp, Queenie Thomas, Gladys Hamer, Eric Bransby Williams, Jameson Thomas

GOLD FROM WEEPAH (1927)
(5 r.) d, William Bertram; lp, Bill Cody, Doris Dawson, Dick La Reno, Joe Harrington

GOLD GRABBERS (1922)
(5 r.) d, Francis Ford; lp, Franklyn Farnum, Shorty Hamilton, Al Hart, Genevieve Berte

GOLD HEELS (1924)
(6 r.) d, William S. Van Dyke; lp, Robert Agnew, Peggy Shaw, Lucien Littlefield, William Norton Bailey

GOLD HUNTERS, THE (1925)
(7 r.) d, Paul Hurst; lp, David Butler, Hedda Nova, Mary Carr, Bull Montana

GOLDEN BED, THE (1925)
(9 r.) d, Cecil B. De Mille; lp, Lillian Rich, Vera Reynolds, Henry Walthall, Rod La Rocque

GOLDEN BEETLE, THE (1914, Ital.)
(4 r.)

GOLDEN CLAW, THE (1915)
(5 r.) d, Reginald Barker; lp, Bessie Barriscale, Frank Mills, Wedgewood Nowell, Truly Shattuck

GOLDEN CLOWN, THE (1927, Swed.)
(8 r.) d, A.W. Sandberg

GOLDEN COCOON, THE (1926)
(7 r.) d, Millard Webb; lp, Huntley Gordon, Helene Chadwick, Richard Tucker, Frank Campeau

GOLDEN DAWN, THE (1921, Brit.)
(6 r.) d, Ralph Dewsbury; lp, Gertrude McCoy, Warwick Ward, Frank Petley, Sydney Fairbrother

GOLDEN DREAMS (1922)
(5 r.) d, Benjamin B. Hampton; lp, Rose Dione, Claire Adams, Norris McKay, Carl Gantvoort

GOLDEN FETTER, THE (1917)
(5 r.) d, Edward J. Le Saint; lp, Wallace Reid, Anita King, Tully Marshall, Guy Oliver

GOLDEN FLAME, THE (1923)
(5 r.) lp, Dick Hatton

GOLDEN FLEECE, THE (1918)
(5 r.) d, Gilbert P. Hamilton; lp, Joe Bennett, Peggy Pearce, Jack Curtis, Harvey Clark

GOLDEN GALLOWS, THE (1922)
(5 r.) d, Paul Scardon; lp, Miss Du Pont, Edwin Stevens, Eve Southern, Jack Mower

GOLDEN GOAL, THE (1918)
(5 r.) d, Paul Scardon; lp, Harry T. Morey, Jean Paige, Florence Deshon, Arthur Donaldson

GOLDEN GOD, THE (1917)
(5 r.) lp, Alma Hanlon, Charles Hutchinson, Mary Doyle

GOLDEN GODDESS, THE (1916)
(5 r.) lp, Marjorie Daw, Wallace D. Coburn, C.M. Giffen

GOLDEN IDIOT, THE (1917)
(4 r.) d, Arthur Berthelet; lp, Bryant Washburn, Virginia Valli, Arthur Metcalfe, Robert Bolder

GOLDEN PRINCESS, THE (1925)
(9 r.) d, Clarence Badger; lp, Betty Bronson, Neil Hamilton, Rockliffe Fellowes, Phyllis Haver

GOLDEN ROSARY, THE (1917)
(5 r.) d, Tom Van Plack; lp, Olga De Costa, Jack Meredith, Betsey Randolph

GOLDEN RULE KATE (1917)
(5 r.) d, Reginald Barker; lp, Louise Glaum, William Conklin, Jack Richardson, Mildred Harris

GOLDEN SEA, THE (1919, Ger.)
(5 r.) d, Fritz Lang; lp, Carl de Vogt, Ressel Orla, Lil Dagover, Paul Morgan

GOLDEN SHACKLES (1928)
(6 r.) d, Dallas M. Fitzgerald; lp, Grant Withers, Priscilla Bonner, LeRoy Mason, Ruth Stewart

GOLDEN SHOWER, THE (1919)
(5 r.) d, John W. Noble; lp, Gladys Leslie, Robert Cummings, Frank Morgan, Estelle Taylor

GOLDEN SILENCE (1923)
(5 r.) d, Paul Hurst; lp, Jack Perrin, Hedda Nova

GOLDEN SNARE, THE (1921)
(6 r.) d, David M. Hartford; lp, Lewis Stone, Wallace Beery, Melbourne MacDowell, Ruth Renick

GOLDEN STRAIN, THE (1925)
(6 r.) d, Victor Schertzinger; lp, Hobart Bosworth, Kenneth Harlan, Madge Bellamy, Lawford Davidson

GOLDEN THOUGHT, A (1924)
(5 r.) lp, Tom Mix

GOLDEN TRAIL, THE (1920)
(5 r.) d, Lewis H. Moomaw, Jean Hersholt; lp, Jane Novak, Jack Livingston, Jean Hersholt, Bert Sprotte

GOLDEN TRAIL, THE (1927)
(5 r.) lp, Dick Carter, Dorothy Wood

GOLDEN WEB, THE (1920, Brit.)
(5 r.) d, Geoffrey H. Malins; lp, Milton Rosmer, Ena Beaumont, Victor Robson, Nina Munro

GOLDEN WEB, THE (1926)
(6 r.) d, Walter Lang; lp, Lillian Rich, Huntley Gordon, Jay Hunt, Lawford Davidson

GOLDEN YUKON, THE (1927)
(7 r.) d, Nell Shipman; lp, Nell Shipman, Alfred Allen, Lillian Leighton, Hugh Thompson

GOLEM, THE (1914, Ger.)
(4 r.) d, Paul Wegener, Henrik Galeen; lp, Paul Wegener, Henrik Galeen, Albert Steinruck, Lydia Salmonoya

GOLF WIDOWS (1928)
(6 r.) d, Erle C. Kenton; lp, Vera Reynolds, Harrison Ford, John Patrick, Sally Rand

GONZAQUE (1923, Fr.)
(? r.) d, Henri Diamant-Berger

GOOD AND EVIL (1921)
(5 r.) lp, Lucy Doraine, Alphonse Fryland, Madeline Nagy, Antoin Tiller

GOOD AS GOLD (1927)
(5 r.) d, Scott Dunlap; lp, Buck Jones, Frances Lee, Carl Miller, Charles French

GOOD BAD BOY (1924)
(5 r.) d, Eddie Cline; lp, Joe Butterworth, Mary Jane Irving, Forrest Robinson, Lucy Beaumont

GOOD FOR NOTHING, THE (1917)
(5 r.) d, Carlyle Blackwell; lp, Carlyle Blackwell, Evelyn Greeley, Muriel Ostriche, Kate Lester

GOOD GRACIOUS ANNABELLE (1919)
(5 r.) d, George Melford; lp, Billie Burke, Herbert Rawlinson, Gilbert Douglas, Crauford Kent

GOOD LOSER, THE (1918)
(5 r.) d, Dick Donaldson; lp, Peggy Pearce, Lee Hill, Arthur Millett, Dick Rosson

GOOD MEN AND BAD (1923)
(5 r.) d, Merrill McCormick; lp, Marin Sais, Steve Carrie, Merrill McCormick, George Guyton

GOOD MEN AND TRUE (1922)
(6 r.) d, Val Paul; lp, Harry Carey, Vola Vale, Thomas Jefferson, Noah Beery

GOOD MORNING JUDGE (1928)
(6 r.) d, William A. Seiter; lp, Reginald Denny, Mary Nolan, Otis Harlan, Dorothy Gulliver

GOOD PROVIDER, THE (1922)
(8 r.) d, Frank Borzage; lp, Vera Gordon, Dore Davidson, Miriam Battista, Vivienne Osborne

GOOD REFERENCES (1920)
(5 r.) d, Roy William Neill; lp, Constance Talmadge, Vincent Coleman, Ned Sparks, Nellie P. Spaulding

GOOD TIME CHARLEY (1927)
(7 r.) d, Michael Curtiz; lp, Helene Costello, Warner Oland, Clyde Cook, Montagu Love

GOOD WOMEN (1921)
(7 r.) d, Louis J. Gasnier; lp, Rosemary Theby, Hamilton Revelle, Irene Blackwell, Earl Schenck

GOOD-BAD WIFE, THE (1921)
(5 r.) d, Vera McCord; lp, Sidney Mason, Dorothy Green, Moe Lee, Leslie Stowe

GOOD-BY GIRLS! (1923)
(5 r.) d, Jerome Storm; lp, William Russell, Carmel Myers, Tom Wilson, Kate Price

GOODBYE (1918, Brit.)
(5 r.) d, Maurice Elvey; lp, Margaret Bannerman, Jessie Winter, Donald Calthrop, Douglas Munro

GOOSE HANGS HIGH, THE (1925)
(6 r.) d, James Cruze; lp, Constance Bennett, Myrtle Stedman, George Irving, Esther Ralston

GORILLA, THE (1927)
(8 r.) d, Alfred Santell; lp, Charlie Murray, Fred Kelsey, Alice Day, Tully Marshall

GOSSIP (1923)
(5 r.) d, King Baggot; lp, Gladys Walton, Ramsey Wallace, Albert Prisco, Freeman Wood

GOVERNOR'S LADY, THE (1923)
(8 r.) d, Harry Millarde; lp, Robert T. Haines, Jane Grey, Ann Luther, Frazer Coulter

GOWN OF DESTINY, THE (1918)
(5 r.) d, Lynn F. Reynolds; lp, Herrera Tejedde, Alma Rubens, Allan Sears, Lillian West

GRAFTERS (1917)
(5 r.) d, Arthur Rosson; lp, Anna Lehr, Jack Devereaux, Frank Currier, Irene Leonard

GRAIL, THE (1923)
(5 r.) d, Colin Campbell; lp, Dustin Farnum, Peggy Shaw, Carl Stockdale, Frances Raymond

GRAND BABYLON HOTEL, THE (1916, Brit.)
(5 r.) d, Frank Wilson; lp, Margaret Blanche, Gerald Lawrence, Lionelle Howard, Stewart Rome

GRAND LARCENY (1922)
(6 r.) d, Wallace Worsley; lp, Claire Windsor, Elliott Dexter, Richard Tucker, Tom Gallery

GRAND PASSION, THE (1918)
(7 r.) d, Ida May Park; lp, Dorothy Phillips, William Stowell, Jack Mulhall, Lon Chaney

GRANDEE'S RING, THE (1915)
(5 r.) lp, Earl Beebe, Helene Wallace, A. Sears Pruden, H. Tudor Morsell

GRANDEUR ET DECADENCE (1923, Fr.)
(? r.) d, Raymond Bernard

GRASP OF GREED, THE (1916)
(5 r.) d, Joseph De Grasse; lp, Louise Lovely, Lon Chaney, Jay Belasco, Gretchen Lederer

GRASS ORPHAN, THE (1922, Brit.)
(6 r.) d, Frank H. Crane; lp, Margaret Bannerman, Reginald Owen, Douglas Munro, Lawford Davidson

GRAUSTARK (1915)
(6 r.) d, Fred E. Wright; lp, Francis X. Bushman, Beverly Bayne, Thomas Commerford, Edna Mayo

GRAUSTARK (1925)
(7 r.) d, Dimitri Buchowetzki; lp, Norma Talmadge, Eugene O'Brien, Marc MacDermott, Roy D'Arcy

GRAY DAWN, THE (1922)
(6 r.) d, Eliot Howe, Jean Hersholt; lp, Carl Gantvoort, Claire Adams, Robert McKim, George Hackathorne

GRAY HORIZON, THE (1919)
(5 r.) d, William Worthington; lp, Sessue Hayakawa, Tsuru Aoki, Bertram Grassby, Eileen Percy

GRAY HORROR, THE (1915)
(4 r.) lp, Joseph Smiley, Lilie Leslie, John Smiley

GRAY TOWERS MYSTERY, THE (1919)
(5 r.) d, John W. Noble; lp, Gladys Leslie, Frank Morgan, Warner Richmond, Warren Chandler

GRAY WOLF'S GHOST, THE (1919)
(5 r.) d, Park Frame, Joseph J. Franz; lp, H.B. Warner, Marin Sais, Edward Peil, Rita Stanwood

GRAZIELLA (1926, Fr.)
(? r.) d, Marcel Vandal

GREASED LIGHTNING (1919)
(5 r.) d, Jerome Storm; lp, Charles Ray, Wanda Hawley, Robert McKim, Willis Marks

GREASED LIGHTNING (1928)
(5 r.) d, Ray Taylor; lp, Ted Wells, Betty Caldwell, Walter Shumway, Lon Poff

GREAT ACCIDENT, THE (1920)
(5 r.) d, Harry Beaumont; lp, Tom Moore, Jane Novak, Andrew Robson, Willard Louis

GREAT ADVENTURE, THE (1921)
(6 r.) d, Kenneth Webb; lp, Lionel Barrymore, Doris Rankin, Octavia Broske, Thomas Braidon

GREAT AIR ROBBERY, THE (1920)
(6 r.) d, Jacques Jaccard; lp, Ormer L. Locklear, Allan Forrest, Francelia Billington, Raymond Ripley

GREAT ALONE, THE (1922)
(6 r.) d, Jacques Jaccard, James Colwell; lp, Monroe Salisbury, Laura Anson, Walter Law, Maria Law

GREAT BRADLEY MYSTERY, THE (1917)
(5 r.) d, Richard Ridgley; lp, Alma Hanlon, Edward Ellis, Florence Short, Bigelow Cooper

GREAT COUP, A (1919, Brit.)
(4 r.) d, George Dewhurst; lp, Stewart Rome, Poppy Wyndham, Gregory Scott, Cameron Carr

GREAT DAY, THE (1921, Brit.)
(5 r.) d, Hugh Ford; lp, Arthur Bourchier, May Palfrey, Marjorie Hume, Bertram Burleigh

GREAT DECEPTION, THE (1926)
(6 r.) d, Howard Higgin; lp, Ben Lyon, Alieen Pringle, Basil Rathbone, Sam Hardy

GREAT DIAMOND MYSTERY, THE (1924)
(5 r.) d, Denison Clift; lp, Shirley Mason, Jackie Saunders, Harry von Meter, John Cossar

GREAT DIAMOND ROBBERY, THE (1914)
(6 r.) d, Daniel V. Arthur; lp, Wallace Eddinger, Gail Kane, Dorothy Arthur, Martin J. Alsop

GREAT DIVIDE, THE (1916)
(5 r.) d, Edgar Lewis; lp, House Peters, Ethel Clayton, Marie Sterling, Hayden Stevenson

GREAT DIVIDE, THE (1925)
(8 r.) d, Reginald Barker; lp, Alice Terry, Conway Tearle, Wallace Beery, Huntly Gordon

GREAT GAY ROAD, THE (1920, Brit.)
(5 r.) d, Norman MacDonald; lp, Stewart Rome, Pauline Johnson, John Stuart, Ernest Spaulding

GREAT IMPERSONATION, THE (1921)
(7 r.) d, George Melford; lp, James Kirkwood, Ann Forrest, Winter Hall, Truly Shattuck

GREAT IMPOSTER, THE (1918, Brit.)
(5 r.) d, F. Martin Thornton; lp, Marie Blanche, Bernard Dudley, Edward O'Neill, Lionel d'Aragon

GREAT JEWEL ROBBERY, THE (1925)
(5 r.) d, John Ince; lp, Herbert Rawlinson, Grace Darmond, Frank Darmond, Carlton Griffin

GREAT LOVER, THE (1920)
(6 r.) d, Frank Lloyd; lp, John Sainpolis, Claire Adams, John Davidson, Alice Hollister

GREAT MAGARAZ, THE (1915, USSR)
(5 r.) d, Vyacheslav Turzhansky; lp, Yevgeni Vakhtangov, M. Goricheva, Turzhansky, Olga Baklanova

GREAT MEN AMONG US (1915)
(4 r.) d, William Parke Sr.; lp, Stuart Paton, William Nally, Paul Iribe

GREAT MOMENT, THE (1921)
(7 r.) d, Sam Wood; lp, Gloria Swanson, Alec B. Francis, Milton Sills, F.R. Butler

GREAT PHYSICIAN, THE (1913)
(? r.) d, Richard Ridgely; lp, Charles Ogle, Mabel Trunnelle, Robert Brower, Helen Couglin

GREAT POISON MYSTERY, THE (1914, Brit.)
(4 r.) d, Frank Wilson; lp, Violet Hopson, Stewart Rome, Cyril Morton, Harry Gilbey

GREAT PRINCE SHAN, THE (1924, Brit.)
(6 r.) d, A.E. Coleby; lp, Sessue Hayakawa, Ivy Duke, Tsuru Aoki, Valia

GREAT PROBLEM, THE (1916)
(5 r.) d, Rex Ingram; lp, Violet Mersereau, Dan Hanlon, Lionel Adams, Kittens Reichert

GREAT REDEEMER, THE (1920)
(5 r.) d, Clarence Brown; lp, House Peters, Marjorie Daw, Joseph Singleton, Jack McDonald

GREAT ROAD, THE (1927, USSR)
(8 r.)

GREAT ROMANCE, THE (1919)
(6 r.) d, Henry Otto; lp, Harold Lockwood, Rubye de Remer, Joseph Granby, Frank Currier

GREAT RUBY, THE (1915)
(5 r.) d, Barry O'Neil; lp, Octavia Handworth, George Soule Spencer, Beatrice Morgan, Eleanor Barry

GREAT SENSATION, THE (1925)
(5 r.) d, Jay Marchant; lp, William Fairbanks, Pauline Garon, Lloyd Whitlock, William Franey

GREAT TURF MYSTERY, THE (1924, Brit.)
(5 r.) d, Walter West; lp, Violet Hopson, James Knight, Warwick Ward, Marjorie Benson

GREAT VICTORY, WILSON OR THE KAISER?, THE (1918)
(7 r.) d, Charles Miller; lp, Creighton Hale, Florence Billings, Fred C. Truesdell, Margaret McWade

GREAT WAR, THE (1927, Ger.)
(7 r.)

GREAT WELL, THE
(SEE: NEGLECTED WOMEN, 1924, Brit.)

GREAT WHITE TRAIL, THE (1917)
(7 r.) d, Leopold D. Wharton; lp, Doris Kenyon, Thomas Holding, Paul Gordon, Hans Roberts

GREAT WHITE WAY, THE (1924)
(10 r.) d, E. Mason Hopper; lp, Anita Stewart, Tom Lewis, T. Roy Barnes, Oscar Shaw

GREATER CLAIM, THE (1921)
(6 r.) d, Wesley Ruggles; lp, Alice Lake, Jack Dougherty, Edward Cecil, De Witt Jennings

GREATER GLORY, THE (1926)
(11 r.) d, Curt Rehfeld; lp, Conway Tearle, Anna Q. Nilsson, May Allison, Ian Keith

GREATER LOVE, THE (1919, Brit.)
(6 r.) d, Geoffrey H. Malins; lp, Ena Beaumont, Victor Robson, Leslie Barrie, Charles Rock

GREATER LOVE HATH NO MAN (1915)
(5 r.) lp, Emmett Corrigan, Mary Martin, Thomas Curran, Mabel Wright

GREATER PROFIT, THE (1921)
(5 r.) d, William Worthington; lp, Edith Storey, Pell Trenton, Willis Marks, Lloyd Bacon

GREATER SINNER, THE (1919)
(7 r.) d, A.J. Blume; lp, James K. Hackett, Ormi Hawley, Irving Cummings, John Shine

GREATER THAN A CROWN (1925)
(5 r.) d, Roy William Neill; lp, Edmund Lowe, Dolores Costello, Margaret Livingston, Ben Hendricks

GREATER THAN ART (1915)
(4 r.) d, John H. Collins; lp, Gertrude McCoy, Edward Earle, Duncan McRae, Lavinia Santell

GREATER THAN LOVE (1921)
(6 r.) d, Fred Niblo, John M. Stahl; lp, Louise Glaum, Mahlon Hamilton, Gertrude Claire, Donald MacDonald

GREATER THAN MARRIAGE (1924)
(7 r.) d, Victor Hugo Halperin; lp, Marjorie Daw, Lou Tellegen, Peggy Kelly, [Frederick] Tyrone Power

GREATER WILL, THE (1915)
(5 r.) d, Harley Knoles; lp, Cyril Maude, Lois Meredith, Will T. Carleton, Montagu Love

GREATER WOMAN, THE (1917)
(5 r.) d, Frank Powell; lp, Marjorie Rambeau, Hassan Mussalli, Aubrey Beattie, Sara Haidez

GREATEST LOVE, THE (1920)
(6 r.) d, Henry Kolker; lp, Vera Gordon, Donald Hall, Raye Dean

GREATEST LOVE OF ALL, THE (1925)
(7 r.) d, George Beban; lp, George Beban, J.W. Johnston, Wanda Lyon, Baby Evelyn

GREATEST MENACE, THE (1923)
(7 r.) d, Albert Rogell; lp, Ann Little, Wilfred Lucas, Robert Gordon, Harry Northrup

GREATEST POWER, THE (1917)
(5 r.) d, Edwin Carewe; lp, Ethel Barrymore, William B. Davidson, Harry S. Northrup, Frank Currier

GREATEST SIN, THE (1922)
(4 r.) lp, Mae Evlyn Lewis, Victor Nix

GREATEST TRUTH, THE (1922, Ger.)
(5 r.) d, Joe May; lp, Mia Mia

GREATHEART (1921, Brit.)
(6 r.) d, George Ridgwell; lp, Cecil Humphreys, Madge Stuart, Ernest Benham, Olive Sloane

GREED (1917)
(5 r.) d, Theodore Marston; lp, Nance O'Neil, Shirley Mason, George Le Guere, Harry Northrup

GREEN CLOAK, THE (1915)
(5 r.) lp, Irene Fenwick, Blanche Aimee, Della Connor, Kathryn Brook

GREEN EYE OF THE YELLOW GOD, THE (1913)
(? r.) d, Richard Ridgely; lp, Charles Ogle

GREEN EYES (1918)
(5 r.) d, Roy William Neill; lp, Dorothy Dalton, Jack Holt, Emory Johnson, Doris Lee

GREEN GOD, THE (1918)
(5 r.) d, Paul Scardon; lp, Harry Morey, Betty Blythe, Arthur Donaldson, George Majeroni

GREEN GODDESS, THE (1923)
(10 r.) d, Sidney Olcott; lp, George Arliss, Alice Joyce, David Powell, Harry T. Morey

GREEN GRASS WIDOWS (1928)
(6 r.) d, Alfred Raboch; lp, Walter Hagen, Gertrude Olmstead, John Harron, Hedda Hopper

GREEN ORCHARD, THE (1916, Brit.)
(5 r.) d, Harold Weston; lp, Gregory Scott, Dora Barton, E. Vassal-Vaughn, Ernie Collins

GREEN SPIDER, THE (1916, USSR)
(5 r.) d, Alexander Volkov; lp, Maria Rutz, Nikolai Tseretelli, Konstantin Khokhlov

GREEN STOCKINGS (1916)
(5 r.) d, Wilfred North; lp, Lillian Walker, Frank Currier, Louise Beaudet, Adele De Garde

GREEN SWAMP, THE (1916)
(4 r.) d, Scott Sidney; lp, Bessie Barriscale, Bruce McRae, J. Barney Sherry, Milton Ross

GREEN TEMPTATION, THE (1922)
(6 r.) d, William D. Taylor; lp, Betty Compson, Mahlon Hamilton, Theodore Kosloff, Neely Edwards

GREEN TERROR, THE (1919, Brit.)
(7 r.) d, W.P. Kellino; lp, Aurele Sydney, Heather Thatcher, W.T. Ellwanger, Cecil du Gue

GREEN-EYED MONSTER, THE (1916)
(5 r.) d, J. Gordon Edwards; lp, Robert B. Mantell, Genevieve Hamper, Stuart Holmes, Charles Crumpton

GREEN-EYED MONSTER, THE (1921)
(8 r.) lp, Jack Austin, Louise Dunbar

GRELL MYSTERY, THE (1917)
(5 r.) d, Paul Scardon; lp, Earle Williams, Miriam Miles, Jean Dumar, Denton Vane

GRETNA GREEN (1915)
(4 r.) d, Thomas Heffron, Hugh Ford; lp, Marguerite Clark, Arthur Hoops, Helen Lutrell, Wilmuth Merkyl

GREY DAWN, THE
(SEE: GRAY DAWN, THE, 1922)

GREY PARASOL, THE (1918)
(5 r.) d, Lawrence Windom; lp, Wellington Cross, Claire Anderson, Joe Bennett, Frank Thorne

GREY STREAK, THE (1927)
(5 r.) lp, William Barrymore

GREY VULTURE, THE (1926)
(5 r.) d, Forrest K. Sheldon

GRIBICHE (1926, Fr.)
(? r.) d, Jacques Feyder; lp, Jean Forest, Francoise Rosay

GRIFFON OF AN OLD WARRIOR (1916, USSR)
(4 r.) d, Yevgeni Bauer; lp, Vera Coralli, Perestiani, Vladimir Strizhevsky

GRIM COMEDIAN, THE (1921)
(6 r.) d, Frank Lloyd; lp, Phoebe Hunt, Jack Holt, Gloria Hope, Bert Woodruff

GRIM JUSTICE (1916, Brit.)
(4 r.) d, Larry Trimble; lp, Florence Turner, Henry Edwards, Malcolm Cherry, Winnington Barnes

GRINNING GUNS (1927)
(5 r.) d, Albert Rogell; lp, Jack Hoxie, Ena Gregory, Robert Milasch, Arthur Morrison

GRIP (1915, Brit.)
(4 r.) d, Maurice Elvey; lp, Leon M. Lion, Elizabeth Risdon, Fred Groves, A.V. Bramble

GRIP OF IRON, THE (1913, Brit.)
(4 r.) d, Arthur Charrington; lp, Fred Powell, Nell Emerald, H. Agar Lyons, Frank E. Petley

GRIP OF IRON, THE (1920, Brit.)
(5 r.) d, Bert Haldane; lp, George Foley, Malvina Longfellow, James Lindsay, Laurence Tessier

GRIP OF JEALOUSY, THE (1916)
(5 r.) d, Joseph De Grasse; lp, Louise Lovely, Lon Chaney, Grace Thompson, Jay Belasco

GRIP OF THE YUKON, THE (1928)
(7 r.) d, Ernst Laemmle; lp, Francis X. Bushman, Neil Hamilton, June Marlowe, Otis Harlan

GROUNDS FOR DIVORCE (1925)
(6 r.) d, Paul Bern; lp, Florence Vidor, Matt Moore, Harry Myers, Louise Fazenda

GROWING BETTER (1923)
(5 r.) lp, William Patton

GRUB STAKE, THE (1923)
(8 r.) d, Bert Van Tuyle; lp, Nell Shipman, Hugh Thompson, Alfred Allen, George Berrell

GRUMPY (1923)
(6 r.) d, William De Mille; lp, Theodore Roberts, May McAvoy, Conrad Nagel, Casson Ferguson

GUARDIAN, THE (1917)
(5 r.) d, Arthur Ashley; lp, Montagu Love, June Elvidge, Arthur Ashley, William Black

GUARDIANS OF THE WILD (1928)
(5 r.) d, Henry MacRae; lp, Rex (a horse), Starlight (a horse), Jack Perrin, Ethlyne Clair

GUARDING BRITAIN'S SECRETS
(SEE: FIENDS OF HELL, THE, 1914, Brit.)

GUARDSMAN, THE (1927, Aust.)
(7 r.) d, Robert Wiene; lp, Maria Corda, Fritz Abel, Biela Friedell, Alma Hasta

GUILT OF SILENCE, THE (1918)
(5 r.) d, Elmer Clifton; lp, Monroe Salisbury, Ruth Clifford, Alfred Allen, Betty Schade

GUILTY (1922)
(5 r.) lp, Bill Miller, May Carson

GUILTY CONSCIENCE, A (1921)
(5 r.) d, David Smith; lp, Antonio Moreno, Betty Francisco, Harry Van Meter, Lila Leslie

GUILTY MAN, THE (1918)
(5 r.) d, Irvin V. Willat; lp, Gloria Hope, Vivian Reed, William Garwood, J.P. Lockney

GUILTY ONE, THE (1924)
(6 r.) d, Joseph Henabery; lp, Agnes Ayres, Edward Burns, Stanley Taylor, Crauford Kent

GULF BETWEEN, THE (1918)
(8 r.) d, Ray Physioc; lp, Niles Welch, Grace Darmond, Herbert Fortier, Violet Axzelle

GULLIVER IN LILLIPUT (1923, Fr.)
(4 r.) d, Albert Mourlan, Raymond Villette; lp, (animated)

GUN GOSPEL (1927)
(7 r.) d, Harry J. Brown; lp, Ken Maynard, Bob Fleming, Romaine Fielding, Virginia Brown Faire

GUN SHY (1922)
(5 r.) d, Alvin J. Neitz; lp, Franklyn Farnum, Florence Gilbert, Andrew Waldron, Robert Kortman

GUN WOMAN, THE (1918)
(5 r.) d, Frank Borzage; lp, Texas Guinan, Ed Brady, Francis McDonald, George Chase

GUNFIGHTER, THE (1917)
(5 r.) d, William S. Hart; lp, William S. Hart, Margery Wilson, Roy Laidlaw, Joseph J. Dowling

GUNFIGHTER, THE (1923)
(5 r.) d, Lynn F. Reynolds; lp, William Farnum, Doris May, L.C. Shumway, J. Morris Foster

GUN-FIGHTIN' GENTLEMAN, A (1919)
(5 r.) d, Jack [John] Ford; lp, Harry Carey, Kathleen O'Connor, J. Barney Sherry, Harry Van Meter

GUN-HAND GARRISON (1927)
(5 r.) d, Edward R. Gordon; lp, Tex Maynard, Ruby Blaine, Jack Anthony, Charles O'Malley

GUNNAR HEDE'S SAGA (1922, Swed.)
(7 r.) d, Mauritz Stiller; lp, Einar Hanson, Mary Johnson, Pauline Brunius, Stina Berg

GUNS OF LOOS, THE (1928, Brit.)
(8 r.) d, Sinclair Hill; lp, Henry Victor, Madeleine Carroll, Bobby Howes, Hermione Baddeley

GUNSAULUS MYSTERY, THE (1921)
(7 r.) d, Oscar Micheaux; lp, Lawrence Chenault, Evelyn Preer, Edward R. Abrams, Louis De Bulger

GUTTER MAGDALENE, THE (1916)
(5 r.) d, George Melford; lp, Fannie Ward, Jack Dean, Charles West, Lucien Littlefield

GUTTERSNIPE, THE (1922)
(5 r.) d, Dallas M. Fitzgerald; lp, Gladys Walton, Walter Perry, Kate Price, Jack Perrin

GUY FAWKES (1923, Brit.)
(7 r.) d, Maurice Elvey; lp, Matheson Lang, Nina Vanna, Hugh Buckler, Shayle Gardner

GWYNETH OF THE WELSH HILLS (1921, Brit.)
(6 r.) d, F. Martin Thornton; lp, Madge Stuart, Ellie Norwood, Lewis Gilbert, R. Henderson Bland

GYPSY BLOOD (1921, Ger.)
(4 r.) d, Ernst Lubitsch; lp, Pola Negri, Harry Liedtke, Magnus Stifer, Fritz Richard

GYPSY PASSION (1922, Fr.)
(? r.) d, Louis Mercanton; lp, Ivor Novello, Rejane, Charles Vanel

GYPSY ROMANCE, THE (1926)
(6 r.) lp, Thur Fairfax, Shannon Day

GYPSY TRAIL, THE (1918)
(5 r.) d, Walter Edwards; lp, Bryant Washburn, Wanda Hawley, Casson Ferguson, Clarence H. Geldert

GYPSY'S TRUST, THE (1917)
(4 r.) d, Edward S. Sloman; lp, William Russell, Charlotte Burton, William Tedmarsh, Rhea Mitchell

HABIT (1921)
(6 r.) d, Edwin Carewe

HACELDAMA (1919, Fr.)
(? r.) d, Julien Duvivier

HAIL THE HERO (1924)
(5 r.) d, James W. Horne; lp, Richard Talmadge

HAIL THE WOMAN (1921)
(8 r.) d, John Griffith Wray; lp, Florence Vidor, Lloyd Hughes, Theodore Roberts, Gertrude Claire

HAINE (1918, Fr.)
(? r.) d, Georges Lacroix

HAIR TRIGGER CASEY (1922)
(5 r.) d, Frank Borzage; lp, Frank Borzage, Ann Little, Chick Morrison, Jack Richardson

HALF A CHANCE (1920)
(7 r.) d, Robert Thornby; lp, Mahlon Hamilton, Lillian Rich, Mary McAllister, Sidney Ainsworth

HALF A ROGUE (1916)
(5 r.) d, Henry Otto; lp, King Baggot, Edna Hunter, Clara Byers, Lottie Ford

HALF AN HOUR (1920)
(5 r.) d, Harley Knoles; lp, Dorothy Dalton, Charles Richman, Albert Barrett, Frank Losee

HALF BREED, THE (1916)
(5 r.) d, Allan Dwan; lp, Douglas Fairbanks, Alma Rubens, Jewel Carmen, Sam De Grasse

HALF BREED, THE (1922)
(6 r.) d, Charles A. Taylor; lp, Wheeler Oakman, Ann May, Mary Anderson, Hugh Thompson

HALF MILLION BRIBE, THE (1916)
(5 r.) d, Edgar Jones; lp, Hamilton Revelle, Marguerite Snow, John Smiley, Carl Brickert

HALF-A-DOLLAR BILL (1924)
(6 r.) d, William S. Van Dyke; lp, Anna Q. Nilsson, William P. Carleton, Raymond Hatton, Mitchell Lewis

HALFBREED (1919, Ger.)
(? r.) d, Fritz Lang; lp, Ressel Orla, Carl de Vogt, Gilda Langer, Carl-Gerrard Schroder

HALF-WAY GIRL, THE (1925)
(8 r.) d, John Francis Dillon; lp, Doris Kenyon, Lloyd Hughes, Hobart Bosworth, Tully Marshall

HAMLET (1921, Ger.)
(8 r.) d, Svend Gade; lp, Asta Nielsen, Eduard Von Winterstein, Mathilde Brandt, Hans Junkermann

HAND AT THE WINDOW, THE (1918)
(5 r.) d, Raymond Wells; lp, Margery Wilson, Joe King, Francis McDonald, Irene Hunt

HAND INVISIBLE, THE (1919)
(5 r.) d, Harry O. Hoyt; lp, Montagu Love, Virginia Hammond, William Sorelle, Marguerite Gale

HAND OF DESTINY, THE (1914)
(4 r.) d, Donald Mackenzie

HAND OF JUSTICE, THE (1915, Den.)
(4 r.)

HAND OF PERIL, THE (1916)
(5 r.) d, Maurice Tourneur; lp, House Peters, June Elvidge, Ralph Delmore, Doris Sawyer

HAND OF THE HUN, THE (1917, Ital.)
(4 r.) d, Giovanni Pastrone; lp, (animated)

HAND OF THE LAW, THE (1915)
(4 r.) d, Edward C. Taylor

HAND THAT ROCKS THE CRADLE, THE (1917)
(6 r.) d, Lois Weber, Phillips Smalley; lp, Phillips Smalley, Lois Weber, Priscilla Dean, Wedgewood Nowell

HANDCUFFS OR KISSES (1921)
(6 r.) George Archainbaud; lp, Elaine Hammerstein, Julia Swayne Gordon, Dorothy Chappell, Robert Ellis

HANDICAP, THE (1925)
(5 r.)

HANDS DOWN (1918)
(5 r.) d, Rupert Julian; lp, Monroe Salisbury, Ruth Clifford, Rupert Julian, W.H. Bainbridge

HANDS OF NARA, THE (1922)
(6 r.) d, Harry Garson; lp, Clara Kimball Young, Count John Orloff, Elliott Dexter, Edwin Stevens

HANDS OF ORLAC, THE (1925, Aust.)
(? r.) d, Robert Wiene; lp, Conrad Veidt, Fritz Kortner, Carmen Cartellieri, Paul Adkonas

HANDS OFF (1921)
(5 r.) d, George E. Marshall; lp, Tom Mix, Pauline Curley, Charles K. French, Lloyd Bacon

HANDS OFF (1927)
(5 r.) d, Ernst Laemmle; lp, Fred Humes, Helen Foster, George Connors, Nelson McDowell

HANDS UP (1917)
(5 r.) d, Tod Browning; lp, Wilfred Lucas, Colleen Moore, Monte Blue, Beatrice Van

HANGMAN'S HOUSE (1928)
(7 r.) d, John Ford; lp, June Collyer, Larry Kent, Earle Foxe, Victor McLaglen

HANTISE (1922, Fr.)
(? r.) d, Jean Kemm

HAPPINESS (1917)
(5 r.) d, Reginald Barker; lp, Enid Bennett, Charles Dunn, Thelma Salter, Andrew Arbuckle

HAPPINESS (1924)
(8 r.) d, King Vidor; lp, Laurette Taylor, Pat O'Malley, Hedda Hopper, Cyril Chadwick

HAPPINESS A LA MODE (1919)
(5 r.) d, Walter Edwards; lp, Constance Talmadge, Harrison Ford, Betty Schade, Myrtle Richelle

HAPPINESS AHEAD (1928)
(8 r.) d, William A. Seiter; lp, Colleen Moore, Edmund Lowe, Charles Sellon, Edythe Chapman

HAPPINESS OF THREE WOMEN, THE (1917)
(5 r.) d, William D. Taylor; lp, House Peters, Myrtle Stedman, L.W. Steers, Daisy Robinson

HAPPY ENDING, THE (1925, Brit.)
(8 r.) d, George A. Cooper; lp, Fay Compton, Jack Buchanan, Joan Barry, Jack Hobbs

HAPPY THOUGH MARRIED (1919)
(5 r.) d, Fred Niblo; lp, Enid Bennett, Douglas MacLean, Philo McCullough, Hallam Cooley

HAPPY WARRIOR, THE (1917, Brit.)
(4 r.) d, F. Martin Thornton; lp, James Knight, Evelyn Boucher, Joan Legge, Minna Grey

HAPPY WARRIOR, THE (1925)
(8 r.) d, J. Stuart Blackton; lp, Malcolm McGregor, Alice Calhoun, Mary Alden, Anders Randolf

HARAKIRI (1919, Ger.)
(8 r.) d, Fritz Lang; lp, Paul Biensfeldt, Lil Dagover, Georg John, Meinhardt Maur

HARBOR PATROL (1924)
(5 r.) lp, Al Ferguson, Virginia Abbot

HARBOUR LIGHTS, THE (1914, Brit.)
(4 r.) d, Percy Nash; lp, Gerald Lawrence, Mercy Hatton, Daisy Cordell, Fred Morgan

HARBOUR LIGHTS, THE (1923, Brit.)
(6 r.) d, Tom Terriss; lp, Tom Moore, Isobel Elsom, Gerald McCarthy, Gibson Gowland

HARD BOILED (1919)
(5 r.) d, Victor L. Schertzinger; lp, Dorothy Dalton, C.W. Mason, Billy Courtright, Gertrude Claire

HARD BOILED (1926)
(6 r.) d, J.G. Blystone; lp, Tom Mix, Helene Chadwick, William Lawrence, Charles Conklin

HARD BOILED HAGGERTY (1927)
(8 r.) d, Charles Brabin; lp, Milton Sills, Molly O' Day, Mitchell Lewis, Arthur Stone

HARD CASH (1921, Brit.)
(5 r.) d, Edwin J. Collins; lp, Dick Webb, Alma Green, Frank Arlton, Cecil Morton York

HARD FISTS (1927)
(5 r.) d, William Wyler; lp, Art Acord, Louise Lorraine, Lee Holmes, Albert J. Smith

HARD HITTIN' HAMILTON (1924)
(5 r.) d, Richard Thorpe; lp, Buffalo Bill, Jr., Hazel Keener, Gordon Russell, William Ryno

HARD ROCK BREED, THE (1918)
(5 r.) d, Raymond Wells; lp, Jack Livingston, Margery Wilson, Jack Curtis, J. Barney Sherry

HARISCHANDRA (1913, India)
(4 r.) d, Dada Phalke

HARP IN HOCK, A (1927)
(6 r.) d, Renaud Hoffman; lp, Rudolph Schildkraut, Junior Coghlan, May Robson, Bessie Love

HARP KING, THE (1920, Brit.)
(5 r.) lp, Nan Wilkie, W.R. Bell, Jack Baker, David Watt

HARPER MYSTERY, THE (1913, Brit.)
(4 r.) d, Larry Trimble; lp, Florence Turner, Coley Goodman, Frank Tennant

HARRIET AND THE PIPER (1920)
(6 r.) d, Bertram Bracken; lp, Anita Stewart, Charles Richman, Ward Crane, Myrtle Stedman

HARSH FATHER, THE (1911, Pol.)
(4 r.) d, Andrezj Marek; lp, Zina Goldstein, Herman Sieracki

HARVEST MOON, THE (1920)
(6 r.) d, J. Searle Dawley; lp, Doris Kenyon, Wilfred Lytell, George A. Lessey, Earl Schenck

HARVESTER, THE (1927)
(8 r.) d, Leo Meehan; lp, Orville Caldwell, Natalie Kingston, Will R. Walling, Jay Hunt

HAS MAN THE RIGHT TO KILL? (1919)
(5 r.)

HASHIMURA TOGO (1917)
(5 r.) d, William C. De Mille; lp, Sessue Hayakawa, Margaret Loomis, Tom Forman, Raymond Hatton

HATE (1917)
(7 r.) d, Walter Richard Hall; lp, Morgan Jones, Adelaide Holland, T. Henderson Murray, Norman Acker

HATE (1922)
(6 r.) d, Joseph Calder; lp, Alice Lake, Conard Nagel, Harry Northrup, Charles Clary

HATE TRAIL, THE (1922)
(5 r.) d, Milburn Morante; lp, George Chesebro, Frank Caffray, Alfred Hewston, Fritzi Rideway

HAUNTED BEDROOM, THE (1919)
(5 r.) d, Fred Niblo; lp, Enid Bennett, Lloyd Hughes, Niles Welch, Dorcas Matthews

HAUNTED CASTLE, THE (1921, Ger.)
(? r.) d, F.W. Murnau; lp, Paul Hartmann, Arnold Korff, Paul Bildt, Olga Tscechova

HAUNTED HOUSE, THE (1917)
(5 r.) d, Albert Parker; lp, Winifred Allen, Dick Rosson, Albert Parker, Albert Day

HAUNTED HOUSE, THE (1928)
(7 r.) d, Benjamin Christensen; lp, Larry Kent, Thelma Todd, Edmund Breese, Sidney Bracy

HAUNTED MANOR, THE (1916)
(5 r.) d, Edwin Middleton; lp, Iva Shepard, Earl O. Schenck, Mathilde Baring, Gertrude Robinson

HAUNTED SHIP, THE (1927)
(5 r.) d, Forrest K. Sheldon; lp, Dorothy Sebastian, Montagu Love, Tom Santschi, Ray Hallor

HAUNTING SHADOWS (1920)
(5 r.) d, Henry King; lp, H.B. Warner, Margaret Livingston, Charles Hill Mailes, Edward Peil

HAVOC, THE (1916)
(5 r.) d, Arthur Berthelet; lp, Gladys Hanson, Lewis S. Stone, Bryant Washburn

HAVOC (1925)
(9 r.) d, Rowland V. Lee; lp, Madge Bellamy, George O'Brien, Walter McGrail, Eulalie Jensen

HAWK, THE (1917)
(5 r.) d, Paul Scardon; lp, Earle Williams, Ethel Grey Terry, Denton Vane, Julia Swayne Gordon

HAWK OF THE HILLS (1929)
(5 r.) d, Spencer Gordon Bennett; lp, Allene Ray, Walter Miller, Robert Chandler, Jack Ganghorn

HAWK'S NEST, THE (1928)
(8 r.) d, Benjamin Christensen; lp, Milton Sills, Montagu Love, Mitchell Lewis, Doris Kenyon

HAXAN
(SEE: WITCHCRAFT THROUGH THE AGES, 1921, Swed.)

HAY FOOT, STRAW FOOT (1919)
(5 r.) d, Jerome Storm; lp, Charles Ray, Doris Lee [May], William Conklin, Spottiswoode Aitken

HAZEL KIRKE (1916)
(5 r.) d, Leopold & Theodore Wharton; lp, Pearl White, Bruce McRae, William Riley Hatch, Allen Murnane

HE COMES UP SMILING (1918)
(5 r.) d, Allan Dwan; lp, Douglas Fairbanks, Marjorie Daw, Herbert Standing, Bull Montana

HE FELL IN LOVE WITH HIS WIFE (1916)
(5 r.) d, William D. Taylor; lp, Florence Rockwell, Forrest Stanley, Page Peters, Lydia Yeamans Titus

HE WHO GETS SLAPPED (1916, USSR)
(5 r.) d, Alexander Ivanov-Gai, I. Schmidt; lp, Illarion Pevtsov, Olga Baklanova, I. Vronsky, A. Nekrasov

HE WHO LAUGHS LAST (1925)
(5 r.) d, Jack Nelson; lp, Kenneth McDonald, Margaret Cloud, David Torrence, Gino Corrado

HEAD OF JANUS, THE (1920, Ger.)
(? r.) d, F.W. Murnau; lp, Conrad Veidt, Bela Lugosi, Margarete Schlegel, Magnus Stifter

HEAD OVER HEELS (1922)
(5 r.) d, Victor Schertzinger; lp, Mabel Normand, Hugh Thompson, Russ Powell, Raymond Hatton

HEAD WINDS (1925)
(6 r.) d, Herbert Blache; lp, House Peters, Patsy Ruth Miller, Richard Travers, Arthur Hoyt

HEADIN' FOR DANGER (1928)
(6 r.) d, Robert North Bradbury; lp, Bob Steele, Jola Mendez, Al Ferguson, Tom Forman

HEADIN' HOME (1920)
(5 r.) d, Lawrence Windom; lp, Babe Ruth, Tom Cameron, James A. Marcus, Ricca Allen

HEADIN' NORTH (1921)
(5 r.) d, Charles Bartlett; lp, Pete Morrison, Jack Walters, Gladys Cooper, Dorothy Dickson

HEADIN' THROUGH (1924)
(5 r.) d, Leo D. Maloney; lp, Leo D. Maloney, Josephine Hill, Horace Carpenter, Robert Williamson

HEADIN' WEST (1922)
(5 r.) d, William J. Craft; lp, Hoot Gibson, Gertrude Short, Charles Le Moyne, Jim Corey

HEADLESS HORSEMAN, THE (1922)
(7 r.) d, Edward Venturini; lp, Will Rogers, Lois Meredith, Ben Hendricks, Jr., Mary Foy

HEADLINES (1925)
(6 r.) d, E.H. Griffith; lp, Alice Joyce, Malcolm McGregor, Virginia Lee Corbin, Harry T. Morey

HEADMASTER, THE (1921, Brit.)
(6 r.) d, Kenelm Foss; lp, Cyril Maude, Margot Drake, Miles Malleson, Marie Illington

HEADS UP, CHARLIE (1926, Ger.)
(? r.) d, Willi Wolff; lp, Anton Pointner, Ellen Richter, Michael Bohnen, Max Gulsdorff

HEADS WIN (1919)
(6 r.) d, Preston Kendall; lp, Baby Ivy Ward

HEAR THE PIPERS CALLING (1918, Brit.)
(5 r.) d, Tom Watts; lp, Hilda Oldfield

HEART AND SOUL (1917)
(5 r.) d, J. Gordon Edwards; lp, Theda Bara, Harry Hilliard, Claire Whitney, Walter Law

HEART BANDIT, THE (1924)
(5 r.) d, Oscar Apfel; lp, Viola Dana, Milton Sills, Gertrude Claire, Wallace MacDonald

HEART BUSTER, THE (1924)
(5 r.) d, Jack Conway; lp, Tom Mix, Esther Ralston, Cyril Chadwick, William Courtwright

HEART IN PAWN, A (1919)
(5 r.) d, William Worthington; lp, Sessue Hayakawa, Vola Vale, Tsuru Aoki

HEART LINE, THE (1921)
(6 r.) d, Frederick A. Thompson; lp, Leah Baird, Jerome Patrick, Frederick Vroom, Ruth Sinclair

HEART O' THE HILLS (1919)
(6 r.) d, Sidney A. Franklin; lp, Mary Pickford, Harold Goodwin, Allen Sears, Claire McDowell

HEART O' THE WEST
(SEE: HEARTS OF THE WEST, 1925)

HEART OF A CHILD, THE (1915, Brit.)
(5 r.) d, Harold Shaw; lp, Edna Flugrath, Edward Sass, Hayford Hobbs, Mary Dibley

HEART OF A CHILD, THE (1920)
(7 r.) d, Ray C. Smallwood; lp, Alla Nazimova, Charles Bryant, Ray Thompson, Nell Newman

HEART OF A CLOWN
(SEE: GOLDEN CLOWN, THE, 1927, Swed.)

HEART OF A FOOL
(SEE: IN THE HEART OF A FOOL, 1920)

HEART OF A GIRL (1918)
(5 r.) d, John G. Adolfi; lp, Barbara Castleton, Irving Cummings, Charles Wellesley, Kate Lester

HEART OF A GIPSY, THE (1919)
(5 r.) d, Henry McRae Webster; lp, Florence Billings, Aida Horton, Mathilda Brundage, Fay Evelyn

HEART OF A HERO, THE (1916)
(5 r.) d, Emile Chautard; lp, Robert Warwick, Gail Kane, Clara Whipple, Alec B. Francis

HEART OF A LION, THE (1918)
(6 r.) d, Frank Lloyd; lp, William Farnum, Wanda Petit [Hawley], Mary Martin, William Courtleigh

HEART OF A PAINTED WOMAN, THE (1915)
(5 r.) lp, Olga Petrova

HEART OF A ROSE, THE (1919, Brit.)
(6 r.) d, Jack Denton; lp, Stella Muir, Henry Victor, Douglas Payne, Edward Thilby

HEART OF A SIREN (1925)
(7 r.) d, Phil Rosen; lp, Barbara La Marr, Conway Tearle, Harry Morey, Paul Doucet

HEART OF A TEMPTRESS
(SEE: HEART OF A SIREN, 1925)

HEART OF A TEXAN, THE (1922)
(5 r.) d, Paul Hurst; lp, Neal Hart, William Quinn, Sarah Bindley, Hazel Maye

HEART OF A WOMAN, THE (1920)
(5 r.) d, Jack Pratt; lp, Mignon Anderson, Jack Richardson, George Fisher, Clara Horton

HEART OF ALASKA (1924)
(5 r.) d, Harold McCracken; lp, Maurice Costello, Marian Swayne

HEART OF BROADWAY, THE (1928)
(6 r.) d, Duke Worne; lp, Pauline Garon, Bobby Agnew, Wheeler Oakman, Oscar Apfel

HEART OF EZRA GREER, THE (1917)
(5 r.) d, Emile Chautard; lp, Frederick Warde, Lelia Frost, George Forth, Lillian Mueller

HEART OF GOLD (1919)
(5 r.) d, Travers Vale; lp, Louise Huff, John Hines, Grace Barton, Marion Barney

HEART OF HUMANITY, THE (1919)
(8 r.) d, Allen Holubar; lp, Dorothy Phillips, William Stowell, Erich von Stroheim, Robert Anderson

HEART OF JENNIFER, THE (1915)
(5 r.) d, James Kirkwood; lp, Hazel Dawn, James Kirkwood, Russell Bassett, Harry Brown

HEART OF JUANITA (1919)
(5 r.) d, George E. Middleton; lp, Beatriz Michelena, Albert Morrison, Andrew Robson, Clarence Arper

HEART OF LINCOLN, THE (1922)
(5 r.) d, Francis Ford; lp, Francis Ford, Grace Cunard, Ella Hall, William Quinn

HEART OF MARYLAND, THE (1915)
(6 r.) d, Herbert Brenon; lp, William E. Shay, Matt Snyder, Herbert Brenon, J. Farrell MacDonald

HEART OF MARYLAND, THE (1927)
(6 r.) d, Lloyd Bacon; lp, Dolores Costello, Jason Robards, Warner Richmond, Helene Costello

HEART OF MIDLOTHIAN, THE (1914, Brit.)
(4 r.) d, Frank Wilson; lp, Flora Morris, Violet Hopson, Alma Taylor, Stewart Rome

HEART OF NEW YORK, THE (1916)
(5 r.) d, Walter MacNamara; lp, Robert T. Haines, Isabelle Macgregor, Thomas Morrissey, Laura Macklan

HEART OF NORA FLYNN, THE (1916)
(5 r.) d, Cecil B. De Mille; lp, Marie Doro, Elliott Dexter, Ernest Joy, Lola May

HEART OF PAULA, THE (1916)
(5 r.) lp, Lenore Ulrich, Velma Lefler, Jack Livingston, Forrest Stanley

HEART OF RACHAEL, THE (1918)
(5 r.) d, Howard Hickman; lp, Bessie Barriscale, Herschel Mayall, Ella Hall, Herbert Heyes

HEART OF ROMANCE, THE (1918)
(5 r.) d, Harry Millarde; lp, June Caprice, Bernard Thornton, George Bunny, Joseph Kilgour

HEART OF SALOME, THE (1927)
(6 r.) d, Victor Schertzinger; lp, Alma Rubens, Walter Pidgeon, Holmes Herbert, Robert Agnew

HEART OF SISTER ANN, THE (1915, Brit.)
(4 r.) d, Harold Shaw; lp, Edna Flugrath, Hayford Hobbs, Guy Newall, Micheline Potous

HEART OF TARA, THE (1916)
(5 r.) d, William J. Bowman; lp, Margaret Gibson, William Clifford, Sherman Bainbridge, Marie James

HEART OF TEXAS RYAN, THE (1917)
(5 r.) d, E.A. Martin; lp, George Fawcett, Bessie Eyton, Frank Campeau, Tom Mix

HEART OF THE HILLS, THE (1916)
(5 r.) d, Richard Ridgeley; lp, Mabel Trunnelle, Conway Tearle, Bigelow Cooper, George A. Wright

HEART OF THE NORTH, THE (1921)
(6 r.) d, Harry Revier; lp, Roy Stewart, George Morrell, Harry von Meter, Roy Justi

HEART OF THE SUNSET (1918)
(7 r.) d, Frank Powell; lp, Anna Q. Nilsson, Herbert Heyes, Robert Tabor, E.L. Fernandez

HEART OF THE WEST
(SEE: HEARTS OF THE WEST, 1925)

HEART OF THE WILDS (1918)
(5 r.) d, Marshall Neilan; lp, Elsie Ferguson, Thomas Meighan, Joseph Smiley, Matt Moore

HEART OF THE YUKON, THE (1927)
(7 r.) d, W.S. Van Dyke; lp, John Bowers, Anne Cornwall, Edward Hearn, Frank Campeau

HEART OF TWENTY, THE (1920)
(5 r.) d, Henry Kolker; lp, ZaSu Pitts, Tom Gallery, Percy Challenger, Hugh Saxon

HEART OF WETONA, THE (1919)
(6 r.) d, Sidney A. Franklin; lp, Norma Talmadge, Thomas Meighan, Fred Huntley, Gladden James

HEART OF YOUTH, THE (1920)
(5 r.) d, Robert G. Vignola; lp, Lila Lee, Buster Irving, Charles Ogle, Fannie Midgley

HEART SPECIALIST, THE (1922)
(5 r.) d, Frank Urson; lp, Mary Miles Minter, Allan Forrest, Roy Atwell, Jack Matheis

HEART STRINGS (1917)
(5 r.) d, Allen Holubar; lp, Allen Holubar, Francelia Billington, Paul Byron, Maude George

HEART STRINGS (1920)
(6 r.) d, J. Gordon Edwards; lp, William Farnum, Gladys Coburn, Betty Hilburn, Paul Cazeneuve

HEART THIEF, THE (1927)
(6 r.) d, Nils Olaf Chrisander; lp, Joseph Schildkraut, Lya De Putti, Robert Edeson, Charles Gerrard

HEART TO HEART (1928)
(7 r.) d, William Beaudine; lp, Mary Astor, Lloyd Hughes, Louise Fazenda, Lucien Littlefield

HEART TO LET, A (1921)
(5 r.) d, Edward Dillon; lp, Justine Johnstone, Harrison Ford, Marcia Harris, Thomas Carr

HEARTACHES (1915)
(4 r.) d, Joseph Kaufman; lp, June Daye, Jessie Terry, Francis Joyner, Helen Greene

HEARTBOUND (1925)
(5 r.) d, Glen Lambert; lp, Ranger Bill Miller, Bess True

HEARTLESS HUSBANDS (1925)
(5 r.) d, Bertram Bracken; lp, John Prince, Gloria Grey, Thomas G. Lingham, Vola Vale

HEARTS AFLAME (1923)
(9 r.) d, Reginald Barker; lp, Frank Keenan, Anna Q. Nilsson, Craig Ward, Richard Headrick

HEARTS AND FLOWERS (1914)
(5 r.) lp, Mrs. Thomas Whiffen, Beulah Poynter

HEARTS AND MASKS (1921)
(5 r.) d, William A. Seiter; lp, Elinor Field, Francis McDonald, Lloyd Bacon, John Cossar

HEARTS AND SADDLES (1919, Brit.)
(5 r.) d, Walter West; lp, Violet Hopson, Stewart Rome, Gregory Scott, Cameron Carr

HEARTS AND SPANGLES (1926)
(6 r.) d, Frank O'Connor; lp, Wanda Hawley, Robert Gordon, Barbara Tennant, Eric Mayne

HEARTS AND SPURS (1925)
(5 r.) d, William S. Van Dyke; lp, Buck Jones, Carol Lombard, William Davidson, Freeman Wood

HEARTS AND THE HIGHWAY (1915)
(5 r.) d, Wilfred North; lp, Lillian Walker, Darwin Karr, Donald Hall, L. Rogers Lytton

HEARTS ARE TRUMPS (1920)
(6 r.) d, Rex Ingram; lp, Winter Hall, Frank Brownlee, Alice Terry, Francelia Billington

HEARTS ASLEEP (1919)
(5 r.) d, Howard Hickman; lp, Bessie Barriscale, George Fisher, Vola Vale, Frank Whitson

HEART'S CRUCIBLE, A (1916)
(5 r.) lp, Cleo Madison, William V. Mong, Edward Hearn, Margaret Whistler

HEART'S DESIRE (1917)
(5 r.) d, Francis J. Grandon; lp, Marie Doro, Albert Roscoe, Mario Majeroni, Jean Gauthier

HEART'S HAVEN (1922)
(6 r.) d, Benjamin B. Hampton; lp, Robert McKim, Claire Adams, Carl Gantvoort, Claire McDowell

HEARTS O' THE RANGE (1921)
(5 r.) d, Milburn Morante; lp, Milburn Morante, Alma Rayford

HEARTS OF LOVE (1918)
(6 r.) d, Charles J. Haydon; lp, Edna Mayo, Gladden James, Frederick Truesdell, Lillian Snyder

HEARTS OF MEN (1915)
(5 r.) d, Perry N. Vekroff; lp, Arthur Donaldson, Beulah Poynter, Frank Longacre, Ethelmary Oakland

HEARTS OF MEN (1928)
(6 r.) d, James P. Hogan; lp, Mildred Harris, Thelma Hill, Cornelius Keefe, Warner Richmond

HEARTS OF MEN, THE
(SEE: HUNS WITHIN OUR GATES, 1918)

HEARTS OF THE WEST (1925)
(5 r.) lp, Lester Cuneo, Annabelle Lee, Charles L. King, Slim Podgett

HEARTS OF THE WOODS (1921)
(? r.) d, Roy Calnek; lp, Clifford Harris, Laurence McGuire, Don Pierson, Anna Lou Allen

HEARTS OF YOUTH (1921)
(? r.) d, Tom Miranda; lp, Harold Goodwin, Lillian Hall, Fred Kirby, George Fisher

HEARTS OR DIAMONDS? (1918)
(5 r.) d, Henry King; lp, William Russell, Charlotte Burton, Howard Davies, Carl Stockdale

HEART'S REVENGE, A (1918)
(5 r.) d, O.A.C. Lund; lp, Sonia Markova, Helen Long, David Herblin, Frank Goldsmith

HEARTS THAT ARE HUMAN (1915, Brit.)
(4 r.) d, A.V. Bramble; lp, Fay Temple, Roy Beard, Somers Bellamy, Kathleen Warwick

HEARTS UNITED (1914)
(4 r.)

HEARTS UP! (1920)
(5 r.) d, Val Paul; lp, Harry Carey, Mignonne Golden, Arthur Millett, Charles Le Moyne

HEARTSEASE (1919)
(5 r.) d, Harry Beaumont; lp, Tom Moore, Helene Chadwick, Larry Steers, Alec B. Francis

HEARTSTRINGS (1917)
(5 r.) d, Allen J. Holubar;

HEAVEN ON EARTH (1927)
(7 r.) d, Phil Rosen; lp, Renee Adoree, Conrad Nagel, Gwen Lee, Julia Swayne

HEDDA GABLER (1917)
(5 r.) d, Frank Powell; lp, Nance O'Neil, Aubrey Beattie, Lillian Paige, Einar Linden

HEEDLESS MOTHS (1921)
(6 r.) d, Robert Z. Leonard; lp, Holmes E. Herbert, Hedda Hopper, Ward Crane, Tom Burroughs

HEIGHTS OF HAZARDS, THE (1915)
(5 r.) d, Harry Lambart; lp, Charles Richman, Eleanor Woodruff, Charles Kent, Hattie De Lara

HEIR OF THE AGES, THE (1917)
(5 r.) d, Edward J. LeSaint; lp, House Peters, Nina Byron, Eugene Palette, John Burton

HEIR TO JENGHIS-KHAN, THE (1928, USSR)
(10 r.) d, Vsevolod Pudovkin; lp, Valeri Inkizhinov, A. Dedintsev, Anna Sudakevich, V. Tsoppi

HEIR TO THE HOORAH, THE (1916)
(5 r.) d, William C. De Mille; lp, Thomas Meighan, Anita King, Edythe Chapman, Horace B. Carpenter

HEIRESS AT "COFFEE DAN'S", THE (1917)
(5 r.) d, Edward Dillon; lp, Bessie Love, Frank Bennett, Max Davidson, Lucille Younge

HEIRESS FOR A DAY (1918)
(5 r.) d, Jack Dillon; lp, Olive Thomas, Joe King, Eugene Burr, Graham Pette [Pettie]

HEIR-LOONS (1925)
(6 r.) d, Grover Jones; lp, Wallace MacDonald, Edith Roberts, Cecille Evans, Frank Campeau

HELD BY THE ENEMY (1920)
(6 r.) d, Donald Crisp; lp, Agnes Ayers, Jack Holt, Wanda Hawley, Lewis Stone

HELD FOR RANSOM (1914)
(4 r.)

HELD IN TRUST (1920)
(6 r.) d, John Ince; lp, May Allison, Darrell Foss, Walter Long, John H. Elliott

HELEN OF FOUR GATES (1920, Brit.)
(6 r.) d, Cecil M. Hepworth; lp, Alma Taylor, James Carew, Gerald Ames, George Dewhurst

HELENE OF THE NORTH (1915)
(5 r.) d, J. Searle Dawley; lp, Marguerite Clark, Frank Losee, Brigham Royce, Conway Tearle

HELEN OF TROY
(SEE: PRIVATE LIFE OF HELEN OF TROY, THE, 1927)

HELIOTROPE (1920)
(6 r.) d, George D. Baker; lp, Diana Allen, Wilfred Lytell, Fred Burton, Julia Swayne Gordon

HELL BENT (1918)
(5 r.) d, Jack [John] Ford; lp, Harry Carey, Neva Gerber, Duke R. Lee, Vester Pegg

HELL CAT, THE (1918)
(6 r.) d, Reginald Barker; lp, Geraldine Farrar, Milton Sills, Tom Santschi, William W. Black

HELL DIGGERS, THE (1921)
(5 r.) d, Frank Urson; lp, Wallace Reid, Lois Wilson, Alexander Broun, Frank Geldert

HELL HATH NO FURY (1917)
(6 r.) d, Charles E. Bartlett; lp, Melbourne McDowell, Joseph King, Robert Warwick, Reeves Eason

HELL MORGAN'S GIRL (1917)
(5 r.) d, Joseph De Grasse; lp, Dorothy Phillips, William Stowell, Lon Chaney, Lilyan Rosine

HELL ROARIN' REFORM (1919)
(5 r.) d, Edward J. LeSaint; lp, Tom Mix, Kathleen Connors, George Berrell, B.M. Turner

HELL SHIP, THE (1920)
(5 r.) d, Scott Dunlap; lp, Madlaine Traverse, Albert Roscoe, Betty Bouton, Dick La Reno

HELL SHIP, THE (1923, Swed.)
(? r.) d, Victor Sjostrom; lp, Victor Sjorstrom, Matheson Lang, Jenny Hasselqvist

HELL-BENT FOR HEAVEN (1926)
(7 r.) d, J. Stuart Blackton; lp, Patsy Ruth Miller, John Harron, Gayne Whitman, Gardner James

HELLCAT, THE (1928, Brit.)
(7 r.) d, Harry Hughes; lp, Mabel Poulton, Eric Bransby Williams, John Hamilton, Pauline Johnson

HELLHOUNDS OF THE WEST (1922)
(5 r.) lp, Dick Hatton, Catherine Craig, Frank Thompson, Willie May Carson

HELLION, THE (1919)
(5 r.) d, George L. Cox; lp, Margarita Fischer, Emory Johnson, Charles Spere, Henry Barrows

HELLION, THE (1924)
(5 r.) d, Bruce Mitchell; lp, J.B. Warner

HELLO BILL! (1915)
(5 r.) lp, George Bickel, Harry Watson, Ben L. Taggart, Ruby Hoffman

HELLO CHEYENE (1928)
(5 r.) d, Eugne Forde; lp, Tom Mix, Caryl Lincoln, Jack Baston, Martin Faust

HELL'S BOARDER
(SEE: HELL'S BORDER, 1922)

HELL'S BORDER (1922)
(5 r.) lp, William Fairbanks

HELL'S CRATER (1918)
(5 r.) d, W.B. Pearson; lp, Grace Cunard, Ray Hanford, Eileen Sedgwick, George McDaniel

HELL'S END (1918)
(5 r.) d, J.W. McLaughlin; lp, William Desmond, Josie Sedgwick, Louis Durham, Dorothy Hagar

HELL'S 400 (1926)
(6 r.) d, John Griffith; lp, Margaret Livingston, Harrison Ford, Henry Kolker, Wallace McDonald

HELL'S HIGHROAD (1925)
(6 r.) d, Rupert Julian; lp, Leatrice Joy, Edmund Burns, Robert Edeson, Julia Faye

HELL'S HOLE (1923)
(6 r.) d, Emmett J. Flynn; lp, Charles Jones, Maurice B. Flynn, Eugene Pallette, George Siegmann

HELL'S OASIS (1920)
(5 r.) d, Neal Hart; lp, Neal Hart, William Quinn, Hal Wilson, Betty Brown

HELL'S RIVER
(SEE: MAN FROM HELL'S RIVER, THE, 1922)

HELLSHIP BRONSON (1928)
(7 r.) d, Joseph E. Henabery; lp, Noah Beery, Mrs. Wallace Reid, Reed Howes, Helen Foster

HELP! HELP! POLICE! (1919)
(5 r.) d, Edward Dillon; lp, George Walsh, Eric Mayne, Henry Hallam, Marie Burke

HELP WANTED (1915)
(5 r.) lp, Lois Meredith, Hobart Bosworth, Owen Moore

HELP YOURSELF (1920)
(5 r.) d, Hugo Ballin; lp, Madge Kennedy, E.J. Radcliffe, Joseph Striker, Helen Greene

HENRY, KING OF NAVARRE (1924, Brit.)
(5 r.) d, Maurice Elvey; lp, Matheson Lang, Gladys Jennings, Henry Victor, Stella St. Audrie

HER ACCIDENTAL HUSBAND (1923)
(6 r.) d, Dallas M. Fitzgerald; lp, Miriam Cooper, Mitchell Lewis, Richard Tucker, Forrest Stanley

HER AMERICAN HUSBAND (1918)
(5 r.) d, E. Mason Hopper; lp, Teddy Sampson, Darrel Foss, Leota Lorraine, Thomas Kurihara

HER AMERICAN PRINCE (1916)
(5 r.) d, D.H. Turner; lp, Ormi Hawley, Bradley Barker

HER ATONEMENT (1915)
(4 r.) lp, Lillian Wiggins

HER BELOVED ENEMY (1917)
(5 r.) d, Ernest Warde; lp, Doris Grey, Wayne Arey, Joseph H. Gilmour, Gladys Leslie

HER BELOVED VILLIAN (1920)
(5 r.) d, Sam Wood; lp, Wanda Hawley, Harrison Ford, Tully Mashall, Ramsey Wallace

HER BENNY (1920, Brit.)
(6 r.) d, A.V. Bramble; lp, Sydney Wood, Babs Reynolds, Charles Buckmaster, Peggy Patterson

HER BETTER SELF (1917)
(5 r.) d, Robert Vignola; lp, Pauline Frederick, Thomas Meighan, Alice Hollister, Maude Turner Gordon

HER BIG ADVENTURE (1926)
(5 r.) d, John Ince; lp, Herbert Rawlinson, Grace Darmond, Vola Vale, Carlton Griffin

HER BIG NIGHT (1926)
(8 r.) d, Melville W. Brown; lp, Laura La Plante, Einar Hansen, ZaSu Pitts, Tully Marshall

HER BITTER CUP (1916)
(5 r.) d, Cleo Madison, Joe King; lp, Cleo Madison, Adele Farrington, William V. Mong, Edward Hearn

HER BLEEDING HEART (1916)
(5 r.) d, Jack Pratt; lp, Rosetta Brice, Richard Buhler, Crauford Kent, Inez Buck

HER BODY IN BOND (1918)
(5 r.) d, Robert Leonard; lp, Mae Murray, Kenneth Harlan, Al Roscoe, Paul Weigel

HER BOY (1918)
(5 r.) d, George Irving; lp, Effie Shannon, Niles Welch, Pauline Curley, Pat O'Malley

HER CODE OF HONOR (1919)
(6 r.) d, John M. Stahl; lp, Florence Reed, William Desmond, Robert Frazer, Irving Cummings

HER COUNTRY FIRST (1918)
(5 r.) d, James Young; lp, Vivian Martin, John Cossar, Florence Oberle, Byrdine Zuber

HER COUNTRY'S CALL (1917)
(5 r.) d, Lloyd Ingraham; lp, Mary Miles Minter, Alan Forrest, George Periolat, Harry A. Barrows

HER CROSS (1919, Brit.)
(5 r.) d, A.V. Bramble; lp, Ivy Close, Lionel Belcher, C. Hargreave Mansell, Alice de Winton

HER DEBT OF HONOR (1916)
(5 r.) d, William Nigh; lp, Valli Valli, William Davidson, William Nigh, J.H. Goldsworthy

HER DECISION (1918)
(5 r.) d, Jack Conway; lp, Gloria Swanson, J. Barney Sherry, Darrel Foss, Ann Kroman

HER DOUBLE CROSS (1917)
(5 r.)

HER DOUBLE LIFE (1916)
(6 r.) d, J. Gordon Edwards; lp, Theda Bara, Stuart Holmes, Walter Law, Lucia Moore

HER EXCELLENCY, THE GOVERNOR (1917)
(5 r.) d, Albert Parker; lp, Wilfred Lukas, Elda Millar [Hedda Hopper], Joseph Kilgour, Regan Houghston

HER FACE VALUE (1921)
(5 r.) d, Thomas N. Heffron; lp, Wanda Hawley, Lincoln Plummer, Dick Rosson, T. Roy Barnes

HER FATHER SAID NO (1927)
(7 r.) d, Jack McKeown; lp, Mary Brian, Danny O'Shea, Al Cooke, Kit Guard

HER FATHER'S GOLD (1916)
(5 r.) d, W. Eugene Moore; lp, Barbara Gilroy, Harris Gordon, Louise Emerald Bates, William Burt

HER FATHER'S KEEPER (1917)
(5 r.) lp, Frank Currier, Irene Howley, Jack Devereaux, Jack Raymond

HER FATHER'S SON (1916)
(5 r.) d, William D. Taylor; lp, Vivian Martin, Alfred Vosburgh, Herbert Standing, Helen Jerome Eddy

HER FINAL RECKONING (1918)
(5 r.) d, Emile Chautard; lp, Pauline Frederick, John Miltern, Robert Cain, Warren Cook

HER FIRST ELOPEMENT (1920)
(5 r.) d, Sam Wood; lp, Wanda Hawley, Jerome Patrick, Nell Craig, Lucien Littlefield

HER GAME (1919)
(5 r.) d, Frank H. Crane; lp, Florence Reed, Conway Tearle, Jed Prouty, Florence Billings

HER GOOD NAME (1917)
(5 r.) lp, Jean Sothern, William H. Turner, Earle Metcalfe, Arthur Housman

HER GREAT HOUR (1916)
(5 r.) d, Stanner E.V. Taylor; lp, Molly McIntyre, Gerda Holmes, Richard Lynn, Martin Alsop

HER GREAT MATCH (1915)
(5 r.) lp, Gail Kane, Vernon Steele, Ned Burton, Clarissa Selwynne

HER GREAT PRICE (1916)
(6 r.) d, Edwin Carewe; lp, Mabel Taliaferro, Henry Mortimer, Richard Barbee, George Pauncefort

HER GREATEST LOVE (1917)
(5 r.) d, J. Gordon Edwards; lp, Theda Bara, Harry Hilliard, Glen White, Walter Law

HER GREATEST PERFORMANCE (1916, Brit.)
(6 r.) d, Fred Paul; lp, Ellen Terry, Dennis Neilson-Terry, Joan Morgan, James Lindsay

HER HALF BROTHER
(SEE: PALS OF THE WEST, 1922)

HER HAPPINESS (1915)
(4 r.) d, Harry Beaumont

HER HONOR THE GOVERNOR (1926)
(7 r.) d, Chet Withey; lp, Pauline Frederick, Carroll Nye, Greta von Rue, Tom Santschi

HER HONOR THE MAYOR (1920)
(5 r.) d, Paul Cazeneuve; lp, Eileen Percy, Ramsey Wallace, Charles Force, William Fletcher

HER HOUR (1917)
(5 r.) d, George Cowl; lp, Kitty Gordon, George Morgan, George MacQuarrie, Edward Burns

HER HUSBAND'S FRIEND (1920)
(5 r.) d, Fred Niblo; lp, Enid Bennett, Rowland Lee, Tom Chatterton, Mae Busch

HER HUSBAND'S HONOR (1918)
(5 r.) d, Burton King; lp, Edna Goodrich, David Powell, Thomas Tamamoto, Barbara Allen

HER HUSBAND'S SECRET (1925)
(7 r.) d, Frank Lloyd; lp, Antonio Moreno, Patsy Ruth Miller, Ruth Clifford, David Torrence

HER HUSBAND'S TRADEMARK (1922)
(5 r.) d, Sam Wood; lp, Gloria Swanson, Richard Wayne, Stuart Holmes, Lucien Littlefield

HER INDISCRETIONS (1927)
(6 r.) lp, Mahlon Hamilton, May Allison

HER INSPIRATION (1918)
(5 r.) d, Robert Thornby

HER KINGDOM OF DREAMS (1919)
(7 r.) d, Marshall Neilan; lp, Anita Stewart, Mahlon Hamilton, Anna Q. Nilsson, Spottiswoode Aitken

HER LIFE AND HIS (1917)
(5 r.) d, Frederick Sullivan; lp, Florence LaBadie, H.E. Herbert, Ethyle Cooke, Sam Niblack

HER LORD AND MASTER (1921)
(6 r.) d, Edward Jose; lp, Alice Joyce, Holmes Herbert, Walter McEwen, Frank Sheridan

HER LOVE STORY (1924)
(7 r.) d, Allan Dwan; lp, Gloria Swanson, Ian Keith, George Fawcett, Echlin Gayer

HER MAJESTY (1922)
(5 r.) d, George Irving; lp, Mollie King, Creighton Hale, Rose Tapley, Neville Percy

HER MAN (1918)
(6 r.) d, Ralph Ince; lp, Elaine Hammerstein, W. Lawson Butt, George Anderson, Carleton Macy

HER MAN O'WAR (1926)
(6 r.) d, Frank Urson; lp, Jetta Goudal, William Boyd, Jimmie Adams, Grace Darmond

HER MARKET VALUE (1925)
(6 r.) d, Paul Powell; lp, Agnes Ayres, George Irving Anders Randolf, Hedda Hopper

HER MARRIAGE LINES (1917, Brit.)
(4 r.) d, Frank Wilson; lp, Stewart Rome, Chrissie White, Violet Hopson, Lionelle Howard

HER MARRIAGE VOW (1924)
(7 r.) d, Millard Webb; lp, Monte Blue, Willard Louis, Beverly Bayne, Margaret Livingston

HER MATERNAL RIGHT (1916)
(5 r.) d, Robert Thornby, John Ince; lp, Kitty Gordon, Zena Keefe, George Ralph, Frank Evans

HER MARTYRDOM (1915)
(4 r.)

HER MISTAKE (1918)
(6 r.) d, Julius Steger

HER MOMENT (1918)
(6 r.) d, Frank Beal; lp, Anna Luther, William Garwood, Bert Hadley, Alida Jones

HER MOTHER'S SECRET (1915)
(5 r.) d, Frederick Thompson; lp, Ralph Kellard, Dorothy Green

HER NAMLESS CHILD (1915, Brit.)
(4 r.) d, Maurice Elvey; lp, Elizabeth Risdon, Fred Groves, A.V. Bramble, M. Gray Murray

HER NEW YORK (1917)
(5 r.) d, O.A.C. Lund; lp, Gladys Hulette, Riley Chamberlin, Carey Hastings, William Parke, Jr.

HER NIGHT OF NIGHTS (1922)
(5 r.) d, Hobart Henley; lp, Marie Prevost, Edward Hearn, Hal Cooley, Betty Francisco

HER NIGHT OF ROMANCE (1924)
(8 r.) d, Sidney A. Franklin; lp, Constance Talmadge, Ronald Colman, Jean Hersholt, Albert Gran

HER OFFICAL FATHERS (1917)
(5 r.) d, Elmer Clifton, Joseph Henabery; lp, Dorothy Gish, Frank Bennett, Sam De Grasse, F.A. Turner

HER ONE MISTAKE (1918)
(5 r.) d, Edward J. LeSaint; lp, Gladys Brockwell, William Scott, Willard Louis, Charles Perley

HER ONLY WAY (1918)
(6 r.) d, Sidney A. Franklyn; lp, Norma Talmadge, Eugene O'Brien, Ramsey Wallace, E.A. Warren

HER OWN MONEY (1922)
(5 r.) d, Joseph Henabery; lp, Ethel Clayton, Warner Baxter, Charles French, Clarence Burton

HER OWN PEOPLE (1917)
(5 r.) d, Scott Sidney; lp, Lenore Ulrich, Howard Davies, Colin Chase, Adelaide Woods

HER OWN STORY (1922)
(5 r.) lp, Sydney Deane, Mildred Elsie Ferguson

HER OWN STORY (1926)
(5 r.) d, Francis Ford; lp, Jack Mower, Mary Carr

HER OWN WAY (1915)
(5 r.) d, Herbert Blache; lp, Florence Reed, Robert Barrat, Fraunie Fraunholz, William A. Morse

HER PENALTY (1921, Brit.)
(4 r.) d, Einar J. Bruun; lp, Stewart Rome, Pauline Peters, Clive Brook, Philip Hewland

HER PRICE (1918)
(5 r.) d, Edmund Lawrence; lp, Virginia Pearson, Edward Rosen, Victor Sutherland, Henri Leone

HER PROPER PLACE (1915)
(4 r.) d, Langdon West

HER PURCHASE PRICE (1919)
(5 r.) d, Howard Hickman; lp, Bessie Barriscale, Albert Roscoe, Joseph Dowling, Kathlyn Williams

HER RECKONING (1915)
(5 r.)

HER REDEMPTION
(SEE: THE GAYEST OF THE GAY, 1924, Brit.)

HER REPUTATION (1923)
(7 r.) d, John Griffith Wray; lp, May McAvoy, Lloyd Hughes, James Corrigan, Casson Ferguson

HER RIGHT TO LIVE (1917)
(5 r.) d, Paul Scardon; lp, Peggy Hyland, Antonio Moreno, Bobby Connelly, Helen Connelly

HER SACRIFICE (1917, USSR)
(5 r.) d, Cheslav Sabinsky; lp, Olga Gzovskaya, Vladimir Gaidrov, Nikolai Panov

HER SACRIFICE (1926)
(6 r.) d, Wilfred Lucas; lp, Gaston Glass, Bryant Washburn, Herbert Rawlinson, Gladys Brockwell

HER SECOND CHANCE (1926)
(7 r.) d, June Mathis; lp, Anna Q. Nilsson, Huntly Gordon, Charlie Murray, Sam De Grasse

HER SECOND HUSBAND (1918)
(5 r.) d, Dell Henderson; lp, Edna Goodrich, William B. Davidson, Richard B. Neill, Miriam Folger

HER SECRET (1917)
(5 r.) d, Perry N. Vekroff; lp, Alice Joyce, Harry Morey, Robert Kelley, Mary Maurice

HER SHATTERED IDOL (1915)
(4 r.) d, John B. O'Brien; lp, Mae Marsh, Robert Harron, Spottiswoode Aitken, Jennie Lee

HER SILENT SACRIFICE (1917)
(5 r.) d, Edward Jose; lp, Alice Brady, Henry Clive, R. Peyton Gibbs, Edmund Pardo

HER SISTER (1917)
(5 r.) d, John B. O'Brien; lp, Olive Tell, David Powell, Eileen Dennes, Anita Rothe

HER SISTER FROM PARIS (1925)
(7 r.) d, Sidney Franklin; lp, Constance Talmadge, Ronald Colman, George K. Arthur, Margaret Mann

HER SISTER'S GUILT (1916)
(5 r.)

HER SOCIAL VALUE (1921)
(6 r.) d, Jerome Storm; lp, Katherine MacDonald, Roy Stewart, Bertram Grassby, Betty Ross Clarke

HER SON (1920, Brit.)
(6 r.) d, Walter West; lp, Violet Hopson, Stewart Rome, Mercy Hatton, Cameron Carr

HER SOUL'S INSPIRATION (1917)
(5 r.) d, Jack Conway; lp, Ella Hall, Marc Robbins, R. Hasset Ryan, Edward Hearn

HER STORY (1922)
(5 r.) d, Allyn B. Carrick; lp, Madge Titheradge

HER STRANGE WEDDING (1917)
(5 r.) d, George Melford; lp, Fannie Ward, Jack Dean, Tom Forman, Billy Elmer

HER STURDY OAK (1921)
(5 r.) d, Thomas N. Heffron; lp, Wanda Hawley, Walter Hiers, Sylvia Ashton, Mayme Kelso

HER SUMMER HERO (1928)
(6 r.) d, James Dugan; lp, Hugh Trevor, Harold Goodwin, Duane Thompson, James Pierce

HERE SURRENDER (1916)
(5 r.) d, Ivan Abramson; lp, Anna Q. Nilsson, William H. Tooker, Wilmuth Merkyl, Rose Coughlan

HER TEMPORARY HUSBAND (1923)
(7 r.) d, John McDermott; lp, Owen Moore, Sydney Chaplin, Sylvia Breamer, Tully Marshall

HER TEMPTATION (1917)
(5 r.) d, Richard Stanton; lp, Gladys Brockwell, Bertram Grassby, Ralph Lewis, James Cruze

HER UNWILLING HUSBAND (1920)
(5 r.) d, Paul Scardon; lp, Blanche Sweet, Albert Roscoe, Edwin Stevens

HER VOCATION (1915)
(4 r.) d, James W. Castle

HER WAYWARD SISTER (1916)
(4 r.) d, Clay M. Greene; lp, June Daye, Blanche Burns, Elizabeth Bobbs, Mimi Yvonne

HER WILD OAT (1927)
(7 r.) d, Marshall Neilan; lp, Colleen Moore, Larry Kent, Hallam Cooley, Gwen Lee

HERE COMES THE BRIDE (1919)
(5 r.) d, John S. Robertson;

HERE HE COMES (1926)
(5 r.) d, Travers Corby; lp, Earl Douglas

HEREDITY (1918)
(5 r.) d, William P.S. Earle; lp, Barbara Castleton, John Bowers, Madge Evans, Jennie Ellison

HERITAGE (1915)
(4 r.) d, Robert Leonard; lp, Robert Leonard, Ella Hall

HERITAGE (1920)
(5 r.) d, William L. Roubert; lp, Matty Roubert, Herbert Standing, Jr., Augusta Perry, Joseph Burke

HERITAGE OF HATE, THE (1916)
(5 r.) d, Burton George; lp, Roberta Wilson, William Quinn, Lillian Concord, Eileen Sedgwick

HERITAGE OF THE DESERT, THE (1924)
(6 r.) d, Irvin Willat; lp, Bebe Daniels, Ernest Torrence, Noah Beery, Lloyd Hughes

HERO FOR A NIGHT, A (1927)
(6 r.) d, William James Craft; lp, Glenn Tryon, Patsy Ruth Miller, Lloyd Whitlock, Burr McIntosh

HERO OF THE CIRCUS, THE (1928, Ital.)
(6 r.) d, Guy Brignone

HERO OF SUBMARINE D-2, THE (1916)
(5 r.) d, Paul Scardon; lp, Charles Richman, James Morrison, Anders Randolf, Charles Wellesley

HERO OF THE BIG SNOWS, A (1926)
(5 r.) d, Herman C. Raymaker; lp, Rin-Tin-Tin, Alice Calhoun, Don Alvarado, Leo Willis

HERO OF THE HOUR, THE (1917)
(5 r.) d, Raymond Wells; lp, Jack Mulhall, Wadsworth Harris, Fritzie Ridgway, Grace MacLean

HERO ON HORSEBACK, A (1927)
(6 r.) d, Del Andrews; lp, Hoot Gibson, Ethlyne Clair, Edwards Davis, Edward Hearn

HEROES AND HUSBANDS (1922)
(6 r.) d, Chet Withey; lp, Katherine MacDonald, Nigel Barrie, Charles Clary, Charles Gerrard

HEROES IN BLUE (1927)
(5 r.) d, Duke Worne; lp, John Bowers, Sally Rand, Gareth Hughes, Ann Brody

HEROES OF THE NIGHT (1927)
(7 r.) d, Frank O'Connor; lp, Cullen Landis, Marion Nixon, Rex Lease, Wheeler Oakman

HEROES OF THE STREET (1922)
(6 r.) d, William Beaudine; lp, Wesley Barry, Marie Prevost, Jack Mulhall, Philo McCullough

HERR ARNES PENGAR
(SEE: SIR ARNE'S TREASURE, 1920, Swed.)

HERR DOKTOR (1917, Fr.)
(? r.) d, Louis Feuillade

HESPER OF THE MOUNTAINS (1916)
(5 r.) d, Wilfred North; lp, Lillian Walker, Donald Hall, Evart Overton, Donald MacBride

HIAWATHA (1913)
(4 r.)

HICKVILLE TO BROADWAY (1921)
(5 r.) d, Carl Harbaugh; lp, Eileen Percy, William Scott, Rosemary Theby, John P. Lockney

HIDDEN ACES (1927)
(5 r.) d, Howard Mitchell; lp, Charles Hutchison, Alice Calhoun, Barbara Tennant, Paul Weigel

HIDDEN CHILDREN, THE (1917)
(5 r.) d, Oscar Apfel; lp, Harold Lockwood, May Allison, Lillian West, Henry Hebert

HIDDEN CODE, THE (1920)
(5 r.) d, Richard Le Strange; lp, Grace Davison, Ralph Osborne, Richard Le Strange, Clayton Davis

HIDDEN FIRES (1918)
(5 r.) d, George Irving; lp, Mae Marsh, Rod La Rocque, Florida Kingsley, Alec B. Francis

HIDDEN HAND, THE (1916, Brit.)
(10 r.) d, Lawrence Cowen; lp, Helene Gingold, Percy Morgan, Marguerite Shelley, Gilbert Esmond

HIDDEN LAW, THE (1916)
(5 r.) lp, William Clifford, Margaret Gibson, Frederick Montague, Robert Kenyon

HIDDEN LIGHT (1920)
(6 r.) d, Abraham S. Schomer; lp, Dolores Cassinelli, J. Brennan, Arthur Donaldson, Gladys Valerie

HIDDEN LOOT (1925)
(5 r.) d, Robert North Bradbury; lp, Jack Hoxie, Olive Hasbrouck, Edward Cecil, Jack Kenney

HIDDEN MENACE, THE (1925)
(5 r.) d, Charles Hutchison; lp, Charles Hutchison

HIDDEN PEARLS (1918)
(5 r.) d, George Melford; lp, Sessue Hayakawa, Margaret Loomis, Florence Vidor, Theodore Roberts

HIDDEN SPRING, THE (1917)
(5 r.) d, E. Mason Hopper; lp, Harold Lockwood, Lester Cuneo, Vera Sisson, Arthur Millett

HIDDEN TRUTH, THE (1919)
(5 r.) d, Julius Steger; lp, Anna Case, Charles Richman, Emma Campbell, Forrest Robinson

HIDDEN VALLEY, THE (1916)
(5 r.) d, Ernest Warde; lp, Mme. Valkyrien [Baroness Dewitz], Boyd Marshall, Ernest Warde, Arthur Bauer

HIDDEN WAY, THE (1926)
(6 r.) d, Joseph De Grasse; lp, Mary Carr, Gloria Grey, Tom Santschi, Arthur Rankin

HIDDEN WOMAN, THE (1922)
(5 r.) d, Allan Dwan; lp, Evelyn Nesbit, Crauford Kent, Murdock MacQuarrie, Ruth Darling

HIER ET AUJOURD'HUI (1918, Fr.)
(? r.) d, Dominique Bernard-Deschamps

HIGH COUNTRY ROMANCE (1915)
(4 r.)

HIGH FINANCE (1917)
(5 r.) d, Otis Turner; lp, George Walsh, Doris Pawn, Charles Clary, Rosita Marstini

HIGH FLYER, THE (1926)
(5 r.) d, Harry J. Brown; lp, Reed Howes, Ethel Shannon, James Bradbury, Ray Hallor

HIGH GEAR JEFFREY (1921)
(? r.) d, Edward Sloman; lp, William Russell, Francelia Billington, Clarence Burton, Al Ferguson

HIGH HAND, THE (1915)
(6 r.) d, William D. Taylor; lp, Carlyle Blackwell, William Brunton, Neva Gerber, Douglas Gerrard

HIGH HAND, THE (1926)
(6 r.) d, Leo Maloney; lp, Leo Maloney, Josephine Hill, Paul Hurst, Murdock MacQuarrie

HIGH HAT (1927)
(7 r.) d, James Ashmore Creelman; lp, Ben Lyon, Mary Brian, Sam Hardy, Lucien Prival

HIGH PLAY (1917)
(5 r.) d, Edward Sloman; lp, William Russell, Francelia Billington, Ashton Dearholt, Lucille Younge

HIGH POCKETS (1919)
(5 r.) d, Ira M. Lowry; lp, Louis Bennison, Katherine MacDonald, William W. Black, Edward Roseman

HIGH ROAD, THE (1915)
(5 r.) d, John W. Noble; lp, Valli Valli, Frank Elliot, C.H. Brennon

HIGH SCHOOL HERO (1927)
(6 r.) d, David Butler; lp, Nick Stuart, Sally Phipps, William N. Bailey, John Darrow

HIGH SIGN, THE (1917)
(5 r.) d, Elmer Clifton; lp, Herbert Rawlinson, Brownie Vernon, Hayward Mack, Edward Brady

HIGH SPEED (1920)
(5 r.) d, Charles Miller; lp, Edward Earle, Gladys Hulette, Roger Lytton, Charles Husted

HIGH SPEED (1924)
(5 r.) d, Herbert Blache; lp, Herbert Rawlinson, Carmelita Geraghty, Bert Roach, Otto Hoffman

HIGH SPEED LEE (1923)
(5 r.) d, Dudley Murphy; lp, Reed Howes

HIGH STAKES (1918)
(5 r.) d, Arthur Hoyt; lp, J. Barney Sherry, Myrtle Rishell, Harvey Clark, Jane Miller

HIGH STEPPERS (1926)
(7 r.) d, Edwin Carewe; lp, Lloyd Hughes, Mary Astor, Dolores Del Rio, Rita Carewe

HIGH TIDE (1918)
(5 r.) d, Gilbert P. Hamilton; lp, Harry Mestayer, Jean Calhoun, Yvonne Pavis, Julia Jackson

HIGHBINDERS, THE (1926)
(6 r.) d, George W. Terwilliger; lp, William T. Tilden, Marjorie Daw, Ben Alexander, George Hackathorne

HIGHEST BID, THE (1916)
(5 r.) d, William Russell; lp, William Russell, Charlotte Burton, Marie Van Tassell, Harry Keenan

HIGHEST BIDDER, THE (1921)
(6 r.) d, Wallace Worsley; lp, Madge Kennedy, Lionel Atwill, Vernon Steele, Ellen Cassity

HIGHEST LAW, THE (1921)
(6 r.) d, Ralph Ince; lp, Ralph Ince, Robert Agnew, Margaret Seddon, Aleen Burr

HIGHEST TRUMP, THE (1919)
(5 r.) d, James Young; lp, Earle Williams, Grace Darmond, Robert Byrem, John Cossar

HIGHWAY OF HOPE, THE (1917)
(5 r.) d, Howard Estabrook; lp, Kathlyn Williams, House Peters, Jim Farley, Harry De Vere

HI-JACKING RUSTLERS (1926)
(5 r.) d, Bennett Cohn; lp, Jack Perrin, Josephine Hill, Billy Lamar, Leonard Trainor

HILDE WARREN AND DEATH (1916, Ger.)
(? r.) d, Joe May; lp, Mia May, Bruno Kastner, Fritz Lang, Georg John

HILL BILLY, THE (1924)
(6 r.) d, George Hill; lp, Jack Pickford, Lucille Ricksen, Frank Leigh, Ralph Yearsley

HILLCREST MYSTERY, THE (1918)
(5 r.) d, George Fitzmaurice; lp, Irene Castle, J.H. Gilmour, Ralph Kellard, Wyndham Standing

HILLS OF HATE (1921)
(5 r.) lp, Jack Hoxie

HILLS OF PERIL (1927)
(5 r.) d, Lambert Hillyer; lp, Buck Jones, Georgia Hale, Albert J. Smith, Buck Black

HINDLE WAKES (1918, Brit.)
(5 r.) d, Maurice Elvey; lp, Norman McKinnel, Colette O'Neil, Hayford Hobbs, Ada King

HINDLE WAKES
(SEE: FANNY HAWTHORNE, 1927, Brit.)

HINDU TOMB, THE
(SEE: MYSTERIES OF INDIA, 1922, Ger.)

HINTON'S DOUBLE (1917)
(5 r.) d, Ernest Warde; lp, Frederick Warde, Kathlyn Adams, Eldean Steuart, Wayne Arey

HIRED MAN, THE (1918)
(5 r.) d, Victor L. Schertzinger; lp, Charles Ray, Doris Lee, Charles French, Robert Gordon

HIS BACK AGAINST THE WALL (1922)
(5 r.) d, Rowland V. Lee; lp, Raymond Hatton, Virginia Valli, Will Walling, Gordon Russell

HIS BIRTHRIGHT (1918)
(5 r.) d, William Worthington; lp, Sessue Hayakawa, Marin Sais, Howard Davies, Mary Anderson

HIS BONDED WIFE (1918)
(5 r.) d, Charles J. Brabin; lp, Emmy Wehlen, Creighton Hale, Frank Currier, John Terry

HIS BRIDAL NIGHT (1919)
(5 r.) d, Kenneth Webb; lp, Alice Brady, Edward Earle, James L. Crane, Daniel Pennell

HIS BROTHER'S KEEPER (1921)
(6 r.) d, Wilfrid North; lp, Albert L. Barrett, Martha Mansfield, Rogers Lytton, Frazer Coulter

HIS BROTHER'S WIFE (1916)
(5 r.) d, Harley Knoles; lp, Carlyle Blackwell, Ethel Clayton, Paul McAllister, Charles Gerard

HIS BUDDY'S WIFE (1925)
(6 r.) d, Tom Terriss; lp, Glenn Hunter, Edna Murphy, Gordon Begg, Harlan Knight

HIS CALL
(SEE: BROKEN CHAINS, 1925, USSR)

HIS CHILDREN'S CHILDREN (1923)
(8 r.) d, Sam Wood; lp, Bebe Daniels, Dorothy Mackaill, James Rennie, George Fawcett

HIS COUNTRY'S HONOUR
(SEE: AVIATOR SPY, THE, 1914, Brit.)

HIS DAUGHTER'S DILEMMA (1916, Brit.)
(5 r.) d, Ralph Dewsbury; lp, Ben Webster, Manora Thew, Philip Hewland, Gwynne Herbert

HIS DAUGHTER'S SECOND HUSBAND (1916)
(5 r.)

HIS DEAREST POSSESSION (1919, Brit.)
(5 r.) d, Henry Edwards; lp, Henry Edwards, Chrissie White, John McAndrews, Esme Hubbard

HIS DEBT (1919)
(5 r.) d, William Worthington; lp, Sessue Hayakawa, Jane Novak, Francis J. McDonald, Fred Montague

HIS DIVORCED WIFE (1919)
(6 r.) d, Douglas Gerrard; lp, Monroe Salisbury, Charles West, Charles Le Moyne, Alfred Allen

HIS DOG (1927)
(7 r.) d, Karl Brown; lp, Joseph Schildkraut, Julia Faye, Crauford Kent, Annabelle Magnus

HIS ENEMY THE LAW (1918)
(5 r.) d, Raymond Wells; lp, Jack Richardson, Irene Hunt, Jack Livingston, Graham Pettie

HIS ENEMY'S DAUGHTER
(SEE: MODERN MONTE CRISTO, A, 1917)

HIS EYES (1916, USSR)
(5 r.) d, Vyacheslav Viskovsky; lp, A. Rudnitsky, M. Moravskaya, Vera Soloviova

HIS FATHER'S WIFE (1919)
(5 r.) d, Frank Crane; lp, June Elvidge, Sam B. Hardy, Malcon Fassatt, W.T. Carleton

HIS FIRST FLAME (1927)
(6 r.) d, Harry Edwards; lp, Harry Langdon, Ruth Hiatt, Natalie Kingston, Vernon Dent

HIS FOREIGN WIFE (1927)
(5 r.) d, John P. McCarthy; lp, Greta von Rue, Edna Murphy, Wallace MacDonald, Charles Clary

HIS FORGOTTEN WIFE (1924)
(6 r.) d, William Seiter; lp, Madge Bellamy, Warner Baxter, Maude Wayne, Hazel Keener

HIS GRACE GIVES NOTICE (1924, Brit.)
(6 r.) d, W.P. Kellino; lp, Nora Swinburne, Henry Victor, John Stuart, Eric Bransby Williams

HIS GREAT CHANCE (1923)
(5 r.) lp, Sandy Burns, Fannetta Burns, Bobby Smart, Tim Moore

HIS GREAT TRIUMPH (1916)
(5 r.) d, William Nigh; lp, William Nigh, Marguerite Snow, Julius D. Cowles, Roy Appelgate

HIS GREATEST BATTLE (1925)
(5 r.) d, Robert J. Horner; lp, Jack Randall, Kit Carson, Jack Richardson, Pauline Curley

HER GREATEST BLUFF (1927, Ger.)
(? r.) d, Harry Piel; lp, Harry Piel, Tony Tetzlaff, Lotte Lorring, Albert Pauling

HIS GREATEST SACRIFICE (1921)
(7 r.) d, J. Gordon Edwards; lp, William Farnum, Alice Fleming, Lorena Volare, Evelyn Greeley

HIS HOUSE IN ORDER (1920)
(5 r.) d, Hugh Ford; lp, Elsie Ferguson, Holmes Herbert, Vernon Steele, Margaret Linden

HIS LAST BULLET (1928)
(5 r.) lp, Al Hoxie

HIS LAST DEFENCE (1919, Brit.)
(5 r.) d, Geoffrey Wilmer; lp, Dennis Neilson-Terry, Mary Glynne, Alfred Bishop, Cyril Raymond

HIS LAST HAUL (1928)
(6 r.) d, Marshall Neilan; lp, Tom Moore, Seena Owen, Charles Mason, Al Roscoe

HIS LAST RACE (1923)
(6 r.) d, Reeves Eason; lp, Rex "Snowy" Baker, Gladys Brockwell, William Scott, Harry Depp

HIS MAJESTY BUNKER BEAN (1918)
(5 r.) d, William D. Taylor; lp, Jack Pickford, Louise Huff, Jack McDonald, Frances Clanton

HIS MAJESTY BUNKER BEAN (1925)
(8 r.) d, Harry Beaumont; lp, Matt Moore, Dorothy Devore, David Butler, George Nichols

HIS MAJESTY THE OUTLAW (1924)
(5 r.) d, Jacques Jaccard; lp, Ben Wilson, Violet La Plante

HIS MAJESTY, THE SCARECROW OF OZ (1914)
(5 r.) d, J. Farrell MacDonald; lp, Frank Moore, Vivian Reed, Fred Woodward, Mae Wells

HIS MOTHER'S BOY (1917)
(5 r.) d, Victor L. Schertzinger; lp, Charles Ray, Doris Lee, William Elmer, Joseph Swickard

HIS MYSTERY GIRL (1923)
(5 r.) d, Robert F. Hill; lp, Herbert Rawlinson, Ruth Dwyer, Margaret Campbell, Jere Austin

HIS NEW YORK WIFE (1926)
(6 r.) d, Albert Kelley; lp, Alice Day, Theodore von Eltz, Ethel Clayton, Fontaine La Rue

HIS NIBS (1921)
(5 r.) d, Gregory La Cava; lp, Charles [Chic] Sale, Colleen Moore, Joseph Dowling, J.P. Lockney

HIS OFFICIAL FIANCEE (1919)
(5 r.) d, Robert G. Vignola; lp, Vivian Martin, Forrest Stanley, Mollie McConnell, Vera Sisson

HIS OLD-FASHIONED DAD (1917)
(4 r.) lp, Daniel Gilfether, Mollie McConnell, Richard Johnson, Lucy Payton

HIS OTHER WIFE (1921, Brit.)
(5 r.) d, Percy Nash; lp, Eileen Magrath, Jack Raymond, Maria Minetti, Dennis Cowles

HIS OWN HOME TOWN (1918)
(5 r.) d, Victor L. Schertzinger; lp, Charles Ray, Katherine MacDonald, Charles French, Otto Hoffman

HIS OWN LAW (1920)
(7 r.) d, J. Parker Read; lp, Hobart Bosworth, Rowland Lee, Jean Calhoun, Frank Brownlee

HIS OWN LAW (1924)
(5 r.) lp, Wesley Barry

HIS OWN PEOPLE (1918)
(5 r.) d, William P.S. Earle; lp, Harry Morey, Gladys Leslie, Arthur Donaldson, William Dunn

HIS PAJAMA GIRL (1921)
(5 r.) lp, Billie Rhodes, Harry Rattenberry, Harry Edwards, George French

HIS PARISIAN WIFE (1919)
(5 r.) d, Emile Chautard; lp, Elsie Ferguson, David Powell, Courtenay Foote, Frank Losee

HIS PEOPLE (1925)
(9 r.) d, Edward Sloman; lp, Rudolph Schildkraut, Rosa Rosanova, George Lewis, Bobby Gordon

HIS PICTURE IN THE PAPERS (1916)
(5 r.) d, John Emerson; lp, Douglas Fairbanks, Loretta Blake, Clarence Handysides, Rene Boucicault

HIS PRIVATE LIFE (1928)
(5 r.) d, Frank Tuttle; lp, Adolphe Menjou, Kathryn Carver, Margaret Livingston, Eugene Pallette

HIS RISE TO FAME (1927)
(6 r.) d, Bernard McEveety; lp, George Walsh, Peggy Shaw, Bradley Barker, Mildred Reardon

HIS ROYAL HIGHNESS (1918)
(5 r.) d, Carlyle Blackwell; lp, Carlyle Blackwell, Evelyn Greeley, Kate Lester

HIS SISTER'S CHAMPION (1916)
(5 r.) d, John H. Collins

HIS SUPREME MOMENT (1925)
(8 r.) d, George Fitzmaurice; lp, Blanche Sweet, Ronald Colman, Kathleen Myers, Belle Bennett

HIS SUPREME SACRIFICE (1922, Brit.)
(5 r.) d, Bert Wynne; lp, Doris Eaton, Warwick Ward, Walter Tennyson, Dorinea Shirley

HIS SWEETHEART (1917)
(5 r.) d, Donald Crisp; lp, George Beban, Helen Jerome Eddy, Harry De Vere, Kathleen Kirkham

HIS TEMPORARY WIFE (1920)
(6 r.) d, Joseph Levering; lp, Mary Boland, Edmund Breese, Rubye De Remer, Eugene Strong

HIS TIGER LADY (1928)
(5 r.) d, Hobart Henley; lp, Adolphe Menjou, Evelyn Brent, Rose Dione, Emil Chautard

HIS TURNING POINT (1915)
(5 r.) lp, Leatrice Joy, Andrew A. Rogers

HIS VINDICATION (1915, Brit.)
(4 r.) d, Ralph Dewsbury; lp, Gerald Ames, Blanche Bryan, Charles Rock, Philip Hewland

HIS WIFE (1915)
(5 r.) d, George Foster Platt; lp, Geraldine O'Brien, H.E. Herbert, Lorraine Huling, Inda Palmer

HIS WIFE'S FRIEND (1920)
(5 r.) d, Joseph De Grasse; lp, Dorothy Dalton, Warren Cook, Henry Mortimer, Richard Neill

HIS WIFE'S GOOD NAME (1916)
(5 r.) lp, Lucille Lee Stewart, Jessie Miller, Huntley Gordon, Frank Currier

HIS WIFE'S HUSBAND (1913, Pol.)
(4 r.) d, Avrom Yitskhok Kaminsky; lp, Vera Zoslovsky, Misha Fishzon, Israel Arko, Isaac Samberg

HIS WIFE'S HUSBAND (1922, Brit.)
(4 r.) d, George A. Cooper; lp, Madge Stuart, Olaf Hytten, M.A. Wetherell, Ralph Forster

HIS WIFE'S HUSBAND (1922)
(6 r.) d, Kenneth Webb; lp, Betty Blythe, Huntley Gordon, Arthur Carewe, George Fawcett

HIS WIFE'S MONEY (1920)
(5 r.) d, Ralph Ince; lp, Eugene O'Brien, Zena Keefe, Ned Hay, Louise Prussing

HIT AND RUN (1924)
(6 r.) d, Edward Sedgwick; lp, Hoot Gibson, Marion Harlan, Cyril Ring, Harold Goodwin

HIT OF THE SHOW (1928)
(7 r.) d, Ralph Ince

HIT OR MISS (1919)
(5 r.) d, Dell Henderson; lp, Carlyle Blackwell, Evelyn Greeley, Charles Sutton, Jack Drumier

HITCHIN' POSTS (1920)
(5 r.) d, Jack [John] Ford; lp, Frank Mayo, Beatrice Burnham, Joe Harris, J. Farrell MacDonald

HIT-THE-TRAIL HOLLIDAY (1918)
(5 r.) d, Marshall Neilan; lp, George M. Cohan, Marguerite Clayton, Robert Broderick, Pat O'Malley

HITTING THE HIGH SPOTS (1918)
(5 r.) d, Charles Swickard; lp, Bert Lytell, Eileen Percy, Winter Hall, Helen Dunbar

HITTING THE TRAIL (1918)
(5 r.) d, Dell Henderson; lp, Carlyle Blackwell, Evelyn Greeley, Joseph Smiley, George McQuarrie

HOARDED ASSETS (1918)
(5 r.) d, Paul Scardon; lp, Harry T. Morey, Betty Blythe, George Majeroni, Robert Gaillard

HOBBS IN A HURRY (1918)
(6 r.) d, Henry King; lp, William Russell, Winifred Westover, Henry Barrows, Richard Morris

HOBSON'S CHOICE (1920, Brit.)
(6 r.) d, Percy Nash; lp, Joe Nightingale, Joan Ritz, Arthur Pitt, Joan Cockram

HOGAN'S ALLEY (1925)
(7 r.) d, Roy Del Ruth; lp, Monte Blue, Patsy Ruth Miller, Willard Louis, Louise Fazenda

HOLD THAT LION (1926)
(6 r.) d, William Beaudine; lp, Douglas MacLean, Walter Hiers, Constance Howard, Cyril Chadwick

HOLD YOUR BREATH (1924)
(6 r.) d, Scott Sidney; lp, Dorothy Devore, Walter Hiers, Tully Marshall, Jimmie Adams

HOLD YOUR HORSES (1921)
(5 r.) d, E. Mason Hopper; lp, Tom Moore, Sylvia Ashton, Naomi Childers, Bertram Grassby

HOLE IN THE WALL, THE (1921)
(6 r.) d, Maxwell Karger; lp, Alice Lake, Allan Forrest, Frank Brownlee, Charles Clary

HOLLOW OF HER HAND, THE
(SEE: IN THE HOLLOW OF HER HAND, 1918)

HOLLYWOOD (1923)
(8 r.) d, James Cruze; lp, Hope Drown, Luke Cosgrave, Mary Astor, Cecil B. De Mille

HOLLYWOOD REPORTER, THE (1926)
(5 r.) d, Bruce Mitchell; lp, Frank Merrill, Charles K. French, Peggy Montgomery, William Hayes

HOLY SINNER, THE (1929)
(6 r.)

HOME (1915, Brit.)
(4 r.) d, Maurice Elvey; lp, Fred Groves, A.V. Bramble, M. Gray Murray, E. Compton Coutts

HOME (1919)
(6 r.) d, Lois Weber; lp, Mildred Harris, Frank Elliott, John Cossar, Clarissa Selwynne

HOME JAMES (1928)
(7 r.) d, William Beaudine; lp, Laura La Plante, Charles Delaney, Aileen Manning, Joan Standing

HOME MADE (1927)
(7 r.) d, Charles Hines; lp, Johnny Hines, Margaret Seddon, De Witt Jennings, Maude Turner Gordon

HOME MAKER, THE (1925)
(8 r.) d, King Baggot; lp, Alice Joyce, Clive Brook, Billy Kent Schaeffer, George Fawcett

HOME STRETCH, THE (1921)
(5 r.) d, Jack Nelson; lp, Douglas MacLean, Beatrice Burnham, Walt Whitman, Margaret Livingston

HOME TALENT (1921)
(5 r.) d, Mack Sennett; lp, Charlie Murray, Ben Turpin, James Finlayson, Eddie Gribbon

HOME TOWN GIRL, THE (1919)
(5 r.) d, Robert G. Vignola; lp, Vivian Martin, Ralph Graves, Lee Phelps, Carmen Phillips

HOME TRAIL, THE (1918)
(5 r.) d, William Wolbert; lp, Nell Shipman, Alfred Whitman, Joe Rickson, Patricia Palmer

HOME WANTED (1919)
(5 r.) d, Tefft Johnson; lp, Madge Evans, W.T. Carleton, Anna Lehr, Jack Drumier

HOMEBREAKER, THE (1919)
(5 r.) d, Victor Schertzinger; lp, Dorothy Dalton, Douglas MacLean, Edwin Stevens, Frank Leigh

HOMECOMING (1929, Ger.)
(8 r.) d, Joe May

HOME-KEEPING HEARTS (1921)
(5 r.) d, Carlyle Ellis; lp, Thomas H. Swinton, Mary Ryan, Louella Carr, Edward Grace

HOMEMAKER, THE (1919, Brit.)
(5 r.) d, George Dewhurst; lp, Manora Thew, Basil Gill, Gwynne Herbert, Peggy Patterson

HOMER COMES HOME (1920)
(5 r.) d, Jerome Storm; lp, Charles Ray, Priscilla Bonner, Otto Hoffman, Ralph McCullough

HOMESPUN FOLKS (1920)
(6 r.) d, John Griffith Wray; lp, Lloyd Hughes, Gladys George, George Webb, Al Filson

HOMESTEADER, THE (1922)
(7 r.) lp, Evelyn Preer

HOMEWARD BOUND (1923)
(7 r.) d, Ralph Ince; lp, Thomas Meighan, Lila Lee, Charles Abbe, William P. Carleton

HONEST HUTCH (1920)
(5 r.) d, Clarence Badger; lp, Will Rogers, Mary Alden, Priscilla Bonner, Tully Marshall

HONEST MAN, AN (1918)
(5 r.) d, Frank Borzage; lp, William Desmond, Ann Kroman, Mary Warren, Graham Pettie

HONESTY-THE BEST POLICY (1926)
(5 r.) d, Chester Bennett; lp, Rockcliffe Fellowes, Pauline Starke, Albert Gran, Johnnie Walker

HONEY BEE, THE (1920)
(6 r.) d, Rupert Julian; lp, Thomas Holding, Nigel Barrie, Marguerite Sylva, Albert Ray

HONEYMOON, THE (1917)
(5 r.) d, Charles Giblyn; lp, Constance Talmadge, Earle Foxe, Maude Turner Gordon, Russell Bassett

HONEYMOON ABROAD (1929, Brit.)
(6 r.) d, Tim Whelan

HONEYMOON EXPRESS, THE (1926)
(7 r.) d, James Flood; lp, Willard Louis, Irene Rich, Holmes Herbert, Helene Costello

HONEYMOON HATE (1927)
(6 r.) d, Luther Reed; lp, Florence Vidor, Tullio Carminati, William Austin, Corliss Palmer

HONEYMOON RANCH (1920)
(5 r.) d, Robin Townley; lp, Allene Ray, Harry McLaughlin, John B. Hagin, Tex O'Reilly

HONEYPOT, THE (1920, Brit.)
(6 r.) d, Fred Leroy Granville; lp, Peggy Hyland, Campbell Gullan, James Lindsay, Lilian Hall Davis

HONNEUR D'ARTISTE (1917, Fr.)
(? r.) d, Jean Kemm

HONOR AMONG MEN (1924)
(5 r.) d, Denison Clift; lp, Edmund Lowe, Claire Adams, Sheldon Lewis, Diana Miller

HONOR BOUND (1920)
(5 r.) d, Jacques Jaccard; lp, Frank Mayo, Edward Coxen, Dagmar Godowsky, Nick De Ruiz

HONOR BOUND (1928)
(7 r.) d, Alfred E. Green; lp, George O'Brien, Estelle Taylor, Leila Hyams, Tom Santschi

HONOR FIRST (1922)
(5 r.) d, Jerome Storm; lp, John Gilbert, Renee Adoree, Hardee Kirkland, Shannon Day

HONOR OF HIS HOUSE, THE (1918)
(5 r.) d, William C. De Mille; lp, Sessue Hayakawa, Florence Vidor, Jack Holt, Mayme Kelso

HONOR OF MARY BLAKE, THE (1916)
(5 r.) d, Edwin Stevens; lp, Violet Meresereau, Tina Marshall, Caroline Harris, Sidney Mason

HONOR SYSTEM, THE (1917)
(10 r.)

HONOR THY NAME (1916)
(5 r.) d, Charles Giblyn; lp, Frank Keenan, Louise Glaum, Charles Ray, Blanche White

HONORABLE ALGY, THE (1916)
(5 r.) d, Raymond B. West; lp, Charles Ray, Margery Wilson, Margaret Thompson, Howard Hickman

HONORABLE FRIEND, THE (1916)
(5 r.) d, Edward J. LeSaint; lp, Sessue Hayakawa, Tsuru Aoki, Raymond Hatton, Goro Kino

HONOR'S ALTAR (1916)
(5 r.) d, Raymond B. West; lp, Bessie Barriscale, Walter Edwards, Lewis S. Stone, Lola May

HONOR'S CROSS (1918)
(6 r.) d, Wallace Worsley; lp, Rhea Mitchell, Edward Coxen, Herschal Mayall, Joseph J. Dowling

HONOUR IN PAWN (1916, Brit.)
(5 r.) d, Harold Weston; lp, Manora Thew, Julian Royce, George Bellamy, Ivan Berlyn

HOODMAN BLIND (1913)
(5 r.) d, James Gordon; lp, Herbert Barrington, Violet Stewart, Mrs. Guy Standing

HOODMAN BLIND
(SEE: MAN OF SORROW, A, 1916)

HOODMAN BLIND (1923)
(6 r.) d, John Ford; lp, David Butler, Gladys Hulette, Regina Connelly, Frank Campeau

HOODOO ANN (1916)
(5 r.) d, Lloyd Ingraham; lp, Mae Marsh, Robert Harron, William H. Brown, Wilbur Higby

HOODOO RANCH (1926)
(5 r.) d, William Bertram; lp, Buddy Roosevelt

HOOF MARKS (1927)
(5 r.) d, Tenny Wright; lp, Jack Donovan, Edward Brady, Edward Cecil, William Steele

HOOK AND HAND (1914)
(4 r.)

HOOP-LA (1919)
(5 r.) d, Louis W. Chaudet; lp, Billie Rhodes, Bertram Grassby, John Cooke, Val Paul

HOOSIER ROMANCE, A (1918)
(5 r.) d, Colin Campbell; lp, Thomas Jefferson, Colleen Moore, Harry McCoy, Edward Robson

HOOSIER SCHOOLMASTER, THE (1924)
(6 r.) d, Oliver L. Sellers; lp, Henry Hull, Jane Thomas, Frank Dane, Mary Foy

HOPE
(SEE: SWEETHEARTS, 1919, Brit.)

HOPE, THE (1920)
(6 r.) d, Herbert Blache; lp, Jack Mulhall, Marguerite de la Motte, Ruth Stonehouse, Frank Elliott

HOPE CHEST, THE (1918)
(5 r.) d, Elmer Clifton; lp, Dorothy Gish, Richard Barthelmess, George Fawcett, Sam De Grasse

HOPPER, THE (1918)
(5 r.) d, Thomas N. Heffron; lp, Irene Hunt, William V. Mong, Thomas Kurihara, George Hernandez

HORNET'S NEST, THE (1919)
(5 r.) d, James Young; lp, Earle Williams, Brinsley Shaw, Vola Vale, Ogden Crane

HORNET'S NEST (1923, Brit.)
(6 r.) d, Walter West; lp, Florence Turner, Fred Wright, Nora Swinburne, James Knight

HORSE ON BROADWAY, A (1926)
(6 r.)

HORSE SENSE (1924)
(5 r.) d, Ward Hayes; lp, Richard Hatton, Marilyn Mills, Elias Bullock, Leon Kent

HORSE SHOES (1927)
(6 r.) d, Clyde Bruckman; lp, Monty Banks, Ernie Wood, Henry Barrows, John Elliott

HORSEMAN OF THE PLAINS, A (1928)
(5 r.) d, Benjamin Stoloff; lp, Tom Mix, Sally Blane, Heinie Conklin, Charles Byer

HORSESHOE LUCK (1924)
(5 r.) d, Joseph Franz; lp, J.B. Warner, Margaret Morris, Harry Todd

HOSTAGE, THE (1917)
(5 r.) d, Robert Thornby; lp, Wallace Reid, Dorothea Abril, Gertrude Short, C.H. Geldert

HOT HEELS (1928)
(6 r.) d, William James Craft; lp, Glenn Tryon, Patsy Ruth Miller, Greta Yoltz, James Bradbury, Sr.

HOTEL IMPERIAL (1927)
(8 r.) d, Mauritz Stiller; lp, Pola Negri, James Hall, George Siegmann, Max Davidson

HOTTENTOT, THE (1922)
(6 r.) d, James W. Horne; lp, Douglas MacLean, Madge Bellamy, Lila Leslie, Martin Best

HOUND OF THE BASKERVILLES, THE (1914, Ger.)
(? r.) d, Rudolf Meinert; lp, Alwin Neuss, Erwin Fichtner, Friedrich Kuhne, Andreas Van Horne

HOUND OF THE BASKERVILLES, THE (1917, Ger.)
(? r.) d, Richard Oswald

HOUND OF THE BASKERVILLES, THE (1921, Brit.)
(6 r.) d, Maurice Elvey; lp, Eille Norwood, Catina Campbell, Rex McDougall, Lewis Gilbert

HOUND OF THE BASKERVILLES, THE (1929, Ger.)
(? r.) d, Richard Oswald; lp, Carlyle Blackwell, Livio Pavanelli, Alexander Mursky, Georges Seroff

HOUND OF THE SILVER CREEK, THE (1928)
(5 r.) d, Stuart Paton; lp, Dynamite (a dog), Edmund Cobb, Gloria Grey, Gladden James

HOUR OF RECKONING, THE (1927)
(6 r.) d, John E. Ince; lp, John E. Ince, Herbert Rawlinson, Grace Darmond, Harry Von Meter

HOUR OF THE TRIAL, THE (1920, Brit.)
(5 r.) d, A.E. Coleby; lp, Cecil Humphreys, Janet Alexander, Maud Yates, Percy Rhodes

HOUSE BEHIND THE CEDARS, THE (1927)
(9 r.) lp, Andrew S. Bishop, Shingzie Howard, William Crowell, Lawrence Chenault

HOUSE BUILT UPON SAND, THE (1917)
(5 r.) d, Ed Morrissey; lp, Lillian Gish, Roy Stewart, William H. Brown, Bessie Buskirk

HOUSE DIVIDED, A (1919)
(5 r.) d, J. Stuart Blackton; lp, Sylvia Breamer, Herbert Rawlinson, Lawrence Grossmith, Shirley Huxley

HOUSE IN THE SNOW-DRIFTS, THE (1928, USSR)
(6 r.) d, Friedrich Ermler; lp, Valeri Solovtsov, Fyodor Nitkin, Yakov Gudkin

HOUSE OF A THOUSAND CANDLES, THE (1915)
(6 r.) d, T.N. Heffron; lp, Grace Darmond, Harry Mestayer, George Backus, John Charles

HOUSE OF DARKENED WINDOWS, THE (1925)
(5 r.) lp, Lark Brownlee

HOUSE OF FEAR, THE (1915)
(5 r.) d, Arnold Daly, Ashley Miller; lp, Arnold Daly, Sheldon Lewis, Ina Hammer, Martin Sabine

HOUSE OF GLASS, THE (1918)
(5 r.) d, Emile Chautard; lp, Clara Kimball Young, Pell Trenton, Corliss Giles, Edward Kimball

HOUSE OF GOLD, THE (1918)
(5 r.) d, Edwin Carewe; lp, Emmy Wehlen, Joseph Kilgour, Hugh Thompson, Helen Lindroth

HOUSE OF LIES, THE (1916)
(5 r.) d, William D. Taylor; lp, Edna Goodrich, Juan de la Cruz, Kathleen Kirkham, Lucille Ward

HOUSE OF MARNEY (1926, Brit.)
(7 r.) d, Cecil M. Hepworth; lp, Alma Taylor, John Longden, James Carew, Patrick Susands

HOUSE OF MIRRORS, THE (1916)
(5 r.) d, Marshall Farnum; lp, Bliss Milford, Frank Mills, Lillian Kemble, J. Frank Glendon

HOUSE OF MIRTH, THE (1918)
(5 r.) d, Albert Capellani; lp, Katherine Harris Barrymore, Joseph Kilgour, Henry Kolker, Christine Mayo

HOUSE OF PERIL, THE (1922, Brit.)
(5 r.) d, Kenelm Foss; lp, Fay Compton, Roy Travers, A.B. Imeson, Madeleine Seymour

HOUSE OF SCANDAL, THE (1928)
(6 r.) d, King Baggot; lp, Pat O'Malley, Dorothy Sebastian, Harry Murray, Gino Corrado

HOUSE OF SHAME, THE (1928)
(6 r.) d, Burton Young; lp, Creighton Hale, Virginia Browne Faire, Lloyd Whittock, Florence Dudley

HOUSE OF SILENCE, THE (1918)
(5 r.) d, Donald Crisp; lp, Wallace Reid, Ann Little, Adele Farrington, Winter Hall

HOUSE OF TEARS, THE (1915)
(5 r.) d, Edwin Carewe; lp, Emily Stevens, Henry Bergman, Walter Hitchcock, Madge Tyrone

HOUSE OF THE GOLDEN WINDOWS, THE (1916)
(5 r.) d, George Melford; lp, Wallace Reid, Cleo Ridgeley, Billy Jacobs, James Neill

HOUSE OF THE TOLLING BELLS, THE (1920)
(6 r.) d, J. Stuart Blackton; lp, May McAvoy, Bruce Gordon, Morgan Thorpe, Edward Elkas

HOUSE OF TOYS, THE (1920)
(6 r.) d, George L. Cox; lp, Seena Owen, Pell Trenton, Helen Jerome Eddy, Lillian Leighton

HOUSE OF WHISPERS, THE (1920)
(5 r.) d, Ernest C. Warde; lp, J. Warren Kerrigan, Joseph Dowling, Fritzi Brunette, Marjorie Wilson

HOUSE ON CEDAR HILL, THE (1926)
(? r.) d, Carlton Moss;

HOUSE ON TRUBNAYA SQUARE (1928, USSR)
(6 r.) d, Boris Barnet; lp, Vera Maretskaya, Vladimir Fogel, Anna Sudakevich, Yelena Tyapkina

HOUSE OPPOSITE, THE (1917, Brit.)
(4 r.) d, Frank Wilson; lp, Matheson Lang, Violet Hopson, Ivy Close, Gregory Scott

HOUSE THAT JAZZ BUILT, THE (1921)
(6 r.) d, Penrhyn Stanlaws; lp, Wanda Hawley, Forrest Stanley, Gladys George, Helen Lynch

HOUSE WITH THE GOLDEN WINDOWS, THE (1916)
(5 r.)

HOUSE WITHOUT CHILDREN, THE (1919)
(6 r.) d, Samuel Brodsky; lp, Richard Travers, Gretchen Hartman, George Fox, Helen Weer [Weir]

HOW BAXTER BUTTED IN (1925)
(7 r.) d, William Beaudine; lp, Dorothy Devore, Matt Moore, Ward Crane, Wilfred Lucas

HOW COULD YOU, CAROLINE? (1918)
(5 r.) d, Frederick Thompson; lp, Bessie Love, James Morrison, Dudley Hawley, Henry Hallam

HOW COULD YOU, JEAN? (1918)
(5 r.) d, William D. Taylor; lp, Mary Pickford, Casson Ferguson, Herbert Standing, Spottiswoode Aitken

HOW COULD YOU UNCLE? (1918, Brit.)
(5 r.) d, Maurice Sandground; lp, Bob Reed, Rowland Hill

HOW KITCHENER WAS BETRAYED (1921, Brit.)
(6 r.) d, Percy Nash; lp, Fred Paul, Peggy Hathaway, Bertram Burleigh, Ion Swinley

HOW MEN LOVE WOMEN (1915, Brit.)
(4 r.) d, Percy Moran; lp, Percy Moran, Marietta de Leyse

HOW TO EDUCATE A WIFE (1924)
(7 r.) d, Monta Bell; lp, Marie Prevost, Monte Blue, Claude Gillingwater, Vera Lewis

HOW TO HANDLE WOMEN (1928)
(6 r.) d, William J. Craft; lp, Glenn Tryon, Marian Nixon, Raymond Keane, Mario Carillo

HOW WOMEN LOVE (1922)
(6 r.) d, Kenneth Webb; lp, Betty Blythe, Gladys Hulette, Julia Swayne Gordon, Katherine Stewart

HUGON THE MIGHTY (1918)
(5 r.) d, Rollin S. Sturgeon; lp, Monroe Salisbury, Margery Bennett, Antrim Short, Thomas H. Persse

HULA (1927)
(6 r.) d, Victor Fleming; lp, Clara Bow, Clive Brook, Arlette Marchal, Arnold Kent

HULDA FROM HOLLAND (1916)
(5 r.) d, John B. O'Brien; lp, Mary Pickford, Frank Losee, John Bowers, Russell Bassett

HUMAN CARGO (1929, Brit.)
(4 r.) d, J. Steven Edwards; lp, David Dunbar, Ella Atherton, Eric Hales, Lionel Roberts

HUMAN COLLATERAL (1920)
(5 r.) d, Lawrence C. Windom; lp, Corinne Griffith, Webster Campbell, Maurice Costello, W.T. Carleton

HUMAN DESIRE, THE (1919)
(6 r.) d, Wilfred North; lp, Anita Stewart, Conway Tearle, Eulalie Jensen, Naomi Childers

HUMAN DRIFTWOOD (1916)
(5 r.) d, Emile Chautard; lp, Robert Warwick, Frances Nelson, Leonore Harris, Alec B. Francis

HUMAN HEARTS (1922)
(7 r.) d, King Baggot; lp, House Peters, Russell Simpson, Gertrude Claire, George Hackathorne

HUMAN LAW (1926, Brit.)
(7 r.) d, Maurice Elvey; lp, Isobel Elsom, Alfred Abel, Paul Richter

HUMAN ORCHID, THE (1916)
(5 r.) d, C.C. Field; lp, Irva Ross, Walter Miller, Charles Graham, Howard Hall

HUMAN PASSIONS (1919)
(6 r.) d, Jacques Tyrol; lp, Lottie Tilford

HUMAN SUFFERING (1923, Jap.)
(4 r.) d, Kensaku Suzuki

HUMAN TERROR, THE (1924)
(5 r.) lp, Alec B. Francis, Margaret Seddon

HUMAN TORNADO, THE (1925)
(5 r.) d, Ben Wilson; lp, Yakima Canutt, Bert Sprotte, Nancy Leeds, Lafe McKee

HUMAN WRECKAGE (1923)
(8 r.) d, John Griffith Wray; lp, Mrs. Wallace Reid, James Kirkwood, Bessie Love, George Hackathorne

HUMANITY (1917)
(6 r.) lp, Bronco Billy Anderson

HUMANIZING MR. WINSBY (1916)
(5 r.) lp, George N. Chesebro, Julius Frankenberg, Arthur Millett, Alice Neice

HUMDRUM BROWN (1918)
(5 r.) d, Rex Ingram; lp, Henry B. Walthall, Mary Charleson, Dorothy Love Clark, Howard Crampton

HUMMING BIRD, THE (1924)
(8 r.) d, Sidney Olcott; lp, Gloria Swanson, Edward Burns, William Ricciardi, Cesare Gravina

HUMORESQUE (1920)
(6 r.) d, Frank Borzage; lp, Vera Gordon, Dore Davidson, Alma Rubens, Gaston Glass

HUNCHBACK AND THE DANCER, THE (1920, Ger.)
(? r.) d, F.W. Murnau; lp, Conrad Veidt, Lyda Salmanova, Sascha Gura

HUNDRETH CHANCE, THE (1920, Brit.)
(7 r.) d, Maurice Elvey; lp, Dennis Neilson-Terry, Mary Glynne, Eille Norwood, Sydney Seaward

HUNGARIAN NABOB, THE (1915)
(4 r.)

HUNGER OF THE BLOOD, THE (1921)
(5 r.) d, Nate Watt; lp, Franklyn Farnum, Ethel Ritchie, Baby Jean O'Rourke

HUNGRY EYES (1918)
(5 r.) d, Rupert Julian; lp, Ruth Clifford, Monroe Salisbury, Rupert Julian, W.H. Bainbridge

HUNGRY HEART, A (1917)
(5 r.) d, Emile Chautard; lp, Alice Brady, Edward Langford, George MacQuarrie, Gerda Holmes

HUNGRY HEART, THE (1917)
(5 r.) d, Robert G. Vignola; lp, Pauline Frederick, Robert Cain, Howard Hall, Eldean Steuart

HUNS WITHIN OUR GATES (1918)
(6 r.) lp, Derwent Hall Caine, Valda Valkyrien, Harry Robinson, Robin Townley

HUNTED WOMAN, THE (1916)
(5 r.) d, S. Rankin Drew; lp, Virginia Pearson, S. Rankin Drew, Frank Currier, George Cooper

HUNTED WOMAN, THE (1925)
(5 r.) d, Jack Conway; lp, Seena Owen, Earl Schenck, Diana Miller, Cyril Chadwick

HUNTIN' TROUBLE (1924)
(5 r.) d, Leo D. Maloney; lp, Leo D. Maloney, Bullet (a dog), Josephine Hill

HUNTING OF THE HAWK, THE (1917)
(5 r.) d, George Fitzmaurice; lp, William Courtenay, Marguerite Snow, Robert Clugston

HUNTRESS OF MEN, THE (1916)
(5 r.) d, Lucius Henderson; lp, Mary Fuller, Joseph W. Girard, Sidney Bracey

HURRICANE HAL (1925)
(4 r.) lp, Jack Meehan

HURRICANE HORSEMAN (1925)
(5 r.) d, Robert Eddy; lp, Wally Wales, Jean Arthur, Vester Pegg, Charles Whitaker

HURRICANE HUTCH IN MANY ADVENTURES (1924, Brit.)
(6 r.) d, Charles Hutchinson; lp, Charles Hutchinson, Warwick Ward, Malcolm Tod, Edith Thornton

HURRICANE'S GAL (1922)
(8 r.) d, Allen Holubar; lp, Dorothy Phillips, Robert Ellis, Wallace Beery, James O. Barrows

HUSBAND AND WIFE (1916)
(5 r.) d, Barry O'Neil; lp, Ethel Clayton, Holbrook Blinn, Gerda Holmes, Madge Evans

HUSBAND HUNTER, THE (1920, Brit.)
(6 r.) d, Fred W. Durrant; lp, C.M. Hallard, Madge Titheradge, Tom Reynolds, Minna Grey

HUSBAND HUNTER, THE (1920)
(5 r.) d, Howard M. Mitchell; lp, Eileen Percy, Emory Johnson, Jane Miller, Harry Dunkinson

HUSBANDS AND WIVES (1920)
(6 r.) d, Joseph Levering; lp, Vivian Martin, Hugh Thompson

HUSH (1921)
(6 r.) d, Harry Garson; lp, Clara Kimball Young, J. Frank Glendon, Kathlyn Williams, Jack Pratt

HUSHED HOUR, THE (1920)
(5 r.) d, Edmund Mortimer; lp, Blanche Sweet, Milton Sills, Wilfred Lucas, Winter Hall

HUTCH OF THE U.S.A. (1924)
(5 r.) d, James Chapin; lp, Charles Hutchison, Edith Thornton, Frank Leigh, Ernest Adams

HUTCH--U.S.A.
(SEE: HUTCH OF THE U.S.A., 1924)

HVEM ER HUN? (1914, Den.)
(4 r.) d, Em Gregers; lp, Em Gregers, Nathalie Krause, Jon Iversen

HYPOCRISY (1916)
(6 r.) d, Kenean Buel; lp, Virginia Pearson, Albert Swenson, John Webb Dillon, Ida Darling

HYPOCRITE, THE (1921)
(7 r.)

HYPOCRITES, THE
(SEE: THE MORALS OF WEYBURY, 1916, Brit.)

HYPOCRITES, THE (1923, Brit.)
(5 r.) d, Charles Giblyn; lp, Wyndham Standing, Mary Odette, Lillian Douglas, Sydney Paxton

I.N.R.I
(SEE: CROWN OF THORNS, 1934)

I ACCUSE (1916)
(5 r.) d, William F. Haddock; lp, Alexander Gaden, Helen Marten, W.J. Butler, Henry W. Pemberton

I ACCUSE
(SEE: J'ACCUSE, 1919)

I AM GUILTY (1921)
(7 r.) d, Jack Nelson; lp, Louise Glaum, Mahlon Hamilton, Claire Du Brey, Joseph Kilgour

I AM THE LAW (1922)
(7 r.) d, Edwin Carewe; lp, Alice Lake, Kenneth Harlan, Rosemary Theby, Gaston Glass

I AM THE MAN (1924)
(7 r.) d, Ivan Abramson; lp, Lionel Barrymore, Seena Owen, Gaston Glass, Martin Faust

I AM THE WOMAN (1921)
(5 r.) d, Francis Ford; lp, Texas Guinan

I BELIEVE (1916, Brit.)
(7 r.) d, George L. Tucker; lp, Milton Rosmer, Edna Flugrath, Barbara Everest, Edward O'Neill

I BELIEVE (1918)
(6 r.)

I CAN EXPLAIN (1922)
(5 r.) d, George D. Baker; lp, Gareth Hughes, Bartine Burkett, Grace Darmond, Herbert Hayes

I FLUNKED, BUT... (1930, Jap.)
(? r.) d, Yasujiro Ozu

I HEAR YOU CALLING ME (1919, Brit.)
(5 r.) d, A.E. Coleby; lp, Janet Alexander, Richard Buttery, Baby Shepherd, Eve Marchew

I WANT MY MAN (1925)
(7 r.) d, Lambert Hillyer; lp, Doris Kenyon, Milton Sills, Phyllis Haver, May Allison

I WAS BORN, BUT... (1932, Jap.)
(8 r.) d, Yasujiro Ozu; lp, Tatsuo Saito, Hideo Sugawara, Tokkan Kozo, Mitsuko Yoshikawa

I WILL (1919, Brit.)
(5 r.) d, George Clark; lp, Guy Newall, Ivy Duke, Dorothy Minto, Cyril Raymond

I WILL REPAY
(SEE: SWORDS AND THE WOMAN, 1923, Brit.)

I WILL REPAY (1917)
(5 r.) d, William P.S. Earle; lp, Corinne Griffith, William Dunn, Mary Maurice, Arthur Donaldson

IDEAL LOVE, THE (1921)
(5 r.)

IDLE HANDS (1920)
(6 r.) d, Frank Reicher; lp, Gail Kane, Thurston Hall, J. Herbert Frank, William Bechtel

IDLE TONGUES (1924)
(6 r.) d, Lambert Hillyer; lp, Percy Marmont, Doris Kenyon, Claude Gillingwater, Lucille Ricksen

IDLE WIVES (1916)
(7 r.) d, Lois Weber, Phillips Smalley; lp, Lois Weber, Phillips Smalley, Mary MacLaren, Charles Perley

IDLER, THE (1914)
(5 r.)

IDOL OF PARIS, THE (1914, Brit.)
(4 r.) d, Maurice Elvey; lp, Elizabeth Risdon, Fred Groves, A.V. Bramble, Gordon Dennis

IDOLATORS (1917)
(5 r.) d, Walter Edwards; lp, Louise Glaum, George Webb, Dorcas Matthews, Rollo Lee Hill

IDOLS OF CLAY (1920)
(7 r.) d, George Fitzmaurice; lp, Mae Murray, David Powell, Dorothy Cumming, George Fawcett

IF I WERE KING (1920)
(8 r.) d, J. Gordon Edwards; lp, William Farnum, Betty Ross Clark, Fritz Leiber, Walter Law

IF MARRIAGE FAILS (1925)
(7 r.) d, John Ince; lp, Jacqueline Logan, Belle Bennett, Clive Brook, Jean Hersholt

IF MY COUNTRY SHOULD CALL (1916)
(5 r.) d, Joseph De Grasse; lp, Dorothy Phillips, Lon Chaney, Helen Leslie, Adele Farrington

IF WINTER COMES (1923)
(12 r.) d, Harry Millarde; lp, Percy Marmont, Arthur Metcalfe, Sidney Herbert, Wallace Kolb

IGNORANCE (1916)
(6 r.) d, J.A. Fitzgerald; lp, Earl Metcalfe, Eleanor Black, Ethel Tully, Arthur W. Mathews

IGNORANCE (1922)
(5 r.) lp, Earl Metcalfe

IL TROVATORE (1914)
(6 r.) d, Charles Simone; lp, Jean Thrall, Agnes Mapes, Morgia Litton, Georgette Leland

I'LL BE THERE (1927)
(5 r.) d, Frank Yaconelli; lp, Earle Douglas

I'LL GET HIM YET (1919)
(5 r.) d, Elmer Clifton

I'LL SAY SO (1918)
(5 r.) d, Raoul Walsh; lp, George Walsh, Regina Quinn, William Bailey, James Black

I'LL SHOW YOU THE TOWN (1925)
(8 r.) d, Harry A. Pollard; lp, Reginald Denny, Marion Nixon, Edward Kimball, Lilyan Tashman

ILL-STARRED BABBLE (1915)
(5 r.) lp, Jackie Saunders

ILLUSION OF LOVE (1929)
(5 r.) lp, John Ho, Florence Lee

ILLUSTRIOUS PRINCE, THE (1919)
(5 r.) d, William Worthington; lp, Sessue Hayakawa, Mabel Ballin, Harry Lonsdale, Beverly Traverse

I'M GLAD MY BOY GREW TO BE A SOLDIER (1915)
(5 r.) d, Frank Beal; lp, Harry Mestayer, Eugenie Besserer, Harry De Vere, Guy Oliver

IMAGE MAKER, THE (1917)
(5 r.) d, Eugene Moore; lp, Valkyrien, Harris Gordon, Arthur Bauer, Inda Palmer

IMAGINARY BARON, THE (1927, Ger.)
(? r.) d, Willi Wolff; lp, Reinhold Schunzel, Henry Bender, Julia Serda, Marlene Dietrich

IMAR THE SERVITOR (1914)
(4 r.) lp, William Garwood

IMMORTAL FLAME, THE (1916)
(5 r.) d, Ivan Abramson; lp, Maude Fealy, Paula Shay, Joseph Burke, James Cooley

IMP, THE (1920)
(5 r.) d, Robert Ellis; lp, Elsie Janis, Ethel Stewart, E.J. Radcliffe, Duncan Penwarden

IMPERFECT LOVER, THE (1921, Brit.)
(7 r.) d, Walter West; lp, Violet Hopson, Stewart Rome, Cameron Carr, Sir Simeon Stuart

IMPERSONATION, THE (1916)
(5 r.) lp, Neva Gerber

IMPOSSIBLE SUSAN (1918)
(5 r.) d, Lloyd Ingraham; lp, Margarita Fischer, Jack Mower, Lloyd Hughes, Hayward Mack

IMPOSTER, THE (1926)
(6 r.) d, Chet Withey; lp, Evelyn Brent, Carroll Nye, James Morrison, Frank Leigh

IN A MOMENT OF TEMPTATION (1927)
(6 r.) d, Philip Carle; lp, Charlotte Stevens, Grant Withers, Cornelius Keefe, Marie Walcamp

IN ANOTHER GIRL'S SHOES (1917, Brit.)
(5 r.) d, G.B. Samuelson, Alexander Butler; lp, Mable Love, Ruby Miller, Leo Belcher, Lionel d'Aragon

IN BONDAGE (1919, Brit.)
(5 r.) d, Rex Wilson; lp, Sydney Fairbrother, Haidee Wright, C.M. Hallard

IN BRONCHO LAND (1926)
(5 r.) d, Archie Ricks; lp, Dick Hatton

IN FULL CRY (1921, Brit.)
(6 r.) d, Einer J. Bruun; lp, Gregory Scott, Pauline Peters, Cecil Mannering, Philip Hewland

IN HIS BROTHER'S PLACE (1919)
(5 r.) d, Harry L. Franklin; lp, Hale Hamilton, Marguerite Snow, Mary McIvor, Emmett C. King

IN HOLLAND (1929)
(5 r.) d, Norman Taurog

IN HONOR'S WEB (1919)
(5 r.) d, Paul Scardon; lp, Harry T. Morey, Agnes Ayres, Gladden James, Robert Gaillord

IN JUDGEMENT OF (1918)
(5 r.) d, Will S. Davis; lp, Anna Q. Nilsson, Franklyn Farnum, Herbert Standing, Edward Alexander

IN LOVE WITH LOVE (1924)
(6 r.) d, Rowland V. Lee; lp, Marguerite De La Motte, Allan Forrest, Harold Goodwin, William Austin

IN MIZZOURA (1914)
(5 r.) lp, Burr McIntosh, Raymond Bond, H.D. Blakemore, William Conlon

IN MIZZOURA (1919)
(5 r.) d, Hugh Ford; lp, Robert Warwick, Eileen Percy, Robert Cain, Monte Blue

IN MUSIC LAND (1928)
(4 r.)

IN PURSUIT OF POLLY (1918)
(5 r.) d, Chester Withey; lp, Billie Burke, Thomas Meighan, Frank Losee, A.J. Herbert

IN SEARCH OF A HERO (1926)
(5 r.) d, Duke Worne; lp, Richard Holt, Jane Thomas, Jimmy Harrison, Gerry O'Dell

IN SEARCH OF A HUSBAND (1915, Brit.)
(4 r.) d, Wilfred Noy; lp, Barbara Conrad, Murray Carrington, Frank Hilton

IN SEARCH OF ARCADY (1919)
(5 r.) d, Bertram Bracken; lp, Billie Rhodes, Wellington Playter, Tom Santschi, Kathleen Kirkham

IN SLUMBERLAND (1917)
(5 r.) d, Irvin Willat; lp, Thelma Salter, Laura Sears, Jack Livingston, J.P. Lockney

IN SOCIETY (1921)
(5 r.) lp, Edith Roberts

IN THE BISHOP'S CARRIAGE (1913)
(? r.) d, Edwin S. Porter, J. Searle Dawley; lp, Mary Pickford, David V. Wall, House Peters

IN THE DARK (1915)
(4 r.)

IN THE DAYS OF THE COVERED WAGON (1924)
(5 r.) lp, Francis Ford

IN THE DAYS OF THE MISSIONS
(SEE: YOKE OF GOLD, A, 1916)

IN THE DAYS OF THE THUNDERING HERD (1914)
(5 r.) d, Colin Campbell

IN THE DEVIL'S BOWL
(SEE: DEVIL'S BOWL, THE, 1923)

IN THE DIPLOMATIC SERVICE (1916)
(5 r.) d, Francis X. Bushman; lp, Francis X. Bushman, Beverly Bayne, Helen Dunbar, Henri Bergman

IN THE FIRST DEGREE (1927)
(6 r.) d, Phil Rosen; lp, Alice Calhoun, Bryant Washburn, Gayne Whitman, Trilby Clark

IN THE GLOAMING (1919, Brit.)
(5 r.) d, Edwin J. Collins; lp, Violet Hopson, Jack Jarman, Cameron Carr, Nicholas Hopson

IN THE GRIP OF SPIES (1914, Brit.)
(4 r.) d, H.O. Martinek; lp, H.O. Martinek, Ivy Montford

IN THE GRIP OF THE SULTAN (1915, Brit.)
(4 r.) d, Leon Bary; lp, Miriam Ferris

IN THE HANDS OF THE LAW (1917)
(5 r.) lp, Lois Meredith

IN THE HEART OF A FOOL (1920)
(6 r.) d, Allan Dwan; lp, Mary Thurman, Anna Q. Nilsson, James Kirkwood, Philo McCullough

IN THE HOLLOW OF HER HAND (1918)
(5 r.) d, Charles Maigne; lp, Alice Brady, Percy Marmont, Myrtle Stedman, Louise Clark

IN THE HOUR OF HIS NEED (1925)
(5 r.)

IN THE KINGDOM OF OIL AND MILLIONS (1916, USSR)
(8 r.) d, B. Svetlov; lp, K. Piontkovskaya, R. Lazareva, Y. Muromsky, Y. Orlitskaya

IN THE NAME OF THE LAW (1922)
(7 r.) d, Emory Johnson; lp, Ben Alexander, Ralph Lewis, Josephine Adair, Claire McDowell

IN THE NAME OF THE PRINCE OF PEACE (1914)
(4 r.) d, J. Searle Dawley

IN THE NIGHT (1920, Brit.)
(5 r.) d, Frankland A. Richardson; lp, C.M. Hallard, Dorothy Fane, Hayford Hobbs, Adelqui Migliar

IN THE PALACE OF THE KING (1915)
(6 r.) d, Fred E. Wright; lp, E.J. Ratcliffe, Richard C. Travers, Arleen Hackett, Lewis Edgard

IN THE PALACE OF THE KING (1923)
(9 r.) d, Emmett Flynn; lp, Blanche Sweet, Edmund Lowe, Hobart Bosworth, Pauline Starke

IN THE PILLORY (1924, USSR)
(6 r.) d, Amo Bek-Nazarov; lp, Nata Vachnadze, Kira Andronikashvili, Akaki Vazadze

IN THE SHADOW (1915)
(5 r.) d, Harry Handworth; lp, Harry Handworth, Marie Boyd, William A. Williams, Octavia Handworth

IN THE SHADOW OF BIG BEN (1914, Brit.)
(4 r.) d, Frank Wilson; lp, Tom Powers, Alma Taylor, Jack Raymond, Henry Vibart

IN THE SPIDER'S WEB (1924)
(5 r.) d, Robert Bondrioz; lp, Howard Hampden, Alice Dean, Charles Vanel, Jean Paul Baer

IN THE WATER (1923)
(5 r.) lp, Donald Mack, Elsie Hanneman

IN THE WEB OF THE GRAFTERS (1916)
(5 r.) d, Murdock MacQuarrie; lp, Edythe Sterling, Norbert A. Myles, Millard K. Wilson, Francis J. MacDonald

IN THE WEST (1923)
(5 r.) d, George Holt; lp, Neva Gerber, Richard Hatton, Arthur Morrison, Elias Bullock

IN THE WHIRLWIND OF REVOLUTION (1922, USSR)
(6 r.) d, Alexander Chargonin; lp, N. Vishnyak, Zoya Barantsevich

IN TREASON'S GRASP (1917)
(5 r.) d, Francis Ford; lp, Grace Cunard, Francis Ford

IN WRONG (1919)
(5 r.) d, James Kirkwood; lp, Jack Pickford, Marguerite de la Motte, Clara Horton, George Dromgold

INCH'ALLAH (1922, Fr.)
(? r.) d, Marco de Gastyne; lp, Stacia Napierkowska

INCOMPARABLE BELLAIRS, THE
(SEE: INCOMPARABLE MISTRESS BELLAIRS, THE, 1914, Brit.)

INCOMPARABLE MISTRESS BELLAIRS, THE (1914, Brit.)
(4 r.) d, Harold Shaw; lp, Edna Flugrath, Gregory Scott, Mercy Hatton, Wyndham Guise

INDESTRUCTIBLE WIFE, THE (1919)
(5 r.) d, Charles Maigne; lp, Alice Brady, Saxon King, Sue Balfour, George Backus

INDIAN SUMMER OF DRY VALLEY JOHNSON, THE (1917)
(4 r.) d, Martin Justice; lp, Carlton King, Jean Paige, Anna Brody

INDIAN TOMB, THE
(SEE: MYSTERIES OF INDIA, 1922, Ger.)

INDISCREET CORINNE (1917)
(5 r.) d, Jack Dillon; lp, Olive Thomas, George Chesebro, Joseph Bennett, Josie Sedgwick

INDISCRETION (1917)
(5 r.) d, Wilfred North; lp, Lillian Walker, Walter McGrail, Richard Wangemann, Katharine Lewis

INDISCRETION (1921)
(6 r.) d, William Davis; lp, Florence Reed, Lionel Atwill, Gareth Hughes

INEVITABLE, THE (1917)
(5 r.) d, Ben Goetz; lp, Anna Q. Nilsson, Chester Barnett, Lucile Dorrington, William Bailey

INFAMOUS LADY, THE (1928, Brit.)
(8 r.) d, Geoffrey Barkas, Michael Barringer; lp, Arthur Wontner, Ruby Miller, Walter Tennyson, Muriel Angelus

INFATUATION (1925)
(7 r.) d, Irving Cummings; lp, Corinne Griffith, Percy Marmont, Malcolm McGregor, Warner Oland

INFELICE (1915, Brit.)
(6 r.) d, Fred Paul, L.C. MacBean; lp, Peggy Hyland, Fred Paul, Bertram Burleigh, Queenie Thomas

INFIDEL, THE (1922)
(6 r.) d, James Young; lp, Katharine MacDonald, Robert Ellis, Joseph Dowling, Boris Karloff

INFINITE SORROW (1922, USSR)
(7 r.) d, Alexander Panteleyev; lp, P. Kirillov, U. Krug, V. Maximov, Y. Chaika

INGEBORG HOLM (1913, Swed.)
(6 r.) d, Victor Sjostrom; lp, Hilda Borgstrom, Aron Lindgren, Eric Lindholm, Georg Gronroos

INHERITANCE (1920, Brit.)
(5 r.) d, Wilfred Noy; lp, Mary Odette, Jack Hobbs, Ursula Hughes, Sir Simeon Stuart

INHERITED PASSIONS (1916)
(7 r.) d, G.P. Hamilton; lp, Dot Farley, William Conklin

INN IN TOKYO, AN (1935, Jap.)
(? r.) d, Yasujiro Ozu

INNER CHAMBER, THE (1915)
(3 r.) p, Wilbert Melville

INNER SHRINE, THE (1917)
(5 r.) d, Frank Reicher; lp, Margaret Illington, Hobart Bosworth, Elliott Dexter, Jack Holt

INNER STRUGGLE, THE (1916)
(5 r.) d, Edward Sloman; lp, Franklin Ritchie, Winnifred Greenwood, Roy Stewart

INNER VOICE, THE (1920)
(7 r.) d, Roy William Neill; lp, E.K. Lincoln, Fuller Mellish, Agnes Ayres, William Riley Hatch

INNOCENCE OF LIZETTE, THE (1917)
(5 r.) d, James Kirkwood; lp, Mary Miles Minter, Eugene Ford, Eugenie Forde, Harvey Clarke

INNOCENT ADVENTURESS, AN (1919)
(5 r.) d, Robert G. Vignola; lp, Vivian Martin, Lloyd Hughes, Edythe Chapman, Gertrude Norman

INNOCENT CHEAT, THE (1921)
(6 r.) d, Ben Wilson; lp, Roy Stewart, Sidney De Gray, George Hernandez, Rhea Mitchell

INNOCENT LOVE (1928)
(6 r.) lp, Gaston Glass, Claire Whitney

INNOCENT MAID, AN (1934, Jap.)
(? r.) d, Yasujiro Ozu

INNOCENT'S PROGRESS (1918)
(5 r.) d, Frank Borzage; lp, Pauline Starke, Jack Livingston, Lillian West, Alice Knowland

INSIDE OF THE CUP, THE (1921)
(7 r.) d, Albert Cappellani; lp, William P. Carleton, David Torrence, Edith Hallor, John Bohn

INSINUATION (1922)
(7 r.) d, Margery Wilson; lp, Margery Wilson, Percy Holton, Bradley Barker, Agnes Neilsen

INSPIRATION (1928)
(7 r.) d, Bernard McEveety; lp, George Walsh, Gladys Frazin, Marguerite Clayton, Earle Larrimore

INSPIRATIONS OF HARRY LARRABEE (1917)
(4 r.) d, Bertram Bracken; lp, Margaret Landis, Clifford Gray, Winnifred Greenwood, Frank Brownlee

INSURRECTION, THE (1915)
(4 r.)

INTERFERIN' GENT, THE (1927)
(5 r.) d, Richard Thorpe; lp, Buffalo Bill, Jr., Olive Hasbrouck, Al Taylor, Harry Todd

INTERLOPER, THE (1918)
(5 r.) d, Oscar Apfel; lp, Kitty Gordon, Irving Cummings, Warren Cook, Isabelle Berwin

INTERNATIONAL MARRIAGE, AN (1916)
(5 r.) d, Frank Lloyd; lp, Rita Jolivet, Marc Robbins, Elliott Dexter, Grace Carlisle

INTO HER KINGDOM (1926)
(7 r.) d, Svend Gade; lp, Corinne Griffith, Einar Hanson, Claude Gillingwater, Charles Crockett

INTO THE PRIMITIVE (1916)
(5 r.) d, T.N. Heffron; lp, Kathlyn Williams, Guy Oliver, Harry Lonsdale

INTRIGUE (1916)
(5 r.) d, Frank Lloyd; lp, Lenore Ulrich, Cecil Van Auker, Howard Davies, Herbert Standing

INTRIGUE (1917)
(5 r.) d, John Robertson; lp, Peggy Hyland, Bobby Connelly, Marc MacDermott, Templer Saxe

INTRIGUE (1921)
(5 r.)

INTRODUCTION TO MARRIAGE (1930, Jap.)
(? r.) d, Yasujiro Ozu

INTRUSION OF ISABEL, THE (1919)
(5 r.) d, Lloyd Ingraham; lp, Mary Miles Minter, Allan Forrest, J. Parks Jones, Lucretia Harris

INVISIBLE BOND, THE (1920)
(5 r.) d, Charles Maigne; lp, Irene Castle, Huntley Gordon, Claire Adams, Fleming Ward

INVISIBLE DIVORCE, THE (1920)
(6 r.) d, Nat C. Deverich, Thomas R. Mills; lp, Leatrice Joy, Walter McGrail, Grace Darmond, Walter Miller

INVISIBLE ENEMY, THE (1916)
(5 r.)

INVISIBLE POWER, THE (1914)
(4 r.) d, George Melford; Cleo Ridgely, William West, Paul Hurst, Thomas Gillette

INVISIBLE WEB, THE (1921)
(? r.) d, Beverly C. Rule

I'PAGLIACCI (1923, Brit.)
(6 r.) d, G.B. Samuelson; lp, Lilian Hall-Davis, Adelqui Millar, Campbell Gullan, Frank Dane

IRISH EYES (1918)
(5 r.) d, William Dowlan; lp, Pauline Starke, Joe King, Ward Caulfield, Virginia Ware

IRISH LUCK (1925)
(7 r.) d, Victor Heerman; lp, Thomas Meighan, Lois Wilson, Cecil Humphreys, Claude King

IRON FIST (1926)
(5 r.) d, J.P. McGowan; lp, Bob Reeves

IRON HAND, THE (1916)
(5 r.) d, Ulysses Davis; lp, Hobart Bosworth, Jane Novak, Maude George, William V. Mong

IRON HEART, THE (1917)
(5 r.) d, George Fitzmaurice; lp, Edwin Arden, Gertrude Berkeley, Forrest Winant, Helene Chadwick

IRON HEART, THE (1920)
(5 r.) d, Dennison Clift, Paul Cezeneuve; lp, Madlaine Traverse, George McDaniel, Edwin Booth Tilton, Melbourne McDowell

IRON RIDER, THE (1920)
(5 r.) d, Scott Dunlap; lp, William Russell, Vola Vale, Arthur Morrison, Wadsworth Harris

IRON STAIR, THE
(SEE: THE BRANDED SOUL, 1920, Brit.)

IRON STRAIN, THE (1915)
(5 r.) d, Reginald Barker; lp, Dustin Farnum, Enid Markey, Charles K. French, Truly Shattuck

IRON TO GOLD (1922)
(5 r.) d, Bernard J. Durning; lp, Dustin Farnum, Marguerite Marsh, William Conklin, William Elmer

IRON TRAIL, THE (1921)
(7 r.) d, Roy William Neill; lp, Wyndham Standing, Thurston Hall, Reginald Denny, Alma Tell

IRON WOMAN, THE (1916)
(6 r.) d, Carl Harbaugh; lp, Nance O'Neil, Einar Linden, Alfred Hickman, Evelyn Brent

IRRESISTIBLE FLAPPER, THE (1919, Brit.)
(4 r.) d, Frank Wilson; lp, Violet Hopson, Ivy Close, Gerald Ames, Basil Gill

IS A MOTHER TO BLAME? (1922)
(5 r.) d, Roy Sheldon;

IS LIFE WORTH LIVING? (1921)
(5 r.) d, Alan Crosland; lp, Eugene O'Brien, Winifred Westover, Arthur Housman, George Lessey

IS MATRIMONY A FAILURE? (1922)
(6 r.) d, James Cruze; lp, T. Roy Barnes, Lila Lee, Lois Wilson, Walter Hiers

ISLAND OF DESIRE, THE (1917)
(5 r.) d, Otis Turner; lp, George Walsh, Anna Luther, Willard Louis, Margaret Gibson [Patricia Palmer]

ISLAND OF DESPAIR, THE (1926, Brit.)
(6 r.) d, Henry Edwards; lp, Matheson Lang, Marjorie Hume, Gordon Hopkirk, Jean Bradin

ISLAND OF ROMANCE, THE (1922, Brit.)
(5 r.) d, Humbertson Wright; lp, Leonard Tremayne, Dora Henwood, Raleigh King

ISLAND OF SURPRISE, THE (1916)
(5 r.) d, Paul Scardon; lp, William Courtenay, Charles Kent, Anders Randolf, Charles Wellesley

ISLAND OF WISDOM, THE (1920, Brit.)
(5 r.) d, Anthony Keith; lp, Margaret Hope, Percy Standing, Anthony Keith, Eva Westlake

ISLAND WIVES (1922)
(5 r.) d, Webster Campbell; lp, Corinne Griffith, Charles Trowbridge, Rockliffe Fellowes, Ivan Christy

ISLE OF DOUBT (1922)
(6 r.) d, Hamilton Smith; lp, Wyndham Standing, Dorothy Mackaill, George Fawcett, Marie Burke

ISLE OF INTRIGUE, THE (1918)
(6 r.) d, Francis Ford; lp, Francis Ford

ISLE OF LIFE, THE (1916)
(5 r.) d, Burton George; lp, Roberta Wilson, Frank Whitson, Hayward Mack, T.D. Crittenden

ISLE OF LOVE, THE (1916)
(5 r.) d, Edwin Middleton; lp, Gertrude McCoy, Earl O. Schenck, Robert Clugston, Iva Shepard

ISLE OF LOVE, THE (1922)
(5 r.) d, Fred J. Balshofer; lp, Julian Eltinge, Alma Francis, Lydia Knott, Rudolph Valentino

ISLE OF OBLIVION (1917, USSR)
(5 r.) d, Vyacheslav Turzhansky; lp, V. Turzhansky, Y. Chaika, V. Elsky

IT HAPPENED IN HONOLULU (1916)
(5 r.) d, Lynn Reynolds; lp, Myrtle Gonzales, Val Paul, George Hernandez, Lule Warrenton

IT HAPPENED IN PARIS (1919)
(5 r.) d, David Hartford; lp, W. Lawson Butt, Hayward Mack, Charles Gunn, Rose Dione

IT HAPPENED OUT WEST (1923)
(5 r.) lp, Franklyn Farnum, Virginia Lee

IT HAPPENED TO ADELE (1917)
(5 r.) d, Van Dyke Brooke; lp, Gladys Leslie, Carey Hastings, Peggy Burke, Charles Emerson

IT IS FOR ENGLAND
(SEE: THE HIDDEN HAND, 1916, Brit.)

IT ISN'T BEING DONE THIS SEASON (1921)
(5 r.) d, George L. Sargent; lp, Corinne Griffith, Sally Crute, Webster Campbell, Charles Wellesley

IT MIGHT HAPPEN TO YOU (1920)
(5 r.) d, Al Santell; lp, Billy Mason, Doris Dare, William Harcourt, Walter Beckwith

IT PAYS TO ADVERTISE (1919)
(5 r.) d, Donald Crisp; lp, Bryant Washburn, Lois Wilson, Walter Hiers, Guy Oliver

ITCHING PALMS (1923)
(6 r.) d, James W. Horne; lp, Tom Gallery, Herschel Mayall, Virginia Fox, Tom Wilson

IT'S A GREAT LIFE (1920)
(5 r.) d, E. Mason Hopper; lp, Cullen Landis, Molly Malone, Clara Horton, Howard Ralston

IT'S EASY TO MAKE MONEY (1919)
(5 r.) d, Edwin Carewe; lp, Bert Lytell, Gertrude Selby, Frank Currier, Stanton Heck

IT'S NEVER TOO LATE TO MEND (1917, Brit.)
(6 r.) d, Dave Aylott; lp, George Leyton, Margaret Hope, George Dewhurst, Charles Vane

IVANHOE (1913, Brit.)
(4 r.) d, Herbert Brenon; lp, King Baggot, Leah Baird, Evelyn Hope, Herbert Brenon

J'ACCUSE (1919, Fr.)
(11 r.) d, Abel Gance; lp, Severin Mars, Romuald Joube, Marise Dauvray, Maxime Desjardins

JACK (1925, Fr.)
(? r.) d, Robert Saidreau

JACK CHANTY (1915)
(5 r.) d, Max Figman; lp, Max Figman, Lolita Robertson, Edwin Harvey, H.A. Livingston

JACKIE (1921)
(5 r.) d, Jack [John] Ford; lp, Shirley Mason, William Scott, Harry Carter, George Stone

JACQUES LANDAUZE (1919, Fr.)
(? r.) d, Andre Hugon

JACQUES OF THE SILVER NORTH (1919)
(6 r.) d, Norval MacGregor; lp, Mitchell Lewis, Fritzi Brunette, C.A. Van Auker, Murdock MacQuarrie

JADE CASKET, THE (1929, Fr.)
(? r.) d, Leon Poirier; lp, Roger Carl, Mlle. Myrga, Mons. Mandaille

JADE CUP, THE (1926)
(5 r.) d, Frank Hall Crane; lp, Evelyn Brent, Jack Luden, Eugene Borden, George Cowl

JADE HEART, THE (1915, Brit.)
(4 r.) d, Dave Aylott; lp, Jack Jarman, Bunty Stewart, Fred Rains, Joyce Templeton

JAFFERY (1915)
(6 r.) d, George Irving; lp, C. Aubrey Smith, Eleanor Woodruff, Paul Doucet, Florence Deshon

JAGUAR'S CLAWS (1917)
(5 r.) d, Marshall Neilan; lp, Sessue Hayakawa, Fritzi Brunette, Tom Moore, Marjorie Daw

J'AI TUE (1924, Fr.)
(? r.) d, Roger Lion; lp, Sessue Hayakawa

JAN OF THE BIG SNOWS (1922)
(5 r.) d, Charles M. Seay; lp, Warner Richmond, Louise Prussing, William Peavy, Baby Eastman Heywood

JANE (1915)
(5 r.) d, Frank Lloyd; lp, Charlotte Greenwood, Sydney Grant, Forrest Stanley, Myrtle Stedman

JANE EYRE (1914)
(4 r.) d, Martin J. Faust; lp, Alberta Roy, Lisbeth Blackstone, Mary Frye Clements, Viola Allen Frayne

JANE SHORE
(SEE: THE STRIFE ETERNAL, 1915, Brit.)

JAPANESE NIGHTINGALE, A (1918)
(5 r.) d, George Fitzmaurice; lp, Fannie Ward, W.E. Lawrence, Yukio Aoyama

JASPER LANDRY'S WILL
(SEE: UNCLE JASPER'S WILL, 1922)

JAWS OF HELL (1928, Brit.)
(9 r.) d, Maurice Elvey, Milton Rosmer; lp, Benita Hume, Cyril McLaglen, Alf Goodard, Miles Mander

JAZZ HOUNDS, THE (1922)
(? r.)

JEALOUSY (1916)
(5 r.) d, Will S. Davis; lp, Valeska Suratt, Herbert Heyes, Claire Whitney, John Charles

JEAN D'AGREVE (1922, Fr.)
(? r.) d, Rene Leprince

JEAN O' THE HEATHER (1916)
(5 r.)

JEANNE DORE (1916, Fr.)
(? r.) d, Louis Mercanton; lp, Sarah Bernhardt

JEANNE OF THE GUTTER (1919)
(5 r.) d, Herbert Blache; lp, Viola Dana, Henry Kolker, Edward Connelly, Darrel Foss

JELF'S
(SEE: A MAN OF HIS WORD, 1915, Brit.)

JERUSALEM DELIVERED (1918, Ital.)
(5 r.)

JES' CALL ME JIM (1920)
(5 r.) d, Clarence Badger; lp, Will Rogers, Irene Rich, Lionel Belmore, Raymond Hatton

JESS (1914)
(4 r.) lp, Ednamae Wilson, Antrim Short, Gertrude Short, Marion Emmons

JESS OF MOUNTAIN COUNTRY (1914)
(4 r.)

JESUS OF NAZARETH (1928)
(6 r.) lp, Philip Van Loan, Anna Lehr, Charles McCaffrey

JEW AT WAR, A (1931, USSR)
(4 r.) d, Grigori Roshal; lp, Vinyamin Zuskin, S. Petrov, E. Pinikova, N. Leonov

JEWEL (1915)
(5 r.) d, Phillips Smalley, Lois Weber; lp, Ella Hall, Rupert Julian, Hilda Hollis Sloman, Lule Warrenton

JEWEL IN PAWN, A (1917)
(5 r.) d, Jack Conway; lp, Ella Hall, Antrim Short, Jack Connolly, Walter Belasco

JEWISH LUCK (1925, USSR)
(8 r.) d, Alexei Granovsky; lp, Solomon Mikhoels, Tamara Adelheim

JILTED JANET (1918)
(5 r.) d, Lloyd Ingraham; lp, Margarita Fischer, Jack Mower, David Howard, Golda Madden

JIM BLUDSO (1917)
(5 r.) d, Wilfred Lucas, Tod Browning; lp, Wilfred Lucas, Olga Grey, George Stone, Charles Lee

JIM LA HOULETTE, ROI DES VOLEURS (1926, Fr.)
(? r.) d, Pierre Colombier; lp, Nicolas Rimsky, Gaby Morlay

JIM, THE PENMAN (1915)
(5 r.) d, Hugh Ford; lp, John Mason, Russell Bassett, Harold Lockwood, Marguerite Leslie

JINX (1919)
(5 r.) d, Victor L. Schertzinger; lp, Mabel Normand, Cullen Landis, Florence Carpenter, Gertrude Claire

JINX JUMPER, THE (1917)
(5 r.) lp, Jack Devereaux, Winifred Allen

JOAN OF FLANDERS
(SEE: WAR BRIDES, 1916)

JOCASTE (1927, Fr.)
(? r.) d, Gaston Ravel

JOCELYN (1922, Fr.)
(? r.) d, Leon Poirier; lp, Armand Tallier, Mlle. Myrga

JOCKEY OF DEATH, THE (1916, Ital.)
(4 r.) d, M. Lind

JOHANNA ENLISTS (1918)
(5 r.) d, William Desmond Taylor; lp, Mary Pickford, Emory Johnson, Anne Schaefer, Fred Huntley

JOHANNES, FILS DE JOHANNES (1918, Fr.)
(? r.) d, Andre Hugon

JOHN ERMINE OF THE YELLOWSTONE (1917)
(5 r.) d, Francis Ford; lp, Francis Ford, Mae Gaston, Burwell Hamrick, John Darkcloud

JOHN FORREST FINDS HIMSELF (1920, Brit.)
(5 r.) d, Henry Edwards; lp, Henry Edwards, Chrissie White, Gerald Ames, Hugh Clifton

JOHN PETTICOATS (1919)
(5 r.) d, Lambert Hillyer; lp, William S. Hart, Winifred Westover, Walt Whitman, George Webb

JOSEPH AND HIS BRETHREN (1915)
(6 r.)

JOSEPH IN THE LAND OF EGYPT (1914)
(4 r.) d, Eugene Moore; lp, James Cruze, Marguerite Snow

JOSSELYN'S WIFE (1919)
(5 r.) d, Howard Hickman; lp, Bessie Barriscale, Nigel Barrie, Kathleen Kirkham, Joseph Dowling

JUCKLINS, THE (1920)
(6 r.) d, George Melford; lp, Mabel Julienne Scott, Monte Blue, Ruth Renick, Charles Ogle

JUDGED BY APPEARANCES (1916, Brit.)
(4 r.) d, Hugh Croise; lp, Nelson Keys, Arthur Playfair

JUDGMENT (1922)
(6 r.) lp, Joe Moore, Eileen Sedgwick

JUDGMENT, THE
(SEE: GUNNAR HEDE'S SAGA, 1922, Swed.)

JUDGMENT HOUSE, THE (1917)
(5 r.) d, J. Stuart Blackton; lp, Conway Tearle, Violet Heming, Wilfred Lucas, Paul Doucet

JULIUS CAESAR (1914, Ital.)
(6 r.) d, George Kleine; lp, Anthony Novelli

JUNGLE GODS (1927)
(7 r.)

JUNGLE LOVERS, THE (1915)
(? r.) d, Lloyd E. Carleton; lp, Bessie Eyton, Edward J. Peil, Richard Morris, Tom Bates

JUNGLE PRINCESS, THE (1923)
(7 r.) lp, Juanita Hansen

JUNGLE TRAIL OF THE SON OF TARZAN (1923)
(6 r.) d, Harry Revier, Arthur Flaven; lp, Dempsey Tabler, Karla Schramm, Gordon Griffith, Kamuela C. Searle

JURY OF FATE, THE (1917)
(5 r.) d, Tod Browning; lp, Mabel Taliaferro, William Sherwood, Frank Fisher Bennett, Charles Fang

JUSTICE (1914, Brit.)
(4 r.) d, Frank Wilson; lp, Alec Worchester, Alma Taylor, Stewart Rome, Harry Royston

JUSTICE (1917, Brit.)
(6 r.) d, Maurice Elvey; lp, Gerald du Mauier, Hilda Moore, Lilian Braithwaite, James Carewe

JUSTICE D'ABORD (1921, Fr.)
(? r.) d, Jacob Protozanoff

JUST A MOTHER (1923)
(5 r.) lp, Burtram Gurleigh, Isabel Elson

JUST A WIFE (1920)
(5 r.) d, Howard Hickman; lp, Roy Stewart, Leatrice Joy, Kathlyn Williams, Albert Van

JUST OUTSIDE THE DOOR (1921)
(5 r.) d, George Irving; lp, Edith Hallor, Betty Blythe, Barney Sherry, Eddie Sutherland

JUST PALS (1920)
(5 r.) d, Jack [John] Ford; lp, Buck Jones, Helen Ferguson, George Stone, Duke R. Lee

JUST PLAIN FOLKS (1925)
(5 r.) d, Robert North Bradbury; lp, Kenneth McDonald

JUST SQAW (1919)
(5 r.) d, George E. Middleton; lp, Beatriz Michelena, William Pike, Andrew Robson, Albert Morrison

JUST TRAVELIN' (1927)
(5 r.) d, Horace B. Carpenter; lp, Bob Burns, Dorothy Donald

KALIA MARDAN (1919, India)
(7 r.)

KANGAROO, THE (1914)
(5 r.)

KARIN, INGMAR'S DAUGHTER (1920, Swed.)
(6 r.) d, Victor Sjostrom; lp, Tore Teja, Victor Sjostrom, Niles Lundell, Vertil Malmstedt

KARL XII
(SEE: CHARLES XII, 1927, Swed.)

KATKA'S REINETTE APPLES (1926, USSR)
(7 r.) d, Eduard Johanson, Andrei Moskin; lp, Veronica Buzhinskaya, B. Chernova, Valeri Solovtsov, Yakov Gudkin

KATORGA (1928, USSR)
(6 r.) d, Yuli Raizman; lp, Vladimir Popov, P. Tamm, Andrei Zhilinsky, Boris Lifanov

KAZAN (1921)
(6 r.) d, Bertram Bracken; lp, Jane Novak, Ben Deeley, William Ryno, Benjamin Haggerty

KEAN (1924, Fr.)
(? r.) d, Alexandre Volkoff; lp, Ivan Mosjoukine, Kenelm Foss, Mary Odette, Nikolai Kolin

KEAN--THE MADNESS OF GENIUS
(SEE: KEAN, 1924, Fr.)

KEEP GOING (1926)
(5 r.) d, John Harvey; lp, Earle Douglas

KEEP TO THE RIGHT (1920)
(5 r.) lp, Mabel Taliaferro, Edith Stockton, Gladden James

KEEPER OF THE BEES, THE (1925)
(7 r.) d, James Leo Meehan; lp, Robert Frazer, Josef Swickard, Martha Mattox, Clara Bow

KEITH OF THE BORDER (1918)
(5 r.) d, Cliff Smith; lp, Roy Stewart, Josie Sedgwick, Norbert Cills, Pete Morrison

KENT THE FIGHTING MAN (1916, Brit.)
(6 r.) d, A.E. Coleby; lp, Billy Wells, Hatty Payne, A.E. Coleby, Arthur Rooke

KENTUCKY COLONEL, THE (1920)
(6 r.) d, William A. Seiter; lp, Joseph J. Dowling, Frederick Vroom, Elinor Field, Francis McDonald

KENTUCKY COURAGE
(SEE: LITTLE SHEPHERD OF KINGDOM COME, THE, 1928)

KENTUCKY PRIDE (1925)
(7 r.) d, John Ford; lp, Henry B. Walthall, J. Farrell MacDonald, Gertrude Astor, Malcolm Waite

KEY OF THE WORLD, THE (1918, Brit.)
(6 r.) d, J.L.V. Leigh; lp, Eileen Molyneux, Heather Thatcher, Eric Harrison, Pat Somerset

KEY TO POWER, THE (1918)
(5 r.) d, William Parke; lp, Claire Adams, Hugh Thompson, J.H. Gilmour, Frazier Nounnan

KEY TO YESTERDAY, THE (1914)
(4 r.) lp, Carlyle Blackwell, Edna Mayo, J. Francis Dillon, John J. Sheehan

KEYS, THE (1917)
(5 r.)

KEYS OF THE RIGHTEOUS, THE (1918)
(5 r.) d, Jerome Storm; lp, Enid Bennett, Earl Rodney, George Nicholls, Joseph Swickard

KID IS CLEVER, THE (1918)
(5 r.) d, Paul Powell; lp, George Walsh, Doris Pawn, Ralph Lewis, A. Burt Wesner

KIDDER & KO. (1918)
(5 r.) lp, Bryant Washburn, Gertrude Selby, Harry Jenkinson, Wadsworth Harris

KILL-JOY, THE (1917)
(4 r.) d, Fred E. Wright; lp, Mary McAllister, Granville Bates, James Fulton, James West

KING COWBOY (1928)
(7 r.) d, Robert De Lacy; lp, Tom Mix, Sally Blane, Lew Meehan, Barney Furey

KING OF CRIME, THE (1914, Brit.)
(4 r.) d, Sidney Northcote; lp, John Lawson, Claudia Guillot

KING OF THE PACK (1926)
(6 r.) d, Frank Richardson; lp, Peter the Great (a dog), Charlotte Stevens, Robert Gordon, Vera Lewis

KING OF THE PEOPLE, A (1917, Brit.)
(5 r.) d, Percy Nash

KING ON MAIN STREET, THE (1925)
(6 r.) d, Monta Bell; lp, Adolphe Menjou, Bessie Love, Greta Nissen, Oscar Shaw

KINGDOM OF HUMAN HEARTS, THE (1921)
(10 r.) d, Wilbert Leroy Cosper; lp, Hugh Metcalfe, Sylvia Edney, Jack Grey, Lana Good

KINGDOM OF TWILIGHT, THE (1929, Brit.)
(8 r.) d, Alexander Macdonald; lp, Wendy Osborne, David Wallace, John Faulkner, Rex Arnot

KINGDOM OF YOUTH, THE (1918)
(5 r.) d, Clarence G. Badger; lp, Madge Kennedy, Tom Moore, Marie de Wolfe, Lee Baker

KING'S HIGHWAY, THE (1927, Brit.)
(8 r.) d, Sinclair Hill; lp, Matheson Lang, Joan Lockton, James Carew, Gerald Ames

KING'S OUTCAST, THE
(SEE: HIS VINDICATION, 1915, Brit.)

KING'S ROMANCE, THE
(SEE: THE REVOLUTIONIST, 1914, Brit.)

KINSMAN, THE (1919, Brit.)
(5 r.) d, Henry Edwards; lp, Henry Edwards, Chrissie White, James Carew, Christine Rayner

KIRA KIRALINA (1927, USSR)
(8 r.) d, Boris Glagolin; lp, Valerskaya, Rubini, Krestinksy, Akitov

KISMET (1916)
(10 r.)

KISS, THE (1921)
(5 r.) d, Jack Conway; lp, George Periolat, William E. Lawrence, J.P. Lockney, Carmel Myers

KISS IN A TAXI, A (1927)
(7 r.) d, Clarence Badger; lp, Bebe Daniels, Chester Conklin, Douglas Gilmore, Henry Kolker

KISS OF DEATH (1916, Swed.)
(4 r.) d, Victor Sjostrom; lp, Victor Sjostrom, Albin Laven, Jeny Tschernichin

KISS OF HATE, THE (1916)
(5 r.) d, William Nigh; lp, Ethel Barrymore, H. Cooper Cliffe, Niles Welch, William L. Abingdon

KISS OR KILL (1918)
(5 r.) d, Elmer Clifton; lp, Herbert Rawlinson, Priscilla Dean, Alfred Allen, Harry Carter

KISSING CUP (1913, Brit.)
(4 r.) d, Jack Hulcup; lp, Alec Worcester, Chrissie White, Cecil Mannering, Flora Morris

KISSING CUP'S RACE (1920, Brit.)
(6 r.) d, Walter West; lp, Violet Hopson, Gregory Scott, Clive Brook, Arthur Walcott

KIT CARSON OVER THE GREAT DIVIDE (1925)
(6 r.) d, Frank S. Mattison; lp, Roy Stewart, Henry B. Walthall, Marguerite Snow, Sheldon Lewis

KITTY (1929, Brit.)
(8 r.) d, Victor Saville; lp, Estelle Brody, John Stuart, Dorothy Cumming, Marie Ault

KITTY KELLY, M.D. (1919)
(5 r.) d, Howard Hickman; lp, Bessie Barriscale, Jack Holt, J.J. Dowling, Wedgewood Nowell

KITTY MACKAY (1917)
(5 r.) d, Wilfred North; lp, Lillian Walker, Jewel Hunt, Charles Kent, Don Cameron

KIVALINA OF THE ICE LANDS (1925)
(6 r.) d, Earl Rossman; lp, Kivalina, Aguvaluk, Nashulik, Tokatoo

KNAVE OF DIAMONDS, THE (1921, Brit.)
(6 r.) d, Rene Plaissetty; lp, Mary Massart, Alec Fraser, Cyril Percival, Olaf Hytten

KNIGHT ERRANT, THE (1922, Brit.)
(5 r.) d, George Ridgwell; lp, Madge Stuart, Rex McDougall, Olaf Hytten, Norma Whalley

KNIGHTS OF THE SQUARE TABLE (1917)
(4 r.) d, Alan Crosland; lp, Paul Kelly, Yale Boss, Andy Clark, Donald McCollan

KNOCK (1926, Fr.)
(? r.) d, Rene Hervil

KOENIGSMARK (1923, Fr.)
(? r.) d, Leonce Perret; lp, Jaque Catelain, Huguette Duflos

KOSHER KITTY KELLY (1926)
(7 r.) d, James Horne; lp, Viola Dana, Tom Forman, Vera Gordon, Kathleen Myers

KREUTZER SONATA, THE (1915)
(5 r.) d, Herbert Brenon; lp, Nance O'Neil, Theda Bara, William Shay, Mimi Yvonne

KULTUR (1918)
(6 r.) d, Edward J. LeSaint; lp, Gladys Brockwell, William Scott, Georgia Woodthorpe, Willard Louis

LA BATAILLE (1923, Fr.)
(? r.) d, Edouard Violet; lp, Sessue Hayakawa

LA BELLE DAME SANS MERCI (1920, Fr.)
(? r.) d, Germaine Dulac

LA BELLE NIVERNAISE (1923, Fr.)
(6 r.) d, Jean Epstein; lp, Blanche Montel, David Evremond, Maurice Touze, Geo Charliot

LA BELLE RUSSE (1919)
(6 r.) d, Charles J. Brabin; lp, Teda Bara, Warburton Gamble, Marian Stewart, Robert Lee Keeling

LA BETE TRAQUEE (1923, Fr.)
(? r.) d, Rene Le Stomptier

LA BLESSURE (1925, Fr.)
(? r.) d, Marco de Gastyne

LA BOHEME
(SEE: LA VIE DE BOHEME, 1916)

LA BOHEME (1926)
(9 r.) d, King Vidor; lp, Lillian Gish, John Gilbert, Renee Adoree, George Hassell

LA BONNE HOTESSE (1918, Fr.)
(? r.) d, Georges Monca

LA BOUQUETIERE DES INNOCENTS (1922, Fr.)
(? r.) d, Jacques Robert

LA BOURASQUE (1920, Fr.)
(? r.) d, Charles Mandru, Charles de Marsan

LA BRIERE (1925, Fr.)
(? r.) d, Leon Poirier; lp, Armand Tallier, Mlle. Myrga, Jose Davert

LA CALOMNIE (1917, Fr.)
(? r.) d, Maurice Mariaud

LA CALVAIRE DE DONA PISA (1925, Fr.)
(? r.) d, Henry Krauss

LA CHATELAINE DU LIBAN (1926, Fr.)
(? r.) d, Marco de Gastyne; lp, Arlette Marchal

LA CHAUSSEE DES GEANTS (1926, Fr.)
(? r.) d, Robert Boudrioz

LA CHAUSSEE DES GEANTS (1926, Fr.)
(? r.) d, Jean Durand

LA CHEVAUCHEE BLANCHE (1923, Fr.)
(? r.) d, Donatien

LA CHEVRE AUX PIEDS D'OR (1926, Fr.)
(? r.) d, Jacques Robert

LA CHUTE DE LA MAISON USHER
(SEE: FALL OF THE HOUSE OF USHER, THE, 1928)

LA CIBLE (1925, Fr.)
(? r.) d, Serge Nadejdine

LA CIGARETTE (1919, Fr.)
(? r.) d, Germaine Dulac; lp, Gabriel Signoret

LA CITE FOUDROYEE (1924, Fr.)
(? r.) d, Luitz-Morat

LA CLE DE VOUTE (1925, Fr.)
(? r.) d, Roger Lion

LA COQUILLE ET LE CLERGYMAN (1928, Fr.)
(? r.) d, Germaine Dulac; lp, Lucien Batalle, Alex Allin, Genica Athanasiou

LA CORDE AU COU (1926, Fr.)
(? r.) d, Robert Saidreau

LA COURSE AU FLAMBEAU (1925, Fr.)
(? r.) d, Luitz-Morat

LA CROISADE (1920, Fr.)
(? r.) d, Rene Le Somptier

LA DAME MASQUEE (1924, Fr.)
(? r.) d, Viatcheslaw Tourjansky

LA DANSEUSE ORCHIDEE (1928, Fr.)
(? r.) d, Leonce Perret; lp, Louise Lagrange

LA DANSEUSE VOILEE (1917, Fr.)
(? r.) d, Maurice Mariaud

LA DETTE (1920, Fr.)
(? r.) d, Gaston Roudes

LA DETTE DE SANG (1923, Fr.)
(? r.) d, Gerard Bourgeois

LA DISTANCE (1918, Fr.)
(? r.) d, Robert Boudrioz

LA DIVINE CROISIERE (1928, Fr.)
(? r.) d, Julien Duvivier

LA DIXIEME SYMPHONIE (1918, Fr.)
(6 r.) d, Abel Gance; lp, Severin-Mars, Jean Toulout, Emmy Lynn, Elizabeth Nizan

LA DOUBLE EXISTENCE DE LORD SAMSEY (1924, Fr.)
(? r.) d, Georges Monca

LA DOULEUR (1925, Fr.)
(? r.) d, Gaston Roudes

LA DUBARRY (1914, Ital.)
(6 r.) d, Edoardo Bencivenga; lp, Leslie Carter, Hamilton Revelle

LA FAUTE DE MONIQUE (1928, Fr.)
(? r.) d, Maurice Gleize

LA FAUTE D'ODETTE MARECHAL (1920, Fr.)
(? r.) d, Henry Roussel; lp, Emmy Lynn

LA FAUTEUIL 47 (1926, Fr.)
(? r.) d, Gaston Ravel

LA FEE DES NEIGES (1920, Fr.)
(? r.) d, Pierre Marodon

LA FEMME AUX DEUX VISAGES (1920, Fr.)
(? r.) d, Pierre Marodon

LA FEMME DE NULLE PART (1922, Fr.)
(? r.) d, Louis Delluc; lp, Eve Francis, Roger Karl, Andre Daven, Gine Avril

LA FEMME SU VOISIN (1929, Fr.)
(? r.) d, Jacques de Baroncelli

LA FEMME ET LE PANTIN (1929, Fr.)
(? r.) d, Jacques de Baroncelli

LA FEMME INCONNUE (1923, Fr.)
(? r.) d, Jacques de Baroncelli

LA FEMME NUE
(SEE: MODEL FROM MONTMARTE, 1926)

LA FEMME REVEE (1929, Fr.)
(? r.) d, Jean Durand

LA FETE ESPAGNOLE (1919, Fr.)
(6 r.) d, Germaine Dulac; lp, Gaston Modot, Jean Toulot, Eve Francis

LA FIANCEE DU DISPARU (1921, Fr.)
(? r.) d, Charles Maudru, Charles de Marsan

LA FILLE BIEN GARDEE (1924, Fr.)
(? r.) d, Louis Feuillade

LA FILLE DE L'EAU (1924, Fr.)
(6 r.) d, Jean Renoir; lp, Catherine Hessling, Pierre Philippe, Pierre Champagne, Maurice Touze

LA FILLE DES CHIFFONNIERS (1922, Fr.)
(? r.) d, Henri Desfontaines

LA FILLE DU PEUPLE (1920, Fr.)
(? r.) d, Camille de Morlhon

LA FIN DE MONTE (1927, Fr.)
(? r.) d, Henri Etievant

LA FLAMBEE DE REVES (1924, Fr.)
(? r.) d, Jacques de Baroncelli

LA FLAMME (1925, Fr.)
(? r.) d, Rene Hervil

LA FLAMME CACHE (1918, Fr.)
(? r.) d, Roger Lion

LA FOLIE DES VAILLANTS (1925, Fr.)
(? r.) d, Germaine Dulac

LA FOLIE DU DOUTE (1923, Fr.)
(? r.) d, Rene Leprince

LA FONTAINE DES AMOURS (1924, Fr.)
(? r.) d, Roger Lion

LA FORET QUI TUE (1924, Fr.)
(? r.) d, Rene Le Somptier

LA FUGITIVE (1918, Fr.)
(? r.) d, Andre Hugon

LA FUGUE DE LILY (1917, Fr.)
(? r.) d, Louis Feuillade

LA GALERIE DES MONSTRES (1924, Fr.)
(? r.) d, Jaque Catelain; lp, Philippe Heriat, Simone Mareuil, Lois Moran, Jean Murat

LA GOSSELINE (1923, Fr.)
(? r.) d, Louis Feuillade

LA GOUTTE DE SANG (1924, Fr.)
(? r.) d, Maurice Mariaud

LA GLU (1927, Fr.)
(? r.) d, Henri Fescourt

LA GRANDE PASSION (1928, Fr.)
(? r.) d, Andre Hugon

LA GUITARE ET LA JAZZ BAND (1922, Fr.)
(? r.) d, Gaston Roudes

LA HURLE (1921, Fr.)
(? r.) d, Georges Champavert

LA JALOUSIE DU BARBOUILLE (1929, Fr.)
(? r.) d, Alberto Cavalcanti

LA JUSTICIERE (1925, Fr.)
(? r.) d, Maurice Gleize

LA LA LUCILLE (1920)
(5 r.) d, Eddie Lyons, Lee Morgan; lp, Eddie Lyons, Lee Moran, Anne Cornwall, Gladys Walton

LA LEGENDE DE SOEUR BEATRIX (1923, Fr.)
(? r.) d, Jacques de Baroncelli

LA LUTTE POUR LA VIE (1920, Fr.)
(? r.) d, Rene Leprince

LA MADONE DES SLEEPINGS (1928, Fr.)
(? r.) d, Maurice Gleize; lp, Claude France, Olaf Fjord

LA MAIN QUI A TUE (1924, Fr.)
(? r.) d, Maurice Gleize;

LA MAISON D'ARGILE (1918, Fr.)
(? r.) d, Gaston Ravel

LA MAISON DU MALTAIS (1927, Fr.)
(? r.) d, Henri Fescourt

LA MAISON DU SOLEIL (1929, Fr.)
(? r.) d, Gaston Roudes

LA MAISON VIDE (1921, Fr.)
(? r.) d, Raymond Bernard; lp, Henri Debain

LA MARCHAND DE PLAISIR (1923, Fr.)
(? r.) d, Jaque Catelain; lp, Marcelle Pradot, Jaque Catelain, Philippe Heriat

LA MARCHE DU DESTIN (1924, Fr.)
(? r.) d, Henri Diamant-Berger

LA MARCHE NUPTIALE (1929, Fr.)
(? r.) d, Andre Hugon; lp, Louise Lagrange, Pierre Blanchar

LA MARCHE TRIOMPHALE (1916, Fr.)
(? r.) d, Maurice Mariaud

LA MARSEILLAISE (1920, Fr.)
(? r.) d, Henri Desfontaines

LA MARTYRE DE STE. MAXENCE (1927, Fr.)
(? r.) d, Donatien

LA MASCOTTE DES POILUS (1918, Fr.)
(? r.) d, Charles Maudru, Charles de Marsan

LA MATERNELLE (1925, Fr.)
(? r.) d, Gaston Roudes

LA MEILLEURE MAITRESSE (1929, Fr.)
(? r.) d, Rene Hervil

LA MERVELILLEUSE VIE DE JEANNE D'ARC (1929, Fr.)
(? r.) d, Marco de Gastyne

LA MONTEE VERS L'ACROPOLE (1920, Fr.)
(? r.) d, Rene Le Somptier; lp, Van Daele, Andre Nox, France Dhelia

LA MORT DU SOLEIL (1922, Fr.)
(? r.) d, Germaine Dulac; lp, Andre Nox, Denise Lorys

LA NIEGE SUR LE PAS (1924, Fr.)
(? r.) d, Henri Etievant

LA NEUVAINE DE COLETTE (1925, Fr.)
(? r.) d, Georges Champavert

LA NOUVELLE ANTIGONE (1916, Fr.)
(? r.) d, Jacques de Baroncelli

LA NUIT DE LA REVANCHE (1924, Fr.)
(? r.) d, Henri Etievant

LA NUIT DE SAINT JEAN (1922, Fr.)
(? r.) d, Robert Saidreau

LA NUIT DU 11 SEPTEMBRE (1922, Fr.)
(? r.) d, Dominique Bernard-Deschamps

LA NUIT DU 13 (1921, Fr.)
(? r.) d, Henri Fescourt

LA NUIT EST A NOUS (1927, Fr.)
(? r.) d, Roger Lion

LA NUIT ROUGE (1924, Fr.)
(? r.) d, Maurice Gleize

LA PAIX CHEZ SOI (1921, Fr.)
(? r.) d, Robert Saidreau

LA PENTE (1928, Fr.)
(? r.) d, Henri Andreani

LA PERE GORIOT (1921, Fr.)
(? r.) d, Jacques de Baroncelli; lp, Gabriel Signoret

LA PETITE CHOCOLATIERE (1927, Fr.)
(? r.) d, Rene Hervil

LA PORTEUSE DE PAIN (1923, Fr.)
(? r.) d, Rene Le Somptier

LA POSSESSION (1929, Fr.)
(? r.) d, Leonce Perret

LA POUPEE (1920, Fr.)
(? r.) d, Henri Etievant

LA PREUVE (1921, Fr.)
(? r.) d, Andre Hugon

LA PRINCESSE AUX CLOWNS (1925, Fr.)
(? r.) d, Andre Hugon

LA PRINCESSE MANDANE (1928, Fr.)
(? r.) d, Germaine Dulac; lp, Ernest Van Duren, Edmonde Guy

LA PROIE (1917, Fr.)
(? r.) d, Georges Monca

LA PROIE DU VENT (1927, Fr.)
(? r.) d, Rene Clair; lp, Charles Vanel, Sandra Milowanoff, Lillian Hall Davis

LA P'TITE DU SIXIEME (1917, Fr.)
(? r.) d, Rene Hervil, Louis Mercanton

LA RAFALE (1920, Fr.)
(? r.) d, Jacques de Baroncelli; lp, Fanny Ward, Gabriel Signoret

LA RESURRECTION DU BOUIF (1922, Fr.)
(? r.) d, Henri Pouctal; lp, Lucien Tramel

LA REVANCHE DU MAUDIT (1929, Fr.)
(? r.) d, Rene Leprince

LA RIPOSTE (1922, Fr.)
(? r.) d, Viatcheslaw Tourjansky

LA RONDE INFERNALE (1927, Fr.)
(? r.) d, Luitz-Morat

LA ROUE (1923, Fr.)
(11 r.) d, Abel Gance; lp, Severin-Mars, Ivy Close, Gabriel de Gravone, Pierre Magnier

LA ROUTE DE DEVOIR (1918, Fr.)
(? r.) d, Georges Monca

LA RUE DU PAVE D'AMOUR (1923, Fr.)
(? r.) d, Andre Hugon

LA RUSE (1922, Fr.)
(? r.) d, Edouard Violet

LA SIN-VENTURA (1922, Fr.)
(? r.) d, Donatien

LA SIRENE DE PIERRE (1922, Fr.)
(? r.) d, Roger Lion

LA SIRENE DES TROPIQUES (1928, Fr.)
(? r.) d, Henri Etievant; lp, Josephine Baker, Pierre Batcheff

LA SULTANE DE L'AMOUR (1919, Fr.)
(? r.) d, Rene Le Somptier, Charles Burguet; lp, Gaston Modot, France Dhelia, Marcel Levesque, Sylvo de Pedrelli

LA SUPREME EPOEE (1919, Fr.)
(? r.) d, Henri Desfontaines

LA SYMPHONIE PATHETIQUE (1929, Fr.)
(? r.) d, Henri Etievant

LA TENTATION (1929, Fr.)
(? r.) d, Jacques de Baroncelli

LA TERRE (1921, Fr.)
(6 r.) d, Andre Antoine; lp, Armand Bour, Jean Herve, Germaine Rouer, Jeanne Briey

LA TERRE DU DIABLE (1921, Fr.)
(? r.) d, Luitz-Morat

LA TERRE PROMISE (1925, Fr.)
(? r.) d, Henry Roussel; lp, Raquel Meller, Maxudian, Tina de Yzarduy, Andre Roanne

LA TOSCA (1918)
(5 r.) d, Edward Jose; lp, Pauline Frederick, Frank Losee, Jules Raucourt, Henry Hebert

LA VENGEANCE DE MALLET (1920, Fr.)
(? r.) d, Georges Lacroix

LA VERITE (1922, Fr.)
(? r.) d, Henry Roussel

LA VESTALE DU GANGE (1927, Fr.)
(? r.) d, Andre Hugon

LA VIE DE BOHEME (1916)
(5 r.) d, Albert Capellani; lp, Alice Brady, Paul Cappellani, Leslie Stowe, June Elvidge

LA VIE D'UNE REINE (1917, Fr.)
(? r.) d, Rene Leprince

LA VIE MIRACULEUSE DE THERESE MARTIN (1929, Fr.)
(? r.) d, Julien Duvivier

LA VIERGE FOLLE (1929, Fr.)
(? r.) d, Luitz-Morat; lp, Emmy Lynn, Jean Angelo, Suzy Vernon

LA VIRGEN DE LA CARIDAD (1930, Cuba)
(? r.) d, Ramon Peon; lp, Diana V. Marde, Miguel de Santos

LA VIVANTE EPINGLE (1921, Fr.)
(? r.) d, Jacques Robert

LA VOIX DE LA MER (1921, Fr.)
(? r.) d, Gaston Roudes

LA VOYANTE (1923, Fr.)
(? r.) d, Louis Mercanton

LA ZOME DE LA MORT (1917, Fr.)
(5 r.) d, Abel Gance; lp, Andree Brabant, Clement, Anthony Gildes, Gaston Modot

L'ABBE CONSTANTIN (1925, Fr.)
(? r.) d, Julien Duvivier

L'ABSOLUTION (1922, Fr.)
(? r.) d, Jean Kemm

LABYRINTH, THE (1915)
(5 r.) d, E. Mason Hopper; lp, Gail Kane, Dolly Larkin, Richard Neal, Edward Roseman

L'ACCUSATEUR (1920, Fr.)
(? r.) d, Edouard Violet

LACE (1928, USSR)
(7 r.) d, Sergei Yutkevich; lp, Nina Shaternikova, Boris Poslavsky, K. Gradopolov, Boris Tenin

LACKEY AND THE LADY, THE (1919, Brit.)
(5 r.) d, Thomas Bentley; lp, Odette Goimbault, Roy Travers, Leslie Howard, Alban Attwood

LAD AND THE LION, THE (1917)
(5 r.) d, Alfred Green; lp, Vivian Reed, Will Machin, Charles LeMoyne, Al W. Filson

LADDER JINX, THE (1922)
(6 r.) d, Jess Robbins; lp, Edward Horton, Margaret Landis, Wilbur Higby, Tully Marshall

LADDER OF LIES, THE (1920)
(5 r.) d, Tom Forman; lp, Ethel Clayton, Clyde Filmore, Jean Acker, Irving Cummings

LADDIE (1920, Brit.)
(5 r.) d, Bannister Merwin; lp, Sydney Fairbrother, C. Jervis Walter, Dorothy Moody, Charles Vane

LADDIE (1926)
(7 r.) d, James Leo Meehan; lp, John Bowers, Bess Flowers, Theodore von Eltz, Eugenia Gilbert

LADIES BEWARE (1927)
(5 r.) d, Charles Giblyn; lp, George O'Hara, Nola Luxford, Florence Wix, Kathleen Myers

LADIES MUST LIVE (1921)
(8 r.) d, George Loane Tucker; lp, Robert Ellis, Mahlon Hamilton, Betty Compson, Leatrice Joy

LADIES' NIGHT IN A TURKISH BATH (1928)
(7 r.) d, Edward Cline; lp, Dorothy Mackaill, Jack Muhall, Sylvia Ashton, James Finlayson

LADIES OF LEISURE (1926)
(6 r.) d, Thomas Buckingham; lp, Elaine Hammerstein, T.Roy Barnes, Robert Ellis, Gertrude Short

LADIES OF THE NIGHT CLUB (1928)
(7 r.) d, George Archainbaud; lp, Ricardo Cortez, Barbara Leonard, Lee Moran, Douglas Gerrard

LADS OF THE VILLAGE, THE (1919, Brit.)
(4 r.) d, Harry Lorraine; lp, Joe Peterman, Jimmy Learmouth, Maudie Dunham, Bernard Dudley

LADY, THE (1925)
(8 r.) d, Frank Borzage; lp, Norma Talmadge, Wallace McDonald, Brandon Hurst, Alf Goulding

LADY AND THE BEARD, THE (1931, Jap.)
(? r.) d, Yasujiro Ozu

LADY AND THE BURGLAR, THE (1915)
(5 r.) d, Herbert Blache; lp, James "Gentleman Jim" Corbett, Claire Whitney

LADY AUDLEY'S SECRET (1920, Brit.)
(5 r.) d, Jack Denton; lp, Margaret Bannerman, H. Manning Haynes, Betty Farquhar, Randolph McLeod

LADY BARNACLE (1917)
(5 r.) d, John H. Collins; lp, Viola Dana, Robert Walker, Augustus Phillips, William B. Davidson

LADY CLARE, THE (1919, Brit.)
(6 r.) lp, Mary Odette, Jack Hobbs, Charles Quartermaine, Sir Simeon Stuart

LADY FREDERICK
(SEE: DIVORCEE, THE, 1919)

LADY FROM LONGACRE, THE (1921)
(5 r.) d, George E. Marshall; lp, William Russell, Mary Thurman, Mathilde Brundage, Robert Klein

LADY IN ERMINE, THE (1927)
(7 r.) d, James Flood; lp, Corinne Griffith, Einar Hansen, Ward Crane, Francis X. Bushman

LADY IN THE LIBRARY, THE (1917)
(4 r.) d, Edgar Jones; lp, Jack Vosburgh, Vola Vale, Robert Weycross, Ella Pitts

LADY JENNIFER (1915, Brit.)
(4 r.) d, James Warry Vickers; lp, Barbara Rutland, Harry Royston

LADY OF QUALITY, A (1913)
(5 r.) d, J. Searle Dawley; lp, Cecilia Loftus, House Peters, Hal Clarendon, Dave Wall

LADY OF QUALITY, A (1924)
(8 r.) d, Hobart Henley; lp, Virginia Valli, Lionel Belmore, Margaret Seddon, Peggy Cartwright

LADY OF RED BUTTE, THE (1919)
(5 r.) d, Victor L. Schertzinger; lp, Dorothy Dalton, Thomas Holding, Tully Marshall, William Courtright

LADY OF THE DUGOUT (1918)
(6 r.) d, William S. Van Dyke; lp, Al Jennings, Frank Jennings, Corinne Grant, Ben Alexander

LADY OF THE HAREM, THE (1926)
(6 r.) d, Raoul Walsh; lp, Ernest Torrence, William Collier, Jr., Greta Nissen, Louise Fazenda

LADY OF THE PHOTOGRAPH, THE (1917)
(5 r.) d, Ben Turbett; lp, Raymond McKee, Royal Byron, Shirley Mason, William Calhoun

LADY OWNER, THE (1923, Brit.)
(6 r.) d, Walter West; lp, Violet Hopson, James Knight, Warwick Ward, Arthur Walcott

LADY RAFFLES (1928)
(6 r.) d, R. William Neill; lp, Estelle Taylor, Roland Drew, Lilyan Tashman, Ernest Hillard

LADY ROSE'S DAUGHTER (1920)
(5 r.) d, Hugh Ford; lp, Elsie Ferguson, David Powell, Frank Losee, Holmes E. Herbert

LADY TETLEY'S DEGREE (1920, Brit.)
(5 r.) d, Fred Paul; lp, Marjorie Hume, Hamilton Stewart, Philip Hewland, Basil Langford

LADY WHO LIED, THE (1925)
(8 r.) d, Edwin Carewe; lp, Lewis Stone, Virginia Valli, Louis Payne, Nita Naldi

LADY WINDERMERE'S FAN (1916, Brit.)
(5 r.) d, Fred Paul; lp, Milton Rosmer, Netta Westcott, Nigel Playfair, Irene Rooke

LADYFINGERS (1921)
(6 r.) d, Bayard Veiller; lp, Bert Lytell, Ora Carew, Frank Elliott, Edythe Chapman

LADY'S NAME, A (1918)
(5 r.) d, Walter Edwards; lp, Constance Talmadge, Harrison Ford, Emory Johnson, Vera Doria

LAFAYETTE, WE COME! (1918)
(6 r.) d, Leonce Perret; lp, E.K. Lincoln, Dolores Cassinelli, Emmett C. King, Ethel Winthrop

L'AFFAIRE DE LA RUE DE LOUREINE (1923, Fr.)
(? r.) d, Henri Diamant-Berger

L'AFFAIRE DU COURRIER DE LYON (1923, Fr.)
(? r.) d, Leon Poirer

L'AFFICHE (1925, Fr.)
(? r.) d, Jean Epstein; lp, Natalie Lissenko, Genica Missirio, Camille Bardou

L'AGONIE DE JERUSALEM (1926, Fr.)
(? r.) d, Julien Duvivier

L'AGONIE DES AIGLES (1921, Fr.)
(? r.) d, Dominique Bernard-Deschamps; lp, Severin-Mars, Gaby Morlay

LAHOMA (1920)
(7 r.) d, Edgar Lewis; lp, Peaches Jackson, Louise Burnham, Beatrice Burnham, Wade Boteler

LAIR OF THE WOLF, THE (1917)
(5 r.) d, Charles Swickard; lp, Gretchen Lederer, Val Paul, Joseph Girard, Chester Bennett

L'ALIBI (1917, Fr.)
(? r.) d, Henri Pouctal

LAMB AND THE LION, THE (1919)
(5 r.) d, Francis J. Grandon; lp, Billie Rhodes, Melbourne McDowell, Al Garcia, William Griffin

L'AME DE PIERRE (1918, Fr.)
(? r.) d, Charles Burguet

L'AME DE PIERRE (1928, Fr.)
(? r.) d, Gaston Roudes

L'AME DU BRONZE (1918, Fr.)
(? r.) d, Henry Roussel; lp, Harry Bauer

L'AME DU MOTEUR: LE CARBURATEUR (1926, Fr.)
(? r.) d, Pierre Colombier

L'AMI FRITZ (1920, Fr.)
(? r.) d, Rene Hervil; lp, Leon Mathot, Huguette Duflos, Maurice de Feraudy

LAMP IN THE DESERT (1922, Brit.)
(6 r.) d, F. Martin Thompson; lp, Gladys Jennings, Lewis Willoughby, George K. Arthur, J.R. Tozer

LAMP OF DESTINY (1919, Brit.)
(5 r.) d, Alexander Butler; lp, Daphne Glenne, Leal Douglas, Judd Green, Florence Nelson

LANCASHIRE LASS, A (1915, Brit.)
(4 r.) d, Frank Wilson; lp, Stewart Rome, Alma Taylor, Tom Powers, William Felton

LAND BEYOND THE LAW, THE (1927)
(7 r.) d, Harry J. Brown; lp, Ken Maynard, Dorothy Dwan, Tom Santschi, Noah Young

LAND JUST OVER YONDER, THE (1916)
(6 r.) lp, George N. Chesebro, Arthur N. Millett, George Best, Elsa Fox

LAND O' LIZARDS (1916)
(5 r.) d, Frank Borzage; lp, Frank Borzage, Anna Little, Jack Richardson, Harvey Clark

LAND OF HOPE, THE (1921)
(5 r.) d, Edward H. Griffith; lp, Alice Brady, Jason Robards, Ben Hendricks, Jr., Schuyler Ladd

LAND OF JAZZ, THE (1920)
(5 r.) d, Jules Furthman; lp, Eileen Percy, Herbert Heyes, George Fisher, Ruth Stonehouse

LAND OF LONG SHADOWS (1917)
(5 r.) d, W.S. Van Dyke; lp, Jack Gardner, Ruth King, C.J. Lionel, Carl Stockdale

LAND OF MY FATHERS (1921, Brit.)
(5 r.) d, Fred Rains; lp, John Stuart, Edith Pearson, Yvonne Thomas, George Leyton

LAND OF MYSTERY, THE (1920, Brit.)
(7 r.) d, Harold Shaw; lp, Edna Flugrath, Norman Tharp, Fred Morgan, Christine Rayner

LAND OF PROMISE, THE (1917)
(5 r.) d, Joseph Kaufman; lp, Billie Burke, Thomas Meighan, Helen Tracy, J.W. Johnston

LAND OF THE LAWLESS (1927)
(5 r.) d, Thomas Buckingham; lp, Jack Padjan, Tom Santschi, Joseph Rickson, Charles Clary

LANDLOPER, THE (1918)
(5 r.) d, George Irving; lp, Harold Lockwood, Pauline Curley, Stanton Heck, William Clifford

LANDON'S LEGACY (1916)
(5 r.) d, Otis Turner; lp, J. Warren Kerrigan, Bertram Grassby, Lois Wilson, Maude George

LANE THAT HAD NO TURNING, THE (1922)
(5 r.) d, Victor Fleming; lp, Agnes Ayres, Theodore Kosloff, Mahlon Hamilton, Wilton Taylor

L'ANGOISSANTE AVENTURE (1920, Fr.)
(? r.) d, Jacob Protozanoff; lp, Ivan Mosjoukine

L'ANNIVERSAIRE (1916, Fr.)
(? r.) d, Georges Monca

L' APACHE (1919)
(6 r.) d, Joseph De Grasse; lp, Dorothy Dalton, Robert Elliott, Macey Harlam, Austin Webber

L'APPEL DU SANG (1920, Fr.)
(? r.) d, Louis Mercanton; lp, Phyllis Neilson Terry, Ivor Novello, Le Bargy, Gabriel de Gravone

L'APRE LUTTE (1917, Fr.)
(? r.) d, Robert Boudrioz

L'ARGENT (1929, Fr.)
(13 r.) d, Marcel L'Herbier; lp, Pierre Alcover, Alfred Abel, Henry Victor, Brigitte Helm

L'ARLESIENNE (1922, Fr.)
(? r.) d, Andre Antoine

LARMES DE CROCODILE (1916, Fr.)
(? r.) d, Maurice Mariaud

L'ARPETE (1929, Fr.)
(? r.) d, Donatien

L'ARRIVISTE (1924, Fr.)
(? r.) d, Andre Hugon

LASCA (1919)
(5 r.) d, Norman Dawn; lp, Edith Roberts, Frank Mayo, Veola Harty, Lloyd Whitlock

LASCIVIOUSNESS OF THE VIPER, THE (1920, Jap.)
(? r.) d, Norimasa Kaeriyama; lp, Tokihiko Okada, Yoko Benizawa

LASH, THE (1916)
(5 r.) d, James A. Young; lp, Marie Doro, Elliott Dexter, James Neill, Thomas Delmar

LASH OF DESTINY, THE (1916)
(5 r.) d, George Terwilliger; lp, Gertrude McCoy, Mabel Julienne Scott, Helen Greene, Duncan McRae

LASH OF JEALOUSY, THE
(SEE: MODERN OTHELLO, A, 1917)

LASH OF PINTO PETE, THE (1924)
(5 r.) d, Francis Ford; lp, Ashton Dearholt

LASH OF POWER, THE (1917)
(5 r.) d, Harry Solter; lp, Carmel Myers, Kenneth Harlan, Helen Wright, Charles Hill Mailes

LASH OF THE LAW (1926)
(5 r.) lp, Bill Bailey

L'ASSOMOIR (1921, Fr.)
(? r.) d, Charles Maudru, Charles de Mansan

LAST ACT, THE (1916)
(5 r.) lp, Bessie Barriscale, Clara Williams, Estelle Allen, Harry Keenan

LAST CARD, THE (1921)
(6 r.) d, Bayard Veiller; lp, May Allison, Albert Roscoe, Stanley Goethals, Frank Elliott

LAST CHALLENGE, THE (1916, Brit.)
(4 r.) d, Harold Shaw; lp, Chesterfield "Billy" Goode, Jem Smith, G.T. Dunning, Toff Wall

LAST CONCERT, THE (1915)
(4 r.) lp, Ellis F. Glickman, Minnie Berlin, Nolan Gane

LAST DOOR, THE (1921)
(5 r.) d, William P.S. Earle; lp, Eugene O'Brien, Charles Craig, Nita Naldi, Helen Pillsbury

LAST FRONTIER, THE (1926)
(8 r.) d, George B. Seitz; lp, William Boyd, Marguerite De La Motte, Jack Hoxie, Junior Coghlan

LAST HOUR, THE (1923)
(7 r.) d, Edward Sloman; lp, Milton Sills, Carmel Myers, Pat O'Malley, Jack Mower

LAST LAP (1928)
(7 r.) d, Bruce Mitchell; lp, Rex Lease, Mildred Harris

LAST MAN, THE (1916)
(5 r.) d, William Wolbert; lp, William Duncan, Corinne Griffith, Mary Anderson, Otto Lederer

LAST MAN, THE (1924)
(5 r.) d, Frederick Reel, Jr.; lp, Bill Patton

LAST MAN ON EARTH, THE (1924)
(7 r.) d, J.G. Blystone; lp, Earle Fox, Grace Cunard, Gladys Tennyson, Derelys Perdue

LAST MOMENT, THE (1923)
(6 r.) lp, Henry Hull, Doris Kenyon, Louis Wolheim, Louis Calhern

LAST MOMENT, THE (1928)
(6 r.) d, Paul Fejos; lp, Otto Matiesen, Julius Molinar, Jr., Lucille La Verne, Anielka Elter

LAST OF HIS PEOPLE, THE (1919)
(5 r.) d, Robert North Bradbury; lp, Mitchell Lewis, Harry Lonsdale, Yvette Mitchell, Catherine Van Buren

LAST OF THE CARNABYS, THE (1917)
(5 r.) d, William Parke; lp, Gladys Hulette, William Parke, Jr., Eugenie Woodward, Paul Everton

LAST OF THE DUANES, THE (1919)
(6 r.) d, J. Gordon Edwards; lp, William Farnum, Louise Lovely, Frankie Raymond, Harry De Vere

LAST OF THE DUANES, THE (1924)
(7 r.) d, Lynn Reynolds; lp, Tom Mix, Marian Nixon, Brinsley Shaw, Frank Nelson

LAST OF THE MAFFIA, THE (1915)
(5 r.) d, Sidney M. Goldin; lp, Jack Clark, Catherine Lee, William Conrad

LAST OUTLAW, THE (1927)
(6 r.) d, Arthur Rosson; lp, Gary Cooper, Jack Luden, Betty Jewel, Herbert Prior

LAST PAYMENT (1921, Ger.)
(6 r.) d, George Jacoby; lp, Pola Negri, Leopold von Ledebour, Henry Liedtke, Reinhold Schunzel

LAST REBEL, THE (1918)
(5 r.) d, Gilbert P. Hamilton; lp, Belle Bennett, Joe King, Walt Whitman, Lillian Langdon

LAST SENTENCE, THE (1917)
(5 r.) d, Ben Turbett; lp, Marc MacDermott, Miriam Nesbitt, Grace Williams, Herbert Prior

LAST TIDE, THE (1931, Brit.)
(5 r.) d, John Argyle; lp, James Benton, Margaret Delane, Grace Johnson

LAST WALTZ, THE (1927, Ger.)
(7 r.) d, Arthur Robinson; lp, Willy Fritsch, Hans Adalbert von Schetlow

LAST WHITE MAN, THE (1924)
(5 r.) d, Frank S. Mattison; lp, Matty Mattison

LATE MATTHEW PASCAL, THE (1925, Fr.)
(11 r.) d, Marcel L'Herbier; lp, Ivan Mosjoukine, Michel Simon Marcelle Pradot, Lois Moran

L'ATLANTIDE (1921, Fr.)
(8 r.) d, Jacques Feyder; lp, Stacia Napierkowska, Jean Angelo, Georges Melchior, Marie-Louise Iribe

L'ATRE (1923, Fr.)
(? r.) d, Robert Boudrioz; lp, Renee Dounis, Charles Vanel, Jacques de Feraudy, Renee Tandil

L'AUBERGE ROUGE (1923, Fr.)
(6 r.) d, Jean Epstein; lp, Gina Manes, Leon Mathot, Jacques Christiany, Curtois

LAUGHING AT DEATH (1929)
(6 r.) d, Wallace W. Fox; lp, Bob Steele, Natalie Joyce, Captain Vic, Kai Schmidt

LAUGHING BILL HYDE (1918)
(5 r.) d, Hobart Henley; lp, Will Rogers, Anna Lehr, John Sainpolis, Clarence Oliver

LAUGHING CAVALIER, THE (1917, Brit.)
(6 r.) d, A.V. Bramble, Eliot Stannard; lp, A.V. Bramble, Mercy Hatton, George Bellamy, Edward O'Neill

LAUNDRY GIRL, THE
(SEE: BECAUSE, 1919, Brit.)

L'AUTRE (1917, Fr.)
(? r.) d, Louis Feuillade

L'AUTRE AILE (1924, Fr.)
(? r.) d, Henri Andreani

L'AVENTURE (1923, Fr.)
(? r.) d, Marco de Gastyne

L'AVENTURE DES MILLIONS (1916, Fr.)
(? r.) d, Louis Feuillade

L'AVENTURIER (1924, Fr.)
(? r.) d, Maurice Mariaud

L'AVOCAT (1925, Fr.)
(? r.) d, Gaston Ravel

LAW AND THE LADY, THE (1924)
(6 r.) d, John L. McCutcheon; lp, Len Leo, Alice Lake, Mary Thurman, [Frederick] Tyrone Power

LAW AND THE MAN (1928)
(6 r.) d, Scott Pembroke; lp, Tom Santschi, Gladys Brockwell, Robert Ellis, Tom Ricketts

LAW AND THE OUTLAW (1925)
(5 r.) lp, Tom Mix

LAW AND THE WOMAN, THE (1922)
(7 r.) d, Penrhyn Stanlaws; lp, Betty Compson, William P. Carleton, Cleo Ridgely, Casson Ferguson

LAW DECIDES, THE (1916)
(7 r.) d, William P.S. Earle; lp, Dorothy Kelly, Harry Morey, Bobby Connelly, Donald Hall

LAW DEMANDS, THE (1924)
(5 r.) d, Harry O. Hoyt; lp, Charles Hutchinson, Leah Baird

LAW DIVINE, THE (1920, Brit.)
(5 r.) d, Challis Sanderson, H.B. Parkinson; lp, H.V. Esmond, Eva Moore, Evelyn Brent, Mary Brough

LAW HUSTLERS, THE
(SEE: LAW RUSTLERS, THE, 1923)

LAW OF COMPENSATION, THE (1917)
(5 r.) d, Julius Steger, Joseph A. Golden; lp, Norma Talmadge, Chester Barnett, Frederick Esmelton, Edwin Stanley

LAW OF COMPENSATION (1927)
(6 r.) d, Julius Steger, Joseph A. Golden; lp, Norma Talmadge, Frederick Esmelton, Chester Barnett, John Charles

LAW OF FEAR (1928)
(5 r.) d, Jerome Storm; lp, Ranger (a dog), Jane Reid, Sam Nelson, Al Smith

LAW OF MEN, THE (1919)
(5 r.) d, Fred Niblo; lp, Enid Bennett, Niles Welch, Andrew Robson, Dorcas Matthews

LAW OF NATURE, THE (1919)
(7 r.) d, David G. Fisher; lp, David G. Fisher, Vincent Coleman, Frances Ne Moyer, Dixie Lee

LAW OF THE GREAT NORTHWEST, THE (1918)
(5 r.) d, Raymond Wells; lp, Margery Wilson, Will Jeffries, Eugene Corey, William Dyer

LAW OF THE NORTH, THE (1917)
(5 r.) d, Burton George; lp, Pat O'Malley, Richard Tucker, Shirley Mason, Charles Sutton

LAW OF THE NORTH, THE (1918)
(5 r.) d, Irvin V. Willat; lp, Charles Ray, Doris Lee, Robert McKim, Gloria Hope

LAW OF THE PLAINS (1929)
(5 r.) lp, Tom Tyler, Natalie Joyce

LAW OF THE YUKON, THE (1920)
(6 r.) d, Charles Miller; lp, Edward Earle, Joseph Smiley, Nancy Deever, Tom Delmar

LAW OR LOYALTY (1926)
(5 r.) d, Lawson Harris

LAW RUSTLERS, THE (1923)
(5 r.) d, Lewis King; lp, William Fairbanks, Edmund Cobb, Joseph Girard, Ena Gregory

LAW THAT DIVIDES, THE (1919)
(5 r.) d, Howard M. Mitchell; lp, Kathleen Clifford, Kenneth Harlan, Gordon Sackville, Corenne Grant

LAW THAT FAILED, THE (1917)
(5 r.) lp, Alma Hanlon, Edward Ellis, John K. Roberts, Florence Short

LAW UNTO HIMSELF, A (1916)
(5 r.) d, Robert Brockwell; lp, Crane Wilbur, Louis Durham, E.W. Harris, Carl Von Schiller

LAWLESS LOVE (1918)
(5 r.) d, Robert Thornby; lp, Jewel Carmen, Henry Woodward, Edward Hearn

LAWLESS MEN (1924)
(5 r.) d, Neal Hart; lp, Neal Hart

LAWLESS TRAILS (1926)
(5 r.) d, Forrest Sheldon; lp, Bruce Gordon, Boris Bullock, Josephine Hill, Bob Williamson

LAW'S LASH, THE (1928)
(5 r.) d, Noel Mason Smith; lp, Klondike (a dog), Robert Ellis, Mary Mayberry, Jack Marsh

LAW'S OUTLAW, THE (1918)
(5 r.) d, Cliff Smith; lp, Roy Stewart, Fritzi Ridgeway, Harry Rattenberry, Norbert Cills

LE BANDEAU SUR LES YEUX (1917, Fr.)
(? r.) d, Louis Feuillade

LE BLED (1929, Fr.)
(8 r.) d, Jean Renior; lp, Jackie Monnier, Diana Hart, Enrique Rivero, Alexandre Arquillere

LE BONHEUR CONJUGAL (1922, Fr.)
(? r.) d, Robert Saidreau

LE BONHEUR DES AUTRES (1919, Fr.)
(? r.) d, Germaine Dulac

LE BONHEUR DU JOUR (1927, Fr.)
(? r.) d, Gaston Ravel

LE BRASIER ARDENT (1923, Fr.)
(? r.) d, Ivan Mosjoukine, Alexander Volkov; lp, Ivan Mosjoukine, Natalie Lissenko

LE CABINET DE L'HOMME NOIR (1924, Fr.)
(? r.) d, Alfred Machin, Henry Wuhlschleger

LE CALVAIRE D'UNE REINE (1919, Fr.)
(? r.) d, Rene Leprince

LE CAPITAINE FRACASSE (1929, Fr.)
(? r.) d, Alberto Cavalcanti

LE CARILLON DE MINUIT (1922, Fr.)
(? r.) d, Jacques de Baroncelli

LE CARNIVAL DES VERITES (1920, Fr.)
(? r.) d, Marcel L'Herbier; lp, Suzanne Despres, Jacque Catelain, Paul Capellani, Claude France

LE CHANSON DU FEU (1917, Fr.)
(? r.) d, Georges Monca

LE CHANT DE L'AMOUR TRIOMPHANT (1923, Fr.)
(? r.) d, Viatcheslaw Tourjansky; lp, Natalie Kovanko, Jean Angelo, Nicolas Koline, Jean D'Yd

LE CHAUFFEUR DE MADEMOISELLE (1928, Fr.)
(? r.) d, Henri Chomette

LE CHEMIN D'ERONA (1921, Fr.)
(? r.) d, Louis Delluc; lp, Durec, Eve Francis

LE CHEMINEAU (1917, Fr.)
(? r.) d, Henry Krauss

LE CHEMINEAU (1926, Fr.)
(? r.) d, Georges Monca

LE CHEVALIER DE GABY (1920, Fr.)
(? r.) d, Charles Burguet

LE CHIFFONNIER DE PARIS (1924, Fr.)
(? r.) d, Serge Nadejdine; lp, Nicolas Koline

LA CINEMA AU SERVICE DE L'HISTOIRE (1927, Fr.)
(? r.) d, Germaine Dulac

LE COUR DES GUEUX (1925, Fr.)
(? r.) d, Alfred Machin, Henry Wuhlschleger

LE COFFRET DE JADE
(SEE: JADE CASKET, THE, 1929)

LE COMTE KOSTIA (1925, Fr.)
(? r.) d, Jacques Robert

LE COUPABLE (1917, Fr.)
(? r.) d, Andre Antoine

LE COSTAUD DES EPINETTES (1923, Fr.)
(? r.) d, Raymond Bernard

LE CREPUSCULE DE COEUR (1916, Fr.)
(? r.) d, Maurice Mariaud

LE CRIME DE LORD ARTHUR SAVILLE (1922, Fr.)
(? r.) d, Rene Hervil

LE CRIME DES HOMMES (1923, Fr.)
(? r.) d, Gaston Roudes

LE CRIME DU BOUIF (1921, Fr.)
(? r.) d, Henri Pouctal; lp, Lucien Tramel

LE DEDALE (1917, Fr.)
(? r.) d, Jean Kemm

LE DEDALE (1927, Fr.)
(? r.) d, Gaston Roudes

LE DELAI (1918, Fr.)
(? r.) d, Jean Kemm

LE DESTIN EST MAITRE (1920, Fr.)
(? r.) d, Jean Kemm

LE DIABLE AU COEUR (1928, Fr.)
(? r.) d, Marcel L'Herbier; lp, Jacque Catelain, Betty Balfour

LE DIABLE DANS LA VILLE (1925, Fr.)
(? r.) d, Germaine Dulac

LE DIAMANT VERT (1917, Fr.)
(? r.) d, Pierre Marodon

LE DIEU DU HASARD (1919, Fr.)
(? r.) d, Henri Pouctal; lp, Gaby Deslys

LE DOUBLE AMOUR (1925, Fr.)
(? r.) d, Jean Epstein

LE DROIT A LA VIE (1917, Fr.)
(5 r.) d, Abel Gance; lp, Paul Vermoyal, Leon Mathot, Andree Brabant, Georges Paulais

LE DROIT DE TUER (1920, Fr.)
(? r.) d, Charles Maudru, Charles de Marsan

LE FANTOME DU MOULIN ROUGE (1925, Fr.)
(? r.) d, Rene Clair; lp, Georges Vaultier, Sandra Milowanoff, Maurice Schutz, Jose Davert

LE FERME DU CHOQUART (1922, Fr.)
(? r.) d, Jean Kemm

LE 15E PRELUDE DE CHOPIN (1922, Fr.)
(? r.) d, Viatcheslaw Tourjansky

LE GAMIN DE PARIS (1923, Fr.)
(? r.) d, Louis Feuillade

LE GARDIN DU FEU (1924, Fr.)
(? r.) d, Gaston Ravel

LE GENTILHOMME COMMERCANT (1918, Fr.)
(? r.) d, Raymond Bernard

LE GEOLE (1921, Fr.)
(? r.) d, Gaston Ravel

LE JARDIN SUR L'ORONTE (1925, Fr.)
(? r.) d, Rene Leprince

LE JOUER D'ECHES
(SEE: CHESS PLAYER, THE, 1930, Fr.)

LE JUIF ERRANT (1926, Fr.)
(? r.) d, Luitz-Morat; lp, Antonin Artaud

LE LAC D'ARGENT (1922, Fr.)
(? r.) d, Gaston Roudes

LE LION DES MOGOLS (1924, Fr.)
(? r.) d, Jean Epstein; lp, Ivan Mosjoukine

LE LOTUS D'OR (1916, Fr.)
(? r.) d, Louis Mercanton

LE LYS ROUGE (1920, Fr.)
(? r.) d, Charles Maudru, Charles de Marsan

LE MALHEUR QUI PASSE (1916, Fr.)
(? r.) d, Louis Feuillade

LE MANOIR DE LA PEUR (1927, Fr.)
(? r.) d, Alfred Machin, Henry Wuhlschleger; lp, Romuald Joube

LE MARIAGE DE MADEMOISELLE BEULEMANS (1927, Fr.)
(? r.) d, Julien Duvivier

LE MARIAGE DE ROSINE (1925, Fr.)
(? r.) d, Pierre Colombier

LE MAUVAIS GARCON (1923, Fr.)
(? r.) d, Henri Diamant-Berger

LE MERCHANT HOMME (1921, Fr.)
(? r.) d, Charles Maudru, Charles de Marsan

LE MENEUR DE JOIES (1929, Fr.)
(? r.) d, Charles Burguet

LE MEURTIER DE THEODORE (1921, Fr.)
(? r.) d, Georges Monca

LE MIRACLE DES LOUPS
(SEE: MIRACLE OD WOLVES, THE, 1925, Fr.)

LE MYSTERE DE LA TOUR EIFFEL (1927, Fr.)
(? r.) d, Julien Duvivier

LE NEGRE BLANC (1925, Fr.)
(? r.) d, Serge Nadejdine

LE NOCTURNE (1919, Fr.)
(? r.) d, Louis Feuillade

LE NOCTURNE (1917, Fr.)
(? r.) d, Maurice Mariaud

LE NOEL DU PERE LATHUILE (1922, Fr.)
(? r.) d, Pierre Colombier

LE NOEL D'UN VAGABOND (1918, Fr.)
(? r.) d, Rene Leprince

LE PASSAGER (1928, Fr.)
(? r.) d, Jacques de Baroncelli

LE PASSE DE MONIQUE (1918, Fr.)
(? r.) d, Louis Feuillade

LE PENSEUR (1920, Fr.)
(? r.) d, Leon Poirier; lp, Andre Nox

LE PETIT CAFE (1919, Fr.)
(? r.) d, Raymond Bernard; lp, Max Linder, Henri Debain

LE PETIT CHOSE (1923, Fr.)
(? r.) d, Andre Hugon

LE PETIT MOINEAU DE PARIS (1923, Fr.)
(? r.) d, Gaston Roudes

LE PORION (1921, Fr.)
(? r.) d, Georges Champavert

LE PREMIERE IDYLLE DE BOUCOT (1920, Fr.)
(? r.) d, Robert Saidreau

LE PRINCE CHARMANT (1925, Fr.)
(? r.) d, Viatcheslaw Tourjansky; lp, Jacque Catelain, Natalie Kovanko, Claude France, Nicolas Koline

LE PRINCE JEAN (1928, Fr.)
(? r.) d, Rene Hervil

LE RAVIN SANS FOND (1917, Fr.)
(? r.) d, Jacques Feyder

LE RAVIN SANS FOND (1917, Fr.)
(? r.) d, Raymond Bernard

LE RAYON INVISIBLE
(SEE: PARIS QUI DORT, 1924)

LE REFLET DE CLAUDE MERCOEUR (1923, Fr.)
(? r.) d, Julien Duvivier

LE REMOUS (1920, Fr.)
(? r.) d, Georges Champavert

LE RETOUR AUX CHAMPS (1918, Fr.)
(? r.) d, Jacques de Baroncelli

LE REVE (1921, Fr.)
(? r.) d, Jacques de Baroncelli; lp, Andree Brabant

LE REVEIL (1925, Fr.)
(? r.) d, Jacques de Baroncelli

LE REVEIL DE MADDALONE (1924, Fr.)
(? r.) d, Henri Etievant

LE ROI DE CAMARGUE (1921, Fr.)
(? r.) d, Andre Hugon; lp, Jean Toulout, Claude Merelle

LE ROI DE CIRQUE (1925, Fr.)
(? r.) d, Edouard Violet; lp, Max Linder

LE ROI DE LA MER (1917, Fr.)
(? r.) d, Jacques de Baroncelli; lp, Gabriel Signoret, Eve Francis, Ginette Darnys

LE ROI DE LA VITESSE (1923, Fr.)
(? r.) d, Henri Diamant-Berger

LE ROMAN D'UN JEUNE HOMME PAUVRE (1927, Fr.)
(? r.) d, Gaston Ravel

LE ROMAN D'UN SPAHI (1917, Fr.)
(? r.) d, Henri Pouctal

LE SANG D'ALLAH (1922, Fr.)
(? r.) d, Luitz-Morat; lp, Gaston Modot

LE SANG DES FINOEL (1922, Fr.)
(? r.) d, Georges Monca

LE SCANDALE (1918, Fr.)
(? r.) d, Jacques de Baroncelli

LE SECRET DE CARGO (1929, Fr.)
(? r.) d, Maurice Mariaud

LE SECRET DE POLICHINELLE (1923, Fr.)
(? r.) d, Rene Hervil

LE SECRET DE ROSETTE LAMBERT (1920, Fr.)
(? r.) d, Raymond Bernard; lp, Lois Meredith, Henri Debain, Sylviane Grey, Charles Dullin

LE SECRET DU 'LONE STAR' (1920, Fr.)
(? r.) d, Jacques de Baroncelli; lp, Fanny Ward, Gabriel Signoret

LE SENS DE LA MORT (1921, Fr.)
(? r.) d, Jacob Protozanoff

LE SIEGE DES TROIS (1918, Fr.)
(? r.) d, Jacques de Baroncelli

LE SOUS MARIN DE CRISTAL (1928, Fr.)
(? r.) d, Marcel Vandal

LE TABLIER BLANC (1917, Fr.)
(? r.) d, Rene Hervil, Louis Mercanton

LE TALISON (1921, Fr.)
(? r.) d, Charles Maudru, Charles de Marsan

LE TAXI 313 x 7 (1922, Fr.)
(? r.) d, Pierre Colombier

LE TOCSIN (1920, Fr.)
(? r.) d, Pierre Marodon

LE TONNERRE (1921, Fr.)
(? r.) d, Louis Delluc

LE TORNOI (1928, Fr.)
(7 r.) d, Jean Renoir; lp, Aldo Nadi, Jackie Monnier, Enrique Rivero, Suzanne Despres

LE TORRENT (1918, Fr.)
(? r.) d, Rene Hervil, Louis Mercanton; lp, Henry Roussel, Gabriel Signoret, Jaque Catelain

LE TOURBILLON DE PARIS (1928, Fr.)
(? r.) d, Julien Duvivier; lp, Lil Dagover

LE TRAIN SANS YEUX (1928, Fr.)
(? r.) d, Alberto Cavalcanti

LE TRAITEMENT DU HOQUET (1918, Fr.)
(? r.) d, Raymond Bernard

LE VALSE DE L'ADIEU (1928, Fr.)
(? r.) d, Henry Roussel; lp, Pierre Blanchar, Marie Bell

LE VENENOSA (1928, Fr.)
(? r.) d, Roger Lion

LE VERTIGE (1917, Fr.)
(? r.) d, Andre Hugon

LE VERTIGE (1926, Fr.)
(? r.) d, Marcel L'Herbier

LE VOYAGE IMAGINAIRE (1926, Fr.)
(? r.) d, Rene Clair; lp, Jean Borlin, Albert Prejean, Jim Gerard, Dolly Davis

LEAD KINDLY LIGHT
(SEE: THE PRODIGAL DAUGHTER, 1916, Brit.)

LEAH KLESCHNA (1913)
(4 r.) d, J. Searle Dawley; lp, Carlotta Nillson, House Peters, Hal Clarendon, Alexander Gaden

LEAH'S SUFFERING (1917, USSR)
(4 r.) d, Joseph Soifer; lp, Solovets, M. Leorov, J. Soifer, A. Lukovsky

LEAP INTO LIFE (1924, Ger.)
(? r.) d, Johannes Guter; lp, Xeni Desni, Walter Rilla, Paul Heidemann, Frida Richard

LEAP YEAR (1921)
(5 r.) lp, Roscoe "Fatty" Arbuckle

LEARNIN' OF JIM BENTON, THE (1917)
(5 r.) d, Cliff Smith; lp, Roy Stewart, Fritzi Ridgeway, Walter Perry, Ed Brady

LEAVE IT TO GERRY (1924)
(6 r.) d, Arvid E. Gillstrom; lp, Billie Rhodes, William Collier, Jr., Claire McDowell, Kate Lester

LEAVE IT TO ME (1920)
(5 r.) d, Emmett J. Flynn; lp, William Russell, Eileen Percy, Marcelle Daley, Hal Cooley

LEAVE IT TO SUSAN (1919)
(5 r.) d, Clarence G. Badger; lp, Madge Kennedy, Wallace MacDonald, Alfred Hollingsworth, Anna Hernandez

LEAVENWORTH CASE, THE (1923)
(6 r.) d, Charles Giblyn; lp, Seena Owen, Martha Mansfield, Wilfred Lytell, Bradley Barker

LEAVES FROM SATAN'S BOOK (1921, Den.)
(7 r.) d, Carl-Theodore Dreyer; lp, Helge Nissen, Halvard Hoff, Jacob Texiere, Erling Hansson

LEAVES OF MEMORY (1914)
(4 r.) d, Donald Mackenzie

L'ECUYERE (1922, Fr.)
(? r.) d, Leonce Perret

LEFT HAND BRAND, THE (1924)
(5 r.) d, Neal Hart; lp, Neal Hart, Fred Burnworth

LEGEND OF GOSTA BERLING (1928, Swed.)
(4 r.) d, Mauritz Stiller; lp, Lars Hanson, Greta Garbo, Jenny Hasselquist, Mona Martenson

LEGION OF DEATH, THE (1918)
(7 r.) d, Tod Browning; lp, Edith Storey, Philo McCullough, Fred Malatesta, Charles Gerard

LEGION OF THE CONDEMNED (1928)
(8 r.) d, William A. Wellman; lp, Gary Cooper, Fay Wray, Barry Norton, Lane Chandler

LEGIONNAIRES IN PARIS (1927)
(6 r.) d, Arvid E. Gillstrom; lp, Al Cooke, Kit Guard, Louise Lorraine, Virginia Sale

L'EMPIRE DU DIAMENT (1921, Fr.)
(? r.) d, Leonce Perret

L'EMPREINTE (1916, Fr.)
(? r.) d, Andre Hugon

L'EMPRISE (1924, Fr.)
(? r.) d, Henri Diamant-Berger

LENA RIVERS (1914)
(5 r.)

LENA RIVERS (1925)
(9 r.) d, Whitman Bennett; lp, Earle Williams, Johnny Walker, Gladys Hulette, Edna Murphy

LEND ME YOUR NAME (1918)
(5 r.) d, Fred J. Balshofer; lp, Harold Lockwood, Bessie Eyton, Pauline Curley, Bert Starkey

L'ENFANT DU CARNAVAL (1921, Fr.)
(? r.) d, Ivan Mosjoukine

L'ENGRENAGE (1923, Fr.)
(? r.) d, Georges Monca

L'ENGRENAGE (1919, Fr.)
(? r.) d, Louis Feuillade

L'ENIGME (1919, Fr.)
(? r.) d, Louis Feuillade

L'ENIGME (1919, Fr.)
(? r.) d, Jean Kemm

L'ENIGME DU MONT AGEL (1924, Fr.)
(? r.) d, Alfred Machin, Henry Wuhlschleger

L'ENVOLEE (1921, Fr.)
(? r.) d, Gaston Ravel

LEOPARD WOMAN, THE (1920)
(6 r.) d, Wesley Ruggles; lp, Louise Glaum, House Peters, Alfred Hollingsworth, Noble Johnson

LEOPARDESS, THE (1923)
(6 r.) d, Henry Kolker; lp, Alice Brady, Edward Langford, Montagu Love, Charles Kent

LEOPARD'S BRIDE, THE (1916)
(5 r.) lp, Margaret Gibson, William Clifford, Brooklyn Keller, Nan Christy

L'EPAVE (1917, Fr.)
(? r.) d, Maurice Mariaud

L'EPERVIER (1924, Fr.)
(? r.) d, Robert Boudrioz; lp, Sylvio de Pedrelli, Nilda du Piessy

L'EPINGLE ROUGE (1921, Fr.)
(? r.) d, Edouard Violet

LES AMOURS DE ROCAMBOLE (1924, Fr.)
(? r.) d, Charles Maudru, Charles de Marsan

LES BLEUS DE L'AMOUR (1918, Fr.)
(? r.) d, Henri Desfontaines

LES CHASSEUR DE CHEZ MAXIM'S (1927, Fr.)
(? r.) d, Roger Lion

LES CHERES IMAGES (1920, Fr.)
(? r.) d, Andre Hugon

LES CLOCHES DE CORNEVILLE (1917, Brit.)
(6 r.) d, Thomas Bentley; lp, Elsie Craven, Moya Mannering, M.R. Morand, Leslie Stiles

LES CINQ GENTLEMEN MAUDITS (1919, Fr.)
(? r.) d, Luitz-Morat

LES CONTES LES MILLES ET UNE NUITS (1922, Fr.)
(? r.) d, Viatcheslaw Tourjansky; lp, Natalie Kovanko, Nicolas Rimsky

LES DAMES DE CROIX-MORT (1917, Fr.)
(? r.) d, Maurice Mariaud

LES DEUX AMOURS (1917, Fr.)
(? r.) d, Charles Burguet

LES DEUX BAISERS (1920, Fr.)
(? r.) d, Gaston Roudes

LES DEUX GOSSES (1924, Fr.)
(? r.) d, Louis Mercanton

LES DEUX MARQUISES (1916, Fr.)
(? r.) d, Jean Kemm

LES DEUX TIMIDES (1929, Fr.)
(6 r.) d, Rene Clair; lp, Pierre Batcheff, Maurice de Feraudy, Vera Flory, Jim Gerald

LES DIEUX ONT SOIF (1926, Fr.)
(? r.) d, Pierre Malodon

LES ECRITS RESTENT (1917, Fr.)
(? r.) d, George Lacroix

LES ELUS DE LA MER (1925, Fr.)
(? r.) d, Gaston Roudes

LES FEMMES COLLANTES (1920, Fr.)
(? r.) d, Georges Monca

LES FEMMES DES AUTRES (1920, Fr.)
(? r.) d, Pierre Marodon

LES FOURCHAMBAULT (1929, Fr.)
(? r.) d, Georges Monca

LES FRERES CORSES (1917, Fr.)
(? r.) d, Andre Antoine

LES GRANDS (1924, Fr.)
(? r.) d, Henri Fescourt

LES HERITIERS DE L'ONCLE JAMES (1924, Fr.)
(? r.) d, Alfred Machin, Henry Wulhschleger

LES LARMES DU PARDON (1919, Fr.)
(? r.) d, Rene Leprince

LES LOUVES (1925, Fr.)
(? r.) d, Robert Boudrioz

LES MAINS FLETRIES (1920, Fr.)
(? r.) d, Edouard Violet

LES MISERABLES (1927, Fr.)
(12 r.) d, Henri Fescourt; lp, Gabriel Gabrio, Sandra Milovanoff, Andree Rolane, Renee Carl

LES MORTS QUI PARLENT (1920, Fr.)
(? r.) d, Pierre Marodon

LES MOUTTES (1919, Fr.)
(? r.) d, Maurice Mariaud

LES MYSTERES DU CIEL (1920, Fr.)
(? r.) d, Gerard Bourgeois

LES NOUVEAUX MESSIEURS (1929, Fr.)
(12 r.) d, Jacques Feyder; lp, Albert Prejean, Gaby Morlay, Henri Roussel

LES NUITS DE CARNAVAL (1922, Fr.)
(? r.) d, Viatcheslaw Tourjansky

LES OMBRES QUI PASSANT (1924, Fr.)
(? r.) d, Alexandre Volkoff; lp, Ivan Mosjoukine, Natalie Lissenko, Andree Brabant, Henry Krauss

LES OPPRIMES (1923, Fr.)
(? r.) d, Henry Roussel; lp, Raquel Meller

LES PETITS (1925, Fr.)
(? r.) d, Gaston Roudes

LES PETITES MARIONETTES (1918, Fr.)
(? r.) d, Louis Feuillade

LES PREMIERES ARMES DE ROCAMBOLE (1924, Fr.)
(? r.) d, Charles Maudru, Charles de Marsan

LES RANTZAU (1924, Fr.)
(? r.) d, Gaston Roudes

LES ROQUEVILLARD (1922, Fr.)
(? r.) d, Julien Duvivier

LES SOEURS ENNEMIES (1917, Fr.)
(? r.) d, Germaine Dulac

LES TERRES D'OR (1925, Fr.)
(? r.) d, Rene Le Somptier

LES TRANSATLANTIQUES (1928, Fr.)
(? r.) d, Pierre Colombier

LES TRAVAILLEURS DE LA MER (1918, Fr.)
(? r.) d, Andre Antoine

LES TROIS GANTS DE LA DAMES EN NOIR (1920, Fr.)
(? r.) d, Pierre Marodon

LES TROIS MASQUES (1921, Fr.)
(? r.) d, Henry Krauss

LES VOLEURS DE GLOIRE (1926, Fr.)
(? r.) d, Pierre Marodon

LES YEUX DE L'AIME (1922, Fr.)
(? r.) d, Roger Lion

L'ESPIONE (1923, Fr.)
(? r.) d, Henri Desfontaines

L'ESPIONE AUX YEUX NOIRS (1926, Fr.)
(? r.) d, Henri Desfontaines

LESS THAN KIN (1918)
(5 r.) d, Donald Crisp; lp, Wallace Reid, Ann Little, Raymond Hatton, Gustav von Seyffertitz

LESS THAN THE DUST (1916)
(7 r.) d, John Emerson; lp, Mary Pickford, David Powell, Frank Losee, Mary Alden

LESSON, THE (1917)
(5 r.) d, Charles Giblyn; lp, Constance Talmadge, Tom Moore, Herbert Heyes, Walter Hiers

LEST WE FORGET (1918)
(7 r.) d, Leonce Perret; lp, Rita Jolivet, Hamilton Revelle, L. Rogers Lytton, Kate Blancke

LET HIM BUCK (1924)
(5 r.) d, Frank Morrow; lp, Dick Carter, Gene Crosby

LET KATHY DO IT (1916)
(5 r.) d, C.M. & S.A. Franklin; lp, Jane Grey, Tully Marshall, Ralph Lewis, Walter Long

LET NO MAN PUT ASUNDER (1924)
(? r.) d, J. Stuart Blackton; lp, Pauline Frederick, Lou Tellegen, Leslie Austen, Helena D'Algy

LET WOMEN ALONE (1925)
(6 r.) d, Paul Powell; lp, Pat O'Malley, Wanda Hawley, Wallace Beery, Ethel Wales

L'ETAU (1920, Fr.)
(? r.) d, Maurice Mariaud

L'ETE DE LA SAINT MARTIN (1920, Fr.)
(? r.) d, Georges Champavert

L'ETERNEL FEMININE (1921, Fr.)
(? r.) d, Roger Lion

L'ETRANGE AVENTURE DU DOCTEUR WORKS (1921, Fr.)
(? r.) d, Robert Saidreau

LET'S BE FASHIONABLE (1920)
(5 r.) d, Lloyd Ingraham; lp, Douglas MacLean, Doris May [Lee], Wade Boteler, Grace Morse

LET'S ELOPE (1919)
(5 r.) d, John S. Robertson; lp, Marguertie Clark, Gaston Glass, Frank Mills, Helen Greene

LET'S FINISH THE JOB (1928)
(5 r.)

LET'S GET A DIVORCE (1918)
(5 r.) d, Charles Giblyn; lp, Billie Burke, John Miltern, Pinna Nesbit, Rod La Rocque

LET'S GO (1923)
(6 r.) d, William K. Howard; lp, Richard Talmadge, Eileen Percy, George Nichols, Tully Marshall

LET'S GO GALLAGHER (1925)
(5 r.) d, Robert De Lacey, James Gruen; lp, Tom Tyler, Barbara Starr, Olin Francis, Sam Peterson

LET'S PRETEND
(SEE: CASTLES IN THE AIR, 1922, Brit.)

L'EVASION (1922, Fr.)
(? r.) d, Georges Champavert

L'EVEIL (1924, Fr.)
(? r.) d, Gaston Roudes

LEW TYLER'S WIVES (1926)
(7 r.) d, Harley Knoles; lp, Frank Mayo, Ruth Clifford, Hedda Hopper, Helen Lee Worthing

L'HEURE TRAGIQUE (1916, Fr.)
(? r.) d, Georges Lacroix

L'HEUREUX MORT (1924, Fr.)
(? r.) d, Serge Nadejdine

L'HOMME A L'HISPANO (1927, Fr.)
(? r.) d, Julien Duvivier

L'HOMME DES BALEARES (1925, Fr.)
(? r.) d, Andre Hugon

L'HOMME DU LARGE (1920, Fr.)
(6 r.) d, Marcel L'Herbier; lp, Jaque Catelain, Roger Karl, Marcelle Pradot, Charles Boyer

L'HOMME DU TRAIN 117 (1923, Fr.)
(? r.) d, Charles Maudru, Charles de Marsan

L'HOMME ET LA POUPEE (1921, Fr.)
(? r.) d, Maurice Mariaud

L'HOMME MERVEILLEUX (1922, Fr.)
(? r.) d, Louis Mercanton

L'HOMME QUI REVIENT DE LION (1917, Fr.)
(? r.) d, Gaston Ravel

L'HOMME SAN VISAGE (1919, Fr.)
(? r.) d, Louis Feuillade

L'HOMME INUSABLE (1923, Fr.)
(? r.) d, Raymond Bernard

LIAR, THE (1918)
(6 r.) lp, Jane Gail, Stanley Walpole

LIAR, THE (1918)
(5 r.) d, Edmund Lawrence; lp, Virginia Pearson, Edward F. Roseman, Victor Sutherland, Alexander Franck

LIBERTINE, THE (1916)
(6 r.) d, Julius Steger, Joseph A. Golden; lp, John Mason, Alma Hamilton, Edward Langford, Marie Alexander

LIBERTY HALL (1914, Brit.)
(? r.) d, Harold Shaw; lp, Ben Webster, Edna Flugrath, O.B. Clarence, Ranee Brooks

L'IBIS BLEU (1919, Fr.)
(? r.) d, Camille de Morlhon

L'IDEE DE FRANCOISE (1923, Fr.)
(? r.) d, Robert Saidreau

L'IDOLE BRISEE (1920, Fr.)
(? r.) d, Maurice Mariaud

LIE, THE (1918)
(5 r.) d, J. Searle Dawley; lp, Elsie Ferguson, David Powell, Betty Howe, John L. Shine

LIFE (1920)
(7 r.) d, Travers Vale; lp, Jack Mower, Arline Pretty, J.H. Gilmore, Rod La Rocque

LIFE AND DEATH OF LIEUTENANT SCHMIDT (1917, USSR)
(5 r.) d, Yakov Poselsky, Alexander Razumni

LIFE AND PASSION OF CHRIST (1921, Fr.)
(7 r.) d, Ferdinand Zecca, Lucien Nonguet

LIFE FOR A LIFE, A (1916, USSR)
(7 r.) d, Yevgeni Bauer; lp, Olga Rakhmanova, Lydia Koreneva, Vera Kholodnaya, Vitold Polonsky

LIFE IN DEATH (1914, USSR)
(? r.) d, Yevgeni Bauer; lp, Ivan Mozhukhin, I. Lashchinilina, P. Biryukov

LIFE IN THE ORANGE GROVES (1920)
(6 r.) d, George L. Cox; lp, Henry Sedley, Marian Skinner Virginia Rumrill, Loyola O'Connor

LIFE LINE, THE (1919)
(6 r.) d, Maurice Tourneur; lp, Jack Holt, Seena Owen, Lew Cody, Pauline Starke

LIFE MASK, THE (1918)
(7 r.) d, Frank H. Crane; lp, Olga Petrova, Thomas Holding, Wyndham Standing, Mathilda Brundage

LIFE OF A LONDON ACTRESS, THE (1919, Brit.)
(5 r.) d, Alexander Butler; lp, Daphne Glenne, James Lindsay, Daisy Cordell, Judd Green

LIFE OF AN ACTRESS, THE (1915, Brit.)
(4 r.) d, Charles Weston; lp, Alice Inward, George Keene, Lily Saxby, George Foley

LIFE OF AN ACTRESS (1927)
(7 r.) d, Jack Nelson; lp, Barbara Bedford, Bert Sprotte, Lydia Knott, John Patrick

LIFE OF "BIG TIM" SULLIVAN, THE (1914)
(4 r.)

LIFE OF GENERAL VILLA, THE (1914)
(7 r.) d, Raoul Walsh

LIFE OF GENEVIEVE, THE (1922)
(6 r.) lp, Lydia Korwin

LIFE OF JOHN BUNYAN-PILGRIM'S PROGRESS (1912)
(5 r.) lp, Warner Oland

LIFE OF LORD KITCHENER, THE (1917, Brit.)
(6 r.) d, Rex Wilson, W. Dane Stanton

LIFE OF MOSES (1909)
(5 r.) d, J. Stuart Blackton

LIFE OF RILEY, THE (1927)
(7 r.) d, William Beaudine; lp, Charlie Murray, George Sidney, Stephen Carr, June Marlowe

LIFE OF SHAKESPEARE, THE
(SEE: LOVES AND ADVENTURES IN THE LIFE OF SHAKESPEARE, 1914, Brit.)

LIFE OF THE PARTY, THE (1920)
(5 r.) d, Joseph Henabery; lp, Roscoe "Fatty" Arbuckle, Winnifred Greenwood, Roscoe Karns, Julia Faye

LIFE OR HONOR? (1918)
(7 r.) d, Edmund Lawrence; lp, Leah Baird, James Morrison, Violet Palmer, Harry Burkhardt

LIFE STORY OF DAVID LLOYD GEORGE, THE (1918, Brit.)
(6 r.) d, Maurice Elvey; lp, Norman Page, Alma Reville, Ernest Thesiger, Douglas Munro

LIFEGUARDSMAN, THE (1916, Brit.)
(4 r.) d, Frank G. Bayly; lp, Annie Saker, Alfred Paumier, Leslie Carter, Alfred Bishop

LIFE'S A FUNNY PROPOSITION (1919)
(5 r.) d, Thomas N. Heffron; lp, William Desmond, Louise Lovely, Jay Belasco, Vera Doria

LIFE'S A STAGE (1929, Brit.)
(6 r.) d, Arthur Phillips; lp, Frank Stanmore, Joy Windsor, Tony Wylde, Gerald Rawlinson

LIFE'S BLIND ALLEY (1916)
(5 r.) d, Thomas Ricketts; lp, Harold Lockwood, May Allison, Nell Franzen, Warren Ellsworth

LIFE'S CROSSROADS (1928)
(6 r.) d, Edgar Lewis; lp, Gladys Hulette, Mahlon Hamilton, William Conklin, William Humphrey

LIFE'S GREATEST GAME (1924)
(7 r.) d, Emory Johnson; lp, Tom Santschi, Jane Thomas, Dickey Brandon, Johnnie Walker

LIFE'S GREATEST PROBLEM (1919)
(6 r.) d, J. Stuart Blackton; lp, Mitchell Lewis, Rubye De Remer, Gus Alexander, Ida Darling

LIFE'S GREATEST QUESTION (1921)
(5 r.) d, Harry Revier; lp, Roy Stewart, Louise Lovely, Harry von Meter, Dorothy Valegra

LIFE'S MOCKERY (1928)
(7 r.) d, Robert F. Hill; lp, Betty Compson, Alec B. Francis, Russell Simpson, Theodore von Eltz

LIFE'S SHADOWS (1916)
(5 r.) d, William Nigh, David Thompson; lp, William Nigh, Irene Howley, Will S. Stevens, Robert Elliott

LIFE'S SHOP WINDOW (1914)
(5 r.) d, Herbert Brenon, Henry Belmar; lp, Claire Whitney, Stuart Holmes, Henry Belmar

LIFE'S TEMPTATIONS (1914)
(4 r.)

LIFE'S TWIST (1920)
(5 r.) d, W. Christy Cabanne; lp, Bessie Barriscale, Walter McGrail, King Baggot, Claire Du Brey

LIFTED VEIL, THE (1917)
(5 r.) d, George D. Baker; lp, Ethel Barrymore, William B. Davidson, Charles French, Frank Gilmore

LIGHT (1915, Brit.)
(4 r.) d, Sidney Morgan; lp, Julian Royce, Mona K. Harrison, Joan Morgan, A. Harding Steerman

LIGHT, THE (1916)
(5 r.) d, William C. Dowlan; lp, Franklin Ritchie, Helen Rosson, George Webb, Eugenie Forde

LIGHT, THE (1919)
(5 r.) d, J. Gordon Edwards; lp, Theda Bara, Eugene Ormonde, Robert Walker, Georges Renevant

LIGHT IN DARKNESS (1917)
(5 r.) d, Alan Crosland; lp, Shirley Mason, Frank Morgan, William Tooker, J. Frank Glendon

LIGHT IN THE CLEARING, THE (1921)
(7 r.) d, T. Hayes Hunter; lp, Eugenie Besserer, Clara Horton, Edward Sutherland, George Hackathorne

LIGHT OF HAPPINESS, THE (1916)
(5 r.) d, John H. Collins; lp, Viola Dana, Robert Walker, Lorraine Frost, George Melville

LIGHT OF THE WESTERN STARS, THE (1925)
(7 r.) d, William K. Howard; lp, Jack Holt, Billie Dove, Noah Beery, Alma Bennett

LIGHT OF WESTERN STARS, THE (1918)
(6 r.) d, Charles Swickard; lp, Dustin Farnum, Winifred Kingston, Bert Appling, Joseph Swickard

LIGHT THAT FAILED, THE (1916)
(5 r.) d, Edward Jose; lp, Robert Edeson, Jose Collins, Lillian Tucker, Claude Fleming

LIGHT THAT FAILED, THE (1923)
(7 r.) d, George Melford; lp, Jacqueline Logan, Percy Marmont, David Torrence, Sigrid Holmquist

LIGHT WITHIN, THE (1918)
(7 r.) d, Larry Trimble; lp, Olga Petrova, Lumsden Hare, Thomas Holding, Clarence Heritage

LIGHT WITHIN, THE
(SEE: DESTINY, 1921, Ger.)

LIGHT WOMAN, A (1920)
(6 r.) d, George L. Cox; lp, Helen Jerome Eddy, Hallam Cooley, Claire Du Brey, Charles Clary

LIGHT WOMAN, A
(SEE: DOLORES, 1928, Brit.)

LIGHTNIN' (1925)
(8 r.) d, John Ford; lp, Jay Hunt, Madge Bellamy, Wallace MacDonald, J. Farrell MacDonald

LIGHTNIN' JACK (1924)
(5 r.) lp, Jack Perrin, Josephine Hill, Lew Meehan, Jack Richardson

LIGHTNIN' SHOT (1928)
(5 r.) d, J.P. McGowan; lp, Buddy Roosevelt, J.P. McGowan, Frank Earle, Carol Lane

LIGHTING (1927)
(7 r.) d, James C. McKay; lp, Jobyna Ralston, Margaret Livingston, Robert Frazier, Guinn Williams

LIGHTING BILL (1926)
(5 r.) d, Louis Chaudet; lp, Bill Bailey, Jean Arthur, Edward Heim, Jack Henderson

LIGHTING RIDER, THE (1924)
(6 r.) d, Lloyd Ingraham; lp, Harry Carey, Virginia Brown Faire, Thomas G. Lingham, Frances Ross

LIGHTING SPEED (1928)
(5 r.) d, Robert North Bradbury; lp, Bob Steele, Mary Mabery, Perry Murdock, Barney Furey

LIGHTS O' LONDON, THE (1914, Brit.)
(4 r.) d, Bert Haldane; lp, Arthur Chesney, Phyllis Relph, Fred Paul, Tom H. MacDonald

LIGHTS OF HOME, THE (1920, Brit.)
(6 r.) d, Fred Paul; lp, George Foley, Nora Hayden, Jack Raymond, Moya Nugent

LIGHTS OF NEW YORK, THE (1922)
(6 r.) d, Charles J. Brabin; lp, Clarence Nordstrom, Margaret Seddon, Marc MacDermott, Estelle Taylor

LIGHTS OF OLD BROADWAY (1925)
(7 r.) d, Monta Bell; lp, Marion Davies, Conrad Nagel, Frank Currier, George K. Arthur

LIGHTS OUT (1923)
(7 r.) d, Al Santell; lp, Ruth Stonehouse, Walter McGrail, Marie Astaire, Theodore von Eltz

LI-HANG LE CRUEL (1920, Fr.)
(? r.) d, Edouard Violet

LIKE WILDFIRE (1917)
(5 r.) d, Stuart Paton; lp, Herbert Rawlinson, Neva Gerber, L.M. Wells, Johnnie Cook

LILAC SUNBONNET, THE (1922, Brit.)
(5 r.) d, Sidney Morgan; lp, Joan Morgan, Warwick Ward, Pauline Peters, Arthur Lennard

L'ILE D'AMOUR (1928, Fr.)
(? r.) d, Jean Durand

L'ILE DE LA MORT (1923, Fr.)
(? r.) d, Donatien

L'ILE ENCHANTEE (1927, Fr.)
(? r.) d, Henry Roussel

LILLIES OF THE FIELD (1924)
(9 r.) d, John Francis Dillon; lp, Corinne Griffith, Conway Tearle, Alma Bennett, Sylvia Breamer

LILLIES OF THE STREETS (1925)
(7 r.) d, Joseph Levering; lp, Virginia Lee Corbin, Wheeler Oakman, Peggy Kelly, Johnnie Walker

LILY, THE (1926)
(7 r.) d, Victor Schertzinger; lp, Belle Bennett, Ian Keith, Reata Hoyt, Barry Norton

LILY OF KILLARNEY (1929, Brit.)
(6 r.) d, George Ridgwell; lp, Cecil Landeau, Pamela Parr, Dennis Wyndham, Barbara Gott

LILY OF POVERTY FLAT, THE (1915)
(5 r.) lp, Beatriz Michelena, Frederick Lewis

LILY OF THE DUST (1924)
(7 r.) d, Dimitri Buchowetski; lp, Pola Negri, Ben Lyon, Noah Beery, Raymond Griffith

L'IMAGE (1926, Fr.)
(? r.) d, Jacques Feyder; lp, Arlette Marchel

LIMITE (1930, Braz.)
(6 r.) d, Mario Peixoto; lp, Iolanda Bernardes, Carmen Santos, Tatiana Rey, Mario Peixoto

LIMITED MAIL, THE (1925)
(7 r.) d, George Hill; lp, Monte Blue, Vera Reynolds, Willard Louis, Tom Gallery

LIMOUSINE LIFE (1918)
(5 r.) d, Jack Dillon; lp, Olive Thomas, Lee Phelps, Joe Bennett, Lillian West

LINCOLN HIGHWAYMAN, THE (1920)
(5 r.) d, Emmett J. Flynn; lp, William Russell, Lois Lee, Frank Brownlee, Jack Connolly

L'INCONNU (1921, Fr.)
(? r.) d, Charles Maudru, Charles de Marsan

L'INHUMAINE (1923, Fr.)
(6 r.) d, Marcel L'Herbier; lp, Georgette Leblanc, Jacque Catelain, Philippe Heriat

LINKED BY FATE (1919, Brit.)
(5 r.) d, Albert Ward; lp, Isobel Elsom, Malcolm Cherry, Clayton Green, Esme Hubbard

L'INONDATION (1924, Fr.)
(? r.) d, Louis Delluc; lp, Philippe Heriat, Ginette Maddie, Van Daele, Eve Francis

L'INSIGNE MYSTERIEUX (1922, Fr.)
(? r.) d, Henri Desfontaines

L'INSTINCT (1917, Fr.)
(? r.) d, Henri Pouctal

L'INSTINCT EST MAITRE (1917, Fr.)
(? r.) d, Jacques Feyder

L'INVITATION AU VOYAGE (1927, Fr.)
(? r.) d, Germaine Dulac; lp, Emmy Gynt, Raymond Dubreil

LION AND THE MOUSE, THE (1914)
(6 r.) d, Barry O'Neil; lp, Ethel Clayton, Gaston Bell, Richard Morris, Carlotta Doty

LION AND THE MOUSE, THE (1919)
(5 r.) d, Tom Terriss; lp, Alice Joyce, Conrad Nagel, Anders Randolf, Henry Hallam

LION'S BREATH, THE (1916)
(? r.) d, Horace Davey; lp, Neal Burns, Billie Rhodes, George French, Ray Gallagher

LION'S BRIDE, THE (1914, Ger.)
(4 r.)

LION'S DEN, THE (1919)
(5 r.) d, George D. Baker; lp, Bert Lytell, Alice Lake, Joseph Kilgour, Edward Connelly

LIQUID GOLD (1919)
(5 r.) d, Aubrey M. Kennedy; lp, Arthur Guy Empey, Harry Lee

L'IRONIE DU DESTIN (1924, Fr.)
(? r.) d, Dimitri Kirsanoff

L'IRONIE DU SORT (1924, Fr.)
(? r.) d, Georges Monca

LISTEN LESTER (1924)
(6 r.) d, William A. Seiter; lp, Louise Fazenda, Harry Myers, Eva Novak, George O'Hara

LITTLE ADVENTURESS, THE (1927)
(7 r.) d, William De Mille; lp, Vera Reynolds, Phyllis Haver, Robert Ober, Theodore Kosloff

LITTLE AMERICAN, THE (1917)
(6 r.) d, Cecil B. DeMille; lp, Mary Pickford, Jack Holt, Raymond Hatton, Hobart Bosworth

LITTLE BIT OF FLUFF, A (1919, Brit.)
(5 r.) d, Kenelm Foss; lp, Ernest Thesiger, Dorothy Minto, Bertie Wright, Kitty Barlow

LITTLE BIT OF FLUFF, A
(SEE: SKIRTS, 1928, Brit.)

LITTLE BIT OF HEAVEN
(SEE: A BIT OF HEAVEN, 1928)

LITTLE BOSS, THE (1919)
(5 r.) d, David Smith; lp, Bessie Love, Wallace MacDonald, Otto Lederer, Harry Russell

LITTLE BOSS, THE (1927)
(5 r.) lp, Ruth Mix

LITTLE BOY SCOUT, THE (1917)
(5 r.) d, Francis J. Grandon; lp, Ann Pennington, Owen Moore, Fraunie Fraunholz, Marcia Harris

LITTLE BREADWINNER, THE (1916, Brit.)
(5 r.) d, Wilfred Noy; lp, Kitty Atfield, Maureen O'Hara

LITTLE BROTHER OF GOD (1922, Brit.)
(7 r.) d, F. Martin Thornton; lp, Victor McLaglen, Valia, Alec Fraser, Fred Raynham

LITTLE BROTHER OF THE RICH, A (1915)
(5 r.) d, Hobart Bosworth, Otis Turner; lp, Hobart Bosworth, Jane Novak, Edmond Brown, Hobart Henley

LITTLE BROTHER OF THE RICH, A (1919)
(6 r.) d, Lynn F. Reynolds; lp, Frank Mayo, Kathryn Adams, J. Barney Sherry, Lilie Leslie

LITTLE BUCKAROO, THE (1928)
(5 r.) d, Louis King; lp, Buzz Barton, Milburn Morante, Kenneth McDonald, Peggy Shaw

LITTLE CHEVALIER, THE (1917)
(4 r.) d, Alan Crosland; lp, Shirley Mason, Ray McKee, Richard Tucker, Freddie Verdi

LITTLE CHILD SHALL LEAD THEM, A (1919, Brit.)
(5 r.) d, Bertram Phillips; lp, Queenie Thomas, Bruce Gordon, Walter Timms

LITTLE CHILD SHALL LEAD THEM, A
(SEE: WHO ARE MY PARENTS?, 1922)

LITTLE CHURCH AROUND THE CORNER, THE (1915)
(5 r.)

LITTLE DAMOZEL, THE (1916, Brit.)
(5 r.) d, Wilfred Noy; lp, Barbara Conrad, Geoffrey Wilmer

LITTLE DIPLOMAT, THE (1919)
(5 r.) d, Stuart Paton; lp, Marie Osborne, Lydia Knott, William Welsh, Jack Connolly

LITTLE DORRIT (1920, Brit.)
(7 r.) d, Sidney Morgan; lp, Lady Tree, Langhorne Burton

LITTLE DUCHESS, THE (1917)
(5 r.) d, Harley Knoles; lp, Madge Evans, Pinna Nesbit, Jack Drumier, James Davis

LITTLE EVE EDGARTON (1916)
(5 r.) d, Robert Z. Leonard; lp, Herbert Rawlinson, Ella Hall, Doris Pawn, Gretchen Lederer

LITTLE FIREBRAND, THE (1927)
(5 r.) d, Charles Hutchison; lp, Edith Thornton, George Fawcett, Lou Tellegen, Eddie Phillips

LITTLE FOOL, THE (1921)
(? r.) d, Philip E. Rosen; lp, Milton Sills, Frances Wadsworth, Nigel Barrie

LITTLE FRENCH GIRL, THE (1925)
(6 r.) d, Herbert Brenon; lp, Alice Joyce, Mary Brian, Neil Hamilton, Esther Ralston

LITTLE GIANT, THE (1926)
(7 r.) d, William Nigh; lp, Glenn Hunter, Edna Murphy, David Higgins, James Bradbury, Jr.

LITTLE GIRL IN A BIG CITY, A (1925)
(6 r.) d, Burton King; lp, Gladys Walton, Niles Welch, Mary Thurman, J. Barney Sherry

LITTLE GIRL NEXT DOOR, THE (1916)
(6 r.) lp, Charles Greenleaf

LITTLE GIRL NEXT DOOR, THE (1923)
(6 r.) d, W.S. Van Dyke; lp, Pauline Starke, James Morrison, Carmel Myers, Mitchell Lewis

LITTLE GIRL THAT HE FORGOT, THE (1914)
(5 r.) lp, Beulah Poynter

LITTLE GREY MOUSE, THE (1920)
(5 r.) d, James P. Hogan; lp, Louise Lovely, Sam De Grasse, Rosemary Theby, Philo McCullough

LITTLE GYPSY, THE (1915)
(5 r.) d, Oscar Apfel; lp, Dorothy Bernard, William Riley Hatch, Thurlow Bergen, Raymond Murray

LITTLE HOUR OF PETER WELLS, THE (1920, Brit.)
(5 r.) d, B.E. Doxat-Pratt; lp, O.B. Clarence, Heather Thatcher, Hebden Foster, Adelqui Migliar

LITTLE INTRUDER, THE (1919)
(5 r.) d, Oscar Apfel; lp, Louise Huff, George MacQuarrie, John Hines, Christine Mayo

LITTLE ITALY (1921)
(5 r.) d, George Terwilliger; lp, Alice Brady, Norman Kerry, George Fawcett, Jack Ridgway

LITTLE JOHNNY JONES (1923)
(7 r.) d, Arthur Rosson; lp, Johnny Hines, Wyndham Standing, Margaret Seddon, Herbert Prior

LITTLE LADY EILEEN (1916)
(5 r.) d, J. Searle Dawley; lp, Marguerite Clark, Vernon Steele, John L. Shine, Harry Lee

LITTLE LOST SISTER (1917)
(5 r.) d, Al Green; lp, Vivian Reed, Bessie Eyton, Marion Warner, Eugenie Besserer

LITTLE MARY SUNSHINE (1916)
(5 r.) d, Henry King; lp, Baby Marie Osborne, Henry King, Marguerite Nichols, Andrew Arbuckle

LITTLE MAYORESS, THE
(SEE: MILL-OWNER'S DAUGHTER, THE, 1916, Brit.)

LITTLE MEENA'S ROMANCE (1916)
(5 r.) d, Paul Powell; lp, Dorothy Gish, Owen Moore, Fred J. Butler, Robert Lawler

LITTLE MEG'S CHILDREN (1921, Brit.)
(5 r.) d, Bert Wynne; lp, Joan Griffiths, Warwick Ward, Hargrave Mansell

LITTLE MICKEY GROGAN (1927)
(6 r.) d, Leo Meehan; lp, Frankie Darrow, Lassie Lou Ahern, Jobyna Ralston, Carroll Nye

LITTLE MINISTER, THE (1921)
(6 r.) d, Penrhyn Stanlaws; lp, Betty Compson, George Hackathorne, Edwin Stevens, Nigel Barrie

LITTLE MINISTER, THE (1922)
(6 r.) d, David Smith; lp, Alice Calhoun, James Morrison, Henry Hebert, Alberta Lee

LITTLE MISS FORTUNE (1917)
(5 r.) d, Joseph Levering; lp, Marian Swayne, Bradley Barker, Hugh Thompson, Lucile Dorrington

LITTLE MISS GROWN-UP (1918)
(5 r.) d, Sherwood McDonald; lp, Gloria Joy, Ethel Pepprell, Mary Northmore, Neil Hardin

LITTLE MISS HAPPINESS (1916)
(5 r.) d, John Adolfi; lp, June Caprice, Harry Hilliard, Zena Keefe, Sara Alexander

LITTLE MISS HAWKSHAW (1921)
(5 r.) d, Eileen Percy, Eric Mayne, Francis Feeney, Frank Clark

LITTLE MISS LONDON (1929, Brit.)
(7 r.) d, Harry Hughes; lp, Pamela Parr, Eric Bransby Williams, Frank Stanmore, Pauline Johnson

LITTLE MISS NO-ACCOUNT (1918)
(5 r.) d, William P.S. Earle; lp, Gladys Leslie, Frank O'Connor, William Calhoun, Eulalie Jensen

LITTLE MISS NOBODY (1917)
(5 r.) d, Harry F. Millarde; lp, Violet Mersereau, Clara Byers, Helen Lindroth, Sidney Mason

LITTLE MISS NOBODY (1923, Brit.)
(6 r.) d, Wilfred Noy; lp, Flora le Breton, John Stuart, Ben Field, Gladys Jennings

LITTLE MISS OPTIMIST (1917)
(5 r.) d, Robert Thornby; lp, Vivian Martin, Tom Moore, Charles West, Ernest Joy

LITTLE MOTHER, THE (1922, Brit.)
(5 r.) d, A.V. Bramble; lp, Florence Turner, John Stuart, Lilian Douglas, Harvey Braban

LITTLE NAPOLEON, THE (1923, Ger.)
(? r.) d, Georg Jacoby; lp, Egon von Hagen, Paul Heidemann, Harry Liedtke, Jacob Tiedtke

LITTLE OLD NEW YORK (1923)
(11 r.) d, Sidney Olcott; lp, Marion Davies, Stephen Carr, J.M. Kerrigan, Harrison Ford

LITTLE ORPHAN (1915)
(5 r.) d, John Gorman; lp, Baby E.M. Gorman, Edward Warren, Violet Wilkey, Harold Goodwin

LITTLE ORPHAN, THE (1917)
(5 r.) d, Jack Conway; lp, Ella Hall, Gertrude Astor, Gretchen Lederer, Jack Conway

LITTLE ORPHANT ANNIE (1919)
(6 r.) d, Colin Campbell; lp, Colleen Moore, Thomas Santschi, Harry Lonsdale, Eugenie Besserer

LITTLE PEOPLE, THE (1926, Brit.)
(7 r.) d, George Pearson; lp, Mona Maris, Frank Stanmore, Gerald Ames, Barbara Gott

LITTLE PIRATE, THE (1917)
(5 r.) d, Elsie Jane Wilson; lp, Zoe Rae, Charles West, Frank Brownlee, Gretchen Lederer

LITTLE PRINCESS, THE (1917)
(5 r.) d, Marshall Neilan; lp, Mary Pickford, Norman Kerry, Theodore Roberts, ZaSu Pitts

LITTLE RED DECIDES (1918)
(5 r.) d, Jack Conway; lp, Barbara Connolly, Goro Kino, Frederick Vroom, Jack Curtis

LITTLE RED RIDING HOOD (1917)
(4 r.)

LITTLE RED SCHOOLHOUSE, THE (1923)
(6 r.) d, John G. Adolfi; lp, Martha Mansfield, Harlan Knight, Sheldon Lewis, E.K. Lincoln

LITTLE ROBINSON CRUSOE (1924)
(7 r.) d, Edward Cline; lp, Jackie Coogan, Will Walling, Tom Santschi, Daniel J. O'Brien

LITTLE ROWDY, THE (1919)
(5 r.) d, Harry Beaumont; lp, Hazel Daly, Harry Hilliard, Sidney Ainsworth

LITTLE RUNAWAY, THE (1918)
(5 r.) d, William P.S. Earle; lp, Gladys Leslie, Edward Earle, Jessie Stevens, Mary Maurice

LITTLE SAMARITAN, THE (1917)
(5 r.) d, Joseph Levering; lp, Marian Swayne, Carl Gerard, Lucile Dorrington, Sam Robinson

LITTLE SHEPHERD OF BARGAIN ROW, THE (1916)
(5 r.) d, Fred E. Wright; lp, Sallie Fisher, Richard C. Travers, John Junior, John Cossar

LITTLE SHEPHERD OF KINGDOM COME, THE (1920)
(5 r.) d, Wallace Worsley; lp, Jack Pickford, Clara Horton, Pauline Starke, J. Parks Jones

LITTLE SHEPHERD OF KINGDOM COME, THE (1928)
(8 r.) d, Alfred Santell; lp, Richard Barthelmess, Molly O'Day, Nelson McDowell, Martha Mattox

LITTLE SHOES (1917)
(5 r.) d, Arthur Berthelet; lp, Henry B. Walthall, Mary Charleson, Patrick Calhoun, Mary V. McAllister

LITTLE SISTER OF EVERYBODY, A (1918)
(5 r.) d, Robert T. Thornby; lp, Bessie Love, George Fisher, Hector Sarno, Joseph J. Dowling

LITTLE SNOB, THE (1928)
(6 r.) d, John G. Adolfi; lp, May McAvoy, Robert Frazier, Alec Francis, Virginia Lee Corbin

LITTLE SUNSET (1915)
(4 r.) lp, Hobart Bosworth, Master Gordon [Gordon Griffith]

LITTLE TERROR, THE (1917)
(5 r.) d, Rex Ingram; lp, Violet Mersereau, Sidney Mason, Mathilde Brundage, Jack Raymond

LITTLE WANDERER, THE (1920)
(5 r.) d, Howard M. Mithcell; lp, Shirley Mason, Raymond McKee, Edwin Booth Tilton, Cecil Van Auker

LITTLE WELSH GIRL, THE (1920, Brit.)
(5 r.) d, Fred Paul; lp, Christine Silver, Humberston Wright, Booth Conway, Adelaide Grace

LITTLE WHITE SAVAGE, THE (1919)
(5 r.) d, Paul Powell; lp, Carmel Myers, Harry Hilliard, William Dyer, Richard Cummings

LITTLE WOMEN (1917, Brit.)
(5 r.) d, G.B. Samuelson, Alexander Butler; lp, Daisy Burrell, Mary Lincoln, Minna Grey, Ruby Miller

LITTLE WOMEN (1919)
(6 r.) d, Harley Knoles; lp, Dorothy Bernard, Isabel Lamon, Lillian Hall, Florence Flinn

LITTLE YANK, THE (1917)
(5 r.) d, George Siegmann; lp, Dorothy Gish, Frank Bennett, Kate Toncray, Allen D. Sears

LITTLE YELLOW HOUSE, THE (1928)
(? r.) d, James Leo Meehan; lp, Orville Caldwell, Martha Sleeper, Lucy Beaumont, William Orlamond

LITTLEST REBEL, THE (1914)
(6 r.) lp, Mimi Yvonne, E.K.[Elmo] Lincoln; Frederick Fleck, William J. Sorrelle

LITTLEST SCOUT (1919)
(5 r.) d, Paula Blackton; lp, Charles Blackton, Violet Blackton

LIVE AND LET LIVE (1921)
(6 r.) d, William Christy Cabanne; lp, Harriet Hammond, George Nichols, Dulcie Cooper, Harris Gordon

LIVE SPARKS (1920)
(5 r.) d, Ernest C. Warde; lp, J. Warren Kerrigan, Fritzi Brunette, Mary Talbot, Roy Laidlow

LIVE WIRE, THE (1925)
(8 r.) d, Charles Hines; lp, Johnny Hines, Edmund Bresse, Mildred Ryan, J. Barney Sherry

LIVE WIRE HICK, A (1920)
(5 r.) d, Henry King; lp, William Russell

LIVING CORPSE, A (1918, USSR)
(6 r.) d, Cheslav Sabinsky; lp, V. Maximov, Vera Kholodnya, Osip Runich

LIVING CORPSE, A (1931, USSR)
(8 r.) d, Fyodor Otsep; lp, Vsevolod Pudovkin, Maria Jacobini, Gustav Diessl, Nata Vachnadze

LIVING DEAD MAN, THE
(SEE: LATE MATTHEW PASCAL, THE, 1924, Fr.)

LIVING LIES (1922)
(5 r.) d, Emile Chautard; lp, Edmund Lowe, Mona Kingsley, Kenneth Hill

LOADED DICE (1918)
(5 r.) d, Herbert Blache; lp, Frank Keenan, Florence Billings, Guy Coombs, Madeline Marshall

L'OBSTACLE (1918, Fr.)
(? r.) d, Jean Kemm

L'OCCIDENT (1928, Fr.)
(? r.) d, Henri Fescourt; lp, Claudia Victrix, Jaque Catelain

LOCKED DOORS (1925)
(7 r.) d, William C. De Mille; lp, Betty Compson, Theodore Roberts, Kathlyn Williams, Theodore von Eltz

LOCKED HEART, THE (1918)
(5 r.) d, Henry King; lp, Gloria Joy, Henry King, Vola Vale, Daniel Gilfether

LOCKED LIPS (1920)
(5 r.) d, William C. Dowlan; lp, Tsuru Aoki, Stanhope Wheatcroft, Magda Lane

LOCKSMITH AND CHANCELLOR (1923, USSR)
(7 r.) d, Vladimir Gardin; lp, I. Khudoleyev, Nikolai Panov, V. Maximov, Zoya Barantsevich

LOCO LUCK (1927)
(5 r.) d, Cliff Smith; lp, Art Acord, Fay Wray, Aggie Herring, William A. Steele

L'OEIL DE SAINT-YVES (1919, Fr.)
(? r.) d, Georges Champavert

L'OEILLET BLANC (1923, Fr.)
(? r.) d, Henri Desfontaines

LOMBARDI, LTD. (1919)
(6 r.) d, Jack Conway; lp, Bert Lytell, Alice Lake, Jean Acker, Juanita Hansen

L'OMBRE DECHIREE (1921, Fr.)
(? r.) d, Leon Poirier; lp, Suzanne Despres

L'OMBRE DU BONHEUR (1924, Fr.)
(? r.) d, Gaston Roudes

L'OMBRE DU PECHE (1922, Fr.)
(? r.) d, Jacob Protozanoff

LONDON FLAT MYSTERY, A (1915, Brit.)
(4 r.) d, Walter West; lp, Vera Cornish, George Foley, Reginald Stevens, Constance Backner

LONDON NIGHTHAWKS (1915, Brit.)
(4 r.) d, Percy Moran; lp, Percy Moran

LONE CHANCE, THE (1924)
(5 r.) d, Howard Mitchell; lp, John Gilbert, Evelyn Brent, John Miljan, Edwin Booth Tilton

LONE FIGHTER (1923)
(5 r.) d, Albert Russell; lp, Vester Pegg, Josephine Hill, Joe Ryan, Jim Gamble

LONE HAND, THE (1922)
(5 r.) d, Reeves Eason; lp, Ed "Hoot" Gibson, Marjorie Daw, Helen Holmes, Hayden Stevenson

LONE HAND SAUNDERS (1926)
(6 r.) d, Reeves Eason; lp, Fred Thomson, Bess Flowers, Billy Butts, Frank Hagney

LONE HAND TEXAS (1924)
(5 r.) lp, Lester Cuneo

LONE HAND WILSON (1920)
(5 r.) d, L.S. McKee, Harry Moody; lp, Lester Cuneo

LONE HORSEMAN, THE (1923)
(5 r.) d, Fred Caldwell; lp, Jack Perrin, Josephine Hill

LONE PATROL, THE (1928)
(5 r.) lp, William Bailey, Jean Dolores

LONE RIDER, THE (1922)
(5 r.) d, Denver Dixon; lp, Denver Dixon, Alma Rayford, Edward Heim, Charles Force

LONE RIDER, THE (1927)
(5 r.) lp, Fred Church

LONE STAR (1916)
(5 r.) d, Edward Sloman; lp, William Russell, Charlotte Burton, Harry Von Meter, Alfred Ferguson

LONE STAR RANGER, THE (1919)
(6 r.) d, J. Gordon Edwards; lp, William Farnum, Louise Lovely, G. Raymond Nye, Charles Clary

LONE STAR RANGER, THE (1923)
(6 r.) d, Lambert Hillyer; lp, Tom Mix, Billie Dove, L.C. Shumway, Stanton Heck

LONE STAR RUSH, THE (1915)
(5 r.) d, Edmund Mitchell; lp, Robert Frazer, Charles Arling, Rupert Julian, Mary Gaston

LONE WOLF, THE (1917)
(8 r.) d, Herbert Brenon; lp, Bert Lytell, Hazel Dawn, Edward Abeles, Alfred Hickman

LONE WOLF, THE (1924)
(6 r.) d, S.E.V. Taylor; lp, Dorothy Dalton, Jack Holt, Wilton Lackaye, [Frederick] Tyrone Power

LONE WOLF RETURNS, THE (1926)
(6 r.) d, Ralph Ince; lp, Bert Lytell, Billie Dove, Freeman Wood, Gustav von Seyffertitz

LONE WOLF'S DAUGHTER, THE (1919)
(7 r.) d, William P.S. Earle; lp, Louise Glaum, Edwin Stevens, Thomas Holding, Bertram Grassby

LONELY HEART (1921)
(5 r.) d, John B. O'Brien; lp, Robert Elliott, Kay Laurell

LONELY LADY OF GROSVENOR SQUARE, THE (1922, Brit.)
(5 r.) d, Sinclair Hill; lp, Betty Faire, Jack Hobbs, Dorothy Fane, Arthur Pusey

LONELY TRAIL, THE (1922)
(5 r.) lp, Fred K. Beauvais, Christina McNulty, W.L. Tremaine, Fred Bezerril

LONELY WOMAN, THE (1918)
(5 r.) d, Thomas N. Heffron; lp, Belle Bennett, Percy Challenger, Lee Hill, Anna Dodge

LONESOME CHAP, THE (1917)
(5 r.) d, Edward J. LeSaint; lp, Louise Huff, House Peters, John Burton, Eugene Pallette

LONESOME CORNERS (1922)
(6 r.) d, Edgar Jones; lp, Edgar Jones, Henry Van Bousen, Edna May Sperl, Walter Lewis

LONESOME HEART (1915)
(4 r.) d, William D. Taylor; lp, Margarita Fischer, William A.Carroll, Lucille Ward, Joseph E. Singleton

LONESOME LADIES (1927)
(6 r.) d, Joseph Henabery; lp, Lewis Stone, Anna Q. Nilsson, Jane Winton, Doris Lloyd

LONESOME TOWN (1916)
(5 r.) d, Thomas N. Heffron; lp, C. William Kolb, Max M. Dill, Harvey Clark, William Tedmarsh

LONG ARM OF MANNISTER, THE (1919)
(7 r.) d, Bertram Bracken; lp, Henry B. Walthall, Helene Chadwick, Olive Ann Alcorn, William H. Clifford

LONG CHANCE, THE (1915)
(6 r.) d, Edward J. LeSaint; lp, Frank Keenan, Fred Church, Harry Blaising, Walter Newman

LONG LANE'S TURNING, THE (1919)
(5 r.) d, L.W. Chaudet; lp, Henry B. Walthall, Mary Charleson, Harry M. O'Connor, Jack Richardson

LONG LOOP, THE
(SEE: LONG LOOP ON THE PECOS, THE, 1927)

LONG LOOP ON THE PECOS, THE (1927)
(6 r.) d, Leo Maloney; lp, Leo Maloney, Eugenia Gilbert, Frederick Dana, Albert Hart

LONG TRAIL, THE (1917)
(5 r.) d, Howard Hansel; lp, Lou Tellegen, Mary Fuller, Winifred Allen, Franklin Woodruff

LOOK OUT GIRL, THE (1928)
(7 r.) d, Dallas M. Fitzgerald; lp, Jacqueline Logan, Ian Keith, William H. Tooker, Lee Moran

LOOK YOUR BEST (1923)
(6 r.) d, Rupert Hughes; lp, Colleen Moore, Antonio Moreno, William Orlamond, Orpha Alba

LOOPED FOR LIFE (1924)
(5 r.) d, Park Frame; lp, Art Acord, Jack Richardson, Marcella Pershing, Charles Adler

LOOT (1919)
(6 r.) d, William C. Dowlan; lp, Joseph Girard, Ora Carew, Frank Thompson, Alfred Allen

L'ORAGE (1917, Fr.)
(? r.) d, Camille de Morlhon

LORD AND LADY ALGY (1919)
(5 r.) d, Harry Beaumont; lp, Tom Moore, Naomi Childers, Leslie Stuart, Frank Leigh

LORD CHUMLEY (1914)
(4 r.) d, James Kirkwood; lp, Henry B. Walthall, Walter Chrystie Miller, Lillian Gish, Charles West

LORD GAVE, THE
(SEE: WORLD'S DESIRE, THE, 1915, Brit.)

LORD LOVELAND DISCOVERS AMERICA (1916)
(5 r.) d, Arthur Maude; lp, Arthur Maude, Constance Crawley, William Carroll, Charles Newton

L'ORDONNANCE (1921, Fr.)
(? r.) d, Viatcheslaw Tourjansky

LORDS OF HIGH DECISION, THE (1916)
(5 r.) d, Jack Harvey; lp, Cyril Scott, Joseph Girard, William Welsh, Joe Daly

LORELEI OF THE SEA (1917)
(6 r.) d, Henry Otto; lp, [Frederick] Tyrone Power, Frances Burnham, Jay Belasco, John Oaker

LORNA DOONE (1920, Brit.)
(5 r.) d, H. Lisle Lucoque; lp, Dennis Wyndham, Bertie Gordon, Roy Raymond, George Bellamy

LORRAINE OF THE LIONS (1925)
(7 r.) d, Edward Sedgwick; lp, Norman Kerry, Patsy Ruth Miller, Fred Humes, Doreen Turner

LORSQU'UNE FEMME VENT (1919, Fr.)
(? r.) d, Georges Monca

LOSS OF THE BIRKENHEAD, THE (1914, Brit.)
(4 r.) d, Maurice Elvey; lp, Elizabeth Risdon, Fred Groves, A.V. Bramble, M. Gray Murray

LOST - A WIFE (1925)
(7 r.) d, William C. De Mille; lp, Adolphe Menjou, Greta Nissen, Robert Agnew, Edgar Norton

LOST AND FOUND
(SEE: LOST AND FOUND ON A SOUTH SEA ISLAND, 1923)

LOST AND FOUND ON A SOUTH SEA ISLAND (1923)
(7 r.) d, R.A. [Raoul] Walsh; lp, House Peters, Pauline Starke, Antonio Moreno, Mary Jane Irving

LOST AND WON (1915, Brit.)
(4 r.) d, Larry Trimble; lp, Florence Turner, Henry Edwards, Edward Lingard, Herbert Dansey

LOST AND WON (1917)
(5 r.) d, James Young; lp, Marie Doro, Elliott Dexter, Carl Stockdale, Mabel Van Buren

LOST AT SEA (1926)
(7 r.) d, Louis J. Gasnier; lp, Huntly Gordon, Lowell Sherman, Jane Novak, Natalie Kingston

LOST AT THE FRONT (1927)
(6 r.) d, Del Lord; lp, George Sidney, Charlie Murray, Natalie Kingston, John Kolb

LOST ATLANTIS
(SEE: MISSING HUSBANDS, 1922, Fr.)

LOST BATTALION, THE (1919)
(8 r.) d, Burton King; lp, Gaston Glass, Helen Ferguson, Marion Coakley, May Robson

LOST BATTALION, THE (1921)
(6 r.) lp, Gaston Glass, Blanche Davenport

LOST CHORD, THE (1925)
(7 r.) d, Wilfred Noy; lp, David Powell, Alice Lake, Dagmar Godowsky, Henry Sedley

LOST EXPRESS, THE (1926)
(5 r.) d, J.P. McGowan; lp, Henry Barrows, Eddie Barry, Martin Turner, Helen Holmes

LOST HOUSE, THE (1915)
(4 r.) d, W. Christy Cabanne; lp, Lillian Gish, Wallace Reid, F.A. Turner, A.D. Sears

LOST IN A BIG CITY (1923)
(8 r.) d, George Irving; lp, John Lowell, Baby Ivy Ward, Jane Thomas, Charles Beyer

LOST IN THE DARK (1914, Ital.)
(7 r.) d, Nino Martoglio; lp, Giovanni Grasso, Virginia Balistrieri, Maria Carmi, Dillo Lombardi

LOST IN TRANSIT (1917)
(5 r.) d, Donald Crisp; lp, George Beban, Helen Jerome Eddy, Frank Bennett, Bob White

LOST LEADER, A (1922, Brit.)
(6 r.) d, George Ridgwell; lp, Robert English, Dorothy Fane, Lily Iris, Lionel D'Aragon

LOST MONEY (1919)
(5 r.) d, Edmund Lawrence; lp, Madlaine Traverse, George McDaniels, Henry Hebert

LOST PARADISE, THE (1914)
(5 r.) d, Oscar Apfel; lp, H.B. Warner, Mabel Van Buren

LOST PRINCESS, THE (1919)
(5 r.) d, Scott Dunlap; lp, Elinor Fair, Albert Ray, George Hernandez, Maggie Halloway Fisher

LOST ROMANCE, THE (1921)
(7 r.) d, William C. De Mille; lp, Jack Holt, Lois Wilson, Fontaine La Rue, Conrad Nagel

LOST SHADOW, THE (1921, Ger.)
(5 r.) d, Paul Wegener; lp, Paul Wegener, Grete Schroder, Lyda Salmanova, Hannes Sturm

LOST TRAIL, THE (1926)
(5 r.) d, J.P. McGowan; lp, Al Hoxie

LOST TRIBE, THE (1924)
(5 r.) lp, Kenneth McDonald

LOST ZEPPELIN, THE (1929)
(7 r.) d, Edward Sloman; lp, Conway Tearle, Virginia Valli, Ricardo Cortez, Duke Martin

LOTTERY MAN, THE (1916)
(5 r.) lp, Thurlow Bergen, Carolyn Lee, Elsie Esmond, Allan Murnane

LOTTERY MAN, THE (1919)
(5 r.) d, James Cruze; lp, Wallace Reid, Wanda Hawley, Harrison Ford, Fanny Midgley

LOTUS BLOSSOM (1921)
(7 r.) d, Frank Grandon; lp, Lasy Tsen Mei, Tully Marshall, Noah Beery, Jack Abbe

LOTUS EATER, THE (1921)
(7 r.) d, Marshall Neilan; lp, John Barrymore, Colleen Moore, Anna Q. Nilsson, Ida Waterman

LOTUS WOMAN, THE (1916)
(5 r.) d, Harry Millarde; lp, Alice Hollister, Harry Millarde, Arthur Albertson, John E. Mackin

LOUDWATER MYSTERY, THE (1921, Brit.)
(5 r.) d, Norman Macdonald; lp, Gregory Scott, Pauline Peters, Clive Brook, Cameron Carr

L'OURAGAN SUR LA MONTAGE (1922, Fr.)
(? r.) d, Julien Duvivier

LOVE (1920)
(6 r.) d, Wesley Ruggles; lp, Louise Glaum, Peggy Cartwright, James Kirkwood, Joseph Kilgour

LOVE AND AMBITION (1917)
(6 r.) d, Edward Warren; lp, Helen Hayes, Howard Hall, Harry Hadfield, Earl Schenck

LOVE AND GLORY (1924)
(7 r.) d, Rupert Julian; lp, Charles De Roche, Wallace MacDonald, Madge Bellamy, Ford Sterling

LOVE AND HATE (1916)
(6 r.) d, James Vincent; lp, Bertha Kalish, Stuart Holmes, Jane Lee, Katherine Lee

LOVE AND JOURNALISM (1916, Swed.)
(? r.) d, Mauritz Stiller; lp, Richard Lund, Jenny Tschernichin-Larsson, Karin Molander, Stina Berg

LOVE AND THE DEVIL (1929)
(7 r.) d, Alexander Korda; lp, Milton Sills, Maria Corda, Ben Bard, Nellie Bly Baker

LOVE AND THE LAW (1919)
(6 r.) d, Edgar Lewis; lp, Ruth Roland, Glenn White, Josephine Hill

LOVE AND THE WOMAN (1919)
(5 r.) d, Tefft Johnson; lp, June Elvidge, Rod LaRoque, Donald Hall, Ed Roseman

LOVE BANDIT, THE (1924)
(6 r.) d, Dell Henderson; lp, Doris Kenyon, Victor Sutherland, Jules Cowles, Christian Frank

LOVE BRAND, THE (1923)
(5 r.) d, Stuart Paton; lp, Roy Stewart, Wilfrid North, Margaret Landis, Arthur Hull

LOVE BURGLAR, THE (1919)
(5 r.) d, James Cruze; lp, Wallace Reid, Anna Q. Nilsson, Raymond Hatton, Wallace Beery

LOVE CALL, THE (1919)
(5 r.) d, Louis William Chaudet; lp, Billie Rhodes, Lloyd Whitlock, Hart Hoxie, William Dyer

LOVE CHEAT, THE (1919)
(5 r.) d, George Archainbaud; lp, June Caprice, Creighton Hale, Edwards Davis, Alfred Hickman

LOVE DARES ALL
(SEE: A SAILOR'S SWEETHEART, 1913, Brit.)

LOVE DEFENDER, THE (1919)
(5 r.) d, Tefft Johnson; lp, June Elvidge, Frank Mayo, Madge Evans, Tefft Johnson

LOVE DOCTOR, THE (1917)
(5 r.) d, Paul Scardon; lp, Earle Williams, Corinne Griffith, Webster Campbell, Evart Overton

LOVE 'EM AND LEAVE 'EM (1926)
(4 r.) d, Frank Tuttle; lp, Evelyn Brent, Lawrence Gray, Louise Brooks, Osgood Perkins

LOVE EXPERT, THE (1920)
(5 r.) d, David Kirkland; lp, Constance Talmadge, Arnold Lucy, John Halliday, Natalie Talmadge

LOVE GAMBLE, THE (1925)
(6 r.) d, Edward Le Saint; lp, Lillian Rich, Robert Frazer, Pauline Garon, Kathleen Clifford

LOVE, HATE AND A WOMAN (1921)
(6 r.) d, Charles Horan; lp, Grace Davison, Ralph Kellard, Robert Frazer, Lila Peck

LOVE - HATE - DEATH (1918, USSR)
(7 r.) d, Ivan Perestiani; lp, Zoya Karabanova, Ivan Perestiani, Richard Boleslawsky

LOVE HERMIT, THE (1916)
(5 r.) lp, William Russell, Charlotte Burton, William Stowell, Harry Von Meter

LOVE, HONOR AND BEHAVE (1920)
(5 r.) d, F. Richard Jones, Earle Kenton; lp, Marie Prevost, George O'Hara, Charles Murray, Ford Sterling

LOVE, HONOR AND ? (1919)
(5 r.) d, Charles Miller; lp, Stuart Holmes, Ellen Cassidy, Corliss Giles, Florence Short

LOVE HOUR, THE (1925)
(7 r.) d, Herman Raymaker; lp, Huntley Gordon, Louise Fazenda, Willard Louis, Ruth Clifford

LOVE HUNGER, THE (1919)
(5 r.) d, William P.S. Earle; lp, Lillian Walker, L.C. Shumway, Herbert Prior, Allene Hale

LOVE HUNGRY (1928)
(6 r.) d, Victor Heerman; lp, Lois Moran, Lawrence Gray, Marjorie Beebe, Edythe Chapman

LOVE IN THE DARK (1922)
(6 r.) d, Harry Beaumont; lp, Viola Dana, Cullen Landis, Arline Pretty, Bruce Guerin

LOVE IN THE WELSH HILLS (1921, Brit.)
(6 r.) d, Bernard Dudley; lp, James Knight, Marjorie Villis, Constance Worth, R. Heaton-Grey

LOVE IN THE WILDERNESS (1920, Brit.)
(6 r.) d, Alexander Butler; lp, Madge Titheradge, C.M. Hallard, Campbell Gullan, Maudie Dunham

LOVE INSURANCE (1920)
(5 r.) d, Donald Crisp' lp, Bryant Washburn, Lois Wilson, Theodore Roberts, Frances Raymond

LOVE IS LOVE (1919)
(5 r.) d, Scott Dunlap; lp, Albert Ray, Elinor Fair, William Ryno, Howard Mack

LOVE LETTERS (1917)
(5 r.) d, Roy William Neill; lp, Dorothy Dalton, Thurston Hall, William Conklin, Dorcas Matthews

LOVE LETTERS (1924)
(5 r.) d, David Soloman; lp, Shirley Mason, Gordon Edwards, Alma Francis, John Miljan

LOVE MADNESS (1920)
(7 r.) d, Joseph Henabery; lp, Louise Glaum, Matt Moore, William Conklin, Noah Beery

LOVE MAGGY (1921, Brit.)
(6 r.) d, Fred Leroy Granville; lp, Peggy Hyland, Campbell Gullan, James Lindsay, Maudie Dunham

LOVE MART, THE (1927)
(8 r.) d, George Fitzmaurice; lp, Billie Dove, Gilbert Roland, Raymond Turner, Noah Beery

LOVE MASK, THE (1916)
(5 r.) d, Frank Reicher; lp, Cleo Ridgely, Wallace Reid, Earle Foxe, Robert Fleming

LOVE MASTER, THE (1924)
(7 r.) d, Laurence Trimble; lp, Strongheart (a dog), Lady Julie (a dog), Lillian Rich, Harold Austin

LOVE ME (1918)
(5 r.) d, Roy William Neil; lp, Dorothy Dalton, Jack Holt, Robert McKim, William Conklin

LOVE NEST, THE (1922)
(? r.) d, Wray Physioc; lp, Bernard Siegel, Jean Scott, Richard Travers, Charles Graham

LOVE NET, THE (1918)
(5 r.) d, Tefft Johnson; lp, Madge Evans, Jack Drumier, Charles Sutton, W.T. Carleton

LOVE NEVER DIES (1916)
(5 r.) d, William Worthington; lp, Ruth Stonehouse, Franklyn Farnum, Dorothy Clark, Maurice Kusell

LOVE NEVER DIES (1921)
(7 r.) d, King Vidor; lp, Lloyd Hughes, Madge Bellamy, Joe Bennett, Lillian Leighton

LOVE OF A STATE COUNCILLOR (1915, USSR)
(5 r.) d, Pyotr Chardynin; lp, V. Elsky, M. Kassatskaya, Vera Coralli

LOVE OF AN ACTRESS, THE (1914, Brit.)
(4 r.) d, Wilfrey Noy; lp, Dorothy Bellew, Evan Thomas

LOVE OF JEANNE NEY, THE (1927, Ger.)
(7 r.) d, G.W. Pabst; lp, Edith Jehanne, Uno Henning, Fritz Rasp, Vladimir Sokolov

LOVE OF PAQUITA, THE (1927)
(6 r.) lp, Marilyn Mills, Floyd Ames, Walter Emerson, Wilbur Mack

LOVE OF SUNYA, THE (1927)
(8 r.) d, Albert Parker; lp, Gloria Swanson, John Boles, Anders Randolf, Andres De Segurola

LOVE OF WOMEN, THE (1915)
(4 r.) d, Joseph Smiley; lp, Lilie Leslie, George Soule Spencer, Jack Standing, William Cohill

LOVE OF WOMEN (1924)
(6 r.) d, Whitman Bennett; lp, Helene Chadwick, Montague Love, Maurice Costello, Mary Thurman

LOVE ON THE RIO GRANDE (1925)
(5 r.) lp, Bill Cody

LOVE ONE ANOTHER (1922, Den.)
(7 r.) d, Carl-Theodor Dreyer; lp, Polina Pickowska, Vladimir Gajdarov, Torleif Reiss, Richard Boleslawski

LOVE OR FAME (1919)
(5 r.) lp, Elaine Hammerstein

LOVE OR JUSTICE (1917)
(5 r.) d, Walter Edwards; lp, Louise Glaum, Jack Richardson, Charles Gunn, J. Barney Sherry

LOVE OR MONEY (1920)
(5 r.) d, Burton King; lp, Virginia Lee, Roger Lytton

LOVE OVER NIGHT (1928)
(6 r.) d, Edward H. Griffith; lp, Rod La Rocque, Jeanette Loff, Richard Tucker, Tom Kennedy

LOVE PIKER, THE (1923)
(7 r.) d, E. Mason Hopper; lp, Anita Stewart, William Norris, Robert Frazer, Carl Gerrard

LOVE PIRATE, THE (1923)
(5 r.) d, Richard Thomas; lp, Melbourne MacDowell, Carmel Myers, Charles Force, Kathryn McGuire

LOVE ROUTE, THE (1915)
(4 r.) d, Allan Dwan; lp, Harold Lockwood, Winifred Kingston, Donald Crisp, Jack Pickford

LOVE SPECIAL, THE (1921)
(5 r.) d, Frank Urson; lp, Wallace Reid, Agnes Ayres, Theodore Roberts, Lloyd Whitlock

LOVE STORY OF ALIETTE BRUNTON, THE (1924, Brit.)
(7 r.) d, Maurice Elvey; lp, Isobel Elsom, Henry Victor, James Carew, Humbertson Wright

LOVE SUBLIME, A (1917)
(5 r.) d, Tod Browning, Wilfred Lucas; lp, Wilfred Lucas, Carmel Myers, Fred Turner, Alice Rae

LOVE THAT DARES, THE (1919)
(5 r.) d, Harry Millarde; lp, Madlaine Traverse, Thomas Santschi, Frank Elliott, Mae Gaston

LOVE THAT LIVES, THE (1917)
(5 r.) d, Robert G. Vignola; lp, Pauline Frederick, John Sainpolis, Pat O'Malley, Joseph Carroll

LOVE, THE ONLY LAW
(SEE: OUTLAW AND HIS WIFE, THE, 1918, Swed.)

LOVE THIEF, THE (1916)
(5 r.) d, Richard Stanton; lp, Gretchen Hartman, Alan Hale, Edwin Cecil, Frances Burnham

LOVE THIEF, THE (1926)
(7 r.) d, John McDermott; lp, Norman Kerry, Greta Nissen, Marc MacDermott, Cissy Fitzgerald

LOVE THRILL, THE (1927)
(6 r.) d, Millard Webb; lp, Laura La Plante, Tom Moore, Bryant Washburn, Jocelyn Lee

LOVE TRAIL, THE (1916, Brit.)
(6 r.) d, Fred Paul, L.C. MacBean; lp, Fred Paul, Agnes Glynne, Bertram Burleigh, Booth Conway

LOVE TRAP, THE (1923)
(6 r.) d, John Ince; lp, Bryant Washburn, Mabel Forrest, Wheeler Oakman, Kate Lester

LOVE WAGER, THE (1927)
(6 r.) d, Clifford Slater Wheeler; lp, Gaston Glass, Lenore Bushman, Lucy Beaumont, Arthur Rankin

LOVE WATCHES (1918)
(5 r.) d, Henri Houry; lp, Corinne Griffith, Denton Vane, Edward Burns, Florence Deshon

LOVE WITHOUT QUESTION (1920)
(6 r.) d, B.A. Rolfe; lp, Olive Tell, James Morrison, Peggy Parr, Mario Majeroni

LOVEBOUND (1923)
(5 r.) d, Henry Otto; lp, Shirley Mason, Albert Roscoe, Richard Tucker, Joseph Girard

LOVELY MARY (1916)
(5 r.) d, Edgar Jones; lp, Mary Miles Minter, Thomas Carrigan, Frank De Vernon, Russell Simpson

LOVER OF CAMILLE, THE (1924)
(8 r.) d, Harry Beaumont; lp, Monte Blue, Willard Louis, Pat Moore, Pierre Gendron

LOVERS? (1927)
(6 r.) d, John M. Stahl; lp, Ramon Novarro, Alice Terry, Edward Martindel, Edward Connelly

LOVERS IN ARABY (1924, Brit.)
(5 r.) d, Adrian Brunel; lp, Annette Benson, Miles Mander, Norman Penrose, Adrian Brunel

LOVERS IN QUARANTINE (1925)
(7 r.) d, Frank Tuttle; lp, Bebe Daniels, Harrison Ford, Alfred Lunt, Eden Gray

LOVES AND ADVENTURES IN THE
LIFE OF SHAKESPEARE (1914, Brit.) (? r.) d, J.B. McDowell, Frank R. Growcott; lp, Albert Ward, Sybil Hare

LOVE'S BATTLE (1920)
(5 r.) d, William James Craft; lp, Joe Moore, Eileen Sedgwick

LOVE'S BOOMERANG (1922)
(6 r.) d, John S. Robertson; lp, Ann Forrest, Bunty Fosse, David Powell, John Miltern

LOVE'S CONQUEST (1918)
(5 r.) d, Edward Jose; lp, Lina Cavalieri, Courtenay Foote, Fred Radcliffe, Frank Lee

LOVE'S CROSS ROADS (1916)
(5 r.) d, Joseph A. Golden; lp, Marie Empress, Marian Swayne, William Huntington, Paul Irving

LOVE'S CRUCIBLE (1916)
(5 r.) d, Emile Chautard; lp, Frances Nelson, Douglas MacLean, June Elvidge, Lumsden Hare

LOVE'S CRUCIBLE (1922, Swed.)
(? r.) d, Victor Sjostrom; lp, Gosta Eckman, Jenny Hasselqvist

LOVE'S FLAME (1920)
(5 r.) d, Carl Louis Gregory; lp, Thomas J. Carrigan, Vivienne Osborne, Cora Williams, Alexis Rene

LOVE'S GREATEST MISTAKE (1927)
(6 r.) d, Edward Sutherland; lp, Evelyn Brent, William Powell, James Hall, Josephine Dunn

LOVE'S HARVEST (1920)
(5 r.) d, Howard Mitchell; lp, Shirley Mason, Raymond McKee, Edwin Booth Tilton, Lile Leslie

LOVE'S INFLUENCE (1922, Brit.)
(5 r.) d, Edward R. Gordon; lp, George K. Arthur, Flora le Breton, Sir Simon Stuart, Bertie White

LOVE'S LARIAT (1916)
(5 r.) d, George E. Marshall, Harry Carey; lp, Harry Carey, Neal Hart, William Quinn, Olive Fuller Golden

LOVE'S LAW (1917)
(5 r.) d, Tefft Johnson; lp, Joan Sawyer, Stuart Holmes

LOVE'S LAW (1918)
(5 r.) d, Francis J. Grandon; lp, Gail Kane, Courtenay Foote, Reed Hamilton, Frederick Jones

LOVE'S MASQUERADE (1922)
(5 r.) d, William P.S. Earle; lp, Conway Tearle, Winifred Westover, Florence Billings, Robert Ellis

LOVES OF AN ACTRESS (1928)
(8 r.) d, Rowland V. Lee; lp, Pola Negri, Nils Asther, Mary McAllister, Richard Tucker

LOVES OF CARMEN (1927)
(9 r.) d, Raoul Walsh; lp, Dolores Del Rio, Victor McLaglen, Don Alvarado, Nancy Nash

LOVES OF COLLEEN BAWN, THE (1924, Brit.)
(7 r.) d, W.P. Kellino; lp, Henry Victor, Colette Brettell, Stewart Rome, Gladys Jennings

LOVES OF LETTY, THE (1920)
(5 r.) d, Frank Lloyd; lp, Pauline Frederick, John Bowers, W. Lawson Butt, Willard Louis

LOVES OF MARY, QUEEN OF SCOTS, THE (1923)
(8 r.) d, Denison Clift; lp, Fay Compton, Gerald Ames, Ivan Samson, John Stuart

LOVE'S OLD SWEET SONG (1923)
(7 r.) d, Oscar Lund; lp, Louis Wolheim, Helen Weir, Donald Gallagher, Helen Lowell

LOVE'S OPTION (1928, Brit.)
(6 r.) d, George Pearson; lp, Dorothy Boyd, Pat Aherne, James Carew, Henry Vibart

LOVE'S PAY DAY (1918)
(5 r.) d, E. Mason Hopper; lp, Pete Morrison, Rosemary Theby, Billy Daye, Lillian West

LOVE'S PILGRIMAGE TO AMERICA (1916)
(5 r.) d, Lawrence Marston; lp, Lulu Glaser, Thomas Keeswald, Sarah Brundage, Henry Norman

LOVE'S PRISONER (1919)
(6 r.) d, Jack Dillon; lp, Olive Thomas, Joe King, William V. Mong

LOVE'S PROTEGE (1920)
(5 r.) lp, Ora Carew

LOVE'S REDEMPTION (1921)
(5 r.) d, Eugene V. Brewster; lp, Dorian Romero, Blanche McGarity, Anetha Getwell, Edwin Markham

LOVE'S WHIRLPOOL (1924)
(6 r.) d, Bruce Mitchell; lp, James Kirkwood, Lila Lee, Robert Agnew, Mathew Betz

LOVETIME (1921)
(5 r.) d, Howard M. Mitchell; lp, Shirley Mason, Raymond McKee, Frances Hatton, Edwin B. Tilton

LOVEY MARY (1926)
(7 r.) d, King Baggot; lp, Bessie Love, William Haines, Mary Alden, Vivia Ogden

LOVIN' FOOL, THE (1926)
(6 r.) d, H.B. Carpenter;

LOVING FOOL, THE
(SEE: LOVIN' FOOL, THE, 1926)

LOVING LIES (1924)
(7 r.) d, W.S. Van Dyke; lp, Evelyn Brent, Monte Blue, Joan Lowell, Charles Gerrard

LOWLAND CINDERELLA, A (1921, Brit.)
(5 r.) d, Sidney Morgan; lp, Joan Morgan, George Foley, Ralph Forbes, Mavis Clare

LOYALTY (1918)
(6 r.) d, Jack Pratt; lp, Betty Brice, Murdock MacQuarrie, Jean Hathaway

LUCETTE (1924, Fr.)
(? r.) d, Louis Feuillade

LUCK AND SAND (1925)
(5 r.) d, Leo Maloney; lp, Leo Maloney, Josephine Hill, Homer Watson, Florence Lee

LUCK IN PAWN (1919)
(5 r.) d, Walter Edwards; lp, Marguerite Clark, Charles Meredith, Leota Lorraine, Richard Wayne

LUCK OF GERALDINE LAIRD, THE (1920)
(5 r.) d, Edward Sloman; lp, Bessie Barriscale, Niles Welch, Boyd Irwin, Dorcas Matthews

LUCK OF THE IRISH, THE (1920)
(7 r.) d, Allan Dwan; lp, James Kirkwood, Anna Q. Nilsson, Harry Northrup, Ward Crane

LUCK OF THE NAVY, THE (1927, Brit.)
(8 r.) d, Fred Paul; lp, Evelyn Laye, Henry Victor, Hayford Hobbs, Robert Cunningham

LUCK TOUCHED MY LEGS (1930, Jap.)
(? r.) d, Yasujiro Ozu

LUCKY CARSON (1921)
(5 r.) d, Wilfred North; lp, Earle Williams, Earl Schenck, Betty Ross Clarke, Gertrude Astor

LUCKY DAN (1922)
(5 r.) d, William K. Howard; lp, Richard Talmadge, George A. Williams, Dorothy Woods, S.E. Jennings

LUCKY DEVIL (1925)
(6 r.) d, Frank Tuttle; lp, Richard Dix, Esther Ralston, Edna May Oliver, Tom Findley

LUCKY FOOL (1927)
(5 r.) lp, Billy West, Kathleen Myers, Virginia Myers

LUCKY LADY, THE (1926)
(6 r.) d, Raoul Walsh; lp, Greta Nissen, Lionel Barrymore, William Collier, Jr., Marc MacDermott

LUCKY LARKIN (1930)
(8 r.) d, Harry J. Brown; lp, Ken Maynard, Nora Lane, James Farley, Harry Todd

LUCKY SPURS (1926)
(5 r.) d, H.B. Carpenter, V.V. Clegg; lp, Bill Patton

LUCRETIA LOMBARD (1923)
(7 r.) d, Jack Conway; lp, Irene Rich, Monte Blue, Marc MacDermott, Norma Shearer

LUNATIC AT LARGE, THE (1921)
(5 r.) d, Henry Edwards; lp, Henry Edwards, Chrissie White, Lyell Johnston, Gwynne Herbert

LUNATIC AT LARGE, THE (1927)
(6 r.) d, Fred Newmeyer; lp, Leon Errol, Dorothy Mackaill, Jack Raymond, Warren Cook

LURE OF AMBITION (1919)
(5 r.) d, Edmund Lawrence; lp, Theda Bara, Thurlow Bergen, William B. Davidson, Dan Mason

LURE OF A WOMAN, THE (1921)
(5 r.) d, J.M. Simms; lp, Regina Taylor, Lenore Jones, John Cobb, Alonzo Nixon

LURE OF CROONING WATER, THE (1920, Brit.)
(6 r.) d, Arthur Rooke; lp, Guy Newall, Ivy Duke, Hugh C. Buckler, Douglas Munro

LURE OF EGYPT, THE (1921)
(6 r.) d, Howard Hickman; lp, Robert McKim, Claire Adams, Joseph J. Dowling, Carl Gantvoort

LURE OF HEART'S DESIRE, THE (1916)
(5 r.) d, Francis J. Grandon; lp, Edmund Breese, Arthur Hoops, John Mahon, Jeanette Horton

LURE OF JADE, THE (1921)
(6 r.) d, Colin Campbell; lp, Pauline Frederick, Thomas Holding, Arthur Rankin, Leon Bary

LURE OF LUXURY, THE (1918)
(5 r.) d, Elsie Jane Wilson; lp, Ruth Clifford, Harry Von Meter, Edward Hearn, Elizabeth Janes

LURE OF MILLIONS (1915, Den.)
(4 r.)

LURE OF NEW YORK, THE (1913)
(4 r.) d, George Rolands

LURE OF THE MASK, THE (1915)
(4 r.) d, Thomas Ricketts; lp, Harold Lockwood, Elsie Jane Wilson, Irving Cummings, Lucy Payton

LURE OF THE MINE (1929)
(5 r.) lp, Montana Bill

LURE OF THE NIGHT CLUB, THE (1927)
(6 r.) d, Thomas Buckingham; lp, Viola Dana, Robert Ellis, Jack Daugherty, Bert Woodruff

LURE OF THE TRACK (1925)
(5 r.) lp, Sheldon Lewis, Maclyn Arbuckle, Dot Farley

LURE OF THE WEST (1925)
(5 r.) d, Alvin J. Neitz; lp, Eileen Sedgwick, Les Bates, Ray Childs, D. Maley

LURING LIGHTS (1915)
(4 r.) lp, Stella Hoban, Corinne Malvern, Helen Lindroth, Frank Woods

LURING LIPS (1921)
(5 r.) d, King Baggot; lp, Darrel Foss, Ramsey Wallace, William Welsh, Carlton King

LURING SHADOWS (1920)
(6 r.) d, Joseph Levering; lp, Aida Norton

LUST OF THE AGES, THE (1917)
(7 r.) d, Harry J. Revier; lp, Lillian Walker, Jack Mower

LUST OF THE RED MAN, THE (1914)
(4 r.) d, G.P. Hamilton; lp, Dot Farley

LUXURY (1921)
(6 r.) d, Marcel Perez; lp, Rubye De Remer, Walter Miller, Frederick Kalgren, Henry Pemberton

LYDIA GILMORE (1916)
(5 r.) d, Edwin S. Porter, Hugh Ford; lp, Pauline Frederick, Vincent Serrano, Thomas Holding, Robert Cain

LYING LIPS (1916)
(5 r.) d, Edward Sloman; lp, Franklin Ritchie, Winnifred Greenwood, Eugenia Forde, Clarence Burton

LYING WIVES (1925)
(7 r.) d, Ivan Abramson; lp, Clara Kimball Young, Richard Bennett, Madge Kennedy, Edna Murphy

LYONS MAIL, THE (1916, Brit.)
(5 r.) d, Fred Paul; lp, Nancy Price, Harry Welchman, James Lindsay, Tom Reynolds

M.A.R.S.
(SEE: RADIO-MANIA, 1923)

MA TANTE D'HONFLEUR (1923, Fr.)
(? r.) d, Robert Saidreau

MABUL (1927, USSR)
(9 r.) d, Yevgeni Ivanov-Barkov; lp, A. Dzyubina, Chechik-Efrati, Benno Schneider, I. Vinyar-Kagur

MACBETH (1916, Ger.)
(5 r.) lp, Arthur Bourchier, Violet Vanbrugh

MACBETH (1916)
(4 r.) d, John Emerson; lp, Sir Herbert Beerbom Tree, Constance Collier, Wilfred Lucas

MACISTE IN HELL (1926, Ital.)
(5 r.) d, Guido Brignone; lp, Umberto Guarracino, Mario Salo, Pauline Polaire, Domenica Serra

MAD HOUR (1928)
(7 r.) d, Joseph C. Boyle; lp, Sally O'Neill, Alice White, Donald Reed, Larry Kent

MAD LOVER, THE
(SEE: MODERN OTHELLO, A, 1917)

MAD MARRIAGE, THE (1925)
(5 r.) d, Frank P. Donovan; lp, Rosemary Davies, Harrison Ford, Maurice Costello, Richard Carle

MAD WHIRL, THE (1925)
(7 r.) d, William A. Seiter; lp, May McAvoy, Jack Mulhall, Myrtle Stedman, Barbara Bedford

MADAM WHO? (1917)
(7 r.) d, Reginald Barker; lp, Bessie Barriscale, Ed Coxen, Howard Hickman, Joseph J. Dowling

MADAME BEHAVE (1925)
(6 r.) d, Scott Sidney; lp, Julian Eltinge, Ann Pennington, Lionel Belmore, David James

MADAME DUBARRY (1918)
(7 r.) d, J. Gordon Edwards; lp, Theda Bara, Charles Clary, Fred Church, Herschal Mayall

MADAME ET SON FILLEUL (1919, Fr.)
(? r.) d, Georges Monca

MADAME FLIRT (1923, Fr.)
(? r.) d, Henri Desfontaines

MADAME JEALOUSY (1918)
(5 r.) d, Robert G. Vignola; lp, Pauline Frederick, Thomas Meighan, Elsie McCloud, Frank Losee

MADAME LA PRESIDENTE (1916)
(5 r.) d, Frank Lloyd; lp, Anna Held, Forrest Stanley, Herbert Standing, Page Peters

MADAME PEACOCK (1920)
(6 r.) d, Ray C. Smallwood; lp, Alla Nazimova, George Probert, John Steppling, William Orlamond

MADAME RECAMIER (1928, Fr.)
(? r.) d, Gaston Ravel; lp, Marie Bell, Francoise Rosay, Van Daele, Francois Rozet

MADAME SANS-GENE (1923)
(6 r.)

MADAME SANS-GENE (1925)
(10 r.) d, Leonce Perret; lp, Gloria Swanson, Emile Drain, Charles De Roche, Madelaine Guitty

MADAME SHERRY (1917)
(5 r.) d, Ralph Dean; lp, Gertrude McCoy, Frank L.A. O'Connor, Lucy Carter, Alfred Deery

MADAME SPHINX (1918)
(5 r.) d, Thomas N. Heffron; lp, Alma Rubens, Wallace MacDonald, Gene Burr, Frank MacQuarrie

MADAME WANTS NO CHILDREN (1927, Ger.)
(6 r.) d, Alexander Korda; lp, Maria Corda, Harry Liedtke, Maria Paudler, Trude Hesterberg

MADAME X (1916)
(5 r.) d, George F. Marion; lp, Dorothy Donnelly, Edwin Fosberg, Ralph Morgan, John Bowers

MADAME X (1920)
(7 r.) d, Frank Lloyd; lp, Pauline Frederick, William Courtleigh, Casson Ferguson, Albert Roscoe

MADCAP, THE (1916)
(5 r.) d, William C. Dowlan; lp, Flora Parker De Haven, Vera Doria, Richard Sterling

MADCAP MADGE (1917)
(5 r.) d, Raymond West; lp, Olive Thomas, Charles Gunn, Dorcas Matthews, Aggie Herring

MADE FOR LOVE (1926)
(7 r.) d, Paul Sloane; lp, Leatrice Joy, Edmund Burns, Ethel Wales, Bertram Grassby

MADEMOISELLE DE LA SEIGLIERE (1921, Fr.)
(? r.) d, Andre Antoine; lp, Hugette Duflos, Romauld Joube, Charles Lamy

MADEMOISELLE JOSETTE MA FEMME (1926, Fr.)
(? r.) d, Gaston Ravel

MADEMOISELLE MIDNIGHT (1924)
(7 r.) d, Robert Z. Leonard; lp, Mae Murray, John Sainpolis, Monte Blue, Robert McKim

MADEMOISELLE MODISTE (1926)
(7 r.) d, Robert Z. Leonard; lp, Corinne Griffith, Norman Kerry, Willard Louis, Dorothy Cumming

MLLE PAULETTE (1918)
(5 r.) d, Raymond Wells; lp, Claire Anderson, Wallace MacDonald, George Pearce, Walter Perry

MADE-TO-ORDER HERO, A (1928)
(5 r.) d, Edgar Lewis; lp, Ted Wells, Marjorie Bonner, Pearl Sindelar, Jack Pratt

MADNESS OF HELEN, THE (1916)
(5 r.) d, Travers Vale; lp, Ethel Clayton, Carlyle Blackwell, Earl Schenck, Jack Drumier

MADNESS OF LOVE, THE (1922)
(5 r.) d, Wray Physioc; lp, Jean Scott, Charles Craig, Bernard Siegel, Willard Cooley

MADONNA OF THE STREETS (1924)
(8 r.) d, Edwin Carewe; lp, Alla Nazimova, Milton Sills, Claude Gillingwater, Courtenay Foote

MAELSTROM, THE (1917)
(5 r.) d, Paul Scardon; lp, Earle Williams, Dorothy Kelly, Denton Vane, John Robertson

MAGDA (1917)
(6 r.) d, Emile Chautard; lp, Clara Kimball Young, Thomas Holding, Valda Valkyrien, Edward Kimball

MAGDALENE OF THE HILLS, A (1917)
(5 r.) d, John W. Noble; lp, Mabel Taliaferro, William Garwood, Frank Montgomery, William B. Davidson

MAGGIE PEPPER (1919)
(5 r.) d, Chester Withey; lp, Ethel Clayton, Elliott Dexter, Winnifred Greenwood, Tully Marshall

MAGIC CLOAK OF OZ, THE (1914)
(5 r.) lp, Violet MacMillan, Mildred Harris, Juanita Hansen, Fred Woodward

MAGIC CUP, THE (1921)
(5 r.) d, John S. Robertson; lp, Constance Binney, Vincent Coleman, Blanche Craig, William H. Strauss

MAGIC EYE, THE (1918)
(5 r.) d, Rea Berger; lp, H.A. Barrows, Claire Du Brey, Zoe Rae, Charles H. Mailes

MAGIC FLAME, THE (1927)
(9 r.) d, Henry King; lp, Ronald Colman, Vilma Banky, Augustino Borgato, Gustav von Seyffertitz

MAGIC GARDEN, THE (1927)
(7 r.) d, J. Leo Meehan; lp, Joyce Coad, Margaret Morris, Philippe De Lacy, Raymond Keane

MAGIC SKIN, THE (1915)
(5 r.) d, Richard Ridgeley; lp, Everett Butterfield, Mabel Trunnelle, Bigelow Cooper, Frank A. Lyon

MAGICIAN, THE (1926)
(7 r.) d, Rex Ingram; lp, Alice Terry, Paul Wegener, Ivan Petrovich, Firmin Gemier

MAGNIFICENT BRUTE, THE (1921)
(5 r.) d, Robert Thornby; lp, Frank Mayo, Dorothy Devore, Percy Challenger, Alberta Lee

MAGNIFICENT MEDDLER, THE (1917)
(5 r.) d, William Wolbert; lp, Mary Anderson, Antonio Moreno, Otto Lederer, George Kunkel

MAID OF BELGIUM, THE (1917)
(5 r.) d, George Archainbaud; lp, Alice Brady, Louise de Rigney, George MacQuarrie, Richard Clarke

MAID OF CEFN YDFA, THE (1914, Brit.)
(4 r.) d, William Haggar, Jr.; lp, William Haggar, Jr., Jenny Haggar

MAIN EVENT, THE (1927)
(7 r.) d, William K. Howard; lp, Vera Reynolds, Rudolph Schildkraut, Julia Faye, Charles Delaney

MAIN STREET (1923)
(9 r.) d, Harry Beaumont; lp, Florence Vidor, Monte Blue, Harry Myers, Robert Gordon

MAINSPRING, THE (1916)
(5 r.) d, Jack Conway; lp, Ben Wilson, Francelia Billington, Wilbur J. Higby, Henry Holland

MAINSPRING, THE (1917)
(4 r.) d, Henry King; lp, Henry King, Ethel Pepperell, Bert Ensminger, Charles Blaisdell

MAISIE'S MARRIAGE (1923, Brit.)
(6 r.) d, Alexander Butler; lp, Lillian Hall Davis, Rex Davis, Sydney Fairbrother, Sam Livesey

MAITRE EVORA (1921, Fr.)
(? r.) d, Gaston Roudes

MAJESTY OF THE LAW, THE (1915)
(5 r.) d, Julia Crawford Ivers; lp, George Fawcett, William Desmond, Charles Ruggles, John Oaker

MAKE-BELIEVE WIFE, THE (1918)
(5 r.) d, John Stuart Robertson; lp, Billie Burke, David Powell, Isabel O'Madigan, Wray Page

MAKERS OF MEN (1925)
(6 r.) d, Forrest Sheldon; lp, Kenneth McDonald, Clara Horton, J.P. McGowan, William Burton

MAKING GOOD (1923)
(5 r.) lp, Pete Morrison, Eileen Sedgwick

MAKING OF BOBBY BURNIT, THE (1914)
(4 r.) d, Oscar Apfel; lp, Edward Abeles, Theodore Roberts, Bessie Barriscale, Raymond Hatton

MAKING OF MADDALENA, THE (1916)
(5 r.) d, Frank Lloyd; lp, Edna Goodrich, Forrest Stanley, Howard Davies, John Burton

MAKING OF O'MALLEY, THE (1925)
(8 r.) d, Lambert Hillyer; lp, Milton Sills, Dorothy Mackaill, Helen Rowland, Warner Richmond

MAKING OVER OF GEOFFREY MANNING, THE (1915)
(4 r.) d, Harry Davenport; lp, Harry T. Morey, L. Rogers Lytton, Belle Bruce, Ned Finley

MALCOLM STRAUSS' SALOME
(SEE: SALOME, 1923)

MALDONE (1928, Fr.)
(9 r.) d, Jean Gremillon; lp, Charles Dullin, Andre Bacque, Annabella, Gencia Athansaiou

MALE WANTED (1923)
(5 r.) lp, Huntley Gordon, Arthur Housman, Diana Allen

MALENCONTRE (1920, Fr.)
(? r.) d, Germaine Dulac

MAMAN COLIBRI (1929, Fr.)
(? r.) d, Julien Duvivier; lp, Maria Jacobini

MAMA'S AFFAIR (1921)
(6 r.) d, Victor Fleming; lp, Constance Talmadge, Effie Shannon, Katherine Kaelred, George Le Guere

MAN, THE (1925, Jap.)
(? r.) d, Kenji Mizoguchi

MAN ALONE, THE (1923)
(5 r.) d, William H. Clifford; lp, Hobart Bosworth, Jamie Gray, William Conklin, George Barnum

MAN AND BEAST (1917)
(5 r.) d, Henry McRae; lp, Eileen Sedgwick, Kingsley Benedict, Harry Clifton, L.M. Wells

MAN AND HIS ANGEL (1916)
(5 r.) d, Burton King; lp, Jane Grey, Willard Deshielle, Edward Mackay, Robert Lee Hill

MAN AND HIS MONEY, A (1919)
(5 r.) d, Harry Beaumont; lp, Tom Moore, Seena Owen, Sidney Ainsworth, Kate Lester

MAN AND HIS SOUL (1916)
(5 r.) d, John W. Noble; lp, Francis X. Bushman, Beverly Bayne, Edward Brennan, Charles H. Prince

MAN AND WIFE (1923)
(5 r.) d, John L. McCutcheon; lp, Maurice Costello, Gladys Leslie, Norma Shearer, Edna May Spooner

MAN AND WOMAN (1920)
(6 r.) d, Charles A. Logue; lp, Diana Allen, Gordon Standing, Joe King, Edwin Sturgis

MAN AND WOMAN (1921)
(6 r.) d, Charles Logue; lp, Diana Allen, Joe King, Edwin Sturges, John L. Shine

MAN BEHIND THE CURTAIN, THE (1916)
(5 r.) d, Courtlandt J. Van Deusen; lp, Lillian Walker, Evart Overton, William Dunn, Templar Saxe

MAN BEHIND "THE TIMES", THE (1917, Brit.)
(4 r.) d, Frank Wilson; lp, Stewart Rome, Chrissie White, Lionelle Howard, Harry Gilbey

MAN BENEATH, THE (1919)
(5 r.) d, William Worthington; lp, Sessue Hayakawa, Helen Jerome Eddy, Pauline Curley, Jack Gilbert

MAN BETWEEN, THE (1923)
(6 r.) d, Finis Fox; lp, Allan Forrest, Edna Murphy, Fred Malatesta, Vola Vale

MAN BY THE ROADSIDE, THE (1923, Ger.)
(? r.) d, Wilhelm Dieterle; lp, Alexander Granach, Wilhelm Dieterle, Heinrich George, Wilhelm Volker

MAN FROM BITTER ROOTS, THE (1916)
(5 r.) d, Oscar Apfel; lp, William Farnum, Betty Schade, Betty Harte, William Burress

MAN FROM BROADWAY (1924)
(5 r.)

MAN FROM BRODNEY'S, THE (1923)
(8 r.) d, David Smith; lp, J. Warren Kerrigan, Alice Calhoun, Wanda Hawley, Pat O'Malley

MAN FROM DOWNING STREET, THE (1922)
(5 r.) d, Edward Jose; lp, Earle Williams, Charles Hill Mailes, Boris Karloff, Betty Ross Clarke

MAN FROM FUNERAL RANGE, THE (1918)
(5 r.) d, Walter Edwards; lp, Wallace Reid, Ann Little, Willis Marks, George McDaniel

MAN FROM GLENGARRY, THE (1923)
(6 r.) d, Henry MacRae; lp, Anders Randolph, Warner P. Richmond, Harlan Knight, Marian Swayne

MAN FROM GOD'S COUNTRY (1924)
(5 r.) d, Alvin J. Neitz; lp, William Fairbanks, Dorothy Revier, Lew Meehan, Milton Ross

MAN FROM HELL'S RIVER, THE (1922)
(5 r.) d, Irving Cummings; lp, Irving Cummings, Eva Novak, Wallace Beery, Frank Whitson

MAN FROM HOME, THE (1922)
(7 r.) d, George Fitzmaurice; lp, James Kirkwood, Anna Q. Nilsson, Geoffrey Kerr, Norman Kerry

MAN FROM LONE MOUNTAIN, THE (1925)
(5 r.) d, Ben Wilson; lp, Ben Wilson

MAN FROM LOST RIVER, THE (1921)
(6 r.) d, Frank Lloyd; lp, House Peters, Fritzi Brunette, Allan Forrest, James Gordon

MAN FROM MANHATTAN, THE (1916)
(5 r.) d, Jack Halloway; lp, William Stowell, Rhea Mitchell, Charles Wheelock, Jo Taylor

MAN FROM MARS, THE
(SEE: RADIO-MANIA, 1923)

MAN FROM MEDICINE HAT, THE
(SEE: MANAGER OF THE B & A, THE, 1916)

MAN FROM MEXICO, THE (1914)
(5 r.) d, Thomas N. Heffron; lp, John Barrymore, Wellington Playter, Harold Lockwood, Fred Annerly

MAN FROM NEVADA, THE (1929)
(5 r.) d, J.P. McGowan; lp, Tom Tyler, Natalie Joyce, Al Ferguson, Alfred Hewston

MAN FROM NEW YORK, THE (1923)
(? r.) lp, Fred Church, Marie Wells, Morgan Jones, W.W. Jones

MAN FROM NOWHERE, THE (1916)
(5 r.) d, Henry Otto; lp, King Baggot, Irene Hunt, Joseph W. Girard, Helen Marten

MAN FROM NOWHERE, A (1920)
(5 r.) d, Francis Ford; lp, Jack Hoxie

MAN FROM NOWHERE, THE (1930)
(5 r.) d, J.P. McGowan; lp, Bob Steele, Ione Reed, Clark Comstock, Bill Nestel

MAN FROM OKLAHOMA, THE (1926)
(5 r.) d, Harry Webb, Forrest Sheldon; lp, Jack Perrin

MAN FROM OREGON, THE (1915)
(5 r.) d, Walter Edwards; lp, Clara Williams, Howard Hickman, Herschal Mayall, Fanny Midgley

MAN FROM RED GULCH, THE (1925)
(6 r.) d, Edmund Mortimer; lp, Harry Carey, Harriet Hammond, Frank Campeau, Mark Hamilton

MAN FROM TEXAS, THE (1921)
(5 r.) d, Ben F. Wilson

MAN FROM THE RIO GRANDE, THE (1926)
(5 r.) lp, George Kesterson, Dorothy Lee

MAN FROM THE WEST, THE (1926)
(5 r.) d, Albert Rogell; lp, Art Acord, Eugenie Gilbert, Irvin Renard, William Welsh

MAN GETTER, THE (1923)
(5 r.) lp, Franklyn Farnum, Peggy O'Day

MAN HUNTER, THE (1919)
(6 r.) d, Frank Lloyd; lp, William Farnum, Louise Lovely, Charles Clary, Marc Robbins

MAN HUNTERS (1923)
(6 r.)

MAN IN BLUE, THE (1925)
(6 r.) d, Edward Laemmle; lp, Herbert Rawlinson, Madge Bellamy, Nick De Ruiz, Andre de Beranger

MAN IN MOTLEY, THE (1916, Brit.)
(5 r.) d, Ralph Dewsbury; lp, Fred Morgan, Hayford Hobbs, Winifred Sadler, Phillip Hewland

MAN IN POSSESSION, THE (1915, Brit.)
(4 r.) d, W.P. Kellino; lp, Billy Merson, Lupino Lane, Winifred Delevanti, Blanche Bella

MAN IN THE ATTIC, THE (1915, Brit.)
(4 r.) d, Ralph Dewsbury; lp, Blanche Bryan, Charles Rock, Philip Hewland, Hubert Willis

MAN IN THE MOONLIGHT, THE (1919)
(6 r.) d, Paul Powell; lp, Monroe Salisbury, William Stowell, Colleen Moore, Alfred Allen

MAN IN THE SADDLE, THE (1926)
(6 r.) d, Lynn Reynolds, Clifford S. Smith; lp, Hoot Gibson, Charles Mailes, Clark Comstock, Fay Wray

MAN IN THE SADDLE, THE
(SEE: A RECKLESS GAMBLE, 1928, Brit.)

MAN IN THE SHADOW, THE (1926)
(6 r.) d, David Hartford; lp, David Torrence, Mary McAllister, Arthur Ranklin, Joseph Bennett

MAN IN THE SHADOWS, THE (1915, Brit.)
(4 r.) d, Charles McEvoy;

MAN INSIDE, THE (1916)
(5 r.) d, John G. Adolfi; lp, Edwin Stevens, Tina Marshall, Charles Burbridge, Justina Huff

MAN LIFE PASSED BY, THE (1923)
(7 r.) d, Victor Schertzinger; lp, Jane Novak, Percy Marmont, Eva Novak, Cullen Landis

MAN MUST LIVE, A (1925)
(7 r.) d, Paul Sloane; lp, Richard Dix, Jacqueline Logan, George Nash, Edna Murphy

MAN NEXT DOOR, THE (1923)
(7 r.) d, Victor Schertzinger; lp, David Torrence, Frank Sheridan, James Morrison, Alice Calhoun

MAN NOBODY KNOWS, THE (1925)
(6 r.) d, Errett LeRoy Kenepp;

MAN O' WARS MAN, THE (1914)
(5 r.) lp, Thomas E. Shea, Dixey Compton

MAN OF ACTION, A (1923)
(6 r.) d, James W. Horne; lp, Douglas MacLean, Marguerite De La Motte, Raymond Hatton, Wade Boteler

MAN OF BRONZE, THE (1918)
(5 r.) d, David M. Hartford; lp, Lewis S. Stone, Marguerite Clayton, Richard Cummings, Harry Von Meter

MAN OF COURAGE (1922)
(? r.) lp, E.K. Lincoln, Spottiswoode Aitken, Fred Bloom, Millicent Fisher

MAN OF HIS WORD, A (1915, Brit.)
(5 r.) d, George Loane Tucker; lp, Henry Ainley, Mary Dibley, Gerald Ames, Charles Rock

MAN OF HONOR, A (1919)
(5 r.) d, Fred J. Balshofer; lp, Harold Lockwood, Bessie Eyton, Stanton Heck, William Clifford

MAN OF MYSTERY, THE (1917)
(5 r.) d, Fred Thompson; lp, E.H. Sothern, Charlotte Ives, Vilda Varesi, Brinsley Shaw

MAN OF QUALITY, A (1926)
(6 r.) d, Wesley Ruggles; lp, George Walsh, Ruth Dwyer, Brian Donlevy, Lucien Prival

MAN OF SHAME, THE (1915)
(5 r.) d, Harry C. Myers; lp, Wilton Lackaye, Rosemary Theby, Harry C. Myers

MAN OF SORROW, A (1916)
(6 r.) d, Oscar Apfel; lp, William Farnum, Dorothy Bernard, Dorothea Wolbert, Fred Huntley

MAN OF STONE, THE (1921)
(5 r.) d, George Archainbaud; lp, Conway Tearle, Betty Howe, Martha Mansfield, Colin Campbell

MAN OF THE FOREST, THE (1921)
(7 r.) lp, Carl Gantvoort, Claire Adams, Robert McKim, Jean Hersholt

MAN OF THE FOREST (1926)
(6 r.) d, John Waters; lp, Jack Holt, Georgia Hale, El Brendel, Warner Oland

MAN ON THE BOX, THE (1914)
(5 r.) d, Cecil B. DeMille, Oscar Apfel, Wilfred Buckland lp, Max Figman, Lolita Robertson

MAN POWER (1927)
(6 r.) d, Clarence Badger; lp, Richard Dix, Mary Brian, Philip Strange, Charles Hill Mailes

MAN RUSTLIN' (1926)
(5 r.) d, Del Andrews; lp, Bob Custer, Florence Lee, Jules Cowles, Sam Allen

MAN SHE BROUGHT BACK, THE (1922)
(5 r.) d, Charles Miller; lp, Earle Foxe, Doris Miller, Frank Losee, Charles Mackay

MAN TAMER, THE (1921)
(5 r.) d, Harry B. Harris; lp, Gladys Walton, Rex De Roselli, William Welsh, C.B. Murphy

MAN THERE WAS, A (1917, Swed.)
(? r.) d, Victor Sjostrom; lp, Victor Sjostrom, Bergliot Husberg, August Falck, Edith Erastoff

MAN TRACKERS, THE (1921)
(5 r.) d, Edward Kull; lp, George Larkin, Josephine Hill, Al Smith, Barney Furey

MAN TRAIL, THE (1915)
(6 r.) d, E.H. Calvert; lp, Richard C. Travers, June Keith, Ernest Maupain, Thomas McLarnie

MAN TRAP, THE (1917)
(5 r.) d, Elmer Clifton; lp, Herbert Rawlinson, Sally Starr, Frank MacQuarrie, Ruby Lafayette

MAN UNCONQUERABLE, THE (1922)
(6 r.) d, Joseph Henabery; lp, Jack Holt, Sylvia Breamer, Clarence Burton, Ann Schaeffer

MAN UNDER COVER, THE (1922)
(5 r.) d, Tod Browning; lp, Herbert Rawlinson, George Hernandez, William Courtwright, George Webb

MAN UPSTAIRS, THE (1926)
(7 r.) d, Roy Del Ruth; lp, Monte Blue, Dorothy Devore, Helen Dunbar, John Roche

MAN WANTED (1922)
(5 r.) d, John Francis Dillon; lp, Arthur Housman, Frank Losee, Flora Finch, Huntley Gordon

MAN WHO BEAT DAN DOLAN, THE (1915)
(4 r.) lp, Willie Ritchie, Betty Marshall

MAN WHO BOUGHT LONDON, THE (1916, Brit.)
(5 r.) d, F. Martin Thornton; lp, E.J. Arundel, Evelyn Boucher, Roy Travers, Nina Leonise

MAN WHO CAME BACK, THE (1924)
(9 r.) d, Emmett Flynn; lp, George O'Brien, Dorothy Mackaill, Cyril Chadwick, Ralph Lewis

MAN WHO COULDN'T BEAT GOD, THE (1915)
(5 r.) d, Maurice Costello, Robert Gaillard; lp, Maurice Costello, Charles Eldridge, Thomas Mills, Robert Gaillard

MAN WHO DARED, THE (1920)
(5 r.) d, Emmett J. Flynn; lp, William Russell, Eileen Percy, Frank Brownlee, Fred Warren

MAN WHO FIGHTS ALONE, THE (1924)
(7 r.) d, Wallace Worsley; lp, William Farnum, Lois Wilson, Edward Horton, Lionel Belmore

MAN WHO FORGOT, THE (1919, Brit.)
(6 r.) d, F. Martin Thornton; lp, James Knight, Marjorie Villis, Bernard Dudley, Evelyn Boucher

MAN WHO FOUND HIMSELF, THE (1915)
(5 r.) d, Frank Crane; lp, Robert Warrick, Paul McAllister, Arline Pretty, E.M. Kimball

MAN WHO FOUND HIMSELF, THE (1925)
(7 r.) d, Alfred E. Green; lp, Thomas Meighan, Virginia Valli, Frank Morgan, Ralph Morgan

MAN WHO HAD EVERYTHING, THE (1920)
(5 r.) d, Alfred Green; lp, Jack Pickford, Priscilla Bonner, Lionel Belmore, Shannon Day

MAN WHO LOST HIMSELF, THE (1920)
(5 r.) d, George D. Baker; lp, William Faversham, Hedda Hopper, Violet Reed, Radcliffe Steele

MAN WHO MADE GOOD, THE (1917, Brit.)
(5 r.) d, Dave Aylott; lp, George Leyton, Lettie Paxton, George Dewhurst, Daisy Cordell

MAN WHO MARRIED HIS OWN WIFE, THE (1922)
(5 r.) d, Stuart Paton; lp, Frank Mayo, Sylvia Breamer, Marie Crisp, Howard Crampton

MAN WHO PAID, THE (1922)
(5 r.) d, Oscar Apfel; lp, Wilfred Lytell, Norma Shearer, Florence Rogan, Fred C. Jones

MAN WHO PLAYED SQUARE, THE (1924)
(7 r.) d, Al Santell; lp, Buck Jones, Ben Hendricks, Jr., David Kirby, Hank Mann

MAN WHO STAYED AT HOME, THE (1915, Brit.)
(4 r.) d, Cecil M. Hepworth; lp, Dennis Eadie, Violet Hopson, Alma Taylor, Lionelle Howard

MAN WHO STAYED AT HOME, THE (1919)
(6 r.) d, Herbert Blache; lp, King Baggot, Claire Whitney, Robert Whittier, Alexandre Herbert

MAN WHO STOOD STILL, THE (1916)
(5 r.) d, Frank Hall Crane; lp, Lew Fields, Doris Kenyon, George Trimble, Edward O'Connor

MAN WHO TOOK A CHANCE, THE (1917)
(5 r.) d, William Worthington; lp, Franklyn Farnum, Agnes Vernon, Lloyd Whitlock, Mark Fenton

MAN WHO VANISHED, THE (1915)
(4 r.)

MAN WHO WAITED, THE (1922)
(5 r.) d, Edward I. Luddy; lp, Frank Braidwood, Inez MacDonald, Jay Morley, Joe Bonner

MAN WHO WAS AFRAID, THE (1917)
(4 r.) d, Fred E. Wright; lp, Bryant Washburn, Ernest Maupian, Margaret Watts, Frankie Raymond

MAN WHO WOKE UP, THE (1918)
(5 r.) d, J.W. McLaughlin; lp, Pauline Starke, Estelle Evans, Darrel Foss, William V. Mong

MAN WHO WON, THE (1918, Brit.)
(6 r.) d, Rex Wilson; lp, Isobel Elsom, Owen Nares, John Kelt, Annie Esmond

MAN WHO WON, THE (1919)
(5 r.) d, Paul Scardon; lp, Harry T. Morey, Maurice Costello, Betty Blythe, Bernard Siegel

MAN WHO WON, THE (1923)
(5 r.) d, William A. Wellman; lp, Dustin Farnum, Jacqueline Gadsden, Lloyd Whitlock, Ralph Cloninger

MAN WHO WOULD NOT DIE, THE (1916)
(5 r.) d, William Russell; lp, William Russell, Charlotte Burton, Harry Keenan, Leona Hutton

MAN WHO WOULDN'T TELL, THE (1918)
(5 r.) d, James Young; lp, Earle Williams, Grace Darmond, Charles Spear, Edward Cecil

MAN WITH THE GLASS EYE, THE (1916, Brit.)
(4 r.) lp, Henry Lonsdale, Mercy Hatton

MAN WITH TWO MOTHERS, THE (1922)
(5 r.) d, Paul Bern; lp, Cullen Landis, Sylvia Breamer, Mary Alden, Hallam Cooley

MAN WITHOUT A CONSCIENCE, THE (1925)
(7 r.) d, James Flood; lp, Willard Louis, Irene Rich, June Marlow, John Patrick

MAN WITHOUT A COUNTRY, THE (1917)
(6 r.) d, Ernest C. Warde; lp, Florence LaBadie, H.J. Herbert, J.H. Gilmour, Carey Hastings

MAN WITHOUT A COUNTRY, THE (1925)
(10 r.) d, Rowland V. Lee; lp, Edward Hearn, Pauline Starke, Lucy Beaumont, Richard Tucker

MAN WITHOUT A HEART, THE (1924)
(6 r.) d, Burton King; lp, Kenneth Harlan, Jane Novak, David Powell, Faire Binney

MAN WITHOUT A SOUL, THE
(SEE: I BELIEVE, 1916, Brit.)

MAN, WOMAN AND SIN (1927)
(7 r.) d, Monta Bell; lp, John Gilbert, Jeanne Eagels, Gladys Brockwell, Marc MacDermott

MAN, WOMAN AND WIFE (1929)
(7 r.) d, Edward Laemmle; lp, Norman Kerry, Pauline Starke, Marion Nixon, Byron Douglas

MAN, WOMAN, MARRIAGE
(SEE: MAN--WOMAN--MARRIAGE, 1921)

MANAGER OF THE B&A, THE (1916)
(5 r.) d, J.P. McGowan; lp, Helen Holmes, Leo D. Maloney, Paul C. Hurst, N.Z. Wood

MANDARIN'S GOLD (1919)
(5 r.) d, Oscar Apfel; lp, Kitty Gordon, Irving Cummings, Warner Oland, George MacQuarrie

MANHANDLED (1924)
(7 r.) d, Allan Dwan; lp, Gloria Swanson, Tom Moore, Lilyan Tashman, Ian Keith

MANHATTAN COCKTAIL (1928)
(8 r.) d, Dorothy Arzner; lp, Nancy Carroll, Richard Arlen, Danny O'Shea, Paul Lukas

MANHATTAN KNIGHT, A (1920)
(5 r.) d, George A. Beranger; lp, George Walsh, Virginia Hammond, William H. Budd, Warren Cook

MANHATTAN MADNESS (1925)
(6 r.) d, John McDermott; lp, Jack Dempsey, Estelle Taylor, George Siegmann, Frank Campeau

MANICURE GIRL, THE (1925)
(6 r.) d, Frank Tuttle; lp, Bebe Daniels, Edmund Burns, Dorothy Cumming, Hale Hamilton

MANNEQUIN (1926)
(7 r.) d, James Cruze; lp, Alice Joyce, Warner Baxter, Dolores Costello, ZaSu Pitts

MANON LESCAUT (1926, Ger.)
(? r.) d, Arthur Robison; lp, Lya de Putti, Vladimir Gaidarov, Eduard Rothauser, Fritz Greiner

MAN'S COUNTRY, A (1919)
(5 r.) d, Henry Kolker; lp, Alma Rubens, Albert Roscoe, Lon Chaney, Joseph Dowling

MAN'S DESIRE (1919)
(5 r.) d, Lloyd Ingraham; lp, Lewis S. Stone, Jane Novak, Jack Curtis, Bill Dyer

MAN'S FATE (1917)
(5 r.) lp, Halsey H. Tower

MAN'S FIGHT, A (1927)
(5 r.)

MAN'S LAW, A (1917)
(5 r.) d, Harry Davenport; lp, Ruth Sinclair, Irving Cummings, Arthur Morrison, Roy Applegate

MAN'S MAKING, THE (1915)
(5 r.) d, Jack Pratt; lp, Richard Buhler, Rosetta Brice, Herbert Fortier, George Clarke

MAN'S MAN, A (1917)
(7 r.) d, Oscar Apfel; lp, J. Warren Kerrigan, Lois Wilson, Kenneth Harlan, Ed Coxen

MAN'S MATE, A (1924)
(6 r.) d, Edmund Mortimer; lp, John Gilbert, Renee Adoree, Noble Johnson, Wilfrid North

MAN'S PAST, A (1927)
(6 r.) d, George Melford; lp, Conrad Veidt, Barbara Bedford, Ian Keith, Arthur Edmund Carew

MAN'S PLAYTHING (1920)
(6 r.) d, Charles T. Horan; lp, Montagu Love, Grace Davison, Stuart Holmes, J.W. Johnston

MAN'S SIZE (1923)
(5 r.) d, Howard M. Mitchell; lp, William Russell, Alma Bennett, Stanton Heck, Charles K. French

MAN'S WOMAN (1917)
(5 r.) d, Travers Vale; lp, Ethel Clayton, Rockcliffe Fellowes, Frank Goldsmith, Justine Cutting

MAN'S WORLD, A (1918)
(5 r.) d, Herbert Blache; lp, Emily Stevens, John Merkyl, Frederick Truesdell, Florence Short

MANSION OF ACHING HEARTS, THE (1925)
(6 r.) d, James P. Hogan; lp, Ethel Clayton, Barbara Bedford, Priscilla Bonner, Philo McCullough

MANSLAUGHTER (1922)
(10 r.) d, Cecil B. DeMille; lp, Thomas Meighan, Leatrice Joy, Lois Wilson, John Miltern

MANTRAP (1926)
(6 r.) d, Victor Fleming; lp, Ernest Torrence, Clara Bow, Percy Marmont, Eugene Pallette

MANTLE OF CHARITY, THE (1918)
(5 r.) d, Edward Sloman; lp, Margarita Fischer, Jack Mower

MAN--WOMAN--MARRIAGE (1921)
(9 r.) d, Allen Holubar; lp, Dorothy Phillips, Ralph Lewis, Margaret Mann, James Kirkwood

MANXMAN, THE (1916, Brit.)
(9 r.) d, George L. Tucker; lp, Henry Ainley, Elizabeth Risdon, Fred Groves, Edward O'Neill

MARBLE HEART, THE (1915)
(4 r.) lp, King Baggot, Frank Smith, Ned Reardon, Jane Fearnley

MARBLE HEART, THE (1916)
(5 r.) d, Kenean Buel; lp, Violet Horner, Walter Miller, Marcelle Carroll

MARCELLINI MILLIONS, THE (1917)
(5 r.) d, Donald Crisp; lp, George Beban, Helen Jerome Eddy, Pietro Sosso, Henry Woodward

MARCH HARE, THE (1921)
(5 r.) d, Maurice Campbell; lp, Bebe Daniels, Grace Morse, Herbert Sherwood, Mayme Kelso

MARCUS GARLAND (1925)
(? r.) lp, Salem Tutt Whitney, Amy Birdsong

MARGARET DAY
(SEE: INGEBORG HOLM, 1913, Swed.)

MARIA MARTEN (1928, Brit.)
(7 r.) d, Walter West; lp, Trilby Clark, Warwick Ward, James Knight, Charles Ashton

MARIA ROSA (1916)
(5 r.) d, Cecil B. DeMille; lp, Geraldine Farrar, Wallace Reid, Pedro de Cordoba, Ernest Joy

MARIAGE D'AMOUR (1917, Fr.)
(? r.) d, Andre Hugon

MARIE, LTD. (1919)
(5 r.) d, Kenneth B. Webb; lp, Alice Brady, Frank Losee, Leslie Austen, Gertrude Hillman

MARION DE LORME (1918, Fr.)
(? r.) d, Henry Krauss

MARIONETTES, THE (1918)
(5 r.) d, Emile Chautard; lp, Clara Kimball Young, Ethel Winthrop, Nigel Barrie, Corliss Giles

MARK OF CAIN, THE (1916)
(5 r.) d, Joseph De Grasse; lp, Lon Chaney, Dorothy Phillips, Frank Whitson, Gilmore Hammond

MARK OF CAIN, THE (1917)
(5 r.) d, George Fitzmaurice; lp, Irene Castle, Antonio Moreno, J.H. Gilmour, Elinore Black

MARK OF THE BEAST (1923)
(6 r.) d, Thomas Dixon; lp, Robert Ellis, Madelyn Clare, Warner Richmond, Gustav von Seyffertitz

MARKED CARDS (1918)
(5 r.) d, Henri D'Elba; lp, Margery Wilson, Wallace MacDonald, Jack Curtis, Rae Godfrey

MARKED MAN, A (1917)
(5 r.) d, Jack [John] Ford; lp, Harry Carey, Molly Malone, Harry Rattenberry, Vester Pegg

MARKED MEN (1920)
(5 r.) d, Jack [John] Ford; lp, Harry Carey, J. Farrell MacDonald, Joe Harris, Ted Brooks

MARKED WOMAN, THE (1914)
(5 r.) d, O.A.C. Lund; lp, Barbara Tennant, R. Radcliffe, Joseph Baker, Walter Connelly

MARKET OF SOULS, THE (1919)
(5 r.) d, Joseph De Grasse; lp, Dorothy Dalton, Holmes Herbert, Philo McCullough, Donald MacDonald

MARLIE THE KILLER (1928)
(5 r.) d, Noel Mason; lp, Klondike (a dog), Francis X. Bushman, Jr., Joseph W. Girard, Blanche Mehaffey

MAROONED HEARTS (1920)
(5 r.) d, George Archainbaud; lp, Conway Tearle, Zena Keefe, Ida Darling, Tom Blake

MARQUIS PREFERRED (1929)
(6 r.) d, Frank Tuttle; lp, Adolphe Menjou, Nora Lane, Chester Conklin, Lucille Powers

MARQUITTA (1927, Fr.)
(7 r.) d, Jean Renoir; lp, Marie-Louise Iribe, Jean Angelo, Henri Debain, Lucien Mancini

MARRIAGE (1927)
(6 r.) d, Roy William Neill; lp, Virginia Valli, Allan Durant, Gladys McConnell, Lawford Davidson

MARRIAGE BOND, THE (1916)
(5 r.) d, Lawrence Marston; lp, Nat C. Goodwin, Margaret Greene, P.J. Rollow, Raymond Bloomer

MARRIAGE BY CONRACT (1928)
(8 r.) d, James Flood; lp, Patsy Ruth Miller, Lawrence Gray, Robert Edeson, Ralph Emerson

MARRIAGE CHANCE, THE (1922)
(6 r.) d, Hampton Del Ruth; lp, Alta Allen, Milton Sills, Henry B. Walthall, Tully Marshall

MARRIAGE CHEAT, THE (1924)
(7 r.) d, John Griffith Wray; lp, Leatrice Joy, Adolphe Menjou, Percy Marmont, Laska Winter

MARRIAGE FOR CONVENIENCE (1919)
(5 r.) d, Sidney Olcott; lp, Catherine Calvert, George Majeroni, Blanche Davenport, Ann May

MARRIAGE IN TRANSIT (1925)
(5 r.) d, Roy William Neill; lp, Edmund Lowe, Carol Lombard, Adolph Milar, Frank Beal

MARRIAGE LIE, THE (1918)
(5 r.) d, Stuart Paton; lp, Carmel Myers, Kenneth Harlan, Harry Carter, William Quinn

MARRIAGE LINES, THE (1921, Brit.)
(6 r.) d, Wilfred Noy; lp, Barbara Hoffe, Lewis Dayton, Sam Livesey, Charles Tilson-Chowne

MARRIAGE MAKER, THE (1923)
(7 r.) d, William De Mille; lp, Agnes Ayres, Jack Holt, Charles De Roche, Robert Agnew

MARRIAGE MARKET, THE (1917)
(5 r.) d, Arthur Ashley; lp, Carlyle Blackwell, June Elvidge, Arthur Ashley, Frederick Truesdell

MARRIAGE MARKET, THE (1923)
(6 r.) d, Edward J. Le Saint; lp, Kate Lester, Mayme Kelso, Pauline Garon, Marc Robbins

MARRIAGE MORALS (1923)
(7 r.) d, William Nigh; lp, Tom Moore, Ann Forrest, Russell Griffin, John Goldsworthy

MARRIAGE OF MOLLY-O, THE (1916)
(5 r.) d, Paul Powell; lp, Mae Marsh, Robert Harron, Kate Bruce, James O'Shea

MARRIAGE OF THE BEAR, THE (1928, USSR)
(7 r.) d, Vladimir Gardin, K.V. Egge; lp, K.V. Eggert, Vera Malanovskaya, Natalya Rosenel, Yuri Zavadsky

MARRIAGE OF WILLIAM ASHE, THE (1916, Brit.)
(5 r.) d, Cecil M. Hepworth; lp, Henry Ainley, Alma Taylor, Stewart Rome, Violet Hopson

MARRIAGE PIT, THE (1920)
(5 r.) d, Frederick A. Thompson; lp, Frank Mayo, Lillian Tucker, Ray Ripley, Frederick Vroom

MARRIAGE RING, THE (1918)
(5 r.) d, Fred Niblo; lp, Enid Bennett, Jack Holt, Robert McKim, Maude George

MARRIAGE SPECULATION, THE (1917)
(5 r.) d, Ashley Miller; lp, Charles Kent, Mildred Manning, Wallace MacDonald

MARRIAGE WHIRL, THE (1925)
(8 r.) d, Alfred Santell; lp, Corinne Griffith, Kenneth Harlan, Harrison Ford, E.J. Ratcliffe

MARRIAGES ARE MADE (1918)
(5 r.) d, Carl Harbaugh; lp, Peggy Hyland, Edwin Stanley, George Clarke, Al Lee

MARRIED? (1926)
(6 r.) d, George Terwilliger; lp, Owen Moore, Constance Bennett, Evangeline Russell, Julia Hurley

MARRIED FLAPPER, THE (1922)
(5 r.) d, Stuart Paton; lp, Marie Prevost, Kenneth Harlan, Philo McCullough, Frank Kingsley

MARRIED FOR MONEY (1915, Brit.)
(4 r.) d, Leon Bary; lp, Gregory Scott, Daisy Cordell, Constance Backner, Frank Tennant

MARRIED IN HASTE (1919)
(5 r.) d, Arthur Rosson; lp, Albert Ray, Elinor Fair, Robert Klein, Don Bailey

MARRIED IN NAME ONLY (1917)
(6 r.) d, Edmund Lawrence; lp, Milton Sills, Gretchen Hartman, William Desmond, Marie Shotwell

MARRIED LIFE (1920)
(5 r.) d, Erle C. Kenton; lp, Ben Turpin, Louise Fazenda, Charles Murray, Ford Sterling

MARRIED LIFE (1921, Brit.)
(5 r.) d, George Treville; lp, Gerald McCarthy, Peggy Hathaway, Roger Treville, Hilda Anthony

MARRIED LOVE
(SEE: MAISIE'S MARRIAGE, 1923, Brit.)

MARRIED PEOPLE (1922)
(6 r.) d, Hugo Ballin; lp, Mabel Ballin, Percy Marmont, Ernest Hilliard, Bobby Clarke

MARRIED VIRGIN, THE (1918)
(6 r.) d, Emmett J. Flynn; lp, Vera Sisson, Kathleen Kirkham, Rodolpho di Valentina [Rudolph Valentino]

MARRY ME (1925)
(6 r.) d, James Cruze; lp, Florence Vidor, Edward Everett Horton, John Roche, Helen Jerome Eddy

MARRY THE POOR GIRL (1921)
(5 r.) d, Lloyd Ingraham; lp, Mrs. Carter De Haven, Carter De Haven

MARRYING MONEY (1915)
(5 r.) d, James Young; lp, Clara Kimball Young, Chester Barnett, William W. Jefferson, Winthrop Chamberlain

MARS CALLING
(SEE: RADIO-MANIA, 1923)

MARSE COVINGTON (1915)
(5 r.) d, Edwin Carewe; lp, Edward Connelly, Louise Huff, John J. Williams

MARTA OF THE LOWLANDS (1914)
(5 r.) d, J. Searle Dawley; lp, Bertha Kalich, Wellington A. Playter, Hal Clarendon, Lillian Kalich

MARTHE (1919, Fr.)
(? r.) d, Gaston Roudes

MARTIN LUTHER, HIS LIFE AND TIME (1924)
(8 r.)

MARTINACHE MARRIAGE, THE (1917)
(4 r.) d, Bert Bracken; lp, Margaret Landis, Philo McCullough, Mollie McConnell, Leota Lorraine

MARTYR SEX, THE (1924)
(5 r.) d, Duke Worne; lp, William Dyer, William Fairbanks, Les Bates, Billie Bennett

MARTYRE (1926, Fr.)
(? r.) d, Charles Burguet

MARTYRDOM OF PHILLIP STRONG, THE (1916)
(5 r.) d, Richard Ridgely; lp, Robert Conness, Mabel Trunnelle, Janet Dawley, Bigelow Cooper

MARUJA
(SEE: GRAY WOLF'S GHOST, THE, 1919)

MARVELOUS MACISTE, THE (1918, Ital.)
(6 r.) lp, Ernesto Pagano, Arline Costello, Louise Farnsworth, Robert Ormand

MARY ELLEN COMES TO TOWN (1920)
(5 r.) d, Elmer Clifton; lp, Dorothy Gish, Ralph Graves, Kate Bruce, Adolphe Lestina

MARY JANE'S PA (1917)
(5 r.) d, William P.S. Earle; lp, Marc MacDermott, Eulalie Jesen, Mildred Manning, Clio Ayres

MARY LAWSON'S SECRET (1917)
(5 r.) d, John B. O'Brien; lp, Charlotte Walker, William Davidson, J.H. Gilmour, N.S. Woods

MARY MORELAND (1917)
(5 r.) d, Frank Powell; lp, Marjorie Rambeau, Robert Elliott, Gene LaMoth, Augusta Burmeister

MARY OF THE MOVIES (1923)
(7 r.) d, John McDermott; lp, Marion Mack, Florence Lee, Mary Kane, Harry Cornelli

MARY REGAN (1919)
(6 r.) d, Lois Weber; lp, Anita Stewart, Frank Mayo, Carl Miller, J. Barney Sherry

MARY-FIND-THE-GOLD (1921, Brit.)
(5 r.) d, George Pearson; lp, Betty Balfour, Hugh E. Wright, Colin Craig, Mabel Poulton

MARY'S ANKLE (1920)
(5 r.) d, Lloyd Ingraham; lp, Douglas MacLean, Doris May, Victor Potel, Neal Burns

MARY'S LAMB (1915)
(5 r.) d, Donald Mackenzie; lp, Richard Carle, Jessie Ralph, Marie Wayne

MARYSE (1917, Fr.)
(? r.) d, Camille de Morlhon; lp, Maryse Dauvray

MASK, THE (1918)
(5 r.) d, Thomas N. Heffron; lp, Claire Anderson, John Gilbert, Rae Godfrey, Grace Marvin

MASK OF LOPEZ, THE (1924)
(5 r.) d, Albert Rogell; lp, Fred Thomson, Wilfred Lucas, David Kirby, Hazel Keener

MASK OF RICHES
(SEE: MASK, THE, 1918)

MASK OF THE KU KLUX KLAN, THE (1923)
(6 r.)

MASKED BRIDE, THE (1925)
(6 r.) d, Christy Cabanne; lp, Mae Murray, Francis X. Bushman, Roy D'Arcy, Basil Rathbone

MASKED DANCER, THE (1924)
(5 r.) d, Burton King; lp, Lowell Sherman, Helene Chadwick, Leslie Austin, Joe King

MASKED HEART, THE (1917)
(5 r.) d, Edward Sloman lp, William Russell, Francelia Billington, William Conklin, Kathleen Kirkham

MASKED LOVER, THE (1928)
(? r.) lp, Jack Hollyday, Muriel Kingston, Lee Timmons

MASTER MAN, THE (1919)
(5 r.) d, Ernest C. Warde; lp, Frank Keenan, Kathleen Kirkham, Joseph J. Dowling, Joseph McManus

MASKED RIDER, THE (1916)
(5 r.) d, Fred J. Balshofer; lp, Harold Lockwood, May Allison, H.W. Willis, John MacDonald

MASKED WOMAN, THE (1927)
(6 r.) d, Silvano Balboni; lp, Anna Q. Nilsson, Holbrook Blinn, Einar Hansen, Charlie Murray

MASKS AND FACES (1917, Brit.)
(6 r.) d, Fred Paul; lp, Sir Johnstone Forbes-Robertson, Irene Vanbrugh, H.B. Irving, Gerald du Maurier

MASKS OF THE DEVIL, THE (1928)
(8 r.) d, Victor Seastrom; lp, John Gilbert, Alma Rubens, Theodore Roberts, Frank Reicher

MASQUERADE BANDIT, THE (1926)
(5 r.) d, Robert De Lacey; lp, Tom Tyler, Dorothy Dunbar, Ethan Laidlaw, Alfred Heuston

MASQUERADER, THE (1922)
(8 r.) d, James Young; lp, Guy Bates Post, Ruth Sinclair, Edward M. Kimball, Herbert Standing

MASTER AND MAN (1915, Brit.)
(4 r.) d, Percy Nash; lp, Gregory Scott, Joan Ritz, Douglas Payne, Daisy Cordell

MASTER AND MAN (1929, Brit.)
(8 r.) d, George A. Cooper; lp, Humberston Wright, Henry de Vries, Betty Siddons, Maurice Braddell

MASTER OF BEASTS, THE (1922)
(5 r.) lp, Charles Vogt, Claire Lotto

MASTER OF GRAY, THE (1918, Brit.)
(5 r.) d, Tom Watts; lp, Athalie Davis, Harry Clifford, Ethel Douglas Ross, Ernest A. Douglas

MASTER OF HIS HOME (1917)
(5 r.) d, Walter Edwards; lp, William Desmond, Alma Reuben, Robert McKim, Joseph J. Dowling

MASTER OF LOVE, THE (1919, Ger.)
(? r.) d, Fritz Lang; lp, Carl de Vogt, Gilda Langer, Erika Unruh, Max Narlinski

MASTER OF MEN, A (1917, Brit.)
(5 r.) d, Wilfred Noy; lp, Malcolm Keen, Dorothy Bellew, Marie Hemingway, Sydney Lewis Ransome

MASTER OF THE HOUSE, THE (1915)
(5 r.) lp, Julius Steger, Austin Webb, Grace Reals, Margot Williams

MASTER OF THE HOUSE (1925, Den.)
(7 r.) d, Carl-Theodore Dreyer; lp, Johannes Meyer, Astrid Holm, Karin Nellemose, Mathilde Nielsen

MASTER OF THE RANGE (1928)
(5 r.) lp, Cliff "Tex" Lyons

MASTER PASSION, THE (1917)
(5 r.) d, Richard Ridgely; lp, Mabel Trunnelle, Robert Conness, A. Lincoln, Helen Strickland

MASTERS OF MEN (1923)
(7 r.) d, David Smith; lp, Earle Williams, Alice Calhoun, Cullen Landis, Wanda Hawley

MASTER SHAKESPEARE, STROLLING PLAYER (1916)
(5 r.) d, Frederick Sullivan; lp, Florence LaBadie, Robert Vaughn, Lawrence Swinburne, Robert Whittier

MATCH-BREAKER, THE (1921)
(5 r.) d, Dallas M. Fitzgerald; lp, Viola Dana, Jack Perrin, Edward Jobson, Julia Calhoun

MATCH-MAKERS, THE (1916)
(3 r.) d, George Ridgwell; lp, Sally Crute, Robert Brower, William Wadsworth, Carlton King

MATE OF THE SALLY ANN, THE (1917)
(5 r.) d, Henry King; lp, Mary Miles Minter, Alan Forrest, George Periolat, Jack Connolly

MATER DOLOROSA (1917, Fr.)
(5 r.) d, Abel Gance; lp, Emmy Lynn, Firmin Gemier, Armand Tallier, Anthony Gildes

MATERNAL SPARK, THE (1917)
(5 r.) d, G.P. Hamilton; lp, Irene Hunt, Rowland Lee, Joey Jacobs, Edwin Jobson

MATERNITY (1917)
(5 r.) d, John B. O'Brien; lp, Alice Brady, Marie Chambers, John Bowers, David Powell

MATING, THE (1915)
(5 r.) d, Scott Sidney; lp, Bessie Barriscale

MATING, THE (1918)
(5 r.) d, Frederick Thompson; lp, Gladys Leslie, Herbert Rawlinson, Forest Robertson, Stephen Carr

MATING CALL, THE (1928)
(7 r.) d, James Cruze; lp, Thomas Meighan, Evelyn Brent, Renne Adoree, Alan Roscoe

MATING OF MARCELLA, THE (1918)
(5 r.) d, Roy William Neill; lp, Dorothy Dalton, Thurston Hall, Juanita Hansen, William Conklin

MATRIMONIAL MARTYR, A (1916)
(5 r.) lp, Ruth Roland, Andrew Arbuckle, Daniel Gilfether, Marguerite Nichols

MATRIMONIAL WEB, THE (1921)
(5 r.) d, Edward Jose; lp, Alice Calhoun, Joseph Striker, William Riley Hatch, Armand Cortez

MATRIMONY (1915)
(5 r.) d, Scott Sidney; lp, Julia Dean, Howard Hickman, Thelma Salter, Louise Glaum

MATT (1918, Brit.)
(5 r.) d, A.E. Coleby; lp, Greta MacDonald, A.E. Coleby, Ernest A. Douglas

MAUPRAT (1926, Fr.)
(? r.) d, Jean Epstein; lp, Nino Constantini, Sandra Milowanoff, Alex Allin, Maurice Schutz

MAYBLOSSOM (1917)
(5 r.) d, Edward Jose; lp, Pearl White, Niles Welch, Hal Ford, Fuller Mellish

MAYOR OF CASTERBRIDGE, THE (1921, Brit.)
(6 r.) d, Sidney Morgan; lp, Fred Groves, Pauline Peters, Warwick Ward, Nell Emerald

MAYOR OF FILBERT, THE (1919)
(7 r.) d, W. Christy Cabanne; lp, Jack Richardson, Belle Bennett, J. Barney Sherry, Ben Alexander

MAYTIME (1923)
(8 r.) d, Louis Gasnier; lp, Ethel Shannon, Harrison Ford, William Norris, Clara Bow

MAZEL TOV (1924)
(8 r.) lp, Molly Picon, Jacob Kalich

MCFADDEN FLATS (1927)
(8 r.) d, Richard Wallace; lp, Charlie Murray, Chester Conklin, Edna Murphy, Larry Kent

MCGUIRE OF THE MOUNTED (1923)
(5 r.) d, Richard Stanton; lp, William Desmond, Louise Lorraine, Willard Louis, Vera James

ME AND CAPTAIN KID (1919)
(5 r.) d, Oscar Apfel; lp, Evelyn Greeley, Raymond McKee, William T. Carleton, Arthur Donaldson

ME AND GOTT
(SEE: ME UND GOTT, 1918)

ME AND ME MOKE
(SEE: ME AND M'PAL, 1916, Brit.)

ME AND M'PAL (1916, Brit.)
(4 r.) d, Harold Shaw; lp, Edna Flugrath, Gerald Ames, Hubert Willis, Sydney Fairbrother

ME, GANGSTER (1928)
(7 r.) d, Raoul Walsh; lp, June Collyer, Don Terry, Anders Randolph, Stella Adams

ME UND GOTT (1918)
(6 r.) d, Wyndham Gittens; lp, Fred Boulk, Paul Weigel, Robert N. Dunbar, Gertrude DeVere

MEA CULPA (1919, Fr.)
(? r.) d, Georges Champavert

MEANEST MAN IN THE WORLD, THE (1923)
(6 r.) d, Edward F. Cline; lp, Bert Lytell, Blanche Sweet, Bryant Washburn, Maryon Aye

MEDDLIN' STRANGER, THE (1927)
(5 r.) d, Richard Thorpe; lp, Wally Wales, Nola Luxford, Charles K. French, Mabel Van Buren

MEDDLING WOMEN (1924)
(7 r.) d, Ivan Abramson; lp, Lionel Barrymore, Sigrid Holmquist, Dagmar Godowsky, Hugh Thompson

MEDICINE BEND (1916)
(5 r.) d, J.P. McGowan; lp, Helen Holmes, J.P. McGowan, Paul C. Hurst, Thomas G. Lingham

MEDICINE MAN, THE (1917)
(5 r.) d, Cliff Smith; lp, Roy Stewart, Ann Kroman, Percy Challenger, Aaron Edwards

MEET THE PRINCE (1926)
(6 r.) d, Joseph Henabery; lp, Joseph Schildkraut, Marguerite De La Motte, Vera Steadman, Julia Faye

MEFIEZ-VOUS DE VOTRE BONNE (1920, Fr.)
(? r.) d, Robert Saidreau

MEG O' THE WOODS (1918, Brit.)
(5 r.) d, Bertram Phillips; lp, Queenie Thomas, Harry Drummond, Alice de Winton, Cameron Carr

MEG OF THE SLUMS (1916, Brit.)
(4 r.) lp, Helena Millais, Bertram Burleigh

MELISSA OF THE HILLS (1917)
(5 r.) d, James Kirkwood; lp, Mary Miles Minter, Spottiswoode Aitken, Allan Forrest, George Periolat

MELODIES (1926)
(5 r.) d, Francis Ford; lp, Jack Mower, Florence Ulrich

MELTING MILLIONS (1917)
(5 r.) d, Otis Turner; lp, George Walsh, Anna Luther, Velma Whitman, Frank Alexander

MELTING POT, THE (1915)
(5 r.) d, George Fitzmaurice; lp, Walker Whiteside, Valentin Grant, Fletcher Harvey

MEMBER OF THE TATTERSALL'S, A (1919, Brit.)
(6 r.) d, Albert Ward; lp, Isobel Elsom, Malcolm Cherry, Campbell Gullan, Tom Reynolds

MEN (1924)
(7 r.) d, Dimitri Buchowetzki; lp, Pola Negri, Robert Frazer, Robert Edeson, Joseph Swickard

MEN AND WOMEN (1925)
(6 r.) d, William De Mille; lp, Richard Dix, Claire Adams, Neil Hamilton, Henry Stephenson

MEN IN THE RAW (1923)
(5 r.) d, George E. Marshall; lp, Jack Hoxie, Marguerite Clayton, Sid Jordan, J. Morris Foster

MEN OF DARING (1927)
(7 r.) d, Albert Rogell; lp, Jack Hoxie, Ena Gregory, Marin Sais, Francis Ford

MEN OF STEEL (1926)
(10 r.) d, George Archainbaud; lp, Milton Sills, Doris Kenyon, May Allison, Victor McLaglen

MEN OF THE DESERT (1917)
(4 r.) d, W.S. Van Dyke; lp, Jack Gardner, Ruth King, Carl Stockman, Bert Woodruff

MEN OF THE NIGHT (1926)
(6 r.) d, Albert Rogell; lp, Herbert Rawlinson, Gareth Hughes, Wanda Hawley, Lucy Beaumont

MEN OF ZANSIBAR, THE (1922)
(5 r.) d, Rowland V. Lee; lp, William Russell, Ruth Renick, Claude Peyton, Harvey Clarke

MEN WHO FORGET (1923)
(5 r.) d, Reuben Gillmer; lp, James Knight, Marjorie Villers, Bernard Dudley, Evelyn Boucher

MEN WHO HAVE MADE LOVE TO ME (1918)
(8 r.) d, Arthur Berthelet; lp, Mary MacLane, Ralph Graves, R. Paul Harvey, Cliff Worman

MEN, WOMEN AND MONEY (1919)
(5 r.) d, George Melford; lp, Ethel Clayton, James Neill, Jane Wolfe, Lew Cody

MEN, WOMEN AND MONEY (1924)
(5 r.) lp, Walter Miller, Marguerite Courtot

MEN WOMEN LOVE (1926)
(? r.)

MENACE, THE (1918)
(5 r.) d, John Robertson; lp, Corinne Griffith, Evart Overton, Herbert Prior, Ned Finley

MENACE OF THE MUTE, THE (1915)
(5 r.) d, Ashley Miller

MENACING PAST, THE (1922)
(5 r.) lp, George Chesebro, Fritzi Ridgeway

MENILMONTANT (1926, Fr.)
(10 r.) d, Dimitri Kirsanoff; lp, Nadia Sibirskaia, Yolande Beaulieu, Guy Belmont, Jean Pasquier

MENSCHEN AM SONNTAG
(SEE: PEOPLE ON SUNDAY, 1929, Ger.)

MENTIONED IN CONFIDENCE (1917)
(4 r.) d, Edgar Jones; lp, R. Henry Grey, Frank Brownlee, Melvin Mayo, Vola Vale

MERCHANT OF VENICE, THE (1914)
(4 r.) d, Phillips Smalley; lp, Lois Weber, Phillips Smalley, Rupert Julian, Douglas Gerrard

MERELY MARY ANN (1916)
(5 r.) d, John Adolfi; lp, Vivian Martin, Sidney Bracy, Harry Hilliard, Niles Welch

MERELY MARY ANN (1920)
(5 r.) d, Edward J. LeSaint; lp, Shirley Mason, Casson Ferguson, Harry Spingler, Georgia Woodthorpe

MERELY MRS. STUBBS (1917, Brit.)
(5 r.) d, Henry Edwards; lp, Henry Edwards, Alma Taylor, Lionelle Howard, Mary Rorke

MERELY PLAYERS (1918)
(5 r.) d, Oscar Apfel; lp, Kitty Gordon, Irving Cummings, George MacQuarrie, Pinna Nesbit

MERES FRANCAISES (1917, Fr.)
(? r.) d, Rene Hervil, Louis Mercanton; lp, Sarah Bernhardt

MERRY CAVALIER, THE (1926)
(5 r.) d, Noel Mason; lp, Richard Talmadge, Charlotte Stevens, William H. Tooker, Joseph Harrington

MERRY-GO ROUND, THE (1919)
(5 r.) d, Edmund Lawrence; lp, Peggy Hyland, Jack Mulhall, Edward Jobson, Edwin B. Tilton

MESSAGE FROM MARS, A (1921)
(6 r.) d, Maxwell Karger; lp, Bert Lytell, Raye Dean, Maude Milton, Leonard Mudie

MESSAGE OF HOPE, THE (1923)
(4 r.)

MESSAGE OF THE MOUSE, THE (1917)
(5 r.) d, J. Stuart Blackton; lp, Anita Stewart, Julia Swayne Gordon, Rudolph Cameron, L. Rogers Lytton.

MESSAGE TO GARCIA, A (1916)
(5 r.) d, Richard Ridgely; lp, Mabel Trunnelle, Robert Conness, Herbert Prior, Robert Kegerreis

MESSALINA (1924, Ital.)
(5 r.) d, Enrico Gauzzoni; lp, Rina de Liguoro, Giovanna Terribili, Lucia Zamissi, Gino Talamo

MESSENGER OF THE BLESSED VIRGIN (1930)
(9 r.)

METROPOLITAN SYMPHONY (1929, Jap.)
(7 r.) d, Kenji Mizoguchi; lp, Shizue Natsukawa, Takako Irie, Isamu Kosugi, Eiji Takaga

MIAMI (1924)
(7 r.) d, Alan Crosland; lp, Betty Compson, Lawford Davidson, Hedda Hopper, J. Barney Sherry

MIARKA, LA FILLE A L'OURSE
(SEE: GYSPY PASSION, 1923, Fr.)

MIARKA, THE DAUGHTER OF THE BEAR
(SEE: GYPSY PASSION, 1923, Fr.)

MICHAEL (1924, Ger.)
(? r.) d, Carl-Theodore Dreyer; lp, Benjamin Christensen, Walter Slezak, Nora Gregor, Robert Garrison

MICHAEL O'HALLORAN (1923)
(7 r.) d, James Leo Meehan; lp, Virginia True Boardman, Ethelyn Irving, Irene Rich, Charles Clary

MICHEL STROGOFF (1926, Fr.)
(6 r.) d, Viatcheslaw Tourjansky; lp, Ivan Mosjoukine, Natalie Kovenko, Henry Debain, Gabriel de Gravonne

MICHELINE (1920, Fr.)
(? r.) d, Jean Kemm

MICROBE, THE (1919)
(5 r.) d, Henry Otto; lp, Viola Dana, Kenneth Harlan, Arthur Maude, Bonnie Hill

MICROSCOPE MYSTERY, THE (1916)
(5 r.) d, Paul Powell; lp, Wilfred Lucas, Constance Talmadge, Fred A. Turner, Pomeroy Cannon

MIDCHANNEL (1920)
(6 r.) d, Harry Garson; lp, Clara Kimball Young, J. Frank Glendon, Edward M. Kimball, Bertram Grassby

MIDDLEMAN, THE (1915, Brit.)
(5 r.) d, George Loane Tucker; lp, Albert Chevalier, Jane Gail, Gerald Ames, Douglas Munro

MIDINETTE (1917, Fr.)
(? r.) d, Rene Hervil, Louis Mercanton

MIDLANDERS, THE (1920)
(6 r.) d, Ida May Park, Joseph De Grasse; lp, Bessie Love, Truman Van Dyke, Frances Raymond, C. Norman Hammond

MIDNIGHT (1922)
(5 r.) d, Maurice Campbell; lp, Constance Binney, William Courtleigh, Sidney Bracey, Arthur S. Hull

MIDNIGHT ACE, THE (1928)
(7 r.) lp, A.B. De Comatheire, Mabel Kelly, Oscar Roy Dugas, Walter Cornick

MIDNIGHT ADVENTURE, THE (1928)
(6 r.) d, Duke Worne; lp, Cullen Landis, Edna Murphy, Ernest Hilliard, Jack Richardson

MIDNIGHT ALARM, THE (1923)
(7 r.) d, David Smith; lp, Alice Calhoun, Percy Marmont, Cullen Landis, Joseph Kilgour

MIDNIGHT AT MAXIM'S (1915)
(4 r.) d, George L. Sargent; lp, Irmgard von Rottenthal, Leo Pirinkoff, Ethel Rose, The Cameron Girls

MIDNIGHT BELL, A (1921)
(6 r.) d, Charles Ray; lp, Charles Ray, Donald MacDonald, Van Dyke Brooke, Doris Pawn

MIDNIGHT BRIDE, THE (1920)
(5 r.) d, William J. Humphrey; lp, Gladys Leslie, James Morrison, Gladden James, Nellie Spaulding

MIDNIGHT BURGLAR, THE (1918)
(5 r.) d, Robert Ensminger; lp, Gloria Joy, Neil Hardin, Ethel Ritchie, Ruth Lackaye

MIDNIGHT FACES (1926)
(5 r.) d, Bennett Cohn; lp, Francis X. Bushman, Jr., Jack Perrin, Kathryn McGuire, Edward Peil, Sr.

MIDNIGHT FIRES
(SEE: MIDNIGHT FACES, 1926)

MIDNIGHT FLOWER, THE (1923)
(5 r.) d, Capt. Leslie T. Peacock; lp, Gaston Glass, Vola Vale

MIDNIGHT FLYER, THE (1925)
(7 r.) d, Tom Forman; lp, Cullen Landis, Dorothy Devore, Buddy Post, Charles Mailes

MIDNIGHT GAMBOLS (1919, Brit.)
(6 r.) d, James McKay; lp, Marie Doro, Godfrey Tearle, Sam Livesey, Mary Jerrold

MIDNIGHT GIRL, THE (1925)
(7 r.) d, Wilfred Noy; lp, Lila Lee, Gareth Hughes, Dolores Cassinelli, Charlotte Walker

MIDNIGHT GUEST, THE (1923)
(5 r.) d, George Archainbaud; lp, Grace Darmond, Mahlon Hamilton, Clyde Fillmore, Pat Harmon

MIDNIGHT KISS, THE (1926)
(5 r.) d, Irving Cummings; lp, Richard Walling, Janet Gaynor, George Irving, Doris Lloyd

MIDNIGHT LIMITED (1926)
(6 r.) d, Oscar Apfel; lp, Gaston Glass, Wanda Hawley, Sam Allen, William Humphrey

MIDNIGHT LOVERS (1926)
(7 r.) d, John Francis Dillon; lp, Lewis Stone, Anna Q. Nilsson, John Roche, Chester Conklin

MIDNIGHT MADNESS (1918)
(5 r.) d, Rupert Julian; lp, Kenneth Harlan, Ruth Clifford, Harry Van Meter, Harry Holden

MIDNIGHT MAN (1917)
(5 r.) d, Elmer Clifton; lp, Jack Mulhall, Ann Kroman, Al McQuarrie, Ward Lamont

MIDNIGHT MOLLY (1925)
(6 r.) d, Lloyd Ingraham; lp, Evelyn Brent, John Dillon, Bruce Gordon, Leon Bary

MIDNIGHT ON THE BARBARY COAST (1929)
(4 r.) d, Robert J. Horner; lp, William Barrymore, Kalla Pasha

MIDNIGHT ROSE (1928)
(6 r.) d, James Young; lp, Lya De Putti, Kenneth Harlan, Henry Kolker, Lorimer Johnston

MIDNIGHT SECRETS (1924)
(5 r.) d, Jack Nelson; lp, George Larkin, Ollie Kirby, Pauline Curley, Jack Richardson

MIDNIGHT SHADOWS (1924)
(5 r.) d, Francis Ford; lp, Edmund Cobb

MIDNIGHT STAGE, THE (1919)
(5 r.) d, Ernest C. Warde; lp, Frank Keenan, Mignon Anderson, Charles Gunn, Maude George

MIDNIGHT SUN, THE (1926)
(9 r.) d, Dimitri Buchowetski; lp, Laura La Plante, George Siegmann, Raymond Keane, George Siegmann

MIDNIGHT THIEVES (1926)
(5 r.) lp, Herbert Rawlinson, Grace Darmond

MIDNIGHT TRAIL, THE (1918)
(5 r.) d, Edward Sloman; lp, William Russell, Francelia Billington, Sidney Dean, Jerome Sheler

MIDSHIPMAN, THE (1925)
(8 r.) d, Christy Cabanne; lp, Ramon Novarro, Harriet Hammond, Wesley Barry, Margaret Seddon

MIDSUMMER NIGHT'S DREAM, A (1928, Ger.)
(8 r.) d, Hans Neumann; lp, Werner Krauss, Valeska Gert, Tamara, Theodor Becker

MIGHT AND THE MAN (1917)
(5 r.) d, Edward Dillon; lp, Elmo Lincoln, Lillian Langdon, Wilbur Higby, Carmel Myers

MIGHTY DEBRAU, THE (1923)
(8 r.)

MIGHTY LAK' A ROSE (1923)
(8 r.) d, Edwin Carewe; lp, James Rennie, Sam Hardy, Anders Randolf, Harry Short

MIGNON (1915)
(5 r.) d, Alex Beyfuss; lp, Beatriz Michelena, House Peters, Clara Beyers

MILADY (1923, Fr.)
(6 r.) d, Henri Diamant-Berger; lp, Aime Simon-Girard, Pierrette Madd, Claude Merelle, Mons. de Max

MILADY O' THE BEAN STALK (1918)
(5 r.) d, William Bertram; lp, Marie Osborne, Jack Connolly, Ellen Cassidy, Sambo

MILE A MINUTE MORGAN (1924)
(5 r.) d, Frank S. Mattison; lp, Matty Mattison, Vivian Rich, Bill Franey, Lafayette McKee

MILE-A-MINUTE KENDALL (1918)
(5 r.) d, William Desmond Taylor; lp, Jack Pickford, Louise Huff, Charles Arling, Jane Wolff

MILE-A-MINUTE MAN, THE (1926)
(5 r.) d, Jack Nelson; lp, William Fairbanks, Virginia Brown Faire, George Periolat, Jane Keckley

MILE-A-MINUTE ROMEO (1923)
(6 r.) d, Lambert Hillyer; lp, Tom Mix, Betty Jewel, J. Gordon Russell, James Mason

MILESTONES (1916, Brit.)
(9 r.) d, Thomas Bentley; lp, Isobel Elsom, Owen Nares, Campbell Gullan, Minna Grey

MILESTONES (1920)
(6 r.) d, Paul Scardon; lp, Lewis Stone, Alice Hollister, Gertrude Robinson, Harvey Clark

MILESTONES OF LIFE (1915)
(4 r.) lp, Mignon Anderson, Louise Rutter

MILKY WAY, THE (1922)
(5 r.) lp, David Butler

MILL ON THE FLOSS, THE (1915)
(5 r.) d, W. Eugene Moore; lp, Mignon Anderson, Harris Gordon, W. Eugene Moore, Fannie Hoyt

MILLION, THE (1915)
(4 r.) lp, Edward Abeles

MILLION A MINUTE, A (1916)
(5 r.) d, John W. Noble; lp, Francis X. Bushman, Beverly Bayne, Robert Cummings, William Bailey

MILLION BID, A (1914)
(5 r.) d, Ralph Ince; lp, Anita Stewart, Julia Swayne, Charles Kent, Harry T. Morey

MILLION BID, A (1927)
(7 r.) d, Michael Curtiz; lp, Dolores Costello, Warner Oland, Malcolm McGregor, Betty Blythe

MILLION DOLLAR DOLLIES, THE (1918)
(5 r.) d, Leonce Perret; lp, Yancsi Dolly, Roszika Dolly, Bradley Barker, Huntley Gordon

MILLION DOLLAR HANDICAP, THE (1925)
(6 r.) d, Scott Sidney; lp, Vera Reynolds, Edmund Burns, Ralph Lewis, Ward Crane

MILLION DOLLAR MYSTERY (1927)
(6 r.) d, Charles J. Hunt; lp, James Kirkwood, Lila Lee, Henry Sedley, Erin La Bissoniere

MILLION FOR MARY, A (1916)
(5 r.) d, Rea Berger; lp, C. William Kolb, Max Dill, Dodo Newton, May Cloy

MILLION TO BURN, A (1923)
(5 r.) d, William Parke; lp, Herbert Rawlinson, Kalla Pasha, Beatrice Burnham, Tom McGuire

MILLIONAIRE, THE (1927)
(7 r.) d, Oscar Micheaux; lp, Grace Smith, J. Lawrence Criner, Cleo Desmond, Lionel Monagas

MILLIONAIRE BABY, THE (1915)
(6 r.) d, Lawrence Marston; lp, Harry Mestayer, John Charles, Grace Darmond, Frederick Hand

MILLIONAIRE COWBOY, THE (1924)
(5 r.) d, Harry Garson; lp, Lefty Flynn, Gloria Grey, Charles Crockett, Frederic Peters

MILLIONAIRE FOR A DAY, A (1921)
(6 r.) d, Wilfred North; lp, Arthur Guy Empey, Harry Burkhardt, Florence Martin, Templar Saxe

MILLIONAIRE ORPHAN, THE (1926)
(5 r.) d, Robert J. Horner; lp, William Barrymore, Jack Richardson, Hal Ferner, Pauline Curley

MILLIONAIRE PIRATE, THE (1919)
(5 r.) d, Rupert Julian; lp, Monroe Salisbury, Ruth Clifford, Clyde Fillmore, Jack Mower

MILLIONAIRE POLICEMAN, THE (1926)
(5 r.) d, Edward J. Le Saint; lp, Herbert Rawlinson, Eva Novak, Eugenie Besserer, Arthur Rankin

MILLIONAIRE VAGRANT, THE (1917)
(5 r.) d, Victor L. Schertzinger; lp, Charles Ray, Sylvia Bremer, J. Barney Sherry, Dorcas Matthews

MILLIONAIRES (1926)
(7 r.) d, Herman C. Raymaker; lp, George Sidney, Louise Fazenda, Vera Gordon, Nat Carr

MILLIONAIRE'S DOUBLE, THE (1917)
(5 r.) d, Harry Davenport; lp, Lionel Barrymore, Evelyn Brent, Harry S. Northrup, H.H. Pattee

MILL-OWNER'S DAUGHTER, THE (1916, Brit.)
(4 r.) d, Fred W. Durrant; lp, Nancy Lewis Waller, Cecil Mannering, Cecil Morton Yorke, Blanche Forsythe

MILLSTONE, THE (1917)
(5 r.)

MIMI TROTTIN (1922, Fr.)
(? r.) d, Henri Andreani

MIND THE PAINT GIRL (1919)
(5 r.) d, Wilfred North; lp, Anita Stewart, Conway Tearle, Victor Steele, Templer Saxe

MIND-THE-PAINT-GIRL (1916)
(5 r.)

MINE OF MISSING MEN (1917)
(? r.) d, Lawrence Trimble

MINE TO KEEP (1923)
(6 r.) d, Ben Wilson; lp, Bryant Washburn, Mabel Forrest, Wheeler Oakman, Charlotte Stevens

MINE WITH THE IRON DOOR, THE (1924)
(8 r.) d, Sam Wood; lp, Pat O'Malley, Dorothy Mackaill, Raymond Hatton, Charlie Murray

MINNIE (1922)
(7 r.) d, Marshall Neilan, Frank Urson; lp, Leatrice Joy, Matt Moore, George Barnum, Josephine Crowell

MINTS OF HELL, THE (1919)
(5 r.) d, Park Frame; lp, William Desmond, Vivian Rich, Edward Jobson, Charles French

MINUIT...PLACE PIGALLE (1928, Fr.)
(? r.) d, Rene Hervil; lp, Nicolas Rimsky, Renee Heribel

MIRACLE, THE (1912, Aust.)
(4 r.) d, Joseph Menchen

MIRACLE BABY, THE (1923)
(6 r.) d, Val Paul; lp, Harry Carey, Margaret Landis, Charles J.L. Mayne, Edward Hearn

MIRACLE OF LIFE, THE (1915)
(4 r.) lp, Margarita Fischer, Joseph E. Singleton, Lucille Ward

MIRACLE OF LIFE, THE (1926)
(5 r.) d, S.E.V. Taylor; lp, Percy Marmont, Mae Busch, Nita Naldi

MIRACLE OF LOVE, A (1916)
(5 r.) d, Lloyd B. Carleton; lp, Dorothy Davenport, Emory Johnson, Richard Morris, Mattie Witting

MIRACLE OF LOVE, THE (1920)
(7 r.) d, Robert Z. Leonard; lp, Lucy Cotton, Jackie Saunders, Wyndham Standing, Percy Standing

MIRACLE OF MANHATTAN, THE (1921)
(5 r.) d, George Archainbaud; lp, Elaine Hammerstein, Matt Moore, Ellen Cassity, Nora Reed

MIRACLE OF MONEY, THE (1920)
(5 r.) d, Hobart Henley; lp, Margaret Seddon, Bess Gearhart Morrison

MIRACLE OF WOLVES, THE (1925, Fr.)
(? r.) d, Raymond Bernard; lp, Charles Dullin, Vanni Marcoux, Yvonne Sergyl, Romauld Joube

MIRACLE-MAKER (1922, USSR)
(6 r.) d, Alexander Panteleyev; lp, Kirillov, Y. Tumanskaya

MIRAGE, THE (1924)
(6 r.) d, George Archainbaud; lp, Florence Vidor, Clive Brook, Alan Roscoe, Vola Vale

MIRANDY SMILES (1918)
(5 r.) d, William C. De Mille lp, Vivian Martin, Douglas MacLean, Lewis Willoughby, Gean Genung

MIRELE EFROS (1912, USSR)
(4 r.) d, Andrzej Marek; lp, Regina Kaminska, Esther Rokhl Kaminska, Ida Kaminska, Gershon Weissman

MIRROR, THE (1917)
(5 r.) d, Frank Powell; lp, Marjorie Rambeau, Robert Elliott, Irene Warfield, Paul Everton

MIRROR OF LIFE, THE (1916)
(5 r.)

MISERICORDE (1917, Fr.)
(? r.) d, Camille de Morlhon

MISFIT EARL, A (1919)
(5 r.) d, Ira W. Lowry; lp, Louis Bennison, Samuel Ross, Charles Brandt, Neil Moran

MISFIT WIFE, THE (1920)
(6 r.) d, Edmund Mortimer; lp, Alice Lake, Forrest Stanley, Billy Gettinger, Frederick Vroom

MISLEADING LADY, THE (1916)
(5 r.) d, Arthur Berthelet; lp, Henry B. Walthall, Edna Mayo, Sidney Ainsworth, Edward Arnold

MISLEADING LADY, THE (1920)
(6 r.) d, George Irving; lp, Bert Lytell, Lucy Cotton, Cyril Chadwick, Frank Currier

MISLEADING WIDOW, THE (1919)
(5 r.) d, John S. Robertson; lp, Billie Burke, James L. Crane, Frank Mills, Madeline Clare

MISMATES (1926)
(7 r.) d, Charles Brabin; lp, Doris Kenyon, Warner Baxter, May Allison, Philo McCullough

MISS ADVENTURE (1919)
(5 r.) d, Lynn F. Reynolds; lp, Peggy Hyland, Edward Burns, Frank Brownlee, George Hernandez

MISS AMBITION (1918)
(5 r.) d, Henry Houry; lp, Corinne Griffith, Walter McGrail, Betty Blythe, Denton Vane

MISS ARIZONA (1919)
(5 r.) d, Otis B. Thayer; lp, Gertrude Bondhill, James O'Neill

MISS CHARITY (1921, Brit.)
(5 r.) d, Edwin J. Collins; lp, Margery Meadows, Dick Webb, Joan Lockton, Ralph Forster

MISS EDITH, DUCHESSE (1928, Fr.)
(? r.) d, Donatien

MISS DECEPTION (1917)
(5 r.) d, Eugene Nowland; lp, Jean Sothern, Jack Newton, Robert Kegerreis, Mary Moore

MISS GEORGE WASHINGTON (1916)
(5 r.) d, J. Searle Dawley; lp, Marguerite Clark, Frank Losee, Niles Welch, Florence Marten

MISS HELYETT (1927, Fr.)
(? r.) d, Georges Monca

MISS INNOCENCE (1918)
(5 r.) d, Harry Millarde; lp, June Caprice, Robert Walker, Marie Shotwell, Frank Beamish

MISS JACKIE OF THE ARMY (1917)
(5 r.) d, Lloyd Ingraham; lp, Margarita Fischer, Jack Mower, L.C. Shumway, Hal Clements

MISS JACKIE OF THE NAVY (1916)
(5 r.) d, Harry Pollard; lp, Margarita Fischer, Jack Mower, J. Gordon Russell, John Steppling

MISS LULU BETT (1921)
(7 r.) d, William C. De Mille; lp, Lois Wilson, Milton Sills, Theodore Roberts, Helen Ferguson

MISS MEND (1926, USSR)
(17 r.) d, Boris Barnet; lp, Natalia Glan, Igor Ilinsky, Vladimir Fogel, Boris Barnet

MISS MISCHIEF MAKER (1918)
(5 r.) d, Sherwood McDonald; lp, Gloria Joy, Nell Saalman, Ruth Lackaye, Edward Jobson

MISS NOBODY (1917)
(5 r.) d, William Parke; lp, Gladys Hulette, Cesare Gravina, A.G. Andrews, William Parke, Jr.

MISS NOBODY (1920)
(5 r.) d, Francis J. Grandon

MISS PAUL REVERE (1922)
(? r.)

MISS PEASANT (1916, USSR)
(4 r.) d, Olga Preobrazhenskaya; lp, A. Miklashevskaya, N. Skryabin, S. Golovin

MISS PETTICOATS (1916)
(5 r.) d, Harley Knoles; lp, Alice Brady, Arthur Asley, Isobel Berwin, Robert Elliott

MISS ROBINSON CRUSOE (1917)
(5 r.) d, William Christy Cabanne; lp, Emmy Wehlen, Walter C. Miller, Harold Entwhistle, Sue Balfour

MISS ROVEL (1920, Fr.)
(? r.) d, Jean Kemm

MISS U.S.A. (1917)
(5 r.) d, Harry Millarde; lp, June Caprice, William Courtleigh, Jr., Frank Evans, Tom Burrough

MISSING (1918)
(5 r.) d, James Young; lp, Thomas Meighan, Sylvia Breamer, Robert Gordon, Winter Hall

MISSING DAUGHTERS (1924)
(7 r.) d, William H. Clifford; lp, Eileen Percy, Pauline Starke, Claire Adams, Eva Novak

MISSING HUSBANDS
(SEE: L'ATLANTIDE, 1921, Fr.)

MISSING LINK, THE (1927)
(7 r.) d, Charles F. Reisner; lp, Syd Chaplin, Ruth Hiatt, Tom McGuire, Crauford Kent

MISSING LINKS, THE (1916)
(5 r.) d, Lloyd Ingraham; lp, Norma Talmadge, Robert Harron, Thomas Jefferson, Elmer Clifton

MIST IN THE VALLEY (1923, Brit.)
(7 r.) d, Cecil M. Hepworth; lp, Alma Taylor, G.H. Mulcaster, James Carew, Esme Hubbard

MISTAKEN ORDERS (1926)
(5 r.) d, J.P. McGowan; lp, Helen Holmes, Jack Perrin, Henry Barrows, Hal Walters

MR. BARNES OF NEW YORK (1922)
(5 r.) d, Victor Schertzinger; lp, Tom Moore, Anna Lehr, Naomi Childers, Lewis Willoughby

MR. BINGLE (1922)
(5 r.) d, Leopold Wharton; lp, Maclyn Arbuckle

MR. DOLAN OF NEW YORK (1917)
(5 r.) d, Raymond Wells; lp, Jack Mulhall, Noble Johnson, Julia Ray, Al McQuarrie

MISTER 44 (1916)
(5 r.) d, Henry Otto; lp, Harold Lockwood, May Allison, Lester Cuneo, Franklin Hall

MR. GILFIL'S LOVE STORY (1920, Brit.)
(5 r.) d, A.V. Bramble; lp, R. Henderson Bland, Mary Odette, Peter Upcher, Dora de Winton

MR. GOODE, THE SAMARITAN (1916)
(5 r.) d, Edward Dillon; lp, De Wolf Hopper, Fay Tincher, Chester Withey, Edward Dillon

MR. GREX OF MONTE CARLO (1915)
(5 r.) d, Frank Reicher; lp, Theodore Roberts, Carlyle Blackwell, Dorothy Davenport, Frank Elliott

MR. LOGAN, USA (1918)
(5 r.) d, Lynn Reynolds; lp, Tom Mix, Kathleen O'Connor, Dick La Reno, Charles Le Moyne

MR. LYNDON AT LIBERTY (1915, Brit.)
(5 r.) d, Harold Shaw; lp, Edna Flugrath, Fred Groves, Harry Welchman, Manora Thew

MR. OPP (1917)
(5 r.) d, Lynn F. Reynolds; lp, Arthur Hoyt, Neva Gerber, George Chesebro, George Hernandez

MR. PIM PASSES BY (1921, Brit.)
(6 r.) d, Albert Ward; lp, Peggy Hyland, Campbell Gullan, Maudie Dunham, Tom Reynolds

MR. POTTER OF TEXAS (1922)
(5 r.) d, Leopold Wharton; lp, Maclyn Arbuckle, Louiszita Valentine, Corinne Uzzell, Robert Frazier

MRS. BALFANE (1917)
(6 r.) d, Frank Powell; lp, Nance O'Neil, Frank Belcher, Robert Elliott, Agnes Eyre [Ayres]

MRS. CASSELL'S PROFESSION (1915, Brit.)
(4 r.) d, Fred W. Durrant; lp, Margaret Belona, Miriam Ferris

MRS. DANE'S CONFESSION (1922, Brit.)
(5 r.) d, Michael Kertes

MRS. DANE'S DANGER (1922, Brit.)
(4 r.) d, Wilifrid North

MRS. DANE'S DEFENSE (1918)
(5 r.) d, Hugh Ford; lp, Pauline Frederick, Frank Losee, Leslie Austen, Maud Turner Gordon

MRS. LEFFINGWELL'S BOOTS (1918)
(5 r.) d, Walter Edwards; lp, Constance Talmadge, Harrison Ford, George Fisher, Fred Goodwins

MRS. PLUM'S PUDDING (1915)
(5 r.) d, Al Christie, Edmund Frazee; lp, Maire Tempest, Eddie Lyons, Lee Moran, W. Grahame Browne

MRS. TEMPLE'S TELEGRAM (1920)
(5 r.) d, James Cruze; lp, Bryant Washburn, Wanda Hawley, Carmen Phillips, Walter Hiers

MRS. WIGGS OF THE CABBAGE PATCH (1914)
(4 r.) lp, Beatriz Michelena, Blanche Chapman, Andrew Robson, House Peters

MRS. WIGGS OF THE CABBAGE PATCH (1919)
(5 r.) d, Hugh Ford; lp, Marguerite Clark, Mary Carr, Vivia Ogden, Gladys Valerie

MITYA (1927, USSR)
(7 r.) d, Nikolai Okhlopkov; lp, Nikolai Okhlopkov, Sergei Minin

MIXED BLOOD (1916)
(5 r.) d, Charles Swickard; lp, Claire McDowell, George Beranger, Roy Stewart, Wilbur Higby

M'LISS (1915)
(5 r.) d, O.A.C. Lund; lp, Barbara Tennant, Howard Estabrook, O.A.C. Lund, Anita Navarro

M'LORD OF THE WHITE ROAD (1923, Brit.)
(7 r.) d, Arthur Rooke; lp, Victor McLaglen, Marjorie Hume, James Lindsay, Fred Wright

MOANA (1926)
(7 r.) d, Robert Flaherty; lp, Ta'avale, Fa'amgase, T'ugaita, Pe'a

MOCCASINS (1925)
(5 r.) d, Robert North Bradbury; lp, Bill Cody, Peggy O'Dare, Mack V. Wright, Frank Austin

MODEL FROM MONTMARTE, THE (1928, Fr.)
(6 r.) d, Leonce Perret; lp, Louise Lagrange, Ivan Petrovich

MODEL'S CONFESSION, THE (1918)
(6 r.) d, Ida May Park; lp, Mary MacLaren, Kenneth Harlan, Edna Earle, Herbert Prior

MODERN CAIN, A (1925)
(? r.) lp, Norman Ward, Ted Williams, Vivian Carrols, Harriett Harris

MODERN DAUGHTERS (1927)
(6 r.) d, Charles J. Hunt; lp, Edna Murphy, Bryant Washburn, Ernest Hilliard, Virginia Lyons

MODERN DU BARRY, A (1928, Ger.)
(? r.) d, Maria Corda, Alfred Abel, Friedrich Kayssler, Julius Von Szoreghy

MODERN ENOCH ARDEN, A (1916)
(4 r.) d, Clarence G. Badger; lp, Joe Jackson, Vivian Edwards, Mack Swain, Hank Mann

MODERN HUSBANDS (1919)
(5 r.) d, Francis J. Grandon; lp, Henry B. Walthall, Ethel Fleming, Neil Hardin, Melbourne McDowell

MODERN JEAN VAL JEAN; OR FRAME UP, A (1930)
(5 r.) lp, Al Hagan

MODERN LORELEI, A
(SEE: LORELEI OF THE SEA, 1917)

MODERN LOVE (1918)
(6 r.) d, Robert Leonard; lp, Mae Murray, George Chesebro, Philo McCullough, Arthur Shirley

MODERN MAGDALEN, A (1915)
(5 r.) d, Will S. Davis; lp, Catherine Countiss, Lionel Barrymore, William H. Tooker, Charles Graham

MODERN MATRIMONY (1923)
(5 r.) d, Victor Heerman; lp, Owen Moore, Alice Lake, Mayme Kelso, Frank Campeau

MODERN MEPHISTO, A (1914)
(6 r.)

MODERN MOTHER GOOSE (1917)
(5 r.)

MODERN MOTHERS (1928)
(6 r.) d, Philip Rosen; lp, Helene Chadwick, Douglas Fairbanks, Jr., Ethel Grey Terry, Barbara Kent

MODERN OTHELLO, A (1917)
(6 r.) d, Leonce Perret; lp, Robert Warwick, Elaine Hammerstein, Valentine Petit, Edward Kimball

MODERN THELMA, A (1916)
(5 r.) d, John G. Adolfi; lp, Vivian Martin, Harry Hilliard, William H. Tooker, Albert Roccardi

MODERN YOUTH (1926)
(5 r.) d, Jack Nelson; lp, Geno Corrado, Olive Kirby, Rhea Mitchell, Charles Clary

MOHICAN'S DAUGHTER, THE (1922)
(5 r.) d, S.E.V. Taylor; lp, Nancy Deaver, Hazel Washburn, Sazon Kling, William Thompson

MOI AUSSI, J'ACCUSE (1920, Fr.)
(? r.) d, Alfred Machin, Henry Wuhlschleger

MOJAVE KID, THE (1927)
(5 r.) d, Robert North Bradbury; lp, Bob Steele, Lillian Gilmore, Buck Connors, Bob Fleming

MOLLY AND I (1920)
(5 r.) d, Howard M. Mitchell; lp, Shirley Mason, Albert Roscoe, Harry Dunkinson, Lile Leslie

MOLLY, GO GET 'EM (1918)
(5 r.) d, Lloyd Ingraham; lp, Margarita Fischer, Hal Clements Jack Mower, True Boardman

MOLLY MAKE-BELIEVE (1916)
(5 r.) d, J. Searle Dawley; lp, Marguerite Clark, Mahlon Hamilton, Dick Gray, Helen Dahl

MOMENT BEFORE, THE (1916)
(5 r.) d, Robert Vignola; lp, Pauline Frederick, Thomas Holding, J.W. Johnston, Frank Losee

MON COEUR AU RALENTI (1928, Fr.)
(? r.) d, Marco de Gastyne

MON CURE CHEZ LES PAUVRES (1925, Fr.)
(? r.) d, Donatien

MON CURE CHEZ LES RICHES (1925, Fr.)
(? r.) d, Donatien

MON ONCLE (1925, Fr.)
(? r.) d, Maurice Mariaud

MON ONCLE BENJAMIN (1923, Fr.)
(? r.) d, Rene Leprince

MONEY (1915)
(5 r.) d, James Keane; lp, Carlotta de Felice

MONEY (1921)
(5 r.) d, Duncan Macrae; lp, Henry Ainley, Faith Bevan, Margot Drake, Sam Wilkinson

MONEY CHANGERS, THE (1920)
(6 r.) d, Jack Conway; lp, Robert McKim, Claire Adams, Roy Stewart, Audrey Chapman

MONEY GOD, OR DO RICHES BRING HAPPINESS, THE (1914)
(5 r.)

MONEY ISN'T EVERYTHING (1918)
(5 r.) d, Edward Sloman; lp, Margarita Fischer, Jack Mower, J. Morris Foster, Wedgwood Nowell

MONEY LENDER, THE (1914)
(4 r.)

MONEY MAD (1918)
(5 r.) d, Hobart Henley; lp, Mae Marsh, Rod La Rocque, John Sainpolis, Macey Harlam

MONEY MADNESS (1917)
(5 r.) d, Henry McRae; lp, Mary MacLaren, Eddie Polo, Don Bailey, Alfred Vosburgh

MONEY MANIAC, THE (1921)
(5 r.) d, Leonce Perret; lp, Robert Elliott, Henry G. Sell, Marcya Capri, Lucy Fox

MONEY MASTER, THE (1915)
(5 r.) lp, Frank Sheridan, Paul McAllister, Calvin Thomas, Sam Reid

MONEY MILL, THE (1917)
(5 r.) d, John Robertson; lp, Dorothy Kelly, Evart Overton, Gordon Gray, Edward Elkas

MONEY TALKS (1926)
(6 r.) d, Archie Mayo; lp, Claire Windsor, Owen Moore, Bert Roach, Ned Sparks

MONEY TO BURN (1922)
(5 r.) d, Rowland V. Lee; lp, William Russell, Sylvia Breamer, Hallam Cooley, Harvey Clark

MONEY TO BURN (1926)
(6 r.) d, Walter Lang; lp, Malcolm McGregor, Dorothy Devore, Eric Mayne, Nina Romano

MONNA VANNA (1923, Ger.)
(9 r.) d, Richard Eichberg; lp, Lee Parry, Paul Wegener, Hans Sturm, Paul Graetz

MONOPOLIST, THE (1915)
(4 r.)

MONSIEUR LE DIRECTEUR (1924, Fr.)
(? r.) d, Robert Saidreau

MONSIEUR LEBIDOIS PROPRIETAIRE (1922, Fr.)
(? r.) d, Pierre Colombier

MONSIEUR LEBUREAU (1920, Fr.)
(? r.) d, Luitz-Morat

M. LECOQ (1915)
(4 r.) lp, Florence LaBadie, William Morris, Julia Blanc, Alphonse Ethier

MONSTER AND THE GIRL, THE (1914)
(4 r.)

MONTANA BILL (1921)
(5 r.) d, Phil Goldstone; lp, William Fairbanks, Maryon Aye, Robert Kortman, Jack Waltemeyer

MONTE CARLO (1926)
(7 r.) d, Christy Cabanne; lp, Lew Cody, Gertrude Olmstead, Roy D'Arcy, Karl Dane

MONTE CARLO (1926)
(? r.) d, Louis Mercanton

MONTE CRISTO (1912)
(4 r.) d, Colin Campbell; lp, Hobart Bosworth, Tom Santschi, Herbert Rawlinson, Eugenie Besserer

MONTE CRISTO (1922)
(10 r.) d, Emmett J. Flynn; lp, John Gilbert, Estelle Taylor, Robert McKim, William V. Mong

MONTE-CRISTO (1929, Fr.)
(? r.) d, Henri Fescourt; lp, Jean Angelo, Lil Dagover, Pierre Batcheff, Gaston Modot

MONTMARTE ROSE (1929)
(6 r.) d, Bernard F. McEvetty, Frederick Hiatt; lp, Marguerite De La Motte, Rosemary Theby, Harry Myers, Paul Ralli

MOON OF ISRAEL (1927, Aust.)
(7 r.) d, Michael Curtiz; lp, Marie Corda, Arlette Marchal, Adelqui Millar, Oscar Beregi

MOONLIGHT AND HONEYSUCKLE (1921)
(5 r.) d, Joseph Henabery; lp, Mary Miles Minter, Monte Blue, Willard Louis, Grace Goodall

MOONLIGHT FOLLIES (1921)
(5 r.) d, King Baggot; lp, Marie Prevost, Lionel Belmore, Marie Crisp, George Fisher

MOONSHINE MENACE, THE (1921)
(5 r.) d, J.P. McGowan

MOONSHINE TRAIL, THE (1919)
(6 r.) d, J. Stuart Blackton; lp, Sylvia Breamer, Robert Gordon, Julia Swayne Gordon, Van Dyke Brooke

MOONSTONE, THE (1915)
(5 r.) d, Frank Crane; lp, Eugene O'Brien, Elaine Hammerstein, Ruth Findlay, William Rozelle

MORAL CODE, THE (1917)
(5 r.) d, Ashley Miller; lp, Anna Q. Nilsson, Walter Hitchcock, Florence Hamilton, Richard Barthelmess

MORAL COURAGE (1917)
(5 r.) d, Romaine Fielding; lp, Muriel Ostriche, Arthur Ashley, Edward Elkas, Clarence Elmer

MORAL DEADLINE, THE (1919)
(5 r.) d, Travers Vale; lp, Frank Mayo, June Elvidge, Ned Burton, Muriel Ostriche

MORAL FABRIC, THE (1916)
(5 r.) d, Raymond B. West; lp, Frank Mills, Edith Reeves, Howard Hickman, Louise Brownell

MORAL LAW, THE (1918)
(5 r.) d, Bertram Bracken; lp, Gladys Brockwell, Colin Chase, Rosita Marstini, Cora Rankin Drew

MORAL SINNER, THE (1924)
(6 r.) d, Ralph Ince; lp, Dorothy Dalton, James Rennie, Alphonse Ethier, Frederick Lewis

MORAL SUICIDE (1918)
(7 r.) d, Ivan Abramson; lp, James Morrison, John Mason, Leah Baird, Anne Luther

MORALS FOR MEN (1925)
(8 r.) d, Bernard Hyman; lp, Conway Tearle, Agnes Ayres, Alyce Mills, Otto Matieson

MORALS OF HILDA, THE (1916)
(5 r.) d, Lloyd B. Carleton; lp, Gretchen Lederer, Emory Johnson, Lois Wilson, Frank Whitson

MORALS OF WEYBURY, THE (1916, Brit.)
(6 r.) d, George Loane Tucker; lp, Elizabeth Risdon, Charles Rock, Cyril Raymond, Douglas Munro

MORAN OF THE MARINES (1928)
(7 r.) d, Frank Strayer; lp, Richard Dix, Ruth Elder, Roscoe Karns, Brooks Benedict

MORAN OF THE MOUNTED (1926)
(5 r.) d, Harry J. Brown; lp, Reed Howes, Sheldon Lewis, J.P. McGowan, Bruce Gordon

MORE DEADLY THAN THE MALE (1919)
(5 r.) d, Robert G. Vignola; lp, Ethel Clayton, Edward Coxen, Herbert Heyes, Hallam Cooley

MORE EXCELLENT WAY, THE (1917)
(5 r.) d, Perry N. Vekroff; lp, Anita Stewart, Charles Richman, Rudolph Cameron, Charles A. Stevenson

MORE PAY - LESS WORK (1926)
(6 r.) d, Albert Ray; lp, Albert Gran, Mary Brian, E.J. Ratcliffe, Charles Rogers

MORE TO BE PITIED THAN SCORNED (1922)
(6 r.) d, Edward Le Saint; lp, J. Frank Glendon, Rosemary Theby, Philo McCullough, Gordon Griffith

MORE TRUTH THAN POETRY (1917)
(5 r.) d, Burton L. King; lp, Olga Petrova, Mahlon Hamilton, Charles Martin, Violet Reed

MORGAN LA SIRENE
(SEE: MORGAN, THE ENCHANTRESS, 1929, Fr.)

MORGANE, THE ENCHANTRESS (1929, Fr.)
(? r.) d, Leonce Perret; lp, Ivan Petrovich, Claire De Lorez, Josyane, Rachel Devirys

MORGAN'S RAIDERS (1918)
(5 r.) d, Wilfred Lucas; lp, Violet Mersereau, William Cavanaugh, Frank Holland, Edward Burns

MORGANSON'S FINISH (1926)
(7 r.) d, Fred Windemere; lp, Anita Stewart, Johnnie Walker, Mahlon Hamilton, Victor Potel

MORMON MAID, A (1917)
(5 r.) d, Robert Leonard; lp, Mae Murray, Hobart Bosworth, Frank Borzage, Edythe Chapman

MORTAL SIN, THE (1917)
(5 r.) d, John H. Collins; lp, Viola Dana, Robert Walker, Augustus Phillips, Henry Leone

MORTGAGED WIFE, THE (1918)
(6 r.) d, Allen Holubar; lp, Dorothy Phillips, Albert Roscoe, William Stowell, Sam De Grasse

MORTMAIN (1915)
(5 r.) d, Theodore Marston; lp, Robert Edeson, Donald Hall, Edward Elkas, Joseph Weber

MOSCOW (1927, USSR)
(6 r.) d, Mikhail Kaufman, Ilya Kopalin

MOSCOW IN OCTOBER (1927, USSR)
(7 r.) d, Boris Barnet;

MOTELE THE WEAVER
(SEE: SIMPLE TAILOR, THE, 1934, USSR)

MOTH, THE (1917)
(5 r.) d, Edward Jose; lp, Norma Talmadge, Eugene O'Brien, Hassard Short, Adolphe Menjou

MOTH AND RUST (1921, Brit.)
(5 r.) d, Sidney Morgan; lp, Sybil Thordike, Malvina Longfellow, Langhorne Burton, Cyril Raymond

MOTHER (1920, USSR)
(4 r.) d, Alexander Razumni; lp, Vladimir Karin, L. Sychova, Ivan Bersenev

MOTHER (1926, USSR)
(6 r.) d, Vsevolod Pudovkin; lp, Vera Baranovskaya, Nikolai Batalov, A. Chistyakov, Ivan Koval-Samborsky

MOTHER (1927)
(7 r.) d, J. Leo Meehan; lp, Belle Bennett, Crauford Kent, William Bakewell, Joyce Coad

MOTHER ETERNAL (1921)
(9 r.) d, Ivan Abramson; lp, Vivian Martin, Thurston Hall, Earl Metcalfe, Jack Sherrill

MOTHER HEART, THE (1921)
(5 r.) d, Howard M. Mitchell; lp, Shirley Mason, Raymond McKee, Edwin Booth Tilton, Cecil Van Auker

MOTHER, I NEED YOU (1918)
(6 r.) d, Frank Beal; lp, Enid Markey, Edward Coxen, G. Raymond Nye, Clarissa Selwynne

MOTHER INSTINCT, THE (1917)
(5 r.) d, Roy William Neill; lp, Enid Bennett, Margery Wilson, Rowland Lee, Jack Gilbert

MOTHER LOVE AND THE LAW (1917)
(7 r.) d, George A. Siegmann; lp, Dollie Ledgerwood Matters, O.A.C. Lund, George A. Siegmund, Mabel Bardine

MOTHER MACHREE (1922)
(7 r.) lp, Amanda Trinkle, James La Para, Jack Hopkins

MOTHER MACHREE (1928)
(7 r.) d, John Ford; lp, Belle Bennett, Neil Hamilton, Philippe De Lacy, Pat Somerset

MOTHER O'MINE (1917)
(5 r.) d, Rupert Julian; lp, Rupert Julian, Ruth Clifford, Ruby Lafayette, Elsie Jane Wilson

MOTHER O' MINE (1921)
(7 r.) d, Fred Niblo; lp, Lloyd Hughes, Betty Ross Clark, Betty Blythe, Joseph Kilgour

MOTHER OF DARTMOOR, THE (1916, Brit.)
(6 r.) d, George L. Tucker; lp, Elizabeth Risdon, Bertram Burleigh, Enid Bell, George Bellamy

MOTHER OF HIS CHILDREN, THE (1920)
(5 r.) d, Edward J. LeSaint; lp, Gladys Brockwell, William Scott, Frank Leigh, Nigel de Brulier

MOTHER'S HEART, A (1914)
(4 r.) lp, Robert Vaughn, Maud Hall Macy

MOTHER'S ORDEAL, A (1917)
(5 r.) d, Will S. Davis; lp, Jean Sothern, Walter Miller, Arthur Housman

MOTHER'S SECRET, A (1918)
(5 r.) d, Douglas Gerrard; lp, Ella Hall, Emory Johnson, Mary Mersch, T.C. Crittenden

MOTHER SHOULD BE LOVED, A (1934, Jap.)
(? r.) d, Yasujiro Ozu

MOTHER'S SIN, A (1918)
(5 r.) d, Thomas R. Mills; lp, Earle Williams, Miriam Miles, Denton Vane, Ernest Maupain

MOTHERHOOD (1917)
(5 r.) d, Frank Powell; lp, Marjorie Rambeau, Paul Everton, Anne Sutherland, Robert Elliott

MOTHERHOOD; LIFE'S GREATEST MIRACLE (1928)
(6 r.) lp, George E. Patton, Adelaide M. Chase

MOTHERLOVE (1916, Brit.)
(5 r.) d, Maurice Elvey; lp, Elizabeth Risdon, Fred Groves, Frank Stanmore, Guy Newall

MOTHERS OF MEN (1917)
(5 r.) d, Willis Robards; lp, Dorothy Davenport, Willis Robards, Katherine Griffith, Arthur Tavares

MOTHERS OF MEN (1920)
(5 r.) d, Edward Jose; lp, Claire Whitney, Lumsden Hare, Gaston Glass, Martha Mansfield

MOTHS (1913)
(5 r.) lp, Maude Fealy, William Russell, Harry Benham, Gerda Holmes

MOTION TO ADJOURN, A (1921)
(6 r.) d, Roy Clements; lp, Harry Rattenberry, Roy Stewart, Sidney D'Albrook, Evelyn Nelson

MOTORING THRU SPAIN (1929)
(4 r.)

MOULDERS OF MEN (1927)
(7 r.) d, Ralph Ince; lp, Conway Tearle, Margaret Morris, Frankie Darro, Rex Lease

MOUNTAIN DEW (1917)
(5 r.) d, Thomas Heffron; lp, Margery Wilson, Charles Gunn, Thomas Washington, Al W. Filson

MOUNTAIN EAGLE, THE
(SEE: FEAR O' GOD, 1926, Brit.)

MOUNTAIN MADNESS (1920)
(5 r.) d, Lloyd Carleton; lp, Mignon Anderson, Edward Coxen, Jack Lott, Grace Pike

MOUNTAIN WOMAN, THE (1921)
(6 r.) d, Charles Giblyn; lp, Pearl White, Corliss Giles, Richard C. Travers, George Barnum

MOUNTAINS OF MANHATTAN (1927)
(6 r.) d, James P. Hogan; lp, Dorothy Devore, Charles Delaney, Kate Price, Bobby Gordon

MOVING GUEST, THE (1927)
(? r.) lp, Al Alt

MOVING IMAGE, THE (1920, Ger.)
(7 r.) d, Fritz Lang; lp, Mia May, Hans Marr, Harry Frank, Rudolf Klein-Rogge

MULHALL'S GREAT CATCH (1926)
(5 r.) d, Harry Garson; lp, Lefty Flynn, Kathleen Myers, Henry Victor, Harry Dunkinson

MUMMY AND THE HUMMINGBIRD, THE (1915)
(5 r.) d, James Durkin; lp, Charles Cherry, Lillian Tucker, William Sorelle, Arthur Hoops

MUM'S THE WORD (1918)
(5 r.)

MURDER OF GENERAL GRYAZNOV, THE (1921, USSR)
(5 r.) d, Ivan Perestiani; lp, Mikhail Chiaureli, Ivan Perestiani, N. Yachmenev, N. Dolidze

MURDOCK TRIAL, THE (1914, Brit.)
(4 r.) d, Larry Trimble; lp, Florence Turner, Frank Tennant, Richard Norton, William Felton

MUSIC MASTER, THE (1927)
(8 r.) d, Allan Dwan; lp, Alec B. Francis, Lois Moran, Neil Hamilton, Norman Trevor

MUST WE MARRY? (1928)
(6 r.) d, Frank S. Mattison; lp, Pauline Garon, Lorraine Eason, Bud Shaw, Vivian Rich

MUTE APPEAL, A (1917)
(5 r.) d, Walter Edwin; lp, Jean Sothern, Donald Cameron, Tom Magrane, Elsie Mason

MUTINY (1917)
(5 r.) d, Lynn F. Reynolds; lp, Myrtle Gonzales, Jack Curtis, George Hernandez, Fred Harrington

MUTINY OF THE ELSINORE, THE (1920)
(6 r.) d, Edward Sloman; lp, Mitchell Lewis, Helen Ferguson, Noah Beery, Casson Ferguson

MY BEST GIRL (1915)
(5 r.) lp, Max Figman, Lois Meredith, Lawrence Peyton, Dick Rosson

MY COUNTRY FIRST (1916)
(6 r.) d, Tom Terriss; lp, Tom Terriss, Helene Ziegfeld, John Hopkins, Alfred Heming

MY FIGHTING GENTLEMAN (1917)
(5 r.) d, Edward Sloman; lp, William Russell, Francelia Billington, Charles Newton, Jack Vosburgh

MY FRIEND FROM INDIA (1927)
(6 r.) d, E. Mason Hopper; lp, Franklin Pangborn, Elinor Fair, Ben Hendricks, Jr., Ethel Wales

MY FRIEND, THE DEVIL (1922)
(8 r.) d, Harry Millarde; lp, Charles Richman, Ben Grauer, William Tooker, Adolph Milar

MY HOME TOWN (1925)
(6 r.) lp, Wesley Barry, Adelaide Rendelle

MY HUSBAND'S FRIEND (1918)
(5 r.) d, Marshall Farnum, James Ormont; lp, Frank Mills, Lillian Kemble, J. Frank Glendon, Jack Curtis

MY HUSBAND'S FRIEND (1922)
(5 r.) lp, Frank Mills

MY HUSBAND'S OTHER WIFE (1919)
(6 r.) d, J. Stuart Blackton; lp, Sylvia Breamer, Robert Gordon, Warren Chandler, May McAvoy

MY LADY FRIENDS (1921)
(6 r.) d, Lloyd Ingraham; lp, Carter De Haven, Thomas G. Lingham, Helen Raymond, Helen Lynch

MY LADY OF WHIMS (1925)
(7 r.) d, Dallas M. Fitzgerald; lp, Clara Bow, Donald Keith, Carmelita Geraghty, Francis McDonald

MY LADY'S DRESS (1917, Brit.)
(9 r.) d, Alexander Butler; lp, Gladys Cooper, Malcolm Cherry, Andre Beaulieu, Alice de Winton

MY LADY'S GARTER (1920)
(5 r.) d, Maurice Tourneur; lp, Sylvia Breamer, Wyndham Standing, Holmes Herbert, Warner Richmond

MY LADY'S LATCHKEY (1921)
(6 r.) d, Edwin Carewe; lp, Katherine MacDonald, Edmund Lowe, Claire Du Brey, Howard Gaye

MY LADY'S LIPS (1925)
(7 r.) d, James P. Hogan; lp, Alyce Mills, William Powell, Clara Bow, Frank Keenan

MY LADY'S SLIPPER (1916)
(5 r.) d, Ralph Ince; lp, Earle Williams, Anita Stewart, George O'Donnell, Albert Roccardi

MY LITTLE BOY (1917)
(5 r.) d, Elsie Jane Wilson; lp, Zoe Rae, Gretchen Lederer, Ella Hall, Emory Johnson

MY LITTLE SISTER (1919)
(5 r.) d, Kenean Buel; lp, Evelyn Nesbit, Leslie Austen, Lillian Hall, Kempton Greene

MY LORD CONCEIT (1921, Brit.)
(6 r.) d, F. Martin Thornton; lp, Evelyn Boucher, Maresco Marisini, Rowland Myles, E.L. Frewen

MY MADONNA (1915)
(5 r.) d, Alice Blache; lp, Olga Petrova, Guy Coombs, Evelyn Dumo, Albert Howson

MY MAN (1924)
(7 r.) d, David Smith; lp, Patsy Ruth Miller, Dustin Farnum, Niles Welch, Margaret Landis

MY NEIGHBOR'S WIFE (1925)
(6 r.) d, Clarence Geldert; lp, E.K. Lincoln, Helen Ferguson, Edwards Davis, Herbert Rawlinson

MY OFFICIAL WIFE (1914)
(6 r.) d, James Young; lp, Clara Kimball Young, Harry T. Morey, Rose Tapley, Earle Williams

MY OFFICIAL WIFE (1926)
(8 r.) d, Paul L. Stein; lp, Irene Rich, Conway Tearle, Jane Winton, Gustav von Seyffertitz

MY OLD DUTCH (1926)
(8 r.) d, Lawrence Trimble; lp, May McAvoy, Pat O'Malley, Cullen Landis, Jean Hersholt

MY OLD KENTUCKY HOME (1922)
(7 r.) d, Ray C. Smallwood; lp, Monte Blue, Julia Swayne Gordon, Frank Currier, Sigrid Holmquist

MY OWN PAL (1926)
(? r.) d, J.G. Blystone; lp, Tom Mix, Olive Borden, Tom Santschi, Virginia Marshall

MY OWN UNITED STATES (1918)
(8 r.) d, John W. Noble; lp, Arnold Daly, Duncan McRae, Charles E. Graham, James Levering

MY PAL (1925)
(5 r.) d, Ward Hayes; lp, Dick Hatton, Marilyn Mills, Star (a horse), Beauty (a horse)

MY PARTNER (1916)
(5 r.) lp, Burr McIntosh, Mary Mantell, James Ryan, Marie Edith Ellis

MY SWEETHEART (1918, Brit.)
(5 r.) d, Meyrick Milton; lp, Margaret Blanche, Concordia Merrill, Randle Ayrton, Bert Wynne

MY UNMARRIED WIFE (1918)
(5 r.) d, George Siegmann; lp, Carmel Myers, Kenneth Harlan, Beatrice Van, Pat Calhoun

MY WIFE (1918)
(5 r.) d, Dell Henderson; lp, Ann Murdock, Rex McDougall, Jules Raucourt, Hubert Druce

MY WIFE AND I (1925)
(7 r.) d, Millard Webb; lp, Irene Rich, Huntly Gordon, John Harron, John Roche

MY WILD IRISH ROSE (1922)
(7 r.) d, David Smith; lp, Pat O'Malley, Helen Howard, Maud Emery, Pauline Starke

MYSTERE D'UNE VIE (1917, Fr.)
(? r.) d, Andre Hugon

MYSTERIES OF INDIA (1922, Ger.)
(8 r.) d, Joe May; lp, Mia May, Conrad Veidt, Erna Morena, Bernhard Gotzke

MYSTERIES OF LONDON, THE (1915, Brit.)
(4 r.) d, A.E. Coleby; lp, Wingold Lawrence, Flora Morris

MYSTERIOUS CLIENT, THE (1918)
(5 r.) d, Fred Wright; lp, Irene Castle, Milton Sills, Warner Oland, Cesare Gravina

MYSTERIOUS GOODS (1923)
(5 r.) d, Charles R. Seeling; lp, George Larkin, Ollie Kirby

MYSTERIOUS MISS TERRY, THE (1917)
(5 r.) d, J. Searle Dawley; lp, Billie Burke, Thomas Meighan, Walter Hiers, Gerald Oliver Smith

MYSTERIOUS MR. TILLER, THE (1917)
(5 r.) d, Rupert Julian; lp, Rupert Julian, Ruth Clifford, Lloyd Whitlock, E.A. Warren

MYSTERIOUS MRS. M, THE (1917)
(5 r.) d, Lois Weber; lp, Mary MacLaren, Harrison Ford, Evelyn Selbie, Willis Marks

MYSTERIOUS MRS. MUSSLEWHITE, THE
(SEE: MYSTERIOUS MRS. M, THE, 1917)

MYSTERIOUS RIDER (1921)
(6 r.) d, Benjamin B. Hampton; lp, Robert McKim, Claire Adams, Carl Gantvoort, James Mason

MYSTERIOUS RIDER, THE (1927)
(6 r.) d, John Waters; lp, Jack Holt, Betty Jewel, Charles Sellon, David Torrence

MYSTERIOUS STRANGER, THE (1925)
(6 r.) d, Jack Nelson; lp, Richard Talmadge, Joseph Swickard, Carmelita Geraghty, Sheldon Lewis

MYSTERY BRAND, THE (1927)
(5 r.) d, Ben Wilson; lp, Ben Wilson, Neva Gerber

MYSTERY CLUB, THE (1926)
(7 r.) d, Herbert Blache; lp, Matt Moore, Edith Roberts, Mildred Harris, Charles Lane

MYSTERY GIRL, THE (1918)
(5 r.) d, William C. De Mille; lp, Ethel Clayton, Henry Woodward, Clarence Burton, Charles West

MYSTERY OF A HANSOM CAB, THE (1915, Brit.)
(6 r.) d, Harold Weston; lp, Milton Rosmer, Fay Temple, A.V. Bramble, Arthur Walcott

MYSTERY OF A LONDON FLAT, THE
(SEE: LONDON FLAT MYSTERY, A, 1915, Brit.)

MYSTERY OF EDWIN DROOD, THE (1914)
(5 r.) d, Tom Terriss; lp, Tom Terriss, Faye Cusick, Alfred Hemming, Paul Sterling

MYSTERY OF NO. 47, THE (1917)
(5 r.) d, Otis B. Thayer; lp, Ralph Herz, Nellie Hartley, Louizetta Valentine, Edgar Murray, Jr.

MYSTERY OF RICHMOND CASTLE, THE (1913)
(4 r.)

MYSTERY OF ROOM 13, THE (1915)
(4 r.) d, George Ridgwell; lp, Lillian Herbert, Marc MacDermott, Guido Colucci, Carlton King

MYSTERY OF SOULS, THE (1911, Ital.)
(4 r.)

MYSTERY OF THE DIAMOND BELT (1914, Brit.)
(4 r.) d, Charles Raymond; lp, Philip Kay, Lewis Carlton, Douglas Payne, Eve Balfour

MYSTERY OF THE FATAL PEARL, THE (1914)
(5 r.)

MYSTERY OF THE GLASS COFFIN, THE (1912, Fr.)
(4 r.)

MYSTERY OF THE LOST RANCH, THE (1925)
(5 r.) d, Harry S. Webb, Tom Gibson; lp, Pete Morrison

MYSTERY OF THE OLD MILL, THE (1914, Brit.)
(4 r.) d, H.O. Martinek; lp, H.O. Martinek, Ivy Montford, Irene Vernon

MYSTERY OF THE YELLOW ROOM, THE (1919)
(5 r.) d, Emile Chautard; lp, William S. Walcott, Edmund Elton, George Cowl, Ethel Grey Terry

MYSTERY RIDER (1928)
(5 r.) d, Robert J. Horner; lp, Pawnee Bill, Jr., Bruce Gordon, Bud Osborne

MYSTERY ROAD, THE (1921, Brit.)
(7 r.) d, Paul Powell; lp, David Powell, Mary Glynne, Ruby Miller, Nadja Ostrovska

MYSTERY VALLEY (1928)
(5 r.) d, J.P. McGowan; lp, Buddy Roosevelt, Carol Lane, Tommy Bay, Jimmy Kane

MYSTIC, THE (1925)
(7 r.) d, Tod Browning; lp, Aileen Pringle, Conway Tearle, Mitchell Lewis, Robert Ober

MYSTIC FACES (1918)
(5 r.) d, E. Mason Hopper; lp, Jack Abbe, Martha Taka, Larry Steers, Liu Chung

MYSTIC HOUR, THE (1917)
(5 r.) d, Richard Ridgely; lp, Alma Hanlon, John Sainpolis, Charles Hutchinson, Florence Short

MYSTIC MIRROR, THE (1928, Ger.)
(7 r.) d, Karl Hoffman, Prof. Teschner; lp, Fritz Rasp, Rina de Ligoure, Felicitas Malten, Albach Retty

NAIDRA, THE DREAM WOMAN (1914, Ger.)
(? r.) d, George Kleine; lp, Mignon Anderson, Riley Chamberlain, Carey L. Hastings, Morris Foster

NAKED TRUTH, THE (1914, Ital.)
(5 r.)

NAKED TRUTH, THE
(SEE: T.N.T., 1924)

NAME THE MAN (1924)
(8 r.) d, Victor Seastrom; lp, Mae Busch, Conrad Nagel, Hobart Bosworth, Creighton Hale

NAMUS (1926, USSR)
(8 r.) d, Amo Bek-Nazarov; lp, S. Abelian, O. Maisurian, A. Khachanian, A. Avetisian

NAN O' THE BACKWOODS (1915)
(4 r.) d, Sidney Olcott; lp, Valentine Grant, Walter Chappen, James Vincent, P.H. O'Malley

NAN WHO COULDN'T BEAT GOD, THE (1915)
(5 r.) lp, Maurice Costello, Thomas Mills, Denton Vane, Edwina Robbins

NANA (1926, Fr.)
(9 r.) d, Jean Renoir; lp, Catherine Hessling, Jean Angelo, Werner Krauss, Raymond Guerin-Catelain

NANCE (1920, Brit.)
(6 r.) d, Albert Ward; lp, Isobel Elsom, James Lindsay, Ivan Samson, Mary Forbes

NANTAS (1924, Fr.)
(? r.) d, Donatien

NAPLES AU BAISER DE FEU (1925, Fr.)
(? r.) d, Serge Nadejdine

NAPOLEON AND JOSEPHINE (1924, Brit.)
(7 r.) d, Alexander Butler

NARAYANA (1920, Fr.)
(? r.) d, Leon Poirier; lp, Van Daele, Marcelle Souty

NARROW PATH, THE (1916)
(5 r.) d, Francis J. Grandon; lp, Violet Mersereau, Lenora Von Ottinger, Nellie Slattery, Anthony Merlo

NARROW TRAIL, THE (1917)
(5 r.) d, Lambert Hillyer, William S. Hart; lp, William S. Hart, Sylvia Breamer, Milton Ross, Robert Kortman

NATASHA ROSTOVA (1915, USSR)
(6 r.) d, Pytor Chardynin; lp, Vera Coralli, Vitold Polonsky, Ivan Mozhukhin, P. Lopukhin

NATIVE COUNTRY (1923, Jap.)
(? r.) d, Kenji Mizoguchi

NATURAL LAW, THE (1917)
(7 r.) d, Charles H. France; lp, Marguerite Courtot, Howard Hall, George Larkin, Jack Ellis

NATURE GIRL, THE (1919)
(5 r.) d, O.A.C. Lund; lp, Violet Mersereau, Donald Stuart, Senorita de Cordoba, Frank Wonderley

NATURE MAN, THE (1915)
(5 r.)

NATURE'S GENTLEMAN (1918, Brit.)
(5 r.) d, F. Martin Thornton; lp, James Knight, Madge Stuart, Arthur Cullin, Cameron Carr

NAUGHTY (1927)
(6 r.) d, Hampton Del Ruth; lp, Pauline Garon, Johnny Harron, Walter Hiers

NAUGHTY BUT NICE (1927)
(7 r.) d, Millard Webb; lp, Colleen Moore, Donald Reed, Claude Gillingwater, Kathryn McGuire

NAUGHTY DUCHESS, THE (1928)
(6 r.) d, Tom Terriss; lp, Eve Southern, H.B. Warner, Duncan Renaldo, Maude Turner Gordon

NAUGHTY HUSBANDS (1930, Brit.)
(6 r.) d, Geoffrey Benstead; lp, Patrick Ludlow, Nigel Cope, James Reardon, Judd Green

NEARER MY GOD TO THEE (1917, Brit.)
(5 r.) d, Cecil M. Hepworth; lp, Henry Edwards, Alma Taylor, A.V. Bramble, Teddy Taylor

NEARLY MARRIED (1917)
(6 r.) d, Chester Withey; lp, Madge Kennedy, Frank Thomas, Mark Smith, Alma Tell

'NEATH WESTERN SKIES (1929)
(5 r.) d, J.P. McGowan; lp, Tom Tyler, Hank Bell, Harry Woods, J.P. McGowan

NECKLACE OF RAMESES, THE (1914)
(4 r.) d, Charles Brabin; lp, Robert Brower, Gertrude Braun, Marc MacDermott, William Betchell

NEDRA (1915)
(5 r.) d, Edward Jose; lp, George Probert, Fania Marinoff, Margaret Greene, Crauford Kent

NE'ER-DO-WELL, THE (1923)
(8 r.) d, Alfred E. Green; lp, Thomas Meighan, Lila Lee, Gertrude Astor, John Miltern

NEGLECTED WOMEN (1924, Brit.)
(6 r.) d, Henry Kolker; lp, Thurston Hall, Seena Owen, Lawford Davidson, Joan Morgan

NENE (1924, Fr.)
(? r.) d, Jacques de Baroncelli; lp, Sandra Milowanoff, Van Daele, France Dhelia, Gaston Modot

NEST OF NOBLEMEN, A (1915, USSR)
(8 r.) d, Vladimir Gardin; lp, Olga Preobrazhenskaya, M. Tamarov, Y. Uvarova, L. Sychova

NEURASTHENIA (1929, USSR)
(6 r.) d, Noah Galkin; lp, Sergei Minin, Y. Yegorova

NEVER TOO LATE (1925)
(5 r.) d, Forrest Sheldon; lp, Francis X. Bushman, Jr., Harriet Loweree, Gino Corrado, Ollie Kirby

NEW ADAM AND EVE, THE (1915)
(4 r.) d, Richard Garrick; lp, Grace Valentine, Charles Richmond,

NEW BABYLON, THE (1929, USSR)
(7 r.) d, Grigori Kozintsev, Leonid Trauberg; lp, Yelena Kuzmina, Pytor Sobolevsky, D. Gutman, Sophie Magarill

NEW GENTLEMEN, THE
(SEE: LES NOUVEAUX MESSIEURS, 1929, Fr.)

NEW MINISTER (1922)
(5 r.) lp, Muriel Kingston

NEW SCHOOL TEACHER, THE (1924)
(6 r.) d, Gregory La Cava; lp, Doris Kenyon, Charles "Chic" Sale, Mickey Bennett, Russell Griffin

NEW TOYS (1925)
(8 r.) d, John S. Robertson; lp, Richard Barthelmess, Mary Hay, Katherine Wilson, Clifton Webb

NEW WIZARD OF OZ, THE
(SEE: HIS MAJESTY, THE SCARECROW OF OZ, 1914)

NEW YEAR'S EVE (1923, Ger.)
(5 r.) d, Lupu Pick; lp, Eugen Klopfer, Edith Posca, Frieda Richard, Karl Harbacher

NEW YORK LUCK (1917)
(5 r.) d, Edward S. Sloman; lp, William Russell, Francelia Billington, Harvey Clark, Clarence Burton

NEXT CORNER, THE (1924)
(7 r.) d, Sam Wood; lp, Conway Tearle, Lon Chaney, Dorothy Mackaill, Ricardo Cortez

NIGGER, THE (1915)
(5 r.) lp, William Farnum, Claire Whitney

NIGHT (1923, Jap.)
(? r.) d, Kenji Mizoguchi

NIGHT BIRD, THE (1928)
(7 r.) d, Fred Newmeyer; lp, Reginald Denny, Betsy Lee, Sam Hardy, Harvey Clark

NIGHT HAWK, THE (1921, Brit.)
(5 r.) d, John Gliddon; lp, Henri de Vries, Malvina Longfellow, Sydney Seaward, Nadja Ostreovska

NIGHT HAWK, THE (1924)
(6 r.) d, Stuart Paton; lp, Harry Carey, Claire Adams, Joseph Girard, Fred Malatesta

NIGHT IN NEW ARABIA, A (1917)
(4 r.) d, Thomas R. Mills; lp, J. Frank Glendon, Patsy De Forest, Horace Vinton, Hattie Delaro

NIGHT MESSAGE, THE (1924)
(5 r.) d, Perley Poore Sheehan; lp, Howard Truesdell, Gladys Hulette, Charles Cruz, Margaret Seddon

NIGHT PATROL, THE
(SEE: CITY OF SHADOWS, 1929, Brit.)

NIGHT RIDERS, THE (1920, Brit.)
(6 r.) d, Alexander Butler; lp, Albert Ray, Maudie Dunham, Andre Beaulieu

NIGHT ROSE, THE (1921)
(6 r.) d, Wallace Worsley; lp, Leatrice Joy, Lon Chaney, John Bowers, Cullen Landis

NIGHTBIRDS OF LONDON, THE (1915, Brit.)
(4 r.) d, Frank Wilson; lp, Stewart Rome, Chrissie White, Violet Hopson, Lionelle Howard

NIKOLAI STAVROGIN (1915, USSR)
(7 r.) d, Yakov Protazanov; lp, Ivan Mozhukhin, Lydia Rindina, A. Ivonin, Pyotr Starkovksy

NINE (1920, Fr.)
(? r.) d, Henri Etievant

NINE POINTS OF THE LAW (1922)
(6 r.) d, Wayne Mack; lp, Helen Gibson, Edward Coxen, Leo Maloney, Aggie Herring

1914 (1915, Brit.)
(4 r.) d, George Loane Tucker; lp, Jane Gail, Hayford Hobbs, Gerald Ames, Sydney Vautier

NINE-TENTHS OF THE LAW (1918)
(6 r.) d, Reaves Eason; lp, Mitchell Lewis, Jimsey Maye, Reaves Eason, Julius Frankenburg

NINETY AND NINE, THE (1916)
(5 r.) d, Ralph W. Ince; lp, Lucille Lee Stewart, William Courtenay, Josephine Lovett, Frank Currier

NINTH OF JANUARY (1925, USSR)
(9 r.) d, Vyacheslav Viskovsky; lp, Yevgeni Boronikhin, Alexei Bogdanovsky, Nikolai Simonov

NITCHEVO (1926, Fr.)
(? r.) d, Jacques de Baroncelli

NO CHILDREN WANTED (1918)
(5 r.) d, Sherwood McDonald; lp, Gloria Joy, Ethel Ritchie, R. Henry Grey, Edward Jobson

NO DEFENSE (1921)
(6 r.) d, William Duncan; lp, William Duncan, Edith Johnson, Jack Richardson, Henry Hebert

NO DEFENSE (1929)
(7 r.) d, Lloyd Bacon; lp, Monte Blue, May McAvoy, Lee Moran, Kathryn Carver

NO GREATER LOVE (1915)
(5 r.)

NO MAN'S LAND (1918)
(5 r.) d, Will S. Davis; lp, Bert Lytell, Anna Q. Nilsson, Eugene Pallette, Charles Arling

NO MAN'S LAW (1925)
(5 r.) d, Del Andrews; lp, Bob Custer, Adalyn Mayer, Ralph McCullough, Bruce Gordon

NO PLACE TO GO (1927)
(7 r.) d, Mervyn LeRoy; lp, Mary Astor, Lloyd Hughes, Hallam Cooley, Myrtle Stedman

NOBODY'S CHILDREN (1926, Ital.)
(10 r.) d, Ugo Del Colle

NOBODY'S GIRL (1920)
(5 r.) d, Francis Grandon; lp, Billie Rhodes, Melbourne McDowell, Mary Alden, Lloyd Bacon

NO-GOOD GUY, THE (1916)
(5 r.) d, Walter Edwards; lp, William Collier, Enid Markey, Charles K. French, Robert Kortman

NOMANDIE (1931)
(4 r.) d, Alexander Singelow

NON-CONFORMIST PARSON, A (1919, Brit.)
(7 r.) d, A.V. Bramble; lp, Gwen Williams, George Keene, Constance Worth, Evan Thomas

NONE SO BLIND (1923)
(6 r.) d, Burton King; lp, Dore Davidson, Zena Keefe, Anders Randolf, Edward Earle

NORTH OF ALASKA (1924)
(5 r.) d, Frank S. Mattison; lp, Matty Mattison, Lorraine Eason, Jack Richardson, Gene Crosby

NORTH OF FIFTY-THREE (1917)
(5 r.) d, Richard Stanton, William Desmond Taylor; lp, Dustin Farnum, Winifred Kingston, William Conklin, Edward Alexander

NORTH OF NOME (1925)
(6 r.) d, Raymond K. Johnston; lp, Robert McKim, Gladys Johnston, Robert N. Bradbury, Howard Webster

NORTH STAR (1925)
(5 r.) d, Paul Powell; lp, Virginia Lee Corbin, Stuart Holmes, Ken Maynard, Harold Austin

NORTHERN LIGHTS (1914)
(5 r.) d, Edgar Lewis; lp, Ivan Shepard, William H. Tooker, Harry Spingler, David Wall

NOT A DRUM WAS HEARD (1924)
(5 r.) d, William Wellman; lp, Charles Jones, Betty Bouton Frank Campeau, Rhody Hathaway

NOT BUILT FOR RUNNIN' (1924)
(5 r.) d, Leo Maloney; lp, Leo Maloney, Josephine Hill, Whitehorse, Milton Fahrney

NOT FOR PUBLICATION (1927)
(7 r.) d, Ralph Ince; lp, Roy Laidlaw, Rex Lease, Jola Mendez, Eugene Strong

NOT FOR SALE (1924)
(5 r.) lp, William Parke, Jr., Dixie Lee, Clayton Fry

NOT GUILTY (1915)
(5 r.) d, Joseph A. Golden; lp, Cyril Scott, Catherine Proctor, Ada Boshell, Mark Ellison

NOT NEGOTIABLE (1918, Brit.)
(4 r.) d, Walter West; lp, Julian Royce, Manora Thew, Gregory Scott, Hubert Woodward

NOT ONE TO SPARE
(SEE: WHICH SHALL IT BE?, 1924)

NOTCH NUMBER ONE (1924)
(5 r.) lp, Ben Wilson, Marjorie Daw

NOTHING BUT LIES (1920)
(6 r.) d, Lawrence C. Windom; lp, Taylor Holmes, Justine Johnstone, Jack McGowan, Rapley Holmes

NOTHING ELSE MATTERS (1920, Brit.)
(6 r.) d, George Pearson; lp, Hugh E. Wright, Moyna McGill, Betty Balfour, George Keene

NOTHING TO BE DONE (1914)
(4 r.) d, Edgar Jones; lp, Charlotte Lambert

NOTORIOUS GALLAGHER
(SEE: HIS GREAT TRIUMPH, 1916)

NOTRA PAUVRE COEUR (1916, Fr.)
(? r.) d, Louis Feuillade

NOTRE DAME D'AMOUR (1922, Fr.)
(? r.) d, Andre Hugon; lp, Jean Toulout, Claude Merelle

NUGGET IN THE ROUGH, A (1918)
(5 r.) lp, Shorty Hamilton

NO.99 (1920)
(5 r.) d, Ernest C. Warde; lp, J. Warren Kerrigan, Fritzi Brunette, Emmett King, Charles Arling

NURSE AND MARTYR (1915, Brit.)
(4 r.) d, Percy Moran; lp, Percy Moran, Cora Lee

NYMPH OF THE FOOTHILLS, A (1918)
(5 r.) d, Fred A. Thompson; lp, Gladys Leslie, Alfred Kappeler, Walter Hiers, Charles A. Stevenson

NYMPH OF THE WOODS, A
(SEE: NYMPH OF THE FOOTHILLS, A, 1918)

O.U. WEST (1925)
(5 r.) d, Harry Garson; lp, Lefty Flynn, Ann May, Milton Ross, Evelyn Francisco

OATH, THE (1921)
(8 r.) d, Raoul Walsh; lp, Miriam Cooper, Robert Fischer, Conway Tearle, Henry Clive

OATH OF THE BIBLE, THE
(SEE: MODERN MEPHISTO, A, 1914)

OBEY THE LAW (1926)
(6 r.) d, Alfred Raboch; lp, Bert Lytell, Edna Murphy, Hedda Hopper, Larry Kent

OBLIGIN' BUCKAROO, THE (1927)
(5 r.) d, Richard Thorpe; lp, Buffalo Bill, Jr., Olive Hasbrouck, Sherry Tansey, Harry Todd

OCEAN WAIF, THE (1916)
(5 r.) d, Alice Blache; lp, Carlyle Blackwell, Doris Kenyon, William Morse, Fraunie Fraunholz

OCTOBER (1928, USSR)
(10 r.) d, Sergei Eisenstein; lp, Nikandrov, N. Popov

ODDS AGAINST
(SEE: LOST AND WON, 1915, Brit.)

OFFICER 444 (1926)
(? r.) d, Ben Wilson, Francis Ford; lp, Ben Wilson, Neva Gerber, Al Ferguson, Phil Ford

OFFICER 666 (1914)
(5 r.) lp, Howard Estabrook, Sidney Seaward, Dan Moyles, Harold Howard

OFFICER 666 (1920)
(5 r.) d, Harry Beaumont; lp, Tom Moore, Jean Calhoun, Jerome Patrick, Harry Dunkinson

OGRE AND THE GIRL, THE (1915)
(4 r.) d, Clay M. Greene; lp, Bernard Siegel, Kempton Greene, James J. Daly, Marie Sterling

OH, BABY! (1926)
(7 r.) d, Harley Knoles; lp, Little Billy, David Butler, Madge Kennedy, Creighton Hale

OH BILLY, BEHAVE (1926)
(5 r.)

OH! CE BAISER (1917, Fr.)
(? r.) d, Rene Hervil, Louis Mercanton

OH, JO! (1921)
(5 r.) d, F. Richard Jones; lp, Dorothy Gish

OH, MABEL BEHAVE (1922)
(5 r.) d, Mack Sennett, Ford Sterling; lp, Mack Sennett, Ford Sterling, Owen Moore, Mabel Normand

OH MARY BE CAREFUL (1921)
(5 r.) d, Arthur Ashley; lp, Madge Kennedy, George Forth, Bernard Thornton, A. Drehle

OH, YOU WOMEN! (1919)
(5 r.) d, John Emerson; lp, Ernest Truex, Louise Huff, Joseph Burke, Bernard Randall

OIL AND ROMANCE (1925)
(5 r.) d, Harry L. Fraser; lp, Gordon Clifford, Charlotte Pierce

OISEAUX DE PASSAGE (1925, Fr.)
(? r.) d, Gaston Roudes

OKLAHOMA COWBOY, AN (1929)
(5 r.) lp, Art Acord, Ione Reed

OLD AND NEW (1930, USSR)
(8 r.) d, Sergei Eisenstein, Grigori Alexandrov; lp, Marfa Lapkina, Vasya Buzenkov, Kostya Vasiliev

OLD BILL OF PARIS
(SEE: CRAINQUEBILLE, 1923, Fr.)

OLD DAD (1920)
(5 r.) d, Lloyd Ingraham; lp, Mildred Harris Chaplin, Irving Cummings, Hazel Howell, Loyola O'Connor

OLD FASHIONED YOUNG MAN, AN (1917)
(5 r.) d, Chester Withey; lp, Robert Harron, Sam De Grasse, Loyola O'Connor, Colleen Moore

OLD FOOL, THE (1923)
(6 r.) d, Edward Venturini; lp, James Barrows, Henry Hunt, Jimmy Mason, Lloyd Hughes

OLD HARTWELL'S CUB (1918)
(5 r.) d, Thomas N. Heffron; lp, William Desmond, Mary Warren, Eugene Burr, Walt Whitman

OLD HEIDELBERG (1915)
(5 r.) d, John Emerson; lp, Wallace Reid, Dorothy Gish, Raymond Wells, Erich Von Stroheim

OLD HOMESTEAD, THE (1916)
(5 r.) d, James Kirkwood; lp, Frank Losee, Creighton Hale, Denman Maley, Louise Huff

OLD HOMESTEAD, THE (1922)
(8 r.) d, James Cruze; lp, Theodore Roberts, George Fawcett, T. Roy Barnes, Fritzi Ridgeway

OLD LADY 31 (1920)
(6 r.) d, John Ince; lp, Emma Dunn, Henry Harmon, Clara Knott, Carrie Clark Ward

OLD LOVES FOR NEW (1918)
(5 r.) d, Raymond Wells; lp, Margery Wilson, Lee Hill, Blanche Gray, George Pearce

OLD NEST, THE (1921)
(8 r.) d, Reginald Barker; lp, Dwight Crittenden, Mary Alden, Nick Cogley, Fanny Stockbridge

OLD OAKEN BUCKET, THE (1921)
(5 r.) d, May Tully; lp, Joseph Smiley, Bobby Connelly, Paul Kelly, Violet Axzelle

OLD ST. PAUL'S
(SEE: WHEN LONDON BURNED, 1915, Brit.)

OLD SWEETHEART OF MINE, AN (1923)
(6 r.) d, Harry Garson; lp, Pat Moore, Elliott Dexter, Mary Jane Irving, Helen Jerome Eddy

OLD WOOD CARVER, THE (1913, Brit.)
(4 r.) d, Hubert Von Herkomer; lp, Maud Milton, May Blaney

OLIVER TWIST (1912)
(5 r.) lp, Nat C. Goodwin, Vinnie Burns, Charles Rogers, Mortimer Martine

O'MALLEY RIDES ALONE (1930)
(5 r.) d, J.P. McGowan; lp, Bob Custer, Phyllis Bainbridge, Martin Cichy, Bud Osborne

OMAR THE TENTMAKER (1922)
(8 r.) d, James Young; lp, Guy Bates Post, Virginia Brown Faire, Nigel De Brulier, Noah Berry

ON BITTER CREEK (1915)
(4 r.) d, Edgar Jones; lp, Edgar Jones, Justina Huff

ON DANGEROUS GROUND (1917)
(5 r.) d, Robert Thornby; lp, Gail Kane, Carlyle Blackwell, William Bailey, Stanhope Wheatcroft

ON DANGEROUS PATHS (1915)
(4 r.) d, John Collins; lp, Viola Dana, Robert Conness

ON HER HONOR (1922)
(5 r.) lp, Marjorie Rambeau

ON HIS MAJESTY'S SECRET SERVICE
(SEE: 0-18 OR A MESSAGE FROM THE SKY, 1914, Brit.)

ON NE BADINE PAS AVEC L'AMOUR (1924, Fr.)
(? r.) d, Gaston Ravel

ON THE BREAD LINE (1915)
(4 r.)

ON THE DOTTED LINE
(SEE: LET WOMEN ALONE, 1925)

ON THE HIGH CARD (1921)
(5 r.) lp, Harry Myers, Tex O'Reilly, Ben Hill, Gene Baker

ON THE JUMP (1918)
(6 r.) d, Raoul Walsh; lp, George Walsh, James Marcus, Frances Burnham, Henry Clive

ON THE LEVEL (1917)
(5 r.) d, George Melford; lp, Fannie Ward, Jack Dean, Harrison Ford, Lottie Pickford

ON THE NIGHT STAGE (1915)
(5 r.) d, Reginald Barker; lp, William S. Hart, Rhea Mitchell, Robert Edeson, Herschal Mayall

ON THE SHELF
(SEE: LET WOMEN ALONE, 1925)

ON THE SPANISH MAIN (1917)
(5 r.) d, Edward A. Salisbury

ON THE STEPS OF THE ALTAR (1916, Brit.)
(4 r.) d, R. Harley West; lp, Harry Lofting, Jack Jarman, Bunty Stewart

ON THE STEPS OF THE THRONE (1913, Ital.)
(4 r.)

ON THE STROKE OF TWELVE (1927)
(6 r.) d, Charles J. Hunt; lp, David Torrence, June Marlowe, Danny O'Shea, Lloyd Whitlock

ON THE THRESHOLD (1925)
(6 r.) d, Renaud Hoffman; lp, Gladys Hulette, Henry B. Walthall, Robert Gordon, Willis Marks

ON THE WARSAW HIGHROAD (1916, USSR)
(4 r.) d, Wladyslaw Starewicz; lp, S. Chaplesky, Z. Valecskaya, S. Zelinsky

ON YOUR TOES (1927)
(6 r.) d, Fred Newmeyer; lp, Reginald Denny, Barbara Worth, Hayden Stevenson, Frank Hagney

ONCE AND FOREVER (1927)
(6 r.) d, Phil Stone; lp, Patsy Ruth Miller, John Harron, Burr McIntosh, Emily Fitzroy

ONCE IN A LIFETIME (1925)
(5 r.) d, Duke Worne; lp, Richard Holt, Mary Beth Milford, Wilbur Higgins, Theodore Lorch

ONCE TO EVERY WOMAN (1920)
(6 r.) d, Allen Holubar; lp, Dorothy Phillips, William Ellingford, Margaret Mann, Emily Chichester

ONCE UPON A TIME (1922, Den.)
(? r.) d, Carl-Theodor Dreyer; lp, Clara Pontoppidan, Svend Methling, Peter Jerndorff, Karen Poulsen

ONE AGAINST MANY (1919)
(6 r.) lp, Anita King

ONE ARABIAN NIGHT (1923, Brit.)
(6 r.) d, Sinclair Hill; lp, George Robey, Julia Kean, Lionelle Howard, Edward O'Neill

ONE EIGHTH APACHE (1922)
(6 r.) d, Ben Wilson; lp, Roy Stewart, Kathleen Kirkham, Wilbur McGaugh, George M. Daniel

ONE GLORIOUS DAY (1922)
(5 r.) d, James Cruze; lp, Will Rogers, Lila Lee, Alan Hale, John Fox

ONE GLORIOUS NIGHT (1924)
(6 r.) d, Scott Dunlap; lp, Elaine Hammerstein, Al Roscoe, Phyllis Haver, Freeman Wood

ONE GLORIOUS SCRAP (1927)
(5 r.) d, Edgar Lewis; lp, Fred Humes, Dorothy Gulliver, Robert McKenzie, Francis Ford

ONE HOUR (1917)
(6 r.) d, Paul McAllister, Edwin L. Hollywood; lp, Zena Keefe, Alan Hale, D.J. Flannigan, Ina Brooks

ONE HOUR BEFORE DAWN (1920)
(6 r.) d, Henry King; lp, H.B. Warner, Anna Q. Nilsson, Augustus Phillips, Frank Leigh

ONE HOUR PAST MIDNIGHT (1924)
(5 r.) d, B.C. Rule

ONE INCREASING PURPOSE (1927)
(8 r.) d, Harry Beaumont; lp, Edmund Lowe, Lila Lee, Holmes Herbert, May Allison

ONE MAN GAME, A (1927)
(5 r.) d, Ernst Laemmle; lp, Fred Humes, Fay Wray, Harry Todd, Clarence Geldert

ONE MAN IN A MILLION (1921)
(6 r.) d, George Beban; lp, George Beban, Helen Jerome Eddy, Irene Rich, Lloyd Whitlock

ONE MAN TRAIL (1926)
(5 r.) lp, Monty Montague, Ena Gregory

ONE MILLION DOLLARS (1915)
(5 r.) d, John W. Noble; lp, William Faversham, Henry Bergman, George LeGuere, Mayme Kelso

ONE MOMENT'S TEMPTATION (1922)
(5 r.) d, A.J. Rooke; lp, James Knight, Marjorie Villers

ONE NIGHT IN ROME (1924)
(7 r.) d, Clarence G. Badger; lp, Laurette Taylor, Tom Moore, Alan Hale, William Humphrey

ONE OF MILLIONS (1914)
(4 r.) d, J. Searle Dawley; lp, Laura Sawyer, Maximilian Jurgens, Gertrude Norman

ONE OF THE FINEST (1919)
(5 r.) d, Harry Beaumont; lp, Tom Moore, Seena Owen, "Peaches" Jackson, Millie McConnell

ONE SHOT RANGER (1925)
(5 r.) lp, Pete Morrison, Betty Goodwin, Lightning (a horse)

ONE THOUSAND DOLLARS (1918)
(5 r.) d, Kenneth Webb; lp, Edward Earle, Agnes Ayres, Florence Deshon, Templar Saxe

ONE TOUCH OF NATURE (1917)
(5 r.) d, Edward H. Griffith; lp, John Drew Bennett, Edward Lawrence, Viola Cain, John J. McGraw

ONE TOUCH OF SIN (1917)
(5 r.) d, Richard Stanton; lp, Gladys Brockwell, Jack Standing, Willard Louis, Sedley Brown

ONE WAY STREET (1925)
(6 r.) d, John Francis Dillon; lp, Ben Lyon, Anna Q. Nilsson, Marjorie Daw, Dorothy Cumming

ONE WEEK OF LIFE (1919)
(5 r.) d, Hobart Henley; lp, Pauline Frederick, Thomas Holding, Sidney Ainsworth, Corinne Barker

ONE WOMAN, THE (1918)
(5 r.) d, Reginald Barker; lp, W. Lawson Butt, Clara Williams, Adda Gleason, Herschel Mayall

ONE WOMAN IDEA, THE (1929)
(7 r.) d, Berthold Viertel; lp, Rod La Rocque, Marceline Day, Shirley Dorman, Sharon Lynn

ONE WONDERFUL NIGHT (1914)
(4 r.) d, E.H. Calvert; lp, Francis X. Bushman, Cyril Leonard, E.H. Calvert, Leo White

ONE WONDERFUL NIGHT (1922)
(5 r.) d, Stuart Paton; lp, Herbert Rawlinson, Lillian Rich, Dale Fuller, Sidney De Grey

ONE-MAN TRAIL, THE (1921)
(5 r.) d, Bernard J. Durning; lp, Buck Jones, Beatrice Burnham, Helene Rosson, James Farley

ONE-THING-AT-A-TIME O'DAY (1919)
(5 r.) d, John Ince; lp, Bert Lytell, Eileen Percy, Joseph Kilgour, Stanton Heck

ONE-WAY TRAIL, THE (1920)
(5 r.) d, Fred Kelsey; lp, Edythe Sterling, Gordon Sackville, Jack Connelly, J. Webster Dill

ONLY MAN, THE (1915, Brit.)
(4 r.) d, W.P. Kellino; lp, Billy Merson, Winifred Delevanti, Fred Dunning, Blanche Bella

ONLY ROAD, THE (1918)
(5 r.) d, Frank Reicher; lp, Viola Dana, Casson Ferguson, Edythe Chapman, Fred Huntley

ONLY THING, THE (1925)
(6 r.) d, Jack Conway; lp, Eleanor Boardman, Conrad Nagel, Edward Connelly, Louis Payne

ONLY WAY OUT, THE (1915)
(4 r.) lp, Rosetta Brice, John Ince, Walter Law, Francis Joyner

ON-THE-SQUARE GIRL, THE (1917)
(5 r.) d, George Fitzmaurice; lp, Mollie King, L. Rogers Lytton, Aimee Dalmores, Donald Hall

OPEN DOOR, THE (1919)
(6 r.) d, Dallas M. Fitzgerald; lp, John P. Wade, Sam J. Ryan, Bob Broderick, Frank Evans

OPEN PLACES (1917)
(5 r.) d, W.S. Van Dyke; lp, Jack Gardner, Ruth King, Carl Stockdale

OPEN RANGE (1927)
(6 r.) d, Clifford S. Smith; lp, Betty Bronson, Lane Chandler, Fred Kohler, Bernard Siegel

OPEN SWITCH, THE (1926)
(5 r.) d, J.P. McGowan; lp, Helen Holmes

OPEN TRAIL, THE
(SEE: RED RIDER, THE, 1925)

OPENED SHUTTERS (1921)
(5 r.) d, William Worthington; lp, Joseph Swickard, Edith Roberts, Joe Singleton, Mai Wells

OPENING NIGHT, THE (1927)
(6 r.) d, Edward H. Griffith; lp, Claire Windsor, John Bowers, E. Alyn Warren, Grace Goodall

OPPORTUNITY (1918)
(5 r.) d, John H. Collins; lp, Viola Dana, Hale Hamilton, Frank Currier, Edward Abeles

ORCHIDS AND ERMINE (1927)
(7 r.) d, Alfred Santell; lp, Colleen Moore, Jack Mulhall, Sam Hardy, Gwen Lee

ORDEAL OF ELIZABETH, THE (1916)
(5 r.) d, Wilfred North; lp, Lillian Walker, Evart Overton, Denton Vane, Ollie Walker

ORDEAL OF ROSETTA, THE (1918)
(5 r.) d, Emile Chautard; lp, Alice Brady, Crauford Kent, Ormi Hawley, Henri Leone

ORPHAN, THE (1920)
(6 r.) d, J. Gordon Edwards; lp, William Farnum, Louise Lovely, Henry J. Hebert, Earl Crain

ORPHAN SALLY (1922)
(5 r.) d, Edward L. Hemmer; lp, Sidney Mason, Flora Finch, Margaret Beecher, Maud Sylvester

ORPHANS OF THE GHETTO (1922)
(6 r.) lp, Arthur Donaldson

OTHELLO (1914, Ital.)
(4 r.)

OTHELLO (1922, Ger.)
(9 r.) d, Dimitri Buchowtzki; lp, Emil Jannings, Lea Von Lenkeffy, Werner Krauss

OTHER, THE (1912, Ger.)
(? r.) d, Max Mack; lp, Albert Basserman, Emmerich Hanus, Hanni Weisse, Relly Ridon

OTHER GIRL, THE (1916)
(5 r.) d, Percy Winter; lp, James J. Corbett, Paul Gilmore, Horace Vinton, Mortimer Martini

OTHER HALF, THE (1919)
(5 r.) d, King Vidor; lp, Florence Vidor, Charles Meredith, ZaSu Pitts, David Butler

OTHER MEN'S DAUGHTERS (1923)
(6 r.) d, Ben Wilson; lp, Bryant Washburn, Mabel Forrest, Kathleen Kirkham, Wheeler Oakman

OTHER MEN'S SHOES (1920)
(7 r.) d, Edgar Lewis; lp, Crauford Kent, Irene Boyle, Stephen Grattan, Jean Armour

OTHER MEN'S WIVES (1919)
(4 r.) d, Victor L. Schertzinger; lp, Dorothy Dalton, Forrest Stanley, Holmes E. Herbert, Dell Boone

OTHER PEOPLE'S MONEY (1916)
(5 r.) d, William Parke; lp, Gladys Hulette, Fraunie Fraunholz, J.H. Gilmour, Yale Benner

OTHER SELF, THE (1918, Aust.)
(4 r.) d, Fritz Freisler; lp, Raoul Aslan, Fritz Kortner, Magda Sonja

OTHER SIDE, THE (1922)
(6 r.) d, Hugh Dierker; lp, Helen Lynch, Fritzi Brunette

OTHER SIDE OF THE DOOR, THE (1916)
(5 r.) d, Thomas Ricketts; lp, Harold Lockwood, May Allison, William Stowell, Harry Von Meter

OTHER WOMAN, THE (1918)
(5 r.) d, Albert Parker; lp, Peggy Hyland, Milton Sills, Anna Lehr, William B. Davidson

OTHER WOMAN, THE (1921)
(5 r.) d, Edward Sloman; lp, Jerome Patrick, Jane Novak, Helen Jerome Eddy, William Conklin

OTHER WOMAN'S STORY, THE (1925)
(6 r.) d, B.F. Stanley; lp, Alice Calhoun, Robert Frazer, Helen Lee Worthing, David Torrence

OTHER WOMEN'S CLOTHES (1922)
(6 r.) d, Hugo Ballin; lp, Mabel Ballin, Raymond Bloomer, Crauford Kent, May Kitson

OTHER WOMEN'S HUSBANDS (1926)
(7 r.) d, Erle C. Kenton; lp, Monte Blue, Marie Prevost, Huntly Gordon, Phyllis Haver

OUR BETTER SELVES (1919)
(5 r.) d, George Fitzmaurice; lp, Fannie Ward, Lewis J. Cody, Charles Hill Mailes, Mary Lee Wise

OUR MUTUAL FRIEND (1921, Swed.)
(8 r.) lp, Catherine Reese, Peter Walton, Albert Fenton, Elvin Milton

OUT OF THE CHORUS (1921)
(5 r.) d, Herbert Blache; lp, Alice Brady, Vernon Steel, Charles Gerard, Emily Fitzroy

OUT OF THE CLOUDS (1921)
(5 r.) d, Leonard Franchon; lp, Al Hart, Jack Mower, Robert Conville

OUT OF THE DEPTHS (1921)
(? r.) d, Otis B. Thayer, Edmund Cobb; lp, Violet Mersereau, Edmund Cobb

OUT OF THE FOG (1919)
(7 r.) d, Albert Capellani; lp, Alla Nazimova, Charles Bryant, Henry Harmon, Nancy Palmer

OUT OF THE NIGHT (1918)
(6 r.) d, James Kirkwood; lp, Catherine Calvert, Herbert Rawlinson, Frederick Esmelton, Emmett King

OUT OF THE RUINS (1915)
(4 r.) d, Ashley Miller; lp, Mabel Trunnelle, Pat O'Malley

OUT OF THE RUINS (1928)
(7 r.) d, John Francis; lp, Richard Barthelmess, Robert Frazer, Marian Nixon, Emile Chautard

OUT OF THE SNOWS (1920)
(6 r.) d, Ralph Ince; lp, Ralph Ince, Zena Keefe, Gladys Coburn, William Hartigan

OUT OF THE STORM (1926)
(7 r.) d, Louis J. Gasnier; lp, Jacqueline Logan, [Frederick] Tyrone Power, Edmund Burns, Montagu Love

OUT OF THE WRECK (1917)
(5 r.) d, William Desmond Taylor; lp, Kathlyn Williams, William Clifford, William Conklin, William Winter Jefferson

OUTCAST, THE (1915)
(4 r.) d, John B. O'Brien; lp, Mae Marsh, Robert Harron, Mary Alden, Spottiswoode Aitken

OUTCAST (1917)
(6 r.) d, Dell Henderson; lp, Ann Murdock, David Powell, Catherine Calvert, Richard Hatteras

OUTCAST (1922)
(7 r.) d, Chester Withey; lp, Elsie Ferguson, David Powell, William David, Mary MacLaren

OUTCAST SOULS (1928)
(6 r.) d, Louis Chaudet; lp, Priscilla Bonner, Charles Delaney, Ralph Lewis, Lucy Beaumont

OUTLAW AND HIS WIFE, THE (1918, Swed.)
(9 r.) d, Victor Sjostrom; lp, Victor Sjostrom, Edith Erastoff

OUTLAW EXPRESS, THE (1926)
(6 r.) d, Leo D. Maloney; lp, Leo Maloney, Joan Renee, Melbourne MacDowell, Albert Hart

OUTLAWED (1921)
(5 r.) d, Alvin J. Neitz; lp, Carlyn Wagner, Bill Patton, Buck Conners, Joseph Rickson

OUTLAW'S PARADISE (1927)
(5 r.) lp, Al Hoxie

OUTSIDER, THE (1917)
(6 r.) d, William C. Dowlan; lp, Emmy Whelen, Herbert Heyes, Florence Short, Virginia Palmer

OVER NIAGRA FALLS (1914)
(4 r.)

OVER NIGHT (1915)
(? r.) d, James Young; lp, Vivian Martin, Sam B. Hardy, Herbert Yost, Florence Morrison

OVER THE GARDEN WALL (1919)
(5 r.) d, David Smith; lp, Bessie Love, Allan Forrest, Otto Lederer, Anne Schaefer

OVER THE HILL (1917)
(5 r.) d, William Parke; lp, Gladys Hulette, William Parke, Jr., Chester Barnett, J.H. Gilmour

OVER THE TOP (1918)
(8 r.) d, Wilfred North; lp, Arthur Guy Empey, Lois Meredith, James Morrison, Arthur Donaldson

OVER THE WIRE (1921)
(6 r.) d, Wesley Ruggles; lp, Alice Lake, Al Roscoe, George Stewart, Alan Hale

OVER THERE (1917)
(6 r.) d, James Kirkwood; lp, Charles Richman, Anna Q. Nilsson, Gertrude Berkeley, Walter Hiers

OVERCOAT, THE (1916)
(5 r.) d, Rea Berger; lp, Rhea Mitchell, William Stowell, Perry Banks, Clarence Burton

OVERCOAT, THE
(SEE: CLOAK, THE, 1926, USSR)

OVERLAND STAGE, THE (1927)
(7 r.) d, Albert Rogell; lp, Ken Maynard, Kathleen Collins, Tom Santschi, Sheldon Lewis

OYSTER PRINCESS, THE (1919, Ger.)
(4 r.) d, Ernst Lubitsch; lp, Ossi Oswalda, Harry Liedtke Victor Janson, Julius Falkenstein

PACE THAT KILLS, THE (1928)
(7 r.) d, Norton S. Parker; lp, Owen Gorin, Thelma Daniels, Florence Turner, Florence Dudley

PADDY O'HARA (1917)
(5 r.) d, Walter Edwards; lp, William Desmond, Mary McIvor, Robert McKim, J.J. Dowling

PADLOCKED (1926)
(7 r.) d, Allan Dwan; lp, Lois Moran, Noah Beery, Louise Dresser, Helen Jerome Eddy

PAGAN, THE (1929)
(7 r.) d, W.S. Van Dyke; lp, Ramon Novarro, Renee Adoree, Dorothy Janis, Donald Crisp

PAGAN GOD, THE (1919)
(5 r.) d, Park Frame; lp, H.B. Warner, Marguerite de la Motte, Jack Abbe, Walter Perry

PAGAN LOVE (1920)
(6 r.) d, Hugo Ballin; lp, Togo Yamamoto, Mabel Ballin, Rockliffe Fellowes, Charlie Fang

PAGAN PASSIONS (1924)
(6 r.) d, Colin Campbell; lp, Wyndham Standing, June Elvidge, Barbara Bedford, Raymond McKee

PAGE MYSTERY, THE (1917)
(5 r.) d, Harley Knoles; lp, Carlyle Blackwell, June Elvidge, Arthur Ashley, Frank Goldsmith

PAGE OF MADNESS, A
(SEE: CRAZY PAGE, A, 1926, Jap.)

PAGLIACCI (1923, Brit.)
(7 r.) d, G.B. Samuelson, S.W. Smith

PAID IN ADVANCE (1919)
(6 r.) d, Allen Holubar; lp, Dorothy Phillips, Joseph Girard, Lon Chaney, Priscilla Dean

PAID IN FULL (1914)
(5 r.) d, Augustus Thomas; lp, William Riley Hatch, Tully Marshall, Caroline French, T. Tamamoto

PAID IN FULL (1919)
(5 r.) d, Emile Chautard; lp, Pauline Frederick, Robert Cain, Wyndham Standing, Frank Losee

PAID TO LOVE (1927)
(7 r.) d, Howard Hawks; lp, George O'Brien, Virginia Valli, J. Farrell MacDonald, Thomas Jefferson

PAINT AND POWDER (1925)
(7 r.) d, Hunt Stromberg; lp, Elaine Hammerstein, Theodore von Eltz, John Sainpolis, Stuart Holmes

PAINTED LADY, THE (1924)
(7 r.) d, Chester Bennett; lp, George O'Brien, Dorothy Mackaill, Harry T. Morey, Lucille Hutton

PAINTED LIE, THE (1917)
(5 r.) d, Crane Wilbur; lp, Crane Wilbur, Harrish Ingraham, Mae Gaston, Ida Lewis

PAINTED LILY, THE (1918)
(5 r.) d, Thomas N. Heffron; lp, Alma Rubens, Francis McDonald, William V. Mong, Jack Richardson

PAINTED LIPS (1918)
(5 r.) d, Edward J. LeSaint; lp, Louise Lovely, Lewis Cody, Hector Dion, Alfred Allen

PAINTED MADONNA, THE (1917)
(5 r.) d, O.A.C. Lund; lp, Sonia Markova, Sidney Mason, William Lampe, David Herblin

PAINTED POST (1928)
(5 r.) d, Eugene Forde; lp, Tom Mix, Natalie Kingston, Philo McCullough, Al St. John

PAINTED TRAIL (1928)
(5 r.) d, J.P. McGowan; lp, Buddy Roosevelt, Betty Baker, Leon De La Mothe, Lafe McKee

PAINTED WORLD, THE (1919)
(5 r.) d, Ralph Ince; lp, Anita Stewart, E.K. Lincoln, Julia Swayne Gordon, Charles Kent

PAIR OF HELLIONS, A (1924)
(6 r.) d, Walter Willis; lp, Ranger Bill Miller, Patricia Palmer, Luther Jones, Mable Turner

PAIR OF SPECTACLES, A (1916, Brit.)
(4 r.) d, Alexander Butler; lp, Sir John Hare, Peggy Hyland, Booth Conway, James le Fane

PAL O'MINE (1924)
(6 r.) d, Edward J. Le Saint; lp, Irene Rich, Josef Swickard, Willard Louis, Albert Roscoe

PALACE AND FORTRESS (1924, USSR)
(10 r.) d, Alexander Ivanovksy; lp, Y. Boronikhin, Y. Korvin-Krukovsky, K. Yakovlev, S. Shishko

PALACE OF PLEASURE, THE (1926)
(6 r.) d, Emmett Flynn; lp, Edmund Lowe, Betty Compson, Henry Kolker, Harvey Clark

PALACE OF THE DARKENED WINDOWS, THE (1920)
(5 r.) d, Henry Kolker; lp, Claire Anderson, Arthur Edmund Carew, Jay Belasco, Christine Mayo

PALACES (1927, Fr.)
(? r.) d, Jean Durand

PALAVER (1926, Brit.)
(7 r.) d, Geoffrey Barkas; lp, Haddon Mason, Reginald Fox, Hilda Cowley, Yiberr

PALISER CASE, THE (1920)
(5 r.) d, William Parke; lp, Pauline Frederick, Albert Roscoe, James Neill, Hazel Brennan

PALLARD THE PUNTER (1919, Brit.)
(7 r.) d, J.L.V. Leigh; lp, Jack Leigh, Heather Thatcher, Lionel d'Aragon, Cecil Morton York

PALM BEACH GIRL, THE (1926)
(7 r.) d, Erle Kenton; lp, Bebe Daniels, Lawrence Gray, Josephine Drake, Marguerite Clayton

PALS (1925)
(5 r.) d, John P. McCarthy; lp, Louise Lorraine, Art Acord, Leon Kent, Andrew Waldron

PALS FIRST (1918)
(6 r.) d, Edwin Carewe; lp, Harold Lockwood, Rubye De Remer, James Lackaye, Frank De Vernon

PALS FIRST (1926)
(7 r.) d, Edwin Carewe; lp, Lloyd Hughes, Dolores Del Rio, Alec Francis, George Cooper

PALS IN BLUE (1924)
(5 r.) lp, Tom Mix

PALS IN PARADISE (1926)
(7 r.) d, George B. Seitz; lp, Marguerite De La Motte, John Bowers, Rudolph Schildkraut, May Robson

PALS IN PERIL (1927)
(5 r.) d, Richard Thorpe; lp, Buffalo Bill Jr., George Ovey, Edward Hearn, Robert Homans

PALS OF THE WEST (1922)
(5 r.) lp, R. Lee Hill, William A. Lowery, M. McWade, Esther Ralston

PAMELA'S PAST (1916)
(5 r.) lp, Maude Fealy, Irving Cummings, Harry Benham, Mignon Anderson

PAMPERED YOUTH (1925)
(7 r.) d, David Smith; lp, Cullen Landis, Ben Alexander, Allan Forrest, Alice Calhoun

PANTHEA (1917)
(6 r.) d, Allan Dwan; lp, Norma Talmadge, L. Roger Lytton, George Fawcett, Earle Foxe

PANTHER WOMAN, THE (1919)
(5 r.) d, Ralph Ince; lp, Olga Petrova, Rockcliffe Fellowes, Vernon Steele, Matilda Baring

PANTS (1917)
(5 r.) d, Arthur Berthelet; lp, Mary McAllister, John Cossar, Arthur Metcalf, Mary Parkin

PAPA HULIN (1916, Fr.)
(? r.) d, Henry Krauss

PAPER DOLL'S WHISPER OF SPRING, A (1926, Jap.)
(? r.) d, Kenji Mizoguchi; lp, Tokihiko Okada, Yoko Umemura

PAPILLON (1920, Fr.)
(? r.) d, Edouard Violet

PAR DESSUS LE MUR (1923, Fr.)
(? r.) d, Pierre Colombier

PARADISE AND PURGATORY (1912, Ital.)
(4 r.)

PARADISE FOR TWO (1927)
(7 r.) d, Gregory La Cava; lp, Richard Dix, Edmund Breese, Betty Bronson, Andre Beranger

PARADISE WITHOUT ADAM (1918, USSR)
(4 r.) d, Vyacheslav Turzhansky

PARASITE, THE (1925)
(6 r.) d, Louis Gasnier; lp, Owen Moore, Madge Bellamy, Bryant Washburn, Mary Carr

PARDNERS (1917)
(5 r.) lp, Charlotte Walker, Richard Tucker, Leo Gordon, Charles Sutton

PARDON MY FRENCH (1921)
(6 r.) d, Sidney Olcott; lp, Vivian Martin, George Spink, Thomas Meegan, Nadine Beresford

PAREMA, CREATURE FROM THE STARWORLD (1922, Aust.)
(5 r.) d, Mano Ziffer-Teschenbruck; lp, Carmen Cartellieri, Viktor Kutschera, Karl Gotz

PARENTAGE (1918)
(7 r.) d, Hobart Henley; lp, Hobart Henley, Anna Lehr, Barbara Castleton, Bert Busby

PARIS (1924, Fr.)
(? r.) d, Rene Hervil; lp, Alibert, Dolly Davis

PARIS (1926)
(6 r.) d, Edmund Goulding; lp, Charles Ray, Joan Crawford, Douglas Gilmore, Michael Visaroff

PARIS AFTER DARK (1923, Ger.)
(7 r.) d, Hans Wierendorf

PARIS ASLEEP
(SEE: PARIS QUI DORT, 1924)

PARIS AT MIDNIGHT (1926)
(7 r.) d, E. Mason Hopper; lp, Jetta Goudal, Lionel Barrymore, Mary Brian, Edmund Burns

PARIS EN CINQ JOURS (1926, Fr.)
(? r.) d, Pierre Colombier; lp, Nicolas Rinsky, Dolly Davis

PARIS GIRLS (1929, Fr.)
(? r.) d, Henry Roussel; lp, Suzy Vernon

PARIS QUI DORT (1924, Fr.)
(4 r.) d, Rene Clair; lp, Henri Rollan, Albert Prejean, Madeleine Rodrigue, Marcel Vallee

PARISH PRIEST, THE (1921)
(6 r.) d, Joseph Franz; lp, William Desmond, Thomas Ricketts, Carl Miller, J. Morris Foster

PARISIAN COBBLER (1928, USSR)
(7 r.) d, Friedrich Ermler; lp, Veronica Buzhinskaya, Fyodor Nikitin, Valeri Solovtsov, Yakov Gudkin

PARISIAN LOVE (1925)
(7 r.) d, Louis Gasnier; lp, Clara Bow, Donald Keith, Lillian Leighton, James Gordon Russell

PARISIAN NIGHTS (1925)
(7 r.) d, Al Santell; lp, Elaine Hammerstein, Gaston Glass, Lou Tellegen, William J. Kelly

PARISIAN ROMANCE, A (1916)
(5 r.) d, Frederick A. Thompson; lp, H. Cooper Cliffe, Dorothy Green, Margaret Skirvin, Angelica Spier

PARISIAN SCANDAL, A (1921)
(5 r.) d, George L. Cox; lp, George Periolat, Lillian Lawrence, Marie Prevost, Beretram Grassby

PARISIAN TIGRESS, THE (1919)
(5 r.) d, Herbert Blache; lp, Viola Dana, Darrel Foss, Henry Kolker, Edward Connelly

PARLOR, BEDROOM AND BATH (1920)
(6 r.) d, Edward Dillon; lp, Ruth Stonehouse, Eugene Pallette, Kathleen Kirkham, Charles H. West

PARSON'S WIDOW, THE (1920, Den.)
(5 r.) d, Carl-Theodor Dreyer; lp, Hildur Carlberg, Einar Rod, Greta Almroth, Olav Aukrust

PART TIME WIFE, THE (1925)
(6 r.) d, Henry McCarty; lp, Alice Calhoun, Robert Ellis, Freeman Wood, Edwards Davis

PARTED BY THE SWORD (1915, Brit.)
(4 r.) d, Percy Moran; lp, Percy Moran, Marietta de Leyse

PARTED CURTAINS (1921)
(6 r.) d, John Bracken; lp, Henry Walthall, Mary Alden, Edward Cecil, Margaret Landis

PARTING OF THE TRAILS (1930)
(4 r.) d, J.P. McGowan; lp, Bob Custer, Vivian Ray, Bobbie Dunn, George A. Miller

PARTNERS AT LAST (1916, Brit.)
(4 r.) d, Ralph Dewsbury; lp, Amy Brandon-Thomas, Charles Rock, Chappel Dossett, Hubert Willis

PARTNERS OF FATE (1921)
(5 r.) d, Bernard Durning; lp, Louise Lovely, William Scott, Rosemary Theby, Philo McCullough

PARTNERS OF THE SUNSET (1922)
(5 r.) d, Robert H. Townley; lp, Allene Ray, Robert Frazer, Mildred Bright, J.W. Johnston

PARTNERS THREE (1919)
(5 r.) d, Fred Niblo; lp, Enid Bennett, Casson Ferguson, John P. Lockney, Robert McKim

PASQUALE (1916)
(5 r.) d, William Desmond Taylor; lp, George Beban, Myrtle Stedman, Helen Jerome Eddy, Page Peters

PASSERS-BY (1916)
(5 r.) d, Stanner E.V. Taylor; lp, Charles Cherry, Mary Charleson, Marguerite Skirvin, Kate Sarjeanston

PASSERS-BY (1920)
(6 r.) d, J. Stuart Blackton; lp, Herbert Rawlinson, Leila Valentine, Ellen Cassity, Pauline Coffyn

PASSIN' THROUGH
(SEE: PASSING THRU, 1921)

PASSING FANCY (1933, Jap.)
(? r.) d, Yasujiro Ozu

PASSING OF THE OKLAHOMA OUTLAWS, THE (1915)
(6 r.) d, William Tilghman; lp, Tom Dolin, Bud Ledbetter, E.D. Nix, Chris Madsen

PASSING OF THE THIRD FLOOR BACK, THE (1918, Brit.)
(6 r.) d, Herbert Brenon; lp, Johnston Forbes-Robertson, Molly Pearson, Ketty Galanta, Augusta Haviland

PASSING OF WOLF MACLEAN, THE (1924)
(5 r.) d, Paul Hurst; lp, Jack Meehan, Mark Fenton, Alma Rayford, Al Hallett

PASSING THRU (1921)
(5 r.) d, William A. Seiter; lp, Douglas MacLean, Madge Bellamy, Otto Hoffman, Cameron Coffey

PASSION (1917)
(5 r.) d, Richard Ridgely; lp, Shirley Mason, George Le Guere, Clifford Bruce, Bigelow Cooper

PASSION FLOWER, THE (1921)
(7 r.) d, Herbert Brenon; lp, Norma Talmadge, Courtenay Foote, Eulalie Jensen, Harrison Ford

PASSION FRUIT (1921)
(6 r.) d, John E. Ince; lp, Doraldina, Edward Earle, Stuart Holmes, Sidney Bracey

PASSION OF A WOMAN TEACHER, THE (1926, Jap.)
(? r.) d, Kenji Mizoguchi

PASSION OF ST. FRANCIS (1932, Ital.)
(5 r.) d, Giulio Antamoro; lp, Alberto Pasquali, Alfredo Robert, Romuald Joube, Franz Salla

PASSION SONG, THE (1928)
(6 r.) d, Harry O. Hoyt; lp, Gertrude Olmsted, Noah Beery, Gordon Elliott, Edgar Washington Blue

PASSIONNEMENT (1921, Fr.)
(? r.) d, Georges Lacroix

PASSION'S PATHWAY (1924)
(6 r.) d, Bertram Bracken; lp, Estelle Taylor, Jean Perry, Wilfred Lucas, Tully Marshall

PASSION'S PLAYGROUND (1920)
(5 r.) d, J.A. Barry; lp, Katherine MacDonald, Norman Kerry, Nell Craig, Edwin Stevens

PASSIONATE PILGRIM, THE (1921)
(7 r.) d, Robert G. Vignola; lp, Matt Moore, Mary Newcomb, Julia Swayne Gordon, Tom Guise

PASSIONATE QUEST, THE (1926)
(7 r.) d, J. Stuart Blackton; lp, May McAvoy, Willard Louis, Louise Fazenda, Gardner James

PASTEBOARD CROWN, A (1922)
(5 r.) d, Travers Vale; lp, Evelyn Greeley, Robert Elliott, Gladys Valerie, Eleanor Woodruff

PASTEBOARD LOVER, THE
(SEE: FAITHLESS LOVER, 1928)

PASTEUR (1922, Fr.)
(? r.) d, Jean Epstein

PATENT LEATHER KID, THE (1927)
(12 r.) d, Alfred Santell; lp, Richard Barthelmess, Molly O'Day, Lawford Davidson, Matthew Betz

PATENT LEATHER PUG, THE (1926)
(5 r.) d, Albert Rogell; lp, Billy Sullivan, Ruth Dwyer, J.P. McGowan

PATH FORBIDDEN, THE (1914)
(5 r.) lp, Octavia Handworth, Gordon De Maine, William A. Williams, John B. Hymer

PATH OF DARKNESS, THE (1916)
(5 r.) lp, Margaret Darwin, Charles Fuller, Harry T. DeVere, Jose Melville

PATH OF HAPPINESS, THE (1916)
(5 r.) lp, Violet Mersereau, Harry Benham, Sidney Bracy, Florence Crawford

PATHS OF FLAME (1926)
(5 r.) lp, George Kesterson, Dorothy Lee

PATH SHE CHOSE, THE (1920)
(5 r.) d, Philip Rosen; lp, Anne Cornwall, J. Farrell MacDonald, Claire Anderson, Dagmar Godowsky

PATH TO THE RAINBOW, THE (1915)
(4 r.) d, Joseph Smiley; lp, Ormi Hawley, Arthur Matthews, Earl Metcalfe, Herbert Fortier

PATRIOT AND THE SPY, THE (1915)
(4 r.) lp, James Cruze, Marguerite Snow, Alphonse Ethier

PATSY (1917)
(5 r.) d, John G. Adolfi; lp, June Caprice, Harry Hilliard, John Smiley, Edna Munsey

PATSY, THE (1928)
(8 r.) d, King Vidor; lp, Marion Davies, Orville Caldwell, Marie Dressler, Dell Henderson

PAUL SLEUTH AND THE MYSTIC SEVEN
(SEE: SECRET SEVEN, THE, 1915, Brit.)

PAUL STREET BOYS (1929)
(5 r.) d, Bela Balogh; lp, Laszlo Gyarfas, Geza Berczy, Erno Verebes, I. Mattyasovsky

PAUPER MILLIONAIRE, THE (1922, Brit.)
(5 r.) d, Frank H. Crane; lp, C.M. Hallard, Katherine Blair, John H. Roberts, Norma Whalley

PAWN OF FATE, THE (1916)
(5 r.) d, Maurice Tourneur; lp, George Beban, Doris Kenyon, Charles W. Charles, John Davidson

PAWN OF FORTUNE, THE (1914)
(5 r.) d, Leopold Wharton

PAWNED (1922)
(5 r.) d, Irvin V. Willat; lp, Tom Moore, Edith Roberts, Charles Gerard, Josef Swickard

PAWNS OF MARS (1915)
(? r.) d, Theodore Marston; lp, Dorothy Kelly, James Morrison, Charles Kent, George Cooper

PAWNS OF PASSION (1929, Fr./USSR)
(7 r.) d, Carmine Gallone; lp, Olga Chekova, Sidney Suberly, Hans Stever, Lola Josane

PAX DOMINE (1923, Fr.)
(? r.) d, Rene Leprince

PAY AS YOU ENTER (1928)
(5 r.) d, Lloyd Bacon; lp, Louise Fazenda, Clyde Cook, William Demarest, Myrna Loy

PAY DAY (1918)
(5 r.) d, Mr.& Mrs. Sidney Drew; lp, Mr.& Mrs. Sidney Drew, Florence Short, Linda Farley, Emily Lorraine

PAY DIRT (1916)
(5 r.) d, Reaves Eason, Henry King; Henry King, Marguerite Nichols, Gordon Sackville, Mollie McConnell

PAY ME (1917)
(5 r.) d, Joseph De Grasse; lp, Dorothy Phillips, Lon Chaney, William Stowell, Ed Brown

PAY OFF, THE (1926)
(5 r.) d, Dell Henderson; lp, Dorothy Drew, Robert McKim

PAYABLE ON DEMAND (1924)
(5 r.) d, Leo Maloney; lp, Leo Maloney, Josephine Hill, Chet Ryan, Jim Corey

PAYING HIS DEBT (1918)
(5 r.) d, Cliff Smith; lp, Roy Stewart, Josie Sedgwick, Dixie Doll, William Ellingford

PAYING THE PIPER (1921)
(6 r.) d, George Fitzmaurice; lp, Dorothy Dickson, Alma Tell, George Fawcett, Rod La Rocque

PAYING THE PRICE (1916)
(5 r.) d, Frank H. Crane; lp, Gail Kane, Robert Cummings, Lydia Knott, George Relph

PAYING THE PRICE (1924)
(5 r.) lp, Owen Lynch, Jean Leslie

PAYING THE PRICE (1927)
(6 r.) d, David Selman; lp, Marjorie Bonner, Priscilla Bonner, John Miljan, George Hackathorne

PAYMENT, THE (1916)
(5 r.) d, Raymond West; lp, Bessie Barriscale, Charles Miller, Katherine Kirkwood, William Desmond

PAYMENT GUARANTEED (1921)
(5 r.) d, George L. Cox; lp, Margarita Fisher, Cecil Van Auker, Hayward Mack, Harry Lonsdale

"PEACE AT ANY PRICE" MAN, THE (1915, Ital.)
(4 r.)

PEACE OF ROARING RIVER, THE (1919)
(5 r.) d, Hobart Henley, Victor Schertzinger; lp, Pauline Frederick, Thomas Holding, Corinne Barker, Lydia Yeamans Titus

PEACEFUL VALLEY (1920)
(7 r.) d, Jerome Storm; lp, Charles Ray, Lydia Knott, Harry Myers, Lincoln Stedman

PEACEMAKER, THE (1922, Brit.)
(4 r.) d, A.E. Coleby; lp, Bob Vallis, Sam Austin, Maud Yates, Minna Leslie

PEACOCK FEATHERS (1925)
(7 r.) d, Svend Gade; lp, Jacqueline Logan, Cullen Landis, Ward Crane, George Fawcett

PEAKS OF DESTINY (1927, Ger.)
(6 r.) d, Arnold Frank; lp, Leni Riefenstahl, Louis Trenker, Ernest Peterson, Frida Richard

PEARL OF ANTILLES, THE (1915)
(5 r.) d, Tom Terriss; lp, Tom Terriss, Lionel Pape

PEARL OF LOVE, THE (1925)
(6 r.) d, Leon E. Dadmun; lp, Betty Balfour, Gladys Leslie, Burr McIntosh, Russell Griffin

PEARL OF PARADISE, THE (1916)
(5 r.) d, Harry Pollard; lp, Margarita Fischer, Harry Pollard, Joseph Harris, Beatrice Van

PEARLS OF DEATH (1914, Brit.)
(4 r.) d, Joe Evans; lp, Joe Evans, Geraldine Maxwell

PEAU DE PECHE (1929, Fr.)
(? r.) d, Marie Epstein, Jean Benoit-Levy; lp, Denise Lorys, "Petit" Jimmy, Simone Mareuil, Maurice Touze

PECHEUR D'ISLANDE (1924, Fr.)
(? r.) d, Jacques de Baroncelli; lp, Charles Vanel, Sandra Milowanoff

PECK O' PICKLES (1916)
(5 r.) d, T.N. Heffron; lp, C. William Kolb, May Cloy, Max M. Dill, Frank Thompson

PEDDLER, THE (1917)
(5 r.) d, Herbert Blache; lp, Joe Welch, Sidney Mason, Catherine Calvert, Kittens Reichert

PEDDLER OF LIES, THE (1920)
(5 r.) d, William C. Dowlan; lp, Frank Mayo, Ora Carew, Ora Devereaux, Harold A. Miller

PEER GYNT (1915)
(? r.) lp, Charles Ruggles, Cyril Maude, Myrtle Stedman

PEG O' MY HEART (1919)
(5 r.) d, William C. De Mille; lp, Wanda Hawley, Thomas Meighan, Theodore Roberts, James Neill

PEG O' MY HEART (1922)
(8 r.) d, King Vidor; lp, Laurette Taylor, Mahlon Hamilton, Russell Simpson, Ethel Grey

PEG O' THE SEA (1917)
(5 r.) d, Eugene Nowland; lp, Jean Sothern

PEGEEN (1920)
(5 r.) d, David Smith; lp, Bessie Love, Edward Burns, Ruth Fuller Golden, Charles Spere

PEGGY DOES HER DARNDEST (1919)
(5 r.) d, George D. Baker; lp, May Allison, Robert Ellis, Rosemary Theby, Frank Currier

PEGGY LEADS THE WAY (1917)
(5 r.) d, Lloyd Ingraham; lp, Mary Miles Minter, Alan Forrest, Andrew Arbuckle, Carl Stockdale

PEGGY OF THE SECRET SERVICE (1925)
(5 r.) d, J.P. McGowan; lp, Peggy O'Day, Eddie Phillips, William H. Ryno, Clarence L. Sherwood

PEGGY PUTS IT OVER (1921)
(5 r.) d, G.V. Seyffertitz; lp, Alice Calhoun, Edward Langford, Leslie Stowe, Charles Mackay

PEGGY REBELS
(SEE: MATE OF THE SALLY ANN, THE, 1917)

PEGGY, THE WILL O' THE WISP (1917)
(5 r.) d, Tod Browning; lp, Mabel Taliaferro, T.J. Kerrigan, W.J. Gross, Sam Ryan

PEN VULTURE, THE
(SEE: PEN VULTURES, 1918)

PEN VULTURES (1918)
(5 r.) lp, Shorty Hamilton

PENAL SERVITUDE
(SEE: KATORGA, 1928, USSR)

PENNY OF TOP HILL TRAIL (1921)
(5 r.) d, Arthur Berthelet; lp, Sam Lauder, Bessie Love, Wheeler Oakman, Raymond Cannon

PENNY PHILANTHROPIST, THE (1917)
(7 r.) d, Guy W. McConnell; lp, Ralph Morgan, Peggy O'Neill, Frank Weed, Margaret Wiggin

PEOPLE ON SUNDAY (1929, Ger.)
(7 r.) d, Robert Siodmak, Fred Zinnemann, Edgar G. Ulmer; lp, Brigitte Borchert, Christl Ehlers

PEOPLE VS. JOHN DOE, THE (1916)
(6 r.) d, Lois Weber; lp, Leah Baird, Harry De More, Evelyn Selbie, Willis Marks

PEOPLE VS. NANCY PRESTON, THE (1925)
(7 r.) d, Tom Forman; lp, Marguerite De La Motte, John Bowers, Frankie Darro, David Butler

PEPPY POLLY (1919)
(5 r.) d, Elmer Clifton; lp, Dorothy Gish, Richard Barthelmess, Edward Peil, Emily Chichester

PERCH OF THE DEVIL (1927)
(7 r.) d, King Baggot; lp, Mae Busch, Pat O'Malley, Jane Winton, Theodore von Eltz

PERCY (1925)
(6 r.) d, Roy William Neill; lp, Charles Ray, Louise Dresser, Joseph Kilgour, Clyde McAtee

PERFECT ALIBI, THE (1924)
(5 r.) lp, Leo Maloney, Bullet (a dog), Leonard Clapham, Jim Corey

PERFECT CLOWN, THE (1925)
(6 r.) d, Fred Newmeyer; lp, Larry Semon, Kate Price, Dorothy Dwan, Joan Meredith

PERFECT DREAMER, THE (1922)
(? r.)

PERFECT FLAPPER, THE (1924)
(7 r.) d, John Francis Dillon; lp, Colleen Moore, Sydney Chaplin, Phyllis Haver, Lydia Knott

PERFECT GENTLEMAN, A (1928)
(6 r.) d, Clyde Bruckman; lp, Monty Banks, Ernest Wood, Henry Barrows, Ruth Dwyer

PERFECT SAP, THE (1927)
(6 r.) d, Howard Higgin; lp, Ben Lyon, Virginia Lee Corbin, Lloyd Whitlock, Diana Kane

PERFECT 36, A (1918)
(5 r.) d, Charles Giblyn; lp, Mabel Normand, Rod La Rocque, Flora Zabelle, Leila Romer

PERFECT WOMAN, THE (1920)
(5 r.) d, David Kirkland; lp, Constance Talmadge, Charles Meredith, Elizabeth Garrison, Joseph Burke

PERIL OF THE RAIL (1926)
(5 r.) d, J.P. McGowan; lp, Helen Holmes, Edward Hearn, Wilfred North, Lloyd Whitlock

PERILOUS VALLEY (1920)
(5 r.) d, Harry Grossman; lp, Frank Goldsmith, Francois Descamps, Claire Du Brey, Bigelow Cooper

PERILS OF DIVORCE (1916)
(5 r.) d, Edwin August; lp, Edna Wallace Hopper, Frank Sheridan, Alec B. Francis, Macey Harlam

PERILS OF PARIS
(SEE: TERREUR, 1924)

PERILS OF PORK PIE, THE (1916, Brit.)
(4 r.) d, W.P. Kellino; lp, Billy Merson, Charles Cohen

PERILS OF TEMPTATION, THE (1915)
(4 r.) lp, Jackie Saunders

PERILS OF THE WEST (1922)
(5 r.) lp, William Hackett

PERIWINKLE (1917)
(5 r.) d, James Kirkwood; lp, Mary Miles Minter, George Fisher, Arthur Howard, Clarence Burton

PERJURY (1921)
(9 r.) d, Harry Millarde; lp, William Farnum, Sally Crute, Wallace Erskine, Alice Mann

PERNICKETY POLLY ANN
(SEE: POLLY ANN, 1917)

PERPETUA
(SEE: LOVE'S BOOMERANG, 1922, Brit.)

PERSISTENT LOVERS, THE (1922, Brit.)
(6 r.) d, Guy Newall; lp, Guy Newall, Ivy Duke, A. Bromley Davenport, Julian Royce

PEST IN FLORENZ (1919, Ger.)
(? r.) d, Otto Rippert; lp, Otto Mannstaedt, Anders Wikman, Karl Bernhard, Franz Knaak

PETER IBBETSON
(SEE: FOREVER, 1921)

PETER THE GREAT (1923, Ger.)
(6 r.) d, Dimitri Buchowetzki; lp, Dagny Servaes, Bernard Goetzke, Emil Jannings, Walter Janssen

PETIT ANGE (1920, Fr.)
(? r.) d, Liutz-Morat

PETIT ANGE ET SON PANTIN (1923, Fr.)
(? r.) d, Luitz-Morat

PETIT HOTEL A LOUER (1923, Fr.)
(? r.) d, Pierre Colombier

PETITE FILLE (1928, Fr.)
(? r.) d, Pierre Colombier

PETTICOAT LOOSE (1922, Brit.)
(5 r.) d, George Ridgwell; lp, Dorinea Shirley, Warwick Ward, Lionelle Howard, Jack Trevor

PETTICOAT PILOT, A (1918)
(5 r.) d, Rollin S. Sturgeon; lp, Vivian Martin, Theodore Roberts, James Neill, Harrison Ford

PETTICOATS AND POLITICS (1918)
(5 r.) d, Howard M. Mitchell; lp, Anita King, R. Henry Grey, Gordon Sackville, Charles Dudley

PETTIGREW'S GIRL (1919)
(5 r.) d, George Melford; lp, Ethel Clayton, Monte Blue, James Mason, Charles Gerrard

PHANTOM, THE (1916)
(5 r.) d, Charles Giblyn; lp, Frank Keenan, Enid Markey, Robert McKim, P.D. Tabler

PHANTOM, THE (1922, Ger.)
(? r.) d, F.W. Murnau; lp, Alfred Abel, Lil Dagover, Aud Egede Nissen, Lya de Putti

PHANTOM BUCCANEER, THE (1916)
(5 r.) d, J. Charles Haydon; lp, Richard C. Travers, Gertrude Glover, Thurlow Brewer, R.P. Thompson

PHANTOM BULLET, THE (1926)
(6 r.) d, Clifford S. Smith; lp, Hoot Gibson, Eileen Percy, Allan Forrest, Pat Harmon

PHANTOM BUSTER, THE (1927)
(5 r.) d, William Bertram; lp, Buddy Roosevelt, Alma Rayford, Charles Whitaker, Boris Karloff

PHANTOM CARRIAGE, THE (1921, Swed.)
(6 r.) d, Victor Sjostrom; lp, Victor Sjostrom, Hilda Borgstrom, Tore Svennberg, Astrid Holm

PHANTOM CHARIOT, THE
(SEE: PHANTOM CARRIAGE, THE, 1920, Swed.)

PHANTOM CITY, THE (1928)
(6 r.) d, Albert Rogell; lp, Ken Maynard, Eugenia Gilbert, James Mason, Charles Mailes

PHANTOM EXPRESS, THE (1925)
(5 r.) d, John Adolfi; lp, Ethel Shannon, George Periolat, David Butler, Frankie Darro

PHANTOM FLYER, THE (1928)
(5 r.) d, Bruce Mitchell; lp, Al Wilson, Lillian Gilmore, Buck Connors, Billy "Red" Jones

PHANTOM FORTUNES, THE (1916)
(5 r.) d, Paul Scardon; lp, Barney Bernard, James Morrison, Lester Bernard, Edward Elkas

PHANTOM HONEYMOON, THE (1919)
(6 r.) d, J. Searle Dawley; lp, Marguerite Marsh, Vernon Steele, Hal Clarendon, Leon Danmun

PHANTOM HORSEMAN, THE (1924)
(5 r.) d, Robert North Bradbury; lp, Jack Hoxie, Lillian Rich, Neil McKinnon, Wade Boteler

PHANTOM HUSBAND, A (1917)
(5 r.) d, Ferris Hartman; lp, Ruth Stonehouse, J.P. Wild, Charles Gunn, Estelle Lasheur

PHANTOM JUSTICE (1924)
(7 r.) d, Richard Thomas; lp, Rod La Rocque, Garry O'Dell, Kathryn McGuire, Frederick Vroom

PHANTOM MELODY, THE (1920)
(6 r.) d, Douglas Gerrard; lp, Monroe Salisbury, Henry Barrows, Ray Gallagher, Charles West

PHANTOM OF THE FOREST, THE (1926)
(6 r.) d, Henry McCarthy; lp, Betty Francisco, Eddie Phillips, James Mason, Frank Foster Davis

PHANTOM OF THE MOULIN ROUGE, THE
(SEE: LE FANTOME DU MOULIN ROUGE, 1925, Fr.)

PHANTOM OF THE TURF (1928)
(6 r.) d, Duke Worne; lp, Helene Costello, Rex Lease, Forrest Stanley, Danny Hoy

PHANTOM RANGER, THE
(SEE: PHANTOM FLYER, THE, 1928)

PHANTOM RIDERS, THE (1918)
(5 r.) d, Jack [John] Ford; lp, Harry Carey, Molly Malone, Buck Connors, Bull Gettinger

PHANTOM SHADOWS (1925)
(5 r.) d, Al Ferguson; lp, Al Ferguson, Lucille Du Bois

PHANTOM SHOTGUN, THE (1917)
(4 r.) d, Harry Harvey; lp, Kathleen Kirkham, R. Henry Grey, Barney Furey, Frank Brownlee

PHANTOM'S SECRET, THE (1917)
(5 r.) d, Charles Swickard; lp, Mignon Anderson, Mark Fenton, Hayward Mack, Dan Leighton

PHIL-FOR-SHORT (1919)
(6 r.) d, Oscar Apfel; lp, Evelyn Greeley, Hugh Thompson, Charles Walcott, James A. Furey

PHILIP HOLDEN - WASTER (1916)
(5 r.) d, George Sargent; lp, Richard Bennett, George Periolat, Adrienne Morrison, Rhea Mitchell

PHROSO (1922, Fr.)
(? r.) d, Louis Mercanton

PICCADILLY JIM (1920)
(5 r.) d, Wesley Ruggles; lp, Owen Moore, Zena Keefe, George Bunny, William T. Hayes

PICTURE OF DORIAN GRAY, THE (1915, USSR)
(8 r.) d, Vsevolod Meyerhold; lp, Varvara Yanova, V. Meyerhold, G. Enriton, P. Belova

PICTURE OF DORIAN GRAY, THE (1917, Ger.)
(? r.) d, Richard Oswald

PIDGIN ISLAND (1916)
(5 r.) d, Fred J. Balshofer; lp, Harold Lockwood, May Allison, Doc Pomeroy Cannon, Lester Cuneo

PIED PIPER MALONE (1924)
(8 r.) d, Alfred E. Green; lp, Thomas Meighan, Lois Wilson, Emma Dunn, Charles Stevenson

PIED PIPER OF HAMELIN, THE (1917, Ger.)
(? r.) d, Paul Wegener; lp, Paul Wegener, Lyda Salmonova, Wilhelm Diegelmann, Jakob Tiedtke

PIERRE ET JEAN (1924, Fr.)
(? r.) d, Donatien

PIERROT PIERRETTE (1924, Fr.)
(? r.) d, Louis Feuillade

PIKOVAJA DAMA
(SEE: QUEEN OF SPADES, 1917, USSR)

PILGRIMS OF THE NIGHT (1921)
(6 r.) d, Edward Sloman; lp, Lewis S. Stone, Rubye De Remer, William V. Mong, Kathleen Kirkham

PILLARS OF SOCIETY (1916)
(5 r.) d, Raoul Walsh; lp, Henry B. Walthall, Mary Alden, Juanita Archer, George Beranger

PILLARS OF SOCIETY (1920, Brit.)
(5 r.) d, Rex Wilson; lp, Ellen Terry, Norman McKinnel, Mary Rorke, Irene Rorke

PILLORY, THE (1916)
(5 r.) d, Frederick Sullivan; lp, Florence LaBadie, Marie Shotwell, Ethyle Cooke, George Marlo

PIMPLE'S THREE WEEKS (1915, Brit.)
(4 r.) d, Charles Weston; lp, Fred Evans

PINCH HITTER, THE (1925)
(7 r.) d, Joseph Henabery; lp, Glen Hunter, Constance Bennett, Jack Drumier, Reginald Sheffield

PINK GODS (1922)
(8 r.) d, Penrhyn Stanlaws; lp, Bebe Daniels, James Kirkwood, Anna Q. Nilsson, Raymond Hatton

PINTO (1920)
(5 r.) d, Victor L. Schertzinger; lp, Mabel Normand, Cullen Landis, Edward Jobson, George Nichols

PINTO KID, THE (1928)
(5 r.) d, Louis King; lp, Buzz Barton, Frank Rice, James Welsh, Gloria Lee

PIONEER TRAILS (1923)
(7 r.) d, David Smith; lp, Cullen Landis, Alice Calhoun, Bertram Grassby, Otis Harlan

PIONEER'S GOLD (1924)
(5 r.) lp, Pete Morrison

PIONEERS OF THE WEST (1927)
(5 r.) lp, Dick Carter, Dorothy Earle

PIONEERS OF THE WEST (1929)
(5 r.) d, J.P. McGowan; lp, Tom Tyler, J.P. McGowan, George Brownhill, Mack V. Wright

PIPER'S PRICE, THE (1917)
(5 r.) d, Joseph De Grasse; lp, Dorothy Phillips, Maude George, William Stowell, Lon Chaney

PIRATE HAUNTS (1917)
(5 r.)

PIT, THE (1915)
(5 r.) d, Maurice Tourneur; lp, Wilton Lackaye, Gail Kane, Milton Sills, Alec B. Francis

PIT-BOY'S ROMANCE, A (1917, Brit.)
(4 r.) d, A.E. Coleby, Arthur Rooke; lp, Jimmy Wilde, Tommy Noble, A.E. Coleby, Arthur Rooke

PITFALL, THE (1915)
(4 r.) d, James W. Horne; lp, Marin Sais, Frank Jonasson, Thomas Lingham, Edward Clisbee

PITFALLS OF A BIG CITY (1919)
(6 r.) d, Frank Lloyd; lp, Gladys Brockwell, William Scott, William Sheer, Neva Gerber

PITFALLS OF PASSION (1927)
(5 r.) d, Leonard Livingstone; lp, Prudence Sutton, Larry O'Dell

PLACE BEYOND THE WINDS, THE (1916)
(5 r.) d, Joseph De Grasse; lp, Dorothy Phillips, Lon Chaney, Jack Mulhall, Joseph De Grasse

PLACE OF THE HONEYMOONS, THE (1920)
(5 r.) d, Kenean Buel; lp, Montagu Love, Emily Stevens, Frankie Mann, Joseph Selman

PLAIN JANE (1916)
(5 r.) d, Charles Miller; lp, Bessie Barriscale, Charles Ray, Mabel Johnson, W. Burgermaster

PLANTER, THE (1917)
(10 r.) d, Thomas Heffron; lp, [Frederick] Tyrone Power, Helen Bateman, Mabel Wiles, Carmen Phillips

PLASTERED IN PARIS (1928)
(6 r.) d, Benjamin Stoloff; lp, Sammy Cohen, Jack Pennick, Lola Salvi, Ivan Linow

PLAY SQUARE (1921)
(5 r.) d, William K. Howard; lp, Johnnie Walker, Edna Murphy, Hayward Mack, Laura La Plante

PLAYING DEAD (1915)
(5 r.) d, Sidney Drew; lp, Mr.& Mrs. Sidney Drew, Donald Hall, Isidor Marcil, Harry English

PLAYING WITH FIRE (1916)
(5 r.) d, Francis J. Grandon; lp, Olga Petrova, Evelyn Brent, Arthur Hoops, Pierre Le May

PLAYING WITH FIRE (1921)
(5 r.) d, Dallas M. Fitzgerald; lp, Gladys Walton, Kathryn McGuire, Eddie Gribbon, Hayward Mack

PLAYING WITH SOULS (1925)
(7 r.) d, Ralph Ince; lp, Jacqueline Logan, Mary Astor, Belle Bennett, Clive Brook

PLAYTHING OF BROADWAY, THE (1921)
(5 r.) d, Jack Dillon; lp, Justine Johnstone, Crauford Kent, Macey Harlam, Edwards Davis

PLAYTHINGS (1918)
(5 r.) d, Douglas Gearrad; lp, Fritzi Brunette, Lewis Cody, Myrtle Reeves, Charles Gerrard

PLEASE GET MARRIED (1919)
(7 r.) d, John Ince; lp, Viola Dana, Antrim Short, Margaret Campbell, Harry Todd

PLEASE HELP EMILY (1917)
(5 r.) d, Dell Henderson; lp, Ann Murdock, Rex McDougall, Hubert Druce, Hal Brown

PLEASURE BEFORE BUSINESS (1927)
(6 r.) d, Frank Strayer; lp, Pat O'Malley, Virginia Brown Faire, Max Davidson, Rosa Rosanova

PLEASURE BUYERS, THE (1925)
(7 r.) d, Chet Withey; lp, Irene Rich, Clive Brook, Gayne Whitman, June Marlowe

PLEASURE SEEKERS (1920)
(6 r.) d, George Archainbaud; lp, Elaine Hammerstein, Webster Campbell, Frank Currier, James A. Furey

PLEBIAN (1915, USSR)
(4 r.) d, Yakov Protazanov; lp, Olga Preobrazhenskaya, Nikolai Radin

PLOUGHSHARE, THE (1915)
(4 r.) d, John H. Collins; lp, Robert Conness, Gertrude McCoy, William West, Richard Peer

PLOW WOMAN, THE (1917)
(5 r.) d, Charles Swickard; lp, Mary MacLaren, Harry De More, L.C. Shumway, Clara Horton

PLUNDERER, THE (1924)
(6 r.) d, George Archainbaud; lp, Frank Mayo, Evelyn Brent, Tom Santschi, James Mason

PLUNGER, THE (1920)
(5 r.) d, Del Henderson; lp, George Walsh, Virginia Valli, Byron Douglas, Richard R. Neill

POIL DE CAROTTE (1926, Fr.)
(? r.) d, Julien Duvivier; lp, Andre Heuze, Fabian Haziza, Charlotte Barbier-Krauss, Henry Krauss

POINT OF VIEW, THE (1920)
(6 r.) d, Alan Crosland; lp, Elaine Hammerstein, Rockliffe Fellowes, Warren Cook, Cornish Beck

POINTING FINGER, THE (1919)
(5 r.) d, Edward Kull, Edward Morrisey; lp, Mary MacLaren, Johnnie Cook, Carl Stockdale, Lydia Knott

POISON PEN, THE (1919)
(5 r.) d, Edwin August; lp, June Elvidge, Earl Metcalfe, Joseph Smiley, Marion Barney

POISONED PARADISE: THE FORBIDDEN STORY OF MONTE CARLO (1924)
(7 r.) d, Louis Gasnier; lp, Kenneth Harlan, Clara Bow

POKER FACES (1926)
(8 r.) d, Harry A. Pollard; lp, Edward Everett Horton, Laura La Plante, George Siegmann, Tom Ricketts

POLIKUSHKA (1919, USSR)
(6 r.) d, Alexander Sanin; lp, Ivan Moskvin, Vera Pashennaya, Yevgeniya Rayevskaya, V. Bulgakov

POLITIC FLAPPER, THE
(SEE: PATSY, THE, 1928)

POLITICIANS, THE (1915)
(5 r.) lp, George Bickel, Harry Watson, Ruby Hoffman, Martin Regan

POLLY ANN (1917)
(5 r.) d, Charles F. Miller; lp, Bessie Love, Rowland Lee, Walt Whitman, John Lockney

POLLY OF THE FOLLIES (1922)
(7 r.) d, John Emerson; lp, Constance Talmadge, Horace Knight, Thomas Carr, Harry Fisher

POLLY OF THE MOVIES (1927)
(7 r.) d, Scott Pembroke; lp, Jason Robards, Gertrude Short, Mary Foy, Corliss Palmer

POLLY PUT THE KETTLE ON (1917)
(5 r.) d, Douglas Gerrard; lp, Douglas Gerrard, Ruth Clifford, Thomas Jefferson, Martha Mattox

POLLY REDHEAD (1917)
(5 r.) d, Jack Conway; lp, Ella Hall, Gertrude Astor, Gretchen Lederer, Helen Wright

POLLY WITH A PAST (1920)
(6 r.) d, Leander De Cordova; lp, Ina Claire, Ralph Graves, Marie Wainwright, Harry Benham

PONJOLA (1923)
(7 r.) d, Donald Crisp; lp, Anna Q. Nilsson, James Kirkwood, Tully Marshall, Joseph Kilgour

POOL OF FLAME, THE (1916)
(5 r.) d, Otis Turner; lp, J. Warren Kerrigan, Lois Wilson, Maude George, Harry Carter

POOR BOOB (1919)
(5 r.) d, Donald Crisp; lp, Bryant Washburn, Wanda Hawley, Dick Rosson, Theodore Roberts

POOR, DEAR MARGARET KIRBY (1921)
(5 r.) d, William P.S. Earle; lp, Elaine Hammerstein, William B. Donaldson, Ellen Cassidy, Helen Lindroth

POOR GIRLS (1927)
(6 r.) d, William James Craft; lp, Dorothy Revier, Edmund Burns, Ruth Stonehouse, Lloyd Whitlock

POOR GIRL'S ROMANCE, A (1926)
(6 r.) d, F. Harmon Weight; lp, Creighton Hale, Gertrude Short, Rosa Rudami, Clarissa Selwyn

POOR LITTLE PEPPINA (1916)
(6 r.) d, Sidney Olcott; lp, Mary Pickford, Eugene O'Brien, Jack Pickford, W.T. Carleton

POOR MILLIONAIRE, THE (1930)
(5 r.) d, George Melford; lp, Richard Talmadge, Constance Howard, George Irving, Frederick Vroom

POOR NUT, THE (1927)
(7 r.) d, Richard Wallace; lp, Jack Mulhall, Charlie Murray, Jean Arthur, Jane Winton

POOR RELATION, A (1921)
(5 r.) d, Clarence Badger; lp, Will Rogers, Sylvia Breamer, Wallace MacDonald, Sydney Ainsworth

POOR RICH MAN, THE (1918)
(5 r.) d, Charles J. Brabin; lp, Francis X. Bushman, Beverly Bayne, Stuart Holmes, Sally Crute

POOR SCHMALTZ (1915)
(4 r.) d, Hugh Ford; lp, Sam Bernard, Dick Bernard, Robert Broderick, Conway Tearle

POOR SIMP, THE (1920)
(5 r.) d, Victor Heerman; lp, Owen Moore, Nell Craig, Vera Lewis, Harry Rattenberry

POPPY (1917)
(8 r.) d, Edward Jose; lp, Norma Talmadge, Eugene O'Brien, Fred Perry, Jack Meredith

POPPY TRAIL, THE (1920)
(5 r.) d, Carl Harbaugh; lp, Herbert Rawlinson

POPULAR SIN, THE (1926)
(7 r.) d, Malcolm St. Clair; lp, Florence Vidor, Clive Brook, Greta Nissen, Philip Strange

PORCELAIN LAMP, THE (1921)
(5 r.) d, Ben Blake; lp, Eugene Borden, Doris Sheerin, Harry Bannister, Herbert Fields

PORI (1930, Ger.)
(4 r.) d, Baron A. Von Dungern; lp, A.P. Von Gontard, Herbert Kluge

PORT OF DOOM, THE (1913)
(4 r.) d, J. Searle Dawley; lp, Laura Sawyer, Peter Lang, Dave Wall, House Peters

PORT OF LOST SOULS (1924, Brit.)
(6 r.) d, Sinclair Hill; lp, Matheson Lang, Joan Lockton, Gordon Hopkirk, Arthur McLaglen

PORT OF MISSING GIRLS, THE (1928)
(8 r.) d, Irving Cummings; lp, Barbara Bedford, Malcolm McGregor, Natalie Kingston, Hedda Hopper

PORT OF MISSING WOMEN, THE (1915, Brit.)
(4 r.) d, Charles Weston; lp, Alice Inward, James Lindsay, Lily Saxby, Gordon Begg

POSSESSION (1922, Brit.)
(7 r.) d, Louis Mercanton; lp, Reginald Owen, Paul Capellani, Max Maxudian, Harrison Brown

POT LUCK PARDS (1924)
(5 r.) lp, Pete Morrison

POT-LUCK PARDS
(SEE: POT LUCK PARDS, 1924)

POTASH AND PERLMUTTER (1923)
(8 r.) d, Clarence Badger; lp, Alexander Carr, Barney Bernard, Vera Gordon, Martha Mansfield

POTS AND PANS PEGGIE (1917)
(5 r.) d, W. Eugene Moore; lp, Gladys Hulette, Wayne Arey, George Marlo, Kathryn Adams

POTTERY GIRL'S ROMANCE, A (1918, Brit.)
(4 r.) d, G. Fletcher Hewitt; lp, Madeleine Tighe

POUR EPOUSER GABY (1917, Fr.)
(? r.) d, Charles Burguet

POUR UNE NUIT (1921, Fr.)
(? r.) d, Jacob Protozanoff

POWDER (1916)
(5 r.) d, Arthur Maude; lp, Constance Crawley, Arthur Maude, Jack Prescott, Jack Farrell

POWER (1928)
(7 r.) d, Howard Higgin; lp, William Boyd, Alan Hale, Jacqueline Logan, Jerry Drew

POWER AND THE GLORY, THE (1918)
(5 r.) d, Lawrence C. Windom; lp, June Elvidge, Frank Mayo, Ricca Allen, Madge Evans

POWER DIVINE, THE (1923)
(5 r.) d, H.G. Moody, William J. Craft; lp, Mary Wynn, Jack Livingston, Caroline Brunson, Ralph Parker

POWER OF A LIE, THE (1922)
(5 r.) d, George Archainbaud; lp, Mabel Julienne Scott, David Torrence, Maude George, Ruby Lafayette

POWER OF DARKNESS, THE (1918, USSR)
(4 r.) d, Cheslav Sabinsky; lp, Pytor Baksheyev, Vera Orlova, Nikolai Panov

POWER OF EVIL, THE (1916)
(6 r.) d, H.M. Horkheimer, H.D. Horkheimer; lp, Margaret Nichols, Lillian West, Henry King, Victory Bateman

POWER OF EVIL (1929, USSR/Armenian)
(6 r.) d, M. Goldvani, P. Barkhoudian; lp, Barbara Matatian

POWER OF LOVE, THE (1922)
(5 r.) d, Nat Deverich; lp, Elliott Sparling, Barbara Bedford, Noah Beery, Aileen Manning

POWER OF SILENCE, THE (1928)
(6 r.) d, Wallace Worsley; lp, Belle Bennett, John Westwood, Marian Douglas, Anders Randolf

POWER OF THE PRESS, THE (1914)
(4 r.) lp, Lionel Barrymore, Alan Hale, Sidney D'Albrook

POWER WITHIN, THE (1921)
(6 r.) d, Lem F. Kennedy; lp, William H. Tooker, Nellie P. Spaulding, Robert Kenyon, Dorothy Allen

POWERS THAT PREY (1918)
(5 r.) d, Henry King; lp, Mary Miles Minter, Alan Forrest, Harvey Clark, Clarence Burton

PRAIRIE KING, THE (1927)
(6 r.) d, Reeves Eason; lp, Hoot Gibson, Barbara Worth, Albert Prisco, Charles Sellon

PRAIRIE MYSTERY, THE (1922)
(5 r.) d, George Edward Hall; lp, Bud Osborne, Pauline Curley

PRAIRIE PIRATE, THE (1925)
(5 r.) d, Edmund Mortimer; lp, Harry Carey, Jean Dumas, Lloyd Whitlock, Trilby Clark

PRAIRIE TRAILS (1920)
(5 r.) d, George Marshall; lp, Tom Mix, Kathleen O'Connor, Gloria Hope, Charles K. French

PRECIOUS PACKET, THE (1916)
(5 r.) d, Donald MacKenzie; lp, Ralph Kellard, Lois Meredith, W. Tabor Wetmore

PREJUDICE (1922)
(9 r.) d, Joseph Belmont; lp, Zena Keefe

PRES DE CRIME (1921, Fr.)
(? r.) d, Charles Maudru, Charles de Marsan

PRESIDENT, THE (1918, Den.)
(? r.) d, Carl-Theodor Dreyer; lp, Halvard Hoff, Elith Pio, Carl Meyer, Olga Raphael-Linden

PRETENDER, THE (1918)
(5 r.) d, Cliff Smith; lp, William Desmond, Ethel Fleming, Gene Burr, Joseph Franz

PRETENDERS, THE (1915)
(4 r.) d, Robert Vignola; lp, Crauford Kent, Marguerite Courtot, Henry Hallam, Joseph Birns

PRETTY SMOOTH (1919)
(6 r.) d, Rollin S. Sturgeon; lp, Priscilla Dean, Francis McDonald, Gertrude Astor, George McDaniels

PREY, THE (1920)
(6 r.) d, George L. Sargent; lp, Alice Joyce, Henry Hallam, Jack McLean, Harry Benham

PREY OF THE DRAGON, THE (1921, Brit.)
(5 r.) d, F. Martin Thornton; lp, Victor McLaglen, Gladys Jennings, Harvey Braban, Hal Martin

PRICE, THE (1915)
(5 r.) d, Joseph A. Golden;

PRICE OF A GOOD TIME, THE (1918)
(7 r.) d, Lois Weber, Phillips Smalley; lp, Mildred Harris, Kenneth Harlan, Anne Schaefer, Helen Rosson

PRICE OF APPLAUSE, THE (1918)
(5 r.) d, Thomas N. Heffron; lp, Jack Livingston, Claire Anderson, Joe King, Walt Whitman

PRICE OF DIVORCE, THE (1928, Brit.)
(8 r.) d, Sinclair Hill; lp, Miriam Seegar, Wyndham Standing, Frances Day, Rex Maurice

PRICE OF FAME, THE (1916)
(5 r.) d, Charles J. Brabin; lp, Marc MacDermott, Naomi Childers, L. Rogers Lytton, Logan Paul

PRICE OF FEAR, THE (1928)
(5 r.) d, Leigh Jason; lp, Bill Cody, Duane Thompson, Tom London, Grace Cunard

PRICE OF HAPPINESS, THE (1916)
(5 r.) d, Edmund Lawrence; lp, Mary Boland, Dave Wall, Marion Singer, Enid Francis

PRICE OF HONOR, THE (1927)
(6 r.) d, E.H. Griffith; lp, Dorothy Revier, Malcolm McGregor, William V. Mong, Gustav von Seyffertitz

PRICE OF HER SILENCE, THE (1915)
(4 r.) lp, Florence LaBadie, Mignon Anderson, Arthur Bauer, Harris Gordon

PRICE OF HER SOUL, THE (1917)
(6 r.) d, Oscar Apfel; lp, Gladys Brockwell, Jack Standing, Monroe Salisbury, Brooklyn Keller

PRICE OF JUSTICE, THE (1914, Brit.)
(4 r.) d, Maurice Elvey; lp, Elizabeth Risdon, Fred Groves, Bottles Winter, A.V. Bramble

PRICE OF JUSTICE, THE (1915)
(4 r.)

PRICE OF MALICE, THE (1916)
(5 r.) d, O.A.C. Lund; lp, Hamilton Revelle, Barbara Tennant, William Davidson, Helen Dunbar

PRICE OF PLEASURE, THE (1925)
(7 r.) d, Edward Sloman; lp, Virginia Valli, Norman Kerry, Louise Fazenda, Kate Lester

PRICE OF POSSESSION, THE (1921)
(5 r.) d, Hugh Ford; lp, Ethel Clayton, Rockliffe Fellowes, Maude Turner Gordon, Reginald Denny

PRICE OF POWER, THE (1916)
(5 r.)

PRICE OF POWER, THE (1916)
(5 r.) lp, Orin Johnson, J. Farrell MacDonald, Marguerite Marsh, Spottiswoode Aitken

PRICE OF PRIDE, THE (1917)
(5 r.) d, Harvey Knoles; lp, Carlyle Blackwell, June Elvidge, Frank Mills, Evelyn Greeley

PRICE OF REDEMPTION, THE (1920)
(6 r.) d, Dallas M. Fitzgerald; lp, Bert Lytell, Seena Owen, Cleo Madison, Landers Stevens

PRICE OF SILENCE, THE (1916)
(5 r.) d, Joseph De Grasse; lp, Dorothy Phillips, Lon Chaney, Vola Smith [Vale], Frank Whitson

PRICE OF SILENCE, THE (1917)
(5 r.) d, Frank Lloyd; lp, William Farnum, Vivian Rich, Charles Clary, Frank Clark

PRICE OF SUCCESS, THE (1925)
(6 r.) d, Tony Gaudio; lp, Alice Lake, Lee Shumway, Gaston Glass, Florence Turner

PRICE OF YOUTH, THE (1922)
(5 r.) d, Ben Wilson; lp, Neva Gerber, Spottiswoode Aitken, Ashton Dearholt, Charles L. King

PRICE SHE PAID, THE (1917)
(7 r.) d, Charles Giblyn; lp, Clara Kimball Young, David Powell, Alan Hale, Louise Beaudet

PRICE SHE PAID, THE (1924)
(6 r.) d, Henry MacRae; lp, Alma Rubens, Frank Mayo, Eugenie Besserer, William Welsh

PRICE WOMAN PAYS, THE (1919)
(6 r.) d, George Terwilliger; lp, Beatriz Michelena, Lois Wilson

PRIDE (1917)
(5 r.) d, Richard Ridgley; lp, Holbrook Blinn, Shirley Mason, George Le Guere, Helen Strickland

PRIDE AND THE MAN (1917)
(5 r.) d, Edward Sloman; lp, William Russell, Francelia Billington, George Fisher, Paul Weigel

PRIDE OF NEW YORK, THE (1917)
(5 r.) d, Raoul Walsh; lp, George Walsh, Regina Quinn, James A. Marcus, William Bailey

PRIDE OF PAWNEE, THE (1929)
(6 r.) d, Robert De Lacy; lp, Tom Tyler, Ethlyne Clair, Barney Furey, Frankie Darrow

PRIMA DONNA'S HUSBAND, THE (1916)
(5 r.) d, Julius Steger, Joseph A. Golden; lp, Holbrook Blinn, Clara Whipple, Kathryn Browne Decker, Freddie Verdi

PRIMAL LAW, THE (1921)
(6 r.) d, Bernard J. Durning; lp, Dustin Farnum, Mary Thurman, Harry Dunkinson, Philo McCullough

PRIMITIVE CALL, THE (1917)
(5 r.) d, Bertram Bracken; lp, Gladys Coburn, Fritz Leiber, John Webb Dillon, George Alan Larkin

PRIMITIVE LOVE (1927)
(6 r.) d, Frank E. Kleinschmidt; lp, Ok-Ba-Ok, Sloca Bruna, Wenga

PRIMITIVE LOVER, THE (1922)
(7 r.) d, Sidney Franklin; lp, Constance Talmadge, Harrison Ford, Kenneth Harlan, Joe Roberts

PRIMITIVE WOMAN, THE (1918)
(5 r.) d, Lloyd Ingraham; lp, Margarita Fisher, Jack Mower, Millard Wilson, Emma Kluge

PRIMROSE PATH, THE (1915)
(5 r.) d, Lawrence Marston; lp, Gladys Hanson, E.H. Sothern, H. Cooper-Willis, Nina Blake

PRIMROSE PATH, THE (1925)
(6 r.) d, Harry O. Hoyt; lp, Wallace MacDonald, Clara Bow, Arline Pretty, Stuart Holmes

PRIMROSE RING, THE (1917)
(5 r.) d, Robert Leonard; lp, Mae Murray, Tom Moore, Winter Hall, Billy Jacobs

PRINCE AND BETTY, THE (1919)
(5 r.) d, Robert Thornby; lp, William Desmond, Mary Thurman, Anita Kay, George Swann

PRINCE AND THE DANCER (1929, Ger.)
(8 r.) d, Max Neufeld; lp, Dina Gralla, Albert Paulig, Werner Pittschau, Anna Kallina

PRINCE AND THE PAUPER, THE (1929, Aust./Czech.)
(6 r.) d, Alexander Kardo; lp, Tibi Lubin, Francis Everth, Francis Herter, Alfred Schreiber

PRINCE CHAP, THE (1916)
(5 r.) d, Marshall Neilan; lp, Marshall Neilan, Mary Charleson, Bessie Eyton, Camille D'Arcy

PRINCE CHAP, THE (1920)
(5 r.) d, William C. De Mille; lp, Thomas Meighan, Lila Lee, Kathlyn Williams, Theodore Kosloff

PRINCE EMBETE (1920, Fr.)
(? r.) d, Georges Monca

PRINCE OF A KING, A (1923)
(6 r.) d, Albert Austin; lp, Dinky Dean, Virginia Pearson, Eric Mayne, John Sainpolis

PRINCE OF BROADWAY, THE (1926)
(6 r.) d, John Gorman; lp, George Walsh, Alyce Mills, Freeman Wood, Robert Roper

PRINCE OF GRAUSTARK, THE (1916)
(5 r.) d, Fred E. Wright; lp, Bryant Washburn, Marguerite Clayton, Ernest Maupain, Sydney Ainsworth

PRINCE OF HEADWAITERS, THE (1927)
(7 r.) d, John Francis Dillon; lp, Lewis Stone, Priscilla Bonner, E.J. Ratcliffe, Lilyan Tashman

PRINCE OF HEARTS, THE (1929)
(6 r.) d, Cliff Wheeler; lp, Norman Kerry, Barbara Worth, John Reinhardt, George Fawcett

PRINCE OF HIS RACE, THE (1926)
(8 r.) d, Roy Calnek; lp, Harry Henderson, William A. Clayton, Jr., Lawrence Chenault, Arline Mickey

PRINCE OF LOVERS, A (1922, Brit.)
(8 r.) d, C.C. Calvert; lp, Howard Gaye, Marjorie Hume, Mary Clare, David Hawthorne

PRINCE OF PEANUTS
(SEE: HOW TO HANDLE WOMEN, 1928)

PRINCE OF PEP, THE (1925)
(5 r.) d, Jack Nelson; lp, Richard Talmadge, Nola Luxford, Carol Wines, Marcella Daly

PRINCE OF TEMPTERS, THE (1926)
(8 r.) d, Lothar Mendes; lp, Lois Moran, Ben Lyon, Lya De Putti, Ian Keith

PRINCE OF THE PLAINS (1927)
(5 r.) d, Robin Williamson; lp, Tex Maynard, Betty Caldwell, Walter Shumway

PRINCE OF THE SADDLE (1926)
(5 r.) lp, Fred Church, Boris Bullock

PRINCE ZILAH (1926, Fr.)
(? r.) d, Gaston Roudes

PRINCESS JONES (1921)
(5 r.) d, G.V. Seyffertitz; lp, Alice Calhoun, Vincent Coleman, Helen du Bois, Robert Lee Keeling

PRINCESS' NECKLACE, THE (1917)
(4 r.) d, Floyd France; lp, William Calhoun, Kathleen Townsend, Wallace MacDonald, Susan Mitchell

PRINCESS OF BAGDAD (1913)
(6 r.) d, Charles L. Gaskill; lp, Helen Gardner

PRINCESS OF BROADWAY, THE (1927)
(6 r.) d, Dallas M. Fitzgerald; lp, Pauline Garon, Dorothy Dwan, Johnny Walker, Harold Miller

PRINCESS OF NEW YORK, THE (1921 US/Brit.)
(5 r.) d, Donald Crisp; lp, David Powell, Mary Glynne, Saba Raleigh, George Bellamy

PRINCESS OF PARK ROW, THE (1917)
(5 r.) d, Ashley Miller; lp, Lillian Walker, Mildred Manning, Wallace MacDonald, William Dunn

PRINCESS OF PATCHES, THE (1917)
(5 r.) d, Al Green; lp, Vivian Reed, Burke Wilbur, Hildor Hoberg, Roy Southerland

PRINCESS OF THE DARK, A (1917)
(5 r.) d, Charles Miller; lp, Enid Bennett, Jack Gilbert, Alfred Vosburgh, Walt Whitman

PRINCESS OF THE DARK (1928)
(? r.)

PRINCESS OLALA
(SEE: ART OF LOVE, THE, 1928, Ger.)

PRINCESS ROMANOFF (1915)
(6 r.) d, Frank Powell

PRINCESS VIRTUE (1917)
(5 r.) d, Robert Z. Leonard; lp, Mae Murray, Lule Warrenton, Wheeler Oakman, Clarissa Selwynne

PRINCESSE LULU (1924, Fr.)
(? r.) d, Donatien

PRINCESSE MASHA (1927, Fr.)
(? r.) d, Rene Leprince; lp, Claudia Victrix

PRINTEMPS D'AMOUR (1927, Fr.)
(? r.) d, Leonce Perret

PRINTER'S DEVIL, THE (1923)
(6 r.) d, William Beaudine; lp, Wesley Barry, Harry Myers, Kathryn McGuire, Louis King

PRISCA (1921, Fr.)
(? r.) d, Gaston Roudes

PRISON WITHOUT WALLS, THE (1917)
(5 r.) d, E. Mason Hopper; lp, Wallace Reid, Myrtle Stedman, William Conklin, Billy Elmer

PRISONER IN THE HAREM, THE (1913)
(4 r.)

PRISONER OF WAR, THE (1918)
(5 r.) lp, Shorty Hamilton, Virginia Harris

PRISONERS OF THE SEA (1929, USSR)
(7 r.) d, M. Werner;

PRISONERS OF THE STORM (1926)
(6 r.) d, Lynn Reynolds; lp, House Peters, Peggy Montgomery, Walter McGrail, Harry Todd

PRIVATE AFFAIRS (1925)
(6 r.) d, Renaud Hoffman; lp, Gladys Hulette, Robert Agnew, Mildred Harris, David Butler

PRIVATE LIFE OF HELEN OF TROY, THE (1927)
(8 r.) d, Alexander Korda; lp, Maria Corda, Lewis Stone, Ricardo Cortez, George Fawcett

PROBATION WIFE, THE (1919)
(6 r.) d, Sidney A. Franklin; lp, Norma Talmadge, Thomas Meighan, Florence Billings, Alec B. Francis

PRODIGAL DAUGHTER, THE (1916, Brit.)
(4 r.) lp, Derra de Moroda, Harry Gilbey

PRODIGAL DAUGHTERS (1923)
(6 r.) d, Sam Wood; lp, Gloria Swanson, Ralph Graves, Vera Reynolds, Theodore Roberts

PRODIGAL JUDGE, THE (1922)
(8 r.) d, Edward Jose; lp, Jean Paige, Maclyn Arbuckle, Ernest Torrence, Earle Foxe

PRODIGAL LIAR, THE (1919)
(5 r.) d, Thomas N. Heffron; lp, William Desmond, Betty Compson, Louis Morrison, Walter Perry

PROFITEER, THE (1919)
(6 r.) d, J.K. Holbrook; lp, Alma Hanlon, Jack Sherrill, Robin H. Townley, Charles Bowell

PROFITEERS, THE (1919)
(5 r.) d, George Fitzmaurice; lp, Fannie Ward, John Miltern, Leslie Stuart, Edwin Stevens

PROMISE, THE (1917)
(5 r.) d, Jay Hunt; lp, Harold Lockwood, May Allison, Lester Cuneo, Paul Willis

PROMISED LAND, THE (1925)
(5 r.)

PROPHET'S PARADISE, THE (1922)
(5 r.) d, Alan Crosland; lp, Eugene O'Brien, Sigrid Holmquist, Bigelow Cooper, Arthur Housman

PROTECT US (1914)
(6 r.)

PROUD HEART
(SEE: HIS PEOPLE, 1925)

PROWLERS OF THE SEA (1928)
(6 r.) d, John G. Adolfi; lp, Carmel Myers, Ricardo Cortez, George Fawcett, Gino Corrado

PROXIES (1921)
(7 r.) d, George D. Baker; lp, Norman Kerry, Zena Keefe, Raye Dean, Jack Crosby

PRUDENCE ON BROADWAY (1919)
(5 r.) d, Frank Borzage; lp, Olive Thomas, Francis McDonald, Harvey Clark, John P. Wild

PRUDENCE THE PIRATE (1916)
(5 r.) d, William Parke; lp, Gladys Hulette, Flora Finch, Riley Chamberlin, William Parke, Jr.

PRUSSIAN CUR, THE (1918)
(7 r.) d, Raoul Walsh; lp, Miriam Cooper, James Marcus, Patrick O'Malley, Leonora Stewart

PUBLIC BE DAMNED (1917)
(5 r.) d, S.E.V. Taylor; lp, Charles Richman, Mary Fuller, Chester Barnett, Joe Smiley

PUBLIC DEFENDER (1917)
(5 r.) d, Burton King; lp, Frank Keenan, Alma Hanlon, Robert Edeson, John Sainpolis

PUBLIC OPINION (1916)
(5 r.) d, Frank Reicher; lp, Blanche Sweet, Earle Foxe, Edythe Chapman, Tom Forman

PUBLIC PROSECUTOR (1917, USSR)
(6 r.) d, Yakov Protazanov; lp, Ivan Mozhukhin, Vera Orlova, Natalia Lisenko

PUBLICITY MADNESS (1927)
(6 r.) d, Albert Ray; lp, Lois Moran, Edmund Lowe, E.J. Ratcliffe, James Gordon

PUDD'NHEAD WILSON (1916)
(5 r.) d, Frank Reicher; lp, Theodore Roberts, Alan Hale, Thomas Meighan, Jane Wolff

PULCINELLA (1925, Fr.)
(? r.) d, Gaston Roudes

PULSE OF LIFE, THE (1917)
(5 r.) d, Rex Ingram; lp, Wedgewood Nowell, Gypsy Hart, Dorothy Barrett, Molly Malone

PUMPKIN (1928, Jap.)
(? r.) d, Yasujiro Ozu

PUPPETS OF FATE (1921)
(6 r.) d, Dallas M. Fitzgerald; lp, Viola Dana, Francis McDonald, Jackie Saunders, Fred Kelsey

PUPPY LOVE (1919)
(5 r.) d, Roy William Neill; lp, Lila Lee, Charles Murray, Harold Goodwin, Helen Dunbar

PURITAN PASSIONS (1923)
(7 r.) d, Frank Tuttle; lp, Glenn Hunter, Mary Astor, Osgood Perkins, Maude Hill

PURITY (1916)
(7 r.) d, Rea Berger; lp, Audrey Munson, Nigel de Brulier, Alfred Hollingsworth, William A. Carroll

PURPLE DAWN (1923)
(5 r.) d, Charles R. Seeling; lp, Bert Sprotte, William E. Aldrich, James B. Leong, Edward Piel

PURPLE HIGHWAY, THE (1923)
(7 r.) d, Henry Kolker; lp, Madge Kennedy, Monte Blue, Vincent Coleman, Pedro De Cordoba

PURPLE LADY, THE (1916)
(5 r.) d, George A. Lessey; lp, Ralph Herz, Irene Howley, Alan Hale, Howard Truesdell

PURPLE LILY, THE (1918)
(5 r.) d, George Kelson; lp, Kitty Gordon, Frank Mayo, Muriel Ostriche, Charles Wellesley

PURSUED (1925)
(5 r.) d, Dell Henderson; lp, Gaston Glass, Dorothy Drew, George Siegmann, Arthur Rankin

PUSUIT OF POLLY
(SEE: IN PURSUIT OF POLLY, 1918)

PUT 'EM UP (1928)
(5 r.) d, Edgar Lewis; lp, Fred Humes, Gloria Grey, Pee Wee Holmes, Tom London

PUT UP YOUR HANDS! (1919)
(5 r.) d, Edward Sloman; lp, Margarita Fischer, George Periolat, Emory Johnson, Hayward Mack

PUTTING ONE OVER (1919)
(5 r.) d, Edward Dillon; lp, George Walsh, Edith Stockton, Ralph J. Locke, Frank Beamish

PUTTING THE BEE IN HERBERT (1917)
(4 r.) d, Floyd France; lp, Harry Benham, Jessie Stevens, William Wadsworth, Ethel Fleming

QUALITY OF FAITH, THE (1916)
(5 r.) d, Richard Garrick; lp, Alexander Gaden, Gertrude Robinson, Lucile Taft, Charles W. Travis

QUAND NOUS ETIONS DEUX (1929, Fr.)
(? r.) d, Leonce Perret

QUARANTINED RIVALS (1927)
(7 r.) d, Archie Mayo; lp, Robert Agnew, Kathleen Collins, John Miljan, Ray Hallor

QUATRE-VINGT TREIZE (1921, Fr.)
(? r.) d, Andre Antoine

QUEEN OF HEARTS, THE (1918)
(5 r.) d, Edmund Lawrence; lp, Virginia Pearson, Joseph Smiley, Victor Sutherland, Edward J. Burns

QUEEN OF SIN, THE
(SEE: QUEEN OF SIN AND THE SPECTACLE OF SODOM AND GOMORRAH, THE, 1923, Aust.)

QUEEN OF SIN AND THE SPECTACLE OF SODOM AND GOMORRAH, THE (1923, Aust.)
(8 r.) d, Michael Kertesz [Curtiz]; lp, Walter Slezak, George Reimers

QUEEN OF SPADES, THE (1916, USSR)
(8 r.) d, Yakov Protazanov; lp, Ivan Mozhukhin, Vera Orlova, Y. Shebuyeva

QUEEN OF SPADES (1925)
(5 r.) d, Harry L. Fraser; lp, Gordon Clifford, Charlotte Pierce

QUEEN OF THE CHORUS (1928)
(6 r.) d, Charles J. Hunt; lp, Virginia Browne Faire, Rex Lease, Lloyd Whitlock, Betty Francisco

QUEEN OF THE MOULIN ROUGE (1922)
(7 r.) d, Ray C. Smallwood; lp, Martha Mansfield, Joseph Striker, Henry Harmon, Fred T. Jones

QUEEN OF THE SCREEN (1916, USSR)
(6 r.) d, Yevgeni Bauer; lp, Vigold Polonsky, V. Yureneva, Grigori Khmara

QUEEN OF THE SEA (1918)
(5 r.) d, John Adolfi; lp, Annette Kellerman, Hugh Thompson, Mildred Keats, Beth Irvine

QUEEN OF THE SMUGGLERS, THE (1914)
(4 r.)

QUEEN O' TURF (1922)
(5 r.) d, John K. Wells; lp, Brownie Vernon, John Faulkner, John Cosgrove, Raymond Lawrence

QUEEN WAS IN THE PARLOUR, THE
(SEE: FORBIDDEN LOVE, 1927, Brit.)

QUEEN X (1917)
(5 r.) d, John B. O'Brien; lp, Edna Goodrich, Hugh Thompson, Lucille Taft, Dora Adams

QUEEN'S SECRET, THE (1919, USSR)
(6 r.) d, Yakov Protazanov; lp, Ivan Mozhukhin, Natalia Lissenko, Nikolai Rimsky, I. Talanov

QUEST, THE (1915)
(5 r.) d, Harry Pollard; lp, Margarita Fischer, Harry Pollard, Joseph E. Singleton, Nan Christy

QUEST OF THE SACRED GEM, THE (1914)
(4 r.) d, George Fitzmaurice; lp, Edna Mayo, William Roselle, Charles Arling, Ernest Truex

QUESTION, THE (1917)
(5 r.) d, Perry N. Vekroff; lp, Alice Joyce, Harry Morey, Charles Kent, Gladden James

QUI A TUE (1919, Fr.)
(? r.) d, Pierre Marodon

QUICK ACTION (1921)
(5 r.) d, Edward Sloman; lp, William Russell

QUICK CHANGE (1925)
(5 r.) d, Dell Henderson; lp, George Larkin

QUICK TRIGGERS (1928)
(5 r.) d, Ray Taylor; lp, Fred Humes, Derelys Perdue, Wilbur Mack, Robert Chandler

QUICKENING FLAME, THE (1919)
(5 r.) d, Travers Vale; lp, Montagu Love, June Elvidge, Mabel Ballin, Albert Hart

QUICKSANDS (1917)
(6 r.) d, George Bellamy; lp, George Dewhurst, Vera Cornish, George Bellamy, Mercy Hatton

QUICKSANDS (1923)
(7 r.) d, Jack Conway; lp, Helene Chadwick, Richard Dix, Alan Hale, Noah Beery

QUICKSANDS OF LIFE (1915, Brit.)
(4 r.) d, J.L.V. Leigh; lp, Malcolm Mortimer

QUINCY ADAMS SAWYER (1922)
(8 r.) d, Clarence G. Badger; lp, John Bowers, Blanche Sweet, Lon Chaney, Barbara La Marr

QUINCY ADAMS SAWYER AND MASON'S CORNER FOLKS (1912)
(4 r.)

QUITTER, THE (1916)
(5 r.) d, Charles Horan; lp, Lionel Barrymore, Marguerite Skirvin, Paul Everton, Charles Prince

QUITTER, THE (1929)
(6 r.) d, Joseph Henabery; lp, Ben Lyon, Dorothy Revier, Fred Kohler, Charles McHugh

QUO VADIS? (1925, Ital.)
(9 r.) d, Arturo Ambrosio; lp, Emil Jannings, Lillian Hall Davis, Elena Di Sangro, Elga Brink

R.S.V.P. (1921)
(6 r.) d, Charles Ray; lp, Charles Ray, Florence Oberle, Harry Myers, Tom McGuire

RACE FOR LIFE, A (1928)
(5 r.) d, D. Ross Lederman; lp, Rin-Tin-Tin, Virginia Brown Faire, Carroll Nye, Bobby Gordon

RACE SUICIDE (1916)
(6 r.) d, George W. Terwilliger; lp, Ormi Hawley, Earl Metcalfe, Octavia Handworth, Kempton Greene

RACE WILD (1926)
(6 r.) d, Oscar Apfel; lp, Rex Lease, Eileen Percy, David Torrence, John Miljan

RACING BLOOD (1926)
(6 r.) d, Frank Richardson; lp, Robert Agnew, Anne Cornwall, John Elliott, Clarence Geldert

RACING FOOL, THE (1927)
(5 r.) d, Harry J. Brown; lp, Reed Howes, Ruth Dwyer, Ernest Hilliard, William Franey

RACING LUCK (1924)
(6 r.) d, Herman C. Raymaker; lp, Monty Banks, Helen Ferguson, Martha Franklin, D.J. Mitsoras

RACING ROMANCE (1927)
(5 r.) lp, William Barrymore

RACING STRAIN (1919)
(5 r.) d, Emmett J. Flynn; lp, Mae Marsh, Clarence Oliver, Clifford Bruce, W.T. Carleton

RADIO FLYER, THE (1924)
(5 r.) d, Harry O. Hoyt; lp, Charles Hutchison, Leah Baird

RADIO-MANIA (1923)
(6 r.) d, Roy William Neill; lp, Grant Mitchell, Margaret Irving, Gertrude Hillman, W.H. Burton

RAFFLES, THE AMATEUR CRACKSMAN (1917)
(7 r.) d, George Irving; lp, John Barrymore, Frederick Perry, H. Cooper Cliffe, Frank Morgan

RAGGED EARL, THE (1914)
(5 r.) d, Lloyd B. Carleton; lp, Andrew Mack, William Conklin, Edward J. Peil, Ormi Hawley

RAGGED PRINCESS, THE (1916)
(5 r.) d, John G. Adolfi; lp, June Caprice, Harry Hilliard, Florence Ashbrook, Jane Lee

RAGGED ROBIN (1924)
(5 r.) d, Frank S. Mattison; lp, Matty Mattison

RAGGEDY QUEEN, THE (1917)
(5 r.) d, Theodore Marston; lp, Violet Mersereau, Grace Barton, Donald Hall, Robert F. Hill

RAIDERS, THE (1916)
(5 r.) d, Charles Swickard; lp, H.B. Warner, Dorothy Dalton, Henry Belmar, Robert McKim

RAIL RIDER, THE (1916)
(5 r.) d, Maurice Tourneur; lp, House Peters, Zena Keefe, Bertram Marburgh, Harry West

RAILROADER, THE (1919)
(5 r.) d, Colin Campbell; lp, Thomas Santschi, Fritzi Brunette, George Fawcett, Virginia Eames

RAINBOW, THE (1917)
(5 r.) d, Ralph Dean; lp, Dorothy Bernard, Robert Conness, Jack Sherrill, Jean Stuart

RAINBOW, THE (1929)
(7 r.) d, Reginald Barker; lp, Dorothy Sebastian, Lawrence Gray, Sam Hardy, Harvey Clarke

RAINBOW GIRL, THE (1917)
(5 r.) d, Rollin S. Sturgeon; lp, Juliette Day, George Fisher, Charles Bennett, Lillian Hayward

RAINBOW RANGE (1929)
(5 r.) lp, Cheyenne Bill

RAINBOW RILEY (1926)
(7 r.) d, Charles Hines; lp, Johnny Hines, Brenda Bond, Bradley Barker, Dan Mason

RAINBOW TRAIL, THE (1918)
(6 r.) d, Frank Lloyd; lp, William Farnum, Ann Forrest, Mary Mersch, William Burress

RAMBLIN' GALOOT, THE (1926)
(5 r.) d, Fred Bain; lp, Buddy Roosevelt, Violet La Plante, Frederick Lee

RAMBLIN' KID, THE (1923)
(6 r.) d, Edward Sedgwick; lp, Hoot Gibson, Laura La Plante, Harold Goodwin, William Welsh

RAMBLING RANGER, THE (1927)
(5 r.) d, Del Henderson; lp, Jack Hoxie, Dorothy Gulliver, C.E. Anderson, Monte Montague, Jr.

RAMUNTCHO (1919, Fr.)
(? r.) d, Jacques de Baroncelli; lp, Rene Lorsay, Yvonne Annie

RANCHERS, THE (1923)
(5 r.) lp, George Elliot;

RANCHERS AND RASCALS (1925)
(5 r.) lp, Leo Maloney, Josephine Hill, Whitehorse, Evelyn Thatcher

RANGE BLOOD (1924)
(5 r.) d, Francis Ford; lp, Edmund Cobb

RANGE BOSS, THE (1917)
(5 r.) d, W.S. Van Dyke; lp, Jack Gardner, Ruth King, Carl Stockdale

RANGE BUZZARDS (1925)
(5 r.) d, Tom Gibson; lp, Pete Morrison

RANGE COURAGE (1927)
(5 r.) d, Ernest Laemmle; lp, Fred Humes, Gloria Grey, Dick Winslow, William A. Steele

RANGE JUSTICE (1925)
(5 r.) d, Ward Hayes; lp, Dick Hatton

RANGE PATROL, THE (1923)
(5 r.) d, H.G. Moody; lp, Jack Livingston, Mary Wynn, Al Ferguson

RANGE PIRATE, THE (1921)
(? r.) d, Leonard Franchon; lp, Al Hart, Jack Mower, Robert Conville

RANGE RAIDERS, THE (1927)
(5 r.) d, Paul Hurst; lp, Al Hoxie

RANGE RIDERS
(SEE: STRAIGHT SHOOTIN,' 1927)

RANGE TERROR, THE (1925)
(5 r.) d, William James Craft; lp, Bob Custer, Thais Valdemar, Claire De Lorez, Boris Bullock

RANGE VULTURES (1925)
(5 r.) lp, Lester Cuneo

RANGELAND (1922)
(5 r.) d, Neal Hart; lp, Ben Corbett, Patrick Megehee, Neal Hart, Max Wesell

RANGER, THE (1918)
(5 r.) lp, Shorty Hamilton

RANGER AND THE LAW, THE (1921)
(5 r.) d, Robert Kelly; lp, Lester Cuneo, Walter I. McCloud, Francelia Billington, Clark Comstock

RANGER BILL (1925)
(5 r.) lp, Dick Carter, Dorothy Wood

RANGER'S OATH (1928)
(5 r.) d, Robert J. Horner; lp, Al Hoxie

RANKS AND PEOPLE (1929, USSR)
(6 r.) d, Yakov Protazanov; lp, Ivan Moskvin, Mikhail Tarkhanov, Vladimir Yershov, Maria Strelkova

RAPID FIRE ROMANCE (1926)
(5 r.) d, Harry J. Brown; lp, Billy Sullivan, Marjorie Bonner, Harry Buckley, Johnny Sinclair

RARIN' TO GO (1924)
(5 r.) d, Richard Thorpe; lp, Buffalo Bill, Jr., Olin Francis, L.J. O'Connor, James Kelly

RASPUTIN (1929, USSR)
(6 r.) d, Nikolai Larin; lp, Gregor Chmara, Vladimir Gaidaroff, Suzanne Delmas, Ernst Ruckert

RASPUTIN (1929, Ger.)
(6 r.) d, Max Neufeld; lp, Max Neufeld, Renati Renee, Eugene Neufeld, Robert Valbar

RASPUTIN (1930)
(4 r.) d, Martin Berger; lp, Nikolai Malikoff, Ervin Kaiser, Diane Karene, Jack Trevor

RASPUTIN, THE BLACK MONK (1917)
(7 r.) d, Arthur Ashley; lp, Montagu Love, June Elvidge, Arthur Ashley, Henry Hull

RASPUTIN, THE HOLY SINNER
(SEE: RASPUTIN, 1929, Ger.)

RATCATCHER, THE
(SEE: PIED PIPER OF HAMELIN, THE, 1917, Ger.)

RATED AT $10.000.000 (1915)
(3 r.) d, Joseph Smiley; lp, Lilie Leslie, Jack Standing, Joseph Smiley, William Cohill

RATTLER, THE (1925)
(5 r.) d, Paul Hurst; lp, Jack Mower, George Williams, Alma Rayford, William Buckley

RAVEN, THE (1915)
(6 r.) d, Charles Brabin; lp, Henry B. Walthall, Warda Howard, Ernest Maupain, Eleanor Thompson

RAWHIDE (1926)
(5 r.) d, Richard Thorpe; lp, Buffalo Bill, Jr., Al Taylor, Molly Malone, Joe Rickson

READIN''RITIN''RITHMETIC (1926)
(5 r.) d, Robert Eddy; lp, Edna Marion, Gordon White

REAPERS, THE (1916)
(5 r.) d, Burton King; lp, John Mason, Clara Whipple, Warner Oland, Pierre LeMay

REASON WHY, THE (1918)
(5 r.) d, Robert G. Vignola; lp, Clara Kimball Young, Milton Sills, Florence K. Billings, Frank Losee

REBELLIOUS BRIDE, THE (1919)
(5 r.) d, Lynn F. Reynolds; lp, Peggy Hyland, George Nichols, George Hernandez, Pell Trenton

RECEIVED PAYMENT (1922)
(5 r.) d, Charles Maigne; lp, Corinne Griffith, Kenneth Harlan, David Torrence, William David

RECKLESS COURAGE (1925)
(5 r.) d, Tom Gibson; lp, Buddy Roosevelt, J.C. Fowler, Helen Foster, William McIllwain

RECKLESS GAMBLE, A (1928, Brit.)
(4 r.) d, Widgey R. Newman; lp, Desmond Roberts, Gladys Dunham, Sir Simeon Stuart, Wally Patch

RECKLESS MOLLYCODDLE, THE (1927)
(5 r.) lp, Richard Holt

RECKLESS MONEY (1926)
(? r.) lp, Sherman H. Dudley, Jr., John La Rue

RECKLESS RIDING BILL (1924)
(5 r.) d, Frank Morrow; lp, Dick Carter, Alys Morrell

RECKLESS SPEED (1924)
(5 r.) d, William James Craft; lp, Frank Merrill, Virginia Warwick, Joseph Girard, Gino Corrado

RECKLESS WIVES (1921)
(? r.) lp, Myra Murray, Leslie Austen, Jane Thomas, Helen McDonald

RECLAIMED (1918)
(5 r.) d, Harry McRae Webster; lp, Mabel Julienne Scott, Niles Welch, Anders Randolf, Fred W. Peters

RECLAMATION, THE (1916)
(5 r.) d, Edward Sloman; lp, Winnifred Greenwood, Franklyn Ritchie, Clarence Burton, Dick La Reno

RECOIL, THE (1917)
(5 r.) d, George Fitzmaurice; lp, William Courtenay, Lillian Greuze, Frank Belcher, Cora Mills Adams

RECOIL, THE (1921)
(5 r.) lp, George Chesebro, Evelyn Nelson, Virginia Morante

RECOIL, THE (1922, Brit.)
(5 r.) d, Geoffrey H. Malins; lp, Eille Norwood, Phyllis Titmuss, Lawrence Anderson, Dawson Millward

RE-CREATION OF BRIAN KENT, THE (1925)
(7 r.) d, Sam Wood; lp, Kenneth Harlan, Helene Chadwick, Mary Carr, ZaSu Pitts

RED ACES (1929, Brit.)
(7 r.) d, Edgar Wallace; lp, Janice Adair, Muriel Angelus, Geoffrey Gwyther, James Raglan

RED BLOOD (1926)
(5 r.) d, J.P. McGowan; lp, Al Hoxie, Nayone Warfield, Lew Meehan, Eddie Barry

RED BLOOD AND BLUE (1925)
(5 r.) d, James C. Hutchinson; lp, Big Boy Williams, Peggy O'Day, John Barley, Fred Butler

RED CLAY (1927)
(5 r.) d, Ernst Laemmle; lp, William Desmond, Marceline Day, Albert J. Smith, Byron Douglas

RED COURAGE (1921)
(5 r.) d, Reaves Eason; lp, Hoot Gibson, Joel Day, Molly Malone, Joe Girard

RED DANCE, THE (1928)
(10 r.) d, Raoul Walsh; lp, Charles Farrell, Dolores Del Rio, Ivan Linow, Boris Charsky

RED FOAM (1920)
(6 r.) d, Ralph Ince; lp, Zena Keefe, Nora Cecil, Peggy Worth

RED GOLD (1930)
(5 r.) lp, Cliff "Tex" Lyons

RED HOT HOOFS (1926)
(5 r.) d, Robert De Lacey; lp, Tom Tyler, Frankie Darro, Dorothy Dunbar, Stanley Taylor

RED HOT LEATHER (1926)
(5 r.) d, Albert Rogell; lp, Jack Hoxie, Ena Gregory, William Malan, Tom Shirley

RED HOT TIRES (1925)
(7 r.) d, Erle C. Kenton; lp, Monte Blue, Patsy Ruth Miller, Fred Esmelton, Lincoln Stedman

RED IMPS (1923, USSR)
(13 r.) d, Ivan Perestiani; lp, Pyotr Yesikovksy, Sofia Jozeffi, Kador Ben-Selim, V. Sutyrin

RED INN, THE
(SEE: L'AUBERGE ROUGE, 1923, Fr.)

RED LANTERN, THE (1919)
(6 r.) d, Albert Capellani; lp, Alla Nazimova, Frank Currier, Darrel Foss, Edward J. Connelly

RED LILY, THE (1924)
(7 r.) d, Fred Niblo; lp, Enid Bennett, Ramon Novarro, Wallace Beery, Frank Currier

RED LOVE (1925)
(6 r.) d, Edgar Lewis; lp, John Lowell, Evangeline Russell, F. Serrano Keating, William Calhoun

RED MAJESTY (1929)
(6 r.) d, Harold Noce

RED PEACOCK, THE (1922, Ger.)
(7 r.) d, Paul Stein; lp, Pola Negri

RED RAIDERS, THE (1927)
(7 r.) d, Albert Rogell; lp, Ken Maynard, Ann Drew, Paul Hurst, J.P. McGowan

RED RIDER, THE (1925)
(5 r.) d, Clifford S. Smith; lp, Jack Hoxie, Mary McAllister, Jack Pratt, Natalie Warfield

RED RIDERS OF CANADA (1928)
(7 r.) d, Robert De Lacy; lp, Patsy Ruth Miller, Charles Byer, Harry Woods, Rex Lease

RED SAUNDERS PLAYS CUPID
(SEE: FIGHTING GRINGO, THE, 1917)

RED SIGNALS (1927)
(? r.) d, J.P.McGowan; lp, Wallace MacDonald, Earle Williams, Eva Novak, J.P. McGowan

RED SWORD, THE (1929)
(7 r.) d, Robert G. Vignola; lp, William Collier, Jr., Marian Nixon, Carmel Myers, Demetrius Alexis

RED TRAIL (1923)
(6 r.) lp, Nora Swinburne

RED VIPER, THE (1919)
(6 r.) d, Jacques Tyrol; lp, Gareth Hughes, Ruth Stonehouse, Jack Gilbert, Irma Harrison

RED VIRGIN, THE (1915)
(4 r.) d, Leon D. Kent; lp, Helen Eddy, L.C. Shumway, Robert Gray, Jay Morley

RED WARNING, THE (1923)
(5 r.) d, Robert North Bradbury; lp, Jack Hoxie, Elinor Field, Fred Kohler, Frank Rice

RED, WHITE AND BLUE BLOOD (1918)
(5 r.) d, Charles J. Brabin; lp, Francis X. Bushman, Beverly Bayne, Willaim H. Tooker, Adella Barker

RED WOMAN, THE (1917)
(5 r.) d, E. Mason Hooper; lp, Gail Kane, Mahlon Hamilton, Ed F. Roseman, June Elvidge

REDEEMED (1915, Brit.)
(4 r.) d, Larry Trimble; lp, Florence Turner, Tom Powers, Maud Stewart, Anthony Keith

REDEEMING LOVE, THE (1917)
(5 r.) d, William Desmond Taylor; lp, Kathlyn Williams, Thomas Holding, Wyndham Standing, Herbert Standing

REDEMPTION (1917)
(6 r.) d, Julius Steger, Joseph A. Golden; lp, Evelyn Nesbit, Russell Thaw, Charles Wellesley, Mary Hall

REDEMPTION OF DAVE DARCEY, THE (1916)
(5 r.) d, Paul Scardon; lp, James Morrison, Belle Bruce, Billie Billings, Emanuel A. Turner

REDEMPTION OF HIS NAME, THE (1918, Brit.)
(5 r.) d, Percy Moran; lp, Aldon Neilson, Jock Hood, Farmer Skein

REDSKIN (1929)
(9 r.) d, Victor Schertzinger; lp, Richard Dix, Gladys Belmont, Jane Novak, Larry Steers

REED CASE, THE (1917)
(5 r.) d, Allen Holubar; lp, Allen Holubar, Louise Lovely, Alfred Allen, Fred Montague

REFORM
(SEE: LIFE'S MOCKERY, 1928)

REFORM CANDIDATE, THE (1915)
(5 r.) d, Frank Lloyd; lp, Macklyn Arbuckle, Forrest Stanley, Myrtle Stedman, Malcolm Blevins

REFUGE (1923)
(6 r.) d, Victor Schertzinger; lp, Katherine MacDonald, Hugh Thompson, J. Gunnis Davis, J. Gordon Russell

REGENERATES, THE (1917)
(5 r.) d, E. Mason Hooper; lp, Walt Whitman, Alma Rubens, Darrel Foss, John Lince

REGENERATING LOVE, THE (1915)
(4 r.) d, George W. Terwilliger; lp, Ormi Hawley, Earl Metcalfe, Kempton Greene, Justina Huff

REGENERATION, THE (1915)
(6 r.) d, Raoul Walsh; lp, Rockliffe Fellowes, Anna Q. Nilsson

REGENERATION (1923)
(5 r.) lp, M. Maxwell, Stella Mayo

REGULAR FELLOW, A (1919)
(5 r.) d, Christy Cabanne; lp, Taylor Holmes, Millicent Fisher, Edna Phillips Holmes, Frank Leigh

REGULAR GIRL, A (1919)
(5 r.) d, James Young; lp, Elsie Janis, Matt Moore, L. Rogers Lytton, Robert Ayerton

RED-HAIRED CUPID, A (1918)
(5 r.) d, Cliff Smith; lp, Roy Stewart, Charles Dorian, Peggy Pearce, Ray Griffith

REDHEAD (1919)
(5 r.) d, Charles Maigne; lp, Alice Brady, Conrad Nagel, Robert Schable, Charles A. Stevenson

REJUVENATION OF AUNT MARY, THE (1914)
(4 r.) d, Eddie Dillon; lp, Del Henderson, Jack Mulhall, Dave Morris

REJUVENATION OF AUNT MARY, THE (1927)
(6 r.) d, Erle C. Kenton; lp, May Robson, Harrison Ford, Phyllis Haver, Franklin Pangborn

REMEMBER (1926)
(6 r.) d, David Selman; lp, Dorothy Phillips, Earl Metcalfe, Lola Todd, Lincoln Stedman

REMEMBRANCE (1922)
(6 r.) d, Rupert Hughes; lp, Claude Gillingwater, Kate Lester, Patsy Ruth Miller, Cullen Landis

REMEMBRANCE (1927, Brit.)
(7 r.) d, Bert Wynne; lp, Rex Davis, Enid Stamp Taylor, Alf Goddard, Hayford Hobbs

REMITTANCE WOMAN, THE (1923)
(6 r.) d, Wesley Ruggles; lp, Ethel Clayton, Rockliffe Fellowes, Mario Carillo, Frank Lanning

REMODELING HER HUSBAND (1920)
(5 r.) d, Lillian Gish; lp, Dorothy Gish, James Rennie, Marie Burke, Downing Clarke

REMORSELESS LOVE (1921)
(5 r.) d, Ralph Ince; lp, Elaine Hammerstein, Niles Welch, Jerry Devine, Ray Allen

RENAISSANCE AT CHARLEROI, THE (1917)
(4 r.) d, Thomas R. Mills; lp, J. Frank Glendon, Eleanor Lawson, Agnes Ayres, Webster Campbell

RENEGADE HOLMES, M.D. (1925)
(5 r.) d, Ben Wilson; lp, Ben Wilson, Marceline Day

RENO DIVORCE, A (1927)
(6 r.) d, Ralph Graves; lp, May McAvoy, Ralph Graves, Hedda Hopper, Robert Ober

RENONCEMENT (1917, Fr.)
(? r.) d, Charles Maudru, Charles de Marsan

RENT FREE (1922)
(5 r.) d, Howard Higgin; lp, Wallace Reid, Lila Lee, Henry Barrows, Gertrude Short

REPUTATION (1917)
(5 r.) d, John B. O'Brien; lp, Edna Goodrich, William Hinckley, Frank Goldsmith, Carey Lee

REQUINS (1917, Fr.)
(? r.) d, Andre Hugon

RESCUING ANGEL, THE (1919)
(5 r.) d, Walter Edwards; lp, Shirley Mason, Forrest Stanley, Arthur Edmund Carew, John Steppling

RESPECTABLE BY PROXY (1920)
(6 r.) d, J. Stuart Blackton; lp, Sylvia Breamer, Robert Gordon, Margaret Barry, William R. Dunn

RESPONDENT, THE
(SEE: SPENDERS, THE, 1921)

RESTITUTION (1918)
(10 r.) d, Howard Gaye; lp, Eugene Corey, Lois Gardner, Alfred Garcia, Frank Whitson

RESTLESS SEX, THE (1920)
(6 r.) d, Robert Z. Leonard; lp, Marion Davies, Ralph Kellard, Carlyle Blackwell, Charles Lane

RESTLESS SOULS (1919)
(5 r.) d, William C. Dowlan; lp, Alma Rubens, Jack Conway, Katherine Adams, Harvey Clark

RESTLESS SOULS (1922)
(5 r.) d, Robert Ensminger; lp, Earle Williams, Francelia Billington, Arthur Hoyt, Martha Mattox

RESTLESS WIVES (1924)
(7 r.) d, Gregory La Cava; lp, Doris Kenyon, James Rennie, Montagu Love, Edmund Breese

RESTLESS YOUTH (1928)
(7 r.) d, Christy Cabanne; lp, Marceline Day, Ralph Forbes, Norman Trevor, Robert Ellis

RESURRECTION (1912)
(4 r.) lp, Blanche Walls

RESURRECTION (1918)
(5 r.) d, Edward Jose; lp, Pauline Frederick, Robert Elliot, John Sainpolis, Jere Austin

RESURRECTION (1927)
(10 r.) d, Edwin Carewe; lp, Rod La Rocque, Dolores Del Rio, Marc MacDermott, Lucy Beaumont

RESURRECTION OF LOVE (1922, Jap.)
(? r.) d, Kenji Mizoguchi

RETALIATION (1929, Chi.)
(11 r.)

RETURN OF BOSTON BLACKIE, THE (1927)
(6 r.) d, Harry O. Hoyt; lp, Corliss Palmer, Raymond Glenn, Rosemary Cooper, Coit Albertson

RETURN OF "DRAW" EGAN, THE (1916)
(5 r.) d, William S. Hart; lp, William S. Hart, Louise Glaum, Margery Wilson, Robert McKim

RETURN OF EVE, THE (1916)
(5 r.) d, Arthur Berthelet; lp, Edna Mayo, Eugene O'Brien, Edward Mawson, Edward Arnold

RETURN OF MARY, THE (1918)
(5 r.) d, Wilfred Lucas; lp, May Allison, Clarence Burton, Claire McDowell, Darrel Foss

RETURN OF MAURICE DONNELLY, THE (1915)
(? r.) d, William Humphrey; lp, Leo Delaney, Leah Baird, Anders Randolph, Mary Maurice

RETURN OF TARZAN, THE (1920)
(7 r.) d, Harry Revier; lp, Gene Pollar, George Romain, Estelle Taylor, Walter Miller

RETURN OF THE LONE WOLF
(SEE: LONE WOLF RETURNS, THE, 1926)

REVEILLE (1924, Brit.)
(8 r.) d, George Pearson; lp, Betty Balfour, Stewart Rome, Ralph Forbes, Sydney Fairbrother

REVELATION (1918)
(7 r.) d, George D. Baker; lp, Alla Nazimova, Charles Bryant, Frank Currier, Syn De Conde

REVELATIONS (1916)
(5 r.) d, Arthur Maude; lp, Constance Crawley, Arthur Maude, William Carroll

REVENGE (1918)
(6 r.) d, Tod Browning; lp, Edith Storey, Wheeler Oakman, Alberta Ballard, Ralph Lewis

REVENGE (1928)
(7 r.) d, Edwin Carewe; lp, Dolores Del Rio, James Marcus, Sophia Ortiga, LeRoy Mason

REVENGEFUL SPIRIT OF EROS, THE (1930, Jap.)
(? r.) d, Yasujiro Ozu

REVOLT, THE (1916)
(5 r.) d, Barry O'Neil; lp, Frances Nelson, Arthur Ashley, Clara Whipple, Lena Schmidt

REVOLUTION
(SEE: REVOLUTIONIST, THE, 1914, Brit.)

REVOLUTIONIST, THE (1914, Brit.)
(4 r.) d, Ernest G. Batley; lp, Fred Morgan, Ethel Bracewell, Henry Victor, George Foley

REVOLUTIONIST (1917, USSR)
(4 r.) d, Yevgeni Bauer; lp, Ivan Perestiani, Vladimir Strizhevsky, Z. Bogdanova

REVOLT IN THE DESERT (1932, USSR)
(5 r.) d, Nicolai Tikhonov; lp, Zinaida Zanoni, Evgraf Zhachovski, I. Kutchenkov

REVOLT OF THE ROBOTS
(SEE: AELITA, 1929, USSR)

REWARD OF FAITH (1929)
(6 r.) d, M. Simon; lp, Andre Carnege, Marcel Charbrie,

REWARD OF PATIENCE, THE (1916)
(5 r.) d, Robert G. Vignola; lp, Louise Huff, John Bowers, Lottie Pickford, Kate Lester

REWARD OF THE FAITHLESS, THE (1917)
(5 r.) d, Rex Ingraham; lp, Wedgewood Nowell, Betty Schade, Claire Du Brey, Richard La Reno

RICH BUT HONEST (1927)
(6 r.) d, Albert Ray; lp, Nancy Nash, Clifford Holland, Charles Morton, J. Farrell McDonald

RICH GIRL, POOR GIRL (1921)
(5 r.) d, Harry B. Harris; lp, Gladys Walton, Gordon McGregor, Harold Austin, Antrim Short

RICH MAN, POOR MAN (1918)
(5 r.) d, J. Searle Dawley; lp, Marguerite Clark, Richard Barthelmess, George Backus, Frederick Warde

RICH MAN'S DAUGHTER, A (1918)
(5 r.) d, Edgar Jones; lp, Louise Lovely, Philo McCullough, Edna Maison, Harry Holden

RICH MAN'S PLAYTHING, A (1917)
(5 r.) d, Carl Harbaugh; lp, Valeska Suratt, Robert Cummings, John Webb Dillon, Edward Martindel

RICH MEN'S SONS (1927)
(6 r.) d, Ralph Graves; lp, Ralph Graves, Shirley Mason, Robert Cain, Frances Raymond

RICH SLAVE, THE (1921)
(6 r.) d, Romaine Fielding; lp, Joseph Smiley, Arthur Elton, Martha Forrest, Mabel Taliaferro

RICHARD THE BRAZEN (1917)
(5 r.) d, Perry N. Vekroff; lp, Harry Morey, Alice Joyce, William Frederic, Franklyn Hanna

RICHARD, THE LION-HEARTED (1923)
(8 r.) d, Chet Withey; lp, Wallace Beery, Charles Gerrard, Kathleen Clifford, Marguerite De La Motte

RICHARD III (1913)
(5 r.) d, Frederick Warde; lp, Frederick Warde

RICHELIEU (1914)
(4 r.) d, Allan Dwan; lp, Murdock MacQuarrie, Pauline Bush, William C. Dowlan, Lon Chaney

RICHEST GIRL, THE (1918)
(5 r.) d, Albert Capellani; lp, Ann Murdock, David Powell, Paul Capellani, Charles Wellesley

RICHTOFEN (1932, Ger.)
(5 r.) d, D. Kortesz, Peter Joseph; lp, George Burghardt, Sybil Moore, Arne Molander, Helga Thomas

RIDDLE GAWNE (1918)
(5 r.) d, William S. Hart, Lambert Hillyer; lp, William S. Hart, Katherine MacDonald, Lon Chaney, Gretchen Lederer

RIDDLE TRAIL, THE (1928)
(5 r.) lp, Cliff "Tex" Lyons

RIDE 'EM HIGH (1927)
(5 r.) d, Richard Thorpe; lp, Buddy Roosevelt, Charles K. French, Olive Hasbrouck, Robert Homans

RIDER OF MYSTERY RANCH (1924)
(5 r.) lp, Art Mix

RIDER OF THE KING LOG, THE (1921)
(7 r.) d, Harry O. Hoyt; lp, Frank Sheridan, Irene Boyle, Richard Travers, Emily Chichester

RIDER OF THE LAW (1919)
(6 r.) d, Jack [John] Ford; lp, Harry Carey, Vester Pegg, Theodore Brooks, Joe Harris

RIDER OF THE LAW (1927)
(5 r.) d, Paul Hurst; lp, Al Hoxie

RIDERS AT NIGHT (1923)
(5 r.) lp, Guin "Big Boy" Williams

RIDERS OF BORDER BAY (1925)
(5 r.) lp, George Kesterson

RIDERS OF THE DARK (1928)
(6 r.) d, Nick Grinde; lp, Tim McCoy, Dorothy Dwan, Rex Lease, Roy D'Arcy

RIDERS OF THE LAW (1922)
(5 r.) d, Robert North Bradbury; lp, Jack Hoxie, Marin Sais

RIDERS OF THE NIGHT (1918)
(5 r.) d, John H. Collins; lp, Viola Dana, George Chesebro, Russell Simpson, Mabel Van Buren

RIDERS OF THE PURPLE SAGE (1918)
(6 r.) d, Frank Lloyd; lp, William Farnum, Mary Mersch, William Scott, Marc Robbins

RIDERS OF THE RANGE (1923)
(5 r.) d, Otis B. Thayer; lp, Edmund Cobb, Frank Gallagher, Clare Hatton, Roy Langdon

RIDERS OF THE SAND STORM (1925)
(5 r.) lp, Guin "Big Boy" Williams, Peggy O'Day

RIDERS OF THE STORM (1929)
(5 r.) d, J.P. McGowan; lp, Yakima Canutt, Ione Reed, Dorothy Vernon, Bobby Dunn

RIDERS OF THE WEST (1927)
(5 r.) d, Ben Wilson; lp, Ben Wilson, Neva Gerber, Ed La Niece, Bud Osborne

RIDERS OF VENGEANCE (1928)
(5 r.) d, Robert J. Horner; lp, Montana Bill

RIDERS UP (1924)
(5 r.) d, Irving Cummings; lp, Crieghton Hale, George Cooper, Kate Price, Robert Brower

RIDIN' COMET (1925)
(5 r.) d, Ben Wilson; lp, Yakima Canutt, Dorothy Woods, Bob Walker, Bill Donovan

RIDIN' DEMON, THE (1929)
(5 r.) d, Ray Taylor; lp, Ted Wells, Kathleen Collins, Lucy Beaumont, Otto Bibber

RIDIN' DOUBLE
(SEE: RIDING DOUBLE, 1924)

RIDIN' EASY (1925)
(5 r.) d, Ward Hayes; lp, Dick Hatton

RIDIN' FOOL (1924)
(5 r.) lp, Lester Cuneo

RIDIN' GENT, A (1926)
(5 r.) d, Bennett Cohn; lp, Jack Perrin

RIDIN' KID FROM POWDER RIVER, THE (1924)
(6 r.) d, Edward Sedgwick; lp, Hoot Gibson, Gladys Hulette, Gertrude Astor, Tully Marshall

RIDIN' LUCK (1927)
(5 r.) d, Edward R. Gordon; lp, Tex Maynard, Ruby Blaine, Jack Anthony, Charles O'Malley

RIDIN' PRETTY (1925)
(5 r.) d, Arthur Rosson; lp, William Desmond, Ann Forrest, Stanhope Wheatcroft, Billy Sullivan

RIDIN' RASCAL, THE (1926)
(5 r.) d, Clifford S. Smith; lp, Art Accord, Olive Hasbrouck, Al Jennings

RIDIN' ROMEO, A (1921)
(5 r.) d, George E. Marshall; lp, Tom Mix, Rhea Mitchell, Pat Chrisman, Sid Jordon

RIDIN' ROWDY, THE (1927)
(5 r.) d, Richard Thorpe; lp, Buffalo Bill Jr., Olive Hasbrouck, Al Hart, Harry Todd

RIDIN' STRAIGHT (1926)
(5 r.) lp, Bob Reeves

RIDIN' STREAK, THE (1925)
(5 r.) d, Del Andrews; lp, Bob Custer, Peggy Udell, Roy Laidlaw, Frank Brownlee

RIDIN' THROUGH
(SEE: STRAIGHT THROUGH, 1925)

RIDIN' THRU (1923)
(5 r.) lp, Dick Hatton

RIDIN' THUNDER (1925)
(5 r.) d, Clifford S. Smith; lp, Jack Hoxie, Katherine Grant, Jack Pratt, Franis Ford

RIDIN' WEST (1924)
(5 r.) d, Harry Webb; lp, Jack Perrin

RIDIN' WILD (1925)
(5 r.) d, Leon De La Motte; lp, Kit Carson, Pauline Curley, Jack Richardson, Walter Maly

RIDING DEMON
(SEE: RIDIN' DEMON, THE, 1929)

RIDING DOUBLE (1924)
(5 r.) d, Leo Maloney; lp, Leo Maloney, Josephine Hill, James Carey, Leonard Clapham

RIDING FOOL (1924)
(5 r.) d, Horace B. Carpenter; lp, Bob Burns, Dorothy Donald

RIDING FOR FAME (1928)
(6 r.) d, Reaves Eason; lp, Hoot Gibson, Ethlyne Clair, Charles K. French, George Summerville

RIDING FOR LIFE (1926)
(5 r.) d, J.P. McGowan; lp, Bob Reeves, Aline Goodwin, Hal Walters, Bob Fleming

RIDING RENEGADE, THE (1928)
(5 r.) d, Wallace W. Fox; lp, Bob Steele, Dorothy Kitchen, Lafe McKee, Bob Fleming

RIDING RIVALS (1926)
(5 r.) d, Richard Thorpe; lp, Wally Wales

RIDING ROMANCE (1926)
(5 r.) d, J.P. McGowan; lp, Al Hoxie, Marjorie Bonner, Arthur Morrison, Steve Clements

RIDING THUNDER
(SEE: RIDIN' THUNDER, 1925)

RIDING TO FAME (1927)
(6 r.) d, A.B. Barringer; lp, George Fawcett, Rosemary Theby, Gladys McConnell, Arthur Rankin

RIGHT DIRECTION, THE (1916)
(5 r.) d, E. Mason Hopper; lp, Vivian Martin, Colin Chase, Herbert Standing, Alfred Hollingsworth

RIGHT ELEMENT, THE (1919, Brit.)
(6 r.) d, Rex Wilson; lp, Campbell Gullan, Miriam Ferris, Tom Reynolds, Mary Rorke

RIGHT MAN, THE (1925)
(5 r.) d, John Harvey; lp, George Larkin

RIGHT OF MARY BLAKE, THE (1916)
(5 r.)

RIGHT OF THE STRONGEST, THE (1924)
(7 r.) d, Edgar Lewis; lp, E.K. [Elmo] Lincoln, Helen Ferguson, George Siegmann, Tom Santschi

RIGHT OF WAY, THE (1915)
(5 r.) d, Jack Noble; lp, William Faversham, Jane Grey, Edward Brennan

RIGHT OF WAY, THE (1920)
(6 r.) d, Jack Dillon; lp, Bert Lytell, H. Gibson Gowland, Leatrice Joy, Virginia Caldwell

RIGHT OFF THE BAT (1915)
(5 r.) d, Hugh Reticker; lp, Mike Donlin, Claire Mersereau, Rita Ross Donlin, Charles Mather

RIGHT TO BE HAPPY, THE (1917)
(5 r.) d, Rupert Julian; lp, Rupert Julian, John Cook, Claire McDowell, Francelia Billington

RIGHT TO HAPPINESS, THE (1919)
(8 r.) d, Allen Holubar; lp, Dorothy Phillips, William Stowell, Robert Anderson, Henry Barrows

RIGHT TO LIVE, THE (1921, Brit.)
(6 r.) d, A.E. Coleby; lp, Phyllis Shannaw, Peter Upcher, Marguerite Hare, H. Nicholls-Bates

RIGHT TO LOVE, THE (1920)
(7 r.) d, George Fitzmaurice; lp, Mae Murray, David Powell, Holmes Herbert, Frank Losee

RIGHT TO STRIKE, THE (1923)
(6 r.) d, Fred Paul; lp, Lilian Hall Davis, Fred Paul, Campbell Gullan, Lauderdale Maitland

RIGHTS OF MAN, THE (1915)
(5 r.) d, John H. Pratt; lp, Richard Buhler, Rosetta Brice, Francis Joyner, George Clarke

RILEY OF THE RAINBOW DIVISION (1928)
(6 r.) d, Robert Ray; lp, Creighton Hale, Al Alt, Pauline Garon, Joan Standing

RILKA (1918, Brit.)
(7 r.) d, F. Martin Thornton; lp, James Knight, Marjorie Villis, Bernard Dudley, Charles Rock

RIMROCK JONES (1918)
(5 r.) d, Donald Crisp; lp, Wallace Reid, Ann Little, Charles Ogle, Paul Hurst

RING OF THE BORGIAS, THE (1915)
(4 r.) d, Langdon West; lp, Margaret Prussing, Cora Linton, Carlton King, Augustus Phillips

RINGING THE CHANGES (1929, Brit.)
(7 r.) d, Leslie Hiscott; lp, Henry Edwards, Margot Landa, James Fenton, Charles Cautley

RINGTAILED RHINOCEROS, THE (1915)
(4 r.) d, George W. Terwilliger; lp, Raymond Hitchcock, Flora Zabelle, Herbert Fortier, Earl Metcalfe

RINTY OF THE DESERT (1928)
(5 r.) d, D. Ross Lederman; lp, Rin-Tin-Tin, Audrey Ferris, Carroll Nye, Paul Panzer

RIO GRANDE (1920)
(7 r.) d, Edwin Carewe; lp, Hector V. Sarno, Rosemary Theby, Georgie Stone, Allan Sears

RIP ROARIN' ROBERTS (1924)
(5 r.) d, Richard Thorpe; lp, Buddy Roosevelt, Brenda Lane, Joe Rickson, Al Richmond

RIP ROARING LOGAN (1928)
(5 r.) d, Robert J. Horner; lp, Al Hoxie

RIP SNORTER, THE (1925)
(5 r.) d, Ward Hayes; lp, Dick Hatton, Archie Ricks, William Rhine, Robert Walker

RISE OF SUSAN, THE (1916)
(5 r.) d, S.E.V. Taylor; lp, Clara Kimball Young, Eugene O'Brien, Warner Oland, Jenny Dickerson

RISING GENERATION, THE (1928, Brit.)
(7 r.) d, Harley Knoles, George Dewhurst; lp, Alice Joyce, Jameson Thomas, Robin Irvine, William Freshman

RISKY BUSINESS (1920)
(5 r.) d, Harry B. Harris; lp, Gladys Walton, Lillian Lawrence, Maude Wayne, Nanine Wright

RISKY BUSINESS (1926)
(7 r.) d, Alan Hale; lp, Vera Reynolds, Ethel Clayton, Kenneth Thomson, Ward Crane

RITZY (1927)
(6 r.) d, Richard Rosson; lp, Betty Bronson, James Hall, William Austin, Joan Standing

RIVAL OF PERPETUA, THE (1915)
(5 r.)

RIVALS (1933, USSR)
(? r.) d, A. Dmitriev; lp, K.I. Chugonov, Gleb Kuznetzov, O.G. Lenskaya, Z. Zononi

RIVER OF LIGHT, THE (1921, Brit.)
(5 r.) d, Dave Aylott;

RIVER OF ROMANCE, THE (1916)
(5 r.) d, Henry Otto; lp, Harold Lockwood, May Allison, Lester Cuneo, Bert Busby

RIVER OF STARS, THE (1921, Brit.)
(5 r.) d, F. Martin Thornton; lp, Philip Anthony, Faith Bevan, Teddy Arundell, W. Dalton Somers

RIVER WOMAN (1929)
(6 r.) d, Joseph Henabery; lp, Lionel Barrymore, Jacqueline Logan, Charles Delaney, Harry Todd

RIVER'S END, THE (1920)
(6 r.) d, Marshall Neilan; lp, Lewis Stone, Marjorie Daw, Jane Novak, J. Barney Sherry

ROAD AGENT (1926)
(5 r.) d, J.P. McGowan; lp, Al Hoxie

ROAD BETWEEN, THE (1917)
(5 r.) d, Joseph Levering; lp, Marian Swayne, Armand Cortez, Bradley Barker, Frank Andrews

ROAD CALLED STRAIGHT, THE (1919)
(5 r.) d, Ira M. Lowry; lp, Louis Bennison, Ormi Hawley, Henry Mortimer, Berton Churchill

ROAD DEMON, THE (1921)
(5 r.) d, Lynn Reynolds; lp, Tom Mix, Claire Anderson, Charles K. French, George Hernandez

ROAD OF AMBITION, THE (1920)
(6 r.) d, William P.S. Earle; lp, Conway Tearle, Florence Billings, Adolph Milar, Arthur Housman

ROAD THROUGH THE DARK, THE (1918)
(5 r.) d, Edmund Mortimer; lp, Clara Kimball Young, Jack Holt, Henry Woodward, Elinor Fair

ROAD TO ARCADY, THE (1922)
(5 r.) d, Burton King; lp, Virginia Lee, Harry Benham, Roger Lytton, Stephen Gratton

ROAD TO BROADWAY, THE (1926)
(6 r.) d, Howard Mitchell; lp, Edith Roberts, Gaston Glass, Ervin Renard

ROAD TO DIVORCE, THE (1920)
(5 r.) d, Philip Rosen; lp, Mary MacLaren, William Ellingford, Alberta Lee, Edward Peil

ROAD TO FRANCE, THE (1918)
(6 r.) d, Dell Henderson; lp, Carlyle Blackwell, Evelyn Greeley, Jack Drumier, Muriel Ostriche

ROAD TO GLORY, THE (1926)
(6 r.) d, Howard Hawks; lp, May McAvoy, Leslie Fenton, Ford Sterling, Rockliffe Fellowes

ROAD TO LOVE, THE (1916)
(5 r.) d, Scott Sidney; lp, Lenore Ulrich, Colin Chase, Lucille Ward, Estelle Allen

ROAD TO ROMANCE, THE (1927)
(7 r.) d, John S. Robertson; lp, Ramon Novarro, Marceline Day, Marc MacDermott, Roy D'Arcy

ROAD TO RUIN, THE (1928)
(6 r.) d, Norton A. Parker; lp, Helen Foster, Grant Withers, Florence Turner, Charles Miller

ROAD TO YESTERDAY, THE (1925)
(10 r.) d, Cecil B. De Mille; lp, Joseph Schildkaut, Jetta Goudal, Vera Reynolds, William Boyd

ROADS OF DESTINY (1921)
(6 r.) d, Frank Lloyd; lp, Pauline Frederick, John Bowers, Richard Tucker, Jane Novak

ROADSIDE IMPRESARIO, A (1917)
(5 r.) d, Donald Crisp; lp, George Beban, Jose Melville, Julia Faye, Harry De Vere

ROARIN' BRONCS (1927)
(5 r.) d, Richard Thorpe; lp, Buffalo Bill Jr., Ann McKay, Harry Todd, Lafe McKee

ROARING ADVENTURE, A (1925)
(5 r.) d, Clifford S. Smith; lp, Jack Hoxie, Mary McAllister, Marin Sais, J. Gordon Russell

ROARING BILL ATWOOD (1926)
(5 r.) d, Bennett Cohn; lp, Dick Hatton

ROARING FIRES (1927)
(6 r.) d, W.T. Lackey; lp, Roy Stewart, Alice Lake, Lionel Belmore, Bert Berkeley

ROARING FORTIES, THE
(SEE: ROBES OF SIN, 1924)

ROARING GUNS (1930)
(5 r.) lp, Al Hoxie

ROARING RIDER (1926)
(5 r.) d, Richard Thorpe; lp, Wally Wales

ROARING ROAD (1926)
(5 r.) d, Paul Hurst; lp, Kenneth McDonald, Jane Thomas

ROBERT'S ADVENTURE IN THE GREAT WAR (1920)
(6 r.) d, Frank C. Griffin

ROBES OF SIN (1924)
(6 r.) d, Russell Allen; lp, Sylvia Breamer, Jack Mower, Lassie Lou Ahern, Bruce Gordon

ROBIN HOOD (1913)
(4 r.) d, Theodore Marston; lp, William Russell, Gerda Holmes, James Cruze, William Garwood

ROBIN HOOD, JR. (1923)
(4 r.) d, Clarence Bricker; lp, Frankie Lee, Peggy Cartwright, Stanley Bingham, Ashley Cooper

ROBINSON CRUSOE (1916)
(5 r.) d, George Marion; lp, Robert P. Gibbs

ROCAMBOLE (1923, Fr.)
(? r.) d, Charles Maudru, Charles de Marsan

ROCK OF AGES (1918, Brit.)
(5 r.) d, Bertram Phillips; lp, Queenie Thomas, Leslie George, Ronald Power, Bernard Vaughan

ROCKING MOON (1926)
(7 r.) d, George Melford; lp, Lilyan Tashman, John Bowers, Rockliffe Fellowes, Laska Winters

ROCKS OF VALPRE, THE (1919, Brit.)
(6 r.) d, Maurice Elvey; lp, Basil Gill, Peggy Carlisle, Cowley Wright, Humberston Wright

RODEO MIXUP, A (1924)
(5 r.) d, Francis Ford; lp, Florence Gilbert, Francis Ford, Helen Hayes, Edmund Cobb

ROGER LA HONTE (1922, Fr.)
(? r.) d, Jacques de Baroncelli

ROGUE AND RICHES (1920)
(6 r.) d, Harry Franklin; lp, Mary MacLaren, Alberta Lee, Robert Walker, Dorothy Abril

ROGUE IN LOVE, A (1916, Brit.)
(4 r.) d, Bannister Merwin; lp, James Reardon

ROGUES AND ROMANCE (1920)
(6 r.) d, George B. Seitz; lp, George B. Seitz, June Caprice, Marguerite Courtot, Harry Semels

ROGUES OF PARIS (1913)
(4 r.) d, Alice Blache; lp, Fraunie Fraunholz, Vinnie Burns

ROGUES OF THE TURF (1923, Brit.)
(6 r.) d, Wilfred Noy; lp, Fred Groves, Olive Sloane, James Lindsay, Marvis Clare

ROGUE'S ROMANCE, A (1919)
(5 r.) d, James Young; lp, Earle Williams, Katherine Adams, Maude George, Brinsley Shaw

ROGUE'S WIFE, A (1915, Brit.)
(4 r.) d, Percy Nash; lp, Gregory Scott, Daisy Cordell, Joan Ritz, Frank Tennant

ROLLING ROAD, THE (1927)
(9 r.) d, Graham Cutts; lp, Carlyle Blackwell, Flora le Breton, A.V. Bramble, Clifford Heatherley

ROLLING STONES (1916)
(5 r.) d, Del Henderson; lp, Owen Moore, Marguerite Courtot, Alan Hale, Denman Maley

ROMAINE KALBRIS (1921, Fr.)
(? r.) d, Georges Monca

ROMANCE (1920)
(7 r.) d, Chet Withey; lp, Doris Keane, Basil Sydney, Norman Trevor, Betty Ross Clarke

ROMANCE AND BRIGHT LIGHTS
(SEE: ROMANCE OF THE UNDERWORLD, 1928)

ROMANCE AND RUSTLERS (1925)
(5 r.) d, Ben Wilson; lp, Yakima Canutt, Dorothy Woods, Harris Gordon, Joe Girard

ROMANCE OF A MILLION DOLLARS, THE (1926)
(6 r.) d, Tom Terriss; lp, Glenn Hunter, Alyce Mills, Gaston Glass, Jane Jennings

ROMANCE OF A ROGUE (1928)
(6 r.) d, King Baggot; lp, H.B. Warner, Anita Stewart, Alfred Fisher, Charles Gerrard

ROMANCE OF A RUSSIAN BALLERINA (1913, USSR)
(4 r.) d, Georg Jacobi, A. Bistritzky; lp, Konstantin Varlamov, Y. Smirnova,

ROMANCE OF ANNIE LAURIE, THE (1920, Brit.)
(5 r.) d, Gerald Somers; lp, Joan Gray, Allan McKelvin

ROMANCE OF BILLY GOAT HILL, A (1916)
(5 r.) d, Lynn F. Reynolds; lp, Myrtle Gonzales, Val Paul, George Hernandez, Fred Church

ROMANCE OF LADY HAMILTON, THE (1919, Brit.)
(7 r.) d, Bert Haldane; lp, Malvina Longfellow, Humberston Wright, Cecil Humphreys, Jane Powell

ROMANCE OF OLD BAGDAD, A (1922, Brit.)
(6 r.) d, Kenelm Foss; lp, Matheson Lang, Manora Thew, Henry Victor, Roy Travers

ROMANCE OF THE MAYFAIR, A (1925, Brit.)
(5 r.) d, Thomas Bentley; lp, Betty Faire, Henry Victor, Molly Johnson, Fred Raynham

ROMANCE OF THE NAVY, A (1915)
(4 r.) lp, Ormi Hawley, Earl Metcalfe

ROMANCE OF THE NILE (1924)
(5 r.)

ROMANCE OF THE UNDERWORLD, A (1918)
(6 r.) d, James Kirkwood; lp, Catherine Calvert, Eugene O'Brien, David Powell, Edwin Forsberg

ROMANCE OF THE UNDERWORLD (1928)
(7 r.) d, Irving Cummings; lp, Mary Astor, Ben Bard, Robert Elliott, John Boles

ROMANCE OF THE WASTELAND (1924)
(5 r.) lp, Art Mix

ROMANCE OF WASTDALE, A (1921, Brit.)
(6 r.) d, Maurice Elvey; lp, Milton Rosmer, Valia Venitskaya, Fred Raynham, Irene Rooke

ROMANCE PROMOTORS, THE (1920)
(5 r.) d, Chester Bennett; lp, Earle Williams, Otis Harlan, Helen Ferguson, Charles Wingate

ROMANTIC ADVENTURESS, A (1920)
(5 r.) d, Harley Knoles; lp, Dorothy Dalton, Charles Meredith, Howard Lang, Augusta Anderson

ROMANTIC AGE, THE (1927)
(6 r.) d, Robert Florey; lp, Eugene O'Brien, Alberta Vaughn, Stanley Taylor, Bert Woodruff

ROMANTIC JOURNEY, THE (1916)
(5 r.) d, George Fitzmaurice; lp, William Courtenay, Alice Dovey, Macey Harlam, Norman Thorp

ROMANTIC ROGUE (1927)
(5 r.) d, Harry J. Brown; lp, Reed Howes, Ena Gregory, James Bradbury, Syd Crossley

ROMANY, THE (1923, Brit.)
(6 r.) d, F. Martin Thornton; lp, Victor McLaglen, Irene Norman, Harvey Braban, Peggy Hathaway

ROMANY LASS, A
(SEE: RILKA; OR THE GYPSY QUEEN, 1927)

ROMANY RYE, THE (1915, Brit.)
(4 r.) d, Percy Nash; lp, Gerald Lawrence, Gregory Scott, Daisy Cordell, Frank Tennant

ROMEO AND JULIET (1916)
(8 r.) d, John W. Noble, Francis X. Bushman; lp, Francis X. Bushman, Beverly Bayne, John Davidson, Ethel Mantell

ROOF TREE, THE (1921)
(5 r.) d, John Francis Dillon; lp, William Russell, Florence Deshon, Sylvia Breamer, Robert Daly

ROOKIES (1927)
(7 r.) d, Sam Wood; lp, Karl Dane, George K. Arthur, Marceline Day, Louise Lorraine

ROOM AND BOARD (1921)
(5 r.) d, Alan Crosland; lp, Constance Binney, Tom Carrigan, Malcolm Bradley, Arthur Housman

ROOT OF EVIL, THE (1919)
(5 r.) d, George Ridgewell; lp, Frances Mann, Philip Yale Drew

ROPED (1919)
(6 r.) d, Jack [John] Ford; lp, Harry Carey, Neva Gerber, Mollie McConnell, Arthur Shirley

ROPED BY RADIO (1925)
(5 r.) lp, George Kesterson, Virginia Warwick

ROPIN' RIDIN' FOOL, A (1925)
(5 r.) lp, Pete Morrison, Martin Turner

ROSALEEN DHU (1920, Brit.)
(4 r.) d, William Powers; lp, William Powers

ROSARY, THE (1915)
(7 r.) d, Colin Campbell; lp, Kathlyn Williams, Wheeler Oakman, Charles Clary, Anna Dodge

ROSARY, THE (1922)
(7 r.) d, Jerome Storm; lp, Lewis S. Stone, Jane Novak, Wallace Beery, Robert Gordon

ROSE FRANCE (1919, Fr.)
(? r.) d, Marcel L'Herbier; lp, Jaque Catelain, Mlle. Aisse

ROSES IN THE DUST (1921, Brit.)
(6 r.) d, C.C. Calvert; lp, Iris Rowe, David Hawthorne, Gordon Craig, Gladys Mason

ROSE O' PARADISE (1918)
(5 r.) d, James Young; lp, Bessie Barriscale, Norman Kerry, Howard Hickman, David M. Hartford

ROSE O' THE RIVER
(SEE: ROSE OF THE RIVER, 1919)

ROSE O' THE SEA (1922)
(7 r.) d, Fred Niblo; lp, Anita Stewart, Rudolph Cameron, Thomas Holding, Margaret Landis

ROSE OF BLOOD, THE (1917)
(6 r.) d, J. Gordon Edwards; lp, Theda Bara, Richard Ordynski, Charles Clary, Herschal Mayall

ROSE OF GRENADE (1916, Ital.)
(6 r.)

ROSE OF KILDARE, THE (1927)
(7 r.) d, Dallas M. Fitzgerald; lp, Helene Chadwick, Pat O'Malley, Henry B. Walthall, Lee Moran

ROSE OF NOME (1920)
(5 r.) d, Edward J. LeSaint; lp, Gladys Brockwell, William Scott, Herbert Prior, Gertrude Ryan

ROSE OF THE ALLEY (1916)
(5 r.) d, Charles Horan, William C. Dowlan; lp, Mary Miles Minter, Thomas J. Carrigan, Daniel B. "Kid" Hogan, Frederick Heck

ROSE OF THE BOWERY (1927)
(6 r.) d, Bertram Bracken; lp, Johnny Walker, Edna Murphy, Mildred Harris

ROSE OF THE DESERT (1925)
(5 r.) lp, Quinn "Big Boy" Williams

ROSE OF THE GOLDEN WEST (1927)
(7 r.) d, George Fitzmaurice; lp, Mary Astor, Gilbert Roland, Gustav von Seyffertitz, Montagu Love

ROSE OF THE RIVER (1919)
(5 r.) d, Robert Thornby; lp, Lila Lee, Darrel Foss, George Fisher, Robert Brower

ROSE OF THE SOUTH (1916)
(5 r.) d, Paul Scardon; lp, Charles Kent, Mary Maurice, Antonio Moreno, Peggy Hyland

ROSE OF THE TENEMENTS (1926)
(7 r.) d, Phil Rosen; lp, Shirley Mason, Johnny Harron, Evelyn Selbie, Sidney Franklin

ROSE OF THE WEST (1919)
(5 r.) d, Harry Millarde; lp, Madlaine Travers, Frank Leigh, Beatrice La Plante, Thomas Santschi

ROSE-MARIE (1928)
(8 r.) d, Lucien Hubbard; lp, Joan Crawford, James Murray, House Peters, Creighton Hale

ROSEMARY (1915)
(5 r.) d, William Bowman, Fred J. Balshofer; lp, Marguerite Snow, Paul Gilmore, Virginia Kraft, William Clifford

ROSEMARY CLIMBS THE HEIGHTS (1918)
(5 r.) d, Lloyd Ingraham; lp, Mary Miles Minter, Allan Forrest, Margaret Shelby, Charlotte Mineau

ROSES OF PICARDY (1918, Brit.)
(4 r.)

ROTTERS, THE (1921, Brit.)
(5 r.) d, A.V. Bramble; lp, Joe Nightingale, Sydney Fairbrother, Sydney Paxton, Margery Meadows

ROUGE AND RICHES (1920)
(5 r.) d, Harry L. Franklin; lp, Mary McLaren, Syn De Conde, Lloyd Whitlock

ROUGED LIPS (1923)
(6 r.) d, Harold Shaw; lp, Viola Dana, Tom Moore, Nola Luxford, Sidney De Gray

ROUGH AND READY (1927)
(5 r.) d, Albert Rogell; lp, Jack Hoxie, Ena Gregory, Jack Pratt, William A. Steele

ROUGH AND READY (1930)
(5 r.) lp, Montana Bill

ROUGH DIAMOND, THE (1921)
(5 r.) d, Edward Sedgwick; lp, Tom Mix, Eva Novak, Hector Sarno, Edwin J. Brady

ROUGH GOING (1925)
(5 r.) d, Wally Van; lp, Franklyn Farnum, Marion Harlan, Vester Pegg, Dora Baker

ROUGH RIDIN' (1924)
(5 r.) d, Richard Thorpe; lp, Buddy Roosevelt, Elsa Benham, Richard Thorpe, Joe Rickson

ROUGH RIDIN' RED (1928)
(5 r.) d, Louis King; lp, Buzz Barton, Frank Rice, James Welch, Bert Moorehouse

ROUGH RIDING ROMANCE (1919)
(5 r.) d, Arthur Rosson; lp, Tom Mix, Juanita Hansen, Pat Chrisman, Spottiswoode Aitken

ROUGH SHOD FIGHTER, A (1927)
(5 r.) lp, William Russell, Francelia Billington

ROUGH STUFF (1925)
(5 r.) d, Dell Henderson; lp, George Larkin

ROUGHNECK, THE (1919)
(5 r.) d, Oscar Apfel; lp, Montagu Love, Barbara Castleton, Frank Mayo, Robert Broderick

ROUNDING UP THE LAW (1922)
(5 r.) d, Charles R. Seeling; lp, Guinn "Big Boy" Williams, Russell Gordon, Chet Ryan, Patricia Palmer

ROYAL AMERICAN, THE (1927)
(5 r.) d, Harry J. Brown; lp, Reed Howes, Nita Martan, Bill Franey, David Kirby

ROYAL BOX, THE (1914)
(4 r.) d, Oscar Eagle

ROYAL DEMOCRAT, A (1919)
(5 r.) lp, Jack Conway, Marguerite Marsh

ROYAL DIVORCE, A (1923, Brit.)
(10 r.) d, Alexander Butler; lp, Gwylim Evans, Gertrude McCoy, Lilian Hall Davis, Gerald Ames

ROYAL LOVE (1915, Brit.)
(4 r.) d, Percy Nash; lp, Joan Ritz, Eve Balfour, Gregory Scott, Frank Tennant

ROYAL PAUPER, THE (1917)
(5 r.) d, Ben Turbett; lp, Francine Larrimore, Herbert Prior, Charles Sutton, Richard Tucker

ROYAL ROMANCE (1917)
(5 r.) d, James Vincent; lp, Virginia Pearson, Irving Cummings, Boyce Coombs, Nora Cecil

ROYAL SCANDAL (1929, Ger.)
(7 r.) d, Hans Behrendt; lp, Werner Krauss, Jenny Jugo

RUBBER HEELS (1927)
(7 r.) d, Victor Heerman; lp, Ed Wynn, Chester Conklin, Thelma Todd, Robert Andrews

RUBE, THE (1925)
(5 r.) lp, Sammy Burns

RUE DE LA PAIX (1927, Fr.)
(? r.) d, Henri Diamant-Berger

RUGGED PATH, THE (1918, Brit.)
(5 r.) lp, Marjorie Villis, Hayford Hobbs, Cameron Carr, Ivy Stanborough

RUGGLES OF RED GAP (1918)
(8 r.) d, Lawrence C. Windom; lp, Taylor Holmes, Frederick Burton, Lawrence D'Orsay, Virginia Valli

RULER OF THE ROAD (1918)
(5 r.) d, Ernest C. Warde; lp, Frank Keenan, Kathryn Lean, Thomas Jackson, Frank Sheridan

RULING PASSION, THE (1916)
(5 r.) d, Herbert Brenon; lp, Claire Whitney, William Shay, Stephen Grattan

RUM RUNNERS, THE (1923)
(5 r.) lp, Leo Maloney

RUMMY, THE (1916)
(5 r.) d, Paul Powell; lp, Wilfred Lucas, Pauline Starke, William H. Brown, James O'Shea

RUMPELSTILSKIN (1915)
(5 r.) d, Reginald Barker; lp, Clyde Tracy, Elizabeth Burbridge, Kenneth Browne, J. Barney Sherry

RUNAWAY, THE (1917)
(5 r.) d, Dell Henderson; lp, Julia Sanderson, Norman Trevor, Ada St. Clair, Dore Plowden

RUNAWAY EXPRESS, THE (1926)
(6 r.) d, Edward Sedgwick; lp, Jack Daugherty, Blanche Mehaffey, Tom O'Brien, Charles K. French

RUNAWAY PRINCESS, THE (1929, Brit.)
(7 r.) d, Frederick Wendhausen, Anthony Asquith; lp, Mady Christians, Paul Cavanagh, Norah Baring, Fred Rains

RUNAWAY ROMANY (1917)
(5 r.) d, George Lederer; lp, Marion Davies, Joseph Kilgour, Matt Moore, Pedro de Cordoba

RUNAWAY WIFE, THE (1915)
(4 r.) lp, Stewart Baird, Justina Wayne, Lowell Stuart, Orlando Daly

RUNNING WILD (1927)
(7 r.) d, Gregory La Cava; lp, W.C. Fields, Mary Brian, Marie Shotwell, Frederick Burton

RUSE OF THE RATTLER, THE (1921)
(5 r.) d, J.P. McGowan; lp, J.P. McGowan, Lillian Rich, Jean Perry, Gordon McGregor

RUSLAN I LUDMILA (1915, USSR)
(6 r.) d, Wladyslaw Starewicz; lp, Ivan Mozhukhin, S. Goslavskaya, A. Bibikov, E. Pukhalsky

RUSSIA (1929, Ger.)
(8 r.) d, Mario Bonnard; lp, Marcella Albani, V. Gaidarov, Wilhelm Dieterle, Louis Ralph

RUSSIA - LAND OF TOMORROW (1919, Brit.)
(5 r.) d, Maurice Sanderground; lp, Eve Balfour, A.B. Imeson, Clifford Cobbe, Bob Reed

RUSTLE OF SILK, THE (1923)
(7 r.) d, Herbert Brenon; lp, Betty Compson, Conway Tearle, Cyril Chadwick, Anna Q. Nilsson

RUSTLER'S END, THE (1928)
(5 r.) lp, Al Hoxie

RUSTLERS OF THE NIGHT (1921)
(? r.) d, Leonard Franchon; lp, Al Hart, Jack Mower, Robert Conville

RUSTLING A BRIDE (1919)
(5 r.) d, Irvin Willat; lp, Lila Lee, Monte Blue, L.C. Shumway, Manuel Ojeda

RUSTLING FOR CUPID (1926)
(5 r.) d, Irving Cummings; lp, George O'Brien, Anita Stewart, Russell Simpson, Edith Yorke

S.O.S. (1928, Brit.)
(7 r.) d, Leslie Hiscott; lp, Robert Loraine, Bramwell Fletcher, Ursula Jeans, Lewis Dayton

S.O.S. PERILS OF THE SEA (1925)
(6 r.) d, James P. Hogan; lp, Elaine Hammerstein, Robert Ellis, William Franey, Pat Harmon

SA GOSSE (1919, Fr.)
(? r.) d, Henri Desfontaines

SA TETE (1930, Fr.)
(? r.) d, Jean Epstein

SABA (1929, USSR)
(7 r.) d, Mikhail Chiaureli; lp, Sandro Djaliashvili, Veriko Andjaparidze, Eka Chavchavadze

SABLE BLESSING, THE (1916)
(5 r.) d, George L. Sargent; lp, Richard Bennett, Rhea Mitchell, Adrienne Morrison, Charles Newton

SABLES (1928, Fr.)
(? r.) d, Dimitri Kirsanoff; lp, Gina Manes, Van Daele, Nadia Sibirskaia

SACKCLOTH AND SCARLET (1925)
(7 r.) d, Henry King; lp, Alice Terry, Orville Caldwell, Dorothy Sebastian, Otto Matiesen

SACRED AND PROFANE LOVE (1921)
(6 r.) d, William Desmond Taylor; lp, Elsie Ferguson, Conrad Nagel, Thomas Holding, Helen Dunbar

SACRED FLAME, THE (1919)
(6 r.) d, Abraham S. Schomer; lp, Emily Stevens, Muriel Ostriche, Maud Hill, Violet Axzelle

SACRED RUBY, THE (1920)
(5 r.) d, Glenn Waite

SACRIFICE (1917)
(5 r.) d, Frank Reicher; lp, Margaret Illington, Jack Holt, Winter Hall, Noah Beery

SACRIFICE (1929, Brit.)
(7 r.) d, Victor Peers; lp, Andree Tourneur, G.H. Mulcaster, Lewis Dayton, Eveline Chipman

SADDLE CYCLONE (1925)
(5 r.) d, Richard Thorpe; lp, Buffalo Bill, Jr., Nell Brantley, Will Hertford, Norbert Myles

SADDLE HAWK, THE (1925)
(6 r.) d, Edward Sedgwick; lp, Hoot Gibson, Marion Nixon, G. Raymond Nye, Josie Sedgwick

SADDLE JUMPERS (1927)
(5 r.) d, Ben Wilson; lp, Dick Hatton

SADDLE KING, THE (1929)
(5 r.) d, Benjamin Franklin Wilson; lp, Cliff "Tex" Lyons, Neva Gerber, Al Ferguson, Glen Cook

SADDLE MATES (1928)
(5 r.) d, Richard Thorpe; lp, Wally Wales, Hank Bell, J. Gordon Russell, Peggy Montgomery

SADIE GOES TO HEAVEN (1917)
(5 r.) d, W.S. Van Dyke; lp, Mary McAllister, Jenny St. George, Russell McDermott, Frankie Raymond

SADIE LOVE (1920)
(5 r.) d, John S. Robertson; lp, Billie Burke, James L. Crane, Ida Waterman, Jed Prouty

SAFE FOR DEMOCRACY
(SEE: LIFE'S GREATEST PROBLEM, 1919)

SAFE GUARDED (1924)
(5 r.) lp, Neal Hart, Eva Novak, George Chesebro, Tommy Ryan

SAFETY CURTAIN, THE (1918)
(5 r.) d, Sidney A. Franklin; lp, Norma Talmadge, Eugene O'Brien, Anders Randolf, Gladden James

SAGA OF GOSTA BERLING, THE (1924, Swed.)
(10 r.) d, Mauritz Stiller; lp, Lars Hanson, Gerda Lundeqvist, Otto Elg-Lundberg, Greta Garbo

SAGE BRUSH HAMLET, A (1919)
(5 r.) d, Joseph J. Franz; lp, William Desmond, Marguerite de la Motte, Florence Gibson, Edward Peil

SAGE HEN, THE (1921)
(6 r.) d, Edgar Lewis; lp, Gladys Brockwell, Wallace MacDonald, Richard Headrick, Lillian Rich

SAGEBRUSH GOSPEL (1924)
(5 r.) d, Richard Hatton; lp, Neva Gerber, Harry von Meter, Richard Hatton, Nellie Franzen

SAGEBRUSH LADY, THE (1925)
(5 r.) d, Horace Davey, H.B. Carpenter; lp, Eileen Sedgwick, Bernie Corbett, Jack Richardson, Eddie Barry

SAGE-BRUSH LEAGUE, THE (1919)
(5 r.) d, Harry A. Gant; lp, Myrta Sterling

SAGEBRUSH TRAIL, THE (1922)
(5 r.) d, Robert T. Thornby; lp, Roy Stewart, Marjorie Daw, Johnny Walker, Wallace Beery

SAGEBRUSHER, THE (1920)
(7 r.) d, Edward Sloman; lp, Roy Stewart, Marguerite de la Motte, Noah Beery, Betty Brice

SAHARA LOVE (1926, Brit.)
(7 r.) d, Sinclair Hill; lp, Marie Colette, John Dehelly, Sybil Rhoda, Gordon Hopkirk

SAILOR TRAMP, A (1922, Brit.)
(6 r.) d, F. Martin Thornton; lp, Victor McLaglen, Pauline Johnson, Hugh E. Wright, Bertie Wright

SAILORS DON'T CARE (1928, Brit.)
(8 r.) d, W.P. Kellino; lp, Estelle Brody, John Stuart, Alf Goddard, Humberston Wright

SAILORS' WIVES (1928)
(6 r.) d, Joseph E. Henabery; lp, Mary Astor, Lloyd Hughes, Earle Foxe, Burr McIntosh

SAINT, DEVIL AND WOMAN (1916)
(5 r.) d, Frederick Sullivan; lp, Florence LaBadie, Wayne Arey, Hector Dion, Ethyle Cooke

SAINTLY SINNER, THE (1917)
(5 r.) d, Raymond B. Wells; lp, Ruth Stonehouse, Alida Hayman, Dorothy Drake, Jack Mulhall

SAINT'S ADVENTURE, THE (1917)
(5 r.) d, Arthur Berthelet; lp, Henry B. Walthall, Mary Charleson, Frankie Raymond, Bert Weston

SAINTS AND SINNERS (1916)
(5 r.) d, James Kirkwood; lp, Peggy Hyland, Albert Tavernier, Estar Banks, Clarence Handysides

SAJENKO THE SOVIET (1929, Ger.)
(6 r.) d, Eric Washneck; lp, Michael Bohnen, Susy Vernon, Walter Rilla, Henry Stuart

SALAMANDER, THE (1916)
(5 r.) lp, John Sainpolis, Ruth Findlay, Ada Boschell

SALAMMBO (1925, Fr.)
(? r.) d, Pierre Malodon

SALESLADY, THE (1916)
(5 r.) d, Frederick Thompson; lp, Hazel Dawn, Irving Cummings, Dorothy Rogers, Clarence Handysides

SALLY BISHOP (1916, Brit.)
(4 r.) d, George Pearson; lp, Aurele Sydney, Marjorie Villis, Peggy Hyland, Alice de Winton

SALLY BISHOP (1923, Brit.)
(7 r.) d, Maurice Elvey; lp, Marie Doro, Henry Ainley, Florence Turner, Sydney Fairbrother

SALLY CASTLETON, SOUTHERNER (1915)
(4 r.) d, Langdon West; lp, Marc MacDermott, Miriam Nesbitt

SALLY IN A HURRY (1917)
(5 r.) d, Wilfred North; lp, Lillian Walker, Don Cameron, Thomas Mills, William Shea

SALLY IN OUR ALLEY (1916, Brit.)
(5 r.) d, Larry Trimble; lp, Hilda Trevelyan, Reginald Owen, Mary Dibley

SALLY IN OUR ALLEY (1916)
(5 r.) d, Travers Vale; lp, Carlyle Blackwell, Muriel Ostriche, Pat Foy, Walter D. Greene

SALLY, IRENE AND MARY (1925)
(6 r.) d, Edmund Goulding; lp, Constance Bennett, Joan Crawford, Sally O'Neil, William Haines

SALLY SHOWS THE WAY
(SEE: ANNIE-FOR-SPITE, 1917)

SALLY'S SHOULDERS (1928)
(7 r.) d, Lynn Shores; lp, Lois Wilson, George Hackathorne, Huntley Gordon, Lucille Williams

SALOME (1919)
(7 r.) d, J. Gordon Edwards; lp, Theda Bara, G. Raymond Nye, Albert Roscoe, Bertram Grassby

SALOME (1923)
(6 r.) d, Malcolm Strauss; lp, Diana Allen, Vincent Coleman, Christine Winthrop

SALOME OF THE TENEMENTS (1925)
(7 r.) d, Sidney Olcott; lp, Jetta Goudal, Godfrey Tearle, Jose Ruben, Lazar Freed

SALT LAKE TRAIL (1926)
(5 r.) lp, George Kesterson, Dorothy Lee

SALT OF THE EARTH (1917)
(5 r.) d, Saul Harrison; lp, Russell Simpson, William Wadsworth, Peggy Adams, Chester Barnett

SALTY SAUNDERS (1923)
(5 r.) d, Neal Hart; lp, Neal Hart

SALVATION JOAN (1916)
(7 r.) d, Wilfred North; lp, Edna Mayo, Harry T. Morey, Dorothy Kelly, Donald Hall

SAM'S BOY (1922, Brit.)
(4 r.) d, Manning Hayes; lp, Johnny Butt, Tom Coventry, Bobbie Rudd, Charles Ashton

SAMSON (1915)
(5 r.) d, Edgar Lewis; lp, William Farnum, Maud Gilbert, Edgar L. Davenport, Agnes Everitt

SAMSON AND DELILAH (1922, Aust.)
(6 r.) d, Alexander Korda; lp, Maria Corda, Franz Herterich, Paul Lukas, Ernst Arndt

SAN FRANCISCO NIGHTS (1928)
(7 r.) d, Roy William Neill; lp, Percy Marmont, Mae Busch, Tom O'Brien, George Stone

SAND BLIND (1925)
(5 r.) d, Jacques Jaccard; lp, Ben Wilson

SANDRA (1924)
(8 r.) d, Arthur H. Sawyer; lp, Barbara La Marr, Bert Lytell, Leila Hyams, Augustin Sweeney

SANDS OF FATE (1914)
(? r.) d, Donald Crisp

SANDS OF SACRIFICE (1917)
(5 r.) d, Edward S. Sloman; lp, William Russell, Francelia Billington, George Periolat, John Gough

SANDS OF TIME, THE (1919, Brit.)
(6 r.) d, Randle Ayrton; lp, Mercy Hatton, Bertram Burleigh, Charles Groves, John Gliddon

SANDY (1918)
(5 r.) d, George Melford; lp, Jack Pickford, Louise Huff, James Neill, Edythe Chapman

SANDY BURKE OF THE U-BAR-U (1919)
(5 r.) d, Ira M. Lowry; lp, Louis Bennison, Virginia Lee, Alphonse Ethier, Herbert Horton

SANS FAMILLE (1925, Fr.)
(? r.) d, Georges Monca

SANTA FE PETE (1925)
(5 r.) d, Harry S. Webb; lp, Pete Morrison

SAP, THE (1926)
(6 r.) d, Erle Kenton; lp, Kenneth Harlan, Heinie Conklin, Mary McAllister, David Butler

SAPHO (1917)
(5 r.) d, Hugh Ford; lp, Pauline Frederick, Thomas Meighan, Frank Losee, John Sainpolis

SAPPHO (1913)
(6 r.) lp, Florence Roberts, Shelly Hull

SARATI-LE-TERRIBLE (1923, Fr.)
(? r.) d, Rene Hervil, Louis Mercanton

SATAN AND THE WOMAN (1928)
(7 r.) d, Burton King; lp, Claire Windsor, Cornelius Keefe, Vera Lewis, Thomas Holding

SATAN IN SABLES (1925)
(8 r.) d, James Flood; lp, Lowell Sherman, John Harron, Pauline Garon, Gertrude Astor

SATAN JUNIOR (1919)
(5 r.) d, Herbert Blache; lp, Viola Dana, Milton Sills, Lloyd Hughes, Alice Knowland

SATAN SANDERSON (1915)
(5 r.) d, J.W. Noble; lp, Orin Johnson, Irene Warfield

SATAN TOWN (1926)
(6 r.) d, Edmund Mortimer; lp, Harry Carey, Kathleen Collins, Charles Clary, Trilby Clark

SATAN TRIUMPHANT (1917, USSR)
(12 r.) d, Yakov Protazanov; lp, Ivan Mozhukhin, Natalia Lisenko, P. Pavlov, A. Chabrov

SATANAS (1919, Ger.)
(? r.) d, F.W. Murnau; lp, Conrad Veidt

SATAN'S PAWN
(SEE: DEVIL, THE, 1915)

SATAN'S PRIVATE DOOR (1917)
(5 r.) d, J. Charles Haydon; lp, Mary Charleson, Webster Campbell, John Cossar, Hazel Daly

SATIN GIRL, THE (1923)
(6 r.) d, Arthur Rosson; lp, Mabel Forrest, Norman Kerry, Marc MacDermott, Clarence Burton

SATIN WOMAN, THE (1927)
(7 r.) d, Walter Lang; lp, Mrs. Wallace Reid [Dorothy Davenport], Rockliffe Fellowes, Alice White

SAUCE FOR THE GOOSE (1918)
(5 r.) d, Walter Edwards; lp, Constance Talmadge, Harrison Ford, Harland Tucker, Vera Doria

SAVAGE, THE (1917)
(5 r.) d, Rupert Julian; lp, Ruth Clifford, Monroe Salisbury, Colleen Moore, Allen Sears

SAVAGE, THE (1926)
(5 r.) d, Fred Newmeyer; lp, Ben Lyon, May McAvoy, Tom Maguire, Philo McCullough

SAVAGE PASSIONS (1927)
(5 r.) lp, Alice Calhoun, Eddie Phillips, Lucy Beaumont

SAVAGE WOMAN, THE (1918)
(5 r.) d, Edmund Mortimer; lp, Clara Kimball Young, Milton Sills, Edward Kimball, Marcia Manon

SAVAGES OF THE SEA (1925)
(5 r.) d, Bruce Mitchell; lp, Frank Merrill, Melbourne MacDowell, Marguerite Snow, Danny Hoy

SAVED BY RADIO (1922)
(6 r.) d, William J. Craft; lp, George Larkin, William Gould, Jacqueline Logan, Harry Northrup

SAVED FROM THE HAREM (1915)
(4 r.) d, Wilbert Melville; lp, George Routh, Violet MacMillan, Melvin Mayo, Adelaide Bronti

SAVED FROM THE SEA (1920, Brit.)
(6 r.) d, W.P. Kellino; lp, Nora Swinburne, Philip Anthony, Cecil Calvert, Wallace Bosco

SAVVA (1919, USSR)
(4 r.) d, Cheslav Sabinsky

SAWDUST DOLL, THE (1919)
(5 r.) d, William Bertram; lp, Marie Osborne, Jack Connolly, Claire DuBrey, William Quinn

SAWDUST PARADISE, THE (1928)
(7 r.) d, Luther Reed; lp, Esther Ralston, Reed Howes, Hobart Bosworth, Tom Maguire

SAWDUST RING, THE (1917)
(5 r.) d, Paul Powell, Charles Miller; lp, Bessie Love, Harold Goodwin, Jack Richardson, Josephine Headley

SAY IT AGAIN (1926)
(8 r.) d, Gregory La Cava; lp, Richard Dix, Alyce Mills, Chester Conklin, "Gunboat" Smith

SAY IT WITH DIAMONDS (1927)
(7 r.) d, Jack Nelson; lp, Betty Compson, Earle Williams, Jocelyn Lee, Armand Kaliz

SAY IT WITH SABLES (1928)
(? r.) d, Frank Capra; lp, Francis X. Bushman, Helene Chadwick, Margaret Livingston, Arthur Rankin

SCALLYWAG, THE (1921, Brit.)
(4 r.) d, Challis Sanderson; lp, Fred Thatcher, Muriel Alexander, Ann Elliott, Hubert Carter

SCANDAL (1917)
(6 r.) d, Charles Giblyn; lp, Constance Talmadge, Harry C. Browne, J. Herbert Frank, Aimee Dalmores

SCANDAL? (1929, USSR)
(7 r.) d, Ivan L. Perestiany; lp, Lena Filkovskaya, Ivan Stalenin, S. Gubin, K. Yakevleva

SCANDAL IN PARIS (1929, Ger.)
(? r.) d, Robert Weine; lp, Lily Damita, Vladimir Gaidrow, Johannes Reimann, Arthur Pusey

SCANDAL MONGERS (1918)
(5 r.) d, Lois Weber, Phillips Smalley; lp, Lois Weber, Phillips Smalley, Rupert Julian, Adele Farrington

SCANDAL PROOF (1925)
(5 r.) d, Edmund Mortimer; lp, Shirley Mason, John Roche, Freeman Wood, Hazel Howell

SCANDAL STREET (1925)
(7 r.) d, Whitman Bennett; lp, Niles Welch, Madge Kennedy, Edwin August, Coit Albertson

SCANDALOUS TONGUES (1922)
(5 r.) d, Victor Schertzinger; lp, Enid Bennett, Fred Niblo

SCAR, THE (1919)
(5 r.) d, Frank Crane; lp, Kitty Gordon, Irving Cummings, Jennie Ellison, Eric Mayne

SCAR HANAN (1925)
(5 r.) d, Ben Wilson; lp, Yakima Canutt, Dorothy Woods, Helen Bruneau, Palmer Morrison

SCAR OF SHAME, THE (1927)
(8 r.) d, Frank Peregini; lp, Harry Henderson, Lucia Lynn Moses, Ann Kennedy, Norman Johnstone

SCARLET AND GOLD (1925)
(5 r.) d, Frank Grandon; lp, Al Ferguson, Lucille Du Bois, Frank Granville, Yvonne Pavis

SCARLET CAR, THE (1918)
(5 r.) d, Joseph De Grasse; lp, Franklyn Farnum, Edith Johnson, Al W. Filson, Lon Chaney

SCARLET CRYSTAL, THE (1917)
(5 r.) d, Charles Swickard; lp, Herbert Rawlinson, Betty Schade, Dorothy Davenport, Raymond Whitaker

SCARLET DAREDEVIL, THE (1928, Brit.)
(8 r.) d, T. Hayes Hunter; lp, Matheson Lang, Juliette Compton, Nelson Keys, Marjorie Hume

SCARLET DROP, THE (1918)
(5 r.) d, Jack [John] Ford; lp, Harry Carey, Molly Malone, Vester Pegg, Betty Schade

SCARLET HONEYMOON, THE (1925)
(5 r.) d, Alan Hale; lp, Shirley Mason, Pierre Gendron, Allan Sears, J. Farrell MacDonald

SCARLET KISS, THE (1920, Brit.)
(5 r.) d, Fred Goodwins; lp, Marjorie Hume, Cyril Raymond, Maud Cressall, Philip Hewland

SCARLET LADY, THE (1922, Brit.)
(6 r.) d, Walter West; lp, Violet Hopson, Lewis Willoughby, Cameron Carr, Arthur Walcott

SCARLET LETTER, THE (1917)
(5 r.) d, Carl Harbaugh; lp, Mary Martin, Stuart Holmes, Kittens Reichert, Dan Mason

SCARLET OATH, THE (1916)
(5 r.) d, Frank Powell, Travers Vale; lp, Gail Kane, Philip Hahn, Carleton Macey, Lillian Paige

SCARLET PIMPERNEL, THE (1917)
(5 r.) d, Richard Stanton; lp, Dustin Farnum, Winifred Kingston, William Burress, Bertram Grassby

SCARLET ROAD, THE (1918)
(5 r.) d, Edward J. LeSaint; lp, Gladys Brockwell, L.C. Shumway, Betty Schade, Charles Clary

SCARLET SAINT (1925)
(7 r.) d, George Archainbaud; lp, Mary Astor, Lloyd Hughes, Frank Morgan, Jed Prouty

SCARLET SHADOW, THE (1919)
(6 r.) d, Robert Z. Leonard; lp, Mae Murray, Martha Mattox, Frank Elliott, Ralph Graves

SCARLET TRAIL, THE (1919)
(5 r.) d, John S. Lawrence; lp, Beth Ivins, Vincent Coleman, Margaret Blanc, John Costello

SCARLET WEST, THE (1925)
(9 r.) d, John G. Adolphi; lp, Robert Frazer, Clara Bow, Robert Edeson, Johnny Walker

SCARLET WOMAN, THE (1916)
(6 r.) d, Edward Lawrence; lp, Olga Petrova, Edward Martindel, Arthur Hoops, Eugene O'Brien

SCARLET WOOING, THE (1920, Brit.)
(5 r.) d, Sidney Morgan; lp, Eve Balfour, George Keene, Marguerite Blanche, Joan Morgan

SCARLET YOUTH (1928)
(7 r.) d, William Hughes Curran; lp, Corliss Palmer, David Findlay, Alphonse Martell, Connie La Mont

SCARRED HANDS (1923)
(5 r.) d, Cliff Smith; lp, Cliff Smith, Eileen Sedgwick

SCARS OF HATE (1923)
(5 r.) d, H.G. Moody; lp, Jack Livingston

SCHEMERS, THE (1922)
(? r.)

SCOFFER, THE (1920)
(7 r.) d, Allan Dwan; lp, James Kirkwood, Mary Thurman, Rhea Mitchell, John Burton

SCHOOL FOR HUSBANDS, A (1917)
(5 r.) d, George Melford; lp, Fannie Ward, Jack Dean, Frank Elliott, Mabel Van Buren

SCHOOL FOR SCANDAL, THE (1914)
(4 r.) d, Kenean Buel; lp, Alice Joyce, James B. Ross, Guy Coombs, Mary Ross

SCHOOL FOR SCANDAL, THE (1923, Brit.)
(6 r.) d, Bertram Phillips; lp, Queenie Thomas, Frank Stanmore, Basil Rathbone, John Stuart

SCHOOL FOR WIVES (1925)
(7 r.) d, Victor Hugo Halperin; lp, Conway Tearle, Sigrid Holmquist, Peggy Kelly, Arthur Donaldson

SCORCHER, THE (1927)
(5 r.) d, Harry J. Brown; lp, Reed Howes, Hank Mann, Harry Allen, Ernest Hilliard

SCORPION'S STING, THE (1915, Brit.)
(4 r.) d, Percy Nash; lp, George Bellamy, Fay Temple, Gregory Scott, Douglas Payne

SCOURGE, THE
(SEE: FORTUNE'S FOOL, 1922, Brit.)

SCRAGS (1930, Brit.)
(6 r.) d, Challis Sanderson; lp, Eric Hales, Bobbie Bradshaw, Augusto Sandoni

SCRAMBLED WIVES (1921)
(7 r.) d, Edward H. Griffith; lp, Marguerite Clark, Leon P. Gendron, Ralph Bunker, Florence Martin

SCRAP IRON (1921)
(7 r.) d, Charles Ray; lp, Charles Ray, Lydia Knott, Vera Steadman, Tom Wilson

SCRAP OF PAPER, THE (1920)
(5 r.) d, Tom Collins; lp, Glen White, William Fredericks, Jane McAlpine, Joseph Striker

SCRAPPIN' KID, THE (1926)
(5 r.) d, Clifford S. Smith; lp, Art Acord, Velma Connor, Jimsy Boudwin, C.E. Anderson

SCRATCH MY BACK (1920)
(6 r.) d, Sidney Olcott; lp, Helene Chadwick, T. Roy Barnes, Lloyd T. Whitlock, Cesare Gravina

SCREAM IN THE NIGHT, A (1919)
(6 r.) d, Burton King, Leander De Cordova; lp, Ruth Budd, Ralph Kellard, Edna Britton, John Webb Dillon

SCULPTOR'S DREAM (1929)
(5 r.) lp, Paul Tellegan

SCUTTLERS, THE (1920)
(6 r.) d, J. Gordon Edwards; lp, William Farnum, Jackie Saunders, Herschal Mayall, G. Raymond Nye

SEA FEVER
(SEE: EN RADE, 1929, Fr.)

SEA FLOWER, THE (1918)
(5 r.) d, Colin Campbell; lp, Juanita Hansen, Alfred Whitman, Fred Huntley, Alfred Allen

SEA HAWK, THE (1924)
(12 r.) d, Frank Lloyd; lp, Milton Sills, Enid Bennett, Lloyd Hughes, Wallace MacDonald

SEA MASTER, THE (1917)
(5 r.) d, Edward S. Sloman; lp, William Russell, Francelia Billington, Joe King, George Ahearn

SEA PANTHER, THE (1918)
(5 r.) d, Thomas N. Heffron; lp, William Desmond, Mary Warren, Jack Richardson, Arthur Millett

SEA PROWLERS
(SEE: PROWLERS OF THE SEA, 1928)

SEA RIDER, THE (1920)
(5 r.) d, Edwin L. Hollywood; lp, Harry T. Morey, Webster Campbell, Van Dyke Brooke, Alice Calhoun

SEA URCHIN, THE (1926, Brit.)
(7 r.) d, Graham Cutts; lp, Betty Balfour, George Hackathorne, W. Cronin Wilson, Haidee Wright

SEA WAIF, THE (1918)
(5 r.) d, Frank Reicher; lp, Louise Huff, John Bowers, Anthony Merlo, Henry Warwick

SEA WOLF, THE (1920)
(7 r.) d, George Melford; lp, Noah Beery, Mabel Julienne Scott, Tom Forman, Raymond Hatton

SEA WOLF, THE (1926)
(7 r.) d, Ralph Ince; lp, Ralph Ince, Claire Adams, Theodore von Eltz, Snitz Edwards

SEA WOMEN, THE
(SEE: WHY WOMEN LOVE, 1925)

SEAL OF SILENCE, THE (1918)
(5 r.) d, Tom Mills; lp, Earle Williams, Grace Darmond, Kate Price, Kathleen Kirkham

SEALED ENVELOPE, THE (1919)
(5 r.) d, Douglas Gerrard; lp, Fritzi Brunette, William Sheer, Joseph Girard, Charles Dorian

SEALED HEARTS (1919)
(5 r.) d, Ralph Ince; lp, Eugene O'Brien, Robert Edeson, Lucille Lee Stewart, John Dean

SEALED LIPS (1925)
(6 r.) d, Antonio Gaudio; lp, Dorothy Revier, Cullen Landis, Lincoln Stedman, Scott Turner

SECLUDED ROADHOUSE, THE (1926)
(5 r.) lp, William Barrymore

SECOND HONEYMOON (1930)
(6 r.) d, Phil Rosen; lp, Josephine Dunn, Edward Earle, Ernest Hilliard, Bernice Elliott

SECOND MATE, THE (1929, Brit.)
(4 r.) d, J. Steven Edwards; lp, David Dunbar, Cecil Barry, Lorna Duveen, Eric Hales

SECOND MRS. TANQUERAY, THE (1916, Brit.)
(6 r.) d, Fred Paul; lp, Sir George Alexander, Hilda Moore, Norman Forbes, Marie Hemingway

SECOND TO NONE (1926, Brit.)
(8 r.) d, Jack Raymond; lp, Moore Marriott, Ian Fleming, Benita Hume, Micky Brantford

SECRET CODE, THE (1918)
(5 r.) d, Albert Parker; lp, Gloria Swanson, J. Barney Sherry, Rhy Alexander, Leslie Stewart

SECRET GARDEN, THE (1919)
(5 r.) d, G. Butler Clonebaugh; lp, Lila Lee, Dick Rosson, Spottiswoode Aitken, Clarence Geldart

SECRET GIFT, THE (1920)
(5 r.) d, Harry L. Franklin; lp, Lee Kohlmar, Rudolph Christians, Doris Baker, Gladys Walton

SECRET KINGDOM, THE
(SEE: BEYOND THE VEIL, 1929, Brit.)

SECRET MAN, THE (1917)
(5 r.) d, Jack [John] Ford; lp, Harry Carey, Edith Sterling, J. Morris Foster, Vester Pegg

SECRET MARRIAGE (1919)
(6 r.) lp, Mary MacLaren

SECRET OF BLACK CANYON, THE (1925)
(5 r.) d, Ward Hayes; lp, Dick Hatton

SECRET OF BLACK MOUNTAIN, THE (1917)
(4 r.) d, Otto Hoffman; lp, Vola Vale, Philo McCullough, Charles Dudley, George Austin

SECRET OF EVE, THE (1917)
(5 r.) d, Perry N. Vekroff; lp, Olga Petrova, Arthur Hoops, William Hinckley, Edward Roseman

SECRET OF THE DESERT (1916, Nor.)
(4 r.)

SECRET OF THE MOOR, THE (1919, Brit.)
(5 r.) d, Lewis Willoughby; lp, Gwen Williams, Philip Hewland, Henry Thompson, Edgar W. Hylton

SECRET OF THE MOUNTAIN, THE (1914)
(4 r.)

SECRET OF THE PUEBLO, THE (1923)
(5 r.) d, Neal Hart; lp, Neal Hart, Hazel Deane, Tom Grimes, Monte Montague

SECRET OF THE STORM COUNTRY, THE (1917)
(5 r.) d, Charles Miller; lp, Norma Talmadge, Herbert Frank, Niles Welch, W.W. Black

SECRET OF THE SWAMP, THE (1916)
(5 r.) d, Lynn F. Reynolds; lp, Myrtle Gonzales, Val Paul, George Hernandez, Fred Church

SECRET ORDERS (1926)
(6 r.) d, Chet Withey; lp, Harold Goodwin, Robert Frazer, Evelyn Brent, John Gough

SECRET ROOM, THE (1915)
(? r.) d, Tom Moore; lp, Tom Moore, Marguerite Courtot, Robert Ellis, Ethel Clifton

SECRET SERVICE (1919)
(6 r.) d, Hugh Ford; lp, Robert Warwick, Wanda Hawley, Theodore Roberts, Edythe Chapman

SECRET SEVEN, THE (1915, Brit.)
(4 r.) d, Charles Calvert; lp, Charles Vane, Lionel d'Aragon

SECRET SORROW (1921)
(6 r.) lp, George Edward Brown, Percy Verwayen, Edna Morton, Lawrence Chenault

SECRET STRINGS (1918)
(5 r.) d, John Ince; lp, Olive Tell, Hugh Thompson, William J. Kelly, John Daly Murphy

SECRET STUDIO, THE (1927)
(6 r.) d, Victor Schertzinger; lp, Olive Borden, Clifford Holland, Noreen Phillips, Ben Bard

SECRET WOMAN, THE (1918, Brit.)
(6 r.) d, A.E. Coleby; lp, Maud Yates, Janet Alexander, Henry Victor, A.E. Coleby

SECRETARY OF FRIVOLOUS AFFAIRS, THE (1915)
(4 r.) d, Thomas Ricketts; lp, Harold Lockwood, May Allison, Hal Clements, Carol Holloway

SECRETS (1924)
(8 r.) d, Frank Borzage; lp, Norma Talmadge, Eugene O'Brien, Harvey Clark, Patterson Dial

SECRETS OF A SOUL (1925, Ger.)
(? r.) d, G.W. Pabst; lp, Werner Krauss, Jack Trevor, Ruth Weyher, Ilka Gruning

SECRETS OF THE NIGHT (1925)
(7 r.) d, Herbert Blache; lp, James Kirkwood, Madge Bellamy, Tom Ricketts, Tom S. Guise

SECRETS OF THE ORIENT (1932, Ger.)
(5 r.) d, Alexander Wolkoff; lp, Dita Parlo, Nikelai Kolin, Marcella Albani, Ivan Petrovich

SECRETS OF THE RANGE (1928)
(5 r.) d, Robert J. Horner; lp, Montana Bill, Betty Gates, Bud Osborne, Carl Berlin

SEE MY LAWYER (1921)
(6 r.) d, Al Christie; lp, T. Roy Barnes, Grace Darmond, Lloyd Whitlock, Jean Acker

SEE YOU IN JAIL (1927)
(6 r.) d, Joseph Henabery; lp, Jack Mulhall, Alice Day, Mack Swain, George Fawcett

SEE YOU LATER (1928)
(5 r.) lp, Earl Douglas, Barbara Luddy

SEEDS OF FREEDOM (1929, USSR)
(6 r.) d, Grigori Roshal; lp, Leonid Leonidov, J. Untershlak, Tamara Adelheim, M. Sinelnikova

SEEDS OF VENGEANCE (1920)
(5 r.) d, Ollie O. Sellers; lp, Bernard Durning, Gloria Hope, Eugenie Besserer, Jack Curtis

SEEING IT THROUGH (1920)
(5 r.) d, Claude H. Mitchell; lp, ZaSu Pitts, Henry Woodward, Edwin Stevens, W.H. Bainbridge

SEEKERS, THE (1916)
(5 r.) d, Otis Turner; lp, Flora Parker De Haven, Paul Byron, Charles Mailes, Edward Hearn

SELF MADE WIDOW (1917)
(5 r.) d, Travers Vale; lp, Alice Brady, John Bowers, Curtis Cooksey, Justine Cutting

SELF STARTER, THE (1926)
(5 r.) d, Harry J. Brown; lp, Reed Howes, Mildred Harris, Sheldon Lewis

SELFISH WOMAN, THE (1916)
(5 r.) d, E. Mason Hopper; lp, Wallace Reid, Cleo Ridgely, Joseph King, Charles Arling

SELFISH YATES (1918)
(5 r.) d, William S. Hart; lp, William S. Hart, Jane Novak, Bert Sprotte, Harry Dunkinson

SELF-MADE FAILURE, A (1924)
(8 r.) d, William Beaudine; lp, Ben Alexander, Lloyd Hamilton, Matt Moore, Patsy Ruth Miller

SELF-MADE MAN, A (1922)
(5 r.) d, Rowland V. Lee; lp, William Russell, Renee Adoree, Mathilde Brundage, James Gordon

SELF-MADE WIFE, THE (1923)
(5 r.) d, Jack Dillon; lp, Ethel Grey Terry, Crauford Kent, Virginia Ainsworth, Phillips Smalley

SELL 'EM COWBOY (1924)
(5 r.) d, Ward Hayes; lp, Ed Lytell, Dick Hatton, Winona Wilkes, Martin Turner

SEN YAN'S DEVOTION (1924, Brit.)
(6 r.) d, A.E. Coleby; lp, Sessue Hayakawa, Tsuru Aoki, Fred Raynham, H. Agar Lyons

SENOR DAREDEVIL (1926)
(7 r.) d, Albert Rogell; lp, Ken Maynard, Dorothy Devore, George Nichols, Josef Swickard

SENORITA (1927)
(7 r.) d, Clarence Badger; lp, Bebe Daniels, James Hall, William Powell, Josef Swickard

SENTIMENTAL TOMMY (1921)
(8 r.) d, John S. Robertson; lp, Gareth Hughes, May McAvoy, Mabel Taliaferro, George Fawcett

SEQUEL TO THE DIAMOND FROM THE SKY (1916)
(8 r.) d, Edward Sloman; lp, William Russell, Charlotte Burton, Rhea Mitchell, William Tedmarsh

SERENADE (1921)
(7 r.) d, Raoul Walsh; lp, Miriam Cooper, George Walsh, Rosita Marstini, James A. Marcus

SERENADE (1927)
(6 r.) d, Harry D'Abbadie; lp, Adolphe Menjou, Kathryn Carver, Lawrence Grant, Lina Basquette

SERGE PANIN (1922, Fr.)
(? r.) d, Charles Maudru, Charles de Marsan

SERPENT'S TOOTH, THE (1917)
(5 r.) d, Rollin S. Sturgeon; lp, Gail Kane, William Conklin, Jane Pascal, Edward Peil

SERVANT IN THE HOUSE, THE (1920)
(8 r.) d, Jack [Hugh Ryan] Conway; lp, Jean Hearsholt, Jack Curtis, Claire Anderson, Clara Horton

SERVANT QUESTION, THE (1920)
(5 r.) d, Dell Henderson; lp, William Collier, Virginia Lee

SERVICE FOR LADIES (1927)
(7 r.) d, Harry D'Arrast; lp, Adolphe Menjou, Kathryn Carver, Charles Lane, Lawrence Grant

SERVICE STAR, THE (1918)
(6 r.) d, Charles Miller; lp, Madge Kennedy, Clarence Oliver, Tammany Young, Maude Turner Gordon

SERVING TWO MASTERS (1921)
(5 r.) lp, Josephine Earle, Dalas Anderson, Pat Somerset, Zoe Palmer

SET FREE (1918)
(5 r.) d, Tod Browning; lp, Edith Roberts, Harry Hilliard, Harold Goodwin, Molly McConnell

SET FREE (1927)
(5 r.) d, Arthur Rosson; lp, Art Acord, Olive Hasbrouck, Claude Payton, Robert McKenzie

SETTLED OUT OF COURT (1925, Brit.)
(9 r.) d, George A. Cooper; lp, Fay Compton, Jack Buchanan, Jeanne de Casalis, Leon Quartermaine

SET-UP, THE (1926)
(5 r.) d, Clifford S. Smith; lp, Art Acord, Alta Allen, Albert Schaeffer, Thomas G. Lingham

SEVEN DAYS (1925)
(7 r.) d, Scott Sidney; lp, Lillian Rich, Creighton Hale, Lilyan Tashman, Mabel Julienne Scott

SEVEN FOOTPRINTS TO SATAN (1929)
(5 r.) d, Benjamin Christensen; lp, Thelma Todd, Creighton Hale, Sheldon Lewis, William V. Mong

SEVEN KEYS TO BALDPATE (1917)
(6 r.) d, Hugh Ford; lp, George M. Cohan, Anna Q. Nilsson, Elda Furry [Hedda Hopper], Corene Uzzell

SEVEN KEYS TO BALDPATE (1925)
(7 r.) d, Fred Newmeyer; lp, Douglas MacLean, Edith Roberts, Anders Randolf, Crauford Kent

SEVEN SINNERS (1925)
(7 r.) d, Lewis Milestone; lp, Marie Prevost, Clive Brook, John Patrick, Charles Conklin

SEVEN SWANS, THE (1918)
(5 r.) d, J. Searle Dawley; lp, Marguerite Clark, Richard Barthelmess, William Danforth, Augusta Anderson

SEVEN YEARS BAD LUCK (1921)
(5 r.) d, Max Linder; lp, Max Linder, Thelma Percy, Alta Allen, Betty Peterson

SEVENTEEN (1916)
(5 r.) d, Robert G. Vignola; lp, Louise Huff, Jack Pickford, Winifred Allen, Madge Evans

SEVENTH BANDIT, THE (1926)
(6 r.) d, Scott R. Dunlap; lp, Harry Carey, James Morrison, Harriet Hammond, John Webb Dillon

SEVENTH NOON, THE (1915)
(5 r.) lp, Ernest Glendinning, Winifred Kingston, George Le Guere, Everett Butterfield

SEVENTH SIN, THE (1917)
(7 r.) d, Theodore Marston; lp, George Le Guere, Ann Murdock, Holbrook Blinn, Shirley Mason

SEX LURE, THE (1916)
(6 r.) d, Ivan Abramson; lp, James Morrison, Louise Vale, Frankie Mann, Donald Hall

SEX MADNESS (1929)
(6 r.) lp, Jack Richardson, Corliss Palmer

SHACKLED (1918)
(5 r.) d, Reginald Barker, Wallace Worsley; lp, Louise Glaum, Jack Gilbert, W. Lawson Butt, Charles West

SHACKLED BY FILM (1918, USSR)
(5 r.) d, Nikandr Turkin; lp, Vladimir Mayakovsky, Lily Brik, Margerita Kibalchich, A. Rebikova

SHACKLED LIGHTING (1925)
(5 r.) lp, Frank Merrill

SHACKLES OF FEAR (1924)
(5 r.) d, Al Ferguson; lp, Al Ferguson, Pauline Curley, Fred Dayton, Les Bates

SHACKLES OF TRUTH (1917)
(5 r.) d, Edward Sloman; lp, William Russell, Francelia Billington, Alfred Vosburgh, Adda Gleason

SHADOW, THE (1916)
(5 r.)

SHADOW, THE (1921)
(5 r.) d, J. Charles Davis, Jack W. Brown; lp, Muriel Ostriche, Walter Miller, Harold Foshay, Helen Courtenay

SHADOW, THE (1921)
(7 r.)

SHADOW BETWEEN, THE (1920, Brit.)
(5 r.) d, George Dewhurst; lp, Doris Lloyd, Lewis Dayton, Sir Simeon Stuart, Cherry Winter

SHADOW OF DOUBT, THE (1916)
(5 r.) d, Ray Physioc; lp, Carlyle Blackwell, Jean Shelby, George Anderson, Lillian Allen

SHADOW OF EVIL (1921, Brit.)
(6 r.) d, James Reardon; lp, Cecil Humphreys, Mary Dibley, Reginald Fox, Gladys Mason

SHADOW OF LIGHTING RIDGE, THE (1921)
(5 r.) d, Wilfred Lucas; lp, Snowy Baker, Wilfred Lucas, Brownie Vernon

SHADOW OF NIGHT, THE
(SEE: MODERN OTHELLO, A, 1917)

SHADOW OF ROSALIE BYRNES, THE (1920)
(5 r.) d, George Archainbaud; lp, Elaine Hammerstein, Edward Langford, Anita Booth, Alfred Hickman

SHADOW OF THE DESERT
(SEE: SHADOW OF THE EAST, 1924)

SHADOW OF THE EAST, THE (1924)
(6 r.) d, George Archainbaud; lp, Frank Mayo, Mildred Harris, Norman Kerry, Bertram Grassby

SHADOW OF THE LAW, THE (1926)
(5 r.) d, Wallace Worsley; lp, Clara Bow, Forrest Stanley, Stuart Holmes, Ralph Lewis

SHADOW ON THE WALL, THE (1925)
(6 r.) d, Reeves Eason; lp, Eileen Percy, Creighton Hale, William V. Mong, Dale Fuller

SHADOW RANGER (1926)
(5 r.) lp, George Kesterson

SHADOWS (1915, Brit.)
(4 r.) d, Harold Weston; lp, Fay Temple, Henry Hargreaves, Ivy Clemow, A.V. Bramble

SHADOWS (1919)
(6 r.) d, Reginald Barker; lp, Geraldine Farrar, Milton Sills, Tom Santschi, Fred Truesdell

SHADOWS AND SUNSHINE (1916)
(5 r.) d, Henry King; lp, Marie Osborne, Henry King, Daniel Gilfether, Lucy Payton

SHADOWS FROM THE PAST (1915)
(4 r.) d, Richard Ridgely; lp, Marc MacDermott, Bigelow Cooper, Mabel Trunnelle, Nellie Grant

SHADOWS OF CHINATOWN (1926)
(5 r.) d, Paul Hurst; lp, Kenneth McDonald, Velma Edele, Elmer Dewey, Ben Corbett

SHADOWS OF FEAR
(SEE: THERESE RAQUIN, 1928)

SHADOWS OF PARIS (1924)
(7 r.) d, Herbert Brenon; lp, Pola Negri, Charles De Roche, Huntley Gordon, Adolphe Menjou

SHADOWS OF SUSPICION (1919)
(5 r.) d, Edwin Carewe; lp, Harold Lockwood, Naomi Childers, Helen Lindroth, Kenneth Kealing

SHADOWS OF THE MOULIN ROUGE, THE (1914)
(4 r.) d, Alice Blache

SHADOWS OF THE NORTH (1923)
(5 r.) d, Robert F. Hill; lp, William Desmond, Virginia Brown Faire, Fred Kohler, William Welsh

SHADOWS OF THE PAST (1919)
(5 r.) d, Ralph Ince; lp, Anita Stewart, Harry T. Morey, Rose Tapley, E.K. Lincoln

SHADOWS OF THE WEST (1921)
(8 r.) d, Paul Hurst; lp, Pat O'Brien, Hedda Nova, Virginia Dale, Seymour Zeliff

SHADOWS OF YOSHIWARA, THE
(SEE: CROSSWAYS, 1928, Jap.)

SHALL WE FORGIVE HER? (1917)
(5 r.) d, Arthur Ashley; lp, June Elvidge, Arthur Ashley, John Bowers, Charles Charles

SHAME (1918)
(7 r.) d, John W. Noble; lp, Zena Keefe, Niles Welch, Fred Stall, Lionel Belmore

SHAMEFUL BEHAVIOR? (1926)
(6 r.) d, Albert Kelley; lp, Edith Roberts, Richard Tucker, Martha Mattox, Harland Tucker

SHAMROCK AND THE ROSE, THE (1927)
(7 r.) d, Jack Nelson; lp, Mack Swain, Olive Hasbrouck, Edmund Burns, Maurice Costello

SHAMROCK HANDICAP, THE (1926)
(6 r.) d, John Ford; lp, Janet Gaynor, Leslie Fenton, J. Farrell MacDonald, Louis Payne

SHANGHAI BOUND (1927)
(6 r.) d, Luther Reed; lp, Richard Dix, Mary Brian, Charles Byer, George Irving

SHANGHAI DOCUMENT, A (1929, USSR)
(6 r.) d, Yakov Blyokh

SHANGHAI ROSE (1929)
(7 r.) d, Scott Pembroke; lp, Irene Rich, William Conklin, Richard Walling, Ruth Hiatt

SHANGHAIED (1927)
(6 r.) d, Ralph Ince; lp, Ralph Ince, Patsy Ruth Miller, Alan Brooks, Gertrude Astor

SHANNON OF THE SIXTH (1914)
(5 r.) d, George Melford; lp, Douglas Gerrard

SHARE AND SHARE ALIKE (1925)
(6 r.) d, Whitman Bennett; lp, Jane Novak, James Rennie, Henry Sands, Cortland Van Deusen

SHARK, THE (1920)
(5 r.) d, Dell Henderson; lp, George Walsh, Mary Hall, Robert Broderick, William G. Nally

SHARK MONROE (1918)
(5 r.) d, William S. Hart; lp, William S. Hart, Katherine MacDonald, Joe Singleton, Berthold Sprotte

SHATTERED DREAMS (1922)
(5 r.) d, Paul Scardon; lp, Miss Du Pont [Patricia Hannon], Bertram Grassby, Herbert Heyes

SHATTERED FAITH (1923)
(6 r.) d, Jesse J. Ormont; lp, Lillian Kemble, Rudolph Cameron, J. Frank Glendon

SHATTERED IDYLL, A (1916, Brit.)
(5 r.) d, Dave Aylott; lp, Peggy Mills, Peter Lewis, Dorothy Dare, Martin Herbert

SHATTERED LIVES (1925)
(6 r.) d, Henry McCarty; lp, Edith Roberts, Robert Gordon, Ethel Wales, Eddie Phillips

SHE (1916, Brit.)
(5 r.) d, Will Barker, H. Lisle Locoque; lp, Alice Delysia, Henry Victor, Sydney Bland, Blanche Forsythe

SHE (1917)
(5 r.) d, Kenean Buel; lp, Valeska Suratt, Ben L. Taggart, Miriam Feuche, Tom Burrough

SHE (1925, Brit.)
(4 r.) d, Leander De Cordova; lp, Betty Blythe, Carlyle Balckwell, Marjorie Statler, Henry George

SHE COULDN'T HELP IT (1921)
(5 r.) lp, Bebe Daniels, Emory Johnson, Wade Boteler, Vera Lewis

SHE DEVIL, THE (1918)
(6 r.) d, J. Gordon Edwards; lp, Theda Bara, Albert Roscoe, Frederick Bond, George A. McDaniel

SHE HIRED A HUSBAND (1919)
(5 r.) d, Jack Dillon; lp, Priscilla Dean, Pat O'Malley, Marian Skinner, Frederick Vroom

SHE LEFT WITHOUT HER TRUNKS (1916)
(4 r.) d, Tefft Johnson; lp, Margaret Loomis, Frank Brownlee

SHE STOOPS TO CONQUER (1914, Brit.)
(4 r.) d, George Loane Tucker; lp, Henry Ainley, Jane Gail, Gregory Scott, Charles Rock

SHE WOLVES (1925)
(6 r.) d, Maurice Elvey; lp, Alma Rubens, Jack Mulhall, Bertram Grassby, Harry Myers

SHEBA (1919, Brit.)
(5 r.) d, Cecil M. Hepworth; lp, Alma Taylor, Gerald Ames, James Carew, Lionelle Howard

SHEEP TRAIL (1926)
(5 r.) d, Harry L. Fraser; lp, Gordon Clifford, Charlotte Pierce

SHEIK OF ARABY, THE (1922)
(5 r.)

SHEIK OF MOJAVE, THE (1928)
(5 r.) lp, Cheyenne Bill

SHEIK'S WIFE, THE
(SEE: VISAGES VOILES...AMES CLOSES, 1921)

SHELL FORTY-THREE (1916)
(5 r.) d, Reginald Barker; lp, H.B. Warner, Enid Markey, Jack [John] Gilbert, George Fisher

SHELL GAME, THE (1918)
(5 r.) d, George D. Baker; lp, Emmy Wehlen, Henry Kolker, Joseph Kilgour, Fanny Cogan

SHELL SHOCKED SAMMY (1923)
(5 r.) d, Frank S. Mattison; lp, Matty Mattison, Mary Anderson, Vivian Rich, Leonard Clapham

SHELTERED DAUGHTERS (1921)
(5 r.) d, Edward Dillon; lp, Justine Johnstone, Riley Hatch, Warner Baxter, Charles Gerard

SHEPHERD KING, THE (1923)
(9 r.) d, J. Gordon Edwards; lp, Violet Mersereau, Edy Darclea, Virginia Lucchetti, Nero Bernardi

SHEPHERD LASSIE OF ARGYLE, THE (1914, Brit.)
(4 r.) d, Larry Trimble; lp, Florence Turner, Rex Davis, Hector Dion, Clifford Pembroke

SHEPHERD OF THE HILLS, THE (1920)
(9 r.) d, Harold Bell Wright; lp, Harry Lonsdale, Catherine Curtis, George McDaniel, Dan Bailey

SHEPHERD OF THE HILLS, THE (1928)
(9 r.) d, Albert Rogell; lp, Alec B. Francis, Molly O'Day, John Boles, Matthew Betz

SHERIFF OF HOPE ETERNAL, THE (1921)
(5 r.) d, Ben Wilson; lp, Jack Hoxie, Marin Sais, Joseph Girard, William Dyer

SHERIFF OF SUN-DOG, THE (1922)
(5 r.) d, Ben Wilson; lp, William Fairbanks, Robert McKenzie, Jim Welch, Florence Gilbert

SHERIFF'S GIRL (1926)
(5 r.) d, Ben Wilson; lp, Fang (a dog), Ben Wilson

SHERIFF'S LASH, THE (1929)
(5 r.) d, Cliff "Tex" Lyons

SHERIFF'S LONE HAND, THE
(SEE: THE COWBOY AND THE FLAPPER, 1924)

SHERIFF'S SON, THE (1919)
(5 r.) d, Victor L. Schertzinger; lp, Charles Ray, Seena Owen, John P. Lockney, Clyde Benson

SHERLOCK HOLMES (1916)
(7 r.) d, Arthur Berthelet; lp, William Gilette, Marjorie Kay, Ernest Maupain, Edward Fielding

SHERRY (1920)
(7 r.) d, Edgar Lewis; lp, Pat O'Malley, Lillian Hall, Harry Spingler, Maggie Halloway

SHE'S MY BABY (1927)
(6 r.) d, Fred Windemere; lp, Robert Agnew, Kathleen Myers, Earle Williams, Grace Carlyle

SHIELD OF SILENCE, THE (1925)
(5 r.) d, Leo Maloney; lp, Leo Maloney, Josephine Hill, Leonard Clapham, Ray Walters

SHIFTING SANDS (1918)
(5 r.) d, Albert Parker; lp, Gloria Swanson, Joe King, Harvey Clark, Leone Carton

SHIFTING SANDS (1922, Brit.)
(7 r.) d, Fred Leroy Granville; lp, Peggy Hyland, Lewis Willoughby, Valia, Gibson Gowland

SHINE GIRL, THE (1916)
(5 r.) d, William Parke; lp, Gladys Hulette, Wayne Arey, Ethelmary Oakland, Warren Cook

SHINING ADVENTURE, THE (1925)
(6 r.) d, Hugo Ballin; lp, Percy Marmont, Mabel Ballin, Ben Alexander, B. Wayne Lamont

SHIP COMES IN, A (1928)
(7 r.) d, William K. Howard; lp, Rudolph Schildkraut, Louise Dresser, Milton Holmes, Linda Landi

SHIP OF DOOM, THE (1917)
(5 r.) d, Wyndham Gittens; lp, Monte Blue, Claire McDowell, Arthur Millett, Aaron Edwards

SHIP OF LOST MEN, THE (1929, Ger.)
(? r.) d, Maurice Tourneur; lp, Fritz Kortner, Marlene Dietrich, Gaston Modot, Robin Irvine

SHIP OF SOULS (1925)
(6 r.) d, Charles Miller; lp, Bert Lytell, Lillian Rich, Gertrude Astor, Earl Metcalf

SHIPS OF THE NIGHT (1928)
(6 r.) d, Duke Worne; lp, Jacqueline Logan, Sojin, Jack Mower, Andy Clyde

SHIPWRECKED (1926)
(6 r.) d, Joseph Henabery; lp, Seena Owen, Joseph Schildkraut, Matthew Betz, Clarence Burton

SHIRAZ (1929)
(8 r.) d, F. Osten, V. Peers; lp, Himansu Rai, Enakshi, Rama Rau, Charu Roy

SHIRLEY (1922, Brit.)
(6 r.) d, A. V. Bramble; lp, Carlotta Breese, Clive Brook, Harvey Braban, Joe Nightingale

SHIRLEY KAYE (1917)
(7 r.) d, Joseph Kaufman; lp, Clara Kimball Young, Corliss Giles, George Fawcett, George Backus

SHOCK PUNCH, THE (1925)
(6 r.) d, Paul Sloane; lp, Richard Dix, Frances Howard, Theodore Babcock, Percy Moore

SHOD WITH FIRE (1920)
(5 r.) d, Emmett J. Flynn; lp, William Russell, Helen Ferguson, Betty Schade, Robert Cain

SHOES (1916)
(5 r.) d, Lois Weber; lp, Mary MacDonald [MacLaren], Harry Griffith, Jessie Arnold, William V. Mong

SHOES THAT DANCED, THE (1918)
(5 r.) d, Frank Borzage; lp, Pauline Starke, Wallace MacDonald, Dick Rosson, Anna Dodge

SHOOTIN' SQUARE (1924)
(5 r.) lp, Jack Perrin, Peggy O'Day

SHOOTING OF DAN MCGREW, THE (1924)
(7 r.) d, Clarence Badger; lp, Barbara La Marr, Lew Cody, Mae Busch, Percy Marmont

SHOOTING STARS (1928)
(7 r.) d, A.V. Bramble, Anthony Asquith, lp, Annette Benson, Brian Aherne, Donald Calthrop, Wally Patch

SHOOTING STRAIGHT (1927)
(5 r.) d, William Wyler; lp, Ted Wells, Garry O'Dell, Buck Connors, Wilbur Mack

SHOP GIRL, THE
(SEE: WINIFRED THE SHOP GIRL, 1916)

SHOPGIRLS; OR, THE GREAT QUESTION (1914, Brit.)
(4 r.) d, Larry Trimble; lp, Florence Turner, Sidney Sinclair, Richard Steele

SHORE ACRES (1914)
(5 r.) d, John H. Pratt; lp, Charles A. Stevenson, William Riley Hatch, Conway Tearle, E.J. Connelly

SHORE ACRES (1920)
(6 r.) d, Rex Ingram; lp, Alice Lake, Robert Walker, Edward Connelly, Frank Brownlee

SHORT SKIRTS (1921)
(5 r.) d, Harry B. Harris; lp, Gladys Walton, Ena Gregory, Jack Mower, Jean Hathaway

SHOT IN THE NIGHT, A (1923)
(5 r.) lp, Walter Holeby, Walter Long, Ruth Freeman, Tom Amos

SHOULD A BABY DIE? (1916)
(5 r.) lp, Arthur Donaldson

SHOULD A DOCTOR TELL? (1923, Brit.)
(7 r.) d, Alexander Butler; lp, Lillian Hall Davis, Henry Vibart, Moyna McGill, Francis Lister

SHOULD A HUSBAND FORGIVE? (1919)
(6 r.) d, Raoul Walsh; lp, Miriam Cooper, Eric Mayne, Vincent Coleman, Lester Chambers

SHOULD A MOTHER TELL? (1915)
(5 r.) d, J. Gordon Edwards; lp, Betty Nansen, Stuart Holmes, Stephen Grattan, Runa Hodges

SHOULD SHE OBEY? (1917)
(7 r.) d, George Siegmann; lp, Billy West, Alice Wilson, Norbert Myles, Gene Genung

SHOULDER ARMS (1917)
(4 r.) d, Charles Chaplin; lp, Charles Chaplin, Edna Purviance, Sydney Chaplin, Jack Wilson

SHOW, THE (1927)
(7 r.) d, Tod Browning; lp, John Gilbert, Renee Adoree, Lionel Barrymore, Edward Connelly

SHOWDOWN, THE (1928)
(8 r.) d, Victor Schertzinger; lp, George Bancroft, Evelyn Brent, Neil Hamilton, Fred Kohler

SHOW OFF, THE (1926)
(7 r.) d, Malcolm St. Clair; lp, Ford Sterling, Lois Wilson, Louise Brooks, Gregory Kelly

SHOW-DOWN, THE (1917)
(5 r.) d, Lynn F. Reynolds; lp, Myrtle Gonzales, George Hernandez, Arthur Hoyt, George Chesebro

SHRIEK OF ARABY, THE (1923)
(5 r.) d, F. Richard Jones; lp, Ben Turpin, Kathryn McGuire, George Cooper, Charles Stevenson

SHRINE OF HAPPINESS, THE (1916)
(5 r.) d, Bertram Bracken; lp, Jackie Saunders, William Conklin, Paul Gilmore

SHULAMITE, THE (1915, Brit.)
(5 r.) d, George Loane Tucker; lp, Norman McKinnel, Manora Thew, Gerald Ames, Mary Dibley

SHUTTLE, THE (1918)
(5 r.) d, Rollin S. Sturgeon; lp, Constance Talmadge, Albert Roscoe, Edith Johnson, E.B. Tilton

SHUTTLE OF LIFE, THE (1920, Brit.)
(4 r.) d, D.J. Williams; lp, C. Aubrey Smith, Evelyn Brent, Jack Hobbs, Gladys Jennings

SI JAMAIS JE TE PINCE (1920, Fr.)
(? r.) d, Georges Monca

SICK ABED (1920)
(5 r.) d, Sam Wood; lp, Wallace Reid, Bebe Daniels, John Steppling, Winnifred Greenwood

SICKLE AND HAMMER (1921, USSR)
(5 r.) d, Vladimir Gardin; lp, Vsevolod Pudovkin, A. Gromov, Andrei Gorchilin, N. Zubova

SIDESHOW, THE (1928)
(7 r.) d, Erle C. Kenton; lp, Marie Prevost, Ralph Graves, Little Billy, Alan Roscoe

SIDEWALKS OF NEW YORK (1923)
(6 r.) d, Lester Park; lp, Hanna Lee, Bernard Siegel, Templar Saxe

SIEGE (1925)
(7 r.) d, Svend Gade; lp, Virginia Valli, Eugene O'Brien, Mary Alden, Marc MacDermott

SIGHT UNSEEN, A (1914)
(6 r.) d, Stanley E.V. Taylor; lp, Marion Leonard

SIGN INVISIBLE, THE (1918)
(6 r.) d, Edgar Lewis; lp, Mitchell Lewis, Mabel Julienne Scott, Hedda Nova, Victor Sutherland

SIGN OF FOUR, THE (1923, Brit.)
(7 r.) d, Maurice Elvey; lp, Eille Norwood, Isobel Elsom, Fred Raynham, Arthur Cullin

SIGN OF THE CACTUS, THE (1925)
(5 r.) d, Clifford S. Smith; lp, Jack Hoxie, Helen Holmes, J. Gordon Russell, Francis Ford

SIGN OF THE CLAW, THE (1926)
(6 r.) d, Reeves Eason; lp, Edward Hearn, Ethel Shannon, Joe Bennett, Peter the Great (a dog)

SIGN OF THE POPPY, THE (1916)
(5 r.) d, Charles Swickard; lp, Hobart Henley, Gertrude Selby, Mina Cunard, Wilbur Higby

SIGN OF THE SPADE, THE (1916)
(5 r.) d, Murdock MacQuarrie; lp, Helene Rosson, Alan Forrest, Warren Ellsworth, Harvey Clarke

SIGN ON THE DOOR, THE (1921)
(7 r.) d, Herbert Brenon; lp, Norma Talmadge, Charles Richman, Lew Cody, David Proctor

SIGNAL FIRES (1926)
(5 r.) lp, Fred Church

SILAS MARNER (1916)
(5 r.) d, Ernest Warde; lp, Frederick Warde, Louise E. Bates, Morgan Jones, Thomas A. Curran

SILAS MARNER (1922)
(7 r.) d, Frank Donovan; lp, Craufurd Kent, Marguerite Courtot, Robert Kenyon, Nona Marden

SILENCE (1926)
(8 r.) d, Rupert Julian; lp, Vera Reynolds, H.B. Warner, Raymond Hatton, Rockliffe Fellowes

SILENCE OF MARTHA, THE
(SEE: MARTHA'S VINDICATION, 1916)

SILENCE OF THE DEAD, THE (1913)
(4 r.)

SILENCE SELLERS, THE (1917)
(5 r.) d, Burton L. King; lp, Olga Petrova, Mahlon Hamilton, Violet Reed, Charles Dungan

SILENT ACCUSER, THE (1914)
(4 r.)

SILENT ACCUSER, THE
(SEE: LOVE PIRATE, THE, 1923)

SILENT ACCUSER, THE (1924)
(6 r.) d, Chester M. Franklin; lp, Eleanor Boardman, Raymond McKee, Earl Metcalfe, Paul Weigel

SILENT AVENGER, THE (1927)
(6 r.) d, James P. Hogan; lp, Charles Delaney, Duane Thompson, David Kirby, George Chesebro

SILENT BARRIER, THE (1920)
(5 r.) d, William Worthington; lp, Sheldon Lewis, Gladys Hulette, Corinne Barker, Florence Dixon

SILENT BATTLE, THE (1916)
(5 r.) d, Jack Conway; lp, J. Warren Kerrigan, Lois Wilson, Maude George, Harry Carter

SILENT COMMAND, THE (1915)
(4 r.) d, Robert Leonard; lp, Robert Leonard, Ella Hall, Harry Carter, Allan Forrest

SILENT GUARDIAN, THE (1926)
(5 r.) d, William Bletcher; lp, Louise Lorraine, Art Acord, Grace Woods, Rex (a dog)

SILENT HERO, THE (1927)
(6 r.) d, Duke Worne; lp, Robert Frazer, Edna Murphy, Ernest Hilliard, Joseph Girard

SILENT HOUSE, THE (1929, Brit.)
(9 r.) d, Walter Forde; lp, Mabel Poulton, Gibb McLaughlin, Arthur Pusey, Gerald Rawlinson

SILENT LADY, THE (1917)
(5 r.) d, Elsie Jane Wilson; lp, Zoe Rae, Gretchen Lederer, Winter Hall, Harry Holden

SILENT LIE, THE (1917)
(5 r.) d, Raoul Walsh; lp, Miriam Cooper, Ralph Lewis, Charles Clary, Monroe Salisbury

SILENT MAN, THE (1917)
(5 r.) d, William S. Hart; lp, William S. Hart, Vola Vale, Robert McKim, J.P. Lockney

SILENT MASTER, THE (1917)
(7 r.) d, Leonce Perret; lp, Robert Warwick, Anna Little, Anna Q. Nilsson, Olive Tell

SILENT PAL (1925)
(6 r.) d, Henry McCarty; lp, Eddie Phillips, Shannon Day, Colin Kenny, Willis Marks

SILENT PARTNER, THE (1917)
(5 r.) d, Marshall Neilan; lp, Blanche Sweet, Thomas Meighan, George Herbert, Ernest Joy

SILENT RIDER, THE (1918)
(5 r.) d, Cliff Smith; lp, Roy Stewart, Ethel Fleming, L. McKee, Leo Willis

SILENT RIDER, THE (1927)
(6 r.) d, Lynn Reynolds; lp, Hoot Gibson, Blanche Mehaffey, Ethan Laidlaw, Otis Harlan

SILENT SANDERSON (1925)
(5 r.) d, Scott R. Dunlap; lp, Harry Carey, Trilby Clark, John Miljan, Gardner James

SILENT SENTINEL (1929)
(5 r.) d, Alvin J. Neitz; lp, Gareth Hughes, Josephine Hill, Walter Maly, Champion (a dog)

SILENT SHELBY
(SEE: LAND O' LIZARDS, 1916)

SILENT SHELDON (1925)
(5 r.) d, Harry Webb; lp, Jack Perrin, Josephine Hill, Martin Turner, Whitehorse

SILENT STRANGER, THE (1924)
(5 r.) d, Albert Rogell; lp, Fred Thomson, Hazel Keener, George Williams, Richard Headrick

SILENT STRENGTH (1919)
(5 r.) d, Paul Scardon; lp, Harry T. Morey, Betty Blythe, Robert Gaillard, Bernard Siegel

SILENT TRAIL (1928)
(5 r.) d, J.P. McGowan; lp, Bob Custer, Peggy Montgomery, John Lowell, J.P. McGowan

SILENT WATCHER, THE (1924)
(8 r.) d, Frank Lloyd; lp, Glenn Hunter, Bessie Love, Hobart Bosworth, Gertrude Astor

SILENT WIRES (1924)
(5 r.) lp, Charles Hutchison

SILENT WITNESS, THE (1917)
(7 r.) d, Harry Lambert, Gerald F. Bacon; lp, Alphie James, Gertrude McCoy, Junius Mathews, Helen May

SILENT WOMAN, THE (1918)
(5 r.) d, Herbert Blache; lp, Edith Storey, Frank Mills, Joseph Kilgour, Lilie Leslie

SILENT YEARS (1921)
(6 r.) d, Louis J. Gasnier; lp, Rose Dione, Tully Marshall, George McDaniel, George Siegmann

SILK BOUQUET, THE (1926)
(8 r.) lp, Jimmy Leong, Anna May Wong

SILK HOSIERY (1920)
(5 r.) d, Fred Niblo; lp, Enid Bennett, Wallace MacDonald, Rose Dione, Derrick Ghent

SILK HUSBANDS AND CALICO WIVES (1920)
(5 r.) d, Alfred E. Green; lp, House Peters, Mary Alden, Mildred Reardon, Edward Kimball

SILK STOCKING SAL (1924)
(5 r.) d, Tod Browning; lp, Evelyn Brent, Robert Ellis, Earl Metcalfe, Alice Browning

SILK STOCKINGS (1927)
(7 r.) d, Wesley Ruggles; lp, Laura La Plante, John Harron, Otis Harlan, William Austin

SILKEN SHACKLES (1926)
(6 r.) d, Walter Morosco; lp, Irene Rich, Huntly Gordon, Bertram Marburgh, Victor Varconi

SILK-LINED BURGLAR, THE (1919)
(6 r.) d, Jack Dillon; lp, Priscilla Dean, Ashton Dearholt, Sam De Grasse, Lillian West

SILKS AND SATINS (1916)
(5 r.) d, J. Searle Dawley; lp, Marguerite Clark, Vernon Steele, Clarence Handysides, Thomas Holding

SILVER BRIDGE, THE (1920, Brit.)
(5 r.) d, Dallas Cairns; lp, Dallas Cairns, Betty Farquhar, Madeleine Meredith, Madge Tree

SILVER FINGERS (1926)
(5 r.) d, J.P. McGowan; lp, George Larkin, Charlotte Morgan, Arthur Morrison, Colin Chase

SILVER GIRL, THE (1919)
(5 r.) d, Frank Keenan, Eliot Howe; lp, Frank Keenan, Catherine Adams, George Hernandez, Donald MacDonald

SILVER GREYHOUND, THE (1919, Brit.)
(5 r.) d, Bannister Merwin; lp, James Knight, Marjorie Villis, Mary Dibley, Frank E. Petley

SILVER HORDE, THE (1920)
(7 r.) d, Frank Lloyd; lp, Curtis Cooksey, Myrtle Stedman, Robert McKim, Betty Blythe

SILVER KING, THE (1919)
(5 r.) d, George Irving; lp, William Faversham, Barbara Castleton, Nadia Gray, Lawrence Johnson

SILVER KING, THE (1929, Brit.)
(8 r.) d, T. Hayes Hunter; lp, Percy Marmont, Jean Jay, Chili Bouchier, Bernard Nedell

SILVER LINING, THE (1919, Brit.)
(6 r.) d, A.E. Coleby; lp, Billy Wells, Ella Milne, Richard Buttery, Warwick Ward

SILVER LINING, THE (1927, Brit.)
(7 r.) d, Thomas Bentley; lp, Marie Ault, Pat Aherne, John Hamilton, Eve Gray

SILVER SPURS (1922)
(5 r.) d, Henry McCarty, Leo Meehan; lp, Lester Cuneo

SILVER TREASURE, THE (1926)
(6 r.) d, Rowland V. Lee; lp, George O'Brien, Jack Rollins, Helena D'Algy, Joan Renee

SIMON THE JESTER (1925)
(7 r.) d, George Melford; lp, Eugene O'Brien, Lillian Rich, Edmund Burns, Henry B. Walthall

SIMONE (1918, Fr.)
(? r.) d, Camille de Morlhon

SIMONE (1926, Fr.)
(? r.) d, Donatien

SIMP, THE (1921)
(? r.) lp, Sherman H. Dudley, Jr., Inez Clough, Edna Morton, Alex K. Shannon

SIMPLE SIMON (1922, Brit.)
(5 r.) d, Henry Edwards; lp, Henry Edwards, Chrissie White, Mary Dibley, Hugh Clifton

SIMPLE SIS (1927)
(7 r.) d, Herman C. Raymaker; lp, Louise Fazenda, Clyde Cook, Myrna Loy, William Demarest

SIMPLE SOULS (1920)
(6 r.) d, Robert Thornby; lp, Blanche Sweet, Charles Meredith, Kate Lester, Herbert Standing

SIMPLE TAILOR, THE (1934, USSR)
(6 r.) d, Vladimir Vilner; lp, M. Leorov, A.D. Goricheva, Y. Mindler, J.K. Kovenberg

SIMPLETTE (1919, Fr.)
(? r.) d, Rene Hervil

SIN CARGO (1926)
(7 r.) d, Louis J. Gasnier; lp, Shirley Mason, Robert Frazer, Earl Metcalfe, Lawford Davidson

SIN FLOOD, THE (1922)
(7 r.) d, Frank Lloyd; lp, Richard Dix, Helene Chadwick, James Kirkwood, John Steppling

SIN TOWN (1929)
(5 r.) d, J. Gordon Cooper; lp, Elinor Fair, Ivan Lebedeff, Hugh Allan, Jack Oakie

SIN WOMAN, THE (1917)
(8 r.) lp, Irene Fenwick, Clifford Bruce, Renie Davies

SIN YE DO, THE (1916)
(5 r.) d, Walter Edwards; lp, Frank Keenan, Margery Wilson, David M. Hartford, Margaret Thompson

SINEWS OF STEEL (1927)
(6 r.) d, Frank O'Connor; lp, Alberta Vaughn, Gaston Glass, Anders Randolf, Paul Weigel

SINGAPORE MUTINY, THE (1928)
(7 r.) d, Ralph Ince; lp, Ralph Ince, Estelle Taylor, James Mason, Gardner James

SINGED WINGS (1915, USSR)
(6 r.) d, Yevgeny Bauer; lp, S. Rassatov, Vera Coralli, Osip Runich, Vitold Polonsky

SINGLE CODE, THE (1917)
(5 r.) d, Thomas Ricketts; lp, Crane Wilbur, Florence Printy, F.A. Johnston, Harrish Ingraham

SINGLE HANDED (1923)
(5 r.) d, Edward Sedgwick; lp, Hoot Gibson, Elinor Field, Percy Challenger, William Steele

SINGLE LIFE (1921, Brit.)
(5 r.) d, Edwin J. Collins; lp, Campbell Gullan, Kathleen Vaughan, Sydney Paxton, Evelyn Hope

SINGLE SHOT PARKER
(SEE: HEART OF TEXAS RYAN, THE, 1917)

SINGLE STANDARD, THE (1914)
(5 r.)

SINGLE WIVES (1924)
(8 r.) d, George Archainbaud; lp, Corinne Griffith, Milton Sills, Kathlyn Williams, Phyllis Haver

SINISTER STREET (1922, Brit.)
(5 r.) d, George Andre Beranger; lp, John Stuart, Amy Verity, Maudie Dunham, Molly Adair

SINKING OF THE LUSITANIA, THE (1918)
(? r.) d, Winsor McCay (animated)

SINLESS SINNER, A
(SEE: MIDNIGHT GAMBOLS, 1919, Brit.)

SINNER OR SAINT (1923)
(6 r.) d, Lawrence Windom; lp, Betty Blythe, William P. Carleton, Gypsy O'Brien, William H. Tooker

SINNERS (1920)
(5 r.) d, Kenneth Webb; lp, Alice Brady, James L. Crane, Agnes Everett, Augusta Anderson

SINNERS IN SILK (1924)
(6 r.) d, Hobart Henley; lp, Adolphe Menjou, Eleanor Boardman, Conrad Nagel, Jean Hersholt

SINS OF HER PARENT (1916)
(5 r.) d, Frank Lloyd; lp, Gladys Brockwell, William Clifford, Carl Von Schiller, George Webb

SINS OF MEN (1916)
(5 r.) d, James Vincent; lp, Stuart Holmes, Dorothy Bernard, Hattie Burks, Stephen Grattan

SINS OF ST. ANTHONY, THE (1920)
(5 r.) d, James Cruze; lp, Bryant Washburn, Margaret Loomis, Lorenza Lazzarini, Guy Oliver

SINS OF THE CHILDREN (1918)
(5 r.) d, John S. Lopez; lp, Alma Hanlon, Stuart Holmes, Beth Tenney

SINS OF THE FATHER (1928)
(8 r.) d, Ludwig Berger; lp, Emil Jannings, Ruth Chatterton, Barry Norton, Jean Arthur

SINS OF THE PARENTS (1914)
(5 r.) lp, Sarah Adler

SINS OF YOUTH, THE (1919, Brit.)
(5 r.) d, Ernest G. Batley; lp, Ernest G. Batley, Dorothy Batley, Sam Livesey, Nancy Bevington

SINS THAT YE SIN, THE (1915)
(5 r.) lp, Gertrude Bondhill

SINS YE DO, THE (1924, Brit.)
(6 r.) d, Fred Leroy Granville; lp, Joan Lockton, Henry Victor, Eileen Dennes, Maie Hanbury

SIR ARNE'S TREASURE (1920, Swed.)
(7 r.) d, Mauritz Stiller; lp, Richard Lund, Eric Stocklassa, Bror Berger, Hjalmar Selander

SIR LUMBERJACK (1926)
(6 r.) d, Harry Garson; lp, Lefty Flynn, Kathleen Myers, Tom Kennedy, William Walling

SIR OR MADAM (1928, Brit.)
(6 r.) d, Carl Boese; lp, Percy Marmont, Ossi Oswalda, Annette Benson, Margot Armand

SIREN, THE (1917)
(5 r.) d, Roland West; lp, Valeska Suratt, Clifford Bruce, Robert Clugston, Curtis Benton

SIREN, THE (1927)
(6 r.) d, Byron Haskin; lp, Tom Moore, Dorothy Revier, Norman Trevor, Jed Prouty

SIREN OF SEVILLE, THE (1924)
(7 r.) d, Jerome Storm; lp, Priscilla Dean, Allan Forrest, Stuart Holmes, Claire De Lorez

SIRENS OF THE SEA (1917)
(5 r.) d, Allen Holubar; lp, Louise Lovely, Carmel Myers, Jack Mulhall, William Quinn

SIREN'S SONG, THE (1919)
(5 r.) d, J. Gordon Edwards; lp, Theda Bara, Albert Roscoe, Alfred Fremont, Ruth Handforth

SIS HOPKINS (1919)
(5 r.) d, Clarence G. Badger; lp, Mabel Normand, John Bowers, Sam De Grasse, Thomas Jefferson

SISTER AGAINST SISTER (1917)
(5 r.) d, James Vincent; lp, Virginia Pearson, Irving Cummings, Walter Law, Maud Hill

SISTER OF SIX, A (1916)
(5 r.) d, C.M. & S.A. Franklin; lp, Bessie Love, Frank Bennett, Ralph Lewis, Ben Lewis

SISTER TO SALOME, A (1920)
(5 r.) d, Edward J. LeSaint; lp, Gladys Brockwell, William Scott, Ben Deely

SISTERS OF EVE (1928)
(6 r.) d, Scott Pembroke; lp, Anita Stewart, Betty Blythe, Creighton Hale, Harold Nelson

SITTING BULL AT THE "SPIRIT LAKE MASSACRE" (1927)
(6 r.) d, Robert North Bradbury; lp, Bryant Washburn, Ann Schaeffer, Jay Morley, Shirley Palmer

SITTING BULL – THE HOSTILE SIOUX INDIAN CHIEF (1914)
(5 r.)

6 1/2 X 11 (1927, Fr.)
(7 r.) d, Jean Epstein; lp, Edmond Van Daele, Suzy Pierson, Nino Constantini, Rene Fert

SIX BEST CELLARS, THE (1920)
(5 r.) d, Donald Crisp; lp, Bryant Washburn, Wanda Hawley, Clarence Burton, Elsa Lorimer

SIX CYLINDER LOVE (1923)
(7 r.) d, Elmer Clifton; lp, Ernest Truex, Florence Eldridge, Donald Meek, Maude Hill

SIX FEET FOUR (1919)
(6 r.) d, Henry King; lp, William Russell, Vola Vale, Charles K. French, Harvey Clark

SIX SHOOTIN' ROMANCE, A (1926)
(5 r.) d, Clifford S. Smith; lp, Jack Hoxie, Olive Hasbrouck, William A. Steele, Carmen Phillips

SIX-FIFTY, THE (1923)
(5 r.) d, Nat Ross; lp, Renee Adoree, Orville Caldwell, Bert Woodruff, Gertrude Astor

SIX-SHOOTER ANDY (1918)
(5 r.) d, S.A. Franklin; lp, Tom Mix, Enid Markey, Herbert Woodruff, Sam De Grasse

SIXTEENTH WIFE, THE (1917)
(5 r.) d, Charles Brabin; lp, Peggy Hyland, Marc MacDermott, George J. Forth, Templer Saxe

SIXTH COMMANDMENT, THE (1924)
(6 r.) d, William Christy Cabanne; lp, William Faversham, Charlotte Walker, John Bohn, Kathleen Martyn

SIXTH OF THE WORLD, A (1926, USSR)
(6 r.) d, Dziga Vertov

SKEDADDLE GOLD (1927)
(5 r.) d, Richard Thorpe; lp, Wally Wales, Betty Baker, Robert Burns, George F. Marion

SKIN DEEP (1922)
(7 r.) d, Lambert Hillyer; lp, Milton Sills, Florence Vidor, Marcia Manon, Charles Clary

SKIN GAME, THE (1920, Brit.)
(6 r.) d, B.E. Doxat-Pratt; lp, Edmund Gwenn, Mary Clare, Helen Haye, Dawson Millward

SKINNER'S BABY (1917)
(4 r.) d, Harry Beaumont; lp, Bryant Washburn, Hazel Daly, James Carroll, U.K. Haupt

SKINNER'S BUBBLE (1917)
(5 r.) d, Harry Beaumont; lp, Bryant Washburn, Hazel Daly, James C. Carroll, Marion Skinner

SKINNING SKINNERS (1921)
(5 r.) d, William Nigh; lp, Johnny Dooley

SKIRTS (1921)
(5 r.) d, Hampton Del Ruth; lp, Clyde Cook, Chester Conklin, Polly Moran, Jack Cooper

SKIRTS (1928, Brit.)
(8 r.) d, Jess Robbins, Wheeler Dryden; lp, Sydney Chaplin, Betty Balfour, Edmond Breon, Nancy Rigg

SKY HIGH CORRAL (1926)
(5 r.) d, Clifford S. Smith; lp, Art Acord, Marguerite Clayton, Duke R. Lee, Jack Mower

SKY MONSTER, THE (1914)
(4 r.)

SKY PIRATE, THE (1926)
(5 r.) lp, Bryant Washburn, Vola Vale, Charles Delaney, Sheldon Lewis

SKY RAIDER, THE (1925)
(7 r.) d, T. Hayes Hunter; lp, Charles Nungesser, Jacqueline Logan, Gladys Walton, Walter Miller

SKY-EYE (1920)
(6 r.) d, Aubrey M. Kennedy; lp, Harry Myers, Russel C. Hunt, Thelma Kenley, Peck Miller

SKYLIGHT ROOM, THE (1917)
(4 r.) d, Martin Justice; lp, Carlton King, Jean Paige, Grace Ashley, Nell Spencer

SKY'S THE LIMIT (1925)
(5 r.) d, I.W. Irving; lp, Bruce Gordon, Charlotte Pierce, Jack Giddings, Melbourne MacDowell

SKYSCRAPER (1928)
(8 r.) d, Howard Higgin; lp, William Boyd, Alan Hale, Sue Carol, Alberta Vaughn

SKYWAYMAN, THE (1920)
(5 r.) d, James P. Hogan; lp, Ormer Locklear, Louise Lovely, Sam De Grasse, Ted McCann

SLACKER, THE (1917)
(7 r.) d, William Christy Cabanne; lp, Emily Stevens, Walter C. Miller, Leo Delaney, Daniel Jarrett

SLAM BANG JIM
(SEE: SNAP JUDGEMENT, 1917)

SLANDER (1916)
(6 r.) d, Will S. Davis; lp, Bertha Kalich, Eugene Ormonde, Mayme Kelso, Edward Van Sloan

SLANDERERS, THE (1924)
(5 r.) d, Nat Ross; lp, Johnnie Walker, Gladys Hulette, Billy Sullivan, George Nichols

SLAUGHTER, THE (1913, USSR)
(4 r.) d, Avrom Yitskhok Kaminsky; lp, Esther Rokhl Kaminska, Gershon Weissman, Jacob Libert, Shmuel Landau

SLAVE, THE (1917)
(5 r.) d, William Nigh; lp, Valeska Suratt, Dan Mason, Violet Palmer, Tom Brooke

SLAVE, THE (1918, Brit.)
(5 r.) d, Arrigo Bocchi; lp, Marie de Lisle, Hayford Hobbs, Charles Vane, Hettie Grossman

SLAVE MARKET, THE (1917)
(5 r.) d, Hugh Ford; lp, Pauline Frederick, Thomas Meighan, Albert Hart, Ruby Hoffman

SLAVE OF FASHION, A (1925)
(6 r.) d, Hobart Henley; lp, Norma Shearer, Lew Cody, William Haines, Mary Carr

SLAVE OF PASSION, SLAVE OF VICE (1914, USSR)
(4 r.) d, M. Martov; lp, Pola Negri, V. Bridzinksy, V. Shavinsky

SLAVE OF VANITY, A (1920)
(6 r.) d, Henry Otto; lp, Pauline Frederick, Nigel Barrie, Willard Louis, Maude Lewis

SLAVER, THE (1927)
(6 r.) d, Harry Revier; lp, Pat O'Malley, Carmelita Geraghty, John Miljan, J.P. McGowan

SLAVES OF PRIDE (1920)
(6 r.) d, George Terwilliger; lp, Alice Joyce, Percy Marmont, Louise Beaudet, Templer Saxe

SLAVES OF SCANDAL (1924)
(5 r.)

SLAVEY STUDENT, THE (1915)
(4 r.) d, John H. Collins; lp, Viola Dana, Pat O'Malley, Marie La Manna

SLEEPING FIRES (1917)
(5 r.) d, Hugh Ford; lp, Pauline Frederick, Thomas Meighan, John Sainpolis, Helen Dahl

SLEEPING LION, THE (1919)
(6 r.) d, Rupert Julian; lp, Monroe Salisbury, Alice Elliot, Sidney Franklin, Marion Skinner

SLEEPING MEMORY, A (1917)
(7 r.) d, George D. Baker; lp, Emily Stevens, Frank Mills, Mario Majeroni, Walter Horton

SLIM PRINCESS, THE (1920)
(5 r.) d, Victor L. Schertzinger; lp, Mabel Normand, Hugh Thompson, Tully Marshall, Russ Powell

SLINGSHOT KID, THE (1927)
(5 r.) d, Louis King; lp, Buzz Barton, Frank Rice, Jeanne Morgan, Buck Connors

SLOTH (1917)
(5 r.) d, Theodore Marston; lp, Charlotte Walker, Jack Meredith, D.J. Flannigan, Jack Crosby

SLOW AS LIGHTING (1923)
(5 r.) d, Grover Jones; lp, Kenneth McDonald, Billy "Red" Jones, Edna Pennington, Gordon Sackville

SLOW DYNAMITE (1925)
(5 r.) d, Frank S. Mattison; lp, Matty Mattison

SLUMS OF TOKYO (1930, Jap.)
(4 r.) d, Teinosuke Kinogasa; lp, A. Techihaya, J. Bandoh, Y. Ogawa, I. Sohma

SMALL BACHELOR, THE (1927)
(7 r.) d, William A. Seiter; lp, Barbara Kent, Andre Beranger, William Austin, Lucien Littlefield

SMALL TOWN GIRL, A (1917)
(5 r.) d, John G. Adolfi; lp, June Caprice, Jane Lee, Bernard Delaney, Ethyle Cooke

SMALL TOWN GUY, THE (1917)
(5 r.) d, Lawrence C. Windom; lp, Taylor Holmes, Helen Ferguson, Fred Tilden, Mark Elliston

SMART SET, A (1919, Brit.)
(5 r.) d, A.V. Bramble; lp, Concordia Merrill, Neville Percy, S.J. Warmington, Doriel Paget

SMART SEX, THE (1921)
(5 r.) d, Fred Leroy Granville; lp, Eva Novak, Frank Braidwood, Geoffrey Webb, Mayre Hall

SMASHED BACK (1927)
(5 r.)

SMASHING BARRIERS (1923)
(6 r.) d, William Duncan; lp, William Duncan, Edith Johnson, Joe Ryan, Walter Rogers

SMASHING THROUGH (1918)
(5 r.) d, Elmer Clifton; lp, Herbert Rawlinson, Sally Starr, Neal Hart, Sam De Grasse

SMILES (1919)
(5 r.) d, Arvid E. Gillstrom; lp, Jane Lee, Katherine Lee, Ethel Fleming, Val Paul

SMILIN' GUNS (1929)
(6 r.) d, Henry MacRae; lp, Hoot Gibson, Blanche Mehaffey, Virginia Pearson, Robert Graves

SMILIN' ON (1923)
(4 r.) d, William J. Craft; lp, Pete Morrison, Gene Crosby

SMILIN' THROUGH (1922)
(8 r.) d, Sidney A. Franklin; lp, Norma Talmadge, Wyndham Standing, Harrison Ford, Alec B. Francis

SMILING ALL THE WAY (1921)
(5 r.) d, Fred J. Butler; lp, David Butler, Leatrice Joy, Frances Raymond, J. Parker McConnell

SMILING BILLY (1927)
(5 r.) d, Duke Worne; lp, Billy Sullivan

SMILING EARTH, THE (1925, Jap.)
(? r.) d, Kenji Mizoguchi

SMILING JIM (1922)
(5 r.) d, Joseph Franz; lp, Franklyn Farnum, Alma Bennett, Percy Challenger, Al Ferguson

SMILING TERROR, THE (1929)
(5 r.) d, Josef Levigard; lp, Ted Wells, Derelys Perdue, Al Ferguson, Bud Osborne

SMILING THROUGH
(SEE: SMILIN' THROUGH, 1922)

SMITH (1917, Brit.)
(4 r.) d, Maurice Elvey; lp, Elizabeth Risdon, Fred Groves, Manora Thew, Guy Newall

SMOKE EATERS, THE (1926)
(6 r.) d, Charles Hunt; lp, Cullen Landis, Wanda Hawley, Edward Cecil, Aryel Darma

SMOKING GUNS (1927)
(5 r.) lp, Al Hoxie, Buddy Roosevelt

SMOKING TRAIL, THE (1924)
(5 r.) d, William Bertram; lp, Bill Patton, William Bertram, Jack House, Tom Ross

SMOOTH AS SATIN (1925)
(6 r.) d, Ralph Ince; lp, Evelyn Brent, Bruce Gordon, Fred Kelsey, Fred Esmelton

SMOULDERING EMBERS (1920)
(5 r.) d, Frank Keenan; lp, Frank Keenan, Jay Belasco, Kate Van Buren, Russ Powell

SMOULDERING FIRES (1925)
(8 r.) d, Clarence Brown; lp, Pauline Frederick, Laura La Plante, Malcolm McGregor, Tully Marshall

SMUDGE (1922)
(5 r.) d, Charles Ray; lp, Charles Ray, Charles K. French, Florence Oberle, Ora Carew

SMUGGLERS, THE (1916)
(5 r.) d, Sidney Olcott; lp, Donald Brian, Cyril Chadwick, Harold Vosburgh, Rita Bori

SNAIL, THE (1918)
(5 r.) lp, Shorty Hamilton, Ethel Grey Terry

SNAP JUDGEMENT (1917)
(5 r.) d, Edward Sloman; lp, William Russell, Francelia Billington, Harvey Clark, Adda Gleason

SNARES OF PARIS (1919)
(5 r.) d, Howard Mitchell; lp, Madlaine Traverse, Charles Arling, Frank Leigh, Joseph Swickard

SNARL, THE (1917)
(5 r.) d, Raymond B. West; lp, Bessie Barriscale, Charles Gunn, Howard Hickman, Aggie Herring

SNARL OF HATE, THE (1927)
(6 r.) d, Noel Mason Smith; lp, Johnnie Walker, Mildred June, Jack Richardson, Wheeler Oakman

SNEAK, THE (1919)
(5 r.) d, Edward J. LeSaint; lp, Gladys Brockwell, William Scott, Alfred Hollingsworth, John Oaker

SNITCHING HOUR, THE (1922)
(5 r.) d, Alan Crosland; lp, Arthur Houseman, Gladys Leslie, Frank Currier, Nita Naldi

SNOB, THE (1921)
(5 r.) d, Sam Wood; lp, Wanda Hawley, Edwin Stevens, Walter Hiers, Sylvia Ashton

SNOB BUSTER, THE (1925)
(5 r.) d, Albert Rogell; lp, Reed Howes, Wilfred Lucas, George French, David Kirby

SNOW IN THE DESERT (1919, Brit.)
(7 r.) d, Walter West; lp, Violet Hopson, Stewart Rome, Poppy Wyndham, Sir Simeon Stuart

SNOW MAIDEN, THE (1914, USSR)
(4 r.) d, Ladislas Starevitch; lp, D. Tchitorina, A. Gromoff, A. Bibikoff

SNOW WHITE (1916)
(4 r.)

SNOW WHITE (1917)
(6 r.) d, J. Searle Dawley; lp, Marguerite Clark, Creighton Hale, Dorothy G. Cumming, Lionel Braham

SNOW BRIDE, THE (1923)
(6 r.) d, Henry Kolker; lp, Alice Brady, Maurice B. Flynn, Mario Majeroni, Nick Thompson

SNOWBIRD, THE (1916)
(6 r.) d, Edwin Carewe; lp, Mabel Taliaferro, Edwin Carewe, James Cruze, Warren Cook

SNOWBOUND (1927)
(6 r.) d, Phil Stone; lp, Betty Blythe, Lillian Rich, Robert Agnew, George Fawcett

SNOWDRIFT (1923)
(5 r.) d, Scott Dunlap; lp, Bert Sprotte, Gertrude Ryan, Colin Chase, Evelyn Selbie

SNOWSHOE TRAIL, THE (1922)
(6 r.) d, Chester Bennett; lp, Jane Novak, Roy Stewart, Lloyd Whitlock, Herbert Prior

SO LONG LETTY (1920)
(6 r.) d, Al Christie; lp, T. Roy Barnes, Colleen Moore, Grace Darmond, Walter Hiers

SO THIS IS MARRIAGE (1924)
(7 r.) d, Hobart Henley; lp, Conrad Nagel, Eleanor Boardman, Lew Cody, Clyde Cook

SOAP GIRL, THE (1918)
(5 r.) d, Martin Justice; lp, Gladys Leslie, Edward Burns, Frank Norcross, Julia Swayne Gordon

SOCIAL AMBITION (1918)
(6 r.) d, Wallace Worsley; lp, Rhea Mitchell, Howard Hickman, Katherine Kirkham, Noah Beery

SOCIAL BRIARS (1918)
(5 r.) d, Henry King; lp, Mary Miles Minter, Alan Forrest, Anne Schaefer, Edmund Cobb

SOCIAL BUCCANEER, THE (1916)
(5 r.) d, Jack Conway; lp, J. Warren Kerrigan, Louise Lovely, Maude George, Harry Carter

SOCIAL EXILE, THE
(SEE: DECLASSEE, 1925)

SOCIAL HIGHWAYMAN, THE (1916)
(5 r.) d, Edwin August; lp, Edwin August, Ormi Hawley, John Sainpolis, Alice Clair Elliott

SOCIAL HYPOCRITES (1918)
(5 r.) d, Albert Capellani; lp, May Allison, Frank Currier, Joseph Kilgour, Henry Kolker

SOCIAL LEPER, THE (1917)
(5 r.) d, Harley Knoles; lp, Carlyle Blackwell, June Elvidge, Arthur Ashley, George MacQuarrie

SOCIAL PIRATE, THE (1919)
(5 r.) d, Dell Henderson; lp, June Elvidge, Laura Burt, Lillian Lawrence, Winifred Leighton

SOCIAL QUICKSANDS (1918)
(5 r.) d, Charles J. Brabin; lp, Francis X. Bushman, Beverly Bayne, Mabel Frenyear, Leslie Stowe

SOCIETY EXILE, A (1919)
(6 r.) d, George Fitzmaurice; lp, Elsie Ferguson, William P. Carlton, Warburton Gamble, Julia Dean

SOCIETY FOR SALE (1918)
(5 r.) d, Frank Borzage; lp, William Desmond, Gloria Swanson, Herbert Prior, Charles Dorian

SOCIETY SECRETS (1921)
(5 r.) d, Leo McCarey; lp, Eva Novak, Gertrude Claire, George Verrell, Clarissa Selwynne

SOCIETY SENSATION, A (1918)
(5 r.) d, Paul Powell; lp, Carmel Myers, Rudolph Valentino, Fred Kelsey, ZaSu Pitts

SOCIETY WOLVES (1916)
(5 r.) d, Tom Terriss; lp, Elaine Terriss, Alfred Heming, Lida Hikox, Louella Knox

SOCIETY'S DRIFTWOOD (1917)
(5 r.) d, Louis William Chaudet; lp, Grace Cunard, Joseph Girard, Charles West, William Musgrave

SODA WATER COWBOY (1927)
(5 r.) d, Richard Thorpe; lp, Wally Wales, Beryl Roberts, J.P. Lockney, Charles Whitaker

SOFT BOILED (1923)
(8 r.) d, J.G. Blystone; lp, Tom Mix, Joseph Girard, Billie Dove, L.C. Shumway

SOFT LIVING (1928)
(6 r.) d, James Tinling; lp, Madge Bellamy, Johnny Mack Brown, Mary Duncan, Joyce Compton

SOFT SHOES (1925)
(6 r.) d, Lloyd Ingraham; lp, Harry Carey, Lillian Rich, Paul Weigel, Francis Ford

SOILED (1924)
(7 r.) d, Fred Windemere; lp, Kenneth Harlan, Vivian Martin, Mildred Harris, Johnny Walker

SOIREE DE REVEILLON (1922, Fr.)
(? r.) d, Pierre Colombier

SOLD APPETITE, THE (1928, USSR)
(7 r.) d, Nikolai Okhlopkov; lp, Ambrose Buchma, M. Tsibulsky, Marie Doucemetier

SOLD FOR MARRIAGE (1916)
(5 r.) d, William Christy Cabanne; lp, Lillian Gish, Frank Bennett, Walter Long, Pearl Elmore

SOLDIER'S OATH, A (1915)
(5 r.) d, Oscar C. Apfel; lp, William Farnum

SOLDIERS OF CHANCE (1917)
(5 r.) d, Paul Scardon; lp, Evart Overton, Miriam Fouche, Julia Swayne Gordon, Charles Kent

SOLDIERS OF FORTUNE (1914)
(6 r.) d, Augustus Thomas; lp, Dustin Farnum, John Sainpolis, John Pratt, Leighton Stark

SOLDIERS OF FORTUNE (1919)
(7 r.) d, Allan Dwan; lp, Norman Kerry, Pauline Starke, Anna Q. Nilsson, Melbourne McDowell

SOLDIER'S SONS (1916)
(4 r.) d, Wilbert Melville; lp, Benjamin Hopkins, L.C. Shumway, Helen Wolcott, Melvin Mayo

SOLITARY SIN, THE (1919)
(6 r.) d, Fred Sullivan; lp, Jack Mulhall, Helene Chadwick, Pauline Curley, Anne Schaefer

SOLOMON IN SOCIETY (1922)
(6 r.) d, Lawrence C. Windom; lp, William H. Strauss, Brenda Moore, Nancy Deaver, Charles Delaney

SOME ARTIST (1919, Brit.)
(5 r.) d, Rex Wilson; lp, Campbell Gullan, Eric Harrison, Cecily Debenham

SOME BOY (1917)
(5 r.) d, Otis Turner; lp, George Walsh, Doris Pawn, Herschal Mayall, Velma Whitman

SOME BRIDE (1919)
(5 r.) d, Henry Otto; lp, Viola Dana, Irving Cummings, Jack Mower, Ruth Sinclair

SOME LIAR (1919)
(5 r.) d, Henry King; lp, William Russell, Eileen Percy, Haywood Mack, Gordon Russell

SOME MOTHER'S BOY (1929)
(6 r.) d, Duke Worne; lp, Mary Carr, Jason Robards, Jobyna Ralston, M.A. Dickinson

SOME PUN'KINS (1925)
(7 r.) d, Jerome Storm; lp, Charles Ray, George Fawcett, Fanny Midgley, Duane Thompson

SOME WAITER! (1916, Brit.)
(4 r.) d, George Carney; lp, George Carney, George Hughes, Robert Chester, Vesta Leonard

SOMEBODY'S DARLING (1925, Brit.)
(9 r.) d, George A. Cooper; lp, Betty Balfour, Rex O'Malley, Fred Raynham, Forrester Harvey

SOMEBODY'S MOTHER (1926)
(5 r.) d, Oscar Apfel; lp, Mary Carr, Rex Lease, Mickey McBan, Kathryn McGuire

SOMEONE IN THE HOUSE (1920)
(6 r.) d, John E. Ince; lp, Edmund Lowe, Vola Vale, Edward Connelly, Howard Crampton

SOMEONE MUST PAY (1919)
(6 r.) d, Ivan Abramson; lp, Gail Kane, Edmund Breese, Jackie Saunders, Hugh Thompson

SOMEONE TO LOVE (1928)
(7 r.) d, F. Richard Jones; lp, Charles "Buddy" Rogers, Mary Brian, William Austin, Jack Oakie

SOMETHING ALWAYS HAPPENS (1928)
(5 r.) d, Frank Tuttle; lp, Esther Ralston, Neil Hamilton, Sojin, Charles Sellon

SOMETHING DIFFERENT (1920)
(5 r.) d, Roy William Neill; lp, Constance Binney, Lucy Fox, Ward Crane, Gertrude Hillman

SOMETHING TO DO (1919)
(5 r.) d, Donald Crisp; lp, Bryant Washburn, Ann Little, Robert Brower, Charles Gerard

SOMEWHERE IN FRANCE (1916)
(5 r.) d, Charles Giblyn; lp, Louise Glaum, Howard Hickman, Fannie Midgley

SOMEWHERE IN GEORGIA (1916)
(6 r.) d, George Ridgwell; lp, Ty Cobb, Elsie McLeod, Harry Fisher, Will Corbett

SON ADVENTURE (1919, Fr.)
(? r.) d, Rene Hervil

SON CRIME (1921, Fr.)
(? r.) d, Albert Dieudonne

SON DESTIN (1919, Fr.)
(? r.) d, George Lacroix

SON HEROS (1917, Fr.)
(? r.) d, Charles Burguet

SON OF A GUN, THE (1919)
(5 r.) lp, Broncho Billy Anderson, A.E. Whitting, Mrs. A.E. Whitting, Joy Lewis

SON OF A GUN (1926)
(5 r.) d, Paul Hurst; lp, Al Hoxie

SON OF DAVID, A (1920, Brit.)
(5 r.) d, Hay Plumb; lp, Poppy Wyndham, Ronald Colman, Arthur Walcott, Constance Backner

SON OF ERIN, A (1916)
(5 r.) d, Julia Crawford Ivers; lp, Dustin Farnum, Winifred Kingston, Jack Livingston, Wilfred McDonald

SON OF HIS FATHER, THE (1917)
(5 r.) d, Victor Schertzinger; lp, Charles Ray, Vola Vale, Robert McKim, George Nichols

SON OF HIS FATHER, A (1925)
(7 r.) d, Victor Fleming; lp, Bessie Love, Warner Baxter, Raymond Hatton, Walter McGrail

SON OF KISSING CUP (1922, Brit.)
(6 r.) d, Walter West; lp, Violet Hopson, Stewart Rome, Cameron Carr, Arthur Walcott

SON OF MADAME SANS GENE (1924, Ital.)
(7 r.)

SON OF SATAN, A (1924)
(7 r.) lp, Andrew S. Bishop, Ida Anderson

SON OF SONTAG, THE (1925)
(5 r.) d, Paul Hurst; lp, Jack Meehan

SON OF STRIFE, A (1917)
(5 r.)

SON OF THE DESERT, A (1928)
(5 r.) d, William Merrill McCormick; lp, William Merrill McCormick, Marin Sais, Robert Burns, Faith Hope

SON OF THE GOLDEN WEST (1928)
(6 r.) d, Eugene Forde; lp, Tom Mix, Sharon Lynn, Tom Lingham, Duke R. Lee

SON OF THE HILLS, A (1917)
(5 r.) d, Harry Davenport; lp, Antonio Moreno, Robert Gaillard, Julia Swayne Gordon, Belle Bruce

SON OF THE IMMORTALS, A (1916)
(5 r.) d, Otis Turner; lp, J. Warren Kerrigan, Bertram Grassby, Lois Wilson, Harry Carter

SON OF THE LAND (1931, USSR)
(4 r.) d, Edward Ioganson; lp, Boris Ivanitski, Vladamir Vikulin, Iona Brokski

SON OF THE SAHARA, A (1924)
(8 r.) d, Edwin Carewe; lp, Claire Windsor, Bert Lytell, Walter McGrail, Rosemary Theby

SON OF WALLINGFORD, THE (1921)
(8 r.) d, George Randolph Chester; lp, Wilfrid North, Tom Gallery, George Webb, Antrim Short

SONG AND DANCE MAN, THE (1926)
(7 r.) d, Herbert Brenon; lp, Tom Moore, Bessie Love, Harrison Ford, Norman Trevor

SONG OF CHINA (1936, Chi.)
(4 r.) d, Lo Ming-yau; lp, Lim Cho-Cho, Shang Kwah-wu, Li Shoh-shoh, Chang Yih

SONG OF SIXPENCE, A (1917)
(5 r.) d, Ralph Dean; lp, Marie Wayne, Robert Conness, Margaret Townsend, Alfred Hemming

SONG OF SONGS, THE (1918)
(5 r.) d, Joseph Kaufman; lp, Elsie Ferguson, Cecil Fletcher, Crauford Kent, Frank Losee

SONG OF THE SOUL, THE (1918)
(5 r.) d, Tom Terriss; lp, Alice Joyce, Percy Standing, Walter McGrail, Bernard Siegel

SONG OF THE SOUL, THE (1920)
(5 r.) d, John W. Noble; lp, Vivian Martin, Fritz Leiber, Charles E. Graham, Ricca Allen

SONG OF TRIUMPHANT LOVE (1915, USSR)
(5 r.) d, Yevgeni Bauer; lp, Vera Kholodnaya, Osip Runich, Vitold Polonsky

SONIA (1921, Brit.)
(6 r.) d, Denison Clift; lp, Evelyn Brent, Clive Brook, Cyril Raymond, Olaf Hytten

SONIA (1928)
(5 r.) d, Hector V. Sarno; lp, Rosa Rosanova, Evelyn Pierce, Hector V. Sarno

SONS OF SATAN, THE (1915, Brit.)
(5 r.) d, George Loane Tucker; lp, Gerald Ames, Blanche Bryan, Hayford Hobbs, Charles Rock

SONS OF THE SEA (1925, Brit.)
(6 r.) d, H. Bruce Woolfe; lp, E. Godfrey, Dorothy Barclay

SONS OF THE WEST (1922)
(5 r.)

SOONER OR LATER (1920)
(5 r.) d, Wesley Ruggles; lp, Owen Moore, Seena Owen, Clifford Gray, Amy Dennis

SORRELL AND SON (1927)
(10 r.) d, Herbert Brenon; lp, H.B. Warner, Anna Q. Nilsson, Mickey McBan, Carmel Myers

SORROWS OF HAPPINESS (1916)
(4 r.) d, Joseph Kaufman; lp, June Daye, Crauford Kent, Inez Buck, Marie Sterling

SORROWS OF LOVE, THE (1916)
(5 r.) d, Charles Giblyn; lp, Bessie Barriscale, William Desmond, Ora Carew, Herschal Mayall

SORROWS OF SATAN, THE (1917)
(5 r.) d, Alexander Butler; lp, Gladys Cooper, Owen Nares, Cecil Humphreys, Lionel d'Aragon

SOUL ADRIFT, A
(SEE: TARNISHED REPUTATIONS, 1920)

SOUL AND BODY (1921)
(6 r.) d, Frank Beal; lp, Ann Luther, William Garland, Frank Brownlee

SOUL ENSLAVED, A (1916)
(5 r.) d, Cleo Madison; lp, Cleo Madison, Irma Sorter, Tom Chatterton, Douglas Gerrard

SOUL FOR SALE, A (1915, Brit.)
(4 r.) d, Thomas Bentley; lp, Austen Camp

SOUL FOR SALE, A (1918)
(6 r.) d, Allen Holubar; lp, Dorothy Phillips, Albert Roscoe, Catherine Kirkwood, Harry Dunkinson

SOUL HARVEST, THE
(SEE: SOULS IN BONDAGE, 1923)

SOUL IN TRUST, A (1918)
(7 r.) d, Gilbert P. Hamilton; lp, Belle Bennett, J. Barney Sherry, Darrel Foss, Lillian West

SOUL MARKET, THE (1916)
(5 r.) d, Francis J. Grandon; lp, Olga Petrova, Arthur Hoops, Wilmuth Merkyl, Fritz De Lint

SOUL MASTER, THE (1917)
(5 r.) d, Marguerite Bertsch; lp, Earle Williams, Billie Billings, Katherine Lewis, Julia Swayne Gordon

SOUL MATES (1916)
(5 r.) d, William Russell; lp, William Russell, Charlotte Burton, Leona Hutton, Harry Keenan

SOUL OF A CHILD, THE (1916)
(5 r.) d, Jack Gorman; lp, Em Gorman, John Dunn, Wellington Playter, Nancy Baring

SOUL OF A MAN, THE (1921)
(6 r.) d, William Nigh;

SOUL OF A WOMAN, THE (1915)
(5 r.) d, Edwin Carewe; lp, Emily Stevens, George LeGuere, Theodore Babcock, Walter Hitchcock

SOUL OF A WOMAN, THE (1922)
(? r.) lp, Jane Novak

SOUL OF BRONZE, THE (1921)
(? r.) lp, Harry Houdini

SOUL OF BUDDHA, THE (1918)
(5 r.) d, J. Gordon Edwards; lp, Theda Bara, Hugh Thompson, Victor Kennard, Anthony Merlo

SOUL OF FRANCE (1929, Fr.)
(8 r.) d, A. Duges, A. Ryder; lp, M. Desjardins, Jean Murat, G. Charlia, Michele Verly

SOUL OF GUILDA LOIS, THE
(SEE: SOUL'S CRUCIFIXION, A, 1919, Brit.)

SOUL OF KURA SAN, THE (1916)
(5 r.) d, Edward J. LeSaint; lp, Sessue Hayakawa, Myrtle Stedman, Tsuru Aoki, George Webb

SOUL OF MAGDALEN, THE (1917)
(5 r.) d, Burton L. King; lp, Olga Petrova, Wyndham Standing, Mahlon Hamilton, Mathilde Brundage

SOUL OF MEXICO (1932, Mex.)
(5 r.) d, David Kirkland; lp, Ernesto Gillen, Alicia Ortiz

SOUL OF SATAN, THE (1917)
(5 r.) d, Otis Turner; lp, Gladys Brockwell, Bertram Grassby, Charles Clary, William Burress

SOUL WITHOUT WINDOWS, A (1918)
(5 r.) d, Travers Vale; lp, Ethel Clayton, Frank Mayo, Richard Clarke, Eugenie Woodward

SOUL-FIRE (1925)
(9 r.) d, John S. Robertson; lp, Richard Barthelmess, Bessie Love, Percy Ames, Charles Esdale

SOULS ADRIFT (1917)
(5 r.) d, Harley Knoles; lp, Ethel Clayton, Milton Sills, John Davidson, Frank de Vernon

SOUL'S AWAKENING, A (1922, Brit.)
(6 r.) d, W.P. Kellino; lp, David Hawthorne, Flora le Breton, Ethel Oliver, Maurice Thompson

SOUL'S CRUCIFIXION, A (1919, Brit.)
(6 r.) d, Frank Wilson; lp, Violet Hopson, Basil Gill, Cameron Carr, Richard Buttery

SOUL'S CYCLE, THE (1916)
(5 r.) d, Ulysses Davis; lp, Margaret Gibson, John Oaker, George Claire, Jr., George Stanley

SOULS FOR SABLES (1925)
(7 r.) d, James C. McKay; lp, Claire Windsor, Eugene O'Brien, Claire Adams, Edith Yorke

SOULS IN BONDAGE (1916)
(5 r.) d, Edgar Lewis; lp, Nance O'Neil, Ida Stanhope, William Corbett, Bernard Siegel

SOULS IN BONDAGE (1923)
(7 r.) d, William H. Clifford; lp, Pat O'Malley, Cleo Madison, Otto Lederer, Eugenia Gilbert

SOULS IN PAWN (1917)
(5 r.) d, Henry King; lp, Gail Kane, Douglas MacLean, Robert Klein, Frank Rickert

SOULS OF MEN (1921)
(? r.) lp, William Jeffries

SOULS ON THE ROAD (1921, Jap.)
(? r.) d, Minoru Murata, Kaoru Osanai; lp, Mikio Hisamatsu, Denmei Suzuki, Haruko Sawamura, Komei Minami

SOULS TRIUMPHANT (1915)
(4 r.) d, John B. O'Brien; lp, Lillian Gish, Wilfred Lucas, Louise Hamilton, Spottiswoode Aitken

SOURCE, THE (1918)
(5 r.) d, Donald Crisp, George Melford; lp, Wallace Reid, Ann Little, Theodore Roberts, James Cruze

SOUS LA MENACE (1916, Fr.)
(? r.) d, Andre Hugon

SOUTH OF PANAMA (1928)
(7 r.) lp, Carmelita Geraghty, Edouard Raquello, Lewis Sargent, Philo McCullough

SOUTH OF SANTA FE (1924)
(5 r.) lp, Art Mix

SOUTH OF THE EQUATOR (1924)
(5 r.) d, William James Craft; lp, Kenneth McDonald, Eugene Corey, Robert Barnes, Virginia Warwick

SOUTH SEA BUBBLE, A (1928, Brit.)
(8 r.) d, T. Hayes Hunter; lp, Ivor Novello, Benita Hume, Annette Benson, S.J. Warmington

SOUTH SEA LOVE (1927)
(7 r.) d, Ralph Ince; lp, Patsy Ruth Miller, Lee Shumway, Alan Brooks, Harry Crocker

SOUTHERN JUSTICE (1917)
(5 r.) d, Lynn F. Reynolds; lp, Myrtle Gonzales, George Hernandez, Jack Curtis, Jean Hersholt

SOUTHERN PRIDE (1917)
(5 r.) d, Henry King; lp, Gail Kane, Cora Drew, Jack Vosburgh, Robert Klein

SOWERS, THE (1916)
(5 r.) d, William C. De Mille; lp, Blanche Sweet, Thomas Meighan, Mabel Van Buren, Ernest Joy

SOWERS AND REAPERS (1917)
(5 r.) d, George D. Baker; lp, Emmy Wehlen, George Stuart Christie, Frank Currier, Peggy Parr

SOWING THE WIND (1916, Brit.)
(5 r.) d, Cecil M. Hepworth; lp, Henry Ainley, Alma Taylor, Stewart Rome, Violet Hopson

SOWING THE WIND (1921)
(9 r.) d, John M. Stahl; lp, Anita Stewart, James Morrison, Myrtle Stedman, Ralph Lewis

SPAN OF LIFE, THE (1914)
(5 r.) d, Edward Mackey; lp, Lionel Barrymore, Gladys Wynne, Lester Chambers

SPANGLES (1926)
(6 r.) d, Frank O'Connor; lp, Marian Nixon, Pat O'Malley, Hobart Bosworth, Gladys Brockwell

SPANGLES (1928, Brit.)
(7 r.) d, George J. Banfield; lp, Fern Andra, Forrester Harvey, Lewis Dayton, A. Bromley Davenport

SPANIARD, THE (1925)
(7 r.) d, Raoul Walsh; lp, Richardo Cortez, Jetta Goudal, Noah Beery, Mathilda Brundage

SPANISH DANCER, THE (1923)
(9 r.) d, Herbert Brenon; lp, Pola Negri, Antonio Moreno, Wallace Beery, Kathlyn Williams

SPANISH JADE, THE (1915)
(6 r.) d, Wilfred Lucas; lp, Betty Belairs, Bess Meredyth

SPANISH JADE (1922, Brit.)
(7 r.) d, John S. Robertson, Tom Geraghty; lp, David Powell, Evelyn Brent, Marc McDermott, Charles de Rochefort

SPARK DIVINE, THE (1919)
(5 r.) d, Tom Terriss; lp, Alice Joyce, William Carlton Jr, Eulalie Jensen, Frank Norcross

SPARKS OF FLINT (1921)
(5 r.) d, Roy Clements; lp, Jack Hoxie

SPARTAKIADA (1929, USSR)
(5 r.) d, I.M. Poselsky, V. Rotov

SPECTRE HAUNTS EUROPE, A (1923, USSR)
(9 r.) d, Vladimir Gardin; lp, Zova Barantsevich, Oleg Froelich, I. Talanov, Vasili Kovrigin

SPEED (1925)
(6 r.) d, Edward J. Le Saint; lp, Betty Blythe, Pauline Garon, William V. Mong, Arthur Rankin

SPEED CLASSIC, THE (1928)
(5 r.) d, Bruce Mitchell; lp, Rex Lease, Mitchell Lewis, Mildred Harris, James Mason

SPEED DEMON, THE (1925)
(5 r.) d, Robert N. Bradbury; lp, Kenneth McDonald, Peggy Montgomery, B. Wayne Lamont, Art Manning

SPEED LIMIT, THE (1926)
(6 r.) d, Frank O'Connor; lp, Raymond McKee, Ethel Shannon, Bruce Gordon, George Chapman

SPEED MADNESS (1925)
(5 r.) d, Bruce Mitchell; lp, Frank Merrill, Clara Horton, Evelyn Sherman, Garry O'Dell

SPEED MANIAC, THE (1919)
(5 r.) d, Edward J. Le Saint; lp, Tom Mix, Eva Novak, Charles K. French, Hayward Mack

SPEED SPOOK, THE (1924)
(7 r.) d, Charles Hines; lp, Johnny Hines, Faire Binney, Edmund Breese, Warner Richmond

SPEED WILD (1925)
(5 r.) d, Harry Garson; lp, Lefty Flynn, Ethel Shannon, Frank Elliott, Ralph McCullough

SPEEDING HOOFS (1927)
(5 r.) d, Louis Chaudet; lp, Dick Hatton

SPEEDING THROUGH (1926)
(6 r.) d, Bertram Bracken; lp, Creighton Hale, Judy King, Helen Lynch

SPEEDING VENUS, THE (1926)
(6 r.) d, Robert Thornby; lp, Priscilla Dean, Robert Frazer, Dale Fuller, Johnny Fox

SPEEDWAY (1929)
(8 r.) d, Harry Beaumont; lp, William Haines, Anita Page, Ernest Torrence, Karl Dane

SPEEDY MEADE (1919)
(5 r.) d, Ira M. Lowry; lp, Louis Bennison, Katherine MacDonald, Neil Moran, Claire Adams

SPEEDY SMITH (1927)
(5 r.) d, Duke Worne; lp, Billy Sullivan, Hazel Deane, Harry Tenbrook, Virginia True Boardman

SPEEDY SPURS (1926)
(5 r.) d, Richard Thorpe; lp, Buffalo Bill Jr., Charles Whittaker Jr., James Welch, Alma Rayford

SPELL OF THE YUKON, THE (1916)
(5 r.) d, Burton L. King; lp, Edmund Breese, Christine Mayo, William Sherwood, Evelyn Brent

SPELLBOUND (1916)
(5 r.) d, H.M. & E.D. Horkheimer; lp, Lois Meredith, William Conklin, Bruce Smith, Edward J. Brady

SPENDER, THE (1919)
(5 r.) d, Charles Swickard; lp, Bert Lytell, Mary Anderson, Thomas Jefferson, Clarence Burton

SPENDER OR THE FORTUNES OF PETER, THE (1915)
(5 r.) d, Donald MacKenzie; lp, George Probert, James McCabe, Sam Ryan, Alma Martin

SPENDERS, THE (1921)
(6 r.) d, Jack Conway; lp, Claire Adams, Robert McKim, Joseph J. Dowling, Niles Welch

SPHINX, THE (1916)
(5 r.) d, John Adolfi; lp, Herbert Kelcey, Effie Shannon, Beatrice Nozes, Charles Compton

SPIDER AND THE FLY, THE (1916)
(5 r.) d, J. Gordon Edwards; lp, Robert Mantell, Genevieve Hamper, Claire Whitney, Walter Miller

SPIDERS, THE (1919, Ger.)
(14 r.) d, Fritz Lang; lp, Carl de Vogt, Ressel Orla, Lil Dagover, Paul Morgan

SPIDER'S WEB, THE (1927)
(7 r.) lp, Lorenzo McLane, Evelyn Preer, Edward Thompson, Grace Smythe

SPINNER O' DREAMS (1918, Brit.)
(5 r.) d, Wilfred Noy; lp, Basil Gill, Odette Goimbault, James Carew, Stella Mervyn Campbell

SPIRIT OF GOOD, THE (1920)
(5 r.) d, Paul Cazeneuve; lp, Madlaine Traverse, Frederick Stanton, Dick La Reno, Charles Smiley

SPIRIT OF ROMANCE, THE (1917)
(5 r.) d, E. Mason Hopper; lp, Vivian Martin, Herbert Standing, Colin Chase, Elinor Hancock

SPIRIT OF '17, THE (1918)
(5 r.) d, William Desmond Taylor; lp, Jack Pickford, Katherine MacDonald, Charles H. Geldert, Edythe Chapman

SPIRIT OF '76, THE (1917)
(12 r.) d, George Siegmann; lp, Adda Gleason, Doris Pawn, Jane Novak, Howard Gaye

SPIRIT OF THE CONQUEROR, OR THE NAPOLEON OF LABOR, THE (1915)
(5 r.)

SPIRIT OF THE U.S.A., THE (1924)
(9 r.) d, Emory Johnson; lp, Johnnie Walker, Mary Carr, Carl Stockdale, Dave Kirby

SPIRIT OF YOUTH, THE (1929)
(7 r.) d, Walter Lang; lp, Dorothy Sebastian, Larry Kent, Betty Francisco, Maurice Murphy

SPITE BRIDE, THE (1919)
(5 r.) d, Charles Giblyn; lp, Olive Thomas, Robert Ellis, Jack Mulhall, Claire Du Brey

SPITFIRE, THE (1914)
(4 r.) lp, Carlyle Blackwell, Violet Mersereau, Redfield Clark, Lionel Adams

SPITFIRE (1922)
(? r.) lp, Edna Morton

SPLENDID COWARD, THE (1918, Brit.)
(6 r.) d, F. Martin Thornton; lp, James Knight, Joan Legge, Roy Travers, Winifred Evans

SPLENDID CRIME, THE (1926)
(6 r.) d, William C. De Mille; lp, Bebe Daniels, Neil Hamilton, Anne Cornwall, Anthony Jowitt

SPLENDID FOLLY (1919, Brit.)
(5 r.) d, Arrigo Bocchi; lp, Manora Thew, Hayford Hobbs, Evelyn Harding, Charles Vane

SPLENDID HAZARD, A (1920)
(6 r.) d, Arthur Rosson; lp, Henry B. Walthall, Rosemary Theby, Norman Kerry, Ann Forrest

SPLENDID ROMANCE, THE (1918)
(5 r.) d, Edward Jose; lp, Enrico Caruso, Ormi Hawley, Charlotte Ives

SPLENDID SINNER, THE (1918)
(6 r.) d, Edwin Carewe; lp, Mary Garden, Hamilton Revelle, Anders Randolf, Hassan Mussalli

SPOILERS, THE (1923)
(8 r.) d, Lambert Hillyer; lp, Milton Sills, Anna Q.Nilsson, Barbara Bedford, Robert Edeson

SPOILERS OF THE WEST (1927)
(6 r.) d, W.S. Van Dyke; lp, Tim McCoy, Marjorie Daw, William Fairbanks, Chief Big Tree

SPORT OF THE GODS, THE (1921)
(7 r.) d, Henry Vernot; lp, Elizabeth Boyer, Edward R. Abrams, George Edward Brown, Leon Williams

SPORTING AGE, THE (1928)
(6 r.) d, Erle C. Kenton; lp, Belle Bennett, Holmes Herbert, Carroll Nye, Josephine Borio

SPORTING BLOOD (1916)
(5 r.) d, Bertram Bracken; lp, Dorothy Bernard, Glen White, DeWitt Jennings, Sidney Bracy

SPORTING CHANCE, A (1919)
(5 r.) d, Henry King; lp, William Russell, Fritzi Brunette, George Periolat, J. Farrell MacDonald

SPORTING CHANCE, A (1919)
(5 r.) d, George Melford; lp, Ethel Clayton, Jack Holt, Anna Q. Nilsson, Herbert Standing

SPORTING CHANCE, THE (1925)
(7 r.) d, Oscar Apfel; lp, Lou Tellegen, Dorothy Phillips, George Fawcett, Theodore von Eltz

SPORTING DOUBLE, A (1922, Brit.)
(5 r.) d, Arthur Rooke; lp, John Stuart, Lillian Douglas, Douglas Munro, Humberston Wright

SPORTING DUCHESS, THE (1915)
(5 r.) d, Barry O'Neil; lp, Rose Coughlan, Ethel Clayton, George Soule Spencer, Rosetta Brice

SPORTING DUCHESS, THE (1920)
(7 r.) d, George Terwilliger; lp, Alice Joyce, Percy Marmont, Gustav von Seyffertitz, Edith Campbell Walker

SPORTING INSTINCT, THE (1922, Brit.)
(5 r.) d, Arthur Rooke; lp, Lillian Douglas, J.R. Tozer, Mickey Brantford, Tom Coventry

SPORTING LIFE (1918)
(7 r.) d, Maurice Tourneur; lp, Ralph Graves, Constance Binney, Warner Richmond, Charles Eldridge

SPORTING LIFE (1925)
(7 r.) d, Maurice Tourneur; lp, Bert Lytell, Marian Nixon, Paulette Duval, Cyril Chadwick

SPORTING LOVER, THE (1926)
(7 r.) d, Alan Hale; lp, Conway Tearle, Barbara Bedford, Ward Crane, Arthur Rankin

SPORTING VENUS, THE (1925)
(7 r.) d, Marshall Neilan; lp, Blanche Sweet, Ronald Colman, Lew Cody, Josephine Crowell

SPORTING WEST (1925)
(5 r.) lp, Guinn "Big Boy" Williams, Peggy O'Day

SPORTING YOUTH (1924)
(7 r.) d, Harry A. Pollard; lp, Reginald Denny, Laura La Plante, Hallam Cooley, Frederick Vroom

SPORTSMAN'S WIFE, A (1921, Brit.)
(7 r.) d, Walter West; lp, Violet Hopson, Gregory Scott, Clive Brook, Mercy Hatton

SPOTLIGHT, THE (1927)
(5 r.) d, Frank Tuttle; lp, Esther Ralston, Neil Hamilton, Nicholas Soussainin, Arlette Marchal

SPOTLIGHT SADIE (1919)
(5 r.) d, Lawrence Trimble; lp, Mae Marsh, Wallace MacDonald, Mary Thurman, Betty Schade

SPOTTED LILY, THE (1917)
(5 r.) d, Harry Solter; lp, Ella Hall, Gretchen Lederer, Victor Rottman, Charles Hill Mailes

SPREADING EVIL, THE (1919)
(7 r.) d, James Keane; lp, Howard Davies, Leo Pierson, Carlyn Wagner, Irene Wylie

SPRING COMES WITH THE LADIES (1932, Jap.)
(? r.) d, Yasujiro Ozu

SPRING FEVER (1927)
(7 r.) d, Edward Sedgwick; lp, William Haines, Joan Crawford, George K. Arthur, George Fawcett

SPURS AND SADDLES (1927)
(5 r.) d, Clifford S. Smith; lp, Art Acord, Fay Wray, Bill Dyer, J. Gordon Russell

SPURS OF SYBIL, THE (1918)
(5 r.) d, Travers Vale; lp, Alice Brady, John Bowers, John Davidson, Iseth Munro

SPY, THE (1914)
(4 r.) d, Otis Turner; lp, Herbert Rawlinson, Edna Maison, William Worthington, Frank Lloyd

SPY, THE (1917)
(7 r.) d, Richard Stanton; lp, Dustin Farnum, Winifred Kingston, Charles Clary, Howard Gaye

SPY OF MME. POMPADOUR (1929, Ger.)
(9 r.) d, Karl Grune; lp, Fritz Kortner, Mona Maris, Dene Morel, H. Malikoff

SQUANDERED LIVES (1920, Brit.)
(6 r.) d, Franklin Dyall; lp, Guy Newall, Ivy Duke, Hugh C. Buckler, C. Lawford Davidson

SQUARE CROOKS (1928)
(6 r.) d, Lewis Seiler; lp, Robert Armstrong, Johnny Mack Brown, Dorothy Dwan, Dorothy Appleby

SQUARE DEAL, A (1917)
(5 r.) d, Harley Knoles; lp, Carlyle Blackwell, June Elvidge, Henry Hull, Charlotte Granville

SQUARE DEAL, A (1918)
(5 r.) d, Lloyd Ingraham; lp, Margarita Fischer, Jack Mower, Val Paul, Constance Johnson

SQUARE DEAL MAN, THE (1917)
(5 r.) d, William S. Hart; lp, William S. Hart, Mary McIvor, Joseph J. Dowling, Mary Jane Irving

SQUARE DEAL SANDERSON (1919)
(5 r.) d, William S. Hart; lp, William S. Hart, Ann Little, Frank Whitson, Lloyd Bacon

SQUARE DECEIVER, THE (1917)
(5 r.) d, Fred J. Balshofer; lp, Harold Lockwood, Pauline Curley, William Clifford, Dora Mills

SQUARE JOE (1921)
(? r.) lp, Joe Jeanette, John Lester Johnson, Marion Moore, Bob Slater

SQUARE SHOOTER, THE (1920)
(5 r.) d, Paul Cazenuve; lp, Buck Jones, Patsy De Forrest, Charles K. French, Al Fremont

SQUAW MAN, THE (1918)
(6 r.) d, Cecil B. De Mille; lp, Elliott Dexter, Ann Little, Katherine MacDonald, Theodore Roberts

SQUAW MAN'S SON, THE (1917)
(5 r.) d, Edward J. Le Saint; lp, Wallace Reid, Dorothy Davenport, Anita King, Donald Bowles

SQUIRE OF LONG HADLEY, THE (1925, Brit.)
(6 r.) d, Sinclair Hill; lp, Marjorie Hume, Brian Aherne, G.H. Mulcaster, Eileen Dennes

SQUIRE PHIN (1921)
(5 r.) d, Leopold Wharton; lp, Maclyn Arbuckle

STABLE COMPANIONS (1922, Brit.)
(6 r.) d, Albert Ward; lp, Clive Brook, Lillian Hall Davis, Robert English, Arthur Pusey

STACKED CARDS (1926)
(5 r.) d, Robert Eddy; lp, Fred Church, Kathryn McGuire, Robert Thurston, John Watson

STAGE COACH DRIVER (1924)
(5 r.) lp, Tom Mix

STAGE ROMANCE, A (1922)
(7 r.) d, Herbert Brenon; lp, William Farnum, Peggy Shaw, Holmes Herbert, Mario Carillo

STAGE STRUCK (1917)
(5 r.) d, Edward Morrissey; lp, Dorothy Gish, Frank Bennett, Kate Toncray, Jennie Lee

STAGE STRUCK (1925)
(7 r.) d, Allan Dwan; lp, Gloria Swanson, Lawrence Gray, Gertrude Astor, Marguerite Evans

STAIN IN THE BLOOD, THE (1916)
(5 r.) d, Murdock MacQuarrie; lp, Edythe Sterling, Norbert A. Myles, Murdock MacQuarrie, Dorothy Nash

STAINLESS BARRIER, THE (1917)
(5 r.) d, Thomas Heffron; lp, Irene Hunt, Jack Livingstone, H.A. Barrows, Rowland Lee

STAKING HIS LIFE (1918)
(5 r.)

STAMPEDE, THE (1921)
(5 r.) d, Francis Ford; lp, Texas Guinan, Francis Ford, Frederick Moore, Jean Carpenter

STAMPEDE (1930, Sudan)
(5 r.) d, Major C. Court Treatt lp, Shekh Fadl, Abd el Aziz, Abd el Nebi, Fatma Idam

STAMPEDE THUNDER (1925)
(5 r.) d, Tom Gibson; lp, Pete Morrison, Betty Goodwin,

STAMPEDIN' TROUBLE (1925)
(5 r.) d, Forrest Sheldon; lp, Bruce Gordon

STAR DUST TRAIL, THE (1924)
(5 r.) d, Edmund Mortimer; lp, Shirley Mason, Bryant Washburn, Thomas R. Mills, Richard Tucker

STAR OF INDIA, THE (1913)
(4 r.)

STAR REPORTER, THE (1921)
(6 r.) d, Duke Worne; lp, Billie Rhodes, Truman Van Dyke, William Horne

STAR ROVER, THE (1920)
(6 r.) d, Edward Sloman; lp, Courtenay Foote, Thelma Percy, Pomeroy "Doc" Cannon, Dwight Crittenden

STARK LOVE (1927)
(7 r.) d, Karl Brown; lp, Helen Munday, Forrest James, Silas Miracle, Reb Grogan

STARLIGHT, THE UNTAMED (1925)
(5 r.) d, Harry Webb; lp, Jack Perrin

STARLIGHT'S REVENGE (1926)
(5 r.) d, Harry Webb; lp, Jack Perrin

STARLIT GARDEN, THE (1923, Brit.)
(6 r.) d, Guy Newall; lp, Guy Newall, Ivy Duke, Valia, A. Bromley Davenport

STATION CONTENT (1918)
(5 r.) d, Arthur Hoyt; lp, Lee Hill, Gloria Swanson, Arthur Millett, Nellie Allen

STATION MASTER, THE (1928, USSR)
(7 r.) d, Yuri Zheliabuzhsky, Ivan Moskvin; lp, I. Moskvin, Vera Malinovskaya, Boris Tamarin

STAY HOME
(SEE: I CAN EXPLAIN, 1922)

STEALERS, THE (1920)
(7 r.) d, William Christy Cabanne; lp, William H. Tooker, Robert Kenyon, Myrtle Morse, Norma Shearer

STEEL KING, THE (1919)
(5 r.) d, Oscar Apfel; lp, Montagu Love, June Elvidge, Charles Mackay, Marion Barney

STEEL PREFERRED (1926)
(7 r.) d, James P. Hogan; lp, Vera Reynolds, William Boyd, Hobart Bosworth, Charlie Murray

STELLA (1921)
(6 r.) d, Edwin J. Collins; lp, Molly Adair, Manning Hayes, Charles Vane, Betty Farquhar

STELLE OF THE ROYAL MOUNTED (1925)
(6 r.) d, David Smith; lp, Bert Lytell, Stuart Holmes, Charlotte Merriam, Sidney De Grey

STEPAN KHALTURIN (1925, USSR)
(7 r.) d, Alexander Ivanovsky; lp, Anotoli Morozov, Angelo Raupenas, A. Sysoyev, N. Schmidthof

STEPMOTHER, THE (1914, Pol.)
(5 r.) d, Avrom Yitskhok Kaminsky; lp, Lea Kompaniejec, Shmuel Landau, M. Shlosberg

STEPPIN' OUT (1925)
(6 r.) d, Frank Strayer; lp, Dorothy Revier, Ford Sterling, Robert Agnew, Cissy Fitzgerald

STEPPING LIVELY (1924)
(6 r.) d, James W. Horne; lp, Richard Talmadge, Mildred Harris, Norval MacGregor, Brinsley Shaw

STEPPING OUT (1919)
(5 r.) d, Fred Niblo; lp, Enid Bennett, Niles Welch, Julia Faye, Gertrude Claire

STEPPING STONE, THE (1916)
(5 r.) d, Reginald Barker; lp, Frank Keenan, Mary Boland, Robert McKim, Margaret Thompson

STICK TO YOUR STORY (1926)
(5 r.) d, Harry J. Brown; lp, Billy Sullivan, Estelle Bradley, Melbourne MacDowell, Bruce Gordon

STICKS
(SEE: BIT OF KINDLING, A, 1917)

STIGMATIZED ONE, THE
(SEE: LOVE ONE ANOTHER, 1922, Den.)

STILL ALARM, THE (1926)
(7 r.) d, Edward Laemmle; lp, Helene Chadwick, William Russell, Richard C. Travers, Edna Marion

STING OF VICTORY, THE (1916)
(5 r.) d, J. Charles Haydon; lp, Henry B. Walthall, Antoinette Walker, Anne Leigh, John Lorenz

STIRRUP CUP SENSATION, THE (1924, Brit.)
(5 r.) d, Walter West; lp, Violet Hopson, Stewart Rome, Cameron Carr, Judd Green

STITCH IN TIME, A (1919)
(5 r.) d, Ralph Ince; lp, Gladys Leslie, Eugene Strong, Agnes Ayres, Charles Walton

STOLEN CHILD, THE (1923)
(5 r.) lp, Matty Roubert

STOLEN GOODS (1915)
(5 r.) d, George Melford; lp, Blanche Sweet, House Peters, Cleo Ridgley, Sydney Deane

STOLEN HEIRLOOMS, THE (1915, Brit.)
(4 r.) d, Charles Raymond; lp, Harry Lorraine, Bert Rex

STOLEN HONOR (1918)
(5 r.) d, Richard S. Stanton; lp, Virginia Pearson, Clay Clement, Ethel Hallor, Walter Law

STOLEN HONOURS (1914, Brit.)
(4 r.) d, Joe Evans; lp, Joe Evans, Fred Evans, Geraldine Maxwell

STOLEN HOURS (1918)
(5 r.) d, Travers Vale; lp, Ethel Clayton, John Bowers, Joseph Herbert, Louise De Rigney

STOLEN KISS, THE (1920)
(5 r.) d, Kenneth Webb; lp, Constance Binney, Rod La Rocque, George Backus, Bradley Barker

STOLEN LOVE (1928)
(7 r.) d, Lynn Shores; lp, Marceline Day, Rex Lease, Owen Moore, Helen Lynch

STOLEN MASTERPIECE, THE (1914, Brit.)
(4 r.) d, H.O. Martinek; lp, H.O. Martinek, Ivy Montford, Douglas Payne

STOLEN MOMENTS (1920)
(6 r.) d, James Vincent; lp, Marguerite Namara, Rudolph Valentino, Andre Davan, Aileen Savage [Pringle]

STOLEN ORDERS (1918)
(8 r.) d, Harley Knoles, George Kelson; lp, Kitty Gordon, Carlyle Blackwell, Montagu Love, June Elvidge

STOLEN PARADISE, THE (1917)
(5 r.) d, Harley Knoles; lp, Ethel Clayton, Edward Langford, Pinna Nesbit, George MacQuarrie

STOLEN PLAY, THE (1917)
(4 r.) d, Harry Harvey; lp, Ruth Roland, Edward J. Brady, William Conklin, Lucy Blake

STOLEN RANCH, THE (1926)
(5 r.) d, William Wyler; lp, Fred Humes, Louise Lorraine, William Norton Bailey, Ralph McCullough

STOLEN SACRIFICE, THE (1916, Brit.)
(4 r.) d, Sidney Morgan; lp, Peggy Richards

STOLEN SECRETS (1924)
(5 r.) d, Irving Cummings; lp, Herbert Rawlinson, Kathleen Myers, Edwards Davis, Henry Herbert

STOLEN TREATY, THE (1917)
(5 r.) d, Paul Scardon; lp, Earle Williams, Corinne Griffith, Denton Vane, Robert Gaillard

STOLEN TRIUMPH, THE (1916)
(5 r.) d, David Thompson; lp, Julius Steger, Harry Burkhardt, Clara Whipple, Clara Blandick

STONE RIDER, THE (1923, Ger.)
(? r.) d, Fritz Wendhausen; lp, Rudolf Klein-Rogge, Georg John, Lucie Mannheim, Fritz Kampers

STOOL PIGEON (1928)
(6 r.) d, Renaud Hoffman; lp, Olive Borden, Charles Delaney, Lucy Beamont, Louis Natheaux

STOOL PIGEON, THE
(SEE: TIP-OFF, THE, 1929)

STOP AT NOTHING (1924)
(5 r.) d, Charles R. Seeling; lp, George Larkin

STOP FLIRTING (1925)
(6 r.) d, Scott Sidney; lp, John T. Murray, Wanda Hawley, Hallam Cooley, Ethel Shannon

STOP, LOOK, AND LISTEN (1926)
(6 r.) d, Larry Semon; lp, Larry Semon, Dorothy Dwan, Mary Carr, William Gillespie

STOP THIEF (1915)
(5 r.) d, George Fitzmaurice; lp, Mary Ryan, Harry Mestayer, Harold Howard, Albert Tavernier

STORM, THE (1916)
(5 r.) d, Frank Reicher; lp, Blanche Sweet, Thomas Meighan, Theodore Roberts, Richard Sterling

STORM BREAKER, THE (1925)
(7 r.) d, Edward Sloman; lp, House Peters, Ruth Clifford, Nina Romano, Ray Hallor

STORM GIRL (1922)
(5 r.) d, Francis Ford; lp, Peggy O'Day, Francis Ford, Phil Ford

STORMY KNIGHT, A (1917)
(5 r.) d, Elmer Clifton; lp, Franklyn Farnum, Jean Hersholt, Agnes "Brownie" Vernon, Hayward Mack

STORY OF FLOATING WEEDS, A (1934, Jap.)
(? r.) d, Yasujiro Ozu; lp, Emiko Yakumo, Takeshi Sakamoto

STORY OF SEVEN WHO WERE HANGED (1920, USSR)
(8 r.) d, Pyotr Chardynin; lp, Loren, Chitorin, Lorenzo, Vostorgov

STORY OF SUSAN, THE (1916)
(5 r.)

STORY OF THE BLOOD RED ROSE, THE (1914)
(4 r.) d, Colin Campbell; lp, Kathlyn Williams, Wheeler Oakman, Charles Clary, Eugenie Besserer

STORY OF THE ROSARY, THE (1920, Brit.)
(5 r.) d, Percy Nash; lp, Malvina Longfellow, Dick Webb, Charles Vane, Frank Tennant

STORY WITHOUT A NAME, THE (1924)
(6 r.) d, Irvin Willat; lp, Agnes Ayres, Antonio Moreno, [Frederick] Tyrone Power, Louis Wolheim

STOWAWAY GIRL, THE (1916)
(5 r.)

STRAIGHT FROM PARIS (1921)
(6 r.) d, Harry Garson; lp, Clara Kimball Young, Bertram Grassby, William P. Carleton, Betty Francisco

STRAIGHT FROM THE SHOULDER (1921)
(6 r.) d, Bernard Durning; lp, Buck Jones, Helen Ferguson, Norman Selby, Frances Hatton

STRAIGHT SHOOTIN' (1927)
(5 r.) d, William Wyler; lp, Ted Wells, Garry O'Dell, Lillian Gilmore, Joe Bennett

STRAIGHT SHOOTING (1917)
(5 r.) d, Jack [John] Ford; lp, Harry Carey, Molly Malone, Duke Lee, George Berrell

STRAIGHT THROUGH (1925)
(5 r.) d, Arthur Rosson; lp, William Desmond, Marguerite Clayton, Albert J. Smith, Ruth Stonehouse

STRAIGHT WAY, THE (1916)
(4 r.) d, Will S. Davis; lp, Valeska Suratt, Herbert Heyes, Glenn White, Claire Whitney

STRAIGHTFORWARD BOY, A (1929, Jap.)
(? r.) d, Yasujiro Ozu

STRANDED (1916)
(5 r.) d, Lloyd Ingraham; lp, De Wolf Hopper, Carl Stockdale, Bessie Love, Frank Bennett

STRANDED IN ARCADY (1917)
(5 r.) d, Frank Crane; lp, Irene Castle, Elliott Dexter, Pell Trenton, George Majeroni

STRANDED IN PARIS (1926)
(7 r.) d, Arthur Rosson; lp, Bebe Daniels, James Hall, Ford Sterling, Iris Stuart

STRANGE BORDER, THE (1920)
(5 r.) d, Clarence Badger; lp, Will Rogers, Jimmy Rogers, Irene Rich, James Mason

STRANGE CASE OF DISTRICT ATTORNEY M. (1930)
(5 r.) d, Rudolph Meinert; lp, Gregor Chmara, Warwick Ward, Jean Angelo, Marie Jacobeni

STRANGE CASE OF PHILIP KENT, THE (1916, Brit.)
(4 r.) d, Fred W. Durrant; lp, Cyril Morton, J. Hastings Batson

STRANGE IDOLS (1922)
(5 r.) d, Bernard J. Durning; lp, Dustin Farnum, Doris Pawn, Philo McCullough, Richard Tucker

STRANGE RIDER, THE (1925)
(5 r.) d, Ward Hayes; lp, Yakima Canutt

STRANGE TRANSGRESSOR, A (1917)
(5 r.) d, Reginald Barker; lp, Louise Glaum, J. Barney Sherry, Colin Chase, Dorcas Matthews

STRANGE WOMAN, THE (1918)
(5 r.) d, Edward J. Le Saint; lp, Gladys Brockwell, William Scott, Charles Clary, Harry Depp

STRANGER, THE (1913, Pol.)
(4 r.) d, Nahum Lipovsky; lp, Regina Kaminska, Jacob Libert, Gershon Weissman, Vera Zoslovsky

STRANGER FROM SOMEWHERE, A (1916)
(5 r.) d, William Worthington; lp, Franklyn Farnum, Agnes Vernon, Claire McDowell, Helen Wright

STRANGER IN CANYON VALLEY, THE (1921)
(5 r.) d, Cliff Smith; lp, Edith Sterling

STRANGER OF THE HILLS, THE (1922)
(5 r.) d, Bruce Mitchell; lp, Edward Coxen, Ethel Ritchie, Charles Farra

STRANGLING THREADS (1923, Brit.)
(7 r.) d, Cecil M. Hepworth; lp, Alma Taylor, Campbell Gullan, James Carew, Mary Dibley

STRATHMORE (1915)
(4 r.) lp, Charles Clary, Elmer Clifton, Francelia Billington, Irene Hunt

STRAUSS' SALOME
(SEE: SALOME, 1923)

STRAUSS, THE WALTZ KING (1929, Ger.)
(6 r.) d, Conrad Weine; lp, Alfred Abel, Imre Hardy, Hermine Sterler, Lillian Ellis

STRAWS IN THE WIND (1924, Brit.)
(6 r.) d, Bertram Phillips; lp, Betty Ross Clarke, Queenie Thomas, Fred Paul, Ivo Dawson

STREAK OF LUCK, A (1925)
(5 r.) d, Richard Thorpe; lp, Buffalo Bill Jr., Dorothy Wood, Nelson McDowell, Bertram Marburgh

STREAM OF LIFE, THE (1919)
(7 r.) d, Horace G. Plympton

STREET, THE (1927, Ger.)
(4 r.) d, Karl Grune; lp, Eugen Klopfer, Aud Edege-Nissen, Leonhard Haskel, Lucie Hoflich

STREET ANGEL (1928)
(9 r.) d, Frank Borzage; lp, Janet Gaynor, Charles Farrell, Guido Trento, Henry Armetta

STREET CALLED STRAIGHT, THE (1920)
(5 r.) d, Wallace Worsley; lp, Milton Sills, Naomi Childers, Charles Clary, Irene Rich

STREET OF ADVENTURE, THE (1921, Brit.)
(5 r.) d, Kenelm Fossi; lp, Lionelle Howard, Margot Drake, H.V. Tollemach, Irene Rooke

STREET OF FORGOTTEN MEN, THE (1925)
(7 r.) d, Herbert Brenon; lp, Percy Marmont, Mary Brian, Neil Hamilton, John Harrigton

STREET OF ILLUSION, THE (1928)
(7 r.) d, Erle C. Kenton; lp, Virginia Valli, Ian Keith, Harry Myers, Kenneth Thomson

STREET OF SEVEN STARS, THE (1918)
(6 r.) d, John B. O'Brien; lp, Doris Kenyon, Hugh Thompson, Carey Hastings, Stephen Carr

STREET OF TEARS, THE (1924)
(5 r.) d, Travers Vale; lp, Tom Santschi, Marguerite Clayton, Gordon Griffith, Barbara Tennant

STREETS OF ILLUSION, THE (1917)
(5 r.) d, William Parke; lp, Gladys Hulette, J.H. Gilmour, William Parke Jr., Richard Barthelmess

STREETS OF LONDON, THE (1929, Brit.)
(4 r.) d, Norman Lee; lp, David Dunbar, Jack Rutherford, Charles Lincoln, Beatrice Duffy

STREETS OF SHANGHAI (1927)
(6 r.) d, Louis Gasnier; lp, Pauline Starke, Kenneth Harlan, Eddie Gribbon, Margaret Livingston

STRENGTH OF DONALD MCKENZIE, THE (1916)
(5 r.) d, William Russell; lp, William Russell, Charlotte Burton, Harry Keenan, George Ahearn

STRENGTH OF THE PINES (1922)
(5 r.) d, Edgar Lewis; lp, William Russell, Irene Rich, Lule Warrenton, Arthur Morrison

STRENGTH OF THE WEAK, THE (1916)
(5 r.) d, Lucius Henderson; lp, Mary Fuller, Edward Davis, Harry Hilliard, Curtis Benton

STRICTLY CONFIDENTIAL (1919)
(5 r.) d, Clarence G. Badger; lp, Madge Kennedy, John Bowers, Robert Bolder, Lydia Yeamans Titus

STRIFE (1919)
(5 r.) lp, George Le Guere

STRIFE ETERNAL, THE (1915, Brit.)
(6 r.) d, Bert Haldane, F. Martin Thornton; lp, Blanche Forsythe, Roy Travers, Robert Purdie, Thos H. MacDonald

STRIKE (1925, USSR)
(7 r.) d, Sergei Eisenstein; lp, Gregori Alexandrov, Maxim Strauch, Mikhail Gomarov, Judith Glizer

STRIKERS, THE (1915)
(4 r.)

STRING BEANS (1918)
(5 r.) d, Victor L. Schertzinger; lp, Charles Ray, Jane Novak, John P. Lockney, Donald McDonald

STRIPED STOCKING GANG, THE
(SEE: MRS. CASSELL'S PROFESSION, 1915, Brit.)

STRIPPED FOR A MILLION (1919)
(5 r.) d, L. de la Parelle; lp, Crane Wilbur, Anita King, J.H. Keller, Gladys Bell

STROKE OF MIDNIGHT, THE
(SEE: PHANTOM CARRIAGE, THE, 1921, Swed.)

STRONG MAN, THE (1917, USSR)
(7 r.) d, Vsevolod Meyerhold; lp, Konstantin Khokhlov, Varvara Yanova, Vsevold Meyerhold, M. Zhdanova

STRONG MAN'S WEAKNESS, A (1917, Brit.)
(4 r.) d, A.E. Coleby; lp, Malvina Longellow, A.E. Coleby, Arthur Rooke, Janet Alexander

STRONG WAY, THE (1918)
(5 r.) d, George Kelson; lp, June Elvidge, John Bowers, Isabel Berwin, Joe Herbert

STRONGER LOVE, THE (1916)
(5 r.) d, Frank Lloyd; lp, Vivian Martin, Edward Peil, Frank Lloyd, Alice Knowland

STRONGER THAN DEATH (1920)
(7 r.) d, Herbert Blache, Charles Bryant; lp, Alla Nazimova, Charles Bryant, Charles French, Margaret McWade

STRONGER VOW, THE (1919)
(6 r.) d, Reginald Barker; lp, Geraldine Farrar, Milton Sills, Kate Lester, Tom Santschi

STRONGER WILL, THE (1928)
(7 r.) d, Bernard McEveetty; lp, Percy Marmont, Rita Carewe, Howard Truesdell, Merle Ferris

STRONGEST, THE (1920)
(5 r.) d, Raoul Walsh; lp, Renee Adoree, Carlo Liten, Harrison Hunter, Florence Malone

STRUGGLE, THE (1916)
(5 r.) d, John Ince; lp, Frank Sheridan, Arthur Ashley, Alfred Loring, Isabelle Vernon

STRUGGLE EVERLASTING, THE (1918)
(5 r.) d, James Kirkwood; lp, Florence Reed, Milton Sills, Irving Cummings, Wellington Playter

STUBBORNESS OF GERALDINE, THE (1915)
(5 r.) d, Gaston Mervale; lp, Laura Nelson Hall, Vernon Steele

STUDENT OF PRAGUE, THE (1913, Ger.)
(5 r.) d, Stellan Rye; lp, Paul Wegener, Lyda Salmanova, John Gottowt, Grete Berger

STUDENT PRINCE IN OLD HEIDELBERG, THE (1927)
(10 r.) d, Ernst Lubitsch; lp, Ramon Novarro, Norma Shearer, Jean Hersholt, Gustav von Seyffertitz

STUDIO GIRL, THE (1918)
(5 r.) d, Charles Giblyn; lp, Constance Talmadge, Earle Foxe, Johnny Hines, Edna Earle

STUDY IN SCARLET, A (1914, Brit.)
(6 r.) d, George Pearson; lp, Fred Paul, James Bargington, Agnes Glynne, Harry Paulo

SUBMARINE (1928)
(9 r.) d, Frank Capra; lp, Jack Holt, Dorothy Revier, Ralph Graves, Clarence Burton

SUBMARINE EYE, THE (1917)
(8 r.) d, Winthrop Kelley; lp, Chester Barnett, Lindsay Hall, Charles Hartley, Edith Conway

SUBSTITUTE WIFE, THE (1925)
(6 r.) d, Wilfred May; lp, Jane Novak, Niles Welch, Coit Albertson, Louise Carter

SUBWAY SADIE (1926)
(7 r.) d, Alfred Santell; lp, Dorothy Mackaill, Jack Mulhall, Charles Murray, Peggy Shaw

SUCCESSFUL ADVENTURE, THE (1918)
(5 r.) d, Harry L. Franklin; lp, May Allison, Harry Hilliard, Christine Mayo, Fred Jones

SUCCESSFUL FAILURE, A (1917)
(5 r.) d, Arthur Rosson; lp, Jack Devereaux, Winifred Allen, George Senaut

SUCH A LITTLE PIRATE (1918)
(5 r.) d, George Melford; lp, Lila Lee, Harrison Ford, Theodore Roberts, Guy Oliver

SUCH IS LIFE (1929, Czech)
(6 r.) d, Karl Junghans; lp, Vera Baranovskaya, Theodor Pistek, Wolfgang Zilzer, Valeska Gert

SUDDEN GENTLEMAN, THE (1917)
(5 r.) d, Thomas N. Heffron; lp, William Desmond, Mary McIvor, Jack Richardson, Margaret Shillingford

SUDDEN JIM (1917)
(5 r.) d, Victor Schertzinger; lp, Charles Ray, Sylvia Bremer, Joseph J. Dowling, Lydia Knott

SUDDEN RICHES (1916)
(5 r.) d, Emile Chautard; lp, Robert Warwick, Gerda Holmes, Clara Whipple, Madge Evans

SUE OF THE SOUTH (1919)
(5 r.) d, W. Eugene Moore; lp, Edith Roberts, James Farley, Ruby Lafayette, George Hackathorne

SUICIDE CLUB, THE (1914, Brit.)
(4 r.) d, Maurice Elvey; lp, Montagu Love, Elizabeth Risdon, Fred Groves, M. Gray Murray

SULTANA, THE (1916)
(5 r.) lp, Ruth Roland, William Conklin, Daniel Gilfether, Charles Dudley

SUMMER GIRL, THE (1916)
(5 r.) d, Edwin August; lp, Mollie King, Arthur Ashley, Dave Ferguson, Ruby Hoffman

SUMURUN (1910, Ger.)
(7 r.)

SUMURUN (1921, Ger.)
(8 r.) d, Ernst Lubitsch; lp, Pola Negri, Ernst Lubitsch, Paul Wegener, Harry Leidtke

SUN DOG TRAILS (1923)
(5 r.) d, Lewis King; lp, William Fairbanks

SUNBEAM, THE (1916)
(5 r.) d, Edwin Carewe; lp, Mabel Taliaferro, Raymond McKee, Gerald Griffin, David Thompson

SUNDOWN (1924)
(9 r.) d, Laurence Trimble; lp, Bessie Love, Roy Stewart, Hobart Bosworth, Arthur Hoyt

SUNDOWN SLIM (1920)
(5 r.) d, Val Paul; lp, Harry Carey, Otto Meyers, Ed Jones, Mignonne

SUNDOWN TRAIL, THE (1919)
(6 r.) d, Rollin S. Sturgeon; lp, Monroe Salisbury, Clyde Fillmore, Alice Elliot, Beatrice Domingues

SUNKEN ROCKS (1919, Brit.)
(5 r.) d, Cecil M. Hepworth; lp, Alma Taylor, Gerald Ames, James Carew, Nigel Playfair

SUNLIGHT'S LAST RAID (1917)
(5 r.) d, William Wolbert; lp, Mary Anderson, Alfred Whitman, V. Howard, Fred Burns

SUNNY JANE (1917)
(5 r.) d, Sherwood MacDonald; lp, Jackie Saunders, Frank Mayo, Cullen Landis, Edward Joleson

SUNNYSIDE UP (1926)
(6 r.) d, Donald Crisp; lp, Vera Reynolds, Edmund Burns, George K. Arthur, ZaSu Pitts

SUNSET JONES (1921)
(5 r.) d, George L. Cox; lp, Charles Clary, James Gordon, Irene Rich, Kathleen O'Connor

SUNSET PASS (1929)
(6 r.) d, Otto Brower; lp, Jack Holt, Nora Lane, John Loder, Christian J. Frank

SUNSET SPRAGUE (1920)
(5 r.) d, Thomas N. Heffron, Paul Cazenuve; lp, Buck Jones, Patsy De Forrest, Henry J. Hebert, Gloria Payton

SUNSET TRAIL (1917)
(5 r.) d, George H. Melford; lp, Vivian Martin, Henry A. Barrows, Harrison Ford, Charles Ogle

SUNSET TRAIL, THE (1924)
(5 r.) d, Ernst Laemmle; lp, William Desmond, Gareth Hughes, Lucille Hutton, S.E. Jennings

SUNSHINE ALLEY (1917)
(6 r.) d, John W. Noble; lp, Mae Marsh, Robert Harron, Dion Titheradge, J.A. Furey

SUNSHINE AND GOLD (1917)
(5 r.) d, Henry King; lp, Marie Osborne, Henry King, Daniel Gilfether, Neil Hardin

SUNSHINE DAD (1916)
(5 r.) d, Edward Dillon; lp, De Wolf Hopper, Fay Tincher, Jewel Carmen, Chester Withey

SUNSHINE HARBOR (1922)
(5 r.) d, Edward L. Hemmer; lp, Margaret Beecher, Howard Hall, Coit Albertson, Ralf Harolde

SUNSHINE NAN (1918)
(5 r.) d, Charles Giblyn; lp, Ann Pennington, John Hines, Richard Barthelmess, Helen Tracy

SUNSHINE OF PARADISE ALLEY (1926)
(7 r.) d, Jack Nelson; lp, Barbara Bedford, Kenneth McDonald, Max Davidson, Nigel Barrie

SUN-UP (1925)
(6 r.) d, Edmund Goulding; lp, Pauline Starke, Conrad Nagel, Lucille La Verne, Sam De Grasse

SUPER SPEED (1925)
(5 r.) d, Albert Rogell; lp, Reed Howes, Mildred Harris, Charles Clary, Sheldon Lewis

SUPERSTITION (1922)
(5 r.) d, Allan Dwan; lp, Jack Deveraux, Veta Searl, Stafford Windsor

SUPREME PASSION, THE (1921)
(6 r.) d, Samuel Bradley; lp, Robert Adams, William Mortimer, Daniel Kelly, George Fox

SUPREME SACRIFICE, THE (1916)
(5 r.) d, Lionel Belmore, Harley Knoles; lp, Robert Warwick, Anna Q. Nilsson, Vernon Steele, Christine Mayo

SUPREME TEMPTATION, THE (1916)
(5 r.) d, Harry Davenport; lp, Antonio Moreno, Dorothy Kelly, Charles Kent, Mary Maurice

SUPREME TEST, THE (1915)
(5 r.) d, Edward J. Le Saint; lp, Henrietta Crosman, Wyndham Standing, Adele Farrington, Stella Razeto

SURE FIRE (1921)
(5 r.) d, Jack [John] Ford; lp, Hoot Gibson, Molly Malone, Breezy Eason Jr., Harry Carter

SUPRISES OF AN EMPTY HOTEL, THE (1916)
(4 r.) d, Theodore Marston; lp, Charles Richman, C. Jay Williams, Arline Pretty, Leo Delaney

SURRENDER (1927)
(8 r.) d, Edward Sloman; lp, Mary Philbin, Ivan Mosjukine, Otto Matieson, Nigel De Brulier

SURVIVAL (1930, Ger.)
(4 r.) d, Manfred Noa; lp, Paul Wegener, Andree LaFayette, Werner Feuterrer, Nien Son Ling

SUSAN ROCKS THE BOAT (1916)
(5 r.) d, Paul Powell; lp, Dorothy Gish, Owen Moore, Fred J. Butler, Fred A. Turner

SUSAN'S GENTLEMAN (1917)
(5 r.) d, Edwin Stevens; lp, Violet Mersereau, Maud Cooling, James O'Neill, William O'Neill

SUSIE SNOWFLAKE (1916)
(5 r.) d, James Kirkwood; lp, Ann Pennington, Leo Delaney, William Courtleigh Jr., William J. Butler

SUSPECT, THE (1916)
(6 r.) d, S. Rankin Drew; lp, Anita Stewart, S. Rankin Drew, Anders Randolf, Bobby Connelly

SUSPENCE (1919)
(6 r.) d, Frank Reicher; lp, Mollie King, Harris Gordon, Howard Truesdale, Ineth Munro

SUSPICION (1918)
(6 r.) d, John M. Stahl; lp, Warren Cook, Wilmuth Merkyl, Grace Davison, Mathilde Brundage

SUSPICIOUS WIFE, A (1914)
(4 r.)

SUSPICIOUS WIVES (1921)
(6 r.) d, John M. Stahl; lp, H.J. Herbert, Mollie King, Ethel Grey Terry, Rod La Rocque

SUZANNE (1916, Fr.)
(? r.) d, Rene Hervil, Louis Mercanton

SWAN, THE (1925)
(6 r.) d, Dimitri Buchowetzki; lp, Frances Howard, Adolphe Menjou, Richardo Cortez, Ida Waterman

SWAT THE SPY (1918)
(5 r.) d, Arvid E. Gillstrom; lp, Jane Lee, Katherine Lee, Charles Slattery, P.C. Hartigan

SWEENEY TODD (1928, Brit.)
(7 r.) d, Walter West; lp, Moore Marriott, Zoe Palmer, Charles Ashton, Iris Darbyshire

SWEEPING AGAINST THE WINDS (1930)
(5 r.) lp, Theodore von Eltz

SWEET ALYSSUM (1915)
(5 r.) d, Colin Campbell; lp, [Frederick] Tyrone Power, Kathlyn Williams, Edith Johnson, Wheeler Oakman

SWEET AND TWENTY (1919, Brit.)
(5 r.) d, Sidney Morgan; lp, Marguertie Blanche, Langhorne Burton, George Keene, Arthur Lennard

SWEET DADDIES (1926)
(7 r.) d, Alfred Santell; lp, George Sidney, Charlie Murray, Vera Gordon, Jobyna Ralston

SWEET KITTY BELLAIRS (1916)
(5 r.) d, James Young; lp, Mae Murray, Tom Forman, Belle Bennett, Joseph King

SWEET LAVENDER (1915, Brit.)
(5 r.) d, Cecil M. Hepworth; lp, Henry Ainley, Chrissie White, Alma Taylor, Stewart Rome

SWEET LAVANDER (1920)
(5 r.) d, Paul Powell; lp, Mary Miles Minter, Harold Goodwin, Milton Sills, Theodore Roberts

SWEET ROSIE O'GRADY (1926)
(7 r.) d, Frank R. Strayer; lp, Shirley Mason, Cullen Landis, E. Alyn Warren, William Conklin

SWEETHEART OF THE DOOMED (1917)
(5 r.) d, Reginald Barker; lp, Louise Glaum, Charles Gunn, Thomas Guise, Roy Laidlaw

SWEETHEARTS (1919, Brit.)
(5 r.) d, Rex Wilson; lp, Isobel Elsom, Malcolm Cherry, Windham Guise

SWIFT SHADOW, THE (1927)
(5 r.) d, Jerome Storm; lp, Josephine Borjo, William Bertram, Sam Nelson, Ranger (a dog)

SWIM, GIRL, SWIM (1927)
(7 r.) d, Clarence Badger; lp, Bebe Daniels, James Hall, Gertrude Ederle, Josephine Dunn

SWINDLER, THE (1919, Brit.)
(5 r.) d, Maurice Elvey; lp, Cecil Humphreys, Marjorie Hume, Neville Percy, Teddy Arundell

SWORD OF DAMOCLES, THE (1920, Brit.)
(5 r.) d, George Ridgwell; lp, Jose Collins, H.V. Esmond, Claude Fleming, Bobbie Andrews

SWORD OF FATE, THE (1921, Brit.)
(5 r.) d, Frances E. Grant; lp, David Hawthorne, Lionel d'Aragon, Dorothy Moody, Sir Simeon Stuart

SWORD OF PENITENCE (1927, Jap.)
(? r.) d, Yasujiro Ozu

SWORDS AND THE WOMAN (1923, Brit.)
(7 r.) d, Henry Kolker; lp, Holmes Herbert, Flora le Breton, Pedro de Cordoba, Ivan Samson

SYBIL (1921, Brit.)
(5 r.) d, Jack Denton; lp, Evelyn Brent, F. Cowley Wright, Hubert Gordon Hopkirk, Harry Gilbey

SYLVIA OF THE SECRET SERVICE (1917)
(5 r.) d, George Fitzmaurice; lp, Irene Castle, Elliott Dexter, Macey Harlam, Susan Willa

SYLVIA ON A SPREE (1918)
(5 r.) d, Harry L. Franklin; lp, Emmy Wehlen, W.I. Percival, Frank Currier, Eugene Acker

SYMBOL OF THE UNCONQUERED (1921)
(7 r.) lp, Lawrence Chenault, Walker Thompson, Iris Hall, E.G. Tatum

SYMPHONY OF LOVE AND DEATH (1914, USSR)
(4 r.) d, V. Turzhansky; lp, Alexander Geirot, A. Michurin, Olga Baklanova

SYNTHETIC SIN (1929)
(7 r.) d, William A. Seiter; lp, Colleen Moore, Antonio Moreno, Edythe Chapman, Kathryn McGuire

SYRIAN IMMIGRANT, THE (1921)
(8 r.) lp, Nicholas S. Haber, Estella Mackintosh

SYV DAGER FOR ELISABETH (1927, Swed.)
(? r.) d, Leif Sinding; lp, Magda Holm, Hakon Hjelde, Ellen Sinding, David Knudsen

T.N.T (THE NAKED TRUTH) (1924)
(7 r.) lp, Jack Mulhall, Helene Chadwick, Leo Pierson, Charles Spere

TABLE TOP RANCH (1922)
(5 r.) d, Paul Hurst; lp, Neal Hart, William Quinn, Hazel Maye

TABLES TURNED (1915)
(5 r.) d, Charles Horan; lp, Emmy Wehlen, H. Cooper Cliffe, J. Frank Glendon, Leslie Austin

TAINTED MONEY (1924)
(5 r.) d, Henry MacRae; lp, William Fairbanks, Eva Novak, Bruce Gordon, Edwards Davis

TAKE THE HEIR (1930)
(4 r.) d, Lloyd Ingraham; lp, Edward Everett Horton, Dorothy Devore, Edyth Chapman, Otis Harlan

TAKING A CHANCE (1928)
(5 r.) d, Norman Z. McLeod; lp, Rex Bell, Lola Todd, Richard Carlyle, Billy Butts

TALE OF A SHIRT (1916, Brit.)
(4 r.) d, W.P. Kellino; lp, Billy Merson, Miss Bijou

TALE OF PRIEST PANKRATI (1918, USSR)
(4 r.) d, Preobrazhensky, Alexander Arkatov; lp, Preobrazhensky, L. Sychova

TALE OF TWO NATIONS, A (1917)
(5 r.) lp, Edwin August, Alice Hayes, James Cooley

TALES OF 1001 NIGHTS
(SEE: LES CONTES LESS MILLES ET UNE NUITS, 1922, Fr.)

TALK OF THE TOWN (1918)
(6 r.) d, Allen Holubar; lp, Dorothy Phillips, William Stowell, Lon Chaney, George Fawcett

TALKER, THE (1925)
(8 r.) d, Alfred E. Green; lp, Anna Q. Nilsson, Lewis S. Stone, Shirley Mason, Ian Keith

TAME CAT, THE (1921)
(5 r.) d, William Bradley; lp, Ray Irwin, Marion Harding

TAMING OF THE WEST, THE (1925)
(6 r.) d, Arthur Rosson; lp, Hoot Gibson, Marceline Day, Morgan Brown, Edwin Booth Tilton

TANGLED HEARTS (1916)
(5 r.) d, Jospeh De Grasse; lp, Louise Lovely, Agnes Vernon, Marjorie Ellison, Georgia French

TANGLED HERDS (1926)
(5 r.) d, William Bertram; lp, Buddy Roosevelt

TANGLED LIVES (1917)
(5 r.) d, J. Gordon Edwards; lp, Genevieve Hamper, Stuart Holmes, Robert B. Mantell, Walter Miller

TANGLED LIVES (1918)
(5 r.) d, Paul Scardon; lp, Betty Blythe, Harry Morey, Jean Paige, Albert Roccardi

TANGLED TRAILS (1921)
(5 r.) d, Charles Bartlett; lp, Neal Hart, Violet Palmer, Gladys Hampton, Jean Bary

TANGO CAVALIER (1923)
(5 r.) d, Charles R. Seeling; lp, George Larkin, Frank Whitson, Doris Dare, Ollie Kirby

TANSY (1921, Brit.)
(6 r.) d, Cecil M. Hepworth; lp, Alma Taylor, Gerald Ames, James Carew, Hugh Clifton

TARAKANOVA (1930, Fr.)
(? r.) d, Raymond Bernard

TARANTULA, THE (1916)
(6 r.) d, George D. Baker; lp, Edith Storey, Antonio Moreno, Eulalie Jensen, L. Rogers Lytton

TARNISH (1924)
(7 r.) d, George Fitzmaurice; lp, May McAvoy, Ronald Colman, Marie Prevost, Albert Gran

TARNISHED REPUTATIONS (1920)
(5 r.) d, Alice Blache [Guy]; lp, Dolores Cassinelli, Albert Roscoe, George Deneubourg, Ned Burton

TARZAN AND THE GOLDEN LION (1927)
(6 r.) d, J.P. McGowan; lp, James Pierce, Frederic Peters, Edna Murphy, Harold Goodwin

TASTE OF LIFE, A (1919)
(5 r.) d, Jack Dillon; lp, Edith Roberts, Harry Todd, Billy Mason

TATTLERS, THE (1920)
(5 r.) d, Howard M. Mitchell; lp, Madlaine Traverse, Howard Scott, Jack Rollens [Rollins], Ben Deely

TAVERN KNIGHT, THE (1920, Brit.)
(7 r.) d, Maurice Elvey; lp, Eille Norwood, Madge Stuart, Cecil Humphreys, Teddy Arundell

TAXI (1919)
(5 r.) d, Lawrence Windom; lp, Taylor Holmes, Lillian Hall, Irene Tams, Maude Eburne

TEA--WITH A KICK (1923)
(6 r.) d, Erle C. Kenton; lp, Doris May, Creighton Hale, Ralph Lewis, Rosemary Theby

TEARIN' INTO TROUBLE (1927)
(5 r.) d, Richard Thorpe; lp, Wally Wales, Olive Hasbrouck, Walter Brennan, Tom Bay

TEARIN' LOOSE (1925)
(5 r.) d, Richard Thorpe; lp, Wally Wales, Jean Arthur, Charles Whitaker, Alfred Hewston

TEARING THROUGH (1925)
(5 r.) d, Arthur Rosson; lp, Richard Talmadge, Kathryn McGuire, Herbert Prior, Frank Elliott

TEARS (1914, USSR)
(4 r.) d, Yevgeni Bauer; lp, V. Yureneva, Ivan Bersenev, A. Barov, N. Pomerantsev

TEARS AND SMILES (1917)
(5 r.) d, William Bertram; lp, Marie Osborne, Philo McCullough, Marian Warner, Katherine MacLaren

TEASER, THE (1925)
(7 r.) d, William A. Seiter; lp, Laura La Plante, Pat O'Malley, Hedda Hopper, Walter McGrail

TEETH (1924)
(7 r.) d, John Blystone; lp, Tom Mix, Lucy Fox, George Bancroft, Edward Piel

TEETH OF THE TIGER, THE (1919)
(5 r.) d, Chester Withey; lp, David Powell, Marguerite Courtot, Templar Saxe, Myrtle Stedman

TELL IT TO SWEENEY (1927)
(6 r.) d, Gregory La Cava; lp, Chester Conklin, George Bancroft, Jack Luden, Doris Hill

TELL IT TO THE MARINES (1918)
(5 r.) d, Arvid E. Gillstrom; lp, Jane Lee, Katherine Lee, Charles Slattery, Edward Bagley

TELLTALE STEP, THE (1917)
(5 r.) lp, Guido Colucci, Shirley Mason, Charles Sutton, Bob Huggins

TEMPERAMENTAL WIFE, A (1919)
(6 r.) d, David Kirkland; lp, Constance Talmadge, Wyndham Standing, Ben Hendricks, Eulalie Jensen

TEMPERED STEEL (1918)
(5 r.) d, Ralph Ince; lp, Olga Petrova, Thomas Holding, J. Herbert Frank, William Carlton

TEMPEST AND SUNSHINE (1916)
(5 r.) d, Carlton S. King; lp, Evelyn Greeley

TEMPETES (1922, Fr.)
(? r.) d, Robert Boudrioz

TEMPLE OF DUSK, THE (1918)
(5 r.) d, James Young; lp, Sessue Hayakawa, Jane Novak, Sylvia Bremer, Louis Willoughby

TEMPLE OF VENUS, THE (1923)
(7 r.) d, Henry Otto; lp, William Walling, Mary Philbin, Mickey McBan, Alice Day

TEMPORAL POWER (1916, Ital.)
(7 r.)

TEMPORARY GENTLEMAN, A (1920, Brit.)
(6 r.) d, Fred W. Durrant; lp, Owen Nares, Madge Titheradge, Tom Reynolds, Maudie Dunham

TEMPORARY SHERIFF (1926)
(5 r.) d, Dick Hatton; lp, Dick Hatton

TEMPTATION (1916)
(5 r.) d, Cecil B. DeMille; lp, Geraldine Farrar, Theodore Roberts, Pedro de Cordoba, Raymond Hatton

TEMPTATION AND THE MAN (1916)
(5 r.) d, Robert F. Hill; lp, Hobart Henley, Sydell Dowling, Bert Bushy, Sidney Bracey

TEMPTATION OF CARLTON EARLYE, THE (1923, Brit.)
(6 r.) d, Wilfred Noy; lp, C. Aubrey Smith, Gertrude McCoy, James Lindsay, Sir Simeon Stuart

TEMPTATION'S HOUR (1916, Brit.)
(4 r.) d, Sidney Morgan; lp, Fanny Tittell-Brune, Eille Norwood, Sydney Fairbrother, Julian Royce

TEMPTATIONS OF A SHOP GIRL (1927)
(6 r.) d, Tom Terriss; lp, Betty Compson, Pauline Garon, Armand Kaliz, Raymond Glenn

TEMPTATIONS OF SATAN, THE (1914)
(5 r.) d, Albert Blache; lp, Binnie Burns, Joseph Levering, James O'Neill

TEMPTRESS, THE (1920, Brit.)
(5 r.) d, George Edwardes Hall; lp, Yvonne Arnaud, Langhorne Burton, John Gliddon, Christine Maitland

10 CONDEMNED (1932, Pol.)
(6 r.) d, Richard Ordynski; lp, Josef Wegrzyn, Karolina Lubienska, Boguslaw Samborski, Zofia Batycka

TEN DAYS (1925)
(5 r.) d, Duke Worne; lp, Richard Holt, Hazel Keener, Victor Potel, Joseph Girard

TEN MODERN COMMANDMENTS (1927)
(7 r.) d, Dorothy Arzner; lp, Esther Ralston, Neil Hamilton, Maude Truax, Romaine Fielding

TEN NIGHTS IN A BARROOM
(SEE: FOLKS FROM WAY DOWN EAST, 1914)

TEN NIGHTS IN A BAR ROOM (1921)
(8 r.) d, Oscar Apfel; lp, Baby Ivy Ward, John Lowell, Nell Clarke Keller, Charles Mackay

TEN NIGHTS IN A BARROOM (1926)
(7 r.) lp, Charles Gilpin, Myra Burwell, Lawrence Chenault, Harry Henderson

TEN OF DIAMONDS (1917)
(5 r.) d, Raymond B. West; lp, Dorothy Dalton, Jack Livingston, J. Barney Sherry, Billy Shaw

TENDERFEET (1928)
(? r.) lp, Spencer Bell, Mildred Washington, Flora Washington, James Robinson

TENDERFOOT, THE (1917)
(5 r.) d, William Duncan; lp, William Duncan, Carol Holloway, Florence Dye, Joe Ryan

TENTACLES OF THE NORTH (1926)
(6 r.) d, Louis Chaudet; lp, Gaston Glass, Alice Calhoun, Al Roscoe, Al Ferguson

TENTH AVENUE (1928)
(7 r.) d, William C. De Mille; lp, Phyllis Haver, Victor Varconi, Joseph Schildkraut, Louis Natheaux

TENTH CASE, THE (1917)
(5 r.) d, George Kelson; lp, June Elvidge, John Bowers, George MacQuarrie, Gladden James

TENTH WOMAN, THE (1924)
(7 r.) d, James Flood; lp, Beverly Bayne, John Roche, June Marlowe, Raymond McKee

TENTS OF ALLAH, THE (1923)
(7 r.) d, Charles A. Logue; lp, Monte Blue, Mary Alden, Frank Currier, Mary Thurman

TERCENTENARY OF THE ROMANOV DYNASTY'S ACCESSION TO THE THRONE (1913, USSR)
(4 r.) d, A. Uralsky, N. Larin; lp, Mikhail Chekhov, L. Sychova

TERESA RAQUIN (1915, Ital.)
(? r.) d, Nino Martoglio; lp, Maria Carmi, Dillo Lombardi, Giacinta Pezzana

TERREUR (1924, Fr.)
(6 r.) d, Edward Jose; lp, Pearl White

TERRIBLE ONE, THE (1915)
(4 r.) d, Wilbert Melville; lp, Velma Whitman, William E. Parsons, George Routh

TERRIBLE REVENGE, A (1913, USSR)
(? r.) d, Wladyslaw Starewicz; lp, Ivan Mozhukhin, O. Obolenskaya, V. Turzhansky, P. Knorr

TERROR, THE (1917)
(5 r.) d, Raymond Wells; lp, Jack Mulhall, Grace MacLean, Virginia Lee, Malcolm Blevins

TERROR, THE (1920)
(5 r.) d, Jacques Jaccard; lp, Tom Mix, Francelia Billington, Lester Cuneo, Charles K. French

TERROR, THE (1926)
(5 r.) d, Clifford Smith; lp, Art Acord, Velma Connor, Dudley Hendricks, C.E. Anderson

TERROR (1928)
(5 r.) d, Louis King; lp, Tom Tyler, Jane Reid, Al Ferguson, Jules Cowles

TERROR ISLAND (1920)
(6 r.) d, James Cruze; lp, Harry Houdini, Lila Lee, Jack Brammall, Rosemary Theby

TERROR MOUNTAIN (1928)
(5 r.) d, Louis King; lp, Tom Tyler, Frankie Darro, Jane Reid, AL Ferguson

TERROR OF PUEBLO, THE (1924)
(5 r.) lp, Art Mix

TESSIE (1925)
(7 r.) d, Dallas M. Fitzgerald; lp, May McAvoy, Bobby Agnew, Lee Moran, Myrtle Stedman

TEST, THE (1915)
(4 r.) d, James W. Castle; lp, Herbert Prior, Charles Sutton, John Sturgeon, Frank McGlyn

TEST, THE (1916)
(5 r.) d, George Fitzmaurice; lp, Jane Grey, Lumsden Hare, Claude Fleming, Carl Harbaugh

TEST OF DONALD NORTON, THE (1926)
(7 r.) d, B. Reeves Eason; lp, George Walsh, [Frederick] Tyrone Power, Robert Graves, Eugenie Gilbert

TEST OF HONOR, THE (1919)
(6 r.) d, John S. Robertson; lp, John Barrymore, Constance Binney, Marcia Manon, Robert Schable

TEST OF LOYALTY, THE (1918)
(? r.)

TEST OF WOMANHOOD, THE (1917)
(5 r.) lp, Stuart Holmes

TESTIMONY (1920, Brit.)
(7 r.) d, Guy Newall; lp, Ivy Duke, David Hawthorne, Lawford Davidson, Mary Rorke

TESTING OF MILDRED VANE, THE (1918)
(5 r.) d, Wilfred Lucas; lp, May Allison, Darrel Foss, George Field, Nigel de Brulier

TEX (1926)
(6 r.) d, Tom Gibson; lp, Ruth Mix, Robert McKim, Gladden James, Francelia Billington

TEXAN, THE (1920)
(5 r.) d, Lynn F. Reynolds; lp, Tom Mix, Gloria Hope, Pat Chrisman, Sid Jordan

TEXAS (1922)
(5 r.) d, William Bertram; lp, Franklyn Farnum

TEXAS BEARCAT, THE (1925)
(5 r.) d, B. Reeves Eason; lp, Bob Custer, Sally Rand, Harry von Meter, Jack Richardson

TEXAS COWBOY, A (1929)
(5 r.) lp, Bob Steele

TEXAS FLASH (1928)
(5 r.) d, Robert J. Horner; lp, Pawnee Bill Jr., Ione Reed, Bud Osborne, Bill Nestel

TEXAS STEER, A (1915)
(5 r.) d, Giles R. Warren; lp, [Frederick] Tyrone Power, John Charles, Grace Darmond, Frances Bayless

TEXAS STEER, A (1915)
(5 r.)

TEXAS STREAK, THE (1926)
(7 r.) d, Lynn Reynolds; lp, Hoot Gibson, Blanche Mehaffey, Alan Roscoe, James Marcus

TEXAS TERROR, THE (1926)
(5 r.) lp, Al Hoxie

TEXAS TOMMY (1928)
(5 r.) d, J.P. McGowan; lp, Bob Custer, Lynn Anderson, Bud Osborne, Mary Mayberry

TEXAS TORNADO, THE (1928)
(5 r.) d, Frank Howard Clark; lp, Tom Tyler, Frankie Darro, Nora Lane, Jack Anthony

TEXAS TRAIL, THE (1925)
(5 r.) d, Scott R. Dunlap; lp, Harry Carey, Ethel Shannon, Charles K. French, Claude Payton

THAIS (1917)
(6 r.) d, Frank Crane; lp, Mary Garden, Hamilton Revelle, Crauford Kent, Lionel Adams

THANK YOU (1925)
(7 r.) d, John Ford; lp, Alec B. Francis, Jacqueline Logan, George O'Brien, J. Farrell MacDonald

THAT CERTAIN THING (1928)
(7 r.) d, Frank Capra; lp, Viola Dana, Ralph Graves, Burr McIntosh, Aggie Herring

THAT DEVIL, BATEESE (1918)
(5 r.) d, William Wolbert; lp, Monroe Salisbury, Adda Gleason, Lamar Johnstone, Lon Chaney

THAT DEVIL QUEMADO (1925)
(5 r.) d, Del Andrews; lp, Fred Thomson, Albert Priscoe, Nola Luxford, Byron Douglas

THAT FRENCH LADY (1924)
(6 r.) d, Edmund Mortimer; lp, Shirley Mason, Theodore von Eltz, Harold Goodwin, Charles Coleman

THAT GIRL MONTANA (1921)
(5 r.) d, Robert Thornby; lp, Blanche Sweet, Mahlon Hamilton, Frank Lanning, Edward Peil

THAT GIRL OKLAHOMA (1926)
(6 r.) lp, Ruth Mix, Bryant Washburn

THAT MAN JACK! (1925)
(5 r.) d, William J. Craft; lp, Bob Custer, Mary Beth Milford, Monte Collins, Hayford Hobbs

THAT MODEL FROM PARIS (1926)
(7 r.) d, Louis J. Gasiner; lp, Marceline Day, Bert Lytell, Eileen Percy, Ward Crane

THAT MURDER IN BERLIN (1929, Ger.)
(7 r.) d, Frederick Feher; lp, Magda Sonya, Carl Goetz, Anton Pointner, Gustav Diesel

THAT NIGHT'S WIFE (1930, Jap.)
(? r.) d, Yasujiro Ozu

THAT OLD GANG OF MINE (1925)
(5 r.) d, May Tully; lp, Maclyn Arbuckle, Brooke Johns, Tommy Brown

THAT SOMETHING (1921)
(5 r.) d, Lawrence Underwood, Margery Wilson; lp, Charles Meredith, Margery Wilson, Nigel De Brulier, Eugenia Drake

THAT SORT (1916)
(5 r.) d, Charles J. Brabin; lp, Warda Howard, Duncan McRae, Ernest Maupain, John Lorenz

THAT WILD WEST (1924)
(5 r.) d, Alvin J. Neitz; lp, William Fairbanks, Dorothy Revier, Jack Richardson, Milton Ross

THAT WOMAN (1922)
(6 r.) d, Harry O. Hoyt; lp, Catherine Calvert, Joseph Bruelle, William Black, George Pauncefort

THAT'S GOOD (1919)
(5 r.) d, Harry L. Franklin; lp, Hale Hamilton, Stella Gray [Grace La Rue], Herbert Prior, James Duffy

THAT'S MY DADDY (1928)
(6 r.) d, Fred Newmeyer; lp, Reginald Denny, Barbara Kent, Lillian Rich, Tom O'Brien

THEIR COMPACT (1917)
(7 r.) d, Edwin Carewe; lp, Francis X. Bushman, Beverly Bayne, Harry S. Northrup, Henry Mortimer

THEIR HOUR (1928)
(6 r.) d, Alfred Raboch; lp, John Harron, Dorothy Sebastian, June Marlowe, John Roche

THEIR MUTUAL CHILD (1920)
(6 r.) d, George L. Cox; lp, Margarita Fischer, Nigel Barrie, Harvey Clark, Margaret Campbell

THELMA (1918, Brit.)
(6 r.) d, A.E. Coleby, Arthur Rooke; lp, Malvina Longfellow, Arthur Rooke, Maud Yates, Marsh Allen

THEN CAME THE WOMAN (1926)
(7 r.) d, David Hartford; lp, Frank Mayo, Cullen Landis, Mildred Ryan, Blanche Craig

THEN I'LL COME BACK TO YOU (1916)
(5 r.) d, George Irving; lp, Alice Brady, Jack Sherrill, Eric Blind, Leo Gordon

THEN YOU'LL REMEMBER ME (1918, Brit.)
(4 r.) d, Edward Waltyre; lp, Lionel D'Aragon, Mabel Hirst, Babby Reynolds

THEODORA (1921, Ital.)
(10 r.) d, Victoria Sardou

THERE ARE NO VILLAINS (1921)
(5 r.) d, Bayard Veiller; lp, Viola Dana, Gaston Glass, Edward Cecil, De Witt Jennings

THERE YOU ARE! (1926)
(6 r.) d, Hugh Herbert; lp, Conrad Nagel, Edith Roberts, George Fawcett, Gwen Lee

THERE'S MILLIONS IN IT (1924)
(6 r.) d, Dennison Clift

THERESE RAQUIN (1928, Fr./Ger.)
(8 r.) d, Jacques Feyder; lp, Gina Manes, Wolfgang Zilzer, Jeanne-Marie Laurent, Hans-Adalbert von Schlettow

THEY LIKE 'EM ROUGH (1922)
(5 r.) d, Harry Beaumont; lp, Viola Dana, William E. Lawrence, Hardee Kirkland, Myrtle Richell

THEY SHALL PAY (1921)
(6 r.) d, Martin Justine; lp, Lottie Pickford, Allan Forrest, Paul Weigel, Lloyd Whitlock

THEY'RE OFF (1917)
(5 r.) d, Roy William Neill; lp, Enid Bennett, Rowland Lee, Melbourne McDowell, Walter Whitman

THEY'RE OFF (1922)
(5 r.) d, Francis Ford; lp, Peggy O'Day, Francis Ford, Martin Turner, Frederick Moore

THIEF (1916, USSR)
(4 r.) d, M. Bonch-Tomashevsky; lp, V. Maximov, Vera Baranovskaya

THIEF, THE (1920)
(6 r.) d, Charles Giblyn; lp, Pearl White, Charles Waldron, Wallace McCutcheon, George Howard

THIEF IN PARADISE, A (1925)
(8 r.) d, George Fitzmaurice; lp, Doris Kenyon, Ronald Colman, Aileen Pringle, Claude Gillingwater

THIEF IN THE DARK, A (1928)
(6 r.) d, Albert Ray; lp, George Meeker, Doris Hill, Gwen Lee, Marjorie Beebe

THIEVES (1919)
(5 r.) d, Frank Beal; lp, Gladys Brockwell, William Scott, Hayward Mack, Jean Calhoun

THIEVES' GOLD (1918)
(5 r.) d, Jack [John] Ford; lp, Harry Carey, Molly Malone, Vester Pegg, John Cook

THIN ICE (1919)
(5 r.) d, Tom R. Mills; lp, Corinne Griffith, Charles Kent, Jack McLean, L. Rogers Lytton

THINGS MEN DO (1921)
(5 r.) d, Robert North Bradbury; lp, Patricia Palmer, Edward Hearn, William Lion West, Gertrude Claire

THINGS WE LOVE, THE (1918)
(5 r.) d, Lou Tellegren; lp, Wallace Reid, Kathlyn Williams, Tully Marshall, Mayme Kelso

THINGS WIVES TELL (1926)
(7 r.) d, Hugh Dierker;

THINK IT OVER (1917)
(5 r.) d, Herbert Blache; lp, Catherine Calvert, Richard Tucker, A. Lloyd Lack, Eugene Borden

THIRD DEGREE, THE (1914)
(5 r.) d, Barry O'Neil; lp, Bernard Siegel, Gaston Bell, George S. Spencer, Robert Dunbar

THIRD DEGREE, THE (1919)
(7 r.) d, Tom Terriss; lp, Alice Joyce, Gladden James, Anders Randolf, Hedda Hopper

THIRD EYE, THE (1929, Brit.)
(7 r.) d, P. Maclean Rogers; lp, Dorothy Seacombe, Ian Harding, Hayford Hobbs, John Hamilton

THIRD GENERATION, THE (1915, Brit.)
(5 r.) d, Harold Shaw; lp, Edna Flugrath, Sydney Vautier, Charles Rock, Hayford Hobbs

THIRD GENERATION, THE (1920)
(5 r.) d, Henry Kolker; lp, Betty Blythe, Mahlon Hamilton, Jack Pratt, Joseph Swickard

THIRD KISS, THE (1919)
(5 r.) d, Robert G. Vignola; lp, Vivian Martin, Harrison Ford, Robert Ellis, Kathleen Kirkham

THIRD WOMAN, THE (1920)
(5 r.) d, Charles Swickard; lp, Carlyle Blackwell, Gloria Hope, Louise Lovely, Myrtle Owen

THIRST
(SEE: DESERT NIGHTS, 1929)

THIRTEENTH CHAIR, THE (1919)
(6 r.) d, Leonce Perret; lp, Alice Calhoun, Yvonne Delva, Creighton Hale, Marie Shotwell

13TH COMMANDMENT, THE (1920)
(5 r.) d, Robert G. Vignola; lp, Ethel Clayton, Charles Meredith, Monte Blue, Anna Q. Nilsson

THIRTEENTH HOUR, THE (1927)
(6 r.) d, Chester Franklin; lp, Lionel Barrymore, Jacquelin Gadsdon, Charles Delaney, Fred Kelsey

THIRTEENTH JUROR, THE (1927)
(6 r.) d, Edward Laemmle; lp, Anna Q. Nilsson, Francis X. Bushman, Walter Pidgeon, Martha Mattox

THIRTIETH PIECE OF SILVER, THE (1920)
(6 r.) d, George L. Cox; lp, Margarita Fischer, King Baggot, Lillian Leighton, Forrest Stanley

THIRTY A WEEK (1918)
(5 r.) d, Harry Beaumont; lp, Tom Moore, Tallulah Bankhead, Alec B. Francis, Brenda Fowler

30 BELOW ZERO (1926)
(5 r.) d, Robert P. Kerr; lp, Buck Jones, Eva Novak, E.J. Ratcliffe, Frank Butler

$30,000 (1920)
(5 r.) d, Ernest C. Warde; lp, J. Warren Kerrigan, Fritzi Brunette, Carl Stockdale, Nancy Chase

THIRTY YEARS BETWEEN (1921)
(? r.) lp, Vera Stewart

THIRTY YEARS LATER (1928)
(7 r.) d, Oscar Micheaux; lp, William Edmonson, A.B. de Comatheire, Mabel Kelly, Ardella Dabney

39 EAST (1920)
(5 r.) d, John S. Robertson; lp, Constance Binney, Reginald Denny, Alison Skipworth, Lucia Moore

THIS FREEDOM (1923, Brit.)
(7 r.) d, Denison Clift; lp, Fay Compton, Clive Brook, John Stuart, Athene Seyler

THIS IS THE LIFE (1917)
(5 r.) d, Raoul A. Walsh; lp, George Walsh, Wanda Petit [Hawley], James A. Marcus, Ralph Lewis

THIS WOMAN (1924)
(7 r.) d, Phil Rosen; lp, Irene Rich, Ricardo Cortez, Louise Fazenda, Frank Elliott

THOROBRED (1922)
(5 r.) d, George Halligan; lp, Helen Gibson, Robert Burns, Otto Nelson, Jack Ganzhorn

THOROUGHBRED, THE (1916)
(5 r.) d, Charles Bartlett; lp, William Russell, Charlotte Burton, Roy Stewart, Lizette Thorne

THOROUGHBRED, THE (1916)
(5 r.) d, Reginald Barker; lp, Frank Keenan, Margaret Thompson, George Fisher, J.J. Dowling

THOROUGHBRED, THE (1925)
(6 r.) d, Oscar Apfel; lp, Maclyn Arbuckle, Theodore von Eltz, Gladys Hulette, Hallam Cooley

THOROUGHBRED, THE (1928, Brit.)
(6 r.) d, Sidney Morgan; lp, Ian Hunter, Louise Prussing, Richard Barclay, H. Agar Lyons

THOSE WHO DANCE (1924)
(8 r.) d, Lambert Hillyer; lp, Blanche Sweet, Bessie Love, Warner Baxter, Robert Agnew

THOSE WHO DARE (1924)
(6 r.) d, John B. O'Brien; lp, John Bowers, Marguerite De La Motte, Joseph Dowling, Claire McDowell

THOSE WHO JUDGE (1924)
(6 r.) d, Burton King; lp, Patsy Ruth Miller, Lou Tellegen, Mary Thurman, Flora Le Breton

THOSE WHO PAY (1918)
(7 r.) d, Raymond B. Wells; lp, Bessie Barriscale, Howard Hickman, Dorcas Matthews, Melbourne McDowell

THOSE WHO TOIL (1916)
(5 r.) d, Edgar Lewis; lp, Nance O'Neil, Herbert Fortier, Victor Sutherland, Tom Tempest

THOU ART THE MAN (1915)
(6 r.) d, S. Rankin Drew; lp, S. Rankin Drew, Virginia Pearson, Joseph Kilgour, George Cooper

THOU ART THE MAN (1916)
(6 r.) d, S. Rankin Drew; lp, S. Rankin Drew, Joseph Kilgour, Virginia Pearson, George Cooper

THOU SHALT HONOR THY WIFE
(SEE: MASTER OF THE HOUSE, 1925, Den.)

THOU SHALT NOT (1919)
(6 r.) d, Charles J. Brabin; lp, Evelyn Nesbit, Ned Burton, Florida Kingsley, Gladden James

THOU SHALT NOT
(SEE: THERESE RAQUIN, 1928, Fr.)

THOU SHALT NOT COVET (1916)
(5 r.) d, Colin Campbell; lp, [Frederick] Tyrone Power, Kathlyn Williams, Guy Oliver, Eugenie Besserer

THOU SHALT NOT KILL (1915)
(5 r.) lp, Rose Coghlan, Charles Coghlan

THOU SHALT NOT LOVE (1922)
(6 r.) lp, Vivian Le Picard

THOU SHALT NOT STEAL (1917)
(5 r.) d, William Nigh; lp, Virginia Pearson, Claire Whitney, Eric Mayne, Mathilde Brundage

THOU SHALT NOT STEAL (1929, Ger.)
(7 r.) d, Victor Jansen; lp, Werner Fuetterer, Dina Gralla, Bruno Kastner, Charlotte Susa

THOUGHT (1916, USSR)
(4 r.) d, Vladimir Gardin; lp, Grigori Khmara, N. Komarovskaya

THOUGHTLESS WOMEN (1920)
(6 r.) d, Daniel Carson Goodman; lp, Alma Rubens, E. Holland, Mercita Esmonde, Lumsden Hare

THOUSAND DOLLAR HUSBAND, THE (1916)
(5 r.) d, James Young; lp, Blanche Sweet, Theodore Roberts, James Neill, Tom Forman

THOUSAND TO ONE, A (1920)
(6 r.) d, Rowland V. Lee; lp, Hobart Bosworth, Ethel Grey Terry, Charles West, Landers Stevens

THREADS OF DESTINY (1914)
(5 r.) d, Joseph W. Smiley; lp, Evelyn Nesbit Thaw, Russell William Thaw, Bernard Siegel, Marguerite Risser

THREADS OF FATE (1917)
(5 r.) d, Eugene Nowland; lp, Viola Dana, Richard Tucker, Robert Whittier, Augustus Phillips

THREE BAD MEN (1926)
(9 r.) d, John Ford; lp, George O'Brien, Olive Borden, Lou Tellegen, J. Farrell MacDonald

THREE BLACK TRUMPS, THE (1915)
(4 r.)

THREE BUCKAROOS, THE (1922)
(5 r.) d, Fred J. Balshofer; lp, Buck Humes, Peggy O'Dare, Monty Montague, "Tex" Keith

THREE DAYS TO LIVE (1924)
(5 r.) d, Tom Gibson; lp, Ora Carew, Jay Morley, Dick La Reno, Hal Stephens

THREE FACES EAST (1926)
(7 r.) d, Rupert Julian; lp, Jetta Goudal, Robert Ames, Henry Walthall, Clive Brook

THREE FRIENDS AND AN INVENTION (1928, USSR)
(6 r.) d, Alexei Popov; lp, S. Lavrentyev, S. Yablokov, Olga Tretyakova, A. Popov

THREE GODFATHERS, THE (1916)
(6 r.) d, Edward J. Le Saint; lp, Stella Razetto, Harry Carey, George Berrell, Frank Lanning

THREE GOLD COINS (1920)
(5 r.) d, Cliff Smith; lp, Tom Mix, Margaret Loomis, Frank Whitson, Bert Hadley

THREE GREEN EYES (1919)
(5 r.) d, Dell Henderson; lp, Carlyle Blackwell, June Elvidge, Evelyn Greeley, Montagu Love

THREE HOURS (1927)
(6 r.) d, James Flood; lp, Corinne Griffith, John Bowers, Hobart Bosworth, Paul Ellis

THREE IN EXILE (1925)
(5 r.) d, Fred Windemere; lp, Louise Lorraine, Art Acord, Tom London, Rex (a dog)

THREE JUMPS AHEAD (1923)
(5 r.) d, Jack [John] Ford; lp, Tom Mix, Alma Bennett, Edward Piel, Joe Girard

THREE KEYS (1925)
(6 r.) d, Edward J. Le Saint; lp, Edith Roberts, Jack Mulhall, Gaston Glass, Virginia Lee Corbin

THREE KINGS, THE (1929, Brit.)
(7 r.) d, Hans Steinhoff; lp, Henry Edwards, Evelyn Holt, Warwick Ward, John Hamilton

THREE LIGHTS, THE
(SEE: DESTINY, 1921, Ger.)

THREE LIVE GHOSTS (1922, Brit.)
(7 r.) d, George Fitzmaurice; lp, Norman Kerry, Anna Q. Nillsson, Edmund Goulding, John Milterne

THREE LOVES (1931, Ger.)
(7 r.) d, Kurt Bernhardt; lp, Marlene Dietrich, Fritz Kortner, Uno Henning, Oscar Simma

THREE MEN AND A GIRL (1919)
(5 r.) d, Marshall Neilan; lp, Marguerite Clark, Richard Barthelmess, Percy Marmont, Jerome Patrick

THREE MEN IN A BOAT (1920, Brit.)
(5 r.) d, Challis Sanderson; lp, Lionelle Howard, Manning Haynes, Johnny Butt, Eva Westlake

THREE MEN IN A CART (1929, Brit.)
(5 r.) d, Arthur Phillips; lp, Frank Stanmore, Tony Wylde, Pat Morton, Joan Morgan

THREE MILES OUT (1924)
(6 r.) d, Irvin Willat; lp, Madge Kennedy, Harrison Ford, Marc MacDermott, Ivan Linow

THREE MILES UP (1927)
(5 r.) d, Bruce Mitchell; lp, Al Wilson, William Malan, Ethlyne Clair, William Clifford

THREE MOUNTED MEN (1918)
(6 r.) d, Jack [John] Ford; lp, Harry Carey, Neva Gerber, Joe Harris, Harry Carter

THREE MUSKETEERS, THE (1914)
(6 r.)

THREE MUST-GET-THERES, THE (1922)
(5 r.) d, Max Linder; lp, Max Linder, Bull Montana, Frank Cooke, Catherine Rankin

THREE O'CLOCK IN THE MORNING (1923)
(6 r.) d, Kenneth Webb; lp, Constance Binney, Edmund Breese, Richard Thorpe, Mary Carr

THREE OF MANY (1917)
(5 r.) d, Reginald Barker; lp, Clara Williams, Charles Gunn, George Fisher

THREE OF US, THE (1915)
(5 r.) d, John W. Noble; lp, Mabel Taliaferro, Creighton Hale, Edwin Carewe, Irving Cummings

THREE OUTCASTS, THE (1929)
(5 r.) d, Clifford Smith; lp, Yakima Canutt, Pete Morrison, Gertrude Short, Lew Short

THREE PALS (1916)
(5 r.) d, Rea Berger; lp, Clarence William Kolb, Max M. Dill, May Cloy

THREE PALS (1926)
(5 r.) d, Wilbur McGaugh; lp, Marilyn Mills, Josef Swickard, William H. Turner, Martin Turner

THREE PASSIONS, THE (1928, Brit.)
(9 r.) d, Rex Ingram; lp, Alice Terry, Ivan Petrovitch, Shayle Gardner, Leslie Faber

THREE SEVENS (1921)
(5 r.) d, Chester Bennett; lp, Antonio Moreno, Jean Calhoun, Emmett King, Geoffrey Webb

THREE WAX MEN
(SEE: WAXWORKS, 1929, Ger.)

THREE WAX WORKS
(SEE: WAXWORKS, 1929, Ger.)

THREE WEEK-ENDS (1928)
(6 r.) d, Clarence Badger; lp, Clara Bow, Neil Hamilton, Harrison Ford, Lucille Powers

THREE WEEKS (1915)
(5 r.) d, Perry N. Vekroff

THREE WEEKS (1924)
(8 r.) d, Alan Crosland; lp, Aileen Pringle, Conrad Nagel, John Sainpolis, H. Reeves Smith

THREE WEEKS IN PARIS (1925)
(6 r.) d, Roy Del Ruth; lp, Matt Moore, Dorothy Devore, Willard Louis, Helen Lynch

THREE WHO PAID (1923)
(5 r.) d, Colin Campbell; lp, Dustin Farnum, Fred Kohler, Bessie Love, Frank Campeau

THREE WHO WERE DOOMED, THE
(SEE: SIR ARNE'S TREASURE, 1921, Swed.)

THREE WISE CROOKS (1925)
(6 r.) d, F. Harmon Weight; lp, Evelyn Brent, Fannie Midgley, John Gough, Bruce Gordon

THREE WOMEN (1924)
(8 r.) d, Ernest Lubitsch; lp, May McAvoy, Pauline Frederick, Marie Prevost, Lew Cody

THREE WORD BRAND (1921)
(7 r.) d, Lambert Hillyer; lp, William S. Hart, Jane Novak, S.J. Bingham, Gordon Russell

THREE X GORDON (1918)
(5 r.) d, Ernest C. Warde; lp, J. Warren Kerrigan, Lois Wilson, John Gilbert, Charles French

THREE-RING MARRIAGE (1928)
(6 r.) d, Marshall Neilan; lp, Mary Astor, Lloyd Hughes, Lawford Davidson, Yola D'Avril

THRILL CHASER, THE (1923)
(6 r.) d, Edward Sedgwick; lp, Hoot Gibson, James Neill, Billie Dove, William E. Lawrence

THRILL CHASER, THE (1928)
(5 r.) d, Robert J. Horner; lp, Pawnee Bill Jr., Boris Bullock, Bill Nestel, Bud Osborne

THRILL HUNTER, THE (1926)
(6 r.) d, Eugene De Rue; lp, William Haines, Kathryn McGuire, Alma Bennett, E.J. Ratcliffe

THRILL SEEKERS, THE (1927)
(6 r.) d, Harry Revier; lp, Jimmy Fulton, Ruth Clifford, Gloria Grey, Sally Long

THRILLING YOUTH (1926)
(5 r.) d, Grover Jones; lp, Billy West, Gloria Grey, George Bunny, Charles Clary

THROUGH A GLASS WINDOW (1922)
(5 r.) d, Maurice Campbell; lp, May McAvoy, Fanny Midgley, Burwell Hamrick, Raymond McKee

THROUGH DANTE'S FLAMES (1914)
(4 r.) lp, Lois Howard, Will S. Davis, Stuart Holmes

THROUGH FIRE AND WATER (1923, Brit.)
(6 r.) d, Thomas Bentley; lp, Clive Brook, Flora le Brenton, Lawford Davidson, Jerrold Robertshaw

THROUGH FIRE TO FORTUNE OR THE SUNKEN VILLAGE (1914)
(5 r.) d, L.B. Carleton; lp, Richard Wangemann, Ormi Hawley

THROUGH STORMY WATERS (1920, Brit.)
(6 r.) d, Frederick Goddard; lp, Eileen Bellamy, George Keene, Harry J. Worth, Fred Morgan

THROUGH THE BACK DOOR (1921)
(6 r.) d, Alfred E. Green; lp, Mary Pickford, Gertrude Astor, Wilfred Lucas, Helen Raymond

THROUGH THE BREAKERS (1928)
(6 r.) d, Joseph C. Boyle; lp, Holmes Herbert, Margaret Livingston, Clyde Cook, Natalie Joyce

THROUGH THE DARK (1924)
(8 r.) d, George Hill; lp, Colleen Moore, Forrest Stanley, Margaret Seddon, Hobart Bosworth

THROUGH THE STORM (1922)
(6 r.) d, Horace G. Plympton; lp, Edith Stockton, Louis Kimball, Mary Worth, Leonard Mudie

THROUGH THE TOILS (1919)
(5 r.) d, Harry O. Hoyt; lp, Montagu Love, Ellen Cassity, Gertrude Le Brandt, John Davidson

THROUGH THE VALLEY OF SHADOWS (1914, Brit.)
(4 r.) d, Larry Trimble; lp, Florence Turner, Edward Lingard, James Lindsay, Clifford Pembroke

THROUGH THE WALL (1916)
(6 r.) d, Rollin S. Sturgeon; lp, Nell Shipman, William Duncan, George Holt, Webster Campbell

THROUGH THE WRONG DOOR (1919)
(5 r.) d, Clarence G. Badger; lp, Madge Kennedy, John Bowers, Herbert Standing, J.Burnell Manly

THROUGH THICK AND THIN (1927)
(5 r.) d, Jack Nelson, Reeves Eason; lp, William Fairbanks, Ethel Shannon, Jack Curtis, George Periolat

THROUGH TURBULENT WATERS (1915)
(4 r.) d, Duncan McRae; lp, Gertrude McCoy, Duncan McRae, Frank Farrington, Bessie Learn

THROW OF THE DICE (1930, Brit.)
(4 r.) d, Frank Osten; lp, Hismansu Ray, Charu Roy, Seeta Devi, Sarada Gupta

THROWING LEAD (1928)
(5 r.) d, Robert J. Horner; lp, Al Hoxie

THROWN TO THE LIONS (1916)
(5 r.) d, Lucius Henderson; lp, Mary Fuller, Finita DeSopia, Joe W. Girard, Clifford Gray

THRU THE EYES OF MEN (1920)
(5 r.) d, Charles Taylor; lp, Frank Mayo, Ben Alexander, Claire McDowell

THRU THE FLAMES (1923)
(5 r.) d, Jack Nelson; lp, Richard Talmadge, Charlotte Pierce, Maine Geary, S.J. Bingham

THUMB PRINT, THE (1914)
(4 r.)

THUNDER ISLAND (1921)
(5 r.) d, Norman Dawn; lp, Edith Roberts, Fred De Silva, Jack O'Brien, Arthur Jasmine

THUNDER MOUNTAIN (1925)
(8 r.) d, Victor Schertzinger; lp, Madge Bellamy, Leslie Fenton, Alec B. Francis, Paul Panzer

THUNDER RIDERS (1928)
(5 r.) d, William Wyler; lp, Ted Wells, Charlotte Stevens, William A. Steele, Bill Dyer

THUNDERBOLT, THE (1919)
(5 r.) d, Colin Campbell; lp, Katherine MacDonald, Thomas Meighan, Spottiswoode Aitken, James Gordon

THUNDERBOLT STRIKES, THE (1926)
(5 r.) lp, Jack Perrin

THUNDERBOLTS OF FATE (1919)
(5 r.) d, Edward Warren; lp, House Peters, Anna Lehr, Ned Burton, Wilfred Lytell

THUNDERBOLT'S TRACKS (1927)
(5 r.) d, J.P. McGowan; lp, Jack Perrin, Pauline Curley, Jack Henderson, Billy Lamar

THUNDERCLAP (1921)
(7 r.) d, Richard Stanton; lp, Mary Carr, J. Barney Sherry, Paul Willis, Violet Mersereau

THUNDERCLOUD, THE (1919, Brit.)
(5 r.) d, Alexander Butler; lp, Unity More, James Lindsay, Mary Dibley, Daisy Cordell

THUNDERGATE (1923)
(7 r.) d, Joseph De Grasse; lp, Owen Moore, Virginia Brown Faire, Edwin Booth Tilton, Sylvia Breamer

THUNDERGOD (1928)
(6 r.) d, Charles J. Hunt; lp, Cornelius Keefe, Lila Lee, Walter Long, Helen Lynch

THUNDERING DAWN (1923)
(7 r.) d, Harry Garson; lp, Winter Hall, J. Warren Kerrigan, Anna Q. Nilsson, Tom Santschi

THUNDERING HERD, THE (1925)
(7 r.) d, William K. Howard; lp, Jack Holt, Lois Wilson, Noah Beery, Raymond Hatton

THUNDERING HOOFS (1922)
(5 r.) d, Francis Ford; lp, Peggy O'Day, Francis Ford, Florence Murth, Phil Ford

THUNDERING HOOFS (1924)
(5 r.) d, Albert Rogell; lp, Fred Thomson, Fred Huntley, Charles Mailes, Charles De Revenna

THUNDERING ROMANCE (1924)
(5 r.) d, Richard Thorpe; lp, Buffalo Bill Jr., Jean Arthur, Rene Picot, Harry Todd

THUNDERING SPEED (1926)
(5 r.) d, Alvin J. Neitz; lp, Eileen Sedgwick

THUNDERING THOMPSON (1929)
(5 r.) d, Benjamin Franklin Wilson; lp, Cheyenne Bill, Neva Gerber, Al Ferguson, Ed La Niece

THUNDERING THROUGH (1925)
(5 r.) d, Fred Bain; lp, Buddy Roosevelt, Jean Arthur, Charles Colby, Lew Meehan

THY NAME IS WOMAN (1924)
(9 r.) d, Fred Niblo; lp, Ramon Novarro, Barbara La Marr, William V. Mong, Wallace MacDonald

THY SOUL SHALL BEAR WITNESS
(SEE: PHANTOM CARRIAGE, THE, 1921, Swed.)

TICKET-OF-LEAVE MAN, THE (1918, Brit.)
(6 r.) d, Bert Haldane; lp, Daphne Glenne, George Foley, Aubrey Fitzmaurice, Wilfred Benson

TIDAL WAVE, THE (1918)
(8 r.) d, William Stoermer

TIDAL WAVE, THE (1920, Brit.)
(6 r.) d, Sinclair Hill; lp, Poppy Wyndham, Sydney Seaward, Pardoe Woodman

TIDE OF EMPIRE (1929)
(8 r.) d, Allan Dwan; lp, Renee Adoree, George Duryea, George Fawcett, William Collier, Jr.

TIDES OF BARNEGAT, THE (1917)
(5 r.) d, Marshall Neilan; lp, Blanche Sweet, Elliott Dexter, Tom Forman, Harrison Ford

TIDES OF PASSION (1925)
(7 r.) d, J. Stuart Blackton; lp, Mae Marsh, Ben Hendricks, Laska Winter, Earl Schenck

TIES OF BLOOD (1921)
(? r.) lp, Inez Clough, Arthur Ray, Harry Pleasant

TIGER LILY, THE (1919)
(5 r.) d, George L. Cox; lp, Margarita Fisher, Emory Johnson, George Periolat, E. Alyn Warren

TIGER LOVE (1924)
(6 r.) d, George Melford; lp, Antonio Moreno, Estelle Taylor, G. Raymond Nye, Manuel Camero

TIGER MAN, THE (1918)
(5 r.) d, William S. Hart; lp, William S. Hart, Jane Novak, Milton Ross, Robert Lawrence

TIGER OF THE SEA, THE (1918)
(7 r.) lp, Nell Shipman

TIGER ROSE (1923)
(8 r.) d, Sidney A. Franklin; lp, Lenore Ulric, Forrest Stanley, Joseph Dowling, Andre de Beranger

TIGER THOMPSON (1924)
(6 r.) d, B. Reeves Eason; lp, Harry Carey, Marguerite Clayton, John Dillon, Jack Richardson

TIGER TRUE (1921)
(5 r.) d, J.P. McGowan; lp, Frank Mayo, Fritzi Brunette, Eleanor Hancock, Al Kaufman

TIGER'S COAT, THE (1920)
(5 r.) d, Roy Clements; lp, Myrtle Stedman, W. Lawson Butt, Tina Modotti, Jiquel Lanoe

TIGER'S CUB (1920)
(6 r.) d, Charles Giblyn; lp, Pearl White, Thomas Carrigan, J. Thornton Baston, John Davidson

TIGRESS, THE (1927)
(6 r.) d, George B. Seitz; lp, Jack Holt, Dorothy Revier, Frank Leigh, Philippe De Lacy

TIGRIS (1913, Ita.)
(4 r.) d, Giovanni Pastrone

'TILL I COME BACK TO YOU (1918)
(6 r.) d, Cecil B. DeMille; lp, Bryant Washburn, Florence Vidor, G. Butler Clonebaugh [Gustav von Seyffertitz]

TILL WE MEET AGAIN (1922)
(6 r.) d, William Christy Cabanne; lp, Julia Swayne Gordon, Mae Marsh, J. Barney Sherry, Walter Miller

TILLERS OF THE SOIL
(SEE: L'ATRE, 1923, Fr.)

TILLIE, A MENONITE MAID (1922)
(5 r.) d, Frank Urson

TILLY OF BLOOMSBURY (1921, Brit.)
(5 r.) d, Rex Wilson; lp, Edna Best, Tom Reynolds, Campbell Kendall, Helen Haye

TIMBER WOLF (1925)
(5 r.) d, William S. Van Dyke; lp, Buck Jones, Elinor Fair, David Dyas, Sam Allen

TIME LOCK NO. 776 (1915)
(6 r.) d, Hal Reid; lp, Joe Welsh, Dora Dean, Edward Carewe, David Wall

TIME LOCKS AND DIAMONDS (1917)
(5 r.) d, Walter Edwards; lp, William Desmond, Gloria Hope, Robert McKim, Roland Lee

TIME, THE COMEDIAN (1925)
(5 r.) d, Robert Z. Leonard; lp, Mae Busch, Lew Cody, Gertrude Olmsted, Rae Ethelyn

TIMES HAVE CHANGED (1923)
(5 r.) d, James Flood; lp, William Russell, Mabel Julienne Scott, Charles West, Martha Mattox

TIMID TERROR, THE (1926)
(5 r.) d, Del Andrews; lp, George O'Hara, Edith Yorke, Doris Hill, Rex Lease

TIN HATS (1926)
(7 r.) d, Edward Sedgwick; lp, Conrad Nagel, Claire Windsor, George Cooper, Bert Roach

TIN PAN ALLEY (1920)
(5 r.) d, Frank Beal; lp, Albert Ray, Elinor Fair, George Hernandez, Louis Natheaux

TINKER, TAILOR, SOLDIER, SAILOR (1918, Brit.)
(7 r.) d, Rex Wilson; lp, Isobel Elsom, Owen Nares, James Lindsay, Tom Reynolds

TINSEL (1918)
(5 r.) d, Oscar Apfel; lp, Kitty Gordon, Muriel Ostriche, Frank Mayo, Anthony Merlo

TINTED VENUS, THE (1921, Brit.)
(5 r.) d, Cecil M. Hepworth; lp, Alma Taylor, George Dewhurst, Maud Cressall, Eileen Dennes

TIP-OFF, THE (1929)
(5 r.) d, Leigh Jason; lp, Bill Cody, George Hackathorne, Duane Thompson, L.J. O'Connor

TIPTOES (1927, Brit.)
(6 r.) d, Herbert Wilcox; lp, Dorothy Gish, Will Rogers, Nelson Keys, John Manners

TIRE AU FLANC (1929, Fr.)
(7 r.) d, Jean Renoir; lp, Georges Pomies, Michel Simon, Fridette, Felix Oudard

TIRED BUSINESS MAN, THE (1927)
(6 r.) d, Allen Dale; lp, Raymond Hitchcock, Dot Farley, Mack Swain, Margaret Quimby

TIT FOR TAT (1922, Brit.)
(5 r.) d, Henry Edwards; lp, Henry Edwards, Chrissie White, Eileen Dennes, Gwynne Herbert

TO A FINISH (1921)
(5 r.) d, Bernard J. Durning; lp, Buck Jones, Helen Ferguson, G. Raymond Nye, Norman Selby

TO HAVE AND TO HOLD (1916)
(5 r.) d, George Melford; lp, Mae Murray, Wallace Reid, Tom Forman, Ronald Bradbury

TO HELL WITH THE KAISER (1918)
(7 r.) d, George Irving; lp, Lawrence Grant, Olive Tell, John Sunderland, Betty Howe

TO HIM THAT HATH (1918)
(5 r.) d, Oscar Apfel; lp, Montagu Love, Gertrude McCoy, Reginald Carrington, George De Carlton

TO HONOR AND OBEY (1917)
(5 r.) d, Otis Turner; lp, Jewel Carmen, Gladys Brockwell, Bertram Grassby, Charles Clary

TO PLEASE ONE WOMAN (1920)
(6 r.) d, Lois Weber; lp, Claire Windsor, Edith Kessler, Edward Burns, George Hackathorne

TO THE DEATH (1917)
(5 r.) d, Burton King; lp, Olga Petrova, Mahlon Hamilton, Wyndham Standing, Henry Leone

TO THE HIGHEST BIDDER (1918)
(5 r.) d, Tom Terriss; lp, Alice Joyce, Percy Standing, Walter McGrail, Edna Murphy

TO THE LADIES (1923)
(6 r.) d, James Cruze; lp, Edward Horton, Theodore Roberts, Helen Jerome Eddy, Louise Dresser

TOAST OF DEATH, THE (1915)
(4 r.) d, Scott Sidney; lp, Herschal Mayall, Harry Keenan, Louise Glaum, J. Frank Burke

TOBY'S BOW (1919)
(5 r.) d, Harry Beaumont; lp, Tom Moore, Doris Pawn, Macey Harlam, Arthur Housman

TODD OF THE TIMES (1919)
(5 r.) d, Eliot Howe; lp, Frank Keenan, Irene Rich, Buddy Post, Aggie Herring

TOGETHER (1918)
(5 r.) d, O.A.C. Lund; lp, Violet Mersereau, Chester Barnett, Barney Randall, Lindsay J. Hall

TOILER, THE (1932, Ital.)
(5 r.) d, Gustavo Sereno; lp, Silvio Orsini, Mina Violetto, Anna Martelli, Tina Renaldi

TOILERS, THE (1919, Brit.)
(5 r.) d, Tom W. Watts; lp, Manora Thew, George Dewhurst, Gwynne Herbert, Ronald Colman

TOILERS OF THE SEA (1923 US/Ital.)
(6 r.) d, Roy William Neill; lp, Lucy Fox, Holmes Herbert, Horace Tesseron, Dell Cawley

TOKIO SIREN, A (1920)
(5 r.) d, Norman Dawn; lp, Tsuru Aoki, Jack Livingston, Goro Kino, Toyo Fujita

TOKYO MARCH (1929, Jap.)
(? r.) d, Kenji Mizoguchi

TOLD AT THE TWILIGHT (1917)
(5 r.) d, Henry King; lp, Marie Osborne, Daniel Gilfether, Henry King, Beatrice Van

TOLD IN THE HILLS (1919)
(6 r.) d, George Melford; lp, Robert Warwick, Ann Little, Tom Forman, Wanda Hawley

TOLL GATE, THE (1920)
(6 r.) d, Lambert Hillyer; lp, William S. Hart, Anna Q. Nilsson, Jack Richardson, Joseph Singleton

TOLL OF LOVE, THE (1914)
(4 r.) lp, Lisbeth Blackstone, Dallas Tyler, Harrish Ingraham, John Charles

TOLL OF THE SEA, THE (1922)
(5 r.) d, Chester M. Franklin; lp, Anna May Wong, Kenneth Harlan, Beatrice Bentley, Baby Marion

TOM BROWN'S SCHOOLDAYS (1916, Brit.)
(6 r.) d, Rex Wilson; lp, Joyce Templeton, Jack Coleman, Jack Hobbs, Evelyn Boucher

TOM JONES (1917, Brit.)
(7 r.) d, Edwin J. Collins; lp, Langhorne Burton, Sybil Arundale, Will Corrie, Wyndham Guise

TOM SAWYER (1917)
(5 r.) d, William Desmond Taylor; lp, Jack Pickford, George Hackathorne, Alice Marvin, Edythe Chapman

TOMBOY, THE (1921)
(5 r.) d, Carl Harbaugh; lp, Eileen Percy, Hal Cooley, Richard Cummings, Paul Kamp

TOMBOY, THE (1924)
(6 r.) d, David Kirkland; lp, Herbert Rawlinson, Dorothy Devore, James Barrows, Lee Moran

TOMMY ATKINS (1928, Brit.)
(8 r.) d, Norman Walker; lp, Lilian Hall Davies, Henry Victor, Walter Butler, Shayle Gardner

TOMORROW'S LOVE (1925)
(6 r.) d, Paul Bern; lp, Agnes Ayres, Pat O'Malley, Raymond Hatton, Jane Winton

TOM'S GANG (1927)
(5 r.) d, Robert De Lacy; lp, Tom Tyler, Sharon Lynn, Frankie Darro, Harry Woods

TONG MAN, THE (1919)
(5 r.) d, William Worthington; lp, Sessue Hayakawa, Helen Jerome Eddy, Marc Robbins, Toyo Fujita

TONGUES OF FLAME (1919)
(5 r.) d, Colin Campbell; lp, Marie Walcamp, Al Whitman, Alfred Allen, Hugh Sutherland

TONGUES OF FLAME (1924)
(7 r.) d, Joseph Henabery; lp, Thomas Meighan, Bessie Love, Eileen Percy, Berton Churchill

TONGUES OF SCANDAL (1927)
(6 r.) d, Roy Clements; lp, Mae Busch, William Desmond, Ray Hallor, Mathilde Brundage

TONI (1928, Brit.)
(6 r.) d, Arthur Maude; lp, Jack Buchanan, Dorothy Boyd, W. Lawson Butt, Moore Marriott

TONIO, SON OF THE SIERRAS (1925)
(5 r.) d, Ben Wilson; lp, Ben Wilson, Neva Gerber, Chief Yowlache, Jim Welch

TONS OF MONEY (1924, Brit.)
(6 r.) d, Frank Crane; lp, Leslie Henson, Flora le Breton, Mary Brough, Clifford Seyler

TONY AMERICA (1918)
(5 r.) d, Thomas N. Heffron; lp, Francis McDonald, Yvonne Pavis, Dorothy Giraci, Rae Godfrey

TOO FAT TO FIGHT (1918)
(6 r.) d, Hobart Henley; lp, Frank McIntyre, Florence Dixon, Henrietta Floyd, Countess De Martimprey

TOO MANY CROOKS (1919)
(5 r.) d, Ralph Ince; lp, Gladys Leslie, Jean Paige, Huntley Gordon, T.J. McGrane

TOO MANY CROOKS (1927)
(6 r.) d, Fred Newmeyer; lp, Mildred Davis, Lloyd Hughes, George Bancroft, El Brendel

TOO MANY KISSES (1925)
(6 r.) d, Paul Sloane; lp, Richard Dix, Frances Howard, William Powell, Frank Currier

TOO MANY MILLIONS (1918)
(5 r.) d, James Cruze; lp, Wallace Reid, Ora Carew, Tully Marshall, Charles Ogle

TOO MANY WIVES (1927)
(5 r.) lp, Norma Shearer

TOO MUCH JOHNSON (1920)
(5 r.) d, Donald Crisp; lp, Bryant Washburn, Lois Wilson, Adele Farrington, C.H. Geldart

TOO MUCH MARRIED (1921)
(5 r.) d, Scott Dunlap; lp, Mary Anderson, Roscoe Karns, Jack Connolly, Mathilde Brundage

TOO MUCH MONEY (1926)
(7 r.) d, John Francis Dillon; lp, Lewis Stone, Anna Q. Nilsson, Robert Cain, Derek Glynne

TOO MUCH WIFE (1922)
(5 r.) d, Thomas N. Heffron; lp, Wanda Hawley, T. Roy Barnes, Arthur Hoyt, Lillian Langdon

TOO MUCH YOUTH (1925)
(5 r.) d, Duke Worne; lp, Richard Holt, Sylvia Breamer, Eric Mayne, Charles K. French

TOO WISE WIVES (1921)
(6 r.) d, Lois Weber; lp, Louis Calhern, Claire Windsor, Phillips Smalley, Mona Lisa

TOP DOG, THE (1918, Brit.)
(6 r.) d, Arrigo Bocchi; lp, Kenelm Foss, Odette Goimbault, Hayford Hobbs, Evelyn Harding

TOP HAND (1925)
(5 r.) lp, Bill Bailey

TOP O' THE MORNING, THE (1922)
(5 r.) d, Edward Laemmle; lp, Gladys Walton, Harry Myers, Doreen Turner, Florence D. Lee

TOP OF THE WORLD, THE (1925)
(7 r.) d, George Melford; lp, James Kirkwood, Anna Q. Nilsson, Joseph Kilgour, Mary Mersch

TOP SERGEANT MULLIGAN (1928)
(6 r.) d, James P. Hogan; lp, Donald Keith, Lila Lee, Wesley Barry, Gareth Hughes

TOPSY AND EVA (1927)
(8 r.) d, Del Lord; lp, Rosetta Duncan, Vivian Duncan, Gibson Gowland, Noble Johnson

TORCH BEARER, THE (1916)
(5 r.) d, William Russell, John Prescott; lp, William Russell, Charlotte Burton, Rena Carlton, Harry Keenan

TORCHBEARER, THE
(SEE: FROM THE WEST, 1920)

TORN SAILS (1920, Brit.)
(5 r.) d, A.V. Bramble; lp, Milton Rosmer, Mary Odette, Geoffrey Kerr, Jose Shannon

TORNADO, THE (1924)
(7 r.) d, King Baggot; lp, House Peters, Ruth Clifford, Richard Tucker, Snitz Edwards

TORRENT, THE (1924)
(6 r.) d, A.P. Younger, Willian Doner; lp, William Fairbanks, Ora Carew, Frank Elliott, Joseph Kilgour

TORTURED HEART, A (1916)
(5 r.) d, Will S. Davis; lp, Virginia Pearson, Stuart Holmes, Stephen Grattan

T'OTHER DEAR CHARMER (1918)
(5 r.) d, William P.S. Earle; lp, Louise Huff, John Bowers, Charles Dungan, Eugenie Woodward

TOTON (1919)
(6 r.) d, Frank Borzage; lp, Olive Thomas, Norman Kerry, Jack Perrin, Francis McDonald

TOUCH OF A CHILD, THE (1918, Brit.)
(5 r.) d, Cecil M. Hepworth; lp, Alma Taylor, Henry Edwards, Stewart Rome, A. Trevor Addinsell

TOUGH GUY, THE (1926)
(6 r.) d, David Kirkland; lp, Fred Thomson, Lola Todd, Robert McKim, William Courtwright

TOWARDS THE LIGHT (1918, Brit.)
(6 r.) d, Henry Edwards; lp, Henry Edwards, Chrissie White, A.V. Bramble, Marsh Allen

TOWER OF JEWELS, THE (1920)
(5 r.) d, Tom Terriss; lp, Corinne Griffith, Webster Campbell, Henry Stephenson, Maurice Costello

TOWN OF CROOKED WAYS, THE (1920, Brit.)
(5 r.) d, Bert Wynne; lp, Edward O'Neill, Poppy Wyndham, Denis Cowles, Cyril Percival

TOWER OF STRENGTH
(SEE: GATES OF DUTY, 1919, Brit.)

TOWN THAT FORGOT GOD, THE (1922)
(9 r.) d, Harry Millarde; lp, Bunny Grauer, Warren Krech, Jane Thomas, Harry Benham

TOYS OF FATE (1918)
(7 r.) d, George D. Baker; lp, Alla Nazimova, Charles Bryant, Frank Currier, Irving Cummings

TRACKED (1928)
(5 r.) d, Jerome Storm; lp, Sam Nelson, Caryl Lincoln, Al Smith, Ranger (a dog)

TRACKED BY THE POLICE (1927)
(6 r.) d, Ray Enright; lp, Rin-Tin-Tin, Jason Robards, Virginia Browne Faire, Tom Santschi

TRACKED IN THE SNOW COUNTRY (1925)
(7 r.) d, Herman C. Raymaker; lp, Rin-Tin-Tin, June Marlowe, David Butler, Mitchell Lewis

TRACKING THE ZEPPELIN RAIDERS (1916, Brit.)
(4 r.)

TRACKS (1922)
(6 r.) d, Joseph Franz; lp, Bill Patton, George Berrell, Francois Dumas, Beatrice Burnham

TRACY THE OUTLAW (1928)
(6 r.) d, Otis B. Thayer; lp, Jack Hoey, Rose Chadwick, Dave Marrell, Jane La Rue

TRAFFIC (1915, Brit.)
(4 r.) d, Charles Raymond; lp, Marjorie Villis, Charles Vane, Alden Lovett, Lily Saxby

TRAFFIC COP, THE (1926)
(5 r.) d, Harry Garson; lp, Lefty Flynn, Kathleen Myers, James Marcus, Adele Farrington

TRAFFIC IN HEARTS (1924)
(6 r.) d, Scott Dunlap; lp, Robert Frazer, Mildred Harris, Don Marion, Charles Wellesley

TRAGEDIES OF THE CRYSTAL GLOBE, THE (1915)
(4 r.) d, Richard Ridgley; lp, Mabel Trunnelle, Bigelow Cooper, Robert Conness

TRAGEDY OF BASIL GRIEVE, THE
(SEE: GREAT POISON MYSTERY, THE, 1914, Brit.)

TRAGEDY OF LOVE (1923, Ger.)
(? r.) d, Joe May; lp, Emil Jannings, Erika Glassner, Mia May, Kurt Vespermann

TRAIL DUST (1924)
(6 r.) d, Gordon Hines; lp, David Dunbar

TRAIL OF COURAGE, THE (1928)
(6 r.) d, Wallace W. Fox; lp, Bob Steele, Marjorie Bonner, Tom Lingham, Jay Morley

TRAIL OF HATE (1922)
(5 r.) d, W. Hughes Curran; lp, Guinn "Big Boy" Williams, Molly Malone, Gordon Russell, Andree Tourneur

TRAIL OF THE CIGARETTE, THE (1920)
(5 r.) d, Tom Collins; lp, Glenn White, Alexander F. Frank, Eugene Acker, Stanley Walpole

TRAIL OF THE HORSE THIEVES, THE (1929)
(5 r.) d, Robert De Lacy; lp, Tom Tyler, Bee Amann, Harry O'Connor, Frankie Darro

TRAIL OF THE LAW (1924)
(5 r.) d, Oscar Apfel; lp, Wilfred Lytell, Norma Shearer, John Morse, George Stevens

TRAIL OF THE LONESOME, THE (1923)
(6 r.) d, Charles Maigne; lp, Mary Miles Minter, Antonio Moreno, Ernest Torrence, Edwin J. Brady

TRAIL OF THE LONESOME PINE, THE (1914)
(5 r.) d, Frank Dear; lp, Dixie Compton, Richard Allen, Frank Dear, Mrs. Stuart Robson

TRAIL OF THE LONESOME PINE, THE (1916)
(5 r.) d, Cecil B. DeMille; lp, Charlotte Walker, Theodore Roberts, Thomas Meighan, Earle Foxe

TRAIL OF VENGEANCE, THE (1924)
(6 r.) d, Al Ferguson; lp, Al Ferguson, Pauline Curley

TRAIL RIDER, THE (1925)
(5 r.) d, William S. Van Dyke; lp, Buck Jones, Nancy Deaver, Lucy Fox, Carl Stockdale

TRAIL RIDERS (1928)
(5 r.) d, J.P. McGowan; lp, Buddy Roosevelt, Lafe McKee, Betty Baker, Pee Wee Holmes

TRAIL TO RED DOG, THE (1921)
(? r.) d, Leonard Franchon; lp, Al Hart, Jack Mower, Robert Conville

TRAIL TO YESTERDAY, THE (1918)
(5 r.) d, Edwin Carewe; lp, Bert Lytell, Anna Q. Nilsson, Harry S. Northrup, Ernest Maupain

TRAILIN' (1921)
(5 r.) d, Lynn F. Reynolds; lp, Tom Mix, Jay Morley, Eva Novak, James Gordon

TRAILIN' BACK (1928)
(5 r.) d, J.P. McGowan; lp, Buddy Roosevelt, Betty Baker, Lafe McKee, Leon De La Mothe

TRAILS OF DESTINY (1926)
(5 r.)

TRAILS OF TREACHERY (1928)
(5 r.) d, Robert J. Horner; lp, Montana Bill

TRAIN WRECKERS, THE (1925)
(5 r.) d, J.P. McGowan; lp, Helen Holmes

TRAINER AND THE TEMPTRESS (1925, Brit.)
(8 r.) d, Walter West; lp, Juliette Compton, James Knight, Stephanie Stephens, Cecil Morton York

TRAITOR (1926, USSR)
(7 r.) d, Abram Room; lp, Nikolai Panov, P. Korizno, David Gutman, Nikolai Okhlopkov

TRANSCONTINENTAL LIMITED (1926)
(7 r.) d, Nat Ross; lp, Johnnie Walker, Eugenia Gilbert, Alec B. Francis, Edith Yorke

TRANSGRESSION (1917)
(5 r.) d, Paul Scardon; lp, Earle Williams, Corinne Griffith, Webster Campbell, Mary Maurice

TRANSGRESSOR, THE (1918)
(8 r.) d, Joseph Levering; lp, Marian Swayne, Ben Lyon, Inez Marcel, Theodore Friebus

TRANSPORT OF FIRE (1931, USSR)
(5 r.) d, Alexander Ivanoff; lp, Gleb Kuzentsov, Fedor Slavski, Nikolay Minchurin, Ksenia Klyaro

TRAP, THE (1918)
(5 r.) d, George Archainbaud; lp, Alice Brady, Curtis Cooksey, Crauford Kent, Robert Cummings

TRAP, THE (1919)
(6 r.) d, Frank Reicher; lp, Olive Tell, Sidney Mason, Jere Austin, Rod La Rocque

TRAPPED (1925)
(5 r.) lp, Carl Miller, Elinor Fair

TRAPPED IN THE AIR (1922)
(5 r.) d, Henry McCarthy, Leo Meehan; lp, Lester Cuneo

TRAVAIL (1920, Fr.)
(? r.) d, Henri Pouctal; lp, Leon Mathot, Hugette Duflos

TRAVELIN' FAST (1924)
(5 r.) lp, Jack Perrin, Jean Arthur, Peggy O'Day, Lew Meehan

TRAVELING SALESMAN, THE (1916)
(5 r.) d, Joseph Kaufman; lp, Frank McIntyre, Doris Kenyon, Harry Northrup, Julia Stuart

TRAVELING SALESMAN, THE (1921)
(5 r.) d, Joseph Henabery; lp, Roscoe "Fatty" Arbuckle, Betty Ross Clark, Frank Holland, Wilton Taylor

TREASON (1917)
(5 r.) d, Allen Holubar; lp, Allen Holubar, Lois Wilson, Dorothy Davenport, Joseph Girard

TREASON (1918)
(5 r.) d, Burton King; lp, Edna Goodrich, Stuart Holmes, Howard Hall, Mildred Clair

TREASURE (1918)
(5 r.) d, Frank Reicher

TREASURE CANYON (1924)
(5 r.) lp, J.B. Warner, Marie Walcamp

TREASURE ISLAND (1917)
(6 r.) d, C.M. & S.A. Franklin; lp, Francis Carpenter, Virginia Lee Corbin, Violet Radcliffe, Lloyd Perl

TREASURE OF ARNE, THE
(SEE: SIR ARNE'S TREASURE, 1921, Swed.)

TREASURE OF HEAVEN, THE (1916, Brit.)
(5 r.) d, A.E. Coleby; lp, Janet Alexander, A.E. Coleby, Langhorne Burton, Arthur Rooke

TREASURE OF THE SEA (1918)
(5 r.) d, Frank Reicher; lp, Edith Storey, Lew Cody, Lewis Willoughby, Joseph Swickard

TREAT 'EM ROUGH (1919)
(5 r.) d, Lynn F. Reynolds; lp, Tom Mix, Jane Novak, Val Paul, Charles LeMoyne

TREE OF KNOWLEDGE, THE (1920)
(5 r.) d, William C. De Mille; lp, Robert Warwick, Kathlyn Williams, Wanda Hawley, Tom Forman

TRELAWNEY OF THE WELLS (1916, Brit.)
(5 r.) d, Cecil M. Hepworth; lp, Alma Taylor, Stewart Rome, Violet Hopson, Lionelle Howard

TREMBLING HOUR, THE (1919)
(6 r.) d, George Siegmann; lp, Kenneth Harlan, Helen Jerome Eddy, Henry Barrows, Willis Marks

TRENT'S LAST CASE (1920, Brit.)
(6 r.) d, Richard Garrick; lp, Gregory Scott, Pauline Peters, Clive Brook, George Foley

TRENT'S LAST CASE (1929)
(6 r.) d, Howard Hawks; lp, Donald Crisp, Raymond Griffith, Raymond Hatton, Marceline Day

TRIAL MARRIAGE (1928)
(6 r.) d, William Curran; lp, Jack Richardson, Corliss Palmer, Paul Power, Ruth Robinson

TRAIL MARRIAGE (1929)
(7 r.) d, Erle C. Kenton; lp, Norman Kerry, Sally Eilers, Jason Robards, Thelma Todd

TRICK OF FATE, A (1919)
(5 r.) d, Howard Hickman; lp, Bessie Barriscale, Alfred Whitman, George Field, Joe Swickard

TRICK OF HEARTS, A (1928)
(6 r.) d, Reeves Eason; lp, Hoot Gibson, Georgia Hale, Heinie Conklin

TRICKS (1925)
(5 r.) d, Bruce Mitchell; lp, Marilyn Mills, J. Frank Glendon, Gladys Moore, Myles McCarthy

TRIFLERS, THE (1920)
(6 r.) d, William Christy Cabanne; lp, Edith Roberts, David Butler, Forrest Stanley, Ben Alexander

TRIFLERS, THE (1924)
(7 r.) d, Louis Gasnier; lp, Mae Busch, Elliott Dexter, Frank Mayo, Walter Hiers

TRIFLING WITH HONOR (1923)
(8 r.) d, Harry A. Pollard; lp, Rockliffe Fellowes, Fritzi Ridgeway, Buddy Messinger, Hayden Stevenson

TRIFLING WOMEN (1922)
(9 r.) d, Rex Ingram; lp, Barbara La Marr, Ramon Novarro, Pomeroy Cannon, Edward Connelly

TRIGGER FINGER (1924)
(5 r.) d, Reeves Eason; lp, Bob Custer, George Field, Margaret Landis, Bill Dyer

TRILBY (1914, Brit.)
(4 r.) d, Harold Shaw; lp, Sir Herbert Tree, Viva Birkett, Ion Swinley, Charles Rock

TRILBY (1923)
(8 r.) d, James Young; lp, Andree Lafayette, Creighton Hale, Arthur Edmund Carew, Philo McCullough

TRIMMED (1922)
(5 r.) d, Harry Pollard; lp, Hoot Gibson, Patsy Ruth Miller, Alfred Hollingsworth, Fred Kohler

TRIMMED IN SCARLET (1923)
(5 r.) d, Jack Conway; lp, Kathlyn Williams, Roy Stewart, Lucille Rickson, Robert Agnew

TRIP TO CHINATOWN, A (1926)
(6 r.) d, Robert P. Kerr; lp, Margaret Livingston, Earle Foxe, J. Farrell MacDonald, Anna May Wong

TRIP TO MARS, A (1920, Den.)
(4 r.)

TRIP TO MARS, A (1920, Ital.)
(5 r.)

TRIP TO PARADISE, A (1921)
(6 r.) d, Maxwell Karger; lp, Bert Lytell, Virginia Valli, Brinsley Shaw, Unice Vin Moore

TRIPLE ACTION (1925)
(5 r.) d, Tom Gibson; lp, Pete Morrison, Trilby Clark, Dolores Gardner, Harry von Meter

TRIPLE PASS (1928)
(5 r.) lp, William Barrymore

TRIPLEPATTE (1922, Fr.)
(? r.) d, Raymond Bernard; lp, Henri Debain

TRIUMPH (1917)
(5 r.) d, Joseph De Grasse; lp, Dorothy Phillips, Lon Chaney, William Stowell, William J. Dyer

TRIUMPH (1924)
(8 r.) d, Cecil B. DeMille; lp, Leatrice Joy, Rod La Rocque, Victor Varconi, Charles Ogle

TRIUMPH OF THE RAT, THE (1926, Brit.)
(8 r.) d, Graham Cutts; lp, Ivor Novello, Isabel Jeans, Nina Vanna, Julie Suedo

TRIUMPH OF THE SCARLET PIMPERNEL
(SEE: SCARLET DAREDEVIL, THE, 1928, Brit.)

TRIUMPH OF THE WEAK, THE (1918)
(5 r.) d, Tom Terriss; lp, Alice Joyce, Walter McGrail, Eulalie Jensen, Adele De Garde

TRIUMPH OF VENUS, THE (1918)
(7 r.) d, Edwin Bower Hesser; lp, Betty Lee, William Sherwood, Phyllis Beveridge, Hassan Mussalli

TRIXIE FROM BROADWAY (1919)
(5 r.) d, Roy William Neill; lp, Margarita Fischer, Emory Johnson, George Periolat, Frank Clark

TROIS JEUNES FILLES (1928, Fr.)
(? r.) d, Robert Boudrioz

TROOP TRAIN, THE
(SEE: LOVE AND THE LAW, 1919)

TROOPER 44 (1917)
(5 r.) d, Roy Gahris; lp, George Soule Spencer, June Daye, Betty Dodsworth, Lynn G. Adams

TROOPER O'NEIL (1922)
(5 r.) d, Scott Dunlap; lp, Charles Jones, Beatrice Burnham, Francis McDonald, Claude Payton

TROPIC MADNESS (1928)
(7 r.) d, Robert Vignola; lp, Leatrice Joy, Lena Malena, George Barraud, Henry Sedley

TROPICAL LOVE (1921)
(5 r.) d, Ralph Ince; lp, Ruth Clifford, Fred Turner, Reginald Denny, Huntley Gordon

TROPICAL NIGHTS (1928)
(6 r.) d, Elmer Clifton; lp, Patsy Ruth Miller, Malcolm McGregor, Ray Hallor, Wallace McDonald

TROUBLE BUSTER, THE (1917)
(5 r.) d, Frank Reicher; lp, Vivian Martin, James Neill, Paul Willis, Charles West

TROUBLE BUSTER, THE (1925)
(5 r.) d, Leo Maloney; lp, Leo Maloney, Josephine Hill, Whitehorse, Evelyn Thatcher

TROUBLE CHASER (1926)
(5 r.)

TROUBLE FOR EDGAR (1915)
(4 r.)

TROUBLE SHOOTER, THE (1924)
(6 r.) d, Jack Conway; lp, Tom Mix, Kathleen Key, Frank Currier, J. Gunnis Davis

TROUBLE TRAIL (1924)
(5 r.) d, George Holt; lp, Neva Gerber, Richard Hatton

TROUBLE WITH WIVES, THE (1925)
(7 r.) d, Malcolm St. Clair; lp, Florence Vidor, Tom Moore, Esther Ralston, Ford Sterling

TROUBLEMAKERS (1917)
(7 r.) d, Kenean Buel; lp, Jane Lee, Katherine Lee, Lillian Concord, Richard Turner

TROUBLES OF A BRIDE (1924)
(5 r.) d, Thomas Buckingham; lp, Robert Agnew, Mildred June, Alan Hale, Bruce Covington

TROUBLESOME WIVES (1928, Brit.)
(6 r.) d, Harry Hughes; lp, Mabel Poulton, Lillian Oldland, Eric Bransby Williams, Reginald Fox

TROUPER, THE (1922)
(5 r.) d, Harry B. Harris; lp, Gladys Walton, Jack Perrin, Thomas Holding, Kathleen O'Connor

TROUPING WITH ELLEN (1924)
(7 r.) d, T. Hayes Hunter; lp, Helene Chadwick, Mary Thurman, Gaston Glass, Basil Rathbone

TROUSERS (1920, Brit.)
(5 r.) d, Bertram Phillips; lp, Queenie Thomas, Jack Leigh, Fred Morgan, Bernard Vaughan

TRUANT HUSBAND, THE (1921)
(5 r.) d, Thomas N. Heffron; lp, Mahlon Hamilton, Betty Blythe, Francelia Billington, Edward Ryan

TRUANT SOUL, THE (1917)
(7 r.) d, Harry Beaumont; lp, Henry B. Walthall, Mary Charleson, Patrick Calhoun, Anna May Walthall

TRUANTS, THE (1922, Brit.)
(6 r.) d, Sinclair Hill; lp, Joan Morgan, Philip Simmonds, Lawford Davidson, Robert English

TRUCKER'S TOP HAND (1924)
(5 r.) d, Neal Hart; lp, Neal Hart

TRUE AS STEEL (1924)
(7 r.) d, Rupert Hughes; lp, Aileen Pringle, Huntley Gordon, Cleo Madison, Eleanor Boardman

TRUE BLUE (1918)
(7 r.) d, Frank Lloyd; lp, William Farnum, Katherine Adams, Charles Clary, Francis Carpenter

TRUE HEAVEN (1929)
(6 r.) d, James Tinling; lp, George O'Brien, Lois Moran, Phillips Smalley, Oscar Apfel

TRUE NOBILITY (1916)
(5 r.) d, Donald MacDonald; lp, Helene Rosson, E. Forrest Taylor, Lizette Thorne, Charles Newton

TRUFFLERS, THE (1917)
(5 r.) d, Fred E. Wright; lp, Nell Craig, Sydney Ainsworth, Ernest Maupain, Richard C. Travers

TRUMPET CALL, THE (1915, Brit.)
(5 r.) d, Percy Nash; lp, Gregory Scott, Joan Ritz, Douglas Payne, Daisy Cordell

TRUMPET ISLAND (1920)
(7 r.) d, Tom Terriss; lp, Marguerite de la Motte, Wallace MacDonald, Hallam Cooley, Joseph Swickard

TRUMPIN' TROUBLE (1926)
(5 r.) d, Richard Thorpe; lp, Buffalo Bill Jr., Bob Fleming, Alma Rayford, Charles Whitaker

TRUNK MYSTERY, THE (1927)
(5 r.) d, Frank Hall Crane; lp, Charles Hutchinson, Alice Calhoun, Richard Neill, Ben Walker

TRUST, THE
(SEE; FEUD GIRL, THE, 1916)

TRUST YOUR WIFE (1921)
(6 r.) d, J.A. Barry; lp, Katherine MacDonald, Dave Winter, Charles Richman, Mary Alden

TRUTH ABOUT HELEN, THE (1915)
(4 r.) d, Frank McGlyn; lp, Robert Conness, Grace Williams, Harry Linson, Augustus Phillips

TRUTH ABOUT HUSBANDS, THE (1920)
(6 r.) d, Kenneth Webb; lp, Anna Lehr, Holmes E. Herbert, Elizabeth Garrison, May McAvoy

TRUTH ABOUT MEN (1926)
(7 r.) d, Elmer Clifton

TRUTH ABOUT WIVES, THE (1923)
(6 r.) d, Lawrence Windom; lp, Betty Blythe, [Frederick] Tyrone Power, William P. Carleton, Ann Luther

TRUTH ABOUT WOMEN, THE (1924)
(6 r.) d, Burton King; lp, Hope Hampton, Lowell Sherman, David Powell, Mary Thurman

TRUTH AND JUSTICE (1916, Brit.)
(4 r.) d, Bert Haldene; lp, Horatio Bottomley, Florence Aliston

TRUTHFUL LIAR, THE (1922)
(6 r.) d, Thomas N. Heffron; lp, Wanda Hawley, Edward Hearn, Charles Stevenson, Casson Ferguson

TRUTHFUL SEX, THE (1926)
(6 r.) d, Richard Thomas; lp, Mae Busch, Huntley Gordon, Ian Keith, Leo White

TRUTHFUL TULLIVER (1917)
(5 r.) d, William S. Hart; lp, William S. Hart, Alma Rubens, Nina Byron, Norbert A. Myles

TRUXTON KING (1923)
(6 r.) d, Jerome Storm; lp, John Gilbert, Ruth Clifford, Frank Leigh, Mickey Moore

TRY AND GET IT (1924)
(6 r.) d, Cullen Tate; lp, Bryant Washburn, Billie Dove, Edward Horton, Joseph Kilgour

TSAR IVAN VASILYEVICH GROZNY (1915, USSR)
(6 r.) d, A. Ivanov-Gai; lp, Fyodor Shalyapin, N. Saltikov, Richard Boleslawski, Boris Sushkevich

TSAR NIKOLAI II (1917, USSR)
(5 r.) d, A. Ivonin, Boris Mikhin; lp, Pytor Baksheyev, Vera Orlova, N. Golosov, M. Kemper

TU M'APPARTIENS (1929, Fr.)
(? r.) d, Maurice Gleize

TURF CONSPIRACY, A (1918, Brit.)
(6 r.) d, Frank Wilson; lp, Violet Hopson, Gerald Ames, Joan Legge, Cameron Carr

TURKISH DELIGHT (1927)
(6 r.) d, Paul Sloane; lp, Julia Faye, Rudolph Schildkraut, Kenneth Thomson, Louis Natheaux

TURKSIB (1930, USSR)
(6 r.) d, Victor Turin

TURMOIL, THE (1916)
(5 r.) d, Edgar Jones; lp, Valli Valli, George Le Guere, Charles Prince, Florida Kingsley

TURMOIL, THE (1924)
(7 r.) d, Hobart Henley; lp, Emmett Corrigan, George Hackathorne, Edward Hearn, Theodore von Eltz

TURN BACK THE HOURS (1928)
(6 r.) d, Howard Bretherton; lp, Myrna Loy, Walter Pidgeon, Sam Hardy, George Stone

TURN IN THE ROAD, THE (1919)
(5 r.) d, King Vidor; lp, George Nichols, Ben Alexander, Lloyd Hughes, Winter Hall

TURN OF THE CARD, THE (1918)
(7 r.) d, Oscar Apfel; lp, J. Warren Kerrigan, Lois Wilson, Eugene Pallette, David M. Hartford

TURN OF THE ROAD, THE (1915)
(5 r.) d, Tefft Johnson; lp, Joseph Kilgour, Naomi Childers, Virginia Pearson, Bobby Connelly

TURN OF THE WHEEL, THE (1918)
(5 r.) d, Reginald Barker; lp, Geraldine Farrar, Herbert Rawlinson, Percy Marmont, Violet Heming

TURN TO THE RIGHT (1922)
(8 r.) d, Rex Ingram; lp, Alice Terry, Jack Mulhall, Harry Myers, George Cooper

TURNED UP (1924)
(5 r.) d, James Chapin; lp, Charles Hutchison, Mary Beth Milford, Crauford Kent, Otto Lederer

TURNING POINT, THE (1920)
(6 r.) d, J.A. Barry; lp, Katherine MacDonald, Leota Lorraine, Nigel Barrie, William V. Mong

TURNING THE TABLES (1919)
(5 r.) d, Elmer Clifton; lp, Dorothy Gish, Raymond Cannon, George Fawcett, Porter Strong

TWAS EVER THUS (1915)
(4 r.) lp, Elsie Janis, Hobart Bosworth, Owen Moore, Myrtle Stedman

TWELVE POUND LOOK, THE (1920, Brit.)
(5 r.) d, Jack Denton; lp, Milton Rosmer, Jessie Winter, Ann Elliott, Nelson Ramsey

$20 A WEEK (1924)
(6 r.) d, Harmon Weight; lp, George Arliss, Taylor Holmes, Edith Roberts, Walter Howe

TWENTY-ONE (1918)
(5 r.) d, William Worthington; lp, Bryant Washburn, Gertrude Selby

TWENTY-ONE (1923)
(7 r.) d, John S. Robertson; lp, Richard Barthelmess, Joe King, Dorothy Cumming, Dorothy Mackaill

23 1/2 HOURS ON LEAVE (1919)
(5 r.) d, Henry King; lp, Douglas MacLean, Doris May, Thomas Guise, Maxfield Stanley

TWILIGHT (1919)
(6 r.) d, J. Searle Dawley; lp, Doris Kenyon, Frank Mills, Sally Crute, George Lessey

TWIN FLAPPERS (1927)
(5 r.) lp, Harry Morey, Muriel Kingston, Marguerite Clayton, James Morrison

TWIN KIDDIES (1917)
(6 r.) d, Henry King; lp, Marie Osborne, Henry King, Ruth Lackaye, Daniel Gilfether

TWIN PAWNS, THE (1919)
(6 r.) d, Leonce Perret; lp, Mae Murray, J.W. Johnston, Warner Oland, Henry G. Sell

TWIN SIX O'BRIEN (1926)
(5 r.) d, Robert J. Horner; lp, Kit Carson, Pauline Curley

TWIN TRIANGLE, THE (1916)
(5 r.) d, Harry Harvey; lp, Jackie Saunders

TWIN TRIGGERS (1926)
(5 r.) d, Richard Thorpe; lp, Buddy Roosevelt, Nita Cavalier, Frederick Lee, Laura Lockhart

TWINKLER, THE (1916)
(5 r.) d, Edward Sloman; lp, William Russell, Charlotte Burton, Clarence Burton, William Carroll

TWINS OF SUFFERING CREEK (1920)
(5 r.) d, Scott Dunlap; lp, William Russell, Louise Lovely, E.A. Warren, Bill Ryno

TWISTED TRIGGERS (1926)
(5 r.) d, Richard Thorpe; lp, Wally Wales, Jean Arthur, Al Richmond, Art Winkler

TWO ARABIAN KNIGHTS (1927)
(9 r.) d, Lewis Milestone; lp, William Boyd, Mary Astor, Louis Wolheim, Michael Vavitch

TWO BRIDES, THE (1919)
(5 r.) d, Edward Jose; lp, Lina Cavalieri, Courtenay Foote, Warburton Gamble, Hal Reid

TWO CAN PLAY (1926)
(6 r.) d, Nat Ross; lp, George Fawcett, Allan Forrest, Clara Bow, Wallace MacDonald

TWO DAYS (1929, USSR)
(6 r.) d, Grigori Stabovoi; lp, Ivan Zamychovsky, Sergei Minin, Y. Gekebush

TWO FISTED BUCKAROO (1926)
(5 r.) lp, Fred Church

TWO FISTED JUSTICE (1924)
(5 r.) d, Dick Hatton; lp, Dick Hatton, Marilyn Mills

TWO FISTED TENDERFOOT, A (1924)
(5 r.) d, J.P. McGowan; lp, Franklyn Farnum

TWO FISTED THOMPSON (1925)
(5 r.) lp, Lester Cuneo

2 GIRLS WANTED (1927)
(7 r.) d, Alfred E. Green; lp, Janet Gaynor, Glenn Tryon, Ben Bard, Marie Mosquini

TWO GUN MURPHY (1928)
(5 r.) lp, Al Hoxie

TWO GUN O'BRIEN (1928)
(5 r.) d, Robert J. Horner; lp, Art Acord

TWO GUN SAP (1925)
(5 r.) lp, Franklyn Farnum

TWO KINDS OF LOVE (1920)
(5 r.) d, Reaves Eason; lp, George McDaniels, Ted Brooks, Jimsy Maye, Reaves Eason

TWO KINDS OF WOMEN (1922)
(6 r.) d, Colin Campbell; lp, Pauline Frederick, Tom Santschi, Charles Clary, Dave Winter

TWO LANCASHIRE LASSES IN LONDON (1916, Brit.)
(5 r.) d, Dave Aylott; lp, Lettie Paxton, Dolly Tree, Wingold Lawrence, Dave Aylott

TWO LITTLE DRUMMER BOYS (1928, Brit.)
(8 r.) d, G.B. Samuelson; lp, Wee Georgie Wood, Alma Taylor, Paul Cavanagh, Walter Butler

TWO LITTLE IMPS (1917)
(5 r.) d, Kenean Buel; lp, Jane Lee, Katherine Lee, Leslie Austen, Edna Hunter

TWO LITTLE WOODEN SHOES (1920, Brit.)
(5 r.) d, Sidney Morgan; lp, Joan Morgan, Langhorne Burton, J. Denton-Thompson, Constance Backner

TWO MEN AND A WOMAN (1917)
(5 r.) d, William Humphrey; lp, James Morrison, Guy Coombs, John Reinhart, Christine Mayo

TWO MEN OF SANDY BAR (1916)
(5 r.) d, Lloyd B. Carleton; lp, Hobart Bosworth, Emory Johnson, Gretchen Lederer, Frank MacQuarrie

TWO MOONS (1920)
(5 r.) d, Edward J. Le Saint; lp, Buck Jones, Carol Holloway, Gus Saville, Bert Sprotte

TWO ORPHANS, THE (1915)
(7 r.) d, Herbert Brenon; lp, Theda Bara, Jean Sothern, Herbert Brenon, William E. Shay

TWO OUTLAWS, THE (1928)
(5 r.) d, Henry MacRae; lp, Jack Perrin, Kathleen Collins, J.P. McGowan, Rex (a dog)

TWO SHALL BE BORN (1924)
(6 r.) d, Whitman Bennett; lp, Jane Novak, Kenneth Harlan, Sigrid Holmquist, Frank Sheridan

TWO SISTERS (1929)
(6 r.) d, Scott Pembroke; lp, Viola Dana, Rex Lease, Claire Du Brey, Tom Lingham

TWO SOULED WOMAN, THE
(SEE: UNTAMEABLE, THE, 1923)

TWO WEEKS (1920)
(5 r.) d, Sidney A. Franklin; lp, Constance Talmadge, Conway Tearle, Reginald Mason, George Fawcett

TWO WEEKS WITH PAY (1921)
(5 r.) d, Maurice Campbell; lp, Bebe Daniels, Jack Mulhall, James Mason, George Periolat

TWO WOMEN (1919)
(5 r.) d, Ralph Ince; lp, Anita Stewart, Earle Williams, Julia Swayne Gordon, Harry Northrup

TWO-BITS SEATS (1917)
(5 r.) d, Lawrence Windom; lp, Taylor Holmes, Marguerite Clayton, Sidney Ainsworth, John Cossar

TWO-FISTED JEFFERSON (1922)
(5 r.) d, Roy Clements; lp, Jack Hoxie, Evelyn Nelson, Claude Payton, Bill White

TWO-FISTED JONES (1925)
(5 r.) d, Edward Sedgwick; lp, Jack Hoxie, Kathryn McGuire, William Steele, Harry Todd

TWO-FISTED SHERIFF, A (1925)
(5 r.) d, Ben Wilson; lp, Takima Canutt, Ruth Stonehouse, Art Walker, Cliff Davidson

TWO-GUN BETTY (1918)
(5 r.) d, Howard Hickman; lp, Bessie Barriscale, L.C. Shumway, Catherine Van Buren, Helen Hawley

TWO-GUN MAN, THE (1926)
(6 r.) d, David Kirkland; lp, Fred Thomson, Joseph Dowling, Spottiswoode Aitken, Sheldon Lewis

TWO-GUN OF THE TUMBLEWEED (1927)
(6 r.) d, Leo Maloney; lp, Leo Maloney, Peggy Montgomery, Josephine Hill, Frederick Dana

TWO-SOUL WOMAN, THE (1918)
(5 r.) d, Elmer Clifton; lp, Priscilla Dean, Joseph Girard, Ashton Dearholt, Evelyn Selbie

TYPHOON LOVE (1926)
(6 r.) d, Norman Dawn; lp, Mitchell Lewis, Ruth Clifford

TYRANT FEAR (1918)
(5 r.) d, Roy William Neill; lp, Dorothy Dalton, Thurston Hall, Melbourne McDowell, William Conklin

TYRANT OF RED GULCH (1928)
(5 r.) d, Robert De Lacy; lp, Tom Tyler, Frankie Darro, Josephine Borio, Harry Woods

U.P. TRAIL, THE (1920)
(7 r.) lp, Kathlyn Williams, Marguerite de la Motte, Roy Stewart, Joseph Dowling

UGLY DUCKLING, THE (1920, Brit.)
(6 r.) d, Alexander Butler; lp, Albert Ray, Florence Turner, Maudie Dunham, William Merrick

ULTUS, THE MAN FROM THE DEAD (1916, Brit.)
(5 r.)

UN AVENTUERIER (1921, Fr.)
(? r.) d, Charles Maudru, Charles de Marsan

UN BON PETIT DIABLE (1923, Fr.)
(? r.) d, Rene Leprince

UN CHATEAU DE LA MORT LENTE (1925, Fr.)
(? r.) d, Donatien

UN CRIME A ETE COMMIS (1919, Fr.)
(? r.) d, Andre Hugon

UN DRAME SOUS NAPOLEON (1921, Fr.)
(? r.) d, Gerard Bourgeois

UN FIL A LA PATTE (1924, Fr.)
(? r.) d, Robert Saidreau

UN FILS D'AMERIQUE (1925, Fr.)
(? r.) d, Henri Fescourt

UN HOMME PASSA (1917, Fr.)
(? r.) d, Henry Roussel

UN MARIAGE DE RAISON (1916, Fr.)
(? r.) d, Louis Feuillade

UN OURS (1921, Fr.)
(? r.) d, Charles Burguet

UN ROMAN D'AMOUR ET D'AVENTURES (1918, Fr.)
(? r.) d, Rene Hervil, Louis Mercanton

UN SOIR (1919, Fr.)
(? r.) d, Robert Boudrioz

UNAFRAID, THE (1915)
(4 r.) d, Cecil B. DeMille; lp, Rita Jolivet, House Peters, Page Peters, Billy Elmer

UNATTAINABLE, THE (1916)
(5 r.) d, Lloyd B. Carleton; lp, Dorothy Davenport, Mattie Witting, Emory Johnson, Richard Morris

UNBEATABLE GAME, THE (1925)
(9 r.) d, J. Law Siple; lp, Rev. Robert R. Jones

UNBELIEVER, THE (1918)
(7 r.) d, Alan Crosland; lp, Raymond McKee, Marguerite Courtot, Kate Lester, Frank De Vernon

UNBLAZED TRAIL (1923)
(5 r.) d, Richard Hatton; lp, Richard Hatton, Vivian Rich, Donald McCollum

UNBROKEN PROMISE, THE (1919)
(5 r.) d, Frank Powell; lp, Jane Miller, Sydney Mason, William Human, John Smiley

UNBROKEN ROAD, THE (1915)
(5 r.) lp, Mary Nash, William H. Tooker, Alexander Gaden, Thomas O'Keefe

UNCANNY ROOM, THE (1915, Ger.)
(4 r.) d, Richard Oswald; lp, Carlyle Blackwell, Tatjana Irrah, Livio Pavanelli, Alexander Mursky

UNCHARTED CHANNELS (1920)
(6 r.) d, Henry King; lp, H.B. Warner, Kathryn Adams, Same De Grasse, Evelyn Selbie

UNCHARTED SEAS (1921)
(6 r.) d, Wesley Ruggles; lp, Alice Lake, Carl Gerard, Rudolph Valentino, Robert Alden

UNCLAIMED GOODS (1918)
(5 r.) d, Rollin S. Sturgeon; lp, Vivian Martin, Harrison Ford, Casson Ferguson, George McDaniel

UNCLE DICK'S DARLING (1920, Brit.)
(5 r.) d, Fred Paul; lp, George Bellamy, Athalie Davis, Humberston Wright, Ronald Power

UNCLE JASPAR'S WILL (1922)
(6 r.) lp, William E. Fountaine, Shingzie Howard

UNCLE SAM AWAKE (1916)
(5 r.)

UNCLE TOM'S CABIN (1918)
(5 r.) d, J. Searle Dawley; lp, Marguerite Clark, J.W. Johnston, Florence Carpenter, Frank Losee

UNCLE TOM'S CABIN (1927)
(13 r.) d, Harry Pollard; lp, James Lowe, Virginia Grey, George Siegmann, Margarita Fisher

UNCONQUERED (1917)
(5 r.) d, Frank Reicher; lp, Fannie Ward, Jack Dean, Hobart Bosworth, Tully Marshall

UNCONQUERED WOMAN (1922)
(5 r.) d, Marcel Perez; lp, Rubye De Remer, Walter Miller, Fred C. Jones, Frankie Mann

UNDER COVER (1916)
(5 r.) d, Robert Vignola; lp, Hazel Dawn, Owen Moore, Frank Losee, William Courtleigh Jr.

UNDER CRIMSON SKIES (1920)
(6 r.) d, Rex Ingram; lp, Elmo Lincoln, Harry Van Meter, Mabel Ballin, Nancy Caswell

UNDER FALSE COLORS (1917)
(5 r.) d, Emile Chautard; lp, Frederick Warde, Jeanne Eagles, Robert Vaughn, Anne Gregory

UNDER HANDICAP (1917)
(7 r.) d, Fred J. Balshofer; lp, Harold Lockwood, Anna Little, William Clifford, Lester Cuneo

UNDER NORTHERN LIGHTS (1920)
(5 r.) d, Jacques Jaccard; lp, William Buckley, Leonard Clapham, Virginia Browne Faire, Herbert Bethew

UNDER OATH (1922)
(5 r.) d, George Archainbaud; lp, Elaine Hammerstein, Mahlon Hamilton, Niles Welch, Carl Gerard

UNDER SOUTHERN SKIES (1915)
(5 r.) d, Lucius Henderson; lp, Mary Fuller, Charles Ogle, Clara Byers, Bert Bushy

UNDER SUSPICION (1916, Brit.)
(6 r.) d, George Loane Tucker; lp, Gerald Ames, Douglas Munro, Laura Cowie, Bert Wynne

UNDER SUSPICION (1918)
(5 r.) d, William S. Davis; lp, Francis X. Bushman, Beverly Bayne, Eva Gordon, Hugh Jeffrey

UNDER SUSPICION (1919)
(6 r.) d, William C. Dowlan; lp, Ora Carew, Forrest Stanley, Frank McQuarrie, Blanche Rose

UNDER THE BLACK EAGLE (1928)
(6 r.) d, W.S. Van Dyke; lp, Ralph Forbes, Marceline Day, Bert Roach, William Fairbanks

UNDER THE GASLIGHT (1914)
(4 r.)

UNDER THE GREENWOOD TREE (1918)
(5 r.) d, Emile Chautard; lp, Elsie Ferguson, Eugene O'Brien, Edward Burns, Mildred Havens

UNDER THE LASH (1921)
(6 r.) d, Sam Wood; lp, Gloria Swanson, Mahlon Hamilton, Russell Simpson, Lillian Leighton

UNDER THE RED ROBE (1915, Brit.)
(4 r.) d, Wilfred Noy; lp, Owen Roughwood, Dorothy Drake, Jackson Wilcox, Sydney Bland

UNDER THE ROUGE (1925)
(6 r.) d, Lewis H. Moomaw; lp, Eileen Percy, Tom Moore, Eddie Phillips, James Mason

UNDER THE SOUTHERN CROSS
(SEE: DEVIL'S PIT, THE, 1930)

UNDER THE TONTO RIM (1928)
(6 r.) d, Herman C. Raymaker; lp, Richard Arlen, Alfred Allen, Mary Brian, Jack Luden

UNDER THE TOP (1919)
(5 r.) d, Donald Crisp; lp, Fred Stone, Ella Hall, Lester Le May, Sylvia Ashton

UNDER THE YOKE (1918)
(5 r.) d, J. Gordon Edwards; lp, Theda Bara, Albert Roscoe, G. Raymond Nye, Edwin B. Tilton

UNDER TWO FLAGS (1916)
(6 r.) d, J. Gordon Edwards; lp, Theda Bara, Hervert Heyes, Stuart Holmes, Stanhope Wheatcroft

UNDER TWO FLAGS (1922)
(8 r.) d, Tod Browning; lp, Priscilla Dean, James Kirkwood, John Davidson, Stuart Holmes

UNDER WESTERN SKIES (1921)
(5 r.) d, George Martin; lp, Wallace Ray, Grace Lloyd

UNDER WESTERN SKIES (1926)
(7 r.) d, Edward Sedgwick; lp, Norman Kerry, Anne Cornwall, Ward Crane, George Fawcett

UNDERCURRENT, THE (1919)
(6 r.) d, Wilfred North; lp, Arthur Guy Empey, Marguerite Courtot, Florence Evelyn Martin, Betty Blythe

UNDERGROUND (1928, Brit.)
(7 r.) d, Anthony Asquith; lp, Elissa Landi, Brian Aherne, Norah Baring, Cyril McLaglen

UNDERSTANDING HEART, THE (1927)
(7 r.) d, Jack Conway; lp, Joan Crawford, Rockliffe Fellowes, Francis X. Bushman Jr., Carmel Myers

UNDERSTUDY, THE (1917)
(4 r.) d, William Bertram; lp, Ethel Ritchie, Neil Hardin, Bruce Smith, Mollie McConnell

UNDERSTUDY, THE (1922)
(5 r.) d, William A. Seiter; lp, Doris May, Wallace MacDonald, Christine Mayo, Otis Harlan

UNDERTOW, THE (1916)
(5 r.) lp, Franklin Ritchie, Helene Rosson, Eugenie Forde, Orral Humphrey

UNDERWORLD OF LONDON, THE (1915, Brit.)
(4 r.) d, Charles Weston; lp, Arthur Finn, Lily Saxby, Winnie Fitch, Harry Webb

UNDINE (1916)
(5 r.) d, Henry Otto; lp, Ida Schnall, Douglas Gerrard, Edna Maison, Carol Stellson

UNDISPUTED EVIDENCE (1922)
(? r.)

UNDRESSED (1928)
(6 r.) d, Philip Rosen; lp, David Torrence, Hedda Hopper, Virginia Brown Faire, Buddy Messenger

UNDYING FLAME, THE (1917)
(5 r.) d, Maurice Tourneur; lp, Olga Petrova, Mahlon Hamilton, Violet Reed, Charles W. Martin

UNE AVENTURE (1922, Fr.)
(? r.) d, Viatcheslaw Tourjansky

UNE ETRANGERE (1924, Fr.)
(? r.) d, Robert Saidreau

UNE FEMME INCONNUE (1918, Fr.)
(? r.) d, Gaston Ravel

UNE FLEUR DANS LES RONCES (1921, Fr.)
(? r.) d, Camille de Morlhon

UNE HISTOIRE DE BRIGANDS (1920, Fr.)
(? r.) d, Donatien

UNE NUIT AGITEE (1920, Fr.)
(? r.) d, Alfred Machin

UNE VIE SANS JOIE
(SEE: CATHERINE, 1924)

UNEASY MONEY (1918)
(? r.) d, Lawrence C. Windom; lp, Taylor Holmes, Virginia Valli, Arthur Bates, Charles Gardner

UNEASY PAYMENTS (1927)
(5 r.) d, David Kirkland; lp, Alberta Vaughn, Jack Luden, Gino Corrado, Gene Stone

UNEXPECTED PLACES (1918)
(5 r.) d, E. Mason Hopper; lp, Bert Lytell, Rhea Mitchell, Colin Kenny, Louis Morrison

UNFAIR SEX, THE (1926)
(5 r.) d, Henri Diamant-Berger; lp, Hope Hampton, Holbrook Blinn, Nita Naldi, Walter Miller

UNFAITHFUL WIFE, THE (1915)
(5 r.) d, J. Gordon Edwards; lp, Robert B. Mantell, Genvieve Hamper, Stuart Holmes

UNFOLDMENT, THE (1922)
(6 r.) d, George Kern; lp, Florence Lawrence, Barbara Bedford, Charles French, William Conklin

UNFORSEEN, THE (1917)
(5 r.) d, John B. O'Brien; lp, Olive Tell, David Powell, Lionel Adams, Fuller Mellish

UNFORTUNATE SEX, THE (1920)
(5 r.) d, Elsier La Maie; lp, Frances Edmonde, George Larkin, Harry van Meter, Katherine Lewis

UNGUARDED GIRLS (1929)
(7 r.) d, William Curran; lp, Paddy O'Flynn, Marcella Arnold, Alphonse Martell, Jean Porter

UNGUARDED WOMEN (1924)
(6 r.) d, Alan Crosland; lp, Bebe Daniels, Richard Dix, Mary Astor, Walter McGrail

UNINVITED GUEST, THE (1924)
(7 r.) d, Ralph Ince; lp, Maurice B. Flynn, Jean Tolley, Mary MacLaren, William Bailey

UNITED STATES SMITH (1928)
(7 r.) d, Joseph Henabery; lp, Eddie Gribbon, Lila Lee, Mickey Bennett, Kenneth Harlan

UNJUSTLY ACCUSED (1913, Norway)
(4 r.)

UNKNOWN, THE (1915)
(5 r.) d, George Melford; lp, Lou Tellegen, Theodore Roberts, Dorothy Davenport, Hal Clements

UNKNOWN DANGERS (1926)
(5 r.) d, Grover Jones; lp, Frank Merrill, Gloria Grey, Eddie Boland, Marcin Asher

UNKNOWN LOVE, THE (1919)
(6 r.) d, Leonce Perret; lp, Dolores Cassinelli, E.K. [Elmo] Lincoln, W. Cook, Robert Elliott

UNKNOWN LOVER, THE (1925)
(7 r.) d, Victor Hugo Halperin; lp, Frank Mayo, Elsie Ferguson, Mildred Harris, Peggy Kelly

UNKNOWN PURPLE, THE (1923)
(7 r.) d, Roland West; lp, Henry B. Walthall, Alice Lake, Stuart Holmes, Helen Ferguson

UNKNOWN QUANTITY, THE (1919)
(5 r.) d, Tom Mills; lp, Corinne Griffith, Huntley Gordon, Harry Davenport, Jack Ridgway

UNKNOWN RIDER, THE (1929)
(5 r.) d, A.R. Meals; lp, Fred Church, Frank Lanning, Mary Lou Winn, Jack Kruger

UNKNOWN SOLDIER, THE (1926)
(8 r.) d, Renaud Hoffman; lp, Charles Emmett Mack, Marguerite De La Motte, Henry B. Walthall, Claire McDowell

UNKNOWN TREASURES (1926)
(6 r.) d, Archie Mayo; lp, Gladys Hulette, Robert Agnew, John Miljan, Bertram Marburgh

UNKNOWN 274 (1917)
(5 r.) d, Harry Millarde; lp, June Caprice, Kittens Reichert, Florence Ashbrook, Tom Burrough

UNKNOWN WIFE, THE (1921)
(5 r.) d, William Worthington; lp, Edith Roberts, Spottiswoode Aitken, Casson Ferguson, Joe Quinn

UNMARRIED (1920, Brit.)
(6 r.) d, Rex Wilson; lp, Gerald du Maurier, Malvina Longfellow, Edmund Gwenn, Mary Glynne

UNMARRIED WIVES (1924)
(6 r.) d, James P. Hogan; lp, Mildred Harris, Gladys Brockwell, Lloyd Whitlock, Bernard Randall

UNMASKED (1929)
(6 r.) d, Edgar Lewis; lp, Robert Warwick, Susan Conroy, Milton Krims, Sam Ash

UNNAMED WOMAN, THE (1925)
(6 r.) d, Harry O. Hoyt; lp, Katherine MacDonald, Herbert Rawlinson, Wanda Hawley, Leah Baird

UNPAINTED WOMAN, THE (1919)
(6 r.) d, Tod Browning; lp, Mary MacLaren, Thurston Hall, David Butler, Laura La Varnie

UNPARDONABLE SIN, THE (1916)
(5 r.) d, Barry O'Neill; lp, Holbrook Blinn, Helen Fulton, Lila Hayward Chester, William A. Norton

UNPARDONABLE SIN, THE (1919)
(9 r.) d, Marshall Neilan; lp, Blanche Sweet, Matt Moore, Wallace Beery, Edwin Stevens

UNPROTECTED (1916)
(5 r.) d, James Young; lp, Blanche Sweet, Theodore Roberts, Tom Forman, Ernest Joy

UNRESTRAINED YOUTH (1925)
(6 r.) d, Joseph Levering; lp, Brandon Tynan, Gardner James, Mildred Arden, Blanche Davenport

UNSEEING EYES (1923)
(9 r.) d, E.H. Griffith; lp, Lionel Barrymore, Seena Owen, Louis Wolheim, Gustav von Seffertitz

UNSEEN ENEMIES (1926)
(5 r.) d, J.P. McGowan; lp, Al Hoxie

UNSEEN FORCES (1920)
(6 r.) d, Sidney A. Franklin; lp, Sylvia Breamer, Conrad Nagel, Sam De Grasse, Sidney A. Franklin

UNSEEN HANDS (1924)
(6 r.) d, Jacques Jaccard; lp, Wallace Beery, Joseph J. Dowling, Fontaine La Rue, Jack Rollins

UNTAMEABLE, THE (1923)
(5 r.) d, Herbert Blache; lp, Gladys Walton, Malcolm McGregor, John Sainpolis, Etta Lee

UNTAMED (1918)
(5 r.) d, Cliff Smith; lp, Roy Stewart, Ethel Fleming, May Giraci, H.N. Dudgeon

UNTAMED, THE (1920)
(6 r.) d, Emmett J. Flynn; lp, Tom Mix, Pauline Starke, George Siegmann, Philo McCullough

UNTAMED JUSTICE (1929)
(7 r.) d, Harry Webb; lp, Gaston Glass, Virginia Browne Faire, David Torrence, Philo McCullough

UNTAMED YOUTH (1924)
(5 r.) d, Emile Chautard; lp, Derelys Perdue, Lloyd Hughes, Ralph Lewis, Emily Fitzroy

UNTIL THE DAY WE MEET AGAIN (1932, Jap.)
(? r.) d, Yasujiro Ozy

UNTIL THEY GET ME (1918)
(5 r.) d, Frank Borzage; lp, Pauline Starke, Joe King, Jack Curtis, Wilbur Higby

UNTO EACH OTHER (1929, Brit.)
(8 r.) d, A.E. Coleby; lp, Frederick Catling, Harry Lorraine, Yvonne Thomas, Josephine Earle

UNTO THOSE WHO SIN (1916)
(5 r.) d, Colin Campbell; lp, Fritzi Brunette, Al W. Filson, Lillian Hayward, Marion Warner

UNVEILING HAND, THE (1919)
(5 r.) d, Frank Crane; lp, Kitty Gordon, Irving Cummings, George MacQuarrie, Frederick Warde

UNWELCOME MRS. HATCH, THE (1914)
(4 r.) d, Allan Dwan; lp, Henrietta Crosman, Harold Lockwood, Walter Craven, Lorraine Huling

UNWELCOME MOTHER, THE (1916)
(5 r.) d, James Vincent; lp, Walter Law, Frank Evans, Tom Burrough, Miss Valkyrien

UNWELCOME WIFE, THE (1915)
(5 r.) d, Ivan Abramson; lp, Malvine Lobel, William McNulty, R.G. Don, Ned Nye

UNWILLING HERO, AN (1921)
(5 r.) d, Clarence G. Badger; lp, Will Rogers, Molly Malone, John Bowers, Darrel Foss

UNWRITTEN CODE, THE (1919)
(5 r.) d, Bernard Durning; lp, Shirley Mason, Matt Moore, Ormi Hawley, Frank O'Connor

UNWRITTEN LAW, THE (1916)
(5 r.) lp, Beatriz Michelena, William Pike, Andrew Robson, Matt Snyder

UNWRITTEN LAW, THE (1925)
(7 r.) d, Edward J. Le Saint; lp, Elaine Hammerstein, Forrest Stanley, William V. Mong, Mary Alden

UP AND AT 'EM (1922)
(5 r.) d, William A. Seiter; lp, Doris May, Hallam Cooley, J. Herbert Frank, Otis Harlan

UP AND GOING (1922)
(5 r.) d, Lynn Reynolds; lp, Cecil Van Auker, Carol Holloway, Tom Mix, Eva Novak

UP FROM THE DEPTHS (1915)
(4 r.) lp, Courtenay Foote, Gladys Brockwell

UP IN MABEL'S ROOM (1926)
(7 r.) d, E. Mason Hopper; lp, Marie Prevost, Harrison Ford, Phyllis Haver, Harry Myers

UP IN MARY'S ATTICK (1920)
(5 r.) d, William H. Watson; lp, Eva Novak, Harry Gribbon, Virginia Stearns, Al Fichlesfield

UP IN THE AIR ABOUT MARY (1922)
(5 r.) lp, Louise Lorraine, Joe Moore, Laura La Varnie, Robert Anderson

UP OR DOWN (1917)
(5 r.) d, Lynn F. Reynolds; lp, George Hernandez, Fritzi Ridgeway, Jack Gilbert, Elwood Bredell

UP ROMANCE ROAD (1918)
(5 r.) d, Henry King; lp, William Russell, Charlotte Burton, John Burton, Joseph Belmont

UP THE LADDER (1925)
(7 r.) d, Edward Sloman; lp, Virginia Valli, Forrest Stanley, Margaret Livingston, Holmes Herbert

UP THE ROAD WITH SALLIE (1918)
(5 r.) d, William Desmond Taylor; lp, Constance Talmadge, Norman Kerry, Kate Toncray, Thomas H. Persse

UPHEAVAL, THE (1916)
(5 r.) d, Charles Horan; lp, Lionel Barrymore, Marguerite Skirvin, Franklyn Hanna, Edgar L. Davenport

UPLAND RIDER, THE (1928)
(6 r.) d, Albert Rogell; lp, Ken Maynard, Marian Douglas, Lafe McKee, Sidney Jarvis

UPLIFTERS, THE (1919)
(5 r.) d, Herbert Blache; lp, May Allison, Pell Trenton, Alfred Hollingsworth, Kathleen Kerrigan

UPPER CRUST, THE (1917)
(5 r.) d, Rollin S. Sturgeon; lp, Gail Kane, Douglas MacLean, Eugenie Forde

UPRISING (1918, USSR)
(5 r.) d, Alexander Razumni, Vladimir Karin

UPSIDE DOWN (1919)
(5 r.) d, Lawrence C. Windom; lp, Taylor Holmes, Anna Lehr, Roy Applegate, Ruby Hoffman

UPSTAGE (1926)
(7 r.) d, Monta Bell; lp, Norma Shearer, Oscar Shaw, Tenen Holtz, Gwen Lee

UPSTAIRS (1919)
(5 r.) d, Victor L. Schertzinger; lp, Mabel Normand, Cullen Landis, Hallam Cooley, Edwin Stevens

UPSTAIRS AND DOWN (1919)
(5 r.) d, Charles Giblyn; lp, Olive Thomas, Rosemary Theby, Mary Charleson, David Butler

UPSTART, THE (1916)
(5 r.) d, Edwin Carewe; lp, Marguerite Snow, George Le Guere, James Lackaye, Frederick Summer

UPSTREAM (1927)
(6 r.) d, John Ford; lp, Nancy Nash, Earle Foxe, Grant Withers, Lydia Yeamans

USURPER, THE (1919)
(5 r.) d, James Young; lp, Earle Williams, Louise Lovely, Bob Russell, Frank Leigh

USURPER, THE (1919, Brit.)
(5 r.) d, Duncan Macrae; lp, Gertrude McCoy, Cecil Warde, Stephen T. Ewart, Geoffrey Kerr

VAGABOND CUB, THE (1929)
(6 r.) d, Louis King; lp, Buzz Barton, Frank Rice, Sam Nelson, Al Ferguson

VAGABOND LUCK (1919)
(5 r.) d, Scott Dunlap; lp, Albert Ray, Elinor Fair, Jack Rollens, John Cossar

VAGABOND PRINCE, THE (1916)
(5 r.) d, Charles Giblyn; lp, H.B. Warner, Dorothy Dalton, Roy Laidlaw, Katherine Kirkwood

VAGABOND TRAIL, THE (1924)
(5 r.) d, William A. Wellman; lp, Charles Jones, Marian Nixon, Charles Coleman, L.C. Shumway

VAGABOND'S REVENGE, A (1915, Brit.)
(5 r.) d, Wallett Waller; lp, Agnes Glynne, Jack Morrison, Lyston Lyle, Alice de Winton

VALENCIA (1926)
(6 r.) d, Dimitri Buchowetzki; lp, Mae Murray, Lloyd Hughes, Roy D'Arcy, Max Barwyn

VALENTINE GIRL, THE (1917)
(5 r.) d, J. Searle Dawley; lp, Marguerite Clark, Frank Losee, Richard Barthelmess, Katherine Adams

VALIANTS OF VIRGINIA, THE (1916)
(5 r.) d, T.N. Heffron; lp, Kathlyn Williams, Arthur Shirley, Edward J. Peil, Virginia Kraft

VALLEY OF DECISION, THE (1916)
(5 r.) d, Rea Berger; lp, Richard Bennett, Adrienne Morrison, Blanche Hanson, George Periolat

VALLEY OF DOUBT, THE (1920)
(6 r.) d, Burton George; lp, Thurston Hall, Arline Pretty, Anna Lehr, Jack Costello

VALLEY OF FEAR, THE (1916, Brit.)
(7 r.) d, Alexander Butler; lp, H.A. Saintsbury, Daisy Burrell, Booth Conway, Jack Macaulay

VALLEY OF FEAR, THE (1917)
(6 r.)

VALLEY OF HATE, THE (1924)
(5 r.) d, Russell Allen; lp, Raymond McKee, Helen Ferguson, Earl Metcalf, Wilfred Lucas

VALLEY OF HELL, THE (1927)
(5 r.) d, Clifford S. Smith; lp, Francis McDonald, Edna Murphy, William Steele, Anita Garvin

VALLEY OF HUNTED MEN, THE (1928)
(5 r.) d, Richard Thorpe; lp, Buffalo Bill Jr., Oscar Apfel, Kathleen Collins, Jack Ganzhorn

VALLEY OF LOST HOPE, THE (1915)
(5 r.) d, Romaine Fielding; lp, Romaine Fielding

VALLEY OF LOST SOULS, THE (1923)
(5 r.) d, Caryl S. Fleming; lp, Muriel Kingston, Victor Sutherland, Anne Hamilton, Edward Roseman

VALLEY OF THE GHOSTS (1928, Brit.)
(5 r.) d, G.B. Samuelson; lp, Miriam Seegar, Ian Hunter, Leo Sheffield, Wallace Bosco

VALLEY OF THE GIANTS, THE (1919)
(5 r.) d, James Cruze; lp, Wallace Reid, Grace Darmond, Will Brunton, Charles Ogle

VALLEY OF THE GIANTS, THE (1927)
(7 r.) d, Charles J. Brabin; lp, Milton Sills, Doris Kenyon, Arthur Stone, George Fawcett

VALLEY OF THE MOON, THE (1914)
(7 r.) d, Hobart Bosworth; lp, Jack Conway, Myrtle Stedman, Hobart Bosworth

VALLEY OF TOMORROW, THE (1920)
(6 r.) d, Emmett J. Flynn; lp, William Russell, Mary Thurman, Harvey Clark, Fred Malatesta

VALLEY OF VANISHING MEN, THE (1924)
(5 r.) d, Neal Hart; lp, Neal Hart

VANDERHOFF AFFAIR, THE (1915)
(4 r.) d, Robert Vignola; lp, Hal Forde, Marguerite Courtot, Henry Hallam, T.J. Dow

VAMP, THE (1918)
(5 r.) d, Jerome Storm; lp, Enid Bennett, Douglas MacLean, Charles French, Robert McKim

VAMPIRE, THE (1915)
(5 r.) lp, Olga Petrova

VANINA (1922, Ger.)
(? r.) d, Arthur Von Gerlach; lp, Paul Hartmann, Paul Wegener, Asta Nielsem

VANISHING AMERICAN, THE (1925)
(10 r.) d, George B. Seitz; lp, Richard Dix, Lois Wilson, Noah Beery, Malcolm McGregor

VANISHING PIONEER, THE (1928)
(6 r.) d, John Waters; lp, Jack Holt, Sally Blane, William Powell, Fred Kohler

VANITY (1917)
(5 r.) d, John B. O'Brien; lp, Emily Whelen, Tom O'Keefe, Edward Martindel, Paul Gordon

VANITY FAIR (1915)
(7 r.) d, Charles Brabin; lp, Leonie Flugrath, Yale Benner, William Wadsworth, Helen Fulton

VANITY FAIR (1923)
(8 r.) d, Hugo Ballin; lp, Mabel Ballin, Hobart Bosworth, George Walsh, Harrison Ford

VANITY POOL, THE (1918)
(5 r.) d, Ida May Park; lp, Mary MacLaren, Thomas Holding, Anna Q. Nilsson, Franklyn Farnum

VANITY'S PRICE (1924)
(6 r.) d, Roy William Neill; lp, Anna Q. Nilsson, Stuart Holmes, Wyndham Standing, Arthur Rankin

VARMINT, THE (1917)
(5 r.) d, William Desmond Taylor; lp, Jack Pickford, Louise Huff, Theodore Roberts, Henry Malvern

VARSITY (1928)
(6 r.) d, Frank Tuttle

VARSITY (1930, Brit.)
(4 r.) d, Stuart Legg; lp, Geoffrey Beaumont, J. Evans Hunter, Barbara Lee, Rene Ray

VEILED ADVENTURE, THE (1919)
(5 r.) d, Walter Edwards; lp, Constance Talmadge, Harrison Ford, Stanhope Wheatcroft, Vera Doria

VEILED MARRIAGE, THE (1920)
(5 r.) d, Kenean Buel; lp, Anna Lehr, Ralph Kellard, Dorothy Walters, John Charles

VEILED WOMAN, THE (1922)
(6 r.) d, Lloyd Ingraham; lp, Marguerite Snow, Edward Coxen, Landers Stevens, Lottie Williams

VEILLE D'ARMES (1925, Fr.)
(? r.) d, Jacques de Baroncelli

VELVET HAND, THE (1918)
(5 r.) d, Douglas Gerrard; lp, Fritzi Brunette, Eugene Corey, Carmen Phillips, Fred Turner

VELVET PAW, THE (1916)
(5 r.) d, Maurice Tourneur; lp, House Peters, Gail Kane, Ned Burton, Frank Goldsmith

VENDEMIAIRE (1919, Fr.)
(7 r.) d, Louis Feuillade; lp, Rene Creste, Edouard Mathe

VENDETTA (1914, Fr.)
(5 r.)

VENDETTA (1921, Ger.)
(6 r.) d, Ernst Lubitsch; lp, Pola Negri, Emil Jannings, Harry Liedtke

VENETIAN LOVERS (1925, Brit.)
(6 r.) d, Walter Niebuhr, Frank A. Tilley; lp, Arlette Marechal, Hugh Miller, John Stuart, Ben Field

VENGEANCE (1918)
(6 r.) d, Travers Vale; lp, Montagu Love, Brabara Castleton, Louise Vale, Henry Warwick

VENGEANCE IS MINE! (1916)
(5 r.) d, Robert R. Broadwell; lp, Crane Wilbur, Carl Von Schiller, Brooklyn Keller, William Jackson

VENGEANCE IS MINE (1918)
(5 r.) d, Frank Crane; lp, Irene Castle, Frank Sheridan, Elliott Dexter, Helen Chadwick

VENGEANCE OF DURAND, THE (1919)
(6 r.) d, Tom Terriss; lp, Alice Joyce, Percy Marmont, Gustav von Seyffertitz, William Bechtel

VENGEANCE OF NANA (1915, Brit.)
(4 r.) d, Charles Weston; lp, Elizabeth Grayson

VENGEANCE OF PIERRE, THE (1923)
(5 r.) lp, Lester Cuneo

VENGEANCE OF THE DEAD (1917)
(4 r.) d, Henry King

VENGEANCE OF THE DEEP (1923)
(5 r.) d, A.B. Barringer; lp, Ralph Lewis, Virginia Browne Faire, Van Mattimore, Harmon MacGregor

VENGEANCE OF THE WEST
(SEE: PAY ME, 1917)

VENGEANCE TRAIL, THE (1921)
(5 r.) d, Charles R. Seeling; lp, Guinn "Big Boy" Williams, Maryon Aye, Charles Arling, Bert Apling

VENT DEBOUT (1923, Fr.)
(? r.) d, Rene Leprince

VENUS (1929, Fr.)
(8 r.) d, Louis Mercanton; lp, Constance Talmadge, Andre Roanne, Jean Murat, Max Manudian

VENUS IN THE EAST (1919)
(5 r.) d, Donald Crisp; lp, Bryant Washburn, Anna Q. Nilsson, Margery Wilson, Guy Oliver

VENUS MODEL, THE (1918)
(5 r.) d, Clarence Badger; lp, Mabel Normand, Rod La Rocque, Alec B. Francis, Alfred Hickman

VENUS OF THE SOUTH SEAS (1924)
(5 r.) d, James R. Sullivan; lp, Annette Kellerman

VENUS OF VENICE (1927)
(7 r.) d, Marshall Neilan; lp, Constance Talmadge, Antonio Moreno, Julanne Johnston, Edward Martindel

VENUS VICTRIX (1917, Fr.)
(? r.) d, Germaine Dulac

VERA, THE MEDIUM (1916)
(? r.) d, G.M. [Bronco Billy] Anderson; lp, Kitty Gordon, Frank Goldsmith, Lowell Sherman, J. Harrison

VERDICT, THE (1925)
(7 r.) d, Fred Windemere; lp, Lou Tellegen, Louise Lorraine, William Collier Jr., Gertrude Astor

VERDICT OF THE DESERT, THE (1925)
(5 r.) d, Neal Hart; lp, Neal Hart

VERDICT OF THE HEART, THE (1915, Brit.)
(4 r.) d, Wilfred Noy; lp, Harry Welchman, Barbara Conrad, Frank Royde

VERDUN, VISIONS D'HISTOIRE (1929, Fr.)
(? r.) d, Leon Poirier; lp, Albert Prejean, Jose Davert, Antonion Artaud, Hans Brausewetter

VERMILION PENCIL, THE (1922)
(5 r.) d, Norman Dawn; lp, Sessue Hayakawa, Ann May, Misao Seki, Sidney Franklin

VERS ABECHER LA MYSTERIEUSE (1924, Fr.)
(? r.) d, Henri Desfontaines

VERY CONFIDENTIAL (1927)
(6 r.) d, James Tinling; lp, Madge Bellamy, Patrick Cunning, Mary Duncan, Joseph Cawthorn

VERY GOOD YOUNG MAN, A (1919)
(5 r.) d, Donald Crisp; lp, Bryant Washburn, Helene Chadwick, Julia Faye, Anna Q. Nilsson

VERY IDEA, THE (1920)
(6 r.) d, Lawrence Windom; lp, Taylor Holmes, Virginia Valli, Betty Ross Clarke, Jack Levering

VERY TRULY YOURS (1922)
(5 r.) d, Harry Beaumont; lp, Shirley Mason, Allan Forrest, Charles Clary, Otto Hoffman

VI OF SMITH'S ALLEY (1921, Brit.)
(6 r.) d, Walter West; lp, Violet Hopson, Cameron Carr, George Foley, Sydney Folker

VIA WIRELESS (1915)
(5 r.) d, George Fitzmaurice; lp, Gail Kane, Bruce McRae, Brandon Hurst, Paul McAllister

VIC DYSON PAYS (1925)
(5 r.) d, Jacques Jaccard; lp, Ben Wilson, Archie Ricks, Neva Gerber, Vic Allen

VICAR OF WAKEFIELD, THE (1913, Brit.)
(4 r.) d, John Douglas; lp, Christine Rayner, Alys Collier

VICAR OF WAKEFIELD, THE (1913, Brit.)
(4 r.) d, Frank Wilson; lp, Violet Hopson, Harry Royston, Warwick Buckland, Chrissie White

VICAR OF WAKEFIELD, THE (1916, Brit.)
(6 r.) d, Fred Paul; lp, Sir John Hare, Laura Cowie, Ben Webster, Marie Illington

VICAR OF WAKEFIELD, THE (1917)
(6 r.) d, Ernest Warde; lp, Frederick Warde, Gladys Leslie, Kathryn Adams, Boyd Marshall

VICE AND VIRTUE; OR, THE TEMPTERS OF LONDON (1915, Brit.)
(4 r.) d, Charles Weston; lp, Rowland Moore, Alice Inward

VICE OF FOOLS, THE (1920)
(5 r.) d, Edward H. Griffith; lp, Alice Joyce, Ellen Cassity, Robert Gordon, Raymond Bloomer

VICKY VAN (1919)
(5 r.) d, Robert G. Vignola; lp, Ethel Clayton, Noah Beery, Emory Johnson, Clarence Geldart

VICTIM, THE (1914)
(? r.) lp, Mae Marsh, Robert Harron

VICTIM, THE (1916)
(5 r.) d, Will S. Davis; lp, Valeska Suratt, Herbert Heyes, Claire Whitney, John Charles

VICTIM, THE (1917)
(9 r.) d, Joseph Levering; lp, Robert T. Haines, Joyce Fair, Inez Marcel, Harry Benham

VICTIM, THE (1921)
(6 r.)

VICTOR, THE (1923)
(5 r.) d, Edward Laemmle; lp, Herbert Rawlinson, Dorothy Manners, Frank Currier, Otis Harlan

VICTORIA CROSS, THE (1916)
(5 r.) d, Edward J. Le Saint; lp, Lou Tellegen, Cleo Ridgely, Ernest Joy, Sessue Hayakawa

VICTORY (1913)
(5 r.)

VICTORY (1919)
(8 r.) d, Maurice Tourneur; lp, Jack Holt, Seena Owen, Wallace Beery, Lon Chaney

VICTORY (1928, Brit.)
(9 r.) d, M.A. Wetherell; lp, Moore Marriott, Walter Butler, Julie Suedo, Marie Ault

VICTORY AND PEACE (1918, Brit.)
(8 r.) d, Herbert Brenon; lp, Matheson Lang, Marie Lohr, James Carew, Ellen Terry

VICTORY OF CONSCIENCE, THE (1916)
(5 r.) d, George Melford, Frank Reicher; lp, Lou Tellegen, Cleo Ridgely, Elliott Dexter, Thomas Delmar

VICTORY OF VIRTUE, THE (1915)
(5 r.) d, Harry McRae Webster; lp, Gerda Holmes, Wilmuth Merkyl, Rapley Holmes, J.H. Gilmour

VIGILANTES (1920)
(7 r.)

VIKING, THE (1929)
(9 r.) d, Roy William Neill; lp, Donald Crisp, Pauline Starke, LeRoy Mason, Anders Randolph

VILLA DESTIN (1921, Fr.)
(? r.) d, Marcel L'Herbier

VILLAGE BLACKSMITH, THE (1922)
(8 r.) d, Jack [John] Ford; lp, William Walling, Virginia True Boardman, Virginia Valli, Ida McKenzie

VILLAGE HOMESTEAD, THE (1915)
(4 r.) d, Joseph Byron Totten; lp, Darwin Karr, Betty Brown, Joseph Byron Totten, Howard Lang

VILLAGE IN CRISIS (1920, USSR)
(4 r.) d, Cheslav Sabinsky

VILLAGE SLEUTH, A (1920)
(5 r.) d, Jerome Storm; lp, Charles Ray, Winifred Westover, Dick Rush, Donald MacDonald

VINGT ANS APRES
(SEE: MILADY, 1923, Fr.)

VIOLETTES IMPERIALES (1924, Fr.)
(? r.) d, Henry Roussel; lp, Raquel Meller, Suzanne Bianchetti, Andre Roanne, San-Juana

VIRGIN, THE (1924)
(6 r.) d, Alvin J. Neitz; lp, Kenneth Harlan, Dorothy Revier, Sam De Grasse, Frank Lackteen

VIRGIN LIPS (1928)
(6 r.) d, Elmer Clifton; lp, Olive Borden, John Boles, Marshall Ruth, Alexander Gill

VIRGIN OF SEMINOLE, THE (1923)
(6 r.) lp, William E. Fontaine, Shingzie Howard

VIRGIN OF STAMBOUL, THE (1920)
(7 r.) d, Tod Browning; lp, Priscilla Dean, Wheeler Oakman, Wallace Beery, Eugenie Forde

VIRGIN PARADISE, A (1921)
(8 r.) d, J. Searle Dawley; lp, Pearl White, Robert Elliott, J. Thornton Baston, Alan Edwards

VIRGIN QUEEN, THE (1923, Brit.)
(7 r.) d, J. Stuart Blackton; lp, Lady Diana Manners, Carlyle Blackwell, Walter Tennyson, Hubert Carrer

VIRGIN WIFE, THE (1926)
(? r.)

VIRGINIA COURTSHIP, A (1921)
(5 r.) d, Frank O'Connor; lp, May McAvoy, Alec B. Francis, Jane Keckley, L.M. Wells

VIRGINIAN OUTCAST (1924)
(5 r.) d, Robert J. Horner; lp, Jack Perrin, Marjorie Daw

VIRGIN'S SACRIFICE, A (1922)
(5 r.) d, Webster Campbell; lp, Corinne Griffith, Curtis Cooksey, David Torrence, Louise Cussing

VIRTUE'S REVOLT (1924)
(6 r.) d, James Chapin; lp, Edith Thornton, Crauford Kent, Betty Morrisey, Charles Cruz

VIRTUOUS LIARS (1924)
(6 r.) d, Whitman Bennett; lp, David Powell, Maurice Costello, Edith Allen, Ralph Kellard

VIRTUOUS MEN (1919)
(7 r.) d, Ralph Ince; lp, E.K. [Elmo] Lincoln, Grace Darling, Clara Joel, Robert W. Cummings

VIRTUOUS MODEL, THE (1919)
(6 r.) d, Albert Capellani; lp, Dolores Cassinelli, Vincent Serrano, Franklyn Farnum, Helen Lowell

VIRTUOUS OUTCAST, THE
(SEE: FAITH, 1916)

VIRTOUS SINNERS (1919)
(5 r.) d, Emmett J. Flynn; lp, Norman Kerry, Wanda Hawley, Harry Holden, David Kirby

VIRTUOUS THIEF, THE (1919)
(5 r.) d, Fred Niblo; lp, Enid Bennett, Niles Welch, Lloyd Hughes, Willis Marks

VIRTUOUS VAMP, A (1919)
(5 r.) d, David Kirkland; lp, Constance Talmadge, Conway Tearle, Harda Belle Daube, Jack Kane

VIRTUOUS WIVES (1919)
(6 r.) d, George Loane Tucker; lp, Anita Stewart, Conway Tearle, Hedda Hooper, Edwin Arden

VISAGE D'ENFANTS (1926, Fr.)
(? r.) d, Jacques Feyder; lp, Jean Forest, Pierette Houyez, Victor Vina, Arlette Peyran

VISAGES VIOLES...AMES CLOSES (1921, Fr.)
(6 r.) d, Henry Roussel; lp, Emmy Lynn, Marcel Vibert, Albert Bras, Gustav Bogaert

VITAL QUESTION, THE (1916)
(5 r.) d, S. Rankin Drew; lp, Charles Kent, George Cooper, Virginia Pearson, Anders Randolf

VIVE LA FRANCE (1918)
(5 r.) d, Roy William Neill; lp, Dorothy Dalton, Edmund Lowe, Frederick Starr, Thomas Guise

VIVIETTE (1918)
(5 r.) d, Walter Edwards; lp, Vivian Martin, Eugene Pallette, Harrison Ford, Kate Toncray

VIVRE (1928, Fr.)
(? r.) d, Robert Boudrioz

VIXEN, THE (1916)
(6 r.) d, J. Gordon Edwards; lp, Theda Bara, Herbert Heyes, A.H. Van Buren, Mary Martin

VOICE FROM THE MINARET, THE (1923)
(7 r.) d, Frank Lloyd; lp, Norma Talmadge, Eugene O'Brien, Edwin Stevens, Winter Hall

VOICE OF CONSCIENCE, THE (1917)
(5 r.) d, Edwin Carewe; lp, Francis X. Bushman, Beverly Bayne, Harry S. Northrup, Maggie Breyer

VOICE OF DESTINY, THE (1918)
(5 r.) d, William Bertram; lp, Marie Osborne, Jack Connolly, Morris Foster, Ellen Cassity

VOICE OF LOVE, THE (1916)
(5 r.) d, Rea Berger; lp, Edward Coxen, Winnifred Greenwood, George Field, Harvey Clark

VOICE OF THE STORM, THE (1929)
(7 r.) d, Lynn Shores; lp, Karl Dane, Martha Sleeper, Hugh Allan, Theodore von Eltz

VOICES (1920)
(5 r.) d, Chester De Vonde; lp, Corliss Giles, Diana Allen, Gilbert Rooney, Henry Sedley

VOICES FROM THE PAST (1915)
(4 r.) d, Joseph Smiley; lp, William Cohill, Lilie Leslie, Dorothy DeWolff, Joseph Smiley

VOLCANO, THE (1919)
(6 r.) d, George Irving; lp, Leah Baird, Edward Langford, W.H. Gibson, Jacob Kingsberry

VOLGA AND SIBERIA (1914, USSR)
(5 r.) d, Vasili Goncharov; lp, P. Lopukhin, Pytor Chardynin, P. Knorr

VOLONTE (1917, Fr.)
(? r.) d, Henri Pouctal

VOLUNTEER, THE (1918)
(5 r.) d, Harley Knoles; lp, Madge Evans, Henry Hull, Muriel Ostriche, Victor Kennard

VOLUNTEER ORGANIST, THE (1914)
(8 r.)

VORTEX, THE (1918)
(5 r.) d, Gilbert P. Hamilton; lp, Joseph King, Mary Warren, Wilbur Higby, Eugene Burr

VORTEX OF FATE, THE (1913)
(4 r.)

VOW, THE (1915)
(4 r.) d, S.E.V. Taylor; lp, Marion Leonard

VOW OF VENGEANCE, THE (1923)
(5 r.) d, H.G. Moody; lp, Jack Livingston

VULGAR YACHTSMEN, THE (1926)
(10 r.) d, Marcel Perez

VULTURE OF GOLD, THE (1914)
(4 r.)

VULTURES OF SOCIETY (1916)
(5 r.) d, E.H. Calvert; lp, Lillian Drew, Marguerite Clayton, E.H. Calvert, Ernest Maupain

WAGER, THE (1916)
(5 r.) d, George D. Baker; lp, Emily Stevens, Lester Chambers, Hugh Jeffrey, Daniel Jarrett

WAGES OF CONSCIENCE (1927)
(5 r.) d, John Ince; lp, Herbert Rawlinson, Grace Darmond, John Ince, Henri La Garde

WAGES OF SIN, THE (1918, Brit.)
(5 r.) d, Arrigo Bocchi; lp, Kenelm Foss, Odette Goimbault, Mary Marsh Allen, Hayford Hobbs

WAGES OF SIN, THE (1922)
(7 r.) lp, Jean Gabriel, Arline Pretty, Pearl Shepard

WAGES OF VIRTUE (1924)
(7 r.) d, Allan Dwan; lp, Gloria Swanson, Ben Lyon, Norman Trevor, Ivan Linow

WAGON SHOW, THE (1928)
(7 r.) d, Harry J. Brown; lp, Ken Maynard, Marian Douglas, Maurice Costello, Fred Malatesta

WAGON TRACKS (1919)
(5 r.) d, Lambert Hillyer; lp, William S. Hart, Jane Novak, Robert McKim, Lloyd Bacon

WAIF, THE (1915)
(5 r.) d, William L. Roubert; lp, Matty Roubert, Morgan Philthorpe, Harry Weise, William Heidloff

WAIFS, THE (1916)
(5 r.) d, Scott Sidney; lp, Jane Grey, William Desmond, Robert Kortman, Carol Holloway

WAIFS (1918)
(5 r.) d, Albert Parker; lp, Gladys Hulette, Creighton Hale, J.H. Gilmour, Walter Hiers

WAIT AND SEE (1928, Brit.)
(6 r.) d, Walter Forde; lp, Walter Forde, Frank Stanmore, Pauline Johnson, Sam Livesey

WAITING SOUL, THE (1917)
(5 r.) d, Burton L. King; lp, Olga Petrova, Mahlon Hamilton, Mathilde Brundage, Wyndham Standing

WAKEFIELD CASE, THE (1921)
(6 r.) d, George Irving; lp, Herbert Rawlinson, John P. Wade, J.H. Gilmore, Charles Dalton

WAKING UP THE TOWN (1925)
(6 r.) d, James Cruze; lp, Jack Pickford, Claire McDowell, Alec B. Francis, Norma Shearer

WALK CHEERFULLY (1930, Jap.)
(? r.) d, Yasujiro Ozu

WALK-OFFS, THE (1920)
(6 r.) d, Herbert Blache; lp, May Allison, Emory Johnson, Effie Conley, Darrel Foss

WALL BETWEEN, THE (1916)
(5 r.) d, John W. Noble; lp, Francis X. Bushman, Beverly Bane, John Davidson

WALL STREET MYSTERY, THE (1920)
(5 r.) d, Tom Collins; lp, Glen White, Jane McAlpine, David Wall, Alexander F. Frank

WALL STREET TRAGEDY, A (1916)
(5 r.) d, Lawrence Marston; lp, Nat C. Goodwin, Richard Neill, Mabel Wright, Mary Norton

WALL STREET WHIZ, THE (1925)
(5 r.) d, Jack Nelson; lp, Richard Talmadge, Marceline Day, Lillian Langdon, Carl Miller

WALLFLOWERS (1928)
(7 r.) d, Leo Meehan; lp, Hugh Trevor, Mabel Julienne Scott, Charles Stevenson, Jean Arthur

WALLOPING KID (1926)
(5 r.) d, Robert J. Horner; lp, Kit Carson, Jack Richardson, Dorothy Ward, Frank Whitson

WALLS OF JERICHO, THE (1914)
(5 r.) d, James K. Hackett; lp, Edmund Breese, Claire Whitney, Walter Hitchcock, Stuart Holmes

WALTZ DREAM, A (1926, Ger.)
(8 r.) d, Ludwig Berger

WANDERER, THE (1926)
(9 r.) d, Raoul Walsh; lp, Greta Nissen, William Collier Jr., Ernest Torrence, Wallace Beery

WANDERER BEYOND THE GRAVE (1915, USSR)
(4 r.) d, V. Turzhansky; lp, Olga Baklanova, V. Turzhansky, A. Virubov, A. Michurin

WANDERER OF THE WASTELAND (1924)
(6 r.) d, Irvin Willat; lp, Jack Holt, Noah Beery, George Irving, Kathlyn Williams

WANDERER OF THE WEST (1927)
(5 r.) d, Joseph E. Zivelli, R.E. Williamson; lp, Tex Maynard, Betty Caldwell, Frank Clark, Walter Shumway

WANDERING DAUGHTERS (1923)
(6 r.) d, James Young; lp, Marguerite De La Motte, William V. Mong, Mabel Van Buren, Marjorie Daw

WANDERING FIRES (1925)
(6 r.) d, Maurice Campbell; lp, Constance Bennett, George Hackathorne, Wallace MacDonald, Effie Shannon

WANDERING FOOTSTEPS (1925)
(6 r.) d, Phil Rosen; lp, Alec B. Francis, Estelle Taylor, Bryant Washburn, Eugenie Besserer

WANDERING HUSBANDS (1924)
(7 r.) d, William Beaudine; lp, James Kirkwood, Lila Lee, Margaret Livingston, Eugene Pallette

WANDERING JEW, THE (1913, Ital.)
(5 r.)

WANDERING JEW, THE (1923, Brit.)
(8 r.) d, Maurice Elvey; lp, Matheson Lang, Hutin Britton, Malvina Longfellow, Isobel Elsom

WANDERING STARS (1927, USSR)
(7 r.) d, G. Gricher-Cherikover; lp, M. Leorov, I. Dubravim, R. Rami-Shor, A. Leorov

WANTED - A BROTHER (1918)
(5 r.) d, Robert Ensminger; lp, Gloria Joy, Mignon LeBrun, H.E. Archer, Daniel Gilfether

WANTED - A HOME (1916)
(5 r.) d, Phillips Smalley, Lois Weber; lp, Mary MacLaren, Nanie Wright, Grace Johnson, Marian Sigler

WANTED - A HUSBAND (1919)
(5 r.) d, Lawrence Windom; lp, Billie Burke, James L. Crane, Margaret Linden, Charles Lane

WANTED - A MOTHER (1918)
(5 r.) d, Harley Knoles; lp, Madge Evans, George MacQuarrie, Gerda Holmes, Alec B. Francis

WANTED - A WIDOW (1916, Brit.)
(4 r.) lp, Donald Calthrop, Leslie Henson, Alfred Bishop, A.E. Matthews

WANTED - A WIFE (1918, Brit.)
(5 r.) d, Percy Nash; lp, Isobel Elsom, Owen Nares, C.M. Hallard, Minna Grey

WANTED AT HEADQUARTERS (1920)
(5 r.) d, Stuart Paton; lp, Eva Novak, Agnes Emerson, Leonard C. Shumway, William Marion

WANTED BY THE LAW (1924)
(5 r.) d, Robert N. Bradbury; lp, J.B. Warner, Dorothy Woods

WAR AND PEACE (1915, USSR)
(10 r.) d, Vladimir Gardin, Yakov Protazanov

WAR AND THE WOMAN (1917)
(5 r.) d, Ernest C. Warde; lp, Florence LaBadie, Ernest C. Warde, Tom Brooke, Wayne Arey

WAR BRIDES (1916)
(8 r.) d, Herbert Brenon; lp, Alla Nazimova, Charles Hutchinson, Charles Bryant, William Bailey

WAR BRIDE'S SECRET, THE (1916)
(6 r.) d, Kenean Buel; lp, Virginia Pearson, Glen White, Walter Law, Robert Vivian

WAR EXTRA, THE (1914)
(4 r.)

WAR OF THE TONGS, THE (1917)
(5 r.) lp, Tom Hing, Lee Gow, Hoo Ching, Lin Neong

WARE CASE, THE (1928, Brit.)
(8 r.) d, Manning Haynes; lp, Stewart Rome, Betty Carter, Ian Fleming, Cameron Carr

WARFARE OF THE FLESH, THE (1917)
(5 r.) d, Edward Warren; lp, Sheldon Lewis, Marie Shotwell, Walter Hampden, Charlotte Ives

WARNED OFF (1928, Brit.)
(7 r.) d, Walter West; lp, Tony Wylde, Chili Bouchier, Queenie Thomas, Evan Thomas

WARNING, THE (1915)
(5 r.) d, Edmund Lawrence; lp, Henry Kolker, Lilie Leslie, Frank Longacre, Mayme Kelso

WARNING, THE (1928, Brit.)
(7 r.) d, Reginald Fogwell; lp, Percy Marmont, Fern Andra, Anne Grey, Pearl Hay

WARNING SHADOWS (1924, Ger.)
(? r.) d, Arthur Robison; lp, Fritz Kortner, Ruth Weyher, Gustav Von Wagenheim, Alexander Granach

WARNING SIGNAL, THE (1926)
(5 r.) d, Charles Hunt; lp, Gladys Hulette, Kent Mead, Lincoln Stedman, Clarence Burton

WARRING MILLIONS, THE (1915)
(7 r.)

WARRIOR GAP (1925)
(5 r.) d, Alvin J. Neitz; lp, Ben Wilson, Neva Gerber, Robert Walker, Jim Welch

WARRIOR STRAIN, THE (1919, Brit.)
(4 r.) d, F. Martin Thornton; lp, Sydney Wood, H. Agar Lyons, Evelyn Boucher, James Edwards Barber

WAR'S WOMEN (1916)
(5 r.) lp, Enid Markey

WAR'S WOMEN (1923)
(5 r.) lp, Frank Keenan

WAS HE GUILTY? (1927)
(5 r.) lp, William Boyd

WAS SHE GUILTY? (1922, Brit.)
(5 r.) d, George Andre Beranger; lp, Gertrude McCoy, Zoe Palmer, Lewis Willoughby, William Freshman

WAS SHE JUSTIFIED? (1922, Brit.)
(6 r.) d, Walter West; lp, Florence Turner, Ivy Close, Lewis Gilbert, Arthur Walcott

WAS SHE TO BLAME? (1915)
(5 r.)

WASP, THE (1918)
(5 r.) d, Lionel Belmore; lp, Kitty Gordon, Rockliffe Fellowes, Charles Gerry, Zadee Burbank

WASTED LIVES (1923)
(5 r.) d, Clarence Geldert; lp, Richard Wayne, Catherine Murphy, Winter Hall, Lillian Leighton

WASTED LOVE (1930, Brit.)
(4 r.) d, Richard Eichberg

WASTED YEARS, THE (1916)
(5 r.) lp, Crane Wilbur, Mae Gaston, Joseph Habelton, M.D. Moran

WASTER, THE (1926)
(5 r.)

WATCHING EYES (1921, Brit.)
(6 r.) d, Geoffrey H. Malins; lp, Ena Beaumont, Geoffrey H. Malins, John Wickens

WATER HOLE, THE (1928)
(7 r.) d, F. Richard Jones; lp, Jack Holt, Nancy Carroll, John Boles, Montague Shaw

WATER LILY, THE (1919)
(5 r.) d, George Ridgwell; lp, Alice Mann, Leatrice Joy

WATER, WATER, EVERYWHERE (1920)
(5 r.) d, Clarence G. Badger; lp, Will Rogers, Irene Rich, Roland V. Lee, Wade Boteler

WATERFRONT (1928)
(7 r.) d, William A. Seiter; lp, Dorothy Mackaill, Jack Mulhall, James Bradbury Sr., Knute Erickson

WATERFRONT WOLVES (1924)
(? r.) d, Tom Gibson; lp, Ora Carew, Jay Morley, Hal Stephens, Dick La Reno

WAX MODEL, THE (1917)
(5 r.) d, E. Mason Hooper; lp, Vivian Martin, Thomas Holding, Helen Jerome Eddy, George Fisher

WAXWORKS (1924, Ger.)
(4 r.) d, Paul Leni; lp, Conrad Veidt, Werner Krauss, Wilhelm Dieterle, John Gottowt

WAY BACK, THE (1915)
(4 r.) d, Carlton King; lp, Miriam Nesbitt, Yale Benner, Frank McGlyn, Robert Walker

WAY MEN LOVE, THE
(SEE: BY DIVINE RIGHT, 1924)

WAY OF A GIRL, THE (1925)
(6 r.) d, Robert G. Vignola; lp, Eleanor Boardman, Matt Moore, William Russell, Mathew Betz

WAY OF A MAN, THE (1921, Brit.)
(7 r.) d, C.C. Calvert; lp, Josphine Earle, Philip Anthony, Lewis Dayton, Cecil du Gue

WAY OF A MAN WITH A MAID, THE (1918)
(5 r.) d, Donald Crisp; lp, Bryant Washburn, Wanda Hawley, Fred Goodwins, Clarence Geldart

WAY OF A WOMAN, THE (1925, Brit.)
(6 r.) d, Geoffrey H. Malins; lp, Marjorie Hume, G.H. Mulcaster, Eric Bransby Williams, Genvieve Townsend

WAY OF THE STRONG, THE (1919)
(5 r.) d, Edwin Carewe; lp, Anna Q. Nilsson, Joe King, Harry S. Northrup, Irene Yeager

WAY OF THE TRANSGRESSOR, THE (1923)
(5 r.) d, William J. Craft; lp, George Larkin, Ruth Stonehouse, Frank Whitson, Al Ferguson

WAY OF THE WORLD, THE (1916)
(5 r.) d, L.B. Carleton; lp, Hobart Bosworth, Dorothy Davenport, Emory Johnson, Gretchen Lederer

WAY OF THE WORLD, THE (1920, Brit.)
(5 r.) d, A.E. Coleby; lp, A.E. Coleby, Gordon Coghill, Charles Vane, Bobs Ronald

WAY OUT, THE (1918)
(5 r.) d, George Kelson; lp, Carlyle Blackwell, June Elvidge, Kate Lester, John Bowers

WAY WOMEN LOVE, THE (1920)
(5 r.) d, Marcel Perez; lp, Rubye De Remer, Rose Mints, Walter Miller, Henry Pemberton

WAYS OF THE WORLD, THE (1915, Brit.)
(4 r.) d, L.C. MacBean

WE AMERICANS (1928)
(9 r.) d, Edward Sloman; lp, George Sidney, Patsy Ruth Miller, George Lewis, Eddie Phillips

WE CAN'T HAVE EVERYTHING (1918)
(6 r.) d, Cecil B. DeMille; lp, Kathlyn Williams, Elliott Dexter, Wanda Hawley, Theodore Roberts

WE MODERNS (1925)
(7 r.) d, John Francis Dillon; lp, Colleen Moore, Jack Mulhall, Carl Miller, Claude Gillingwater

WE SHOULD WORRY (1918)
(5 r.) d, Kenean Buel; lp, Jane Lee, Katherine Lee, Rubye De Remer, William Pike

WE WOMEN (1925, Brit.)
(5 r.) d, W.P. Kellino; lp, John Stuart, Reginald Bach, Nina Vanna, Charles Ashton

WEAKER SEX, THE (1917)
(5 r.) d, Raymond B. West; lp, Dorothy Dalton, Charles Ray, Louise Glaum, Robert McKim

WEAKER VESSEL, THE (1919)
(6 r.) d, Paul Powell; lp, Mary MacLaren, Anne Schaefer, John Mackay, Johnnie Cooke

WEAKNESS OF MAN, THE (1916)
(5 r.) d, Barry O'Neill; lp, Holbrook Blinn, Eleanor Woodruff, Richard Wangemann, Charles D. Mackey

WEAKNESS OF STRENGTH, THE (1916)
(5 r.) d, Harry Revier; lp, Edmund Breese, Ormi Hawley, Clifford Bruce, Evelyn Brent

WEARY DEATH, THE
(SEE: DESTINY, 1921, Ger.)

WEAVER OF DREAMS (1918)
(5 r.) d, John H. Collins

WEAVERS OF LIFE (1917)
(6 r.) d, Edward Warren; lp, Helen Hayes, Howard Hall, Earl Schenck, Beatrice Allen

WEB OF CHANCE, THE (1919)
(5 r.) d, Alfred E. Green; lp, Peggy Hyland, Harry Ham, E.B. Tilton, William Machin

WEB OF DECEIT, THE (1920)
(6 r.) d, Edwin Carewe; lp, Dolores Cassinelli, Letty Ford, Hugh Cameron, Franklyn Hanna

WEB OF DESIRE, THE (1917)
(5 r.) d, Emile Chautard; lp, Ethel Clayton, Rockliffe Fellowes, Doris Field, Richard Turner

WEB OF LIFE, THE (1917)
(5 r.) lp, Hilda Nord, James Cruze, George Soule Spencer, Billy Quirk

WEBS OF STEEL (1925)
(5 r.) d, J.P. McGowan; lp, Helen Holmes

WEDDING BELLS (1921)
(6 r.) d, Chet Withey; lp, Constance Talmadge, Harrison Ford, Emily Chichester, Ida Darling

WEDLOCK (1918)
(5 r.) d, Wallace Worsley; lp, Louise Glaum, John Gilbert, Herschal Mayall, Charles Gunn

WEE LADY BETTY (1917)
(5 r.) d, Charles Miller; lp, Bessie Love, Frank Borzage, Charles K. French, Walter Perkins

WEE MACGREGOR'S SWEETHEART, THE (1922, Brit.)
(5 r.) d, Gearge Pearson; lp, Betty Balfour, Donald Macardle, Nora Swinburne, Cyril Percival

WEEK END HUSBANDS (1924)
(7 r.) d, E.H. Griffith; lp, H.J. Herbert, Alma Rubens, Montague Love, Maurice Costello

WEEK-END, THE (1920)
(6 r.) d, George L. Cox; lp, Margarita Fischer, Milton Sills, Bertram Grassby, Mary Lee Wise

WELCOME HOME (1925)
(6 r.) d, James Cruze; lp, Luke Cosgrave, Warner Baxter, Lois Wilson, Ben Hendricks

WELCOME TO OUR CITY (1922)
(5 r.) d, Robert H. Townley; lp, Maclyn Arbuckle, Bessie Emerick, Fred Dalton, Bessie Wharton

WE'RE ALL GAMBLERS (1927)
(7 r.) d, James Cruze; lp, Thomas Meighan, Marietta Millner, Cullen Landis, Philo McCullough

WE'RE IN THE NAVY NOW (1926)
(6 r.) d, Edward Sutherland; lp, Wallace Beery, Raymond Hatton, Chester Conklin, Tom Kennedy

WEST IS EAST
(SEE: WEST VS. EAST, 1922)

WEST IS WEST (1920)
(5 r.) d, Val Paul; lp, Harry Carey, Charles LeMoyne, Joe Harris, Ted Brooks

WEST OF ARIZONA (1925)
(5 r.) d, Tom Gibson; lp, Pete Morrison, Betty Goodwin

WEST OF BROADWAY (1926)
(6 r.) d, Robert Thornby; lp, Priscilla Dean, Arnold Gray, Majel Coleman, Walter Long

WEST OF PARADISE (1928)
(5 r.) lp, Cheyenne Bill

WEST OF THE MOJAVE (1925)
(5 r.) d, Harry L. Fraser; lp, Gordon Clifford

WEST OF THE PECOS (1922)
(5 r.) d, Neal Hart; lp, Neal Hart, William Quinn, Max Wessel, Sarah Bindley

WEST OF THE RIO GRANDE (1921)
(5 r.) d, Robert H. Townley; lp, Harry McLaughlin, Allene Ray, John Hagin, "Tex" O'Reilly

WEST OF THE SACRED GEM, THE (1914)
(4 r.)

WEST OF THE WATER TOWER (1924)
(8 r.) d, Rollin Sturgeon; lp, Glenn Hunter, May McAvoy, Ernest Torrence, George Fawcett

WEST VS. EAST (1922)
(5 r.) d, Marcel Perez; lp, Pete Morrison, Dorothy Wood, Gene Crosby, Renee Danti

WESTBOUND LIMITED, THE (1923)
(7 r.) d, Emory Johnson; lp, Ralph Lewis, Claire McDowell, Ella Hall, Johnny Harron

WESTERN ADVENTURER, A (1921)
(5 r.) lp, William Fairbanks

WESTERN BLOOD (1918)
(5 r.) d, Lynn Reynolds; lp, Tom Mix, Victoria Forde, Frank Clark, Barney Furey

WESTERN BLOOD (1923)
(5 r.) d, Robert Hunter; lp, Pete Morrison

WESTERN ENGAGEMENT, A (1925)
(5 r.) d, Paul Hurst; lp, Dick Hatton

WESTERN FEUDS (1924)
(5 r.) d, Francis Ford; lp, Edmund Cobb, Florence Gilbert, Al McCormick, Kathleen Calhoun

WESTERN GOVERNOR'S HUMANITY, A (1915)
(4 r.) d, Romaine Fielding; lp, Gov. W.P. Hunt, Vinnie Burns, Romaine Fielding, Jack Lawton

WESTERN GRIT (1924)
(5 r.) d, Ad Cook; lp, Lester Cuneo, Alma Deer, Joe Bonner, Raye Hampton

WESTERN HONOR
(SEE: MAN FROM NOWHERE, THE, 1930)

WESTERN JUSTICE (1923)
(5 r.) d, Fred Caldwell; lp, Josephine Hill

WESTERN METHODS (1929)
(5 r.) lp, Fred Church

WESTERN PLUCK (1926)
(5 r.) d, Travers Vale; lp, Art Accord, Marceline Day, Ray Ripley, Robert Rose

WESTERN PROMISE (1925)
(5 r.) lp, Lester Cuneo

WESTERN SPEED (1922)
(5 r.) d, Scott Dunlap; lp, Charles Jones, Eileen Percy, Jack McDonald, J.P. Lockney

WESTERN THOROUGHBRED, A (1922)
(5 r.) lp, Harry McCabe

WESTERN TRAILS (1926)
(5 r.) d, H.B. Carpenter; lp, Bill Patton

WESTERN WALLOP, THE (1924)
(5 r.) d, Clifford Smith; lp, Jack Hoxie, Margaret Landis, James Gordon Russell, Charles Brinley

WESTERN YESTERDAYS (1924)
(5 r.) d, Francis Ford; lp, Florence Gilbert, Edmund Cobb, William White, Ashton Dearholt

WESTERNERS, THE (1919)
(5 r.) d, Edward Sloman; lp, Roy Stewart, Robert McKim, Mildred Manning, Graham Pettie

WESTWARD HO! (1919, Brit.)
(6 r.) d, Percy Nash; lp, Renee Kelly, Charles Quartermaine, Eric Harrison, Booth Conway

WHARF RAT, THE (1916)
(5 r.) d, Chester [Chet] Withey; lp, Mae Marsh, Robert Harron, Spottiswoode Aitken, Lillian Langdon

WHAT A WIFE LEARNED (1923)
(7 r.) d, John Griffith Wray; lp, John Bowers, Milton Sills, Marguerite De La Motte, Evelyn McCoy

WHAT AM I BID? (1919)
(6 r.) d, Robert Z. Leonard; lp, Mae Murray, Ralph Graves, Willard Louis, Chief Dark Cloud

WHAT BECOMES OF THE CHILDREN? (1918)
(6 r.) d, Walter Richard Stahl; lp, Corra Beach, Walter Shumway, Morgan Jones, Billy Sullivan

WHAT DOES A WOMAN NEED MOST (1918)
(6 r.)

WHAT EIGHTY MILLION WOMEN WANT (1913)
(4 r.)

WHAT EVERY WOMAN LEARNS (1919)
(5 r.) d, Fred Niblo; lp, Enid Bennett, Milton Sills, Irving Cummings, William Conklin

WHAT EVERY WOMAN WANTS (1919)
(5 r.) d, Jesse D. Hampton; lp, Grace Darmond, Forrest Stanley, Wilfred Lucas, Hedda Nova

WHAT HAPPENED AT 22 (1916)
(5 r.) d, George Irving; lp, Frances Nelson, Arthur Ashley, Gladden James, Frank Burbeck

WHAT HAPPENED TO FATHER (1915)
(5 r.) d, C. Jay Williams; lp, Frank Daniels, Bernice Berner, Adele Kelly, Anna Laughlin.

WHAT HAPPENED TO JONES (1920)
(5 r.) d, James Cruze; lp, Bryant Washburn, Margaret Loomis, Morris Foster, Frank Jonasson

WHAT HAPPENED TO JONES (1915)
(5 r.) d, Travers Vale; lp, Fred Mace, Josie Sadler, Mary Charleson, William Manderville

WHAT LOVE CAN DO (1916)
(5 r.) d, Jay Hunt; lp, Adele Farrington, C.N. Hammond, Mina Cunard, O.C. Jackson

WHAT LOVE FORGIVES (1919)
(5 r.) d, Perry N. Vekroff; lp, Barbara Castleton, John Hines, John Bowers, Bobby Connelly

WHAT LOVE WILL DO (1921)
(5 r.) d, William K. Howard; lp, Edna Murphy, Johnnie Walker, Glen Cavender, Barbara Tennant

WHAT LOVE WILL DO (1923)
(5 r.) d, Robert North Bradbury; lp, Kenneth McDonald, Marguerite Clayton

WHAT MONEY CAN BUY (1928, Brit.)
(6 r.)

WHAT MONEY CAN'T BUY (1917)
(5 r.) d, Lou Tellegen; lp, Jack Pickford, Louise Huff, Theodore Roberts, Hobart Bosworth

WHAT NEXT? (1928, Brit.)
(8 r.) d, Walter Forde; lp, Walter Forde, Pauline Johnson, Frank Stanmore, Douglas Payne

WHAT PRICE BEAUTY (1928)
(5 r.) d, Thomas Buckingham; lp, Nita Naldi, Pierre Gendron, Virginia Pearson, Dolores Johnson

WHAT PRICE FAME (1928)
(7 r.)

WHAT PRICE LOVE (1927)
(6 r.) d, Harry Revier; lp, Jane Novak, Charles Clary, Mahlon Hamilton, George Nordelli

WHAT PRICE LOVING CUP? (1923, Brit.)
(5 r.) d, Walter West; lp, Violet Hopson, James Knight, James Lindsay, Marjorie Benson

WHAT SHALL I DO? (1924)
(6 r.) d, John G. Adolfi; lp, Dorothy Mackaill, John Harron, Louise Dresser, William V. Mong

WHAT SHALL WE DO WITH HIM? (1919)
(5 r.) d, Harry Revier;

WHAT THE BUTLER SAW (1924, Brit.)
(6 r.) d, George Dewhurst; lp, Irene Rich, Pauline Garon, Guy Newall, Cecil Morton York

WHAT THREE MEN WANTED (1924)
(5 r.) d, Paul Burns; lp, Miss Du Pont [Patricia Hannon], Jack Livingston, Catherine Murphy

WHAT WILL PEOPLE SAY (1915)
(5 r.) d, Alice Blache; lp, Olga Petrova, Fraunie Fraunholz, Fritz de Lint, Charles Dungan

WHAT WOMEN LOVE (1920)
(6 r.) d, Nate C. Watt; lp, Annette Kellerman, Ralph Lewis, Wheeler Oakman, Carl Ullman

WHAT WOMEN WANT (1920)
(5 r.) d, George Archainbaud; lp, Louise Huff, Van Dyke Brooke, Howard Truesdale, Betty Browne

WHAT WOULD A GENTLEMAN DO? (1918, Brit.)
(5 r.) d, Wilfred Noy; lp, Stanley Logan, Queenie Thomas, A.B. Imeson, Dora de Winton

WHAT WOULD YOU DO? (1920)
(5 r.) d, Edmund Lawrence, Dennison Clift; lp, Madlaine Travers, George McDaniel, Frank Elliott, Charles K. French

WHATEVER THE COST (1918)
(5 r.) d, Robert Ensminger; lp, Anita King, Stanley Pembroke, Bruce Smith, Charles Dudley

WHAT'S BRED...COMES OUT IN THE FLESH (1916, Brit.)
(4 r.) d, Sidney Morgan; lp, Janet Alexander, Lauderdale Maitland, Frank Tennant, Richard Norton

WHAT'S HIS NAME? (1914)
(5 r.) d, Cecil B. DeMille; lp, Max Figman, Lolita Robertson, Sydney Deane, Fred Montague

WHAT'S WORTHWHILE? (1921)
(6 r.) d, Lois Weber; lp, Claire Windsor, Arthur Stuart Hull, Mona Lisa, Louis Calhern

WHAT'S WRONG WITH THE WOMEN? (1922)
(7 r.) d, Roy William Neill; lp, Wilton Lackaye, Montagu Love, Rod La Rocque, Huntley Gordon

WHAT'S YOUR HUSBAND DOING? (1919)
(5 r.) d, Lloyd Ingraham; lp, Douglas MacLean, Doris May, Walter Hiers, William Buckley

WHAT'S YOUR REPUTATION WORTH? (1921)
(6 r.) d, Webster Campbell; lp, Corinne Griffith, Percy Marmont, Leslie Roycroft, George Howard

WHEATS AND TARES (1915)
(5 r.)

WHEEL, THE (1925)
(8 r.) d, Victor Schertzinger; lp, Margaret Livingston, Harrison Ford, Claire Adams, Mahlon Hamilton

WHEEL OF CHANCE (1928)
(7 r.) d, Alfred Santell; lp, Richard Barthelmess, Bodil Rosing, Warner Oland, Ann Schaeffer

WHEEL OF DEATH, THE (1916, Brit.)
(4 r.) d, A.E. Coleby; lp, Arthur Rooke, Joan Legge, Frank Rosbert Cheroka, Charles Vane

WHEEL OF THE LAW, THE (1916)
(5 r.) d, George D. Baker; lp, Emily Stevens, Frank Mills, Raymond McKee, Edwin Holt

WHEELS OF CHANCE, THE (1922, Brit.)
(5 r.) d, Harold M. Shaw; lp, George K. Arthur, Olwen Roose, Gordon Parker, Bertie Wright

WHEN A DOG LOVES (1927)
(5 r.) d, J.P. McGowan; lp, Harold Goodwin, Helen Foster, Mickey McBan, Ranger (a dog)

WHEN A GIRL LOVES (1919)
(6 r.) d, Lois Weber, Phillips Smalley; lp, Mildred Harris, William Stowell, Wharton Jones, Alfred Paget

WHEN A GIRL LOVES (1924)
(6 r.) d, Victor Hugo Halperin; lp, Agnes Ayres, Percy Marmont, Robert McKim, Kathlyn Williams

WHEN A MAN LOVES (1920)
(5 r.) d, Chester Bennett; lp, Earle Williams, Margaret Loomis, Thomas Guise, Barbara Tennant

WHEN A MAN LOVES (1927)
(10 r.) d, Alan Crosland; lp, John Barrymore, Dolores Costello, Warner Oland, Sam De Grasse

WHEN A MAN RIDES ALONE (1919)
(5 r.) d, Henry King; lp, William Russell, Lule Warrenton, Carl Stockdale, Olga Grey

WHEN A MAN SEES RED (1917)
(6 r.) d, Frank Lloyd; lp, William Farnum, Jewel Carmen, Lulu May Bower, Marc Robbins

WHEN A MAN'S A MAN (1924)
(7 r.) d, Edward F. Cline; lp, John Bowers, Marguerite De La Motte, Robert Frazer, June Marlowe

WHEN A WOMAN LOVES (1915)
(5 r.)

WHEN A WOMAN STRIKES (1919)
(5 r.) d, Roy Clements; lp, Rosemary Theby, Ben Wilson, Neva Gerber, Murdock MacQuarrie

WHEN ARIZONA WON (1919)
(5 r.) lp, Shorty Hamilton, Virginia Harris

WHEN BABY FORGOT (1917)
(5 r.) d, W. Eugene Moore; lp, Marie Osborne, Fred Newburg, Margaret Nichols, Lee Hill

WHEN BEARCAT WENT DRY (1919)
(6 r.) d, Oliver L. Sellers; lp, Vangie Valentine, Lon Chaney, Walt Whitman, Bernard Durning

WHEN DANGER CALLS (1927)
(5 r.) d, Charles Hutchison; lp, William Fairbanks, Eileen Sedgwick, Ethan Laidlaw, Sally Long

WHEN DANGER SMILES (1922)
(5 r.) d, William Duncan; lp, William Duncan, Edith Johnson, James Farley, Henry Herbert

WHEN DAWN CAME (1920)
(7 r.) d, Colin Campbell; lp, Lee C. Shumway, Colleen Moore, James O. Barrows, Kathleen Kirkham

WHEN DESTINY WILLS (1921)
(? r.) d, R.C. Baker; lp, Grace Davidson

WHEN DOCTORS DISAGREE (1919)
(5 r.) d, Victor L. Schertzinger; lp, Mabel Normand, Walter Hiers, George Nichols, Fritzi Ridgeway

WHEN DREAMS COME TRUE (1929)
(6 r.) d, Duke Worne; lp, Helene Costello, Rex Lease, Claire McDowell, Danny Hoy

WHEN EAST MEETS WEST (1915, Brit.)
(4 r.) d, Wilfred Noy; lp, Dorothy Bellew

WHEN FALSE TONGUES SPEAK (1917)
(5 r.) d, Carl Harbaugh; lp, Virginia Pearson, Carl Harbaugh, Hardee Kirkland, Claire Whitney

WHEN FATE DECIDES (1919)
(5 r.) d, Harry Millarde; lp, Madlaine Traverse, William Conklin, Clyde Fillmore, Claire DuBrey

WHEN FATE LEADS TRUMP (1914)
(5 r.) d, Harry Handworth; lp, Octavia Handworth, Gordon De Maine, William A. Williams, Tom Tempest

WHEN HUSBANDS DECEIVE (1922)
(6 r.) d, Wallace Worsley; lp, Leah Baird, William Conklin, Jack Mower, Eulalie Jensen

WHEN HUSBANDS FLIRT (1925)
(6 r.) d, William A. Wellman; lp, Dorothy Revier, Forrest Stanley, Tom Ricketts, Ethel Wales

WHEN IT STRIKES HOME (1915)
(5 r.) d, Perry N. Vekroff; lp, Grace Washburn, Edwin August, Muriel Ostriche, William Bailey

WHEN IT WAS DARK (1919, Brit.)
(7 r.) d, Arrigo Bocchi; lp, Manora Thew, Hayford Hobbs, George Butler, Charles Vane

WHEN KNIGHTS WERE BOLD (1916, Brit.)
(5 r.) d, Maurice Elvey; lp, James Welch, Janet Ross, Gerald Ames, Hayford Hobbs

WHEN KNIGHTS WERE BOLD (1929, Brit.)
(7 r.) d, Tim Whelan; lp, Nelson Keys, Miriam Seegar, Eric Bransby Williams, Wellington Briggs

WHEN LAW COMES TO HADES (1923)
(5 r.) lp, Noah Beery, Eileen Sedgwick, Edward W. Borman

WHEN LONDON BURNED (1915, Brit.)
(4 r.) d, Wilifred Noy; lp, Lionelle Howard, R. Juden, P.G. Ebbutt, J. Cooper

WHEN LONDON SLEEPS (1914, Brit.)
(4 r.) d, Ernest G. Batley; lp, Lillian Wiggins, Douglas Mars, George Foley

WHEN LOVE CAME TO GAVIN BURKE (1918)
(4 r.) d, Fred O'Donovan; lp, Brian Magowan, Kathleen Murphy

WHEN LOVE COMES (1922)
(6 r.) d, William A. Seiter; lp, Helen Jerome Eddy, Harrison Ford, Fannie Midgley, Claire Du Brey

WHEN LOVE GROWS COLD (1925)
(7 r.) d, Harry O. Hoyt; lp, Natacha Rambova, Clive Brook, Sam Hardy, Kathryn Hill

WHEN LOVE IS KING (1916)
(5 r.) d, Ben Turbett; lp, Richard Tucker, Carrol McComas, Bigelow Cooper, Vivian Perry

WHEN LOVE IS YOUNG (1922)
(5 r.) lp, Russell Simpson, Zena Keefe

WHEN LOVE WAS BLIND (1917)
(5 r.) d, Frederick Sullivan; lp, Florence LaBadie, Thomas Curran, Inda Palmer, Boyd Marshall

WHEN MEN ARE TEMPTED (1918)
(5 r.) d, William Wolbert; lp, Mary Anderson, Alfred Whitman, R. Bradbury, Otto Lederer

WHEN MEN DESIRE (1919)
(5 r.) d, J. Gordon Edwards; lp, Theda Bara, Fleming Ward, G. Raymond Nye, Florence Martin

WHEN MY SHIP COMES IN (1919)
(5 r.) d, Robert Thornby; lp, Jane Grey, William J. Kelly, Nigel Barrie, Frank Andrews

WHEN PARIS SLEEPS (1917, Brit.)
(5 r.) d, A.V. Bramble; lp, A.V. Bramble, Ivy Martinek, Pauline Peters, Ernie Collins

WHEN QUACKEL DID HYDE (1920)
(4 r.) d, Charles Gramlich; lp, Charlie Joy, Edgar Jones

WHEN ROMANCE RIDES (1922)
(5 r.) d, Eliot Howe; lp, Claire Adams, Carl Gantvoort, Jean Hersholt, Harry Van Meter

WHEN THE CLOCK STRUCK NINE (1921)
(? r.)

WHEN THE DESERT CALLS (1922)
(6 r.) d, Ray C. Smallwood; lp, Violet Heming, Robert Frazer, Sheldon Lewis, Huntley Gordon

WHEN THE DESERT SMILES (1919)
(5 r.) d, Neal Hart; lp, Neal Hart, Fred Kelsey, Awretha Pickering, Vester Pegg

WHEN THE DOOR OPENED (1925)
(7 r.) d, Reginald Barker; lp, Jacqueline Logan, Walter McGrail, Margaret Livingston, Robert Cain

WHEN THE LAD CAME HOME (1922)
(5 r.) lp, Harry Myers, Ali Raby

WHEN THE LAW RIDES (1928)
(5 r.) d, Robert De Lacy; lp, Tom Tyler, Jane Reid, Frankie Darro, Harry O'Connor

WHEN THE STRINGS OF THE HEART SOUND (1914, USSR)
(4 r.) d, Boris Sushkevich; lp, Yevgeni Vakhtangov, Mikhail Chekhov, Olga Baklanova, Boris Sushkevich

WHEN WE WERE TWENTY-ONE (1915)
(5 r.) d, Edwin S. Porter, Hugh Ford; lp, William Elliott, Charles Waldron, Marie Empress, Helen Lutrell

WHEN WE WERE TWENTY-ONE (1921)
(? r.) d, Henry King; lp, H.B. Warner, Claire Anderson, James Morrison, Christine Mayo

WHEN WILL WE DEAD AWAKEN? (1918, USSR)
(6 r.) d, Yakov Poselsky; lp, Mikhail Doronin, S. Volkhovskaya, L. Zhukov

WHEN WINTER WENT (1925)
(5 r.) d, Reginald Morris; lp, Raymond Griffith, Charlotte Merriam

WHEN WOMAN HATES (1916, Brit.)
(6 r.) d, Albert Ward; lp, Henry Lonsdale, Mercy Hatton, Jose Brooks

WHEN YOU AND I WERE YOUNG (1918)
(5 r.) d, Alice Blache; lp, Alma Hanlon, Harry Benham, Florence Short, Robert Mantell Jr.

WHERE AMBITION LEADS (1919, Brit.)
(5 r.) d, Billy Asher; lp, Donalda Campbell, Gerald Ivas, Ernie Collins, Sha Lebosi

WHERE ARE MY CHILDREN? (1916)
(5 r.) d, Lois Weber, Phillips Smalley; lp, [Frederick] Tyrone Power, Helen Riaume, Marie Walcamp

WHERE ARE THE DREAMS OF YOUTH? (1932, Jap.)
(? r.) d, Yasujiro Ozu

WHERE BONDS ARE LOOSED (1919)
(6 r.) d, David G. Fischer; lp, Dixie Lee, Arthur Behrens, David G. Fischer

WHERE D'YE GET THAT STUFF? (1916)
(5 r.) lp, Edna Aug

WHERE IS MY FATHER? (1916)
(7 r.) d, Joseph Adelman; lp, May Ward, William Sorrelle, Ed F. Roseman, George Henry

WHERE IS MY WANDERING BOY TONIGHT? (1922)
(7 r.) d, James P. Hogan, Millard Webb; lp, Cullen Landis, Carl Stockdale, Virginia True Boardman, Patsy Ruth Miller

WHERE IS THIS WEST? (1923)
(5 r.) d, George E. Marshall; lp, Jack Hoxie, Mary Philbin, Bob McKenzie, Sid Jordan

WHERE LOVE IS (1917)
(5 r.) lp, Ann Murdock, Henry Stanford, Shirley Mason, Bigelow Cooper

WHERE LOVE LEADS (1916)
(5 r.) d, Frank C. Griffin; lp, Ormi Hawley, Rockliffe Fellowes

WHERE ROMANCE RIDES (1925)
(5 r.) d, Ward Hayes; lp, Dick Hatton, Marilyn Mills, Roy Laidlaw, Jack Richardson

WHERE THE NORTH BEGINS (1923)
(6 r.) d, Chester M. Franklin; lp, Claire Adams, Walter McGrail, Pat Hartigan, Myrtle Owen

WHERE THE NORTH HOLDS SWAY (1927)
(5 r.) d, Bennett Cohn; lp, Jack Perrin, Starlight (a horse)

WHERE THE PAVEMENT ENDS (1923)
(8 r.) d, Rex Ingram; lp, Edward Connelly, Alice Terry, Ramon Novarro, Harry T. Morey

WHERE THE RAINBOW ENDS (1921, Brit.)
(5 r.) d, H. Lisle Lucoque; lp, Babs Farren, B. Cave Chinn, Muriel Pointer, Eric Gray

WHERE THE WEST BEGINS (1919)
(5 r.) d, Henry King; lp, William Russell, Eileen Percy, J. Cullen Landis, Frederick Vroom

WHERE THE WEST BEGINS (1928)
(5 r.) d, Robert J. Horner; lp, Pawnee Bill Jr., Boris Bullock, Bud Osborne

WHERE THE WORST BEGINS (1925)
(6 r.) d, John McDermott; lp, Ruth Roland, Alec B. Francis, Matt Moore, Grace Darmond

WHERE TRAILS BEGIN (1927)
(6 r.) d, Noel Mason Smith; lp, Johnnie Walker, Charlotte Stevens, Albert J. Smith, Hughie Mack

WHERE WAS I? (1925)
(7 r.) d, William A. Seiter; lp, Reginald Denny, Marion Nixon, Pauline Garon, Lee Moran

WHICH SHALL IT BE? (1924)
(5 r.) d, Renaud Hoffman; lp, Willis Marks, Ethel Wales, David Torrence, Paul Weigel

WHICH WOMAN? (1918)
(5 r.) d, Tod Browning; lp, Ella Hall, Priscilla Dean, Eddie Sutherland, Edward Jobson

WHILE FIRE RAGED (1914)
(5 r.)

WHILE JUSTICE WAITS (1922)
(5 r.) d, Bernard J. Durning; lp, Dustin Farnum, Irene Rich, Earl Metcalf, Junior Delameter

WHILE LONDON SLEEPS (1922, Brit.)
(5'r.) d, Graham Cutts; lp, Hilda Bayley, Flora le Breton, Ward McAllister, Cyril Raymond

WHILE LONDON SLEEPS (1926)
(6 r.) d, H.P. Bretherton; lp, Rin-Tin-Tin, Helene Costello, Walter Merrill, John Patrick

WHILE PARIS SLEEPS (1923)
(6 r.) d, Maurice Tourneur; lp, Lon Chaney, Mildred Manning, Jack Gilbert, Hardee Kirkland

WHILE THE DEVIL LAUGHS (1921)
(5 r.) d, George W. Hill; lp, Louise Lovely, William Scott, G. Raymond Nye, Edwin Booth Tilton

WHIMS OF SOCIETY, THE (1918)
(5 r.) d, Travers Vale; lp, Ethel Clayton, Frank Mayo, Frank Beamish, Jack Drumier

WHIP, THE (1917)
(8 r.) d, Maurice Tourneur; lp, Irving Cummings, Alma Hanlon, Paul McAllister, June Elvidge

WHIP, THE (1928)
(7 r.) d, Charles J. Brabin; lp, Dorothy Mackaill, Ralph Forbes, Anna Q. Nilsson, Lowell Sherman

WHIPPING BOSS, THE (1924)
(6 r.) d, J.P. McGowan; lp, Wade Boteler, Eddie Phillips, J.P. McGowan, Lloyd Hughes

WHIRL OF LIFE, THE (1915)
(6 r.) d, Oliver D. Bailey; lp, Vernon Castle, Irene Castle, Ruth Gordon

WHIRLPOOL, THE (1918)
(5 r.) d, Alan Crosland; lp, Alice Brady, Holmes E. Herbert, J.H. Gilmour, William Davidson

WHIRLPOOL OF DESTINY, THE (1916)
(5 r.) d, Otis Turner; lp, Flora Parker De Haven, Jack Mulhall, Bertram Grassby, Nanine Wright

WHIRLPOOL OF YOUTH, THE (1927)
(6 r.) d, Rowland V. Lee; lp, Lois Moran, Vera Voronina, Donald Keith, Alyce Mills

WHIRLWIND RANGER, THE (1924)
(5 r.) d, Richard Hatton; lp, Richard Hatton, Neva Gerber

WHISPER MARKET, THE (1920)
(5 r.) d, George L. Sargent; lp, Corinne Griffith, George MacQuarrie, Eulalie Jensen, Jacob Kingsbury

WHISPERED NAME, THE (1924)
(5 r.) d, King Baggot; lp, Ruth Clifford, Charles Clary, William E. Lawrence, May Mersch

WHISPERING CANYON (1926)
(6 r.) d, Tom Forman; lp, Jane Novak, Robert Ellis, Lee Shumway, Josef Swickard

WHISPERING CHORUS, THE (1918)
(6 r.) d, Cecil B. DeMille; lp, Kathlyn Williams, Raymond Hatton, Elliott Dexter, Edythe Chapman

WHISPERING DEVILS (1920)
(6 r.) d, Harry Garson; lp, Conway Tearle, Rosemary Theby, Sam Southern, Esther Ralston

WHISPERING PALMS (1923)
(5 r.) lp, Val Cleary, Gladys Hulette

WHISPERING SAGE (1927)
(5 r.) d, Scott R. Dunlap; lp, Buck Jones, Natalie Joyce, Emile Chautard, Carl Miller

WHISPERING SHADOWS (1922)
(6 r.) d, Emil Chautard; lp, Lucy Cotton, Charles A. Stevenson, Philip Merivale, Robert Barrat

WHISPERING SMITH (1916)
(5 r.) d, J.P. McGowan; lp, Helen Holmes, J.P. McGowan, Belle Hutchinson, Paul C. Hurst

WHISPERING WIRES (1926)
(6 r.) d, Albert Ray; lp, Anita Stewart, Edmund Burns, Charles Clary, Otto Matieson

WHISPERING WOMEN (1921)
(5 r.) d, James Keane; lp, Walter Davis, Esther Welty, Clara Heller, Everett Moran

WHISTLE, THE (1921)
(6 r.) d, Lambert Hillyer; lp, William S. Hart, Frank Brownlee, Myrtle Stedman, Georgie Stone

WHISTLING JIM (1925)
(5 r.) d, Wilbur McGaugh; lp, Guinn "Big Boy" Williams, Peggy O'Day, Dan Peterson

WHITE CARGO (1929, Brit.)
(8 r.) d, J.B. Williams, Arthur Barnes; lp, Leslie Faber, Gypsy Rhouma, John Hamilton, Maurice Evans

WHITE CAT, THE
(SEE: UNTAMEABLE, THE, 1923)

WHITE CIRCLE, THE (1920)
(5 r.) d, Maurice Tourneur; lp, Spottiswoode Aitken, Janis Wilson, Harry S. Northrup, Jack Gilbert

WHITE DESERT, THE (1925)
(7 r.) d, Reginald Barker; lp, Claire Windsor, Pat O'Malley, Robert Frazer, Frank Currier

WHITE DOVE, THE (1920)
(5 r.) d, Henry King; lp, H.B. Warner, James O. Barrows, Claire Adams, Herbert Greenwood

WHITE EAGLE, THE (1928, USSR)
(6 r.) d, Yakov Protazanov; lp, Vasili Kachalov, Vsevolod Meyerhold, Anna Sten, Ivan Chuyelyov

WHITE FANG (1925)
(6 r.) d, Lawrence Trimble; lp, Theodore von Eltz, Ruth Dwyer, Matthew Betz, Walter Perry

WHITE FLAME (1928)
(6 r.) lp, Mahlon Hamilton, William V. Mong, Eileen Sedgwick

WHITE HEAT (1926, Brit.)
(7 r.) d, Thomas Bentley; lp, Juliette Compton, Wyndham Standing, Vesta Sylva, Walter Butler

WHITE HEATHER, THE (1919)
(6 r.) d, Maurice Tourneur; lp, Ralph Graves, Mabel Ballin, Holmes E. Herbert, Ben Alexander

WHITE HELL (1922)
(5 r.) d, Bernard Feikel; lp, Richard Travers, Muriel Kingston, J. Thornton Baston, Ruth La Marr

WHITE HEN, THE (1921, Brit.)
(5 r.) d, Frank Richardson; lp, Mary Glynne, Leslie Faber, Pat Somerset, Cecil Humphreys

WHITE HOPE, THE (1915, Brit.)
(4 r.) d, Frank Wilson; lp, Stewart Rome, Violet Hopson, Lionelle Howard, John MacAndrews

WHITE HOPE, THE (1922, Brit.)
(6 r.) d, Frank Wilson; lp, Violet Hopson, Stewart Rome, Frank Wilson, John McAndrews

WHITE LIES (1920)
(5 r.) d, Edward J. Le Saint; lp, Gladys Brockwell, William Scott, Josephine Crowell, Evans Kirk

WHITE MAN (1924)
(7 r.) d, Louis Gasnier; lp, Kenneth Harlan, Alice Joyce, Walter Long, Clark Gable

WHITE MAN'S LAW, THE (1918)
(5 r.) d, James Young; lp, Sessue Hayakawa, Florence Vidor, Jack Holt, Herbert Standing

WHITE MASKS, THE (1921)
(5 r.) d, George Holt; lp, Franklyn Farnum, Al Hart, Virginia Lee, Shorty Hamilton

WHITE MICE (1926)
(6 r.) d, Edward H. Griffith; lp, Jacqueline Logan, William Powell, Ernest Hilliard, Bigelow Cooper

WHITE MOLL, THE (1920)
(7 r.) d, Harry Millarde; lp, Pearl White, Richard C. Travers, Jack Thornton Baston, Walter Lewis

WHITE MONKEY, THE (1925)
(7 r.) d, Phil Rosen; lp, Barbara La Marr, Thomas Holding, Henry Victor, George F. Marion

WHITE MOTH, THE (1924)
(7 r.) d, Maurice Tourneur; lp, Barbara La Marr, Conway Tearle, Charles De Roche, Ben Lyon

WHITE OUTLAW, THE (1929)
(5 r.) d, Robert J. Horner; lp, Art Acord, Lew Meehan, Walter Maly, Howard Davies

WHITE PANTHER, THE (1924)
(5 r.) d, Alvin J. Neitz; lp, Gertrude McConnell, Phil Burke, Lois Scott, Frank Whitson

WHITE PEBBLES (1927)
(5 r.) d, Richard Thorpe; lp, Wally Wales, Olive Hasbrouck, Walter Maly, Tom Bay

WHITE RAVEN, THE (1917)
(6 r.) d, George D. Baker

WHITE RIDER, THE (1920)
(5 r.) d, William J. Craft; lp, Joe Moore, Eileen Sedgwick, S.W. Williams, Robert Craft

WHITE ROSETTE, THE (1916)
(5 r.) d, Donald MacDonald; lp, E. Forrest Taylor, Helene Rosson, Eugenia Forde, Harry Von Meter

WHITE SCAR, THE (1915)
(5 r.) d, Hobart Bosworth; lp, Hobart Bosworth, Anna Lehr, Jane Novak, Frank Newburg

WHITE SHADOW, THE
(SEE: WHITE SHADOWS, 1924, Brit.)

WHITE SHADOWS (1924, Brit.)
(5 r.) d, Graham Cutts; lp, Betty Compson, Clive Brook, Henry Victor, A.B. Imeson

WHITE SHEEP, THE (1924)
(6 r.) d, Hal Roach; lp, Glenn Tryon, Blanche Mehaffey, Jack Gavin, Robert Kortman

WHITE SHEIK, THE (1928, Brit.)
(9 r.) d, Harley Knoles; lp, Lilian Hall Davis, Jameson Thomas, Warwick Ward, Clifford McLaglen

WHITE SHOULDERS (1922)
(6 r.) d, Tom Forman; lp, Katherine MacDonald, Lillian Lawrence, Tom Forman, Bryant Washburn

WHITE SIN, THE (1924)
(6 r.) d, William Seiter; lp, Madge Bellamy, John Bowers, Francelia Billington, Hal Cooley

WHITE SISTER, THE (1915)
(6 r.) d, Fred E. Wright; lp, Viola Allen, Richard C. Travers, Camille D'Arcy, Thomas Commerford

WHITE SLAVE, THE (1929)
(6 r.) lp, Charles Vanel, Lucille Barns

WHITE SLIPPERS
(SEE: PORT OF LOST SOULS, THE, 1924, BRIT.)

WHITE STAR, THE (1915, Brit.)
(5 r.) d, Bertram Phillips; lp, Queenie Thomas, Norman Howard, Rowland Moore, Arthur Walcott

WHITE TERROR, THE (1915)
(4 r.) d, Stuart Paton; lp, Hobart Henley, Frances Nelson, Allen Holubar, William Welsh

WHITE THUNDER (1925)
(5 r.) d, Ben Wilson; lp, Yakima Canutt, William H. Turner, Lew Meehan, George Lessey

WHITE TIGER (1923)
(7 r.) d, Tod Browning; lp, Priscilla Dean, Matt Moore, Raymond Griffith, Wallace Beery

WHITHER THOU GOEST (1917)
(5 r.) d, Raymond B. West; lp, Orin Johnson, Rhea Mitchell, Tom Chatterton, Ida Lewis

WHO AM I? (1921)
(5 r.) d, Henry Kolker; lp, Claire Anderson, Gertrude Astor, Niles Welch, George Periolat

WHO ARE MY PARENTS? (1922)
(9 r.) d, J. Searle Dawley; lp, Roger Lytton, Peggy Shaw, Florence Bilings, Ernest Hilliard

WHO CARES? (1919)
(5 r.) d, Walter Edwards; lp, Constance Talmadge, Harrison Ford, Spottiswoode Aitken, California Truman

WHO CARES (1925)
(6 r.) d, David Kirkland; lp, Dorothy Devore, William Haines, Lloyd Whitlock, Beverly Bayne

WHO GOES THERE? (1917)
(5 r.) d, William P.S. Earle; lp, Harry Morey, Corinne Griffith, Arthur Donaldson, Mary Maurice

WHO IS THE MAN? (1924, Brit.)
(6 r.) d, Walter Summers; lp, Isobel Elsom, Langhorne Burton, Lewis Dayton, John Gielgud

WHO IS TO BLAME? (1918)
(5 r.) d, Frank Borzage; lp, Jack Livingston, Maud Wayne, Jack Abbe, Lillian West

WHO KILLED JOE MERRION? (1915)
(4 r.) d, Tefft Johnson; lp, Joseph Kilgour, S. Rankin Drew, Rose Tapley, J. Herbert Frank

WHO KILLED WALTON? (1918)
(5 r.) d, Thomas N. Heffron; lp, J. Barney Sherry, Mary Mersch, Edwin Brady, Dora Rodgers

WHO KNOWS? (1918)
(6 r.)

WHO LOVED HIM BEST? (1918)
(5 r.) d, Dell Henderson; lp, Edna Goodrich, Herbert Evans, Frank Otto, Charles Martin

WHO SHALL TAKE MY LIFE? (1918)
(7 r.) d, Colin Campbell; lp, Thomas Santschi, Fritzi Brunette, Bessie Eyton, Ed Coxen

WHO VIOLATES THE LAW (1915)
(4 r.)

WHO WAS THE OTHER MAN? (1917)
(5 r.) d, Francis Ford; lp, Francis Ford, Mae Gaston, Beatrice Van, Duke Worne

WHO WILL MARRY ME? (1919)
(5 r.) d, Paul Powell; lp, Carmel Myers, Thurston Hall, William Dyer, Betty Schade

WHOLE DAMN WAR, THE
(SEE: WHOLE DARN WAR, THE, 1928)

WHOLE DARN WAR, THE (1928)
(5 r.)

WHOLE TOWN'S TALKING, THE (1926)
(7 r.) d, Edward Laemmle; lp, Edward Everett Horton, Virginia Lee Corbin, Trixie Friganza, Otis Harlan

WHOM GOD HATH JOINED (1919, Fr.)
(4 r.)

WHOM SHALL I MARRY (1926)
(6 r.) lp, Wanda Hawley, Elmo Lincoln, Mary Carr

WHOM THE GODS DESTROY (1916)
(5 r.) d, William P.S. Earle, J. Stuart Blackton; lp, Alice Joyce, Harry T. Morey, Marc MacDermott, Charles Kent

WHOM THE GODS WOULD DESTROY (1915)
(4 r.) d, Joseph W. Smiley

WHOM THE GODS WOULD DESTROY (1919)
(7 r.) d, Frank Borzage; lp, Jack Muhall, Pauline Starke, Kathryn Adams, Harvey Clark

WHO'S CHEATING? (1924)
(5 r.) d, Joseph Levering; lp, Dorothy Chappell, Ralph Kellard, Zena Keefe, Montagu Love

WHO'S WHO IN SOCIETY (1915)
(4 r.) lp, Kate Sargeantson, William H. Power, Dan Moyles, Della Connor

WHO'S YOUR BROTHER? (1919)
(5 r.) d, John G. Adolfi; lp, Edith Taliaferro, Frank Burbeck, E. Coit Albertson, Paul Panzer

WHO'S YOUR FRIEND (1925)
(5 r.) d, Forrest K. Sheldon; lp, Francis X. Bushman, Jimmy Aubrey, Patricia Palmer, Hal Thompson

WHO'S YOUR NEIGHBOR? (1917)
(6 r.) d, S. Rankin Drew; lp, Evelyn Brent, Christine Mayo, Frank Morgan, Anders Randolf

WHO'S YOUR SERVANT? (1920)
(5 r.) lp, Lois Wilson, Yukio Aoyama, Andrew Robson, Albert Morrison

WHOSE WIFE? (1917)
(5 r.) d, Rollin S. Sturgeon; lp, Gail Kane, Elizabeth Taylor, Edward Peil, Harry von Meter

WHOSO DIGGETH A PIT (1915, Brit.)
(4 r.) d, Ralph Dewsbury; lp, Gerald Ames, Charles Rock, Gwynne Herbert, Mary Dibley

WHOSO FINDETH A WIFE
(SEE: WHOSO TAKETH A WIFE, 1916)

WHOSO IS WITHOUT SIN (1916, Brit.)
(5 r.) d, Fred Paul; lp, Hilda Moore, Milton Rosmer, Flora Morris, Ronald Squire

WHOSO TAKETH A WIFE (1916)
(5 r.) d, Frank H. Crane; lp, Jean Sothern, Leo Delaney, George Henry Trader, Ida Brooks

WHOSOEVER SHALL OFFEND (1919, Brit.)
(6 r.) d, Arrigo Bocchi; lp, Kenelm Foss, Odette Goimbault, Mary Marsh Allen, Hayford Hobbs

WHY AMERICA WILL WIN (1918)
(7 r.) d, Richard Stanton; lp, Harris Gordon, Olaf Skavlan, A. Alexander, R.A. Faulkner

WHY ANNOUNCE YOUR MARRIAGE? (1922)
(5 r.) d, Alan Crosland; lp, Elaine Hammerstein, Niles Welch, Frank Currier, Arthur Housman

WHY BLAME ME?
(SEE: HER MOMENT, 1918)

WHY CHANGE YOUR WIFE? (1920)
(7 r.) d, Cecil B. DeMille; lp, Gloria Swanson, Thomas Meighan, Bebe Daniels, Theodore Kosloff

WHY GERMANY MUST PAY (1919)
(6 r.) d, Charles Miller; lp, Creighton Hale, Florence Billings, Fred C. Truesdell, Margaret McWade

WHY GIRLS GO BACK HOME (1926)
(6 r.) d, James Flood; lp, Patsy Ruth Miller, Clive Brook, Jane Winton, Myrna Loy

WHY GIRLS LEAVE HOME (1921)
(7 r.) d, William Nigh; lp, Anna Q. Nilsson, Maurine Powers, Julia Swayne Gordon, Corinne Barker

WHY I WOULD NOT MARRY (1918)
(6 r.) d, Richard Stanton; lp, Lucy Fox, William Davidson, Corinne Barker, John W. Dillon

WHY MEN FORGET (1921, Brit.)
(6 r.) d, Denison Clift; lp, Milton Rosmer, Evelyn Brent, Warwick Ward, Bettina Campbell

WHY MEN LEAVE HOME (1924)
(8 r.) d, John M. Stahl; lp, Lewis Stone, Helene Chadwick, Mary Carr, William V. Mong

WHY NOT MARRY? (1922)
(5 r.) d, John S. Lopez; lp, Albert Edward, Margery Wilson, Fred C. Jones, George A. Wright

WHY SAILORS GO WRONG (1928)
(6 r.) d, Henry Lehrman; lp, Sammy Cohen, Ted McNamara, Sally Phipps, Carl Miller

WHY SMITH LEFT HOME (1919)
(5 r.) d, Donald Crisp lp, Bryant Washburn, Lois Wilson, Mayme Kelso, Winter Hall

WHY TRUST YOUR HUSBAND? (1921)
(5 r.) d, George E. Marshall; lp, Eileen Percy, Harry Myers, Ray Ripley, Harry Dunkinson

WHY WOMEN LOVE (1925)
(7 r.) d, Edwin Carewe; lp, Blanche Sweet, Bert Sprotte, Robert Frazer, Charles Murray

WHY WOMEN REMARRY (1923)
(5 r.) d, John Gorman; lp, Milton Sills, Ethel Grey Terry, William Lowery, Marion Feducha

WICKED DARLING, THE (1919)
(6 r.) d, Tod Browning; lp, Priscilla Dean, Wellington Playter, Lon Chaney, Spottiswoode Aitken

WICKEDNESS PREFERRED (1928)
(6 r.) d, Hobart Henley; lp, Lew Cody, Aileen Pringle, Mary McAllister, Bert Roach

WIDE OPEN (1927)
(5 r.) d, John Wesley Grey; lp, Dick Grace, Grace Darmond, Lionel Belmore, Ernest Hilliard

WIDECOMBE FAIR (1928, Brit.)
(6 r.) d, Norman Walker; lp, William Freshman, Marguerite Allan, Wyndham Standing, Violet Hopson

WIDOW BY PROXY (1919)
(5 r.) d, Walter Edwards; lp, Marguerite Clark, Brownie Vernon, Gertrude Norman, Gertrude Claire

WIDOW TWAN-KEE
(SEE: ONE ARABIAN NIGHT, 1923, Brit.)

WIDOW'S MIGHT, THE (1918)
(5 r.) d, William C. De Mille; lp, Julian Eltinge, Florence Vidor, Gustav von Seyffertitz, Mayme Kelso

WIFE BY PROXY, A (1917)
(5 r.), Mabel Taliaferro, Robert Walker, Sally Crute, Fred Jones

WIFE HE BOUGHT, THE (1918)
(5 r.) d, Harry Solter; lp, Carmel Myers, Kenneth Harlan, Howard Crampton, Sydney Dean

WIFE HUNTERS, THE (1922)
(? r.) d, Bob White;

WIFE IN NAME ONLY (1923)
(5 r.) d, George W. Terwilliger; lp, Mary Thurman, Arthur Housman, Edmund Lowe, William Tucker

WIFE LOST (1928, Jap.)
(? r.) d, Yasujiro Ozu

WIFE NUMBER TWO (1917)
(5 r.) d, William Nigh; lp, Valeska Suratt, Eric Mayne, Mathilde Brundage, John Goldsworthy

WIFE OF THE CENTAUR (1924)
(7 r.) d, King Vidor; lp, Eleanor Boardman, John Gilbert, Aileen Pringle, Kate Lester

WIFE OF THE PHARAOH, THE (1922, Ger.)
(6 r.) d, Ernst Lubitsch; lp, Emil Jannings, Harry Liedtke, Lyda Salmonova, Paul Wegener

WIFE ON TRAIL, A (1917)
(5 r.) d, Ruth Ann Baldwin; lp, Mignon Anderson, Leo Pierson, L.M. Wells, Julia Jackson

WIFE OR COUNTRY (1919)
(5 r.) d, E. Mason Hooper; lp, Harry Mestayer, Gloria Swanson, Jack Richardson, Gretchen Lederer

WIFE TRAP, THE (1922)
(6 r.) d, Robert Wullner

WIFE WHO WASN'T WANTED, THE (1925)
(7 r.) d, James Flood; lp, Irene Rich, Huntly Gordon, John Harron, Gayne Whitman

WIFE'S RELATIONS, THE (1928)
(6 r.) d, Maurice Marshall; lp, Shirley Mason, Gaston Glass, Ben Turpin, Armand Kaliz

WIFE'S ROMANCE, A (1923)
(6 r.) d, Thomas N. Heffron; lp, Clara Kimball Young, Lewis Dayton, Louise Bates Mortimer, Albert Roscoe

WIFE'S SACRIFICE, A (1916)
(5 r.) d, J. Gordon Edwards; lp, Robert B. Mantell, Stuart Holmes, Claire Whitney, Walter Miller

WILD BEAUTY (1927)
(6 r.) d, Henry MacRae; lp, June Marlowe, Hugh Allan, Scott Seaton, Hayes Robinson

WILD BILL HICKOK (1923)
(7 r.) d, William S. Hart; lp, William S. Hart, Ethel Grey Terry, Kathleen O'Connor, James Farley

WILD BORN (1927)
(5 r.) d, Edward R. Gordon; lp, Tex Maynard, Ruby Blaine, Charles Schaeffer, Jack Anthony

WILD BULL'S LAIR, THE (1925)
(6 r.) d, Del Andrews; lp, Fred Thomson, Catherine Bennett, Herbert Prior, Tom Carr

WILD CAT OF PARIS, THE (1919)
(6 r.) d, Joseph De Grasse; lp, Priscilla Dean, Edward Cecil, Louis Darclay, Lucille Furness

WILD GEESE (1927)
(7 r.) d, Phil Stone; lp, Belle Bennett, Russell Simpson, Eve Southern, Donald Keith

WILD GIRL, THE (1917)
(5 r.) d, Howard Estabrook; lp, Eva Tanguay, Stuart Holmes, Dean Raymond

WILD GIRL OF THE SIERRAS, A (1916)
(5 r.) d, Paul Powell; lp, Mae Marsh, Robert Harron, Wilfred Lucas, Maizie Radford

WILD GOOSE CHASE (1919)
(5 r.) d, Harry Beaumont; lp, Hazel Daly, Matt Moore, Raymond Hatton, Lucien Littlefield

WILD HEATHER (1921, Brit.)
(6 r.) d, Cecil M. Hepworth; lp, Chrissie White, Gerald Ames, G.H. Mulcaster, George Dewhurst

WILD HORSE MESA (1925)
(8 r.) d, George B. Seitz; lp, Jack Holt, Noah Beery, Billie Dove, Douglas Fairbanks Jr.

WILD HORSE STAMPEDE, THE (1926)
(5 r.) d, Albert Rogell; lp, Jack Hoxie, Fay Wray, William Steele, Marin Sais

WILD JUSTICE (1925)
(6 r.) d, Chester Franklin; lp, George Sherwood, Frank Hagney, Frances Teague, Peter the Great (a dog)

WILD LIFE (1918)
(5 r.) d, Henry Otto; lp, William Desmond, Josie Sedgwick, Dot Hagar, Ed Brady

WILD OATS (1915, Brit.)
(4 r.) d, Harold Weston; lp, Arthur Finn, Fay Temple, A.V. Bramble, M. Gray Murray

WILD OATS (1916)
(5 r.) lp, Malcolm Duncan, Alma Hanlon, William Anker, Herbert Heyes

WILD OATS (1919)
(7 r.) d, C. Jay Williams; lp, William Jefferson, Leslie Hunt

WILD ORANGES (1924)
(7 r.) d, King Vidor; lp, Virginia Valli, Frank Mayo, Ford Sterling, Nigel De Brulier

WILD PARTY, THE (1923)
(5 r.) d, Herbert Blache; lp, Gladys Walton, Robert Ellis, Freeman Wood, Dorothy Revier

WILD PRIMROSE (1918)
(5 r.) d, Fred Thompson; lp, Gladys Leslie, Richard Barthelmess, Eulalie Jensen, Claude Gillingwater

WILD STRAIN, THE (1918)
(5 r.) d, William Wolbert; lp, Nell Shipman, Alfred Whitman, Otto Lederer, Edward Alexander

WILD SUMAC (1917)
(5 r.) d, William V. Mong; lp, Margery Wilson, Edwin J. Brady, Frank Brownlee, Wilbur Higby

WILD TO GO (1926)
(5 r.) d, Robert De Lacey; lp, Tom Tyler, Frankie Darrow, Fred Burns, Ethan Laidlaw

WILD WEST ROMANCE (1928)
(5 r.) d, R. Lee Hough; lp, Rex Bell, Caryl Lincoln, Neil Neely, Billy Butts

WILD WEST SHOW, THE (1928)
(6 r.) d, Del Andrews; lp, Hoot Gibson, Dorothy Gulliver, Allan Forrest, Gale Henry

WILD, WILD SUSAN (1925)
(6 r.) d, Edward Sutherland; lp, Bebe Daniels, Rod La Rocque, Henry Stephenson, Jack Kane

WILD WINSHIP'S WIDOW (1917)
(5 r.) d, Charles Miller; lp, Dorothy Dalton, Rowland Lee, Joe King, Lillian Hayward

WILD WOMEN (1918)
(5 r.) d, Jack [John] Ford; lp, Harry Carey, Molly Malone, Vester Pegg, Edgar Jones

WILD YOUTH (1918)
(5 r.) d, George H. Melford; lp, Louise Huff, Theodore Roberts, Jack Mulhall, James Cruze

WILDCAT, THE (1917)
(5 r.) d, Sherwood MacDonald; lp, Jackie Saunders, Daniel Gilfether, Mollie McConnell, Arthur Shirley

WILDCAT, THE (1924)
(5 r.) lp, Robert Gordon

WILDCAT, THE (1926)
(5 r.) d, Harry L. Frazer; lp, Gordon Clifford

WILDCAT JORDAN (1922)
(5 r.) d, Al Santell; lp, Richard Talmadge, Eugenia Gilbert, Harry Van Meter, Jack Waltemeyer

WILDERNESS TRAIL, THE (1919)
(5 r.) d, Edward J. Le Saint; lp, Tom Mix, Colleen Moore, Sid Jordan, Frank Clark

WILDERNESS TRAIL, THE
(SEE: SYMBOL OF THE UNCONQUERED, 1921)

WILDFIRE (1915)
(5 r.) d, Edwin Middleton; lp, Lillian Russell, Lionel Barrymore, Sam J. Ryan, Georgie Mack

WILDFIRE (1925)
(7 r.) d, T. Hayes Hunter; lp, Aileen Pringle, Edna Murphy, Holmes Herbert, Edmund Breese

WILDFLOWER (1914)
(4 r.) d, Allan Dwan; lp, Marguerite Clark, Harold Lockwood, James Cooley, Jack Pickford

WILDNESS OF YOUTH (1922)
(8 r.) d, Ivan Abramson; lp, Virginia Pearson, Harry T. Morey, Mary Anderson, Joseph Striker

WILFUL YOUTH (1927)
(6 r.) d, Dallas M. Fitzgerald; lp, Edna Murphy, Kenneth Harlan, Jack Richardson, Walter Perry

WILL, THE (1921, Brit.)
(5 r.) d, A.V. Bramble; lp, Milton Rosmer, Evangeline Hilliard, J. Fisher White, Alec Fraser

WILL AND A WAY, A (1922, Brit.)
(4 r.) d, Manning Hayes; lp, Ernest Hendrie, Pollie Emery, Johnny Butt, Cynthia Murtagh

WILL O' THE WISP, THE (1914)
(4 r.) lp, Jackie Saunders

WILL OF HER OWN, A (1915, Brit.)
(4 r.) d, Maurice Elvey; lp, Elizabeth Risdon, Fred Groves, Hilda Sims, Ernest Cox

WILL OF THE PEOPLE, THE
(SEE: STRONG MAN'S WEAKNESS, A, 1917, Brit.)

WILL YOU BE STAYING FOR SUPPER? (1919)
(5 r.) d, Kenneth Webb; lp, Harry Lonsdale, Mary Jane Irving, Clara Whipple, John Burkell

WILLIAM TELL (1925)
(12 r.)

WILLOW TREE, THE (1920)
(6 r.) d, Henry Otto; lp, Viola Dana, Edward Connelly, Pell Trenton, Harry Dunkinson

WILLY REILLY AND HIS COLLEEN BAWN (1918, Brit.)
(5 r.) d, Fred O'Donovan; lp, Brian Magowan, Kathleen Murphy

WILSON OR THE KAISER?
(SEE: GREAT VICTORY, WILSON OR THE KAISER?, 1918)

WIN, LOSE OR DRAW (1925)
(5 r.) d, Leo Maloney; lp, Leo Maloney, Roy Watson, Whitehorse, Josephine Hill

WIN THAT GIRL (1928)
(6 r.) d, David Butler; lp, David Rollins, Sue Carol, Tom Elliott, Roscoe Karns

WINCHESTER WOMAN, THE (1919)
(6 r.) d, Wesley Ruggles; lp, Alice Joyce, Percy Marmont, Robert Middlemass, Jean Armour

WINDING ROAD, THE (1920)
(7 r.) d, Bert Haldane, Frank Wilson; lp, Cecil Humphreys, Edith Pearson, Annesley Hely, Jack Jarman

WINDING TRAIL, THE (1921)
(5 r.) d, George Martin; lp, Marjorie Clifford, Buck Manning, William V. Mong

WINDING TRAIL, THE (1918)
(5 r.) d, John H. Collins; lp, Viola Dana, Clifford Bruce, Hayward Mack, Mabel Van Buren

WINDJAMMER, THE (1926)
(5 r.) d, Harry J. Brown; lp, Billy Sullivan

WINDOW IN PICCADILLY, A (1928, Brit.)
(8 r.) d, Sidney Morgan; lp, De Groot, Joan Morgan, John Hamilton, James Carew

WINDS OF CHANCE (1925)
(10 r.) d, Frank Lloyd; lp, Anna Q. Nilsson, Ben Lyon, Viola Dana, Hobart Bosworth

WINDS OF THE PAMPAS (1927)
(6 r.) d, Arthur Varney; lp, Ralph Cloninger, Harry Holden, Vesey O'Davoren, Edwards Davis

WINE (1924)
(7 r.) d, Louis J. Gasnier; lp, Clara Bow, Forrest Stanley, Huntley Gordon, Myrtle Stedman

WINE GIRL, THE (1918)
(5 r.) d, Stuart Paton; lp, Carmel Myers, Rex De Rosselli, Kenneth Harlan, E.A. Warren

WINE OF LIFE, THE (1924, Brit.)
(6 r.) d, Arthur Rooke; lp, Betty Carter, Clive Brook, James Carew, Juliette Compton

WINE OF YOUTH (1924)
(7 r.) d, King Vidor; lp, Eleanor Boardman, James Morrison, Niles Welch, Creighton Hale

WINGED HORSEMAN, THE (1929)
(6 r.) d, Arthur Rosson, Reeves Eason; lp, Hoot Gibson, Mary Elder, Charles Schaeffer, Allan Forrest

WINGED IDOL, THE (1915)
(5 r.) d, Walter Edwards; lp, Katherine Kaelred, House Peters, Clara Williams, Harry Keenan

WINGED MYSTERY, THE (1917)
(5 r.) d, Joseph De Grasse; lp, Franklyn Farnum, Claire Du Brey, Rosemary Theby, Charles Hill Mailes

WINGS OF A SERF (1926, USSR)
(7 r.) d, Yuri Tarich, Leonid Leonidov; lp, Leonid Leonidov, I. Klyukvin, Nikolai Prozorovsky, Korsh

WINGS OF THE MORNING, THE (1919)
(6 r.) d, J. Gordon Edwards; lp, William Farnum, Louise Lovely, Herschel Mayall, Frank Elliott

WINGS OF YOUTH (1925)
(6 r.) d, Emmett Flynn; lp, Ethel Clayton, Madge Bellamy, Charles Farrell, Freeman Wood

WINIFRED THE SHOP GIRL (1916)
(5 r.) d, George D. Baker; lp, Edith Storey, Antonio Moreno, Lillian Burns, John Costello

WIN(K)SOME WIDOW, THE (1914)
(4 r.) d, James Young; lp, Cissy Fitzgerald, Wally Van, L. Rogers Lytton, Hughie Mack

WINNER, THE (1926)
(5 r.) d, Harry J. Brown; lp, Billy Sullivan, Lucille Hutton, Tom O'Brien, Ben Walker

WINNER TAKE ALL (1924)
(6 r.) d, William S. Van Dyke; lp, Buck Jones, Peggy Shaw, Edward Hearn, Lilyan Tashman

WINNER TAKES ALL (1918)
(5 r.) d, Elmer Clifton; lp, Monroe Salisbury, Betty Schade, Alfred Allen, Helen Jerome Eddy

WINNERS OF THE WILDERNESS (1927)
(7 r.) d, W.S. Van Dyke; lp, Tim McCoy, Joan Crawford, Edward Connelly, Roy D'Arcy

WINNING A CONTINENT (1924)
(6 r.) d, Harold Shaw; lp, Percy Marmont, Edna Flugrath, Harold Shaw

WINNING A WOMAN (1925)
(5 r.) lp, Jack Perrin, Josephine Hill

WINNING GIRL, THE (1919)
(5 r.) d, Robert G. Vignola; lp, Shirley Mason, Niles Welch, Theodore Roberts, Harold Goodwin

WINNING GRANDMA (1918)
(5 r.) d, William Bertram; lp, Marie Osborne, J. Morris Foster, Ruth King, William Quinn

WINNING HIS FIRST CASE (1914)
(4 r.)

WINNING OAR, THE (1927)
(6 r.) d, Bernard McEveety; lp, George Walsh, Dorothy Hall, William Cain, Arthur Donaldson

WINNING OF BEATRICE, THE (1918)
(5 r.) d, Harry L. Franklin; lp, May Allison, Hale Hamilton, Frank Currier, Stephen Grattan

WINNING OF SALLY TEMPLE, THE (1917)
(5 r.) d, George Melford; lp, Fannie Ward, Jack Dean, Walter Long, Horace B. Carpenter

WINNING OF THE WEST (1922)
(5 r.)

WINNING THE FUTURITY (1926)
(6 r.) d, Scott Dunlap; lp, Cullen Landis, Clara Horton, Henry Kolker, Pat Harmon

WINNING WALLOP, THE (1926)
(5 r.) d, Charles Hutchinson; lp, William Fairbanks, Shirley Palmer, Charles K. French, Melvin McDowell

WINNING WITH WITS (1922)
(5 r.) d, Howard M. Mitchell; lp, Barbara Bedford, William Scott, Harry S. Northrup, Edwin B. Tilton

WIRELESS (1915, Brit.)
(4 r.) d, Harry Lorraine; lp, Harry Lorraine, Violet Graham, Jack Wayho, Bert Rex

WISE GUY, THE (1926)
(8 r.) d, Frank Lloyd; lp, Mary Astor, James Kirkwood, Betty Compson, George F. Marion

WISE KID, THE (1922)
(5 r.) d, Tod Browning; lp, Gladys Walton, David Butler, Hallam Cooley, Hector Sarno

WISE VIRGIN, THE (1924)
(6 r.) d, Lloyd Ingraham; lp, Patsy Ruth Miller, Edythe Chapman, Lucy Fox, Matt Moore

WISE WIFE, THE (1927)
(6 r.) d, E. Mason Hopper; lp, Phyllis Haver, Tom Moore, Fred Walton, Jacqueline Logan

WISHING RING MAN, THE (1919)
(5 r.) d, David Smith; lp, Bessie Love, J. Frank Glendon, Jean Hathaway, Claire Du Brey

WISP O' THE WOODS (1919, Brit.)
(5 r.) d, Lewis Willoughby; lp, Constance Worth, Evan Thomas, S.J. Warmington, Eric Maturin

WIT WINS (1920)
(6 r.) d, Burton King; lp, Florence Billings, Hugh Thompson, E.J. Radcliffe, John Nichols

WITCH, THE (1916)
(5 r.) d, Frank Powell; lp, Nance O'Neil, Alfred Hickman

WITCH WOMAN, THE (1918)
(5 r.) d, Travers Vale; lp, Ethel Clayton, Frank Mayo, John Ardizoni, Jack Drumier

WITCHCRAFT (1916)
(5 r.) d, Frank Reicher; lp, Fannie Ward, Jack Dean, Paul Weigel, Lillian Leighton

WITCHCRAFT THROUGH THE AGES (1921, Swed.)
(7 r.) d, Benjamin Christensen; lp, Benjamin Christensen, Maren Pedersen, Clara Pontoppidan, Emmy Schonfield

WITCHING EYES, THE (1929)
(? r.)

WITCHING HOUR, THE (1916)
(7 r.) d, George Irving; lp, C. Aubrey Smith, Robert Conness, Marie Shotwell, Jack Sherrill

WITCH'S LURE, THE (1921)
(5 r.) lp, Davide

WITH ALL HER HEART (1920, Brit.)
(5 r.) d, Frank Wilson; lp, Milton Rosmer, Mary Odette, Jack Vincent, J. Hastings Batson

WITH BRIDGES BURNED (1915)
(4 r.) d, Ashley Miller

WITH DAVY CROCKETT AT THE FALL OF THE ALAMO
(SEE: DAVY CROCKETT AT THE FALL OF THE ALAMO, 1926)

WITH GENERAL CUSTER AT LITTLE BIG HORN
(SEE: GENERAL CUSTER AT LITTLE BIG HORN, 1926)

WITH HOOPS OF STEEL (1918)
(5 r.) d, Eliot Howe; lp, Henry B. Walthall, Mary Charleson, William DeVaull, Joseph J. Dowling

WITH KIT CARSON OVER THE GREAT DIVIDE
(SEE: KIT CARSON OVER THE GREAT DIVIDE, 1925)

WITH NAKED FISTS (1923)
(5 r.) lp, Tom Kennedy, Leonard Clapham

WITH NEATNESS AND DISPATCH (1918)
(5 r.) d, William S. Davis; lp, Francis X. Bushman, Beverly Bayne, Frank Currier, Walter Miller

WITH SITTING BULL AT THE SPIRIT LAKE MASSACRE
(SEE: SITTING BULL AT THE "SPIRIT LAKE MASSACRE", 1927)

WITH THIS RING (1925)
(6 r.) d, Fred Windermere; lp, Alyce Mills, Forrest Stanley, Lou Tellegen, Donald Keith

WITH WINGS OUTSPREAD (1922)
(5 r.) lp, Fred Terry, Walter Franklin, Madeline Cassinelli

WITHIN THE CUP (1918)
(7 r.) d, Raymond B. West; lp, Bessie Barriscale, George Fisher, Edward Coxen, Aggie Herring

WITHIN THE LAW (1917)
(8 r.) d, William P.S. Earle; lp, Alice Joyce, Harry Morey, Adele De Garde, Anders Randolf

WITHIN THE LAW (1923)
(8 r.) d, Frank Lloyd; lp, Norma Talmadge, Lew Cody, Jack Mulhall, Eileen Percy

WITHOUT A SOUL (1916)
(5 r.) lp, Clara Kimball Young, Alec B. Francis, Edward M. Kimball, Irene Tams

WITHOUT BENEFIT OF CLERGY (1921)
(6 r.) d, James Young; lp, Virginia Brown Faire, Thomas Holding, Evelyn Selbie, Otto Lederer

WITHOUT COMPROMISE (1922)
(6 r.) d, Emmett J. Flynn; lp, William Farnum, Lois Wilson, Robert McKim, Tully Marshall

WITHOUT HONOR (1918)
(5 r.) d, E. Mason Hopper; lp, Margery Wilson, Arthur Moon, Walt Whitman, Darrel Foss

WITHOUT MERCY (1925)
(7 r.) d, George Melford; lp, Dorothy Phillips, Rockcliffe Fellowes, Vera Reynolds, Robert Ames

WITHOUT ORDERS (1926)
(5 r.) d, Leo Maloney; lp, Leo Maloney, Josephine Hill, Whitehorse, Bud Osborne

WITHOUT WARNING
(SEE: STORY WITHOUT A NAME, THE, 1924)

WITNESS FOR THE DEFENSE, THE (1919)
(5 r.) d, George Fitzmaurice; lp, Elsie Ferguson, Vernon Steele, Warner Oland, Wyndham Standing

WITS VS. WITS (1920)
(5 r.) d, Harry Grossman; lp, Marguerite Marsh, E. Coit Albertson, Charles Middleton, Bernard Randall

WIVES AND OTHER WIVES (1919)
(5 r.) d, Lloyd Ingraham; lp, Mary Miles Minter, Colin Chase, George Periolat, William Garwood

WIVES AT AUCTION (1926)
(6 r.) d, Elmer Clifton; lp, Edna Murphy, Gaston Glass

WIVES OF MEN (1918)
(6 r.) d, John M. Stahl; lp, Florence Reed, Frank Mills, Mathilde Brundage, Edgar P. Lewis

WIVES OF THE PROPHET, THE (1926)
(7 r.) d, J.A. Fitzgerald; lp, Orville Caldwell, Alice Lake, Violet Mersereau, Harlan Knight

WIZARD, THE (1927)
(6 r.) d, Richard Rosson; lp, Edmund Lowe, Lelia Hyams, Gustav von Seyffertitz, E.H. Calvert

WIZARD OF THE SADDLE (1928)
(5 r.) d, Frank Howard Clark; lp, Buzz Barton, Milburn Morante, James Ford, Duane Thompson

WOLF, THE (1914)
(5 r.) d, Barry O'Neill; lp, George Soule Spencer, Ethel Clayton, Ferdinand Tidmarsh, Gaston Bell

WOLF, THE (1919)
(6 r.) d, James Young; lp, Earle Williams, Jane Novak, Brinsley Shaw, George Nichols

WOLF AND HIS MATE, THE (1918)
(5 r.) d, Edward J. LeSaint; lp, Louise Lovely, Hart Hoxie, Betty Schade, George R. Odell

WOLF BLOOD (1925)
(6 r.) d, George Chesebro; lp, Marguerite Clayton, George Chesebro, Ray Hanford, Roy Watson

WOLF FANGS (1927)
(6 r.) d, Lewis Seiler; lp, Caryl Lincoln, Charles Morton, Frank Rice, Thunder (a dog)

WOLF HUNTERS, THE (1926)
(6 r.) d, Stuart Paton; lp, Robert McKim, Virginia Browne Faire, Alan Roscoe, Mildred Harris

WOLF LOWRY (1917)
(5 r.) d, William S. Hart; lp, William S. Hart, Margery Wilson, Aaron Edwards, Carl Ullman

WOLF MAN, THE (1924)
(6 r.) d, Edmund Mortimer; lp, John Gilbert, Norma Shearer, Alma Francis, George Barraud

WOLF MAN (1924)
(5 r.) lp, J.B. Warner

WOLF OF DEBT, THE (1915)
(4 r.) d, Jack Harvey; lp, Violet Mersereau, William Garwood, Fanny Hayes, Brinsley Shaw

WOLF WOMAN, THE (1916)
(5 r.) d, Irvin Willat, Walter Edwards; lp, Louise Glaum, Charles Ray, Howard Hickman, Marjory Temple

WOLFE OR THE CONQUEST OF QUEBEC (1914)
(5 r.) d, Sidney Olcott; lp, Gene Gaunthier, Barry O'Brien, James B. Ross

WOLFHEART'S REVENGE (1925)
(5 r.) lp, Guinn "Big Boy" Williams, Wolfheart (a dog)

WOLF-MAN, THE (1915)
(4 r.) lp, Ralph Lewis, Jack Brammall, Richard Cummings, William Hinckley

WOLF'S FANGS, THE (1922)
(5 r.) d, Oscar Apfel; lp, Wilfred Lytell, Nancy Deaver, Manilla Martans

WOLF'S TRACKS (1923)
(5 r.) lp, Jack Hoxie

WOLF'S TRAIL (1927)
(5 r.) d, Francis Ford; lp, Edmund Cobb, Dixie Lamont, Edwin Terry, Joe Bennett

WOLVES OF THE AIR (1927)
(6 r.) d, Francis Ford; lp, Johnnie Walker, Lois Boyd, Maurice Costello, Mildred Harris

WOLVES OF THE BORDER (1918)
(5 r.) d, Cliff Smith; lp, Roy Stewart, Josie Sedgwick, Frank McQuarrie, Jack Curtis

WOLVES OF THE BORDER (1923)
(5 r.) d, Alvin J. Neitz; lp, Franklyn Farnum, William Dyer, William Lester, Andrew Waldron

WOLVES OF THE CITY (1929)
(5 r.) d, Leigh Jason; lp, Bill Cody, Sally Blane, Al Ferguson, Monty Montague

WOLVES OF THE DESERT (1926)
(5 r.) d, Ben Wilson; lp, Ben Wilson

WOLVES OF THE NIGHT (1919)
(7 r.) d, J. Gordon Edwards; lp, William Farnum, Louise Lovely, G. Raymond Nye, Charles Clary

WOLVES OF THE NORTH (1921)
(5 r.) d, Norman Dawn; lp, Herbert Heyes, Percy Challenger, Eva Novak, Starke Patterson

WOLVES OF THE RAIL (1918)
(5 r.) d, William S. Hart; lp, William S. Hart, Vola Vale, C. Norman Hammond, Melbourne McDowell

WOLVES OF THE RANGE (1921)
(5 r.) lp, Jack Livingston

WOLVES OF THE ROAD (1925)
(5 r.) d, Ward Hayes; lp, Yakima Canutt

WOLVES OF THE STREET (1920)
(6 r.) d, Otis B. Thayer; lp, Edmund F. Cobb, Vida Johnson

WOMAN (1919)
(7 r.) d, Maurice Tourneur; lp, Florence Billings, Ethel Hallor, Warren Cook, Chester Barnett

WOMAN ABOVE REPROACH, THE (1920)
(5 r.) lp, Florence Chase

WOMAN AGAINST THE WORLD, A (1928)
(6 r.) d, George Archainbaud; lp, Harrison Ford, Georgia Hale, Lee Moran, Harvey Clark

WOMAN ALONE, A (1917)
(5 r.) d, Harry Davenport; lp, Alice Brady, Edward T. Langford, Edward M. Kimball, Justine Cutting

WOMAN AND OFFICER 26, THE (1920, Brit.)
(5 r.) d, Harry Lorraine; lp, Marguerite de Belabre, Jeffrey Julian, Harry Lorraine, Jack Mullins

WOMAN AND THE BEAST, THE (1917)
(5 r.) d, Ernest C. Warde; lp, Marie Shotwell, Alphonse Ethier, Fred Eric, Kathryn Adams

WOMAN AND THE LAW (1918)
(7 r.) d, Raoul Walsh; lp, Miriam Cooper, Ramsay Wallace, Peggy Hopkins, George Humbert

WOMAN AND THE PUPPET, THE (1920)
(7 r.) d, Reginald Barker; lp, Geraldine Farrar, Lou Tellegen, Dorothy Cumming, Bertram Grassby

WOMAN AND WIFE (1918)
(5 r.) d, Edward Jose; lp, Alice Brady, Elliott Dexter, Helen Greene, Helen Lindroth

WOMAN BENEATH, THE (1917)
(5 r.) d, Travers Vale; lp, Ethel Clayton, Curtis Cooksey, Isabelle Berwin, Frank De Vernon

WOMAN BETWEEN FRIENDS, THE (1918)
(5 r.) d, Tom Terriss; lp, Alice Joyce, Marc MacDermott, Robert Walker, Bernard Siegel

WOMAN BREED, THE (1922)
(6 r.) lp, Pauline Frederick

WOMAN CONQUERS, THE (1922)
(6 r.) d, Tom Forman; lp, Katherine MacDonald, Bryant Washburn, Mitchell Lewis, June Elvidge

WOMAN DISPUTED, THE (1928)
(9 r.) d, Henry King; lp, Norma Talmadge, Gilbert Roland, Arnold Kent, Boris De Fas

WOMAN ETERNAL, THE (1918)
(7 r.) d, Ralph Ince; lp, Elaine Hammerstein, W. Lawson Butt, George Cooper, Violet Palmer

WOMAN FROM CHINA, THE (1930, Brit.)
(7 r.) d, Edward Dryhurst; lp, Julie Suedo, Gibb McLaughlin, Frances Cuyler, Tony Wylde

WOMAN FROM HELL, THE (1929)
(6 r.) d, A. F. Erickson; lp, Mary Astor, Robert Armstrong, Dean Jagger, Roy D'Arcy

WOMAN FROM MOSCOW, THE (1928)
(7 r.) d, Ludwig Berger; lp, Pola Negri, Norman Kerry, Paul Lukas, Otto Matiesen

WOMAN GAME, THE (1920)
(6 r.) d, William P.S. Earle; lp, Elaine Hammerstein, Jere Austin, Louis Broughton, Florence Billings

WOMAN GIVES, THE (1920)
(6 r.) d, Roy William Neill; lp, Norma Talmadge, Edmund Lowe, John Halliday, Lucille Lee Stewart

WOMAN GOD FORGOT, THE (1917)
(6 r.) d, Cecil B. DeMille; lp, Geraldine Farrar, Wallace Reid, Hobart Bosworth, Raymond Hatton

WOMAN GOD SENT, THE (1920)
(7 r.) d, Larry Trimble; lp, Zena Keefe, Warren Cook, Joe King, William Fredericks

WOMAN HATER, THE (1925)
(7 r.) d, James Flood; lp, Helene Chadwick, Clive Brook, John Harron, Helen Dunbar

WOMAN HE LOVED, THE (1922)
(5 r.) d, Edward Sloman; lp, William V. Mong, Marcia Manon, Eddie Sutherland, Mary Wynn

WOMAN HE MARRIED, THE (1922)
(7 r.) d, Fred Niblo; lp, Anita Stewart, Darrel Foss, Donald MacDonald, William Conklin

WOMAN I LOVE, THE (1929)
(7 r.) d, George Melford; lp, Margaret Morris, Robert Frazer, Leota Lorraine, Norman Kerry

WOMAN IN BLACK, THE (1914)
(4 r.) d, Lawrence Marston; lp, Lionel Barrymore, Millicent Evans, Alan Hale, Charles Hill Mailes

WOMAN IN CHAINS, THE (1923)
(7 r.) d, William P. Burt; lp, E.K. [Elmo] Lincoln, William H. Tooker, Natasha Rambova, Martha Mansfield

WOMAN IN 47, THE (1916)
(5 r.) d, George Irving; lp, Alice Brady, William Raymond, John Warwick, George D. Melville

WOMAN IN HIS HOUSE, THE (1920)
(6 r.) d, John M. Stahl; lp, Mildred Harris Chaplin, Ramsey Wallace, Thomas Holding, George Fisher

WOMAN IN PAWN, A (1927, Brit.)
(7 r.) d, Edwin Greenwood; lp, Gladys Jennings, John Stuart, Lauderdale Maitland, Chili Bouchier

WOMAN IN POLITICS, THE (1916)
(5 r.) d, W. Eugene Moore; lp, Mignon Anderson, Arthur Bauer, Ernest Howard, George Marlo

WOMAN IN ROOM 13, THE (1920)
(5 r.) d, Frank Lloyd; lp, Pauline Frederick, Charles Clary, John Bowers, Charles Arling

WOMAN IN THE CASE, A (1916)
(5 r.) d, Hugh Ford; lp, Pauline Frederick, Alan Hale, Paul Gordon, Marie Chambers

WOMAN IN THE NIGHT, A (1929)
(8 r.) d, Victor Saville

WOMAN IN THE SUITCASE, THE (1920)
(6 r.) d, Fred Niblo; lp, Enid Bennett, William Conklin, Claire McDowell, Dorcas Matthews

WOMAN IN WHITE, THE (1917)
(5 r.) d, Ernest C. Warde; lp, Florence LaBadie, Richard Neil, Gertrude Dallas, Arthur Bower

WOMAN IN WHITE, THE (1929, Brit.)
(7 r.) d, Herbert Wilcox; lp, Blanche Sweet, Haddon Mason, Cecil Humphreys, Louise Prussing

WOMAN MICHAEL MARRIED, THE (1919)
(5 r.) d, Henry Kolker; lp, Bessie Barriscale, Jack Holt, Marcia Manon, Tom Guise

WOMAN NEXT DOOR, THE (1915)
(5 r.) lp, Irene Fenwick, Camilla Dalberg, Della Connor, Richie Ling

WOMAN NEXT DOOR, THE
(SEE: VICKY MAN, THE, 1919)

WOMAN OF BRONZE, THE (1923)
(6 r.) d, King Vidor; lp, Clara Kimball Young, John Bowers, Kathryn McGuire, Edwin Stevens

WOMAN OF FLESH, A (1927)
(6 r.) lp, Charles Richardson, Edith Hampton

WOMAN OF HIS DREAM, THE (1921, Brit.)
(4 r.) d, Harold Shaw; lp, Mary Dibley, Alec Fraser, Sydney Seaward, Fred Thatcher

WOMAN OF IMPULSE, A (1918)
(5 r.) d, Edward Jose; lp, Lina Cavalieri, Gertrude Robinson, Raymond Bloomer, Robert Cain

WOMAN OF LIES (1919)
(5 r.) d, Gilbert Hamilton; lp, June Elvidge, Earl Metcalfe, Charles Mackay, Gaston Glass

WOMAN OF NO IMPORTANCE, A (1921, Brit.)
(5 r.) d, Denison Clift; lp, Fay Compton, Milton Rosmer, Ward McAllister, Lilian Walker

WOMAN OF PLEASURE, A (1919)
(7 r.) d, Wallace Worsley; lp, Blanche Sweet, Wilfred Lucas, Wheeler Oakman, Spottiswoode Aitken

WOMAN OF PLEASURE (1924, Jap.)
(? r.) d, Kenji Mizoguchi

WOMAN OF REDEMPTION, A (1918)
(5 r.) d, Travers Vale; lp, June Elvidge, Charles H. Martin, John Bowers, Alec Shannon

WOMAN ON THE INDEX, THE (1919)
(5 r.) d, Hobart Henley; lp, Pauline Frederick, Wyndham Standing, Jere Austin, Willard Mack

WOMAN OF THE IRON BRACELETS, THE (1920, Brit.)
(5 r.) d, Sidney Morgan; lp, Eve Balfour, George Keene, Margaret Blanche, George Bellamy

WOMAN OF THE SEA, A (1926)
(? r.) d, Josef von Sternberg; lp, Edna Purviance, Eve Southern, Gayne Whitman

WOMAN OF THE WORLD, A (1925)
(7 r.) d, Malcolm St. Clair; lp, Pola Negri, Charles Emmett Mack, Holmes Herbert, Blanche Mehaffey

WOMAN OF TOKYO (1933, Jap.)
(? r.) d, Yasujiro Ozu

WOMAN OF TOMORROW (1914, USSR)
(4 r.) d, Pyotr Chardynin; lp, V. Yureneva, Ivan Mozhukhin, M. Morskaya

WOMAN ON THE JURY, THE (1924)
(7 r.) d, Harry O. Hoyt; lp, Sylvia Breamer, Frank Mayo, Lew Cody, Bessie Love

WOMAN PAYS, THE (1915)
(5 r.) d, Edgar Jones; lp, Valli Valli, Edward Brennan, Marie Empress, John E. Bowers

WOMAN REDEEMED, A (1927, Brit.)
(8 r.) d, Sinclair Hill; lp, Joan Lockton, Brian Aherne, Stella Arbenina, James Carew

WOMAN THE GERMANS SHOT (1918)
(6 r.) d, John G. Adolfi; lp, Julia Arthur, Creighton Hale, J.W. Johnston, William Tooker

WOMAN THERE WAS, A (1919)
(5 r.) d, J. Gordon Edwards; lp, Theda Bara, Robert Elliott, William B. Davidson, Claude Payton

WOMAN THOU GAVEST ME, THE (1919)
(6 r.) d, Hugh Ford; lp, Katherine MacDonald, Milton Sills, Jack Holt, Theodore Roberts

WOMAN TO WOMAN (1923, Brit.)
(7 r.) d, Graham Cutts; lp, Betty Compson, Clive Brook, Josephine Earle, Marie Ault

WOMAN UNDER COVER, THE (1919)
(6 r.) d, George Siegmann; lp, Fritzi Brunette, George McDaniels, Harry Spingler, Fontaine La Rue

WOMAN UNDER OATH, THE (1919)
(5 r.) d, John M. Stahl; lp, Florence Reed, Hugh Thompson, Gareth Hughes, David Powell

WOMAN UNTAMED, THE (1920)
(5 r.) d, Jack Pratt; lp, Doraldina, Jay Morlay, Dark Cloud

WOMAN, WAKE UP! (1922)
(6 r.) d, Marcus Harrison; lp, Florence Vidor, Charles Meredith, Louis Calhern

WOMAN WHO BELIEVED, THE (1922)
(6 r.) d, John Harvey; lp, Walter Miller, Ann Luther

WOMAN WHO DARED, THE
(SEE: SOUL FOR SALE, A, 1915, Brit.)

WOMAN WHO DARED, THE (1916)
(7 r.) d, George E. Middleton; lp, Beatriz Michelena, Andrew Robson, William Pike, Albert Morrison

WOMAN WHO DID, THE (1915, Brit.)
(6 r.) d, Walter West; lp, Eve Balfour, Thos. H. MacDonald, George Foley, Lily Saxby

WOMAN WHO DID, A (1914)
(4 r.)

WOMAN WHO GAVE, THE (1918)
(5 r.) d, Kenean Buel; lp, Evelyn Nesbit, Irving Cummings, Russell Thaw, Robert Walker

WOMAN WHO INVENTED LOVE, THE (1918, USSR)
(10 r.) d, Vyacheslav Viskovksy; lp, Vera Kholodnaya, V. Maximov, Osip Runich, I. Khudoleyev

WOMAN WHO LIED, THE (1915)
(4 r.) p, Lucius Henderson

WOMAN WHO OBEYED, THE (1923, Brit.)
(6 r.) d, Sidney Morgan; lp, Hilda Bayley, Stewart Rome, Henry de Vries, Valia

WOMAN WHO TOUCHED THE LEGS, THE (1926, Jap.)
(? r.) d, Yutaka Abe; lp, Tokihiko Okada, Yoko Umemura

WOMAN WHO UNDERSTOOD, A (1920)
(5 r.) d, William Parke; lp, Bessie Barriscale, Forrest Stanley, Dorothy Cumming, Thomas Holding

WOMAN WHO WAS FORGOTTEN, THE (1930)
(8 r.) d, Richard Thomas; lp, LeRoy Mason, Belle Bennett, Jack Mower, Gladys McConnell

WOMAN WHO WAS NOTHING, THE (1917, Brit.)
(5 r.) d, Maurice Elvey; lp, Lilian Braithwaite, Madge Titheradge, George Tully, Leon M. Lion

WOMAN WITH A DAGGER (1916, USSR)
(5 r.) d, Yakov Protazanov; lp, Ivan Mozhukhin, Olga Gzovskaya, Nikolai Panov, Zoya Karabanova

WOMAN WITH FOUR FACES, THE (1923)
(6 r.) d, Herbert Brenon; lp, Betty Compson, Richard Dix, George Fawcett, Theodore von Eltz

WOMAN WITH THE FAN, THE (1921, Brit.)
(5 r.) d, Rene Plaissetty; lp, Mary Massart, Alec Fraser, Cyril Percival, Paulette del Baye

WOMAN! WOMAN! (1919)
(5 r.) d, Kenean Buel; lp, Evelyn Nesbit, Clifford Bruce, Gareth Hughes, William H. Tooker

WOMANHOOD (1917)
(7 r.) d, J. Stuart Blackton

WOMAN-PROOF (1923)
(8 r.) d, Alfred E. Green; lp, Thomas Meighan, Lila Lee, John Sainpolis, Louise Dresser

WOMAN'S AWAKENING, A (1917)
(5 r.) d, Chester Withey; lp, Seena Owen, Kate Bruce, A.D. Sears, Spottiswoode Aitken

WOMAN'S DARING, A (1916)
(5 r.) d, Edward Sloman; lp, Edward Coxen, Winnifred Greenwood, George Field, Charles Newton

WOMAN'S EXPERIENCE, A (1918)
(6 r.) d, Perry N. Vekroff; lp, Mary Boland, Sam Hardy, Lawrence McGill, Robert Cain

WOMAN'S FAITH, A (1925)
(7 r.) d, Edward Laemmle; lp, Alma Rubens, Percy Marmont, Jean Hersholt, ZaSu Pitts

WOMAN'S FIGHT, A (1916)
(5 r.) d, Herbert Blache; lp, Geraldine O'Brien, Thurlow Bergen

WOMAN'S FOOL, A (1918)
(5 r.) d, Jack [John] Ford; lp, Harry Carey, Molly Malone, Millard K. Wilson, Ed Jones

WOMAN'S HEART, A (1926)
(6 r.) d, Phil Rosen; lp, Enid Bennett, Gayne Whitman, Edward Earle, Mabel Julienne Scott

WOMAN'S HONOR, A (1916)
(5 r.) d, Roland West; lp, Jose Collins, Arthur Donaldson, Armand Cortez

WOMAN'S LAW, THE (1916)
(5 r.) d, Lawrence D. McGill; lp, Florence Reed, Duncan McRae, Anita d'Este Scott, Jack Curtis

WOMAN'S LAW (1927)
(6 r.) d, Dallas M. Fitzgerald; lp, Pat O'Malley, Lillian Rich, Ernest Wood, John Cossar

WOMAN'S PAST, A (1915)
(5 r.) d, Frank Powell; lp, Nance O'Neil, Alfred Hickman

WOMAN'S POWER, A (1916)
(5 r.) d, Robert W. Thornby; lp, Mollie King, Douglas MacLean, Charles Mitchell, N.J. Thompson

WOMAN'S RESURRECTION, A (1915)
(5 r.)

WOMAN'S SACRIFICE, A
(SEE: VIRGIN'S SACRIFICE, A, 1922)

WOMAN'S SIDE, THE (1922)
(6 r.) d, J.A. Barry; lp, Katherine MacDonald, Edward Burns, Henry Barrows, Dwight Crittenden

WOMAN'S TRIUMPH, A (1914)
(4 r.) d, J. Searle Dawley; lp, Laura Sawyer, Betty Harte, Hal Clarendon, Wellington A. Playter

WOMAN'S WAY, A (1916)
(5 r.) d, Barry O'Neill; lp, Carlyle Blackwell, Ethel Clayton, Montagu Love, Edith Cambell Walker

WOMAN'S WAY, A (1928)
(6 r.) d, Edmund Mortimer; lp, Margaret Livingston, Warner Baxter, Armand Kaliz, Mathilde Comont

WOMAN'S WEAPONS (1918)
(5 r.) d, Robert G. Vignola; lp, Ethel Clayton, Elliott Dexter, Vera Doria, James Neill

WOMAN'S WOMAN, A (1922)
(8 r.) d, Charles Giblyn; lp, Mary Alden, Louise Lee, Dorothy Mackaill, Holmes E. Herbert

WOMEN AND DIAMONDS (1924, Brit.)
(5 r.) d, F. Martin Thornton; lp, Victor McLaglen, Madge Stuart, Florence Turner, Norman Whalley

WOMEN AND GOLD (1925)
(6 r.) d, James P. Hogan; lp, Frank Mayo, Sylvia Breamer, William Davidson, Frankie Darrow

WOMEN ARE STRONG (1924, Jap.)
(? r.) d, Kenji Mizoguchi

WOMEN FIRST (1924)
(5 r.) d, Reeves Eason; lp, William Fairbanks, Eva Novak, Lydia Knott, Bob Rhodes

WOMEN IN CHAINS, THE
(SEE: WOMAN IN CHAINS, THE, 1923)

WOMEN LOVE DIAMONDS (1927)
(7 r.) d, Edmund Goulding; lp, Pauline Starke, Owen Moore, Lionel Barrymore, Cissy Fitzgerald

WOMEN MEN FORGET (1920)
(5 r.) d, John M. Stahl; lp, Mollie King, Edward Langford, Frank Mills, Lucy Fox

WOMEN MEN LIKE (1928)
(6 r.) lp, Alice Lake

WOMEN MEN LOVE (1921)
(6 r.) d, Samuel R. Bradley; lp, William Desmond, Marguerite Marsh, Martha Mansfield, Charlotte Naulting

WOMEN MEN MARRY (1922)
(6 r.) d, Edward Dillon; lp, E.K. [Elmo] Lincoln, Florence Dixon, Charles Hammond, Hedda Hopper

WOMEN OF RYAZAN (1927, USSR)
(6 r.) d, Olga Preobrazhenskaya; lp, Kuzma Yastrebetsky, G. Bobynin, Yelena Maximova, Emma Tsessarskaya

WOMEN ON THE FIRING LINE (1933, Jap.)
(? r.) d, Yasujiro Ozu

WOMEN WHO DARE (1928)
(7 r.) d, Burton King; lp, Helene Chadwick, Charles Delaney, Frank Beal, Jack Richardson

WOMEN WHO GIVE (1924)
(8 r.) d, Reginald Barker; lp, Barbara Bedford, Frank Keenan, Renee Adoree, Robert Frazer

WOMEN WHO WAIT
(SEE: FORBIDDEN LOVE, 1921)

WOMEN WHO WIN (1919, Brit.)
(6 r.) d, Percy Nash, Fred W. Durrant; lp, Unity More, Mary Dibley, Mary Forbes, Minna Grey

WOMEN'S WARES (1927)
(6 r.) d, Arthur Gregor; lp, Evelyn Brent, Bert Lytell, Larry Kent, Gertrude Short

WOMEN'S WEAPONS
(SEE: WOMAN'S WEAPONS, 1918)

WON IN THE CLOUDS (1928)
(5 r.) d, Bruce Mitchell; lp, Al Wilson, Helen Foster, Frank Rice, George French

WONDER MAN, THE (1920)
(7 r.) d, John G. Adolfi; lp, Georges Carpentier, Faire Binney, Florence Billings, Downing Clarke

WONDERFUL ADVENTURE, THE (1915)
(6 r.) d, Frederick Thompson; lp, William Farnum, Dorothy Green, Mary G. Martin

WONDERFUL CHANCE, THE (1920)
(5 r.) d, George Archainbaud; lp, Eugene O'Brien, Tom Blake, Rudolph Valentino, Martha Mansfield

WONDERFUL THING, THE (1921)
(7 r.) d, Herbert Brenon; lp, Norma Talmadge, Harrison Ford, Julia Hoyte, Howard Truesdale

WONDERFUL WOOING, THE
(SEE: WAY OF A WOMAN, THE, 1925, Brit.)

WONDERFUL YEAR, THE (1921, Brit.)
(6 r.) d, Kenelm Foss; lp, Mary Odette, Lionelle Howard, Randle Ayrton, Margot Drake

WONDERS OF THE SEA (1922)
(6 r.) d, J. Ernest Williamson; lp, J. Ernest Williamson, Richard Ross, Asa Cassidy, Lulu McGrath

WOOD NYMPH, THE (1916)
(5 r.) d, Paul Powell; lp, Marie Doro, Frank Campeau, Wilfred Lucas, Charles West

WOODPIGEON PATROL, THE (1930, Brit.)
(4 r.) d, Ralph Smart, F.R. Lucas; lp, Arthur Villiesid, Maurice Walter, J.A. Hewson, Lord Baden-Powell

WOOING OF PRINCESS PAT, THE (1918)
(5 r.) d, William P.S. Earle; lp, Gladys Leslie, J. Frank Glendon, Bigelow Cooper, William Dunn

WORDS AND MUSIC BY... (1919)
(5 r.) d, Scott Dunlap; lp, Albert Ray, Elinor Fair, Robert Bolder, Eugene Pallette

WORKING OF A MIRACLE, THE (1915)
(4 r.) d, Ashley Miller

WORLD AFLAME, THE (1919)
(6 r.) d, Ernest C. Warde; lp, Frank Keenan, Kathleen Kerrigan, Clark Marshall, Janice Wilson

WORLD AGAINST HIM, THE (1916)
(5 r.) d, Frank Hall Crane; lp, E.K. [Elmo] Lincoln, June Elvidge, Ruth Findlay, John Sainpolis

WORLD AND HIS WIFE, THE (1920)
(7 r.) d, Robert G. Vignola; lp, Alma Rubens, Montagu Love, Gaston Glass, Pedro de Cordoba

WORLD AND ITS WOMAN, THE (1919)
(7 r.) d, Frank Lloyd; lp, Geraldine Farrar, Lou Tellegen, May Giraci, Francis Marion

WORLD AND THE WOMAN, THE (1916)
(5 r.) d, Eugene Moore; lp, Jeanne Eagles, Boyd Marshall, Thomas A. Curran, Wayne Arey

WORLD APART, THE (1917)
(5 r.) d, William Desmond Taylor; lp, Wallace Reid, Myrtle Stedman, John Burton, Eugene Pallette

WORLD AT HER FEET, THE (1927)
(6 r.) d, Luther Reed; lp, Florence Vidor, Arnold Kent, Margaret Quimby, Richard Tucker

WORLD FOR SALE, THE (1918)
(5 r.) d, J. Stuart Blackton; lp, Conway Tearle, Ann Little, Norbert Wicki, W.W. Bittner

WORLD OF FOLLY, A (1920)
(5 r.) d, Frank Beal; lp, Vivian Rich, Aaron Edwards, Philo McCullough, Daisy Robinson

WORLD OF TODAY, THE (1915)
(6 r.) lp, Sylvia Ormonde, Alfred Ryden, Harry Fredericks, Richard A. Stratton

WORLD, THE FLESH AND THE DEVIL, THE (1914, Brit.)
(5 r.) d, F. Martin Thornton; lp, Frank Esmond, Stella St. Audrie, Warwick Wellington, Charles Carter

WORLD TO LIVE IN, THE (1919)
(5 r.) d, Charles Maigne; lp, Alice Brady, Virginia Hammond, Zyllah Shannon, W.T. Carleton Jr.

WORLDLY GOODS (1924)
(6 r.) d, Paul Bern; lp, Agnes Ayres, Pat O'Malley, Victor Varconi, Edythe Chapman

WORLDLY MADONNA, THE (1922)
(6 r.) d, Harry Garson; lp, Clara Kimball Young, William P. Carleton, Richard Tucker, George Hackathorne

WORLD'S A STAGE, THE (1922)
(6 r.) d, Colin Campbell; lp, Dorothy Phillips, Bruce McRae, Kenneth Harlan, Otis Harlan

WORLDS APART (1921)
(6 r.) d, Alan Crosland; lp, Eugene O'Brien, Olive Tell, William H. Tooker, Florence Billings

WORLD'S APPLAUSE, THE (1923)
(8 r.) d, William De Mille; lp, Bebe Daniels, Lewis Stone, Kathlyn Williams, Adolphe Menjou

WORLD'S DESIRE, THE (1915, Brit.)
(4 r.) d, Sidney Morgan; lp, Lilian Braithwaite, Fred Groves, A.V. Bramble, Joan Morgan

WORLD'S GREAT SNARE, THE (1916)
(5 r.) d, Joseph Kaufman; lp, Pauline Frederick, Irving Cummings, Ferdinand Tidmarsh, Frank Evans

WORMWOOD (1915)
(5 r.) d, Marshall Farnum; lp, Ethel Kaufman, John Sainpolis, Charles Arthur

WOULD YOU BELIEVE IT! (1929, Brit.)
(5 r.) d, Walter Forde; lp, Walter Forde, Pauline Fohnson, Arthur Stratton, Albert Brouett

WOULD YOU FORGIVE? (1920)
(5 r.) d, Scott Dunlap; lp, Vivian Rich, Tom Chatterton, Ben Deely, Lilie Leslie

WRAITH OF THE TOMB, THE
(SEE: AVENGING HAND, THE, 1915, Brit.)

WRATH (1917)
(5 r.) d, Theodore Marston; lp, H.B. Warner, Shirley Mason, George Le Guere, Edith Hallor

WRATH OF LOVE (1917)
(5 r.) d, James Vincent; lp, Virginia Pearson, Irving Cummings, Louise Bates, Nellie Slattery

WRECK, THE (1919)
(5 r.) d, Ralph Ince

WRECK, THE (1927)
(6 r.) d, William J. Craft; lp, Shirley Mason, Malcolm McGregor, Francis McDonald, James Bradbury Jr.

WRECK OF THE HESPERUS, THE (1927)
(7 r.) d, Elmer Clifton; lp, Sam De Grasse, Virginia Bradford, Francis Ford, Frank Marion

WRECKAGE (1925)
(6 r.) d, Scott R. Dunlap; lp, May Allison, Holmes Herbert, John Miljan, Rosemary Theby

WRECKER, THE (1928, Brit.)
(7 r.) d, Geza M. Bolvary; lp, Carlyle Blackwell, Benita Hume, Joseph Striker, Winter Hall

WRECKER OF LIVES, THE (1914, Brit.)
(4 r.) d, Charles Calvert; lp, Jack Leigh, Una Tristram, Lionel D'Aragon, Edward Sydney

WRIGHT IDEA, THE (1928)
(7 r.) d, Charles Hines; lp, Johnny Hines, Louise Lorraine, Edmund Breese, Walter James

WRITING ON THE WALL, THE (1916)
(5 r.) d, Tefft Johnson; lp, Joseph Kilgour, Virginia Pearson, Robert Gaillard, Naomi Childers

WRONG DOERS, THE (1925)
(7 r.) d, Hugh Dierker; lp, Lionel Barrymore, Anne Cornwall, Henry Hull, Henry Sedley

WRONG DOOR, THE (1916)
(5 r.) d, Carter De Haven; lp, Flora Parker De Haven, Carter De Haven, Ernie Shields, Helen Hayward

WRONG MR. WRIGHT, THE (1927)
(7 r.) d, Scott Sidney; lp, Jean Hersholt, Enid Bennett, Dorothy Devore, Edgar Kennedy

WRONG WOMAN, THE (1915)
(4 r.) d, Richard Ridgely

WRONG WOMAN, THE (1920)
(6 r.) d, Ivan Abramson; lp, Olive Tell, Montagu Love, Jack Crosby, Guy Coombs

WRONGS RIGHTED (1924)
(5 r.) lp, Tom Gallery, Clara Horton

WUTHERING HEIGHTS (1920, Brit.)
(6 r.) d, A.V. Bramble; lp, Milton Rosmer, Colette Brettel, Warwick Ward, Anne Trevor

WYOMING (1928)
(5 r.) d, W.S. Van Dyke; lp, Tim McCoy, Dorothy Sebastian, Charles Bell, William Fairbanks

WYOMING TORNADO (1929)
(5 r.) lp, Art Acord

WYOMING WILDCAT, THE (1925)
(5 r.) d, Robert De Lacey; lp, Tom Tyler, Billie Bennett, Ethan Laidlaw, Virginia Southern

YANKEE CONSUL, THE (1924)
(6 r.) d, James W. Horne; lp, Arthur Stuart Hull, Douglas MacLean, Patsy Ruth Miller, Stanhope Wheatcroft

YANKEE DOODLE, JR. (1922)
(5 r.) d, Jack Pratt; lp, J. Frank Glendon, Zelma Morgan, Edward M. Kimball, Victor Sarno

YANKEE FROM THE WEST, A (1915)
(4 r.) d, George Siegmann; lp, Signe Auen, Wallace Reid, Tom Wilson

YANKEE GIRL, THE (1915)
(5 r.) d, Phillips Smalley; lp, Blanche Ring, Herbert Standing, Howard Davies, Harry Fisher Jr.

YANKEE GO-GETTER, A (1921)
(5 r.) d, Duke Worne; lp, Neva Gerber, James Morrison, Joseph Girard, Ashton Dearholt

YANKEE MADNESS (1924)
(5 r.) d, Charles R. Seeling; lp, George Larkin, Billie Dove, Walter Long, Earl Schenck

YANKEE PLUCK (1917)
(5 r.) d, George Archainbaud; lp, Ethel Clayton, Montagu Love, Edward Langford, Johnny Hines

YANKEE PRINCESS, A (1919)
(5 r.) d, David Smith; lp, Bessie Love, Robert Gordon, George Pierce, Aggie Herring

YANKEE SPEED (1924)
(6 r.) d, Robert N. Bradbury; lp, Kenneth McDonald, Jay Hunt, Richard Lewis, Milton Fahrney

YANKEE WAY, THE (1917)
(5 r.) d, Richard Stanton; lp, George Walsh, Enid Markey, Joseph Dowling, Charles Elder

YAQUI, THE (1916)
(5 r.) d, Lloyd B. Carleton; lp, Hobart Bosworth, Golda Coldwell, Dorothy Clark, Charles H. Hickman

YASMINA (1926, Fr.)
(? r.) d, Andre Hugon; lp, Leon Mathot, Hugette Duflos

YEARS OF THE LOCUST, THE (1916)
(5 r.) d, George Melford; lp, Fannie Ward, Walter Long, Jack Dean, H.M. Best

YEKATERINA IVANOVNA (1915, USSR)
(7 r.) d, A. Uralsky; lp, Maria Germanova, N. Massalitinov, M. Durasova, Ican Bersenev

YELLOW BULLET, THE (1917)
(4 r.) d, Harry Harvey; lp, Robyn Adair, Lucy Payton, Bruce Smith, Neil Hardie

YELLOW CLAW, THE (1920, Brit.)
(6 r.) d, Rene Plaissetty; lp, Kitty Fielder, Norman Page, Harvey Braban, Sydney Seaward

YELLOW CONTRABAND (1928)
(6 r.) d, Leo Maloney; lp, Leo Maloney, Greta Yoltz, Noble Johnson, Tom London

YELLOW DOG, THE (1918)
(6 r.) d, Colin Campbell; lp, Arthur Hoyt, Clara Horton, Ralph Graves, Antrim Short

YELLOW LILY, THE (1928)
(8 r.) d, Alexander Korda; lp, Billie Dove, Clive Brook, Gustav von Seyffertitz, Marc MacDermott

YELLOW MEN AND GOLD (1922)
(6 r.) d, Irvin V. Willat; lp, Richard Dix, Helene Chadwick, Henry Barrows, Rosemary Theby

YELLOW PASSPORT, THE (1916)
(5 r.) d, Edwin August; lp, Clara Kimball Young, John Sainpolis, Alec B. Francis, John Boyle

YELLOW PAWN, THE (1916)
(5 r.) d, George Melford; lp, Cleo Ridgley, Wallace Reid, William Conkiln, Tom Forman

YELLOW STOCKINGS (1928, Brit.)
(8 r.) d, Theodor Komisarjevsky; lp, Percy Marmont, Marjorie Mars, Georges Galli, Enid Stamp-Taylor

YELLOW STREAK, A (1915)
(5 r.) d, William Nigh; lp, Lionel Barrymore, Irene Howley, Dorothy Gwynne, J.H. Goldsworthy

YELLOW STREAK, A (1927)
(5 r.) d, Ben Wilson; lp, Ben Wilson, Neva Gerber

YELLOW TAIFUN, THE (1920)
(6 r.) d, Edward Jose; lp, Anita Stewart, Ward Crane, Donald MacDonald, Joseph Kilgour

YELLOW TICKET, THE (1918)
(5 r.) d, William Parke; lp, Fannie Ward, Milton Sills, Warner Oland, Armand Kaliz

YELLOW TRAFFIC, THE (1914)
(4 r.) lp, Olaf Skavlan, Fay Cusick, Albert Lang, William V. Mong

YELLOW TYPHOON, THE (1920)
(6 r.) d, Edward Jose; lp, Anita Stewart, Ward Crane, Donald McDonald, Joseph Kilgour

YELLOWBACK, THE (1929)
(7 r.) d, Jerome Storm; lp, Tom Moore, Irma Harrison, Tom Santschi, William Martin

YES OR NO? (1920)
(7 r.) d, Roy William Neill; lp, Norma Talmadge, Rockliffe Fellowes, Lowell Sherman, Gladden James

YOKE OF GOLD, A (1916)
(5 r.) d, Lloyd B. Carleton; lp, Emory Johnson, Dorothy Davenport, Alfred Allen, Richard Morris

YOLANDA (1924)
(11 r.) d, Robert G. Vignola; lp, Marion Davies, Lyn Harding, Holbrook Blinn, Maclyn Arbuckle

YORK STATE FOLKS (1915)
(5 r.) d, Harry Jackson; lp, James Lackaye, Ray L. Royce, Edith Offutt, Amy Dennis

YOSEMITE TRAIL, THE (1922)
(5 r.) d, Bernard J. Durning; lp, Dustin Farnum, Irene Rich, Walter McGrail, Frank Campeau

YOU AND I
(SEE: OUTLAW AND HIS WIFE, THE, 1918, Swed.)

YOU ARE GUILTY (1923)
(5 r.) d, Edgar Lewis; lp, James Kirkwood, Doris Kenyon, Robert Edeson, Mary Carr

YOU ARE IN DANGER
(SEE: LITTLE GIRL NEXT DOOR, THE, 1923)

YOU CAN'T BEAT THE LAW (1928)
(6 r.) d, Charles J. Hunt; lp, Lila Lee, Cornelius Keefe, Warner Richmond, Betty Francisco

YOU CAN'T BELIEVE EVERYTHING (1918)
(5 r.) d, Jack Conway; lp, Gloria Swanson, Darrel Foss, Jack Richardson, Edward Peil

YOU CAN'T FOOL YOUR WIFE (1923)
(6 r.) d, George Melford; lp, Leatrice Joy, Nita Naldi, Lewis Stone, Pauline Garon

YOU CAN'T GET AWAY WITH IT (1923)
(6 r.) d, Rowland V. Lee; lp, Percy Marmont, Malcolm McGregor, Betty Bouton, Barbara Tennant

YOU CAN'T KEEP A GOOD MAN DOWN (1922)
(6 r.)

YOU FIND IT EVERYWHERE (1921)
(5 r.) d, Charles Horan; lp, Catherine Calvert, Herbert Rawlinson, Macey Harlam, Riley Hatch

YOU KNOW WHAT SAILORS ARE (1928, Brit.)
(8 r.) d, Maurice Elvey; lp, John Longden, Alf Goddard, Cyril McLaglen, Chili Bouchier

YOU NEVER CAN TELL (1920)
(5 r.) d, Chester M. Franklin; lp, Bebe Daniels, Jack Mulhall, Edward Martindel, Helen Dunbar

YOU NEVER KNOW (1922)
(5 r.) d, Robert Ensminger; lp, Earle Williams, Gertrude Astor, George Field, Claire Du Brey

YOU NEVER KNOW WOMEN (1926)
(6 r.) d, William A. Wellman; lp, Florence Vidor, Lowell Sherman, Clive Brook, El Brendel

YOU NEVER KNOW YOUR LUCK (1919)
(5 r.) d, Frank Powell; lp, House Peters, Claire Whitney, Bertram Marburgh, Marion Dyer

YOU NEVER SAID SUCH A GIRL (1919)
(5 r.) d, Robert G. Vignola; lp, Vivian Martin, Harrison Ford, Mayme Kelso, Willis Marks

YOU'D BE SURPRISED (1926)
(6 r.) d, Arthur Rosson; lp, Raymond Griffith, Dorothy Sebastian, Earle Williams, Edward Martindel

YOUNG AMERICA (1918)
(7 r.) d, Arthur Berthelet; lp, Madelyn Clare, Helen MacDonald, Howard Smith, William Wadsworth

YOUNG APRIL (1926)
(7 r.) d, Donald Crisp; lp, Joseph Schildkraut, Rudolph Schildkraut, Bessie Love, Bryant Washburn

YOUNG DIANA, THE (1922)
(7 r.) d, Albert Capellani, Robert G. Vignola; lp, Marion Davies, Maclyn Arbuckle, Forrest Stanley, Gypsy O'Brien

YOUNG IDEAS (1924)
(5 r.) d, Robert F. Hill; lp, Laura La Plante, T. Roy Barnes, Lucille Ricksen, James O. Barrows

YOUNG LOCHINVAR (1923, Brit.)
(5 r.) d, W.P. Kellino; lp, Owen Nares, Gladys Jennings, Dick Webb, Cecil Morton York

YOUNG MISS (1930, Jap.)
(? r.) d, Yasujiro Ozu; lp, Tokihiko Okada, Sumiko Kurishima, Tatsuo Saito

YOUNG MRS. WINTHROP (1920)
(5 r.) d, Walter Edwards; lp, Ethel Clayton, Harrison Ford, Helen Dunbar, Winnifred Greenwood

YOUNG MOTHER HUBBARD (1917)
(4 r.) d, Arthur Berthelet; lp, Mary McAllister, William Clifford, Granville Bates, Carolyn Irwin

YOUNG RAJAH, THE (1922)
(8 r.) d, Philip Rosen; lp, Rudolph Valentino, Wanda Hawley, Pat Moore, Charles Ogle

YOUNG ROMANCE (1915)
(4 r.) d, George Melford; lp, Edith Taliaferro, Tom Forman, Frederick Wilson, Ernest Garcia

YOUNG WOODLEY (1929, Brit.)
(8 r.) d, Thomas Bentley; lp, Robine Irvine, Marjorie Hume, Sam Livesey, Gerald Rawlinson

YOUR ACQUAINTANCE (1927, USSR)
(6 r.) d, Lev Kuleshov; lp, Alexandra Khokhlova, B. Ferdinandov, Vasilchikov, A. Chekulayeva

YOUR BEST FRIEND (1922)
(7 r.) d, William Nigh; lp, Vera Gordon, Harry Benham, Stanley Price, Belle Bennett

YOUR FRIEND AND MINE (1923)
(6 r.) d, Clarence G. Badger; lp, Enid Bennett, Huntly Gordon, Willard Mack, Rosemary Theby

YOUR GIRL AND MINE (1914)
(7 r.) d, Giles Warren; lp, Olive Wyndham, Katherine Kaelred, Sidney Booth, Katherine Henry

YOUR OBEDIENT SERVANT (1917)
(5 r.) d, Edward H. Griffith; lp, Peggy Adams, Pat O'Malley

YOUR WIFE AND MINE (1919)
(6 r.) lp, Eve Dorrington

YOU'RE FIRED (1919)
(5 r.) d, James Cruze; lp, Wallace Reid, Wanda Hawley, Henry Woodward, Theodore Roberts

YOU'RE FIRED (1925)
(5 r.) lp, Bill Bailey

YOURS TO COMMAND (1927)
(5 r.) d, David Kirkland; lp, George O'Hara, Shirley Palmer, William Burress, Dot Farley

YOUTH (1917)
(5 r.) d, Romaine Fielding; lp, Carlyle Blackwell, June Elvidge, Johnny Hines, George Cowl

YOUTH AND ADVENTURE (1925)
(6 r.) d, James W. Horne; lp, Richard Talmadge, Pete Gordon, Joseph Girard, Margaret Landis

YOUTH MUST HAVE LOVE (1922)
(5 r.) d, Joseph Franz; lp, Shirley Mason, Cecil Van Auker, Wallace MacDonald, Landers Stevens

YOUTH OF FORTUNE, A (1916)
(5 r.) d, Otis Turner; lp, Carter De Haven, Flora Parker, Harry Carter, J. Hope

YOUTHFUL CHEATERS (1923)
(6 r.) d, Frank Tuttle; lp, William Calhoun, Glenn Hunter, Martha Mansfield, Marie Burke

YOUTHFUL FOLLY (1920)
(5 r.) d, Alan Crosland; lp, Olive Thomas, Crauford Kent, Helen Gill, Hugh Huntley

YOUTH'S DESIRE (1920)
(5 r.) lp, Joseph Bennett, Doris Baker

YOUTH'S ENDEARING CHARM (1916)
(6 r.) d, William C. Dowlan; lp, Mary Miles Minter, Wallace MacDonald, Harry Von Meter, Gertrude Le Brandt

YOUTH'S GAMBLE (1925)
(5 r.) d, Albert Rogell; lp, Reed Howes, James Thompson, Margaret Morris, Wilfred Lucas

YVETTE (1928, Fr.)
(? r.) d, Alberto Cavalcanti

YVONNE FROM PARIS (1919)
(5 r.) d, Emmett J. Flynn; lp, Mary Miles Minter, Allan Forrest, Vera Lewis, J. Barney Sherry

ZAZA (1923)
(7 r.) d, Allan Dwan; lp, Gloria Swanson, H.B. Warner, Ferdinand Gottschalk, Lucille La Verne

ZEEBRUGGE (1924, Brit.)
(7 r.) d, H. Bruce Woolfe, A.V. Bramble;

ZEPPELIN'S LAST RAID, THE (1918)
(5 r.) d, Thomas H. Ince

0-18 OR A MESSAGE FROM THE SKY (1914, Brit.)
(4 r.) d, George L. Tucker; lp, Jane Gail, Douglas Munro, Gerald Ames, Edward O'Neill

ZERO HOUR, THE (1918)
(5 r.) d, Travers Vale; lp, June Elvidge, Frank Mayo, Henry Warwick, Armand Kaliz

ZERO HOUR, THE (1923)
(5 r.) lp, Lester Cuneo

ZISKA LA DANSEUSE ESPIONNE (1922, Fr.)
(? r.) d, Henri Andreani

ZOLLENSTEIN (1917)
(4 r.) d, Edgar Jones; lp, Vola Vale, Monroe Salisbury, Daniel Gilfether, William Elder

ZON (1920, Fr.)
(? r.) d, Robert Boudrioz

ZONGAR (1918)
(5 r.) d, Bernarr MacFadden; lp, George Larkin, Dolores Cassinelli, Jack Hopkins, Grace Davidson

ZVENIGORA (1928, USSR)
(6 r.) d, Alexander Dovshenko; lp, Semyon Svashenko, Mikola Nademsky, Alexander Podorozhny

ZYTE (1916, Fr.)
(? r.) d, Rene Leprince